W9-CNL-343

General Editors: Frank Kermode and John Hollander

VOLUME II

From Blake to Auden

Romantic Poetry and Prose

HAROLD BLOOM AND LIONEL TRILLING
Yale University Columbia University

Victorian Prose and Poetry

LIONEL TRILLING AND HAROLD BLOOM

Modern British Literature

FRANK KERMODE AND JOHN HOLLANDER
Cambridge University Hunter College

THE OXFORD ANTHOLOGY OF ENGLISH LITERATURE

MAJOR AUTHORS EDITION
Volume I

The Oxford Anthology of English Literature

MAJOR AUTHORS EDITION

VOLUME I

From Beowulf to Johnson

Medieval English Literature

J. B. TRAPP
Warburg Institute

The Literature of Renaissance England

JOHN HOLLANDER AND FRANK KERMODE
Hunter College — Cambridge University

The Restoration and the Eighteenth Century

MARTIN PRICE
Yale University

NEW YORK
OXFORD UNIVERSITY PRESS
LONDON TORONTO 1975

Library of Congress Catalogue Card Number: 74-22882

Selections from the following works were made possible by the kind permission of their respective publishers and representatives:

Beowulf: The Oldest English Epic, translated by Charles W. Kennedy. Copyright 1940 by Oxford University Press, Inc.; renewed 1968 by Charles W. Kennedy. Reprinted by permission of the publisher.
James Boswell: *Boswell's London Journal 1762–1763,* edited by Frederick A. Pottle. Copyright 1950 by Yale University. Reprinted by permission of McGraw-Hill Book Company and William Heinemann Ltd., Publishers.
William Shakespeare: *Othello* from *The Riverside Shakespeare,* edited by G. Blakemore Evans *et al.* Copyright © 1974 by Houghton Mifflin Company. Reprinted by permission of the publisher.

Printed in the United States of America

Preface
to the Major Authors Edition

This special edition of *The Oxford Anthology* is not merely an abridgment of the earlier collection. With the help and advice of many academics from around the country, the editors have shaped this edition to the special needs of teachers who prefer the so-called Major Authors approach to English literature. Thirty authors from the *Beowulf*-poet to W. H. Auden have been selected from the larger version, but significant additions have been made so that the student may have access to a broader range of material by several of these figures. For example: a tragedy by Shakespeare, *Othello,* now accompanies *The Tempest;* the whole of Book I of *The Faerie Queene* appears here; four complete books of *Paradise Lost* (I, II, IV, IX) are reprinted where only two exist in the larger edition; *Gulliver's Travels* is given in its entirety, as is Tennyson's *In Memoriam.* Upon closer examination, the teacher will find several shorter works—*Eloisa to Abelard, Lamia, The Palace of Art* are a few—anthologized just for this edition. In the interests of space-saving and at the request of many teachers, two noteworthy deletions were made: a group of Blake's later poems and Lawrence's *St. Mawr;* the latter novella has been replaced by the shorter, more familiar *Odour of Chrysanthemums.*

But it must be noted that these changes have been adopted without impinging on those qualities which have made the first version of *The Oxford Anthology of English Literature* an enormous success. The commentary, annotations, and illustrations have been only slightly altered for this edition. As for the annotations, the editors have never been afraid to be lively or even speculative. They have consistently tried to avoid usurping the teacher's role, as providing standard or definitive readings might do. On the other hand, the commentary goes beyond merely providing a lowest common denominator of information by suggesting interpretive directions and levels along which the teacher is free to move or not; and of course the teacher always has the freedom to disagree. The editors have been neither prudish nor portentous in their tone, nor have they sought—in the interests of some superficial consistency, but with leaden effect—to efface their personal styles.

Each contributing editor has worked and taught in at least one period or field outside the one for which he is, in this anthology, principally responsible, and none has ever allowed specialization to reduce his broader commitment to humane studies more largely considered. Thus we were able to plan a work which called for an unusual degree of cross reference and collaboration. During a crucial phase in the preparation of the text, the editors held daily discussions of their work for a period of months. By selection, allusion, comparison, by direction and indirection, we contrived to preserve continuity between epochs, and to illuminate its character. At the same time, the close cooperation of the various editors has precluded the possibility of common surrender to any single dominating literary theory; and the teacher need have no fear that he must prepare to do battle with some critical Hydra showing a head on every page.

A word about the pictures. They are not to be thought of simply as illustrations, and certainly not as mere decorations, but rather as part of the anthologized material. Throughout, the reader is introduced to the relations between poem as speaking picture, and picture as mute poem. Aside from contextual and anecdotal illustration, of which there is indeed a good deal, the pictorial examples allow teachers, or students on their own, to explore some of the interrelations of texts and the visual arts in all periods, whether exemplified in Renaissance emblems or in contemporary illustrations of Victorian poems.

Texts have all been based on the best modern editions, which happen quite often to be published by the Oxford University Press. Spelling and punctuation have been modernized throughout, save in two instances: the texts of Spenser and Blake two poets whose spelling and punctuation are so far from idiosyncrasies to be silently normalized that they constitute attempts to refashion poetic language. In the medieval section a modern verse translation of *Beowulf* by C. W. Kennedy has been adopted.

Glossaries of literary and historical terms in all periods have been provided, sometimes keyed to the annotations, sometimes supplementing the larger headnotes. These, it will be noticed, seek to illuminate the immediate contexts of the literature of a period rather than to provide a dense précis of its social, political, and economic history. Similarly, the reading lists at the end of each volume are not exhaustive bibliographies; in the happy instance where a teacher finds an extensive bibliography advisable, he or she will want to supply one.

Finally, an inevitable inadequate word of acknowledgment. To the English Department of Dartmouth College the editors are deeply indebted for having so generously and hospitably provided a place in which to work together for a sustained period. The staff of the Dartmouth College Library was extraordinarily helpful and attentive.

All of the editors would like to extend a note of gratitude to the many academics throughout the United States who willingly made suggestions as to what should be included as well as excluded. A special note of thanks to Jim Cox (Dartmouth College), Paul Dolan (State University of New York at Stony Brook), Michael Rewa (University of Delaware), William Stephany (University of Vermont), Henry Vittum (Plymouth State College), and Bernard Knab (Greater Hartford Community College), for their challenging and helpful comments.

And finally to the entire staff of the New York branch of the Oxford University Press, who have done more than could be humanly expected in connection with the planning and execution of this book. We would especially like to thank our editor John Wright, as well as Leona Capeless and her staff, Mary Ellen Evans, Patricia Cristol, Joyce Berry, Deborah Zwecher, and Jean Shapiro. An unusual but very deserved note of thanks to the Production people, especially Gerard S. Case, Leslie Phillips, and Ann Boudreau; and to the designer, Frederick Schneider, whose excellent work speaks for itself.

New York
November 1974

Frank Kermode
John Hollander

BRITISH ISLES
10°W
5°W
0°
60°N
55°N
50°N
N
Atlantic Ocean
North Sea
SCOTLAND
Clyde
Glasgow
Edinburgh
Belfast
IRELAND
Shannon
Dublin
Irish Sea
LAKE DISTRICT
YORKSHIRE
York
Hull
Blackpool
Leeds
Manchester
Liverpool
Sheffield
MERCIA
Trent
Nottingham
Norwich
EAST ANGLIA
WALES
Birmingham
Avon
ENGLAND
Severn
Oxford
Thames
Bristol
London
Southampton
KENT
WESSEX
English Channel
FRANCE
Miles
0
50
100
150
A. KARL

Contents

* An asterisk indicates that a work does not appear in its entirety.

THE RENAISSANCE, 269

Eighteenth Century

Later Eighteenth Century

Medieval English Literature

Medieval English Literature

HISTORICAL BACKGROUND

Britain's first experience of a literate civilization came in 55 B.C., when Julius Caesar's military expedition from across the Channel initiated the Romanization of this part of the known world. Settled by Celtic tribes from Gaul in the fifth century B.C., Britain had hitherto been, for Rome, the remotest of countries, known only from traders' reports and garbled accounts. Caesar's two brief forays in successive years established Roman dominion and opened up the island. "Corn, cattle, gold, silver and iron; also hides, slaves and clever hunting dogs" were the British commodities that could help to maintain the Roman standard of living, while in return British chieftains received food, drink, furniture, and household equipment of a luxury never before available to them.

For nearly a century Britain remained a trading outpost of the Roman Empire. Not until after 43 A.D., under the Emperor Claudius, did the island come fully under Roman political and military domination. Even then, remoter areas in Scotland retained independence, and Ireland, never conquered by Rome, was free to continue its Celtic tradition.

Roman conquest meant that Roman civic organization created an urban civilization on the Roman model within the conglomeration of small local Celtic tribal units. The Romans encouraged the chiefs and leading families to adopt their way of life and to have their sons educated in the Roman manner. Walled towns were laid out in the Roman style, some at the old tribal centers, some outside the walls of Roman fortresses, some as settlements of discharged veterans. In the countryside, villas replaced older farm complexes and served as rural centers.

Roman civilization in Britain managed to weather the first raids of Saxon pirates in the late third century, but once the Roman forces were withdrawn (*c.* 410) it soon collapsed under the impact of much larger armed migration. During the first half of the fifth century the Angles, Saxons, and Jutes descended on the country in great numbers from northern Germany and Jutland or the Jutish Peninsula. The initial wave of this migration is dated 449 by many Anglo-Saxon writers, on the basis of a statement by the Venerable Bede (*c.* 673–735), the first historian of the English church and people. According to Bede, the Britain of his time comprised four nations—English, British (Welsh), Picts, and Scots—each having its own language yet united in the study of God's truth by the fifth—Latin. When the English invasion began, the Picts inhabited the northernmost parts of the island, the modern Scotland, the Scots (confusingly) occupied Ireland, and the Britons held possession of all the island of Britain to the south of the Firth of Forth. The invaders, according to race, settled in the South-East (the Jutes, in Kent and on the Isle of Wight); in Essex (north of Kent: "East Saxony"), Sussex (south of Kent: "South Saxony," and Wessex (South-West as far as Gloucestershire and Devon, "West Saxony"); and in the North-East (East Anglia), North (Northumbria) and North-West (Mercia), these last three being occupied by the Angles.

While Bede's division corresponds too closely to the political divisions of his day to be entirely reliable, it is a useful guide. It is valuable particularly as suggesting the disunity within unity of these pagan Germanic invaders, a disunity reflected in the cultural differences that continued throughout the Anglo-Saxon and Middle English periods. It is important to remember that despite centralizing influences English provincial cultures remained vigorous. Canterbury, in Kent, the town from which Roman Christianity spread from the sixth century, is today the primatial Anglican see of England and was throughout the Middle Ages a notable literary and artistic center, besides being later a place of pilgrimage. Winchester, the chief town of the Anglo-Saxon kingdom of Wessex, was highly influential in both the visual and the verbal arts during the later Anglo-Saxon period, as well as being a city where Norman kings held court. Superb manuscripts were produced in later medieval East Anglia, and manuscript writing and illumination and wood and stone carving, as well as literary studies, flourished in late seventh- and early eighth-century Northumbria. Later, in the fourteenth century, poems in the West Midland dialect and plays in the Northern sustained the standard of provincial culture in regions remote (by medieval reckoning) from the capital. A pilgrim to Canterbury took four days to cover the sixty miles from London; the West Midland area where *Sir Gawain and the Green Knight* was written was more than twice as far from the metropolis.

In the fifth century this flourishing England provincial and metropolitan culture was of course far in the future. The invaders were a hardy, warlike race, their characteristics still resembling those of the Germans as described by Tacitus (see Headnote to *Beowulf*, below). An index of their success is the degree to which the Celtic languages were supplanted: only a very few words of Celtic origin survived to find their way into later medieval and modern English. The English drove the Britons from their land and brought much more of the land under the plow; basically, however, like Tacitus's Germans, they were not prone to group themselves into large social organisms—let alone urban societies—or to maintain the quite elaborate communications system between groups that would have been possible if they had taken over existing towns with their connecting Roman roads.

A centralized urban society developed only very slowly among the small, oligarchic, local units of the various English kingdoms. For long, chieftains and petty kings moved with their courts from one royal estate to the other, expecting and receiving generous hospitality. Their counselors, chosen by them and not elected by any democratic process, served one month in three and retired to their estates for the other two. Gradually, more permanent establishments evolved, kingdoms grew in size and strength, and learning and the arts of peace began to flourish. The kingdoms of Northumbria, Mercia, and Wessex rose to a dominant position in the seventh, eighth, and ninth-tenth centuries respectively.

During the eighth century the nascent civilization of the English was already menaced by the Norwegian sea-raiders, who sacked the Northumbrian monastery of Lindisfarne in 793. The Danes made great inroads into England during the next two hundred years. In 870 they came down by land to attack the southwestern kingdom of Wessex; when later defeated by King Alfred the Great they retired, to be confined by treaty to the territory in the North and East Midlands known as the Danelaw. A century and a half later, a Danish king, Canute, succeeded to the throne of Wessex and ruled a great part of England.

Throughout the Anglo-Saxon period and for centuries thereafter, the Church remained the most powerful force in the written culture of the English nation. Since St. Augustine's mission from Rome had landed in Canterbury in 597, the English church had flourished, although the Roman Christianity represented by Augustine had been in doctrinal conflict with Celtic Christianity, which had earlier evangelized the North and the South-West. The two were notably at loggerheads about the date of Easter, and their differences were not settled until the Synod held at Whitby Abbey in Northumbria in 664, when Canterbury won the day. Later during the same century, Englishmen began to evangelize heathen Germany, and finally in the eighth brought that entire territory to Christianity.

The importance of the Church and of its monastic, predominantly Latin, culture for the cultural life of Anglo-Saxon England can hardly be overemphasized. In the development of a beautiful script for the writing of texts, in the decoration and illumination of manuscripts, as well as in scholarship and the arts of architecture and sculpture, Church patronage was paramount. This was especially so of monastic patronage: a monastic community was a small town in itself, in this respect a kind of equivalent of the country villa of Roman times, with a community existing on the fruit of its own toil and on charitable benefactions.

THE NORMAN CONQUEST AND LATER

The men who followed Duke William of Normandy to England in 1066, to assert his right to the West-Saxon throne, were the descendants of Scandinavians who had landed on the north coast of France a century and a half before. Nominally subjects of the French king and speaking the French language, the Normans comprised virtually an independent state, with territorial ambitions and a Viking joy in war. During the same century in which they conquered England they founded states in South Italy and Sicily.

These invaders, like the Romans before them, were a compact, efficient army, many of them mercenaries, rather than half a nation on the move like the Angles, Saxons, and Jutes. Immediately on landing, William won the decisive Battle of Hastings, to become—by right of conquest as well as by family—King of England and Duke of Normandy. For four hundred years, until the end of the Hundred Years' War between England and France (1453), this dual kingdom was the most powerful state in Europe. Its territories on the French side of the Channel were greatly extended by William the Conqueror's successors. The kings of England gave at least as much of their time and attention to their French dominions as to their English, held their court at least as often in France as in England, and regularly engaged in military operations on French soil.

The Normans brought to England their northern dialect of the French language, and their social and political dominance imposed this dialect on the almost exclusively Germanic (with borrowings from Latin) language of the conquered English as the norm of educated and aristocratic communication. Latin remained the language of learning, and Old English continued to be spoken and written; but the machinery of government and the law functioned in French. Throughout the Middle Ages, French taste in literature and the arts prevailed, especially in southern English noble and royal circles. The language that grew up in this situation was an amalgam known as Middle English: its syntax and grammar largely remained English while its vocabulary was greatly augmented by French.

Before the coming of the Normans the English had created a society remarkable for a degree of civilization that had continued to flourish in spite of Danish invasions. After the Danish wars of the ninth century the Kingdom of Wessex had established a military and cultural ascendancy over the whole country, but the kingdoms of Mercia and Northumbria, as well as the Norse kingdom of York, survived in a shadow form in 1066. Despite the ascendancy of Wessex, and the existence of a consistent and workable system of law, local government, and taxation throughout the land, England before the Norman Conquest was by no means a close-knit unity. The Frenchmen, as the conquered called the conquerors, imposed themselves on England, driving the older English aristocracy from the court and to a lower position in society in general, and creating one kingdom from many.

William the Conqueror's method of asserting his power (binding on the whole realm) was orderly, simple, autocratic—and novel to the English. Every inch of the land was declared to be the king's; retaining great estates for himself, he distributed the remainder among his followers, who held it as his tenants only in return for the performance of exactly defined services. Within this feudal system the Norman barons were free to govern and exploit their lands as they wished. They were encouraged to build strongholds, and William himself saw to it that a castle, with a constable (a noble vassal of the king), was erected in every county town and at strategic points throughout the country. These great stone fortresses, on ground naturally or artificially elevated, with moats around them and stockades for an outer defense, became the symbol of Norman power. The English had never seen anything like them.

William also took care to know, by means of a systematic enquiry made in the 1080's and recorded in Doomsday Book, the feudal obligation of each of his vassals. He also took care to strengthen the towns already established during the Anglo-Saxon period, as centers of trade, justice, and administration in peace, and defense in war. Ports such as Southampton on the south coast and London on the navigable River Thames gradually came into greater prominence because of their advantages in these respects. London, already a major town in Roman days, had become by the beginning of the thirteenth century a community strong and rich enough to turn the scale in a dispute—according as it supported the barons against the king (as in 1215 against King John) or vice versa. It was by far the largest, wealthiest, and most powerful town in England, and the administrative and cultural hub of the country as well.

By the fourteenth century the English kingdom—in the British Isles and in France—was at the height of its political strength and economic prosperity. The power of Edward III (*d.* 1377), the military exploits of his eldest son the Black Prince, and the political and cultural influence of his fourth son, John of Gaunt, are among the outstanding features of English life at the time. Even though social unrest and political strife were prevalent during the reign of Richard II (deposed 1399), these did not destroy the social and economic conditions in which literature and the arts could flourish.

Though the power and influence of the King of England tended to concentrate itself in the south, both because of its proximity to the French territories of the king and because of the metropolis of London and the ports of the south coast, mercantile centers in the provinces also came to prosper. The Yorkshire farms and towns in the north grew rich on the production of wool, and the eastern and western counties, on weaving and the export trade. The rising well-to-do bourgeois society of London and of these provincial towns began to exert an influence on taste. The most obvious example in literature is the fourteenth-century mystery play in the north and the Midlands. The exactions of great landowners in pursuit of more profitable means of farming became a staple source of the literature of social complaint.

One of the most distinctive features of the later Middle Ages in England and in Europe was the change that came about in institutions of education. The first universities were founded in Europe during the twelfth century. Their curricula included civil and canon (ecclesiastical) law, the Latin classics, the newly revived Aristotelian philosophy, especially logic (in Latin translation), mathematics, and medicine. Until the late twelfth century an English boy acquired his education either in a school—perhaps attached to a cathedral but in any case licensed by the bishop of the diocese, or in a royal or noble household whose life he shared, or an abbey or monastery, where he was trained by the monks. Little care was taken for the education of girls. The late twelfth century saw the beginnings of the University of Oxford (its constituent colleges were not founded until later); and Cambridge was founded during the early thirteenth century. These two remained the only English universities for more than five hundred years.

After elementary schooling in cathedral, court, or abbey, a boy would enter university at the age of about fourteen, and spend seven years or so equipping himself for a career in the church or the administration of the realm. From the last years of the thirteenth century onward, he had another choice. During the reign of Edward I (1272–1307) the laws of England became the object of serious study and definition and at about the same time the "common" or civil lawyers began to group themselves into societies known as Inns of Court. In these "Inns" the senior members lived, studied, and taught; and there a boy could be sent as an alternative to university or for post-university education.

In the thousand years between the coming of the Anglo-Saxons in the fifth century and the waning of the Middle Ages in the fifteenth, England had advanced from a land conquered and sparsely populated by a alien race to a civilization in full flower. From a country divided among many petty rulers, she had become one powerful kingdom, commercially prosperous, with a unified legal system and the beginnings of parliamentary government by two houses, Lords and Commons. At various times architecture, sculpture, painting, and the minor arts had all been brought to a point where they excelled what the rest of Europe had to offer. By the end of the fifteenth century, however, she was beginning to lag behind in the arts and in scholarship. Italy, in particular, was now the leader: when Gothic was still the style of England, Italian Renaissance painters, sculptors, and architects were producing the masterpieces that set the standard for the next three hundred years. In learning, too, England was retardataire. But vernacular literature, both popular and courtly, was still her great glory, and she had already produced, in Geoffrey Chaucer, a great European poet who united both French and English traditions, as well as other English masters working in a poetic that was the lineal descendant of Old English verse techniques.

ANGLO-SAXON (OLD ENGLISH) LITERATURE

It is no accident that much of Old English literature is in verse. All cultures find their first verbal artistic expression in rhythmic utterance, the organization into less free, more formal repetitive patterns of the basic prosodic structures of language. These patterns are first used in ritual, that is to say, in the oral realization of a solemn or joyful effect, involving the raising and fulfilling of an exalted expectation, sometimes with the aid of music, sometimes without. This often occurs at a preliterate stage, since poetry depends less than prose on the written word. Nevertheless, all poems seek and some are felt to have—or else they would never be written down at all—a validity beyond the single performance, as well as a dimension and an influence that go beyond the merely verbal and either imitate or command some basic and universal pattern or harmony.

While any artistic utterance seeks the condition of permanence, oral poetry always retains something of the occasional quality of performance. Chief among the accidents of time as they affect the transmission of literature, especially medieval literature, is the point in its development at which a text was committed to writing. Sometimes the act of writing down crystallized and solidified the text; sometimes it allowed it an existence of continued change as spoken art—as in the popular ballads. To a certain extent this is true of all literature: the form in which we read a modern poem or novel is the form in which the author was finally obliged to give it to the publisher—which may or may not be "final." Its transmission, even in a literate society that produces multiple copies of books by mechanical means—Western society as it has been since the invention of printing—is not entirely straightforward. Still, modern texts are comparatively stable and the range of variant conditions remains relatively narrow, growing narrower the nearer we approach our own times.

We can say little with certainty about date of composition or authorship of many of the poems from this period. We have more information about the poets and other authors of the later Middle Ages, but never as much as we should like—and it is surprising how frequently we are unable to give even the name of an author to some of the most remarkable works of the fourteenth century.

To go back to the time when the earliest poetry of the English people is thought to have been composed, we must pick an arbitrary date, say about 500 A.D., when the migration of the Germanic tribes was more or less complete. The written records we possess from that time amount only to a handful of inscriptions, serving a no longer definable magical function, expressed in pagan characters known as runes. Runes continue to appear on Christian monuments, such as the Ruthwell Cross (Fig. 23), on which a portion of the poem *The Dream of the Rood* is carved, and on such objects as the Franks Casket (Fig. 22); yet with very few exceptions they are not used in the transcription of any extant manuscript texts. The vernacular manuscripts originating in the seventh century used an alphabet based on the Latin script of the Irish missionaries to England, with a few extra characters for Anglo-Saxon sounds having no equivalent in Latin (Fig. 4).

By the seventh century the physical means for recording texts and enough trained scribes to write them were in existence, particularly in Northumbria. The Lindisfarne Gospels (Fig. 5), now in the British Museum, are only one witness to the skill and sophistication exercised at the end of the seventh century and the beginning of the eighth. On the other hand, the manuscripts in which Old English poetry is preserved are almost all unique, and almost none of them were written until the end of the tenth century. Scribal effort, in other words, had been expended on the new learning in the new language of culture—Latin—rather than on what we now think of as the earliest monuments of our literature, the heroic poetry of the Anglo-Saxon people. This means that many poems, in the form in which we have them, were not written down until perhaps two and one-half centuries after their composition. On the other hand, certain works, such as *The Battle of Maldon,* which commemorates a historical event of 991, must have been copied into a manuscript almost as soon as composed. Most scholars think that earlier manuscripts of the earlier poems must have existed, and that they were probably transcribed in various dialects rather than only in the literary West Saxon in which the tenth-century versions are expressed. We cannot be sure, but it seems likely that *Beowulf,* for example, was given a form approximating that which we know, by a singer or singers at some time during the eighth century. The poet was probably binding together materials from an earlier time and adding to them. During the Anglo-Saxon period, however, it looks as though the transcription of works which were predominantly secular, or only indirectly didactic—especially those based on pagan materials and pagan codes of value and behavior—must have taken a very secondary place to the writing of sacred works.

Throughout the Middle Ages, in all Europe, the Bible was by far the most frequently copied text, either in itself or in the many liturgical books for which it formed the basis. Without the Christian missionaries from Ireland and Rome, the impulse toward a written culture in England would have come far later; yet the culture that the missionaries brought with them and in which they educated their converts was primarily a sacred one, Latin not English, learned rather than popular. Those who came under its influence were more likely to busy themselves with Latin verse and prose (especially Christian) than with the vernacular. Since Latin was the common language of learned Europe, Englishmen could make a European reputation in that language: St. Aldhelm of Malmesbury (640–709), in Wessex; the Venerable Bede (c.653–735) scholar, grammarian, poet, encyclopedist, Scripture commentator, hagiographer, and historian, monk of Jarrow in Northumbria; and Alcuin of York (735–804) did exactly that. After a distinguished career in his native York, Alcuin spent most of the last twenty years of his life as principal educator to the Emperor Charlemagne and the Frankish court.

By translation from the Latin, too, the most beneficial works of the new faith could be made available—the Bible itself, the *Pastoral Care* and the *Dialogues* of St. Gregory the Great, the *Consolation of Philosophy* of Boethius (a pagan philosopher, d. c.524, then thought to be Christian). This was the ambition of King Alfred, in Wessex during the later ninth century; and though there is evidence that he was an admirer of *Beowulf,* there is stronger evidence that he was more an admirer of piety and learning, which he wished to see flourish in a kingdom at peace and secure from the attacks of Scandinavian marauders.

The further development of the Alfredian program during the late tenth- and early eleventh-century movement which goes under the name of the Benedictine Revival is associated especially with the name of St. Dunstan, Archbishop of Canterbury from 959 to 988, whose program of monastic reform brought education, learning, and the arts into still closer contact than ever before in England. In its beginnings the Benedictine Revival was primarily Latin in character, but in its wake was produced some of the greatest vernacular work of the entire medieval period, in both the visual and the verbal arts. The inspiration is classical and Mediterranean, the finished product characteristically English. With a writer such as Ælfric (955–1020), it is no longer a matter of saving oneself for Latin or of producing a stiff rendering of Latin into Old English, but rather of a highly conscious, fully mastered rhetorical art in Old English prose. So too, in the manuscript illumination of the century preceding the Norman Conquest: in the Benedictional of St. Æthelwold, St. Dunstan's collaborator (Fig. 6), a Mediterranean model has been assimilated into a style recognizably national and entirely independent and self-assured. A later example still, with influences from Byzantium, is seen in Fig. 7, from the St. Albans Psalter of the first quarter of the twelfth century.

The Benedictine Revival was the summing up and crowning of a process that had begun in the sixth century and had produced a large body of English prose by the time of the Norman Conquest in 1066. Much of this prose consists of sermons or of works of devotion or morality, private and public. Some is legal and administrative, some annalistic, like the sometimes lively (and often dull) narrative of the *Anglo-Saxon Chronicle*. Some pieces, like the translations of the Greek romance of *Apollonius of Tyre* and of the *Marvels of the East,* seem to exist for the sake of the tale alone. Most of it would have been intended for reading aloud, since only a small proportion of the population could read and write; and some of the sermons, in particular, must have been delivered with a sense of performance almost as great as that of poetry. But it is unlikely that such prose was intended to be memorized to the same extent as verse, even in an age when men's verbal memories were more exercised and more tenacious than they are today. It is recorded of King Alfred that as a boy he received a coveted book of poetry as a reward for memorizing its entire contents after having them read to him.

By comparison with the mass of prose writings, the amount of Old English verse that survives is small. Some of it is religious: *The Dream of the Rood,* brief and highly wrought, is perhaps its high point. Much consists of what is loosely described as heroic: that is to say, it takes as its basic assumptions the older Germanic pagan insistence on the virtues of courage in battle and endurance in the face of all the ills that beset a man as he passes from youth to old age. Its greatest monument is *Beowulf,* its most perfect epitome *The Battle of Maldon*—a late, fully crystallized statement of the heroic ideal which is also a memorial for an aged English leader against the Danes.

Though it is probable that poetry, the older literary form, took second place in the monastic scriptoria to English and Latin prose, the poetic gift was always held in high esteem among the English. The singer of tales, the *scop,* with a repertoire part memorized and part improvised, and accompanying his verses on the harp, was an important member of a noble household. He could expect his stock-in-trade to command a receptive audience, his listeners themselves versed in, and hence appreciative of, his poetic skills. Performances by such trained and (so to speak) professional minstrels, as well as by the guests themselves in turn, were an important feature of any feast.

While we have the names of many scholars and prose writers of the Anglo-Saxon period, and even considerable biographical information about a good number, we can name only three poets, all of them Christian and active in a monastic ambience. Cædmon is one, Aldhelm another; six lines of vernacular poetry survive from one, none at all from the second. Of the third, Cynewulf, we know little, except that he has left us about twenty-six hundred lines of verse, including a long poem, *Elene* (on St. Helena and the finding of the True Cross). More survives from what is known as the school of Cynewulf, all of it seemingly written by ecclesiastics during the late eighth and early ninth centuries. Its subject matter is religious—saints' lives, Gospel stories, and Christian allegory. Works such as *The Phoenix,* adapted from pseudo-Lactantius, and *The Dream of the Rood,* the latter chiefly because of resemblance to *Elene* in subject, are often called Cynewulfian. Though the *Dream* has a depth and richness and is of a quality that sets it above the other work of Cynewulf and his "school," there are enough resemblances between the two in style and diction to make the comparison useful.

The remainder of the Old English poetic corpus is anonymous and untitled. In a very few cases, such as the Riddles, to have given a title would have been to destroy the point of the game, which was to describe a familiar object in language as figurative and impenetrable as possible, provoking admiration for poetic skill in the making and surprised pleasure at the solution. This delight in figurative diction is one of the chief characteristics of Old English poetry—as indeed of medieval literature in general. For the medieval poet, richness and difficulty of language were not to be avoided, but rather to be cultivated. Rhetoric and ornament were not the terms of abuse that they have become in modern times. Old English poetry, naturally, does not bear the strong impress of Latin rhetorical theory and practice that marks later English medieval verse and prose. But it loves ornament, repeated in patterns—just as Anglo-Saxon art did (Figs. 5–6, 21). It preserves a careful balance between what is strange and what is familiar and it orders its rhythms and effects according to metrical and structural principles that are strict in operation. Particularly in a heroic epic like *Beowulf,* but also in shorter elegiac poems, it achieves an effect of carefully contrived and ordered ceremonial performance. Like oral poetry in general, it is essentially an art of preservation rather than of innovation, using and re-using traditional materials. The hearer or reader is made to feel that he is on familiar ground as he recognizes the highly conventional—the word is again not one of abuse in medieval times—figurative vocabulary, with its formulaic repetitions and fossilized poetic terms, and the poet's use of one incident to convey the parallel implications of another.

One of the chief marks distinguishing the literature of medieval and Renaissance Europe from that of our day is its profound belief in the didactic and exemplary value of the verbal work of art. *Beowulf* is a poem of praise punctuated, in a manner typical of Old English poetry, by passages of Christian and pagan moralizing. In one sense it can be very loosely called an allegory of the perpetual struggle of light against dark, good against evil. Over and above the pleasure it was undoubtedly expected to give its audience, the weight of the poem is thrown into the attempt to move and persuade this audience that Beowulf's example is one that it would be admirable to follow if one wished for fame in this generation and the generations to come.

MIDDLE ENGLISH LITERATURE

This belief survives the changes in both the language itself and the forms of English literature as they develop during the centuries succeeding the Norman Conquest. If anything, it becomes stronger, as influences from other literatures, especially French, begin to assert themselves. The language of English poetry and prose becomes more recognizably our own. Both are refined and augmented by contact with and imitation of the French language and the new narrative and lyrical poetic that came into being in France during the twelfth century. Latin culture continues to play a large part in the formation of English literature, but for at least four centuries France becomes the dominant outside influence. Its power is greater for the fact that for so much of the time England was first of all a province of the Dukes of Normandy and later the ruler of large tracts of France. The influence of France on England was often direct, but often, and in some respects more significantly, it was indirect, acting as the intermediary between English and Latin or Italian literature. Frequently, instead of going to originals for translation or adaptation, an English writer went to a French version.

From the century or so after the Norman Conquest we now possess comparatively little literature in English. The works written at the beginning of what historians call the Middle English period—from a little before 1200 to the end of the fifteenth century—suggest, however, that the tradition of vernacular writing was continuous and that there was constant interaction between Latin, French, and English. English prose works of religious instruction have a continuous tradition from Anglo-Saxon times to the end of the Middle Ages—the late twelfth-century *Ancrene Riwle* (a manual for women religious recluses) is an early example of devout impulse and sophisticated performance. In secular literature the Latin and French form of verse debate is naturalized in the lively late-twelfth-century rhyming poem *The Owl and the Nightingale,* in which the two birds put the case respectively for the solemn and the joyous ways of life. Layamon, at about the same time, is the first writer to give substance in English to what becomes one of the most potent myths of the English Middle Ages and Renaissance: the legendary history of King Arthur and his ancestor Brutus, eponymous founder of Britain, and descendant of Aeneas, the Trojan hero and founder of Rome. Layamon writes in an alliterative measure that is the intermediary between Old English poetic and the verse of the alliterative revival in the West and North-West Midlands in the fourteenth century (Langland and the *Gawain*-Poet).

During the twelfth century the English poet and the English writer of devotional prose, in particular, came to have at their disposal, either directly or through French, a much larger range of classical literature and literary theory—and, increasingly, of medieval adaptations of them—than ever before. Their enlarged education gave them access to the sources of knowledge contained in the liberal arts—the *trivium* (grammar, rhetoric, and logic) and the *quadrivium* (astronomy, arithmetic, geometry, and music)—as well as to the poets and rhetoricians of Rome. The development of the Latin liturgy and of the literature of devotion and religious instruction, in both verse and prose, enormously enlarged their sacred range.

France provided a recognized classification of the materials of secular story. The "matter of France," less important for England, yielded the stories of Charlemagne, Roncevaux, Roland, and the rest; the "matter of Britain" (i.e. Brittany) comprised the Arthurian legend and the so-called Breton lays, of which Chaucer's *Franklin's Tale* is an adaptation; and the "matter of Rome," including the Troy story (Rome being a Trojan foundation), the story of Thebes, and the stories of Alexander the Great, was the largest in scope and most influential of all. While many of these stories, especially those of the "matter of Rome," were available in Latin, it was their French versions that made them the narrators' basic material, the inexhaustible well from which they could draw. It was never thought to be the poet's task to make it new: these stories were worth the telling again and again. They are the tales that displace the Germanic heroic legends.

The romances—ancestors of the novel—that are made from them differ from the oral epic poetry which they supplant almost as much in the manner of their telling as in their matter. They reflect a different society from the earlier Germanic variety, and a new valuation of social activity. Bravery in battle becomes less an end in itself, less the prime opportunity to win reputation, so that it occupies relatively less space in the social experience and consequently in literature. As the institution of chivalry comes into being, warlike courage begins to function, still importantly but less prominently, as part of a larger and more sophisticated pattern of social activity. The virtues of chivalry were in part an elaboration and refinement of the older pagan heroic ideals of the conduct befitting a man of good birth. Courage and generosity, the keeping of an oath remained, as they still remain, part of the groundwork of virtuous behavior, but they were incorporated in a system of values radically transformed by Christian ethics and a philosophy of love. True courtesy, honor, the practice of the ideal of knighthood, implied the exercise in their various aspects of the "cardinal" virtues of prudence, fortitude, temperance, and justice, controlled and enriched by the "theological"—faith, hope, and charity. All these words and concepts had a much wider and less institutionalized application than they do today; they embraced such other virtues as generosity, honor, good temper, friendliness, truth, and their various manifestations. In the world of the romances and, at a lower pitch, in the real world, fame and life everlasting were to be won by the practice of these virtues in the service of the Christian faith and of both a heavenly lady—the Virgin Mary—and an earthly.

The matter of Britain, especially, and the matter of Rome are deployed to tell stories of true lovers, to explore the nature of their thoughts and actions, in a context of martial adventure and fairy magic, and often at great length. The nature of love itself, religious and profane, becomes a subject for exploration by philosophers and poets, who picked up some of what had been written about its theory and practice by Plato and by the Latin and Arabic authors through whom Plato became known to the Middle Ages; and by the love poets of ancient Rome, especially Ovid. In philosophy, the investigation is carried on most remarkably during the twelfth century by the school of Chartres in the north; in poetry by the Provençal poets of the south, who shape the new genre of love lyric. The first of these secular poets of France known to us by name is William, Duke of Aquitaine (1071–1127), who already had behind him a tradition of classical and medieval love poetry in Latin and Arabic-Spanish for which there are no more than one or two parallels in the earlier Germanic languages. The troubadour poets, in their exploration of love's nature and transforming power and of the anguish of love-longing, evolve the notion of *fin' amors:* gracious love, noble and ennobling, love-worship, for which nineteenth-century scholars coined the term "courtly love." Nothing illustrates better the change from an old Germanic to a typical European medieval society than this complex of ideas in which women, love, and praise of women occupy a dominant position.

The same change in values is apparent in the songs that deal less with love as a state of being than with imagined love-encounters: the *alba*—the song of lovers' prearranged secret meeting by night and their despairing parting at dawn, and the *pastourelle*—the song of lovers' chance meeting by day and what comes of it, as well as in the other varieties of love lyric. The lyrical stanzaic form in which many of these songs are expressed had already been developed in Latin religious poetry of the ninth century. Rhyme, too, is first to be found in Latin poetry and is transferred from that to the vernacular. Throughout the early development of medieval lyric poetry there is constant interplay between Latin and vernacular, sacred and secular. Religious poetry, in particular, exploits the notion of *figura,* either in its narrower typological sense or in the broader and universal, in which Eve or the Maiden in the Moor can stand for all women, all humanity.

Some of the developing poetic genres reflect the growing taste, in a society where women were assuming a considerable role, for what much later came to be called polite literature. The *carole* is one example: a dance-song in which the leader sang the verse and the rest of the dancers, men and women, the refrain. It was a graceful musical diversion for a festival, a winter evening, or a summer afternoon; and typical of its age in that it was inseparable from its musical accompaniment. The *fabliau* is another example, wittier, more polished than the popular prose "merry tale." The longer comic beast fable or poem—the ironic, satiric counterpart of the chivalric romance, as in the cycle of stories concerned with Reynard the Fox—is a third. More important, often longer still, and most characteristic is the allegorical poem, such as the *Romance of the Rose,* exploring the nature of love and of many other philosophical matters, by means of a story whose characters are personifications of the qualities of a lover and his mistress, of Nature herself, of Fortune, and of the other abstractions which preside over a systematic view of human life.

At the same time as these French poetic forms and modes of thought were passing into currency in England, a huge body of prose was being produced, particularly in the field of moral instruction and exhortation—treatises, sermons, meditations. A vast increase in these works came with the thirteenth-century rise of the friars, the Mendicant Orders, vowed to poverty. Prayer, penance, and (for the Dominicans) the preaching of God's word was their major obligation; and the volume of their (and others') sermons continues to expand throughout the Middle Ages.

Another form that seems to have developed earlier in France than in England was the religious drama, which emerged into vigorous life in northern provincial centers of England—York, Wakefield, Coventry and Chester—in the fourteenth century. The drama was the vehicle of bourgeois piety and religious instruction in a half-secular context. It displayed the whole scheme of salvation, from the Creation and the Fall of Man to the Resurrection and the Harrowing of Hell, its production being under the control of the tradesmen's guilds and the solemnity of its message tempered with the beginnings of dramatic comedy. Later still, dramatized moral instruction was presented in morality plays.

When French literary genres passed into English they underwent changes of various kinds. Romances, for example, tended to be shorn of their speculative and spiritualized dimensions, and the Arthurian stories of *Sir Gawain and the Green Knight* or Malory's *Morte Darthur* are more down-to-earth than their French counterparts.

Some fourteenth-century English works have no French equivalent. One is *Piers Plowman,* which preserves the older English verse technique of the alliterative long line and conducts its investigation of the nature of goodness and of the ordering of a truly Christian society in such a way as to leave no room for doubt in the reader's mind that this is what the poem is really about. We can be sure of this, as we cannot be quite sure what the author of *Sir Gawain and the Green Knight* intended us to take from his poem.

Even taking into account exceptions like *Piers Plowman* and allowing for the changes wrought by English variations on originally French forms and themes, English medieval literature is strongly tinctured with French. It is the measure of Chaucer's greatness that he has assimilated the French tradition and made it his own. His shorter lyrics can deal with the values of "courtly love" seriously or satirically; his *Troilus and Criseyde,* the greatest romance in our language, investigates the experience of love in depth and at length; his *Book of the Duchess, Parliament of Fowls,* and *House of Fame* show his self-assurance in handling the allegorical vision; his Franklin's Tale is a perfectly balanced work of art in its transformation of the fairy "matter of Britain" into an exploration of love and its obligations; his Miller's Tale is a perfectly judged *fabliau;* his Pardoner's Tale and Nun's Priest's Tale are literary transformations of sermons, exactly adjusted to the characters of their tellers. The Nun's Priest's Tale holds in equilibrium the animal-story-for-moral-instruction of the *Bestiary,* the sermon, and the rhetorical mode, in a magnificently managed parody of genres and of manner.

At the other end of the scale of sophistication are some of the short lyrics of moral and religious instruction. These, and their less direct and simple companions in the lyric genre, emphasize the fact that by far the largest part of what was written during the Middle Ages was intended for instruction, direct or indirect. This is true of all medieval fiction—or at least of most of it:

> St. Paul saith that all that written is
> To our doctrine it is ywrit, iwis . . .

If a fourteenth-century Englishman had been asked to defend himself against the old Platonic or the Christian-ascetic charge leveled at the artist—that he made fictions that were lies—he might have replied (as one in fact did) that St. Paul did not mean that everything that is written for our "doctrine" (teaching) is or need be true. He meant that, if we take it aright, everything that is written can give us useful instruction. If what we feign in our fictions has some signification and is not merely empty, then it is not a lie but indeed a figure of the truth.

The same Englishman would not have doubted that if his treatise or his fiction was to be fully effective it ought to be constructed with true rhetorical decorum, employing the tropes—the figures of thought and of speech inherited by medieval authors from the classics—to bring home story and lesson with all its force. He would have been especially concerned that his language should be rich and strong enough to support the weight of the doctrine and the richness of the effect that he wished it to carry. It would never have occurred to him to speak of "mere rhetoric" or "mere ornament." Only the greatest poet of the English Middle Ages, Chaucer himself, can afford to demonstrate his independence of a tradition he respects.

The generations following Chaucer's saw an increasing concern with richness of diction and—at its best as in the work of the "Scottish Chaucerians"—an exuberance of rhetoric that were to help the English language toward its triumph in the sixteenth century. Didactic and exemplary verse and prose flourished as perhaps never before during the reign of the pious Henry VI (1422–61). In the turbulent period of the Wars of the Roses (1455–85), when the throne of England was being battled for—the twilight of the Middle Ages—two literary figures stand out: the reprobate knight, Sir Thomas Malory, author of the *Morte Darthur,* and the thriving bourgeois, William Caxton.

Caxton not only brought printing to England but moreover was Malory's first printer. Both were deeply concerned with the values of an aristocratic, chivalric social system that was already in decline. For a hundred years the English archer had displaced the mounted knight as the architect of England's military strength. The commercial and professional men of the cities were thrusting themselves forward to form the beginnings of the English urban middle class, while the smaller landowners were also rising in power and wealth. Malory chose to write of the legendary, knightly King Arthur and his followers, providing the last medieval expression of the myth that was to serve the Tudor dynasty (1485–1603, founded by Henry VII) so well and to reach its finest expression in Edmund Spenser's *Faerie Queene*. Caxton, too, concerned himself with chivalric codes and practices, but still more with the provision of entertaining and edifying literature in a strengthened, refined, and uniform English. The printing press made more copies of a given work available to more people than had ever before been possible: a whole culture changed with the end of the era of the hand-produced book. The process by which the writer's audience became a reading, rather than a read-to, public had begun.

VERSIFICATION

The reader coming to Old and Middle English poetry for the first time will find a great deal that is unfamiliar and disconcerting in its verse techniques. He has been led, by his reading in the verse of the sixteenth to the twentieth century, to expect that poetry will be written in a regular series of lines, rhyming or not rhyming, with regularly alternating stresses and a strict attention to form. Modern free-verse techniques will have done something to prepare him for what he will find in this selection from poets who wrote before Chaucer, and from two of Chaucer's contemporaries; yet the close-knit accentual patterns of Old English verse are much firmer and stricter in their requirements than the modifications of such patterns that have been used by modern poets.

The Old English poets built their poems of single-line units of accentual verse, each single line divided at its center by a pause or caesura. Rhyme, either to link two half-lines or to hold together single lines in couplets, stanzaic forms, or verse paragraphs, is almost unknown among them. Instead of rhyme they developed alliteration—that is, the choice of words beginning with the same sound.

A song I sing   of sorrow unceasing

is a translation of one typical line in an Old English poem. Such a line contains four main stresses, two on either side of the caesura, here marked by a space. The line is welded into a unit by the fact that both stressed words of the first half begin with the same sound as the first stress of the second half. Further, the same sound is picked up again in the second element of the second stressed word of the second half-line.

This is only one of the line patterns used by Old English poets. The poet had the further option that any vowel could alliterate with any other vowel. But he was strictly limited as to the number of the patterns of half-line that he could employ, by the number of unstressed syllables that he was allowed and by the patterns in which they might be placed, and by other prescriptions.

The metrical effect of Old English poetry is of a disciplined series of dignified (though not slow-moving), single utterances in a regular and very marked rhythm, taut and carefully timed. Heightened and pointed by being sung or chanted to the accompaniment of a harp, Old English verse must have achieved in recitation—for it was predominantly oral in character, like most vernacular poetry written throughout the Middle Ages—a tone equal to that of the best of its kind.

After the Norman Conquest, French literary models came to supplant the older English tradition of unrhymed alliterative verse. The chief differences between the two were that French verse employed rhyme, and later stanza form, and was written in a pattern of metrical feet—that is, with alternating stressed and unstressed syllables. But the older tradition was not immediately and entirely supplanted by the new. What happened was that its patterns of alliteration became looser and more permissive of extra syllables and more accents to the line. Rhyme is still not employed, though some poets combine the rhymed and the alliterative techniques and there is still a strongly marked caesura in the middle of each line. To either side of the break there are deviations and license. Often, the line consists of the basic four stresses, but as often it has five or six or even more. The alliteration may be the bare minimum—one stress in each half-line; or it may run through almost every stress in the line. There are no norms for the number of unstressed syllables, so that short lines like

> And had leave to lie   all their life after

may occur next to lines like

> To each a tale that they told   their tongue was tempered to lie.

The effect of control that a poet such as Langland can give the alliterative measure is exceptional—and even Langland slips into formlessness from time to time. When Langland came to use the alliterative meter it was already out of fashion: it was his achievement to give it new life. The same may be said of the poet of *Sir Gawain and the Green Knight,* also writing in a center of provincial culture remote from the capital and, as far as can be told, making a conscious effort to revive the form. In his other poems the *Gawain* poet uses rhyme; and even in *Sir Gawain* he organizes the poem into unrhymed blocks, each of them marked off and in a sense summed up by the "bob" (a two- or three-syllable half-line) rhyming with one of the rhymes of the four-line "wheel" that follows it. So he gives an impression of a tighter and more organized form to his poem, especially since these little comments form a kind of synopsis-commentary to the whole. Rhetorically as well as metrically he holds his poem together in the large unit, however free his treatment of the single alliterating line.

Both before and after Chaucer there is much rhymed verse in Middle English in which the meter is irregular and shambling and seemingly constructed after no metrical principle except a rough approximation to an uneven rhythm. But there is a good deal of sophistication in stanzaic form; and even a poem that appears to be largely imitating the rhythms of common speech (such as the *Second Shepherd's Play*), keeps a firm and regular stanza. But one cannot have the same expectation of disciplined variety in regularity that is to become the norm in the sixteenth century, nor the feeling of deliberate and rhetorically controlled irregularity that one has from John Skelton—as will be illustrated later in this volume.

When one comes to Chaucer's verse, however, the situation changes. There were, in his day, poets who could handle with entire competence the meters and stanzaic forms of the French tradition, even the very forms and meters that Chaucer uses. But none have his variety, whether in the octosyllabic couplets (already naturalized in English) that he adopted from his French models; or the lyric forms also taken over from French; or the various stanzaic patterns, especially the rhyme royal (iambic pentameters, rhyming *ababbcc* in a seven-line stanza) of *Troilus and Criseyde* and the *Parliament of Fowls*. Chaucer's greatest achievement was with a verse form that he may have introduced into England and certainly naturalized there—the heroic couplet in which most of the *Canterbury Tales* are written. To state that this basic unit consists of ten- or eleven-syllable iambic pentameters rhyming in twos

> In Flaundres whilom was a compaignye
> Of yonge folk that haunteden folye . . .

gives no notion of the variations, the force, and the richness Chaucer imparts to it. He is able to give an effect of even greater metrical fluidity and variety than if he were using a stanzaic form, maintaining the metrical units of line and couplet while building the large unit of sentence and paragraph from it, playing off sentence structure against the rhythm of the verse. The rhythms of speech provide a constant counterpoint to the accentuation of the meter, the verse running in the smooth, rising rhythm of the iambic pentameter, always varied, never monotonous. It is incomparable poetry for reading aloud.

Old English Poetry

Beowulf

The finest surviving long poem in Old English has come down to us in a single manuscript, now MS. Cotton Vitellius A.XV in the British Museum, transcribed in the West Saxon dialect at the end of the tenth century, at least two centuries after its composition. We still do not know the name of its author, and it was not given the title *Beowulf* until 1805 and not printed until 1815.

We need not be surprised at this. Almost all Old English poetry is untitled and anonymous: we know the names of only two poets whose work survives—Cædmon and Cynewulf, and of Cædmon's poetry we possess only the few lines presented at the head of the present selection. Almost all Old English poems survive in a single manuscript, often in a copy that includes other texts composed at an earlier or a later date. Most of these manuscripts were written down in the West Saxon dialect at about the end of the tenth century, when the full force of the monastic revival had made itself felt and the literary culture of England had reached its high point.

It is not clear just how far the fact that most of the Old English poetry we possess was transcribed about this time and in this dialect reflects a conscious program aimed at preserving, in a written "literary standard" language, what was thought to be best. We know that *Beowulf* was admired in the ninth century, by King Alfred among others, and that poets then used it to strengthen their own work. The author of *The Battle of Maldon,* at the end of the tenth century, borrowed from *Beowulf,* and an anonymous sermon-writer used the description of Grendel's mere.

Nor is it clear how much Old English poetry, for want of such copying down, has been lost. It is generally assumed that a great deal has perished without trace, leaving a remainder of a scant 30,000 lines—about the length of some single poems of a few centuries later. There must have been other manuscripts of many, if not all, of the poems, often earlier and in other dialects.

We possess *Beowulf* only because the unique manuscript survived the fire of 1731, which destroyed or damaged much of the remarkable library of Sir Robert Cotton (1571–1631), in which the *Beowulf* manuscript then was. But the scorching that it then received caused its edges to crumble, so that some of the text was already lost when the Icelandic scholar G. J. Thorkelin came to make the transcriptions which were completed in 1787. All modern editions of the poem use Thorkelin's transcripts to reconstruct, as far as possible, the words and letters that are missing from the manuscript as it is today. The text is divided into forty-three fitts or sections, with line-endings and, less frequently, half-line endings, indicated by punctuation. The arrangement of the text as verse is the work of modern editors.

Scholars agree that the Cotton manuscript of *Beowulf* does not represent the first occasion on which the poem was written down. Its reputation suggests that there must have been earlier manuscripts, perhaps transcribed in West Mercia, the modern West Midlands, or further north, in Northumbria, where the poem may well have been composed. We do not know the date of the first of these, though archaic verbal forms suggest that a written version existed by the middle of the eighth century.

No evidence so far, however, is conclusive for date and place of composition. Some have put the composition earlier than the eighth century, but most agree that the Christian coloring of the diction and of some of the subject matter of the poem reflects an audience and a poet to whom Christianity and the usages of the church have been familiar long and thoroughly enough for the one to use and the other to catch allusions to the Bible and Christian literature—to Cain, to the giants, to the Devil as the "old enemy" or the "enemy of mankind." This can hardly have been before the eighth century. By 664, the date of the Synod of Whitby, at which important differences between the Celtic church and the Roman church in England were settled, Christianity was the dominant religion in the country—but thirty years later bishops still found it necessary to prescribe penance for those who sacrificed to devils (i.e. the Germanic pagan gods). Moreover, the poem can hardly be earlier than the work of the Northumbrian poet Cædmon, which must have been dictated between 658 and 680 and which established many of the modes of Christian heroic poetry. It may be of a specific poem by Cædmon that the *Beowulf* poet is thinking when he makes Hrothgar's *scop* or minstrel sing of the Creation of the World. Some scholars feel that *Beowulf* would fit best the Christian culture of Northumbria at this time, the golden age of the Venerable Bede (c. 673–735), one of the greatest European scholars of the early Middle Ages. This was the civilization that produced the superb Lindisfarne Gospels, now in the British Museum (Fig. 5), and the Northumbrian crosses of Ruthwell (Fig. 23) and Bewcastle. Such monuments are Christian in a sense in which *Beowulf* is not: a fairer comparison with the poem is the whalebone box in the British Museum known as the Franks Casket—a more provincial work, on which scenes from Germanic legend mingle with Christian scenes: the Germanic smith of the gods, Weland, and the Adoration of the Magi side by side (Fig. 22).

Other scholars, now in the majority, argue for a West Mercian origin for the poem, which may imply a date sometime in the eighth century. Strong support for West Mercia as *Beowulf*'s place of composition comes from the supposition that the poem was written for the court of Offa the Great, king of Mercia from 757 to 796. This Offa's ancestor, Offa the Angle, is especially praised by the *Beowulf* poet in an episode whose structural function seems to be to commend Queen Hygd, Hygelac's consort, by comparing her with the cruel queen of the earlier Offa.

Beowulf, the longest surviving Old English poem, is a somber masterpiece, the first great English work in the oral, primary epic mode. English as it is in language, and written in English as it must have been, it makes mention only twice, or perhaps three times, of an Englishman. It must have been written when English and Scandinavian events were of enough mutual interest for an English audience to grasp their implications, perhaps a time when the Germanic tribes still retained a consciousness of common origins and history. Scholars agree that, as far as can be told from other evidence, including the archaeological, the *Beowulf* poet has got his Swedish history—for example—right. English-Scandinavian relations must still have been close in the eighth century: we find at Sutton Hoo, dating from about 670, a mixture of English and Scandinavian cultures in both the manner of the burial and the goods in the burial mounds.

The hero of the poem is a Geat, a prominent member of a tribe known by that name from only a few other sources, but said by the poet to be ancient and powerful. Earlier scholarship identified the Geats with the Jutes (whose name in Old English was Eotan), who came either from Jutland or from the country east of the Lower Rhine. Modern opinion more strongly favors their being the Gautar, who seem to have lived in what is now southern Sweden. It is also possible that they are the Getae, believed in late classical and medieval times to inhabit southern Scandinavia, a land as remote and forbidding as Scythia, thought to have been their original home. These Getae, founding fathers of the Germanic nations as legend made them out, would be a fitting people to be the heroes of a poem set in a remote and indefinite Germanic heroic past. (See map, Fig. 2.)

Identification cannot be pressed too far nor historical consistency demanded in a poem which relies so much on indirectness and allusion, on the atmosphere of far away and long ago, shaded, deliberately darkened, and misty—a time when men still fought the evil creatures of the dark which they believed to threaten and beset them hard. An English poet is writing about the common heroic past of the Germanic race: the tribes who take part in the action are out there somewhere, distant in time and space. This is an essential assumption of the poet's art.

Nevertheless, a kind of historical and geographical frame for *Beowulf* clearly exists. The Danes, neighbors of the Geats, inhabit the island which is now Zealand: that is historical fact. The Geats come to their aid, led by Beowulf, from what is now southeast Sweden. North of the Geats are the Swedes and other tribes—again historical fact. South of the Danes, on the European mainland, are the Heathobards, sworn enemies, while farther to the west, at the extreme edge of the Merovingian domain, in Frisia, are the Hetware, the Atuarii, raided by Hygelac the Geat, who finds defeat and death among them.

This raid is the one piece of hard history in *Beowulf*. According to Frankish historians such as Gregory of Tours (c. 540–594), one Chlochilaicus was killed on such a raid in about 520. But the mode of the poem is such that this may mean that all Hygelac's doings—even much of the poem's action—have a historical basis, or it may not: we cannot tell. We can safely say that Grendel and his dam are fabulous monsters of the night—and so is the dragon, though sober historical sources record a dragon in England as late as the end of the eighth century, and men went on believing in the physical existence of such creatures for many centuries after. The supernatural elements might belong to almost any age. The incidents of the digressions, elliptically and allusively told, clearly cannot all be referred to the same limited portion of time. If we ask the date of the events of *Beowulf,* rather than the date at which the poem was composed, the best answer is that some belong to the early sixth century and others are probably older, while others again are fabulous. To expect a more exact answer is as pointless as to try to fix the direction and distance of Beowulf's swimming match with Breca, or how many suits of armor Beowulf actually carried as he swam home after the fatal conclusion of Hygelac's raid. We are dealing with a poem, not a piece of history.

Nevertheless, the poem embodies and takes as the basis of its characters' actions a social system and a set of behavioral assumptions which were common to the Germanic peoples of history. These were set out in their earliest, simplest, and most clearly recorded form by the first-century Roman historian Tacitus, in his *Germania*. These Germans, Tacitus says, are a warrior race, fierce and cruel, setting courage above all the other virtues, finding their deepest shame in cowardice, ready to use any end to gain the victory: "To retreat, provided that you return to the attack, is thought to be cunning, not cowardly." They choose their leaders for courage and demand that they continue to set a courageous example. They have a profound belief in Fate and in casting lots to foresee the future. Their warlike character is seen in the fact that all come to their assemblies and transact their business fully armed—and a young men enters manhood when he is publicly equipped (after due proof of valor), with spear and shield. Young and old group themselves round the chief as his retinue, the companions or *comitatus*. Their numbers and their bravery lend him power. He holds their allegiance by courage and generosity: his keenest disgrace is to be outdone by retainer or enemy. The companions, having sworn him allegiance, must not fall short: they must die on the battlefield rather than leave it—especially once the chieftain is killed (cf. the praise of Wiglaf in *Beowulf* and the close of *The Battle of Maldon*). "The chieftain battles for victory, the companions fight for their chief," Tacitus goes on. If the young men find no fighting at home, they seek it abroad, for they have no taste for peace. They are grasping and demanding, which encourages war and plunder to maintain the supply of what they value—horses, arms and armor, jewelry, collars. They live not in cities, but in scattered houses, each house a community. Monogamous, reverencing their women for the gift of holiness and prophecy they find in them, the men bring the dowry. Women bring men weapons, and their exchange of gifts symbolizes the holiest of bonds, the sharing of burdens. Germanic reverence for women is mirrored in their recognition of an especially close tie between a man and his sister's son—a tie as close as that between father and son.

Everyone is bound to continue the feuds and the friendships of his father and his family. Feuds are often concluded by payment of tribute, and even murder can be paid for, in money and goods (*wergild*), so that—for a time—the dishonor is wiped out.

The Germans love to feast and entertain, holding it sinful to turn a man from the door. If a host cannot continue to give the visitor the hospitality he deserves, he sends him on to another. Drinking bouts of a day and a night are commonplace and the quarrels they engender are settled by blows. Banquets have peaceful, ceremonial functions, too: they are the setting to discuss truces, form marriage alliances, make new chiefs, decide for peace or war. Feasts are chosen as a time for making such decisions because the heart is then open and exalted. At these feasts a sort of "juice extracted from barley or grain" washes down plain food: there is no excess in their eating. Their addiction to gambling may lead them to gamble away their freedom; if this happens, they go uncomplainingly into slavery, as a point of "honor." Slaves are agricultural serfs rather than household or body servants, and even when freed seldom rise to positions of influence. Usury is unknown. The land is tilled communally and shares in it are allotted according to rank.

Death is attended by no pomp, though their great men are cremated, after the pagan usage, on a pyre on which arms and armor, and sometimes also horses, are placed. Over the body is raised a barrow, a high mound of earth. Excessive mourning is frowned on: women are permitted to express their grief, but men hide it in their hearts.

Physically, these men are hardy, tough and trained, savage and vigorous, placing their trust in courage, the one thing they see as sure, though like all that is mortal, it is subject to fortune and chance. Some are hardy, sea-going people, their ships, oar-propelled, having a prow at each end for easier putting into land. Some tribes wear the images of boars for protection (Fig. 20).

Tacitus is writing of the Germanic tribes of the end of the first century A.D., three hundred and fifty years before some of them migrated to England, nearly five hundred before Pope Gregory the Great sent St. Augustine of Canterbury to bring Roman Christianity to the country, nearly six hundred before it can be said that England was Christian, and perhaps a little more before *Beowulf* was written down. Nevertheless, Tacitus tells us much about the world of *Beowulf* and of heroic poetry in general. His picture of warrior societies close-knit in small units by the ties of blood and of mutual duty between lord and retainer, finding in the ethos of the *comitatus* the most effective of social bonds and in courage the only possible stance in response to the harsh and inescapable decrees of fate and the duties of life—this picture is closely relevant to the poem. The virtues of such a society, like its vices, are fierce and combative. There is dignity, but it is martial dignity: renown can be won in battle and nowhere else. Age is more poignant in that it lessens appetite for battle and chances of success in it. Ancestry counts for much, for this is an aristocratic society, but each generation must confirm by its own courage the family's title to consideration.

This was the society to which Roman Christianity came with the arrival of St. Augustine in England in 597. The progress of the new religion was sporadic. Areas like Essex were notably slow to accept conversion, and there especially pagan practices and much of the pagan flavor of everyday life must have long remained. *Beowulf,* at least in the form in which we have it, reflects the usages of a pagan society of an indeterminate period before the Christian conversion and perhaps a time near the migration of the Angles, Saxons, and Jutes to England about the middle of the fifth century, with later accretions. The poet, almost certainly a Christian, is perhaps, like a less sophisticated Virgil, recalling to his people a past which is heroic but legendary, indeterminate, undifferentiated, and therefore ever present.

The poet's allusive, apparently unstructured technique—regular in oral poetry—seems to expect an audience conversant with its own legendary past, with details of this and other stories. He is touching on the known to awaken resonances which will enhance what he is saying. The digressions concerning the feud between Danes and Heathobards, the Fight at Finnsburg, Hygelac's fatal expedition against the Frisians and the Hetware, the story of Sigemund and the dragon, in addition to the story of Offa and his cruel queen—are all intended not to stop the march of the narrative but to reinforce its episodic, disjointed progress. The poet counts on his audience to apply the associations of these to the other events of the poem. All tragic in their outcome, they prepare the hearers, singly and cumulatively, for the tragic outcome, in human terms, of *Beowulf*. The allusions are planted with skill to bring home the transitoriness of human glory and human life, the forward seeping of the menacing dark. At the height of exultation, the poet will slip in the hint of deadliness that lurks in all actions—often in an understatement that strikes us as flat or banal, but achieves its strong effect from the narrowness of its ironic range. Hrothgar's high hall, Heorot, glitters with gold—but its future destruction in the Heathobard feud is foretold within the first hundred lines of the poem and recalled seven hundred lines later. Hrothgar's brother, Hrothulf, who will be the betrayer of his blood, breaker of loyalty, instigator of civil war in Denmark, usurper, sits enthroned in Heorot with Hrothgar—but an allusion to his future treachery will be taken up later by Queen Wealhtheow's poignant expression of trust and confidence in her brother-in-law. These are two of the lesser digressions. The greater episodes operate in the same way. Hygelac's piracy is frequently referred to after its first mention about a third of the way through the poem.

On that first occasion, a pang of mortality strikes Beowulf as he looks at the splendid neck-ring he has been given by Hrothgar as part of his reward for victory over Grendel. It reminds him of the magic necklace of the fire dwarfs which Hygelac took with him on his last raid. Later, just before Beowulf's own fatal last encounter with the dragon, his own behavior at the time of the raid is recounted—his superhuman feat of swimming back with thirty suits of armor, his punctilious refusal of the throne, his protection of Hygelac's widowed queen and of the rightful heir, the young Heardred, as well as his own final ascent of the throne when Heardred had been killed in fighting against the Swedes. He has fulfilled all that a hero should do—and the audience is intended to have in mind at this moment that heroic as he has been, magnanimous and good, especially by contrast with Hrothulf's behavior in a similar situation, he has now grown old and his end is near. Nor is it only his destruction that the audience is aware to be looming, but the annihilation of the whole Geatish race at the hands of the Swedes, once Beowulf, the protector hero of the Geats, has been taken from them. The poet manages to deal even-handed justice to Beowulf the hero and Beowulf the mortal, exalting him only to deepen the tragedy.

So, too, he throws into relief by example and counter-example the qualities of spirit and action in which the heroic society found its fulfillment, the duties that it enjoined upon its members. The lay that the *scop* (bard) sings in Heorot of the Fight at Finnsburg and the story of the strife between Danes and Heathobards mirror the overriding necessity for vengeance to be taken by a member of the *comitatus* for the killing of the lord—a necessity that justifies dissemblance and treachery, as it overrides any attempt to compose the feud. The power of social obligation is too strong for single human instance: strife and violence, restrained for a time by material or spiritual generosity, hasten the death which is every man's lot. The details of these two stories parallel each other, foreshadowing the strife between Geats and Swedes with its fatal outcome.

These digressions, by which the poet binds his poem together, throwing the reference forward and backward, seem to modern taste to slow the pace. Meditative, moralizing passages from the poet himself, or from such characters as Hrothgar, also deepen the elegiac tone. The language—formalized, traditional, often arranged in elaborately parallel double statement—and the steady dignity of the style keep the movement of the poem deliberate and exalted. To this effect the mode of performance—chanting aloud to the accompaniment of a stringed instrument—must have greatly contributed.

The poetic vocabulary of *Beowulf* is remarkable for the large number of words it contains of the same or very similar meaning—words for "warrior," for example—which could be brought into play according to the demands of expressing a precise meaning or to the more mechanical needs of rhythm and alliteration. Compound nouns and adjectives are also plentiful and are found, like many of the simple words, only in poetry, the more exalted medium than prose: rain-hard, shower-hard, enmity-hard, fire-hard, iron-hard; ring-bestower, battle-flasher (for sword) are examples. They are one way in which the poet sustains the promise of a performance arresting and rich made with the opening word of his poem: "Hwæt!", "Lo!", the formulaic call to silence and attention. Still more characteristic and important are the condensed metaphors (Old English is not rich in the conventional metaphor or simile and has no equivalent of the extended Homeric simile) known as *kennings* (an Old Norse word).

The stateliness of the language, its tonal resources—we must always imagine it as it would have sounded—enhance and justify the slowness of the action and drive home the realization that *Beowulf* is essentially a poem of praise, elegiac only because its hero is human. Its mode is the superlative. Essentially it is a poem in praise of earthly life and the glory that a man may win in it by courage, and magnanimity—*lof* (reputation) is one of its key words—even as he realizes that life is short, passing, and often bitter.

There is no trace of any confidence in a greater triumph, in a life after death, such as raises even the simplest narratives of the passions of saints to a kind of epic level and is characteristic of the literature of Christian heroism. Nevertheless, scholarly opinion agrees to call *Beowulf* a Christian poem in that it was written by a Christian and many parts of it would be intelligible only to a Christian audience—particularly its Christian moralizing and many of its allusions. But given the relatively short time that had elapsed since Christianity had come to Britain, and given the firm structure of social institutions and ethical and religious assumptions already existing, we could hardly expect that a heroic poem of such a time would be permeated with the spirit of the New Testament. *Beowulf* is not a poem of Grace, but of the Law: its morality is nearer that of the Old Testament, partly perhaps because of direct influence, partly owing to a joint participation in the epic genre. All the biblical references that it contains are to the Old Testament. It is the power and glory of God the Creator that move the poet and his characters to joy in the Creation or to at least sporadic recognition of his will as equivalent to Fate, just as they are moved to fear of judgment, to certainty that the souls of giants and monsters, Grendel and his dam, will fall to Hell and the Devil. while those of believers will go to God. The bloodthirsty monster Grendel is made the descendant of Cain, the first murderer, and the sword which Beowulf catches up to kill Grendel's mother has its blade decorated with the destruction of the Old Testament giants by the Flood. None of these allusions, nor even the moralizing sermon of Hrothgar, give us any reason to suppose that the poet thought of Beowulf as passing to immortality in a Christian Heaven.

Beowulf is a tragedy, as it must be: a gigantic elegy for its hero in which the moments of glory serve only to emphasize the completeness and inevitability of his end. In its broadest dimension, it is a tragedy of the human predicament: more narrowly, of the warrior's situation. A Germanic hero's fulfillment is not reached in victory alone, but in unflinching courage in all circumstances, most of all when the odds—adversaries, conditions, age, and the rest—are stacked against him and he must die. A glorious death is the only fitting close to a glorious life. We are meant to feel the contrast between Hrothgar, a good king, generous and firm, but now old and lacking the true heroic spirit which would send him out to battle with this enemy of his land (at the beginning of the poem), and Beowulf, Hrothgar's rescuer, who dies in his moment of triumph over the enemy of his people, at the poem's end. The hero knows that his fate has long been decided and he knows it at every moment of his life, with every successive battle. He can only trust, as encounter follows encounter, that his doom is not yet written and that therefore his courage will suffice for one more occasion. These occasions, with the shadow of the human condition lengthening as the hero passes from fierce and aggressive youth to fierce and unyielding old age, are the stuff of the poem.

The poet who produced *Beowulf* and the audience which heard it recited were aristocratic and of considerable literary and artistic cultivation. Of their standard of material culture, the frequent reference to splendor of ornament is witness enough, even if we did not have from the poem's period the masterpieces of Northumbrian stone sculpture and manuscript illumination (Figs. 23, 5), the earlier jewelry and other objects from Sutton Hoo (Figs. 9, 11, 13–17, 19), and the richly decorated metal work of other centers (Figs. 18, 21). We can get some idea, too, of what the musical instrument ment to which the poem was later recited probably looked like—from manuscripts (Fig. 10) and from the present reconstruction of the Sutton Hoo instrument (Fig. 11). Some notion of the arms and armor of the period 650–1050 can be got from surviving fragments and from manuscripts (Figs. 8, 9, 18–21).

Of the level of literary culture little need be added to what has already been said in the General Introduction. Poet and audience may well have known Virgil's *Aeneid* and there are many allusions which would be lost on those unfamiliar with the writings of the Fathers of the Church and the Bible itself. The audience that enjoyed *Beowulf* must have had a considerable body of heroic verse to compare with it, as well as a body of other verse of great skill in the handling of feeling and incident, of the formal, exalted, "distanced" language and the narrow though varied metrical range which are the media of Old English poetry.

The translation used here is by Charles W. Kennedy, and appears below as it was first published in 1940, with the exception of the numbering of lines. The line numbers are not those of the original poem but serve merely as a guide.

GENEALOGICAL TABLES

I. The Danes (Scyldings; East-, South-, Spear-Danes; Honor-, Victor-Scyldings; Ingwines)

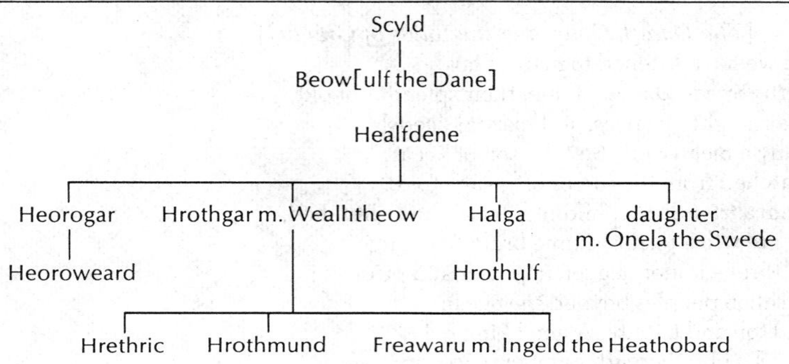

II. The Geats (Weders, Sea-Geats; Hrethlings)

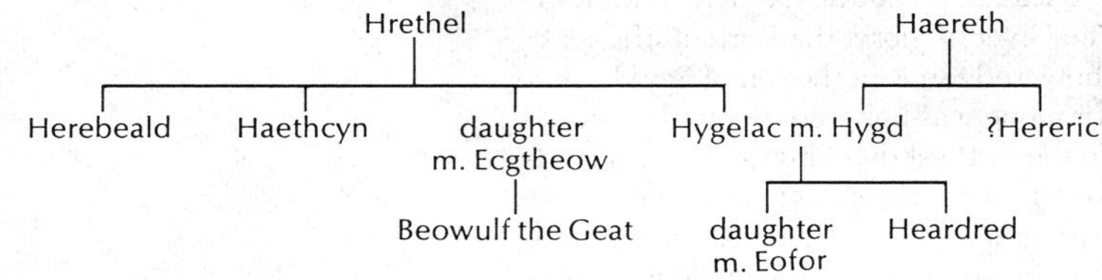

III. The Half-Danes and The Frisians

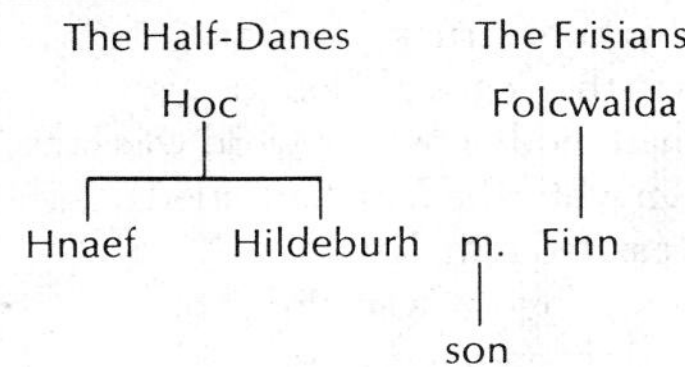

IV. The Heathobards

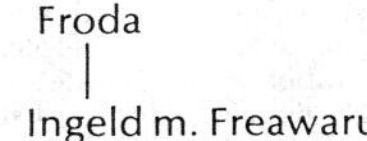

V. The Swedes (Scylfings; Battle-Scylfings)

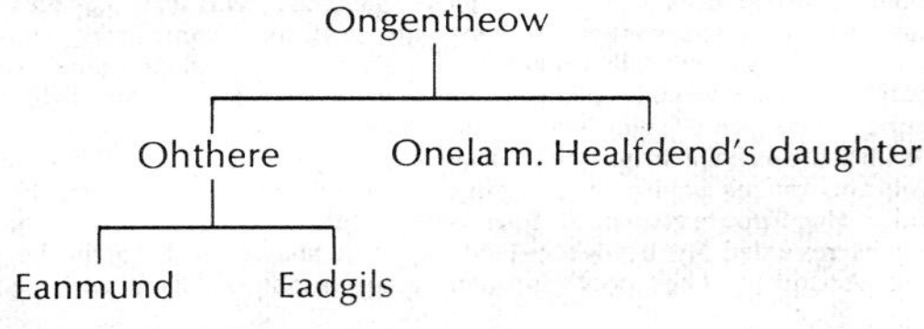

Beowulf

[*The Danish Court and the Raids of Grendel*]

Lo! we have listened to many a lay
Of the Spear-Danes'° fame, their splendor of old,
Their mighty princes, and martial deeds!
Many a mead-hall° Scyld,° son of Sceaf,
Snatched from the forces of savage foes.
From a friendless foundling, feeble and wretched,
He grew to a terror as time brought change.
He throve under heaven in power and pride
Till alien peoples beyond the ocean
Paid toll and tribute. A good king he!
To him thereafter an heir was born,
A son of his house, whom God had given
As stay to the people; God saw the distress
The leaderless nation had long endured.
The Giver of glory, the Lord of life,
Showered fame on the son of Scyld;
His name was honored, Beowulf° known,
To the farthest dwellings in Danish lands.
So must a young man strive for good
With gracious gifts from his father's store,
That in later seasons, if war shall scourge,
A willing people may serve him well.°
'Tis by earning honor a man must rise
In every state. Then his hour struck,
And Scyld passed on to the peace of God.
As their leader had bidden, whose word was law
In the Scylding° realm which he long had ruled,
His loving comrades carried him down
To the shore of ocean; a ring-prowed ship,°
Straining at anchor and sheeted with ice,

Spear-Danes The Danes are given various epithets in the course of the poem—perhaps partly to help out alliteration, partly as an aid to characterization—e.g. Bright-, Half-, Ring-, Spear-, North-, East-, South- and West-Danes.
mead-hall rather "mead-bench," i.e. he conquered other tribes and took away the symbol of the independence of the chief, the high bench in the hall from which he dispensed gifts and justice
Scyld The arrival and departure of the mysterious Scyld, eponymous hero of the Danes (Scyldings: men of the shield, sons of Scyld), form a prologue to the poem, and Scyld's life is perhaps intended to be a parallel to the career of Beowulf in capsule form. Scyld is well known in Scandinavian tradition: the poet's account of how he came, young, weak, and friendless to the coast of Denmark and founded a mighty dynasty is, however, unique and makes Scyld into a figure frequent in folktale: the apparently poor foundling, whose royalty is revealed by his later deeds (cf. Theseus and Arthur). The poet is also planting at the beginning a sense of the dignity and antiquity of the Danish race, drawing out, by suggestion, its genealogies and at the same time implying that this great and ancient people, in all its strength and power, will be found to be helpless against the attacks of the monster Grendel, against whom only the greater hero from outside, Beowulf, can deliver Hrothgar and his Danes. Beowulf's stature is thus magnified.
Beowulf not Beowulf the Geat, who is the hero of the poem, but a Danish king whom most now agree to call Beow or Beo, the Dane, grandfather of Hrothgar
So . . . well (ll. 19–22) the first of the poet's moralizing comments, pauses in the motion of the poem, statements of the heroic virtues which its action exemplifies
Scylding Danish
ring-prowed ship It is not quite certain what "ring-prowed" means. Ships were broad, with a tall prow and stern, and of shallow draft, so that they could easily be beached and dragged up on land (Fig. 12).

Rode in the harbor, a prince's pride.
Therein they laid him, their well-loved lord,
Their ring-bestower, in the ship's embrace,°
The mighty prince at the foot of the mast
Amid much treasure and many a gem
From far-off lands. No lordlier ship
Have I ever heard of, with weapons heaped,
With battle-armor, with bills and byrnies.°
On the ruler's breast lay a royal treasure
As the ship put out on the unknown deep.
With no less adornment they dressed him round,
Or gift of treasure, than once they gave
Who launched him first on the lonely sea
While still but a child. A golden standard
They raised above him, high over head,
Let the wave take him on trackless seas.
Mournful their mood and heavy their hearts;
Nor wise man nor warrior knows for a truth
Unto what haven that cargo came.
　　Then Beowulf ruled o'er the Scylding realm,
Beloved and famous, for many a year—
The prince, his father, had passed away—
Till, firm in wisdom and fierce in war,
The mighty Healfdene held the reign,
Ruled, while he lived, the lordly Scyldings.
Four sons and daughters were seed of his line,
Heorogar and Hrothgar, leaders of hosts,
And Halga, the good. I have also heard
A daughter was Onela's consort° and queen,
The fair bed-mate of the Battle-Scylfing.
　　To Hrothgar was granted glory in war,
Success in battle; retainers bold
Obeyed him gladly; his band increased
To a mighty host. Then his mind was moved
To have men fashion a high-built hall,
A mightier mead-hall than man had known,
Wherein to portion to old and young
All goodly treasure that God had given,
Save only the folk-land,° and lives of men.°

ship's embrace The sea burial of Scyld reflects earlier pagan Scandinavian practice, but by the time *Beowulf* was written ship burials on land, with the dead chieftain surrounded by rich possessions and a barrow, or burial-mound, heaped above, were common.

bills and byrnies swords and coats of ring-mail

Onela's consort The text being defective at this point we can only conjecture that Onela the Swede is referred to, and we are not given the name of Healfdene's daughter, Onela's wife. Onela was son of Ongentheow (ll. 2750 ff.), His nephews Eadgils and Eanmund rebelled against him (ll. 2466 ff.) and took refuge at the Geatish court. Onela pursued them there and killed the young Geatish king Heardred. Eanmund was also killed. Later, Beowulf helps Eadgils in a punitive expedition against Onela, who is slain (ll. 2261 ff.).

folk-land public common land, which Germanic law gave by inalienable right to be held by the community at large for grazing

men i.e. men's bodies; the reference is unclear

His word was published to many a people
Far and wide o'er the ways of earth
To rear a folk-stead richly adorned;
The task was speeded, the time soon came
That the famous mead-hall was finished and done.
To distant nations its name was known,
The Hall of the Hart;° and the king kept well
His pledge and promise to deal out gifts,
Rings at the banquet. The great hall rose
High and horn-gabled,° holding its place
Till the battle-surge of consuming flame
Should swallow it up; the hour was near
That the deadly hate of a daughter's husband
Should kindle to fury and savage feud.°
    Then an evil spirit who dwelt in the darkness
Endured it ill that he heard each day
The din of revelry ring through the hall,
The sound of the harp, and the scop's° sweet song.
A skillful bard sang the ancient story
Of man's creation;° how the Maker wrought
The shining earth with its circling waters;
In splendor established the sun and moon
As lights to illumine the land of men;
Fairly adorning the fields of earth
With leaves and branches; creating life
In every creature that breathes and moves.
So the lordly warriors lived in gladness,
At ease and happy, till a fiend from hell
Began a series of savage crimes.
They called him Grendel, a demon grim
Haunting the fen-lands, holding the moors,
Ranging the wastes, where the wretched wight
Made his lair with the monster kin;
He bore the curse of the seed of Cain°
Whereby God punished the grievous guilt
Of Abel's murder. Nor ever had Cain

Hart Heorot, probably situated near modern Lejre, on the north coast of Zealand, not far from Roskilde, the ancient seat of Danish kingship. The royalty of the hall is emphasized by its name, Hart or Stag, a symbol of kingship—see the stag on the Sutton Hoo scepter (Fig. 17).

horn-gabled rather "wide-gabled"

consuming flame . . . feud (ll. 80–83) Heorot stood until it was burned to the ground, probably during an attack by Ingeld, king of the Heathobards, on Hrothgar, which the poet later describes (ll. 1893 ff). The poet is using his characteristic device of "tragic anticipation" for an audience already familiar with the story: the contrast is made between the present magnificence of Hrothgar's mead-hall and its later fate.

scop's the singer of tales, the bard chanting stories in verse at the feast to the sound of the harp

creation i.e. all created good (cf. "Cædmon's Hymn"), and man, sinless and perfect.

seed of Cain The first murderer—Genesis 4:8 ff. The giant race before Noah's flood (Genesis 6:4) is taken by the Biblical commentators, from very early times, to be not merely strong but also cruel and cunning—cf. Genesis 6:5: "And God saw that the wickedness of man was great in the earth." The giants were thought to spring from the union of the descendants of Cain the wrongdoer with the descendants of the righteous Seth.

Cause to boast of that deed of blood;
God banished him far from the fields of men;
Of his blood was begotten an evil brood,
Marauding monsters and menacing trolls,
Goblins and giants who battled with God
A long time. Grimly He gave them reward!
Then at the nightfall the fiend drew near
Where the timbered mead-hall towered on high,
To spy how the Danes fared after the feast.
Within the wine-hall he found the warriors
Fast in slumber,° forgetting grief,
Forgetting the woe of the world of men.
Grim and greedy the gruesome monster,
Fierce and furious, launched attack,
Slew thirty spearmen asleep in the hall,
Sped away gloating, gripping the spoil,
Dragging the dead men home to his den.
Then in the dawn with the coming of daybreak
The war-might of Grendel was widely known.
Mirth was stilled by the sound of weeping;
The wail of the mourner awoke with day.
And the peerless hero, the honored prince,
Weighed down with woe and heavy of heart,
Sat sorely grieving for slaughtered thanes,
As they traced the track of the cursed monster.
From that day onward the deadly feud
Was a long-enduring and loathsome strife.
Not longer was it than one night later
The fiend returning renewed attack
With heart firm-fixed in the hateful war,
Feeling no rue for the grievous wrong.
'Twas easy thereafter to mark the men
Who sought their slumber elsewhere afar,
Found beds in the bowers,° since Grendel's hate
Was so baldly blazoned in baleful signs.
He held himself at a safer distance
Who escaped the clutch of the demon's claw.
So Grendel raided and ravaged the realm,
One against all, in an evil war
Till the best of buildings was empty and still.
'Twas a weary while! Twelve winters' time
The lord of the Scyldings had suffered woe,
Sore affliction and deep distress.

slumber The mead-hall was the place of honor and of communal living for the lord's close companions, the *comitatus,* who also slept there. This was a mark of the lord's generous hospitality and of the companions' acceptance of their honorable vassalage.

bowers the small separate rooms elsewhere in the building complex rather than the central hall

And the malice of Grendel, in mournful lays,
Was widely sung by the sons of men,
The hateful feud that he fought with Hrothgar—
Year after year of struggle and strife,
An endless scourging, a scorning of peace
With any man of the Danish might.
No strength could move him to stay his hand,
Or pay for his murders;° the wise knew well
They could hope for no halting of savage assault.
Like a dark death-shadow° the ravaging demon,
Night-long prowling the misty moors,
Ensnared the warriors, wary or weak.
No man can say how these shades of hell
Come and go on their grisly rounds.
With many an outrage, many a crime,
The fierce lone-goer, the foe of man,
Stained the seats of the high-built house,
Haunting the hall in the hateful dark.
But throne or treasure he might not touch,
Finding no favor or grace with God.°
Great was the grief of the Scylding leader,
His spirit shaken, while many a lord
Gathered in council considering long
In what way brave men best could struggle
Against these terrors of sudden attack.
From time to time in their heathen temples
Paying homage they offered prayer
That the Slayer of souls° would send them succor
From all the torment that troubled the folk.
Such was the fashion and such the faith
Of their heathen hearts that they looked to hell,
Not knowing the Maker, the mighty Judge,
Nor how to worship the Wielder of glory,
The Lord of heaven, the God of hosts.
Woe unto him who in fierce affliction
Shall plunge his soul in the fiery pit
With no hope of mercy or healing change;
But well with the soul that at death seeks God,
And finds his peace in his Father's bosom.
The son of Healfdene° was heavy-hearted,
Sorrowfully brooding in sore distress,

pay . . . murders i.e. pay *wergild*, lit., "man-money," the money payment which Germanic law prescribed for a killer to buy peace from the dead man's family; payable only for the life of a free man, it varied according to the social status of the victim

death-shadow The word is used elsewhere of Satan, but Grendel throughout preys on bodies, not, like the Devil (l. 176), on souls.

Finding . . . God The sense is difficult, but seems to apply to Grendel and mean that, since he does not obey the laws of God or of man he cannot share in either human or divine gifts.

Slayer of souls the Devil. The Danes are here pointedly thought of as pagan idolaters.

son of Healfdene Hrothgar

Finding no help in a hopeless strife;
Too bitter the struggle that stunned the people,
The long oppression, loathsome and grim.

[*The Coming of Beowulf*]

Then tales of the terrible deeds of Grendel
Reached Hygelac's thane° in his home with the Geats;
Of living strong men he was the strongest,
Fearless and gallant and great of heart.°
He gave command for a goodly vessel
Fitted and furnished; he fain would sail
Over the swan-road to seek the king
Who suffered so sorely for need of men.
And his bold retainers found little to blame
In his daring venture, dear though he was;
They viewed the omens, and urged him on.
Brave was the band he had gathered about him,
Fourteen stalwarts seasoned and bold,
Seeking the shore where the ship lay waiting,
A sea-skilled mariner sighting the landmarks.
Came the hour of boarding; the boat was riding
The waves of the harbor under the hill.
The eager mariners mounted the prow;
Billows were breaking, sea against sand.
In the ship's hold snugly they stowed their trappings,
Gleaming armor and battle-gear;
Launched the vessel, the well-braced bark,
Seaward bound on a joyous journey.
Over breaking billows, with bellying sail
And foamy beak, like a flying bird
The ship sped on, till the next day's sun
Showed sea-cliffs shining, towering hills
And stretching headlands. The sea was crossed,
The voyage ended, the vessel moored.
And the Weder° people waded ashore
With clatter of trappings and coats of mail;
Gave thanks to God that His grace had granted
Sea-paths safe for their ocean-journey.
Then the Scylding coast-guard watched from the sea-cliff
Warriors bearing their shining shields,
Their gleaming war-gear, ashore from the ship.
His mind was puzzled, he wondered much
What men they were. On his good horse mounted,

Hygelac's thane Beowulf the Geat, hero of the poem. The word "thane," originally meaning "servant," by this time meant "a royal vassal of some consequence." Beowulf was bound to Hygelac by his obligation both as a companion and as an especially close kinsman. He was Hygelac's sister's son and would therefore be regarded as in a special relationship with his uncle.

Of living . . . heart For the poet, Beowulf's heroic magnanimity is sufficient reason for his going to Hrothgar's help.

Weder Weder-Geats or "Storm-loving" Geats—Beowulf's people

Hrothgar's thane made haste to the beach,
Boldly brandished his mighty spear
With manful challenge: 'What men are you,
Carrying weapons and clad in steel,
Who thus come driving across the deep
On the ocean-lanes in your lofty ship?
Long have I served as the Scylding outpost,
Held watch and ward at the ocean's edge
Lest foreign foemen with hostile fleet
Should come to harry our Danish home,
And never more openly sailed to these shores
Men without password, or leave to land.
I have never laid eyes upon earl on earth
More stalwart and sturdy than one of your troop,
A hero in armor; no hall-thane° he
Tricked out with weapons, unless looks belie him,
And noble bearing. But now I must know
Your birth and breeding, nor may you come
In cunning stealth upon Danish soil.
You distant-dwellers, you far sea-farers,
Hearken, and ponder words that are plain:
'Tis best you hasten to have me know
Who your kindred and whence you come.'
The lord of the seamen gave swift reply,
The prince of the Weders unlocked his word-hoard:
'We are sprung of a strain of the Geatish stock,
Hygelac's comrades and hearth-companions.°
My father was famous in many a folk-land,
A leader noble, Ecgtheow° his name!
Many a winter went over his head
Before death took him from home and tribe;
Well nigh every wise man remembers him well
Far and wide on the ways of earth.
With loyal purpose we seek your lord,
The prince of your people, great Healfdene's son.
Be kindly of counsel; weighty the cause
That leads us to visit the lord of the Danes;
Nor need it be secret, as far as I know!
You know if it's true, as we've heard it told,
That among the Scyldings some secret scather,
Some stealthy demon in dead of night,
With grisly horror and fiendish hate
Is spreading unheard-of havoc and death.
Mayhap I can counsel the good, old king
What way he can master the merciless fiend,

no hall-thane i.e. not merely splendid-looking on ceremonial occasions, but tough and powerful in battle

hearth-companions the *heorthwerod,* the close companions of the lord

Ecgtheow Nothing is known of Beowulf's father.

If his coil of evil is ever to end
And feverish care grow cooler and fade—
Or else ever after his doom shall be
Distress and sorrow while still there stands
This best of halls on its lofty height.'
Then from the saddle the coast-guard spoke,
The fearless sentry: 'A seasoned° warrior
Must know the difference between words and deeds,
If his wits are with him. I take your word
That your band is loyal° to the lord of the Scyldings.
Now go your way with your weapons and armor,
And I will guide you; I'll give command
That my good retainers may guard your ship,
Your fresh-tarred floater, from every foe,
And hold it safe in its sandy berth,
Till the curving prow once again shall carry
The loved man home to the land of the Geat.
To hero so gallant shall surely be granted
To come from the swordplay sound and safe.'
Then the Geats marched on; behind at her mooring,
Fastened at anchor, their broad-beamed boat
Safely rode on her swinging cable.
Boar-heads° glittered on glistening helmets
Above their cheek-guards, gleaming with gold;
Bright and fire-hardened the boar held watch
Over the column of marching men.
Onward they hurried in eager haste
Till their eyes caught sight of the high-built hall,
Splendid with gold, the seat of the king,
Most stately of structures under the sun;
Its light shone out over many a land.
The coast-guard showed them the shining hall,
The home of heroes; made plain the path;
Turned his horse; gave tongue to words:
'It is time to leave you! The mighty Lord
In His mercy shield you and hold you safe
In your bold adventure. I'll back to the sea
And hold my watch against hostile horde.'

[*Beowulf's Welcome at Hrothgar's Court*]

The street had paving of colored stone;
The path was plain to the marching men.
Bright were their byrnies, hard and hand-linked;
In their shining armor the chain-mail sang

seasoned *scearp*, more likely "acute, keen-witted." The sentry is courteously apologizing for his challenge.
loyal friendly
Boar-heads images of boars placed on Germanic helmets as a protection to the wearers in the material sense—giving extra protection against a blow at the head or upper part of the face—and to invoke the strength and cunning of the boar for the wearer

As the troop in their war-gear tramped to the hall.
The sea-weary sailors set down their shields,
Their wide, bright bucklers along the wall,
And sank to the bench. Their byrnies rang.
Their stout spears stood in a stack together
Shod with iron and shaped of ash.
'Twas a well-armed troop! Then a stately warrior°
Questioned the strangers about their kin:
'Whence come you bearing your burnished shields,
Your steel-gray harness and visored helms,
Your heap of spears? I am Hrothgar's herald,
His servant-thane. I have never seen strangers,
So great a number, of nobler mien.
Not exiles,° I ween, but high-minded° heroes
In greatness of heart have you sought out Hrothgar.'
Then bold under helmet the hero made answer,
The lord of the Weders, manful of mood,°
Mighty of heart: 'We are Hygelac's men,
His board-companions; Beowulf is my name.
I will state my mission to Healfdene's son,
The noble leader, your lordly prince,
If he will grant approach to his gracious presence.'
And Wulfgar answered, the Wendel° prince,
Renowned for merit° in many a land,
For war-might and wisdom: 'I will learn the wish
Of the Scylding leader, the lord of the Danes,
Our honored ruler and giver of rings,
Concerning your mission, and soon report
The answer our leader thinks good to give.'
He swiftly strode to where Hrothgar sat
Old and gray with his earls about him;
Crossed the floor and stood face to face
With the Danish king; he knew courtly custom.°
Wulfgar saluted his lord and friend:°
'Men from afar have fared to our land
Over ocean's margin—men of the Geats,
Their leader called Beowulf—seeking a boon,
The holding of parley, my prince, with thee.
O gracious Hrothgar, refuse not the favor!

stately warrior a proud-hearted and haughty—rather than stately—warrior, who is later named as Wulfgar
exiles i.e. you do not come seeking a new lord and protector because you have lost or been dismissed by your old one; cf. "The Wanderer" below
high-minded brave
mood mind, heart
Wulfgar . . . Wendel perhaps a Vandal, but more likely a man from Vendel in Sweden or Vendill in Jutland, Denmark (where the Vandals may have left pockets of settlement); he is a foreign prince serving Hrothgar—like Beowulf, and recognizing the likeness—from heroic magnanimity and love of adventure, not from necessity
merit courage
courtly custom the usage of the *comitatus*
friend This emphasizes the close but not carefully defined nature of the relationship. The obligations of allegiance and friendship are the ties that bind lord and man together, not, as in the later feudal system, a more exactly set-out complex of legal obligation.

In their splendid war-gear they merit well
The esteem of earls;° he's a stalwart leader
Who led this troop to the land of the Danes.'
Hrothgar spoke, the lord of the Scyldings:
'Their leader I knew when he still was a lad.
His father was Ecgtheow; Hrethel° the Geat
Gave him° in wedlock his only daughter.
Now is their son come, keen for adventure,
Finding his way to a faithful friend.
Sea-faring men who have voyaged to Geatland
With gifts of treasure° as token of peace,
Say that his hand-grip has thirty men's strength.
God, in His mercy, has sent him to save us—
So springs my hope—from Grendel's assaults.
For his gallant courage I'll load him with gifts!
Make haste now, marshal the men to the hall,
And give them welcome to Danish ground.'
Then to the door went the well-known warrior,°
Spoke from the threshold welcoming words:
'The Danish leader, my lord, declares
That he knows your kinship; right welcome you come,
You stout sea-rovers, to Danish soil.
Enter now, in your shining armor
And vizored helmets, to Hrothgar's hall.
But leave your shields and the shafts of slaughter
To wait the issue and weighing of words.'
Then the bold one rose with his band around him,
A splendid massing of mighty thanes;
A few stood guard as the Geat gave bidding
Over the weapons stacked by the wall.
They followed in haste on the heels of their leader
Under Heorot's roof. Full ready and bold
The helmeted warrior strode to the hearth;°
Beowulf spoke; his byrny glittered,
His war-net woven by cunning of smith:
'Hail! King Hrothgar! I am Hygelac's thane,
Hygelac's kinsman. Many a deed
Of honor and daring I've done in my youth.
This business of Grendel was brought to my ears
On my native soil. The sea-farers say
This best of buildings, this boasted hall,
Stands dark and deserted when sun is set,

earls originally men of the higher class of society; later use, in poetry, gives it the sense of "warriors"
Hrethel king of the Geats, father of Hygelac, grandfather of Beowulf
him Ecgtheow, Beowulf's father
gifts of treasure The giving of gifts to followers and to equals was the obligation and the pleasure of Germanic chieftains, see Tacitus, *Germania*, 15.
warrior Wulfgar
strode . . . hearth rather "took up his stand inside the hall"

When darkening shadows gather with dusk.
The best of my people, prudent and brave,
Urged me, King Hrothgar, to seek you out;
They had in remembrance my courage and might.
Many had seen me come safe from the conflict,
Bloody from battle; five foes I bound
Of the giant kindred, and crushed their clan.
Hard-driven in danger and darkness of night
I slew the nicors° that swam the sea,
Avenged the woe they had caused the Weders,
And ended their evil—they needed the lesson!
And now with Grendel, the fearful fiend,
Single-handed I'll settle the strife!
Prince of the Danes, protector of Scyldings,
Lord of nations, and leader of men,
I beg one favor—refuse me not,
Since I come thus faring from far-off lands—
That I may alone with my loyal earls,
With this hardy company, cleanse Hart-Hall.
I have heard that the demon in proud disdain
Spurns all weapons; and I too scorn—
May Hygelac's heart have joy of the deed—
To bear my sword, or sheltering shield,
Or yellow buckler, to battle the fiend.
With hand-grip only I'll grapple with Grendel;
Foe against foe I'll fight to the death,
And the one who is taken must trust to God's grace!
The demon, I doubt not, is minded to feast
In the hall unaffrighted, as often before,
On the force of the Hrethmen,° the folk of the Geats.
No need then to bury the body he mangles!
If death shall call me, he'll carry away
My gory flesh to his fen-retreat
To gorge at leisure and gulp me down,
Soiling the marshes with stains of blood.
There'll be little need longer to care for my body!
If the battle slays me, to Hygelac send
This best of corselets that covers my breast,
Heirloom of Hrethel, and Wayland's work,°
Finest of byrnies. Fate goes as Fate must!'

Hrothgar spoke, the lord of the Scyldings:
'Deed of daring and dream of honor
Bring you, friend Beowulf, knowing our need!
Your father once fought the greatest of feuds,

nicors water monsters

Hrethmen Perhaps a name for the Geats; it may not be a proper name at all but a compound noun meaning "glorious warriors."

Wayland's work i.e. a mail-shirt which is both ancient and excellent. Wayland or Weland, the cunning smith of the gods in Germanic legend, was a magician in his own right; see "Deor's Lament."

Laid Heatholaf° low, of the Wylfing line;°
And the folk of the Weders refused him shelter
For fear of revenge.° Then he fled to the South-Danes,
The Honor-Scyldings beyond the sea.
I was then first governing Danish ground,
As a young lad ruling the spacious realm,
The home-land of warriors. Heorogar° was dead,
The son of Healfdene no longer living,
My older brother, and better than I!
Thereafter by payment composing the feud,
O'er the water's ridge I sent to the Wylfing
Ancient treasure; he° swore me oaths!
It is sorrow sore to recite to another
The wrongs that Grendel has wrought in the hall,
His savage hatred and sudden assaults.
My war-troop is weakened, my hall-band is wasted;
Fate swept them away into Grendel's grip.
But God may easily bring to an end
The ruinous deeds of the ravaging foe.
Full often my warriors over their ale-cups
Boldly boasted,° when drunk with beer,
They would bide in the beer-hall the coming of battle,
The fury of Grendel, with flashing swords.
Then in the dawn, when the daylight strengthened,
The hall stood reddened and reeking with gore,
Bench-boards wet with the blood of battle;
And I had the fewer of faithful fighters,
Beloved retainers, whom Death had taken.
Sit now at the banquet, unbend your mood,
Speak of great deeds as your heart may spur you!'
Then in the beer-hall were benches made ready
For the Geatish heroes. Noble of heart,
Proud and stalwart, they sat them down
And a beer-thane° served them; bore in his hands
The patterned ale-cup, pouring the mead,°
While the scop's sweet singing was heard in the hall.
There was joy of heroes, a host at ease,
A welcome meeting of Weder and Dane.

Heatholaf not otherwise known

Wylfing line lit. "Wolves' sons"—Germanic tribe which lived on the southern shores of the Baltic

revenge i.e. Ecgtheow could not pay the necessary *wergild,* so that Heatholaf's people would have the obligation to take revenge; fear of this caused the Geats to refuse Beowulf's father leave to stay with them.

Heorogar Danish king, elder brother of Hrothgar

he Ecgtheow; Hrothgar had composed the feud by sending ancient prized treasure to the Wylfings, and Ecgtheow presumably swore an oath of friendship and good conduct.

boasted formal boasting, especially of future exploits, protestations of what would be done: a prominent feature of Germanic warriors' feasting

beer-thane the cup-bearer, the butler of later chivalric society—an important person in the household of the chieftain

mead a drink made from fermented honey; but the Old English word used here means literally "sweet drink," which may be beer

[*Unferth Taunts Beowulf*]

Then out spoke Unferth,° Ecglaf's son,
Who sat at the feet of the Scylding lord,
Picking a quarrel—for Beowulf's quest,
His bold sea-voyaging, irked him sore;
He bore it ill that any man other
In all the earth should ever achieve
More fame under heaven than he himself:
'Are you the Beowulf that strove with Breca°
In a swimming match in the open sea,
Both of you wantonly tempting the waves,
Risking your lives on the lonely deep
For a silly boast? No man could dissuade you,
Nor friend nor foe, from the foolhardy venture
Of ocean-swimming; with outstretched arms
You clasped the sea-stream, measured her streets,
With plowing shoulders parted the waves.
The sea-flood boiled with its wintry surges,
Seven nights you toiled in the tossing sea;
His strength was the greater, his swimming the stronger!
The waves upbore you at break of day
To the stretching beach of the Battle-Ræmas;°
And Breca departed, beloved of his people,
To the land of the Brondings, the beauteous home,
The stronghold fair, where he governed the folk,
The city and treasure; Beanstan's son°
Made good his boast to the full against you!
Therefore, I ween, worse fate shall befall,
Stout as you are in the struggle of war,
In deeds of battle, if you dare to abide
Encounter with Grendel at coming of night.'
Beowulf spoke, the son of Ecgtheow:
'My good friend Unferth, addled with beer
Much have you made of the deeds of Breca!
I count it true that I had more courage,
More strength in swimming than any other man.
In our youth we boasted—we were both of us boys—
We would risk our lives in the raging sea.
And we made it good! We gripped in our hands
Naked swords, as we swam in the waves,
Guarding us well from the whales' assault.
In the breaking seas he could not outstrip me,

Unferth Hrothgar's courtier, a type of the "wicked counsellor," sets out to mock Beowulf, but is put down by the hero. His name means "Peace-spoiler" and he here tries to cast doubt on Beowulf's ability to deal with Grendel.

Breca Tales of swimming matches and other such trials of strength occur in later Germanic literature: they usually involve endurance rather than speed. Breca's name may mean "rush, storm": he is known from other Germanic myths. His people, the Brondings, are not.

Battle-Ræmas Heatho-Ræmas, a tribe living in Norway, north of modern Oslo

Beanstan's son Breca

Nor would I leave him. For five nights long
Side by side we strove in the waters
Till racing combers wrenched us apart,
Freezing squalls, and the falling night,
And a bitter north wind's icy blast.
Rough were the waves; the wrath of the sea-fish
Was fiercely roused; but my firm-linked byrny,
The gold-adorned corselet that covered my breast,
Gave firm defense from the clutching foe.
Down to the bottom a savage sea-beast
Fiercely dragged me and held me fast
In a deadly grip; none the less it was granted me
To pierce the monster with point of steel.
Death swept it away with the swing of my sword.
    The grisly sea-beasts again and again
Beset me sore; but I served them home
With my faithful blade as was well-befitting.
They failed of their pleasure to feast their fill
Crowding round my corpse on the ocean-bottom!
Bloody with wounds, at the break of day,
They lay on the sea-beach slain with the sword.
No more would they cumber the mariner's course
On the ocean deep. From the east came the sun,
Bright beacon of God, and the seas subsided;
I beheld the headlands, the windy walls.
Fate often delivers an undoomed earl°
If his spirit be gallant! And so I was granted
To slay with the sword-edge nine of the nicors.
I have never heard tell of more terrible strife
Under dome of heaven in darkness of night,
Nor of man harder pressed on the paths of ocean.
But I freed my life from the grip of the foe
Though spent with the struggle. The billows bore me,
The swirling currents and surging seas,
To the land of the Finns.° And little I've heard
Of any such valiant adventures from you!
Neither Breca nor you in the press of battle
Ever showed such daring with dripping swords—
Though I boast not of it! But you stained your blade
With blood of your brothers,° your closest of kin;

Fate . . . undoomed earl i.e. a warrior not singled out for death by Fate. Fortune favors the brave, but only as Fate preordains: Fate is inescapable. This concept permeates the entire poem. It is typically pagan Germanic and especially typical of Old English poetry.

land of the Finns often identified with Finnmarken, in northern Norway, but probably the territory of the Lapps (frequently called Finns in Old English poetry) in southwest Sweden

you stained . . . brothers Beowulf turns Unferth's taunts in a devastating way: if this Danish spokesman is a boaster and a fratricide, Grendel has nothing to fear from the people he represents. Unferth might have retorted that his fratricide was the result of the *comitatus* system, where a brother serving one lord might have to fulfill his obligation to that lord by killing a brother serving another. But the blood-tie was always very strong—and the poet leaves Beowulf in possession of the field.

And for that you'll endure damnation in hell,
Sharp° as you are! I say for a truth,
Son of Ecglaf, never had Grendel
Wrought such havoc and woe in the hall,
That horrid demon so harried your king,
If your heart were as brave as you'd have men think!
But Grendel has found that he never need fear
Revenge from your people, or valiant attack
From the Victor-Scyldings; he takes his toll,
Sparing none of the Danish stock.
He slays and slaughters and works his will
Fearing no hurt at the hands of the Danes!
But soon will I show him the stuff of the Geats,
Their courage in battle and strength in the strife;
Then let him who may go bold to the mead-hall
When the next day dawns on the dwellings of men,
And the sun in splendor shines warm from the south.'
Glad of heart was the giver of treasure,
Hoary-headed and hardy in war;
The lordly leader had hope of help
As he listened to Beowulf's bold resolve.
There was revel of heroes and high carouse,
Their speech was happy; and Hrothgar's queen,
Of gentle manners, in jewelled splendor
Gave courtly greeting° to all the guests.
The high-born lady first bore the beaker
To the Danish leader, lord of the land,
Bade him be blithe at the drinking of beer;
Beloved of his people, the peerless king
Joined in the feasting, had joy of the cup.
Then to all alike went the Helming° lady
Bearing the beaker to old and young,
Till the jewelled queen with courtly grace
Paused before Beowulf, proffered the mead.
She greeted the Geat and to God gave thanks,
Wise of word, that her wish was granted;
At last she could look to a hero for help,
Comfort in evil. He took the cup,
The hardy warrior, at Wealhtheow's hand
And, eager for battle, uttered his boast;
Beowulf spoke, the son of Ecgtheow:
'I had firm resolve when I set to sea
With my band of earls in my ocean-ship,
Fully to work the will of your people

sharp keen-witted
courtly greeting The Queen's social graces are emphasized: she knows what is due to each person according to his rank and attainments.

Helming the ruling family of the Wylfings—of which Helm was the founder—to which Hrothgar's queen, Wealhtheow, belongs

Or fall in the struggle slain by the foe.
I shall either perform deeds fitting an earl
Or meet in this mead-hall the coming of death!'
Then the woman was pleased with the words he uttered,
The Geat-lord's boast; the gold-decked queen
Went in state to sit by her lord.

[*Beowulf Slays Grendel*]

In the hall as of old were brave words spoken,
There was noise of revel; happy the host
Till the son of Healfdene would go to his rest.
He knew that the monster would meet in the hall
Relentless struggle when light of the sun
Was dusky with gloom of the gathering night,
And shadow-shapes crept in the covering dark,
Dim under heaven. The host arose.
Hrothgar graciously greeted his guest,
Gave rule of the wine-hall, and wished him well,
Praised the warrior in parting words:
'Never to any man, early or late,
Since first I could brandish buckler and sword,
Have I trusted this ale-hall save only to you!
Be mindful of glory, show forth your strength,
Keep watch against foe! No wish of your heart
Shall go unfulfilled if you live through the fight.'
Then Hrothgar withdrew with his host of retainers,
The prince of the Scyldings, seeking his queen,
The bed of his consort. The King of Glory
Had stablished a hall-watch, a guard against Grendel,
Dutifully serving the Danish lord,
The land defending from loathsome fiend.
The Geatish hero put all his hope
In his fearless might and the mercy of God!
He stripped from his shoulders the byrny of steel,
Doffed helmet from head; into hand of thane
Gave inlaid° iron, the best of blades;
Bade him keep well the weapons of war.
Beowulf uttered a gallant boast,
The stalwart Geat, ere he sought his bed:
'I count myself nowise weaker in war
Or grapple of battle than Grendel himself.
Therefore I scorn to slay him with sword,
Deal deadly wound, as I well might do!
Nothing he knows of a noble fighting,
Of thrusting and hewing and hacking of shield,
Fierce as he is in the fury of war.

inlaid "engraved," "patterned"; the reference is not necessarily to the blade, but may be to hilt or pommel

In the shades of darkness we'll spurn the sword
If he dares without weapon to do or to die.
And God in His wisdom shall glory assign,
The ruling Lord, as He deems it right.'
Then the bold in battle bowed down to his rest,
Cheek pressed pillow; the peerless thanes
Were stretched in slumber around their lord.
Not one had hope of return to his home,
To the stronghold or land where he lived as a boy.
For they knew how death had befallen the Danes,
How many were slain as they slept in the wine-hall.
But the wise Lord wove them fortune in war,
Gave strong support to the Weder people;
They slew their foe by the single strength
Of a hero's courage. The truth is clear,
God rules forever the race of men.
Then through the shades of enshrouding night
The fiend came stealing; the archers slept
Whose duty was holding the horn-decked hall—
Though one was watching—full well they knew
No evil demon could drag them down
To shades under ground if God were not willing.°
But the hero watched awaiting the foe,
Abiding in anger the issue of war.
From the stretching moors, from the misty hollows,
Grendel came creeping, accursed of God,
A murderous ravager minded to snare
Spoil of heroes in high-built hall.
Under clouded heavens he held his way
Till there rose before him the high-roofed house,
Wine-hall of warriors gleaming with gold.
Nor was it the first of his fierce assaults
On the home of Hrothgar; but never before
Had he found worse fate or hardier hall-thanes!
Storming the building he burst the portal,
Though fastened of iron, with fiendish strength;
Forced open the entrance in savage fury
And rushed in rage o'er the shining floor.
A baleful glare from his eyes was gleaming
Most like to a flame. He found in the hall
Many a warrior sealed in slumber,
A host of kinsmen. His heart rejoiced;
The savage monster was minded to sever
Lives from bodies ere break of day,
To feast his fill of the flesh of men.
But he was not fated to glut his greed

God . . . willing Here it is God, not Fate, who has pre-decided the issue.

With more of mankind when the night was ended!
    The hardy kinsman of Hygelac waited
To see how the monster would make his attack.
The demon delayed not, but quickly clutched
A sleeping thane in his swift assault,
Tore him in pieces, bit through the bones,
Gulped the blood, and gobbled the flesh,
Greedily gorged on the lifeless corpse,
The hands and the feet. Then the fiend stepped nearer,
Sprang on the Sea-Geat lying outstretched,
Clasping him close with his monstrous claw.
But Beowulf grappled and gripped him hard,
Struggled up on his elbow; the shepherd of sins
Soon found that never before had he felt
In any man other in all the earth
A mightier hand-grip; his mood was humbled,
His courage fled; but he found no escape!
He was fain to be gone; he would flee to the darkness,
The fellowship of devils. Far different his fate
From that which befell him in former days!
The hardy hero, Hygelac's kinsman,
Remembered the boast he had made at the banquet;
He sprang to his feet, clutched Grendel fast,
Though fingers were cracking, the fiend pulling free.
The earl pressed after; the monster was minded
To win his freedom and flee to the fens.
He knew that his fingers were fast in the grip
Of a savage foe. Sorry the venture,
The raid that the ravager made on the hall.
    There was din in Heorot. For all the Danes,
The city-dwellers, the stalwart Scyldings,
That was a bitter spilling of beer!°
The walls resounded, the fight was fierce,
Savage the strife as the warriors struggled.
The wonder was that the lofty wine-hall
Withstood the struggle, nor crashed to earth,
The house so fair; it was firmly fastened
Within and without with iron bands
Cunningly smithied; though men have said
That many a mead-bench gleaming with gold
Sprang from its sill as the warriors strove.
The Scylding wise men had never weened
That any ravage could wreck the building,
Firmly fashioned and finished with bone,
Or any cunning° compass its fall,

bitter . . . beer the characteristic Old English grimly allusive poetic understatement: i.e. that was no feast, such as the hall had been built for

cunning skill

Till the time when the swelter and surge of fire
Should swallow it up in a swirl of flame.
Continuous tumult filled the hall;
A terror fell on the Danish folk
As they heard through the wall the horrible wailing,
The groans of Grendel, the foe of God
Howling his hideous hymn of pain,
The hell-thane shrieking in sore defeat.
He was fast in the grip of the man who was greatest
Of mortal men in the strength of his might,
Who would never rest while the wretch was living,
Counting his life-days a menace to man.
Many an earl of Beowulf brandished
His ancient iron° to guard his lord,
To shelter safely the peerless prince.
They had no knowledge, those daring thanes,
When they drew their weapons to hack and hew,
To thrust to the heart, that the sharpest sword,
The choicest iron in all the world,
Could work no harm to the hideous foe.
On every sword he had laid a spell,
On every blade; but a bitter death
Was to be his fate; far was the journey
The monster made to the home of fiends.
Then he who had wrought such wrong to men,
With grim delight as he warred with God,
Soon found that his strength was feeble and failing
In the crushing hold of Hygelac's thane.
Each loathed the other while life should last!
There Grendel suffered a grievous hurt,
A wound in the shoulder, gaping and wide;
Sinews snapped and bone-joints broke,
And Beowulf gained the glory of battle.
Grendel, fated, fled to the fens,
To his joyless dwelling, sick unto death.
He knew in his heart that his hours were numbered,
His days at an end. For all the Danes
Their wish was fulfilled in the fall of Grendel.
The stranger from far, the stalwart and strong,
Had purged of evil the hall of Hrothgar,
And cleansed of crime; the heart of the hero
Joyed in the deed his daring had done.
The lord of the Geats made good to the East-Danes
The boast he had uttered; he ended their ill,
And all the sorrow they suffered long
And needs must suffer—a foul offense.

ancient iron a sword, sometimes with a name, which was of especially good quality and strength and would be handed down as a prized heirloom from generation to generation

The token was clear when the bold in battle
Laid down the shoulder and dripping claw—
Grendel's arm—in the gabled hall!

[*The Joy of the Danes and the Lay of Sigemund*]

When morning came, as they tell the tale,
Many a warrior hastened to hall,
Folk-leaders faring from far and near
Over wide-running ways, to gaze at the wonder,
The trail of the demon. Nor seemed his death
A matter of sorrow to any man
Who viewed the tracks of the vanquished monster
As he slunk weary-hearted away from the hall,
Doomed and defeated and marking his flight
With bloody prints to the nicors' pool.
The crimson currents bubbled and heaved
In eddying reaches reddened with gore;
The surges boiled with the fiery blood.
But the monster had sunk from the sight of men.
In that fenny covert the cursed fiend
Not long thereafter laid down his life,
His heathen spirit; and hell received him.

Then all the comrades, the old and young,
The brave of heart, in a blithesome band
Came riding their horses home from the mere.°
Beowulf's prowess was praised in song;
And many men stated that south or north,
Over all the world, or between the seas,
Or under the heaven, no hero was greater,
More worthy of rule. But no whit they slighted
The gracious Hrothgar, their good old king.
Time and again they galloped their horses,
Racing their roans° where the roads seemed fairest;
Time and again a gleeman° chanted,
A minstrel mindful of saga and lay.
He wove his words in a winsome° pattern,
Hymning the burden of Beowulf's feat,
Clothing the story in skillful verse.

All tales he had ever heard told he sang of Sigemund's° glory,
Deeds of the Wælsing° forgotten, his weary roving and wars,

mere pond, lake
roans horses of mixed color
gleeman *scop,* bard
winsome pleasing, beautiful
Sigemund Germanic hero, son of Wæls, well known from the Old Norse *Volsungasaga* and the German *Nibelungenlied.* The Old Norse tradition makes him father of Fitela. Here he slays the dragon who guards the treasure: in the other two versions his son Sigurd or Siegfried does so. The story is meant to set up resonances—of Sigurd-Siegfried-Sigemund's dragon-slaying, taking away of the treasure, of the curse that was on the treasure, and of his tragic fate—which the audience will apply to Beowulf. The parallel with Beowulf's past and future life, the proleptic reference to his death in battle with the dragon and the melancholy sense that even the greatest and bravest of heroes must grow old and meet death, would all be present in the minds of the listeners.
Wælsing son of Wæls, Sigemund-Sigurd

Feuds and fighting unknown to men, save Fitela° only,
Tales told by uncle to nephew when the two were companions,
What time they were bosom-comrades in battle and bitter strife.
Many of monster blood these two had slain with the sword-edge;
Great glory Sigemund gained that lingered long after death,
When he daringly slew the dragon that guarded the hoard of gold.
Under the ancient rock the warrior ventured alone,
No Fitela fighting beside him; but still it befell
That his firm steel pierced the worm,° the point stood fast in the wall;
The dragon had died the death! And the hero's daring
Had won the treasure to have and to hold as his heart might wish.
Then the Wælsing loaded his sea-boat, laid in the breast of the ship
Wondrous and shining treasure; the worm dissolved in the heat.
Sigemund was strongest of men in his deeds of daring,
Warrior's shield and defender, most famous in days of old
After Heremod's° might diminished, his valor and vigor in war,
Betrayed in the land of the Jutes to the hands of his foemen, and slain.
Too long the surges of sorrow swept over his soul; in the end
His life was a lingering woe to people and princes.
In former days his fate was mourned by many a warrior
Who had trusted his lord for protection from terror and woe,
Had hoped that the prince would prosper, wielding his father's wealth,
Ruling the tribe and the treasure, the Scylding city and home.
Hygelac's kinsman had favor and friendship of all mankind,
But the stain of sin sank deep into Heremod's heart.

Time and again on their galloping steeds
Over yellow roads they measured the mile-paths;
Morning sun mounted the shining sky
And many a hero strode to the hall,
Stout of heart, to behold the wonder.
The worthy ruler, the warder of treasure,
Set out from the bowers with stately train;
The queen with her maidens paced over the mead-path.°

Then spoke Hrothgar; hasting to hall
He stood at the steps, stared up at the roof
High and gold-gleaming; saw Grendel's hand:
'Thanks be to God for this glorious sight!
I have suffered much evil, much outrage from Grendel,
But the God of glory works wonder on wonder.
I had no hope of a haven from sorrow
While this best of houses stood badged with blood,
A woe far-reaching for all the wise

Fitela nephew and son of Sigurd, by his sister Signy, who had seduced her brother in disguise in order to bear a true Volsung son who could revenge the wrongs done to her and to her family

worm dragon; the word once meant reptile, serpent, of any kind

Heremod See ll. 1596 ff. The intention is to contrast the savagery and tyranny of this king, his early goodness and later evil-doing and failure, with Beowulf, who has already been exalted by the comparison with Sigemund-Sigurd.

paced . . . mead-path i.e. walked from their apartments to the mead-hall

Who weened that they never could hold the hall
Against the assaults of devils and demons.
But now with God's help this hero has compassed
A deed our cunning could no way contrive.
Surely that woman may say with truth,
Who bore this son, if she still be living,
Our ancient God showed favor and grace
On her bringing-forth! O best of men,
I will keep you, Beowulf, close to my heart
In firm affection; as son to father
Hold fast henceforth to this foster-kinship.°
You shall know not want of treasure or wealth
Or goodly gift that your wish may crave,
While I have power. For poorer deeds
I have granted guerdon,° and graced with honor
Weaker warriors, feebler in fight.
You have done such deeds that your fame shall flourish
Through all the ages! God grant you still
All goodly grace as He gave before.'
        Beowulf spoke, the son of Ecgtheow:
'By the favor of God we won the fight,
Did the deed of valor, and boldly dared
The might of the monster. I would you could see
The fiend himself lying dead before you!
I thought to grip him in stubborn grasp
And bind him down on the bed of death,
There to lie straining in struggle for life,
While I gripped him fast lest he vanish away.
But I might not hold him or hinder his going
For God did not grant it, my fingers failed.
Too savage the strain of his fiendish strength!
To save his life he left shoulder and claw,
The arm of the monster, to mark his track.
But he bought no comfort; no whit thereby
Shall the wretched ravager racked with sin,
The loathsome spoiler, prolong his life.
A deep wound holds him in deadly grip,
In baleful bondage; and black with crime
The demon shall wait for the day of doom
When the God of glory shall give decree.'
        Then slower of speech was the son of Ecglaf,°
More wary of boasting of warlike deeds,
While the nobles gazed at the grisly claw,
The fiend's hand fastened by hero's might
On the lofty roof. Most like to steel

foster-kinship tie regarded as equivalent to the bond of blood
guerdon reward
then slower . . . Ecglaf Unferth, now discomfited and unable to taunt Beowulf at all

Were the hardened nails, the heathen's hand-spurs,
Horrible, monstrous; and many men said
No tempered sword, no excellent iron,
Could have harmed the monster or hacked away
The demon's battle-claw dripping with blood.

[*The Feast and the Lay of Finnsburg*]

In joyful haste was Heorot decked
And a willing host of women and men
Gaily dressed and adorned the guest-hall.
Splendid hangings with sheen of gold
Shone on the walls, a glorious sight
To eyes that delight to behold such wonders.
The shining building was wholly shattered
Though braced and fastened with iron bands;
Hinges were riven; the roof alone
Remained unharmed when the horrid monster,
Foul with evil, slunk off in flight,
Hopeless of life. It is hard to flee
The touch of death, let him try who will;
Necessity urges the sons of men,
The dwellers on earth, to their destined place
Where the body, bound in its narrow bed,
After the feasting is fast in slumber.
Soon was the time when the son of Healfdene
Went to the wine-hall; he fain would join
With happy heart in the joy of feasting.
I never have heard of a mightier muster
Of proud retainers around their prince.
All at ease they bent to the benches,
Had joy of the banquet; their kinsmen bold,
Hrothgar and Hrothulf,° happy of heart,
In the high-built hall drank many a mead-cup.
The hall of Hrothgar was filled with friends;
No treachery yet had troubled the Scyldings.
Upon Beowulf, then, as a token of triumph,
Hrothgar bestowed a standard of gold,
A banner embroidered, a byrny and helm.
In sight of many, a costly sword
Before the hero was borne on high;
Beowulf drank of many a bowl.
No need for shame in the sight of heroes
For gifts so gracious! I never have heard
Of many men dealing in friendlier fashion,
To others on ale-bench, richer rewards,
Four such treasures fretted with gold!

Hrothulf Danish prince, nephew of Hrothgar, son of his brother Halga. Hrothulf seems to have usurped the throne after Hrothgar's death.

On the crest of the helmet a crowning wreath,
Woven of wire-work,° warded the head
Lest tempered swordblade, sharp from the file,
Deal deadly wound when the shielded warrior
Went forth to battle against the foe.
Eight horses also with plated headstalls
The lord of heroes bade lead into hall;
On one was a saddle skillfully fashioned
And set with jewels, the battle-seat
Of the king himself, when the son of Healfdene
Would fain take part in the play of swords;
Never in fray had his valor failed,
His kingly courage, when corpses were falling.
And the prince of the Ingwines° gave all these gifts
To the hand of Beowulf, horses and armor;
Bade him enjoy them! With generous heart
The noble leader, the lord of heroes,
Rewarded the struggle with steeds and with treasure,
So that none can belittle, and none can blame,
Who tells the tale as it truly happened.
Then on the ale-bench to each of the earls
Who embarked with Beowulf, sailing the sea-paths,
The lord of princes dealt ancient heirlooms,
Gift of treasure, and guerdon of gold
To requite his slaughter whom Grendel slew,
As he would have slain others, but all-wise God
And the hero's courage had conquered Fate.
The Lord ruled over the lives of men
As He rules them still. Therefore understanding
And a prudent spirit are surely best!
He must suffer much of both weal and woe
Who dwells here long in these days of strife.
Then song and revelry rose in the hall;
Before Healfdene's leader the harp was struck
And hall-joy wakened; the song was sung,
Hrothgar's gleeman rehearsed the lay
Of the sons of Finn when the terror befell them:

Hnæf° of the Scyldings, the Half-Dane, fell in the Frisian slaughter;
Nor had Hildeburh cause to acclaim the faith of the Jutish folk,

crowning . . . wire-work rather, as on the Sutton Hoo helmet, which is Swedish work, a metal ridge adorned with wire-work running from the top of the head to the nose (Fig. 19)
Ingwines lit. "friends of Ing," i.e. Danes
Hnæf Hnæf, king of the Danes, who had succeeded his father, King Hoc, had gone with his retainers on a visit to his sister Hildeburh and her husband Finn, king of the Frisians (or Jutes) at their home, Finnsburg. During the festivities, Jutish treachery—according to the poet—provoked a fight in which Hnæf and his sister's son, his closest kinsman, though half Jute, were killed. They were cremated on the same pyre and a truce was made. Hengest, the new Danish king, stayed the winter with Finn, meditating revenge for the death of Hnæf. Two Danish warriors then provoked another battle, in which Finn was killed. The Danes returned home, taking plunder and Hildeburh with them.
The *scop*'s version, since he is a Dane singing to his fellow Danes, lays the blame for the initial bloodshed on the Jutes. He tells it as a piece of old Danish lore, a story that would be familiar to his hearers, in an oblique and highly allusive manner, designed to set up reso-

Blameless, bereft of her brothers in battle, and stripped of her sons
Who fell overcome by their fate and wounded with spears!
Not for nothing Hoc's daughter bewailed death's bitter decree,
In the dawn under morning skies, when she saw the slaughter of kinsmen
In the place where her days had been filled with the fairest delights
of the world.
Finn's thanes were slain in the fight, save only a few;
Nor could he do battle with Hengest or harry his shattered host;
And the Frisians made terms with the Danes, a truce, a hall for their dwelling,
A throne, and a sharing of rights with the sons of the Jutes,
And that Finn, the son of Folcwalda, each day would honor the Danes,
The host of Hengest, with gifts, with rings and guerdon of gold,
Such portion of plated treasure as he dealt to the Frisian folk
When he gladdened their hearts in the hall. So both were bound by the truce.°
And Finn swore Hengest with oaths that were forceful and firm
He would rightfully rule his remnant, follow his council's decree,
And that no man should break the truce, or breach it by word or by will,
Nor the lordless in malice lament they were fated to follow
The man who had murdered their liege; and, if ever a Frisian
Fanned the feud with insolent speech, the sword should avenge° *it.*
Then a funeral pyre° *was prepared, and gold was drawn from the hoard,*
The best of the Scylding leaders° *was laid on the bier;*
In the burning pile was a gleaming of blood-stained byrnies,
The gilded swine° *and the boar-helm hard from the hammer,*
Many a warrior fated with wounds and fallen in battle.
And Hildeburh bade that her son be laid on the bier of Hnæf,
His body consumed in the surging flame at his uncle's shoulder.
Beside it the lady lamented, singing her mournful dirge.°
The hero was placed on the pyre;° *the greatest of funeral flames*
Rolled with a roar to the skies at the burial barrow.
Heads melted and gashes gaped, the mortal wounds of the body,
Blood poured out in the flames; the fire, most greedy of spirits,
Swallowed up all whom battle had taken of both their peoples.
Their glory was gone! The warriors went to their homes,
Bereft of their friends, returning to Friesland,° *to city and strong-hold.*
Then Hengest abode with Finn all the slaughter-stained winter,
But his heart longed ever for home, though he could not launch on the sea

---

nances in the minds of his hearers. We should know far less of the background if we did not have the story in the much more straightforward narrative of the independent fragment known as the Fight at Finnsburg.

Some think that the allusiveness is carried still further and that the Finnsburg lay is a kind of forecast of the treachery by which Hrothulf, Hrothgar's nephew, usurped the Danish throne from the rightful heirs, Hrothgar's sons, after the death of the old king.

truce This involved Hengest's taking service with the man who had killed his lord—a crime against the Germanic code and only to be justified because it served the final end of revenge.

avenge i.e. settle the dispute

pyre According to the older pagan custom the dead man's precious possessions were burned with him.

best . . . leaders i.e. Hnæf

swine boar-image on the helmet

dirge This was the pagan custom; cf. the woman at Beowulf's funeral, below; and Tacitus, *Germania*, 27.

hero . . . pyre probably a reference to Hildeburh's son

Friesland i.e. Frisian or Jutish country

His ring-stemmed ship, for the billows boiled wtih the storm,
Strove with the wind, and the winter locked ocean in bonds of ice;
Till a new Spring shone once more on the dwellings of men,
The sunny and shining days which ever observe their season.
The winter was banished afar, and fair the bosom of earth.
Then the exile longed to be gone, the guest from his dwelling,
But his thoughts were more on revenge than on voyaging over the wave,
Plotting assault on the Jutes, renewal of war with the sword.
So he spurned not° the naked hint when Hunlafing laid in his lap
The battle-flasher, the best of blades, well known to the Jutes!
In his own home death by the sword befell Finn, the fierce-hearted,
When Guthlaf and Oslaf° requited the grim attack,
The woe encountered beyond the sea, the sorrow they suffered,
Nor could bridle the restive spirits within their breasts!
Then the hall was reddened with blood and bodies of foemen,
Finn killed in the midst of his men, and the fair queen taken.
The Scylding warriors bore to their ships all treasure and wealth,
Such store as they found in the home of Finn of jewels and gems.
And the noble queen they carried across the sea-paths,
Brought her back to the Danes, to her own dear people.
So the song was sung, the lay recited,
The sound of revelry rose in the hall.
Stewards poured wine from wondrous vessels;
And Wealhtheow, wearing a golden crown,
Came forth in state where the two were sitting,
Courteous comrades, uncle and nephew,
Each true to the other in ties of peace.°
Unferth, the orator,° sat at the feet
Of the lord of the Scyldings; and both showed trust
In his noble mind, though he had no mercy
On kinsmen in swordplay; the Scylding queen spoke:
'My sovereign lord, dispenser of treasure,
Drink now of this flagon, have joy of the feast!
Speak to the Geats, O gold-friend of men,
In winning words as is well-befitting;
Be kind to the Geat-men and mindful of gifts
From the gold you have garnered from near and far.°
You have taken as son, so many have told me,
This hardy hero. Heorot is cleansed,
The gleaming gift-hall. Rejoice while you may

So . . . not This passage can be interpreted in several ways. As translated it seems to mean that the son of Hunlaf the Dane, who had taken part in the Danish-Frisian feud, placed a naked sword in Hengest's lap, as a token of allegiance and a reminder that the deaths of Hnæf and of Hunlaf in the fight at Finnsburg are still unavenged. The action is also a pledge that the son of Hunlaf will take part in the revenge, when it is taken. "Battle-flasher" may be the name of a special sword or a *kenning* (condensed metaphor) for any sword.

Guthlaf . . . Oslaf These two Danish warriors, brothers of Hunlaf, seem to have begun the second fight at Finnsburg.

peace perhaps a reference by ironic contrast to the usurpation and strife after Hrothgar's death

orator spokesman, counsellor, again represented as sitting in the place of honor

Be kind . . . far an incitement to generosity: the best sense that can be made of this obscure and difficult passage; the text may be corrupt

In lavish bounty, and leave to your kin
People and kingdom when time shall come,
Your destined hour, to look on death.
I know the heart of my gracious Hrothulf,
That he'll safely shelter and shield our sons
When you leave this world, if he still is living.
I know he will favor with gracious gifts
These boys of ours, if he bears in mind
The many honors and marks of love
We bestowed upon him while he still was a boy.'
She turned to the bench where her boys were sitting,
Hrethric and Hrothmund,° the sons of heroes,
The youth together; there the good man sat,
Beowulf of the Geats, beside the two brothers.
Then the cup was offered with gracious greeting,
And seemly presents of spiraled gold,
A corselet, and rings, and the goodliest collar°
Of all that ever were known on earth.
In the hoarding of heroes beneath the sky
I have never heard tell of a worthier treasure
Since Hama bore off to the shining city
The Brosings' jewel,° setting and gems,
Fled from Eormanric's cruel craft
And sought the grace of eternal glory.
Hygelac,° the Geat, grandson of Swerting
Wore the ring in the last of his raids,
Guarding the spoil under banner in battle,
Defending the treasure. Overtaken by Fate,
In the flush of pride he fought with the Frisians
And met disaster. The mighty prince
Carried the ring o'er the cup of the waves,
The precious jewel, and sank under shield.
Then his body fell into Frankish hands,
His woven corselet and jewelled collar,
And weaker warriors plundered the dead
After the carnage and welter of war.
The field of battle was covered with corpses
Of Geats who had fallen, slain by the sword.
The sound of revelry rose in the hall;
Wealhtheow spoke to the warrior host:
'Take, dear Beowulf, collar and corselet,
Wear these treasures with right good will!

Hrethric and Hrothmund sons of Hrothgar and Wealhtheow
collar torc, neck-ring, of gold
Brosings' jewel This was a necklace, which had, according to Old Norse legend, been made for the goddess Freyja, wife of Odin and goddess of love, fecundity, and death, by the Brisingas. The legend of how Hama, apparently, stole the necklace from Eormanric, king of the Ostrogoths—the historical Eormanric died about 375—is not otherwise known. In Norse legend Freyja loses the necklace through the treachery of Loki.
Hygelac cf. ll. 194 ff. and ll. 2222 ff., 2742 ff.

Thrive and prosper and prove your might!
Befriend my boys with your kindly counsel;
I will remember and I will repay.
You have earned the undying honor of heroes
In regions reaching as far and wide
As the windy walls that the sea encircles.
May Fate show favor while life shall last!
I wish you wealth to your heart's content;
In your days of glory be good to my sons!
Here each hero is true to other,
Gentle of spirit, loyal to lord,
Friendly thanes and a folk united,
Wine-cheered warriors who do my will.'

[*The Troll-Wife° Avenges Grendel*]

Then she went to her seat. At the fairest of feasts
Men drank of the wine-cup, knowing not Fate,
Nor the fearful doom that befell the earls
When darkness gathered, and gracious Hrothgar
Sought his dwelling and sank to rest.
A host of heroes guarded the hall
As they oft had done in the days of old.
They stripped the benches and spread the floor
With beds and bolsters. But one of the beer-thanes
Bowed to his hall-rest doomed to death.
They set at their heads their shining shields,
Their battle-bucklers; and there on the bench
Above each hero his towering helmet,
His spear and corselet hung close at hand.
It was ever their wont to be ready for war
At home or in field, as it ever befell
That their lord had need. 'Twas a noble race!
Then they sank to slumber. But one paid dear
For his evening rest, as had often happened
When Grendel haunted the lordly hall
And wrought such ruin, till his end was come,
Death for his sins; it was easily seen,
Though the monster was slain, an avenger survived
Prolonging the feud, though the fiend had perished.
The mother of Grendel, a monstrous hag,
Brooded over her misery, doomed to dwell
In evil waters and icy streams
From ancient ages when Cain had killed
His only brother, his father's son.
Banished and branded with marks of murder
Cain fled far from the joys of men,
Haunting the barrens, begetting a brood

Troll-Wife i.e. woman evil-spirit

Of grisly monsters; and Grendel was one,
The fiendish ogre who found in the hall
A hero on watch, and awaiting the fray.
The monster grappled; the Geat took thought
Of the strength of his might, that marvelous gift
Which the Lord had given; in God he trusted
For help and succor and strong support,
Whereby he humbled the fiend from hell,
Destroyed the demon; and Grendel fled,
Harrowed in heart and hateful to man,
Deprived of joy, to the place of death.
But rabid and raging his mother resolved
On a dreadful revenge for the death of her son!
She stole to the hall where the Danes were sleeping,
And horror fell on the host of earls
When the dam of Grendel burst in the door.
But the terror was less as the war-craft is weaker,
A woman's strength, than the might of a man
When the hilted sword, well shaped by the hammer,
The blood-stained iron of tempered edge,
Hews the boar from the foeman's helmet.
Then in the hall was the hard-edged blade,
The stout steel, brandished above the benches;
Seizing their shields men stayed not for helmet
Or ample byrny, when fear befell.
As soon as discovered, the hag was in haste
To fly to the open, to flee for her life.
One of the warriors she swiftly seized,
Clutched him fast and made off to the fens.
He was of heroes the dearest to Hrothgar,
The best of comrades between two seas;
The warrior brave, the stout-hearted spearman,
She slew in his sleep. Nor was Beowulf there;
But after the banquet another abode
Had been assigned to the glorious Geat.
There was tumult in Heorot. She tore from its place
The blood-stained claw. Care was renewed!
It was no good bargain when both in turn
Must pay the price with the lives of friends!
Then the white-haired warrior, the aged king,
Was numb with sorrow, knowing his thane
No longer was living, his dearest man dead.
Beowulf, the brave, was speedily summoned,
Brought to the bower; the noble prince
Came with his comrades at dawn of day
Where the wise king awaited if God would award
Some happier turn in these tidings of woe.
The hero came tramping into the hall

With his chosen band—the boards resounded—
Greeted the leader, the Ingwine lord,
And asked if the night had been peaceful and pleasant.
    Hrothgar spoke, the lord of the Scyldings:
'Ask not of pleasure; pain is renewed
For the Danish people. Æschere° is dead!
Dead is Yrmenlaf's elder brother!
He was my comrade, closest of counsellors,
My shoulder-companion as side by side
We fought for our lives in the welter of war,
In the shock of battle when boar-helms crashed.
As an earl should be, a prince without peer,
Such was Æschere, slain in the hall
By the wandering demon! I know not whither
She fled to shelter, proud of her spoil,
Gorged to the full. She avenged the feud
Wherein yesternight you grappled with Grendel
And savagely slew him because so long
He had hunted and harried the men of my folk.
He fell in the battle and paid with his life.
But now another fierce ravager rises
Avenging her kinsman, and carries it far,
As it seems to many a saddened thane
Who grieves in his heart for his treasure-giver.
This woe weighs heavy! The hand lies still
That once was lavish of all delights.
    Oft in the hall I have heard my people,
Comrades and counsellors, telling a tale
Of evil spirits their eyes have sighted,
Two mighty marauders who haunt the moors.
One shape, as clearly as men could see,
Seemed woman's likeness, and one seemed man,
An outcast wretch of another world,
And huger far than a human form.
Grendel my countrymen called him, not knowing
What monster-brood spawned him, what sire begot.
Wild and lonely the land they live in,
Wind-swept ridges and wolf-retreats,
Dread tracts of fen where the falling torrent
Downward dips into gloom and shadow
Under the dusk of the darkening cliff.
Not far in miles lies the lonely mere
Where trees firm-rooted and hung with frost
Overshroud the wave with shadowing gloom.
And there a portent appears each night,
A flame in the water; no man so wise

Æschere not otherwise known

Who knows the bound of its bottomless depth.
The heather-stepper, the horned stag,
The antlered hart hard driven by hounds,
Invading that forest in flight from afar
Will turn at bay and die on the brink
Ere ever he'll plunge in that haunted pool.
'Tis an eerie spot!° Its tossing spray
Mounts dark to heaven when high winds stir
The driving storm, and the sky is murky,
And with foul weather the heavens weep.
On your arm only rests all our hope!
Not yet have you tempted those terrible reaches
The region that shelters that sinful wight.
Go if you dare! I will give requital
With ancient treasure and twisted gold,
As I formerly gave in guerdon of battle,
If out of that combat you come alive.'
Beowulf spoke, the son of Ecgtheow:
'Sorrow not, brave one! Better for man
To avenge a friend than much to mourn.
All men must die; let him who may
Win glory ere death. That guerdon is best
For a noble man when his name survives him.
Then let us rise up, O ward of the realm,
And haste us forth to behold the track
Of Grendel's dam. And I give you pledge
She shall not in safety escape to cover,
To earthy cavern, or forest fastness,
Or gulf of ocean, go where she may.
This day with patience endure the burden
Of every woe, as I know you will.'
Up sprang the ancient, gave thanks to God
For the heartening words the hero had spoken.

[*Beowulf Slays the Troll-Wife*]

Quickly a horse was bridled for Hrothgar,
A mettlesome charger with braided mane;
In royal splendor the king rode forth
Mid the trampling tread of a troop of shieldmen.
The tracks lay clear where the fiend had fared
Over plain and bottom and woodland path,
Through murky moorland making her way
With the lifeless body, the best of thanes
Who of old with Hrothgar had guarded the hall.

eerie spot lit. "that is no pleasant spot." There are general resemblances to the visit to the underworld in the sixth book of Virgil's *Aeneid* and to the apocryphal *Vision of St. Paul,* but there are many features here for which the poet seems to have drawn on a typically Northern winter scene. There are also parallels with the Old Norse saga of Grettir. Later, an English sermon, perhaps of the ninth or earlier tenth century, draws on this passage in *Beowulf* for a description of an icy Hell.

By a narrow path the king pressed on
Through rocky upland and rugged ravine,
A lonely journey, past looming headlands,
The lair of monster and lurking troll.
Tried retainers, a trusty few,
Advanced with Hrothgar to view the ground.
Sudden they came on a dismal covert
Of trees that hung over hoary stone,
Over churning water and blood-stained wave.
Then for the Danes was the woe the deeper,
The sorrow sharper for Scylding earls,
When they first caught sight, on the rocky sea-cliff,
Of slaughtered Æschere's severed head.
The water boiled in a bloody swirling
With seething gore as the spearmen gazed.
The trumpet sounded a martial strain;
The shield-troop halted. Their eyes beheld
The swimming forms of strange sea-dragons,
Dim serpent shapes in the watery depths,
Sea-beasts sunning on headland slopes;
Snakelike monsters that oft at sunrise
On evil errands scour the sea.
Startled by tumult and trumpet's blare,
Enraged and savage, they swam away;
But one the lord of the Geats brought low,
Stripped of his sea-strength, despoiled of life,
As the bitter bow-bolt pierced his heart.
His watery-speed grew slower, and ceased,
And he floated, caught in the clutch of death.
Then they hauled him in with sharp-hooked boar-spears,
By sheer strength grappled and dragged him ashore,
A wondrous wave-beast; and all the array
Gathered to gaze at the grisly guest.
    Beowulf donned his armor for battle,
Heeded not danger; the hand-braided byrny,
Broad of shoulder and richly bedecked,°
Must stand the ordeal of the watery depths.
Well could that corselet defend the frame
Lest hostile thrust should pierce to the heart.
Or blows of battle beat down the life.
A gleaming helmet guarded his head
As he planned his plunge to the depths of the pool
Through the heaving waters—a helm adorned
With lavish inlay and lordly chains,
Ancient work of the weapon-smith
Skillfully fashioned, beset with the boar,

richly bedecked "Strongly made" is more accurate.

That no blade of battle might bite it through.
Not the least or the worst of his war-equipment
Was the sword° the herald of Hrothgar° loaned
In his hour of need—Hrunting° its name—
An ancient heirloom, trusty and tried;
Its blade was iron, with etched design,
Tempered in blood of many a battle.
Never in fight had it failed the hand
That drew it daring the perils of war,
The rush of the foe. Not the first time then
That its edge must venture on valiant deeds.
But Ecglaf's stalwart son was unmindful
Of words he had spoken while heated with wine,
When he loaned the blade to a better swordsman.
He himself dared not hazard his life
In deeds of note in the watery depths;
And thereby he forfeited honor and fame.
Not so with that other undaunted spirit
After he donned his armor for battle.
Beowulf spoke, the son of Ecgtheow:
'O gracious ruler, gold-giver to men,
As I now set forth to attempt this feat,
Great son of Healfdene, hold well in mind
The solemn pledge we plighted of old,
That if doing your service I meet my death
You will mark my fall with a father's love.
Protect my kinsmen, my trusty comrades,
If battle take me. And all the treasure
You have heaped on me bestow upon Hygelac,
Hrothgar beloved! The lord of the Geats,
The son of Hrethel, shall see the proof,
Shall know as he gazes on jewels and gold,
That I found an unsparing dispenser of bounty,
And joyed, while I lived, in his generous gifts.
Give back to Unferth the ancient blade,
The sword-edge splendid with curving scrolls,
For either with Hrunting I'll reap rich harvest
Of glorious deeds, or death shall take me.'
After these words the prince of the Weders
Awaited no answer, but turned to the task,
Straightway plunged in the swirling pool.
Nigh unto a day he endured the depths
Ere he first had view of the vast sea-bottom.
Soon she found, who had haunted the flood,
A ravening hag, for a hundred half-years,

sword The text calls it "gleaming with venom twigs," which may mean that the blade had a serpentine pattern.

herald of Hrothgar Unferth

Hrunting perhaps meaning Thruster

Greedy and grim, that a man was groping
In daring search through the sea-troll's home.
Swift she grappled and grasped the warrior
With horrid grip, but could work no harm,
No hurt to his body; the ring-locked byrny
Cloaked his life from her clutching claw;
Nor could she tear through the tempered mail
With her savage fingers. The she-wolf bore
The ring-prince down through the watery depths
To her den at the bottom; nor could Beowulf draw
His blade for battle, though brave his mood.
Many a sea-beast, strange sea-monsters,
Tasked him hard° with their menacing tusks,
Broke his byrny and smote him sore.
Then he found himself in a fearsome hall
Where water came not to work him hurt,
But the flood was stayed by the sheltering roof.
There in the glow of firelight gleaming
The hero had view of the huge sea-troll.
He swung his war-sword with all his strength,
Withheld not the blow, and the savage blade
Sang on her head its hymn of hate.
But the bold one found that the battle-flasher
Would bite no longer, nor harm her life.
The sword-edge failed at his sorest need.
Often of old with ease it had suffered
The clash of battle, cleaving the helm,
The fated warrior's woven mail.
That time was first for the treasured blade
That its glory failed in the press of the fray.
But fixed of purpose and firm of mood
Hygelac's earl was mindful of honor;
In wrath, undaunted, he dashed to earth
The jewelled sword with its scrolled design,
The blade of steel; staked all on strength,
On the might of his hand, as a man must do
Who thinks to win in the welter of battle
Enduring glory; he fears not death.
The Geat-prince joyed in the straining struggle,
Stalwart-hearted and stirred to wrath,
Gripped the shoulder of Grendel's dam
And headlong hurled the hag to the ground.
But she quickly clutched him and drew him close,
Countered the onset with savage claw.
The warrior staggered, for all his strength,
Dismayed and shaken and borne to earth.

Tasked him hard i.e. tore at him

She knelt upon him and drew her dagger,
With broad bright blade, to avenge her son,
Her only issue. But the corselet's steel
Shielded his breast and sheltered his life
Withstanding entrance of point and edge.
Then the prince of the Geats would have gone his journey,
The son of Ecgtheow, under the ground;
But his sturdy breast-net, his battle-corselet,
Gave him succor, and holy God,
The Lord all-wise, awarded the mastery;
Heaven's Ruler gave right decree.
Swift the hero sprang to his feet;
Saw 'mid the war-gear a stately sword,
An ancient war-brand of biting edge,
Choicest of weapons worthy and strong,
The work of giants,° a warrior's joy,
So heavy no hand but his own could hold it,
Bear to battle or wield in war.
Then the Scylding warrior, savage and grim,
Seized the ring-hilt and swung the sword,
Struck with fury, despairing of life,
Thrust at the throat, broke through the bone-rings;
The stout blade stabbed through her fated flesh.
She sank in death; the sword was bloody;
The hero joyed in the work of his hand.
The gleaming radiance shimmered and shone
As the candle of heaven shines clear from the sky.
Wrathful and resolute Hygelac's thane
Surveyed the span of the spacious hall;
Grimly gripping the hilted sword
With upraised weapon he turned to the wall.
The blade had failed not the battle-prince;
A full requital he firmly planned
For all the injury Grendel had done
In numberless raids on the Danish race,
When he slew the hearth-companions of Hrothgar,
Devoured fifteen of the Danish folk
Clasped in slumber, and carried away
As many more spearmen, a hideous spoil.
All this the stout-heart had stern requited;
And there before him bereft of life
He saw the broken body of Grendel
Stilled in battle, and stretched in death,
As the struggle in Heorot smote him down.
The corpse sprang wide as he struck the blow,
The hard sword-stroke that severed the head.
Then the tried retainers, who there with Hrothgar

work of giants i.e. huge, old, and powerful

Watched the face of the foaming pool,
Saw that the churning reaches were reddened,
The eddying surges stained with blood.
And the gray, old spearmen spoke of the hero,
Having no hope he would ever return
Crowned with triumph and cheered with spoil.
Many were sure that the savage sea-wolf
Had slain their leader. At last came noon.
The stalwart Scyldings forsook the headland;
Their proud gold-giver departed home.
But the Geats sat grieving and sick in spirit,
Stared at the water with longing eyes,
Having no hope they would ever behold
Their gracious leader and lord again.
Then the great sword, eaten with blood of battle,
Began to soften and waste away
In iron icicles, wonder of wonders,
Melting away most like to ice
When the Father looses the fetters of frost,
Slackens the bondage that binds the wave,
Strong in power of times and seasons;
He is true God! Of the goodly treasures
From the sea-cave Beowulf took but two,
The monster's head and the precious hilt
Blazing with gems; but the blade had melted,
The sword dissolved, in the deadly heat,
The venomous blood of the fallen fiend.

[*Beowulf Returns to Heorot*]

Then he who had compassed the fall of his foes
Came swimming up through the swirling surge.
Cleansed were the currents, the boundless abyss,
Where the evil monster had died the death
And looked her last on this fleeting world.
With sturdy strokes the lord of the seamen
To land came swimming, rejoiced in his spoil,
Had joy of the burden he brought from the depths.
And his mighty thanes came forward to meet him,
Gave thanks to God they were granted to see
Their well-loved leader both sound and safe.
From the stalwart hero his helmet and byrny
Were quickly loosened; the lake lay still,
Its motionless reaches reddened with blood.
Fain of heart men fared o'er the footpaths,
Measured the ways and the well-known roads.
From the sea-cliff's brim the warriors bore
The head of Grendel, with heavy toil;
Four of the stoutest, with all their strength,

Could hardly carry on swaying spear
Grendel's head to the gold-decked hall.
Swift they strode, the daring and dauntless,
Fourteen Geats, to the Hall of the Hart;
And proud in the midst of his marching men
Their leader measured the path to the mead-hall.
The hero entered, the hardy in battle,
The great in glory, to greet the king;
And Grendel's head by the hair was carried
Across the floor where the feasters drank—
A terrible sight for lord and for lady—
A gruesome vision whereon men gazed!
　　Beowulf spoke, the son of Ecgtheow:
'O son of Healfdene, lord of the Scyldings!
This sea-spoil wondrous, whereon you stare,
We joyously bring you in token of triumph!
Barely with life surviving the battle,
The war under water, I wrought the deed
Weary and spent; and death had been swift
Had God not granted His sheltering strength.
My strong-edged Hrunting, stoutest of blades,
Availed me nothing. But God revealed—
Often His arm has aided the friendless—
The fairest of weapons hanging on wall,
An ancient broadsword; I seized the blade,
Slew in the struggle, as fortune availed,
The cavern-warders. But the war-brand old,
The battle-blade with its scrolled design,
Dissolved in the gush of the venomous gore;
The hilt alone I brought from the battle.
The record of ruin, and slaughter of Danes,
These wrongs I avenged, as was fitting and right.
Now I can promise you, prince of the Scyldings,
Henceforth in Heorot rest without rue
For you and your nobles; nor need you dread
Slaughter of follower, stalwart or stripling,°
Or death of earl, as of old you did.'
Into the hand of the aged leader,
The gray-haired hero, he gave the hilt,
The work of giants, the wonder of gold.
At the death of the demons the Danish lord
Took in his keeping the cunning craft,
The wondrous marvel, of mighty smiths;
When the world was freed of the ravaging fiend,
The foe of God, and his fearful dam

stalwart or stripling i.e. member of the *duguth*, the tried and seasoned warriors; or the *geogoth*, the young retainers

Marked with murder and badged° with blood,
The bound hilt passed to the best of kings
Who ever held sceptre beside two seas,
And dealt out treasure in Danish land!
Hrothgar spoke, beholding the hilt,
The ancient relic whereon was etched
An olden record of struggle and strife,
The flood that ravaged the giant race,°
The rushing deluge of ruin and death.
That evil kindred were alien to God,
But the Ruler avenged with the wrath of the deep!
On the hilt-guards, likewise, of gleaming gold
Was rightly carven in cunning runes,
Set forth and blazoned, for whom that blade,
With spiral tooling and twisted hilt,
That fairest of swords, was fashioned and smithied.
Then out spoke Hrothgar, Healfdene's son,
And all the retainers were silent and still:
'Well may he say, whose judgment is just,
Recalling to memory men of the past,
That this earl was born of a better stock!
Your fame, friend Beowulf, is blazoned abroad
Over all wide ways, and to every people.
In manful fashion have you showed your strength,
Your might and wisdom. My word I will keep,
The plighted friendship we formerly pledged.
Long shall you stand as a stay to your people,
A help to heroes, as Heremod° was not
To the Honor-Scyldings, to Ecgwela's° sons!
Not joy to kindred, but carnage and death,
He wrought as he ruled o'er the race of the Danes.
In savage anger he slew his comrades,
His table-companions, till, lawless and lone,
An odious outcast, he fled from men.
Though God had graced him with gifts of strength,
Over all men exalting him, still in his breast
A bloodthirsty spirit was rooted and strong.
He dealt not rings to the Danes for glory;
His lot was eternal torment of woe,
And lasting affliction. Learn from his fate!
Strive for virtue! I speak for your good;
In the wisdom of age I have told the tale.
'Tis a wondrous marvel how mighty God°

badged marked, distinguished by
The flood . . . race Noah's flood, which overwhelmed the wicked race of giants
Heremod see above, ll. 841 ff. His name means "Warlike disposition." King of the Danes before Scyld, he seems to have given promise of being a splendid king, but he turned out to be cruel, avaricious, and oppressive.
Ecgwela's a Danish king, otherwise unknown: his name means "Sword-wealth"
'Tis . . . God Hrothgar seizes the occasion to moralize the encounter—cf. the earlier Heremod digression above—in terms of spiritual attack and defense, the transitoriness of human life and happiness.

In gracious spirit bestows on men
The gift of wisdom, and goodly lands,
And princely power! He rules over all!
He suffers a man of lordly line
To set his heart on his own desires,
Awards him fullness of worldly joy,
A fair home-land, and the sway of cities,
The wide dominion of many a realm,
An ample kingdom, till, cursed with folly,
The thoughts of his heart take no heed of his end.
He lives in luxury, knowing not want,
Knowing no shadow of sickness or age;
No haunting sorrow darkens his spirit,
No hatred or discord deepens to war;
The world is sweet, to his every desire,
And evil assails not—until in his heart
Pride overpowering gathers and grows!
The warder slumbers, the guard of his spirit;
Too sound is that sleep, too sluggish the weight
Of worldly affairs, too pressing the Foe,
The Archer who looses the arrows of sin.
    Then is his heart pierced, under his helm,
His soul in his bosom, with bitter dart.
He has no defense for the fierce assaults
Of the loathsome Fiend. What he long has cherished
Seems all too little! In anger and greed
He gives no guerdon of plated rings.
Since God has granted him glory and wealth
He forgets the future, unmindful of Fate.
But it comes to pass in the day appointed
His feeble body withers and fails;
Death descends, and another seizes
His hoarded riches and rashly spends
The princely treasure, imprudent of heart.
Beloved Beowulf, best of warriors,
Avoid such evil and seek the good,
The heavenly wisdom. Beware of pride!
Now for a time you shall feel the fullness
And know the glory of strength, but soon
Sickness or sword shall strip you of might,
Or clutch of fire, or clasp of flood,
Or flight of arrow, or bite of blade,
Or relentless age; or the light of the eye
Shall darken and dim, and death on a sudden,
O lordly ruler, shall lay you low.
    A hundred half-years I've been head of the Ring-Danes,
Defending the folk against many a tribe
With spear-point and sword in the surges of battle
Till not one was hostile 'neath heaven's expanse.

But a loathsome change swept over the land,
Grief after gladness, when Grendel came,
That evil invader, that ancient foe!
Great sorrow of soul from his malice I suffered;
But thanks be to God who has spared me to see
His bloody head at the battle's end!
Join now in the banquet; have joy of the feast,
O mighty in battle! And the morrow shall bring
Exchange of treasure in ample store.'
Happy of heart the Geat leader hastened,
Took seat at the board as the good king bade.
Once more, as of old, brave heroes made merry
And tumult of revelry rose in the hall.
Then dark over men the night shadows deepened;
The host all arose, for Hrothgar was minded,
The gray, old Scylding, to go to his rest.
On Beowulf too, after labor of battle,
Came limitless longing and craving for sleep.
A hall-thane graciously guided the hero,
Weary and worn, to the place prepared,
Serving his wishes and every want
As befitted a mariner come from afar.
The stout-hearted warrior sank to his rest;
The lofty building, splendid and spacious,
Towered above him. His sleep was sound
Till the black-coated raven, blithesome of spirit,
Hailed the coming of Heaven's bliss.°

[*The Parting of Beowulf and Hrothgar*]

Then over the shadows uprose the sun.
The Geats were in haste, and eager of heart
To depart to their people. Beowulf longed
To embark in his boat, to set sail for his home.
The hero tendered the good sword Hrunting
To the son of Ecglaf,° bidding him bear
The lovely blade; gave thanks for the loan,
Called it a faithful friend in the fray,
Bitter in battle. The greathearted hero
Spoke no word in blame of the blade!
Arrayed in war-gear, and ready for sea,
The warriors bestirred them; and, dear to the Danes,
Beowulf sought the high seat of the king.
The gallant in war gave greeting to Hrothgar;
Beowulf spoke, the son of Ecgtheow:
'It is time at last to tell of our longing!
Our homes are far, and our hearts are fain
To seek again Hygelac over the sea.

Heaven's bliss i.e. the sun

son of Ecglaf Unferth

You have welcomed us royally, harbored us well
As a man could wish; if I ever can win
Your affection more fully, O leader of heroes,
Swift shall you find me to serve you again!
If ever I learn, o'er the levels of ocean,
That neighboring nations beset you sore,
As in former days when foemen oppressed,
With thanes by the thousand I will hasten to help.
For I know that Hygelac, lord of the Geats,
Prince of the people, though young in years,
Will favor and further by word and deed
That my arm may aid you, and do you honor,
With stout ash-spear and succor of strength
In the press of need. And if princely Hrethric°
Shall purpose to come to the court of the Geats,
He will find there a legion of loyal friends.
That man fares best to a foreign country
Who himself is stalwart and stout of heart.'
Hrothgar addressed him, uttered his answer:
'Truly, these words has the Lord of wisdom
Set in your heart, for I never have harkened
To speech so sage from a man so young.
You have strength, and prudence, and wisdom of word!
I count it true if it come to pass
That point of spear in the press of battle,
Or deadly sickness, or stroke of sword,
Shall slay your leader, the son of Hrethel,
The prince of your people, and you still live,
The Sea-Geats could have no happier choice
If you would be willing to rule the realm,
As king to hold guard o'er the hoard and the heroes.
The longer I know you, the better I like you,°
Beloved Beowulf! You have brought it to pass
That between our peoples a lasting peace
Shall bind the Geats to the Danish-born;
And strife shall vanish, and war shall cease,
And former feuds, while I rule this realm.
And many a man, in the sharing of treasure,
Shall greet another with goodly gifts
O'er the gannet's° bath. And the ring-stemmed ship
Shall bear over ocean bountiful riches
In pledge of friendship. Our peoples, I know,
Shall be firm united toward foe and friend,
Faultless in all things, in fashion of old.'
Then the son of Healfdene, shelter of earls,
Bestowed twelve gifts on the hero in hall,

Hrethric eldest son of Hrothgar
The longer . . . you lit. "The temper of your heart pleases me more the more I see of it . . ."
gannet's sea-bird's

Bade him in safety with bounty of treasure
Seek his dear people, and soon return.
The peerless leader, the Scylding lord,
Kissed the good thane and clasped to his bosom
While tears welled fast from the old man's eyes.
Both chances he weighed in his wise, old heart,
But greatly doubted if ever again
They should meet at council or drinking of mead.
Nor could Hrothgar master—so dear was the man—
His swelling sorrow; a yearning love
For the dauntless hero, deep in his heart,
Burned through his blood. Beowulf, the brave,
Prizing his treasure and proud of the gold,
Turned away, treading the grassy plain.
The ring-stemmed sea-goer, riding at anchor,
Awaited her lord. There was loud acclaim
Of Hrothgar's gifts, as they went their way.
He was a king without failing or fault,
Till old age, master of all mankind,
Stripped him of power and pride of strength.

[*Beowulf Returns to Geatland*]

Then down to the sea came the band of the brave,
The host of young heroes in harness of war,
In their woven mail; and the coast-warden viewed
The heroes' return, as he heeded their coming!
No uncivil greeting he gave from the sea-cliff
As they strode to ship in their glistening steel;
But rode toward them and called their return
A welcome sight for their Weder kin
There on the sand the ring-stemmed ship,
The broad-bosomed bark, was loaded with war-gear,
With horses and treasure; the mast towered high
Over the riches of Hrothgar's hoard.
A battle-sword Beowulf gave to the boatwarden
Hilted with gold; and thereafter in hall
He had the more honor because of the heirloom,
The shining treasure. The ship was launched.
Cleaving the combers of open sea
They dropped the shoreline of Denmark astern.
A stretching sea-cloth, a bellying sail,
Was bent on the mast; there was groaning of timbers;
A gale was blowing; the boat drove on.
The foamy-necked plunger plowed through the billows,
The ring-stemmed ship through the breaking seas,
Till at last they sighted the sea-cliffs of Geatland,
The well-known headlands; and, whipped by the wind,
The boat drove shoreward and beached on the sand.
Straightway the harbor-watch strode to the seashore;

Long had he watched for the well-loved men,
Scanning the ocean with eager eyes!
The broad-bosomed boat he bound to the shingle
With anchor ropes, lest the rip of the tide
Should wrench from its mooring the comely craft.
    From the good ship Beowulf bade them bear
The precious jewels and plated gold,
The princely treasure.° Not long was the path
That led to where Hygelac, son of Hrethel,
The giver of treasure, abode in his home
Hard by the sea-wall, hedged by his thanes.
Spacious the castle, splendid the king
On his high hall-seat; youthful was Hygd,°
Wise and well-born—though winters but few
Hæreth's daughter had dwelt at court.
She was noble of spirit, not sparing in gifts
Of princely treasure to the people of the Geats.

    Of the pride of Thryth,° and her crimes, the fair folk-queen was free;
Thryth, of whose liegemen none dared by day, save only her lord,
Lift up his eyes to her face, lest his fate be a mortal bondage,
Seizure and fetters and sword, a blow of the patterned blade
Declaring his doom, and proclaiming the coming of death.
That is no way of a queen, nor custom of lovely lady,
Though peerless her beauty and proud, that a weaver of peace°
Should send a dear man to his death for a feigned affront.
But the kinsman of Hemming° at last made an end of her evil.
For men at the drinking of mead tell tale of a change,
How she wrought less ruin and wrong when, given in marriage
Gleaming with jewels and gold, to the high-born hero and young,
Over the fallow° flood she sailed, at her father's bidding
Seeking the land of Offa, and there while she lived,
Famed for goodness, fulfilled her fate on the throne.
She held high love for her lord, the leader of heroes,
The best, I have heard, of mankind or the children of men

treasure A gift to Beowulf would have at least to be formally offered to his lord, who could remit it to him.

Hygd Hygelac's queen, a young woman, daughter of Hæreth, is suddenly introduced into the narrative. She may have married Beowulf after Hygelac's death. Later, she offers the Geat throne to Beowulf in place of her young son Heardred.

Thryth "Strength." Some investigators take the name to be Modthryth. Thryth seems to be a version of the cruel queen who puts to death all except one who look at her. She is the equivalent of Brunhild in another Germanic romance, the *Nibelungenlied*. The male exception, in such tales, is sometimes the father of the cruel woman, or the hero who conquers her (for another, in the case of Brunhild). The digression is probably meant to throw Hygd's virtues into high relief by comparison with Thryth's evil nature.

weaver of peace a woman, one of whose functions it would be to heal differences—or, more specifically, a king's daughter given in marriage to seal a peace or alliance

kinsman of Hemming King Offa, husband of Thryth. According to an Anglian legend, he was the ancestor of another ruler, named Offa: the king of Mercia, one of the Anglo-Saxon kingdoms. Nothing more is known of his kinsman, Hemming. The use of Thryth to praise Hygd *per contrariam* modulates into a praise by direct comparison of the reformed Thryth, after her marriage to Offa, with Hygd. A version of the legend of Offa and Thryth (the Constance legend), with the cruelties reversed, is later told by Chaucer's Man of Law. Offa and his kinsmen are the only Englishmen mentioned in the poem.

fallow gray-brown

Between the two seas; for Offa, the stalwart, was honored
For his gifts and his greatness in war. With wisdom he governed;
And from him Eomær descended, Hemming's kinsman, grandson of Garmund,°
Stalwart and strong in war, and the helper of heroes.

Then the hero strode with his stalwart band
Across the stretches of sandy beach,
The wide sea-shingle. The world-candle shone,
The hot sun hasting on high from the south.
Marching together they made their way
To where in his stronghold the stout young king,
Ongentheow's slayer,° protector of earls,
Dispensed his treasure. Soon Hygelac heard
Of the landing of Beowulf, bulwark of men,
That his shoulder-companion had come to his court
Sound and safe from the strife of battle.
The hall was prepared, as the prince gave bidding,
Places made ready for much travelled men.
And he who came safe from the surges of battle
Sat by the side of the king himself,
Kinsman by kinsman; in courtly speech
His liege lord greeted the loyal thane
With hearty welcome. And Hæreth's daughter
Passed through the hall-building pouring the mead,
With courtesy greeting the gathered host,
Bearing the cup to the hands of the heroes.
In friendly fashion in high-built hall
Hygelac questioned his comrade and thane;
For an eager longing burned in his breast
To hear from the Sea-Geats the tale of their travels.
'How did you fare in your far sea-roving,
Beloved Beowulf, in your swift resolve
To sail to the conflict, the combat in Heorot,
Across the salt waves? Did you soften at all
The sorrows of Hrothgar, the weight of his woe?
Deeply I brooded with burden of care
For I had no faith in this far sea-venture
For one so beloved. Long I implored
That you go not against the murderous monster,
But let the South Danes settle the feud
Themselves with Grendel. To God be thanks
That my eyes behold you unharmed and unhurt.'
Beowulf spoke, the son of Ecgtheow:
'My dear lord Hygelac, many have heard°

Eomær . . . Garmund Little or nothing is known of these two.

Ongentheow's slayer Hygelac did not kill Ongentheow with his own hands, though he led the Geats in their attack on Ongentheow's people, the Scylfings. The full story is told below (ll. 2749 ff.).

many . . . heard lit. "from many it is not concealed"

Of that famous grapple 'twixt Grendel and me,
The bitter struggle and strife in the hall
Where he formerly wrought such ruin and wrong,
Such lasting sorrow for Scylding men!
All that I avenged! Not any on earth
Who longest lives of that loathsome brood,
No kin of Grendel cloaked in his crime,
Has cause to boast of that battle by night!
First, in that country, I fared to the hall
With greeting for Hrothgar; Healfdene's kinsman
Learned all my purpose, assigned me a place
Beside his own son. 'Twas a happy host!
I never have seen under span of heaven
More mirth of heroes sitting at mead!
The peerless queen, the peace-pledge° of peoples,
Passed on her round through the princely hall;
There was spurring of revels, dispensing of rings,
Ere the noble woman went to her seat.
At times in the host the daughter of Hrothgar
Offered the beaker to earls in turn;
Freawaru men called her, the feasters in hall,
As she held out to heroes the well-wrought cup.
Youthful and gleaming with jewels of gold
To the fair son of Froda° the maiden is plighted.
For the Scylding leader, the lord of the land,
Deems it wise counsel, accounting it gain,
To settle by marriage the murderous feud,
The bloody slaughter! But seldom for long
Does the spear go ungrasped when a prince has perished,
Though the bride in her beauty be peerless and proud!
Ill may it please the Heathobard prince
And all his thanes, when he leads his lady
Into the hall, that a Danish noble
Should be welcomed there by the Heathobard host.
For on him shall flash their forefathers' heirlooms,°
Hard-edged, ring-hilted, the Heathobards' hoard
When of old they had war-might, nor wasted in battle
Their lives and the lives of their well-loved thanes.
Then an aged spearman° shall speak at the beer-feast,
The treasure beholding with sorrow of heart,
Remembering sadly the slaughter of men,

peace-pledge i.e. her marriage had been part of a peace settlement between nations

son of Froda Froda was king of the Heathobards, an unidentified Germanic tribe. Freawaru, Hrothgar's daughter, had been betrothed to Ingeld, Froda's son, in pledge of peace between the Danes and the Heathobards. The poet's purpose in putting the story of the Danish-Heathobard feud into the mouth of Beowulf is much debated: it may be intended as a sort of prophecy or as a display of political wisdom on the part of the Geat, who can see the dangers of Hrothgar's attempt to settle the feud by marriage.

heirlooms Armor and ornaments that had been Heathobard property before they were captured by the Danes; they will remind the Heathobards of vengeance untaken.

spearman a Heathobard

Grimly goading the young hero's spirit,
Spurring to battle, speaking this word:
"Do you see, my lord, the sword of your father,
The blade he bore to the last of his fights,
The pride of his heart as, under his helmet,
The Scyldings slew him, the savage Danes,
When Withergyld° fell, and after the slaughter,
The fall of heroes, they held the field?
And now a son of those bloody butchers,
Proud in his trappings, tramps into hall
And boasts of the killing, clothed with the treasure
That is yours by your birthright to have and to hold?"
Over and over the old man will urge him,
With cutting reminders recalling the past
Till it comes at last that the lady's thane,°
For the deeds of his father, shall forfeit his life
In a bloody slaughter, slain by the sword,
While the slayer goes scatheless knowing the land.
On both sides then shall sword-oaths be broken
When hate boils up within Ingeld's heart,
And his love of his lady grows cooler and lessens
Because of his troubles. I count not true
Heathobard faith, nor their part in the peace,
Nor their friendship firm to the Danish folk.
I must now speak on, dispenser of treasure,
Further of Grendel, till fully you know
How we fared in that fierce and furious fight!
When the jewel of heaven had journeyed o'er earth,
The wrathful demon, the deadly foe,
Stole through the darkness spying us out
Where still unharmed we guarded the gold-hall.
But doom in battle and bitter death
Were Handscio's° fate! He was first to perish
Though girded with weapon and famous in war.
Grendel murdered him, mangled his body,
Bolted the dear man's bloody corpse.
No sooner for that would the slaughterous spirit,
Bloody of tooth and brooding on evil,
Turn empty-handed away from the hall!
The mighty monster made trial of my strength
Clutching me close with his ready claw.
Wide and wondrous his huge pouch° hung
Cunningly fastened, and fashioned with skill
From skin of dragon by devil's craft.
Therein the monster was minded to thrust me

Withergyld a Heathobard warrior
lady's thane a Dane attendant on Freawaru
Handscio's a Geat warrior companion of Beowulf's
pouch lit. "glove"; a huge glove is carried by trolls in Old Norse stories

Sinless and blameless, and many beside.
But it might not be, when I rose in wrath,
And fronted the hell-fiend face to face.
Too long is the tale how I took requital
On the cursed foe for his every crime,
But the deeds I did were a lasting honor,
Beloved prince, to your people's name.
He fled away, and a fleeting while
Possessed his life and the world's delights;
But he left in Heorot his severed hand,
A bloody reminder to mark his track.
Humbled in spirit and wretched in heart
Down he sank to the depths of the pool.
When the morrow fell, and we feasted together,
The Scylding ruler rewarded me well
For the bloody strife, in guerdon bestowing
Goodly treasure of beaten gold.
There was song and revel. The aged Scylding
From well-stored mind spoke much of the past.
A warrior sang to the strains of the glee-wood,°
Sometimes melodies mirthful and joyous,
Sometimes lays that were tragic and true.
And the great-hearted ruler at times would tell
A tale of wonder in fitting words.
Heavy with years the white-haired warrior
Grieved for his youth and the strength that was gone;
And his heart was moved by the weight of his winters
And many a memory out of the past.
All the long day we made merry together
Till another night came to the children of men,
And quickly the mother of Grendel was minded
To wreak her vengeance; raging with grief
She came to the hall where the hate of the Weders
Had slain her son. But the hideous hag
Avenged his killing; with furious clutch
She seized a warrior—the soul of Æschere,
Wise and aged, went forth from the flesh!
Not at all could the Danes, when the morrow dawned,
Set brand° to his body or burn on the bale°
Their well-loved comrade. With fiendish clasp
She carried his corpse through the fall of the force.°
That was to Hrothgar, prince of the people,
Sorest of sorrows that ever befell!
For your sake the sad-hearted hero° implored me
To prove my valor and, venturing life,°

glee-wood harp
brand i.e. firebrand
bale funeral pyre
force waterfall, cascade
hero Hrothgar
venturing life lit. "by your life," perhaps "for your sake"

To win renown in the watery depths.
He promised reward. Full well is it known
How I humbled the horrible guard of the gulf.
Hand to hand for a space we struggled
Till the swirling eddies were stained with blood;
With cleaving sword-edge I severed the head
Of Grendel's hag in that hall of strife.
Not easily thence did I issue alive,
But my death was not fated; not yet was I doomed!
Then the son of Healfdene, the shelter of earls,
Gave many a treasure to mark the deed.
The good king governed with courtly custom;
In no least way did I lose reward,
The meed° of my might; but he gave me treasure,
Healfdene's son, to my heart's desire.
These riches I bring you, ruler of heroes,
And warmly tender with right good will.
Save for you, King Hygelac, few are my kinsmen,
Few are the favors but come from you.'
Then he bade men bring the boar-crested headpiece,
The towering helmet, and steel-gray sark,°
The splendid war-sword, and spoke this word:
'The good king Hrothgar gave me this gift,
This battle-armor, and first to you
Bade tell the tale of his friendly favor.
He said King Heorogar,° lord of the Scyldings,
Long had worn it, but had no wish
To leave the mail to his manful son,
The dauntless Heoroweard, dear though he was!
Well may you wear it! Have joy of it all.'
As I've heard the tale, he followed the trappings
With four bay° horses, matched and swift,
Graciously granting possession of both,
The steeds and the wealth. 'Tis the way of a kinsman,
Not weaving in secret the wiles of malice
Nor plotting the fall of a faithful friend.
To his kinsman Hygelac, hardy in war,
The heart of the nephew was trusty and true;
Dear to each was the other's good!
To Hygd, as I've heard, he presented three horses
Gaily saddled, slender and sleek,
And the gleaming necklace Wealhtheow gave,
A peerless gift from a prince's daughter.
With the gracious guerdon, the goodly jewel,
Her breast thereafter was well bedecked.

meed reward
sark shirt of mail

Heorogar Hrothgar's brother and predecessor as king of the Danes
bay lit. "apple-fallow"—bright brown

So the son of Ecgtheow bore himself bravely,
Known for his courage and courteous deeds,
Strove after honor, slew not his comrades
In drunken brawling; nor brutal his mood.
But the bountiful gifts which the Lord God gave him
He held with a power supreme among men.
He had long been scorned,° when the sons of the Geats
Accounted him worthless; the Weder lord
Held him not high among heroes in hall.
Laggard they deemed him, slothful° and slack.
But time brought solace for all his ills!
Then the battle-bold king, the bulwark of heroes,
Bade bring a battle-sword banded with gold,
The heirloom° of Hrethel; no sharper steel,
No lovelier treasure, belonged to the Geats.
He laid the war-blade on Beowulf's lap,
Gave him a hall and a stately seat
And hides° seven thousand. Inherited lands
Both held by birth-fee, home and estate.°
But one held rule o'er the spacious realm,
And higher therein his order and rank.

[*The Fire-Dragon and the Treasure*]

It later befell in the years that followed
After Hygelac sank in the surges of war,
And the sword slew Heardred° under his shield
When the Battle-Scylfings, those bitter fighters,
Invaded the land of the victor-folk
Overwhelming Hereric's nephew in war,
That the kingdom came into Beowulf's hand.
For fifty winters he governed it well,
Aged and wise with the wisdom of years,
Till a fire-drake° flying in darkness of night
Began to ravage and work his will.
On the upland heath he guarded a hoard,
A stone barrow lofty. Under it lay
A path concealed from the sight of men.
There a thief broke in on the heathen treasure,
Laid hand on a flagon all fretted with gold,

scorned We have no other information on Beowulf's younger, feebler days. The scorned weakling who grows into a mighty hero is a frequent figure in folktales.
slothful weak
heirloom i.e. inherited by Hrothgar from his father
hides a huge tract of land. A hide was basically the area of land required for the subsistence of one free peasant family and its dependents, or, alternatively, as much land as could be worked by one plow in one year. Thus the size varies with the peasant's standard of living in different parts of the country from 40 to 120 acres. The gift to Beowulf is a princely one.
Inherited . . . estate Both Hygelac and Beowulf had inherited land, a house, and the estate that went with it.
Heardred The story is told more fully below. Heardred, Hygelac's son, succeeded his father as king, but was killed by the Swedes (Battle-Scylfings) on his own territory. Hereric was probably his maternal uncle, Hygd's brother.
fire-drake a fiery dragon, such as the *Anglo-Saxon Chronicle* records as having been seen in the late 8th century.

As the dragon discovered, though cozened in sleep
By the pilferer's cunning. The people soon found
That the mood of the dragon was roused to wrath!°
    Not at all with intent, of his own free will,
Did he ravish the hoard, who committed the wrong;
But in dire distress the thrall° of a thane,
A guilty fugitive fleeing the lash,
Forced his way in. There a horror befell him!
Yet the wretched exile escaped from the dragon,
Swift in retreat when the terror arose.
A flagon he took. There, many such treasures
Lay heaped in that earth-hall where the owner of old
Had carefully hidden the precious hoard,
The countless wealth of a princely clan.
Death came upon them in days gone by
And he who lived longest, the last of his line,
Guarding the treasure and grieving for friend,
Deemed it his lot that a little while only
He too might hold that ancient hoard.
A barrow new-built near the ocean billows
Stood cunningly° fashioned beneath the cliff;
Into the barrow the ring-warden bore
The princely treasure, the precious trove
Of golden wealth, and these words he spoke:
'Keep thou, O Earth, what men could not keep—
This costly treasure—it came from thee!
Baleful slaughter has swept away,
Death in battle, the last of my blood;
They have lived their lives; they have left the mead-hall.
Now I have no one to wield the sword,
No one to polish the plated cup,
The precious flagon—the host is fled.
The hard-forged helmet fretted with gold
Shall be stripped of its inlay; the burnishers sleep
Whose charge was to brighten the battle-masks.
Likewise the corselet that countered in war
'Mid clashing of bucklers the bite of the sword—
Corselet and warrior decay into dust;
Mailed coat and hero are moveless and still.
No mirth of gleewood, no music of harp,
No good hawk swinging in flight through the hall;
No swift steed stamps in the castle yard;
Death has ravished an ancient race.'
So sad of mood he bemoaned his sorrow,

There . . . wrath (ll. 2087–91) The manuscript is badly damaged at this point; so it is possible only to guess at the precise meaning of the text.

thrall a slave escaping from his master

cunningly lit. "made difficult of access"

Lonely and sole survivor of all,
Restless by day and wretched by night
Till the clutch of death caught at his heart.
Then the goodly treasure was found unguarded
By the venomous dragon enveloped in flame,
The old naked night-foe flying in darkness,
Haunting the barrows; a bane that brings
A fearful dread to the dwellers of earth.
His wont is to hunt out a hoard under ground
And guard heathen gold, growing old with the years.
But no whit for that is his fortune more fair!
For three hundred winters this waster of peoples
Held the huge treasure-hall under the earth
Till the robber aroused him to anger and rage,
Stole the rich beaker and bore to his master,
Imploring his lord for a compact of peace.
So the hoard was robbed and its riches plundered;
To the wretch was granted the boon that he begged;
And his liege-lord first had view of the treasure,
The ancient work of the men of old.
Then the worm awakened and war was kindled,
The rush of the monster along the rock,
When the fierce one found the tracks of the foe;
He had stepped too close in his stealthy cunning
To the dragon's head. But a man undoomed
May endure with ease disaster and woe
If he has His favor who wields the world.
Swiftly the fire-drake sought through the plain
The man who wrought him this wrong in his sleep.
Inflamed and savage he circled the mound,
But the waste was deserted—no man was in sight.
The worm's mood was kindled to battle and war;
Time and again he returned to the barrow
Seeking the treasure-cup. Soon he was sure
That a man had plundered the precious gold.
Enraged and restless the hoard-warden waited
The gloom of evening. The guard of the mound
Was swollen with anger; the fierce one resolved
To requite with fire the theft of the cup.
Then the day was sped as the worm desired;
Lurking no longer within his wall
He sallied forth surrounded with fire,
Encircled with flame. For the folk of the land
The beginning was dread as the ending was grievous
That came so quickly upon their lord.
Then the baleful stranger belched fire and flame,
Burned the bright dwellings—the glow of the blaze
Filled hearts with horror. The hostile flier

Was minded to leave there nothing alive.
From near and from far the war of the dragon,
The might of the monster, was widely revealed
So that all could see how the ravaging scather
Hated and humbled the Geatish folk.
Then he hastened back ere the break of dawn
To his secret den and the spoil of gold.
He had compassed the land with a flame of fire,
A blaze of burning; he trusted the wall,
The sheltering mound, and the strength of his might—
But his trust betrayed him! The terrible news
Was brought to Beowulf, told for a truth,
That his home was consumed in the surges of fire,
The goodly dwelling and throne of the Geats.
The heart of the hero was heavy with anguish,
The greatest of sorrows; in his wisdom he weened
He had grievously angered the Lord Everlasting,
Blamefully broken the ancient law.
Dark thoughts stirred in his surging bosom,
Welled in his breast, as was not his wont.
The flame of the dragon had levelled the fortress,
The people's stronghold washed by the wave.
But the king of warriors, prince of the Weders,
Exacted an ample revenge for it all.
The lord of warriors and leader of earls
Bade work him of iron a wondrous shield,
Knowing full well that wood could not serve him
Nor linden defend him against the flame.
The stalwart hero was doomed to suffer
The destined end of his days on earth;
Likewise the worm, though for many a winter
He had held his watch o'er the wealth of the hoard.
The ring-prince scorned to assault the dragon
With a mighty army, or host of men.
He feared not the combat, nor counted of worth
The might of the worm, his courage and craft,
Since often aforetime, beset in the fray,
He had safely issued from many an onset,
Many a combat and, crowned with success,
Purged of evil the hall of Hrothgar
And crushed out Grendel's loathsome kin.

Nor was that the least of his grim engagements
When Hygelac fell, great Hrethel's son;
When the lord of the people, the prince of the Geats,
Died of his wounds in the welter of battle,
Perished in Friesland, smitten with swords.
Thence Beowulf came by his strength in swimming;
Thirty sets of armor he bore on his back

As he hasted to ocean. The Hetware° men
Had no cause to boast of their prowess in battle
When they gathered against him with linden shields.
But few of them ever escaped his assault
Or came back alive to the homes they had left;
So the son of Ecgtheow swam the sea-stretches,
Lonely and sad, to the land of his kin.
Hygd then tendered him kingdom and treasure,
Wealth of riches and royal throne,
For she had no hope with Hygelac dead
That her son could defend the seat of his fathers
From foreign foemen. But even in need,
No whit the more could they move the hero
To be Heardred's liege,° or lord of the land.
But he fostered Heardred with friendly counsel,
With honor and favor among the folk,
Till he came of age and governed the Geats.
Then the sons of Ohthere° fleeing in exile
Sought out Heardred over the sea.
They had risen against the lord of the Scylfings,
Best of the sea-kings, bestower of rings,
An illustrious prince in the land of the Swedes.
So Heardred fell. For harboring exiles
The son of Hygelac died by the sword.
Ongentheow's son,° after Heardred was slain,
Returned to his home, and Beowulf held
The princely power and governed the Geats.
He was a good king, grimly requiting
In later days the death of his prince.
Crossing the sea with a swarming host
He befriended Eadgils,° Ohthere's son,
In his woe and affliction, with weapons and men;
He took revenge in a savage assault,
And slew the king. So Ecgtheow's son
Had come in safety through all his battles,
His bitter struggles and savage strife,
To the day when he fought with the deadly worm.
With eleven comrades, kindled to rage
The Geat lord went to gaze on the dragon.
Full well he knew how the feud arose,
The fearful affliction; for into his hold

Hetware men i.e. the Atuarii
Heardred's liege Beowulf, though free to do so, refused to usurp the Geatish throne which rightfully belonged to Hygelac's son Heardred. Instead, he acted as the young king's counsellor and protector.
sons of Ohthere the Swedes Eanmund and Eadgils, driven into exile by their uncle Onela, who had usurped the throne of Ohthere and made himself king of the Scylfings (Swedes). Heardred took them into the protection of the Geat court and was attacked by Onela for this act of hospitality, and killed, along with Eanmund. Beowulf then ruled the kingdom, and acted as Eadgils's protector.
Ongentheow's son Onela
befriended Eadgils Beowulf helped Eadgils to get back the Swedish throne from Onela. It is not clear whether it is Eadgils or Beowulf who kills Onela.

From hand of finder the flagon had come.
The thirteenth man in the hurrying throng
Was the sorrowful captive who caused the feud.
With woeful spirit and all unwilling
Needs must he guide them, for he only knew
Where the earth-hall stood near the breaking billows
Filled with jewels and beaten gold.
The monstrous warden, waiting for battle,
Watched and guarded the hoarded wealth.
No easy bargain for any of men
To seize that treasure! The stalwart king,
Gold-friend of Geats, took seat on the headland,
Hailed his comrades and wished them well.
Sad was his spirit, restless and ready,
And the march of Fate immeasurably near;
Fate that would strike, seek his soul's treasure,
And deal asunder the spirit and flesh.
Not long was his life encased in the body!
Beowulf spoke, the son of Ecgtheow:
'Many an ordeal I endured in youth,
And many a battle. I remember it all.
I was seven winters old when the prince of the people,
The lord of the treasure-hoard, Hrethel the king,
From the hand of my father had me and held me,
Recalling our kinship with treasure and feast.
As long as he lived I was no less beloved,
As thane in his hall, than the sons of his house,
Herebeald and Hæthcyn and Hygelac, my lord.
For the eldest brother the bed of death
Was foully fashioned by brother's deed
When Hæthcyn let fly a bolt from his horn-bow,°
Missed the mark, and murdered his lord;
Brother slew brother with bloody shaft—
A tragic deed and beyond atonement,
A foul offense to sicken the heart!
Yet none the less was the lot of the prince
To lay down his soul and his life, unavenged.°
Even so sad and sorrowful is it,
And bitter to bear, to an old man's heart,
Seeing his young son swing on the gallows.°
He wails his dirge and his wild lament
While his son hangs high, a spoil to the raven;
His aged heart can contrive no help.
Each dawn brings grief for the son that is gone

horn-bow Either a bow tipped with a horn or curved like a horn; the bow was not a common Anglo-Saxon weapon.

unavenged The crime could not be wiped out by *wergild* or by vengeance since it was unwitting and the king was father of both parties.

gallows Similarly, since no *wergild* or vengeance could be exacted for an executed criminal, his father could only mourn.

And his heart has no hope of another heir,
Seeing the one has gone to his grave.
In the house of his son he gazes in sorrow
On wine-hall deserted and swept by the wind,
Empty of joy. The horsemen and heroes
Sleep in the grave. No sound of the harp,
No welcoming revels as often of old!
He goes to his bed with his burden of grief;
To his spirit it seems that dwelling and land
Are empty and lonely, lacking his son.
So the helm of the Weders° yearned after Herebeald
And welling sadness surged in his heart.
He could not avenge the feud on the slayer
Nor punish the prince for the loathsome deed,
Though he loved him no longer, nor held him dear.
Because of this sorrow that sore befell
He left life's joys for the heavenly light,
Granting his sons, as a good man will,
Cities and land, when he went from the world.
Then across the wide water was conflict and war,
A striving and struggle of Swedes and Geats,
A bitter hatred, when Hrethel died.
Ongentheow's sons° were dauntless and daring,
Cared not for keeping of peace overseas;
But often around Hreosnabeorh° slaughtered and slew.
My kinsmen avenged the feud and the evil,
As many have heard, though one of the Weders
Paid with his life—a bargain full bitter!
Hæthcyn's° fate was to fall in the fight.
It is often recounted, a kinsman with sword-edge
Avenged in the morning the murderer's deed
When Ongentheow met Eofor. Helm split asunder;
The aged Scylfing° sank down to his death.
The hand that felled him remembered the feud
And drew not back from the deadly blow.
For all the rich gifts that Hygelac gave me
I repaid him in battle with shining sword,
As chance was given. He granted me land,
A gracious dwelling and goodly estate.
Nor needed he seek of the Gifths,° or the Spear-Danes,
Or in Swedish land, a lesser in war

helm . . . Weders protector (helmet) of the Geats, i.e. Hrethel
Ongentheow's sons Onela and Ohthere, of the Swedish royal family
Hreosnabeorh a hill in Geat territory
Hæthcyn a prince of the Geats, second son of Hrethel, who had accidentally killed his elder brother Herebeald with an arrow and therefore succeeded his father on the throne. Hæthcyn was killed by Ongentheow, the Swedish king (see below) in battle at Ravenswood and was succeeded by Hygelac. Eofor avenged Hæthcyn's death by killing Ongentheow.
aged Scylfing Ongentheow
Gifths an East Germanic tribe, the Gepidae, having affinities with the Goths. They originally lived near the delta of the Vistula, but moved in the third century down to Hungary. Here they still seem to be thought of as a Baltic people.

To fight for pay; in the press of battle
I was always before him alone in the van.
So shall I bear me while life-days last,
While the sword holds out that has served me well
Early and late since I slew Dæghrefn,°
The Frankish hero, before the host.
He brought no spoil from the field of battle,
No corselet of mail to the Frisian king.
Not by the sword the warden of standards,
The stalwart warrior, fell in the fight.
My battle-grip shattered the bones of his body
And silenced the heart-beat. But now with the sword,
With hand and hard blade, I must fight for the treasure.'

[*Beowulf and Wiglaf Slay the Dragon*]

For the last time Beowulf uttered his boast:
'I came in safety through many a conflict
In the days of my youth; and now even yet,
Old as I am, I will fight this feud,
Do manful deeds, if the dire destroyer
Will come from his cavern to meet my sword.'
The king for the last time greeted his comrades,
Bold helmet-bearers and faithful friends:
'I would bear no sword nor weapon to battle
With the evil worm, if I knew how else
I could close with the fiend, as I grappled with Grendel.
From the worm I look for a welling of fire,
A belching of venom, and therefore I bear
Shield and byrny. Not one foot's space
Will I flee from the monster, the ward of the mound.
It shall fare with us both in the fight at the wall
As Fate shall allot, the lord of mankind.
Though bold in spirit, I make no boast
As I go to fight with the flying serpent.
Clad in your corselets and trappings of war,
By the side of the barrow abide you to see
Which of us twain may best after battle
Survive his wounds. Not yours the adventure,
Nor the mission of any, save mine alone,
To measure his strength with the monstrous dragon
And play the part of a valiant earl.
By deeds of daring I'll gain the gold
Or death in battle shall break your lord.'
Then the stalwart rose with his shield upon him,
Bold under helmet, bearing his sark
Under the stone-cliff; he trusted the strength

Dæghrefn a Frankish (Huga) warrior, standard bearer, and perhaps slayer of Hygelac on his last expedition; killed by Beowulf at that time

Of his single might. Not so does a coward!
He who survived through many a struggle,
Many a combat and crashing of troops,
Saw where a stone-arch stood by the wall
And a gushing stream broke out from the barrow.
Hot with fire was the flow of its surge,
Nor could any abide near the hoard unburned,
Nor endure its depths, for the flame of the dragon.
Then the lord of the Geats in the grip of his fury
Gave shout of defiance; the strong-heart stormed.
His voice rang out with the rage of battle,
Resounding under the hoary stone.
Hate was aroused; the hoard-warden knew
'Twas the voice of a man. No more was there time
To sue for peace; the breath of the serpent,
A blast of venom, burst from the rock.
The ground resounded; the lord of the Geats
Under the barrow swung up his shield
To face the dragon; the coiling foe
Was gathered to strike in the deadly strife.
The stalwart hero had drawn his sword,
His ancient heirloom of tempered edge;
In the heart of each was fear of the other!
The shelter of kinsmen stood stout of heart
Under towering shield as the great worm coiled;
Clad in his war-gear he waited the rush.
In twisting folds the flame-breathing dragon
Sped to its fate. The shield of the prince
For a lesser while guarded his life and his body
Than heart had hoped. For the first time then
It was not his portion to prosper in war;
Fate did not grant him glory in battle!
Then lifted his arm the lord of the Geats
And smote the worm with his ancient sword
But the brown° edge failed as it fell on bone,
And cut less deep than the king had need
In his sore distress. Savage in mood
The ward of the barrow countered the blow
With a blast of fire; wide sprang the flame.
The ruler of Geats had no reason to boast;
His unsheathed iron, his excellent sword,
Had weakened as it should not, had failed in the fight.
It was no easy journey for Ecgtheow's son
To leave this world and against his will
Find elsewhere a dwelling! So every man shall
In the end give over this fleeting life.
Not long was the lull. Swiftly the battlers

brown lit. "bright," "shining"

Renewed their grapple. The guard of the hoard
Grew fiercer in fury. His venomous breath
Beat in his breast. Enveloped in flame
The folk-leader suffered a sore distress.
No succoring band of shoulder-companions,
No sons of warriors aided him then
By valor in battle. They fled to the forest
To save their lives; but a sorrowful spirit
Welled in the breast of one of the band.
The call of kinship can never be stilled
In the heart of a man who is trusty and true.
His name was Wiglaf,° Weohstan's° son,
A prince of the Scylfings, a peerless thane,
Ælfhere's° kinsman; he saw his king
Under his helmet smitten with heat.
He thought of the gifts which his lord had given,
The wealth and the land of the Wægmunding line
And all the folk-rights his father had owned;
Nor could he hold back, but snatched up his buckler,
His linden shield and his ancient sword,
Heirloom of Eanmund, Ohthere's son,
Whom Weohstan slew with the sword in battle,
Wretched and friendless and far from home.
The brown-hued° helmet he bore to his kinsmen,
The ancient blade and the byrny of rings.
These Onela° gave him—his nephew's arms—
Nor called for vengeance, nor fought the feud,
Though Weohstan had slaughtered his brother's son.°
He° held the treasures for many half-years,
The byrny and sword, till his son was of age
For manful deeds, as his father before him.
Among the Geats he gave him of war-gear
Countless numbers of every kind;
Then, full of winters, he left the world,
Gave over this life. And Wiglaf, the lad,

Wiglaf The passage seems at first contradictory about the origins of Wiglaf in that he is said to be both Swede (Scylfing) and Geat (the Wægmundings were the Geat family to which Beowulf belonged). But the poet may mean that the young Wiglaf is of Swedish royal blood and now under the protection of Beowulf, as one of his household. This system of putting children, sometimes as young as seven years old, to be brought up in another family was common among Germanic peoples.

Weohstan's Wiglaf's father, a Swede, may also have changed his allegiance and become a vassal of Beowulf's. Previously, he had taken part in Swedish King Onela's attack on Heardred, king of the Geats, and himself killed Eanmund, whom Heardred was protecting, receiving Eanmund's sword and armor as the spoils of war. Wiglaf had inherited Eanmund's sword from his father and was now using it against the dragon.

Ælfhere not otherwise known

brown-hued lit. "shining bright"

Onela All the spoils of war belonged by right to the lord, who apportioned them among his followers.

Nor called . . . brother's son The remark has nothing to do with *wergild*: in the heroic age the normal thing would have been for Eanmund's killing to be avenged in blood by his uncle Onela, but Eanmund, having fought against his uncle, has forfeited this family right and Onela is, on the contrary, grateful to Weohstan for killing his kinsman, so that he rewards Weohstan instead of demanding retribution from him.

he Weohstan

Was to face with his lord the first of his battles,
The hazard of war. But his heart did not fail
Nor the blade of his kinsman weaken in war,
As the worm soon found when they met in the fight!
    Wiglaf spoke in sorrow of soul,
With bitter reproach rebuking his comrades: °
'I remember the time, as we drank in the mead-hall,
When we swore to our lord who bestowed these rings
That we would repay for the war-gear and armor,
The hard swords and helmets, if need like this
Should ever befall him. He chose us out
From all the host for this high adventure,
Deemed us worthy of glorious deeds,
Gave me these treasures, regarded us all
As high-hearted bearers of helmet and spear—
Though our lord himself, the shield of his people,
Thought single-handed to finish this feat,
Since of mortal men his measure was most
Of feats of daring and deeds of fame.
Now is the day that our lord has need
Of the strength and courage of stalwart men.
Let us haste to succor his sore distress
In the horrible heat and the merciless flame.
God knows I had rather the fire should enfold
My body and limbs with my gold-friend and lord.
Shameful it seems that we carry our shields
Back to our homes ere we harry the foe
And ward the life of the Weder king.
Full well I know it is not his due
That he alone, of the host of the Geats,
Should suffer affliction and fall in the fight.
One helmet and sword, one byrny and shield,
Shall serve for us both in the storm of strife.'
Then Wiglaf dashed through the deadly reek
In his battle-helmet to help his lord.
Brief were his words: 'Beloved Beowulf,
Summon your strength, remember the vow
You made of old in the years of youth
Not to allow your glory to lessen
As long as you lived. With resolute heart,
And dauntless daring, defend your life
With all your force. I fight at your side!'
    Once again the worm, when the words were spoken,
The hideous foe in a horror of flame,
Rushed in rage at the hated men.
Wiglaf's buckler was burned to the boss

comrades a typical *comitatus* speech

In the billows of fire; his byrny of mail
Gave the young hero no help or defense.
But he stoutly pressed on under shield of his kinsman
When his own was consumed in the scorching flame.
Then the king once more was mindful of glory,
Swung his great sword-blade with all his might
And drove it home on the dragon's head.
But Nægling° broke, it failed in the battle,
The blade of Beowulf, ancient and gray.
It was not his lot that edges of iron
Could help him in battle; his hand was too strong,
Overtaxed, I am told, every blade with its blow.
Though he bore a wondrous hard weapon to war,
No whit the better was he thereby!
 A third time then the terrible scather,
The monstrous dragon inflamed with the feud,
Rushed on the king when the opening offered,
Fierce and flaming; fastened its fangs
In Beowulf's throat; he was bloodied with gore;
His life-blood streamed from the welling wound.
 As they tell the tale, in the king's sore need
His shoulder-companion showed forth his valor,
His craft° and courage, and native strength.
To the head of the dragon he paid no heed,
Though his hand was burned as he helped his king.
A little lower the stalwart struck
At the evil beast, and his blade drove home
Plated° and gleaming. The fire began
To lessen and wane. The king of the Weders
Summoned his wits; he drew the dagger
He wore on his corselet, cutting and keen,
And slit asunder the worm with the blow.
So they felled the foe and wrought their revenge;
The kinsmen together had killed the dragon.
So a man should be when the need is bitter!
That was the last fight Beowulf fought;
That was the end of his work in the world.

[*Beowulf's Death*]

The wound which the dragon had dealt him began
To swell and burn; and soon he could feel
The baneful venom inflaming his breast.
The wise, old warrior sank down by the wall
And stared at the work of the giants of old,°
The arches of stone and the standing columns
Upholding the ancient earth-hall within.

Nægling Beowulf's sword
craft skill in battle
plated or ornamented
work . . . old ancient buildings, usually taken to be Roman ruins

His loyal thane, the kindest of comrades,
Saw Beowulf bloody and broken in war;
In his hands bore water and bathed his leader,
And loosened the helm from his dear lord's head.
Beowulf spoke, though his hurt was sore,
The wounds of battle grievous and grim.
Full well he weened that his life was ended,
And all the joy of his years on earth;
That his days were done, and Death most near:
'My armor and sword I would leave to my son
Had Fate but granted, born of my body,
An heir to follow me after I'm gone.
For fifty winters I've ruled this realm,
And never a lord of a neighboring land
Dared strike with terror or seek with sword.
In my life I abode by the lot assigned,
Kept well what was mine, courted no quarrels,
Swore no false oaths. And now for all this
Though my hurt is grievous, my heart is glad.
When life leaves body, the Lord of mankind
Cannot lay to my charge the killing of kinsmen!
Go quickly, dear Wiglaf, to gaze on the gold
Beneath the hoar stone. The dragon lies still
In the slumber of death, despoiled of his hoard.
Make haste that my eyes may behold the treasure,
The gleaming jewels, the goodly store,
And, glad of the gold, more peacefully leave
The life and the realm I have ruled so long.'
Then Weohstan's son, as they tell the tale,
Clad in his corselet and trappings of war,
Hearkened at once to his wounded lord.
Under roof of the barrow he broke his way.
Proud in triumph he stood by the seat,
Saw glittering jewels and gold on the ground,
The den of the dragon, the old dawn-flier,
And all the wonders along the walls.
Great bowls and flagons of bygone men
Lay all unburnished and barren of gems,
Many a helmet ancient and rusted,
Many an arm-ring cunningly wrought.
Treasure and gold, though hid in the ground,
Override man's wishes, hide them who will!
High o'er the hoard he beheld a banner,°
Greatest of wonders, woven° with skill,
All wrought of gold; its radiance lighted
The vasty ground and the glittering gems.

banner The word may mean a standard, not a flag.

woven "Worked" is more accurate.

But no sign of the worm! The sword-edge had slain him.
As I've heard the tale, the hero unaided
Rifled those riches of giants of old,
The hoard in the barrow, and heaped in his arms
Beakers and platters, picked what he would
And took the banner, the brightest of signs.
The ancient sword with its edge of iron
Had slain the worm who watched o'er the wealth,
In the midnight flaming, with menace of fire
Protecting the treasure for many a year
Till he died the death. Then Wiglaf departed
In haste returning enriched with spoil.
He feared, and wondered if still he would find
The lord of the Weders alive on the plain,
Broken and weary and smitten with wounds.
With his freight of treasure he found the prince,
His dear lord, bloody and nigh unto death.
With water he bathed him till words broke forth
From the hoard of his heart and, aged and sad,
Beowulf spoke, as he gazed on the gold:
'For this goodly treasure whereon I gaze
I give my thanks to the Lord of all,
To the Prince of glory, Eternal God,
Who granted me grace to gain for my people
Such dower of riches before my death.
I gave my life for this golden hoard.
Heed well the wants, the need of my people;
My hour is come, and my end is near.
Bid warriors build, when they burn my body,
A stately barrow on the headland's height.
It shall be for remembrance among my people
As it towers high on the Cape of the Whale,°
And sailors shall know it as Beowulf's Barrow,
Sea-faring mariners driving their ships
Through fogs of ocean from far countries.'
Then the great-hearted king unclasped from his throat
A collar of gold, and gave to his thane;
Gave the young hero his gold-decked helmet,
His ring and his byrny, and wished him well.
'You are the last of the Wægmunding line.
All my kinsmen, earls in their glory,
Fate has sent to their final doom,
And I must follow.' These words were the last
The old king spoke ere the pyre received him,

Cape of the Whale Hrones-næs, a headland on the coast of Geatland. The almost literal parallel with the make-up and position of the funeral pyre here with that of Achilles and Patroclus in the *Odyssey* (XXIV. 80 ff.) has often been noticed. Earlier, cremation of Germanic chieftains was less elaborate; see Tacitus, *Germania*, 27.

The leaping flames of the funeral blaze,
And his breath went forth from his bosom, his soul
Went forth from the flesh, to the joys of the just.
    Then bitter it was for Beowulf's thane
To behold his loved one lying on earth
Suffering sore at the end of life.
The monster that slew him, the dreadful dragon,
Likewise lay broken and brought to his death.
The worm no longer could rule the hoard,
But the hard, sharp sword, the work of the hammer,
Had laid him low; and the winged dragon
Lay stretched near the barrow, broken and still.
No more in the midnight he soared in air,
Disclosing his presence, and proud of his gold;
For he sank to earth by the sword of the king.
But few of mankind, if the tales be true,
Has it prospered much, though mighty in war
And daring in deed, to encounter the breath
Of the venomous worm or plunder his wealth
When the ward of the barrow held watch o'er the mound.
Beowulf bartered his life for the treasure;
Both foes had finished this fleeting life.
    Not long was it then till the laggards in battle
Came forth from the forest, ten craven in fight,
Who had dared not face the attack of the foe
In their lord's great need. The shirkers in shame
Came wearing their bucklers and trappings of war
Where the old man lay. They looked upon Wiglaf.
Weary he sat by the side of his leader
Attempting with water to waken his lord.
It availed him little; the wish was vain!
He could not stay his soul upon earth,
Nor one whit alter the will of God.
The Lord ruled over the lives of men
As He rules them still. With a stern rebuke
He reproached the cowards whose courage had failed.
Wiglaf addressed them, Weohstan's son;
Gazed sad of heart on the hateful men:
'Lo! he may say who would speak the truth
That the lord who gave you these goodly rings,
This warlike armor wherein you stand—
When oft on the ale-bench he dealt to his hall-men
Helmet and byrny, endowing his thanes
With the fairest he found from near or from far—
That he grievously wasted these trappings of war
When battle befell him. The king of the folk
Had no need to boast of his friends in the fight.
But the God of victory granted him strength

To avenge himself with the edge of the sword
When he needed valor. Of little avail
The help I brought in the bitter battle!
Yet still I strove, though beyond my strength,
To aid my kinsman. And ever the weaker
The savage foe when I struck with my sword;
Ever the weaker the welling flame!
Too few defenders surrounded our ruler
When the hour of evil and terror befell.
Now granting of treasure and giving of swords,
Inherited land-right and joy of the home,
Shall cease from your kindred. And each of your clan
Shall fail of his birthright when men from afar
Hear tell of your flight and your dastardly deed.
Death is better for every earl
Than life besmirched with the brand of shame!'

[*The Messenger Foretells the Doom of the Geats*]

Then Wiglaf bade tell the tidings of battle
Up over the cliff in the camp of the host
Where the linden-bearers° all morning long
Sat wretched in spirit, and ready for both,
The return, or the death, of their dear-loved lord.
Not long did he hide, who rode up the headland,
The news of their sorrow, but spoke before all:
'Our leader lies low, the lord of the Weders,
The king of the Geats, on the couch of death.
He sleeps his last sleep by the deeds of the worm.
The dreadful dragon is stretched beside him
Slain with dagger-wounds. Not by the sword
Could he quell the monster or lay him low.
And Wiglaf is sitting, Weohstan's son,
Bent over Beowulf, living by dead.
Death watch he keeps in sorrow of spirit
Over the bodies of friend and foe.

Now comes peril of war when this news is rumored abroad,
The fall of our king known afar among Frisians and Franks!
For a fierce feud rose with the Franks when Hygelac's warlike host
Invaded the Frisian fields, and the Hetware vanquished the Geats,
Overcame with the weight of their hordes, and Hygelac fell in the fray;
It was not his lot to live on dispensing the spoils of war.
And never since then of the Franks had we favor or friend.
And I harbor no hope of peace or faith from the Swedish folk,
For well is it known of men that Ongentheow° slew with the sword
Hæthcyn, the son of Hrethel, near Ravenswood, in the fight

linden-bearers shield-bearers, warriors
Ongentheow See ll. 2342 ff. for the battle at Ravenswood.

When the Swedish people in pride swept down on the Geats.°
And Ohthere's aged father,° *old and a terror in battle,*
Made onslaught, killing their king, and rescued his queen,°
Ohthere's mother and Onela's, aged, bereft of her gold.
He followed the flying foe till, lordless and lorn,
They barely escaped into Ravenswood. There he beset them,
A wretched remnant of war, and weary with wounds.
And all the long hours of the night he thundered his threats
That some on the morrow he would slay with the edge of the sword,
And some should swing on the gallows for food for the fowls!°
But hope returned with the dawn to the heavy-hearted
When they heard the sound of the trumpets and Hygelac's horn,
As the good king came with his troops marching up on their track.
Then was a gory meeting of Swedes and Geats;
On all sides carnage and slaughter, savage and grim,
As the struggling foemen grappled and swayed in the fight.
And the old earl Ongentheow, crestfallen and cowed,
Fled with his men to a fastness, withdrew to the hills.
He had tasted Hygelac's strength, the skill of the hero in war,
And he had no hope to resist or strive with the sea-men,
To save his hoard from their hands, or his children, or wife.
So the old king fled to his fortress; but over the plain
Hygelac's banners swept on in pursuit of the Swedes,
Stormed to the stronghold's defenses, and old Ongentheow°
Was brought to bay with the sword, and subject to Eofor's will!
Wulf, son of Wonred, in wrath then struck with his sword,
And the blood in streams burst forth from under the old man's hair.
Yet the aged Scylfing was all undaunted and answered the stroke
With a bitter exchange in the battle; and Wonred's brave son
Could not requite the blow, for the hero had cleft his helmet,
And, covered with blood, he was forced to bow; he fell to the earth.
But his death was not doomed, and he rallied, though the wound was deep.
Then Hygelac's hardy thane,° *when his brother lay low,*
Struck with his ancient blade, a sturdy sword of the giants,
Cut through the shield-wall, cleaving the helmet. The king,
The folk-defender, sank down. He was hurt unto death.
Then were many that bound Wulf's wounds when the fight was won,
When the Geats held the ground of battle; as booty of war
Eofor stripped Ongentheow of iron byrny and helm,
Of sword-blade hilted and hard, and bore unto Hygelac

Swedish . . . Geats The Swedes had perhaps first provoked a battle—now the Geats had made an expedition in revenge.
father Ongentheow
queen The Geats, under their king, Hæthcyn, are at first successful and capture Ongentheow's queen. Then Ongentheow rescues her and kills Hæthcyn, after which he drives the Geatish forces into Ravenswood. Then Hygelac, Hæthcyn's brother and successor, arrives with reinforcements, and Ongentheow in his turn is driven to take refuge and is killed. The next stages in the Geat-Swedish war have already been told at ll. 2464 ff. and 2246 ff.
fowls carrion birds
Ongentheow Ongentheow first fells, but does not kill, Wulf, one of the sons of Wonred, who has wounded him. Wonred's other son, Eofor, then kills Ongentheow and strips him of his armor and ornaments.
thane Eofor

The old man's trappings of war. And Hygelac took the treasures,
Promising fair rewards, and this he fulfilled.
The son of Hrethel, the king of the Geats, when he came to his home,
Repaid with princely treasure the prowess of Eofor and Wulf;
Gave each an hundred thousand° of land and linked rings,
And none could belittle or blame. They had won the honor in war.
He gave to Eofor also the hand of his only daughter
To be a pledge of good will, and the pride of his home.

This is the fighting and this the feud,
The bitter hatred, that breeds the dread
Lest the Swedish people should swarm against us°
Learning our lord lies lifeless and still.
His was the hand that defended the hoard,
Heroes, and realm against ravaging foe,
By noble counsel and dauntless deed.
Let us go quickly to look on the king
Who brought us treasure, and bear his corpse
To the funeral pyre. The precious hoard
Shall burn with the hero. There lies the heap
Of untold treasure so grimly gained,
Jewels and gems he bought with his blood
At the end of life. All these at the last
The flames shall veil and the brands devour.
No man for remembrance shall take from the treasure,
Nor beauteous maiden adorn her breast
With gleaming jewel; bereft of gold
And tragic-hearted many shall tread
A foreign soil, now their lord has ceased
From laughter and revel and rapture of joy.
Many a spear in the cold of morning
Shall be borne in hand uplifted on high.
No sound of harp shall waken the warrior,
But the dusky raven despoiling the dead
Shall clamor and cry and call to the eagle
What fare he found at the carrion-feast
The while with the wolf he worried the corpses.'°
    So the stalwart hero had told his tidings,
His fateful message; nor spoke amiss
As to truth or telling. The host arose;
On their woeful way to the Eagles' Ness°
They went with tears to behold the wonder.

hundred thousand If this meant 100,000 hides or measures of land (see above), it would equal the size of Geatland itself: probably the meaning is "the value of 100,000 (coins) in land and gold."

Lest . . . us The point of the Ravenswood story: the messenger fears that, once the death of Beowulf becomes known, the Swedes will renew their attacks on the Geats, now without their protector.

eagle . . . corpses See "The Wanderer" (ll. 74–75).

Eagles' Ness Earna-næs, perhaps modern Swedish Ornäs—the promontory near the scene of Beowulf's battle with the dragon

They found the friend, who had dealt them treasure
In former days, on the bed of death,
Stretched out lifeless upon the sand.
The last of the good king's days was gone;
Wondrous the death of the Weder prince!
They had sighted first, where it lay outstretched,
The monstrous wonder, the loathsome worm,
The horrible fire-drake, hideous-hued,
Scorched with the flame. The spread of its length
Was fifty foot-measures! Oft in the night
It sported in air, then sinking to earth
Returned to its den. Now moveless in death
It had seen the last of its earthly lair.
Beside the dragon were bowls and beakers,
Platters lying, and precious swords
Eaten with rust, where the hoard had rested
A thousand winters in the womb of earth.
That boundless treasure of bygone men,
The golden dower, was girt with a spell
So that never a man might ravage the ring-hall
Save as God himself, the Giver of victory—
He is the Shelter and Shield of men—
Might allow such man as seemed to Him meet,
Might grant whom He would, to gather the treasure.
His way of life, who had wickedly hoarded
The wealth of treasure beneath the wall,
Had an evil end, as was widely seen.
Many the dragon had sent to death,
But in fearful fashion the feud was avenged!
'Tis a wondrous thing when a warlike earl
Comes to the close of his destined days,
When he may no longer among his kinsmen
Feast in the mead-hall. So Beowulf fared
When he sought the dragon in deadly battle!
Himself he knew not what fate was in store
Nor the coming end of his earthly life.
The lordly princes who placed the treasure
Had cursed it deep to the day of doom,
That the man who plundered and gathered the gold
Might pay for the evil imprisoned in hell,
Shackled in torment and punished with pain,
Except the invader should first be favored
With the loving grace of the Lord of all!
Then spoke Wiglaf, Weohstan's son:
'Often for one man many must sorrow
As has now befallen the folk of the Geats.
We could not persuade the king by our counsel,
Our well-loved leader, to shun assault

On the dreadful dragon guarding the gold;
To let him lie where he long had lurked
In his secret lair till the world shall end.
But Beowulf, dauntless, pressed to his doom.
The hoard was uncovered; heavy the cost;
Too strong the fate that constrained the king!
I entered the barrow, beholding the hoard
And all the treasure throughout the hall;
In fearful fashion the way was opened,
An entrance under the wall of earth.
Of the hoarded treasure I heaped in my arms
A weighty burden, and bore to my king.
He yet was living; his wits were clear.
Much the old man said in his sorrow;
Sent you greeting, and bade you build
In the place of burning a lofty barrow,
Proud and peerless, to mark his deeds;
For he was of all men the worthiest warrior
In all the earth, while he still might rule
And wield the wealth of his lordly land.
Let us haste once more to behold the treasure,
The gleaming wonders beneath the wall.
I will show the way that you all may see
And closely scan the rings and the gold.
Let the bier be ready, the pyre prepared,
When we come again to carry our lord,
Our leader beloved, where long he shall lie
In the kindly care of the Lord of all.'

[*Beowulf's Funeral*]

Then the son of Weohstan, stalwart in war,
Bade send command to the heads of homes
To bring from afar the wood for the burning
Where the good king lay: 'Now gleed° shall devour,
As dark flame waxes, the warrior prince
Who has often withstood the shower of steel
When the storm of arrows, sped from the string,
Broke over shield, and shaft did service,
With feather-fittings guiding the barb.'
Then the wise son of Weohstan chose from the host
Seven thanes of the king, the best of the band;
Eight heroes together they hied to the barrow
In under the roof of the fearful foe;
One of the warriors leading the way
Bore in his hand a burning brand.
They cast no lots who should loot the treasure

gleed fire

When they saw unguarded the gold in the hall
Lying there useless; little they scrupled
As quickly they plundered the precious store.
Over the sea-cliff into the ocean
They tumbled the dragon, the deadly worm,
Let the sea-tide swallow the guarder of gold.
Then a wagon was loaded with well-wrought treasure,
A countless number of every kind;
And the aged warrior, the white-haired king,
Was borne on high to the Cape of the Whale.
The Geat folk fashioned a peerless pyre
Hung round with helmets and battle-boards,°
With gleaming byrnies as Beowulf bade.
In sorrow of soul they laid on the pyre
Their mighty leader, their well-loved lord.
The warriors kindled the bale° on the barrow,
Wakened the greatest of funeral fires.
Dark o'er the blaze the wood-smoke mounted;
The winds were still, and the sound of weeping
Rose with the roar of the surging flame
Till the heat of the fire had broken the body.
With hearts that were heavy they chanted their sorrow,
Singing a dirge for the death of their lord;
And an aged woman with upbound locks
Lamented for Beowulf, wailing in woe.°
Over and over she uttered her dread
Of sorrow to come, of bloodshed and slaughter,
Terror of battle, and bondage, and shame.
The smoke of the bale-fire rose to sky!
The men of the Weder folk fashioned a mound
Broad and high on the brow of the cliff,
Seen from afar by seafaring men.
Ten days they worked on the warrior's barrow
Inclosing the ash of the funeral flame
With a wall as worthy as wisdom could shape.
They bore to the barrow the rings and the gems,
The wealth of the hoard the heroes had plundered.
The olden treasure they gave to the earth,
The gold to the ground, where it still remains
As useless to men as it was of yore.
Then round the mound rode the brave in battle,°
The sons of warriors, twelve in a band,
Bemoaning their sorrow and mourning their king.

battle-boards i.e. shields
bale pyre, bonfire
And . . . woe (ll. 2948–49) The manuscript is damaged at this point, but the word "Geatish" has been deciphered as describing the woman. Some take this to mean that Beowulf had married Hygelac's widow, Hygd.
round . . . battle See the account in the sixth-century Gothic historian Jordanes of the funeral of Attila the Hun; and Virgil's *Aeneid* XI.182–212.

They sang their dirge and spoke of the hero
Vaunting his valor and venturous deeds.
So is it proper a man should praise
His friendly lord with a loving heart,
When his soul must forth from the fleeting flesh.
So the folk of the Geats, the friends of his hearth,
Bemoaned the fall of their mighty lord;
Said he was kindest of worldly kings,
Mildest, most gentle, most eager for fame.

8th century 1815

GEOFFREY CHAUCER

c. 1343–1400

Geoffrey Chaucer was born into a well-to-do bourgeois family, in London, about 1343. Of his life he himself tells us almost nothing in his poetry, but from the documents, by which it has been possible to piece together the career of moderately distinguished public service which he made for himself, we know a good many details.

His family name goes back to the thirteenth century in the London area, and the Chaucers were already prosperous members of the rising commercial class in the days of Geoffrey's grandfather. Chaucer's father, a wine merchant, was a member of the growing number of men in the commercial centers of England, especially in London, who were beginning to exert a powerful effect on the structure of English society. They were commoners who were advancing in wealth, office-holding, and social prestige to a position above the ordinary, but were excluded from the aristocracy by birth, and from the country gentry by their city occupations. They were somewhere in between: the beginnings of the English middle class.

There was no place in their thinking—or in Chaucer's—for the leveling doctrines of John Ball, the fourteenth-century social agitator: ". . . matters cannot go well in England and never will until all things be in common, and there shall be neither serfs nor gentlemen, but we shall all be equal. . . ." A father from Chaucer's stratum of society would wish to advance his son's interests. He would send him first to school and then either to the University (which would often mean that the son was intended for the priesthood, the third order of English society); or he would place him in a noble household, where he might have the chance to continue his education in a less formal and devout way. In his early teens, Geoffrey Chaucer was made a page in the household of one of England's most considerable noblemen, Prince Lionel, third son of King Edward III, and later Duke of Clarence. The connections he made there must have served him well in later life and we know that his talents kept him in association with members of the aristocracy. His first great patron was John of Gaunt, fifth son of the king and the most powerful noble in England, who may also have been his friend. From the successive kings, Edward III, Richard II, and Henry IV, Chaucer received offices, grants of money, and other privileges for his services in various capacities. He married well; his wife Philippa was a member of the households of both Queen

Philippa and of the third wife of John of Gaunt, and was probably the daughter of a knight. A Thomas Chaucer, probably their son, rose to public prominence and Alice Chaucer, possibly their granddaughter, married into the aristocracy not once but twice. From this tangle of connections, it emerges that the family was steadily rising in its social position.

Geoffrey Chaucer was the chief agent in this rise. The fact that his family had money and had been able to give him certain advantages obviously helped greatly, but his abilities also kept him on the road to advancement. In 1359 he went on one of Edward III's many expeditions against the French, was taken prisoner, and ransomed the following year; he then probably spent some time in study of the law, was made "valet" to the King in 1367 (an honor, not a servant's position), went on diplomatic missions to France several times, to Flanders in 1377 and to Italy in 1372–73 and 1378. In 1374 he was given a rent-free London house and made Controller of the Customs and Subsidies on Wool, Skins, and Hides for the Port of London. This was a lucrative office, for the wool trade was England's most important at the time. Other Customs appointments followed, but in 1386 Chaucer seems to have fallen on less good times and gone to live in Kent—perhaps only at Greenwich, now a suburb of London, a little way down the river. He had meantime become a public man of modest importance, being Justice of the Peace for Kent in 1385 and Knight of the Shire (representative in parliament) for Kent in 1386. After a short time in apparently rather straitened circumstances, he received in 1389 the office of Clerk of the King's Works, which put him in charge of the buildings and their repair at ten of the royal residences, of preparing places for tournaments, and of the walls, ditches, and sewers along a stretch of the Thames. There were later appointments, grants of wine, of money, and of privileges. In 1399, he rented a house in London again, near Westminster Abbey. He died the following year.

These bare facts about Chaucer's career indicate that he was given considerable responsibilities and, presumably, that he discharged them well. But they are the record, in the main, of a public servant's career; not a poet's. This is hardly surprising, since official documents are not the most obvious place to look for critical remarks on poetry, but it is significant because it indicates that the professional man-of-letters has not yet begun to emerge. The functioning of such a person depended upon the growth of a much larger reading public (even in 1533, Sir Thomas More estimated that fewer than four people in ten in England could read), the establishment of a system of printing and publishing, and an enlarged demand for dramatic performance. On the other hand, Chaucer provides a pattern of the writer which will serve for England for two centuries after his lifetime: the poet, whether a cleric or not, who holds ecclesiastical or secular office as a means to gain the leisure to write. A further—and often the most important—source of livelihood would be the dedication of poems to rich or noble patrons, and we know that Chaucer did just that with his first major poem, *The Book of the Duchess,* written in 1369–70 to commemorate the death of Blanche, Duchess of Lancaster, wife of John of Gaunt.

This position of the writer in his society is also a European one, especially in France and Italy. The new status that poets were now claiming is reflected in the ceremony—which Chaucer and all Europe knew about—performed on the Capitol at Rome in 1341, when Francesco Petrarca ("Francis Petrarch, the laureate poet," as Chaucer calls him) had himself formally crowned as a poet with a laurel garland. Petrarch thought he was reviving an ancient Roman custom, admirable because ancient and Roman and therefore pointing the way to the resuscitation of Roman virtue and glory. He also made a speech on the occasion, proclaiming the nobility and dignity of poetry and therefore of the poet, who was necessary to society because he could confer immortality on others as well as upon himself by his verses, and because beneath what seemed poetic fancies and dreams there lurked profound truth. The poet, indeed, was a moral philosopher, as Petrarch held: what he wrote would tend toward the inculcation of virtue in all its aspects.

Petrarch's Coronation Oration has been called "the first manifesto of the Renaissance," and the influence of the concept of the poet that it embodies is clear through to Sir Philip Sidney and even to the last English Renaissance poet, John Milton. But it has, in its serious statement of the poet's role, relevance to Chaucer, the first English poet to write in a manner that is as self-aware as it is self-assured and controlled. Petrarch's example as a poet meant much, consciously and unconsciously, to Chaucer. The first translation of a Petrarch sonnet into English (see below) is embedded in Chaucer's *Troilus and Criseyde,* and there are other indications in his work of his admiration for his Italian mentor. This is not to say that Chaucer would agree with all Petrarch's solemn claims: he was too much the satirist for that. Nor would he hold Petrarch's beliefs about the moral value of poetry as simply and directly as did Petrarch. His poetic method of slipping into and out of one of his characters—especially in *The Canterbury Tales*—often makes it difficult to hold in the mind exactly where he himself stands. We must balance his statement in the Retraction of the *Tales,* where he specifically disowns all in his work which tends toward the encouragement of sin, against the superb, controlled irony of the Clerk's Tale of patient Griselda; she endures in resignation and obedience to her husband all the trials he puts upon her, even to having her children taken from her and given up for dead, and to being put away by him. For Petrarch, this story was an exhortation to the Christian to be as steadfast for God as Griselda had been for her husband under her tribulations. Chaucer, by his very inclusion of the tale in his dramatic framework, has already lowered the story's tone and mode. But, fully in control of his manipulation, he raises the tone of the story again by giving it to the unworldly, idealist Clerk (see the General Prologue, ll. 287 ff.), who reiterates Petrarch's point and then goes on to concede that such absolute patience is a thing of the past and we must now do the best we can with what we have. Chaucer himself adds his ironic comment: a man should not try his wife's patience as hard as that "in trust to finde / Grisildis, for in certein he shall faile."

The Clerk's Tale operates at several levels: for the Clerk it is a moral tale, of trials and their endurance, turned so that it is also a hit at the Wife of Bath and her termagant ways, but it is capped by Chaucer's final encouragement—ironical, too—to sturdy wives to stand no nonsense from husbands. We must here, as always, make up our own minds as to how far we can identify anything that Chaucer says in *The Canterbury Tales* with Chaucer's own views, and judge for ourselves the extent of his irony and detachment. His intention is basically serious, even in the comic tales, but this is not to say that his poems are all moral allegories, lessons as directly applied as Petrarch would apply the Clerk's Tale.

Of the great Italians besides Petrarch, Chaucer was most indebted to Boccaccio and to Dante, but it is now becoming clear that much, though not all, of the influence on him that was formerly thought to be directly from the Italian, came via the French. This is natural: English culture for nearly three centuries before Chaucer and for nearly a century after him, relied heavily on France as a model. For a good part of those centuries, the two countries were, if not one kingdom, at least intimately connected in friendship or enmity. French was still the language of the English court, and in the manners and courtesies of polite society, especially in literature and in music, French practice was still the norm for imitation and modification.

Chaucer's youth, passed in a court milieu where such matters would be taken for granted, must have exposed him to French models, but in attempting to say just what these were and when and how he read and used them, we come up against one of our major difficulties with the poet: we simply do not know, except by inference, when exactly he wrote most of his works, major and minor. In general, his translations and direct imitations are reckoned to be early—the part of the incomplete English translation of the *Roman de la Rose* which is thought to be his, and some short poems, are given to the 1360's. The *Roman de la Rose* was a vast French poem of the thirteenth century, its first half a dream exploration of the process of falling in love according to the approved courtly canons, which had made of human love a deeply refining and ennobling influence on the spirit. This part was the work of Guillaume de Lorris (see below, The Other World: Paradise). To this was added, by Jean de Meun, an immense encyclopedic continuation, dealing with matters such as love, women, nobility, society and its foundations, the clergy, providence, fortune, the nature of dreams, sorcery, and the physical sciences. Chaucer frequently drew on these materials.

The Book of the Duchess (which can be dated exactly to 1369–70), uses a traditional English octosyllabic meter but often borrows directly from Jean Froissart, the French historian and poet who was Chaucer's almost exact contemporary, and from the French poet and musician Guillaume de Machaut (c. 1300–1377). It is an elegy and a dream vision at once. Sleepless, as the dreamer in such visions so often pictures himself, he reads and re-tells Ovid's story of Ceix and Alcyone from the *Metamorphoses* (the legend of how the kingfisher came into being), falls asleep, and dreams of a May morning encounter in the forest with a Man in Black, who tells his sorrow. Such dream visions were a highly fashionable literary form at the time. They allowed the poet to distance his illusion from his reader; they prepared the reader for the unrealities he might encounter, notably the personification of abstract qualities used to explore the nature of an experience or emotion; and they vouched, in one sense, for the validity of the vision. (See below, the Nun's Priest's Tale.)

The Book of the Duchess is an exquisitely turned evocation of grief at the death of Blanche "who every day hir beauté newed," already an assured and skillful poem combining French material with the literature of the ancient world. Of the classical writers who must have formed a part of Chaucer's education, by far the most important for him was Ovid, as both the poet of love and the poet of mythology, even the ancient poet most resembling him in temperament, with his characteristic blend of tenderness and satire, his love of a story. On no other classical author does Chaucer draw so heavily for material and for suggestions. He knew his Virgil, too, especially the *Aeneid,* but the *Eclogues* and the *Georgics* as well. Lucan and Statius (see below, the epilogue to *Troilus and Criseyde*), who were much admired in the Middle Ages, he knew and used also, but it seems probable that much of his knowledge of the Roman poets came from French translations and adaptations.

In the 1370's or early 1380's, again using a French version to help him, Chaucer translated the Latin work which influenced him most profoundly. This was the *Consolation of Philosophy* of Boethius, the Roman statesman, philosopher, and polymath put to death by the Emperor Theodoric in 524 A.D. Boethius wrote influential works on music, on geometry, on arithmetic—which became standard textbooks in medieval education for three of the four subjects of the quadrivium (see Glossary)—and on the philosophy of Aristotle. But his chief work, for the Middle Ages and for Chaucer, was the *Consolation,* a work of Stoic doctrine, teaching detachment from the troubles and difficulties of daily life and the patient bearing of adversity, which had the greater reputation because it was thought that Boethius was a Christian. Cast in the form of a vision, in alternate verse and prose, it tells how Boethius, in prison, was visited by the Lady Philosophy, who showed him how the afflictions of life—from which one must not try simply to escape—were transitory and could be borne once one had determined to put one's trust in absolute good and not allow oneself to come under the domination of Fortune, worldly good. Evil itself, Philosophy taught, could have no existence, since it has no part in absolute good: the evil of the world is therefore illusory. (See below, the Nun's Priest's Tale, ll. 472 ff.). The use Chaucer made of the *Consolation* to construct the philosophical framework for his *Troilus and Criseyde* makes it clear that Boethius's thought had for him the status of philosophic explanation as well as a guide to conduct and consolation in adversity.

At some time before he translated Boethius, Chaucer had tried his hand at a poem which one can already call typically Chaucerian, but which remains fragmentary: *The House of Fame.* The work owes much to many writers—Macrobius on dreams (see below, the Nun's Priest's Tale, ll. 353 ff.), Ovid and Virgil—but especially to Dante. It contains some of the best and most moving lines that Chaucer ever wrote and it has many echoes of Dante, transformed by the lively Chaucerian technique. Indeed, it has elements of burlesque Dante; and it may well be that Chaucer left it off because he did not feel himself equal to the *tour de force* he was attempting. Later, using Dante's words in the conclusion to *Troilus and Criseyde,* he was to show that he could intermittently rise, in all seriousness, to something like Dante's grave exaltation. But he could not keep it up.

Though it is true that Chaucer often used Italian literature, through French versions, it was only during the 1370's that it came to be a major influence on his poetry. Certainly his interest must have derived in part from his visits to Italy. The Italian author who most influenced him was Giovanni Boccaccio (1313–75), best known among his contemporaries for his Latin collections of exemplary lives, *The Falls of Princes* and *Of Famous Ladies,* but also a poet and prose writer of genius in Italian. To Boccaccio, directly or indirectly, Chaucer is indebted for a long passage in *The Parliament of Fowls.* This extended poem is a debate about the nature of love (a *demande d'amours*) in dream allegory form, as argued by birds with the intervention of Dame Nature, on St. Valentine's day. More importantly, Boccaccio provided the plot for one of the greatest love poems in the language, Chaucer's Troy-romance, *Troilus and Criseyde,* which is based, perhaps via the French *Roman de Troyle,* on Boccaccio's *Il Filostrato.* Chaucer never acknowledges this; indeed he never anywhere acknowledges that he has taken anything from Boccaccio, though the debt is enormous. But his poem is far more than Boccaccio, good as Boccaccio's story is. Chaucer transformed it into a more profound work—partly because of the Boethian philosophic character which he gave it, partly because of the depth and subtlety of his insight, and partly because of the unforgettable trio of characters he created from the much more conventional figures of Boccaccio's poem: Pandarus, Troilus, and Criseyde. Like *The Parliament of Fowls* the poem is also an exploration of the nature of earthly love, but played out this time by human actors, not personified abstractions or birds. Troilus has put himself on the wheel of Fortune through love of Criseyde and, through her fickleness, he comes to see the falseness of earthly love: this is his final vision. We, however, cannot forget the glory and the sweetness that have gone before—and Chaucer does not mean us to.

THE CANTERBURY TALES

There is no way of avoiding the feeling that all that has gone before in Chaucer's poetic career merely leads up to *The Canterbury Tales*. Chronologically, the *Tales* are his final achievement, though it looks as if he had long before worked out drafts of some of the stories which he proposed to use (the "tragedies" of the Monk's Tale, the Second Nun's Tale of St. Cecilia, an early version of the Knight's Tale—for the plot of which he was again indebted to Boccaccio). In terms of artistry the *Tales* represent the peak of his gigantic and varied talent, his fullest and most mature production. Chaucer seems to have given to this great poem the major part of his poetic time for the last fifteen or so years of his life. The only interruptions seem to have been his *Treatise on the Astrolabe* and, quite early in the period, a somewhat half-hearted attempt, in *The Legend of Good Women,* at a poem on the Ovidian model concerning women who were martyrs to their faithful love.

The *Tales* are certainly the expression of Chaucer's fully matured genius; yet even if he had never written them he would have done enough to make it clear that he has no superior as an English poet except Shakespeare. He dwarfs his contemporaries —and the poets of the next hundred and fifty years—in the same way as Shakespeare dwarfs his. The isolation of Chaucer's performance, indeed, makes it all the more astonishing. Nothing in the tradition of English poetry prepares us for him, and it appears, though he obviously knew a good deal of what had been written in English before and around him, that he did not find it very helpful. He acknowledges a debt to his older London contemporary, John Gower, "moral Gower"—or rather he dispatches his *Troilus and Criseyde,* perhaps ironically, to Gower for "correction." But he does not seem, anywhere, really to owe anything to any other writer in English—and the kind of poem that he can produce is entirely beyond the reach of any other writer of the time, let alone of the careful, often charming, but pedestrian Gower. It is easy to exaggerate the picture either way and to see—for example, in his mockery of the jog-trot of English romances in his own virtuoso piece, the Tale of Sir Thopas—more knowledge of English poetry than in fact he possessed. Throughout his life his models seem to have been French. His genius was to transform those models and naturalize them in English as thoroughly as he did—verse forms, meters, literary modes and all—to absorb influences from a number of literatures and make himself the first English poet fit to stand with the best that the rest of Europe could produce.

There were many respects in which he shared European preoccupations, one of the most important being the conscious artistry of his verse. As with any great poet, this is partly a matter for which instinct must account. But it is also partly a matter of self-awareness in the handling of subject and verse, so as to produce the maximum effect of "sentence and solas": profit and delight. One means of doing this was to imitate the ancient poets, to show oneself truly worthy to be in their company, inheritor of their poetic. This is one of the things that Petrarch was asserting in his Coronation Oration: Chaucer proclaims it in the epilogue to *Troilus and Criseyde,* with his humble recommendation of the book to the great classical poets. They represent the solid block of tradition behind any true poet. Remembrance of the past, constant remaking of its great stories—stories of Troy, Alexander, Rome, Thebes, Britain—was the essential task of the poet—and this, not any slavish desire for simple support, is the reason for the stress constantly laid on the necessity for authority and example in medieval literature—"auctoritee" and "ensaumple": "And if that olde bokes weren aweye, / Yloren were of remembrance the keye."

Chaucer's sense of the imperfections of his language and his treatment of the stories is not a modesty topos (see Glossary), still less mock modesty: it is the index of a deep concern for literary art: "The lyf so short, the craft so long to lerne," as he says in *The Parliament of Fowls.* Similarly, his conscious parodies of rhetoric (see Glossary) and rhetoricians are the index of his concern for the effects and effectiveness of language. Even when they mock, they mock something which is conceded to be necessary: "The dayes honour and the hevenes ye, / The nyghtes foo. . . ." Chaucer means us to recognize these rhetorical *traductiones* ("conceits"), piled up in *frequentatio* (repetition of the same structure) and with *polysyndeton* (use of the same syntactical scheme). The joke that he then springs on us, "al this clepe I the sonne," is a kind of double-take: he pretends to be amazed that he has been writing rhetoric all the time, mocking himself too for seeing that he is doing so. So too in the famous lament for "black Friday" in the Nun's Priest's Tale, where Chaucer, in the character of the Nun's Priest, is parodying a famous rhetorical set piece without implying that all such set pieces are pompous and useless. Chaucer is a profoundly rhetorical poet, with an explicit concern for his craft. Some of his uses of it are self-mocking, but for every one of these we can discover a hundred where the ordinary devices recommended by the rhetoricians—for beginning an argument, inventing arguments or incidents, varying a theme, making it both effective and pleasant—are being deployed. It is important to remember that rhetoric, for Chaucer, meant effective writing, not bombast, and that when he called a fellow poet "rhetor," it was a compliment.

The question of Chaucer's rhetoric—now taking the word in its widest sense—is much complicated in *The Canterbury Tales* by the dramatic illusion of the tellers within a framework of tales, the double fiction being simultaneously maintained. There was nothing new in the notion of framing a set of stories by putting them into the mouths of different tellers, and collections of such stories were composed from the fifth century A.D. onward. They were common enough in later medieval times. Boccaccio had arranged the hundred tales of his *Decameron* among ten men and women who had left the city for fear of the plague. Each told a tale on ten successive days. Boccaccio's fellow countryman Giovanni Sercambi, probably about 1374, also put together a set of such tales, told by one narrator on a journey and sometimes varied to fit the locality the travelers had reached at a given stage of their journey. We do not know whether Chaucer knew either Boccaccio's or Sercambi's collection—though he certainly knew an analogous use of the framing device by Gower in his *Confessio*

Amantis (The Lover's Confession). His exploitation of the device is a brilliant variation on other uses: unlike Boccaccio, he fits tale to teller; unlike Sercambi and Gower, he provides more than one narrator. It is possible that Chaucer's pilgrim-framework was the result of what he could see himself at any moment, especially from his house at Greenwich, where he was living when he began the *Tales* in earnest—a party of pilgrims on the road to the shrine of St. Thomas Becket at Canterbury, England's most famous and most frequented place of pilgrimage, within easy reach of London. Such pilgrimages were well known, even notorious, for the convoys in which they were made, and the diversions and tale-telling that went on by the way. (Fig. 35)

As he tells us, through the Host in the Prologue, Chaucer had originally planned some one hundred and twenty tales, two for each pilgrim on the way to Canterbury and two more for the way back. Like many ambitious plans, this was severely curtailed in the execution. Before his death at age fifty-seven—which was considered advanced in Chaucer's day—he had completed only twenty-two, had left two more uncompleted, and had done a certain amount of shuffling of tales from those for whom they were originally intended. The result, especially after the addition of the links between tales, with the backchat between pilgrims, the tensions, anger, insults, alliances, and friendships these reveal between teller and teller, tale and tale, is the richest and most complex collection of its kind in any language.

The cheerful, lively General Prologue, with its descriptions of all the pilgrims and the relationships that exist between them before the beginning of the pilgrimage, is followed by the grave, chivalric tale of the Knight—a story of Athens long ago, and the knightly contest of Palemon and Arcite for the love of Emily, a tale perfectly proportioned to its teller. So too, is the Miller's *fabliau* (see Headnote and Glossary) about a stupid carpenter cuckolded by his dapper young lodger, told with force and gusto and rousing the anger of the Reeve, himself a carpenter by trade and resenting the implication that one of his fellow workmen should be treated in this way. The Reeve's turn comes immediately, and he takes advantage of it to tell another *fabliau* about a miller who is outwitted by two students whom he has tried to cheat. Not only do they get back their bread which the miller has stolen, but they manage to lay both his wife and daughter. Later, the Friar and the Summoner also quarrel and each tells a tale against the profession of the other. These are single examples of pairing, but there is one instance where something more seems to have been intended. This occurs in the group of tales known as the Marriage Group: the Wife of Bath, with her militant feminism and aggression and her curious tale of faery love and "maistry," begins it. Then, in the usual order of the *Tales,* we have the disagreement between Summoner and Friar and their opposing tales—and then, to counter the Wife and to calm the atmosphere, the gentle, cool, placid tale of the Clerk, about the patient Griselda and obedience in marriage—followed, to keep the tone from staying too cool, by Chaucer's ironic *envoi* (see Glossary). There follows the Merchant's Tale about the old man, January, who married a young wife, May, and was cuckolded for it—another *fabliau* of cleverness and quick-thinking, its pace much quicker than the Clerk's. Finally comes the moving, sober, simple tale of the Franklin. Since we do not know the exact order of tales that Chaucer had in mind, we cannot be sure that his intention was that these particular tales should function as a close-knit group or should run through the series as a kind of counterpoint, or thematic unifier.

The problem about discovering thematic unity in *The Canterbury Tales* is that we cannot be sure that this was what Chaucer meant us to find. The headlinks give us some clues, but the unfinished state of the work makes it impossible to know whether the sequence is due to chance or design. In the manuscripts the tales are grouped into a number of blocks or fragments, but the order of these is far from invariable. The General Prologue and the tales of the Knight, Miller, Reeve, and Cook (unfinished) are always a beginning; the Parson's Tale and the Retraction always come last. Within that framework, order varies. Here the General Prologue and the tales of the Miller, Nun's Priest, Pardoner, Wife of Bath, and Franklin are presented; this corresponds with the grouping of some manuscripts. It presents the general introduction, followed by two comic tales, one a *fabliau,* one a burlesque beast fable with a final serious "morality." Then comes the self-portrait of the much-married Wife of Bath, and her tale; and the deeply serious and affecting tale of the Franklin; with the dark moral apologue of the Pardoner, preceded by the teller's devastating self-portrait, for a finale.

Of all Chaucer's works, *The Canterbury Tales* has always been the most popular. We can only guess at when exactly most of the tales were composed, for neither Chaucer nor his scribes give us any help. The more than eighty manuscripts, mostly of the fifteenth century, and Caxton's two editions of about 1478 and 1484, besides many other early printings, are indications of how well the poet's successors thought of his great poem.

CHAUCER'S ENGLISH

Chaucer gave both prestige and currency to the English spoken in London at his time, but this was not the only dialect of the language in which works of literature were composed during the fourteenth century. In particular, the regional dialects of the West and North of England and the North-West Midland of the time had a literature of their own, in a language which would often have been next to unintelligible to a Southern reader. This literature is often of great stature—Langland's *Piers Plowman* was originally written in the dialect of the West; the works of the *Gawain*-poet were written in North-West Midland. In the fourteenth and fifteenth centuries, too, the cycles of mystery plays were composed in the Northern dialect (Chaucer makes one of the students speak it in the Reeve's Tale). The comic scenes in *The Second Shepherds' Play* use the difference to set the affected Southern speech of the character Mak against the plain, blunt Northern outspokenness of the shepherds. The difficulty that one part of the country had in understanding another was still present in Caxton's day (see below, his Preface to the *Aeneid*). These two fifteenth-century examples of dialect difference indicate the continuance of the problem: despite Chaucer, London English was not established as the English norm overnight—and considerable dialect differences remain, even today. (The longer Middle English texts in this volume which are not written in the London dialect have been modernized or translated.)

Chaucer, along with John Gower and other London authors of the fourteenth century, took the English of London just at a time when it was beginning to assert itself as the major dialect and carried it farther along the road. Their use of it represents the true beginning of modern standard English. Hitherto, French had been the language of cultured entertainment, and Latin the language of scholarly instruction—and up to a point remained so until the sixteenth century. Gower, in fact, wrote in French and Latin as well as in English. The fifteenth and sixteenth centuries see a conscious effort on the part of poets, prose writers, and their printers alike to bring English to a level of richness and expressive subtlety where it can compete with both French and Latin on equal terms (see Caxton's Prefaces below).

The London English that Chaucer used was a composite, made up of the dialects of the neighboring counties, chiefly of the East Midlands, but with some South-Eastern (Kentish) features and a few South-Western. It is so much the ancestor of modern English that there is comparatively little in vocabulary, syntax, and grammar that is not easily recognizable to a modern reader. The elaborate system of inflections which had characterized Old English and earlier Middle English was being leveled, and unstressed final -e was becoming a silent letter. Most of Chaucer's vocabulary is still recognizable, even though the spelling often differs considerably from the modern: *dayeseye* for "daisy," for example; or *defaute,* a French spelling for "default." Spelling is not uniform, and the same word may be spelled in different ways: thus, *mone, moone,* for "moon." About a third of Chaucer's vocabulary is French. There are differences in sense between Chaucer's vocabulary and ours: *parcel,* for example, for "part"; *chalange* for "claim"; *lust* for "pleasure." *"Him thoughte," "me thoughte"* do not mean "he (or I) thought" but "it seemed to him/me."

The best way to understand Chaucer is to read him aloud. Though we cannot hope to recover the exact manner in which his language was spoken, we can achieve a reasonably good notion of it. Reading aloud minimizes the difficulties of understanding Chaucer, which lie in the different meanings of much of his vocabulary and the subtlety of his poetry, rather than in his grammar or syntax. The merest skeleton of these two is therefore given below, but the pronunciation is dealt with rather more fully.

PRONUNCIATION

The chief points to note about Chaucerian pronunciation are:

Vowels

Stressed short vowels are pronounced as in Modern English, with the exception of *a,* which is open, i.e. a "rounder" sound than in modern "man," as in Modern French *patte,* and *u* (often spelled *o* as in *love*), which has only the sound of modern *put.* A vowel is always short when it is followed by two consonants. Otherwise, it may be short or long: modern pronunciation is a good guide.

Long vowels are pronounced as they are in modern Italian or French. A long vowel can be recognized as long if it is doubled in spelling (*maad, reed, wood*); or if it occurs in a stressed position at the end of a word (*he, mo, wisly*). *A, e, o* are long if followed by a single consonant plus -e (*made, rede, wode*).

a as in Modern English "father": *fader, maad.*

e as in Modern English "air": *ese, heed;* or as in Modern French "été": nede, theef.

> (A practical guide here is modern spelling: Chaucer's words with the open sound as in modern "air" tend to be spelled today with *ea: ease; head;* those with the close sound to be spelled with *ee* or *ie: need, thief.* In the early stages of familiarizing oneself with Chaucerian pronounciation, it may be best to ignore the distinction and use only the pronunciation as in "air.")

i(y) as in Modern English "machine": *sire, slyde.*

o as in Modern English "note": *oo, stoon;* or as in Modern French "chose": *do, good.* (Modern English sometimes spells the open sound *oa: boat;* and the closed *oo.* Again, the best advice to the beginner is to ignore the distinction and use only the pronunciation as in *boat.*)

u generally spelled *ou, ow* as in Modern English "rude": *luce.* (In words of French origin, such as *aventure,* the French pronunciation of *u* is kept.)

Diphthongs combine the two elements, as given above:

ai (*ay*), *ei* (*ey*) are midway between Modern English "play" and "aisle": *fair, way, veines, wey.*

au (*aw*) as in Modern English "house": *baume, bawd.* (In words of French origin, such as *daunce,* it is pronounced as in *haunt.*)

eu (*ew*) as in Modern English "few": *newe, knew;* or as in Modern English "lewd": *fewe, lewed.*

Unstressed vowels (chiefly final -e).
as in Modern English "about."

By Chaucer's time, final unstressed -e was probably not sounded in everyday speech, but in verse it is sounded or not, according to the demands of the meter. It is usually elided, i.e. merged into the following word, if that word begins with a vowel. It is usually sounded before the caesura or at the end of a line.

Consonants

All consonants are pronounced, except the initial *h-* in some words of French origin: *honour.* Both elements of initial *gn, kn, wr* are pronounced *g-naw, g-nof, k-nyt, k-now, w-rap, w-recche.* Similarly both elements of *lk, lf, lm: folk, half, palmer.* The combination *gh* is pronounced gutturally like German *-ch.*

GRAMMAR

The features of Chaucerian grammar on which the modern reader needs most guidance are:

Nouns and adjectives. Almost all older case-endings have disappeared, and those that remain are similar to those surviving in Modern English. The plural of most nouns ends in *-es* or *-s;* with an occasional *-en* plural (*eyen,* or *yën* for "eyes") and an occasional uninflected plural (*pound, yeer*). The possessive case ends in *-es* or *-s.* Adjectives add -e to their final consonant in certain circumstances.

Pronouns. Both *thou* and *you* are used, *you* sometimes to signify respectful or formal use of language. The third person singular uses *his* for the possessive of *it;* and the plural uses *hem, here, hir*(e) for the objective and possessive of they.

Adverbs are formed from adjectives by adding -e, or *-lich*(e), *-ly.*

Verbs. Infinitives end in -e or *-en.*

Present participles usually end in -ing(e), *-yng*(e), with an occasional *-and.*

Past participles end in *-en* or -e and often begin with *y-.* Chaucer uses several different forms: *sworn, swore, ysworn, yswore, comen.*

Present indicative ends in *-e, -est, -eth* for the first three persons of the singular, and all these endings may be contracted after a final vowel or final *-d* or *-t. Lith, lieth, lyeth,* and *last, laste, lasteth* may all be found. All persons of the plural end in -e(*n*).

Past definite. The plural usually ends in -e or -en. *Goon* (go) has two forms for the past: *yede* and *wente.*

SYNTAX

Chaucer's syntax is often oral syntax, sometimes tortuous and inverted, full of omissions and with occasional superfluous words and constructions, but not difficult. One major point to note is that in Chaucer, as in Middle English in general, negatives do not cancel each other out as they do in Modern English. They intensify, so that "That nevere . . . / Ne sholde upon him take no maistrie" is a strong negative. Another important point is the frequent use of impersonal constructions: *him list* for "it pleased him," *me thoughte* for "it seemed to me." Another is the frequent use of auxiliary verbs: *gan* is used to form a simple past tense: *gan slyde* means "did slide," or "slid," and it may be used also to express a sense of beginning. *Do* is used in the sense of "make"—*do me lyve:* "make me live"; go in the sense of "let us"—*go we soupe:* "let us have supper."

The text is based on that of W. W. Skeat, first published in 1894–97, with readings introduced from other sources. For the General Prologue, the helpful text of Phyllis M. Hodgson, 1969, has been much drawn upon. As an aid to the reader, an e which has now become silent has been printed e where the meter requires it to be pronounced as a syllable; an acute accent indicates an *e* pronounced like modern French *é;* and accentuation which differs from Modern English is marked thus: *àppearence.*

It is hoped that this will encourage the reader to recite Chaucer's verse aloud, following the indications for pronunciation given above. This was the way in which many of Chaucer's contemporaries would have made their acquaintance with his works, for they were composed with recitation in mind (Fig. 24).

The Canterbury Tales

General Prologue

With the General Prologue, as with all Chaucer's works, the difficulty is to know art from nature, and to see how Chaucer, from the mass of conventions in which he worked, achieved an utterly unconventional and original masterpiece, the first and the greatest of its kind in our literature. We cannot say what gave him the idea of building his great poem out of a slice of society which is typical but not entirely representative. We do not know whether he began with the notion of a set of tales told by pilgrims, or whether he had written a number of stories before deciding to link them together in this way. We do not know whether the General Prologue, as we have it, is a final version or only the draft for one: we can only say that it was probably written in the 1380's.

The Prologue opens with a rhetorical passage which at once poses a problem. It is a hymn to the regenerative power of the sun and to the rise of the sap in nature, the rebirth of the dead year that sends men and women to seek spiritual regeneration at a place of pilgrimage and physical and mental recreation during the journey. It is often praised as a miracle of naturalistic description: this *is* how it happens. Yet it is thoroughly conventional in two ways. First, a hymn to Spring was a recognized literary commonplace, especially for beginning a poem. Second, it is not, as is so often claimed, utterly lifelike: for example, March is not a dry month in England and the description of it as such is part of a literary convention that, far from being English, goes back to classical literature. Yet the life and vigor are undoubtedly there, in this perfectly wrought, eighteen-line verse paragraph, the striking beginning recommended by rhetorical theory which at once engages the reader and then modulates gently into the lower rhetorical mode of the portraits that are to follow.

The portraits themselves are as difficult to characterize as the opening passage. They are types, without doubt, and intended in their total to represent contemporary English society, with the exception of the higher nobility, who would go on pilgrimage with their own train and not in a company. If we were dealing with an attempt at naturalistic description, we should expect to find more than one representative of each profession or each rank. Yet the characters are so individual that they seem to ride out of the pages. Are we to conclude that they are portraits drawn from life? So many exact details are given for so many of them that Chaucer must, at the very least, be making some reference to existing persons, the point of which is now lost to us but would have been understood by his listeners or his readers. It may be that there is more to it than that: the Host has been identified with an actual innkeeper, and people living in Chaucer's day have been found whose characters would certainly fit the characters that Chaucer gives in the Prologue. He may have taken hints from contemporary men and women who were known to him personally or by repute to diversify the types he was drawing.

Once more our difficulty is to know what is convention and what is not. The tender and delicate portrait of the Prioress, for example, plays with the tension between the heavenly love to which she is vowed and the earthly love which shows in her love of small, delicate, pretty things, and on the ambiguities of applying a single language to both. She is described in terms that fit a heroine of romance—some of her features are a direct imitation of the features of Leisure/Idleness in the *Roman de la*

Rose, and the description of her table manners is derived from the same text. The ambiguities of her character are typical human ambiguities. Her own gentleness is matched by the gentleness of the portrait: the satire is light, controlled, unwounding. She is individual and type in one, lovingly and gently yet satirically placed in relation to the other ecclesiastics of the pilgrimage. Later, Chaucer will intensify the portrait by means of her pitiful tale of the murdered little boy, Hugh of Lincoln, just as he will poke gentle fun at the young, modest, learned Clerk—the type of the earnest young scholar—in his tale. Here the irony and satiric method are quiet, caressing, indirect. For the "noble ecclesiast" who is the Pardoner, or the worldly Monk and begging Friar, much harsher ironic treatment is reserved. As types, they are set against what a religious man ought to be; as characters they are set against what the other religious characters in the Prologue actually are. We are intended to see both how they fall short of what should be—that is, of their profession—and of the example they might take from the pious, decent Parson.

In the Parson and the Plowman, his brother, Chaucer has taken stock types from another sort of literature. In the contemporary prose and poetry of social complaint and criticism, the Plowman in particular figures as critic and as the example of the true laborer, against whose simple piety, scrupulousness in performing his allotted task, poverty, and oppressed condition may be measured the surface devotion, cynicism, neglect of duty, money-grubbing, and love of power of those who profess to be his betters. The same holds true, to a lesser extent, of the country priest—whom Chaucer significantly makes the Plowman's brother.

In presenting his characters Chaucer—like a modern author drawing on present-day psychology—frequently uses the psychological theory of his time, which gave the planets in a man's horoscope at birth, and their positions at different times during his life, an influence on the kind of man he was. Similarly, the bodily fluids, or humors, of which he was composed—blood, phlegm, choler (bile), and melancholy (black bile)—with their "qualities" of hot, cold, dry, and moist, according to their mixture in him, would determine character and behavior. One could, too, according to the theory of the time, read the signs of character in the face (physiognomy, physiognomics) or the outward bodily characteristics (see Fig. 37). The Wife of Bath's horoscope would predispose her to the lasciviousness she glories in. The description of the Miller's physical traits can be interpreted to mean that he is bold, angry, shameless, and talkative. The Summoner's appearance is both the result and the expression of his lecherous temperament. The Pardoner's spiritual degeneracy is partly due to his physical state: he is a eunuch born. The Franklin's love of rich food and wine and hospitality might be deduced from the combination of humors which make up his temperament: blood predominates, so that he is red-faced, outgoing, confident, generous, quick to anger.

Yet to say this about the kind of detail from all sources that Chaucer uses for his descriptions of the pilgrims is not to arrive at the heart of his mystery. It is merely an indication of how incomparably rich were the materials on which he was able to draw and how remarkably he handles them. The poet William Blake has the last word: "Of Chaucer's characters . . . some of the names or titles are altered by time, but the characters themselves remain forever unaltered."

General Prologue

Here biginneth the Book of the Tales of Caunterbury.

Whan that Aprille° with hise shourės> sote>	*showers / sweet*
The droghte of March hath percėd> to the rote,	*pierced*
And bathėd every veyne° in swich licour	
Of which vertu engendrėd is the flour;	
Whan Zephirus° eek> with his sweetė breeth>	*also / breath*
Inspirėd hath in every holt> and heeth>	*wood/ field*
The tendre croppės,> and the yongė sonne°	*shoots*
Hath in the Ram his halfė cours yronne,>	*run*
And smalė fowlės> maken melodye	*birds*
That slepen al the night with open iye°	
(So priketh hem> Nature in hir corages)>:	*them / their hearts*
Thanne longen> folk to goon> on pilgrimages,	*long / go*
And palmeres° for to seken straungė strondes,>	*foreign shores*
To fernė halwės, couthe in sondry londes;°	
And specially from every shirės ende	
Of Engėlond to Caunterbury° they wende,>	*go*
The holy blisful> martir for to seeke,	*blessed*
That hem hath holpen> whan that they were seke.>	*helped / sick*
Bifel> that in that seson> on a day,	*It happened / season*
In Southwerk° at the Tabard as I lay	
Redy to wenden> on my pilgrimage	*go*
To Caunterbury with ful devout corage,	
At nyght was come into that hostelrye>	*inn*
Wel nine and twenty in a companye,	
Of sondry folk, by aventure> yfalle	*chance*
In felawship,> and pilgrimes were they alle	*companionship*
That toward Caunterbury wolden> ryde.	*wished to*
The chambres> and the stables weren wyde,	*bedrooms*
And wel we weren esėd attė beste.°	
And shortly, whan the sonnė was to reste,	
So hadde I spoken with hem everichon>	*every one*
That I was of hir felawship> anon,>	*company / at once*
And madė forward> erly for to ryse,	*agreement*

Aprille the traditional Spring opening. Zephirus, Nature, and the zodiacal dating are part of the stock of the medieval poet.

veyne vein (of plants), sap vessel; thus, "And bathed every vein in such a liquid, by the power of which the flower is begotten"

Zephirus the West wind

yonge sonne young, because just passed out of the first zodiacal sign (Fig. 37) of the solar year, Aries, the Ram, which in Chaucer's time was thought to govern March 12 to April 11

open iye i.e. do not sleep at all in Spring

palmeres originally, pilgrims who carried a palm leaf to show that they had been to the Holy Land; later applied to all pilgrims

To ferne . . . londes to far-off shrines, famous ones, in various countries

Caunterbury the most popular medieval place of pilgrimage in England because of the tomb there of St. Thomas Becket, murdered in the Cathedral in 1170 and canonized 1174

Southwerk Southwark, then a suburb of London on the south bank of the Thames, stood at the beginning of the road to Dover and Canterbury. The Tabard, now destroyed, was a famous inn. Its sign would have shown the short, sleeveless surcoat worn by knights and heralds, called a tabard.

And wel . . . beste and we were made comfortable in the best manner

To take oure wey theras> I yow devyse.> — *where / tell*
But natheles,> whil I have tyme and space,° — *nevertheless*
Er> that I ferther in this talė pace>, — *before / pass*
Me thynketh it acordaunt to resoùn°
To tellė yow al the condicioùn°
Of ech of hem,> so as it semėd me, — *them*
And whiche> they weren, and of what degree,> — *who / status*
And eek in what array° that they were inne;
And at a knyght then wol I first biginne.

KNYGHT

A knyght ther was, and that a worthy> man, — *distinguished*
That fro the tymė that he first bigan
To riden out, he lovėd chivalrie,
Trouthe and honoùr, fredom and curteisie.°
Ful worthy> was he in his lordės werre,> — *brave / war*
And therto hadde he riden, no man ferre,> — *further*
As wel in Cristendom as in hethenesse,> — *pagan lands*
And evere honoured for his worthynesse.
At Alisaundre° he was whan it was wonne.
Ful oftė tyme he hadde the bord bigonne°
Aboven allė nacions in Pruce;
In Lettow hadde he reysėd,> and in Ruce, — *campaigned*
No Cristen man so ofte of his degree.
In Gernade at the seege eek hadde he be
Of Algezir, and riden in Belmarye.
At Lyeys was he, and at Satalye,
Whan they were wonne; and in the Gretė See°
At many a noble armee> hadde he be. — *invading force*
At mortal batailles° hadde he been fiftene,
And foughten for oure feith at Tramissene°
In lystės° thriės, and ay> slayn his foo.> — *always / enemy*
This ilkė> worthy knyght hadde been also — *same*
Somtymė> with the lord of Palatye — *formerly*
Agayn> another hethen in Turkye. — *against*

tyme and space an oral formula; the words carry less than their full value: "while I can"
resoun perhaps French *raison*, right; or Latin *ratio*, rhetorical order; or reason
condicioun whole state of being, inner and outer
array dress or order
Trouthe . . . curteisie knightly virtues; see Chaucer's *balade*, "Truth," below. *Trouthe* here is integrity; *fredom* is liberality, material and spiritual; *curteisie* is well-bred behavior.
Alisaundre The Knight had fought against all three of the great enemies of 14th-century Christendom: the Saracens in the Middle East (Christians captured Alexandria in Egypt, 1365 (Fig. 36); Attalia (Sattalye) in Turkey, 1361; Ayas (Lyes in Armenia, 1367); sometimes in alliance with the pagan "Lord of Palatye," the Turkish sultan, against other infidels—a not infrequent Christian-heathen alliance; the Moors in Spain and North Africa (Granada, Algeciras, Ben-Marin, 1344 and after); the barbarians of Lithuania (Lettow; to 1385), and the Tartars of Russia.
bord bigonne taken the head of the table at a banquet; perhaps of the Teutonic Order of Knights in (East) Prussia
Gretė See Mediterranean
batailles tournaments between champions fought to the death, for a decision between armies
Tramissene Tlemçen, Algeria, then a Berber stronghold
lystes space enclosed by barriers for tournaments or jousts (Fig. 48)

And everemore˃ he hadde a sovereyn prys,˃ — *always / reputation*
And though that he were worthy, he was wys,˃ — *prudent*
And of his port˃ as meeke as is a mayde. — *behavior*
He nevere yet no vilainye ne sayde
In al his lyf unto no maner wight.°
He was a verray,˃ parfit,˃ gentil knyght. — *true / perfect*
But for to tellen yow of his array,˃ — *equipage*
His hors° were godė, but he was nat gay.˃ — *gaudy*
Of fustian he werėd a gypoun°
Al bismoterėd˃ with his habergeoun, — *rust-stained*
For he was late˃ ycome from his viage,˃ — *just / expedition*
And wentė for to doon his pilgrimage.

SQUIER°

With hym ther was his sone, a young squièr,
A lovyere, and a lusty˃ bachelèr, — *lively*
With lokkės crulle,˃ as they were layd in presse.˃ — *curled / crimped*
Of twenty yeer of age he was, I gesse.
Of his statùre he was of evene˃ lengthe, — *moderate*
And wonderly deliver,˃ and greet of strengthe. — *agile*
And he hadde been somtyme in chyvachie°
In Flaundres, in Artoys, and Picardye,
And born hym˃ weel, as of so litel space,° — *carried himself*
In hope to stonden˃ in his lady grace. — *stand well*
Embrouded˃ was he, as it were a mede˃ — *embroidered / meadow*
Al ful of fresshė flowrės, whyte and reede.°
Syngyng he was, or floytinge° al the day.
He was as fressh as is the month of May.
Short was his gowne, with slevės longe and wyde.
Wel coude he sitte on hors and fairė ryde.
He coudė songės make, and wel endite,˃ — *write poetry*
Juste˃ and eek daunce, and weel portraye˃ and write. — *joust / draw*
So hoote he lovėde, that by nightertale
He slepte namore than dooth a nightingale.
Curteis he was, lowly, and servysable,
And carf biforn his fader at the table.°

He nevere . . . wight Middle English uses an accumulation of negatives to strengthen, not cancel each other out; thus, "He never yet, in all his life, said anything base to anyone of any kind."
hors horses; an uninflected plural
gypoun jupon, the close-fitting tunic worn under a coat of mail (*habergeoun*). His was of a thick, coarse cloth (*fustian*).
squier properly speaking not yet a knight but one who served a knight. Later he is called *bacheler*, a young knight who has not yet set up his own banner and is still in the service of a senior knight.
chyvachie cavalry campaigns, perhaps the single one of 1383 during the Hundred Years' War between England and France
as of . . . space considering the short time he had campaigned
whyte and reede stock phrase: "of all colors"
floytinge whistling or playing the flute or pipe
So hoote . . . table (ll. 97–100) "So hotly did he love, that at night-time he slept no more than a nightingale. He was courtly of behavior, modest and ready to serve; and he carved in front of his father at the table." To carve the roast, so that his lord was fittingly served, was a frequently mentioned duty of a squire.

YEMAN°

A yeman hadde he, and servaùnts namo˃ — *no more*
At that tyme, for him liste˃ ridė so; — *it pleased*
And he was clad in cote and hood of grene.°
A sheef of pecok arwės, bright and kene,
Under his belt he bar˃ ful thriftily,˃ — *carried / handily*
(Wel coude he dresse˃ his takel˃ yemanly: — *see to / gear*
His arwes droupėd noght with fetherės lowe°)
And in his hand he baar˃ a myghty bowe.° — *bore*
A not-heed° hadde he, with a brown visage.˃ — *face*
Of wodėcraft˃ wel coude he al the usage. — *woodmanship*
Upon his arm he bar a gay bracer,°
And by his syde, a swerd and a bokeler,°
And on that other syde, a gay daggere,
Harneisėd˃ wel, and sharp as point of spere; — *mounted*
A Cristofre° on his brest, of silver shene;˃ — *shining*
An horn he bar,˃ the bawdrik° was of grene. — *bore*
A forster˃ was he soothly,˃ as I gesse. — *forester / truly*

PRIORESSE°

Ther was also a nonne,˃ a prioresse, — *nun*
That of hir smiling was ful simple and coy.°
Hire gretteste ooth˃ was but 'by Saint Loy.'° — *greatest oath*
And she was clepėd˃ Madame Eglentyne.° — *called*
Ful wel she song the service divine,
Entunėd˃ in hir nose ful semėly.˃ — *intoned / becomingly*
And Frensh she spak ful faire and fetisly,˃ — *prettily*
After the scole˃ of Stratford-attė-Bowe,° — *style*
For Frensh of Paris was to hir unknowe.
At metė˃ wel ytaught was she withalle:˃ — *meal-time / moreover*
She leet˃ no morsel from hir lippės falle, — *let*
Ne wette hir fingrės in hir saucė depe;
Wel coude she carie a morsel, and wel kepe˃ — *take care*
That no drope ne fille˃ upon hir brist.˃ — *fell / breast*
In curteisie was set ful muchel hir list.°

Yeman a yeoman or free man, a commoner attending the knight as his only other servant. A knight was obliged to have a retinue, to uphold his dignity. This knight makes do with squire and yeoman.
he . . . grene The yeoman was dressed in the huntsman's Lincoln green, and had a sheaf of arrows with peacock feathers tucked into his belt.
lowe Peacock feathers tended to disturb the flight of the arrow, but the yeoman can counteract this.
bowe the long-bow was 6 feet tall
not-heed close-cropped head
bracer guard on the left forearm, to prevent friction from the bow-string
swerd . . . bokeler sword and small round shield
Cristofre medal of St. Christopher, patron of travelers
bawdrik baldric, strap worn round the waist or diagonally across the body
Prioresse mother superior of a nunnery
simple and coy sincere and demure; monastic rule enjoined that laughter should be controlled, unaffected, and silent. *Simple and coy* is a stock phrase in medieval literature when a lover is praising his mistress.
Loy St. Eligius (Eloi), patron of goldsmiths and carters
Eglentyne sweetbriar
Stratford-atte-Bowe anglicized French, learned at the Benedictine nunnery of St. Leonard's, Kent
In . . . list her pleasure was strongly fixed on polite behavior

Hir overlippė wypėd she so clene
That in hir coppe> ther was no ferthyng> sene *cup / morsel*
Of grecė,> whan she dronken hadde hir draughte. *grease*
Ful semėly after hir mete she raughte.°
And sikerly, she was of greet desport,°
And ful plesaùnt, and amyable of port,> *bearing*
And peyned hire to countrefetė cheere
Of court, and to been estatlich of manere,
And to ben holden digne of reverence.°
But for to speken of hire conscience,
She was so charitable and so pitous,> *full of pity*
She woldė wepe, if that she sawe a mous
Caught in a trappe, if it were deed> or bledde.> *dead / bleeding*
Of> smalė houndės hadde she that she fedde *some*
With rosted flesh,> or milk and wastel breed.° *meat*
But sore wepte she, if any of hem were deed,
Or if men smoot> it with a yerdė> smerte.> *struck / stick / hard*
And al was conscience> and tendre herte. *soft feelings*
Ful semėly hir wimpel pinchėd was,°
Hir nose tretys,> hir eyen greye as glas,° *well-made*
Hir mouth ful smal, and therto> softe and reed.> *also / red*
But sikerly> she hadde a fair forheed— *certainly*
It was almoost a spannė brood,° I trowe;> *believe*
For, hardily,> she was nat undergrowe. *assuredly*
Ful fetis> was hir cloke, as I was war.> *well-made / aware*
Of smal coral,° aboute hire arm she bar
A paire of bedės,° gauded al with grene,
And theron heng> a brooch of gold ful shene,> *hung / bright*
On which ther was first write a crownėd A,°
And after, *Amor vincit omnia.*°

NONNE AND III PREESTES

Another nonnė with hir haddė she
That was hir chapėleyne,> and preestės thre.° *chaplain*

Ful . . . raughte very politely she reached for her food
And . . . desport and certainly, she was of great charm
And . . . reverence (ll. 139–41) and took pains to imitate the behavior of court and to be dignified of manner and to be considered worthy of reverence
wastel breed cake-bread; French *gâteau;* superior quality white bread
Ful . . . was Her wimple was pleated very becomingly. The wimple was a nun's close linen head covering, which should have covered her forehead and the sides of her face.
greye as glas conventional phrase. Gray was the conventional color for a medieval beauty's eyes.
spanne distance from thumb to extended little finger
coral not only jewelry but then believed a preservative of health, physical and spiritual
paire of bedes Rosary. *Bedes* originally meant prayers, and each bead represented an *Ave Maria;* the *gaudes,* representing a *Pater Noster,* marked off each ten beads.
A Nuns were normally forbidden ornaments.
Amor . . . omnia Latin: "Love conquers all"
thre Only one Nun's Priest tells a tale. A nunnery might have more than one priest, to offer mass and to hear confessions, which a woman could not do.

MONK

A monk ther was, a fair> for the maistrie,° *fine one*
An outridere,° that lovedė venerie,°
A manly man, to been an abbot able.
Ful many a deyntee> hors hadde he in stable, *fine*
And whan he rood,> men myghte his brydel heere *rode*
Gynglen> in a whistlynge wynd als cleere, *jingle*
And eek> as loude, as dooth the chapel belle *also*
Ther as> this lord was kepere° of the celle. *where*
The reule> of Saint Maure° or of Saint Beneit, *rule*
Bycause that it was old, and somdel streit>— *somewhat strict*
This ilkė> monk leet oldė thyngės pace,° *same*
And heeld after the newė world the space.> *meanwhile*
He yaf nat of> that text a pullėd> hen *gave not for / plucked*
That seith> that hunters beth> nat holy men,° *says / are*
Ne that a monk, whan he is recchėlees,> *negligent*
Is likned til> a fissh that is waterlees.° *like to a*
This is to seyn,> a monk out of his cloystre— *say*
But thilkė> text heeld he nat worth an oystre *that very*
And I seyde his opinioùn was good.
What> sholde he studie, and make hymselven wood,> *why / mad*
Upon a book in cloystre alwey to poure,°
Or swynken> with his handės, and laboùre, *toil*
As Austyn° bit?> How shal the world be served? *bids*
Lat Austyn have his swink to him reserved!°
Therfore, he was a pricasour> aright: *hard rider*
Grehoundes> he hadde as swift as fowel> in flight; *greyhounds / bird*
Of priking° and of hunting for the hare
Was al his lust;> for no cost wolde he spare. *pleasure*
I seigh> his slevės purfiled> at the hond *saw / trimmed*
With grys,> and that the fyneste of a lond. *gray fur*
And for to festne> his hood under his chyn, *fasten*
He hadde of gold wroght> a ful curious> pyn; *made / elaborate*
A love-knotte° in the gretter> ende ther was. *larger*
His heed was balled,> that shoon as any glas, *bald*
And eek his face, as it hadde been anoint.
He was a lord ful fat, and in good poynt;°
Hise eyen stepe,> and rollynge in his heed, *prominent*

for the maistrie surpassing all others
outridere a monk who rides out to supervise the monastery's property outside its immediate limits
venerie hunting, but also sexual pursuit
kepere supervisor of an outlying house or dependent community
Saint Maure (Maurus) credited with introducing the monastic *Rule* of St. Benedict (Beneit) to France
pace go their way
That . . . holy men St. Jerome (*c.* 342–420) and St. Augustine (354–430) condemn hunting.
waterlees Wyclif, Gower, and Langland use the comparison.
poure pore. The Benedictines were great supporters of study.
Austyn St. Augustine, on whose writings the Augustinian rule was based, believed in monastic labor.
Lat . . . reserved! Let Augustine have the toil (that he talks so much about) kept for himself alone!
priking literally, following the tracks of. *Prick* is the footprint or track of the hare; or the verb may simply here mean *riding*, as Spenser thought.
love-knotte strands of gold tied to signify the affection of lovers
in good poynt in good condition, plump

That stemėd as a forneys of a leed;°
His bootės souple,> his hors in greet estat.> *supple / array*
Now certeinly he was a fair prelat.°
He was nat pale, as a forpynėd goost.> *pined-away ghost*
A fat swan loved he best of any roost,
His palfrey> was as brown as is a berye. *saddle horse*

FRERE°

A frere ther was, a wantown° and a merye,
A limitour,° a ful solempnė> man. *imposing*
In alle the ordrės foure° is noon that can> *knows*
So muche of daliaùnce> and fair langàge. *flirtation*
He haddė maad ful many a mariàge
Of yongė wommen at his ownė cost.
Unto his ordre he was a noble post.> *support*
And wel biloved and famulier> was he *intimate*
With frankeleyns° overal> in his contree,> *throughout / district*
And with worthy wommen of the toun—
For he had power of confessioùn,
As seyde hymself, more than a curàt,> *parish priest*
For of> his ordre he was licenciat.° *by*
Ful swetėly herde he confessioùn,°
And plesaunt was his absolucioùn.
He was an esy> man to yeve> penaunce *indulgent / give*
Ther as> he wiste> to have a good pitaunce. *where / expected*
For unto a poure> ordre for to yive *poor*
Is signė that a man is wel yshrive;> *absolved*
For if he yaf,> he dorstė> make avaunt> *gave / dared / boast*
He wistė> that a man was repentaùnt; *knew*
For many a man so hard is of his herte,
He may nat wepe, althogh hym sorė smerte.°
Therfore, in stede of wepynge and preyères,> *prayers*
Men moot yeve silver to the pourė freres.
His tipet° was ay farsėd> ful of knyves *always stuffed*
And pynnės, for to yeven fairė wyves.> *women*
And certeinly, he hadde a mery note;

That . . . leed that glowed like a furnace under a cauldron
prelat a churchman of the upper ranks, who has received preferment
Frere Chaucer's portrait is composed of the regular accusations against the friars, the mendicant (begging) religious orders founded during the spiritual revival of the 13th century. Vowed to poverty and to preaching, they had multiplied and become rich by Chaucer's time.
wantown Ranges in meaning from "playful" to "lascivious."
limitour religious field-worker (begging, hearing confessions, burying, preaching) within the district (*limitatio*) assigned to his convent
ordres foure Dominicans, Franciscans, Carmelites, Augustinians
frankeleyns See l. 333.
licenciat licensed by the church to hear confessions
confessioùn The sinner who comes to confession must satisfy the confessor that he is contrite before being granted absolution. He must then perform an act of mortification imposed by the confessor, to express remorse and good intentions. This friar would impose a light penance on those able to give pious donations ("pitaunce") to his order: to be ready to part with money was to him a sure sign of repentance.
hym sore smerte he is greatly pained
tipet the long narrow piece of cloth, part of hood or sleeve, which could be used as pocket

Wel coude he singe, and pleyen on a rote;°
Of yeddinges he bar utterly the pris.°
His nekkė whit was as the flour-de-lys.°
Therto,˃ he strong was as a champioùn.° *moreover*
He knew the tavernes wel in every toun,
And everich˃ hostiler˃ and tappestere *every / innkeeper*
Bet than a lazar or a beggestere;°
For unto swich a worthy man as he
Acorded nat, as by his facultee,°
To have with sikė˃ lazars aqueyntaùnce. *sick*
It is nat honeste,˃ it may nat avaunce,˃ *good / get one anywhere*
For to deelen with no swich poraille,°
But al with riche, and sellers of vitaille.˃ *food and drink*
And overal ther as˃ profit sholde arise, *wherever*
Curteis˃ he was, and lowely˃ of servyse. *courteous / humble*
Ther nas no man nowher so vertuous.˃ *capable*
He was the bestė beggere in his hous;˃ *friary*
And yaf a certeyn fermė for the graunt°
Noon of his bretheren cam ther in his haunt.
For thogh a widwe˃ haddė noght a sho,˃ *widow / shoe*
So plesaunt was his '*In principio*,'°
Yet wolde he have a ferthyng˃ er he wente. *farthing*
His purchas was wel bettre than his rente.°
And rage he coude, as it were right a whelp.°
In lovė-dayes° ther coude he muchel˃ help, *much*
For ther he was nat lyk a cloisterer°
With a thredbare cope,˃ as is a poure scoler,˃ *cape / scholar*
But he was lyk a maister,° or a Pope.
Of double worsted° was his semicope,°
That rounded as a belle out of the presse.˃ *mould*
Somwhat he lipsėd,˃ for his wantownesse,˃ *lisped / affectation*
To make his English sweete upon his tonge;
And in his harping, whan that he hadde songe,˃ *sung*
Hise eyen twynkled in his heed aryght,˃ *truly*

rote stringed instrument
Of . . . pris for ballads, he took the prize entirely
flour-de-lys lily; more often used of a woman
champioùn literally, a knight specially chosen to fight in a tournament to the death
tappestere . . . beggestere tapster, better than a leper or a beggar. The ending *-ere* is normally feminine, but a tapster can be either male or female: barman or barmaid.
as . . . facultee in view of his profession
poraille poor people, whom a friar was bound by his vows to comfort and succor. The Franciscan rule was based on the Gospel injunction "Sell all thou hast and give to the poor."
And yaf . . . graunt He paid a certain sum for the monopoly of practicing in his district. This line and the next do not occur in all manuscripts and the accusation of "farming" is not supported by the historical facts.
'In principio' the opening words of St. John's gospel: "In the beginning [was the word . . .]"; constantly quoted by the friars to justify their preaching and also used by them as a salutation
purchas . . . rente His pickings on the side were better than the income he was authorized to collect.
And rage . . . whelp and he knew how to frolic like a puppy
love-dayes days set aside for amicable settlement of legal disputes by arbitration out of court. Clergy were forbidden to take part, except on behalf of the poor.
cloisterer a member of a religious order confined to the monastery
maister master, university graduate or teacher
double worsted expensive, heavy woolen cloth
semicope short (half-length) cloak

As doon> the sterrės> in the frosty nyght. — *do / stars*
This worthy limitour was cleped> Huberd. — *called*

MARCHANT

A marchant was ther, with a forkėd berd,> — *beard*
In mottėlee,° and hye on horse he sat,
Upon his heed a Flaundrish> bevere hat,° — *Flemish*
His bootės claspėd faire> and fetisly.> — *neatly / elegantly*
His resòns> he spak ful solempnėly,> — *sayings / pompously*
Souninge> alway th'encrees of his winning. — *publishing*
He wolde the see were kept for any thyng°
Bitwixė Middelburgh° and Orėwelle.
Wel coude he in eschaungė sheeldės° selle.
This worthy man ful wel his wit bisette:> — *ingenuity employed*
Ther wistė> no wight that he was in dette, — *knew*
So estatly> was he of his governaunce,> — *impressive / conduct*
With his bargàynes,> and with his chevisaunce.> — *bargaining / loans*
Forsothe,> he was a worthy man withalle; — *In truth*
But sooth to seyn, I noot how men hym calle.°

CLERK° OF OXENFORD

A clerk ther was of Oxenford also,
That unto logik° haddė longe ygo.
As leenė was his hors as is a rake,
And he nas nat> right fat I undertake, — *was not*
But lookėd holwe,> and therto sobrely.> — *hollow / grave*
Ful thredbare was his overeste> courtepy,° — *outermost*
For he hadde geten> hym yet no benefice,> — *gotten / church living*
Ne was so worldly for to have office.°
For hym was lever> have at his beddes heed — *more pleasing*
Twenty bookės, clad in blak or reed,
Of Aristotle° and his philosophie,
Than robės riche, or fithele,> or gay sautrie.° — *fiddle*
But al be> that he was a philosòphre, — *although*
Yet haddė he but litel gold° in cofre.> — *coffer*
But al that he mighte of his freendės hente,> — *get*

mottelee parti-colored cloth
bevere hat an expensive fur hat
He wolde . . . thyng he wished the sea policed, at all costs
Middelburgh Middelburg, in Holland, almost opposite Orwell, in Suffolk; both were important ports for the import and export of wool and cloth, the basis of English trade with Flanders at the time.
sheeldes *écus* (French coins). The Merchant was a successful illegal speculator in enemy currency.
But sooth . . . calle but, to tell the truth, I don't know what he was called
Clerk literally, cleric, advanced student (at Oxford). A clerk professed his intention of entering the priesthood before going to university. He might remain there in minor orders all his life, going no farther up the ladder in the church, and seeking no post outside. Many university scholars were clerks and the word gained the connotation of "learned man."
logik the art of reasoning and argument. The Clerk is long past the elementary stage of his education, and is an accomplished logician.
courtepy short jacket
office a secular, administrative post such as many clerics took to make their living
Aristotle The rediscovered Aristotle, in Latin translation, formed the basis of the university curriculum.
sautrie psaltery, a stringed instrument, played with the hand
But . . . gold "Philosophy" could also mean "alchemy"; so the Clerk did not have the philosopher's stone to turn base metal into gold.

On bookės and on lernynge he it spente,
And bisily gan for the soulės preye°
Of hem that yaf> hym wherwith to scoleye.> — *gave / study*
Of studie took he most cure> and most heede. — *care*
Noght o> word spak he morė than was neede, — *one*
And that was seyd in forme and reverence,°
And short, and quyk,> and ful of hy sentence.° — *lively*
Souninge in> moral vertu was his speche, — *tending towards*
And gladly wolde he lerne and gladly teche.

SERGEANT OF LAWE°

A sergeant of the lawė, war> and wys,> — *cautious / prudent*
That often haddė been at the Parvys°
Ther was also, ful riche of excellence.
Discreet he was, and of greet reverence°—
He semėd swich, his wordes weren so wise.
Justice he was ful often in assise°
By patente,° and by pleyn commissioùn.°
For his science,> and for his heigh renoun, — *knowledge*
Of fees and robės hadde he many oon.
So greet a purchasour> was nowher noon: — *property speculator*
Al was fee simple° to hym in effect;> — *virtually*
His purchasing mighte nat been infect.> — *proved invalid*
Nowher so bisy a man as he ther nas,> — *was not*
And yet he semėd bisier than he was.
In termės hadde he caas and doomės alle
That from the tyme of Kyng William° were yfalle.> — *had occurred*
Therto, he coude endite> and make a thing,> — *compose / deed*
Ther coudė no wight pinche> at his writyng; — *complain*
And every statut coude he pleyn> by rote. — *complete*
He rood but hoomly,> in a medlee> cote — *unpretentiously / parti-colored*
Girt with a ceint> of silk, with barrės> smale. — *belt / stripes*
Of his array telle I no lenger tale.

FRANKELEYN°

A frankėleyn was in his companye,
Whit was his beerd, as is the dayėsye.> — *daisy*
Of his complexioùn he was sangwyn.°

gan . . . preye prayed. The Middle English *gan* and *can* are often used to form a simple past tense.
reverence in due form, with decorum and respect
sentence Latin: *sententia* (moral) significance; weighty, memorable saying
Sergeant of Lawe a lawyer of high rank and competence, who could also act as judge
Parvys area in front of a church, where lawyers and their clients met
of greet reverence highly respected
assise judicial sessions held periodically throughout England
patente "open [letter]": the royal letter of appointment, to be displayed to all
pleyn commissioùn full commission, full authority to adjudicate
fee simple i.e. land owned outright, with no legal complications
termes . . . William Either he had memorized all the cases and decisions since the reign of William the Conqueror (1066–87) or he had the legal yearbooks from that time to his.
Frankeleyn originally "free (*franc*) man." Many rose to be wealthy landowners equivalent to the gentry, and important figures in their district.
sangwyn sanguine; his constitution or temperament (*complexioùn*) dominated by the humor of blood

Wel loved he by the morwe˃ a sop in wyn;° *in the morning*
To liven in delit° was evere his wone,˃ *habit*
For he was Epicurus° ownė sone,
That heeld opinioùn that pleyn˃ delit *full*
Was verraily˃ felicitee parfit. *truly*
An housholdere, and that a greet, was he;
Saint Julian° he was in his contree.˃ *district*
His breed, his ale, was alweys after oon;°
A bettre envynėd° man was nowher noon;
Withoutė bakė mete was never his hous
Of fish and flesh, and that so plentevous,˃ *plentiful*
It snewėd˃ in his hous of mete˃ and drynke, *snowed / food*
Of allė deyntees˃ that men coudė thynke. *dainties*
After˃ the sondry sesons of the yeer, *according to*
So chaunged he his mete and his soper.˃ *supper*
Ful many a fat partrich hadde he in muwe,˃ *coop*
And many a breem and many a luce in stewe.°
Wo was his cook but if˃ his saucė were *unless*
Poynaunt˃ and sharp, and redy al his geere. *piquant*
His table dormant in his halle° alway
Stood redy covered˃ al the longė day.° *set*
At sessioùns ther was he lord and sire;°
Ful oftė tyme he was knyght of the shire.°
An anlas,˃ and a gipser˃ al of silk *dagger / purse*
Heeng˃ at his girdel,˃ whit as mornė milk. *hung / belt*
A shirreve° hadde he been, and a countour.°
Was nowher swich a worthy vavasour.°

HABERDASSHERE,° CARPENTER, WEBBE, DYERE, TAPICER

An haberdasshere and a carpenter
A webbe,˃ a dyere and a tapycer,˃— *weaver / tapestry-maker*
And they were clothed alle in o lyveree°
Of a solempne˃ and a greet fraternitee. *dignified*
Ful fresh and newe hir geere apikėd˃ was; *adorned*

sop in wyn piece of fine toasted bread, soaked in spiced wine
delit sensuous pleasure
Epicurus (342–270 B.C.) Greek philosopher, for whom absence of pain because of virtuous living was the supreme good. The popular form of his doctrine is that pleasure itself is the true end of life.
Saint Julian patron saint of hospitality
after oon of one standard
envyned stocked with wine
breem . . . stewe and many a carp and pike in his fishpond
halle the main living room
Stood . . . day Medieval tables were usually on trestles, set up as required and then taken down. The Franklin's was permanently established and permanently loaded.
At . . . sire He took the chair at the (quarterly) sessions of the justices of the peace.
knyght of the shire county member of parliament, not necessarily a dubbed knight; Chaucer was himself such a representative, for the county of Kent in 1386
shirreve sheriff; next to the lord-lieutenant, the most important administrative officer of the county, whose revenue he had to collect and take to the exchequer.
countour "auditor," "accountant"; also "special pleader"—a county official
vavasour a member of the landed gentry, below the aristocracy
Haberdasshere dealer in needles, tapes, buttons; or in hats. Chaucer never wrote tales for any of the characters listed here.
lyveree livery; the (uniform) clothes of their guild, a group of tradesmen with common commercial interests and social and religious observances

Hir knivės were ychaped> noght with bras *mounted*
But al with silver; wroght ful clene and weel
Hire girdles and hir pouches everydeel.> *in every part*
Wel semėd ech of hem a fair burgeys> *burgher*
To sitten in a yeldhalle,> on a deÿs.> *guildhall / dais*
Everich,> for the wisdom that he can, *each*
Was shaply> for to been an alderman.° *fit*
For catel> haddė they ynogh and rente,> *property / income*
And eek hir wyvės wolde it wel assente;
And ellės certeyn werė they to blame.
It is ful fair to been yclept 'Madame',
And goon to vigiliės° al bifore,
And have a mantel royalliche ybore.

COOK

A cook they haddė with hem for the nones°
To boille the chikens with the marybones,> *marrowbones*
And poudrė-marchant° tart, and galyngale.°
Wel coude he knowe> a draughte of Londoun ale. *recognize*
He coude roste and sethe,> and broille and frye, *boil*
Maken mortreux,> and wel bake a pye.> *thick soups / meat-pie*
But greet harm was it, as it thoughtė> me, *seemed to*
That on his shine> a mormal° haddė he. *shin*
For blankmanger,° that made he with the beste.

SHIPMAN

A shipman was ther, wonynge> fer by> weste; *living / in the*
For aught I woot,> he was of Dertėmouthe.° *know*
He rood upon a rouncy,° as he couthe,> *as best he could*
In a gowne of falding> to the knee. *coarse wool*
A daggere hangynge on a laas> hadde he *strap*
Aboute his nekke, under his arm adoun.
The hote somer hadde mad his hewe> al brown. *color*
And certeinly he was a good felawe.
Ful many a draughte of wyn had he ydrawe°
Fro Burdeux-ward,° whil that the chapman sleep.> *merchant slept*
Of nycė> conscience took he no keep.> *fastidious / heed*
If that he faught, and hadde the hyer> hond, *upper*
By water he sente hem hoom to every lond.°

alderman leading member of town council
vigilies vigils; eves of saints' days; ceremonies on the evenings before guild festivals, in which the aldermen's wives would take the head of the procession
for the nones oral formula, without much meaning: "then"
poudre-marchant sharp spicy flavoring in powder form
galyngale a preparation of sweet spices
mormal ulcer associated with dirty living (in all senses)
blankmanger chopped creamed chicken, flavored with sugar and spice
Dertemouthe Dartmouth; a port in Devon, on the southwest coast of England, still used as a naval base
rouncy a cob or short-legged horse
ydrawe drawn, i.e. dishonestly
Burdeux-ward from Bordeaux, the great wine-shipping port on the west coast of France
By water . . . lond i.e. he threw his captives overboard

But of his craft,˃ to rekene wel his tydes, *calling*
His stremės,˃ and his daungers hym bisides,° *currents*
His herberwe,˃ and his moone,° his lodemenage,° *haven*
Ther nas noon swich from Hull° to Cartage.°
Hardy he was and wys to undertake.
With many a tempest hadde his berd been shake.
He knew wel alle the havenes,˃ as they were, *harbors*
Fro Gootlond to the Cape of Fynystere,°
And every cryke˃ in Britaigne° and in Spayne. *inlet*
His barge yclepėd was the Maudelayne.°

DOCTOUR OF PHISIK

With us ther was a doctour of phisik.˃ *medicine*
In al this world ne was ther noon hym lik,
To speke of phisik and of surgerye.
For he was grounded in astronomye,°
He kepte˃ his paciėnt a ful greet deel *treated*
In hourės,° by his magyk natureel.°
Wel coude he fortunen the ascendent°
Of hise ymagės for his paciėnt.
He knew the cause of everich maladye,
Were it of hoot, or coold, or moyste, or drye,
And where they engendred, and of what humour.°
He was a verray, parfit° practisour.˃ *practitioner*
The cause yknowe,˃ and of his harm the roote, *known*
Anon he yaf the sikė man his boote.˃ *remedy*
Ful redy hadde he hise apothecaries
To sende hym droggės˃ and his letuaries,° *drugs*

hym bisides all around him
moone i.e. phases of the moon
lodemenage navigation, pilotage
Hull port in Yorkshire, on the northeast coast of England
Cartage Cartagena, on the Mediterranean coast of Spain
Gootlond . . . Fynystere Gotland (island in the Baltic Sea) to Cape Finisterre, the westernmost point of Spain
Britaigne Brittany. The piling up of these names marks out the regular English sea-trade area: their cumulative meaning is "everywhere on the sea."
Maudelayne Magdalene, a popular name for a ship
astronomye astrology (see Glossary and Fig. 37); the movements of the planets insofar as they were thought to affect the constitutions of men
houres the astrologically favorable or unfavorable planetary (not clock) times for treatment of disease, governed by the conjunctions of the planets in zodiacal or other houses
natureel "Natural" magic was the harnessing of the natural and supernatural forces of created things to produce a desired result; as opposed to "black" magic, which involved the invocation of evil spirits.
fortunen the ascendent The ascendant was any one of the 360° of the zodiac rising above the horizon at a given moment. The doctor knew how to calculate the best time to make the talismanic images concentrating the forces which would help his patient recover. A degree of the zodiac favorable to a given disease in given circumstances and governing a given part of the body had to be ascendant and the planetary conjunctions in it also auspicious.
hoot . . . humour. All matter was held to contain the four primary contrasting qualities, hot and cold, moist and dry, in varying proportions, and the physician's aim was to keep them in harmonious and healthy balance in the patient's body. Man's constitution was composed of the four humors or vital fluids (the doctrine goes back to ancient Greek medicine): blood (hot and moist); phlegm (cold and moist); black bile (melancholy: cold and dry); yellow bile (choler: hot and dry). Their proportions, determined by the planetary conjunctions at a man's birth, in turn determined his temperament. Disturbance of their proportions caused disease: an excess of one humor or one quality had to be reduced by a medicine which would apply its contrary.
verray, parfit true and consummate
letuaries electuaries; medicinal pastes or preserves

For ech of hem made other for to wynne°—
Hir frendshipe nas nat newė to bigynne.
Wel knew he the olde Esculapius,°
And Deïscorides, and eek Rufus,
Olde Ypocras, Haly, and Galien,
Serapion, Razis, and Avicen,
Averrois, Damascien, and Constantyn,
Bernard, and Gatesden, and Gilbertyn.
Of his dietė mesurable> was he, *moderate*
For it was of no superfluitee,
But of greet norissing,> and digestible. *nourishment*
His studie was but litel on the Bible.
In sangwin and in pers° he clad was al,
Lynėd with taffata and with sendal;> *silk*
And yet he was but esy of dispence;> *expenditure*
He keptė that he wan> in pestilence. *gained*
For> gold in phisik is a cordial,° *because*
Therfore he lovėde gold in special.

THE WYF OF BATHE

A good-wyf° was ther, of bisidė° Bathe,
But she was somdel> deef and that was scathe.> *somewhat / a pity*
Of clooth-makyng she haddė swich an haunt,> *practice*
She passed> hem of Ypres and of Gaunt.° *surpassed*
In al the parisshe wif ne was ther noon
That to the offring bifore hire sholdė goon;°
And if ther dide, certeyn so wrooth> was she *angry*
That she was out of allė charitee.
Hir coverchiefs> ful fynė were of ground;> *head-drapery / in texture*
I dorstė> swere they weyeden° ten pound *dare / weighed*

made other . . . wynne gave the other an opportunity of profit
Esculapius This catalogue of medical authorities, perhaps drawn from a medieval encyclopedia, is not chronological. Aesculapius, the mythical founder of medicine, had treatises attributed to him in the Middle Ages, but is probably here only for the authority of his name. He was supposedly the son of Apollo, god of healing, and was already worshiped in Greece in the 6th century B.C. Dioscorides and Rufus of Ephesus were Greeks who flourished in the 1st and 2nd century A.D. and wrote on pharmacy and on anatomy respectively. Ypocras is the Greek, Hippocrates of Cos, 5th century B.C., the first scientific writer on medicine; Haly may be either of two famous 10th-century Arab doctors who played a large part in transmitting Greek medicine to the West. Galen, most influential of all, was court physician under Marcus Aurelius (2nd century A.D.) and wrote in Greek on many other topics besides medicine. Serapion is a name owned by a Greek (2nd century B.C.), a Damascus Christian (9th century), and an Arab (11th or 12th). Rhazes, also alchemist and philosopher, lived in Baghdad (9th to 10th century) and wrote a medical encyclopedia. Avicenna, the 11th-century Arab, and Averroes, the 12th-century Spanish Arab, were both famous philosophers who wrote on medicine. John of Damascus is a shadowy figure, perhaps of the 9th century. Constantine the African brought Arabic medicine to Salerno, a famous Italian medical school, in the 11th century. Bernard Gordon and John of Gaddesden were 14th-century authorities; Gilbertus Anglicus, 13th.
sangwin . . . pers scarlet and in Persian blue (a bluish gray)
cordial Potable (drinking) gold was sometimes used in medicine—perhaps for the heart (cordial)—but the joke here is at the doctor's expense.
good-wyf woman of some means and standing
biside just outside; the center of Bath's textile industry was the parish of St. Michael's without the North Gate
Ypres . . . Gaunt Flemish towns, famous for fine cloth; or *hem of* may refer to natives of these towns working in England.
to the offring . . . goon should make her offering in church before her

That on a Sonday were upon hir heed.
Hir hosen weren of fyn scarlet reed,
Ful streite yteyd,> and shoes ful moiste> and newe. *tightly laced / soft*
Bold was hir face, and fair and reed of hewe.
She was a worthy womman al hir lyve.
Housbondes at chirchė dore she haddė fyve,°
Withouten other companye in youthe—
But therof nedeth nat to speke as nowthe.> *just now*
And thriės> hadde she been at Jerusalem;° *three times*
She haddė passed many a straungė> strem; *foreign*
At Rome she haddė been, and at Boloigne,
In Galice at Seint Jame, and at Coloigne;°
She coudė> much of wandrynge° by the weye— *knew*
Gat-tothėd° was she, soothly> for to seye. *truly*
Upon an amblere° esily° she sat,
Ywimpled° wel, and on hir heed an hat
As brood as is a bokėler or a targe;°
A foot-mantel> aboute hir hipės large, *riding-skirt*
And on hir feet a paire of sporės> sharpe. *spurs*
In felawschip wel coude she laughe and carpe.> *talk*
Of> remedies° of love she knew per chaunce, *about*
For she coude of that art the oldė daunce.°

PERSOUN OF A TOUN

A good man was ther of religioùn,
And was a pourė persoun> of a toun, *parson*
But riche he was of holy thoght and werk.
He was also a lernėd man, a clerk,°
That Cristės gospel trewėly> wolde preche; *faithfully*
Hise parisshens> devoutly wolde he teche. *parishioners*
Benigne he was, and wonder> diligent, *marvelously*
And in adversitee ful paciėnt.
And swich> he was yprevėd> oftė sithes.> *such / proved / times*
Ful looth were hym to cursen for hise tithes,°
But rather wolde he yeven,> out of doute,° *give*
Unto his pourė parisshens aboute

Housbondes . . . fyve See John 4:18 and the Wife's Prologue below; *at church dore* refers to the fact that medieval marriages were performed outside the church door; nuptial mass was then celebrated within.

Jerusalem The greatest of all pilgrimages would take a full year.

Rome . . . Coloigne These are the chief European centers of pilgrimage: Rome; Galicia, in northwest Spain, which has the shrine of St. James the Greater at Compostela; Cologne, which has the tomb of the Three Kings; and Boulogne with its famous image of the Virgin.

She . . . wandrynge She left no pilgrimage undone, but she also strayed from the path of virtue

Gat-tothed Teeth set wide apart, according to medieval physiognomics, betokened a traveling woman—in both senses.

amblere comfortable horse, pacing, not trotting

esily comfortably, perhaps astride

Ywimpled The wimple covered head, sides of face and neck: it was by this time rather old-fashioned for a laywoman; see l. 151.

bokeler . . . targe small round shields

remedies an allusion to Ovid, the Roman poet (1st century A.D.), writer of *The Remedies of Love* and other lovers' manuals of the Middle Ages; but probably also meaning that she was expert in love potions

the olde daunce a literal translation of the French phrase; so, "All the old routine"

clerk learned man. See l. 287.

looth . . . tithes He was unwilling to excommunicate (*cursen*) anyone for non-payment of tithes.

out of doute without doubt, surely

Of his offring,° and eek of his substaunce.> *property*
He coude in litel thyng have suffisaunce.> *enough*
Wyd was his parisshe, and houses fer asonder,
But he ne leftė> nat, for reyn ne thonder, *neglected*
In siknesse nor in meschief,> to visìte *misfortune*
The ferreste> in his parisshe, muche and lite,° *farthest*
Upon his feet, and in his hand a staf.
This noble ensample> to his sheep° he yaf, *example*
That first he wroghte,> and afterward he taughte. *did*
Out of the gospel° he tho> wordės caughte,> *those / took*
And this figùre he added eek therto,
That if gold rustė, what shal iren do?
For if a preest be foul, on whom we truste,
No wonder is a lewėd> man to ruste. *simple*
And shame it is, if a preest take keep,> *heed*
A shiten> shepherde and a clenė sheep. *filthy*
Wel oghte a preest ensample for to yive,
By his clennesse, how that his sheep sholde live.
He settė nat his benefice to hyre°
And leet> his sheep encombred in the myre *left*
And ran to Londoun, unto Saint Poules,°
To seken hym a chaunterie° for soules,
Or with a bretherhed° to been withholde;> *supported*
But dwelte at hoom, and keptė wel his folde,
So that the wolf ne made it nat miscarie.
He was a shepherde, and no mercenarie.
And though he holy were, and vertuous,
He was to synful men nat despitous,> *contemptuous*
Ne of his spechė daungerous> ne digne,> *disdainful / superior*
But in his teching discreet and benygne.
To drawen folk to hevene by fairnesse,
By good ensample, was his bisynesse:
But> it were> any persone obstinat, *if / there were*
What so he were, of heigh or lowe estat,
Hym wolde he snybben> sharply for the nonys.> *rebuke / at any time*
A bettre preest I trowe> that nowher noon ys. *believe*
He waited> after no pompe and reverence,> *looked for / deference*
Ne makėd hym a spicėd conscience,°
But Cristės loore> and hise apostles twelve° *teaching*
He taughte, but first he folwed it himselve.

offring Whatever the people gave at mass was the property of the parish priest.
muche and lite great and small
sheep See John 10:1–14 for the parable of the Good Shepherd.
gospel Matthew 5:19(?)
benefice to hyre It was common practice to hire a substitute priest at a small wage and, pocketing the difference, take other employment as well.
Saint Poules St. Paul's Cathedral, London
chaunterie endowment providing for perpetual masses for the soul of the donor and his nominees
bretherhed Guilds (see l. 366) often had their own chaplain.
Ne . . . conscience either "did not cultivate a too-scrupulous conscience" or "did not pretend to a heightened sense of right and wrong"
apostles twelve [the teaching of] his twelve apostles [also]

PLOWMAN

With hym ther was a plowman, was his brother,
That hadde ylad> of dong> ful many a fother.> *carried / dung / load*
A trewė swinker> and a good was he, *toiler*
Lyvynge in pees> and parfit charitee. *peace*
God loved he best with al his holė> herte *whole*
At allė tymės, thogh hym gamed or smerte,°
And thanne his neighėbore right as himselve.°
He woldė thresshe, and therto dyke> and delve, *dig ditches*
For Cristės sake, for every pourė wight,
Withouten hire,> if it lay in his might.> *wages / power*
Hise tithės payėd he ful faire and wel,
Bothe of his propre> swink> and his catel.> *own / work / possessions*
In a tabard> he rood upon a mere.° *smock*

Ther was also a reve and a millere,
A somnour, and a pardoner also,
A maunciple,> and myself—ther were namo.> *steward / no more*

MILLER

The miller was a stout carl° for the nones.
Ful big he was of brawn,> and eek of bones. *muscle*
That provėd wel,> for overal> ther he cam, *was clear / wherever*
At wrastling he wolde have alwey the ram.°
He was short-sholdred,> brood,> a thikkė knarre.° *stocky / broad*
Ther was no dore that he ne wolde heve of> harre,> *lift off / hinges*
Or breke it at a renning> with his heed.> *running / head*
His berd as any sowe or fox was reed,°
And therto brood, as though it were a spade.
Upon the cop° right of his nose he hade
A werte,> and theron stood a tuft of herys,> *wart / hairs*
Reed as the bristlės of a sowės erys.> *ears*
Hise nosėthirlės> blakė were and wyde. *nostrils*
A swerd and a bokeler bar> he by his syde. *bore*
His mouth as greet was as a greet forneys.> *oven*
He was a janglere,> and a goliardeys,° *noisy babbler*
And that was moost of sinne and harlotries.°
Wel coude he stelen corn, and tollen thries;°

thogh . . . smerte whether it made him happy or afflicted him
God . . . himselve (ll. 535–37) See Matthew 22:37–39: "Thou shalt love the lord thy God . . . Thou shalt love thy neighbor as thyself."
mere mare: a lower-class mount
carl fellow, usually of the lower class
ram the usual prize at a wrestling match
knarre a knot in wood: so a tough, knotty man; physiognomically, an angry lecherous bully
reed A red beard or head was not to be trusted, according to physiognomic theory. Judas, the arch-traitor, was said to have had red hair; see also Reynard the Fox.
cop bridge, top, or tip
goliardeys from *goliards,* the student and clerical authors of satirical Latin verse in the 12th and 13th centuries, who called their leader and patron, a mythical figure, Golias. Their writings were often scurrilous, and *goliardeys* here has come to mean a teller of dirty jokes.
harlotries i.e. obscenities. Harlot was not applied only to women in the Middle Ages.
tollen . . . thries take his toll three times, instead of once. The Miller's payment was a percentage of what he ground.

And yet he hadde a thombe of gold,° pardee.> *by heaven*
A whit cote and a blew hood werėd> he. *wore*
A baggėpipe wel coude he blowe and sowne,> *sound*
And therwithal> he broghte us out of towne. *therewith*

MAUNCIPLE

A gentil maunciple° was ther of a Temple,°
Of which achatours> mightė take exemple *buyers*
For to be wise> in bying of vitaille;> *thrifty / victuals*
For whether that he payde, or took by taille,°
Algate> he wayted> so in his achat> *always / watched / buying*
That he was ay biforn,> and in good staat.> *ahead / financial position*
Now is nat that of God a ful fair grace
That swich a lewėd> mannės wit shal pace> *unlearned / surpass*
The wisdom of an heep of lernėd men?
Of maistrės> hadde he mo than thriės ten *masters*
That weren of lawe expert and curious,> *subtle*
Of whiche ther weren a doseyne> in that hous *dozen*
Worthy to been stiwardes of rente> and lond *income*
Of any lord that is in Engėlond,
To make hym lyvė by his propre good;°
In honour dettėlees, but> he were wood,> *unless / mad*
Or lyve as scarsly> as hym list> desire; *frugally / it pleases*
And able for to helpen al a shire
In any cas> that mightė falle or happe; *event*
And yet this manciple sette hir aller cappe.°

REVE°

The reve was a sclendrė> colerik° man. *slim*
His berd was shave as ny> as ever he can; *close*
His heer> was by his erės> round yshorn; *hair / ears*
His top was dokkėd° lyk a preest biforn.
Ful longė were his leggės, and ful lene,
Ylyk> a staf, ther was no calf ysene.> *like / visible*
Wel coude he kepe a gerner> and a bynne; *granary*
Ther was noon auditour coude of hym wynne.> *get the better of*
Wel wiste> he by the droghte and by the reyn> *knew in advance / rain*
The yeldynge of his seed and of his greyn.> *grain*

thombe of gold See the proverb: "An honest miller has a golden thumb" ; i.e. there are no honest millers.
maunciple steward at one of the Inns of Court (societies of lawyers in London) or at a college
Temple an Inn of Court, perhaps specifically the Middle or Inner Temple, whose quarters in London had formerly been occupied by the Knights Templars
by taille by tally, on credit. Credit was recorded by cutting (Fr. *tailler*) notches on a stick.
To . . . good keep him from bankruptcy by making him live without borrowing
sette . . . cappe made fools of them all

Reve Usually a man of lowly origin, elected by his fellow peasants for a term as a foreman on the manor. He looked after fields and woods, saw that work was done, collected dues, and gave annual account of all. On larger estates he would be subordinate to a bailiff, who in turn was subordinate to a steward.
colerik having an excess of the humor choler (see l. 422) making him suspicious, prone to anger. Physiognomically, he is avaricious and lustful.
dokked cropped; a sign of low social status in a layman. Clergy wore their hair cut short or tonsured as a token of humility.

His lordės sheep, his neet,˃ his dayerye,˃ *cattle / dairy*
His swyn, his hors, his stoor,˃ and his pultrye *produce*
Was hoolly˃ in this revės governyng, *wholly*
And by his covenant yaf the rekenyng,°
Sin˃ that his lord was twenty yeer of age. *since*
Ther coude no man bringe hym in arrerage.°
Ther nas baillif, ne herde,° nor other hyne,°
That he ne knew his sleighte and his covyne.°
They were adrad˃ of hym as of the deeth.° *afraid*
His wonyng˃ was ful faire upon an heeth;˃ *house / common*
With grenė treës shadwed was his place.
He coudė bettre than his lord purchace:˃ *buy*
Ful riche he was astorėd prively.˃ *stocked stealthily*
His lord wel coude he plesen subtilly,
To yeve and lene˃ hym of his ownė good,˃ *lend / property*
And have a thank, and yet a cote° and hood.
In youthe he haddė lerned a good mister:˃ *trade*
He was a wel good wrighte,˃ a carpenter. *craftsman*
This revė sat upon a ful good stot,°
That was al pomely˃ grey, and hightė˃ Scot. *dapple / was named*
A long surcote of pers upon he hade,°
And by his syde he bar˃ a rusty blade. *bore*
Of Northfolk° was this reve of which I telle,
Biside a toun men clepen Baldėswelle.˃ *Bawdswell*
Tukkėd˃ he was, as is a frere, aboute. *hitched up*
And ever he rood the hindreste˃ of oure route.˃ *hindmost / group*

SOMNOUR°

A somnour was ther with us in that place,
That hadde a fyr-reed˃ cherubinnės° face, *fiery red*
For sawcėfleem˃ he was, with eyėn narwe. *pimply*
As hoot he was, and lecherous as a sparwe,°
With scallėd˃ browės blake and pilėd° berd *scabby*
Of his visagė children were aferd.˃ *afraid*
Ther nas quiksilver, litarge, ne brimstoon,
Boras, ceruce, ne oille of tartre noon,°

And by . . . rekenyng according to his covenant [he] gave his account
arrerage find him in arrears, short on his accounts
herde herd, shepherd
hyne hind, farm laborer
sleighte . . . covyne cunning, quickness and guile, fraud
the deeth most frequently the plague, the most feared of epidemics. The Black Death (1348–49, 1360, 1379) was strong in men's memories.
cote Clothing was sometimes given as part of wages, sometimes as a bonus.
stot a favorite Norfolk breed of horse
A . . . hade He had on a long overcoat of Persian blue.
Northfolk Norfolk
Somnour A summoner bore the citation to a person, clergy or lay, required to appear in an ecclesiastical court, for offenses against canon law and morals; and had to make sure that he obeyed. By Chaucer's time, summoner was a byword for corruption.
cherubinnes Cherubim were fiery red (Ezekiel 1:13); physiognomically, the summoner is a drunken lecher.
As hoot . . . sparwe As hot and lecherous as a sparrow. This bird was a byword for those qualities; see Skelton, *Philip Sparrow* below.
piled straggling or falling out in patches
quiksilver . . . noon The medieval name for the summoner's skin disease was *alopecia,* thought to be sexual in origin; the remedies—mercury, peroxide of lead, sulphur, borax, white-lead ointment, oil of tartar—suggest that he may have been syphilitic.

Ne oynėment that woldė clense and byte,
That hym myghte helpen of his whelkės˃ white, *pimples*
Nor of the knobbės sittinge on his chekes.
Wel loved he garleek, oynons, and eek lekes,°
And for to drinken strong wyn, reed as blood.
Thanne wolde he speke and crie as he were wood.˃ *mad*
And whan that he wel dronken hadde the wyn,
Than wolde he spekė no word but Latyn.
A fewė termės hadde he, two or three,
That he had lernėd out of som decree—
No wonder is, he herde it al the day;
And eek ye knowen wel how that a jay˃ *jackdaw*
Can clepen˃ 'Watte'° as wel as kan the Pope. *say*
But whoso coude in other thyng hym grope,˃ *question*
Thanne hadde he spent al his philosophie;˃ *learning*
Ay˃ *'Questio quid iuris,'*° wolde he crie. *always*
He was a gentil harlot° and a kinde;
A bettre felawe sholdė men noght fynde:
He woldė suffre˃ for a quart of wyn *permit*
A good felawe to have his concubyn
A twelf monthe, and excuse hym attė fulle.°
Ful privėly a fynch eek coude he pulle.°
And if he fond owher˃ a good felawe, *found anywhere*
He woldė techen hym to have noon awe,˃ *fear*
In swich˃ cas, of the erchėdekenės curs,° *such*
But if˃ a mannės soule were in his purs; *unless*
For in his purs he sholde ypunisshed be.
'Purs is the erchėdekenės Helle,'° seyde he.
But wel I woot he lyėd right indede;
Of cursing˃ oghte ech gilty man him drede, *excommunication*
For curs wol slee˃ right as assoilling˃ saveth, *kill / absolution*
And also war hym of a *Significavit*.°
In daunger˃ hadde he at his owene gise˃ *in his power / at will*
The yongė girlės° of the diocise,
And knew hir conseil,˃ and was al hir reed.˃ *secrets / advisor*
A gerland hadde he set upon his heed
As greet as it were for an alė-stake.°
A bokėleer hadde he maad hym of a cake.˃ *loaf of bread*

garleek . . . lekes pimple-inducing foods, with bad moral connotations (Numbers 11:5)
Watte common name for tame, "talking" jackdaw
Questio . . . iuris "I ask, what is the law [on this matter]": a legal catchphrase, common in the ecclesiastical courts
harlot rascal. See l. 563.
atte fulle i.e. completely. Sexual offenses were dealt with by the ecclesiastical courts, and the Summoner had no authority to use his discretion.
fynche . . . pulle "pluck a pigeon": have sex with a woman
erchedekenes curs excommunication by the archdeacon
Purs . . . Helle i.e. a man is punished only in his purse
And also . . . Significavit And also beware of a writ for imprisonment. The church courts could not imprison: for this they had to call in the civil authorities. *Significavit* was the first word of the writ which did this.
girles perhaps in its other meaning of "young people" of both sexes
ale-stake a pole, with a "bush" of green leaves on it to symbolize refreshment, marked an alehouse (Fig. 39)

PARDONER°

With hym ther was a gentil pardoner
Of Rouncivale,° his freend and his compeer,> — *companion*
That streight was comen fro the court of Rome.
Ful loude he song> 'Com hider, love, to me!'° — *sang*
This somnour bar to hym a stif> burdoun;° — *strong*
Was nevere tromp> of half so greet a soun. — *trumpet*
This pardoner hadde heer as yelow as wex,
But smothe it heng, as dooth a strike of flex;> — *hank of flax*
By ounces,> henge hise lokkės that he hadde, — *thin strands*
And therwith he hise shuldres overspradde;> — *overspread*
But thinne it lay, by colpons,> oon and oon. — *in "rats'-tails"*
But hood, for jolitee, ywered> he noon, — *wore*
For it was trussėd up in his walet.> — *pack*
Hym thoughte he rood al of the newe jet;> — *fashion*
Dischevelee,> save his cappe, he rood al bare. — *with hair loose*
Swiche glaringe° eyen hadde he as an hare.
A vernicle° hadde he sowed upon his cappe.
His walet lay biforn hym in his lappe,
Bretful> of pardoun, come from Rome al hoot.> — *brimful / hot*
A voys he hadde as smal as hath a goot.> — *goat*
No berd hadde he, ne nevere sholdė have;
As smothe it was as it were late yshave.
I trowe he were a geldyng or a mare.
But of his craft, fro Berwyk into Ware,°
Ne was ther swich another pardoner.
For in his male> he hadde a pilwe-beer,> — *pack / pillow-case*
Which that he seydė was Oure Lady veyl.
He seyde he hadde a gobet of the seyl> — *piece / sail*
That Seïnt Peter hadde, whan that he wente
Upon the see, til Jesu Crist hym hente.°
He hadde a croys of latoun,° ful of stones,
And in a glas he haddė piggės bones.
But with thisė relikes, whan that he fond> — *found*
A pourė persoun> dwellynge upon lond,> — *parson / up country*
Upon a day he gat> hym more moneye — *got*
Than that the persoun gat in monthės tweye.

Pardoner A seller of "pardons," indulgences, papal bulls allowing some remittance of penance in return for money. Later, such bulls came to be regarded as giving some exemption from Purgatory and, by the simple, as guaranteeing forgiveness of sins. Unscrupulous salesmen used them to gain money for the church, specific institutions in it—and themselves.
Rouncivale St. Mary Roncevall, near Charing Cross in London, an English branch of an important Spanish religious house
'Com . . . me!' presumably a popular song
burdoun either burden, i.e. refrain, or accompaniment
glaringe staring, bulging
vernicle Pilgrims to Rome bought a small replica of the handkerchief (in St. Peter's) with which St. Veronica was said to have wiped away the sweat from Christ's face on the road to Calvary, on which occasion the likeness of his features had been miraculously transferred to the handkerchief.
Berwyk . . . Ware the length of England (Berwick on Tweed in Northumberland to Ware in Hertfordshire, near London)
That . . . hente either before Christ took Peter as a disciple; or when he tried to walk on the waters (Matthew 14:28–31)
croys of latoun cross made of a brassy base metal, to be passed off as gold (as the pig's bones were to be passed off as saints' relics)

And thus, with feynėd> flatery and japes,> *false / tricks*
He made the persoun and the peple his apes.> *dupes*
But trewėly to tellen attė laste,
He was in chirche a noble ecclesiaste;
Wel coude he rede a lessoun or a storie,> *sacred narrative*
But alderbest> he song an offertorie; *best of all*
For wel he wistė, whan that song was songe,
He mostė> preche and wel affile> his tonge *must / sharpen*
To wynnė silver, as he ful wel coude;
Therfore he song so meriely and loudė.

Now have I told you shortly> in a clause> *briefly / short space*
Th'estat, th'array, the nombre, and eek the cause
Why that assembled was this companye
In Southwerk, at this gentil hostelrye
That highte the Tabard, fastė> by the Belle.° *close*
But now is tymė to yow for to telle
How that we baren> us that ilkė> nyght, *behaved / same*
Whan we were in that hostelrie alight;
And after wol I telle of oure viage,> *journey*
And al the remenaunt> of oure pilgrimage. *remainder*
But first I pray yow, of youre curteisye,
That ye n'arette> it nat my vileinye,> *attribute / ill-breeding*
Thogh that I pleynly speke in this matere,
To tellė yow hir wordės and hir cheere,> *behavior*
Ne thogh I speke hir wordės proprely.> *exactly*
For this ye knowen also> wel as I, *as*
Whoso shal telle a tale after a man,
He moot reherce> as ny> as evere he kan *must repeat / near*
Everich a word, if it be in his charge,> *power*
Al> speke he never so rudėliche> or large,> *although / coarsely / broadly*
Or ellis> he moot> telle his tale untrewe, *else / must*
Or feynė> thyng, or fyndė wordės newe. *falsify*
He may nat spare, althogh he were his brother;
He moot as wel seye o word as another.
Crist spak hymself ful brode> in holy writ, *plainly*
And wel ye woot no vileynye is it.
Eek Plato seïth, whoso can hym rede,
'The wordės mote be cosin to the dede.'°
Also I prey yow to foryeve it me,
Al> have I nat set folk in hir degree *although*
Heere in this tale, as that they sholdė stonde.
My wit is short, ye may wel understonde.
Greet cherė made oure host° us everichon,
And to the soper sette he us anon.

Belle another pilgrim inn. See l. 20.
Plato . . . dede' in Plato's *Timaeus,* which Chaucer might have read in Latin translation, though he probably found it in Boethius
host Harry Bailly, the landlord of the Tabard

He servėd us with vitaille˃ at the beste. *victuals*
Strong was the wyn, and wel to drynke us leste.˃ *it pleased*

A semely man oure hostė was withalle
For to han been a marchal° in an halle.
A largė˃ man he was, with eyen stepe˃— *broad / prominent*
A fairer burgeys˃ was ther noon in Chepe°— *burgher*
Boold of his speche, and wys, and wel ytaught,
And of manhod hym lakkedė right naught.°
Eek therto he was right a mery˃ man, *pleasant*
And after soper pleyen˃ he bigan, *to jest*
And spak of mirthe, amongės othere thynges—
Whan that we haddė maad oure rekeninges°—
And seydė thus: 'Now, lordinges,˃ trewėly, *ladies and gentlemen*
Ye been to me right welcome, hertėly.˃ *sincerely*
For by my trouthe, if that I shal nat lye,
I saugh nat this yeer so mery a compaunye
At onės in this herberwe˃ as is now. *inn*
Fayn˃ wolde I doon yow mirthė, wiste˃ I how. *willingly / knew*
And of a mirthe I am right now bithoght,
To doon yow ese,˃ and it shal costė noght. *pleasure*
Ye goon to Caunterbury—God yow speede!
The blisful martir quitė˃ yow youre mede!˃ *pay / reward*
And wel I woot, as ye goon by the weye,
Ye shapen˃ yow to talen˃ and to pleye; *intend / tell tales*
For trewėly, confort ne myrthe is noon
To ridė by the weye doumb as the stoon.˃ *stone*
And therfore wol I maken yow disport,
As I seyde erst,˃ and doon yow som confort. *before*
And if yow liketh alle, by oon assent,
For to stonden at˃ my jugėment, *abide by*
And for to werken˃ as I shal yow seye, *do*
Tomorwe, whan ye riden by the weye,
Now, by my fader˃ soulė that is deed, *father's*
But if˃ ye be merye, I wol yeve yow myn heed.˃ *unless / head*
Hold up youre hond, withouten morė speche.'
Oure counseil was nat longė for to seche.˃ *seek*
Us thoughte it was noght worth to make it wys,°
And graunted hym, withouten moore avys,˃ *deliberation*
And bad hym seye his verdit as hym leste.
'Lordinges,' quod he, 'now herkneth for the beste;
But taak it nought, I prey yow, in desdeyn.˃ *disdain*
This is the poynt, to speken short and pleyn,
That ech of yow, to shortė˃ with oure weye *shorten*

marchal master of ceremonies in a [lord's] hall
Chepe Cheapside, in the City of London, the commercial center
naught unlike the Pardoner
Whan . . . rekeninges after we had paid our bills
Us . . . wys it seemed to us not worthwhile to make a business of it

In this viage, shal tellė talės tweye°
To Caunterbury-ward, I mene it so,
And homward, he shal tellen othere two,
Of aventures that whilom> han bifalle. *once upon a time*
And which of yow that bereth hym best of alle,
That is to seyn, that telleth in this cas
Tales of best sentènce> and moost solas,> *profit / delight*
Shal have a soper at oure aller cost°
Heere in this placė, sitting by this post,> *inn sign*
Whan that we come agayn fro Caunterbury.
And for to makė yow the morė mery,
I wol myselven goodly> with yow ryde, *willingly*
Right at myn owene cost, and be youre gyde.
And whoso wole my jugėment withseye> *contradict*
Shal paye al that we spenden by the weye.
And if ye vouchėsauf that it be so,
Tel me anon, withouten wordės mo,> *more*
And I wol erly shapė> me therfore.' *prepare*
  This thyng was graunted, and ourė othes swore
With ful glad herte, and preyden> hym also *begged*
That he wolde vouchėsauf for to do so,
And that he woldė been oure governour,
And of oure talės juge and reportour,> *bringer of verdict*
And sette a soper, at a certeyn pris,> *price*
And we wol> reulėd been at his devys *will*
In heigh and lowe;> and thus by oon assent *completely*
We been acorded to his jugėment.
And therupon the wyn was fet> anon; *fetched*
We dronken, and to restė wente echon> *everyone*
Withouten any lenger taryinge.> *delay*
  Amorwe,> whan that day gan° for to springe, *in the morning*
Up roos oure hoost and was oure aller cok,°
And gadrede> us togidre,> alle in a flok, *gathered / together*
And forth we riden,> a litel moore than pas,> *rode / walking pace*
Unto the Watering of Saint Thomas.°
And there oure hoost bigan his hors areste,> *stopped*
And seyde: 'Lordynges, herkneth, if yow leste!> *it please*
Ye woot youre forward, and I it yow recorde.°
If even-song and morwe-song accorde,> *morning-song agree*
Lat se now who shal tellė the firste tale.
As evere mote> I drynkė wyn or ale, *may*
Whoso be rebel to my jugėment
Shal paye for al that by the wey is spent.

ech . . . tweye Less than a quarter of this number of tales was written.
at . . . cost at the cost of us all
gan an auxiliary, to make simple past tense
oure aller cok the rooster who woke us all
Watering . . . Thomas watering-place for horses, two miles on the way
Ye . . . recorde you know your agreement, and I recall it to you

Now draweth cut,° er that we ferrer twinne;> *travel farther*
He which that hath the shorteste shal biginne.
Sire Knyght,' quod he, 'my mayster and my lord,
Now draweth cut, for that is myn accord.> *agreement*
Cometh neer,' quod he, 'my lady Prioresse.
And ye, sire Clerk, lat be youre shamefastnesse,> *modesty*
Ne studieth noght. Ley hond to, euery man.'
  Anon to drawen every wight bigan,
And shortly, for to tellen as it was,
Were it by aventure,> or sort,> or cas,> *luck / fate / chance*
The sothe> is this, the cut fil> to the knyght, *truth / fell*
Of which ful blithe and glad was every wyght,
And telle he moste> his tale, as was resoùn,> *must / right*
By forward and by composicioùn,> *compact*
As ye han herd. What nedeth wordės mo?
And whan this goode man saugh that it was so,
As he that wys was and obedient
To kepe his forward by his free assent,
He seyde, 'Syn I shal biginne the game,
What, welcome be the cut, a> Goddės name! *in*
Now lat us ryde, and herkneth what I seye.'
  And with that word we ryden forth oure weye,
And he bigan with right a mery cheere> *face*
His tale anon, and seyde in this manere.°

Here endeth the prolog of this book

c. 1385–1400 1478

The Miller's Prologue and Tale

Chaucer has skillfully planted in the General Prologue a notion of what sort of tale we can expect from the bag-piping Miller. His drunken thrusting forward of himself to tell the next tale as soon as the grave, sober Knight has done with his is another pointer. The Reeve, slender, choleric man that he is—timid and prone to ineffectual anger on account of his constitution and his advanced age—also senses what is up: this is going to be a tale of old age, youth, carpentry, and cuckoldry, and, as an elderly carpenter and perhaps a cuckold himself, he bursts into fury. But the great, thick Miller coarsely puts the poor man aside and begins.

What we get is one of Chaucer's several *fabliaux:* a dirty story told with wit and point. The *fabliau* developed in France in the thirteenth century—though such verse tales exist in both Latin and the vernacular from an earlier period—and was hardly used there after the early fourteenth. French *fabliaux* are realistic, short, plain in style, and rapid in narration, but they are a skillful and courtly and not a popular or folk literary form. Rather, they are an aristocratic mocking of the antics of the lower classes: amoral, not pornographic. Chaucer's are among the few written in English, another example of his ability to take a convention and work in it to masterly effect.

cut lot. Straws of different lengths would be used.
in this manere Some manuscripts read "as ye may heere"—which will remind us that Chaucer's poetry was intended for reading aloud.

This is the literary mode in which Chaucer is working in such tales as the Miller's, the Reeve's, and the Merchant's—and to some extent in the Wife of Bath's Prologue. What we have holds the two requirements of the *fabliau* genre perfectly in balance: the dirty story which we might expect from the Miller, and the aristocratically brutal and polished tone. Chaucer has woven together what were probably two disparate narratives (one German, the other Italian in origin); both arrive at their climax at the same moment in one of the great comic scenes of English literature.

Prologue

Here folwen the wordes bitwene the Host and the Millere

Whan that the Knight had thus his tale ytold,
In al the routė˃ nas ther yong ne old — *group*
That he ne seyde it was a noble storie,
And worthy for to drawen˃ to memorie; — *recall*
And namėly˃ the gentils° everichoon. — *especially*
Our Hoste lough˃ and swoor, 'So moot I goon, — *laughed*
This gooth aright; unbokeled is the male;°
Lat see now who shal telle another tale:
For trewėly, the game is wel bigonne.
Now telleth ye, sir Monk, if that ye conne,˃ — *can*
Somwhat, to quytė˃ with the Knightės tale.' — *requite*
The Miller, that fordronken° was al pale,
So that unnethe˃ upon his hors he sat, — *with difficulty*
He nolde avalen˃ neither hood ne hat, — *would not take off*
Ne abydė no man for his curteisie,
But in Pilàtės vois° he gan to crye,
And swoor by armės and by blood and bones,°
'I can˃ a noble talė for the nones, — *know*
With which I wol now quyte the Knightės tale.'
Our Hostė saugh˃ that he was dronke of ale, — *saw*
And seyde: 'Abydė, Robin, my leve˃ brother, — *dear*
Som bettrė man shal telle us first another:
Abyde, and lat us werken thriftily.'˃ — *sensibly*
'By Goddes soul,' quod he, 'that wol nat I ;
For I wol speke, or ellės go my wey.'
Our Hoste answerde: 'Tel on, a devel wey!°
Thou art a fool, thy wit is overcome.'
'Now herkneth,' quod the Miller, 'alle and some˃! — *one*

gentils the better born among the pilgrims, to whom a chivalrous tale would most appeal
'So moot . . . male' as I may walk (i.e. continue able to walk), this is going well; the pack is unstrapped
fordronken completely drunk; or, reading "for dronken": because of being drunk
Pilates vois a high, harsh voice, like that used for Pontius Pilate in the mystery plays
by armes . . . bones i.e. by Christ's arms, blood, and bones. See the Pardoner's Tale, l. 188.
devel wey i.e. in the Devil's name; originally a strengthening of "away," the parts divided as in "unto the gardinward," l. 464.

But first I make a protestacioùn°
That I am dronke, I knowe it by my soun;> *how I sound*
And therfore, if that I misspeke or seye,
Wyte> it the ale of Southwerk, I yow preye; *blame it on*
For I wol telle a legende° and a lyf
Bothe of a carpenter, and of his wyf,
How that a clerk hath set the wrightės cappe.'°
  The Reve answerde and seydė, 'Stint> thy clappe,> *stop / babble*
Lat be thy lewėd> dronken harlotrye.° *ignorant*
It is a sinne and eek> a greet folye *also*
To apeiren> any man, or him diffame, *injure*
And eek to bringen wyvės in swich fame.> *reputation*
Thou mayst ynogh of othere thingės seyn.'
  This dronken Miller spak ful sone ageyn,
And seydė, 'Levė> brother Osėwold, *dear*
Who hath no wyf, he is no cokewold.°
But I sey nat therfore that thou art oon;
Ther been ful godė wyvės many oon,> *a one*
And ever a thousand gode ayeyns oon badde,
That knowestow wel thyself, but if> thou madde.> *unless / are mad*
Why artow angry with my talė now?
I have a wyf, pardee, as well as thou,
Yet nolde> I, for the óxen in my plough, *would not*
Taken upon me more than ynough,
As demen of myself that I were oon;°
I wol belevė wel that I am noon.
An housbond shal> nat been inquisitif *must*
Of Goddės privetee,> nor of his wyf. *secrets*
So> he may findė Goddės foyson> there, *provided / plenty*
Of the remenant nedeth nat enquere.>' *enquire*
  What sholde I morė seyn, but this Millere
He nolde his wordės for no man forbere,
But tolde his cherlės> tale in his manere; *lout's*
M'athinketh that I shal reherce it here.°
And therfore every gentil wight I preye,
For Goddės love, demeth nat that I seye
Of evel entente, but that> I moot> reherce *because / must*
Hir talės allė, be they bettre or werse,
Or ellės falsen som of my matere.
And therfore, whoso list it nat yhere,> *to listen*
Turne over the leef, and chese> another tale; *choose*
For he shal finde ynowė,> grete and smale, *plenty*

protestacioun formal, public avowal
legende usually a holy story, a saint's life
clerk . . . cappe scholar made a fool of the workman
harlotrye obscenity, low conduct of all kinds
Who . . . cokewold Only the man who has no wife cannot be a cuckold.
As . . . oon to think that I myself were one, i.e. a cuckold
M'athinketh . . . here I regret that I must tell it here

Of storial° thing that toucheth gentillesse,
And eek moralitee and holinesse;
Blameth nat me if that ye chese amis.
The Miller is a cherl, ye knowe wel this;
So was the Reve, and otherė many mo,
And harlotrye they tolden bothė two.
Avyseth> yow and putte me out of blame; *consider*
And eek men shal nat make ernèst of game.°

Here endeth the prologe

Tale

Here biginneth the Millere his Tale

Whylom> ther was dwellinge at Oxenford *once*
A richė gnof,> that gestės heeld to bord,° *boor*
And of his craft he was a carpenter.
With him ther was dwellinge a poore scoler,
Had lernėd art, but al his fantasye°
Was turnėd for to lerne astrologye,
And coude a certeyn of conclusioùns°
To demen by interrogacioùns,
If that men axėd> him in certein houres, *asked*
Whan that men sholde have droghte or ellės shoures,
Or if men axėd him what sholde bifalle
Of every thing; I may nat rekene hem alle.
  This clerk was clepėd> hendė° Nicholas. *called*
Of dernė love he coude and of solas;°
And therto he was sleigh> and ful privee,> *sly / secretive*
And lyk a mayden mekė for to see.
A chambre hadde he in that hostelrye
Allone, withouten any companye,
Ful fetisly ydight> with herbės swote;> *adorned / sweet*
And he himself as swete as is the rote> *root*
Of licorys, or any cetewale.°

storial literally, historical; thus, not a made-up story but something refined, moral, exemplary, based on what really happened, told for pleasure and instruction

And eek . . . game and also one must not make serious tales of jokes

bord literally, table. The carpenter took in boarders, some of them students.

fantasye originally the mental process of sense perception: so, all his intellectual effort, with overtones of disapproval. This poor scholar had passed through the trivium and gone on to the quadrivium (see Glossary).

coude . . . conclusiouns i.e. and knew a certain number of conclusions or propositions, the use of which would allow him to determine astrologically the answers to such questions as "At this or that time, shall we have drought or rain?"

hende agreeable, handsome

Of derne . . . solas He knew all about love-in-secret and what pleasure was. That is, he knew all the refinements of concealment, to protect the lady's reputation (and his own), and the whole range of meaning of solace (comfort from the lady in and out of bed).

cetewale setwall, zedoary, an aromatic Eastern root. Licorice root was proverbially sweet.

His *Almageste*° and bokės grete and smale,
His astrelabie,° longinge for> his art,> *belonging to / craft*
His augrim stonės° layen faire apart,
On shelvės couchėd,> at his beddes heed: *laid*
His presse ycovered with a falding reed.°
And al above ther lay a gay sautrye,°
On which he made a-nightės melodye
So swetėly that al the chambre rong;> *rang*
And *Angelus ad virginem*° he song;
And after that he song the *Kingės Note;*°
Ful often blessėd was his mery throte.
And thus this swetė clerk his tymė spente
After his freendės finding and his rente.°
  This carpenter had wedded newe> a wyf *recently*
Which that he lovede morė than his lyf;
Of eightėtenė yeer she was of age.
Jalous he was, and heeld hir narwe> in cage, *closely*
For she was wilde and yong, and he was old,°
And demed himself ben lyk a cokėwold.°
He knew nat Catoun,° for his wit was rude,
That bad man sholdė wedde his sìmilitude.°
Men sholdė wedden after> hir estaat,> *according to / condition*
For youthe and elde> is often at debaat. *age*
But sith that he was fallen in the snare,
He moste endure, as other folk, his care.
  Fair was this yongė wyf, and therwithal
As any wesele hir body gent and smal.°
A ceynt she werede barrėd al of silk,°
A barmclooth> eek as whyt as mornė milk *apron*
Upon hir lendės,> ful of many a gore.> *loins / pleat*
Whyt was hir smok,> and brouded> al bifore *undergarment / embroidered*
And eek bihinde, on hir coler> aboute, *collar*
Of> col-blak silk, withinne and eek withoute. *with*
The tapės> of hir whytė voluper> *ribbons / cap*

Almageste the astronomical treatise of Claudius Ptolemy, the Greek astronomer and geographer; see the Wife of Bath's Prologue, l. 188
atrelabie astrolabe; an astronomical instrument for taking observations of the sun, moon, and planets, measuring heights and distances, determining latitudes and longitudes, and preparing horoscopes
augrim stones stones or counters for use on an abacus
his presse . . . reed his large, shelved, doorless cupboard curtained off with coarse woolen cloth ("falding") of red
sautrye psaltery; a stringed instrument played with the hand
Angelus ad virginem "The Angel to the Virgin," the first words of a famous hymn on the Annunciation
Kinges Note "The King's Tune" has not been identified. Nicholas could sing sacred or secular songs to order and be thanked for either—his gay voice ("throte") was often blessed by his listeners.
After . . . rente He lived on what his friends provided for him and his own income.
For . . . old See Chaucer's Merchant's Tale, his "courtly" treatment of the old husband-young wife theme.
And . . . cokėwold and thought himself likely to be a cuckold
Catoun Dionysius Cato, 4th-century author of verses of moral instruction, the *Distichs*, a popular medieval schoolbook
bad . . . similitude a bad man should marry someone like him. This particular proverb occurs in a supplement to the *Distichs*.
As . . . smal her body graceful and slim as a weasel's
A . . . silk She wore a belt, with cross-stripes, of silk.

Were of the samė suyte° of hir coler;
Hir filet brood> of silk, and set ful hye; *headband broad*
And sikerly> she hadde a likerous> yë. *certainly / wanton*
Ful smale ypullėd° were hir browės two,
And tho were bent, and blake as any sloo.
She was ful more blisful on to see
Than is the newė perėjonette° tree;
And softer than the wolle> is of a wether.° *wool*
And by hir girdel> heeng> a purs of lether *belt / hung*
Tasseld with silk, and perlėd with latoun.°
In al this world, to seken up and doun,
There nis no man so wys, that coudė thenche> *imagine*
So gay a popelote,> or swich> a wenche. *poppet / such*
Ful brighter was the shyning of hir hewe
Than in the Towr the noble° yforgėd newe.
But of hir song, it was as loude and yerne> *lively*
As any swalwė sittinge on a berne.> *barn*
Therto she coudė skippe and makė game,
As any kide or calf folwinge his dame.> *mother*
Hir mouth was swete as bragot or the meeth,°
Or hord of apples leyd in hay or heeth.> *heather*
Winsinge> she was, as is a joly> colt, *skittish / lively*
Long as a mast, and upright> as a bolt.> *straight / arrow*
A brooch she baar upon hir lowe coler,
As brood as is the bos> of a bocler.> *boss / round shield*
Hir shoes were lacėd on hir leggės hye;
She was a prymėrole,° a piggės-nye°
For any lord to leggen> in his bedde,° *lay*
Or yet for any good yeman to wedde.
  Now sire, and eft> sire, so bifel the cas, *again*
That on a day this hendė Nicholas
Fil> with this yongė wyf to rage> and pleye, *happened / sport*
Whyl that hir housbond was at Osėneye,°
As clerkės ben ful subtile> and ful queynte;> *clever / inventive*
And privėly he caughte hir by the queynte,°
And seyde, 'Ywis,> but if> ich> have my wille, *surely / unless / I*
For dernė love of thee, lemman, I spille.'°
And heeld> hir hardė by the haunchė-bones, *held*

suyte literally, suit, following; i.e. the ribbons of her cap matched her collar
smale ypulled plucked to a narrow line
perejonette early-ripe pear, in bloom. Its fruit was also delicate and sweet.
wether strictly, a castrated ram; here used simply for sheep
perled . . . latoun spangled with brass. Latoun was a base brassy metal, imitation gold; see the General Prologue, l. 701.
Towr . . . noble The Tower of London held the principal mint of the kingdom at the time. The noble, also called an angel, was a gold coin worth two-thirds of a pound.
bragot . . . meeth Bragget, honey and ale fermented together; meeth is mead, also a fermented honey drink.
prymerole a primrose, a cowslip
pigges-nye pig's eye, a charming little eye; so, a doll
lord . . . wedde The lord need not marry her, but the yeoman would have to be honorable.
Oseneye Osney, now a suburb of Oxford, then some distance from the city, site of Osney abbey, for which the carpenter did work
queynte pudendum. See the Wife of Bath's Prologue, l. 338, and Fig. 39
For derne . . . spille for my hidden love of you, darling, I'm dying

And seydė, 'Lemman, love me al at ones,> *on the spot*
Or I wol dyen, also> God me save!> *so*
And she sprong as a colt doth in the trave,°
And with hir heed she wryėd> faste awey, *twisted*
And seyde, 'I wol nat kisse thee, by my fey,> *faith*
Why, lat be,' quod she, 'lat be, Nicholas,
Or I wol crye out "Harrow"° and "allas!"
Do wey your handės for your curteisye!'
  This Nicholas gan mercy for to crye,
And spak so faire, and profred hir so faste,°
That she hir love him graunted attė laste,
And swoor hir ooth, by Seint Thomas° of Kent,
That she wol been at his comandėment,
Whan that she may hir leyser° wel espye.
'Myn housbond is so ful of jalousye,
That but ye waytė> wel and been privee,> *watch / discreet*
I woot right wel I nam> but deed,' quod she. *am not*
'Ye mostė been ful derne, as in this cas.'
  'Nay therof care> thee noght,' quod Nicholas, *worry*
'A clerk had litherly biset his whyle,°
But if he coude a carpenter bigyle.'
And thus they been acorded and ysworn
To wayte> a tyme, as I have told biforn. *look for*
Whan Nicholas had doon thus everydeel,
And thakkėd> hir aboute the lendes> weel, *patted / loins*
He kist hir swete, and taketh his sautrye,
And pleyeth faste, and maketh melodye.
  Than fil> it thus, that to the parish chirche, *happened*
Cristės ownė werkės for to wirche,> *do*
This godė wyf wente on an haliday;°
Hir forheed shoon as bright as any day,
So was it wasshen whan she leet> hir werk. *gave over*
  Now was ther of that chirche a parish clerk,
The which that was yclepėd> Absolon.° *called*
Crul> was his heer, and as the gold it shoon, *curled*
And strouted as a fannė large and brode.°
Ful streight and even lay his joly shode,°
His rode> was reed, his eyen greye as goos;> *complexion / goose-feather*

sprong . . . trave shied as a colt does in the trave—i.e. in the frame used to keep restive horses still while being shod
'Harrow' French *haro:* a cry of distress; see ll. 404, 717.
profred . . . faste offered himself so often
Thomas St. Thomas Becket, the premier saint of England; see General Prologue, l. 16; and below, l. 353.
leyser time to spare, opportunity
A clerk . . . whyle A clerk would have made poor use of his time.
haliday holy day, saint's day or feast day
Absolon For the name and the emphasis on the beauty of the hair, see Chaucer's *balade,* "Hide Absolon," and, for the original Absalom, II Samuel 14:26: " . . . he weighed the hair of his head at two hundred shekels, after the king's weight." Absalom is a traditional type of masculine beauty.
And strouted . . . brode and spread out wide and broad like a winnowing fan; i.e. a flat shovel or wide-mouthed basket for separating grain from chaff by throwing it in the air
Ful . . . shode The beautiful parting of his hair was very straight and exact.

With Powlės window corven on his shoes,°
In hoses> rede he wentė fetisly.> *stockings / elegantly*
Yclad he was ful smal° and proprėly,
Al in a kirtel> of a light wachet;° *tunic*
Ful faire and thikkė been the poyntės° set.
And therupon he hadde a gay surplys°
As whyt as is the blosme upon the rys.> *bough*
A mery child he was, so God me save,
Wel coude he laten blood and clippe and shave,°
And make a chartre of lond or acquitaunce.°
In twenty manere> coude he trippe and daunce *ways*
After the scole of Oxenfordė tho,°
And with his leggės casten> to and fro, *fling*
And pleyen songės on a small rubìble;°
Therto he song somtyme a loud quinible;°
And as wel coude he pleye on his giterne.°
In al the toun nas brewhous ne taverne
That he ne visited with his solas,> *gaiety*
Ther any gaylard tappesterė° was.
But sooth to seyn, he was somdel squaymous> *squeamish*
Of farting, and of spechė daungerous.> *disdainful*
   This Absolon, that joly> was and gay, *frisky*
Gooth with a sencer> on the haliday, *censer*
Sensinge the wyvės of the parish faste;
And many a lovely look on hem he caste,
And namely> on this carpenterės wyf. *especially*
To loke on hir him thoughte a mery lyf,
She was so propre and swete and likerous.°
I dar wel seyn, if she had been a mous,
And he a cat, he wolde hir hente> anon. *pounce on*
   This parish clerk, this joly Absolon,
Hath in his hertė swich a love-longinge,°
That of no wyf ne took he noon offringe—
For curteisye, he seyde, he woldė> noon. *wished for*
The moone, whan it was night, ful brightė shoon,> *shone*
And Absolon his giterne hath ytake,
For paramours,° he thoghtė for to wake.> *revel*

With . . . shoos Windowed shoes were shoes with uppers cut and latticed so as to resemble windows. *Powles,* St. Paul's Cathedral in London, is Chaucer's invention in the context.
smal neatly, with close-fitting clothes
wachet a light blue, sky-color
poyntes tagged laces to fasten the tunic, hold up the hose, and otherwise perform the function of buttons
surplys overgarment, loose robe
Wel . . . shave He knew well how to let blood, cut hair and shave: i.e. he was a skillful barber-surgeon; this knowledge would be part of a learned man's equipment.
And . . . acquitaunce He was a good conveyancer also, who could draw up a title to land or a legal release.
After . . . tho It is not clear whether Oxford then, or at any time, had a great reputation for, or special style of, dancing.
rubìble a two-stringed musical instrument played with a bow; a kind of fiddle
quinible the highest pitch of the voice
giterne a kind of guitar
gaylard tappestere lively, gay barmaid. Tappestere, the ending suggests, is probably feminine here.
propre . . . likerous handsome and sweet and toothsome
love-longinge lovesickness, lover's melancholy
paramours being in love

And forth he gooth, jolif and amorous,
Til he cam to the carpenterės hous
A litel after cokkės hadde ycrowe;
And dressėd him up by a shot windòwe°
That was upon the carpenterės wal.
He singeth in his vois gentil and smal,°
'Now, derė lady, if thy willė be,
I preyė yow that ye wol rewe> on me,' — *pity*
Ful wel acordaunt to his giterninge.°
This carpenter awook, and herde him singe,
And spak unto his wyf, and seyde anon,
'What! Alison! heerestow nat Absolon
That chaunteth thus under our bourės> wal?' — *bedroom*
And she answerde hir housbond therwithal,
'Yis, God wot, John, I here it everydel.'> — *all*
  This passeth forth: what wol ye bet than wel?°
Fro day to day this joly Absolon
So woweth> hir, that him is wo bigon. — *woos*
He waketh> al the night and al the day; — *stays awake*
He kembed> hise lokkės brode,> and mad him gay; — *combed / spreading*
He woweth> hir by menės and brocage,° — *woos*
And swoor he woldė been hir ownė page;> — *servant*
He singeth, brokkinge> as a nightingale; — *trilling*
He sente hir pimènt,° meeth, and spycėd ale,
And wafres,> pyping hote out of the glede;> — *wafers / coals*
And for she was of towne,> he profrėd mede;> — *townswoman / bribery*
For som folk wol ben wonnen for richesse,
And som for strokes,> and som for gentillesse. — *blows*
  Somtyme, to shewe his lightnesse and maistrye,°
He pleyeth Heròdės on a scaffold hye.°
But what availleth him as in this cas?
She loveth so this hendė Nicholas,
That Absolon may blowe the bukkės horn;°
He ne hadde for his labour but a scorn;
And thus she maketh Absolon hir ape,°
And al his ernest turneth til a jape.> — *joke*
Ful sooth is this provèrbe, it is no lye,
Men seyn right thus, 'Alwey the nyė slye
Maketh the ferrė levė to be looth.'°

And . . . windòwe He placed himself by a casement. A shot-window was a window opening on hinges, like a shutter.
smal fine and delicate
Ful . . . giterninge in excellent accord with his guitar-playing
what wol . . . wel would you have things go better than well?
menes and brocage intermediaries and go-betweens
pimènt wine sweetened with honey and mixed with spices
lightnesse . . . maistrye quickness and mastery, virtuosity
pleyeth . . . hye Takes the part of Herod in a nativity play, on a high platform stage; this would imply a change of character, for Herod is usually shown as a blustering bully.
blowe . . . horn blow the buck's horn, i.e. get nowhere
she . . . ape she makes light of, makes a fool of Absolon
'Alwey . . . looth' "Always the clever man who is close at hand makes the distant, dear one unloved."

For though that Absolon be wood˃ or wrooth,˃ *mad / enraged*
Bycausė that he fer was from hir sighte,
This nyė˃ Nicholas stood in his lighte. *nearby*
Now bere thee wel,° thou hendė Nicholas!
For Absolon may waille and singe 'Allas!'
And so bifel it on a Saterday,
This carpenter was goon til˃ Osėnay; *to*
And hendė Nicholas and Alisoun
Acordėd been to this conclusioun,
That Nicholas shal shapen˃ him a wyle˃ *fix up / trick*
This sely˃ jalous housbond to bigyle; *poor innocent*
And if so be the gamė wente aright,
She sholdė slepen in his arm al night;
For this was his desyr and hir˃ also. *hers*
And right anon, withouten wordės mo,
This Nicholas no lenger woldė tarie,
But doth ful softe unto his chambre carie
Bothe mete˃ and drinkė for a day or tweye; *food*
And to hir housbonde bad hir for to seye,
If that he axėd˃ after Nicholas, *asked*
She sholdė seye she nistė˃ where he was: *did not know*
Of al that day she saugh him nat with yë;
She trowėd˃ that he was in maladye, *believed*
For, for no cry, hir maydė coude him calle;
He nolde answère, for nothing that mighte falle.
This passeth forth al thilkė˃ Saterday, *that*
That Nicholas stille° in his chambre lay,
And eet˃ and sleep,˃ or didė what him leste,˃ *ate / slept / pleased*
Til Sonday, that the sonnė gooth to reste.
This sely carpenter hath greet mervayle
Of Nicholas, or what thing mighte him ayle,
And seyde, 'I am adrad,˃ by Saint Thomas, *afraid*
It stondeth nat aright with Nicholas.
God shildė˃ that he deydė˃ sodeynly! *avert / is dead*
This world is now ful tikel,˃ sikerly;˃ *unstable / certainly*
I saugh˃ today a cors˃ yborn to chirche *saw / corpse*
That now, on Monday last, I saugh him wirche.˃ *at work*
Go up,' quod he unto his knave˃ anoon, *boy*
'Clepe˃ at his dore, or knokkė with a stoon,˃ *call / stone*
Loke how it is, and tel me boldėly.'
This knavė gooth him up ful sturdily,
And at the chambre dore, whyl that he stood,
He cryde and knokkėd as that he were wood:˃ *mad*
'What how! what do ye, maister Nicholay?
How may ye slepen al the longė day?'
But al for noght, he herdė nat a word;

bere thee wel conduct yourself well **stille** all the time

An hole he fond, ful lowe upon a bord,
Ther as the cat was wont in for to crepe;
And at that hole he lookėd in ful depe,
And at the laste he hadde of him a sighte.
This Nicholas sat gaping ever uprighte,
As he had kykėd° on the newė mone.°
Adown he gooth, and tolde his maister sone> — *at once*
In what array> he saugh this ilkė> man. — *condition / same*
This carpenter to blessen him> bigan, — *cross himself*
And seyde, 'Help us, Sainte Fridėswyde!°
A man woot litel what him shal bityde.
This man is fallė, with his astromye,°
In som woodnesse> or in som agonye; — *insanity*
I thoghte ay wel how that it sholdė be!°
Men sholde> nat knowe of Goddės privetee.> — *must / secrets*
Ye,> blessėd be alwey a lewėd> man, — *yes / ignorant*
That noght but oonly his bilevė can!> — *creed knows*
So ferde> another clerk with astromye; — *fared*
He walkėd in the feeldės for to prye> — *look*
Upon the sterrės,> what ther sholde bifalle, — *stars*
Til he was in a marlė-pit° yfalle;
He saugh nat that. But yet, by Saint Thomas,
Me reweth sore> of hendė Nicholas. — *I greatly pity*
He shal be rated of> his studying, — *scolded for*
If that I may, by Jesus, hevenė king!
Get me a staf, that I may underspore,°
Whyl that thou, Robin, hevest> up the dore. — *lift*
He shal> out of his studying, as I gesse.' — *must*
And to the chambre dore he gan him dresse.> — *address himself*
His knavė was a strong carl> for the nones,° — *tough*
And by the haspe he haf> it up atones;> — *heaved / at once*
Into the floor the dorė fil anon.
This Nicholas sat ay as stille as stoon,°
And ever gaped upward into the air.
This carpentėr wende> he were in despair,° — *thought*
And hente> him by the sholdres mightily, — *seized*
And shook him harde, and crydė spitously,> — *vehemently*

kyked Scots "keeked," i.e. looked, peeped. Many of Chaucer's words stay in use longer in the North of England and in Scotland than in the South.
newe mone i.e. as if he had gone mad
Frideswyde St. Frideswide, an Anglo-Saxon saint, *d.* 735, patron saint of the city and University of Oxford
astromye Like Nowelis for Noah's, this mispronunciation is meant to emphasize the carpenter's lack of education; see l. 349.
I thoghte . . . be I knew all along that it would be like this
marle-pit pit from which marl, a clayey soil used as a fertilizer, is dug. The story of the astronomer Thales, to whom this accident happened, first occurs in Plato, and there are medieval versions.
underspore pry up; they are going to lift the door off its hinges
for the nones oral formula, with little meaning here
stille as stoon silent and still. "Still" keeps some of its older meaning in this proverbial comparison.
despair the condition of the sinner who falls into inactive melancholy because he believes that his sins are too great for God's mercy to forgive

'What! Nicholay! what, how! what! loke adown!
Awake, and thenk on Cristės passioùn;
I crouchė thee from elvės and fro wightes!'°
Therwith the night-spel seyde he anon rightes°
On fourė halvės> of the hous aboute, *sides*
And on the threshfold> of the dore withoute: *threshold*
'Jesu Crist, and seynt Benedight,°
Blesse this hous from every wikkėd wight,
For nightės verye,° the white Pater-noster!°
Where wentėstow,> Seynte Petres soster?'° *did you go*
  And attė laste this hendė Nicholas
Gan for to sykė> sore, and seyde, 'Allas! *sigh*
Shal al the world be lost eftsonės> now?' *again*
  This carpenter answerdė, 'What seystow?
What! thenk on God, as we don, men that swinke.'> *toil*
  This Nicholas answerdė, 'Fecche me drinke;
And after wol I speke in privetee
Of certeyn thing that toucheth me and thee;
I wol telle it non other man, certeyn.'
  This carpenter goth doun, and comth ageyn,
And broghte of mighty ale a largė quart;
And whan that ech of hem had dronke his part,
This Nicholas his dorė fastė shette,> *shut*
And doun the carpenter by him he sette.
  He seydė, 'John, myn hostė lief> and dere, *beloved*
Thou shalt upon thy trouthė> swere me here, *oath*
That to no wight thou shalt this conseil wreye;> *secret betray*
For it is Cristės conseil that I seye,
And if thou telle it man,> thou are forlore;> *anyone / lost*
For this vengaùnce thou shalt han> therfore, *have*
That if thou wreyė me, thou shalt be wood!'°
'Nay, Crist forbede it, for His holy blood!'
Quod tho this sely man, 'I nam no labbe,
Ne, though I seye, I nam nat lief to gabbe.°
Sey what thou wolt, I shal it never telle
To child ne wyf, by Him that harwed Helle!'°

I crouche . . . wightes I cross you; i.e. defend you (with the sign of the cross) from supernatural beings and wicked creatures of all kinds. Elves are not necessarily small in Chaucer's English.
Therwith . . . rightes Then he said the night-charm at once. This was a formula to protect the house from evil influence while the occupants were asleep. Children's blessings, such as: "Matthew, Mark, Luke, and John / Bless the bed that I lie on," belong to this family.
Benedight St. Benedict, founder of Western monasticism
For . . . verye This may mean: against the evil spirits of night. The reading, *nerye* for *verye* can be made to give the sense: save [us] from the [perils of the] night.
white Pater-noster the white Lord's Prayer, most likely the prayer said against the powers of darkness on going to bed
Seynte Petres soster uncertain significance
if . . . wood if you betray me, you will go mad
Ne . . . gabbe I am no blabberer nor, though I say it myself, do I like to gossip.
by . . . Helle through Christ who harrowed Hell. The harrowing of Hell (Fig. 7), the descent of Christ to bring the just out of Limbo, got its English name from the outcry (harrow, see l. 178 above) of the devils as their doors were beaten down and they were defeated. It was an episode in several cycles of mystery plays.

'Now John,' quod Nicholas, 'I wol nat lye;
I have yfounde in myn astrologye,
As I have lokėd in the moonė bright,°
That now, a Monday next, at quarter-night,°
Shal falle a rayn and that so wilde and wood,> *fierce*
That half so greet was never Noës° flood.
This world,' he seyde, 'in lasse> than in an hour *less*
Shal al be dreynt,> so hidous is the shour; *drowned*
Thus shal mankyndė drenche> and lese> hir lyf.' *drown / lose*
This carpenter answerde, 'Allas, my wyf!
And shal she drenche? Allas! myn Alisoun!'
For sorwe of this he fil almòst adoun,°
And seyde, 'Is ther no remedie in this cas?'
'Why, yis, for> Gode,' quod hendė Nicholas, *before*
'If thou wolt werken after lore and reed;°
Thou mayst nat werken after thyn owene heed.> *head*
For thus seith Salomon, that was ful trewe,> *wise*
"Werk al by conseil, and thou shalt nat rewe."°
And if thou werken wolt by good conseil,
I undertake, withouten mast and seyl,> *sail*
Yet shal I saven hir and thee and me.
Hastow nat herd how savėd was Noë,
Whan that our Lord had warned him biforn
That al the world with water sholde be lorn?'> *lost*
'Yis,' quod this carpenter, 'ful yore> ago.' *long*
'Hastow nat herd,' quod Nicholas, 'also
The sorwe> of Noë with his felawshipe,> *difficulty / company*
Er that he mightė gete his wyf to shipe?°
Him had be lever,> I dar wel undertake, *rather*
At thilkė tyme, than alle hise wetherės blake,°
That she hadde had a ship hirself allone.
And therfore, wostou> what is best to done? *do you know*
This asketh> haste, and of an hastif> thing *requires / urgent*
Men may nat preche or maken tarying.
Anon go gete us faste into this in> *lodging*
A kneding trogh, or elles a kimelin,°
For ech of us, but loke that they be large,> *broad-bottomed*
In which we mowė> swimme> as in a barge, *may float*
And han therinne vitaillė suffisànt> *provisions sufficient*

moone bright On the importance of the moon in prognostication, see Franklin's Tale, l. 421.
quarter-night If this is the end of the first quarter of the night, i.e. about 9 p.m., the time-scheme of the story would be wrong; perhaps therefore, at the beginning of the last quarter, about 3 a.m.
Noës Noah's; *Noë* is the usual Latin form.
For sorwe . . . adoun for sorrow at this he almost fell down
If . . . reed if you will act according to learning and counsel
"Werk . . . rewe" do nothing without advice; and when thou hast once done, repent not (Ecclesiasticus 32:19, then attributed to Solomon)
Er . . . shipe Noah's difficulties in getting his wife on to the Ark provided the comic relief in the mystery plays on the Flood.
wetheres blake black rams (or wethers; see above, l. 141); i.e. his most highly prized sheep
A kneding trogh . . . kimelin a dough-trough or else a brewing vat

But for a day; fy on the remenant!°
The water shal aslake> and goon away *diminish*
Aboutė pryme° upon the nextė day.
But Robin may nat wite> of this, thy knave, *know*
Ne eek thy maydė Gille I may nat save;
Axė nat why, for though thou askė me,
I wol nat tellen Goddės privetee.
Suffiseth thee, but if> thy wittės madde,> *unless / are crazy*
To han> as greet a grace> as Noë hadde. *have / favor*
Thy wyf shal I wel saven, out of doute.
Go now thy wey, and speed thee heeraboute.
  'But whan thou hast, for hir and thee and me,
Ygeten us thise kneding-tubbės three,
Than shaltow hange hem in the roof ful hye,
That no man of our purveyaùncė° spye.
And whan thou thus hast doon as I have seyd,
And hast our vitaille faire in hem ylayd,
And eek an ax, to smyte the corde atwo> *in two*
When that the water comth, that we may go,
And broke an hole an heigh,> upon the gable, *up high*
Unto the gardinward,° over the stable,
That we may frely passen forth our way
Whan that the gretė showr is goon away
Than shaltow swimme as myrie,> I undertake, *carefree*
As doth the whytė doke> after hir drake. *duck*
Than wol I clepe,> "How! Alison! how! John! *call*
Be myrie, for the flood wol passe anon."> *soon*
And thou wolt seyn, "Hayl, maister Nicholay!
Good morwe, I se thee wel, for it is day."
And than shul we be lordės al our lyf
Of al the world, as Noë and his wyf.
  But of o thyng I warnė thee ful right,
Be wel avysėd,> on that ilkė night *careful*
That we ben entred into shippės bord,
That noon of us ne spekė nat a word,
Ne clepe, ne crye, but been in his prayere;
For it is Goddės ownė hestė dere.> *commandment precious*
  Thy wyf and thou mote hangė fer atwinne,> *far apart*
For that bitwixė yow shal be no sinne°
No more in looking than ther shal in dede;
This ordinance is seyd, go, God thee spede!
Tomorwe at night, whan men ben alle aslepe,
Into our kneding-tubbės wol we crepe,
And sitten ther, abyding Goddės grace.

fy . . . remenant no bother about the rest
Aboute pryme First thing in the morning; prime was the first of the canonical divisions of the day, 6 a.m. to 9 a.m.
purveyaùnce advance preparations
Unto the gardinward looking toward the garden
For . . . sinne at this second flood you must be as entirely pure as Noah, without even a venial sin on your conscience

Go now thy wey, I have no lenger space>   *time*
To make of this no lenger sermoning.
Men seyn thus, "Send the wyse, and sey nothing";°
Thou art so wys, it nedeth thee nat teche;
Go, save our lyf, and that I thee biseche.'
  This sely carpenter goth forth his wey.
Ful ofte he seith 'Allas' and 'Weylawey,'
And to his wyf he tolde his privėtee;
And she was war,> and knew it bet> than he,   *forewarned / better*
What al this queyntė cast> was for to seye. >   *subtle plan / meant*
But nathėlees she ferde> as she wolde deye,   *acted*
And seyde, 'Allas! go forth thy wey anon,
Help us to scape,> or we ben lost echon;>   *escape / each one*
I am thy trewė verray> wedded wyf;   *faithful true*
Go, derė spouse, and help to save our lyf.'
  Lo! which a greet thyng is affeccioùn!°
Men may dye of imaginacioùn,
So depė> may impressioùn be take.   *deeply*
This sely carpenter biginneth quake;
Him thinketh verraily> that he may see   *truly*
Noës flood come walwing> as the see   *rolling*
To drenchen> Alisoun, his hony dere.   *drown*
He wepeth, weyleth, maketh sory chere,
He syketh> with ful many a sory swogh.>   *sighs / groan*
He gooth and geteth him a kneding-trogh,
And after that a tubbe and a kimelin,
And privėly he sente hem to his in,>   *house*
And heng> hem in the roof in privetee.   *hung*
His ownė hand he madė laddres three,
To climben by the rongės> and the stalkes>   *rungs / uprights*
Unto the tubbės hanginge in the balkes,>   *rafters*
And hem vitailled,> bothė trogh and tubbe,   *victualed*
With breed and chese, and good ale in a jubbe,>   *jug*
Suffysinge right ynogh> as for a day.   *in plenty*
But er that he had maad al this array,>   *arrangement*
He sente his knave, and eek his wenche> also,   *maidservant*
Upon his nede° to London for to go.
And on the Monday, whan it drow to> night,   *approached*
He shette> his dore withoutė candel-light,   *shut*
And dressėd> al thing as it sholdė be.   *arranged*
And shortly, up they clomben> allė three;   *climbed*
They sitten stillė wel a furlong-way.°
  'Now, Pater-noster, clom!'° seyde Nicholay,
And 'Clom,' quod John, and 'Clom,' seyde Alisoun.

"Send . . . nothing" proverbial: a word to the wise is enough
affeccioun the faculty of the soul concerned with emotion, desire, will; here emotional excitement or disturbance
Upon his nede for something he wanted; on an errand
furlong-way a short time—the time it takes to walk a furlong (1/8 mile)
Pater . . . clom Our Father, hush!

This carpenter seyde his devocioùn,
And stille he sit,> and biddeth> his preyere, *sits / prays*
Awaytinge on the reyn, if he it here.> *might hear*
  The dedė sleep, for wery bisinesse,
Fil> on this carpenter right, as I gesse, *descended*
Aboutė corfew tyme,° or litel more;
For travail> of his goost> he groneth sore, *affliction / spirit*
And eft> he routeth,> for his heed mislay.° *then / snores*
Doun of the laddrė stalketh> Nicholay, *climbs stealthily*
And Alisoun, ful softe adoun she spedde;
Withouten wordės mo, they goon to bedde
Theras> the carpenter is wont to lye. *where*
Ther was the revel and the melodye;
And thus lyth> Alison and Nicholas, *lie*
In bisinesse of mirthe and of solas,> *pleasure*
Til that the belle of Laudės° gan to ringe,
And frerės in the chauncel> gonnė singe. *chancel*
  This parish clerk, this amorous Absolon,
That is for love alwey so wo bigon,
Upon the Monday was at Osėneye
With companye, him to disporte and pleye,
And axėd upon cas> a cloisterer° *by chance*
Ful privėly after John the carpenter;
And he drough> him apart out of the chirche, *drew*
And seyde, 'I noot,> I saugh him here nat wirche> *don't know / work*
Sin Saterday; I trow that he be went
For timber, ther our abbot hath him sent;
For he is wont for timber for to go,
And dwellen at the grange° a day or two;
Or ellės he is at his hous, certeyn;
Wher that he be, I can nat sothly> seyn.' *truly*
  This Absolon ful joly> was and light,> *frisky / gay*
And thoghtė, 'Now is tymė wake> al night; *to wake*
For sikirly I saugh him nat stiringe
Aboute his dore sin day bigan to springe.
So moot> I thryve, I shal, at cokkės crowe,° *may*
Ful prively knokken at his windowe
That stant> ful lowe upon his bourės> wal. *stands / bedroom*
To Alison now wol I tellen al
My love-longing, for yet I shal nat misse
That at the lestė wey> I shal hir kisse. *at least*

corfew tyme about dusk, when the town gates would be shut; perhaps 8 p.m.
his heed mislay his head lay awry
Laudes lauds; the first office (church service) of the day, usually between 3 and 4 a.m., before day actually broke
cloisterer a member of a religious order living in a convent or monastery; here an Augustinian canon of Osney Abbey
grange barn or granary; but here an outlying farm belonging to the Abbey
at cokkes crowe a vague indication of time. First cockcrow was not long after midnight; second about 3 a.m., about the time of lauds. So the time scheme works—just about lauds, when Nicholas and Alison were finishing their bouts, Absolon arrives.

Som maner confort shal I have, parfay,˃ *in faith*
My mouth hath icchėd° al this longė day;
That is a signe of kissing attė leste.
Al night me mette˃ eek, I was at a feste. *dreamed*
Therfor I wol gon slepe an houre or tweye,
And al the night than wol I wake and pleye.'
  Whan that the firstė cok hath crowe, anon
Up rist˃ this joly lover Absolon, *rises*
And him arrayeth gay, at point devys.°
But first he cheweth greyn° and lycorys,
To smellen swete, er he had kembed˃ his heer. *combed*
Under his tonge a trewė love° he beer,˃ *bore*
For therby wende he to ben gracïoùs.
He rometh˃ to the carpenterės hous, *walks*
And stille he stant under the shot windowe;
Unto his brest it raughte,˃ it was so lowe; *reached*
And softe he cogheth with a semisoun˃— *low voice*
'What do ye, hony-comb, swete Alisoun?
My fairė brid,° my swetė cinamome,
Awaketh, lemman˃ myn, and speketh to me! *darling*
Wel litel thenken ye upon my wo,
That for your love I swetė˃ ther˃ I go. *sweat / wherever*
No wonder is thogh that I swelte˃ and swete; *swelter*
I moorne˃ as doth a lamb after the tete.˃ *long / teat*
Ywis,˃ lemman, I have swich love-longinge, *indeed*
That lyk a turtel° trewe is my moorninge;
I may nat ete na morė than a mayde.'
  'Go fro the window, Jakkė fool,' she sayde,
'As help me God, it wol nat be "Com ba˃ me," *kiss*
I love another, and elles I were to blame,
Wel bet˃ than thee, by Jesu, Absolon! *better*
Go forth thy wey, or I wol caste a ston,
And lat me slepe, a twenty devel wey!'°
  'Allas,' quod Absolon, 'and weylawey!
That trewė love was ever so yvel biset!˃ *hardly used*
Than kissė me, sin it may be no bet,
For Jesus love and for the love of me.'
  'Wiltow˃ than go thy wey therwith?' quod she. *will you*
  'Ye, certės, lemman,' quod this Absolon.
  'Thanne make thee redy,' quod she, 'I come anon.'
And unto Nicholas she seydė stille,˃ *quietly*
'Now hust,˃ and thou shalt laughen al thy fille.' *hush*
  This Absolon doun sette him on his knees,

My . . . icched Divination from involuntary movements was widely practiced in ancient times and in the Middle Ages.
at point devys very neatly and elegantly; to perfection
greyn grain of Paris or Paradise, a seed used as spice; like licorice, a sweetener of the breath
trewe love probably a four-leafed sprig of herb-paris, with a flower or berry in the middle, and looking like a true-love knot
brid bird, most likely; or perhaps bride
turtel turtledove, proverbially true to its mate, and pining away at its absence or death
a . . . wey for twenty devils' sake

And seyde, 'I am a lord at alle degrees;°
For after this I hope ther cometh more!
Lemman, thy grace, and swetė brid,> thyn ore>!' *bird / favor*
The window she undoth, and that in haste,
'Have do,' quod she, 'com of, and speed thee faste,
Lest that our neighėborės thee espye.'
This Absolon gan wype his mouth ful drye;
Derk was the night as pich, or as the cole,
And at the window out she putte hir hole,
And Absolon, him fil no bet ne wers,°
But with his mouth he kiste hir naked ers> *ass*
Ful savourly,> er he was war of this. *with great relish*
Abak he sterte,> and thoghte it was amis, *jumped*
For wel he wiste a womman hath no berd;> *beard*
He felte a thing al rough and long yherd,> *haired*
And seydė, 'Fy! allas! what have I do?'
'Teehee!' quod she, and clapte the window to;
And Absolon goth forth a sory pas.°
'A berd, a berd!' quod hendė Nicholas,
'By Goddės corpus,> this goth faire and weel!' *body*
This sely> Absolon herde every deel, *poor*
And on his lippe he gan for anger byte;
And to himself he seyde, 'I shal thee quyte>!' *pay back*
Who rubbeth now, who froteth> now his lippes *scrubs*
With dust, with sond,> with straw, with clooth, with chippes, *sand*
But Absolon, that seith ful ofte, 'Allas!
My soule bitake I unto Sathanas,
But me wer lever than al this town,' quod he,
'Of this despyt awroken for to be!°
Allas!' quod he, 'allas! I ne hadde ybleynt!'> *turned away*
His hotė> love was cold and al yqueynt;> *hot / quenched*
For fro that tyme that he had kiste hir ers,
Of paramours he settė nat a kers,°
For he was helėd of his maladye;
Ful oftė paramours he gan deffye,> *give up*
And weep> as dooth a child that is ybete. *wept*
A softė paas° he wente over> the strete *across*
Until> a smith men clepėd Daun Gerveys,° *to*
That in his forgė smithėd plough harneys;> *equipment*
He sharpeth shaar° and culter bisily.
This Absolon knokketh al esily,> *quietly*

at alle degrees in all ways, completely
him . . . wers it happened to him neither better nor worse: i.e. it happened just like this
sory pas at a sad pace; walking dejectedly
My soule . . . be (ll. 642–44) I would give my soul to Satan. That is, I'll be damned, if I wouldn't rather have my revenge than be the owner of this whole town.
Of . . . kers On love of women he set no value at all; *kers* is cress, a worthless piece of vegetation.
softe paas quiet walk, quietly
Daun Gerveys Master Gervase (*Daun* is short for *dominus,* master). It is still before daybreak, but many would already be at work; and smiths were notorious early workers.
shaar plowshare, the blade that turns the turf over on its side; *culter,* coulter, the tip on the share which cuts the turf vertically

And seyde, 'Undo, Gerveys, and that anon.'
  'What, who artow?' 'It am I, Absolon.'
'What, Absolon! for Cristės swetė tree,> *cross*
Why rysė ye so rathe,> ey, Benedicite!> *early / bless me*
What ayleth yow? som gay gerl, God it woot,
Hath broght yow thus upon the viritoot;°
By Seÿnt Note,° ye woot wel what I mene.'
  This Absolon ne roghtė> nat a bene> *cared / bean*
Of al his pley, no word agayn he yaf;> *returned*
He haddė morė tow on his diståf°
Than Gerveys knew, and seydė, 'Freend so dere,
That hotė culter in the chimenee> here, *fireplace*
As lene° it me, I have therwith to done,
And I wol bringe it thee agayn ful sone.'
  Gerveys answerde, 'Certės, were it gold,
Or in a pokė nobles alle untold,°
Thou sholdest have, as I am trewė smith;
Ey, Cristės foo!° what wol ye do therwith?'
  'Therof,' quod Absolon, 'be as be may;
I shal wel telle it thee tomorwe day'—
And caughte the culter by the coldė stele.> *handle*
Ful softe out at the dore he gan to stele,
And wente unto the carpenterės wal.
He cogheth first, and knokketh therwithal
Upon the windowe, right as he dide er.> *before*
  This Alison answerde, 'Who is ther
That knokketh so? I warante° it a theef.'
  'Why, nay,' quod he, 'God woot, my swetė leef,> *dear*
I am thyn Absolon, my derėling!
Of gold,' quod he, 'I have thee broght a ring;
My moder> yaf it me, so God me save, *mother*
Ful fyn it is, and therto wel ygrave;> *engraved*
This wol I gevė> thee, if thou me kisse!' *give*
  This Nicholas was risen for to pisse,
And thoghte he wolde amenden> al the jape,> *better / jest*
He sholdė kisse his ers er that he scape.
And up the windowe dide> he hastily, *put*
And out his ers he putteth privėly
Over the buttok, to the haunchė-bon;
And therwith spak this clerk, this Absolon,
'Spek, swetė brid,> I noot> nat wher thou art.' *bird / don't know*
  This Nicholas anon leet flee> a fart, *let fly*
As greet as it had been a thonder-dent,> *thunder-clap*

viritoot meaning unknown; perhaps, on the prowl
Seynt Note Neot, a 9th-century Saxon saint
He . . . distaf proverbial phrase: he had more flax to spin into linen thread; i.e. he had plenty of other things to think of
As lene please lend
Or . . . untold or gold coins all uncounted in a bag; for *nobles*, see l. 148
Cristes foo by Christ's foe, i.e. the Devil; or short for "by Christ's foot"; cf. l. 17
warante guarantee or wager

That with the strook he was almost yblent;> *blinded*
And he was redy with his iren hoot,> *hot*
And Nicholas amidde> the ers he smoot.> *in the middle of / smote*
  Of gooth the skin an handė-brede> aboute, *hand's breadth*
The hotė culter brendė so his toute,> *rump*
And for the smert he wendė for> to dye. *expected*
As he were wood,> for wo he gan to crye: *crazy*
'Help! water! water! help, for Goddės herte!'
  This carpenter out of his slomber sterte,
And herde oon cryen 'Water' as he were wood,
And thoghte, 'Allas! now comth Nowelis° flood!'
He sit him up withouten wordes mo,
And with his ax he smoot the corde atwo,
And down goth al; he fond neither to selle,
Ne breed ne ale, til he cam to the celle
Upon the floor;° and ther aswowne> he lay. *unconscious*
  Up sterte> hir Alison, and Nicholay, *jumped*
And cryden 'Out' and 'Harrow' in the strete.
The neighėborės, bothė smale and grete,
In ronnen,> for to gauren> on this man, *ran / gape*
That yet aswowne he lay, bothe pale and wan;
For with the fal he brosten> hadde his arm; *broken*
But stonde he moste> unto his owne harm. *must*
For whan he spak, he was anon bore doun> *overcome*
With> hendė Nicholas and Alisoun. *by*
They tolden every man that he was wood,
He was agast so of 'Nowelis flood'
Thurgh fantasye,> that of his vanitee> *imagination / folly*
He hadde yboght him kneding-tubbės three,
And hadde hem hangėd in the roof above;
And that he preyėd hem, for Goddės love,
To sitten in the roof, par companye.°
  The folk gan laughen at his fantasye;
Into the roof they kyken> and they gape, *peer*
And turnėd al his harm unto a jape.
For what so that this carpenter answerde,
It was for noght, no man his reson> herde; *argument*
With othės grete he was so sworn adoun,> *sworn under*
That he was holden> wood in al the toun; *held*
For every clerk anon right> heeld> with other. *at once / sided*
They seyde, 'The man is wood, my leve brother';
And every wight gan laughen of this stryf.> *fuss*

Nowelis Noah's; like astromye, l. 343, this is a mispronunciation of the carpenter's, confusing Noah with Nowel, Christmas.

he . . . floor He found no opportunity to sell bread or ale until he reached the floorboards; i.e. he went down with a great rush. "Celle" and "floor" seem to mean the same thing; or "celle" is the floor, and "floor" the ground beneath it. Perhaps "celle" means the house's main room, above which the carpenter had been suspended.

par companye for company's sake; to keep him company

Thus swyvėd> was the carpenterės wyf, *screwed*
For al his keping> and his jalousye; *guarding*
And Absolon hath kist hir nether yë;> *lower eye*
And Nicholas is scalded in the toute.
This tale is doon, and God save al the route!> *company*

Here endeth the Millere his tale.

The Nun's Priest's Prologue and Tale

The Nun's Priest is one of the characters in the *Tales* of whom we know least: in the General Prologue he is one of three priests, given a bare mention after the Prioress. But only one Nun's Priest tells a tale; and our only description of him comes from the Host, who calls him brawny and a "tread-fowl" (Fig. 28).

His tale, which may have been written at any time after 1381 (there is a reference in it to the Peasants' Revolt of that year), is based on an animal fable which Chaucer probably found in one of the popular collections of stories concerning Reynard the Fox and his tricks which had begun to be built into beast epics in the twelfth century. The idea of presenting a story in which beasts act as human beings—and so giving some sort of moral lesson from a world thus turned upside down—goes back as far as Greek literature, and is associated with the name of Aesop, in the sixth century B.C. In these fables the fox is always the embodiment of deceit.

Preachers naturally found such stories useful in sermons. These would open with a text from the Bible or other sacred work, out of which flowed the *exordium,* the arresting beginning, and next the illustrative *exemplum.* Then came the application of its story (the *moralitee*) to the moral lives of the audience, and finally the *peroration,* the finale, with its exhortation to a better life. This is the classic model for an oration and the rhetorical principle on which a medieval sermon was built. The Nun's Priest's Tale is, in the mouth of its teller, such a sermon, in perfectly conventional form, with the lesson firmly stated at the end: don't trust flatterers.

The Nun's Priest's Tale is, however, far more than sermon or moral lesson: it is yet another illustration of that quality which makes Chaucer one of the greatest poets in the language: his ability to work within a convention and transform it. Here he has taken two conventions—the theory and practice of rhetoric and the beast fable—and put this superbly witty and lively comedy into the mouth of a nobody, an ordinary priest. Moreover, he seems to have intended it to follow immediately upon the tale told by a somebody: the sleek, huntsman Monk, whose pedestrian, lifeless series of "tragedies" make a dramatic contrast with the lively, witty, erudite tale of the Nun's Priest.

The Nun's Priest's Tale too is peopled with its great men—but they are barnyard animals. Chaunticleer displays vast learning on dreams—at least that is what he would wish us to think—claiming for himself, noblest of birds, the privilege of visions that, in the technical language of dream classification at the time, are truly prophetic. These are not the foolish, invalid dreams that come from physical causes such as his wife, with her lesser nature, thinks that his dream of the fox has been. They do not, he claims, result from something he has eaten or because of some excess of one or other humor (or bodily fluid): that sort of dream is for lesser mortals. But Chaunticleer is not quite on top of his subject: the joke is, in fact, that he has not perceived the true relation between what happens of necessity and what happens through free will. Someone so noble cannot quite be bound by his dream: he flies down and is lost.

The comedy of knowledge is seen also in Pertelote, but her learning though correct and full according to the medical theory of the day, is practical and down-to-earth. She is the complete feminine materialist, downright and doubly annoying to a masculine mind such as Chaunticleer's, which thinks it sees more deeply into the true nature of things.

Chaunticleer's vainglorious learning and Pertelote's sympathetic wisdom are subtly deployed to keep the story slow and even-paced in its first part; all the bustle and action are at the end. This skillful rhetorical design in Chaucer's hands contrasts with the continuous parody of rhetorical inflation that goes on throughout the poem, especially in Chaunticleer's speeches and finally in the stream of *exempla* which flows from the climactic moment of the poem. Constantly, as the poem goes on, the simplest matters are treated in a highly ornamental manner. Long illustrative stories are introduced. *Sententiae* are bandied about. Chaucer's parody of rhetoric is presented with the maximum rhetorical sophistication and force, in the first true mock-heroic masterpiece in English.

The question has often been asked whether there is not a great deal more to this story of a cock and a hen than meets the eye. The Nun's Priest's words, "Saint Paul saith that al that writen is / To oure doctrine it is ywrit, ywis," state one of the most consistently held notions about literature during the entire Middle Ages. Should we then see in the poem an indirect meaning or application other than the warning against flatterers issued by the teller of the tale? It has been read as a much more sophisticated allegory of the friars (the fox), the secular clergy, i.e. parish priests, and other ecclesiastics not bound by a rule (Chaunticleer), and the Church (the widow); or as the Christian (Chaunticleer) carried off by the Devil or seduced by the heretic (the fox), as in the *Bestiary*. The first of these readings develops from the application of methods of interpreting the Bible that were not widely used in England in Chaucer's day, and suffers from inconsistencies. The second, simpler explanation has more to recommend it—but everyone must make up his own mind about these explanations and the view of medieval literature that they imply.

Two other Reynard and Chaunticleer stories are added here. The selections from the *Bestiary* show another mode of moralizing the animal kingdom, which is a great deal more literal and crude than Chaucer's. The selection from Caxton shows how far the notion of the fox as a deceitful animal was turned to the specific purposes of satire against the clergy (Fig. 34).

The Prologue

The prologue of the Nonne Preestes Tale

'Ho!' quod the Knight, 'good sir, namore of this,
That ye han seyd is right ynough, ywis,
And mochel˃ more; for litel hevinesse˃ — *much / sadness*
Is right ynough to mochel˃ folk, I gesse. — *many*

I seye for me, it is a greet disese> *distress*
Wheras men han ben in greet welthe and ese,> *comfort*
To heren of hir sodeyn> fall, allas! *sudden*
And the contrarie is joie and greet solas,> *relief*
As whan a man hath been in poore estaat,°
And clymbeth up, and wexeth> fortunat, *grows*
And ther abydeth in prosperitee,
Swich thing is gladsom, as it thinketh me,
And of swich thing were goodly for to telle.'
'Ye,' quod our hoste, 'by Seint Poulės° belle,
Ye seye right sooth; this monk, he clappeth> loude, *prattles*
He spak how 'Fortune covered with a cloude'
I noot> never what, and als> of a 'Tragedie' *know not / also*
Right now ye herde, and pardė!° no remedie
It is for to biwaillė,> ne compleyne *bewail*
That that is doon; and als it is a peyne,
As ye han seyd,> to here> of hevinesse. *said / hear*
Sir Monk, namore of this, so God yow blesse!
Your tale anoyeth> al this companye; *displeases*
Swich talking is nat worth a boterflye;
For therin is ther no desport> ne game.> *recreation / pleasure*
Wherfor, sir Monk, or Dan° Piers by your name,
I preye yow hertėly, telle us somwhat elles,> *else*
For sikerly,> nere° clinking of your belles, *certainly*
That on your brydel hange on every syde,
By heven> king, that for us allė dyde,> *Heaven's / died*
I sholde er this han fallen doun for slepe,
Although the slough> had never been so depe; *mire*
Than had your talė al be told in vayn.
For certeinly, as that thisė clerkės> seyn, *learned men*
'Wheras> a man may have noon audience, *when*
Noght helpeth it to tellen his sentence.'> *matter, wisdom*
And wel I woot the substance is in me,°
If any thing shal wel reported be.
Sir, sey> somwhat of hunting, I yow preye.' *say*
'Nay,' quod this monk, 'I have no lust> to pleye;> *pleasure / jest*
Now let another telle, as I have told.'
Than spak our host, with rudė speche and bold,
And seyde unto the Nonnės Preest anon,> *at once*
'Com neer,> thou preest, com hider,> thou Sir John,° *closer / hither*
Tel us swich thing as may our hertės glade,> *gladden*
Be blythė, though thou ryde upon a jade.> *wretched horse*

estaat state, status. The image does not necessarily involve Fortune's wheel (see below and Fig. 41) but may do so.
Seint Poules St. Paul's Cathedral, the chief church of London
parde i.e. *par dieu*, by God
Dan Dan = *dominus*, master; a title of respect, especially for a religious and/or learned man
nere were it not for
wel . . . me i.e. and I know very well I have the capacity to understand; or: I know very well I understand the meat of the matter
Sir John the regular nickname for a priest

What though thyn hors be bothė foule> and lene,> *dirty / lean*
If he wol serve thee, rekkė> nat a bene;> *care / bean*
Look that thyn herte be mery evermo.'
'Yis, sir,' quod he, 'yis, host, so mote I go,
But> I be mery, ywis,> I wol be blamed.' *unless / indeed*
And right anon his tale he hath attamed,> *broached*
And thus he seyde unto us everichon,
This swetė preest, this goodly man, Sir John.

Explicit°

The Tale

Here biginneth the Nonne Preestes Tale of the Cok and Hen, Chauntėcleer and Pertėlote.

A povre> widwe, somdel stape> in age, *poor / advanced*
Was whylom> dwelling in a narwe> cotage, *formerly / little*
Bisyde a grovė, stonding in a dale.> *valley*
This widwe, of which I telle yow my tale,
Sin thilkė> day that she was last a wyf, *since the same*
In paciėnce ladde> a ful simple lyf, *led*
For litel was hir catel° and hir rente;> *income*
By housbondrye,> of such as God hir sente, *economy*
She fond° hirself, and eek> hir doghtren> two. *also / daughters*
Three largė sowės hadde she, and namo,> *no more*
Three kyn,> and eek a sheep that hightė> Malle. *cows / was called*
Ful sooty was hir bour, and eek hir halle,°
In which she eet> ful many a sclendre> meel. *ate / frugal*
Of poynaunt sauce hir neded never a deel.°
No deyntee morsel passėd thurgh hir throte;
Hir dyete was accordant> to hir cote.> *according / cottage*
Replecciou̇n> ne made hir never syk;> *over-eating / sick*
Attempree> dyete was al hir phisyk,> *temperate / medicine*
And exercyse, and hertės suffisaunce.> *heart's contentment*
The goutė lette> hir nothing for to daunce, *hindered*
Napoplexye shentė> nat hir heed; *injured*
No wyn> ne drank she, neither whyt ne reed; *wine*
Hir bord> was servėd most with whyt and blak, *table*
Milk and brown breed,> in which she fond no lak,> *bread / defect*

Explicit Literally, it is finished.
catel chattels, property
fond found, provided for: see Miller's Tale, l. 112
bour . . . halle The widow's house probably had only one room serving as living room and bedroom for the widow, her daughters, and assorted livestock. Chaucer describes the little cottage in terms of a grand house, in which the hall was the large room where household and guests assembled for food and entertainment; the bower, originally the private apartments, by Chaucer's time was a usual term for bedroom.
Of poynaunt . . . deel she did not need even a touch of piquant sauce to provoke an appetite

Seynd° bacoun, and somtyme an ey> or tweye, *egg*
For she was, as it were, a maner deye.°
  A yerd> she hadde, enclosėd al aboute *yard*
With stikkės, and a dryė dich> withoute, *ditch*
In which she hadde a cok,> hight> Chauntėcleer,° *rooster / called*
In al the land, of crowing, nas> his peer.> *was not / equal*
His vois was merier> than the mery orgon> *gayer / organ*
On messė-dayes> that in the chirchė gon;° *mass-days*
Wel sikerer> was his crowing in his logge,> *surer / lodge*
Than is a clokke, or an abbèy orlogge.°
By nature knew he ech ascencioùn
Of equinoxial° in thilkė toun;
For whan degrees fiftenė were ascended,
Thanne crew he, that it mighte nat ben amended.> *bettered*
His comb was redder than the fyn coral,
And batailed,> as it were a castel wal. *battlemented*
His bile> was blak, and as the jeet> it shoon; *bill / jet*
Lyk asur° were his leggės, and his toon;> *toes*
His naylės> whytter than the lilie flour, *claws*
And lyk the burnėd> gold was his coloùr. *burnished*
This gentil> cok hadde in his governaùnce *noble*
Sevene hennės, for to doon al his plesaùnce,> *pleasure*
Whiche were his sustres> and his paramoùrs, *sisters*
And wonder lyk> to him, as of coloùrs. *amazingly like*
Of whiche the faireste hewėd> on hir throte> *colored / throat*
Was cleped> faire damoyselė° Pertėlote. *called*
Curteis° she was, discreet, and debonaire,
And compaignable, and bar> hirself so faire, *bore*
Sin thilkė day that she was seven night old,
That trewėly> she hath the herte in hold> *firmly / keeping*
Of Chauntėcleer, loken> in every lith;> *locked / limb*
He loved hir so, that wel was him therwith.°
But such a joye was it to here> hem singe, *hear*
Whan that the brightė sonnė gan to springe,> *rise*
In swete accord, 'My lief is faren in londe.'°
For thilkė tyme, as I have understonde,> *heard*
Bestės and briddės> coudė speke and singe. *birds*
  And so befel,> that in a dawėninge,> *it happened / dawn*

Seynd singed, i.e. broiled; or perhaps fat, as in French *saindoux*, lard
maner deye a kind of dairywoman
Chauntecleer the usual name for the cock in the Reynard story, from his clear singing voice
gon The verb is plural, because "orgon" was frequently plural, on the analogy of Latin *organa*, literally a set of pipes.
orlogge the great public clock, often giving astronomical information as well as time
equinoxial The equinoxial circle or celestial equator, thought to make a complete rotation round the earth every natural (24-hour) day, at the rate of 15° per hour. So Chaunticleer crowed every hour, on the hour.
asur lapis lazuli; bright blue
damoysele Literally, young (unmarried) woman, especially of good family. The word signals Chaucer's description of the hen-heroine, called Pinte in other Reynard stories, in terms of the lady in a poem of courtly love.
Curteis full of courtly qualities, refined in manners
wel . . . therwith all was well with him for it; he was perfectly happy
'My . . . londe' My dear one has gone away; a popular song of the time.

As Chauntėcleer among his wyvės alle
Sat on his perchė, that was in the halle,
And next him sat this fairė Pertėlote,
This Chauntėcleer gan gronen> in his throte, *(did) groan*
As man that in his dreem is drecchėd> sore. *afflicted*
And whan that Pertėlote thus herde him rore,> *roar*
She was agast,> and seyde, 'O hertė dere, *afraid*
What eyleth> yow, to grone in this manere? *ails*
Ye been a verray> sleper, fy for shame!' *fine*
And he answerde and seydė thus, 'Madame,
I pray yow, that ye take it nat agrief:°
By God, me mette> I was in swich meschief> *I dreamed / trouble*
Right now, that yet myn herte is sore afright.> *frightened*
Now God,' quod he, 'my swevene recche aright,°
And keep my body out of foul prisoun!
Me mette,> how that I romėd> up and down *dreamed / walked*
Withinne our yerde, wheras> I sawe a beste, *where*
Was lyk an hound, and wolde han maad areste
Upon my body, and wolde han had me deed.°
His colour was bitwixe yellow and reed;
And tippėd was his tail, and bothe his eres,> *ears*
With blak, unlyk the remnant> of his heres;> *rest / hairs*
His snowtė smal,> with glowinge eyen tweye.> *narrow / two*
Yet of his look for fere almost I deye;> *die*
This causėd me my groning, doutėles.'
'Avoy!'> quod she, 'fy on yow, hertėles!> *fie / coward*
Allas!' quod she, 'for, by that God above,
Now han ye lost myn herte and al my love;
I can nat love a coward, by my faith.
For certės,> what so any womman seith, *indeed*
We alle desyren, if it mightė be,
To han housbondės° hardy,> wyse, and free,> *brave / generous*
And secree,> and no nigard, ne no fool, *discreet*
Ne him that is agast> of every tool,> *afraid / weapon*
Ne noon avauntour,° by that God above!
How dorste> ye seyn> for shame unto your love, *dare / say*
That any thing mightė make yow aferd?> *afraid*
Have ye no mannės herte, and han a berd?> *beard*
Allas! and conne> ye been agast of swevenis?> *can / dreams*
Nothing, God wot, but vanitee,> in sweven is. *emptiness*
Swevenes° engendren> of replecciouns,> *grow / over-eating*

take . . . agrief don't take my groaning amiss
my . . . aright interpret my dream well, i.e. make it be a dream that presages good fortune
wolde . . . deed (ll. 134–35) wanted (i.e. tried) to make seizure of my body and kill me. There is a tinge of legal process about "areste."
housbondes Pertelote describes the sort of husband she approves of in terms of the male ideal of courtly love.
avauntour either a boaster in general, or merely one who boasts of success in love, a crime against the code
Swevenes Learned argument now ensues about the nature, cause, and meaning of Chaunticleer's dream. Pertelote, down-to-earth, wise in practical things, attributes it to indigestion or to a possibly consequent overplus of one of the humors: Chaunticleer has been on the wrong

And ofte of fume,° and of complecciouns,°
Whan humours been to habundant° in a wight.
Certės this dreem, which ye han met tonight,> *dreamed last night*
Cometh of the gretė superfluitee
Of yourė redė colera,° pardee,
Which causeth folk to dreden in here dremes
Of arwes,> and of fyr with redė lemes,> *arrows / flames*
Of gretė bestės, that they wol hem byte,
Of contek,> and of whelpės grete and lyte;° *strife*
Right as the humour of malèncolye°
Causeth ful many a man, in sleep, to crye,
For fere of blakė beres,> or bolės> blake, *bears / bulls*
Or ellės, blakė develės wole hem take.
Of othere humours coude I telle also,
That warken many a man in sleep ful wo;
But I wol passe as lightly> as I can. *rapidly*
  Lo Catoun,° which that was so wys a man,
Seyde he nat thus, ne do no fors° of dremes?
Now, sire,' quod she, 'whan we flee> fro the bemes,> *fly / rafters*
For Goddės love, as tak som laxatyf;
Up> peril of my soule, and of my lyf, *upon*
I counseille yow the beste, I wol nat lye,
That bothe of colere and of malèncolye
Ye purgė yow; and for> ye shul nat tarie, *so that*
Though in this toun is noon apothecarie,
I shal myself to herbės techen> yow, *direct*
That shul ben for your hele,> and for your prow;> *health / advantage*
And in our yerd tho> herbes shal I finde, *these*
The whiche han of hir propretee, by kinde,> *nature*
To purgen yow binethe, and eek above.°
Forget not this, for Goddės owene love!

---

diet. He needs only digestives followed by laxatives. There is danger, but to health only, not to life, and not from some exterior disaster. The dream is a natural dream, rising from his bodily state, not a dream sent from above, or below, to prophesy or deceive; not even a dream rising from a disturbance of the mind or emotions. "Peck it up, there's nothing wrong with you," the verse runs rapidly on. Pertelote's rhetoric is plain and to the point: she is for experience, not authority.

fume exhalation: either the vapor rising to the mind from the decoction or digestion of food and drink in the stomach, hastening the process begun by fermentation in wine or beer; or stomach gas, indigestion; or the vapor rising from one of the four humors, not counteracted by its opposite humors and so disturbing the psychosomatic balance

complecciouns i.e. the individual combinations of bodily fluids or humors (General Prologue, l. 423), of which behavior, temperament, and outward appearance were both the signs and the result

habundant a learned spelling; it was wrongly thought that the word abundant was connected with Latin *habere*, to have

superfluitee . . . colera An excess of the humor of red choler, bile (hot and dry) mixed with blood (hot and moist). Medieval medical authorities such as Arnold of Villanova (13th century) agree with Pertelote's categories of things appearing in the dreams of men so afflicted (see the Wife of Bath's Prologue, l. 587). Choler was the humor of anger, hence the dreams of strife and aggression.

whelpes . . . lyte dogs, big and little

malencolye melancholy, black bile, thought to be secreted in the liver, causing a man to dream fearfully of black, sad, and menacing things

Catoun Dionysius Cato; cf. the Miller's Tale, l. 119

ne . . . fors Attach no importance, take no notice. "Cato's" advice is a Stoic philosopher's. Pertelote quotes only this single elementary authority by name.

To purgen . . . above purging both downward (laxative, aperient) and upward (emetic or snuff-like) to bring your humors into balance; or merely, to clear your stomach and your head

Ye been ful colerik of complecciouǹ.
Warė> the sonne in his ascencioùn *beware lest*
Ne fynde yow nat repleet> of humours hote;° *over-full*
And if it do, I dar wel leye> a grote,° *wager*
That ye shul have a fevere terciane,°
Or an agù,> that may be youre bane.> *ague / death*
A day or two ye shul have digestyves°
Of wormės, er ye take your laxatyves,°
Of lauriol, centaure, and fumėtere,
Or ellės of ellebor, that groweth there,
Of catapuce, or of gaytrės beryis,
Of erbe yvė, growing in our yerd, ther mery is;°
Pekke hem up right as they growe, and ete hem in.
Be mery, housbond, for your fader kin!> *father's lineage*
Dredeth no dreem; I can say yow namore.'
'Madame,' quod he, 'graunt mercy> of your lore.> *thank you / teaching*
But nathėlees, as touching daun Catoun,°
That hath of wisdom such a greet renoun,
Though that he bad no dremės for to drede,
By God, men may in oldė bokės rede
Of many a man, more of auctoritee
Than ever Catoun was, so mote I thee,> *thrive*
That al the rėvers seyn of his sentence,> *opinion*
And han wel founden by experience,
That dremės ben significacioùns,
As wel of joye as tribulacioùns
Thàt folk enduren in this lyf present.
Ther nedeth make of this noon argument;
The verray> prevė> sheweth it in dede. *actual / experience*
Oon of the gretteste auctour° that men rede
Seith thus, that whylom> two felawės wente *formerly*
On pilgrimage, in a ful good entente;
And happėd so, thay come into a toun,
Wheras ther was swich congregacioun
Of peple, and eek so streit of herbergage,°
That they ne founde as muche as o cotage,

humours hote Hot humors (choler and blood) would be super-heated by the sun, especially when it was high in the heavens, so that further imbalance would be caused in a man in whom they were already in dangerous disproportion.
grote an English silver coin, worth only a small sum
terciane a tertian ague or fever, in which the paroxysm recurred on alternate days. Pertelote's diagnosis is medically impeccable.
digestyves Gentler in action than harsh laxatives, they absorb or dissipate bile, whether red or black. In the Middle Ages worms were used in human medicine.
laxatyves Pertelote offers a depth-charge rather than a purge, acting both upward and downward. Laureole causes vomiting, centaury purges the bowels, fumitory the urine; hellebore purges choler downward, catapuce is a general cathartic, and so are gaiter-berries and bitter herb-ivy.
ther mery is where it is agreeable, pleasant
Catoun Chaunticleer despises Pertelote and Master Cato, her one elementary authority, and his rhetoric is grave and stately.
Oon . . . auctour Either the greatest author, or one of the greatest; probably Cicero, one of the great ancient authorities on such matters, who tells the story which follows in his *Of Divination*. Valerius Maximus (see the Wife of Bath's Prologue, l. 648) also has it; Chaucer may have got it from another medieval source.
So . . . herbergage such a shortage of lodgings

In which they bothė mighte yloggėd> be. *lodged*
Wherfor thay mosten,> of necessitee, *must*
As for that night, departen> compaignye; *part*
And ech of hem goth to his hostelrye,
And took his logging as it woldė falle.> *happen*
That oon of hem was loggėd in a stalle,
Fer> in a yerd, with oxen of the plough; *isolated*
That other man was loggėd wel ynough,
As was his aventure,> or his fortune, *luck*
That us governeth alle as in commune.°
 And so bifel, that, longe er it were day,
This man mette> in his bed, theras he lay, *dreamed*
How that his felawe gan upon him calle,
And seyde, "Allas! for in an oxės stalle
This night I shal be mordred> ther I lye. *murdered*
Now help me, derė brother, er I dye;
In allė hastė com to me," he sayde.
This man out of his sleep for fere abrayde;> *leapt*
But whan that he was waknėd of his sleep,
He turnėd him, and took of this no keep;> *notice*
Him thoughte his dreem nas but a vanitee.
Thus twyës in his sleping dremėd he.
And attė thriddė tyme yet his felawe
Cam, as him thoughte, and seide, "I am now slawe;> *slain*
Bihold my blody woundės, depe and wyde!
Arys> up erly in the morwė tyde,> *rise / morning*
And at the west gate of the toun," quod he,
"A cartė ful of donge> ther shaltow see, *dung*
In which my body is hid ful privėly;
Do> thilkė carte aresten> boldėly. *have / stopped*
My gold causėd my mordre, sooth to sayn";
And tolde him every poynt how he was slayn,
With a ful pitous> facė, pale of hewe. *pitiful*
And trustė wel, his dreem he fond> ful trewe; *found*
For on the morwe,> as sone as it was day, *morning*
To his felawės in> he took the way; *lodging*
And whan that he cam to this oxės stalle,
After his felawe he bigan to calle.
 The hostiler> answerėd him anon, *innkeeper*
And seydė, "Sire, your felawe is agon,> *gone*
As sone as day he wente out of the toun."
This man gan fallen in suspecioùn,
Remembring on his dremės that he mette,> *dreamed*
And forth he goth, no lenger wolde he lette,> *stay*
Unto the west gate of the toun, and fond
A dong carte, as it were to dongė> lond, *manure*

That . . . commune that has power over each and every one of us

That was arrayėd˃ in the samė wyse *ordered*
As he han herd the dedė˃ man devyse;˃ *dead / describe*
And with an hardy herte he gan to crye
Vengeaunce and justice of this felonye:—
"My felawe mordrėd is this same night,
And in this carte he lyth˃ gapinge upright.˃ *lies / on his back*
I crye out on the ministres,˃" quod he, *governors*
"That sholden kepe and reulen this citee;
Harrow!˃ allas! her lyth˃ my felawe slayn!" *help / lies*
What sholde I more unto this talė sayn?
The peple out sterte,˃ and caste the cart to grounde, *rushed out*
And in the middel of the dong they founde
The dedė man, that mordred was al newe.˃ *recently*
  O blisful˃ God, that art so just and trewe! *blessed*
Lo, how that thou biwreyest˃ mordre alway! *uncover*
Mordre wol out, that see we day by day.
Mordre is so wlatsom˃ and abhominable° *loathsome*
To God, that is so just and resonable,
That he ne wol nat suffre it helėd˃ be; *hidden*
Though it abyde a yeer, or two, or three,
Mordre wol out, this my conclusioun.
And right anoon, ministrės of that toun
Han hent˃ the carter, and so sore him pyned,˃ *taken / tortured*
And eek the hostiler so sore engyned,˃ *racked*
That thay biknewe˃ hir wikkednesse anoon, *confessed*
And were anhangėd˃ by the nekkė-boon. *hanged*
  Here may men seen that dremės been to drede.˃ *be feared*
And certės, in the samė book° I rede,˃ *read*
Right in the nexte chapìtre after this,
(I gabbė˃ nat, so have I joye or blis,) *babble*
Two men that wolde han passėd over see,
For certeyn cause, into a fer˃ contree, *far*
If that the wind ne hadde been contrarie,
That made hem in a citee for to tarie,
That stood ful mery˃ upon an haven˃ syde. *pleasant / harbor*
But on a day, agayn˃ the eventyde, *toward*
The wind gan chaunge, and blew right as hem leste.°
Jolif˃ and glad they wente unto hir reste, *in good spirits*
And casten˃ hem ful erly for to saille; *intended*
But to that oo˃ man fil˃ a greet mervaille. *one / happened*
That oon of hem, in sleping as he lay,
Him mette a wonder dreem, agayn the day;°
Him thoughte a man stood by his beddės syde,

abhominable The spelling is due to the belief that the word meant inhuman (Latin *ab:* non + *homo:* a man).

same book See l. 218: Cicero, and the other authorities; all have this story, but not in the next chapter.

The . . . leste the wind did change and blew just as they wanted

Him . . . day he dreamed a very strange dream, just before day. Such waking dreams were often thought of as having special importance as prophecies.

And him comaunded, that he sholde abyde,> — *stay*
And seyde him thus, "If thou to-morwe wende,> — *go*
Thou shalt be dreynt;> my tale is at an ende." — *drowned*
He wook, and tolde his felawe what he mette,> — *dreamed*
And preydė him his viage> for to lette;> — *voyage / stop*
As for that day, he preyde him to abyde.
His felawė, that lay by his beddės syde,
Gan for to laughe, and scornėd him ful faste.
"No dreem," quod he, "may so myn herte agaste,> — *frighten*
That I wol lettė> for to do my thinges.> — *delay / business*
I settė not a straw by thy dreminges,
For swevenes been but vanitees and japes.
Men dreme alday> of owlės or of apes,° — *constantly*
And eke of many a masė> therwithal; — *bewilderment*
Men dreme of thing that nevere was ne shal.> — *shall be*
But sith I see that thou wolt heer abyde,
And thus forsleuthen wilfully thy tyde,°
God wot it reweth me;> and have good day." — *makes me sorry*
And thus he took his leve, and wente his way.
But er that he hadde halfe his cours ysayled,
Noot I nat why, ne what mischaunce it ayled,
But casuelly the shippės botmė rente,°
And ship and man under the water wente
In sighte of otherė shippės it byside,
That with hem saylėd at the samė tyde.
And therfor, fairė Pertėlote so dere,
By swiche ensamples° oldė maistow> lere,> — *may you / learn*
That no man sholdė been to recchėlees> — *regardless*
Of dremės, for I sey thee, doutėless,
That many a dreem ful sore is for to drede.
　Lo, in the lyf of Saint Kenelm,° I rede,
That was Kenulphus sone, the noble king
Of Mercenrike,> how Kenelm mette a thing; — *Mercia*
A lyte> er he was mordrėd, on a day, — *little*
His mordrė in his avisioùn> he say.> — *dream / saw*
His norice> him expounėd every del> — *nurse / part*
His sweven, and bad him for to kepe him> wel — *himself*
For> traisoun; but he nas but seven yeer old, — *for fear of*
And therfore litel talė hath he told°

owles . . . apes foolish, absurd things
And thus . . . tyde either: And thus you deliberately miss your chance (or: the tide) for pure idleness; or: And thus you deliberately and idly waste your time
Noot I . . . rente I do not know why, nor what misfortune befell it, but by some accident the ship's bottom split
ensamples *exempla,* examples; the more ancient, the more effective as illustrations
Kenelm The last two dreams that Chaunticleer has told from Cicero are not fully prophetic, nor of the best and most trustworthy sort. He therefore gives examples of true visions, experienced by men who are more his equals. St. Kenelm became king of Mercia at the age of 7, in 821. His high-born innocence was allowed a dream of himself sitting high in a splendid tree, which one of his best friends cut down, whereupon his soul flew to heaven in the form of a bird. This was a true prophecy of his murder on the orders of his aunt.
litel . . . told he took little account

Of any dreem, so holy was his herte.
By God, I haddė lever than my sherte
That ye had rad his legende, as have I.°
Dame Pertėlote, I sey yow trewėly,
Macrobeus, that writ the *Avisioùn*°
In Affrike of the worthy Cipioùn,
Affermeth˃ dremes, and seïth that they been — *confirms*
Warning of thingės that men after seen.
  And forthermore, I pray yow loketh wel
  In the Olde Testament, of Danièl,°
If he held˃ dremės any vanitee. — *considered*
Reed eek of Joseph,° and ther shul ye see
Wher˃ dremės ben somtyme˃ (I sey nat alle) — *whether / sometimes*
Warning of thingės that shul after falle.
Loke of Egipt the king, daun˃ Pharäo,° — *Lord*
His bakere and his botėler˃ also, — *butler*
Wher they ne feltė noon effect in dremes.
Whoso wol seken actes of sondry remes,˃ — *realms*
May rede of dremės many a wonder thing.
  Lo Cresus,° which that was of Lydė king,
Mette he nat that he sat upon a tree,
Which signified he sholde anhangėd˃ be? — *hanged*
Lo heer Andromacha,° Ectorės wyf,
That day that Ector sholdė lese˃ his lyf, — *lose*
She dremėd on the samė night biforn,
How that the lyf of Ector sholde be lorn,˃ — *lost*
If thilkė day he wente into bataille;
She warnėd him, but it mighte nat availle;
He wentė for to fightė nathelees,

I . . . have I I had rather than my shirt; i.e. I'd give my shirt if you had read his life (legend: a saint's life), as I have

Avisioun The *Somnium Scipionis*, the *Dream of Scipio*, or *Avisioun of Cipioun* forms part of Cicero's *On the State* (*De Republica*), which was unknown to the Middle Ages. What they had was the long commentary on the *Dream* (*avisioun* or *visio* was the technical term for a true, prophetic vision experienced by a notable historical person), by Macrobius, written about 400, which was the source of much of the information available to the Middle Ages on the nature of dreams. The story is told of how Scipio Africanus Minor, in Africa, was taken, in his dream, by his grandfather Scipio, the conqueror of Hannibal, up to heaven through the spheres of the universe, and shown a vision of his future as final conqueror of Carthage, as well as how insignificant is worldly glory when compared with strictly virtuous conduct, mortal with immortal. (Cf. the *envoi* to Chaucer's *Troilus and Criseyde*, below.) Macrobius discusses the nature of dreams and, at greater length, the nature of virtue: medieval science and literature used the discussion of dreams a great deal; medieval moral theology used the discussion of the virtues at least as much.

Daniel The Bible, more authoritative still, is now added to the authority of the classics, with a general reference to the prophetic visions described in Daniel 5 ff.

Joseph Genesis 37:5ff.: Joseph's dream of his brothers' sheaves bowing down to him, signifying his future exaltation

Pharäo Genesis 40–41: Joseph's exposition of the dreams of Pharaoh's imprisoned butler and baker, signifying that the first would be restored to favor and the second executed; and of Pharaoh's dream of the seven fat and the seven lean cows, signifying years of plenty and of famine in Egypt.

Cresus Croesus, king of Lydia. Chaucer's version differs from others current: he refers to it more than once.

Andromacha Andromache, Hector's wife; her dream is not in Homer or any ancient "authority" for the Trojan War: it occurs in Dares the Phrygian, a late Latin author whom the Middle Ages believed to be more reliable than Homer in Trojan matters and on whom the medieval Troy romances which Chaucer knew are partly based. Andromache's dream also occurs in these romances.

But he was slayn anoon˃ of Achilles. *at once*
But thilkė tale is al too long to telle,
And eek it is ny day, I may nat dwelle.
Shortly I seye, as for conclusioùn,
That I shal han of this avisioùn°
Adversitee; and I seye forthermore,
That I ne telle of laxatyves no store,°
For they ben venimous,˃ I woot it wel; *poisonous*
I hem defye, I love hem never a del.˃ *bit*
  Now let us speke of mirthe, and stinte˃ al this; *cease*
Madàmė Pertėlote, so have I blis,°
Of o thing God hath sent me largė grace;
For whan I see the beautee of your face,
Ye ben so scarlet reed˃ about your yën,˃ *red / eyes*
It maketh al my dredė for to dyen;˃ *die (down)*
For, also siker as In principio,
Mulier est hominis confusio;°
Madàme, the sentence˃ of this Latin is— *meaning*
Womman is mannės joye and al his blis.
For wan I fele anight your softė syde,
Albeit that I may nat on you ryde,
For that our perche is maad so narwe, alas!
I am so ful of joye and of solas˃ *delight*
That I defye bothė sweven and dreem.'°
And with that word he fley˃ down fro the beem, *flew*
For it was day, and eek his hennės alle;
And with a 'Chuk' he gan hem for to calle,
For he had founde a corn, lay˃ in the yerd. *that lay*
Royal he was, he was namore aferd;˃ *afraid*
He fethered Pertėlote twenty tyme,
And trad as oftė, er that it was pryme.°
He loketh as it were a grim leoùn;
And on his toos he rometh up and doun,
Him deynėd˃ not to sette his foot to grounde. *he deigned*
He chukketh, whan he hath a corn yfounde,
And to him rennen˃ thanne his wyvės alle. *run*
Thus royal, as a prince is in his halle,
Leve I this Chauntėcleer in his pastùre;
And after wol I tell his adventùre.
  Whan that the month in which the world bigan,

Shortly . . . avisioun Chaunticleer insists again that his was a truly prophetic dream: Briefly I say, in conclusion, that I shall have ill-fortune from this divinely-inspired vision.
ne . . . store I set no store whatever by laxatives. The several negatives intensify.
so . . . blis as I hope to go to heaven
For also . . . confusio For, as sure as "In the beginning," woman is the ruination of man. *In principio,* the first words of St. John's Gospel, were thought to possess a special truth. See General Prologue, l. 256.
sweven and dreem A distinction between true visions and mere insignificant dreams may be intended, but Chaucer's usage is not consistent or definite enough to be sure.
He fethered . . . pryme He embraced Pertelote twenty times and screwed her as often, before prime. Prime is the time—see the Miller's Tale, l. 446 above—between 6 a.m. and 9 a.m.

That hightė March, whan God first makėd man,°
Was complet, and ypassed were also,
Sin March bigan, thritty dayes and two,°
Bifel that Chauntėcleer, in al his pryde,
His seven wyvės walking by his syde,
Caste up his eyen to the brightė sonne,
That in the signe of Taurus hadde yronne
Twenty degrees and oon, and somwhat more;
And knew by kynde,> and by noon other lore, *nature*
That it was pryme, and crew with blisful stevene.> *voice*
'The sonne,' he sayde 'is clomben> up on hevene *has climbed*
Fourty degrees and oon, and more, ywis.> *indeed*
Madamė Pertėlote, my worldės blis,
Herkneth thise blisful briddės> how they singe, *birds*
And see the fresshė flourės how they springe;
Ful is myn herte of revel and solas.'
But sodeinly him fil> a sorweful cas;> *befell / chance*
For ever the latter ende of joye is wo.
God woot that worldly joye is sone ago;
And if a rethor° coudė faire endyte,> *write*
He in a cronique saufly> mighte it wryte, *chronicle safely*
As for a sovereyn notabilitee.°
Now every wys man, lat him herkne me;
This storie is also> trewe, I undertake, *as*
As is the book of Launcelot de Lake,°
That wommen holde in ful gret reverence.
Now wol I torne agayn to my sentence.> *purport*
A col-fox,° ful of sly iniquitee,
That in the grove hadde wonėd> yerės three, *lived*
By heigh imaginacioùn forncast,°
The samė night thurghout the heggės brast> *hedges burst*
Into the yerd, ther Chauntėcleer the faire
Was wont, and eek his wyvės, to repaire;
And in a bed of wortės> stille he lay, *vegetables*

whan . . . man The common opinion was that the Creation took place at the spring equinox.
thritty . . . two This may be elaborate rhetorical parody. It is not certain whether we are intended to read April 3 or May 3. May 3 would be appropriate, since it is an unlucky "Egyptian" day (two or three days each month were marked as "evil" or "Egyptian" because of God's plagues on Egypt)—see the Franklin's Tale, l. 198. Chaucer also uses this day in his Knight's Tale, and in *Troilus and Criseyde*. On that day the sun would have passed through about 20° of Taurus, the Bull, the second zodiacal sign. It would be 40° high in the sky, from the horizon, at about 9 a.m.
rethor Rhetorician, i.e. polished writer; Chaucer (or the Nun's Priest) is making a tacit and insincere apology for lack of polish in writing; reinforcing, perhaps, the effect of the elaborate dating and timing just past.
sovereyn notabilitee something worthy of the most careful note—an important *sententia*
Launcelot de Lake The false lover of Queen Guinevere in the popular Arthurian romances (Dante put him into *Inferno*). The Nun's Priest is bringing home his little lesson to the ladies, for whose reading the stories of Lancelot were intended; to them these romances seemed true as well as beautiful. The Priest is also having a little private joke at the ladies' expense.
col-fox a fox with much black fur, or with black markings
forncast Predestined by divine planning. The Nun's Priest shifts to an attempt to reach a more exalted plane: he feels it necessary to argue the matter of whether Chaunticleer's fate was predestined or not; and he becomes the counterweight to Chaunticleer's valuation of his dream.

Til it was passėd undern° of the day,
Wayting> his tyme> on Chauntėcleer to falle, — *watching / opportunity*
As gladly doon thise homicydes alle,
That in awayt liggen to mordre men.°
O false mordrer, lurking in thy den!
O newė Scariot,° newė Genilon!°
False dissimilour,> O Greek Sinon,° — *dissembler*
That broghtest Troye al outrely> to sorwe! — *completely*
O Chauntėcleer, acursėd be that morwe,
That thou into that yerd flough> fro the bemes! — *flew*
Thou were ful wel ywarnėd by thy dremes,
That thilkė day was perilous to thee.
But what that God forwoot mot> nedes be, — *foreknows must*
After> the opinioùn of certeyn clerkis.° — *according to*
Witnesse on him, that any perfit> clerk is, — *perfect*
That in scole is gret altercacioùn
In this matere, and greet disputisoùn,°
And hath ben of an hundred thousand men.
But I ne can not bulte> it to the bren,> — *sift / bran*
As can the holy doctour Augustyn,
Or Boece, or the bishop Bradwardyn,
Whether that Goddės worthy forwiting> — *noble foreknowledge*
Streyneth> me nedely> for to doon a thing, — *constrains / necessarily*
('Nedely' clepe I simple necessitee);
Or ellės, if free choys be graunted me
To do that samė thing, or do it noght,
Though God forwoot> it, er that it was wroght; — *foreknew*
Or if his witing> streyneth nevere a del — *knowledge*
But by necessitee condicionel.°
I wol not han to do of swich matere;

undern literally, the intervening or middle period, of morning or afternoon; here mid-morning
As gladly . . . men as all such murderers usually (or: willingly) do, that lie in ambush to murder men
Scariot The Nun's Priest shifts into top preaching gear, and Chaucer into another mock-heroic mode, with a list of traitors and deceivers, beginning with the worst, Judas Iscariot, betrayer of Christ.
Genilon Ganelon, the traitor who caused the defeat of Charlemagne and the death of Roland in the medieval French epic *The Song of Roland*
Sinon the Greek decoy, who persuaded the Trojans to drag the Wooden Horse into Troy
After . . . clerkis The matter of free-will and predestination, of how much freedom of choice a man can have, given an all-knowing Creator, had been much discussed by Christian philosophers, especially by St. Augustine in his early 5th-century controversy with Pelagius. Augustine takes the side of predestination. Boethius (Boece) the early 6th-century Roman philosopher, whose *Consolation of Philosophy* Chaucer translated, evolved a solution (see below). Thomas Bradwardine, Archbishop of Canterbury, *d.* 1349, came in on the side of Augustine in his *On the Cause of God*, during a renewal of the controversy in the 14th century. The Nun's Priest says modestly that he cannot completely sift out the flour from the husks (bran) and decide who is right and who wrong.
Witnesse . . . disputisoun (ll. 466–68). Any fully educated man can bear witness that in the schools (i.e. philosophical faculties of the universities) there is great argument and dispute on the matter.
condicionel Boethius's solution to the question was to divide necessity, predestination, and God's foreknowledge into two categories, simple and conditional. Strictly speaking, God foreknows everything, so that man has no full and true freedom of choice, but only a limited degree. Men are mortal and must die, by simple necessity. Man has no voice in the matter. But he is not constrained by necessity to walk, though if he does so, he does so necessarily. His necessary walking is conditional on his free choice whether to walk or stay still. See Boethius, *On the Consolation of Philosophy*, Bk. 5.

My tale is of a cok, as ye may here,
That took his counseil of his wyf, with sorwe,°
To walken in the yerd upon that morwe
That he had met> the dreem, that I yow tolde. — *dreamed*
Wommennės counseils> been ful oftė colde;° — *advice*
Wommennės counseil broghte us first to wo,
And made Adam fro Paradys to go,
Ther as he was ful mery,> and wel at ese. — *content*
But for I noot,> to whom it mighte displese, — *know not*
If I counseil of wommen woldė blame,
Passe over, for I seyde it in my game.> — *jest*
Rede auctours, wher they trete of swich matere,
And what thay seyn of wommen ye may here.
Thise been the cokkės wordės, and nat myne;
I can noon harm of no womman divyne.> — *discover*
 Faire in the sond,> to bathe hir merily, — *dust*
Lyth Pertelote, and alle hir sustrės by,
Agayn> the sonne; and Chauntėcleer so free> — *in / noble*
Song merier than the mermayde in the see;
For *Phisiologus*° seith sikerly,> — *certainly*
How that they singen wel and merily.
And so bifel that, as he caste his yë,
Among the wortės, on a boterflye,> — *butterfly*
He was war of this fox that lay ful lowe.
Nothing ne liste him thannė for to crowe,°
But cryde anon, 'Cok, cok,' and up he sterte,> — *leapt*
As man that was affrayėd> in his herte. — *frightened*
For naturelly a beest desyreth flee
Fro his contrarie,° if he may it see,
Though he never erst> had seyn it with his yë. — *before*
 This Chauntėcleer, whan he gan him espye,
He wolde han fled, but that the fox anon
Seyde, 'Gentil sire, allas! wher wol ye gon?
Be ye affrayed of me that am your freend?
Now certės, I were worsė than a feend,
If I to yow wold> harm or vileinye. — *intended*
I am nat come your counseil> for t'espye; — *secrets*
But trewėly, the cause of my cominge
Was only for to herkne how that ye singe.
For trewėly ye have as mery a stevene> — *voice*
As any aungel hath, that is in hevene;

with sorwe sad to say
colde chilly, comfortless
Phisiologus A book, not a man: the *Bestiary*. First written in Greek in Alexandria, 2nd century A.D., it was translated into Latin in the 4th or 5th, and attributed to one Theobaldus. Later, it was translated into the medieval European languages. It consisted of descriptions of real and fabulous creatures, with moralizations (see below). The Mermaids or Sirens, who lure sailors to destruction with the sweetness of their song, represented destructive worldly and fleshly delights.
Nothing . . . crowe he had no desire at all to crow, then
contrarie opposite, natural enemy; every creature was supposed to have an opposite to whom it felt antipathy by nature

Therwith ye han in musik more felinge
Than hadde Boece,° or any that can singe.
My lord your fader (God his soulė blesse!)
And eek your moder, of hir gentilesse,> — *courtesy*
Han in myn hous ybeen, to my gret ese;
And certės, sire, ful fayn> wolde I yow plese. — *gladly*
But for men speke of singing, I wol saye,
So mote I broukė wel° myn eyen tweye,
Save yow, I herdė never man so singe,
As dide your fader in the morweninge;
Certes, it was of> herte, al that he song.> — *from the / sang*
And for to make his voys the morė strong,
He wolde so peyne him, that with bothe his yën
He moste winke,° so loudė he wolde cryen,
And stonden on his tiptoon therwithal,
And strecchė forth his nekkė long and smal.
And eek he was of swich discreciòun,
That ther nas no man in no regiòun
That him in song or wisdom mightė passe.
I have wel rad in *Daun Burnel the Asse,*°
Among his vers, how that ther was a cok,
For that a preestės sone yaf him a knok
Upon his leg, whyl he was yong and nyce,> — *foolish*
He made him for to lese> his benefyce.° — *lose*
But certeyn, ther nis no comparisoùn
Bitwix the wisdom and discrecioùn
Of yourė fader, and of his subtiltee.
Now singeth, sire, for seïnte> charitee, — *sainted*
Let see, conne> ye your fader countrefete>?' — *can / imitate*
This Chauntėcleer his wingės gan to bete,
As man that coude his tresoun> nat espye, — *deceit*
So was he ravisshed with his flaterye.
Allas! ye lordės, many a fals flatour> — *flatterer*
Is in your courtes, and many a losengeour,> — *fawner*
That plesen yow wel morė, by my feith,
Than he that soothfastnesse> unto yow seith. — *truth*
Redeth Ecclesiaste° of flaterye;
Beth war, ye lordės, of hir trecherye.
This Chauntėcleer stood hye upon his toos,
Strecching his nekke, and heeld his eyen cloos,

Therwith . . . Boece Boethius's *On Music* was a standard medieval textbook.
So . . . brouke wel as I may properly enjoy the use of
He wolde . . . winke he would take such pains that he had to close both his eyes
Daun . . . Asse Master Burnellus, the hero of *The Mirror of Fools,* a satirical poem by Nigel Wireker (12th century); a donkey dissatisfied with the length of his tail, he roamed the world looking for a longer one
For that . . . benefyce (ll. 548–50) Because a priest's son gave him a blow on his leg, when he was young and foolish, the cock caused him to lose his benefice by refusing to crow at the proper time and wake the young man on the morning he was to be ordained, so that he was late and missed his chance.
Ecclesiaste Ecclesiasticus 12:10–11, 16: Never trust thine enemy . . . take good heed and beware of him . . .

And gan to crowė loudė for the nones;°
And Daun Russel° the fox sterte up at ones,
And by the gargat hentė> Chauntėcleer. *throat grabbed*
And on his bak toward the wode him beer,> *bore*
For yet ne was ther no man that him sewed.> *pursued*
O destinee, that mayst nat been eschewed!> *escaped*
Allas, that Chauntėcleer fleigh> fro the bemes! *flew*
Allas, his wyf ne roghtė nat° of dremes!
And on a Friday° fil al this meschaunce.
O Venus, that art goddesse of plesaunce,
Sin that thy servant was this Chauntėcleer,
And in thy service dide al his powèr,
More for delyt, than world to multiplye,°
Why woldestow suffre him on thy day° to dye?
O Gaufred,° dere mayster soverayn,
That, whan thy worthy King Richard was slayn
With shot,° compleynedest his deth so sore,
Why ne hadde I now thy sentence> and thy lore,> *wisdom / learning*
The Friday for to chide, as diden ye?
(For on a Friday soothly slayn was he.)
Than wolde I shewe yow how that I coude pleyne> *lament*
For Chauntėclerės drede, and for his peyne.
  Certes, swich cry ne lamentacioùn
Was never of ladies maad, whan Ilioùn> *Troy*
Was wonne, and Pirrus with his streitė swerd,°
Whan he hadde hent King Priam by the berd,
And slayn him (as saith us *Eneydos*),°
As maden alle the hennės in the clos,> *enclosure*
Whan they had seyn> of Chauntėcleer the sighte. *seen*
But sovereynly> Dame Pertėlotė shrighte,> *royally / shrieked*
Ful louder than dide Hasdrubalės° wyf,
Whan that hir housbond haddė lost his lyf,
And that the Romayns haddė brend> Cartage; *burned*
She was so ful of torment and of rage,> *violent grief*
That wilfully into the fyr she sterte,
And brende hirselven with a stedfast herte.

for the nones on this occasion
Daun Russel Master Red
roghte nat cared not for, took no account of
Friday traditionally an unlucky day of the week —and an "Egyptian" day (May 3) as well; see l. 424
More . . . multiplye more for the pleasure than to increase the population
thy day Friday is the day of the planet and goddess Venus; French *vendredi,* Italian *venerdi.*
Gaufred Geoffrey of Vinsauf, a 12th-century rhetorician, whose treatise on Latin poetics, *Poetria Nova,* published soon after the death of Richard I, Coeur-de-Lion, contained, as a model of a lament, verses on the death of that king. Friday is a day of mischance, especially because Richard was killed on it, and its very existence is lamented and scolded. Chaucer, and the Nun's Priest, are again professing weakness as rhetoricians.
shot a missile, actually an arrow
Pirrus . . . swerd Pyrrhus, with his naked (Latin: *stricta*) sword. Pyrrhus was the Greek who killed King Priam of Troy when the Greeks sacked the city.
as . . . Eneydos As Virgil's *Aeneid* tells us (II.550–53). Chaucer may have taken his references to Troy, Carthage, and Rome from Geoffrey's treatise cited above.
Hasdrubales See the Franklin's Tale, ll. 691 ff; this Hasdrubal was not Hannibal's brother, but the King of Carthage who committed suicide when his city was burned by the Romans in 146 B.C.

O woful hennės, right so cryden ye,
As, whan that Nero° brendė the citee
Of Romė, cryden senatourės wyves,
For that hir housbondes losten alle hir lyves;
Withouten gilt this Nero hath hem slayn.
Now wol I tornė to my tale agayn.
  This sely> widwe, and eek hir doghtres two, *poor*
Herden thise hennės crye and maken wo,
And out at dorės sterten> they anoon, *rushed*
And syen> the fox toward the grovė goon, *saw*
And bar upon his bak the cok away;
And cryden, 'Out! Harrow!> and weylaway! *help*
Ha, ha, the fox!' and after him they ran,
And eek with stavės many another man;
Ran Colle° our dogge, and Talbot, and Gerland,°
And Malkin,° with a distaf in hir hand;
Ran cow and calf, and eek the verray hogges
So were they fered> for berking of the dogges *afraid*
And shouting of the men and wimmen eke,
They ronnė> so, hem thoughte hir hertė breke.> *ran / would burst*
They yellėden as feendės> doon in helle; *devils*
The dokės> cryden as men wolde hem quelle;> *ducks / kill*
The gees for ferė flowen> over the trees; *flew*
Out of the hyvė cam the swarm of bees;
So hidous was the noyse, a! Benedicitė!
Certės,> he Jakkė Straw,° and his meynee,> *surely / company*
Ne madė never shoutės half so shrille,
Whan that they wolden any Fleming kille,
As thilkė day was maad upon the fox.
Of bras thay broghten bemės,> and of box,> *trumpets / boxwood*
Of horn, of boon,> in whiche they blewe and pouped,> *bone / tooted*
And therwithal thay shrykėd> and they houped;> *shrieked / whooped*
It semėd as that heven sholdė falle.
Now, godė men, I pray yow herkneth alle!
  Lo, how fortune turneth> sodeinly *overturns*
The hope and pryde eek of hir enemy!
This cok, that lay upon the foxes bak,
In al his drede, unto the fox he spak,
And seydė, 'Sire, if that I were as ye,

Nero Nero, wishing to re-enact the burning of Troy, set fire to Rome in 64 A.D. and enjoyed the laments that he heard from the dying and the survivors of all classes. He had previously put to death many innocent patricians.
Colle a common dog's name
Talbot, and Gerland two other dogs, or perhaps two men
Malkin traditional name for a maidservant
Jakke Straw One of the leaders of the Peasants' Revolt of 1381. Foreigners working and trading in London were commonly held to be doing native Englishmen out of their jobs and were therefore attacked. The Flemings were mainly cloth-workers (see the General Prologue, l. 450), and many were killed "with the usual row"—as a contemporary chronicler puts it. "Meynee" often has the sense of rabble. The Nun's Priest is bringing the noise and strife of his story close home to his hearers.

Yet sholde I seyn (as wis God helpė me°):
"Turneth agayn, ye proudė cherlės alle!
A verray pestilence upon yow falle!
Now am I come unto this wodės syde,
Maugree your heed,° the cok shal heer abyde;
I wol him ete, in feith, and that anon."'
The fox answerde, 'In feith, it shal be don;'
And as he spak that word, al sodeinly
This cok brak from his mouth deliverly,> *nimbly*
And heighe upon a tree he fleigh anon.
And whan the fox saugh that he was ygon,
'Allas!' quod he, 'O Chauntėcleer, allas!
I have to yow,' quod he, 'ydoon trespas,
Inasmuche as I makėd yow aferd,
Whan I yow hente, and broghte out of the yerd;
But, sire, I dide it in no wikke> entente; *evil*
Com doun, and I shal telle yow what I mente.
I shal seye sooth to yow, God help me so.'
'Nay than,' quod he, 'I shrewe> us bothė two, *curse*
And first I shrewe myself, bothe blood and bones,
If thou bigylė me ofter than ones.
Thou shalt namore, thurgh thy flaterye,
Do> me to singe and winkė with myn yë. *cause*
For he that winketh, whan he sholdė see,
Al wilfully, God lat him never thee>!' *thrive*
'Nay,' quod the fox, 'but God yeve him meschaunce,
That is so undiscreet of governaunce,> *self-control*
That jangleth> whan he sholdė holde his pees.' *babbles*
Lo, swich it is for to be recchėlees,> *reckless*
And necligent, and truste on flaterye.
But ye that holden this tale a folye,
As of a fox, or of a cok and hen,
Taketh the moralitee,° good men.
For Saint Paul° seith, that al that writen is,
To our doctryne it is ywrite, ywis.
Taketh the fruyt, and lat the chaf be stille.
Now, godė God, if that it be thy wille,
As seith my Lord,° so make us alle good men;
And bringe us to his heighė blisse. Amen.

Here is ended the Nonne Preestes Tale.

as wis . . . me as surely as God may help me.
Maugree your heed in spite of your head; for anything you can do about it
moralitee Morality, lesson. The Nun's Priest winds up in a little confusion, but makes his point: this tale has a lesson for us all.
Saint Paul Romans 15:4: "For whatsoever things were written aforetime were written for our learning that we through patience and comfort of the scriptures might have hope." The Nun's Priest stops to drive home the moral lesson, turning his story into a sermon.
Lord i.e. Christ

Two Cock-and-Fox Stories

Here are two stories, one heavily moralizing the habits of the cock and the fox, one telling the story of Chaunticleer and Reynard as part of a long series of the fox's tricks and adventures.

The first, from the *Bestiary* (*Physiologus,* see l. 505n above), paints the kind of *moralitee* that the Nun's Priest would expect his hearers to have at the back of their minds. Such *exempla,* illustrative stories, were much used by preachers. Our text is a free modern version of a fifteenth-century Latin translation.

The second is from Caxton's translation from the Dutch in his *Reynard the Fox,* printed in 1481, which goes back ultimately to the French *Roman de Renart* (late twelfth century). There are more than forty such tales in Caxton's book. Caxton still moralizes the story, but he gives it none of Chaucer's wit and spirit; his public wanted stories and stories alone. The fox as a sham cleric was a regular feature of Reynard literature.

The text, based on the edition of 1481, is modernized in spelling and punctuation.

From The Bestiary—

Of the Fox

The nature or characteristic of the fox is as follows. The fox is an animal with a heart full of tricks and deceptions; for when it wishes to catch rooks and crows it stretches itself out on the ground and closes its eyes as if it had been lying dead for many days. The rooks and crows, greedy to dine off the corpse, come and begin to tear at it. Then the fox, quickly jumping up, seizes them and gobbles them up.

Morality In the fox we see the Devil, full of guile, who deceives sinners as the fox deceives birds like rooks and crows. The Devil cannot deceive good, honest, and holy men because they are clothed in the righteousness of virtue. . . .

Of the Cock

The nature or characteristic of the cock is that the more the night approaches, the louder it crows; and when day approaches, it sings more often.

Morality We should imitate its character, and the nearer the night approaches with its perils and doubts and with the Devil at hand, we should sing loudly and devoutly, asking the aid of God to defend us from all perils; and when the dawn is near, we should pray to God as often as we can. . . .

Another characteristic of the cock is that when it wishes to crow, it strikes itself with its wings three times beforehand.

Morality This shows that a man ought to beat himself on the breast for the blame of his sins and offenses before praying, so that he can sing better and more righteously his praises of God. . . .

From William Caxton's The History of Reynard the Fox

How the Cock Complained on Reynard

Chanticleer came forth and smote piteously his hands and his feathers; and on each side of the bier went twain sorrowful hens. That one was called Cantart and that other good hen, Crayant; they were two the fairest hens that were between

Holland[1] and Ardennes. These hens bare each of them a burning taper which was long and strait.[2] These two hens were Coppen's sisters, and they cried so piteously, 'Alas and weleaway!'[3] for the death of their dear sister Coppen. Two young hens bare the bier, which cackled so heavily[4] and wept so loud for the death of Coppen their mother, that it was far heard. Thus came they together before the King.

And Chanticleer then said, 'Merciful lord, my lord the King, please it you to hear our complaint and abhor the great scathe[5] that Reynard hath done to me and my children that here stand. It was so that in the beginning of April, when the weather is fair, as that I was hardy[6] and proud because of the great lineage that I am come of, and also had.[7] For I had eight fair sons and seven fair daughters which my wife had hatched, and they were all strong and fat and went in a yard which was walled round about, in which was a shed wherein were six great dogs which had totore[8] and plucked many a beast's skin in such wise as my children were not afraid. On whom Reynard the Thief had great envy because they were so secure that he could none get of them. How well oft-times hath this fell[9] thief gone round about this wall and hath laid for us in such wise that the dogs have been set on him and have hunted him away. And once they leapt on him upon the bank, and that cost him somewhat for his theft. I saw that his skin smoked.[10] Nevertheless, he went his way.[11] God amend it![12]

'Thus were we quit of Reynard a long while. At last came he in likeness of an hermit,[13] and brought to me a letter for to read, sealed with the King's seal, in which stood written that the King had made peace over all in his realm, and that all manner beasts and fowls should do none harm nor scathe to one another. Yet said he to me more, that he was a cloisterer or a closed recluse[14] become, and that he would receive great penance for his sins. He showed me his slavin and pilch and an hair shirt thereunder;[15] and then said he, "Sir Chanticleer, after this time be no more afraid of me nor take no heed, for I

1. The northern coastal country, not the United Netherlands now called Holland, and the Ardennes, in the southern Netherlands; thus, from north to south, anywhere.
2. Slender.
3. Happiness is gone, alas!
4. Sorrowfully.
5. Harm.
6. Bold.
7. The great lineage that I am sprung from and that is sprung from me.
8. Torn to pieces.
9. Fierce.
10. I saw the dust rise from his skin.
11. He got away.
12. God see that things go better next time.
13. In the guise of a hermit.
14. Both words mean a member of a monastic order, prevented by religious vows from leaving the monastery or receiving visitors, except by special dispensation.
15. A slavin was a pilgrim's mantle; a pilch, originally an outer garment of dressed skin with the hair still on it, but later merely of leather or coarse wool. The hair shirt, which was woven of animal hair, was worn next to the skin by penitents and religious to mortify the flesh. There is a sort of joke here at Chanticleer's gullibility: Reynard's innermost shirt would naturally be of hair.

now will eat no more flesh.[16] I am forthon so old that I would fain remember my soul.[17] I will now go forth, for I have yet to say my sext, none, and mine evensong.[18] To God, I betake[19] you." Then went Reynard thence, saying his Credo;[20] and laid him under an hawthorn.

'Then I was glad and merry, and also took no heed, and went to my children and clucked them together, and went without the wall for to walk, whereof is much harm come to us. For Reynard lay under a bush and came creeping between us and the gate, so that he caught one of my children and laid him in his male.[21] Whereof we have great harm; for since he hath tasted of him there might never hunter nor hound save nor keep him from us. He hath waited by night and day in such wise that he hath stolen so many of my children that of fifteen I have but four; in such wise hath this thief forslongen[22] them. And yet yesterday was Coppen my daughter, that here lieth upon the bier, with the hounds rescued. This complain I to you, gracious King; have pity on my great and unreasonable damage and loss of my fair children!'

1481

The Wife of Bath's Prologue and Tale

The Wife of Bath's horoscope, as she herself states it in her Prologue, gives astrological clues to her character that would have been recognized by Chaucer's contemporaries. Her zodiacal sign is Taurus, one of the "mansions" of the planet Venus, the love star. Taurus was just rising above the horizon when the Wife was born but, most unfortunately, Mars, the warlike planet, was in conjunction with Venus at the same time. The sign just rising above the eastern horizon, the ascendant, was held to govern a nativity; and if only Venus had been alone in Taurus, the Wife would have been everything that was gentle, playful, loving, slim, and beautiful. But the effect of Mars turned gentleness to fierceness, play to aggression, love to insatiability, and slim, blonde beauty to heavier, fleshier, darker charms. The Wife is thus still an attractive woman, but more of a handful (Fig. 29).

All this we should have been led to expect, too, from her description in the General Prologue—her proud behavior, her confident skill in her trade, her roving eye—all add to and help to round out the picture into what has always been rightly thought one of Chaucer's most lifelike characters. But she also, like the Prioress, has a literary prototype in the *Roman de la Rose:* the Duenna, protectress, imparter of the secrets of catching men, and ironic commentator.

16. That is, I will make the religious observance of fasting by eating no meat.
17. Moreover, so old that I wish to be mindful of my soul.
18. The meeting must have taken place in the forenoon, since the canonical hours mentioned begin at noon. The recitation of the Divine Office, as contained in the Breviary, was (and is) obligatory for anyone in major orders in the Catholic Church. The office of sext was recited at the sixth hour (noon) after prime (the first hour, 6 a.m.); nones at the ninth (3 p.m.) and evensong (vespers) shortly before sunset.
19. Commend.
20. Creed, from the opening words *Credo in unum Deum* ("I believe in God"), the confession of faith; part of the mass. Reynard repeats it as an act of pretended devotion.
21. Bag.
22. Swallowed down.

It is characteristic of the Wife that, when her turn comes to tell a tale, she prefaces it with a great comic account of her life and marryings, dealing first with the question of whether her own successive experiences of marriage can be justified from Scripture —and in the eyes of the church and of society. Her experience falls foul of the authority of St. Jerome (c. 342–420), the most famous and influential representative of the tradition which, beginning in the unquestioning acceptance of male superiority in pre-classical societies, passes into Greek and Roman thought as explicit anti-feminism. *The Golden Book of Marriage* is attributed to Theophrastus (c. 372–287 B.C.), the pupil of Aristotle, but we know of it only from its use by later Christian writers, who drew on it for ammunition. They also drew—and so perhaps did Chaucer—on the savage sixth satire of the Roman poet Juvenal (c. 60–140 A.D.) directed against women. But it was the Fathers of the Christian Church, especially St. Jerome, who saw in the biblical account of Eden and its loss the first example of man brought to destruction by woman. Justification of their attitude was found in the pagan philosophy in which they had been educated, and the dispraise of women became the subject of works designed to encourage male and female chastity. The Fathers' great Christian weapon was St. Paul's First Epistle to the Corinthians, chapter 7, which figures largely in the Wife's Prologue. St. Jerome's tract, *Adversus Jovinianum* (Against Jovinian), written about A.D. 400, is the most comprehensive and influential statement of the anti-feminist case. Jovinian, a monk, had ventured to suggest that fasting and chastity were not necessarily higher states than reasonable indulgence in food, drink, and sex. Jerome refuted him with authorities, eloquence, and abuse. Jerome's tract was, however, only the beginning of a long tradition of Christian anti-feminist literature which Chaucer uses in the Wife's Prologue.

In presenting all this, Chaucer is operating in his accustomed mode of transformation. The Wife, we feel, has made out her case for successive remarriages with the brand of defiance that is conscious of running counter to social and religious pressures, hinting that part of her excuse must be that she is Venerian by temperament. Then, as the anti-feminist stories begin to flow and she warms to the description of her fifth husband, Jankin, and his little ways, her stature as Chaucer's character grows. Our sympathy for her as a representative of slandered womanhood increases. In the end, she stands unharmed by the whole tide of it. She is life itself, ready for another husband, or whatever the future has in store.

The tale that Chaucer gives her to tell is a version of the ancient and widely diffused folk-tale of the Loathly Lady: the repulsive hag, whom a vow or an obligation forces a young man to accept as his wife. The lady has received her ill-favored shape by enchantment and must keep it until true courtesy frees her from it; in some versions she has assumed it as a matter of choice. In each case, the true perceptions and the courtesy of the man who has somehow, wittingly or unwittingly, put himself in her power are tested. He has to show either that he is not led astray by outward unattractiveness, or that his obligation of noble behavior toward women is fulfilled, before the happy ending to the tale can ensue.

At least one other version of the story was current in Chaucer's day. This was the tale of Florent in the first book of John Gower's *Confessio Amantis* (Lover's Confession). It is also probable that more versions of it were available, such as those in the ballad *The Marriage of Sir Gawain* and the poem *The Wedding of Sir Gawain and Dame Ragnell*. The versions involving Sir Gawain turn on his knightly perfection. In accepting the loathly bride, he demonstrates his true nobility, holding to the obligation that courtesy has conferred on him. "He wolde algate his trowthe holde"—he wanted in all ways to keep faith—as the ballad puts it.

None of these versions, including Chaucer's, is derived from the other, yet all are clearly interrelated, in spite of minor differences. Chaucer's tale, in the Wife's mouth, becomes an *exemplum* of her view of what the marital situation should be, and what it is unlikely to be in male-dominated society without active intervention by women themselves. As the Wife tells it, the story illustrates the validity of the admission she has exhorted from her husband in her Prologue: "Myn owene trewe wyf, / Do as thee lust the terme of al thy lyf." The hero of the story, instead of being King Arthur, or Gawain, the flower of courtesy, is a rogue, who has to solve a riddle in order to exculpate himself from a rape. Having put himself into the Loathly Lady's power, in order to answer the Queen's riddle, he must acknowledge the superiority of the woman. To the Wife this is all quite plain and as it should be; there is no suggestion, as there is in the Gawain poems, that sovereignty is yielded out of *gentilesse,* in accordance with the subtler modes of another female retort to male domination: the code of courtly love (see Glossary). The terms of the choice offered the knight have been slanted by Chaucer to fit the wife's character; they emphasize the nature of the submission that any man—even in an illustrative fiction—must make if he comes within her orbit. This knight is not offered the plain choice between beauty and ugliness: he must choose rather between a mate who is ugly but faithful and one who is beautiful and unfaithful. Things turn out fairly well for him in the end: he yields his authority to her, but his wife is both beautiful and obedient. She is the correlative of the discussion of *gentilesse.* In the overriding fiction of the *Tales,* however, the Wife has the last word, in her final prayer for young, vigorous husbands—and for mastery over them. Her Prologue and this final prayer for men apt to be mastered bracket her tale and give it its predominant tinge, so well suited to the teller, of feminine militancy in the face of male provocation. The final prayer lowers the level on which the nature of nobility is so high-mindedly discussed in the tale—but this does not mean that Chaucer does not intend the discussion to be taken seriously.

At the end of the Wife of Bath's Tale, there is added, by the editor, an example of another use than Chaucer's of one of the Wife's fifth husband's favorite stories (Prologue, ll. 763–70). It is a modern English translation of a fifteenth-century story from the *Gesta Romanorum* (Deeds of the Romans), with its moralization given in a summary form. The *Gesta Romanorum* is a collection of tales, perhaps composed in Franciscan circles, for use by preachers and others. It may be of English origin and was probably first put together about 1300.

This particular short tale is chosen as an illustration of how, given the firm intention of moralizing in a certain direction, any story can be turned into an allegory. The corollary of this is that we cannot say of any allegorical interpretation that it is impossible: someone, at some time, may have used it. Medieval allegory did not, of course, always function in such a crude and *ad hoc* fashion: it drew on a long and rich tradition of the allegorization of Scripture. But if we wish to see allegorical meanings in the *Tales,* we must carefully distinguish between the possible and the likely and bear in mind the complication of the fictional mode of the *Tales,* placed as they are in the mouths of so many different tellers.

Prologue

The Prologe of the Wyves Tale of Bathe

Experience, though noon auctoritee°
Were in this world, is right ynough for me
To speke of wo that is in mariàge;
For, lordinges,> sith I twelve yeer was of age, *ladies and gentlemen*
Thonkėd be God that is eterne on lyve,> *alive*
Housbondes at chirchėdore° I have had fyve;
(For I so oftė have ywedded be);
And alle were worthy men in hir degree.> *rank*
But me was told certeyn, nat longe agon> is, *ago*
That sith> that Crist ne wente nevėr but onis> *since / once*
To wedding, in the Cane° of Galilee,
That by the same ensample> taughte he me *example*
That I ne sholdė wedded be but ones.
Herkne eek,> lo! which> a sharp word for the nones° *also / what*
Besyde a welle> Jesus, God and man, *well*
Spak in repreve> of the Samaritan:° *reproof*
'Thou hast yhad fyve housbondės,' quod he,
'And thilkė> man, the which that hath now thee, *the same*
Is noght thyn housbond;' thus seyde he certeyn.
What that he mente therby, I can nat seyn;
But that I axe,> why that the fifthė man *ask*
Was noon housbond to the Samaritan?
How manye mighte she have in mariàge?
Yet herde I never tellen in myn age
Upon this nombre diffinicioùn;°
Men may devyne> and glosen> up and doun. *guess / interpret*
But wel I woot expres,> withoutė lye, *know expressly*
God bad us for to wexe° and multiplye;
That gentil> text can I wel understonde. *noble*
Eek wel I woot he seÿde, myn housbonde
Sholde lete> fader and moder, and take me;° *leave*
But of no nombre mencion made he,
Of bigamye or of octogamye;°

Experience . . . auctoritee The Wife begins by making her position clear. A good plain woman, she sets herself against contemporary respect for learning. She will use no book-learning, no citations of authorities, to make her case. In the event she quotes much of it, though she finally answers it by an act of violence.
chirchedore See the General Prologue, l. 460; the wedding ceremony was performed outside the church door, in public, after which nuptial mass was celebrated within the church.
Cane Cana, in Galilee, where the miracle of water into wine was performed (John 2:1ff.). The question of whether a woman could marry more than once was much discussed.
for the nones for the nonce, on the occasion, to the purpose—but a conventional formula, with little meaning
Samaritan John 4:16 ff. Jesus's retort to the Samaritan woman at the well was that she had had five husbands, but that her sixth man was not her husband. The passage was often cited in such discussions. The Wife adapts it slightly to her own case: she has had five husbands—but not yet six.
diffinicioun definition, but also carrying the sense of finite number, limit; neither five nor any other number has been laid down
wexe increase; Genesis 1:28: "Be fruitful and multiply and replenish the earth."
Sholde . . . take me Matthew 19:5
octogamye Chaucer took the word from St. Jerome. Here, bigamy and octogamy mean two and eight successive, not simultaneous, marriages.

Why sholdė men speke of it vileinye?> *evil*
 Lo, here the wysė king, dan° Salomon;
I trowe he haddė wyvės mo than oon.
As woldė God it leveful were to me
To be refresshėd half so ofte as he!°
Which yifte° of God hadde he for alle his wyvis!
No man hath swich,> that in this world alyve is. *such*
God woot, this noble king, as to my wit,> *knowledge*
The firstė night had many a mery fit> *bout*
With ech of hem, so wel was him on lyve!°
Blessed be God that I have wedded fyve
Of whiche I havė pykėd out the beste,°
Both of here nether> purs and of here cheste.> *lower / coffer*
Diversė scolės maken parfyt clerkes:> *perfect learned men*
And diverse practyk° in many sondry werkes
Maketh the werkman parfit sikerly;> *surely*
Of five husbondės scoleying> am I. *schooling*
Welcome the sixte, whan that ever he shal.°
Forsothe,> I wol nat kepe me chaste in al; *in truth*
Whan myn housbond is fro the world ygon,
Som Cristen man shal weddė me anon;
For thanne, th'Apostle° seith, that I am free
To wedde, a Goddes half, wher it lyketh> me. *it pleases*
He seith that to be wedded is no sinne;
Bet> is to be wedded than to brinne.> *better / burn*
What rekketh me,> thogh folk seye vileinye *do I care*
Of shrewėd> Lamech° and his bigamye? *cursed*
I woot> wel Abraham was an holy man, *know*
And Jacob eek, as ferforth as I can;°
And ech of hem hadde wyvės mo than two;
And many another holy man also.
 When saugh> ye ever, in any maner age, *saw*
That hyė God defended> marïage *forbade*
By expres word? I pray you, telleth me;
Or wher comanded he virginitee?
I woot as wel as ye, it is no drede,> *doubt*

dan Latin, *dominus,* master: Lord Solomon; he had 700 wives, besides 300 concubines (I Kings 11:3)
As wolde . . . he (ll. 37–38) Would to God it were permitted to me to take recreation half as often as he!
Which yifte what a gift
so wel . . . lyve such a happy life he led
beste I have picked out the best both in their balls and their bank balance; or perhaps: I have drawn out all their substance from either of these places
practyk practice, practical work
whan . . . shal whenever he shall turn up
th'Apostle St. Paul: I Corinthians 7:39 ("The wife is bound by the law as long as her husband liveth; but if her husband be dead, she is at liberty to be married to whom she will; only in the Lord"); *Bet is . . . brinne* I Corinthians 7:8–9 ("I say therefore to the unmarried and widows . . . if they cannot contain, let them marry: for it is better to marry than to burn").
Lamech Genesis 4:19–24; great-great-grandson of Cain. Lamech was a murderer and the first man to divide one flesh between two wives. The Wife is careful of the example of this villain; she prefers to invoke the example of the virtuous patriarchs Abraham and Jacob, both polygamists, but not—at least—murderers.
ferforth . . . can as far as I know

Th'Apostel,° whan he speketh of maydenhede;˃ *virginity*
He seyde, that precept therof hadde he noon.
Men may conseille a womman to been oon,˃ *single*
But conseilling is no comandėment;
He putte it in our owene jugėment.
For haddė God comanded maydenhede,
Thanne hadde he dampnėd˃ wedding with the dede;° *condemned*
And certės,˃ if ther were no seed ysowe,° *certainly*
Virginitee, wherof than sholde it growe?
Paul dorstė nat comanden attė˃ leste *at the*
A thing of which his maister yaf˃ noon heste.˃ *gave / command*
The dart° is set up for virginitee;
Cacche who so may, who renneth˃ best lat see. *runs*
  But this word is nat take of° every wight,
But ther˃ as God list˃ give it of his might. *where / it pleases*
I woot wel, that th'Apostel was a mayde;˃ *virgin*
But natheless, thogh that he wroot and sayde,°
He wolde˃ that every wight were swich˃ as he,° *wished / such*
Al nis but conseil to virginitee;
And for to been a wyf, he yaf me leve
Of indulgence;° so it is no repreve˃ *reproof*
To weddė me,° if that my makė˃ dye— *mate*
Withoute excepcioùn of bigamye°—
Al were it good no womman for to touche°
(He mente as in his bed or in his couche,
For peril is bothe fyr˃ and tow˃ t'assemble— *fire / flax*
Ye knowe what this ensample may resemble°).
This is al and som,° he heeld virginitee
More parfit than wedding in frelėtee.°
Freletee clepe˃ I, but if˃ that he and she *call (it) / unless*
Wolde leden al hir lyf in chastitee.
  I graunte it wel, I havė noon envye,
Thogh maydenhedė prèferre bigamye;˃ *surpass remarriage*
Hem lyketh˃ to be clene in body and goost,˃ *pleases / spirit*
Of myn estaat˃ I nil nat make no boost. *condition*

th'Apostel St. Paul: I Corinthians 7:25 ("Now concerning virgins, I have no commandment of the Lord"). The recommendation of virginity and the institution of monasticism rest on the tradition of the church, not on Scripture—but the church holds that its tradition is of equal authority.
with . . . dede when he did (the other); at the same time
if ther . . . ysowe if no seed were sown; the argument is used by St. Jerome
dart spear, apparently as a prize in a race, perhaps "set up" for the winner to take (*cacche*) at the finish line. Chaucer is translating St. Jerome, and perhaps making a sexual pun.
take of received, understood by
wroot and sayde wrote and said. This sort of meaningless doublet, perhaps the survival of an oral formula, is a favorite with Chaucer's successors.
He . . . he I Corinthians 7:7 ("For I would that all men were even as myself [i.e. chaste]")
indulgence I Corinthians 7:6 ("I speak this by [your] permission [indulgence], not of commandment")
wedde me marry me. The verb is still reflexive; I Corinthians 7:39 again.
Withoute . . . bigamye so that no exception can be taken to my second marriage
touche I Corinthians 7:1
Ye . . . resemble you know what this figure means
al and som the sum total of it
in freletee for the frailty of our humanity

For wel ye knowe, a lord in his houshold,
He hath nat every vessel al of gold;
Somme been of tree,> and doon hir lord servyse. *wood*
God clepeth> folk to him in sondry wyse, *calls*
And everich hath of God a propre yifte,°
Som> this, som that—as him lyketh shifte.> *one / command*
  Virginitee is greet perfeccioùn,
And continence eek with devocioùn.
But Crist, that of perfeccioùn is welle,> *fountain-head*
Bad nat every wight he sholde go selle
All that he hadde, and give it to the pore,
And in swich wyse folwe him and his fore.°
He spak to hem that wolde live parfitly;> *perfectly*
And lordinges, by your leve, that am nat I.
I wol bistowe the flour of al myn age
In the actės and in fruit of marïage.
  Telle me also, to what conclusioùn> *end*
Were membres maad> of generacioùn, *made*
And of so parfit wis a wright ywroght?°
Trusteth right wel, they wer nat maad for noght.
Glose> whoso wole, and seye bothe up and doun, *comment*
That they were makėd for purgacioùn> *purging*
Of urine, and our bothė thingės smale> *narrow*
Were eek to knowe a femele from a male,
And for noon other causė: sey ye no?
The experience woot wel it is noght so.
So that the clerkės be nat with me wrothe,
I sey this, that they makėd been for bothe,
This is to seye, for office,° and for ese
Of engendrure, ther> we nat God displese. *procreation where*
Why sholde men ellės in hir bokės sette,
That man shal yeldė> to his wyf hir dette? *pay*
Now wherwith sholde he make his payėment,
If he ne used his sely° instrument?
Than were they maad, upon> a creätùre, *in*
To purge uryne, and eek for engendrùre.
  But I seye noght that every wight is holde,> *bound*
That hath swich harneys> as I to yow tolde, *tackle*
To goon and usen hem in engendrùre;
Than sholde men take of chastitee no cure.> *care*
Crist was a mayde,> and shapen as a man, *virgin*
And many a saint, sith that the world bigan:
Yet lived they ever in parfit chastitee.

propre yifte a gift of his own; his individual bent: I Corinthians 7:7
fore track, footsteps. Matthew 19:21 is the source for ll. 114–16.
And of . . . ywroght One reading would give here: And for what purpose was a creature made. The sense of the reading adopted—and so perfectly wise a Maker made—translates St. Jerome.
office might mean urinating, but more frequently means excretion; the sense here is more general: for natural functions
sely little, innocent

I nil envyė no virginitee;
Lat hem be breed> of purėd> whetė seed, *bread / refined*
And lat us wyvės hoten> barly breed; *be called*
And yet with barly breed, Mark° tellė can,
Our Lord Jesu refresshėd many a man.
In swich estaat as God hath clepėd° us
I wol persèvere, I nam nat precious.> *choosy*
In wyfhode> I wol use myn instrument *wifehood*
As frely> as my Maker hath it sent. *liberally*
If I be daungerous,° God yeve> me sorwe! *give*
Myn housbond shal it have bothe eve and morwe,> *morning*
Whan that him list> com forth and paye his dette. *it pleases him*
An housbonde I wol have, I nil nat° lette,
Which shal be bothe my dettour> and my thral,> *debtor / slave*
And have his tribulatioùn withal°
Upon his flessh, whyl that I am his wyf.
I have the power duringe al my lyf
Upon his propre> body, and noght he.° *own*
Right thus the Apostel tolde° it unto me;
And bad our housbondes for to love us weel.
Al this sentence> me lyketh every deel.> *matter / every part*
Up sterte> the Pardoner, and that anon,> *started / at once*
'Now dame,' quod> he, 'by God and by Saint John, *said*
Ye been a noble prechour in this cas!
I was aboute to wedde a wyf; allas!
What> sholde I bye it on my flesh so dere? *why*
Yet hadde I lever> wedde no wyf to-yere!'° *rather*
'Abyde!' quod she, 'my tale is nat bigonne;
Nay, thou shalt drinken of another tonne> *barrel*
Er that I go, shal savoure> wors than ale. *taste*
And whan that I have told thee forth my tale
Of tribulacioùn in marïage,
Of which I am expert in al myn age,
This to seyn, myself have been the whippe;
Than maystow chese> whether thou wolt sippe *choose*
Of thilkė tonne> that I shal abroche.> *barrel / broach*
Bewar of it, er thou too ny> approache; *near*
For I shal telle ensamples mo than ten.
Whoso that nil> be war by otherė men, *will not*
By him shul otherė men corrected be.
The samė wordės wryteth Ptholomee;°

Mark miracle of the loaves and fishes, when about 5000 were fed with five loaves. Mark (8:5) does not say that they were barley-loaves; John (6:9) does.
cleped called; see I Corinthians 7:20
daungerous careful, difficult of access
nil nat will not; double negative, intensifying
withal moreover; see I Corinthians 7:28
I have . . . he I Corinthians 7:4
tolde Ephesians 5:25
to-yere literally, this year, but meaning next year, sometime, never
Ptholomee Claudius Ptolemy, the most influential ancient astronomer, an Alexandrian Greek of the 2nd century A.D. whose chief work is the *Almagest*. This proverb does not appear in it, but is included in a collection of sayings attributed to him in the Middle Ages.

Rede in his *Almageste*, and take it there.’
‘Dame, I wolde praye yow, if your wil it were,’
Seyde this Pardoner, ‘as ye bigan,
Telle forth your talė, spareth for no man,
And teche us yongė men of your praktike.’› *practice*
‘Gladly,’ quod she, ‘sith it may yow lyke.› *please*
But yet I praye to al this companye,
If that I speke after my fantasye,°
As taketh not agrief› of that I seye; *offense*
For myn ententė nis but for to pleye.› *divert*
Now sires, now wol I tellė forth my tale.
As ever mote I drinken wyn or ale,
I shal seye sooth, tho› housbondes that I hadde, *those*
As three of hem were gode› and two were badde. *good*
The threė men were gode, and riche, and olde;
Unnethė› mightė they the statut› holde *scarcely / covenant*
In which that they were bounden unto me.
Ye woot› wel what I mene of this, pardee! *know*
As help me God, I laughė whan I thinke
How pitously anight I made hem swinke;› *toil*
And by my fey,› I tolde of it no stoor.° *faith*
They had me yeven hir› gold and hir tresoor; *given their*
Me neded nat do lenger› diligence *longer*
To winne hir love, or doon hem reverence.
They lovėd me so wel by God above,
That I ne tolde no dayntee of hir love!°
A wys womman wol sette hir ever in oon:°
To gete hir lovė, theras› she hath noon. *where*
But sith I hadde hem hoolly› in myn hond, *completely*
And sith they hadde me yeven› all hir lond, *given*
What› sholde I taken heed hem for to plese, *why*
But it were for my profit and myn ese?
I sette hem so a-werkė,› by my fey, *to work*
That many a night they songen› weilawey!› *sang / alas*
The bacoun was nat fet› for hem, I trowe, *fetched*
That som men han in Essex at Dunmowe.°
I governed hem so wel, after› my lawe, *according to*
That ech of hem ful blisful› was and fawe› *happy / glad*
To bringė me gaye thingės fro the fayre.
They were ful glad whan I spak to hem fayre;
For God it woot, I chidde› hem spitously.› *chided / unmercifully*
Now herkneth, hoẉ I bar me° proprely,

fantasye strictly, a specific faculty of the mind, imagination; thus, “as I feel like”
I . . . stoor I did not take much account of it; or perhaps: I gained no money by it (since I’d already got it from them)
That I . . . love i.e. I needed to take no special pains to get their love
A wys . . . in oon a sensible woman will set herself one object
Dunmowe At this town and elsewhere a flitch or side of bacon was offered to any couple who could prove they had not quarreled or regretted their marriage during the year just past.
bar me behaved myself

Ye wysė wyvės, that can understonde.
Thus shulde ye speke and bere hem wrong on honde;°
For half so boldėly can ther no man
Swere and lyen> as a womman can. *lie*
I sey nat this by> wyves that ben wyse,> *about / careful*
But if> it be whan they hem misavyse.> *unless / go wrong*
A wys wyf, if that she can hir good,°
Shal beren him on hond the cow is wood,°
And takė witnesse of hir owene mayde
Of hir assent;° but herkneth how I sayde.
"Sir olde kaynard,> is this thyn array>° *dotard*
Why is my neighėborės wyf so gay?
She is honoùred over al ther> she goth;> *wherever / goes*
I sitte at hoom, I have no thrifty cloth.> *good clothes*
What dostow> at my neighėborės hous? *do you*
Is she so fair? artow so amorous?
What rowne> ye with our mayde? Benedicitė!° *whisper*
Sir oldė lechour, lat thy japes> be! *tricks*
And if I have a gossib> or a freend, *confidant*
Withouten gilt, thou chydest as a feend,> *fiend*
If that I walke or pleye unto his hous!
Thou comest hoom as dronken as a mous,
And prechest on thy bench, with yvel preef!°
Thou seist to me, it is a greet meschief> *misfortune*
To wedde a poorė womman, for costage;> *because of expense*
And if that she be riche, of heigh parage,> *descent*
Than seistow> that it is a tormentrye *you say*
To suffre hir pryde and hir malėncolye.°
And if that she be fair, thou verray knave,
Thou seyst that every holour> wol hir have; *adulterer*
She may no whyle in chastitee abyde,
That is assaillėd upon ech a side.
Thou seyst, som folk desyre us for richesse,
Somme for our shap, and somme for our fairnesse;
And som, for she can outher> singe or daunce, *either*
And som, for gentillesse> and daliaunce;> *kindness / favor*
Som, for hir handės and hir armės smale;> *slender*
Thus goth al to the devel by> thy tale. *according to*
Thou seyst, men may nat kepe> a castel wal; *hold*
It may so longe assailled been overal.> *everywhere*
And if that she be foul, thou seïst that she

bere . . . on honde pretend that they have insulted you
wys . . . good clever wife, if she knows what's good for her
Shal . . . wood Shall make him believe the chough is mad. Cf. Chaucer's Manciple's Tale: an anti-feminist *exemplum*. The chough or jackdaw, a talking bird. tells a husband that his wife has been unfaithful. She has been, but she persuades him that the bird is crazy and he wrings its neck.
And take . . . assent and she will call her own maid, who sides with her, to witness
array way of going on
Benedicite bless me
yvel preef bad luck to you
malencolye melancholy, excess of black bile; thus, indifference

Coveiteth˃ every man that she may se; *longs for*
For as a spaynel˃ she wol on him lepe, *spaniel*
Til that she findė som man hir to chepe;˃ *buy*
Ne noon so grey goos goth ther in the lake,
As, seïstow, that wol been withoute make.˃ *mate*
And seÿst, it is an hard thing for to welde˃ *control*
A thing that no man wol, his thankės,˃ helde.˃ *willingly / hold*
Thus seïstow, lorel,˃ whan thow goost to bedde; *wretch*
And that no wys˃ man nedeth for to wedde, *prudent*
Ne no man that entendeth˃ unto hevene. *hopes for*
With wildė thonder-dint˃ and firy levene˃ *thunderbolt / lightning*
Mote thy welkėd nekkė be to-broke!°
Thow seÿst that dropping˃ houses, and eek smoke, *leaking*
And chyding wyves, maken men to flee
Out of hir owene hous; a! Benedicitė!
What eyleth˃ swich an old man for to chyde? *ails*
Thow seyst, we wyvės wol our vyces hyde
Til we be fast,° and than we wol hem shewe;
Wel may that be a proverbe of a shrewe!˃ *scoundrel*
Thou seïst, that oxen, asses, hors,° and houndes,
They been assayėd at diversė stoundes;˃ *times*
Bacins, lavours,˃ er that men hem bye, *washbasins*
Sponės and stoles,˃ and al swich housbondrye,˃ *stools / household goods*
And so been˃ pottės, clothės, and array;˃ *are / ornaments*
But folk of wyvės maken noon assay
Til they be wedded; oldė dotard shrewe!
And than, seïstow, we wol oure vices shewe.
Thou seïst also, that it displeseth me
But if that thou wolt preysė my beautee.
And but thou poure alwey˃ upon my face, *gaze*
And clepė˃ me 'Faire dame' in every place; *call*
And but thou make a feste˃ on thilkė˃ day *feast / the same*
That I was born, and make me fresh and gay,
And but thou do to my norìce˃ honoùr, *nurse*
And to my chamberere˃ withinne my bour,˃ *chambermaid / room*
And to my fadres˃ folk and his allyes;˃ *father's / relatives*
Thus seïstow, olde barel ful of lyes!
And yet of our apprentice Janekyn,
For his crisp heer,˃ shyninge as gold so fyn, *curly hair*
And for he squiereth me bothe up and doun,
Yet hastow caught a fals suspecioun;
I wol˃ hym noght, thogh thou were deed˃ tomorwe. *want / dead*

Mote . . . to-broke may your withered neck be broken; to- intensifies
fast firmly tied, married
hors Horses. The complaint that one can have a good look at a horse one is buying, but not at a prospective wife, goes back as far as the Roman poet Horace (65–8 B.C.). Sir Thomas More's solution may be found in *Utopia*, Bk. ii. Chaucer here, as he has done earlier, and as he goes on doing, is borrowing from Theophrastus, *The Golden Book of Marriage*, quoted by St. Jerome, perhaps, through a French reworking —in this case Eustache Deschamps' *Mirror of Marriage*.

But tel me this, why hydėstow, with sorwe,°
The keyės of thy cheste awey fro me?
It is my good> as wel as thyn, pardee. *property*
What wenestow> make an idiot of our dame? *think you to*
Now by that lord, that called is Saint Jame,°
Thou shalt not bothė, thogh that thou were wood,> *angry*
Be maister of my body and of my good;
That oon thou shalt forgo, maugree thyne yën;°
What nedeth thee of me to enquere> or spyën? *enquire*
I trowė, thou woldst loke> me in thy chiste!> *lock / money-chest*
Thou sholdest seye, 'Wyf, go wher thee liste,> *it pleases*
Tak your disport, I wol nat leve> no talis; *believe*
I knowe yow for a trewė wyf, dame Alis.'
We love no man that taketh keep> or charge> *heed / notice*
Wher that we goon, we wol> ben at our large.> *want / liberty*
Of allė men yblessed moot he be,
The wyse astrologien° Dan Ptholome,
That seith this proverbe in his *Almageste,*
'Of allė men his wisdom is the hyeste,
That rekketh> never who hath the world in honde.' *cares*
By this proverbė thou shalt understonde,
Have thou ynogh,° what thar> thee recche> or care *need / trouble*
How merily> that othere folkės fare? *happily*
For certeyn, oldė dotard, by your leve,
Ye shul have queyntė° right ynough> at eve. *plenty*
He is to greet a nigard that wol werne> *refuse*
A man to lighte his candle at his lanterne;
He shal have never the lassė> light, pardee; *less*
Have thou ynough, thee thar nat pleynė thee.
Thou seÿst also, that if we make us gay
With clothing and with precïous array,
That it is peril of our chastitee;
And yet, with sorwe, thou most enforcė> thee, *reinforce*
And seye thise wordės in the Apostle's name,
'In habit,> maad with chastitee and shame, *clothes*
Ye wommen shul> apparaille yow,' quod he,° *must*
'And noght in tressėd heer and gay perree,
As perlės, ne with gold, ne clothės riche;'
After thy text, ne after thy rubriche°

with sorwe literally, with sorrow; thus, damn it
Jame St. James (the Great), patron saint of Spain; see the General Prologue, l. 468. The Wife had made the pilgrimage to Santiago de Compostela.
maugree . . . yën despite (Fr. malgré) your eyes; i.e. damn your eyes
astrologien The line between astrologers and astronomers is hard to draw in the Middle Ages, but Ptolemy was by all counts an astronomer. For his aphorism, see l. 188n above; its sense is: he is the wisest of men who does not care if others have much wealth.
Have . . . ynogh if you have enough
queynte pudendum. It would not be in the Wife's nature to use a polite expression, but the form she uses may be a kind of genteelism, a variant spelling of *cuinte;* see her use of *quoniam, bele chose, chambre of Venus* below.
he I Timothy 2:9 ("modest apparel, with shamefastness and sobriety; not with braided hair or gold or pearls, or costly array"); "perree" (Fr. *pierrerie*) is jewelry
rubriche the opening words or headings in a manuscript, written in red to give the reader an orientation; thus, direction

I wol nat wirche as muchel> as a gnat.° *much*
Thou seydest this, that I was lyk a cat;°
For whoso woldė senge> a cattės skin, *singe*
Thanne wolde the cat wel dwellen in his in;> *house*
And if the cattės skin be slyk and gay,
She wol nat dwelle in housė half a day,
But forth she wole, er> any day be dawed,> *before / dawned*
To shewe hir skin, and goon a-caterwawed;> *caterwauling*
This is to seye, if I be gay, sir shrewe,
I wol renne> out, my borel> for to shewe. *run / clothes*
  Sire oldė fool, what eyleth> thee to spyën? *ails*
Thogh thou preye Argus,° with his hundred yën,
To be my wardė-cors,> as he can> best, *bodyguard / knows how*
In feith, he shal nat kepe me but me lest;> *unless it pleases me*
Yet coude I make his berd,° so moot I thee.> *thrive*
  Thou seydest eek, that ther ben thingės three,
The whichė thingės troublen al this erthe,
And that no wight ne may endure the ferthe;> *fourth*
O leve> sir shrewė, Jesu shorte> thy lyf! *dear / shorten*
Yet prechestow, and seyst, an hateful wyf
Yrekenėd> is for oon of thise meschances.> *reckoned / misfortunes*
Been ther none othere maner resemblances
That ye may lyknė your paràbles to,°
But if a sely wyf be oon> of tho>? *one / them*
  Thou lykenest eek wommanes love to helle,
To bareyne> land, ther> water may not dwelle. *barren / where*
Thou lyknest it also to wildė fyr;°
The more it brenneth,> the more it hath desyr *burns*
To consume every thing that brent> wol be. *burned*
Thou seyst, that right> as wormės° shende> a tree, *just / destroy*
Right so a wyf destroyeth hir housbonde;
This knowė they that been to wyvės bonde."> *bound*
  Lordinges, right thus, as ye have understonde,
Bar I stifly myne olde housbondes on honde,°
That thus they seyden in hir dronkenesse;
And al was fals, but that I took witnesse
On Janekin and on my nece also.
O Lord, the peyne I dide hem and the wo,
Ful giltėlees,> by Goddės swetė pyne!> *innocent / sufferings*
For as an hors I coudė byte and whyne.°

I . . . gnat i.e. I don't care a fly for them
cat a singed cat dwells at home (a proverb)
Argus Argus, unsleeping because of his hundred eyes, was set by Juno to watch Io, whom Jupiter was currently involved with; but Mercury charmed him asleep and killed him. Do what you like in the way of watching, says the Wife, it will do you no good.
make his berd outwit him
Been . . . to i.e. are there no other similarities you can apply your moral tales to rather than to a poor, innocent woman?
wilde fyr Wild fire was a naphtha preparation that was especially fierce and difficult to put out.
wormes grubs, crawling creatures of all kinds
Bar . . . honde I pressed my pretense on my old husbands
byte and whyne bite when in a bad temper and whinny when in a good

I coudė pleyne,> thogh I were in the gilt,> *complain / wrong*
Or ellės oftentyme hadde I ben spilt.> *ruined*
Whoso that first to millė comth, first grint;> *grinds*
I pleynėd first, so was our werre ystint.> *ceased*
They were ful glad to excusen hem ful blyve> *quickly*
Of thing of which they never agilte hir lyve.°
   Of wenches wolde I beren him on honde,
Whan that for syk unnethės> mighte he stonde. *sickness scarcely*
Yet tikled it his hertė, for that he
Wende> that I hadde of him so greet chiertee.> *thought / love*
I swoor that al my walkinge out by nighte
Was for to espyė wenches that he dighte;> *laid*
Under that colour> hadde I many a mirthe. *pretense*
For al swich wit is yeven> us in our birthe; *given*
Deceitė, weping, spinning God hath yive
To wommen kindėly,> whyl> they may live. *by nature / as long as*
And thus of o thing I avauntė me,> *boast*
Atte ende I hadde the bettre in ech degree,
By sleighte,> or force, or by som maner thing, *cleverness*
As by continuel murmur> or grucching;> *complaint / grumbling*
Namely> abeddė hadden they meschaunce, *especially*
Ther wolde I chyde and do hem no plesaunce;> *pleasure*
I wolde no lenger in the bed abyde,
If that I felte his arm over my syde,
Til he had maad his raunson> unto me; *payment*
Than wolde I suffre him do his nycetee.> *folly*
And therfore every man this tale I telle,
Winne whoso> may, for al is for to selle. *whoever*
With empty hand men may none hawkės lure;
For winning> wolde I al his lust endure, *profit*
And makė me a feynėd appetyt;
And yet in bacon° hadde I never delyt;
That made me that ever I wolde hem chyde.
For thogh the Pope had seten> hem biside, *sat*
I wolde nat spare hem at hir owene bord.> *table*
For by my trouthe, I quitte> hem word for word. *requited*
As help me verray God omnipotent,
Thogh I right now sholde make my testament,
I ne owe hem nat a word that it nis quit.
I broghte it so aboutė by my wit,
That they moste yeve it up, as for the beste;°
Or ellės hadde we never been in reste.
For thogh he lokėd as a wood leoùn,> *raging lion*
Yet sholde he faille of his conclusioùn.> *purpose*

Of thing . . . lyve of something of which they were never guilty in their lives
bacon old, dried, tough, pig's meat; cf. Lechery in *Dr. Faustus*, scene VI, ll. 151–52: "I am she who likes an inch of raw mutton better than an ell of dried stockfish."
as . . . beste and make the best of it

Thanne wolde I seyė, "Godė lief,˃ tak keep˃ *dear one / note*
How mekely loketh Wilkin ourė sheep;°
Com neer, my spouse, lat me ba˃ thy cheke! *kiss*
Ye sholdė been al pacïent and meke,
And han a swetė spycėd˃ conscience, *delicate*
Sith ye so preche of Jobės pacience.
Suffreth alwey, sin ye so wel can preche;
And but˃ ye do, certein we shal yow teche *unless*
That it is fair˃ to have a wyf in pees. *good*
Oon of us two moste bowen, doutėless;
And sith a man is more resonable°
Than womman is, ye moste been suffrable.˃ *long-suffering*
What ayleth yow to grucchė˃ thus and grone? *grumble*
Is it for ye wolde have my queynte allone?
Why taak it al, lo, have it everydeel;˃ *all*
Peter!° I shrewe˃ yow but˃ ye love it weel! *curse / unless*
For if I woldė selle my belė chose,˃ *fair thing*
I coudė walke as fresh˃ as is a rose; *sweet*
But I wol kepe it for your owene tooth.˃ *enjoyment*
Ye be to blame, by God, I sey yow sooth."
Swiche maner wordės haddė we on honde.°
Now wol I speken of my fourthe housbonde.
My fourthė housbonde was a revelour,
This is to seyn, he hadde a paramour;˃ *mistress*
And I was yong and ful of ragerye,˃ *passion*
Stiborn˃ and strong, and joly as a pye.˃ *vigorous / magpie*
Wel coude I dauncė to an harpe smale,°
And singe, ywis,˃ as any nightingale, *indeed*
Whan I had dronke a draughte of swetė wyn.
Metellius,° the foulė cherl, the swyn,
That with a staf birafte˃ his wyf hir lyf, *bereft*
For˃ she drank wyn, thogh˃ I hadde been his wyf, *because / if*
He sholdė nat han daunted me fro drinke;
And, after wyn, on Venus moste˃ I thinke: *most*
For al so siker˃ as cold engendreth hayl, *sure*
A likerous mouth moste han a likerous tayl.°
In womman vinolent° is no defence:
This knowen lechours by experience.
But, Lord Crist! whan that it remembreth° me

How . . . sheep i.e. you, old lamb, how patient you look
And . . . resonable Men were held to be more rational, more capable of intellectual operations, than women.
Peter by St. Peter
Swiche . . . honde this was the kind of words we dealt in
smale perhaps, gracefully; or an adjective going with "harp," in reference to its thin, elegant, graceful sound
Metellius For this anti-husband story, the Wife reaches into another bin of *exempla* much used in the Middle Ages—the handbook, by Valerius Maximus (1st century A.D.), of Greek and Roman history.
A likerous . . . tayl A gluttonous mouth means a lecherous tail. Gluttony and lechery go together in the moral treatises of the time, and sin in Eden is often shown as a combination of the two in 14th-century art.
vinolent full of wine
whan . . . me impersonal construction: when I look back and recollect it all

Upon my youthe, and on my jolitee,
It tikleth me aboute myn hertė rote.˃ *heart's root*
Unto this day it dooth myn hertė bote˃ *good*
That I have had my world as in my tyme.
But age, allas! that al wol envenyme,˃ *poison*
Hath me biraft˃ my beautee and my pith;˃ *deprived / strength*
Lat go, farewel, the Devil go therwith!
The flour is goon, ther is namore to telle,
The bren,˃ as I best can,° now moste I selle; *bran*
But yet to be right mery wol I fonde.˃ *try*
Now wol I tellen of my fourthe housbonde.
  I seye, I hadde in hertė greet despyt˃ *contempt*
That he of any other had delyt.
But he was quit,˃ by God and by Saint Joce!° *repaid*
I made him of the samė wode a croce;°
Nat of my body in no foul manere,
But certeinly, I madė folk swich chere,
That in his owene grece˃ I made him frye *fat*
For angre, and for verray jalousye.
By God, in erthe I was his purgatorie,°
For which I hope his soulė be in glorie.
For God it woot, he sat ful ofte and song˃ *sang*
Whan that his shoo ful bitterly him wrong.°
Ther was no wight, save God and he, that wiste,˃ *knew*
In many wysė, how sorė I him twiste.˃ *wrung*
He deyde˃ whan I cam fro Jerusalem, *died*
And lyth ygrave˃ under the rode-beem,° *buried*
Al˃ is his tombė noght so curious˃ *although / splendid*
As was the sepulcre of him, Darius,°
Which that Appellės wroghtė subtilly;˃ *skillfully*
It nis but waste to burie him preciously.˃ *expensively*
Lat him fare wel,˃ God yevė˃ his soule reste, *go in peace / give*
He is now in the grave and in his cheste.˃ *coffin*
  Now of my fifthė housbond wol I telle.
God lete his soulė never come in helle!
And yet was he to me the mostė shrewe;˃ *vicious*
That fele I on my ribbės al by rewe,°
And ever shal, unto myn ending day.

can as best I can—but still with a hint of the old meaning of "can": I know best how it is done

Joce a Breton saint; Chaucer found a knight with the same name in the French of Jean de Meun (d. 1305)

I . . . croce I made him a staff (crutch, not cross) of the same wood [to beat him with]; cf. l. 493: I made him fry in his own fat

I . . . purgatorie Matrimony as purgatory on earth was a frequent concept in medieval literature; the consolation for its pains was that, unlike heaven and hell, it did not retain people forever.

Whan . . . wrong when his shoe pinched him most painfully; the figure, in relation to marriage, goes back to St. Jerome, at least

rode-beem a beam across a church at the chancel-area, separating nave from choir, with the crucifix (rood) mounted on its middle

Darius king of the Persians (d. 330 B.C.), defeated by Alexander the Great, whose court painter was Apelles. Medieval versions of the story of Alexander make him magnanimously order from Apelles splendid tombs of marble, gold, and silver for Darius and his queen.

by rewe in a row, each one

But in our bed he was so fresh> and gay, *lively*
And therwithal so wel coude he me glose,> *flatter*
Whan that he wolde han> my belė chose, *have*
That thogh he hadde me bet> on every boon,> *beaten / bone*
He coudė winnen agayn my love anoon.> *at once*
I trowe I loved him bestė, for that he
Was of his lovė daungerous> to me. *sparing*
We wommen han, if that I shal nat lye,
In this matere a queyntė fantasye;> *fancy*
Wayte what° thing we may nat lightly have,
Therafter wol we crye al day and crave.
Forbede us thing, and that desyren we;
Prees> on us faste,> and thannė wol we flee. *press / hard*
With daunger° outė> we al our chaffàre;> *display / wares*
Greet prees> at market maketh derė wàre,> *crowd / goods*
And too greet cheep> is holde at litel prys;> *bargain / value*
This knoweth every womman that is wys.
  My fifthė housbonde, God his soule blesse!
Which that I took for love and no richesse,
He somtyme> was a clerk° of Oxenford, *formerly*
And had left scole, and wente at hoom to bord> *as boarder*
With my gossib,° dwellinge in oure toun,
God have hir soule! hir name was Alisoun.
She knew myn herte and eek my privetee> *secrets*
Bet> than our parisshe preest, so moot I thee!> *better / thrive*
To hir biwreyėd> I my conseil> al. *disclosed / secrets*
For had myn housbonde pissėd on a wall,
Or doon a thing that sholde han cost his lyf,
To hir, and to another worthy wyf,
And to my nece,° which that I lovėd weel,
I wolde han told his conseil every deel.> *part*
And so I dide ful often, God it woot,> *knows*
That made his face ful often reed> and hoot> *red / hot*
For verray shame, and blamed himself for he
Had told to me so greet a privetee.
  And so bifel that onės, in a Lente,> *Lent*
(So often tymes I to my gossib wente,
For ever yet I lovede to be gay,
And for to walke, in March, Averille, and May,
Fro hous to hous, to herė sondry talės),
That Jankin clerk, and my gossib Dame Alis,
And I myself, into the feldės wente.
Myn housbond was at London al that Lente;
I hadde the bettre leyser> for to pleye,° *opportunity*

Wayte what whatever
daunger care, parsimony; caution
clerk See the General Prologue, l. 287.
gossib literally, God-relation: God-child, God-parent: thus, anyone to whom one is especially close
nece niece or cousin
pleye She should have passed Lent in religious observances.

And for to see, and eek for to be seye> *seen*
Of lusty> folk; what wiste I wher my grace *lively*
Was shapen for to be, or in what place?°
Therefore I made my visitacioùns,
To vigilies° and to processioùns,
To preching eek and to thise pilgrimàges,
To pleyes of miracles° and mariàges,
And wered upon my gayė scarlet gytes.°
Thise wormės, ne thise mothės, ne thise mites,
Upon my peril,° frete> hem never a deel;> *ate / part*
And wostow> why? for they were used weel.> *know you / much*
Now wol I tellen forth what happėd me.
I seye, that in the feeldės walked we,
Til trewėly we hadde swich daliànce,> *pleasure*
This clerk and I, that of my purveyànce°
I spak to him, and seyde him, how that he,
If I were widwe, sholdė weddė me.
For certeinly, I sey for no bobance,> *without boasting*
Yet was I never withouten purveyànce> *prospect*
Of mariage, nof> otherė thingės eek. *nor of*
I holde a mouses herte> nat worth a leek,° *life*
That hath but oon hol for to stertė> to, *escape*
And if that faillė, thanne is al ydo.°
I bar him on honde,> he hadde enchanted> me; *pretended / bewitched*
My damė> taughtė me that soutiltee.> *mother / trick*
And eek I seyde, I mette> of him al night; *dreamed*
He wolde han slayn me as I lay up-right,> *on my back*
And al my bed was ful of verray> blood, *real*
But yet I hope that he shal do me good;
For blood bitokeneth gold,° as me was taught.
And al was fals, I dremed of it right naught,> *nothing*
But as I folwėd ay> my damės lore,> *always / teaching*
As wel of this as of other thingės more.
But now sir, lat me see, what I shal seyn?
Aha! by God, I have my tale ageyn.
Whan that my fourthė housbond was on bere,> *bier*
I weep algate,> and madė sory chere,> *anyway / behavior*
As wyvės moten,> for it is usàge,> *must / custom*
And with my coverchief covered my visàge;

what . . . place I didn't know where my good luck was ordained to be; or: how could I know where my favor was destined to be bestowed
vigilies feasts or festivals on the eves of saints' days
miracles plays based on the historical books of the Bible and on legends of the saints
And . . . gytes and wore upon [me] my bright scarlet gowns
peril an oath: upon peril of my soul; damn me!
purveyance providing for my future (so that I wouldn't ever be without a husband—but you can't sleep with me until I'm a widow and we can be married)
leek The accumulation of little worthless things is meant to emphasize her own provident vigor, with a probable pun on *hole*. The mouse with only one place to go was proverbial.
thanne . . . al ydo then it is all up
blood . . . gold This was regular doctrine in the medieval books on the interpretation of dreams: one red thing (blood) betokens another (red gold); cf. the Nun's Priest's Tale.

But for that I was purveyed of˃ a make,˃ *provided with / mate*
I weep˃ but smal, and that I undertake. *wept*
To chirchė was myn housbond born amorwe˃ *carried in the morning*
With˃ neighėbores, that for him maden sorwe; *by*
And Jankin, ourė clerk, was oon of tho.
As help me God, whan that I saugh˃ him go *saw*
After the bere, me thoughte he hadde a paire
Of leggės and of feet so clene˃ and faire,˃ *neat / handsome*
That al myn herte I yaf unto˃ his hold.˃ *into / keeping*
He was, I trowe, a twenty winter old,
And I was fourty, if I shal seye sooth;
But yet I hadde alwey a coltės tooth.°
Gat-tothed° I was, and that bicam˃ me weel; *suited*
I hadde the prente˃ of Seÿnt Venus' seel.˃ *imprint / seal*
As help me God, I was a lusty˃ oon, *good-looking*
And faire and riche, and yong, and wel bigoon;˃ *fortunate*
And trewėly, as myne housbondes tolde me,
I had the bestė quoniam° mighte be.
For certės, I am al Venerien
In felinge,˃ and myn herte is Marcien.° *feelings*
Venus me yaf my lust, my likerousnesse,˃ *lecherousness*
And Mars yaf me my sturdy hardinesse.˃ *boldness*
Myn ascendent was Taur,° and Mars therinne.
Allas! allas! that ever love was sinne!
I folwed ay myn inclinacioùn˃ *bent*
By vertu of my constellacioùn;
That madė me I coudė noght withdrawe
My chambre of Venus from a good felawe.
Yet have I Martės mark upon my face,°
And also in another privee˃ place. *secret*
For, God so wis˃ be my savacioùn,˃ *surely / salvation*
I ne loved never by no discrecioùn,
But ever folwedė myn appetyt;
Al were he short or long, or blak or whyt,
I took no kepe,˃ so that he lyked˃ me, *heed / pleased*

coltes tooth a young appetite
Gat-tothed See the General Prologue, l. 470.
quoniam Latin: whereas, whatever; another of the Wife's coy words for pudendum
Venerien . . . Marcien influenced by the planets Venus and Mars; thus, lustful and bold
Taur The Wife's ascendant (the sign of the zodiac just rising in the east at her birth) was Taurus, the Bull: therefore, she would be industrious, energetic, prudent, a money-maker, one who usually comes out on top; florid, bold-eyed, wide-mouthed, short-legged, big-buttocked; gossipy, given to love affairs. Venus in her mansion of Taurus makes people cheerful, with good figures, attractive, lovable, passionate and voluptuous, lovers of fine clothes: there is, essentially, no evil in them. Mars, masculine, baleful, and angry, in conjunction (*constellacioùn*) with Venus in Taurus counteracts these good influences and has made the Wife into the holy terror that she is. She cannot keep her chamber of Venus from a good man. Between them, then, Taurus and Mars take away or change for the worse her most agreeable characteristics.
Yet . . . face Every person was thought to have placed on him, at conception or birth, a (birth) mark representing the ascendant sign and dominant star of the moment, by which his fortunes were ruled. They would appear on that part of the body ruled by a particular sign or planet. The Wife's sign, as she was born in Taurus, should be on the neck; she has also the "print of Saint Venus's seal," l. 610, a red mark, probably, on the thigh; and Mars's mark, a scar on the face and on the thigh or groin ("another privee place").

How pore> he was, ne eek of what degree. *poor*
What sholde I seye, but, at the monthės ende,
This joly> clerk Jankin, that was so hende,> *handsome / pleasant*
Hath weddėd me with greet solempnitee,> *ceremony*
And to him yaf I al the lond> and fee> *property / money*
That ever was me yeven therbifore;
But afterward repented me ful sore.
He noldė suffre> nothing of my list.> *allow / pleasure*
By God, he smoot me onės> on the list,° *once*
For that I rente> out of his book a leef, *tore*
That of the strook myn erė wex> al deef.> *became / deaf*
Stiborn> I was as is a leonesse, *fierce*
And of my tonge a verray jangleresse,> *babbler*
And walke I wolde, as I had doon biforn,> *before*
From hous to hous, although he had it sworn.> *forbidden*
For which he oftentymės woldė preche,
And me of oldė Romayn gestės° teche,
How he, Simplicius Gallus,° lefte his wyf,
And hir forsook for terme> of al his lyf, *duration*
Noght but for open-heeded> he hir say> *hatless / saw*
Lokinge out at his dore> upon a day.> *door / one day*
Another Romayn° tolde he me by name,
That, for> his wyf was at a somerės> game *because / summer's*
Withoute his witing,> he forsook hir eke. *knowledge*
And than wolde he upon> his Bible seke> *in / seek*
That ilkė> proverbe of Ecclesiaste,° *same*
Wher he comandeth and forbedeth faste,> *absolutely*
Man shal nat suffre> his wyf go roule> aboute; *allow / gad*
Than wolde he seye right thus, withouten doute,
"Whoso that buildeth his hous al of salwes,> *willow-twigs*
And priketh> his blindė hors over the falwes,> *rides / plowed ground*
And suffreth his wyf to go seken halwės,> *shrines*
Is worthy to been hangėd on the galwės>!" *gallows*
But al for noght, I settė noght an hawe°
Of his proverbės nof> his oldė sawe,> *nor of / sayings*
Ne I wolde nat of him corrected be.
I hate him that my vices telleth me,
And so do mo,> God woot! of us than I. *more*
This made him with me wood> al outrely;> *furious / completely*
I noldė noght forbere> him in no cas. *endure*

list i.e. cheek. To rhyme two words that look the same but have different meanings was thought good, as in French *rime riche*.
gestes Latin: (*res*) *gestae*, things done; the regular medieval word for stories of feats of arms
Gallus This story is from Valerius Maximus; see l. 466 above.
Romayn P. Sempronius Sophus, from the same chapter in Valerius
Ecclesiaste Ecclesiasticus 25:25: "Give . . . neither a wicked woman liberty to gad abroad." The clerk is threatening the Wife with authorities from the two most powerful sources known to the Middle Ages—the classics and the Bible. They are not just moral tales: all carry the specific threat of divorce.
I . . . hawe I give not a hawthorn berry

Now wol I seye yow sooth, by Seint Thomas,°
Why that I rente out of his book a leef,
For which he smoot me so that I was deef.
He hadde a book that gladly, night and day,
For his desport> he woldė rede alway.> *recreation / always*
He clepėd> it Valerie° and Theofraste,° *called*
At whichė book he lough> alwey ful faste.> *laughed / much*
And eek ther was somtyme> a clerk> at Rome, *once / scholar*
A cardinal, that hightė> Saint Jerome, *was called*
That made a book agayn> Jovinian;° *against*
In whichė book eek ther was Tertulan,°
Crisippus,° Trotula,° and Helowys,°
That was abbessė nat fer> fro Parỳs; *far*
And eek the Parables of Salomon,°
Ovydes Art,° and bokės many on,
And allė thise wer bounden in o volume.
And every night and day was his custume,> *custom*
Whan he had leyser> and vacacioùn> *lesiure / free time*
From other worldly occupacioùn,
To reden on this book of wikked wyves.> *women*
He knew of hem mo legendės and lyves
Than been of godė wyvės in the Bible.
For trusteth wel, it is an impossible> *impossibility*
That any clerk wol spekė good of wyves,
But if> it be of holy seintės lyves, *unless*
Ne of noon other womman never the mo.°
Who peyntedė the leoun, tel me who?°
By God, if wommen haddė writen stories,
As clerkės han withinne hir oratories,> *cells*
They wolde han writen of men more wikkednesse

Seint Thomas St. Thomas Becket of Canterbury, the premier saint of England; see General Prologue, l. 16

Valerie The clerk had a manuscript, perhaps specially written for him, containing a number of related texts teaching him the ways and wiles of women. Valerie is not Valerius Maximus, but the *Letter of Valerius to Rufinus About Not Marrying* by Walter Map (12th century).

Theofraste Theophrastus' work *On Marriage,* mentioned and used by St. Jerome; see l. 291n

Jovinian For the Jovinian-Jerome controversy see the Headnote. The Wife uses St. Jerome freely, against his sense, for her defense of herself; and, in his sense, for her and Jankin's examples of unchastity. Cf. Dorigen, in the Franklin's Tale, ll. 659 ff.

Tertulan Tertullian (*c.* 160–*c.* 220), Father of the Church, who wrote *An Exhortation to Chastity, On Having Only One Husband,* and *On Modesty*

Crisippus perhaps the Stoic philosopher

Trotula probably never existed; she was thought to have been the author of books on gynecology and pediatrics, as well as on cosmetics, and to have been active in the famous medical center Salerno, in southern Italy, during the 11th century

Helowys Héloïse (d. 1164), the secret wife of Peter Abélard, the great Parisian philosopher who was castrated by Héloïse's uncle, Fulbert, for seducing her. She became a nun, and was later prioress of Argenteuil, near Paris. The correspondence of Héloïse and Abélard has been preserved: it was famous in the Middle Ages.

Parables of Salomon the Proverbs of Solomon—not merely the biblical book Proverbs, but a compendium from all those biblical books of which Solomon was, or was thought to be, the author, including Ecclesiasticus and Wisdom

Ovydes Art the *Ars Amatoria* (Art of Love) by the Roman poet Ovid (43 B.C.–*c.*18 A.D.), the lover's textbook, for his time, the Middle Ages, and the Renaissance

Ne . . . mo a heavy negative line: and nothing at all of any other woman

Who . . . who In one of the Aesopic fables a lion, seeing a picture of a lion being killed by a man, points out that all depends on the point of view; a lion would paint a man being killed by a lion.

Than all the mark of Adam° may redresse.
The children of Mercurie and of Venus°
Been in hir wirking> ful contrarious;> *occupations / opposed*
Mercurie loveth wisdom and science,> *knowledge*
And Venus loveth ryot> and dispence.> *debauchery / expenditure*
And, for hir diverse disposicioùn,
Ech falleth in otherės exaltacioùn;°
And thus, God woot! Mercury is desolat
In Pisces, wher Venus is exaltat;
And Venus falleth ther Mercurie is reysed;> *exalted*
Therfore no womman of no clerk is preysed.
The clerk, whan he is old, and may noght do
Of Venus werkės worth his oldė sho,°
Than sit> he doun, and writ> in his dotàge *sits / writes*
That wommen can nat kepe hir mariàge!> *marriage-vows*
  But now to purpos,> why I toldė thee *point*
That I was beten for a book, pardee.
Upon a night Jankin, that was our syre,> *lord*
Redde on his book, as he sat by the fyre,
Of Eva° first, that, for hir wikkednesse,
Was al mankindė broght to wrecchednesse,> *destruction*
For which that Jesu Crist himself was slayn,
That boghte> us with his hertės blood agayn. *redeemed*
Lo, here expres> of womman may ye finde, *made clear*
That womman was the los> of al mankinde. *destruction*
  Tho> redde he me how Sampson° loste his heres,> *then / hair*
Slepinge, his lemman kitte> hem with hir sheres; *lover cut*
Thurgh whichė tresoun> loste he bothe his yën.> *betrayal / eyes*
  Tho> redde he me, if that I shal nat lyen, *then*
Of Hercules and of his Dianyre,°
That causėd him to sette himself afyre.
  Nothing forgat he the penaùnce and wo
That Socrates had with hise wyvės two;°

mark of Adam the image of Adam: men; cf. the Franklin's Tale, l. 172

The children . . . Venus I.e. those born under the influence of each. It is not clear whether Chaucer means that the operations of the planets are different or that the occupations of those born under them differ. Mercury was the planetary god of knowledge and eloquence; his children are scholars, painters, sculptors, skilled metalworkers and so on. Venus was the planetary goddess of love and lovers; her children are courtiers, weavers, and dyers. But Chaucer may simply mean clerks (Mercury) and women (Venus).

exaltacioun The zodiacal sign in which a planet's influence is greatest: it is at the same time the dejection of another planet whose nature is contrary. Venus (female: pleasure) is in exaltation *(exaltat)* in Pisces, the fishes; Mercury (male: wisdom) is therefore in dejection (*desolat*) in the same sign.

of . . . sho a clerk is not worth his own old shoe in the occupations of Venus

Eva the primal female sinner. This spelling of her name is frequently used because, backward, it spells *Ave*, the salutation to Mary at the Annunciation, the beginning of our salvation. Most of the examples which follow are common knowledge, or come from St. Jerome's *Against Jovinian*, Walter Map (l. 677n), or the *Romance of the Rose*.

Sampson the story of Samson and Delilah, Judges 16

Dianyre Deianeira caused the death of her unfaithful husband Hercules, by giving him the shirt of the centaur Nessus, previously killed by Hercules for trying to rape her. The shirt had been poisoned by Nessus' blood and gave Hercules such burning pain that he preferred to build a funeral pyre and die in its flames.

wo . . . two The Athenian philosopher was famous for his patience and had, according to Jerome and others, two wives, of whom Xantippe, the second, tormented him continually.

How Xantippe caste pisse upon his heed; *head*
This sely man sat stille, as he were deed; *poor*
He wyped his heed, namore dorste he seyn *dared*
But 'Er that thonder stinte, comth of a reyn.' *ceases / rain*
  Of Phasipha,° that was the quene of Crete—
For shrewėdnesse, him thoughte the talė swete— *nastiness*
Fy! spek namore—it is a grisly thing— *speak*
Of hir horrìble lust and hir lyking. *pleasure*
  Of Clitėmistra,° for hir lecherye,
That falsly made hir housbond for to dye,
He redde it with ful good devocioùn.
  He tolde me eek for what occasioùn
Amphiorax° at Thebės loste his lyf;
Myn housbond hadde a legende of his wyf,
Eriphilem, that for an ouche of gold
Hath prively unto the Grekės told *secretly*
Wher that hir housbonde hidde him in a place,
For which he hadde at Thebės sory grace. *sad treatment*
  Of Livia° tolde he me, and of Lucye,°
They bothė made hir housbondes for to dye;
That oon for love, that other was for hate;
Livia hir housbond, on an even late, *evening*
Empoysoned hath, for that she was his fo.
Lucya, likerous, loved hir housbond so, *lecherous*
That, for he sholde alwey upon hir thinke, *so*
She yaf him swich a maner lovė drinke,
That he was deed, er it were by the morwe; *dead / morning*
And thus algatės housbondės han sorwe. *all ways*
  Than tolde he me, how oon Latumius°
Compleynėd to his felawe Arrius, *companion*
That in his gardin growėd swich a tree, *such*
On which, he seyde, how that his wyvės three
Hangėd hemself for hertė despitoùs.°
"O leve brother," quod this Arrius, *dear / said*
"Yif me a plante of thilkė blissed tree, *cutting*
And in my gardin planted shal it be!"
  Of latter date, of wyvės hath he red,
That somme han slayn hir housbondes in hir bed,
And lete hir lechour dighte hir al the night *let / lay*

Phasipha Pasiphaë, queen of Minos of Crete, fell in love with a bull and bore by him the Minotaur, half-man, half-bull.
Clitemistra Clytemnestra, Agamemnon's queen; she and her lover, Aegisthus, killed her husband on his return to Greece after the Trojan War.
Amphiorax Amphiareus, in hiding so as not to go to the siege of Thebes, was betrayed by his wife, Eriphyle, for a necklace (*ouche*) of gold and diamonds, and had to go on the expedition, where he knew himself fated to die. He was swallowed up in an earthquake at Thebes.
Livia Wife of Drusus, son of the Roman Emperor Tiberius. She poisoned her husband at the prompting of her lover Sejanus (23 A.D.).
Lucye Lucilia, wife of the Roman poet Lucretius (1st century B.C.), gave her husband a love-potion to keep him true to her. It killed him quickly: see Tennyson's *Lucretius*.
Latumius The story is told by Walter Map (l. 677n), who gives the name as Pacuvius; and it is in the *Gesta Romanorum* (see below) with a moralization. It comes, ultimately, from Cicero's *De Oratore*.
for . . . despitoùs for the malice of their hearts

Whyl that the corps> lay in the floor upright.> *corpse / on its back*
And somme han drivė> naylės° in hir brayn *driven*
Whyl that they slepte, and thus they han hem slayn.
Somme han hem yevė> poysoun in hir drinke. *given*
He spak more harm than hertė may bithinke.> *imagine*
And therwithal, he knew of mo> proverbes *more*
Than in this world ther growen gras or herbes.
"Bet> is," quod he, "thyn habitacioùn *better*
Be with a leoun or a foul dragoùn,°
Than with a womman usinge> for to chyde. *accustomed*
Bet is," quod he, "hye> in the roof abyde° *high*
Than with an angry wyf doun in the hous;
They been so wikkėd and contrarious;> *contrary*
They haten> that hir housbondes loveth ay." *hate*
He seyde, "A womman cast> hir shame away, *casts*
Whan she cast of> hir smok";° and forthermo, *off*
"A fair womman, but> she be chaast also, *unless*
Is lyk a gold ring in a sowės nose."°
Who woldė wenen,> or who wolde suppose *imagine*
The wo that in myn hertė was, and pyne>? *torment*
And whan I saugh> he woldė never fyne> *saw / finish*
To reden on this cursėd book al night,
Al sodeynly three levės have I plight> *plucked*
Out of his book, right as he radde,> and eke, *read*
I with my fist so took him on the cheke,
That in our fyr he fil> bakward adoun.> *fell / down*
And he up stirte> as dooth a wood> leoùn, *jumped / raging*
And with his fist he smoot> me on the heed,> *struck / head*
That in the floor I lay as I were deed.
And when he saugh how stillė that I lay,
He was agast,> and wolde han fled his way, *afraid*
Til attė laste out of my swogh> I breyde:> *swoon / burst*
"O! hastow slayn me, falsė theef?" I seyde,
"And for my land thus hastow mordred> me? *murdered*
Er I be deed, yet wol I kissė thee."
And neer> he cam, and knelėd faire adoun, *closer*
And seydė, "Derė suster° Alisoun,
As help me God, I shal thee never smyte;
That I have doon, it is thyself to wyte.> *blame*
Foryeve it me, and that I thee biseke."> *beg*
And yet eftsones> I hit him on the cheke, *again*
And seydė, "Theef, thus muchel> am I wreke;> *much / revenged*
Now wol I dye, I may no lenger> speke." *longer*

nayles Joel killed the tyrant Sisera thus (Judges 4:21).
Bet . . . dragoùn Ecclesiasticus 25:16
Bet . . . abyde Proverbs 21:9
A . . . smok from *Against Jovinian;* Jerome took it from the Greek historian Herodotus (died *c.* 425 B.C.)
A fair . . . nose See Proverbs 11:22: "As a jewel of gold in a swine's snout, so is a fair woman who is without discretion."
suster term of affection

But attė laste, with muchel care> and wo, *trouble*
We fille acorded,> by us selven two. *fell agreed*
He yaf me al the brydel> in myn hond *bridle*
To han the governance of hous and lond,
And of his tonge> and of his hond also; *tongue*
And made him brenne his book anon right tho.°
And whan that I hadde geten> unto me, *gotten*
By maistrie,> al the soveraynėtee,> *mastering / sovereignty*
And that he seyde, "Myn owene trewė wyf,
Do as thee lust> the terme> of al thy lyf, *pleases / duration*
Keep thyn honour, and keep eek myn estaat">— *possessions*
After that day we hadden never debaat.
God help me so, I was to him as kinde
As any wyf from Denmark unto Inde,> *India*
And also trewe, and so was he to me.
I prey to God that sit> in magestee, *sits*
So blesse his soulė, for His mercy dere!
Now wol I seye my tale, if ye wol here."> *hear*

Biholde the wordes bitween the Somonour and the Frere

The Frerė lough,> whan he hadde herd al this, *laughed*
'Now, dame,' quod he, 'so have I joye or blis,
This is a long preamble of a tale!'
And whan the Somnour herde the Frerė gale,> *exclaim*
'Lo!' quod the Somnour, 'Goddės armės two!
A frere wol entremette him evermo.°
Lo, godė men, a flye and eek a frere
Wol falle in every dish and eek matere.°
What spekestow of preambulacioùn?
What! amble, or trotte, or pees,° or go sit doun;
Thou lettest> our disport> in this manere.' *hinderest / enjoyment*
'Ye, woltow so, sir Somnour?' quod the Frere,
'Now, by my feith, I shal, er that I go,
Telle of a Somnour swich a tale or two,
That alle the folk shal laughen in this place.'
'Now ellės,° Frerė, I bishrewe> thy face,' *curse*
Quod this Somnoùr, 'and I bishrewė me,
But if I tellė talės two or thre
Of frerės er I come to Sidingborne,°
That I shal make thyn hertė for to morne;
For wel I woot thy pacience is goon.'
Our Hostė crydė 'Pees! and that anoon!'
And seydė, 'Lat the womman telle hir tale

And made . . . tho and I made him burn his book on the spot
A frere . . . evermo a friar will always be meddling
a flye . . . matere a proverb
pees be still; some prefer the reading "pisse"
Now elles now otherwise; i.e. now unless
Sidingborne Sittingbourne, in Kent, about 40 miles from London, more than two-thirds of the way to Canterbury. The pilgrim-journey to Canterbury usually took three days and part of a fourth.

Ye fare as folk that dronken been of ale.
Do, dame, tel forth your tale, and that is best.'
'Al redy, sir,' quod she, 'right as yow lest,˃ *it pleases*
If I have licence of this worthy Frere.'
'Yis, dame,' quod he, 'tel forth, and I wol here.'

Here endeth the Wyf of Bathe hir Prologe.

Tale

Here biginneth the Tale of the Wyf of Bathe

In tholdė dayės of the king Arthoùr,
Of which that Britons˃ speken greet honoùr, *Bretons*
All was this land fulfild of fayėrye.°
The elf-queen, with hir joly companye,
Douncėd ful ofte in many a grenė mede;˃ *meadow*
This was the olde opinion, as I rede.
I speke of manye hundred yeres ago;
But now can no man see none elvės mo.
For now the gretė charitee and prayeres
Of limitours° and othere holy freres,
As thikke as motės in the sonnė-beem,
That serchen every lond and every streem,
Blessinge hallės, chambres, kichenes, boures,
Citees, burghės,° castels, hyė toures,
Thropės, bernės, shipnės, dayėryes,°
This maketh that ther been no fayėryes.
For ther as wont to walken was an elf,
Ther walketh now the limitour himself
In undermelės° and in morweninges,˃ *mornings*
And seÿth his matins and his holy thinges
As he goth in his limitacioùn.°
Wommen may go saufly˃ up and doun, *safely*
In every bush, or under every tree;
Ther is noon other incubus but he,
And he ne wol doon hem but dishonoùr.°
And so bifel it, that this King Arthoùr
Hadde in his hous a lusty bacheler,

All . . . fayerye i.e. this land was teeming with supernatural creatures
limitours friars licensed to beg and hear confessions within a certain district; cf. the General Prologue, l. 209
burghes literally, boroughs; i.e. towns
Thropes . . . dayeryes thorps (i.e. villages), barns, stables, dairies
undermeles The word could mean mid-mornings or mid-afternoons: here it seems to be the latter.
And . . . limitacioun And says his morning prayers and his holy office as he goes about his district. All clergy were bound to repeat the office at the required hours; friars were allowed to do so as they walked or rode.
Ther . . . dishonour There is no other incubus now but the friar—and he only dishonors them (without making them conceive). An incubus was an evil spirit (or fallen angel) who got children on women.

That on a day cam rydinge fro river;°
And happėd> that, allone as she was born, *it chanced*
He saugh a maydė walkinge him biforn,
Of whichė mayde anon, maugree hir heed,°
By verray force he rafte> hir maydenheed; *took*
For which oppressioùn> was swich clamoùr *rape*
And swich pursute> unto the King Arthoùr, *appeal*
That dampnėd was this knight for to be deed°
By cours of lawe, and sholde han lost his heed
Paraventure,> swich was the statut> tho; *perhaps / law*
But that the quene and othere ladies mo
So longė preyėden the king of grace,
Til he his lyf him graunted in the place,
And yaf him to the quene al at hir wille,
To chesė,> whether she wolde him save or spille.° *choose*
The quene thanketh the king with al hir might,
And after this thus spak she to the knight,
Whan that she saugh hir tyme,> upon a day: *opportunity*
'Thou standest yet,' quod she, 'in swich array,> *state*
That of thy lyf yet hastow no suretee.> *certainty*
I grante thee lyf, if thou canst tellen me
What thing is it that wommen most desyren?
Be war, and keep thy nekkė-boon> from yren.> *neck-bone / iron*
And if thou canst nat tellen it anon,
Yet wol I yeve> thee levė for to gon *give*
A twelf-month and a day, to seche> and lere> *seek / learn*
An answere suffisànt in this matere.
And suretee> wol I han, er that thou pace,> *pledge / go*
Thy body for to yelden in this place.'
Wo was this knight and sorwefully he syketh;> *sighs*
But what! he may nat do al as him lyketh.
And at the laste, he chees> him for to wende, *chose*
And come agayn, right at the yerės ende,
With swich answere as God wolde him purveye;> *provide*
And taketh his leve, and wendeth forth his weye.
He seketh every hous and every place,
Wheras he hopeth for to findė grace,
To lernė, what thing wommen loven most;
But he ne coude arryven in no cost,> *region*
Wheras he mightė finde in this matere
Two creätùrės àccordinge in fere.°
Somme seydė,> wommen loven best richesse, *said*
Somme seydė, honour, somme seyde, jolynesse;°
Somme, riche array, somme seyden, lust> abedde, *pleasure*

fro river i.e. from hawking for wild-fowl by the river-side
maugree hir heed literally, in spite of her head; thus, despite anything she could do
That . . . deed that this knight was condemned to death
save or spille spare or put to death
accordinge in fere agreeing together
jolynesse good looks, happiness

And oftė tyme to be widwe and wedde.
  Somme seydė, that our hertės been most esed,
Whan that we been yflatered and yplesed.
He gooth ful ny the sothe,˃ I wol nat lye; *truth*
A man shal winne us best with flaterye;
And with attendance, and with bisinesse,˃ *assiduity*
Been we ylymėd,˃ bothė more and lesse. *ensnared*
  And sommė seyn, how that we loven best
For to be free, and do right as us lest,˃ *it pleases*
And that no man repreve˃ us of our vyce, *reprove*
But seye that we be wyse, and no thing nyce.˃ *silly*
For trewėly, ther is noon of us alle,
If any wight wol clawe us on the galle,˃ *sore place*
That we nil kikė,˃ for˃ he seith us sooth; *kick / since*
Assay, and he shal finde it that so dooth.
For be we never so vicioùs withinne,
We wol˃ been holden˃ wyse, and clene of sinne. *want / thought*
  And sommė seyn, that greet delyt han we
For to ben holden stable and eek secree,°
And in o purpos stedefastly to dwelle,
And nat biwreyė˃ thing that men us telle. *disclose*
But that tale is nat worth a rakė-stele;˃ *rake-handle*
Pardee, we wommen connė nothing hele;˃ *hide*
Witnesse on Myda;° wol ye here the tale?
  Ovyde, amongės otherė thingės smale,
Seyde, Myda hadde, under his longė heres,
Growinge upon his heed two asses eres,
The which vycė˃ he hidde, as he best mighte, *defect*
Ful subtilly˃ from every mannės sighte, *cleverly*
That, save his wyf, ther wiste of it namo.˃ *no more*
He loved hir most, and trusted hir also;
He preyėde hir, that to no creätùre
She sholdė tellen of his disfigùre.˃ *disfigurement*
  She swoor him 'nay, for al this world to winne,
She noldė do that vileinye or sinne,
To make hir housbond han so foul a name;
She nolde nat telle it for hir owene shame.'
But nathėlees, hir thoughtė˃ that she dyde,˃ *it seemed / was dying*
That she so longė sholde a conseil˃ hyde; *secret*
Hir thoughte it swal˃ so sore aboute hir herte, *swelled*
That nedėly som word hir moste asterte;°
And sith she dorste telle it to no man,
Doun to a mareys fastė˃ by she ran; *marsh close*
Til she came there, hir hertė was afyre,

For . . . secree to be thought stable and discreet
Myda See Ovid, *Metamorphoses* XI. 174–93. Midas, King of Phrygia, had been given asses' ears by Apollo because he thought the music of Pan's pipes superior to that of the god's lyre. In Ovid's story, he was actually betrayed by his barber.
nedely . . . asterte necessarily some word must escape her

And, as a bitore bombleth in the myre,°
She leyde hir mouth unto the water doun:
'Biwreye> me nat, thou water, with thy soun,'> *betray / sound*
Quod she, 'to thee I telle it, and namo;> *no other*
Myn housbond hath longe asses erės two!
Now is myn herte all hool,> now is it oute; *whole*
I mighte no lenger kepe it, out of doute.'
Heer may ye se, thogh we a tyme abyde,
Yet out it moot,> we can no conseil hyde; *must*
The remenant of the tale if ye wol here,
Redeth Ovyde, and ther ye may it lere.> *learn*
  This knight, of which my tale is specially,
Whan that he saugh> he mighte nat come therby, *saw*
This is to seye, what wommen loven moost,
Withinne his brest ful sorweful was the goost;> *spirit*
But hoom he gooth, he mightė nat sojourne.> *stay*
The day was come, that hoomward moste> he tourne, *must*
And in his wey it happėd him to ryde,
In al this care, under> a forest syde, *by*
Wheras he saugh upon a daunce go
Of ladies foure and twenty, and yet mo;
Toward the whichė daunce he drow ful yerne,°
In hopė that som wisdom sholde he lerne.
But certeinly, er he came fully there,
Vanisshed was this daunce, he nistė> where. *knew not*
No creatùrė saugh he that bar> lyf, *bore*
Save on the grene he saugh sittinge a wyf;> *woman*
A fouler wight> ther may no man devyse.> *creature / imagine*
Agayn> the knight this oldė wyf gan ryse, *before*
And seyde, 'Sir knight, heer-forth ne lyth> no wey.> *lies / road*
Tel me, what that ye seken, by your fey?> *faith*
Paraventure it may the bettre be;
Thise oldė folk can muchel> thing,' quod she. *know much*
  'My levė mooder,'> quod this knight, certeyn, *dear mother*
'I nam> but deed, but if that I can seyn *am*
What thing it is that wommen most desyre;
Coude ye me wisse, I wolde wel quyte your hyre.'°
  'Plighte me thy trouthe, heer in myn hand,' quod she,
'The nextė thing that I requerė> thee, *ask*
Thou shalt it do, if it lye in thy might;
And I wol telle it yow er it be night.'
'Have heer my trouthė,' quod the knight, 'I grante.'
  'Thannė,' quod she, 'I dar me wel avante,> *boast*
Thy lyf is sauf,> for I wol stonde therby, *safe*

bitore . . . myre A bittern makes a booming sound in the mud. The bittern, a kind of small heron, was thought to make its characteristic bellowing cry by plunging its beak into the mud.

drow . . . yerne approached very eagerly

Coude . . . hyre if you could make me know, I would pay you a good reward for it

Upon my lyf, the queen wol seye as I.
Lat see which is the proudeste of hem alle,
That wereth on a coverchief or a calle,°
That dar seye nay, of that I shal thee teche;
Lat us go forth withouten lenger speche.'
Tho rounėd she a pistel in his ere,°
And bad him to be glad, and have no fere.
  Whan they be comen to the court, this knight
Seyde, 'He had holde his day, as he hadde hight,> *promised*
And redy was his answere,' as he sayde.
Ful many a noble wyf, and many a mayde,
And many a widwe, for that they ben wyse,
The quene hirself sittinge as a justyse,
Assembled been, his answere for to here;
And afterward this knight was bode> appere. *bidden*
  To every wight commanded was silènce,
And that the knight sholde telle in audience,°
What thing that worldly wommen loven best.
This knight ne stood nat stille> as doth a best,> *silent / beast*
But to his questioùn anon answerde
With manly voys, that al the court it herde:
  'My ligė> lady, generally,' quod he, *liege*
'Wommen desyren to have sovereyntee> *dominion*
As wel over hir housbond as hir love,
And for to been in maistrie him above;
This is your moste desyr, thogh ye me kille,
Doth as yow list, I am heer at your wille.'°
  In al the court ne was ther wyf ne mayde,
Ne widwe, that contraried> that he sayde, *contradicted*
But seyden, 'He was worthy han> his lyf.' *to keep*
  And with that word up stirte> the oldė wyf, *started*
Which that the knight saugh sittinge in the grene:
'Mercy,' quod she, 'my sovereyn lady quene!
Er that your court departė, do me right.
I taughtė this answère unto the knight;
For which he plightė me his trouthė there,
The firstė thing I wolde of him requere,
He wolde it do, if it lay in his might.
Bifore the court than preye I thee, sir knight,'
Quod she, 'that thou me take unto thy wyf;
For wel thou wost> that I have kept> thy lyf. *knowest / saved*
If I sey fals, sey nay, upon thy fey!'
  This knight answerde, 'Allas! and weylawey!

That . . . calle that wears upon her head-covering or caul; the caul was a close-fitting netted cap or headdress
Tho rouned . . . ere then she whispered a short lesson (epistle) in his ear

in audience in formal hearing
thogh . . . wille even if you kill me (for saying it), do as pleases you, I am at your disposal here

I woot right wel that swich was my biheste.> *promise*
For Goddės love, as chees> a newe requeste; *choose*
Tak al my good, and lat my body go.'
'Nay than,' quod she, 'I shrewe> us bothė two! *curse*
For thogh that I be foul, and old, and pore,
I nolde for al the metal, ne for ore,
That under erthe is grave,> or lyth> above, *buried / lies*
But if thy wyf I were, and eek thy love.'
'My love?' quod he; 'nay, my dampnacioùn!> *damnation*
Allas! that any of my nacioùn°
Sholde ever so foulė disparàgėd> be!' *disgraced*
But al for noght, the ende is this, that he
Constreynėd> was, he nedės moste hir wedde; *forced*
And taketh his olde wyf, and gooth to bedde.
Now wolden som men seye, paraventùre,
That, for my necligence, I do no cure°
To tellen yow the joye and al th'array°
That at the festė was that ilkė day.
To whichė thing shortly answere I shal;
I seye, ther nas no joye ne feste at al,
Ther nas but hevinesse and muchė sorwe;
For privėly he wedded hir on a morwe,> *morning*
And al day after hidde him as an oule;
So wo was him, his wyf lookėd so foule.
Greet was the wo the knight hadde in his thoght,
Whan he was with his wyf abedde ybroght;
He walweth,> and he turneth to and fro. *tosses*
His oldė wyf lay smylinge evermo,
And seyde, 'O derė housbond, Benedicitė!> *bless me*
Fareth> every knight thus with his wyf as ye? *behaves*
Is this the lawe of King Arthùrės hous?
Is every knight of his so dangerous?> *unapproachable*
I am your owenė love and eek your wyf;
I am she, which that savėd hath your lyf;
And certės, yet dide I yow never unright;
Why fare ye thus with me this firstė night?
Ye faren lyk a man had lost his wit;
What is my gilt? for Goddes love, tel me it,
And it shal been amended, if I may.'
'Amended?' quod this knight, 'allas! nay, nay!
It wol nat been amended never mo!
Thou art so loothly,> and so old also, *hateful*
And therto comen of so lowe a kinde,> *nature*
That litel wonder is, thogh I walwe and winde.> *toss and turn*
So woldė God myn hertė woldė breste!'> *break*

nacioùn birth; i.e. family
for . . . cure because of my negligence, I do not take the trouble
th'array the arrangements, special preparations

'Is this,' quod she, 'the cause of your unreste?'
'Ye, certainly,' quod he, 'no wonder is.'
'Now, sire,' quod she, 'I coude amende al this,
If that me liste, er it were dayės three,
So wel ye mightė bere yow° unto me.
But for ye speken of swich gentillesse°
As is descended out of old richesse,
That therfore sholden ye be gentil men,
Swich arrogàncė is nat worth an hen.
Loke who that is most vertuous alway,
Privee and apert,° and most entendeth ay°
To do the gentil dedės that he can,
And tak him for the grettest> gentil man. *greatest*
Crist wol,> we clayme of him our gentillesse, *wishes that*
Nat of our eldrės for hir old richesse.°
For thogh they yeve us al hir heritage,
For which we clayme to been of heigh parage,> *descent*
Yet may they nat biquethė, for nothing,
To noon of us hir vertuous living,
That made hem gentil men ycallėd be;
And bad us folwen hem in swich degree.°
  Wel can the wysė poete of Florènce,
That hightė> Dant,° speken in this sentènce;> *is called / wisdom*
Lo in swich maner rym is Dantės tale:
"Ful selde> up ryseth by his branches smale *seldom*
Prowesse> of man, for God, of his goodnesse, *excellence*
Wol that of him we clayme our gentillesse";
For of our eldrės may we nothing clayme
But temporel thing, that man may hurte and mayme.
  Eek every wight wot this as wel as I,
If gentillesse were planted naturelly
Unto a certeyn linage, doun the lyne,
Privee ne apert, than wolde they never fyne> *cease*
To doon of gentillesse the faire offyce;> *function*
They mightė do no vileinye or vyce.°
  Tak fyr,> and ber> it in the derkeste hous *fire / bear*
Bitwix this and the mount of Caucasus,°
And lat men shette> the dorės and go thenne;> *shut / thence*
Yet wol the fyr as fairė lye° and brenne,> *burn*
As twenty thousand men mighte it biholde;

bere yow behave
gentillesse gentleness, noble kindness; see Chaucer's poem below
Privee and apert in private and in public
entendeth ay always sets himself
Nat . . . richesse not from our ancestors, because of their ancient wealth
And . . . degree and they commanded us to follow them to that state
Dant Dante. The quotation is from his *Purgatorio* VII.121 ff. and emphasizes that gentilesse is not the inevitable result of noble blood and "old richesse."
If gentillesse . . . vyce (ll. 1140–44) If gentilesse were naturally implanted in a family and merely transmitted from father to son, then none of that family could ever do evil.
Caucasus i.e. to the furthest, coldest, and darkest of places
lye blaze; i.e. it is the nature of fire to be bright and warm, whether we are looking at it or not

His office naturel° ay wol it holde,
Up˃ peril of my lyf, til that it dye. *upon*
 Heer may ye see wel, how that genterye°
Is nat annexėd˃ to possessioùn,° *tied*
Sith folk ne doon hir operacioùn
Alwey, as dooth the fyr, lo! in his kinde.˃ *nature*
For, God it woot, men may wel often finde
A lordės sone˃ do shame and vileinye; *son*
And he that wol han prys of his gentrye°
For he was boren˃ of a gentil hous, *born*
And hadde hise eldrės noble and vertuous,
And nil himselven do no gentil dedis,
Ne folwe his gentil auncestre that deed˃ is, *dead*
He nis nat gentil, be he duk or erl;
For vileyns sinful dedės make a cherl.
For gentillessė nis but renomee˃ *renown*
Of thyne auncestres, for hir heigh bountee,°
Which is a strangė˃ thing to thy persone. *foreign*
Thy gentillessė cometh fro God allone;
Than comth our verray gentillesse of grace,
It was nothing biquethe us with our place.
 Thenketh how noble, as seith Valerius,°
Was thilkė Tullius Hostilius,°
That out of povert˃ roos to heigh noblesse. *poverty*
Redeth Senek,° and redeth eek Boëce,°
Ther shul ye seen expres that it no drede˃ is, *doubt*
That he is gentil that doth gentil dedis;
And therfore, leve˃ housbònd, I thus conclude, *dear*
Al˃ were it that myne auncestres were rude,˃ *although / lowly*
Yet may the hyė God, and so hope I,
Grantė me grace to liven vertuously.
Thanne am I gentil, whan that I biginne
To liven vertuously and weyvė˃ sinne. *leave off*
 And theras ye of povert me repreve,
The hyė God, on whom that we bileve,
In wilful˃ povert chees˃ to live his lyf. *voluntary / chose*
And certės every man, mayden, or wyf,
May understonde that Jesus, Hevenė king,
Ne wolde nat chese a viciouѕ living.
Glad povert is an honest˃ thing, certèyn; *honorable*
This wol Senek and otherė clerkės seyn.

office naturel the function which belongs to it by nature
genterye noble conduct, gentilesse
possessioun worldly riches, hereditary wealth
he . . . gentrye he that wants to have reputation on account of gentle birth
For . . . bountee what you claim as your nobility is only due to your ancestors, because of their great goodness
Valerius Valerius Maximus, 1st century A.D. Roman author of a book of *exempla* for rhetoricians
Tullius Hostilius Tullus Hostilius, the third king of Rome, 673–642 B.C., who began life as a shepherd, according to the story, and is used by Valerius as an example of rags-to-riches
Senek Lucius Annaeus Seneca, *c.*5 B.C.–65 A.D., Roman Stoic philosopher and dramatist; see his *Moral Epistles* 44
Boëce Boethius

Whoso that halt him payd of° his poverte,
I holde him riche, al hadde he nat a sherte.> *shirt*
He that coveyteth is a povrė wight,°
For he wolde han that is nat in his might.
But he that noght hath, ne covèyteth have,
Is riche, although ye holde him but a knave.
  Verray> povert, it singeth proprely;> *true / appropriately*
Juvenal seith of povert merily:
"The povrė man, whan he goth by the weye,
Bifore the thevės he may singe and pleye."°
Povert is hateful good, and, as I gesse,
A ful greet bringer out of bisiness;°
A greet amender eek of sapience> *wisdom*
To him that taketh it in pacience.
Povert is this, although it seme elenge:> *hard to bear*
Possessioùn, that no wight wol chalenge.> *claim*
Povert ful oftė, whan a man is lowe,
Maketh° his God and eek himself to knowe.
Povert a spectacle> is, as thinketh me, *eyeglass*
Thurgh which he may his verray frendės see.
And therfore, sire, sin that I noght> yow greve, *ought not*
Of my povert namore ye me repreve.> *reproach*
  Now, sire, of eldė> ye reprevė me; *old age*
And certės, sire, thogh noon auctoritee
Were in no book, ye gentils of honour
Seyn that men sholde an old wight doon favour,
And clepe him fader,> for your gentillesse; *father*
And auctours> shal I finden, as I gesse. *authorities*
  Now ther ye seye, that I am foul and old,
Than drede you noght to been a cokėwold;> *cuckold*
For filthe and eldė, also moot I thee,°
Been gretė wardeyns> upon chastitee. *guardians*
But nathelees, sin I knowe your delyt,
I shal fulfille your worldly appetyt.
  Chese now,' quod she, 'oon of thise thingės tweye,
To han me foul and old til that I deye,
And be to yow a trewė humble wyf,
And never yow displese in al my lyf,
Or ellės ye wol han me yong and fair,
And take your aventure> of the repair° *chance*
That shal be to your hous, bycause of me,
Or in som other placė, may wel be.
Now chese yourselven, whether> that yow lyketh.' *which*

Whoso . . . of whoever is contented with
He . . . wight he that covets more money is a poor person, i.e. the true pauper
Juvenal . . . pleye Juvenal, *Satire* X. 22
bisinesse Preoccupations. Most of these definitions are taken ultimately from the favorite medieval moral text, *Hadrian and Epictetus*, an apocryphal dialogue between the Emperor and the Philosopher. Chaucer probably got them from the 13th-century encyclopedist Vincent of Beauvais.
Maketh makes him
also . . . thee as I may thrive
repair frequenting, resort

This knight avyseth him> and sorė syketh,> *considers / sighs*
But attė laste he seyde in this manere,
'My lady and my love, and wyf so dere,
I put me in your wysė governance;
Cheseth> yourself, which may be most plesance,> *choose / pleasure*
And most honour to yow and me also.
I do no fors the whether° of the two;
For as yow lyketh,> it suffiseth> me.' *it pleases / satisfies*
'Thanne have I gete> of yow maistrye,' quod she, *got*
'Sin I may chese, and governe as me lest?'> *pleases*
'Ye, certės, wyf,' quod he, 'I holde it best.'
'Kis me,' quod she, 'we be no lenger wrothe;
For, by my trouthe, I wol be to yow bothe,
This is to seyn, ye, bothė fair and good.
I prey to God that I mot sterven wood,°
But> I to yow be also> good and trewe *unless / as*
As ever was wyf, sin that the world was newe.
And, but I be to morn> as fair to sene *tomorrow morning*
As any lady, emperyce, or quene,
That is bitwixe the est and eke the west,
Doth with my lyf and deeth right as yow lest.
Cast up the curtin, loke how that it is.'
And whan the knight saugh verraily al this,
That she so fair was, and so yong therto,
For joye he hente> hir in his armės two, *took*
His hertė bathėd in a bath of blisse;
A thousand tyme arewe> he gan hir kisse. *in succession*
And she obeyėd him in every thing
That mightė doon him plesance> or lyking.> *happiness / pleasure*
And thus they live, unto hir lyvės ende,
In parfit> joye; and Jesu Crist us sende *perfect*
Housbondes mekė, yonge, and fresshe abedde,
And grace t'overbyde> hem that we wedde. *outlast*
And eek I preyė Jesu shorte> hir lyves *shorten*
That wol nat be govèrnėd by hir wyves;
And olde and angry nigardes of dispence,> *paying*
God sende hem sonė> verray> pestilence. *at once / true*

Here endeth the Wyves Tale of Bathe

From Gesta Romanorum

Of Hanging

Valerius tells us that a man named Paletinus one day burst into a flood of tears; and, calling his son and his neighbours around him, said, 'Alas! alas! I have now growing in my garden a fatal tree, on which my first poor wife hung herself, then my second, and after that my third. Have I not therefore cause

I . . . whether I do not care which **mot . . . wood** may die crazy

for the wretchedness I exhibit?' 'Truly,' said one who was called Arrius, 'I marvel that you should weep at such an unusual instance of good fortune! Give me, I pray you, two or three sprigs of that gentle tree, which I will divide with my neighbours, and thereby afford every man an opportunity of indulging the laudable wishes of his spouse.' Paletinus complied with his friend's request; and ever after found this remarkable tree the most productive part of his estate.

Application

My beloved, the tree is the cross of Christ. The man's three wives are, pride, lusts of the heart, and lusts of the eyes, which ought to be thus suspended and destroyed. He who solicited a part of the tree is any good Christian.

The Franklin's Prologue and Tale

The Franklin's Tale is about *gentilesse,* true nobility and virtue (see Chaucer's short poem of that title). It explores the relation between *trouthe,* or integrity, the central notion of the short "balade of good counsel" and the keeping of an oath, which is part of *gentilesse;* and demonstrates how *fredom,* or generosity, if exercised by all those involved in a situation, will bring it to good issue. Perhaps Chaucer means to suggest, in the Franklin's preoccupation with the idea, a sense of the social position he occupies as a member of the rising country gentry, aspiring to the aristocracy.

According to the Franklin, his tale is an old "Breton lay," a literary genre first popularized in twelfth-century France as a short narrative romance in verse, usually on a theme of love, promises, and magical occurrences. Though many of the motifs of the tale occur in extant lays, the exact source of Chaucer's tale has not been discovered—and even the exact placing of the scene in a locality in Brittany paradoxically tells against it. There are extant fourteenth-century English poems of the "lay" type, but the form was at that date somewhat old-fashioned. Chaucer may be giving us some suggestion of the kind of man the Franklin was by putting into his mouth an out-of-date form set in the long ago.

The plot of the tale is probably taken either from Boccaccio's *Il Filocolo* or from his *Decameron* (it appears in both works); but the germ of the story goes back very much farther in time and can be found in a widely diffused Eastern folk-tale in which a woman's unconsidered promise to a second lover puts her in the same embarrassing position as Dorigen. Her first lover advises her to keep her promise, and her second then releases her from it. The question is asked, as it is in Boccaccio, which of the three showed the greatest generosity.

Chaucer's treatment of the story, with the mass of astrological and magical detail laid onto, but never obscuring, the delicate articulation of its central moral content, is not the statement of a question about love (*questione d'amore*). It is an exploration of the basis of marriage, refining some of the questions that have already been raised by the Wife of Bath, the Clerk, and the Merchant. Dorigen, opting for love in marriage of the most idealistic kind, is brought to realize that virtue is not single and cannot be exercised in isolation, so that virtues may come into conflict with each other as well as with vices.

Prologue

The Prologe of the Frankeleyns Tale

Thise oldė gentil Britons in hir dayes
Of diverse adventùrės maden layes,
Rymeyėd in hir firstė Briton tonge;°
Which layės with hir instruments they songe,
Or ellės redden> hem for hir pleasunce;> *read / pleasure*
And oon of hem have I in remembraùnce,
Which I shal seyn with good wil as I can.
  But, sirės, bycause I am a burel> man, *plain*
At my biginning first I yow biseche
Have me excusėd of my rudė speche;°
I lernėd never rethoryk, certeyn;
Thing that I speke, it moot> be bare and pleyn. *must*
I sleep never on the mount of Pernaso,°
Ne lernėd Marcus Tullius Cithero.°
Coloùrs ne knowe I none, withouten drede,°
But swiche> coloùrs as growen in the mede>, *such / meadow*
Or ellės swiche as men dye or peynte.
Coloùrs of rethoryk ben me to queynte;> *ingenious*
My spirit feeleth noght of swich matere
But if yow list,> my talė shul ye here. *it pleases*

Thise . . . tonge (ll. 1–3) These noble old Bretons, in their own day, made lays about various happenings, written in rhyme in their earliest Breton language.

rude speche This is the conventional Chaucerian disclaimer, in an age where ornateness and enrichment of the language was highly thought of, whether the poet speaks in his own person or through the mouth of one of his characters. The Franklin speaks as a good plain man, who never knew rhetoric. As so often in Chaucer, the character is here made to protest his unfitness as an orator by using the exact form in which a skilled orator would do the same thing: *diminution* of oneself, to begin; then varying of the theme (ll. 10–19); with elegant circumlocution in the oblique references to poetry; and a play on the word *color* (ornament of style / natural color / artificial color), a figure of speech known as *adnomination.* The Franklin uses a slightly stiff and elaborate rhetoric for his higher-flown moments, but in general his narrative is direct.

Pernaso Parnassus, the double-peaked mountain in Phocis, Greece; sacred to Apollo, god of music and poetry; to his servants the nine Muses, daughters of Memory and guardians of poetry, music, dance, and learning; and to Dionysus (Bacchus), god of wine and song. Chaucer took the bit about sleeping on Parnassus (and the exact form of the word) from the Roman satirist Persius (34–62 A.D.): it was a very popular quotation.

Cithero Marcus Tullius Cicero (106–43 B.C.), the Roman statesman and writer, the best-known and most used of all classical rhetoricians in the Middle Ages. So, says the Franklin, I am eloquent in neither poetry nor prose.

withouten drede conventional oral formula: "without fear," hence, "certainly"

Tale

Here biginneth the Frankeleyns Tale

In Armorik,° that callėd is Britayne,
Ther was a knight that loved and dide his payne°
To serve a lady in his bestė wyse;> — *manner*
And many a labour, many a greet empryse> — *enterprise*
He for his lady wroghte,> er she were wonne. — *did*
For she was oon the faireste° under sonne,
And eek> therto come of so heigh kinrede,> — *also / ancestry*
That wel unnethės dorste> this knight, for drede, — *hardly dared*
Telle hir his wo, his peyne, and his distresse.
But attė laste, she, for his worthinesse,
And namely> for his meke obeÿsaùnce,> — *especially / obedience*
Hath swich a pitee caught of his penaùnce,
That privėly> she fil of his accord — *secretly*
To take him for hir housbonde and hir lord,
Of swich lordshipe as men han over hir wyves.
And for to lede the more in blisse hir lyves,
Of his free will he swoor hir as a knight,
That never in al his lyf he, day ne night,
Ne sholde upon him takė no maistrye°
Agayn hir wil, ne kythe> hir jalousye, — *show*
But hir obeye, and folwe hir will in all
As any lovere to his lady shall;
Save that the name of soveraynėtee,
That wolde he have for shame of his degree.°
  She thankėd him, and with ful greet humblesse> — *meekness*
She seyde: 'Sire, sith> of your gentillesse° — *since*
Ye profre> me to have so large> a reyne, — *offer / loose*
Ne woldė never God bitwixe us tweyne,
As in my gilt,> were outher> werre or stryf. — *responsibility / either*
Sir, I wol be your humble trewė wyf,
Have heer my trouthe, til that myn hertė breste.> — *break*
Thus been they bothe in quiete and in reste.
  For o thing, sirės, saufly> dar I seye,> — *confidently / say*
That frendės everich> other moot> obeye, — *each / must*
If they wol longė holden> companye. — *keep*
Love wol nat ben constreynėd by maistrye;

Armorik Armorica (*Ar vor,* land by the sea) was the old name for Brittany, before, so the legend goes, it was named Little Britain "beyond the sea," to emphasize its links with Greater Britain. Chaucer uses this bit of recondite, ancient information to enhance the "once upon a time" atmosphere of the Franklin's romance of magic and true nobility.

payne The hero's pains, service, and undertakings for the lady; the woe, pain and distress he suffers in silence because he loves her; and his entire submission, mark him as the courtly lover.

oon the faireste either "one of the most beautiful" or "the most beautiful"

no maistrye i.e. his love would tame his natural masculine desire for domination, mastery

Save . . . degree only that he wished to have the title of ruler, so as not to bring shame on his status (as a husband); love might make them equal, but the ordinary and courtly appearances must be kept up

gentillesse magnanimous behavior becoming a man of true nobility in birth and feeling; it is self, not birth, that is important

Whan maistriė comth, the god of love anon
Beteth˃ hise winges, and farewel! he is gon!	*beats*
Love is a thing as any spirit free;
Wommen of kinde˃ desiren libertee,	*nature*
And nat to ben constreynėd as a thral;˃	*slave*
And so don men, if I soth˃ seyen shal.˃	*truth / must*
Loke who that is most pacient in love,
He is at his avantage al above.
Pacience is an heigh vertù, certeyn,
For it venquisseth, as thise clerkės seyn,°
Thingės that rigour sholdė never atteyne.
For every word men may nat chyde or pleyne.
Lerneth to suffre, or elles, so moot I goon,
Ye shul it lerne, wherso ye wole or noon.°
For in this world, certein, ther no wight is,
That he ne dooth or seith somtyme amis.
Irė, siknesse, or constellacioùn,°
Wyn,˃ wo, or chaunginge of complexioùn˃	*wine / constitution*
Causeth ful ofte to doon amis or speken.
On every wrong a man may nat be wreken.˃	*revenged*
After˃ the tymė,˃ moste be temperaunce	*according to / occasion*
To every wight that can on˃ governaunce.	*is wise in*
And therfore hath this wysė worthy knight,
To live in esė, suffrance˃ hir bihight,˃	*permission / promised*
And she to him ful wisly˃ gan to˃ swere	*firmly / did*
That never sholde ther be defaute° in here.˃	*her*
  Heer may men seen an humble wys accord;
Thus hath she take hir servant and hir lord,°
Servant in love, and lord in mariàge;
Than was he bothe in lordship and servage;
Servage? nay, but in lordshipe above,
Sith he hath bothe his lady and his love;
His lady, certės,˃ and his wyf also,	*indeed*
The which that˃ lawe of love acordeth˃ to.	*who / agrees*
And whan he was in this prosperitee,˃	*happiness*
Hoom with his wyf he gooth to his contree,
Nat fer fro Penmark,° ther his dwelling was,
Wheras he liveth in blisse and in solas.˃	*comfort*
  Who coudė telle, but˃ he had wedded be,	*unless*

Pacience . . . seyn a glance at the Clerk's Tale of the patient Griselda, with overtones from the Bible (Proverbs 16:32; James 1:4), and at such collections of moral precepts for schools as the *Distichs of Cato* (see the Miller's Tale, l. 119)
Lerneth . . . noon learn to bear things, or else, as true as I walk, you will have to learn it, whether you want to or not
constellacioun the combination of the planets, at any given time, was thought to influence every aspect of earthly life
defaute anything lacking
servant . . . lord The knight's love is better than love within the courtly conventions, for he has the best of both worlds, his mistress also being his wife.
Penmark Penmarc'h just south of Brest, in Brittany; its headland, like much of the coast of Brittany, has a rocky shore, with a chain of granite rocks out to sea. Chaucer may have seen the place or heard it described, since the rocks of Brittany were proverbial, and lay on a much-used trade route.

The joye, the ese, and the prosperitee
That is bitwixe an housbonde and his wyf?
A yeer and more lasted his blisful lyf,
Til that the knight of which I speke of thus,
That of Kayrrud° was cleped˃ Arveragus,° — *called*
Shoop˃ him to goon, and dwelle a yeer or tweyne˃ — *arranged / two*
In Engėlond, that cleped was eek˃ Briteyne,° — *also*
To seeke in armės worship and honour;
For al his lust˃ he sette in swich labour; — *pleasure*
And dwellėd ther two yeer, the book seith thus.
  Now wol I stinte˃ of this Arveragus, — *cease*
And speken I wole of Dorigene° his wyf,
That loveth hir housbonde as hir hertės lyf.
For his absence wepeth she and syketh,˃ — *sighs*
As doon thise noble wyvės° whan hem lyketh.˃ — *it pleases*
She moorneth,˃ waketh, waileth, fasteth, pleyneth;˃ — *mourns / complains*
Desyr of his presènce hir so distreyneth,˃ — *constrains*
That al this wydė world she sette˃ at noght. — *valued*
Hir frendės, whiche that knewe hir hevy thoght,
Conforten hir in al that ever they may;
They prechen hir, they telle hir night and day,
That causėlees she sleeth˃ hirself, allas! — *is killing*
And every confort possible in this cas
They doon to hir with al hir bisinesse,˃ — *diligence*
Al for to make hir leve hir hevinesse.
  By proces,˃ as ye knowen everichoon,˃ — *gradually / everyone*
Men may so longė graven˃ in a stoon,° — *engrave*
Til som figùre therinne emprented˃ be. — *imprinted*
So longe han they confòrted hir, til she
Receyvėd hath, by hope and by resoùn,˃ — *reason*
The emprenting of hir consolacioùn,
Thurgh which hir gretė sorwe gan aswage;˃ — *diminish*
She may nat alwey duren˃ in swich rage.˃ — *endure / great grief*
  And eek Arveragus, in al this care,˃ — *sorrow*
Hath sent hir lettres hoom of his welfare,
And that he wol come hastily˃ agayn; — *soon*
Or ellės hadde this sorwe hir hertė slayn.
  Hir freendės sawe hir sorwe gan to slake,˃ — *slacken*
And preyėde hir on knees, for Goddės sake,

Kayrrud A Celtic name, *kaer* is a fortified place; *rud* may mean red. The name does not occur near Penmarc'h.
Arveragus Latinized form of a Celtic name; Chaucer may have taken it from Geoffrey of Monmouth's 12th-century chronicle (*Historia Regum Britanniae*), where the name of Aurelius also occurs. Some scholars have suggested that Chaucer found the idea for this tale in the chronicle, but the evidence is inconclusive.
Briteyne See l. 21.
Dorigene a Breton name
For . . . wyves The Squire had already told a story involving a wife's grief at separation, reinforcing some remarks in the tale of his father, the Knight.
graven . . . stoon Chaucer refines the image which he probably found in Boccaccio. Constant dripping wears away a stone, as Boccaccio says, but in this courtly context the patience and delicacy needed by the gem-engraver are paralleled by the same qualities in Dorigen's friends when they try to console her. This is the atmosphere of the poem.

To come and romen> hir in companye, — *go about*
Awey to dryve hir derkė fantasye.> — *gloomy imaginings*
And finally, she graunted that requeste;
For wel she saugh> that it was for the beste. — *saw*
  Now stood hir castel fastė by the see,
And often with hir freendės walketh she
Hir to disporte upon the bank on heigh,
Wheras she many a ship and bargė seigh.> — *saw*
Seilinge> hir cours, wheras hem listė> go; — *sailing / it pleased*
But than was that a parcel> of hir wo. — *part*
For to hirself ful ofte 'Allas!' seith she,
'Is ther no ship, of so manye as I see,
Wol bringen hom my lord? than were myn herte
Al warisshed> of his bittre peynės smerte.>' — *cured / sharp*
  Another tyme ther wolde she sitte and thinke,
And caste hir eyen dounward fro the brinke.
But whan she saugh the grisly rokkės blake,°
For verray fere so wolde hir hertė quake,
That on hir feet she mighte hir noght sustene.> — *sustain*
Than wolde she sitte adoun upon the grene,
And pitously> into the see biholde, — *pitifully*
And seyn> right thus, with sorweful sykės> colde: — *say / sighs*
  '釘ternė God, that thurgh thy purveyaùnce> — *foreknowledge*
Ledest the world by certein governaùnce,
In ydel,> as men seyn, ye nothing make; — *vain*
But, Lord, thise grisly feendly> rokkės blake, — *hostile*
That semen rather a foul confusioùn
Of werk than any fair creacioùn
Of swich a parfit wys God and a stable,> — *sure*
Why han ye wroght this werk unresonable?
For by this werk, south, north, ne west, ne eest,
Ther nis yfostrėd> man, ne brid,> ne beest; — *helped / bird*
It dooth no good, to my wit,> but anoyeth.> — *knowledge / harms*
See ye nat, Lord, how mankinde it destroyeth?
An hundred thousand bodies of mankinde
Han rokkės slayn, al be they nat in minde,> — *remembered*
Which mankinde is so fair part of thy werk
That thou it madest lyk to thyn owene merk.°
Than semėd it ye hadde a greet chiertee> — *love*
Toward mankinde; but how than may it be
That ye swiche menės> make, it to destroyen, — *means*

rokkes blake Black rocks; Dorigen's meditation, in her sorrow at being parted from Arveragus, with its accumulation of evil and hellishness as she looks at the rocks, is on the theme of how a good Creator could bring himself to create sorrow, evil, and misshapenness. He must have known what He was about, since He has "purveyaunce" (l. 157): foreknowledge, providence. Boethius (born *c.*480 A.D.) explains this in *The Consolation of Philosophy*. The godhead, perfect and single, is outside all His creation, though it is He who keeps all creation in being. Everything, even the causes of things, have true existence only within God's mind and as far as they are part of the plan of the universe which is in His mind and is called Providence. See Romans 8:28ff.

merk Likeness, image (Genesis 1:27: "So God created man in his own image"). *Merk* originally meant the image or likeness on a coin.

Which menės do no good, but ever anoyen?> *hurt*
I woot wel clerkes wol seÿn, as hem leste,> *it pleases*
By arguments,° that al is for the beste,
Though I ne can the causes nat yknowe.
But thilkė God, that madė wind to blowe,
As kepe my lord!° this my conclusioùn;
To clerkės lete> I al disputisoùn.> *leave / dispute*
But woldė God that alle thise rokkės blake
Were sonken> into Hellė for his sake! *sunken*
Thise rokkės sleen myn hertė for the fere.>" *fear*
Thus wolde she seyn, with many a pitous tere.
Hir freendės sawe that it was no disport> *pleasure*
To romen> by the see, but disconfòrt; *walk*
And shopen> for to pleyen> somwher elles. *arranged / amuse themselves*
They leden hir by riverės and by welles,> *pools*
And eek in otherė places delitables;> *pleasant*
They dauncen, and they pleyen at ches and tables.°
So on a> day, right in the morwė> tyde, *one / morning*
Unto a gardin that was ther bisyde,
In which that they had maad hir ordinaùnce> *orders*
Of vitaille> and of other purveyaùnce,> *food / prearrangements*
They goon and pleye hem al the longė day.
And this was on the sixtė morwe of May,°
Which May had peynted with his softė shoures
This gardin° ful of levės and of floures;
And craft of mannės hand so curiously> *ingeniously*
Arrayėd> hadde this gardin, trewėly, *laid out*
That never was ther gardin of swich prys,> *excellence*
But if> it were the verray Paradys. *unless*
The odour of flourės and the fresshė sighte
Wolde han maad any hertė for to lighte> *lighten*
That ever was born, but if too gret siknesse,
Or too gret sorwe helde it in distresse;
So ful it was of beautee with plesaunce.
At after diner gonnė> they to daunce, *began*
And singe also, save Dorigen allone,
Which made alwey hir còmpleint and hir mone;> *moan*

arguments Arguments, causes, conclusions are all terms in Scholastic logic: a mild bit of sarcasm by Dorigen on "explainers."
But . . . lord but may that same God as made winds blow, preserve my master
ches . . . tables chess and backgammon; the latter a board game, played by two opponents with dice and "men"
sixte . . . May The sixth morning of May. Two or three days in each month were marked as "evil" or "Egyptian" (because of God's plagues on Egypt) days in medieval calendars. May 6 is sometimes one. On such a day it was thought especially dangerous to fall ill or begin anything in which one hoped to be successful. See Nun's Priest's Tale, l. 424.
gardin The garden setting is meant to recall, with a hint of coming disaster, the exemplar of all gardens, the Garden of Eden, where Adam and Eve, our first parents, were said to have spent only one brief hour, before the first sin and their expulsion (Fig. 56). Medieval literature teems with descriptions of such lovely spots *(loci amoeni)*, especially in a love context: they give solace for pain physical, mental, and spiritual. Chaucer's description may have been borrowed from the French of Guillaume de Machaut (*c.* 1300–1377); it balances the description of the rocks, above.

For she ne saugh him on the daunċe go,
That was hir housbonde and hir love also.
But nathėlees she moste a tyme abyde,
And with good hopė lete hir sorwe slyde.
  Upon this daunce, amongės othere men,
Dauncėd a squyer° biforen Dorigen,
That fressher˃ was and jolyer of array, *handsomer*
As to my doom,˃ than is the monthe of May.° *judgment*
He singeth, daunceth, passinge˃ any man *surpassing*
That is, or was, sith˃ that the world bigan. *since*
Therwith he was, if men sholde him discryve,˃ *describe*
Oon of the bestė faringe˃ man on lyve; *most handsome*
Yong, strong, right vertuous,˃ and riche and wys, *accomplished*
And wel biloved, and holden in gret prys.˃ *esteem*
And shortly, if the sothe˃ I tellen shal, *truth*
Unwiting˃ of this Dorigen at al, *unknown*
This lusty squyer, servant to Venus,°
Which that yclepėd˃ was Aurelius, *called*
Had loved hir best of any creatùre
Two yeer and more, as was his aventùre,˃ *fortune*
But never dorste he telle hir his grevaùnce;˃ *distress*
Withouten coppe he drank al his penaùnce.°
He was despeyrėd, nothing dorste he seye,
Save in his songės somwhat wolde he wreye˃ *disemble*
His wo, as in a general compleyning;
He seyde he loved, and was biloved nothing.
Of swich materė made he manye layes,
Songės, compleintės, roundels, virėlayes,°
How that he dorstė nat his sorwe telle,
But languissheth, as a Furie° dooth in Helle;
And die he moste, he seyde, as dide Ekko°
For Narcisus, that dorste nat telle hir wo.
In other manere than ye here˃ me seye, *hear*
Ne dorste he nat to hir his wo biwreye;˃ *reveal*
Save that, paràventure,˃ somtyme at daunces, *by chance*
Ther yongė folk kepen hir observaùnces,

squyer The squire has a Romano-British name (Aurelius) to suggest the long ago; and may be intended to recall Chaucer's Squire.
That fressher . . . May conventional description of a young man; in medieval calendars May is sometimes shown as a brightly dressed squire on horseback
Venus goddess of love
Withouten . . . penaunce perhaps "without measure he took his medicine" (*coppe*-cup); or "under difficulties"; or "he drank his penance eagerly"; i.e. scooping it up with his hands instead of using a cup—a reference to the contraries of love
layes . . . virelayes All these are varieties of the short lyrical love-song, of which the complaint could also deal with religious love. Lays and songs are general terms, meaning the same thing in this context: "lay" is not used in the technical sense of l. 2. The complaint bewails lack of success in love; see Chaucer's satirical *Complaint to His Purse* below. It was a French genre, like the roundel (rondeau) and virelay (see Glossary).
Furie The three Furies were daughters of Pluto, king of the underworld, who pursued evil-doers: always in pain themselves (*languissheth*), because in hell; see Skelton, *Philip Sparrow*, l. 74, below.
Ekko The nymph Echo loved Narcissus, who preferred his own reflected self to her. She took to the woods and pined away for grief, until there was nothing left of her but her voice.

It may wel be he lokėd on hir face
In swich a wyse, as man that asketh grace;
But nothing wistė˃ she of his entente. *knew*
Nathėlees, it happėd, er˃ they thennės wente, *before*
Bycausė that he was hir neighėbour,
And was a man of worship and honour,
And hadde yknowen him of tymė yore,°
They fille in˃ speche; and forth more and more *fell into*
Unto his purpose drough˃ Aurelius, *moved*
And whan he saugh his tyme, he seydė thus:
'Madame,' quod he, 'by God that this world made,
So˃ that I wiste it mighte your hertė glade,˃ *if / delight*
I wolde, that day that your Arveragus
Wente over the see, that I, Aurelius,
Had went ther˃ never I sholde have come agayn; *gone where*
For wel I woot˃ my service is in vayn. *know*
My guerdon˃ is but bresting˃ of myn herte; *reward / breaking*
Madame, reweth˃ upon my peynės smerte;˃ *have pity / sharp*
For with a word ye may me sleen˃ or save, *slay*
Heer at your feet God wolde that I were grave!˃ *buried*
I ne have as now no leyser˃ more to seye; *leisure*
Have mercy, swete, or ye wol do˃ me deye˃!' *make / die*
She gan to loke upon Aurelius:
'Is this your wil,' quod she, 'and sey ye thus?
Never erst,'˃ quod she, 'ne wiste I what ye mente. *before*
But now, Aurelie, I knowe your entente,
By thilkė God that yaf˃ me soule and lyf, *gave*
Ne shal I never been untrewė wyf
In word ne werk,˃ as far as I have wit: *deed*
I wol ben his to whom that I am knit;
Tak this for fynal answer as of me.'
But after that in pley˃ thus seydė she: *jest*
'Aurelie,' quod she, 'by heighė God above,
Yet wolde I grauntė yow to been your love,
Sin I yow see so pitously complayne;
Loke what day that, endėlong˃ Britayne, *all along*
Ye remove alle the rokkės, stoon by stoon,°
That they ne lettė˃ ship ne boot˃ to goon: *hinder / boat*
I seye, whan ye han maad the coost˃ so clene *coast*
Of rokkės, that ther nis no stoon ysene,
Than wol I love yow best of any man,
Have heer my trouthe,˃ in al that ever I can.' *word*
'Is ther non other grace in yow?' quod he.
'No, by that Lord,' quod she, 'that makėd me!

And hadde . . . yore and she had known him for some time past

stoon by stoon Every one. Dorigen's condition is an extravagant parody (to emphasize her love for Arveragus) of the tasks that heroines of the romance would lay on their lovers; but with the connotation "sooner shall you move these rocks than me."

For wel I woot that it shal never bityde.˃ *happen*
Lat swiche foliės out of your hertė slyde.
What deyntee˃ sholde a man han in his lyf *pleasure*
For to go love another mannės wyf,
That hath hir body whan so that him lyketh?'
  Aurelius ful oftė sorė syketh;˃ *sighs*
Wo was Aureliė, whan that he this herde,
And with a sorweful herte he thus answerde:
  'Madame,' quod he, 'this were an inpossìble!˃ *impossibility*
Than moot I dye of sodein˃ deth horrìble.' *sudden*
And with that word he turnėd him anoon.˃ *at once*
Tho come hir othere freendės many oon,
And in the aleyes romeden˃ up and doun, *paths walked*
And nothing wiste of this conclusioùn,
But sodeinly bigonnė revel˃ newe *began diversion*
Til that the brightė sonnė loste his hewe;˃ *color*
For th'orisonte˃ hath reft˃ the sonne his light; *the horizon / taken*
(This is as muche to seye as it was night).
And hoom they goon in joye and in solas,
Save only wrecche Aurelius, allas!
He to his hous is goon with sorweful herte;
He seeth he may nat fro his deeth asterte.˃ *escape*
Him semėd that he felte his hertė colde;
Up to the hevene his handės he gan holde,
And on his knowės˃ bare he sette˃ him doun, *knees / put*
And in his raving˃ seyde his orisoùn.˃ *delirium / prayer*
For verray wo out of his wit˃ he breyde.˃ *mind / went*
He nistė˃ what he spak, but thus he seyde; *knew not*
With pitous˃ herte his pleynt hath he bigonne *sad*
Unto the goddes, and first unto the sonne:
  He seyde, 'Appollo,° god and governour
Of every plauntė, herbė, tree and flour,
That yevest,˃ after thy declinacioùn,° *gives*
To ech of hem his tyme and his sesoùn,
As thyn herberwė˃ chaungeth lowe or hye; *position*
Lord Phebus, cast thy merciable˃ yë *merciful*
On wrecche Aurelie, which that am but lorn.˃ *lost*
Lo, lord! my lady hath my deeth ysworn
Withoutė gilt,° but thy benignitee
Upon my dedly˃ herte have som pitee! *doomed*
For wel I woot,˃ lord Phebus, if yow lest, *know*
Ye may me helpen, save my lady, best.°
Now voucheth sauf˃ that I may yow devyse˃ *grant / show*
How that I may been holpe˃ and in what wyse. *helped*

Appollo Apollo (Phoebus), god of light, the sun
after thy declinacioun according to your celestial latitude or seasonal position in the sky; *herberwe* (l. 327) is literally lodging
Withoute gilt i.e. when I am innocent
Ye may . . . best you can be my best helper of anyone, except my lady

Your blisful suster, Lucina° the shene,> *shining*
That of the see is chief goddesse and quene,
Though Neptunus° have deitee in the see,
Yet emperesse aboven him is she:
Ye knowen wel, lord, that right as hir desyr
Is to be quiked> and lightned of your fyr,> *enlivened / fire*
For which she folweth yow ful bisily,> *assiduously*
Right so the see desyreth naturelly
To folwen hir, as she that is goddesse
Bothe in the see and riveres more and lesse.
Wherfore, lord Phebus, this is my requeste—
Do this miracle, or do myn hertė breste—
That now, next at this opposicioùn,°
Which in the signe shal be of the Leoùn,°
As preyeth hir so greet a flood to bringe,
That fyve fadme> at the leeste it oversprynge> *fathoms / rise above*
The hyeste rokke in Armorik Briteyne;
And lat this flood endurė yerės tweyne;
Than certės to my lady may I seye:
"Holdeth> your heste,° the rokkės been aweye." *keep / promise*
Lord Phebus, dooth this miracle for me;
Preye hir she go no faster cours than ye;°
I seye, preyeth your suster that she go
No faster cours than ye thise yerės two.
Than shal she been evene attė fulle alway,
And spring-flood> lastė bothė night and day. *spring-tide*
And, but> she vouchėsauf> in swiche manere *unless / grant*
To grauntė me my sovereyn lady dere,
Prey hir to sinken every rok adoun
Into hir owene derkė regioùn
Under the ground, ther Pluto° dwelleth inne,
Or nevermo shal I my lady winne.
Thy temple in Delphos° wol I barefoot seke;
Lord Phebus, see the terės on my cheke,
And of my peyne have som compassioùn.'
And with that word in swowne> he fil adoun, *swoon*

Lucina I.e. the triple goddess of the universe, manifesting herself as Luna (the moon) in the skies; Diana on earth; Proserpina (Hecate) in the underworld. He means the moon, who governs the tides of the sea and depends upon the sun for her light. The sun is to use his influence with the moon to bring a lasting spring tide, and cover the rocks. Lucina was that manifestation of the goddess who presided over childbirth.
Neptunus Neptune, god of the sea
opposicioun i.e. 180° apart, at full moon, when the influence of sun and moon reinforce each other to bring about the spring tides, and the water is higher than normal at both rise and ebb
Leoun The sun's power is greatest when it is in the zodiacal sign of Leo, the Lion, because that is its own mansion or house. But the sun was, on May 6, in Taurus, the Bull; and Aurelius is ready to wait until July for his miracle, which will be most effective because the sun will be in Leo and the moon in opposition in Aquarius, the Water-carrier, an appropriate sign for a flood.
Lord . . . ye The sun is being asked to slow the moon's pace (28-day orbit) to his own (1-year orbit) for two years, so that their oppositions will continue and the tide remain at flood all that time.
Pluto god of the underworld, husband of Proserpina-Luna
Delphos Delphi, in a valley of Mt. Parnassus, the chief shrine of Apollo and the seat of the most famous ancient oracle; Aurelius vows to make a barefoot pilgrimage there.

And longė tyme he lay forth> in a traunce. *continually*
His brother, which that knew of his penaunce,> *pain*
Up caughte him and to bedde he hath him broght.
Dispeyrèd> in this torment and this thoght *despairing*
Lete> I this woful creätùrė lye; *let*
Chese he, for me, whether he wol live or dye.°
Arveragus, with hele> and greet honour, *prosperity*
As he that was of chivalrye the flour,
Is comen hoom, and othere worthy men.
O blisful artow> now, thou Dorigen, *art thou*
That hast thy lusty housbonde in thyne armes,
The fresshė knight, the worthy man of armes,
That loveth thee, as his owene hertės lyf.
Nothing list him to been imaginatyf> *suspicious*
If any wight had spoke, whyl he was oute,> *abroad*
To hire of love; he hadde of it no doute.
He noght entendeth> to no swich matere, *attends*
But daunceth, justeth,> maketh hir good chere; *jousts*
And thus in joye and blisse I lete hem dwelle,
And of the syke> Aurelius wol I telle. *sick*
In langour and in torment furious
Two yeer and more lay wrecche Aurelius,
Er any foot he mighte on erthė goon;
Ne confort in this tymė hadde he noon,
Save of his brother, which that was a clerk;> *learned man*
He knew of al this wo and al this werk.
For to non other creätùre certeyn
Of this matère he dorstė no word seyn.
Under his brest he bar it more secree> *secret*
Than ever dide Pamphilus° for Galathee.
His brest was hool,> withoutė for to sene, *whole*
But in his herte ay> was the arwe> kene. *ever / arrow*
And wel ye knowe that of a sursanure°
In surgerye is perilous the cure,
But> men mighte touche the arwe, or come therby. *unless*
His brother weep and waylėd privėly,
Til attė laste him fil in remembraunce,
That whyl he was at Orliens° in Fraunce,
As yongė clerkės, that been likerous> *eager*

Chese . . . dye let him choose, as far I am concerned, whether he live or die

Pamphilus One of the catalogue of famous and unfortunate lovers. The name is a corruption of Polyphemus, the Sicilian Cyclops who loved and was rejected by the nymph Galatea. Pamphilus himself is the timid hero of the medieval Latin comic poem *Pamphilus de Amore,* who cannot make his girl without personal instruction from Venus and the help of a madam.

sursanure a wound healed only on the outside, with the cause of the wound (arrow) sealed inside and causing suppuration. Chaucer has enlarged a hint from *Pamphilus de Amore.*

Orliens The schools of Orleans, in France, had been famous since perhaps the 6th century; the University was founded in the early 13th century. Its reputation for learning, especially in the law, fostered the legend that some had acquired magical knowledge by deep study there. The equation, learned men/philosophers = magicians/alchemists, was easily made in the Middle Ages and later—see l. 853. With Orleans and its magicians, compare Oxford and Roger ("Friar") Bacon, or Wittenberg and Dr. Faustus.

To reden artės that been curious,°
Seken in every halke and every herne
Particuler sciėnces for to lerne,°
He him remembred that, upon a day,
At Orliens in studie a book he say> *saw*
Of magik naturel,° which his felawe,> *companion*
That was that tyme a bacheler of lawe,
Al> were he ther to lerne another craft,> *although / profession*
Had privėly° upon his desk ylaft;
Which book spak muchel> of the operaciouns,° *much*
Touchinge the eighte and twenty mansiouns
That longen to the mone, and swich folye,
As in our dayės is nat worth a flye;
For holy chirchės° feith in our bileve> *belief*
Ne suffreth noon illusion us to greve.> *harm*
And whan this book was in his remembraunce,
Anon for joye his hertė gan to daunce,
And to himself he seydė privėly:> *privately*
'My brother shal be warisshed> hastily; *cured*
For I am siker> that ther be sciėnces, *sure*
By whichė men make diverse apparėnces
Swiche as thise subtile tregetourės° pleye.
For ofte at festės have I wel herd seye,
That tregetours, withinne an hallė large,
Have maad come in a water and a barge,
And in the hallė rowen up and doun.
Somtyme hath semėd come a grim leoun;> *lion*
And somtyme flourės springe as in a mede;
Somtyme a vyne, and grapės whyte and rede;
Somtyme a castel, al of lym and stoon;
And whan hem lykėd, voyded> it anoon. *emptied*
Thus semėd it to every mannės sighte.
Now than conclude I thus, that if I mighte
At Orliens som old felawe yfinde,> *find*
That hadde this monės mansiòns in minde,
Or other magik naturel above,> *in addition*
He sholde wel make my brother han his love.

artes . . . curious books of instruction that are recondite, or: arts that are occult
Seken . . . lerne seek, in every hiding-place and corner to learn out-of-the-way knowledge
magik naturel See General Prologue, l. 418.
prively i.e. he had left it hidden, so that he would not be known to have it
operaciouns Magical workings concerning the 28 mansions of the moon, one for each day of the lunar month (see Astrology in the Glossary). Moreover, as the nearest planet to earth the moon is the most powerful planetary influence to be manipulated; as possessing the shortest orbit it is the trickiest to manipulate; as the planet of darkness the most obvious for magic. The position of the moon was vital for any astrological purpose.
chirches The church naturally condemned any attempt to alter the course of a nature preordained and created by God, who was the only truth. The truth of astrology could never be more than apparent. Magical operations were permitted, as long as they were natural and not black, but they could only be rational, scientific demonstrations of God's wonders and purposes, not imitations or disturbances of them.
tregetoures Conjurors, illusionists; also used for jugglers, sleight-of-hand entertainers. The brother is unknowingly insulting the noble craft of true magicians, who claim to work on a larger scale.

For with an apparènce a clerk may make
To mannės sighte, that alle the rokkės blake
Of Britaigne weren yvoyded> everichon, *swept away*
And shippės by the brinkė comen and gon,
And in swich forme endure a day or two;
Than were my brother warisshed> of his wo. *cured*
Than moste she nedės holden hir biheste,
Or ellės he shal shame hir atte leste.'
  What> sholde I make a lenger tale of this? *why*
Unto his brotherės bed he comen is,
And swich confort he yaf him for to gon
To Orliens, that he up stirte> anon, *jumped*
And on his wey forthward thanne is he fare,> *gone*
In hope for to ben lissėd> of his care. *cured*
  Whan they were come almost to that citee,
But if> it were a two furlong° or three, *all but*
A yong clerk rominge by himself they mette,
Which that in Latin thriftily> hem grette, *well*
And after that he seyde a wonder thing:
'I knowe,' quod he, 'the cause of your coming';
And er they ferther any fotė> wente, *foot*
He tolde hem al that was in hir entente.
  This Briton> clerk him askėd of felawes *Breton*
The whiche that he had knowe in oldė dawes;> *days*
And he answerde him that they dede were,
For which he weep ful oftė many a tere.
  Doun of his hors Aurelius lighte> anon, *alighted*
And forth with this magicien is he gon
Hoom to his hous, and made hem wel at ese.
Hem lakkėd no vitaìlle that mighte hem plese;
So wel arrayėd hous as there was oon
Aurelius in his lyf saugh never noon.°
  He shewed him, er he wentė to sopeer,> *supper*
Forestės, parkės ful of wildė deer;
Ther saugh he hertės> with hir hornės hye, *harts*
The gretteste that ever werė seyn with yë.
He saugh of hem an hondred slayn with houndes,
And somme with arwes blede of bittre woundes.°
He saugh, whan voided> were thise wildė deer, *gone*
Thise fauconers> upon a fair river,> *falconers / river bank*
That with hir hawkės han the heron slayn.
  Tho saugh he knightės jousting in a playn;
And after this, he dide him swich plesaunce,
That he him shewed his lady on a daunce
On which himself he dauncėd, as him thoughte.> *it seemed*

furlong one-eighth mile
never noon intensifying double negative: Aurelius never saw such a well-ordered (or: well-supplied) house in his life as that one

He sough . . . woundes he saw a hundred of them killed (after hunting) with dogs; and some bleeding with painful arrow-wounds

And whan this maister, that this magik wroughte,> *did*
Saugh it was tyme, he clapte his handės two,
And farewel! al our revel° was ago.> *gone*
And yet remoeved they never out of the hous,
Whyl they saugh al this sightė merveillous,
But in his studie, theras his bookės be,
They seten stille, and no wight but they three.
  To him this maister callėd his squyėr,
And seyde him thus: 'Is redy our sopėr?
Almost an houre it is, I undertake,> *swear*
Sith I yow bad our soper for to make,
Whan that thise worthy men wenten with me
Into my studie, theras my bookės be.'
  'Sire,' quod this squyer, 'whan it lyketh> yow, *pleases*
It is al redy, though ye wol> right now.' *want it*
'Go we than soupe,' quod he, 'as for the beste;°
This amorous folk somtyme mote> han reste.' *must*
  At after-soper fille they in tretee,> *discussion*
What sommė sholde this maistres guerdon> be, *master's reward*
To remoeven alle the rokkės of Britayne,
And eek from Gerounde° to the mouth of Sayne.
  He made it straunge,> and swoor, so God him save, *difficult*
Lasse than a thousand pound he wolde nat have,
Ne gladly for that somme he wolde nat goon.
  Aurelius, with blisful herte anoon,
Answerdė thus, 'Fy on a thousand pound!
This wydė world, which that men seye is round,°
I wolde it yeve, if I were lord of it.
This bargayn is ful drive,> for we ben knit. *complete*
Ye shal be payėd trewely, by my trouthe!> *word of honor*
But loketh now, for no necligence or slouthe,> *laziness*
Ye tarie> us heer no lenger than to-morwe.' *delay*
'Nay,' quod this clerk, 'have heer my feith to borwe.> *as pledge*
  To bedde is goon Aurelius whan him leste,
And wel ny al that night he hadde his reste;
What for his labour and his hope of blisse,
His woful herte of penaunce hadde a lisse.> *relief*
  Upon the morwe, whan that it was day,
To Britaigne tokė they the rightė> way, *direct*
Aurelius, and this magicien bisyde,
And been descended ther> they wolde abyde; *where*
And this was, as the bokės me remembre,> *tell*
The coldė frosty seson of Decembre.

revel See Prospero, in *The Tempest* IV.i; overall, Chaucer and Shakespeare often say much the same thing about the ennobling power of love.
Go . . . beste let us go sup, said he, it is the best thing
Gerounde the river Gironde, as far south of Penmarc'h as the river Seine is north
world . . . round See *Rosemounde* below and see Fig. 54.

Phebus wex old, and hewėd lyk latoùn,
That in his hotė declinatioùn
Shoon as the burnėd gold with stremės brighte;°
But now in Capricorn adoun he lighte,› *alighted*
Wheras he shoon ful pale, I dar wel seyn.› *say*
The bittre frostės, with the sleet and reyn,
Destroyėd hath the grene in every yerd.› *yard*
Janus sit by the fyr, with double berd,°
And drinketh of his bugle-horn the wyn.
Biforn him stant brawn° of the tuskėd swyn,
And 'Nowel'° cryeth every lusty› man. *jocund*
Aurelius, in al that ever he can,
Doth to his maister chere› and reverence,› *entertainment / respect*
And preyeth him to doon his diligence
To bringen him out of his peynės smerte,
Or with a swerd that he wolde slitte his herte.
This subtil› clerk swich routhe› had of this man, *skilled / pity*
That night and day he spedde› him that› he can, *hastened / as much as*
To wayte› a tyme› of his conclusioùn;° *watch / opportunity*
This is to seye, to make illusioùn,
By swich an apparènce of jogelrye›— *conjuring*
I ne can› no termės of astrologye— *know*
That she and every wight sholde wene› and seye,› *think / say*
That of Britaigne the rokkės were aweye,
Or ellės they were sonken under grounde.
So attė laste he hath his tyme yfounde
To maken his japės and his wrecchednesse°
Of swich a supersticious cursednesse.
His tables Toletanès° forth he broght,

Phebus . . . brighte (ll. 537–39) The sun grew old and latten-colored, he who in his hot position shone, with bright beams, like burnished gold. (For latten, and the same base metal-gold comparison, see the General Prologue, l. 701.) The sun has declined from its highest latitude in Cancer (summer solstice) to its lowest in Capricorn (Figs. 43, 45, winter solstice—December 12 in the 14th century). So Aurelius has had to wait even longer for the miracle he wanted (l. 350).
Janus . . . berd Janus sits by the fire, with his double face (literally, "beard"). Janus, the Roman god of comings-in and goings-out, had two faces, one looking forward, the other back. He gave his name to the month of January and represents the turn of the year.
brawn boar's flesh; a boar was a traditional, prized Christmas dish
'Nowel' A greeting for Christmas, the great feast, lasting from Christmas Day to Twelfth Night. "Nowel" = Latin: *natalis*, birthday. The cry ends this gay, homely little interlude and we return to serious, high-flown magical endeavor.
conclusioun object and end of his "operation"
japes . . . wrecchednesse tricks and wickednesses, so diabolically cursed
Toletanes I.e. of Toledo, in Spain; astronomical tables, for calculating the positions of the heavenly bodies; also called Alfonsine tables, having been made by order of Alfonso X of Castile about 1272. The magician was up-to-date: these were the most accurate available. The pile-up of technical terms reinforces the impression of competence and we are expected to be bullied into respect by its mysteries. *Collect* years show the amount of a planet's motion over more than 20 years; *expans* years over a period of anything less than that. *Rotes* are tables for making astrological propositions; *geres* are paraphernalia; *centre* is part of an astrolabe; *argument* is an astronomical mathematical quantity from which another may be deduced. *Proportioneels convenients* are fitting proportionals, to find planetary movements during part of a year. The eighth sphere was the sphere of the fixed stars. The magician allows for its slow rotation. *Alnath* was in the eighth sphere, at the beginning of the constellation Aries, below the stable Aries in the ninth sphere—the sign of the zodiac—so that the two were out of kilter. The mass of astrological terms goes on—Alnath was also the first mansion of the moon; *face* and *terme* (l. 580) seem to be divisions of the zodiacal sign.

Ful wel corrected, ne ther lakkėd noght,
Neither his collect ne his expans yeres,
Ne his rotės, ne his othere geres,
As been his centres and his arguments,
And his proporcionels convenients
For his equaciòns in every thing.
And, by his eightė spere in his wirking,
He knew ful wel how fer Alnath was shove
Fro the heed of thilkė fixe Aries above
That in the ninthė speere considered is;
Ful subtilly˃ he calculėd˃ al this. *skillfully / calculated*
  Whan he had founde his firstė mansioùn,
He knew the remenant˃ by proporcioùn;˃ *rest / adjustment*
And knew the arysing of his monė˃ weel, *moon*
And in whos face, and terme, and every deel;
And knew ful weel the monės mansioùn
Acordaunt˃ to his operacioùn, *answering*
And knew also his othere observaùnces˃ *rites*
For swiche illusiouns and swiche meschaunces˃ *evil doings*
As hethen folk usėd in thilkė dayes;
For which no lenger˃ makėd he delayes, *longer*
But thurgh his magik, for a wyke or tweye,
It semed that alle the rokkės were aweye.
  Aurelius, which that yet despeirėd˃ is *desperate*
Wher˃ he shal han his love or fare amis, *whether*
Awaiteth night and day on this miracle;
And whan he knew that ther was noon obstàcle,
That voided were thise rokkės everichon,
Doun to his maistres feet he fil anon,
And seyde, 'I woful wrecche, Aurelius,
Thankė yow, lord, and lady myn Venus,
That me han holpen˃ fro my carės colde': *helped*
And to the temple his wey forth hath he holde,˃ *taken*
Wheras he knew he sholde his lady see.
And whan he saugh his tyme, anon right˃ he, *at once*
With dredful˃ herte and with ful humble chere,˃ *fearful / appearance*
Salewėd˃ hath his sovereyn lady dere: *saluted*
  'My rightė lady,' quod this woful man,
'Whom I most drede and love as I best can,
And lothest˃ were of al this world displese, *most reluctant*
Nere it° that I for yow have swich disese,˃ *pain*
That I moste dyen˃ heer at your foot anon, *die*
Noght wolde I telle how me is wo bigon;
But certės outher˃ moste I dye or pleyne; *either*
Ye slee me giltėlees for verray peyne.
But of my deeth, thogh that ye have no routhe,˃ *pity*

Nere it were it not

Avyseth> yow, er that ye breke your trouthe. *consider*
Repenteth yow, for thilkė God above,
Er ye me sleen> bycause that I yow love. *slay*
For, madame, wel ye woot> what ye han hight;> *know / promised*
Nat that I chalange> any thing of right *claim*
Of yow my sovereyn lady, but your grace;
But in a gardin yond, at swich a place,
Ye woot right wel what ye bihighten> me; *promised*
And in myn hand your trouthė plighten> ye *word gave*
To love me best. God woot, ye seydė so,
Al be that I unworthy be therto.
Madame, I speke it for the honour of yow,
More than to save myn hertės lyf right now:
I have do so as ye comanded me;
And if ye vouchėsauf,> ye may go see. *grant*
Doth as yow list, have your biheste> in minde, *promise*
For quik> or deed, right ther ye shul me finde; *living*
In yow lyth al, to do> me live or deye— *make*
But wel I woot the rokkės been aweye!'
He taketh his leve, and she astonied> stood, *stunned*
In al hir facė nas a drope of blood;
She wendė> never han come in swich a trappe: *expected*
'Allas!' quod she, 'that ever this sholde happe!> *chance*
For wende I never, by possibilitee,
That swich a monstre° or merveille mighte be!
It is agayns the process of natùre':
And hoom she gooth a sorweful creäture.
For verray fere unnethė> may she go, *scarcely*
She wepeth, wailleth, all a day or two,
And swowneth,> that it routhė> was to see; *swoons / pity*
But why it was, to no wight toldė she;
For out of toune was goon Arveragus.
But to hirself she spak, and seydė thus,
With facė pale and with ful sorweful chere,
In hir compleynt,° as ye shul after here.
'Allas,' quod she, 'on thee, Fortune,° I pleyne,
That unwar> wrappėd hast me in thy cheyne; *unawares*
Fro which, t'escape, woot I no socoùr> *help*
Save only deeth or ellės dishonoùr;
Oon of thise two bihoveth> me to chese.> *it is necessary / choose*
But nathėlees, yet have I lever> to lese> *rather / lose*
My lyf than of my body have a shame,
Or knowe myselven fals,> or lese my name,> *false / reputation*
And with my deth I may be quit,> ywis. *freed*

monstre unnatural thing
compleynt see l. 239 above
Fortune The Roman goddess, taken over by the Middle Ages to help explain the existence of wrong and injustice in the world; blind and capricious, she offers and takes away her gifts of exterior goods and is not to be trusted (Fig. 41).

Hath ther nat many a noble wyf, er this,
And many a mayde yslayn hirself, allas!
Rather than with hir body doon trespas?
  Yis, certės, lo, thise stories° beren witnesse;
Whan thretty tyraunts,° ful of cursednesse,
Had slayn Phidoun in Athenes, attė feste,> — *at the feast*
They comanded his doghtrės for t'areste,
And bringen hem biforn hem in despyt> — *contempt*
Al naked, to fulfille hir foul delyt,> — *pleasure*
And in hir fadrės> blood they made hem daunce — *fathers'*
Upon the pavement. God yeve hem mischaunce!
For which thise woful maydens, ful of drede,
Rather than they wolde lese hir maydenhede,
They privėly> ben stirt> into a welle, — *stealthily / leaped*
And dreynte> hemselven, as the bokės telle. — *drowned*
  They of Messenė° lete enquere> and seke — *caused to enquire*
Of Lacedomie fifty maydens eke,
On whiche they wolden doon hir lecherye;
But was ther noon of al that companye
That she nas slayn, and with a good entente
Chees> rather for to dyė than assente — *chose*
To be oppressėd> of hir maydenhede. — *raped*
Why sholde I thanne to dyė been in drede?
  Lo, eek, the tiraunt Aristoclides
That loved a mayden, heet> Stimphalides, — *called*
Whan that hir fader slayn was on a night,
Unto Dianės temple goth she right,> — *straight*
And hente> the image in hir handės two, — *took*
Fro which imagė wolde she never go.
No wight ne mighte hir handes of it arace,> — *tear*
Til she was slayn right in the selvė> place. — *same*
Now sith that maydens hadden swich despyt> — *scorn*

stories All these *exempla* of maids, wives, and widows come from the most famous anti-feminist work of the Middle Ages, St. Jerome's late 4th-century treatise *Against Jovinian* (see the Wife of Bath's Prologue, l. 679). Chaucer makes the Franklin use this text as a counterblast to the Wife, who tears from it anything that will support her case for generation; Dorigen is more scrupulous and uses only Jerome's own stories in praise of womanly virtue. Chaucer follows Jerome very closely, but Jerome's versions are often garbled.

tyraunts The Thirty Tyrants began a reign of of terror in Athens when they seized power at the end of the Peloponnesian War (404 B.C.). Pheidon was one of them. The long list that now follows isolates, as *exempla* do, a single trait or incident; these are not intended to be a comment on the character of Aurelius or to cast him in the role of a monster who combines the worst features of all these would-be rapists. It is a list of women who had kept faith.

Messene The men of Messene attempted to rape fifty Spartan virgins; Aristoclides killed Stymphalis for refusing to sleep with him; Hasdrubal's wife (see the Nun's Priest's Tale, l. 591) joined her husband in death when Carthage was taken; Lucretia killed herself after her rape by Tarquinius Sextus; Miletus was sacked by the Gauls; Abradates' wife Panthea killed herself on his corpse; Demotion's daughter died rather than marry another after her fiancé's death; Scedasus' two daughters killed themselves after being raped by two Spartans—and so on, through Nicanor, Nicerates, Alcibiades: Alcestis, who accepted death in place of her husband; Penelope, the wife of Odysseus, who kept herself by tricks from the suitors who laid siege to her in her husband's absence; Laodameia, who joined her husband Protesilaus in the shades when he was killed by Hector at Troy; Portia, wife of Brutus, the conspirator; Artemisia, who built the mausoleum at Halicarnassus for her husband and was honored throughout barbarian lands for it; Teuta, queen of Illyria; Bilia, who was a martyr for her husband; Rhodogone and Valeria, who both refused a second marriage.

To been defouled with mannės foul delyt,
Wel oghte a wyf rather hirselven slee˃ — *slay*
Than be defoulėd, as it thinketh˃ me. — *seems*
  What shal I seyn of Hasdrubalės wyf,
That at Cartage birafte˃ hirself hir lyf˃ — *took*
For whan she saugh that Romayns wan˃ the toun, — *won*
She took hir children alle, and skipte˃ adoun — *jumped*
Into the fyr, and chees rather to dye
Than any Romayn dide hir vileinye.
  Hath nat Lucresse yslayn hirself, allas!
At Romė, whannė she oppressėd was
Of Tarquin, for hir thoughte it was a shame
To liven whan she haddė lost hir name?
  The sevene maydens of Milesie also
Han slayn hemself, for verray drede and wo,
Rather than folk of Gaule hem sholde oppresse.
Mo than a thousand stories, as I gesse,
Coude I now telle as touchinge this matere.
  Whan Habradate was slayn, his wyf so dere
Hirselven slow,˃ and leet hir blood to glyde˃ — *slew / flow*
In Habradatės woundės depe and wyde,
And seyde, "My body, at the leestė way,
Ther shal no wight defoulen, if I may."˃ — *can help it*
  What sholde I mo ensamples heerof sayn,
Sith that so manye han hemselven slayn
Wel rather than they wolde defoulėd be?
I wol conclude, that it is bet˃ for me — *better*
To sleen myself, than been defoulėd thus.
I wol be trewe unto Arveragus,
Or rather sleen myself in som manere,
As dide Democionės doghter dere,˃ — *dear*
Bycause that she wolde nat defoulėd be.
  O Cedasus! it is ful greet pitee,
To reden how thy doghtren deyde,˃ allas! — *daughters died*
That slowe hemselven for swich maner cas.˃ — *happening*
  As greet a pitee was it, or wel more,
The Theban mayden, that for Nichanore
Hirselven slow,˃ right for swich maner wo. — *slew*
  Another Theban mayden dide right so;
For oon of Macedoine hadde hir oppressed,
She with hir deeth hir maydenhede redressed.
  What shal I seye of Niceratės wyf,
That for swich cas birafte hirself hir lyf?
  How trewe eek was to Alcebiades
His love, that rather for to dyen chees˃ — *chose*
Than for to suffre his body unburied be!
Lo which˃ a wyf was Alcestė,' quod she. — *what*
  'What seith Omer of gode˃ Penalopee? — *good*

Al Grecė knoweth of hir chastitee.
Pardee, of Laodomya is writen thus,
That whan at Troye was slayn Protheselaus,
No lenger wolde she live after his day.
The same of noble Porcia telle I may;
Withoutė Brutus coudė she nat live,
To whom she hadde al hool> hir hertė yive. *completely*
The parfit> wyfhod of Arthemesye *perfect*
Honourėd is thurgh al the Barbarye.
O Teuta, queen! thy wyfly chastitee
To allė wyvės may a mirour be.
The samė thing I seye of Bilia,
Of Rodogone, and eek Valeria.'
Thus pleynėd Dorigene a day or tweye,
Purposinge> ever that she woldė deye. *intending*
But nathėlees, upon the thriddė> night, *third*
Hom> cam Arveragus, this worthy knight, *home*
And askėd hir, why that she weep so sore?
And she gan wepen ever lenger the more.°
'Allas!' quod she, 'that ever was I born!
Thus have I seyd,' quod she, 'thus have I sworn'—
And told him al as ye han herd bifore;
It nedeth nat reherce> it yow namore. *tell*
This housbond with glad chere,> in freendly wyse, *look*
Answerde and seyde as I shal yow devyse.> *tell*
'Is ther oght ellės,> Dorigen, but this?' *else*
'Nay, nay,' quod she 'God help me so, as wys
This is to muche, and it were Goddės wille.'°
'Ye, wyf,' quod he, 'lat slepen that is stille;
It may be wel, paràventure,> yet to-day. *perhaps*
Ye shul your trouthė holden, by my fay!> *faith*
For God so wisly have mercy on me,°
I hadde wel lever ystikėd> for to be, *rather stabbed*
For verray love which that I to yow have,
But if ye sholde your trouthė kepe and save.
Trouthe is the hyeste> thing that man may kepe.' *highest*
But with that word he brast> anon to wepe, *burst*
And seyde, 'I yow forbede, up> peyne of deeth,> *on / death*
That never, whyl thee lasteth lyf ne breeth,
To no wight tel thou of this aventùre>— *happening*
As I may best, I wol my wo endure—
Ne make no contenance> of hevinesse,> *appearance / sadness*
That folk of yow may demen harm> or gesse.' *suspect evil*
And forth he cleped> a squyer and a mayde: *called*

And she . . . more and she wept more and more, the longer she went on

God help . . . wille God help me, this is too much, even if it is God's will

For God . . . me as surely as God will have mercy on me

'Goth forth anon with Dorigen,' he sayde,
'And bringeth hir to swich a place anon.'
They take hir leve, and on hir wey they gon;
But they ne wistė why she thider wente.
He noldė no wight tellen his entente.
  Paràventure an heep> of yow, ywis,> *lot / indeed*
Wold holden him a lewėd> man in this, *stupid*
That he wol putte his wyf in jupartye;> *jeopardy*
Herkneth the tale, er ye upon hir crye.
She may have bettre fortune than yow semeth;
And whan that ye han herd the talė, demeth.> *judge*
  This squyer, which that highte Aurelius,
On Dorigen that was so amorous,> *in love*
Of aventùrė> happėd hir to mete *chance*
Amidde the toun, right in the quikkest> strete, *busiest*
As she was boun> to goon the wey forthright> *ready / direct*
Toward the gardin theras she had hight.> *promised*
And he was to the gardinward° also;
For wel he spyed, whan she woldė go
Out of hir hous to any maner> place. *kind of*
But thus they mette, of aventure or grace;°
And he saleweth> hir with glad entente,> *salutes / mind*
And askėd of hir whiderward> she wente? *whither*
  And she answerde, half as she were mad,
'Unto the gardin, as myn housbond bad,
My trouthe for to holde, allas! allas!'
  Aurelius gan wondren on this cas,> *chance*
And in his herte had greet compassioùn
Of hir and of hir lamentacioùn,
And of Arveragus, the worthy knight,
That bad hir holden al that she had hight,
So looth> him was his wyf sholde breke hir trouthe; *hateful to*
And in his herte he caughte of this greet routhe,> *compassion*
Consideringe the beste on every syde,
That fro his lust yet were him lever abyde> *rather abstain*
Than doon so heigh a cherlish> wrecchednesse *mean*
Agayns franchyse> and allė gentillesse;> *generosity / courtesy*
For which in fewė wordės seyde he thus:
  'Madame, seyth> to your lord Arveragus, *say*
That sith I see his gretė gentillesse
To yow, and eek I see wel your distresse,
That him were lever han shame (and that were routhe)
Than ye to me sholde brekė thus your trouthe,
I have wel lever ever to suffre wo°

gardinward toward the garden
of . . . grace by chance or (God's) grace—a favorite conventional formula, meaning: however it happened
I have . . . wo I had much rather suffer unhappiness forever

Than I departe> the love bitwix yow two. *part*
I yow relessė,> madame, into your hond *release*
Quit,> every surement> and every bond,° *paid / security*
That ye han maad to me as heerbiforn,> *heretofore*
Sith thilkė tymė which that ye were born.
My trouthe I plighte, I shal yow never repreve> *reproach*
Of no biheste.> And here I take my leve, *promise*
As of the treweste and the bestė wyf
That ever yet I knew in al my lyf.
But every wyf be war of hir biheste,
On Dorigene remembreth attė leste.
Thus can a squyer doon a gentil> dede, *noble*
As well as can a knight, withouten drede.'
  She thonketh him upon hir knees al bare,
And hoom unto hir housbond is she fare,> *gone*
And tolde him al as ye han herd me sayd.> *say*
And be ye siker,> he was so weel apayd, *sure*
That it were inpossìble me to wryte.
  What sholde I lenger> of this cas endyte?> *longer / write*
Arveragus and Dorigene his wyf
In sovereyn> blissė leden forth hir lyf. *supreme*
Never eft ne was ther angre hem bitwene;
He cherisseth hir as though she were a quene;
And she was to him trewe for evermore.
Of thise two folk ye gete of me namore.
  Aurelius, that his cost hath al forlorn,> *lost*
Curseth the tyme that ever he was born:
'Allas,' quod he, 'allas! that I bihighte> *promised*
Of purėd> gold a thousand pound of wighte> *refined / weight*
Unto this philosòphre°! how shal I do?
I see namore but that I am fordo.> *undone*
Myn heritagė moot> I nedės selle, *must*
And been a begger. Heer may I nat dwelle,
And shamen al my kinrede in this place,
But> I of him may getė bettre grace. *unless*
But nathėlees, I wol of him assaye,> *attempt*
At certeyn dayės, yeer by yeer, to paye,
And thankė him of his grete curteisye;
My trouthė wol I kepe, I wol nat lye.'
  With hertė soor> he gooth unto his cofre,> *sore / coffer*
And broghtė gold unto this philosòphre,
The value of fyve hundred pound, I gesse,
And him bisecheth,> of his gentillesse, *begs*
To graunte him dayės of the remenaunt,°

I yow . . . bond legal language: a solemn, formal renunciation, in contractual terms; with puns on the meanings of the words in the terminology of courtly love

philosòphre wise man; often a magician/alchemist (see l. 410)

dayes . . . remenaunt time to pay the rest

And seydė, 'Maister, I dar wel make avaunt,> *boast*
I faillėd never of my trouthe as yit;> *so far*
For sikerly> my dettė shal be quit> *certainly / paid*
Towardės yow, however that I fare
To goon abeggėd> in my kirtle> bare. *begging / tunic*
But woldė ye vouchesauf, upon seurtee,> *surety*
Two yeer or three for to respyten> me, *give respite*
Than were I wel. For ellės moot I selle
Myn heritage; ther is namore to telle.'
This philosòphre sobrely> answerde, *gravely*
And seyde thus, whan he thisė wordės herde:
'Have I nat holden covenant unto thee?'
'Yes, certės, wel and trewėly,' quod he.
'Hastow nat had thy lady as thee lyketh?'
'No, no,' quod he, and sorwefully he syketh.> *sighs*
'What was the causė? tel me if thou can.'
Aurelius his tale anon bigan,
And tolde him al, as ye han herd bifore;
It nedeth nat to yow reherce> it more. *tell*
He seide, 'Arveragus, of gentillesse,
Had lever dye in sorwe and in distresse
Than that his wyf were of hir trouthė fals.'
The sorwe of Dorigen he tolde him als,> *also*
How looth hir was to been a wikked wyf,
And that she lever had lost that day hir lyf,
And that hir trouthe she swoor,> thurgh innocence. *swore*
'She never erst herde speke of apparènce;°
That made me han> of hir so greet pitee. *have*
And right as frely> as he sente hir me, *generously*
As frely sente I hir to him ageyn.
This al and som,° ther is namore to seyn.'
This philosòphre answerde, 'Levė brother,
Everich of yow dide gentilly til> other. *nobly to*
Thou art a squyer, and he is a knight;
But God forbedė, for his blisful might,
But if a clerk coude doon a gentil dede
As wel as any of yow, it is no drede!°
Sire, I relessė thee thy thousand pound,
As thou right now were cropen out of the ground,°
Ne never er> now ne haddest knowen me. *before*
For sire, I wol nat take a peny of thee
For al my craft,> ne noght for my travaille.> *work / trouble*
Thou hast ypayėd wel for my vitaille.
It is ynogh, and farewel, have good day.'

'She . . . apparence she never before had heard so much as talk of illusions (such as Aurelius had had conjured up)
al and som i.e. everything
But God . . . drede (ll. 902–4) but God forbid, in his blessed power, that a learned man can't do a courteous deed—there's no doubt (he can)
As thou . . . ground as if you'd just come out of a hole in the ground

And took his hors, and forth he gooth his way.
  Lordinges, this question wolde I aske now,
Which was the mostė free,˃ as thinketh yow˃ *generous*
Now telleth me, er that ye ferther wende.
I can˃ namore, my tale is at an ende. *can say*

Here is ended the Frankeleyns Tale

The Pardoner's Prologue and Tale

Chaucer's portrait of the Pardoner in the General Prologue has prepared us for his Tale, but not fully for either the open cynicism of his behavior or the dark power of his story. His Prologue here, with its direct self-revelation—a technique that Chaucer does not often employ in the *Tales*—is followed by the long, indirect comment of his tale, an impressive demonstration of his abilities to preach upon his favorite theme: "Love of money is the root of evil." In the Epilogue the virtuoso feels that he ought to improve the occasion by attempting to do a little business.

From the General Prologue it is clear that this ecclesiastical fund-raiser is a rogue and a cheat, with his fake relics and pious threats, though Chaucer concedes his ability as a performer in church—an ability to be borne out by his tale. We need no more than Chaucer's description to let us know this; in the General Prologue, he seems to have reserved his most direct picture of villainy for the last, his portrait of the Pardoner. The Pardoner is a born eunuch, whom medieval character psychology made out much worse than a man who had merely been castrated. Eunuchs were, according to the doctrine, always evil-natured, foolish, lustful, and presumptuous, but those who had been born so were much worse; they could be recognized from their lack of beard, long scrawny necks and thin bodies, high voices, and prominent, rolling, lecherous eyes—physical defects indicating defects of character. Inclined to lechery, but unable to fulfill their desires, they are reduced, like the Pardoner in his Prologue, to boasting of them; he openly confesses he is a "ful vicious man" (Fig. 31).

The audience would have been familiar with the activities of this man, both from literature (the figure of Hypocrisy in the *Roman de la Rose* is strongly similar) and from life. Pardoners were already a source of some embarrassment to the Church, which licensed them to sell "pardons" to raise money for church purposes. Unscrupulous pardoners claimed more for their wares than they were authorized to do, and ordinary people believed them. What they were licensed to sell was partial remission of penance for sin, granted by papal authority through a "bull" or written proclamation—that is to say, a man could show his remorse for sin by a charitable contribution instead of by performing some act commanded by his confessor. Gradually, the notion grew up—encouraged by such corrupt practitioners as Chaucer's Pardoner—that exemption from purgatory (the place or state of expiation before admission to heaven) could be so purchased. A pardon was never intended by the Church to grant forgiveness of sins, but ignorant people could be made to believe that it did.

A pardoner was officially appointed and could operate only with the permission of the bishop, who could also license him to preach—a source of much dispute with the friars, who earned part of their livelihood from the same source. In practice, he would often display and sell relics—bodily parts of Christ or the saints or objects associated with them—which were venerated and thought by the simple to give the entree to heaven.

The Pardoner's demonstration of his powers as a preacher is one of the most economical and powerful of *The Canterbury Tales.* It is cast in the form of a set sermon on the desire for money as the root of all evil, opening with a denunciation of the sins of the tavern—drunkenness, gluttony, lechery, blasphemy, and gambling, with the implication that one sin leads to another, that all are related—but reserving his main theme, or *exemplum,* until the audience has been thoroughly drawn into the story (Fig. 38).

The story itself, like many tales that found their way to Europe in the Middle Ages, is Eastern in origin and known in many versions, medieval and modern: it is used by Kipling in his *The King's Ankus.* The irony of it is centered on the fact that three hardened sinners, who have never given a Christian thought to Death, set out in anger and drunkenness to find this murdering creature and kill him. Their ignorance of what they do and what they seek is continually played on; they cannot realize that they are attempting the thing that only Christ and belief in Christ can do, give victory over death and the grave.

The wordes of the Host to the Phisicien and the Pardoner

Oure Hostė gan to swere> as he were wood;> *did swear / mad*
'Harrow!°' quod he, 'by naylės and by blood!°
This was a fals cherl and a fals justise.°
As shamful deeth as hertė may devyse
Come to thise juges and hir advocats!
Algate> this sely° mayde is slayn, allas! *anyway*
Allas! to derė boghtė she beautee!
Wherfore I seye al day,> as men may see *always*
That yiftės of Fortùne or of Natùre°
Ben cause of deeth to many a creatùre.
Hire beautee was hire deth, I dar wel sayn.
Allas! so pitously as she was slayn!
Of bothė yiftės that I speke> of now *spoke*
Men han ful oftė morė harm than prow.> *profit*
But trewėly, myn owene maister dere,
This is a pitous talė for to heere.
But nathėlees, passe over, is no fors.> *it is no matter*

Harrow help!; here an expression only of astonishment; see the Miller's Tale, l. 178, and the Nun's Priest's Tale, l. 614
by nayles . . . blood By the nails that held Christ on the cross, and by His blood; or, by God's fingernails; but see l. 365. The Pardoner's Tale will later reprove such oaths.
This . . . justise The Host is referring to the Physician's Tale, which has just been told, of Appius and Virginia. Appius Claudius, the Roman magistrate, wanted the beautiful maiden Virginia as his mistress, and, in a trumped-up law-suit, adjudged her to be the slave of an unscrupulous dependent of his (*cherl:* plebeian, low-born man). Virginia's father killed her on the spot, to preserve her chastity.
sely defenseless, innocent
yiftes . . . Natùre the gifts of Nature are usually youth, beauty, and so on; the gifts of Fortune are wealth and high rank. The distinction is a frequent topos in medieval and Renaissance literature.

I pray to God, so save thy gentil cors,> *body*
And eek thyne urinals and thy jordanes,°
Thyn ypocras,° and eek thy galianes,°
And every boist> ful of thy letuarie;° *box*
God blesse hem, and oure lady Seïnte Marie!
So mot I theen,> thou art a propre man, *as I may thrive*
And lyk a prelat,° by Saïnt Ronyan!°
Seyde I nat wel? I can nat speke in terme;> *technically*
But wel I woot> thou doost> myn herte to erme,° *know / make*
That I almost have caught a cardinacle.°
By corpus bonės!° but> I have triacle,° *unless*
Or elles a draughte of moiste and corny° ale,
Or but I here anon> a mery tale, *quickly*
Myn herte is lost for pitee of this mayde.
Thou bel amy,° thou Pardoner,' he seyde,
'Telle us som myrthe or japės° right anon.'
'It shal be doon,' quod he, 'by Saint Ronyon!
But first,' quod he, 'heere at this alėstake°
I wol bothe drinke, and eten of a cake.'
But right anon thise gentils gonne to crye,
'Nay, lat hym telle us of no ribaudye!> *ribaldry*
Telle us som moral thing, that we may lere> *learn*
Som wit,° and thannė wol we gladly here.'
'I graunte, ywis,'> quod he, 'but I mot thinke *certainly*
Upon som honest> thing while that I drinke.' *a respectable*

urinals . . . jordanes Urinals are glass phials used for collecting urine; jordans are here probably round-bellied glass vessels used when urine was to be diagnosed. Or, jordan may here mean chamber-pot: the Host, in his pride at being able to "speak good," may be either mixing up his terms a bit, or he may be mocking the Physician as a looker into urine-pots.
ypocras corruption of the name of Hippocrates, the founder of Greek medicine. It was red wine mixed with spices and sugar, strained through a cloth, and taken as a pleasant drink after food and as a kind of tonic.
galianes either "medicines" or, perhaps, Galen's works; possibly a blunder of the Host's, but certainly connected with the great Greco-Roman doctor Galen (2nd century A.D.), whose name was usually spelled Galien in the Middle Ages
letuarie electuary: medicine in the form of conserve or paste, to be mixed with syrup or other liquid
prelat church dignitary
Ronyan either St. Ronan or St. Ninian; or there may be a pun on runnion (sexual organ)
erme grieve
cardinacle a confusion between cardiacle (the reading of some manuscripts), i.e. cardiac spasm or pain, and cardinal
By . . . bones a blasphemous oath, an illiterate conflation of God's bones! and Corpus Dei! (God's body!)
triacle the best restorative medicine: *theriakon* was originally a remedy for snake-bite and other poisons, and contained the flesh of the snake that had bit one
moiste and corny fresh, new, and malty
bel amy fair friend
som . . . japes something diverting or some jokes
alestake the pole sticking out at an angle from an alehouse wall, with a green bush or garland on it as a sign that refreshment is available (Fig. 39); *cake:* piece of bread
wit knowledge; something that will improve us mentally and morally

Here folweth The Prologe of the Pardoners Tale

Radix malorum est Cupiditas: Ad Thimotheum, sexto.°

'Lordings,> quod he, 'in chirchės> whan I preche, *ladies and gentlemen / churches*
I peynė me> to han an hauteyn° speche, *take pains*
And ringe it out as round as gooth a belle,
For I can al by rotė> that I telle. *know all by heart*
My theme° is alwey oon,> and ever was— *one*
Radix malorum est Cupiditas.
First I pronouncė whennės> that I come, *whence*
And than my bullės° shewe I, alle and somme.> *one and all*
Our ligė lordės seel° on my patente,°
That shewe I first, my body to warente,°
That no man be so bold, ne preest ne clerk,°
Me to destourbe> of Cristės holy werk; *hinder*
And after that than telle I forth my tales:°
Bullės of popės and of cardinales,
Of patriarkes, and bishoppės I shewe;
And in Latyn I speke a wordės fewe,
To saffron> with my predicacioùn,> *color / preaching*
And for to stire> men to devocioùn. *incite*
Than shewe I forth my longė cristal stones,°
Ycrammėd ful of cloutės> and of bones; *rags*
Reliks° been they, as wenen> they, echoon.> *think / each one*
Than have I in latoùn° a sholder-boon
Which that was of an holy Jewės° shepe.
"Good men," seye I, "Tak of my wordės kepe;> *heed*
If that this boon> be wasshe in any welle,° *bone*
If cow, or calf, or sheep, or oxė swelle
That any worm hath ete, or worm ystonge,°

Radix . . . sexto "The love of money is the root of evil" (I Timothy 6:10)
hauteyn loud; the word has overtones of exaltation, pride
theme Text. The medieval preacher regularly announced his text, made a sort of introduction (pro-theme), then an exposition or dilatation; followed by an *exemplum* or story which would illustrate the theme; next came an application or peroration, in which the lesson was drawn; and then a closing formula. Not all sermons were arranged to such an exact scheme, and these parts tend to run into each other, but most are built around theme, exposition, *exemplum*, and application. The Pardoner's Tale is more directly a sermon than the Nun's Priest's, but both are in the genre.
bulles papal mandates, permitting the sale of indulgences and setting out their benefits; and perhaps also his bishop's confirmations, which he would carry as his credentials
lordes seel i.e. the pope's or bishop's seal on his official license
patente document open for inspection by anyone
warente warrant; to protect against violence from other clergy or their hirelings who might try to stop him by violence
preest ne clerk no member of the clergy whatever
And . . . tales and after that I carry on with my stories
stones glass jars or encasings
Reliks Trade in false relics was both frequent and a regular object of satire.
latoun Base brassy metal; see the General Prologue, l. 701. The sheep's shoulder-blade was mounted in this imitation gold.
Jewes one of the Old Testament patriarchs, who were pastoralists
welle well, pool, or spring
That . . . ystonge That has eaten any worm or any snake has bitten. Diseases of cattle were thought to come from eating worms; see Milton's *Lycidas*, l. 46. Worm in the second half of the clause probably has its older meaning of serpent.

Tak water of that welle, and wash his tonge,
And it is hool anon;> and forthermore, *sound at once*
Of pokkės> and of scabbe, and every sore *pox*
Shal every sheep be hool, that of this welle
Drinketh a draughte. Tak kepe eek> what I telle, *notice also*
If that the good-man,° that the bestės oweth,> *beasts owns*
Wol every wike,> er that the cok him croweth,° *week*
Fastinge, drinken of this welle a draughte,
As thilkė> holy Jewe our eldrės taughte, *the same*
His bestės and his stoor° shal multiplye.
And, sirs, also it heleth> jalousye; *heals*
For, though a man be falle in jalous rage,
Let maken with this water his potage,> *soup*
And never shal he more his wyf mistriste,> *mistrust*
Though he the sooth> of hir defautė wiste;> *truth / infidelity knew*
Al had she> taken preestės two or three. *even though she had*
  Heer is a miteyn° eek,> that ye may see. *also*
He that his hond wol> putte in this miteyn, *will*
He shal have multiplying of his greyn,> *grain*
Whan he hath sowen, be it whete> or otes,> *wheat / oats*
So that> he offrė pens, or ellės grotes.° *as long as*
  Good men and wommen, o> thing warne I yow, *one*
If any wight> be in this chirchė now, *person*
That hath doon sinnė horrible, that he
Dar nat,> for shame, of it yshriven be,° *dare not*
Or any womman, be she yong or old,
That hath ymaad hir housbond cokėwold,> *cuckold*
Swich folk shul have no powėr ne no grace
To offren° to my reliks in this place.
And whoso findeth him out of swich> blame, *such*
He wol com up and offre in Goddes name,
And I assoille> him by the auctoritee> *absolve / authority*
Which that by bulle ygraunted was to me."
  By this gaude> have I wonnė, yeer by yeer, *trick*
An hundred mark° sith> I was Pardoner. *since*
I stondė lyk a clerk in my pulpet,
And whan the lewėd peple is doun yset,°
I prechė, so as ye han herd bifore,
And telle an hundred falsė japės> more. *deceptions*
Than peyne I me> to strecchė forth the nekke, *take pains*

good-man worthy man, man of substance
er . . . croweth before cock-crow
stoor property, produce, what he has stored in his barns
miteyn a sower's glove
pens . . . grotes pennies or else groats, i.e. silver coins worth four pennies
yshriven be confess it, be shriven of it
Swich . . . offren such people shall not have the power nor the favor to make offerings in reverence to my relics; unconfessed persons cannot receive the sacraments, or worship at my shrine
mark The mark was worth 13s. 4d., two-thirds of a pound; 100 marks was a large sum, about five times Chaucer's salary from the king; and ten times a schoolmaster's salary.
whan . . . yset when the congregation has sat down; *lewėd:* simple, lay, uneducated. *Yset* may imply that medieval churches had seats for the congregation; but they may well have either brought their own or sat on the floor.

SCOTLAND
Danish and Norse occupied territory north of this Line.
N
NORTHUMBRIA
IRELAND
ISLE OF MAN
KINGDOM OF YORK
York
WIRRAL
Lincoln
Chester
WALES
ENGLISH MERCIA
EAST ANGLIA
Coventry
Cambridge
MALVERN HILLS
Maldon
Oxford
London
KENT
Canterbury
WESSEX
Winchester
Hastings
Southampton
ISLE OF WIGHT
Miles
0
50
100
A. Karl

1. Medieval England.

2. The Geography of Beow
After F. Klaeber, *Beowulf*.

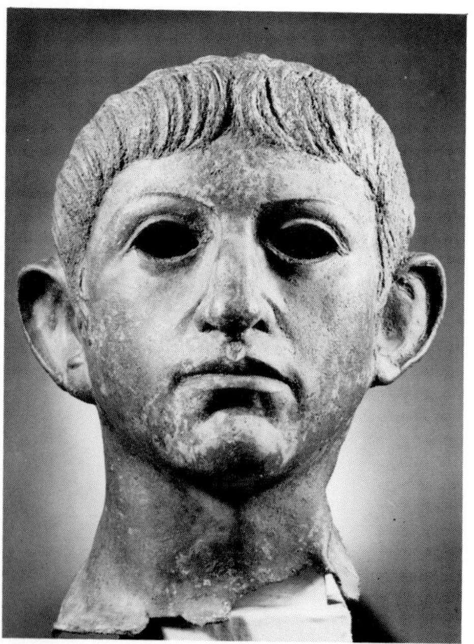

3. The Emperor Claudius, under whom the Romans conquered Britain, 43 A.D. Roman bronze, first century A.D.

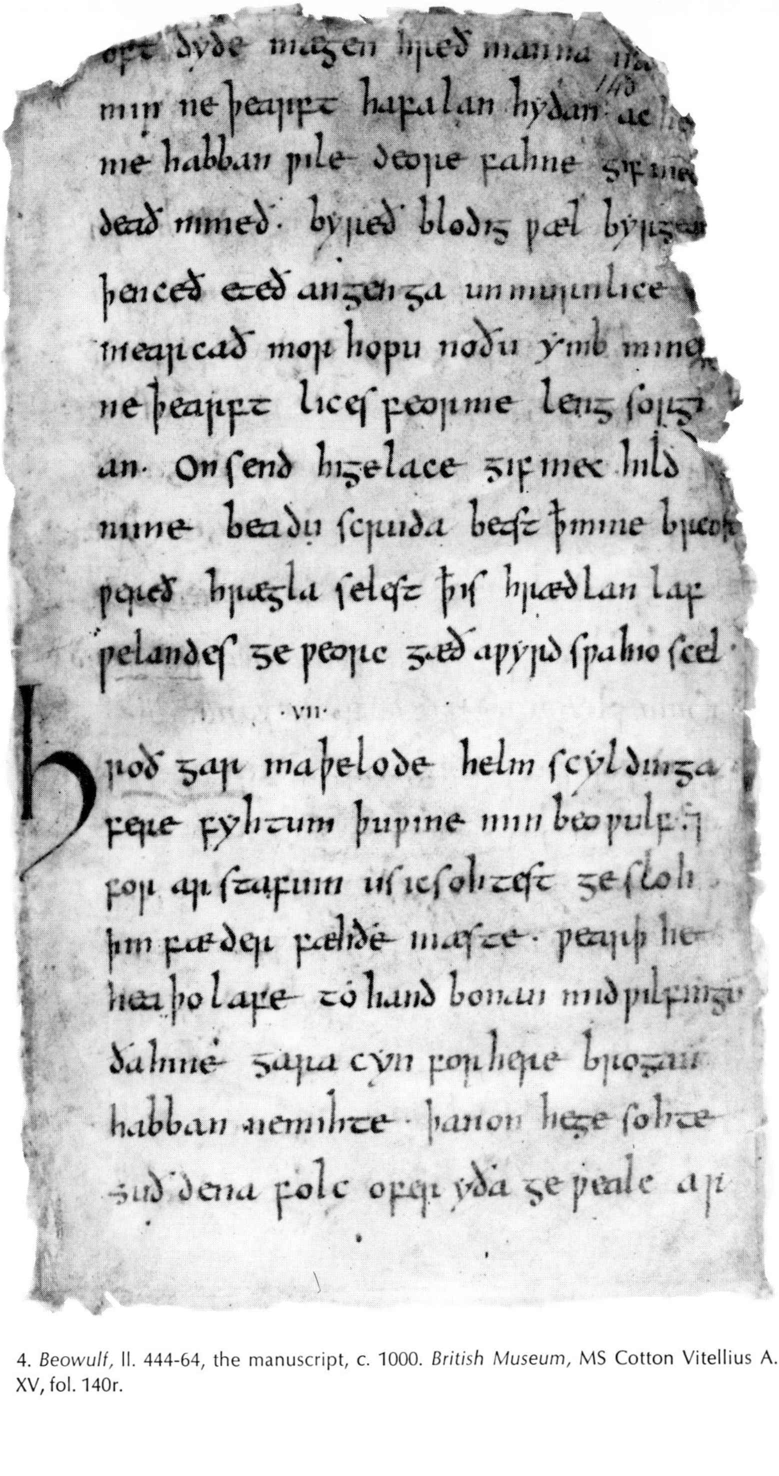
oft dyde mægen hreð manna na
min ne þearft hafalan hydan· ac he
me habban wile d[r]eore fahne gif mec
deað nimeð· byreð blodig wæl byrgean
þenceð eteð angenga unmurnlice
mearcað mor hopu no ðu ymb mines
ne þearft lices feorme leng sorgi
an· Onsend higelace gif mec hild
nime beadu scruda betst þæt mine breo
wereð hrægla selest þæt is hrædlan laf
welandes geweorc gæð a wyrd swa hio scel·
·VII·
Hroð gar maþelode helm scyldinga
fere fyhtum þu wine min beowulf 7
for ar stafum usic sohtest gesloh
þin fæder fæhðe mæste· wearþ he
heaþo lafe to handa bonan mid wilfingu
ða hine gara cyn for here brogan
habban ne mihte· þanon he gesohte
suð dena folc ofer yða gewealc ar

4. *Beowulf,* ll. 444-64, the manuscript, c. 1000. *British Museum,* MS Cotton Vitellius A. XV, fol. 140r.

5. Cruciform Carpet-page, with interlace ornament, from Lindisfarne Gospels. Northumbria, c. 700. *British Museum,* MS Cotton Nero D. IV, fol. 26v.

6. The Annunciation, from the Benedictional of St. Æthelwold, Bishop of Winchester 975-80. Winchester, c. 975. *British Museum*, MS Add. 49598, fol. 5v.

7. The Harrowing of Hell, from an English Psalter. First quarter of twelfth century. Hildesheim, *St. Godehard*, p. 49.

8. Goliath threatening David, from a Winchester Psalter. English, c. 1050. *Britisn Museum,* MS Cotton Tiberius C. VI, fol. 9r.

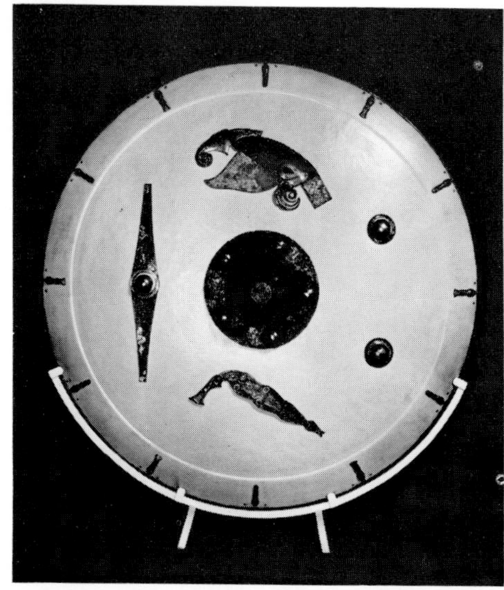

9. Sutton Hoo: Shield (front view, reconstruction). ?First half of the seventh century. *British Museum.*

10. David as Musician, from a Canterbury Psalter. English, c. 750. *British Museum,* MS Cotton Vespasian A. I, fol. 30v.

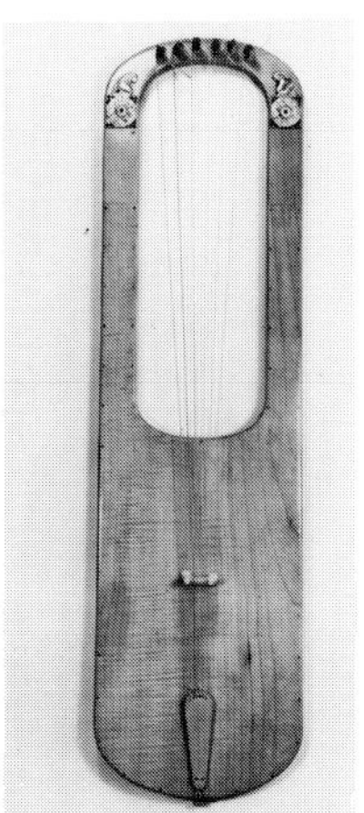

11. Sutton Hoo: the Harp as at present reconstructed. ?First half of seventh century. *British Museum.*

12. The Oseberg Ship. Viking luxury ship, not a warship. From a barrow in Norway, c. 800. Oslo, *Universitetets Oldsaksamling.*

13. Sutton Hoo: Purse-lid of gold, enamel, glass, and garnet. ?English, first half of seventh century, *British Museum.*

14. Sutton Hoo: the great gold Belt Buckle, with ornament of interlaced snakes and animals. English, first half of seventh century. *British Museum.*

15. Sutton Hoo: Shoulder Clasps, one of a pair, of gold, garnet, and enamel. ?English, first half of seventh century. *British Museum.*

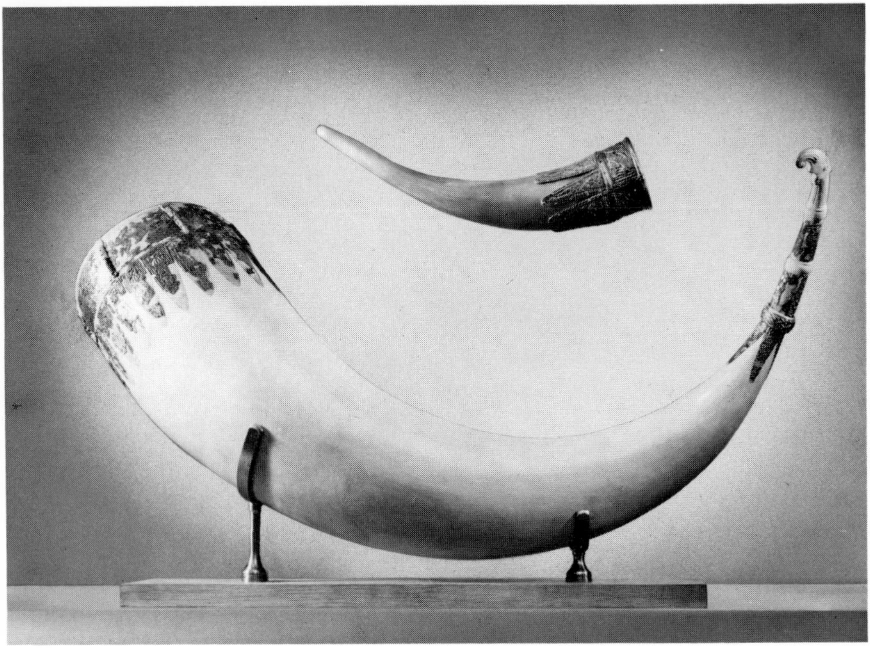

16. Sutton Hoo: large and small Drinking Horns. ?Early seventh century. These horns are reconstructions made soon after the excavation of the find and now thought to be mistaken. The larger horn, with a capacity of six imperial quarts, a greatest diameter of 7.2 inches, and a circumference of 41.5 inches along the outer curve, would have been too heavy and clumsy, when full, for even the most heroic warrior to bring to his lips. *British Museum.*

17. Sutton Hoo: Stag, height about 4″ from the head of the Scepter. ?First half of seventh century. *British Museum.*

18. Sword with inlaid decoration. English, ninth or tenth century. *British Museum.*

19. Sutton Hoo: the Helmet. Swedish work, early sixth century. *British Museum.*

20. Boar Crest, from Benty Grange Helmet. English, seventh century. Sheffield, *City Museum.*

21. The Fetter Lane Sword Pommel, with snake design. English, ninth century. *British Museum.*

22. The Franks Casket (front) of whalebone ivory, is carved in relief. Northumbrian workmanship, early eighth century. *Left:* a scene from the story of Weland; *Right:* the Adoration of the Magi; both surrounded by a runic inscription in the Northumbrian dialect of Old English. *British Museum.*

23. Christ and Mary Magdalene, stone relief from the Ruthwell Cross, Ruthwell, Dumfriesshire. (The runes of the *Dream of the Rood* are not shown.) Northumbrian, ?early eighth century.

24. Chaucer reading his poem *Troilus and Criseyde* at court. English, c. 1410. Cambridge, *Corpus Christi College*, MS 61, fol. lv.

OF PAINTING IN OYLE 1410 THIS WAS PAINTED BEFORE, IN

25. Richard II, with Saints Edmund, Edward the Confessor, and John the Baptist, adoring the Virgin and Child (Wilton Diptych). English, *c.* 1395-1405. London, *The National Gallery.*

26. *Upper left:* Geoffrey Chaucer, from the Ellesmere MS of the *Canterbury Tales.* English c. 1410. His clothes and the pen case hung around his neck identify him as a man of letters. San Marino, California, *Henry E. Huntington Library,* MS 26. c.9, fol. 159v. 27. *Upper right:* The Miller, fol. 34v. 28. *Lower left:* The Nun's Priest, fol. 185. 29. *Lower right:* The Wife of Bath, fol. 72.

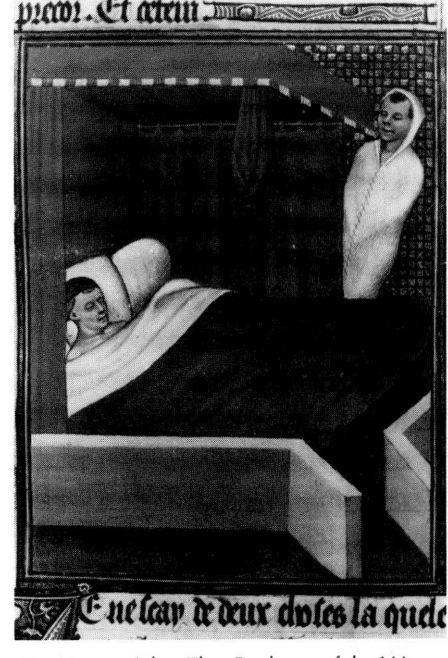

30. *Upper left:* The Franklin, fol. 129v. 31. *Upper right:* The Pardoner, fol. 144. 32. *Lower left:* Friar confessing a nun, from Luttrell Psalter. English, c. 1340. *British Museum,* MS Add. 42130, fol. 74. 33. *Lower right:* The Drowned Man warns Simonides in a dream not to sail, from Boccaccio, *De casibus virorum illustrium.* French, 1409-14. Paris, *Bibliothèque de l'Arsenal,* MS 5193, fol. 76v.

34. Reynard as a bishop, preaching to the birds; and Reynard escaping with a goose, chased by the farmer's wife, from the Smithfield Decretals. English, c. 1340. *British Museum,* MS Royal 10.E.IV, fol. 49v.

35. St. Thomas Becket taking ship from England (*above*) and his martyrdom in Canterbury Cathedral (*below*), on a Limoges enamel *châsse* (case for relics, etc.). French, thirteenth century. *British Museum.*

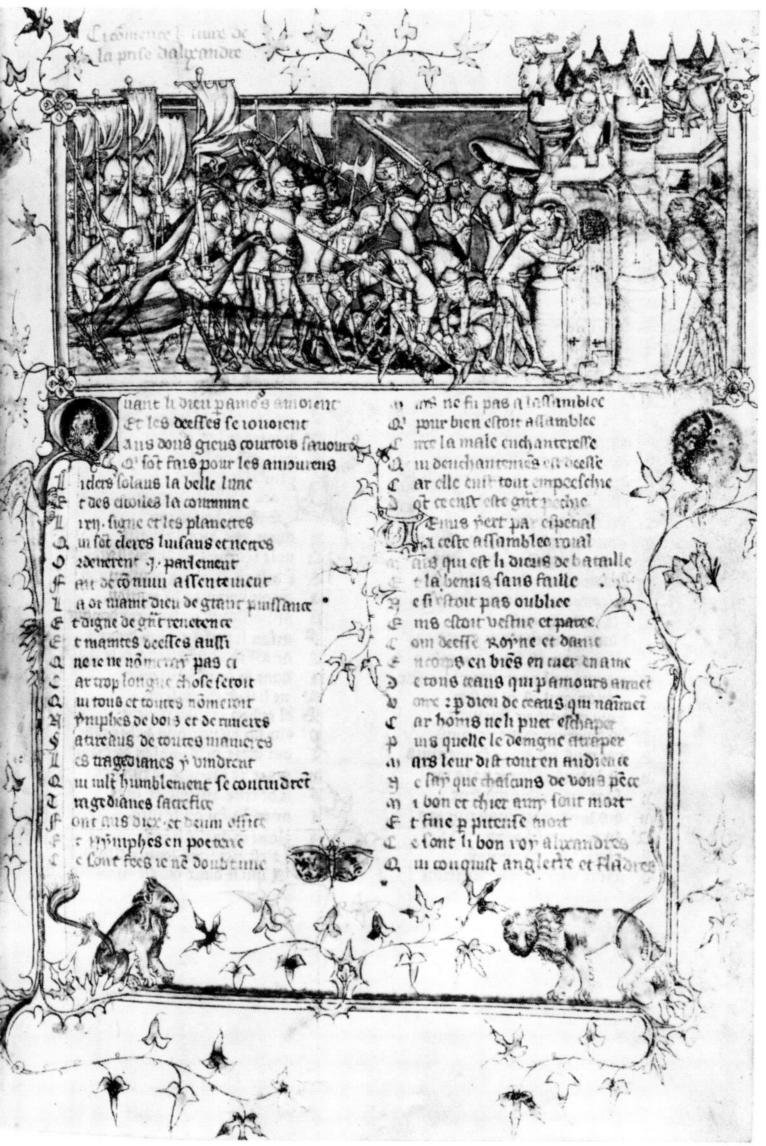

36. The Capture of Alexandria, in which the Knight took part. French, fourteenth century. Paris, *Bibliotheque Nationale,* MS franç. 1584, fol. 309.

37. Zodiac Man and Vein Man, with the Qualities. By the Brothers Limbourg; from the *Très Riches Heures du duc de Berry.* Franco-Flemish, before 1416. Chantilly, *Musée Condé,* MS 65 (1284), fol. 14v. *Photo Giraudon.*

An important part of the physician's skill was to know the correct time of year, month, or day in which treatment, especially by bloodletting, would be feasible and effective by virtue of a favorable relation between macrocosm and microcosm: planets, zodiacal signs, qualities, humors, sex, and parts of the body. The zodiacal sign of the Ram governs the head, so that a time when the sun was in the Ram would be favorable for treating that part. Taurus governed the neck, Gemini the shoulders and arms, and so on. In this miniature, the "qualities," hot, cold, moist, and dry, which are combined in the "humors," blood, phlegm, choler, and melancholy, are associated with zodiacal signs and with male and female sexes in the corners, which are the cardinal points of the compass.

38. The Buying of the Poison and the Deaths of the "Rioters," from Chaucer's Pardoner's Tale. English wood-relief, c. 1400. London, private collection.

39. Lechery. English, mid-fourteenth century. The man's gesture (which is also that of Nicholas of Chaucer's Miller's Tale) is obviously associated with lechery, as is the tavern before which the couple stand, with its ale-bush. *British Museum,* Taymouth Hours, fol. 177.

40. Swearing and Gambling: "rioters" tear Christ's body apart. Broughton, Bucks., wall-painting in St. Lawrence Church. English c. 1430. *Royal Commission on Historical Monuments, Crown Copyright.*

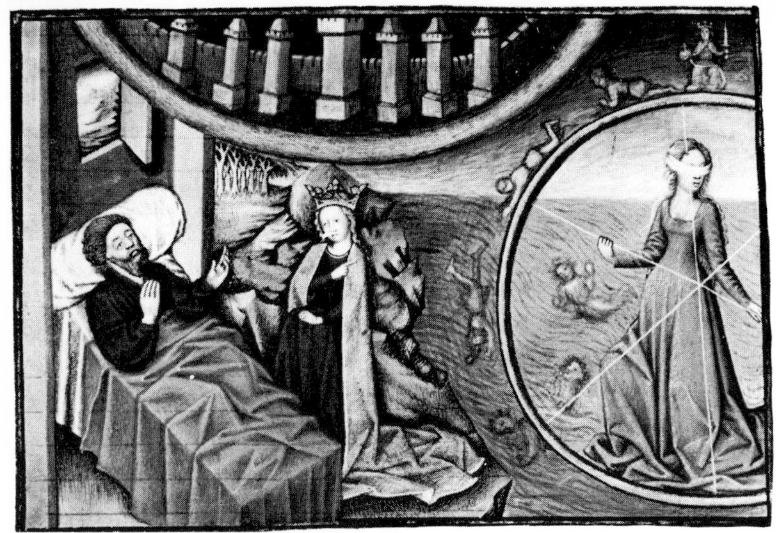

41. Philosophy and Blind Fortune with her Wheel, from Boethius, *De Consolatione Philosophiae* (trans. Jean de Meun). French, *c.* 1450-60. *British Museum,* MS Add. 10341, fol. 31v.

42. The Great Hall of Penshurst Place, Kent, built by the London merchant Sir John Pulteney (d. 1349). *A. F. Kersting.*

43. A New Year feast in the court of Jean duc de Berry, with the sun in his chariot in the zodiacal signs of Capricorn and Aquarius (January), and a tournament in the background. By the Brothers Limbourg; from the *Très Riches Heures du duc de Berry,* Chantilly, *Musée Condé*, MS 65 (1284), fol. 1v. *Giraudon.*

44. A Castle, with the vintage being gathered, and the sun in the signs of Virgo and Libra (September). Begun by the Brothers Limbourg before 1416, and completed by Jean Colombe c. 1485; from the *Très Riches Heures du duc de Berry*, Chantilly, *Musée Condé*, MS 65 (1284), fol. 9v. *Giraudon*.

45. A Boar Hunt, with the sun in Sagittarius and Capricorn (December). By the Brothers Limbourg; from the *Très Riches Heures du duc de Berry*, Chantilly, *Musée Condé*, MS 65 (1284), fol. 12v. *Giraudon.*

46. King Arthur, from the Berry tapestry of the Nine Worthies. French, late fourteenth century. *New York, the Cloisters, Metropolitan Museum of Art.*

47. The Round Table. From *Lancelot,* Rouen, Dupré, 1488.

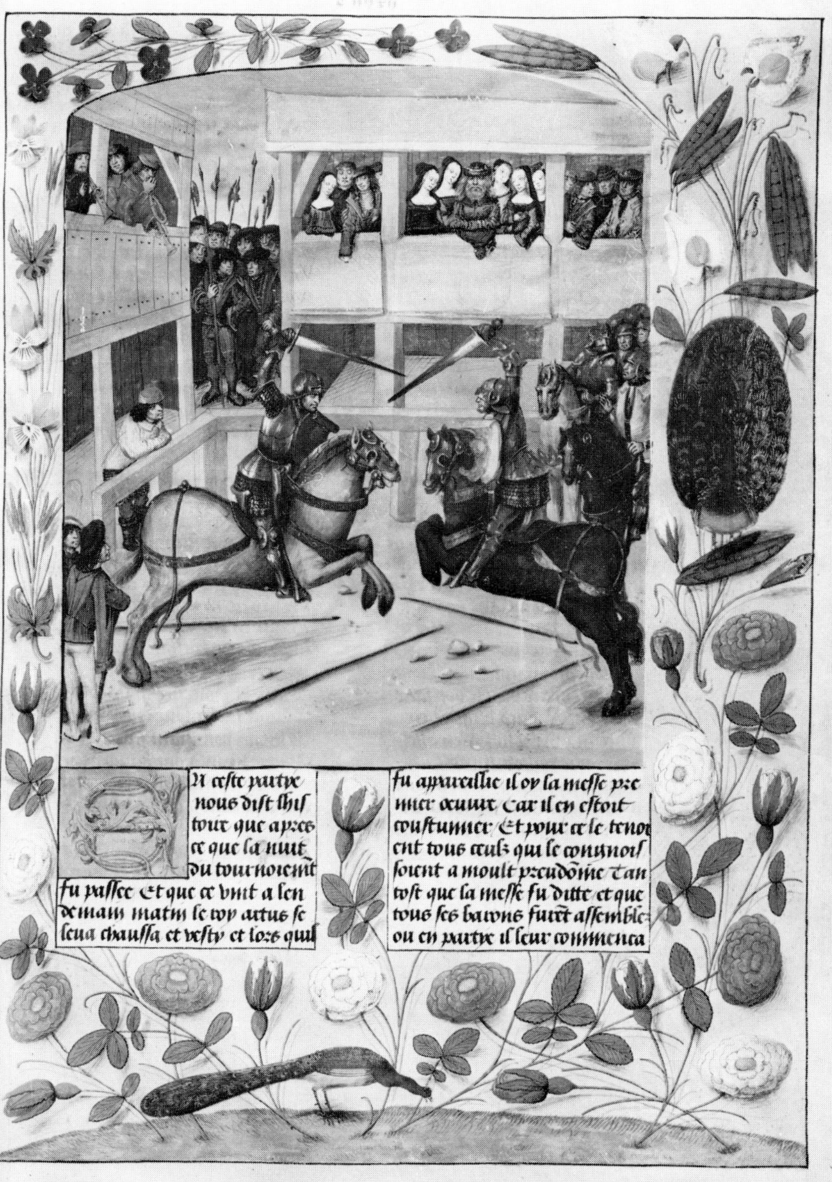

48. A Joust before King Arthur. By the so-called Master of Edward IV, from a Flemish manuscript of (?) Hélie de Borron, *Guiron le courtois*, c. 1480-1500. Oxford, *Bodleian Library*, MS Douce 383, fol. 16r.

49. The Annunciation to the Shepherds. By the Brothers Limbourg. *Très Riches Heures du duc de Berry,* Chantilly, *Musée Condé,* MS 65 (1284), fol. 48r. *Giraudon.*

50. The Last Judgment. By the Brothers Limbourg; from *Très Riches Heures du duc de Berry,* Chantilly, *Musée Condé,* MS 65 (1284), fol. 34r. *Giraudon.*

51. Nuns in choir. From the Psalter of King Henry VI, probably made in Paris c. 1340. *British Museum*, MS Cotton Domitian A. XVII, fol. 177v.

52. Death in True Piety, from *Ars Moriendi,* Netherlandish block-book, 1466. The soul of the penitent received into Heaven by the mediation of Christ, with Mary, John, and Mary Magdalene below the Cross. The confessor places a candle in the dying man's hand, while the frustrated devils exclaim in fury and despair.

53. The Nave of Canterbury Cathedral, looking east. Begun in 1379, the nave pictured replaced an earlier one of the eleventh century. It is one of the great monuments of English religious architecture of Chaucer's lifetime, the second half of the fourteenth century. Its tall and elegant design gives it an effect of spareness and economy, to which the assured simplicity of its lierne vaulting—less extravagant than that of West Country examples—adds the finishing touch. *A. F. Kersting.*

54. *Mappa mundi* (mappemonde), from Jean Mansel, *La Fleur des histoires*. Flemish, c. 1455. Brussels, *Bibliothèque Royale*, MS 9231, fol. 281v.

Other maps are much more detailed. This is more schematic and decorative than utilitarian: it shows earth surrounded by the other elements (water, air, and fire) in concentric circles, and the starry heaven outside them. As usual, the East is at the top with the phoenix in the woods of Paradise, Noah's Ark on Mt. Ararat, and the sons of Noah (from whom post-diluvial man is sprung) on the three then-known continents: Sem on Asia, Ham (Cham) on Africa, and Japhet on Europe.

55. Paradise. By the Brothers Limbourg; from the *Très Riches Heures du duc de Berry,* Chantilly, *Musée Condé,* MS 65 (1284), fol. 25v. *Giraudon.*

Paradise, high in the mountains, walled with the Fountain of Life at the center; Eve tempted by the Serpent "with a lady visage"; Eve tempting Adam; Adam pointing to Eve as the source of the trouble as God rebukes them; the Expulsion by the fiery angel.

And est and west upon the peple I bekke,> *nod my head*
As doth a dowvė> sitting on a berne.> *dove / barn*
Myn hondės and my tongė goon so yerne.> *eagerly*
That it is joye to see my bisinesse.> *activity*
Of avaryce and of swich cursednesse
Is al my preching, for to make hem free> *open-handed*
To yeve her pens,> and namely> unto me. *money / especially*
For my entente is nat but> for to winne,> *only / gain*
And nothing for correccioùn of sinne.
I rekkė> never, whan that they ben beried,> *care / buried*
Though that her soulės goon a blakėberied!°
For certės, many a predicacioùn
Comth oftetyme of yvel entencioùn;°
Som for plesaunce> of folk and flaterye, *pleasure*
To been avauncėd> by ipocrisye, *promoted*
And som for veyne gloriè,> and som for hate. *vainglory*
For, whan I dar non otherweyes debate,°
Than wol I stinge him with my tongė smerte> *sharply*
In preching, so that he shal nat asterte> *escape*
To been defamėd falsly, if that he
Hath trespased° to my brethren or to me.
For, though I tellė noght his propre> name, *actual*
Men shal wel knowė that it is the same
By signės and by othere circumstances.
Thus quyte> I folk that doon us displesànces;> *repay / annoyances*
Thus spitte I out my venim under hewe> *color*
Of holynesse, to semė holy and trewe.
But shortly myn entente I wol devyse;> *describe*
I preche of nothing but for coveityse.°
Therfor my theme is yet, and ever was—
Radix malorum est cupiditas.
Thus can I preche agayn that samė vyce
Which that I use, and that is avaryce.
But, though myself be gilty in that sinne,
Yet can I maken other folk to twinne> *separate*
From avaryce, and sorė to repente.
But that is nat my principal entente.
I prechė nothing> but for coveityse; *not at all*
Of this matere it oughte ynogh suffyse.°
Than telle I hem ensamples° many oon
Of oldė stories, longė tyme agoon:
For lewėd> peple loven talės olde; *simple*

goon a-blakeberied go blackberrying, wander anywhere, to Hell, for all I care
many . . . entencioùn good preaching often comes from bad intention; i.e. even my badness can be turned to good by Christ; see ll. 173–74
whan . . . debate when I dare attack in no other way
trespased sinned against, injured
I . . . coveityse I preach about nothing except for covetousness
Of . . . suffyse that's enough of that
ensamples *exempla*

Swich thingės can they wel reporte> and holde.> *repeat / remember*
What> trowė> ye, the whylės I may preche, *believe*
And winnė gold and silver for> I teche, *because*
That I wol live in povert wilfully?°
Nay, nay, I thoghte> it never trewėly! *intended*
For I wol preche and begge in sondry londes;
I wol not do no labour with myn hondes,
Ne makė baskettes,° and live therby,
Because I wol nat beggen ydelly.°
I wol non of the apostles counterfete;°
I wol have money, wollė,> chese,> and whete,> *wool / cheese / wheat*
Al were it yeven of the povrest page,°
Or of the povrest widwe in a village,
Al sholde hir children stervė° for famyne.
Nay! I wol drinke licour of the vyne,
And have a joly wenche in every toun.
But herkneth,> lordings, in conclusioùn; *listen*
Your lyking> is that I shal telle a tale. *pleasure*
Now have I dronke a draughte of corny ale;
By God, I hope I shal yow telle a thing
That shal, by resoun, been at> your lyking. *to*
For, though myself be a ful vicious man,
A moral talė° yet I yow telle can,
Which I am wont to prechė, for to winne.> *gain*
Now holde your pees, my tale I wol beginne.'

The Tale

In Flaundres whylom> was a companye *once upon a time*
Of yongė folk, that haunteden> folye, *practiced*
As ryot, hasard, stewės,° and tavernes,
Wheras, with harpės, lutės, and giternes,°
They daunce and pleye at dees> bothe day and night, *dice*
And ete also and drinken over hir might,> *capacity*
Thurgh which they doon the devel sacrifyse
Within that develes temple, in cursed wyse
By superfluitee> abhominàble;° *overindulgence*

wilfully gladly, voluntarily. Glad Poverty, to be content with what one has, is the reply to Fortune.
make baskettes St. Paul the Hermit is said to have made his living thus.
Because . . . ydelly I will not be a beggar in idleness, or without making money—a hit, like the preceding few lines, at the friars, the preaching orders who were his rivals in supporting themselves by charitable contributions
counterfete imitate; i.e. by giving up all to follow Christ, which was the precept on which the Franciscan Order was founded
Al . . . page although it were given by the poorest servant-lad
Al . . . sterve even though her children should die (of famine)
For . . . tale See ll. 121–22.
ryot . . . stewes riotous living, gambling, brothels
g释ernes kind of guitar
abhominable thus spelled because supposed to mean inhuman

Hir othės> been so grete and so dampnàble,> *oaths / damnable*
That it is grisly for to here hem swere;
Our blissed Lordės body they to-tere,°
Hem thoughtė Jewės rente> him noght ynough; *tore*
And ech of hem at otherės sinnė lough.> *laughed*
And right anon than comen tombesterės°
Fetys> and smale,> and yongė fruytesterės, *well-made / slim*
Singers with harpės, baudės, wafererės,
Whiche been the verray> develės officerės *true*
To kindle and blowe the fyr of lecherye,
That is annexėd unto glotonye;°
The Holy Writ° take I to my witnesse,
That luxurie> is in wyn and dronkenesse. *lechery*
  Lo, how that dronken Loth,° unkindely,> *unnaturally*
Lay by his doghtrės two, unwitingly;
So dronke he was, he nistė> what he wroghte. *did not know*
  Heròdės, whoso wel the stories soghte,°
Whan he of wyn was replet at his feste,> *feast*
Right at his owenė table he yaf> his heste> *gave / command*
To sleen> the Baptist John ful giltėlees.> *slay / innocent*
  Senek° seith eek> a good word doutėlees; *also*
He seith, he can no differencė finde
Bitwix a man that is out of his minde
And a man which that is dronkėlewe,> *drunk*
But that woodnesse, yfallen in a shrewe,°
Persevereth lenger than doth dronkenesse.
O glotonyė, ful of cursednesse,> *evil*
O causė first° of our confusioùn,> *downfall*
O original of our dampnacioùn,> *damnation*
Til Crist had boght> us with his blood agayn! *redeemed*
Lo, how derė,> shortly for to sayn, *dearly*
Aboght> was thilkė> cursed vileinye; *paid for / same*
Corrupt> was al this world for glotonye! *corrupted*
  Adam our fader,> and his wyf also, *father*
Fro Paradys to labour and to wo
Were driven for that vyce, it is no drede;> *doubt*
For whyl that Adam fasted, as I rede,°
He was in Paradys; and whan that he

to-tere tear to pieces, by oaths referring to God or Christ's body and limbs (Fig. 40).
tombesteres Dancing girls; *fruytesteres,* fruit sellers; and *wafereres,* cake vendors. But the *tombesteres* may be male tumblers and the *wafereres* male pastry cooks, confectioners; the *baudes*—prostitutes—too can be male or female.
annexed . . . glotonye That is a near neighbor to gluttony. From the first sin in Eden, which combined them, lechery and gluttony are close cousins, not to be separated, as Chaucer says in the Parson's Tale. (See Fig. 39.)
Holy Writ Ephesians 5:18
Loth Lot, who slept with his daughters while drunk (Genesis 19:32 ff.)
Heròdes . . . soghte Herod, whoever looks up the stories properly (see Mark 6:17–29 and Matthew 14:1–11)
Senek Lucius Annaeus Seneca (*c.*4 B.C.–*c.*65 A.D.), Roman Stoic philosopher and dramatist, in his *Moral Letters,* 83:18
But . . . shrewe except that madness, come upon a wicked man
cause first i.e. by Eve's eating the forbidden fruit and giving it to Adam
rede in St. Jerome's *Against Jovinian,* for which see the Wife of Bath's Prologue, l. 681

Eet˃ of the fruyt defended˃ on the tree, *ate / forbidden*
Anon° he was outcast to wo and peyne.
O glotonye, on thee wel oghte us pleyne!˃ *cry out*
O, wiste a man˃ how many maladyes *if only one knew*
Folwen of èxcesse and of glotonyes,
He woldė been the morė mesuràble˃ *moderate*
Of his dietė, sittinge at his table.
Allas! the shortė throte, the tendrė mouth,°
Maketh that, Est and West, and North and South,
In erthe, in eir,˃ in water men to swinke˃ *air / toil*
To gete a glotoun deyntee˃ mete and drinke! *delicious*
Of this matere, o Paul,° wel canstow trete,˃ *can you write*
'Mete unto wombe, and wombe eek unto mete,
Shal God destroyen bothe,' as Paulus seith.
Allas! a foul thing is it, by my feith,
To seye˃ this word, and fouler is the dede, *say*
Whan man so drinketh of the whyte and rede,°
That of his throte he maketh his privee,˃ *privy*
Thurgh thilkė cursėd superfluitee.˃ *excess*
  The apostel° weping seith ful pitously,˃ *sadly*
'Ther walken many of whiche yow told have I,
I seye it now weping with pitous voys,
That they been enemys of Cristės croys,
Of whiche the ende is deeth, wombe˃ is her god.' *stomach*
O wombe! O bely! O stinking cod,°
Fulfild˃ of donge˃ and of corrupcioùn! *filled full / dung*
At either ende of thee foul is the soun.˃ *sound*
How greet labour and cost is thee to finde!˃ *provide for*
Thise cokės,° how they stampe,˃ and streyne, and grinde, *pound*
And turnen substaunce into accident,°
To fulfille al thy likerous° talent!
Out of the hardė bonės knokkė they
The mary,˃ for they castė noght awey *marrow*
That may go thurgh the golet˃ softe and swote;˃ *gullet / sweetly*

Anon It was a frequent opinion that Adam and Eve spent only one hour together in Paradise.
shorte . . . mouth little throat and soft mouth; or: the brief pleasure of swallowing—a paraphrase of a passage in St. Jerome's *Against Jovinian*
Paul I Corinthians 6:13 ("Meats for the belly and the belly for meats; but God shall destroy them both")
whyte and rede both kinds of wine
apostel St. Paul, Philippians 3:18 ("For many walk, of whom I have told you often, and now tell you even weeping, that they are the enemies of the cross of Christ: whose end is destruction, whose God is their belly")
cod Bag; more frequently used of the scrotum. The discourse on gluttony is from Pope Innocent III's (1160–1216) *De Contemptu Mundi* (On Despising the World), a tract against earthly pleasures.
cokes The passage on the cooks is a close paraphrase of Innocent III.
substaunce . . . accident This philosophic pun is also in Innocent III. In Aristotelian (and so in Scholastic) philosophy, substance is the permanent, inherent, and essential; accident is the changeable and outward, which can be changed without affecting the substance. In ordinary usage, substance is material; in this case, food. So the cooks change substance (the meat, etc.) into its attributes of flavor, taste, smell, etc., the essential into the non-essential. Chaucer may be glancing at the controversies of his day between the opposing philosophic schools of Realists and Nominalists; or at the alchemists, whose aim was to find a way of changing substance.
likerous greedy, fond of choice food; *talent* [evil] inclination, desire, appetite

Of spicerye,˃ of leef, and bark, and rote˃ *spices / root*
Shal been his sauce ymakėd, by delyt˃ *through pleasure*
To make him yet a newer appetyt.
But certės, he that haunteth swich delyces˃ *pleasures*
Is deed,˃ whyl that he liveth in tho˃ vyces.° *dead / those*
  A lecherous thing is wyn, and dronkėnesse°
Is ful of stryving˃ and of wrecchednesse.˃ *quarreling / evil*
O dronkė man, disfigured is thy face,
Sour is thy breeth, foul artow˃ to embrace, *are you*
And thurgh thy dronkė nose semeth the soun˃ *sound*
As though thou seydest ay˃ 'Sampsoun, Sampsoun'; *always*
And yet, God wot,˃ Sampsoun drank never no wyn.° *knows*
Thou fallest, as it were a stikėd swyn;˃ *stuck pig*
Thy tonge is lost, and al thyn honest cure;°
For dronkenesse is verray sepulture˃ *true burial*
Of mannės wit and his discrecioùn.
In whom that drinke hath dominacioùn,
He can no conseil° kepe, it is no drede.˃ *doubt*
Now kepe yow fro the whyte and fro the rede,
And namely˃ fro the whytė wyn of Lepe,° *especially*
That is to selle˃ in Fish-strete or in Chepe.° *for sale*
This wyn of Spaynė crepeth subtilly°
In otherė wynės, growing fastė˃ by, *close*
Of which ther ryseth swich fumositee,°
That whan a man hath dronken draughtės three,
And weneth˃ that he be at hoom in Chepe, *believes*
He is in Spaynė, right at the toune of Lepe,
Nat at the Rochel, ne at Burdeux toun;
And thannė wol he seye, 'Sampsoun, Sampsoun.'
  But herkneth, lordings, o word, I yow praye,
That alle the sovereyn actės,˃ dar I seye, *supreme deeds*
Of victories in the Oldė Testament,
Thurgh verray God, that is omnipotent,
Were doon in abstinence and in preyère;
Loketh˃ the Bible, and ther ye may it lere.˃ *look at / learn*
  Loke, Attila,° the gretė conquerour,
Deyde in his sleep, with shame and dishonoùr,

But . . . vyces I Timothy 5:6 ("But she that liveth in pleasure is dead while she liveth"). Quotations from St. Paul, often also used by St. Jerome and Innocent III, are continually interwoven.
dronkenesse Proverbs 20:1 ("Wine is a mocker, strong drink is raging")
Sampsoun . . . wyn Judges 13:4,7; Samson's mother is commanded to drink no wine, and told that her son will be a Nazarite, a sect denying itself wine and strong drink.
cure care for decent behavior, self-respect
conseil secrets, discretion
Lepe a town near Cadiz, Spain, famous for strong wines
Chepe Fish Street and either Eastcheap, near it, or Cheapside; all streets in the City of London, the commercial center
This . . . subtilly a joke about either the mixing of stronger, cheaper Spanish wines with the finer French wines exported from Bordeaux and La Rochelle; or simply selling Spanish wines as French
fumositee See the Nun's Priest's Tale, l. 158.
Attila leader of the Huns—invaders of Italy in the 5th century—who died drunk, of a burst blood vessel, on the last of his many wedding nights

Bledinge ay˃ at his nose in dronkénesse; *continually*
A capitayn shoulde live in sobrenesse.
And over˃ al this, avyseth˃ yow right wel *above / consider*
What was comaunded unto Lamuel°—
Nat Samuel, but Lamuel, seye I—
Redeth the Bible, and finde it expresly
Of wyn-yeving˃ to hem that han justyse.° *wine-serving*
Namore of this, for it may wel suffyse.
And now that I have spoke of glotonye,
Now wol I yow defenden hasardrye.˃ *forbid gambling*
Hasard is verray moder˃ of lesinges,˃ *mother / lies*
And of deceite, and cursed forsweringes,°
Blasphemė of Crist, manslaughtre, and wast˃ also *waste*
Of catel° and of tyme; and forthermo,
It is repreve˃ and contrarie of honoùr *reproach*
For to ben holde a commune hasardoùr.˃ *gambler*
And ever the hyër he is of estaat,˃ *status*
The more is he holden desolaat.˃ *abandoned*
If that a prince useth hasardrye,
In allė governaunce and policye
He is, as by commune opinioùn,
Yholde˃ the lasse in reputacioùn. *considered*
Stilbon,° that was a wys˃ embassadoùr, *prudent*
Was sent to Corinthe, in ful greet honoùr,
Fro Lacidomie,˃ to make hir alliaùnce. *Sparta*
And whan he cam, him happedė, par chaunce,°
That alle the grettest that were of that lond,
Pleyinge attė hasard° he hem fond.
For which, as sone as it mightė be,
He stal him˃ hoom agayn to his contree, *stole away*
And seyde, 'Ther wol I nat lesė˃ my name; *lose*
Ne I wol nat take on me so greet defame,˃ *dishonor*
Yow for to allye unto none hasardoùrs.
Sendeth otherė wyse embassadoùrs;
For, by my trouthe, me were lever˃ dye, *I had rather*
Than I yow sholde to hasardoùrs allye.
For ye that been so glorious in honoùrs
Shul nat allyen yow with hasardoùrs
As by my will, ne as by my tretee.'˃ *treaty*
This wyse philosòphre thus seyde he.
Loke eek˃ that, to the king Demetrius° *also*

Lamuel Proverbs 31:4–5; Lemuel's mother told him: "It is not for kings to drink wine . . . nor for princes strong drink."
han justyse have judicial power
forsweringes Perjury; the passage is imitated from the Latin *Policraticus,* a mirror for princes by John of Salisbury (*c.*1115–80).
catel chattels, possessions, material wealth
Stilbon This story is also in John of Salisbury, where the ambassador's name is Chilon. Stilbon was a name for the planet Mercury.
him . . . chaunce it happened to him, by chance
hasard here, dice
Demetrius Probably Demetrius Nicator, king of the Parthians, an Asian people; his story is also in the *Policraticus.* Chaucer may have confused him with another Demetrius, and got the name Stilbon above, from a passage in Seneca, where the two are mentioned together.

The king of Parthės, as the book seith us,
Sente him a paire of dees> of gold in scorn,   *dice*
For he hadde usėd hasard therbiforn;
For which he heeld his glorie or his renoùn
At no value or reputacioùn.
Lordės may finden other maner pley>   *kind of pastime*
Honeste ynough to dryve the day awey.>   *pass the time*
  Now wol I speke of othės> false and grete   *oaths*
A word or two, as oldė bokės trete.
Gret swering is a thing abhominàble,
And false swering is yet more reprevàble.>   *reprehensible*
The heighė God forbad swering at al,
Witnesse on Mathew;° but in special
Of swering seith the holy Jeremye,°
'Thou shalt seye sooth thyn othės, and nat lye,
And swere in dome, and eek in rightwisnesse';
But ydel swering is a cursėdnesse.
Bihold and see, that in the firstė table°
Of heighė Goddės hestės> honurable,   *commandments*
How that the seconde heste of Him is this—
'Tak nat my name in ydel or amis.'
Lo, rather> he forbedeth swich swering   *sooner*
Than homicyde or many a cursed thing;
I seye that, as by ordre, thus it stondeth;
This knoweth that His hestės understondeth,°
How that the second° heste of God is that.
And forther-over,> I wol thee telle al plat,>   *moreover / flat*
That vengeance shal nat parten> from his hous,   *depart*
That of his othes> is too outrageous.°   *oaths*
'By Goddės precious herte, and by his nayles,°
And by the blode of Crist that is in Hayles,°
Seven is my chaunce,> and thyn is cink> and treye;>   *throw / five / three*
By Goddės armės, if thou falsly pleye,
This dagger shal thurghout thyn herte go'—
This fruyt cometh of the bicchėd bonės° two,
Forswering,> irė, falsnesse, homicyde.   *perjury*
Now, for the love of Crist that for us dyde,
Leveth your othės, bothė grete and smale;
But, sirs, now wol I tellė forth my tale.
  Thise ryotourės> three, of whiche I telle,   *revelers*

Mathew Matthew 5:34 ("But I say unto you, swear not at all")
Jeremye Jeremiah 4:2 ("And thou shalt swear: [As] the Lord liveth, in truth, in judgment (*dome*) and in righteousness")
table of the Law, the Ten Commandments, written on two tablets of stone; the first tablet contained the first four, concerning duty toward God
This . . . understondeth this he knows who understandeth his (God's) commandments
second according to the Vulgate; in the English Bible, the third Commandment
outrageous See Ecclesiaticus 23:12.
nayles See above, l. 2; nails of the Cross, often shown with Christ's pierced heart.
Hayles Hailes, an abbey in Gloucestershire, supposed to possess a phial of Christ's blood
bicched bones bitched, or damned, dice

Longe erst er> prymė° rong of any belle, *before*
Were set hem in a taverne for to drinke;
And as they satte, they herde a bellė clinke
Biforn a cors,> was caried to his grave; *corpse*
That oon of hem gan callen° to his knave,> *servant*
'Go bet,'° quod he, 'and axė redily,> *ask promptly*
What cors is this that passeth heer forby;> *nearby*
And look> that thou reporte his namė wel.' *be sure*
'Sir,' quod this boy, 'it nedeth never-a-del.°
It was me told, er ye cam heer, two houres;
He was, pardee,° an old felawe> of youres; *companion*
And sodeynly he was yslayn tonight,> *last night*
For-dronkė,° as he sat on his bench upright;
Ther cam a privee> theef, men clepeth> Deeth, *secret / call*
That in this contree al the peple sleeth,> *slays*
And with his spere° he smoot his herte atwo,> *in two*
And wente his wey withouten wordės mo.
He hath a thousand slayn this pestilence:> *during this plague*
And, maister, er ye come in his presence,
Me thinketh that it werė necessarie
For to be war> of swich an adversarie: *be careful*
Beth redy for to meete him evermore.
Thus taughtė me my dame,> I sey namore.' *mother*
'By saintė Marie,' seyde this taverner,> *innkeeper*
'The child seith sooth, for he hath slayn this yeer,
Henne> over a myle, within a greet village, *hence*
Both man and womman, child and hyne,> and page *farm-laborer*
I trowe> his habitacioùn be there; *believe*
To been avysėd> greet wisdom it were, *forewarned*
Er that he dide a man a dishonoùr.'
'Ye, Goddės armės,' quod this ryotour,
'Is it swich peril with him for to meete?
I shal him seke by wey and eek by streete,°
I make avow to Goddės dignė> bones! *worshipful*
Herkneth, felawes, we three been al ones;> *of one mind*
Lat ech of us holde up his hond til> other, *to the*
And ech of us bicomen otherės brother,
And we wol sleen> this falsė traytour Deeth; *slay*
He shal be slayn, which that so many sleeth,
By Goddės dignitee,> er it be night.' *reverence*
Togidres han thise three her trouthės plight,°

pryme some time between 6 a.m. and 9 a.m.; or just after sunrise; see the Miller's Tale, l. 446, and the Nun's Priest's Tale, ll. 412, 431
gan callen did call
bet better, i.e. as fast as you can
it . . . never-a-del it isn't the least bit necessary
pardee indeed (literally, *par Dieu,* by God)
For-dronke blind drunk
spere Death's dart
by wey . . . streete by path and paced road; by highway and byway; everywhere
her . . . plight pledged their words, swearing to be as brothers by blood

To live and dyen ech of hem for other,
As though he were his owene yboren> brother. — *born*
And up they sterte> al dronken, in this rage, — *leapt*
And forth they goon towardės that village,
Of which the taverner had spoke biforn,
And many a grisly> ooth than han they sworn, — *terrible*
And Cristės blessėd body° they to-rente>— — *tore apart*
'Deeth shal be deed,> if that they may him hente.'> — *dead / catch*
  Whan they han goon nat fully half a myle,
Right as they wolde han troden> over a style, — *stepped*
An old man° and a povrė> with hem mette. — *poor*
This oldė man ful mekėly hem grette,> — *greeted*
And seydė thus, 'Now, lordės, God yow see!'> — *protect*
  The proudest of thise ryotourės three
Answerde agayn, 'What! carl,> with sory grace,° — *churl*
Why artow> al forwrappėd> save thy face> — *are you / completely swathed*
Why livestow so longe in so greet age?'
  This oldė man gan loke in his visàge,
And seydė thus, 'For> I ne can nat finde — *because*
A man, though that I walkėd into Inde,°
Neither in citee nor in no village,
That woldė chaunge his youthė for myn age;
And therfore moot> I han myn agė stille,> — *must / always*
As longė time as it is Goddės wille.
  Ne deeth, allas! ne wol nat han my lyf;
Thus walke I, lyk a restėlees caityf,> — *captive*
And on the ground, which is my modrės> gate, — *mother's*
I knokkė with my staf, bothe erly and late,
And seyė, "Levė> moder, leet me in! — *dear*
Lo, how I vanish, flesh, and blood, and skin!
Allas! whan shul my bonės been at reste?
Moder, with yow woldė I chaunge> my cheste, — *exchange*
That in my chambre longė tymė hath be,
Ye! for an heyrė clowt to wrappė me!"°
But yet to me she wol nat do that grace,
For which ful pale and welkėd> is my face. — *withered*
  But, sirs, to yow it is no curteisye
To speken to an old man vileinye,> — *roughness*
But> he trespasse in worde, or elles in dede. — *unless*
In Holy Writ ye may yourself wel rede,°

body See Fig. 40.
old man seemingly Chaucer's invention. In the Italian version there is a hermit, fleeing from Death as the riotors go to meet him.
with . . . grace with wretched looks, or, an imprecation: Devil take it
Inde India, an image of remoteness, the Far East. Chaucer makes his old man a version of the legendary Wandering Jew, Ahasuerus, who was condemned to walk the earth eternally for having refused a resting place to Christ on the road to Calvary. To find death would be for him a release.
Moder . . . me (ll. 448–50) Mother, I should like to exchange with you my chest [earthly possessions], which has long been in my bedroom, even for a hair-cloth to wrap myself in; i.e. he asks Earth to take him, in a common shroud
rede Leviticus 19:32: "Thou shalt rise up before the hoary head."

"Agayns> an old man, hoor> upon his heed, *before / white*
Ye sholde aryse"; wherfor I yeve> yow reed,> *give / advice*
Ne dooth unto an old man noon harm now,
Namorė than ye wolde men dide to yow
In agė, if that ye so longe abyde;
And God be with yow, wher ye go or ryde.°
I moot go thider as I have to> go.' *where I must*
'Nay, oldė cherl, by God, thou shalt nat so,'
Seydė this other hasardour anon;
'Thou partest nat so lightly,> by Saint John! *easily*
Thou spak right now of thilkė traitour Deeth,
That in this contree alle our frendės sleeth.
Have heer my trouthe,> as thou art his aspye,> *word / spy*
Tel wher he is, or thou shalt it abye,> *pay for it*
By God, and by the holy sacrament!°
For soothly thou art oon of his assent,°
To sleen us yongė folk, thou falsė theef!'
'Now, sirs,' quod he, 'if that yow be so leef> *wishful*
To findė Deeth, turne up this crookėd wey,
For in that grove I laft> him, by my fey,> *left / faith*
Under a tree, and ther he wol abyde;
Nat for your boost> he wol him nothing hyde. *boasting*
See ye that ook?> Right ther ye shul him finde. *oak*
God savė yow, that boghte agayn> mankinde, *redeemed*
And yow amende!'° Thus seyde this oldė man.
And everich> of thise ryotourės ran, *each*
Til he cam to that tree, and ther they founde
Of florins° fyne of golde ycoynėd rounde
Wel ny an eightė busshels, as hem thoughte.
No lenger thanne after Deeth they soughte,
But ech of hem so glad was of that sighte,
For that the florins been so faire and brighte,
That doun they sette hem by this precious hord.
The worste of hem he spake the firstė word.
'Brethren,' quod he, 'tak kepė what I seye;
My wit is greet, though that I bourde> and pleye. *jest*
This tresor hath Fortune unto us yiven,> *given*
In mirthe and jolitee our lyf to liven,
And lightly> as it comth, so wol we spende. *easily*
Ey! Goddės precious dignitee!> who wende> *reverence / expected*
To-day, that we sholde han so fair a grace?
But mighte this gold be cariėd fro this place
Hoom to myn hous, or ellės unto youres—
For wel ye woot that al this gold is oures—

wher . . . ryde whether you walk or ride; an oral formula: whatever you do
sacrament Eucharist
oon . . . assent one of those who accept him; one of his following

And . . . amende bring you to better state
florins originally coined in Florence. In Chaucer's time the English florin, worth 6s. 8d. (one-third of a pound), was relatively new.

Than werė we in heigh felicitee.
But trewėly, by daye it may nat be;
Men woldė seyn that we were thevės stronge,> *violent*
And for our owenė tresor doon us honge.> *have us hanged*
This tresor moste ycariėd be by nighte
As wysly> and as slyly as it mighte. *carefully*
Wherfore I rede> that cut° among us alle *advise*
Be drawe, and lat se wher the cut wol falle;
And he that hath the cut with hertė blythe
Shal rennė> to the toune, and that ful swythe,> *run / quickly*
And bringe us breed and wyn ful privėly.> *secretly*
And two of us shul kepen> subtilly *guard*
This tresor wel; and, if he wol nat tarie,
Whan it is night, we wol this tresor carie
By oon assent,> wheras us thinketh best.' *agreement*
That oon of hem the cut broughte in his fest,> *closed fist*
And bad hem drawe, and loke wher it wol falle;
And it fil> on the yongeste of hem alle; *fell*
And forth toward the toun he wente anon.
And also> sone as that he was gon, *as*
That oon of hem spak thus unto that other,
'Thou knowest wel thou art my swornė brother,
Thy profit wol I tellė thee anon.
Thou woost wel that our felawe is agon;> *gone*
And heer is gold, and that ful greet plentee,
That shal departed> been among us three. *divided*
But nathėles, if I can shape> it so *arrange*
That it departed were among us two,
Hadde I nat doon a freendės torn> to thee?' *turn*
That other answerde, 'I noot> how that may be; *do not know*
He woot how that the gold is with us tweye,
What shal we doon, what shal we to him seye?'
'Shal it be conseil?'> seyde the firstė shrewe,> *secret / villain*
'And I shal tellen thee, in wordės fewe,
What we shal doon, and bringe it wel aboute.'
'I grauntė,' quod that other, 'out of doute,
That, by my trouthe, I wol thee nat biwreye.'> *expose*
'Now,' quod the firste, 'thou woost wel we be tweye,> *two*
And two of us shul strenger> be than oon. *must stronger*
Look whan that he is set,> and right anoon *seated*
Arys,> as though thou woldest with him pleye; *get up*
And I shal ryve> him thurgh the sydes tweye *pierce*
Whyl that thou strogelest with him as in game,
And with thy dagger look thou do the same;
And than shal al this gold departed be,
My derė freend, bitwixen me and thee;

cut lot; see the General Prologue, l. 837. They draw lots to see who will go to town.

Than may we bothe our lustės˃ al fulfille, *desires*
And pleye at dees˃ right at our owene wille.' *dice*
And thus acorded˃ been thise shrewės tweye *agreed*
To sleen˃ the thridde, as ye han herd me seye. *slay*
  This yongest, which that wente unto the toun,
Ful ofte in herte he rolleth up and doun
The beautee of thise florins newe and brighte.
'O Lord!' quod he, 'if so were that I mighte
Have al this tresor to myself allone,
Ther is no man that liveth under the trone˃ *throne*
Of God, that sholdė live so mery as I!'
And attė laste the Feend,˃ our enemy, *devil*
Putte in his thought that he shold poyson beye,˃ *buy*
With which he mightė sleen his felawes tweye;
For why the Feend fond him in swich lyvinge,°
That he had levė˃ him to sorwe bringe, *leave*
For this was outrėly˃ his fulle entente *utterly*
To sleen hem bothe, and never to repente.
And forth he gooth, no lenger wolde he tarie,
Into the toun, unto a pothecarie,˃ *apothecary*
And preyėd him, that he him woldė selle
Som poyson, that he mighte his rattės quelle;˃ *kill*
And eek ther was a polcat˃ in his hawe,˃ *polecat / yard*
That, as he seyde, his capouns hadde yslawe,˃ *slain*
And fayn˃ he woldė wreke˃ him, if he mighte, *gladly / revenge*
On vermin,° that destroyėd˃ him by nighte. *ruined*
  The pothecarie answerde, 'And thou shalt have
A thing that, also˃ God my soulė save, *as*
In al this world ther nis no creätùre,
That ete or dronke hath of this confitùre˃ *mixture*
Noght but the mountance˃ of a corn˃ of whete, *amount / grain*
That he ne shal his lyf anon forlete;˃ *lose*
Ye, sterve˃ he shal, and that in lassė whyle *die*
Than thou wolt goon a paas˃ nat but a myle; *at walking pace*
This poyson is so strong and violent.'
  This cursed man hath in his hond yhent˃ *taken*
This poyson in a box, and sith˃ he ran *then*
Into the nextė strete, unto a man,
And borwed of him largė botels three;
And in the two his poyson pourėd he;
The thridde he keptė clenė for his drinke.
For al the night he shoop˃ him for to swinke˃ *intended / toil*
In caryinge of the gold out of that place.
And whan this ryotour, with sory grace,
Had filled with wyn his gretė botels three,

For why . . . lyvinge because the Devil found him in such a state of life that he had leave to bring him to grief. Since God foreordains all, the Devil can only act with His permission.
vermin any reptile or marauding animal

To his felawes agayn repaireth he.
  What nedeth it to sermone of it more?
For right as they had cast> his deeth bifore,   *plotted*
Right so they han him slayn, and that anon.
And whan that this was doon, thus spak that oon,
'Now lat us sitte and drinke, and make us merie,
And afterward we wol his body berie.'>   *bury*
And with that word it happėd him, par cas,>   *by chance*
To take the botel ther> the poyson was,   *where*
And drank, and yaf his felawe drinke also,
For which anon they storven> bothė two.   *died*
  But, certės, I suppose that Avicen°
Wroot never in no canon, ne in no fen,
Mo wonder signės° of empoisoning
Than hadde thise wrecchės two, er> hir ending.   *before*
Thus ended been thise homicydės two,
And eek the false empoysoner also.

  O cursed sinnė,° ful of cursednesse!
O traytours homicyde, o wikkednesse!
O glotonye, luxurie,> and hasardrye!   *lechery*
Thou blasphemoùr of Crist with vileinye
And othės> grete, of usage> and of pryde!   *oaths / habit*
Allas! mankinde, how may it bityde,>   *happen*
That to thy creatoùr which that thee wroghte,>   *made*
And with his precious hertė-blood thee boghte,>   *redeemed*
Thou art so fals and so unkinde,> allas!°   *unnatural*
  Now, goode men, God forgeve yow your trespas,
And ware> yow fro the sinne of avaryce.   *guard*
Myn holy pardoun may yow alle waryce,>   *preserve*
So that ye offre nobles° or sterlinges,°
Or ellės silver brochės, sponės, ringes.
Boweth your heed> under this holy bulle!   *head*
Cometh up, ye wyves, offreth of your wolle!>   *wool*
Your name I entre heer in my rolle anon;
Into the blisse of hevene shul ye gon;
I yow assoilė,> by myn heigh power,   *absolve*
Yow that wol offre, as clene and eek as cleer
As ye were born and, lo, sirs, thus I preche.
And Jesu Crist, that is our soulės leche,>   *physician*

Avicen Avicenna (d. 1037), the Arab philosopher and physician, whose *Canon of Medicine,* divided into fens or sections, was a standard textbook and included a section on poisons. Cf. the General Prologue, l. 434.
wonder signes extraordinary symptoms
sinne The Pardoner turns to the application of his *exemplum* and to his *peroration:* exclamation upon the horror of sin, followed by invitation to repent—on the Pardoner's terms.
Allas! mankinde . . . allas (ll. 614–17) an imitation of the Reproach of Christ, part of the Office for the fourth Sunday in Lent and often made into English lyric verse; Christ addresses man from the Cross: "Man, full dearly I have thee bought / How is it that thou lov'st me not? . . ."
nobles gold, valuable coins; see the Miller's Tale, l. 148
sterlinges silver pennies, less valuable, 80 to the noble

So grauntė yow his pardon to receyve;
For that is best; I wol yow nat deceyve.
But sirs, o word forgat I in my tale,
I have relikes and pardon in my male,˃ *bag*
As faire as any man in Engėlond,
Whiche were me yeven by the popės hond.
If any of yow wol, of devocioùn,
Offren, and han myn absolucioùn,
Cometh forth anon, and kneleth heer adoun,
And mekėly receyveth my pardoùn:
Or ellės, taketh pardon as ye wende,˃ *go*
Al newe and fresh, at every tounės ende,
So that ye offren alwey newe and newe˃ *again and again*
Nobles and pens, which that be gode and trewe.°
It is an honour˃ to everich that is heer, *good thing*
That ye mowe have a suffisant˃ pardoneer *competent*
T'assoillė yow, in contree as ye ryde,
For aventurės˃ which that may bityde. *chances*
Peràventure˃ ther may falle oon or two *perhaps*
Doun of his hors, and breke his nekke atwo.
Look which a seuretee˃ is it to yow alle *safeguard*
That I am in your felaweship yfalle,
That may assoille yow, bothė more and lasse,°
Whan that the soule shal fro the body passe.
I redė˃ that our hoste heer shal biginne, *counsel*
For he is most envolupėd˃ in sinne. *wrapped*
Com forth, sir Hoste, and offre first anon,
And thou shalt kisse the reliks everichon,
Ye, for a grote! unbokel˃ anon thy purs.' *unbuckle*

'Nay, nay,' quod he, 'than have˃ I Cristės curs! *would have*
Lat be,' quod he, 'it shal nat be, so theech!˃ *may I thrive*
Thou woldest make me kissė thyn old breech,˃ *breeches*
And swere it were a relik of a saint,
Thogh it were with thy fundement depeint!˃ *stained*
But by the croys which that Saint Eleynė° fond,
I wolde I hadde thy coillons˃ in myn hond *testicles*
In stede of relikes or of seintuarie;˃ *reliquary*
Lat cutte hem of, I wol thee helpe hem carie;
Thay shul be shrynėd in an hoggės tord.'˃ *turd*
This pardoner answerdė nat a word;
So wrooth he was, no word ne wolde he seye.
'Now,' quod our Host, 'I wol no lenger pleye
With thee, ne with noon other angry man.'

Nobles . . . trewe Nobles and pennies, good and not forgeries. The debasement of currency, by forgery and otherwise, was a continual problem.

more and lasse great and small; everybody
Eleyne St. Helena, mother of the Emperor Constantine the Great, and said to have discovered the true Cross

But right anon the worthy Knight bigan,
Whan that he saugh that al the peple lough,> *laughed*
'Namore of this, for it is right ynough;
Sir Pardoner, be glad and mery of chere;
And ye, sir Host, that been to me so dere,
I prey yow that ye kisse the Pardoner.°
And Pardoner, I prey thee, drawe thee neer,
And, as we diden, lat us laughe and pleye.'
Anon they kiste, and riden forth hir weye.

Here is ended the Pardoners Tale

Retraction

Heere taketh the makere of this book his leve

Now preye I to hem alle that herkne[1] this litel tretys[2] or rede, that if ther be any thyng in it that liketh[3] hem, that therof they thanken oure Lord Jhesu Crist, of whom procedeth al wit[4] and al goodnesse. And if ther be any thyng that displese hem, I preye hem also that they arrette it to the defaute of myn unkonnynge,[5] and nat to my wyl, that wolde ful fayn have seyd bettre if I hadde had konnynge. For oure book[6] seith, 'Al that is writen is writen for oure doctrine,'[7] and that is myn entente. Wherfore I biseke[8] yow mekely, for the mercy of God, that ye preye for me that Crist have mercy on me and foryeve me my giltes; and namely[9] of my translacions and enditynges[10] of worldly vanitees, the whiche I revoke in my retracciouns: as is the book of Troilus;[11] the book also of Fame;[12] the book of the xxv. Ladies;[13] the book of the Duchesse; the book of Seint Valentynes day of the Parlement of Briddes;[14] the tales of Caunterbury, thilke that sownen into[15] synne; the book of the Leoun;[16] and many another book, if they were in my remembrance, and many

kisse the Pardoner Kissing between men, especially as a sign of peace-making, was normal. The Knight and the Host use the familiar "thou" when addressing the Pardoner, but the more formal "you" with each other.

1. Hear, listen to.
2. Treatise.
3. Pleases.
4. Knowledge.
5. Ascribe it to my defect of lack of skill.
6. The Bible.
7. Romans 15:4; see the Nun's Priest's Tale, l. 675.
8. Beseech.
9. Especially.
10. Verses.
11. *Troilus and Criseyde.*
12. *The House of Fame.*
13. *The Legend of Good Women.*
14. Birds, i.e. *The Parliament of Fowls.*
15. Tend toward.
16. This has not survived and we do not know what it was.

a song and many a leccherous lay; that Crist for his grete mercy foryeve me the synne. But of the translacion of Boece de Consolacione,[17] and othere bookes of legendes of saintes, and omelies,[18] and moralitee, and devocioun, that thanke I oure Lord Jhesu Crist and his blisful[19] Mooder, and alle the saintes of hevene, bisekynge hem that they from hennes forth[20] unto my lyves ende sende me grace to biwayle my giltes, and to studie to the salvacioun of my soule, and graunte me grace of verray penitence, confessioun and satisfaccioun to doon in this present lyf, thurgh the benigne grace of hym that is kyng of kynges and preest over alle preestes, that boghte[21] us with the precious blood of his herte; so that I may been oon of hem at the day of doom[22] that shulle be saved. *Qui cum patre et Spiritu Sancto vivit et regnat Deus per omnia secula.*[23] *Amen.*

Heere is ended the book of the tales of Caunterbury, compiled by Geffrey Chaucer, of whos soule Jhesu Crist have mercy. Amen.

c. 1400

Shorter Poems

In many ways the handful of short poems that Chaucer wrote are the best introduction to his genius and to some of the basic concepts of his world of thought. The metric and the verse forms of all of the short poems are borrowed from French, the concepts that they play with are ultimately French; yet each is individually Chaucerian, with his characteristic witty turn. The first two here given, "Gentilesse" and "Truth," are *balades* on the French model, rhyming stanzas with refrain, seriously exploring the moral virtues of their titles. The roundel from *The Parliament of Fowls* is a "straight" performance, and so is Troilus's song, translated from a sonnet by Petrarch into the French *rime royal* of the long poem from which it is taken. The *balade* from *The Legend of Good Women* is a serious, rhetorical amassing of examples of true ladies, but "To Rosemounde" is a parody of the courtly love lyric, and "The Complaint to His Purse" a turning upside-down of all the values of the courtly code of love, expressed in the strictest and most exact form of the love complaint. "To Adam" is a biting comment on the fallibility of scribes, written as if it were one of those rhyming tags by which manuscript copyists congratulate themselves on the completion of their task.

17. Boethius, *De Consolatione Philosophiae* (Of the Consolation of Philosophy).
18. Homilies.
19. Blessed.
20. Henceforth.
21. Bought, redeemed.
22. Judgment.
23. "Who, with the Father and the Holy Ghost, lives and reigns, God in all eternity"; a doxology, or praise to God, at completion of a prayer or intercession.

Gentilesse°

The firstė stok,° fader> of gentilesse— *father*
What man that claymeth gentil for to be
Must followe his trace, and alle his wittės° dresse
Vertu to sewe,> and vyces for to flee. *follow*
For unto vertu longeth dignitėe,> *belongs rank*
And noght the revers, saufly dar> I deme,> *safely dare / judge*
Al were he mytre, croune, or diademe.°

This firstė stok was ful of rightwisnesse,> *righteousness*
Trewe of his word, sobre, pitous,> and free,> *merciful / generous*
Clene of his gost,> and lovėd besinesse,> *pure in spirit / industry*
Ageinst the vyce of slouthe,> in honestee;> *sloth / righteousness*
And, but> his heir love vertu, as dide he, *unless*
He is noght gentil, thogh he richė seme,°
Al were he mytre, croune, or diademe.

Vyce may wel be heir to old richesse;
But ther may no man, as men may wel see,
Bequethe his heir his vertuous noblesse
That is appropred> unto no degree, *assigned solely*
But to the firstė fader in magestee,
That maketh him his heyre that can him queme,> *please*
Al were he mytre, croune, or diademe.
c. 1385

Truth

Flee fro the prees> and dwell with soothfastnesse;> *throng / truth*
  Suffice unto thy good, though it be smal;
For hord> hath hate, and climbing tikelnesse,> *hoarding / insecurity*
  Prees hath envye, and welė blent overal;°
  Savour no more than thee behovė shal.°
    Wirche> wel thyself, that other folk canst rede;> *act / advise*
    And Trouthė shal delivere, it is no drede.°

Tempest thee not al crokėd to redresse,°
  In trust of hir that turneth as a bal°—

Gentilesse Four important discussions of the sources and nature of *gentilesse* are Boethius, *De Consolatione Philosophiae* III, prose 6 and meter 6; Dante, *Convivio,* tract. 4; the *Roman de la Rose,* ll. 18607–896; and Chaucer's Wife of Bath's Tale, ll. 1109–64.
stok Literally, trunk, stem (of a tree); thus, founder of a family or line of descent. The reference is probably to Christ, the perfection of humanity and the New Adam, i.e. the repairer of the perfect condition of humanity possessed by Adam before the Fall.
Must . . . wittes he must follow in his footsteps and dispose all his wits, i.e. the five senses of sight, hearing, smell, taste, touch
Al . . . diademe even if he should wear miter, crown, or diadem—i.e. should be a prince of the church, a king, or a nobleman
thogh . . . seme though he is outwardly rich
Prees . . . overal the crowd is full of striving, and prosperity blinds one completely
Savour . . . shal taste no more than you ought
And . . . drede And truth shall make you free, there is no fear; see the words of Christ to his disciples, John 8:32: "And ye shall know the truth and the truth shall make you free."
Tempest . . . redresse do not harass yourself to set right all that is not straight
hir . . . bal Fortune, unstable and continually turning. She is sometimes, a little later, shown as sitting on a ball which is balanced on a knife edge.

For grete rest stant˃ in litel bisinesse;˃ — *stands / agitation*
  And elk be ware to sporne ayen an al;°
  Strive not as doth the crokkė with the wal.°
    Dauntė˃ thyself, that dauntest otheres dede;˃ — *govern / deed*
    And Trouthė shal delivere, it is no drede.

That thee is sent, receive in buxumnesse;˃ — *with good grace*
  The wrestling for this worlde asketh˃ a fal: — *asks for*
Here is none home, here nis but wildernesse:
  Forth, pilgrim,° forth! Forth, beest,° out of thy stal!˃ — *stall*
  Know thy countree,˃ look up,° thank God of˃ al. — *(heavenly) homeland / for*
    Hold the high way and let thy gost˃ thee lede; — *spirit*
    And Trouthė shal delivere, it is no drede.

Envoy

Therfore, thou Vache,° leve thyn olde wrecchednesse˃ — *evil condition*
  Unto the world; leve˃ now to be thrall.˃ — *cease / slave*
Crye Him mercy° that of His heigh goodnesse
  Made thee of nought, and in especial
  Draw unto him, and praye in general,
    For thee and eek for othere, hevenlich meede.˃ — *reward*
    And Trouthė shal delivere, it is no drede.
    c. 1390

Roundel° *from* The Parliament of Fowls

Now welcome, somer, with thy sunnė softe,˃ — *warm*
That hast this wintres wedres overshake˃ — *storms shaken off*
And driven away the longė nightės blake!

Saint Valentin,° that art ful hy on-lofte,˃ — *aloft*
Thus singen smalė fowlės˃ for thy sake: — *birds*
  'Now welcome, somer, with thy sunnė softe,
  That hast this wintres wedres overshake!'

Wel han they causė for to gladden ofte,°
Sith˃ ech of hem recovered hath his make;˃ — *since / mate*
Ful blissful mowe˃ they singė when they wake: — *may*
  'Now welcome, somer, with thy sunnė softe,

al awl; i.e. be careful not to kick against the pricks (Acts 9:5)
Strive . . . wal Do not contend, or you will be broken, like an earthenware pot against a wall. See the Aesopic fable of the metal and earthen pots.
pilgrim Life as a pilgrimage was an especially popular image in the Middle Ages.
beest Animals, not having reason, could not be expected to behave reasonably, i.e. virtuously. A man who does not behave reasonably reduces himself to the condition of an animal. Chaucer now begins to play with this notion.
look up A quadruped's head hung down, which was held to be a sign of its lack of rationality. If it were rational, it would look up.
Vache you cow (Fr. *vache*), i.e. beast; probably with a pun on the name of Sir Philip de la Vache
Crye . . . mercy Beg mercy of Him; or: thank Him, who fashioned you from nothing
Roundel a short poem, also called a triolet—developed in France—in which the first lines recur as a refrain; see the Franklin's Tale, l. 240
Saint Valentin The traditional association of St. Valentine with courtship has no foundation except that his day, February 14, was a Roman fertility festival at the beginning of spring.
Wel . . . ofte they have good reason to rejoice often

That hast this wintres wedres overshake
And driven away the longė nightės blake!'
1382–83

From Troilus and Criseyde

Book I

CANTUS TROILI°

'If no love is,> O God, what fele I so? *there is*
And if love is, what thing and whiche is he?
If love be good, from whennes> comth my wo? *whence*
If it be wikke,> a wonder thinketh me,° *bad*
When every torment and adversitee
That cometh of him, may to me savory> thinke; *pleasant*
For ay> thurst I, the more that I it drinke. *ever*

And if that at myn owene lust> I brenne,> *pleasure / burn*
Fro whennes cometh my wailing and my pleynte?> *complaint*
If harme agree me,° wher-to pleyne I thenne?
I noot,> ne why unwery that I faynte. *do not know*
O quikė> deeth, o swetė harm° so queynte, *living / curious*
How may of thee in me swich quantitee,°
But if that I consentė that it be?

And if that I consentė, I wrongfully
Compleyne, y-wis;> thus possėd° to and fro, *certainly*
Al sterėlees° withinne a boot am I
Amid the see,> bytwixen> windės two, *sea / between*
That in contrarie stonden> evermo. *opposition stand*
Allas! what is this wonder> maladye? *strange*
For hete> of cold, for cold of hete, I dye.' *heat*
c. 1385

Cantus Troili the song of Troilus, now fallen in love with Criseyde, a translation from the Italian of Petrarch's Sonnet LXXXVIII to Laura, "S'amor non è," "amplified" to three *Troilus*-stanzas. It is the first English work based on any of Petrarch's Italian poetry, complete with mistranslations.
a wonder . . . me it seems to me very strange (a marvel)
If . . . me if hurt gives me pleasure
quike . . . harm rhetorical use of contradictory terms (oxymoron), especially common in Petrarch and in ancient, medieval, and Renaissance love poetry
How may . . . quantitee How can there be such a quantity of you [the contrasts of love] in me, unless I consent to it?
possed pushed; thus, tossed
sterelees i.e., completely rudderless in a boat. The image of the sea-tossed lover is a favorite one in classical and Petrarchan poetry.

From Book 5: The Finale°

Go, litel book, go litel myn tragedie,
Ther˃ God thy maker yet er that he° dye, *where*
So sendė might to make° in som comedie!
But litel book, ne making thou n'envye,°
But subgit˃ be to allė poesye; *subject*
And kis the steppes, wheras thou seëst pace˃ *pass*
Virgile, Ovyde, Omer, Lucan, and Stace.

And for˃ ther is so greet diversitee *since*
In English and in wryting of our tonge,
So preye˃ I God that noon miswrytė thee, *pray*
Ne thee mismetre for defaute of tonge.°
And red˃ wherso thou be, or ellės songe, *read*
That thou be understonde˃ I God beseche! *understood*
But yet to purpos of my rather speche.°

The wrathe, as I began yow for to seye,
Of Troïlus, the Grekes boughten dere;˃ *paid for dearly*
For thousandės his hondės˃ maden deye,˃ *hands / die*
As he that was withouten any pere,˃ *equal*
Save Ector,° in his tyme, as I can here.°
But weylaway, save only Goddės wille!°
Dispitously him slough the fiers Achille.°

And whan that he was slayn in this manere,
His lightė goost ful blisfully is went
Up to the holownesse˃ of the eighth spere.° *concavity*
In convers letinge˃ every element; *leaving behind*
And ther he saugh,˃ with ful avysėment,˃ *saw / in full view*
The erratik sterrės, herkeninge armonye˃ *hearing harmony*
With sownės˃ fulle of hevenish˃ melodye. *sounds / heavenly*

And down from thenės˃ faste he gan avyse˃ *thence / did consider*
This litel spot of erthe, that with the see˃ *sea*

Finale Chaucer slips in and out of this *envoi* or conclusion, in which he gathers up and seals his story, claims kinship with the poetic masters of past and present, and sums up the "morality" to which his whole poem has been leading. Like Troilus, he surveys his doings in the world below the spheres: imperfect as they are, his tenderness cannot quite condemn them.

he i.e. Chaucer, the "maker" of this book

make match with, not turn into; the pun is intended

n'envye Do not be envious, take your place below the Roman and Greek poets Virgil, Ovid, Homer, Lucan (author of the *Pharsalia*, 39–65 A.D.) and Statius (author of the *Thebaid*, *Achilleid*, and *Silvae*, 61–96 A.D.). The reputation of the last two was higher in the Middle Ages than it is today.

defaute of tonge Chaucer recognizes the effect of dialect and linguistic change.

But . . . speche Back to the purport of my earlier words—i.e. back to my story of Troilus.

Ector Hector, the Trojan champion

as I can here as I understand

But . . . wille alas for everything, unless God wills it

Achille Achilles, the Greek hero: without mercy, the fierce Achilles slew him.

spere Troilus' insubstantial soul travels joyfully from the earth up through the concentric spheres of the planets (erratic, i.e. moving, stars), until he can hear the perfect music they make as they pass on their courses. Sitting in heaven, leaving behind all the elements of which matter is composed (air, fire, earth, and water), he can see the true nature of things.

Enbracėd° is, and fully gan despyse
This wrecched world, and held al> vanitee *everything*
To> rèspect of the pleyn> felicitee *in / absolute*
That is in hevene above; and at the laste,
Ther> he was slayn, his loking doun he caste; *to where*

And in himself he lough> right at the wo *laughed*
Of hem that wepten for his deeth so faste;
And dampnėd> al our werk> that folweth so *damned / doings*
The blindė lust,> the which that may not> laste, *pleasure / cannot*
And sholden al our herte on hevene caste.°
And forth he wentė, shortly for to telle,
Ther> as Mercùrie° sorted> him to dwelle. *where / allotted*

Swich fyn> hath, lo, this Troïlus for love, *ending*
Swich fyn hath al his gretė worthinesse;> *valiance*
Swich fyn hath his estat reäl above,°
Swich fyn his lust,> swich fyn hath his noblesse;> *pleasure / nobility*
Swich fyn hath falsė worldės brotelnesse.> *brittleness*
And thus bigan his lovinge of Criseyde,
As I have told, and in this wyse> he deyde.> *manner / died*

O yongė fresshė folkės, he or she,
In which that love up groweth with your age,
Repeyreth> hoom from worldly vanitee,° *return*
And of your herte up casteth the visage
To thilkė> God that after his image *that same*
Yow made, and thinketh al nis> but a fayre> *is nothing / show*
This world, that passeth sone as flourės fayre.

And loveth him, the which that right for love
Upon a cros, our soules for to beye,> *redeem*
First starf,> and roos,> and sit in hevene above; *died / ascended*
For he nil falsen no wight,> dar I seye, *will deceive no-one*
That wol his herte al hoolly> on him leye.> *wholly / set*
And sin> he best to love is, and most meke, *since*
What nedeth feynėd> lovės for to seke? *false*

Lo here, of payens corsėd> oldė rytes, *pagans cursed*
Lo here, what alle hir> goddės may availle; *their*
Lo here, these wrecched worldės appetytes;
Lo here, the fyn> and guerdon> for travaille> *end / reward / toil*
Of Jove, Appollo, of Mars,° of swich rascaille!> *riff-raff*
Lo here, the forme of oldė clerkės> speche *learned men*
In poetrye, if ye hir bokės seche.

Enbraced i.e. encircled; see Fig. 55
And . . . caste i.e. when we ought to set our whole heart on heaven
Mercurie Mercury, messenger of the gods, who led souls where they were to live henceforth
estat . . . above i.e. exalted, royal condition
Repeyreth . . . vanitee The repudiation of earthly love for heavenly was a literary convention, but one that was also deeply felt.
Jove . . . Mars Jupiter, ruler of the gods; Apollo, god of the sun, of music and poetry; Mars, god of war

O moral Gower,° this book I directe
To thee, and to thee, philosophical Strode,°
To vouchensauf, ther nede is, to corecte,
Of your benignitees and zelės gode.
And to that sothfast> Crist, that starf on rode,> *true / cross*
With al myn herte of mercy ever I preye;
And to the Lord right thus I speke and seye:

Thou oon, and two, and three,° eterne on lyve,> *eternally living*
That regnest ay in three and two and oon,
Uncircumscript, and al mayst circumscryve,> *embrace*
Us from visìble and invisìble foon> *foes*
Defende: and to thy mercy, everychoon,> *everyone*
So make us, Jesus, for thy gracė, digne,> *worthy*
For love of mayde and moder> thyn benigne! Amen. *mother*

Explicit Liber Troili et Criseydis.°

1380–86

Balade *from* The Legend of Good Women°

Hide, Absolon,° thy giltė> tresses clere;> *golden / shining*
Ester, lay thou thy meekness al adoun;°
Hide, Jonathas,° al thy frendly manère;
  Penalopee° and Marcia Catoùn,°
  Make of your wifhood no comparisoùn;
    Hide ye your beautés, Isoude° and Eleyne:°
    My lady comth, that al this may disteine.> *outshine*

Thy fairė body let it not appere,
  Lavine;° and thou, Lucresse° of Romė toun,
And Polixene,° that boughten> love so dere,> *bought / dearly*
  And Cleopatre,° with al thy passioùn,
  Hide ye your trouthe> of love and your renoùn; *fidelity*
    And thou, Tisbé,° that hast> for love swich> peine: *had / such*
    My lady comth, that al this may disteine.

Gower John Gower (1325?–1408), Chaucer's senior and—in a sense—poetic master, author of the *Confessio Amantis* (Lover's Confession)

Strode probably the Oxford philosopher Ralph Strode

three an adaptation of Dante, *Paradiso* XIV. 28–30

Explicit . . . Criseydis Here ends the book of Troilus and Criseyde.

The Legend . . . Women For a discussion of this poem, see the Headnote to Chaucer. Though *The Legend* is the first English poem in heroic couplets, this lyric in *balade* form occurs in it.

Absolon Absalom, famed for the beauty of his hair; see the Miller's Tale, l. 128

Ester . . . adoun Esther, resign your title to graciousness. Esther was the beautiful Jewish maiden whom King Ahasuerus chose as his queen instead of Queen Vashti.

Jonathas Jonathan, David's friend, the pattern of "friendliness"

Penalopee Penelope, the patient and loyal wife of Ulysses

Marcia Catoun daughter of Cato of Utica, who refused to remarry

Isoude Isolde, who gave up husband and life for love of Tristram

Eleyne Helen, wife of Menelaus, who ran off with Paris and provoked the Trojan War

Lavine Lavinia, wife of Aeneas

Lucresse Lucretia, who killed herself after her rape by Tarquin

Polixene Polyxena, who stayed with her father Priam and was killed with him

Cleopatra, Cleopatra, mistress of Julius Caesar and Mark Antony, who killed herself at Antony's death

Tisbé Thisbe, who killed herself because she thought her lover Pyramus dead

Hero,° Dido,° Laodamia,° alle y-fere,˃ *together*
And Phillis,° hanging for thy Demophoun,
And Canacee,° espiėd˃ by thy chere,˃ *found out / appearance*
Ysiphilee,° betraisėd with˃ Jasoùn, *betrayed by*
Make of your trouthė˃ neither bost˃ ne soun;˃ *fidelity / boast / vaunt*
Nor Ypermestre° or Adriane,° ye tweine:˃ *two*
My lady comth, that al this may disteine.
c. 1385

To Rosemounde°

Madame, ye ben of al beautė shryne
As fer as cercled is the mappėmounde,°
For as the cristal° glorious ye shyne,
And likė ruby ben your chekės rounde.
Therwith ye ben so mery and so jocoùnde°
That at a revel whan that I see you daunce,
It is an oynėment˃ unto my wounde, *ointment*
Thogh ye to me ne do no daliaùnce.°

For thogh I wepe of terės˃ ful a tyne,˃ *tears / vat*
Yet may that wo myn hertė nat confounde;
Your semy voys, that ye so smal out-twyne,°
Maketh my thoght in joy and blis habounde.°
So curteisly° I go, with lovė bounde,
That to myself I sey, in my penaùnce,°
'Suffyseth me to love you, Rosemounde,
Thogh ye to me ne do no daliaùnce.'

Hero Hero of Sestos, loved by Leander
Dido Dido of Carthage, lover of Aeneas
Laodamia Laodameia, wife of Protesilaus, who accompanied him to the shades
Phillis Phyllis, who hanged herself when her lover Demophon abandoned her
Canacee committed suicide when her incest with her brother Macaraeus was discovered
Ysiphilee Hypsipyle, pregnant and abandoned by Jason, leader of the Argonauts
Ypermestre Hypermnestra, who refused to murder her husband
Adriane Ariadne, abandoned wife of Theseus. Both she and Hypermnestra had abandoned their fathers for love.
To Rosemounde This *balade* is a virtuoso parody of the love lyric in which the lady is the subject of extravagant comparisons. The movement of the verse is perfectly under control, and rhyme and rhetoric are also handled masterfully, so that absurdity is allowed to creep in only at intervals: the vat of tears and the fish swimming in sauce.
mappemounde map of the world, see Fig. 55; you are the shrine of all the beauty that is within the circle of the whole world
cristal Jewel imagery is usual in such contexts and is much used by Chaucer's imitators.
jocounde gay and elegant
ye . . . daliaunce you do not give me any kindness; *daliaunce:* consenting, encouraging behavior from the lady to the lover
Your . . . out-twyne your little voice, which you so delicately spin out
habounde to be abundant; the word was thought to be connected with Latin *habere,* to have
curteisly courteously, like a true lover
penaunce sad state, because my love is not returned

Nas never pyk walwed in galauntyne°
As I in love am walwed and ywounde,> *wound about*
For which ful ofte I of myself divyne> *discover*
That I am trewė Tristam° the secoùnde.
My love may not refreydė nor affounde;°
I brenne> ay in an amorous plesaùnce.> *burn / pleasure*
Do what you lyst,> I wil your thral> be founde, *(it) pleases you / slave*
Thogh ye to me ne do no daliaùnce.
c. 1385?

The Complaint° of Chaucer to His Purse

To you, my purse, and to non other wight> *creature*
Compleyne I, for ye be my lady dere!
I am so sory,> now that ye be light, *sad*
That certės,> but> ye make me hevy chere, *certainly / unless*
Me were as leef be leyd upon my bere;°
For which unto your mercy thus I crye:
Beth hevy again, or ellės mot> I dye! *must*

Now voucheth> sauf this day, or> it be night, *grant / before*
That I of yow the blisful soun> may here, *blessed sound*
Or see your colour, lik the sonnė bright,
That of yelownesse hadde never pere.> *equal*
Ye be my lif, ye be myn hertės stere,> *steersman*
Quene of comfòrt and of good companye:
Beeth hevy ageyne, or ellės mot I dye!

Now purse, that been to me my livės lyght
And saviour, as doun in this world here,
Out of this tounė helpe me thurgh your might,
Syn> that ye wol nat ben my tresorere;> *since / treasurer*
For I am shave> as nye> as any frere.° *shaven / close*
But yet I pray unto your curtesie:
Beth hevy agen,> or ellės mot I dye! *again*

pyk . . . galauntyne pike, smothered in galantine. It was usual to serve pike covered with this pickle sauce made of bread, vinegar, and cinnamon.

Tristam Tristram, the lover of Isolde, type of the true and constant in love

refreyde . . . affounde be cooled again and chilled

Complaint In conventional three-stanza *balade* form, with an envoi addressing it to a royal or noble patron, in the hope of reward; see the Franklin's Tale, l. 240. Chaucer's witty request is imitated from the French. It was successful, since a few days after his accession in 1399 Henry IV renewed and augmented the pension granted to the poet by Richard II in 1394.

Me . . . bere I'd just as soon be dead

For . . . frere A friar's head was tonsured, i.e. shaven.

Envoy [to Henry IV]

O conquerour of Brutės Albyon,°
Which that by line˃ and free eleccioùn˃ *lineage / choice*
Been verray˃ king, this song to you I sende; *true*
And ye, that mowėn˃ alle oure harmes amende, *may*
Have minde˃ upon my supplicacioùn! *remember*
1399

To Adam, His Scribe

Adam scrivein,˃ if ever it thee bifalle *scribe*
Boèce° or *Troilus*° for to writen newe,
Under thy long lokkes thou most˃ have the scalle˃ *may you / scab*
But after my making thou write more trewe!°
So ofte a-daye˃ I mot˃ thy werk renewe, *each day / must*
It to correcte and eek˃ to rubbe and scrape; *also*
And al is through thy negligence and rape.˃ *haste*
c. 1390

O . . . Albyon The legend was that Brutus, great-grandson of Aeneas, founder of Rome, brought Trojans to Britain (Albion) and founded New Troy (London) as his capital.

Boèce Chaucer's translation of Boethius, *De Consolatione Philosophiae*
Troilus *Troilus and Criseyde*
But . . . trewe unless you copy accurately [according to] what I have composed

The Renaissance

The Renaissance

RENAISSANCE AND RENASCENCES

As a historical term, the "Renaissance" can mean a good many things, most of them having to do with what was happening to Europe half a millennium ago. Used purely to refer to a rebirth of interest in, and knowledge of, some of the ideas and discursive forms of classical antiquity which had been lost for a thousand years, it could, of course, be pushed back even farther. Some scholars have found in the design of some of the great Gothic architecture of the twelfth century the operation of principles of proportion and numerical order which we usually associate with the kind of neo-classical architecture called "humanist." An economic historian might be far more excited about what was happening to the production of woolen cloth in the fourteenth century than about some of the changes two centuries later in the ritualized behavior —religious, political, and linguistic—of the people who used and were enriched by that cloth.

The invention (1454) of movable-block printing (for texts, as distinguished from carved woodcuts for pictures, which had come earlier) and the discovery (1492) of the New World across the western oceans were both crucial events in the history of the shaking-loose of European culture from the political and conceptual structures in which it had lived for so long. And yet, artists and thinkers in fourteenth- and early fifteenth-century Italy were taking leaps of the eye, hand, and mind which would remain unexcelled in other realms of human activity for nearly a hundred years. The relation between discovery and invention is always a complex one, rather like a matter of deciding on the precedence of chicken over egg: the discovery of certain properties of the ground lens leads to the invention of a telescope which leads to the discovery of Jupiter's moons, but the chain has no beginning and never ends. It is even harder to trace the links between the social and technological events during the period from 1450 to 1650, say, and the aspects of the human imagination which, if they are being born again, are appearing in a new form. Wherever one tries to pin down the life-span of the period—in Italy, earlier; in Northern Europe, later—whether in painting, sculpture, and architecture, or in music, or in the technologies of exploration and economic expansion, it will begin and end differently. But there is a trace of common self-awareness in the name itself, for the general rebirth which, by consensus, all historians of all fields continue, when talking generally, to use.

The word "Renaissance" was probably employed in this context for the first time by Giorgio Vasari (1511–74), the Italian painter and architect who is today best known for his *Lives of the Most Excellent Painters, Sculptors and Architects* (1568), in a passage in which he was arguing for the modern view, which was not necessarily that of the early Renaissance, that an artist is not a mere handicraftsman, but a learned and imaginative figure—a "creator" in our sense, rather than a "maker." The community of artists could feel this sense of itself, and its recent history (Vasari saw the predecessor of the painting of his age in Giotto, as the Elizabethan writers in England would, as we shall see, look back to Chaucer). A general sense, of newness and freshness, all over Europe and in every sphere of activity, however, is the literary dream of the nineteenth century. The unique problem of England's Renaissance with respect to the Continent is a result of her twofold alienation from sources of influence during the fifteenth century: she was Northern and she was insular. England had no "quattrocento" like Italy's, and no local traditions in the arts like those of the very great painters of Flanders in the fifteenth century, or like the Flemish musicians who were so to influence the Italian Renaissance composers. John Dunstable, who died in 1453, was the last English practitioner of the arts to have much of an impact on the Continent for more than a century and a half. Scotland, which in the fifteenth century had a much more exciting literary culture than England, maintained very close ties with France—Mary, Queen of Scots (1542–87) was half-French, and married to the Dauphin of France—and in a particular way was thereby less insular. Scotland's intellectual traditions, as manifested, for example, in its approach to the Reformation, and in its subsequent educational system, were quite different from England's.

The literary and intellectual culture of England, during a period which overlapped only at the beginning what is called the Renaissance in Italy, was a complex product of the energies and talents of individual men and of the institutions, conventions, and styles which were open to them as instruments for those energies. To try to understand Shakespeare's genius as a function of a historical moment seems hopeless; to try to understand why, from 1590 to around 1610, the genius of a middle-class, self-educated man from Warwickshire might have flowered in the theater, to such a degree that some of the greatest wisdom of his age might be embodied in popular plays, is not. More than in any other period in recent history, the sixteenth and seventeenth centuries represent the use of what would look to us like imprisoning conventions—linguistic and intellectual patterns—in order to escape from other conventions which had preceded their use, and for so long a time that they resembled Nature, that they were all there was. The radical, humanistic notion of *originality* involved going back to true sources, to origins (today we would call this being "derivative," but our view reflects an intervening cultural phase of Romantic elevation of the notion of the self). In contemplating this long historical moment, then, we must try to understand the ways in which these new conventions—of everything from verse forms and rhyme schemes to ways of making sense out of something shown one—are used and transformed by major talents, and are beautifully exemplified by minor ones. (It is always instructive to learn how something which one truly admires in a great writer is merely a phrase, a turn, a strategy, an element of style, which he shares with even his tedious contemporaries, and that what we have admired is simply what defines our distance from his historical period.) All these conventions would themselves have arisen by adaptation or outright borrowing of ancient, or contemporary European, ones. It may seem strange that in the evolution of a great literary culture an important part might be played by the struggle, not totally successful, of a courtier and diplomat to translate and paraphrase some Italian love poems written two hundred years before. But Sir Thomas Wyatt's getting Petrarch's *Rime* (or sonnets) into English was just the kind of act which, unlike the action of vast, impersonal forces massively taking place over decades, has observable, and traceable, consequences for the individual human imagination.

By the English Renaissance, historians of literature and culture mean the period from about 1509 to 1660, the reign of the Tudor Henry VIII and his children and the first two Stuarts, and the revolutionary government of the Commonwealth which was brought about by troubles boiling up in the reigns of the Stuarts. Culturally speaking, there is a great deal of continuity in English life after the restoration of Charles II to the throne until the end of the century, though the lives and careers of individual writers and thinkers stretch across its chronological boundaries. Literary history is always concerned with self-consciousness, or at least with self-awareness; what an age thinks of itself defines it as an age, and the Restoration, with its Frenchified court fashions, its irreversibly altered Parliament, its Royal Society, and its integration of the lives of Court and Town (London) is really a part of the Europe of the Enlightenment. But there are other continuities, like the one between the convictions of the earliest Tudor humanists, Bacon's visions of the Institution of Reason in the middle of that period, and Milton's final and total presentation of the humanist program in the broadest sense. (This might be called attempting to transform the future of man by refocusing the light of his past.) It is such traditions, too, which help to shape this century and a half of both evolution and violent change.

HUMANISM

One of the important things to remember about the sixteenth century in England is that the New Learning, the interest in and access to classical culture, did not become fully associated with courtly life and patronage until late in the period of Elizabeth's reign. In Italy there were not only many local princes and wealthy families, as in Florence, or corporate municipalities, like Venice, but also the princes of the church in Rome to encourage the arts of splendor and, for a long while, of enlightenment. In England there was a court intent on its international and religious politics, for some time involved in a kind of cold war with Spain; and although it did support some humanistic scholarship, it was unable to bring together the arts and learning in anything like European fashion until the last years of Elizabeth's reign. The great Italian families had subsidized scholarship as well as pageantry; in England the early classical learning was the work and dream of the universities and of schoolmasters.

The rise of humanism can itself certainly be pushed back farther into history. Petrarch's Laureate Oration in 1341 was a dramatic instance in the career of that great precursor not only of Renaissance lyric poetry and its personal muses but also of classical scholarship. (Petrarch himself discovered texts of Cicero and Quintilian, the Roman rhetorician who became so important for the shape of written style later on.) But when the Dutch scholar Desiderius Erasmus (1466–1536), as he called himself—in a made-up Greek-Latin name both halves of which meant "lovable"—came to England, first to Oxford and then, later, to Cambridge in 1509, the new approach to classical learning that had emerged in Europe was only beginning to take hold. The use of Cicero's Latin rather than that of the medieval church, the study of Greek and even of Hebrew, the publication, editing, commentary upon, and appreciation of texts by classical authors became part of a vast institution for shifting the grounds of authority in human affairs. In the intellectual sphere this consisted of a turning from the rigid logical and rhetorical systems of scholasticism (see Glossary), in their day instruments of light, but by the fifteenth century more like walls. The use of classical models for prose style and for kinds of verse was far more than merely a stylistic change. They were assertions of the learned mind's unchallengeable right to make its own contract with classical learning, unmediated by the systems of medieval scholasticism.

THE REFORMATION

If some humanist scholars like Erasmus and, in England, Sir Thomas More, could remain in the church, there were others who could not. All across sixteenth-century Europe, we can observe a parallel to the humanist program in the various movements to substitute for the authority of the Roman Catholic Church a previously unthinkable notion of Christianity, of civilization, as something not necessarily embodied therein. In 1517, Martin Luther tacked his ninety-five theses to the door of his church in Wittenberg. In 1532, John Calvin's *Institutes of the Christian Religion* was published in Switzerland. In 1535, Henry VIII was able to designate himself the Supreme Head of the Church of England. In 1558, the Scottish reformer John Knox returned to his native country from Geneva, and the Calvinist character of the church in Scotland was firmly established; in the North, the Highlanders remained Roman Catholic, but elsewhere the "kirk" (as it is called in Scots) was Presbyterian. The Church of England itself, it must be remembered, was still by no means truly reformed. By confiscating the wealth of the monasteries Henry VIII dotted the English countryside with ruins, but it was only at the end of his reign that he began to build upon them, and over the bones of men like Sir Thomas More, who, as Lord Chancellor, refused to acknowledge, in place of the papal authority, a king who had broken with it over a divorce refused. In 1539 the Great Bible was in use in churches, but it was not until the brief reign of his son Edward VI (from 1547 to 1553) that the famous English Prayer Book, over which so much fighting would be done in less than a hundred years, was made available for a purely English liturgy. The Book of Common Prayer was published in 1549; four years later the Articles of Faith made the English church a Protestant one beyond doubt. Mass had become a communion service, and worship and Scripture had been brought over into the vernacular.

Thomas Cranmer, the Archbishop of Canterbury under whom all this was happening, and who had allowed the burning of various sorts of deviationists—too papal in outlook, or too Protestant—was himself one of the victims of the next monarch's reign. Mary Tudor, Henry's daughter by Catharine of Aragon and wife of Philip II, was Roman Catholic, and until her sister Elizabeth's accession in 1558, a compensatory reaction raged. Catholicism and the influence of Spanish power were two fears that plagued England until the succeeding reign of James. Despite its own mode of reformation, the English church still thought of itself as Catholic, and it was groups of reformers within it, whom we loosely designate as Puritan, who sought continuously to make it less so. They ranged from those who wanted to do away with bishops altogether, to those who merely wanted to stem the drift toward re-alliance with Rome which seemed to them to be a natural movement toward decay. Some of the more extreme of them fled en masse to Holland, which, since it had became independent of Spain, was a haven for religious refugees of all sorts. Others stayed behind, suffering various changes of fortune in the early decades of the seventeenth century. In general, it should be remembered that the English church was seeking throughout this period to maintain a kind of balance between two strong forces, Rome and the more thoroughgoing consequences of Geneva, home of Calvinism.

In 1603, James VI of Scotland became king of England (he was the great-grandson of Henry VII's daughter, Margaret). He had already planted some of the seeds of later discontent by introducing (in 1600) bishops into Scotland, much to the hatred of the Presbyterians there. Almost forty years later, his son Charles allowed his Puritan-persecuting Archbishop of Canterbury, William Laud, to try again to Anglicize the Scottish church, and precipitated the fighting known as the "Bishops' War" (1639). Charles's attempts to raise more money for its continuance led to the calling of the Long Parliament, which eventually beheaded both Archbishop Laud (1645) and the King (1649). Throughout the reigns of the first two Stuarts, the dangers of Rome and Spain were not a matter of universal national consciousness as they had been under Elizabeth, but when the Catholicism of Charles I's French wife, Henrietta Maria, helped to jeopardize national trust in him as Defender of the (English) Faith, Puritan factions in Parliament and Presbyterian ones in Scotland and England united for a while in maintaining the course and safety of the Reformation. For an absolutely committed mid-seventeenth-century Protestant like John Milton, the Reformation continued through the course of the Commonweath, and through the eventual conflicts between the powerful, official Presbyterian party (which had become for him the abrogator of freedom) and the more liberal congregationalist faction called the Independents. The Reformation must be seen as an institutional process which, after it had succeeded in establishing Protestant churches, continued, like a kind of permanent revolution, to unfold in the individual positions and visions of particular religious thinkers. Its primary movement, from the time of its beginning in the sixteenth century, was toward the *internalization* of institutions: individual conscience, rather than the structure of a church hierarchy to mediate between God and Man; an identification of Christ as the Light of the World with an inner light within men, and so forth. It was a process which continued later in the seventeenth and eighteenth centuries, in such manifestations as millenarian sects, the Quakers, and, later on, in the religious revival among a rising middle class, which eventually gave rise to Methodism within the Church of England itself.

It should also be briefly observed that the Roman church's own reaction to the rise of Protestantism, the Counter Reformation as it is called, produced a new approach to what Protestantism had isolated from other parts of life as *religion* (rather than the totality of spiritual life in its infusion of the material life, which marked the organic quality of medieval Christianity). The Council of Trent, which met sporadically between 1545 and 1563 to reformulate the doctrine of the Roman church, initiated this trend toward reform of some of the material abuses attacked by the early Protestants, as well as toward new modes of religiousness, including missionary work and more practical popular religious instruction—the Jesuits were instrumental in this. But English hopes that the Council would see the way to some kind of *via media* (or "middle way"), not unlike Richard Hooker's "Anglicanism," were disappointed, and in the end the Council sharpened the differences between the Roman and the Reformed churches. There was an English interest (because a Protestant one) in the Thirty Years' War in Germany (ended 1648), and at times an almost paranoid fear of the Jesuits; aside from these the Counter Reformation remained a curiosity of Continental faith.

A NEW IMAGE OF THE WORLD

Another revision of authority previously vested in an older order occurred in connection with the mixture of invention and discovery mentioned earlier. The explorations of the New World for purposes of economic development and, particularly in England's case, the undermining of Spanish colonial power in the West Indies by naval strength brought with them one kind of opening up. Another was in the exploration of the conceptual new world of the cosmos. The Ptolemaic cosmology which had prevailed since classic times was being gradually undermined, during the sixteenth and seventeenth centuries, by new discoveries which could not be accommodated to it as they previously had been (see Glossary: Astronomy and Astrology). Without cataloguing the scientific developments of the period under discussion, we may observe in one sequence of revisions of the older world picture some of the sorts of change which might affect the life of the mind for all men of thought. The Ptolemaic model of the universe corresponded to observed phenomena by positing transparent spheres of huge magnitude, moving concentrically about the earth, each carrying a heavenly body, or, the last but outside one, all the fixed stars which do not move in relation to each other. Circles and spheres were traditional symbols of perfection, and in order to maintain both the idea of a perfectly constructed universe and the actuality of what happened in the sky night after night, astronomers since classical times had been forced to adapt and change the model slightly; for example, they built so-called "epicycles," or circular reroutings, onto the circular path of the planets. But the basic idea of planned and patterned circularity was there. In the year of his death, the Polish astronomer Nicolaus Copernicus (1473–1543) published his treatise *On the Revolution of the Spheres*, which put the sun, not the earth, at the center of the model, but left the notion of circular paths of motion about it. This meant asserting that what "really" happened in the sky was not what "apparently" happened, but that a picture of reality with concentric circles on it, no matter how disturbing in its decentralization of the earth—and, by implication, of humanity—in the divine scheme, could still look orderly.

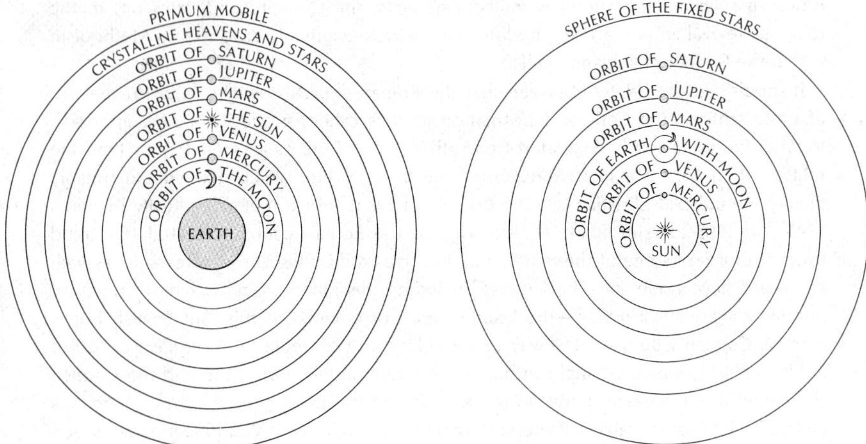

The Ptolemaic World-System

Copernican World System, 1543

Johannes Kepler (1571–1630) wrecked that order when he formulated his laws of planetary motion, published in 1609: the planets, he showed, moved in elliptical orbits, not circular ones, with the sun at one of the foci of the ellipse. But he showed a kind of beautiful regularity in their motion which to us, today, looks as mysteriously contrived as any nest of circles. The planets move more quickly when nearer the sun, more slowly when far away; but these changes in speed are so orderly that the planets, as he put it, sweep out "equal areas in equal times." That means merely this: if we take two points on the elliptical path that are, say, one planetary month apart, and then take two more at the other end of the orbit, at the "fast end" they will be farther apart than at the distant one. Now, if we draw lines from those points toward the sun, at one of the foci of the ellipse, we will get two pie-shaped wedges, one long and thinnish, the other shorter and fatter. But their areas will always be equal. Moreover, Kepler showed, the square of its periodic time at any point around its ellipse will be proportional to the cube of its mean distance from the sun.

Kepler's Second Law

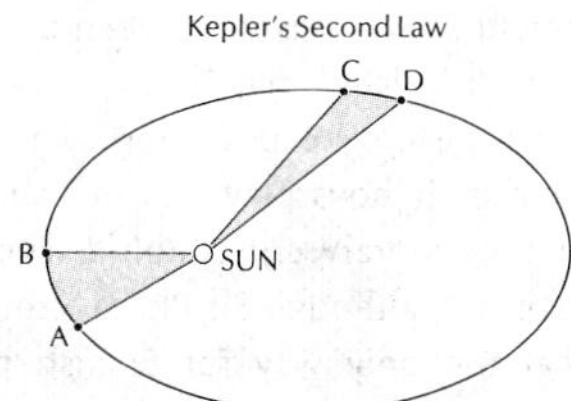

If the time taken to travel A-B and C-D is the same, then the two shaded bits, different in shape, will always be equal in area.

These are elegances of order which it takes a bit more than simple arithmetic to comprehend as orderly at all. But one more shift or dislocation of the idea of orderliness occurs during the seventeenth century which we might glance at. For Kepler, these were "laws," but if one could not show *why* they were true, then, no matter how carefully formulated, they might recede into the status of phenomena again. This is what finally happened. Galileo Galilei (1564–1642) discovered that the earth's gravitational pull on all objects could be mathematically described as an accelerating force (this is aside from the astronomical observations for which he was so famous—his perfecting of the refracting telescope led him to conclude that the moon shone by reflected light, that Jupiter had four satellites, that the Milky Way was the massed effect of countless stars, etc.). Sir Isaac Newton (1642–1727) would finally take a huge conceptual leap, and argue that the gravity which Galileo had described was *not* just a local peculiarity of the surface of the earth, but applied as a force acting between any two or more bodies, anywhere. Kepler's Second Law, then, could be shown to be an effect which would have to be true, given the gravitational situation of the sun and the planet in question. With such a notion, any connection between simple observation of what were called the "appearances," obvious to any reasonable man, and the proper explanation or mathematical model, was gone. By the end of the English Renaissance, science (or "natural philosophy" as it was called) had become a special sort of explanation, given in totally different sorts of language from moral, or metaphysical, or even psychological accounts.

Cosmology, banishing the older astrology, was, of course, not the only kind of revision of the older picture of the world. Alchemy, with its highly symbolic interpretation of the realities behind natural processes, gave way to chemistry, whose concerns had been mostly a by-product of the true, religious alchemical quest. The inner structure of the human totality, with its humors and spirits which reflected in their composition the basic four-part grouping of elements in the universe, gave way to specific biological answers to clearly defined questions. The whole program sketched out in Francis Bacon's dream of methods for reaching truth began to be, with the establishment of the Royal Society in 1660, an actuality.

THE INSTRUMENT OF PROSE

Just as the new science would need mathematical languages in which to express complicated relationships, the far more general problem of human discourse required a new sort of language as well. The humanist program had started with Latin, and the Classics generally; it soon moved to a rebuilding of the vernacular. There are really two phases to this development in the sixteenth century: the first established the authority of antiquity, the second insisted that it could be fulfilled in the vernacular. Schoolmasters like Richard Mulcaster (head of the Merchant Taylors' School and teacher of Spenser) might have their boys play ball in Latin, and by the 1590's there were still debates going on among literary critics about whether English poetry should be written in classical meters or not, although Sir Philip Sidney had argued persuasively in his *Defence of Poesie* that the only way for English poets to be truly like the classical ones they so admired was by being themselves. The modes of eloquence were, of course, prose and verse. It is hard for a twentieth-century reader, with his built-in notion that prose is plain, universal, and ordinary and that verse is special, ornate, and idiosyncratic, to understand how this was not true, really, until the end of the seventeenth century. An ordinarily competent sonnet, for example, written as a dedicatory poem to some friend's book on anything from logic to gardening, would be truly anonymous in character—unless a considerable poet with a marked style were to put it to such a purpose, those verses would constitute the equivalent of a formal, common prose in our day and before. Any literate person might have learned in school to compose verses in Latin and, later on, in Greek. To do so in English was no indication of special poetic gifts.

The prose styles of the sixteenth and seventeenth centuries were in a state of flux just because of the phases of the humanist learning mentioned above. The first style taught for English prose was modeled on Cicero—elaborate, balanced, ornate, with many dependent clauses and rounded periods. In one of its more affected and personal styles, it developed into the so-called Euphuistic prose (see Headnote to John Lyly) of the last decades of the sixteenth century. But in sermons, treatises, tracts, and even translations of foreign authors, the so-called Senecan prose favored by Bacon, a livelier, jumpier style involving short sentences and sudden turns and variations of pace, began to replace it. The spoken language could not enter the written one to shape and extend its resources as easily as one might think. There was no prose fiction in our sense of the word, and even a picaresque romance of great brilliance and linguistic power like Thomas Nashe's *The Unfortunate Traveller* (1594) is written in a prose more highly patterned than most contemporary verse today. It is, indeed, through the verse and occasional prose of the theater on the one hand, and in certain kinds of song texts which contain more of the music of speech than they allow for the addition of melody on the other, that the spoken word begins to inform the written one.

TRANSLATIONS; THE EXAMPLE OF MONTAIGNE

One of the ways in which the resources of the language could be augmented was a natural concomitant of decreasing insularity through translation of the classical and contemporary European authors who both might and might not be read in the original. The English Bible was a matter of necessity to the reform not only of liturgy but of the relation of even the simplest of men to God's word. Translations of secular authors served two purposes: in the case of, say, Sir Thomas North's very important translation of Plutarch's *Parallel Lives* (1579) from the Greek, to which fewer people would have access than to Latin. The fragments of the *Aeneid* done into verse by the Earl of Surrey (1517–47) were more than merely toying with a new verse form (the blank verse which he borrowed from the Italian), but a kind of act of commitment to a literary tradition that he and the other earlier Tudor writers were trying to join. Getting the great works of other languages into English meant also creating a canon, a basic body of almost *scriptural* secular works, which would have the same power and general reference as biblical texts. Arthur Golding's Ovid of 1567 and George Chapman's Homer (*Iliad,* 1611; *Odyssey,* 1616) were verse translations of the first importance. But perhaps the most important piece of Elizabethan translation, as far as the subsequent history of English prose was concerned, was the version by the linguistic scholar John Florio (c. 1553–1625) of the *Essays* of Montaigne.

Michel Eyquem de Montaigne (1533–92) was a scholar, lawyer, and skeptical philosopher who retired to his tower near Bordeaux to meditate and put together those commonplace books or scraps of quotations with an added commentary which eventually outgrew the quotations, and became his meditational trials, or essays into thought. His is the final blow struck against dogmatism, and he is the predecessor, writing from his book-lined study, not only of French philosophers of subsequent centuries but, in Florio's translation, of many English writers as well. Bacon knew him, and so did Burton, Shakespeare, Donne, Ralegh, Ben Jonson, and many others. His vision of the contemplative life, vastly different from that of medieval Christianity, saw a new kind of relation between man's mind and the thoughts of others, and he defined solitude in a new way:

> A man that is able may have wives, children, goods, and chiefly health, but not so tie himself unto them that his felicity depend on them. We should reserve a storehouse for ourselves, what need soever chance, altogether ours and wholly free, wherein we may hoard up and establish true liberty and principal retreat and solitariness, wherein we must go alone to ourselves to take our ordinary entertainment, and so privately that no acquaintance or communication of any strange thing may therein find place; there to discourse, to meditate and laugh, as without wife, without children and goods, without train or servants, that if by any occasion they be lost it seem not strange to us to pass it over. We have a mind moving and turning in itself; it may keep itself company; it hath wherewith to offend and defend, wherewith to receive and wherewith to give. . . . [*Of Solitude*]

This "storehouse" (*arrière-boutique*—"back of the shop," Montaigne calls it) becomes for humanist meditative writers more than merely a locale, a room, a place, but rather a whole region of the mind, a condition of relation to thought and nature. But perhaps one of the most famous and resonant examples of Montaigne's concept of what was in his phrase "the human condition" and its dignity is to be found in his famous essay "Of Cannibals," in which he broods over the meaning of civilization itself. In 1562 at Rouen he had met some natives of the New World, and in his essay of about 1580 he describes the condition of some of these inhabitants of the tropical Americas, and goes on to remark that "there is nothing in that nation that is either barbarous or savage, unless men call that barbarism which is not common to them." The whole following passage is of great interest and merit:

> As indeed we have no other aim of truth and reason than the example and *Idea* of the opinions and customs of the country we live in. There is ever perfect religion, perfect policy,[1] perfect and complete use of all things. They are even savage, as we call those fruits wild which nature of herself and of her ordinary progress hath produced; whereas indeed they are those which ourselves have altered by our artificial devices and diverted from their common order, we should rather term savage. In those are the true and most profitable virtues and natural properties most lively and vigourous, which in these we have bastardised, applying them to the pleasure of our corrupted taste. And if, notwithstanding, in diverse fruits of those countries that were never tilled we shall find that in respect of ours they are most excellent and as delicate unto our taste, there is no reason art should gain the point of honour of our great and puissant[2] mother nature. We have so much by our inventions surcharged the beauties and riches of her works that we have altogether overchoked her. Yet, wherever her purity shineth she makes our vain and frivolous enterprises wonderfully ashamed.
>
> Ivies spring better of their own accord,
> Unhaunted plots much fairer trees afford.
> Birds by no art much sweeter notes record.
> Propertius[3] I *Elegies* ii 10.
>
> All our endeavour or wit cannot so much as reach to represent the nest of the least birdlet, its contexture,[4] beauty, profit and use, no nor the web of a silly[5] spider. *All things,* saith *Plato, are produced either by nature, by fortune. or by art: the greatest and fairest by one or other of the two first, the least and imperfect by the last.* Those nations seem, therefore, so barbarous unto me, because they have received very little fashion from human wit and are yet near their original naturality. The laws of nature do yet command them, which are but little bastardised by ours; and that with such purity as I am sometimes grieved the knowledge of it came no sooner to light, at what time there were men that better than we could have judged of it. I am sorry *Lycurgus*[6] and *Plato* had it not, for meseemeth that what in those nations we see by experience doth not only exceed all the pictures wherewith licentious Poesy had proudly embellished the golden age, and all her quaint inventions to feign a happy condition of man, but also the conception and desire of Philosophy. They could not imagine a genuity[7] so pure and simple as we see it by experience, nor ever believe our society might be maintained with so little art and human combination. It is a nation, would I answer *Plato,* that hath no kind of traffic, no knowledge of Letters, no intelligence of numbers, no name of

1. Government.
2. Capable.
3. Sextus Propertius, Roman elegiac poet (*c.* 54 B.C.–*c.* 2 B.C.).
4. Structure.
5. Simple.
6. As framer of the constitution of Sparta; Plato, as propounder of a Utopian republic (in *Laws* X).
7. Nature.

> magistrate nor of politic superiority; no use of service, of riches or of poverty; no contracts, no successions, no partitions, no occupation but idleness; no respect of kindred but common, no apparel but natural, no manuring[8] of lands, no use of wine, corn, or metal. The very words that import lying, falsehood, treason, dissimulations, covetousness, envy, detraction, and pardon, were never heard of amongst them. How dissonant would he find his imaginary commonwealth from this perfection![9]

COMMONPLACES

Montaigne's meditative prose was a great instrument for both the transmission of knowledge and the discovery of the self. It arose from commentary on texts of other authors, and it should be observed that this process of taking off from a text, obviously basic to scriptural commentaries and those of classical scholars, and the fundamental method of homiletic prose, the sermons of both Anglican and Puritan divines throughout this period, was an intellectual operation of a much more general character. In a way, there remained an unbroken tradition going back to medieval times of beginning all exposition with a text from tradition; if there was not a particular passage from biblical or classical sources, there might be one of a number of received ideas, set themes or topics, the response to which on the part of the writer would generate *copy* (from *copia* or "plenty"). Thus, the notion of the *theatrum mundi,* that "all the world's a stage" was one topic; the concept of the *locus amoenus* or "lovely place," the garden associated with pastoral ideal realms, Eden, and various classical gardens was another. And in a peculiar way the presence of classical mythology, whether embodied in particular formulations or quotations from Ovid or Virgil, or passed through a filter of received tradition and interpretive commentary, was always available. It is only the philosophical tradition of the seventeenth century which begins, as a counterpart to the raising of scientific questions based only on observed phenomena, to produce discourse based only upon the topic questions posed by self-awareness. Montaigne had, while still surrounded by his books, allowed their light to strike a spark of questioning ("Who am I? What do I know? What is what I know good for?") in him. His French follower, René Descartes (1596–1650), would carry this even farther by wondering what, if anything, it was possible to be absolutely certain of. Thomas Hobbes (1588–1679), although his view of the lives of Montaigne's noble savages was vastly different, also stems from him in a different way. (See the Glossary: *Rhetoric.*)

LANGUAGE AND THE THEATER

The theater in the sixteenth century blended a native, vernacular popular tradition with a learned one. Latin plays based on the tragedies of Seneca were written and acted in schools; it was not until an English drama with recognizable links to that classical tradition developed that any truly public theater was able to emerge. In 1561, an English blank-verse tragedy called *Gorboduc,* by Thomas Norton and Thomas Sackville, was played first at the Inner Temple and then before the Queen, as a kind

8. Cultivation.

9. The foregoing passage seems to be imitated in Shakepeare's *The Tempest,* II.i.54 ff. It is interesting that Florio's Protestant reticence leads him not to translate the quotation which follows: "Men sprung from the Gods" (from Seneca's *Epistles* XC).

of warning to her to beget an heir, so that the English throne would be safe from the disasters of division portrayed in the play. The Inns of Court—the Middle Temple, Inner Temple, Gray's Inn, and Lincoln's Inn—were the London law schools whose students and fellows contributed so much to the intellectual and cultural life of the city of London. The two universities were producing students who, after classical studies and training in rhetoric, might often read law before going into government service. Younger sons of noble families and older ones of the merchant classes and yeomanry shared a background in classical learning and a sense of sophistication that made the dining halls of the Inns of Court a breeding ground for the theater that would later come outdoors. An outdoor theater was built in London in 1576, and from then until 1642, in the more generally public theaters built south of the Thames, and in the more private coteries of the Inns of Court, a great theatrical tradition arose and flourished. Traveling companies of actors, writing and producing their own plays, attached to the household of some nobleman for protection against ordinances hostile to strolling players, moved about the country; but the theaters bred their own companies and audiences with their own expectations and, consequently, styles produced to meet them. There were also intimate, learned court plays which, in the early years of James's reign, developed into the court masque, a unique and totally unreconstructable lost theatrical realm. During this period of almost seventy years, the English stage developed a complex literary and political history of its own, and at this point it will only be remarked again how that history was the function of contributions as various as those of song-and-dance clowns on the one hand, and learned poets like Christopher Marlowe, who brought to blank-verse tragedy a kind of poetic style nurtured on non-dramatic (epic and elegiac) classical verse in English, on the other. The stage remained, despite the Puritan attacks upon it, a public institution which attracted the interests and energies of men as diverse as the highly learned, ideologically neoclassical Ben Jonson and the prosaic, popularly entertaining Thomas Dekker (c. 1570–c. 1641), who attacked Jonson (his erstwhile collaborator) in a broad satiric onslaught. It reflected the rest of the literary culture of the nation which surrounded it in all of its phases (the Jacobean tragedies of John Webster and Cyril Tourneur will be recognized even by the beginning student of the period as having more to do with the world of John Donne's later poems and sermons, and with Burton's *Anatomy of Melancholy,* than with the literary conventions of the 1590's). When the theaters finally closed, by order of the Puritan Parliament in 1642, a whole chapter in the development of English imaginative language came to an end.

THE FORMS OF VERSE

In some periods of change, the question of forms of activity can seem to matter more than content. In the practical history of the Reformation in England, the form of a prayer book could be defended with force of arms; in the literary history of the 1580's and 90's, arguments about verse forms could conceal debates about larger issues. One such argument was about how literally classical English verse should be. Upholders of quantitative scansion tried to establish Latin and Greek traditions in the actual structure of English poetry; their opponents maintained that analogues of classical forms were the only appropriate ones. But the two sides agreed that there were ways of working from classical models of form, as well as of reference and allusion. The case of the English heroic couplet is a good instance of this. During the later decades of the sixteenth century, the rhymed pairs of iambic pentameter lines in English served various purposes: closing scenes in blank-verse drama, closing the English form of the sonnet, translating (as with Marlowe's *Hero and Leander)* classical heroic verse, which in Greek or Latin was in unrhymed hexameters. After Wyatt and Surrey the so-called "fourteener,"

A line that rumbles on like this for just a bit too long

when used in couplets, had a classical ring to it, for it was "long" like the hexameter. Golding's Ovid is in this meter. But the pentameter couplet began to eclipse the longer ones, both for translating and, even more important, *standing for,* heroic verse. Then, too, there were the forms of epigram and satire. In classical verse, these are written in unrhymed "elegiac" couplets, a longer hexameter followed by a shorter pentameter. The English heroic couplet served for this as well. By the beginning of the seventeenth century the form was doing both jobs—so much so, that Ben Jonson, careful neoclassicist that he was, indented the second line of his couplets when used in epigrams, to stand for the classical couplets, but had them printed flush left when they stood for heroic hexameters. By the mid-century, the heroic couplet was so entrenched as the verse mode of both heroic and elegiac that Milton had to apologize, in a second printing, for the blank verse which he had used for the epic meter of *Paradise Lost.*

The later sixteenth century and the early seventeenth century saw a proliferation of lyric forms for verse, and with them, an ever varying set of relations between what the forms stood for, or suggested, about the poet's intention, and what the forms did in the way of affecting the language of the poem. Sir Philip Sidney's great experiments in the songs from the *Arcadia* developed in two directions the possibilities of using the formal structures of verse to control tone of voice and the structure of poetic discourse. One of these moved toward a patterning of surface, a decorative draping of grammatical parallelisms and mirrorings over the basic shape of a line. The other involved the opposition between line structure, its fixed number of stressed and unstressed syllables, and the ways in which the sound of a speaking voice would push against those patterns. From one of these directions the Spenserian diction branches off; from the other, the sonnets of Shakespeare and the lyrics of Donne. It should be remembered that there was, up through the turn of the seventeenth century, a strong general sense of formal discovery and invention, and that between the pre-1590's verse of the kind which C. S. Lewis has called "drab" and the carefully controlled and measured "plain style" of some of Ben Jonson's verse and that of his followers, there are not only a few decades of literary development, but changing assumptions about the relation of imagery, density of thought, and allusion to the verse forms in which they were set out.

While the Elizabethan literary debates frequently centered on the ways in which style should mirror intention, Jacobean and Caroline poets moved in one of three directions. Either they helped to make a tradition of the strong lines of John Donne—the so-called Metaphysical school, or they took the course that ran, through what Alexander Pope would call in the next century "Denham's strength and Waller's sweetness"—the contrived elegance in the way in which tone of voice is submerged in the formality of verse, and the tact with which imagery is introduced and led away from in poetry of statement or praise—to the Augustan style of John Dryden. There was also a third tradition (and it must be understood that individual poets often drew upon more than one stream) which had a curious fate—Spenser's followers in the early seventeenth century, Michael Drayton, William Browne, Giles and Phineas Fletcher, all interested in extended mythological poems, found themselves running against a tide. They were more admired in the nineteenth century than in our day, which is still influenced by the reinterpretation of the seventeenth century brought about by the influence of T. S. Eliot in his poetry and criticism. The only poem attributed to John Donne in Palgrave's *Golden Treasury of Songs and Lyrics,* a major Victorian anthology, is not by Donne at all. The minor Spenserians, poets of great skill and more than charm, will one day again be read with interest.

Some of the literary history of the last forty years may lead the beginning student of seventeenth-century poetry to believe that "lines" meant factions. This was not true, although occasionally the rhetoric of criticism might make it seem so. The cavalier poets, for example, while united in their loyalty to the king and the church, differed widely in how much Donne's wit and energy (Thomas Carew, for example, pledges himself to these), and how much Jonson's elegance and firm tactfulness characterized their verse. The Spenserian tradition ends up in Milton, a very great poet of the Puritan faction, and perhaps rightly so, Spenser's vision being radical and Protestant. But Andrew Marvell, a major talent and a devoted political servant of the Commonwealth, extends the styles of cavalier verse in developing his own. Many of the seventeenth-century lyric poets were clergymen, and the student cannot help but notice how many poets in the line of Donne were, like him, in holy orders; when they were, they were Anglican and, when the fighting started, Royalist.

THE CIVIL WAR

The Revolution was the second major center of upheaval in the period we have been calling the English Renaissance, the first being the turbulent fluctuations of Catholic and Anglican power in the mid-sixteenth century and the ensuing uneasiness about Rome and Spain which lasted well into Elizabeth's reign. Even after the defeat of the Armada (1588), the Elizabethan court was marked by uncertainty, rapid changes in the wind of favor, and the lack of norms of approach to preferment and finding appropriate governmental posts; thus a well-connected and useful man like Francis Bacon could get nowhere in the court of Elizabeth, and it was only with the accession of James that, particularly for men of letters, there was more of an official openness.

James's tutor, as a boy, had been the Great Scotch humanist George Buchanan (another of whose pupils, earlier on, had been Montaigne). James, however, did not respond with any sympathy to the teachings of his former tutor's tract *De Jure Regni* (On the Law of the Realm), in which the rule of kings is subjected to popular will and welfare. Instead, he formulated a doctrine of the divine right of kings. Intellectual, learned, and contentious, James was impractically given to the elevation of his favorites; men like Robert Carr (who became involved in a major scandal when he arranged for the murder of Sir Thomas Overbury), and, after him, the Duke of Buckingham, whom James ennobled as he did many others, engendered some mistrust.

The court of his son Charles was marked by a certain royal grandeur without the intellectual cast of his father's: Charles was a great patron of painters (Van Dyck and Rubens) and a collector of pictures—many of which Cromwell subsequently sold; and he preferred the pure spectacle and stage effects of Inigo Jones, the great stage designer, in his masques, or court entertainments, to the allegorical visions of Ben Jonson for which that spectacle had been originally employed. Despite his almost spiritual sense of the condition of kingship, he agreed, three years after ascending the throne in 1628, to Parliament's Petition of Right, in order to secure its vote on funds he needed. The Petition, although aimed at specific grievances such as the king's ability to declare martial law, and certain taxing privileges, in fact established the supremacy of parliamentary law over regal power. Charles largely ignored its provisions, and from 1629 until 1640 he ruled without calling any Parliament at all. A war with France made him unpopular, as did an attempt to extend to inland counties with no use for ships a tax known as *ship-money* (traditionally a levy only on certain port cities to help finance the royal support of shipping). But Charles needed money, and called what turned out to be a short, querulous session of Parliament lasting for three weeks in 1640. Several months later the so-called Long Parliament, under whom Charles was eventually beheaded, was called into session.

The Long Parliament drafted a Grand Remonstance against Charles, in his absence, in 1641; his attempt, early in 1642, to arrest five members of Parliament brought on war that year. After four years of fighting, Charles surrendered, was imprisoned, escaped and was recaptured, and finally, after trial at Westminster as "the tyrant, traitor and murderer, Charles Stuart," was executed in 1649. The parliamentary government which succeeded him had split into two factions, a Presbyterian one and an Independent one, under Oliver Cromwell (1599–1658). For a while Parliament had been dominated by the first, while Cromwell had control of the army; but fearful that the Presbyterian faction might finally return power to the crown, Cromwell took virtual control of the nation. An Instrument of Government in 1653 named him Lord Protector and formally established a Commonwealth.

During all this, Royalist refugees, aristocratic and clerical, and those who were neither but were ideologically committed to established power, like Thomas Hobbes, had fled to France, and a circle of English émigrés remained there for various lengths of time. Charles II, who had himself crowned in 1651 in Scotland, attempted to lead an attacking force into England that year, was defeated, and joined the rest of the exiles in France after a dramatic forty days of escape through England. Following nine years of exile, the wave of political confusion after Cromwell's death and during the tenure of Richard Cromwell, his son, allowed Charles to return to England. He landed at Dover on May 29, 1660, his thirtieth birthday.

The continuities of English town and country life had been far less disturbed by the events of the past two decades—the closing of the theaters being a notable exception—than had institutions of power and patronage. Strongly Anglican clergyman and fellows of Oxford and Cambridge colleges had lost their posts. But largely, the Restoration signaled the donning of new styles, new fashions or, as the fashionably French word went, "modes." The tight lacing of Elizabethan corsets had given way, after lasting through the Jacobean reign, to a loosening of line of dress and of hair; this had been associated with Cavalier rather than with "Roundhead" or Puritan factions in the time of the Civil War, and came back to Restoration fashion with a vengeance. But traces of the world view which such styles of costume reflect are evident in the literature, primarily in the poetry, of the 1630's and after; for the imagination, outward styles can be seen as the objectification of states of mind. The peculiar paradoxes of English cultural styles during this whole period—particularly with respect to Continental ones—remain fascinating. King's College Chapel, in Cambridge, finished in 1539, remains a triumph of late English gothic architecture; when it was dedicated, the high-

Renaissance triumph of St. Peter's in Rome was already under construction. The peculiar blending of the gothic and the baroque temperaments which we find in John Donne, those strange remnants of medievalism in Shakespeare, are reflected in the seventeenth-century façade of the chapel of Peterhouse, Cambridge, whose gothic arched long window is surmounted, on the outside, by a typically seventeenth-century baroque broken pediment. These co-existing and contrasting strands of tradition, the pulls and tensions of orthodoxy and Protestantism, royalism and republicanism, insularlity and cosmopolitanism, make for a complex and often slightly awkward picture. But perhaps by virtue of this very awkwardness, this being out of phase with so many normative developments of European cultural history, the magnificent aspects of the earliest humanist programs continued to flower and bear fruit in a visionary mid-century literature well after it should have. The massive geniuses of Shakespeare, Spenser, and Milton, concentrated in this brief time, are enough for any culture's life history.

EDMUND SPENSER

1552–1599

Spenser was born in London in 1552, or soon after that date. Though connected with a noble family of Spencers, he was not himself richly born, and went to school as a "poore scholler." His school was the Merchant Taylors', then a new humanist foundation, and his headmaster was Richard Mulcaster, famous for his learning and his insistence that the boys study not only Latin, Greek, and Hebrew, but also English.

In 1569, assisted by a charitable grant, Spenser went to Pembroke Hall, Cambridge, a strongly Puritan college. He was a sizar, which meant that he had free meals in return for doing jobs about the college. His studies were in rhetoric, logic, and philosophy, and he would have had to take part in formal disputations. In the usual way he was graduated B.A. after four years and took the three-year M.A. course, including philosophy, astronomy, Greek, and mathematics. These studies were based on ancient authors—there was no formal study of modern languages.

Spenser had published poetry even before going to university—his translations of Petrarch and Du Bellay appeared in John Vandernoodt's *Theatre of Voluptuous Worldlings* in 1569. But the learning that was considered essential to poetry—Harvey was to insist that the heroic poet needed to be "a curious and universal scholar"—Cambridge provided, together with the warm ecclesiastical controversy that left its mark on his poetry, especially *The Shepheardes Calender.* His poetic interests were also developed by his friendship with Gabriel Harvey, a Fellow of the College. Harvey was a farmer's son, and at once learned and likable, pedantic and amusing. Later he became famous for his acrimonious pamphleteering exchanges with Thomas Nashe. At this time he shared with Spenser an interest in English versification, and wanted to introduce into English the quantitative prosody of Latin. His exchange of letters with Spenser on this point was published in 1580. Spenser experimented with quantitative meters, and sent them to Harvey with a request for fuller instruction, adding that Sidney and others were also trying them out. Little came of this, but Harvey happened in replying to mention some works by Spenser, whether complete, in progress, or projected; there seems to have been a large body of work, virtually all of which has perished. Harvey remarked that he preferred Spenser's Nine Comedies to a part of *The Faerie Queene* then in existence. He hoped Spenser would give up the attempt to write like Ariosto, regretting that he would not write prophetic and visionary poetry on the lines of St. John's Revelation. This indicates that what Harvey saw was not a part of Book I, which is largely based on Revelation, but something now embedded in Books III or IV. Replying, Spenser speaks of the "Areopagus." This group consisted of himself, Sidney, and Dyer, and was dedicated to the reform of English poetry; but he soon abandoned the attempt to introduce classical meter. Indeed he had already written the *Calender,* which, however experimental in language and techniques, is in the native tradition.

After being graduated M.A. in 1576, Spenser visited his noble kinsmen in Lancashire, and seems to have met Rosalind, a girl whom Harvey teases him about, and who figures in the *Calender* and even, many years later, in *Colin Clouts Come Home Againe.* In 1577 he probably made his first trip to Ireland, and returned to enter the service of the powerful Earl of Leicester—hence his acquaintance with Leicester's nephew Philip Sidney. He married Machabyas Childe in 1579, the year of the *Calender,* which he dedicated to Sidney. Sidney admired it, with reservations concerning the "old rustic language," which he expressed in his *Defence of Poesie*.

Now familiar with the court, Spenser began a bold satire, *Mother Hubberds Tale*, a beast fable with strong political implications—he was of the party which disliked Lord Burleigh and opposed the projected marriage of the Queen to the Duc d'Alençon. In 1580 he became secretary to Lord Grey de Wilton, the new Lord Deputy of Ireland; and apart from visits to London he spent the rest of his life in that country. Elizabeth's handling of the Irish problem is one of the least glorious aspects of her reign. Ireland was virtually a colony, harshly exploited by the English; and Spenser was as colonialist as the rest of them. The new men, coming in to serve their own interests, got on neither with the Catholic poor nor the old Anglo-Irish ruling class; they tried to impose Protestantism, English justice, and the kind of agriculture profitable to themselves on a nation that wanted none of them. The ensuing uprisings Lord Grey suppressed with great severity, and Spenser approved of this, as Book V of *The Fairie Queene* and, more explicitly, his prose work, *A Vewe of the Present State of Ireland*, written in 1596, show. He accompanied Grey on military expeditions intended to pacify the Irish, and may well have seen him in action as Justice, with his troops in the role of Talus (the impersonal agent of Justice in Book V). But Grey felt he had inadequate support in London, and resigned, amid much ill-feeling and backbiting, in 1582. Spenser stayed on, at first in Dublin, then, from 1588, on the 3000-acre estate he had acquired at Kilcolman, adjacent to the larger estate of Ralegh.

Spenser, though much involved with his job, made a literary friend in Lodowick Bryskett, another civil servant, and in Bryskett's book, *A Discourse of Civil Life*, published in 1606, we hear of a conversation between Spenser, Bryskett, and others, in which Spenser declines to discourse on moral philosophy because he has in hand a poem on that very subject, "in *heroical verse* under the title of a *Faerie Queene* . . . assigning to every vertue a Knight to be the patron and defender of the same." Even if Bryskett is using hindsight here, it would seem that Spenser in Dublin had decided on the general scheme and was writing the poem.

In 1589 his neighbor Ralegh induced Spenser to visit London with him, and to bring along the first three books of the big poem. The Queen liked them, and awarded him a pension of £50, quite a good sum at the time, though he was disappointed, as we see from *Colin Clout* and from the Proem to Book IV. They were published in 1590, and Spenser followed up their success by publishing several poems in the following year, among them the mythological fable *Muiopotmos*, the satire *Mother Hubberds Tale*, and *Daphnaida*, an elegy.

Back in Ireland, he was involved in difficult law-suits, but remained very productive. If the attribution is correct, he translated the pseudo-Platonic dialogue *Axiochus*, published in 1592. He courted and in 1594 married Elizabeth Boyle, and the publication of *Amoretti* (the sonnet sequence of about 1591–94) and the marriage poem *Epithalamion* followed in 1595. That year also saw the publication of *Colin Clout* and *Astrophell*, his elegy for Sidney. Meanwhile he was finishing Books IV, V, and VI of *The Faerie Queene*, which were published, together with the earlier books, in 1596. His interest in contemporary affairs was never greater than in these later Irish years, when he inserted very late into *The Faerie Queene* (V.xi) a piece of political allegory involving the Earl of Essex and Henry IV of France, and wrote the *Vewe*. In 1596 James VI of Scotland, who was to succeed Elizabeth in 1603, demanded Spenser's punishment for libeling his mother, Mary Queen of Scots, in the portrait of Duessa before

Mercilla (V.ix). No action was taken. Other works of this period were the *Fowre Hymnes* and *Prothalamion,* written for the double marriage of the daughters of the Earl of Worcester, a friend of Essex.

The continuation of *The Faerie Queen* brought Spenser no reward from the Queen, and after a spell in London he went back to Ireland, becoming Sheriff of Cork in 1598. The much-feared rebellion of Tyrone, who was later to help discredit Essex himself, broke out in 1598; Kilcolman was sacked, and Spenser fled to Cork and then to London. There, on January 6, 1599, he died, probably not, as Jonson said, "for lack of bread," but certainly much reduced. Essex paid for his funeral in Westminister Abbey, and poets threw elegies into his grave, near Chaucer's. The Queen ordered him a monument, but it was not erected; the Countess of Dorset provided one in 1620. It got Spenser's dates wrong, but contained the famous eulogy, "The Prince of Poets in His Tyme." It was restored in marble in 1778, with the dates corrected, and is still in the Abbey.

It is not easy to form a definite view of the personality of Spenser. He was scholarly in a poet's way; he was ambitious, and had, till the final debacle, a pretty successful worldly career. He must have been exceptionally industrious, combining diligence in his job with diligence in poetry, from which he sought material reward as well as glory. He was a literary adventurer, seeking in the past models for entirely original modern achievements, much as the voyagers did. He, like some of his poetry, constituted a reconciliation of opposites. His views on Ireland seem cruel, yet he was gentle. He had strong opinions on the subjection of women, as Book V shows, yet he broke off the composition of his major work to write *Epithalamion,* and most of his lifework is an act of worship offered to a woman. He was oppressed by signs of returning chaos in the world, but celebrated love as an inexhaustible source of beauty and order. He valued peace and courtesy, yet supported the war party. These real and apparent oppositions are characteristic of his great poem, and perhaps also of his personality.

The text of Spenser used here is that of J. C. Smith and E. de Selincourt in the Oxford Standard Authors. Punctuation, capitalization, and use of italic are unchanged, but *u* and *v* have been changed to conform to modern usage, and *j* replaces *i* in such words as *joy.*

The Faerie Queene

Heroic poetry, which in the Renaissance was taken by most commentators to be the highest kind, was necessarily associated with the growth of nationalist feelings, since it attempted to achieve in the vernacular what Virgil had done for the Roman empire in Latin. This explains Spenser's interest not only in the ancient models but also in modern Italian and French poetry—he would learn what he could from renaissances that flowered earlier than the English. But it also explains why *The Faerie Queene*, for all its dreamy Romance landscape and narrative, is very much a poem of its moment. He was celebrating national or imperial power, and did so not only by placing its origins in a fictive British past but by justifying modern policies, ecclesiastical, political, and military. He had to make his poem relevant to the glories, real and imaginary, of the reign he chose to represent as climactic in history; but he could not ignore the dark side of the picture.

The Acts of Supremacy and Uniformity of 1559 gave the country a foundation of peace and order but alienated recusants. The loss of Calais in 1558 marked the end of English power in France; henceforth England would be more narrowly nationalistic, and its church, with the Queen at its head, reflected this development. It became the chief Protestant power and engaged in a long and mostly cold war with Spain, the chief Catholic power. Meanwhile the cities grew larger and the great men grew greater, but the reign of Elizabeth ended with years that were glorious only in some ways; they were also melancholy, anxious, and beset by social and economic problems.

Elizabeth was a great but difficult woman. Her failure to marry and produce an heir meant that over the long period when this was no longer even a possibility her reign was under threat of the Catholic Stuart claims, represented in life by Mary Queen of Scots, and in Spenser's poem by Duessa. Mary was beheaded in 1587, the Armada defeated in 1588; but the succeeding thirteen years continued to be anxious, and the last of the favorites, Essex, was executed in 1601 for rebelliously declaring his interest in the succession of Mary's son, James VI of Scotland.

The celebration of the Virgin Queen, which Spenser and others carried to such heights, was in origin a way of making the best of a bad situation, and was intimately, though not obviously, related to foreign and ecclesiastical policy, which would arguably have been much easier if the Queen had lost her virginity, since the disputed succession made all the problems more acute. The religious situation was political, and vice versa. When Elizabeth succeeded to the throne in 1558, the country had just lived through her father's dispute with Rome, the brief period of triumphant Protestantism under Edward VI, and the Catholic reaction under Mary. Elizabeth was by no means an extreme Protestant, and the settlement of 1559 was a compromise, which for years pleased neither Protestant nor Catholic. The church now claimed, in fact, to be both—a Catholic church purged by Protestant action, with the Queen as its governor. Conformity was required by law. The clergy had mostly changed doctrines with each new reign; they were undistinguished, often venal, and easily exploited by the great laymen who had made fortunes out of the dissolution of the monasteries. The new (or, as propaganda said, very old) church was in poor condition. It was rescued by a brilliant intellectual enterprise: Archbishop Jewel's apology for the church, Archbishop Parker's history of it, and Hooker's justification of its middle way in broad historical and theological terms created a myth which Spenser and others accepted. The English church was older than Rome, having been founded soon after the Crucifixion by

Joseph of Arimathaea, and it was ruled by an empress who inherited the powers of Constantine, the emperor who Christianized the Roman empire. So, from the doctrinal confusion and worldly corruption he commented on in the *Calender,* Spenser moved on to the heroic situation of a nation in all respects the heir of Rome, a church which had restored primitive purity in an apocalyptic manner, and an empress who concentrated the universal empire in her reign over one people. Rejecting both the extremes, the Catholic enemy who threatened both inside and outside England, and the Puritanism he had known at Cambridge, with its mistrust of bishops and the Prayer Book, Spenser found himself in a position to write an Anglican epic. The enemy therein is, primarily, Catholicism, the usurping papacy (antichrist); in his myth they are destroyers of paradise, types of the perfidy and duplicity which beset fallen humanity. Truth is England, Falsehood Rome.

This is stated most clearly in Book I. But Spenser never calls the British restoration of Truth perfect. And the strength of the whole poem arises in part from his reconciling incompatible feelings and attitudes to his subject. The court is the fount of courtesy, but also corrupt. The world which has seen the restoration of the true church is also evil and decaying. A polarity of light and dark is essential to his mind. He delights in the changing forms and colors of life, while allowing that movement belongs to time, not eternity, and color to earth, not heaven. He celebrates fertility and generation, but allows that it is inseparable from "fleshly slime" (III.vi.3). Life is not only delightful, it is also a trial or initiation, a total temptation. Time, which makes the world changeable and delightful to the senses, is the drudge of eternity, and our main business is with that.

Whatever his stated subject, Spenser confronts a virtue with its opposites, dark with light; he invents myth after myth to celebrate opposites, and develops his great technical variety in order to accommodate them. The very length of the poem, its diffuseness, are functions of his need to make contraries meet in one: past and present, concord and discord, good and evil, time and eternity, light and dark. The inclusiveness of the poem is its most remarkable virtue. It lacks the gravity of Virgil, the speed and power of Ariosto, but as a "continued allegory" it has no rival. Spenser aims, as heroic poets were supposed to, at educating a gentleman in the virtues. But in doing so he used his allegorical powers to much greater effect than Ariosto and Tasso, even with all the help they got from their commentators, had wanted or been able to do. Sometimes he is simple, as in the House of Alma or the House of Holiness. Sometimes the allegory is thin, sometimes frankly popular, as in parts of the First Book, which are little different in design from the popular allegories of Lord Mayors' shows or celebrations of the Queen's birthday, or her reception at some country house. The symbolism of the First Book is especially popular; but Spenser is capable of deepening it until it remembles the learned allegory of Ben Jonson in his masques, so that Spenser is both "homely, churchwardenly," as C. S. Lewis calls him, and a profound philosophical allegorist, with elaborate allegorical programs that have still not been worked out.

The allegory, then, is multiform, sometimes thin, sometimes thick, always an aspect of a syncretic myth-making operation which for Spenser was the poet's way to tell the truth about everything—and that means about the state of affairs in the England of the 1580's and 1590's as well as in the whole frame of the world. Hence the blend, strange to us, of topicality and ethical generality; hence the sudden moves from shallow to very deep water. In a sense it could be said that this habitual allegorizing at one level or another makes Spenser more "medieval" than, say, Tasso; if so, the issue is not very important. The England of the Renaissance did retain, in spite of its efforts to be modern and humanist, much of the medieval spirit, and Chaucer was as important to Spenser as any other poet. But there was nevertheless a true modernism in Spenser's experimental, past-rifling methods. An employment of every resource—Ovidian mythologizing, heroic convention, symbolism and allegory of whatever kind—to speak about the world as it is, about deep problems which, rightly expressed, are reflected in the movements from day to day of politicians and religious leaders, is in that sense modern.

A poem, to do all that, must have readers who understand its peculiar languages and its ways of achieving flexibility. Spenser's language is not modern; it corresponds to his device of thrusting all the action back into a remote past, where connections are easier to make, life being simpler. Thus did the Elizabethans restore in show and tournament the old language and symbolism of chivalry. The archaism of *The Faerie Queene* increases its range of meaning; the vagueness of its fairyland allows Spenser to fluctuate, as in a myth or a dream, between vagueness and sharp definition at will. The reader must collaborate: *The Faerie Queene* is a world and a great one to all who learn to move in it.

A Letter of the Authors

Spenser returned to London with Ralegh in 1589–90, and presumably wrote this Letter specially for the publication of Books I through III in 1590. Perhaps he did so in haste, for, valuable as it is, it contains some puzzles and inaccuracies. The account of Book II seems to conflict with the facts of the poem. The reference to "the twelve private morall vertues, as Aristotle hath devised" and again to Magnificence and "the xii other vertues" has long been debated. Is it twelve or thirteen? In any case Aristotle's *Nicomachean Ethics* has no such list of virtues; and furthermore the six Spenser actually treated—seven if one counts Constancy—do not match Aristotle; for example, Temperance is an Aristotelian virtue but Holiness is not. Perhaps the mistake about Book II arose from haste—in setting down the part of Guyon's story which precedes the narrative as we have it, he neglected to make the two exactly consistent. As to the virtues, he may have been thinking more loosely than at first appears when he spoke of using Aristotle's *Ethics*—or some of the many Christianizing commentaries on the book—as a scheme from which he could vary.

These difficulties do not cancel the great value of the Letter. Here is a summary of its argument: 1. mode of the work: allegory; 2. moral intention: justification of subject and method; 3. defense of allegorical poetry as morally beneficial ("ensample" better than "rule"); 4. "general intention" of portrait of Arthur and of the Faerie Queene and other "shadowings" of Elizabeth; 5. the other knights of the first three books; 6. difference between poetry and historiography—stories of Books I through III as they would be in a chronicle rather than a poem; 7. "other adventures intermedled"; 8. conclusion: the Letter tries to establish the general design of a poem that might without this explanation seem "tedious and confused."

The Letter, in its general claims, is in the tradition of Renaissance apologias for epic poetry; see Sidney's remarks in the *Defence*. The object is to fashion gentlemen; moral precepts are easier to swallow if the pill is coated. The choice of Arthur fits the rule that the hero should be both great and of a remote time (more, he was an official ancestor of the Tudors and the last emperor of Britain before them; thus he was a hero of the type used by Virgil and the Italian heroic poets of the sixteenth century). Homer and, more importantly, Virgil provide models; Ariosto and Tasso maintained and modified their tradition in modern times; to cover all the ground he would need twenty-four books.

Teaching "by ensample," Spenser needs an exemplary hero. His Arthur, however, cannot be to Elizabeth what Aeneas was to Augustus, and the sex of his monarch led him into various "dark conceits." Arthur is Magnificence, which includes all the other virtues. Elizabeth is first the Faerie Queene, Glory, for which gentlemen should strive; secondly, "a most vertuous and beautifull Lady." The division reflects her two "persons," political and natural (Gloriana and Belphoebe), a division that goes deep in English constitutional theory. She is also present in other female characters. As for the knights, they have a virtue apiece; Spenser found some difficulty in working Arthur into a scheme already so elaborate.

In the "historiographical" rendering, Spenser allows only an occasional hint of allegorical intention—as when he speaks of Red Cross's armour as that of the soldier of Christ (*miles Christi,* Ephesians 6). He also states that some episodes are "accidents" rather than "intendments"—scenes and narratives that developed along the way without belonging to the master plan; but this does not mean that they have no allegorical meanings; Britomart, Marinell and Florimell, and Belphoebe certainly have, and so do "many the like."

Everybody wishes Spenser had said a bit more, and said it more clearly, in this Letter; but it is the first commentary ever written on the poem, and comes from the best-informed commentator; so it is certainly worth study.

A Letter of the Authors

expounding his *whole intention in the course of this worke: which* for that it giveth great light to the Reader, for the better understanding is hereunto annexed.

To the Right noble, and Valorous, Sir Walter Ralegh knight, Lo. Wardein of the Stanneryes, and her Majesties liefetenaunt of the County of Cornewayll.

Sir knowing how doubtfully[1] all Allegories may be construed, and this booke of mine, which I have entituled the Faery Queene, being a continued Allegory, or darke conceit,[2] I have thought good as well for avoyding of gealous [3] opinions

1. Ambiguously.
2. Homer and Virgil were interpreted as continuously allegorical; allegorical readings were attached to Ariosto by the poet himself and his commentators; Tasso insisted on his moral allegory. So it was right for heroic poetry to be allegorical, to have a meaning or meanings below the surface and therefore "dark." These meanings Spenser calls "conceits," meaning something between the modern "concepts" and the now obsolete "acute metaphorical discoveries." In a poem so long and loosely structured as *The Faerie Queene* the conceits cannot be uniformly dark—the allegorical significances vary from the transparent to the unfathomable.
3. Hostile, envious.

and misconstructions, as also for your better light in reading therof, (being so by you commanded,) to discover unto you the general intention and meaning, which in the whole course thereof I have fashioned, without expressing of any particular [4] purposes or by-accidents therein occasioned. The generall end therefore of all the booke is to fashion a gentleman or noble person in vertuous and gentle discipline: Which for that I conceived shoulde be most plausible and pleasing, being coloured with an historicall fiction, the which the most part of men delight to read, rather for variety of matter, then for profite of the ensample: I chose the historye of king Arthure, as most fitte for the excellency of his person, being made famous by many mens former workes, and also furthest from the daunger of envy, and suspition of present time. In which I have followed all the antique Poets historicall, first Homere, who in the Persons of Agamemnon and Ulysses hath ensampled a good governour and a vertuous man, the one in his Ilias, the other in his Odysseis: [5] then Virgil, whose like intention was to doe in the person of Aeneas: after him Ariosto [6] comprised them both in his Orlando: and lately Tasso [7] dissevered them againe, and formed both parts in two persons, namely that part which they in Philosophy call Ethice, or vertues of a private man, coloured in his Rinaldo.[8] The other named Politice in his Godfredo.[9] By ensample of which excellente Poets, I labour to pourtraict in Arthure, before he was king, the image of a brave knight, perfected in the twelve private morall vertues, as Aristotle hath devised, the which is the purpose of these first twelve bookes: which if I finde to be well accepted, I may be perhaps encoraged, to frame the other part of polliticke vertues in his person, after that hee came to be king. To some I know this Methode will seeme displeasaunt, which had rather have good discipline delivered plainly in way of precepts, or sermoned at large, as they use, then thus clowdily enwrapped in Allegoricall devises. But such, me seeme, should be satisfide with the use of these dayes, seeing all things accounted by their showes, and nothing esteemed of, that is not delightfull and pleasing to commune sence. For this cause is Xenophon [10] preferred before Plato, for that the one in the exquisite depth of his judgement, formed a Commune welth such as it should be, but the other in the person of Cyrus and the Persians fashioned a government such as might best be: So much more profitable and gratious is doctrine by ensample, then by rule. So have I laboured to doe in the person of Arthure: whome I conceive after his long education by Timon, to whom he was by Merlin delivered to be brought up, so soone as he was borne of the Lady Igrayne, to have seene in a dream or vision the Faery Queene, with

4. As opposed to general, meaning the "accidents" mentioned near the end of the letter.
5. *Iliad, Odyssey.*
6. Lodovico Ariosto (1474–1533), author of *Orlando Furioso* (1532), the formative heroic poem of the Renaissance; Spenser is closest to it in the many interlinked stories of Bks. III and IV.
7. Torquato Tasso (1544–95), author of *Gerusalemme Liberata* (1581), owing much to Ariosto but made graver and more explicitly Christian by the influence of the Counter-Reformation.
8. Hero of Tasso's poem in its dealings with personal morality.
9. Godfrey of Boulogne, hero of Tasso's poem in its dealings with political morality.
10. Xenophon's *Cyropaedia, The Education of Cyrus,* and Plato's *Republic;* see Sidney's *Defence of Poesie.*

whose excellent beauty ravished, he awaking resolved to seeke her out, and so being by Merlin armed, and by Timon throughly instructed, he went to seeke her forth in Faerye land.[11] In that Faery Queene I meane glory in my generall intention, but in my particular I conceive the most excellent and glorious person of our soveraine the Queene, and her kingdome in Faery land. And yet in some places els, I doe otherwise shadow[12] her. For considering she beareth two persons,[13] the one of a most royall Queene or Empresse, the other of a most vertuous and beautifull Lady, this latter part in some places I doe expresse in Belphœbe, fashioning her name according to your owne excellent conceipt of Cynthia,[14] (Phœbe and Cynthia being both names of Diana.) So in the person of Prince Arthure I sette forth magnificence in particular, which vertue for that (according to Aristotle and the rest) it is the perfection of all the rest, and conteineth in it them all, therefore in the whole course I mention the deedes of Arthure applyable to that vertue, which I write of in that booke. But of the xii. other vertues, I make xii. other knights the patrones, for the more variety of the history: Of which these three bookes contayn three, The first of the knight of the Redcrosse, in whome I expresse Holynes: The seconde of Sir Guyon, in whom I sette forth Temperaunce: The third of Britomartis a Lady knight, in whome I picture Chastity. But because the beginning of the whole worke seemeth abrupte and as depending upon other antecedents, it needs that ye know the occasion of these three knights severall adventures. For the Methode of a Poet historical is not such, as of an Historiographer. For an Historiographer discourseth of affayres orderly as they were donne, accounting as well the times as the actions, but a Poet thrusteth into the middest,[15] even where it most concerneth him, and there recoursing to the thinges forepaste, and divining of thinges to come, maketh a pleasing Analysis of all. The beginning therefore of my history, if it were to be told by an Historiographer, should be the twelfth booke, which is the last, where I devise that the Faery Queene kept her Annuall feaste xii. dayes, uppon which xii. severall dayes, the occasions of the xii. severall adventures hapned, which being undertaken by xii. severall knights, are in these xii books severally handled and discoursed. The first was this. In the beginning of the feast, there presented him selfe a tall clownishe[16] younge man, who falling before the Queen of Faries desired a boone (as the manner then was) which during that feast she might not refuse: which was that hee might have the atchievement of any adventure, which during that feaste should happen, that being graunted, he rested him on the floore, unfitte through his rusticity for a better place. Soone after entred a faire Ladye in mourning weedes, riding on a white Asse, with a dwarfe behind her leading a warlike steed, that bore the Armes of a knight, and his speare in the dwarfes hand. Shee falling before the Queene of Faeries, com-

11. "By the Faery land of the poem I mean England."
12. Portray.
13. Referring to the doctrine that the monarch had two persons, one private and mortal, one political and immortal ("the king is dead, long live the king"). Elizabeth is therefore represented as both Queen and Empress, and most virtuous and beautiful lady.
14. Ralegh's poem to the Queen, *Cynthia;* like Phoebe and Diana, a name of the goddess of the moon and of chastity.
15. *In medias res,* as Horace (*Ars Poetica,* 148) advises.
16. Rustic, unpolished.

playned that her father and mother an ancient King and Queene, had bene by an huge dragon many years shut up in a brasen Castle, who thence suffred them not to yssew: and therefore besought the Faery Queene to assygne her some one of her knights to take on him that exployt. Presently [17] that clownish person upstarting, desired that adventure: whereat the Queene much wondering, and the Lady much gainesaying,[18] yet he earnestly importuned his desire. In the end the Lady told him that unlesse that armour which she brought, would serve him (that is the armour of a Christian man specified by Saint Paul v. Ephes.) that he could not succeed in that enterprise, which being forthwith put upon him with dewe furnitures [19] thereunto, he seemed the goodliest man in al that company, and was well liked of the Lady. And eftesoones taking on him knighthood, and mounting on that straunge Courser, he went forth with her on that adventure: where beginneth the first booke, vz.

A gentle knight was pricking on the playne, &c.

The second day ther came in a Palmer bearing an Infant with bloody hands, whose Parents he complained to have bene slayn by an Enchaunteresse called Acrasia: and therfore craved of the Faery Queene, to appoint him some knight, to performe that adventure, which being assigned to Sir Guyon, he presently went forth with that same Palmer: which is the beginning of the second booke and the whole subject thereof. The third day there came in, a Groome who complained before the Faery Queene, that a vile Enchaunter called Busirane had in hand a most faire Lady called Amoretta, whom he kept in most grievous torment, because she would not yield him the pleasure of her body. Whereupon Sir Scudamour the lover of that Lady presently tooke on him that adventure. But being unable to performe it by reason of the hard Enchauntments, after long sorrow, in the end met with Britomartis, who succoured him, and reskewed his love.

But by occasion hereof, many other adventures are intermedled,[20] but rather as Accidents, then intendments. As the love of Britomart, the overthrow of Marinell, the misery of Florimell, the vertuousnes of Belphœbe, the lasciviousnes of Hellenora, and many the like.

Thus much Sir, I have briefly overronne [21] to direct your understanding to the wel-head of the History, that from thence gathering the whole intention of the conceit, ye may as in a handfull gripe al the discourse, which otherwise may happily [22] seeme tedious and confused. So humbly craving the continuaunce of your honorable favour towards me, and th'eternall establishment of your happines, I humbly take leave.

23. January. 1589.
Yours most humbly affectionate.
Ed. Spenser.

17. At once.
18. Protesting.
19. Equipment.
20. Mixed in.
21. Run through.
22. Perchance.

Book I

Spenser probably did not begin here; the parts of the work that Harvey saw in 1580 must, if they survive at all, be in the middle books, for the work in which Spenser was then attempting to "overgo" Ariosto can have had nothing to do with the Revelation of St. John, a topic which Harvey recommends, and which is central to Book I as we now have it. When he did settle to Book I he made it very different in tone, and also made it much more self-contained than the more Ariostan books; in fact, I is even more so than II, which is to a great degree modeled on it, and V, the other Book that comes closest.

Red Cross is the greatest of the knights, a saint rather than a mere hero, and occasionally the image of Christ. The historical scope of the Book (extended by more or less "dark conceits") is the whole history of the world from the Fall to the final overthrow of Satan. Its theology and religion are more directly expressed than in the other Books, and it speaks with far more urgency to the great themes of history, and notably the vicissitudes of the church on earth, than they.

Red Cross is St. George, slayer of the dragon; a figure who is both a type of Christ and a droll figure in folkplay and popular pageant, hero of great works of art and of the antique Mummers Play; patron saint of England. He rides into Spenser's poem, *in medias res,* with his usual pageant companions, the lady on the ass and the lamb. The scene is vague and dreamlike, and we can already see what Coleridge meant when he spoke of "the marvellous independence and true imaginative absence of all particular space and time" in *The Faerie Queene.* But that is only a half-truth. These characters from the village play and the Lord Mayor's Show, in their narrative of nightmare apparitions, dreamlike transfigurations, apparently fitful meanings, are going to serve a story which deals with the history of the human condition as it appeared in an age of apocalyptic climax, the late 1580's. We have the same fancy in our day, but do not express it, as Spenser did and Virgil had done, in a heroic poem about human destiny in the context of earthly power and heavenly providence; nor would we give the story a milieu of Arthurian romance, though we might envy the way in which it enables the poet to achieve those strange transitions and condensations which so remind us of the Freudian dreamwork.

Red Cross, though of the elect, is a sinner, everyman. Spenser emphasizes his fall into sin and despair by echoing the anti-Romanist article of his church: "that we are justified by faith alone is a most wholesome doctrine." Given grace to repent, Red Cross undertakes the imitation of Christ, redeems the parents of Una (Adam and Eve), slays the old Dragon, and harrows hell—becomes, in short, Christ, the object of his imitation, and marries his Bride, Una, the True Church (i.e. the Church of England). Such are the transformations of Spenser's world, and they are prepared for in the opening lines. Red Cross, who wears the apocalyptic "bloudie Cross" (Christ wore it in the battle in heaven, as shown in illuminated manuscripts of Revelation), is also called "Right faithful true," which, *fidelis et verax,* is the title of Christ in Revelation (19:11). And Red Cross, St. George, is also England, defender of the true faith.

Revelation is the ultimate source. Una is "the woman clothed with the sun" (Revelation 12:1), traditionally identified with the true church; Spenser speaks of her "sunshyny face" (I.xii.23) as the medieval illuminators showed her in a glory of light. She, like her prototype, flees into the wilderness (Revelation 12:6). Duessa plays multiplicity to Una's integrity, but is also the Whore of Babylon, the Scarlet Woman

(Revelation 17); the best possible illustrations of Spenser's eighth canto, where she rides the Beast, are in the medieval apocalypses. She is also the Church of Rome in the allegories of Reformation propaganda. Archimago is antichrist, the Beast from the Land of Revelation, the papacy. The tree and the water, representing the two out of the Catholic seven sacraments retained by the reformed church (communion and baptism) refresh Red Cross in his three-day battle with the Dragon; they come from Revelation 22. And these are only samples of Spenser's allusions to Revelation.

If one thinks of the number of times it has happened both before and after Spenser, it will seem less strange that reference should be made to Revelation—a vision of the end of the world—for historical and political purposes. The last book of the Bible was thought to contain in prophetic form the whole history of the church, and Spenser followed an English tradition when he favored a Protestant interpretation and one which made the true Catholic church the Church of England, the primitive church now restored after centuries of Romanist disfigurement. Una is that church, and also its head, Elizabeth I, who replaced the papacy which had usurped the royal chief priests, her ancestors, for so long. The overthrow of the antichrist Archimago and the false fallen church, Duessa, amounts to a restoration of Eden.

Thus Spenser embodies in his dreamlike romance story the imperial and ecclesiastical pretensions of the last of the Tudors. He associates his empress with a triumphant restoration of the true church on earth, and with the reuniting of church and state by a queen who liked to be thought of as a second Constantine, the emperor who 1200 years earlier had Christianized the Roman empire. The presumptuous bishops of Rome had set apart the secular and religious powers, but they had been ousted from England and a new emperor, a new Constantine, ruled all.

As Virgil had celebrated the culmination of empire in the *Aeneid,* so would Spenser in *The Faerie Queene,* and especially in Book I. But to do so he chooses not courtly or difficult materials; rather he builds into his heroic pattern the familiar figures and almost equally familiar interpretations of Revelation, and explains how universal history justifies the worship of imperial Elizabeth.* It is not surprising that when Colin Clout read the poem to her she "gan to take delight . . . and it desired at timely hours to hear."

* The dedication ran as follows: "To the most high, mightie and magnificent empresse renowmed for pietie, vertue, and all gratious government Elizabeth by the grace of God Queene of England Fraunce and Ireland and of Virginia, defendour of the faith, &c. Her Most humble servaunt Edmund Spenser doth in all Humilitie Dedicate, Present and Consecrate these his labours to live with the eternitie of her fame."

The First Booke of The Faerie Queene

Contayning, the Legende of the Knight of the Red Crosse, or *Of Holinesse*

1 Lo I the man, whose Muse whilome˃ did maske, *formerly*
As time her taught, in lowly Shepheards weeds,˃ *clothes*
Am now enforst a far unfitter taske,

For trumpets sterne to chaunge mine Oaten reeds,°
And sing of Knights and Ladies gentle˃ deeds; *noble*
Whose prayses having slept in silence long,°
Me, all too meane, the sacred Muse areeds˃ *counsels*
To blazon broad emongst her learned throng:
Fierce warres and faithfull loves shall moralize my song.

2 Helpe then, O holy Virgin chiefe of nine,°
Thy weaker˃ Novice to performe thy will, *too weak*
Lay forth out of thine everlasting scryne˃ *record chest*
The antique rolles, which there lye hidden still,
Of Faerie knights and fairest *Tanaquill*,˃ *Gloriana*
Whom that most noble Briton Prince° so long
Sought through the world, and suffered so much ill,
That I must rue his undeserved wrong:
O helpe thou my weake wit, and sharpen my dull tong.

3 And thou most dreaded impe˃ of highest *Jove*, *child*
Faire *Venus* sonne,° that with thy cruell dart
At that good knight so cunningly didst rove,˃ *shoot*
That glorious fire it kindled in his hart,
Lay now thy deadly Heben˃ bow apart, *ebony*
And with thy mother milde, come to mine ayde:
Come both, and with you bring triumphant *Mart*,°
In loves and gentle jollities arrayd,
After his murdrous spoiles and bloudy rage allayd.˃ *calmed*

4 And with them eke,˃ O Goddesse heavenly bright,° *also*
Mirrour of grace and Majestie divine,
Great Lady of the greatest Isle, whose light
Like *Phœbus* lampe° throughout the world doth shine,
Shed thy faire beames into my feeble eyne˃, *eyes*
And raise my thoughts too humble and too vile,
To thinke of that true glorious type° of thine,
The argument of mine afflicted stile:
The which to heare, vouchsafe, O dearest dred° a-while.

For trumpets . . . reeds He changes from the shepherd's pipe of pastoral to the trumpets of heroic poetry. This first stanza imitates the proem to Virgil's *Aeneid*. On Virgil's model it became prescriptive for an epic poet to prepare himself with pastoral.
And sing . . . long imitating the opening of Ariosto's *Orlando Furioso*
O holy . . . nine Calliope, chief of the Muses, presided over eloquence and heroic poetry; represented in art with a trumpet in the right hand, a book in the left.
most . . . Prince Arthur
sonne Cupid
Mart Mars, god of war and lover of Venus
Goddesse . . . bright Queen Elizabeth
Phœbus lamps the sun
true . . . type Gloriana, symbol of Queen Elizabeth
dearest dred object of greatest awe

Canto i°

The Patron of true Holinesse,
  Foule Errour doth defeate:
Hypocrisie him to entrappe,
  Doth to his home entreate.

1 A Gentle Knight was pricking˃ on the plaine, *spurring*
  Y cladd in mightie armes and silver shielde,
  Wherein old dints of deepe wounds did remaine,
  The cruell markes of many' a bloudy fielde;
  Yet armes till that time did he never wield:°
  His angry steede did chide his foming bitt,
  As much disdayning to the curbe to yield:
  Full jolly˃ knight he seemd, and faire did sitt, *brave*
As one for knightly giusts˃ and fierce encounters fitt. *jousts*

2 But on his brest a bloudie Crosse he bore,
  The deare remembrance of his dying Lord,
  For whose sweete sake that glorious badge he wore,
  And dead as living ever him ador'd:
  Upon his shield the like was also scor'd,
  For soveraine hope, which in his helpe he had:
  Right faithfull true° he was in deede and word,
  But of his cheere˃ did seeme too solemne sad; *expression*
Yet nothing did he dread, but ever was ydrad.˃ *dreaded*

3 Upon a great adventure he was bond,˃ *bound*
  That greatest *Gloriana* to him gave,
  That greatest Glorious Queene of *Faerie* lond,
  To winne him worship, and her grace to have,
  Which of all earthly things he most did crave;
  And ever as he rode, his hart did earne˃ *yearn*
  To prove his puissance˃ in battell brave *strength*
  Upon his foe, and his new force to learne;
Upon his foe, a Dragon horrible and stearne.

4 A lovely Ladie° rode him faire beside,
  Upon a lowly Asse more white then snow,
  Yet she much whiter, but the same did hide
  Under a vele, that wimpled˃ was full low, *folded*
  And over all a blacke stole she did throw,
  As one that inly mournd: so was she sad,

Canto i When Red Cross and his companions seek shelter they enter a wood, symbol of the errors of human existence. Despite the lady's warning that he places too much confidence in unaided human strength, the knight provokes and fights with Error (heresy, corrupter of pure doctrine). In his difficulty he is advised "Add faith unto your force"—a tenet of the true religion which allowed no justification by works alone—and he forces Error to spew forth its heretical brood. His victory at the outset foreshadows the victory over the dragon at the end, as Christ's victory over Satan in the wilderness foreshadowed the final overthrow of the old dragon; but his lapse foretells the sins that lie ahead also. His first encounter with religious deceit and hypocrisy of the papal kind that plagued England till the Reformation follows immediately.

armes . . . wield He is wearing the old arms of the Christian soldier (see Headnote to Bk. I) for the first time.

Right . . . true See Headnote.

Ladie Una, her radiance concealed by a veil

And heavie sat upon her palfrey slow:
Seemed in heart some hidden care she had,
And by her in a line> a milke white lambe she lad. *leash*

5 So pure an innocent, as that same lambe,
She was in life and every vertuous lore,
And by descent from Royall lynage came
Of ancient Kings and Queenes, that had of yore
Their scepters stretcht from East to Westerne shore,
And all the world in their subjection held;°
Till that infernal feend with foule uprore
Forwasted> all their land, and them expeld: *destroyed*
Whom to avenge, she had this Knight from far compeld.> *summoned*

6 Behind her farre away a Dwarfe° did lag,
That lasie seemd in being ever last,
Or wearièd with bearing of her bag
Of needments at his backe. Thus as they past,
The day with cloudes was suddeine overcast,
And angry *Jove* an hideous storme of raine
Did poure into his Lemans lap° so fast,
That every wight> to shrowd> it did constrain, *creature / shelter*
And this faire couple eke to shroud themselves were fain.

7 Enforst to seeke some covert nigh at hand,
A shadie grove not far away they spide,
That promist ayde the tempest to withstand:
Whose loftie trees yclad with sommers pride,
Did spred so broad, that heavens light did hide,
Not perceable with power of any starre:
And all within were pathes and alleies wide,
With footing worne, and leading inward farre:
Faire harbour that them seems; so in they entred arre.

8 And foorth they passe, with pleasure forward led,
Joying to heare the birdes sweete harmony,
Which therein shrouded from the tempest dred,
Seemd in their song to scorne the cruell sky.
Much can> they prayse the trees so straight and hy, *did*
The sayling Pine,° the Cedar proud and tall,
The vine-prop Elme, the Poplar never dry,
The builder Oake, sole king of forrests all,
The Aspine good for staves, the Cypresse funerall.

by descent . . . held Una is both the true and primitive church and the daughter of Eden. She is the unfallen world (her name means One, the primal unity before numbers) and the church while still universal; Duessa is multiplicity and even on her own claim her father rules only the west (I.ii.22). The point is, politically, to establish, as Elizabethan churchmen always did, the truth of the position that the English church was older and purer than the Roman, which had usurped it.

Dwarfe perhaps signifies her human needs, as the lamb signifies her purity

Lemans lap mistress's lap; the earth

sayling Pine used by shipbuilders. This epic catalogue of trees is probably developed here from Chaucer's *Parliament of Fowls.*

9 The Laurell, meed> of mightie Conquerors *prize*
And Poets sage, the Firre that weepeth still,> *always*
The Willow worne of forlorne Paramours,
The Eugh> obedient to the benders will, *yew*
The Birch for shaftes, the Sallow> for the mill, *willow*
The Mirrhe sweete bleeding in the bitter wound,°
The warlike Beech, the Ash for nothing ill,
The fruitfull Olive, and the Platane> round, *plane-tree*
The carver Holme,° the Maple seeldom inward sound.

10 Led with delight, they thus beguile the way,
Untill the blustring storme is overblowne;
When weening> to returne, whence they did stray, *thinking*
They cannot finde that path, which first was showne,
But wander too and fro in wayes unknowne,
Furthest from end then, when they neerest weene,
That makes them doubt, their wits be not their owne:
So many pathes, so many turnings seene,
That which of them to take, in diverse doubt they been.

11 At last resolving forward still to fare,
Till that some end they finde or> in or out, *either*
That path they take, that beaten seemd most bare,
And like to lead the labyrinth about;> *out of*
Which when by tract they hunted had throughout,
At length it brought them to a hollow cave,
Amid the thickest woods. The Champion stout> *brave*
Eftsoones> dismounted from his courser brave,> *at once / splendid*
And to the Dwarfe a while his needlesse spere he gave.

12 Be well aware, quoth then that Ladie milde,
Least suddaine mischiefe ye too rash provoke:
The danger hid, the place unknowne and wilde,
Breedes dreadfull doubts: Oft fire is without smoke,
And perill without show: therefore your stroke
Sir knight with-hold, till further triall made.
Ah Ladie (said he) shame were to revoke
The forward footing for> an hidden shade: *because of*
Vertue gives her selfe light, through darkenesse for to wade.°

13 Yea but (quoth she) the perill of this place
I better wot> then you, though now too late *know*
To wish you backe returne with foule disgrace,
Yet wisedome warnes, whilest foot is in the gate,
To stay the steppe, ere forcèd to retrate.
This is the wandring wood, this *Errours den*,°

Mirrhe . . . wound Its resins were extracted for perfume from cuts in the bark.
carver Holme holm-oak used for carving
Vertue . . . wade Compare the misplaced confidence of the Elder Brother in Milton's *Comus*, ll. 372–73: "Virtue could see to do what Virtue would / By her own radiant light . . ."
Errours den Error stands for heresy; old heresies breed new ones which feed on them; Spenser remembers Revelation 9:7–10.

A monster vile, whom God and man does hate:
Therefore I read> beware. Fly fly (quoth then *counsel*
The fearefull Dwarfe:) this is no place for living men.

14 But full of fire and greedy hardiment,> *courage*
The youthfull knight could not for ought be staide,
But forth unto the darksome hole he went,
And lookèd in: his glistring armor made
A litle glooming light, much like a shade,
By which he saw the ugly monster plaine,
Halfe like a serpent horribly displaide,
But th'other halfe did womans shape retaine,
Most lothsom, filthie, foule, and full of vile disdaine.

15 And as she lay upon the durtie ground,
Her huge long taile her den all overspred,
Yet was in knots and many boughtes> upwound, *bends*
Pointed with mortall sting. Of her there bred
A thousand yong ones, which she dayly fed,
Sucking upon her poisonous dugs, eachone
Of sundry shapes, yet all ill favorèd:
Soone as that uncouth> light upon them shone, *unfamiliar*
Into her mouth they crept, and suddain all were gone.

16 Their dam upstart, out of her den effraide,> *scared*
And rushed forth, hurling her hideous taile
About her cursèd head, whose folds displaid
Were stretcht now forth at length without entraile.> *coils*
She lookt about, and seeing one in mayle
Armèd to point,> sought back to turne againe; *fully*
For light she hated as the deadly bale,> *harm*
Ay wont in desert darknesse to remaine,
Where plaine none might her see, nor she see any plaine.

17 Which when the valiant Elfe° perceiv'd, he lept
As Lyon fierce upon the flying pray,
And with his trenchand> blade her boldly kept *sharp*
From turning backe, and forcèd her to stay:
Therewith enrag'd she loudly gan to bray,
And turning fierce,> her speckled taile advaunst, *fiercely*
Threatning her angry sting, him to dismay:
Who nought aghast, his mightie hand enhaunst>: *raised*
The stroke down from her head unto her shoulder glaunst.

18 Much daunted with that dint, her sence was dazd,
Yet kindling rage, her selfe she gathered round,
And all attonce her beastly body raizd
With doubled forces high above the ground:

Elfe fairy (Harvey's early reference is to the *Elvish Queen*)

Tho> wrapping up her wrethèd sterne arownd, *then*
Lept fierce upon his shield, and her huge traine> *tail*
All suddenly about his body wound,
That hand or foot to stirre he strove in vaine:
God helpe the man so wrapt in *Errours* endlesse traine.> *deceit*

19 His Lady sad to see his sore constraint,
Cride out, Now now Sir knight, shew what ye bee,
Add faith unto your force, and be not faint:
Strangle her, else she sure will strangle thee.
That when he heard, in great perplexitie,
His gall did grate for griefe> and high disdaine, *anger*
And knitting all his force got one hand free,
Wherewith he grypt her gorge with so great paine,
That soone to loose her wicked bands did her constraine.

20 Therewith she spewd out of her filthy maw> *stomach*
A floud of poyson horrible and blacke,
Full of great lumpes of flesh and gobbets raw,
Which stunck so vildly,> that it forst him slacke *vilely*
His grasping hold, and from her turne him backe:
Her vomit full of bookes and papers was,°
With loathly frogs and toades, which eyes did lacke,°
And creeping sought way in the weedy gras:
Her filthy parbreake> all the place defilèd has. *vomit*

21 As when old father *Nilus* gins to swell
With timely pride above the *Aegyptian* vale,
His fattie> waves do fertile slime outwell, *greasy*
And overflow each plaine and lowly dale:
But when his later spring> gins to avale,> *flood / subside*
Huge heapes of mudd he leaves, wherein there breed
Ten thousand kindes of creatures, partly male
And partly female of his fruitfull seed;
Such ugly monstrous shapes elsewhere may no man reed.>° *see*

22 The same so sore annoyèd has the knight,
That welnigh chokèd with the deadly stinke,
His forces faile, ne> can no longer fight. *nor*
Whose corage when the feend perceiv'd to shrinke,
She pourèd forth out of her hellish sinke
Her fruitfull cursèd spawne of serpents small,
Deformèd monsters, fowle, and blacke as inke,
Which swarming all about his legs did crall,
And him encombred sore, but could not hurt at all.

vomit . . . was referring to the voluminousness of religious controversy, especially in the 16th century

loathly . . . lacke Revelation 16:13: "And I saw three unclean spirits like frogs come out of the mouth of the dragon, and out of the mouth of the beast, and out of the mouth of the false prophet."

As when . . . reed (stanza 21) The Nile floods which ensure the fertility of the valley, were supposed on subsiding to leave behind such creatures as crocodiles, bred from the mud.

23 As gentle Shepheard in sweete even-tide,
When ruddy *Phœbus* gins to welke> in west, *fade*
High on an hill, his flocke to vewen wide,
Markes which do byte their hasty supper best;
A cloud of combrous gnattes do him molest,
All striving to infixe their feeble stings,
That from their noyance> he no where can rest, *irritation*
But with his clownish hands their tender wings
He brusheth oft, and oft doth mar their murmurings.

24 Thus ill bestedd,> and fearefull more of shame, *situated*
Then> of the certaine perill he stood in, *than*
Halfe furious> unto his foe he came, *mad*
Resolv'd in minde all suddenly to win,
Or soone to lose, before he once would lin;> *stop*
And strooke at her with more than manly force,
That from her body full of filthie sin
He raft> her hatefull head without remorse; *cut*
A streame of cole black bloud forth gushèd from her corse.

25 Her scattred brood, soone as their Parent deare
They saw so rudely falling to the ground,
Groning full deadly, all with troublous feare,
Gathred themselves about her body round,
Weening their wonted entrance to have found
At her wide mouth: but being there withstood
They flockèd all about her bleeding wound,
And suckèd up their dying mothers blood,
Making her death their life, and eke her hurt their good.°

26 That detestáble sight him much amazde,
To see th'unkindly Impes> of heaven accurst, *young, brood*
Devoure their dam; on whom while so he gazd,
Having all satisfide their bloudy thurst,
Their bellies swolne he saw with fulnesse burst,
And bowels gushing forth: well worthy end
Of such as drunke her life, the which them nurst;
Now needeth him no lenger labour spend,
His foes have slaine themselves, with whom he should contend.

27 His Ladie seeing all, that chaunst, from farre
Approcht in hast to greet his victorie,
And said, Faire knight, borne under happy starre,
Who see your vanquisht foes before you lye;
Well worthy be you of that Armorie,°
Wherein ye have great glory wonne this day,
And proov'd your strength on a strong enimie,

Making . . . good heresy as finally self-destructive

Armorie the armor of the *miles Christi*

Your first adventure: many such I pray,
And henceforth ever wish, that like succeed it may.

28 Then mounted he upon his Steede againe,
And with the Lady backward> sought to wend;> — *back / go*
That path he kept, which beaten was most plaine,
Ne ever would to any by-way bend,
But still> did follow one unto the end, — *always*
The which at last out of the wood them brought.
So forward on his way (with God to frend)
He passèd forth, and new adventure sought;
Long way he travellèd, before he heard of ought.

29 At length they chaunst to meet upon the way
An agèd Sire,° in long blacke weedes> yclad, — *garments*
His feete all bare, his beard all hoarie gray,
And by his belt his booke he hanging had;
Sober he seemde, and very sagely sad,> — *grave*
And to the ground his eyes were lowly bent,
Simple in shew, and voyde of malice bad,
And all the way he prayèd, as he went,
And often knockt his brest, as one that did repent.

30 He faire the knight saluted, louting> low, — *bowing*
Who faire him quited,> as that courteous was: — *responded*
And after asked him, if he did know
Of straunge adventures, which abroad did pas.
Ah my deare Sonne (quoth he) how should, alas,
Silly> old man, that lives in hidden cell, — *simple*
Bidding his beades all day for his trespas,
Tydings of warre and worldly trouble tell?
With holy father sits not with such things to mell.> — *meddle*

31 But if of daunger which hereby doth dwell,
And homebred evill ye desire to heare,
Of a straunge man I can you tidings tell,
That wasteth all this countrey farre and neare.
Of such (said he) I chiefly do inquere,
And shall you well reward to shew the place,
In which that wicked wight> his dayes doth weare:> — *creature / pass*
For to all knighthood it is foule disgrace,
That such a cursèd creature lives so long a space.

32 Far hence (quoth he) in wastfull wildernesse
His dwelling is, by which no living wight
May ever passe, but thorough> great distresse. — *through*
Now (sayd the Lady) draweth toward night,
And well I wote,> that of your later> fight — *know / recent*

agèd Sire The black-magician hermit occurs in other romances, but Spenser makes Archimago allegorical of the papacy; various popes were accused by Protestant historians of black magic.

Ye all forwearied be: for what so strong,
But wanting> rest will also want of might? *lacking*
The Sunne that measures heaven all day long,
At night doth baite> his steedes the *Ocean* waves emong. *refresh*

33 Then with the Sunne take Sir, your timely rest,
And with new day new worke at once begin:
Untroubled night they say gives counsell best.
Right well Sir knight ye have advisèd bin,
(Quoth then that agèd man;) the way to win
Is wisely to advise:> now day is spent; *consider*
Therefore with me ye may take up your In> *lodging*
For this same night. The knight was well content:
So with that godly father to his home they went.

34 A little lowly Hermitage it was,
Downe in a dale, hard by a forests side,
Far from resort of people, that did pas
In travell to and froe: a little wyde> *away*
There was an holy Chappell edifyde,
Wherein the Hermite dewly wont to say
His holy things each morne and eventyde:
Thereby a Christall streame did gently play,
Which from a sacred fountaine wellèd forth alway.

35 Arrivèd there, the little house they fill,
Ne looke for entertainement,> where none was: *food*
Rest is their feast, and all things at their will;> *as they wish*
The noblest mind the best contentment has.
With faire discourse the evening so they pas:
For that old man of pleasing wordes had store,
And well could file his tongue as smooth as glas;
He told of Saintes and Popes, and evermore
He strowd an *Ave-Mary* after and before.

36 The drouping Night thus creepeth on them fast,
And the sad humour> loading their eye liddes, *heavy moisture*
As messenger of *Morpheus*° on them cast
Sweet slombring deaw, the which to sleepe them biddes.
Unto their lodgings then his guestes he riddes:> *leads*
Where when all drownd in deadly> sleepe he findes, *death-like*
He to his study goes, and there amiddes
His Magick bookes and artes of sundry kindes,
He seekes out mighty charmes, to trouble sleepy mindes.

37 Then choosing out few wordes most horrible,
(Let none them read) thereof did verses frame,
With which and other spelles like terrible,
He bad awake blacke *Plutoes* griesly Dame,°

Morpheus god of dreams

Plutoes . . . Dame Hecate, goddess of witchcraft, wife of Pluto, god of the underworld

And cursed heaven, and spake reprochfull shame
Of highest God, the Lord of life and light;
A bold bad man, that dar'd to call by name
Great *Gorgon,*° Prince of darknesse and dead night,
At which *Cocytus* quakes, and *Styx*° is put to flight.

38 And forth he cald out of deepe darknesse dred
Legions of Sprights, the which like little flyes
Fluttring about his ever damnèd hed,
A-waite whereto their service he applyes,°
To aide his friends, or fray> his enimies: *frighten*
Of those he chose out two, the falsest twoo,
And fittest for to forge true-seeming lyes;
The one of them he gave a message too,
The other by him selfe staide other worke to doo.

39 He making speedy way through spersèd> ayre, *dispersed*
And through the world of waters wide and deepe,
To *Morpheus* house doth hastily repaire.
Amid the bowels of the earth full steepe,
And low, where dawning day doth never peepe,
His dwelling is; there *Tethys*° his wet bed
Doth ever wash, and *Cynthia*° still> doth steepe *forever*
In silver deaw his ever-drouping hed,
Whiles sad Night over him her mantle black doth spred.

40 Whose double gates° he findeth lockèd fast,
The one faire fram'd of burnisht Yvory,
The other all with silver overcast;
And wakefull dogges before them farre do lye,
Watching to banish Care their enimy,
Who oft is wont to trouble gentle Sleepe.
By them the Sprite doth passe in quietly,
And unto *Morpheus* comes, whom drownèd deepe
In drowsie fit he findes: of nothing he takes keepe.> *heed*

41 And more, to lulle him in his slumber soft,
A trickling streame from high rocke tumbling downe
And ever-drizling raine upon the loft,
Mixt with a murmuring winde, much like the sowne> *sound*
Of swarming Bees, did cast him in a swowne:> *faint*
No other noyse, nor peoples troublous cryes,
As still are wont t'annoy the wallèd towne,
Might there be heard: but carelesse Quiet lyes,
Wrapt in eternall silence farre from enemyes.

Gorgon Demogorgon, the original god, who dwelt in darkness
Cocytus . . . Styx two of the five rivers of hell
A-waite . . . applyes wait to find out what job he wants them to do
Tethys wife of Ocean
Cynthia moon goddess
double gates In *Odyssey* XIX the two gates of sleep were of ivory and horn (here silver); false dreams issued from the ivory gate, true ones from the gate of horn.

42 The messenger approching to him spake,
But his wast wordes returnd to him in vaine:
So sound he slept, that nought mought› him awake. *might*
Then rudely he him thrust, and pusht with paine,
Whereat he gan to stretch: but he againe
Shooke him so hard, that forcèd him to speake.
As one then in a dreame, whose dryer› braine *too dry*
Is tost with troubled sights and fancies weake,
He mumbled soft, but would not all his silence breake.

43 The Sprite then gan more boldly him to wake,
And threatned unto him the dreaded name
Of *Hecate:* whereat he gan to quake,
And lifting up his lumpish head, with blame› *pain*
Halfe angry askèd him, for what he came.
Hither (quoth he) me *Archimago* sent,
He that the stubborne Sprites can wisely tame,
He bids thee to him send for his intent
A fit› false dreame, that can delude the sleepers sent.› *suitable / senses*

44 The God obayde, and calling forth straight way
A diverse› dreame out of his prison darke, *deceptive*
Delivered it to him, and down did lay
His heavie head, devoide of carefull carke,› *worry*
Whose sences all were straight benumbd and starke.› *paralyzed*
He backe returning by the Yvorie dore,
Remounted up as light as chearefull Larke,
And on his litle winges the dreame he bore
In hast unto his Lord, where he him left afore.

45 Who all this while with charmes and hidden artes,
Had made a Lady of that other Spright,
And fram'd of liquid ayre her tender partes
So lively, and so like› in all mens sight, *lifelike*
That weaker› sence it could have ravisht quight: *too weak*
The maker selfe for all his wondrous witt,
Was nigh beguilèd with so goodly sight:
Her all in white he clad, and over it
Cast a blacke stole, most like to seeme for *Una* fit.

46 Now when that ydle› dreame was to him brought, *mischievous*
Unto that Elfin knight he bad him fly,
Where he slept soundly void of evill thought,
And with false shewes abuse his fantasy,°
In sort as he him schoolèd privily:°
And that new creature borne without her dew,› *unnaturally*
Full of the makers guile, with usage sly

fantasy imagination (in sleep the reason no longer controls it)

In sort . . . privily in the manner in which he had secretly taught him

He taught to imitate that Lady trew,˃ *honest*
Whose semblance she did carrie under feignèd hew.˃ *form*

47 Thus well instructed, to their worke they hast,
And comming where the knight in slomber lay,
The one upon his hardy head him plast,
And made him dreame of loves and lustfull play,
That nigh his manly hart did melt away,
Bathèd in wanton blis and wicked joy:
Then seemèd him his Lady by him lay,
And to him playnd,˃ how that false wingèd boy° *complained*
Her chast hart had subdewd, to learne Dame pleasures toy.˃ *love play*

48 And she her selfe of beautie soveraigne Queene,
Faire *Venus* seemde unto his bed to bring
Her, whom he waking˃ evermore did weene˃ *when awake / believe*
To be the chastest flowre, that ay˃ did spring *ever*
On earthly braunch, the daughter of a king,
Now a loose Leman˃ to vile service bound: *mistress*
And eke the *Graces*° seemed all to sing,
Hymen iô Hymen,° dauncing all around,
Whilst freshest *Flora*° her with Yvie girlond crownd.

49 In this great passion of unwonted lust,
Or wonted feare of doing ought amis,
He started up, as seeming to mistrust
Some secret ill, or hidden foe of his:
Loe there before his face his Lady is,
Under blake stole hyding her bayted hooke,
And as halfe blushing offred him to kis,
With gentle blandishment and lovely looke,
Most like that virgin true, which for her knight him took.

50 All cleane dismayd to see so uncouth˃ sight, *unfamiliar*
And halfe enragèd at her shamelesse guise,
He thought have˃ slaine her in his fierce despight:˃ *to have / contempt*
But hasty heat tempring with sufferance˃ wise, *patience*
He stayde his hand, and gan himselfe advise˃ *consider*
To prove his sense, and tempt her faignèd truth.
Wringing her hands in wemens pitteous wise,
Tho˃ can˃ she weepe, to stirre up gentle ruth,˃ *then / did / pity*
Both for her noble bloud, and for her tender youth.

51 And said, Ah Sir, my liege Lord and my love,
Shall I accuse the hidden cruell fate,

false . . . boy Cupid
Graces Aglaia, Thalia, Euphrosyne (see VI.x. 22): daughters of Venus by Bacchus; here expressing in the false vision amity and joy as at marriage. Renaissance mythography held that "the unity of Venus is unfolded in the trinity of the Graces."
Hymen iô Hymen ritual shout at Roman wedding, invoking the god of marriage
Flora goddess of flowers; present with the Graces and Venus in Botticelli's *Primavera*

And mightie causes wrought in heaven above,
Or the blind God, that doth me thus amate,> *cast down*
For> hopèd love to winne me certaine hate? *instead of*
Yet thus perforce he bids me do, or die.
Die is my dew: yet rew> my wretched state *pity*
You, whom my hard avenging destinie
Hath made judge of my life or death indifferently.

52 Your owne deare sake forst me at first to leave
My Fathers kingdome, There she stopt with teares;
Her swollen hart her speach seemd to bereave,
And then againe begun, My weaker years> *extreme youth*
Captiv'd to fortune and frayle worldly feares,
Fly to your faith for succour and sure ayde:
Let me not dye in languor and long teares.
Why Dame (quoth he) what hath ye thus dismayd?
What frayes ye, that were wont to comfort me affrayd?

53 Love of your selfe, she said, and deare constraint> *strong compulsion*
Lets me not sleepe, but wast the wearie night
In secret anguish and unpittied plaint,
Whiles you in carelesse sleepe are drownèd quight.
Her doubtfull> words made that redoubted knight *questionable*
Suspect her truth: yet since no' untruth he knew,
Her fawning love with foule disdainefull spight
He would not shend,> but said, Deare dame I rew, *reprove*
That for my sake unknowne such griefe unto you grew.

54 Assure your selfe, it fell not all to ground;
For all so deare as life is to my hart,
I deeme your love, and hold me to you bound;
Ne let vaine feares procure your needlesse smart,
Where cause is none, but to your rest depart.
Not all content, yet seemd she to appease
Her mournefull plaintes, beguilèd of her art,
And fed with words, that could not chuse but please,
So slyding softly forth, she turnd as to her ease.

55 Long after lay he musing at her mood,
Much griev'd to thinke that gentle Dame so light,
For whose defence he was to shed his blood.
At last dull wearinesse of former fight
Having yrockt a sleepe his irkesome spright,> *spirit*
That troublous dreame gan freshly tosse his braine,
With bowres, and beds, and Ladies deare delight:
But when he saw his labour all was vaine,
With that misformèd> spright he backe returnd againe. *illicitly created*

Canto ii

[In canto ii, Red Cross, deceived by the demonic imitator of Una, is parted from the Truth; when he sees the spirit-Una again, this time in bed with a "young Squire" (another demon), he abandons her and leaves with the Dwarf. Una goes in pursuit, and is met by Archimago disguised as Red Cross—a false St. George. Meanwhile Red Cross meets a scarlet lady, Duessa (doubleness, duplicity, and multiplicity in contrast to Una's unfallen singleness), in the company of Sans Foy (Faithless). Red Cross kills the knight and consoles the lady, who tells him she is the daughter of the Roman ruler of the West; that is, as we gather from her scarlet dress (she is the Whore of Babylon) and her miter, she is the Roman church. (Una, the true and single church, is the daughter of one who ruled both East and West: the primitive universal church.) Duessa explains her relation to the false trinity of brothers, Sans Foy, Sans Joy, and Sans Loy (faithless, loveless, lawless), and falsely calls herself Fidessa. Despite the warning of Fradubio, Red Cross believes her; his lapse into sin and error also signifies the desertion by England of the true and original faith.]

The guilefull great Enchaunter parts
The Redcrosse Knight from Truth:
Into whose stead faire falsehood steps,
And works him wofull ruth.

1 By this the Northerne wagoner had set
His sevenfold teme behind the stedfast starre,°
That was in Ocean waves yet never wet,
But firme is fixt, and sendeth light from farre
To all, that in the wide deepe wandring arre:
And chearefull Chaunticlere˃ with his note shrill — *cock*
Had warnèd once, that *Phœbus* fiery carre˃ — *chariot*
In hast was climbing up the Easterne hill,
Full envious that night so long his roome˃ did fill. — *place*

2 When those accursèd messengers of hell,
That feigning dreame, and that faire-forgèd Spright
Came to their wicked maister, and gan tell
Their bootelesse˃ paines, and ill succeeding night: — *unavailing*
Who all in rage to see his skilfull might
Deluded˃ so, gan threaten hellish paine — *frustrated*
And sad *Proserpines*° wrath, them to affright.
But when he saw his threatning was but vaine,
He cast about, and searcht his balefull˃ bookes againe. — *pernicious*

3 Eftsoones˃ he tooke that miscreated faire, — *forthwith*
And that false other Spright, on whom he spred

the Northerne . . . starre The Constellation Boötes and the Big Dipper (the seven stars in the constellation Ursa Major) had set behind the Pole Star.

Proserpines Proserpina was the queen of hell

A seeming body of the subtile aire,
Like a young Squire, in loves and lusty-hed
His wanton dayes that ever loosely led,
Without regard of armes and dreaded fight:
Those two he tooke, and in a secret bed,
Covered with darknesse and misdeeming˃ night, *misjudging*
Them both together laid, to joy˃ in vaine delight. *take joy in*

4 Forthwith he runnes with feignèd faithfull hast
Unto his guest, who after troublous sights
And dreames, gan now to take more sound repast,˃ *rest*
Whom suddenly he wakes with fearefull frights,
As one aghast with feends or damnèd sprights,
And to him cals, Rise rise unhappy Swaine,˃ *young man*
That here wex˃ old in sleepe, whiles wicked wights˃ *grow / persons*
Have knit themselves in *Venus* shamefull chaine;
Come see, where your false Lady doth her honour staine.

5 All in amaze he suddenly up start˃ *leapt up*
With sword in hand, and with the old man went;
Who soone him brought into a secret part,
Where that false couple were full closely ment˃ *joined*
In wanton lust and lewd embracèment:
Which when he saw, he burnt with gealous fire,
The eye of reason was with rage yblent,˃ *blinded*
And would have slaine them in his furious ire,
But hardly˃ was restreinèd of that agèd sire. *with difficulty*

6 Returning to his bed in torment great,
And bitter anguish of his guiltie sight,
He could not rest, but did his stout heart eat,
And wast his inward gall with deepe despight,˃ *anger*
Irkesome˃ of life, and too long lingring night. *sick*
At last faire *Hesperus*° in highest skie
Had spent his lampe, and brought forth dawning light
Then up he rose, and clad him hastily;
The Dwarfe him brought his steed: so both away do fly.

7 Now when the rosy-fingred Morning faire,
Weary of aged *Tithones*° saffron bed,
Had spred her purple robe through deawy˃ aire, *dewy*
And the high hils *Titan*° discoverèd,
The royall virgin shooke off drowsy-hed,˃ *drowsiness*
And rising forth out of her baser bowre,
Lookt for her knight, who far away was fled,

Hesperus morning star
Tithones . . . bed Tithonus became the lover of Eos, the dawn; she conferred immortality on him but could not prevent his growing old.
Titan the sun

And for her Dwarfe, that wont to wait each houre;
Then gan she waile and weepe, to see that woefull stowre.˃ *difficult situation*

8 And after him she rode with so much speede
As her slow beast could make; but all in vaine:
For him so far had borne his light-foot steede,
Prickèd˃ with wrath and fiery fierce disdaine,˃ *spurred / indignation*
That him to follow was but fruitless paine;
Yet she her weary limbes would never rest,
But every hill and dale, each wood and plaine
Did search, sore grievèd in her gentle brest,
He so ungently left her, whom she lovèd best.

9 But subtill *Archimago*, when his guests
He saw divided into double parts,
And *Una* wandring in woods and forrests,
Th'end of his drift,˃ he praisd his divelish arts, *object of his scheme*
That had such might over true meaning harts;
Yet rests not so, but other meanes doth make,
How he may worke unto her further smarts:
For her he hated as the hissing snake,
And in her many troubles did most pleasure take.

10 He then devisde himselfe how to disguise;
For by his mightie science˃ he could take *magic art*
As many formes and shapes in seeming wise;˃ *in appearance*
As ever *Proteus*° to himselfe could make:
Sometime a fowle, sometime a fish in lake,
Now like a foxe, now like a dragon fell,˃ *terrible*
That of himselfe he oft for feare would quake,
And oft would flie away. O who can tell
The hidden power of herbes, and might of Magicke spell?

11 But now seemde best, the person to put on
Of that good knight, his late beguilèd guest:
In mighty armes he was yclad anon,
And silver shield: upon his coward brest
A bloudy crosse, and on his craven crest
A bounch˃ of haires discolourd˃ diversly: *bunch / dyed*
Full jolly˃ knight he seemde, and well addrest,˃ *handsome / fitted out*
And when he sate upon his courser free,˃ *noble*
Saint George himself ye would have deemèd him to be.

12 But he the knight, whose semblaunt˃ he did beare, *semblance*
The true *Saint George* was wandred far away,

Proteus Greek old man of the sea, who could change shape at will

Still flying from his thoughts and gealous feare;
Will was his guide, and griefe led him astray.
At last him chaunst to meete upon the way
A faithlesse Sarazin all arm'd to point,˃ *fully armed*
In whose great shield was writ with letters gay
Sans foy: full large of limbe and every joint
He was, and carèd not for God or man a point.

13 He had a faire companion of his way,
A goodly Lady clad in scarlot red,
Purfled˃ with gold and pearle of rich assay,˃ *fringed / valuation*
And like˃ a *Persian* mitre on her hed *a thing like*
She wore, with crownes and owches˃ garnishèd, *clasps, ornaments*
The which her lavish lovers to her gave;
Her wanton palfrey˃ all was overspred *saddle horse*
With tinsell˃ trappings, woven like a wave, *glittering*
Whose bridle rung with golden bels and bosses˃ brave. *knobs*

14 With faire disport˃ and courting dalliaunce *diversion*
She intertainde her lover all the way:
But when she saw the knight his speare advaunce,
She soone left off her mirth and wanton play,
And bad her knight addresse him to the fray:
His foe was nigh at hand. He prickt with pride
And hope to winne his Ladies heart that day,
Forth spurrèd fast: adowne his coursers side
The red bloud trickling staind the way, as he did ride.

15 The knight of the *Redcrosse* when him he spide,
Spurring so hote with rage dispiteous,˃ *cruel*
Gan fairely couch˃ his speare, and tówards ride: *lower for attack*
Soone meete they both, both fell˃ and furious, *fierce*
That daunted with their forces hideous,
Their steeds do stagger, and amazèd stand,
And eke themselves too rudely rigorous,
Astonied˃ with the stroke of their owne hand, *stunned*
Do backe rebut,˃ and each to other yeeldeth land. *recoil*

16 As when two rams stird with ambitious pride,
Fight for the rule of the rich fleecèd flocke,
Their hornèd fronts so fierce on either side
Do meete, that with the terrour of the shocke
Astonied both, stand sencelesse as a blocke,
Forgetfull of the hanging victory:˃ *victory in the balance*
So stood these twaine, unmovèd as a rocke,
Both staring fierce, and holding idèly˃ *uselessly*
The broken reliques of their former cruelty.

17 The *Sarazin* sore daunted with the buffe˃ *blow*
Snatcheth his sword, and fiercely to him flies;

Who well it wards, and quyteth˃ cuff with cuff: *repays*
Each others equal puìssaunce˃ envies,° *strength*
And through their iron sides with cruell spies
Does seeke to perce: repining˃ courage yields *fretful*
No foote to foe. The flashing fier flies
As from a forge out of their burning shields,
And streames of purple bloud new dies the verdant fields.

18 Curse on that Crosse (quoth then the *Sarazin*)
That keepes thy body from the bitter fit;
Dead long ygoe˃ I wote˃ thou haddest bin, *ago / know*
Had not that charme from thee forwarnèd it:
But yet I warne thee now assurèd sitt,
And hide thy head. Therewith upon his crest
With rigour so outragèous˃ he smitt, *violent*
That a large share it hewd out of the rest,
And glauncing downe his shield, from blame˃ him fairely blest.˃
injury / saved

19 Who thereat wondrous wroth, the sleeping spark
Of native vertue˃ gan eftsoones revive, *strength*
And at his haughtie helmet making mark,
So hugely stroke, that it the steel did rive,˃ *split*
And cleft his head. He tumbling downe alive,
With bloudy mouth his mother earth did kis,
Greeting his grave: his grudging˃ ghost did strive *complaining*
With the fraile flesh; at last it flitted is,
Whither the soules do fly of men, that live amis.

20 The Lady when she saw her champion fall,
Like the old ruines of a broken towre,
Staid not to waile his woefull funerall,
But from him fled away with all her powre;
Who after her as hastily gan scowre,˃ *run*
Bidding the Dwarfe with him to bring away
The *Sarazins* shield, signe of the conqueroure.
Her soone he overtooke, and bad to stay,
For present cause was none of dread her to dismay.

21 She turning backe with ruefull countenaunce,
Cride, Mercy mercy Sir vouchsafe to show
On silly˃ Dame, subject to hard mischaunce, *innocent*
And to your mighty will. Her humblesse low
In so ritch weedes and seeming glorious show,
Did much emmove˃ his stout heroïcke heart, *move*
And said, Deare dame, your suddein overthrow
Much rueth˃ me; but now put feare apart, *moves to pity*
And tell, both who ye be, and who that tooke your part.

envies rhymes with "flies"

22 Melting in teares, then gan she thus lament;
The wretched woman, whom unhappy howre
Hath now made thrall to your commandèment,
Before that angry heavens list˃ to lowre,˃ *chose / frown*
And fortune false betraide me to your powre
Was, (O what now availeth that I was!)
Borne the sole daughter of an Emperour,
He that the wide West under his rule has,
And high hath set his throne, where *Tiberis*˃ doth pas. *Tiber*

23 He in the first flowre of my freshest age,
Betrothèd me unto the onely haire
Of a most mighty king, most rich and sage;
Was never Prince so faithfull and so faire,
Was never Prince so meeke and debonaire;˃ *courteous*
But ere my hopèd day of spousall˃ shone, *marriage day*
My dearest Lord fell from high honours staire,
Into the hands of his accursed fone,˃ *foes*
And cruelly was slaine, that shall I ever mone.

24 His blessed body spoild˃ of lively breath, *robbed*
Was afterward, I know not how, convaid
And fro me hid: of whose most innocent death
When tidings came to me unhappy maid,
O how great sorrow my sad soule assaid.˃ *assailed*
Then forth I went his woefull corse˃ to find, *body*
And many years throughout the world I straid,
A virgin widow, whose deepe wounded mind
With love, long time did languish as the striken hind.

25 At last it chauncèd this proud *Sarazin*
To meete me wandring, who perforce me led
With him away, but yet could never win
The Fort, that Ladies hold in soveraigne dread.°
There lies he now with foule dishonour dead,
Who whiles he liv'de, was callèd proud *Sans foy*,
The eldest of three brethren, all three bred
Of one bad sire, whose youngest is *Sans joy*,
And twixt them both was borne the bloudy bold *Sans loy*.

26 In this sad plight, friendlesse, unfortunate,
Now miserable I *Fidessa* dwell,
Craving of you in pitty of my state,
To do none˃ ill, if please ye not do well. *no*
He in great passion all this while did dwell,
More busying his quicke eyes, her face to view,

The Fort . . . dread maidenhood, held in supreme reverence

Then his dull eares, to heare what she did tell;
And said, Faire Lady hart of flint would rew˃ *pity*
The undeservèd woes and sorrowes, which ye shew.

27 Henceforth in safe assuraunce may ye rest,
Having both found a new friend you to aid,
And lost an old foe, that did you molest:
Better new friend then an old foe is˃ said. *it is*
With chaunge of cheare˃ the seeming simple maid *countenance*
Let fall her eyen, as shamefast˃ to the earth, *modest*
And yeelding soft, in that she nought gain-said,
So forth they rode, he feining seemely merth,
And she coy lookes: so dainty˃ they say maketh derth. *such fastidiousness*

28 Long time they thus together traveilèd,
Till weary of their way, they came at last,
Where grew two goodly trees, that faire did spred
Their armes abroad, with gray mosse overcast,
And their greene leaves trembling with every blast,
Made a calme shadow far in compasse round:
The fearfull Shepheard often there aghast
Under them never sat, ne wont there sound
His mery oaten pipe, but shund th'unlucky ground.

29 But this good knight soone as he them can˃ spie, *did*
For the coole shade him thither hastly got:
For golden *Phœbus*° now ymounted hie,
From fiery wheeles of his faire chariot
Hurlèd his beame so scorching cruell hot,
That living creature mote˃ it not abide; *could*
And his new Lady it endurèd not.
There they alight, in hope themselves to hide
From the fierce heat, and rest their weary limbs a tide.˃ *spell*

30 Faire seemely pleasaunce each to other makes,
With goodly purposes˃ there as they sit: *conversation*
And in his falsèd˃ fancy he her takes *deceived*
To be the fairest wight, that livèd yit;
Which to expresse, he bends his gentle wit,
And thinking of those braunches greene to frame
A girlond for her dainty forehead fit,
He pluckt a bough; out of whose rift˃ there came *broken end*
Small drops of gory bloud, that trickled downe the same.

31 Therewith a piteous yelling voyce was heard,
Crying, O spare with guilty hands to teare

Phoebus sun god

My tender sides in this rough rynd embard,> *confined*
But fly, ah fly far hence away, for feare
Least> to you hap, that happened to me heare, *lest*
And to this wretched Lady, my deare love,
O too deare love, love bought with death too deare.
Astond> he stood, and up his haire did hove,>
astonished / stand on end
And with that suddein horror could no member move.

32 At last whenas the dreadfull passion> *passion of fear*
Was overpast, and manhood well awake,
Yet musing at the straunge occasiòn,
And doubting much his sence, he thus bespake;
What voyce of damnèd Ghost from *Limbo* lake,
Or guilefull spright wandring in empty aire,
Both which fraile men do oftentimes mistake,
Sends to my doubtfull eares these speaches rare,
And ruefull plaints, me bidding guiltlesse bloud to spare?

33 Then groning deepe, Nor damnèd Ghost, (quoth he,)
Nor guilefull sprite to thee these wordes doth speake,
But once a man *Fradubio,* now a tree,
Wretched man, wretched tree; whose nature weake,
A cruell witch her cursèd will to wreake,
Hath thus transformd, and plast> in open plaines, *placed*
Where *Boreas* doth blow full bitter bleake,
And scorching Sunne does dry my secret vaines:
For though a tree I seeme, yet cold and heat me paines.

34 Say on *Fradubio* then, or> man, or> tree, *either / or*
Quoth then the knight, by whose mischievous arts
Art thou misshapèd thus, as now I see?
He oft finds med'cine, who his griefe imparts;> *makes known*
But double griefs afflict concealing harts,
As raging flames who> striveth to suppresse. *him who*
The author then (said he) of all my smarts,> *pains*
Is one *Duessa* a false sorceresse,
That many errant> knights hath brought to wretchednesse. *wandering*

35 In prime of youthly yeares, when corage> hot *desire*
The fire of love and joy of chevalree
First kindled in my brest, it was my lot
To love this gentle Lady, whom ye see,
Now not a Lady, but a seeming tree;
With whom as once I rode accompanyde,
Me chauncèd of a knight encountred bee,
That had a like> faire Lady by his syde, *equally*
Like a faire Lady, but did fowle *Duessa* hyde.

36 Whose forgèd beauty he did take in hand,
All other Dames to have exceeded farre;
I in defence of mine did likewise stand,
Mine, that did then shine as the Morning starre:
So both to battell fierce arraungèd arre,
In which his harder˃ fortune was to fall — *very hard*
Under my speare: such is the dye˃ of warre: — *chance*
His Lady left as a prise martiall,˃ — *spoil of battle*
Did yield her comely person, to be at my call.

37 So doubly lov'd of Ladies unlike˃ faire, — *in different ways*
Th'one seeming such, the other such indeede,
One day in doubt I cast˃ for to compare, — *planned*
Whether˃ in beauties glorie did exceede; — *which*
A Rosy girlond was the victors meede:˃ — *reward*
Both seemde to win, and both seemde won to bee,
So hard the discord was to be agreede.
Frælissa was as faire, as faire mote˃ bee, — *could*
And ever false *Duessa* seemde as faire as shee.

38 The wicked witch now seeing all this while
The doubtfull ballaunce equally to sway,
What not by right, she cast to win by guile,
And by her hellish science˃ raisd streight way — *magic art*
A foggy mist, that overcast the day,
And a dull blast, that breathing on her face,
Dimmèd her former beauties shining ray,
And with foule ugly forme did her disgrace:˃ — *disfigure*
Then was she faire alone, when none was faire in place.°

39 Then cride she out, Fye, fye, deformèd wight,
Whose borrowed beautie now appeareth plaine
To have before bewitchèd all mens sight;
O leave her soone, or let her soone be slaine.
Her loathly visage viewing with disdaine,
Eftsoones I thought her such, as she me told,
And would have kild her; but with faignèd paine,
The false witch did my wrathfull hand withhold;
So left her, where she now is turnd to treèn mould.°

40 Thens forth I tooke *Duessa* for my Dame,
And in the witch unweeting˃ joyd long time, — *unwitting*
Ne ever wist,˃ but that she was the same, — *knew*
Till on a day (that day is every Prime,˃ — *springtime*
When Witches wont do penance for their crime)
I chaunst to see her in her proper hew,˃ — *shape, form*
Bathing her selfe in origane and thyme:°

when . . . place when there was no beautiful person around to judge her by
treèn mould shape of a tree
origane . . . thyme herbs used as remedies for skin diseases

A filthy foule old woman I did vew,
That ever to have toucht her, I did deadly rew.

41 Her neather˃ partes misshapen, monstruous, *lower*
Were hidd in water, that˃ I could not see, *so that*
But they did seeme more foule and hideous,
Then womans shape man would beleeve to bee.
Thens forth from her most beastly companie
I gan refraine, in minde to slip away,
Soone as appeard safe opportunitie:
For danger great, if not assur'd decay˃ *death*
I saw before mine eyes, if I were knowne to stray.

42 The divelish hag by chaunges of my cheare˃ *countenance*
Perceiv'd my thought, and drownd in sleepie night,
With wicked herbes and ointments did besmeare
My bodie all, through charmes and magicke might,
That all my senses were bereavèd quight:
Then brought she me into this desert waste,
And by my wretched lovers side me pight,˃ *placed*
Where now enclosed in wooden wals full faste,
Banisht from living wights, our wearie dayes we waste.

43 But how long time, said then the Elfin knight,
Are you in this misformèd house to dwell?
We may not chaunge (quoth he) this evil plight,
Till we be bathèd in a living well;
That is the terme prescribèd by the spell.
O how, said he, mote˃ I that well out find, *can*
That may restore you to your wonted well?˃ *well-being*
Time and suffised˃ fates to former kynd˃ *satisfied / nature*
Shall us restore, none else from hence may us unbynd.

44 The false *Duessa*, now *Fidessa* hight,˃ *called*
Heard how in vaine *Fradubio* did lament,
And knew well all was true. But the good knight
Full of sad feare and ghastly dreriment,˃ *grief*
When all this speech the living tree had spent,
The bleeding bough did thrust into the ground,
That from the bloud he might be innocent,
And with fresh clay did close the wooden wound:
Then turning to his Lady, dead with feare her found.

45 Her seeming dead he found with feignèd feare,
As˃ all unweeting˃ of that˃ well she knew,
As if / unknowing / that which
And paynd himselfe with busie care to reare
Her out of carelesse˃ swowne.˃ Her eyelids blew *unconscious / swoon*

And dimmèd sight with pale and deadly˃ hew *death-like*
At last she up gan lift: with trembling cheare
Her up he tooke, too simple˃ and too trew, *innocent*
And oft her kist. At length all passèd feare,°
He set her on her steede, and forward forth did beare.

Canto iii°

Forsaken Truth long seekes her love,
And makes the Lyon mylde,
Marres blind Devotions mart,˃ and fals *business*
In hand of leachour vylde.˃ *vile*

1 Nought is there under heav'ns wide hollownesse,
That moves more deare compassion of mind,
Then beautie brought t'unworthy˃ wretchednesse *undeserved*
Through envies snares or fortunes freakes˃ unkind: *whims*
I, whether lately through her brightnesse blind,
Or through alleageance and fast fealtie,
Which I do owe unto all woman kind,
Feele my heart perst˃ with so great agonie, *pierced*
When such I see, that all for pittie I could die.

2 And now it is empassionèd so deepe,
For fairest *Unaes* sake, of whom I sing,
That my fraile eyes these lines with teares do steepe,
To thinke how she through guilefull handeling,
Though true as touch,˃ though daughter of a king, *touchstone*
Though faire as ever living wight was faire,
Though nor in word nor deede ill meriting,
Is from her knight divorcèd in despaire
And her due loves deriv'd˃ to that vile witches share.˃ *transferred / portion*

3 Yet she most faithfull Ladie all this while
Forsaken, wofull, solitarie mayd
Farre from all peoples prease,˃ as in exile, *press*
In wildernesse and wastfull˃ deserts strayd, *waste*
To seeke her knight; who subtilly betrayd
Through that late vision, which th'Enchaunter wrought,
Had her abandoned. She of nought affrayd,
Through woods and wastnesse wide him daily sought;
Yet wishèd tydings none of him unto her brought.

4 One day nigh wearie of the yrkesome˃ way, *painful*
From her unhastie beast she did alight,

At length . . . feare her fear having quite passed
Canto iii Una, protected by a lion, shelters in the House of Blind Devotion (the Roman faith, attended by superstition and clerical greed). Archimago, dressed as Red Cross, joins her, but is defeated in combat by Sans Loy, who kills the lion and takes Una captive.

And on the grasse her daintie limbes did lay
In secret shadow, farre from all mens sight:
From her faire head her fillet˃ she undight,˃ *headband / unfastened*
And laid her stole aside. Her angels face
As the great eye of heaven shynèd bright,
And made a sunshine in the shadie place;
Did never mortall eye behold such heavenly grace.°

5 It fortunèd out of the thickest wood
A ramping˃ Lyon rushèd suddainly, *bounding*
Hunting full greedie after salvage˃ blood; *wild*
Soone as the royall virgin he did spy,
With gaping mouth at her ran greedily,
To have attonce devour'd her tender corse:˃ *body*
But to the pray when as he drew more ny,
His bloudie rage aswagèd with remorse,˃ *pity*
And with the sight amazd, forgat his furious forse.°

6 In stead thereof he kist her wearie feet,
And lickt her lilly hands with fawning tong,
As˃ he her wrongèd innocence did weet.˃ *as if / know of*
O how can beautie maister the most strong,
And simple truth subdue avenging wrong?
Whose yeelded pride and proud submissìon,
Still dreading death, when she had markèd long,
Her hart gan melt in great compassìon,
And drizling teares did shed for pure affectìon.

7 The Lyon Lord of everie beast in field,
Quoth she, his princely puissance doth abate,
And mightie proud to humble weake does yield,
Forgetfull of the hungry rage, which late
Him prickt, in pittie of my sad estate:˃ *condition*
But he my Lyon, and my noble Lord,
How does he find in cruell hart to hate
Her that him lov'd, and ever most adord,
As the God of my life? why hath he me abhord?

8 Redounding˃ teares did choke th'end of her plaint, *overflowing*
Which softly ecchoed from the neighbour wood;
And sad to see her sorrowfull constraint˃ *affliction*
The kingly beast upon her gazing stood;
With pittie calmd, downe fell his angry mood.
At last in close hart shutting up her paine,
Arose the virgin borne of heavenly brood,˃ *lineage*
And to her snowy Palfrey got againe,
To seeke her strayèd Champion, if she might attain.˃ *overtake*

er angels face . . . grace (ll. 6–9) a compari-
n of Una to The Woman Clothed with the
un (Revelation 12:1)

forgat . . . forse The lion who will not hurt a virgin is common in medieval literature. Allegorically this figure may represent natural law.

9 The Lyon would not leave her desolate,
But with her went along, as a strong gard
Of her chast person, and a faithfull mate
Of her sad troubles and misfortunes hard:
Still˃ when she slept, he kept both watch and ward, *always*
And when she wakt, he waited diligent,
With humble service to her will prepard:
From her faire eyes he tooke commaundement,
And ever by her lookes conceivèd her intent.

10 Long she thus traveiled through deserts wyde,
By which she thought her wandring knight shold pas,
Yet never shew of living wight espyde;
Till that at length she found the troden gras,
In which the tract˃ of peoples footing was, *track*
Under the steepe foot of a mountaine hore;˃ *gray*
The same she followes, till at last she has
A damzell spyde slow footing her before,
That on her shoulders sad˃ a pot of water bore. *heavily laden*

11 To whom approching she to her gan call,
To weet,˃ if dwelling place were night at hand; *know*
But the rude˃ wench her answer'd nought at all, *simple, uncultivated*
She could not heare, nor speake, nor understand;
Till seeing by her side the Lyon stand,
With suddaine feare her pitcher downe she threw,
And fled away: for never in that land
Face of faire Ladie she before did vew,
And that dread Lyons looke her cast in deadly˃ hew. *deathlike*

12 Full fast she fled, ne ever lookt behynd,
As if her life upon the wager lay,
And home she came, whereas˃ her mother blynd *where*
Sate in eternall night: nought could she say,
But suddaine catching hold, did her dismay
With quaking hands, and other signes of feare:
Who full of ghastly fright and cold affray,˃ *fear*
Gan shut the dore. By this arrivèd there
Dame *Una,* wearie Dame, and entrance did requere.˃ *request*

13 Which when none yeelded, her unruly Page
With his rude˃ clawes the wicket˃ open rent, *rough / gate*
And let her in; where of his cruell rage
Nigh dead with feare, and faint astonishment,○
She found them both in darkesome corner pent;
Where that old woman day and night did pray

faint astonishment a terror so great as to make her feel faint

Upon her beades devoutly penitent;
Nine hundred *Pater nosters* every day,
And thrise nine hundred *Aves* she was wont to say.

14 And to augment her painefull pennance more,
Thrise every weeke in ashes she did sit,
And next her wrinkled skin rough sackcloth wore,
And thrise three times did fast from any bit:˃ *bite of food*
But now for feare her beads she did forget.
Whose needlesse dread for to remove away,
Faire *Una* framèd words and count'nance fit:
Which hardly˃ doen,˃ at length she gan them pray, *with difficulty / done*
That in their cotage small that night she rest her may.

15 The day is spent, and commeth drowsie night,
When every creature shrowded is in sleepe;
Sad *Una* downe her laies in wearie plight,
And at her feet the Lyon watch doth keepe:
In stead of rest, she does lament, and weepe
For the late losse of her deare lovèd knight,
And sighes, and grones, and evermore does steepe
Her tender brest in bitter teares all night,
All night she thinks too long, and often lookes for light.

16 Now when *Aldeboran* was mounted hie
Above the shynie *Cassiopeias* chaire,°
And all in deadly sleepe did drownèd lie,
One knockèd at the dore, and in would fare;
He knockèd fast, and often curst, and sware,
That readie entrance was not at his call:
For on his backe a heavy load he bare
Of nightly stelths and pillage severall,
Which he had got abroad by purchase˃ criminall. *means of acquisition*

17 He was to weete˃ a stout and sturdie thiefe, *to wit*
Wont to robbe Churches of their ornaments,
And poore mens boxes˃ of their due reliefe, *poor-boxes*
Which given was to them for good intents;
The holy Saints of their rich vestiments
He did disrobe, when all men carelesse slept,
And spoild˃ the Priests of their habiliments,˃ *robbed / vestments*
Whiles none the holy things in safety kept;
Then he by cunning sleights˃ in at the window crept. *tricks*

18 And all that he by right or wrong could find,
Unto this house he brought, and did bestow

Aldeboran . . . chaire Cassiopeia's Chair is a constellation of five stars shaped like a rough *W*. Aldebaran is a star in the constellation Taurus, emitting alternate red and green light.

Upon the daughter of this woman blind,
Abessa° daughter of *Corceca*° slow,˃ *dull*
With whom he whoredome usd, that few did know,
And fed her fat with feast of offerings,
And plentie, which in all the land did grow;
Ne sparèd he to give her gold and rings:
And now he to her brought part of his stolen things.

19 Thus long the dore with rage and threats he bèt,˃ *beat*
Yet of those fearefull women none durst rize,
The Lyon frayèd˃ them, him in to let: *frightened*
He would no longer stay him to advize,˃ *reflect*
But open breakes the dore in furious wize,˃ *manner*
And entring is; when that disdainfull˃ beast *angry*
Encountring fierce, him suddaine doth surprize,
And seizing˃ cruell clawes on trembling brest, *fastening*
Under his Lordly foot him proudly hath supprest.

20 Him booteth not˃ resist, nor succour call, *It avails him not to*
His bleeding hart is in the vengers hand,
Who streight him rent in thousand peeces small,
And quite dismembred hath: the thirstie land
Drunke up his life; his corse left on the strand.
His fearefull friends weare out the wofull night,
Ne dare to weepe, nor seeme to understand
The heavie hap,˃ which on them is alight,˃ *bad luck / has alighted*
Affraid, least˃ to themselves the like mishappen might. *lest*

21 Now when broad day the world discoverèd has,
Up *Una* rose, up rose the Lyon eke,
And on their former journey forward pas,
In wayes unknowne, her wandring knight to seeke,
With paines farre passing that long wandring *Greeke*,°
That for his love refusèd deitie;
Such were the labours of this Lady meeke,
Still seeking him, that from her still did flie,
Then furthest from her hope, when most she weenèd˃ nie.
thought herself to be

22 Soone as she parted thence, the fearefull twaine,
That blind old woman and her daughter deare
Came forth, and finding *Kirkrapine*° there slaine,
For anguish great they gan to rend their heare,
And beat their brests, and naked flesh to teare.

Abessa probably standing for absenteeism in the clergy (Latin, *abesse:* to be away)
Corceca Blind Devotion
long . . . Greeke Odysseus (Ulysses) gave up the immortality offered him by Calypso and returned to his wife Penelope.

Kirkrapine Church robbery. It is not clear whether Spenser had in mind the spoliation of monasteries and churches during the Reformation or, more likely, the charge that the clergy had in the old days robbed the church by converting its wealth to their own use.

And when they both had wept and wayld their fill,
Then forth they ranne like two amazèd deare,
Halfe mad through malice, and revenging will,
To follow her, that was the causer of their ill.

23 Whom overtaking, they gan loudly bray,
With hollow howling, and lamenting cry,
Shamefully at her rayling all the way,
And her accusing of dishonesty,
That was the flowre of faith and chastity;
And still amidst her rayling, she did pray,
That plagues, and mischiefs, and long misery
Might fall on her, and follow all the way,
And that in endless error she might ever stray.

24 But when she saw her prayers nought prevaile,
She backe returnèd with some labour lost;
And in the way as she did weepe and waile,
A knight her met in mighty armes embost,> *enclosed*
Yet knight was not for all his bragging bost,> *boast*
But subtill *Archimag*, that *Una* sought
By traynes> into new troubles to have tost: *snares*
Of that old woman tydings he besought,
If that of such a Ladie she could tellen ought.

25 Therewith she gan her passion to renew,
And cry, and curse, and raile, and rend her heare,> *hair*
Saying, that harlot she too lately knew,
That causd her shed so many a bitter teare,
And so forth told the story of her feare:
Much seemèd he to mone her haplesse chaunce,
And after for that Ladie did inquere;
Which being taught, he forward gan advaunce
His fair enchaunted steed, and eke his charmèd launce.

26 Ere long he came, where *Una* traveild slow,
And that wilde Champion wayting> her besyde: *watching*
Whom seeing such, for dread he durst not show
Himselfe too nigh at hand, but turnèd wyde> *aside*
Unto an hill; from whence when she him spyde,
By his like seeming shield, her knight by name
She weend it was, and tòwards him gan ryde:
Approching nigh, she wist> it was the same, *thought*
And with faire fearefull humblesse> towards him shee came. *humility*

27 And weeping said, Ah my long lackèd Lord,
Where have ye been thus long out of my sight?
Much fearèd I to have bene quite abhord,
Or ought have done, that ye displeasen might,

That should as death unto my deare hart light:
For since mine eye your joyous sight did mis,
My chearefull day is turnd to chearelesse night,
And eke my night of death the shadow is;
But welcome now my light, and shining lampe of blis.

28 He thereto meeting said, My dearest Dame,
Farre be it from your thought, and fro my will,
To thinke that knighthood I so much should shame,
As you to leave, that have me lovèd still,
And chose in Faery court of meere˃ goodwill, *pure*
Where noblest knights were to be found on earth:
The earth shall sooner leave her kindly˃ skill *natural*
To bring forth fruit, and make eternall derth,
Then I leave you, my liefe,˃ yborne of heavenly berth. *beloved*

29 And sooth˃ to say, why I left you so long, *truth*
Was for to seeke adventure in strange place,
Where *Archimago* said˃ a felon strong *said to be*
To many knights did daily worke disgrace;˃ *harm*
But knight he now shall never more deface:˃ *destroy*
Good cause of mine excuse; that mote˃ ye please *may*
Well to accept, and evermore embrace
My faithfull service, that by land and seas
Have vowd you to defend, now then your plaint appease.˃ *subdue*

30 His lovely˃ words her seemd due recompence *loving*
Of all her passèd paines: one loving howre
For many yeares of sorrow can dispence:
A dram of sweet is worth a pound of sowre:
She has forgot, how many a wofull stowre˃ *hardship*
For him she late endur'd; she speakes no more
Of past: true is, that true love hath no powre
To looken backe; his eyes be fixt before.
Before her stands her knight, for whom she toyld so sore.

31 Much like, as when the beaten marinere,
That long hath wandred in the *Ocean* wide,
Oft soust˃ in swelling *Tethys*° saltish teare, *soaked*
And long time having tand his tawney hide
With blustring breath of heaven, that none can bide,
And scorching flames of fierce *Orions* hound,°
Soone as the port from farre he has espide,
His chearefull whistle merrily doth sound,
And *Nereus*° crownes with cups; his mates him pledg around.

Tethys wife of Oceanus, and as such identified with the sea
Orions hound Sirius, the Dog Star—ascendant in July and August, thus associated with heat
Nereus Aegean Sea god to whom sailors offered libations

32 Such joy made *Una,* when her knight she found;
And eke th'enchaunter joyous seemd no lesse,
Then the glad marchant, that does vew from ground
His ship farre come from watrie wildernesse,
He hurles out vowes, and *Neptune* oft doth blesse:
So forth they past, and all the way they spent
Discoursing of her dreadfull late distresse,
In which he askt her what the Lyon ment:
Who told her all that fell> in journey as she went. *happened*

33 They had not ridden farre, when they might see
One pricking> tòwards them with hastie heat, *spurring*
Full strongly armd, and on a courser free,
That through his fiercenesse fomèd all with sweat,
And the sharpe yron> did for anger eat, *bit*
When his hot ryder spurd his chauffed> side; *chafed*
His looke was sterne, and seemèd still to threat
Cruell revenge, which he in hart did hyde,
And on his shield *Sans loy* in bloudie lines was dyde.

34 When nigh he drew unto this gentle payre
And saw the Red-crosse, which the knight did beare,
He burnt in fire, and gan eftsoones> prepare *at once*
Himselfe to battell with his couchèd> speare. *lowered for attack*
Loth was that other, and did faint through feare,
To taste th'untryèd dint of deadly steele;
But yet his Lady did so well him cheare,
That hope of new good hap he gan to feele;
So bent> his speare, and spurnd his horse with yron heele. *aimed*

35 But that proud Paynim> forward came so fierce, *pagan*
And full of wrath, that with his sharp-head speare
Through vainely crossèd shield he quite did pierce,
And had his staggering steede not shrunke for feare,
Through shield and bodie eke> he should him beare:> *also / thrust*
Yet so great was the puissance of his push,
That from his saddle quite he did him beare:
He tombling rudely> downe to ground did rush, *awkwardly*
And from his gorèd wound a well of bloud did gush.

36 Dismounting lightly from his loftie steed,
He to him lept, in mind to reave> his life, *snatch away*
And proudly said, Lo there the worthie meed> *reward*
Of him, that slew *Sansfoy* with bloudie knife;
Henceforth his ghost freed from repining> strife *fretful*
In peace may passen over *Lethe*° lake,

Lethe the river of forgetfulness in Hades

When mourning altars purgd with enemies life,
The blacke infernall *Furies* doen˃ aslake:˃ *do / pacify*
Life from *Sansfoy* thou tookst, *Sansloy* shall from thee take.

37 Therewith in haste his helmet gan unlace,
Till *Una* cride, O hold that heavie hand,
Deare Sir, what ever that thou be in place:°
Enough is, that thy foe doth vanquisht stand
Now at thy mercy: Mercie not withstand:˃ *withhold*
For he is one˃ the truest knight alive, *one of (knights)*
Though conquered now he lie on lowly land,
And whilest him fortune favourd, faire did thrive
In bloudie field: therefore of life him not deprive.

38 Her piteous words might not abate his rage,
But rudely˃ rending up his helmet, would *roughly*
Have slaine him straight: but when he sees his age,
And hoarie head of *Archimago* old,
His hastie hand he doth amazèd hold,
And halfe ashamèd, wondred at the sight:
For the old man well knew he, though untold,
In charmes and magicke to have wondrous might,
Ne ever wont in field, ne in round lists˃ to fight. *jousting enclosures*

39 And said, Why *Archimago,* lucklesse syre,
What doe I see? what hard mishap is this,
That hath thee hither brought to taste mine yre?
Or thine the fault, or mine the error is,
In stead of foe to wound my friend amis?
He answered nought, but in a traunce still lay,
And on those guilefull dazèd eyes of his
The cloud of death did sit. Which doen away,°
He left him lying so, ne would no longer stay.

40 But to the virgin comes, who all this while
Amasèd stands, her selfe so mockt˃ to see *deceived*
By him, who has the guerdon˃ of his guile, *reward*
For so misfeigning her true knight to bee:
Yet is she now in more perplexitie,
Left in the hand of that same Paynim bold,
From whom her booteth not˃ at all to flie; *it avails her not*
Who by her cleanly garment catching hold,
Her from her Palfrey pluckt, her visage to behold.

41 But her fierce servant full of kingly awe
And high disdaine, whenas his soveraine Dame
So rudely handled by her foe he sawe,

what . . . place whoever you are **Which doen away** when his swoon was over

With gaping jawes full greedy at him came,
And ramping˃ on his shield, did weene˃ the same — *leaping / expect (to)*
Have reft˃ away with his sharpe rending clawes. — *torn*
But he was stout, and lust did now inflame
His corage more, that from his griping pawes
He hath his shield redeem'd,˃ and foorth his swerd he drawes. — *recovered*

42 O then too weake and feeble was the forse
Of salvage˃ beast, his puissance to withstand: — *savage*
For he was strong, and of so mightie corse,˃ — *body*
As ever wielded speare in warlike hand,
And feates of armes did wisely˃ understand. — *skillfully*
Eftsoones he percèd through his chaufèd˃ chest — *heated*
With thrilling˃ point of deadly yron brand,˃ — *piercing / sword*
And launcht˃ his Lordly hart: with death opprest — *lanced, pierced*
He roar'd aloud, whiles life forsooke his stubborne brest.°

43 Who now is left to keepe the forlorne maid
From raging spoile of lawlesse victors will?
Her faithfull gard remov'd, her hope dismaid,
Her selfe a yeelded pray to save or spill.
He now Lord of the field, his pride to fill,
With foule reproches, and disdainfull spight
Her vildly˃ entertaines,˃ and will or nill,˃
vilely / deals with / willy-nilly
Beares her away upon his courser light:
Her prayers nought prevaile, his rage is more of might.˃ — *all the greater*

44 And all the way, with great lamenting paine,
And piteous plaints she filleth his dull˃ eares, — *deaf*
That stony hart could riven have in twaine,
And all the way she wets with flowing teares:
But he enrag'd with rancor, nothing heares.
Her servile beast yet would not leave her so,
But followes her farre off, ne ought he feares,
To be partaker of her wandring woe,
More mild in beastly kind,˃ then that her beastly foe. — *nature*

Canto iv°

To sinfull house of Pride, Duessa
guides the faithfull knight,
Where brothers death to wreak˃ Sansjoy — *avenge*
doth chalenge him to fight.

whiles life . . . brest The death of the lion suggests the inadequacy of natural law.

Canto iv Duessa leads Red Cross into the House of Pride, ruled over by Lucifera (Pride, which was the sin of Lucifer) and her six counselors, representing the six other deadly sins. There follows a pageant of the Seven Deadly Sins, fairly conventional in detail but vigorously handled. Red Cross challenges Sans Joy, but Lucifer postpones their fight; they will meet next day in the lists. Duessa attaches herself to Sans Joy.

1 Young knight, what ever that dost armes professe,
And through long labours huntest after fame,
Beware of fraud, beware of ficklenesse,
In choice, and change of thy deare lovèd Dame,
Least thou of her beleeve too lightly blame,
And rash misweening˃ doe thy hart remove: *misunderstanding*
For unto knight there is no greater shame,
Then lightnesse and inconstancie in love;
That doth this *Redcrosse* knights ensample plainly prove.

2 Who after that he had fair *Una* lorne,˃ *abandoned*
Through light misdeeming of her loialtie,
And false *Duessa* in her sted˃ had borne, *place*
Callèd *Fidess,*' and so supposd to bee;
Long with her traveild, till at last they see
A goodly building, bravely garnishèd,
The house of mightie Prince it seemd to bee:
And towards it a broad high way that led,
All bare through peoples feet, which thither traveilèd.

3 Great troupes of people traveild thitherward
Both day and night, of each degree and place,˃ *rank*
But few returnèd, having scapèd˃ hard,˃ *escaped / with difficulty*
With balefull˃ beggerie, or foule disgrace, *miserable*
Which ever after in most wretched case,
Like loathsome lazars,˃ by the hedges lay. *lepers*
Thither *Duessa* bad him bend his pace:
For she is wearie of the toilesome way,
And also nigh consumèd is the lingring day.

4 A stately Pallace built of squarèd bricke,
Which cunningly was without morter laid,
Whose wals were high, but nothing strong, nor thick,
And golden foile all over them displaid,
That purest skye with brightnesse they dismaid:
High lifted up were many loftie towres,
And goodly galleries farre over laid,˃ *placed high above*
Full of faire windowes, and delightfull bowres;
And on the top a Diall told the timely howres.°

5 It was a goodly heape˃ for to behould, *building*
And spake the praises of the workmans wit;
But full great pittie, that so faire a mould˃ *shape*
Did on so weake foundation ever sit:
For on a sandie hill, that still did flit,˃ *give way*
And fall away, it mounted was full hie,

And on . . . howres indicating that the inhabitants of this house, which aspires to rivalry with heaven, are nevertheless subject to earthly time

That every breath of heaven shakèd it:
And all the hinder parts, that few could spie,
Were ruinous and old, but painted cunningly.

6 Arrivèd there they passèd in forth right;˃ *at once*
For still to all the gates stood open wide,
Yet charge of them was to a Porter hight˃ *entrusted*
Cald *Malvenù,*° who entrance none denide:
Thence to the hall, which was on every side
With rich array and costly arras˃ dight:˃ *tapestry / bedecked*
Infinite sorts of people did abide
There waiting long, to win the wishèd sight
Of her, that was the Lady of that Pallace bright.

7 By them they passe, all gazing on them round,
And to the Presence˃ mount; whose glorious vew *royal reception hall*
Their frayle amazèd senses did confound:
In living Princes court none ever knew
Such endlesse richesse, and so sumptuous shew;
Ne *Persia* selfe, the nourse of pompous pride
Like ever saw. And there a noble crew
Of Lordes and Ladies stood on every side,
Which with their presence faire, the place much beautifide.

8 High above all a cloth of State was spred,
And a rich throne, as bright as sunny day,
On which there sate most brave embellishèd
With royall robes and gorgèous array,
A mayden Queene, that shone as *Titans* ray,°
In glistring gold, and peerelesse pretious stone:
Yet her bright blazing beautie did assay˃ *attempt*
To dim the brightnesse of her glorious throne,
As envying her selfe, that too exceeding shone.

9 Exceeding shone, like *Phœbus* fairest childe,°
That did presume˃ his fathers firie wayne,˃ *take over / chariot*
And flaming mouthes of steedes unwonted wilde
Through highest heaven with weaker hand to rayne;˃ *rein*
Proud of such glory and advancement vaine,
While flashing beames do daze his feeble eyen,
He leaves the welkin way˃ most beaten plaine, *way through the sky*

Malvenù "Ill-come"—the opposite of "Welcome"
Titans ray Titan is Phoebus, the sun god.

Phoebus . . . childe Phaeton, who tried to drive the chariot of his father, the sun god

And rapt˃ with whirling wheeles, inflames the skyen,˃ *carried away / skies*
With fire not made to burne, but fairely for to shyne.

10 So proud she shynèd in her Princely state,
Looking to heaven; for earth she did disdayne,
And sitting high; for lowly˃ she did hate: *all that is lowly*
Lo underneath her scornefull feete, was layne
A dreadfull Dragon with an hideous trayne,˃ *tail*
And in her hand she held a mirrhour bright,
Wherein her face she often vewèd fayne,
And in her selfe-lov'd semblance tooke delight;
For she was wondrous faire, as any living wight.°

11 Of griesly *Pluto* she the daughter was,
And sad *Proserpina*° the Queene of hell;
Yet did she thinke her pearelesse worth to pas˃ *surpass*
That parentage, with pride so did she swell,
And thundring *Jove*, that high in heaven doth dwell,
And wield the world, she claymèd for her syre,
Or if that any else did *Jove* excell:
For to the highest she did still aspyre,
Or if ought higher were then that, did it desyre.

12 And proud *Lucifera* men did her call,
That made her selfe a Queene, and crownd to be,
Yet rightfull kingdome she had none at all,
Ne heritage of native soveraintie,
But did usurpe with wrong and tyrannie
Upon the scepter, which she now did hold:
Ne ruld her Realmes with lawes, but pollicie,˃ *political trickery*
And strong advizement of six wisards old,
That with their counsels bad her kingdome did uphold.

13 Soone as the Elfin knight in presence came,
And false *Duessa* seeming Lady faire,
A gentle Husher,˃ *Vanitie* by name *usher*
Made rowme, and passage for them did prepaire:
So goodly brought them to the lowest staire
Of her high throne, where they on humble knee
Making obeyssance, did the cause declare,
Why they were come, her royall state to see,
To prove˃ the wide report of her great Majestee. *test*

For she . . . wight She is Lucifera, named for Lucifer (Satan), who was also beautiful.

Proserpina abducted by Pluto and made to spend half the year as his queen

14 With loftie eyes, halfe loth to looke so low,
She thankèd them in her disdainefull wise,
Ne other grace vouchsafèd them to show
Of Princesse worthy, scarse them bad˃ arise. *bade*
Her Lordes and Ladies all this while devise˃ *prepare*
Themselves to setten forth to straungers sight:
Some frounce˃ their curlèd haire in courtly guise, *wave*
Some prancke˃ their ruffes, and others trimly dight˃ *show off / arrange*
Their gay attire: each others greater pride does spight.

15 Goodly they all that knight do entertaine,
Right glad with him to have increast their crew:
But to *Duess'* each one himselfe did paine
All kindnesse and faire courtesie to shew;
For in that court whylome˃ her well they knew; *formerly*
Yet the stout Faerie mongst the middest crowd
Thought all their glorie vaine in knightly vew,
And that great Princesse too exceeding prowd,
That to strange knight no better countenance allowd.

16 Suddein upriseth from her stately place
The royall Dame, and for her coche˃ doth call: *coach*
All hurtlen˃ forth, and she with Princely pace, *jostle*
As faire *Aurora*° in her purple pall,˃ *cloak*
Out of the East the dawning day doth call:
So forth she comes: her brightnesse brode˃ doth blaze; *abroad*
The heapes of people thronging in the hall,
Do ride each other, upon her to gaze:
Her glorious glitterand˃ light doth all mens eyes amaze. *glittering*

17 So forth she° comes, and to her coche does clyme,
Adornèd all with gold, and girlonds gay,
That seemd as fresh as *Flora* in her prime,
And strove to match, in royall rich array,
Great *Junoes* golden chaire, the which they say
The Gods stand gazing on, when she does ride
To *Joves* high house through heavens braspavèd way
Drawne of faire Pecocks,° that excell in pride,
And full of *Argus* eyes° their tailes dispredden wide.

Aurora goddess of dawn
she Lucifera
Pecocks Juno's chariot was represented as drawn by peacocks.
Argus eyes Argus had 100 eyes, and so Juno put him to watch over Io, a paramour of Jupiter's; Jupiter had Mercury lull all the eyes to sleep and kill Argus; Juno put his eyes on the peacock's tail.

18 But this was drawne of six unequall˃ beasts, *dissimilar*
On which her six sage Counsellours did ryde,
Taught to obay their bestiall beheasts,°
With like conditions to their kinds˃ applyde: *natures*
Of which the first, that all the rest did guyde,
Was sluggish *Idlenesse* the nourse of sin;
Upon a slouthfull Asse he chose to ryde,
Arayd in habit blacke, and amis˃ thin, *hood*
Like to an holy Monck, the service to begin.

19 And in his hand his Portesse˃ still he bare, *breviary*
That much was worne, but therein little red,
For of devotion he had little care,
Still drownd in sleepe, and most of his dayes ded;
Scarse could he once uphold his heavie hed,
To looken, whether it were night or day:
May seeme the wayne˃ was very evill led, *coach, car*
When such an one had guiding of the way,
That knew not, whether right he went, or else astray.

20 From wordly cares himselfe he did esloyne,˃ *withdraw*
And greatly shunnèd manly exercise,
From every worke he chalengèd essoyne˃, *excuse*
For contemplation sake: yet otherwise,
His life he led in lawlesse riotise;
By which he grew to grievous malady;
For in his lustlesse˃ limbs through evill guise˃ *feeble / way of life*
A shaking fever raignd continually:
Such one was *Idlenesse*, first of this company.

21 And by his side rode loathsome *Gluttony*,
Deformèd creature, on a filthie swyne,
His belly was up-blowne with luxury,
And eke with fatnesse swollen were his eyne,
And like a Crane° his necke was long and fyne,˃ *thin*
With which he swallowed up excessive feast,
For want whereof poore people oft did pyne;˃ *starve*
And al the way, most like a brutish beast,
He spuèd up his gorge, that all did him deteast.

22 In greene vine leaves he was right fitly clad;
For other clothes he could not weare for heat,
And on his head an yvie girland had,
From under which fast trickled downe the sweat:
Still as he rode, he somewhat˃ still did eat, *something*
And in his hand did beare a bouzing can,
Of which he supt so oft, that on his seat

Taught . . . beheasts i.e. they were instructed to obey the animals, not control them
Crane Like most of the other detail, this is traditional; Gluttony was represented as having a long thin crane's neck, for the better enjoyment of food.

His dronken corse he scarse upholden can,
In shape and life more like a monster, then a man.°

23 Unfit he was for any worldly thing,
And eke unhable once˃ to stirre or go,˃ *at all / walk*
Not meet to be of counsell to a king,
Whose mind in meat and drinke was drownèd so,
That from his friend he seldome knew his fo:
Full of diseases was his carcas blew,˃ *livid*
And a dry˃ dropsie through his flesh did flow: *thirst-producing*
Which by misdiet daily greater grew:
Such one was *Gluttony*, the second of that crew.

24 And next to him rode lustfull *Lechery*,
Upon a bearded Goat, whose rugged haire,
And whally˃ eyes (the signe of gelosy,) *green-tinged*
Was like the person selfe, whom he did beare:
Who rough, and blacke, and filthy did appeare,
Unseemely man to please faire Ladies eye;
Yet he of Ladies oft was lovèd deare,
When fairer faces were bid standen by:˃ *aside*
O who does know the bent of womens fantasy?

25 In a greene gowne he clothèd was full faire,
Which underneath did hide his filthinesse,
And in his hand a burning hart he bare,
Full of vaine follies, and new fanglenesse˃: *vain novelty*
For he was false, and fraught with ficklenesse,
And learnèd had to love with secret lookes,
And well could˃ daunce, and sing with ruefulnesse, *knew how to*
And fortunes tell, and read in loving bookes,
And thousand other wayes, to bait his fleshly hookes.

26 Inconstant man, that lovèd all he saw,
And lusted after all, that he did love,
Ne would his looser˃ life be tide to law, *too loose*
But joyd weake wemens hearts to tempt and prove˃ *try*
If from their loyall loves he might them move;
Which lewdnesse fild him with reprochfull paine
Of that fowle evill,˃ which all men reprove, *syphilis*
That rots the marrow, and consumes the braine:
Such one was *Lecherie*, the third of all this traine.

27 And greedy *Avarice* by him did ride,
Upon a Camell loaden all with gold;
Two iron coffers hong on either side,
With precious mettall full, as they might hold,

In greene . . . man (stanza 22) modeled on Silenus, gluttonous and drunken attendant of Bacchus

And in his lap an heape of coine he told;> *counted*
For of his wicked pelfe his God he made,
And unto hell him selfe for money sold;
Accursed usurie was all his trade,
And right and wrong ylike in equall ballaunce waide.

28 His life was nigh unto deaths doore yplast,
And thred-bare cote, and cobled shoes he ware,
Ne scarse good morsell all his life did tast,
But both from backe and belly still did spare,
To fill his bags, and richesse to compare;> *acquire*
Yet chylde ne kinsman living had he none
To leave them to; but thorough> daily care *through*
To get, and nightly feare to lose his owne,
He led a wretched life unto him selfe unknowne.

29 Most wretched wight, whom nothing might suffise,
Whose greedy lust did lacke in greatest store,> *plenty*
Whose need had end, but no end covetise,
Whose wealth was want, whose plenty made him pore,
Who had enough, yet wishèd ever more;
A vile disease, and eke in foote and hand
A grievous gout tormented him full sore,
That well he could not touch, nor go, nor stand:
Such one was *Avarice,* the fourth of this faire band.

30 And next to him malicious *Envie* rode,
Upon a ravenous wolfe, and still did chaw
Betweene his cankred teeth a venemous tode,
That all the poison ran about his chaw;> *jaw*
But inwardly he chawèd his owne maw> *guts*
At neighbours wealth, that made him ever sad;
For death it was, when any good he saw,
And wept, that cause of weeping none he had,
But when he heard of harme, he wexèd wondrous glad. *grew*

31 All in a kirtle of discolourd say> *serge*
He clothèd was, ypainted full of eyes;
And in his bosome secretly there lay
An hatefull Snake, the which his taile uptyes
In many folds, and mortall sting implyes.> *enfolds*
Still as he rode, he gnasht his teeth, to see
Those heapes of gold with griple> Covetyse, *grasping*
And grudgèd at the great felicitie
Of proud *Lucifera,* and his owne companie.

32 He hated all good workes and vertuous deeds,
And him no lesse, that any like did use,°
And who with gracious bread the hungry feeds,

that . . . use that did such good deeds

His almes for want of faith he doth accuse;
So every good to bad he doth abuse:
And eke the verse of famous Poets witt
He does backebite, and spightfull poison spues
From leprous mouth on all, that ever writt:
Such one vile *Envie* was, that fifte in row did sitt.

33 And him beside rides fierce revenging *Wrath,*
Upon a Lion, loth for to be led;
And in his hand a burning brond> he hath, *sword*
The which he brandisheth about his hed;
His eyes did hurle forth sparkles fiery red,
And starèd sterne on all, that him beheld,
As ashes pale of hew and seeming ded;
And on his dagger still his hand he held,
Trembling through hasty rage, when choler> in him sweld. *anger*

34 His ruffin> raiment all was staind with blood, *disorderly*
Which he had spilt, and all to rags yrent,> *torn*
Through unadvizèd> rashnesse woxen wood;> *unreflecting / mad*
For of his hands he had no government,
Ne car'd for> bloud in his avengement: *cared about*
But when the furious fit was overpast,
His cruell facts> he often would repent; *deeds*
Yet wilfull man he never would forecast,> *foretell*
How many mischieves should ensue his heedlesse hast.

35 Full many mischiefes follow cruell *Wrath;*
Abhorrèd bloudshed, and tumultuous strife,
Unmanly murder, and unthrifty scath,> *damage*
Bitter despight, with rancours rusty knife,
And fretting griefe the enemy of life;
All these, and many evils moe> haunt ire, *more*
The swelling Splene, and Frenzy raging rife,
The shaking Palsey, and Saint *Fraunces* fire:> *erysipelas*
Such one was *Wrath,* the last of this ungodly tire.

36 And after all, upon the wagon beame> *shaft*
Rode *Sathan,* with a smarting whip in hand,
With which he forward lasht the laesie teme,
So oft as *Slowth* still in the mire did stand.
Huge routs of people did about them band,
Showting for joy, and still before their way
A foggy mist had covered all the land;
And underneath their feet, all scattered lay
Dead sculs and bones of men, whose life had gone astray.

37 So forth they marchen in this goodly sort,
To take the solace> of the open aire, *recreation*
And in fresh flowring fields themselves to sport;

Emongst the rest rode that false Lady faire,
The fowle *Duessa,* next unto the chaire
Of proud *Lucifera,* as one of the traine:
But that good knight would not so nigh repaire,
Him selfe estraunging from their joyaunce vaine,
Whose fellowship seemd far unfit for warlike swaine.

38 So having solacèd themselves a space
With pleasaunce of the breathing˃ fields yfed, *fragrant*
They backe returnèd to the Princely Place;
Whereas˃ an errant˃ knight in armes yclad, *where / wandering*
And heathnish shield, wherein with letters red
Was writ *Sans joy,* they new arrivèd find:
Enflam'd with fury and fiers hardy-hed,˃ *boldness*
He seemd in hart to harbour thoughts unkind,
And nourish bloudy vengeaunce in his bitter mind.

39 Who when the shamèd shield of slaine *Sans foy*
He spide with that same Faery champions page,
Bewraying˃ him, that did of late destroy *accusing*
His eldest brother, burning all with rage
He to him leapt, and that same envious gage˃ *envied token*
Of victors glory from him snatcht away:
But th'Elfin knight, which ought˃ that warlike wage,˃ *owned / reward*
Disdaind to loose the meed˃ he wonne in fray, *reward*
And him rencountring˃ fierce, reskewd the noble pray. *engaging*

40 Therewith they gan to hurtlen˃ greedily,˃ *jostle / fiercely*
Redoubted˃ battaile ready to darrayne,˃ *terrible / engage in*
And clash their shields, and shake their swords on hy,
That with their sturre they troubled all the traine;˃ *company*
Till that great Queene upon eternall paine
Of high displeasure, that ensewen˃ might, *ensue*
Commaunded them their fury to refraine,
And if that either to that shield had right,
In equall lists they should the morrow next it fight.

41 Ah dearest Dame, (quoth then the Paynim bold,)
Pardon the errour of enragèd wight,
Whom great griefe made forget the raines to hold
Of reasons rule, to see this recreant knight,
No knight, but treachour˃ full of false despight *traitor*
And shamefull treason, who through guile hath slayn
The prowest˃ knight, that ever field did fight, *bravest*
Even stout *Sans foy* (O who can then refrayn?)
Whose shield he beares renverst,˃ the more to heape disdayn.
upside down

42 And to augment the glorie of his guile,
His dearest love the faire *Fidessa* loe
Is there possessèd of the traytour vile,
Who reapes the harvest sowen by his foe,
Sowen in bloudy field, and bought with woe:
That brothers hand shall dearely well requight
So be, O Queene, you equall> favour showe. *impartial*
Him litle answerd th'angry Elfin knight;
He never meant with words, but swords to plead his right.

43 But threw his gauntlet as a sacred pledge,
His cause in combat the next day to try:
So been they parted both, with harts on edge,
To be aveng'd each on his enimy.
That night they pas in joy and jollity,
Feasting and courting both in bowre and hall;
For Steward was excessive *Gluttonie,*
Which doen, the Chamberlain *Slowth* did to rest them call.

44 Now whenas darkesome night had all displayd> *spread out*
Her coleblacke curtein over brightest skye,
The warlike youthes on dayntie couches layd,
Did chace away sweet sleepe from sluggish eye,
To muse on meanes of hopèd victory.
But whenas *Morpheus*° had with leaden mace
Arrested all that courtly company,
Up-rose *Duessa* from her resting place,
And to the Paynims lodging comes with silent pace.

45 Whom broad awake she finds, in troublous fit,> *mood*
Forecasting,> how his foe he might annoy, *planning*
And him amoves> with speaches seeming fit: *moves*
Ah deare *Sans joy,* next dearest to *Sans foy,*
Cause of my new griefe, cause of my new joy,
Joyous, to see his ymage in mine eye,
And greev'd, to thinke how foe did him destroy,
That was the flowre of grace and chevalrye;
Lo his *Fidessa* to thy secret faith I flye.

46 With gentle wordes he can> her fairely greet, *did*
And bad say on> the secret of her hart. *bade her tell*
Then sighing soft, I learne that litle sweet
Oft tempred is (quoth she) with muchell> smart: *great*
For since my brest was launcht> with lovely dart *pierced*
Of deare *Sansfoy,* I never joyèd howre,
But in eternall woes my weaker> hart *too weak*
Have wasted, loving him with all my powre,
And for his sake have felt full many an heavie stowre.> *anxious time*

Morpheus god of sleep

47 At last when perils all I weenèd past,
And hop'd to reape the crop of all my care,
Into new woes unweeting I was cast,
By this false faytor,˃ who unworthy ware — *villain, impostor*
His worthy shield, whom he with guilefull snare
Entrappèd slew, and brought to shamefull grave.
Me silly˃ maid away with him he bare, — *innocent, simple*
And ever since hath kept in darksome cave,
For that˃ I would not yeeld, that˃ to *Sans-foy* I gave. — *because / that which*

48 But since faire Sunne hath sperst˃ that lowring clowd, — *dispersed*
And to my loathèd life now shewes some light,
Under your beames I will me safely shrowd,
From dreaded storme of his disdainfull spight:
To you th'inheritance belongs by right
Of brothers prayse, to you eke longs˃ his love. — *belongs*
Let not his love, let not his restlesse spright
Be unreveng'd, that calles to you above
From wandring *Stygian* shores,° where it doth endlesse move.

49 Thereto said he, Faire Dame be nought dismaid
For sorrowes past; their griefe is with them gone:
Ne yet of present perill be affraid;
For needlesse feare did never vantage˃ none, — *profit*
And helplesse˃ hap it booteth not to mone. — *unavoidable*
Dead is *Sans-foy*, his vitall˃ paines are past, — *relating to life*
Though greevèd ghost for vengeance deepe do grone:
He lives, that shall him pay his dewties˃ last, — *rites*
And guiltie Elfin bloud shall sacrifice in hast.

50 O but I feare the fickle freakes˃ (quoth shee) — *whims*
Of fortune false, and oddes of armes in field.
Why dame (quoth he) what oddes can ever bee,
Where both do fight alike, to win or yield?
Yea but (quoth she) he beares a charmèd shield,
And eke enchaunted armes, that none can perce,
Ne none can wound the man, that does them wield.
Charmd or enchaunted (answerd he then ferce˃) — *fiercely*
I no whit reck, ne you the like need to reherce.˃ — *recount*

51 But faire *Fidessa*, sithens˃ fortunes guile, — *since*
Or enimies powre hath now captivèd you,
Returne from whence ye came, and rest a while
Till morrow next, that I the Elfe subdew,
And with *Sans-foyes* dead dowry you endew.˃ — *endow*
Ay me, that is a double death (she said)

Stygian shores the banks of the Styx, a river in hell which dead souls must cross

With proud foes sight my sorrow to renew:
Where ever yet I be, my secrete aid
Shall follow you. So passing forth she him obaid.

Canto v°

The faithfull knight in equall field
subdewes his faithlesse foe,
Whom false Duessa saves, and for
his cure to hell does goe.

1 The noble hart, that harbours vertuous thought,
And is with child of glorious great intent,
Can never rest, untill it forth have brought
Th'eternall brood of glorie excellent:°
Such restlesse passion did all night torment
The flaming corage of that Faery knight,
Devizing,˃ how that doughtie turnament *planning*
With greatest honour he atchieven might;
Still˃ did he wake, and still did watch for dawning light. *always*

2 At last the golden Orientall gate
Of greatest heaven gan to open faire,
And *Phœbus* fresh, as bridegrome to his mate,
Came dauncing forth, shaking his deawie haire:
And hurld his glistring beames through gloomy aire.
Which when the wakeful Elfe perceiv'd, streight way
He started up, and did him selfe prepaire,
In sun-bright armes, and battailous˃ array: *warlike*
For with that Pagan proud he combat will that day.

3 And forth he comes into the commune hall,
Where earely waite him many a gazing eye,
To weet˃ what end to straunger knights may fall. *learn*
There many Minstrales maken melody,
To drive away the dull melàncholy,
And many Bardes, that to the trembling chord
Can tune their timely˃ voyces cunningly, *measured*
And many Chroniclers, that can record
Old loves, and warres for Ladies doen by many a Lord.

4 Soone after comes the cruell Sarazin,
In woven maile all armèd warily,
And sternly lookes at him, who not a pin
Does care for looke of living creatures eye.

Canto v In this canto, Duessa's attempt to find help for Sansfoy is the occasion of an elaborate digression on hell and the punishment of presumption and pride.

The noble . . . excellent (ll. 1–4) i.e. virtue must be exhibited in action, or it will wither—a commonplace frequently expressed in, for example, Shakespeare

They bring them wines of *Greece* and *Araby*,
And daintie spices fetcht from furthest *Ynd*,
To kindle heat of corage privily:˃ *inwardly*
And in the wine a solemne oth they bynd
T'observe the sacred lawes of armes, that are assynd.˃ *prescribed*

5 At last forth comes that far renowmèd Queene,
With royall pomp and Princely majestie;
She is ybrought unto a palèd˃ greene, *fenced*
And placèd under stately canapee,˃ *canopy*
The warlike feates of both those knights to see.
On th'other side in all mens open vew
Duessa placèd is, and on a tree
Sans-foy his shield is hangd with bloudy hew:
Both those the lawrell girlonds to the victor dew.

6 A shrilling trompet sownded from on hye,
And unto battaill bad them selves addresse:
Their shining shieldes about their wrestes˃ they tye, *wrists*
And burning blades about their heads do blesse,˃ *brandish*
The instruments of wrath and heavinesse:
With greedy force each other doth assayle,
And strike so fiercely, that they do impresse
Deepe dinted furrowes in the battred mayle;
The yron walles to ward their blowes are weake and fraile.

7 The Sarazin was stout, and wondrous strong,
And heapèd blowes like yron hammers great:
For after bloud and vengeance he did long.
The knight was fiers, and full of youthly heat:
And doubled strokes, like dreaded thunders threat:
For all for prayse and honour he did fight.
Both stricken strike, and beaten both do beat,
That from their shields forth flyeth firie light,
And helmets hewen deepe, shew marks of eithers might.

8 So th'one for wrong, the other strives for right:
As when a Gryfon° seizèd of˃ his pray, *in possession of*
A Dragon fiers encountreth in his flight,
Through widest ayre making his ydle way,
That would his rightfull ravine˃ rend away: *booty, prey*
With hideous horrour both together smight,
And souce˃ so sore, that they the heavens affray:˃
strike heavily / frighten
The wise Southsayer seeing so sad sight,
Th'amazèd vulgar˃ tels of warres and mortall fight. *common people*

Gryfon the griffin, legendary monster with a man's body and an eagle's head and wings

9 So th'one for wrong, the other strives for right,
And each to deadly shame would drive his foe:
The cruell steele so greedily doth bight
In tender flesh, that streames of bloud down flow,
With which the armes, that earst˃ so bright did show, *previously*
Into a pure vermillion now are dyde:
Great ruth in all the gazers harts did grow,
Seeing the gorèd woundes to gape so wyde.
That victory they dare not wish to either side.

10 At last the Paynim chaunst to cast his eye,
His suddein eye, flaming with wrathfull fyre,
Upon his brothers shield, which hong thereby:
Therewith redoubled was his raging yre,
And said, Ah wretched sonne of wofull syre,
Doest thou sit wayling by black *Stygian* lake,
Whilest here thy shield is hangd for victors hyre,˃ *reward*
And sluggish german˃ doest thy forces slake,˃ *brother / slacken*
To after-send his foe, that him may overtake?

11 Goe caytive Elfe, him quickly overtake,
And soone redeeme from his long wandring woe;
Goe guiltie ghost, to him my message make,
That I his shield have quit˃ from dying foe. *redeemed*
Therewith upon his crest he stroke him so,
That twise he reelèd, readie twise to fall;
End of the doubtfull battell deemèd tho˃ *then*
The lookers on, and lowd to him can˃ call *did*
The false *Duessa,* Thine the shield, and I, and all.

12 Soone as the Faerie heard his Ladie speake,
Out of his swowning dreame he gan awake,
And quickning faith, that earst was woxen weake,°
The creeping deadly cold away did shake:
Tho˃ mov'd with wrath, and shame, and Ladies sake, *then*
Of all attonce he cast avengd to bee,
And with so'exceeding furie at him strake,
That forcèd him to stoupe upon his knee;
Had he not stoupèd so, he should have cloven bee,

13 And to him said, Goe now proud Miscreant,
Thy selfe thy message doe to german deare,
Alone he wandring thee too long doth want:
Goe say, his foe thy shield with his doth beare.
Therewith his heavie hand he high gan reare,
Him to have slaine; when loe a darkesome clowd
Upon him fell: he no where doth appeare,

earst . . . weake had previously grown weak

But vanisht is. The Elfe him cals alowd,
But answer none receives: the darknes him does shrowd.°

14 In haste *Duessa* from her place arose,
And to him running said, O prowest˃ knight, *most valiant*
That ever Ladie to her love did chose,˃ *choose*
Let now abate the terror of your might,
And quench the flame of furious despight,
And bloudie vengeance; lo th'infernall powres
Covering your foe with cloud of deadly night,
Have borne him hence to *Plutoes* balefull bowres.
The conquest yours, I yours, the shield, and glory yours.

15 Not all so satisfide, with greedie eye
He sought all round about, his thirstie blade
To bath in bloud of faithlesse enemy;
Who all that while lay hid in secret shade:
He stands amazèd, how he thence should fade.
At last the trumpets Triumph sound on hie,
And running Heralds humble homage made,
Greeting him goodly with new victorie,
And to him brought the shield, the cause of enmitie.

16 Wherewith he goeth to that soveraine Queene,
And falling her before on lowly knee,
To her makes present of his service seene:
Which she accepts, with thankes, and goodly gree,˃ *goodwill*
Greatly advauncing˃ his gay chevalree. *praising*
So marcheth home, and by her takes the knight,
Whom all the people follow with great glee,
Shouting, and clapping all their hands on hight,
That all the aire it fils, and flyes to heaven bright.

17 Home is he brought, and laid in sumptuous bed:
Where many skilfull leaches˃ him abide, *physicians*
To salve his hurts, that yet still freshly bled.
In wine and oyle they wash his woundès wide,
And softly can˃ embalme on every side. *did*
And all the while, most heavenly melody
About the bed sweet musicke did divide,°
Him to beguile of griefe and agony:
And all the while *Duessa* wept full bitterly.

18 As when a wearie traveller that strayes
By muddy shore of broad seven-mouthèd *Nile*,
Unweeting of the perillous wandring wayes,
Doth meet a cruell craftie Crocodile,

darknes . . . shrowd This divine device for the protection of a favorite is anticipated in ancient epic and in Italian romance.

divide "Division" is breaking the melody into smaller phrases.

Which in false griefe hyding his harmefull guile,
Doth weepe full sore, and sheddeth tender teares:
The foolish man, that pitties all this while
His mournefull plight, is swallowd up unwares,
Forgetfull of his owne, that mindes anothers cares.

19 So wept *Duessa* untill eventide,
That shyning lampes in *Joves* high house were light:
Then forth she rose, ne lenger would abide,
But comes unto the place, where th'Hethen knight
In slombring swownd˃ nigh voyd of vitall spright,˃ *swoon / spirit of life*
Lay cover'd with inchaunted cloud all day:
Whom when she found, as she him left in plight,
To wayle his woefull case she would not stay,
But to the easterne coast of heaven makes speedy way.

20 Where griesly *Night,*° with visage deadly sad,
That *Phœbus* chearefull face durst never vew,
And in a foule blacke pitchie mantle clad,
She findes forth comming from her darkesome mew,˃ *den*
Where she all day did hide her hated hew.
Before the dore her yron charet˃ stood, *chariot*
Alreadie harnessèd for journey new;
And coleblacke steedes yborne of hellish brood,
That on their rustie bits did champ, as they were wood.˃ *mad*

21 Who when she saw *Duessa* sunny bright,
Adornd with gold and jewels shining cleare,
She greatly grew amazèd at the sight,
And th'unacquainted˃ light began to feare: *unfamiliar*
For never did such brightnesse there appeare,
And would have backe retyrèd to her cave,
Untill the witches speech she gan to heare,
Saying, Yet O thou dreaded Dame, I crave
Abide, till I have told the message, which I have.

22 She stayd, and foorth *Duessa* can proceede,
O thou most auncient Grandmother of all,
More old then *Jove,* whom thou at first didst breede,
Or that great house of Gods cælestiall,
Which wast begot in *Dæmogorgons*° hall,
And sawst the secrets of the world unmade,˃ *before it was made*
Why suffredst thou thy Nephewes˃ deare to fall *descendants*
With Elfin sword, most shamefully betrade?
Lo where the stout *Sansjoy* doth sleepe in deadly shade.

Night Here Spenser depends, for his allegorical description of Night, on the mythographical handbooks of the time, and perhaps especially on Natalis Comes, *Mythologiae.*

Dæmogorgon mysterious ancestor of the gods

23 And him before, I saw with bitter eyes
The bold *Sansfoy* shrinke underneath his speare;
And now the pray of fowles in field he lyes,
Nor wayld of friends, nor laid on groning beare,˃ *bier*
That whylome was to me too dearely deare.
O what of Gods then boots it to be borne,
In old *Aveugles* sonnes° so evill heare?˃ *fare so ill*
Or who shall not great *Nightès* children scorne,
When two of three her˃ Nephews are so fowle forlorne? *of her three*

24 Up then, up dreary Dame, of darknesse Queene,
Go gather up the reliques of thy race,
Or else goe them avenge, and let be seene,
That dreaded *Night* in brightest day hath place,
And can the children of faire light deface.˃ *destroy*
Her feeling speeches some compassion moved
In hart, and chaunge in that great mothers face:
Yet pittie in her hart was never proved
Till then: for evermore she hated, never loved.

25 And said, Deare daughter rightly may I rew
The fall of famous children borne of mee,
And good successes, which their foes ensew:˃ *follow*
But who can turne the streame of destinee,
Or breake the chayne of strong necessitee,
Which fast is tyde to *Joves* eternall seat?°
The sonnes of Day he favoureth, I see,
And by my ruines thinkes to make them great:
To make one great by others losse, is bad excheat.˃ *exchange*

26 Yet shall they not escape so freely all;
For some shall pay the price of others guilt:
And he the man that made *Sansfoy* to fall,
Shall with his owne bloud price˃ that he hath split. *pay for*
But what art thou, that telst of Nephews kilt?˃ *killed*
I that do seeme not I, *Duessa* am,
(Quoth she) how ever now in garments gilt,
And gorgeous gold arayd I to thee came;
Duessa I, the daughter of Deceipt and Shame.

27 Then bowing downe her agèd backe, she kist
The wicked witch, saying; In that faire face
The false resemblance of Deceipt, I wist
Did closely lurke; yet so true-seeming grace
It carried, that I scarce in darkesome place
Could it discerne, though I the mother bee

Aveugles sonnes the Sons of Night (the Blind One)
chayne . . . seat This chain is mentioned first in Homer (*Iliad* VIII) but was commonplace; see, for a different use of it, I.ix.1 below.

Of falshood, and root of *Duessaes* race.
O welcome child, whom I have longd to see,
And now have seene unwares.> Lo now I go with thee. *without knowing it*

28 Then to her yron wagon she betakes,
And with her beares the fowle welfavourd witch:
Through mirkesome aire her readie way she makes.
Her twyfold> Teme, of which two blacke as pitch, *twofold*
And two were browne, yet each to each unlich,> *unlike*
Did softly swim away, ne ever stampe,
Unlesse she chaunst their stubborne mouths to twitch;
Then foming tarre, their bridles they would champe,
And trampling the fine element, would fiercely rampe.> *prance*

29 So well they sped, that they be come at length
Unto the place, whereas the Paynim lay,
Devoid of outward sense, and native strength,
Coverd with charmèd cloud from vew of day,
And sight of men, since his late luckelesse fray.
His cruell wounds with cruddy> bloud congealed, *clotted*
They binden up so wisely,> as they may, *skillfully*
And handle softly, till they can be healed:
So lay him in her charet, close in night concealed.

30 And all the while she stood upon the ground,
The wakefull dogs did never cease to bay,
As giving warning of th'unwonted sound,
With which her yron wheeles did them affray,
And her darke griesly looke them much dismay;
The messenger of death, the ghastly Owle
With drearie shriekes did also her bewray;> *reveal*
And hungry Wolves continually did howle,
At her abhorrèd face, so filthy and so fowle.

31 Thence turning backe in silence soft they stole,
And brought the heavie corse with easie pace
To yawning gulfe of deepe *Avernus*° hole.
By that same hole an entrance darke and bace
With smoake and sulphure hiding all the place,
Descends to hell: there creature never past,
That backe returnèd without heavenly grace;
But dreadfull *Furies*, which their chaines have brast,> *burst*
And damnèd sprights sent forth to make ill> men aghast. *wicked*

32 By that same way the direfull dames doe drive
Their mournefull charet, fild with rusty> blood, *rust-colored*

Avernus lake near Naples, traditionally an entrance to hell (as in Virgil, *Aeneid* VI)

And downe to *Plutoes* house are come bilive:˃ *soon*
Which passing through, on every side them stood
The trembling ghosts with sad amazèd mood,
Chattring their yron teeth, and staring wide
With stonie eyes; and all the hellish brood
Of feends infernall flockt on every side,
To gaze on earthly wight, that with the Night durst ride.

33 They pas the bitter waves of *Acheron*,°
Where many soules sit wailing woefully,
And come to fiery flood of *Phlegeton*,
Whereas the damnèd ghosts in torments fry,
And with sharpe shrilling shriekes doe bootlesse˃ cry, *unavailingly*
Cursing high *Jove*, the which them thither sent.
The house of endlesse paine is built thereby,
In which ten thousand sorts of punishment
The cursèd creatures doe eternally torment.

34 Before the threshold dreadfull *Cerberus*°
His three deformèd heads did lay along,
Curlèd with thousand adders venemous,
And lillèd˃ forth his bloudie flaming tong: *lolled*
At them he gan to reare his bristles strong,
And felly˃ gnarre,˃ untill dayes enemy *fiercely / snarl*
Did him appease; then downe his taile he hong
And suffered them to passen quietly:
For she in hell and heaven had power equally.

35 There was *Ixion* turnèd on a wheele,
For daring tempt the Queene of heaven to sin;
And *Sisyphus* an huge round stone did reele˃ *roll*
Against an hill, ne might from labour lin;˃ *cease*
There thirstie *Tantalus* hong by the chin;
And *Tityus* fed a vulture on his maw;
Typhœus joynts were stretchèd on a gin,˃ *rack*
Theseus condemn'd to endlesse slouth by law,
And fifty sisters water in leake vessels draw.°

36 They all beholding worldly wights in place,˃ *there*
Leave off their worke, unmindfull of their smart,˃ *pain*
To gaze on them; who forth by them doe pace,
Till they be come unto the furthest part:
Where was a Cave ywrought by wondrous art,

Acheron one of the four rivers of Hades; Phlegeton (l. 35) is another.
Cerberus three-headed dog guarding the gates of Hades
There was . . . draw The sufferings of Ixion, who lay with Hera; of Sisyphus, who was disrespectful to Zeus; of Tantalus, who revealed the secrets of the gods; of Tityus, who assaulted the Titaness Leto; of Typhoeus, who attacked Zeus; of Theseus, who revealed the mysteries; and of the fifty daughters of Danaus, forty-nine of whom sacrilegiously murdered their husbands, were all in consequence of their disrespect of the gods.

Deepe, darke, uneasie, dolefull, comfortlesse,
In which sad *Æsculapius*° farre a part
Emprisond was in chaines remedilesse,
For that *Hippolytus*° rent corse he did redresse.˃ *cure*

37 *Hippolytus* a jolly˃ huntsman was, *brave*
That wont in charet chace the foming Bore;
He all his Peeres in beautie did surpas,
But Ladies love as losse of time forbore:
His wanton stepdame lovèd him the more,
But when she saw her offred sweets refused
Her love she turnd to hate, and him before
His father fierce of treason false accused,
And with her gealous termes his open˃ eares abused. *credulous*

38 Who all in rage his Sea-god syre besought,
Some cursèd vengeance on his sonne to cast:
From surging gulf two monsters straight were brought,
With dread whereof his chasing steedes aghast,
Both charet swift and huntsman overcast.
His goodly corps on ragged cliffs yrent,˃ *torn*
Was quite dismembred, and his members chast
Scattered on every mountaine, as he went,
That of *Hippolytus* was left no moniment.

39 His cruell stepdame seeing what was donne,
Her wicked dayes with wretched knife did end,
In death avowing th'innocence of her sonne.
Which hearing his rash Syre, began to rend
His haire, and hastie tongue, that did offend:
Tho gathering up the relicks of his smart°
By *Dianes* meanes, who was *Hippolyts* frend,
Them brought to *Æsculape,* that by his art
Did heale them all againe, and joynèd every part.

40 Such wondrous science˃ in mans wit to raine *skill*
When *Jove* avizd,˃ that could the dead revive, *considered*
And fates expirèd could renew againe,
Of endlesse life he might him not deprive,
But unto hell did thrust him downe alive,
With flashing thunderbolt ywounded sore:
Where long remaining, he did alwaies strive
Himselfe with salves to health for to restore,
And slake the heavenly fire, that ragèd evermore.

Aesculapius god of medicine and son of Apollo, punished for coming too close to giving immortality to men
Hippolytus His story is best known from Euripides and Racine, though Spenser used Ovid, Virgil, and the mythographical handbooks.
relicks . . . smart the remains of Hippolytus

41 There auncient Night arriving, did alight
From her nigh wearie˃ waine, and in her armes *exhausted*
To *Æsculapius* brought the wounded knight:
Whom having softly disarayd of armes,
Tho gan to him discover all his harmes,
Beseeching him with prayer, and with praise,
If either salves, or oyles, or herbes, or charmes
A fordonne˃ wight from dore of death mote raise, *ruined*
He would at her request prolong her nephews daies.

42 Ah Dame (quoth he) thou temptest me in vaine,
To dare the thing, which daily yet I rew,
And the old cause of my continued paine
With like attempt to like end to renew.
Is not enough, that thrust from heaven dew
Here endlesse penance for one fault I pay,
But that redoubled crime with vengeance new
Thou biddest me to eeke?˃ Can Night defray˃ *increase / appease*
The wrath of thundring *Jove*, that rules both night and day?

43 Not so (quoth she) but sith that˃ heavens king *since*
From hope of heaven hath thee excluded quight,
Why fearest thou, that canst not hope for thing,
And fearest not, that more thee hurten might,
Now in the powre of everlasting Night?
Goe to˃ then, O thou farre renowmèd sonne *come on*
Of great *Apollo*, shew thy famous might
In medicine, that else˃ hath to thee wonne *already*
Great paines, and greater praise, both never to be donne.˃ *ended*

44 Her words prevaild: And then the learnèd leach˃ *physician*
His cunning hand gan to his wounds to lay,
And all things else, the which his art did teach:
Which having seene, from thence arose away
The mother of dread darknesse, and let stay
Aveugles sonne there in the leaches cure,˃ *care*
And backe returning tooke her wonted way,
To runne her timely race, whilst *Phœbus* pure
In westerne waves his wearie wagon did recure.˃ *refresh*

45 The false *Duessa* leaving noyous˃ Night, *harmful*
Returnd to stately pallace of dame Pride:
Where when she came, she found the Faery knight
Departed thence, albe˃ his woundes wide *although*
Not throughly˃ heald, unreadie were to ride. *thoroughly*
Good cause he had to hasten thence away;
For on a day his wary Dwarfe had spide,
Where in a dongeon deepe huge numbers lay
Of caytive˃ wretched thrals, that waylèd night and day. *captive*

46 A ruefull sight, as could be seene with eie;
Of whom he learnèd had in secret wise
The hidden cause of their captivitie,
How mortgaging their lives to *Covetise,*˃ *covetousness*
Through wastfull Pride, and wanton Riotise,
They were by law of that proud Tyrannesse°
Provokt with *Wrath,* and *Envies* false surmise,
Condemnèd to that Dongeon mercilesse,
Where they should live in woe, and die in wretchednesse.

47 There was that great proud king of *Babylon,*°
That would compell all nations to adore,
And him as onely God to call upon,
Till through celestiall doome throwne out of dore,
Into an Oxe he was transform'd of yore:
There also was king *Crœsus,*° that enhaunst˃ *exalted*
His heart too high through his great riches store;
And proud *Antiochus,*° the which advaunst
His cursèd hand gainst God, and on his altars daunst.

48 And them long time before, great *Nimrod*° was,
That first the world with sword and fire warrayd;˃ *harassed*
And after him old *Ninus*° farre did pas
In princely pompe, of all the world obayd;
There also was that mightie Monarch layd
Low under all, yet above all in pride,
That name of native syre˃ did fowle upbrayd,˃ *natural father / disgrace*
And would as *Ammons* sonne° be magnifide,
Till scornd of God and man a shamefull death he dide.

49 All these together in one heape were throwne,
Like carkases of beasts in butchers stall.
And in another corner wide were strowne
The antique ruines of the *Romaines* fall:
Great *Romulus* the Grandsyre of them all,
Proud *Tarquin,* and too lordly *Lentulus,*
Stout *Scipio,* and stubborne *Hanniball,*
Ambitious *Sulla,* and sterne *Marius,*
High *Cæsar,* great *Pompey,* and fierce *Antonius.*°

50 Amongst these mighty men were wemen mixt,
Proud wemen, vaine, forgetfull of their yoke:˃ *marriage obligations*

Tyrannesse Lucifera
king of Babylon Nebuchadnezzar (Daniel 3–4)
Croesus 6th-century (B.C.) king of Lydia, famous for his wealth
Antiochus Antiochus IV, king of Syria in second century B.C., who tried to crush the Jewish religion
Nimrod grandson of Noah, "a mighty hunter," who offended God by building the Tower of Babel
Ninus founder of Nineveh
Ammons sonne Alexander the Great, who claimed to be the son of Jupiter Ammon, and died after a prolonged drinking bout
Great Romulus . . . Antonius (ll. 5–9) great names of Roman history, from that of the founder to that of Mark Antony, whose defeat at Actium by Octavius ensured the Augustan age and the Empire

The bold *Semiramis,*° whose sides transfixt
With sonnes owne blade, her fowle reproches spoke;
Faire *Sthenobœa,*° that her selfe did choke
With wilfull cord, for wanting of˃ her will; *not getting*
High minded *Cleopatra,*° that with stroke
Of Aspes sting her selfe did stoutly kill:
And thousands moe˃ the like, that did that dongeon fill. *more*

51 Besides the endlesse routs of wretched thralles,
Which thither were assembled day by day,
From all the world after their wofull falles,
Through wicked pride, and wasted wealthes decay.
But most of all, which in that Dongeon lay
Fell from high Princes courts, or Ladies bowres,
Where they in idle pompe, or wanton play,
Consumèd had their goods, and thriftlesse howres,
And lastly throwne themselves into these heavy stowres.

52 Whose case when as the carefull˃ Dwarfe had tould, *sorrowful*
And made ensample˃ of their mournefull sight *example*
Unto his maister, he no lenger would
There dwell in perill of like painefull plight,
But early rose, and ere that dawning light
Discovered had the world to heaven wyde,
He by a privie Posterne˃ tooke his flight, *gate*
That of no envious eyes he mote be spyde:
For doubtlesse death ensewd, if any him descryde.

53 Scarse could he footing find in that fowle way,
For many corses, like a great Lay-stall˃ *rubbish dump*
Of murdred men which therein strowèd lay,
Without remorse,˃ or decent funerall: *pity*
Which all through that great Princesse° pride did fall
And came to shamefull end. And them beside
Forth ryding underneath the castell wall,
A donghill of dead carkases he spide,
The dreadfull spectacle˃ of that sad house of *Pride.* *image*

Canto vi°

From lawlesse lust by wondrous grace
fayre Una is releast:
Whom salvage nation does adore,
and learnes her wise beheast.˃ *bidding*

Semiramis wife of Ninus
Sthenoboea or Anteia, wife of Proetus, king of Argus, who loved Bellerophon, rider of Pegasus
Cleopatra whose suicide after Actium made her, like the other women, a victim of passion and ambition
Princesse Princess's (Lucifera's)

Canto vi The "salvage nation," which first rescues and then worships Una (and later her ass), indicates the inadequacy of natural religion, as well as demonstrating that to worship is instinctive. Satyrane is a blend of civility and nature, a stronger though still an inadequate servant of Truth. The story of his inconclusive battle with Sansloy is adapted from Ariosto.

1 As when a ship, that flyes faire under saile,
An hidden rocke escapèd hath unwares,
That lay in waite her wrack for to bewaile,˃ *bring about*
The Marriner yet halfe amazèd stares
At perill past, and yet in doubt˃ ne dares *fear*
To joy at his foole-happie˃ oversight: *lucky*
So doubly is distrest twixt joy and cares
The dreadlesse courage of this Elfin knight,
Having escapt so sad ensamples in his sight.

2 Yet sad he was that his too hastie speed
The faire *Duess'* had forst him leave behind;
And yet more sad, that *Una* his deare dreed˃ *loved one*
Her truth had staind with treason so unkind;˃ *unnatural*
Yet crime in her could never creature find,
But for his love, and for her owne selfe sake,
She wandred had˃ from one to other *Ynd,*° *would have*
Him for to seeke, ne ever would forsake,
Till her unwares the fierce *Sansloy* did overtake.

3 Who after *Archimagoes* fowle defeat,
Led her away into a forrest wilde,
And turning wrathfull fire to lustfull heat,
With beastly sin thought her to have defilde,
And made the vassall of his pleasures vilde.˃ *vile*
Yet first he cast˃ by treatie, and by traynes,˃ *tried / tricks*
Her to perswade, that stubborne fort to yilde:
For greater conquest of hard love he gaynes,
That workes it to his will, then he that it constraines.

4 With fawning wordes he courted her a while,
And looking lovely,˃ and oft sighing sore, *lovingly*
Her constant hart did tempt with diverse guile:
But wordes, and lookes, and sighes she did abhore,
As rocke of Diamond stedfast evermore.
Yet for to feed his fyrie lustfull eye,
He snatcht the vele, that hong her face before;
Then gan her beautie shine, as brightest skye,
And burnt his beastly hart t'efforce˃ her chastitye. *gain by force*

5 So when he saw his flatt'ring arts to fayle,
And subtile engines bet from batteree,°
With greedy force he gan the fort assayle,
Whereof he weend possessèd soone to bee,
And win rich spoile of ransackt chastetee.
Ah heavens, that do this hideous act behold,

one to other Ynd from the East to the West Indies

bet from batteree beaten back from their assault

Sylvanus god of fields and forests

And heavenly virgin thus outragèd see,
How can ye vengeance just so long withhold,
And hurle not flashing flames upon that Paynim bold?

6 The pitteous maiden carefull˃ comfortlesse, *oppressed by cares*
Does throw out thrilling˃ shriekes, and shrieking cryes, *piercing*
The last vaine helpe of womens great distresse,
And with loud plaints importuneth the skyes,
That molten starres do drop like weeping eyes;
And *Phœbus* flying so most shamefull sight,
His blushing face in foggy cloud implyes;˃ *enfolds*
And hides for shame. What wit of mortall wight
Can now devise to quit˃ a thrall from such a plight? *save*

7 Eternall providence exceeding thought,
Where none appeares can make her selfe a way:
A wondrous way it for this Lady wrought,
From Lyons clawes to pluck the gripèd pray.
Her shrill outcryes and shriekes so loud did bray,
That all the woodes and forestes did resownd;
A troupe of *Faunes* and *Satyres* far away
Within the wood were dauncing in a rownd,
Whiles old *Sylvanus*° slept in shady arber sownd.

8 Who when they heard that pitteous strainèd voice,
In hast forsooke their rurall meriment,
And ran towards the far rebownded noyce,
To weet,˃ what wight so loudly did lament. *find out*
Unto the place they come incontinent:˃ *immediately*
Whom when the raging Sarazin espide,
A rude, misshapen, monstrous rablement,
Whose like he never saw, he durst not bide,
But got his ready steed, and fast away gan ride.

9 The wyld woodgods arrivèd in the place,
There find the virgin dolefull desolate,
With ruffled rayments, and faire blubbred face,
As her outrageous foe had left her late,
And trembling yet through feare of former hate;
All stand amazèd at so uncouth˃ sight, *strange*
And gin to pittie her unhappie state,
All stand astonied at her beautie bright,
In their rude eyes unworthie of so wofull plight.

10 She more amaz'd, in double dread doth dwell;
And every tender part for feare does shake:
As when a greedie Wolfe through hunger fell
A seely˃ Lambe farre from the flocke does take, *innocent*

Of whom he meanes his bloudie feast to make,
A Lyon spyes fast running towards him,
The innocent pray in hast he does forsake,
Which quit from death yet quakes in every lim
With chaunge of feare, to see the Lyon looke so grim.

11 Such fearefull fit assaid her trembling hart,
Ne word to speake, ne joynt to move she had:
The salvage nation feele her secret smart,
And read her sorrow in her count'nance sad;
Their frowning forheads with rough hornes yclad,
And rusticke horror˃ all a side doe lay, *roughness*
And gently grenning,˃ shew a semblance glad *grinning*
To comfort her, and feare to put away,
Their backward bent knees teach˃ her humbly to obay. *teach*

12 The doubtfull Damzell dare not yet commit
Her single˃ person to their barbarous truth,˃ *unprotected / good faith*
But still twixt feare and hope amazd does sit,
Late learnd˃ what harme to hastie trust ensu'th, *taught*
They in compassion of her tender youth,
And wonder of her beautie soveraine,
Are wonne with pitty and unwonted ruth,
And all prostrate upon the lowly plaine,
Do kisse her feete, and fawne on her with count'nance faine.˃ *glad*

13 Their harts she ghesseth˃ by their humble guise,˃ *estimates / conduct*
And yields her to extremitie of time;˃ *needs of the moment*
So from the ground she fearelesse doth arise,
And walketh forth without suspect of crime:
They all as glad, as birdes of joyous Prime,˃ *springtime*
Thence lead her forth, about her dauncing round,
Shouting, and singing all a shepheards ryme,
And with greene braunches strowing all the ground,
Do worship her, as Queene, with olive girlond cround.

14 And all the way their merry pipes they sound,
That all the woods with doubled Eccho ring,
And with their hornèd feet do weare the ground,
Leaping like wanton kids in pleasant Spring.
So towards old *Sylvanus* they her bring;
Who with the noyse awakèd, commeth out,
To weet the cause, his weake steps governing,
And agèd limbs on Cypresse stadle˃ stout, *staff*
And with an yvie twyne his wast is girt about.

15 Far off he wonders, what them makes so glad,

Or˃ *Bacchus* merry fruit° they did invent,˃ *whether / find*
Or *Cybeles* franticke rites° have made them mad;
They drawing nigh, unto their God present
That flowre of faith and beautie excellent.
That God himselfe vewing that mirrhour˃ rare, *example*
Stood long amazd, and burnt in his intent;
His owne faire *Dryope*° now he thinkes not faire,
And *Pholoe*° fowle, when her to this he doth compaire.

16 The woodborne people fall before her flat,
And worship her as Goddesse of the wood;
And old *Sylvanus* selfe bethinkes not, what
To thinke of wight so faire, but gazing stood,
In doubt to deeme her borne of earthly brood;
Sometimes Dame *Venus* selfe he seemes to see,
But *Venus* never had so sober mood;
Sometimes *Diana* he her takes to bee,
But misseth bow, and shaftes, and buskins˃ to her knee. *boots*

17 By vew of her he ginneth to revive
His ancient love, and dearest *Cyparisse*,°
And calles to mind his pourtraiture alive;˃ *appearance when alive*
How faire he was, and yet not faire to this,
And how he slew with glauncing dart amisse˃ *accidentally*
A gentle Hynd, the which the lovely boy
Did love as life, above all worldly blisse;
For griefe whereof the lad n'ould˃ after joy,˃ *would not / be glad*
But pynd away in anguish and selfe-wild annoy.˃ *vexation*

18 The wooddy Nymphes, faire *Hamadryades*°
Her to behold do thither runne apace,
And all the troupe of light-foot *Naiades*,°
Flocke all about to see her lovely face:
But when they vewèd have her heavenly grace,
They envie her in their malitious mind,
And fly away for feare of fowle disgrace:
But all the *Satyres* scorne their woody kind,
And henceforth nothing faire, but her on earth they find.

19 Glad of such lucke, the luckelesse lucky maid,
Did her content to please their feeble eyes,
And long time with that salvage people staid,
To gather breath in many miseries.
During which time her gentle wit she plyes,˃ *applies*

Bacchus merry fruit grapes for wine
Cybeles franticke rites This goddess (Rhea) was orgiastically worshiped.
Dryope wife of Faunus, perhaps identified with Sylvanus
Pholoe nymph loved by Pan (also a wood god)
Cyparisse Cyparissus, who was changed into a cypress (Ovid, *Metamorphoses* X)
Hamadryades wood nymphs
Naiades water nymphs

To teach them truth, which worshipt her in vaine,> *foolishly*
And made her th'Image of Idolatryes;> *made an idol of her*
But when their bootlesse zeale she did restraine
From her own worship, they her Asse would worship fayn.> *wanted to worship*

20 It fortunèd a noble warlike knight
By just occasion to that forrest came,
To seeke his kindred, and the lignage right,> *true*
From whence he tooke his well deservèd name:
He had in armes abroad wonne muchell fame,
And fild far landes with glorie of his might,
Plaine, faithfull, true, and enimy of shame,
And ever lov'd to fight for Ladies right,
But in vaine glorious frayes he litle did delight.

21 A Satyres sonne yborne in forrest wyld,
By straunge adventure> as it did betyde;> *chance / happen*
And there begotten of a Lady myld,
Faire *Thyamis* the daughter of *Labryde*,
That was in sacred bands of wedlocke tyde
To *Therion*,° a loose unruly swayne;
Who had more joy to raunge the forrest wyde,
And chase the salvage beast with busie payne,
Then serve his Ladies love, and wast in pleasures vayne.

22 The forlorne mayd did with loves longing burne,
And could not lacke> her lovers company, *do without*
But to the wood she goes, to serve her turne,
And seeke her spouse, that from her still does fly,
And followes other game and venery:> *hunting*
A Satyre chaunst her wandring for to find,
And kindling coles of lust in brutish eye,
The loyall links of wedlocke did unbind,
And made her person thrall unto his beastly kind.

23 So long in secret cabin there he held
Her captive to his sensuall desire,
Till that with timely fruit her belly sweld,
And bore a boy unto that salvage sire:
Then home he suffred her for to retire,
For ransome leaving him the late borne child;
Whom till to ryper yeares he gan aspire,
He noursled up> in life and manners wilde, *reared*
Emongst wild beasts and woods, from lawes of men exilde.

Thyamis . . . Therion names deriving from the Greek words for "passion," "turbulent," and "wild beast"

24 For all he taught the tender ymp,˃ was but — *child*
To banish cowardize and bastard feare;
His trembling hand he would him force to put
Upon the Lyon and the rugged Beare,
And from the she Beares teats her whelps to teare;
And eke wyld roring Buls he would him make
To tame, and ryde their backes not made to beare;
And the Robuckes in flight to overtake,
That every beast for feare of him did fly and quake.

25 Thereby so fearelesse, and so fell he grew,
That his owne sire and maister˃ of his guise˃ — *teacher / way of life*
Did often tremble at his horrid vew,˃ — *frightening appearance*
And oft for dread of hurt would him advise,
The angry beasts not rashly to despise,
Nor too much to provoke; for he would learne˃ — *teach*
The Lyon stoup to him in lowly wise,
(A lesson hard) and make the Libbard˃ sterne˃ — *leopard / fierce*
Leave roaring, when in rage he for revenge did earne.˃ — *yearn*

26 And for to make his powre approvèd more, — *demonstrated*
Wyld beasts in yron yokes he would compell;
The spotted Panther, and the tusked Bore,
The Pardale˃ swift, and the Tigre cruell; — *leopard*
The Antelope, and Wolfe both fierce and fell;
And them constraine in equall teme° to draw.
Such joy he had, their stubborne harts to quell,
And sturdie courage tame with dreadfull aw,
That his beheast they fearèd, as a tyrans law.

27 His loving mother came upon a day
Unto the woods, to see her little sonne;
And chaunst unwares to meet him in the way,
After his sportes, and cruell pastime donne,
When after him a Lyonesse did runne,
That roaring all with rage, did lowd requere˃ — *demand*
Her children deare, whom he away had wonne:
The Lyon whelpes she saw how he did beare,
And lull in rugged armes, withouten childish feare.

28 The fearefull Dame all quakèd at the sight,
And turning backe, gan fast to fly away,
Untill with love revokt˃ from vaine affright, — *called back*
She hardly yet perswaded was to stay,
And then to him these womanish words gan say;
Ah *Satyrane*, my dearling, and my joy,
For love of me leave off this dreadfull play;

in equall teme as paired members of a team

To dally thus with death, is no fit toy,
Go find some other play-fellowes, mine own sweet boy.

29 In these and like delights of bloody game
He traynèd was, till ryper yeares he raught,˃ *reached*
And there abode, whilst any beast of name˃ *known*
Walkt in that forest, whom he had not taught
To feare his force: and then his courage haught˃ *proud*
Desird of forreine foemen to be knowne,
And far abroad for straunge adventures sought:
In which his might was never overthrowne,
But through all Faery lond his famous worth was blown.˃ *reported*

30 Yet evermore it was his manner faire,
After long labours and adventures spent,
Unto those native woods for to repaire,
To see his sire and ofspring˃ auncient. *origin*
And now he thither came for like intent;
Where he unwares the fairest *Una* found,
Straunge Lady, in so straunge habiliment,
Teaching the Satyres, which her sat around,
Trew sacred lore, which from her sweet lips did redound.˃ *proceed*

31 He wondred at her wisedome heavenly rare,
Whose like in womens wit he never knew;
And when her curteous deeds he did compare,˃ *consider*
Gan her admire, and her sad sorrowes rew,
Blaming of Fortune, which such troubles threw,
And joyd to make proofe of her crueltie
On gentle Dame, so hurtlesse, and so trew:
Thenceforth he kept her goodly company,
And learnd her discipline of faith and veritie.

32 But she all vowd˃ unto the *Redcrosse* knight, *dedicated*
His wandring perill closely˃ did lament, *privately*
Ne in this new acquaintaunce could delight,
But her deare heart with anguish did torment,
And all her wit in secret counsels spent,
How to escape. At last in privie wise
To *Satyrane* she shewèd her intent;
Who glad to gain such favour, gan devise,
How with that pensive Maid he best might thence arise.˃ *leave*

33 So on a day when Satyres all were gone,
To do their service to *Sylvanus* old,
The gentle virgin left behind alone
Se led away with courage stout and bold.
Too late it was, to Satyres to be told,

Or ever hope recover her againe:
In vaine he seekes that having cannot hold.
So fast he carried her with carefull paine,
That they the woods are past, and come now to the plaine.

34 The better part now of the lingring day,
They traveild had, when as they farre espide
A wearie wight forwandring> by the way, *wandering along*
And towards him they gan in hast to ride,
To weet of newes, that did abroad betide,
Or tydings of her knight of the *Redcrosse*.
But he them spying, gan to turne aside,
For feare as seemd, or for some feignèd losse;
More greedy they of newes, fast tòwards him do crosse.

35 A silly man, in simple weedes forworne,> *worn out*
And soild with dust of the long drièd way;
His sandales were with toilesome travell torne,
And face all tand with scorching sunny ray,
As he had traveild many a sommers day,
Through boyling sands of *Arabie* and *Ynde*;
And in his hand a *Jacobs* staffe, to stay> *support*
His wearie limbes upon: and eke behind,
His scrip> did hang, in which his needments he did bind. *small bag*

36 The knight approching nigh, of him inquerd
Tydings of warre, and of adventures new;
But warres, nor new adventures none he herd.
Then *Una* gan to aske, if ought he knew,
Or heard abroad of that her champion trew,
That in his armour bare a croslet> red. *small cross*
Aye me, Deare dame (quoth he) well may I rew
To tell the sad sight, which mine eies have red:> *seen*
These eyes did see that knight both living and eke ded.

37 That cruell word her tender hart so thrild,> *pierced*
That suddein cold did runne through every vaine,
And stony horrour all her sences fild
With dying> fit, that downe she fell for paine. *deathlike*
The knight her lightly rearèd up againe,
And comforted with curteous kind reliefe:
Then wonne from death, she bad him tellen plaine
The further processe> of her hidden griefe; *account*
The lesser pangs can> beare, who hath endur'd the chiefe. *he can*

38 Then gan the Pilgrim thus, I chaunst> this day, *chanced*
This fatall day, that shall I ever rew,
To see two knights in travell on my way

(A sory sight) arraung'd in battall new,˃ *beginning their combat*
Both breathing vengeaunce, both of wrathfull hew:
My fearefull flesh did tremble at their strife,
To see their blades so greedily imbrew,˃ *soak in blood*
That drunke with bloud, yet thristed˃ after life: *thirsted*
What more? the *Redcrosse* knight was slaine with Paynim knife.

39 Ah dearest Lord (quoth she) how might that bee.
And he the stoutest knight, that ever wonne?˃ *conquered*
Ah dearest dame (quoth he) how might I see
The thing, that might not be, and yet was donne?
Where is (said *Satyrane*) that Paynims sonne,
That him of life, and us of joy hath reft?
Not far away (quoth he) he hence doth wonne˃ *dwell*
Foreby˃ a fountaine, where I late him left *close by*
Washing his bloudy wounds, that through the steele were cleft.

40 Therewith the knight thence marchèd forth in hast,
Whiles *Una* with huge heavinesse˃ opprest, *grief*
Could not for sorrow follow him so fast;
And soone he came, as he the place had ghest,˃ *guessed*
Whereas that *Pagan* proud him selfe did rest,
In secret shadow by a fountaine side:
Even he it was, that earst would have supprest˃ *forced*
Faire *Una*: whom when *Satyrane* espide,
With fowle reprochfull words he boldly him defide.

41 And said, Arise thou cursèd Miscreaunt,
That hast with knightlesse guile and trecherous train
Faire knighthood fowly shamèd, and doest vaunt
That good knight of the *Redcrosse* to have slain:
Arise, and with like treason now maintain˃ *defend*
Thy guilty wrong, or else thee guilty yield.
The Sarazin this hearing, rose amain,˃ *at once*
And catching up in hast his three square˃ shield, *triangular*
And shining helmet, soone him bucklèd to the field.

42 And drawing nigh him said, Ah misborne Elfe,
In evil houre thy foes thee hither sent,
Anothers wrongs to wreake upon thy selfe:
Yet ill thou blamest me, for having blent˃ *tainted*
My name with guile and traiterous intent;
That *Redcrosse* knight, perdie,˃ I never slew, *by God*
But had he beene, where earst his armes were lent,
Th'enchaunter vaine his errour should not rew:
But thou his errour shalt, I hope now proven trew.°

But thou trew He means that it would have been better for Archimago if Red Cross had been inside the armour that appeared to be his, and that he is glad Satyrane is about to be just as unwise as Archimago had been.

43 Therewith they gan, both furious and fell,
To thunder blowes, and fiersly to assaile,
Each other bent his enimy to quell,
That with their force they perst both plate and maile,
And made wide furrowes in their fleshes fraile,
That it would pitty> any living eie. *cause to pity*
Large floods of bloud adowne their sides did raile;> *flow*
But floods of bloud could not them satisfie:
Both hungred after death: both chose to win, or die.

44 So long they fight, and fell revenge pursue,
That fainting each, themselves to breathen let,
And oft refreshèd, battell oft renue:
As when two Bores with rancling malice met,
Their gory sides fresh bleeding fiercely fret,
Till breathlesse both them selves aside retire,
Where foming wrath, their cruell tuskes they whet,
And trample th'earth, the whiles they may respire;> *breathe again*
Then backe to fight againe, new breathèd and entire.> *restored*

45 So fiersly, when these knights had breathèd once,
They gan to fight returne, increasing more
Their puissant force, and cruell rage attonce,
With heapèd strokes more hugely, then before,
That with their drerie> wounds and bloudy gore *bloody*
They both deformèd, scarsely could be known.
By this sad *Una* fraught with anguish sore,
Let with their noise, which through the aire was thrown,
Arriv'd, where they in erth their fruitles bloud had sown.

46 Whom all so soone as that proud Sarazin
Espide, he gan revive the memory
Of his lewd lusts, and late attempted sin,
And left the doubtfull battell hastily,
To catch her, newly offred to his eie:
But *Satyrane* with strokes him turning, staid,
And sternely bad him other businesse plie,
Then hunt the steps of pure unspotted Maid:
Wherewith he all enrag'd, these bitter speaches said.

47 O foolish faeries sonne, what furie mad
Hath thee incenst, to hast thy dolefull fate?
Were it not better, I that Lady had,
Then that thou hadst repented it too late?
Most sencelesse man he, that himselfe doth hate,
To love another. Lo then for thine ayd
Here take thy lovers token on thy pate.
So they to fight; the whiles the royall Mayd
Fled farre away, of that proud Paynim sore afrayd.

48 But that false *Pilgrim,* which that leasing> told, *lie*
Being in deed old *Archimage,* did stay
In secret shadow, all this to behold,
And much rejoycèd in their bloudy fray:
But when he saw the Damsell passe away
He left his stond,> and her pursewd apace, *place*
In hope to bring her to her last decay,> *ruin*
But for to tell her lamentable cace,
And eke this battels end,° will need another place.

Canto vii°

The Redcrosse knight is captive made
By Gyaunt proud opprest,
Prince Arthur meets with Una great-
ly with those newes distrest.

1 What man so wise, what earthly wit so ware,> *aware*
As to descry the crafty cunning traine,> *stratagem*
By which Deceipt doth maske in visour> faire, *mask*
And cast> her colours dyèd deepe in graine,> *devise / thoroughly*
To seeme like Truth, whose shape she well can faine,
And fitting gestures to her purpose frame,
The guiltlesse man with guile to entertaine?
Great maistresse of her art was that false Dame,
The false *Duessa,* clokèd with *Fidessaes* name.

2 Who when returning from the drery *Night,*
She fownd not in that perilous house of *Pryde,*
Where she had left, the noble *Redcrosse* knight,
Her hopèd pray, she would no lenger bide,
But forth she went, to seeke him far and wide.
Ere long she fownd, whereas he wearie sate,
To rest him selfe, foreby> a fountaine side, *close by*
Disarmèd all of yron-coted Plate,
And by his side his steed the grassy forage ate.

3 He feedes upon the cooling shade, and bayes> *bathes*
His sweatie forehead in the breathing wind,
Which through the trembling leaves full gently playes
Wherein the cherefull birds of sundry kind
Do chaunt sweet musick, to delight his mind:
The Witch approching gan him fairely greet,

eke . . . battels end This battle never ends; Satyrane disappears from the poem, returning only in Bk III.

Canto vii A crucial canto, as the seventh often is in *The Faerie Queene*. Red Cross succumbs, and only Grace, in the person of Arthur, can save him; the saint is Everyman. But he is also England under the domination of Rome. The apocalyptic imagery (from Revelation) was regularly used by Protestant historians and especially by Foxe in *Acts and Monuments,* the great propagandistic history of the Elizabethan Settlement.

And with reproch of carelesnesse unkind
Upbrayd, for leaving her in place unmeet,˃ *unsuitable*
With fowle words tempring faire, soure gall with hony sweet.

4 Unkindnesse past, they gan of solace˃ treat,˃ *pleasure / talk*
And bathe in pleasaunce of the joyous shade,
Which shielded them against the boyling heat,
And with greene boughes decking a gloomy glade,
About the fountaine like a girlond made;
Whose bubbling wave did ever freshly well,
Ne ever would through fervent sommer fade:
The sacred Nymph, which therein wont to dwell,
Was out of *Dianes* favour, as it then befell.

5 The cause was this:° one day when *Phœbe*˃ fayre *Diana*
With all her band was following the chace,
This Nymph, quite tyr'd with heat of scorching ayre
Sat downe to rest in middest of the race:
The goddesse wroth gan fowly her disgrace,˃ *revile*
And bad the waters, which from her did flow,
Be such as she her selfe was then in place.
Thenceforth her waters waxèd dull and slow,
And all that drunke thereof, did faint and feeble grow.

6 Hereof this gentle knight unweeting was,
And lying downe upon the sandie graile,˃ *gravel*
Drunke of the streame, as cleare as cristall glas;
Eftsoones his manly forces gan to faile,
And mightie strong was turnd to feeble fraile.
His chaungèd powres at first themselves not felt,
Till crudled˃ cold his corage gan assaile, *curdled, frozen*
And chearefull bloud in faintnesse chill did melt,
Which like a fever fit through all his body swelt.˃ *burned*

7 Yet goodly court he made still to his Dame,
Pourd out in loosnesse on the grassy grownd,
Both carelesse of his health, and of his fame:
Till at the last he heard a dreadfull sownd,
Which through the wood loud bellowing, did rebownd,
That all the earth for terrour seemd to shake,
And trees did tremble. Th'Elfe therewith astownd,˃ *astonished*
Upstarted lightly from his looser˃ make,˃ *wanton / companion*
And his unready weapons gan in hand to take.

8 But ere he could his armour on him dight,˃ *put*
Or get his shield, his monstrous enimy

The cause was this a characteristic Ovidian invention

With sturdie steps came stalking in his sight,
An hideous Geant horrible and hye,
That with his talnesse seemd to threat the skye,
The ground eke gronèd under him for dreed;
His living like saw never living eye,
Ne durst behold: his stature did exceed
The hight of three the tallest sonnes of mortall seed.

9 The greatest Earth his uncouth mother was,
And blustring *Æolus*° his boasted sire,
Who with his breath, which through the world doth pas,
Her hollow womb did secretly inspire,˃ *breathe into*
And fild her hidden caves with stormie yre,
That she conceiv'd; and trebling the dew time,
In which the wombes of women do expire;˃ *give birth*
Brought forth this monstrous masse of earthly slime,
Puft up with emptie wind, and fild with sinfull crime.

10 So growen great through arrogant delight
Of th'high descent, whereof he was yborne,
And through presumption of his matchlesse might,
All other powres and knighthood he did scorne.
Such now he marcheth to this man forlorne,
And left to losse: his stalking steps are stayde˃ *supported*
Upon a snaggy˃ Oke, which he had torne *knotty*
Out of his mothers bowelles, and it made
His mortall mace, wherewith his foemen he dismayde.

11 That when the knight he spide, he gan advance
With huge force and insúpportáble˃ mayne,˃ *irresistible / strength*
And tówards him with dreadfull fury praunce;˃ *swagger*
Who haplesse, and eke hopelesse, all in vaine
Did to him pace, sad battaile to darrayne,˃ *offer*
Disarmd, disgrast, and inwardly dismayde,
And eke so faint in every joynt and vaine,
Through that fraile fountaine, which him feeble made,
That scarsely could he weeld his bootlesse˃ single blade. *useless*

12 The Geant strooke so maynly˃ mercilesse, *mightily*
That could have overthrowne a stony towre,
And were not˃ heavenly grace, that him did blesse, *had it not been for*
He had beene pouldred˃ all, as thin as flowre: *pulverized*
But he was wary of that deadly stowre,˃ *danger*
And lightly lept from underneath the blow:
Yet so exceeding was the villeins powre,
That with the wind it did him overthrow,
And all his sences stound,˃ that still he lay full low. *stunned*

Aeolus god of the winds

13 As when that divelish yron Engin wrought
In deepest Hell, and framd by *Furies* skill,
With windy Nitre and quick Sulphur fraught, *filled*
And ramd with bullet round, ordaind to kill,
Conceiveth fire, the heavens it doth fill *ignites*
With thundring noyse, and all the ayre doth choke,
That none can breath, nor see, nor heare at will,
Through smouldry cloud of duskish stincking smoke,
That th'onely breath him daunts, who hath escapt the stroke. *merely the breath*

14 So daunted when the Geaunt saw the knight,
His heavie hand he heavèd up on hye,
And him to dust thought to have battred quight,
Until *Duessa* loud to him gan crye;
O great *Orgoglio,*° greatest under skye,
O hold thy mortall hand for Ladies sake,
Hold for my sake, and do him not to dye, *do not kill him*
But vanquisht thine eternall bondslave make,
And me thy worthy meed unto thy Leman take. *reward / lover*

15 He hearkned, and did stay from further harmes,
To gayne so goodly guerdon, as she spake: *reward*
So willingly she came into his armes,
Who her as willingly to grace did take, *favor*
And was possessèd of his new found make. *mate*
Then up he tooke the slombred sencelesse corse,
And ere he could out of his swowne awake,
Him to his castle brought with hastie forse,
And in a Dongeon deepe him threw without remorse. *pity*

16 From that day forth *Duessa* was his deare,
And highly honourd in his haughtie eye,
He gave her gold and purple pall to weare, *cloak*
And triple crowne set on her head full hye,
And her endowd with royall majestye:
Then for to make her dreaded more of men,
And peoples harts with awfull terrour tye,
A monstrous beast ybred in filthy fen
He chose, which he had kept long time in darksome den.°

17 Such one it was, as that renowmèd Snake°
Which great *Alcides* in *Stremona* slew,
Long fostred in the filth of *Lerna* lake,

Orgoglio is Pride, and Red Cross must overcome this greatest of sins before he can attain to sanctity.
He gave . . . den (ll. 3–9) Duessa, wearing the triple crown of the papacy, in purple and riding the beast, is the Scarlet Woman of Revelation, and thus the Roman Catholic religion (Revelation 17:4).
renowmèd Snake the Lernæan hydra, which had nine heads, and was slain by Hercules (Alcides) as one of his labors

Whose many heads out budding ever new,
Did breed him endlesse labour to subdew:
But this same Monster much more ugly was;
For seven great heads out of his body grew,
An yron brest, and backe of scaly bras,
And all embrewd> in bloud, his eyes did shine as glas. *soaked*

18 His tayle was stretchèd out in wondrous length,
That to the house of heavenly gods it raught,> *reached*
And with extorted> powre, and borrow'd strength, *stolen*
The ever-burning lamps from thence it brought,
And prowdly threw to ground, as things of nought;°
And underneath his filthy feet did tread
The sacred things, and holy heasts> foretaught. *commands*
Upon this dreadfull Beast with sevenfold head
He set the false *Duessa,* for more aw and dread.

19 The wofull Dwarfe, which saw his maisters fall,
Whiles he had keeping of his grasing steed,
And valiant knight become a caytive thrall,
When all was past, tooke up his forlorne weed,> *abandoned attire*
His mightie armour, missing most at need;
His silver shield, now idle maisterlesse;
His poynant> speare, that many made to bleed, *sharp*
The ruefull moniments> of heavinesse,> *memorials / grief*
And with them all departes, to tell his great distresse.

20 He had not travaild long, when on the way
He wofull Ladie, wofull *Una* met,
Fast flying from the Paynims greedy pray,> *clutches*
Whilest *Satyrane* him from pursuit did let:> *hinder*
Who when her eyes she on the Dwarfe had set,
And saw the signes, that deadly tydings spake,
She fell to ground for sorrowfull regret,
And lively breath her sad brest did forsake,
Yet might her pitteous hart be seene to pant and quake.

21 The messenger of so unhappie newes
Would faine have dyde: dead was his hart within,
Yet outwardly some little comfort shewes:
At last recovering hart, he does begin
To rub her temples, and to chaufe> her chin, *rub, chafe*
And every tender part does tosse and turne:
So hardly he the flitted life does win,> *persuade*
Unto her native prison to retourne:
Then gins her grievèd ghost> thus to lament and mourne. *spirit*

His tayle . . . nought (ll. 1–5) "And his tail drew the third part of the stars from heaven, and did cast them to the earth" (Revelation 12:3).

22 Ye dreary instruments of dolefull sight,
That doe this deadly spectacle behold,
Why do ye lenger feed on loathèd light,
Or liking> find to gaze on earthly mould,> *pleasure* *pleasure / form*
Sith> cruell fates the carefull threeds unfould, *since*
The which my life and love together tyde?
Now let the stony dart of senselesse cold
Perce to my hart, and pas through every side,
And let eternall night so sad sight fro me hide.

23 O lightsome day, the lampe of highest *Jove,*
First made by him, mens wandring wayes to guyde,
When darknesse he in deepest dongeon drove,
Henceforth thy hated face for ever hyde,
And shut up heavens windowes shyning wyde:
For earthly sight can nought but sorrow breed,
And late repentance, which shall long abyde.
Mine eyes no more on vanitie shall feed,
But seelèd up> with death, shall have their deadly meed. *blinded*

24 Then downe againe she fell unto the ground;
But he her quickly rearèd up againe:
Thrise did she sinke adowne in deadly swownd,
And thrise he her reviv'd with busie paine:
At last when life recover'd had the raine,> *mastery*
And over-wrestlèd his strong enemie,
With foltring> tong, and trembling every vaine, *faltering*
Tell on (quoth she) the wofull Tragedie,
The which these reliques sad present unto mine eie.

25 Tempestuous fortune hath spent all her spight,
And thrilling sorrow throwne his utmost dart;
Thy sad tongue cannot tell more heavy plight,
Then that I feele, and harbour in mine hart:
Who hath endur'd the whole, can beare each part.
If death it be, it is not the first wound,
That launchèd> hath my brest with bleeding smart. *pierced*
Begin, and end the bitter balefull stound;> *pain*
If lesse, then that I feare, more favour I have found.

26 Then gan the Dwarfe the whole discourse declare,
The subtill traines of *Archimago* old;
The wanton loves of false *Fidessa* faire,
Bought with the bloud of vanquisht Paynim bold:
The wretched payre transform'd to treèn mould;> *the shape of trees*
The house of Pride, and perils round about;
The combat, which he with *Sansjoy* did hould;
The lucklesse conflict with the Gyant stout,
Wherein captiv'd, of life or death he stood in doubt.

27 She heard with patience all unto the end,
And strove to maister sorrowfull assay,˃ *the assault of sorrow*
Which greater grew, the more she did contend,
And almost rent her tender hart in tway;˃ *in two*
And love fresh coles unto her fire did lay:
For greater˃ love, the greater is the losse. *the greater the*
Was never Ladie lovèd dearer day,
Then she did love the knight of the *Redcrosse*;
For whose deare sake so many troubles her did tosse.

28 At last when fervent sorrow slakèd was,
She up arose, resolving him to find
Alive or dead: and forward forth doth pas,
All as the Dwarfe the way to her assynd:˃ *showed*
And evermore in constant carefull˃ mind *sorrowful*
She fed her wound with fresh renewèd bale;˃ *grief*
Long tost with stormes, and bet˃ with bitter wind, *beaten*
High over hils, and low adowne the dale,
She wandred many a wood, and measurd many a vale.

29 At last she chauncèd by good hap to meet
A goodly knight,° faire marching by the way
Together with his Squire, arayèd meet:˃ *fittingly*
His glitterand armour shinèd farre away,
Like glauncing light of *Phœbus* brightest ray;
From top to toe no place appearèd bare,
That deadly dint of steele endanger may:
Athwart his brest a bauldrick˃ brave he ware, *belt*
That shynd, like twinkling stars, with stons most pretious rare.

30 And in the midst thereof one pretious stone
Of wondrous worth, and eke of wondrous mights,
Shapt like a Ladies head, exceeding shone,
Like *Hesperus*° emongst the lesser lights,
And strove for to amaze the weaker sights;
Thereby his mortall blade full comely hong
In yvory sheath, ycarv'd with curious˃ slights;˃ *skillful / designs*
Whose hilts were burnisht gold, and handle strong
Of mother pearle,˃ and bucklèd with a golden tong. *mother-of-pearl*

31 His haughtie˃ helmet, horrid˃ all with gold, *proud / bristling*
Both glorious brightnesse, and great terrour bred;
For all the crest a Dragon did enfold
With greedie pawes, and over all did spred

A goodly knight Arthur, representing, according to the Letter to Ralegh, the virtue of Magnificence, which contains all the others. He bears emblems of the Virgin (or Gloriana) and of the Dragon (conquered in Revelation by the knight "faithful and true"). His armour is "the whole armour of God" (Ephesians 6:11, 13). Theologically he is divine Grace, without which the sinner cannot be redeemed.
Hesperus the evening and morning star

His golden wings: his dreadfull hideous hed
Close couchèd on the bever,˃ seem'd to throw *vizor*
From flaming mouth bright sparkles fierie red,
That suddeine horror to faint harts did show;
And scaly tayle was stretcht adowne his backe full low.

32 Upon the top of all his loftie crest,
A bunch of haires discolourd˃ diversely, *dyed*
With sprinclèd pearle, and gold full richly drest,
Did shake, and seem'd to daunce for jollity,
Like to an Almond tree ymounted hye
On top of greene *Selinis*° all alone,
With blossomes brave bedeckèd daintily;
Whose tender locks do tremble every one
At every little breath, that under heaven is blowne.

33 His warlike shield all closely cover'd was,
Ne might of mortall eye be ever seene;
Not made of steele, nor of enduring bras,
Such earthly mettals soone consumèd bene:
But all of Diamond perfect pure and cleene
It framèd was, one massie entire mould,
Hewen out of Adamant rocke with engines keene,
That point of speare it never percen could,
Ne dint of direfull sword divide the substance would.

34 The same to wight he never wont disclose,
But when as monsters huge he would dismay,
Or daunt unequall armies of his foes,
Or when the flying heavens he would affray;˃ *frighten*
For so exceeding shone his glistring ray,
That *Phœbus* golden face it did attaint,˃ *dim*
As when a cloud his beames doth over-lay;
And silver *Cynthia* wexèd pale and faint,
As when her face is staynd with magicke arts constraint.°

35 No magicke arts hereof had any might,
Nor bloudie wordes of bold Enchaunters call,
But all that was not such,° as seemd in sight,
Before that shield did fade, and suddeine fall:
And when him list˃ the raskall˃ routes˃ apall,
when he pleased / worthless / crowds
Men into stones therewith he could transmew,˃ *transmute*
And stones to dust, and dust to nought at all;
And when him list the prouder lookes subdew,
He would them gazing blind, or turne to other hew.˃ *shape*

Selinis city in Asia Minor, celebrated for palms
As when . . . constraint The power to dim the moon (doubtless related to superstitions concerning eclipses) is a feature of the tradition of magic.

36 Ne let it seeme, that credence this exceedes,
For he that made the same, was knowne right well
To have done much more admirable˃ deedes. *wonderful*
It *Merlin* was, which whylome˃ did excell *formerly*
All living wightes in might of magicke spell:
Both shield, and sword, and armour all he wrought
For this young Prince, when first to armes he fell;
But when he dyde, the Faerie Queene it brought
To Faerie lond, where yet it may be seene, if sought.

37 A gentle youth, his dearely loved Squire°
His speare of heben˃ wood behind him bare, *ebony*
Whose harmefull head, thrice heated in the fire,
Had riven many a brest with pikehead square;
A goodly person, and could menage˃ faire *handle*
His stubborne steed with curbèd canon bit,˃ *smooth round bit*
Who under him did trample as the aire,
And chauft,˃ that any on his backe should sit; *chafed*
The yron rowels into frothy fome he bit.

38 When as this knight nigh to the Ladie drew,
With lovely˃ court he gan her entertaine; *loving*
But when he heard her answeres loth, he knew
Some secret sorrow did her heart distraine:˃ *oppress*
Which to allay, and calme her storming paine,
Faire feeling˃ words he wisely˃ gan display, *compassionate / skillfully*
And for her humour fitting purpose˃ faine, *conversation*
To tempt the cause it selfe for to bewray;˃ *reveal*
Wherewith emmov'd, these bleeding words she gan to say.

39 What worlds delight, or joy of living speach
Can heart, so plung'd in sea of sorrowes deepe,
And heapèd with so huge misfortunes, reach?
The carefull cold beginneth for to creepe,
And in my heart his yron arrow steepe,
Soone as I thinke upon my bitter bale:˃ *sorrow*
Such helplesse harmes yts better hidden keepe,
Then˃ rip up griefe, where it may not availe, *than*
My last left comfort is, my woes to weepe and waile.

40 Ah Ladie deare, quoth then the gentle knight,
Well may I weene, your griefe is wondrous great;
For wondrous great griefe groneth in my spright,
Whiles thus I heare you of your sorrows treat.
But wofull Ladie let me you intrete,
For to unfold the anguish of your hart:

Squire Timias (from the Greek for "honored"), an important figure in later parts of the poem.

Mishaps are maistred by advice discrete,˃ *discrete, wise*
And counsell mittigates the greatest smart;
Found never helpe, who˃ never would his hurts impart. *he who*

41 O but (quoth she) great griefe will not be tould,
And can more easily be thought, then said.
Right so; (quoth he) but he, that never would,
Could never: will to might gives greatest aid.
But griefe (quoth she) does greater grow displaid,
If then it find not helpe, and breedes despaire.
Despaire breedes not (quoth he) where faith is staid.˃ *firm*
No faith so fast (quoth she) but flesh does paire.˃ *weaken*
Flesh may empaire˃ (quoth he) but reason can repaire. *impair*

42 His goodly reason, and well guided speach
So deepe did settle in her gratious thought,
That her perswaded to disclose the breach,
Which love and fortune in her heart had wrought,
And said; Faire Sir, I hope good hap hath brought
You to inquire the secrets of my griefe,
Or that your wisedome will direct my thought,
Or that your prowesse can me yield reliefe:
Then heare the storie sad, which I shall tell you briefe.

43 The forlorne Maiden, whom your eyes have seene
The laughing stocke of fortunes mockeries,
Am th'only daughter of a King and Queene,
Whose parents deare, whilest equall˃ destinies *impartial*
Did runne about, and their felicities
The favourable heavens did not envy,
Did spread their rule through all the territories,
Which *Phison* and *Euphrates* floweth by,
And *Gehons*° golden waves doe wash continually.

44 Till that˃ their cruell cursed enemy, *until*
An huge great Dragon horrible in sight,
Bred in the loathly lakes of *Tartary*,
With murdrous ràvine,˃ and devouring might *plunder*
Their kingdome spoild, and countrey wasted quight:
Themselves, for feare into his jawes to fall,
He forst to castle strong to take their flight,
Where fast embard in mightie brasen wall,
He has them now foure yeres° besiegd to make them thrall.

45 Full many knights adventurous and stout
Have enterprizd˃ that Monster to subdew; *endeavored*

Phison . . . Euphrates . . . Gehon three of the four rivers of Paradise (see Genesis 2:11–14)
foure yeres See Revelation 12:1–6: "the woman clothed with the sun . . . fled into the wilderness . . . a thousand two hundred and threescore days"

From every coast that heaven walks about,
Have thither come the noble Martiall crew,
That famous hard atchievements still pursew,
Yet never any could that girlond win,
But all still shronke, and still he greater grew:
All they for want of faith, or guilt of sin,
The pitteous pray of his fierce crueltie have bin.

46 At last yledd with farre reported praise,
Which flying fame throughout the world had spred,
Of doughtie knights, whom Faery land did raise,
That noble order hight˃ of Maidenhed,° *called*
Forthwith to court of *Gloriane*° I sped,
Of *Gloriane* great Queene of glory bright,
Whose kingdomes seat *Cleopolis*° is red,˃ *called*
There to obtaine some such redoubted knight,
That Parents deare from tyrants powre deliver might.

47 It was my chance (my chance was faire and good)
There for to find a fresh unprovèd knight,
Whose manly hands imbrew'd in guiltie blood
Had never bene, ne ever by his might
Had throwne to ground the unregarded right:
Yet of his prowesse proofe he since hath made
(I witnesse am) in many a cruell fight;
The groning ghosts of many one dismaide˃ *defeated*
Have felt the bitter dint of his avenging blade.

48 And ye the forlorne reliques of his powre,
His byting sword, and his devouring speare,
Which have endurèd many a dreadfull stowre,
Can speake his prowesse, that did earst you beare,
And well could rule: now he hath left you heare,
To be the record of his ruefull losse,˃ *unlucky loss*
And of my dolefull disaventurous deare:
O heavie record of the good *Redcrosse*,
Where have you left your Lord, that could so well you tosse?˃ *handle*

49 Well hopèd I, and faire beginnings had,
That he my captive langour˃ should redeeme, *powerless captivity*
Till all unweeting, an Enchaunter bad
His sence abusd, and made him to misdeeme
My loyalty, not such as it did seeme;
That˃ rather death desire, then such despight. *I that*
Be judge ye heavens, that all things right esteeme,

order . . . Maidenhed the Most Noble Order of the Garter
Gloriane allegorical equivalent of Elizabeth I

Cleopolis allegorical equivalent of London (*kleos*, "fame"; *polis*, "city")

How I him lov'd, and love with all my might,
So thought I eke of him, and thinke I thought aright.

50 Thenceforth me desolate he quite forsooke,
To wander, where wilde fortune would me lead,
And other bywaies he himself betooke,
Where never foot of living wight did tread,
That brought not backe the balefull body dead;°
In which him chauncèd false *Duessa* meete,
Mine onely foe, mine onely deadly dread,
Who with her witchcraft and misseeming˃ sweete, *false appearance*
Inveigled him to follow her desires unmeete.˃ *improper*

51 At last by subtill sleights she him betraid
Unto his foe, a Gyant huge and tall,
Who him disarmèd, dissolute,˃ dismaid, *enfeebled*
Unwares surprisèd, and with mightie mall˃ *club*
The monster mercilesse him made to fall,
Whose fall did never foe before behold;
And now in darkesome dungeon, wretched thrall,
Remèdilesse, for aie˃ he doth him hold; *for ever*
This is my cause of griefe, more great, then may be told.

52 Ere she had ended all, she gan to faint:
But he her comforted and faire bespake,
Certes,˃ Madàme, ye have great cause of plaint, *certainly*
That stoutest heart, I weene, could cause to quake.
But be of cheare, and comfort to you take:
For till I have acquit˃ your captive knight, *freed*
Assure your selfe, I will you not forsake.
His chearefull words reviv'd her chearelesse spright,
So forth they went, the Dwarfe them guiding ever right.

Canto viii°

Faire virgin to redeeme her deare
brings Arthur to the fight:
Who slayes the Gyant, wounds the beast,
and strips Duessa quight.

1 Ay me, how many perils doe enfold
The righteous man, to make him daily fall?
Were not, that heavenly grace doth him uphold,
And stedfast truth acquite˃ him out of all. *deliver*
Her love is firme, her care continuall,
So oft as he through his owne foolish pride,
Or weaknesse is to sinfull bands˃ made thrall: *bonds*

That . . . dead i.e. all who did so venture were brought back dead
Canto viii The account of Orgoglio's overthrow by Arthur, and the details of his castle, continue the apocalyptic figures of canto vii, and develop the traditional Protestant attack on Rome.

Else should this *Redcrosse* knight in bands have dyde,
For whose deliverance she this Prince doth thither guide.

2 They sadly traveild thus, untill they came
Nigh to a castle builded strong and hie:
Then cryde the Dwarfe, lo yonder is the same,
In which my Lord my liege doth lucklesse lie,
Thrall> to that Gyants hatefull tyrannie: *slave*
Therefore, deare Sir, your mightie powres assay.> *try*
The noble knight alighted by and by
From loftie steede, and bad the Ladie stay,
To see what end of fight should him befall that day.

3 So with the Squire, th'admirer of his might,
He marchèd forth towards that castle wall;
Whose gates he found fast shut, ne> living wight *nor*
To ward> the same, nor answere commers call. *guard*
Then tooke that Squire an horne of bugle small,°
Which hong adowne his side in twisted gold,
And tassels gay. Wyde wonders° over all
Of that same hornes great vertues weren told,
Which had approvèd> bene in uses manifold. *proved*

4 Was never wight, that heard that shrilling sound,
But trembling feare did feele in every vaine;
Three miles it might be easie heard around,
And Ecchoes three answerd it selfe againe:
No false enchauntment, nor deceiptfull traine> *trickery*
Might once abide the terror of that blast,
But presently was voide and wholly vaine:
No gate so strong, no locke so firme and fast,
But with that percing noise flew open quite, or brast.> *burst*

5 The same before the Geants gate he blew,
That all the castle quakèd from the ground,
And every dore of freewill open flew.
The Gyant selfe dismaièd with that sownd,
Where he with his *Duessa* dalliance> fownd, *love making*
In hast came rushing forth from inner bowre,
With staring countenance sterne, as one astownd,
And staggering steps, to weet, what suddein stowre> *tumult*
Had wrought that horror strange, and dar'd his dreaded powre.

6 And after him the proud *Duessa* came,
High mounted on her manyheaded beast,°
And every head with fyrie tongue did flame,
And every head was crownèd on his creast,
And bloudie mouthèd with late cruell feast.

horne . . . small small wild ox's horn
Wyde wonders from the *Chanson de Roland;* such horns had been featured in Romance
High . . . beast See Headnote to Bk. I.

That when the knight beheld, his mightie shild
Upon his manly arme he soone addrest,> *adjusted*
And at him fiercely flew, with courage fild,
And eger greedinesse through every member thrild.

7 Therewith the Gyant buckled him to fight,
Inflam'd with scornefull wrath and high disdaine,
And lifting up his dreadfull club on hight,
Allarm'd with ragged snubbes> and knottie graine, *snags*
Him thought at first encounter to have slaine.
But wise and warie was that noble Pere>, *peer*
And lightly leaping from so monstrous maine,> *force*
Did faire avoide the violence him nere;
It booted nought, to thinke, such thunderbolts to beare.

8 Ne shame he thought to shunne so hideous might:
The idle stroke, enforcing furious way,
Missing the marke of his misaymèd sight
Did fall to ground, and with his> heavie sway *its*
So deepely dinted in the driven clay,
That three yardes deepe a furrow up did throw:
The sad earth wounded with so sore assay,> *onslaught*
Did grone full grievous underneath the blow,
And trembling with strange feare, did like an earthquake show.

9 As when almightie *Jove* in wrathfull mood,
To wreake> the guilt of mortall sins is bent, *punish*
Hurles forth his thundring dart with deadly food,> *hatred (feud)*
Enrold in flames, and smouldring dreriment,
Through riven cloudes and molten firmament;
The fierce threeforkèd engin> making way, *weapon*
Both loftie towres and highest trees hath rent,
And all that might his> angrie passage stay, *its*
And shooting in the earth, casts up a mount of clay.

10 His boystrous> club, so buried in the ground, *vast*
He could not rearen up again so light,
But that the knight him at avantage found,
And whiles he strove his combred clubbe to quight> *free*
Out of the earth, with blade all burning bright
He smote off his left arme, which like a blocke
Did fall to ground, depriv'd of native might;
Large streames of bloud out of the trunckèd stocke
Forth gushed, like fresh water streame from riven rocke.

11 Dismaièd with so desperate deadly wound,
And eke impatient of unwonted paine,
He loudly brayd with beastly yelling sound,
That all the fields rebellowèd againe;
As great a noyse, as when in Cymbrian> plaine *Danish*

An heard of Bulles, whom kindly˃ rage doth sting, *natural*
Do for the milkie mothers want complaine,°
And fill the fields with troublous bellowing,
The neighbour woods around with hollow murmur ring.

12 That when his deare *Duessa* heard, and saw
The evill stownd,˃ that daungerd her estate, *blow*
Unto his aid she hastily did draw
Her dreadfull beast, who swolne with bloud of late
Came ramping forth with proud presumpteous gate,
And threatned all his heads like flaming brands.˃ *torches*
But him the Squire made quickly to retrate,
Encountring fierce with single˃ sword in hand, *only*
And twixt him and his Lord did like a bulwarke stand.

13 The proud *Duessa* full of wrathfull spight,
And fierce disdaine, to be affronted so,
Enforst her purple beast with all her might
That stop˃ out of the way to overthroe, *hindrance*
Scorning the let˃ of so unequall foe: *obstruction*
But nathemore˃ would that courageous swayne *nevertheless . . . not*
To her yeeld passage, gainst his Lord to goe,
But with outrageous strokes did him restraine,
And with his bodie bard the way atwixt them twaine.

14 Then tooke the angrie witch her golden cup,°
Which still she bore, replete with magick artes;
Death and despeyre did many thereof sup,
And secret poyson through their inner parts,
Th'eternall bale˃ of heavie wounded harts; *grief*
Which after charmes and some enchauntments said,
She lightly sprinkled on his weaker˃ parts; *too weak*
Therewith his sturdie courage soone was quayd,˃ *subdued*
And all his senses were with suddeine dread dismayd.

15 So downe he fell before the cruell beast,
Who on his necke his bloudie clawes did seize,
That life nigh crusht out of his panting brest:
No powre he had to stirre, nor will to rize.
That when the carefull˃ knight gan well avise,˃ *watchful / notice*
He lightly left the foe, with whom he fought,
And to the beast gan turne his enterprise;
For wondrous anguish in his hart it wrought,
To see his lovèd Squire into such thraldome brought.

16 And high advauncing his bloud-thirstie blade,
Stroke one of those deformèd heads so sore,°

Do . . . complaine lament the absence of cows
golden cup Revelation 17:4; the Whore carries "a golden cup in her hand full of abominations and filthiness of her fornication"
Stroke . . . sore Revelation 13:3: "And I saw one of his heads as it were wounded to death"; the passage is related to the prophecy of the bruising of the serpent's head (fulfilled at the Crucifixion) in Genesis 3:15.

That of his puissance proud ensample made;
His monstrous scalpe downe to his teeth it tore,
And that misformèd shape mis-shapèd more:
A sea of bloud gusht from the gaping wound,
That> her gay garments staynd with filthy gore, *which*
And overflowèd all the field around;
That over shoes in bloud he waded on the ground.

17 Thereat he roarèd for exceeding paine,
That to have heard, great horror would have bred,
And scourging th'emptie ayre with his long traine,> *tail*
Through great impatience> of his grievèd hed *pain*
His gorgeous ryder from her loftie sted> *place*
Would have cast downe, and trod in durtie myre,
Had not the Gyant soone her succourèd;
Who all enrag'd with smart and franticke yre,
Came hurtling in full fierce, and forst the knight retyre.

18 The force, which wont in two to be disperst,
In one alone left> hand he now unites, *remaining*
Which is through rage more strong then both were erst;> *formerly*
With which his hideous club aloft he dites,> *raises*
And at his foe with furious rigour smites,
That strongest Oake might seeme to overthrow:
The stroke upon his shield so heavie lites,
That to the ground it doubleth him full low:
What mortall wight could ever beare so monstrous blow?

19 And in his fall his shield, that covered was,
Did loose his vele by chaunce, and open flew:
The light whereof, that heavens light did pas,> *surpass*
Such blazing brightnesse through the aier threw,
That eye mote> not the same endure to vew. *might*
Which when the Gyaunt spyde with staring eye,
He downe let fall his arme, and soft withdrew
His weapon huge, that heavèd was on hye
For to have slaine the man, that on the ground did lye.

20 And eke the fruitfull-headed> beast, amaz'd *many-headed*
At flashing beames of that sunshiny shield,
Became starke blind, and all his senses daz'd,
That downe he tumbled on the durtie field,
And seem'd himselfe as conquerèd to yield.
Whom when his maistresse proud perceiv'd to fall,
Whiles yet his feeble feet for faintnesse reeld,
Unto the Gyant loudly she gan call,
O helpe Orgoglio, helpe, or else we perish all.

21 At her so pitteous cry was much amoov'd
Her champion stout, and for to ayde his frend,

Againe his wonted angry weapon proov'd:> *tried*
But all in vaine: for he has read his end
In that bright shield, and all their forces spend
Themselves in vaine: for since that glauncing sight,
He hath no powre to hurt, nor to defend;
As where th'Almighties lightning brond does light,
It dimmes the dazèd eyen, and daunts the senses quight.

22 Whom when the Prince, to battell new addrest,
And threatning high his dreadfull stroke did see,
His sparkling blade about his head he blest,> *waved*
And smote off quite his right leg by the knee,
That downe he tombled; as an agèd tree,
High growing on the top of rocky clift,
Whose hartstrings with keene steele nigh hewen be,
The mightie trunck halfe rent, with ragged rift
Doth roll adowne the rocks, and fall with fearefull drift.> *impact*

23 Or as a Castle rearèd high and round,
By subtile engins and malitious slight> *artifice*
Is underminèd from the lowest ground,
And her foundation forst, and feebled quight,
At last downe falles, and with her heapèd hight
Her hastie ruine does more heavie make,
And yields it selfe unto the victours might;
Sich was this Gyaunts fall, that seemd to shake
The stedfast globe of earth, as it for feare did quake.

24 The knight then lightly leaping to the pray,
With mortall steele him smot againe so sore,
That headlesse his unweldy bodie lay,
All wallowd in his owne fowle bloudy gore,
Which flowèd from his wounds in wondrous store.
But soone as breath out of his breast did pas,
That huge great body, which the Gyaunt bore,
Was vanisht quite, and of that monstrous mas
Was nothing left, but like an emptie bladder was.

25 Whose grievous fall, when false *Duessa* spide,
Her golden cup she cast unto the ground,
And crownèd mitre rudely threw aside;
Such piercing griefe her stubborne hart did wound,
That she could not endure that dolefull stound,> *affliction*
But leaving all behind her, fled away:
The light-foot Squire her quickly turnd around,
And by hard meanes enforcing her to stay,
So brought unto his Lord, as his deservèd pray.

26 The royall Virgin, which beheld from farre,
In pensive plight, and sad perplexitie,

The whole atchievement> of this doubtfull warre, *course*
Came running fast to greet his victorie,
With sober gladnesse, and myld modestie,
And with sweet joyous cheare him thus bespake;
Faire braunch of noblesse, flowre of chevalrie,
That with your worth the world amazèd make,
How shall I quite> the paines, ye suffer for my sake? *repay*

27 And you fresh bud of vertue springing fast,°
Whom these sad eyes saw nigh unto deaths dore,
What hath poore Virgin for such perill past,
Wherewith you to reward? Accept therefore
My simple selfe, and service evermore;
And he that high does sit, and all things see
With equall> eyes, their merites to restore,> *just / reward*
Behold what ye this day have done for mee,
And what I cannot quite, requite with usuree.> *interest*

28 But sith> the heavens, and your faire handeling> *since / conduct*
Have made you maister of the field this day,
Your fortune maister eke with governing,°
And well begun end all so well, I pray,
Ne let that wicked woman scape away;
For she it is, that did my Lord bethrall,
My dearest Lord, and deepe in dongeon lay,
Where he his better dayes hath wasted all.
O heare, how piteous he to you for ayd does call.

29 Forthwith he gave in charge unto his Squire,
That scarlot whore to keepen carefully;
Whiles he himselfe with greedie> great desire *eager*
Into the Castle entred forcibly,
Where living creature none he did espye;
Then gan he lowdly through the house to call:
But no man car'd to answere to his crye.
There raignd a solemne silence over all,
Nor voice was heard, nor wight was seene in bowre or hall.

30 At last with creeping crooked pace forth came
An old old man, with beard as white as snow,
That on a staffe his feeble steps did frame,
And guide his wearie gate both too and fro:
For his eye sight him failed long ygo,
And on his arme a bounch of keyes he bore,
The which unusèd rust did overgrow:
Those were the keyes of every inner dore,
But he could not them use, but kept them still in store.

And . . . fast addressed to the squire, Timias

Your . . . governing now take advantage of your fortune, too, by exercising foresight

31 But very uncouth sight was to behold,
How he did fashion his untoward pace,
For as he forward moov'd his footing old,
So backward still was turnd his wrincled face,
Unlike to men, who ever as they trace,
Both feet and face one way are wont to lead.
This was the auncient keeper of that place,
And foster father of the Gyant dead;
His name *Ignaro*° did his nature right aread.> *reveal*

32 His reverend haires and holy gravitie
The knight much honord, as beseemèd well,
And gently askt, where all the people bee,
Which in that stately building wont to dwell.
Who answerd him full soft, he could not tell.
Againe he askt, where that same knight was layd,
Whom great *Orgoglio* with his puissaunce fell
Had made his caytive thrall;> againe he sayde, *slave*
He could not tell: ne ever other answere made.

33 Then askèd he, which way he in might pas:
He could not tell, againe he answerèd.
Thereat the curteous knight displeasèd was,
And said, Old sire, it seemes thou hast not red> *understood*
How ill it sits with> that same silver hed *becomes*
In vaine to mocke, or mockt in vaine to bee:
But if thou be, as thou art pourtrahèd
With natures pen, in ages grave degree,> *solemn status*
Aread> in graver wise, what I demaund of thee. *answer*

34 His answere likewise was, he could not tell.
Whose sencelesse speach, and doted ignorance
When as the noble Prince had markèd well,
He ghest his nature by his countenance,
And calmd his wrath with goodly temperance.
Then to him stepping, from his arme did reach
Those keyes, and made himselfe free enterance.
Each dore he openèd without any breach;
There was no barre to stop, nor foe him to empeach.> *hinder*

35 There all within full rich arayd he found,
With royall arras and resplendent gold.
And did with store of every thing abound,
That greatest Princes presence might behold.
But all the floore (too filthy to be told)
With bloud of guiltlesse babes, and innocents trew,
Which there were slaine, as sheepe out of the fold,

Ignaro This Ignorance reflects Spenser's contempt for blind devotion—he showed it in canto iv; Ignaro is silent and pious but lives with and fosters Worldly Pride.

Defilèd was, that dreadfull was to vew,
And sacred ashes over it was strowèd new.

36 And there beside of marble stone was built
An Altare, carv'd with cunning imagery,
On which true Christians bloud was often spilt,
And holy Martyrs often doen to dye,> *put to death*
With cruell malice and strong tyranny.
Whose blessèd sprites from underneath the stone
To God for vengeance cryde continually,°
And with great griefe were often heard to grone,
That hardest heart would bleede, to heare their piteous mone.

37 Through every rowme he sought, and every bowr,
But no where could he find that wofull thrall:
At last he came unto an yron doore,
That fast was lockt, but key found not at all
Emongst that bounch, to open it withall;
But in the same a little grate was pight,> *placed*
Through which he sent his voyce, and lowd did call
With all his powre, to weet, if living wight
Were housèd therewithin, whom he enlargen> might. *set free*

38 Therewith an hollow, dreary, murmuring voyce
These piteous plaints and dolours did resound;
O who is that, which brings me happy choyce
Of death, that here lye dying every stound,> *moment*
Yet live perforce in balefull darkenesse bound?
For now three Moones have changèd thrice° their hew,> *shape*
And have beene thrice hid underneath the ground,
Since I the heavens chearefull face did vew,
O welcome thou, that doest of death bring tydings trew.

39 Which when that Champion heard, with percing point
Of pitty deare> his hart was thrillèd> sore, *great / pierced*
And trembling horrour ran through every joynt,
For ruth of gentle knight so fowle forlore:> *lost*
Which shaking off, he rent that yron dore,
With furious force, and indignation fell;
Where entred in, his foot could find no flore,
But all a deepe descent, as darke as hell,
That breathèd ever forth a filthie banefull smell.

40 But neither darkenesse fowle, nor filthy bands,> *bonds*
Nor noyous> smell his purpose could withhold, *noxious*

Whose . . . continually At the opening of the Fifth Seal St. John "saw under the altar the souls of them that were slain for the word of God . . . And they cried with a loud voice, saying, How long, O Lord, holy and true, dost thou not judge and avenge our blood . . . ?" (Revelation 6:9–10); in this canto the apocalyptic theme is unusually evident.

three Moones . . . thrice three months, representing the three centuries between Pope Gregory VII and Wyclif during which England was supposed to have been under the domination of the papacy

(Entire affection hateth nicer> hands) *too fastidious*
But that with constant zeale, and courage bold,
After long paines and labours manifold,
He found the meanes that Prisoner up to reare;
Whose feeble thighes, unhable to uphold
His pinèd corse,> him scarse to light could beare, *wasted corpse*
A ruefull spectacle of death and ghastly drere.> *wretchedness*

41 His sad dull eyes deepe sunck in hollow pits,
Could not endure th'unwonted sunne to view;
His bare thin cheekes for want of better bits,> *food*
And empty sides deceivèd of their dew,
Could make a stony hart his hap> to rew; *luck*
His rawbone armes, whose mighty brawnèd bowrs> *muscles*
Were wont to rive steele plates, and helmets hew,
Were cleane consum'd, and all his vitall powres
Decayd, and all his flesh shronk up like withered flowres.

42 Whom when his Lady saw, to him she ran
With hasty joy: to see him made her glad,
And sad to view his visage pale and wan,
Who earst> in flowres of freshest youth was clad. *formerly*
Tho when her well of teares she wasted had,
She said, Ah dearest Lord, what evill starre
On you hath fround, and pourd his influence bad,
That of your selfe ye thus berobbèd arre,
And this misseeming hew> your manly looks doth marre? *appearance*

43 But welcome now my Lord, in wele or woe,
Whose presence I have lackt too long a day;
And fie on Fortune mine avowèd foe,
Whose wrathfull wreakes> them selves do now alay.> *injuries / diminish*
And for these wrongs shall treble penaunce pay
Of treble good: good growes of evils priefe.> *test, experience*
The chearelesse man, whom sorrow did dismay,
Had no delight to treaten> of his griefe; *talk*
His long endurèd famine needed more reliefe.

44 Faire Lady, then said that victorious knight,
The things, that grievous were to do, or beare,
Them to renew, I wote, breeds no delight;°
Best musicke breeds delight in loathing eare:°
But th'onely good, that growes of passèd feare,
Is to be wise, and ware> of like agein. *wary*
This dayes ensample hath this lesson deare

Them . . . delight remembering the famous line (*Aeneid* II.3), in which Aeneas answers Dido's request that he should tell the story of his adventures: *Infandum, regina, jubes renovare dolorem* ("Queen, you are commanding me to renew unspeakable grief")

Best . . . eare although fine music can produce pleasure even in the ear that resists it (this is not true of the knight's story)

Deepe written in my heart with yron pen,
That blisse may not abide in state of mortall men.

45 Henceforth sir knight, take to you wonted strength,
And maister these mishaps with patient might;
Loe where your foe lyes stretcht in monstrous length,
And loe that wicked woman in your sight,
The roote of all your care, and wretched plight,
Now in your powre, to let her live, or dye.
To do her dye (quoth *Una*) were despight,
And shame t'avenge so weake an enimy;
But spoile her of her scarlot robe, and let her fly.

46 So as she bad, that witch they disaraid,
And robd of royall robes, and purple pall,
And ornaments that richly were displaid;
Ne sparèd they to strip her naked all.
Then when they had despoild her tire˃ and call,˃ *dress / headdress*
Such as she was, their eyes might her behold,
That her misshapèd parts did them appall,
A loathly, wrinckled hag, ill favoured, old,
Whose secret filth good manners biddeth not be told.

47 Her craftie head was altogether bald,
And as in hate of honorable eld,˃ *old age*
Was overgrowne with scurfe and filthy scald;˃ *scabs*
Her teeth out of her rotten gummes were feld,˃ *fallen*
And her sowre breath abhominably smeld;
Her drièd dugs, like bladders lacking wind,
Hong downe, and filthy matter from them weld;
Her wrizled˃ skin as rough, as maple rind, *wrinkled*
So scabby was, that would have loathd all womankind.

48 Her neather parts, the shame of all her kind,˃ *womenkind*
My chaster Muse for shame doth blush to write;
But at her rompe she growing had behind
A foxes taile,° with dong all fowly dight;˃ *covered*
And eke her feete most monstrous were in sight;
For one of them was like an Eagles claw,
With griping talaunts armd to greedy fight,
The other like a Beares uneven˃ paw: *rough*
More ugly shape yet never living creature saw.

49 Which when the knights beheld, amazd they were,
And wondred at so fowle deformèd wight.
Such then (said *Una*) as she seemeth here,
Such is the face of falshood, such the sight
Of fowle *Duessa*, when her borrowed light

Foxes taile The fox was associated in contemporary polemic with the Catholic clergy; the text was Song of Songs 2:15, supported by Luke 13:32, where Jesus calls Herod a fox.

Is laid away, and counterfesaunce˃ knowne. *deception*
Thus when they had the witch disrobèd quight,°
And all her filthy feature open showne,
They let her goe at will, and wander wayes unknowne.

50 She flying fast from heavens hated face,
And from the world that her discovered wide,
Fled to the wastfull wildernesse apace,
From living eyes her open shame to hide,
And lurkt in rocks and caves long unespide.
But that faire crew of knights, and *Una* faire
Did in that castle afterwards abide,
To rest them selves, and weary powres repaire,
Where store they found of all, that dainty was and rare.°

Canto ix

[In canto ix we hear Arthur's story of his love for Gloriana. He exchanges gifts, Arthur's symbolizing the Eucharist, and Red Cross's the New Testament, and Arthur leaves. Red Cross then meets Sir Trevisan, fleeing from the Cave of Despair; he goes to the Cave and meets Despair, to whom he almost succumbs. In terms of the spiritual allegory this passage describes a great crisis in the career of what Milton calls the "wayfaring" Christian soul; despair is the greatest single threat to it. In terms of the historical allegory, following the exposure of Duessa, it means the relapse into Romanism under Queen Mary, before the Elizabethan Settlement established the true church for ever.]

His loves and lignage Arthur tells:
The knights knit friendly bands:
Sir Trevisan flies from Despayre,
Whom Redcrosse knight withstands.

1 O goodly golden chaine,° wherewith yfere˃ *together*
The vertues linkèd are in lovely wize:
And noble minds of yore allyèd were,
In brave poursuit of chevalrous emprize,˃ *enterprise*
That none did others safèty despize,
Nor aid envy˃ to him, in need that stands, *grudge*
But friendly each did others prayse devize
How to advaunce with favourable hands,
As this good Prince redeemd the *Redcrosse* knight from bands.˃ *bonds*

2 Who when their powres, empaird˃ through labour long, *weakened*
With dew repast they had recurèd˃ well, *restored*
And that weake captive wight now wexèd strong,
Them list˃ no lenger there at leasure dwell, *they wished*
But forward fare, as their adventures fell,

disrobèd quight Revelation 17:16: "these shall hate the whore, and shall make her desolate and naked . . . ".

store . . . rare They confiscate the viciously acquired wealth of Orgoglio and Duessa, which figures the confiscation of monastic wealth in the reign of Henry VIII.

chaine See I.v.25 and note.

But ere they parted, *Una* faire besought
That straunger knight his name and nation tell;
Least˃ so great good, as he for her had wrought, *lest*
Should die unknown, and buried be in thanklesse thought.

3 Faire virgin (said the Prince) ye me require
A thing without˃ the compas of my wit: *outside*
For both the lignage and the certain˃ Sire, *true*
From which I sprong, from me are hidden yit.
For all so soone as life did me admit
Into this world, and shewèd heavens light,
From mothers pap˃ I taken was unfit:˃ *breast / untimely*
And streight deliverèd to a Faery knight,
To be upbrought in gentle˃ thewes˃ and martiall might. *noble/manners*

4 Unto old *Timon*° he me brought bylive,˃ *forthwith*
Old *Timon*, who in youthly yeares hath beene
In warlike feates th'expertest man alive,
And is the wisest now on earth I weene;
His dwelling is low in a valley greene,
Under the foot of *Rauran*° mossy hore;˃ *gray with moss*
From whence the river *Dee*° as silver cleene
His tombling billowes rolls with gentle rore:
There all my dayes he traind me up in vertuous lore.

5 Thither the great Magicien *Merlin* came,
As was his use, ofttimes to visit me:
For he had charge my discipline to frame,
And Tutours nouriture˃ to oversee. *education*
Him oft and oft I askt in privitie,
Of what loines and what lignage I did spring:
Whose aunswere bad me still assurèd bee,
That I was sonne and heire unto a king,
As time in her just terme° the truth to light should bring.

6 Well worthy impe,˃ said then the Lady gent,˃ *scion / gentle*
And Pupill fit for such a Tutours hand.
But what adventure, or what high intent
Hath brought you hither into Faery land,
Aread˃ Prince *Arthur*, crowne of Martiall band? *tell*
Full hard it is (quoth he) to read aright
The course of heavenly cause, or understand
The secret meaning of th'eternall might,
That rules mens wayes, and rules the thoughts of living wight.

Timon Honor (*Greek*)
Rauran a hill in northwest Wales. The Tudors, a Welsh family, claimed descent from King Arthur, last king of all ancient Britain; the claim was an important element in their propaganda, for essentially their claim to the throne was shaky.
Dee river of North Wales, often associated with the ancient Britons—Milton speaks of its "wizard stream" in *Lycidas*.
just terme due season; alluding to the saying *veritas filia temporis*, "truth is the daughter of time"

7 For whither he through fatall˃ deepe foresight — *ordained by fate*
Me hither sent, for cause to me unghest,˃ — *unguessed*
Or that fresh bleeding wound, which day and night
Whilome˃ doth rancle in my riven brest, — *continuously*
With forcèd fury following his˃ behest, — *its*
Me hither brought by wayes yet never found,
You to have helpt I hold my selfe yet blest.
Ah curteous knight (quoth she) what secret wound
Could ever find, to grieve the gentlest hart on ground?˃ — *in the world*

8 Deare Dame (quoth he) you sleeping sparkes awake,
Which troubled once, into huge flames will grow,
Ne ever will their fervent fury slake,
Till living moysture into smoke do flow,
And wasted˃ life do lye in ashes low. — *consumed*
Yet sithens˃ silence lesseneth not my fire, — *since*
But told it flames, and hidden it does glow,
I will revele, what ye so much desire:
Ah Love, lay downe thy bow, the whiles I may respire.˃ — *breathe, rest*

9 It was in freshest flowre of youthly yeares,
When courage first does creepe in manly chest,
Then first the coale of kindly˃ heat appeares — *natural*
To kindle love in every living brest;
But me had warnd old *Timons* wise behest,
Those creeping flames by reason to subdew,
Before their rage grew to so great unrest,
As miserable lovers use to rew,
Which still wex old in woe, whiles woe still wexeth new.

10 That idle˃ name of love, and lovers life, — *foolish, vain*
As losse of time, and vertues enimy
I ever scornd, and joyd to stirre up strife,
In middest of their mournfull Tragedy,
Ay˃ wont˃ to laugh, when them I heard to cry, — *always / accustomed*
And blow the fire, which them to ashes brent:˃ — *burnt*
Their God° himselfe, griev'd at my libertie,˃ — *immunity*
Shot many a dart at me with fiers intent,
But I them warded all with wary government.˃ — *self-control*

11 But all in vaine: no fort can be so strong,
Ne fleshly brest can armèd be so sound,
But will at last be wonne with battrie˃ long, — *siege*
Or unawares at disadvantage found;
Nothing is sure that growes on earthly ground:
And who most trustes in arme of fleshly might,
And boasts, in beauties chaine not to be bound,

God Cupid

Doth soonest fall in disaventrous> fight, *disastrous*
And yeeldes his caytive neck to victours most> despight. *greatest*

12 Ensample make of him your haplesse joy,> *love (Red Cross)*
And of my selfe now mated,> as ye see; *defeated*
Whose prouder vaunt that proud avenging boy
Did soone plucke downe, and curbd my libertie.
For on a day prickt> forth with jollitie *urged*
Of looser> life, and heat of hardiment,> *too loose / boldness*
Raunging the forest wide on courser free,
The fields, the floods, the heavens with one consent
Did seeme to laugh on me, and favour mine intent.

13 For-wearied with my sports, I did alight
From loftie steed, and downe to sleepe me layd;
The verdant gras my couch did goodly dight,> *adorn*
And pillow was my helmet faire displayd:
Whiles every sence the humour> sweet embayd,> *moisture / bathed*
And slombring soft my hart did steale away,
Me seemèd, by my side a royall Mayd
Her daintie limbes full softly down did lay:
So faire a creature yet saw never sunny day.°

14 Most goodly glee> and lovely blandishment *pleasure*
She to me made, and bad me love her deare,
For dearely sure her love was to me bent,
As when just time expirèd should appeare.
But whether dreames delude, or true it were,
Was never hart so ravisht with delight,
Ne living man like words did ever heare,
As she to me delivered all that night;
And at her parting said, She Queene of Faeries hight.> *was called*

15 When I awoke, and found her place devoyd,> *empty*
And nought but pressèd gras, where she had lyen,
I sorrowed all so much, as earst I joyd,
And washèd all her place with watry eyen.
From that day forth I lov'd that face divine;
From that day forth I cast> in carefull mind, *resolved*
To seeke her out with labour, and long tyne,> *toil*
And never vow to rest, till her I find,
Nine monethes I seeke in vaine yet ni'll> that vow unbind. *will not*

16 Thus as he spake, his visage wexèd pale,
And chaunge of hew great passion did bewray;> *reveal*
Yet still he strove to cloke his inward bale,> *sorrow*

Me seemèd . . . day The theme of the fairy lover who visits a sleeping knight is Celtic in origin.

And hide the smoke, that did his fire display,
Till gentle *Una* thus to him gan say;
O happy Queene of Faeries, that hast found
Mongst many, one that with his prowesse may
Defend thine honour, and thy foes confound:
True Loves are often sown, but seldom grow on ground.

17 Thine, O then, said the gentle *Redcrosse* knight,
Next to that Ladies love, shalbe the place,
O fairest virgin, full of heavenly light,
Whose wondrous faith, exceeding earthly race,
Was firmest fixt in mine extremest case.˃ *emergency*
And you, my Lord, the Patrone of my life,
Of that great Queene may well gaine worthy grace:
For onely worthy you through prowes priefe˃ *test of valor*
Yf living man mote worthy be, to be her liefe.˃ *beloved*

18 So diversly discoursing of their loves,
The golden Sunne his glistring head gan shew,
And sad remembraunce now the Prince amoves,
With fresh desire his voyage˃ to pursew: *journey*
Als˃ *Una* earnd˃ her traveill to renew. *also / yearned*
Then those two knights, fast friendship for to bynd,
And love establish each to other trew,
Gave goodly gifts, the signes of gratefull mynd,
And eke as pledges firme, right hands together joynd.

19 Prince *Arthur* gave a boxe of Diamond sure,˃ *flawless*
Embowd with gold and gorgeous ornament,
Wherein were closd few drops of liquor pure,
Of wondrous worth, and vertue excellent,
That any wound could heale incontinent:˃ *at once*
Which to requite, the *Redcrosse* knight him gave
A booke, wherein his Saveours testament
Was writ with golden letters rich and brave;
A worke of wondrous grace, and able soules to save.°

20 Thus beene they parted, *Arthur* on his way
To seeke his love, and th'other for to fight
With *Unaes* foe, that all her realme did pray.˃ *prey upon*
But she now weighing the decayèd plight,
And shrunken synewes of her chosen knight,
Would not a while her forward course pursew,
Ne bring him forth in face of dreadfull fight,
Till he recovered had his former hew:˃ *shape*
For him to be yet weake and wearie well she knew.

Prince . . . save This exchange of gifts is variously explained. Some say that Arthur gives the Eucharist, Red Cross the New Testament. More probably the reference is to the English coronation rite, at which the king is anointed with holy oil; Edward VI, Elizabeth's brother, was the first to be given a New Testament.

21 So as they traveild, lo they gan espy
An armèd knight towards them gallop fast,
That seemèd from some fearèd foe to fly,
Or other griesly thing, that him agast.˃ *terrified*
Still as he fled, his eye was backward cast,
As if his feare still followed him behind;
Als flew his steed, as he his bands˃ had brast,˃ *bonds / burst*
And with his wingèd heeles did tread the wind,
As he had beene a fole of *Pegasus*° his kind.

22 Nigh as he drew, they might perceive his head
To be unarmd, and curld uncombèd heares
Upstaring˃ stiffe, dismayd with uncouth˃ dread; *bristling / unheard of*
Nor drop of bloud in all his face appeares
Nor life in limbe: and to increase his feares,
In fowle reproch of knighthoods faire degree,˃ *rank*
About his neck an hempen rope he weares,
That with his glistring armes does ill agree;
But he of rope or armes has now no memoree.

23 The *Redcrosse* knight toward him crossèd fast,
To weet, what mister wight˃ was so dismayd: *kind of man*
There him he finds all sencelesse and aghast,
That of him selfe he seemd to be afrayd;
Whom hardly he from flying forward stayd,
Till he these wordes to him deliver might;
Sir knight, aread˃ who hath ye thus arayd, *say*
And eke from whom make ye this hasty flight:
For never knight I saw in such misseeming˃ plight. *unbecoming*

24 He answerd nought at all, but adding new
Feare to his first amazment, staring wide
With stony eyes, and hartlesse˃ hollow hew, *disheartened*
Astonisht stood, as one that had aspide
Infernall furies, with their chaines untide.
Him yet againe, and yet againe bespake
The gentle knight; who nought to him replide,
But trembling every joynt did inly quake,
And foltring˃ tongue at last these words seemd forth to shake. *faltering*

25 For Gods deare love, Sir knight, do me not stay;
For loe he comes, he comes fast after mee.
Eft˃ looking backe would faine have runne away; *again*
But he him forst to stay, and tellen free
The secret cause of his perplexitie:
Yet nathemore˃ by his bold hartie speach, *none the more*
Could his bloud-frosen hart emboldned bee,

Pegasus the winged horse that sprang from the blood of Medusa

But through his boldnesse rather feare did reach,
Yet forst, at last he made through silence suddein breach.

26 And am I now in safetie sure (quoth he)
From him, that would have forcèd me to dye?
And is the point of death now turnd fro mee,
That I may tell this haplesse history?
Feare nought: (quoth he) no daunger now is nye.
Then shall I you recount a ruefull cace,
(Said he) the which with this unlucky eye
I late beheld, and had not greater grace
Me reft from it, had been partaker of the place.°

27 I lately chaunst (Would I had never chaunst)
With a faire knight to keepen companee,
Sir *Terwin* hight, that well himselfe advaunst
In all affaires, and was both bold and free,
But not so happie as mote happie bee:
He lov'd, as was his lot, a Ladie gent,˃ *gracious*
That him againe˃ lov'd in the least degree: *in return*
For she was proud, and of too high intent,˃ *ambition*
And joyd to see her lover languish and lament.

28 From whom returning sad and comfortlesse,
As on the way together we did fare,
We met that villen (God from him me blesse˃) *protect*
That cursèd wight, from whom I scapt whyleare,˃ *recently*
A man of hell, that cals himself *Despaire*:°
Who first us greets, and after faire areedes˃ *tells*
Of tydings strange, and of adventures rare:
So creeping close, as Snake in hidden weedes,
Inquireth of our states, and of our knightly deedes.

29 Which when he knew, and felt our feeble harts
Embost with bale,˃ and bitter byting griefe, *enveloped in sorrow*
Which love had launchèd with his deadly darts,
With wounding words and termes of foule repriefe˃ *reproof*
He pluckt from us all hope of due reliefe,
That earst us held in love of lingring life;
Then hopelesse hartlesse, gan the cunning thiefe
Perswade us die, to stint˃ all further strife: *end*
To me he lent this rope, to him a rustie knife.

30 With which sad instrument of hastie death,
That wofull lover, loathing lenger light,
A wide way made to let forth living breath.
But I more fearefull, or more luckie wight,

had . . . place would myself have experienced the fate of my companion
Despaire the sin held to be a denial of God's mercy. Red Cross must also pass through this temptation.

Dismayd with that deformèd dismall sight,
Fled fast away, halfe deade with dying feare:
Ne yet assur'd of life by you, Sir knight,
Whose like infirmitie like chaunce may beare:
But God you never let˃ his charmèd speeches heare. *may God never allow you*

31 How may a man (said he) with idle˃ speach *empty*
Be wonne, to spoyle˃ the Castle of his health? *despoil*
I wote (quoth he) whom triall late did teach,
That like would not° for all this worldès wealth:
His subtill tongue, like dropping honny, mealt'th˃ *melts*
Into the hart, and searcheth every vaine,
That ere one be aware, by secret stealth
His powre is reft, and weaknesse doth remaine.
O never Sir desire to try˃ his guilefull traine.˃ *test / trickery*

32 Certes˃ (said he) hence shall I never rest, *indeed*
Till I that treachours art have heard and tride;
And you Sir knight, whose name mote I request,
Of grace do me unto his cabin guide.
I that hight *Trevisan* (quoth he) will ride
Against my liking backe, to doe you grace:
But nor for gold nor glee˃ will I abide *glitter*
By you, when ye arrive in that same place;
For lever had˃ I die, then see his deadly face. *rather would*

33 Ere long they come, where that same wicked wight°
His dwelling has, low in an hollow cave,
Farre underneath a craggie clift ypight,˃ *placed*
Darke, dolefull, drearie, like a greedie grave,
That still for carrion carcases doth crave:
On top whereof aye dwelt the ghastly Owle,
Shrieking his balefull note, which ever drave
Farre from that haunt all other chearefull fowle;
And all about it wandring ghostes did waile and howle.

34 And all about old stockes and stubs of trees,
Whereon nor fruit, nor leafe was ever seene,
Did hang upon the ragged rocky knees;˃ *crags*
On which had many wretches hangèd beene,
Whose carcases were scattered on the greene,
And throwne about the cliffs. Arrivèd there,
That bare-head knight for dread and dolefull teene,˃ *grief*
Would faine have fled, ne durst approchen neare,
But th'other forst him stay, and comforted in feare.

I wote . . . not I know one . . . who wouldn't . . . **wight** Despair

35 That darkesome cave they enter, where they find
That cursèd man, low sitting on the ground,
Musing full sadly in his sullein mind;
His griesie> lockes, long growen, and unbound, *gray*
Disordred hong about his shoulders round,
And hid his face; through which his hollow eyne
Lookt deadly dull, and starèd as astound;
His raw-bone cheekes through penurie and pine,> *hunger*
Were shronke into his jawes, as> he did never dine. *as though*

36 His garments nought but many ragged clouts,> *cloths*
With thornes together pind and patchèd was,
The which his naked sides he wrapt abouts;
And him beside there lay upon the gras
A dreary corse, whose life away did pas,
All wallowd in his owne yet> luke-warme blood, *still*
That from his wound yet wellèd fresh alas;
In which a rustie knife fast fixèd stood,
And made an open passage for the gushing flood.

37 Which piteous spectacle, approving> trew *proving*
The wofull tale that *Trevisan* had told,
When as the gentle *Redcrosse* knight did vew,
With firie zeale he burnt in courage bold,
Him to avenge, before his bloud were cold,
And to the villein said, Thou damnèd wight,
The author of this fact,> we here behold, *deed*
What justice can but judge against thee right,
With thine owne bloud to price> his bloud, here shed in sight? *pay for*

38 What franticke fit (quoth he) hath thus distraught
Thee, foolish man, so rash a doome> to give? *judgment*
What justice ever other judgement taught,
But he should die, who merites not to live?
None else to death this man despayring drive,> *drove*
But his owne guiltie mind deserving death.
Is then unjust to each his due to give?
Or let him die, that loatheth living breath?
Or let him die at ease, that liveth here uneath?> *uneasy*

39 Who travels by the wearie wandring way,
To come unto his wishèd home in haste,
And meetes a flood, that doth his passage stay,
Is not great grace to helpe him over past,> *to pass over*
Or free his feet, that in the myre sticke fast?
Most envious man, that grieves at neighbours good,
And fond,> that joyest in the woe thou hast, *foolish*
Why wilt not let him passe, that long hath stood
Upon the banke, yet wilt thy selfe not passe the flood?

40 He there does now enjoy eternall rest
And happie ease, which thou doest want and crave,
And further from it daily wanderest:
What if some litle paine the passage have,
That makes fraile flesh to feare the bitter wave?
Is not short paine well borne, that brings long ease,
And layes the soule to sleepe in quiet grave?
Sleepe after toyle, port after stormie seas,
Ease after warre, death after life° does greatly please.

41 The knight much wondred at his suddeine> wit, *quick*
And said, The terme of life is limited,
Ne may a man prolong, nor shorten it;
The souldier may not move from watchfull sted,> *post*
Nor leave his stand, untill his Captaine bed.> *orders*
Who life did limit by almightie doome,> *judgment*
(Quoth he) knowes best the terms establishèd;
And he, that points> the Centonell his roome,> *appoints / post*
Doth license him depart at sound of morning droome.

42 Is not his deed, what ever thing is donne,
In heaven and earth? did not he all create
To die againe? all ends that was begonne.
Their times in his eternall booke of fate
Are written sure, and have their certaine date.> *termination*
Who then can strive with strong necessitie,
That holds the world in his> still chaunging state, *its*
Or shunne the death ordaynd by destinie?
When houre of death is come, let none aske whence, nor why.

43 The lenger life, I wote> the greater sin, *think*
The greater sin, the greater punishment:
All those great battels, which thou boasts to win,
Through strife, and bloud-shed, and avengèment,
Now praysd, hereafter deare thou shalt repent:
For life must life, and bloud must bloud repay.
Is not enough thy evill life forespent?
For he, that once hath missèd the right way,
The further he doth goe, the further he doth stray.

44 Then do no further goe, no further stray,
But here lie downe, and to thy rest betake,
Th'ill to prevent, that life ensewen may.°
For what hath life, that may it lovèd make,
And gives not rather cause it to forsake?
Feare, sicknesse, age, losse, labour, sorrow, strife,
Paine, hunger, cold, that makes the hart to quake;

death . . . life This is Despair's "suddeine wit"—he smuggles this item, which is not parallel to the others, into his list; all his subsequent arguments have the same kind of rhetorical plausibility.

that . . . may that may follow life

And ever fickle fortune rageth rife,
All which, and thousands mo› do make a loathsome life. *more*

45 Thou wretched man, of death hast greatest need,
If in true ballance thou wilt weigh thy state:
For never knight, that darèd warlike deede,
More lucklesse disaventures did amate:› *overthrow*
Witnesse the dongeon deepe, wherein of late
Thy life shut up, for death so oft did call;
And though good lucke prolongèd hath thy date,
Yet death then, would the like mishaps forestall,
Into the which hereafter thou maiest happen fall.

46 Why then doest thou, O man of sin, desire
To draw thy dayes forth to their last degree?
Is not the measure of thy sinfull hire› *service to sin*
High heapèd up with huge iniquitie,
Against the day of wrath, to burden thee?
Is not enough, that to this Ladie milde
Thou falsèd hast thy faith with perjurie,
And sold thy selfe to serve *Duessa* vilde,› *vile*
With whom in all abuse thou hast thy selfe defilde?

47 Is not he just, that all this doth behold
From highest heaven, and beares an equall› eye? *impartial*
Shall he thy sins up in his knowledge fold,
And guiltie be of thine impietie?
Is not his law, Let every sinner die:
Die shall all flesh?° what then must needs be donne,
Is it not better to doe willinglie,
Then linger, till the glasse be all out ronne?
Death is the end of woes: die soone, O faeries sonne.

48 The knight was much enmovèd with his speach,
That as a swords point through his hart did perse,
And in his conscience made a secret breach,
Well knowing true all, that he did reherse› *recount*
And to his fresh remembrance did reverse› *bring back*
The ugly vew of his deformèd crimes,
That all his manly powres it did disperse,
As he were charmèd with inchaunted rimes,
That oftentimes he quakt, and fainted oftentimes.

49 In which amazement, when the Miscreant
Perceivèd him to waver weake and fraile,
Whiles trembling horror did his conscience dant,› *daunt*
And hellish anguish did his soule assaile,

Is . . . flesh Despair naturally omits to mention that God modified this sentence, or that He forbade suicide.

To drive him to despaire, and quite to quaile,> *be dismayed*
He shew'd him painted in a table> plaine, *picture*
The damnèd ghosts, that doe in torments waile,
And thousand feends that doe them endlesse paine
With fire and brimstone, which for ever shall remaine.

50 The sight whereof so throughly him dismaid,
That nought but death before his eyes he saw,
And ever burning wrath before him laid,
By righteous sentence of th'Almighties law:
Then gan the villein him to overcraw,> *exult over*
And brought unto him swords, ropes, poison, fire,
And all that might him to perdition draw;
And bad him choose, what death he would desire:
For death was due to him, that had provokt Gods ire.°

51 But when as none of them he saw him take,
He to him raught> a dagger sharpe and keene, *handed*
And gave it him in hand: his hand did quake,
And tremble like a leafe of Aspin> greene, *poplar*
And troubled bloud through his pale face was seene
To come, and goe with tydings from the hart,
As it a running messenger had beene.
At last resolv'd to worke his finall smart,
He lifted up his hand, that backe again did start.

52 Which when as *Una* saw, through every vaine
The crudled> cold ran to her well of life, *congealed*
As in a swowne:> but soone reliv'd> againe, *faint / revived*
Out of his hand she snatcht the cursèd knife,
And threw it to the ground, enragèd rife,> *deeply*
And to him said, Fie, fie, faint harted knight,
What meanest thou by this reprochfull strife?
Is this the battell, which thou vauntst to fight
With that fire-mouthèd Dragon, horrible and bright?

53 Come, come away, fraile, feeble, fleshly wight,
Ne let vaine words bewitch thy manly hart,
Ne divelish thoughts dismay thy constant spright.
In heavenly mercies hast thou not a part?
Why shouldst thou then despeire, that chosen art?°
Where justice growes, there grows eke greater grace,°
The which doth quench the brond of hellish smart,> *pain*

death . . . ire Red Cross has been deceived into the desperate belief that his sins are unforgivable and that he should therefore anticipate the judgment of God.

chosen art theological: he is one of God's Elect, chosen before the creation for heaven. This "single" predestinarianism—there is election to salvation but not to damnation—is the less rigid form of the Calvinist doctrine: see *Paradise Lost* III.183 ff.: "Some I have chosen of peculiar grace / Elect above the rest; so is my will; / The rest shall hear me call, and oft be warned / Their sinful state, and to appease betimes / The incensed deity, while offered grace / Invites. . . ."

where . . . grace Una reminds him of the fact Despair wanted him to forget: God's justice is followed by even greater grace.

And that accurst hand-writing doth deface.
Arise, Sir knight arise, and leave this cursèd place.

54 So up he rose, and thence amounted˃ streight. *mounted*
Which when the carle˃ beheld, and saw his gust *churl*
Would safe depart, for all his subtill sleight,
He chose an halter from among the rest,
And with it hung himselfe, unbid˃ unblest. *unprayed for*
But death he could not worke himselfe thereby;
For thousand times he so himselfe had drest,˃ *prepared*
Yet nathelesse it could not doe him die,˃ *kill him*
Till he should die his last, that is eternally.

Canto x°

Her faithfull knight faire Una brings
to house of Holinesse,
Where he is taught repentance, and
the way to heavenly blesse.˃ *bliss*

1 What man is he, that boasts of fleshly might,
And vaine assurance of mortality;˃ *mortal life*
Which all so soone, as it doth come to fight,
Against spirituall foes, yeelds by and by,
Or from the field most cowardly doth fly?
Ne let the man ascribe it to his skill,
That thorough˃ grace hath gainèd victory. *through*
If any strength we have, it is to ill,
But all the good is Gods, both power and eke will.°

2 By that, which lately hapned, *Una* saw,
That this her knight was feeble, and too faint;
And all his sinews woxen˃ weake and raw, *grown*
Through long emprisonment, and hard constraint,
Which he endurèd in his late restraint,
That yet he was unfit for bloudie fight:
Therefore to cherish him with diets daint,˃ *dainty*
She cast to bring him, where he chearen˃ might, *restored to health and spirits*
Till he recovered had his˃ late decayèd plight. *from his*

3 There was an auntient house not farre away,
Renowned throughout the world for sacred lore,

Canto x The House of Holiness is an elaborate allegorical set-piece; Red Cross meets the Three Theological Virtues, Fidelia, Speranza, and Charissa (Faity, Hope, and Charity), sketched with their emblematical attributes and called the daughters of Caelia (Heaven). He undergoes penance and, in the allegory of the beadsmen, performs the Seven Corporal Works of Mercy. This prepares him for Contemplation, who shows him, from the top of a holy mountain, the Heavenly Jerusalem, which he compares with its earthly counterpart Cleopolis (London). Now he acquires his saint's name and reluctantly departs to finish his quest.

If any . . . will A doctrine of importance in the Reformed churches: see Ephesians 2:8–9.

And pure unspotted life: so well they say
It governed was, and guided evermore,
Through wisedome of a matrone grave and hore;˃ *gray-haired*
Whose onely joy was to relieve the needes
Of wretched soules, and helpe the helpelesse pore:
All night she spent in bidding of her bedes,˃
telling her beads (saying her prayers)
And all the day in doing good and godly deedes.

4 Dame *Cælia*° men did her call, as thought
From heaven to come, or thither to arise,
The mother of three daughters, well upbrought
In goodly thewes,˃ and godly exercise: *qualities*
The eldest two most sober, chast, and wise,
Fidelia° and *Speranza*° virgins were,
Though spousd, yet wanting wedlocks solemnize;˃ *solemnization*
But faire *Charissa*° to a lovely fere˃ *mate*
Was linckèd, and by him had many pledges˃ dere. *children*

5 Arrivèd there, the dore they find fast lockt;
For it was warely watchèd night and day,
For feare of many foes: but when they knockt,°
The Porter opened unto them streight way:
He was an agèd syre, all hory gray,
With lookes full lowly cast, and gate˃ full slow, *gait*
Wont on a staffe his feeble steps to stay,˃ *support*
Hight *Humiltà.*° They passe in stouping low;
For streight and narrow was the way,° which he did show.

6 Each goodly thing is hardest to begin,
But entred in a spacious court they see,
Both plaine, and pleasant to be walkèd in,
Where them does meete a francklin˃ faire and free, *landowner*
And entertaines with comely courteous glee,
His name was *Zele*, that him right well became,
For in his speeches and behavior hee
Did labour lively to expresse the same,
And gladly did them guide, till to the Hall they came.

7 There fairely them receives a gentle Squire,
Of milde demeanure, and rare courtesie,
Right cleanly clad in comely sad˃ attire; *dark*
In word and deede that shew'd great modestie,
And knew his good˃ to all of each degree, *proper conduct*
Hight *Reverence*. He them with speeches meet

Caelia "heavenly"
Fidelia "faith"
Speranza "hope"
Charissa "charity" (love); always represented with many children in allegorical representations of the Theological Virtues (see I Corinthians 13:13)
knockt Matthew 7:7
Humiltà "humility"
streight . . . way Matthew 7:14

Does faire entreat; no courting nicetie,˃ *affected manners*
But simple true, and eke unfainèd sweet,
As might become a Squire so great persons to greet.

8 And afterwards them to his Dame he leades,
That agèd Dame, the Ladie of the place:
Who all this while was busie at her beades:
Which doen, she up arose with seemely grace,
And tòward them full matronely did pace.
Where when that fairest *Una* she beheld,
Whom well she knew to spring from heavenly race,
Her hart with joy unwonted inly sweld,
As feeling wondrous comfort in her weaker eld.˃ *old age*

9 And her embracing said, O happie earth,
Whereon thy innocent feet doe ever tread,
Most vertuous virgin borne of heavenly berth,
That to redeeme thy woefull parents head,
From tyrans˃ rage, and ever-dying dread,˃ *tyrant's / perpetual fear of death*
Hast wandred through the world now long a day;
Yet ceasest not thy wearie soles to lead,
What grace hath thee now hither brought this way?
Or doen˃ thy feeble feet unweeting˃ hither stray? *do / unwittingly*

10 Strange thing it is an errant knight to see
Here in this place, or any other wight,
That hither turnes his steps. So few there bee,
That chose˃ the narrow path, or seeke the right: *choose*
All keepe the broad high way, and take delight
With many rather for to go astray,
And be partakers of their evill plight,
Then with a few to walke the rightest way;
O foolish men, why haste ye to your owne decay?

11 Thy selfe to see, and tyred limbs to rest,
O matrone sage (quoth she) I hither came,
And this good knight his way with me addrest,˃ *directed*
Led with thy prayses and broad-blazèd fame,
That up to heaven is blowne. The auncient Dame
Him goodly greeted in her modest guise,
And entertaynd them both, as best became,
With all the court'sies,˃ that she could devise, *courtesies*
Ne wanted ought, to shew her bounteous or wise.

12 Thus as they gan of sundry things devise,˃ *converse*
Loe two most goodly virgins° came in place,

two . . . virgins The description of Faith and Hope, like that of Charity (see note on stanza 4), conforms to the traditional iconography.

Ylinkèd arme in arme in lovely˃ wise, *loving*
With countenance demure, and modest grace,
They numbred even steps and equall pace:
Of which the eldest, that *Fidelia* hight,
Like sunny beames threw from her Christall face,
That could have dazd the rash beholders sight,
And round about her head did shine like heavens light.

13 She was araièd all in lilly white,
And in her right hand bore a cup of gold,
With wine and water fild up to the hight,
In which a Serpent did himselfe enfold,°
That horrour made to all, that did behold;
But she no whit did chaunge her constant mood:˃ *expression*
And in her other hand she fast did hold
A booke, that was both signd and seald with blood,°
Wherein darke things were writ, hard to be understood.

14 Her younger sister, that *Speranza* hight,
Was clad in blew, that her beseemèd well;
Not all so chearefull seemèd she of sight,
As was her sister; whether dread did dwell,
Or anguish in her hart, is hard to tell:
Upon her arme a silver anchor° lay,
Whereon she leanèd ever, as befell:
And ever up to heaven, as she did pray,
Her stedfast eyes were bent, ne swarvèd˃ other way. *swerved*

15 They seeing *Una,* towards her gan wend,
Who them encounters with like courtesie;
Many kind speeches they betwene them spend,
And greatly joy each other well to see:
Then to the knight with shamefast˃ modestie *bashful*
They turne themselves, at *Unaes* meeke request,
And him salute with well beseeming glee;
Who faire them quites,˃ as him beseemèd best, *replies to*
And goodly gan discourse of many a noble gest.˃ *feat of arms*

16 Then *Una* thus; But she your sister deare;
The deare *Charissa* where is she become?˃ *what has become of her?*
Or wants she health, or busie is elsewhere?
Ah no, said they, but forth she may not come:
For she of late is lightned of her wombe,
And hath encreast the world with one sonne more,

cup . . . enfold the sacrament of Holy Communion. The serpent is related typologically to the brazen serpent held up by Moses (Numbers 21:8–9).

booke . . . blood The New Testament

anchor the normal attribute of Hope

That her to see should be but troublesome.
Indeede (quoth she) that should her trouble sore,
But thankt be God, and her encrease so evermore.

17 Then said the agèd *Cælia*, Deare dame,
And you good Sir, I wote that of your toyle,
And labours long, through which ye hither came,
Ye both forwearied be: therefore a whyle
I read you˃ rest, and to your bowres recoyle.˃ *advise you to / withdraw*
Then callèd she a Groome, that forth him led
Into a goodly lodge, and gan despoile˃ *undress*
Of puissant armes, and laid in easie bed;
His name was meeke *Obedience* rightfully ared.˃ *understood*

18 Now when their wearie limbes with kindly rest,
And bodies were refresht with due repast,
Faire *Una* gan˃ *Fidelia* faire request, *did*
To have her knight into her schoolehouse plaste,
That of her heavenly learning he might taste,
And heare the wisedome of her words divine.
She graunted, and that knights so much agraste,˃ *graced / favored*
That she him taught celestiall discipline,
And opened his dull eyes, that light mote in them shine.

19 And that her sacred Booke, with bloud ywrit,
That none could read, except she did them teach,
She unto him disclosèd every whit,
And heavenly documents˃ thereout˃ did preach, *teaching / from it*
That weaker wit of man could never reach,
Of God, of grace, of justice, of free will,
That wonder was to heare her goodly speach:
For she was able, with her words to kill,
And raise againe to life the hart, that she did thrill.˃ *pierce*

20 And when she list poure out her larger spright,˃ *spirit*
She would commaund the hastie Sunne to stay,
Or backward turne his course from heavens hight;
Sometimes great hostes of men she could dismay,
Dry-shod to passe, she parts the flouds in tway;˃ *two*
And eke huge mountaines from their native seat
She would commaund, themselves to beare away,
And throw in raging sea with roaring threat.
Almightie God her° gave such powre, and puissance great.

her that is, Faith, which can "move mountains" (Matthew 21:21) and which enabled Joshua to make the sun stand still (Joshua 10:12), Hezekiah to make it run backward, Gideon to win his great victory (Judges 7:7), and Moses to part the waters of the Red Sea

21 The faithfull knight now grew in litle space,
By hearing her, and by her sisters lore,
To such perfection of all heavenly grace,
That wretched world he gan for to abhore,
And mortall life gan loath, as thing forlore,˃ *abandoned*
Greev'd with remembrance of his wicked wayes,
And prickt with anguish of his sinnes so sore,
That he desirde to end his wretched dayes:
So much the dart of sinfull guilt the soule dismayes.

22 But wise *Speranza* gave him comfort sweet,
And taught him how to take assurèd hold
Upon her silver anchor, as was meet;
Else had his sinnes so great, and manifold
Made him forget all that *Fidelia* told.
In this distressèd doubtfull agonie,
When him his dearest *Una* did behold,
Disdeining life, desiring leave to die,
She found her selfe assayld with great perplexitie.

23 And came to *Cælia* to declare her smart,˃ *pain*
Who well acquainted with that commune plight,
Which sinfull horror˃ workes in wounded hart, *horror of sin*
Her wisely comforted all that she might,
With goodly counsell and advisement right;
And streightway sent with carefull diligence,
To fetch a Leach,˃ the which had great insight *physician*
In that disease of grievèd conscìence,
And well could cure the same; His name was *Patience*.

24 Who comming to that soule-diseasèd knight,
Could hardly him intreat,˃ to tell his griefe: ○ *persuade*
Which knowne, and all that noyd˃ his heavie spright *troubled*
Well searcht, eftsoones he gan apply reliefe
Of salves and med'cines, which had passing priefe,˃ *efficacy*
And thereto added words of wondrous might:
By which to ease he him recurèd briefe,˃ *quickly*
And much asswag'd the passion˃ of his plight, *suffering*
That he his paine endur'd, as seeming now more light.

25 But yet the cause and root of all his ill,
Inward corruption, and infected sin,
Not purg'd nor heald, behind remainèd still,

tell his griefe confession, to be followed by absolution and penance

And festring sore did rankle yet within,
Close> creeping twixt the marrow and the skin, *secretly*
Which to extirpe,> he laid him privily *root out*
Downe in a darksome lowly place farre in,
Whereas he meant his còrrosives to apply,
And with streight> diet tame his stubborne malady. *strict*

26 In ashes and sackcloth he did array
His daintie corse, proud humors> to abate, *passions*
And dieted with fasting every day,
The swelling of his wounds to mitigate,
And made him pray both earely and eke late:
And ever as superfluous flesh did rot
Amendment readie still at hand did wayt,
To pluck it out with pincers firie whot,> *hot*
That soone in him was left no one corrupted jot.

27 And bitter *Penance* with an yron whip,
Was wont him once to disple> every day: *scourge*
And sharpe *Remorse* his hart did pricke and nip,
That drops of bloud thence like a well did play;
And sad *Repentance* usèd to embay> *bathe*
His bodie in salt water smarting sore,
The filthy blots of sinne to wash away.
So in short space they did to health restore
The man that would not live, but earst> lay at deathes dore. *formerly*

28 In which his torment often was so great,
That like a Lyon he would cry and rore,
And rend his flesh, and his owne synewes eat.
His owne dear *Una* hearing evermore
His ruefull shriekes and gronings, often tore
Her guiltlesse garments, and her golden heare,
For pitty of his paine and anguish sore;
Yet all with patience wisely she did beare;
For well she wist, his crime could else be never cleare.

29 Whom thus recover'd by wise Patience,
And trew *Repentance* they to *Una* brought:
Who joyous of his curèd conscience,
Him dearely kist, and fairely eke besought
Himselfe to chearish,> and consuming thought *cheer up*
To put away out of his carefull brest.
By this *Charissa,* late in child-bed brought,
Was woxen strong, and left her fruitfull nest;
To her faire *Una* brought this unacquainted guest.°

To her . . . guest Red Cross comes now to the Virtue without which Faith and Hope profit one nothing.

30 She was a woman in her freshest age,
Of wondrous beauty, and of bountie rare,
With goodly grace and comely personage,
That was on earth not easie to compare;
Full of great love, but *Cupids* wanton snare
As hell she hated, chast in worke and will;
Her necke and breasts were ever open bare,
That ay thereof her babes might sucke their fill;
The rest was all in yellow robes arayèd still.

31 A multitude of babes about her hong,
Playing their sports, that joyd her to behold,
Whom still she fed, whiles they were weake and young,
But thrust them forth still, as they wexèd old:
And on her head she wore a tyre˃ of gold, *headdress*
Adornd with gemmes and owches˃ wondrous faire, *jewels*
Whose passing price uneath˃ was to be told;˃ *scarcely / estimated*
And by her side there sate a gentle paire
Of turtle doves, she sitting in an yvorie chaire.

32 The knight and *Una* entring, faire her greet,
And bid her joy of that her happie brood;
Who them requites with court'sies seeming meet,
And entertaines with friendly chearefull mood.
Then *Una* her besought, to be so good,
As in her vertuous rules to schoole her knight,
Now after all his torment well withstood,
In that sad house of *Penaunce,* where his spright
Had past the paines of hell, and long enduring night.

33 She was right joyous of her just request,
And taking by the hand that Faeries sonne,
Gan him instruct in every good behest,
Of love, and righteousness, and well to donne,˃ *do*
And wrath, and hatred warèly to shonne,˃ *shun*
That drew on men Gods hatred, and his wrath,
And many soules in dolours˃ had fordonne:˃ *miseries / ruined*
In which when him she well instructed hath,
From thence to heaven she teacheth him the ready path.

34 Wherein his weaker wandring steps to guide,
An auncient matrone she to her does call,
Whose sober lookes her wisedome well descride:˃ *made known*
Her name was *Mercie,* well knowne over all,
To be both gratious, and eke liberall:

To whom the carefull charge of him she gave,
To lead aright, that he should never fall
In all his wayes through this wide worldès wave,
That Mercy in the end his righteous soule might save.

35 The godly Matrone by the hand him beares
Forth from her presence, by a narrow way,
Scattred with bushy thornes, and ragged breares,˃ *briars*
Which still˃ before him she remov'd away, *ever*
That nothing might his ready passage stay:
And ever when his feet encombred were,
Or gan to shrinke, or from the right to stray,
She held him fast, and firmely did upbeare,
As carefull Nourse her child from falling oft does reare.

36 Eftsoones unto an holy Hospitall,
That was fore by˃ the way, she did him bring, *beside*
In which seven Bead-men˃ that had vowed all *men who pray for others*
Their life to service of high heavens king
Did spend their dayes in doing godly thing:
Their gates to all were open evermore,
That by the wearie way were traveiling,
And one sate wayting ever them before,
To call in commers-by, that needy were and pore.

37 The first of them that eldest was, and best,
Of all the house had charge and government,
As Guardian and Steward of the rest:
His office was to give entertainement
And lodging, unto all that came, and went:
Not unto such, as could him feast againe,
And double quite,˃ for that he on them spent, *repay*
But such, as want of harbour˃ did constraine: *shelter*
Those for Gods sake his dewty was to entertaine.

38 The second was as Almner˃ of the place, *almoner, distributor of alms*
His office was, the hungry for to feed,
And thristy give to drinke, a worke of grace:
He feard not once him selfe to be in need,
Ne car'd to hoord for those, whom he did breede:°
The grace of God he layd up still in store,
Which as a stocke he left unto his seede;
He had enough, what need him care for more?
And had he lesse, yet some he would give to the pore.

those . . . breede his own family

39 The third had of their wardrobe custodie,
In which were not rich tyres,> nor garments gay, *headdresses*
The plumes of pride, and wings of vanitie,
But clothes meet> to keepe keene could> away, *suitable / cold*
And naked nature seemely to aray;
With which bare wretched wights he dayly clad,
The images of God in earthly clay;
And if that no spare cloths to give he had,
His owne coate he would cut, and it distribute glad.

40 The fourth appointed by his office was,
Poore prisoners to relieve with gratious ayd,
And captives to redeeme with price of bras,> *money*
From Turkes and Sarazins, which them had stayd;> *detained*
And though they faultie were, yet well he wayd,
That God to us forgiveth every howre
Much more then that, why> they in bands> were layd, *for which / bonds*
And he that harrowd hell° with heavie stowre,> *trouble*
The faultie soules from thence brought to his heavenly bowre.

41 The fift had charge sicke persons to attend,
And comfort those, in> point of death which lay; *at the*
For them most needeth comfort in the end,
When sin, and hell, and death do most dismay
The feeble soule departing hence away.
All is but lost, that living we bestow,
If not well ended at our dying day.
O man have mind of that last bitter throw;> *pang, throe*
For as the tree does fall, so lyes it ever low.

42 The sixt had charge of them now being dead,
In seemely sort their corses to engrave,> *bury*
And deck with dainty flowres their bridall bed,
That to their heavenly spouse both sweet and brave> *fair*
They might appeare, when he their soules shall save,
The wondrous workemanship of Gods owne mould,> *image*
Whose face he made all beasts to feare, and gave
All in his hand, even dead we honour should.
Ah dearest God me graunt, I dead be not defould.> *defiled*

43 The seventh now after death and buriall done,
Had charge the tender Orphans of the dead
And widowes ayd, least> they should be undone:> *lest / ruined*
In face of judgement> he their right would plead, *in courts of law*
Ne ought the powre of mighty men did dread

he . . . hell Christ's "harrowing of hell"—between Crucifixion and Resurrection—was a popular theme in medieval literature.

In their defence, nor would for gold or fee
Be wonne their rightfull causes downe to tread:
And when they stood in most necessitee,
He did supply their want, and gave them ever free.> *freely*

44 There when the Elfin knight arrived was,
The first and chiefest of the seven, whose care
Was guests to welcome, towardes him did pas:
Where seeing *Mercie,* that his steps up bare,> *supported*
And always led, to her with reverence rare
He humbly louted> in meeke lowlinesse, *bowed*
And seemely welcome for her did prepare:
For of their order she was Patronesse,
Albe> *Charissa* were their chiefest founderesse. *although*

45 There she awhile him stayes, him selfe to rest,
That to the rest> more able he might bee: *remainder of task*
During which time, in every good behest
And godly worke of Almes and charitee
She him instructed with great industree;
Shortly therein so perfect he became,
That from the first unto the last degree,
His mortall life he learnèd had to frame
In holy righteousnesse, without rebuke or blame.

46 Thence forward by that painfull way they pas,
Forth to an hill, that was both steepe and hy;
On top whereof a sacred chappell was,
And eke a litle Hermitage thereby,
Wherein an agèd holy man did lye,
That day and night said his devotión,
Ne> other worldly busines did apply; *nor*
His name was heavenly *Contemplatión*;
Of God and godnesse was his meditatión.

47 Great grace that old man to him given had;
For God he often saw from heavens hight,
All> were his earthly eyen both blunt and bad, *although*
And through great age had lost their kindly> sight, *natural*
Yet wondrous quick and persant> was his spright, *penetrating*
As Eagles eye, that can behold the Sunne:
That hill they scale with all their powre and might,
That his frayle thighes nigh wearie and fordonne> *tired out*
Gan faile, but by her helpe the top at last he wonne.

48 There they do finde that godly aged Sire,
With snowy lockes adowne his shoulders shed,
As hoarie frost with spangles doth attire
The mossy braunches of an Oke halfe ded.

Each bone might through his body well be red,> *seen*
And every sinew seene through his long fast:
For nought he car'd his carcas long unfed;
His mind was full of spirituall repast,
And pyn'd> his flesh, to keepe his body low and chast. *starved*

49 Who when these two approaching he aspide,
At their first presence grew agrievèd sore,
That forst him lay his heavenly thoughts aside;
And had he not that Dame° respected more,> *greatly*
Whom highly he did reverence and adore,
He would not once have movèd for the knight.
They him saluted standing far afore;> *far off*
Who well them greeting, humbly did requight,
And askèd, to what end they clomb that tedious height.

50 What end (quoth she) should cause us take such paine,
But that same end, which every living wight
Should make his marke, high heaven to attaine?
Is not from hence the way, that leadeth right
To that most glorious house, that glistreth bright
With burning starres, and everliving fire,
Whereof the keyes are to thy hand behight> *entrusted*
By wise *Fidelia*? she doth thee require,
To shew it to this knight, according> his desire. *granting*

51 Thrise happy man, said then the father grave,
Whose staggering steps thy steady hand doth lead,
And shewes the way, his sinfull soule to save.
Who better can the way to heaven aread,> *show*
Then thou thy selfe, that was both borne and bred
In heavenly throne, where thousand Angels shine?
Thou doest the prayers of the righteous sead> *offspring*
Present before the majestie divine,
And his avenging wrath to clemencie incline.

52 Yet since thou bidst, thy pleasure shalbe donne.
Then come thou man of earth, and see the way,
That never yet was seene of Faeries sonne,
That never leads the traveiler astray,
But after labours long, and sad delay,
Brings them to joyous rest and endlesse blis.
But first thou must a season fast and pray,
Till from her bands the spright assoilèd> is, *released*
And have her strength recur'd> from fraile infirmitis. *recovered*

53 That done, he leads him to the highest Mount;
Such one, as that same mighty man of God,°

Dame Mercy, who is leading Red Cross
man of God Moses, who parted the Red Sea for the Israelites in flight from Egypt (Exodus 14:21 ff.)

That bloud-red billowes like a wallèd front
On either side disparted˃ with his rod, *parted*
Till that his army dry-foot through them yod,˃ *went*
Dwelt fortie dayes upon; where writ in stone
With bloudy letters by the hand of God,
The bitter doome of death and balefull mone
He did receive, whiles flashing fire about him shone.°

54 Or like that sacred hill, whose head full hie,
Adornd with fruitfull Olives all arownd,
Is, as it were for endlesse memory
Of that deare Lord, who oft thereon was fownd,
For ever with a flowring girlond crownd:
Or like that pleasaunt Mount, that is for ay
Through famous Poets verse each where˃ renownd, *everywhere*
On which the thrise three learnèd Ladies° play
Their heavenly notes, and make full many a lovely lay.

55 From thence, far off he unto him did shew
A litle path, that was both steepe and long,
Which to a goodly Citie led his vew;
Whose wals and towres were builded high and strong
Of perle and precious stone, that earthly tong
Cannot describe, nor wit of man can tell;
Too high a ditty for my simple song;
The Citie of the great king hight it˃ well, *it is called*
Wherein eternall peace and happinesse doth dwell.

56 As he thereon stood gazing, he might˃ see *could*
The blessed Angels to and fro descend
From highest heaven,° in gladsome companee,
And with great joy into that Citie wend,
As commonly˃ as friend does with his frend. *familiarly*
Whereat he wondred much, and gan enquere,
What stately building durst so high extend
Her loftie towres unto the starry sphere,
And what unknowen nation there empeoplèd˃ were. *established*

57 Faire knight (quoth he) *Jerusalem* that is,
The new *Jerusalem*,° that God has built
For those to dwell in, that are chosen his,
His chosen people purg'd from sinfull guilt,
With pretious bloud, which cruelly was spilt
On cursèd tree, of that unspotted lam,
That for the sinnes of all the world was kilt:

where writ . . . shone Moses received the tablets of the Law on Mount Sinai (Exodus 24:12 ff.).
thrise . . . Ladies the nine Muses, who lived on Parnassus
to and fro . . . heaven Jacob dreamed he saw a ladder stretching from earth to heaven, with "the angels of God ascending and descending on it" (Genesis 28:12).
new Jerusalem Hebrews 12:22–23; the Heavenly City, here compared not with Jerusalem but Gloriana's capital, in effect London

Now are they Saints all in that Citie sam,˃ *together*
More deare unto their God, then younglings to their dam.

58 Till now, said then the knight, I weenèd˃ well, *thought*
That great *Cleopolis,*° where I have beene,
In which that fairest *Faerie Queene* doth dwell,
The fairest Citie was, that might be seene;
And that bright towre all built of christall cleene,˃ *clear*
Panthea,° seemd the brightest thing, that was:
But now by proofe˃ all otherwise I weene; *test*
For this great Citie that does far surpas,
And this bright Angels towre quite dims that towre of glas.

59 Most trew, then said the holy agèd man;
Yet is *Cleopolis* for earthly frame,˃ *structure*
The fairest peece, that eye beholden can:
And well beseemes all knights of noble name,
That covett in th'immortall booke of fame,
To be eternizèd, that same to haunt.˃ *frequent*
And doen their service to that soveraigne Dame,
That glorie does to them for guerdon graunt:
For she is heavenly borne, and heaven may justly vaunt.˃ *claim*

60 And thou faire ymp, sprong out from English race,
How ever now accompted Elfins sonne,°
Well worthy doest thy service for her grace,
To aide a virgin desolate foredonne.˃ *ruined*
But when thou famous victorie hast wonne,
And high emongst all knights hast hong thy shield,
Thenceforth the suit˃ of earthly conquest shonne,˃ *pursuit / avoid*
And wash thy hands from guilt of bloudy field:
For bloud can nought but sin, and wars but sorrowes yield.

61 Then seeke this path, that I to thee presage,˃ *point out*
Which after all˃ to heaven shall thee send; *finally*
Then peaceably thy painefull pilgrimage
To yonder same *Jerusalem* do bend,
Where is for thee ordaind a blessèd end:
For thou emongst those Saints, whom thou doest see,
Shalt be a Saint, and thine owne nations frend
And Patrone: thou Saint *George* shalt called bee,
Saint *George* of mery England, the signe of victoree.

62 Unworthy wretch (quoth he) of so great grace,
How dare I thinke such glory to attaine?
These that have it attaind, were in like cace

Cleopolis London
Panthea feminine version of Pantheon; a royal palace, perhaps Greenwich, may be in Spenser's mind
How . . . sonne Spenser wants Red Cross now to be known as English; in the next stanza he becomes, explicitly, St. George, patron saint of England, slayer of the dragon, knight faithful true, and type of Christ. For explanation see stanzas 64–66.

(Quoth he) as wretched, and liv'd in like paine.
But deeds of armes must I at last be faine,> *willing*
And Ladies love to leave so dearely bought?
What need of armes, where peace doth ay remaine,
(Said he) and battailes none are to be fought?
As for loose loves are vaine, and vanish into nought.

63 O let me not (quoth he) then turne againe
Backe to the world, whose joyes so fruitlesse are;
But let me here for aye in peace remaine,
Or streight way on that last long voyage fare,
That nothing may my present hope empare.> *impair*
That may not be° (said he) ne maist thou yit> *yet*
Forgo that royall maides bequeathèd care,°
Who did her cause into thy hand commit,
Till from her cursèd foe thou have her freely quit.

64 Then shall I soone, (quoth he) so God me grace,
Abet> that virgins cause disconsolate, *uphold*
And shortly backe returne unto this place,
To walke this way in Pilgrims poore estate.
But now aread, old father, why of late
Didst thou behight> me borne of English blood, *call*
Whom all a Faeries sonne doen nominate?
That word shall I (said he) avouchen> good, *prove*
Sith to thee is unknowne the cradle of thy brood.

65 For well I wote, thou springst from ancient race
Of *Saxon* kings, that have with mightie hand
And many bloudie battailes fought in place> *there*
High reard their royall throne in *Britane* land,
And vanquisht them, unable to withstand:
From thence a Faerie thee unweeting> reft,> *unconscious / stole*
There as thou slepst in tender swadling band,
And her base Elfin brood there for thee left.
Such men do Chaungelings call, so chaungd by Faeries theft.

66 Thence she thee brought into this Faerie lond,
And in an heapèd furrow did thee hyde,
Where thee a Ploughman all unweeting> fond, *unexpectedly*
As he his toylesome teme that way did guyde,
And brought thee up in ploughmans state to byde,
Whereof *Georgos*° he thee gave to name;
Till prickt with courage, and thy forces pryde,°
To Faery court thou cam'st to seeke for fame,
And prove thy puissaunt armes, as seemes thee best became.

That . . . be Spenser uses the familar idea that in life there must be a balance of the active and the contemplative.

royall . . . care charge of that royal maid, which has been entrusted to you
Georgos Greek for "farmer"
forces pryde confidence of your own strength

67 O holy Sire (quoth he) how shall I quight
The many favours I with thee have found,
That hast my name and nation red aright,
And taught the way that does to heaven bound?˃ *lead*
This said, adowne he lookèd to the ground,
To have returnd, but dazèd were his eyne,
Through passing˃ brightnesse, which did quite confound *surpassing*
His feeble sence, and too exceeding shyne.
So darke are earthly things compard to things divine.

68 At last whenas himselfe he gan to find,
To *Una* back he cast him to retire;
Who him awaited still with pensive mind.
Great thankes and goodly meed˃ to that good syre, *reward*
He thence departing gave for his paines hyre.
So came to *Una*, who him joyd to see,
And after litle rest, gan him desire,
Of her adventure mindfull for to bee.
So leave they take of *Cælia*, and her daughters three.

Canto xi

[The eleventh canto describes the battle of Red Cross with the Dragon. The fight takes three days; it is a type (see Glossary) of the victory of Christ over Satan in the Last Days. On the first, things go badly for the knight; the heat of battle makes his Christian armor intolerable to him. He is revived by water from the Well of Life, described in Revelation 22 and related to the river of Paradise, which "went out of Eden to water the garden" (Genesis 2:10); it is the type of the sacrament of Baptism, one of the two sacraments admitted, out of the Roman Catholic seven, by the Reformed church. The second day's fighting goes better at first, but the knight is again driven back, to be revived this time by the Tree of Life, representing the sacrament of Communion. On the third and last day, the Dragon is killed.]

The knight with that old Dragon fights
two dayes incessantly:
The third him overthrowes, and gayns
most glorious victory.

1 High time now gan it wex for *Una* faire,
To thinke of those her captive Parents deare,
And their forwasted˃ kingdome to repaire: *ravaged*
Whereto whenas they now approchèd neare,
With hartie words her knight she gan to cheare,
And in her modest manner thus bespake;
Deare knight, as deare, as ever knight was deare,
That all these sorrowes suffer for my sake,
High heaven behold the tedious toyle, ye for me take.

2 Now are we come unto my native soyle,
And to the place, where all our perils dwell;
Here haunts that feend, and does his dayly spoyle,
Therefore henceforth be at your keeping> well, *on guard*
And ever ready for your foeman fell.
The sparke of noble courage now awake,
And strive your excellent selfe to excell;
That shall ye evermore renowmèd make,
Above all knights on earth, that batteill undertake.

3 And pointing forth, lo yonder is (said she)
The brasen towre in which my parents deare
For dread of that huge feend emprisond be,
Whom I from far see on the walles appeare,
Whose sight my feeble> soule doth greatly cheare: *saddened*
And on the top of all I do espye
The watchman wayting tydings glad to heare,
That O my parents might I happily
Unto you bring, to ease you of your misery.

4 With that they heard a roaring hideous sound,
That all the ayre with terrour fillèd wide,
And seemd uneath> to shake the stedfast ground. *almost*
Eftsoones that dreadfull Dragon they espide,
Where stretcht he lay upon the sunny side
Of a great hill, himself like a great hill.
But all so soone, as he from far descride
Those glistring armes, that heaven with light did fill,
He rousd himselfe full blith,> and hastned them untill.> *joyfully / toward them*

5 Then bad the knight his Lady yede aloofe,> *move aside*
And to an hill her selfe with draw aside,
From whence she might behold that battailles proof> *trial*
And eke be safe from daunger far descryde:
She him obayd, and turnd a little wyde.> *aside*
Now O thou sacred Muse,° most learnèd Dame,
Faire ympe> of *Phœbus*, and his agèd bride,° *child*
The Nourse of time, and everlasting fame,
That warlike hands ennoblest with immortall name;

6 O gently come into my feeble brest,
Come gently, but not with that mighty rage,
Wherewith the martiall troupes thou doest infest,
And harts of great Heroës doest enrage,
That nought their kindled courage may aswage,

sacred Muse Clio, muse of history
agèd bride Mnemosyne ("memory"), mother of the muses. While classical tradition makes Zeus their father, Spenser follows the *Mythologiae* of Conti in having them sired by Apollo.

Soone as thy dreadfull trompe begins to sownd;
The God of warre with his fiers equipage
Thou doest awake, sleepe never he so sownd,
And scarèd nations doest with horrour sterne astownd.

7 Faire Goddesse lay that furious fit˃ aside, *mood*
Till I of warres and bloudy *Mars* do sing,
And Briton fields with Sarazin bloud bedyde,
Twixt that great faery Queene and Paynim king,
That with their horrour heaven and earth did ring,
A worke° of labour long, and endlesse prayse:
But now a while let downe that haughtie˃ string, *high-toned*
And to my tunes thy second tenor° rayse,
That I this man of God his godly armes may blaze.˃ *blazon, proclaim*

8 By this the dreadfull Beast° drew nigh to hand,
Halfe flying, and halfe footing in his hast,
That with his largenesse measurèd much land,
And made wide shadow under his huge wast;
As mountaine doth the valley overcast.
Approching nigh, he rearèd high afore
His body monstrous, horrible, and vast,
Which to increase his wondrous greatnesse more,
Was swolne with wrath, and poyson, and with bloudy gore.

9 And over all˃ with brasen scales was armd, *everywhere*
Like plated coate of steele, so couchèd neare,˃ *closely set*
That nought mote perce, ne might his corse be harmd
With dint of sword, nor push of pointed speare;
Which as an Eagle, seeing pray appeare,
His aery plumes doth rouze,˃ full rudely dight,˃ *shake / arranged*
So shakèd he, that horrour was to heare,
For as the clashing of an Armour bright,
Such noyse his rouzèd scales did send unto the knight.

10 His flaggy˃ wings when forth he did display, *drooping*
Were like two sayles, in which the hollow wynd
Is gathered full, and worketh speedy way:
And eke the pennes,˃ that did his pineons bynd, *quills*
Were like mayne-yards, with flying canvas lynd,
With which whenas him list the ayre to beat,
And there by force unwonted passage find,
The cloudes before him fled for terrour great,
And all the heavens stood still amazèd with his threat.

A worke probably Spenser's intended epic of wars and "of politic virtues" mentioned in the Letter to Ralegh

second tenor a less excited style, more appropriate to an epic of internalized moral conflict. The musical metaphors are conventional in the Renaissance, with ancient Greek musical modes standing for poetic levels.

dreadfull Beast a type of the great beast of Revelation. Spenser alludes also to the serpent of Mars vanquished by Cadmus in Ovid's *Metamorphoses* III.

11 His huge long tayle wound up in hundred foldes,
Does overspred his long bras-scaly backe,
Whose wreathèd boughts˃ when ever he unfoldes, *coils*
And thicke entangled knots adown does slacke,
Bespotted as with shields of red and blacke,
It sweepeth all the land behind him farre,
And of three furlongs does but litle lacke;
And at the point two stings in-fixèd arre,
Both deadly sharpe, that sharpest steele exceeden farre.

12 But stings and sharpest steele did far exceed°
The sharpnesse of his cruell rending clawes;
Dead was it sure, as sure as death in deed,
What ever thing does touch his ravenous pawes,
Or what within his reach he ever drawes.
But his most hideous head my toung to tell
Does tremble: for his deepe devouring jawes
Wide gapèd, like the griesly mouth of hell,
Through which into his darke abisse all ravin˃ fell. *prey*

13 And that more wondrous was, in either jaw
Three ranckes of yron teeth enraungèd were,
In which yet trickling bloud and gobbets˃ raw *lumps of flesh*
Of late devourèd bodies did appeare,
That sight thereof bred cold congealèd feare:
Which to increase, and all atonce to kill,
A cloud of smoothering smoke and sulphur seare˃ *burning*
Out of his stinking gorge forth steemèd still,
That all the ayre about with smoke and stench did fill.

14 His blazing eyes, like two bright shining shields,
Did burne with wrath, and sparkled living fyre;
As two broad Beacons, set in open fields,
Send forth their flames farre off to every shyre,
And warning give, that enemies conspyre,
With fire and sword the region to invade;
So flam'd his eyne with rage and rancorous yre:
But farre within, as in a hollow glade,
Those glaring lampes were set, that made a dreadfull shade.

15 So dreadfully he towards him did pas,˃ *pace*
Forelifting up aloft his speckled brest,
And often bounding on the brusèd gras,
As for great joyance of his newcome guest.
Eftsoones he gan advance his haughtie crest,

did far exceed were far exceeded by. The details of the dragon's appearance allude to those in Revelation 13:2.

As chauffèd> Bore his bristles doth upreare, *enraged*
And shoke his scales to battell readie drest;
That made the *Redcrosse* knight nigh quake for feare,
As bidding bold defiance to his foeman neare.

16 The knight gan fairely couch> his steadie speare, *set for charging*
And fiercely ran at him with rigorous might:
The pointed steele arriving rudely theare,
His harder hide would neither perce, nor bight,> *bite*
But glauncing by forth passèd forward right;
Yet sore amovèd> with so puissant push, *moved*
The wrathfull beast about him turnèd light,
And him so rudely passing by, did brush
With his long tayle, that horse and man to ground did rush.

17 Both horse and man up lightly rose againe,
And fresh encounter towards him addrest:
But th'idle stroke yet backe recoyld in vaine,
And found no place his deadly point to rest.
Exceeding rage enflam'd the furious beast,
To be avengèd of so great despight;> *outrage*
For never felt his imperceable brest
So wondrous force, from hand of living wight;
Yet had he prov'd> the powre of many a puissant knight. *tested*

18 Then with his waving wings displayèd wyde,
Himselfe up high he lifted from the ground,
And with strong flight did forcibly divide
The yielding aire, which nigh too feeble found
Her flitting partes, and element unsound,> *weak*
To beare so great a weight: he cutting way
With his broad sayles, about him soarèd round:
At last low stouping> with unweldie sway, *swooping down like a hawk*
Snatcht up both horse and man, to beare them quite away.

19 Long he them bore above the subject> plaine, *set below*
So farre as Ewghen> bow a shaft may send, *yew*
Till struggling strong did him at last constraine,
To let them downe before his flightès end:
As hagard> hauke presuming to contend *wild*
With hardie fowle, above his hable might,> *ability*
His wearie pounces> all in vaine doth spend, *claws*
To trusse> the pray too heavie for his flight; *seize*
Which comming downe to ground, does free it selfe by fight.

20 He so disseizèd of his gryping grosse,°
The knight his thrillant> speare againe assayd *piercing*

He . . . grosse when he was dispossessed of his heavy grip

In his bras-plated body to embosse,˃ *plunge*
And three mens strength unto the stroke he layd;
Wherewith the stiffe beame quakèd, as affrayd,
And glauncing from his scaly necke, did glyde
Close under his left wing, then broad displayd.
The percing steele there wrought a wound full wyde,
That with the uncouth smart˃ the Monster lowdly cryde. *unfamiliar pain*

21 He cryde, as raging seas are wont to rore,
When wintry storme his wrathfull wreck does threat,
The rolling billowes beat the ragged shore,
As they the earth would shoulder from her seat,
And greedie gulfe does gape, as he would eat
His neighbour element˃ in his revenge: *the earth*
Then gin the blustring brethren˃ boldly threat, *winds*
To move the world from off his stedfast henge,˃ *axis*
And boystrous battell make, each other to avenge.

22 The steely head stucke fast still in his flesh,
Till with his cruell clawes he snatcht the wood,
And quite a sunder broke. Forth flowèd fresh
A gushing river of blacke goarie blood,
That drownèd all the land, whereon he stood;
The streame thereof would drive a water-mill.
Trebly augmented was his furious mood
With bitter sense˃ of his deepe rooted ill, *feeling*
That flames of fire he threw forth from his large nosethrill.˃ *nostril*

23 His hideous tayle then hurlèd he about,
And therewith all enwrapt the nimble thyes
Of his froth-fomy steed, whose courage stout
Striving to loose the knot, that fast him tyes,
Himselfe in streighter bandes too rash implyes,˃ *too quickly entangles*
That to the ground he is perforce constraynd
To throw his rider: who can˃ quickly ryse *did*
From off the earth, with durty bloud distaynd,˃ *stained*
For that reprochfull fall right fowly he disdaynd.

24 And fiercely tooke his trenchand˃ blade in hand, *cutting*
With which he stroke so furious and so fell,
That nothing seemd the puissance could withstand:
Upon his crest the hardned yron fell,
But his more hardned crest was armd so well,
That deeper dint therein it would not make;
Yet so extremely did the buffe˃ him quell,˃ *buffet, blow / daunt*
That from thenceforth he shund the like to take,
But when he saw them come, he did them still forsake.

25 The knight was wrath to see his stroke beguyld,
And smote againe with more outrageous might;
But backe againe the sparckling steele recoyld,
And left not any marke, where it did light;
As if in Adamant rocke it had bene pight.˃ *thrust*
The beast impatient of his smarting wound,
And of so fierce and forcible despight,
Thought with his wings to stye˃ above the ground; *rise*
But his late wounded wing unserviceable found.

26 Then full of griefe and anguish vehement,
He lowdly brayd, that like was never heard,
And from his wide devouring oven sent
A flake of fire, that flashing in his beard,
Him all amazd, and almost made affeard:
The scorching flame sore swingèd˃ all his face, *singed*
And through his armour all his bodie seard,
That he could not endure so cruell cace,
But thought his armes to leave, and helmet to unlace.

27 Not that great Champion° of the antique world,
Whom famous Poetes verse so much doth vaunt,
And hath for twelve huge labours high extold,
So many furies and sharpe fits did haunt,
When him the poysoned garment did enchaunt
With *Centaures* bloud, and bloudie verses charm'd,
As did this knight twelve thousand dolours˃ daunt, *pains*
Whom fyrie steele now burnt, that earst˃ him arm'd, *previously*
That erst him goodly arm'd, now most of all him harm'd.

28 Faint, wearie, sore, emboylèd, grievèd, brent
With heat, toyle, wounds, armes, smart, and inward fire
That never man such mischiefes did torment;
Death better were, death did he oft desire,
But death will never come, when needes require.
Whom so dismayd when that his foe beheld,
He cast to suffer him no more respire,
But gan his sturdie sterne about to weld,
And him so strongly stroke, that to the ground him feld.

29 It fortunèd (as faire it then befell)
Behind his backe unweeting,˃ where he stood, *not noticed*
Of auncient time there was a springing well,
From which fast trickled forth a silver flood,
Full of great vertues, and for med'cine good.
Whylome,˃ before that cursèd Dragon got *formerly*

Champion Hercules, who when he put on the shirt soaked in the blood of Nessus, suffered horrible pain (see Ovid, *Metamorphoses* IX. 134–272). Mythographers drew a parallel between his suffering and that of Christ on the cross, which is being enacted by Red Cross here.

That happie land, and all with innocent blood
Defyld those sacred waves, it rightly hot> *was called*
The well of life, ne yet his> vertues had forgot. *its*

30 For unto life the dead it could restore,
And guilt of sinfull crimes cleane wash away,
Those that with sicknesse were infected sore,
It could recure,> and agèd long decay *cure*
Renew, as one were borne that very day.
Both *Silo* this, and *Jordan* did excell,
And th'English *Bath,* and eke the german *Spau,*
Ne can *Cephise,* nor *Hebrus*° match this well:
Into the same the knight backe overthrowen, fell.

31 Now gan the golden *Phœbus* for to steepe
His fierie face in billowes of the west,
And his faint steedes watred in Ocean deepe,
Whiles from their journall> labours they did rest, *daily*
When that infernall Monster, having kest> *cast*
His wearie foe into that living well,
Can> high advance his broad discolourèd brest, *did*
Above his wonted pitch, with countenance fell,
And clapt his yron wings, as victor he did dwell.> *remain*

32 Which when his pensive Ladie saw from farre,
Great woe and sorrow did her soule assay,> *assault*
As weening that the sad end of the warre,
And gan to highest God entirely> pray, *earnestly*
That fearèd chance from her to turne away;
With folded hands and knees full lowly bent
All night she watcht, ne once adowne would lay
Her daintie limbs in her sad dreriment,> *sorrow*
But praying still> did wake, and waking did lament. *always*

33 The morrow next gan early to appeare,
That> *Titan*> rose to runne his daily race; *when / the sun*
But early ere the morrow next gan reare
Out of the sea faire *Titans* deawy face,
Up rose the gentle virgin from her place,
And lookèd all about, if she might spy
Her lovèd knight to move his manly pace:
For she had great doubt of his safèty,
Since late she saw him fall before his enemy.

34 At last she saw, where he upstarted brave
Out of the well, wherein he drenchèd lay;

Silo . . . Hebrus Siloam, the stream by which Jesus cured a blind man (John 9:7); Jordan, the crossing of which saved the Jews; Bath in England and Spa in Germany have therapeutic waters; Cephisus and the Thracian Hebrus were renowned for the purity of their waters.

As Eagle fresh out of the Ocean wave,°
Where he hath left his plumes all hoary gray,
And deckt himselfe with feathers youthly gay,
Like Eyas> hauke up mounts unto the skies, *fledgling*
His newly budded pineons to assay,
And marveiles at himselfe, still as he flies:
So new this new-borne knight to battell new did rise.

35 Whom when the damnèd feend so fresh did spy,
No wonder if he wondred at the sight,
And doubted, whether his late enemy
It were, or other new supplièd knight.
He, now to prove his late renewèd might,
High brandishing his bright deaw-burning° blade,
Upon his crested scalpe so sore did smite,
That to the scull a yawning wound it made:
The deadly dint his dullèd senses all dismaid.

36 I wote> not, whether the revenging steele *know*
Were hardned with that holy water dew,
Wherein he fell, or sharper edge did feele,
Or his baptizèd hands now greater grew;
Or other secret vertue did ensew;
Else never could the force of fleshly arme,
Ne molten mettall in his bloud embrew:> *steep*
For till that stownd> could never wight him harme, *time*
By subtilty, nor slight, nor might, nor mighty charme.

37 The cruell wound enragèd him so sore,
That loud he yellèd for exceeding paine;
As hundred ramping Lyons seem'd to rore,
Whom ravenous hunger did thereto constraine:
Then gan he tosse aloft his stretchèd traine,
And therewith scourge the buxome> aire so sore, *yielding*
That to his force to yeelden it was faine;
Ne ought> his sturdie strokes might stand afore, *nothing*
That high trees overthrew, and rocks in peeces tore.

38 The same advauncing high above his head,
With sharpe intended> sting so rude him smot, *stretched out*
That to the earth him drove, as stricken dead,
Ne living wight would have him life behot:°

Eagle . . . wave "thy youth is renewed like the eagle's" (Psalms 103:5). The eagle, in bestiary lore, was supposed when old to fly toward the sun and burn off his old feathers before plunging into water and renewing his youth; cf. Milton, *Areopagitica*.

deaw-burning shining with "that holy water dew" of the next stanza

Ne living . . . behot No living person would have thought him to be alive.

The mortall sting his angry needle shot
Quite through his shield, and in his shoulder seasd,
Where fast it stucke, ne would there out be got:
The griefe thereof him wondrous sore diseasd,˃ *distressed*
Ne might his ranckling paine with patience be appeasd.

39 But yet more mindfull of his honour deare,
Then of the grievous smart, which him did wring,˃ *torment*
From loathèd soile he can him lightly reare,˃ *quickly reared himself*
And strove to loose the farre infixèd sting:
Which when in vaine he tryde with struggeling,
Inflam'd with wrath, his raging blade he heft,˃ *heaved*
And strooke so strongly, that the knotty string
Of his huge taile he quite a sunder cleft,
Five joynts thereof he hewd, and but the stump him left.

40 Hart cannot thinke, what outrage, and what cryes,
With foule enfouldred˃ smoake and flashing fire, *black as a thunder-cloud*
The hell-bred beast threw forth unto the skyes,
That all was coverèd with darknesse dire:
Then fraught with rancour, and engorgèd˃ ire, *congested*
He cast at once him to avenge for all,
And gathering up himselfe out of the mire,
With his uneven wings did fiercely fall
Upon his sunne-bright shield, and gript it fast withall.

41 Much was the man encombred with his hold,
In feare to lose his weapon in his paw,
Ne wist yet, how his talants˃ to unfold; *talons*
Nor harder was from *Cerberus*° greedie jaw
To plucke a bone, then from his cruell claw
To reave˃ by strength the gripèd gage˃ away: *wrench away / prize*
Thrise he assayd it from his foot to draw,
And thrise in vaine to draw it did assay,
It booted nought to thinke, to robbe him of his pray.

42 Tho˃ when he saw no power might prevaile, *then*
His trustie sword he cald to his last aid,
Wherewith he fiercely did his foe assaile,
And double blowes about him stoutly laid,
That glauncing fire out of the yron plaid;
As sparckles from the Andvile˃ use to fly, *anvil*
When heavie hammers on the wedge are swaid;˃ *swung*
Therewith at last he forst him to unty˃ *loosen*
One of his grasping feete, him to defend thereby.

Cerberus the three-headed watchdog at the entrance to hell, defeated by Hercules

43 The other foot, fast fixèd on his shield,
Whenas no strength, nor stroks mote him constraine
To loose, ne yet the warlike pledge to yield,
He smot thereat with all his might and maine,
That nought so wondrous puissance might sustaine;
Upon the joynt the lucky steele did light,
And made such way, that hewd it quite in twaine;
The paw yet missèd not his minisht˃ might, *decreased*
But hong still on the shield, as it at first was pight.˃ *placed*

44 For griefe˃ thereof, and divelish despight, *pain*
From his infernall fournace forth he threw
Huge flames, that dimmèd all the heavens light,
Enrold˃ in duskish smoke and brimstone blew; *wrapped up*
As burning *Aetna*° from his boyling stew˃ *caldron*
Doth belch out flames, and rockes in peeces broke,
And ragged ribs of mountaines molten new,˃ *newly*
Enwrapt in coleblacke clouds and filthy smoke,
That all the land with stench, and heaven with horror choke.

45 The heate whereof, and harmefull pestilence
So sore him noyd,˃ that forst him to retire *hurt*
A little backward for his best defence,
To save his bodie from the scorching fire,
Which he from hellish entrailes did expire.˃ *exhale*
It chaunst (eternall God that chaunce did guide)
As he recoylèd backward, in the mire
His nigh forwearied feeble feet did slide,
And downe he fell, with dread of shame sore terrified.

46 There grew a goodly tree him faire beside,
Loaden with fruit and apples rosie red,
As they in pure vermilion had beene dide,˃ *dyed*
Whereof great vertues over all˃ were red:˃ *everywhere / told*
For happie life to all, which thereon fed,
And life eke everlasting did befall:
Great God it planted in that blessèd sted˃ *place*
With his almightie hand, and did it call
The tree of life, the crime of our first fathers fall.°

47 In all the world like was not to be found,
Save in that soile, where all good things did grow,
And freely sprong out of the fruitfull ground,
As incorrupted Nature did them sow,
Till that dread Dragon all did overthrow.°

Aetna great Sicilian volcano
The tree . . . fall planted next to the Tree of the Knowledge of Good and Evil in Eden (Genesis 2:9). Its benefits were lost through Adam's fall; it grows in the New Jerusalem (Revelation 22:2).
Till . . . overthrow referring to Satan, who caused the Fall

Another like faire tree eke grew thereby,
Whereof who so did eat, eftsoones did know
Both good and ill: ° O mornefull memory:
That tree through one mans fault hath doen us all to dy.

48 From that first tree forth flowd, as from a well,
A trickling streame of Balme,° most soveraine˃ *curative*
And daintie deare,˃ which on the ground still fell, *precious*
And overflowèd all the fertill plaine,
As it had deawèd bene with timely raine:
Life and long health that gratious ointment gave,
And deadly woundes could heale, and reare againe
The senselesse corse appointed˃ for the grave. *prepared*
Into that same he fell: which did from death him save.

49 For nigh thereto the ever damnèd beast
Durst not approch, for he was deadly made,°
And all that life preservèd, did detest:
Yet he it oft adventur'd˃ to invade. *tried*
By this the drouping day-light gan to fade,
And yeeld his roome to sad succeeding night,
Who with her sable mantle gan to shade
The face of earth, and wayes of living wight,
And high her burning torch set up in heaven bright.

50 When gentle *Una* saw the second fall
Of her deare knight, who wearie of long fight,
And faint through losse of bloud, mov'd not at all,
But lay as in a dreame of deepe delight,
Besmeard with pretious Balme, whose vertuous might˃ *effective power*
Did heale his wounds, and scorching heat alay,
Againe she stricken was with sore affright,
And for his safetie gan devoutly pray;
And watch the noyous˃ night, and wait for joyous day. *harmful*

51 The joyous day gan early to appeare,
And faire *Aurora*° from the deawy bed
Of agèd *Tithone* gan her selfe to reare,
With rosie cheekes, for shame as blushing red;°
Her golden lockes for haste were loosely shed
About her eares, when *Una* her did marke
Clymbe to her charet,˃ all with flowers spred, *chariot*
From heaven high to chase the chearelesse darke;
With merry note her loud salutes the mounting larke.

Whereof . . . ill This is the Tree of Knowledge of Good and Evil, of which Eve and Adam ate the fruit (Genesis 3:1–6).

Balme This balm is related in typology to the healing blood of Christ.

deadly made His being had affinity with death, not life.

Aurora the goddess of dawn whose mortal lover, Tithonus, was given eternal life, but not eternal youth

for shame . . . red blushing red as if for shame

52 Then freshly up arose the doughtie knight,
All healèd of his hurts and woundès wide,
And did himselfe to battell readie dight;˃ *prepared*
Whose early foe awaiting him beside
To have devourd, so soone as day he spyde,
When now he saw himselfe so freshly reare,
As if late fight had nought him damnifyde,˃ *damaged*
He woxe˃ dismayd, and gan his fate to feare; *grew*
Nathless˃ with wonted rage he him advauncèd neare. *nevertheless*

53 And in his first encounter, gaping wide,
He thought attonce him to have swallowd quight,
And rusht upon him with outragious pride;
Who him r'encountring˃ fierce, as hauke in flight, *engaging*
Perforce rebutted˃ backe. The weapon bright *drove*
Taking advantage of his open jaw,
Ran through his mouth with so importune˃ might, *violent*
That deepe emperst˃ his darksome hollow maw, *pierced*
And back retyrd, his life bloud forth with all did draw.

54 So downe he fell, and forth his life did breath,
That vanisht into smoke and cloudès swift;
So downe he fell, that th'earth him underneath
Did grone, as feeble so great load to lift;
So downe he fell, as an huge rockie clift,˃ *cliff*
Whose false foundation waves have washt away,
With dreadfull poyse˃ is from the mayneland rift, *weight*
And rolling downe, great *Neptune* doth dismay;
So downe he fell, and like an heapèd mountaine lay.

55 The knight himselfe even trembled at his fall,
So huge and horrible a masse it seem'd;
And his deare Ladie, that beheld it all,
Durst not approch for dread, which she misdeem'd,˃ *misjudged*
But yet at last, when as the direfull feend
She saw not stirre, off-shaking vaine affright,
She nigher drew, and saw that joyous end:
Then God she praysd, and thankt her faithfull knight,
That had atchiev'd so great a conquest by his might.

Canto xii

[In the final canto, Red Cross, fully confirmed as a type of Christ, harrows hell, restores Eden, and takes Una (the true church) as his betrothed bride. Details of the marriage feast derive both from Revelation and perhaps from contemporary Elizabethan pageantry. Una appears in her full glory—as the true ancient church appears in the Church of England. Archimago arrives with a lying letter from Duessa, but is exposed and cast into a dungeon, like his prototype in Revelation, "that old serpent, which is the Devil, and Satan," who is "bound . . . a thousand years, and cast . . . into the bottomless pit" (Revelation 20:1–2). Finally, Red Cross resumes his knightly role and returns to the service of Gloriana for six more years.]

Faire Una to the Redcrosse knight
betrouthèd is with joy:
Though false Duessa it to barre
her false sleights doe imploy.

1 Behold I see the haven nigh at hand,
To which I meane my wearie course° to bend;
Vere˃ the maine shete, and beare up with˃ the land, *let out/turn toward*
The which afore is fairely to be kend,˃ *observed*
And seemeth safe from stormes, that may offend;
There this faire virgin wearie of her way
Must landed be, now at her journeyes end:
There eke my feeble barke a while may stay,
Till merry˃ wind and weather call her thence away. *favorable*

2 Scarsely had *Phœbus* in the glooming East
Yet harnessèd his firie-footed teeme,
Ne reard above the earth his flaming creast,
When the last deadly smoke aloft did steeme,
That signe of last outbreathèd life did seeme
Unto the watchman on the castle wall;
Who thereby dead that balefull Beast did deeme,
And to his Lord and Ladie lowd gan call,
To tell, how he had seene the Dragons fatall fall.

3 Uprose with hastie joy, and feeble speed
That agèd Sire, the Lord of all that land,
And lookèd forth, to weet,˃ if true indeed *know*
Those tydings were, as he did understand,
Which whenas true by tryall he out fond,˃ *found out*
He bad to open wyde his brazen gate,
Which long time had bene shut, and out of hond˃ *at once*
Proclaymèd joy and peace through all his state;
For dead now was their foe, which them forrayèd˃ late. *ravaged*

4 Then gan triumphant Trompets sound on hie,
That sent to heaven the ecchoèd report
Of their new joy, and happie victorie
Gainst him, that had them long opprest with tort,˃ *wrong*
And fast imprisonèd in siegèd fort.
Then all the people, as in solemne feast,

wearie course the course of the "feeble barke" of the poem itself, a nautical metaphor used by many Latin, medieval, and Renaissance poets as a pacing device in narrative

To him assembled with one full consort,˃ *company*
Rejoycing at the fall of that great beast,
From whose eternall bondage now they were releast.

5 Forth came that auncient Lord and aged Queene,
Arayd in antique robes downe to the ground,
And sad habiliments right well beseene;°
A noble crew about them waited round
Of sage and sober Peres, all gravely gownd;
Whom farre before did march a goodly band
Of tall young men, all hable˃ armes to sownd,˃ *able / wield*
But now they laurell braunches bore in hand;
Glad signe of victorie and peace in all their land.

6 Unto that doughtie Conquerour they came,
And him before themselves prostrating low,
Their Lord and Patrone˃ loud did him proclame, *protector*
And at his feet laurell boughes did throw.
Soone after them all dauncing on a row
The comely virgins came, with girlands dight,˃ *adorned*
As fresh as flowres in medow greene do grow,
When morning deaw upon their leaves doth light:
And in their hands sweet Timbrels˃ all upheld on hight.˃ *tambourines / high*

7 And them before, the fry˃ of children young *swarms*
Their wanton sports and childish mirth did play,
And to the Maydens sounding tymbrels sung
In well attunèd notes, a joyous lay,
And made delightfull musicke all the way,
Until they came, where that faire virgin stood;
As faire *Diana* in fresh sommers day
Beholds her Nymphes, enraung'd˃ in shadie wood, *ranged about*
Some wrestle, some do run, some bathe in christall flood.

8 So she beheld those maydens meriment
With chearefull vew; who when to her they came,
Themselves to ground with gratious humblesse˃ bent, *humility*
And her ador'd by honorable name,
Lifting to heaven her everlasting fame:
Then on her head they set a girland greene,
And crownèd her twixt earnest and twixt game;˃ *half in play*
Who in her selfe-resemblance well beseene,°
Did seeme such, as she was, a goodly maiden Queene.

9 And after, all the raskall many˃ ran, *the mob*
Heapèd together in rude rablement,˃ *tumult*

sad . . . beseene sober costume appropriate to the occasion

selfe-resemblance well beseene appropriately resembling her true self

To see the face of that victorious man:
Whom all admired, as from heaven sent,
And gazd upon with gaping wonderment.
But when they came, where that dead Dragon lay,
Stretcht on the ground in monstrous large extent,
The sight with idle˃ feare did them dismay, *baseless*
Ne durst approch him nigh, to touch, or once assay.

10 Some feard, and fled; some feard and well it faynd;˃ *disguised*
One that would wiser seeme, then all the rest,
Warnd him not touch, for yet perhaps remaynd
Some lingring life within his hollow brest,
Or in his wombe might lurke some hidden nest
Of many Dragonets, his fruitfull seed;
Another said, that in his eyes did rest
Yet sparckling fire, and bad thereof take heed;
Another said, he saw him move his eyes indeed.

11 One mother, when as her foolehardie chyld
Did come too neare, and with his talants˃ play, *talons*
Halfe dead through feare, her litle babe revyld,˃ *scolded*
And to her gossips gan in counsell˃ say; *friends in private*
How can I tell, but that his talents may
Yet scratch my sonne, or rend his tender hand?
So diversly themselves in vaine they fray;˃ *frighten*
Whiles some more bold, to measure him nigh stand,
To prove how many acres he did spread of land.

12 Thus flockèd all the folke him round about,
The whiles that hoarie˃ king, with all his traine, *gray-haired*
Being arrivèd, where that champion stout
After his foes defeasance˃ did remaine, *defeat*
Him goodly greetes, and faire does entertaine,˃ *receive*
With princely gifts of yvorie and gold,
And thousand thankes him yeelds for all his paine.
Then when his daughter deare he does behold,
Her dearely doth imbrace, and kisseth manifold.

13 And after to his Pallace he them brings,
With shaumes,˃ and trompets, and with Clarions sweet; *oboes*
And all the way the joyous people sings,
And with their garments strowes the pavèd street:
Whence mounting up, they find purveyance meet˃ *proper provision*
Of all, that royall Princes court became,
And all the floore was underneath their feet
Bespred with costly scarlot˃ of great name, *rich cloth*
On which they lowly sit, and fitting purpose˃ frame. *conversation*

14 What needs me tell their feast and goodly guize, *deportment*
In which was nothing riotous nor vaine?
What needs of daintie dishes to devize,˃ *tell*
Of comely services, or courtly trayne?˃ *retinue*
My narrow leaves cannot in them containe
The large discourse of royall Princes state.
Yet was their manner then but bare and plaine:
For th'antique world excesse and pride did hate;
Such proud luxurious pompe is swollen up but late.

15 Then when with meates and drinkes of every kinde
Their fervent appetites they quenchèd had,
That auncient Lord gan fit occasion finde,
Of straunge adventures, and of perils sad,
Which in his travell him befallen had,
For to demaund of his renowmèd guest:
Who then with utt'rance grave, and count'nance sad,
From point to point, as is before exprest,
Discourst his voyage long, according˃ his request. *agreeing to*

16 Great pleasure mixt with pittifull˃ regard, *sympathetic*
That godly King and Queene did passionate,˃ *feelingly express*
Whiles they his pittifull adventures heard,
That oft they did lament his lucklesse state,
And often blame the too importune fate,
That heapd on him so many wrathfull wreakes:˃ *injuries*
For never gentle knight, as he of late,
So tossed was in fortunes cruell freakes;˃ *changes*
And all the while salt teares bedeawd˃ the hearers cheaks. *bedewed*

17 Then said that royall Pere in sober wise;°
Deare Sonne, great beene the evils, which ye bore
From first to last in your late enterprise,
That I note,° whether prayse, or pitty more:
For never living man, I weene, so sore
In sea of deadly daungers was distrest;
But since now safe ye seisèd˃ have the shore, *reached*
And well arrivèd are, (high God be blest)
Let us devize of ease and everlasting rest.

18 Ah dearest Lord, said then that doughty knight,
Of ease or rest I may not yet devize;
For by the faith, which I to armes have plight,
I bounden am streight after this emprize,˃ *enterprise*
As that your daughter can ye well advize,
Backe to returne to that great Faerie Queene,
And her to serve six yeares in warlike wize,˃ *wise*

Then . . . wise Una's father is commenting on Red Cross's story of his adventures.

I note I don't know whether to

Gainst that proud Paynim king,° that workes her teene:> *woe*
Therefore I ought> crave pardon, till I there have beene. *must*

19 Unhappie falles that hard necessitie,
(Quoth he) the troubler of my happie peace,
And vowèd foe of my felicitie;
Ne I against the same can justly preace:> *press*
But since that band> ye cannot now release, *bond*
Nor doen undo; (for vowes may not be vaine)
Soone as the terme of those six yeares shall cease,
Ye then shall hither backe returne againe,
The marriage to accomplish vowd betwixt you twain.

20 Which for my part I covet to performe,
In sort as> through the world I did proclame, *just as*
That who so kild that monster most deforme,
And him in hardy battaile overcame,
Should have mine onely daughter to his Dame,> *wife*
And of my kingdome heire apparaunt bee:
Therefore since now to thee perteines the same,
By dew desert of noble chevalree,
Both daughter and eke kingdome, lo I yield to thee.

21 Then forth he called that his daughter faire,
The fairest *Un'* his onely daughter deare,
His onely daughter, and his onely heyre;
Who forth proceeding with sad> sober cheare,> *solemn / appearance*
As bright as doth the morning starre appeare
Out of the East, with flaming lockes bedight,
To tell that dawning day is drawing neare,
And to the world does bring long wishèd light;
So faire and fresh that Lady shewd her selfe in sight.

22 So faire and fresh, as freshest flowre in May;
For she had layd her mournefull stole aside,
And widow-like sad wimple> throwne away, *veil*
Wherewith her heavenly beautie she did hide,
Whiles on her wearie journey she did ride;
And on her now a garment she did weare,
All lilly white, withoutten spot, or pride,> *ornament*
That seemd like silke and silver woven neare,
But neither silke nor silver therein did appeare.°

23 The blazing brightnesse of her beauties beame,
And glorious light of her sunshyny face°

Paynim king the enemies of the true church, both the Romans and the Turks
But . . . appeare The bride of the Lamb was arrayed in fine linen (Revelation 19:7–8).
glorious . . . face Una, the woman clothed with the sun (Revelation 12:1), has now ended her time in the wilderness (12:6) and survived the persecution of the dragon (12:4); she emerges reclothed with the sun, the Bride of Christ, who, as the New Jerusalem, has a "light . . . like unto a stone most precious" (Revelation 21:11).

To tell, were as to strive against the streame.
My ragged rimes are all too rude and bace,
Her heavenly lineaments for to enchace.˃ *adorn*
Ne wonder; for her owne deare lovèd knight,
All˃ were she dayly with himselfe in place,˃ *although / in the same place*
Did wonder much at her celestiall sight:
Oft had he seene her faire, but never so faire dight.

24 So fairely dight, when she in presence came,
She to her Sire made humble reverence,
And bowèd low, that˃ her right well became, *so that it*
And added grace unto her excellence:
Who with great wisedome, and grave eloquence
Thus gan to say. But eare˃ he thus had said, *before*
With flying speede, and seeming great pretence,˃ *importance*
Came running in, much like a man dismaid,
A Messenger with letters, which his message said.

25 All in the open hall amazèd stood,
At suddeinnesse of that unwarie˃ sight, *unexpected*
And wondred at his breathlesse hastie mood.
But he for nought would stay his passage right˃ *direct*
Till fast˃ before the king he did alight; *close*
Where falling flat, great humblesse he did make,
And kist the ground, whereon his foot was pight;˃ *placed*
Then to his hands that writ he did betake,
Which he disclosing, red thus, as the paper spake.

26 To thee, most mighty king of *Eden* faire,
Her greeting sends in these sad lines addrest,
The wofull daughter, and forsaken heire
Of that great Emperour of all the West;
And bids thee be advizèd for the best,
Ere thou thy daughter linck in holy band
Of wedlocke to that new unknowen guest:
For he already plighted his right hand
Unto another love, and to another land.

27 To me sad mayd, or rather widow sad,
He was affiauncèd long time before,
And sacred pledges he both gave, and had,
False erraunt knight, infámous, and forswore:
Witnesse the burning Altars, which˃ he swore, *by which*
And guiltie heavens of his bold perjury,°
Which though he hath polluted oft of yore,
Yet I to them for judgement just do fly,
And them conjure˃ t'avenge this shamefull injury. *beseech*

guiltie . . . perjury heavens tainted by the guilt of his perjury

28 Therefore since mine he is, or free or bond,
Or false or trew, or living or else dead,
Withhold, O soveraine Prince, your hasty hond
From knitting league with him, I you aread;> *advise*
Ne weene> my right with strength adowne to tread, *don't think*
Through weakenesse of my widowhed, or woe:
For truth is strong, her rightfull cause to plead,
And shall find friends, if need requireth soe,
So bids thee well to fare, Thy neither friend, nor foe, *Fidessa.*

29 When he these bitter byting words had red,
The tydings straunge did him abashèd make,
That still he sate long time astonishèd
As in great muse, ne word to creature spake.
At last his solemne silence thus he brake,
With doubtfull eyes fast fixèd on his guest;
Redoubted knight, that for mine onely sake
Thy life and honour late adventurest,
Let nought be hid from me, that ought to be exprest.

30 What meane these bloudy vowes, and idle threats,
Throwne out from womanish impatient mind?
What heavens? what altars? what enragèd heates> *passions*
Here heapèd up with termes of love unkind,
My conscience cleare with guilty bands° would bind?
High God be witnesse, that I guiltlesse ame.
But if your selfe, Sir knight, ye faultie find,
Or wrappèd be in loves of former Dame,
With crime do not it cover, but disclose the same.

31 To whom the *Redcrosse* knight this answere sent,
My Lord, my King, be nought hereat dismayd,
Till well ye wote by grave intendiment,> *consideration*
What woman, and wherefore doth me upbrayd
With breach of love, and loyalty betrayd.
It was in my mishaps, as hitherward
I lately traveild, that unwares I strayd
Out of my way, through perils straunge and hard;
That day should faile me, ere I had them all declard.

32 There did I find, or rather I was found
Of this false woman, that *Fidessa* hight,
Fidessa hight the falsest Dame on ground,> *anywhere*
Most false *Duessa,* royall richly dight,
That easie was t'invegle> weaker> sight: *deceive / too weak*
Who by her wicked arts, and wylie skill,

guilty bands illicit bonds

Too false and strong for earthly skill or might,
Unwares me wrought unto her wicked will,
And to my foe betrayd, when least I fearèd ill.

33 Then steppèd forth the goodly royall Mayd,
And on the ground her selfe prostrating low,
With sober countenaunce thus to him sayd;
O pardon me, my soveraigne Lord, to show
The secret treasons, which of late I know
To have bene wroght by that false sorceresse.
She onely she it is, that earst> did throw *previously*
This gentle knight into so great distresse,
That death him did awaite in dayly wretchednesse.

34 And now it seemes, that she subornèd hath
This craftie messenger with letters vaine,
To worke new woe and improvided> scath,> *unlooked-for / harm*
By breaking of the band betwixt us twaine;
Wherein she usèd hath the practicke paine> *artful skill*
Of this false footman, clokt with simplenesse,
Whom if ye please for to discover plaine,
Ye shall him *Archimago* find, I ghesse,
The falsest man alive; who tries shall find no lesse.

35 The king was greatly movèd at her speach,
And all with suddein indignation fraight,> *burdened*
Bad on that Messenger rude hands to reach.
Eftsoones the Gard, which on his state did wait,
Attacht> that faitor> false, and bound him strait: *seized / impostor*
Who seeming sorely chauffèd> at his band, *chafed*
As chained Beare, whom cruell dogs do bait,
With idle> force did faine> them to withstand, *futile / wish*
And often semblaunce made to scape out of their hand.

36 But they him layd full low in dungeon deepe,°
And bound him hand and foote with yron chains.
And with continuall watch did warely keepe;
Who then would thinke, that by his subtile trains
He could escape fowle death or deadly paines?
Thus when that Princes wrath was pacifide,
He gan renew the late forbidden banes,> *banns*
And to the knight his daughter deare he tyde,
With sacred rites and vowes for ever to abyde.

they . . . deepe "And he laid hold on the dragon, that old serpent, which is the devil, and Satan, and bound him a thousand years, and cast him into the bottomless pit, and shut him up, and set a seal upon him, that he should deceive the nations no more, till the thousand years should be fulfilled: and after that he must be loosed a little season" (Revelation 20:1–3). Hence Archimago's escape, and the fact that history does not end at this point.

37 His owne two hands the holy knots did knit,
That none but death for ever can devide;
His owne two hands, for such a turne most fit,
The housling> fire did kindle and provide, *sacramental*
And holy water° thereon sprinckled wide;
At which the bushy Teade> a groome did light, *torch*
And sacred lampe in secret chamber hide,
Where it should not be quenchèd day nor night,
For feare of evill fates, but burnen ever bright.

38 Then gan they sprinckle all the posts with wine,
And made great feast to solemnize that day;
They all perfumde with frankencense divine,
And precious odours fetcht from far away,
That all the house did sweat with great aray:> *adornment*
And all the while sweete Musicke did apply
Her curious> skill, the warbling notes to play, *intricate*
To drive away the dull Meláncholy;
The whiles one sung a song of love and jollity.

39 During the which there was an heavenly noise
Heard sound through all the Pallace pleasantly,
Like as it had bene many an Angels voice,
Singing before th'eternall majesty,
In their trináll triplicities° on hye;
Yet wist no creature, whence that heavenly sweet> *delight*
Proceeded, yet each one felt secretly> *inwardly*
Himselfe thereby reft of his sences meet,> *proper*
And ravishèd with rare impression> in his sprite. *sensation*

40 Great joy was made that day of young and old,
And solemne feast proclaimd throughout the land,
That their exceeding merth may not be told:
Suffice it heare by signes to understand
The usuall joyes at knitting of loves band.
Thrise happy man the knight himselfe did hold,
Possessèd of his Ladies hart and hand,
And ever, when his eye did her behold,
His heart did seeme to melt in pleasures manifold.

41 Her joyous presence and sweet company
In full content he there did long enjoy,
Ne wicked envie, ne vile gealosy
His deare delights were able to annoy:
Yet swimming in that sea of blisfull joy,
He nought forgot, how he whilome> had sworne, *formerly*

fire . . . water These rituals are borrowed from the ancient Roman marriage ceremony.

trináll triplicities The angels were ranked in three groups of three orders.

In case he could that monstrous beast destroy, *did*
Unto his Farie Queene backe to returne:
The which he shortly did, and *Una* left to mourne.

42 Now strike your sailes ye jolly Mariners,
For we be come unto a quiet rode,> *harbor*
Where we must land some of our passengers,
And light this wearie vessell of her lode.
Here she a while may make her safe abode,
Till she repairèd have her tackles spent,> *worn out*
And wants supplide. And then againe abroad
On the long voyage whereto she is bent:
Well may she speede and fairely finish her intent.

1590

Book II

The main theme of the Legend of Temperance is the control of the passions by the higher powers of the mind. In the *Nicomachean Ethics* Aristotle had distinguished between temperance and continence; the latter presupposes, as the former does not, the existence of strong desires that have to be overcome. Guyon seems to represent a mixture of these two virtues, and Spenser, who probably derived his knowledge of the *Ethics* from editions with Christian commentaries, does not keep rigidly to Aristotle's scheme. Temperance, in Christian thought, was one of the four cardinal virtues, the others being Prudence, Fortitude, and Justice; these, added to the theological virtues (Faith, Hope, and Charity), made up the seven which were set against the Seven Deadly Sins. Christian Temperance, like the other virtues, had its own emblems —the set square, the bridle, the wine mixed with water, or the mixing bowl itself— and Spenser uses them all. The very name of Guyon derives from that one of the four rivers of Eden—Gehon—which was allegorically associated with Temperance.

However, there are Aristotelian elements in the syncretic mix. Aristotle, as usual, defines the virtue as a mean between its excess and its deficiency, and Spenser uses this, together with the doctrine that the passions, which temperance and continence oppose, are divided into the angry and the desirous, the irascible and the concupiscible. Spenser illustrates this division by concentrating on the irascible in the first six cantos and on the concupiscible in the second six. Even the condition Guyon finally attains to—

Heroic Virtue—is mentioned by Aristotle as the opposite—there is, exceptionally, no mean between them—of bestiality.

The conflicts involving Guyon take place in the human being; so there is much less supernatural activity in this than in the First Book, which it otherwise so closely parallels in design. Primarily Book II has to do with the moral activity of men in the natural world. (Temperance was a pagan virtue; holiness was known only to Christians, by revelation.) Guyon must keep to the golden mean, and has the Palmer, representing Right Reason, to aid him most of the time. Thus he is lower than Red Cross, a saint, and more like a pagan hero, such as Aeneas, whom he resembles also in his visit to the underworld. But it would be wrong to suggest that Spenser excludes Christianity. As we shall see, the quest of Guyon has strong Christian implications. The Second Book is an interesting example of a Renaissance phenomenon, the syncretic blend of pagan and Christian, set in a medieval (romance) form.

The Second Booke of The Faerie Queene

Contayning,
The Legend of Sir Guyon,
or
Of Temperaunce

1 Right well I wote> most mighty Soveraine, *know*
That all this famous antique history,
Of some th'aboundance of an idle braine
Will judgèd be, and painted forgery,
Rather then matter of just> memory, *true*
Sith> none, that breatheth living aire, does know, *since*
Where is that happy land of Faery,
Which I so much do vaunt,> yet no where show, *publicize*
But vouch> antiquities, which no body can know. *assert*

2 But let that man with better sence advize,> *consider*
That of the world least part to us is red:> *made known*
And dayly how through hardy enterprize,
Many great Regions are discoverèd,
Which to late age were never mentionèd.
Who ever heard of th'Indian *Peru*?
Or who in venturous vessell measurèd
The *Amazons* huge river now found trew?°
Or fruitfullest *Virginia*° who did ever vew?

3 Yet all these were, when no man did them know;
Yet have from wisest ages hidden beene:
And later times things more unknowne shall show.

The Amazons . . . trew It was first navigated (in part) in 1540.

Virginia named for Elizabeth, the Virgin Queen, on Ralegh's return in 1584.

Why then should witlesse man so much misweene˃ *wrongly suppose*
That nothing is, but that which he hath seene?
What if within the Moones faire shining spheare?
What if in every other starre unseene
Of other worldes he happily˃ should heare? *by chance*
He wonder would much more: yet such to some appeare.

4. Of Faerie lond yet if he more inquire,
By certaine signes here set in sundry place
He may it find; ne let him then admire,˃ *be surprised*
But yield˃ his sence to be too blunt and bace, *confess*
That no'te without an hound fine footing trace.°
And thou, O fairest Princesse under sky,
In this faire mirrhour maist behold thy face,
And thine owne realmes in lond of Faery,
And in this antique Image thy great auncestry.

5 The which O pardon me thus to enfold
In covert vele, and wrap in shadowes light,
That feeble eyes your glory may behold,
Which else could not endure those beames bright,
But would be dazled with exceeding light.
O pardon, and vouchsafe with patient eare
The brave adventures of this Faery knight
The good Sir *Guyon* gratiously to heare,
In whom great rule of Temp'raunce goodly doth appeare.

[The first canto of Book II, like that of I, establishes the nature of the quest assigned to the knight of the Book, Guyon, whose "Legend" is Temperance. The escaped Archimago directs Guyon and the Palmer to Duessa, posing as a girl raped by Red Cross; but the knights recognize each other before Guyon prosecutes her revenge. They converse and part, Red Cross wishing Guyon luck as he sets out "like race to run." Beside a fountain they find Amavia with her baby Ruddymane, so called because his hands are stained with her blood. Amavia dies beside the body of her husband Mordant, victim of the enchantress Acrasia (Incontinence). Mordant (Mortdant: deathgiver) was like Adam infected by concupiscence with original sin. The fountain stands for divine law, which provides sin with its occasion to produce concupiscence in men (Romans 7:7). The burial of Amavia and Mordant represents the death of the Old Man. Ruddymane is baptized, but carries the stain contracted by his father. Guyon at first thinks it is a simple case of intemperance; the deeper Christian meaning is revealed to him by the Palmer in canto xi. The destruction of the Bower of Bliss in xii is not just the overthrow of incontinence, but of sin in the human heart. Spenser is building Temperance into a Christian rather than a pagan (Aristotelian) scheme.

The second canto offers a schematic allegory of the doctrine of the mean, in the House of Medina. Medina is the mean, her sisters Elissa ("deficient") and Perissa

no'te . . . trace can't follow the tracks without a hunting dog

("excessive") are the extremes. They have lovers who share their qualities; Perissa's is San Loy. Canto iii introduces Braggadocchio, who steals Guyon's horse, and Belphoebe—it is a sort of first installment of Book III. In the fourth canto Spenser deals with irascibility as the enemy of temperance; Furor (Anger) is bound, and Occasio (occasion, opportunity) has her tongue locked up. Other characters are Atin (Strife), Pyrochles ("fire disturbed" = incontinent anger), and Cymochles, his brother ("wave disturbed" = incontinent sex); these last two return later.

In canto v, amid more instances of anger and its occasions, Guyon overthrows Pyrochles. In vi there is a transition from irascibility to concupiscence, and Spenser starts it with the moralization: "A Harder lesson, to learne Continence / In joyous pleasure, then in grievous paine." Guyon, now without his Palmer, falls in with Phaedria (Greek, "glittering," but Spenser himself calls her "immodest Merth".) She sails about on the Idle Lake—loose mirth floating on idleness leads, says Spenser to "loose desire." She sings to her victim Cymochles of the beauty and plenty of the paradise she inhabits on a floating island (a forecast of the Bower of Bliss). Guyon, though courteous, has no difficulty in rejecting her charms. There is an inconclusive bout between Guyon and Cymochles; and we see Pyrochles, trying to drown himself to extinguish his anger, saved by Archimago. The rejection of sensual pleasure by Guyon, though easy, is part of the pattern of rejections that is completed in the seventh canto; note that he undergoes these temptations without the aid of the Palmer.]

Book II, Canto vii

This is the crucial canto of Book II. Mammon is the god of money, but of more than money: "God of the world and worldlings" he says; of all, in fact, that the virtuous soul must resist, including fame, power, and improper knowledge. The scheme of the canto has much in common with that of *Paradise Regained,* and of Marvell's "Dialogue Between the Resolved Soul and Created Pleasure." During his three-day tour of Mammon's underground realm, Guyon is followed by a terrible fiend who will tear him to pieces if he once weakens. He has no difficulty in rejecting riches, having chosen "another bliss . . . another end." Nor does he have much of a struggle at the Temple of Philotime ("love of earthly honor"), because he has plighted his troth to another lady ("heavenly honor"). The final temptation is that of the Garden of Proserpina: this is the temptation of forbidden knowledge—here, as in Milton and Marvell, the climactic temptation. Unmoved, he has undergone, like Christ in the wilderness, the *total* temptation (the temptation of sex came with Phaedria), and Mammon, his time expired, has to take him back to the light. Only then does he require succor, as Christ received it after his trial.

This is one of the great cantos; Lamb said that "the transitions in this episode are every whit as violent as in the most extravagant dream, and yet the waking judgment ratifies them." Its interpretation is, however, disputed. Some believe Guyon should not have accompanied Mammon, and that his doing so illustrates his inability to avoid the occasion of temptation. His error would be comparable to that of Red Cross in the Cave of Despair. But Milton, despite his error in thinking that the Palmer was with

Guyon, is likely to be right in his reading, when he says, in *Areopagitica,* that "our sage and serious poet Spenser . . . describing true temperance under the person of Guyon, brings him in with his palmer through the cave of Mammon, and the bower of earthly bliss, that he might see and know, and yet abstain."

In this episode Guyon is not being tempted by his own desires but by an external enemy; he is no more seeking the occasion of sin than Christ in the wilderness. His reward for withstanding the total temptation is Heroic Virtue, in the sense given to this term by the church when adapting it from Aristotle's *Ethics;* he now has a habit of good conduct that is second nature, and it fits him for deeds beyond the scope of the ordinarily virtuous man; he occupies a middle ground between such a man and a saint. As the victory over sin in the wilderness prepared Christ for the victory over death on the Cross, so Guyon's victory over Mammon makes possible the destruction of the Bower of Bliss. His faint, requiring angelic succor, is therefore not a sign of moral weakness, but of exhaustion at the end of this ordeal of initiation.

Canto vii

Guyon findes Mammon in a delve,
 Sunning his threasure hore:
Is by him tempted, and led downe,
 To see his secret store.

1 As Pilot well expert in perilous wave,
 That to a stedfast starre his course hath bent,
 When foggy mistes, or cloudy tempests have
 The faithfull light of that faire lampe yblent,> *blinded*
 And cover'd heaven with hideous dreriment,
 Upon his card> and compas firmes his eye, *chart*
 The maisters> of his long experiment,> *agents / experience*
 And to them does the steddy helme apply,
Bidding his wingèd vessell fairely forward fly:

2 So *Guyon* having lost his trusty guide,°
 Late left beyond that *Ydle lake,* proceedes
 Yet on his way, of none accompanide;
 And evermore himselfe with comfort feedes,
 Of his owne vertues, and prayse-worthy deedes.°
 So long he yode,> yet no adventure found, *went*
 Which fame of her shrill trompet worthy reedes:> *considers*
 For still he traveild through wide wastfull ground,
That nought but desert wildernesse shew'd all around.

3 At last he came unto a gloomy glade,
 Cover'd with boughes and shrubs from heavens light,
 Whereas he sitting found in secret shade
 An uncouth,> salvage, and uncivile wight, *strange*
 Of griesly hew,> and fowle ill favour'd sight;> *shape / appearance*

lost . . . guide The absence of the Palmer is presumably to allow Guyon to undergo these tests without the help of a guide external to himself who would always represent the reasonable attitude, and so shield Guyon from the spiritual pressures besetting him; Jesus in the wilderness had no supernatural aid, was as if only a man.

And evermore . . . deedes sometimes thought very smug, but he is cheering himself up by counting all the support he has

His face with smoke was tand, and eyes were bleard,
His head and beard with sout were ill bedight,
His cole-blacke hands did seeme to have beene seard
In smithes fire-spitting forge, and nayles like clawes appeard.

4 His yron coate all overgrowne with rust,
Whose underneath envelopèd with gold,
Whose glistring glosse darkned with filthy dust,
Well yet appearèd, to have beene of old
A worke of rich entayle,> and curious mould, *carving*
Woven with antickes> and wild Imagery: *strange figures*
And in his lap a masse of coyne he told,> *counted*
And turnèd upsidowne, to feede his eye
And covetous desire with his huge threasury.

5 And round about him lay on every side
Great heapes of gold, that never could be spent:
Of which some were rude owre,> not purifide *ore*
Of *Mulcibers*° devouring element;
Some others were new driven,> and distent> *smelted / beaten*
Into great Ingoes,> and to wedges square; *ingots*
Some in round plates withouten moniment;> *engraving*
But most were stampt, and in their metall bare
The antique shapes of kings and kesars> straunge and rare. *emperors*

6 Soone as he *Guyon* saw, in great affright
And hast he rose, for to remove aside
Those pretious hils from straungers envious sight,
And downe them pourèd through an hole full wide,
Into the hollow earth, them there to hide.
But *Guyon* lightly to him leaping, stayd
His hand, that trembled, as one terrifyde;
And though him selfe were at the sight dismayd,
Yet him perforce restraynd, and to him doubtfull sayd.

7 What art thou man, (if man at all thou art)
That here in desert hast thine habitaunce,
And these rich heapes of wealth doest hide apart
From the worldes eye, and from her right usaunce?
Thereat with staring eyes fixèd askaunce,
In great disdaine, he answerd; Hardy Elfe,
The darest vew my direfull countenaunce,
I read> thee rash, and heedlesse of thy selfe, *perceive*
To trouble my still> seate,> and heapes of pretious pelfe. *quiet / place*

8 God of the world and worldlings I me call,
Great *Mammon,*° greatest god below the skye,

Mulcibers Mulciber was Vulcan, the smith god; his element was fire.
Mammon "No man can serve two masters . . . Ye cannot serve God and mammon" (Matthew 6:24); his name means "wealth"; one has to choose between the world and heaven.

That of my plenty poure out unto all,
And unto none my graces do enuye:
Riches, renowme, and principality,
Honour, estate, and all this worldes good,
For which men swinck> and sweat incessantly, *labor*
Fro me do flow into an ample flood,
And in the hollow earth have their eternall brood.

9 Wherefore if me thou deigne to serve and sew,> *follow*
At thy command lo all these mountains bee;
Or if to thy great> mind, or greedy vew *ambitious*
All these may not suffise, there shall to thee
Ten times so much be numbred francke and free.
Mammon (said he) thy godheades vaunt° is vaine,
And idle offers of thy golden fee;
To them, that covet such eye-glutting gaine,
Proffer thy giftes, and fitter servaunts entertaine.

10 Me ill besits,> that in der-doing armes,° *besets*
And honours suit> my vowèd dayes do spend, *pursuit*
Unto thy bounteous baytes, and pleasing charmes,
With which weake men thou witchest, to attend:
Regard of worldly mucke doth fowly blend,> *defile*
And low abase the high heroicke spright,
That joyes for crownes and kingdomes to contend;
Faire shields, gay steedes, bright armes be my delight.
Those be the riches fit for an advent'rous knight.

11 Vaine glorious Elfe (said he) doest not thou weet,
That money can thy wantes at will supply?
Shields, steeds, and armes, and all things for thee meet
It can purvay in twinckling of an eye;
And crownes and kingdomes to thee multiply.
Do not I kings create, and throw the crowne
Sometimes to him, that low in dust doth ly?
And him that raignd, into his rowme thrust downe,
And whom I lust,> do heape with glory and renowne? *please*

12 All otherwise (said he) I riches read,> *understand*
And deeme them roote of all disquietnesse;°
First got with guile, and then preserv'd with dread,
And after spent with pride and lavishnesse,
Leaving behind them griefe and heavinesse.
Infinite mischiefes of them do arize,
Strife, and debate, bloudshed, and bitternesse,
Outrageous wrong, and hellish covetize,
That noble heart as great dishonour doth despize.

godheades vaunt boast of divinity
der-doing armes feats of high courage
roote . . . disquietnesse "the love of money is the root of all evil" (I Timothy 6:10)

13 Ne thine be kingdomes, ne the scepters thine;
But realmes and rulers thou doest both confound,
And loyall truth to treason doest incline;
Witnesse the guiltlesse bloud pourd oft on ground,
The crownèd often slain, the slayer cround,
The sacred Diademe in peeces rent
And purple robe> gorèd with many a wound; *imperial cloak*
Castles surprizd, great cities sackt and brent:
So mak'st thou kings, and gaynest wrongfull governement.

14 Long were to tell the troublous stormes, that tosse
The private state,> and make the life unsweet: *private life*
Who swelling sayles in Caspian sea doth crosse,
And in frayle wood on *Adrian*> gulfe doth fleet,> *Adriatic / float*
Doth not, I weene, so many evils meet.
Then *Mammon* wexing wroth, And why then, said,
Are mortall men so fond and undiscreet,
So evil thing to seeke unto their ayd,
And having not complaine, and having it upbraid?> *reproach it*

15 Indeede (quoth he) through fowle intemperaunce,
Frayle men are oft captiv'd to covetise:
But would they thinke, with how small allowaunce
Untroubled Nature doth her selfe suffise,°
Such superfluities they would despise,
Which with sad cares empeach> our native joyes: *impair*
At the well head the purest streames arise:
But mucky filth his> braunching armes annoyes,> *its / fouls*
And with uncomely weedes the gentle wave accloyes.> *clogs*

16 The antique> world,° in his first flowring youth, *ancient*
Found no defect in his Creatours grace,
But with glad thankes, and unreprovèd truth,
The gifts of soveraigne bountie did embrace:
Like Angels life was then mens happy cace;
But later ages pride, like corn-fed steed,
Abusd her plenty, and fat swolne encreace
To all licentious lust, and gan exceed
The measure of her meane, and naturall first need.

17 Then gan a cursèd hand the quiet wombe
Of his great Grandmother with steele to wound,
And the hid treasures in her sacred tombe,
With Sacriledge to dig. Therein he found
Fountaines of gold and silver to abound,

Untroubled . . . suffice Boethius, *The Consolation of Philosophy* II.5, was the classical statement of this idea.
The antique world also based on the famous passage in Boethius, *The Consolation of Philosophy* II.5, *Felix nimium prior aetas* ("Too happy was that first age"); Boethius was translated into English by two sovereigns, Alfred and Elizabeth. Spenser also knew well the opening pages of Ovid's *Metamorphoses,* which describe the Golden Age and the subsequent decline.

Of which the matter of his huge desire
And pompous pride eftsoones> he did compound; *forth with*
Then avarice gan through his veines inspire> *breathe*
His greedy flames, and kindled life-devouring fire.

18 Sonne (said he then) let be thy bitter scorne,
And leave the rudenesse of that antique age
To them, that liv'd therein in state forlorne;
Thou that doest live in later times, must wage
Thy workes for wealth, and life for gold engage.
If then thee list my offred grace to use,
Take what thou please of all this surplusage;
If thee list not, leave have thou to refuse:
But thing refused, do not afterward accuse.

19 Me list not> (said the Elfin knight) receave *I choose not*
Thing offred, till I know it well be got,°
Ne wote> I, but thou didst these goods bereave *nor know*
From rightfull owner by unrighteous lot,> *division*
Or that bloud guiltinesse or guile them blot.
Perdy> (quoth he), yet never eye did vew, *indeed*
Ne toung did tell, ne hand these handled not,
But safe I have them kept in secret mew,> *den*
From heavens sight, and powre of all which them pursew.

20 What secret place (quoth he) can safely hold
So huge a masse, and hide from heavens eye?
Or where hast thou thy wonne,> that so much gold *dwelling*
Thou canst preserve from wrong and robbery?
Cóme thou (quoth he) and see. So by and by
Through that thicke covert he him led, and found
A darkesome way, which no man could descry
That deepe descended through the hollow ground,
And was with dread and horrour compassèd around.

21 At length they came into a larger space,
That stretcht it selfe into an ample plaine,
Through which a beaten broad high way did trace,
That streight did lead to *Plutoes* griesly raine:> *hideous realm*
By that wayes side, there sate infernall Payne,°
And fast beside him sat tumultuous Strife:
The one in hand an yron whip did straine,> *grip*
The other brandishèd a bloudy knife,
And both did gnash their teeth, and both did threaten life.

22 On thother side in one consort there sate,
Cruell Revenge, and rancorous despight,

Me list . . . well got Aristotle, *Nicomachean Ethics* IV, says a good man will not take money from a tainted source; the concept was Christianized (as we see from the reply of Jesus to Satan in *Paradise Regained*) on an offer of food—Satan asks "wouldst thou not eat?" and the reply is "Thereafter as I like the giver" (II.321).

Payne These simple allegories are based on the description of hell in Virgil, *Aeneid* VI.273 ff.

Disloyall Treason, and hart-burning Hate,
But gnawing Gealosie out of their sight
Sitting alone, his bitter lips did bight,
And trembling Feare still to and fro did fly,
And found no place, where safe he shroud˃ him might, *shelter*
Lamenting Sorrow did in darknesse lye,
And Shame his ugly face did hide from living eye.

23 And over them sad Horrour with grim hew,˃ *shape*
Did alwayes sore, beating his yron wings;
And after him Owles and Night-ravens flew,
The hatefull messengers of heavy things,
Of death and dolour telling sad tidings;
Whiles sad *Celeno,*° sitting on a clift,˃ *cliff*
A song of bale and bitter sorrow sings,
That hart of flint a sunder could have rift:˃ *split*
Which having ended, after him she flyeth swift.

24 All these before the gates of *Pluto* lay,
By whom they passing, spake unto them nought.
But th'Elfin knight with wonder all the way
Did feed his eyes, and fild his inner thought.
At last him to a litle dore he brought,
That to the gate of Hell, which gapèd wide,
Was next adjoyning, ne them parted ought:°
Betwixt them both was but a little stride,
That did the house of Richesse from hell-mouth divide.

25 Before the dore sat self-consuming Care,
Day and night keeping wary watch and ward,
For feare least Force or Fraud should unaware
Breake in, and spoile the treasure there in gard:
Ne would he suffer Sleepe once thither-ward
Approch, albe his drowsie den were next;
For next to death is Sleepe to be compard:
Therefore his house is unto his annext;
Here Sleep, there Richesse, and Hel-gate them both betwext.°

26 So soone as *Mammon* there arriv'd, the dore
To him did open, and affoorded way;
Him followed eke Sir *Guyon* evermore,
Ne darkensse him, ne daunger might dismay.
Soone as he entred was, the dore streight way
Did shut, and from behind it forth there lept

Celeno a Harpy; in Virgil, *Aeneid* III.219 ff., an image of rapacity; she speaks like a prophetess of doom (cf. *Tempest* III.iii, the apparition of Ariel as Harpy before the "three men of sin")

ne . . . ought i.e. there was nothing between them

Here . . . betwext Spenser arranges the "houses" and hell-mouth as if in a picture or in a pageant; the "hell-mouth" was familiar on the popular stage, a large-toothed aperture, partly a whale's, partly a devil's mouth.

An ugly feend,° more fowle then dismall day,
The which with monstrous stalke behind him stept,
And ever as he went, dew watch upon him kept.

27 Well hopèd he, ere long that hardy guest,
If ever covetous hand, or lustfull eye,
Or lips he layd on thing, that likt> him best, *pleased*
Or ever sleepe his eye-strings did untye,
Should be his pray. And therefore still> on hye *always*
He over him did hold his cruell clawes,
Threatning with greedy gripe to do him dye
And rend in peeces with his ravenous pawes,
If ever he transgrest the fatal *Stygian*° lawes.

28 That houses forme within was rude and strong,
Like an huge cave hewne out of rocky clift,
From whose rough vaut> the ragged breaches> hong, *vault / fissures*
Embost with massy gold of glorious gift,> *quality*
And with rich metall loaded every rift,
That heavy ruine> they did seeme to threat; *fall*
And over them *Arachne*° high did lift
Her cunning web, and spred her subtile net,
Enwrappèd in fowle smoke and clouds more blacke then Jet.

29 Both roofe, and floore, and wals were all of gold,
But overgrowne with dust and old decay,
And hid in darkenesse, that none could behold
The hew> thereof: for vew of chearefull day *appearance*
Did never in that house it selfe display,
But a faint shadow of uncertain light;
Such as a lamp, whose life does fade away:
Or as the Moone cloathèd with clowdy night,
Does shew to him, that walkes in feare and sad affright.

30 In all that rowme was nothing to be seene,
But huge great yron chests and coffers strong,
All bard with double bends, that none could weene> *think*
Them to efforce> by violence or wrong; *break open*
On every side they placèd were along.
But all the ground with sculs was scatterèd,
And dead mens bones, which round about were flong,
Whose lives, it seemèd, whilome> there were shed, *formerly*
And their vile carcases now left unburièd.

feend Probably Eurynomos, described first by Pausanias (*Description of Greece* X.28) but accessible in the well-known manual of Cartari, *Imagini degli Dei* (many 16th-century editions). He tore his victims to pieces. In the Eleusinian mystery ritual the candidate was followed by a similar fury and forbidden to turn around; this stresses the initiatory element in Guyon's visit to the Cave of Mammon. The Eleusinian rite involved three days in "hell." Hercules, the type-hero for Guyon, was an initiate. Of course the ancient mystery rituals were given Christian significances.

Stygian referring to Styx, the infernal river, and thus to hell

Arachne the spider

31 They forward passe, ne *Guyon* yet spoke word,
Till that they came unto an yron dore,
Which to them openèd of his owne accord,
And shewd of richesse such exceeding store,
As eye of man did never see before;
Ne ever could within one place be found,
Through all the wealth, which is, or was of yore,
Could gatherèd be through all the world around,
And that above were added to that under ground.

32 The charge thereof unto a covetous Spright
Commaunded was, who thereby did attend,
And warily awaited day and night,
From other covetous feends it to defend,
Who it to rob and ransacke did intend.> *wish*
Then *Mammon* turning to that warriour, said;
Loe here the worldès blis, loe here the end,
To which all men do ayme, rich to be made:
Such grace now to be happy, is before thee laid.

33 Certes (said he) I n'ill> thine offred grace, *do not want*
Ne to be made so happy do intend:
Another blis before mine eyes I place,
Another happinesse, another end.
To them, that list, these base regardes I lend:> *give*
But I in armes, and in atchievements brave,
Do rather choose my flitting houres to spend,
And to be Lord of those, that riches have,
Then them to have my selfe, and be their servile sclave.

34 Thereat the feend his gnashing teeth did grate,
And griev'd, so long to lacke his greedy> pray; *eagerly desired*
For well he weenèd, that so glorious bayte
Would tempt his guest, to take thereof assay:> *trial*
Had he so doen, he had him snatcht away,
More light then Culver> in the Faulcons fist. *dove*
Eternall God thee save from such decay.
But whenas *Mammon* saw his purpose mist,
Him to entrap unwares another way he wist.

35 Thence forward he him led, and shortly brought
Unto another rowme,° whose dore forthright,
To him did open, as it had beene taught:
Therein an hundred raunges weren pight,> *placed*
And hundred fornaces all burning bright;
By every fornace many feends did bide,
Deformèd creatures, horrible in sight,

rowme This is Mammon's forge, based on the forges of the Cyclops in Virgil, *Aeneid* VIII.418.

And every feend his busie paines applide,
To melt the golden metall, ready to be tride.> *refined*

36 One with great bellowes gatherèd filling aire,
And with forst wind the fewell did inflame;
Another did the dying bronds repaire
With yron toungs, and sprinckled oft the same
With liquid waves, fiers *Vulcans* rage to tame,
Who maistring them, renewd his former heat;
Some scumd the drosse, that from the metall came;
Some stird the molten owre with ladles great;
And every one did swincke,> and every one did sweat. *labor*

37 But when as earthly wight they present saw,
Glistring in armes and battailous aray,
From their whot> worke they did themselves withdraw *hot*
To wonder at the sight: for till that day,
They never creature saw, that came that way.
Their staring eyes sparckling with fervent fire,
And ugly shapes did nigh the man dismay,
That were it not for shame, he would retire,
Till that him thus bespake their soveraigne Lord and sire.

38 Behold, thou Faeries sonne, with mortall eye,
That> living eye before did never see: *that which*
The thing, that thou didst crave so earnestly,
To weet, whence all the wealth late shewd by mee,
Proceeded, lo now is reveald to thee.
Here is the fountaine of the worldès good:
Now therefore, if thou wilt enrichèd bee,
Avise thee> well, and chaunge thy wilfull mood, *consider*
Least> thou perhaps hereafter wish, and be withstood. *lest*

39 Suffise it then, thou Money God (quoth hee)
That all thine idle offers I refuse.
All that I need I have; what needeth mee
To covet more, then I have cause to use?
With such vaine shewes thy worldlings vile abuse:
But give me leave to follow mine emprise.> *enterprise*
Mammon was much displeased, yet no'te he> chuse, *he could not*
And beare the rigour of his bold mesprise,> *scorn*
And thence him forward led, him further to entise.

40 He brought him through a darksome narrow strait,
To a broad gate, all built of beaten gold:
The gate was open, but therein did wait
A sturdy villein, striding stiffe and bold,
As if that highest God defie he would;
In his right hand an yron club he held,
But he himselfe was all of golden mould,

Yet had both life and sence, and well could weld> *wield*
That cursèd weapon, when his cruell foes he queld.

41 *Disdayne* he callèd was, and did disdaine
To be so cald, and who so did him call:
Sterne was his looke, and full of stomacke> vaine, *pride*
His portaunce> terrible, and stature tall, *bearing*
Far passing th'hight of men terrestriall;
Like an huge Gyant of the *Titans* race,
That made him scorne all creatures great and small,
And with his pride all others powre deface>: *abash*
More fit amongst blacke fiendes, then men to have his place.

42 Soone as those glitterand armes he did espye,
That with their brightnesse made that darknesse light,
His harmefull club he gan to hurtle> hye, *brandish*
And threaten batteill to the Faery knight;
Who likewise gan himselfe to batteill dight,> *prepare*
Till *Mammon* did his hasty hand withhold,
And counseld him abstaine from perilous fight:
For nothing might abash the villein bold,
Ne mortall steele emperce his miscreated mould.

43 So having him with reason pacifide,
And the fiers Carle> commaunding to forbeare, *churl*
He brought him in. The rowme° was large and wide,
As it some Gyeld> or solemne Temple weare: *guildhall*
Many great golden pillours did upbeare
The massy roofe, and riches huge sustayne,
And every pillour deckèd was full deare> *richly*
With crownes and Diademes, and titles vaine,
Which mortall Princess wore, whiles they on earth did rayne.

44 A route of people there assemblèd were,
Of every sort and nation under skye,
Which with great uprore preacèd to draw nere *pressed*
To th'upper part, where was advauncèd hye
A stately siege> of soveraigne majestye; *throne*
And thereon sat a woman° gorgeous gay,
And richly clad in robes of royaltye,
That> never earthly Prince in such aray *such that*
His glory did enhaunce, and pompous pride display.

45 Her face right wondrous faire did seeme to bee,
That> her broad beauties beam great brightnes threw *so that*
Through the dim shade, that all men might it see:
Yet was not that same her owne native hew,> *form*

The rowme Passing by Disdain, protector of the privileged, Guyon now embarks on the temptation of false honor and wordly power in the temple of Philotime ("love of honor"); Spenser makes the temple rather like a great monarch's court.

woman Philotime, a corrupt earthly version of heavenly honor, to which Guyon is committed

But wrought by art and counterfetted shew,
Thereby more lovers unto her to call;
Nath'lesse˃ most heavenly faire in deed and vew *nevertheless*
She by creation was, till she did fall;
Thenceforth she sought for helps, to cloke her crime withall.

46 There, as in glistring glory she did sit,
She held a great gold chaine° ylinckèd well,
Whose upper end to highest heaven was knit,
And lower part did reach to lowest Hell;
And all that preace˃ did round about her swell, *crowd*
To catchen hold of that long chaine, thereby
To clime aloft, and others to excell:
That was *Ambition,* rash desire to sty.˃ *ascend*
And every lincke thereof a step of dignity.

47 Some thought to raise themselves to high degree,
By riches and unrightèous reward,
Some by close shouldring,˃ some by flatteree; *intriguing*
Others through friends, others for base regard;˃ *bribery*
And all by wrong wayes for themselves prepard.
Those that were up themselves, kept others low,
Those that were low themselves, held others hard,
Ne suffered them to rise or greater grow,
But every one did strive his fellow downe to throw.

48 Which whenas *Guyon* saw, he gan inquire,
What meant that preace about that Ladies throne,
And what she was that did so high aspire.
Him *Mammon* answerèd; That goodly one,
Whom all that folke with such contention,
Do flocke about, my deare, my daughter is;
Honour and dignitie from her alone
Derivèd are, and all this worldès blis
For which ye men do strive: few get, but many mis.

49 And faire *Philotime* she rightly hight,˃ *is called*
The fairest wight that wonneth˃ under skye, *lives*
But that this darksome neather world her light
Doth dim with horrour and deformitie,
Worthy of heaven and hye felicitie,
From whence the gods have her for envy thrust:
But sith thou hast found favour in mine eye,
Thy spouse I will her make, if that thou lust,˃ *wish*
That she may thee advance for workes and merites just.

gold chaine When attached to the throne of Zeus in Homer's *Iliad* (VIII.19 ff.) the golden chain became, for later allegorists, a symbol of the order of divine creation with its grades and hierarchies; Philotime's gold chain is a human and wicked parody, representing only the struggle for worldly power; every link is a "step of dignity," that is, a degree of social rank by which earthly ambition seeks to ascend.

50 Gramercy *Mammon* (said the gentle knight)
For so great grace and offred high estate;
But I, that am fraile flesh and earthly wight,
Unworthy match for such immortall mate
My self well wote,˃ and mine unequall fate;˃ *know / inferior destiny*
And were I not, yet is my trouth yplight,
And love avowd to other Lady° late,˃ *lately*
That to remove the same I have no might:˃ *power*
To chaunge love causelesse is reproch to warlike knight.

51 *Mammon* emmovèd was with inward wrath;
Yet forcing it to faine,˃ him forth thence led *to dissimulate it*
Through griesly shadowes by a beaten path,
Into a gardin° goodly garnishèd
With hearbs and fruits, whose kinds mote˃ not be red:˃ *can / told*
Not such, as earth out of her fruitfull woomb
Throwes forth to men, sweet and well savourèd,
But direfull deadly blacke both leafe and bloom,
Fit to adorne the dead, and decke the drery toombe.

52 There mournfull *Cypresse* grew in greatest store,
And trees of bitter *Gall*, and *Heben*˃ sad, *ebony*
Dead sleeping *Poppy*, and blacke *Hellebore*,
Cold *Coloquintida*, and *Tetra* mad,
Mortall *Samnitis*, and *Cicuta* bad,°
With which th' unjust *Atheniens* made to dy
Wise *Socrates*, who thereof quaffing glad
Pourd out his life, and last Philosophy
To the faire *Critias*° his dearest Belamy.˃ *friend*

53 The *Gardin* of *Proserpina* this hight;˃ *was named*
And in the midst thereof a silver seat,°
With a thicke Arber goodly over dight,˃ *placed overhead*

other Lady Guyon courteously rejects the offer on the ground that he is betrothed to another lady, meaning the true "love of honor" in the heaven from which Philotime has fallen (see stanza 45 and, for Mammon's version of her fall, stanza 49).

gardin The Garden of Proserpina is the setting for Guyon's last temptation, which completes the others, so that they add up to a total temptation like that of Jesus in the wilderness. This is the temptation of *curiosity* (forbidden knowledge). The garden is based on the Grove of Persephone in Homer, *Odyssey* X; Spenser fills it with deathly herbs, taking a hint from Pausanias, (*Description of Greece* X.30). The herbs are appropriate to Proserpina in her character as Hecate, patroness of poisons.

Dead sleeping . . . bad Poppy is the source of narcotics; hellebrore is a plant supposed to cure madness; coloquintida is bitter-apple; tetra is deadly nightshade; samnitis is the savine-tree used to procure abortions; cicuta is hemlock.

Critias Though once a disciple, Critias was an enemy of Socrates; Spenser seems confused about what happens in Plato's *Phaedo*. Many involved explanations of this have been offered, and some say Spenser evidently did not know his Plato. But there is a simple explanation: Socrates speaks his last words to Crito; Crito closes his eyes. The dialogue *Crito* also deals with the last days of Socrates. Crito was a very old friend of the philosopher.

silver seat Not a simple invitation to sloth but the forbidden seat of the Eleusinian mysteries—the *mystes* could not sit in it lest they should seem to be imitating the mourning Ceres as she rested on her search for her daughter Proserpina. For his attempt to rape Proserpina Theseus was punished (*Aeneid* VI. 617–18) by perpetual imprisonment in an underworld chair; Pausanias describes a painting (XXIX.9) which shows Theseus in the Chair of Forgetfulness, now a punishment for knowing too much of forbidden matters. Spenser somehow discovered this allegorical sense; it fits his theme of initiation into the mystery (of Heroic Virtue) and goes well, of course, in the Garden of Proserpina.

In which she often usd from open heat
Her selfe to shroud,> and pleasures to entreat,> *shelter / occupy herself with*
Next thereunto did grow a goodly tree,
With braunches broad dispred and body great,
Clothèd with leaves, that none the wood mote> see *could*
And loaden all with fruit as thicke as it might bee.

54 Their fruit were golden apples° glistring bright,
That goodly was their glory to behold,
On earth like never grew, ne living wight
Like ever saw, but> they from hence were sold;> *unless / brought*
For those, which *Hercules* with conquest bold
Got from great *Atlas* daughters,° hence began,
And planted there, did bring forth fruit of gold:
And those with which th'*Eubœan* young man wan> *won*
Swift *Atalanta,*° when through craft he her out ran.

55 Here also sprong that goodly golden fruit,
With which *Acontius*° got his lover trew,
Whom he had long time sought with fruitlesse suit:
Here eke that famous golden Apple grew,
The which emongst the gods false *Ate*° threw;
For which th'*Idæan* Ladies disagreed,
Till partiall *Paris* dempt> it *Venus* dew, *judged*
And had of her, faire *Helen* for his meed,
That many noble *Greekes* and *Trojans* made to bleed.

56 The warlike Elfe much wondred at this tree,
So faire and great, that shadowèd all the ground,
And his broad braunches, laden with rich fee,
Did stretch themselves without> the utmost bound *beyond*
Of this great gardin, compast with a mound,
Which over-hanging, they themselves did steepe,
In a blacke flood which flow'd about it round;
That is the river of *Cocytus*° deepe,
In which full many soules do endlesse waile and weepe.

golden apples These are underworld fruit that must not be eaten (the *mala Punica,* Punic apples or pomegranates, were Proserpina's food of the dead), but Spenser adds that the famous apples of myth all descended from them. The forbidden fruit represents a temptation like that of Eve's apple, which was eaten out of appetite, vainglory, and curiosity. Spenser relates its mythological descendants to the temptation of forbidden knowledge.

Hercules . . . daughters The apples of the Hesperides; Hercules in his eleventh labor had to get them from the tree of the daughters of Atlas (Hesperides); they were protected by a dragon. They became emblems of astronomical knowledge.

th'Eubœan . . . Atalanta Hippomenes won his race with the swift Atalanta by throwing golden apples in her way; she stopped to pick them up and was beaten. These apples were Hesperidean. Atalanta had desecrated the shrine of the Great Mother (an image of the blasphemy of forbidden knowledge).

Acontius He wrote on an apple "I swear by Artemis that I will marry Acontius"; Cydippe picked the apple up, read the message aloud, and was bound by the oath, though she tried blasphemously to get out of it.

Ate goddess of Discord. She produced the apple which was the prize to be awarded by Paris to the most beautiful of three goddesses; in return for Helen he gave it to Venus. His abduction of Helen caused the Trojan War. Allegorically this apple was a symbol of insane contempt for divine wisdom.

Cocytus river of hell

57 Which to behold, he clomb up to the banke,
And looking downe, saw many damnèd wights,
In those sad waves, which direfull deadly stanke,
Plongèd continually of> cruell Sprights, *by*
That with their pitteous cryes, and yelling shrights,> *shrieks*
They made the further shore resounden> wide: *echo*
Emongst the rest of those same ruefull sights,
One cursèd creature he by chaunce espide,
That drenchèd lay full deepe, under the Garden side.

58 Deepe was he drenchèd to the upmost chin,
Yet gapèd still, as coveting to drinke
Of the cold liquor, which he waded in,
And stretching forth his hand, did often thinke
To reach the fruit, which grew upon the brincke:
But both the fruit from hand, and floud from mouth
Did flie abacke, and made him vainely swinke:> *labor*
The whiles he sterv'd> with hunger and with drouth *died*
He daily dyde, yet never throughly> dyen couth.> *completely / could*

59 The knight him seeing labour so in vaine,
Askt who he was, and what he ment thereby:
Who groning deepe, thus answerd him againe;
Most cursèd of all creatures under skye,
Lo *Tantalus,*° I here tormented lye:
Of whom high *Jove* wont> whylome> feasted bee, *was accustomed / once*
Lo here I now for want of food doe dye:
But if that thou be such, as I thee see,
Of grace I pray thee, give to eat and drinke to mee.

60 Nay, nay, thou greedie *Tantalus* (quoth he)
Abide the fortune of thy present fate,
And unto all that live in high degree,
Ensample be of mind intemperate,
To teach them how to use their present state.
Then gan the cursèd wretch aloud to cry,
Accusing highest *Jove* and gods ingrate,
And eke blaspheming heaven bitterly,
As authour of unjustice, there to let him dye.

61 He lookt a little further, and espyde
Another wretch, whose carkasse deepe was drent> *submerged*
Within the river, which the same did hyde:
But both his hands most filthy feculent,> *foul*

Tantalus His punishment derives from *Odyssey* XI. A type of avarice, but also of intemperate and blasphemous knowledge, for he served the gods a dish made of the body of his son Pelops in order to test their immortality; also, as a guest of Jupiter, he heard secrets of divine knowledge and reported them to men. Ovid says he revealed the Eleusinian secrets, and Pausanias shows him suffering in hell with those who revealed or despised these mysteries. Guyon in stanza 60 says he is an example of "mind intemperate"; Spenser is not talking about greed or avarice.

Above the water were on high extent,> *extended*
And faynd> to wash themselves incessantly: *pretended*
Yet nothing cleaner were for such intent,
But rather fowler seemèd to the eye;
So lost his labour vaine and idle industry.

62 The knight him calling, askèd who he was,
Who lifting up his head, him answerd thus:
I *Pilate*° am the falsest Judge, alas,
And most unjust, that by unrighteous
And wicked doome, to Jewes despiteous
Delivered up the Lord of life to die,
And did acquite a murdrer felonous;
The whiles my hands I washt in puritie,
The whiles my soule was soyld with foule iniquitie.

63 Infinite moe,> tormented in like paine *more*
He there beheld, too long here to be told:
Ne *Mammon* would there let him long remaine,
For terrour of the tortures manifold,
In which the damnèd soules he did behold,
But roughly him bespake. Thou fearefull foole,
Why takest not of that same fruit of gold,
Ne sittest downe on that same silver stoole,
To rest thy wearie person, in the shadow coole.

64 All which he did, to doe him deadly fall
In frayle intemperance through sinfull bayt;
To which if he inclinèd had at all,
That dreadfull feend, which did behind him wayt,
Would him have rent in thousand peeces strayt:
But he was warie wise in all his way,
And well perceivèd his deceiptfull sleight,
Ne suffred lust his safetie to betray:
So goodly did beguile the Guyler> of the pray. *deceiver*

65 And now he has so long remainèd there,
That vitall powres gan wexe both weake and wan,
For want of food, and sleepe, which two upbeare,
Like mightie pillours, this fraile life of man,
That none without the same enduren can.
For now three dayes of men were full outwrought,> *completed*
Since he this hardie enterprize began:
For thy> great *Mammon* fairely he besought, *therefore*
Into the world to guide him backe, as he him brought.

Pilate the type of judicial corruption. When Christ said "To this end was I born, and for this cause came I into the world, that I should bear witness unto the truth. Every one that is of the truth heareth my voice," Pilate replied "What is truth?" (John 18:37–38); by releasing Barabbas he denied divine truth.

66 The God, though loth, yet was constraind t'obay,
For lenger time, then that, no living wight
Below the earth, might suffred be to stay:
So backe againe, him brought to living light.
But all so soone as his enfeebled spright
Gan sucke this vitall aire into his brest,
As overcome with too exceeding might,
The life did flit away out of her nest,
And all his senses were with deadly fit opprest.

From Canto viii°

Sir Guyon laid in swowne is by
Acrates sonnes despoyld,
Whom Arthur soone hath reskewed
And Paynim brethren foyld.

1 And is there care in heaven? and is there love
In heavenly spirits to these creatures bace,
That may compassion of their evils move?
There is: else much more wretched were the cace
Of men, then beasts. But O th' exceeding grace
Of highest God, that loves his creatures so,
And all his workes with mercy doth embrace,
That blessèd Angels, he sends to and fro,
To serve to wicked man, to serve his wicked foe.°

2 How oft do they, their silver bowers leave,
To come to succour us, that succour want?> *lack*
How oft do they with golden pineons,> cleave *wings*
The flitting> skyes, like flying Pursuivant,> *changing / messenger*
Against foule feends to aide us millitant?
They for us fight, they watch and dewly ward,
And their bright Squadrons round about us plant,
And all for love, and nothing for reward:
O why should heavenly God to men have such regard?°

[In canto viii the Palmer returns, but Arthur has to rescue Guyon from the attack of Pyrochles and Cymochles, perhaps representing the threat of a temporary insurrection of irascibility and concupiscence in his weakened state. Canto ix has a full-scale allegorical treatment of the House of Alma (the soul), also called the House of Temperance. The well-regulated human body is here described under the transparent allegory of a great house with its services, interconnections, sewers, etc. But it is besieged by enemies; and in xi (the interven-

Canto viii Spenser opens with a passage commenting on the fact that Guyon, in his faint, is tended by an angel (stanzas 5–8). So was Christ after his victory over sin in the wilderness; he had overcome, says St. Augustine, temptation by the lust of the flesh; by vainglory; and by curiosity. These are all the temptations. (Augustine says this in a Homily on Psalm 8, which Spenser quotes in these stanzas.) Guyon is now confirmed in Heroic Virtue, having withstood his initiatory trial; his virtues are now those of the purged soul, a little lower than sanctity, which Red Cross achieved, but higher than ordinary virtues, and qualifying for the category first invented by Aristotle, and later Christianized, namely, Heroic Virtue.

blessèd . . . foe "ministering spirits, sent forth to minister for them who shall be heirs of salvation" (Hebrews 1:14)

O why . . . regard "What is man, that thou art mindful of him? and the son of man, that thou visitest him?" (Psalms 8:4)

ing canto is a long account of Elizabeth's legendary ancient British ancestors) Spenser describes the siege, the assault on the human body of its enemies, led by Maleger (Latin: *aeger,* sick). This is one of the great passages of *The Faerie Queene;* Maleger is Spenser's most nightmarish figure—"like a ghost he seemed, whose grave clothes were unbound"—and Arthur's combat with this unkillable but apparently lifeless shadow has real horror. It represents the unstoppable onslaught of ills brought on by Adam's intemperance.

Canto xii brings Guyon to the climax of his quest, the Bower of Bliss, home of Acrasia, Intemperance herself. But it takes a long voyage to get there, and the account of it serves to recapitulate much of the Book. Guyon and the Palmer sail past Phaedria, for example, and many other *exempla* of intemperance. At the Bower they encounter many spurious beauties provided by art to conceal the truth that it is an evil structure calling for merciless purgation. The Porter is Genius, but not the benign Genius of "life and generation" we meet in *Epithalamion;* in fact he is the exact opposite, "the foe of life," and Guyon knocks over his winebowl and breaks his staff. Within, the Bower is a false version of the Earthly Paradise.]

From Canto xii

50 Thus being entred, they behold around
A large and spacious plaine, on every side
Strowèd with pleasauns,> whose faire grassy ground *pleasances*
Mantled with greene, and goodly beautifide
With all the ornaments of *Floraes* pride,
Wherewith her mother Art, as halfe in scorne
Of niggard Nature, like a pompous bride
Did decke her, and too lavishly adorne,
When forth from virgin bowre she comes in th' early morne.

51 Thereto the Heavens alwayes Joviall,°
Lookt on them lovely, still in stedfast state,
Ne suffred storme nor frost on them to fall,
Their tender buds or leaves to violate,
Nor scorching heat, nor cold intemperate°
T'afflict the creatures, which therein did dwell,
But the milde aire with season moderate
Gently attempred, and disposd so well,
That still it breathèd forth sweet spirit and holesome smell.

52 More sweet and holesome, then the pleasaunt hill
Of *Rhodope,*° on which the Nimphe, that bore
A gyaunt babe, her selfe for griefe did kill;

Joviall under the influence of the planet Jupiter, producing joy and happiness

Nor . . . intemperate Spenser represents the place somewhat conventionally as an Earthly Paradise and, like Milton in *Paradise Lost* IV, enforces the idea by saying that this is better than all the others; but he includes various indications—not only Guyon's determination to have nothing to do with the pleasures of the place—to suggest that it is the scene of abuses as well as of the natural plenty proper to paradises. Hence the "wanton wreathings"; but especially he places Excess in the foreground, for the lavish gifts of nature are being abused, as later they are by Comus.

Rhodope mountain in Thrace into which Rhodope was turned for claiming to be more beautiful than Juno; she bore Neptune a giant son

Or the Thessalian *Tempe,*° where of yore
Faire *Daphne*° *Phœbus* hart with love did gore;
Or *Ida,*° where the Gods lov'd to repaire,
When ever they their heavenly bowres forlore;
Or sweet *Parnasse,* the haunt of Muses faire;
Or *Eden* selfe, if ought with *Eden* mote> compaire. *can*

53 Much wondred *Guyon* at the faire aspect
Of that sweet place, yet suffred no delight
To sincke into his sence, nor mind affect,
But passèd forth, and lookt still forward right,
Bridling his will, and maistering his might:
Till that he came unto another gate;
No gate, but like one, being goodly dight
With boughes and braunches, which did broad dilate
Their clasping armes, in wanton wreathings intricate.

54 So fashionèd a Porch with rare device,
Archt over head with an embracing vine,
Whose bounches hanging downe, seemed to entice
All passers by, to tast their lushious wine,
And did themselves into their hands incline,
As freely offering to be gatherèd:
Some deepe empurpled as the *Hyacint,*> *sapphire*
Some as the Rubine,> laughing sweetly red, *ruby*
Some like faire Emeraudes, not yet well ripenèd.

55 And them amongst, some were of burnisht gold,
So made by art, to beautifie the rest,
Which did themselves emongst the leaves enfold,
As lurking from the vew of covetous guest,
That the weake bowes, with so rich load opprest,
Did bow adowne, as over-burdenèd.
Under that Porch a comely dame did rest,
Clad in faire weedes,> but fowle disorderèd, *garments*
And garments loose, that seemd unmeet for womanhed.

56 In her left hand a Cup of gold she held,
And with her right the riper fruit did reach,
Whose sappy liquor, that with fulnesse sweld,
Into her cup she scruzd,> with daintie breach *squeezed*
Of her fine fingers, without fowle empeach,> *detriment*
That so faire wine-presse made the wine more sweet:
Thereof she usd to give to drinke to each,
Whom passing by she happenèd to meet:
It was her guise,> all Straungers goodly so to greet. *manner*

Tempe Orpheus by his music led trees to the mountain valley in Thessaly, famous for its groves and walks.

Daphne She escaped Phoebus Apollo in Tempe by being turned into a laurel.

Ida Cretan mountain, frequented by gods during the Trojan war

57 So she to *Guyon* offred it to tast;
Who taking it out of her tender hond,
The cup to ground did violently cast,
That all in peeces it was broken fond,
And with the liquor stainèd all the lond:
Whereat *Excesse* exceedingly was wroth,
Yet no'te> the same amend, ne yet withstond, *could not*
But suffrèd him to passe, all were she loth;
Who nought regarding her displeasure forward goth.

58 There the most daintie Paradise on ground,
It selfe doth offer to his sober eye,
In which all pleasures plenteously abound,
And none does others happinesse envye:
The painted flowres, the trees upshooting hye,
The dales for shade, the hilles for breathing space,
The trembling groves, the Christall running by;
And that, which all faire workes doth most aggrace,
The art, which all that wrought, appearèd in no place.°

59 One would have thought, (so cunningly, the rude,
And scornèd parts were mingled with the fine,)
That nature had for wantonesse ensude> *imitated*
Art, and that Art at nature did repine;
So striving each th' other to undermine,
Each did the others worke more beautifie;
So diff'ring both in willes, agreed in fine:> *in the end*
So all agreed through sweete diversitie,
This Gardin to adorne with all varietie.

60 And in the midst of all, a fountaine stood,
Of richest substaunce, that on earth might bee,
So pure and shiny, that the silver flood
Through every channell running one might see;
Most goodly it with curious imageree
Was over-wrought, and shapes of naked boyes,
Of which some seemd with lively jollitee,
To fly about, playing their wanton toyes,> *games*
Whilest others did them selves embay> in liquid joyes. *bathe*

61 And over all, of purest gold was spred,
A trayle of yvie in his native hew:> *appearance*
For the rich mettall was so colourèd,
That wight, who did not well avis'd it vew,
Would surely deeme it to be yvie trew;
Low his lascivious armes adown did creepe,
That themselves dipping in the silver dew,

The art . . . place exactly translated from Tasso, *Gerusalemme Liberata* (the main inspiration of this canto). Spenser's meaning is not that art is lower than nature, as some critics say; the fault in the paradise lies in the human uses to which it is put, not in its design.

Their fleecy flowres they tenderly did steepe,
Which drops of Christall seemd for wantonès to weepe.

62 Infinit streames continually did well
Out of this fountaine, sweet and faire to see,
The which into an ample laver> fell, *basin*
And shortly grew to so great quantitie,
That like a little lake it seemd to bee;
Whose depth exceeded not three cubits hight,
That through the waves one might the bottom see,
All pav'd beneath with Jaspar shining bright,
That seemd the fountaine in that sea did sayle upright.

63 And all the margent round about was set,
With shady Laurell trees, thence to defend> *fend off*
The sunny beames, which on the billowes bet,> *beat*
And those which therein bathèd, mote offend.
As *Guyon* hapned by the same to wend,
Two naked Damzelles he therein espyde,
Which therein bathing, seemèd to contend,
And wrestle wantonly, ne car'd to hyde,
Their dainty parts from vew of any, which them eyde.

64 Sometimes the one would lift the other quight
Above the waters, and then downe againe
Her plong, as over maisterèd by might,
Where both awhile would covered remaine,
And each the other from to rise> restraine; *rising*
The whiles their snowy limbes, as through a vele,
So through the Christall waves appearèd plaine:
Then suddeinly both would themselves unhele,> *uncover*
And th'amarous sweet spoiles to greedy eyes revele.

65 As that faire Starre,° the messenger of morne,
His deawy face out of the sea doth reare:
Or as the *Cyprian* goddesse,° newly borne
Of th'Oceans fruitfull froth, did first appeare:
Such seemèd they, and so> their yellow heare *in the same way*
Christalline humour> dropped downe apace. *water*
Whom such when *Guyon* saw, he drew him neare,
And somewhat gan relent his earnest pace,
His stubborne brest gan secret pleasaunce to embrace.°

66 The wanton Maidens him esyping, stood
Gazing a while at his unwonted guise;> *behavior*
Then th'one her selfe low duckèd in the flood,

faire Starre the Morning Star (Venus)
Cyprian goddesse Venus, born of the union of Saturn's semen and the ocean
His stubborne . . . embrace Guyon's momentary lust for the girls in the fountain recalls the lapses of his pagan (but Christianized) prototype Hercules; but Right Reason (the Palmer) enables temperance to overcome concupiscence.

Abasht, that her a straunger did avise:> *look at*
But th'other rather higher did arise,
And her two lilly paps aloft displayd,
And all, that might his melting hart entise
To her delights, she unto him bewrayd:> *displayed*
The rest hid underneath, him more desirous made.

67 With that, the other likewise up arose,
And her faire lockes, which formerly were bownd
Up in one knot, she low adowne did lose:> *unloose*
Which flowing long and thick, her cloth'd arownd,
And th'yvorie in golden mantle gown:
So that faire spectacle from him was reft,
Yet that, which reft it, no lesse faire was fownd:
So hid in lockes and waves from lookers theft,
Nought but her lovely face she for his looking left.

68 Withall she laughèd, and she blusht withall,
That blushing to her laughter gave more grace,
And laughter to her blushing, as did fall:
Now when they spide the knight to slacke his pace,
Them to behold, and in his sparkling face
The secret signes of kindled lust appeare,
Their wanton meriments they did encreace,
And to him beckned, to approach more neare,
And shewd him many sights, that courage> cold could reare. *desire*

69 On which when gazing him the Palmer saw,
He much rebukt those wandring eyes of his,
And counseld well, him forward thence did draw.
Now are they come nigh to the *Bowre of blis*
Of her fond favorites so nam'd amis:
When thus the Palmer; Now Sir, well avise;
For here the end of all our travell is:
Here wonnes> *Acrasia*, whom we must surprise, *lives*
Else she will slip away, and all our drift> despise. *plans*

70 Eftsoones they heard a most melodious sound,
Of all that mote delight a daintie eare,
Such as attonce might not on living ground,
Save in this Paradise, be heard elsewhere:
Right hard it was, for wight, which did it heare,
To read,> what manner musicke that mote bee: *tell*
For all that pleasing is to living eare,
Was there consorted in one harmonee,
Birdes, voyces, instruments, windes, waters, all agree.

71 The joyous birdes shrouded in chearefull shade,
Their notes unto the voyce attempred sweet;
Th'Angelicall soft trembling voyces made

To th'instruments divine respondence meet;
The silver sounding instruments did meet
With the base˃ murmure of the waters fall: *bass*
The waters fall with difference discreet,
Now soft, now loud, unto the wind did call:
The gentle warbling wind low answerèd to all.°

72 There, whence that Musick seemèd heard to bee,
Was the faire Witch her selfe now solacing,
With a new Lover, whom through sorceree
And witchcraft, she from farre did thither bring:
There she had him now layd a slombering,
In secret shade, after long wanton joyes:
Whilst round about them pleasauntly did sing
Many faire Ladies, and lascivious boyes,
That ever mixt their song with light licentious toyes.

73 And all that while, right over him she hong,
With her false eyes fast fixèd in his sight,
As seeking medicine, whence she was stong,°
Or greedily depasturing˃ delight: *consuming*
And oft inclining downe with kisses light,
For feare of waking him, his lips bedewed,
And through his humid eyes did sucke his spright,
Quite molten into lust and pleasure lewd;
Wherewith she sighèd soft, as if his case she rewd.

74 The whiles some one did chaunt this lovely lay;°
Ah see, who so faire thing doest faine to see,
In springing flowre the image of thy day;
Ah see the Virgin Rose, how sweetly shee
Doth first peepe forth with bashfull modestee,
That fairer seemes, the lesse ye see her may;
Lo see soone after, how more bold and free
Her bared bosome she doth broad display;
Loe see soone after, how she fades, and falles away.

75 So passeth, in the passing of a day,
Of mortall life the leafe, the bud, the flowre,
Ne more doth flourish after first decay,
That earst was sought to decke both bed and bowre,

The joyous . . . all This stanza of natural and artificial harmony Spenser developed from Tasso, *Gerusalemme Liberata* XVI.2, though that leaves out the instruments and voices; however, Tasso includes these when he writes a rather similar stanza (XVIII.8); hence if Spenser is really, as some critics say, making the combination of artificial and natural music seem sinister, Tasso, whose sinister intent is hard to see, preceded him.

seeking . . . stong seeking a cure from that which hurt her

lay Translated from Tasso (XVI.14–15), where it is sung by a bird. The theme—*carpe diem*, seize the day—is ancient, and so is the group of figures attached to the rose. The beauty of the "lovely lay" emphasizes, like the beauty of the approaches to the Bower, the powerful forces against which Temperance must fight. The theme occurs in many poems which have not the moralistic context of Spenser's, but Comus's use of the rose-figure in Milton's masque is very like this one (ll. 742–43).

Of many a Ladie, and many a Paramowre:
Gather therefore the Rose, whilest yet is prime,
For soone comes age, that will her pride deflowre:
Gather the Rose of love, whilest yet is time,
Whilest loving thou mayst lovèd be with equall crime.> *sin*

76 He ceast, and then gan all the quire of birdes
Their diverse notes t'attune unto his lay,
As in approvance of his pleasing words.
The constant paire heard all, that he did say,
Yet swarvèd> not, but kept their forward way, *swerved*
Through many covert groves, and thickets close,
In which they creeping did at last display> *discover*
That wanton Ladie, with her lover lose,
Whose sleepie head she in her lap did soft dispose.

77 Upon a bed of Roses she was layd,
As faint through heat, or dight to pleasant sin,
And was arayd, or rather disarayd,
All in a vele of silke and silver thin,
That hid no whit her alablaster> skin, *alabaster*
But rather shewd more white, if more might bee:
More subtile web *Arachne* cannot spin,
Nor the fine nets, which oft we woven see
Of scorchèd deaw, do not in th'aire more lightly flee.

78 Her snowy brest was bare to readie spoyle
Of hungry eies, which n'ote> therewith be fild, *could not*
And yet through languor of her late sweet toyle,
Few drops, more cleare then Nectar, forth distild,
That like pure Orient perles adowne it trild,
And her faire eyes sweet smyling in delight,
Moystenèd their fierie beames, with which she thrild
Fraile harts, yet quenchèd not; like starry light
Which sparckling on the silent waves, does seeme more bright.

79 The young man sleeping by her, seemd to bee
Some goodly swayne of honorable place,
That certes it great pittie was to see
Him his nobilitie so foule deface;
A sweet regard, and amiable grace,
Mixèd with manly sternnesse did appeare
Yet sleeping, in his well proportiond face,
And on his tender lips the downy heare
Did now but freshly spring, and silken blosomes beare.

80 His warlike armes, the idle instruments
Of sleeping praise, were hong upon a tree,
And his brave shield, full of old moniments,> *figures*
Was fowly ra'st,> that none the signes might see; *erased*

Ne for them, ne for honour carèd hee,
Ne ought, that did to his advauncement tend,
But in lewd loves, and wastfull luxuree,
His dayes, his goods, his bodie he did spend:
O horrible enchantment, that him so did blend.˃ *blind*

81 The noble Elfe, and carefull Palmer drew
So nigh them, minding nought, but lustfull game,
That suddein forth they on them rusht, and threw
A subtile˃ net,° which onely˃ for the same *fine / specially*
The skilfull Palmer formally˃ did frame.˃ *expressly / design*
So held them under fast, the whiles the rest
Fled all away for feare of fowler shame.
The faire Enchauntresse, so unwares opprest,
Tryde all her arts, and all her sleights, thence out to wrest.

82 And eke her lover strove: but all in vaine;
For that same net so cunningly was wound,
That neither guile, nor force might it distraine.˃ *break*
They tooke them both, and both them strongly bound
In captive bandes, which there they readie found:
But her in chaines of adamant he tyde;
For nothing else might keepe her safe and sound;
But *Verdant*° (so he hight) he soone untyde,
And counsell sage in steed thereof˃ to him applyde. *of constraint*

83 But all those pleasant bowres and Pallace brave,
Guyon broke downe, with rigour pittilesse;
Ne ought their goodly workmanship might save
Them from the tempest of his wrathfulnesse,
But that their blisse he turn'd to balefulnesse:
Their groves he feld, their gardins did deface,
Their arbers spoyle, their Cabinets˃ suppresse, *bowers*
Their banket houses burne, their buildings race,˃ *raze*
And of the fairest late, now made the fowlest place.

84 Then led they her away, and eke that knight
They with them led, both sorrowfull and sad:
The way they came, the same retourn'd they right,
Till they arrivèd, where they lately had
Charm'd those wild-beasts,° that rag'd with furie mad.
Which now awaking, fierce at them gan fly,
As in their mistresse reskew, whom they lad;
But them the Palmer soone did pacify.
Then *Guyon* askt, what meant those beastes, which there did ly.

net borrowed from *Odyssey* VIII. 276 ff., where Hephaestus (Vulcan) traps his wife Aphrodite (Venus) in bed with Ares (Mars) by a similar stratagem

Verdant perhaps because in the spring of his life; perhaps "spring (or life)-giving," as Mordant, Acrasia's earlier lover, was "death-giving"

wild-beasts They met these beasts on the way in stanza 39.

85 Said he, These seeming beasts are men indeed,
Whom this Enchauntresse hath transformèd thus,
Whylome> her lovers, which her lusts did feed, *formerly*
Now turned into figures hideous,
According to their mindes like monstruous.°
Sad end (quoth he) of life intemperate,
And mournefull meed of joyes delicious:
But Palmer, if it mote thee so aggrate,> *please*
Let them returnèd be unto their former state.

86 Streight way he with his vertuous staffe them strooke,
And streight of beasts they comely men became;
Yet being men they did unmanly looke,
And starèd ghastly, some for inward shame,
And some for wrath, to see their captive Dame:
But one above the rest in speciall,
That had an hog beene late, hight *Grille*° by name,
Repinèd greatly, and did him miscall,
That had from hoggish forme him brought to naturall.

87 Said *Guyon*, See the mind of beastly man,
That hath so soone forgot the excellence
Of his creation, when he life began,
That now he chooseth, with vile difference,
To be a beast, and lacke intelligence.
To whom the Palmer thus, The donghill kind
Delights in filth and foule incontinence:
Let *Grill* be *Grill*, and have his hoggish mind,
But let us hence depart, whilest wether serves and wind.

1590

Book III

Book III is the Legend of Chastity, a Book of Love, and very different structurally from I and II, being in this regard closely linked to IV. It may be that parts of it are earlier than I and II, and belong to a time when Spenser was much more interested in writing a poem like Ariosto's *Orlando Furioso,* which has, though with greater pace and dash, a similar interweaving of many stories. Spenser here combines the tales of Britomart and Artegall, Marinell and Florimell, Belphoebe and Timias, with that of Scudamour and Amoret and many others. Amoret is chaste married love, and Scuda-

According . . . monstruous Acrasia is modeled on Homer's Circe, who turns men into beasts. Allegorically, the cup she offers gives a man his choice between two extremes between which, according to Aristotle, there is no mean: Bestiality and Heroic Virtue. Acrasia's victims chose Bestiality, and so are transformed into beasts.

Grille According to Plutarch, in his *Whether the Beasts Have Use of Reason,* one of Odysseus' comrades refused to be turned back into a man. This was Gryllus. The story was known in England from a book called *Circe,* translated from Italian and published in 1557. Guyon uses Grille as an occasion to reflect on the willingness of some men to forgo their rank above the beast and next to the angels; the Palmer abandons him, since some men do, through incontinence, lose even the desire to be restored to humanity.

mour finally achieves her at the end of the Book, but only in the 1590 edition of Books I to III; in 1596 Spenser canceled the last five stanzas and replaced them by three new ones postponing the union.

In Book III Elizabeth is celebrated in her second person, not as Queen but as "a most virtuous and beautifull Lady," namely Belphoebe. Spenser can include in a treatment of love philosophical considerations wider and higher than relations between men and women; he glories in love as the bringer of fertility and order in the whole world. Thus the Virgin Queen can be the patroness and exemplar of plenty, fertility, order, while remaining a devotee of virginity; her twin sister, Amoret, expresses the other kind of chastity, which is consistent with married love.

The cosmic and moral implications of love are present also in the parts of the Book Spenser calls, in the Letter to Ralegh, "Accidents"; one is "the over-throw of Marinell, the misery of Florimell," a story that runs on into Book V. Florimell is based on Ariosto's Angelica, who is always being chased and who has an evil double, as Florimell has a Snowy Florimell imitating her. Her allegorical significance is not clear, but she seems to be a type of the beauty of natural creation, the opposite but also the complement of the chaotic sea (Marinell) out of which Love was born.

[In the opening canto Spenser follows his now established procedure—the departing Guyon meets the knight of the new Book, the maiden warrior Britomart, and she beats him in fight because Chastity, her virtue, is higher than Temperance, Guyon's. But she presides over the Book much less firmly than Guyon over his, and comes into her own only at the end. The first canto also contains a key to the whole Book in the account of Castle Joyeous, the abode of Malecasta, which is full of emblems of unchastity. Britomart defeats Malecasta's champions. Cantos ii and iii establish the relation between Britomart and Artegall (knight of Justice in Book V) to Elizabeth, and iv is about Marinell and Florimell and ends with a beautiful apostrophe to Night. Canto v describes the healing of the squire Timias by Belphoebe (probably a reference to the quarrel between Ralegh and the Queen). Canto vi is the "core" canto, and one of the most important in the entire poem.]

Book III, Canto vi

This canto, which has strong associations with the Mutability Cantos, contains a charming, newly invented myth and a philosophical allegory which is not only hard to interpret but also, in some respects, central to the poem, and the source of much that we consider "Spenserian"; if *The Faerie Queene* in any sense adds up to a great poem much depends upon these stanzas; they tell us about the color of the poet's mind and the way he had learned to speak a philosophy of life through mythological fictions.

The Garden of Adonis is about the great opposites that everybody knows about in his own life; we experience continuity but also change; we know that humanity, like plant life, survives, but also that as individuals we die. In short, life is mutable but also constant. The Renaissance poet will express this felt knowledge by making a myth which brings the opposites into a unity. Spenser will explain that the forms are sempiternal, that is, perpetual though lacking the final immutable stillness of eternity.

They are deathless but do not possess being-for-ever. The matter which these forms assume is separated from them by death. He represents the forms as plants in a nursery garden, and the matter that clothes them comes from a chaos like that which God used as material for the creation. This matter is eternal; love produces its union with form, so that the world is stocked with generated beings; and Time produces their separation. The generative *cycle* is quasi-immortal; the individual elements of it are not.

Consequently the species, neither eternal nor of time, occupies a third realm in between them. It partakes both of mutability and the unchangingness of the eternal: "by succession made perpetuall, / Transformed oft and chaunged diverslie." The symbol of this realm is Adonis; he is the entire biological cycle, dying and living on, in time and out of it.

Like all myths, as Claude Lévi-Strauss sees them, Spenser's is not an answer to a problem, but a way of containing it, making it humanly acceptable. Through culture man is aware of and dreads death; here culture and nature confront each other, and the myth allows the mind to condone the confrontation: the problem is not solved but acceptably formulated. So essential is this problem to Spenser's whole view of the world that he restates it in an analogous myth in Book VII.

It is disastrous to try to give this canto exact philosophical meanings. It is a myth, and the use of philosophical concepts and language is incidental to that kind of explanation. But a few notes on the more abstract-sounding stanzas may be helpful. The seminary (as described in stanzas 33–38) is analogous to the Platonic *anima mundi* or world-soul, from which come the forms that give created things their characteristic shapes ("hews") when joined with matter from chaos. When Spenser says "the substance is eterne" he is not trying, as a philosopher using such language would, to distinguish between "matter" and "substance"; for him they mean much the same thing, substance being a little more specific, and meaning matter in so far as it has a relation to form.

When Spenser says that it is the forms which suffer under time, and that if it were otherwise the voluptuous delights of the garden would be immortal, we understand him well enough without troubling to ask why, since the wearing out of the forms takes place in "the state of life," there has to be an allegorical figure of Time inside the garden as well. The introduction of that figure into an Earthly Paradise is in itself a myth; it represents the confrontation of human knowledge of fact and human hope.

It is Adonis himself, in the famous stanza 47, who elicits from Spenser his most determined effort to spell out discursively the knowledge which is implicit in his myth. Adonis was killed by the boar, but lives. Instead of representing him in the traditional way as dying annually and annually reviving, like vegetation, Spenser crushes together his mortality and immortality; in explaining this he has to be aphoristic: "All be he subject to mortalitie, / Yet is eterne in mutabilitie, / And by succession made perpetuall." For this reason he is called "the Father of all formes"; he represents the condition under which, though the living die, they still have life. Meanwhile the additional myth of Cupid and Psyche relates the pleasure of generation to the most exalted idea of love, seen as following the mutable course of the passion in life and in time. In the Mutability Cantos the relation of eternity to time is more fully considered.

Canto vi°

The birth of faire Belphœbe and
Of Amoret is told.
The Gardins of Adonis° fraught
With pleasures manifold.

1 Well may I weene, faire Ladies, all this while
Ye wonder, how this noble Damozell°
So great perfections did in her compile,
Sith that in salvage> forests she did dwell, *wild*
So farre from court and royall Citadell,
The great schoolmistresse of all curtesy:
Seemeth that such wild woods should far expell
All civill usage and gentility,
And gentle sprite deforme with rude rusticity.

2 But to this faire *Belphœbe*° in her berth
The heavens so favourable were and free,> *unencumbered*
Looking with myld aspect° upon the earth,
In th'*Horoscope* of her nativitee,
That all the gifts of grace and chastitee
On her they pourèd forth of plenteous horne;°
Jove laught on *Venus* from his soveraigne see,> *throne*
And *Phœbus* with faire beames did her adorne,
And all the *Graces*° rockt her cradle being borne.

3 Her berth was of the wombe of Morning dew,
And her conception of the joyous Prime> *spring*
And all her whole creation did her shew
Pure and unspotted from all loathly crime,> *sin*
That is ingenerate> in fleshly slime. *inborn*
So was this virgin borne, so was she bred,
So was she trayned up from time to time,°
In all chast vertue, and true bounti-hed
Till to her dew perfection she was ripenèd.

4 Her mother was the faire *Chrysogonee,*°
The daughter of *Amphisa,*° who by race
A Faerie was, yborne of high degree,
She bore *Belphœbe,* she bore in like cace
Faire *Amoretta* in the second place:
These two were twinnes, and twixt them two did share
The heritage of all celestiall grace.

Gardins of Adonis originally little pots of flowers which sprang up and in a few days withered, symbols of the death of Adonis used by women who mourned him, like Thammuz, as a god who died and was annually revived. Spenser hardly has them in mind when he constructs his big allegory of what is "eterne in mutabilitie."

Damozell Belphoebe

Belphœbe "handsome-radiant"

aspect This is the relative position of the planets as it determines their influence (see *Astronomy and Astrology* in the Glossary).

pourèd . . . horne as if from a cornucopia

Graces See I.i.48n.

from time to time through the stages of growth

Chrysogonee "golden-born"

Amphisa "of double nature" (natural and supernatural)

That all the rest it seem'd they robbèd bare
Of bountie, and of beautie, and all vertues rare.

5 It were a goodly storie,° to declare,
By what straunge accident faire *Chrysogone*
Conceiv'd these infants, and how them she bare,
In this wild forrest wandring all alone,
After she had nine moneths fulfild and gone:
For not as other wemens commune brood,
They were enwombèd in the sacred throne
Of her chaste bodie, nor with commune food,
As other wemens babes, they suckèd vitall blood.

6. But wondrously they were begot, and bred
Through influence of th'heavens fruitfull ray,
As it in antique bookes is mentionèd.
It was upon a Sommers shynie day,
When *Titan* faire his beamès did display,
In a fresh fountaine, farre from all mens vew,
She bath'd her brest, the boyling heat t' allay;
She bath'd with roses red, and violets blew,
And all the sweetest flowres, that in the forrest grew.

7 Till faint through irkesome wearinesse, adowne
Upon the grassie ground her selfe she layd
To sleepe, the whiles a gentle slombring swowne> *faint*
Upon her fell all naked bare displayd;
The sunne-beames bright upon her body playd,
Being through former bathing mollifide,> *softened*
And pierst into her wombe, where they embayd> *pervaded*
With so sweet sence and secret power unspide,
That in her pregnant flesh they shortly fructifide.

8 Miraculous may seeme to him, that reades
So straunge ensample of conceptión;
But reason teacheth that the fruitfull seades
Of all things living, through impressión
Of the sunbeames in moyst complexión,
Doe life conceive and quickned are by> kynd: *according to*
So after *Nilus* inundatión,°
Infinite shapes of creatures men do fynd,
Informèd in the mud, on which the Sunne hath shynd.

9 Great father he of generation
Is rightly cald, th'author of life and light;
And his faire sister for creation
Ministreth matter fit, which tempred right

storie This is a myth of Spenser's invention, made to give a narrative explanation of the sinless birth of Belphoebe and Amoret, and their separate and different educations.

Nilus inundation See I.i.21n.

With heate and humour,˃ breedes the living wight. *moisture*
So sprong these twinnes in wombe of *Chrysogone*,
Yet wist she nought thereof, but sore affright,
Wondred to see her belly so upblone,
Which still increast, till she her terme had full outgone.

10 Whereof conceiving shame and foule disgrace,
Albe˃ her guiltlesse consciènce her cleard, *although*
She fled into the wildernesse a space,
Till that unweeldy burden she had reard,
And shund dishonor, which as death she feard:
Where wearie of long travell, downe to rest
Her selfe she set, and comfortably cheard,˃ *encouraged*
There a sad cloud of sleepe her overkest,˃ *overcast*
And seizèd every sense with sorrow sore opprest.

11 It fortunèd, faire *Venus* having lost
Her little sonne, the wingèd god of love,
Who for some light displeasure, which him crost,
Was from her fled, as flit˃ as ayerie Dove, *swift*
And let her blisfull bowre of joy above,
(So from her often he had fled away,°
When she for ought him sharpely did reprove,
And wandred in the world in strange aray,
Disguiz'd in thousand shapes, that none might him bewray.˃) *reveal*

12 Him for to seeke, she left her heavenly hous,
The house of goodly formes and faire aspects,
Whence all the world derives the glorious
Features of beautie, and all shapes select,
With which high God his workmanship hath deckt;
And searchèd every way, through which his wings
Had borne him, or his tract˃ she mote˃ detect: *track / could*
She promist kisses sweet, and sweeter things
Unto the man, that of him tydings to her brings.

13 First she him sought in Court, where most he used
Whylome˃ to haunt, but there she found him not; *formerly*
But many there she found, which sore accused
His falsehood, and with foule infámous blot
His cruell deedes and wicked wyles did spot:
Ladies and Lords she every where mote heare
Complayning, how with his empoysned shot
Their wofull harts he wounded had whyleare,˃ *earlier*
And so had left them languishing twixt hope and feare.

14 She then the Citties sought from gate to gate,
And every one did aske, did he him see;

So . . . away Spenser is imitating an idyll of the Alexandrian poet Moschus, called *Love the Runaway*. Venus seeks Cupid in court, city, and country, the three divisions of society, and must now try the wilds.

And every one her answerd, that too late
He had him seene, and felt the crueltie
Of his sharpe darts and whot artillerie;
And every one threw forth reproches rife
Of his mischíevous deedes, and said, That hee
Was the disturber of all civill> life, *city*
The enimy of peace, and author of all strife.

15 Then in the countrey she abroad him sought,
And in the rurall cottages inquirèd,
Where also many plaints to her were brought,
How he their heedlesse harts with love had fyrèd,
And his false venim through their veines inspyrèd;
And eke the gentle shepheard swaynes, which sat
Keeping their fleecie flockes, as they were hyrèd,
She sweetly heard complaine, both how and what
Her sonne had to them doen; yet she did smile thereat.

16 But when in none of all these she him got,
She gan avize,> where else he mote> him hyde: *consider / might*
At last she her bethought, that she had not
Yet sought the salvage woods and forrests wyde,
In which full many lovely Nymphes abyde,
Mongst whom might be, that he did closely lye,
Or that the love of some of them him tyde:
For thy,> she thither cast her course t'apply, *wherefore*
To search the secret haunts of *Dianes* company.

17 Shortly unto the wasteful woods she came,
Whereas she found the Goddesse with her crew,
After late chace of their embrewèd> game, *blood-stained*
Sitting beside a fountaine in a rew,> *row*
Some of them washing with the liquid dew
From off their dainty limbes the dustie sweat,
And soyle which did deforme their lively hew;> *form*
Others lay shaded from the scorching heat;
The rest upon her person gave attendance great.

18 She having hong upon a bough on high
Her bow and painted quiver, had unlaste
Her silver buskins from her nimble thigh,
And her lancke loynes ungirt, and brests unbraste,
After her heat the breathing cold to taste;
Her golden lockes, that late in tresses bright
Embreaded were for hindring of her haste,
Now loose about her shoulders hong undight,> *loose*
And were with sweet *Ambrosia* all besprinckled light.

19 Soone as she *Venus* saw behind her backe,
She was asham'd to be so loose surprized,

And woxe halfe wroth against her damzels slacke,
That had not her thereof before avized,˃ *warned*
But suffred her so carelesly disguized˃ *adorned*
Be overtaken. Soone her garments loose
Upgath'ring, in her bosome she comprized,˃ *drew together*
Well as she might, and to the Goddesse rose,
Whiles all her Nymphes did like a girlond her enclose.°

20 Goodly she gan faire *Cytherea* greet, *Venus*
And shortly askèd her, what cause her brought
Into that wildernesse for her unmeet,˃ *unsuitable*
From her sweete bowres, and beds with pleasures fraught:
That suddein change she strange adventure thought.
To whom halfe weeping, she thus answerèd,
That she her dearest sonne *Cupído* sought,
Who in his frowardnesse˃ from her was fled; *peevishness*
That she repented sore, to have him angerèd.

21 Thereat *Diana* gan to smile, in scorne
Of her vaine plaint, and to her scoffing sayd;
Great pittie sure, that ye be so forlorne
Of your gay sonne, that gives ye so good ayd
To your disports:˃ ill mote ye bene apayd˃ *sports / requited*
But she was more engrievèd, and replide;
Faire sister, ill beseemes it to upbrayd
A dolefull heart with so disdainfull pride;
The like that mine, may be your paine another tide.˃ *time*

22 As you in woods and wanton wildernesse
Your glory set, to chace the salvage beasts,
So my delight is all in joyfulnesse,
In beds, in bowres, in banckets, and in feasts:
And ill becomes you with your loftie creasts,˃ *helmets*
To scorne the joy, that *Jove* is glad to seeke;
We both are bound to follow heavens beheasts,
And tend our charges with obeisance meeke:
Spare, gentle sister, with reproch my paine to eeke.˃ *augment*

23 And tell me, if that ye my sonne have heard,
To lurke emongst your Nymphes in secret wize;
Or keepe˃ their cabins: much I am affeard, *watch*
Least he like one of them him selfe disguize,
And turne his arrowes to their exercize:
So may he long himselfe full easie hide:
For he is faire and fresh in face and guize,˃ *appearance*
As any Nymph (let not it be envyde.)˃ *grudged*
So saying every Nymph full narrowly she eyde.

Whiles . . . enclose The story of Venus surprising Diana is adapted from that of Actaeon, who did so in Ovid, *Metamorphoses* III; and this line is almost a translation of III.180.

24 But *Phœbe* therewith sore was angerèd,
And sharply said; Goe Dame, goe seeke your boy,
Where you him lately left, in *Mars* his bed;
He comes not here, we scorne his foolish joy,
Ne lend we leisure to his idle toy:˃ *game*
But if I catch him in this company,
By *Stygian* lake I vow, whose sad annoy˃ *injuriouness*
The Gods doe dread, he dearely shall abye.˃ *pay for it*
Ile clip his wanton wings, that he no more shall fly.

25 Whom when as *Venus* saw so sore displeased,
She inly sory was, and gan relent,
What she had said: so her she soone appeased,
With sugred words and gentle blandishment,
Which as a fountaine from her sweet lips went,
And wellèd goodly forth, that in short space
She was well pleasd, and forth her damzels sent,
Through all the woods, to search from place to place,
If any tract of him or tydings they mote trace.

26 To search the God of love, her Nymphes she sent
Throughout the wandring forrest every where:
And after them her selfe eke with her went
To seeke the fugitive, both farre and nere,
So long they sought, till they arrivèd were
In that same shadie covert, whereas lay
Faire *Crysogone* in slombry traunce whilere:
Who in her sleepe (a wondrous thing to say)
Unwares had borne two babes, as faire as springing day.

27 Unwares she them conceiv'd, unwares she bore:
She bore withouten paine, that she conceived
Withouten pleasure: ne her need implore
Lucinaes aide: ° which when they both perceived,
They were through wonder nigh of sense bereaved,
And gazing each on other, nought bespake:
At last they both agreed, her seeming grieved˃ *unwell*
Out of her heavy swowne not to awake,
But from her loving side the tender babes to take.

28 Up they them tooke, each one a babe uptooke,
And with them carried, to be fosterèd;
Dame *Phœbe* to a Nymph her babe betooke,
To be upbrought in perfect Maydenhed,
And of her selfe her name *Belphœbe* red:˃ *gave*
But *Venus* hers thence farre away convayd,
To be upbrought in goodly womanhed,

Lucinaes aide Juno, in the capacity of patron of women in labor, was called Lucina.

And in her litle loves stead,˃ which was strayd, *place*
Her *Amoretta* cald,° to comfort her dismayd.

29 She brought her to her joyous Paradize,
Where most she wonnes,˃ when she on earth does dwel. *lives*
So faire a place, as Nature can devize:
Whether in *Paphos,*° or *Cytheron*° hill,
Or it in *Gnidus*° be, I wote not well;
But well I wote by tryall,˃ that this same *experience*
All other pleasant places doth excell,
And callèd is by her lost lovers name
The *Gardin* of *Adonis,* farre renowmd by fame.

30 In that same Gardin all the goodly flowres,
Wherewith dame Nature doth her beautifie,
And decks the girlonds of her paramoures,
Are fetcht: there is the first seminarie˃ *seed nursery*
Of all things, that are borne to live and die,
According to their kindes. Long worke it were,
Here to account the endlesse progenie
Of all the weedes,˃ that bud and blossome there; *plants*
But so much as doth need, must needs be counted here.

31 It sited was in fruitfull soyle of old,
And girt in with two walles on either side;
The one of yron, the other of bright gold,
That none might thorough˃ breake, nor overstride: *through*
And double gates it had, which opened wide,
By which both in and out men moten˃ pas; *could*
Th'one faire and fresh, the other old and dride:
Old *Genius* the porter of them was,
Old *Genius,* the which a double nature has.

32 He letteth in, he letteth out to wend,˃ *go*
All that to come into the world desire;
A thousand thousand naked babes attend
About him day and night, which do require,
That he with fleshly weedes would them attire:
Such as him list, such as eternall fate
Ordainèd hath, he clothes with sinfull mire,°
And sendeth forth to live in mortall state,
Till they againe returne backe by the hinder gate.

33 After that they againe returnèd beene,
They in that Gardin planted be againe;

And in . . . cald Lacking Cupid (Amor), she called the baby Amoretta.
Paphos town in Cyprus, sacred to Venus
Cytheron mountain where Venus was worshiped
Gnidus Cnidus in Doria, where stood the statue of Venus by Praxiteles

sinful mire flesh; matter; so called because the world is fallen, but also because, in neoplatonism, matter is evil in so far as it is remote from spirit

And grow afresh, as they had never seene
Fleshly corruption, nor mortall paine.
Some thousand yeares so doen they there remaine;
And then of him are clad with other hew,> *forms*
Or sent into the chaungefull world againe,
Till thither they returne, where first they grew:
So like a wheele around they runne from old to new.

34 Ne needs there Gardiner to set, or sow,
To plant or prune: for of their owne accord
All things, as they created were, doe grow,
And yet remember well the mightie word,
Which first was spoken by th'Almightie lord,
That bad them to increase and multiply:°
Ne doe they need with water of the ford,
Or of the clouds to moysten their roots dry;
For in themselves eternall moisture they imply.> *contain*

35 Infinite shapes of creatures there are bred,
And uncouth> formes, which none yet ever knew, *unknown, strange*
And every sort is in a sundry> bed *separate*
Set by it selfe, and ranckt in comely rew:> *row*
Some fit for reasonable soules° t'indew,> *put on*
Some made for beasts, some made for birds to weare,
And all the fruitfull spawne of fishes hew
In endlesse rancks along enraungèd were,
That seem'd the *Oceán* could not containe them there.

36 Daily they grow, and daily forth are sent
Into the world, it to replenish more;
Yet is the stocke not lessenèd, nor spent,
But still remaines in everlasting store,
As it at first created was of yore,
For in the wide wombe of the world there lyes,
In hatefull darkenesse and in deepe horrore,
An huge eternal *Chaos*, which supplyes
The substances of natures fruitfull progenyes.

37 All things from thence doe their first being fetch,
And borrow matter, whereof they are made,
Which when as forme and feature it does ketch,> *take*
Becomes a bodie, and doth then invade> *enter*
The state of life, out of the griesly> shade. *ghastly*
That substance is eterne, and bideth so,
Ne when the life decayes, and forme does fade,
Doth it consume, and into nothing go,
But chaungèd is, and often altred to and fro.

increase and multiply Genesis 1:22

reasonable soules human souls; below them there is no reason

38 The substance is not chaunged, nor alterèd,
But th'only> forme and outward fashión;> *only the / appearance*
For every substance is conditioned
To change her hew, and sundry formes to don,
Meet for her temper and complexión:
For formes are variable and decay,
By course of kind,> and by occasión;> *nature / accident*
And that faire flowre of beautie fades away,
As doth the lilly fresh before the sunny ray.

39 Great enimy to it, and to all the rest,
That in the *Gardin* of *Adonis* springs,
Is wicked *Time*, who with his scyth addrest,> *equipped*
Does mow the flowring herbes and goodly things,
And all their glory to the ground downe flings,
Where they doe wither, and are fowly mard:
He flyes about, and with his flaggy> wings *drooping*
Beates downe both leaves and buds without regard,
Ne ever pittie may relent his malice hard.

40 Yet pittie often did the gods relent,
To see so faire things mard, and spoylèd quight:
And their great mother *Venus* did lament
The losse of her deare brood, her deare delight:
Her hart was pierst with pittie at the sight,
When walking through the Gardin, them she spyde,
Yet no'te> she find redresse for such despight. *knew not how to*
For all that lives, is subject to that law:
All things decay in time, and to their end do draw.

41 But were it not, that *Time* their troubler is,
All that in this delightfull Gardin growes,
Should happie be, and have immortall bliss.
For here all plentie, and all pleasure flowes,
And sweet love gentle fits emongst them throwes,
Without fell rancor, or fond gealosie;
Franckly each paramour> his leman> knowes. *lover / mistress*
Each bird his mate, ne any does envie> *resent*
Their goodly meriment, and gay felicitie.

42 There is continuall spring, and harvest there
Continuall, both meeting at one time: °
For both the boughes doe laughing blossomes beare,
And with fresh colours decke the wanton Prime,> *spring*
And eke attonce the heavy trees they clime,
Which seeme to labour under their fruits lode:
The whiles the joyous birdes make their pastime

Continuall . . . time another feature of the Earthly Paradise. To contrast this with the Bower of Bliss in II.xii is a favorite topic: here is good generative sexuality, where God's commandment to increase and multiply is obeyed with joy and not corrupted by sinister luxury.

Emongst the shadie leaves, their sweet abode,
And their true loves without suspition> tell abrode. *fear*

43 Right in the middest of that Paradise,
There stood a stately Mount, on whose round top
A gloomy grove of mirtle trees did rise,
Whose shadie boughes sharpe steele did never lop,
Nor wicked beasts their tender buds did crop,
But like a girlond compassèd the hight,
And from their fruitfull sides sweet gum did drop,
That all the ground with precious deaw bedight,
Threw forth most dainty odours, and most sweet delight.

44 And in the thickest covert of that shade,
There was a pleasant arbour, not by art.
But of the trees owne inclination> made, *bending*
Which knitting their rancke> braunches part to part, *luxuriant*
With wanton yvie twyne entrayld athwart,
And Eglantine, and Caprifole> emong, *honeysuckle*
Fashiond above within their inmost part,
That nether> *Phœbus* beams could through them throng, *neither*
Nor *Aeolus* sharp blast could worke them any wrong.

45 And all about grew every sort of flowre,
To which sad lovers were transformed of yore;
Fresh *Hyacinthus,*° *Phœbus* paramoure,
And dearest love,
Foolish *Narcisse,*° that likes the watry shore,
Sad *Amaranthus,*° made a flowre but late,
Sad *Amaranthus,* in whose purple gore
Me seemes I see *Amintas*° wretched fate,
To whom sweet Poets verse hath given endlesse date.

46 There wont faire *Venus* often to enjoy
Her deare *Adonis* joyous company,
And reape sweet pleasure of the wanton boy;
There yet, some say, in secret he does ly,
Lappèd in flowres and pretious spycery,
By her hid from the world, and from the skill> *knowledge*
Of *Stygian* Gods,> which doe her love envy; *gods of hell*
But she her selfe, when ever that she will,
Possesseth him, and of his sweetnesse takes her fill.

47 And sooth it seemes they say: for he may not
For ever die, and ever burièd bee
In balefull night, where all things are forgot;

Hyacinthus killed while playing quoits with Apollo, who made the flower that sprang from his blood an emblem of his mourning

Narcisse Narcissus, who died of self-love and was transformed into a flower

Amaranthus from the flower so called because it does not fade; there is no myth of Amaranthus

Amintas a pastoral name for Sir Philip Sidney, whose death was celebrated by many elegies

All be> he subject to mortalitie, *even though*
Yet is eterne in mutabilitie,
And by succession made perpetuall,
Transformèd oft, and chaungèd diverslie:
For him the Father of all formes, they call;
Therefore needs mote he live, that living gives to all.

48 There now he liveth in eternall blis,
Joying his goddesse, and of her enjoyd:
Ne feareth he henceforth that foe of his,
Which with his cruell tuske him deadly cloyd:> *pierced*
For that wilde Bore, the which him once annoyd,> *injured*
She firmely hath emprisonèd for ay,
That her sweet love his malice mote avoyd,
In a strong rocky Cave, which is they say,
Hewen underneath that Mount, that none him losen> may. *loose*

49 There now he lives in everlasting joy,
With many of the Gods in company,
Which thither haunt,> and with the wingèd boy *visit*
Sporting himselfe in safe felicity:
Who when he hoth with spoiles and cruelty
Ransackt the world, and in the wofull harts
Of many wretches set his triumphes hye,
Thither resorts, and laying his sad darts
Aside, with faire *Adonis* playes his wanton parts.

50 And his true love faire *Psyche*° with him playes,
Faire *Psyche* to him lately reconcyld,
After long troubles and unmeet upbrayes,> *unsuitable reproaches*
With which his mother *Venus* her revyld,
And eke himselfe her cruelly exyld:
But now in stedfast love and happy state
She with him lives, and hath him borne a chyld,
Pleasure,° that doth both gods and men aggrate,
Pleasure, the daughter of *Cupid* and *Psyche* late.

51 Hither great *Venus* brought this infant faire,
The younger daughter of *Chrysogonee,*
And unto *Psyche* with great trust and care
Committed her, yfosterèd to bee,
And trainèd up in true feminitee:
Who no lesse carefully her tenderèd,
Then her owne daughter *Pleasure,* to whom shee

Psyche (Greek, "breath" and "soul") The myth of Cupid and Psyche originates in *The Golden Ass* of Apuleius, and from the outset had allegorical significance; Psyche is the Soul, joined, after many trials, with the love of God. **Pleasure** Apuleius called the daughter of Cupid and Psyche Voluptas (Pleasure). See Milton's adaptation, in which he had Spenser much in mind, in the Epilogue to *Comus*. Cupid visits Psyche only at night and she never sees him; trying to do so, she spills hot oil from a lamp on the sleeping god, and he leaves her. In her search for him she has to perform almost impossible tasks set by Venus, but finally succeeds.

Made her companion, and her lessonèd
In all the lore of love, and goodly womanhead.

52 In which when she to perfect ripenesse grew,
Of grace and beautie noble Paragone,> *model*
She brought her forth into the worldes vew,
To be th'ensample of true love alone,
And Lodestarre of all chaste affectióne,
To all faire Ladies, that doe live on ground.
To Faery court she came, where many one
Admyred her goodly haveour,> and found *behavior*
His feeble hart wide launchèd> with loves cruell wound. *pierced*

53 But she to none of them her love did cast,
Save to the noble knight Sir *Scudamore,*
To whom her loving hart she linkèd fast
In faithfull love, t'abide for evermore,
And for his dearest sake endurèd sore,
Sore trouble of an hainous enimy;
Who her would forcèd have to have forlore> *abandoned*
Her former love, and stedfast loialty,
As ye may elsewhere read that ruefull history.

. . .

[The remainder of Book III continues Florimell's story, and introduces other *exempla* of love. So, in canto vii, Satyrane rescues the Squire of Dames, who has been set the impossible task of finding many chaste women (this has humor, somewhat rare in Spenser). The ninth canto contains the story of Malbecco, an impotent miser who keeps a jealous eye on his pretty young wife Hellenore. Satyrane says knowingly: "Extremely mad the man I surely deeme, / That weenes with watch and hard restraint to stay / A womans will, which is disposed to go astray" (stanza 6). And go astray she does, with Paridell, Satyrane's traveling companion. (The girl's name derives from that of Helen, Paridell's from Paris.) At first Malbecco will not let them into his house, though the weather is very bad. Britomart shows up, fights with Paridell, forms an allegiance with him, and finally succeeds with him in making Malbecco let them in. They sit at the table. The dinner is the occasion for an intense flirtation between Hellenore and Paridell, and a discourse on the history of the Trojans after the fall of their city; they founded first Rome and then London.]

From Canto ix

27 They sate to meat, and *Satyrane* his chaunce
Was her before,° and *Paridell* besyde;
But he him selfe° sate looking still askaunce,
Gains *Britomart,* and ever closely eyde
Sir *Satyrane,* that glaunces might not glyde:

his chaunce . . . before it happened that he sat opposite her **he him selfe** Malbecco

But his blind eye, that syded *Paridell,*
All his demeasnure,> from his sight did hyde: *behavior*
On her faire face so did he feede his fill,
And sent close messages of love to her at will.

28 And ever and anone, when none was ware,
With speaking lookes, that close embassage> bore, *message*
He rov'd> at her, and told his secret care: *shot*
For all that art he learnèd had of yore.
Ne was she ignoraunt of that lewd lore,
But in his eye his meaning wisely red,
And with the like him answerd evermore:
She sent at him one firie dart, whose hed
Empoisned was with privy lust, and gealous dred.

29 He from that deadly throw made no defence,
But to the wound his weake hart opened wyde;
The wicked engine> through false influence, *weapon*
Past through his eyes, and secretly did glyde
Into his hart, which it did sorely gryde.> *pierce*
But nothing new to him was that same paine,
Ne paine at all; for he so oft had tryde
The powre thereof, and lov'd so oft in vaine,
That thing of course he counted,° love to entertaine.

30 Thenceforth to her he sought to intimate
His inward griefe, by meanes to him well knowne,
Now *Bacchus* fruit out of the silver plate
He on the table dasht, as overthrowne,
Or of the fruitfull liquor overflowne,
And by the dauncing bubbles did divine,
Or therein write to let his love be showne;
Which well she red out of the learnèd line,
A sacrament prophane in mistery of wine.°

31 And when so of his hand the pledge she raught,°
The guilty cup she fainèd to mistake,°
And in her lap did shed her idle draught,
Shewing desire her inward flame to slake:
By such close signes they secret way did make
Unto their wils, and one eyes watch escape;
Two eyes him needeth, for to watch and wake,
Who lovers will deceive. Thus was the ape,
By their faire handling, put into *Malbeccoes* cape.°

That . . . counted he regarded such suffering as a necessary part of
A sacrament . . . wine based on Ovid's account of Paris and Helen in a similar situation, *Heroides* XVII.75 ff., where the word *Amo* ("I love you") is traced in wine. The sacrament is "profane" because of the use of wine in the communion service, where it relates to divine love and the blood of Christ.
of . . . raught took the winecup from his hand
mistake not get good hold of
ape . . . cape Malbecco was made a fool of

32 Now when of meats and drinks they had their fill,
Purpose was movèd by that gentle Dame,
Unto those knights adventurous, to tell
Of deeds of armes, which unto them became,
And every one his kindred, and his name.
Then *Paridell,* in whom a kindly> pryde *natural*
Of gracious speach, and skill his words to frame
Abounded, being glad of so fit tyde> *occasion*
Him to commend to her, thus spake, of all well eyde.

33 *Troy,* that art now nought, but an idle name,
And in thine ashes buried low dost lie,
Though whilome> far much greater then thy fame, *formerly*
Before that angry Gods, and cruell skye
Upon thee heapt a direfull destinie,
What boots it boast thy glorious descent,
And fetch from heaven thy great Genealogie,
Sith all thy worthy prayses being blent,> *defiled*
Their of-spring hath embaste,> and later glory shent.> *debased / disgraced*

34 Most famous Worthy of the world, by whome
That warre was kindled, which did *Troy* inflame,
And stately towres of *Ilion* whilome
Brought unto balefull ruine, was by name
Sir *Paris* far renowmd through noble fame,
Who through great prowesse and bold hardinesse,
From *Lacedæmon*° fetcht the fairest Dame,> *Helen*
That ever *Greece* did boast, or knight possesse,
Whom *Venus* to him gave for meed> of worthinesse. *reward*

35 Faire *Helene,* flowre of beautie excellent,
And girlond of the mighty Conquerours,
That madest many Ladies deare lament
The heavie losse of their brave Paramours,
Which they far off beheld from *Trojan* toures,°
And saw the fieldes of faire *Scamander*° strowne
With carcases of noble warrioures,
Whose fruitlesse lives were under furrow sowne,
And *Xanthus*° sandy bankes with bloud all overflowne.

36 From him my linage I derive aright,
Who long before the ten yeares siege of *Troy,*
Whiles yet on *Ida* he a shepheard hight,> *was called*
On faire *Oenone*° got a lovely boy,
Whom for remembraunce of her passèd joy,

Lacedæmon Sparta, where Helen was the wife of the king, Menelaus
toures Helen and the other ladies watched the fighting from the towers of Troy
Scamander river flowing through the plain before Troy
Xanthus another name for Scamander
Oenone nymph of Ida, and first love of Paris before he was awarded Helen (see Tennyson, *Oenone*)

She of his Father *Parius* did name;
Who, after *Greekes* did *Priams* realme° destroy,
Gathred the *Trojan* reliques° sav'd from flame,
And with them sayling thence, to th'Isle of *Paros* came.

37 That was by him cald *Paros*, which before
Hight *Nausa*, there he many yeares did raine,
And built *Nausicle*° by the *Pontick*° shore,
The which he dying left next in remaine
To *Paridas* his sonne.
From whom I *Paridell* by kin descend;
But for faire Ladies love, and glories gaine,
My native soile have left, my dayes to spend
In sewing> deeds of armes, my lives and labours end. *pursuing*

38 Whenas the noble *Britomart* heard tell
Of *Trojan* warres, and *Priams* Citie sackt,°
The ruefull story of Sir *Paridell*,
She was empassiond at that piteous act,
With zelous envy of Greekes cruell fact,> *deed*
Against that nation, from whose race of old
She heard, that she was lineally extract:
For noble *Britons* sprong from *Trojans* bold,
And *Troynovant*° was built of old *Troyes* ashes cold.

39 Then sighing soft awhile, at last she thus:
O lamentable fall of famous towne,
Which raignd so many yeares victorious,
And of all *Asie* bore the soveraigne crowne,
In one sad night consumd, and throwen downe:
What stony hart, that heares thy haplesse fate,
Is not empierst with deepe compassiowne,
And makes ensample of mans wretched state,
That floures so fresh at morne, and fades at evening late?

40 Behold, Sir, how your pitifull complaint
Hath found another partner of your payne:
For nothing may impresse so deare constraint,> *distress*
As countries cause, and commune foes disdayne
But if it should not grieve you, backe agayne
To turne your course, I would to heare desyre,
What to *Aeneas* fell; sith that men sayne
He was not in the Cities wofull fyre
Consum'd, but did him selfe to safètie retyre.

Priams realme Troy
Trojan reliques the palladium, on which the safety of Troy depended, and which Aeneas (not Paris) saved and took to Rome
Nausicle the city of Nausa
Pontick Black Sea
Priams . . . sackt Spenser is varying the story as he knew it from Virgil's *Aeneid* and other sources.
Troynovant New Troy = London. It was a commonplace in popular history and also in propaganda that the British were descended from the Trojans, just as the Romans were—a myth shared by many other countries.

41 *Anchyses* sonne begot of *Venus* faire,°
(Said he,) out of the flames for safegard fled,
And with a remnant did to sea repaire,
Where he through fatall errour° long was led
Full many yeares, and weetlesse wanderèd
From shore to shore, emongst the Lybicke> sands, *Libyan*
Ere rest he found. Much there he sufferèd,
And many perils past in forreine lands,
To save his people sad from victours vengefull hands.

42 At last in *Latium*° he did arrive,
Where he with cruell warre was entertaind
Of th'inland folke, which sought him backe to drive,
Till he with old *Latinus* was constraind,
To contract wedlock: (so the fates ordaind.)
Wedlock contract in bloud, and eke in blood
Accomplishèd, that many deare> complaind:° *sadly*
The rivall slaine, the victour through the flood
Escapèd hardly, hardly praisd his wedlock good.

43 Yet after all, he victour did survive,
And with *Latinus* did the kingdome part.
But after, when both nations gan to strive,
Into their names the title to convart,
His sonne *Iülus* did from thence depart,
With all the warlike youth of *Trojans* bloud,
And in long *Alba*° plast his throne apart,
Where faire it florishèd, and long time stoud,
Till *Romulus* renewing it,° to *Rome* remoud.

44 There there (said *Britomart*) a fresh appeard
The glory of the later world to spring,
And *Troy* againe out of her dust was reard,
To sit in second seat of soveraigne king,
Of all the world under her governing.
But a third kingdome yet is to arise,
Out of the *Trojans* scatterèd of-spring,
That in all glory and great enterprise,
Both first and second *Troy* shall dare to equalise.

45 It *Troynovant* is hight, that with the waves
Of wealthy *Thamis*> washèd is along, *Thames*
Upon whose stubborne neck, whereat he raves
With roring rage, and sore him selfe does throng,> *crush*

Anchyses . . . faire Aeneas
fatall errour wanderings decreed by fate
Latium part of Italy near the Tiber
Wedlock . . . complaind refers to the wars between Aeneas and Latinus, king of Latium, and their settlement by Aeneas' marriage with Lavinia, daughter of Latinus; Juno said this would result in bloodshed, because Turnus of the Rutilians wanted Lavinia. Turnus tried to expel Aeneas, but was killed by him.
long Alba city built in Latium by Aeneas' son Ascanius, extending along the hill Albinus
it the Trojan dynasty, which now moved to Rome

That all men feare to tempt his billowes strong,
She fastned hath her foot, which standes so hy,
That it a wonder of the world is song
In forreine landes, and all which passen by,
Beholding it from far, do thinke it threates the skye.

46 The *Trojan Brute*° did first that Citie found,
And Hygate made the meare˃ thereof by West, *boundary*
And *Overt*˃ gate by North: that is the bound *open*
Toward the land; two rivers bound the rest.
So huge a scope at first him seemèd best,
To be the compasse of his kingdomes seat:
So huge a mind could not in lesser rest,
Ne in small meares containe his glory great,
That *Albion*° had conquerèd first by warlike feat.

47 Ah fairest Lady knight, (said *Paridell*)
Pardon I pray my heedlesse oversight,
Who had forgot, that whilome˃ I heard tell *once*
From agèd *Mnemon;*° for my wits bene light.
Indeed he said (if I remember right,)
That of the antique *Trojan* stocke, there grew
Another plant, that raught˃ to wondrous hight, *reached*
And far abroad his mighty branches threw,
Into the utmost Angle of the world he knew.

48 For that same *Brute*, whom much he did advaunce˃ *praise*
In all his speach, was *Sylvius* his sonne,
Whom having slaine, through luckles arrowes glaunce
He fled for feare of that he had misdonne,
Or else for shame, so fowle reproch to shonne,
And with him led to sea an youthly trayne,
Where wearie wandring they long time did wonne,˃ *dwell*
And many fortunes prov'd in th'*Ocean* mayne,
And great adventures found, that now were long to sayne.˃ *say*

49 At last by fatall course they driven were
Into an Island spatious and brode,
The furthest North, that did to them appeare:
Which after rest they seeking far abrode,
Found it the fittest soyle for their abode,
Fruitfull of all things fit for living foode,
But wholy wast, and void of peoples trode,
Save an huge nation of the Geaunts broode,°
That fed on living flesh, and druncke mens vitall blood.

50 Whom he through wearie wars and labours long,
Subdewd with losse of many *Britons* bold:

Brute Brutus, in legendary history the first king of Britain, and great-grandson of Aeneas
Albion Britain
Mnemon Memory personified
Geaunts broode Brutus, arriving in Britain found it populated only by giants.

In which the great *Goemagot*° of strong
Corineus,° and *Coulin*° of *Debon*° old
Were overthrowne, and layd on th'earth full cold,
Which quakèd under their so hideous masse,
A famous history to be enrold
In everlasting moniments˃ of brasse, *records*
That all the antique Worthies merits far did passe.

51 His worke great *Troynovant,* his worke is eke
Faire *Lincolne,* both renowmèd far away,
That who from East to West will endlong seeke,
Cannot two fairer Cities find this day,
Except *Cleopolis:*° so heard I say
Old *Mnemon.* Therefore Sir, I greet you well
Your countrey kin, and you entirely pray
Of pardon for the strife, which late befell
Betwixt us both unknowne. So ended *Paridell.*

52 But all the while, that he these speaches spent,
Upon his lips hong faire Dame *Hellenore,*
With vigilant regard, and dew attent,˃ *attention*
Fashioning worlds of fancies evermore
In her fraile wit, that now her quite forlore:˃ *deserted*
The whiles unwares away her wondring eye,
And greedy eares her weake hart from her bore:
Which he perceiving, ever privily
In speaking, many false belgardes˃ at her let fly. *loving looks*

53 So long these knights discoursed diversly,
Of straunge affaires, and noble hardiment,
Which they had past with mickle jeopardy,
That now the humid night was farforth spent,
And heavenly lampes were halfendeale˃ ybrent: *half*
Which th'old man seeing well, who too long thought
Every discourse and every argument,
Which by the houres he measurèd, besought
Them go to rest. So all unto their bowres were brought.

[In canto x Paridell outwits Malbecco, and elopes with "this second Hellene," having stolen his wealth and set fire to his house. Malbecco, fruitlessly pursuing them, falls in with the sham knight Braggadocchio and his servant Trompart, who take up his cause. Paridell abandons Hellenore, who is discovered by Malbecco in a new role, as the queen of a group of satyrs, greatly enjoying their sexual performances; she turns Malbecco down, and he goes off, finding

Goemagot Gogmagog: giant, later split into Gog and Magog, whose effigies stand outside the Guildhall in the City of London
Corineus Trojan who conquered Gogmagog and was awarded Cornwall for his pains
Coulin a giant
Debon the hero who overcame Coulin, and was awarded Devonshire (Spenser had already made these points about Corineus and Debon in II.xii.12)
Cleopolis here the city of Gloriana, temporarily distinct from London (Troynovant)

himself a cave, where he lives miserably and for ever; for "he has quight / Forgot he was a man, and *Gealosie* is hight." So ends one of the oddest and most lascivious of Spenser's "accidents."

Canto xi brings Britomart to the aid of Scudamour, lamenting the imprisonment of Amoret in the house of Busirane, an enchanter named for Busiris, a cruel pharaoh who slew all strangers. To enter one must pass through a flame; Britomart does so, but Scudamour cannot, his desires not being sufficiently pure. Britomart, inside, inspects Busirane's tapestries, dealing with Jupiter's love affairs, and those of the other gods. There is also an altar dedicated to Cupid, "Victor of the Gods," at which the inhabitants of the house blasphemously worship. The motto *Be bold* is emblazoned everywhere, except in one place, where it reads *Be not too bold*, which seems to refer to an English nursery rhyme—behind *that* door are skeletons and tubs of blood. Britomart prepares her weapons. She is about to perform for Unchastity what Guyon did for Intemperance.]

Book III, Canto xii

Allegorically the Mask of Cupid represents the disordered passions which intervene in love relationships, as between Amoret and Scudamour—she, though the perfect bride, tormented by the charms of Busirane, he out of control and unable to act for her preservation. Spenser emphasizes that the procession of Cupid's attendants is a masque, that is, a show of allegorical figures with allegorical intent, presented as a dance which displays their attributes. Masques were courtly entertainments, and involved dancing in which the characters of the masque joined with the audience; but here he is content with that part of the presentation which exhibited, in the known language of symbols, some complex moral proposition. In this respect it could be called a pageant with equal correctness. In fact some of Spenser's allegorical detail is borrowed from Petrarch's pageant *The Triumph of Love*. The "triumph" was a Renaissance courtly form related to the masque.

Although there is a real debt to courtly entertainments of a kind he must often have seen, Spenser is here, no more than anywhere else, willing to tie himself strictly to what could be presented in such a show, as the plight of Amoret sufficiently proves. With the masque itself Spenser combines the story of Britomart's intrusion, which is the stuff of romantic narrative: the storm, the fire, the arras depicting Cupid's triumphs, the baffling of the hero by a closed door, the reversal of the enchanter's charms, and the extinguishing of the fire are all romance themes.

Cupid here has a different aspect from that displayed in the allegory of Cupid and Psyche in III.vi. Spenser uses Venus in similarly contradictory (or complementary) ways. The cruelty of the wrong kind of love, in which passion predominates, is his theme. He wanted, as in the last cantos of Books I and II, a great set piece, this time an image of the love in which chastity has no part, but which succumbs to passion and madness; and he has his knight come in and abolish this image, and take prisoner the enchanter who forged it.

From Canto xii

The maske of Cupid, and th'enchaunted
  Chamber are displayd.
Whence Britomart redeemes faire
  Amoret, through charmes decayd.

1 Tho when as chearelesse Night ycovered had
  Faire heaven with an universall cloud,
  That every wight dismayd with darknesse sad,
  In silence and in sleepe themselves did shroud,
  She heard a shrilling Trompet sound aloud,
  Signe of nigh battell, or got victory;
  Nought therewith daunted was her courage proud,
  But rather stird to cruell enmity,
Expecting ever, when some foe she might descry.

2 With that, an hideous storme of winde arose,
  With dreadfull thunder and lightning atwixt,
  And an earth-quake, as if it streight would lose
  The worlds foundations from his centre fixt;
  A direfull stench of smoke and sulphure mixt
  Ensewd, whose noyance fild the fearefull sted,> *place*
  From the fourth houre of night untill the sixt;
  Yet the bold *Britonesse* was nought ydred,
Though much emmov'd, but stedfast still perseverèd.

3 All suddenly a stormy whirlwind blew
  Throughout the house, that clappèd every dore,
  With which that yron wicket open flew,
  As it with mightie levers had bene tore:
  And forth issewd, as on the ready flore
  Of some Theàtre, a grave personage,
  That in his hand a branch of laurell bore,
  With comely haveour and count'nance sage,
Yclad in costly garments, fit for tragicke Stage.

4 Proceeding to the midst, he still did stand,
  As if in mind he somewhat had to say,
  And to the vulgar beckning with his hand,
  In signe of silence, as to heare a play,
  By lively actions he gan bewray> *expound*
  Some argument of matter passionèd;
  Which doen, he backe retyrèd soft away,
  And passing by, his name discoverèd,
Ease,° on his robe in golden letters cypherèd.

5 The noble Mayd, still standing all this vewd,
  And merveild at his strange intendiment,> *design*

Ease is the "presenter" of the masque, as the Attendant Spirit is of Milton's *Comus;* he makes the preliminary announcement stating the theme.

With that a joyous fellowship issewd
Of Minstrals, making goodly meriment,
With wanton Bardes, and Rymers impudent,
All which together sung full chearefully
A lay of loves delight, with sweet concent.> *harmony*
After whom marcht a jolly company,
In manner of a maske, enragèd orderly.

6 The whiles a most delitious harmony,
In full straunge notes was sweetly heard to sound,
That the rare sweetnesse of the melody
The feeble senses wholly did confound,
And the fraile soule in deepe delight nigh dround:
And when it ceast, shrill trompets loud did bray,
That their report did farre away rebound,> *echo*
And when they ceast, it gan againe to play,
The whiles the maskers marchèd forth in trim aray.

7 The first was *Fancy,*° like a lovely boy,
Of rare aspect, and beautie without peare;
Matchable either to that ympe> of *Troy,* *child*
Whom Jove did love, and chose his cup to beare,°
Or that same daintie lad, which was so deare
To great *Alcides,*° that when as he dyde,
He wailèd womanlike with many a teare,
And every wood, and every valley wyde
He fild with *Hylas*° name; the Nymphes eke *Hylas* cryde.

8 His garment neither was of silke nor say,> *fine wool*
But painted plumes, in goodly order dight,
Like as the sunburnt *Indians* do aray
Their tawney bodies, in their proudest plight.> *attire*
As those same plumes, so seemd he vaine and light,
That by his gate> might easily appeare; *gait*
For still he far'd as dauncing in delight,
And in his hand a windy fan did beare,
That in the idle aire he mov'd still here and there.

9 And him beside marcht amorous *Desyre,*
Who seemd of riper yeares, then th'other Swaine,
Yet was that other swayne this elders syre,
And gave him being, commune to them twaine:
His garment was disguisèd> very vaine,> *worn / foolishly*
And his embrodered Bonet sat awry;
Twixt both his hands few sparkes he close did straine,

Fancy, fantasy, imagination, especially strong in lovers; he wears feathers, symbols of lightness and uncertainty

ympe . . . beare Ganymede, cupbearer of Jupiter, very beautiful

Alcides Hercules

Hylas Hercules' page, abducted by nymphs; for this Hercules mourned

Which still he blew, and kindled busily,
That soone they life conceiv'd, and forth in flames did fly.

10 Next after him went *Doubt*, who was yclad
In a discolour'd cote, of straunge disguyse,> — *fashion*
That at his backe a brode Capuccio> had, — *hood*
And sleeves dependant *Albanese*-wyse:°
He lookt askew with his mistrustfull eyes,
And nicely> trode, as thornes lay in his way, — *delicately*
Or that the flore to shrinke he did avyse,> — *consider*
And on a broken reed he still> did stay — *ever*
His feeble steps, which shrunke, when hard theron he lay.> — *trod*

11 With him went *Daunger*,° cloth'd in raggèd weed,
Made of Beares skin, that him more dreadfull made,
Yet his owne face was dreadfull, ne did need
Straunge> horrour, to deforme his griesly shade; — *external*
A net in th'one hand, and a rustie blade
In th'other was, this Mischiefe, that Mishap;
With th'one his foes he threatned to invade,> — *stab*
With th'other he his friends ment to enwrap:
For whom he could not kill, he practizd to entrap.

12 Next him was *Feare*, all arm'd from top to toe,
Yet thought himselfe not safe enough thereby,
But feard each shadow moving to and fro,
And his owne armes when glittering he did spy,
Or clashing heard, he fast away did fly,
As ashes pale of hew, and wingyheeld;
And evermore on daunger fixt his eye,
Gainst whom he alwaies bent a brasen shield,
Which his right hand unarmèd fearefully did wield.

13 With him went *Hope* in rancke, a handsome Mayd,
Of chearefull looke and lovely to behold;
In silken samite> she was light arayd, — *rich silk*
And her faire lockes were woven up in gold;
She alway smyld, and in her hand did hold
An holy water Sprinckle, dipt in deowe,
With which she sprinckled favours manifold,
On whom she list, and did great liking sheowe,
Great liking unto many, but true love to feowe.> — *few*

14 And after them *Dissemblance*> and *Suspect*> — *dissimulation / suspicion*
Marcht in one rancke, yet an unequall paire:
For she was gentle, and of milde aspect,
Courteous to all, and seeming debonaire,

Albanese-wyse in the Albanian fashion (?)
Daunger a regular attendant on Love. It means, in this context, the unapproachability of a lady, her creation around herself of hostility toward a lover; in IV.x.17 and also here it has to do with the withholding of love from a suitor.

Goodly adornèd, and exceeding faire:
Yet was that all but painted, and purloynd,
And her bright browes were deckt with borrowed haire:
Her deedes were forgèd, and her words false coynd,
And alwaies in her hand two clewes of silke she twynd.

15 But he was foule, ill favourèd, and grim,
Under his eyebrowes looking still askaunce;
And ever as *Dissemblance* laught on him,
He lowrd on her with daungerous eyeglaunce;
Shewing his nature in his countenance;
His rolling eyes did never rest in place,
But walkt each where, for feare of hid mischaunce,
Holding a lattice° still˃ before his face, *always*
Through which he still did peepe, as forward he did pace.

16 Next him went *Griefe*, and *Fury* matcht yfere,˃ *together*
Griefe all in sable sorrowfully clad,
Downe hanging his dull head, with heavy chere,
Yet inly being more, then˃ seeming sad: *than*
A paire of Pincers in his hand he had,
With which he pinchèd people to the hart,
That from thenceforth a wretched life they lad,
In wilfull languor and consuming smart,
Dying each day with inward wounds of dolours dart.

17 But *Fury* was full ill appareilèd
In rags, that naked nigh she did appeare,
With ghastly lookes and dreadfull drerihed,˃ *gloom*
For from her backe her garments she did teare,
And from her head oft rent her snarlèd heare:
In her right hand a firebrand she did tosse
About her head, still roming here and there;
As a dismayèd Deare in chace embost,˃ *hard pressed*
Forgetfull of his safety, hath his right way lost.

18 After them went *Displeasure* and *Pleasance*,
He looking lompish and full sullein sad,
And hanging downe his heavy countenance;
She chearefull fresh and full of joyance glad,
As if no sorrow she ne felt ne drad;
That evill matchèd paire they seemd to bee:
An angry Waspe th'one in a viall had
Th'other in hers an hony-lady Bee;
Thus marchèd these sixe couples forth in faire degree.

19 After all these there marcht a most faire Dame,°
Led of two grysie˃ villeins, th'one *Despight*,˃ *grim / spite*

lattice Suspect carries it because of a pun on the Italian *gelosia* or French *jalousie*, meaning both "jealousy" and "Venetian blind."

Dame Amoret; the picture of her is reminiscent of some in the emblem books (see Glossary).

The other clepèd *Cruelty* by name:
She dolefull Lady, like a dreary Spright,
Cald by strong charmes out of eternall night,
Had deathes owne image figurd in her face,
Full of sad signes, fearefull to living sight;
Yet in that horror shewd a seemely grace,
And with her feeble feet did move a comely pace.

20 Her brest all naked, as net> ivory, *pure*
Without adorne of gold or silver bright,
Wherewith the Craftesman wonts it beautify,
Of her dew honour was despoylèd quight,
And a wide wound therein (O ruefull sight)
Entrenchèd deepe with knife accursèd keene,
Yet> freshly bleeding forth her fainting spright, *still*
(The worke of cruell hand) was to be seene,
That dyde in sanguine red her skin all snowy cleene.

21 At that wide orifice her trembling hart
Was drawne forth, and in silver basin layd,
Quite through transfixèd with a deadly dart,
And in her bloud yet steeming fresh embayd.> *bathed*
And those two villeins, which her steps upstayd,
When her weake feete could scarcely her sustaine,
And fading vitall powers gan to fade,
Her forward still with torture did constraine,
And evermore encreasèd her consuming paine.

22 Next after her the winged God himselfe
Came riding on a Lion ravenous,
Taught to obay the menage> of that Elfe, *handling*
That man and beast with powre imperious
Subdeweth to his kingdome tyrannous:
His blindfold eyes° he bad a while unbind,
That his proud spoyle of that same dolorous
Faire Dame he might behold in perfect kind;
Which seene, he much rejoyced in his cruell mind.

23 Of which full proud, himselfe up rearing hye,
He lookèd round about with sterne disdaine;
And did survay his goodly company:
And marshalling the evill ordered traine,
With that the darts which his right hand did straine,
Full dreadfully he shooke that all did quake,
And clapt on hie his coulourd wingès twaine,
That all his many> it affraide did make: *company*
Tho> blinding him> againe, his way he forth did take. *then / himself*

blindfold eyes Cupid was never blindfolded in antiquity; later he was so represented to imply the blindness of erotic choice, though in more mystical writings his blindness was said to show that love is above the intellect.

24 Behinde him was *Reproch, Repentance, Shame;*
Reproch the first, *Shame* next, *Repent* behind:
Repentance feeble, sorrowfull, and lame:
Reproch despightfull, carelesse, and unkind;
Shame most ill favourd, bestiall, and blind:
Shame lowrd, *Repentance* sigh'd, *Reproch* did scould;
Reproch sharpe stings, *Repentance* whips entwind,
Shame burning brond-yrons in her hand did hold:
All three to each unlike, yet all made in one mould.

25 And after them a rude confusèd rout
Of persons flockt, whose names is> hard to read: *it is*
Emongst them was sterne *Strife,* and *Anger* stout,
Unquiet *Care,* and fond *Unthriftihead,*
Lewd *Losse of Time,* and *Sorrow* seeming dead,
Inconstant *Chaunge,* and false *Disloyaltie,*
Consuming *Riotise,* and guilty *Dread*
Of heavenly vengeance, faint *Infirmitie,*
Vile *Povertie,* and lastly *Death* with infamie.

26 There were full many moe like maladies,
Whose names and natures I note readen well,> *cannot well say*
So many moe, as there be phantasies
In wavering wemens wit, that none can tell,
Or paines in love, or punishments in hell;
All which disguizèd marcht in masking wise,
About the chamber with that Damozell,
And then returnèd, having marchèd thrise,
Into the inner roome, from whence they first did rise.

27 So soone as they were in, the dore streight way
Fast lockèd, driven with that stormy blast,
Which first it opened; and bore all away.
Then the brave Maid, which all this while was plast
In secret shade, and saw both first and last,
Issewèd forth, and went unto the dore,
To enter in, but found it lockèd fast:
It vaine she thought with rigorous uprore
For to efforce, when charmes had closèd it afore.

28 Where force might not availe, there sleights and art
She cast to use, both fit for hard emprize;
For thy> from that same roome not to depart *because*
Till morrow next, she did her selfe avize,> *counsel*
When that same Maske againe should forth arize.
The morrow next appeard with joyous cheare,
Calling men to their daily exercize,
Then she, as morrow fresh, her selfe did reare
Out of her secret stand, that day for to out weare.

29 All that day she outwore in wandering,
And gazing on that Chambers ornament,
Till that againe the second evening
Her covered with her sable vestiment,
Wherewith the worlds faire beautie she hath blent:˃ *extinguished*
Then when the second watch was almost past,
That brasen dore flew open, and in went
Bold *Britomart*, as she had late forecast,˃ *planned*
Neither of idle shewes, nor of false charmes aghast.

30 So soone as she was entred, round about
She cast her eies, to see what was become
Of all those persons, which she saw without:
But lo, they streight were vanisht all and some,˃ *entirely*
Ne living wight she saw in all that roome,
Save that same woefull Ladie, both whose hands
Were bounden fast, that did her ill become,
And her small wast girt round with yron bands,
Unto a brasen pillour, by the which she stands.

31 And her before the vile Enchaunter sate,
Figuring straunge charácters of his art,
With living bloud he those charácters wrate,
Dreadfully dropping from her dying hart,
Seeming transfixèd with a cruell dart,
And all perforce to make her him to love.
Ah who can love the worker of her smart?˃ *pain*
A thousand charmes he formerly did prove;˃ *try*
Yet thousand charmes could not her stedfast heart remove.

32 Soone as that virgin knight he saw in place,
His wicked bookes in hast he overthrew,
Not caring his long labours to deface,˃ *spoil*
And fiercely ronning to that Lady trew,
A murdrous knife out of his pocket drew,
The which he thought, for villeinous despight,
In her tormented bodie to embrew:˃ *plunge*
But the stout Damzell to him leaping light,
His cursèd hand withheld, and maisterèd his might.

33 From her, to whom his fury first he ment,˃ *intended*
The wicked weapon rashly he did wrest,
And turning to her selfe his fell intent,
Unwares it strooke into her snowie chest,
That little drops empurpled her faire brest.
Exceeding wroth therewith the virgin grew,
Albe˃ the wound were nothing deepe imprest, *although*
And fiercely forth her mortall blade she drew,
To give him the reward for such vile outrage dew.

34 So mightily she smote him, that to ground
He fell halfe dead; next stroke him should have slaine,
Had not the Lady, which by him stood bound,
Dernely> unto her callèd to abstaine, *dismally*
From doing him to dy. For else her paine
Should be remedilesse, sith> none but hee, *since*
Which wrought it, could the same recure> againe. *cure*
Therewith she stayd her hand, loth stayd to bee;
For life she him envyde,> and long'd revenge to see. *begrudged*

35 And to him said, Thou wicked man, whose meed
For so huge mischiefe, and vile villany
Is death, or if that ought do death exceed,
Be sure, that nought may save thee from to dy,
But if that thou this Dame doe presently
Restore unto her health, and former state;
This doe and live, else die undoubtedly.
He glad of life, that lookt for death but late,
Did yield himselfe right willing to prolong his date.

36 And rising up, gan streight to overlooke
Those cursèd leaves, his charmes backe to reverse;
Full dreadfull things out of that balefull booke
He red, and measur'd many a sad verse,
That horror gan the virgins hart to perse,
And her faire locks up starèd stiffe on end,
Hearing him those same bloudy lines reherse;
And all the while he red, she did extend
Her sword high over him, if ought> he did offend. *lest in anyway*

37 Anon she gan perceive the house to quake,
And all the dores to rattle round about;
Yet all that did not her dismaièd make,
Nor slacke her threatfull hand for daungers dout,> *fear*
But still with stedfast eye and courage stout
Abode, to weet what end would come of all.
At last that mightie chaine, which round about
Her tender waste was wound, adowne gan fall,
And that great brasen pillour broke in peeces small.

38 The cruell steele, which thrild> her dying hart, *pierced*
Fell softly forth, as of his owne accord,
And the wyde wound, which lately did dispart> *divide*
Her bleeding brest, and riven bowels gor'd,
Was closèd up, as it had not bene bor'd,
And every part to safèty full sound,
As she were never hurt, was soone restor'd:
Tho> when she felt her selfe to be unbound, *then*
And perfect hole,> prostrate she fell unto the ground. *whole*

39 Before faire *Britomart*, she fell prostrate,
Saying, Ah noble knight, what worthy meed
Can wretched Lady, quit˃ from wofull state, *redeemed*
Yield you in liew of this your gratious deed?
Your vertue selfe her owne reward shall breed,
Even immortall praise, and glory wyde,
Which I your vassall, by your prowesse freed,
Shall through the world make to be notifyde,
And goodly well advance,˃ that goodly well was tryde.˃ *make known / proved*

40 But *Britomart* uprearing her from ground,
Said, Gentle Dame, reward enough I weene
For many labours more, then I have found,
This, that in safety now I have you seene,
And meane of your deliverance have beene:
Henceforth faire Lady comfort to you take,
And put away remembrance of late teene;
In stead thereof know, that your loving Make,˃ *mate*
Hath no lesse griefe endurèd for your gentle sake.

41 She much was cheard to heare him mentiònd,
Whom of all living wights she lovèd best.
Then laid the noble Championesse strong hond
Upon th'enchaunter, which had her distrest
So sore, and with foule outrages opprest:
With that great chaine, wherewith not long ygo
He bound that pitteous Lady prisoner, now relest,
Himselfe she bound, more worthy to be so,
And captive with her led to wretchednesse and wo.

42 Returning backe, those goodly roomes, which erst˃ *recently*
She saw so rich and royally arayd,
Now vanisht utterly, and cleane subverst˃ *overthrown*
She found, and all their glory quite decayd,
That sight of such a chaunge her much dismayd.
Thence forth descending to that perlous Porch,
Those dreadfull flames she also found delayd,˃ *quenched*
And quenchèd quite, like a consumèd torch,
That erst all entrers won˃ so cruelly to scorch. *used*

43 More° easie issew˃ now, then entrance late *exit*
She found: for now that fainèd dreadfull flame,

More The following three stanzas were inserted in the edition of 1596 to replace the five with which Spenser had originally ended the Book. In the first version Britomart finds Scudamour, as usual, in distress, but when he sees Amoret in good health he runs to her and embraces her. They seemed grown together like a hermaphrodite, and Britomart half envies them, knowing that she is to be denied such happiness. Spenser makes no use of these stanzas when Scudamour and Amoret finally do meet again in IV.ix. It has been suggested (see Proem to IV) that he changed them because he was afraid of offending Burleigh any further; but more probably he had further use, in the interlocking stories that also make up Book IV, for Scudamour and Amoret.

Which chokt the porch of that enchaunted gate,
And passage bard to all, that thither came,
Was vanisht quite, as it were not the same,
And gave her leave at pleasure forth to passe.
Th'Enchaunter selfe, which all that fraud did frame,
To have efforst the love of that faire lasse,
Seeing his worke now wasted deepe engrievèd was.

44 But when the victoresse arrivèd there,
Where late she left the pensife *Scudamore,*
With her owne trusty Squire, both full of feare,
Neither of them she found where she them lore:> *left*
Thereat her noble hart was stonisht sore;
But most faire *Amoret,* whose gentle spright
Now gan to feede on hope, which she before
Conceivèd had, to see her owne deare knight,
Being thereof beguyld was fild with new affright.

45 But he sad man, when he had long in drede
Awayted there for *Britomarts* returne,
Yet saw her not nor signe of her good speed,
His expectation to despaire did turne,
Misdeeming sure that her those flames did burne;
And therefore gan advize> with her old Squire, *decide*
Who her deare nourslings losse no lesse did mourne,
Thence to depart for further aide t'enquire:
Where let them wend at will, whilest here I doe respire.> *take a breather*

1590

Book IV

It may be that in the course of writing Book IV Spenser found that the Ariostan scheme of interlocked stories was less suitable to his purposes than the more monolithic organization of I and II. Book IV is the least compelling part of the poem, despite its connections with the brilliant Book III. It is the Legend of Friendship, and attempts to express the Renaissance mystique of friendship; the simplest expression Spenser gives it occurs in the opening stanza of canto ix:

Hard is the doubt, and difficult to deeme,
When all three kinds of love together meet,
And do dispart> the heart with powre extreme, *divide*
Whether> shall weigh the balance down; to weet *which*
The deare affection unto kindred sweet,
Or raging fire of love to woman kind,
Or zeale of friends combynd with vertues meet.
But of them all the band> of vertuous mind *bond*
Me seemes the gentle hart should most assurèd bind.

For naturall affection soone doth cesse,
 And quenchèd is with *Cupids* greater flame:
 But faithfull friendship doth them both suppresse,
 And them with maystring discipline doth tame,
 Through thoughts aspyring to eternall fame.
 For as the soule doth rule the earthly masse,
 And all the service of the bodie frame,
 So love of soule doth love of bodie passe,
No lesse than perfect gold surmounts the meanest brasse.

This is the kind of friendship that makes Shakespeare's Valentine, in *Two Gentlemen of Verona,* offer to give up his girl Silvia to his friend Proteus, who has just tried to rape her; except that Spenser always insists that true friendship is between virtuous equals.

The nominal heroes of this book are Cambel and Triamond, borrowed from Chaucer's unfinished Squire's Tale; but Spenser diversifies that story in order to provide many different examples of love and friendship. Many of these are carried over from III: the False Florimell, Florimell and Marinell, Britomart and Artegall, Timias and Belphoebe, Scudamour and Amoret. Guyon and Braggadocchio, Satyrane and Archimago also return. The cancellation of the original conclusion made it possible to continue Scudamour's adventures, and to show him in the House of Care, a famous passage which is given below.

In the Proem to IV, which serves as an introduction to the second installment of the whole poem, Books IV through VI, Spenser refers to the censure of Lord Burleigh, Elizabeth's Lord Chancellor and the most powerful man in England, and offers a spirited defense, saying that his work is not for such readers but for those who, like the Queen, understand love, and the utility of examples which show what is right by exposing what is wrong.

The Fourth Booke of The Faerie Queene

Contayning, The Legend of Cambel and Triamond, or *Of Friendship*

1 The rugged forhead that with grave foresight
 Welds> kingdomes causes, and affaires of state,° *wields*
 My looser rimes (I wote) doth sharply wite,> *blame*
 For praising love, as I have done of late,
 And magnifying> lovers deare debate; *glorifying*
 By which fraile youth is oft to follie led,
 Through false allurement of that pleasing baite,
 That better were in vertues disciplèd,
Then with vaine poemes weeds> to have their fancies fed. *blooms*

The rugged . . . state William Cecil, Lord Burleigh

2 Such ones ill judge of love, that cannot love,
Ne in their frosen hearts feele kindly˃ flame: *natural*
For thy˃ they ought not thing unkowne reprove, *therefore*
Ne naturall affection faultlesse blame,
For fault of few that have abusd the same.
For it of honor and all vertue is
The roote, and brings forth glorious flowres of fame,
That crowne true lovers with immortall blis,
The meed of them that love, and do not live amisse.

3 Which who so list looke backe to former ages,
And call to count the things that then were donne,
Shall find, that all the workes of those wise sages,
And brave exploits which great Heroès wonne,
In love were either ended or begunne:
Witnesse the father of Philosophie,
Which to his *Critias*,° shaded oft from sunne,
Of love full manie lessons did apply,
The which these Stoicke censours cannot well deny.

4 To such therefore I do not sing at all,
But to that sacred Saint my soveraigne Queene,
In whose chast breast all bountie naturall,
And treasures of true love enlockèd beene,
Bove all her sexe that ever yet was seene;
To her I sing of love, that loveth best,
And best is lov'd of all alive I weene:
To her this song most fitly is addrest,
The Queene of love, and Prince of peace from heaven blest.

5 Which that she may the better deigne to heare,
Do thou dred infant, *Venus* dearling dove,°
From her high spirit chase imperious feare,
And use of awfull Majestie remove:
In sted thereof with drops of melting love,
Deawd with ambrosiall kisses, by thee gotten
From thy sweete smyling mother from above,
Sprinckle her heart, and haughtie courage˃ soften, *spirit*
That she may hearke to love, and reade this lesson often.

[In this Book Atè (Strife) and Concord contend for mastery. Atè fills Scudamour with rage and misery by persuading him that Britomart has stolen the affections of Amoret. It is in this frame of mind that Scudamour enters the House of Care. Care is a blacksmith who makes instruments to torment the unquiet soul.]

Critias meaning Crito; see II.vii.52n **dove** Cupid

From Canto v

32 So as they travellèd, the drouping night
Covered with cloudie storme and bitter showre,
That dreadfull seem'd to every living wight,
Upon them fell, before her timely howre;
That forcèd them to seeke some covert bowre,
Where they might hide their heads in quiet rest,
And shrowd their persons from that stormie stowre.
Not farre away, not meete for any guest
They spide a little cottage, like some poore mans nest.

33 Under a steepe hilles side it placèd was,
There where the mouldred earth had cav'd the banke;
And fast beside a little brooke did pas
Of muddie water, that like puddle stanke,
By which few crookèd sallowes> grew in ranke: *willows*
Whereto approaching nigh, they heard the sound
Of many yron hammers beating ranke,> *violently*
And answering their wearie turnes around,
That seemèd some blacksmith dwelt in that desert ground.

34 There entring in, they found the goodman selfe,
Full busily unto his worke ybent;
Who was to weet a wretched wearish> elfe, *wizened*
With hollow eyes and rawbone cheekes forspent,
As if he had in prison long bene pent:
Full blacke and griesly did his face appeare,
Besmeard with smoke that nigh his eye-sight blent;> *blinded*
With rugged beard, and hoarie shaggèd heare,
The which he never wont to combe, or comely sheare.

35 Rude was his garment, and to rags all rent,
Ne better had he, ne for better cared:
With blistred hands emongst the cinders brent,
And fingers filthie, with long nayles unpared,
Right fit to rend the food, on which he fared.
His name was *Care;* a blacksmith by his trade,
That neither day nor night from working spared,
But to small purpose yron wedges made;
Those be unquiet thoughts, that carefull minds invade.

36 In which his worke he had sixe servants prest,
About the Andvile standing evermore,
With huge great hammers, that did never rest
From heaping stroakes, which thereon sousèd> sore: *struck*
All sixe strong groomes, but one then other more;
For by degrees they all were disagreed;
So likewise did the hammers which they bore,
Like belles in greatnesse orderly succeed,
That he which was the last, the first did farre exceede.

37 He like a monstrous Gyant seem'd in sight,
Farre passing *Bronteus*, or *Pyracmon*° great,
The which in *Lipari*° doe day and night
Frame thunderbolts for *Joves* avengefull threate.
So dreadfully he did the andvile beat,
That seem'd to dust he shortly would it drive:
So huge his hammer and so fierce his heat,
That seem'd a rocke of Diamond it could rive,
And rend a sunder quite, if he thereto list strive.

38 Sir *Scudamour* there entring, much admired
The manner of their worke and wearie paine;
And having long beheld, at last enquired
The cause and end thereof: but all in vaine;
For they for nought would from their worke refraine,
Ne let his speeches come unto their eare.
And eke the breathfull bellowes blew amaine,˃ *powerfully*
Like to the Northren winde, that˃ none could heare: *so that*
Those *Pensifenesse* did move; and *Sighes* the bellows weare.

39 Which when that warriour saw, he said no more,
But in his armour layd him downe to rest:
To rest he layd him downe upon the flore,
(Whylome˃ for ventrous Knights the bedding best) *formerly*
And thought his wearie limbs to have redrest.
And that old agèd Dame,° his faithfull Squire,
Her feeble joynts layd eke a downe to rest;
That needed much her weake age to desire,
After so long a travell, which them both did tire.

40 There lay Sir *Scudamour* long while expecting,
When gentle sleepe his heavie eyes would close;
Oft chaunging sides, and oft new place electing,
Where better seem'd he mote himselfe repose;
And oft in wrath he thence againe uprose;
And oft in wrath he layd him downe againe.
But wheresoever he did himselfe dispose,
He by no meanes could wishèd ease obtaine:
So every place seem'd painefull, and ech changing vaine.

41 And evermore, when he to sleepe did thinke,
The hammers sound his senses did molest;
And evermore, when he began to winke,
The bellowes noyse disturb'd his quiet rest,
Ne suffred sleepe to settle in his brest.
And all the night the dogs did barke and howle
About the house, at sent˃ of stranger guest: *scent*

Bronteus . . . Pyracmon two of the Cyclops who forged the thunderbolts of Zeus
Lipari Lipara, one of the Lipari islands off Sicily
agèd Dame Glaucè, serving as squire to Scudamour

And now the crowing Cocke, and now the Owle
Lowde shriking him afflicted to the very sowle.

42 And if by fortune any litle nap
Upon his heavie eye-lids chaunst to fall,
Eftsoones one of those villeins him did rap
Upon his headpeece with his yron mall;> *mallet*
That he was soone awakèd therewithall,
And lightly started up as one affrayd;
Or as if one him suddenly did call.
So oftentimes he out of sleepe abrayd,> *awoke*
And then lay musing long, on that him ill apayd.> *pleased*

43 So long he muzèd, and so long he lay,
That at the last his wearie sprite opprest
With fleshly weaknesse, which no creature may
Long time resist, gave place to kindly rest,
That all his senses did full soone arrest:
Yet in his soundest sleepe, his dayly feare
His ydle braine gan busily molest,
And made him dreame those two° disloyall were:
The things that day most minds, at night doe most appeare.

44 With that, the wicked carle the maister Smith
A paire of redwhot yron tongs did take
Out of the burning cinders, and therewith
Under his side him nipt, that forst to wake,
He felt his hart for very paine to quake,
And started up avengèd for to be
On him, the which his quiet slomber brake:
Yet looking round about him none could see;
Yet did the smart remaine, though he himselfe did flee.

45 In such disquiet and hartfretting payne,
He all that night, that too long night did passe.
And now the day out of the Ocean mayne
Began to peepe above this earthly masse,
With pearly dew sprinkling the morning grasse:
Then up he rose like heavie lumpe of lead,
That in his face, as in a looking glasse,
The signes of anguish one mote plainely read,
And ghesse the man to be dismayd with gealous dread.

46 Unto his lofty steede he clombe anone,
And forth upon his former voiage fared,
And with him eke that agèd Squire attone;> *together*
Who whatsoever perill was prepared,
Both equall paines and equall perill shared:
The end whereof and daungerous event

those two Britomart and Amoret

Shall for another canticle be spared.
But here my wearie teeme nigh over spent
Shall breath it selfe awhile, after so long a went.> *journey*

[In the sixth canto Britomart and Artegall fall in love; upon their union depend not only the future happiness of Britain but much of Spenser's Fifth Book. In vii Belphoebe saves Amoret from the attentions of a wicked "salvage" man (some are good, some bad as Caliban). He represents the intrusion of bestial lust into the world of love, a fallen world in which virtuous friendship is nobler than the love of women. Yet the core of the Book is really not any example of male friendship but Scudamour's account, in canto x, of his first wooing and winning of Amoret. He forces access into the Temple of Venus, past Doubt, Delay, and Danger, who make for the unapproachability of virtuous women, and comes upon a paradise of pleasure and innocent friendship. In the Temple itself, Concord reconciles the passions of love and hate, as she holds together the conflicting elements in the frame of the world. The goddess now appears as Hermaphrodite, symbolizing the union of opposites in the love of man and woman (Spenser had used the idea figuratively in the original conclusion to Book III). The prayer of the lover to Venus is based on the great invocation to Venus of Lucretius in his *De Rerum Natura:* "alma Venus, Venus genetrix," giver of pleasure and fertility throughout the creation. Scudamour echoes him. In the lap of Womanhood, flanked by appropriate female qualities, he sees Amoret; the goddess smiles on him and he leads his woman away. This is an allegory of proper courtship; a little forcefulness is required to break down the good customary prohibitions. It is also an allegory of love as Spenser understands it, for instance in *Epithalamion* and Book III of *The Faerie Queene*. It is a power transcending physical relations, being the source of order and fertility in all things. As it affects men and women it is a source of delight, but needs checks, and is subject to being overbalanced by sexual passion; this episode is a flashback, and precedes the disasters of Book III, in which Scudamour is parted from Amoret by Busirane, who stands for the unregulated desire that came between them on their wedding night. At the end of Book IV he still hasn't got her back.]

From Canto x

23 In such luxurious plentie of all pleasure,
It seem'd a second paradise° to ghesse,
So lavishly enricht with natures threasure,
That if the happie soules, which doe possesse
Th'Elysian fields, and live in lasting blesse,
Should happen this with living eye to see,
They soone would loath their lesser happinesse,
And wish to life return'd againe to bee,
That in this joyous place they mote have joyance free.

24 Fresh shadowes, fit to shroud from sunny ray;
Faire lawnds, to take the sunne in season dew;

second paradise We have now seen several such paradises; note how their purport changes with the context, just as does the significance of Cupid and Venus.

Sweet springs, in which a thousand Nymphs did play;
Soft rombling brookes, that gentle slomber drew;
High rearèd mounts, the lands about to vew;
Low looking dales, disloignd˃ from common gaze; *distant*
Delightfull bowres, to solace lovers trew;
False Labyrinthes, fond runners eyes to daze;
All which by nature made did nature selfe amaze.

25 And all without were walkes and alleyes dight˃ *adorned*
With divers trees, enrang'd in even rankes;
And here and there were pleasant arbors pight.˃ *placed*
And shadie seates, and sundry flowring bankes,
To sit and rest the walkers wearie shankes,
And therein thousand payres of lovers walkt,
Praysing their god, and yeelding him great thankes,
Ne ever ought but of their true loves talkt,
Ne ever for rebuke or blame of any balkt.˃ *stopped*

26 All these together by themselves did sport
Their spotlesse pleasures, and sweet loves content.
But farre away from these, another sort
Of lovers linckèd in true harts consent;
Which lovèd not as these, for like intent,
But on chast vertue grounded their desire,
Farre from all fraud, or faynèd blandishment;
Which in their spirits kindling zealous fire,
Brave thoughts and noble deeds did evermore aspire.

27 Such were great *Hercules,* and *Hylas*° deare;
Trew *Jonathan,* and *David*° trustie tryde;
Stout *Theseus,* and *Pirithous*° his feare;˃ *companion*
Pylades and *Orestes*° by his syde;
Myld *Titus* and *Gesippus*° without pryde;
Damon and *Pythias* whom death could not sever:°
All these and all that ever had bene tyde
In bands of friendship, there did live for ever,
Whose lives although decay'd, yet loves decayèd never.

28 Which when as I, that never tasted blis,
Nor happie howre, beheld with gazefull eye,
I thought there was none other heaven then this;
And gan their endlesse happinesse envye,
That being free from feare and gealosye,

Hylas boy lover of Hercules; he was either drowned or carried away by nymphs
Jonathan, and David I Samuel 18
Theseus, and Pirithous a friendship cemented by war against the Centaurs and by the attempted rape of Proserpina from the underworld
Pylades and Orestes the classical type of friendship; Pylades helped Orestes revenge his father Agamemnon by killing his mother Clytemnestra and her lover Aegisthus
Titus and Gesippus The story of Titus and Giseppus is in the Tenth Day of Boccaccio's *Decameron;* Titus accused himself of a murder for which Giseppus had accepted responsibility.
Damon . . . sever Damon stood as hostage for his friend Pythias when the latter was under sentence of death.

Might frankely there their loves desire possesse;
Whilest I through paines and perlous jeopardie,
Was forst to seeke my lifes deare patronesse:
Much dearer be the things, which come through hard distresse.

29 Yet all those sights, and all that else I saw,
Might not my steps withhold, but that forthright
Unto that purposd place I did me draw,
Where as my love was lodgèd day and night:
The temple of great *Venus,* that is hight
The Queene of beautie, and of love the mother,
There worshippèd of every living wight;
Whose goodly workmanship farre past all other
That ever were on earth, all were they˃ set together. *as if they were*

30 Not that same famous Temple of *Diane,*°
Whose hight all *Ephesus* did oversee,
And which all *Asia* sought with vowes prophane,
One of the worlds seven wonders sayd to bee,
Might match with this by many a degree:
Nor that, which that wise King of *Jurie* framed,
With endlesse cost, to be th'Almighties see;˃ *abode*
Nor all that else through all the world is named
To all the heathen Gods, might like to this be clamed.

31 I much admyring that so goodly frame,
Unto the porch approcht, which open stood;
But therein sate an amiable Dame,
That seem'd to be of very sober mood,
And in her semblant˃ shewed great womanhood: *appearance*
Strange was her tyre;˃ for on her head a crowne *headdress*
She wore much like unto a Danisk hood,°
Poudred with pearle and stone, and all her gowne
Enwoven was with gold, that raught˃ full low a downe. *reached*

32 On either side of her, two young men stood,
Both strongly arm'd, as fearing one another;
Yet were they brethren both of halfe the blood,
Begotten by two fathers of one mother,
Though of contrarie natures each to other:
The one of them hight *Love,* the other *Hate,*
Hate was the elder, *Love* the younger brother;
Yet was the younger stronger in his state
Then th'elder, and him maystred still in all debate.

33 Nathlesse that Dame so well them tempred both,
That she them forcèd hand to joyne in hand,
Albe that *Hatred* was thereto full loth,

Temple of Diane Acts 19

Danisk hood Danish headdress, perhaps distinctive in shape

And turn'd his face away, as he did stand,
Unwilling to behold that lovely band.> *bond*
Yet she was of such grace and vertuous might,
That her commaundment he could not withstand,
But bit his lip for felonous despight,
And gnasht his yron tuskes at that displeasing sight.

34 *Concord*° she cleepèd> was in common reed,> *called / speech*
Mother of blessèd *Peace,* and *Friendship* trew;
They both her twins, both borne of heavenly seed,
And she her selfe likewise divinely grew;
The which right well her workes divine did shew:
For strength, and wealth, and happinesse she lends,
And strife, and warre, and anger does subdew:
Of litle much, of foes she maketh frends,
And to afflicted minds sweet rest and quiet sends.

35 By her the heaven is in his course contained,
And all the world in state unmovèd stands,
As their Almightie maker first ordained.
And bound them with inviolable bands;
Else would the waters overflow the lands,
And fire devoure the ayre, and hell them quight,> *revenge, pay back*
But that she holds them with her blessèd hands.
She is the nourse of pleasure and delight,
And unto *Venus* grace the gate doth open right.°

36 By her I entring halfe dismayèd was,
But she in gentle wise me entertayned,
And twixt her selfe and *Love* did let me pas;
But *Hatred* would my entrance have restrayned,
And with his club me threatned to have brayned,
Had not the Ladie with her powrefull speach
Him from his wicked will uneath> refrayned; *with difficulty*
And th'other eke his malice did empeach,> *hinder*
Till I was throughly past the perill of his reach.

37 Into the inmost Temple thus I came,
Which fuming all with frankensence I found,
And odours rising from the altars flame,
Upon an hundred marble pillors round
The roofe up high was rearèd from the ground,
All deckt with crownes, and chaynes, and girlands gay,
And thousand pretious gifts worth many a pound,
The which sad lovers for their vowes did pay;
And all the ground was strow'd with flowres, as fresh as May.

Concord Placing her between love and hate as mediator, Spenser is remembering the ancient principle that concord issues from the resolution of discords; it is stated in Boethius, *The Consolation of Philosophy* II.8, which he knew, and also by Chaucer in *Troilus and Criseyde* III.1751 ff., and The Knight's Tale, ll. 2990 ff. Spenser puts it into the *Hymne of Heavenly Love,* ll. 76 ff.

unto . . . right without the resolution of the discord of opposites there can be no love between men and women

38 An hundred Altars round about were set,
All flaming with their sacrifices fire,
That with the steme thereof the Temple swet,˃ *sweated*
Which rould in clouds to heaven did aspire,
And in them bore true lovers vowes entire:
And eke an hundred brasen caudrons bright,
To bath in joy and amorous desire,
Every of which was to a damzell hight;˃ *assigned*
For all the Priests were damzels, in soft linnen dight.

39 Right in the midst the Goddesse selfe did stand
Upon an altar of some costly masse,
Whose substance was uneath˃ to understand: *difficult*
For neither pretious stone, nor durefull brasse,
Nor shining gold, nor mouldring clay it was;
But much more rare and pretious to esteem,
Pure in aspect, and like to christall glasse,
Yet glasse was not, if one did rightly deeme,
But being faire and brickle,˃ likest glasse did seeme. *brittle*

40 But it in shape and beautie did excell
All other Idoles, which the heathen adore,
Farre passing that, which by surpassing skill
Phidias did make in *Paphos* Isle° of yore,
With which that wretched Greeke, that life forlore,˃ *abandoned*
Did fall in love: yet this much fairer shined,
But covered with a slender veile afore;
And both her feete and legs together twyned
Were with a snake, whose head and tail were fast combyned.

41 The cause why she was covered with a vele,
Was hard to know, for that her Priests the same
From peoples knowledge labour'd to concele.
But sooth it was not sure for womanish shame,
Nor any blemish, which the worke mote blame;˃ *disfigure*
But for, they say, she hath both kinds in one,
Both male and female, both under one name:°
She syre and mother is her selfe alone,
Begets and eke conceives, ne needeth other none.

42 And all about her necke and shoulders flew
A flocke of litle loves, and sports, and joyes,
With nimble wings of gold and purple hew;
Whose shapes seem'd not like to terrestriall boyes,
But like to Angels playing heavenly toyes;˃ *games*

that . . . Isle the statue made by Praxiteles at Cnidos, which first showed Venus naked; a youth fell in love with it
Both . . . name The name is Hermaphroditus, son of Hermes and Aphrodite, who was made one body with the nymph Salmacis in love. The Venus of this name sums up the male-female generative process over which the goddess traditionally presides; as Spenser puts it in *Colin Clout,* ll. 801–2: "For Venus selfe doth solely couples seem, / Both male and female through commixture join'd." Hairy Venuses in women's dress are recorded in antiquity.

The whilest their eldest brother was away,
Cupid their eldest brother; he enjoyes
The wide kingdome of love with Lordly sway,
And to his law compels all creatures to obay.

43 And all about her altar scattered lay
Great sorts˃ of lovers piteously complayning, *groups*
Some of their losse, some of their loves delay,
Some of their pride, some paragons disdayning,
Some fearing fraud, some fraudulently fayning,
As every one had cause of good or ill.
Amongst the rest some one through loves constrayning,
Tormented sore, could not containe it still,
But thus brake forth, that all the temple it did fill.

44 Great *Venus*, Queene of beautie and of grace,
The joy of Gods and men, that under skie
Doest fayrest shine, and most adorne thy place,
That with thy smyling looke doest pacifie
The raging seas, and makst the stormes to flie;
Thee goddesse, thee the winds, the clouds doe feare,
And when thou spredst thy mantle forth on hie,
The waters play and pleasant lands appeare,
And heavens laugh, and al the world shews joyous cheare.

45 Then doth the dædale° earth throw forth to thee
Out of her fruitfull lap aboundant flowres,
And then all living wights, soone as they see
The spring breake forth out of his lusty bowres,
They all doe learne to play the Paramours;
First doe the merry birds, thy prety pages
Privily prickèd with thy lustfull powres,
Chirpe loud to thee out of their leavy cages,
And thee their mother call to coole their kindly rages.

46 Then doe the salvage beasts begin to play
Their pleasant friskes, and loath their wonted food;
The Lyons rore, the Tygres loudly bray,
The raging Buls rebellow through the wood,
And breaking forth, dare tempt the deepest flood,
To come where thou doest draw them with desire:
So all things else, that nourish vitall blood,
Soone as with fury thou doest them inspire,
In generation seeke to quench their inward fire.

47 So all the world by thee at first was made,
And dayly yet thou doest the same repayre:

dædale intricately constructed, as if by Daedalus, the great artificer who built the labyrinth at Cnossos

Ne ought on earth that merry is and glad,
Ne ought on earth that lovely is and fayre,
But thou the same for pleasure didst prepayre.
Thou art the root of all that joyous is,
Great God of men and women, queene of th'ayre,
Mother of laughter, and welspring of blisse,
O graunt that of my love at last I may not misse.

48 So did he say: but I with murmure soft,
That none might heare the sorrow of my hart,
Yet inly groning deepe and sighing oft,
Besought her to graunt ease unto my smart,
And to my wound her gratious help impart.
Whilest thus I spake, behold with happy eye
I spyde, where at the Idoles feet apart
A bevie of fayre damzels close did lye,
Wayting when as the Antheme should° be sung on hye.

49 The first of them did seeme of ryper yeares,
And graver countenance then all the rest;
Yet all the rest were eke her equall peares,
Yet unto her obayèd all the best.
Her name was *Womanhood,* that she exprest
By her sad> semblant> and demeanure wyse: *serious / appearance*
For stedfast still her eyes did fixèd rest,
Ne rov'd at randon after gazers guyse,> *fashion*
Whose luring baytes oftimes doe heedlesse harts entyse.

50 And next to her sate goodly *Shamefastnesse,*
Ne ever durst her eyes from ground upreare,
Ne never once did looke up from her desse,> *dais*
As if some blame of evill she did feare,
That in her cheekes made roses oft appeare.
And her against sweet *Cherefulnesse* was placed,
Whose eyes like twinkling stars in evening cleare,
Were deckt with smyles, that all sad humors chaced,
And darted forth delights, the which her goodly graced.

51 And next to her sate sober *Modestie,*
Holding her hand upon her gentle hart;
And her against sate comely *Curtesie,*
That unto every person knew her part;
And her before was seated overthwart> *opposite*
Soft *Silence,* and submisse> *Obedience,* *submissive*
Both linckt together never to dispart,> *part*
Both gifts of God not gotten but from thence,
Both girlonds° of his Saints against their foes offence.

Wayting . . . should waiting for the anthem to be

girlonds adornments (which protect them from foes)

52 Thus sate they all a round in seemely rate:> *manner*
And in the midst of them a goodly mayd,
Even in the lap of *Womanhood* there sate,
The which was all in lilly white arayd,
With silver streames amongst the linnen stray'd;
Like to the Morne, when first her shyning face
Hath to the gloomy world it selfe bewray'd,
That same was fayrest *Amoret* in place,
Shyning with beauties light, and heavenly vertues grace.

53 Whom soone as I beheld, my hart gan throb,
And wade in doubt, what best were to be donne:
For sacrilege me seem'd the Church to rob,
And folly seem'd to leave the thing undonne,
Which with so strong attempt I had begonne.
Tho> shaking off all doubt and shamefast feare, *then*
Which Ladies love I heard had never wonne
Mongst men of worth, I to her steppèd neare,
And by the lilly hand her labour'd up to reare.

54 Thereat that formost matrone me did blame,
And sharpe rebuke, for being over bold;
Saying it was to Knight unseemely shame,
Upon a recluse> Virgin to lay hold, *in seclusion*
That unto *Venus* services were sold.> *given*
To whom I thus, Nay but it fitteth best,
For *Cupids* man with *Venus* mayd to hold,
For ill your goddesse services are drest
By virgins, and her sacrifices let to rest.

55 With that my shield I forth to her did show,
Which all that while I closely had conceld;
On which when *Cupid* with his killing bow
And cruell shafts emblazond she beheld,
At sight thereof she was with terror queld,
And said no more: but I which all that while
The pledge of faith, her hand engagèd held,
Like warie Hynd> within the weedie soyle, *laborer*
For no intreatie would forgoe so glorious spoyle.

56 And evermore upon the Goddesse face
Mine eye was fixt, for feare of her offence,
Whom when I saw with amiable grace
To laugh at me, and favour my pretence,> *claim*
I was emboldned with more confidence,
And nought for nicenesse> nor for envy sparing, *scrupulousness*
In presence of them all forth led her thence,
All looking on, and like astonisht staring,
Yet to lay hand on her, not one of all them daring.

57 She often prayd, and often me besought,
Sometime with tender teares to let her goe,
Sometime with witching smyles: but yet for nought,
That ever she to me could say or doe,
Could she her wishèd freedome fro me wooe;
But forth I led her through the Temple gate,
By which I hardly past with much adoe:
But that same Ladie which me friended late
In entrance, did me also friend in my retrate.

58 No lesse did *Daunger* threaten me with dread,
When as he saw me, maugre˃ all his powre, *despite*
That glorious spoyle of beautie with me lead,
Then *Cerberus*, when *Orpheus* did recoure˃ *recover*
His Leman° from the Stygian Princes boure.
But evermore my shield did me defend,
Against the storme of every dreadfull stoure˃: *conflict*
Thus safely with my love I thence did wend.
So ended he his tale, where I this Canto end.

1596

[The main business of the concluding cantos is to bring together Florimell and Marinell. Canto xi is a big set-piece, which Spenser had possibly had for some years in a drawer, describing the marriage of the rivers Thames and Medway. It fits, in general, the theme of concord resolving discord, but emphasizes the loose-knit quality of IV; the union of Florimell and Marinell (of sea and land) also fits the theme, but neither the characters nor the theme have the centrality and the climactic quality one finds at the conclusion of the earlier books. However, Alastair Fowler, in his study of the numerological patterns of *The Faerie Queene* (*Spenser and the Numbers of Time*, 1964), claims that on the basis of such patterns he sees the fourth "as in many ways the most unified of all the books of *The Faerie Queene*."]

Book VI

Book VI is the legend of Courtesy; the knight Calidore must quest after the Blatant Beast. As in I, II, and V, the knight meets his predecessor in canto i, and in this opening there is a seed of all the rest. After encountering many *exempla* of courtesy and discourtesy Calidore drops out, rather as Red Cross did, in mid-course, going into a "pastoral truancy" and neglecting his quest. But the tone of the Book is new; it lacks deep allegories like those in the "core" cantos of earlier Books. Instead Spenser includes something quite different, the scene in which the Graces appear to Colin Clout, as given below.

Spenser means more by "courtesy" than agreeableness of manner. In his Proem he distinguishes between that, and something more noble and inclusive. Courtesy is a gentleman's or nobleman's standard of conduct, the virtue which poems of this kind

Leman Eurydice, temporarily brought back from the underworld by the music of her husband Orpheus

were meant to develop, when they undertook, as Spenser did in the Letter to Ralegh, "to fashion a gentleman or noble person in vertuous and gentle discipline." Gentle birth was a prerequisite for its possession; even courteous savages will turn out to have been well born. Of course, the gentle can fall into discourtesy.

Courtesy, in the full sense of "civility" or "gentleness" given it by the Elizabethans, is *noblesse oblige*—what makes for decency, honor, and harmony in civil and military life. It was a fashionable subject, and courtesy books abounded, Castiglione's *The Courtier,* which Hoby translated into English, being only the most famous. Their precepts—aimed at fashioning gentlemen by example and ethical instruction—Spenser takes over in this Book, translating them into a romance narrative which, more than his others, approximates to the mood and style of Greek romance, and especially to the novella *Daphnis and Chloe* of Longus (probably 3rd century B.C.). He was also remembering the courtesy of Sidney, and the example of his prose-epic *Arcadia.* There is every reason to think that Shakespeare in turn was affected by Book VI when he wrote his final plays.

Calidore is bound to put down slander and evil speaking at its source, but also to demonstrate the gentleness of the gentleman: to be mild when that is appropriate, to champion women, show politeness to inferiors, and oppose all manifestations of discourtesy. In the course of some strange stories we see him doing this, chastising a churl for cutting off people's hair, righting the wrongs of ladies. He meets Childe Tristram, a wild young man of the forest, and at once detects his royal birth. He tends a wounded knight, and, by a knightly equivocation, saves a lady, caught in a compromising position with her lover, from her father's anger. Stumbling on a secluded pair of lovers, he manages to convince them that his intentions are innocent, and when the lady, Serena, is carried off by the Blatant Beast, he rescues her. The lover, Calepine, then takes Serena to the castle of Sir Turpine, a discourteous knight who refuses them admittance. Turpine and Calepine fight, and Calepine is saved by a courteous "salvage man," who also turns out to have been nobly born. The savage cures Calepine's wounds, but the knight gets lost, and Serena, traveling now with the savage, meets Arthur with Timias (Ralegh), who is being slandered (an allusion to Ralegh's fall into royal disfavor when he secretly married the lady-in-waiting Elizabeth Throckmorton). Timias and Serena are cured of the wound of slander by a hermit's psychological counseling; Arthur and the savage defeat Turpine and courteously allow him and his wife Blandina to live; but on a recurrence of treachery Arthur hangs Turpine by his heels from a tree. Meanwhile Timias and Serena meet Mirabella, who is undergoing a grotesque punishment for treating her lovers discourteously. Timias is captured by Disdain, and Arthur frees him. Calepine turns up just in time to save Serena from a band of cannibals who are admiring her naked body as a prelude to consuming it—this is one of the most sensual passages in the poem; the prurience of these savages represents a great enemy of courtesy.

Having neglected Calidore for a long time, Spenser now returns to him, describing his "truancy," his sojourn in the idyllic pastoral retreat of Pastorella and her (supposed) father Meliboee. The knight lives the life of pastoral content, described by Meliboee in lines (ix.20–21) that may have been in Shakespeare's mind when he conducted his lighthearted but searching examination of the pastoral conventions in *As You Like It.* Meliboee attacks gardens, emblems of the interference of art with nature, rather as Marvell's Mower does (see below). Calidore accepts the pastoral life, and when a rustic swain of Pastorella's grows jealous, he treats him with courtesy. The girl begins to love Calidore, but Spenser reminds us that his time is not his own, and that he should not be "Unmyndful of his vow and high beheast." Yet it is in the midst of this premature retirement from the life of action that he is blessed with the vision of the maidens dancing around the three Graces to the music of Colin Clout, representing Spenser himself.

The Graces usually appear in a group, usually with one facing the spectator. Here (in vi. x. 1–28) they represent the civil delight which good love spreads through human society—they are often associated with Venus—and are the opposites of the vices associated with discourtesy. The presence of Colin makes this a rare autobiographical interlude, strangely occurring at a crucial point in the Book; Spenser places his own love at the center, and shows himself singing her praises. He seems to be saying that his labors on the huge poem were interrupted by the personal matters described in the *Amoretti* and *Epithalamion,* poems which must have caused him to break off the epic in Book VI. He himself has been guilty of a "pastoral truancy," and in stanza 27 he asks pardon of the Queen for introducing this passage in praise of her "poore handmayd," for, after all, he had spent his life celebrating her greater glory. The girl is almost certainly Elizabeth Boyle, though some say she is the Rosalind of *The Shepheardes Calender* and *Colin Clout;* the tone of the poet's praise of her, mediator of delight and virtue through love, is close to that of *Epithalamion.*

From Canto x

Calidore sees the Graces daunce,
  To Colins melody:
The whiles his Pastorell is led,
  Into captivity.

1 Who now does follow the foule *Blatant Beast,*
  Whilest *Calidore* does follow that faire Mayd,
  Unmyndfull of his vow and high beheast,
  Which by the Faery Queene was on him layd,
  That he should never leave, nor be delayd
  From chacing him, till he had it attchieved?
  But now entrapt of love, which him betrayd,
  He mindeth more, how he may be relieved
With grace from her, whose love his heart hath sore engrieved.

2 That from henceforth he meanes no more to sew> *follow*
  His former quest, so full of toile and paine;
  Another quest, another game in vew
  He hath, the guerdon> of his love to gaine: *reward*
  With whom he myndes for ever to remaine,
  And set his rest amongst the rusticke sort,
  Rather then hunt still after shadowes vaine
  Of courtly favour, fed with light report
Of every blaste, and sayling alwaies in the port.°

3 Ne certes mote he greatly blamèd be,
  From so high step to stoupe unto so low.

sayling . . . port prevented by headwinds from getting anywhere

For who had tasted once (as oft did he)
The happy peace, which there doth overflow,
And prov'd the perfect pleasures, which doe grow
Amongst poore hyndes,˃ in hils, in woods, in dales, *country folk*
Would never more delight in painted show
Of such false blisse, as there is set for stales,˃ *baits*
T'entrap unwary fooles in their eternall bales.˃ *evils*

4 For what hath all that goodly glorious gaze
Like to one sight, which *Calidore* did vew?
The glaunce whereof their dimmèd eies would daze,
That never more they should endure the shew
Of that sunne-shine, that makes them looke askew.
Ne ought in all that world of beauties rare,
(Save onely *Glorianaes* heavenly hew˃ *form*
To which what can compare?) can it compare;°
The which as commeth now, by course I will declare.

5 One day as he did raunge the fields abroad,
Whilest his faire *Pastorella* was elsewhere,
He chaunst to come, far from all peoples troad,˃ *tread*
Unto a place, whose pleasaunce did appere
To passe all others, on the earth which were:
For all that ever was by natures skill
Devized to worke delight, was gathered there,
And there by her were pourèd forth at fill,
As if this to adorne, she all the rest did pill.˃ *plunder*

6 It was an hill plaste in an open plaine,
That round about was bordered with a wood
Of matchlesse hight, that seem'd th'earth to disdaine,
In which all trees of honour stately stood,
And did all winter as in sommer bud,°
Spredding pavilions for the birds to bowre,
Which in their lower braunches sung aloud;
And in their tops the soring hauke did towre,˃ *perch high*
Sitting like King of fowles in majesty and powre.

7 And at the foote thereof, a gentle flud
His silver waves did softly tumble downe,
Unmard with ragged mosse or filthy mud,
Ne mote wylde beastes, ne mote the ruder clowne
Thereto approach, ne filth mote therein drowne:
But Nymphes and Faeries by the bancks did sit,
In the woods shade, which did the waters crowne,
Keeping all noysome things away from it,
And to the waters fall tuning their accents fit.

can . . . compare can rival it

all winter . . . bud yet another view of the Earthly Paradise

8 And on the top thereof a spacious plaine
Did spred it selfe, to serve to all delight,
Either to daunce, when they to daunce would faine,
Or else to course about their bases light;°
Ne ought there wanted, which for pleasure might
Desirèd be, or thence to banish bale:
So pleasauntly the hill with equall hight,
Did seeme to overlooke the lowly vale;
Therefore it rightly cleepèd was mount *Acidale*.°

9 They say that *Venus*, when she did dispose
Her selfe to pleasaunce, usèd to resort
Unto this place, and therein to repose
And rest her selfe, as in a gladsome port,
Or with the Graces there to play and sport;
That even her owne Cytheron,° though in it
She usèd most to keepe her royall court,
And in her soveraine Majesty to sit,
She in regard hereof° refusde and thought unfit.

10 Unto this place when as the Elfin Knight
Approcht, him seemèd that the merry sound
Of a shrill pipe he playing heard on hight,
And many feete fast thumping th'hollow ground,
That through the woods their Eccho did rebound.
He nigher drew, to weete what mote it be;
There he a troupe of Ladies dauncing found
Full merrily, and making gladfull glee,
And in the midst of Shepheard piping he did see.

11 He durst not enter into th'open greene,
For dread of them unwares to be descryde,
For breaking of their daunce, if he were seene;
But in the covert of the wood did byde,
Beholding all, yet of them unespyde.
There he did see, that pleasèd much his sight,
That even he himselfe his eyes envyde,
An hundred naked maidens lilly white,
All raungèd in a ring, and dauncing in delight.

12 All they without were raungèd in a ring,
And dauncèd round; but in the midst of them
Three other Ladies did both daunce and sing,
The whilest the rest them round about did hemme,
And like a girlond did in compasse stemme

to course . . . light to play the game of prisoner's base
Acidale the name of the Muses' fountain (see *Epithalamion*, l. 310) but here transferred to the hill because of its association with Greek *akades*, "carefree," or because of Latin *acies*, sight, view, here combined with *dale*
Cytheron Cythera, Venus' island, was sometimes confused with the mountain Citheron in Greece.
in regard hereof compared with this

And in the middest of those same three, was placed
Another Damzell, as a precious gemme,
Amidst a ring most richly well enchaced,
That with her goodly presence all the rest much graced.

13 Looke how the Crowne, which *Ariadne* wore
Upon her yvory forehead that same day,
That *Theseus* her unto his bridale bore,
When the bold *Centaures* made that bloudy fray,
With the fierce *Lapithes*, which did them dismay;
Being now placèd in the firmament,
Through the bright heaven doth her beams display,
And is unto the starres an ornament,
Which round about her move in order excellent.°

14 Such was the beauty of this goodly band,
Whose sundry parts were here too long to tell:
But she that in the midst of them did stand,
Seem'd all the rest in beauty to excell,
Crownd with a rosie girlond, that right well
Did her beseeme. And ever, as the crew
About her daunst, sweet flowres, that far did smell,
And fragrant odours they uppon her threw;
But most of all, those three did her with gifts endew.

15 Those were the Graces, daughters of delight,
Handmaides of *Venus*, which are wont to haunt˃ *sojourn*
Uppon this hill, and daunce there day and night:
Those three to men all gifts of grace do graunt,
And all, that *Venus* in her selfe doth vaunt,
Is borrowèd of them. But that faire one,
That in the midst was placed paravaunt,˃ *in foremost place*
Was she to whom that shepheard pypt alone,
That made him pipe so merrily, as never none.

16 She was to weete˃ that jolly Shepheards lasse, *to wit*
Which pipèd there unto that merry rout,
That jolly shepheard, which there pipèd, was
Poore *Colin Clout* (who knowes not *Colin Clout*?)
He pypt apace, whilest they him daunst about.
Pype jolly shepheard, pype thou now apace
Unto thy love, that made thee low to lout:˃ *bow*
Thy love is present there with thee in place,
Thy love is there advaunst to be another Grace.

17 Much wondred *Calidore* at this straunge sight,
Whose like before his eye had never seene,
And standing long astonishèd in spright,

Looke how . . . excellent (stanza 13) refers to the constellation, but the fight Spenser mentions occurred at the wedding of Pirithous and Hippodamia

And rapt with pleasaunce, wist not what to weene;
Whether it were the traine of beauties Queene,
Or Nymphes, or Faeries, or enchaunted show,
With which his eyes mote have deluded beene.
Therefore resolving, what it was, to know,
Out of the wood he rose, and toward them did go.

18 But soone as he appearèd to their vew,
They vanisht all away out of his sight,
And cleane were gone, which way he never knew;
All save the shepheard, who for fell despight
Of that displeasure, broke his bag-pipe quight,
And made great mone for that unhappy turne.
But *Calidore,* though no lesse sory wight,
For that mishap, yet seeing him to mourne,
Drew neare, that he the truth of all by him mote learne.

19 And first him greeting, thus unto him spake,
Haile jolly shepheard, which thy joyous dayes
Here leadest in this goodly merry make,> *merrymaking*
Frequented of these gentle Nymphes alwayes,
Which to thee flocke, to heare thy lovely layes;
Tell me, what mote these dainty Damzels be,
Which here with thee doe make their pleasant playes?
Right happy thou, that mayst them freely see:
But why when I them saw, fled they away from me?

20 Not I so happy, answerd then that swaine,
As thou unhappy, which them thence didst chace,
Whome by no meanes thou canst recall againe,
For being gone, none can them bring in place,
But whom they of themselves list so to grace.
Right sory I, (saide then Sir *Calidore,*)
That my ill fortune did them hence displace.
But since things passèd none may now restore,
Tell me, what were they all, whose lacke thee grieves so sore.

21 Tho> gan that shepheard thus for to dilate; *then*
Then wote thou shepheard, whatsoever thou bee,
That all those Ladies, which thou sawest late,
Are *Venus* Damzels, all within her fee,> *service*
But differing in honour and degree:
They all are Graces, which on her depend,
Besides a thousand more, which ready bee
Her to adorne, when so she forth doth wend:
But those three in the midst, doe chiefe on her attend.

22 They are the daughters of sky-ruling Jove,
By him begot of faire *Eurynome,*°

Eurynome daughter of Ocean and mother of the Graces

The Oceans daughter, in this pleasant grove,
As he this way comming from feastfull glee,
Of *Thetis* wedding with *Æacidee*,°
In sommers shade him selfe here rested weary.
The first of them hight mylde *Euphrosyne*,
Next faire *Aglaia*, last *Thalia* merry:
Sweete Goddesses all three which me in mirth do cherry.> *cheer*

23 These three on men all gracious gifts bestow,
Which decke the body or adorne the mynde,
To make them lovely or well favoured show,
As comely carriage, entertainement> kynde, *behavior to others*
Sweete semblaunt,> friendly offices that bynde, *demand*
And all the complements of curtesie:
They teach us, how to each degree and kynde
We should our selves demeane,> to low, to hie; *conduct*
To friends, to foes, which skill men call Civility.

24 Therefore they alwaies smoothly seeme to smile,
That we likewise should mylde and gentle be,
And also naked are, that without guile
Or false dissemblaunce all them plaine may see,
Simple and true from covert malice free:
And eeke them selves so in their daunce they bore,
That two of them still froward> seem'd to bee, *turned away*
But one still tòwards shew'd her selfe afore;
That good should from us goe, then come in greater store.

25 Such were those Goddesses, which ye did see;
But that fourth Mayd, which there amidst them traced,
Who can aread,> what creature mote she bee, *tell*
Whether a creature, or a goddesse graced
With heavenly gifts from heven first enraced?> *implanted*
But what so sure she was, she worthy was,
To be the fourth with those three other placed:
Yet was she certes but a countrey lasse,
Yet she all other countrey lasses farre did passe.

26 So farre as doth the daughter of the day,°
All other lesser lights in light excell,
So farre doth she in beautyfull array,
Above all other lasses beare the bell,> *gains victory*
Ne lesse in vertue that beseemes her well,
Doth she exceede the rest of all her race,
For which the Graces that here wont to dwell,
Have for more honor brought her to this place,
And gracèd her so much to be another Grace.

Æacidee Peleus, son of Aeacus, whose wedding (he married Thetis) was attended by the gods

daughter of the day the evening (and morning) star, Venus

27 Another Grace she well deserves to be,
In whom so many Graces gathered are,
Excelling much the meane of her degree;
Divine resemblaunce, beauty soveraine rare,
Firme Chastity, that spight ne blemish dare;
All which she with such courtesie doth grace,
That all her peres cannot with her compare,
But quite are dimmèd when she is in place.
She made me often pipe and now to pipe apace.> *copiously*

28 Sunne of the world, great glory of the sky,
That all the earth doest lighten with thy rayes,
Great *Gloriana,* greatest Majesty,
Pardon thy shepheard, mongst so many layes,
As he hath sung of thee in all his dayes,
To make one minime> of thy poore handmayd, *musical note*
And underneath thy feete to place her prayse,
That when thy glory shall be farre displayd
To future age of her this mention may be made.

. . .

1596

[The pastoral calm is abruptly broken when brigands attack the settlement and carry off Pastorella, Meliboee, and others. Then the brigands fight with slavers, and all their prisoners are killed except Pastorella, whom Calidore rescues from under a heap of bodies. The courtesy of innocence, he has discovered, is too vulnerable; in the wicked world we have there must be men of chivalry perpetually ready for the defense of innocence and courtesy. Pastorella, identified by a birthmark, is restored to her noble parents; Calidore captures the Blatant Beast, but it escapes, and, says Spenser, waxes even more mischievous and outrageous, not even sparing poets.

On this inconclusive note, introduced as a sad afterthought in the last four stanzas, the unfinished poem comes to a stop, except for the fragment of another Book which was published in 1609. This is made up of the Two Cantos of Mutability, and the publisher guesses that they are part of a legend of Constancy, labeling them cantos vi, vii, and viii 1–2 of that Book.]

Two Cantos of Mutability

It appears most likely that Spenser wrote these as the "core" cantos, leaving the rest of the work, which would have to be devoted more to narrative, for later completion; for example, there is no reason why the Garden of Adonis canto in Book III should not have been written separately and in advance. The view that these are early and rejected drafts seems incomprehensible, considering that they contain Spenser's finest philosophical poetry.

Canto vi proposes the topic of Change or Mutability, opposite of Constancy, and calls Mutability a daughter of the Titans (charged in Book V with the guilt of having brought rebellion and intemperance into the world). She has altered the original order of creation, defaced Nature and Justice, and brought death into life; she is, in fact under one aspect, the image of the disaster of the Fall. Having ruined earth, she aspires to the heavens which are beyond the moon, below which her power is admitted by all. First she claims the moon, whose sphere is the border between the two worlds; an eclipse strikes terror and creates the fear that Chaos is coming again. Mercury investigates for Jupiter, who explains to the heavenly powers that a Titan's daughter is again challenging them. Mutability arrives to state her claim. Jupiter admires her beauty, but chides her, asserting his obvious preeminence. She claims a hearing in a higher court, that of Nature, and a hearing is appointed, to be held on Arlo Hill in Spenser's Ireland.

Spenser now makes a myth, based on Ovid, to explain why this beautiful place (used in the previous Book as the dancing place of the Graces) should have lost some of its original loveliness and innocence. Then, in canto vii, the hearing is described.

The success of these cantos depends on Spenser's ability to convert philosophical explanations into myths of his own devising, and therefore fitting the basic patterns of his imagination. Scholarship has said much about the sources—in Ovid, Lucretius, the neo-platonists, in Boethius, the mainstay of medieval philosophy, and even in the thought of Spenser's contemporary, Giordano Bruno, who spent some time in London and Oxford before being condemned as a heretic by the Inquisition. Probably he depended on no particular source—philosophically, what he says on this subject both here and in III.vi is not very different from the speech of Theseus at the end of Chaucer's Knight's Tale: God is stable and eternal, but has decreed that "speces of thinges and progressiouns / Shullen enduren by successiouns, / And nat eterne be, withoute lye." But the whole joint development of thought and myth—or thought-in-myth—is Spenserian.

Ovid, the classic poet of mutability (his greatest work is the *Metamorphoses*), was in Spenser's mind; he borrowed from Ovid not only Nature (again see the opening lines of the *Metamorphoses*), trimming it with other material from the long tradition, but also three strands of narrative: the challenge of Mutability, the story of Faunus in vi, and the pageant of times and seasons in vii. From Ovid he also borrowed a speech attributed to Pythagoras on the subject of change. But he is not a "classical" poet; he admits medieval elements, and also understands things in a Christian sense. The relation of Time and Eternity—the root problem, since time is the agent of change—he sees in a Christian light, remembering the great medieval commonplaces. Here the answer is quite like that of III.vi. Adonis, though "subject to mortalitee / Yet is eterne in mutabilitie, / And by succession made perpetuall." Boethius said that "all things rejoice to return again to their own nature," and that in the long run they do not change except insofar as change may bring them to the perfection potential in their natures. This also implies change and decay; but the two things are complementary, and mutability is the servant of the eternality of things.

Mutability may reflect, as Spenser often does, contemporary convictions of the rapid decay of the world, but she also represents something that delighted him, which is why he makes her beautiful, and why this myth goes very deep with him. "All change is sweet," he says in *Muiopotmos,* and, at the very end of the poem, "for all that moveth, doth in *Change* delight." The beauty and variety of the physical world are a consequence of mutability. Thus Mutability has the better arguments, and Jupiter merely storms; Nature ends the dispute only by means of a mysterious answer, but one in which gnomic language underlines what mythological invention has already achieved, the reconciliation of opposites.

From Canto vii

3 Now, at the time that was before agreed,
The Gods assembled all on *Arlo*° hill;
As well those that are sprung of heavenly seed,
As those that all the other world doe fill,
And rule both sea and land unto their will:
Onely th'infernall Powers might not appeare;
As well for horror of their count'naunce ill,
As for th'unruly fiends which they did feare;
Yet *Pluto* and *Proserpina*° were present there.

4 And thither also came all other creatures,
What-ever life or motion doe retaine,
According to their sundry kinds of features;
That *Arlo* scarsly could them all containe;
So full they fillèd every hill and Plaine:
And had not *Natures* Sergeant (that is *Order*)
Them well disposèd by his busie paine,
And raungèd farre abroad in every border,
They would have causèd much confusion and disorder.

5 Then forth issewed (great goddesse) great dame *Nature*°
With goodly port and gracious Majesty;
Being far greater and more tall of stature
Then any of the gods or Powers on hie:
Yet certès by her face and physnomy,
Whether she man or woman inly were,
That could not any creature well descry:
For, with a veile that wimpled> every where *covered*
Her head and face was hid, that mote to none appeare.

6 That some doe say was so by skill devizèd,
To hide the terror of her uncouth> hew, *unknown*
From mortall eyes that should be sore agrizèd;> *horrified*
For that her face did like a Lion shew,
That eye of wight could not indure to view:
But others tell that it so beautious was,
And round about such beames of splendor threw,
That it the Sunne a thousand times did pass,
Ne could be seene, but like an image in a glass.

Arlo hill near Spenser's estate at Kilcolman
Pluto and Proserpina king and queen of hell
dame Nature As he suggests, Spenser owes something to Alanus, *De Planctu Naturae*, and more directly to Chaucer's *Parliament of Fowls* for this figure. The veil and the hermaphroditism probably come from Plutarch's Isis and Osiris, on which he also drew for III.vi and V.x vii; and just as the philosophical argument partly parallels that of III.vi, so the presentation of the figure of Nature is reminiscent of the hermaphrodite Venus of IV.x. Here he succeeds marvelously in attributing to Nature beauty and terror, mystery and authority, fertility and order.

7 That well may seemen true: for, well I weene
That this same day, when she on *Arlo* sat,
Her garment was so bright and wondrous sheene,> *fair*
That my fraile wit cannot devize to what
It to compare, nor finde like stuffe to that,
As those three sacred *Saints,* though else most wise,
Yet on mount *Thabor* quite their wits forgat,
When they their glorious Lord in strange disguise
Transfigur'd sawe;° his garments so did daze their eyes.

8 In a fayre Plaine upon an equall> Hill, *symmetrical*
She placèd was in a pavilión;
Not such as Craftes-men by their idle> skill *vain*
Are wont for Princes states to fashión:
But th'earth her self of her owne motión,
Out of her fruitfull bosome made to growe
Most dainty trees; that, shooting up anon,
Did seeme to bow their bloosming heads full lowe,
For homage unto her, and like a throne did shew.

9 So hard it is for any living wight,
All her array and vestiments to tell,
That old *Dan Geffrey*° (in whose gentle spright
The pure well head of Poesie did dwell)
In his *Foules parley*° durst not with it mel,
But it transferd to *Alane,*° who he thought
Had in his *Plaint of kindes*° describ'd it well:
Which who will read set forth so as it ought,
Go seek he out that *Alane* where he may be sought.

10 And all the earth far underneath her feete
Was dight with flowres, that voluntary grew
Out of the ground, and sent forth odours sweet;
Tenne thousand mores> of sundry sent and hew, *roots, plants*
That might delight the smell, or please the view;
The which, the Nymphes, from all the brooks thereby
Had gathered, which° they at her foot-stoole threw;
That richer seem'd then any tapestry,
That Princes bowres adorne with painted imagery.

11 And *Mole*° himself, to honour her the more,
Did deck himself in freshest faire attire,

those three . . . sawe Matthew 17:1–2, Mark 9:6: "And after six days Jesus taketh Peter, James and John his brother, and bringeth them up into a high mountain apart, and was transfigured before them: and his face did shine with the sun, and his raiment was white as the light . . . they were sore afraid"
Dan Geffrey Chaucer
Foules parley *The Parliament of Fowls*
Alane Alanus de (ab) Insulis, Alain de l'Isle (c.1128–1203), French Cistercian theologian, author of satirical poem cited in the following line.
Plaint of kinds *De Planctu Naturae;* Chaucer says: "And right as Aleyn, in the Pleynt of Kinde, / Devyseth Nature of aray and face, / In swich aray men mighten hir ther finde" (*The Parliament of Fowls,* ll. 316–18)
which redundant syntactically, and also metrically if one says *gatherèd*
Mole forest near Kilcolman

And his high head, that seemeth alwaies hore
With hardned frosts of former winters ire,
He with an Oaken girlond now did tire,> *dress*
As if the love of some new Nymph late seene,
Had in him kindled youthfull fresh desire,
And made him change his gray attire to greene;
Ah gentle *Mole!* such joyance hath thee well beseene.> *become*

12 Was never so great joyance since the day,
That all the gods whylome> assembled were, *once*
On *Hæmus hill*° in their divine array,
To celebrate the solemne bridall cheare,
Twixt *Peleus,* and dame *Thetis*° pointed> there; *appointed*
Where *Phœbus* self, that god of Poets hight,
They say did sing the spousall hymne full cleere,
That all the gods were ravisht with delight
Of his celestiall song, and Musicks wondrous might.

13 This great Grandmother of all creatures bred
Great *Nature,* ever young yet full of eld,
Still mooving, yet unmovèd from her sted;> *position*
Unseene of any, yet of all beheld;°
Thus sitting in her throne as I have teld,
Before her came dame *Mutabilitie;*
And being lowe before her presence feld,> *fallen*
With meek obaysance and humilitie,
Thus gan her plaintif Plea, with words to amplifie;

14 To thee O greatest goddesse, onely> great, *alone*
An humble suppliant loe, I lowely fly
Seeking for Right, which I of thee entreat;
Who Right to all dost deale indifferently,
Damning all Wrong and tortious> Injurie, *wrongful*
Which any of thy creatures doe to other
(Oppressing them with power, unequally)
Sith of them all thou art the equall> mother, *impartial*
And knittest each to each, as brother unto brother.

15 To thee therefore of this same *Jove* I plaine,> *complain*
And of his fellow gods that faine to be,
That challenge> to themselves the whole worlds raign; *claim*
Of which, the greatest part is due to me,
And heaven it selfe by heritage in Fee:> *right of inheritance*
For, heaven and earth I both alike do deeme,
Sith heaven and earth are both alike to thee;

Hæmus hill hill in Thessaly
Peleus . . . Thetis See XI.x.22n.
ever young . . . beheld This reconciliation of opposites in Nature states the main theme of the Mutability Cantos, and one of Spenser's most radically important poetic preoccupations. Furthermore, in her ability to be "Still mooving, yet unmovèd from her sted," Nature contains the secret answer to Mutability, who cannot understand the possibility of reconciling stillness and movement, or time and eternity.

And, gods no more then men thou doest esteeme:
For, even the gods to thee, as men to gods do seeme.

16 Then weigh, O soveraigne goddesse, by what right
These gods do claime the worlds whole soverainty;
And that> is onely> dew unto thy might *that which / solely*
Arrogate to themselves ambitiously:
As for the gods owne principality,
Which *Jove* usurpes unjustly; that to be
My heritage, *Jove's* self cannot deny,
From my great Grandsire *Titan,* unto mee,
Deriv'd by dew descent; as is well knowen to thee.

17 Yet mauger> *Jove,* and all his gods beside, *in spite of*
I doe possesse the worlds most regiment;> *rule*
As, if ye please it into parts divide,
And every parts inholders> to convent,> *tenants / summon*
Shall to your eyes appeare incontinent.> *immediately*
And first, the Earth (great mother of us all)
That only> seems unmov'd and permanent, *alone*
And unto *Mutability* not thrall;
Yet is she chang'd in part, and eeke in generall.°

18 For, all that from her springs, and is ybredde,
How-ever fayre it flourish for a time,
Yet see we soone decay; and, being dead,
To turne again unto their earthly slime:
Yet, out of their decay and mortall crime,°
We daily see new creatures to arize;
And of their Winter spring another Prime,> *spring*
Unlike in forme, and chang'd by strange disguise:
So turne they still about, and change in restlesse wise.

19 As for her tenants; that is, man and beasts,
The beasts we daily see massácred dy,
As thralls and vassalls unto mens beheasts:> *commands*
And men themselves doe change continually,
From youth to eld, from wealth to poverty,
From good to bad, from bad to worst of all.
Ne doe their bodies only flit and fly:
But eeke their minds (which they immortall call)
Still change and vary thoughts, as new occasions fall.

20 Ne is the water in more constant case;
Whether those same on high, or these belowe.°
For, th'Ocean moveth stil,> from place to place; *always*

Yet . . . generall The arguments of Mutability derive partly from the teaching of Pythagoras in Ovid, *Metamorphoses* XV, on the theme *omnia mutantur,* all things are changed.

mortall crime This is the association, inevitable in the period, between mutability and the consequences of the Fall.

on high . . . belowe Genesis 1:7

And every River still doth ebbe and flowe:
Ne any Lake, that seems most still and slowe;
Ne Poole so small, that can his smoothnesse holde,> *maintain*
When any winde doth under heaven blowe;
With which, the clouds are also tost and roll'd;
Now like great Hills; and, streight, like sluces, them unfold.

21 So likewise are all watry living wights
Still tost, and turnèd, with continuall change.
Never abyding in their stedfast plights.> *fixed conditions*
The fish, still floting, doe at randon range,
And never rest; but evermore exchange
Their dwelling places, as the streames them carrie:
Ne have the watry foules a certaine grange,> *dwelling*
Wherein to rest, ne in one stead> do tarry; *place*
But flitting still doe flie, and still their places vary.

22 Next is the Ayre: which who feeles not by sense
(For, of all sense it is the middle meane)°
To flit still? and, with subtill influence
Of this thin spirit,° all creatures to maintaine,
In state of life? O weake life! that does leane
On thing so tickle> as th'unsteady ayre; *unstable*
Which every howre is chang'd, and altred cleane> *completely*
With every blast that bloweth fowle or faire:
The faire doth it prolong; the fowle doth it impaire.

23 Therein the changes infinite beholde,
Which to her creatures every minute chaunce;
Now, boyling hot: streight, friezing deadly cold:
Now, faire sun-shine, that makes all skip and daunce:
Streight, bitter storms and balefull countenance,
That makes them all to shiver and to shake:
Rayne, hayle, and snowe do pay> them sad penance, *inflict on*
And dreadfull thunder-claps (that makes them quake)
With flames and flashing lights that thousand changes make.

24 Last is the fire: which, though it live for ever,
Ne can be quenchèd quite; yet, every day,
Wee see his parts, so soone as they do sever,
To lose their heat, and shortly to decay;
So, makes himself his owne consuming pray.
Ne any living creatures doth he breed:°
But all, that are of others bredd,° doth slay;
And, with their death, his cruell life dooth feed;
Nought leaving but their barren ashes, without seede.

middle meane medium, e.g. for scent and hearing
spirit monosyllabic
Ne . . . breed The salamander was sometimes excepted.
of others bredd bred of the other elements

25 Thus, all these fower° (the which the ground-work bee
Of all the world, and of all living wights)
To thousand sorts of *Change* we subject see.
Yet are they chang'd (by other wondrous slights˃) *tricks*
Into themselves,˃ and lose their native mights; *each other*
The Fire to Aire, and th'Ayre to Water sheere,˃ *bright*
And Water into Earth: yet Water fights
With Fire, and Aire with Earth approaching neere:
Yet all are in one body, and as one appeare.

26 So, in them all raignes *Mutabilitie*;
How-ever these, that Gods themselves do call,
Of them doe claime the rule and soverainty:
As, *Vesta*, of the fire æthereall;°
Vulcan, of this, with us so usuall;°
Ops,° of the earth; and *Juno* of the Ayre;
Neptune, of Seas; and Nymphes, of Rivers all.
For, all those Rivers to me subject are:
And all the rest, which they usurp, be all my share.

27 Which to approven true, as I have told,
Vouchsafe, O goddesse, to thy presence call
The rest which doe the world in being hold:
As, times and seasons of the yeare that fall:
Of all the which, demand in generall,
Or judge thy selfe, by verdit˃ of thine eye, *verdict*
Whether to me they are not subject all.
Nature did yeeld thereto; and by-and-by,
Bade *Order* call them all, before her Maiesty.

. . .

[There follows a lavish pageant of the Seasons, the Months, Day and Night, the Hours, and Life and Death. Mutability resumes her plea.]

47 When these were past, thus gan the *Titanesse*;
Lo, mighty mother, now be judge and say,
Whether in all thy creatures more or lesse˃ *greater or smaller*
CHANGE doth not raign and beare the greatest sway:
For, who sees not, that *Time* on all doth pray?
But *Times* do change and move continually.
So nothing here long standeth in one stay:
Wherefore, this lower world who can deny
But to be subject still to *Mutabilitie*?

48 Then thus gan *Jove*; Right true it is, that these
And all things else that under heaven dwell
Are chaung'd of *Time*, who doth them all disseise˃ *deprive*

fower the four elements, earth, water, air, fire, of which everything is constituted
Vesta . . . æthereall Vesta, goddess of holy fire, and so of the celestial fires of the heavens
Vulcan . . . usual Vulcan the smith, so god of the fire on earth, which is used for manufacture
Ops identified with Rhea and Gaea, names of the earth goddess

Of being: But, who is it (to me tell)
That *Time* himselfe doth move and still compell
To keepe his course? Is not that namely wee
Which poure that vertue˃ from our heavenly cell, *influence*
That moves them all, and makes them changèd be?
So them we gods doe rule, and in them also thee.

49 To whom, thus *Mutability:* The things
Which we see not how they are mov'd and swayd,
Ye may attribute to your selves as Kings,
And say they by your secret powre are made:
But what we see not, who shall us perswade?
But were they so, as ye them faine to be,
Mov'd by your might, and ordred by your ayde;
Yet what if I can prove, that even yee.
Your selves are likewise chang'd, and subject unto mee?

50 And first, concerning her that is the first,
Even you faire *Cynthia*,° whom so much ye make
Joves dearest darling, she was bread and nurst
On *Cynthus* hill, whence she her name did take:
Then is she mortall borne, how-so ye crake;˃ *boast*
Besides, her face and countenance every day
We changèd see, and sundry forms partake,
Now hornd, now round, now bright, now brown and gray:
So that *as changefull as the Moone* men use to say.

51 Next, *Mercury*, who though he lesse appeare
To change his hew,˃ and alwayes seeme as one; *form*
Yet, he his course doth altar˃ every yeare, *alter*
And is of late far out of order gone:°
So *Venus* eeke, that goodly Paragone,
Though faire all night, yet is she darke all day;
And *Phœbus* self, who lightsome is alone,˃ *alone is*
Yet is he oft eclipsèd by the way,
And fills the darkned world with terror and dismay.

52 Now *Mars* that valiant man is changèd most:
For, he some times so far runs out of square,
That he his way doth seem quite to have lost,
And cleane without his usuall sphere to fare;
That even these Star-gazers stonisht are
At sight thereof, and damne their lying bookes:
So likewise, grim Sir *Saturne* oft doth spare

Cynthia moon goddess, so called from Cynthus, a mountain in Delos. Spenser treats the moon as a planet, and goes on to deal with the other six of the old system: Mercury, Venus, the sun, Mars, Saturn, and Jupiter.

out of order gone See Proem to Book V, where Spenser confines his remarks on eccentric orbits to the sun, Mars, and Saturn. That Mercury, much harder to observe, was also eccentric, was a fairly recent discovery, and perhaps Spenser caught up with it between the writing of V and of these cantos. Of course all such eccentricities were consequent upon the mistaken view that planetary orbits were circular (see also the opening lines of Donne's "Good Friday, 1613. Riding Westward").

His sterne aspect, and calme his crabbèd lookes:
So many turning cranks these have, so many crookes.°

53 But you *Dan Jove,* that only constant are,
And King of all the rest, as ye do clame,
Are you not subject eek to this misfare?˃ *misfortune*
Then let me aske you this withouten blame,˃ *offense*
Where were ye borne? some say in *Crete* by name,
Others in *Thebes*, and others other-where;°
But wheresoever they comment˃ the same, *lyingly invent*
They all consent that ye begotten were,
And borne here in this world, ne other can appeare.

54 Then are ye mortall borne, and thrall to me,
Unlesse the kingdome of the sky yee make˃ *argue*
Immortall, and unchangeable to bee;
Besides, that power and vertue which ye spake,
That ye here worke, doth many changes take,
And your owne natures change: for, each of you.
That vertue have, or this, or that to make,
Is checkt and changèd from his nature trew,
By others opposition or obliquid view.°

55 Besides, the sundry motions of your Spheares,
So sundry waies and fashions as clerkes faine,
Some in short space, and some in longer yeares;
What is the same but alteration plaine?
Onely the starrie skie° doth still remaine:
Yet do the Starres and Signes therein still move,°
And even it self is mov'd, as wizards saine.°
But all that moveth, doth mutation love:
Therefore both you and them to me I subject prove.

56 Then since within this wide great *Universe*
Nothing doth firme and permanent appeare,
But all things tost and turnèd by transverse:˃ *haphazardly*
What then should let,˃ but I aloft should reare *hinder*
My Trophee, and from all, the triumph beare?
Now judge then (O thou greatest goddesse trew!)

cranks . . . crooks turnings and windings (alluding to the progressively more complex hypotheses of epicycles introduced to justify the Ptolemaic system in the light of observed eccentricities)
some . . . other-where There were conflicting traditions about Jupiter's birthplace, Crete, Thebes, and Arcadia being claimants: Natalis Comes, the Renaissance mythographer known to Spenser, sums up the matter as "very contentious."
each of you . . . view The influences of which the planets are capable are qualified and changed by their action on one another; *opposition* is the relation between two planets when their longitude differs by 180 degrees; an *obliquid* relation is more obliquely directed.
the starry skie the "crystalline" sphere of the fixed stars, held to be immutable and pure
Starres . . . move The movement referred to resulted from the effect on terrestrial observation of the precession of the equinoxes (cf. V, Proem).
it self . . . saine the crystalline sphere itself moves, according to astronomers. Ptolemy said that "inasmuch as the stars maintain their relative distances we may justly call them fixed, yet inasmuch as the whole sphere to which they are attached is in motion, the word 'fixed' is but little appropriate."

According as thy selfe doest see and heare,
And unto me addoom> that is my dew; *adjudicate*
That is the rule of all, all being rul'd by you.

57 So having ended, silence long ensewed,
Ne *Nature* to or fro spake for a space,
But with firme eyes affixt, the ground still viewed.
Meane while, all creatures, looking in her face,
Expecting th'end of this so doubtfull case,
Did hang in long suspence what would ensew,
To whether> side should fall the soveraigne place: *which*
At length, she looking up with chearefull view,
The silence brake, and gave her doome in speeches few.

58 I well consider all that ye have sayd,
And find that all things stedfastnes doe hate
And changèd be: yet being rightly wayd> *considered*
They are not changèd from their first estate;
But by their change their being doe dilate:
And turning to themselves at length againe,
Doe worke their owne perfection so by fate:
Then over them Change doth not rule and raigne;
But they raigne over change, and doe their states maintaine.

59 Cease therefore daughter further to aspire,
And thee content thus to be rul'd by me:
For thy decay thou seekst by thy desire;°
But time shall come that all shall changèd bee,
And from thenceforth, none no more change shall see.
So was the *Titaness* put downe and whist,> *silenced*
And *Jove* confirm'd in his imperiall see.> *throne*
Then was that whole assembly quite dismist,
And *Natur's* selfe did vanish, whither no man wist.> *knew*

The viii. Canto, unperfite> *unfinished*

1 When I bethinke me on that speech whyleare,> *recent*
Of *Mutability*, and well it way:
Me seemes, that though she all unworthy were
Of the Heav'ns Rule; yet very sooth to say,
In all things else she beares the greatest sway.
Which makes me loath this state of life so tickle,> *unstable*
And love of things so vaine to cast away;
Whose flowring pride, so fading and so fickle,
Short> *Time* shall soon cut down with his consuming sickle. *who shortens*

2 Then gin I thinke on that which Nature sayd,
Of that same time when no more *Change* shall be,

For . . . desire by your own wish to subject everything to mutability you unwittingly seek your own decay, since you will have to be mutable too

But stedfast rest of all things firmely stayd
Upon the pillours of Eternity,
That is contrayr to *Mutabilitie*:
For, all that moveth, doth in *Change* delight:
But thence-forth all shall rest eternally
With Him that is the God of Sabbaoth° hight:> *called*
O that great Sabbaoth God, graunt me that Sabaoths sight.°

1609

Amoretti

Amoretti means "little cupids"; Spenser's sonnet sequence, published in 1595 with the *Epithalamion*, is not only a collection of "little loves" (or expressions thereof), but a carefully constructed series of glimpses into the quasi-fictional sonnet world, part private and autobiographical, part mythological and shared with Sidney, Daniel, Drayton, and Shakespeare. Spenser married Elizabeth Boyle before the publication of the collection, and the poems seem to comprehend this cycle of courtship and marriage, interlaced with the cycle of the secular and liturgical year and even of phases of poetic work (numbers 33 and 80 refer to the unfinished *Faerie Queene*). Spenser's form combines French and English verse traditions in linking the sonnet quatrains with common rhymes (the interlocking of *The Faerie Queene* stanza) and maintaining or breaking the octave-sestet division at will (abab bcbc cdcd ee). Rhetorically less dynamic than the sonnets of Sidney or Shakespeare, they nevertheless present in a subtle way a variety of tones and stances.

From Amoretti

I

Happy ye leaves° when as those lilly hands,
which hold my life in their dead doing> might, *killing*
shall handle you and hold in loves soft bands,
lyke captives trembling at the victors sight.
And happy lines, on which with starry light,
those lamping> eyes will deigne sometimes to look *flashing*
and reade the sorrowes of my dying spright,> *spirit*
written with teares in harts close> bleeding book. *secret*
And happy rymes bath'd in the sacred brooke,
of *Helicon*° whence she derivèd is,
when ye behold that Angels blessèd looke,
my soules long lackèd foode, my heavens blis.

God of Sabbath God of Hosts
Sabaoths sight Spenser may mean "grant me sight of the Lord on the last day," but more probably he means *Sabbath* in the sense of eternity—the stillness that will follow the tumult of the six days of the world's history.
leaves pages of the book of the *Amoretti;* similarly the "lines" and "rymes"
the sacred . . . Helicon the fountain of Hippocrene on Mt. Helicon, sacred to the Muses, the mythical "source" (which word itself originally means "spring") of poetry, here "sacred" because of the Petrarchan heavenly associations with the sonneteer's muse

Leaves, lines, and rymes, seeke her to please alone,
whom if ye please, I care for other none.

1595

XV

Ye tradefull Merchants, that with weary toyle,
do seeke most pretious things to make your gain;
and both the Indias° of their treasures spoile,
what needeth you to seeke so farre in vaine?
For loe my love doth in her selfe containe
all this worlds riches that may farre be found,
if Saphyres,° loe her eies be Saphyres° plaine,> *clear*
if Rubies, loe hir lips be Rubies sound:
If Pearles, hir teeth be pearles both pure and round;
if Yvorie, her forhead yvory weene;> *beautiful*
if Gold, her locks are finest gold on ground;
if silver, her faire hands are silver sheene.
But that which fairest is, but few behold,
her mind adornd with vertues manifold.

1595

XVI

One day as I unwarily did gaze
on those fayre eyes my loves immortall light:
the whiles my stonisht hart stood in amaze,
through sweet illusion of her lookes delight.
I mote> perceive how in her glauncing sight, *could*
legions of loves° with little wings did fly:
darting their deadly arrowes fyry bright,
at every rash beholder passing by.
One of those archers closely> I did spy, *secretly*
ayming his arrow at my very hart:
when suddenly with twincle> of her eye, *blink*
the Damzell broke his misintended dart.
Had she not so doon, sure I had bene slayne,
yet as it was, I hardly> scap't with paine. *scarcely*

1595

LIV

Of this worlds Theatre° in which we stay,
My love lyke the Spectator ydly sits

Indias both East and West Indies
Saphyres This blazon of the Lady's beauties may stem from the comparisons of those of the beloved to rare artifacts in the Song of Songs 5:10–16, but it also reflects a contemporary convention: it is hard to believe that Shakespeare's Sonnet CXXX is not, particularly in ll. 3–4, parodying this poem.
loves The "amoretti," little cupids, fly along the "eyebeams" which interlock two lovers' gazes (see Donne, "The Ecstasy," for a complex use of this lore; behind Spenser's use of it lies the serious doctrine in his own *Hymne in Honour of Beautie*, ll. 231–45).
worlds Theatre The *theatrum mundi* commonplace, likening reality to a play, God to the author and director, the world to a set, and people to actors (the final curtain is, inevitably, Apocalypse), goes back originally to Plato; it is most familiar through Jaques's "All the world's a stage" speech in *As You Like It*, although it is uncommon in Petrarchan sonnets.

beholding me that all the pageants° play,
disguysing diversly my troubled wits.
Sometimes I joy when glad occasion fits,
and mask in myrth lyke to a Comedy:
soone after when my joy to sorrow flits,
I waile and make my woes a Tragedy.
Yet she beholding me with constant eye,
delights not in my merth> nor rues my smart:° *mirth*
but when I laugh she mocks, and when I cry
she laughs, and hardens evermore her hart.
What then can move her? if nor merth nor mone,> *moan*
she is no woman, but a sencelesse stone.

1595

LXIII

After long stormes and tempests sad assay,°
Which hardly I endurèd heretofore:
in dread of death and daungerous dismay,
with which my silly barke° was tossèd sore:
I doe at length descry the happy shore,
in which I hope ere long for to arryve;
fayre soyle it seemes from far and fraught with store°
of all that deare and daynty is alyve.
Most happy he that can at last atchyve
the joyous safety of so sweet a rest:
whose least delight sufficeth to deprive
remembrance of all paines which him opprest.
All paines are nothing in respect of this,
all sorrowes short that gaine eternall blisse.

1595

LXIV

Comming to kisse her lyps, (such grace I found)
me seemd I smelt a gardin of sweet flowres:°
that dainty odours from them threw around
for damzels fit to decke their lovers bowres.
Her lips did smell lyke unto Gillyflowers,
her ruddy cheekes lyke unto Roses red:
her snowy browes lyke budded Bellamoures,
her lovely eyes lyke Pincks> but newly spred. *carnations*
Her goodly bosome lyke a Strawberry bed,
her neck lyke to a bounch of Cullambynes:> *columbine*
her brest lyke lillyes, ere theyr leaves be shed,
her nipples lyke yong blossomd Jessemynes.> *jasmines*

pageants parts in the productions
rues my smart pities my sorrow
sad assay painful encounter (with storms)
silly barke innocent or simple ship: this is a commonplace (see Wyatt's "My Galley Chargèd with Forgetfullness")
fraught with store bounteously supplied
gardin of sweet flowres another sort of blazon or catalogue, going back to another source in Song of Songs (4:12–15), describing the lover as an enclosed garden

Such fragrant flowres doe give most odorous smell,
but her sweet odour did them all excell.

1595

LXXV

One day I wrote her name upon the strand,> *beach*
but came the waves and washèd it away:
agayne I wrote it with a second hand,
but came the tyde, and made my paynes his pray.> *prey*
Vayne man, sayd she, that doest in vaine assay,
a mortall thing so to immortalize,
for I my selve shall lyke to this decay,
and eek> my name bee wypèd out lykewize. *also*
Not so, (quod I) let baser things devize> *contrive*
to dy in dust, but you shall live by fame:
my verse your vertues rare shall eternize,°
and in the hevens wryte your glorious name.
Where whenas death shall all the world subdew,
our love shall live, and later life renew.

1595

Epithalamion

Epithalamion was published with the *Amoretti* in 1595. An epithalamion is a marriage song, and Spenser combines conventional features of the genre with strong personal applications, for he wrote the poem about his own wedding, to his second wife, Elizabeth Boyle. The wedding songs of Catullus are the type, and, as in Jonson in the masque *Hymenaei* and Herrick later, there are ceremonies and figures belonging more to a Roman than an English wedding; but Spenser, in the Renaissance manner, blends with these purely Christian figures, and also breaks with tradition in making the bridegroom the singer of the song.

In apparently freely flowing stanzas, Spenser invokes the Muses and follows the events of the wedding day, much in the Latin manner; the effect is of controlled abundance, an ordered joy appropriate to marriage and that desire of generation which is the honorable gift of the earthly Venus. And this effect is not impaired by the knowledge, recently achieved, that the poem has an elaborate hidden numerological structure. A. Kent Hieatt has demonstrated that the twenty-three stanzas and the envoy stand for the hours of the day, the last eight being the night hours, for the day of the wedding is the summer solstice. The day hours have the refrain, "The woods shall to me answer"; the night hours, "The woods no more shall answer." There are 365 long lines, one for each day of the year. There are other evidences of strict design, but the demands it made on Spenser did not prevent his achieving what C. S. Lewis calls "festal sublimity," any more than similar patterns, even more recently discovered in *The Faerie Queene,* cramp or diminish it.

eternize Poetry's ability to perpetuate beautiful lives in myth even longer than can statues or inscriptions in stone is an old theme (cf. Shakespeare's Sonnet LV: "Not marble, nor the gilded monuments"), and especially suited to the delight sonnet sequences took in referring to themselves.

Epithalamion

Ye learnèd sisters° which have oftentimes
Beene to me ayding, others° to adorne:
Whom ye thought worthy of your gracefull° rymes,
That even the greatest did not greatly scorne
To heare theyr names sung in your simple layes,
But joyèd in theyr prayse.
And when ye list˃ your owne mishaps to mourne, *choose*
Which death, or love, or fortunes wreck did rayse,
Your string could soone to sadder tenor° turne,
And teach the woods and waters to lament
Your dolefull dreriment.˃ *grief*
Now lay those sorrowfull complaints aside,
And having all your heads with girland crownd,
Helpe me mine owne loves prayses to resound,
Ne let the same of any be envide˃ *grudged*
So Orpheus did for his owne bride,°
So I unto my selfe alone will sing,
The woods shall to me answer and my Eccho ring.

Early before the worlds light giving lampe,
His golden beame upon the hils doth spred,
Having disperst the nights unchearefull dampe,
Doe ye awake, and with fresh lusty hed,˃ *vigor*
Go to the bowre of my belovèd love,
My truest turtle dove,
Bid her awake; for Hymen° is awake,
And long since ready forth his maske to move,°
With his bright Tead˃ that flames with many a flake,˃ *torch / spark*
And many a bachelor to waite on him,
In theyr fresh garments trim.
Bid her awake therefore and soone her dight,˃ *dress*
For lo the wishèd day is come at last,
That shall for al the paynes and sorrowes past,
Pay to her usury˃ of long delight: *interest*
And whylest she doth her dight,
Doe ye to her of joy and solace sing,
That all the woods may answer and your eccho ring.

Bring with you all the Nymphes that you can heare°
Both of the rivers and the forrests greene:
And of the sea that neighbours to her neare,°
Al with gay girlands goodly wel beseene.˃ *provided*

learnèd sisters the Muses
others e.g. Queen Elizabeth
gracefull conferring grace
sadder tenor graver mood, deeper note
So . . . bride Orpheus can plausibly be supposed to have provided an epithalamion for Eurydice.
Hymen god of marriage
his maske to move to lead the procession of revelers
that . . . heare that can hear you
sea . . . neare Elizabeth Boyle had been staying at Youghal near the sea.

And let them also with them bring in hand,
Another gay girland
For my fayre love of lillyes and of roses,
Bound truelove wize° with a blew silke riband.
And let them make great store of bridale poses,
And let them eeke bring store of other flowers
To deck the bridale bowers.
And let the ground whereas> her foot shall tread, *where*
For feare the stones her tender foot should wrong
Be strewed with fragrant flowers all along,
And diapred> lyke the discolorèd> mead. *strewn with flowers / multicolored*
Which done, doe at her chambre dore awayt,
For she will waken strayt,
The whiles doe ye this song unto her sing,
The woods shall to you answer and your Eccho ring.

Ye Nymphes of Mulla° which with carefull heed,
The silver scaly trouts doe tend full well;
And greedy pikes which use therein to feed,
(Those trouts and pikes all others doo excell)
And ye likewise which keepe the rushy lake,
Where none doo fishes take,
Bynd up the locks the which hang scatterd light,
And in his waters which your mirror make,
Byhold your faces as the christall bright,
That when you come whereas my love doth lie,
No blemish she may spie.
And eke ye lightfoot mayds which keepe the deere,
That on the hoary mountayne use to towre,°
And the wylde wolves which seeke them to devoure,
With your steele darts doo chace from comming neer
Be also present heere,
To helpe to decke her and to help to sing,
That all the woods may answer and your eccho ring.

Wake, now my love, awake; for it is time,
The Rosy Morne long since left Tithones bed,°
All ready to her silver coche to clyme,
And Phœbus gins to shew his glorious hed.
Hark how the cheerefull birds do chaunt theyr laies
And carroll of loves praise.
The merry Larke hir mattins sings aloft,
The thrush replyes, the Mavis> descant° playes. *thrush*
The Ouzell> shrills, the Ruddock> warbles soft, *blackbird / robin*
So goodly all agree with sweet consent,

truelove wize in a love knot
Mulla now the river Awbeg, which flows near Kilcolman
towre live high up
Tithones bed Tithonus is the husband of the Dawn; this is a stock expression, going back to Homer.
descant melody or counterpoint written above a simple musical theme. The concert (or "consort") of birds is a medieval convention.

To this dayes merriment.
Ah my deere love why doe ye sleepe thus long,
When meeter were that ye should now awake,
T'awayt the comming of your joyous make,> *mate*
And hearken to the birds lovelearnèd song,
The deawy leaves among.
For they of joy and pleasance to you sing,
That all the woods them answer and theyr eccho ring.

My love is now awake out of her dreame,
And her fayre eyes like stars that dimmèd were
With darksome cloud, now shew theyr goodly beams
More bright then Hesperus his head doth rere.
Come now ye damzels, daughters of delight,
Helpe quickly her to dight.
But first come ye fayre houres which were begot
In Joves sweet paradice, of Day and Night,°
Which doe the seasons of the yeare allot,
And al that ever in this world is fayre
Doe make and still> repayre. *ever*
And ye three handmayds of the Cyprian Queene,°
The which doe still adorne her beauties pride,
Helpe to addorne my beautifullest bride:
And as ye her array, still throw betweene
Some graces to be seene,
And as ye use> to Venus, to her sing, *do as a rule*
The whiles the woods shal answer and your eccho ring.

Now is my love all ready forth to come,
Let all the virgins therefore well awayt,
And ye fresh boyes that tend upon her groome
Prepare your selves; for he is comming strayt.
Set all your things in seemely good aray
Fit for so joyfull day,
The joyfulst day that ever sunne did see.
Faire Sun, shew forth thy favourable ray,
And let thy lifull> heat not fervent be *life-bestowing*
For feare of burning her sunshyny face,
Her beauty to disgrace.
O fayrest Phœbus, father of the Muse,
If ever I did honour thee aright,
Or sing the thing, that mote thy mind delight,
Doe not thy servants simple boone refuse,
But let this day let this one day be myne,
Let all the rest be thine.
Then I thy soverayne prayses loud wil sing,
That all the woods shal answer and theyr eccho ring.

of Day and Night more usually of Zeus and Themis—a little invention of Spenser's

three . . . Queene the Graces, attendant on Venus, as in *The Faerie Queene* VI.x

Harke how the Minstrels gin to shrill aloud
Their merry Musick that resounds from far,
The pipe, the tabor, and the trembling Croud,˃ *fiddle*
That well agree withouten breach or jar.˃ *discord*
But most of all the Damzels doe delite,
When they their tymbrels smyte,
And thereunto doe daunce and carrol sweet,
That all the sences they doe ravish quite,
The whyles the boyes run up and downe the street,
Crying aloud with strong confusèd noyce,˃ *noise*
As if it were one voyce.
Hymen io Hymen,° Hymen they do shout,
That even to the heavens theyr shouting shrill
Doth reach, and all the firmament doth fill,
To which the people standing all about,
As in approvance doe thereto applaud
And loud advaunce her laud,˃ *praise*
And evermore they Hymen Hymen sing,
That al the woods them answer and theyr eccho ring.

Loe where she comes along with portly˃ pace *stately*
Lyke Phœbe° from her chamber of the East,
Arysing forth to run her mighty race,
Clad all in white, that seemes a virgin best.
So well it her beseemes˃ that ye would weene *becomes*
Some angell she had beene.
Her long loose yellow locks lyke golden wyre,
Sprinckled with perle, and perling flowres a tweene,
Doe lyke a golden mantle her attyre,
And being crownèd with a girland greene,
Seeme lyke some mayden Queene.
Her modest eyes abashèd to behold
So many gazers, as on her do stare,
Upon the lowly ground affixèd are.
Ne dare lift up her countenance too bold,
But blush to heare her prayses sung so loud,
So farre from being proud.
Nathlesse doe ye still loud her prayses sing.
That all the woods may answer and your eccho ring.

Tell me ye merchants daughters did ye see
So fayre a creature in your towne before,
So sweet, so lovely, and so mild as she,
Adornd with beautyes grace and vertues store,
Her goodly eyes° lyke Saphyres shining bright,

Hymen io Hymen traditional wedding cry (see *The Faerie Queen* I.i.48)

Phoebe moon goddess, who borrows from her brother Phoebus the sun, "which is as a bridegroom coming out of his chamber, and rejoiceth as a strong man to run a race" (Psalms 15:5): Spenser transfers all this to the virgin bride.

goodly eyes This begins a conventional catalogue of beauties known as the blazon; cf. Sonnet XV of the *Amoretti*.

Her forehead yvory white,
Her cheekes lyke apples which the sun hath rudded,˃ *reddened*
Her lips lyke cherryes charming men to byte,
Her brest like to a bowle of creame uncrudded,˃ *uncurdled*
Her paps lyke lyllies budded,
Her snowie necke lyke to a marble towre,
And all her body like a pallace fayre,
Ascending uppe with many a stately stayre,
To honors seat and chastities sweet bowre.°
Why stand ye still ye virgins in amaze,
Upon her so to gaze,
Whiles ye forget your former lay to sing,
To which the woods did answer and your eccho ring.

But if ye saw that which no eyes can see,
The inward beauty of her lively spright,˃ *spirit*
Garnisht with heavenly guifts of high degree,
Much more then would ye wonder at that sight,
And stand astonisht lyke to those which red˃ *saw*
Medusaes mazeful hed.°
There dwels sweet love and constant chastity,
Unspotted fayth and comely womanhood,
Regard of honour and mild modesty,
There vertue raynes as Queen in royal throne,
And giveth lawes alone.°
The which the base affections˃ doe obay, *passions*
And yeeld theyr services unto her will,
Ne thought of thing uncomely ever may
Thereto approach to tempt her mind to ill.
Had ye once seene these her celestial threasures,
And unrevealèd pleasures,
Then would ye wonder and her prayses sing,
That al the woods should answer and your echo ring.

Open the temple gates unto my love,
Open them wide that she may enter in,
And all the postes adorne° as doth behove,˃ *as is fitting*
And all the pillours deck with girlands trim,
For to recyve this Saynt with honour dew,
That commeth in to you.
With trembling steps and humble reverence,
She commeth in, before th'almighties vew,
Of her ye virgins learne obedience,
When so ye come into those holy places,
To humble your proud faces:

honors . . . bowre the head, which controls the rest
Medusaes . . . hed Medusa was a Gorgon, whose terrible head turned the beholder to stone; the bride's spirit would be awe-inspiring.
giveth . . . alone alone commands
postes adorne Roman wedding custom, surviving in poetry

Bring her up to th'high altar, that she may
The sacred ceremonies there partake,
The which do endlesse matrimony make,
And let the roring Organs loudly play
The praises of the Lord in lively notes,
The whiles with hollow throates
The Choristers the joyous Antheme sing,
That al the woods may answere and their eccho ring.

Behold whiles she before the altar stands
Hearing the holy priest that to her speakes
And blesseth her with his two happy hands,
How the red roses flush up in her cheekes,
And the pure snow with goodly vermill stayne,
Like crimsin dyde in grayne,> *thoroughly*
That even th'Angels which continually,
About the sacred Altare doe remaine,°
Forget their service and about her fly;
Ofte peeping in her face that seemes more fayre,
The more they on it stare.
But her sad> eyes still fastened on the ground, *grave*
Are governèd with goodly modesty,
That suffers not one looke to glaunce awry,
Which may let in a little thought unsownd.
Why blush ye love to give to me your hand,
The pledge of all our band?> *bond*
Sing ye sweet Angels, Alleluya sing,°
That all the woods may answere and your eccho ring.

Now al is done; bring home the bride againe,
Bring home the triumph of our victory,
Bring home with you the glory of her gaine,> *of gaining her*
With joyance bring her and with jollity.
Never had man more joyfull day then this,
Whom heaven would heape with blis.
Make feast therefore now all this live long day,
This day for ever to me holy is,
Poure out the wine without restraint or stay,
Poure not by cups, but by the belly full,
Poure out to all that wull,> *want*
And sprinkle all the postes and wals with wine,°
That they may sweat, and drunken be withall.
Crowne ye God Bacchus with a coronall,> *garland*
And Hymen also crowne with wreathes of vine,
And let the Graces daunce unto the rest;
For they can doo it best:

remaine Revelation 7:11
Sing . . . sing Revelation 19:1. Spenser remembers the marriage in Revelation, which was so important in the conclusion of *The Faerie Queene* I.
sprinkle . . . wine another Roman custom

The whiles the maydens doe theyr carroll sing,
To which the woods shal answer and theyr eccho ring.

Ring ye the bels, ye yong men of the towne,
And leave your wonted> labors for this day: *usual*
This day is holy; doe ye write it downe,
That ye for ever it remember may.
This day the sunne is in his chiefest hight,
With Barnaby the bright,°
From whence declining daily by degrees,
He somewhat loseth of his heat and light,
When once the Crab behind his back he sees.°
But for this time it ill ordainèd was,
To chose the longest day in all the yeare,
And shortest night, when longest fitter weare:
Yet never day so long, but late> would passe. *at last*
Ring ye the bels, to make it weare away,
And bonefiers° make all day,
And daunce about them, and about them sing
That all the woods may answer, and your eccho ring.

Ah when will this long weary day have end,
And lende me leave to come unto my love?
How slowly do the houres theyr numbers spend?
How slowly does sad Time his feathers move?
Hast thee O fayrest Planet° to thy home
Within the Westerne fome:
Thy tyrèd steedes long since have need of rest.
Long though it be, at last I see it gloome,> *darken*
And the bright evening star with golden creast
Appeare out of the East.
Fayre childe of beauty, glorious lampe of love
That all the host of heaven in rankes doost lead,
And guydest lovers through the nightes dread,
How chearefully thou lookest from above,
And seemst to laugh atweene thy twinkling light
As joying in the sight
Of these glad many which for joy doe sing,
That all the woods them answer and their eccho ring.

Now ceasse ye damsels your delights forepast;> *over*
Enough is it, that all the day was youres:
Now day is doen, and night is nighing fast:
Now bring the Bryde into the brydall boures.
Now night is come, now soone her disaray,

the sunne . . . bright St. Barnabas day, June 11, was till the revision of the calendar the summer solstice.

the Crab . . . sees The sun moved out of Cancer into Leo in mid-June.

bonefiers midsummer bonfires, a surviving pagan custom

Planet The sun was regarded as a planet in Ptolemaic astronomy.

And in her bed her lay;
Lay her in lillies and in violets,
And silken courteins over her display,> *spread*
And odourd sheetes, and Arras> coverlets. *tapestry*
Behold how goodly my faire love does ly
In proud humility;
Like unto Maia,° when as Jove her tooke,
In Tempe,° lying on the flowry gras,
Twixt sleepe and wake, after she weary was,
With bathing in the Acidalian° brooke.
Now it is night, ye damsels may be gon,
And leave my love alone,
And leave likewise your former lay to sing:
The woods no more shal answere, nor your eccho ring.

Now welcome night, thou night so long expected,
That long daies labour doest at last defray,> *pay for*
And all my cares, which cruell love collected,
Hast sumd in one, and cancellèd for aye:
Spread thy broad wing over my love and me,
That no man may us see,
And in thy sable mantle us enwrap,
From feare of perrill and foule horror free.
Let no false treason seeke us to entrap,
Nor any dread disquiet once annoy
The safety of our joy:
But let the night be calme and quietsome,
Without tempestuous storms or sad afray:
Lyke as when Jove with fayre Alcmena lay,
When he begot the great Tirynthian groome:°
Or lyke as when he with thy selfe° did lie,
And begot Majesty.°
And let the mayds and yongmen cease to sing:
Ne let the woods them answer, nor theyr eccho ring.

Let no lamenting cryes, nor dolefull teares,
Be heard all night within nor yet without:
Ne let false whispers, breeding hidden feares,
Breake gentle sleepe with misconceivèd dout.
Let no deluding dreames, nor dreadful sights
Make sudden sad affrights;
Ne let housefyres, nor lightnings helpelesse> harmes, *incurable*

Maia one of the seven Pleiades; she gave birth to Hermes (Mercury) after the encounter described
Tempe beautiful vale in Thessaly
Acidalian Acidalia was a fountain sacred to Venus.
Lyke . . . groome Alcmena, wife of Amphitryon, spent a night of love, magically prolonged to the length of three nights, with Jupiter, and conceived Hercules, who was born at Tiryns and served as a super-groom in the cleaning of the Augean stables.
thy selfe Night
begot Majesty Spenser made up this little myth himself.

Ne let the Pouke,° nor other evill sprights,
Ne let mischívous witches with theyr charmes,
Ne let hob Goblins, names whose sence we see not,
Fray us with things that be not,
Let not the shriech Oule, nor the Storke be heard:
Nor the night Raven° that still˃ deadly yels, *ever*
Nor damnèd ghosts cald up with mighty spels,
Nor griesly vultures make us once affeard:
Ne let th'unpleasant Quyre of Frogs still˃ croking *always*
Make us to wish theyr choking.
Let none of these theyr drery accents sing;
Ne let the woods them answer, nor theyr eccho ring.

But let stil Silence trew night watches keepe,
That sacred peace may in assurance rayne,
And tymely sleep, when it is tyme to sleepe,
May poure his limbs forth on your° pleasant playne,
The whiles an hundred little wingèd loves,°
Like divers fethered doves,
Shall fly and flutter round about your bed,
And in the secret darke, that˃ none reproves, *when*
Their prety stealthes shal worke, and snares shal spread
To filch away sweet snatches of delight,
Conceald through covert night.
Ye sonnes of Venus, play your sports at will,
For greedy pleasure, carelesse of your toyes,˃ *tricks*
Thinks more upon her paradise of joyes,
Then what ye do, albe it good or ill.
All night therefore attend your merry play,
For it will soone be day:
Now none doth hinder you, that say or sing,
Ne will the woods now answer, nor your Eccho ring.

Who is the same, which at my window peepes?
Or whose is that faire face, that shines so bright,
Is it not Cinthia,° she that never sleepes,
But walkes about high heaven al the night?
O fayrest goddesse, do thou not envy
My love with me to spy:
For thou likewise didst love, though now unthought,˃ *unremembered*
And for a fleece of woll, which privily,
The Latmian shephard° once unto thee brought,
His pleasures with thee wrought.
Therefore to us be favorable now;

Pouke puck, Robin Goodfellow, mischievous and malevolent fairy
Oule . . . Storke . . . night Raven birds of ill-omen, all foretelling death except the stork, believed to avenge adultery
your Night's
loves cupids, "amoretti"
Cinthia the moon; there was a new moon on June 9, two days before the wedding
Latmian shephard Endymion lay with Diana on Mount Latmos; in most versions it was Pan who won her with a fleece of wool.

And sith of wemens labours thou hast charge,
And generation goodly dost enlarge,
Encline thy will t'effect our wishfull vow,
And the chast wombe informe with timely seed,
That may our comfort breed:
Till which we cease our hopefull hap> to sing, *luck*
Ne let the woods us answere, nor our Eccho ring.

And thou great Juno, which with awful might
The lawes of wedlock still dost patronize,°
And the religion> of the faith first plight> *bond / pledged*
With sacred rites hast taught to solemnize:
And eeke for comfort often callèd art
Of women in their smart,> *labor pains*
Eternally bind thou this lovely band,
And all thy blessings unto us impart.
And thou glad Genius,° in whose gentle hand,
The bridale bowre and geniall° bed remaine,
Without blemish or staine,
And the sweet pleasures of theyr loves delight
With secret ayde doest succour and supply,
Till they bring forth the fruitfull progeny,
Send us the timely fruit of this same night.
And thou fayre Hebe,° and thou Hymen free,
Grant that it may so be.
Til which we cease your further prayse to sing,
Ne any woods shal answer, nor your Eccho ring.

And ye high heavens, the temple of the gods,
In which a thousand torches flaming bright
Doe burne, that to us wretched earthly clods,
In dreadful darknesse lend desirèd light;
And all ye powers which in the same remayne,
More then we men can fayne,
Poure out your blessing on us plentiously,
And happy influence upon us raine,
That we may raise a large posterity,
Which from the earth, which they may long possesse,
With lasting happinesse,
Up to your haughty pallaces may mount,
And for the guerdon of theyr glorious merit
May heavenly tabernacles there inherit,
Of blessèd Saints for to increase the count.
So let us rest, sweet love, in hope of this,

Juno . . . patronize *Juno pronuba,* goddess of marriage. Lucina, on whom women called in childbirth, was a name applied to both Diana and Juno.

Genius the patron of generation, as in *The Faerie Queene* III.vi 31–33

geniall Latin expression for marriage bed, place of generation

Hebe goddess of youth, not traditionally associated with weddings

And cease till then our tymely joyes to sing,
The woods no more us answer, nor our eccho ring.

Song made in lieu of many ornaments,°
With which my love should duly have bene dect,˃ *decked*
Which cutting off through hasty accidents,°
Ye would not stay your dew time to expect,
But promist both to recompens,
Be unto her a goodly ornament,
And for short time an endlesse moniment.°

1595

ornaments wedding presents; the envoy makes apologetic reference to the occasion of the poem
hasty accidents accidents of haste (perhaps the date had to be brought forward)
short . . . moniment immortal record of the one day it records and schematically represents

WILLIAM SHAKESPEARE

1564–1616

Shakespeare was baptized on April 26, 1564, at Stratford-on-Avon, Warwickshire. His father John was a Stratford tradesman, called in legal documents a "glover," but also a dealer in timber and wool, the main commodity of the nearby Cotswold area. A man of substance and father of eight children, John owned property in Stratford, and was an official of the town, but he suffered a period of reverses, some possibly caused by his recusancy—he remained Catholic when it was dangerous and costly to do so. He got over this, and in 1596 he was granted the arms of a gentleman, probably at William Shakespeare's request. He died in 1601.

Shakespeare almost certainly attended Stratford Grammar School, where the teaching was mostly of Latin grammar and rhetoric, and where he would have read Terence, the Latin dramatist from whom the rules of dramatic structure—which he knew but did not slavishly obey—ultimately derived. He went to neither university, but married the pregnant Anne Hathaway, eight years his senior, in November 1582; their daughter Susanna was christened in May 1583, and their twins, Judith and Hamnet, in February 1585.

Nothing is known about his going to London, but he almost certainly was there by 1589; by 1592 he had written *Henry VI* and was well enough known to be attacked as an upstart actor by the pamphleteer Greene in his *Groatsworth of Wit*.

The London theaters closed when deaths from plague reached a certain figure each week, and there was an especially bad epidemic in the years 1592–94. During this time the existing companies went on tour, collapsed, and lost their principal writers. Shakespeare wrote his narrative poems, *Venus and Adonis* and *The Rape of Lucrece*, during this time. Both poems were dedicated to the Earl of Southampton (1573–1624), a patron of literature and the friend of the Queen's favorite, the Earl of Essex, in whose rebellion (1601) Southampton was to take part. Although he is a favored candidate for the role of dedicatee and friend in Shakespeare's *Sonnets*, no positive connection between them other than the dedications of *Venus and Adonis* and *The Rape of Lucrece* has ever been proved. Evidently, however, during the plague years Shakespeare was seeking or enjoying the protection of this powerful nobleman.

When the plague abated, the companies sorted themselves out into two—the Admiral's Men and the Lord Chamberlain's Men (named for their official sponsors at court—they were in fact liveried servants of these aristocrats). The great actor Alleyn went to the Admiral's Men; Burbage, his rival, to the Lord Chamberlain's. Shakespeare joined Burbage, and remained with the company for the rest of his working life. When King James I took it over (1603) as the King's Men he became, technically, a servant of the king. The grant of arms to his father in 1596 made Shakespeare himself a gentleman, and in the following year he was rich enough to buy a large house in Stratford.

Before the formation of the Lord Chamberlain's Men Shakespeare had probably written *Henry VI, Richard II,* and *Titus Andronicus.* His early plays for the new company were *The Comedy of Errors, The Taming of the Shrew, The Two Gentlemen of Verona,* and *Love's Labour's Lost.* He must have been extremely busy in this period, as "sharer" (shareholder) in the company, actor, and principal playwright. By 1599 he had also written *Romeo and Juliet, Richard II, King John, The Merchant of Venice,* the two parts of *Henry IV, Henry V, Much Ado About Nothing,* and *The Merry Wives of Windsor.*

In 1599 the lease of their house, The Theatre, expired, and in an operation of considerable ingenuity and enterprise Shakespeare's company forestalled the demolition men sent in by the landlord, rapidly dismantled the building, and shipped it across the Thames to Bankside, where they built a new playhouse with the old timbers and called it The Globe. Shakespeare was registered as owner of one-tenth share. In this theater were played most of his masterpieces, including all the main tragedies: *Julius Caesar, Hamlet, Othello, King Lear, Macbeth, Antony and Cleopatra, Coriolanus,* and *Timon of Athens* (if it was performed at all). The Globe also saw the première of *As You Like It* and *Twelfth Night,* of the "problem" plays, *Troilus and Cressida, All's Well That Ends Well,* and *Measure for Measure,* and Shakespeare's final plays, *Pericles, Cymbeline, The Winter's Tale,* and *The Tempest.* There were two more works, in which Shakespeare was a collaborator, *Two Noble Kinsmen* and *Henry VIII,* during a performance of which the theater burnt down when a blank cannon shot set fire to the thatch, on June 29, 1613.

In the preceding few years, from about 1609, the King's Men had also performed indoors in the more sophisticated Blackfriars Theatre; this certainly affected the kind of play they wanted and got from Shakespeare and the younger playwrights Beaumont and Fletcher. But The Globe was his true arena, the "wooden O" which contained and fed his imagination.

Shakespeare retired to Stratford around 1610; *The Winter's Tale* and *The Tempest* were probably written there. He continued his business life, and records of lawsuits—Shakespeare appears always to have enjoyed litigation—survive from the period between his retirement and his death, at the age of fifty-two, on April 23, 1616.

Shakespeare apparently took little care to be published, except with *Venus and Adonis* and *The Rape of Lucrece;* even the authorized quartos of the plays published during his life time are badly and carelessly printed. The *Sonnets* were published without his consent or care, and his mysterious poem "The Phoenix and Turtle," which appeared in an anthology in 1601, is almost the only work he willingly published after 1593. A great part of his work remained in manuscript until his colleagues John Heminges and Henry Condell brought out in 1623 the collection we now call the First Folio. This large book contains, in texts of varying authority, all the plays we now attribute to Shakespeare except *Pericles,* which was added in the third edition (Third Folio) of 1664.

The Sonnets

Shakespeare's sonnets were written over an indeterminate period and published together in 1609, after the vogue of sonneteering was over. Unlike Spenser's *Amoretti* or Sidney's *Astrophel and Stella* they revolve about no central mythical lady, named and constantly invoked; instead, we have a constellation of three figures providing a far greater ironic and dramatic range than the traditional relation of lover-poet to lady-muse. A blond young aristocrat, a dark lady, and a rival poet, none totally trustworthy, all ambiguously admirable, inhabit these sonnets, which, throughout, are haunted by the theme of time and its effects on people, things and buildings, human relationships. They attracted much misguided critical attention because of the belief that they were autobiographical and because of the mystery (but probably trivial import) of the dedication to an unknown "Mr. W. H." Their compact language, range of tone, profound word-play, and intense moral vision are unsurpassed by any of the regular sonnet sequences of Sidney, Spenser, or Drayton. The early poems of the cycle urge the young man to marry and have children; later on, there is a group addressed to the lady; toward the end, obvious complications occur.

XII

When I do count the clock that tells the time,°
And see the brave° day sunk in hideous night;
When I behold the violet past prime,°
And sable curls o'er-silvered all with white;
When lofty trees I see barren of leaves,
Which erst from heat did canopy the herd,
And summer's green all girded up° in sheaves
Borne on the bier with white and bristly beard;°
Then of thy beauty do I question make
That thou among the wastes of time° must go,
Since sweets° and beauties do themselves forsake°
And die as fast as they see others grow;
  And nothing 'gainst Time's scythe can make defence
  Save breed° to brave° him when he takes thee hence.

XVIII

Shall I compare thee to a summer's day?°
Thou art more lovely and more temperate:
Rough winds do shake the darling buds of May,
And summer's lease hath all too short a date:°

count . . . time mark the passage of the hours
brave resplendent, finely attired
past prime faded
girded up with a girdle about his waist, the image being that of an old man being carried to his grave
And summer's . . . beard the green corn, now ripe, harvested, the imagery making the sheaves a conceited image of death
wastes of time the things time has destroyed
sweets blossoms
forsake undo
breed offspring
brave defy
day may mean the period (or season) of a summer, as in the expression "in my day"
date the period of a lease

Sometime too hot the eye of heaven shines,
And often is his gold complexion dimmed,
And every fair from fair sometime declines,
By chance or nature's changing course untrimmed;°
But thy eternal summer shall not fade
Nor lose possession of that fair thou owest,°
Nor shall Death brag thou wander'st in his shade,
When in eternal lines° to time thou growest:°
So long as men can breathe or eyes can see,
So long lives this, and this gives life to thee.

XIX

Devouring Time, blunt thou the lion's paws,
And make the earth devour her own sweet brood;
Pluck the keen teeth from the fierce tiger's jaws,
And burn the long-lived phoenix in her blood;°
Make glad and sorry seasons as thou fleet'st,
And do whate'er thou wilt, swift-footed Time,
To the wide world and all her fading sweets:°
But I forbid thee one most heinous crime—
Oh carve not with thy hours my love's fair brow
Nor draw no lines there with thine ántique° pen;
Him in thy course untainted do allow
For beauty's pattern to succeeding men.
Yet do thy worst, old Time: despite thy wrong
My love shall in my verse ever live young.

XX

A woman's face with nature's own hand painted
Hast thou, the master-mistress° of my passion;
A woman's gentle heart, but not acquainted
With shifting change as is false women's fashion;
An eye more bright than theirs, less false in rolling,°
Gilding the object whereupon it gazeth;
A man in hue° all hues in his controlling,
Which steals men's eyes and women's souls amazeth:
And for a woman wert thou first created,—
Till nature as she wrought thee fell a-doting,
And by addition me of thee defeated,°

untrimmed stripped of beauty
that . . . owest that beauty thou possessest (ownest)
lines such as the lines of this poem and the other sonnets
growest becomes a part of
phoenix . . . blood The first three lines describe Time's action on living things that change and die; the phoenix also comes to the end of its years, although it is instantly reborn from its own funeral pyre.
sweets flowers
ántique ancient, with a play on "antic" or "fantastic"
master-mistress both the oxymoron "boy-girl" and, as if unhyphenated, "sovereign mistress"
rolling roving
hue form
defeated defrauded

By adding one thing° to my purpose nothing.
But since she pricked° thee out for women's pleasure,
Mine be thy love and thy love's use° their treasure.

XXIX

When, in disgrace with Fortune and men's eyes,
I all alone beweep my outcast state,°
And trouble deaf heaven with my bootless° cries,
And look upon myself and curse my fate,
Wishing me like to one more rich in hope,
Featured like him,° like him with friends possessed,
Desiring this man's art and that man's scope,
With what I most enjoy contented least;
Yet in these thoughts myself almost despising
Haply I think on thee, and then my state,
Like to the lark at break of day arising
From sullen° earth, sings hymns at heaven's gate:
For thy sweet love remembered such wealth brings
That then I scorn to change my state with kings.

XXX

When to the sessions° of sweet silent thought
I summon up remembrance of things past,
I sigh the lack of many a thing I sought,
And with old woes new wail my dear time's waste:
Then can I drown an eye, unused to flow,
For precious friends hid in death's dateless° night,
And weep afresh love's long since cancelled woe,
And moan the expense° of many a vanished sight:
Then can I grieve at grievances foregone,°
And heavily° from woe to woe tell° o'er
The sad account of fore-bemoanèd moan,
Which I new pay as if not paid before.
But if the while I think on thee, dear friend,°
All losses are restored and sorrows end.

XXXIII

Full many a glorious morning have I seen
Flatter° the mountain tops with sovereign eye,
Kissing with golden face the meadows green,

one thing male sex
pricked selected; also "prick" as in modern slang for penis
use sexual practice
state Here, as in all the sonnets, the meaning shifts from "condition in life" through "state of being" (l. 10) to "stately."
bootless unavailing
like him like yet another person
sullen dull, heavy
sessions of a law court. The legal conceit turns on words like "dateless," "cancelled," "expense," "account," etc., and suggests the poet being called to account, as steward, for the estate of his life.
dateless endless
expense loss
foregone gone by
heavily sadly
tell reckon
dear friend the first use of this term in the *Sonnets*
Flatter brighten, cheer up (as the sovereign's smile would a courtier)

Gilding pale streams with heavenly alchemy,
Anon permit the basest clouds to ride
With ugly rack° on his celestial face,
And from the fórlorn world his visage hide,
Stealing unseen to west with this disgrace:°
Even so my sun one early morn did shine
With all triumphant° splendour on my brow;
But out alack, he was but one hour mine:
The region° cloud hath masked him from me now.
  Yet him for this my love no whit disdaineth:
  Suns of the world may stain,° when heaven's sun staineth.

LIII

What is your substance, whereof are you made,
That millions of strange shadows° on you tend?
Since every one hath, every one, one shade,
And you, but one, can every shadow lend.
Describe Adonis, and the counterfeit
Is poorly imitated after you;
On Helen's cheek all art of beauty set,°
And you in Grecian tires° are painted new.
Speak of the spring and foison° of the year:
The one doth shadow of your beauty show,
The other as your bounty doth appear,
And you in every blessèd shape we know.
  In all external grace you have some part,
  But you like none, none you for constant heart.

LV

Not marble, nor the gilded monuments
Of princes shall outlive this powerful rhyme;
But you shall shine more bright in these contents
Than unswept stone besmeared with sluttish time.°
When wasteful° war shall statues overturn,
And broils° root out the work of masonry,
Nor Mars his sword° nor war's quick° fire shall burn
The living record of your memory.
'Gainst death and all oblivious° enmity

rack drifting; a mass of clouds driven before the wind; cf. *The Tempest* IV.i.156
this disgrace i.e. the concealing clouds
triumphant glorious
region region of the air
stain grow dim
strange shadows external, foreign images. The word-play is on "shadow and substance" meaning "appearance vs. reality"; in l. 10, the word takes on its modern sense of "cast shade."
On Helen's . . . set put the best makeup on the face of the most beautiful woman ever
tires attire, costume, dress
foison autumnal harvest
unswept . . . time The stone bore an inscription to the dead man, the letters of which had become obscured ("sluttish" = dirty) in the course of time.
wasteful destructive
broils battles
Nor . . . sword "Destroy" is understood.
quick lively
oblivious bringing to oblivion

Shall you pace forth: your praise° shall still find room
Even in the eyes of all posterity
That wear this world out° to the ending doom.
So, till the judgment that yourself arise,
You live in this,° and dwell in lovers' eyes.

LXIV

When I have seen by Time's fell hand defaced
The rich proud cost of outworn buried age;
When sometime lofty towers I see down razed,
And brass eternal° slave to mortal° rage;
When I have seen the hungry ocean gain
Advantage on the kingdom of the shore,
And the firm soil win of the watery main,
Increasing store° with loss and loss with store;
When I have seen such interchange of state,°
Or state itself confounded to decay,
Ruin hath taught me thus to ruminate
That Time will come and take my love away.
This thought is as a death, which cannot choose
But weep to have that which it fears to lose.

LXVI

Tired with all these for restful death I cry
As to behold Desert° a beggar born,
And needy Nothing trimmed in jollity,°
And purest Faith° unhappily forsworn,
And gilded Honour shamefully misplaced,
And maiden Virtue rudely strumpeted,°
And right Perfection wrongfully disgraced,
And Strength by limping Sway disablèd,
And Art made tongue-tied by Authority,
And Folly, Doctor-like,° controlling° Skill,
And simple Truth miscalled Simplicity,°
And captive Good attending captain Ill:
Tired with all these, from these would I be gone
Save that, to die, I leave my love alone.

praise glory
wear . . . out outlast
this these lines of poetry
brass eternal Eternal brass as opposed, syntactically, to "mortal rage"—this patterning of noun-adjective:adjective-noun, called chiasmus, is typically Elizabethan.
mortal both "deadly" and "subject to death"
store abundance
state condition; also "estate"; also "grandeur" (as in the next line)
Desert a personification of one who is deserving
jollity fine costume
Faith fidelity; also True Religion
strumpeted called a whore
Doctor-like pedant-like
controlling also with a sense of rebuking, censuring
Simplicity stillness

LXXIII

That time of year thou mayst in me behold
When yellow leaves, or none, or few, do hang
Upon those boughs which shake against the cold,
Bare ruined choirs where late the sweet birds sang: °
In me thou see'st the twilight of such day
As after sunset fadeth in the west,
Which by and by black night doth take away,
Death's second self that seals up all in rest:
In me thou see'st the glowing of such fire
That on the ashes of his youth doth lie
As the death-bed whereon it must expire,
Consumed with that which it was nourished by: °
This thou perceivest, which makes thy love more strong
To love that well which thou must leave ere long.

LXXXVI

Was it the proud full sail of his° great verse,
Bound for the prize of all-too-precious you,
That did my ripe thoughts in my brain inhearse,°
Making their tomb the womb wherein they grew?
Was it his spirit, by spirits taught to write
Above a mortal pitch, that struck me dead?
No, neither he, nor his compeers by night
Giving him aid, my verse astonishèd:
He, nor that affable familiar ghost°
Which nightly gulls° him with intelligence,°
As victors of my silence cannot boast,
I was not sick of any fear from thence:
But when your countenance filled up his line,
Then lacked I matter; that° enfeebled mine.

LXXXVII

Farewell—thou art too dear° for my possessing,
And like enough thou knowest thy estimate: °
The charter° of thy worth gives thee releasing;
My bonds in thee are all determinate.°
For how do I hold thee but by thy granting?
And for that riches where is my deserving?

Bare . . . sang The trees are likened to arching ruins, half-opened to the sky, of the choirs of gothic monastery churches; the sweet birds literally sang in the summer trees, and, figuratively, sang as choir boys, perhaps, in the choir stalls of the church in the image; notice the sequence in the quatrains of autumn—sundown—dying fire.
Consumed . . . by "consumed with life," as with passion; also perhaps consumed by the nourishing fire; the image is one of embers hotter than they look
his some rival poet: George Chapman has been suggested
inhearse entomb
familiar ghost some spirit attending the rival; perhaps a poetic predecessor
gulls deceives
intelligence secret information
that "that this was true"
dear expensive; also, "aristocratic"
estimate worth
charter privilege
determinate ended

The cause of this fair gift in me is wanting,
And so my patent° back again is swerving.°
Thy self thou gavest, thy own worth then not knowing;
Or me, to whom thou gavest it, else mistaking:°
So thy great gift, upon misprision° growing,
Comes home again on better judgment making.°
Thus have I had thee as a dream doth flatter:
In sleep a king, but waking no such matter.

XCIV

They that have power to hurt and will do none,
That do not do the thing they most do show,°
Who moving others are themselves as stone,
Unmovèd, cold, and to temptation slow;
They rightly do inherit heaven's graces,°
And husband nature's riches from expense;°
They are the lords and owners of their faces,
Others but stewards° of their excellence.
The summer's flower is to the summer sweet,
Though to itself it only live and die;
But if that flower with base infection meet,
The basest weed outbraves° his dignity:
For sweetest things turn sourest by their deeds.
Lilies that fester smell far worse than weeds.°

XCVII

How like a winter hath my absence been
From thee, the pleasure of the fleeting year!
What freezings have I felt, what dark days seen!—
What old December's bareness everywhere!
And yet this time removed° was summer's time:
The teeming autumn big with rich increase°
Bearing the wanton° burthen of the prime,°
Like widowed wombs after their lords' decease.
Yet this abundant issue seemed to me
But hope of orphans, and unfathered fruit;
For summer and his pleasures wait on° thee,
And thou away the very birds are mute;
Or if they sing, 'tis with so dull a cheer
That leaves look pale, dreading the winter's near.

patent grant of a monopoly
is swerving returns to you
mistaking overestimating
misprision misjudgment
on better judgment making on your judging better
show look as if they could do
heaven's graces the favors of heaven
husband . . . expense protect from wastefulness
stewards officials who manage estates for the owners; "their" refers to "they" in l. 1
outbraves makes a finer show than
Lilies . . . weeds a line from an old play
time removed time of separation
increase offspring, crops
wanton playful; luxuriant
prime spring
wait on attend, as at court

CVI

When in the chronicle of wasted time
I see descriptions of the fairest wights,°
And beauty making beautiful old rhyme
In praise of ladies dead and lovely knights,
Then in the blazon° of sweet beauty's best—
Of hand, of foot, of lip, of eye, of brow—
I see their antique pen would have expressed
Even such a beauty as you master now.
So all their praises are but prophecies
Of this our time, all you prefiguring;
And for they looked but with divining eyes
They had not skill enough your worth to sing:
For we which now behold these present days
Have eyes to wonder, but lack tongues to praise.

CVII

Not mine own fears, nor the prophetic soul
Of the wide world dreaming on things to come
Can yet the lease° of my true love control,
Supposed as forfeit to a cónfined doom.
The mortal moon hath her eclipse endured,°
And the sad augurs mock their own presage;
Incertainties now crown themselves assured,
And peace proclaims olives° of endless age.
Now with the drops of this most balmy time
My love looks fresh; and Death to me subscribes,
Since spite of him I'll live in this poor rhyme
While he insults o'er° dull and speechless tribes:
And thou in this shalt find thy monument
When tyrants' crests and tombs of brass are spent.

CXVI

Let me not to the marriage of true minds
Admit impediments:° love is not love
Which alters when it alteration finds,
Or bends with the remover to remove.°
Oh no! it is an ever-fixèd mark°
That looks on tempests and is never shaken;
It is the star to every wandering bark,
Whose worth's unknown although his height be taken.°

wights people
blazon poetic cataloguing of a person's beauties and virtues, publicly displayed
lease period or term of lease
The mortal moon . . . endured Some historical crisis has passed—whether the Spanish Armada, sailing in a crescent (defeated in 1588), a lunar eclipse, or some crisis of the Queen—making "mortal" mean "deadly" or "able to die."
olives olive branch of peace (ever since the dove flew back to Noah's ark with one when the flood had abated)
insults o'er triumphs over
Let . . . impediments an echo of the marriage service. The "impediments" are change of circumstance (l. 3) and inconstancy (l. 4).
bends . . . remove withdraws when its object does
an . . . mark a beacon
height be taken altitude be known

Love's not Time's fool, though rosy lips and cheeks
Within his bending° sickle's compass come;
Love alters not with his brief hours and weeks,
But bears it out° even to the edge of doom.
If this be error and upon me proved,
I never writ, nor no man ever loved.

CXXI

'Tis better to be vile than vile esteemed,
When not to be receives reproach of being,
And the just pleasure lost which is so deemed°
Not by our feeling but by others' seeing.
For why should others' false adulterate eyes
Give salutation to my sportive blood?°
Or on my frailties why are frailer spies,
Which in their wills count bad what I think good?
No: I am that I am,° and they that level°
At my abuses reckon up their own;
I may be straight though they themselves be bevel;°
By their rank° thoughts my deeds must not be shown,—
Unless this general evil° they maintain:
All men are bad and in their badness reign.

CXXIX

The expense of spirit in a waste of shame°
Is lust° in action; and till action, lust°
Is perjured, murderous, bloody, full of blame,
Savage, extreme, rude,° cruel, not to trust;
Enjoyed no sooner but despisèd straight;
Past reason hunted; and no sooner had,
Past reason hated, as a swallowed bait
On purpose laid to make the taker mad;
Mad in pursuit, and in possession so;
Had, having, and in quest to have, extreme;
A bliss in proof;° and proved, a very woe;
Before, a joy proposed; behind, a dream.
All this the world well knows, yet none knows well
To shun the heaven that leads men to this hell.

bending bent; also "causing the grass of youthful beauty to bend"
bears it out endures
so deemed either "vile," in which case the unjust condemnation of the love by outsiders wrecks its pleasure; or "just pleasure," in which case the outsiders ("others") approve of the love although the sonneteer doesn't
Give salutation . . . blood mockingly hail my sexual activity
I am that I am I am what I am (apparently echoing the words of God from the burning bush to Moses, Exodus 3:14)
level aim a weapon
bevel crooked
rank lewd
general evil i.e. the following moral formula: "All men are bad . . ." etc.
The expense . . . shame abstractly, characterizing lust; concretely, sexual "spending" (orgasm) to no purpose in a shameful waste (the theme of *post coitum triste*—"sorrow after sex")
lust grammatical subject of the first sentence
rude brutal
in proof experienced

CXXX

My mistress' eyes are nothing like the sun;
Coral is far more red than her lips' red;
If snow be white, why then her breasts are dun;°
If hairs be wires, black wires grow on her head;
I have seen roses damasked,° red and white,
But no such roses see I in her cheeks;
And in some perfumes is there more delight
Than in the breath that from my mistress reeks;°
I love to hear her speak, yet well I know
That music hath a far more pleasing sound;
I grant I never saw a goddess go
(My mistress when she walks treads on the ground).
And yet by heaven I think my love as rare
As any she belied with false compare.

CXXXV

Whoever hath her wish, thou hast thy *Will*,°
And *Will* to boot, and *Will* in overplus:
More than enough am I that vex thee still,
To thy sweet *Will* making addition thus.
Wilt thou whose *Will* is large and spacious
Not once vouchsafe to hide my *Will* in thine?
Shall *Will* in others seem right gracious,
And in my *Will* no fair acceptance shine?
The sea, all water, yet receives rain still,
And in abundance addeth to his store:
So thou being rich in *Will* add to thy *Will*
One *Will* of mine to make thy large *Will* more.
Let no unkind no fair° beseechers kill;
Think all but one, and me in that one *Will*.

CXXXVIII

When my love swears that she is made of truth°
I do believe her, though I know she lies,°
That she might think me some untutored youth
Unlearnèd in the world's false subtleties.
Thus vainly thinking that she thinks me young,
Although she knows my days are past the best,
Simply° I credit her false-speaking tongue:
On both sides thus is simple truth suppressed.

dun tan. The whole poem is an anti-blazon, actually a Petrarchan "anti-Petrarchan" device.
roses damasked pink roses, but also perhaps patterned in the symbolic colors of passion and purity
reeks emanates (with no sense of "stinks")
Will volition; desire; passionate feeling ("wit and will" meant something like "thought and feeling"); the auxiliary verb; and, in this sonnet, both the poet's own name, and sexual member (but of both sexes—as if modern slang "dick" meant both penis and vagina)
fair legitimate
made of truth "faithful to me," as well as "truth-telling"
she lies "sleeps around," as well as "tells lies"
Simply like a simpleton, unconditionally, absolutely

But wherefore says she not she is unjust?°
And wherefore say not I that I am old?
Oh, love's best habit° is in seeming trust,
And age, in love,° loves not to have years told.
Therefore I lie with her,° and she with me,
And in our faults by lies we flattered be.

CXLIV

Two loves I have, of comfort and despair,
Which like two spirits do suggest me still:°
The better angel is a man right fair,°
The worser spirit a woman coloured ill.°
To win me soon to hell, my female evil
Tempteth my better angel from my side,
And would corrupt my saint to be a devil,
Wooing his purity with her foul pride.
And whether that my angel be turned fiend
Suspect I may, yet not directly tell;
But being both from me, both to each friend,
I guess one angel in another's hell:°
Yet this shall I ne'er know, but live in doubt
Till my bad angel fire my good one out.°

CXLVI

Poor soul, the centre of my sinful earth,°
(Foiled by)° these rebel powers that thee array,°
Why dost thou pine within and suffer dearth,
Painting thy outward walls so costly gay?
Why so large cost, having so short a lease,
Dost thou upon thy fading mansion spend?
Shall worms, inheritors of this excess,
Eat up thy charge? Is this thy body's end?
Then, soul, live thou upon thy servant's loss,
And let that° pine to aggravate° thy store;
Buy terms° divine in selling hours of dross;
Within be fed, without be rich no more:
So shalt thou feed on Death, that feeds on men,
And Death once dead there's no more dying then.°

unjust unfaithful
habit costume
in love also, "in re love"
lie with her "lie to her"; also, "sleep with her"
suggest me still tempt me ever
fair light-haired and -complexioned; beautiful; honest (modern "fair" as "just")
coloured ill a brunette
hell the prison zone in barley-break, a game like prisoner's base; also, as in a story in the *Decameron* of Giovanni Boccaccio (1313–75), "the devil in hell" as his sexual member in hers
fire . . . out reject him; also, to give him venereal disease (only when the friend shows signs of this will it be clear that he slept with her)
earth flesh, body
(Foiled by) an emendation; the original phrase is a misprint
array both "deck out" and "afflict"
that "that one," the servant body
aggravate increase
terms years or decades of a lease
And Death . . . then Cf. I Corinthians 15:54–55.

Othello

Othello no less than the other great tragedies invents its own idiom. The voice of the Moor has its own orotundity, verging, as some infer, on hollowness; the dialect of Iago is appropriate to the archetypal Shakespearean evildoer. Venice, Cyprus, and the sea between give the work its particular local splendor, as of a great and typical action occurring on the outposts of civilization. For all its relative tautness of structure and simplicity of action, *Othello* enacts its story of a great man's fall into the barbarism of human nature against a scene no less regal than that of *Hamlet, Lear,* or *Macbeth*. And like these it accommodates many interpretations.

Othello was not published until 1622, but cannot be later than 1604 in composition. It was the next tragedy after *Hamlet* (1600) and preceded *King Lear* (1605). The source of *Othello* is a *novella* by Giraldi Cinthio. No English translation was available, and some think that Shakespeare read the work in a French version by Gabriel Chappuys (Paris, 1584). Such evidence of verbal indebtedness as can be found tends to show that he looked at Cinthio's Italian, and so does his account of the wounding of Cassio. Cinthio had recommended that tragic writers should choose plots from stories of modern life, and Shakespeare took his advice, choosing a story by the man who had called fiction the mythology of the modern world, more in touch with the values and interests of a contemporary audience than were the old Greek myths.

But Shakespeare did not find in the tale the same values as Cinthio. Each, of course, exploits its themes of love, jealousy, and revenge. But to Cinthio the point of the story is, briefly, that Desdemona made an unhappy choice in marrying a man so different from her in every way—unsuitable by reason of race, creed, and education. Shakespeare indeed emphasizes the color difference, but he firmly establishes Othello as a Christian, and allows the original moral of the story to degenerate into an aspect of the partial or evil interpretations put upon the events by disaffected or incompetent observers: Cinthio's moral is expressed only by Brabantio and Iago.

Shakespeare allowed this story to change as it germinated in his mind, so that the resemblances that remain have almost the look of accidents. He ennobles the Moor, both in character and in birth, and gives to the love between him and his wife a quality of exaltation and spirituality lacking in Cinthio. At the same time he allows them no quiet married life in Venice; their marriage now begins among the tensions and alarms of a remote and embattled Cyprus. Shakespeare's Iago, though he would seduce her if he could, is so far from being in love with Desdemona that he specifically declares himself contemptuous of the very notion as he observes it in Roderigo. In the play the lovers are reunited, one might almost say married, in Cyprus; in Cinthio they travel safely in the same ship, without alarms. Emilia becomes the waiting-woman of Desdemona, and has no three-year-old child, as in Cinthio (Iago as the father of a tender infant is an improbable consideration). The handkerchief plays a different part. In Cinthio, Iago is responsible neither for Cassio's drunken indiscretion nor for his use of Desdemona as pleader. Roderigo is an entirely new invention. The end of the story is quite changed.

To read Cinthio's little story gives one a sharpened sense of the scope of Shakespeare's mind, and also of the essentially dramatic character of his imagination. One thinks, for instance, of the development of hints and accidental suggestions into the magnificent III.iii, so audacious, so capable of bearing the weight of this great idea; and one thinks too of the famous problem of "double time" in this play. For good reasons Shakespeare wanted an intense concentration of event—the blissful reunion at Cyprus; the consummation of the marriage, interrupted by the Cassio brawl; and the next day a rapid darkening of the scene: Othello blasted, reduced from a type of magnanimity to a grotesque dupe by unsuspected wickedness and his own ignorance of men. That the events are crushed into brief time Shakespeare frequently forces us to notice. From the landing in Cyprus the whole story unfolds in a space of one and a half days. He gives Iago a much more active part in arranging disasters than Cinthio's Ensign; improviser as Iago is, he makes capital out of anything, sometimes so absurdly that for Othello simply to "send for" or meet Cassio would put an end to his schemes. But there is no time. Othello murders his wife on the second night in Cyprus.

The difficulty—and Shakespeare was clearly aware of it—arises from the fact that this leaves no time for her to have had "stol'n hours of lust," certainly not to have enjoyed them repeatedly, as Iago alleges. In such allusions to frequent adultery as III.iii.340–43 and V.ii.211–12, Shakespeare slides over from Short to Long Time very successfully; the audience is not invited to consider that Othello is forgetting that Desdemona was not in the same ship as Cassio, and has had no chance since. We accept it as possible for her to have been unfaithful, though we know she was not. The trick depends upon the conventions of Elizabethan drama in respect of the treatment of time, which is habitually episodic and extensive, more as in a novel than as in a classical play. Although Shakespeare, for his purpose, can remind us that only a short time is elapsing, we shall, in the immediate absence of such reminders, assume that the action has picked out only significant spots of time, in the usual way. Thus he gets the advantages of both systems. It should be remembered that he could have avoided the problem altogether, as Boito does in his libretto for Verdi's opera. But he wanted not only plausibility but also pace and sudden shocking contrasts; he wanted white to be suddenly blackened, not to pass through indeterminate grays of growing suspicion and meanness. In the rapid progress of its plot, and the violence of its thematic oppositions, *Othello* stands in extraordinary contrast with *Hamlet*, its hesitant, deliberately delaying predecessor.

"Double time" is a classical topic of *Othello* criticism; one of its uses is to remind us that the play, more largely considered, is characterized by a kind of imaginative duplicity. Thus one can isolate a plot of monumental and satisfying simplicity without forgetting that the text can be made to support very different interpretations. The richness of the tragedy derives from uncanceled suggestions, from latent subplots operating in terms of imagery as well as character, even from hints of large philosophical and theological contexts which are not fully developed.

In the simplest terms, one could describe the main business of the play thus. Othello is a magnanimous soldier, dedicated to an unquestioned code of conduct that belongs to the field of honor rather than to the city. Considered in relation to this sphere of action, he is a complete man, self-controlled, superbly sure of his powers, and totally honest (to use the word in its broadest sense). His marriage to Desdemona, founded upon her just understanding of his virtue, is a triumph over appearances; it is grounded in reality and independent of such accidents as color or the easy lusts of the flesh; it is more like the love of Adam and Eve before the Fall than after. The archaic grandeur of Othello's diction (as in the long speeches to the Senate in I.iii) and the extreme innocence of Desdemona (as the courtly Cassio celebrates it in II.i) are ways of emphasizing these simple themes; one may see them ideally reflected in the music Verdi wrote for Otello's heroic entry, and the soaring purity of his Desdemona.

Othello has lived for nine months or so (I.iii.84) in the city. It is notable for its wealth, its power, and its justice; but also it is not Eden but a fallen world. The order in which we are allowed to see the events occur is not without its simple importance; and the first thing we see in Venice is baseness—the whining of Roderigo, the envy and the sharp low talk of Iago, and profane shouting outside a senator's house. The climate of Othello's love may be fertile, but it is plagued with flies; and before we learn that he and Desdemona love each other in total honesty, we hear them described as old black ram and white ewe, or the beast with two backs. There is room for another and more worldly view of the honesty of Desdemona's proceedings; Iago and Brabantio express it. Her penetrating to the truth of Othello under an appearance conventionally thought repulsive can seem less a result of her purity of response than of some pagan witchcraft of his. It is precisely because such a union must appear to the disenchanted worldly eye perverse or absurd that Iago can destroy it. He represents a sort of metropolitan knowingness, a pride in being without illusion and a power to impose upon others an illusory valuation of himself. He converts to his own uses all the praise of honesty which properly belongs to Othello and Desdemona.

It has often been said that Shakespeare's idea of a truly evil man is one in whom, to quote the famous critic, A. C. Bradley, "evil is [seen to be] compatible with, and even appears to ally itself easily with, exceptional powers of will and intellect." Iago is the most striking instance. He is provided with motives for hating Othello—the false suspicion of his adultery with Emilia, and the promotion of Cassio—but the much-maligned formula "motiveless malignity" has something to recommend it. Over the ancient figure of the Vice—a familiar shape for abstract evil—Iago wears the garb of a modern devil. Iago's naturalistic ethic, as expounded to Roderigo at the close of Act I, is a wicked man's version of Montaigne, an instance of the way in which men convert to evil the precepts of a common sense supported by no act of faith. The reason that commands the sensuality of an unfallen Adam or an unfallen Othello controls also the carnal stings of an Iago, but for ends that become entirely and monstrously selfish.

The storm divides the lovers and reunites them in an absolute content, honorably and courteously celebrated by Cassio; but again their nuptial night is disturbed by a civic brawl, and this time courtesy is permanently dishonored. Cassio, cashiered, thinks he has lost what Othello is soon really to lose, his reputation: "I have lost the immortal part of myself, and what remains is bestial" (II.iii.239–40). (We must think of "reputation" as meaning not merely the good word of others, but that self-respect which is indispensable to social beings and without which they cannot function well in private or public life. Without it, a man is no more than a beast.) The object of Iago's wit is to make Othello see Desdemona and love as deceitful and bestial; to destroy the harmonies of honor and replace them with more lifelike discords.

Dramaturgically, the central problem of the enterprise was to make plausible the corruption of Othello's mind. It is very important to see that Othello's self-estimate—"one not easily jealious, but, being wrought, / Perplexed in the extreme" (V.ii.345–46)—is, as Bradley says, "perfectly just," and perfectly consistent with the release of unsuspected grossness of language and imagery under the shock of discovering infidelity in the loved one. The peculiar pain of sexual jealousy is deeply involved with the excremental aspect of the sexual organs, and the emotion in betrayal in a supremely intimate trust is involved with agonizing associations of filth and animality. This kind of shock has no necessary connection with temperamental jealousy—that is, holding a partner in habitual suspicion. There are similarities, of course—neither the permanently jealous man, nor the man who suffers the single shock of a discovered infidelity, easily bears the thought that he keeps "a corner in the thing [he loves] / For others' uses" (III.iii.272–73). But Othello's is the case of the man who knows nothing of the infernal power of jealousy till he is suddenly and by evil led into an unsuspected area of human experience, an area where innocence merely increases the pain and shock. And it is worth noting that Shakespeare, who shows with incomparable authority the surrender of Othello's mind to these dark experiences, shows him also restored to dignity, though still terribly in error, in the scene of Desdemona's murder (Shakespeare's honorable murderers always behave like priests at a sacrifice) and in the self-recognition of the closing moments.

All these effects, however, depend on the success of the temptation—or corruption—scene, III.iii. There are expert witnesses who read this scene as evidence that Othello succumbs too quickly, that he is a hollow man ironically represented as incapable of dealing with reality except in the narrow selection of it made by conventional men of honor. There may be, in the stream, an eddy or two that can be interpreted thus; but that this reading perverts the main movement of the play there is surely little doubt. The whiteness of Desdemona blackened, we see the white and tranquil mind of Othello darkened by atavistic shock and disgust—"where's that palace whereinto foul things / Sometimes intrude not," (III.iii.137–38). This must happen quickly, yet not implausibly; there is the basic technical problem, and Shakespeare solves it with intelligence and resource. Iago hints, is disarmed by Desdemona's innocent candor. She pleads, is indulgently heard, and departs:

OTHELLO Excellent wretch! Perdition catch my soul
But I do love thee! and when I love thee not,
Chaos is come again.
IAGO My noble lord—

Iago at once begins again, and within a hundred lines his wit has ensnared Othello. As J. C. Maxwell says, the central speech is Othello's at lines 177–92, and I can do no more than echo his very penetrating remarks on it. Othello's demand for ocular proof to settle the matter of Desdemona's fidelity is logically absurd, since there could be no such proof of *fidelity;* evidence can be only on the other side.

> Once Othello's mind is turned in this direction, Iago can consolidate his position by infecting Othello with his own gross visualizing lust; he can do so in part by insisting on what Othello will *not* be able to see (III.iii.395–409), and he also has in reserve the one tangible and visible token, the handkerchief. It is not introduced until all the ground has been prepared for its transformation. In the world to which the love of Othello and Desdemona belongs, it is a token of unquestioning faith. In the world into which Iago has initiated Othello, it becomes merely divorce-court evidence.[1]

Henceforth Desdemona appears to Othello "a super-subtle Venetian," an inhabiter of the fallen world; he himself, as he later recognizes, becomes for a time "an erring barbarian." He accepts, though with horror, Iago's version of the world; he begins to use Iago's gross vocabulary. There is the singularly horrible opening of Act IV, a crescendo of prurience which ends with Othello's lapse from an unbearable consciousness. Thereafter follows a passage that dreadfully adapts a scene from farce, as Othello eavesdrops on Cassio and Bianca; then the public display of his disgraced condition before the Venetian envoys, and the "brothel" scene.

1. "Shakespeare: The Middle Plays," in *The Age of Shakespeare*, ed. Boris Ford, 1955, p. 225.

Out of the confusion of the last act one certainty emerges, and that in the mind of Othello himself. It is no use asking the devil why he ensnares souls; but one can at least see what it is to be fallen, one's occupation gone. Othello's final speech is perhaps not the whole story, but neither is it untruthful. He has behaved like the Turk (used throughout the play as an enemy of civility and grace, a type of cunning and disorder). He has become that person of different "clime, complexion, and degree" whom it was wanton of Desdemona to marry. He has beaten a Venetian and traduced the state. So he punishes himself as he punished the Turk. Apart from Gratiano's "All that is spoke is marr'd," there is no reference to the impropriety of this act in the Christian Othello; this is not to Shakespeare's purpose. Othello is self-recognized as a Turk. He is an enemy of Venice, and the justice he carries out is that of the city, ideally considered.

Othello and "Otello"

Given the "operatic" and rhetorical qualities of *Othello* and its hero, it is interesting to consider the transformation of Shakespeare's play into the great opera composed by Giuseppe Verdi in 1887, toward the end of his career. The many cuts, simplifications, and reductions in its nonetheless remarkable libretto by Arrigo Boito (1842–1918) cast useful light, too, on the complexities of the original. In general, the simplifications allow the music itself to do the dramatic, emotional, and symbolic work of the complex plot and time structure, and much of the imagery, of the play. Boito's libretto starts out, for example, with Act II of the original, omitting Venice entirely (just as, so Joseph Kerman in his *Opera as Drama* reminds us, Samuel Johnson had recommended), and making the storm a matter of the highest prominence and importance. Iago's malignity, too, is made far less a conjectural matter; for example, he is given the following forthright *credo,* a statement of his faith, toward the beginning of Act II of *Otello:*

> I believe in a cruel God who created me in his image, whom I name in anger;
> I am born of a vile seed, a vile atom of matter.
>
> I am wicked because human, and I feel the primordial slime in me.
> Yes, this is my creed!
>
> I believe—with as devout a heart as the old woman before the altar—
> That the evil of my thoughts and deeds fulfills my destiny.
>
> I believe that justice is an actor, a clown in his face and in his heart,
> That he is all lies: tears, kisses, glances, honor, and sacrifice.
>
> And I believe that Man is Fortune's fool,
> Issuing from the germ of the cradle
> Making for the worm of the grave.
>
> Death comes after all this mockery.
> —And then? Death is Nothingness,
> And the old lie of Heaven.

At the very end of the opera's second act, the last 35 lines or so of Shakespeare's Act III, scene iii, with Iago and Othello together, become an extraordinary duet. It begins with Verdi's Otello calling out (as in Sh. III.iii.451) "Ah! *sangue! sangue! sangue!*" ("Oh, blood, blood, blood!"). Then, on his knees, he sings,

> Yes, I swear by the marble heavens,
> By the spinning lights above!
> By the dark, destroying sea!

My rage and wrath shall speedily blaze forth,
By this hand which I raise and extend!

Verdi's Iago intervenes with a phrase that, in the original Italian, completes the rhyme scheme even as the music completes the melodic pattern. He sings the next stanza to what turns out to be the melody to which Otello's first stanza was but a harmony part, a discovery confirmed in the final stanza—a repeat of the words of the first—which they sing together. As a musical metaphor for the way in which Iago, as it were, "calls the tune" for Othello's action, it is masterful.

(Iago) —No, don't get up yet! *(He kneels himself.)*
Witness the sun which shines
And warms and animates us,
The abundant earth and the vast breath of the All-Creator,
That to Otello I consecrate body, mind, and soul,
And to this bloody business, the weapons of will!

The text reprinted here is taken from *The Riverside Shakespeare,* edited by G. Blakemore Evans. Its principles of elision differ from those of the remainder of the *Oxford Anthology* (e.g., "capp'd" appears instead of "capped," "unhoused" instead of "unhousèd"). The spelling, however, has been re-anglicized.

The Tragedy of Othello, the Moor of Venice

The Scene: Venice; a seaport in Cyprus

Names of the Actors

DUKE OF VENICE
BRABANTIO, *a senator, father to Desdemona*
[*Other*] SENATORS
GRATIANO, *brother to Brabantio* } *two noble Venetians*
LODOVICO, *kinsman to Brabantio* } *two noble Venetians*
OTHELLO, *the Moor, in the military service of Venice*
CASSIO, *an honorable lieutenant*
IAGO, *an ensign, a villain*
RODERIGO, *a gull'd gentleman*
MONTANO, *governor of Cyprus before Othello*
CLOWN, *servant to Othello*
DESDEMONA, *daughter to Brabantio and wife to Othello*
EMILIA, *wife to Iago*
BIANCA, *a courtezan*
GENTLEMEN *of Cyprus,* SAILORS, OFFICERS, MESSENGERS, HERALD, MUSICIANS, *and* ATTENDANTS

ACT I

SCENE I [*Venice. A Street.*]

Enter RODERIGO *and* IAGO.

RODERIGO Tush, never tell me! I take it much unkindly
That thou, Iago, who hast had my purse
As if the strings were thine, shouldst know of this.°

IAGO ['Sblood,]° but you'll not hear me.
If ever I did dream of such a matter,
Abhor me.

RODERIGO Thou toldst me thou didst hold him in thy hate.

IAGO Despise me if I do not. Three great ones of the city,
In personal suit to make me his lieutenant,
Off-capp'd to him; and, by the faith of man,
I know my price, I am worth no worse a place.
But he (as loving his own pride and purposes)
Evades them with a bumbast° circumstance°
Horribly stuff'd with epithites of war,°
And in conclusion,
Nonsuits° my mediators; for, 'Certes,'° says he,
'I have already chose my officer.'
And what was he?
Forsooth, a great arithmetician,°

this i.e. Othello's marriage to Desdemona
'Sblood by God's (Christ's) blood
bumbast bombast, a cotton material used for padding; here, inflated. The figure is continued in *stuff'd* (l. 14).
circumstance circumlocution, rigmarole
epithites of war military jargon (*epithites,* a variant spelling of *epithets,* expressions, terms)
Nonsuits refuses
Certes certainly
arithmetician i.e. one adept at figures, not at fighting (cf. l. 31)

One Michael Cassio, a Florentine
(A fellow almost damn'd in a fair wife),°
That never set a squadron in the field,
Nor the division° of a battle° knows
More than a spinster°—unless the bookish theoric,
Wherein the toged° consuls° can propose°
As masterly as he. Mere prattle, without practice,
Is all his soldiership. But he, sir, had th' election;
And I, of whom his° eyes had seen the proof
At Rhodes, at Cyprus, and on other grounds
Christen'd and heathen, must be belee'd and calm'd°
By debitor and creditor°—this counter-caster,°
He (in good time!)° must his lieutenant be,
And I (God bless the mark!) his Moorship's ancient.°

RODERIGO By heaven, I rather would have been his hangman.°

IAGO Why, there's no remedy. 'Tis the curse of service;
Preferment° goes by letter and affection,°
And not by old gradation,° where each second
Stood heir to th' first. Now, sir, be judge yourself
Whether I in any just term° am affin'd°
To love the Moor.

RODERIGO I would not follow him then.

IAGO O, sir, content you;°
I follow him to serve my turn upon him.
We cannot all be masters, nor all masters
Cannot be truly follow'd. You shall mark
Many a duteous and knee-crooking knave
That (doting on his own obsequious bondage)
Wears out his time, much like his master's ass,
For nought but provender, and when he's old, cashier'd.°
Whip me such honest knaves. Others there are
Who, trimm'd in forms and visages of duty,°
Keep yet their hearts attending on themselves,
And throwing but shows of service on their lords,
Do well thrive by them; and when they have lin'd their coats,
Do themselves homage. These fellows have some soul,
And such a one do I profess myself. For, sir,
It is as sure as you are Roderigo,

almost . . . wife unexplained. Perhaps Shakespeare originally intended to follow his source Cinthio in giving Cassio a wife. There is no evidence that Cassio has yet met Bianca.
division arrangement
battle battalion
spinster i.e., housewife (one of whose duties was spinning)
toged wearing togas (dressed for the council-chamber, not the battlefield)
consuls senators
propose talk
his i.e. Othello's
be . . . calm'd have the wind taken out of my sails and be left becalmed
debitor and creditor i.e. bookkeeper
counter-caster accountant; literally, one who calculates with the aid of metal counters
in good time ironic
ancient ensign, standard-bearer
his hangman the one to hang him
Preferment advancement
letter and affection private recommendation and favoritism
old gradation seniority, as in the good old days
term respect
affin'd bound
content you calm yourself
cashier'd dismissed
trimm'd . . . duty wearing the manners and countenance of humble service

Were I the Moor, I would not be Iago.
In following him, I follow but myself;
Heaven is my judge, not I for love and duty,
But seeming so, for my peculiar° end;
For when my outward action doth demonstrate
The native act and figure° of my heart
In complement extern,° 'tis not long after
But I will wear my heart upon my sleeve
For daws to peck at: I am not what I am.

RODERIGO What a full fortune does the thick-lips° owe°
If he can carry't thus!°

IAGO Call up her father.
Rouse him, make after him, poison his delight,
Proclaim him in the streets; incense her kinsmen,
And though he in a fertile climate dwell,°
Plague him with flies.° Though that his joy be joy,
Yet throw such changes of vexation° on't,
As it may lose some colour.°

RODERIGO Here is her father's house, I'll call aloud.

IAGO Do, with like timorous° accent and dire yell
As when, by night and negligence,° the fire
Is spied in populous cities.

RODERIGO What ho! Brabantio, Signior Brabantio, ho!

IAGO Awake! what ho, Brabantio! thieves, thieves!
Look to your house, your daughter, and your bags!
Thieves, thieves!

[*Enter* BRABANTIO] *above* [*at a window*].

BRABANTIO What is the reason of this terrible summons?
What is the matter there?

RODERIGO Signior, is all your family within?

IAGO Are your doors lock'd?

BRABANTIO Why? Wherefore ask you this?

IAGO 'Zounds,° sir, y' are robb'd! For shame, put on your gown;
Your heart is burst, you have lost half your soul;
Even now, now, very now, an old black ram
Is tupping your white ewe. Arise, arise!
Awake the snorting° citizens with the bell,
Or else the devil will make a grandsire of you.
Arise, I say!

BRABANTIO What, have you lost your wits?

RODERIGO Most reverend signior, do you know my voice?

BRABANTIO Not I; what are you?

RODERIGO My name is Roderigo.

peculiar private
figure shape
complement extern external show corresponding to these hidden motives
thick-lips i.e. Othello
owe own
carry't thus carry this off
though . . . dwell i.e. though his general situation is a fortunate one (*climate,* region, country)
flies i.e. petty annoyances
changes of vexation vexatious changes
some colour i.e. some of its fresh gloss
timorous terrifying
by . . . negligence at night and as the result of negligence
'Zounds by God's (Christ's) wounds
snorting snoring

BRABANTIO The worser welcome;
I have charg'd thee not to haunt about my doors.
In honest plainness thou hast heard me say
My daughter is not for thee; and now, in madness
(Being full of supper and distemp'ring draughts),
Upon malicious bravery dost thou come
To start my quiet.

RODERIGO Sir, sir, sir—

BRABANTIO But thou must needs be sure
My spirits and my place have in their power
To make this bitter to thee.

RODERIGO Patience, good sir.

BRABANTIO What tell'st thou me of robbing? This is Venice;
My house is not a grange.

RODERIGO Most grave Brabantio,
In simple and pure soul I come to you.

IAGO 'Zounds, sir, you are one of those that will not serve God, if the devil bid you. Because we come to do you service, and you think we are ruffians, you'll have your daughter cover'd with a Barbary horse, you'll have your nephews neigh to you; you'll have coursers for cousins, and gennets for germans.

BRABANTIO What profane wretch art thou?

IAGO I am one, sir, that comes to tell you your daughter and the Moor are now making the beast with two backs.

BRABANTIO Thou art a villain.

IAGO You are a senator.

BRABANTIO This thou shalt answer; I know thee, Roderigo.

RODERIGO Sir, I will answer any thing. But I beseech you,
If't be your pleasure and most wise consent
(As partly I find it is) that your fair daughter,
At this odd-even and dull watch o' th' night,
Transported with no worse nor better guard
But with a knave of common hire, a gundolier,
To the gross clasps of a lascivious Moor—
If this be known to you, and your allowance,
We then have done you bold and saucy wrongs;
But if you know not this, my manners tell me
We have your wrong rebuke. Do not believe
That, from the sense of all civility,
I thus would play and trifle with your reverence.
Your daughter (if you have not given her leave),
I say again, hath made a gross revolt,

distemp'ring disordering, intoxicating
Upon malicious bravery with hostile intent to defy me
start startle
grange isolated farmhouse
simple sincere
nephews i.e. grandsons
coursers horses
cousins kinsmen
gennets Spanish horses
germans close relatives
villain base fellow
answer be held answerable for
odd-even i.e. about midnight, when there is scarcely any distinction between the end of one day and the beginning of the next
with by
But than
gundolier gondolier
allowance approval
saucy insolent
from . . . civility contrary to all sense of decency

Tying her duty, beauty, wit, and fortunes
In an extravagant° and wheeling° stranger°
Of here and every where. Straight° satisfy yourself.
If she be in her chamber or your house,
Let loose on me the justice of the state
For thus deluding you.

BRABANTIO Strike on the tinder, ho!
Give me a taper! Call up all my people!
This accident° is not unlike my dream,
Belief of it oppresses me already.
Light, I say, light! *Exit above.*

IAGO Farewell; for I must leave you.
It seems not meet, nor wholesome to my place,
To be producted° (as, if I stay, I shall)
Against the Moor; for I do know the state
(How ever this may gall him with some check)°
Cannot with safety cast° him, for he's embark'd
With such loud reason° to the Cyprus wars
(Which even now stands in act)° that, for their souls,
Another of his fadom° they have none
To lead their business; in which regard,°
Though I do hate him as I do hell-pains,
Yet, for necessity of present life,
I must show out a flag and sign of love,
Which is indeed but sign. That you shall surely find him,
Lead to the Sagittary° the raised search;°
And there will I be with him. So farewell. *Exit.*

Enter [below] BRABANTIO *[in his night-gown°] with* SERVANTS *and torches.*

BRABANTIO It is too true an evil; gone she is;
And what's to come of my despised time°
Is nought but bitterness. Now, Roderigo,
Where didst thou see her?—O unhappy girl!—
With the Moor, say'st thou?—Who would be a father!—
How didst thou know 'twas she?—O, she deceives me
Past thought!—What said she to you?—Get moe° tapers;
Raise all my kindred.—Are they married, think you?

RODERIGO Truly, I think they are.

BRABANTIO O heaven! how got she out? O treason of the blood!°
Fathers, from hence trust not your daughters' minds

extravagant expatriate; literally, wandering beyond his due limits
wheeling roving
stranger foreigner
Straight straightway
accident occurrence
producted produced, brought forward (to give evidence)
gall . . . check bring on him some irritating rebuke (*gall* = rub sore)
cast dismiss
loud reason i.e. evident rightness of choice
stands in act are under way
fadom fathom, i.e. capability
in which regard because of which consideration
Sagittary an inn (so called because its sign bore the conventional figure of Sagittarius, the Archer—a Centaur shooting an arrow)
raised search party of searchers who have been roused from their beds
night-gown dressing gown
what's . . . time the hateful remainder of my life
moe more
of the blood within the family

By what you see them act. Is there not charms°
By which the property° of youth and maidhood
May be abus'd?° Have you not read, Roderigo,
Of some such thing?

RODERIGO Yes, sir, I have indeed.

BRABANTIO Call up my brother.—O would you had had her!—
Some one way, some another.—Do you know
Where we may apprehend her and the Moor?

RODERIGO I think I can discover° him, if you please
To get good guard and go along with me.

BRABANTIO Pray you lead on. At every house I'll call
(I may command at most).°—Get weapons, ho!
And raise some special officers of night.—
On, good Roderigo, I will deserve° your pains. *Exeunt.*

SCENE II [*Venice. Another street.*]

Enter OTHELLO, IAGO, ATTENDANTS *with torches.*

IAGO Though in the trade° of war I have slain men,
Yet do I hold it very stuff° o' th' conscience
To do no contriv'd° murder. I lack iniquity
Sometimes to do me service. Nine or ten times
I had thought t' have yerk'd° him here under the ribs.

OTHELLO 'Tis better as it is.

IAGO Nay, but he prated,
And spoke such scurvy and provoking terms
Against your honor,
That with the little godliness I have
I did full hard forbear him.° But I pray you, sir,
Are you fast married? Be assur'd of this,
That the magnifico is much belov'd,
And hath in his effect a voice potential°
As double° as the Duke's. He will divorce you,
Or put upon you what restraint or grievance
The law (with all his might to enforce it on)
Will give him cable.°

OTHELLO Let him do his spite;
My services which I have done the signiory°
Shall out-tongue his complaints. 'Tis yet to know°—
Which, when I know that boasting is an honour,
I shall provulgate°—I fetch my life and being
From men of royal siege,° and my demerits°

charms magic spells
property nature
abus'd deceived
discover uncover, bring to light
I . . . most I can be sure of help from most of them.
deserve i.e. reward.
trade i.e. actual business
stuff material, substance
contriv'd premeditated
yerk'd stabbed
did . . . him had a hard time keeping my hands off him
potential powerful
double of double strength (like the Duke's voting power in the Senate)
cable scope (cf. "give one rope enough")
signiory Venetian government
yet to know not yet public knowledge
provulgate make publicly known
siege seat, i.e. rank
demerits deserts, merits

May speak, unbonneted,° to as proud a fortune
As this that I have reach'd; for know, Iago,
But that I love the gentle Desdemona,
I would not my unhoused° free condition
Put into circumscription and confine
For the sea's worth.° But look, what lights come yond?

Enter CASSIO *with* OFFICERS *and torches.*

IAGO Those are the raised father and his friends.
You were best go in.
OTHELLO Not I; I must be found.
My parts,° my title,° and my perfect soul°
Shall manifest me rightly. Is it they?
IAGO By Janus,° I think no.
OTHELLO The servants of the Duke? and my lieutenant?
The goodness of the night upon you, friends!
What is the news?
CASSIO The Duke does greet you, general,
And he requires your haste-post-haste appearance,
Even on the instant.
OTHELLO What is the matter,° think you?
CASSIO Something from Cyprus, as I may divine;
It is a business of some heat. The galleys
Have sent a dozen sequent° messengers
This very night at one another's heels;
And many of the consuls, rais'd and met,
Are at the Duke's already. You have been hotly call'd for;
When, being not at your lodging to be found,
The Senate hath sent about three several quests
To search you out.
OTHELLO 'Tis well I am found by you.
I will but spend a word here in the house,
And go with you. [*Exit.*]
CASSIO Ancient, what makes he° here?
IAGO Faith, he to-night hath boarded a land carract.°
If it prove lawful prize,° he's made for ever.
CASSIO I do not understand.
IAGO He's married.
CASSIO To who?

[*Enter* OTHELLO.]

IAGO Marry,° to—Come, captain, will you go?
OTHELLO Have with you.°

unbonneted Explained either as "without taking my hat off, i.e. on equal terms" (the opposite of the word's expected meaning, but in *Coriolanus*, II.ii.27, *bonneted* = took off their caps) or as a parenthetical "I say it in all due modesty."
unhoused unconfined
the sea's worth all the treasure in the sea
parts qualities, personal merits
title position
perfect soul clear conscience, conviction that I have done no wrong
Janus the two-faced god (dear to Iago)
matter business
sequent one after another
makes he is he doing
carract carrack, large trading ship
prize booty
Marry indeed (originally, the name of the Virgin Mary used as an oath)
Have with you a formula equivalent to "Yes, let's go"

CASSIO Here comes another troop to seek for you.

Enter BRABANTIO, RODERIGO, *with* OFFICERS [*with*] *torches* [*and weapons*].

IAGO It is Brabantio. General, be advis'd,°
He comes to bad intent.

OTHELLO Holla, stand there!

RODERIGO Signior, it is the Moor.

BRABANTIO Down with him, thief!

[*They draw on both sides.*]

IAGO You, Roderigo! come, sir, I am for you.

OTHELLO Keep up° your bright swords, for the dew will rust them.
Good signior, you shall more command with years
Than with your weapons.

BRABANTIO O thou foul thief, where hast thou stow'd my daughter?
Damn'd as thou art, thou hast enchanted° her,
For I'll refer me to all things of sense,°
If she in chains of magic were not bound,
Whether a maid so tender, fair, and happy,
So opposite to marriage that she shunn'd
The wealthy curled darlings of our nation,
Would ever have, t' incur a general mock,
Run from her guardage to the sooty bosom
Of such a thing as thou—to fear,° not to delight!
Judge me the world, if 'tis not gross in sense,°
That thou hast practis'd on° her with foul charms,
Abus'd her delicate youth with drugs or minerals
That weakens motion.° I'll have't disputed on,°
'Tis probable, and palpable to thinking.
I therefore apprehend and do attach° thee
For an abuser of the world, a practicer
Of arts inhibited° and out of warrant.°
Lay hold upon him, if he do resist
Subdue him at his peril.

OTHELLO Hold your hands,
Both you of my inclining,° and the rest.
Were it my cue to fight, I should have known it
Without a prompter. Whither will you that I go
To answer this your charge?

BRABANTIO To prison, till fit time
Of law and course of direct° session
Call thee to answer.

OTHELLO What if I do obey?
How may the Duke be therewith satisfied,

advis'd on your guard
Keep up sheathe
enchanted bewitched, cast a spell upon
refer . . . sense submit my case to the court of ordinary common sense
fear frighten
gross in sense obvious to perception (synonymous with *palpable to thinking* in l. 76)
practis'd on plotted against
motion the mental powers
I'll . . . on I'll submit it to experts for judgment
attach arrest
inhibited prohibited
out of warrant unwarrantable, illegal
inclining party
direct regular

Whose messengers are here about my side,
Upon some present business of the state,
To bring me to him?

OFFICER
'Tis true, most worthy signior;
The Duke's in council, and your noble self
I am sure is sent for.

BRABANTIO
How? the Duke in council?
In this time of the night? Bring him away;°
Mine's not an idle° cause. The Duke himself,
Or any of my brothers of the state,
Cannot but feel this wrong as 'twere their own;
For if such actions may have passage free,
Bond-slaves and pagans shall our statesmen be. *Exeunt.*

SCENE III [*Venice. A council chamber.*]

Enter DUKE [*and*] SENATORS [*set at a table, with lights*] *and* OFFICERS.

DUKE There's no composition° in these news
That gives them credit.

1 SENATOR
Indeed, they are disproportioned;
My letters say a hundred and seven galleys.

DUKE And mine, a hundred forty.

2 SENATOR
And mine, two hundred!
But though they jump° not on a just° accompt°
(As in these cases where the aim° reports,
'Tis oft with difference), yet do they all confirm
A Turkish fleet, and bearing up to Cyprus.

DUKE Nay, it is possible enough to judgment.
I do not so secure me in the error
But the main article I do approve°
In fearful° sense.

SAILOR (*within*) What ho, what ho, what ho!

Enter SAILOR

OFFICER A messenger from the galleys.

DUKE
Now? what's the business?

SAILOR The Turkish preparation° makes for Rhodes,
So was I bid report here to the state
By Signior Angelo. [*Exit* SAILOR.]

DUKE How say you by° this change?

1 SENATOR
This cannot be
By no assay of reason;° 'tis a pageant°
To keep us in false gaze.° When we consider
Th' importancy of Cyprus to the Turk,

away right along
idle trivial
composition consistency
jump agree
just exact
accompt accounting, number
the aim i.e. conjecture
so . . . approve take such assurance from the discrepancy that I don't accept the central item
fearful alarming
preparation force prepared for war; here, fleet (so also at l. 221 below)
by about
assay of reason test of common sense
pageant mere show
in false gaze looking in the wrong direction

And let ourselves again but understand
That, as it more concerns the Turk than Rhodes,
So may he with more facile question bear it,°
For that it stands not in such warlike brace,°
But altogether lacks th' abilities
That Rhodes is dress'd in—if we make thought of this,
We must not think the Turk is so unskillful°
To leave that latest° which concerns him first,
Neglecting an attempt of ease and gain°
To wake and wage° a danger profitless.

DUKE Nay, in all confidence, he's not for Rhodes.

OFFICER Here is more news.

Enter a MESSENGER.

MESSENGER The Ottomites, reverend and gracious,
Steering with due course toward the isle of Rhodes,
Have there injointed them with an after fleet.

1 SENATOR Ay, so I thought. How many, as you guess?

MESSENGER Of thirty sail; and now they do restem
Their backward course, bearing with frank appearance°
Their purposes toward Cyprus. Signior Montano,
Your trusty and most valiant servitor,
With his free duty° recommends° you thus,
And prays you to believe him. [*Exit* MESSENGER.]

DUKE 'Tis certain then for Cyprus.
Marcus Luccicos, is not he in town?

1 SENATOR He's now in Florence.

DUKE Write from us to him, post-post-haste. Dispatch!

1 SENATOR Here comes Brabantio and the valiant Moor.

Enter BRABANTIO, OTHELLO, CASSIO, IAGO, RODERIGO, *and* OFFICERS.

DUKE Valiant Othello, we must straight employ you
Against the general° enemy Ottoman.
[*To* BRABANTIO.] I did not see you; welcome, gentle° signior,
We lack'd your counsel and your help to-night.

BRABANTIO So did I yours. Good your Grace, pardon me:
Neither my place, nor aught I heard of business,
Hath rais'd me from my bed, nor doth the general care
Take hold on me; for my particular° grief
Is of so flood-gate° and o'erbearing nature
That it engluts° and swallows other sorrows,
And it is still itself.

DUKE Why? what's the matter?

with . . . it capture it more easily
brace readiness
unskillful unable to weigh the situation, undiscriminating
latest last
of . . . gain that will yield easy success
wage risk
with frank appearance openly, without disguising their intention
his free duty i.e. expressions of unwavering loyalty
recommends informs
general universal, i.e. of all Christendom
gentle noble
particular private
flood-gate i.e. overwhelming (like the onrushing water when floodgates are opened)
engluts engulfs

BRABANTIO My daughter! O, my daughter!
ALL Dead?
BRABANTIO Ay, to me:
She is abus'd,° stol'n from me, and corrupted
By spells and medicines bought of mountebanks;
For nature so prepost'rously to err°
(Being not deficient,° blind, or lame of sense)°
Sans° witchcraft could not.
DUKE Who e'er he be that in this foul proceeding
Hath thus beguil'd your daughter of herself,
And you of her, the bloody book of law
You shall yourself read in the bitter letter
After your own sense;° yea, though our proper° son
Stood in your action.°
BRABANTIO Humbly I thank your Grace.
Here is the man—this Moor, whom now, it seems,
Your special mandate for the state affairs
Hath hither brought.
ALL We are very sorry for't.
DUKE [*To* OTHELLO.] What, in your own part, can you say to this?
BRABANTIO Nothing, but this is so.
OTHELLO Most potent, grave, and reverend signiors,
My very noble and approv'd° good masters:
That I have ta'en away this old man's daughter,
It is most true; true I have married her;
The very head and front of my offending°
Hath this extent, no more. Rude° am I in my speech,
And little bless'd with the soft phrase of peace;
For since these arms of mine had seven years' pith,°
Till now some nine moons wasted, they have us'd
Their dearest action in the tented field;
And little of this great world can I speak
More than pertains to feats of broils and battle,
And therefore little shall I grace my cause
In speaking for myself. Yet (by your gracious patience)
I will a round° unvarnish'd tale deliver
Of my whole course of love—what drugs, what charms,
What conjuration, and what mighty magic
(For such proceeding I am charg'd withal)°
I won his daughter.
BRABANTIO A maiden, never bold;

abus'd deceived, deluded
err suffer aberration
deficient defective
sense reason
Sans without
After . . . sense giving it your own interpretation
proper own
Stood . . . action were the one who faced your charges
approv'd proved
The very . . . offending i.e. my offense at the utmost
Rude unpolished
pith strength
round plain
withal with

Of spirit so still and quiet that her motion
Blush'd at herself;° and she, in spite of nature,
Of years, of country, credit,° every thing,
To fall in love with what she fear'd to look on!
It is a judgment main'd,° and most imperfect,
That will confess° perfection so could err
Against all rules of nature, and must° be driven
To find out practices° of cunning hell
Why this should be. I therefore vouch° again
That with some mixtures pow'rful o'er the blood,°
Or with some dram (conjur'd to this effect)°
He wrought upon her.

DUKE To vouch this is no proof,
Without more wider° and more overt test
Than these thin habits° and poor likelihoods
Of modern° seeming° do prefer° against him.

1 SENATOR But, Othello, speak.
Did you by indirect and forced courses
Subdue and poison this young maid's affections?
Or came it by request, and such fair question°
As soul to soul affordeth?

OTHELLO I do beseech you,
Send for the lady to the Sagittary,
And let her speak of me before her father.
If you do find me foul in her report,
The trust, the office I do hold of you,
Not only take away, but let your sentence
Even fall upon my life.

DUKE Fetch Desdemona hither.
[*Exeunt two or three.*]

OTHELLO Ancient, conduct them; you best know the place. [*Exit* IAGO.]
And, till she come, as truly as to heaven
I do confess the vices of my blood,°
So justly° to your grave ears I'll present
How I did thrive in this fair lady's love,
And she in mine.

DUKE Say it, Othello.

OTHELLO Her father lov'd me, oft invited me;
Still° question'd me the story of my life
From year to year—the battles, sieges, fortunes,
That I have pass'd.

her . . . herself any stirring of her feelings made her blush (as if it were improper)
credit reputation
main'd maimed
confess aver, declare
must i.e. the unmaimed judgment must
practices plots
vouch affirm
blood passions
conjur'd . . . effect made thus efficacious by spells
more wider fuller
thin habits thin clothing, i.e. slight appearances
modern commonplace, insignificant
seeming supposition
prefer present
question conversation
vices . . . blood my human failings
justly exactly, truthfully
Still continually

I ran it through, even from my boyish days
To th' very moment that he bade me tell it;
Wherein I spoke of most disastrous chances:
Of moving accidents° by flood and field,
Of hair-breadth scapes i' th' imminent deadly° breach,°
Of being taken by the insolent foe
And sold to slavery, of my redemption thence
And portance° in my travel's history;
Wherein of antres° vast and deserts idle,°
Rough quarries,° rocks, and hills whose heads touch heaven,
It was my hint° to speak—such was my process—°
And of the Cannibals that each other eat,
The Anthropophagi,° and men whose heads
Do grow beneath their shoulders. These things to hear
Would Desdemona seriously incline;
But still the house affairs would draw her thence,
Which ever as she could with haste dispatch,
She'ld come again, and with a greedy ear
Devour up my discourse. Which I observing,
Took once a pliant° hour, and found good means
To draw from her a prayer of earnest heart
That I would all my pilgrimage dilate,°
Whereof by parcels° she had something heard,
But not intentively.° I did consent,
And often did beguile her of her tears,
When I did speak of some distressful stroke
That my youth suffer'd. My story being done,
She gave me for my pains a world of sighs;
She swore, in faith 'twas strange, 'twas passing strange;
'Twas pitiful, 'twas wondrous pitiful.
She wish'd she had not heard it, yet she wish'd
That heaven had made her such a man. She thank'd me,
And bade me, if I had a friend that lov'd her,
I should but teach him how to tell my story,
And that would woo her. Upon this hint° I spake:
She lov'd me for the dangers I had pass'd,
And I lov'd her that she did pity them.
This only is the witchcraft I have us'd.
Here comes the lady; let her witness it.

Enter DESDEMONA, IAGO, ATTENDANTS.

DUKE I think this tale would win my daughter too.
Good Brabantio.

accidents events
imminent deadly threatening death
breach gap made in fortifications
portance behavior
antres caves
idle barren, empty
Rough quarries rugged stone-masses
hint occasion
process proceeding (?) or story (?)
Anthropophagi man-eaters
pliant convenient, favorable
dilate relate in detail
by parcels by snatches, in bits and pieces
intentively with continuous attention
hint opportunity

Take up this mangled matter at the best;°
Men do their broken weapons rather use
Than their bare hands.

BRABANTIO I pray you hear her speak.
If she confess that she was half the wooer,
Destruction on my head if my bad blame
Light on the man! Come hither, gentle mistress.
Do you perceive in all this noble company
Where most you owe obedience?

DESDEMONA My noble father,
I do perceive here a divided duty:
To you I am bound for life and education;°
My life and education both do learn° me
How to respect° you; you are the lord of duty;
I am hitherto your daughter.° But here's my husband;
And so much duty as my mother show'd
To you, preferring you before her father,
So much I challenge° that I may profess
Due to the Moor, my lord.

BRABANTIO God be with you!° I have done.
Please it your Grace, on to the state affairs.
I had rather to adopt a child than get° it.
Come hither, Moor:
I here do give thee that with all my heart
Which but thou hast already, with all my heart
I would keep from thee. For your sake,° jewel,
I am glad at soul I have no other child,
For thy escape° would teach me tyranny,
To hang clogs° on them. I have done, my lord.

DUKE Let me speak like yourself,° and lay a sentence,°
Which as a grise° or step, may help these lovers
Into your favour.
When remedies° are past, the griefs are ended
By seeing the worst, which° late on hopes° depended.
To mourn a mischief° that is past and gone
Is the next° way to draw new mischief on.
What cannot be preserv'd when Fortune takes,
Patience her injury a mock'ry makes.°

Take . . . best make the best of this badly damaged situation
education rearing
learn teach
respect regard
I . . . daughter until now I have owed all my obedience to you as my father
challenge claim
God . . . you good-bye
get beget
For your sake because of what you have done
escape transgression
clogs blocks of wood hung on criminals or animals to prevent their running away
like yourself as you should
sentence maxim, moral saying
grise degree, step
remedies i.e. hopes of remedy
which i.e. the griefs
hopes anticipations
mischief injury
next nearest
Patience . . . makes patient endurance of the loss makes a mockery of Fortune's intended injury

The robb'd that smiles steals something from the thief;
He robs himself that spends a bootless° grief.

BRABANTIO So let the Turk of Cyprus us beguile,
We lose it not, so long as we can smile.
He bears the sentence well that nothing bears
But the free° comfort which from thence he hears;
But he bears both the sentence and the sorrow
That, to pay grief, must of poor patience° borrow.
These sentences, to sugar or to gall,
Being strong on both sides, are equivocal.
But words are words; I never yet did hear
That the bruis'd heart was pierced° through the ear.
I humbly beseech you proceed to th' affairs of state.

DUKE The Turk with a most mighty preparation° makes for Cyprus. Othello, the fortitude° of the place is best known to you; and though we have there a substitute° of most allow'd° sufficiency, yet opinion, a sovereign mistress of effects,° throws a more safer voice on you.° You must therefore be content to slubber° the gloss of your new fortunes with this more stubborn° and boist'rous expedition.

OTHELLO The tyrant custom, most grave senators,
Hath made the flinty and steel couch of war
My thrice-driven° bed of down. I do agnize°
A natural and prompt alacrity°
I find in hardness;° and do undertake
This present wars against the Ottomites.
Most humbly therefore bending to your state,°
I crave fit disposition° for my wife,
Due reference of place° and exhibition,°
With such accommodation and besort°
As levels with her breeding.

DUKE If you please,
Be't at her father's.

BRABANTIO I will not have it so.

OTHELLO Nor I.

DESDEMONA Nor I; I would not there reside,
To put my father in impatient thoughts
By being in his eye. Most gracious Duke,
To my unfolding lend your prosperous° ear,

bootless unavailing
free i.e. unmixed with sorrow
poor patience i.e. endurance, which hasn't much to lend
pierced i.e. relieved as by a surgeon's lancet. Some editors adopt Warburton's emendation *pieced* = mended.
preparation fleet
fortitude military strength
substitute representative
allow'd acknowledged
opinion . . . effects public opinion, the ultimate arbiter of what is to be done
throws . . . you gives you the reputation of being safer
slubber sully
stubborn rough
thrice-driven thrice-winnowed (to obtain the smallest and softest feathers)
agnize recognize
alacrity readiness
hardness hardship
state i.e. authority
fit disposition suitable provision
reference of place assignment of residence
exhibition allowance of money
besort suitable company
prosperous favorable

And let me find a charter° in your voice
T' assist my simpleness.

DUKE What would you, Desdemona?

DESDEMONA That I did love the Moor to live with him,
My downright° violence,° and storm of fortunes,°
May trumpet to the world. My heart's subdu'd
Even to° the very quality° of my lord.
I saw Othello's visage in his mind,
And to his honours and his valiant parts°
Did I my soul and fortunes consecrate.
So that, dear lords, if I be left behind,
A moth° of peace, and he go to the war,
The rites° for why I love him are bereft me,
And I a heavy interim shall support
By his dear° absence. Let me go with him.

OTHELLO Let her have your voice.
Vouch with me, heaven, I therefore beg it not
To please the palate of my appetite,
Nor to comply with heat (the young affects
In me defunct)° and proper° satisfaction;
But to be free and bounteous to her mind.
And heaven defend° your good souls, that you think
I will your serious and great business scant
For° she is with me. No, when light-wing'd toys
Of feather'd Cupid seel° with wanton dullness°
My speculative and offic'd instruments,°
That° my disports corrupt and taint my business,
Let housewives make a skillet of my helm,
And all indign° and base adversities
Make head° against my estimation!°

DUKE Be it as you shall privately determine,
Either for her stay or going; th' affair cries haste,
And speed must answer it.

1 SENATOR You must away to-night.

DESDEMONA To-night, my lord?

DUKE This night.

OTHELLO With all my heart.

charter authorization, privilege
downright plain, open
violence i.e. boldly aggressive action, breach of customary behavior
storm of fortunes taking my fortune by storm
subdu'd Even to brought completely into accord with
quality (1) nature, character; (2) profession, mode of life
parts qualities
moth mere idle consumer, parasite
rites perhaps to be taken as a variant spelling of *rights,* i.e. all the rights (including love-rites) involved in sharing his life to the full
dear heartfelt
Nor . . . defunct nor to serve sexual appetite—since the excesses of youthful passion are in me over and done with
proper personal, private
defend forbid
For because
seel blind (literally, sew shut the eyelids of a hawk to tame it)
wanton dullness dullness produced by sexual indulgence
My . . . instruments my faculties of perception when they have duties to perform. *Speculative* means literally "having power to see," and the line has been explained by some annotators as referring to the eyes, but it probably refers to the powers of mental perception, the "mind's eye."
That so that
indign unworthy, shameful
Make head raise an armed force
estimation reputation

DUKE At nine i' th' morning here we'll meet again.
Othello, leave some officer behind,
And he shall our commission bring to you;
And such things else of quality and respect°
As doth import° you.

OTHELLO So please your Grace, my ancient;
A man he is of honesty° and trust.
To his conveyance I assign my wife,
With what else needful your good Grace shall think
To be sent after me.

DUKE Let it be so.
Good night to every one. [*To* BRABANTIO.] And, noble signior,
If virtue no delighted° beauty lack,
Your son-in-law is far more fair than black.

1 SENATOR Adieu, brave Moor, use Desdemona well.

BRABANTIO Look to her, Moor, if thou hast eyes to see;
She has deceiv'd her father, and may thee.

Exeunt [DUKE, SENATORS, OFFICERS, *etc.*].

OTHELLO My life upon her faith! Honest Iago,
My Desdemona must I leave to thee.
I prithee let thy wife attend on her,
And bring them after in the best advantage.°
Come, Desdemona, I have but an hour
Of love, of wordly° matter and direction,
To spend with thee. We must obey the time.

Exit [*with* DESDEMONA].

RODERIGO Iago—

IAGO What say'st thou, noble heart?

RODERIGO What will I do, think'st thou?

IAGO Why, go to bed and sleep.

RODERIGO I will incontinently° drown myself.

IAGO If thou dost, I shall never love thee after.
Why, thou silly gentleman?

RODERIGO It is silliness to live, when to live is torment; and then have we a prescription° to die, when death is our physician.

IAGO O villainous!° I have look'd upon the world for four times seven years, and since I could distinguish betwixt a benefit and an injury, I never found man that knew how to love himself. Ere I would say I would drown myself for the love of a guinea hen, I would change my humanity with a baboon.

RODERIGO What should I do? I confess it is my shame to be so fond, but it is not in my virtue° to amend it.

IAGO Virtue? a fig! 'tis in ourselves that we are thus or thus.° Our bodies are

of . . . respect pertaining to your rank and privilege
import concern
honesty honor
delighted delightful
in . . . advantage at . . . opportunity
wordly worldly (a variant spelling)
incontinently at once
prescription (1) perfect right; (2) doctor's order
villainous wretched nonsense
virtue nature
'tis . . . thus it is in our own power to make ourselves what we will

our gardens, to the which our wills are gardeners; so that if we will plant nettles or sow lettuce, set hyssop° and weed up tine,° supply it with one gender° of herbs or distract it with many, either to have it sterile with idleness or manur'd with industry—why, the power and corrigible° authority of this lies in our wills. If the beam° of our lives had not one scale of reason to poise° another of sensuality, the blood and baseness° of our natures would conduct us to most prepost'rous conclusions. But we have reason to cool our raging motions,° our carnal stings, our unbitted lusts; whereof I take this that you call love to be a sect or scion.°

RODERIGO It cannot be.

IAGO It is merely a lust of the blood and a permission of the will. Come, be a man! Drown thyself? drown cats and blind puppies! I have profess'd me thy friend, and I confess me knit to thy deserving with cables of perdurable toughness. I could never better stead° thee than now. Put money in thy purse; follow thou the wars; defeat thy favour° with an usurp'd° beard. I say put money in thy purse. It cannot be long that Desdemona should continue her love to the Moor—put money in thy purse—nor he his to her. It was a violent commencement in her, and thou shalt see an answerable sequestration°—put but money in thy purse. These Moors are changeable in their wills°—fill thy purse with money. The food that to him now is as luscious as locusts,° shall be to him shortly as acerb° as the coloquintida.° She must change for youth; when she is sated with his body, she will find the error of her choice. She must have change, she must; therefore put money in thy purse. If thou wilt needs damn thyself, do it a more delicate way than drowning. Make° all the money thou canst. If sanctimony° and a frail vow betwixt an erring° barbarian and a super-subtle° Venetian be not too hard for my wits and all the tribe of hell, thou shalt enjoy her; therefore make money. A pox of drowning thyself, it is clean out of the way. Seek thou rather to be hang'd in compassing thy joy than to be drown'd and go without her.

RODERIGO Wilt thou be fast° to my hopes, if I depend on the issue?

IAGO Thou art sure of me—go make money. I have told thee often, and I retell thee again and again, I hate the Moor. My cause is hearted;° thine hath no less reason. Let us be conjunctive° in our revenge against him. If thou canst cuckold him, thou dost thyself a pleasure, me a sport. There are many events in the womb of time which will be deliver'd.

hyssop a fragrant herb
tine tares, wild grasses
gender kind
corrigible corrective
beam balance
poise counterbalance
blood and baseness base passions
motions desires, appetites
sect or scion cutting or offshoot
stead serve, help
defeat thy favour alter your appearance
usurp'd to which you have no right (because you are scarcely old enough to grow it)
answerable sequestration correspondingly abrupt ending (or separation)
wills lusts
locusts the sweet fruit of the carob tree
acerb bitter
coloquintida colocynth or "bitter apple," used as a purgative
Make raise, get together
sanctimony religious bond or ceremony
erring vagabond
super-subtle highly refined and sensitive
fast true
hearted rooted in my heart, i.e. deeply and passionately felt
conjunctive united

Traverse,° go, provide thy money. We will have more of this to-morrow.
Adieu.

RODERIGO Where shall we meet i' th' morning?

IAGO At my lodging.

RODERIGO I'll be with thee betimes.

IAGO Go to, farewell. Do you hear,° Roderigo?

RODERIGO What say you?

IAGO No more of drowning, do you hear?

RODERIGO I am chang'd.

IAGO Go to, farewell. Put money enough in your purse.

RODERIGO I'll sell all my land. *Exit.*

IAGO Thus do I ever make my fool my purse;
For I mine own gain'd knowledge should profane
If I would time expend with such a snipe°
But for my sport and profit. I hate the Moor,
And it is thought abroad° that 'twixt my sheets
H'as done my office. I know not if't be true,
But I, for mere suspicion in that kind,
Will do as if for surety.° He holds me well,
The better shall my purpose work on him.
Cassio's a proper° man. Let me see now:
To get his place and to plume up my will°
In double knavery—How? how?—Let's see—
After some time, to abuse Othello's ear
That he is too familiar with his wife.
He hath a person and a smooth dispose°
To be suspected—fram'd to make women false.
The Moor is of a free and open nature,
That thinks men honest that but seem to be so,
And will as tenderly° be led by th' nose
As asses are.
I have't. It is engend'red. Hell and night
Must bring this monstrous birth to the world's light. [*Exit.*]

ACT II

SCENE I [*A seaport in Cyprus. An open place near the quay.*]
Enter MONTANO *and two* GENTLEMEN.

MONTANO What from the cape can you discern at sea?

1 GENTLEMAN Nothing at all, it is a high-wrought flood.
I cannot, 'twixt the heaven and the main,
Descry a sail.

MONTANO Methinks the wind hath spoke aloud at land,

Traverse forward
Do you hear just a minute, one more thing
snipe woodcock; used contemptuously of an insignificant or silly person
it . . . abroad there is gossip
do . . . surety act as if on the basis of proved fact
proper handsome
plume . . . will pamper my ego
dispose bearing
tenderly readily

A fuller blast ne'er shook our battlements.
If it hath ruffian'd so upon the sea,
What ribs of oak, when mountains melt on them,
Can hold the mortise?° What shall we hear of this?

2 GENTLEMAN A segregation° of the Turkish fleet:
For do but stand upon the foaming shore,
The chidden billow seems to pelt the clouds,
The wind-shak'd surge, with high and monstrous mane,°
Seems to cast water on the burning Bear,
And quench the guards° of th' ever-fixed Pole;
I never did like molestation view
On the enchafed flood.

MONTANO If that the Turkish fleet
Be not enshelter'd and embay'd, they are drown'd;
It is impossible to bear it out.

Enter a [*third*] GENTLEMAN.

3 GENTLEMAN News, lads! our wars are done.
The desperate tempest hath so bang'd the Turks,
That their designment° halts.° A noble ship of Venice
Hath seen a grievous wrack and sufferance°
On most part of their fleet.

MONTANO How? is this true?

3 GENTLEMAN The ship is here put in,
A Veronesa;° Michael Cassio,
Lieutenant to the warlike Moor Othello,
Is come on shore; the Moor himself at sea,
And is in full commission here for Cyprus.

MONTANO I am glad on't; 'tis a worthy governor.

3 GENTLEMAN But this same Cassio, though he speak of comfort
Touching the Turkish loss, yet he looks sadly,
And prays the Moor be safe; for they were parted
With foul and violent tempest.

MONTANO Pray heaven he be;
For I have serv'd him, and the man commands
Like a full soldier. Let's to the sea-side, ho!
As well to see the vessel that's come in
As to throw out our eyes for brave Othello,
Even till we make the main and th' aerial blue
An indistinct regard.°

3 GENTLEMAN Come, let's do so;
For every minute is expectancy
Of more arrivance.

hold the mortise hold their joints together
segregation dispersion
mane Many editors prefer *main* = power. F1 *Maine* and Q1 *mayne* are ambiguous.
guards two stars in the Little Bear, in line with the pole star
designment plan
halts is lame
sufferance damage
Veronesa If this word means "Veronese," there is difficulty about applying it either to the ship, which has just been described as "of Venice," or to Cassio, who is called a Florentine at I.i.20. Perhaps it is the lost name of a particular type of ship.
An indistinct regard indistinguishable to the sight

Enter CASSIO.

CASSIO Thanks you,° the valiant of this warlike isle,
That so approve° the Moor! O, let the heavens
Give him defense against the elements,
For I have lost him on a dangerous sea.

MONTANO Is he well shipp'd?

CASSIO His bark is stoutly timber'd, and his pilot
Of very expert and approv'd allowance;°
Therefore my hopes (not surfeited to death)
Stand in bold cure.° *Within,* 'A sail, a sail, a sail!'

[*Enter a* MESSENGER.]

CASSIO What noise?

[MESSENGER] The town is empty; on the brow o' th' sea
Stands ranks of people, and they cry, "A sail!"

CASSIO My hopes do shape him for the governor.

[*A shot.*]

2 GENTLEMAN They do discharge their shot of courtesy;
Our friends at least.

CASSIO I pray you, sir, go forth,
And give us truth who 'tis that is arriv'd.

2 GENTLEMAN I shall. *Exit.*

MONTANO But, good lieutenant, is your general wiv'd?

CASSIO Most fortunately: he hath achiev'd a maid
That paragons description° and wild fame;
One that excels the quirks° of blazoning° pens,
And in th' essential vesture of creation
Does tire the ingener.°

Enter [SECOND] GENTLEMAN.

How now? who has put in?

2 GENTLEMAN 'Tis one Iago, ancient to the general.

CASSIO H'as had most favorable and happy speed:
Tempests themselves, high seas, and howling winds,
The gutter'd° rocks and congregated sands,
Traitors ensteep'd° to enclog the guiltless keel,
As having sense of beauty, do omit°
Their mortal° natures, letting go safely by
The divine Desdemona.

MONTANO What is she?

CASSIO She that I spake of, our great captain's captain,
Left in the conduct of the bold Iago,

Thanks you thanks to you
approve commend, admire
expert . . . allowance i.e. of acknowledged and proved skill
my . . . cure since I have not had to indulge my hopes so long that they are near death, I am confident that they will be fulfilled
paragons description surpasses whatever praise is uttered of her
quirks conceits, flourishes
blazoning listing her beauties
in . . . ingener in her native beauty defeats all attempts of the inventive poet to praise her adequately
gutter'd jagged
ensteep'd submerged
omit give up, do not act in accordance with
mortal deadly

Whose footing° here anticipates our thoughts
A se'nnight's speed. Great Jove, Othello guard,
And swell his sail with thine own pow'rful breath,
That he may bless this bay with his tall ship,
Make love's quick pants in Desdemona's arms,
Give renew'd fire to our extincted spirits,
And bring all Cyprus comfort!

Enter DESDEMONA, IAGO, RODERIGO, *and* EMILIA, [*with* ATTENDANTS].

O, behold,
The riches° of the ship is come on shore!
You men of Cyprus, let her have your knees.
Hail to thee, lady! and the grace of heaven,
Before, behind thee, and on every hand,
Enwheel thee round!

DESDEMONA I thank you, valiant Cassio.
What tidings can you tell me of my lord?

CASSIO He is not yet arriv'd, nor know I aught
But that he's well and will be shortly here.

DESDEMONA O, but I fear—How lost you company?

CASSIO The great contention of the sea and skies
Parted our fellowship.

Within, 'A sail, a sail!' [*A shot.*]

But hark! a sail.

2 GENTLEMAN They give their greeting to the citadel.
This likewise is a friend.

CASSIO See for the news.

[*Exit* SECOND GENTLEMAN.]

Good ancient, you are welcome. [*To* EMILIA.] Welcome, mistress.
Let it not gall your patience, good Iago,
That I extend° my manners; 'tis my breeding
That gives me this bold show of courtesy.

[*Kissing her.*]

IAGO Sir, would she give you so much of her lips
As of her tongue she oft bestows on me,
You would have enough.

DESDEMONA Alas! she has no speech.

IAGO In faith, too much;
I find it still, when I have list° to sleep.
Marry, before your ladyship, I grant,
She puts her tongue a little in her heart,
And chides with thinking.°

EMILIA You have little cause to say so.

IAGO Come on, come on; you are pictures° out a' doors,
Bells° in your parlors, wild-cats in your kitchens,

footing landing, arrival
riches Singular (from French *richesse*)
extend show
list inclination
with thinking i.e. without speaking her thoughts
pictures i.e. painted
Bells i.e. with tongues going like bell-clappers

Saints in your injuries,° devils being offended,
Players° in your huswifery,° and huswives° in your beds.

DESDEMONA O, fie upon thee, slanderer!

IAGO Nay, it is true, or else I am a Turk:
You rise to play, and go to bed to work.

EMILIA You shall not write my praise.

IAGO No, let me not.

DESDEMONA What wouldst write of me, if thou shouldst praise me?

IAGO O gentle lady, do not put me to't,
For I am nothing if not critical.°

DESDEMONA Come on, assay.°—There's one gone to the harbour?

IAGO Ay, madam.

DESDEMONA I am not merry; but I do beguile
The thing I am° by seeming otherwise.—
Come, how wouldst thou praise me?

IAGO I am about it, but indeed my invention
Comes from my pate as birdlime° does from frieze,°
It plucks out brains and all. But my Muse labors,
And thus she is deliver'd:
If she be fair and wise, fairness and wit,
The one's for use, the other useth it.

DESDEMONA Well prais'd! How if she be black° and witty?

IAGO If she be black, and thereto have a wit,
She'll find a white° that shall her blackness hit.°

DESDEMONA Worse and worse.

EMILIA How if fair and foolish?

IAGO She never yet was foolish that was fair,
For even her folly° help'd her to an heir.

DESDEMONA These are old fond° paradoxes to make fools laugh i' th' alehouse. What miserable praise hast thou for her that's foul and foolish?

IAGO There's none so foul and foolish thereunto,
But does foul pranks which fair and wise ones do.

DESDEMONA O heavy ignorance! thou praisest the worst best. But what praise couldst thou bestow on a deserving woman indeed—one that in the authority° of her merit, did justly put on the vouch° of very malice itself?

IAGO She that was ever fair, and never proud,
Had tongue at will, and yet was never loud,
Never lack'd gold, and yet went never gay,°
Fled from her wish, and yet said, 'Now I may';°
She that being ang'red, her revenge being nigh,

Saints . . . injuries when you offend, you do it with an air of sanctity
Players actors, i.e. people making a pretense (?) or perfunctory triflers (?)
huswifery household management
huswives hussies, wantons
critical censorious
assay try
The thing I am my anxious self
birdlime sticky substance used to catch birds
frieze coarse wool
black brunette
white with a pun on *wight*, "person"
hit suit, fit (with sexual quibble)
folly with second sense "wantonness"
fond foolish
foul ugly
in the authority by virtue
put . . . vouch compel the favorable testimony
gay extravagantly dressed
Fled . . . may did not indulge herself even though she was free to do so

Bade her wrong stay,° and her displeasure fly;
She that in wisdom never was so frail
To change the cod's head for the salmon's tail;°
She that could think, and nev'r disclose her mind,
See suitors following, and not look behind:
She was a wight (if ever such wight were)—

DESDEMONA To do what?

IAGO To suckle fools and chronicle small beer.°

DESDEMONA O most lame and impotent conclusion! Do not learn of him, Emilia, though he be thy husband. How say you, Cassio? is he not a most profane and liberal° counsellor?

CASSIO He speaks home,° madam. You may relish him more in° the soldier than in the scholar.

IAGO *Aside.* He takes her by the palm; ay, well said,° whisper. With as little a web as this will I ensnare as great a fly as Cassio. Ay, smile upon her, do; I will gyve° thee in thine own courtship.° You say true, 'tis so indeed. If such tricks as these strip you out of your lieutenantry, it had been better you had not kiss'd your three fingers so oft, which now again you are most apt to play the sir° in. Very good; well kiss'd! an excellent courtesy!° 'Tis so indeed. Yet again, your fingers to your lips? Would they were clyster-pipes° for your sake! [*Trumpets within.*]—The Moor! I know his trumpet.

CASSIO 'Tis truly so.

DESDEMONA Let's meet him and receive him.

CASSIO Lo, where he comes!

Enter OTHELLO *and* ATTENDANTS.

OTHELLO O my fair warrior!

DESDEMONA My dear Othello!

OTHELLO It gives me wonder great as my content
To see you here before me. O my soul's joy!
If after every tempest come such calms,
May the winds blow till they have waken'd death!
And let the labouring bark climb hills of seas
Olympus-high, and duck again as low
As hell's from heaven! If it were now to die,
'Twere now to be most happy; for I fear
My soul hath her content so absolute
That not another comfort like to this
Succeeds in unknown fate.

DESDEMONA The heavens forbid
But that our loves and comforts should increase
Even as our days do grow!

wrong stay sense of injury cease
change . . . tail Obscure. Perhaps "give up something common but valuable in exchange for something showy but worthless," but more probably a sexual innuendo
suckle . . . beer tend babies and keep petty household accounts
liberal free-spoken
home bluntly
in in the character of
well said well done
gyve fetter, entangle
courtship display of courtly manners
sir gentleman, gallant
courtesy bow
clyster-pipes enema tubes

OTHELLO Amen to that, sweet powers!
I cannot speak enough of this content,
It stops me here; it is too much of joy.
And this, and this, the greatest discords be
[*They kiss.*]
That e'er our hearts shall make!

IAGO [*Aside.*] O, you are well tun'd now!
But I'll set down the pegs° that make this music,
As honest as I am.

OTHELLO Come; let us to the castle.
News, friends: our wars are done; the Turks are drown'd.
How does my old acquaintance of this isle?
Honey, you shall be well desir'd° in Cyprus,
I have found great love amongst them. O my sweet,
I prattle out of fashion,° and I dote
In mine own comforts. I prithee, good Iago,
Go to the bay and disembark my coffers.°
Bring thou the master° to the citadel;
He is a good one, and his worthiness
Does challenge° much respect. Come, Desdemona,
Once more, well met at Cyprus.

Exeunt OTHELLO *and* DESDEMONA [*with all but* IAGO *and* RODERIGO].

IAGO [*To an* ATTENDANT, *as he is going out.*] Do thou meet me presently at the harbour.—Come [hither]. If thou be'st valiant (as they say base men° being in love have then a nobility in their natures more than is native to them), list me. The lieutenant to-night watches on the court of guard.° First, I must tell thee this: Desdemona is directly in love with him.

RODERIGO With him? why, 'tis not possible.

IAGO Lay thy finger thus;° and let thy soul be instructed. Mark me with what violence she first lov'd the Moor, but for bragging and telling her fantastical lies. To love him still° for prating—let not thy discreet heart think it. Her eye must be fed; and what delight shall she have to look on the devil?° When the blood is made dull with the act of sport, there should be, again to inflame it and to give satiety a fresh appetite, loveliness in favor,° sympathy° in years, manners, and beauties—all which the Moor is defective in. Now for want of these requir'd conveniences,° her delicate tenderness will find itself abus'd, begin to heave the gorge,° disrelish and abhor the Moor; very nature will instruct her in it and compel her to some second choice. Now, sir,

set . . . pegs i.e. untune the instrument (and so produce discords)
desir'd welcomed, loved
out of fashion irrelevantly (?) or unconventionally (?)
coffers baggage
master ship's captain
challenge claim, deserve
base men even men of low birth
watches . . . guard has charge of the watch
thus i.e. on your lips
still always
the devil traditionally black
favor face, appearance
sympathy similarity, correspondence
conveniences compatibilities
heave the gorge feel nauseated

this granted (as it is a most pregnant° and unforc'd position), who stands so eminent in the degree of this fortune as Cassio does? a knave very voluble; no further conscionable° than in putting on the mere form of civil and humane° seeming, for the better compass of his salt° and most hidden loose affection?° Why, none, why, none—a slipper° and subtle knave, a finder-out of occasion; that has an eye can stamp° and counterfeit advantages,° though true advantage never present itself; a devilish knave. Besides, the knave is handsome, young, and hath all those requisites in him that folly° and green° minds look after; a pestilent complete knave, and the woman hath found him° already.

RODERIGO I cannot believe that in her, she's full of most bless'd condition.°

IAGO Bless'd fig's-end! The wine she drinks is made of grapes. If she had been bless'd, she would never have lov'd the Moor. Bless'd pudding!° Didst thou not see her paddle with the palm of his hand? Didst not mark that?

RODERIGO Yes, that I did; but that was but courtesy.

IAGO Lechery, by this hand; an index° and obscure prologue to the history of lust and foul thoughts. They met so near with their lips that their breaths embrac'd together. Villainous thoughts, Roderigo! When these mutualities° so marshal the way, hard at hand° comes the master and main exercise, th' incorporate° conclusion. Pish! But, sir, be you rul'd by me. I have brought you from Venice. Watch° you to-night; for the command, I'll lay't upon you.° Cassio knows you not. I'll not be far from you. Do you find some occasion to anger Cassio, either by speaking too loud, or tainting° his discipline, or from what other course you please, which the time shall more favorably minister.

RODERIGO Well.

IAGO Sir, he's rash° and very sudden in choler, and happily° may strike at you—provoke him that he may; for even out of that will I cause these of Cyprus to mutiny,° whose qualification shall come into no true taste° again but by the displanting of Cassio. So shall you have a shorter journey to your desires by the means I shall then have to prefer them; and the impediment most profitably remov'd, without the which there were no expectation of our prosperity.

RODERIGO I will do this, if you can bring it to any opportunity.

IAGO I warrant thee.° Meet me by and by at the citadel. I must fetch his necessaries ashore. Farewell.

RODERIGO Adieu. *Exit.*

pregnant obvious
conscionable bound by considerations of conscience
civil and humane polite and courteous
salt lewd
affection passion
slipper slippery
stamp coin, manufacture
advantages opportunities
folly wantonness
green youthful, lusty
found him sized him up
condition disposition, character
pudding sausage
index table of contents at beginning of a book
mutualities exchanges
hard at hand very soon after
incorporate carnal
Watch serve as a member of the watch
lay't upon you arrange for your orders
tainting discrediting
rash impetuous
happily haply, perhaps
mutiny riot
whose . . . taste whose anger will not be acceptably diluted
I warrant thee I guarantee you'll have opportunity

IAGO That Cassio loves her, I do well believe't;
That she loves him, 'tis apt and of great credit.°
The Moor (howbeit that I endure him not)
Is of a constant, loving, noble nature,
And I dare think he'll prove to Desdemona
A most dear husband. Now I do love her too,
Not out of absolute lust (though peradventure
I stand accomptant° for as great a sin),
But partly led to diet my revenge,
For that I do suspect the lusty Moor
Hath leap'd into my seat; the thought whereof
Doth (like a poisonous mineral) gnaw my inwards;
And nothing can or shall content my soul
Till I am even'd with him, wife for wife;
Or failing so, yet that I put the Moor
At least into a jealousy so strong
That judgment cannot cure. Which thing to do,
If this poor trash of Venice, whom I trace°
For his quick hunting, stand the putting on,°
I'll have our Michael Cassio on the hip,°
Abuse him to the Moor in the rank garb°
(For I fear Cassio with my night-cap too),
Make the Moor thank me, love me, and reward me,
For making him egregiously an ass,
And practising upon° his peace and quiet
Even to madness. 'Tis here; but yet confus'd,
Knavery's plain face is never seen till us'd. *Exit.*

SCENE II [*Cyprus. A street.*]

Enter Othello's HERALD *with a proclamation;* [*people following*].

HERALD It is Othello's pleasure, our noble and valiant general, that upon certain tidings now arriv'd, importing the mere perdition° of the Turkish fleet, every man put himself into triumph; some to dance, some to make bonfires, each man to what sport and revels his addiction leads him; for besides these beneficial news, it is the celebration of his nuptial. So much was his pleasure should be proclaim'd. All offices° are open, and there is full liberty of feasting from this present hour of five till the bell have told eleven. Heaven bless the isle of Cyprus and our noble general Othello! *Exeunt.*

apt . . . credit likely and credible
accomptant accountable
trace Obscure. The meaning must be something like "train," or "check to make more eager"; the latter is the sense of Steevens' widely accepted emendation *trash,* meaning to hang weights on a hound to prevent his hunting too fast.
stand . . . on perform properly when the moment comes for me to set him on
on the hip in a position where I can throw him (wrestling term)
rank garb coarse fashion
practicing upon plotting against
mere perdition utter destruction
offices kitchens, food storerooms, etc.

SCENE III [*Cyprus. The citadel.*]

Enter OTHELLO, DESDEMONA, CASSIO, *and* ATTENDANTS.

OTHELLO Good Michael, look you to the guard to-night.
Let's teach ourselves that honourable stop,
Not to outsport° discretion.

CASSIO Iago hath direction what to do;
But notwithstanding with my personal eye
Will I look to't.

OTHELLO Iago is most honest.
Michael, good night. To-morrow with your earliest
Let me have speech with you. [*To* DESDEMONA.] Come, my dear love,
The purchase made, the fruits are to ensue;
That profit's yet to come 'tween me and you.—
Good night. *Exit* [*with* DESDEMONA *and* ATTENDANTS].

Enter IAGO.

CASSIO Welcome, Iago; we must to the watch.

IAGO Not this hour,° lieutenant; 'tis not yet ten o' th' clock. Our general cast° us thus early for the love of his Desdemona; who let us not therefore blame. He hath not yet made wanton the night with her; and she is sport for Jove.

CASSIO She's a most exquisite lady.

IAGO And I'll warrant her, full of game.

CASSIO Indeed she's a most fresh and delicate creature.

IAGO What an eye she has! Methinks it sounds a parley° to provocation.

CASSIO An inviting eye; and yet methinks right modest.

IAGO And when she speaks, is it not an alarum° to love?

CASSIO She is indeed perfection.

IAGO Well—happiness to their sheets! Come, lieutenant, I have a stope° of wine, and here without are a brace of Cyprus gallants that would fain have a measure to the health of black Othello.

CASSIO Not to-night, good Iago. I have very poor and unhappy brains for drinking. I could well wish courtesy would invent some other custom of entertainment.

IAGO O, they are our friends—but one cup, I'll drink for you.

CASSIO I have drunk but one cup to-night—and that was craftily qualified° too—and behold what innovation° it makes here.° I am infortunate in the infirmity, and dare not task my weakness with any more.

IAGO What, man? 'Tis a night of revels, the gallants desire it.

CASSIO Where are they?

IAGO Here, at the door; I pray you call them in.

CASSIO I'll do't, but it dislikes me.° *Exit.*

IAGO If I can fasten but one cup upon him,
With that which he hath drunk to-night already,

outsport carry our sports beyond
Not this hour not for an hour yet
cast dismissed
parley trumpet signal for a conference
alarum trumpet signal to arms
stope stoup, large drinking vessel
craftily qualified cannily diluted
innovation insurrection
here i.e. in his head
it dislikes me I don't care for it

He'll be as full of quarrel and offense
As my young mistress' dog.° Now, my sick fool Roderigo,
Whom love hath turn'd almost the wrong side out,
To Desdemona hath to-night carous'd°
Potations pottle-deep;° and he's to watch.
Three else° of Cyprus, noble swelling° spirits
That hold their honours in a wary distance,°
The very elements° of this warlike isle,
Have I to-night fluster'd with flowing cups,
And they watch too. Now 'mongst this flock of drunkards
Am I to put our Cassio in some action
That may offend the isle. But here they come.

Enter CASSIO, MONTANO, *and* GENTLEMEN; [SERVANTS *follow with wine*].

If consequence do but approve my dream,°
My boat sails freely, both with wind and stream.°

CASSIO 'Fore God, they have given me a rouse° already.

MONTANO Good faith, a little one; not past a pint, as I am a soldier.

IAGO Some wine ho!
[*Sings.*°]

And let me the canakin clink, clink;
And let me the canakin clink.
A soldier's a man;
O, man's life's but a span;°
Why then let a soldier drink.

Some wine, boys!

CASSIO 'Fore God, an excellent song.

IAGO I learn'd it in England, where indeed they are most potent in potting; your Dane, your German, and your swag-bellied Hollander—Drink ho!—are nothing to your English.

CASSIO Is your Englishman so exquisite in his drinking?

IAGO Why, he drinks you, with facility, your Dane dead drunk; he sweats not to overthrow your Almain;° he gives your Hollander a vomit ere the next pottle can be fill'd.

CASSIO To the health of our general!

MONTANO I am for it, lieutenant; and I'll do you justice.°

IAGO O sweet England!
[*Sings.*°]

King Stephen was and-a worthy peer,
His breeches cost him but a crown;

my . . . dog a young lady's pet dog (likely to be spoiled)
carous'd drunk off
pottle-deep to the bottom of the tankard (a pottle was a two-quart vessel)
else others
swelling proud
hold . . . distance are very touchy about their honor
very elements typical products
If . . . dream if the sequel corresponds to my fond hope
stream current
rouse drink
Sings probably an old drinking song
span i.e. brief stretch of time
Almain German
do you justice match you in drinking that toast
Sings from an old ballad also alluded to in *The Tempest*, IV.i.220

He held them sixpence all too dear,
With that he call'd the tailor lown;°
He was a wight of high renown,
And thou art but of low degree.
'Tis pride° *that pulls the country down,*
Then take thy auld cloak about thee.

Some wine ho!

CASSIO 'Fore God, this is a more exquisite song than the other.

IAGO Will you hear't again?

CASSIO No; for I hold him to be unworthy of his place that does those things. Well, God's above all; and there be souls must be sav'd, and there be souls must not be sav'd.

IAGO It's true, good lieutenant.

CASSIO For mine own part—no offense to the general, nor any man of quality—I hope to be sav'd.

IAGO And so do I too, lieutenant.

CASSIO Ay; but by your leave, not before me; the lieutenant is to be sav'd before the ancient. Let's have no more of this; let's to our affairs.—God forgive us our sins!—Gentlemen, let's look to our business. Do not think, gentlemen, I am drunk: this is my ancient, this is my right hand, and this is my left hand. I am not drunk now; I can stand well enough, and I speak well enough.

[ALL] Excellent well.

CASSIO Why, very well then; you must not think then that I am drunk. *Exit.*

MONTANO To th' platform, masters, come, let's set the watch.

IAGO You see this fellow that is gone before:
He's a soldier fit to stand by Caesar
And give direction; and do but see his vice,
'Tis to his virtue a just equinox,°
The one as long as th' other. 'Tis pity of him.
I fear the trust Othello puts him in,
On some odd time of his infirmity,
Will shake this island.

MONTANO But is he often thus?

IAGO 'Tis evermore the prologue to his sleep.
He'll watch the horologe a double set°
If drink rock not his cradle.

MONTANO It were well
The general were put in mind of it.
Perhaps he sees it not, or his good nature
Prizes the virtue that appears in Cassio,
And looks not on his evils. Is not this true?

Enter RODERIGO.

IAGO [*Aside to him.*] How now, Roderigo?
I pray you, after the lieutenant, go. [*Exit* RODERIGO.]

lown rascal
pride ostentation, extravagance
just equinox exact counterpart (of dark against light)
watch . . . set stay awake twice round the clock

MONTANO And 'tis great pity that the noble Moor
Should hazard such a place as his own second
With° one of an ingraft° infirmity;
It were an honest action to say
So to the Moor.

IAGO Not I, for this fair island.
I do love Cassio well; and would do much
To cure him of this evil. [*Cry within:* 'Help! help!']
But hark, what noise?

Enter CASSIO *pursuing* RODERIGO.

CASSIO 'Zounds, you rogue! you rascal!

MONTANO What's the matter, lieutenant?

CASSIO A knave teach me my duty? I'll beat the knave into a twiggen° bottle.

RODERIGO Beat me?

CASSIO Dost thou prate, rogue? [*Striking* RODERIGO.]

MONTANO Nay, good lieutenant; I pray you, sir, hold your hand. [*Staying him.*]

CASSIO Let me go, sir, or I'll knock you o'er the mazzard.°

MONTANO Come, come—you're drunk.

CASSIO Drunk? [*They fight.*]

IAGO [*Aside to* RODERIGO.] Away, I say; go out and cry a mutiny. [*Exit* RODERIGO.]
Nay, good lieutenant—God's will, gentlemen—
Help ho!—lieutenant—sir—Montano—sir—
Help, masters!—Here's a goodly watch indeed! [*A bell rung.*]
Who's that which rings the bell? *Diablo,* ho!
The town will rise. God's will, lieutenant, hold!
You'll be asham'd for ever.

Enter OTHELLO *and* ATTENDANTS.

OTHELLO What is the matter here?

MONTANO 'Zounds, I bleed still,
I am hurt to th' death. He dies. [*Assailing* CASSIO *again.*]

OTHELLO Hold, for your lives!

IAGO Hold ho! Lieutenant—sir—Montano—gentlemen—
Have you forgot all place of sense° and duty?
Hold! the general speaks to you; hold, for shame!

OTHELLO Why, how now ho? from whence ariseth this?
Are we turn'd Turks, and to ourselves do that
Which heaven hath forbid the Ottomites?°
For Christian shame, put by this barbarous brawl.
He that stirs next to carve for his own rage°

hazard . . . With take risks with a position as important as that of his own deputy by appointing
ingraft ingrained, inveterate
twiggen wicker-covered
mazzard head
place of sense i.e. the ordinary decencies. Some editors adopt Hanmer's emendation *sense of place.*
Which . . . Ottomites i.e. by wrecking their fleet
carve . . . rage indulge his own impulse

Holds his soul light;° he dies upon his motion.
Silence that dreadful bell, it frights the isle
From her propriety.° What is the matter, masters?
Honest Iago, that looks dead with grieving,
Speak: who began this? On thy love, I charge thee!

IAGO I do not know. Friends all, but now, even now;
In quarter,° and in terms like bride and groom
Devesting them for bed; and then, but now
(As if some planet had unwitted men),
Swords out, and tilting one at other's breast,
In opposition bloody. I cannot speak
Any beginning to this peevish odds;°
And would in action glorious I had lost
Those legs that brought me to a part of it.

OTHELLO How comes it, Michael, you are thus forgot?°

CASSIO I pray you pardon me, I cannot speak.

OTHELLO Worthy Montano, you were wont to be civil;
The gravity and stillness of your youth
The world hath noted, and your name is great
In mouths of wisest censure.° What's the matter
That you unlace° your reputation thus,
And spend your rich opinion° for the name
Of a night-brawler? Give me answer to it.

MONTANO Worthy Othello, I am hurt to danger.
Your officer, Iago, can inform you—
While I spare speech, which something now offends° me—
Of all that I do know, nor know I aught
By me that's said or done amiss this night,
Unless self-charity be sometimes a vice,
And to defend ourselves it be a sin
When violence assails us.

OTHELLO Now by heaven,
My blood° begins my safer guides° to rule,
And passion, having my best judgment collied,°
Assays to lead the way. 'Zounds, if I stir,
Or do but lift this arm, the best of you
Shall sink in my rebuke. Give me to know
How this foul rout began; who set it on;
And he that is approv'd in this offense,°
Though he had twinn'd with me, both at a birth,
Shall lose me. What, in a town of war,
Yet wild, the people's hearts brimful of fear,

light of small value
propriety natural temper (of calmness and order)
quarter bounds
peevish odds childish quarrel
are thus forgot have forgotten yourself in this way
censure judgment
unlace lay open
opinion reputation
offends pains
blood anger
safer guides i.e. rational controls
collied darkened
approv'd . . . offense found guilty

To manage° private and domestic quarrel?
In night, and on the court and guard of safety?°
'Tis monstrous. Iago, who began't?

MONTANO If partially affin'd,° or leagu'd in office,
Thou dost deliver more or less than truth,
Thou art no soldier.

IAGO Touch me not so near;
I had rather have this tongue cut from my mouth
Than it should do offense to Michael Cassio;
Yet I persuade myself, to speak the truth
Shall nothing wrong him. Thus it is, general:
Montano and myself being in speech,
There comes a fellow crying out for help,
And Cassio following him with determin'd sword
To execute upon him. Sir, this gentleman
Steps in to Cassio and entreats his pause;
Myself the crying fellow did pursue,
Lest by his clamor (as it so fell out)
The town might fall in fright. He, swift of foot,
Outran my purpose; and I return'd the rather°
For that I heard the clink and fall of swords,
And Cassio high in oath; which till to-night
I ne'er might say before. When I came back
(For this was brief), I found them close together
At blow and thrust, even as again they were
When you yourself did part them.
More of this matter cannot I report.
But men are men; the best sometimes forget.
Though Cassio did some little wrong to him,
As men in rage strike those that wish them best,
Yet surely Cassio, I believe, receiv'd
From him that fled some strange indignity
Which patience could not pass.°

OTHELLO I know, Iago,
Thy honesty and love doth mince° this matter,
Making it light to Cassio. Cassio, I love thee,
But never more be officer of mine.

Enter DESDEMONA *attended.*

Look if my gentle love be not rais'd up!
I'll make thee an example.

DESDEMONA What is the matter, dear?

OTHELLO All's well now, sweeting;
Come away to bed. [*To* MONTANO.] Sir, for your hurts,
Myself will be your surgeon.—Lead him off.

manage carry on
on . . . safety i.e. at the very headquarters on which the security of the town depends
partially affin'd biased (in Cassio's favor) because of your connection with him
rather sooner, i.e. more speedily
pass pass over
mince cut fine, i.e. try to make light of

Iago, look with care about the town,
And silence those whom this vild brawl distracted.
Come, Desdemona, 'tis the soldiers' life
To have their balmy slumbers wak'd with strife.

Exit [*with* DESDEMONA *and* ATTENDANTS].

IAGO What, are you hurt, lieutenant?

CASSIO Ay, past all surgery.

IAGO Marry, God forbid!

CASSIO Reputation, reputation, reputation! O, I have lost my reputation! I have lost the immortal part of myself, and what remains is bestial. My reputation, Iago, my reputation!

IAGO As I am an honest man, I had thought you had receiv'd some bodily wound; there is more sense° in that than in reputation. Reputation is an idle and most false imposition;° oft got without merit, and lost without deserving. You have lost no reputation at all, unless you repute yourself such a loser. What, man, there are more ways to recover° the general again. You are but now cast° in his mood,° a punishment more in policy° than in malice,° even so as one would beat his offenseless dog to affright an imperious lion.° Sue to him again, and he's yours.

CASSIO I will rather sue to be despis'd than to deceive so good a commander with so slight,° so drunken, and so indiscreet an officer. Drunk? and speak parrot?° and squabble? swagger? swear? and discourse fustian° with one's own shadow? O thou invisible spirit of wine, if thou hast no name to be known by, let us call thee devil!

IAGO What was he that you follow'd with your sword? What had he done to you?

CASSIO I know not.

IAGO Is't possible?

CASSIO I remember a mass of things, but nothing distinctly; a quarrel, but nothing wherefore. O God, that men should put an enemy in their mouths to steal away their brains! that we should, with joy, pleasance, revel, and applause, transform ourselves into beasts!

IAGO Why, but you are now well enough. How came you thus recover'd?

CASSIO It hath pleas'd the devil drunkenness to give place to the devil wrath: one unperfectness shows me another, to make me frankly despise myself.

IAGO Come, you are too severe a moraler. As the time, the place, and the condition of this country stands, I could heartily wish this had not befall'n; but since it is as it is, mend it for your own good.

CASSIO I will ask him for my place again, he shall tell me I am a drunkard! Had I as many mouths as Hydra,° such an answer would stop them all. To be now a sensible° man, by and by a fool, and presently a beast! O strange! Every inordinate cup is unbless'd, and the ingredient is a devil.

sense physical sensation
imposition i.e. something laid on from outside; what others say of him, and not the man himself
recover regain the favor of
cast dismissed
mood anger
policy expediency
malice ill will
as . . . lion proverbial
slight worthless
speak parrot talk nonsense
fustian gibberish
Hydra many-headed snake killed by Hercules as one of his twelve labors
sensible in possession of one's faculties

IAGO Come, come; good wine is a good familiar° creature, if it be well us'd; exclaim no more against it. And, good lieutenant, I think you think I love you.

CASSIO I have well approv'd° it, sir. I drunk!

IAGO You, or any man living, may be drunk at a time,° man. I'll tell you what you shall do. Our general's wife is now the general—I may say so in this respect, for that he hath devoted and given up himself to the contemplation, mark,° and denotement° of her parts° and graces. Confess yourself freely to her; importune her help to put you in your place again. She is of so free,° so kind, so apt,° so bless'd a disposition, she holds it a vice° in her goodness not to do more than she is requested. This broken joint between you and her husband entreat her to splinter;° and my fortunes against any lay° worth naming, this crack of your love shall grow stronger than it was before.

CASSIO You advise me well.

IAGO I protest,° in the sincerity of love and honest kindness.

CASSIO I think it freely; and betimes in the morning I will beseech the virtuous Desdemona to undertake for me. I am desperate of my fortunes if they check me here.

IAGO You are in the right. Good night, lieutenant, I must to the watch.

CASSIO Good night, honest Iago. *Exit* CASSIO.

IAGO And what's he then that says I play the villain,
When this advice is free° I give, and honest,
Probal to thinking,° and indeed the course
To win the Moor again? For 'tis most easy
Th' inclining Desdemona to subdue
In any honest suit; she's fram'd as fruitful°
As the free elements. And then for her
To win the Moor, were't to renounce his baptism,
All seals and symbols of redeemed sin,
His soul is so enfetter'd to her love,
That she may make, unmake, do what she list,
Even as her appetite shall play the god
With his weak function.° How am I then a villain,
To counsel Cassio to this parallel° course,
Directly to his good? Divinity° of hell!
When devils will the blackest sins put on,
They do suggest° at first with heavenly shows,
As I do now; for whiles this honest fool
Plies Desdemona to repair his fortune,
And she for him pleads strongly to the Moor,

familiar domestic, serviceable
approv'd tested and found true
at a time at some time, on some occasion
mark marking, observing
denotement noting
parts good qualities
free generous
apt willing
vice defect
splinter bind up with splints
lay wager
protest declare
free free from guile
Probal to thinking something that thought would show to be true
fruitful generous
function mental faculties
parallel conforming with these facts
Divinity theology
suggest tempt

I'll pour this pestilence into his ear—
That she repeals° him for her body's lust,
And by how much she strives to do him good,
She shall undo her credit with the Moor.
So will I turn her virtue into pitch,
And out of her own goodness make the net
That shall enmesh them all.

Enter RODERIGO.

How now, Roderigo?

RODERIGO I do follow here in the chase, not like a hound that hunts, but one that fills up the cry.° My money is almost spent; I have been to-night exceedingly well cudgell'd; and I think the issue will be, I shall have so much experience for my pains; and so, with no money at all and a little more wit, return again to Venice.

IAGO How poor are they that have not patience!
What wound did ever heal but by degrees?
Thou know'st we work by wit, and not by witchcraft,
And wit depends on dilatory time.
Does't not go well? Cassio hath beaten thee,
And thou by that small hurt hast cashier'd Cassio.
Though other things grow fair against the sun,
Yet fruits that blossom first will first be ripe.
Content thyself a while. By the mass, 'tis morning;
Pleasure and action make the hours seem short.
Retire thee, go where thou art billeted.
Away, I say, thou shalt know more hereafter.
Nay, get thee gone. [*Exit* RODERIGO.] Two things are to be done:
My wife must move for Cassio to her mistress—
I'll set her on—
Myself a while to draw the Moor apart,
And bring him jump° when he may Cassio find
Soliciting his wife. Ay, that's the way;
Dull not device° by coldness and delay. *Exit.*

ACT III

SCENE I [*The citadel.*]

Enter CASSIO [*with*] MUSICIANS.

CASSIO Masters, play here, I will content° your pains;
Something that's brief; and bid "Good morrow, general."
[*They play, and enter the*] CLOWN.

CLOWN Why, masters, have your instruments been in Naples, that they speak i' th' nose thus?°

repeals recalls, i.e. seeks to reinstate
cry pack
jump at the precise moment
device plotting
content requite
speak . . . thus sound like a man whose nose has been affected by syphilis (a disease supposed to have originated in Naples).

I MUSICIAN How, sir? how?

CLOWN Are these, I pray you, wind instruments?

I MUSICIAN Ay, marry, are they, sir.

CLOWN O, thereby hangs a tail.

I MUSICIAN Whereby hangs a tale, sir?

CLOWN Marry, sir, by many a wind instrument that I know. But, masters, here's money for you; and the general so likes your music, that he desires you for love's sake to make no more noise with it.

I MUSICIAN Well, sir, we will not.

CLOWN If you have any music that may not° be heard, to't again; but (as they say) to hear music the general does not greatly care.

I MUSICIAN We have none such, sir.

CLOWN Then put up your pipes in your bag, for I'll away. Go, vanish into air, away! *Exeunt* MUSICIANS.

CASSIO Dost thou hear, mine honest friend?

CLOWN No, I hear not your honest friend; I hear you.

CASSIO Prithee keep up° thy quillets.° There's a poor piece of gold for thee. If the gentlewoman that attends the general's wife be stirring, tell her there's one Cassio entreats her a little favor of speech.° Wilt thou do this?

CLOWN She is stirring, sir. If she will stir hither, I shall seem to notify unto her.

CASSIO Do, good my friend. *Exit* CLOWN.

Enter IAGO. In happy time,° Iago.

IAGO You have not been a-bed then?

CASSIO Why, no; the day had broke
Before we parted. I have made bold, Iago,
To send in to your wife. My suit to her
Is that she will to virtuous Desdemona
Procure me some access.

IAGO I'll send her to you presently;
And I'll devise a mean to draw the Moor
Out of the way, that your converse and business
May be more free.

CASSIO I humbly thank you for't. *Exit* [IAGO].
I never knew a Florentine° more kind and honest.

Enter EMILIA.

EMILIA Good morrow, good lieutenant. I am sorry
For your displeasure;° but all will sure be well.
The general and his wife are talking of it,
And she speaks for you stoutly. The Moor replies
That he you hurt is of great fame in Cyprus,

may not cannot
keep up do not bring out
quillets quibbles, puns
a little . . . speech the favor of a brief conference
In happy time opportunely met
a Florentine i.e. even a Florentine, one of my own townsmen
displeasure loss of favor

And great affinity;° and that in wholesome wisdom
He might not but refuse you. But he protests he loves you,
And needs no other suitor but his likings
To take the safest occasion° by the front°
To bring you in again.

CASSIO Yet I beseech you,
If you think fit, or that it may be done,
Give me advantage of some brief discourse
With Desdemona alone.

EMILIA Pray you come in.
I will bestow you where you shall have time
To speak your bosom° freely.

CASSIO I am much bound to you. [*Exeunt.*]

SCENE II [*The citadel.*]

Enter OTHELLO, IAGO, *and* GENTLEMEN.

OTHELLO These letters give, Iago, to the pilot,
And by him do my duties° to the Senate.
That done, I will be walking on the works;°
Repair there to me.

IAGO Well, my good lord, I'll do't.

OTHELLO This fortification, gentlemen, shall we see't?

GENTLEMEN We'll wait upon your lordship. *Exeunt.*

SCENE III [*The garden of the citadel.*]

Enter DESDEMONA, CASSIO, *and* EMILIA.

DESDEMONA Be thou assur'd, good Cassio, I will do
All my abilities in thy behalf.

EMILIA Good madam, do. I warrant it grieves my husband
As if the cause were his.

DESDEMONA O, that's an honest fellow. Do not doubt, Cassio,
But I will have my lord and you again
As friendly as you were.

CASSIO Bounteous madam,
What ever shall become of Michael Cassio,
He's never any thing but your true servant.

DESDEMONA I know't; I thank you. You do love my lord;
You have known him long, and be you well assur'd
He shall in strangeness° stand no farther off
Than in a politic° distance.

CASSIO Ay, but, lady,
That policy may either last so long,

affinity family connections
occasion opportunity
front forelock
bosom most private concerns
do my duties send my dutiful respects
works fortifications
strangeness aloofness
politic dictated by policy

Or feed upon such nice and waterish diet,°
Or breed itself so out of circumstances,°
That I being absent and my place supplied,°
My general will forget my love and service.

DESDEMONA Do not doubt° that; before Emilia here,
I give thee warrant of thy place. Assure thee,
If I do vow a friendship,° I'll perform it
To the last article. My lord shall never rest,
I'll watch him tame,° and talk him out of patience;°
His bed shall seem a school, his board a shrift,°
I'll intermingle every thing he does
With Cassio's suit. Therefore be merry, Cassio,
For thy solicitor shall rather die
Than give thy cause away.°

Enter OTHELLO *and* IAGO.

EMILIA Madam, here comes my lord.

CASSIO Madam, I'll take my leave.

DESDEMONA Why, stay, and hear me speak.

CASSIO Madam, not now; I am very ill at ease,
Unfit for mine own purposes.

DESDEMONA Well, do your discretion. *Exit* CASSIO.

IAGO Hah? I like not that.

OTHELLO What dost thou say?

IAGO Nothing, my lord; or if—I know not what.

OTHELLO Was not that Cassio parted from my wife?

IAGO Cassio, my lord? No, sure, I cannot think it,
That he would steal away so guilty-like,
Seeing your coming.

OTHELLO I do believe 'twas he.

DESDEMONA How now, my lord?
I have been talking with a suitor here,
A man that languishes in your displeasure.

OTHELLO Who is't you mean?

DESDEMONA Why, your lieutenant, Cassio. Good my lord,
If I have any grace or power to move you,
His present reconciliation° take;
For if he be not one that truly loves you,
That errs in ignorance and not in cunning,°
I have no judgment in an honest face.
I prithee call him back.

OTHELLO Went he hence now?

feed . . . diet require so little to keep it alive (*nice* = trivial)
breed . . . circumstances be revived by some accident or other.
supplied filled
doubt fear
friendship friendly act
watch him tame keep him awake till he capitulates (as in training a hawk)
talk . . . patience keep talking until he can't endure it any longer
shrift confessional
away up
reconciliation repentance
in cunning wittingly

DESDEMONA Yes, faith; so humbled
That he hath left part of his grief with me
To suffer with him. Good love, call him back.
OTHELLO Not now, sweet Desdemona, some other time.
DESDEMONA But shall't be shortly?
OTHELLO The sooner, sweet, for you.
DESDEMONA Shall't be to-night at supper?
OTHELLO No, not to-night.
DESDEMONA To-morrow dinner then?
OTHELLO I shall not dine at home;
I meet the captains at the citadel.
DESDEMONA Why then to-morrow night, or Tuesday morn;
On Tuesday noon, or night; on We'n'sday morn.
I prithee name the time, but let it not
Exceed three days. In faith, he's penitent;
And yet his trespass, in our common reason
(Save that they say the wars must make example
Out of her° best), is not almost° a fault
T' incur a private check.° When shall he come?
Tell me, Othello. I wonder in my soul
What you would ask me that I should deny,
Or stand so mamm'ring° on. What? Michael Cassio,
That came a-wooing with you, and so many a time,
When I have spoke of you dispraisingly,
Hath ta'en your part—to have so much to do°
To bring him in!° By'r lady, I could do much—
OTHELLO Prithee no more; let him come when he will;
I will deny thee nothing.
DESDEMONA Why, this is not a boon;
'Tis as I should entreat you wear your gloves,
Or feed on nourishing dishes, or keep you warm,
Or sue to you to do a peculiar profit°
To your own person. Nay, when I have a suit
Wherein I mean to touch your love indeed,
It shall be full of poise° and difficult weight,
And fearful to be granted.
OTHELLO I will deny thee nothing;
Whereon,° I do beseech thee, grant me this,
To leave me but a little to myself.
DESDEMONA Shall I deny you? No. Farewell, my lord.
OTHELLO Farewell, my Desdemona, I'll come to thee straight.
DESDEMONA Emilia, come.—Be as your fancies teach you;
What e'er you be, I am obedient. *Exit* [*with* EMILIA].
OTHELLO Excellent wretch! Perdition catch my soul

her *Wars* was frequently construed as a singular. See I.i.148–49, I.iii.232, III.iii.349–50.
not almost scarcely
a private check even a private rebuke
mamm'ring hesitating
to do ado, fuss
bring him in restore him to your favor
peculiar profit personal benefit
poise weight
Whereon in return for which

But I do° love thee! and when I love thee not,
Chaos is come again.

IAGO My noble lord—

OTHELLO What dost thou say, Iago?

IAGO Did Michael Cassio, when you woo'd my lady,
Know of your love?

OTHELLO He did, from first to last. Why dost thou ask?

IAGO But for a satisfaction of my thought,
No further harm.

OTHELLO Why of thy thought, Iago?

IAGO I did not think he had been acquainted with her.

OTHELLO O yes, and went between us very oft.

IAGO Indeed!

OTHELLO Indeed? ay, indeed. Discern'st thou aught in that?
Is he not honest?

IAGO Honest, my lord?

OTHELLO Honest? ay, honest.

IAGO My lord, for aught I know.

OTHELLO What dost thou think?

IAGO Think, my lord?

OTHELLO Think, my lord? By heaven, thou echo'st me,
As if there were some monster in thy thought
Too hideous to be shown. Thou dost mean something.
I heard thee say even now, thou lik'st not that,
When Cassio left my wife. What didst not like?
And when I told thee he was of my counsel°
In my whole course of wooing, thou criedst, 'Indeed!'
And didst contract and purse thy brow together,
As if thou then hadst shut up in thy brain
Some horrible conceit. If thou dost love me,
Show me thy thought.

IAGO My lord, you know I love you.

OTHELLO I think thou dost;
And for I know thou'rt full of love and honesty,
And weigh'st thy words before thou giv'st them breath,
Therefore these stops of thine fright me the more;
For such things in a false disloyal knave
Are tricks of custom; but in a man that's just
They're close dilations,° working from the heart,
That passion cannot rule.°

IAGO For Michael Cassio,
I dare be sworn I think that he is honest.

OTHELLO I think so too.

IAGO Men should be what they seem,
Or those that be not, would they might seem none!

OTHELLO Certain, men should be what they seem.

But I do if I do not
of my counsel in my confidence
close dilations expressions of secret thought
passion cannot rule the man because of his impassioned state cannot control

IAGO Why then I think Cassio's an honest man.
OTHELLO Nay, yet there's more in this.
I prithee speak to me as to° thy thinkings,
As thou dost ruminate, and give thy worst of thoughts
The worst of words.
IAGO Good my lord, pardon me:
Though I am bound to every act of duty,
I am not bound to that all slaves are free to.°
Utter my thoughts? Why, say they are vild and false,
As where's that palace whereinto foul things
Sometimes intrude not? Who has that breast so pure
But some uncleanly apprehensions°
Keep leets° and law-days and in sessions sit
With meditations lawful?°
OTHELLO Thou dost conspire against thy friend, Iago,
If thou but think'st him wrong'd, and mak'st his ear
A stranger to thy thoughts.
IAGO I do beseech you,
Though I perchance am vicious in my guess
(As I confess it is my nature's plague
To spy into abuses, and oft my jealousy°
Shapes faults that are not), that your wisdom then,°
From one that so imperfectly conjects,
Would take no notice, nor build yourself a trouble
Out of his scattering and unsure observance.
It were not for your quiet nor your good,
Nor for my manhood, honesty, and wisdom,
To let you know my thoughts.
OTHELLO 'Zounds, what dost thou mean?
IAGO Good name in man and woman, dear my lord,
Is the immediate jewel of their souls.
Who steals my purse steals trash; 'tis something, nothing;
'Twas mine, 'tis his, and has been slave to thousands;
But he that filches from me my good name
Robs me of that which not enriches him,
And makes me poor indeed.
OTHELLO By heaven, I'll know thy thoughts.
IAGO You cannot, if° my heart were in your hand,
Nor shall not, whilst 'tis in my custody.
OTHELLO Ha?
IAGO O, beware, my lord, of jealousy!
It is the green-ey'd monster which doth mock
The meat it feeds on.° That cuckold lives in bliss

as to with respect to
that . . . to that which even a slave is not bound to
apprehensions thoughts
leets sessions of local courts
With meditations lawful along with innocent thoughts
jealousy suspicion
then on that account
if even if
meat . . . on i.e. the heart of the man who suffers it

Who, certain of his fate, loves not his wronger;
But O, what damned minutes tells he o'er
Who dotes, yet doubts; suspects, yet strongly loves!

OTHELLO O misery!

IAGO Poor and content is rich, and rich enough,
But riches fineless° is as poor as winter
To him that ever fears he shall be poor.
Good God, the souls of all my tribe defend
From jealousy!

OTHELLO Why? why is this?
Think'st thou I'ld make a life of jealousy?
To follow still the changes of the moon
With fresh suspicions? No! to be once in doubt
Is once° to be resolv'd. Exchange me for a goat,
When I shall turn the business of my soul
To such exsufflicate and blown° surmises,
Matching thy inference. 'Tis not to make me jealious°
To say my wife is fair, feeds well, loves company,
Is free of speech, sings, plays, and dances well;
Where virtue is, these are more virtuous.
Nor from mine own weak merits will I draw
The smallest fear or doubt° of her revolt,°
For she had eyes, and chose me. No, Iago,
I'll see before I doubt; when I doubt, prove;°
And on the proof, there is no more but this—
Away at once with love or jealousy!

IAGO I am glad of this, for now I shall have reason
To show the love and duty that I bear you
With franker spirit; therefore (as I am bound)
Receive it from me. I speak not yet of proof.
Look to your wife, observe her well with Cassio,
Wear your eyes thus, not jealous nor secure.°
I would not have your free and noble nature,
Out of self-bounty,° be abus'd; look to't.
I know our country disposition well:
In Venice they do let God see the pranks
They dare not show their husbands; their best conscience
Is not to leave't undone, but keep't unknown.

OTHELLO Dost thou say so?

IAGO She did deceive her father, marrying you,
And when she seem'd to shake and fear your looks,
She lov'd them most.

OTHELLO And so she did.

IAGO Why, go to then.

fineless boundless
once once for all
exsufflicate and blown Both adjectives may mean "blown-up, inflated," or the phrase may mean "spat-out and fly-blown."
jealious jealous, suspicious
doubt suspicion
revolt unfaithfulness
prove test
secure culpably free of anxiety, overconfident
self-bounty inherent goodness

She that so young could give out such a seeming
To seel her father's eyes up, close as oak,°
He thought 'twas witchcraft—but I am much to blame;
I humbly do beseech you of your pardon
For too much loving you.

OTHELLO I am bound° to thee for ever.

IAGO I see this hath a little dash'd your spirits.

OTHELLO Not a jot, not a jot.

IAGO I' faith, I fear it has.
I hope you will consider what is spoke
Comes from my love. But I do see y' are mov'd.
I am to pray you not to strain my speech
To grosser issues° nor to larger reach°
Than to suspicion.

OTHELLO I will not.

IAGO Should you do so, my lord,
My speech should fall into such vild success°
Which my thoughts aim'd not. Cassio's my worthy friend—
My lord, I see y' are mov'd.

OTHELLO No, not much mov'd:
I do not think but Desdemona's honest.°

IAGO Long live she so! and long live you to think so!

OTHELLO And yet how nature erring from itself—

IAGO Ay, there's the point; as (to be bold with you)
Not to affect° many proposed matches
Of her own clime,° complexion, and degree,
Whereto we see in all things nature tends—
Foh, one may smell in such, a will° most rank,
Foul disproportions,° thoughts unnatural.
But (pardon me) I do not in position°
Distinctly speak of° her, though I may fear
Her will, recoiling to her better judgment,°
May fall to match° you with her country forms,°
And happily° repent.

OTHELLO Farewell, farewell!
If more thou dost perceive, let me know more;
Set on thy wife to observe. Leave me, Iago.

IAGO [*Going.*] My lord, I take my leave.

OTHELLO Why did I marry? This honest creature, doubtless,
Sees and knows more, much more, than he unfolds.

IAGO [*Returning.*] My lord, I would I might entreat your honour
To scan this thing no farther; leave it to time.

oak a close-grained wood
bound indebted
issues conclusions
reach scope
success effect
honest chaste
affect desire, look with favor on
clime region, country
will desire, appetite
disproportions abnormality
in position i.e. in arguing thus
Distinctly speak of refer specifically to
recoiling . . . judgment reverting to a more natural preference
match compare
her country forms the appearance of her countrymen
happily haply, perchance

Although 'tis fit that Cassio have his place—
For sure he fills it up with great ability—
Yet if you please to hold him off awhile,
You shall by that perceive him and his means.
Note if your lady strain his entertainment°
With any strong or vehement importunity;
Much will be seen in that. In the mean time,
Let me be thought too busy in my fears
(As worthy cause I have to fear I am)
And hold her free,° I do beseech your honour.

OTHELLO Fear not my government.°

IAGO I once more take my leave. *Exit.*

OTHELLO This fellow's of exceeding honesty,
And knows all qualities,° with a learned spirit,
Of human dealings. If I do prove her haggard,°
Though that her jesses° were my dear heart-strings,
I'ld whistle her off, and let her down the wind°
To prey at fortune.° Haply, for° I am black,
And have not those soft parts of conversation°
That chamberers° have, or for I am declin'd
Into the vale of years (yet that's not much),
She's gone. I am abus'd, and my relief
Must be to loathe her. O curse of marriage!
That we can call these delicate creatures ours,
And not their appetites! I had rather be a toad
And live upon the vapour of a dungeon
Than keep a corner in the thing I love
For others' uses. Yet 'tis the plague of great ones,
Prerogativ'd° are they less than the base;
'Tis destiny unshunnable, like death.
Even then this forked plague° is fated to us
When we do quicken.° Look where she comes:

Enter DESDEMONA *and* EMILIA.

If she be false, O then heaven mocks itself!
I'll not believe't.

DESDEMONA How now, my dear Othello?
Your dinner, and the generous° islanders
By you invited, do attend your presence.

OTHELLO I am to blame.

strain his entertainment repeatedly urge his reappointment
free guiltless
government conduct, self-control
qualities types, conditions
haggard wild (a term from falconry)
jesses leather straps on the hawk's legs, by which it was fastened to the leash held by the falconer
down the wind To release the hawk downwind was to court its loss.
at fortune at random
for because
soft . . . conversation pleasing qualities of social behavior
chamberers gallants
Prerogativ'd privileged
forked plague curse of cuckold's horns
quicken begin to live
generous noble

DESDEMONA Why do you speak so faintly?
Are you not well?
OTHELLO I have a pain upon my forehead, here.
DESDEMONA Faith, that's with watching,° 'twill away again.
Let me but bind it hard, within this hour
It will be well.
OTHELLO Your napkin° is too little;
[*He puts the handkerchief from him, and it drops.*]
Let it alone.° Come, I'll go in with you.
DESDEMONA I am very sorry that you are not well. *Exit* [*with* OTHELLO].
EMILIA I am glad I have found this napkin;
This was her first remembrance from the Moor.
My wayward° husband hath a hundred times
Woo'd me to steal it; but she so loves the token
(For he conjur'd her she should ever keep it)
That she reserves it evermore about her
To kiss and talk to. I'll have the work ta'en out,°
And give't Iago. What he will do with it
Heaven knows, not I;
I nothing but° to please his fantasy.°

Enter IAGO.

IAGO How now? what do you here alone?
EMILIA Do not you chide; I have a thing for you.
IAGO You have a thing for me? It is a common thing—
EMILIA Hah?
IAGO To have a foolish wife.
EMILIA O, is that all? What will you give me now
For that same handkerchief?
IAGO What handkerchief?
EMILIA What handkerchief?
Why, that the Moor first gave to Desdemona,
That which so often you did bid me steal.
IAGO Hast stol'n it from her?
EMILIA No, faith; she let it drop by negligence,
And to th' advantage,° I, being here, took't up.
Look, here 'tis.
IAGO A good wench, give it me.
EMILIA What will you do with't, that you have been so earnest
To have me filch it?
IAGO [*Snatching it*]. Why, what is that to you?
EMILIA If it be not for some purpose of import,
Give't me again. Poor lady, she'll run mad
When she shall lack it.

with watching from lack of sleep
napkin handkerchief
Let it alone don't trouble yourself about it
wayward capricious
work ta'en out pattern copied
I nothing but my only thought is
fantasy fancy, whim
to th' advantage upon the opportunity

IAGO Be not acknown on't;° I have use for it.
Go, leave me. *Exit* EMILIA.
I will in Cassio's lodging lose this napkin,
And let him find it. Trifles light as air
Are to the jealious confirmations strong
As proofs of holy writ; this may do something.
The Moor already changes with my poison:
Dangerous conceits are in their natures poisons,
Which at the first are scarce found to distaste,
But with a little act° upon the blood
Burn like the mines of sulphur.

Enter OTHELLO. I did say so.

Look where he comes! Not poppy, nor mandragora,°
Nor all the drowsy syrups of the world
Shall ever medicine thee to that sweet sleep
Which thou ow'dst° yesterday.

OTHELLO Ha, ha, false to me?

IAGO Why, how now, general? No more of that.

OTHELLO Avaunt, be gone! thou hast set me on the rack.
I swear 'tis better to be much abus'd
Than but to know't a little.

IAGO How now, my lord?

OTHELLO What sense had I in° her stol'n hours of lust?
I saw't not, thought it not; it harm'd not me.
I slept the next night well, fed well, was free° and merry;
I found not Cassio's kisses on her lips.
He that is robb'd, not wanting° what is stol'n,
Let him not know't, and he's not robb'd at all.

IAGO I am sorry to hear this.

OTHELLO I had been happy, if the general camp,
Pioners° and all, had tasted her sweet body,
So I had nothing known. O now, for ever
Farewell the tranquil mind! farewell content!
Farewell the plumed troops and the big° wars
That makes ambition virtue! O, farewell!
Farewell the neighing steed and the shrill trump,
The spirit-stirring drum, th' ear-piercing fife,
The royal banner, and all quality,°
Pride,° pomp,° and circumstance° of glorious war!
And O you mortal° engines,° whose rude throats

Be . . . on't pretend not to know of it
with . . . act after they have acted for a little while
mandragora an opiate, made of the mandrake
ow'dst didst own
in of
free carefree
wanting missing
Pioners the lowest rank of soldier, primarily used for manual labor, not fighting
big stately
quality character, attributes
Pride proud display
pomp dignity
circumstance ceremonial splendor
mortal deadly
engines instruments of war; here, cannon

Th' immortal Jove's dread clamors counterfeit,
Farewell! Othello's occupation's gone.

IAGO Is't possible, my lord?

OTHELLO Villain, be sure thou prove my love a whore;
[*Taking him by the throat.*]
Be sure of it. Give me the ocular proof,
Or by the worth of mine eternal soul,
Thou hadst been better have been born a dog
Than answer my wak'd wrath!

IAGO Is't come to this?

OTHELLO Make me to see't; or (at the least) so prove it
That the probation° bear no hinge nor loop
To hang a doubt on; or woe upon thy life!

IAGO My noble lord—

OTHELLO If thou dost slander her and torture me,
Never pray more; abandon all remorse;°
On horror's head horrors accumulate;
Do deeds to make heaven weep, all earth amaz'd;°
For nothing canst thou to damnation add
Greater than that.

IAGO O grace! O heaven forgive me!
Are you a man? Have you a soul? or sense?
God buy you;° take mine office. O wretched fool,
That lov'st to make thine honesty a vice!°
O monstrous world! Take note, take note, O world,
To be direct and honest is not safe.
I thank you for this profit,° and from hence
I'll love no friend, sith° love breeds such offense.°

OTHELLO Nay, stay. Thou shouldst be° honest.

IAGO I should be° wise—for honesty's a fool
And loses that it works for.

OTHELLO By the world,
I think my wife be honest, and think she is not;
I think that thou are just, and think thou art not.
I'll have some proof. Her name, that was as fresh
As Dian's visage, is now begrim'd and black
As mine own face. If there be cords, or knives,
Poison, or fire, or suffocating streams,
I'll not endure it. Would I were satisfied!

IAGO I see, sir, you are eaten up with passion;
I do repent me that I put it to you.
You would be satisfied?

OTHELLO Would? nay, and I will.

IAGO And may; but how? How satisfied, my lord?

probation proof
remorse pity
amaz'd utterly confounded
God buy you God be with you, i.e. good-bye
vice flaw, failing
profit valuable lesson
sith since
offense injury (to the one who loves)
Thou shouldst be all indications point to the fact that you are
should be ought to be

Would you, the supervisor,° grossly gape on?
Behold her topp'd?

OTHELLO Death and damnation! O!

IAGO It were a tedious difficulty, I think,
To bring them to that prospect; damn them then,
If ever° mortal eyes do see them bolster°
More° than their own. What then? How then?
What shall I say? Where's satisfaction?
It is impossible you should see° this,
Were they as prime° as goats, as hot as monkeys,
As salt° as wolves in pride,° and fools as gross
As ignorance made drunk. But yet, I say,
If imputation and strong circumstances
Which lead directly to the door of truth
Will give you satisfaction, you might have't.

OTHELLO Give me a living reason she's disloyal.

IAGO I do not like the office;
But sith I am ent'red in this cause so far
(Prick'd to't by foolish honesty and love),
I will go on. I lay with Cassio lately,
And being troubled with a raging tooth,
I could not sleep.
There are a kind of men, so loose of soul,
That in their sleeps will mutter their affairs;
One of this kind is Cassio.
In sleep I heard him say, 'Sweet Desdemona,
Let us be wary, let us hide our loves';
And then, sir, would he gripe° and wring my hand;
Cry, 'O sweet creature!' then kiss me hard,
As if he pluck'd up kisses by the roots
That grew upon my lips; then laid his leg
Over my thigh, and sigh'd, and kiss'd, and then
Cried, "Cursed fate that gave thee to the Moor!"

OTHELLO O monstrous! monstrous!

IAGO Nay, this was but his dream.

OTHELLO But this denoted a foregone conclusion.°

IAGO 'Tis a shrewd doubt,° though it be but a dream,
And this may help to thicken° other proofs
That do demonstrate thinly.

OTHELLO I'll tear her all to pieces.

IAGO Nay, yet be wise; yet we see nothing done;
She may be honest yet. Tell me but this,
Have you not sometimes seen a handkerchief
Spotted with strawberries in your wive's° hand?

supervisor onlooker, spectator
damn . . . ever to condemn them only if
bolster go to bed together
More other (eyes)
see i.e. contrive to be an actual witness of
prime lustful
salt lecherous
pride heat
gripe grip, clasp
foregone conclusion act already performed
shrewd doubt strong reason for suspicion
thicken substantiate
wive's wife's

OTHELLO I gave her such a one; 'twas my first gift.
IAGO I know not that; but such a handkerchief
(I am sure it was your wive's) did I to-day
See Cassio wipe his beard with.
OTHELLO If it be that—
IAGO If it be that, or any that was hers,
It speaks against her with the other proofs.
OTHELLO O that the slave° had forty thousand lives!
One is too poor, too weak for my revenge.
Now do I see 'tis true. Look here, Iago,
All my fond love thus do I blow to heaven.
'Tis gone.
Arise, black vengeance, from the hollow hell!
Yield up, O love, thy crown and hearted° throne
To tyrannous hate! Swell, bosom, with thy fraught,°
For 'tis of aspics'° tongues!
IAGO Yet be content.
OTHELLO O blood, blood, blood!
IAGO Patience, I say; your mind perhaps may change.
OTHELLO Never, Iago. Like to the Pontic Sea,°
Whose icy current and compulsive course
Nev'r feels retiring ebb, but keeps due on
To the Propontic and the Hellespont,
Even so my bloody thoughts, with violent pace,
Shall nev'r look back, nev'r ebb to humble love,
Till that a capable° and wide revenge
Swallow them up. [*He kneels.*] Now by yond marble° heaven,
In the due reverence of a sacred vow
I hear engage my words.
IAGO Do not rise yet. [IAGO *kneels.*]
Witness, you ever-burning lights above,
You elements that clip° us round about,
Witness that here Iago doth give up
The execution° of his wit, hands, heart,
To wrong'd Othello's service! Let him command,
And to obey shall be in me remorse,
What bloody business ever.° [*They rise.*]
OTHELLO I greet thy love,
Not with vain thanks, but with acceptance bounteous,
And will upon the instant put thee to't:
Within these three days let me hear thee say
That Cassio's not alive.
IAGO My friend is dead; 'tis done at your request.
But let her live.

the slave i.e. Cassio
hearted established in my heart
fraught burden
aspics' asps'
Pontic Sea Black Sea
capable capacious, comprehensive
marble shining (?) or enduring, changeless (cf. *marble-constant,* in *Anthony and Cleopatra,* V.ii.240)
clip embrace
execution action
to . . . ever i.e. in Othello's service even the cruellest acts will be as allowable as if they were gentle and prompted by pity (*remorse*)

OTHELLO Damn her, lewd minx!° O, damn her, damn her!
Come go with me apart, I will withdraw
To furnish me with some swift means of death
For the fair devil. Now art thou my lieutenant.
IAGO I am your own for ever. *Exuent.*

SCENE IV [*Before the citadel.*]

Enter DESDEMONA, EMILIA, *and* CLOWN.

DESDEMONA Do you know, sirrah,° where Lieutenant Cassio lies?°
CLOWN I dare not say he lies any where.
DESDEMONA Why, man?
CLOWN He's a soldier, and for me to say a soldier lies, 'tis stabbing.
DESDEMONA Go to! where lodges he?
CLOWN To tell you where he lodges, is to tell you where I lie.
DESDEMONA Can any thing be made of this?
CLOWN I know not where he lodges, and for me to devise a lodging and say he lies here, or he lies there, were to lie in mine own throat.°
DESDEMONA Can you inquire him out, and be edified by report?
CLOWN I will catechize the world for him, that is, make questions, and by them answer.
DESDEMONA Seek him, bid him come hither. Tell him I have mov'd° my lord on his behalf, and hope all will be well.
CLOWN To do this is within the compass of man's wit, and therefore I will attempt the doing it. *Exit* CLOWN.
DESDEMONA Where should I lose° the handkerchief, Emilia?
EMILIA I know not, madam.
DESDEMONA Believe me, I had rather have lost my purse
Full of crusadoes;° and but my noble Moor
Is true of mind, and made of no such baseness
As jealious creatures are, it were enough
To put him to ill thinking.
EMILIA Is he not jealious?
DESDEMONA Who, he? I think the sun where he was born
Drew all such humours° from him.
EMILIA Look where he comes.

Enter OTHELLO.

DESDEMONA I will not leave him now till Cassio
Be call'd to him.—How is't with you, my lord?
OTHELLO Well, my good lady. [*Aside.*] O, hardness to dissemble!—
How do you, Desdemona?
DESDEMONA Well, my good lord.
OTHELLO Give me your hand. This hand is moist, my lady.

minx wanton
sirrah term of address to inferiors
lies lodges
lie . . . throat tell a gross and deliberate lie
mov'd urged, made suit to
should I lose could I have lost
crusadoes Portuguese coins stamped with a cross
humours bodily fluids (which were thought to determine temperament)

DESDEMONA It [yet] hath felt no age nor known no sorrow.
OTHELLO This argues fruitfulness and liberal heart;
Hot, hot, and moist. This hand of yours requires
A sequester° from liberty: fasting and prayer,
Much castigation,° exercise devout,
For here's a young and sweating devil here
That commonly rebels. 'Tis a good hand,
A frank° one.
DESDEMONA You may, indeed, say so;
For 'twas that hand that gave away my heart.
OTHELLO A liberal hand. The hearts of old gave hands;
But our new heraldry is hands, not hearts.°
DESDEMONA I cannot speak of this. Come now, your promise.
OTHELLO What promise, chuck?°
DESDEMONA I have sent to bid Cassio come speak with you.
OTHELLO I have a salt and sorry rheum° offends me;
Lend me thy handkerchief.
DESDEMONA Here, my lord.
OTHELLO That which I gave you.
DESDEMONA I have it not about me.
OTHELLO Not?
DESDEMONA No, faith, my lord.
OTHELLO That's a fault. That handkerchief
Did an Egyptian to my mother give;
She was a charmer,° and could almost read
The thoughts of people. She told her, while she kept it,
'Twould make her amiable,° and subdue my father
Entirely to her love; but if she lost it,
Or made a gift of it, my father's eye
Should hold her loathed, and his spirits should hunt
After new fancies. She, dying, gave it me,
And bid me, when my fate would have me wiv'd,
To give it her.° I did so; and take heed on't,
Make it a darling like your precious eye.
To lose't or give't away were such perdition°
As nothing else could match.
DESDEMONA Is't possible?
OTHELLO 'Tis true; there's magic in the web° of it.
A sibyl,° that had numb'red in the world
The sun to course two hundred compasses,
In her prophetic fury° sew'd the work;
The worms were hallowed that did breed the silk,

sequester sequestration, separation
castigation corrective discipline, penance
frank Desdemona takes this as meaning "generous," but Othello may have in mind also the meanings "lusty, vigorous" and "open, unable to conceal secrets." So *liberal* in l. 40 means both "generous" and "licentious."
our . . . hearts under our newfangled heraldry, hands (given in marriage) no longer signify that hearts are given also
chuck a term of endearment, related to *chick*
salt . . . rheum distressing watering of the eyes
charmer magician
amiable desirable
her i.e. to my wife
perdition loss
web fabric
sibyl prophetess
prophetic fury the divine frenzy which enabled her to prophesy

And it was dy'd in mummy° which the skillful
Conserv'd° of maidens' hearts.

DESDEMONA I' faith! is't true?

OTHELLO Most veritable, therefore look to't well.

DESDEMONA Then would to God that I had never seen't!

OTHELLO Ha? wherefore?

DESDEMONA Why do you speak so startingly and rash?°

OTHELLO Is't lost? Is't gone? Speak, is't out o' th' way?

DESDEMONA Heaven bless us!

OTHELLO Say you?

DESDEMONA It is not lost; but what and if° it were?

OTHELLO How?

DESDEMONA I say, it is not lost.

OTHELLO Fetch't, let me see't.

DESDEMONA Why, so I can, sir, but I will not now.
This is a trick to put me from my suit.
Pray you let Cassio be receiv'd again.

OTHELLO Fetch me the handkerchief, my mind misgives.

DESDEMONA Come, come;
You'll never meet a more sufficient° man.

OTHELLO The handkerchief!

DESDEMONA I pray talk me of Cassio.

OTHELLO The handkerchief!

DESDEMONA A man that all his time
Hath founded his good fortunes on your love,
Shar'd dangers with you—

OTHELLO The handkerchief!

DESDEMONA I' faith, you are to blame.

OTHELLO 'Zounds! *Exit* OTHELLO.

EMILIA Is not this man jealious?

DESDEMONA I nev'r saw this before.
Sure, there's some wonder in this handkerchief;
I am most unhappy in the loss of it.

EMILIA 'Tis not a year or two shows us a man:
They are all but stomachs, and we all but° food;
They eat us hungerly, and when they are full
They belch us.

Enter IAGO *and* CASSIO.

Look you, Cassio and my husband!

IAGO There is no other way: 'tis she must do't;
And lo the happiness!° Go, and importune her.

DESDEMONA How now, good Cassio, what's the news with you?

CASSIO Madam, my former suit. I do beseech you
That by your virtuous° means I may again

mummy fluid drawn from embalmed bodies
Conserv'd prepared
startingly and rash disjointedly and impetuously
and if if
sufficient able, complete
but nothing but
happiness good luck
virtuous efficacious

Exist, and be a member of his love
Whom I, with all the office° of my heart,
Entirely honour. I would not be delay'd.
If my offense be of such mortal° kind
That nor my service past, nor present sorrows,
Nor purpos'd merit in futurity,°
Can ransom me into his love again,
But° to know so must be my benefit;
So shall I clothe me in a forc'd content,
And shut myself up in some other course,
To fortune's alms.°

DESDEMONA Alas, thrice-gentle Cassio,
My advocation is not now in tune.
My lord is not my lord; nor should I know him
Were he in favour° as in humour alter'd.
So help me every spirit sanctified,
As I have spoken for you all my best,
And stood within the blank° of his displeasure
For my free speech! You must awhile be patient.
What I can do, I will; and more I will
Than for myself I dare. Let that suffice you.

IAGO Is my lord angry?

EMILIA He went hence but now;
And certainly in strange unquietness.

IAGO Can he be angry? I have seen the cannon
When it hath blown his ranks into the air,
And like the devil from his very arm
Puff'd his own brother—and is he angry?
Something of moment then. I will go meet him.
There's matter in't indeed, if he be angry.

DESDEMONA I prithee do so, *Exit* IAGO.
Something sure of state,
Either from Venice, or some unhatch'd practise°
Made demonstrable here in Cyprus to him,
Hath puddled° his clear spirit; and in such cases
Men's natures wrangle with inferior things,
Though great ones are their object. 'Tis even so;
For let our finger ache, and it endues°
Our other healthful members even to a sense
Of pain. Nay, we must think men are not gods,
Nor of them look for such observancy°
As fits the bridal. Beshrew me° much, Emilia,
I was (unhandsome° warrior as I am)

office devoted service
mortal fatal
purpos'd . . . futurity intention to serve well in the future
But merely
fortune's alms pittances handed out by Fortune to beggars
favour appearance
blank center of a target, i.e. direct line of aim
unhatch'd practise plot not yet ready for execution
puddled muddied
endues makes conformable
observancy devoted attention
Beshrew me a very mild imprecation
unhandsome unskillful

Arraigning his unkindness with° my soul;
But now I find I had suborn'd the witness,°
And he's indicted falsely.

EMILIA Pray heaven it be state matters, as you think,
And no conception nor no jealious toy°
Concerning you.

DESDEMONA Alas the day, I never gave him cause.

EMILIA But jealious souls will not be answer'd so;
They are not ever jealious for the cause,
But jealious for they're jealious. It is a monster
Begot upon itself,° born on itself.

DESDEMONA Heaven keep the monster from Othello's mind!

EMILIA Lady, amen.

DESDEMONA I will go seek him. Cassio, walk hereabout;
If I do find him fit, I'll move your suit
And seek to effect it to my uttermost.

CASSIO I humbly thank your ladyship.

Exeunt [DESDEMONA *and* EMILIA].

Enter BIANCA.

BIANCA 'Save you,° friend Cassio!

CASSIO What make you from home?
How is't with you, my most fair Bianca?
Indeed, sweet love, I was coming to your house.

BIANCA And I was going to your lodging, Cassio.
What? keep a week away? seven days and nights?
Eightscore eight hours? and lovers' absent hours,
More tedious than the dial eightscore times?
O weary reck'ning!

CASSIO Pardon me, Bianca.
I have this while with leaden thoughts been press'd,
But I shall in a more continuate° time
Strike off this score° of absence. Sweet Bianca,

[*Giving her* DESDEMONA'S *handkerchief.*]

Take me this work out.

BIANCA O Cassio, whence came this?
This is some token from a newer friend;
To the felt absence now I feel a cause.
Is't come to this? Well, well.

CASSIO Go to, woman!
Throw your vild guesses in the devil's teeth,
From whence you have them. You are jealious now
That this is from some mistress, some remembrance;
No, by my faith, Bianca.

with before the bar of
suborn'd the witness caused the witness to lie, i.e. misinterpreted Othello's behavior
toy fancy
Begot . . . itself i.e. spontaneously generated, without cause
'Save you God save you
continuate uninterrupted
Strike . . . score settle this account

BIANCA Why, whose is it?
CASSIO I know not, neither; I found it in my chamber.
I like the work well; ere it be demanded°
(As like enough it will) I would have it copied.
Take it, and do't, and leave me for this time.
BIANCA Leave you? Wherefore?
CASSIO I do attend here on the general,
And think it no addition,° nor my wish,
To have him see me woman'd.
BIANCA Why, I pray you?
CASSIO Not that I love you not.
BIANCA But that you do not love me.
I pray you bring me on the way a little,
And say if I shall see you soon at night.
CASSIO 'Tis but a little way that I can bring you,
For I attend here; but I'll see you soon.
BIANCA 'Tis very good; I must be circumstanc'd.° *Exeunt omnes.*

ACT IV

SCENE I [*Before the citadel.*]

Enter OTHELLO *and* IAGO.

IAGO Will you think so?
OTHELLO Think so, Iago?
IAGO What,
To kiss in private?
OTHELLO An unauthoriz'd kiss!
IAGO Or to be naked with her friend in bed
An hour, or more, not meaning any harm?
OTHELLO Naked in bed, Iago, and not mean harm?
It is hypocrisy against the devil.
They that mean virtuously, and yet do so,
The devil their virtue tempts, and they tempt heaven.
IAGO If they do nothing, 'tis a venial slip;
But if I give my wife a handkerchief—
OTHELLO What then?
IAGO Why then 'tis hers, my lord, and being hers,
She may, I think, bestow't on any man.
OTHELLO She is protectress of her honour too;
May she give that?
IAGO Her honour is an essence that's not seen;
They have it very oft° that have it not.
But for the handkerchief—
OTHELLO By heaven, I would most gladly have forgot it.

demanded inquired for
addition credit
be circumstanc'd yield to circumstances, accept your conditions

They . . . oft i.e. often individuals are credited with it

Thou saidst (O, it comes o'er my memory,
As doth the raven o'er the infectious house,
Boding to all) he had my handkerchief.

IAGO Ay; what of that?

OTHELLO That's not so good now.

IAGO What
If I had said I had seen him do you wrong?
Or heard him say—as knaves be such abroad,
Who having by their own importunate suit,
Or voluntary dotage of some mistress,
Convinced or supplied° them, cannot choose
But they must blab—

OTHELLO Hath he said any thing?

IAGO He hath, my lord, but be you well assur'd,
No more than he'll unswear.

OTHELLO What hath he said?

IAGO Faith, that he did—I know not what he did.

OTHELLO What? what?

IAGO Lie—

OTHELLO With her?

IAGO With her? On her; what you will.

OTHELLO Lie with her? lie on her? We say lie on her, when they belie her. Lie with her! 'Zounds, that's fulsome! Handkerchief—confessions—handkerchief! To confess, and be hang'd for his labour—first to be hang'd, and then to confess. I tremble at it. Nature would not invest herself in such shadowing° passion° without some instruction.° It is not words that shakes me thus. Pish! Noses, ears, and lips. Is't possible? Confess? Handkerchief? O devil! *Falls in a trance.*

IAGO Work on,
My medicine, work! Thus credulous fools are caught,
And many worthy and chaste dames even thus
(All guiltless) meet reproach.—What ho! my lord!
My lord, I say! Othello!
How now, Cassio?

Enter CASSIO.

CASSIO What's the matter?

IAGO My lord is fall'n into an epilepsy.
This is his second fit; he had one yesterday.

CASSIO Rub him about the temples.

IAGO No, forbear,
The lethargy° must have his° quiet course;
If not, he foams at mouth, and by and by
Breaks out to savage madness. Look, he stirs.
Do you withdraw yourself a little while,

Convinced or supplied conquered or satisfied
shadowing coming over one like a shadow, i.e. overwhelming suddenly (?) or filling the imagination with shapes and figures (?)
passion paroxysm of emotion
instruction prompting, cause
lethargy coma
his its

He will recover straight. When he is gone,
I would on great occasion speak with you. [*Exit* CASSIO.]
How is it, general? Have you not hurt your head?°

OTHELLO Dost thou mock me?

IAGO I mock you not, by heaven.
Would you would bear your fortune like a man!

OTHELLO A horned man's a monster and a beast.

IAGO There's many a beast then in a populous city,
And many a civil° monster.

OTHELLO Did he confess it?

IAGO Good sir, be a man;
Think every bearded fellow that's but yok'd°
May draw° with you. There's millions now alive
That nightly lie in those unproper° beds
Which they dare swear peculiar;° your case is better.
O, 'tis the spite of hell, the fiend's arch-mock,
To lip a wanton in a secure° couch,
And to suppose her chaste! No, let me know,
And knowing what I am, I know what she shall be.

OTHELLO O, thou art wise; 'tis certain.

IAGO Stand you a while apart,
Confine yourself but in a patient list.°
Whilst you were here o'erwhelmed with your grief
(A passion most unsuiting such a man),
Cassio came hither. I shifted him away,
And laid good 'scuses upon your ecstasy;°
Bade him anon return and here speak with me,
The which he promis'd. Do but encave yourself,
And mark the fleers,° the gibes, and notable° scorns
That dwell in every region of his face,
For I will make him tell the tale anew:
Where, how, how oft, how long ago, and when
He hath, and is again to cope° your wife.
I say, but mark his gesture. Marry, patience,
Or I shall say y' are all in all in spleen,°
And nothing of a man.

OTHELLO Dost thou hear, Iago,
I will be found most cunning in my patience;
But (dost thou hear) most bloody.

IAGO That's not amiss,
But yet keep time in all. Will you withdraw? [OTHELLO *withdraws.*]
Now will I question Cassio of Bianca,
A huswife° that by selling her desires

hurt your head Othello takes this as alluding to the cuckold's horns
civil i.e. among the citizenry, city-dwelling
yok'd married
draw pull (like oxen under the yoke)
unproper not their own
peculiar their own
secure free from suspicion
in . . . list within the bounds of patience
ecstasy trance
fleers sneers
notable obvious
cope encounter with
spleen considered the seat of sudden and capricious impulses
huswife hussy

Buys herself bread and clothes. It is a creature
That dotes on Cassio (as 'tis the strumpet's plague
To beguile many and be beguil'd by one);
He, when he hears of her, cannot restrain
From the excess of laughter. Here he comes.

Enter CASSIO.

As he shall smile, Othello shall go mad;
And his unbookish° jealousy must conster°
Poor Cassio's smiles, gestures, and light behaviours
Quite in the wrong. How do you now, lieutenant?

CASSIO The worser that you give me the addition°
Whose want even kills me.

IAGO Ply Desdemona well, and you are sure on't.
[*Speaking lower.*] Now, if this suit lay in Bianca's pow'r,
How quickly should you speed!

CASSIO Alas, poor caitiff!°

OTHELLO Look how he laughs already!

IAGO I never knew woman love man so.

CASSIO Alas, poor rogue, I think, i' faith, she loves me.

OTHELLO Now he denies it faintly,° and laughs it out.

IAGO Do you hear, Cassio?

OTHELLO Now he importunes him
To tell it o'er. Go to, well said, well said.

IAGO She gives it out that you shall marry her.
Do you intend it?

CASSIO Ha, ha, ha!

OTHELLO Do you triumph, Roman?° do you triumph?

CASSIO I marry her! What? a customer!° Prithee bear some charity to my wit, do not think it so unwholesome.° Ha, ha, ha!

OTHELLO So, so, so, so; they laugh that wins.

IAGO Faith, the cry goes that you marry her.

CASSIO Prithee say true.

IAGO I am a very villain else.

OTHELLO Have you scor'd° me? Well.

CASSIO This is the monkey's own giving out. She is persuaded I will marry her, out of her own love and flattery,° not out of my promise.

OTHELLO Iago beckons° me; now he begins the story.

CASSIO She was here even now; she haunts me in every place. I was the other day talking on the seabank with certain Venetians, and thither comes the bauble,° and by this hand, falls me thus about my neck—

OTHELLO Crying, "O dear Cassio!" as it were; his gesture imports it.

CASSIO She hangs, and lolls, and weeps upon me; so hales and pulls me. Ha, ha, ha!

unbookish uninstructed, unpracticed
conster construe, interpret. The figure is of a person trying to translate a language he is ignorant of.
addition title
caitiff wretch
faintly not very earnestly
Roman exultant fellow (suggested by *triumph*)
customer prostitute
unwholesome unsound
scor'd scored off, beaten
own . . . flattery self-love and self-satisfaction
beckons signals
bauble plaything

OTHELLO Now he tells how she pluck'd him to my chamber. O, I see that nose of yours, but not that dog I shall throw it to.

CASSIO Well, I must leave her company.

IAGO Before me! look where she comes.

Enter BIANCA.

CASSIO 'Tis such another fitchew!° marry, a perfum'd one!—What do you mean by this haunting of me?

BIANCA Let the devil and his dam haunt you! What did you mean by that same handkerchief you gave me even now? I was a fine fool to take it. I must take out the work? A likely piece of work, that you should find it in your chamber, and know not who left it there! This is some minx's token, and I must take out the work? There, give it your hobby-horse.° Wheresoever you had it, I'll take out no work on't.

CASSIO How now, my sweet Bianca? how now? how now?

OTHELLO By heaven, that should be my handkerchief!

BIANCA An'° you'll come to supper to-night, you may; an' you will not, come when you are next prepar'd for. *Exit.*

IAGO After her, after her.

CASSIO Faith, I must, she'll rail in the streets else.

IAGO Will you sup there?

CASSIO Faith, I intend so.

IAGO Well, I may chance to see you; for I would very fain speak with you.

CASSIO Prithee come; will you?

IAGO Go to; say no more. [*Exit* CASSIO.]

OTHELLO [*Advancing.*] How shall I murther him, Iago?

IAGO Did you perceive how he laugh'd at his vice?

OTHELLO O Iago!

IAGO And did you see the handkerchief?

OTHELLO Was that mine?

IAGO Yours, by this hand. And to see how he prizes the foolish woman your wife! She gave it him, and he hath giv'n it his whore.

OTHELLO I would have him nine years a-killing. A fine woman! a fair woman! a sweet woman!

IAGO Nay, you must forget that.

OTHELLO Ay, let her rot, and perish, and be damn'd to-night, for she shall not live. No, my heart is turn'd to stone; I strike it, and it hurts my hand. O, the world hath not a sweeter creature! she might lie by an emperor's side and command him tasks.

IAGO Nay, that's not your way.°

OTHELLO Hang her, I do but say what she is. So delicate with her needle! an admirable musician! O, she will sing the savageness out of a bear. Of so high and plenteous wit and invention!

IAGO She's the worse for all this.

OTHELLO O, a thousand, a thousand times. And then of so gentle a condition!°

fitchew polecat (thought to be very lecherous as well as strong-smelling)
hobby-horse woman of easy virtue
An' and, i.e. if
your way your proper course, the direction your mind should take
of . . . condition so nobly born and bred

IAGO Ay, too gentle.°

OTHELLO Nay, that's certain. But yet the pity of it, Iago! O Iago, the pity of it, Iago!

IAGO If you are so fond° over her iniquity, give her patent° to offend, for if it touch not you, it comes near nobody.

OTHELLO I will chop her into messes.° Cuckold me!

IAGO O, 'tis foul in her.

OTHELLO With mine officer!

IAGO That's fouler.

OTHELLO Get me some poison, Iago, this night. I'll not expostulate with her, lest her body and beauty° unprovide my mind again. This night, Iago.

IAGO Do it not with poison; strangle her in her bed, even the bed she hath contaminated.

OTHELLO Good, good; the justice of it pleases; very good.

IAGO And for Cassio, let me be his undertaker.° You shall hear more by midnight.

OTHELLO Excellent good. [*A trumpet.*] What trumpet is that same?

IAGO I warrant, something from Venice.

Enter LODOVICO, DESDEMONA, *and* ATTENDANTS.

'Tis Lodovico—
This comes from the Duke. See, your wife's with him.

LODOVICO God save you, worthy general!

OTHELLO With all my heart,° sir.

LODOVICO The Duke and the senators of Venice greet you.
[*Gives him a letter.*]

OTHELLO I kiss the instrument of their pleasures. [*Opens the letter and reads.*]

DESDEMONA And what's the news, good cousin Lodovico?

IAGO I am very glad to see you, signior;
Welcome to Cyprus.

LODOVICO I thank you. How does Lieutenant Cassio?

IAGO Lives, sir.

DESDEMONA Cousin, there's fall'n between him and my lord
An unkind breach; but you shall make all well.

OTHELLO Are you sure of that?

DESDEMONA My lord?

OTHELLO [*Reads.*] 'This fail you not to do, as you will—'

LODOVICO He did not call; he's busy in the paper.
Is there division 'twixt my lord and Cassio?

DESDEMONA A most unhappy one. I would do much
T' atone° them, for the love I bear to Cassio.

OTHELLO Fire and brimstone!

DESDEMONA My lord?

OTHELLO Are you wise?

DESDEMONA What, is he angry?

gentle generous with her favors
fond dotingly foolish
patent license
messes portions of food, i.e. little pieces
body and beauty physical beauty
be his undertaker undertake to dispatch him
With . . . heart I heartily thank you
atone reconcile

LODOVICO May be th' letter mov'd him;
For as I think, they do command him home,
Deputing Cassio in his government.
DESDEMONA [By my troth], I am glad on't.
OTHELLO Indeed?
DESDEMONA My lord?
OTHELLO I am glad to see you mad.
DESDEMONA Why, sweet Othello?
OTHELLO [*Striking her.*] Devil!
DESDEMONA I have not deserv'd this.
LODOVICO My lord, this would not be believ'd in Venice,
Though I should swear I saw't. 'Tis very much,
Make her amends; she weeps.
OTHELLO O devil, devil!
If that the earth could teem with° woman's tears,
Each drop she falls° would prove a crocodile.
Out of my sight.
DESDEMONA I will not stay to offend you. [*Going.*]
LODOVICO Truly, an obedient lady:
I do beseech your lordship call her back.
OTHELLO Mistress!
DESDEMONA My lord?
OTHELLO What would you with her, sir?
LODOVICO Who, I, my lord?
OTHELLO Ay, you did wish that I would make her turn.
Sir, she can turn, and turn; and yet go on
And turn again; and she can weep, sir, weep;
And she's obedient, as you say, obedient;
Very obedient.—Proceed you in your tears.—
Concerning this, sir—O well-painted passion!—
I am commanded home.—Get you away;
I'll send for you anon.—Sir, I obey the mandate,
And will return to Venice.—Hence, avaunt!° [*Exit* DESDEMONA.]
Cassio shall have my place. And, sir, to-night
I do entreat that we may sup together.
You are welcome, sir, to Cyprus.—Goats and monkeys!° *Exit.*
LODOVICO Is this the noble Moor whom our full Senate
Call all in all sufficient? Is this the nature
Whom passion could not shake? whose solid virtue
The shot of accident nor dart of chance
Could neither graze nor pierce?
IAGO He is much chang'd.
LODOVICO Are his wits safe?° Is he not light of brain?
IAGO He's that he is; I may not breathe my censure

teem with be made pregnant by
falls lets fall
avaunt begone
Goats and monkeys Cf. III.iii.403.
safe sound

What he might be.° If what he might he is not,
I would to heaven he were!°

LODOVICO What? strike his wife?

IAGO Faith, that was not so well; yet would I knew
That stroke would prove the worst!

LODOVICO Is it his use?°
Or did the letters work upon his blood,°
And new-create this fault?

IAGO Alas, alas!
It is not honesty in me to speak
What I have seen and known. You shall observe him,
And his own courses will denote him so
That I may save my speech. Do but go after,
And mark how he continues.

LODOVICO I am sorry that I am deceiv'd in him. *Exeunt.*

SCENE II [*The citadel.*]

Enter OTHELLO *and* EMILIA.

OTHELLO You have seen nothing then?

EMILIA Nor ever heard—nor ever did suspect.

OTHELLO Yes, you have seen Cassio and she together.

EMILIA But then I saw no harm, and then I heard
Each syllable that breath made up between them.

OTHELLO What? did they never whisper?

EMILIA Never, my lord.

OTHELLO Nor send you out o' th' way?

EMILIA Never.

OTHELLO To fetch her fan, her gloves, her mask, nor nothing?

EMILIA Never, my lord.

OTHELLO That's strange.

EMILIA I durst, my lord, to wager she is honest;
Lay down my soul at stake. If you think other,
Remove your thought; it doth abuse your bosom.
If any wretch have put this in your head,
Let heaven requite it with the serpent's curse!°
For if she be not honest, chaste, and true,
There's no man happy; the purest of their wives
Is fould as slander.

OTHELLO Bid her come hither; go. *Exit* EMILIA.
She says enough; yet she's a simple bawd
That cannot say as much.° This is a subtile whore,

censure . . . be i.e. opinion as to whether he is insane
I . . . were i.e. because otherwise his behavior is unpardonable
use habit
blood passions
the serpent's curse the curse laid by God on the serpent that tempted Eve. Emilia implies that the crime of a slanderer of Desdemona, who is as innocent as Eve was before the fall, would be of the same magnitude.
she's . . . much the bawd who cannot say as much is a stupid one

A closet° lock and key of villainous secrets;
And yet she'll kneel and pray; I have seen her do't.

Enter DESDEMONA *and* EMILIA.

DESDEMONA My lord, what is your will?
OTHELLO Pray you, chuck, come hither.
DESDEMONA What is your pleasure?
OTHELLO Let me see your eyes;
Look in my face.
DESDEMONA What horrible fancy's this?
OTHELLO [*To* EMILIA.] Some of your function,° mistress;
Leave procreants alone, and shut the door;
Cough, or cry 'hem,' if anybody come.
Your mystery, your mystery;° nay, dispatch. *Exit* EMILIA.
DESDEMONA Upon my knee, what doth your speech import?
I understand a fury in your words,
But not the words.
OTHELLO Why? what art thou?
DESDEMONA Your wife, my lord; your true
And loyal wife.
OTHELLO Come swear it, damn thyself,
Lest being like one of heaven, the devils themselves
Should fear to seize thee; therefore be double damn'd:
Swear thou art honest.
DESDEMONA Heaven doth truly know it.
OTHELLO Heaven truly knows that thou art false as hell.
DESDEMONA To whom, my lord? With whom? How am I false?
OTHELLO Ah, Desdemon! Away, away, away!
DESDEMONA Alas the heavy day! Why do you weep?
Am I the motive° of these tears, my lord?
If happily you my father do suspect
An instrument of this your calling back,
Lay not your blame on me. If you have lost him,
Why, I have lost him too.
OTHELLO Had it pleas'd heaven
To try me with affliction, had they° rain'd
All kind of sores and shames on my bare head,
Steep'd me in poverty to the very lips,
Given to captivity me and my utmost hopes,
I should have found in some place of my soul
A drop of patience; but, alas, to make me
The fixed figure for the time of scorn°
To point his slow unmoving finger° at!
Yet could I bear that too, well, very well;

closet place where private papers could be locked up
Some . . . function go about your bawd's business (of standing watch outside the door)
mystery trade
motive moving force, cause
they i.e. the gods
time of scorn scornful world
slow unmoving finger A troublesome phrase; perhaps the meaning is that the finger points steadily and is slow to alter its aim, or that it rises slowly to its aim and then remains fixed.

But there, where I have garner'd up my heart,
Where either I must live or bear no life;
The fountain° from the which my current runs
Or else dries up: to be discarded thence!
Or keep it as a cestern° for foul toads
To knot and gender in! Turn° thy complexion there,°
Patience, thou young and rose-lipp'd cherubin—
Ay, here look grim as hell!

DESDEMONA I hope my noble lord esteems me honest.

OTHELLO O ay, as summer flies are in the shambles,
That quicken even with blowing.° O thou weed!
Who art so lovely fair and smell'st so sweet
That the sense aches at thee, would thou hadst never been born!

DESDEMONA Alas, what ignorant sin have I committed?

OTHELLO Was this fair paper, this most goodly book,
Made to write 'whore' upon? What committed?
Committed? O thou public commoner,°
I should make very forges of my cheeks,
That would to cinders burn up modesty,
Did I but speak thy deeds. What committed?
Heaven stops the nose at it, and the moon winks;°
The bawdy wind, that kisses all it meets,
Is hush'd within the hollow mine of earth
And will not hear't. What committed?
Impudent° strumpet!

DESDEMONA By heaven, you do me wrong.

OTHELLO Are not you a strumpet?

DESDEMONA No, as I am a Christian.
If to preserve this vessel for my lord
From any other foul unlawful touch
Be not to be a strumpet, I am none.

OTHELLO What, not a whore?

DESDEMONA No, as I shall be sav'd.

OTHELLO Is't possible?

DESDEMONA O, heaven forgive us!

OTHELLO I cry you mercy° then.
I took you for that cunning whore of Venice
That married with Othello.—[*Raising his voice.*] You, mistress,

Enter EMILIA.

That have the office opposite to Saint Peter,
And keeps the gate of hell! You, you! ay, you!
We have done our course; there's money for your pains.
I pray you turn the key and keep your counsel. *Exit.*

fountain source, spring
cestern cistern
Turn change
there at that point, when that happens
quicken . . . blowing come to life as soon as the eggs are deposited
commoner prostitute
winks shuts her eyes
Impudent shameless
cry you mercy beg your pardon

EMILIA Alas, what does this gentleman conceive?
How do you, madam? how do you, my good lady?
DESDEMONA Faith, half asleep.
EMILIA Good madam, what's the matter with my lord?
DESDEMONA With who?
EMILIA Why, with my lord, madam.
DESDEMONA Who is thy lord?
EMILIA He that is yours, sweet lady.
DESDEMONA I have none. Do not talk to me, Emilia;
I cannot weep, nor answers have I none
But what should go by water.° Prithee to-night
Lay on my bed my wedding-sheets—remember;
And call thy husband hither.
EMILIA Here's a change indeed! *Exit.*
DESDEMONA 'Tis meet I should be us'd so, very meet.
How have I been behav'd, that he might stick
The small'st opinion° on my least misuse?°

Enter IAGO *and* EMILIA.

IAGO What is your pleasure, madam? How is't with you?
DESDEMONA I cannot tell. Those that do teach young babes
Do it with gentle means and easy tasks.
He might have chid me so; for in good faith
I am a child to chiding.
IAGO What is the matter, lady?
EMILIA Alas, Iago, my lord hath so bewhor'd her,
Thrown such despite and heavy terms upon her,
That true hearts cannot bear it.
DESDEMONA Am I that name, Iago?
IAGO What name, fair lady?
DESDEMONA Such as she said my lord did say I was.
EMILIA He call'd her whore. A beggar in his drink
Could not have laid such terms upon his callet.°
IAGO Why did he so?
DESDEMONA I do not know; I am sure I am none such.
IAGO Do not weep, do not weep. Alas the day!
EMILIA Hath she forsook so many noble matches?
Her father? and her country? and her friends?
To be call'd whore? Would it not make one weep?
DESDEMONA It is my wretched fortune.
IAGO Beshrew him for't!
How comes this trick° upon him?
DESDEMONA Nay, heaven doth know.
EMILIA I will be hang'd if some eternal° villain,
Some busy and insinuating° rogue,

go by water be rendered by tears
opinion censure
my least misuse the slightest misconduct on my part
callet whore
trick odd behavior
eternal inveterate
insinuating worming his way into favor

Some cogging,° cozening° slave, to get some office,
Have not devis'd this slander. I will be hang'd else.

IAGO Fie, there is no such man; it is impossible.

DESDEMONA If any such there be, heaven pardon him!

EMILIA A halter pardon him! and hell gnaw his bones!
Why should he call her whore? Who keeps her company?
What place? what time? what form?° what likelihood?
The Moor's abus'd by some most villainous knave,
Some base notorious knave, some scurvy fellow.
O heaven, that such companions° thou'dst unfold,°
And put in every honest hand a whip
To lash the rascals naked through the world
Even from the east to th' west!

IAGO Speak within door.°

EMILIA O fie upon them! Some such squire he was
That turn'd your wit the seamy side without,°
And made you to suspect me with the Moor.

IAGO You are a fool; go to.

DESDEMONA Alas, Iago,
What shall I do to win my lord again?
Good friend, go to him; for by this light of heaven,
I know not how I lost him. Here I kneel:
If e'er my will did trespass 'gainst his love,
Either in discourse of thought° or actual deed,
Or that mine eyes, mine ears, or any sense
Delighted them in any other form;
Or that I do not yet, and ever did,
And ever will (though he do shake me off
To beggarly divorcement) love him dearly,
Comfort forswear me! Unkindness may do much,
And his unkindness may defeat° my life,
But never taint my love. I cannot say 'whore.'
It does abhor me° now I speak the word;
To do the act that might the addition° earn,
Not the world's mass of vanity could make me.

IAGO I pray you be content; 'tis but his humour.°
The business of the state does him offense,
And he does chide with you.

DESDEMONA If 'twere no other—

IAGO It is but so, I warrant. [*Trumpets within.*]
Hark how these instruments summon to supper!
The messengers of Venice stays the meat.°
Go in, and weep not; all things shall be well.

Exeunt DESDEMONA *and* EMILIA.

cogging cheating
cozening deceiving
form shape, i.e. specific circumstances
companions fellows
unfold expose
within door i.e. less loudly
seamy side without wrong side out
discourse of thought process of thinking
defeat destroy
abhor me fill me with abhorrence
addition designation
humour mood
stays the meat wait to dine

Enter RODERIGO.

How now, Roderigo?

RODERIGO I do not find that thou deal'st justly with me.

IAGO What in the contrary?

RODERIGO Every day thou daff'st me° with some device, Iago, and rather, as it seems to me now, keep'st from me all conveniency° than suppliest me with the least advantage of hope. I will indeed no longer endure it; nor am I yet persuaded to put up° in peace what already I have foolishly suff'red.

IAGO Will you hear me, Roderigo?

RODERIGO Faith, I have heard too much; for your words and performances are no kin together.

IAGO You charge me most unjustly.

RODERIGO With nought but truth. I have wasted myself out of my means. The jewels you have had from me to deliver Desdemona would half have corrupted a votarist.° You have told me she hath receiv'd them and return'd me expectations and comforts of sudden respect° and acquaintance, but I find none.

IAGO Well, go to; very well.

RODERIGO Very well! go to! I cannot go to, man, nor 'tis not very well. By this hand, I think it is scurvy, and begin to find myself fopp'd° in it.

IAGO Very well.

RODERIGO I tell you 'tis not very well. I will make myself known to Desdemona. If she will return me my jewels, I will give over my suit and repent my unlawful solicitation; if not, assure yourself I will seek satisfaction of you.

IAGO You have said now.

RODERIGO Ay; and said nothing but what I protest intendment of doing.

IAGO Why, now I see there's mettle in thee, and even from this instant do build on thee a better opinion than ever before. Give me thy hand, Roderigo. Thou hast taken against me a most just exception; but yet I protest I have dealt most directly in thy affair.

RODERIGO It hath not appear'd.

IAGO I grant indeed it hath not appear'd; and your suspicion is not without wit and judgment. But, Roderigo, if thou hast that in thee indeed, which I have greater reason to believe now than ever (I mean purpose, courage, and valour), this night show it. If thou the next night following enjoy not Desdemona, take me from this world with treachery and devise engines for° my life.

RODERIGO Well; what is it? Is it within reason and compass?

IAGO Sir, there is especial commission come from Venice to depute Cassio in Othello's place.

RODERIGO Is that true? Why then Othello and Desdemona return again to Venice.

daff'st me puttest me off
conveniency i.e. opportunity to meet Desdemona
put up tolerate, stomach
votarist nun
sudden respect immediate consideration
fopp'd made a fool of, duped
engines for plots against

IAGO O no; he goes into Mauritania and taketh away with him the fair Desdemona, unless his abode be ling'red here by some accident; wherein none can be so determinate° as the removing of Cassio.

RODERIGO How do you mean, removing him?

IAGO Why, by making him uncapable of Othello's place: knocking out his brains.

RODERIGO And that you would have me to do?

IAGO Ay; if you dare do yourself a profit and a right. He sups to-night with a harlotry,° and thither will I go to him—he knows not yet of his honourable fortune. If you will watch his going thence (which I will fashion to fall out between twelve and one), you may take him at your pleasure. I will be near to second your attempt, and he shall fall between us. Come, stand not amaz'd at it, but go along with me; I will show you such a necessity in his death that you shall think yourself bound to put it on him. It is now high supper-time, and the night grows to waste.° About it.

RODERIGO I will hear further reason for this.

IAGO And you shall be satisfied. *Exeunt.*

SCENE III [*The citadel.*]

Enter OTHELLO, LODOVICO, DESDEMONA, EMILIA, *and* ATTENDANTS.

LODOVICO I do beseech you, sir, trouble yourself no further.
OTHELLO O, pardon me; 'twill do me good to walk.
LODOVICO Madam, good night; I humbly thank your ladyship.
DESDEMONA Your honour is most welcome.
OTHELLO Will you walk, sir?
O, Desdemona!
DESDEMONA My lord?

OTHELLO Get you to bed on th' instant, I will be return'd forthwith. Dismiss your attendant there. Look't be done.

DESDEMONA I will, my lord.

Exeunt [OTHELLO, LODOVICO, *and* ATTENDANTS].

EMILIA How goes it now? He looks gentler than he did.
DESDEMONA He says he will return incontinent,°
And hath commanded me to go to bed,
And bid me to dismiss you.
EMILIA Dismiss me?
DESDEMONA It was his bidding; therefore, good Emilia,
Give me my nightly wearing, and adieu.
We must not now displease him.
EMILIA I would you had never seen him!
DESDEMONA So would not I. My love doth so approve him,
That even his stubbornness,° his checks, his frowns—
Prithee unpin me—have grace and favour° in them.
EMILIA I have laid those sheets you bade me on the bed.

determinate effectual
harlotry slut
grows to waste is being wasted
incontinent at once
stubbornness roughness
favour attractiveness

DESDEMONA All's one. Good faith, how foolish are our minds!
If I do die before thee, prithee shroud me
In one of these same sheets.

EMILIA Come, come; you talk.°

DESDEMONA My mother had a maid call'd Barbary;
She was in love, and he she lov'd prov'd mad,°
And did forsake her. She had a song of "Willow,"°
An old thing 'twas, but it express'd her fortune,
And she died singing it. That song to-night
Will not go from my mind; I have much to do
But to° go hang my head all at one side
And sing it like poor Barbary. Prithee dispatch.

EMILIA Shall I go fetch your night-gown?

DESDEMONA No, unpin me here.
This Lodovico is a proper man.

EMILIA A very handsome man.

DESDEMONA He speaks well.

EMILIA I know a lady in Venice would have walk'd barefoot to Palestine for a touch of his nether lip.

DESDEMONA [*Singing.*]
The poor soul sat sighing by a sycamore tree,
Sing all a green willow;
Her hand on her bosom, her head on her knee,
Sing willow, willow, willow.
The fresh streams ran by her, and murmur'd her moans,
Sing willow, willow, willow;
Her salt tears fell from her, and soft'ned the stones,
Sing willow—
Lay by these—
[*Singing.*] *—willow, willow—*
Prithee hie thee;° he'll come anon—
[*Singing.*]
Sing all a green willow must be my garland.
Let nobody blame him, his scorn I approve—
Nay, that's not next. Hark, who is't that knocks?

EMILIA It's the wind.

DESDEMONA [*Singing.*]
I call'd my love false love; but what said he then?
Sing willow, willow, willow;
If I court moe women, you'll couch with moe men.—
So get thee gone, good night. Mine eyes do itch;
Doth that bode weeping?

EMILIA 'Tis neither here nor there.

DESDEMONA I have heard it said so. O, these men, these men!
Dost thou in conscience° think—tell me, Emilia—

talk i.e. prattle idly
mad wild, i.e. untrue
Willow symbolic of disappointed love
I . . . to it's all I can do not to
hie thee make haste
in conscience sincerely, truly

That there be women do abuse their husbands
In such gross kind?

EMILIA There be some such, no question.

DESDEMONA Wouldst thou do such a deed for all the world?

EMILIA Why, would not you?

DESDEMONA No, by this heavenly light!

EMILIA Nor I neither by this heavenly light;
I might do't as well i' th' dark.

DESDEMONA Wouldst thou do such a deed for all the world?

EMILIA The world's a huge thing; it is a great price°
For a small vice.

DESDEMONA Good troth, I think thou wouldst not.

EMILIA By my troth, I think I should, and undo't when I had done't. Marry, I would not do such a thing for a jòint-ring,° nor for measures of lawn,° nor for gowns, petticoats, nor caps, nor any petty exhibition;° but, for all the whole world—'ud's° pity, who would not make her husband a cuckold to make him a monarch? I should venture purgatory for't.

DESDEMONA Beshrew me, if I would do such a wrong
For the whole world.

EMILIA Why, the wrong is but a wrong i' th' world; and having the world for your labour, 'tis a wrong in your own world, and you might quickly make it right.

DESDEMONA I do not think there is any such woman.

EMILIA Yes, a dozen; and as many to th' vantage° as
would store the world they play'd for.
But I do think it is their husbands' faults
If wives do fall. Say that they slack their duties,°
And pour our treasures into foreign laps;°
Or else break out in peevish° jealousies,
Throwing restraint upon us; or say they strike us,
Or scant° our former having° in despite:°
Why, we have galls;° and though we have some grace,
Yet have we some revenge. Let husbands know
Their wives have sense° like them; they see, and smell,
And have their palates both for sweet and sour,
As husbands have. What is it that they do
When they change us for others? Is it sport?
I think it is. And doth affection breed it?
I think it doth. Is't frailty that thus errs?
It is so too. And have not we affections,
Desires for sport, and frailty, as men have?
Then let them use us well; else let them know,
The ills we do, their ills instruct us so.

price prize
joint-ring cheap ring made in separable halves
lawn fine linen
exhibition gift
'ud's a corruption of *God's*
to th' vantage in addition
duties marital duties
foreign laps i.e. the laps of other women
peevish silly, childish
scant reduce
having allowance
despite spite
galls tempers, the capacity to resent such treatment
sense bodily senses

DESDEMONA Good night, good night. God me such uses send,°
Not to pick bad from bad, but by bad mend.° *Exeunt.*

ACT V

SCENE I [*A street near the citadel.*]

Enter IAGO *and* RODERIGO.

IAGO Here, stand behind this bulk,° straight will he come.
Wear thy good rapier bare, and put it home.
Quick, quick, fear nothing; I'll be at thy elbow.
It makes us, or it mars us, think on that,
And fix most firm thy resolution.
RODERIGO Be near at hand, I may miscarry in't.
IAGO Here, at thy hand; be bold, and take thy stand. [*Retires.*]
RODERIGO I have no great devotion to the deed,
And yet he hath given me satisfying reasons.
'Tis but a man gone. Forth my sword; he dies.
IAGO I have rubb'd this young quat° almost to the sense,°
And he grows angry. Now, whether he kill Cassio,
Or Cassio him, or each do kill the other,
Every way makes my gain. Live Roderigo,
He calls me to a restitution large
Of gold and jewels that I bobb'd° from him
As gifts to Desdemona;
It must not be. If Cassio do remain,
He hath a daily beauty in his life
That makes me ugly; and besides, the Moor
May unfold me to him; there stand I in much peril.
No, he must die. Be't so. I hear him coming.

Enter CASSIO.

RODERIGO I know his gait, 'tis he.—Villain, thou diest!
[*Makes a pass at* CASSIO.]
CASSIO That thrust had been mine enemy indeed,
But that my coat° is better than thou know'st.
I will make proof of thine. [*Draws, and wounds* RODERIGO.]
RODERIGO O, I am slain.
[IAGO *from behind wounds* CASSIO *in the leg, and exit.*]
CASSIO I am maim'd for ever. Help ho! murther, murther! [*Falls.*]

Enter OTHELLO.

OTHELLO The voice of Cassio! Iago keeps his word.

me . . . send i.e. enable me to make it my practice
Not . . . mend not to use others' ill conduct as an excuse for behaving likewise, but rather to learn from it how to behave otherwise.
bulk shop-stall protruding into the street
quat pimple, small boil
sense quick
bobb'd swindled
coat Possibly he wears a rapier-proof vest under his outer clothing.

RODERIGO O, villain that I am!
OTHELLO It is even so.
CASSIO O, help ho! light! a surgeon!
OTHELLO 'Tis he!—O brave° Iago, honest and just,
That hast such noble sense of thy friend's wrong!
Thou teachest me. Minion,° your dear lies dead,
And your unblest fate hies.° Strumpet, I come.
Forth of my heart those charms, thine eyes, are blotted;
Thy bed, lust-stain'd, shall with lust's blood be spotted. [*Exit* OTHELLO.]

Enter LODOVICO *and* GRATIANO.

CASSIO What ho! no watch? no passage?° Murther, murther!
GRATIANO 'Tis some mischance, the voice is very direful.
CASSIO O, help!
LODOVICO Hark!
RODERIGO O wretched villain!
LODOVICO Two or three groan. 'Tis heavy° night;
These may be counterfeits; let's think't unsafe
To come in to the cry without more help.
RODERIGO Nobody come? Then shall I bleed to death.

Enter IAGO [*with a light*].

LODOVICO Hark!
GRATIANO Here's one comes in his shirt, with light and weapons.
IAGO Who's there? Whose noise is this that cries on° murther?
LODOVICO We do not know.
IAGO Did not you hear a cry?
CASSIO Here, here! for heaven° sake help me!
IAGO What's the matter?
GRATIANO This is Othello's ancient, as I take it.
LODOVICO The same indeed, a very valiant fellow.
IAGO What are you here that cry so grievously?
CASSIO Iago? O, I am spoil'd,° undone by villains!
Give me some help.
IAGO O me, lieutenant! what villains have done this?
CASSIO I think that one of them is hereabout,
And cannot make away.
IAGO O treacherous villains!
[*To* LODOVICO *and* GRATIANO.] What are you there? Come in, and give some help.
RODERIGO O, help me there!
CASSIO That's one of them.
IAGO O murd'rous slave! O villain! [*Stabs* RODERIGO.]
RODERIGO O damn'd Iago! O inhuman dog!
IAGO Kill men i' th' dark?—Where be these bloody thieves?—

brave excellent, noble
Minion hussy
hies approaches rapidly
passage passers-by
heavy dark
cries on cries out
heaven heaven's
spoil'd destroyed

How silent is this town!—Ho, murther, murther!—
What may you be? Are you of good or evil?
LODOVICO As you shall prove us, praise us.
IAGO Signior Lodovico?
LODOVICO He, sir.
IAGO I cry you mercy. Here's Cassio hurt by villains.
GRATIANO Cassio?
IAGO How is't, brother?
CASSIO My leg is cut in two.
IAGO Marry, heaven forbid!
Light, gentlemen! I'll bind it with my shirt.

Enter BIANCA.

BIANCA What is the matter ho? Who is't that cried?
IAGO Who is't that cried?
BIANCA O my dear Cassio, my sweet Cassio!
O Cassio, Cassio, Cassio!
IAGO O notable strumpet! Cassio, may you suspect
Who they should be that have thus mangled you?
CASSIO No.
GRATIANO I am sorry to find you thus; I have been to seek you.
IAGO Lend me a garter. So.—O for a chair
To bear him easily hence!
BIANCA Alas, he faints! O Cassio, Cassio, Cassio!
IAGO Gentlemen all, I do suspect this trash
To be a party in this injury.—
Patience awhile, good Cassio.—Come, come;
Lend me a light. Know we this face or no?
Alas, my friend and my dear countryman
Roderigo! No—yes, sure—O heaven, Roderigo!
GRATIANO What, of Venice?
IAGO Even he, sir; did you know him?
GRATIANO Know him? ay.
IAGO Signior Gratiano? I cry your gentle pardon;
These bloody accidents must excuse my manners
That so neglected you.
GRATIANO I am glad to see you.
IAGO How do you, Cassio? O, a chair, a chair!
GRATIANO Roderigo!
IAGO He, he, 'tis he. [*A chair brought in.*] O, that's well said:° the chair.
Some good man bear him carefully from hence,
I'll fetch the general's surgeon. [*To* BIANCA.] For you, mistress,
Save you your labour.—He that lies slain here, Cassio,
Was my dear friend. What malice° was between you?
CASSIO None in the world; nor do I know the man.
IAGO [*To* BIANCA.] What? look you pale?—O, bear him out o' th' air.°
[CASSIO *and* RODERIGO *are borne off.*]

well said well done
malice enmity
out . . . air Fresh air was considered bad for wounds.

Stay you, good gentlemen.—Look you pale, mistress?—
Do you perceive the gastness° of her eye?—
Nay, an' you stare, we shall hear more anon.—
Behold her well; I pray you look upon her.
Do you see, gentlemen? Nay, guiltiness will speak,
Though tongues were out of use.

[*Enter* EMILIA.]

EMILIA Alas, what is the matter? What is the matter, husband?
IAGO Cassio hath here been set on in the dark
By Roderigo and fellows that are scap'd.
He's almost slain, and Roderigo quite dead.
EMILIA Alas, good gentleman! alas, good Cassio!
IAGO This is the fruits of whoring. Prithee, Emilia,
Go know of Cassio where he supp'd to-night.
[*To* BIANCA.] What, do you shake at that?
BIANCA He supp'd at my house, but I therefore shake not.
IAGO O, did he so? I charge you go with me.
EMILIA O fie upon thee, strumpet!
BIANCA I am no strumpet, but of life as honest
As you that thus abuse me.
EMILIA As I? Fough, fie upon thee!
IAGO Kind gentlemen, let's go see poor Cassio dress'd.
Come, mistress, you must tell 's another tale.
Emilia, run you to the citadel,
And tell my lord and lady what hath happ'd.—
Will you go on afore? [*Aside.*] This is the night
That either makes me, or foredoes° me quite. *Exeunt.*

SCENE II [*The citadel.*]

Enter OTHELLO [*with a light*] *and* DESDEMONA *in her bed* [*asleep.*]

OTHELLO It is the cause, it is the cause,° my soul;
Let me not name it to you, you chaste stars,
It is the cause. Yet I'll not shed her blood,
Nor scar that whiter skin of hers than snow,
And smooth as monumental alablaster,°
Yet she must die, else she'll betray more men.
Put out the light, and then put out the light:
If I quench thee, thou flaming minister,
I can again thy former light restore,
Should I repent me;° but once put out thy light,
Thou cunning'st pattern of excelling nature,
I know not where is that Promethean° heat

gastness terror
foredoes destroys
the cause the crime (not the criminal). Othello sees himself as an agent of justice, not an avenger of his own honor.
alablaster alabaster
repent me change my mind
Promethean i.e. divine (since Prometheus brought down fire from heaven)

That can thy light relume.° When I have pluck'd thy rose,
I cannot give it vital growth again,
It needs must wither. I'll smell thee on the tree. [*Kisses her.*]
O balmy breath, that dost almost persuade
Justice to break her sword! One more, one more.
Be thus when thou art dead, and I will kill thee
And love thee after. One more, and that's the last.
So sweet was ne'er so fatal. I must weep,
But they are cruel° tears. This sorrow's heavenly,
It strikes where it doth love.° She wakes.

DESDEMONA Who's there? Othello?

OTHELLO Ay, Desdemona.

DESDEMONA Will you come to bed, my lord?

OTHELLO Have you pray'd to-night, Desdemon?

DESDEMONA Ay, my lord.

OTHELLO If you bethink yourself of any crime°
Unreconcil'd as yet to heaven and grace,
Solicit for it straight.

DESDEMONA Alack, my lord, what may you mean by that?

OTHELLO Well, do it, and be brief, I will walk by.
I would not kill thy unprepared spirit,
No, heaven forefend!° I would not kill thy soul.

DESDEMONA Talk you of killing?

OTHELLO Ay, I do.

DESDEMONA Then heaven
Have mercy on me!

OTHELLO Amen, with all my heart!

DESDEMONA If you say so, I hope you will not kill me.

OTHELLO Humh!

DESDEMONA And yet I fear you; for you're fatal then
When your eyes roll so. Why I should fear I know not,
Since guiltiness I know not; but yet I feel I fear.

OTHELLO Think on thy sins.

DESDEMONA They are loves I bear to you.

OTHELLO Ay, and for that thou diest.

DESDEMONA That death's unnatural that kills for loving.
Alas, why gnaw you so your nether lip?
Some bloody passion shakes your very frame.
These are portents; but yet I hope, I hope,
They do not point on° me.

OTHELLO Peace, and be still!

DESDEMONA I will so. What's the matter?

OTHELLO That handkerchief which I so lov'd, and gave thee,
Thou gav'st to Cassio.

relume rekindle
cruel unrelenting
This . . . love Cf. Hebrews 12:6: "For whom the Lord loveth he chasteneth. . ."
crime sin
forefend forfend, forbid
point on point to, aim at

DESDEMONA No, by my life and soul!
Send for the man, and ask him.
OTHELLO Sweet soul, take heed,
Take heed of perjury, thou art on thy death-bed.
DESDEMONA Ay, but not yet to die.
OTHELLO Yes, presently:°
Therefore confess thee freely of thy sin;
For to deny each article with oath
Cannot remove nor choke the strong conception°
That I do groan withal. Thou art to die.
DESDEMONA Then Lord have mercy on me!
OTHELLO I say, amen.
DESDEMONA And have you mercy too! I never did
Offend° you in my life; never lov'd Cassio
But with such general warranty° of heaven
As I might love. I never gave him token.
OTHELLO By heaven, I saw my handkerchief in 's hand.
O perjur'd woman, thou dost stone° my heart,
And mak'st me call what I intend to do
A murther, which I thought a sacrifice.°
I saw the handkerchief.
DESDEMONA He found it then;
I never gave it him. Send for him hither;
Let him confess a truth.
OTHELLO He hath confess'd.
DESDEMONA What, my lord?
OTHELLO That he hath us'd thee.
DESDEMONA How? unlawfully?
OTHELLO Ay.
DESDEMONA He will not say so.
OTHELLO No—his mouth is stopp'd;
Honest Iago hath ta'en order for't.°
DESDEMONA O, my fear interprets. What, is he dead?
OTHELLO Had all his hairs been lives, my great revenge
Had stomach for them all.
DESDEMONA Alas, he is betray'd and I undone!
OTHELLO Out, strumpet! weep'st thou for him to my face?
DESDEMONA O, banish me, my lord, but kill me not!
OTHELLO Down, strumpet!
DESDEMONA Kill me to-morrow, let me live to-night!
OTHELLO Nay, an' you strive—°
DESDEMONA But half an hour!
OTHELLO Being done,° there is no pause.
DESDEMONA But while I say one prayer!
OTHELLO It is too late. *Smothers her.*

presently at once
conception i.e. conviction of your guilt
Offend wrong
warranty approval, allowance
stone turn to stone
sacrifice i.e. offering to justice
ta'en order for't taken steps to effect it
strive struggle
Being done since all is over

DESDEMONA O Lord, Lord, Lord!
EMILIA (*At the door* [*within*].) My lord, my lord! What ho! my lord, my lord!
OTHELLO What noise is this? Not dead? not yet quite dead?
I that am cruel am yet merciful,
I would not have thee linger in thy pain.
So, so.
EMILIA (*within*) What ho! my lord, my lord!
OTHELLO Who's there?
EMILIA [*within*] O, good my lord, I would speak a word with you!
OTHELLO Yes.—'Tis Emilia.—By and by.—She's dead.
'Tis like she comes to speak of Cassio's death;
The noise was high.° Hah, no more moving?
Still as the grave. Shall she come in? Were't good?
I think she stirs again. No. What's best to do?
If she come in, she'll sure speak to my wife.
My wife, my wife! what wife? I have no wife.
O insupportable° O heavy hour!
Methinks it should be now a huge eclipse
Of sun and moon, and that th' affrighted globe
Did yawn° at alteration.°
EMILIA *Within.* I do beseech you
That I may speak with you. O, good my lord!
OTHELLO I had forgot thee. O, come in, Emilia.—
Soft,° by and by, let me the curtains draw.—
Where art thou? [*Unlocks the door.*]
What's the matter with thee now?

Enter EMILIA.

EMILIA O, my good lord, yonder's foul murthers done!
OTHELLO What? now?
EMILIA But now, my lord.
OTHELLO It is the very error° of the moon,
She comes more nearer earth than she was wont,
And makes men mad.
EMILIA Cassio, my lord, hath kill'd a young Venetian
Call'd Roderigo.
OTHELLO Roderigo kill'd?
And Cassio kill'd?
EMILIA No, Cassio is not kill'd.
OTHELLO Not Cassio kill'd? Then murther's out of tune,
And sweet revenge grows harsh.
DESDEMONA O, falsely, falsely murder'd!
EMILIA O Lord, what cry is that?
OTHELLO That? what?

The noise was high i.e. it caused a great commotion. Many editors, following Q1, read *The noise was here*, referring to the noise in the bed (l. 86).
yawn It was commonly believed that eclipses were accompanied by earthquakes.
alteration the great change on earth
Soft wait a moment
error aberration, deviation from the normal course

EMILIA Out,° and alas, that was my lady's voice.
Help, help, ho, help! O lady, speak again!
Sweet Desdemona, O sweet mistress, speak!
DESDEMONA A guiltless death I die.
EMILIA O, who hath done this deed?
DESDEMONA Nobody; I myself. Farewell!
Commend me to my kind lord. O, farewell! [*Dies.*]
OTHELLO Why, how should she be murd'red?
EMILIA Alas! who knows?
OTHELLO You heard her say herself, it was not I.
EMILIA She said so; I must needs report the truth.
OTHELLO She's like a liar gone to burning hell:
'Twas I that kill'd her.
EMILIA O, the more angel she,
And you the blacker devil!
OTHELLO She turn'd to folly, and she was a whore.
EMILIA Thou dost belie her, and thou art a devil.
OTHELLO She was false as water.
EMILIA Thou art rash° as fire to say
That she was false. O, she was heavenly true!
OTHELLO Cassio did top her; ask thy husband else.
O, I were damn'd beneath all depth in hell
But that I did proceed upon just grounds
To this extremity. Thy husband knew it all.
EMILIA My husband?
OTHELLO Thy husband.
EMILIA That she was false to wedlock?
OTHELLO Ay, with Cassio. Nay, had she been true,
If heaven would make me such another world
Of one entire and perfect chrysolite,°
I'ld not have sold her for it.
EMILIA My husband?
OTHELLO Ay, 'twas he that told me on her first.
An honest man he is, and hates the slime
That sticks on filthy deeds.
EMILIA My husband?
OTHELLO What needs this iterance,° woman? I say thy husband.
EMILIA O mistress, villainy hath made mocks with° love!
My husband say she was false?
OTHELLO He, woman:
I say thy husband; dost understand the word?
My friend, thy husband, honest, honest Iago.
EMILIA If he say so, may his pernicious soul
Rot half a grain a day! He lies to th' heart.
She was too fond of her most filthy bargain.
OTHELLO Hah?

Out exclamation of grief
rash impetuous
chrysolite topaz
iterance repetition
with at

EMILIA Do thy worst!
This deed of thine is no more worthy heaven
Than thou wast worthy her.

OTHELLO Peace, you were best.

EMILIA Thou hast not half that pow'r to do me harm
As I have to be hurt.° O gull,° O dolt,
As ignorant as dirt! Thou hast done a deed—
I care not for thy sword, I'll make thee known,
Though I lost twenty lives. Help, help, ho, help!
The Moor hath kill'd my mistress! Murther, murther!

Enter MONTANO, GRATIANO, *and* IAGO, [*with others*].

MONTANO What is the matter? How now, general?

EMILIA O, are you come, Iago? You have done well,
That men must lay their murthers on your neck.

GRATIANO What is the matter?

EMILIA Disprove this villain, if thou be'st a man.
He says thou toldst him that his wife was false.
I know thou didst not; thou'rt not such a villain.
Speak, for my heart is full.

IAGO I told him what I thought, and told no more
Than what he found himself was apt° and true.

EMILIA But did you ever tell him she was false?

IAGO I did.

EMILIA You told a lie, an odious, damned lie;
Upon my soul, a lie, a wicked lie.
She false with Cassio? did you say with Cassio?

IAGO With Cassio, mistress. Go to, charm° your tongue.

EMILIA I will not charm my tongue; I am bound to speak.
My mistress here lies murthered in her bed—

ALL O heavens forefend!

EMILIA And your reports have set the murder on.

OTHELLO Nay, stare not, masters, it is true indeed.

GRATIANO 'Tis a strange truth.

MONTANO O monstrous act!

EMILIA Villainy, villainy, villainy!
I think upon't, I think—I smell't—O villainy!
I thought so then°—I'll kill myself for grief—
O villainy! villainy!

IAGO What, are you mad? I charge you get you home.

EMILIA Good gentlemen, let me have leave to speak.
'Tis proper I obey him; but not now.
Perchance, Iago, I will ne'er go home.

OTHELLO O, O, O! [OTHELLO *falls on the bed.*]

EMILIA Nay, lay thee down and roar;

be hurt i.e. endure hurt
gull dupe
apt credible
charm i.e. silence, as if with a magic spell
I . . . then See IV.ii.130–33.

For thou hast kill'd the sweetest innocent
That e'er did lift up eye.

OTHELLO [*Rising.*] O, she was foul!
I scarce did know you, uncle; there lies your niece,
Whose breath, indeed, these hands have newly stopp'd.
I know this act shows horrible and grim.

GRATIANO Poor Desdemon! I am glad thy father's dead.
Thy match was mortal to him, and pure grief
Shore° his old thread° in twain. Did he live now,
This sight would make him do a desperate turn,°
Yea, curse his better angel from his side,
And fall to reprobance.°

OTHELLO 'Tis pitiful; but yet Iago knows
That she with Cassio hath the act of shame
A thousand times committed. Cassio confess'd it,
And she did gratify his amorous works
With that recognizance° and pledge of love
Which I first gave her. I saw it in his hand;
It was a handkerchief, an antique token
My father gave my mother.

EMILIA O God! O heavenly God!

IAGO 'Zounds, hold your peace.

EMILIA 'Twill out, 'twill out! I peace?
No, I will speak as liberal° as the north:°
Let heaven and men and devils, let them all,
All, all, cry shame against me, yet I'll speak.

IAGO Be wise, and get you home.

EMILIA I will not. [IAGO *offers to stab* EMILIA.]

GRATIANO Fie,
Your sword upon a woman?

EMILIA O thou dull Moor, that handkerchief thou speak'st of
I found by fortune, and did give my husband;
For often, with a solemn earnestness
(More than indeed belong'd° to such a trifle),
He begg'd of me to steal't.

IAGO Villainous whore!

EMILIA She gave it Cassio? No, alas, I found it,
And I did give't my husband.

IAGO Filth, thou liest!

EMILIA By heaven, I do not, I do not, gentlemen.
O murd'rous coxcomb,° what should such a fool
Do with so good a wife?

OTHELLO Are there no stones in heaven
But what serves for the thunder?°—Precious villain!

[*The* MOOR *runs at* IAGO; MONTANO *disarms* OTHELLO; IAGO *kills his wife.*]

Shore sheared, cut
thread i.e. thread of life
turn act
to reprobance into damnation
recognizance token
liberal unrestrainedly
as the north as the north wind blows
belong'd was appropriate
coxcomb fool
for the thunder i.e. as thunderbolts

GRATIANO The woman falls; sure he hath kill'd his wife.
EMILIA Ay, ay! O, lay me by my mistress' side. [*Exit* IAGO.]
GRATIANO He's gone, but his wife's kill'd.
MONTANO 'Tis a notorious° villain. Take you this weapon
Which I have here recover'd° from the Moor.
Come guard the door without; let him not pass,
But kill him rather. I'll after that same villain,
For 'tis a damned slave.
Exit [with all but OTHELLO *and* EMILIA*].*
OTHELLO I am not valiant neither,
But every puny whipster° gets my sword.
But why should honour° outlive honesty?°
Let it go all.
EMILIA What did thy song bode, lady?
Hark, canst thou hear me? I will play the swan,
And die in music. [*Sings.*] 'Willow, willow, willow.'
Moor, she was chaste; she lov'd thee, cruel Moor;
So come my soul to bliss, as I speak true;
So speaking as I think, alas, I die. [*Dies.*]
OTHELLO I have another weapon in this chamber;
It was a sword of Spain, the ice-brook's temper—°
O, here it is. Uncle, I must come forth.
GRATIANO [*Within*] If thou attempt it, it will cost thee dear:
Thou hast no weapon, and perforce must suffer.
OTHELLO Look in upon me then and speak with me,
Or naked° as I am I will assault thee.

[*Enter* GRATIANO.]

GRATIANO What is the matter?
OTHELLO Behold, I have a weapon;
A better never did itself sustain
Upon a soldier's thigh. I have seen the day
That with this little arm, and this good sword,
I have made my way through more impediments
Than twenty times your stop.° But (O vain boast!)
Who can control his fate? 'tis not so now.
Be not afraid though you do see me weapon'd;
Here is my journey's end, here is my butt°
And very sea-mark° of my utmost sail.
Do you go back dismay'd? 'Tis a lost° fear;
Man but a rush° against Othello's breast,
And he retires. Where should Othello go?

notorious exceptional, egregious
recover'd taken away
whipster insignificant or contemptible person
honour i.e. personal prowess and courage, and one's reputation for them
honesty inward integrity
the ice-brook's temper i.e. its steel tempered in icy water
naked unarmed
stop power to stop
butt goal
sea-mark beacon or other object marking the entrance to a harbor; hence, destination, end
lost idle, unnecessary
Man . . . rush hold a mere reed

Now—how dost thou look now? O ill-starr'd wench,
Pale as thy smock! when we shall meet at compt,°
This look of thine will hurl my soul from heaven,
And fiends will snatch at it. Cold, cold, my girl?
Even like thy chastity. O cursed, cursed slave!
Whip me, ye devils,
From the possession of this heavenly sight!
Blow me about in winds! roast me in sulphur!
Wash me in steep-down gulfs of liquid fire!
O Desdemon! dead, Desdemon! dead!
O, O!

Enter LODOVICO, CASSIO [*in a chair*], MONTANO, *and* IAGO [*guarded*], *with* OFFICERS.

LODOVICO Where is this rash° and most unfortunate man?
OTHELLO That's he that was Othello; here I am.
LODOVICO Where is that viper? Bring the villain forth.
OTHELLO I look down towards his feet;° but that's a fable.°
If that thou be'st a devil, I cannot kill thee. [*Wounds* IAGO.]
LODOVICO Wrench his sword from him.
IAGO I bleed, sir, but not kill'd.
OTHELLO I am not sorry neither, I'ld have thee live;
For in my sense,° 'tis happiness to die.
LODOVICO O thou Othello, that was once so good,
Fall'n in the practise° of a damned slave,
What shall be said to thee?
OTHELLO Why, any thing:
An honourable murderer, if you will;
For nought I did in hate, but all in honour.
LODOVICO This wretch hath part confess'd his villainy.
Did you and he consent in Cassio's death?
OTHELLO Ay.
CASSIO Dear general, I never gave you cause.
OTHELLO I do believe it, and I ask your pardon.
Will you, I pray, demand that demi-devil
Why he hath thus ensnar'd my soul and body?
IAGO Demand me nothing; what you know, you know:
From this time forth I never will speak word.
LODOVICO What? not to pray?
GRATIANO Torments will ope your lips.
OTHELLO Well, thou dost best.
LODOVICO Sir, you shall understand what hath befall'n,
Which, as I think, you know not. Here is a letter
Found in the pocket of the slain Roderigo,
And here another. The one of them imports

compt accounting, i.e. Judgment Day
rash overhasty
I . . . feet i.e. to see if they are cloven, as the devil's were thought to be
that's a fable i.e. the fact that your feet aren't cloven doesn't prove that you aren't a devil
in my sense i.e. to one who feels as I do
practise plotting

The death of Cassio to be undertook
By Roderigo.

OTHELLO Most heathenish and most gross!°

CASSIO O villain!

LODOVICO Now here's another discontented paper,
Found in his pocket too; and this it seems
Roderigo meant t' have sent this damned villain;
But that, belike, Iago in the nick
Came in and satisfied him.

OTHELLO O thou pernicious caitiff!—
How came you, Cassio, by that handkerchief
That was my wive's?

CASSIO I found it in my chamber:
And he himself confess'd it but even now,
That there he dropp'd it for a special purpose
Which wrought to° his desire.

OTHELLO O fool, fool, fool!

CASSIO There is besides, in Roderigo's letter,
How he upbraids Iago, that he made him
Brave° me upon the watch, whereon it came
That I was cast; and even but now he spake
(After long seeming dead) Iago hurt him,
Iago set him on.

LODOVICO You must forsake this room and go with us.
Your power and your command is taken off,
And Cassio rules in Cyprus. For this slave,
If there be any cunning cruelty
That can torment him much, and hold him long,
It shall be his. You shall close prisoner rest,
Till that the nature of your fault be known
To the Venetian state. Come, bring away.

OTHELLO Soft you; a word or two before you go.
I have done the state some service, and they know't—
No more of that. I pray you, in your letters,
When you shall these unlucky deeds relate,
Speak of me as I am; nothing extenuate,°
Nor set down aught in malice. Then must you speak
Of one that lov'd not wisely but too well;
Of one not easily jealious, but being wrought,°
Perplexed° in the extreme; of one whose hand,
Like the base Indian,° threw a pearl away
Richer than all his tribe; of one whose subdu'd eyes,
Albeit unused to the melting mood,

gross monstrous
wrought to worked toward, fitted in with
Brave defy, behave insolently toward
extenuate tone down (literally, make thin)
wrought worked upon
Perplexed bewildered, distraught
Indian. This, the Q1 reading, relates to the not unfamiliar notion of an Indian ignorant of the value of some precious object he finds. (*Base* = low in the scale of civilization.) A few editors prefer to read *Judean*, after F1; this is taken as an allusion to Judas, or to Herod the Great, who in a fit of jealousy had his beloved wife Mariamne killed.

Drops tears as fast as the Arabian trees
Their medicinable° gum. Set you down this;
And say besides, that in Aleppo once,
Where a malignant and a turban'd Turk
Beat a Venetian and traduc'd the state,
I took by th' throat the circumcised dog,
And smote him—thus. [*He stabs himself.*]

LODOVICO O bloody period!°

GRATIANO All that is spoke is marr'd.

OTHELLO I kiss'd thee ere I kill'd thee. No way but this,
Killing myself, to die upon a kiss. [*Falls on the bed and*] *dies.*

CASSIO This did I fear, but thought he had no weapon;
For he was great of heart.

LODOVICO [*To* IAGO.] O Spartan dog,°
More fell° than anguish, hunger, or the sea!
Look on the tragic loading of this bed;
This is thy work. The object° poisons sight
Let it be hid. Gratiano, keep° the house,
And seize upon° the fortunes of the Moor,
For they succeed on you. To you, Lord Governor,
Remains the censure° of this hellish villain,
The time, the place, the torture, O, enforce it!
Myself will straight aboard, and to the state
This heavy act with heavy heart relate. *Exeunt.*

medicinable medicinal
period conclusion
Spartan dog a kind of bloodhound, noted for its silence as well as its skill
fell cruel
object sight, spectacle
keep remain in
seize upon take legal possession of
censure judgment, sentence

The Tempest

The first play in the First Folio is *The Tempest,* although it was the last Shakespeare wrote unaided. The publishers took exceptional care with its preparation, as if, in putting it at the head of the section of comedies, and so first in the book, they were treating it as a showpiece.

Ever since it was discovered to be the last of Shakespeare's plays, *The Tempest* has attracted special attention as a kind of culmination of his work, the final statement of the greatest of dramatists. The attempts of nineteenth- and twentieth-century critics to find in it an allegory of Shakespeare's life or thoughts vary in subtlety and constitute an enormous range of interpretations. Perhaps we should react to these not by choosing one against the others but by arguing that the very fact of its lending itself, however partially, to such allegories, proves the play to have the rare quality of *suggesting* to the spectator or reader that he must make his own contribution, must complete the work in his own imagination. The play is perhaps the most remarkable example of qualities all good Shakespeareans learn to attribute to his finest work: patience and reticence. Patience is that ability to suffer and survive interpretation without which no work of art can achieve classic status and have direct relevance to the lives of successive generations. Reticence is the quality of not speaking out, not simplifying the text to the point where its meanings become more or less explicit, but leaving unsettled potential conflicts and complexities of meaning. Anyone who studies Verdi's *Otello,* great masterpiece though it is, will see that in comparison Shakespeare's *Othello* is *reticent.* Anyone who knows the history of *King Lear* criticism will understand the sense in which *King Lear* is *patient. The Tempest,* so resistant to interpretation, so full of possible but never fully spoken meanings, exemplifies both characteristics; which is why it preserves its unique status in the canon of Shakespeare's work.

It is, of course, possible to relate it to other plays of Shakespeare, and especially to the romances—*Pericles, Cymbeline,* and *The Winter's Tale,* with which it is usually classified. These works all came into being because of the revival of an old form of dramatic romance. The element of masque, the dominant form of courtly entertainment in King James's reign, which is particularly strong in *The Tempest,* suggests not only that the King's Men were often engaged for masques at court but also that the play may have been written with the Blackfriars Theatre in mind; for these things, with their scenes and machines, their dancing and music, could be done better in the smaller, artificially-lighted indoor theater with its courtly audiences than in the big open-air house. If we speak of *The Tempest* as a romance, we need to bear all this in mind: the dramatic romance was not a subtle or courtly form, but it rapidly became so in the years leading up to *The Tempest.*

The history of the changes whereby simple romance could be made adequate to the purposes of Shakespeare in *The Tempest* may be seen from his own work. *Pericles* is formally an adaptation of a simpler romance narrative enormously sophisticated by Shakespeare in the interests of the beautiful scene of recognition between Marina and Pericles which is its climax. *Cymbeline* displays examples of Shakespeare's most mature and difficult blank verse, but also exploits with a deliberate false naïveté the Romance themes of lost sons and miraculous multiple recognitions. *The Winter's Tale* dramatizes a romantic novella, changing out of recognition its naïve philosophy but preserving its extensive Romance chronology and also developing its "pastoral" possibilities; again the climax is a miraculous recognition scene, more improbable than anything in the novella.

The Tempest is the story of a magician prince and his daughter put to sea in a leaky boat and taking possession of an island where, twelve years later, amid fantastic displays of the prince's supernatural powers, the wrongs of the past are righted at the final recognition. But this time Shakespeare has taken up the themes of royal children, of marvelous rescue from death, of reconciliation a generation later between enemies —in a different way. He has made the form *intensive;* this play alone of Shakespeare's is played in something like the same time as that taken by the events it enacts, and the text draws our attention to this. Such tautness of dramatic form—which nevertheless allows multiple plotting, a masque, and spectacular and climactic *coups de théâtre* like the apparition of Ariel as a Harpy—makes this play, for all its thematic resemblances to the other romances, uniquely surprising in design and suggestive in meaning. Nowhere else does Shakespeare use so much music, so many pantomimic devices, yet there is always a sense of the imminence of the catastrophe. Nowhere else does he juxtapose so abruptly verses which enact the turbulent human passions of anger, remorse, and fear—the verse, one might say, of *Coriolanus* and parts of *Cymbeline*—with the limpid, stylized grief of Ferdinand ("This music crept by me upon the waters") and the unearthly songs of Ariel. *The Tempest* is, finally, *sui generis,* the only play of its kind, and nothing we can learn about it will alter that.

At the level of fact, as of reasonable conjecture, we can, however, offer some relevant information. Shakespeare in 1610 evidently saw certain accounts, both published and unpublished, of a wreck in the Bermudas a year earlier. He had read a lot about voyages to the New World, but this occurrence was especially interesting because he knew people connected with the Virginia Company; the *Sea-Adventure* was bound for Virginia when she ran ashore in a gale and was lodged between two rocks; the colonists escaped with their lives and much of the ship's stores. William Strachey's *True Reportory of the Wrack,* written in 1610 but not published till 1625, gives the most important account of the wreck and subsequent adventures. Shakespeare uses Strachey's description of St. Elmo's fire in Ariel's account of the storm, as well as other borrowings.

The importance of these allusions is not that Shakespeare was being very topical, but that the New World colonies deeply stirred his imagination. The Virginia Company had, of course, an economic interest which was served best by regarding the colonies as the natural domain of the European Christian. One of the books Shakepeare read calls the natives "human beasts." When Prospero says he was set upon his island "to be the lord on it" (V.i.162), he is talking like a colonist; when he discovers that on Caliban's "nature / Nurture will never stick," he is repeating what many colonial adventurers had reported; and when Caliban complains that he had been helpful with fresh water and fish-dams we recall that this was also admitted by the colonists, who added that the natives soon turned treacherous.

In this way *The Tempest* alludes to the new colonial problem; it also repeats some of the moralizations of the adventurers, who called the wreck a "tragicall comaedie," and rejoiced that what had seemed "a punishment against evil" was "but a medicine." Discussing the quarrels and mutinies in Virginia, they showed they had learned the lesson that "every inordinate soul soon becomes his own punishment." (Compare Gonzalo's "their great guilt . . . now 'gins to bite the spirits," III.iii.104–6.) Strachey calls the Bermudas "these unfortunate (yet fortunate) Ilands"—for all their terrors they proved a place of deliverance. (Compare Gonzalo's expressions in V.i.206 ff.)

But *The Tempest* does not take place in the New World—the island is somewhere between Tunis and Naples in the Mediterranean—and like everybody else Shakespeare interpreted the astonishing news from America in accordance with already existing Old World ideas. For example, Caliban, though his name is probably an anagram of "cannibal," is based on the wild man or *Wodewose* of European tradition—treacherous, lecherous, without language. It was easy to relate the savages to this type, which was traditionally held to be in an intermediate position between man and beast, natural in a bad sense. However, there are, for example in Spenser, good and bad wild men; and the travelers and others who speculated on the matter were divided into those who believed that "natural" men—without Christianity or civility—would be better and more beautiful, or wickeder and more ugly, than Europeans. Montaigne, whose essay "Of Cannibals" is paraphrased by Gonzalo in II.i.143 ff., was of the first party. Shakespeare is more ambiguous. Prospero's "Art," represented by his magical powers, is incapable of civilizing Caliban ("You taught me language; and my profit on't / Is, I know how to curse," I.ii.365–66), and Caliban is the dupe of Stephano and a traitor to his lord. He was given the same education as Miranda, but tried to rape her and was unrepentant. Yet he is not as base as the wicked Italians, who illustrate the saying *corruptio optimi pessima,* the corruption of the best is the worst corruption. Miranda's "brave new world" is the old one, in which man, though redeemed and beautiful in comparison with the world of mere nature, can be corrupt. Although art as well as grace can be added to nature, as by grafting finer fruit is made to grow on natural stocks, there is a corruption worse than the natural; and this the art of Prospero must try to purge. The purity possible to those who live above nature is Miranda's; her assurance that beautiful souls inhabit beautiful bodies ('There's nothing ill can dwell in such a temple," I.ii.460, and "How beauteous mankind is!," V.i.183) is not in accord with the facts, any more than the notion of the noble savage. And Prospero, having failed with Caliban, must try with the Italian noblemen. He does not, it appears, wholly succeed.

Prospero has a "project," like an alchemist; the action of the play represents the climactic stage of the experiment. He saves his enemies, unharmed, from a tempest of his own causing; and will, if he can, regenerate them and by a marriage union prevent further strife. He is technically in charge of the whole experiment, stage-managing, or "presenting" the wanderings of the various parties, the great apparition of Ariel, the masques, the punishment of the vulgar rebels, and the final confrontation with Alonso and Sebastian. But Shakespeare will not allow the play to become too inertly schematic. Prospero is passionate, even bad-tempered. His excitement in the long expository scene (I.ii) is reflected in the disturbed verses which recount the past, his severe admonitions to Miranda, his nervous rage with Caliban and harshness to Ariel. So, later, his mind is "troubled" (IV.i.160); he rejoices in having his enemies at his mercy (IV.i.263), but also speaks the great lines from Ovid which are his farewell to magic arts, and the famous elegiac set piece after the masque. He is naggingly insistent about the need for Miranda and Ferdinand not to anticipate marriage; and his forgiveness of his brother Antonio is hardly in the mood of gentle reconciliation occasionally called characteristic in these romances—"most wicked sir, whom to call brother / Would even infect my mouth" (V.i.130–31). Miranda's more innocent reactions he learns to treat pityingly.

Such are the cross-currents of meaning and tone that make it impossible for anybody to announce boldly what *The Tempest* is about. Like all the best plays of Shakespeare, it is reticent on that point. When you think it may declare itself as having a particular theme, it frustrates the expectation by suddenly modulating into a different narrative manner, a different verse style. Thus the stage realism of the opening scene is followed by the scene of Prospero's agitated reminiscence, and when that threatens to become a forceful account of some political usurpation, the verse shifts it into a new mode of fairy tale at I.ii.44. Soon we meet Ariel and Caliban, for each of whom Shakespeare invented an idiomatic poetry; and then Ferdinand (I.ii.390), his strange water-music deriving from Ariel's uncanny song, "Full fadom five." This is a slight indication of the range of the play's voices; one needs to add the cheerful solemnity of Gonzalo's, the guilty sorrow of Alonso's, the Macbeth-like whispers of Antonio's and Sebastian. Ariel speaks as scourge and minister as well as fretful sprite, Caliban as a native of a good place and not only as a savage, Prospero as artist but also as fallible, vindictive, regretful man. Miranda's are the expressions of a perfectly innocent high-born wonder no less true for its brokenness; Ferdinand greets her as a goddess, she him as a god, and it is Prospero who suggests that there is ignorance in this innocence. The play does not imply that he must be right, and it does not call him wrong; it leaves us to follow, and choose between, the swirling changes of tone and emphasis, the clues that cross each other and prevent any from becoming dominant, ideological. This is the reticence that accompanies the classic's patience, and this marvelous play, so well endowed with both, may stand here as representative of Shakespeare's highest achievements.

The Tempest

The Scene, an uninhabited Island

Names of the Actors

ALONSO, *King of Naples*
SEBASTIAN, *his brother*
PROSPERO, *the right Duke of Milan*
ANTONIO *his brother, the usurping Duke of Milan*
FERDINAND, son to the King of Naples
GONZALO, *an honest old Counsellor*
ADRIAN *and* FRANCISCO, *Lords*
CALIBAN, *a savage and deformed slave*
TRINCULO, *a jester*
STEPHANO, *a drunken butler*

MASTER OF A SHIP
BOATSWAIN
MARINERS
MIRANDA, *daughter to Prospero*
ARIEL, *an airy spirit*
IRIS, CERES, JUNO, NYMPHS, REAPERS — SPIRITS

ACT I

SCENE I [*On a ship at sea*]:° *a tempestuous noise of thunder and lightning heard.*

Enter a SHIP-MASTER *and a* BOATSWAIN.

SHIP-MASTER Boatswain!

BOATSWAIN Here, master: what cheer?

SHIP-MASTER Good: speak to the mariners: fall to it, yarely,° or we run ourselves aground: bestir, bestir. *Exit.*

Enter MARINERS.

BOATSWAIN Heigh, my hearts! cheerly, cheerly, my hearts! yare, yare! Take in the topsail. Tend to the master's whistle.° Blow till thou burst thy wind, if room° enough!

Enter ALONSO, SEBASTIAN, ANTONIO, FERDINAND, GONZALO, *and others.*

ALONSO Good boatswain, have care. Where's the master? Play the men.°

BOATSWAIN I pray now, keep below.

ANTONIO Where is the master, boatswain?

BOATSWAIN Do you not hear him? You mar our labour: keep your cabins: you do assist the storm.

GONZALO Nay, good, be patient.

BOATSWAIN When the sea is. Hence! What cares these roarers° for the name of King? To cabin: silence! trouble us not.

[On a ship at sea] Square brackets in stage directions mean that the words enclosed are editorial additions to the copy-text, which is that of the First Folio of 1623, here called F.
yarely briskly
whistle used for giving orders by the Master
room sea-room
Play the men be courageous; or, make the men work (*ply* the men)
cares care
roarers toughs, hooligans (meaning the waves)

GONZALO Good, yet remember whom thou hast aboard.

BOATSWAIN None that I more love than myself. You are a counsellor; if you can command these elements to silence, and work the peace of the presence,° we will not hand a rope more; use your authority: if you cannot, give thanks you have lived so long, and make yourself ready in your cabin for the mischance of the hour, if it so hap. Cheerly, good hearts! Out of our way, I say. *Exit.*

GONZALO I have great comfort from this fellow: methinks he hath no drowning mark° upon him; his complexion is perfect gallows.° Stand fast, good Fate, to his hanging: make the rope of his destiny our cable, for our own doth little advantage.° If he be not born to be hanged, our case is miserable. *Exeunt.*

Re-enter BOATSWAIN.

BOATSWAIN Down with the topmast! yare! lower, lower! Bring her to try with main-course° [*A cry within*]. A plague upon his howling! they are louder than the weather or our office.

Re-enter SEBASTIAN, ANTONIO, *and* GONZALO.

Yet again! what do you here? Shall we give o'er, and drown? Have you a mind to sink?

SEBASTIAN A pox o' your throat, you bawling, blasphemous, incharitable dog!

BOATSWAIN Work you, then.

ANTONIO Hang, cur! hang, you whoreson, insolent noise-maker. We are less afraid to be drowned than thou art.

GONZALO I'll warrant him for° drowning, though the ship were no stronger than a nutshell, and as leaky as an unstanched wench.°

BOATSWAIN Lay her a-hold,° a-hold! set her two courses;° off to sea again; lay her off.

Enter MARINERS *wet.*

MARINERS All lost, to prayers, to prayers! all lost!

BOATSWAIN What, must our mouths be cold?

GONZALO The King and Prince at prayers, let's assist them,
For our case is as theirs.

SEBASTIAN I'm out of patience.

ANTONIO We are merely° cheated of our lives by drunkards:
This wide-chapped rascal,—would thou mightst lie drowning
The washing of ten tides!

GONZALO He'll be hanged yet,
Though every drop of water swear against it,

presence F has *present,* but *presence* (meaning the immediate vicinity of the king and court) is probable; his counselors would be responsible for keeping order in this area.
drowning mark mole or other blemish thought to indicate by its position the person's likeliest mode of death, here drowning
perfect gallows he will hang rather than drown
little advantage helps us little
Bring . . . main-course make her heave to
for i.e. against
unstanched wench loose (literally "leaky") woman
a-hold hove-to
courses sails; lacking sea-room to heave to, he tries to take the ship to sea
merely absolutely

And gape at wid'st to glut him.
[*A confused noise within:* 'Mercy on us!'—
'We split, we split!'—'Farewell, my wife and children!'—
'Farewell, brother!'—'We split, we split, we split!']

ANTONIO Let's all sink wi' the King.

SEBASTIAN Let's take leave of him. *Exeunt* ANTONIO *and* SEBASTIAN

GONZALO Now would I give a thousand furlongs of sea for an acre of barren ground, long heath, broom, furze,° anything. The wills above be done! but I would fain die a dry death. *Exeunt.*

SCENE II [*The Island. Before* PROSPERO's *Cell.*]

Enter PROSPERO *and* MIRANDA.

MIRANDA If by your Art, my dearest father, you° have
Put the wild waters in this roar, allay them.
The sky, it seems, would pour down stinking pitch,
But that the sea, mounting to the welkin's° cheek,
Dashes the fire out. O, I have suffered
With those that I saw suffer! a brave vessel,
(Who had, no doubt, some noble creature in her,)
Dashed all to pieces. O, the cry did knock
Against my very heart! Poor souls, they perished!
Had I been any god of power, I would
Have sunk the sea within the earth, or ere
It should the good ship so have swallowed, and
The fraughting° souls within her.

PROSPERO Be collected:
No more amazement:° tell your piteous° heart
There's no harm done.

MIRANDA O, woe the day!

PROSPERO No harm.
I have done nothing but in care of thee,
Of thee, my dear one; thee, my daughter, who
Art ignorant of what thou art; nought knowing
Of whence I am, nor that I am more better°
Than Prospero, master of a full poor cell,
And thy no greater father.

MIRANDA More to know
Did never meddle° with my thoughts.

PROSPERO 'Tis time
I should inform thee farther. Lend thy hand,
And pluck my magic garment from me.—So:
Lays down his mantle.
Lie there, my Art.° Wipe thou thine eyes; have comfort.

broom, furze F has *browne firrs.*
you deferential, used by Miranda to her father, who usually addresses her as "thou"
welkin's firmament's
fraughting forming the cargo
amazement terror
piteous full of pity
more better of higher rank
meddle mingle
my Art i.e. the robe, symbol of his art

The direful spectacle of the wrack,° which touched
The very virtue° of compassion in thee,
I have with such provision in mine Art
So safely ordered, that there is no soul°—
No, not so much perdition° as an hair
Betid° to any creature in the vessel
Which thou heard'st cry, which thou saw'st sink. Sit down;
For thou must now know farther.

MIRANDA You have often
Begun to tell me what I am, but stopped,
And left me to bootless inquisition,°
Concluding 'Stay: not yet.'

PROSPERO The hour's now come;
The very minute bids thee ope thine ear;
Obey, and be attentive. Canst thou remember
A time before we came unto this cell?
I do not think thou canst, for then thou wast not
Out° three years old.

MIRANDA Certainly, sir, I can.

PROSPERO By what? by any other house or person?
Of any thing the image tell me, that
Hath kept with thy remembrance.

MIRANDA 'Tis far off,
And rather like a dream than an assurance
That my remembrance warrants.° Had I not
Four or five women once that tended me?

PROSPERO Thou hadst, and more, Miranda. But how is it
That this lives in thy mind? What seest thou else
In the dark backward and abysm of time?°
If thou rememberest aught ere thou camest here,
How thou camest here thou mayst.

MIRANDA But that I do not.

PROSPERO Twelve year since, Miranda, twelve year since,
Thy father was the Duke of Milan, and
A prince of power.

MIRANDA Sir, are not you my father?

PROSPERO Thy mother was a piece° of virtue, and
She said thou wast my daughter; and thy father
Was Duke of Milan; and his only heir
And princess, no worse issued.

MIRANDA O the heavens!
What foul play had we, that we came from thence?
Or blessed was't we did?

wrack wreck
virtue essence
soul Prospero is about to say something like "lost," but changes the direction of his sentence.
perdition loss
Betid happened
bootless inquisition fruitless inquiry
Out fully
an assurance . . . warrants a certainty my memory guarantees
backward . . . time dark abyss of time past
piece perfect specimen

PROSPERO Both, both, my girl:
By foul play, as thou say'st, were we heaved thence,
But blessedly holp° hither.

MIRANDA O, my heart bleeds
To think o' the teen° that I have turned you to,
Which is from° my remembrance! Please you, farther.

PROSPERO My brother, and thy uncle, called Antonio,—
I pray thee, mark me, that a brother should
Be so perfidious!—he whom next thyself
Of all the world I loved, and to him put
The manage of my state; as at that time
Through all the signories it was the first,
And Prospero the prime duke, being so reputed
In dignity, and for the liberal Arts
Without a parallel; those being all my study,
The government I cast upon my brother,
And to my state grew stranger, being transported
And rapt in secret studies° thy false uncle—
Dost thou attend me?

MIRANDA Sir, most heedfully.

PROSPERO Being once perfected how to grant suits,
How to deny them, who to advance, and who
To trash for over-topping,° new created
The creatures that were mine, I say, or changed 'em,
Or else new formed 'em; having both the key
Of officer and office, set all hearts i' the state
To what tune pleased his ear;° that now he was
The ivy which had hid my princely trunk,
And sucked my verdure out on it.° Thou attend'st not?

MIRANDA O, good sir, I do.

PROSPERO I pray thee, mark me.
I, thus neglecting worldly ends, all dedicated
To closeness and the bettering of my mind
With that which, but by being so retired,
O'er-prized all popular rate, in my false brother
Awaked an evil nature; and my trust,
Like a good parent, did beget of him
A falsehood in its contrary, as great

holp helped
teen trouble
from absent from
My brother . . . studies (ll. 66–77) Prospero loses the thread of this speech, which may be summarized: My brother Antonio—note his amazing treachery—the person I loved best in the world except for you, so that I entrusted him with the management of my estate, which was the chief one in North Italy and I the senior duke by virtue of my position and my learning . . . to this brother I delegated the government, caring not for my dukedom but for my studies.
trash for over-topping keep in check for being over-bold; "trash" means a cord used in training hounds
set . . . ear The musical image grows out of the word *key*.
Being . . . on it (ll. 79–87) having mastered the art of dealing with suitors, advancing some, disappointing others, so arranging things that those already in office by my favor became his dependents—having got the measure of all the jobs and the men who did them, he ran the state exactly as he pleased; he was to me as ivy to the noble oak, concealing and enfeebling it

As my trust was; which had indeed no limit,
A confidence sans bound.° He being thus lorded,°
Not only with what my revénue yielded,
But what my power might else exact,° like one
Who having into° truth, by telling of it,°
Made such a sinner of his memory,
To credit his own lie, he did believe
He was indeed the duke; out o' the substitution,
And executing the outward face of royalty,
With all prerogative;°—hence his ambition growing,—
Dost thou hear?

MIRANDA Your tale, sir, would cure deafness.

PROSPERO To have no screen between this part he played
And him he played it for,° he needs will be
Absolute Milan.° Me, poor man, my library
Was dukedom large enough: of temporal° royalties
He thinks me now incapable; confederates,
So dry° he was for sway, wi' the King of Naples
To give him annual tribute, do him homage,
Subject his coronet to his crown, and bend
The dukedom, yet unbowed,—alas, poor Milan!—
To most ignoble stooping.

MIRANDA O the heavens!

PROSPERO Mark his condition,° and the event;° then tell me
If this might be a brother.

MIRANDA I should sin
To think but nobly of my grandmother:
Good wombs have borne bad sons.

PROSPERO Now the condition.
This King of Naples, being an enemy
To me inveterate, hearkens my brother's suit;
Which was, that he, in lieu o' the premises°
Of homage and I know not how much tribute,
Should presently° extirpate me and mine
Out of the dukedom, and confer fair Milan,
With all the honours, on my brother: whereon,
A treacherous army levied, one midnight
Fated to the purpose, did Antonio open

I . . . sans bound (ll. 89–97) the fact of my retirement, in which I neglected wordly affairs and gave myself to secret studies of a kind beyond the understanding and esteem of the people, brought out a bad side in my brother's nature; consequently the great, indeed boundless, trust I placed in him gave rise on his part to a disloyalty equally great, just as it can happen that a virtuous father may have a vicious son
lorded made a lord of
else exact otherwise extort
into unto
it i.e. his own lie
executing . . . prerogative carrying out the public duties of royalty with full power
him . . . for i.e. himself
Absolute Milan Duke, not merely Duke's substitute
temporal worldly, as opposed to spiritual
dry thirsty
condition terms on which the deal with Naples was concluded
event outcome
in lieu o' the premises in return for the undertaking
presently immediately

The gates of Milan; and, i' the dead of darkness,
The ministers° for the purpose hurried thence
Me and thy crying self.

MIRANDA Alack, for pity!
I, not remembering how I cried out then,
Will cry it o'er again: it is a hint°
That wrings mine eyes to it.

PROSPERO Hear a little further,
And then I'll bring thee to the present business
Which now's upon us; without the which, this story
Were most impertinent.°

MIRANDA Wherefore did they not
That hour destroy us?

PROSPERO Well demanded, wench:
My tale provokes that question. Dear, they durst not,
So dear the love my people bore me; nor set
A mark so bloody on the business; but
With colours fairer painted their foul ends.
In few,° they hurried us aboard a bark,
Bore us some leagues to sea; where they prepared
A rotten carcass of a butt,° not rigged,
Nor tackle, sail, nor mast; the very rats
Instinctively have quit it: there they hoist us,
To cry to the sea that roared to us; to sigh
To the winds, whose pity, sighing back again,
Did us but loving wrong.

MIRANDA Alack, what trouble
Was I then to you!

PROSPERO O, a cherubin
Thou wast that did preserve me. Thou didst smile,
Infusèd with a fortitude from heaven,
When I have decked° the sea with drops full salt,
Under my burthen groaned; which raised in me
An undergoing stomach,° to bear up
Against what should ensue.

MIRANDA How came we ashore?

PROSPERO By Providence divine.
Some food we had, and some fresh water, that
A noble Neapolitan, Gonzalo,
Out of his charity,° who being then appointed
Master of this design, did give us, with
Rich garments, linens, stuffs and necessaries,
Which since have steaded much;° so, of his gentleness,

ministers those employed
hint occasion
impertinent not to the purpose
In few to be brief
butt tub (contemptuous); a clumsy boat
decked adorned; note the intrusion here of an artificial, conceited manner
undergoing stomach spirit of endurance
charity love, but in a wider sense than the modern
steaded much stood us in good stead

Knowing I loved my books, he furnished me
From mine own library with volumes that
I prize above my dukedom.

MIRANDA Would I might
But ever° see that man!

PROSPERO Now I arise:
Sit still, and hear the last of our sea-sorrow.
Here in this island we arrived; and here
Have I, thy schoolmaster, made thee more profit
Than other princess'° can, that have more time
For vainer hours, and tutors not so careful.

MIRANDA Heavens thank you for it! And now, I pray you, sir,
For still 'tis beating in my mind, your reason
For raising this sea-storm?

PROSPERO Know thus far forth.
By accident most strange, bountiful Fortune
(Now my dear lady) hath mine enemies
Brought to this shore; and by my prescience°
I find my zenith doth depend upon
A most auspicious star,° whose influence
If now I court not, but omit, my fortunes
Will ever after droop. Here cease more questions:
Thou art inclined to sleep; 'tis a good dulness,
And give it way: I know thou canst not choose.

MIRANDA *sleeps.*

Come away, servant, come. I am ready now.
Approach, my Ariel, come.

Enter ARIEL.

ARIEL All hail, great master! grave sir, hail! I come
To answer thy best pleasure; be it to fly,
To swim, to dive into the fire, to ride
On the curled clouds, to thy strong bidding task
Ariel and all his quality.°

PROSPERO Hast thou, spirit,
Performed to point° the tempest that I bade thee?

ARIEL To every article.
I boarded the king's ship; now on the beak,°
Now in the waist,° the deck,° in every cabin,
I flamed amazement:° sometime I'd divide,
And burn in many places; on the topmast,
The yards and boresprit,° would I flame distinctly,

But ever only someday
princess' princesses
prescience foreknowledge
my zenith . . . star I am reaching the highest point in my fortunes—my star is in its most favorable aspect
quality attendant spirits
to point exactly
beak prow
waist amidships
deck poop
flamed amazement struck terror by appearing as flames (as lightning and St. Elmo's fire)
boresprit bowsprit

Then meet and join. Jove's lightnings, the precursors
O' the dreadful thunder-claps, more momentary
And sight-outrunning were not: the fire and cracks
Of sulphurous roaring the most mighty Neptune
Seem to besiege, and make his bold waves tremble,
Yea, his dread trident shake.

PROSPERO My brave spirit!
Who was so firm, so constant, that this coil°
Would not infect his reason?

ARIEL Not a soul
But felt a fever of the mad, and played
Some tricks of desperation. All but mariners
Plunged in the foaming brine, and quit the vessel,
Then all afire with me: the King's son, Ferdinand,
With hair up-staring,°—then like reeds, not hair,—
Was the first man that leaped; cried, 'Hell is empty,
And all the devils are here.'

PROSPERO Why, that's my spirit!
But was not this nigh shore?

ARIEL Close by, my master.

PROSPERO But are they, Ariel, safe?

ARIEL Not a hair perished;
On their sustaining° garments not a blemish,
But fresher than before: and, as thou bad'st me.
In troops I have dispersed them 'bout the isle.
The King's son have I landed by himself;
Whom I left cooling of the air with sighs
In an odd angle° of the isle, and sitting,
His arms in this sad knot.°

PROSPERO Of the King's ship,
The mariners, say how thou hast disposed,
And all the rest o' the fleet.

ARIEL Safely in harbour
Is the King's ship; in the deep nook, where once
Thou call'dst me up at midnight to fetch dew
From the still-vexed Bermoothes,° there she's hid:
The mariners all under hatches stowed;
Who, with a charm joined to their suffered labour,°
I have left asleep: and for the rest o' the fleet,
Which I dispersed, they all have met again,
And are upon the Mediterranean flote,°
Bound sadly home for Naples;
Supposing that they saw the King's ship wracked,
And his great person perish.

coil turmoil
up-staring standing on end
sustaining upholding
angle corner
in . . . knot folded
still-vexed Bermoothes always stormy Bermudas
suffered labour the labor they have undergone
flote sea

PROSPERO Ariel, thy charge
Exactly is performed: but there's more work.
What is the time o' the day?
ARIEL Past the mid season.
PROSPERO At least two glasses.° The time 'twixt six and now
Must by us both be spent most preciously.
ARIEL Is there more toil? Since thou dost give me pains,
Let me remember thee what thou hast promised,
Which is not yet performed me.
PROSPERO How now? moody?
What is it thou canst demand?
ARIEL My liberty.
PROSPERO Before the time be out? no more!
ARIEL I prithee,
Remember I have done thee worthy service;
Told thee no lies, made no mistakings,° served
Without or° grudge or grumblings: thou didst promise
To bate° me a full year.
PROSPERO Dost thou forget
From what a torment I did free thee?
ARIEL No.
PROSPERO Thou dost, and think'st it much to tread the ooze°
Of the salt deep,
To run upon the sharp wind of the north,
To do me business in the veins o' the earth°
When it is baked° with frost.
ARIEL I do not, sir.
PROSPERO Thou liest, malignant thing! Hast thou forgot
The foul witch Sycorax, who with age and envy°
Was grown into a hoop?° hast thou forgot her?
ARIEL No, sir.
PROSPERO Thou hast. Where was she born? speak; tell me.
ARIEL Sir, in Argier.°
PROSPERO O, was she so? I must
Once in a month recount what thou hast been,
Which thou forget'st. This damned witch Sycorax,
For mischiefs manifold, and sorceries terrible
To enter human hearing, from Argier,
Thou knowest, was banished: for one thing she did°
They would not take her life. Is not this true?
ARIEL Ay, sir.
PROSPERO This blue-eyed° hag was hither brought with child,

glasses hours; turns of the hourglass
made no mistakings F has *made thee no mistakings.*
or either
bate let me off
ooze slimy bottom
veins o' the earth Contemporary cosmology held that there were subterranean waters in the earth like veins and arteries in the body.
baked hardened
envy malignity
grown into a hoop bent double
Argier Algiers
one thing she did some good service; or, being with child
blue-eyed sign of exhaustion or pregnancy

And here was left by the sailors. Thou, my slave,
As thou report'st thyself, wast then her servant;
And, for° thou wast a spirit too delicate
To act her earthy° and abhorred commands,
Refusing her grand hests,° she did confine thee,
By help of her more potent ministers,°
And in her most unmitigable rage,
Into a cloven pine; within which rift
Imprisoned thou didst painfully remain
A dozen years; within which space she died,
And left thee there; where thou didst vent° thy groans
As fast as mill-wheels strike. Then was this island—
Save for the son that she did litter here,
A freckled whelp hag-born—not honoured with
A human shape.

ARIEL Yes, Caliban her son.

PROSPERO Dull thing, I say so; he, that Caliban,
Whom now I keep in service. Thou best knowest
What torment I did find thee in; thy groans
Did make wolves howl, and penetrate the breasts
Of ever-angry bears: it was a torment
To lay upon the damned, which Sycorax
Could not again undo: it was mine Art,
When I arrived and heard thee, that made gape
The pine, and let thee out.

ARIEL I thank thee, master.

PROSPERO If thou more murmur'st, I will rend an oak,
And peg thee in his knotty entrails, till
Thou hast howled away twelve winters.

ARIEL Pardon, master:
I will be correspondent° to command,
And do my spriting gently.°

PROSPERO Do so; and after two days
I will discharge thee.

ARIEL That's my noble master!
What shall I do? say what; what shall I do?

PROSPERO Go make thyself like a nymph o' the sea:
Be subject to
No sight but thine and mine; invisible
To every eyeball else. Go take this shape,
And hither come in it: go: hence
With diligence. *Exit* ARIEL.
Awake, dear heart, awake! thou hast slept well;
Awake!

for because
earthy Sycorax and Caliban are associated with earth, Ariel with air and fire.
hests commands
ministers demonic agents
vent utter
correspondent compliant
gently without complaint

MIRANDA The strangeness of your story put
Heaviness° in me.

PROSPERO Shake it off. Come on;
We'll visit Caliban my slave, who never
Yields us kind answer.

MIRANDA 'Tis a villain, sir,
I do not love to look on.

PROSPERO But, as 'tis,
We cannot miss° him: he does make our fire,
Fetch in our wood, and serves in offices°
That profit us. What, ho! slave! Caliban!
Thou earth, thou! speak.

CALIBAN [*Within*] There's wood enough within.

PROSPERO Come forth, I say! there's other business for thee;
Come, thou tortoise! when?

Re-enter ARIEL *like a water-nymph.*

Fine apparition! My quaint° Ariel,
Hark in thine ear.

ARIEL My lord, it shall be done. *Exit.*

PROSPERO Thou poisonous slave, got by the devil himself°
Upon thy wicked dam, come forth!

Enter CALIBAN.

CALIBAN As wicked° dew as e'er my mother brushed
With raven's feather° from unwholesome fen
Drop on you both! a south-west° blow on ye
And blister you all o'er!

PROSPERO For this, be sure, tonight thou shalt have cramps,
Side-stitches that shall pen thy breath up; urchins°
Shall for that vast of night that they may work,
All exercise on thee;° thou shalt be pinched
As thick as honeycomb, each pinch more stinging
Than bees that made 'em.°

CALIBAN I must eat my dinner.
This island's mine, by Sycorax my mother,
Which thou tak'st from me. When thou camest first,
Thou strok'st me, and made much of me; wouldst give me
Water with berries° in it; and teach me how

Heaviness drowiness
miss do without
offices services
quaint elegant, ingenious
got . . . himself Caliban was the result of a union between witch and devil.
wicked baneful
raven's feather The raven (*corax*) was a bird of ill-omen.
south-west the pestilence-bearing wind
urchins hedgehogs, goblins in the shape of hedgehogs
Shall for . . . thee shall, during the dead of night which is the period during which they are allowed to operate, all torment you
'em the cells of the honeycomb
berries The Bermudan castaways used berries to make drinks.

To name the bigger light, and how the less,°
That burn by day and night: and then I loved thee,
And showed thee all the qualities o' the isle,
The fresh springs, brine-pits, barren place and fertile:
Cursed be I that did so! All the charms
Of Sycorax, toads, beetles, bats,° light on you!
For I am all the subjects that you have,
Which first was mine own King: and here you sty me°
In this hard rock, whiles you do keep from me
The rest o' the island.

PROSPERO Thou most lying slave,
Whom stripes° may move, not kindness! I have used thee,
Filth as thou art, with human care; and lodged thee
In mine own cell, till thou didst seek to violate
The honour of my child.

CALIBAN O ho, O ho! would it had been done!
Thou didst prevent me; I had peopled else
This isle with Calibans.

MIRANDA Abhorrèd slave,
Which any print° of goodness wilt not take,
Being capable of° all ill! I pitied thee,
Took pains to make thee speak, taught thee each hour
One thing or other: when thou didst not, savage,
Know thine own meaning, but wouldst gabble like
A thing most brutish, I endowed thy purposes
With words that made them known. But thy vile race,°
Though thou didst learn, had that in it which good natures
Could not abide to be with; therefore wast thou
Deservedly confined into this rock,
Who hadst deservèd more than a prison.

CALIBAN You taught me language; and my profit on it
Is, I know how to curse. The red plague° rid° you
For learning me your language!

PROSPERO Hag-seed, hence!
Fetch us in fuel; and be quick, thou 'rt best,
To answer other business.° Shrug'st thou, malice?°
If thou neglect'st, or dost unwillingly
What I command, I'll rack thee with old° cramps,
Fill all thy bones with achès, make thee roar,
That beasts shall tremble at thy din.

CALIBAN No, 'pray thee.
[*Aside*] I must obey: his Art is of such power,

bigger light . . . less sun and moon; see Genesis 1:16
toads, beetles, bats all associated with witches
sty me keep me pent up
stripes lashes
print impression
capable of apt to receive the impression of
race hereditary nature; contrasted with the "good natures" of the next line
red plague bubonic plague; called after the color of the sores
rid destroy
thou'rt . . . business it will be best for you to do the jobs assigned you
malice malicious thing
old severe

It would control° my dam's god, Setebos,°
And make a vassal of him.

PROSPERO So, slave; hence! *Exit* CALIBAN.

Re-enter ARIEL, *invisible, playing and singing;* FERDINAND *following.*

ARIEL'S SONG

Come unto these yellow sands,
And then take hands:
Courtsied when you have and kissed
The wild waves whist:°
Foot it featly° here and there,
And sweet sprites bear
The burthen. Hark, hark.

Burthen° dispersedly.° *Bow-wow.*

ARIEL *The watch dogs bark:*

Burthen dispersedly. *Bow-wow.*

ARIEL *Hark, hark! I hear*
The strain of strutting chanticleer

Cry—Burthen dispersedly. *Cock a diddle dow.*

FERDINAND Where should this music be? i' the air or the earth?
It sounds no more: and, sure, it waits upon°
Some god o' the island. Sitting on a bank,
Weeping again° the King my father's wrack,
This music crept by me upon the waters,
Allaying both their fury and my passion
With its sweet air: thence° I have followed it,
Or it hath drawn me rather. But 'tis gone.
No, it begins again.

ARIEL *sings.*

Full fadom° five thy father lies;
Of his bones are coral made;
Those are pearls that were his eyes:
Nothing of him that doth fade,
But doth suffer a sea-change
Into something rich and strange.°
Sea-nymphs hourly ring his knell:

Burthen: *Ding-dong.*

ARIEL *Hark! now I hear them,—Ding-dong, bell.*

control overcome
Setebos Patagonian god mentioned by a travel writer
Courtsied . . . whist either "when you have curtsied to and kissed your partner, the sea remaining quiet," or, "when you have curtsied and kissed the sea into silence"
featly gracefully
Burthen refrain
dispersedly not in unison
waits upon attends
again indicates intensity as well as repetition
thence from the water's edge
fadom fathom
Nothing . . . strange Every part of his body that is otherwise doomed to decay is transformed into some rich or rare sea-substance.

Full fad - om five thy fa - ther lies; of his
bones are cor - al made; those are pearls that were his eyes
noth - ing of him that doth fade, but doth suf - fer a
sea - change In - to some- thing rich and strange. Sea nymphs hour-ly
ring his knell; Hark, now I hear them, Hark now I hear them,
Ding, Dong Bell Ding Dong Ding Dong Bell

Ding Dong Ding Dong Bell
Ding Dong Ding Dong Bell.

This setting of "Full Fadom Five", like that of "Where the Bee Sucks" in Act V (for voice and unfigured bass line), is by Robert Johnson (1583?–1633), a composer known for his music for plays and masques. These settings may well have been written for the first production, although they were first published in an arrangement for three voices in John Wilson's *Cheerful Airs* (1659). The unfigured bass simply gave the lowest musical line; the songs could be sung as given, with a bass viol accompaniment, or with a lute (filling in other lines and chords), or by a group of instruments (this is a little like the modern practice of printing a popular song with guitar chords). In "Full Fadom Five" there is a fugue-like imitation in the voice and bass parts, and we can be certain that other instruments took up the melody as well. The effect of the whole would be that of chiming bells.

FERDINAND The ditty° does remember° my drowned father.
This is no mortal business, nor no sound
That the earth owes:°—I hear it now above me.
PROSPERO The fringèd curtains of thine eye advance,°
And say what thou seest yond.
MIRANDA What is it? a spirit?
Lord, how it looks about! Believe me, sir,
It carries a brave° form. But 'tis a spirit.
PROSPERO No, wench; it eats and sleeps and hath such senses
As we have, such. This gallant which thou seest
Was in the wrack; and, but° he's something stained
With grief (that's beauty's canker°) thou mightst call him
A goodly person: he hath lost his fellows,
And strays about to find 'em.
MIRANDA I might call him
A thing divine; for nothing natural°
I ever saw so noble.
PROSPERO [*Aside*] It goes on,° I see,
As my soul prompts it. Spirit, fine spirit! I'll free thee
Within two days for this.
FERDINAND Most sure the goddess°
On whom these airs attend! Vouchsafe my prayer

ditty words of the song
remember commemorate
owes owns
fringèd curtains . . . advance eyelids . . . lift up
brave splendid
but except that
canker disease of roses
natural in the realm of nature as opposed to spirit
It goes on my plan (that Miranda should love Ferdinand) is working out
Most sure the goddess virtually a translation of Virgil's *O dea certe, Aeneid* I.328, often used in romance. Miranda's response (ll. 430–31) is also modeled on the passage.

May know if you remain upon this island;
And that you will some good instruction give
How I may bear me° here: my prime° request,
Which I do last pronounce, is, O you wonder!°
If you be maid or no?

MIRANDA No wonder, sir;
But certainly a maid.

FERDINAND My language! heavens!
I am the best of them that speak this speech,
Were I but where 'tis spoken.

PROSPERO How? the best?
What wert thou, if the King of Naples heard thee?

FERDINAND A single° thing, as I am now, that wonders
To hear thee speak of Naples. He does hear me;
And that he does I weep: myself am Naples,°
Who with mine eyes, never since at ebb, beheld
The King my father wracked.

MIRANDA Alack, for mercy!

FERDINAND Yes, faith, and all his lords; the Duke of Milan
And his brave° son being twain.

PROSPERO [*Aside*] The Duke of Milan
And his more braver daughter could control° thee,
If now 'twere fit to do it. At the first sight
They have changed eyes.° Delicate Ariel,
I'll set thee free for this. [*To* FERDINAND] A word, good sir;
I fear you have done yourself some wrong:° a word.

MIRANDA Why speaks my father so ungently? This
Is the third man° that e'er I saw; the first
That e'er I sighed for: pity move my father
To be inclined my way!°

FERDINAND O, if a virgin,
And your affection not gone forth, I'll make you
The Queen of Naples.

PROSPERO Soft, sir! one word more.
[*Aside*] They are both in either's powers: but this swift business
I must uneasy make, lest too light winning°
Make the prize light.° [*To* FERDINAND] One word more; I charge thee
That thou attend me: thou dost here usurp
The name thou ow'st° not; and hast put thyself
Upon this island as a spy, to win it
From me, the lord on it.

bear me conduct myself
prime most important
wonder a play on Miranda's name, which Ferdinand doesn't yet know
single solitary
myself am Naples Ferdinand thinks his father is dead and that he himself is King of Naples.
brave gallant. There is no further mention of Antonio's son in the play and this may be a slip.
control confute
changed eyes fallen in love
you have done yourself some wrong ironically polite way of saying "You're mistaken"
third man the others are Prospero and Caliban
inclined my way persuaded to my wishes
light winning easy success
light undervalued
ow'st ownest

FERDINAND No, as I am a man.
MIRANDA There's nothing ill can dwell in such a temple:°
If the ill spirit have so fair a house,
Good things will strive to dwell with it.°
PROSPERO Follow me.
Speak not you for him: he's a traitor. Come;
I'll manacle thy neck and feet together:
Sea-water shalt thou drink; thy food shall be
The fresh-brook mussels, withered roots, and husks
Wherein the acorn cradled. Follow.
FERDINAND No;
I will resist such entertainment° till
Mine enemy has more power.
He draws, and is charmed from moving.
MIRANDA O dear father,
Make not too rash a trial of him, for
He's gentle, and not fearful.°
PROSPERO What! I say,
My foot my tutor?° Put thy sword up, traitor;
Who mak'st a show, but dar'st not strike, thy conscience
Is so possessed with guilt: come from thy ward;°
For I can here disarm thee with this stick°
And make thy weapon drop.
MIRANDA Beseech you, father.
PROSPERO Hence! hang not on my garments.
MIRANDA Sir, have pity;
I'll be his surety.
PROSPERO Silence! one word more
Shall make me chide thee, if not hate thee. What!
An advocate for an impostor! hush!
Thou think'st there is° no more such shapes as he,
Having seen but him and Caliban: foolish wench!
To° the most of men this is a Caliban,
And they to him are angels.
MIRANDA My affections°
Are then most humble; I have no ambition
To see a goodlier° man.
PROSPERO Come on; obey:
Thy nerves° are in their infancy again,
And have no vigour in them.

There's nothing . . . temple Conventional neoplatonic doctrine—that the beautiful body houses a beautiful soul—is expressed by Miranda though qualified by Prospero later; but for the same reason Caliban and Sycorax are ugly.
Good things . . . with it suggesting that this is absurd
entertainment hospitality (ironical)
gentle . . . fearful high-born and not cowardly
My foot my tutor? shall you, so much my inferior, presume to instruct me? (Prospero thinks of himself as the head)
come from thy ward abandon your posture of defense
stick magic staff
is are
To in comparison with
affections feelings
goodlier more handsome
nerves sinews

FERDINAND So they are:
My spirits,° as in a dream, are all bound up.
My father's loss, the weakness which I feel,
The wrack of all my friends, nor° this man's threats,
To whom I am subdued, are° but light to me,
Might I but through my prison once a day
Behold this maid: all corners else o' the earth
Let liberty make use of;° space enough
Have I in such a prison.

PROSPERO [*Aside*] It works. [*To* FERDINAND] Come on.
[*To* ARIEL] Thou hast done well, fine Ariel! Follow me;
Hark what thou else shalt do me.

MIRANDA Be of comfort;
My father's of a better nature, sir,
Than he appears by speech: this is unwonted°
Which now came from him.

PROSPERO Thou shalt be as free
As mountain winds: but then exactly do
All points of my command.

ARIEL To the syllable.

PROSPERO Come, follow. Speak not for him. *Exeunt.*

ACT II

SCENE I [*Another part of the Island.*]

Enter ALONSO, SEBASTIAN, ANTONIO, GONZALO, ADRIAN, FRANCISCO, *and others.*

GONZALO Beseech you, sir, be merry; you have cause,
So have we all, of joy; for our escape
Is much beyond our loss. Our hint of° woe
Is common; every day, some sailor's wife,
The masters of some merchant,° and the merchant,°
Have just our theme of woe; but for the miracle,
I mean our preservation, few in millions
Can speak like us: then wisely, good sir, weigh
Our sorrow with our comfort.

ALONZO Prithee, peace.

SEBASTIAN [*Aside to* ANTONIO] He receives comfort like cold porridge.°

ANTONIO [*Aside to* SEBASTIAN] The visitor° will not give him o'er° so.

spirits energies; animal spirits, which convey nourishment and so strength to the body
nor Grammar confused; it would be clear if this were *and*.
are Read *would be*.
all corners . . . use of those who are free may have all the rest of the world; my prison, if I could see Miranda, would be all the space I needed
unwonted unaccustomed
hint of occasion for
some merchant some merchant vessel
merchant owner of the vessel
porridge made of pease; so there is a pun on Alonso's word, "peace"
visitor one who comforts the infirm
give him o'er cease to administer his advice

SEBASTIAN [*Aside to* ANTONIO] Look, he's winding up the watch of his wit; by and by it will strike.°

GONZALO Sir,—

SEBASTIAN [*Aside to* ANTONIO] One: tell.°

GONZALO When every grief is entertained that's offered,
Comes to the entertainer°—

SEBASTIAN A dollar.°

GONZALO Dolour comes to him, indeed: you have spoken truer than you purposed.

SEBASTIAN You have taken it wiselier° than I meant you should.

GONZALO Therefore, my lord,—

ANTONIO Fie, what a spendthrift is he of his tongue!

ALONZO I prithee, spare.°

GONZALO Well, I have done: but yet,—

SEBASTIAN He will be talking.

ANTONIO Which, of he or Adrian, for a good wager, first begins to crow?

SEBASTIAN The old cock.

ANTONIO The cockerel.°

SEBASTIAN Done. The wager?

ANTONIO A laughter.°

SEBASTIAN A match!

ADRIAN Though this island seem to be desert,—

ANTONIO Ha, ha, ha!

SEBASTIAN So: you're paid.°

ADRIAN Uninhabitable, and almost inaccessible,—

SEBASTIAN Yet,—

ANTONIO He could not miss it.

ADRIAN It must needs be of subtle, tender and delicate temperance.°

ANTONIO Temperance° was a delicate wench.

SEBASTIAN Ay, and a subtle; as he most learnedly delivered.

ADRIAN The air breathes upon us here most sweetly.

SEBASTIAN As if it had lungs, and rotten ones.

ANTONIO Or as 'twere perfumed by a fen.

GONZALO Here is everything advantageous to life.

ANTONIO True; save means to live.

SEBASTIAN Of that there's none, or little.

GONZALO How lush and lusty° the grass looks! how green!

ANTONIO The ground, indeed, is tawny.°

SEBASTIAN With an eye of green° in it.

ANTONIO He misses not much.

strike Striking or "repeating" watches were invented about 1510.
tell count
When . . . entertainer he who makes a point of accepting every occasion for grief that presents itself gets—
dollar sum of money (punning on the word Gonzalo speaks next)
wiselier more cleverly, more sagely
spare your words
cockerel i.e. Adrian
A laughter The winner is to have the right to laugh at the loser.
paid Antonio has had his laugh; in F Sebastian is given l. 35, Antonio l. 36.
temperance climate
Temperance a (Puritan) woman's name
lush and lusty fresh and luxuriant
tawny parched brown
eye of green having green patches

SEBASTIAN No; he doth but mistake° the truth totally.

GONZALO But the rarity of it is,—which is indeed almost beyond credit,°—

SEBASTIAN As many vouched rarities° are.

GONZALO That our garments, being, as they were, drenched in the sea, hold, notwithstanding, their freshness and glosses, being rather new-dyed than stained with salt water.

ANTONIO If but one of his pockets could speak, would it not say he lies?

SEBASTIAN Ay, or very falsely pocket up° his report.

GONZALO Methinks our garments are now as fresh as when we put them on first in Afric, at the marriage of the King's fair daughter Claribel to the King of Tunis.

SEBASTIAN 'Twas a sweet marriage, and we prosper well° in our return.

ADRIAN Tunis was never graced before with such a paragon to their Queen.

GONZALO Not since widow Dido's° time.

ANTONIO Widow! a pox o' that! How came that widow in? widow Dido!

SEBASTIAN What if he had said 'widower Æneas'° too? Good Lord, how you take it!

ADRIAN 'Widow Dido' said you? you make me study of that:° she was of Carthage, not of Tunis.°

GONZALO This Tunis, sir, was Carthage.

ADRIAN Carthage?

GONZALO I assure you, Carthage.

ANTONIO His word is more than the miraculous harp.°

SEBASTIAN He hath raised the wall, and houses too.

ANTONIO What impossible matter will he make easy next?

SEBASTIAN I think he will carry this island home in his pocket, and give it his son for an apple.

ANTONIO And, sowing the kernels of it in the sea, bring forth more islands.

GONZALO Ay.°

ANTONIO Why, in good time.

GONZALO Sir,° we were talking that our garments seem now as fresh as when we were at Tunis at the marriage of your daughter, who is now Queen.

ANTONIO And the rarest that e'er came there.

SEBASTIAN Bate,° I beseech you, widow Dido.

ANTONIO O, widow Dido! ay, widow Dido.

GONZALO Is not, sir, my doublet as fresh as the first day I wore it? I mean, in a sort.°

mistake punning on *miss* in previous line
credit belief
vouched rarities strange travelers' tales, vouched for by the teller
pocket up conceal (referring to the remark about Gonzalo's pocket, which could act as mouthpiece for the suit and tell a different story)
we prosper well ironical, of course
widow Dido's She was the widow of Sychaeus when she met Aeneas, but the expression is found ridiculous.
widower Æneas Aeneas was a widower just as Dido was a widow—why not mention that, too?
study of that give some thought to that
Tunis The site of the ancient Carthage was near to, but not identical with, that of modern Tunis; so Gonzalo is wrong.
more . . . harp Only the *walls* of Thebes rose to the music of Amphion's harp, whereas Gonzalo, by identifying Carthage and Tunis, fabricates a whole city.
Ay Gonzalo reaffirms his position on Tunis and Carthage (F has *I*).
Sir he addresses the King
Bate make an exception of
sort up to a point

ANTONIO That sort was well fished for.°

GONZALO When I wore it at your daughter's marriage?

ALONSO You cram these words into mine ears against
The stomach of my sense.° Would I had never
Married my daughter there! for, coming thence,
My son is lost, and, in my rate,° she too,
Who is so far from Italy removed
I ne'er again shall see her. O thou mine heir
Of Naples and of Milan, what strange fish
Hath made his meal on thee?

FRANCISCO Sir, he may live:
I saw him beat the surges° under him,
And ride upon their backs; he trod the water,
Whose enmity he flung aside, and breasted
The surge most swoln that met him; his bold head
'Bove the contentious waves he kept, and oared
Himself with his good arms in lusty stroke
To the shore, that o'er his wave-worn basis° bowed,
As stooping to relieve him: I not doubt
He came alive to land.

ALONSO No, no, he's gone.

SEBASTIAN Sir, you may thank yourself for this great loss,
That would not bless our Europe with your daughter,
But rather loose° her to an African;
Where she, at least, is banished from your eye,
Who hath cause to wet the grief on it.°

ALONSO Prithee, peace.

SEBASTIAN You were kneeled to, and importuned otherwise,
By all of us; and the fair soul herself
Weighed° between loathness° and obedience, at
Which end o' the beam should bow. We have lost your son,
I fear, for ever: Milan and Naples have
Mo° widows in them of this business' making
Than we bring men to comfort them:
The fault's your own.

ALONSO So is the dearest° o' the loss.

GONZALO My lord Sebastian,
The truth you speak doth lack some gentleness,
And time° to speak it in: you rub the sore,
When you should bring the plaster.°

SEBASTIAN Very well.

That . . . for the word "sort" was a lucky catch, and saved Gonzalo from an outright lie
stomach of my sense The King compares Gonzalo's persistence in plying him with consolations to that of a man who forces food on a reluctant recipient.
rate estimation
surges waves
basis base
loose mate (contemptuous)
Who . . . on it obscure: probably "weep for the grief her loss has caused you"
Weighed balanced
loathness reluctance
Mo more
dearest bitterest
time appropriate time
plaster dressing

ANTONIO And most chirurgeonly.°
GONZALO It is foul weather in us all, good sir,
When you are cloudy.
SEBASTIAN Foul° weather?
ANTONIO Very foul.
GONZALO Had I plantation° of this isle, my lord,—
ANTONIO He'd sow it with nettle-seed.
SEBASTIAN Or docks, or mallows.°
GONZALO And were the King on it, what would I do?
SEBASTIAN 'Scape being drunk for want of wine.
GONZALO I' the commonwealth° I would by contraries°
Execute all things; for no kind of traffic°
Would I admit; no name of magistrate;
Letters° should not be known; riches, poverty,
And use of service,° none; contract, succession,°
Bourn,° bound of land, tilth,° vineyard, none;
No use of metal, corn, or wine, or oil;
No occupation;° all men idle, all;
And women too, but innocent and pure:
No sovereignty;—
SEBASTIAN Yet he would be King on it.
ANTONIO The latter end of his commonwealth forgets the beginning.
GONZALO All things in common° Nature should produce
Without sweat or endeavour: treason, felony,
Sword, pike, knife, gun, or need of any engine,°
Would I not have; but Nature should bring forth,
Of its own kind, all foison,° all abundance,
To feed my innocent people.
SEBASTIAN No marrying 'mong his subjects?
ANTONIO None, man; all idle; whores and knaves.
GONZALO I would with such perfection govern, sir,
To excel the Golden Age.
SEBASTIAN 'Save his Majesty!
ANTONIO Long live Gonzalo!
GONZALO And,—do you mark me, sir?
ALONSO Prithee, no more: thou dost talk nothing° to me.
GONZALO I do well believe your highness; and did it to minister occasion° to these gentlemen, who are of such sensible° and nimble lungs that they always use to laugh at nothing.

chirurgeonly surgeon-like
Foul The point of this exchange is lost—perhaps Sebastian looks mockingly at the fineness of the weather.
plantation colonization; Antonio takes it in the other sense of "planting"
nettle-seed . . . docks . . . mallows common English weeds
commonwealth The passage that follows is based on Montaigne's essay "Of Cannibals" as translated by John Florio.
by contraries doing the opposite of what is usually done
traffic trade
Letters literacy
use of service the employment of servants
succession inheritance of property
Bourn boundry
tilth tillage
occupation working at a trade
in common for ownership
engine military weapon
foison abundance
nothing empty nonsense
minister occasion afford opportunity
sensible sensitive

ANTONIO 'Twas you we laughed at.

GONZALO Who in this kind of merry fooling am nothing to you: so you may continue, and laugh at nothing still.

ANTONIO What a blow was there given!

SEBASTIAN An it had not fallen flat-long.°

GONZALO You are gentlemen of brave mettle;° you would lift the moon out of her sphere, if she would continue in it five weeks without changing.°

Enter ARIEL (*invisible*) *playing solemn music.*

SEBASTIAN We would so, and then go a-batfowling.°

ANTONIO Nay, good my lord, be not angry.

GONZALO No, I warrant you; I will not adventure° my discretion so weakly. Will you laugh me asleep, for I am very heavy?°

ANTONIO Go sleep, and hear us.°

All sleep except ALONSO, SEBASTIAN, *and* ANTONIO

ALONSO What, all so soon asleep! I wish mine eyes
Would, with themselves, shut up my thoughts: I find
They are inclined to do so.

SEBASTIAN Please you, sir,
Do not omit° the heavy offer of it:
It seldom visits sorrow; when it doth,
It is a comforter.

ANTONIO We two, my lord,
Will guard your person while you take your rest,
And watch your safety.

ALONSO Thank you.—Wondrous heavy.

ALONSO *sleeps. Exit* ARIEL.

SEBASTIAN What a strange drowsiness possesses them!

ANTONIO It is the quality° o' the climate.

SEBASTIAN Why
Doth it not then our eyelids sink? I find not
Myself disposed to sleep.

ANTONIO Nor I; my spirits are nimble.
They fell together all, as by consent;
They dropped, as by a thunder-stroke. What might,
Worthy Sebastian?—O, what might?—No more:—
And yet methinks I see it in thy face,
What thou shouldst be: the occasion speaks° thee; and
My strong imagination sees a crown
Dropping upon thy head.

SEBASTIAN What, art thou waking?°

ANTONIO Do you not hear me speak?

flat-long with the flat of the sword
brave mettle fine spirit
you would lift . . . changing you'd have the moon out of the heavens if she'd stay still a little longer
a-batfowling hunting birds with a light (in this case, the moon), toward which they fly and are beaten down with clubs
adventure risk
heavy drowsy
hear us hear us laughing
omit neglect
quality characteristic
occasion speaks opportunity invites
waking awake

SEBASTIAN I do; and surely
It is a sleepy language, and thou speak'st
Out of thy sleep. What is it thou didst say?
This is a strange repose, to be asleep
With eyes wide open; standing, speaking, moving,
And yet so fast asleep.

ANTONIO Noble Sebastian,
Thou let'st thy fortune sleep—die, rather; wink'st°
Whiles thou art waking.

SEBASTIAN Thou dost snore distinctly;
There's meaning in thy snores.

ANTONIO I am more serious than my custom: you
Must be so too, if heed me; which to do
Trebles thee o'er.°

SEBASTIAN Well, I am standing water.°

ANTONIO I'll teach you how to flow.°

SEBASTIAN Do so: to ebb
Hereditary sloth instructs me.

ANTONIO O,
If you but knew how you the purpose cherish°
Whiles thus you mock it! how, in stripping it,
You more invest it!° Ebbing men, indeed,
Most often do so near the bottom run
By their own fear of sloth.

SEBASTIAN Prithee, say on:
The setting of thine eye and cheek° proclaim
A matter° from thee; and a birth, indeed,
Which throes° thee much to yield.

ANTONIO Thus, sir:
Although this lord of weak remembrance,° this,
Who shall be of as little memory
When he is earthed,° hath here almost persuaded,—
For he's a spirit of persuasion, only
Professes to persuade,°—the King his son's alive,
'Tis is as impossible that he's undrowned
As he that sleeps here swims.

SEBASTIAN I have no hope°
That he's undrowned.

ANTONIO O, out of that 'no hope'
What great hope have you! no hope that way is
Another way so high a hope, that even

wink'st closest thine eyes
Trebles thee o'er triples thy greatness
standing water slack water between tides
flow continuing the tide figure—flow rather than ebb
cherish value, enhance
invest it clothe it (while you think that by playing it cool you're stripping or minimizing it)
setting . . . cheek serious look on your face
A matter something of weight
throes gives pain
weak remembrance poor memory
Who shall . . . earthed who will himself be unremembered when he is buried
Professes to persuade makes a profession of persuasion
hope expectation. Antonio takes it in a more modern sense.

Ambition cannot pierce a wink beyond,
But doubt discovery there.° Will you grant with me
That Ferdinand is drowned?

SEBASTIAN He's gone.

ANTONIO Then tell me,
Who's the next heir of Naples?

SEBASTIAN Claribel.

ANTONIO She that is Queen of Tunis; she that dwells
Ten leagues beyond man's life;° she that from Naples
Can have no note,° unless the sun were post,°—
The man i' the moon's too slow,—till new-born chins
Be rough and razorable; she that from whom°
We all were sea-swallowed, though some cast° again,
And by that destiny to perform an act
Whereof what's past is prologue; what to come,
In yours and my discharge.°

SEBASTIAN What stuff is this! how say you?
'Tis true, my brother's daughter's Queen of Tunis;
So is she heir of Naples; 'twixt which regions
There is some space.

ANTONIO A space whose every cubit°
Seems to cry out, 'How shall that Claribel
Measure us° back to Naples? Keep in Tunis,
And let Sebastian wake.' Say this were death
That now hath seized them;° why, they were no worse
Than now they are. There be that can rule Naples
As well as he that sleeps; lords that can prate
As amply and unnecessarily
As this Gonzalo; I myself could make
A chough of as deep chat.° O, that you bore°
The mind that I do! what a sleep were this
For your advancement! Do you understand me?

SEBASTIAN Methinks I do.

ANTONIO And how does your content
Tender° your own good fortune?

SEBASTIAN I remember
You did supplant your brother Prospero.

ANTONIO True:
And look how well my garments sit upon me;
Much feater° than before: my brother's servants

Ambition . . . there Ambition cannot set its eye on higher object (than the crown) and even there must have difficulty in discerning the goal
Ten leagues . . . life ten leagues farther than one might journey in a lifetime
note communication
post messenger
from whom in coming from whom
cast vomited forth
perform . . . act . . . prologue . . . discharge theatrical expressions; "to discharge a part" was the common phrase
cubit ancient measure; 18 to 22 inches
us i.e. the cubits
Keep stay (the cubits address Claribel)
them the sleepers
I myself . . . chat I could teach a jackdaw to talk as profoundly as he does
bore had
Tender regard
feater more gracefully

Were then my fellows; now they are my men.
SEBASTIAN But for your conscience.
ANTONIO Ay, sir; where lies that? if 'twere a kibe,°
'Twould put me to my slipper:° but I feel not
This deity in my bosom: twenty consciences,
That stand 'twixt me and Milan, candied° be they,
And melt, ere they molest! Here lies your brother,
No better than the earth he lies upon,
If he were that which now he's like, that's dead;
Whom I, with this obedient steel, three inches of it,
Can lay to bed for ever; whiles you, doing thus,
To the perpetual wink° for aye might put
This ancient morsel,° this Sir Prudence, who
Should not upbraid our course. For all the rest,
They'll take suggestion° as a cat laps milk;
They'll tell the clock to any business that
We say befits the hour.°
SEBASTIAN Thy, case, dear friend,
Shall be my precedent; as thou got'st Milan,
I'll come by Naples. Draw thy sword: one stroke
Shall free thee from the tribute which thou payest;
And I the King shall love thee.
ANTONIO Draw together;
And when I rear my hand, do you the like,
To fall it° on Gonzalo.
SEBASTIAN O, but one word. *They talk apart.*

Re-enter ARIEL *invisible, with music and song.*

ARIEL My master through his Art foresees the danger
That you, his friend,° are in; and sends me forth,—
For else his project dies,—to keep them living.
Sings in GONZALO*'s ear.*

While you here do snoring lie,
Open-eyed conspiracy
His time doth take.
If of life you keep a care,
Shake off slumber, and beware:
Awake, Awake!

ANTONIO Then let us both be sudden.°
GONZALO [*Waking*] Now, good angels
Preserve the King! *The others wake.*
ALONSO Why, how now? ho; awake?—Why are you drawn?

kibe sore, usually on the heel
put in slipper force me to wear a slipper
candied frozen solid
perpetual wink everlasting sleep
ancient morsel Gonzalo
suggestion prompting
tell . . . hour pretend that whatever we propose is opportune
fall it let it fall
friend Gonzalo
sudden prompt in action

Wherefore this ghastly looking?

GONZALO What's the matter?

SEBASTIAN Whiles we stood here securing your repose,
Even now, we heard a hollow burst of bellowing
Like bulls, or rather lions: did it not wake you?
It struck mine ear most terribly.

ALONSO I heard nothing.

ANTONIO O, 'twas a din to fright a monster's ear,
To make an earthquake! sure, it was the roar
Of a whole herd of lions.

ALONSO Heard you this, Gonzalo?

GONZALO Upon mine honour, sir, I heard a humming,°
And that a strange one too, which did awake me:
I shaked you, sir, and cried: as mine eyes opened,
I saw their weapons drawn:—there was a noise,
That's verily.° 'Tis best we stand upon our guard,
Or that we quit this place: let's draw our weapons.

ALONSO Lead off this ground; and let's make further search
For my poor son.

GONZALO Heavens keep him from these beasts!
For he is, sure, i' the island.

ALONSO Lead away.

ARIEL Prospero my lord shall know what I have done:
So, King, go safely on to seek thy son. *Exeunt.*

SCENE II [*Another part of the Island.*]

Enter CALIBAN *with a burthen of wood. A noise of thunder heard.*

CALIBAN All the infections that the sun sucks up°
From bogs, fens, flats, on Prosper fall, and make him
By inch-meal° a disease! his spirits hear me,
And yet I needs must curse. But they'll nor pinch,
Fright me with urchin-shows,° pitch me i' the mire,
Nor lead me, like a firebrand,° in the dark
Out of my way, unless he bid 'em: but
For every trifle are they set upon me;
Sometime like apes, that mow° and chatter at me,
And after bite me; then like hedgehogs, which
Lie tumbling in my barefoot way, and mount
Their pricks° at my footfall; sometime am I
All wound° with adders, who with cloven tongues
Do hiss me into madness.

humming he heard Ariel's song
verily (to speak) truly
sucks up Disease-bearing mists were thought to be sucked from bogs and fens by the sun.
inch-meal inch by inch
urchin-shows apparitions of goblins
firebrand will-o'-the-wisp, *ignis fatuus*
mow make faces
pricks quills
wound twined about with

Enter TRINCULO.

Lo, now, lo!
Here comes a spirit of his, and to torment me
For bringing wood in slowly. I'll fall flat;
Perchance he will not mind me.

TRINCULO Here's neither bush nor shrub, to bear off° any weather at all, and another storm brewing; I hear it sing i' the wind: yond same black cloud, yond huge one, looks like a foul bombard° that would shed his liquor. If it should thunder as it did before, I know not where to hide my head: yond same cloud cannot choose but fall by pailfuls. What have we here? a man or a fish? dead or alive? A fish: he smells like a fish; a very ancient and fish-like smell; a kind of, not of the newest Poor-John.° A strange fish! Were I in England° now, as once I was, and had but this fish painted,° not a holiday fool there but would give a piece of silver: there would this monster make a man;° any strange beast there makes a man: when they will not give a doit° to relieve a lame beggar, they will lay out ten to see a dead Indian.° Legged like a man! and his fins like arms! Warm o' my troth! I do now let loose my opinion, hold it no longer: this is no fish, but an islander, that hath lately suffered° by a thunderbolt. [*Thunder*] Alas, the storm is come again! my best way is to creep under his gaberdine;° there is no other shelter hereabout: misery acquaints a man with strange bed-fellows. I will here shroud till the dregs of the storm be past.

Enter STEPHANO, *singing: a bottle in his hand.*

I shall no more to sea, to sea,
Here shall I die ashore,—

This is a very scurvy tune to sing at a man's funeral; well, here's my comfort. *Drinks. Sings.*

The master, the swabber, the boatswain, and I,
The gunner, and his mate,
Loved Mall,° Meg, and Marian, and Margery,
But none of us cared for Kate:
For she had a tongue with a tang,
Would cry to a sailor, Go hang!
She loved not the savour of tar nor of pitch;
Yet a tailor might scratch her where'er she did itch.
Then to sea, boys, and let her go hang!

This is a scurvy tune too: but here's my comfort. *Drinks.*

CALIBAN Do not torment me:—O!

bear off ward off
bombard large leather bottle
Poor-John dried hake, a fish similar to cod
England where exhibitions of monsters were popular
painted on a board and hung outside a fair-booth
make a man make a man's fortune (with pun on the other sense)
doit small coin
Indian Indians were often so exhibited, and usually died early.
suffered been killed
gaberdine cloak
Mall diminutive form of Mary

STEPHANO What's the matter? Have we devils here? Do you put tricks upon us with salvages° and men of Ind,° ha? I have not scaped drowning, to be afeard now of your four legs; for it hath been said, As proper a man° as ever went on four legs cannot make him give ground; and it shall be said so again, while Stephano breathes at' nostrils.

CALIBAN The spirit torments me:—O!

STEPHANO This is some monster of the isle with four legs, who hath got, as I take it, an ague.° Where the devil should he learn° our language? I will give him some relief, if it be but for that. If I can recover° him, and keep him tame, and get to Naples with him, he's a present° for any emperor that ever trod on neat's leather.°

CALIBAN Do not torment me, prithee; I'll bring my wood home faster.

STEPHANO He's in his fit now, and does not talk after the wisest. He shall taste of my bottle: if he have never drink wine afore, it will go near to remove his fit. If I can recover him, and keep him tame, I will not take too much for him;° he shall pay for him that hath him and that soundly.

CALIBAN Thou dost me yet but little hurt; thou wilt anon, I know it by thy trembling:° now Prosper works upon thee.

STEPHANO Come on your ways; open your mouth; here is that which will give language to you, cat:° open your mouth; this will shake your shaking, I can tell you, and that soundly: you cannot tell who's your friend: open your chaps° again.

TRINCULO I should know that voice: it should be—but he is drowned; and these are devils:—O defend me!

STEPHANO Four legs and two voices,—a most delicate monster! His forward voice, now, is to speak well of his friend; his backward voice is to utter foul speeches and to detract.° If all the wine in my bottle will recover him, I will help° his ague. Come:—Amen!° I will pour some in thy other mouth.

TRINCULO Stephano!

STEPHANO Doth thy other mouth call me? Mercy, mercy! This is a devil, and no monster: I will leave him; I have no long spoon.°

TRINCULO Stephano! If thou beest Stephano, touch me, and speak to me; for I am Trinculo,—be not afeard,—thy good friend Trinculo.

STEPHANO If thou beest Trinculo, come forth: I'll pull thee by the lesser legs: If any be Trinculo's legs, these are they. Thou art very Trinculo indeed! How camest thou to be the siege° of this moon-calf?° can he vent° Trinculos?

salvages savages
men of Ind Indians
As proper a man as fine a fellow
ague fever
should he learn can he have learned
recover restore
present Great men of the period liked to collect dwarfs and other unusual species.
neat's-leather cowhide (the expression was proverbial)
I will . . . for him no price I get for him will be too much
trembling Caliban takes this as a sign that the tormentor is in process of being possessed prior to starting work on him.
cat alluding to the proverb "Ale (liquor) will make a cat speak"
chaps jaws
detract slander
help cure
Amen that's enough for one mouth
long spoon proverb: "He that would eat with the devil must have a long spoon"
siege excrement
moon-calf monstrosity, deformed by the influence of the moon
vent excrete

TRINCULO I took him to be killed with a thunder-stroke. But art thou not drowned, Stephano? I hope, now, thou art not drowned. Is the storm over-blown? I hid me under the dead moon-calf's gaberdine for fear of the storm. And art thou living, Stephano? O Stephano, two Neapolitans scaped!

STEPHANO Prithee, do not turn me about; my stomach is not constant.°

CALIBAN [*Aside*] These be fine things,° an if° they be not sprites.
That's a brave° god, and bears celestial liquor:
I will kneel to him.

STEPHANO How didst thou scape? How camest thou hither? swear, by this bottle, how thou camest hither. I escaped upon a butt of sack,° which the sailors heaved o'erboard, by this bottle! which I made of the bark of a tree with mine own hands, since I was cast ashore.

CALIBAN I'll swear, upon that bottle, to be thy true subject; for the liquor is not earthly.

STEPHANO Here; swear, then, how thou escapedst.

TRINCULO Swum ashore, man, like a duck: I can swim like a duck, I'll be sworn.

STEPHANO Here, kiss the book.° Though thou canst swim like a duck, thou art made like a goose.

TRINCULO O Stephano, hast any more of this?

STEPHANO The whole butt, man: my cellar is in a rock by the seaside, where my wine is hid. How now, moon-calf! how does thine ague?

CALIBAN Hast thou not dropped from heaven?

STEPHANO Out o' the moon,° I do assure thee: I was the man i' the moon when time was.°

CALIBAN I have seen thee in her, and I do adore thee:
My mistress showed me thee, and thy dog, and thy bush.

STEPHANO Come, swear to that; kiss the book: I will furnish it anon with new contents: swear.

TRINCULO By this good light, this is a very shallow monster; I afeard of him? A very weak monster! The man i' the moon! A most poor credulous monster! Well drawn,° monster, in good sooth!°

CALIBAN I'll show thee every fertile inch° o' the island; and I will kiss thy foot: I prithee, be my god.

TRINCULO By this light, a most perfidious and drunken monster! when his god's asleep, he'll rob his bottle.

CALIBAN I'll kiss thy foot; I'll swear myself thy subject.

STEPHANO Come on, then; down, and swear.

TRINCULO I shall laugh myself to death at this puppy-headed monster. A most scurvy monster! I could find in my heart to beat him,—

constant steady
fine things Note the similarity of Caliban's reaction to the sight of Trinculo and Stephano, and Miranda's to the noblemen, especially Ferdinand.
an if if
brave fine
sack sherry-like wine; such a butt is mentioned in one of the narratives of the Bermuda wreck
kiss the book Trinculo raises the bottle to his lips.
Out o' the moon Stephano was not the first voyager to tell this to the natives.
when time was once upon a time
Well drawn a good pull at the wine
in good sooth truly
every fertile inch Twelve years earlier he had done this for Prospero.

STEPHANO Come, kiss.

TRINCULO But that the poor monster's in drink. An abominable monster!

CALIBAN I'll show thee the best springs; I'll pluck thee berries;
I'll fish for thee, and get thee wood enough.
A plague upon the tyrant° that I serve!
I'll bear him no more sticks, but follow thee,
Thou wondrous man.

TRINCULO A most ridiculous monster, to make a wonder of a poor drunkard!

CALIBAN I prithee, let me bring thee where crabs° grow;
And I with my long nails will dig thee pig-nuts;°
Show thee a jay's nest, and instruct thee how
To snare the nimble marmoset;° I'll bring thee
To clustering filberts,° and sometimes I'll get thee
Young scamels° from the rock. Wilt thou go with me?

STEPHANO I prithee now, lead the way, without any more talking. Trinculo, the King and all our company else being drowned, we will inherit° here: here; bear my bottle: fellow Trinculo, we'll fill him by and by again.

CALIBAN *Sings drunkenly.*

Farewell, master; farewell, farewell!

TRINCULO A howling monster; a drunken monster!

CALIBAN *No more dams I'll make for fish;*
Nor fetch in firing
At requiring;
Nor scrape trenchering,° nor wash dish:
'Ban, 'Ban, Cacaliban
Has a new master:—get a new man.

Freedom, high-day!° high-day, freedom! freedom, high-day, freedom!

STEPHANO O brave monster! lead the way. *Exeunt.*

ACT III

SCENE I [*Before* PROSPERO*'s Cell.*]

Enter FERDINAND, *bearing a log.*

FERDINAND There be some sports are painful, and their labour
Delight in them sets off:° some kinds of baseness
Are nobly undergone; and most poor° matters
Point to rich ends. This my mean task
Would be as heavy to me as odious, but
The mistress which I serve quickens° what's dead,

tyrant usurper
crabs crab-apples
pig-nuts earthnuts
marmoset small monkey (called "good meat" by colonists)
filberts trees bearing hazel nuts
scamels The word is not recorded elsewhere: either a bird or a shellfish.
inherit take possession
trenchering "trenchers" (dishes) collectively; cf. housing, clothing
high-day meaningless cry of joy and pleasure
There . . . off in some arduous sports the pleasure they give cancels our pains
most poor the poorest
quickens gives life to

And makes my labour pleasures: O, she is
Ten times more gentle than her father's crabbed,°
And he's composed of harshness. I must remove
Some thousands of these logs, and pile them up,
Upon a sore injunction:° my sweet mistress
Weeps when she sees me work, and says, such baseness
Had never like executor.° I forget:
But these sweet thoughts do even refresh my labours,
Most busy least when I do it.°

Enter MIRANDA; *and* PROSPERO [*at a distance, unseen*].

MIRANDA Alas, now, pray you,
Work not so hard: I would the lightning had
Burnt up those logs that you are enjoined° to pile!
Pray, set it down, and rest you: when this burns,
'Twill weep° for having wearied you. My father
Is hard at study; pray, now, rest yourself:
He's safe for these three hours.

FERDINAND O most dear mistress,
The sun will set before I shall discharge°
What I must strive to do.

MIRANDA If you'll sit down,
I'll bear your logs the while: pray give me that;
I'll carry it to the pile.

FERDINAND No, precious creature;
I had rather crack my sinews, break my back,
Than you should such dishonour undergo,
While I sit lazy by.

MIRANDA It would become me
As well as it does you: and I should do it
With much more ease; for my good will is to it,
And yours it is against.

PROSPERO Poor worm, thou art infected!°
This visitation° shows it.

MIRANDA You look wearily.

FERDINAND No, noble mistress: 'tis fresh morning with me
When you are by at night. I do beseech you,—
Chiefly that I might set it in my prayers,—
What is your name?

MIRANDA Miranda.—O my father,
I have broke your hest° to say so!

FERDINAND Admired° Miranda!

crabbed bad-tempered
Upon . . . injunction under a severe penalty
Had . . . executor was never carried out by so noble a person
Most busy . . . it F: *Most busie lest, when I do it;* unsolved crux, perhaps corrupt, perhaps meaning "My work is hardest when I think of her least"
enjoined commanded
weep by exuding sap
discharge fulfill
infected by love, as by the plague
visitation visit; also used of a plague epidemic
hest order
admired playing on the meaning of her name: "worthy of admiration"

Indeed the top of admiration! worth
What's dearest to the world! Full many a lady
I have eyed with best regard,° and many a time
The harmony of their tongues hath into bondage
Brought my too diligent ear: for several° virtues°
Have I liked several women; never any
With so full soul, but some defect in her
Did quarrel with the noblest grace° she owed,°
And put it to the foil:° but you, O you,
So perfect and so peerless, are created
Of every creature's best!°

MIRANDA I do not know
One of my sex: no woman's face remember,
Save, from my glass, mine own; nor have I seen
More that I may call men than you, good friend,
And my dear father: how features are abroad,°
I am skilless of;° but, by my modesty,
The jewel in my dower, I would not wish
Any companion in the world but you;
Nor can imagination form a shape,
Besides yourself, to like of.° But I prattle
Something too wildly, and my father's precepts
I therein do forget.

FERDINAND I am, in my condition,°
A prince, Miranda; I do think, a King;
I would not so!—and would no more endure
This wooden slavery° than to suffer
The flesh-fly blow° my mouth. Hear my soul speak:
The very instant that I saw you, did
My heart fly to your service; there resides,
To make me slave to it; and for your sake
Am I this patient log-man.

MIRANDA Do you love me?

FERDINAND O heaven, O earth, bear witness to this sound,
And crown what I profess with kind event,°
If I speak true! if hollowly,° invert
What best is boded me° to mischief! I,
Beyond all limit of what else i' the world,
Do love, prize, honour you.

MIRANDA I am a fool
To weep at what I am glad of.

best regard attentive gaze
several different
virtues qualities
noblest grace finest attribute
owed owned
put . . . foil spoiled, overthrew it
every creature's best a common Elizabethan love-compliment
abroad out in the world
skilless of ignorant of
like of be pleased with
condition rank
wooden slavery menial task of wood-carrying
blow foul, sully
kind event favorable outcome
hollowly insincerely
What . . . me the best fortune has in store for me

PROSPERO Fair encounter
Of two most rare affections!° Heavens rain grace
On that which breeds between 'em!°

FERDINAND Wherefore weep you?

MIRANDA At mine unworthiness, that dare not offer
What I desire to give; and much less take
What I shall die to want.° But this is trifling;°
And all the more it° seeks to hide itself,
The bigger bulk it shows. Hence, bashful cunning!
And prompt me, plain and holy innocence!
I am your wife, if you will marry me;
If not, I'll die your maid:° to be your fellow
You may deny me; but I'll be your servant,
Whether you will or no.

FERDINAND My mistress, dearest;
And I thus humble ever.

MIRANDA My husband, then?

FERDINAND Ay, with a heart as willing
As bondage e'er of freedom:° here's my hand.

MIRANDA And mine, with my heart in it: and now farewell
Till half an hour hence.

FERDINAND A thousand thousand!°

Exeunt. FERDINAND *and* MIRANDA *severally.*

PROSPERO So glad of this as they I cannot be,
Who are surprised with all;° but my rejoicing
At nothing can be more. I'll to my book;
For yet, ere supper-time, must I perform
Much business appertaining.° *Exit.*

SCENE II [*Another part of the Island.*]

Enter CALIBAN, STEPHANO, *and* TRINCULO.

STEPHANO Tell not me;°—when the butt is out, we will drink water; not a drop before: therefore bear up, and board 'em.° Servant-monster, drink to me.

TRINCULO Servant-monster! the folly° of this island! They say there's but five upon this isle: we are three of them; if the other two be brained° like us, the state totters.

STEPHANO Drink, servant-monster, when I bid thee: thy eyes are almost set° in thy head.

affections dispositions
that which . . . 'em i.e. love and/or children
want be without
trifling using words unequal to her true feelings
it her love
maid with two senses, "virgin" and "servant"
with . . . freedom as eagerly as the captive longs for freedom
thousand "farewells"
surprised with all taken unawares by all these developments (or *withal*, by this)
appertaining relating (to the marriage and what must lead up to it)
Tell not me don't talk to me (about saving liquor)
bear up and board 'em naval order, here meaning "drink up"
folly freak
brained equipped with brains
set disappearing, like the setting sun. Trinculo takes it in a different sense.

TRINCULO Where should they be set else? he were a brave monster indeed, if they were set in his tail.

STEPHANO My man-monster hath drowned his tongue in sack: for my part, the sea cannot drown me; I swam, ere I could recover° the shore, five-and-thirty leagues off and on. By this light, thou shalt be my lieutenant, monster, or my standard.°

TRINCULO Your lieutenant, if you list; he's no standard.

STEPHANO We'll not run,° Monsieur Monster.

TRINCULO Nor go° neither; but you'll lie,° like dogs, and yet say nothing neither.

STEPHANO Moon-calf, speak once in thy life, if thou beest a good moon-calf.

CALIBAN How does thy honour? Let me lick thy shoe: I'll not serve him, he is not valiant.

TRINCULO Thou liest, most ignorant monster: I am in case° to justle a constable.° Why, thou deboshed° fish, thou, was there ever man a coward that hath drunk so much sack as I to-day? Wilt thou tell a monstrous lie, being but half a fish and half a monster?

CALIBAN Lo, how he mocks me! wilt thou let him, my lord?

TRINCULO 'Lord,' quoth he? That a monster should be such a natural!°

CALIBAN Lo, lo, again! bite him to death, I prithee.

STEPHANO Trinculo, keep a good tongue in your head: if you prove a mutineer,—the next tree! The poor monster's my subject, and he shall not suffer indignity.

CALIBAN I thank my noble lord. Wilt thou be pleased to hearken once again to the suit I made to thee?

STEPHANO Marry, will I: kneel and repeat it; I will stand, and so shall Trinculo.

Enter ARIEL, *invisible*.

CALIBAN As I told thee before, I am subject to a tyrant,° a sorcerer, that by his cunning hath cheated me of the island.

ARIEL Thou liest.

CALIBAN Thou liest, thou jesting monkey,° thou:
I would my valiant master would destroy thee!
I do not lie.

STEPHANO Trinculo, if you trouble him any more in 's tale, by this hand, I will supplant° some of your teeth.

TRINCULO Why, I said nothing.

STEPHANO Mum, then, and no more. Proceed.

CALIBAN I say, by sorcery he got this isle;
From me he got it. If thy greatness will
Revenge it on him,—for I know thou dar'st,
But this thing° dare not,—

recover reach
standard standard-bearer, but as Caliban can hardly stand, Trinculo puns on the word
run from the enemy; but also because they are staggering
go walk
lie lie down; tell lies
in case in a condition
justle a constable Trinculo is drunk enough to rough up a law officer.
deboshed debauched
natural idiot
tyrant usurper
Thou liest . . . monkey Caliban thinks the previous remark came from Trinculo.
supplant uproot
this thing Trinculo

STEPHANO That's most certain.

CALIBAN Thou shalt be lord of it, and I'll serve thee.

STEPHANO How now shall this be compassed?° Canst thou bring me to the party?°

CALIBAN Yea, yea, my lord: I'll yield him thee asleep,
Where thou mayst knock a nail into his head.

ARIEL Thou liest; thou canst not.

CALIBAN What a pied° ninny's this! Thou scurvy patch!°
I do beseech thy greatness, give him blows,
And take his bottle from him: when that's gone,
He shall drink nought but brine; for I'll not show him
Where the quick freshes° are.

STEPHANO Trinculo, run into no further danger: interrupt the monster one word further, and, by this hand, I'll turn my mercy out o' doors, and make a stock-fish° of thee.

TRINCULO Why, what did I? I did nothing. I'll go farther off.

STEPHANO Didst thou not say he lied?

ARIEL Thou liest.

STEPHANO Do I so? take thou that. [*Beats him.*] As you like this, give me the lie° another time.

TRINCULO I did not give the lie. Out o' your wits, and hearing too? A pox o' your bottle! this can sack and drinking do. A murrain° on your monster, and the devil take your fingers!

CALIBAN Ha, ha, ha!

STEPHANO Now, forward with your tale.—Prithee, stand further off.°

CALIBAN Beat him enough: after a little time,
I'll beat him too.

STEPHANO Stand farther.—Come, proceed.

CALIBAN Why, as I told thee, 'tis a custom with him
I' the afternoon to sleep: there° thou mayst brain him,
Having first seized his books; or with a log
Batter his skull, or paunch° him with a stake,
Or cut his wezand° with thy knife. Remember
First to possess° his books; for without them
He's but a sot,° as I am, nor hath not
One spirit to command: they all do hate him
As rootedly as I. Burn but° his books.
He has brave útensils,°—for so he calls them,—
Which, when he has a house, he'll deck withal.°
And that° most deeply to consider is

compassed brought about
party person concerned
pied particolored (referring to jester's motley)
patch fool, jester
freshes springs of fresh water
stock-fish salted cod, beaten with a club before cooking
give me the lie call me a liar
murrain disease of cattle
stand further off to Trinculo, to prevent him from interrupting; or to Caliban because he smells
there at that time
paunch disembowel
wezand windpipe
possess seize
sot ignoramus
Burn but only be sure to burn; burn only
utensils household goods
deck withal furnish it with
that that which is

The beauty of his daughter; he himself
Calls her a nonpareil:° I never saw a woman,
But only Sycorax my dam and she;
But she as far surpasseth Sycorax
As greatest does least.

STEPHANO Is it so brave a lass?

CALIBAN Ay, lord; she will become thy bed, I warrant,
And bring thee forth brave brood.

STEPHANO Monster, I will kill this man: his daughter and I will be king and queen,—save our graces!—and Trinculo and thyself shall be viceroys. Dost thou like the plot,° Trinculo?

TRINCULO Excellent.

STEPHANO Give me thy hand: I am sorry I beat thee; but, while thou livest, keep a good tongue in thy head.

CALIBAN Within this half hour will he be asleep:
Wilt thou destroy him then?

STEPHANO Ay, on mine honour.

ARIEL This will I tell my master.

CALIBAN Thou mak'st me merry; I am full of pleasure:
Let us be jocund: will you troll the catch°
You taught me but while-ere?°

STEPHANO At thy request, monster, I will do reason, any reason.°—Come on, Trinculo, let us sing. *Sings.*

Flout 'em and scout° 'em,
And scout 'em and flout 'em;
Thought is free.°

CALIBAN That's not the tune.

ARIEL *plays the tune on a tabor° and pipe.*

STEPHANO What is this same?

TRINCULO This is the tune of our catch, played by the picture of Nobody.°

STEPHANO If thou beest a man, show thyself in this likeness: if thou beest a devil, take it as thou list.°

TRINCULO O, forgive me my sins!

STEPHANO He that dies pays all debts: I defy thee. Mercy upon us!

CALIBAN Art thou afeard?

STEPHANO No, monster, not I.

CALIBAN Be not afeard; the isle is full of noises,°
Sounds and sweet airs, that give delight, and hurt not.
Sometimes a thousand twangling instruments
Will° hum about mine ears; and sometime voices,
That, if I then had waked° after long sleep,

nonpareil without an equal
plot in the modern sense; but *plot* was also the summary of a play's action
troll the catch sing the round
while-ere a short time ago
any reason anything within reason
scout on first occurrence F reads *cout* (jeer at), which is possible
Thought is free thought can't be censored (proverbial)
tabor little drum
picture of Nobody Personifying Nobody was a very old joke, and pictures of Nobody usually consist of empty suits of clothes.
take it as thou list take it anyway you like (old saying: "the devil take it")
noises music
Will . . . had waked . . . Will . . . methought . . . waked . . . cried Note illogical sequence of tenses for special effect.

Will° make me sleep again: and then, in dreaming,
The clouds methought° would open; and show riches
Ready to drop upon me; that, when I waked,°
I cried° to dream again.

STEPHANO This will prove a brave kingdom to me, where I shall have my music for nothing.

CALIBAN When Prospero is destroyed.

STEPHANO That shall be by and by: I remember the story.

TRINCULO The sound is going away; let's follow it, and after do our work.

STEPHANO Lead, monster; we'll follow. I would I could see this taborer; he lays it on.

TRINCULO Wilt come?° I'll follow, Stephano. *Exeunt.*

SCENE III [*Another part of the Island.*]

Enter ALONSO, SEBASTIAN, ANTONIO, GONZALO, ADRIAN, FRANCISCO, etc.

GONZALO By 'r lakin,° I can go no further, sir;
My old bones ache: here's a maze trod, indeed,
Through forth-rights° and meanders!° By your patience,
I needs must rest me.

ALONSO Old lord, I cannot blame thee,
Who am myself attached° with weariness,
To the dulling of my spirits:° sit down, and rest.
Even here I will put off° my hope, and keep it
No longer for my flatterer: he is drowned
Whom thus we stray to find; and the sea mocks
Our frustrate° search on land. Well, let him go.

ANTONIO [*Aside to* SEBASTIAN] I am right glad that he's so out of hope.
Do not, for one repulse, forego the purpose
That you resolved to effect.

SEBASTIAN [*Aside to* ANTONIO] The next advantage
Will we take throughly.°

ANTONIO [*Aside to* SEBASTIAN] Let it be tonight;
For, now they are oppressed with travel, they
Will not, nor cannot, use such vigilance
As when they are fresh.

SEBASTIAN [*Aside to* ANTONIO] I say, tonight: no more.

Solemn and strange music; and PROSPER *on the top*° (*invisible*).° *Enter several strange Shapes, bringing in a banquet;*° *and dance about it with gentle actions of salutations; and inviting the King, etc., to eat,*° *they depart.*

Wilt come? addressed to Caliban
lakin "Ladykin," i.e. the Virgin Mary
forth-rights straight paths
meanders winding paths
attached seized
spirits vital powers
put off divest myself of
frustrate vain
throughly thoroughly
on the top on the upper stage, or possibly in a higher place
(**invisible**) not, of course, to the audience
banquet a light meal; stage magicians often conjured up banquets
to eat Banquets could stand allegorically for all voluptuous temptation and for that which the virtuous man would refuse to partake of.

ALONSO What harmony is this? My good friends, hark!
GONZALO Marvellous sweet music!
ALONSO Give us kind keepers,° heavens!—What were these?
SEBASTIAN A living drollery.° Now I will believe
That there are unicorns; that in Arabia
There is one tree, the phoenix' throne; one phoenix°
at this hour reigning there.
ANTONIO I'll believe both;
And what does else want credit,° come to me,
And I'll be sworn 'tis true: travellers ne'er did lie,°
Though fools at home condemn 'em.
GONZALO If in Naples
I should report this now, would they believe me?
If I should say, I saw such islanders,—
For, certes,° these are people of the island,—
Who, though they are of monstrous° shape, yet, note,
Their manners° are more gentle, kind, than of
Our human generation you shall find
Many, nay, almost any.
PROSPERO [*Aside*] Honest° lord,
Thou hast said well; for some of you there present
Are worse than devils.
ALONSO I cannot too much muse°
Such shapes, such gesture, and such sound, expressing—
Although they want the use of tongue—a kind
Of excellent dumb discourse.
PROSPERO [*Aside*] Praise in departing.°
FRANCISCO They vanished strangely.
SEBASTIAN No matter, since
They have left their viands° behind; for we have stomachs.°—
Will it please you taste of what is here?
ALONSO Not I.
GONZALO Faith, sir, you need not fear. When we were boys,
Who would believe that there were mountaineers
Dew-lapped like bulls, whose throats had hanging at 'em
Wallets of flesh?° or that there were such men
Whose heads stood in their breasts?° which now we find

keepers guardian angels
living drollery puppet show in which the figures are alive
unicorns . . . phoenix frequent wonders in travelers' tales, myth, and folklore. There was only one Phoenix, in the "sole Arabian tree"; it renewed itself from the ashes of its funeral pyre.
want credit is difficult to believe
travellers . . . lie The lies of travelers were famous.
certes certainly
monstrous unnatural
manners in a wider sense than ours
Honest honorable
muse wonder at
Praise in departing "don't praise your host till the entertainment's over" (proverbial)
viands food
stomachs appetites
Wallets of flesh exaggerated account of goiter found in some mountain areas; "wallet" is cognate with "wattle"
heads . . . breasts These monsters go back beyond Mandeville to Pliny; and Othello on his travels met "men whose heads / Do grow beneath their shoulders."

Each putter-out of five for one° will bring us
Good warrant of.

ALONSO I will stand to, and feed,
Although my last: no matter, since I feel
The best° is past. Brother, my lord the duke,
Stand to, and do as we.

Thunder and lightning. Enter ARIEL *like a Harpy;° claps his wings upon the table; and, with a quaint device,° the banquet vanishes.*

ARIEL You are three men of sin, whom Destiny,—
That hath to instrument° this lower world
And what is in it,—the never-surfeited° sea
Hath caused to belch up you; and on this island,
Where man doth not inhabit,—you 'mongst men
Being most unfit to live. I have made you mad;
And even with such-like valour° men hang and drown
Their proper° selves.

ALONSO, SEBASTIAN, *etc., draw their swords.*

You fools! I and my fellows
Are ministers° of Fate: the elements,
Of whom your swords are tempered, may as well
Wound the loud winds, or with bemocked-at-stabs
Kill the still-closing° waters, as diminish
One dowle° that's in my plume: my fellow-ministers
Are like° invulnerable.° If° you could hurt,
Your swords are now too massy° for your strengths,
And will not be uplifted. But remember—
For that's my business to you—that you three
From Milan did supplant good Prospero:
Exposed unto the sea, which hath requit° it,
Him and his innocent child: for which foul deed
The powers, delaying, not forgetting, have
Incensed the seas and shores, yea, all the creatures,°
Against your peace. Thee of thy son, Alonso,
They have bereft; and do pronounce by me

putter-out . . . one Travelers could take out a form of insurance, leaving a premium which would be forfeited if they failed to return, but which would be repaid fivefold if they came back with proof that they had reached the stated destination.
best best part of my life
Harpy In Virgil's *Aeneid* III.255 ff. harpies devour and befoul the food of Aeneas and his friends, and the harpy Celaeno speaks a prophecy on which Ariel's is ultimately based; allegorically the harpy confronted a man with his guilty past.
quaint device ingenious contrivance. Perhaps Ariel, descending in a "machine," covered the table with his wings, and a stagehand, concealed under the table, removed a panel and whisked the banquet out of sight below.
to instrument as its instrument
never-surfeited A surfeit—eating too much—would be a normal cause of belching up, but the sea is always hungry, and a special intervention of Destiny was necessary to cause it to vomit forth the "men of sin" on this occasion.
such-like valour a false courage, of the kind that leads people to suicide
proper own
ministers agents
still-closing that always close up again
dowle small feather
like likewise
invulnerable as were Virgil's harpies
If even if
massy heavy
requit paid back
Incensed roused
creatures created things

Ling'ring perdition°—worse than any death
Can be at once—shall step by step attend
You and your ways; whose wraths to guard you from—
Which here, in this most desolate isle, else° falls°
Upon your heads,—is nothing but heart-sorrow
And a clear° life ensuing.

He vanishes in thunder; then, to soft music, enter the Shapes again, and dance, with mocks and mows,° and carrying out the table.

PROSPERO Bravely° the figure of this Harpy hast thou
Performed, my Ariel; a grace it had devouring: °
Of my instruction hast thou nothing bated°
In what thou hadst to say: so, with good life°
And observation strange,° my meaner ministers°
Their several kinds have done.° My high charms work,
And these mine enemies are all knit up
In their distractions:° they now are in my power;
And in these fits I leave them, while I visit
Young Ferdinand,—whom they suppose is drowned,—
And his and mine loved darling. *Exit.*

GONZALO I' the name of something holy, sir, why stand you
In this strange stare?

ALONSO O, it is monstrous, monstrous!
Methought the billows spoke, and told me of it;
The winds did sing it to me; and the thunder,
That deep and dreadful organ-pipe, pronounced
The name of Prosper: it did bass my trespass.°
Therefor my son i' the ooze° is bedded; and
I'll seek him deeper than e'er plummet sounded,
And with him there lie mudded. *Exit.*

SEBASTIAN But one fiend at a time,
I'll fight their legions o'er.°

ANTONIO I'll be thy second.

Exeunt SEBASTIAN *and* ANTONIO.

GONZALO All three of them are desperate: their great guilt,
Like poison given to work a great time after,°
Now 'gins to bite the spirit. I do beseech you,

Ling'ring perdition slow wasting away
else otherwise
falls fall
clear blameless
mocks and mows mocking gestures and grimaces
Bravely finely
a grace . . . devouring either: it was graceful in the act of devouring the banquet (Virgil's harpies do so, but Ariel presumably merely caused it to disappear); or: it had a devouring (ravishing) grace
bated left out
good life a comment on Ariel's powers as an actor
observation strange unusual attentiveness
meaner ministers the spirits, subservient to Ariel, who played in the banquet scene
Their . . . done have performed the tasks their natures suited them for
knit up . . . distractions entangled in their madness
bass my trespass provide the bass part in the chorus in which nature described my sin
ooze sea mud
o'er to the last
Like poison . . . after The Elizabethan was credulous about poisons, especially in the hands of Italians, and it was thought possible that there were some that acted after a long interval.

That are of suppler joints, follow them swiftly,
And hinder them from what this ecstasy°
May now provoke them to.

ADRIAN Follow, I pray you. *Exeunt omnes.*

ACT IV

SCENE I [*Before* PROSPERO'*s Cell.*]

Enter PROSPERO, FERDINAND, *and* MIRANDA.

PROSPERO If I have too austerely punished you,
Your compensation makes amends; for I
Have given you here a third of mine own life,°
Or that for which I live; who once again
I tender° to thy hand: all thy vexations
Were but my trials of thy love, and thou
Hast strangely° stood the test: here, afore Heaven,
I ratify this my rich gift. O Ferdinand,
Do not smile at me that I boast her off,°
For thou shalt find she will outstrip all praise,
And make it halt° behind her.

FERDINAND I do believe it
Against an oracle.°

PROSPERO Then, as my gift,° and thine own acquisition
Worthily purchased,° take my daughter: but
If thou dost break her virgin-knot° before
All sanctimonious° ceremonies may
With full and holy rite be ministered,
No sweet aspersion° shall the heavens let fall
To make this contract grow;° but barren hate,
Sour-eyed disdain and discord shall bestrew°
The union of your bed with weeds so loathly
That you shall hate it both: therefore take heed,
As Hymen's lamp shall light you.°

FERDINAND As I hope
For quiet days, fair issue° and long life,

ecstasy madness
a third . . . life Either he thinks of Miranda, his dead wife, and himself as the whole; or Miranda, Milan, and himself; or that he has spent a third of his life bringing up Miranda; or that he has a third of his life to come, and that Miranda alone gives it value.
tender hand over
strangely wonderfully well
boast her off cry up her praises
halt limp
Against an oracle even if an oracle should declare otherwise
gift F: *guest*
purchased earned, won
break her virgin-knot take her maidenhead; from the symbolic loosening of the girdle in Roman custom, *virgineam dissoluit zonam,* "he untied her virgin belt or girdle"
sanctimonious holy
aspersion sprinkling (ritual sense)
grow into a happy and fruitful marriage
bestrew flowers—not weeds—were customarily scattered on the bridal bed
As . . . light you as you hope that the torch of the marriage god will burn clear as a good omen at your marriage; F has *lamps*
issue children

With such love as 'tis now, the murkiest den,
The most opportune place, the strong'st suggestion°
Our worser genius° can,° shall never melt
Mine honour into lust, to° take away
The edge of that day's celebration
When I shall think, or° Phoebus' steeds are foundered,°
Or Night kept chained below.°

PROSPERO Fairly spoke.
Sit, then, and talk with her; she is thine own.
What, Ariel! my industrious servant, Ariel!

Enter ARIEL.

ARIEL What would my potent master? here I am.

PROSPERO Thou and thy meaner fellows your last service
Did worthily perform; and I must use you
In such another trick.° Go bring the rabble,°
O'er whom I give thee power, here to this place:
Incite them to quick motion; for I must
Bestow upon the eyes of this young couple
Some vanity° of mine Art: it is my promise,
And they expect it from me.

ARIEL Presently?°

PROSPERO Ay, with a twink.°

ARIEL Before you can say, 'come,' and 'go,'
And breathe twice, and cry, 'so, so,'
Each one, tripping on his toe,
Will be here with mop and mow.°
Do you love me, master? no?

PROSPERO Dearly, my delicate Ariel. Do not approach
Till thou dost hear me call.

ARIEL Well, I conceive.° *Exit.*

PROSPERO Look thou be true;° do not give dalliance°
Too much the rein: the strongest oaths are straw
To the fire in' the blood: be more abstemious,
Or else, good night your vow!

FERDINAND I warrant you, sir;
The white cold virgin snow upon my heart
Abates the ardour of my liver.°

PROSPERO Well.
Now come, my Ariel! bring a corollary,°

suggestion temptation
worser genius bad angel; everybody had a good one and a bad one
can is capable of
to so as to
or either
foundered gone lame
below below the horizon, from which it ascends at sunset
trick magic device
rabble the inferior spirits
vanity trifle
Presently at once
with a twink in the twinkling of an eye
mop and mow grin and grimace
conceive understand
true faithful to your promise
dalliance lovemaking
liver thought to be the seat of the passion of love
corollary extra man, supernumerary

Rather than want° a spirit: appear, and pertly!°
No tongue! all eyes! be silent. *Soft music.*

Enter IRIS.°

IRIS *Ceres, most bounteous lady, thy rich leas°*
Of wheat, rye, barley, vetches, oats, and pease;
Thy turfy mountains, where live nibbling sheep,
And flat meads thatched with stover,° them to keep;
Thy banks with pionèd and twillèd° brims,
Which spongy April° at thy hest betrims,°
To make cold° nymphs chaste crowns; and thy broom-groves,°
Whose shadow the dismissèd bachelor° loves,
Being lass-lorn;° thy pole-clipt° vinëyard;
And thy sea-marge,° sterile and rocky-hard,
Where thou thyself dost air;—the queen o' th' sky,
Whose wat'ry arch° and messenger° am I,
Bids thee leave these;° and with her sovereign grace,

JUNO *descends.°*

Here, on this grass-plot, in this very place,
To come and sport:—her peacocks° fly amain:°
Approach, rich Ceres, her to entertain.

Enter CERES.

CERES *Hail, many-coloured messenger, that ne'er*
Dost disobey the wife of Jupiter;
Who, with thy saffron° wings, upon my flowers
Diffusest honey-drops, refreshing showers;
And with each end of thy blue bow dost crown
My bosky° acres and my unshrubbed down,°
Rich scarf to my proud earth; why hath thy queen
Summoned me hither, to this short-grassed green?

IRIS *A contract of true love to celebrate;*
And some donation° freely to estate°
On the blest lovers.

want lack
pertly smartly
Enter Iris What follows is a reduced form of court masque appropriate to a betrothal; it cannot end, as masques should, with a dance involving the spectators; however, it is what was called a "show," as was the spectacular episode in III.iii.
Ceres goddess of grain and harvest
leas meadows
thatched . . . stover covered with a growth of grass used as winter fodder.
pionèd and twillèd Meaning is uncertain but most likely man-made embankments with branches laid criss-cross on the top.
spongy April April is traditionally a showery month.
betrims adorns
cold sexually pure
broom-groves gorse-clumps (perhaps)
dismissèd bachelor rejected lover
lass-lorn deprived of his girl
pole-clipt pruned
sea-marge seashore
wat'ry arch rainbow
messenger Iris traditionally had this role.
these the places mentioned
Juno descends presumably begins her descent from the roof
peacocks sacred to Juno, whose chariot they drew
amain swiftly
saffron yellow
bosky wooded
unshrubbed down hilly country without trees
donation gift
estate bestow

CERES *Tell me, heavenly bow,*
If Venus or her son, as thou dost know,
Do now attend the queen? Since they did plot
The means that dusky Dis° my daughter got,
Her and her blind boy's° scandalled° company
I have forsworn.

IRIS *Of her society*
Be not afraid: I met her deity
Cutting the clouds towards Paphos,° and her son
Dove-drawn° with her. Here thought they to have done
Some wanton charm upon this man and maid,
Whose vows are, that no bed-right shall be paid°
Till Hymen's torch be lighted: but in vain;
Mars's hot minion° is returned again;
Her waspish-headed° son has broke his arrows,
Swears he will shoot no more, but play with sparrows,°
And be a boy right out.°

CERES *Highest queen of state,*
Great Juno comes; I know her by her gait.

JUNO *How does my bounteous sister? Go with me*
To bless this twain, that they may prosperous be,
And honoured in their issue.

They sing:

JUNO *Honour, riches, marriage-blessing,*
Long continuance, and increasing,
Hourly joys be still° upon you!
Juno sings her blessings on you.

CERES *Earth's increase, foison° plenty,*
Barns and garners never empty;
Vines with clust'ring bunches growing;
Plants with goodly burthen bowing;
Spring come to you at the farthest
In the very end of harvest!°
Scarcity and want shall shun you;
Ceres' blessing so is on you.

FERDINAND This is a most majestic vision, and
Harmonious charmingly. May I be bold
To think these spirits?

dusky Dis Pluto; dusky because king of the underworld; he abducted Persephone (Proserpina in Latin) to be his queen for half the year
blind boy's Cupid's
scandalled tainted with scandal, disgraceful
Paphos center of the cult of Venus, in Cyprus
Dove-drawn doves were sacred to Venus and drew her chariot
bed-right . . . paid marital intercourse take place
hot minion lustful mistress
waspish-headed peevish
sparrows also associated with Venus, and thought to be lustful
right out outright, altogether
still always
foison harvest
Spring . . . harvest i.e. may you have no winter

PROSPERO Spirits, which by mine Art
I have from their confines° called to enact
My present fancies.°

FERDINAND Let me live here ever;
So rare a wondered father and a wise°
Makes this place Paradise.

JUNO and CERES whisper, and send IRIS on employment.

Sweet, now, silence!
Juno and Ceres whisper seriously;
There's something else to do: hush, and be mute,
Or else our spell is marred.

IRIS *You nymphs, called Naiads, of the windring° brooks,*
With your sedged crowns° and ever-harmless looks,
Leave your crisp° channels, and on this green land
Answer your summons; Juno does command:
Come, temperate° nymphs, and help to celebrate
A contract of true love; be not too late.

Enter certain NYMPHS.

You sunburned sicklemen,° of August weary,
Come hither from the furrow, and be merry:
Make holiday; your rye-straw hats put on,
And these fresh° nymphs encounter every one
In country footing.°

Enter certain Reapers, properly habited: they join with the Nymphs in a graceful dance; towards the end whereof PROSPERO starts suddenly, and speaks; after which, to a strange, hollow, and confused noise, they heavily° vanish.

PROSPERO [*Aside*] I had forgot that foul conspiracy
Of the beast Caliban and his confederates
Against my life: the minute of their plot
Is almost come. [*To the SPIRITS*] Well done! avoid;° no more!

FERDINAND This is strange: your father's in some passion
That works° him strongly.

MIRANDA Never till this day
Saw I him touched with anger, so distempered.

PROSPERO You do look, my son, in a moved sort,°
As if you were dismayed: be cheerful, sir.
Our revels° now are ended. These our actors,

confines natural limits
fancies imaginative entertainments
wondered . . . wise father so to be wondered at (or so capable of producing wonders) and also wise (some copies of F have *wife*, which creates an analogy between the island and the Garden of Eden, with Prospero as God the Father and Miranda as Eve)
windring portmanteau of "wandering" and "winding"
sedged crowns garlands of sedge
crisp covered with little waves
temperate chaste (which is why Naiads, nymphs of the cool water, are summoned)
sicklemen reapers
fresh young
encounter . . . footing partner in a country dance
heavily dejectedly
avoid begone
works agitates
moved sort troubled state
revels common name for such entertainments

As I foretold you, were all spirits, and
Are melted into air, into thin air:
And, like the baseless fabric° of this vision,
The cloud-capped towers, the gorgeous palaces,
The solemn temples, the great globe itself,
Yea, all which it inherit,° shall dissolve,
And, like this insubstantial pageant° faded,
Leave not a rack° behind. We are such stuff
As dreams are made on;° and our little life
Is rounded with° a sleep. Sir, I am vexed;°
Bear with my weakness; my old brain is troubled:
Be not disturbed with my infirmity:
If you be pleased, retire into my cell,
And there repose: a turn or two I'll walk,
To still my beating° mind.

FERDINAND, MIRANDA We wish your peace. *Exeunt.*

PROSPERO Come with a thought.° I thank thee. Ariel: come.

Enter ARIEL.

ARIEL Thy thoughts I cleave to.° What's thy pleasure?

PROSPERO Spirit,
We must prepare to meet with Caliban.

ARIEL Ay, my commander: when I presented° Ceres,
I thought to have told thee of it; but I feared
Lest I might anger thee.

PROSPERO Say again, where didst thou leave these varlets?°

ARIEL I told you, sir, they were red-hot with drinking;
So full of valour that they smote the air
For breathing in their faces; beat the ground
For kissing of their feet; yet always bending°
Towards their project. Then I beat my tabor;
At which, like unbacked° colts, they pricked their ears,
Advanced° their eyelids, lifted up their noses
As° they smelt music: so I charmed their ears,
That, calf-like, they my lowing followed, through
Toothed briers, sharp furzes, pricking goss,° and thorns,
Which entered their frail shins: at last I left them
I' the filthy-mantled° pool beyond your cell,
There dancing up to the chins, that the foul lake

baseless fabric structure without foundation. The comparison that follows between "revels" and the whole world was an old commonplace, here given powerful elegiac expression; cf. Spenser, *Amoretti,* Sonnet 54.
inherit possess, occupy
pageant term applied to elaborate and temporary allegorical show
rack cloud
on of
rounded with rounded off by; or, crowned with
vexed emotionally troubled
beating agitated
Come with a thought Prospero has only to think his wish that Ariel should come.
Thy thoughts . . . cleave to Ariel confirms this.
presented acted the part of Ceres; or, as Iris, the "presenter" of the masque, introduced Ceres
varlets rascals
bending directly their way
unbacked unbroken
Advanced opened
As As if
goss gorse
filthy-mantled covered with filthy scum

O'erstunk their feet.°
PROSPERO This was well done, my bird.
Thy shape invisible retain thou still:
The trumpery° in my house, go bring it hither,
For stale° to catch these thieves.
ARIEL I go, I go. *Exit.*
PROSPERO A devil, a born devil, on whose nature
Nurture° can never stick; on whom my pains,
Humanely taken, all, all lost, quite lost;
And as with age his body uglier grows,
So his mind cankers.° I will plague them all,
Even to roaring.

Re-enter ARIEL, *loaden with glistering apparel, etc.*

Come, hang them on this line.°
PROSPERO *and* ARIEL *remain, invisible.*

Enter CALIBAN, STEPHANO, *and* TRINCULO, *all wet.*

CALIBAN Pray you, tread softly, that the blind mole may not
Hear a foot fall: we now are near his cell.

STEPHANO Monster, your fairy, which you say is a harmless fairy, has done little better than played the Jack° with us.
with us.

TRINCULO Monster, I do smell all horse-piss; at which my nose is in great indignation.

STEPHANO So is mine. Do you hear, monster? If I should take displeasure against you, look you,—

TRINCULO Thou wert but a lost monster.

CALIBAN Good my lord, give me thy favour still.
Be patient, for the prize I'll bring thee to
Shall hoodwink this mischance:° therefore speak softly.
All's hushed as midnight yet.

TRINCULO Ay, but to lose our bottles in the pool,—

STEPHANO There is not only disgrace and dishonour in that, monster, but an infinite loss.

TRINCULO That's more to me than my wetting: yet this is your harmless fairy, monster.

STEPHAN I will fetch off my bottle, though I be o'er ears for my labour.

CALIBAN Prithee, my King, be quiet. Seest thou here,
This is the mouth o' the cell: no noise, and enter.
Do that good mischief which may make this island
Thine own for ever, and I, thy Caliban,
For aye thy foot-licker.

O'erstunk their feet smelled worse than their feet
trumpery rubbishy clothes
stale bait, decoy
Nurture education, civility
cankers grows diseased
line lime-tree
played the Jack played the knave; played the jack o' lantern (will-o'-the-wisp)
hoodwink this mischance put this mischance out of sight

STEPHANO Gives me thy hand. I do begin to have bloody thoughts.

TRINCULO O King Stephano! O peer! O worthy Stephano!° look what a wardrobe here is for thee!

CALIBAN Let it alone, thou fool; it is but trash.

TRINCULO O, ho, monster! we know what belongs to a frippery.° O King Stephano!

STEPHANO Put off that gown, Trinculo; by this hand, I'll have that gown.

TRINCULO Thy grace shall have it.

CALIBAN The dropsy drown this fool!° what do you mean
To dote thus on such luggage?° Let 't° alone,
And do the murther first: if he awake,
From toe to crown he'll fill our skins with pinches,
Make us strange stuff.°

STEPHANO Be you quiet, monster. Mistress line, is not this my jerkin? Now is the jerkin under the line: now, jerkin, you are like to lose your hair, and prove a bald jerkin.°

TRINCULO Do, do;° we steal by line and level,° an't like your grace.

STEPHANO I thank thee for that jest; here's a garment for it: wit shall not go unrewarded while I am King of this country. 'Steal by line and level' is an excellent pass of pate;° there's another garment for it.

TRINCULO Monster, come, put some lime° upon your fingers, and away with the rest.

CALIBAN I will have none on it: we shall lose our time,
And all be turned to barnacles,° or to apes
With foreheads villainous° low.

STEPHANO Monster, lay-to your fingers: help to bear this away where my hogshead of wine is, or I'll turn you out of my kingdom: go to, carry this.

TRINCULO And this.

STEPHANO Ay, and this.

A noise of hunters heard. Enter divers Spirits, in shape of dogs and hound, hunting them about; PROSPERO *and* ARIEL *setting them on.*

PROSPERO Hey, Mountain, hey!

ARIEL Silver! there it goes, Silver!

PROSPERO Fury, Fury! there, Tyrant,° there! hark, hark!

CALIBAN, STEPHANO, *and* TRINCULO *are driven out.*

Go charge my goblins that they grind their joints

O King . . . Stephano refers to old ballad "King Stephen was a worthy peer," which Iago sings in *Othello*.
frippery old-clothes shop. Trinculo is saying he knows the contents of such shops, and denies that these clothes are of that kind.
The dropsy . . . fool Dropsy is an excessive accumulation of fluid in the body. Caliban wants him to drown internally since he escaped drowning in the sea.
luggage encumbrance
Let't F has "let's"
strange stuff when he's done with us we'll look even stranger than the clothes
Now is . . . bald jerkin The jerkin is under the tree (line=equator) and diseases contracted in the tropics caused loss of hair.
Do, do expressing some kind of amusement at the joke?
steal . . . level according to the rule, systematically (carrying on the punning on *line*)
an't like if it please
pass of pate thrust of wit
lime birdline
barnacles a kind of geese, supposed to hatch from barnacles on ships' timbers
villainous wretchedly
Mountain . . . Silver . . . Fury . . . Tyrant names of hounds

With dry convulsions;° shorten up their sinews
With aged cramps;° and more pinch-spotted° make them
Than pard° or cat o' mountain.°

ARIEL Hark, they roar!

PROSPERO Let them be hunted soundly. At this hour
Lies° at my mercy all mine enemies:
Shortly shall all my labours end, and thou
Shalt have the air at freedom: for a little
Follow, and do me service. *Exeunt.*

ACT V

SCENE I [*Before the Cell of* PROSPERO.]

Enter PROSPERO *in his magic robes, and* ARIEL.

PROSPERO Now does my project gather to a head:°
My charms crack not;° my spirits obey; and time
Goes upright with his carriage.° How's the day?

ARIEL On the sixth hour; at which time, my lord,
You said our work should cease.

PROSPERO I did say so,
When first I raised the tempest. Say, my spirit,
How fares the King and his followers?

ARIEL Confined together
In the same fashion as you gave in charge,
Just as you left them; all prisoners, sir,
In the line-grove which weather-fends° your cell;
They cannot budge till your release.° The King,
His brother, and yours, abide all three distracted.
And the remainder mourning over them,
Brimful of sorrow and dismay; but chiefly
Him that you termed, sir, 'The good old lord, Gonzalo';
His tears runs° down his beard, like winter's drops
From eaves of reeds.° Your charm so strongly works° 'em,
That if you now beheld them, your affections
Would become tender.

PROSPERO Dost thou think so, spirit?

ARIEL Mine would, sir, were I human.°

PROSPERO And mine shall.
Hast thou, which art but air, a touch, a feeling
Of their afflictions, and shall not myself,

dry convulsions convulsions in which bone grinds on bone
aged cramps cramps such as the aged suffer
pinch-spotted bruised all over with pinches from the goblins
pard leopard
cat' o' mountain catamount, lynx
Lies lie
project . . . head experiment reach its final phase (alchemical)
crack not don't go wrong (the alchemist's retort might "crack" at this point)
time . . . carriage time's burden is light; we are near the end
weather-fends protects from the weather
your release you release them
runs run
reeds a thatched roof
works moves, agitates
were I human Ariel, a spirit of air, can only imagine human feelings.

One of their kind, that relish all as sharply
Passion as they,° be kindlier° moved than thou art?
Though with their high wrongs° I am struck to the quick,
Yet with my nobler° reason 'gainst my fury
Do I take part: the rarer° action is
In virtue° than in vengeance: they being penitent,
The sole drift of my purpose doth extend
Not a frown further.° Go release them, Ariel:
My charms I'll break, their senses I'll restore,
And they shall be themselves.

ARIEL I'll fetch them, sir. *Exit.*

PROSPERO Ye elves° of hills, brooks, standing lakes, and groves;
And ye that on the sands with printless foot°
Do chase the ebbing Neptune,° and do fly him
When he comes back; you demi-puppets° that
By moonshine do the green sour ringlets° make,
Whereof the ewe not bites; and you whose pastime
Is to make midnight mushrooms,° that rejoice
To hear the solemn curfew;° by whose aid—
Weak masters° though ye be—I have bedimmed
The noontide sun, called forth the mutinous winds,
And 'twixt the green sea and the azured vault°
Set roaring war: to the dread rattling thunder
Have I given fire, and rifted Jove's stout oak
With his own bolt; the strong-based promontory
Have I made shake, and by the spurs° plucked up
The pine and cedar: graves at my command
Have waked their sleepers, oped, and let 'em forth
By my so potent Art. But this rough magic
I here abjure; and, when I have required
Some heavenly music,—which even now I do,—
To work mine end upon their senses, that
This airy charm is for, I'll brake my staff,
Bury it certain fadoms in the earth,
And deeper than did ever plummet sound
I'll drown my book.° *Solemn music.*

Re-enter ARIEL *before: then* ALONSO, *with a frantic gesture,° attended by* GONZALO; SEBASTIAN *and* ANTONIO *in like manner, attended by* ADRIAN

relish . . . they am wholly as sensitive as they to suffering
kindlier more suitably to human nature
high wrongs great injuries inflicted on me
nobler i.e. nobler than passion
rarer finer
virtue as contrasted with *vengeance,* the Christian virtue of forgiveness
Not a frown further no further than I have gone, not by so much as a look of displeasure
Ye elves . . . ll. 33–58. In this farewell to magic Shakespeare paraphrases very closely Ovid, *Metamorphoses* VII.197–209, using the original as well as Golding's translation.
printless foot foot that leaves no print
Neptune ocean
demi-puppets quasi-puppets; elves the size of puppets
green sour ringlets "fairy rings," caused by mycelium under the surface. Apparently sheep do not avoid them.
mushrooms grow overnight, so their nurture is attributed to elves
curfew After curfew tolls, spirits and elves can walk abroad.
masters the magician's demonic agents
azured vault blue sky
spurs roots
book which is necessary to his magic
gesture demeanor

and FRANCISCO: *they all enter the circle which* PROSPERO *had made, and there stand charmed; which* PROSPERO *observing, speaks:*

A solemn air, and the best comforter
To an unsettled fancy, cure thy brains,
Now useless, boiled° within thy skull! There stand,
For you are spell-stopped.
Holy Gonzalo, honourable man,
Mine eyes, even sociable to the show of thine,
Fall fellowly drops.° The charm dissolves apace;
And as the morning steals upon the night,
Melting the darkness, so their rising senses
Begin to chase the ignorant fumes that mantle°
Their clearer reason. O good Gonzalo,
My true preserver, and a loyal sir
To him thou follow'st! I will pay° thy graces
Home° both in word and deed. Most cruelly
Didst thou, Alonso, use me and my daughter:
Thy brother was a furtherer in the act.
Thou art pinched for it now, Sebastian. Flesh and blood,
You, brother mine, that entertained° ambition,
Expelled remorse and nature; whom,° with Sebastian—
Whose inward pinches therefore are most strong—
Would here have killed your King; I do forgive thee,
Unnatural though thou art. Their understanding
Begins to swell;° and the approaching tide
Will shortly fill the reasonable shore,°
That now lie° foul and muddy. Not one of them
That yet looks on me, or would know me: Ariel,
Fetch me the hat and rapier in my cell:
I will discase me,° and myself present
As I was sometime° Milan:° quickly, spirit;

ARIEL *sings and helps to attire him.*

Thou shalt ere long be free.

Where the bee sucks, there suck I:
In a cowslip's bell lie;
There I couch° when owls do cry.
On the bat's back I do fly
After summer° merrily.
Merrily, merrily shall I live now
Under the blossom that hangs on the bough.

boiled seething; F: *boile*
Mine eyes . . . drops my eyes, in sympathy with the tears visible in yours, let fall sympathetic drops
mantle shroud, obscure
pay repay
Home thoroughly
entertained welcomed
whom who
swell rise like the tide
reasonable shore shore of reason, now empty and dry
lie lies
discase me take off my cloak
sometime formerly
Milan Duke of Milan
couch lie
After summer in pursuit of summer

Where the bee sucks there suck I In a cow-slip's
bell I lie; There I couch when owls do cry, on the
bat's back I do fly, af-ter sum-mer mer-ri-ly
Mer-ri-ly Mer-ri-ly Shall I live now
un-der the blos-som that hangs on the bough.
Mer-ri-ly, Mer-ri-ly shall I live now,

This setting of "Where the Bee Sucks" is by Robert Johnson. (See Note on "Full Fadom Five," Act I, Scene II.)

PROSPERO Why, that's my dainty Ariel! I shall miss thee;
But yet thou shalt have freedom: so, so, so.
To the King's ship, invisible as thou art:
There shalt thou find the mariners asleep
Under the hatches; the master and the boatswain
Being awake,° enforce them to this place,
And presently, I prithee.

ARIEL I drink the air° before me, and return
Or ere your pulse twice beat. *Exit.*

GONZALO All torment, trouble, wonder and amazement
Inhabits here: some heavenly power guide us
Out of this fearful country!

PROSPERO Behold, sir King,
The wrongèd Duke of Milan, Prospero:
For more assurance° that a living Prince
Does now speak to thee, I embrace thy body;
And to thee and thy company I bid
A hearty welcome.

ALONSO Whether° thou be'st he or no,
Or some enchanted trifle° to abuse° me,
As late I have been, I not know: thy pulse
Beats, as of flesh and blood; and, since I saw thee,
The affliction of my mind amends, with which,
I fear, a madness held me: this must crave—
An if this be at all—a most strange story.
Thy dukedom I resign, and do entreat
Thou pardon me my wrongs.—But how should Prospero
Be living and be here?

PROSPERO First, noble friend,
Let me embrace thine age, whose honour cannot
Be measured or confined.

GONZALO Whether this be
Or be not, I'll not swear.

PROSPERO You do yet taste

Being awake having awakened them
drink the air devour the way
For more assurance to make thee more sure
Whether F: *Where*
enchanted trifle apparition raised by an enchanter
abuse delude, deceive

Some subtleties° o' the isle, that will not let you
Believe things certain.° Welcome, my friends all!
[*Aside to* SEBASTIAN *and* ANTONIO] But you, my brace of lords, were I so minded,
I here could pluck° his highness' frown upon you,
And justify° you traitors: at this time
I will tell no tales.

SEBASTIAN [*Aside*] The devil speaks in him.

PROSPERO No.
For you, most wicked sir, whom to call brother
Would even infect my mouth, I do forgive
Thy rankest fault,—all of them; and require
My dukedom of thee, which perforce, I know,
Thou must restore.

ALONSO If thou be'st Prospero,
Give us particulars of thy preservation;
How thou hast met us here, whom three hours since°
Were wracked upon this shore; where I have lost—
How sharp the point of this remembrance is!—
My dear son Ferdinand.

PROSPERO I am woe° for it, sir.

ALONSO Irreparable is the loss; and patience
Says it is past her cure.

PROSPERO I rather think
You have not sought her help, of whose soft grace
For the like loss I have her sovereign° aid,
And rest myself content.

ALONSO You the like loss!

PROSPERO As great to me as late;° and, súpportable
To make the dear° loss, have I means much weaker°
Than you may call to comfort you, for I
Have lost my daughter.

ALONSO A daughter?
O heavens, that they were living both in Naples,
The King and Queen there! that° they were, I wish
Myself were mudded in that oozy bed
Where my son lies. When did you lose your daughter?

PROSPERO In this last tempest. I perceive, these lords
At this encounter do so much admire,°
That they devour their reason,° and scarce think

taste . . . subtleties The normal meaning of *subtleties* is qualified by a secondary sense, "elaborate confections of sugar," hence the word *taste*.
things certain real, non-magical things
pluck bring down
justify prove
three hours since calling attention to the short time taken by the events of the play
woe sorry
sovereign all-healing
As great to me as late as great to me and as recent (as yours to you)
dear heavy
much weaker Alonso has a child left; or, Miranda will live at Naples
that provided that
admire wonder
devour their reason are open-mouthed with wonder

Their eyes do offices of truth,° their words
Are natural breath:° but, howsoe'er you have
Been justled from your senses, know for certain
That I am Prospero, and that very duke
Which was thrust forth of° Milan; who most strangely
Upon this shore, where you were wracked, was landed,
To be the lord on it. No more yet of this;
For 'tis a chronicle of day by day,
Not a relation for a breakfast, nor
Befitting this first meeting. Welcome, sir;
This cell's my court: here have I few attendants,
And subjects none abroad:° pray you, look in.
My dukedom since you have given me again,
I will requite you with as good a thing;
At least bring forth a wonder,° to content ye
As much as me my dukedom.

Here PROSPERO *discovers°* FERDINAND *and* MIRANDA *playing at chess.*

MIRANDA Sweet lord, you play me false.°
FERDINAND No, my dearest love,
I would not for the world.
MIRANDA Yes, for a score of kingdoms you should wrangle,
And I would call it fair play.°
ALONSO If this prove
A vision° of the island, one dear son
Shall I twice lose.
SEBASTIAN A most high miracle!°
FERDINAND Though the seas threaten, they are merciful;
I have cursed them without cause.
ALONSO Now all the blessings
Of a glad father compass thee about!
Arise,° and say how thou cam'st here.
MIRANDA O, wonder!
How many goodly creatures are there here!
How beauteous mankind is! O brave new world,
That has such people in it!
PROSPERO 'Tis new to thee.
ALONSO What is this maid with whom thou wast at play?
Your eld'st° acquaintance cannot be three hours:°
Is she the goddess that hath severed us,
And brought us thus together?
FERDINAND Sir, she is mortal;

do offices of truth report the world truly
natural breath the ordinary speech of human beings
of from
abroad outside this cell, about the island
wonder apparently announcing another "trick," really about to display Miranda (the wonder) and Ferdinand
discovers draws back a curtain to display
play me false cheat me
fair . . . play i.e. if we were playing for a stake of twenty kingdoms you'd cheat and I'd call it fair play
vision illusion
miracle Sebastian has the right reaction.
Arise Ferdinand has knelt for a paternal blessing.
eld'st longest
three hours another reminder

But by immortal Providence she's mine:
I chose her when I could not ask my father
For his advice, nor thought I had one. She
Is daughter to this famous Duke of Milan,
Of whom so often I have heard renown,
But never saw before; of whom I have
Received a second life; and second father
This lady makes him to me.

ALONSO I am hers:°
But, O, how oddly will it sound that I
Must ask my child forgiveness!

PROSPERO There, sir, stop:
Let us not burthen our remembrance'° with
A heaviness° that's gone.

GONZALO I have inly wept,
Or should have spoke ere this. Look down, you gods,
And on this couple drop a blessed crown!
For it is you that have chalked forth° the way
Which brought us hither.

ALONSO I say, Amen, Gonzalo!

GONZALO Was Milan° thrust from Milan, that his issue
Should become Kings of Naples! O, rejoice
Beyond a common joy, and set it down
With gold on lasting pillars: in one voyage
Did Claribel her husband find at Tunis,
And Ferdinand, her brother, found a wife
Where he himself was lost, Prospero his dukedom
In a poor isle, and all of us ourselves
When no man was his own.°

ALONSO [*To* FERDINAND *and* MIRANDA] Give me your hands:
Let grief and sorrow still° embrace° his heart
That doth not wish you joy!

GONZALO Be it so! Amen!

Re-enter ARIEL, *with the Master and Boatswain amazedly following.*

O, look, sir, look, sir! here is more of us:
I prophesied, if a gallows were on land,
This fellow could not drown. Now, blasphemy,°
That swear'st grace o'erboard,° not an oath on shore?
Hast thou no mouth by land? What is the news?

BOATSWAIN The best news is, that we have safely° found
Our King, and company; the next, our ship—

hers her father
remembrance' F: *remembrances*
heaviness sadness
chalked forth marked out
Was . . . (ll. 205–12) Gonzalo, rejoicing that all the ills resulting from the crime against Prospero should be canceled, and good come of them, has a sort of exaltation, and this speech greatly affects the overall tone of the play.
no man was his own nobody was in command of himself; now they have found themselves again
still always
embrace cling to
blasphemy blasphemous fellow
swear'st grace o'erboard by thy profanity drivest grace out of the ship
safely in a state of safety

Which, but three glasses° since, we gave out split—
Is tight and yare° and bravely rigged, as when
We first put out to sea.
ARIEL [*Aside to* PROSPERO] Sir, all this service
Have I done since I went.
PROSPERO [*Aside to* ARIEL] My tricksy° spirit!
ALONSO These are not natural events; they strengthen
From strange to stranger.° Say, how came you hither?
BOATSWAIN If I did think, sir, I were well awake,
I'd strive to tell you. We were dead of sleep,°
And—how we know not—all clapped under hatches;
Where, but even now, with strange and several° noises
Of roaring, shrieking, howling, jingling chains,
And mo° diversity of sounds, all horrible,
We were awaked; straightway, at liberty;°
Where we, in all our trim,° freshly beheld
Our royal, good, and gallant ship; our master
Cap'ring° to eye her:—on a trice,° so please you,
Even in a dream, were we divided from them,
And were brought moping° hither.
ARIEL [*Aside to* PROSPERO] Was it well done?
PROSPERO [*Aside to* ARIEL] Bravely,° my diligence.° Thou shalt be free.
ALONSO This is as strange a maze as e'er men trod;
And there is in this business more than nature
Was ever conduct of:° some oracle°
Must rectify our knowledge.
PROSPERO Sir, my liege,
Do not infest° your mind with beating° on
The strangeness of this business; at picked° leisure
Which shall be shortly single,° I'll resolve you,°
Which to you shall seem probable,° of every
These happened accidents;° till when, be cheerful,
And think of each thing well.° [*Aside to* ARIEL] Come hither, spirit:
Set Caliban and his companions free;
Untie the spell. [*Exit* ARIEL] How fares my gracious sir?
There are yet missing of your company
Some few odd lads that you remember not.

three glasses three hours (another reminder)
yare shipshape, ready for sea
tricksy nimble, clever
strengthen . . . stranger increase in strangeness
of sleep asleep
several separate, different
mo more
at liberty no longer confined under hatches
in all our trim our clothes in good shape; some read *her trim* and refer the phrase to the ship
Cap'ring dancing for joy
on a trice in an instant
moping dazed
Bravely splendidly
diligence diligent one
more . . . of more than unaided nature could arrange
oracle source of more than natural information
infest torment, annoy
beating dwelling agitatedly
picked leisure a free time we shall choose
single continuous
resolve you explain to you
Which . . . probable in a manner you'll accept as plausible
every . . . accidents each one of these occurrences
think . . . well give a favorable interpretation to everything

Re-enter ARIEL, *driving in* CALIBAN, STEPHANO, *and* TRINCULO, *in their stolen apparel.*

STEPHANO Every man shift for all the rest,° and let no man take care for himself; for all is but fortune.—Coragio,° bully-monster, coragio!

TRINCULO If these be true spies° which I wear in my head, here's a goodly sight.

CALIBAN O Setebos, these be brave spirits indeed!
How fine° my master is! I am afraid
He will chastise me.

SEBASTIAN Ha, ha!
What things are these, my lord Antonio?
Will money buy 'em?

ANTONIO Very like; one of them
Is a plain fish, and, no doubt, marketable.

PROSPERO Mark but the badges° of these men, my lords,
Then say if they be true.° This mis-shapen knave,
His mother was a witch; and one so strong
That could control the moon, make flows and ebbs,
And deal in her command, without her power.°
These three have robbed me; and this demi-devil—
For he's a bastard one°—had plotted with them
To take my life. Two of these fellows you
Must know and own;° this thing of darkness I
Acknowledge mine.

CALIBAN I shall be pinched to death.

ALONSO Is not this Stephano, my drunken butler?

SEBASTIAN He is drunk now: where had he wine?

ALONSO And Trinculo is reeling ripe:° where should they
Find this grand liquor that hath gilded 'em?°—
How comest thou in this pickle?°

TRINCULO I have been in such pickle,° since I saw you last, that, I fear me, will never out of my bones: I shall not fear fly-blowing.°

SEBASTIAN Why, how now, Stephano!

STEPHANO O, touch me not;—I am not Stephano, but a cramp.

PROSPERO You'ld be King o' the isle, sirrah?

STEPHANO I should have been a sore° one, then.

ALONSO This is as strange a° thing as e'er I looked on.

Every man . . . rest inversion of the saying, "Every man for himself"
Coragio courage
true spies trustworthy eyes
fine Prospero is magnificently dressed in ducal robes.
badges device indicating to which lord a servant belonged (the stolen clothes are thus a proof of the conspirators' dishonesty)
true honest
deal . . . power act in the moon's sphere of authority with a power beyond that of the moon herself (the witch Medea in Ovid's *Metamorphoses* VII.207 had this power)
demi-devil . . . one Caliban was begotten by the devil on a witch; he is a half-devil and a bastard.
own acknowledge
reeling ripe so drunk he reeled as he walked
grand liquor . . . 'em The "grand liquor" is sack, but here Alonso alludes to the elixir the alchemists make gold; "gilded" refers to this metaphor but also means "flushed."
pickle mess
pickle preservative
fly-blowing being pickled, he is safe from the flies that corrupt fresh meat
sore severe; also aching
as strange a F: *a stranger*

Pointing to CALIBAN.

PROSPERO He is disproportioned in his manners°
As in his shape. Go, sirrah, to my cell;
Take with you your companions; as you look
To have my pardon, trim it handsomely.
CALIBAN Ay, that I will; and I'll be wise hereafter,
And seek for grace.° What a thrice-double ass
Was I, to take this drunkard for a god,
And worship this dull fool!
PROSPERO Go to; away!
ALONSO Hence, and bestow your luggage° where you found it.
SEBASTIAN Or stole it, rather.
PROSPERO Sir, I invite your Highness and your train
To my poor cell, where you shall take your rest
For this one night; which, part of it, I'll waste°
With such discourse as, I not doubt, shall make it
Go quick away: the story of my life,
And the particular accidents° gone by
Since I came to this isle: and in the morn
I'll bring you to your ship, and so to Naples,
Where I have hope to see the nuptial°
Of these our dear-beloved solemnized;
And thence retire me to my Milan, where
Every third thought shall be my grave.
ALONSO I long
To hear the story of your life, which must
Take° the ear strangely.
PROSPERO I'll deliver° all;
And promise you calm seas, auspicious gales,
And sail° so expeditious, that shall catch
Your royal fleet far off.° [*Aside to* ARIEL] My Ariel, chick,°
That is thy charge: then to the elements°
Be free, and fare thou well! Please you, draw near. *Exeunt omnes.*

EPILOGUE°

Spoken by PROSPERO.

Now my charms are all o'erthrown,
And what strength I have's mine own,

manners conduct, morality
grace pardon, favor
luggage rubbish, encumbrance
waste spend
accidents incidents
nuptial nuptials, wedding ceremony
Take captivate
deliver tell
sail voyage
far off far off though it already is
chick term of endearment
elements Ariel's natural habitat
Epilogue Although this is valuable material for those who would read the play as an allegory, it is basically the traditional appeal for applause, expressed in figures derived from the action of the play that has just ended. The actor who played Prospero has now, he says, no power to release himself from a spell which can only be broken when the audience applauds; and he prays for this as a grace that will help him avoid the sin of despair and set him free of his faults (as an actor). This he asks in the language of the Lord's Prayer; as the audience hopes for pardon itself, so it should award it to him.

Which is most faint: now, 'tis true,
I must be here confined° by you,
Or sent to Naples. Let me not,
Since I have my dukedom got,
And pardoned the deceiver, dwell
In this bare island by your spell;
But release me from my bands°
With the help of your good hands:°
Gentle breath° of yours my sails
Must fill, or else my project° fails,
Which was to please. Now I want
Spirits to enforce, Art to enchant;
And my ending is despair,
Unless I be relieved by prayer,°
Which pierces° so, that it assaults
Mercy itself,° and frees° all faults.
As you from crimes° would pardoned be,
Let your indulgence° set me free. *Exit.*
1611 1623

JOHN DONNE
1572–1631

Donne was born early in 1572, son of a prosperous London merchant and a mother not only Catholic but connected by marriage to Sir Thomas More; her brother, Jasper Heywood, translator of Seneca, was imprisoned for his part in a Jesuit mission to England, and Donne's own brother Henry died in prison in 1593 after being arrested for concealing a priest. The poet was justified in claiming that his family had suffered heavily "for obeying the teachers of the Roman Doctrine" (*Pseudo-Martyr,* an anti-Jesuit polemic of 1610). His early education was Catholic, and although he came to reject it (especially in its Jesuit form) his thinking and his temperament were affected by his Catholic training throughout his life.

As a Catholic, Donne could not take a degree, though he spent three years at Oxford, and three at Cambridge; in the early 1590's he was a student at the Inns of Court, in

confined as Ariel was
bands bonds
hands their clapping would break the spell
Gentle breath kindly comment on the performance
project his, parallel to but distinct from, Prospero's
prayer the petition he is now making
pierces is so penetrating
assaults Mercy itself "Prayers . . . break open heaven's gate" was a proverb.
frees wins pardon for
crimes sins
indulgence kindness; also remission for sins

London, then more a university than a law school; he studied law, languages, and theology from four in the morning till ten, and in his spare time was, we are told, a great visitor of ladies and a theatergoer. In these years he wrote the Elegies and Satires, and some of the *Juvenilia* and of the *Songs and Sonnets*. He traveled in Europe and took part in two naval expeditions before becoming, in 1598, secretary to the powerful Sir Thomas Egerton; but his good prospects of worldly success were ended by his secret marriage with Ann More, Egerton's niece, in 1601. For years he lived miserably and sought patronage—Lucy, Countess of Bedford and Sir Robert Drury were among his most important benefactors—and worked at anti-Romanist polemic as assistant to Morton, a clergyman who was to become the bishop of Durham. In 1610 his financial difficulties were eased; he published *Pseudo-Martyr* and the satire *Ignatius His Conclave,* also directed against the Jesuits. To this period belong also the two *Anniversaries* commemorating Elizabeth Drury (1611, 1612) and *Biathanatos,* a casuistic work on suicide which he did not publish. His chief theological work, *Essays in Divinity,* was written in 1614 but remained unpublished till after his death.

Although he had probably declared for the Anglican religion by 1602, Donne resisted royal pressure to take orders until 1615, after which his ecclesiastical advancement was rapid. Henceforth he wrote few poems—even the *Holy Sonnets* are, for the most part, earlier than the date of his ordination. His wife died in 1617, at a time when he was achieving fame as a preacher. He became Dean of St. Paul's in 1621, and so completed the rejection of "the mistress of my youth, Poetry" for "the wife of mine age, Divinity." In 1623 he had a serious illness, during which he wrote his *Devotions upon Emergent Occasions* and two famous hymns. But the great sermons—ten volumes of them in the standard edition—were his chief work in these years. They often allude to his own life—the deaths of his wife and daughter, his own departure abroad, his remorse at past sins, even, in the famous *Death's Duel,* preached to King Charles I in Lent 1631, his own death. His friend Walton made much of his histrionic composure on his deathbed, and did much to confirm the traditional view of Donne as a sort of St. Augustine, who, after a wild youth, settled for preaching, piety, and remorse. This is too simple, for Donne was an ambitious man, a man with many friends in the world; there must have been a certain piquancy in the thought that the libertine poems still circulating around London had come from the pen of the somber and powerful preacher in St. Paul's; yet the same intellectual ambitions and interests, the same wit, animate both. "Wit / He did not banish, but transplanted it," says one of his elegists; for wit was certainly a quality as highly valued in sermons as in love poems.

The best way to understand what is meant by Donne's "wit" is to work at the poems. For they require work; they depend upon one's understanding how the fantastic argument is advanced by the pseudo-logic of analogy and far-fetched allusion. After that one can begin to admire the complexity of tone, the countercurrents of secondary meaning, the ingenuity of the prodigally invented stanza forms, and the "masculine persuasive force," as Donne himself called it, of the language. To be thus "harsh"—Donne's own word again—was a duty imposed on satirists; to be conceited and harsh was a requirement of the funeral elegy, of which Donne wrote many. What is more unusual is the employment of "strong lines" and scholastic argument in love poetry, especially in a poet whose voice is capable of combining a masculine tenderness with colloquial power and both with obscure argument. Such combination—of apparent spontaneity and fine-drawn ratiocination, of amorous élan with verse forms of wantonly ingenious difficulty—characterize the finest of the poems to a degree that sets them apart from all predecessors and imitators, no matter how cogently resemblances are argued.

This does not mean, of course, that Donne was an absolute innovator. Many of his poems are on topics which occur in other sixteenth- and early seventeenth-century verse—"The Flea" and "The Dream," for example—and the conceits of Petrarchanism, like some standard emblems, recur, though in modified forms. Donne was harsher than the others—Jonson scolded him for it—and also wittier and more skeptical.

It might also be said that he was more "modern"; but this is a difficult concept. Wit, the *discordia concors,* was not modern. Nor was obscurity—Jonson said Donne would perish for not being understood, but he is much less obscure than his contemporary Chapman, and even the mellifluous Spenser is on occasion virtually impenetrable. Furthermore, the modernity of Donne's references to "new philosophy"—specifically Copernicanism—has been much exaggerated; his chief sources of learned imagery are the doctrines of the Schoolmen, law, and alchemy. For all his learning he was traditionally skeptical about the power of the human mind to know truth.

Where, then, does this modernity, so much admired by the nineteenth and twentieth centuries, lie? Partly in the new cult of an old wit, which affected poetry and preaching throughout Europe in these years; partly in a new kind of obscurity, deriving not from a manipulation of secret mythic meanings but from the representation of passionate thinking; partly from a skepticism which, despite its deep religious roots, took a modern form in Montaigne and Donne. Donne's rejection of the learning that depends on unaided human sense is essential to his religion; we see it expressed with extravagance in the lines here extracted from the *Second Anniversary,* and with more gravity in the Easter-Day Sermon. In the same way he distinguished between human "custom," which has no divine support, and the law; and his ultimate rejection of the church of Rome depended on this distinction. But when erotic poetry is subjected to the same skepticism the effect is very different; for "custom" is what controls normal "bourgeois" sexual relations, and "law" is natural inclination. In short, the skeptic can, in these matters, reject convention and the vast superstructure of human sanctions as matters of opinion, not of true knowledge of the natural law. The consequence of this rejection is libertine poetry.

Yet even libertine poetry is ancient; and in the Elegies, the warmest of his poems, Donne is imitating Ovid. Nor is his amorous verse all concerned with the paradoxes and problems that arise from the conflict of desire with authority; he often has a recognizably more serious tone, and draws on the lore of Renaissance Platonism to illustrate the union of lovers' souls and the relationship between soul and body.

All we can say, then, is that Donne's modern contained much of the past, as modernity always does. What, in the end, preserves him is that his poetry is full of his powerful mind; and that the projection of his mind into poetry is immediate and, whatever the subject, witty or passionate or both.

It would not do to end this brief general introduction without a word more about Donne's religion, which preoccupied him through most of his life and long survived his active career as a poet. The third Satire is an urgent statement of the importance, there and then, of discovering a true religion. His choice of the English church as nearest to the true primitive and catholic was no doubt made possible by the labors of Hooker and other apologists. Donne held to the English middle course, the *via media,* supporting all attempts to persuade others to join it, for the rest of his life.

His chosen church avoided the errors of Rome, but maintained its contact with the ancient learning and forms; it cherished tradition without accumulated error, the Fathers but not their follies. He rejected the extreme Calvinists with detestation, but, like them, knew his Augustine. He saw the dangers of learned controversy: "It is the text that saves us; the interlineary glosses, and the marginal notes, and the *variae lectiones,* controversies and perplexities, undo us." Although his sermons seem very learned, it is worth noticing that he patiently explains his meanings, and repeats the explanations; he was an enormously popular preacher, and his distinction as a churchman lies in that and in his piety, for he was not a distinguished theologian. The wit—fineness of mind—and passion of the erotic poetry lived on, not only into the religious poetry but, suitably adapted to a larger audience, into the great sermons also. "His fancy," said his biographer Izaak Walton, "was unimitably high, equalled only by his great wit . . . He was by nature highly passionate." The words will serve to explain why, as beneficiaries of the twentieth-century revival of Donne and the scholarship which has cleared his text and illustrated his meanings, we continue to value him so highly, and perhaps occasionally to marvel that the smallish city of London, in one lifetime, contained such different poets as Marlowe, Spenser, Shakespeare, Jonson, and Donne.

We sometimes hear of a School of Donne, and there were certainly admirers and imitators, of whom the best was also the last of any merit, Abraham Cowley (1618–67). What will not do is to include the other so-called Metaphysical poets—men of the stature and idiosyncrasy of Herbert, Vaughan, Crashaw, Marvell—under such a heading. The conceit of Donne degenerated into a joke; the ultimate ancestor of such a work as the young Dryden's *Elegy on Lord Hastings* may be the conceit-powered funeral elegies of Donne, or even the *Anniversaries,* but a remarkable decline has occurred.

At the same time the concept of wit underwent important changes. As an admired quality it was no longer primarily a matter of acuteness, the power to make unforeseen metaphors and arguments; the concept grew more general, closer to Pope's "What oft was thought. . . ." So conceited, "strong-lined" poetry went out of fashion, as did "Senecan" prose and the witty sermon. Dr. Johnson's study of Donne's wit in his *Life of Cowley,* hostile, penetrating, even in its way just, shows him conversant with the Donnean idea of wit, but also disapproving; the best he can say is that to write as these men did it "was at least necessary to think." Pope knew the Satires, but smoothed them out, and Donne's poetry came to be thought of as at best interesting primitive work. The revival, depending on atrocious texts, was an achievement of the nineteenth century; Coleridge read deeply in the verse and prose, saying some harsh things about the verse but soliciting admiration also, especially for "The Ecstasy" and *Satire 3.* Later Browning, and George Eliot, and then many poets of the later years of the century, helped to build up a cult. Grierson's edition of 1912 made good texts and informed commentary available, and by the time T. S. Eliot wrote his famous essay "The Metaphysical Poets" in 1923, there were easily available ways of speaking and writing about this exciting poet. These we tend, wrongly, to attribute to Eliot himself. For a while modern criticism treated the disappearance of Donne's colloquial intensity from English poetry as a symptom of a general cultural disaster, called by Eliot a "dissociation of sensibility"; later he revised his views on Donne, and somewhat changed that concept, in itself neither original nor historically valid; but the association of Donne with it, and with critical campaigns against Milton, still persists in some quarters. It is not harmless, for it imposes false ways of reading both Donne and Milton, which is why these notes say so little, and that skeptically, about the cultural and scientific crisis identified with Donne's verse, and so much, relatively, about Donne's own skepticism.

From Juvenilia: Or Paradoxes and Problems°

Problem: Why Does the Pox So Much Affect to Undermine the Nose?°

Paracelsus° perchance saith true, that every disease hath his exaltation° in some part certain. But why this in the nose? Is there so much mercy in this disease that it provides that one should not smell his own stink? Or hath it but the common fortune that, being begot and bred in obscurest and secretest places (because therefore his serpentine crawling and insinuation should not be suspected nor seen), he comes soonest into great place, and is more able to destroy the worthiest member than a disease better born? Perchance as mice defeat elephants° by gnawing their *proboscis* (which is their nose), this wretched Indian vermin practiceth to do the same upon us. Or as the ancient furious custom and connivancy° of some laws that° one might cut off their nose whom he deprehended in adultery, was but a type of this; and that now, more charitable laws having taken away all revenge from particular hands, this common magistrate and executioner is come to do the same office invisibly? Or by withdrawing this conspicuous part, the nose, it warns us from all adventuring upon that coast—for it is as good a mark to take in a flag, as to hang one out. Possibly Heat, which is more potent and active than Cold, thought herself injured, and the Harmony of the World out of tune, when Cold was able to show the high-way to noses in Muscovia, except she found the means to do the same in other countries. Or because by the consent of all, there is an analogy, proportion and affection between the nose and that part where this disease is first contracted, and therefore Heliogabalus° chose not his minions° in the bath but by the nose. And Albertus° had a knavish meaning when he preferred great noses. And the licentious poet° was *Naso Poeta*. I think this reason is nearest truth:° that the nose is most compassionate with this part

Paradoxes and Problems The paradox was a fashionable exercise throughout Europe, and Donne's early interest in it is reflected in some of the *Songs and Sonnets*.

Why Does . . . Nose While the point of the "paradox" as a literary exercise was to argue contrary to the received view, the problem of these "problems" was to produce as many ingenious and funny "explanations" as possible for a phenomenon that, presumably, could not be explained. The pox, syphilis, frequently resulted in facial disfigurement; as the erotic and mercantile disease (it was believed to have been brought to Europe from the Caribbean by explorers) it led to much grim humor.

Paracelsus (Theophrastus Bombastus von Hohenheim, 1493–1541), Swiss alchemist and physician

exaltation most powerful manifestation

mice . . . elephants or so the belief was

connivancy literally, "winking at," overlooking, and pretending not to

that so that

deprehended apprehended

Heliogabalus (204–222 A.D.), wildly depraved Roman emperor

minions literally, "cuties," male sexual partners

Albertus St. Albertus Magnus (Albert von Böllstadt, 1193?–1280), scholastic philosopher and St. Thomas Aquinas's teacher

licentious poet Ovid, whose full name was Publius Ovidius Naso

nearest truth He certainly does not; this is like the "But seriously, now," of the stand-up comic.

—except this be nearer: that it is reasonable that this disease in particular should affect the most eminent and perspicuous part, which in general doth affect to take hold of the most eminent and conspicuous men.

1633

Elegies

The chief model of the Elizabethan love elegy was the *Amores* of Ovid; Marlowe had made these fashionable, and the tradition was crossed with that of the witty, paradoxical, Italian love poetry of the period. Donne's Elegies, of which two are given here, belong to his early twenties, being attributable to the early 1590's, when he was a student at Lincoln's Inn. He outdoes Ovid in his witty dedication to physical pleasure; and the Elegies differ from the *Songs and Sonnets* not only in their adherence to the iambic pentameter couplet but in the unspiritual ruthlessness that for the most part characterizes their attitude to love. Not all the Elegies have the sexual directness and plain-spokenness of these two, but they will serve to demonstrate one extreme of his love poetry.

Elegy XVIII: Love's Progress°

Whoever loves, if he do not propose
The right true end of love, he's one that goes
To sea for nothing but to make him sick.
And love's a bear-whelp° born, if we o'er-lick
Our love, and force it new strange shapes to take,
We err, and of a lump a monster make.
Were not a calf a monster that were grown
Faced like a man, though better than his own?°
Perfection is in unity: prefer°
One woman first, and then one thing in her.
I, when I value gold, may think upon
The ductileness, the application,°
The wholesomeness, the ingenuity,°
From rust, from soil, from fire ever free,
But if I love it, 'tis because 'tis made
By our new nature,° use, the soul of trade.
All these in women we might think upon
(If women had them) and yet love but one.
Can men more injure women than to say
They love them for that, by which they are not they?

Love's Progress refused a license in 1633; first printed in 1661 and with Donne's other poems in 1669
bear-whelp supposed to be born a shapeless lump which the mother licked into shape
though . . . own even though a man's face is in itself better than a calf's
prefer choose
application uses it is put to
ingenuity noble quality
new nature human custom (or, as he calls it, *use*)

Makes virtue woman? must I cool my blood
Till I both be, and find one, wise and good?
May barren angels love so. But if we
Make love to woman, virtue is not she,
As beauty's not, nor wealth. He that strays thus
From her to hers,° is more adulterous
Than if he took her maid. Search every sphere
And firmament, our Cupid is not there.°
He's an infernal god and underground
With Pluto dwells, where gold and fire° abound.
Men to such gods, their sacrificing coals
Did not in altars lay, but pits and holes.
Although we see celestial bodies move
Above the earth, the earth we till and love:
So we her airs contemplate, words and heart,
And virtues; but we love the centric part.°
  Nor is the soul more worthy, or more fit
For love than this,° as infinite as it.
But in attaining this desirèd place
How much they stray, that set out at the face!
The hair a forest is of ambushes,
Of springes, snares, fetters and manacles;
The brow becalms us when 'tis smooth and plain,
And when 'tis wrinkled, shipwrecks us again;
Smooth, 'tis a paradise, where we would have
Immortal stay, and wrinkled 'tis our grave.
The nose like to the first meridian° runs
Not 'twixt an east and west, but 'twixt two suns;
It leaves a cheek, a rosy hemisphere
On either side, and then directs us where
Upon the Islands Fortunate° we fall,
(Not faint Canary,° but ambrosial°)
Her swelling lips; to which when we are come,
We anchor there, and think ourselves at home,
For they seem all: there sirens' songs, and there
Wise Delphic oracles do fill the ear;
There in a creek where chosen pearls do swell,
The remora,° her cleaving tongue doth dwell.
These, and the glorious promontory, her chin
O'erpast; and the strait Hellespont between

from her to hers from her essential self to her mere attributes
Search . . . there no heavenly body is called after Cupid
gold with fire Deep in the earth, in the realm of the god of hell, are gold and heat, both necessary to love.
pits and holes . . . centric part *doubles entendres*
this the vagina
springes small traps for game
first meridian first circle of longitude, which (at the Canary Islands) divided the eastern and western hemispheres
Islands Fortunate mythical happy islands west of Gibraltar; usually identified with the Canaries
faint Canary the light sweet wine of the Canaries
ambrosial Ambrosia was the food of the gods.
remora sucking-fish, supposed to be able to stop ships

The Sestos and Abydos° of her breasts,
(Not of two lovers,° but two loves the nests)
Succeeds a boundless sea, but yet thine eye
Some island moles may scattered there descry;
And sailing towards her India,° in that way
Shall at her fair Atlantic navel stay;
Though thence the current be thy pilot made,
Yet ere thou be where thou wouldst be embayed,
Thou shalt upon another forest set,
Where many shipwreck, and no further get.
When thou art there, consider what this chase
Misspent by thy beginning at the face.
  Rather set out below, practise my art,
Some symmetry° the foot hath with that part
Which thou dost seek, and is thy map for that
Lovely enough to stop, but not stay at:
Least subject to disguise and change it is;
Men say the Devil never can change his.°
It is the emblem that hath figurèd
Firmness;° 'tis the first part that comes to bed.
Civility, we see, refined the kiss
Which at the face begun, transplanted is
Since to the hand, since to the imperial knee,
Now at the papal foot delights to be.°
If kings think that the nearer way,° and do
Rise from the foot, lovers may do so too;
For as free spheres° move faster far than can
Birds, whom the air resists, so may that man
Which goes this empty and ethereal way,
Than if at beauty's elements he stay.
Rich Nature hath in women wisely made
Two purses,° and their mouths aversely° laid;
They then, which to the lower tribute owe,
That way which that exchequer looks, must go.
He which doth not, his error is as great,
As who by clyster° gave the stomach meat.

1669

Sestos and Abydos towns on the opposite shores of the Hellespont
two lovers Hero and Leander
India the orient, source of riches
symmetry likeness of shape
his his cloven foot
emblem . . . firmness The foot was used as an emblem of *firmitas*.
Civility . . . to be polite manners have made our kissing more subservient; kissing on the face descends to hand-kissing, then to kissing the emperor's knee and the pope's foot
the nearer way the shortest way to what they want
free spheres the heavenly bodies, which encounter no resistance from the air
Two purses the mouth and the vagina
aversely at different angles
clyster enema

Elegy XIX: To His Mistress Going to Bed°

Come, Madam, come, all rest my powers defy,
Until I labour, I in labour lie.
The foe oft-times having the foe in sight,
Is tired with standing° though they never fight.
Off with that girdle, like heaven's zone° glistering,
But a far fairer world encompassing.
Unpin that spangled breastplate° which you wear,
That the eyes of busy fools may be stopped there.
Unlace yourself, for that harmonious chime°
Tells me from you, that now 'tis your bed time.
Off with that happy busk,° which I envy,
That still can be, and still can stand so nigh.
Your gown going off, such beauteous state reveals,
As when from flowery meads the hill's shadow steals.
Off with that wiry coronet° and show
The hairy diadem which on you doth grow;
Now off with those shoes, and then safely tread
In this love's hallowed temple, this soft bed.
In such white robes heaven's angels used to be
Received by men; thou angel bring'st with thee
A heaven like Mahomet's paradise;° and though°
Ill spirits walk in white, we easily know
By this these angels from an evil sprite:
Those set our hairs, but these our flesh upright.
  Licence my roving hands, and let them go
Before, behind, between, above, below.
O my America, my new found land,
My kingdom, safeliest when with one man manned,°
My mine of precious stones, my empery,°
How blessed am I in this discovering thee!
To enter in these bonds,° is to be free;
Then where my hand is set, my seal shall be.°
  Full nakedness, all joys are due to thee.
As souls unbodied, bodies unclothed must be,
To taste whole joys.° Gems which you women use
Are like Atalanta's balls,° cast in men's views,

To His Mistress Going to Bed refused license in 1633; published 1669
standing waiting to fight; here: having an erection
heaven's zone Orion's belt (*zona* = girdle)
spangled breastplate stomacher, which covered the breast and was often jeweled
chime she had a chiming watch
busk corset
wiry coronet band of metal worn round the brow
Mahomet's paradise a place of sensual bliss (for men)
though even though
manned inhabited, served
empery empire
these bonds her arms
where . . . shall be having signed the contract he will seal it; having put his hand on her sex he will complete that transaction also
As souls . . . whole joys as souls must be divested of bodies to taste heavenly joy, so bodies must be divested of clothes
Atalanta's balls Hippomenes defeated the unbeatable Atalanta in a race by throwing three golden apples in her path; she stopped to pick them up.

That when a fool's eyes lighteth on a gem,
His earthly soul may covet theirs, not them.
Like pictures, or like books' gay coverings made
For laymen,° are all women thus arrayed;
Themselves are mystic books, which only we
Whom their imputed grace will dignify°
Must see revealed. Then since I may know,
As liberally, as to a midwife, show
Thyself: cast all, yea, this white linen hence,
There is no penance due to innocence.°
  To teach thee, I am naked first, why then
What need'st thou have more covering than a man.

1669

Songs and Sonnets

First published in 1633, two years after Donne's death, these poems circulated in manuscript during the poet's lifetime. Their first audience was a small, sophisticated, no doubt rather "fast" group of like-minded young men, willing to be tested by fantastic argument, admiring what Donne himself called, in a squib called *The Courtier's Library,* "itchy outbreaks of far-fetched wit." This much may be said without prejudice to the great variety of tone in the poems: they all ask one to admire their ingenuity, their skill in overcoming the difficulties placed in the way of complicated argument by the arbitrarily difficult stanza forms. Yet some really are "songs," and were sung; others fail, as so many of the poems of later poets who imitated them fail, by being nothing but ingenious. The selection of poems that follows excludes several such relative failures.

Nevertheless, it would be dangerous to argue that only the more "serious" poems are good; just as it is dangerous to divide the poems, as some do, into two groups, rakish poems written before 1600, more subtle and serious poems written after 1602. Occasionally dates can be conjectured; some of these dates are after 1600, and the tone of the poems is different from that of the more libertine Elegies, which belong to the 1590's. But there is no certainty, and for that reason no dates of composition are appended to the poems in this selection.

The Good Morrow

  I wonder by my troth, what thou and I
    Did, till we loved? were we not weaned till then,
  But sucked on country° pleasures, childishly?

laymen who cannot understand the contents
imputed grace . . . dignify to the elect women will impute the grace necessary to this revelation, as Christ, in Calvinist doctrine, imputes to his elect the grace necessary to salvation
There . . . innocence the white linen of penitence is inappropriate, since you are doing no sin. Another much-favored reading is: "Here is no penance, much less innocence"—you are neither a penitent nor an innocent, and so have no occasion to wear white.
country rustic

Or snorted° we in the seven sleepers' den?°
'Twas so; but this,° all pleasures fancies be.
If ever any beauty I did see,
Which I desired, and got, 'twas but a dream of thee.

And now good morrow to our waking souls,
Which watch not one another out of fear;
For love, all love of other sights controls,°
And makes one little room, an every where.
Let sea-discoverers to new worlds have gone,
Let maps° to others, worlds on worlds have shown,
Let us possess one world, each hath one, and is one.

My face in thine eye, thine in mine appears,
And true plain hearts do in the faces rest;
Where can we find two better hemispheres°
Without sharp north, without declining west?
Whatever dies, was not mixed equally;°
If our two loves be one, or, thou and I
Love so alike that none do slacken, none can die.°

1633

The Sun Rising°

Busy old fool, unruly sun,
Why dost thou thus,
Through windows, and through curtains call on us?
Must to thy motions lovers' seasons run?
Saucy pedantic wretch, go chide
Late school-boys, and sour prentices,
Go tell court-huntsmen,° that the King will ride,
Call country ants° to harvest offices;°
Love, all alike, no season knows, nor clime,
Nor hours, days, months, which are the rags° of time.

Thy beams, so reverend, and strong
Why shouldst thou think?
I could eclipse and cloud them with a wink,
But that I would not lose her sight so long:
If her eyes have not blinded thine,

snorted snored
seven sleepers' den Seven young Christians were walled up in a cave during the persecution of Decius (249) and did not die but slept for 187 years.
but this except for this
controls inhibits
maps charts of the heavens
two better hemispheres together they make the whole world, and as hemispheres they lack the disadvantages of the geographical ones, which have to include the cold north and the west where the sun sets
Whatever . . . equally Death, in Galen's teaching, results from imbalance of elements within the body.
Love . . . die each matches the perfection of the other's love to a degree that prevents either from waning; neither can die
The Sun Rising follows the tradition, beginning with Ovid, of the lover's address to the sun, but differs in its irreverence.
court-huntsmen who hunt with King James, and also hunt office
country ants rural drudges
offices tasks
rags fragments, divisions

Look, and tomorrow late, tell me,
Whether both the Indias° of spice and mine
Be where thou left'st them, or lie here with me.
Ask for those kings whom thou saw'st yesterday,
And thou shalt hear, All here in one bed lay.

She is all states, and all princes, I,
Nothing else is.
Princes do but play us; compared to this,
All honour's mimic; all wealth alchemy.°
Thou sun art half as happy as we,
In that the world's contracted thus;
Thine age asks ease, and since thy duties be
To warm the world, that's done in warming us.
Shine here to us, and thou art everywhere;
This bed thy centre° is, these walls, thy sphere.

1633

The Canonization°

For God's sake hold your tongue, and let me love,
Or chide my palsy, or my gout,
My five grey hairs, or ruined fortune flout,
With wealth your state, your mind with arts improve,
Take you a course,° get you a place,°
Observe his Honour,° or his Grace,°
Or the King's real, or his stamped face°
Contemplate; what you will, approve,°
So you will let me love.

Alas, alas, who's injured by my love?
What merchant's ships have my sighs° drowned?
Who says my tears° have overflowed his ground?
When did my colds° a forward spring remove?
When did the heats° which my veins fill
Add one more to the plaguy bill?°
Soldiers find wars, and lawyers find out still
Litigious men, which quarrels move,
Though she and I do love.

both the Indias the East and West Indies, the first for perfumes and spices, the second for gold
alchemy fake gold
centre of his universe; that around which he revolves
The Canonization The martyrs of love become saints.
Take . . . course get yourself a career
place appointment at court
his Honor some lord
his Grace some bishop
King's . . . face the King in person (as to a sycophant) or as he appears on money (as to a businessman)
approve try, experience
sighs . . . tears . . . colds . . . heats the conventional Petrarchan hyperboles for lovesickness used as an argument that their love affects nobody else's business
plaguy bill lists of plague victims posted weekly

Call us what you will, we are made such by love;
  Call her one, me another fly,
We are tapers too,° and at our own cost die,°
  And we in us find the Eagle and the Dove.
    The Phoenix riddle° hath more wit
    By us; we two being one, are it.
So to one neutral thing both sexes fit,°
  We die and rise the same, and prove
  Mysterious by this love.

We can die by it, if not live by love,
  And if unfit for tombs and hearse
Our legend be, it will be fit for verse;
  And if no piece of chronicle° we prove,
    We'll build in sonnets° pretty rooms;
    As well a well-wrought urn° becomes
The greatest ashes, as half-acre tombs,°
  And by these hymns, all shall approve°
  Us canonized for love:

And thus invoke us;° 'You whom reverend love
  Made one another's hermitage;
You, to whom love was peace, that now° is rage;
  Who did the whole world's soul contract, and drove
    Into the glasses of your eyes
    (So made such mirrors, and such spies,
That they did all to you epitomize),
  Countries, towns, courts:° beg from above°
  A pattern° of your love!'

1633

Lovers' Infiniteness°

If yet I have not all thy love,
Dear, I shall never have it all,
I cannot breathe one other sigh, to move,
Nor can entreat one other tear to fall.
All my treasure, which should purchase thee,

fly . . . tapers too not only moths but flames
die with the common double meaning: have orgasm
Eagle . . . Dove the predatory and the meek
Phoenix riddle The Phoenix was reborn out of its own ashes, not by sex, and so contained in one individual the male and female principles; cf. Shakespeare, *The Phoenix and Turtle*.
So . . . fit in such measure do both sexes meet in one neutral thing (that)
die and rise with secondary sexual sense
Mysterious worthy of reverence, like religious mysteries
chronicle history
sonnets love poems
urn . . . tombs taking the urn as the love lyric, the tomb as the chronicle of worldly achievement
approve allow
invoke us pray to them as saints
now in the world you have left
Who did . . . courts who reduced the entire animating principle of the world to yourselves, concentrated all society into your own eyes, which accordingly mirrored and epitomized it
beg from above pray on behalf (for)
pattern model
Lovers' Infiniteness the three-stage argument often found in Donne

Sighs, tears, and oaths, and letters I have spent,
Yet no more can be due to me,
Than at the bargain made was meant.
If then thy gift of love were partiàl,
That some to me, some should to others fall,
Dear, I shall never have thee all.

Or if then thou gavest me all,
All was but all, which thou hadst then;
But if in thy heart, since, there be or shall
New lòve created be, by other men,
Which have their stocks entire, and can in tears,
In sighs, in oaths, and letters outbid me,
This new love may beget new fears,
For, this love was not vowed by thee.
And yet it was, thy gift being general,
The ground, thy heart is mine; whatever shall
Grow there, dear, I should have it all.

Yet I would not have all yet,
He that hath all can have no more,
And since my love doth every day admit
New growth, thou shouldst have new rewards in store;
Thou canst not every day give me thy heart,
If thou canst give it, then thou never gav'st it:
Love's riddles° are, that though thy heart depart,
It stays at home, and thou with losing sav'st it:°
But we will have a way more liberal,
Than changing hearts, to join them, so we shall
Be one, and one another's all.

1633

Song°

Sweetest love, I do not go,
For weariness of thee,
Nor in hope the world can show
A fitter love for me;
But since that I
Must die at last, 'tis best,
To use my self in jest
Thus by feigned deaths to die.

Yesternight the sun went hence,
And yet is here today,
He hath no desire nor sense,

riddles paradoxes. They are adapted from Matthew 16:25: ". . . whosoever will save his life shall lose it."

Song Like several other Donne poems, this one exists in a contemporary musical setting.

Nor half so short a way:
Then fear not me,
But believe that I shall make
Speedier journeys, since I take
More wings and spurs than he.

O how feeble is man's power,
That if good fortune fall,
Cannot add another hour,
Nor a lost hour recall!
But come bad chance,
And we join to it our strength,
And we teach it art and length,
Itself o'er us to advance.°

When thou sigh'st, thou sigh'st not wind,
But sigh'st my soul away,
When thou weep'st, unkindly kind,
My life's blood doth decay.
It cannot be
That thou lov'st me, as thou say'st,
If in thine my life thou waste,
Thou art the best of me.°

Let not thy divining° heart
Forethink me any ill,
Destiny may take thy part,
And may thy fears fulfil;
But think that we
Are but turned aside to sleep;
They who one another keep
Alive, ne'er parted be.

1633

A Fever°

Oh do not die, for I shall hate
All women so when thou art gone,
That thee I shall not celebrate
When I remember, thou wast one.

But yet thou canst not die, I know,
To leave this world behind, is death;
But when thou from this world wilt go,
The whole world vapours with thy breath.

But come . . . advance but if bad luck comes we lend it our strength, and teach it how to torment us protractedly, so that it triumphs over us

the best of me in expending her soul in sighs and tears she is wasting him, since she is his life

divining prophetic, foreseeing

A Fever The basic conceit—that the death of a mistress destroys the world—is Petrarchan.

Or if, when thou, the world's soul,° go'st,
  It stay, 'tis but thy carcase then,
The fairest woman, but thy ghost,
  But corrupt worms, the worthiest men.

Oh wrangling schools, that search what fire
  Shall burn this world,° had none the wit
Unto this knowledge to aspire,
  That this her fever might be it?

And yet she cannot waste by this,
  Nor long bear this torturing wrong,
For much corruption needful is
  To fuel such a fever long.°

These burning fits but meteors be,
  Whose matter in thee is soon spent.
Thy beauty, and all parts, which are thee,
  Are unchangeable firmament.°

Yet 'twas of my mind, seizing thee,
  Though it in thee cannot persévér.°
For I had rather owner be
  Of thee one hour, than all else ever.

1633

Air and Angels°

Twice or thrice had I loved thee,
Before I knew thy face or name;
So in a voice, so in a shapeless flame,
Angels affect us oft, and worshipped be;
  Still° when, to where thou wert, I came,
Some lovely glorious nothing° I did see,
  But since my soul, whose child love is,
Takes limbs of flesh, and else could nothing do,°
  More subtle° than the parent is
Love must not be, but take a body too,
  And therefore what thou wert, and who

world's soul anima mundi, a Platonic concept
what fire . . . world The Stoics, and later the Schoolmen, disputed the nature of the final conflagration.
much . . . long The heat of fevers was thought to proceed from corruption caused by conflict between elements in the body.
These burning . . . firmament Meteors were thought to be exhaled from the earth and consumed in the sphere of fire (cf. *Dr. Faustus* vi.61.); their corruptibility is contrasted with the incorruptibility of the heavens.
seizing taking possession of (legal)
persévér persist
Air and Angels The argument of the poem depends on the difference of purity between air and angels: air, the purest form of matter, cannot be quite as pure as angels, which are spirit. One of Donne's most difficult poems.
Still always
some . . . nothing He saw her as he might an angel, without the specific form angels take on when, to be visible to those they visit, they wear a "body of air"; the point is that his first love for her lacked this physical or material element.
could nothing do Cf. end of "The Ecstasy"; the soul acts through the senses.
subtle ethereal

I bid love ask, and now
That it assume thy body, I allow,
And fix itself in thy lip, eye, and brow.

Whilst thus to ballast love I thought,
And so more steadily to have gone,
With wares which would sink admiration,
I saw, I had love's pinnace° overfraught,
Every thy hair for love to work upon
Is much too much, some fitter must be sought;
For, nor° in nothing, nor in things
Extreme, and scatt'ring bright, can love inhere;
Then as an angel, face and wings
Of air, not pure as it, yet pure doth wear,
So thy love may be my love's sphere;°
Just such disparity
As is 'twixt air and angels' purity,
'Twixt women's love and men's will ever be.°

1633

The Anniversary

All kings, and all their favourites,
All glory of honours, beauties, wits
The sun itself, which makes times as they pass,
Is elder by a year now than it was
When thou and I first one another saw:
All other things to their destruction draw,
Only our love hath no decay;
This, no tomorrow hath, nor yesterday,
Running it never runs from us away,
But truly keeps his first, last, everlasting day.

Two graves must hide thine and my corse,
If one might, death were no divorce,
Alas, as well as other princes, we
(Who prince enough in one another be),
Must leave at last in death, these eyes, and ears,
Oft fed with true oaths, and with sweet salt tears;
But souls where nothing dwells but love
(All other thoughts being inmates°) then shall prove°
This, or a love increasèd there above,°
When bodies to their graves, souls from their graves remove.

pinnace small ship; now he has gone too far in associating love with specific physical detail
nor neither
sphere in the relation of the planet (material) to the angel-intelligence (spiritual) which informs and guides it
Just . . . ever be The compromise, whereby love is not reduced to materiality—the woman's way—nor left in an angelic shapelessness and spirituality—men's way—is represented by the angel wearing his body of air.
inmates lodgers
prove experience
above in heaven

And then we shall be throughly blessed,
But we no more, than all the rest.°
Here upon earth, we are kings, and none but we
Can be such kings, nor of such subjects° be;
Who is so safe as we? where none can do
Treason to us, except one of us two.
True and false fears let us refrain,
Let us love nobly, and live, and add again
Years and years unto years, till we attain
To write threescore; this is the second of our reign.

1633

The Dream°

Dear love, for nothing less than thee
Would I have broke this happy dream,
It was a theme
For reason, much too strong for phantasy,°
Therefore thou waked'st me wisely; yet
My dream thou brokest not, but continued'st it;
Thou art so truth,° that thoughts of thee suffice,
To make dreams truths, and fables histories;
Enter these arms, for since thou thought'st it best,
Not to dream all my dream, let's act the rest.

As lightning, or a taper's light,
Thine eyes, and not thy noise waked me;
Yet I thought thee
(For thou lov'st truth) an angel, at first sight,
But when I saw thou saw'st my heart,
And knew'st my thoughts, beyond an angel's art,°
When thou knew'st what I dreamed, when thou knew'st when
Excess of joy would wake me, and cam'st then,
I must confess, it could not choose but be
Profane,° to think thee anything but thee.

Coming and staying showed thee, thee,
But rising makes me doubt, that now,
Thou art not thou.
That love is weak, where fear's as strong as he;
'Tis not all spirit, pure, and brave,

no more . . . rest the doctrine that in heaven each is blessed with contentment according to his capacity
of such subjects subjects of such kings
The Dream based on the topic of the waking to find at one's bedside a mistress of whom one has been dreaming; as old as Ovid, but here newly handled
too strong . . . phantasy The fantasy or imagination continues to produce images in sleep, when the reason cannot process them.
truth so absolutely the truth itself (many editions read *true*)
knew'st . . . art not even angels, but only God himself, can read one's inmost thoughts
Profane with a hint that she is more God than angel

If mixture it of fear, shame, honour,° have.
Perchance as torches which must ready be,
Men light and put out,° so thou deal'st with me,
Thou cam'st to kindle, goest to come;° then I
Will dream that hope again, but else would die.

1633

A Valediction: Of Weeping

Let me pour forth
My tears before thy face, whilst I stay here,°
For thy face coins them,° and thy stamp they bear,
And by this mintage they are something worth,
For thus they be
Pregnant of thee;
Fruits of much grief they are, emblems° of more,
When a tear falls, that thou° falls which it bore,
So thou and I are nothing then, when on a divers shore.°

On a round ball
A workman that hath copies by, can lay
An Europe, Afric, and an Asia,
And quickly make that, which was nothing, all,°
So doth each tear,
Which thee doth wear,
A globe, yea world by that impression grow,
Till thy tears mixed with mine do overflow
This world, by waters sent from thee, my heaven dissolvèd so.°

O more than moon,°
Draw not up seas to drown me in thy sphere,
Weep me not dead, in thine arms, but forbear
To teach the sea, what it may do too soon;
Let not the wind
Example find,
To do me more harm, than it purposeth;
Since thou and I sigh one another's breath,
Whoe'er sighs most, is cruellest, and hastes the other's death.

1633

honour as usual in Donne, the enemy of love
torches . . . put out A torch that has been burning ignites more easily.
come come back
whilst I stay here while I'm still with you
coins them Each tear, bearing her reflected image, is like a coin.
emblems prophetic images (the next lines explain why)
that thou that image of you
on a divers shore in different countries
nothing, all By pasting maps of the countries of the world on a blank globe he is converting nothing (the zero of the globe) into everything (the world).
Till . . . dissolved so Their tears combine to form a flood and inundate the world of the tear—it is a world because it bears her image. She is his heaven, which dissolves as the sky did for the Flood.
more than moon She is more powerful than the moon and should not raise a tide that would drown him.

Love's Alchemy°

Some that have deeper digged love's mine than I,
Say, where his centric happiness doth lie:
    I have loved, and got,° and told,°
But should I love, get, tell, till I were old,
I should not find that hidden mystery;
    Oh, 'tis imposture all:
And as no chemic yet the elixir got,
    But glorifies his pregnant pot,
    If by the way to him befall
Some odoriferous thing, or medicinal,°
  So, lovers dream a rich and long delight,
  But get a winter-seeming summer's night.

Our ease, our thrift, our honour, and our day,°
Shall we, for this vain bubble's shadow pay?
    Ends love in this, that my man,°
Can be as happy as I can; if he can
Endure the short scorn of a bridegroom's play?
    That loving wretch that swears,
'Tis not the bodies marry, but the minds,
    Which he in her angelic finds,
    Would swear as justly, that he hears,
In that day's° rude hoarse minstrelsy, the spheres.°
Hope not for mind in women; at their best
  Sweetness and wit, they are but mummy, possessed.°

1633

The Flea°

Mark but this flea, and mark in this,
How little that which thou deny'st me is;
Me it sucked first, and now sucks thee,
And in this flea, our two bloods mingled be;
Confess it, this cannot be said°

Love's Alchemy entitled *Mummy* in many MSS
got acquired
told counted
no chemic . . . medicinal No alchemist ever achieved the quintessence, but all the same praises his fertile retort if, along the way, he makes a chance discovery, of a perfume or a medicine (a common remark about alchemists).
winter-seeming . . . night at once short and cold
our day our life wasted day by day in sexual acts
man servant
short scorn brief indignity
that day's the wedding day's
the spheres the music of the spheres
mummy, possessed like a dead body (from which the soul has departed) occupied by a demon; i.e. even when they seem to have wit, they are only well-preserved flesh with substitute (and devilish) minds
The Flea an ancient theme for ribald love-poems, dating back to Ovid (cf. *Dr. Faustus* vi.111.); but Donne's treatment, making the flea a symbol of the desired union of his and his mistress's blood, is original. The action of the poem is in three stages: first, the poet draws a moral from the flea; second, the woman proposes to kill it; third, she has done so. He makes the maximum capital out of each stage by fertility of argument.
said called

A sin, or shame, or loss of maidenhead,
Yet this enjoys before it woo,
And pampered swells with one blood made of two,
And this, alas, is more than we would do.°

Oh stay, three lives in one flea spare,
Where we almost, nay more than married are.
This flea is you and I, and this
Our marriage bed, and marriage temple is;
Though parents grudge, and you, we are met,
And cloistered in these living walls of jet.
Though use° make you apt to kill me,
Let not to this, self murder added be,
And sacrilege, three sins° in killing three.

Cruel and sudden, hast thou since
Purpled thy nail, in blood of innocence?
In what could this flea guilty be,
Except in that drop which it sucked from thee?
Yet thou triumph'st, and say'st that thou
Find'st not thyself, nor me the weaker now;
'Tis true, then learn how false, fears be;
Just so much honour, when thou yield'st to me,
Will waste, as this flea's death took life from thee.

1633

A Nocturnal upon S. Lucy's Day, Being the Shortest Day°

'Tis the year's midnight, and it is the day's,
Lucy's, who scarce seven hours herself unmasks,
The sun is spent, and now his flasks°
Send forth light squibs,° no constant rays;
The world's whole sap is sunk:
The general balm° the hydroptic° earth hath drunk,
Whither, as to the bed's-feet,° life is shrunk,
Dead and interred; yet all these seem to laugh,
Compared with me, who am their epitaph.

Study me then, you who shall lovers be
At the next world, that is, at the next spring:°

more . . . do They don't want an ensuing pregnancy.
use habit
three sins murder, suicide, sacrilege
A Nocturnal upon S. Lucy's Day . . . December 13, then the shortest day of the year, the winter solstice, when the sun entered the sign of the Goat (Capricorn). The Gregorian calendar was not adopted in England till 1752, by which eleven days were added to the date. St. Lucy's festival is celebrated with lights and candles.
flasks The stars were thought to store up the sun's light as flasks store gunpowder.
light squibs weak flashes
sap . . . balm preservative essences of living things
hydroptic pathologically thirsty
bed's-feet A patient huddling at the foot of the bed was thought to be near death.
world . . . spring spring as *renovatio mundi*, rebirth of the world

For I am every dead thing,
In whom love wrought new alchemy.°
For his art did express°
A quintessence° even from nothingness,°
From dull privations, and lean emptiness;
He ruined me,° and I am re-begot
Of absence, darkness, death;° things which are not.

All° others, from all° things, draw all° that's good,
Life, soul, form, spirit, whence they being have;
I, by love's limbeck,° am the grave
Of all,° that's nothing.° Oft a flood
Have we two wept, and so
Drowned the whole world, us two;° oft did we grow
To be two chaoses, when we did show
Care to aught else;° and often absences
Withdrew our souls; and made us carcases.

But I am by her death (which word wrongs her)
Of the first nothing, the elixir grown;°
Were I a man, that I were one,
I needs must know; I should prefer,
If I were any beast,
Some ends, some means; yea plants, yea stones detest,
And love,° all, all some properties invest;°
If I an ordinary nothing were,
As° shadow, a light, and body must be here.

But I am none;° nor will my sun° renew.
You lovers, for whose sake, the lesser sun°
At this time to the Goat is run
To fetch new lust,° and give it you,
Enjoy your summer all;
Since she enjoys her long night's festival,°

new alchemy which, unlike the old, is concerned with the principle of deadness rather than the principle of life
express distill, extract (alchemical)
quintessence elixir, principle
from nothingness unlike "old" alchemy, which dealt with allness
He ruined me he broke down my substance (alchemical)
I am . . . death I am reconstituted by the forms of nothingness ("re-begot" is alchemical)
limbeck alembic, the distilling flask used by alchemists
All . . . nothing the basic conceit of the poem
Oft a flood . . . us two By weeping they have drowned the images of each other in their eyes (see "Valediction: Of Weeping" above); "flood" is another alchemical term.
show . . . else concerned ourselves about matters external to us, so causing our souls which having given form to our material bodies, to vacate them, leaving them chaoses
Of the first . . . grown become the quintessence not of chaos but of the primal nothing which preceded the institution of chaos (matter without form) by God
Were I . . . love If I were a man I should know it, because men have a rational soul; if a beast, I should have a sensitive soul, and make certain choices; if a plant, with only a vegetative soul, I could choose nutriment. Even (magnetic) stones, with no souls at all, attract and repel.
all . . . invest everything else is endowed with *some* properties
As such as
none usage to suggest absolute nothingness
my sun his lady
lesser sun the sun
to the Goat . . . lust to the sign of Capricorn to bring back lust, always associated with the goat
long night's festival dark sleep of death, which this, the longest night of the year, fittingly commemorates

Let me prepare towards her,° and let me call
This hour her virgil, and her eve, since this
Both the year's, and the day's deep midnight is.

1633

The Bait

Come live with me, and be my love,
And we will some new pleasures prove
Of golden sands, and crystal brooks,
With silken lines, and silver hooks.

There will the river whispering run
Warmed by thy eyes, more than the sun.
And there th'enamoured fish will stay,
Begging themselves they may betray.

When thou wilt swim in that live bath,
Each fish, which every channel hath,
Will amorously to thee swim,
Gladder to catch thee, than thou him.

If thou, to be so seen, be'st loth,
By sun, or moon, thou darkenest both,
And if myself have leave to see,
I need not their light, having thee.

Let others freeze with angling reeds,
And cut their legs, with shells and weeds,
Or treacherously poor fish beset,
With strangling snare, or windowy net:

Let coarse bold hands, from slimy nest
The bedded fish in banks out-wrest,
Or curious traitors, sleavesilk flies°
Bewitch poor fishes' wandering eyes.

For thee, thou need'st no such deceit,
For thou thyself art thine own bait,
That fish, that is not catched thereby,
Alas, is wiser far than I.

1633

prepare towards her fit myself by meditation for her feast
vigil service the night before a festival
The Bait A reply—by no means the first—to Marlowe's *The Passionate Shepherd to His Love* (cf. Ralegh's *Reply*). Walton quotes all three in *The Compleat Angler,* Donne's being of course especially appropriate; Walton thought it showed Donne "could make soft and smooth verses when he thought fit." It is also a piscatory pastoral, substituting the world of the fisherman for that of the shepherd.
sleavesilk flies artificial flies made of silk thread separable into finer filaments

The Apparition

When by thy scorn,° O murderess, I am dead,
And that thou think'st thee free
From all solicitation from me,
Then shall my ghost come to thy bed,
And thee, feigned vestal,° in worse arms shall see;
Then thy sick taper will begin to wink,
And he whose thou art then, being tired before,
Will, if thou stir, or pinch to wake him, think
Thou call'st for more,
And in false sleep will from thee shrink,
And then poor aspen° wretch, neglected thou
Bathed in a cold quicksilver sweat wilt lie
A verier ghost than I;
What I will say, I will not tell thee now,
Lest that preserve thee; and since my love is spent,
I had rather thou shouldst painfully repent,
Than by my threatenings rest still innocent.

1633

A Valediction: Forbidding Mourning

As virtuous men pass mildly away,
And whisper to their souls, to go,
Whilst some of their sad friends do say,
The breath goes now, and some say, no:

So let us melt, and make no noise,
No tear-floods, nor sigh-tempests move,
'Twere profanation of our joys
To tell the laity our love.

Moving of th' earth° brings harms and fears,
Men reckon what it did and meant,
But trepidation of the spheres,°
Though greater far, is innocent.°

Dull súblunary° lovers' love
(Whose soul is sense°) cannot admit
Absence, because it doth remove
Those things which elemented° it.

by thy scorn Donne takes up the Petrarchan theme of the lover dying of his mistress's scorn but gives it new dramatic force.
vestal holy virgin
aspen trembling (like a poplar leaf in the wind)
Moving of th'earth earthquakes
trepidation of the spheres libration of the ninth or crystalline sphere, which accounted for the precession of the equinoxes
innocent does no harm
sublunary below the moon, therefore more corrupt than the heavens
Whose soul is sense not mind; it therefore requires contact
elemented composed

But we by a love, so much refined,
That our selves know not what it is,
Inter-assurèd of the mind,
Care less, eyes, lips, and hands to miss.

Our two souls therefore, which are one,
Though I must go, endure not yet
A breach, but an expansion,
Like gold to aery thinness beat.

If they be two, they are two so
As stiff twin compasses° are two,
Thy soul the fixed foot, makes no show
To move, but doth, if th'other do.

And though it in the centre sit,
Yet when the other far doth roam,
It leans, and hearkens after it,
And grows erect, as that comes home.

Such wilt thou be to me, who must
Like the other foot, obliquely run;
Thy firmness makes my circle just,
And makes me end, where I begun.°

1633

The Ecstasy°

Where, like a pillow on a bed,
A pregnant bank swelled up, to rest
The violet's reclining head,°
Sat we two, one another's best;

Our hands were firmly cemented
With a fast balm, which thence did spring,°
Our eye-beams twisted, and did thread
Our eyes, upon one double string;°

compasses a familiar emblem, denoting constancy in change
end . . . begun complete circle
The Ecstasy The title means "standing outside," as the souls here are represented as doing; long periods of this were thought inadvisable, though the experience offered unmediated knowledge of divine truth. The argument concerns the power of the ecstatic joint soul of the lovers to know the truth about love when outside their bodies, but the man urges a return to the physical. Opinion is divided about the full tone and sense of the poem: to some it is a central statement of the poet's love-metaphysic, and deeply serious; to others it is an example of what Dryden called his power to "perplex the minds of the fair sex with the nice speculations of philosophy." At one extreme is the reading which takes the last line as referring merely to the return of the souls to the inanimate bodies; at the other, the view that the whole poem is a fantastic seduction. In fact the opinion that the last line connotes sexual activity does not imply cynicism, and there is no good reason not to treat the poem as both serious *and* persuasive to love. See also William Cartwright's "No Platonic Love."
Where . . . head a traditional, though quickly sketched, *locus amoenus:* setting for pastoral or garden love-making or love-talk
Our . . . spring sweat; a moist palm was an index of sexual desire
Our . . . string The light-rays, thought of as emerging from the eyes, twist together so that the eyes are like beads on a string.

So to intergraft° our hands, as yet
Was all our means to make us one,
And pictures in our eyes to get°
Was all our propagatiòn.°

As 'twixt two equal armies, Fate
Suspends uncertain victory,°
Our souls, (which to advance their state,°
Were gone out), hung 'twixt her, and me.

And whilst our souls negotiate° there,
We like sepulchral statues lay;
All day, the same our postures were,
And we said nothing, all the day.

If any, so by love refined,
That he soul's language understood,
And by good love were grown all mind,
Within convenient distance stood,

He (though he knew not which soul spake
Because both meant, both spake the same)
Might thence a new concoction° take,
And part far purer than he came.

This ecstasy doth unperplex
(We said) and tell us what we love,°
We see by this, it was not sex,
We see we saw not what did move:°

But as all several° souls contain
Mixture of things, they know not what,°
Love, these mixed souls doth mix again,
And makes both one, each this and that.°

A single violet transplant,
The strength, the colour, and the size,
(All which before was poor, and scant,)
Redoubles still, and multiplies.°

When love, with one another so
Interinanimates two souls,

intergraft graft one on the other; grafting—cf. Marvell, "Mower against Gardens"—was a sexual figure
pictures . . . get The reflection of one's face in an eye into which one is gazing was sometimes called a baby—hence *get* = beget.
propagatiòn five syllables
'twixt . . . victory The uncertainty of the outcome of a battle is represented by an image of Victory hanging between them.
state dignity
negotiate as in a parley before battle
concoction purification of metals by heat, of the physique by refinement of the animal spirits; see below
what we love the true object of their love
what did move what the true motive was
several distinct
Mixture . . . what the functions of the soul being both physical and spiritual, it must be of compounded nature which we cannot know exactly
Love . . . that The new single soul, made up of two, is also mixed, but has advantages explained later: that the two souls of lovers become one is a Platonic commonplace.
A single . . . multiplies either the violet propagates itself on transplantation, or grows richer double flowers

That abler soul, which thence doth flow,
Defects of loneliness controls.°

We then, who are this new soul, know,
Of what we are composed, and made,
For, th'atomies° of which we grow,
Are souls, whom no change can invade.°

But O alas, so long, so far
Our bodies why do we forbear?
They are ours, though they are not we, we are
The intelligences, they the sphere.°

We owe them thanks, because they thus,
Did us, to us, at first convey,
Yielded their forces, sense,° to us,
Nor are dross to us, but allay.°

On man heaven's influence works not so,
But that it first imprints the air,°
So soul into the soul may flow,
Though it to body first repair.

As our blood labours to beget
Spirits, as like souls as it can,°
Because such fingers need° to knit
That subtle° knot, which makes us man:

So must pure lovers' souls descend
T'affections,° and to faculties,°
Which sense may reach and apprehend,°
Else a great prince in prison lies.°

To our bodies turn we then, that so
Weak men on love revealed may look;°
Love's mysteries in souls do grow,
But yet the body is his book.°

And if some lover, such as we,
Have heard this dialogue of one,

Defects . . . controls overcomes the imperfections of separateness
atomies components
Are . . . invade Unlike the body, the soul is not subject to change; this completes the argument for the advantages of pure soul-union, and there is now a sharp turn in the poem.
we are . . . sphere Souls are to bodies as the angel-intelligence-spirit is to the planet—matter—it controls; cf. "Air and Angels" above.
forces, sense They have given up their power of movement to enable the souls to experience non-physical union.
dross . . . allay not the waste left over after metallurgical refinement but that which, in an alloy, makes the gold serviceable
heaven's . . . air The influence of the stars on men was held to occur through the medium of air; and angels (cf. "Air and Angels") took a body of air, "not pure as it," when appearing to men.
Spirits . . . can The animal spirits, "concocted" or refined from the blood, serve as a medium between matter and spirit, body and soul.
need are needed
subtle fine, impalpable
affections feelings, passions
faculties power of the body
Which . . . apprehend with which sense has contact and relation
Else . . . lies otherwise the new soul is impotent, has no agents
weak . . . look As the truths of religions accommodate themselves to weak men through revelation, so physical activity will make evident a love which otherwise would not be so.
body is his book as the Bible makes evident the truths of religion

Let him still mark us, he shall see
  Small change, when we are to bodies gone.°

1633

The Funeral

Whoever comes to shroud me, do not harm
    Nor question much
That subtle wreath of hair, which crowns my arm;
The mystery, the sign you must not touch,
    For 'tis my outward soul,
Viceroy to that, which then to heaven being gone,
    Will leave this to control,
And keep these limbs, her° provinces, from dissolution.

For if the sinewy thread° my brain lets fall
    Through every part,
Can tie those parts, and make me one of all;°
These hairs which upward grew, and strength and art
    Have from a better brain,
Can better do it; except° she meant that I
    By this should know my pain,
As prisoners then are manacled, when they're condemned to die.

Whate'er she meant by it, bury it with me,
    For since I am
Love's martyr, it might breed idolatry,
If into others' hands these relics came;
    As 'twas humility
To afford to it all that a soul can do,°
    So, 'tis some bravery,°
That since you would save none of me, I bury some of you.

1633

Farewell to Love°

  Whilst yet to prove,°
I thought there was some deity in love
  So did I reverence, and gave
Worship; as atheists at their dying hour
Call, what they cannot name, an unknown power,

some lover . . . gone The refined lover of line 21 will see that there is little difference between our loving before and after we used our bodies.
her the soul's
sinewy thread the nerves by which the brain transmits messages to the body
make . . . all unite my several parts into a whole person
except unless
To afford . . . do to credit it with the powers of a soul
bravery bravado
Farewell to Love Not positively ascribed to Donne in the 1633 edition; it is probably by him but may represent a draft rather than a finished poem.
Whilst . . . prove while still inexperienced

As ignorantly did I crave:
Thus when
Things not yet known are coveted by men,
Our desires give them fashion,° and so
As they wax lesser, fall, as they size, grow.°

But, from late° fair
His highness sitting in a golden chair,°
Is not less cared for after three days
By children, than the thing° which lovers so
Blindly admire, and with such worship woo;
Being had, enjoying it decays:°
And thence,
What before pleased them all, takes but one sense,°
And that so lamely, as it leaves behind
A kind of sorrowing dullness to the mind.°

Ah cannot we,
As well as cocks and lions° jocund be,
After such pleasures? Unless wise
Nature decreed (since each such act, they say,
Diminisheth the length of life a day)
This; as she would man should despise
The sport,
Because that other curse of being short,
And only for a minute made to be
Eager, desires to raise posterity.°

Since so,° my mind
Shall not desire what no man else can find,
I'll no more dote and run
To pursue things which had endamaged me.
And when I come where moving beauties° be,
As men do when the summer's sun
Grows great,
Though I admire their greatness, shun their heat;
Each place can afford shadows. If all fail,
'Tis but applying worm-seed° to the tail.°

1633

Our . . . fashion we imagine them to accord with our wishes
As . . . grow they decline as our desire reduces, grow as our desire expands
late some recent
His highness . . . chair gingerbread effigy of a prince sold to children at a fair
the thing sex
Being . . . decays once had, the enjoyment of it wanes
What . . . sense what formerly pleased all the senses now captivates only one (touch)
A kind . . . mind referring to the saying "omne animal post coitum triste" (all animals are sad after sex)
cocks and lions The medical authority Galen exempts these animals from the general rule.
Unless . . . posterity perhaps the most difficult passage in Donne, and possibly corrupt—"unless nature, because every act of sex is said to reduce one's life by a day, wisely arranged that men should feel contemptuous of sex when the act is over; since its other disadvantage (its brevity) would otherwise lead us to do it too often." Here "desires to raise posterity" is taken to mean "wants the act to beget other successive acts."
so it is so
moving beauties beauties who rouse my desire
worm-seed an anaphrodisiac
tail penis

The Relic°

When my grave is broke up again
Some second guest to entertain,
(For graves have learned that woman-head°
To be to more than one a bed)
And he that digs it, spies
A bracelet of bright hair about the bone,
Will he not let us alone,
And think that there a loving couple lies,
Who thought that this device might be some way
To make their souls, at the last busy day,°
Meet at this grave, and make a little stay?

If this fall° in a time, or land,
Where mis-devotion° doth command,
Then, he that digs us up, will bring
Us, to the Bishop, and the King,
To make us relics; then
Thou shalt be a Mary Magdalen,° and I
A something else° thereby;
All women shall adore us, and some men;
And since at such time, miracles are sought,
I would have that age by this paper° taught
What miracles we harmless lovers wrought.

First, we loved well and faithfully,
Yet knew not what we loved, nor why,
Difference of sex no more we knew,
Than our guardian angels° do;
Coming and going,° we
Perchance might kiss, but not between those meals;
Our hands ne'er touched the seals,
Which nature, injured by late law, sets free:°
These miracles we did; but now alas,
All measure, and all language, I should pass,
Should I tell what a miracle she was.

1633

The Relic Cf. "The Funeral"; the situation is the same, but at a somewhat later time.
woman-head woman-like behavior
last busy day the Resurrection
this fall the digging up of my body should happen
mis-devotion false religious practices, such as the use of relics
a Mary Magdalen in art represented as having golden hair, and in her youth could have given lovers such tokens
a something else contemptuous for Mary's lover; or, scandalously, "Jesus Christ," represented in that role
this paper this poem
guardian angels having no sexuality
Coming and going arriving and departing
seals . . . free prohibitions on sexual conduct which do not exist in nature, but which law and custom have, at a later time of the world, imposed

Satire III

Donne wrote five satires in the 1590's, a time when they were greatly in vogue (publication of satire was inhibited in 1598). Partly because of a mistaken etymology which related satire to *Satyr,* the Elizabethan practitioners affected a very rough style, harsh and "snarling," as appropriate to an uncouth natural speaker commenting on the evil sophistication of city life. Hence the violently misplaced accents, hypermetric syllables, and forced rhymes, not to speak of the farfetched images and emphasis on vice and ugliness, of Donne's satires. The ancient model was Horace, whose satires are colloquial in manner and have similar themes, but are not, in this sense, "harsh."

The third Satire is unlike the others, not in manner but in theme. It concerns the necessity for choosing a religion, a necessity nonetheless paramount because the decision is not one to be made hastily. This was Donne's own position as a young man; he said he "used no inordinate haste, nor precipitation, in binding my conscience to any local religion" (*Pseudo-Martyr*), but nevertheless regarded the choice as of great urgency. He seems to have regarded himself as Protestant from about the turn of the century; this poem probably belongs to 1595. It is unique in the impassioned immediacy of its religious argument; it is part satiric railing against men's unwillingness to give priority to their most urgent concerns, part sarcasm at the expense of contemporary religious follies, and partly virile exhortation. Above all it considers, in the very voice of urgent meditation, the harsh and solemn necessity of choice imposed upon the serious Christian in an age when doctrinal differences were reflected in political power-struggles. It reminds us that the poet of the Elegies was, at the same time, profoundly concerned to use his mind and poetic powers on what seemed to him the greatest single issue, that of the true religion.

Satire III

Kind pity chokes my spleen;° brave scorn° forbids
Those tears to issue which swell my eye-lids,
I must not laugh, nor weep sins, and be wise;°
Can railing° then cure these worn° maladies?
Is not our mistress fair religion,
As worthy of all our soul's devotion,
As virtue was to the first blinded age?°
Are not heaven's joys as valiant to assuage
Lusts, as earth's honour° was to them? Alas,
As we do them in means, shall they surpass
Us in the end, and shall thy father's spirit
Meet blind philosophers in heaven, whose merit

spleen the source of scornful laughter
brave scorn the flaunting scorn of the satirist
I must . . . wise If I'm to be wise I mustn't, it seems, either laugh about sins or weep over them
railing ranting, shouting down
worn hackneyed
first blinded age Before Christ the philosophers, denied the light of revelation, worshipped virtue; we should surely think as well of religion as they did of virtue.
earth's honour which was all they had, whereas we have the bliss of heaven

Of strict life may be imputed faith,° and hear
Thee, whom he taught so easy ways and near
To follow, damned? O if thou dar'st, fear this;
This fear great courage, and high valour is.
Dar'st thou aid mutinous Dutch,° and dar'st thou lay
Thee in ships' wooden sepulchres, a prey
To leaders' rage, to storms, to shot, to dearth?
Dar'st thou dive seas, and dungeons° of the earth?
Hast thou courageous fire to thaw the ice
Of frozen north discoveries?° and thrice
Colder than salamanders,° like divine
Children in th'oven,° fires of Spain, and the line,°
Whose countries limbecks° to our bodies be,
Canst thou for gain bear? and must every he
Which cries not, 'Goddess!' to thy mistress, draw,
Or eat thy poisonous words? courage of straw!
O desperate coward, wilt thou seem bold, and
To thy foes and his° (who made thee to stand
Sentinel in his world's garrison) thus yield,
And for forbidden wars, leave th'appointed field?
Know thy foes: the foul Devil, he, whom thou
Strivest to please, for hate, not love, would allow
Thee fain, his whole realm to be quit;° and as
The world's all parts wither away and pass,
So the world's self, thy other loved foe, is
In her decrepit wane,° and thou loving this,
Doest love a withered and worn strumpet; last,
Flesh (itself's death)° and joys which flesh can taste,
Thou lovest; and thy fair goodly soul, which doth
Give this flesh power to taste joy, thou dost loathe.
Seek true religion. O where? Mirreus°
Thinking her unhoused here, and fled from us,
Seeks her at Rome, there, because he doth know
That she was there a thousand years ago,
He loves her rags° so, as we here obey
The statecloth where the Prince sate yesterday.°
Crants° to such brave° loves will not be enthralled,

blind . . . faith though not justified by faith, since they lived before Christ, they may be in heaven because their pagan virtues qualify them—are imputed to them as faith
mutinous Dutch The Dutch resisted their Spanish overlords, and the English sometimes assisted them.
dungeon mines, caves
frozen . . . discoveries attempts to find a northwest passage to the Pacific
salamanders lizards supposed to live in fire
divine . . . oven Shadrach, Meshach, and Abednego, who survived the ordeal of the fiery furnace into which Nebuchadnezzar cast them
fires . . . line the Inquisition and tropical heat
limbecks alchemical stills
his God's
the foul . . . quit Satan, whom you try to please, would willingly grant you his whole kingdom, but for hate, not love
decrepit wane Donne often recurs to the view that the world is declining into its last age.
(itself's death) the sins of the flesh bring about its destruction
Mirreus the Romanist; perhaps latinized from "Mreo," anagram of "Rome"
rags ceremonial survivals
statecloth . . . yesterday the canopy over the chair of state; the throne was reverenced even in the monarch's absence
Crants Calvinist
brave showy

But loves her only, who at Geneva° is called
Religiòn, plain, simple, sullen, young,
Contemptuous, yet unhandsome; as among
Lecherous humours,° there is one that judges
No wenches wholesome, but coarse country drudges.
Graius° stays still at home here, and because
Some preachers, vile ambitious bawds,° and laws
Still new like fashions,° bid him think that she
Which dwells with us, is only° perfect, he
Embraceth her, whom his godfathers will
Tender to him, being tender,° as wards still
Take such wives as their guardians offer, or
Pay values.° Careless Phrygius° doth abhor
All, because all cannot be good, as one
Knowing some women whores, dares marry none.
Gracchus° loves all as one, and thinks that so
As women do in divers countries go
In divers habits, yet are still one kind,
So does, so is religion; and this blind-
ness too much light breeds;° but unmovèd thou
Of force must one, and forced but one allow;
And the right; ask thy father° which is she,
Let him ask his; though truth and falsehood be
Near twins, yet truth a little elder is;°
Be busy to seek her, believe me this,
He's not of none, nor worst, that seeks the best.°
To adore, or scorn an image, or protest,°
May all be bad; doubt wisely; in strange way°
To stand inquiring right, is not to stray;
To sleep, or run wrong is. On a huge hill,
Cragged, and steep, Truth stands, and he that will
Reach her, about must, and about must go;
And what the hill's suddenness resists, win so;°
Yet strive so, that before age, death's twilight,
Thy soul rest, for none can work in that night,°

Geneva center of Calvinism
lecherous humours men of lecherous tastes
Graius Greek; perhaps because the Greeks worshipped "an unknown God"—Acts 17–23 —and sought novelty
ambitious bawds pimps seeking advancement by selling their girl
Still . . . fashions always changing, like fashions (the variety of English laws aimed at securing conformity)
only alone
Tender . . . tender offer to him in his infancy
Pay values Wards who refused the marriage proposed for them by their guardians had to pay a fine; so, under the Act of Uniformity of 1559, did people who refused to attend the parish church.
Phrygius who turns against all religion
Gracchus named for the Roman Gracchi, who were democrats; a liberal, unwisely tolerant
bindness . . . breeds too much light breeds this blindness
ask thy father "Ask thy father and he will show thee," Deuteronomy 32:7
a little elder is the need is to get back to the facts of the true primitive church; heresy is almost but not quite as old
He's . . . best he's not of no religion, nor of the worst religion, who seeks the best religion
protest be Protestant
in strange way on an unfamilar road
And what . . . so thus achieve what the steepness of the hill tries to prevent
that night "the night cometh, when no man can work" (John 9:4)

To will implies delay, therefore now do.
Hard deeds, the body's pains; hard knowledge too
The mind's endeavours reach,° and mysteries
Are like the sun, dazzling, yet plain to all eyes.°
Keep the truth which thou hast found; men do not stand
In so ill case° here, that God hath with his hand
Signed king's blank-charters° to kill whom they hate,
Nor are they vicars,° but hangmen to Fate.
Fool and wretch, wilt thou let thy soul be tied
To man's laws, by which she shall not be tried
At the last day? Or will it then boot thee
To say a Philip,° or a Gregory,°
A Harry,° or a Martin° taught thee this?
Is not this excuse for mere° contraries,
Equally strong; cannot both sides say so?
That thou mayest rightly obey power, her bounds know;
Those past, her nature, and name is changed;° to be
Then humble to her is idolatry.
As streams are, power is; those blessed flowers that dwell
At the rough stream's calm head, thrive and prove well,
But having left their roots, and themselves given
To the stream's tyrannous rage, alas are driven
Through mills, and rocks, and woods, and at last, almost
Consumed in going, in the sea are lost:
So perish souls, which more choose men's unjust
Power from God claimed, than God himself to trust.

from MS. 1802

The Second Anniversary

Donne wrote two *Anniversaries* to commemorate the death at fourteen of Elizabeth Drury in 1610. The girl's father, Sir Robert, was his benefactor, but he never met the girl. These strange poems—Donne's longest, and interesting experiments in the prolongation during lengthy structured works of the fantastic conceited style of the funeral elegy—were regarded at the time as excessive; Ben Jonson is reported as saying that "Donne's Anniversary was profane and full of blasphemies; that he had told Mr. Donne, if it had been written of the Virgin Mary it had been something; to which he answered, that he described the Idea of a Woman, and not as she was."

The poems, especially the second, use an elaborate system of linked formal meditations. The first, *An Anatomy of the World,* treats the girl as the embodiment of all that

Hard deeds . . . reach as the labor of the body achieves severe physical tasks, so that of the mind achieves hard knowledge
mysteries . . . eyes the fact that we can never comprehend them doesn't alter the fact that they are visibly there
so ill case such an evil condition
blank-charters Richard II made wealthy men sign promises to pay money to him, and to leave the sum blank; here the idea is extended to death warrants which could be filled in at the whim of the ruler.
vicars deputies
Philip Philip II of Spain
Gregory Pope Gregory VII (who in the 11th century established papal power over secular rulers) or Gregory XIII or Gregory XIV (contemporary popes)
Harry Henry VIII
Martin Luther
mere absolute
nature . . . changed to tyranny

men forfeited at the Fall, and imagines the world as a corpse following the departure of its soul. The second, *The Progress of the Soul,* dwells on the advantages enjoyed by the soul after death by comparison with "the incommodities of the soul in this life." The extract is from a section dealing with a theme Donne often treated, the uselessness and partiality of earthly knowledge in comparison with the full knowledge of essentials that the soul will achieve in heaven.

From The Second Anniversary

Poor soul, in this thy flesh what dost thou know?
Thou know'st thyself so little, as thou know'st not,
How thou didst die, nor how thou wast begot.
Thou neither know'st, how thou at first cam'st in,
Nor how thou took'st the poison of man's sin.°
Nor dost thou, (though thou know'st, that thou art so)
By what way thou art made immortal, know.
Thou art too narrow, wretch, to comprehend
Even thyself; yea though thou wouldst but bend
To know thy body. Have not all souls thought
For many ages, that our body is wrought
Of air, and fire, and other elements?
And now they think of new ingredients,°
And one soul thinks one, and another way
Another thinks, and 'tis an even lay.
Know'st thou but how the stone doth enter in
The bladder's cave, and never break the skin?
Know'st thou how blood, which to the heart doth flow,
Doth from one ventricle to th'other go?°
And for the putrid stuff, which thou dost spit,
Know'st thou how thy lungs have attracted it?
There are no passages, so that there is
(For aught thou know'st) piercing of substances.°
And of those many opinions which men raise
Of nails and hairs,° dost thou know which to praise?
What hope have we to know our selves, when we
Know not the least things, which for our use be?
We see in authors, too stiff to recant,
A hundred controvèrsies of an ant;
And yet one watches, starves, freezes, and sweats,
To know but catechisms and alphabets
Of unconcerning° things, matters of fact;

how . . . sin whether from the parents or by direct infusion—an old controversy
new ingredients The old Galenist view was that earth, water, and fire were balanced in man; the Paracelsan novelty lay in making the constituents chemical, e.g. sulfur, mercury, etc.
blood . . . go Harvey's discoveries were published in 1628.
piercing of substances transmission of matter through solid resistances
opinions . . . hairs whether or no they were organic or waste matter
unconcerning trivial; a magnificent statement of the argument

How others on our stage their parts did act;
What Caesar did, yea, and what Cicero said.
Why grass is green, or why our blood is red,
Are mysteries which none have reached unto.
In this low form,° poor soul, what wilt thou do?
When wilt thou shake off this pedántery,
Of being taught by sense and fantasy?°
Thou look'st through spectacles; small things seem great
Below; but up unto the watch-tower get,
And see all things despoiled of fallacies:
Thou shalt not peep through lattices of eyes,
Nor hear through labyrinths of ears, nor learn
By circuit,° or collections° to discern.
In heaven thou straight know'st all, concerning it,°
And what concerns it not, shalt straight forget.

1612

The Holy Sonnets

It seems probable that all these sonnets, except for three in the Westmoreland manuscript, belong to about 1609–11, that is, before Donne's ordination. These other three are later: one on the death of his wife (1617), one on the defeat of the Protestants at the battle of the White Mountain in 1620, and one uncertain, but presumably late. Of the remaining sixteen, four are additional to the two sequences of six which appeared in the first edition of 1633. Their order in that edition is the correct one, as Dame Helen Gardner showed when she restored and justified it in her 1952 Oxford edition of Donne's *Divine Poems*.

The first six, here represented by II, IV, V, and VI, are meditations on the Last Judgment; the second six, of which only X is given here, meditate on the Atonement and on the love owed by man to God and to his neighbor, and plead the intervention of God in the subject's life. The Jesuit meditation, based on the prescriptions of St. Ignatius Loyola, was designed to involve all the powers of the soul, including the senses, in the contemplation of some religious object or moment—the subject's own deathbed, for example, or the Crucifixion, or, as in IV, the Last Judgment. Donne adapts this form of meditation to an Italian sonnet form, usually with a clear break at the *volta,* after the eighth line, and a change of tone in the sestet, which is quieter and more reflective than the octave. It was admirably suited to his powers, providing for passionate and excited as well as for devotional language and rhythms.

II

Oh my black soul! now thou art summonèd
By sickness, death's herald, and champion;
Thou art like a pilgrim, which abroad hath done
Treason, and durst not turn° to whence he is fled,
Or like a thief, which till death's doom be read,

low form humble condition
sense and fantasy by the evidence of the senses as treated by the fancy or imagination, i.e. by fallible human instruments
circuit roundabout processes
collections inferences
it heaven
turn return

Wisheth himself deliverèd from prison;
But damned and haled to executiòn,
Wisheth that still he might be imprisonèd;
Yet grace, if thou repent, thou canst not lack;
But who shall give thee that grace to begin?°
Oh make thyself with holy mourning black,
And red with blushing, as thou art with sin;
Or wash thee in Christ's blood, which hath this might
That being red, it dyes red souls to white.

IV

At the round earth's imagined corners,° blow
Your trumpets, angels, and arise, arise
From death, you numberless infinities
Of souls, and to your scattered bodies go,
All whom the flood did, and fire shall o'erthrow,
All whom war, dearth, age, agues, tyrannies,
Despair, law, chance, hath slain, and you whose eyes,
Shall behold God, and never taste death's woe.°
But° let them sleep, Lord, and me mourn a space,
For, if above all these, my sins abound,
'Tis late to ask abundance of thy grace,°
When we are there; here on this lowly ground,
Teach me how to repent; for that's as good
As if thou hadst sealed° my pardon, with thy blood.

V

If poisonous minerals, and if that tree,
Whose fruit threw death on else immortal us,
If lecherous goats, if serpents envious
Cannot be damned;° alas, why should I be?
Why should intent or reason, born in me,
Make sins, else equal, in me more heinous?
And mercy being easy, and glorious
To God, in his stern wrath, why threatens he?
But who am I,° that dare dispute with thee
O God? Oh! of thine only worthy blood,°
And my tears, make a heavenly lethean° flood,
And drown in it my sin's black memory;
That thou remember them, some claim as debt,°
I think it mercy, if thou wilt forget.

grace to begin prevenient grace, without which the repentance which gains further grace is impossible
imagined corners Revelation 7:1
never . . . woe I Corinthians 15:51–52
But the characteristic change of tone for the sestet
sins . . . grace Romans 6:1
sealed confirmed
If . . . be damned Only men, who have reason, can be damned; cf. *Dr. Faustus* XVIII. 171 ff.
But who am I Changing tone in sestet, he reproves himself for arguing with God's dispensations.
thine . . . blood thy blood which is alone worthy
lethean Lethe was the river of Hades out of which souls drank forgetfulness of their previous existence.
That . . . debt some ask for their sins to be remembered, and so included in the debt Christ discharged

VI

Death be not proud, though some have callèd thee
Mighty and dreadful, for, thou art not so,
For, those, whom thou think'st, thou dost overthrow,
Die not, poor death, nor yet canst thou kill me;
From rest and sleep, which but thy pictures be,
Much pleasure, then from thee, much more must flow,°
And soonest our best men with thee do go,°
Rest of their bones, and soul's delivery.
Thou art slave to fate, chance, kings, and desperate men,
And dost with poison, war, and sickness dwell,
And poppy,° or charms can make us sleep as well,
And better than thy stroke; why swell'st thou then?
One short sleep past, we wake eternally,
And death shall be no more, Death thou shalt die.

X

Batter my heart, three-personed° God; for, you
As yet but knock, breathe, shine, and seek to mend;
That I may rise, and stand, o'erthrow me, and bend
Your force, to break, blow, burn, and make me new.
I, like an usurped town, to another due,°
Labour to admit you, but oh, to no end,
Reason your viceroy in me, me should defend,
But is captived, and proves weak or untrue,
Yet dearly I love you,° and would be loved fain,
But am bethrothed unto your enemy,
Divorce me, untie, or break that knot again,
Take me to you, imprison me, for I
Except you enthral° me, never shall be free,
Nor ever chaste, except you ravish me.

XIX

Oh, to vex° me, contraries meet in one:
Inconstancy unnaturally hath begot
A constant habit; that when I would not
I change in vows, and in devotiòn.
As humorous° is my contritiòn
As my profane love,° and as soon forgot:
As riddlingly distempered,° cold and hot,

From rest . . . flow if we derive pleasure from rest and sleep, which are only images of death, how much more should we get from death itself
soonest . . . go the good die without fuss
swell's puff yourself up
poppy opiate
three-personed the trinity
to another due owing allegiance to someone other than the usurper, in this case the devil
Yet . . . you For the sestet the figure changes to one of love, marriage, and rape.
enthral take prisoner
vex trouble
humorous changeable, whimsical
As . . . love rare instance of Donne's relating sacred and profane love
riddlingly distempered puzzlingly disproportioned

As praying, as mute; as infinite, as none.
I durst not view heaven yesterday; and today
In prayers, and flattering speeches I court God:
Tomorrow I quake with true fear of his rod.
So my devout fits come and go away
Like a fantastic ague:° save that here
Those are my best days, when I shake with fear.°

1633

Good Friday, 1613. Riding Westward°

Let man's soul be a sphere, and then, in this,
The intelligence that moves, devotion is,
And as the other spheres, by being grown
Subject to foreign motions, lose their own,
And being by others hurried every day,
Scarce in a year their natural form obey:
Pleasure or business, so, our souls admit
For their first mover, and are whirled by it.°
Hence is't, that I am carried towards the west
This day, when my soul's form° bends toward the east.
There I should see a sun, by rising set,°
And by that setting endless day beget;°
But that Christ on this Cross, did rise and fall,
Sin had eternally benighted all.
Yet dare I almost be glad, I do not see
That spectacle of too much weight for me.
Who sees God's face, that is self life,° must die;°
What a death were it then to see God die?°
It made his own lieutenant° Nature shrink,
It made his footstool crack,° and the sun wink.
Could I behold those hands which span the poles,
And turn° all spheres at once, pierced with those holes?
Could I behold that endless height which is
Zenith° to us, and to our antipodes,°

fantastic ague capricious fever; agues, caused by malaria, struck at intervals
best . . . fear the difference from an ague is that in that case one's worst days are the days on which one shakes
Good Friday, 1613. . . . a meditation actually composed on a journey taken that day from Warwickshire to Montgomery in Wales
Let . . . whirled by it as the angel-intelligence moves its heavenly body, so the devotion moves man's soul; and as the regular motion of heavenly bodies is affected by external forces, so that they are rarely in their proper orbits, so the forces of business or pleasure take over from devotion and move us in directions not proper to us
soul's form devotion
by rising set . . . beget Christ coming into the world and dying; by so doing he creates the possibility of eternal life
self life the essence of life
must die Exodus 33:20
die the *rime riche,* unusual in English verse
lieutenant deputy
footstool crack Isaiah 66:1 and, for the earthquake at the Crucifixion, Matthew 27:51
turn An alternative reading, "tune," would make this refer to the music of the spheres.
Zenith . . . antipodes the highest point to us and also to those who inhabit the other side of the world

Humbled below us? or that blood which is
The seat of all our souls, if not of his,°
Made dirt of dust,° or that flesh which was worn,
By God, for his apparel, ragged, and torn?
If on these things I durst not look, durst I
Upon his miserable mother cast mine eye,
Who was God's partner here, and furnished thus
Half of that sacrifice, which ransomed us?
Though these things, as I ride, be from mine eye,
They are present yet unto my memory,
For that looks towards them; and thou look'st towards me,
O Saviour, as thou hang'st upon the tree;
I turn my back to thee, but to receive
Corrections, till thy mercies bid thee leave.
O think me worth thine anger, punish me,
Burn off my rusts, and my deformity,
Restore thine image,° so much, by thy grace,
That thou mayst know me, and I'll turn my face.

1633

Hymn to God My God, in My Sickness°

Since I am coming to that holy room,°
  Where, with thy choir of saints for evermore,
I shall be made thy music; as I come
  I tune the instrument here at the door,
  And what I must do then, think now before.

Whilst my physicians by their love° are grown
  Cosmographers, and I their map, who lie
Flat on this bed, that by them may be shown
  That this is my south-west discovery°
  Per fretum febris,° by these strains to die,

I joy, that in these straits, I see my west;°
  For, though their currents yield return to none,
What shall my west hurt me? As west and east
  In all flat maps (and I am one) are one,
  So death doth touch the resurrection.

The seat . . . of his whether or no the blood is, as some say, the seat of the soul, Christ's blood is certainly the seat of ours
Made . . . dust turned into mud by mixing with dust
Restore thine image (by punishment) make anew your likeness in me
Hymn to God, in My Sickness According to Walton this was written by Donne on his deathbed, but more likely it dates, like "A Hymn to God the Father," from his illness of 1623.
holy room heaven
love attentive care to his body
Cosmographers geographers
south-west discovery The south is hot, the west "declining"—cf. "The Good Morrow"—and so the discovery of a southwest passage to the East is an emblem of death by fever.
Per fretum febris *fretum* is both "heat" and "strait": through the hot strait of fever
my west my death (his east will be the resurrection)

Is the Pacific Sea° my home? Or are
  The eastern riches?° Is Jerusalem?°
Anyan,° and Magellan, and Gibraltàr,
  All straits, and none but straits, are ways to them,°
  Whether where Japhet dwelt, or Cham, or Shem.°

We think that Paradise and Calvary,
  Christ's cross, and Adam's tree, stood in one place;°
Look Lord, and find both Adams met in me;
  As the first Adam's sweat surrounds my face,
  May the last Adam's blood my soul embrace.

So, in his purple wrapped receive me Lord,
  By these his thorns° give me his other crown;
And as to others' souls I preached thy word,
  Be this my text, my sermon to mine own,
  Therefore that° he may raise the Lord throws down.

1635

A Hymn to God the Father°

I

Wilt thou forgive that sin where I begun,
  Which is my sin, though it were done before?°
Wilt thou forgive that sin, through which I run,°
  And do run still:° though still° I do deplore?
    When thou hast done, thou hast not done,°
      For I have more.

II

Wilt thou forgive that sin which I have won
  Others to sin? and, made my sin their door?
Wilt thou forgive that sin which I did shun
  A year, or two, but wallowed in a score?
    When thou hast done, thou hast not done,
      For I have more.

Pacific Sea which could stand for heavenly peace
eastern riches standing for heaven
Jerusalem standing, as always, for the Heavenly City
Anyan Annam, then thought of as a strait dividing Asia from America
All straits . . . to them all the ways to heaven are "straits"
Japhet . . . Cham . . . Shem The world was divided between the sons of Noah: Japhet got Europe, Ham Africa, and Shem Asia.
Paradise . . . one place This myth is recorded elsewhere, but seems not to have been widespread, though Donne refers to it twice.
these his thorns the poet's sufferings which resemble Christ's
Therefore that in order that
A Hymn to God the Father according to Walton, written during the serious illness of 1623 which also produced the *Devotions*. A contemporary musical setting by John Hilton survives.
my sin . . . before the sin of his parents, by which original sin was transmitted to him
run ran
still always
When . . . done When you've done that you've not finished / When you've done that you've still not gained Donne

III

I have a sin of fear, that when I have spun
My last thread, I shall perish on the shore;
But swear by thy self, that at my death thy son°
Shall shine as he shines now, and heretofore;
And, having done that, thou hast done,
I fear no more.

1633

Devotions upon Emergent Occasions

From Meditation X

This is Nature's nest of Boxes: the Heavens contain the earth, the earth, cities, cities, men. And all these are concentric: the common center to them all is decay, ruin; only that is eccentric which was never made; only that place or garment rather, which we can imagine, but not demonstrate—that light which is the very emanation of the light of God, in which the saints shall dwell, with which the saints shall be apparelled—only that bends not to this center, this ruin; that which was not made of Nothing is not threatened with this annihilation. All other things are, even angels, even our souls: they move upon the same poles, they bend to the same center, and if they were not made immortal by preservation, their nature could not keep them from sinking to this center, annihilation.

Meditation XVII

Nunc lento sonitu dicunt, Morieris [1]
Now this bell, rolling softly for another, says to me, Thou must die

Perchance he for whom this bell [2] tolls may be so ill as that he knows not it tolls for him; and perchance I may think myself so much better than I am, as that they who are about me and see my state, may have caused it to toll for me, and I know not that. The church is catholic, universal; so are all her actions; all that she does belongs to all. When she baptizes a child, that action concerns me, for that child is thereby connected to that Head which is my Head too, and engraffed [3] into that body, whereof I am a member.[4] And when she buries a man, that action concerns me. All mankind is of one author, and is one volume; when one man dies, one chapter is not torn out of the book, but trans-

thy son a pun which makes Christ = the sun

1. Literally, "Now they say with their slow sounding, 'Thou shalt die.' "
2. Passing-bell.
3. Grafted.
4. The church.

lated[5] into a better language, and every chapter must be so translated; God employs several translators; some pieces are translated by age, some by sickness, some by war, some by justice; but God's hand is in every translation; and his hand shall bind up all our scattered leaves again for that library where every book shall lie open to one another. As therefore the bell that rings to a sermon calls not upon the preacher only, but upon the congregation to come, so this bell calls us all; but how much more me, who am brought so near the door by this sickness. There was a contention as far as a suit[6] (in which both piety and dignity, religion and estimation,[7] were mingled) which of the religious orders should ring to prayers first in the morning; and it was determined, that they should ring first that rose earliest. If we understand aright the dignity of this bell that tolls for our evening prayer, we would be glad to make it ours by rising early, in that application, that it might be ours as well as his whose indeed it is. The bell doth toll for him that thinks it doth; and though it intermit[8] again, yet from that minute that that occasion wrought upon him, he is united to God. Who casts not[9] up his eye to the sun when it rises? But who takes off his eye from a comet when that breaks out? Who bends not[9] his ear to any bell which upon any occasion rings? But who can remove it from that bell which is passing a piece of himself out of this world? No man is an island, entire of itself; every man is a piece of the continent, a part of the main;[10] if a clod be washed away by the sea, Europe is the less, as well as if a promontory were, as well as if a manor[11] of thy friend's or of thine own were. Any man's death diminishes me, because I am involved in mankind; and therefore never send to know for whom the bell tolls; it tolls for thee. Neither can we call this a begging of misery or a borrowing of misery, as though we were not miserable enough of ourselves, but must fetch in more from the next house, in taking upon us the misery of our neighbours. Truly it were an excusable covetousness if we did; for affliction is a treasure, and scarce any man hath enough of it. No man hath affliction enough that is not matured and ripened by it, and made fit for God by that affliction. If a man carry treasure in bullion, or in a wedge of gold, and have none coined into current monies, his treasure will not defray him as he travels. Tribulation is treasure in the nature of it, but it is not current money in the use of it, except we get nearer and nearer our home, heaven, by it. Another man may be sick too, and sick to death, and this affliction may lie in his bowels, as gold in a mine, and be of no use to him; but this bell, that tells me of his affliction, digs out and applies that gold to me, if by this consideration of another's danger, I take mine own into contemplation, and so secure myself by making my recourse to my God, who is our only security.

1624

5. Punning on the etymological sense, "carried over."
6. Which went as far as legal action.
7. Self-esteem.
8. Break off.
9. These words may be intrusive; the sense is stronger without them.
10. Mainland.
11. Estate.

Sermons

By the end of his life, when he was Dean of St. Paul's, Donne's chief fame was as a preacher. His sermons form a vast bulk, and nowadays they are mostly read by scholars seeking, and finding, enlightenment concerning what they value more highly, namely, the poems; but they are, in themselves, a great achievement. They are not all of equal importance or profundity; some were for learned audiences, some for large; some are relatively perfunctory, some terrifying. The liturgical season, the particular occasion, affect the tone. Like most preachers of his time, Donne was preoccupied by sin and death; he confesses his melancholy and his desire for extinction. "I preach the sense of God's indignation on mine own soul." But there is joy also, and humanity. Above all there is a learned wit, which relates the old to the young Donne, and both to the other great preachers of his day. He followed the general scheme employed in the very long sermons of the time, but expected his audience, in the midst of their instruction, to follow his puns and allusions, as well as to respond to the immense eloquence he could produce when he thought fit.

It is impossible to select one brief passage and expect it to give any notion of Donne the preacher; the famous final sermon *Death's Duel* is not really characteristic, and too many anthologists have, by choosing only purple passages, given a positively false impression. What follows here is from a fine but not spectacular sermon on a central biblical text. There is just about enough of it to enable the reader to see how Donne handled a text, and how he defined and enriched his theme for an audience which, though made up of better listeners than any preacher could find today, nevertheless needed the preacher's summations, repetitions and explanations, if they were to follow him.

From A Sermon Preached at St. Paul's for Easter-Day, 1628

> 'For now we see through a glass darkly, but then face to face; now I know in part, but then I shall know even as also I am known.'[1]

These two terms in our text, *nunc* and *tunc,* now and then, now in a glass, then face to face, now in part, then in perfection, these two secular[2] terms, of which one designs the whole age of this world from the creation to the dissolution thereof, for all that is comprehended in this word *now,* and the other designs the everlastingness of the next world, for that incomprehensibleness is comprehended in the other word *then*—these two words that design two such ages are now met in one day, in this day in which we celebrate all resurrections in the root in the resurrection of our Lord and Saviour Christ Jesus blest forever. For the first term, *now,* 'Now in a glass, now in part,' is intended most especially of that very act which we do now at this present, that is, of the ministry of the Gospel, of declaring God in his ordinance, of preaching his word, 'Now,' in

1. I Corinthians 13:12–"glass" = "mirror."
2. Relating to ages.

this ministry of his Gospel, 'we see in a glass, we know in part'; and then the *then,* the time of seeing face to face and knowing as we are known is intended of that time which we celebrate this day, the day of resurrection, the day of judgement, the day of the actual possession of the next life. So that this day this whole Scripture is fulfilled in your ears; for now, now in this preaching, you have some sight, and then, then when that day comes which in the first root thereof we celebrate this day, you shall have a perfect sight of all; 'Now we see through a glass,' etc.

That therefore you may the better know him when you come to see him face to face than by having seen him in a glass now, and that your seeing him now in his ordinance[3] may prepare you to see him then in his essence, proceed we thus in the handling of these words. First, that there is nothing brought into comparison, into consideration, nothing put into the balance, but the sight of God, the knowledge of God; it is not called a better sight, nor a better knowledge, but there is no other sight, no other knowledge proposed or mentioned or intimated or imagined but this; all other sight is blindness, all other knowledge is ignorance;[4] and then we shall see how there is a twofold sight of God and a twofold knowledge of God proposed to us here; a sight and a knowledge here in this life, and another manner of sight and another manner of knowledge in the life to come; for here we see God *in speculo,* in a glass, that is, by reflection, and here we know God *in ænigmate,* says our text, darkly, so we translate it, that is, by obscure presentations, and therefore it is called a knowledge but in part; but in heaven our sight is face to face, and our knowledge is to know as we are known.

For our sight of God here, our theatre, the place where we sit and see him, is the whole world, the whole house and frame of nature, and our medium, our glass, is the book of creatures, and our light, by which we see him, is the light of natural reason. And then for our knowledge of God here, our place, our academy, our university is the church, our medium is the ordinance of God in his church, preaching and sacraments; and our light is the light of faith. Thus we shall find it to be for our sight and for our knowledge of God here. But for our sight of God in heaven, our place, our sphere is heaven itself, our medium is the patefaction,[5] the manifestation, the revelation of God himself, and our light is the light of glory. And then for our knowledge of God there, God himself is all; God himself is the place, we see him in him; God is our medium, we see him by him; God is our light; not a light which is his, but a light which is he; not a light which flows from him, no, nor a light which is in him, but that light which is he himself. Lighten our darkness, we beseech thee, O Lord, O Father of lights, that in thy light we may see light,[6] that now we see this through this thy glass, thy ordinance, and by the good of this hereafter face to face.

The sight is so much the noblest of all the senses as that it is all the senses.[7] As the reasonable soul of man, when it enters, becomes all the soul of man, and

3. Explained in next paragraph.
4. See *The Second Anniversary,* ll. 254 ff.
5. Making plain.
6. Psalms 36:9.
7. The usual view; the senses ran down from sight through hearing, smell, taste, and touch.

he hath no longer a vegetative and a sensitive soul but all is that one reasonable soul;[8] so, says St. Augustine, and he exemplifies it by several pregnant places of Scripture, *Visus per omnes sensus recurrit,* all the senses are called seeing; as there is *videre et audire,* 'St. John turned to see the sound';[9] and there is *gustate et videte,* 'Taste and see how sweet the Lord is';[10] and so of the rest of the senses, all is sight. Employ then this noblest sense upon the noblest object, see God; see God in everything, and then thou needst not take off thine eye from beauty, from riches, from honour, from anything. St. Paul speaks here of a diverse seeing of God. Of seeing God in a glass, and seeing God face to face; but of not seeing God at all, the apostle speaks not at all.

When Christ took the blind man by the hand,[11] though he had then begun his cure upon him, yet he asked him if he saw aught. Something he was sure he saw; but it was a question whether it were to be called a sight, for he saw men but as trees. The natural man[12] sees beauty and riches and honour, but yet it is a question whether he sees them or no, because he sees them but as a snare. But he that sees God in them sees them to be beams and evidences of that beauty, that wealth, that honour, that is in God, that is in God himself. The other blind man that importuned Christ, 'Jesus, thou son of David, have mercy upon me,' when Christ asked him, 'What wilt thou that I shall do unto thee?' had presently that answer, 'Lord, that I may receive my sight';[13] and we may easily think that if Christ had asked him a second question, 'What wouldst thou see when thou hast received thy sight?' he would have answered, 'Lord, I will see thee'; for when he had his sight and Christ said to him, 'Go thy way,' he had no way to go from Christ, but, as the text says there, 'He followed him.' All that he cared for was seeing, all that he cared to see was Christ. Whether he would see a peace or a war may be a statesman's problem; whether he would see plenty or scarcity of some commodity may be a merchant's problem; whether he would see Rome or Spain grow in greatness may be a Jesuit's problem; but whether I had not rather see God than anything is no problematical matter. All sight is blindness, that was our first; all knowledge is ignorance till we come to God, is our next consideration.

The first act of will is love, says the School;[14] for till the will love, till it would have something, it is not a will. But then, *amare nisi nota non possumus;* it is impossible to love anything till we know it. First our understanding must present it as *verum,* as a known truth, and then our will embraces it as *bonum,* as good, and worthy to be loved. Therefore the philosopher[15] concludes easily, as a thing that admits no contradiction, that naturally all men desire to know, that they may love. But then, as the addition[16] of an honest man varies the signification with the profession and calling of the man—for he is an honest man at court that oppresses no man with his power, and at the exchange he is

8. Man has the first, which comprehends the others; animals the second and third.
9. Revelation 1:12.
10. Psalms 34:8.
11. Mark 8:23.
12. Man without religion, seeing by the light of nature.
13. Mark 10:46–51.
14. The scholastic philosophy.
15. St. Augustine.
16. Description.

the honest man that keeps his word, and in an army the valiant man is the honest man—so the addition of learning and understanding varies with the man; the divine, the physician, the lawyer are not qualified, not denominated by the same kind of learning. But yet, as it is for honesty, there is no honest man at court or exchange or army if he believe not in God; so there is no knowledge in the physician nor lawyer if he know not God. Neither does any man know God except he know him so as God hath made himself known, that is, in Christ. Therefore, as St. Paul desires to know nothing else,[17] so let no man pretend to know anything but Christ crucified; that is, crucified for him, made his. In the eighth verse of this chapter he says, 'Prophecy shall fail, and tongues shall fail, and knowledge shall vanish'; but this knowledge of God in Christ made mine, by being crucified for me, shall dwell with me forever. And so from this general consideration all sight is blindness, all knowledge is ignorance, but of God, we pass to the particular consideration of that twofold sight and knowledge of God expressed in this text, 'Now we see through a glass,' etc.

First then we consider—before we come to our knowledge of God—our sight of God in this world, and that is, says our apostle, *in speculo*, 'We see as in a glass.' But how do we see in a glass? Truly, that is not easily determined. The old writers in the optics said that when we see a thing in a glass, we see not the thing itself but a representation only; all the later men say we do see the thing itself but not by direct but by reflected beams. It is a useless labour for the present to reconcile them. This may well consist with both, that as that which we see in a glass assures us that such a thing there is, for we cannot see a dream in a glass, nor a fancy, nor a chimera, so this sight of God, which our apostle says we have in a glass, is enough to assure us that a God there is.

This glass is better than the water; the water gives a crookedness and false dimensions to things that it shows; [18] as we see by an oar when we row a boat, and as the poet describes a wry and distorted face, *qui faciem sub aqua, Phœbe, natantis habes,* that he looked like a man that swam under water. But in the glass which the apostle intends we may see God directly, that is, see directly that there is a God. And therefore St. Cyril's addition in this text is a diminution; *videmus quasi in fumo,* says he, we see God as in a smoke; we see him better than so; for it is a true sight of God, though it be not a perfect sight, which we have this way. This way our theatre, where we sit to see God, is the whole frame of nature; our medium, our glass in which we see him is the creature; and our light by which we see him is natural reason.

Aquinas calls this theatre, where we sit and see God, the whole world; and David compasses the world and finds God everywhere and says at last, 'Whither shall I fly from thy presence? If I ascend up into heaven, thou art there'; [19] at Babel they thought to build to heaven; but did any man ever pretend to get above heaven? Above the power of the winds, or the impression of other malignant meteors, some high hills are got. But can any man get above the power of God? 'If I take the wings of the morning, and dwell in the uttermost parts of the sea, there thy right hand shall hold me and lead me.' If we sail to the waters above the firmament, it is so too. Nay, take a place which

17. I Corinthians 2:2.
18. The phenomenon of refraction.
19. Psalms 139:8.

God never made, a place which grew out of our sins, that is, hell; yet, 'If we make our bed in hell, God is there too.' It is a woeful inn to make our bed in, hell; and so much the more woeful as it is more than an inn, an everlasting dwelling. But even there God is; and so much more strangely than in any other place because he is there without any emanation of any beam of comfort from him who is the God of all consolation or any beam of light from him who is the Father of all lights. In a word, whether we be in the eastern parts of the world, from whom the truth of religion is passed, or in the western, to which it is not yet come; whether we be in the darkness of ignorance, or darkness of the works of darkness, or darkness of oppression of spirit in sadness; the world is the theatre that represents God, and everywhere every man may, nay, must see him.

The whole frame of the world is the theatre, and every creature the stage, the medium, the glass in which we may see God. 'Moses made the laver in the tabernacle of the looking glasses of women.'[20] Scarce can you imagine a vainer thing—except you will except the vain lookers-on in the action—than the looking glasses of women; and yet Moses brought the looking glasses of women to a religious use, to show them that came in the spots of dirt which they had taken by the way, that they might wash themselves clean before they passed any farther.

There is not so poor a creature but may be the glass to see God in. The greatest flat glass that can be made cannot represent anything greater than it is. If every gnat that flies were an archangel, all that could but tell me that there is a God; and the poorest worm that creeps tells me that. If I should ask the basilisk,[21] how camest thou by those killing eyes? he would tell me, thy God made me so; and if I should ask the slow-worm, how camest thou to be without eyes? he would tell me, thy God made me so. The cedar is no better a glass to see God in than the hyssop[22] upon the wall; all things that are, are equally removed from being nothing; and whatsoever hath any being is by that very being a glass in which to see God, who is the root and the fountain of all being. The whole frame of nature is the theatre, the whole volume of creatures is the glass, and the light of nature, reason, is our light; which is another circumstance.

Of these words, John 1:9, 'That was the true light that lighteth every man that cometh into the world,' the slackest sense that they can admit gives light enough to see God by. If we spare St. Chrysostom's sense, that that light is the light of the Gospel and of grace, and that that light considered in itself and without opposition in us does enlighten, that is, would enlighten every man if that man did not wink[23] at that light; if we forbear St. Augustine's sense, that light enlightens every man, that is, every man that is enlightened is enlightened by that light; if we take but St. Cyril's sense, that this light is the light of natural reason, which, without all question, 'enlighteneth every man that comes into the world'; yet have we light enough to see God by that light in the theatre of nature and in the glass of creatures. God affords no man the comfort, the false comfort of atheism. He will not allow a pretending atheist the power to flatter

20. Exodus 38:8: "laver" = washbowl.
21. Fabulous dragon that killed by looking at its victim.
22. Aromatic herb.
23. Close his eyes.

himself so far as seriously to think there is no God. He must pull out his own eyes and see no creature before he can say, he sees no God; he must be no man and quench his reasonable soul before he can say to himself, there is no God. The difference between the reason of man and the instinct of the beast is this, that the beast does but know, but the man knows that he knows.[24] The bestial atheist will pretend that he knows there is no God; but he cannot say that he knows that he knows it; for his knowledge will not stand the battery[25] of an argument from another nor a ratiocination from himself. He dares not ask himself, who is it that I pray to in a sudden danger if there be no God? Nay, he dares not ask, who is it that I swear by in a sudden passion if there be no God? Whom do I tremble at and sweat under at midnight and whom do I curse by next morning if there be no God? It is safely said in the School, *media perfecta ad quæ ordinantur,* how weak soever those means which are ordained by God seem to be, and be indeed in themselves, yet they are strong enough to those ends and purposes for which God ordained them.

And so for such a sight of God as we take the apostle to intend here, which is to see that there is a God, the frame of nature, the whole world is our theatre, the book of creatures is our medium, our glass, and natural reason is light enough. But then for the other degree, the other notification of God, which is the knowing of God, though that also be first to be considered in this world, the means is of a higher nature than served for the sight of God; and yet whilst we are in this world it is but *in ænigmate,* in an obscure riddle, a representation, darkly, and in part, as we translate it.

As the glass which we spoke of before was proposed to the sense, and so we might see God, that is, see that there is a God, this *ænigma* that is spoken of now, this dark similitude and comparison, is proposed to our faith; and so far we know God, that is, believe in God in this life but by enigmas, by dark representations and allusions. Therefore says St. Augustine that Moses saw God, in that conversation which he had with him in the mount, *sevocatus ab omni corporis sensu,* removed from all benefit and assistance of bodily senses—he needed not that glass, the help of the creature; and more than so, *ab omni significativo ææenigmate spiritus,* removed from all allusions or similitudes or representations of God which might bring God to the understanding and so to the belief; Moses knew God by a more immediate working than either sense or understanding or faith. Therefore says that father, *per speculum et ænigma,* by this which the apostle calls a glass and this which he calls *ænigma,* a dark representation, *intelliguntur omnia accommodata ad notificandum deum,* he understands all things by which God hath notified himself to man, by the glass to his reason, by the *ænigma* to his faith. And so for this knowing of God by way of believing in him—as for seeing him our theatre was the world, the creature was our glass, and reason was our light—our academy to learn this knowledge is the church, our medium is the ordinance and institution of Christ in his church, and our light is the light of faith in the application of those ordinances in that church.

This place then where we take our degrees in this knowledge of God, our

24. See "A Nocturnal upon S. Lucy's Day," ll. 30–31.
25. Assault.

academy, our university for that, is the church; for, though as there may be some few examples given of men that have grown learned who never studied at university; so there may be some examples of men enlightened by God and yet not within that covenant which constitutes the church; yet the ordinary place for degrees is the university, and the ordinary place for illumination in the knowledge of God is the church. Therefore did God, who ever intended to have his kingdom of heaven well peopled, so powerfully, so miraculously enlarge his way to it, the church, that it prospered as a wood which no feeling, no stubbing could destroy. We find in the acts of the church five thousand martyrs executed in a day; and we find in the Acts of the Apostles five thousand brought to the church by one sermon; still our christenings were equal to our burials at least. . . .

1628 1640

JOHN MILTON

1608–1674

The shape of a very great poetic career must always be discerned against a historical background even as the effects of powerful forming forces within it are being understood. The intentions of Chaucer, Shakespeare, and Spenser to live a life of art, and their visions of the route along which they would move, must all be read from the inner biography of their poetry itself. In the case of Milton, both the historical determinants and the informing energies from within are documented for us, and in inner and outer biography together. From his university days on, he was possessed of a self-awareness as a poet that could still, without limitation or qualification, transcend self-consciousness in a way that became almost impossible in literary history after, and perhaps because of, him. He planned when young not only to become a poet but to become a major one, and lived a consecrated life; yet he did not shrink from responding to the demands of a historical moment, and at a crucial high point in his creative career was ready to abandon the service of his poetic imagination, to stand and wait, while his activities and errands were all in the service of the Commonwealth, the Just City of men in whose possibility his vision encouraged him to believe.

The Renaissance and Reformation which continued in England through the middle of the seventeenth century surrounded him in childhood. His father, John Milton senior, was the Protestant son of a recusant Catholic yeoman who had disinherited him; he came to London and became moderately wealthy as a moneylender and scrivener, or notary. Sacrifice and inconvenience tend to strengthen piety, and Milton's continuation of his family's devoted Protestantism remained no easy and habitual matter, but a commitment which flourished, rather than suffered, in the high winds of doctrinal controversy that buffeted his post-university years. His father was a musician of some competence as well; and his general culture may have aided an imaginative generosity about a son who decided to give himself a six-year postgraduate course at home, leading to no degree or to anything else save for possible distant laurels.

Milton's education formally began at St. Paul's School in London, under a scholarly and imaginative master, in late 1620 or early 1621; but he started soon after to extend his own education at home with voluminous and extensive reading, and shortly thereafter additional formal tutoring followed, in classics and modern languages as well. He was at Cambridge for the spring term of 1625, matriculating at Christ's College and taking his B.A. in the spring of 1629, despite some slight altercation with a tutor in 1626 that seems to have resulted in a suspension for a brief time. While at Cambridge, he produced an impressive body of Latin verse and prose, the latter being represented by a group of oratorical exercises, or *Prolusions,* which show more than a mechanical approach to rhetorical problems. Indeed, in such pieces as the first one, delivered in college and debating the claims of day and night to be more excellent, we see the beginnings of a kind of mythopoetic thinking which is more than a mere brilliant assemblage of classical texts, just as the problematic part of the exercise seems a far cry from the undergraduate scholastic jugglings of Donne (in his *Paradoxes and Problems*). The germ of the *L'Allegro—Il Penseroso* pairing may indeed lie in the ability of Milton's mind, evidenced by this early work, to generate energies from conflict. His Latin verses of the time were mostly elegiac, commendatory, funerary, or half-serious epistolary, but his longish, mock-heroic poem on the Gunpowder Plot, written for the annual university Guy Fawkes Day celebrations, was extremely ambitious and unusually powerful. After some talented but tentatively conventional exercises in Jacobean poetic in English—funeral elegy was an accessible mode, and from the experimental vigor of his fancy, no nearby death was safe—he produced, in December of 1629, an unquestionably major poem of its moment, his *On the Morning of Christ's Nativity.* Its handling of the harmonization of various modes of angelic and celestial harmony, in the presentation of the heavenly voices heard by the Bethlehem shepherds, is brilliant at one level; but its treatment of the main theme of the phasing-out of pagan mythology by the birth of a new truth is more than that. The poem's vision is so fine that it is unable to avoid even a feeling of pathetic generosity for the gentler among the displaced: "With flower-inwoven tresses torn / The Nymphs in twilight shade of tangled thickets mourn." It represents the first clear instance of the direction Milton's poetic career is to take thenceforth, following neither the Tribe of Ben into the realms of gracefulness, nor the "strong lines" of Donne's school into the tense regions of wit, erotic or divine. "If the Athenians, as some say, made their small deeds great and renowned by their eloquent writers, England hath had her noble achievements made small by the unskillful handling of monks and mechanics," he would write in 1642 in *The Reason of Church Government,* in a spirited passage of self-defense in the midst of his pamphleteering. But the conviction behind this started to flower early on, while in continued residence at Cambridge for his Master of Arts degree, reading Italian and writing sonnets in it, and, in 1631, producing *L'Allegro* and *Il Penseroso.* After taking his M.A. in 1632, Milton moved back home to continue preparing himself for major eloquence; first in a suburb west of London, then, in about 1635, at the family's country estate at Horton, in Buckinghamshire, near Windsor.

It was at Horton that Milton's fierce period of reading and creative concentration began to focus on specific large goals. In 1634, through his friendship with the musician Henry Lawes, who was tutor to the children of the Earl of Bridgewater, he got a chance to write a public piece of some magnitude. *Comus* (or, *A Masque Presented at Ludlow Castle,* as the 1637 printed version calls it) enabled him not only to address himself to the exposition of a virtue that was far from being what he would call in *Areopagitica* "fugitive and cloistered," but also to import into the transitory conventions of court masque some of the Shakespearean and Spenserian language and modes of representation that lyric poetry had not allowed him, up till then, to attempt. Similarly with the great programmatic force of *Lycidas,* in 1637.

From the spring of 1638 until the middle of the summer of 1639, Milton was in Italy, traveling in Tuscany and to Rome and Naples; he went about some in society, met musicians and patrons and even, in Florence, Galileo. In general, Italy had come to stand, in its language and poetry, as a region of the creative imagination for him; he was fortunate, this being so, that his experience of the actuality was so pleasant. In 1640 he moved to London and set up as a private schoolmaster; his first pupils were his nephews, Edward and John Phillips. But his concerns began to move toward public conflict, for London was a center of the struggle between Parliament on the one hand, and king and bishops on the other. Milton was on the brink of moving into some of his grandest fields of accomplishment—"not to make verbal curiosities the end (that were a toilsome vanity), but to be an interpreter and relater of the best and sagest things among mine own citizens throughout this island in the mother dialect"—as he would put it two years later in *The Reason of Church Government.* But the crucial issues raging about him, and about the principles to which he felt so committed, would have betrayed any task in the realm of epic or major drama which he might have set himself. From 1641, when he published his first tract against the institution of bishops, until twenty years after, when those bishops had been reinstituted with the Restoration of the monarchy, Milton devoted himself to prose, to argument, to armed mental fight. Writing with what he referred to as his "left hand," he produced a major series of prose works in defense of various religious, political, and moral freedoms, moving with a majority Puritan consensus in his anti-episcopal writings and then finding that the Presbyterian cause could itself become the oppressive one. In the next phase of his life, during which he married Mary Powell in 1642 (she left him in a fit of incompatibility after three months, but returned in 1645 to live with him until her death in childbirth seven years later), Milton wrote tracts in favor of divorce on the grounds of disharmony rather than only for adultery, and a brilliant short essay, *Of Education,* which supported the reformation of the still predominantly scholastic educational systems which prevailed in Europe. Such a reformation had indeed been going on at Milton's own school, St. Paul's, whose more "Platonic" tradition of humanist training had been established by Erasmus, John Colet, and William Lily. Then, too, there were the influential educational theories of John Amos Comenius (1592–1670), the Czech educator who likewise opposed the arbitrariness and wearisome stuffiness of older methods, but whose own methods and curricula aimed at a more pragmatic and less imaginatively self-fulfilling kind of literacy. Milton's argument for the centrality of humanist literary and philosophical disciplines itself made use, in an almost Baconian way, of the very methods whose inculcation it desired to foster. Thus, Milton urges that logic be employed to lead toward a flowering of intellectual activity in the arts of rhetoric, but that poetry be made an instrument in that process, "as being less subtle and fine, but more simple, sensuous and passionate"; and thus, in setting out the very aims of education themselves, earlier in the treatise, he leaps to the heart of biblical example:

> The end then of learning is to repair the ruins of our first parents by regaining to know God aright, and out of that knowledge to love him, to imi-

> tate him, to be like him, as we may the nearest by possessing our souls of true virtue, which being united to the heavenly grace of faith makes up the highest perfection. But because our understanding cannot in this body found itself but on sensible things, nor arrive so clearly to the knowledge of God and things invisible as by orderly conning over the visible and inferior creature, the same method is necessarily to be followed in all discreet teaching. And seeing every nation affords not experience and tradition enough for all kind of learning, therefore we are chiefly taught the languages of those who have at any time been most industrious after wisdom; so that language is but the instrument conveying to us things useful to be known. And though a linguist should pride himself to have all the tongues that Babel cleft the world into, yet, if he have not studied the solid things in them as well as the words and lexicons, he were nothing so much to be esteemed a learned man as any yeoman or tradesman competently wise in his mother dialect only.

Of Education and *Areopagitica* appeared in 1644. The following year, amid more pamphleteering, Milton published a volume of his verse, *Poems of Mr. John Milton,* including the sonnets which he had been writing during the 1640's as his only poetry. It would not be until after service to the Commonwealth as Secretary for Foreign Tongues to the Council of State (from 1649 until 1655, three years after his blindness had become total), and after a long series of prose works, that he was able, under the most adverse of circumstances, to get on with his deferred epic task. In 1649, *The Tenure of Kings and Magistrates* had argued, shortly after the execution of Charles I, for the divine right of removing kings; later that year, he attacked in *Eikonoklastes* the roots of a Royalist cult which was attempting to make the martyred Charles into a kind of saint. His first and second *Defences of the English People* apeared in 1651 and 1654; *The Ready and Easy Way to Establish a Free Commonwealth* was published on the brink of the Restoration in 1660.

The return of a Stuart monarch to the throne brought with it more than disappointment for Milton; he was in danger from royal prosecution, both as a propagandist for the Commonwealth cause and as a formal member of its government. He actually went into hiding in the summer of 1660 until the general pardon of August of that year, in which he was finally included. For some reason he was arrested and imprisoned briefly at the end of the year, probably in November, but by December he was granted a full pardon and had no further fear that personal action would be taken against him.

It was during these last years of his life that Milton was finally to fulfill himself. Despite his total blindness, which dated from 1651–52, he was able to dictate *Paradise Lost,* finish it by 1665, continue on to *Paradise Regained* and, if most critics are correct in their view of its date of composition, *Samson Agonistes,* all of which were published in these last fourteen years of Milton's life. He was blind, and poorer than he had been with a state salary to augment his inheritance; he had seen the Commonwealth for which he had labored submerged in what looked to be an irreversible current of reaction; and yet he was able to concentrate all of his visionary and creative energies for a poetic accomplishment which ranks with Virgil's and Dante's in its organization of the knowledge and the spirit of its age. Like them, too, he evolved from received materials a fable powerful enough to be able to insist that it was not merely a fable, but an image of evolving human consciousness itself. Milton's major poems are the crowning fulfillment, too, of a life of learning as well as of the exercise of mental and moral combat; William Hazlitt remarked that Milton's learning has "the effect of intuition," and certainly in *Paradise Lost* he was able to include all that he knew without a sense of intrusion. His precursors (Virgil, Dante, Spenser among them) were an unalloyed imaginative aid to him. He was able to take what he needed from them without moving into their shadows; Hazlitt could perceive in him "a mighty intellect that, the nearer it approaches to others, the more distinct it becomes from them." Milton's last years were spent in continuing work, including revisions of the 1667 *Paradise Lost,* the second edition of which appeared in the year of his death, 1674.

L'Allegro and Il Penseroso

L'Allegro and Il Penseroso are of an unprecedented form in English poetry, related only to what was called a *synkriseis,* or debating situation, in classical literature (of which Milton's own college exercise, a prose oration on "Whether Day or Night Is More Excellent," is an example), and to analogous treatments, in Renaissance paintings and prints, of pairs of allegorical figures, such as Nature and Grace—the first, nude and associated with Eve, the second robed, and associated with Mary. Milton's two spirits are his own, compounded by his myth-making from traditional figures, but transformed by their milieu and its details. *L'Allegro* is a picture of a kind not yet invented: imagine a film version of a series of paintings like Botticelli's *Primavera* (Spring), with different scenes, but connected by the presence of one figure. She is Euphrosyne, one of the three Graces, naked (like her sisters, considered to be aspects of Venus). *Il Penseroso,* dark-robed, derives from personified Melancholy; a somber muse, neither the self-creating and self-consuming obsession of Burton in his dark tower of books, nor the massive, brooding angel of Albrecht Dürer's great engraving. The introductory verses to Burton's *Anatomy of Melancholy* may have suggested the tetrameter couplets as a meter (their refrain rhymes "melancholy" alternately with "folly" and "jolly"), but the modulation of their rhythms in the two poems is most flexible. Each poem opens with a half-serious banishment of a parody version of the spirit in the other lyric; in the main portion of each, the complementary treatment of light and dark, sound and silence, society and solitude, is subtle and complex. (See Figs. 15–18).

L'Allegro

Hence, loathèd Melancholy,°
Of Cerberus° and blackest Midnight born,
In Stygian cave forlorn
'Mongst horrid shapes, and shrieks, and sights unholy,
Find out some uncouth° cell,
Where brooding darkness spreads his jealous wings,
And the night-raven sings;
There under ebon shades and low-browed rocks,
As ragged as thy locks
In dark Cimmerian° desert ever dwell.
But come, thou goddess fair and free,
In heaven yclept Euphrosyne,°
And by men heart-easing Mirth,
Whom lovely Venus at a birth°
With two sister Graces more
To ivy-crownèd Bacchus bore;
Or whether° (as some sager sing)
The frolic wind that breathes the spring,
Zephyr, with Aurora° playing,
As he met her once a-Maying,
There on beds of violets blue,
And fresh-blown roses washed in dew,
Filled her with thee, a daughter fair,
So buxom,° blithe, and debonair.°
Haste thee, Nymph, and bring with thee
Jest and youthful Jollity,
Quips and cranks,° and wanton wiles,
Nods and becks° and wreathèd smiles,
Such as hang on Hebe's° cheek,
And love to live in dimple sleek;
Sport that wrinkled Care derides,°
And Laughter holding both his sides.
Come, and trip it as ye go
On the light fantastic toe,
And in thy right hand lead with thee
The mountain nymph, sweet Liberty;

loathèd Melancholy See Headnote.
Cerberus three-headed watchdog of Hades, whose cave by the river Styx, Virgil says (*Aeneid* VI.418), is full of the shrieking souls of dead children
uncouth unknown
Cimmerian proverbially dark region, home of the cave of Morpheus, one of the three sons of sleep
yclept Euphrosyne called Euphrosyne, or "Mirth." She was one of the three Graces usually thought of as daughters of Zeus and Hera; her sisters were Aglaia ("Brightness") and Thalia ("Flowering") (see *The Faerie Queene* VI.x.21–24).
Venus at a birth other fables make the Graces daughters of Venus and Bacchus
Or whether In the tone of a commentator on mythology, Milton adduces yet another parentage, made up by him for this poem; in a sense, the new parentage redefines the meaning of the Grace.
Aurora goddess of the dawn
buxom compliant
debonair gracious
cranks word-play jokes
becks gestures of beckoning, or "come-on"
Hebe's the Olympian barmaid and youth goddess
derides "Care" is the object.

And if I give thee honour due,
Mirth, admit me of thy crew,
To live with her, and live with thee,
In unreprovèd pleasures free;
To hear the lark begin his flight,
And singing startle the dull night,
From his watch-tower in the skies,°
Till the dappled dawn doth rise;
Then to come in spite of sorrow
And at my window bid good-morrow,
Through the sweet-briar or the vine,
Or the twisted eglantine;
While the cock with lively din
Scatters the rear of darkness thin,
And to the stack or the barn door
Stoutly struts his dames before;
Oft listening how the hounds and horn
Cheerly rouse the slumbering morn,
From the side of some hoar° hill,
Through the high wood echoing shrill;
Sometime walking, not unseen,°
By hedgerow elms, on hillocks green,
Right against the eastern gate,
Where the great sun begins his state,°
Robed in flames and amber light,
The clouds in thousand liveries dight;°
While the ploughman near at hand
Whistles o'er the furrowed land,
And the milkmaid singeth blithe,
And the mower whets his scythe,
And every shepherd tells his tale°
Under the hawthorn in the dale.
Straight mine eye hath caught new pleasures,
Whilst the landscape round it measures:
Russet lawns and fallows gray,
Where the nibbling flocks do stray;
Mountains on whose barren breast
The labouring clouds° do often rest;
Meadows trim with daisies pied,°
Shallow brooks and rivers wide.
Towers and battlements it° sees

To hear . . . skies The poetic power of the skylark results from the intensity of his song, filling the sky which, because of the small size and great altitude of the singer, looks empty.
hoar not frosty, but gray from morning mist
Sometime . . . unseen Cf. *Il Penseroso*, l. 65.
state royal progress or tour
liveries dight gay costumes clad
tells his tale counts his tally (of sheep); perhaps "recounts his story"
labouring clouds unlike the barren hills, they will bring forth rain
daisies pied variegated daisies; like many other phrases in these poems, quoted from Shakespeare (the cuckoo's song from *Love's Labour's Lost* V.ii.882–85)
it "mine eye" (from l. 69)

Bosomed high in tufted trees,
Where perhaps some beauty lies,
The cynosure° of neighbouring eyes.
Hard by, a cottage chimney smokes
From betwixt two agèd oaks,
Where Corydon and Thyrsis met
Are at their savoury dinner set
Of herbs and other country messes,
Which the neat-handed Phillis dresses;
And then in haste her bower° she leaves,
With Thestylis to bind the sheaves;
Or if the earlier season lead,
To the tanned haycock in the mead.
Sometimes with secure° delight
The upland hamlets will invite,
When the merry bells ring round,
And the jocund rebecs° sound
To many a youth and many a maid
Dancing in the chequered shade;
And young and old come forth to play
On a sunshine holiday,
Till the livelong daylight fail:
Then to the spicy nut-brown ale,
With stories told of many a feat,
How fairy Mab the junkets eat;°
She was pinched and pulled, she said,
And he, by friar's lantern° led,
Tells how the drudging goblin sweat
To earn his cream-bowl duly set,
When in one night, ere glimpse of morn,
His shadowy flail hath threshed the corn
That ten day-labourers could not end;
Then lies him down the lubber fiend,°
And stretched out all the chimney's length,
Basks at the fire his hairy strength;
And crop-full out of doors he flings,
Ere the first cock his matin rings.
Thus done the tales, to bed they creep,
By whispering winds soon lulled asleep.
Towered cities please us then,°

cynosure the constellation Ursa Minor, containing Polaris; thus, a proverbial center of attention
bower cottage
secure carefree
rebecs primitive fiddles
eat ate. "Mab" is the fairy queen from Mercutio's speech in *Romeo and Juliet* I.iv. 55–95.
friar's lantern the will-o'-the-wisp
lubber fiend spirit who is a lob, or household drudge. Puck, in *Midsummer Night's Dream* II.i.16 and 40, is called "lob of spirits" and "Hobgoblin."
Towered . . . then Here comes the shift from glad day to glad night, paralleled at almost exactly the same point (l. 121) in *Il Penseroso* by the dawning of sad day. The interpenetration of the spirits of the poems is important: *L'Allegro's* night is full of illuminations, comic theater, songs, and festivals, while *Il Penseroso's* day is shadowed and shrouded.

And the busy hum of men,
Where throngs of knights and barons bold
In weeds° of peace high triumphs hold,
With store of ladies, whose bright eyes
Rain influence,° and judge the prize
Of wit or arms, while both contend
To win her grace whom all commend.
There let Hymen° oft appear
In saffron robe, with taper clear,
And pomp, and feast, and revelry,
With masque and antique pageantry:
Such sights as youthful poets dream
On summer eves by haunted stream.
Then to the well-trod stage anon,
If Jonson's learnèd sock° be on,
Or sweetest Shakespeare, Fancy's child,°
Warble his native wood-notes wild;
And ever against eating° cares
Lap me in soft Lydian airs,°
Married to immortal verse,
Such as the meeting soul may pierce
In notes with many a winding bout°
Of linkèd sweetness long drawn out,
With wanton heed and giddy cunning,
The melting voice through mazes running,
Untwisting all the chains that tie
The hidden soul of harmony;
That Orpheus' self may heave his head
From golden slumber on a bed
Of heaped Elysian flowers, and hear
Such strains as would have won the ear
Of Pluto, to have quite set free
His half-regained Eurydice.
These delights if thou canst give,
Mirth, with thee I mean to live.°

1631–32? 1645

weeds costumes
Rain influence See *Astrology* in the Glossary. The ladies are out of Petrarchan poetry—the conceit about the eyes of the beloved being stars is a cliché.
Hymen god of marriage, as a character in a masque
learnèd sock The sock, or low shoe, was emblematic of classical comedy; cf. *Il Penseroso*, l. 102.
sweetest . . . child In the earlier poem "On Shakespeare" Milton alluded to this spontaneous creativity; the juxtaposition of "learnèd" Jonson and "native" Shakespeare is a commonplace.
eating (adjectival)
soft Lydian airs melodies of a delightful and relaxing sort (the Lydian mode or key, in Greek tradition, was "lax," the Dorian "manly," the Phrygian "wild," etc., in the same way in which we think of minor as being "sad" and major "happy"; in addition, "airs" means breezes).
bout turn, or possibly, return. Milton may be thinking of the Italian aria, or solo air, with its turning ornamentations, and *ritornello*, or *da capo* repeat.
These delights . . . live yet one more response—here to the closing lines of Marlowe's "The Passionate Shepherd"

Il Penseroso

Hence, vain deluding Joys,°
The brood of Folly without father bred,
How little you bestead,°
Or fill the fixèd mind with all your toys;
Dwell in some idle brain,
And fancies fond with gaudy shapes possess,
As thick and numberless
As the gay motes that people the sunbeams,
Or likest hovering dreams,
The fickle pensioners of Morpheus' train.°
But hail, thou Goddess sage and holy,
Hail, divinest Melancholy,
Whose saintly visage is too bright
To hit the sense of human sight,
And therefore to our weaker view
O'erlaid with black, staid Wisdom's hue;
Black, but such as in esteem
Prince Memnon's sister° might beseem,
Or that starred Ethiop queen° that strove
To set her beauty's praise above
The sea-nymphs, and their powers offended.
Yet thou art higher far descended:
Thee bright-haired Vesta° long of yore
To solitary Saturn bore—
His daughter she (in Saturn's reign
Such mixture was not held a stain).
Oft in glimmering bowers and glades
He met her, and in secret shades
Of woody Ida's inmost grove,
While yet there was no fear of Jove.°
Come, pensive Nun, devout and pure,
Sober, steadfast, and demure,
All in a robe of darkest grain,°
Flowing with majestic train,
And sable stole of cypress lawn°
Over thy decent shoulders drawn.
Come, but keep thy wonted state,
With even step and musing gait,
And looks commercing with the skies,

deluding Joys See Headnote.
bestead help
pensioners . . . train attendants on Morpheus, god of dreams, son of Sleep
Memnon's sister Himera, an Ethiopian princess in Homer
Ethiop queen Cassiopeia who, in one version of her legend, was transformed into a constellation because she boasted so of her daughter Andromeda's beauty
Vesta usually virginal, Roman goddess of the hearth. Milton invents this myth of her incestuous parentage.
Jove Jupiter's childhood was spent on Mt. Ida on Crete; later, he overthrew Saturn, his father (or Zeus and his father Cronos, in Greek).
grain color
cypress lawn black, fine linen

Thy rapt soul sitting in thine eyes;
There held in holy passion still,
Forget thyself to marble, till
With a sad° leaden downward cast
Thou fix them on the earth as fast.
And join with thee calm Peace and Quiet,
Spare Fast, that oft with gods doth diet,
And hears the Muses in a ring
Aye round about Jove's altar sing;
And add to these retired Leisure,°
That in trim gardens takes his pleasure;
But first, and chiefest, with thee bring
Him that yon soars on golden wing,
Guiding the fiery-wheelèd throne,
The Cherub Contemplatïon;°
And the mute Silence hist° along,
'Less Philomel will deign a song,
In her sweetest, saddest plight,°
Smoothing the rugged brow of Night,
While Cynthia° checks her dragon yoke
Gently o'er th' accustomed oak.
Sweet bird, that shunn'st the noise of folly,
Most musical, most melancholy!
Thee, chauntress, oft the woods among
I woo to hear thy even-song;
And missing thee, I walk unseen
On the dry smooth-shaven green,
To behold the wandering moon
Riding near her highest noon,
Like one that had been led astray
Through the heaven's wide pathless way;
And oft, as if her head she bowed,
Stooping through a fleecy cloud.
Oft on a plat° of rising ground
I hear the far-off curfew sound
Over some wide-watered shore,
Swinging slow with sullen° roar;
Or if the air will not permit,
Some still removèd place will fit,
Where glowing embers through the room
Teach light to counterfeit a gloom,°

sad serious
Leisure See Marvell's "The Garden" for an instance of this theme of retirement.
Contemplatïon The diaeresis mark indicates that the diphthong is separated into two vowels sounds, here giving the word five syllables.
hist to whisper "hist!"—meaning "come along!"
'Less . . . plight the nightingale, changed form of Philomela whose brother-in-law raped her and tore out her tongue; her metamorphosis made her the bird of sad song
Cynthia the moon goddess; "dragon yoke" because a chariot drawn by dragons is Hecate's and Hecate is the antithetical form of the moon enchantress
plat plot
sullen solemn, religious
Teach . . . gloom This contrasts with the lighting of interiors at night in *L'Allegro*.

Far from all resort of mirth,
Save the cricket on the hearth,
Or the bellman's drowsy charm,°
To bless the doors from nightly harm:
Or let my lamp at midnight hour
Be seen in some high lonely tower,°
Where I may oft outwatch the Bear,°
With thrice great Hermes,° or unsphere
The spirit of Plato° to unfold
What worlds or what vast regions hold
The immortal mind that hath forsook
Her mansion in this fleshly nook;
And of those daemons that are found
In fire, air, flood, or under ground,
Whose power hath a true consent
With planet or with element.°
Sometime let gorgeous Tragedy
In sceptred pall come sweeping by,
Presenting Thebes, or Pelops' line,°
Or the tale of Troy divine,
Or what (though rare) of later age
Ennobled hath the buskined° stage.
But, O sad Virgin, that thy power
Might raise Musaeus° from his bower,
Or bid the soul of Orpheus sing
Such notes as, warbled to the string,
Drew iron tears down Pluto's cheek
And made hell grant what love did seek;°
Or call up him° that left half told
The story of Cambuscan bold,
Of Camball and of Algarsife,
And who had Canace to wife,
That owned the virtuous ring and glass,
And of the wondrous horse of brass,
On which the Tartar king did ride;
And if aught else great bards beside

bellman's . . . charm the chant of the night-watchman calling the hours

high lonely tower This is the central point of contemplative vision in the poem; it has been associated by critics with Isaiah's watchtower (Isaiah 21:8), and Plato's notion, in the *Republic* 560b, of a high place, or "acropolis" of the soul. The tower is ascended not like the major prophetic mountains, but, as here, to devote to the night skies the same attentive gaze as that which, in *L'Allegro,* follows the "live-long daylight."

outwatch the Bear Ursa Major, the Big Dipper, never sets; thus, to work all night.

thrice great Hermes Hermes Trismegistus, supposed author of neoplatonist writings, actually from Alexandria in the third and fourth centuries A.D. (See *Platonism* in the Glossary.)

unsphere . . . Plato to call Plato's ghost back from its home in the highest sphere of heaven

With planet . . . element Evil or marginal spirits were classified according to which of the four elements composed them, and with particular heavenly bodies.

Thebes, or Pelops' line the Oedipus cycle and the tales of the house of Atreus (Thyestes, Agamemnon, Orestes, etc.)

buskined booted with the emblematic footwear of tragedy; cf. *L'Allegro,* l. 132

Musaeus mythical Greek poet (fictionally associated by Marlowe with his actual, late 5th-century A.D. author in *Hero and Leander*)

what . . . seek Eurydice; cf. *L'Allegro,* ll. 145–50

him Chaucer; the half-told story, The Squire's Tale

In sage and solemn tunes have sung,
Of tourneys and of trophies hung,
Of forests and enchantments drear,
Where more is meant than meets the ear.°
Thus, Night, oft see me in thy pale career,°
Till civil-suited° Morn appear,
Not tricked and frounced° as she was wont
With the Attic boy° to hunt,
But kerchiefed in a comely cloud,
While rocking winds are piping loud,
Or ushered with a shower still,
When the gust hath blown his fill,
Ending on the rustling leaves,
With minute° drops from off the eaves.
And when the sun begins to fling
His flaring beams, me, Goddess, bring
To archèd walks of twilight groves,
And shadows brown° that Sylvan loves,
Of pine or monumental oak,
Where the rude axe with heavèd stroke
Was never heard the nymphs to daunt,
Or fright them from their hallowed haunt.
There in close covert by some brook,
Where no profaner eye may look,
Hide me from Day's garish eye,
While the bee with honied thigh,
That at her flowery work doth sing,
And the waters murmuring
With such consort° as they keep,
Entice the dewy-feathered Sleep;
And let some strange mysterious dream
Wave at his wings in airy stream
Of lively portraiture displayed,
Softly on my eyelids laid.
And as I wake, sweet music breathe
Above, about, or underneath,
Sent by some Spirit to mortals good,
Or the unseen Genius of the wood.
But let my due feet never fail
To walk the studious cloister's pale,°
And love the high embowèd° roof,

Where more . . . ear the corpus of allegorical romance: particularly Spenser (see *Areopagitica*), but also Tasso and Ariosto
Thus, Night . . . career a deliberately placed pentameter line, breaking the rhythm: it moves away from the praise of dead poets, and is, perhaps, a hidden defiance of Mirth
civil-suited simply dressed
frounced with hair curled
Attic boy Cephalus
minute falling once a minute (not "tiny")
brown standard term for "dark" in pastoral diction
consort other polyphonic parts (sung by leaves, sad birds, etc.)
pale enclosure
embowèd vaulted

With antique° pillars' massy proof,°
And storied windows richly dight,°
Casting a dim religious light.
There let the pealing organ blow
To the full-voiced quire below,
In service high and anthems clear,
As may with sweetness, through mine ear,
Dissolve me into ecstasies,
And bring all heaven before mine eyes.
And may at last my weary age
Find out the peaceful hermitage,
The hairy gown and mossy cell,
Where I may sit and rightly spell°
Of every star that heaven doth shew,
And every herb that sips the dew,
Till old experience do attain
To something like prophetic strain.
These pleasures, Melancholy, give,
And I with thee will choose to live.

1631–32? 1645

Sonnets

Milton started writing sonnets while still at Cambridge, but they were never of the traditionally Petrarchan sequence type (e.g. *Astrophel and Stella, Delia, Ideas Mirror*) that had gone out of fashion more than forty years earlier. His poems developed under the influence of the Italian sonnets of Giovanni della Casa and, in his later ones, of Tasso's *Sonnetti Eroici;* he learned particularly from their syntax, their placing of nouns and adjectives, and strong enjambments. Five of Milton's first six sonnets were in Italian; later on, he used the form in a more public, proclamatory, and even denunciatory manner—as a kind of ode in miniature. Based on the Italian sonnet form divided into octave-sestet sections (rather than the more logically schematic quatrain and couplet pattern used by Shakespeare), Milton's sonnets nevertheless grew to override that central division. They developed a flow of utterance building to a high (rather than to the kind of shutting-off that an epigrammatic or neat ending effects). Wordsworth likened their self-contained homogeneous character to that of a drop of dew. Their rhymes aside, these sonnets were a study for the eventual blank-verse paragraphs of *Paradise Lost.*

antique antic, grotesque
proof impenetrability
dight decorated (stained-glass)
spell decipher the meaning, read. At the end of the poem, Melancholy is left with a kind of resolute, scientific patience, a healthy introspection fulfilled in looking outward, not like Dürer's angel of the imagination whose abandoned scientific instruments lie around her.

Sonnet I°

O nightingale, that on yon bloomy spray
Warblest at eve, when all the woods are still,
Thou with fresh hope the lover's heart dost fill,
While the jolly Hours° lead on propitious May;
Thy liquid notes that close the eye of day,°
First heard before the shallow cuckoo's bill,
Portend success in love; O if Jove's will
Have linked that amorous power to thy soft lay,
Now timely sing, ere the rude bird of hate°
Foretell my hopeless doom in some grove nigh,
As thou from year to year hast sung too late
For my relief, yet hadst no reason why:
Whether the Muse or Love call thee his mate,°
Both them I serve, and of their train am I.

1629–30? 1645

Sonnet VII

How soon hath time, the subtle thief of youth,
Stolen on his wing my three and twentieth year!°
My hasting days fly on with full career,
But my late spring no bud or blossom° showeth.
Perhaps my semblance° might deceive° the truth,
That I to manhood am arrived so near,
And inward ripeness doth much less appear,
That some more timely-happy spirits° endueth.
Yet be it less or more, or soon or slow,
It shall be still° in strictest measure even
To that same lot, however mean or high,
Toward which time leads me, and the will of heaven;
All is, if I have grace to use it so,
As ever° in my great task-master's eye.

1631 1645

Sonnet I Milton's first sonnet in English, a response to the self-generated occasion of answering the song of the nightingale: he has never been in love, he has never written the kind of poetry he was going to demand of himself—what can the nightingale *mean,* then, as an emblem as well as by its song?
Hours daughters of Jupiter and Themis (see Spenser's *Epithalamion,* I.98, 280)
eye of day the sun; a vestigial Petrarchanism
bird of hate the cuckoo. In medieval tradition, to hear him sing before the nightingale was a bad omen for a lover.
Whether . . . mate The sexes here are a bit confused, but "mate" merely implies mythological association: whether the nightingale is a myth of poetry (as in Ovid's story of the raped, mute Philomela, restored to her voice through change), or whether, as in popular tradition, the night-bird of love.

three and twentieth year thus, the poem written for his 24th birthday, a confrontation with his own inactivity and of his prolonged scholarly and imaginative apprenticeship
bud or blossom poetry (a 17th-century commonplace)
semblance appearance
deceive prove false
timely-happy spirits He is thinking of Cambridge friends, perhaps, who at his age seem more mature, fulfilled, and fashionable as poets; scholars have proposed his friend Charles Diodati, Thomas Randolph, Abraham Cowley, and even Spenser, as historical candidates.
still always
ever eternity. The last two lines probably mean "All time is, if I have grace to use it so, as eternity in the sight of God."

Sonnet VIII

When the Assault Was Intended to the City°

Captain or colonel,° or knight in arms,
Whose chance on these defenseless doors may seize,
If deed of honour did thee ever please,
Guard them, and him within protect from harms;
He can requite thee, for he knows the charms
That call fame on such gentle acts as these,
And he can spread thy name o'er lands and seas,
Whatever clime the sun's bright circle warms.
Lift not thy spear against the Muses' bower:
The great Emathian conqueror bid spare
The house of Pindarus,° when temple and tower
Went to the ground; and the repeated air°
Of sad Electra's poet had the power
To save the Athenian walls from ruin bare.
1642 1642

Sonnet XVII

When I consider how my light is spent,
Ere half my days,° in this dark world and wide,
And that one talent° which is death to hide
Lodged with me useless, though my soul more bent
To serve therewith my maker, and present
My true account, lest he, returning, chide.
'Doth God exact day-labour, light denied?'
I fondly ask; but Patience, to prevent°
That murmur, soon replies: 'God doth not need
Either man's work or his own gifts; who best
Bear his mild yoke,° they serve him best; his state

When . . . City The assault was of Royalist troops on London, from which King Charles's army was turned back on November 13, 1642, at Turnham Green, and the poem is written as if to be posted on the author's door.
colonel here trisyllabic: cur-o-nel
Pindarus Alexander the Great reportedly spared Pindar's house when he burned Thebes.
air song, here the first chorus of Euripides' *Electra*, recited ("repeated") by an Athenian officer in 404 B.C., so moving the victorious Spartans that they spared Athens
half my days Since there is some controversy over the dating of this sonnet, "half my days" does not necessarily mean 35, midpoint of the biblical life-span of "threescore years and ten," but perhaps half of Milton's mature life, or half the span of his father, who died at 84; some scholars would put it earlier, and have the "spent" light indicate the onset of his blindness, which was gradually overcoming him between 1644 and 1652.
one talent Our modern word is derived from a word meaning a weight of gold, a sum of money equivalent to about $30,000 (if a silver talent, about $6,000), thus a possession or disposition. However, our modern use is shaped by the central allusion of this poem, the parable of the Kingdom of Heaven in Matthew 25:14–30, in which a lord gives his servants various sums of money. The good ones use their talents to double the value by investment, but the "wicked and slothful servant" hides his in the ground and is rebuked when his master returns, asking for a true account. Milton's talent, for writing a great poem, seems to be burying itself in darkness against his will.
prevent forestall
Bear . . . yoke Milton is alluding to Matthew 11:29–30.

Is kingly—thousands° at his bidding speed
And post o'er land and ocean without rest:
They also serve who only stand and wait.'
1652? 1673

Sonnet XVIII

On the Late Massacre in Piedmont°

Avenge, O Lord, thy slaughtered saints, whose bones
Lie scattered on the Alpine mountains cold,
Even them who kept thy truth so pure of old
When all our fathers worshipped stocks and stones,°
Forget not; in thy book° record their groans
Who were thy sheep, and in their ancient fold
Slain by the bloody Piemontese that rolled
Mother with infant down the rocks. Their moans
The vales redoubled to the hills, and they
To heaven. Their martyred blood and ashes sow
O'er all the Italian fields, where still doth sway
The triple tyrant,° that from these may grow
A hundredfold,° who, having learnt thy way,
Early may fly the Babylonian° woe.
1655 1673

Sonnet XIX

Methought I saw my late espousèd saint°
Brought to me like Alcestis° from the grave,
Whom Jove's great son to her glad husband gave,
Rescued from death by force, though pale and faint.
Mine, as whom washed from spot of child-bed taint
Purification in the old Law° did save,

Thousands of angels
On . . . Piedmont The Vaudois, an early Protestant sect formed in the 12th century, lived in Alpine villages and were tolerated by the Dukes of Savoy, until the then Duke, Charles Emmanuel II, sent an army to remove them. On April 24, 1655, many were massacred, including prisoners.
stocks and stones gods of wood or stone
book the Book of Life in Revelation 5:1ff.
triple tyrant the triple-crowned pope
A hundredfold The army harvested by Cadmus from dragon's teeth he sowed combines with the seeds of the sower (Matthew 13:8) which "fell into good ground, and brought forth fruit, some an hundredfold."
Babylonian Just as the author of Revelation had encoded imperial Rome as Babylon, so did Puritan writers with the papal city.
saint a spirit in heaven, in this case, probably Katherine Woodcock, Milton's second wife, although some scholars, dating the sonnet earlier, apply it to Mary Powell, the first Mrs. Milton, who died in childbirth
Alcestis wife of Admetus who chose to die in his place and who, in Euripides' drama, was returned to him by Heracles, who wrestled with Death to win her back; Alcestis was veiled on her return, and Katherine also, in that Milton had never seen her face, being blind at their marriage
Law In Leviticus, the postpartum condition is deemed unclean for 66 days, and the woman must be purified; if this is literal, it might apply to Mary Powell; if figurative, to Katherine (from the Greek *kathara*, "pure"), who died the day after the feast of the Purification of the Virgin.

And such as yet once more I trust to have
Full sight of her in heaven without restraint,
Came vested all in white,° pure as her mind.
Her face was veiled, yet to my fancied sight
Love, sweetness, goodness in her person shined
So clear as in no face with more delight.
But O as to embrace me she inclined,
I waked, she fled, and day brought back my night.
1658 1673

Comus

The proper but less familiar title of *Comus* is "A Masque Presented at Ludlow Castle, 1634," and it comes down to us in printed editions (an anonymous one of 1637 and, later, in the *Poems* of 1645) as well as in manuscripts which suggest what the actual version was like. It was written as an entertainment for the household of the Earl of Bridgewater, who had recently been made Lord President of Wales; Milton's friend, the composer Henry Lawes, was employed there as tutor to the Earl's three children, Alice, fifteen, and John and Thomas, eleven and nine. *Comus* is not strictly a masque, but it partakes of many elements of that major seventeenth-century form of symbolic entertainment, particularly in the relation of the masquing figures, or members of the courtly audience who in fact participate in the emblematic dances, and those mythological roles. In *Comus* the roles of the Lady, her younger brothers, and the Attendant Spirit were played by the children and their tutor; the monsters attending Comus dance in a version of the "antimasque" or grotesque prelude or interlude that in Ben Jonson's masques provided different sorts of contrast to the main fiction. But the heart of masque is dancing, and the heart of *Comus* is language; the mythological "action" in it occurs through no staggering effects of stage machinery, in which one realm or world "becomes" another, but in the great speeches of Comus and the Lady, and in the recitations and songs of the Spirit and the goddess Sabrina. Milton's poetic language is notably Shakespearean: his phrases echo *A Midsummer Night's Dream, The Tempest, The Winter's Tale,* and other plays, and the syntax and the texture of the blank verse throughout constantly remind us of the earlier poet. Word-forms and archaisms are modeled on, but not actually borrowed from, Spenser.

Most critics today like to think of *Comus* as pastoral drama, objectifying platonistic tradition and stemming from Tasso's *Aminta* (see Samuel Daniel's "A Pastoral" and the analogous passage from Guarini's *Il Pastor Fido* adapted by Fanshawe). Here, the allegory of chastity is embodied in the powers to resist deforming magic that a young girl's virginity possesses. (It must be understood that lifelong virginity is not what Milton, or Spenser, thought chastity to be, but that for a certain kind of symbolic dramaturgy, that complex virtue seemed best represented by the power of virginity, as a state, to preserve itself delicately and forcefully.) Chastity's antagonist is worthy of her, making trial rather than crudely assaulting; he is Comus, a transformed version of both the handsome young reveler from classical lore, and Ben Jonson's big-bellied

white With this word the rhymes shift from those on the long ā sound to long ī; the last line "waked . . . night" recapitulates this shift.

mockery of pleasure. Milton makes him the son of Circe, who, in the *Odyssey*, changed men who behaved like pigs into the swine they "really" were. Circe was the first satirist, in a sense, and the worse a person was, the more monstrous his transformed shape would be. But Comus is also a suave, learned seducer, master of the conventional *carpe diem* arguments which overran Caroline love poetry and which Milton augmented, presumably after more exposure to them, in his printed text.

The magic herb *haemony* which the "shepherd lad" (l. 619) produces is an example of Milton's kind of myth-making in his early poems; scholars are in doubt about its exact traditional source, but it is clearly modeled on the moly plant used against Circe in Homer, and may derive its name from Greek words for blood (thus associating it with the power of sacrificial blood, in both pagan and Christian story), or with the name of Thessaly, from which magic herbs came. In any event, it is a resonant name for a substance whose power, though limited, must be defined by the poem's own moral realm.

Comus

THE PERSONS

The Attendant Spirit, afterwards in the habit of Thyrsis
Comus with his crew
The Lady
First Brother
Second Brother
Sabrina the Nymph

The chief persons which presented were
The Lord Brackley
Mr. Thomas Egerton his Brother
The Lady Alice Egerton

The first scene discovers a wild wood.
[THE ATTENDANT SPIRIT *descends or enters*]

Before the starry threshold of Jove's court
My mansion is, where those immortal shapes
Of bright aërial Spirits live ensphered
In regions mild of calm and serene air,
Above the smoke and stir of this dim spot
Which men call Earth, and with low-thoughted care,
Confined and pestered° in this pinfold° here,
Strive to keep up a frail and feverish being,
Unmindful of the crown that Virtue gives,
After this mortal change,° to her true servants
Amongst the enthronèd gods on sainted seats.
Yet some there be that by due steps aspire
To lay their just hands on that golden key

pestered crowded together
pinfold pen for farm animals

mortal change death

That opes the palace of Eternity:
To such my errand is, and but for such
I would not soil these pure ambrosial weeds°
With the rank vapours of this sin-worn mould.°
  But to my task. Neptune, besides the sway
Of every salt flood and each ebbing stream,
Took in, by lot, 'twixt high and nether Jove°
Imperial rule of all the sea-girt isles
That like to rich and various gems inlay
The unadornèd bosom of the deep,
Which he, to grace his tributary gods,
By course° commits to several government,
And gives them leave to wear their sapphire crowns
And wield their little tridents;° but this isle,
The greatest and the best of all the main,
He quarters° to his blue-haired deities;
And all this tract° that fronts the falling sun
A noble peer° of mickle° trust and power
Has in his charge, with tempered awe° to guide
An old and haughty nation° proud in arms—
Where his fair offspring, nursed in princely lore,
Are coming to attend their father's state
And new-entrusted sceptre, but their way
Lies through the pérplexed° paths of this drear wood,°
The nodding horror of whose shady brows
Threats the forlorn and wandering passenger.
And here their tender age might suffer peril,
But that by quick command from sovereign Jove
I was dispatched for their defence and guard;
And listen why, for I will tell ye now
What never yet was heard in tale or song
From old or modern bard, in hall or bower.
  Bacchus, that first from out the purple grape
Crushed the sweet poison of misusèd wine,
After the Tuscan mariners transformed,°
Coasting the Tyrrhene shore, as the winds listed,
On Circe's° island fell (Who knows not Circe,
The daughter of the Sun? whose charmèd cup

ambrosial weeds heavenly garments
mould the earth, the body in which he incarnates
Neptune . . . Jove Zeus, high Jove, and Hades or Pluto, nether Jove, ruled the realms of the sky and the dead; over the third realm, the sea, Neptune ruled.
By course duly
tridents Neptune's three-pronged spear
quarters deals out
this tract Wales, and Bridgewater's counties in England
peer the Earl of Bridgewater
mickle great
awe awesomeness
nation the Welsh
pérplexed tangled
wood The dark wood at the opening of Dante's *Inferno* and Book I of Spenser's *Faerie Queene* represents the moral difficulties and obscurities of life.
mariners transformed by Bacchus, whom they had captured, into dolphins. The construction is latinate *(post nautas mutatos)*, an early instance of what was to become a dominant feature of Milton's diction.
Circe's See Headnote.

Whoever tasted, lost his upright shape,
And downward fell into a groveling swine).
This nymph that gazed upon his clustering locks,
With ivy berries wreathed, and his blithe youth,
Had by him, ere he parted thence, a son
Much like his father, but his mother more,
Whom therefore she brought up and Comus° named;
Who, ripe and frolic° of his full-grown age,
Roving the Celtic and Iberian fields,
At last betakes him to this ominous wood,
And, in thick shelter of black shades embowered,
Excels his mother at her mighty art,
Offering to every weary traveller
His orient° liquor in a crystal glass,
To quench the drouth of Phoebus,° which as they taste
(For most do taste through fond intemperate thirst)
Soon as the potion works, their human countenance,
The express resemblance of the gods,° is changed
Into some brutish form of wolf, or bear,
Or ounce,° or tiger, hog, or bearded goat,
All other parts remaining as they were;°
And they, so perfect is their misery,
Not once perceive their foul disfigurement,
But boast themselves more comely than before
And all their friends, and native home forget
To roll with pleasure in a sensual sty.
Therefore when any favoured of high Jove
Chances to pass through this adventurous glade,
Swift as the sparkle of a glancing° star
I shoot from heaven to give him safe convoy,
As now I do—but first I must put off
These my sky-robes, spun out of Iris' woof,°
And take the weeds° and likeness of a swain
That to the service of this house belongs,
Who with his soft pipe and smooth-dittied song
Well knows to still the wild winds when they roar,
And hush the waving woods;° nor of less faith,°
And in this office of his mountain watch
Likeliest, and nearest to the present aid

Comus See Headnote.
frolic joyful
orient sparkling
drouth of Phoebus thirst caused by the sun
The express . . . gods "God created man in his image" (Genesis 1:27)
ounce lynx
All . . . were Necessities of production (animal-head masks are easier to manage than animal suits) and emblematic meaning (the head, the highest, most divine and least animal part of man, is reduced to the bestial status of his lower organs and limbs) here combine to produce the monsters of Comus's retinue.
glancing shooting
Iris' woof rainbow fabric
weeds costume; cf. l. 16
That . . . woods Henry Lawes, a composer and tutor, playing the part of the Spirit, is likened to Orpheus, whose music was indeed so commanding.
nor of less faith no less loyal

Of this occasion. But I heard the tread
Of hateful steps; I must be viewless° now.

[COMUS *enters with a charming-rod in one hand, his glass in the other; with him a rout of monsters headed like sundry sorts of wild beasts, but otherwise like men and women, their apparel glistering. They come in making a riotous and unruly noise, with torches in their hands.*]

COMUS The star° that bids the shepherd fold°
Now the top of heaven doth hold,
And the gilded car° of day
His glowing axle doth allay°
In the steep Atlantic stream,
And the slope sun his upward beam
Shoots against the dusky pole,
Pacing toward the other goal
Of his chamber in the east.
Meanwhile welcome joy and feast,
Midnight shout and revelry,
Tipsy dance and jollity.
Braid your locks with rosy twine
Dropping odours, dropping wine.
Rigour now is gone to bed,
And Advice with scrupûlous head,
Strict Age, and sour Severity,
With their grave saws° in slumber lie.
We that are of purer fire
Imitate the starry quire,
Who in their nightly watchful spheres
Lead in swift round the months and years.°
The sounds and seas with all their finny drove
Now to the moon in wavering morris° move,
And on the tawny sands and shelves
Trip the pert fairies and the dapper elves;
By dimpled brook and fountain brim
The wood-nymphs, decked with daisies trim,
Their merry wakes° and pastimes keep:
What hath night to do with sleep?
Night hath better sweets to prove,
Venus now wakes, and wakens Love.
Come, let us our rites begin;
'Tis only daylight that makes sin,
Which these dun shades will ne'er report.

viewless invisible
star Hesperus, the Evening Star
fold pen up the sheep
car chariot
allay cool
saws maxims
the starry . . . years The heavenly motions, imaged as "the music of the spheres" in antiquity and later, were also thought of by Plato in *Timaeus* 40 as a great dance of the spheres (see *Astronomy* in the Glossary).
morris morris dance (from "Moorish")
wakes night-long ceremonies

Hail, goddess of nocturnal sport,
Dark-veiled Cotytto,° to whom the secret flame
Of midnight torches burns; mysterious dame,
That ne'er art called but when the dragon womb
Of Stygian darkness spits her thickest gloom,
And makes one blot of all the air,
Stay thy cloudy ebon chair
Wherein thou rid'st with Hecat',° and befriend
Us thy vowed priests, till utmost end
Of all thy dues be done, and none left out
Ere the blabbing eastern scout,
The nice Morn° on the Indian steep,°
From her cabined loop-hole peep,
And to the tell-tale Sun descry°
Our concealed solemnity.°
Come, knit hands, and beat the ground,
In a light fantastic round.°

[*The Measure*°]

Break off, break off, I feel the different pace
Of some chaste footing near about this ground.
Run to your shrouds° within these brakes and trees;
Our number may affright: some virgin sure
(For so I can distinguish by mine art)
Benighted in these woods. Now to my charms
And to my wily trains;° I shall ere long
Be well stocked with as fair a herd as grazed
About my mother Circe. Thus I hurl
My dazzling spells into the spongy air,
Of power to cheat the eye with blear° illusion,
And give it false presentments,° lest the place
And my quaint habits° breed astonishment,
And put the damsel to suspicious flight,
Which must not be, for that's against my course;
I, under fair pretence of friendly ends,
And well-placed words of glozing° courtesy
Baited with reasons not unplausible,
Wind me into the easy-hearted man,
And hug him into snares. When once her eye
Hath met the virtue° of this magic dust,

Cotytto Thracian goddess whose nocturnal rites were reputedly wildly lascivious
Hecat' Hecate, the witch goddess
nice Morn the overly fastidious goddess Aurora
Indian steep the Himalayas
descry reveal
solemnity celebration
round ring dance
Measure the antic dance of what would, in a traditional masque, have been the antimasque, or grotesque counterpart of the main dance and mythology
shrouds hiding places
trains allurements
blear deceiving
false presentments fake visions
quaint habits strange costume
glozing flattering
virtue power

I shall appear some harmless villager
Whom thrift keeps up about his country gear.
But here she comes; I fairly° step aside,
And hearken, if I may, her business here.

[THE LADY *enters*]

LADY This way the noise was, if mine ear be true,
My best guide now. Methought it was the sound
Of riot and ill-managed merriment,
Such as the jocund flute or gamesome pipe
Stirs up among the loose unlettered hinds,°
When for their teeming° flocks, and granges° full,
In wanton dance they praise the bounteous Pan,°
And thank the gods amiss. I should be loth
To meet the rudeness and swilled insolence
Of such late wássailers;° yet O where else
Shall I inform my unacquainted feet
In the blind mazes of this tangled wood?
My brothers, when they saw me wearied out
With this long way, resolving here to lodge
Under the spreading favour of these pines,
Stepped as they said to the next thicket side
To bring me berries, or such cooling fruit
As the kind hospitable woods provide.
They left me then when the grey-hooded Even,
Like a sad votarist in palmer's weed,°
Rose from the hindmost wheels of Phoebus' wain.°
But where they are, and why they came not back,
Is now the labour of my thoughts; 'tis likeliest
They had engaged their wandering steps too far,
And envious darkness, ere they could return,
Had stole them from me—Else, O thievish Night,
Why shouldst thou, but for some felonious end,
In thy dark lantern thus close up the stars
That Nature hung in heaven, and filled their lamps
With everlasting oil, to give due light
To the misled and lonely traveller?
This is the place, as well as I may guess,
Whence even now the tumult of loud mirth
Was rife, and perfect in my listening ear,
Yet naught but single° darkness do I find.
What might this be? A thousand fantasies
Begin to throng into my memory

fairly silently
hinds farmhands
teeming both overflowing or abundant
granges barns
Pan god of woods and shepherds
wássailers revelers
votarist . . . weed pilgrim to the Holy Land
wain wagon
single absolute

Of calling shapes, and beckoning shadows dire,
And airy tongues that syllable men's names
On sands and shores and desert wildernesses.
These thoughts may startle well, but not astound
The virtuous mind, that ever walks attended
By a strong siding° champion, Conscïence.
O welcome, pure-eyed Faith, white-handed Hope,
Thou hovering angel girt with golden wings,
And thou unblemished form of Chastity,
I see ye visibly, and now believe
That He, the supreme Good, to whom all things ill
Are but as slavish officers of vengeance,
Would send a glistering guardian if need were
To keep my life and honour unassailed.
Was I deceived, or did a sable cloud
Turn forth her silver lining on the night?
I did not err, there does a sable cloud
Turn forth her silver lining on the night,°
And casts a gleam over this tufted grove.
I cannot hallo to my brothers, but
Such noise as I can make to be heard farthest
I'll venture, for my new-enlivened spirits
Prompt me; and they perhaps are not far off.

SONG°

Sweet Echo, sweetest nymph that liv'st unseen
Within thy airy shell°
By slow Maeander's margent° green,
And in the violet-embroidered vale
Where the lovelorn nightingale
Nightly to thee her sad song mourneth well:
Canst thou not tell me of a gentle pair
That likest thy Narcissus are?
O if thou have
Hid them in some flowery cave,
Tell me but where,
Sweet queen of parley,° daughter of the sphere;
So mayest thou be translated to the skies,
And give resounding grace° to all heaven's harmonies.

siding defending
Was I . . . night This exact repetition in answer to a rhetorical question may seem almost ludicrous, but (1) these lines were not in the acting script; (2) they have a rhetorical source in Ovid (*Fasti* V.549) for their use on the page; and (3) they do serve to indicate the Lady's calm self-possession.
Song The Lady's song to Echo is a prayer for amplification (by natural acoustic means) of her call, and also a song to her solitariness; unlike operatic "echo scenes" there is no audible answer from hidden chorus or whatever, but the effects on Comus are quite apparent.
shell personified echoes inhabit caverns; "shell" has the sense both of "cell" or cave, and of the higher "shell" of the arched sky
Maeander's margent the margin, or bank of a (hence) "meandering" river in Asia Minor
parley discourse
resounding grace "grace" also in the musical sense of embellishments like trills

Sweet Ech - o, sweet - est nymph, that liv'st un-seen
With-in thy air - y shell, By slow Me-an-der's mar - gent
green, And in the vi - o - let - em - broi-dered vale
Where the love-lorn Night-in - gale night - ly to thee her sad
Song mourn - eth well. Canst thou not tell me
of a gen - tle pair That lik - est thy Nar-cis - sus are?

O if thou have hid them in some flow - 'ry cave.
Tell me but where sweet Queen of Par - ly, Daugh-
- ter of the Sphere, So may'st thou be trans - lat - ed to the skies,
And give re-sound-ing grace to all heav'ns har - mo - nies.

Lawes's setting of this song uses in its last line Milton's earliest version of the text, which he later rewrote.

COMUS [*Aside*] Can any mortal mixture of earth's mould
Breathe such divine enchanting ravishment?
Sure something holy lodges in that breast,
And with these raptures moves the vocal air
To testify° his hidden residence;
How sweetly did they float upon the wings
Of silence, through the empty-vaulted night,
At every fall° smoothing the raven down
Of darkness till it smiled. I have oft heard
My mother Circe with the Sirens three,°
Amidst the flowery-kirtled Naiades,°
Culling their potent herbs and baleful drugs,
Who as they sung would take the prisoned soul

testify attest to
fall musical cadence
Circe . . . three Milton means the sirens whose song bewitched sailors; in Milton, they attend Circe, but not in Homer.
flowery-kirtled Naiades fresh-water nymphs, perhaps dressed in pond lilies

And lap it in Elysium; Scylla° wept,
And chid her barking waves into attention,
And fell Charybdis murmured soft applause.
Yet they in pleasing slumber lulled the sense,
And in sweet madness robbed it of itself;
But such a sacred and home-felt° delight,
Such sober certainty of waking bliss,
I never heard till now. I'll speak to her,
And she shall be my queen. Hail, foreign wonder,
Whom certain these rough shades did never breed,
Unless° the goddess that in rural shrine
Dwellest here with Pan or Sylvan, by blest song
Forbidding every bleak unkindly fog
To touch the prosperous growth of this tall wood.
LADY Nay, gentle shepherd, ill is lost that praise
That is addressed to unattending ears;
Not any boast of skill, but éxtreme shift
How to regain my severed company
Compelled me to awake the courteous Echo
To give me answer from her mossy couch.
COMUS What chance, good lady, hath bereft you thus?
LADY Dim darkness and this leafy labyrinth.°
COMUS Could that divide you from near-ushering guides?
LADY They left me weary on a grassy turf.
COMUS By falsehood, or discourtesy, or why?
LADY To seek i' th' valley some cool friendly spring.
COMUS And left your fair side all unguarded, lady?
LADY They were but twain, and purposed quick return.
COMUS Perhaps forestalling night prevented them.
LADY How easy my misfortune is to hit!°
COMUS Imports their loss,° beside the present need?
LADY No less than if I should my brothers lose.
COMUS Were they of manly prime, or youthful bloom?
LADY As smooth as Hebe's° their unrazored lips.
COMUS Two such I saw, what time the laboured ox
In his loose traces from the furrow came,°
And the swinked hedger° at his supper sat;
I saw them under a green mantling vine
That crawls along the side of yon small hill,
Plucking ripe clusters from the tender shoots;
Their port° was more than human, as they stood.
I took it for a faëry vision

Scylla . . . Charybdis The monster and, across the strait of Messina from her, the whirlpool—all these Odyssean allusions are associated with Circe.
home-felt deeply felt
Unless unless you are
Dim . . . labyrinth This line-for-line dialogue imitates the stichomythia of Greek drama.
hit guess
Imports their loss does losing them matter
Hebe's the youth goddess and Olympian cup-bearer
what time . . . came Unyoking the oxen is a symbol of nightfall in Homer and Virgil.
swinked hedger tired hedge-cutter
port bearing

Of some gay creatures of the element,°
That in the colours of the rainbow live
And play i' th' plighted° clouds. I was awe-strook,
And as I passed, I worshipped; if those you seek,
It were a journey like the path to heaven
To help you find them.
LADY Gentle villager,°
What readiest way would bring me to that place?
COMUS Due west it rises from this shrubby point.
LADY To find out that, good shepherd, I suppose,
In such a scant allowance of star-light,
Would overtask the best land-pilot's art
Without the sure guess of well-practised feet.
COMUS I know each lane and every alley green,
Dingle° or bushy dell of this wild wood,
And every bosky bourn° from side to side
My daily walks and ancient neighbourhood,
And if your stray attendance° be yet lodged,
Or shroud° within these limits, I shall know
Ere morrow wake or the low-roosted lark
From her thatched pallet° rouse; if otherwise,
I can conduct you, lady, to a low
But loyal cottage, where you may be safe
Till further quest.
LADY Shepherd, I take thy word,
And trust thy honest-offered courtesy,
Which oft is sooner found in lowly sheds
With smoky rafters, than in tap'stry halls
And courts of princes, where it first was named,
And yet is most pretended. In a place
Less warranted than this, or less secure,
I cannot be, that I should fear to change it.
Eye me, blest Providence, and square my trial
To my proportioned strength. Shepherd, lead on.
[*Exeunt*]

[*The two Brothers*]

ELDER BROTHER Unmuffle, ye faint stars, and thou, fair moon,
That wont'st to love the traveller's benison,
Stoop thy pale visage through an amber cloud,
And disinherit° Chaos, that reigns here
In double night of darkness and of shades;

element in this case, air
plighted folded
Gentle villager Comus is, of course, disguised as a Shropshire countryman, to trap the Lady's own "gentleness" which would assume no connection between rusticity or humble condition and evil.
Dingle hollow
bosky bourn bushy brook
attendance attendants
shroud hide themselves
pallet straw bed
disinherit dispossess

Or if your influence be quite dammed up
With black usurping mists, some gentle taper
Though a rush-candle from the wicker hole
Of some clay habitation, visit us
With thy long levelled rule of streaming light,
And thou shalt be our star of Arcady,
Or Tyrian Cynosure.°

SECOND BROTHER Or if our eyes
Be barred that happiness, might we but hear
The folded flocks penned in their wattled cotes,°
Or sound of pastoral reed with oaten stops,°
Or whistle from the lodge, or village cock
Count the night-watches to his feathery dames,
'Twould be some solace yet, some little cheering,
In this close dungeon of innumerous° boughs.
But O that hapless virgin, our lost sister,
Where may she wander now, whither betake her
From the chill dew, amongst rude burrs and thistles?
Perhaps some cold bank is her bolster now,
Or 'gainst the rugged bark of some broad elm
Leans her unpillowed head fraught with sad fears.
What if in wild amazement and affright,
Or, while we speak, within the direful grasp
Of savage hunger or of savage heat?

ELDER BROTHER Peace, brother, be not over-exquisite°
To cast° the fashion of uncertain evils;
For grant they be so, while they rest unknown,
What need a man forestall his date of grief,
And run to meet what he would most avoid?
Or if they be but false alarms of fear,
How bitter is such self-delusïon?
I do not think my sister so to seek,°
Or so unprincipled in virtue's book,
And the sweet peace that goodness bosoms ever,
As that the single° want of light and noise
(Not being in danger, as I trust she is not)
Could stir the constant mood of her calm thoughts,
And put them into misbecoming plight.
Virtue could see to do what Virtue would
By her own radiant light, though sun and moon
Were in the flat sea sunk. And Wisdom's self
Oft seeks to sweet retired solitude,

star . . . Cynosure Ursa Major or Ursa Minor (containing the pole star); Greek mariners steered by the first, Phoenicians by the second
wattled cotes sheepfolds of interwoven branches
pastoral . . . stops The reed flute symbolized pastoral poetry; cf. the "oaten pipe" of Colin Clout in Spenser, *The Shepheards Calender,* January Eclogue, l. 72, and the "oaten flute" in *Lycidas,* l. 33.
innumerous numberless
over-exquisite too subtle
cast forecast
so to seek so lacking (here, virtue)
single mere

Where with her best nurse, Contemplatïon,
She plumes her feathers, and lets grow her wings,
That in the various bustle of resort
Were all to-ruffled,° and sometimes impaired.
He that has light within his own clear breast
May sit i' th'centre° and enjoy bright day,
But he that hides a dark soul and foul thoughts
Benighted walks under the mid-day sun;
Himself is his own dungeon.

SECOND BROTHER 'Tis most true
That musing meditation most affects
The pensive secrecy of desert cell,
Far from the cheerful haunt of men and herds,
And sits as safe as in a senate-house;
For who would rob a hermit of his weeds,
His few books, or his beads, or maple dish,
Or do his grey hairs any violence?
But beauty, like the fair Hesperian tree
Laden with blooming gold,° had need the guard
Of dragon-watch with unenchanted° eye
To save her blossoms and defend her fruit
From the rash hand of bold Incontinence.
You may as well spread out the unsunned heaps
Of miser's treasure by an outlaw's den,
And tell me it is safe, as bid me hope
Danger will wink on opportunity,
And let a single helpless maiden pass
Uninjured in this wild surrounding waste.
Of night or loneliness it recks me not;°
I fear the dread events that dog them both,
Lest some ill-greeting touch attempt the person
Of our unowned° sister.

ELDER BROTHER I do not, brother,
Infer as if I thought my sister's state
Secure without all doubt or controversy;
Yet where an equal poise of hope and fear
Does arbitrate the event, my nature is
That I incline to hope rather than fear,
And gladly banish squint° suspicïon.
My sister is not so defenceless left
As you imagine; she has a hidden strength
Which you remember not.

SECOND BROTHER What hidden strength,

to-ruffled ruffled up
centre of the earth
blooming gold the golden apples of the Hesperides
unenchanted unenchantable (Milton liked this phrase so much that he reinserted it here after having cut it from another place in the MS.; cf. similar latinate use of participle in l. 215)
it recks me not I don't care
unowned unguarded
squint squinting

Unless the strength of heaven, if you mean that?
ELDER BROTHER I mean that too, but yet a hidden strength
Which, if heaven gave it, may be termed her own
—'Tis chastity, my brother, chastity:
She that has that is clad in cómplete steel,
And like a quivered° nymph with arrows keen
May trace huge forests and unharboured heaths,
Infamous hills and sandy perilous wilds,
Where, through the sacred rays of chastity,
No savage fierce, bandit, or mountaineer
Will dare to soil her virgin purity.
Yea, there where very desolation dwells,
By grots and caverns shagged with horrid shades,
She may pass on with unblenched° majesty,
Be it not done in pride or in presumption.
Some say no evil thing that walks by night
In fog or fire,° by lake or moorish fen,
Blue meagre hag, or stubborn unlaid° ghost
That breaks his magic chains at curfew time,
No goblin or swart fairy of the mine,
Hath hurtful power o'er true virginity.
Do ye believe me yet, or shall I call
Antiquity from the old schools° of Greece
To testify the arms of chastity?
Hence had the huntress Dian her dread bow,
Fair silver-shafted queen for ever chaste,
Wherewith she tamed the brinded° lioness
And spotted mountain pard,° but set at naught
The frivolous bolt of Cupid; gods and men
Feared her stern frown, and she was queen o' th' woods.
What was that snaky-headed Gorgon shield
That wise Minerva wore,° unconquered virgin,
Wherewith she freezed her foes to cóngealed stone,
But rigid looks of chaste austerity,
And noble grace that dashed brute violence
With sudden adoration and blank awe?
So dear to heaven is saintly chastity
That when a soul is found sincerely so,
A thousand liveried angels lackey° her,
Driving far off each thing of sin and guilt,
And in clear dream and solemn visïon
Tell her of things that no gross ear can hear,

quivered carrying a quiver of arrows; a nymph of Diana, the virgin goddess of the hunt
unblenched undismayed
fire *ignis fatuus:* will-o'-the-wisp or phosphorescent light
unlaid unexorcised
schools philosophical traditions
brinded tawny
pard panther
Minerva wore Athena (Minerva) had Medusa's petrifying head on her shield because, said a Renaissance mythographer, no one can turn his eyes against wisdom with impunity.
lackey attend

Till oft converse with heavenly habitants
Begin to cast a beam on the outward shape,
The unpolluted temple of the mind,
And turns it by degrees to the soul's essence,
Till all be made immortal. But when lust,
By unchaste looks, loose gestures, and foul talk,
But most by lewd and lavish act of sin,
Lets in defilement to the inward parts,
The soul grows clotted by contagion,°
Imbodies and imbrutes, till she quite lose
The divine property of her first being.
Such are those thick and gloomy shadows damp
Oft seen in charnel vaults and sepulchres
Lingering, and sitting by a new-made grave,
As loth to leave the body that it loved,
And linked itself by carnal sensuality
To a degenerate and degraded state.

SECOND BROTHER How charming is divine philosophy!
Not harsh and crabbèd, as dull fools suppose,
But musical as is Apollo's lute,
And a perpetual feast of nectared sweets,
Where no crude surfeit reigns.

ELDER BROTHER List! list, I hear
Some far-off hallo break the silent air.

SECOND BROTHER Methought so too; what should it be?

ELDER BROTHER For certain,
Either some one like us night-foundered° here,
Or else some neighbour woodman, or at worst,
Some roving robber calling to his fellows.

SECOND BROTHER Heaven keep my sister! Again, again, and near!
Best draw, and stand upon our guard.

ELDER BROTHER I'll hallo;
If he be friendly, he comes well; if not,
Defense is a good cause, and Heaven be for us.

[THE ATTENDANT SPIRIT, *habited like a shepherd*]

That hallo I should know; what are you? speak.
Come not too near, you fall on iron stakes° else.

SPIRIT What voice is that? my young lord? speak again.

SECOND BROTHER O brother, 'tis my father's shepherd, sure.

ELDER BROTHER Thyrsis,° whose artful strains have oft delayed
The huddling brook° to hear his madrigal,

The soul . . . contagion Plato's *Phaedo* 81 provides the doctrine for this explanation of why ghosts are always the souls of those who made of their bodies a prison while alive.
night-foundered sunk in night
iron stakes swords
Thyrsis name of a pastoral singer from Theocritus and Virgil; it is the Attendant Spirit in disguise, or rather incarnated as a literary figure whose name Milton might have used to praise Henry Lawes, who is playing the part
huddling brook its waves crowd together to stop and listen

And sweetened every musk-rose of the dale,
How camest thou here, good swain? Hath any ram
Slipped from the fold, or young kid lost his dam,
Or straggling wether° the pent flock forsook?
How couldst thou find this dark sequestered nook?
SPIRIT O my loved master's heir, and his next° joy,
I came not here on such a trivial toy
As a strayed ewe, or to pursue the stealth
Of pilfering wolf; not all the fleecy wealth
That doth enrich these downs is worth a thought
To this my errand, and the care it brought.
But O my virgin lady, where is she?°
How chance she is not in your company?
ELDER BROTHER To tell thee sadly,° shepherd, without blame
Or our neglect, we lost her as we came.
SPIRIT Ay me unhappy, then my fears are true.
ELDER BROTHER What fears, good Thyrsis? Prithee briefly shew.
SPIRIT I'll tell ye. 'Tis not vain or fabulous°
(Though so esteemed by shallow ignorance)
What the sage poets, taught by the heavenly Muse,
Storied of old in high immortal verse
Of dire Chimeras and enchanted isles,
And rifted rocks whose entrance leads to hell—
For such there be, but unbelief is blind.
Within the navel° of this hideous wood,
Immured in cypress shades, a sorcerer dwells,
Of Bacchus and of Circe born, great Comus,
Deep skilled in all his mother's witcheries,
And here to every thirsty wanderer
By sly enticement gives his baneful cup,
With many murmurs° mixed, whose pleasing poison
The visage quite transforms of him that drinks,
And the inglorious likeness of a beast
Fixes instead, unmoulding reason's mintage
Charáctered° in the face; this have I learnt
Tending my flocks hard by i' th' hilly crofts°
That brow° this bottom glade, whence night by night
He and his monstrous rout are heard to howl
Like stabled wolves, or tigers at their prey,
Doing abhorrèd rites to Hecate
In their obscurèd haunts of inmost bowers.

wether castrated ram
next nearest and dearest
where is she? The Spirit clearly knows (see ll. 561–76) and the question is rhetorical in a way, drawing the audience's attention to the following long description.
sady seriously
fabulous mythical. The Spirit is here stating a basic position of Renaissance mythography, namely, that not only did these old stories have ethical and psychological significance, but that they represented slightly misshapen versions of biblical truths.
navel center
murmurs incantations
Charactered imprinted
crofts small farms
brow overlook

Yet have they many baits and guileful spells
To inveigle and invite the unwary sense
Of them that pass unweeting° by the way.
This evening late, by then° the chewing flocks
Had ta'en their supper on the savoury herb
Of knot-grass dew-besprent, and were in fold,
I sat me down to watch upon a bank
With ivy canopied, and interwove
With flaunting honeysuckle, and began,
Wrapped in a pleasing fit of melancholy,
To meditate my rural minstrelsy,°
Till fancy had her fill. But ere a close°
The wonted roar was up amidst the woods,
And filled the air with barbarous dissonance,
At which I ceased, and listened them a while,
Till an unusual stop of sudden silence
Gave respite to the drowsy frighted steeds
That draw the litter of close-curtained Sleep.
At last a soft and solemn-breathing sound
Rose like a steam of rich distilled perfumes,
And stole upon the air, that even Silence
Was took ere she was ware, and wished she might
Deny her nature and be never more,
Still to be so displaced. I was all ear,
And took in strains that might create a soul
Under the ribs of Death, but O ere long
Too well I did perceive it was the voice
Of my most honoured lady, your dear sister.
Amazed I stood, harrowed with grief and fear,
And 'O poor hapless nightingale,' thought I,
'How sweet thou sing'st, how near the deadly snare!'
Then down the lawns I ran with headlong haste
Through paths and turnings often trod by day,
Till guided by mine ear I found the place
Where that damned wizard, hid in sly disguise
(For so by certain signs I knew), had met
Already, ere my best speed could prevent,
The aidless innocent lady, his wished prey,
Who gently asked if he had seen such two,
Supposing him some neighbour villager;
Longer I durst not stay, but soon I guessed
Ye were the two she meant; with that I sprung
Into swift flight, till I had found you here;
But further know I not.

SECOND BROTHER O night and shades,

unweeting heedless
by then when

To meditate . . . minstrelsy to play a shepherd's pipe
close musical cadence

How are ye joined with hell in triple knot
Against the unarmèd weakness of one virgin
Alone and helpless! Is this the confidence
You gave me, brother?

ELDER BROTHER Yes, and keep it still,
Lean on it safely; not a period°
Shall be unsaid, for me—against the threats
Of malice or of sorcery, or that power
Which erring men call chance, this I hold firm:
Virtue may be assailed, but never hurt,
Surprised by unjust force, but not enthralled,
Yea, even that which mischief meant most harm
Shall in the happy trial prove most glory.
But evil on itself shall back recoil,
And mix no more with goodness, when at last,
Gathered like scum, and settled to itself,
It shall be in eternal restless change
Self-fed and self-consumèd;° if this fail,
The pillared firmament is rottenness,
And earth's base built on stubble. But come, let's on.
Against the opposing will and arm of heaven
May never this just sword be lifted up;
But for that damned magician, let him be girt
With all the grisly legïons that troop
Under the sooty flag of Acheron,°
Harpies° and Hydras,° or all the monstrous forms
'Twixt Africa and Ind, I'll find him out,
And force him to restore his purchase° back,
Or drag him by the curls to a foul death,
Cursed as his life.

SPIRIT Alas, good venturous youth,
I love thy courage yet, and bold emprise,°
But here thy sword can do thee little stead;
For other arms and other weapons must
Be those that quell the might of hellish charms.
He with his bare wand can unthread thy joints,
And crumble all thy sinews.

ELDER BROTHER Why, prithee, shepherd,
How durst thou then thyself approach so near
As to make this relation?

SPIRIT Care and utmost shifts
How to secure the lady from surprisal
Brought to my mind a certain shepherd lad,
Of small regard to see to, yet well skilled

period sentence
But evil . . . self-consumed Cf. *Paradise Lost* II.795–802.
Acheron one of the rivers of Hades; hell itself
Harpies horrible birds with women's faces
Hydras nine-headed monsters of the species killed by Hercules
purchase prey
emprise enterprise

In every virtuous° plant and healing herb
That spreads her verdant leaf to the morning ray.
He loved me well, and oft would beg me sing;
Which when I did, he on the tender grass
Would sit, and hearken even to ecstasy,
And in requital ope his leathern scrip,°
And show me simples° of a thousand names,
Telling their strange and vigorous faculties;
Amongst the rest a small unsightly root,
But of divine effect, he culled me out;
The leaf was darkish, and had prickles on it,
But in another country, as he said,
Bore a bright golden flower, but not in this soil:
Unknown, and like esteemed, and the dull swain
Treads on it daily with his clouted shoon,°
And yet more med'cinal is it than that moly°
That Hermes once to wise Ulysses gave;
He called it haemony,° and gave it me,
And bade me keep it as of sovereign use
'Gainst all enchantments, mildew blast, or damp,
Or ghastly Furies' apparitïon;
I pursed it up, but little reckoning made,
Till now that this extremity compelled,
But now I find it true; for by this means
I knew the foul enchanter though disguised,
Entered the very lime-twigs° of his spells,
And yet came off. If you have this about you
(As I will give you when we go), you may
Boldly assault the necromancer's hall,
Where if he be, with dauntless hardihood
And brandished blade rush on him, break his glass,
And shed the luscious liquor on the ground,°
But seize his wand. Though he and his cursed crew
Fierce sign of battle make, and menace high,
Or like the sons of Vulcan vomit smoke,
Yet will they soon retire, if he but shrink.

ELDER BROTHER Thyrsis, lead on apace, I'll follow thee,
And some good angel bear a shield before us.

The scene changes to a stately palace, set out with all manner of deliciousness: soft music, tables spread with all dainties. COMUS *appears*

virtuous pharmacologically potent
scrip bag
simples medicinal herbs; called so because used uncompounded
clouted shoon hobnailed shoes
moly Hermes gave Odysseus this magic plant as an antidote to the transforming spells of Circe.
haemony See Headnote.
lime-twigs Twigs, smeared with lime, were used to trap birds.
And shed . . . ground one of many Spenserian reminiscences in this work; in the Bower of Bliss, Guyon breaks the cup of excess "And with the liquor stainèd all the lond" (*The Faerie Queene* II.xii.57); by this allusion, the overthrow of Comus is made to parallel Acrasia's in moral significance

with his rabble, and THE LADY *set in an enchanted chair, to whom he offers his glass, which she puts by, and goes about to rise.*

COMUS Nay, lady, sit; if I but wave this wand,
Your nerves° are all chained up in alabaster,°
And you a statue, or as Daphne° was
Root-bound, that fled Apollo.
LADY Fool, do not boast;
Thou canst not touch the freedom of my mind
With all thy charms, although this corporal rind
Thou hast immanacled,° while heaven sees good.
COMUS Why are you vexed, lady? why do you frown?
Here dwell no frowns, nor anger; from these gates
Sorrow flies far: see, here be all the pleasures
That fancy can beget on youthful thoughts,
When the fresh blood grows lively, and returns
Brisk as the April buds in primrose season.
And first behold this cordial julep here
That flames and dances in his crystal bounds
With spirits of balm and fragrant syrups mixed.
Not that nepenthes which the wife of Thone
In Egypt gave to Jove-born Helena°
Is of such power to stir up joy as this,
To life so friendly, or so cool to thirst.
Why should you be so cruel to yourself,
And to those dainty limbs which Nature lent
For gentle usage and soft delicacy?
But you invert the covenants of her trust,
And harshly deal like an ill borrower
With that which you received on other terms,
Scorning the unexempt conditïon
By which all mortal frailty must subsist,
Refreshment after toil, ease after pain,
That have been tired all day without repast,
And timely rest have wanted; but, fair virgin,
This will restore all soon.
LADY 'Twill not, false traitor,
'Twill not restore the truth and honesty
That thou hast banished from thy tongue with lies.
Was this the cottage and the safe abode
Thou told'st me of? What grim aspécts are these,
These ugly-headed monsters? Mercy guard me!
Hence with thy brewed enchantments, foul deceiver;
Hast thou betrayed my credulous innocence

nerves muscles
alabaster marble
Daphne Fleeing Apollo's desiring grasp, she turned into a laurel bush.
immanacled chained up

nepenthes . . . Helena In the *Odyssey* IV. 219–32 Helen gives her husband Menelaus an Egyptian drug of an opium-like sort to drive away his grief.

With vizored falsehood and base forgery,°
And wouldst thou seek again to trap me here
With lickerish° baits fit to ensnare a brute?
Were it a draught for Juno when she banquets,
I would not taste thy treasonous offer; none
But such as are good men can give good things,
And that which is not good is not delicious
To a well-governed and wise appetite.
COMUS O foolishness of men! that lend their ears
To those budge° doctors of the Stoic fur,°
And fetch their precepts from the Cynic tub,°
Praising the lean and sallow Abstinence.
Wherefore did Nature pour her bounties forth
With such a full and unwithdrawing hand,
Covering the earth with odours, fruits, and flocks
Thronging the seas with spawn innumerable,
But all to please and sate the curious taste?
And set to work millions of spinning worms,
That in their green shops weave the smooth-haired silk
To deck her sons, and that no corner might
Be vacant of her plenty, in her own loins
She hutched° the all-worshipped ore and precious gems
To store her children with. If all the world
Should in a pet of temperance feed on pulse,°
Drink the clear stream, and nothing wear but frieze,°
The All-giver would be unthanked, would be unpraised,
Not half his riches known, and yet despised;
And we should serve him as a grudging master,
As a penurious niggard of his wealth,
And live like Nature's bastards, not her sons,
Who would be quite surcharged with her own weight,
And strangled with her waste fertility;
The earth cumbered, and the winged air darked with plumes;
The herds would over-multitude their lords,
The sea o'erfraught would swell, and the unsought diamonds
Would so emblaze the forehead of the deep,°
And so bestud with stars, that they below
Would grow inured to light, and come at last
To gaze upon the sun with shameless brows.
List, lady, be not coy, and be not cozened°
With that same vaunted name 'Virginity':

forgery deception
lickerish pleasing to the taste, but also with a sense of "lecherous"
budge stiff, pompous (from the fur "budge" on academic gowns)
Stoic fur here, Stoic school or persuasion—Comus is sneering at philosophic asceticism
Cynic tub Diogenes the Cynic also scorned the things of this world; unlike the Stoics Epictetus and Seneca, his views were unsupported by theories of the relation of soul to body and he lived in a tub.
hutched laid away
pulse peas, beans, lentils, etc.
frieze coarse woolen cloth
deep the middle of the earth, specifically the outer layer where mining takes place, and where precious stones were thought to reproduce themselves like living organisms
cozened cheated

Beauty is Nature's coin, must not be hoarded,
But must be current, and the good thereof
Consists in mutual and partaken bliss,
Unsavoury in the enjoyment of itself.
If you let slip time, like a neglected rose
It withers on the stalk with languished head.
Beauty is Nature's brag,° and must be shown
In courts, at feasts, and high solemnities
Where most may wonder at the workmanship;
It is for homely features to keep home,
They had their name thence; coarse complexïons
And cheeks of sorry grain° will serve to ply
The sampler, and to tease° the housewife's wool.
What need a vermeil°-tinctured lip for that,
Love-darting eyes, or tresses like the morn?
There was another meaning in these gifts,
Think what, and be advised; you are but young yet.
LADY I had not thought to have unlocked my lips
In this unhallowed air, but that this juggler
Would think to charm my judgment, as mine eyes,
Obtruding false rules pranked° in reason's garb.
I hate when vice can bolt° her arguments,
And virtue has no tongue to check her pride.
Impostor, do not charge most innocent Nature,
As if she would her children should be riotous
With her abundance; she, good cateress,
Means her provision only to the good,
That live according to her sober laws
And holy dictate of spare Temperance.
If every just man that now pines with want
Had but a moderate and beseeming share
Of that which lewdly pampered luxury
Now heaps upon some few with vast excess,
Nature's full blessings would be well dispensed
In unsuperfluous even proportïon,
And she no whit encumbered with her store;
And then the Giver would be better thanked,
His praise due paid, for swinish gluttony
Ne'er looks to heaven amidst his gorgeous feast,
But with besotted base ingratitude
Crams, and blasphemes his Feeder. Shall I go on?
Or have I said enough? To him that dares
Arm his profane tongue with contemptuous words
Against the sun-clad power of Chastity,
Fain would I something say, yet to what end?

brag boast
grain color
tease comb
vermeil vermilion
pranked decked out
bolt sift; refine

Thou hast nor ear nor soul to apprehend
The sublime notion and high mystery°
That must be uttered to unfold the sage
And serious doctrine of Virginity,
And thou art worthy that thou shouldst not know
More happiness than this thy present lot.
Enjoy your dear wit and gay rhetoric
That hath so well been taught her dazzling fence;°
Thou art not fit to hear thyself convinced.°
Yet should I try, the uncontrollèd worth
Of this pure cause would kindle my rapt° spirits
To such a flame of sacred vehemence
That dumb things would be moved to sympathize,
And the brute Earth would lend her nerves, and shake,
Till all thy magic structures, reared so high,
Were shattered into heaps o'er thy false head.
COMUS She fables not. I feel that I do fear
Her words set off by some superior power;
And though not mortal, yet a cold shuddering dew
Dips me all o'er, as when the wrath of Jove
Speaks thunder and the chains of Erebus°
To some of Saturn's crew.° I must dissemble,
And try her yet more strongly. Come, no more,
This is mere moral babble, and direct
Against the canon laws of our foundation;
I must not suffer this, yet 'tis but the lees°
And settlings of a melancholy blood;
But this will cure all straight; one sip of this
Will bathe the drooping spirits in delight
Beyond the bliss of dreams. Be wise, and taste.

[THE BROTHERS *rush in with swords drawn, wrest his glass out of his hand, and break it against the ground; his rout make sign of resistance, but are all driven in;* THE ATTENDANT SPIRIT *comes in*]

SPIRIT What, have you let the false enchanter scape?
O ye mistook, ye should have snatched his wand
And bound him fast; without his rod reversed,°
And backward mutters of dissevering power,
We cannot free the lady that sits here

mystery Milton writes elsewhere, quoting I Corinthians 6:13, of "unfolding those chaste and high mysteries . . . that 'the body is for the Lord and the Lord for the body' " (*Apology for Smectymnuus*, Columbia Edition, Vol. 3, p. 306).
fence fencing, i.e. debating
convinced refuted
rapt transported
Erebus in Hesiod's account of creation, the son of Chaos, and the original darkness that existed before there was light
Saturn's crew Zeus (Jupiter) overthrew his ruling father Cronus, or Saturn, and imprisoned him in the underworld, Tartarus.
lees dregs of wine, here likened to the melancholy humor of blood
rod reversed In Ovid, *Metamorphoses* XIV.300, Circe's spells are undone by reversing the motion of the wand that cast them; the spells of Spenser's Busyrane are also revoked in this manner (*The Faerie Queene* III.xii.36).

In stony fetters fixed and motionless;
Yet stay, be not disturbed; now I bethink me,
Some other means I have which may be used,
Which once of Meliboeus° old I learnt,
The soothest shepherd that e'er piped on plains.
  There is a gentle Nymph not far from hence,
That with moist curb sways the smooth Severn° stream;
Sabrina is her name, a virgin pure;
Whilom she was the daughter of Locrine,
That had the sceptre from his father Brute.°
She, guiltless damsel, flying the mad pursuit
Of her enragèd stepdame Guendolen,
Commended her fair innocence to the flood
That stayed her flight with his cross-flowing course;
The water-nymphs that in the bottom played
Held up their pearlèd wrists and took her in,
Bearing her straight to aged Nereus'° hall,
Who, piteous of her woes, reared her lank head,
And gave her to his daughters to imbathe
In nectared lavers° strewed with asphodel,°
And through the porch and inlet of each sense
Dropped in ambrosial oils, till she revived
And underwent a quick immortal change,
Made goddess of the river. Still she retains
Her maiden gentleness, and oft at eve
Visits the herds along the twilight meadows,
Helping all urchin blasts,° and ill-luck signs
That the shrewd meddling elf delights to make,
Which she with precious vialed liquors heals;
For which the shepherds at their festivals
Carol her goodness loud in rustic lays,
And throw sweet garland wreaths into her stream
Of pansies, pinks, and gaudy daffodils.
And, as the old swain° said, she can unlock
The clasping charm and thaw the numbing spell,
If she be right invoked in warbled song;
For maidenhood she loves, and will be swift
To aid a virgin such as was herself
In hard-besetting need: this will I try,
And add the power of some adjuring verse.

Meliboeus Milton's pastoral name for Spenser

Severn the river rising in Wales and flowing through Shropshire to the sea. Sabrina is her mythical personification, whose story Spenser tells in *The Faerie Queene* II.x.19; Milton transforms her into a local spirit for Ludlow Castle and makes her powers more complex and potent than those of a mere water nymph.

Brute in British mythology, Aeneas' great-grandson, who founded Britain

Nereus' father of the Nereids or sea nymphs

lavers basins

asphodel the undying flower growing in the Elysian fields (see Chapman's Homer)

urchin blasts boils or infections caused by the fairies

old swain Meliboeus

SONG

Sabrina fair,
Listen where thou art sitting
Under the glassy, cool, translucent wave,
In twisted braids of lilies knitting
The loose train of thy amber-dropping hair;
Listen for dear honour's sake,
Goddess of the silver lake,
Listen and save.

Listen and appear to us
In name of great Oceanus,°
By the earth-shaking Neptune's mace,°
And Tethys'° grave majestic pace,
By hoary Nereus'° wrinkled look,
And the Carpathian wizard's hook,°
By scaly Triton's° winding shell,
And old soothsaying Glaucus'° spell,
By Leucothea's° lovely hands,
And her son that rules the strands,
By Thetis'° tinsel-slippered feet,
And the songs of Sirens sweet,
By dead Parthenope's° dear tomb,
And fair Ligea's golden comb,°
Wherewith she sits on diamond rocks
Sleeking her soft alluring locks;
By all the nymphs that nightly dance
Upon thy streams with wily glance,
Rise, rise, and heave thy rosy head
From thy coral-paven bed,
And bridle in thy headlong wave,
Till thou our summons answered have.
Listen and save.

[*Sabrina rises, attended by water-nymphs, and sings*]

By the rushy-fringèd bank,
Where grows the willow and the osier dank,
My sliding chariot stays,°

Oceanus god of the river of ocean which, in Greek mythology, circled the earth
mace trident
Tethys' his wife
Nereus' See l. 835n.
Carpathian . . . hook the crook of Proteus, shepherd of Poseidon's (Neptune's) seals
Triton's Triton was Neptune's trumpeter, who played a conch; "winding" means "being blown upon" as well as "twisting."
Glaucus' He became a sea god and prophet.
Leucothea's "bright goddess" who helps Odysseus in *Odyssey* V
Thetis' a Nereid, married to Peleus and mother of Achilles
Parthenope's one of the sirens
Ligea's . . . comb another siren. Virgil mentions her hair, and Milton puts her in standard mermaid position, sitting on the rocks, combing her hair.
sliding chariot stays Her "chariot" is the water itself, awaiting her in the sense that it is always there, rushing by; the chariot of water is the subject of l. 895.

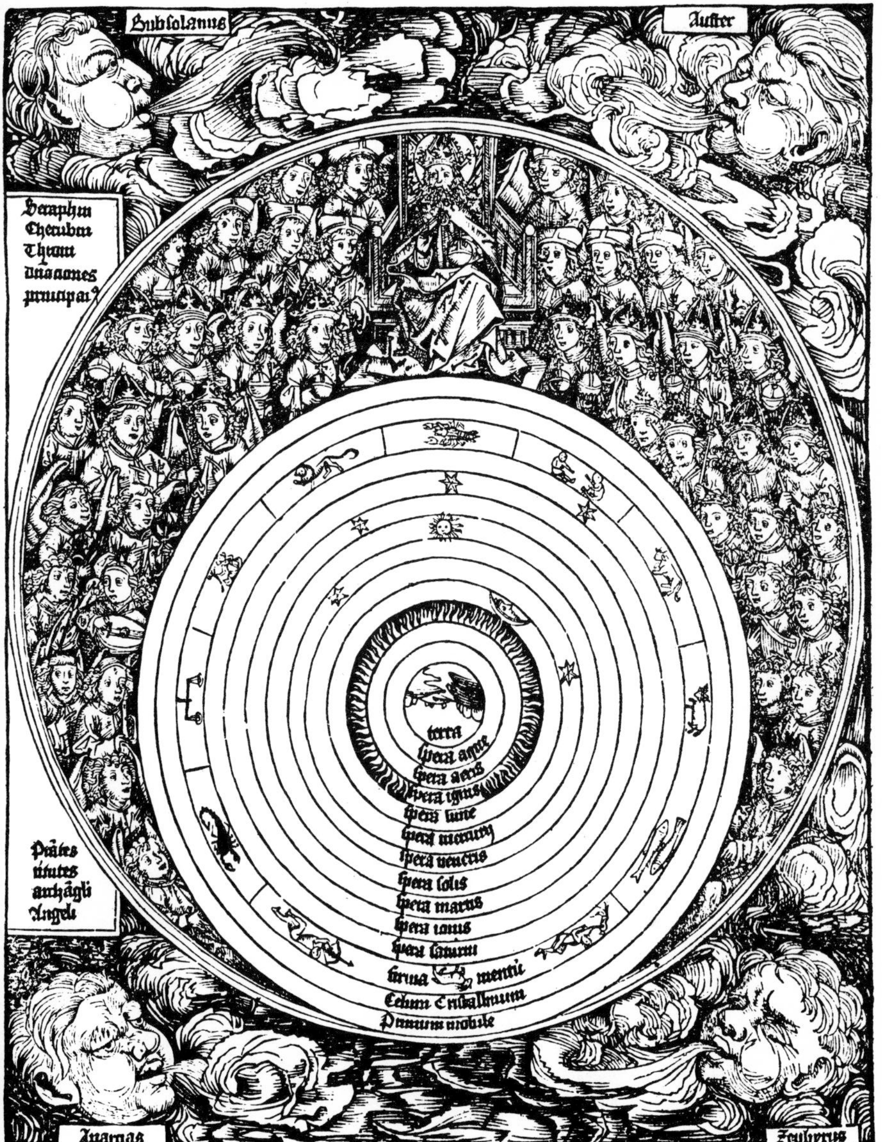

1. The "Ptolemaic" Universe: the spheres from earth to Prime Mover, with God at the top, surrounded by choiring angels, and with the four winds in their corners. From Hartmann Schedel, *Liber Chronicarum* ("Nuremberg Chronicle"), 1493.

2. *Sir Thomas More and His Household* (c. 1527), by Hans Holbein the Younger (1497/8–1543), the German artist who served as court painter to Henry VIII. *Oeffentliche Kunstsammlung,* Basel.

3. *Sir Thomas Elyot* (c. 1527–28), also drawn by Holbein. *By permission of Her Majesty the Queen, Copyright reserved.*

4. Guidobaldo da Montefeltro as a boy, with his father Federigo, Duke of Urbino, painted about 1476 by the Flemish artist Joos van Wassenhove called Justus van Ghent (active c. 1460–80). *Anderson-Art Reference Bureau.*

5. Raphael's portrait of Baldassare Castiglione (c. 1514–15). *Photo Bulloz.*

6. Allegory in Portraiture: Sir John Luttrell (1550), after the painting by Hans Eworth (c. 1520–73). Here shown wading waist-high amid shipwreck, Luttrell, a naval adventurer, looks up at the allegorical figure of Peace surrounded by her attendants. On his wrist is a bracelet with a Latin motto, which would be translated "Money deterred him not, nor did danger wreck him." On the rock at the left are the English verses:

> More than the rock amid the raging seas
> The constant heart no danger dreads, nor fears.

It has recently been suggested that the allegory of Peace also refers specifically to a treaty made with France in 1550. *Luttrell Estates, Ltd.*

7. *Queen Elizabeth I and the Three Goddesses* (1569), by the monogrammist "HE." Like so much mythological poetry and, in particular, like the masques and entertainments of the Jacobean period, this emblematic painting portrays the Queen as Paris, in the famous episode from Greek mythology in which he awards the apple to Aphrodite (Venus) and is rewarded with Helen of Troy—and the Trojan War. Here the Queen awards the prize (the apple "for the fairest" as her orb of power) to herself; the goddesses are, *left to right,* Juno (crowned but with her scepter cast down and with her left shoe come off), Minerva (armed), and Venus (nude, as always, and accompanied by Cupid). In the background is Windsor Castle. *By permission of Her Majesty the Queen, Copyright reserved.*

8. Queen Elizabeth (*c.* 1592), by Marcus Gheeraerts the Younger (1561–1635). The so-called "Ditchley Portrait," probably commemorating an entertainment given the Queen at his house in Oxfordshire by Sir Henry Lee, her Master of the Armoury and probable author of the sonnet appearing in fragmentary form on the right. It hails her as "The prince of light," toward which the figure of the Queen faces, away from stormy clouds ("Thunder, the image of that power divine," says the inscription). She stands on a map of England, with her feet near Ditchley, in fact. *National Portrait Gallery,* London.

9. Sir Walter Ralegh (1588); to the right of his head, a crescent moon facing downward, perhaps in allusion to Queen Elizabeth as Cynthia, the moon goddess and muse of Ralegh's unfinished cycle of poems. The painter has not been definitely identified. *National Portrait Gallery.*

10. A Burning Lover. A miniature by Nicholas Hilliard (c. 1547–1619) depicting a man in his shirt, conventionally ear-ringed, holding a locket probably containing his mistress's picture, and surrounded by the metaphorical fires of his passion. *Victoria and Albert Museum, London.*

11. A Courtly Sonneteer. This Hilliard miniature, c. 1588, shows an unidentified young man leaning against a tree among roses. The Latin motto, *Dat poenas laudata fides,* proclaims that the lover's vaunted faith in love has given him suffering, a typical formula. *Victoria and Albert Museum.*

12. An Elizabethan Musing, c. 1590. This later miniature by Isaac Oliver (1568?–1617) shows a young man beneath a tree in solitude away from the social life in the house and garden behind him. It has been suggested that the melancholy with which the figure is tinged has some relation to that of the figure of Democritus (also seated beneath a tree) on the title page of Burton's *Anatomy of Melancholy* (see Fig. 17). *By permission of Her Majesty the Queen, Copyright reserved.*

MR. WILLIAM

SHAKESPEARES

COMEDIES,
HISTORIES, &
TRAGEDIES.

Publiſhed according to the True Originall Copies.

LONDON
Printed by Iſaac Iaggard, and Ed. Blount. 1623.

13. Shakespeare, engraving by Martin Droeshout (b. 1601) on a title page of the First Folio. *The Granger Collection.*

14. Frontispiece of *The Tempest*, from Rowe's edition of Shakespeare, 1709. *The New York Public Library*.

15. Two nineteenth-century lithographs of Edmund Kean (1789-1833) as Othello. Notice the classical pose in the upper one (c. 1835). The "fantasy-oriental" costumes of both pictures are more alike than the different graphic styles suggest. *The Folger Library*.

16. John Donne (c. 1595), as a melancholic lover—"that picture of mine" he said in disposing of it in his will, "which was taken in the shadows." The large, floppy hat and the undone collar were both marks of the distracted lover in a usually tightly laced age. The inscription, to an unidentified lady, implores her to light up his shadow: *Illumina tenebras nostras domina* (Enlighten our darkness, lady)—a parody, in fact, of the Latin text translated in the (Anglican) Book of Common Prayer as "Lighten our darkness, we beseech thee, Lord." *National Portrait Gallery.*

17. *Melancholy.* The celebrated engraving by Albrecht Dürer (1471–1528), with its emblematic bat, dog, abandoned scientific and speculative instruments, makes of this brooding, dark angel as personal a myth of the internalized imagination as Milton's in "Il Penseroso" or Burton's in the *Anatomy. The Metropolitan Museum of Art, Harris Brisbane Dick Fund, 1943,* New York.

18. *The Anatomy of Melancholy*, title page of the 1628 edition. Surrounding the text are images of melancholic types: on the *left*, the Lover; on the *right*, the Hypochondriac; *above, center*, the Scholar. The Lover may be compared, for his hat and crossed arms, with the portrait of Donne in Figure 15. "Democritus Jr.," the pseudonymous Burton, appears at lower center. *New York Public Library, Arents Collection*.

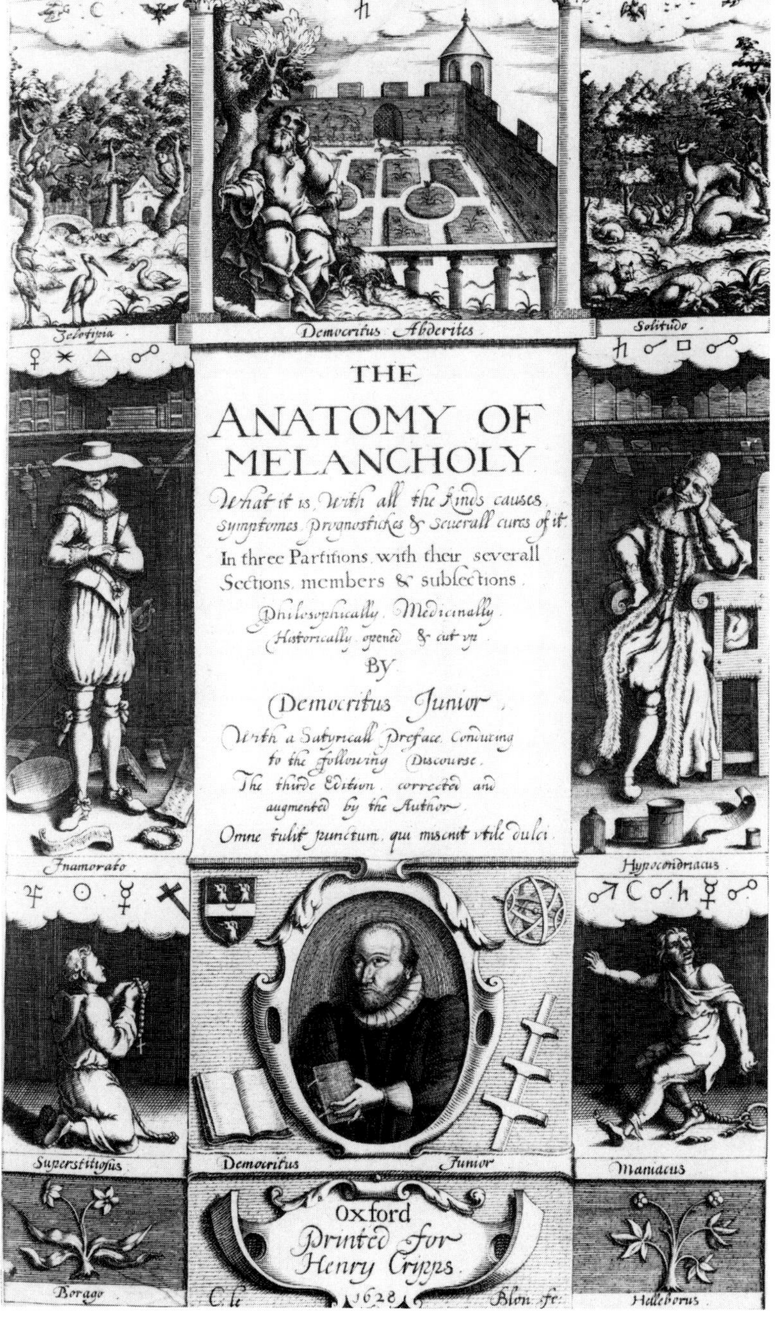

HEERE *Melancholly* mufing in his fits,
Pale vifag'd, of complexion cold and drie,
All folitarie, at his ftudie fits,
Within a wood, devoid of companie:
Saue Madge the Owle, and melancholly Puffe,
Light-loathing Creatures, hatefull, ominous.

His mouth, in figne of filence, vp is bound,
For *Melancholly* loues not many wordes:
One foote on Cube is fixt vpon the ground,
The which him plodding *Conftancie* affordes:
A fealed Purfe he beares, to fhew no vice,
So proper is to him, as *Avarice*.

T 1. *Sanguis*

19. *Melancholy.* Notice that the text gives readings of various elements of the picture.

Emblems of the Four Temperaments from Henry Peacham's emblem book *Minerva Brittana,* 1610. *Yale University Library,* New Haven, Conn.

THE Aierie *Sanguine*, in whose youthfull cheeke,
The *Pestane Rose*, and *Lilly* doe contend:
By nature is benigne, and gentlie meeke,
To Musick, and all merriment a frend;
As seemeth by his flowers, and girlondes gay,
Wherewith he dightes him, all the merry May.

And by him browzing, of the climbing vine,
The lustfull *Goate* is seene, which may import,
His pronenes both to women, and to wine,
Bold, bounteous, frend vnto the learned sort;
For studies fit, best louing, and belou'd,
Faire-spoken, bashfull, seld in anger moou'd.

Cholera

20. *The Sanguine Temperament.*

NEXT *Choller* ſtandes, reſembling moſt the fire,
Of ſwarthie yeallow, and a meager face;
With Sword a late, vnſheathed in his Ire:
Neere whome, there lies, within a little ſpace,
A ſterne ei'de Lion, and by him a ſheild,
Charg'd with a flame, vpon a crimſon feild.

We paint him young, to ſhew that paſſions raigne,
The moſt in heedles, and vnſtaied youth:
That Lion ſhowes, he ſeldome can refraine,
From cruell deede, devoide of gentle ruth:
Or hath perhaps, this beaſt to him aſſign'd,
As bearing moſt, the braue and bounteous mind.

21. *The Choleric.*

HEERE *Phlegme* ſits coughing on a Marble ſeate,
As Citie-vſurers before their dore:
Of Bodie groſſe, not through exceſſe of meate,
But of a Dropſie, he had got of yore:
His ſlothfull hand, in's boſome ſtill he keepes,
Drinkes, ſpits, or nodding, in the Chimney ſleepes.

Beneath his feete, there doth a *Tortoiſe* crall,
For floweſt pace, Sloth's Hieroglyphick here,
For Phlegmatique, hates Labour moſt of all,
As by his courſe araiment, may appeare:
Nor is he better furniſhed I find,
With Science, or the virtues of the mind.

Ad

22. *The Phlegmatic.*

HEARE what's the reason why a man we call
A little world? and what the wiser ment
By this new name? two lights Cœlestiall
Are in his head, as in the Element:
Eke as the wearied Sunne at night is spent,
So seemeth but the life of man a day,
At morne hee's borne, at night he flits away.

Of heate and cold as is the Aire composed,
So likewise man we see breath's whot and cold,
His bodie's earthy: in his lunges inclosed,
Remaines the Aire: his braine doth moisture hold,
His heart and liver, doe the heate infold:
Of Earth, Fire, Water, Man thus framed is,
Of Elements the threefold Qualities.

23. Man the Microcosm, another emblem from *Minerva Brittana*. Compare with the treatment of the human microcosm in Donne's "I am a little world made cunningly," and in Browne and Ralegh. *Yale University Library.*

40 *Bivium virtutis & vitij.*

WHEN HERCVLES, was dowtfull of his waie,
Incloſed rounde, with vertue, and with vice:
With reaſons firſte, did vertue him aſſaie,
The other, did with pleaſures him entice:
They longe did ſtriue, before he coulde be wonne,
Till at the lengthe, ALCIDES thus begonne.

Oh pleaſure, thoughe thie waie bee ſmoothe, and faire,
And ſweete delightes in all thy courtes abounde:
Yet can I heare, of none that haue bene there,
That after life, with fame haue bene renoumde:
For honor hates, with pleaſure to remaine,
Then houlde thy peace, thow waſtes thio winde in vaine.

But heare, I yeelde oh vertue to thie will,
And vowe my ſelfe, all labour to indure,
For to aſcende the ſteepe, and craggie hill,
The toppe whereof, whoe ſo attaines, is ſure
For his rewarde, to haue a crowne of fame:
Thus HERCVLES, obey'd this ſacred dame.

Virgil. in Fragm. de littera y.
Quiſquis enim duros caſus virtutis amore Vicerit, ille ſibi laudémque decúſque parabit.
At qui deſidiã luxúmque ſequetur inertem, Dum fugit oppoſitos incauta mente labores, Turpis, inópſque ſimul, miſerabile tranſiget æuum.

Pœna

24. The Choice of Hercules, a mythological emblem expounded in an almost homiletic way, from Geoffrey Whitney's *Choice of Emblems,* 1586. See also Ben Johnson's *Pleasure Reconciled to Virtue. Yale University Library.*

146

By Studiousnesse, *in* Vertue's *waies*
Men gaine an universall-praise.

12
VIRTUTE AC STUDIO PER ORBEM FAMA PERPETUA COMPARATUR.
Per Orbem
Virtus

ILLVSTR. XII. *Book.* 3

WHen *Emblems*, of too many parts consist,
Their Author was no choice *Emblematist*:
But, is like those, that wast whole *howres*, to tell
What, in three *minutes*, might be said as well.
Yet, when each member is interpreted,
Out of these vulgar *Figures*, you may read
A *Morall*, (altogether) not unfit
To be remembred, ev'n, by *men of wit*.
And, if the *Kernell* proove to be of worth,
No matter from what shell we drew it forth.
The *Square* whereon the *Globe* is placed, here,
Must *Vertue* be; That *Globe* upon the *Square*,
Must meane the *World*; The *Figure*, in the *Round*,
(Which in appearance doth her *Trumpet* sound)
Was made for *Fame*; The *Booke* she beares, may show,
What *Breath* it is, which makes her *Trumpet* blow:
The *Wreath*, inclosing all, was to intend
A glorious *Praise*, that never shall have end:
And, these, in one summ'd up, doe seeme to say;
That, (if men *study* in a *vertuous-way*)
The *Trumpet* of a never-ceasing *Fame*,
Shall through the *world* proclaime their praisefull *Name*.
Now *Reader*, if large *Fame*, be thy ambition,
This *Emblem* doth informe, on what condition
She may be gain'd. But, (herein, me beleeve)
Thy *studie* for meere-praise, will thee deceive:
And, if thy *Vertues*, be, but onely, those
For which the vulgar *Fame*, her *Trumpet* blowes,
Thy *Fame's* a blast; Thy *Vertues*, Vices be;
Thy *Studie's* vaine; and, *shame* will follow thee.

Above

25. Study and Fame. George Wither's *A Collection of Emblems*, 1635, contains this rather plodding reading of a complex symbol. It may amuse the modern reader to follow it step by step.

If Safely, *thou deſire to goe,*
Bee not too ſwift, *nor* overſlow.

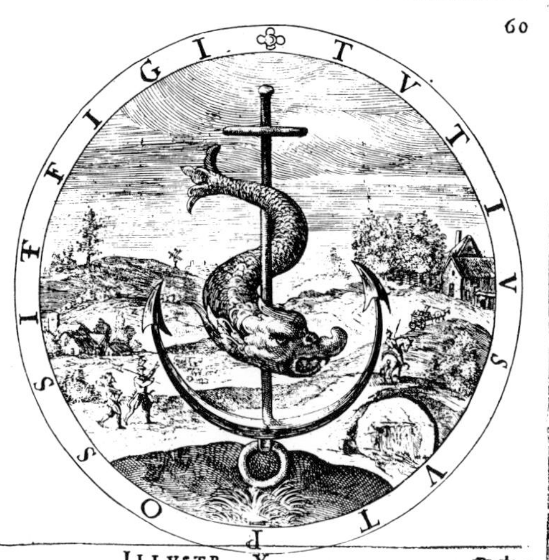

ILLVSTR. X. *Book.* 2

OVr *Elders,* when their meaning was to ſhew
A *native-ſpeedineſſe* (in Emblem wiſe)
The picture of a *Dolphin-Fiſh* they drew;
Which, through the waters, with great ſwiftneſſe, flies.
An *Anchor,* they did figure, to declare
Hope, ſtayedneſſe, or a *grave-deliberation:*
And therefore when thoſe two, united are,
It giveth us a two-fold Intimation.
For, as the *Dolphin* putteth us in minde,
That in the Courſes, which we have to make,
Wee ſhould not be, to *ſlothfulneſſe* enclin'd;
But, ſwift to follow what we undertake:
So, by an *Anchor* added thereunto,
Inform'd wee are, that, to maintaine our *ſpeed,*
Hope, muſt bee joyn'd therewith (in all we doe)
If wee will undiſcouraged proceed.
It ſheweth (alſo) that, our *ſpeedineſſe,*
Muſt have ſome *ſtaydneſſe*; leſt, when wee ſuppoſe
To proſecute our aymes with good ſucceſſe,
Wee may, by *Raſhneſſe,* good endeavors loſe.
They worke, with moſt ſecuritie, that know
The *Times,* and beſt *Occaſions* of *delay*;
When, likewiſe, to be neither *ſwift,* nor *ſlow*;
And, when to practiſe all the *ſpeed,* they may.
For, whether calme, or ſtormie-paſſages,
(Through this life's *Ocean*) ſhall their *Bark* attend;
This *double Vertue,* will procure their eaſe:
And, them, in all neceſſities, befriend.
By *Speedineſſe,* our works are timely wrought;
By *Staydneſſe,* they, to paſſe are, ſafely, brought.

They,

26. *Festina Lente* (Make haste slowly). The device of a dolphin curled about an anchor appears first in classical times and as ascribed to the Emperor Augustus. In the Renaissance it becomes a dialectical resolution of the opposites of anchored steadfastness and joyful, bounding motion. The great Venetian printer Aldus Manutius used it as his device. This version, from Wither's book of emblems, uses the conventional symbolism of the anchor as Hope and, later, as Faith.

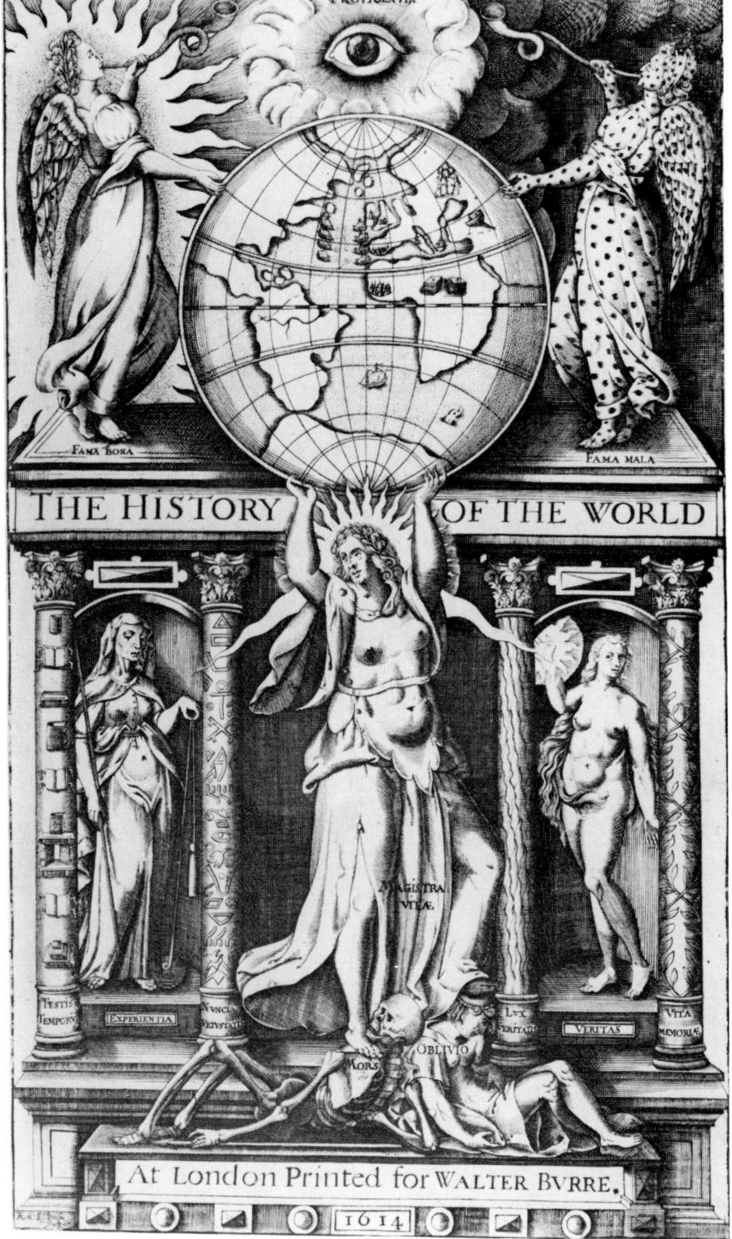
PROVIDENTIA
FAMA BONA
FAMA MALA
THE HISTORY OF THE WORLD
MAGISTRA VITÆ
TESTIS TEMPORV
EXPERIENTIA
NVNCIA VETVSTATI
LVX VERITATI
VERITAS
VITA MEMORIÆ
MORS
OBLIVIO
At London Printed for WALTER BVRRE.
1614

27. Emblem and Poem

The engraved title page of Ralegh's *History of the World,* 1614, shows an allegorical figure of History, labeled in Latin "mistress of life" and bearing aloft the globe, which remains beneath the Eye of Providence; History tramples Death and Oblivion, and is attended by Experience and Truth (naked as always). Ben Jonson wrote the poem "The Mind of the Frontispiece to a Book" to accompany, and gloss, the picture:

From Death and dark Oblivion, ne'er the same
　　The Mistress of Man's life, grave History
Raising the World to Good or Evil Fame
　　Doth vindicate it to eternity.
Wise Providence would so: that nor the good
　　Might be defrauded, nor the great secured,
But both might know their ways were understood
　　When Vice alike in time with Virtue dured.
Which makes that (lighted by the beamy hand
　　Of Truth that searcheth the most hidden springs
And guided by Experience, whose straight wand
　　Doth mete, whose line doth sound, the depth of things),
She cheerfully supporteth what she rears
　　Assisted by no strengths but are her own,
Some note of which each varied pillar bears,
　　By which, as proper titles, she is known:
Time's witness, Herald of Antiquity,
　　The Light of Truth, and Life of Memory.

New York Public Library, Rare Book Division.

28. The young Milton, at age twenty or twenty-one, in 1629. *National Portrait Gallery*.

Melpomene
Erato
IOANNIS MILTONI ANGLI EFFIGIES ANNO ÆTATIS VIGESI: PRI:
Urania
Clio
Ἀμαθεῖ γεγράφθαι χειρὶ τήνδε μὲν εἰκόνα
Φαίης τάχ' ἂν, πρὸς εἶδος αὐτοφυὲς βλέπων·
Τὸν δ' ἐκτυπωτὸν οὐκ ἐπιγνόντες φίλοι
Γελᾶτε φαύλου δυσμίμημα ζωγράφου.
W.M. sculp:

29. Milton at thirty-six or thirty-seven, the frontispiece to the *Poems*, 1645, as engraved by William Marshall. In reaction Milton wrote the Greek inscription at the bottom: "This picture was drawn by an unskillfull hand (you'd say,) looking at its original and not recognizing the true copy [pun on *engraving*]. Friends, laugh at the bad picture by a worthless engraver." *New York Public Library, Rare Book Division*.

30. *King Charles I on Horseback.* Sir Anthony Van Dyck (1599–1641), who lived in England from 1632 until his death, served as painter to Charles I, a great collector and connoisseur. Van Dyck's various portraits of him capture a range of the King's qualities, such as hauteur and refinement; in this equestrian portrait (163?) he is depicted in a manner derived from Titian's Emperor Charles V, but not literally denoting the head of a conquering army so much as suggesting, with almost Platonist imagery, a higher soul controlling powerful passions. *National Gallery,* London.

31. *Charles I and James, Duke of York, 1647*. Portrait by Sir Peter Lely (1618–80) of the doomed King and his heir suggested an almost emblematic reading to the Cavalier poet Richard Lovelace, who wrote of it:

> See what a clouded Majesty! and eyes
> Whose glory through their mist doth brighter rise!
> See what an humble bravery doth shine,
> And grief triumphant breaking through each line; . . .
> That mightiest Monarchs by this shaded book
> May copy out their proudest, richest look.

From "To My Worthy Friend Mr. Peter Lilly"

Country Life, London.

32. The Cavalier Temper. Though most often thought of as a court painter to Charles II, the Dutch artist Sir Peter Lely, who came to London in 1643, was active during the Commonwealth as well. This exotic vision of nymphs at a fountain seems an apt counterpart to the poetic world of Thomas Carew's "A Rapture." *Dulwich College Picture Gallery,* London.

33. St. Teresa in Ecstasy

His is the dart must make the death
Whose stroke shall taste thy hallowed breath;
A dart thrice dipped in that rich flame
Which writes thy spouse's radiant name
Upon the roof of heaven. . . .

From Richard Crashaw's "A Hymn to the Name and Honour of the Admirable Saint Teresa, . . ."

The great baroque vision of *The Ecstasy of St. Teresa* by Gianlorenzo Bernini (1598–1680) (in the Cornaro Chapel of Santa Maria della Vittoria, in Rome) took form in 1645–52, and its amazing theatrical use of natural lighting from above to play about flesh, drapery, and gilded, carved rays of celestial light parallels Crashaw's imagery in representing the rapid transience of the ecstatic moment. Compare with Crashaw's "The Flaming Heart." *Alinari-Scala.*

34. Oliver Cromwell, painted by Robert Walker (c. 1605–60) in a format derived, like Lely's of Charles I and his son, from Van Dyck's division of the scene into two areas, one backed by hanging drapery, the other by outdoor sky. It is ironic that Walker should have used the courtly pictorial conventions to depict the Court's destroyer. *National Portrait Gallery*

35. Rubens's Ceiling, detail of the center end panel representing *The Benefits of the Government of James I.* James crowned and wreathed by angelic figures; *below* Minerva (as Wisdom) defends the throne against Mars (as War) who crushes the King's enemies. Mercury, *left*, points toward their Hell, and above him Peace embraces Plenty. *Department of the Environment, Crown Copyright reserved.*

36. Interior view of the Banqueting House, Whitehall, designed by Inigo Jones (1573–1652) and completed in 1622 for James I. It was the scene of court masques by Ben Jonson and others until 1635, at which time the ceiling by Peter Paul Rubens (1577–1640), commissioned by Charles I was installed. *A. F. Kersting.*

Thick set with agate, and the azurn° sheen
Of turkis° blue, and emerald green,
That in the channel strays.
Whilst from off the waters fleet
Thus I set my printless feet
O'er the cowslip's velvet head,
That bends not as I tread.
Gentle swain, at thy request
I am here.

SPIRIT Goddess dear,
We implore thy powerful hand
To undo the charmèd band
Of true virgin here distressed,
Through the force and through the wile
Of unblest enchanter vile.
SABRINA Shepherd, 'tis my office best
To help ensnarèd chastity.
Brightest lady, look on me;
Thus I sprinkle on thy breast
Drops that from my fountain pure
I have kept of precious cure,
Thrice upon thy finger's tip,
Thrice upon thy rubied lip;
Next this marble venomed seat,
Smeared with gums of glutinous heat,
I touch with chaste palms moist and cold.
Now the spell hath lost his hold,
And I must haste ere morning hour
To wait in Amphitrite's° bower.

[SABRINA *descends, and* THE LADY *rises out of her seat*]

SPIRIT Virgin, daughter of Locrine,
Sprung of old Anchises' line,°
May thy brimmèd waves for this
Their full tribute never miss
From a thousand petty rills,
That tumble down the snowy hills;
Summer drouth or singèd air
Never scorch thy tresses fair,
Nor wet October's torrent flood
Thy molten crystal fill with mud,
May thy billows roll ashore
The beryl and the golden ore,
May thy lofty head be crowned

azurn azure
turkis turquoise
Amphitrite's Neptune's wife's
Virgin . . . line Sabrina is the daughter of Locrine, who is the great-granddaughter of Aeneas, who is the son of Anchises; see l. 828n.

With many a tower and terrace round,
And here and there thy banks upon
With groves of myrrh and cinnamon.
  Come, lady, while heaven lends us grace,
Let us fly this cursèd place,
Lest the sorcerer us entice
With some other new device.
Not a waste or needless sound
Till we come to holier ground;
I shall be your faithful guide°
Through this gloomy covert wide,
And not many furlongs thence
Is your father's residence,
Where this night are met in state
Many a friend to gratulate
His wished presence, and beside
All the swains that there abide
We shall catch them at their sport,
With jigs and rural dance resort;
We shall catch them at their sport,
And our sudden coming there
Will double all their mirth and cheer.
Come let us haste, the stars grow high,
But Night sits monarch yet in the mid sky.

The scene changes, presenting Ludlow Town and the President's Castle; then come in Country Dancers, after them THE ATTENDANT SPIRIT, *with the* TWO BROTHERS *and* THE LADY.

SONG

SPIRIT *Back, shepherds, back, enough your play*
Till next sunshine holiday;
Here be without duck° or nod
Other trippings to be trod
Of lighter toes, and such court guise
As Mercury did first devise
With the mincing Dryades°
On the lawns and on the leas.

[*This second song presents them to their father and mother*]

Noble Lord, and Lady bright,
I have brought ye new delight.

faithful guide Double meanings begin to emerge here as the Spirit, played by their tutor Henry Lawes, leads the Earl of Bridgewater's children (as the Brothers and the Lady) out of the dark wood in whose mythological realm the whole of the action has taken place, and into the transformed scene of "Ludlow Town" and the castle where the very masque is itself being given. What is underlined is how Lawes has indeed been their "guide" in their education, and the act of presenting them to their father occurs both within the fiction of the masque and outside it, as a kind of graduation ceremony.

duck bow or curtsy in country dancing

Dryades dryads, wood nymphs

Here behold so goodly grown
Three fair branches of your own;
Heaven hath timely° tried their youth,
Their faith their patience, and their truth,
And sent them here through hard assays
With a crown of deathless praise,
To triumph in victorious dance
O'er sensual folly and intemperance.

[*The dances ended,* THE SPIRIT *epiloguizes*]

SPIRIT To the ocean now I fly,°
And those happy climes that lie
Where day never shuts his eye,
Up in the broad fields of the sky.
There I suck the liquid air
All amidst the gardens fair
Of Hesperus, and his daughters three
That sing about the golden tree:°
Along the crispèd° shades and bowers
Revels the spruce and jocund Spring;
The Graces° and the rosy-bosomed Hours°
Thither all their bounties bring,
That there eternal summer dwells,
And west winds with musky wing
About the cedarn alleys fling
Nard and cassia's balmy smells.°
Iris° there with humid bow
Waters the odorous banks that blow°
Flowers of more mingled hue
Than her purfled° scarf can shew,
And drenches with Elysian dew
(List, mortals, if your ears be true)
Beds of hyacinth and roses,
Where young Adonis° oft reposes,
Waxing well of his deep wound
In slumber soft, and on the ground

timely early
To . . . fly The ocean which surrounds the earth, and which contains such islands as those of the Hesperidean gardens, but this is also an ocean of heavenly sky, in which drift islands of light. This vision, like so many Renaissance earthly paradises, combines many elements from classical mythology: the Elysian fields and the Hesperides were often associated, and Milton has assimilated the vision of Venus and Adonis from Spenser's Garden of Adonis (in *The Faerie Queene* III.vi) as well. In the performance of the masque, the Spirit opened with a version of these lines, presenting his realm of origin in a more detailed way.
golden tree on which the golden apples grew
crispèd curled
Graces Euphrosyne, Aglaia, Thalia; see Spenser, *The Faerie Queene* VI.x
Hours goddesses of seasonal cycle and changing times, frequently associated with spring
Nard and cassia's balmy smells spikenard and a cinnamon-like bark
Iris the rainbow
blow cause to blossom
purfled with a decorated border
Adonis Here Venus and Adonis seem to be in a more transitional state than in Spenser, where they lie at the world's center of generation; here, Adonis is recovering from his wound, asleep, and Venus ("the Assyrian queen") sits "sadly" by; upon recovery, Adonis will presumably advance beyond this phase of representing wounded sexual love.

Sadly sits the Assyrian queen;
But far above in spangled sheen
Celestial Cupid,° her famed son, advanced,
Holds his dear Psyche sweet entranced
After her wandering labours long,
Till free consent the gods among
Make her his eternal bride,
And from her fair unspotted side
Two blissful twins are to be born,
Youth and Joy; so Jove hath sworn.
But now my task is smoothly done,
I can fly, or I can run
Quickly to the green earth's end,
Where the bowed welkin° slow doth bend,
And from thence can soar as soon
To the corners of the moon.
Mortals that would follow me,
Love Virtue, she alone is free;
She can teach ye how to climb
Higher than the sphery chime;°
Or if Virtue feeble were,
Heaven itself would stoop to her.
1634 1637

Lycidas

Lycidas is a pastoral elegy, but its relation to that tradition is most complex. Milton's college acquaintance Edward King was drowned in the Irish Sea in August 1637. *Lycidas* is Milton's response not so much to his death, which Dr. Johnson and many critics since have assumed, as to being asked to contribute a poem to a memorial volume, *Justa Edouardo King* (1638), of which the other contributions, such as John Cleveland's extravagant effusion, could easily lead one to believe that sincerity and eloquence frequently avoid each other's company. Milton's contribution is a very great poem about the death of The Poet by drowning; the consolation that all elegies must offer comes in this case from the unfolding realization that it is not Poetry which has died. Starting with his own feeling of unripeness for a major poetic task, the poem moves through a series of confrontations—with the chosen form of pastoral elegy and its symbolic devices; with the possible demands of epic poetry someday, perhaps, to be faced; and, finally, with a kind of floating processional of emblematic personages, each of whom is to disclaim responsibility for The Poet's death. This sequence is

Cupid Venus' son, he is "advanced" by being elevated to this higher realm; in the imagery of Christian Platonism, Cupid or Eros could be made to stand for heavenly love, and Apuleius' 2nd-century A.D. story of Cupid and Psyche came to be interpreted as Christ's love for the human soul. Spenser, following Apuleius, makes them the parents of Pleasure (*The Faerie Queene* III.vi.50); here, Milton gives them Youth and Joy.

bowed welkin the sky's curved vault

sphery chime the music of the spheres, supposedly produced by the movements of the crystalline heavenly spheres, each carrying one of the planets or all the fixed stars, as they moved through the ether (see *Music of the Spheres* in the Glossary). Above these would be heaven.

rather like a pageant or masque worked into a solo invocation (the model for this is Spenser's *Epithalamion,* made in "lieu of many ornaments" for Spenser's own wedding, and containing ceremony within an expanded kind of lyric poem). All the personages—classical, Christian, local, and made-up spirits—are relevant to the drowned *pastor*—which means "shepherd" (or poet, in pastoral symbolism) as well as "priest." Water nymphs and local deities are finally followed by the fisherman-priest, St. Peter, who denounces a corrupt clergy even more blatantly than Apollo had previously attacked easy, vulgar poetic successes.

The poem keeps shifting back to pastoral elegy from its digressions, and throughout there runs, like a stream of water itself, the myth of the Arcadian river god Alpheus (standing for pastoral poetry), reputedly ran underground and undersea to mix with his beloved Arethusa, a Sicilian fountain (Sicily, home of Theocritus, was the official home of pastoral). The rivers, lakes, and streams in *Lycidas* are all beneficent presences associated with poetic and religious traditions; the estranging salt water of tears and drowning sea is hostile. Central also is the myth of Orpheus floating down the Hebrus (see ll. 58 ff.) as a type of deliverance.

The verse is a brilliant adaptation of the Italian *canzone,* using ten- and six-syllabled lines for the Italian seven and eleven, irregular rhyming schemes, and occasional blank lines to build up its strophic paragraphs, moving at the end to two rhymed couplets just before a final stanza of *ottava rima.* This last replaces the *commiato* or usual formal address of the canzona to itself (as in Spenser's at the end of *Epithalamion*) with a stanza reminiscent of Renaissance epic narrative, distancing and framing the whole poem.

Lycidas

In this monody the author bewails a learned friend, unfortunately drowned in his passage from Chester on the Irish Seas, 1637. And by occasion foretells the ruin of our corrupted clergy, then in their height.°

Yet once more, O ye laurels,° and once more,
Ye myrtles brown,° with ivy never sere,°
I come to pluck your berries harsh and crude,
And with forced fingers rude
Shatter your leaves before the mellowing year.
Bitter constraint, and sad occasion dear,°
Compels me to disturb your season due:
For Lycidas° is dead, dead ere his prime,
Young Lycidas, and hath not left his peer.

In this monody . . . height This note was added in an edition of 1645, after there was no danger from the church's censors. "By occasion" is a conventional one: Renaissance eclogues frequently used the bucolic mask for denouncing clerical abuses.

laurels sacred to Apollo, and the crown of poetic achievement. Myrtle is Venus', and ivy Bacchus', crown; the point is that poetry lives in the realm of all three of these deities, as Petrarch said in his Oration of 1341.

brown dark

ivy never sere All these plants are evergreen.

dear in both senses of "precious" and "dire"

Lycidas the name of a shepherd in Theocritus and Virgil, of a man who nearly drowned in Lucan's *Pharsalia,* and of the fisherman-swain in the first of Sannazaro's piscatory eclogues, which substituted Neapolitan marine life for a bucolic realm

Who would not sing for Lycidas? He knew
Himself to sing, and build the lofty rhyme.
He must not float upon his watery bier
Unwept, and welter° to the parching wind,
Without the meed of some melodious tear.°
  Begin then, Sisters of the sacred well°
That from beneath the seat of Jove doth spring,
Begin, and somewhat loudly sweep the string.
Hence with denial vain, and coy° excuse,
So may some gentle Muse
With lucky words favour my destined urn,
And as he passes turn,
And bid fair peace be to my sable° shroud.
For we were nursed upon the self-same hill,
Fed the same flock, by fountain, shade, and rill.
  Together both, ere the high lawns appeared
Under the opening eyelids of the morn,
We drove afield, and both together heard
What time the grey-fly winds° her sultry horn,
Battening° our flocks with the fresh dews of night,
Oft till the star that rose, at evening, bright
Toward heaven's descent had sloped his westering wheel.
Meanwhile the rural ditties were not mute,
Tempered to the oaten flute;°
Rough Satyrs danced, and Fauns with cloven heel
From the glad sound would not be absent long,
And old Damaetas° loved to hear our song.
  But O the heavy change, now thou art gone,
Now thou art gone, and never must return!
Thee, Shepherd, thee the woods and desert caves,
With wild thyme and the gadding° vine o'ergrown,
And all their echoes mourn.
The willows and the hazel copses green
Shall now no more be seen
Fanning their joyous leaves to thy soft lays.
As killing as the canker° to the rose,
Or taint-worm to the weanling herds that graze,
Or frost to flowers, that their gay wardrobe wear,
When first the white-thorn blows;°
Such, Lycidas, thy loss to shepherd's ear.
  Where were ye, Nymphs, when the remorseless deep
Closed o'er the head of your loved Lycidas?

welter be tossed about
the meed . . . tear the recompense of some elegiac poem
Sisters . . . well the Muses; their well on Mt. Helicon was Aganippe
coy reticent
sable black
winds blows
Battening fattening
oaten flute instrument symbolic of pastoral poetry
Damaetas pastoral name, perhaps for some Cambridge tutor
gadding wandering
canker a kind of worm
white-thorn blows hawthorn blossoms

For neither were ye playing on the steep°
Where your old bards, the famous Druids, lie,
Nor on the shaggy top of Mona° high,
Nor yet where Deva° spreads her wizard stream.
Ay me, I fondly° dream,
Had ye been there!—for what could that have done?
What could the Muse herself that Orpheus bore,°
The Muse herself, for her enchanting son
Whom universal nature did lament,
When by the rout that made the hideous roar
His gory visage down the stream was sent,
Down the swift Hebrus to the Lesbian shore?
  Alas! what boots° it with uncessant care
To tend the homely slighted shepherd's trade,
And strictly meditate the thankless Muse?
Were it not better done as others use,
To sport with Amaryllis° in the shade,
Or with° the tangles of Neaera's hair?
Fame is the spur that the clear spirit doth raise
(That last infirmity of noble mind)
To scorn delights, and live laborious days;
But the fair guerdon when we hope to find,
And think to burst out into sudden blaze,
Comes the blind Fury° with the abhorrèd shears,
And slits the thin-spun life. 'But not the praise,'
Phoebus replied, and touched my trembling ears:°
'Fame° is no plant that grows on mortal soil,
Nor in the glistering foil°
Set off to the world, nor in broad rumour lies,
But lives and spreads aloft by those pure eyes
And perfect witness of all-judging Jove;
As he pronounces lastly on each deed,
Of so much fame in heaven expect thy meed.'
  O fountain Arethuse,° and thou honoured flood,

steep mountain slope, perhaps on the island of Bardsey ("Bards' island")
Mona the island of Anglesey
Deva the river Dee, "wizard" because it was reputed to shift its channel
fondly foolishly
the Muse . . . bore Calliope. Orpheus was torn apart by Thracian Bacchantes and his head floated down the river Hebrus, and it was fabled that all of nature went into mourning for him.
boots profits
Amaryllis The poet-swain Tityrus in Virgil's First Eclogue writes poems that "teach the woods to echo" his girl's name, Amaryllis; she and Neaera, also known to Milton from classical tradition for her beautiful hair, stand for the objects of the fashionable erotic Caroline verse which it would be so much easier, and safer, to write than an ambitious work on the death of poets.
with Perhaps this is a form of the verb *"withe,"* "to twist."
blind Fury Atropos, nastiest of the Fates, cut the thread of life which her sisters had spun and measured; Milton calls her a "Fury" here as if to evoke a feeling of bungled retribution, of punishment for no crime.
touched . . . ears So Apollo tweaked Virgil's ear, warning him against over-ambition, Milton's allusion to whom being hardly modest, but contrasting heroic poetry with Pan's pastoral.
Fame Apollo properly defines it as immortal glory, whose acquisition cannot be arranged for
foil gold or silver leaf set under jewels before modern faceting could make them brilliant enough
Arethuse See Headnote; the juxtaposition with Mincius, a river of Lombardy associated with Virgil and his *Eclogues,* signals a return of the poem to a pastoral key, after the distant major ("that strain I heard") of Apollo's pronouncement.

Smooth-sliding Mincius, crowned with vocal reeds,
That strain I heard was of a higher mood.
But now my oat° proceeds,
And listens to the herald of the sea°
That came in Neptune's plea.
He asked the waves, and asked the felon winds,
What hard mishap hath doomed this gentle swain?
And questioned every gust of rugged wings
That blows from off each beakéd promontory—
They knew not of his story,
And sage Hippotades° their answer brings,
That not a blast was from his dungeon strayed;
The air was calm, and on the level brine
Sleek Panope° with her all sisters played.
It was that fatal and perfidious bark,
Built in the eclipse, and rigged with curses dark,
That sunk so low that sacred head of thine.
Next Camus,° reverend sire, went footing slow,
His mantle hairy, and his bonnet sedge,°
Inwrought with figures dim, and on the edge
Like to that sanguine flower° inscribed with woe.
'Ah, who hath reft,' quoth he, 'my dearest pledge?'°
Last came, and last did go,
The Pilot° of the Galilean lake;
Two massy keys he bore of metals twain
(The golden opes, the iron shuts amain°).
He shook his mitred locks, and stern bespake:
'How well could I have spared for thee, young swain,
Enow of such as for their bellies' sake
Creep and intrude and climb into the fold!
Of other care they little reckoning make
Than how to scramble at the shearers' feast,
And shove away the worthy bidden guest.
Blind mouths!° that scarce themselves know how to hold
A sheep-hook, or have learned aught else the least
That to the faithful herdman's art belongs!
What recks° it them? What need they? They are sped;°
And when they list,° their lean and flashy songs

oat See l. 33n.
herald of the sea Triton, blowing his shell
Hippotades Aeolus, wind god
Panope standing for all the Nereids, or sea nymphs
Camus the river Cam, standing for his university, Cambridge
sedge plants growing near water
sanguine flower the blood-colored hyacinth, which sprang up from the blood of the young man Apollo had accidentally killed, the streaks on its leaves reading like AI AI, Greek sounds of woe
pledge child
Pilot St. Peter, fisherman, the first bishop, to whom Jesus gave "the keys of the kingdom of heaven" (Matthew 16:19)
amain mightily
Blind mouths a startling and intense characterization of inauthentic bishops and corrupted clergy in general. John Ruskin's reading of it, in *Sesame and Lilies* I.22, remains the best: he points out that a *bishop* ("episcopus") is someone who oversees, and a pastor is someone who feeds, nurtures a flock. "The most unbishoply character a man can have is therefore to be blind. The most unpastoral is, instead of feeding, to want to be fed—to be a Mouth."
recks matters
are sped have more than enough
list want

Grate on their scrannel° pipes of wretched straw
The hungry sheep look up, and are not fed,
But swoln with wind, and the rank mist they draw,
Rot inwardly, and foul contagion spread,
Besides what the grim wolf° with privy paw
Daily devours apace, and nothing said;
But that two-handed engine° at the door
Stands ready to smite once, and smite no more.'
Return, Alphéus,° the dread voice is past
That shrunk thy streams; return, Sicilian Muse,
And call the vales, and bid them hither cast
Their bells and flowerets of a thousand hues.
Ye valleys low where the mild whispers use°
Of shades and wanton winds and gushing brooks,
On whose fresh lap the swart star° sparely looks,
Throw hither all your quaint enamelled eyes,
That on the green turf suck the honied showers,
And purple all the ground with vernal flowers.
Bring the rathe° primrose that forsaken dies,
The tufted crowtoe, and pale jessamine,
The white pink, and the pansy freaked° with jet,
The glowing violet,
The musk-rose, and the well-attired woodbine,
With cowslips wan that hang the pensive° head,
And every flower that sad embroidery wears.
Bid amaranthus all his beauty shed,
And daffadillies fill their cups with tears,
To strew the laureate hearse where Lycid lies.
For so to interpose a little ease,
Let our frail thoughts dally with false surmise;
Ay me! whilst thee the shores and sounding seas
Wash far away, where'er thy bones are hurled,
Whether beyond the stormy Hebrides,
Where thou perhaps under the whelming° tide
Visit'st the bottom of the monstrous world;
Or whether thou, to our moist vows denied,
Sleep'st by the fable of Bellerus° old,

scrannel thin and squeaky-sounding
grim wolf the Roman Catholic Church, particularly in the person of the Jesuits, who can only devour (make converts) when the shepherd fails his flock
two-handed engine "Engine" usually means a device, and many scholars have suggested that Milton's visionary instrument of retribution is some kind of sword or axe, of symbolic nature in that it is identified in some scriptural or later text as such; others have suggested everything from two houses of Parliament to the two keys Peter holds. Some sort of sword seems most probable, and possibly one which combines the attributive significances of many of the single candidates proposed.
Alphéus See Headnote; the modulation is back to pastoral again, which the complexities of the poem's seriousness lead it to keep fleeing (where there is leisure for demonstrated grief, there is little room for the true fictions).
use are used to go
swart star Sirius
rathe early
freaked capriciously dressed
pensive The Latin words for "think" and "hang" are related, and Milton is reminding us of this.
whelming tossing
Bellerus mythical giant, perhaps invented by Milton, who would have given his name to Bellerium, the Roman designation of Land's End in Cornwall

Where the great Vision of the guarded mount°
Looks toward Namancos and Bayona's hold:°
Look homeward, Angel,° now, and melt with ruth;°
And, O ye dolphins,° waft the hapless youth.
  Weep no more, woeful shepherds, weep no more,
For Lycidas, your sorrow, is not dead,
Sunk though he be beneath the watery floor;
So sinks the day-star° in the ocean bed,
And yet anon repairs his drooping head,
And tricks his beams, and with new-spangled ore
Flames in the forehead of the morning sky:
So Lycidas sunk low, but mounted high,
Through the dear might of him that walked the waves,°
Where, other groves and other streams along,
With nectar pure his oozy locks he laves,
And hears the unexpressive nuptial song
In the blest kingdoms meek of joy and love.
There entertain him all the saints above,
In solemn troops and sweet societies
That sing, and singing in their glory move,
And wipe the tears for ever from his eyes.
Now, Lycidas, the shepherds weep no more;
Henceforth thou art the Genius° of the Shore,
In thy large recompense, and shalt be good
To all that wander in that perilous flood.
  Thus sang the uncouth° swain to the oaks and rills,
While the still morn went out with sandals grey;
He touched the tender stops of various quills,°
With eager thought warbling his Doric lay.°
And now the sun had stretched out all the hills,
And now was dropped into the western bay;
At last he rose, and twitched his mantle blue:
Tomorrow to fresh woods, and pastures new.

1637 1645

guarded mount St. Michael's Mount, off Cornwall
Namancos . . . hold the mountains of Namancos and the fortress of Bayona, on the coast of Spain
Angel the archangel Michael, patron of mariners, looking across the water from the top of St. Michael's Mount (as he is from the top of Mont St. Michel off Brittany)
ruth pity
dolphins The poet-musician Arion was carried to safety over the waves by a dolphin; also, Melicertes (see *Comus*, l. 876n) was carried to shore by a dolphin and became the sea god Palaemon; dolphins are here invoked to carry the drowned poet over into myth.
day-star the sun
walked the waves Christ, of course (Matthew 14:25–26)
Genius in the sense of *genius loci*, the local spirit inhabiting and protecting a particular spot
uncouth awkward; also perhaps in the older sense of "unknown"
quills hollow stems of reeds in Pan's pipe
Doric lay rustic, pastoral song

Paradise Lost

Milton's blindness and the return of king and bishops combined to make of the 1660's an inner and outer darkness out of which, like a night bird and like a blind prophet, he could respond vocally to an inner light. The abandoned confrontation with epic was his first task. Early notes for a tragedy to be called *Adam Unparadised* proved more potent seeds than those of ideas specifically for heroic narrative—the Arthurian subject, for example, toward which English poetic vision has continued to gaze. Brought up for consideration in two of his early Latin poems (*Damon's Epitaph* and *Manso*), it is one of those alternatives to the poem's subject whose rejection is explained in IX.25–40. *Paradise Lost* was composed in the early 1660's, dictated in stretches of up to forty lines at once during days otherwise filled with walking, playing music, and being read to. It was published in 1667, originally in ten books which, considered in pairs, reflected the five-act structure of neoclassical drama. In 1674, the second edition reorganized the poem into an epic pattern of twelve books, but it required very little actual revision to do so.

Paradise Lost is a Renaissance, Protestant, English epic, confronting, containing, and reinterpreting the Homeric, Virgilian, Dantesque, and Spenserian poems which precede it. It enlists their aid in the poetic realization of a perfect state of man, and the fall from that perfection into a state of human reality. Whereas in Homeric epic the similes and other arts of language are employed to explain to an audience what a vanished heroic age was really like, Milton's analogous task was to describe Paradise in the kind of language that had developed in human history only since, and because of, the loss of it. The very form of his poem is an avowal of the nature of that task.

It begins with a literal "fall" to prefigure the metaphorical, but more general, Fall of Man—the dropping of Satan from heaven to the bottom of everything (save, as we soon see, the depths of his own thoughts) in hell. The once glorious leader of a rebellion against God evinces, in Book I, some of the virtues of the human heroic—energy, resolution, wit, power of command, what looks like imagination. It is only when we remember that these virtues—along with physical strength, competitiveness, craft, and enterprise, for example—are rather like spiritual crutches with which Fallen Man was supplied, that we can put into proper perspective the inverted heroics of Satan and the world of Pandemonium. Satan's perversion of activity brings about the primary (but, in the narrative, chronologically secondary) human one; this relation is like that of prophecy to fulfillment, if we read it correctly, of "shadowy type" (as Milton puts it in the terms used by biblical interpreters) to truth, or, an another way, of thought to action. The puzzle of the attractiveness and intensity of Books I and II, and the static, doctrinal quality of Book III (which directly treats of God and heaven) has been observed since William Blake's first perception of it ("Milton was of the Devil's party without knowing it") to represent the effects of unavowed forces in Milton's imagination. Critics since remain divided even about the proper language in which to describe the puzzle, let alone about how to solve it. Is Satan hero? Villain? Hero-villain from the Jacobean stage? Embodiment of energy or only of evil? Attractive because he speaks to our condition of vitality? Or only because we are fallen sinners who cannot respond without interest and pleasure to the embodiment of our worst fault?

The way in which Satan's fall introduces Adam's (and thereby, ours) is not only an act of obeisance to the classical epic tradition of starting *in medias res* ("in the midst of things"), rather than with true causal beginnings: rather is it at the heart of Milton's poetic method. Classical, biblical, and contemporary allusions, at the poem's beginning, to events which, in human time, are yet to occur, light up this world of events prior to all events. Classical myths in relation to their later interpretations are constantly and thematically present, and patristic biblical commentary, with its typological readings of earlier events in the light of later ones, provides both details and larger models. The complex relation *Satan—Adam—Christ,* for instance, is almost a typological triangle, and there are many interesting parallels to this. By alluding, for example, in the description of Satan's spear in Book I, to Ovid's Golden Age, Milton underlines Satan's destructive role: Renaissance mythographers associated Saturn, who ruled the Age of Gold in Hesiod and Ovid, and who taught men to farm and who was cast, by Zeus, out of the sky, with Adam. Momentary connections like this abound in *Paradise Lost,* where they have both local and general application.

Milton's language and style in the poem both reflect this too. His similes are always powerfully complex; they never merely compare the recounted to the familiar with respect to one quality or attribute (like Homeric similes), but always imply others, of a different sort or quality, as well. His references look forward and back, within and beyond the poem: the reader's knowledge of human history, Man's past, lies in the visionary future of the poem's events, and even the use of particular words shows an awareness of this. The unfallen world, the pre-historical dimension, has to be rendered in concepts themselves created by history. Milton compensates for this somewhat by associating the etymological meaning of a word with the unfallen domain, and the more common, ordinary sense of it with the world of biological-historical mankind. Other concepts—*crooked:straight, stand:rise:fall, up:down*—have this double role in the poem, an early use of a term in Paradise being "infected," as Christopher Ricks has called it, with the figurative moral meanings they would, in human vernaculars, come to have.

Milton's latinate syntax, attacked by T. S. Eliot and other associates in a modernist cause for its betrayal of the values of English speech, is by no means only latinate. His placing of adjectives (as in I. 18: "the upright heart and pure"), where the sequence *first adjective–noun–second adjective* is itself a miniature narrative or argument, is all Italian. Constructions like "Tree of Prohibition" (meaning "prohibited tree" primarily, but with complex overtones) are Hebrew. If Greek syntax were less like English, so that its use might set up new possibilities for enriching the forward movement of subject-predicate word order in English, there might have been more adaptations of it. The language of *Paradise Lost,* in fact, even echoes itself, time and again: phrases from earlier parts appear in later ones, and it is almost as if the story of Satan's fall were a minor epic lying in the background of the poem's central world —that of Books IV through IX: the region of Eden and the stories and lessons learned there.

Milton's poetic line is the blank verse of English stage tragedy, a counterpart of classical hexameters first used by Surrey for his *Aeneid* translation (but without, at the time, setting up a tradition). In a prose statement about the form of the poem, added to the second printing of the first edition purportedly because of complaints from readers that the poem was not in heroic couplets, Milton says something very revealing. "The sense variously drawn out from one verse to another," he declares, will do the work of orchestrating his line endings better than rhyme can. He refers to the enjambment (the way in which line-breaks cut into the syntactic flow, thus manipulating sense). We see this in the very first line of the poem, and throughout. In

IV.25 we are told of how conscience, in Satan, "wakes the bitter memory / Of what he was, what is, and what must be"—and here the new line starts—"Worse"; the very drama of discovery that the familiar liturgical *is–was–will be* phrasing is violated, and that the verb "be" is auxiliary (predicating, and not identifying), is part of the poetic action.

Milton's ambition in *Paradise Lost* was nothing short of the highest—as he does not shrink from acknowledging. The poem's influence on subsequent English poetry is only beginning to be fully understood today, and it remains perhaps the last poem which could equal, if only as an intellectual achievement, any other accomplishment —even Newton's *Principia*—of its century, or of our age.

Paradise Lost

Book I

Of man's first disobedience, and the fruit°
Of that forbidden tree, whose mortal taste
Brought death into the world, and all our woe,
With loss of Eden, till one greater Man°
Restore us, and regain the blissful seat,
Sing, heavenly Muse,° that on the secret top
Of Oreb, or of Sinai,° didst inspire
That shepherd who first taught the chosen seed
In the beginning how the heavens and earth
Rose out of Chaos; or if Sion hill
Delight thee more, and Siloa's brook° that flowed
Fast by the oracle of God, I thence
Invoke thy aid to my adventurous song,
That with no middle flight intends to soar
Above the Aonian mount,° while it pursues
Things unattempted yet in prose or rhyme.
And chiefly thou, O Spirit, that dost prefer
Before all temples the upright heart and pure,
Instruct me, for thou knowest; thou from the first
Wast present, and with mighty wings outspread
Dove-like sat'st brooding on the vast abyss
And mad'st it pregnant:° what in me is dark
Illumine, what is low raise and support;

Of . . . fruit The opening line's structure, with "disobedience," the commanding polysyllabic word framed by monosyllables, culminates in the "fruit" which, because of the enjambment, suggests both "results" and the fruit of "that forbidden tree," both the general and concrete meanings; notice also the end words of the first three lines, whose sequence "fruit–taste-woe" is the plot of the Fall.
one greater Man Christ, the "second Adam"
heavenly Muse invoking Urania, Muse of the most elevated vision, whom he will actually name only at the beginning of Book VII
Oreb . . . Sinai where Moses ("That shepherd") heard the word of God (Exodus 3:1) and received the law.
Siloa's brook in Jerusalem, near the temple
Aonian mount Helicon, the hill of the Muses: Milton's epic will fly beyond antiquity
mad'st it pregnant The creation of the world as told in Genesis, the impregnation of Mary by the descending dove of the Holy Spirit, and the secondary creation of Milton's own great poem are here brought together.

That to the highth of this great argument
I may assert eternal providence,
And justify the ways of God to men.
  Say first, for heaven hides nothing from thy view,
Nor the deep tract of hell, say first what cause
Moved our grand° parents in that happy state,
Favoured of heaven so highly, to fall off
From their creator, and transgress his will
For one restraint, lords of the world besides?
Who first seduced them to that foul revolt?
The infernal serpent;° he it was whose guile,
Stirred up with envy and revenge, deceived
The mother of mankind, what time his pride
Had cast him out from heaven, with all his host
Of rebel angels, by whose aid aspiring°
To set himself in glory above his peers,
He trusted to have equalled the Most High,
If he opposed; and with ambitious aim
Against the throne and monarchy of God
Raised impious war in heaven and battle proud
With vain attempt. Him the Almighty Power
Hurled headlong flaming from the ethereal sky
With hideous ruin° and combustion down
To bottomless perdition, there to dwell
In adamantine° chains and penal fire,
Who° durst defy the omnipotent to arms.
Nine times the space that measures day and night
To mortal men, he with his horrid crew
Lay vanquished, rolling in the fiery gulf
Confounded though immortal. But his doom
Reserved him to more wrath; for now the thought
Both of lost happiness and lasting pain
Torments him; round he throws his baleful eyes,
That witnessed° huge affliction and dismay
Mixed with obdúrate pride and steadfast hate.
At once as far as angels' ken° he views
The dismal situation waste and wild:
A dungeon horrible, on all sides round
As one great furnace flamed, yet from those flames
No light, but rather darkness visible°

grand great, but also the parents of all the parents who would ever live
infernal serpent Only in the last book of the Bible, Revelation 12:9 and 20:2, is the wily serpent of Genesis associated with the rebel angel, Satan.
aspiring one of very few lines in *Paradise Lost* with a feminine, or unstressed, ending
ruin downfall
adamantine of the hardest substance imaginable; there is a hint of Prometheus, chained to his rock, too
Who he who
witnessed bore witness to
angels' ken their range of vision
darkness visible Light in all its forms—heavenly, created, the light of physical sight denied a blind man, symbolic light of reason, and divine creative power—is far too important in *Paradise Lost* to allow Milton to be careless with it: whatever makes things visible in hell, it is not light.

Served only to discover sights of woe,
Regions of sorrow, doleful shades, where peace
And rest can never dwell, hope never comes°
That comes to all; but torture without end
Still urges,° and a fiery deluge, fed
With ever-burning sulphur unconsumed:
Such place eternal justice had prepared
For those rebellious, here their prison ordained
In utter° darkness, and their portion set
As far removed from God and light of heaven
As from the centre thrice to the utmost pole.
O how unlike the place from whence they fell!
There the companions of his fall, o'erwhelmed
With floods and whirlwinds of tempestuous fire,
He soon discerns, and weltering° by his side
One next himself in power, and next in crime,
Long after known in Palestine, and named
Beelzebub.° To whom the arch-enemy,
And thence in heaven called Satan,° with bold words
Breaking the horrid silence thus began:
'If thou beest he . . . but O how fallen! how changed
From him, who in the happy realms of light
Clothed with transcendent brightness didst outshine
Myriads though bright—if he whom mutual league,
United thoughts and counsels, equal hope
And hazard in the glorious enterprise,
Joined with me once, now misery hath joined
In equal ruin: into what pit thou seest
From what highth fallen, so much the stronger proved
He with his thunder, and till then who knew
The force of those dire arms? Yet not for those,
Nor what the potent victor in his rage
Can else inflict, do I repent or change,
Though changed in outward lustre that fixed mind
And high disdain, from sense of injured merit,°
That with the mightiest raised me to contend,
And to the fierce contention brought along
Innumerable force of spirits armed
That durst dislike his reign, and me preferring,
His utmost power with adverse power opposed
In dubious battle on the plains of heaven,
And shook his throne.° What though the field be lost?

hope never comes echoing Dante, over the entrance to whose hell is inscribed: "Abandon hope all ye who enter here" (*Inferno* III.4–6)
urges presses
utter also in the sense of "outer"
weltering tossing
Beelzebub Hebrew for "lord of the flies"; Satan's lieutenant here
Satan The name in Hebrew means "enemy, opponent, adversary."
merit an important word: for Satan, it means "power," for Christ, goodness; cf.II.6 and 21
And shook his throne a lie—in the description of the war in heaven in Bk. VI, we learn that it was because of the chariot of the Son that "The steadfast Empyrean shook throughout." In this and subsequent speeches, one can view Satan as a crude liar or as a suffering, deposed leader, enthusiastically self-deceived.

All is not lost; the unconquerable will,
And study° of revenge, immortal hate,
And courage never to submit or yield:
And what is else not to be overcome?
That glory never shall his wrath or might
Extort from me. To bow and sue for grace
With suppliant knee, and deify his power—
Who° from the terror of this arm so late
Doubted° his empire—that were low indeed,
That were an ignominy° and shame beneath
This downfall; since by fate the strength of gods°
And this empyreal substance cannot fail,°
Since through experience of this great event,
In arms not worse, in foresight much advanced,
We may with more successful hope resolve
To wage by force or guile eternal war
Irreconcilable to our grand foe,
Who now triumphs, and in the excess of joy
Sole reigning holds the tyranny of heaven.'
 So spake the apostate Angel, though in pain,
Vaunting aloud, but racked with deep despair;
And him thus answered soon his bold compeer:
 'O Prince, O chief of many thronèd powers,°
That led the embattled seraphim to war
Under thy conduct, and in dreadful deeds
Fearless, endangered heaven's perpetual king,
And put to proof his high supremacy,
Whether upheld by strength, or chance, or fate;
Too well I see and rue the dire event,
That with sad overthrow and foul defeat
Hath lost us heaven, and all this mighty host
In horrible destruction laid thus low,
As far as gods and heavenly essences
Can perish: for the mind and spirit remains
Invincible, and vigour soon returns,
Though all our glory extinct,° and happy state
Here swallowed up in endless misery.
But what if he our conqueror (whom I now
Of force° believe almighty, since no less
Than such could have o'erpowered such force as ours)
Have left us this our spirit and strength entire
Strongly to suffer and support our pains,

study search for
Who I who
Doubted feared for
ignominy pronounced "ignomy"
gods As a relativist in theology and a Hobbesian in political theory, Satan thinks of God as being one of a collection of pagan deities; it is axiomatic that He is not.
substance cannot fail even the vanquished rebels are immortal (see l. 53, above)
thronèd powers Medieval angelology distinguished nine angelic orders: seraphim, cherubim, thrones, dominations, virtues, powers, principalities, angels, and archangels. Beelzebub obliquely invokes these now, but will trot out most of the list later, in his public rhetoric.
extinct extinguished
Of force perforce

That we may so suffice° his vengeful ire,
Or do him mightier service as his thralls
By right of war, whate'er his business be,
Here in the heart of hell to work in fire,
Or do his errands in the gloomy deep?
What can it then avail though yet we feel
Strength undiminished, or eternal being
To undergo eternal punishment?'
Whereto with speedy words the arch-fiend replied:
'Fallen cherub, to be weak is miserable,
Doing or suffering: but of this be sure,
To do aught good never will be our task,
But ever to do ill our sole delight,
As being the contrary to his high will
Whom we resist. If then his providence
Out of our evil seek to bring forth good,
Our labour must be to pervert that end,
And out of good still to find means of evil;°
Which ofttimes may succeed, so as perhaps
Shall grieve him, if I fail not,° and disturb
His inmost counsels from their destined aim.
But see the angry victor hath recalled
His ministers of vengeance and pursuit
Back to the gates of heaven; the sulphurous hail
Shot after us in storm, o'erblown hath laid°
The fiery surge, that from the precipice
Of heaven received us falling, and the thunder,
Winged with red lightning and impetuous rage,
Perhaps hath spent his shafts, and ceases now
To bellow through the vast and boundless deep.
Let us not slip° the occasion, whether scorn
Or satiate fury yield it from our foe.
Seest thou yon dreary plain, forlorn and wild,
The seat of desolation, void of light,
Save what the glimmering of these livid flames
Casts pale and dreadful? Thither let us tend
From off the tossing of these fiery waves,
There rest, if any rest can harbour there,
And reassembling our afflicted° powers,
Consult how we may henceforth most offend°
Our enemy, our own loss how repair,
How overcome this dire calamity,
What reinforcement we may gain from hope;

suffice appease
If then . . . evil These lines frame the notion of the *felix culpa*, or fortunate fall: out of their evil God will bring forth human and divine good; they also introduce Satan's dialectical juggling of divine concepts and their opposites; later on, it will get more tortured and desperate.
if I fail not unless I'm wrong
laid reduced
slip let go by
afflicted cast down
offend injure

If not, what resolution from despair.'
—Thus Satan talking to his nearest mate
With head uplift above the wave, and eyes
That sparkling blazed;° his other parts besides
Prone on the flood, extended long and large
Lay floating many a rood,° in bulk as huge
As whom the fables name of monstrous size,
Titanian° or Earth-born, that warred on Jove,
Briareos or Typhon, whom the den
By ancient Tarsus held, or that sea-beast
Leviathan,° which God of all his works
Created hugest that swim the ocean stream:
Him haply slumbering on the Norway foam,
The pilot of some small night-foundered° skiff,
Deeming some island, oft, as seamen tell,
With fixèd anchor in his scaly rind
Moors by his side under the lee, while night
Invests° the sea, and wishèd morn delays:
So stretched out huge in length the arch-fiend lay
Chained on the burning lake; nor ever thence
Had risen or heaved his head, but that the will
And high permission of all-ruling heaven
Left him at large to his own dark designs,
That with reiterated crimes he might
Heap on himself damnation, while he sought
Evil to others, and enraged might see
How all his malice served but to bring forth
Infinite goodness, grace and mercy shown
On man by him seduced, but on himself
Treble confusion, wrath and vengeance poured.
　Forthwith upright he rears from off the pool
His mighty stature; on each hand the flames
Driven backward slope their pointing spires, and rolled
In billows, leave i' th' midst a horrid° vale.
Then with expanded wings he steers his flight
Aloft, incumbent° on the dusky air
That felt unusual weight, till on dry land
He lights, if it were land that ever burned
With solid, as the lake with liquid fire;
And such appeared in hue;° as when the force

With head . . . blazed There is a premonition of Satan's later—chosen—shape here, a touch of the sea serpent.
rood rod, the unit of length: 5.5 yards
Titanian The Titans and the Giants both attacked the Olympian gods (Briareos represents the first, Typhon the second).
Leviathan the great sea beast of Scripture (Job 41, Isaiah 27:1, and elsewhere), thought of as a whale. The story about the whale's being mistaken for an island is from the medieval bestiaries; every simile emphasizing Satan's magnitude or power in Books I and II of *Paradise Lost* will also show something false, illusory, or, as here, untrustworthy about it.
night-foundered sunk in night
Invests enfolds
horrid in the Latin sense, "bristling," with a touch of the modern sense
incumbent weighing down
hue surface color and texture

Of subterranean wind transports a hill
Torn from Pelorus,° or the shattered side
Of thundering Aetna, whose combustible
And fuelled entrails thence conceiving fire,
Sublimed° with mineral fury, aid the winds,
And leave a singèd bottom all involved°
With stench and smoke: such resting found the sole
Of unblest feet. Him followed his next° mate,
Both glorying to have scaped the Stygian flood°
As gods, and by their own recovered strength,
Not by the sufferance of supernal power.
'Is this the region, this the soil, the clime,'
Said then the lost archangel, 'this the seat°
That we must change for heaven, this mournful gloom
For that celestial light? Be it so, since he
Who now is sovereign can dispose and bid
What shall be right: farthest from him is best,
Whom reason hath equalled, force hath made supreme
Above his equals. Farewell, happy fields,
Where joy for ever dwells: hail, horrors! hail,
Infernal world! and thou, profoundest hell,
Receive thy new possessor: one who brings
A mind not to be changed by place or time.
The mind is its own place, and in itself
Can make a heaven of hell, a hell of heaven.°
What matter where, if I be still the same,
And what I should be, all but less than he
Whom thunder hath made greater? Here at least
We shall be free; the Almighty hath not built
Here for his envy, will not drive us hence:
Here we may reign secure, and in my choice
To reign is worth ambition, though in hell:
Better to reign in hell than serve in heaven.°
But wherefore let we then our faithful friends,
The associates and co-partners of our loss,
Lie thus astonished on the oblivious pool,°
And call them not to share with us their part
In this unhappy mansion, or once more
With rallied arms to try what may be yet

Pelorus Cape Faro, near the volcano Aetna in Sicily
Sublimed vaporized; a term from alchemy meaning the refining of metals by fire
involved entwined
next closest
Stygian flood the "fiery gulf" of l. 52
seat proper place
The mind . . . heaven This sounds both like great self-reliance and courageous resolve, and like a bad mistake in denying the external, local existence of heaven and hell; the dramatic irony is that after twisting good and evil, rise and fall, up and down, heaven and hell into each other, Satan will complain, in his great speech on Mt. Niphates (IV.32–113), of the hell within him.
Better . . . heaven again, on the surface, a slogan asserting human dignity; but Satan is not human, heaven commands no "servitude," and what kind of kingdom hell is becomes clear
astonished . . . pool stupefied on the lake of forgetfulness

Regained in heaven, or what more lost in hell?'
So Satan spake, and him Beelzebub
Thus answered: 'Leader of those armies bright,
Which but the omnipotent none could have foiled,
If once they hear that voice, their liveliest pledge
Of hope in fears and dangers, heard so oft
In worst extremes, and on the perilous edge°
Of battle when it raged, in all assaults
Their surest signal, they will soon resume
New courage and revive, though now they lie
Grovelling and prostrate on yon lake of fire,
As we erewhile, astounded and amazed;
No wonder, fallen such a pernicious highth!'
He scarce had ceased when the superior fiend
Was moving toward the shore; his ponderous shield,
Ethereal temper,° massy, large, and round,
Behind him cast; the broad circumference
Hung on his shoulders like the moon,° whose orb
Through optic glass the Tuscan artist° views
At evening from the top of Fesole,
Or in Valdarno,° to descry new lands,
Rivers or mountains in her spotty globe.
His spear, to equal which the tallest pine
Hewn on Norwegian hills, to be the mast
Of some great ammiral,° were but a wand,
He walked with to support uneasy steps
Over the burning marl, not like those steps
On heaven's azure; and the torrid clime
Smote on him sore besides, vaulted with fire.
Nathless° he so endured, till on the beach
Of that inflamèd sea, he stood and called
His legions, angel forms, who lay entranced,
Thick as° autumnal leaves that strow the brooks
In Vallombrosa,° where the Etrurian shades
High over-arched embower; or scattered sedge
Afloat, when with fierce winds Orion armed°
Hath vexed the Red Sea° coast, whose waves o'erthrew

perilous edge front line
Ethereal temper tempered by ethereal flame
like the moon In this sequence of similes, the grandeur of Satan's appearance and his authenticity are simultaneously developed; the moon, to which his shield is compared, looks startlingly huge through the artificial magnification of a telescope, and unlike the shield of Achilles in Homer (*Iliad* XIX) it does not have an emblem of human civilization upon it.
Tuscan artist Galileo Galilei (1564–1642); Milton had actually visited him
Fesole . . . Valdarno Fiesole and the Arno valley, both near Florence
ammiral admiral's flagship. Like the shield, the comparison is to something technological, hence from fallen human life, and, in this case, quotes Ovid, *Metamorphoses* I, to remind us that Satan will be doing the equivalent of wrenching the Golden Age into an Iron one, in which trees will become masts of ships. There is also a covert allusion to the blind Polyphemus, "of light bereft," in whose hand a pine tree guides and steadies his steps (Virgil, *Aeneid* III. 658–59).
Nathless nevertheless
Thick as also, dead as
Vallombrosa shady, wooded valley near Florence
Orion armed associated with seasonal storms
Red Sea in Hebrew, "sea of sedge"

Busiris° and his Memphian chivalry,
While with perfidious hatred they pursued
The sojourners of Goshen,° who beheld
From the safe shore their floating carcasses
And broken chariot wheels;° so thick bestrown,
Abject° and lost lay these, covering the flood,
Under amazement of° their hideous change.
He called so loud that all the hollow deeps
Of hell resounded: 'Princes, Potentates,
Warriors, the flower of heaven, once yours, now lost,
If such astonishment° as this can seize
Eternal Spirits; or have ye chosen this place
After the toil of battle to repose
Your wearied virtue,° for the ease you find
To slumber here, as in the vales of heaven?
Or in this abject posture have ye sworn
To adore the conqueror, who now beholds
Cherub and seraph rolling in the flood
With scattered arms and ensigns, till anon
His swift pursuers from heaven gates discern
The advantage, and descending tread us down
Thus drooping, or with linkèd thunderbolts
Transfix us to the bottom of this gulf?
Awake, arise, or be for ever fallen!'
They heard, and were abashed, and up they sprung
Upon the wing, as when men wont to watch
On duty, sleeping found by whom they dread,
Rouse and bestir themselves ere well awake.
Nor did they not perceive the evil plight
In which they were, or the fierce pains not feel;
Yet to their general's voice they soon obeyed
Innumerable. As when the potent rod
Of Amram's son° in Egypt's evil day
Waved round the coast, up called a pitchy cloud
Of locusts, warping° on the eastern wind,
That o'er the realm of impious Pharaoh hung
Like night, and darkened all the land of Nile:
So numberless were those bad angels seen
Hovering on wing under the cope° of hell
'Twixt upper, nether, and surrounding fires;
Till, as a signal given, the uplifted spear

Busiris Pharaoh in Exodus
Goshen place of safety on the east of the Red Sea
chariot wheels again, a remarkable simile purporting to show how thick, numerous, and densely massed were Satan's troops, but reminding us of corpses and a defeated army that pursued Israel as Satan does Adam
abject cast down
amazement of stupefaction *of* and *at*
astonishment immobilization
virtue power, strength
Amram's son Moses
locusts, warping one of the ten plagues with which God smote the Egyptians (Exodus 10:12–13); "warping" here means "swerving"
cope canopy

Of their great Sultan waving to direct
Their course, in even balance down they light
On the firm brimstone, and fill all the plain;
A multitude, like which the populous North
Poured never from her frozen loins, to pass
Rhene or the Danaw,° when her barbarous sons
Came like a deluge on the south, and spread
Beneath Gibraltar to the Libyan sands.
Forthwith from every squadron and each band
The heads and leaders thither haste where stood
Their great commander; godlike shapes and forms
Excelling human, princely dignities,
And powers that erst° in heaven sat on thrones;
Though of their names in heavenly records now
Be no memorial, blotted out and razed
By their rebellion from the books of life.°
Nor had they yet among the sons of Eve
Got them new names, till wandering o'er the earth,
Through God's high sufferance for the trial of man,
By falsities and lies the greatest part
Of mankind they corrupted to forsake
God their creator, and the invisible
Glory of him that made them to transform
Oft to the image of a brute, adorned
With gay religions° full of pomp and gold,
And devils to adore for deities:
Then were they known to men by various names,
And various idols through the heathen world.
  Say, Muse, their names then known,° who first, who last,
Roused from the slumber on that fiery couch,
At their great emperor's call, as next in worth
Came singly where he stood on the bare strand,
While the promiscuous crowd stood yet aloof.
  The chief were those who from the pit of hell,
Roaming to seek their prey on earth, durst fix
Their seats long after next the seat of God,
Their altars by his altar, gods adored
Among the nations round, and durst abide

Rhene . . . Danaw Rhine and Danube. The whole image compares Satan to a leader of Asiatic barbarian raiders.

erst formerly

books of life God's ledgers, in which the Good are enrolled

gay religions pagan ceremonies

names then known This invocation follows those of Homer and Virgil (*Iliad* II and *Aeneid* VII) introducing their famous catalogues: Homer's, a list of the ships bearing all the Greek captains and princes allied against Troy; Virgil's, of the followers of Turnus banded against Aeneas and thereby against Rome and the inevitability of history. Milton's list of demons includes names of devils from Hebraic and Christian folklore, as well as a multitude of pagan gods, whose mythological ancestry, following patristic tradition, Milton locates in fallen angels. In human history they would (or, from this point on in the poem's time scheme, they *will*) come to be false gods. This is Milton's visionary alternative to what might be a modern anthropologist's observation that the gods of a conquered people may persist, in changed form as demons or fairies or the like, under the imposed religion—or to a psychologist's suggestion that vanquished, suppressed memories of trauma return as the false gods of dream and hysterical symptom.

Jehovah thundering out of Sion, throned
Between the cherubim; yea, often placed
Within his sanctuary itself their shrines,
Abominations; and with cursèd things
His holy rites and solemn feasts profaned,°
And with their darkness durst affront his light.
First Moloch,° horrid king besmeared with blood
Of human sacrifice, and parents' tears,
Though for the noise of drums and timbrels loud
Their children's cries unheard, that passed through fire°
To his grim idol. Him the Ammonite
Worshiped in Rabba and her watery plain,
In Argob and in Basan,° to the stream
Of utmost Arnon. Nor content with such
Audacious neighbourhood, the wisest heart
Of Solomon he led by fraud to build
His temple right against the temple of God
On that opprobrious hill,° and made his grove
The pleasant valley of Hinnom,° Tophet thence
And black Gehenna called, the type of hell.
Next Chemos,° the óbscene dread of Moab's sons,
From Aroer° to Nebo, and the wild
Of southmost Abarim; in Hesebon
And Horonaim, Seon's realm, beyond
The flowery dale of Sibma clad with vines,
And Elealè° to the Asphaltic pool:°
Peor his other name, when he enticed
Israel in Sittim on their march from Nile
To do him wanton rites, which cost them woe.°
Yet thence his lustful orgies he enlarged
Even to that hill of scandal,° by the grove
Of Moloch homicide, lust hard by hate;
Till good Josiah drove them thence to hell.°
With these came they who, from the bordering flood
Of old Euphrates to the brook° that parts
Egypt from Syrian ground, had general names
Of Baalim and Ashtaroth,° those male,

profaned like the kings of Judah who lapsed into idolatry (2 Kings 16, 17, 21)
Moloch (literally in Semitic, "king"). Alastair Fowler points out that Moloch heads the list of twelve Satanic disciples which follow: Moloch, Baal, Ashtoreth, Tammuz, Dagon, Osiris, Isis, Horus, Belial, Titan, Saturn, Jupiter.
passed through fire See 2 Kings 23:10.
Rabba . . . Basan the royal city of the Ammonites, and the regions east of the Jordan, all conquered by the Israelites
opprobrious hill the Mount of Olives, called "opprobrious" because of Solomon's idolatry there. See below, ll.416, 443.
Hinnom valley near Jerusalem where sacrifices were made to Moloch
Chemos Moabite god associated with Moloch (1 Kings, 11:17)
From Aroer . . . Elealè formerly Moabite places mostly mentioned in Numbers and assigned by Moses to Reuben and God
Asphaltic pool the Dead Sea
woe a plague (Numbers 25:9)
hill of scandal the Mount of Olives
good Josiah . . . hell Josiah's abolition of idolatry is chronicled in 2 Kings 22–23.
brook the river Besor, the boundary between Palestine and Egypt
Baalim and Ashtaroth These are plural forms in Hebrew of the names Baal and Ashtoreth, the Phoenician and Canaanitish sun god and moon goddess worshipped in various aspects. See below, l.438.

These feminine.—For spirits when they please
Can either sex assume, or both; so soft
And uncompounded is their essence pure,
Not tied or manacled with joint or limb,
Nor founded on the brittle strength of bones,
Like cumbrous flesh; but in what shape they choose,
Dilated° or condensed, bright or obscure,
Can execute their airy purposes,
And works of love or enmity fulfill.
For those the race of Israel oft forsook
Their living strength, and unfrequented left
His righteous altar, bowing lowly down
To bestial gods; for which their heads as low
Bowed down in battle, sunk before the spear
Of despicable foes. With these in troop
Came Astoreth,° whom the Phoenicians called
Astarte, queen of heaven, with crescent horns;
To whose bright image nightly by the moon
Sidonian virgins paid their vows and songs;
In Sion also not unsung, where stood
Her temple on the offensive mountain, built
By that uxorious king,° whose heart though large,
Beguiled by fair idolatresses, fell
To idols foul. Thammuz° came next behind,
Whose annual wound in Lebanon allured
The Syrian damsels to lament his fate
In amorous ditties all a summer's day,
While smooth Adonis from his native rock
Ran purple to the sea, supposed with blood
Of Thammuz yearly wounded: the love-tale
Infected Sion's daughters with like heat,
Whose wanton passions in the sacred porch
Ezekiel saw, when by the vision led
His eye surveyed the dark idolatries
Of alienated Judah. Next came one
Who mourned in earnest, when the captive ark
Maimed his brute image, head and hands lopped off
In his own temple, on the grunsel° edge,
Where he fell flat, and shamed his worshipers:
Dagon° his name, sea monster, upward man
And downward fish; yet had his temple high
Reared in Azotus, dreaded through the coast
Of Palestine, in Gath and Ascalon,

Dilated expanded
Astoreth Astarte, the Sidonian (Phoenician) moon goddess, combined attributes of the Greek Artemis, Hecatè, and Aphrodite
uxurious King Solomon
Thammuz Syrian counterpart of the Greek Adonis, sometimes seen as Astarte's lover. In July the Lebanese river named for him ran red, supposedly with the blood of the young dead god. In Ezekiel 8:12–14, "women weeping for Tammuz" is a typical instance of idolatry.
grunsel threshold
Dagon Philistine fish-god, undone in Samuel 5:15

And Accaron and Gaza's frontier bounds.
Him followed Rimmon,° whose delightful seat
Was fair Damascus, on the fertile banks
Of Abbana and Phárphar, lucid streams.
He also against the house of God was bold:
A leper once he lost and gained a king,
Ahaz his sottish° conqueror, whom he drew
God's altar to disparage and displace
For one of Syrian mode, whereon to burn
His odious offerings, and adore the gods
Whom he had vanquished. After these appeared
A crew who under names of old renown,
Osiris, Isis, Orus, and their train,
With monstrous shapes and sorceries abused
Fanatic Egypt and her priests, to seek
Their wandering gods° disguised in brutish forms
Rather than human. Nor did Israel scape
The infection when their borrowed gold composed
The calf in Oreb;° and the rebel king°
Doubled that sin in Bethel and in Dan,
Likening his Maker to the grazèd ox—
Jehovah, who in one night when he passed
From Egypt marching, equaled with one stroke
Both her first-born and all her bleating gods.
Belial° came last, than whom a spirit more lewd
Fell not from heaven, or more gross to love
Vice for itself. To him no temple stood
Or altar smoked; yet who more oft than he
In temples and at altars, when the priest
Turns atheist, as did Eli's sons,° who filled
With lust and violence the house of God?
In courts and palaces he also reigns
And in luxurious cities, where the noise
Of riot ascends above their loftiest towers,
And injury and outrage; and when night
Darkens the streets, then wander forth the sons
Of Belial, flown° with insolence and wine.
Witness the streets of Sodom, and that night
In Gibeah,° when the hospitable door
Exposed a matron to avoid worse rape.

Rimmon a Syrian god. Naaman, a Syrian general cured of leprosy by the rough waters of Jordan rather than by the "lucid streams," renounced Rimmon for the God of Israel; Ahaz, king of Judah, was an apostate to his cult.
sottish foolish
wandering gods Ovid (*Metamorphoses* V.319–31) retells the myth of the Olympian gods who flee from Typhoeus, a giant, and hide in bestial shapes in Egypt.
Oreb Horeb, where the golden calf was worshiped (Exodus 32)
rebel king Jereboam set up two golden calves
Belial not worshiped as a pagan god. His name means "iniquity," and such biblical phrases as "sons of Belial" were used in Milton's day to indicate the wicked. Milton personifies him as suave and erotic.
Eli's sons They polluted the Temple.
flown flooded
Gibeah In Judges 19–31 a concubine of a Levite household is given over to a crowd of "sons of Belial" in order that the male inhabitants within be spared homosexual rape.

These were the prime in order and in might;
The rest were long to tell, though far renowned,
The Ionian gods, of Javan's issue° held
Gods, yet confessed later than Heaven and Earth,
Their boasted parents; Titan, Heaven's first-born,
With his enormous° brood, and birthright seized
By younger Saturn; he from mightier Jove,
His own and Rhea's son, like measure found;
So Jove usurping reigned. These, first in Crete
And Ida known, thence on the snowy top
Of cold Olympus ruled the middle air,
Their highest heaven; or on the Delphian cliff,°
Or in Dodona,° and through all the bounds
Of Doric land;° or who with Saturn old
Fled over Adria to the Hesperian fields,
And o'er the Celtic roamed the utmost isles.°
All these and more came flocking, but with looks
Downcast and damp, yet such wherein appeared
Obscure some glimpse of joy, to have found their chief
Not in despair, to have found themselves not lost
In loss itself; which on his countenance cast
Like doubtful hue. But he, his wonted pride
Soon recollecting, with high words, that bore
Semblance of worth, not substance, gently raised
Their fainting courage, and dispelled their fears.
Then straight commands that at the warlike sound
Of trumpets loud and clarions be upreared
His mighty standard; that proud honor claimed
Azazel° as his right, a cherub tall;
Who forthwith from the glittering staff unfurled
The imperial ensign, which full high advanced
Shone like a meteor streaming to the wind,
With gems and golden luster rich emblazed,
Seraphic arms and trophies, all the while
Sonorous metal blowing martial sounds;°
At which the universal host upsent
A shout that tore hell's concave,° and beyond
Frighted the reign of Chaos and old Night.
All in a moment through the gloom were seen
Ten thousand banners rise into the air
With orient colours waving; with them rose

Javan's issue Some writers held that Javan, son of Japhet, son of Noah, sired the line of Ionian (Greek) gods.
enormous Titanic: Heaven and Earth (Uranus and Ge) bred titans, giants and gods, according to Greek tradition. "Titan" himself, according to a later story, fought against his younger brother Saturn.
Delphian cliff oracle of Apollo at Delphi
Dodona where there was an oracle of Zeus
Doric land southern Greece
Adria . . . utmost isles In various versions of the myth, the exiled Saturn wandered across the Adriatic Sea to Italy, thence variously to Britain, Ireland, or Iceland.
Azazel in Jewish cabbalistic tradition, one of the four standard-bearers in Satan's legion
Sonorous . . . sounds a most effective chiasmus (see *Rhetoric* in the Glossary) of sound and meaning
concave i.e. concave vault

A forest huge of spears; and thronging helms
Appeared, and serried shields in thick array
Of depth immeasurable. Anon they move
In perfect phalanx to the Dorian mood°
Of flutes and soft recorders, such as raised
To highth of noblest temper heroes old
Arming to battle, and instead of rage
Deliberate valour breathed, firm and unmoved
With dread of death to flight or foul retreat,
Nor wanting power to mitigate and swage,°
With solemn touches,° troubled thoughts, and chase
Anguish and doubt and fear and sorrow and pain
From mortal or immortal minds. Thus they,
Breathing united force with fixèd thought,
Moved on in silence to soft pipes that charmed
Their painful steps o'er the burnt soil; and now
Advanced in view they stand, a horrid° front
Of dreadful length and dazzling arms, in guise
Of warriors old with ordered spear and shield,
Awaiting what command their mighty Chief
Had to impose. He through the armèd files
Darts his experienced eye, and soon traverse°
The whole battalion views, their order due,
Their visages and stature as of gods;
Their number last he sums. And now his heart
Distends with pride, and hardening in his strength
Glories; for never, since created man,°
Met such embodied force as named with these
Could merit more than that small infantry°
Warred on by cranes: though all the giant brood
Of Phlegra with the heroic race were joined
That fought at Thebes and Ilium,° on each side
Mixed with auxiliar gods; and what resounds
In fable or romance of Uther's son°
Begirt with British and Armoric° knights;
And all who since, baptized or infidel,°
Jousted in Aspramont or Montalban,
Damasco, or Marocco, or Trebisond,
Or whom Biserta sent from Afric shore

Dorian mood The so-called Dorian mode or key in Greek music connoted order and vigor (as the minor keys of classical music are considered "sad"); the flutes, instead of the trumpets, suggest accounts like that of Plutarch of the Spartans marching to battle, and the whole effect is of heroic valor.
swage assuage
touches passages of music
horrid bristling (with spears)
traverse across
since created man since man was created (Latin construction)
small infantry the Pygmies, mentioned later at l.780
Thebes and Ilium epic battles of the so-called "Seven against Thebes" and the Trojan war
Uther's son King Arthur
Armoric Breton
baptized or infidel the Christian and Saracen combatants in the medieval legends of Charlemagne; all the places listed below, ll.581–587, refer to romances about them. In none of these stories was Charlemagne killed at a battle of Fontarabbia (the battle of Roncevaux).

When Charlemain with all his peerage fell
By Fontarabbia. Thus far these beyond
Compare of mortal prowess, yet observed°
Their dread commander. He above the rest
In shape and gesture proudly eminent
Stood like a tower; his form had yet not lost
All her original brightness, nor appeared
Less than archangel ruined, and the excess
Of glory obscured: as when the sun new risen
Looks through the horizontal misty air
Shorn of his beams,° or from behind the moon
In dim eclipse disastrous twilight sheds
On half the nations, and with fear of change
Perplexes monarchs. Darkened so, yet shone
Above them all the archangel; but his face
Deep scars of thunder had intrenched, and care
Sat on his faded cheek, but under brows
Of dauntless courage, and considerate° pride
Waiting revenge. Cruel his eyes, but cast
Signs of remorse and passion to behold
The fellows of his crime, the followers rather
(Far other once beheld in bliss), condemned
For ever now to have their lot in pain,
Millions of Spirits for his fault amerced°
Of heaven, and from eternal splendours flung
For his revolt, yet faithful how they stood,
Their glory withered: as when heaven's fire
Hath scathed the forest oaks or mountain pines,
With singèd top their stately growth though bare
Stands on the blasted heath. He now prepared
To speak; whereat their doubled ranks they bend
From wing to wing, and half enclose him round
With all his peers: attention held them mute.
Thrice he assayed, and thrice in spite of scorn,
Tears such as angels weep° burst forth; at last
Words interwove with sighs found out their way:
'O myriads of immortal Spirits, O Powers
Matchless, but with the Almighty, and that strife
Was not inglorious, though the event was dire,
As this place testifies, and this dire change
Hateful to utter. But what power of mind
Foreseeing or presaging, from the depth
Of knowledge past or present, could have feared
How such united force of gods, how such

observed honored
shorn of his beams in an eclipse, and thus traditionally presaging destruction; but suggesting the doom of a ruler (here, Satan) as well
considerate considered
amerced deprived
tears such as angels weep i.e. given their conditional corporeality (these are not human tears, however)

As stood like these, could ever know repulse?
For who can yet believe, though after loss,
That all these puissant legions, whose exile
Hath emptied heaven,° shall fail to re-ascend
Self-raised, and repossess their native seat?
For me, be witness all the host of heaven,
If counsels different,° or danger shunned
By me, have lost our hopes. But he who reigns
Monarch in heaven, till then as one secure
Sat on his throne, upheld by old repute,
Consent or custom,° and his regal state
Put forth at full, but still his strength concealed,
Which tempted our attempt, and wrought our fall.
Henceforth his might we know, and know our own,
So as not either to provoke, or dread
New war, provoked; our better part remains
To work in close° design, by fraud or guile,
What force effected not, that he no less
At length from us may find, who overcomes
By force hath overcome but half his foe.
Space may produce new worlds; whereof so rife
There went a fame° in heaven that he ere long
Intended to create, and therein plant
A generation, whom his choice regard
Should favor equal to the sons of heaven.
Thither, if but to pry, shall be perhaps
Our first eruption, thither or elsewhere;
For this infernal pit shall never hold
Celestial spirits in bondage, nor the abyss
Long under darkness cover. But these thoughts
Full counsel must mature. Peace is despaired,
For who can think submission? War then, war
Open or understood must be resolved.'
  He spake; and to confirm his words, out flew
Millions of flaming swords, drawn from the thighs
Of mighty cherubim; the sudden blaze
Far round illumined hell. Highly they raged
Against the highest, and fierce with graspèd arms
Clashed on their sounding shields the din of war,
Hurling defiance toward the vault of heaven.

emptied heaven This is palpably untrue.
different differing
Consent or custom Satan's argument is one with which Milton would himself have concurred (against divine right of kingship), had it been applied to the English throne. Satan's argument that God rules in heaven by convention, rather than by nature, is based on his tragic mistake.
close secret
fame rumor; in Milton's version, the rumor, *before* the revolt, that God intended to create the world *after* it

There stood a hill not far whose grisly top
Belched fire and rolling smoke; the rest entire
Shone with a glossy scurf,° undoubted sign
That in his womb was hid metallic ore,
The work of sulphur.° Thither winged with speed
A numerous brígade hastened: as when bands
Of pioneers with spade and pickaxe armed
Forerun the royal camp, to trench a field
Or cast a rampart. Mammon° led them on,
Mammon, the least erected° Spirit that fell
From heaven, for even in heaven his looks and thoughts
Were always downward bent, admiring more
The riches of heaven's pavement, trodden gold,
Than aught divine or holy else enjoyed
In vision beatific.° By him first
Men also, and by his suggestion taught,
Ransacked° the centre, and with impious hands
Rifled the bowels of their mother earth
For treasures better hid. Soon had his crew
Opened into the hill a spacious wound
And digged out ribs of gold. Let none admire°
That riches grow in hell; that soil may best
Deserve the precious bane. And here let those
Who boast in mortal things, and wondering tell
Of Babel,° and the works of Memphian° kings,
Learn how their greatest monuments of fame,
And strength and art are easily outdone
By spirits reprobate,° and in an hour
What in an age they with incessant toil
And hands innumerable scarce perform.
Nigh on the plain in many cells prepared,
That underneath had veins of liquid fire
Sluiced from the lake, a second multitude
With wondrous art founded the massy ore,
Severing each kind, and scummed the bullion dross.
A third as soon had formed within the ground
A various mould, and from the boiling cells
By strange conveyance filled each hollow nook,
As in an organ from one blast of wind

scurf scaly incrustation: gold ore is seen as a skin disease of hell's rocks
sulphur essential, in alchemy, to the production of metals
Mammon in Aramaic, "wealth," but in medieval tradition standing for the realm of this world. Milton's conception of him as a Pluto-like mining god is based on Spenser's Cave of Mammon (see *The Faerie Queene* II.vii); cf. Matthew 6:24.
erected uplifted
vision beatific the direct vision of God by the saints which constitutes paradise
Ransacked This word, and "Rifled" below, suggest the aggressive violence of mining, as opposed to the nurturing of agriculture; the truer, "vegetable" gold of the earth's fruits, rather than her guts, will be seen in Paradise (IV. 220).
admire wonder
Babel the tower of Babel (Genesis 11:1–9) and all of Babylon's famous structures, all emblems of pride and presumption
Memphian Egyptian
reprobate rejected

To many a row of pipes the sound-board breathes.
Anon out of the earth a fabric huge
Rose like an exhalation,° with the sound
Of dulcet symphonies and voices sweet,
Built like a temple, where pilasters round
Were set, and Doric pillars overlaid
With golden architrave; nor did there want
Cornice or frieze, with bossy° sculptures graven;
The roof was fretted° gold. Not Babylon,
Nor great Alcairo° such magnificence
Equalled in all their glories, to enshrine
Belus or Serapis° their gods, or seat
Their kings, when Egypt with Assyria strove
In wealth and luxury. The ascending pile
Stood fixed her stately highth, and straight the doors
Opening their brazen folds discover wide
Within, her ample spaces, o'er the smooth
And level pavement; from the archèd roof
Pendent by subtle magic many a row
Of starry lamps and blazing cressets° fed
With naphtha and asphaltus° yielded light
As from a sky. The hasty multitude
Admiring entered, and the work some praise,
And some the architect: his hand was known
In heaven by many a towered structure high,
Where sceptred angels held their residence,
And sat as princes, whom the súpreme king
Exalted to such power, and gave to rule,
Each in his hierarchy, the orders bright.
Nor was his name unheard or unadored
In ancient Greece, and in Ausonian land°
Men called him Mulciber;° and how he fell
From heaven, they fabled, thrown by angry Jove
Sheer o'er the crystal battlements: from morn
To noon he fell, from noon to dewy eve,
A summer's day; and with the setting sun
Dropped from the zenith like a falling star,
On Lemnos the Aégean isle. Thus they relate,
Erring; for he with this rebellious rout
Fell long before; nor aught availed him now

exhalation also, like a comet or meteor. This whole passage suggests a description of a masque transformation scene—rapid, illusory, dramatically impressive; the accompanying music hints at the power of Amphion raising the walls of Thebes to music, while the architectural details are those of massive, baroque architecture.
bossy in relief
fretted patterned, interlaced carving
Alcairo ancient Memphis
Belus or Serapis Baal or Osiris
cressets iron baskets
asphaltus pitch asphalt
Ausonian land Italy (its old Greek name)
Mulciber Hephaestus, Vulcan. Milton sums up the Homeric story (*Iliad* I.590–94) of his day-long, leisurely fall, almost as if a pleasant trip, then snaps in (l. 747) the corrective to what seems far too sweet a fable.

To have built in heaven high towers;° nor did he scape
By all his engines,° but was headlong sent
With his industrious crew to build in hell.
  Meanwhile the wingèd heralds by command
Of sovereign power, with awful ceremony
And trumpet's sound, throughout the host proclaim
A solemn council forthwith to be held
At Pandemonium,° the high capitol
Of Satan and his peers; their summons called
From every band and squarèd regiment
By place or choice the worthiest; they anon
With hundreds and with thousands trooping came
Attended. All access was thronged, the gates
And porches wide, but chief the spacious hall
(Though like a covered field, where champions bold
Wont ride in armed, and at the Soldan's° chair
Defied the best of paynim° chivalry
To mortal combat or career with lance)
Thick swarmed, both on the ground and in the air,
Brushed with the hiss of rustling wings. As bees
In springtime, when the sun with Taurus° rides,
Pour forth their populous youth about the hive
In clusters; they among fresh dews and flowers
Fly to and fro, or on the smoothèd plank,
The suburb of their straw-built citadel,
New rubbed with balm, expatiate° and confer
Their state affairs: so thick the airy crowd
Swarmed° and were straitened; till the signal given,
Behold a wonder! they but now who seemed
In bigness to surpass earth's giant sons,
Now less than smallest dwarfs, in narrow room
Throng numberless, like that pygmean race
Beyond the Indian mount, or fairy elves,
Whose midnight revels by a forest side
Or fountain some belated peasant sees,
Or dreams he sees, while overhead the moon
Sits arbitress, and nearer to the earth
Wheels her pale course; they on their mirth and dance
Intent, with jocund music charm his ear;°

heaven high towers The reversed syntax reflects the climax-capping of adding height to heaven.
engines devices (machinery and machinations)
Pandemonium in Greek, "all demons"
Soldan's Sultan's
paynim pagan
Taurus the sun is in Taurus from mid-April to mid-May
expatiate amble about
so thick . . . Swarmed Again, the density, busy-ness, and multitude of the bees show us those qualities of Satan's legions, but the scale is reduced to a *tiny* model of human industry and social organization (although a traditional one), and the "straw-built citadel" is both literal about straw beehives and figurative about vast structures (like Roman churches with hive-shaped domes) "built on straw."
fairy elves . . . ear (ll. 781–87) no longer reduced in size (bees, pygmies), but are now as illusory as spooks that the simple see. We are now in the English countryside for a moment, to give us a breath of pragmatic fresh air (as Chaucer does with his introduction of January in The Franklin's Tale); there are echoes of *A Midsummer Night's Dream.*

At once with joy and fear his heart rebounds.
Thus incorporeal spirits to smallest forms
Reduced their shapes immense, and were at large,°
Though without number still, amidst the hall
Of that infernal court. But far within,
And in their own dimensions like themselves,
The great seraphic lords and cherubim
In close° recess and secret conclave sat,
A thousand demi-gods and golden seats,
Frequent° and full. After short silence then
And summons read, the great consult° began.

Book II

High on a throne of royal state, which far
Outshone the wealth of Ormus° and of Ind,
Or where the gorgeous East with richest hand
Showers on her kings barbaric pearl and gold,
Satan exalted sat, by merit° raised
To that bad eminence; and from despair
Thus high uplifted beyond hope, aspires
Beyond thus high,° insatiate to pursue
Vain war with heaven, and by success° untaught,
His proud imaginations thus displayed:
'Powers and dominions,° deities of heaven,
For since no deep within her gulf can hold
Immortal vigour, though oppressed and fallen,
I give not heaven for lost. From this descent
Celestial virtues° rising will appear
More glorious and more dread than from no fall,
And trust themselves to fear no second fate.
Me though just right and the fixed laws of heaven
Did first create your leader, next, free choice,
With what besides, in council or in fight,
Hath been achieved of merit, yet this loss,
Thus far at least recovered, hath much more
Established in a safe unenvied throne
Yielded with full consent. The happier state
In heaven, which follows dignity, might draw
Envy from each inferior; but who here
Will envy whom the highest place exposes
Foremost to stand against the thunderer's° aim
Your bulwark, and condemns to greatest share

at large The pun is quite deliberate.
close secret
Frequent crowded
consult debate
Ormus island city in the Persian gulf
merit power (see I.98n and II.21)
from despair . . . high again, the patterned syntax reflects the overreaching of Satan's will
success the outcome, implying neither good nor bad results; cf. II.123
Powers and dominions He still uses their angelic titles (see I.128n).
virtues capabilities; also, the angelic order
the thunderer's Zeus, Jupiter; again, a false reduction of God

Of endless pain? Where there is then no good
For which to strive, no strife can grow up there
From faction; for none sure will claim in hell
Precedence, none whose portion is so small
Of present pain that with ambitious mind
Will covet more. With this advantage then
To union, and firm faith, and firm accord,
More than can be in heaven, we now return
To claim our just inheritance of old,
Surer to prosper than prosperity
Could have assured us;° and by what best way,
Whether of open war or covert guile,
We now debate; who can advise, may speak.
He ceased, and next him Moloch,° sceptred king,
Stood up, the strongest and the fiercest Spirit
That fought in heaven, now fiercer by despair.
His trust was with the Eternal to be deemed
Equal in strength, and rather than be less
Cared not to be at all; with that care lost
Went all his fear: of God, or hell, or worse
He recked not, and these words thereafter spake:
'My sentence° is for open war. Of wiles,
More unexpert, I boast not: them let those
Contrive who need, or when they need, not now.
For while they sit contriving, shall the rest,
Millions that stand° in arms and longing wait
The signal to ascend, sit lingering here,
Heaven's fugitives, and for their dwelling-place
Accept this dark opprobrious den of shame,
The prison of his tyranny who reigns
By our delay? No, let us rather choose,
Armed with hell flames and fury, all at once
O'er heaven's high towers° to force resistless way,
Turning our tortures into horrid arms
Against the torturer; when to meet the noise
Of his almighty engine he shall hear
Infernal thunder, and for lightning see
Black fire and horror shot with equal rage
Among his angels, and his throne itself
Mixed with Tartarean° sulphur and strange fire,

Surer . . . assured us This shaping of words—a b b a—called a "chiasmus," or "crossing," exemplifies Satan's use of rhetorical devices common in the Renaissance.
Moloch One of the better known of Milton's devils who later enter history as pagan gods; he becomes a Canaanite idol to whom children are sacrificed and is introduced in I.392–96 as the "horrid king besmeared with blood / Of human sacrifice, and parents' tears / Though for the noise of drums and timbrels loud / Their children's cries unheard, that passed through fire / To his grim idol."
sentence decision; cf. l. 291
stand metaphorically, as in "standing army," but notice the sequence of words in these lines: "sit . . . stand . . . ascend . . . sit"
towers echoing I.749
Tartarean hellish. This is gunpowder, artillery being an infernal parody of God's thunder and an appropriate revenge.

His own invented torments. But perhaps
The way seems difficult and steep to scale
With upright wing against a higher foe?
Let such bethink them, if the sleepy drench
Of that forgetful lake benumb not still,
That in our proper motion we ascend
Up to our native seat; descent and fall
To us is adverse. Who but felt of late,
When the fierce foe hung on our broken rear
Insulting,° and pursued us through the deep,
With what compulsion and laborious flight
We sunk thus low? The ascent is easy then;
The event is feared; Should we again provoke
Our stronger, some worse way his wrath may find
To our destruction, if there be in hell
Fear to be worse destroyed: what can be worse
Than to dwell here, driven out from bliss, condemned
In this abhorrèd deep to utter woe;
Where pain of unextinguishable fire
Must exercise° us without hope of end
The vassals of his anger, when the scourge
Inexorably, and the torturing hour
Calls us to penance? More destroyed than thus
We should be quite abolished and expire.
What fear we then? What doubt we to incense
His utmost ire? Which to the highth enraged
Will either quite consume us, and reduce
To nothing this essential,° happier far
Than miserable to have eternal being;
Or if our substance be indeed divine,
And cannot cease to be, we are at worst
On this side nothing; and by proof we feel
Our power sufficient to disturb his heaven,
And with perpetual inroads to alarm,
Though inaccessible, his fatal° throne;
Which if not victory is yet revenge.'
He ended frowning, and his look denounced°
Desperate revenge, and battle dangerous
To less than gods. On the other side up rose
Belial, in act more graceful and humane;
A fairer person lost not heaven; he seemed
For dignity composed and high exploit:
But all was false and hollow, though his tongue
Dropped manna,° and could make the worse appear

Insulting assaulting, as well as jeering
exercise torture
essential essence. Angelic substance is immaterial; cf. I.138.
fatal by fate; cf. I.116
denounced threatened
manna the heavenly food supplied to the wandering Israelites (Exodus 16:14–16); this is sarcastic, modeled on "dripping honey"

The better reason, to perplex and dash
Maturest counsels: for his thoughts were low;
To vice industrious, but to nobler deeds
Timorous and slothful: yet he pleased the ear,
And with persuasive accent thus began:
'I should be much for open war, O Peers,
As not behind in hate, if what was urged
Main reason to persuade immediate war
Did not dissuade me most, and seem to cast
Ominous conjecture on the whole success:
When he who most excels in fact° of arms,
In what he counsels and in what excels
Mistrustful, grounds his courage on despair
And utter dissolution, as the scope
Of all his aim, after some dire revenge.
First, what revenge? The towers of heaven are filled
With armèd watch, that render all access
Impregnable; oft on the bordering deep
Encamp their legions, or with óbscure wing
Scout far and wide into the realm of Night,
Scorning surprise. Or could we break our way
By force, and at our heels all hell should rise
With blackest insurrection, to confound
Heaven's purest light, yet our great enemy
All incorruptible would on his throne
Sit unpolluted, and the ethereal mould
Incapable of stain would soon expel
Her mischief, and purge off the baser fire,°
Victorious. Thus repulsed, our final hope
Is flat despair; we must exasperate
The almighty victor to spend all his rage,
And that must end us, that must be our cure,
To be no more. Sad cure! for who would lose,
Though full of pain, this intellectual being,
Those thoughts that wander through eternity,°
To perish rather, swallowed up and lost
In the wide womb of uncreated Night,
Devoid of sense and motion? And who knows,
Let this be good, whether our angry foe
Can give it, or will ever? How he can
Is doubtful; that he never will is sure.
Will he, so wise, let loose at once his ire,
Belike° through impotence, or unaware,
To give his enemies their wish, and end

fact deed, feat
baser fire Heavenly light has been a refining fire in this passage, burning off even the lower, hellish sort.

for who . . . eternity An overtone of Hamlet's "To be or not to be" soliloquy may be discerned here.
Belike doubtless

Them in his anger, whom his anger saves
To punish endless? *Wherefore cease we then?*
Say they who counsel war; *We are decreed,*
Reserved, and destined to eternal woe;
Whatever doing, what can we suffer more,
What can we suffer worse?° Is this then worst,
Thus sitting, thus consulting, thus in arms?
What when we fled amain, pursued and strook
With heaven's afflicting thunder, and besought
The deep to shelter us? This hell then seemed
A refuge from those wounds—or when we lay
Chained on the burning lake?° That sure was worse.
What if the breath that kindled those grim fires
Awaked should blow them into sevenfold rage
And plunge us in the flames? or from above
Should intermitted vengeance arm again
His red right hand° to plague us? What if all
Her stores were opened and this firmament
Of hell should spout her cataracts of fire,
Impendent horrors, threatening hideous fall
One day upon our heads; while we perhaps
Designing or exhorting glorious war,
Caught in a fiery tempest shall be hurled
Each on his rock transfixed, the sport and prey
Of racking whirlwinds, or for ever sunk
Under yon boiling ocean, wrapped in chains;
There to converse with everlasting groans,
Unrespited, unpitied, unreprieved,
Ages of hopeless end? This would be worse.
War therefore, open or concealed, alike
My voice dissuades; for what can force or guile
With him, or who deceive his mind, whose eye
Views all things at one view? He from heaven's highth
All these our motions° vain, sees and derides;
Not more almighty to resist our might
Than wise to frustrate all our plots and wiles.
Shall we then live thus vile, the race of heaven
Thus trampled, thus expelled to suffer here
Chains and these torments? Better these than worse,
By my advice; since fate inevitable
Subdues us, and omnipotent decree,
The victor's will. To suffer, as to do,°

What . . . worse He will keep answering this rhetorical question in his own rhetorically brilliant speech.
burning lake an echo of I.52
red right hand quoted from Horace (*Odes* I.2), where it is used of civil war. This passage (to l. 186) also echoes classical accounts of Zeus' vanquishing the Titans.
motions plans
To suffer, as to do chimes against Satan's "Doing or suffering" (I.158) and the words of the Roman Mucius Scaevola, as he burned his right hand in the flames to show his captors his inner resources

Our strength is equal, nor the law unjust
That so ordains: this was at first resolved,
If we were wise, against so great a foe
Contending, and so doubtful what might fall.
I laugh when those who at the spear are bold
And venturous, if that fail them, shrink and fear
What yet they know must follow, to endure
Exile, or ignominy,° or bonds, or pain,
The sentence of their conqueror. This is now
Our doom; which if we can sustain and bear,
Our súpreme foe in time may much remit
His anger, and perhaps, thus far removed,
Not mind us not offending, satisfied
With what is punished; whence these raging fires
Will slacken, if his breath stir not their flames.
Our purer essence then will overcome
Their noxious vapour, or enured° not feel,
Or changed at length, and to the place conformed
In temper and in nature, will receive
Familiar the fierce heat, and void of pain;
This horror will grow mild, this darkness light,°
Besides what hope the never-ending flight
Of future days may bring, what chance, what change
Worth waiting, since our present lot appears
For happy° though but ill, for ill not worst,
If we procure not to ourselves more woe.'
  Thus Belial with words clothed in reason's garb,
Counselled ignoble ease, and peaceful sloth,
Not peace; and after him thus Mammon° spake—
  'Either to disenthrone the king of heaven
We war, if war be best, or to regain
Our own right lost: him tŏ unthrone we then
May hope when everlasting fate shall yield
To fickle chance, and Chaos judge the strife:°
The former, vain to hope, argues as vain
The latter; for what place can be for us
Within heaven's bound, unless heaven's lord supreme
We overpower? Suppose he should relent
And publish grace to all, on promise made
Of new subjection; with what eyes could we
Stand in his presence humble, and receive
Strict laws imposed, to celebrate his throne
With warbled hymns, and to his Godhead sing
Forced halleluiahs; while he lordly sits
Our envied sovereign, and his altar breathes

ignominy See I.115n.
enured accustomed to
light not dark; not heavy
For happy as for happiness
Mammon See I.680.
strife between fate and chance

Ambrosial odours and ambrosial flowers,
Our servile offerings? This must be our task
In heaven, this our delight; how wearisome
Eternity so spent in worship paid
To whom we hate. Let us not then pursue
By force impossible, by leave obtained
Unácceptáble—though in heaven—our state
Of splendid vassalage, but rather seek
Our own good from ourselves, and from our own
Live to ourselves, though in this vast recess,
Free, and to none accountable, preferring
Hard liberty° before the easy yoke
Of servile pomp. Our greatness will appear
Then most conspicuous, when great things of small,
Useful of hurtful, prosperous of adverse
We can create, and in what place soe'er
Thrive under evil, and work ease out of pain
Through labour and endurance. This deep world
Of darkness do we dread? How oft amidst
Thick clouds and dark doth heaven's all-ruling sire
Choose to reside, his glory unobscured,
And with the majesty of darkness round
Covers his throne; from whence deep thunders roar,
Mustering their rage, and heaven resembles hell?
As he our darkness, cannot we his light
Imitate when we please? This desert soil
Wants not her hidden lustre, gems and gold;
Nor want we skill or art, from whence to raise
Magnificence; and what can heaven show more?
Our torments also may in length of time
Become our elements, these piercing fires
As soft as now severe, our temper changed
Into their temper; which must needs remove
The sensible° of pain. All things invite
To peaceful counsels, and the settled state
Of order, how in safety best we may
Compose° our present evils, with regard
Of what we are and where, dismissing quite
All thoughts of war. Ye have what I advise.'
He scarce had finished, when such murmur filled
The assembly as when hollow rocks retain
The sound of blustering winds, which all night long
Had roused the sea, now with hoarse cadence lull

Hard liberty Mammon's declaration of independence cannot help but move the lover of human freedom, even one who appreciates the prophecy of the relation of individual liberty to the institution of wealth as acted out in the history of Western capitalism. In the context of the debate—Moloch's primitive, heroic violence and Belial's guileful parody of medieval quietism—Mammon's exhortation (ll. 269–73 below) to his fellows to produce light of their own follows as a version of what Max Weber called the Protestant ethic.
sensible felt part
Compose arrange

Seafaring men o'erwatched, whose bark by chance
Or pinnace anchors in a craggy bay
After the tempest. Such applause was heard
As Mammon ended, and his sentence° pleased,
Advising peace; for such another field
They dreaded worse than hell: so much the fear
Of thunder and the sword of Michaël°
Wrought still within them; and no less desire
To found this nether empire, which might rise
By policy,° and long procéss of time,
In emulation opposite to heaven.
Which when Beelzebub° perceived, than whom,
Satan except, none higher sat, with grave
Aspect he rose, and in his rising seemed
A pillar of state; deep on his front° engraven
Deliberation sat and public care;
And princely counsel in his face yet shone,
Majestic though in ruin: sage he stood,
With Atlantean° shoulders fit to bear
The weight of mightiest monarchies; his look
Drew audience and attention still as night
Or summer's noontide air, while thus he spake:
'Thrones and imperial powers, offspring of heaven,
Ethereal virtues—or these titles now
Must we renounce, and changing style be called
Princess of hell? For so the popular vote
Inclines, here to continue, and build up here
A growing empire; doubtless; while we dream
And know not that the King of heaven hath doomed
This place our dungeon, not our safe retreat
Beyond his potent arm, to live exempt
From Heaven's high jurisdiction, in new league
Banded against his throne, but to remain
In strictest bondage, though thus far removed,
Under the inevitable curb, reserved
His captive multitude. For he, be sure,
In highth or depth, still first and last° will reign
Sole king, and of his kingdom lose no part
By our revolt, but over hell extend
His empire, and with iron sceptre° rule
Us here, as with his golden those in heaven.
What° sit we then projecting peace and war?

sentence opinion; cf. l. 51
Michaël archangel who commanded God's army in Bk. VI
policy statecraft, with Machiavellian overtones
Beelzebub See I.81.
front forehead
Atlantean Atlas-like
first and last "I am Alpha and Omega, the first and the last" (Revelation 1:11)
iron sceptre standing for hard, stern justice, as opposed to the gold of equity and mercy; also perhaps with an echo of Psalms 2:9, "Thou shalt break them with a rod of iron."
What why

War hath determined° us, and foiled with loss
Irreparable; terms of peace yet none
Vouchsafed or sought; for what peace will be given
To us enslaved, but custody severe,
And stripes, and arbitrary punishment
Inflicted? And what peace can we return,
But to our power° hostility and hate,
Untamed reluctance, and revenge though slow,
Yet ever plotting how the conqueror least
May reap his conquest, and may least rejoice
In doing what we most in suffering feel?
Nor will occasion want, nor shall we need
With dangerous expedition to invade
Heaven, whose high walls fear no assault or siege
Or ambush from the deep. What if we find
Some easier enterprise? There is a place
(If ancient and prophetic fame in heaven
Err not), another world, the happy seat
Of some new race called man, about this time
To be created like to us, though less
In power and excellence, but favored more°
Of him who rules above; so was his will
Pronounced among the gods,° and by an oath,
That shook heaven's whole circumference, confirmed.
Thither let us bend all our thoughts, to learn
What creatures there inhabit, of what mold
Or substance, how endued,° and what their power,
And where their weakness, how attempted° best,
By force or subtlety. Though heaven be shut,
And heaven's high arbitrator sit secure
In his own strength, this place may lie exposed,
The utmost border of his kingdom, left
To their defence who hold it; here perhaps
Some advantageous act may be achieved
By sudden onset, either with hell fire
To waste his whole creation, or possess
All as our own, and drive as we were driven,
The puny° habitants; or if not drive,
Seduce them to our party, that their God
May prove their foe, and with repenting hand
Abolish his own works. This would surpass
Common revenge, and interrupt his joy
In our confusion, and our joy upraise

determined with an overtone of "given us determination"
to our power to the limits of our power
favored more not true, but a self-fulfilling prophecy in that belief that it is so prompts the fallen angels to join Satan in the action that will undo them even further
among the gods Beelzebub is talking as though God's oath were taken in some Homeric conclave of pagan deities.
endued endowed with attributes
attempted got at
puny both in the sense of "weak" and (later) that of "created" or "born" (from French, *puis né*)

In his disturbance; when his darling sons,
Hurled headlong to partake with us, shall curse
Their frail original,° and faded bliss,
Faded so soon. Advise if this be worth
Attempting, or to sit in darkness here
Hatching vain empires.'—Thus Beelzebub
Pleaded his devilish counsel, first devised
By Satan, and in part proposed; for whence,
But from the author of all ill, could spring
So deep a malice, to confound the race
Of mankind in one root, and earth with hell
To mingle and involve,° done all to spite
The great Creator? But their spite still serves
His glory to augment. The bold design
Pleased highly those infernal states,° and joy
Sparkled in all their eyes; with full assent
They vote: whereat his speech he thus renews:
'Well have ye judged, well ended long debate,
Synod of gods, and like to what ye are,
Great things resolved; which from the lowest deep
Will once more lift us up, in spite of fate,
Nearer our ancient seat;° perhaps in view
Of those bright confines, whence with neighbouring arms
And opportune excursion we may chance
Re-enter heaven; or else in some mild zone
Dwell not unvisited of heaven's fair light
Secure, and at the brightening orient beam
Purge off this gloom; the soft delicious air
To heal the scar of these corrosive fires
Shall breathe her balm. But first whom shall we send
In search of this new world, whom shall we find
Sufficient? Who shall tempt° with wandering feet
The dark unbottomed infinite abyss
And through the palpable obscure° find out
His uncouth° way, or spread his airy flight
Upborne with indefatigable wings
Over the vast abrupt,° ere he arrive
The happy isle; what strength, what art can then
Suffice, or what evasion bear him safe
Through the strict senteries° and stations thick
Of angels watching round? Here he had need
All circumspection, and we now no less
Choice in our suffrage; for on whom we send,
The weight of all and our last hope relies.'
This said, he sat; and expectation held

original Adam, also identified as the "one root" in l. 383 below
involve entangle
states estates of the realm, as represented in a parliament
seat home
tempt try
palpable obscure "darkness which may be felt" (Exodus 10:21)
uncouth unknown
abrupt like "obscure," above, used as a noun
senteries sentries

His look suspense,° awaiting who appeared
To second, or oppose, or undertake
The perilous attempt: but all sat mute,
Pondering the danger with deep thoughts; and each
In other's countenance read his own dismay
Astonished. None among the choice and prime
Of those heaven-warring champions could be found
So hardy as to proffer or accept
Alone the dreadful voyage, till at last
Satan, whom now transcendent glory raised
Above his fellows, with monarchal pride
Conscious of highest worth, unmoved thus spake:
'O Progeny of heaven, empyreal Thrones,
With reason hath deep silence and demur°
Seized us, though undismayed. Long is the way
And hard, that out of hell leads up to light;
Our prison strong, this huge convex° of fire,
Outrageous to devour, immures us round
Ninefold, and gates of burning adamant
Barred over us prohibit all egress.
These passed, if any pass, the void profound
Of unessential° Night receives him next
Wide gaping, and with utter loss of being
Threatens him, plunged in that abortive° gulf.
If thence he scape into whatever world,
Or unknown region, what remains him less
Than unknown dangers and as hard escape?
But I should ill become this throne, O Peers,
And this imperial sovereignty, adorned
With splendour, armed with power, if aught proposed
And judged of public moment, in the shape
Of difficulty or danger could deter
Me from attempting. Wherefore do I assume
These royalties, and not refuse to reign,
Refusing° to accept as great a share
Of hazard as of honour, due alike
To him who reigns, and so much to him due
Of hazard more, as he above the rest
High honour sits? Go therefore, mighty Powers,
Terror of heaven, though fallen; intend° at home,
While here shall be our home, what best may ease
The present misery, and render hell
More tolerable, if there be cure or charm
To respite or deceive,° or slack the pain
Of this ill mansion; intermit no watch

suspense suspended
demur hesitation
convex convex vault
unessential without substance
abortive both aborting and, as a gulf that yields or produces nothing, aborted
Refusing if I refuse
intend consider
deceive beguile

Against a wakeful foe, while I abroad
Through all the coasts of dark destruction seek
Deliverance for us all: this enterprise
None shall partake with me.' Thus saying rose
The monarch, and prevented all reply;
Prudent, lest from his resolution raised°
Others among the chief might offer now
(Certain to be refused) what erst they feared;
And so refused might in opinion stand
His rivals, winning cheap the high repute
Which he through hazard huge must earn. But they
Dreaded not more the adventure than his voice
Forbidding, and at once with him they rose;
Their rising all at once was as the sound
Of thunder heard remote. Towards him they bend
With awful° reverence prone; and as a god
Extol him equal to the highest in heaven.
Nor failed they to express how much they praised,
That for the general safety he despised
His own: for neither do the spirits damned
Lose all their virtue; lest bad men should boast
Their specious deeds on earth, which glory excites,
O close° ambition varnished o'er with zeal.
  Thus they their doubtful consultations dark
Ended rejoicing in their matchless Chief:
As when from mountain tops the dusky clouds
Ascending, while the north wind sleeps, o'erspread
Heaven's cheerful face, the louring element°
Scowls o'er the darkened landscape snow or shower;
If chance° the radiant sun with farewell sweet
Extend his evening beam, the fields revive,
The birds their notes renew, and bleating herds
Attest their joy, that hill and valley rings.
O shame to men! Devil with devil damned
Firm concord holds, men only disagree
Of creatures rational, though under hope
Of heavenly grace; and God proclaiming peace,
Yet live in hatred, enmity, and strife
Among themselves, and levy cruel wars,
Wasting the earth, each other to destroy:
As if (which might induce us to accord)°
Man had not hellish foes enow° besides,
That day and night for his destruction wait.
  The Stygian council thus dissolved; and forth
In order came the grand infernal peers;
Midst came their mighty paramount,° and seemed

raised encouraged
awful full of awe
close secret
element the sky
If chance if by chance
accord agree
enow enough
paramount ruler

Alone the antagonist of heaven, nor less
Than hell's dread emperor, with pomp supreme
And god-like imitated state;° him round
A globe° of fiery seraphim enclosed
With bright emblazonry and horrent° arms.
Then of their session ended they bid cry
With trumpet's regal sound the great result.
Toward the four winds four speedy cherubim
Put to their mouths the sounding alchemy°
By herald's voice explained; the hollow abyss
Heard far and wide, and all the host of hell
With deafening shout returned them loud acclaim.
Thence more at ease their minds and somewhat raised°
By false presumptuous hope, the rangèd powers°
Disband, and wandering each his several way
Pursues, as inclination or sad choice
Leads him perplexed, where he may likeliest find
Truce to his restless thoughts, and entertain°
The irksome hours, till his great chief return.
Part on the plain, or in the air sublime°
Upon the wing, or in swift race contend,
As at the Olympian games or Pythian fields;°
Part curb their fiery steeds, or shun the goal
With rapid wheels, or fronted brígades form:
As when to warn proud cities war appears
Waged in the troubled sky, and armies rush
To battle in the clouds; before each van
Prick forth the airy knights, and couch their spears,
Till thickest legions close; with feats of arms
From either end of heaven the welkin° burns.
Others with vast Typhoean° rage more fell
Rend up both rocks and hills, and ride the air
In whirlwind; hell scarce holds the wild uproar;
As when Alcides° from Oechalia crowned
With conquest, felt the envenomed robe, and tore
Through pain up by the roots Thessalian pines,°
And Lichas from the top of Oeta threw
Into the Euboic sea. Others more mild,

state ceremonial royal trappings
globe phalanx
horrent bristling
alchemy metallic alloy
raised heartened
rangèd powers ranked armies
entertain pass away
sublime raise up
Olympian . . . fields This introduces the heroic games.
welkin sky
Typhoean titanic (see I.199); also, through "typhon" (influencing "typhoon" later on), a whirlwind
Alcides Hercules, whose wife sent him a poisoned robe, went mad with the pain and hurled his friend Lichas, the mere bringer of the gift, into the Euboean sea.
tore . . . pines Not only does the wrenched syntax "imitate" the heroic action described (mostly by separating "tore" and "up"), but the whole of l. 544 itself is symmetrically patterned, with a pun on "pain" and "pine" (meaning "pain" as a noun, as well).

Retreated in a silent valley, sing°
With notes angelical to many a harp
Their own heroic deeds and hapless fall
By doom of battle; and complain that fate
Free virtue should enthrall to force or chance.
Their song was partial,° but the harmony
(What could it less when spirits immortal sing?)
Suspended° hell, and took with ravishment
The thronging audience. In discourse more sweet
(For eloquence the soul, song charms the sense)
Others apart sat on a hill retired,
In thoughts more elevate, and reasoned° high
Of providence, foreknowledge, will, and fate,
Fixed fate, free will, foreknowledge absolute,
And found no end, in wandering mazes lost.°
Of good and evil much they argued then,
Of happiness and final misery,
Passion and apathy, and glory and shame,
Vain wisdom all, and false philosophy—
Yet with a pleasing sorcery could charm
Pain for a while or anguish, and excite
Fallacious hope, or arm the obdurèd° breast
With stubborn patience as with triple steel.
Another part, in squadrons and gross° bands,
On bold adventure to discover wide
That dismal world, if any clime perhaps
Might yield them easier habitation, bend
Four ways their flying march, along the banks
Of four infernal rivers that disgorge
Into the burning lake their baleful streams:
Abhorrèd Styx,° the flood of deadly hate;
Sad Acheron of sorrow, black and deep;
Cocytus, named of lamentation loud
Heard on the rueful stream; fierce Phlegethon,
Whose waves of torrent fire inflame with rage.
Far off from these a slow and silent stream,
Lethe, the river of oblivion, rolls
Her watery labyrinth,° whereof who drinks
Forthwith his former state and being forgets,
Forgets both joy and grief, pleasure and pain.
Beyond this flood a frozen continent

sing epics, like their own versions of *Paradise Lost* VI
partial one-sided; also, possibly "in parts," or polyphonic musically
Suspended held rapt
reasoned a prophetic vision of fallen classical philosophy, particularly of Stoicism
wandering mazes lost as in the syntax and the twisting repetitions of abstract philosophical concepts, their way to truth forever lost
obdurèd hardened
gross massive
Abhorrèd Styx Each of these four rivers of the classical Hades has its name translated and explained.
labyrinth ironically paralleling the labyrinthine mazes of pagan thought, l. 561

Lies dark and wild, beat with perpetual storms
Of whirlwind and dire hail, which on firm land
Thaws not, but gathers heap, and ruin seems
Of ancient pile;° all else deep snow and ice,
A gulf profound as that Serbonian° bog
Betwixt Damiata and Mount Casius old,
Where armies whole have sunk; the parching air
Burns frore,° and cold performs the effect of fire.
Thither by harpy-footed Furies haled,
At certain revolutions all the damned
Are brought; and feel by turns the bitter change
Of fierce extremes, extremes by change more fierce,
From beds of raging fire to starve° in ice
Their soft ethereal warmth, and there to pine
Immovable, infixed, and frozen round,
Periods of time; thence hurried back to fire.
They ferry over this Lethean sound
Both to and fro, their sorrow to augment,
And wish and struggle, as they pass, to reach
The tempting stream, with one small drop to lose
In sweet forgetfulness all pain and woe,
All in one moment, and so near the brink;
But fate withstands, and to oppose the attempt
Medusa° with Gorgonian terror guards
The ford, and of itself the water flies
All taste of living wight, as once it fled
The lip of Tantalus.° Thus roving on
In cónfused march forlorn, the adventurous bands,
With shuddering horror pale, and eyes aghast,
Viewed first their lamentable lot, and found
No rest. Through many a dark and dreary vale
They passed, and many a region dolorous,
O'er many a frozen, many a fiery alp,°
Rocks, caves, lakes, fens, bogs, dens, and shades of death,°
A universe of death, which God by curse
Created evil, for evil only good,
Where all life dies, death lives, and Nature breeds,
Perverse, all monstrous, all prodigious things,
Abominable, inutterable, and worse
Than fables yet have feigned, or fear conceived,
Gorgons and Hydras, and Chimeras° dire.

pile building
Serbonian the quicksands which lay between Lake Serbonis and Damiata, near the Nile delta, renowned in antiquity for their danger to armies
frore frozen
starve Only the syntax is misleading: "to starve their warmth to death in ice."
Medusa one of the snaky-haired Gorgons whose look turns men to stone
Tantalus In the *Odyssey,* Odysseus sees Tantalus, desperately thirsty, standing in a pool that always drops below his mouth when he tries to drink from it; cf. *The Faerie Queene* I.v.35.
alp any mountain
Rocks . . . death again, a mimetic line, its list of monosyllables tiring to get through, and slow
Hydras, and Chimeras many-headed beasts, and fire-breathing, triple-bodied (lion-serpent-goat) monsters

Meanwhile the adversary of God and man,
Satan, with thoughts inflamed of highest design,
Puts on swift wings, and toward the gates of hell
Explores° his solitary flight; sometimes
He scours the right-hand coast, sometimes the left;
Now shaves with level wing the deep, then soars
Up to the fiery concave towering high:
As when far off at sea a fleet descried
Hangs in the clouds, by equinoctial winds
Close sailing from Bengala,° or the isles
Of Ternate and Tidore,° whence merchants bring
Their spicy drugs: they on the trading flood
Through the wide Ethiopian to the Cape°
Ply° stemming nightly toward the pole. So seemed
Far off the flying fiend. At last appear
Hell bounds high reaching to the horrid° roof,
And thrice threefold the gates; three folds were brass,
Three iron, three of adamantine rock,
Impenetrable, impaled° with circling fire,
Yet unconsumed. Before the gates there sat
On either side a formidable shape;
The one seemed woman to the waist, and fair,
But ended foul in many a scaly fold
Voluminous° and vast, a serpent armed
With mortal sting. About her middle round
A cry° of hell-hounds never ceasing barked
With wide Cerberean mouths full loud, and rung
A hideous peal; yet, when they list, would creep,
If aught disturbed their noise, into her womb,
And kennel there, yet there still barked and howled,
Within unseen. Far less abhorred than these
Vexed Scylla bathing in the sea that parts
Calabria from the hoarse Trinacrian° shore;
Nor uglier follow the Night-hag,° when called
In secret, riding through the air she comes,
Lured with the smell of infant blood, to dance
With Lapland witches, while the labouring° moon
Eclipses at their charms. The other shape—
If shape it might be called that shape had none°

Explores tests out
Bengala Bengal
Ternate and Tidore islands of the Moluccas, or "spice islands"
Ethiopian to the Cape Indian Ocean to the Cape of Good Hope
Ply beat to windward
horrid bristling
impaled not "spiked," but "enclosed"
Voluminous coiled
cry pack. Part of the description evokes Spenser's Error (*The Faerie Queene* I.i.14–15).
Trinacrian Sicilian. In the *Odyssey,* the monster Scylla and the whirlpool Charybdis control the strait of Messina.
Night-hag Hecate
labouring undergoing eclipse
that shape had none Nobody can know what death is like; only the dead, who cannot know or tell, have seen it. Having Satan—and thus the reader—encounter Sin and Death before knowing who they are, is a higher kind of allegorizing: were they both labeled with their identities they would be more easily avoided. Cf. *The Faerie Queene* VII.vii.46.

Distinguishable in member, joint, or limb,
Or substance might be called that shadow seemed,
For each seemed either—black it stood as Night,
Fierce as ten Furies, terrible as hell,
And shook a dreadful dart; what seemed his head
The likeness of a kingly crown had on.
Satan was now at hand, and from his seat
The monster moving onward came as fast
With horrid strides; hell trembled as he strode.
The undaunted fiend what this might be admired,
Admired, not feared; God and his Son except,
Created thing naught valued he nor shunned;
And with disdainful look thus first began:
'Whence and what art thou, execrable shape,
That darest, though grim and terrible, advance
Thy miscreated front athwart my way
To yonder gates? Through them I mean to pass,
That be assured, without leave asked of thee.
Retire, or taste thy folly, and learn by proof,
Hell-born, not to contend with spirits of heaven.'
To whom the goblin full of wrath replied:
'Art thou that traitor angel, art thou he,
Who first broke peace in heaven and faith, till then
Unbroken, and in proud rebellious arms
Drew after him the third part of heaven's sons
Conjured° against the highest, for which both thou
And they, outcast from God, are here condemned
To waste eternal days in woe and pain?
And reckonest thou thyself with spirits of heaven,
Hell-doomed, and breathest defiance here and scorn
Where I reign king, and to enrage thee more,
Thy king and lord? Back to thy punishment,
False fugitive, and to thy speed add wings,
Lest with a whip of scorpions I pursue
Thy lingering, or with one stroke of this dart
Strange horror seize thee, and pangs unfelt before.'
So spake the grisly terror, and in shape,
So speaking and so threatening, grew tenfold
More dreadful and deform. On the other side,
Incensed with indignation Satan stood
Unterrified, and like a comet burned,
That fires the length of Ophiuchus° huge
In the arctic sky, and from his horrid hair°
Shakes pestilence and war. Each at the head

Conjured sworn together. The "third part of the stars of heaven" were thrown to earth by the dragon in Revelation 12:3–4.

Ophiuchus "serpent-bearer," a large and prominent constellation of the northern sky

horrid hair "Comet" means "long-haired" star, and comets were portents of disaster; the Latin *horrere* means "to bristle."

Levelled his deadly aim; their fatal hands
No second stroke intend; and such a frown
Each cast at the other, as when two black clouds
With heaven's artillery fraught, come rattling on
Over the Caspian, then stand front to front
Hovering a space, till winds the signal blow
To join their dark encounter in mid-air:°
So frowned the mighty combatants that hell
Grew darker at their frown, so matched they stood;
For never but once more was either like
To meet so great a foe.° And now great deeds
Had been achieved, whereof all hell had rung,
Had not the snaky sorceress that sat
Fast by hell gate, and kept the fatal key,
Risen, and with hideous outcry rushed between.
'O father, what intends thy hand,' she cried,
'Against thy only son? What fury, O son,
Possesses thee to bend that mortal dart
Against thy father's head? And knowest for whom?
For him who sits above and laughs the while
At thee ordained his drudge, to execute
Whate'er his wrath, which he calls justice, bids,
His wrath which one day will destroy ye both.'
She spake, and at her words the hellish pest
Forbore; then these to her Satan returned:
'So strange thy outcry, and thy words so strange
Thou interposest, that my sudden hand
Prevented spares to tell thee yet by deeds
What it intends; till first I know of thee,
What thing thou art, thus double-formed, and why
In this infernal vale first met thou callest
Me father, and that phantasm callest my son.
I know thee not, nor ever saw till now
Sight more detestable than him and thee.'
To whom thus the portress of hell gate replied:
'Hast thou forgot me then, and do I seem
Now in thine eye so foul? Once deemed so fair
In heaven, when at the assembly, and in sight
Of all the seraphim with thee combined
In bold conspiracy against heaven's king,
All on a sudden miserable pain
Surprised thee; dim thine eyes, and dizzy swum
In darkness, while thy head flames thick and fast
Threw forth, till on the left side opening wide,
Likest to thee in shape and countenance bright,

mid-air the middle region of atmospheric phenomena and air demons (as opposed to a more visionary domain of sky)

so great a foe Christ, conquering them

Then shining heavenly fair, a goddess armed
Out of thy head I sprung.° Amazement seized
All the host of heaven; back they recoiled afraid
At first, and called me *Sin,* and for a sign
Portentous held me; but familiar grown,
I pleased, and with attractive graces won
The most averse, thee chiefly, who full oft
Thyself in me thy perfect image viewing
Becamest enamoured; and such joy thou tookest
With me in secret, that my womb conceived
A growing burden. Meanwhile war arose,
And fields were fought in heaven; wherein remained
(For what could else?) to our almighty foe
Clear victory, to our part loss and rout
Through all the empyrean: down they fell
Driven headlong from the pitch° of heaven, down
Into this deep, and in the general fall
I also; at which time this powerful key
Into my hand was given, with charge to keep
These gates for ever shut, which none can pass
Without my opening. Pensive here I sat
Alone, but long I sat not, till my womb,
Pregnant by thee, and now excessive grown,
Prodigious motion felt and rueful throes.
At last this odious offspring whom thou seest,
Thine own begotten, breaking violent way
Tore through my entrails, that with fear and pain
Distorted, all my nether shape thus grew
Transformed; but he my inbred enemy
Forth issued, brandishing his fatal dart
Made to destroy. I fled, and cried out *Death!*
Hell trembled at the hideous name, and sighed
From all her caves, and back resounded *Death!*
I fled, but he pursued (though more, it seems,
Inflamed with lust than rage) and swifter far,
Me overtook, his mother, all dismayed,
And in embraces forcible and foul
Engendering with me, of that rape begot
These yelling monsters that with ceaseless cry
Surround me, as thou sawest, hourly conceived
And hourly born, with sorrow infinite
To me; for when they list, into the womb
That bred them they return, and howl and gnaw
My bowels, their repast; then bursting forth

Out . . . sprung like Athena, Wisdom, from the forehead of Zeus, to show the birth of Mind. Similarly, Sin proceeds from Satan's thought, not, for example, from his guts, or by normal engendering; additionally, in the anti-Trinity of Father, Daughter, and Unholy Monster, she is the second term.
pitch high point

Afresh, with conscious terrors vex me round,
That rest or intermission none I find.°
Before mine eyes in opposition sits
Grim Death my son and foe, who sets them on,
And me his parent would full soon devour
For want of other prey, but that he knows
His end with mine involved; and knows that I
Should prove a bitter morsel, and his bane,
Whenever that shall be; so fate pronounced.
But thou, O father, I forewarn thee, shun
His deadly arrow; neither vainly hope
To be invulnerable in those bright arms,
Though tempered heavenly, for that mortal dint,°
Save he who reigns above, none can resist.'
  She finished, and the subtle Fiend his lore
Soon learned, now milder, and thus answered smooth:
'Dear daughter, since thou claimest me for thy sire,
And my fair son here showest me, the dear pledge°
Of dalliance had with thee in heaven, and joys
Then sweet, now sad to mention, through dire change
Befallen us unforeseen, unthought of, know
I come no enemy, but to set free
From out this dark and dismal house° of pain
Both him and thee, and all the heavenly host
Of spirits that in our just pretences° armed
Fell with us from on high. From them I go
This uncouth errand sole, and one for all
Myself expose with lonely steps to tread
The unfounded° deep, and through the void immense
To search with wandering quest a place foretold
Should be, and, by concurring signs, ere now
Created vast and round, a place of bliss
In the purlieus° of heaven, and therein placed
A race of upstart creatures, to supply
Perhaps our vacant room, though more removed,
Lest heaven surcharged° with potent multitude
Might hap to move new broils. Be this or aught
Than this more secret now designed, I haste
To know, and this once known, shall soon return,
And bring ye to the place where thou and Death
Shall dwell at ease, and up and down unseen
Wing silently the buxom° air, embalmed
With odours; there ye shall be fed and filled

These yelling . . . find (ll. 795–802). Cf. *The Faerie Queene* I.i.15.
dint blow of a sword
pledge child
house hell, as in Job 30:23
pretences legal claims
unfounded bottomless
purlieus bordering region, but with an implication of a licentious neighborhood
surcharged overburdened
buxom unresisting

Immeasurably; all things shall be your prey.'
He ceased, for both seemed highly pleased, and Death
Grinned horrible a ghastly smile, to hear
His famine should be filled, and blessed his maw
Destined to that good hour. No less rejoiced
His mother bad, and thus bespake her sire:
'The key of this infernal pit by due°
And by command of heaven's all-powerful king
I keep, by him forbidden to unlock
These adamantine gates; against all force
Death ready stands to interpose his dart,
Fearless to be o'ermatched by living might.
But what owe I to his commands above
Who hates me, and hath hither thrust me down
Into this gloom of Tartarus profound,
To sit in hateful office here confined,
Inhabitant of heaven and heavenly-born,
Here in perpetual agony and pain,
With terrors and with clamours compassed round
Of mine own brood, that on my bowels feed?
Thou art my father, thou my author, thou
My being gavest me; whom should I obey
But thee, whom follow? Thou wilt bring me soon
To that new world of light and bliss, among
The gods who live at ease, where I shall reign
At thy right hand voluptuous,° as beseems
Thy daughter and thy darling, without end.'
Thus saying, from her side the fatal key,
Sad instrument of all our woe, she took;
And towards the gate rolling her bestial train,
Forthwith the huge portcullis° high up drew,
Which but herself not all the Stygian powers
Could once have moved; then in the key-hole turns
The intrícate wards,° and every bolt and bar
Of massy iron or solid rock with ease
Unfastens. On a sudden open fly
With impetuous recoil and jarring sound
The infernal doors, and on their hinges grate
Harsh thunder, that the lowest bottom shook
Of Erebus.° She opened, but to shut
Excelled her power; the gates wide open stood,
That with extended wings a bannered host
Under spread ensigns marching might pass through
With horse and chariots ranked in loose array;

due right
At thy right hand voluptuous a parody of the Nicene Creed: "who sittest on the right hand of the Father" and "whose kingdom shall be without end"
portcullis (*lit.* sliding door) iron grate suspended from gateway of a castle or fortified place and lowered to prevent entry
wards of the lock
Erebus hell

So wide they stood, and like a furnace mouth
Cast forth redounding° smoke and ruddy flame.
Before their eyes in sudden view appear
The secrets of the hoary deep, a dark
Illimitable ocean without bound,
Without dimension; where length, breadth, and highth,
And time and place are lost; where eldest Night
And Chaos, ancestors of Nature, hold
Eternal anarchy, amidst the noise
Of endless wars, and by confusion stand.
For Hot, Cold, Moist, and Dry,° four champions fierce,
Strive here for mastery, and to battle bring
Their embryon atoms; they around the flag
Of each his faction, in their several clans,
Light-armed or heavy, sharp, smooth, swift or slow,
Swarm populous, unnumbered as the sands
Of Barca or Cyrene's° torrid soil,
Levied° to side with warring winds, and poise°
Their lighter wings. To whom these most adhere,
He rules a moment; Chaos umpire sits,
And by decision more embroils the fray
By which he reigns; next him high arbiter
Chance governs all. Into this wild abyss—
The womb of nature and perhaps her grave,
Of neither sea, nor shore, nor air, nor fire,
But all these in their pregnant causes mixed
Confusedly, and which thus must ever fight,
Unless the almighty maker them ordain
His dark materials to create more worlds—
Into this wild abyss the wary fiend
Stood on the brink of hell and looked a while,
Pondering his voyage; for no narrow frith°
He had to cross. Nor was his ear less pealed°
With noises loud and ruinous (to compare
Great things with small) than when Bellona° storms,
With all her battering engines bent to raze
Some capital city; or less than if this frame
Of heaven were falling, and these elements
In mutiny had from her axle torn
The steadfast earth. At last his sail-broad vans°
He spreads for flight, and in the surging smoke
Uplifted spurns the ground; thence many a league

redounding overflowing
Hot . . . Dry the four elements (see Glossary) or, rather, the four primary qualities of which the elements are assembled. In the realm of Chaos there are none of the basic conceptual qualities of time, space, individuation, by which we make sense out of phenomena.
Barca or Cyrene's cities of Cyrenaica, west of Egypt
Levied lifted
poise weigh down
frith firth, estuary
pealed assailed with noise
Bellona Roman goddess of war
vans wings

As in a cloudy chair ascending rides
Audacious, but that seat soon failing, meets
A vast vacuity: all unawares
Fluttering his pennons° vain plumb down he drops
Ten thousand fadom° deep, and to this hour
Down had been falling, had not by ill chance
The strong rebuff of some tumultuous cloud
Instinct° with fire and nitre hurried him
As many miles aloft. That fury stayed,
Quenched in a boggy Syrtis,° neither sea,
Nor good dry land, nigh foundered on he fares,
Treading the crude consistence, half on foot,
Half flying; behoves him now both oar and sail.
As when a gryphon through the wilderness
With wingèd course o'er hill or moory° dale,
Pursues the Arimaspian,° who by stealth
Had from his wakeful custody purloined
The guarded gold: so eagerly the fiend
O'er bog or steep, through strait, rough, dense, or rare,
With head, hands, wings, or feet pursues his way,
And swims or sinks, or wades, or creeps, or flies.°
At length a universal hubbub wild
Of stunning sounds and voices all confused,
Borne through the hollow dark, assaults his ear
With loudest vehemence; thither he plies,
Undaunted to meet there whatever power
Or spirit of the nethermost abyss
Might in that noise reside, of whom to ask
Which way the nearest coast of darkness lies
Bordering on light; when straight behold the throne
Of Chaos, and his dark pavilion spread
Wide on the wasteful° deep; with him enthroned
Sat sable-vested Night, eldest of things,
The consort of his reign; and by them stood
Orcus and Ades,° and the dreaded name
Of Demogorgon;° Rumor next and Chance,
And Tumult and Confusion all embroiled,
And Discord with a thousand various mouths.
To whom Satan turning boldly, thus: 'Ye powers
And spirits of this nethermost abyss,
Chaos and ancient Night, I come no spy,
With purpose to explore or to disturb
The secrets of your realm, but by constraint

pennons wings
fadom fathoms
instinct impelled
Syrtis gulf off Tripoli noted for its quicksand shores
moory swampy
Arimaspian one of a tribe of one-eyed people who, in classical folklore, steal gold from the griffins who guard it
O'er bog . . . or flies (ll.948–50) The imitative effect of this profusion of monosyllables points up the confusion of Satan's journey through Chaos.
wasteful desolate
Orcus and Ades Orcus = Roman for the Greek Pluto or Hades; Ades = Hades
Demogorgon in Renaissance tradition, progenitor of all the gods of darkness

Wandering this darksome desert, as my way
Lies through your spacious empire up to light,
Alone, and without guide, half lost, I seek
What readiest path leads where your gloomy bounds
Confine with° heaven; or if some other place
From your dominion won, the ethereal King
Possesses lately, thither to arrive
I travel this profound; direct my course;
Directed, no means recompense it brings
To your behoof, if I that region lost,
All usurpation thence expelled, reduce
To her original darkness and your sway
(Which is my present journey), and once more
Erect the standard there of ancient Night;
Yours be the advantage all, mine the revenge.'
  Thus Satan; and him thus the Anarch° old
With faltering speech and visage incomposed°
Answered: 'I know thee, stranger, who thou art,
That mighty leading angel, who of late
Made head against heaven's King, though overthrown.
I saw and heard, for such a numerous host
Fled not in silence through the frighted deep
With ruin upon ruin, rout on rout,
Confusion worse confounded; and heaven gates
Poured out by millions her victorious bands
Pursuing, I upon my frontiers here
Keep residence; if all I can will serve
That little which is left so to defend,
Encroached on still through our° intestine broils
Weakening the scepter of old Night: first hell
Your dungeon stretching far and wide beneath;
Now lately heaven and earth, another world
Hung o'er my realm, linked in a golden chain°
To that side heaven from whence your legions fell.
If that way be your walk, you have not far;
So much the nearer danger;° go and speed;
Havoc and spoil and ruin are my gain.'
  He ceased; and Satan stayed not to reply,
But glad that now his sea should find a shore,
With fresh alacrity and force renewed
Springs upward like a pyramid of fire
Into the wild expanse, and through the shock
Of fighting elements, on all sides round
Environed, wins his way; harder beset

Confine with border on
Anarch Chaos, monarch of an anarchic realm
incomposed discomposed
our Perhaps this should be amended to "your."
golden chain a powerful and traditional symbol of order and necessity in the universe, first appearing in Homer's *Iliad* VIII.18–27, where Zeus' chain is envisioned as connecting earth and sea with Olympus. Milton himself treats this elsewhere as an image of harmony; see also Spenser, *The Faerie Queene* II.vii.46, and l. 1051, below.
danger harm

And more endangered than when Argo° passed
Through Bosporus betwixt the justling rocks,
Or when Ulysses on the larboard shunned
Charybdis, and by the other whirlpool steered.
So he with difficulty and labour hard
Moved on, with difficulty and labour he;
But he once passed, soon after when man fell,
Strange alteration! Sin and Death amain°
Following his track, such was the will of heaven,
Paved after him a broad and beaten way
Over the dark abyss, whose boiling gulf
Tamely endured a bridge of wondrous length
From hell continued reaching the utmost orb
Of this frail world; by which the Spirits perverse
With easy intercourse pass to and fro
To tempt or punish mortals, except whom
God and good angels guard by special grace.
  But now at last the sacred influence
Of light appears, and from the walls of heaven
Shoots far into the bosom of dim Night
A glimmering dawn; here nature° first begins
Her farthest verge, and Chaos to retire
As from her outmost works a broken foe,
With tumult less and with less hostile din,
That Satan with less toil and now with ease
Wafts on the calmer wave by dubious light,
And like a weather-beaten vessel holds°
Gladly the port, though shrouds and tackle torn;
Or in the emptier waste, resembling air,
Weighs his spread wings, at leisure to behold
Far off the empyreal heaven, extended wide
In circuit, undetermined square or round,
With opal towers and battlements adorned
Of living° sapphire, once his native seat;
And fast by hanging in a golden chain
This pendant world,° in bigness as a star
Of smallest magnitude close by the moon.
Thither full fraught° with mischievous revenge,
Accurst, and in a cursèd hour, he hies.

From *Book III*

[The Muse is again invoked, here as light itself, which resulted from the first act of creation (Genesis 1:3) but which also, in another aspect, coexisted with its creator from the beginning. The original of all creative acts for Milton is the lighting up of darkness—transforming a chaotic world by ex-

Argo the ship of Jason and the Argonauts on their quest for the Golden Fleece
amain immediately
nature the created universe, as opposed to the dark chaos surrounding it
holds head for
living uncut
pendant world not the earth but the whole universe, hanging inside the larger space of pre-creation
fraught freighted

plaining it—and the physical reduction of general created light into the sun and moon was the shaping of an attribute of this power. The present exordium is a lyric spell spun to help the poet move from his description of hell, where all the energies of heroic, epical poetry aided him, to scenes in heaven, whose static and doctrinal character would pose a different sort of challenge.]

Hail, holy Light, offspring of heaven first-born,
Or of the eternal coeternal beam
May I express thee unblamed? since God is light,
And never but in unapproachèd light
Dwelt from eternity, dwelt then in thee,
Bright effluence of bright essence increate.
Or hearest thou rather° pure ethereal stream,°
Whose fountain who shall tell? Before the sun,
Before the heavens thou wert, and at the voice
Of God, as with a mantle didst invest
The rising world of waters dark and deep,
Won from the void and formless infinite.
Thee I revisit now with bolder wing,
Escaped the Stygian pool,° though long detained
In that obscure sojourn, while in my flight
Through utter° and through middle darkness° borne
With other notes° than to the Orphéan lyre
I sung of Chaos and eternal Night,
Taught by the heavenly Muse to venture down
The dark descent, and up to reascend,
Though hard and rare. Thee I revisit safe,
And feel thy sovereign vital lamp; but thou
Revisit'st not these eyes, that roll in vain
To find thy piercing ray, and find no dawn;
So thick a drop serene° hath quenched their orbs,
Or dim suffusion° veiled. Yet not the more
Cease I to wander where the Muses haunt
Clear spring, or shady grove, or sunny hill,
Smit with the love of sacred song; but chief
Thee, Sion,° and the flowery brooks beneath
That wash thy hallowed feet, and warbling flow,
Nightly I visit;° nor sometimes forget
Those other two equalled with me in fate,
So were I° equalled with them in renown,

hearest thou rather would you rather be called?
stream like poetry in classical myth, an outbreak of expression
Stygian pool hell, the lower darkness
utter outer
middle darkness Chaos
other notes because he (his poetry) would not merely make an Orphean visit to the underworld, nor would his Muse be lost to him there
drop serene translates the Latin medical term for his blindness, *gutta serena.*
suffusion cataract
Sion Hebrew poetry, rather than Helicon, or Greek
Nightly I visit This theme of composing at night, literally and figuratively, is taken up again at VII. 29.
So were I would that I were

Blind Thamyris and blind Maeonides,°
And Tiresias and Phineus° prophets old:
Then feed on thoughts that voluntary move
Harmonious numbers,° as the wakeful bird
Sings darkling,° and in shadiest covert hid
Tunes her nocturnal note. Thus with the year
Seasons return; but not to me returns
Day, or the sweet approach of even or morn,
Or sight of vernal bloom, or summer's rose,
Or flocks, or herds, or human face divine;°
But cloud instead, and ever-during dark
Surrounds me, from the cheerful ways of men
Cut off, and for the book of knowledge° fair
Presented with a universal blank°
Of Nature's works to me expunged and razed,
And wisdom at one entrance° quite shut out.
So much the rather thou, celestial Light,
Shine inward, and the mind through all her powers
Irradiate, there plant eyes, all mist from thence
Purge and disperse, that I may see and tell
Of things invisible to mortal sight. . . .

[The world of Book III is unveiled with God enthroned in heaven, where all the angels "stood thick as stars"; at his right hand is his Son, to whom he points out the tiny image of distant Satan, about to alight, insect-like (as he appears from heaven), on the outside of the world. Telling the Son of the Satanic plan, God points out that Man will nevertheless be responsible for the foreknown, but not foreordained Fall ("he had of me / All he could have: I made him just and right, / Sufficient to have stood, though free to fall"). When the Father insists that justice must be done, the Son offers himself as a sacrifice for human eternal life: "Behold me then, me for him, life for life / I offer, on me let thine anger fall: / Account me man." God accepts, describing the incarnation and passion, ordains "Be thou in Adam's room / The head of all mankind, though Adam's son. / As in him perish all men, so in thee / As from a second root shall be restored." An angelic choir celebrates this ordination. The action then cuts to Satan, alighting now vulture-like upon the world, passing through a Limbo of Vanity where, blown by winds, types of folly abound. He moves into the orb of the sun (descending, as he must, from the outermost sphere of the Ptolemaic structure down toward the central earth),

Thamyris . . . Maeonides a mythical Thracian bard, blinded for his presumption, and Homer (from Maeonia)
Tiresias . . . Phineus Tiresias was the blind seer of antiquity, Phineus a blinded Thracian king who prophesied.
Harmonious numbers beautiful lines of verse
darkling in the dark. This bird is the nightingale, with whom is associated mute suffering transformed into poetic song.
human face divine The word order makes the adjectives play different roles, defining and attributing, and in reading the phrase we progress from low to high; Blake used this compound as a model for a crucial phrase of his own: "human form divine."
book of knowledge Nature, which, for the hieroglyphic-minded, was a book to be read and understood (see *Emblem* in the Glossary)
blank a blank page, a whiteness
one entrance too fragile a one: see Samson's staggering eloquence on this matter in *Samson Agonistes* ll. 90–96

encounters Uriel, "God's light," the guardian of that region, disguises himself and is able by fraud to discover the whereabouts of Eden, and alights on Mount Niphates.]

Book IV

O for that warning voice, which he who saw
The Apocalypse° heard cry in heaven aloud,
Then when the dragon, put to second rout,
Came furious down to be revenged on men,
'Woe to the inhabitants on earth!' that now,
While time was, our first parents had been warned
The coming of their secret foe, and scaped,
Haply so scaped, his mortal snare; for now
Satan, now first inflamed with rage, came down,
The tempter ere the accuser of mankind,
To wreak° on innocent frail man his loss
Of that first battle, and his flight to hell:
Yet not rejoicing in his speed, though bold,
Far off and fearless, nor with cause to boast,
Begins his dire attempt, which nigh the birth
Now rolling, boils in his tumultuous breast,
And like a devilish engine° back recoils
Upon himself; horror and doubt distract
His troubled thoughts, and from the bottom stir
The hell within him, for within him hell
He brings, and round about him, nor from hell°
One step no more than from himself can fly
By change of place. Now conscience wakes despair
That slumbered, wakes the bitter memory
Of what he was, what is, and what must be
Worse; of worse deeds worse sufferings must ensue.
Sometimes towards Eden which now in his view
Lay pleasant,° his grieved look he fixes sad,
Sometimes towards heaven and the full-blazing sun,
Which now sat high in his meridian tower.°
Then much revolving, thus in sighs began:
'O thou° that with surpassing glory crowned
Look'st from thy sole dominion like the god

he . . . Apocalypse St. John, warning in Revelation 12:7–12 of another battle in heaven between "the dragon" and Michael; would that he could so prophetically warn, Milton pleads.
wreak avenge
devilish engine artillery, invented by Satan's forces in the war; also, "engine" (in a sense related to "ingenious") as a plan or scheme, for which the word "recoils" is metaphoric, suggesting the re-coiling or twisting of snaky thought, of dialectic; cf. II.65
The hell within . . . hell This beautifully arranged line with its chiasmus (see II.39–40n) mocks by its static order the churning of Satan's inner state, an ironic fulfillment of his statement in I.254–55 about the mind's being "its own place"; cf. *Doctor Faustus* V.120–21.
pleasant In Hebrew, Eden means "delight."
meridian tower It is noon, and the Fall will occur at noon with light at its height and despite guarding enlightenment.
O thou the sun. According to Milton's nephew Edward Phillips in his *Life of Milton*, these lines were originally composed as the opening lines of the tragedy about the Fall that *Paradise Lost* was once to have been.

Of this new world; at whose sight all the stars
Hide their diminished heads; to thee I call,
But with no friendly voice, and add thy name,
O sun, to tell thee how I hate thy beams
That bring to my remembrance from what state
I fell, how glorious once above thy sphere;
Till pride and worse ambition threw me down
Warring in heaven against heaven's matchless king.
Ah wherefore? He deserved no such return
From me, whom he created what I was°
In that bright eminence,° and with his good
Upbraided none; nor was his service hard.
What could be less than to afford him praise,
The easiest recompense, and pay him thanks,
How due! Yet all his good proved ill in me,
And wrought but malice; lifted up so high
I sdained° subjection, and thought one step higher
Would set me highest, and in a moment quit°
The debt immense of endless gratitude,
So burdensome still paying, still° to owe;
Forgetful what from him I still received,
And understood not that a grateful mind
By owing owes not, but still pays, at once
Indebted and discharged; what burden then?
O had his powerful destiny ordained
Me some inferior angel, I had stood
Then happy; no unbounded hope had raised
Ambition. Yet why not? Some other power
As great might have aspired, and me though mean
Drawn to his part; but other powers as great
Fell not, but stand unshaken, from within
Or from without, to all temptations armed.
Hadst thou the same free will and power to stand?
Thou hadst. Whom hast thou then or what to accuse,
But heaven's free love dealt equally to all?
Be then his love accurst, since love or hate,
To me alike, it deals eternal woe.
Nay cursed be thou, since against his thy will
Chose freely what it now so justly rues.
Me miserable! which way shall I fly
Infinite wrath, and infinite despair?
Which way I fly is hell; myself am hell;°

whom he . . . was Satan admits this here, but denies it in his public, political oratory elsewhere.
that bright eminence Notice the echo of the reciprocal epithet in the narrator's lines in II.6.
sdained disdained
quit pay off
still continually
Which way . . . hell echoing IV.20, and Marlowe's *Doctor Faustus* III.76: "Why, this is hell, nor am I out of it" and, later on, V.120–121: "Hell hath no limits, nor is circumscribed / In one self place, but where we are is hell"; cf. also I.225 and IX.122–23

And in the lowest deep a lower deep
Still threatening to devour me opens wide,
To which the hell I suffer seems a heaven.°
O then at last relent: is there no place
Left for repentance, none for pardon left?
None left but by submission; and that word
Disdain forbids me, and my dread of shame
Among the spirits beneath, whom I seduced
With other promises and other vaunts
Than to submit, boasting I could subdue
The omnipotent.° Ay me, they little know
How dearly I abide that boast so vain,
Under what torments inwardly I groan;
While they adore me on the throne of hell,
With diadem and sceptre high advanced,
The lower still I fall, only supreme
In misery; such joy ambition finds.
But say I could repent and could obtain
By act of grace° my former state; how soon
Would highth recall high thoughts, how soon unsay
What feigned submission swore: ease would recant
Vows made in pain, as violent and void.
For never can true reconcilement grow
Where sounds of deadly hate have pierced so deep;
Which would but lead me to a worse relapse
And heavier fall: so should I purchase dear
Short intermission bought with double smart.
This knows my punisher; therefore as far
From granting he, as I from begging peace.
All hope excluded thus, behold instead
Of us outcast, exiled, his new delight,
Mankind created, and for him this world.
So farewell hope, and with hope farewell fear,
Farewell remorse! All good to me is lost;
Evil, be thou my good;° by thee at least
Divided empire with heaven's king I hold
By thee, and more than half perhaps will govern;
As man ere long, and this new world shall know.'
Thus while he spake, each passion dimmed his face
Thrice changed with° pale, ire, envy, and despair,
Which marred his borrowed visage,° and betrayed
Him counterfeit, if any eye beheld.

the hell . . . heaven Local and general, concrete and abstract, literal ad figurative uses of words have become all mixed up in Satan's tangled thought.
None left . . . omnipotent (ll. 81–86) Cf. ll. 388–92 below.
act of grace formal pardon, not an admission of right

Evil . . . good Again, the dramatic irony here is crushing: at IX.121–23 he realizes, almost with disgust, that his command has been obeyed; cf. I.165.
changed with changed to
borrowed visage explained in III.636 to be that of a "stripling cherub"

For heavenly minds from such distempers foul
Are ever clear. Whereof he soon aware,
Each perturbation smoothed with outward calm,
Artificer of fraud; and was the first
That practised falsehood under saintly show,
Deep malice to conceal, couched with revenge:
Yet not enough had practised to deceive
Uriel° once warned, whose eye pursued him down
The way he went, and on the Assyrian mount°
Saw him disfigured, more than could befall
Spirit of happy sort: his gestures fierce
He marked and mad demeanour, then alone,
As he supposed, all unobserved, unseen.
So on he fares, and to the border comes
Of Eden, where delicious Paradise,
Now nearer, crowns with her enclosure green
As with a rural mound the champaign head°
Of a steep wilderness, whose hairy sides
With thicket overgrown, grotesque° and wild,
Access denied; and overhead up grew
Insuperable highth of loftiest shade,
Cedar, and pine, and fir, and branching palm,
A sylvan scene, and as the ranks ascend
Shade above shade, a woody theatre
Of stateliest view. Yet higher than their tops
The verdurous wall of Paradise up sprung;
Which to our general sire° gave prospect large°
Into his nether empire neighbouring round.
And higher than that wall a circling row
Of goodliest trees loaden with fairest fruit,
Blossoms and fruits at once° of golden hue,
Appeared, with gay enamelled colours mixed;
On which the sun more glad impressed his beams
Than in fair evening cloud, or humid bow,
When God hath showered the earth; so lovely seemed
That landscape. And of pure now purer air
Meets his approach, and to the heart inspires
Vernal delight and joy, able to drive
All sadness but despair; now gentle gales
Fanning their odoriferous wings dispense

Uriel In III.623 ff. this archangel is deceived by Satan's disguise.
Assyrian mount Mount Niphates, on which this soliloquy occurs, and which Milton makes the scene of Christ's temptation in *Paradise Regained*
champaign head a treeless plateau. The imagery of the human body persists in the following lines.
grotesque grotto-like
general sire Adam
large broad

Blossoms and fruits at once This description assembles images of pastoral perfection from such myths as the Hesperides (cf. *Comus* ll. 980–81), the Elysian fields, the Golden Age, and Spenser's Garden of Adonis (*The Faerie Queene* III.vi); in Eden, the spring of beauty and promise, the fall of ripeness and fulfillment, coexist with no intervening extreme seasons, which will come into being with the Fall, and the origin of biological "nature."

Native perfumes, and whisper whence they stole
Those balmy spoils. As when to them who sail
Beyond the Cape of Hope,° and now are past
Mozambic,° off at sea north-east winds blow
Sabaean° odours from the spicy shore
Of Araby the Blest, with such delay
Well pleased they slack their course, and many a league
Cheered with the grateful smell old ocean smiles;
So entertained those odorous sweets the fiend
Who came their bane, though with them better pleased
Than Asmodëus° with the fishy fume,
That drove him, though enamoured, from the spouse
Of Tobit's son, and with a vengeance sent
From Media post to Egypt, there fast bound.
   Now to the ascent of that steep savage° hill
Satan had journeyed on, pensive and slow;
But further way found none, so thick entwined,
As one continued brake, the undergrowth
Of shrubs and tangling bushes had perplexed
All path of man or beast that passed that way.
One gate there only was, and that looked east
On the other side; which when the arch-felon saw,
Due entrance he disdained, and in contempt
At one slight bound high overleaped all bound
Of hill or highest wall, and sheer within
Lights on his feet. As when a prowling wolf,
Whom hunger drives to seek new haunt for prey,
Watching where shepherds pen their flocks at eve
In hurdled cotes° amid the field secure,
Leaps o'er the fence with ease into the fold;
Or as a thief bent to unhoard the cash
Of some rich burgher, whose substantial doors,
Cross-barred and bolted fast, fear no assault,
In at the window climbs, or o'er the tiles:
So clomb° this first grand thief into God's fold;
So since into his church lewd° hirelings climb.
Thence up he flew, and on the Tree of Life,
The middle tree and highest there that grew,
Sat like a cormorant;° yet not true life
Thereby regained, but sat devising death°
To them who lived; nor on the virtue thought

Hope Good Hope
Mozambic Mozambique
Sabaean Sheban, from modern Yemen
Asmodëus a nasty demon, driven off by Tobias, Tobit's son, on Raphael's advice, by means of a stink-bomb (Tobit 7:6)
savage wooded
hurdled cotes crowded folds
clomb climbed
lewd ignorant and uneducated, as well as vile. Milton is attacking, in the same ecclesiastical pastoral imagery as in *Lycidas*, "hirelings," or salaried clergy.
cormorant literally "sea-crow"; emblem of greed
death both "death in general" and, reading on across the enjambment, the deaths of Adam and Eve

Of that life-giving plant, but only used
For prospect, what well used had been the pledge
Of immortality. So little knows
Any, but God alone, to value right
The good before him, but perverts best things
To worst abuse, or to their meanest use.
  Beneath him with new wonder now he views
To all delight of human sense exposed
In narrow room Nature's whole wealth,° yea more,
A heaven on earth, for blissful Paradise
Of God the garden was, by him in the east
Of Eden planted; Eden stretched her line
From Auran° eastward to the royal towers
Of great Seleucia,° built by Grecian kings,
Or where the sons of Eden long before
Dwelt in Telassar.° In this pleasant soil
His far more pleasant garden God ordained;
Out of the fertile ground he caused to grow
All trees of noblest kind for sight, smell, taste;
And all amid them stood the Tree of Life,
High eminent, blooming ambrosial fruit
Of vegetable gold,° and next to life
Our death,° the Tree of Knowledge, grew fast by,
Knowledge of good bought dear by knowing ill.°
Southward through Eden went a river large,
Nor changed his course, but through the shaggy hill
Passed underneath engulfed, for God had thrown
That mountain as his garden mould, high raised
Upon the rapid current, which through veins
Of porous earth with kindly thirst up drawn,
Rose a fresh fountain, and with many a rill
Watered the garden; thence united fell
Down the steep glade, and met the nether flood,
Which from his darksome passage now appears,
And now divided into four main streams
Runs diverse, wandering° many a famous realm
And country whereof here needs no account;
But rather to tell how, if art could tell,
How from that sapphire fount the crispèd brooks,
Rolling on orient pearl and sands of gold,

Nature's whole wealth all the fruitfulness that was ever to be was there (see *The Faerie Queene* III.vi.30)
Auran a town in northwestern Mesopotamia; see Genesis 11:31
Seleucia built as a capital city by Alexander the Great's viceroy for Syria, Seleucus
Telassar a city in Mesopotamia, mentioned in II Kings 19:12 as a land ruined by war
vegetable gold the figurative "gold" of grain and natural fruitfulness; also in the sense of "vegetative" (cf. I.685–87)
life . . . death perhaps the most startling enjambment in the poem. Reading along, we expect something like "*and next to life / the brightest gift* . . . etc., and then realize, with a shock, that the juxtaposition of the two Trees in Paradise, reinforced by "Our," means a good deal more.
Knowledge . . . ill Cf. *Areopagitica,* note 28.
wandering wandering through

With mazy error° under pendant shades
Ran nectar, visiting each plant, and fed
Flowers worthy of Paradise, which not nice art
In beds and curious knots,° but Nature boon°
Poured forth profuse on hill and dale and plain,
Both where the morning sun first warmly smote
The open field, and where the unpierced shade
Embrowned° the noontide bowers. Thus was this place,
A happy rural seat of various view;
Groves whose rich trees wept odorous gums and balm,
Others whose fruit burnished with golden rind
Hung amiable, Hesperian fables true,°
If true, here only, and of delicious taste.
Betwixt them lawns, or level downs, and flocks
Grazing the tender herb, were interposed,
Or palmy hillock, or the flowery lap
Of some irriguous° valley spread her store,
Flowers of all hue, and without thorn the rose.°
Another side, umbrageous° grots and caves
Of cool recess, o'er which the mantling vine
Lays forth her purple grape, and gently creeps
Luxuriant; meanwhile murmuring waters fall
Down the slope hills, dispersed, or in a lake,
That to the fringèd bank with myrtle° crowned
Her crystal mirror holds, unite their streams.
The birds their quire apply; airs, vernal airs,°
Breathing the smell of field and grove, attune
The trembling leaves, while universal Pan,°
Knit with the Graces and the Hours in dance,
Led on the eternal spring. Not that fair field
Of Enna, where Prosérpine° gathering flowers,
Herself a fairer flower by gloomy Dis
Was gathered, which cost Ceres all that pain

mazy error "Error" in Latin means "wandering," with no negative moral sense; this is an unfallen usage (see Headnote) as well as the first instance of unfallen, beautiful twisting, turning, and curling imagery, later to be corrupted.
curious knots labyrinthine patterns in which flowerbeds were frequently laid out; is Milton remembering the beneficent "curious knots" of Pleasure and Virtue in Jonson's masque? See *Pleasure Reconciled to Virtue.*
boon bountiful
Embrowned darkened
Hesperian fables true as if the golden apples of the Hesperides were a fiction mistakenly based on the truth of Paradise's "vegetable gold"
irriguous irrigated
the rose a traditional interpretation; in Genesis 3:18 part of Adam's curse involves the origins of thorns and thistles
umbrageous shadowy
myrtly sacred to Venus. The mirror is also her emblem, and they both partake of the unfallen, pre-erotic sensual joy of this bower.
airs songs, melodies. Notice the whole musical sequence of waters, birds, and leaves; cf. its perverted version in Spenser's *Bower of Bliss,* an artfully faked Eden (*The Faerie Queene* II. xii).
Pan In Greek, his name means "all, everything"; the classical figures here are metaphorical for the forces of unfallen nature.
Prosérpine Persephone (Proserpine), daughter of Demeter (Ceres), the harvest goddess, carried to the underworld by Dis (Pluto) to be his queen. Ceres sought her throughout the world, which in sympathy became barren. When she was finally restored, it was only for half the year (hence, spring and summer), because while Queen of the Underworld, she had eaten seven pomegranate seeds. Renaissance mythographers seized on the obvious parallels to Eve, who, in Bk. IX, will be "gathered" by Satan while "gathering flowers."

To seek her through the world; nor that sweet grove
Of Daphne° by Orontes, and the inspired
Castalian spring, might with this Paradise
Of Eden strive; nor that Nyseian isle°
Girt with the river Triton, where old Cham,
Whom Gentiles Ammon call and Libyan Jove,
Hid Amalthea and her florid son
Young Bacchus from his stepdame Rhea's eye;
Nor where Abassin kings their issue guard,
Mount Amara,° though this by some supposed
True Paradise, under the Ethiop line°
By Nilus' head, enclosed with shining rock,
A whole day's journey high, but wide remote
From this Assyrian garden, where the fiend
Saw undelighted all delight, all kind
Of living creatures new to sight and strange.
  Two of far nobler shape erect and tall,
God-like erect, with native honour° clad
In naked majesty seemed lords of all,
And worthy seemed, for in their looks divine
The image of their glorious maker shone,
Truth, wisdom, sanctitude severe and pure,
Severe but in true filial freedom placed;
Whence true authority in men; though both
Not equal, as their sex not equal seemed;
For contemplation he and valour formed,
For softness she and sweet attractive grace;
He for God only, she for God in him.
His fair large front° and eye sublime° declared
Absolute rule; and hyacinthine locks°
Round from his parted forelock manly hung
Clustering, but not beneath his shoulders broad:
She as a veil down to the slender waist
Her unadornèd golden tresses wore
Dishevelled, but in wanton° ringlets waved
As the vine curls her tendrils, which implied
Subjection, but required with gentle sway,°

Daphne a grove near the river Orontes, famous for its oracle

Nyseian isle Nysa in Tunisia, where Ammon (Jupiter) hid the infant Dionysus (Bacchus) from his wife, Rhea (Ops)

Amara where Abyssinian princes were brought up

Ethiop line the equator

native honour The natural dignity of being complete in their skin; the very concepts "nakedness" and "nudity" would be as meaningless if applied to them here as to a lion or a human fetus; see l. 314. Milton suggests that the "honour" as used in fallen human society, whether of women or of "gentlemen," is as inferior to this original honor as fallen is to "original Justice." Fallen "honour," the "honour dishonourable" against which Milton rages in l.314, is a show, or mask of virtue, more like "reputation."

front forehead

sublime upward-looking

hyacinthine locks probably not referring to color, but to curliness, and invoking the doomed beauty of Hyacinth, Apollo's beloved. The curling hair in this passage is an emblem of luxuriant sensuality and uncorrupted complexity (like the "curious knots," l. 242), as well as "Subjection."

wanton unrestrained

sway influence

And by her yielded, by him best received,
Yielded with coy° submission, modest pride,
And sweet reluctant amorous delay.
Nor those mysterious parts were then concealed;
Then was not guilty shame; dishonest shame
Of Nature's works, honour dishonourable,°
Sin-bred, how have ye troubled all mankind
With shows instead, mere shows of seeming pure,
And banished from man's life his happiest life,
Simplicity and spotless innocence!
So passed they naked on, nor shunned the sight
Of God or angel, for they thought no ill;
So hand in hand° they passed, the loveliest pair
That ever since in love's embraces met,
Adam the goodliest man of men since born
His sons, the fairest of her daughters Eve.
Under a tuft of shade that on a green
Stood whispering soft, by a fresh fountain side
They sat them down; and after no more toil
Of their sweet gardening labour than sufficed
To recommend cool Zephyr, and made ease
More easy,° wholesome thirst and appetite
More grateful, to their supper fruits they fell,
Nectarine fruits which the compliant boughs
Yielded them, sidelong as they sat recline°
On the soft downy bank damasked° with flowers.
The savoury pulp they chew, and in the rind
Still as they thirsted scoop the brimming stream;
Nor gentle purpose,° nor endearing smiles
Wanted,° nor youthful dalliance, as beseems
Fair couple linked in happy nuptial league,
Alone as they. About them frisking played
All beasts of the earth, since wild, and of all chase°
In wood or wilderness, forest or den;
Sporting the lion ramped, and in his paw
Dandled the kid; bears, tigers, ounces, pards,°
Gambolled before them; the unwieldy elephant
To make them mirth used all his might, and wreathed
His lithe proboscis; close° the serpent sly

coy reticent
honour dishonourable In this context, even the thought of sexual shame, of guilt about bodies, of covering up genitalia, disgusts Milton, and his meditation gives way to indignation.
hand in hand Clasped hands appear in emblem books in pictures of Faith, Concord, and Married Love; but see also *Paradise Lost* XII.648, and intervening glimpses of the pair at 488, 689, and 739 of Bk. IV, VIII.510, IX.385 and 1037.
easy comfortable
recline recumbent
damasked patterned
gentle purpose polite discourse
Wanted were lacking
of all chase of every habitat, part of "Nature's whole wealth" (l. 207)
ounces, pards lynxes, leopards
close Close by (in the garden and in the line of verse) the serpent's "curious knot" of motion, uninfected yet by Satan's possession of it, is a sort of emblem requiring prophecy, or a fallen reader, correctly to understand (thus, "proof unheeded").

Insinuating,° wove with Gordian twine
His braided train, and of his fatal guile
Gave proof unheeded; others on the grass
Couched, and now filled with pasture gazing sat,
Or bedward ruminating; for the sun
Declined was hasting now with prone career
To the ocean isles,° and in the ascending scale°
Of heaven the stars that usher evening rose:
When Satan still in gaze, as first he stood,
Scarce thus at length failed speech recovered sad:
'O hell! what do mine eyes with grief behold!
Into our room° of bliss thus high advanced
Creatures of other mould, earth-born perhaps,
Not spirits, yet to heavenly spirits bright
Little inferior; whom my thoughts pursue
With wonder, and could love, so lively shines
In them divine resemblance, and such grace
The hand that formed them on their shape hath poured.
Ah gentle pair, ye little think how nigh
Your change approaches, when all these delights
Will vanish and deliver ye to woe,
More woe, the more your taste is now of joy;
Happy, but for so happy ill secured
Long to continue, and this high seat your heaven
Ill fenced, for heaven, to keep out such a foe
As now is entered; yet no purposed foe
To you whom I could pity thus forlorn,
Though I unpitied. League with you I seek,
And mutual amity so strait,° so close,
That I with you must dwell, or you with me
Henceforth; my dwelling haply may not please,
Like this fair Paradise, your sense, yet such
Accept your maker's work; he gave it me,
Which I as freely give;° hell shall unfold,°
To entertain you two, her widest gates,
And send forth all her kings; there will be room,
Not like these narrow limits, to receive
Your numerous offspring; if no better place,
Thank him who puts me loth to this revenge
On you who wrong me not, for him who wronged.
And should I at your harmless innocence
Melt, as I do, yet public reason just,
Honour and empire with revenge enlarged

Insinuating winding
ocean isles the Azores; see l. 592
scale both Libra, now rising, and the heavens' balance of light and darkness in the then eternal equinox
room region, space
strait intimate
freely give not only half-sarcastic, but echoing Matthew 10:8
hell shall unfold At Isaiah 14:9 the destruction of Babylon is envisaged in these terms, but Satan is offering Adam and Eve part of his kingdom, as Dis had given Proserpine his.

By conquering this new world, compels me now
To do what else though damned I should abhor.'
  So spake the fiend, and with necessity—
The tyrant's plea—excused his devilish deeds.
Then from his lofty stand on that high tree
Down he alights among the sportful herd
Of those four-footed kinds, himself now one,
Now other, as their shape served best his end
Nearer to view his prey, and unespied
To mark what of their state he more might learn
By word or action marked. About them round
A lion now he stalks with fiery glare;
Then as a tiger, who by chance hath spied
In some purlieu° two gentle fawns at play,
Straight° couches close, then rising, changes oft
His couchant watch, as one who chose his ground
Whence rushing he might surest seize them both
Gripped in each paw; when Adam first of men
To first of women Eve thus moving speech,
Turned him° all ear to hear new utterance flow—
  'Sole partner and sole part° of all these joys,
Dearer thyself than all, needs must the power
That made us, and for us this ample world,
Be infinitely good, and of his good
As liberal and free as infinite,
That raised us from the dust and placed us here
In all this happiness, who at his hand
Have nothing merited, nor can perform
Aught whereof he hath need; he who requires
From us no other service than to keep
This one, this easy charge, of all the trees
In Paradise that bear delicious fruit
So various, not to taste° that only Tree
Of Knowledge, planted by the Tree of Life,
So near grows death to life,° whate'er death is,
Some dreadful thing no doubt; for well thou knowest
God hath pronounced it death to taste that Tree,
The only sign of our obedience left
Among so many signs of power and rule
Conferred upon us,° and dominion given
Over all other creatures that possess
Earth, air, and sea. Then let us not think hard
One easy prohibition, who enjoy
Free leave so large to all things else, and choice

purlieu borders of a forest
Straight immediately; also, "tightly" (punning on "strait")
him Satan
Sole partner and sole part only partner and principal part
not to taste the commandment at Genesis 2:16–17
death to life See ll. 220–21.
Conferred upon us at Genesis 1:28

Unlimited of manifold delights;
But let us ever praise him, and extol
His bounty, following our delightful task
To prune these growing plants, and tend these flowers,
Which were it toilsome, yet with thee were sweet.'
To whom thus Eve replied, 'O thou for whom
And from whom I was formed flesh of thy flesh,
And without whom am to no end, my guide
And head,° what thou hast said is just and right.
For we to him indeed all praises owe,
And daily thanks, I chiefly who enjoy
So far the happier lot, enjoying thee
Pre-eminent by so much odds,° while thou
Like consort to thyself canst nowhere find.
That day I oft remember, when from sleep
I first awaked, and found myself reposed
Under a shade of flowers, much wondering where
And what I was, whence thither brought, and how.
Not distant far from thence a murmuring sound
Of waters issued from a cave and spread
Into a liquid plain,° then stood unmoved
Pure as the expanse of heaven; I thither went
With unexperienced thought, and laid me down
On the green bank, to look into the clear
Smooth lake, that to me seemed another sky.°
As I bent down to look, just opposite
A shape within the watery gleam appeared
Bending to look on me: I started back,
It started back, but pleased I soon returned,
Pleased it returned as soon with answering looks
Of sympathy and love; there I had fixed
Mine eyes till now, and pined with vain desire,
Had not a voice thus warned me:° "*What thou seest,*
What there thou seest, fair creature, is thyself,
With thee it came and goes; but follow me,
And I will bring thee where no shadow stays°
Thy coming, and thy soft embraces, he
Whose image thou art, him thou shalt enjoy
Inseparably thine; to him shalt bear

head echoing I Corinthians 11:3: "The head of every man is Christ; and the head of the woman is the man . . . ," but also combining the two in a kind of single human body, an image suggested for the garden itself, ll. 134 ff.
by so much odds by so much
liquid plain The first mirror forms when "murmuring" water stops and reflects.
another sky There is only the subtlest hint here ("another sky": "another heaven") of the idolatry implict in the use of mirrors; in the fallen world, mirrors are emblems of Venus and of the other nude figure, personified Vanitas, "vanity."
warned me Narcissus, Eve's prototype here who fell in love with his own image (like Eve, not knowing it was himself), died when he discovered the truth—the only warning had been from the blind seer Tiresias, in the boy's childhood, that he would die when he knew himself; Eve is not abandoned to his fate, at least at this point.
no shadow stays no illusory image awaits

Multitudes like thyself, and thence be called
Mother of human race." What could I do
But follow straight, invisibly thus led?
Till I espied thee, fair indeed and tall,
Under a platane;° yet methought less fair,
Less winning soft, less amiably mild,
Than that smooth watery image; back I turned,
Thou following cried'st aloud, "Return, fair Eve,
Whom fli'st thou? Whom thou fli'st, of him thou art,
His flesh, his bone;° to give thee being I lent
Out of my side to thee, nearest my heart,
Substantial life, to have thee by my side
Henceforth an individual° solace dear.
Part of my soul° I seek thee, and thee claim
My other half." With that thy gentle hand
Seized mine, I yielded, and from that time see°
How beauty is excelled by manly grace
And wisdom, which alone is truly fair.'
So spake our general mother, and with eyes
Of conjugal attraction unreproved,
And meek surrender, half embracing leaned
On our first father; half her swelling breast
Naked met his under the flowing gold
Of her loose tresses hid. He in delight
Both of her beauty and submissive charms
Smiled with superior love, as Jupiter
On Juno smiles, when he impregns° the clouds
That shed May flowers; and pressed her matron lip
With kisses pure. Aside the devil turned
For envy,° yet with jealous leer malign
Eyed them askance, and to himself thus plained:
'Sight hateful, sight tormenting! thus these two
Imparadised in one another's arms,
The happier Eden,° shall enjoy their fill
Of bliss on bliss, while I to hell am thrust,
Where neither joy nor love, but fierce desire,
Among our other torments not the least,
Still unfulfilled with pain of longing pines;°
Yet let me not forget what I have gained
From their own mouths. All is not theirs, it seems;

platane plane tree
His flesh, his bone Here, and at l. 441, the reference is to Genesis 2:23.
individual undividable
Part of my soul a musical and rhetorical resonance, if not a pun, from l. 411
see Again, the enjambment brings a surprise—"see / How," or "know," "understand"; Eve never really totally "*sees*" wisdom as fairer than beauty.
impregns impregnates
envy Part of the torment of Hell is sexual deprivation, a practice common to various sorts of imprisonment in most Christian societies.
Imparadised . . . Eden Satan is almost at his most pitiable at this poignant moment, for it is only after the Fall that human love will be able (and be forced) to "imparadise" the lovers. Here, at this unfallen moment, when the two are *in Paradise*, literally, he sees them as they will be in Bk. XII (see ll. 614–19).
pines tortures

One fatal tree there stands, of Knowledge called,
Forbidden them to taste. Knowledge forbidden?
Suspicious, reasonless. Why should their lord
Envy them that? Can it be sin to know?
Can it be death? And do they only stand
By ignorance, is that their happy state,
The proof of their obedience and their faith?
O fair foundation laid whereon to build
Their ruin!° Hence I will excite their minds
With more desire to know, and to reject
Envious commands, invented with design
To keep them low whom knowledge might exalt
Equal with gods. Aspiring to be such,
They taste and die: what likelier can ensue?
But first with narrow search I must walk round
This garden, and no corner leave unspied;
A chance but chance may lead where I may meet
Some wandering Spirit of heaven, by fountain side,
Or in thick shade retired, from him to draw
What further would be learnt. Live while ye may,
Yet happy pair; enjoy, till I return,
Short pleasures, for long woes are to succeed.'
So saying, his proud step he scornful turned,
But with sly circumspection, and began
Through wood, through waste, o'er hill, o'er dale, his roam.°
Meanwhile in utmost longitude, where heaven
With earth and ocean meets, the setting sun
Slowly descended, and with right aspéct
Against the eastern gate of Paradise
Levelled his evening rays. It was a rock
Of alabaster, piled up to the clouds,
Conspicuous far, winding with one ascent
Accessible from earth, one entrance high;
The rest was craggy cliff, that overhung
Still as it rose, impossible to climb.
Betwixt these rocky pillars Gabriel° sat,
Chief of the angelic guards, awaiting night;
About him exercised° heroic games
The unarmèd youth of heaven, but nigh at hand
Celestial armoury, shields, helms, and spears,
Hung high, with diamond flaming and with gold.
Thither came Uriel, gliding through the even
On a sunbeam, swift as a shooting star
In autumn thwarts the night, when vapours fired
Impress the air, and shows the mariner

ruin both "destruction" and the wreckage, or remnants, of that destruction ("ruins")
roam walk

Gabriel one of the four archangels in apocryphal tradition assigned to Paradise as guards
exercised played

From what point of his compass to beware
Impetuous winds. He thus began in haste:
'Gabriel, to thee thy course by lot hath given
Charge and strict watch that to this happy place
No evil thing approach or enter in;
This day at highth of noon came to my sphere
A Spirit, zealous, as he seemed, to know
More of the Almighty's works, and chiefly man,
God's latest image.° I described° his way
Bent all on speed, and marked his airy gait;
But in the mount that lies from Eden north,
Where he first lighted, soon discerned his looks
Alien from heaven, with passions foul obscured.
Mine eye pursued him still, but under shade
Lost sight of him; one of the banished crew,
I fear, hath ventured from the deep, to raise
New troubles; him thy care must be to find.'
To whom the wingèd warrior thus returned:
'Uriel, no wonder if thy perfect sight,
Amid the sun's bright circle where thou sit'st,
See far and wide. In at this gate none pass
The vigilance° here placed, but such as come
Well known from heaven; and since meridian hour
No creature thence. If spirit of other sort,
So minded, have o'erleaped these earthy bounds°
On purpose, hard thou knowest it to exclude
Spiritual substance with corporeal bar.
But if within the circuit of these walks,
In whatsoever shape he lurk, of whom
Thou tell'st, by morrow dawning I shall know.'
So promised he, and Uriel to his charge
Returned on that bright beam, whose point now raised
Bore him slope downward to the sun now fallen
Beneath the Azores—whether the prime orb,°
Incredible how swift, had thither rolled
Diurnal, or this less volúble° earth
By shorter flight to the east, had left him there
Arraying with reflected purple and gold
The clouds that on his western throne attend.
Now came still evening on, and twilight grey
Had in her sober livery all things clad;
Silence accompanied,° for beast and bird,
They to their grassy couch, these to their nests
Were slunk, all but the wakeful nightingale—

latest image The first image was Christ, the Son.
described perceived
The vigilance Gabriel
o'erleaped . . . bounds reminding us of the easy joke back at l. 181
prime orb the sun, in the Ptolemaic system. Milton allows for both accounts, as if either might be a distorting reduction of an actual Edenic sunset.
volúble rapidly revolving; see ll. 661–64
Silence accompanied in both a musical and a general sense

She all night long her amorous descant° sung:
Silence was pleased.° Now glowed the firmament
With living sapphires; Hesperus° that led
The starry host, rode brightest, till the moon
Rising in clouded majesty, at length
Apparent queen° unveiled her peerless light,
And o'er the dark her silver mantle threw;
  When Adam thus to Eve: 'Fair consort, the hour
Of night, and all things now retired to rest
Mind us of like repose, since God hath set
Labour and rest, as day and night to men
Successive, and the timely dew of sleep
Now falling with soft slumbrous weight inclines
Our eyelids; other creatures all day long
Rove idle, unemployed, and less need rest;
Man hath his daily work° of body or mind
Appointed, which declares his dignity,
And the regard of heaven on all his ways;
While other animals unactive range,
And of their doings God takes no account.
Tomorrow ere fresh morning streak the east
With first approach of light, we must be risen,
And at our pleasant labour, to reform
Yon flowery arbours, yonder alleys green,
Our walk at noon, with branches overgrown,
That mock our scant manuring,° and require
More hands than ours to lop their wanton° growth.
Those blossoms also, and those dropping gums,
That lie bestrown unsightly and unsmooth,
Ask riddance, if we mean to tread with ease;
Meanwhile, as nature wills, night bids us rest.'
  To whom thus Eve with perfect beauty adorned:
'My author and disposer,° what thou bid'st
Unargued I obey; so God ordains.
God is thy law, thou mine; to know no more
Is woman's happiest knowledge and her praise.
With thee conversing I forget all time,
All seasons° and their change, all please alike.
Sweet is the breath of morn, her rising sweet,
With charm° of earliest birds; pleasant the sun
When first on this delightful land he spreads
His orient beams, on herb, tree, fruit, and flower,

descant highest free contrapuntal part
Silence was pleased at her pupil?
Hesperus the Evening Star
Apparent queen manifestly the queen (of the sky, now that she has risen), who rules this whole part of Bk. IV, from the opening Virgilian night-piece just concluded (see the selection from the Earl of Surrey's *Aeneid* translation) to the love scene which follows
daily work Even in Paradise there is gardening to do, not to be confused with agriculture, done "with the sweat of thy brow."
manuring cultivating
wanton luxuriant (like Eve's hair at l. 306)
My . . . disposer In Books IX through XII these formal titles of address are not used.
seasons times of day (it is always spring and fall at once in Eden)
charm song

Glistering with dew; fragrant the fertile earth
After soft showers; and sweet the coming on
Of grateful evening mild, then silent night
With this her solemn bird° and this fair moon,
And these the gems of heaven, her starry train:
But neither breath of morn when she ascends
With charm of earliest birds, nor rising sun
On this delightful land, nor herb, fruit, flower,
Glistering with dew, nor fragrance after showers,
Nor grateful evening mild, nor silent night
With this her solemn bird, nor walk by moon
Or glittering starlight without thee is sweet.
But wherefore all night long° shine these, for whom
This glorious sight, when sleep hath shut all eyes?'
To whom our general ancestor replied:
'Daughter of God and man, accomplished° Eve,
Those have their course to finish, round the earth,
By morrow evening, and from land to land
In order, though to nations yet unborn,
Ministering light prepared, they set and rise;
Lest total darkness should by night regain
Her old possession,° and extinguish life
In nature and all things; which these soft fires
Not only enlighten, but with kindly° heat
Of various influence° foment and warm,
Temper or nourish, or in part shed down
Their stellar virtue on all kinds that grow
On earth, made hereby apter to receive
Perfection from the sun's more potent ray.
These then, though unbeheld in deep of night,
Shine not in vain, nor think, though men were none,
That heaven would want spectators, God want praise;
Millions of spiritual creatures walk the earth
Unseen, both when we wake, and when we sleep:
All these with ceaseless praise his works behold
Both day and night—how often from the steep
Of echoing hill or thicket have we heard
Celestial voices to the midnight air,
Sole, or responsive each to other's note,°
Singing their great creator; oft in bands
While they keep watch, or nightly rounding walk,
With heavenly touch of instrumental sounds
In full harmonic number joined, their songs

solemn bird the nightingale
wherefore all night long Eve's question is innocent, straightforward, reasonable, personal, and anticlimactically deadly to the cadence of the ode she has just recited.
accomplished Cf. *Samson Agonistes*, l. 230.
Her old possession Chaos originally reigned in darkness; creation of light meant a dispossession of her rule.
kindly natural
influence See *Astrology* in the Glossary.
responsive . . . note in antiphonal choirs

Divide° the night, and lift our thoughts to heaven.'
  Thus talking, hand in hand alone they passed
On to their blissful bower;° it was a place
Chosen by the sovereign planter, when he framed
All things to man's delightful use; the roof
Of thickest covert was inwoven shade,
Laurel and myrtle,° and what higher grew
Of firm and fragrant leaf; on either side
Acanthus, and each odorous bushy shrub
Fenced up the verdant wall; each beauteous flower,
Iris all hues, roses, and jessamine
Reared high their flourished° heads between, and wrought
Mosaic; under foot the violet,
Crocus, and hyacinth with rich inlay
Broidered the ground, more coloured than with stone
Of costliest emblem. Other creature here,
Beast, bird, insect, or worm durst enter none;
Such was their awe of man. In shadier bower
More sacred and sequestered, though but feigned,°
Pan or Silvanus never slept, nor nymph
Nor Faunus haunted. Here in close recess
With flowers, garlands, and sweet-smelling herbs
Espousèd Eve decked first her nuptial bed,
And heavenly quires the hymenean sung,
What day the genial angel° to our sire
Brought her in naked beauty more adorned,
More lovely than Pandora,° whom the gods
Endowed with all their gifts, and O too like
In sad event, when to the unwiser son
Of Japhet° brought by Hermes, she ensnared
Mankind with her fair looks, to be avenged
On him who had stole Jove's authentic° fire.
  Thus at their shady lodge arrived, both stood,
Both turned, and under open sky adored
The God that made both sky, air, earth, and heaven
Which they beheld, the moon's resplendent globe
And starry pole: 'Thou also mad'st the night,

Divide by marking off the watches of the night, and also by playing "divisions" or melodic improvisations
blissful bower not the artificial Bower of Bliss (*The Faerie Queene* II.xii), but a brilliant reversal of Spenser's construct of false love, where art imitates nature deceptively. In the following lines, natural beauties triumph over artificiality by anticipating it.
Laurel and myrtle Apollo's plant and Venus' entwined together, making an emblem of married attributes such as male-female, wisdom-beauty
flourished flowered
feigned fictionalized; see Sidney's discussion of "the feigned image of poesie" in *The Defence of Poetry*
genial angel nuptial, generative spirit, parallel to Old Genius at the boundary of the Garden of Adonis, *The Faerie Queene* III.vi
Pandora another Greek Eve-parallel. Her name means "all gifts," and she was given to the Titan Epimetheus ("after-knowledge"), brother of Prometheus ("fore-knowledge") who stole fire from Olympus for mankind; she opened a box she was forbidden to and loosed evils and miseries on the world.
Japhet Iapetus, father of the two Titans above
authentic original

Maker omnipotent, and thou the day,
Which we in our appointed work employed
Have finished happy in our mutual help
And mutual love, the crown of all our bliss
Ordained by thee, and this delicious place
For us too large, where thy abundance wants
Partakers, and uncropped falls to the ground.
But thou hast promised from us two a race
To fill the earth, who shall with us extol
Thy goodness infinite, both when we wake,
And when we seek, as now, thy gift of sleep.'
  This said unanimous, and other rites
Observing none, but adoration pure
Which God likes best, into their inmost bower
Handed° they went; and eased the putting off
These troublesome disguises which we wear,
Straight side by side were laid, nor turned, I ween,
Adam from his fair spouse, nor Eve the rites
Mysterious° of connubial love refused;
Whatever hypocrites austerely talk
Of purity and place and innocence,
Defaming as impure what God declares
Pure, and commands to some, leaves free to all.
Our Maker bids increase; who bids abstain
But our destroyer, foe to God and man?
Hail, wedded Love, mysterious law, true source
Of human offspring, sole propriety°
In Paradise of all things common else.
By thee adulterous lust was driven from men
Among the bestial herds to range; by thee
Founded in reason, loyal, just, and pure,
Relations dear, and all the charities°
Of father, son, and brother first were known.
Far be it that I should write thee sin or blame,
Or think thee unbefitting holiest place,
Perpetual fountain of domestic sweets,
Whose bed is undefiled and chaste pronounced,
Present or past, as saints and patriarchs used.
Here Love his golden shafts° employs, here lights
His constant lamp, and waves his purple wings,
Reigns here and revels; not in the bought smile
Of harlots, loveless, joyless, unendeared,
Casual fruition; nor in court amours,
Mixed dance, or wanton masque, or midnight ball,

Handed hand in hand (see l. 321n)
Mysterious The representation of unfallen sex is indeed tinged with mystery, and Milton will be able only to insist, as he does below, that it transcends fallen eroticism, and that its mysteries are re-created in human marriage.
propriety domain of belonging, of possessing
charities loves
golden shafts Cupid had golden arrows of desire and leaden ones of disaffection.

Or serenate,° which the starved lover° sings
To his proud fair, best quitted with disdain.
These lulled by nightingales, embracing slept,
And on their naked limbs the flowery roof
Showered roses, which the morn repaired. Sleep on,
Blest pair; and O yet happiest if ye seek
No happier state, and know° to know no more.
Now had night measured with her shadowy cone
Half way up hill this vast sublunar vault,
And from their ivory port° the cherubim
Forth issuing at the accustomed hour stood armed
To their night-watches in warlike parade,
When Gabriel to his next in power thus spake:
'Uzziel, half these draw off, and coast the south
With strictest watch; these other wheel the north;
Our circuit meets full west.' As flame they part,
Half wheeling to the shield, half to the spear.°
From these, two strong and subtle spirits he called
That near him stood, and gave them thus in charge:
'Ithuriel and Zephon, with winged speed
Search through this garden; leave unsearched no nook,
But chiefly where those two fair creatures lodge,
Now laid perhaps asleep secure of harm.
This evening from the sun's decline arrived
Who° tells of some infernal spirit seen
Hitherward bent (who could have thought?) escaped
The bars of hell, on errand bad no doubt:
Such where ye find, seize fast, and hither bring.'
So saying, on he led his radiant files,
Dazzling the moon; these to the bower direct
In search of whom they sought. Him there they found
Squat like a toad, close at the ear of Eve,
Assaying by his devilish art to reach
The organs of her fancy, and with them forge
Illusions as he list, phantasms and dreams,
Or if, inspiring venom, he might taint
The animal spirits° that from pure blood arise
Like gentle breaths from rivers pure, thence raise
At least distempered, discontented thoughts,
Vain hopes, vain aims, inordinate desires
Blown up with high conceits° engendering pride.
Him thus intent Ithuriel with his spear

serenate serenade
starved lover Milton's point is that fallen Eros, here imaged in Ovidian, courtly, and Cavalier love, flourishes in a world of sexual denial, of loss.
know know enough
ivory port through the gates of ivory came false dreams, through gates of horn, true ones; the Cherubim will interfere with the Satanically induced false dream
Half . . . spear to left and right
Who one who
animal spirits See *Renaissance Psychology* in the Glossary.
conceits ideas

Touched lightly; for no falsehood can endure
Touch of celestial temper, but returns
Of force to its own likeness. Up he starts
Discovered and surprised. As when a spark
Lights on a heap of nitrous powder,° laid
Fit for the tun° some magazine to store
Against a rumoured war, the smutty grain
With sudden blaze diffused, inflames the air:
So started up in his own shape the fiend.
Back stepped those two fair angels half amazed
So sudden to behold the grisly king,
Yet thus, unmoved with fear, accost him soon:
 'Which of those rebel spirits adjudged to hell
Com'st thou, escaped thy prison; and transformed,
Why sat'st thou like an enemy in wait
Here watching at the head of these that sleep?'
 'Know ye not then,' said Satan, filled with scorn,
'Know ye not me? Ye knew me once no mate
For you, there sitting where ye durst not soar;
Not to know me argues yourselves unknown,
The lowest of your throng; or if ye know,
Why ask ye, and superfluous begin
Your message, like to end as much in vain?'
To whom thus Zephon, answering scorn with scorn:
'Think not, revolted Spirit, thy shape the same,
Or undiminished brightness, to be known
As when thou stood'st in heaven upright and pure;
That glory then, when thou no more wast good,
Departed from thee, and thou resemblest now
Thy sin and place of doom obscure° and foul.
But come, for thou, be sure, shalt give account
To him who sent us, whose charge is to keep
This place inviolable, and these° from harm.'
 So spake the cherub, and his grave rebuke,
Severe in youthful beauty, added grace
Invincible. Abashed the devil stood,
And felt how awful° goodness is, and saw
Virtue in her shape how lovely; saw, and pined
His loss; but chiefly to find here observed
His lustre visibly impaired; yet seemed
Undaunted. 'If I must contend,' said he,
'Best with the best, the sender not the sent;
Or all at once; more glory will be won,
Or less be lost.' 'Thy fear,' said Zephon bold,

nitrous powder gunpowder
tun keg
obscure dark (whereas "dark," as in I Corinthians 13:12, and Spenser's phrase "dark conceit," means "obscure" in the modern sense of "hard to make out")
these Adam and Eve, asleep
awful awe-engendering

'Will save us trial what the least can do
Single against thee wicked, and thence weak.'
The fiend replied not, overcome with rage;
But like a proud steed reined, went haughty on,
Champing his iron curb. To strive or fly
He held it vain; awe from above had quelled
His heart, not else dismayed. Now drew they nigh
The western point, where those half-rounding guards
Just met, and closing stood in squadron joined
Awaiting next command. To whom their chief
Gabriel from the front thus called aloud:
'O friends, I hear the tread of nimble feet
Hasting this way, and now by glimpse discern
Ithuriel and Zephon through the shade,
And with them comes a third, of regal port,
But faded splendour wan, who by his gait
And fierce demeanour seems the prince of hell,
Not likely to part hence without contést;
Stand firm, for in his look defiance lours.'
He scarce had ended, when those two approached
And brief related whom they brought, where found,
How busied, in what form and posture couched.
To whom with stern regard thus Gabriel spake:
'Why hast thou, Satan, broke the bounds prescribed
To thy transgressions, and disturbed the charge
Of others,° who approve not to transgress
By thy example, but have power and right
To question thy bold entrance on this place;
Employed it seems to violate sleep, and those
Whose dwelling God hath planted here in bliss?'
To whom thus Satan, with contemptuous brow:
'Gabriel, thou hadst in heaven the esteem of wise,
And such I held thee; but this question asked
Puts me in doubt. Lives there who loves his pain?
Who would not, finding way, break loose from hell,
Though thither doomed? Thou wouldst thyself, no doubt,
And boldly venture to whatever place
Farthest from pain, where thou mightst hope to change
Torment with ease, and soonest recompense
Dole° with delight, which in this place I sought;
To thee no reason, who knowest only good,
But evil hast not tried. And wilt object°
His will who bound us? Let him surer bar
His iron gates, if he intends our stay
In that dark durance°—thus much what was asked.

charge Of others their responsibility (Adam and Eve)
Dole distress
object make legal objection about
durance confinement

The rest is true, they found me where they say;
But that implies not violence or harm.'
  Thus he in scorn. The warlike angel moved,
Disdainfully half smiling thus replied:
'O loss of one in heaven to judge of wise,°
Since Satan fell, whom folly overthrew,
And now returns him from his prison scaped,°
Gravely in doubt whether to hold them wise
Or not, who ask what boldness brought him hither
Unlicensed from his bounds in hell prescribed;
So wise he judges it to fly from pain
However,° and to scape his punishment.
So judge thou still, presumptuous, till the wrath,
Which thou incurrest by flying, meet thy flight
Sevenfold, and scourge that wisdom back to hell,
Which taught thee yet no better, that no pain
Can equal anger infinite provoked.
But wherefore thou alone? Wherefore with thee
Came not all hell broke loose? Is pain to them
Less pain, less to be fled, or thou than they
Less hardy to endure? Courageous chief,
The first in flight from pain, hadst thou alleged
To thy deserted host this cause of flight,
Thou surely hadst not come sole fugitive.'
  To which the fiend thus answered frowning stern:
'Not that I less endure, or shrink from pain,
Insulting angel, well thou knowest I stood°
Thy fiercest, when in battle to thy aid
The blasting volleyed thunder made all speed
And seconded thy else not dreaded spear.
But still thy words at random, as before,
Argue thy inexperience what behoves,
From hard assays° and ill successes past,
A faithful leader, not to hazard all
Through ways of danger by himself untried.
I therefore, I alone first undertook
To wing the desolate abyss, and spy
This new-created world, whereof in hell
Fame° is not silent, here in hope to find
Better abode, and my afflicted° powers
To settle here on earth, or in mid-air;
Though for possession put to try once more
What thou and thy gay legions dare against,
Whose easier business were to serve their Lord

O loss . . . wise What a loss . . . wisdom!
returns . . . scaped returns himself from his escape
However whichever way
stood withstood
assays attempts
Fame rumor
afflicted outcast

High up in heaven, with songs to hymn his throne,
And practiced distances to cringe, not fight.'
  To whom the warrior angel soon replied:
'To say and straight unsay, pretending first
Wise to fly pain, professing next the spy,
Argues no leader but a liar traced,°
Satan, and couldst thou "faithful" add? O name,
O sacred name of faithfulness profaned!
Faithful to whom? To thy rebellious crew?
Army of fiends, fit body to fit head;
Was this your discipline and faith engaged,
Your military obedience, to dissolve
Allegiance to the acknowledged power supreme?
And thou sly hypocrite, who now wouldst seem
Patron of liberty, who more than thou
Once fawned, and cringed, and servilely adored
Heaven's awful monarch? Wherefore but in hope
To dispossess him, and thyself to reign?
But mark what I areed° thee now: Avaunt!
Fly thither whence thou fled'st. If from this hour
Within these hallowed limits thou appear,
Back to the infernal pit I drag thee chained,
And seal thee so, as henceforth not to scorn
The facile° gates of hell too slightly barred.'
  So threatened he, but Satan to no threats
Gave heed, but waxing more in rage replied:
  'Then when I am thy captive talk of chains,
Proud limitary° cherub, but ere then
Far heavier load thyself expect to feel
From my prevailing arm, though heaven's king
Ride on thy wings, and thou with thy compeers,
Used to the yoke, drawest his triumphant wheels
In progress through the road of heaven star-paved.'
  While thus he spake, the angelic squadron bright
Turned, fiery red, sharpening in moonèd horns°
Their phalanx, and began to hem him round
With ported spears, as thick as when a field
Of Ceres° ripe for harvest waving bends
Her bearded grove of ears, which way the wind
Sways them; the careful° ploughman doubting stands
Lest on the threshing-floor his hopeful sheaves
Prove chaff. On the other side Satan alarmed°
Collecting all his might dilated° stood,

traced disclosed
areed advise
facile easily opened
limitary frontier-guard (with a bit of a snarl)
moonèd horns crescent-shaped
Ceres here, the goddess standing for the grain itself
careful anxious, even as God, the thresher and winnower, might be for the outcome of this renewed combat. This image is reinforced shortly by that of God as weigher.
alarmed aroused
dilated into more ethereal condition by Ithuriel's spear

Like Teneriffe or Atlas unremoved:°
His stature reached the sky, and on his crest
Sat Horror plumed; nor wanted in his grasp
What seemed both spear and shield. Now dreadful deeds
Might have ensued, nor only Paradise
In this commotion, but the starry cope°
Of heaven perhaps, or all the elements
At least had gone to wrack, disturbed and torn
With violence of this conflict, had not soon
The Eternal to prevent such horrid fray
Hung forth in heaven his golden scales,° yet seen
Betwixt Astraea° and the Scorpion sign,
Wherein all things created first he weighed,
The pendulous round earth with balanced air
In counterpoise, now ponders° all events,
Battles and realms. In these he put two weights,
The sequel° each of parting and of fight;
The latter quick up flew, and kicked the beam;
Which Gabriel spying, thus bespake the fiend:
'Satan, I know thy strength, and thou knowest mine,
Neither our own but given; what folly then
To boast what arms can do, since thine no more
Than heaven permits, nor mine, though doubled now
To trample thee as mire. For proof look up,
And read thy lot in yon celestial sign
Where thou art weighed,° and shown how light, how weak,
If thou resist.' The fiend looked up and knew
His mounted scale aloft: nor more; but fled
Murmuring, and with him fled the shades of night.

From *Book V*

Now Morn her rosy steps in the eastern clime
Advancing, sowed the earth with orient pearl,
When Adam waked, so customed—for his sleep
Was airy light, from pure digestion bred,
And temperate vapours° bland, which the only° sound
Of leaves and fuming rills, Aurora's fan,°
Lightly dispersed, and the shrill matin song
Of birds on every bough—so much the more

Teneriffe . . . unremoved peak in the Canary islands, and the Atlas range in Morocco, both unremovable
cope canopy
golden scales the constellation Libra now, at midnight, at the zenith; also reminiscent of the Homeric golden scales in which Zeus weighed the destinies of Greek and Trojans, Achilles and Hector, and, in Virgil, Aeneas and Turnus
Astraea the constellation Virgo was formed when Astraea, or Justice, left the world at the end of the Golden Age
ponders weighs, with an overtone of "considers"
sequel consequence
thou art weighed "—in the balance, and art found wanting," the warning to Belshazzar in the Book of Daniel 5:27
vapours a medical term referring to the exhalations of digestion
only mere
Aurora's fan the leaves

His wonder was to find unwakened Eve
With tresses discomposed, and glowing cheek,
As through unquiet rest. He on his side
Leaning half-raised, with looks of cordial love
Hung over her enamoured, and beheld
Beauty, which whether waking or asleep
Shot forth peculiar graces;° then with voice
Mild, as when Zephyrus on Flora breathes,
Her hand soft touching, whispered thus: 'Awake,
My fairest,° my espoused, my latest found,
Heaven's last best gift, my ever new delight,
Awake, the morning shines, and the fresh field
Calls us; we lose the prime,° to mark how spring
Our tended plants, how blows° the citron grove,
What drops the myrrh, and what the balmy° reed,
How Nature paints her colours, how the bee
Sits on the bloom extracting liquid sweet.'
  Such whispering waked her, but with startled eye
On Adam, whom embracing, thus she spake:
  'O sole in whom my thoughts find all repose,
My glory, my perfection, glad I see
Thy face, and morn returned, for I this night—
Such night till this I never passed—have dreamed,
If dreamed, not as I oft am wont, of thee,
Works of day past, or morrow's next design,
But of offence and trouble, which my mind
Knew never till this irksome night. Methought
Close at mine ear one called me forth to walk
With gentle voice; I thought it thine. It said:
"*Why sleep'st thou, Eve? Now is the pleasant time,*
The cool, the silent, save where silence yields
To the night-warbling bird, that now awake
Tunes sweetest his° *love-laboured song; now reigns*
Full-orbed the moon, and with more pleasing light
Shadowy sets off the face of things;° *in vain,*
If none regard; heaven wakes with all his eyes,°
Whom to behold but thee, Nature's desire,
In whose sight all things joy, with ravishment
Attracted by thy beauty still to gaze?"
I rose as at thy call, but found thee not;
To find thee I directed then my walk;
And on, methought, alone I passed through ways
That brought me on a sudden to the tree

peculiar graces graces peculiar to her
Awake, My fairest echoes the morning song in the Song of Songs 2:10.
prime early morning hours
blows blooms
balmy yielding aromatic resin
his The nightingale is, normally, "she" (because the transformed Philomela), but here is masculine by association with Satan.
Shadowy . . . things This serenade (evening song), the opposite of Adam's aubade (morning song), praises moonlight's qualities of ambiguity, soft vagueness, and outline-blurring.
all his eyes the stars

Of interdicted° knowledge. Fair it seemed,
Much fairer to my fancy than by day;
And as I wondering looked, beside it stood
One shaped and winged like one of those from heaven
By us oft seen; his dewy locks distilled
Ambrosia; on that tree he also gazed;
And "*O fair plant,*" said he, "*with fruit surcharged,*
Deigns none to ease thy load and taste thy sweet,
Nor god,° *nor man; is knowledge so despised?*
Or envy, or what reserve forbids to taste?
Forbid who will, none shall from me withhold
Longer thy offered good, why else set here?"
This said he paused not, but with venturous arm
He plucked, he tasted; me damp horror chilled
At such bold words vouched with a deed so bold.
But he thus, overjoyed: "*O fruit divine,*°
Sweet of thyself, but much more sweet thus cropped,
Forbidden here, it seems, as only fit
For gods, yet able to make gods of men;
And why not gods of men, since good, the more
Communicated, more abundant grows,
The author not impaired, but honoured more?
Here, happy creature, fair angelic Eve,
Partake thou also; happy though thou art,
Happier thou may'st be, worthier canst not be;
Taste this, and be henceforth among the gods
Thyself a goddess, not to earth confined,
But sometimes in the air, as we; sometimes
Ascend to heaven, by merit thine, and see
What life the gods live there, and such live thou."
So saying, he drew nigh, and to me held,
Even to my mouth of that same fruit held part
Which he had plucked; the pleasant savoury smell
So quickened appetite that I, methought,
Could not but taste. Forthwith up to the clouds
With him I flew, and underneath beheld
The earth outstretched immense, a prospect wide
And various. Wondering at my flight and change
To this high exaltation, suddenly
My guide was gone, and I, methought, sunk down,
And fell asleep; but O how glad I waked
To find this but a dream!'° Thus Eve her night
Related, and thus Adam answered sad:°

interdicted forbidden
god spirit, as at l. 117, below
O fruit divine Satan's voice mistakenly overemphasizes the power of the fruit itself which, "well used" (IV.200), would have remained uneaten.
but a dream as Eve recounts it, a prophetic one, having its fulfillment in Bk. IX, when details of the temptation of Eve will echo those of her narration here. This non-biblical dream raises interesting interpretive questions: if a "true dream," is Eve already lost? if a false one (see IV.778n.), then a necessary educational experience?
sad serious

'Best image of myself and dearer half,
The trouble of thy thoughts this night in sleep
Affects me equally; nor can I like
This uncouth° dream, of evil sprung, I fear;
Yet evil whence? In thee can harbour none,
Created pure. But know that in the soul
Are many lesser faculties° that serve
Reason as chief; among these fancy next
Her office holds; of all external things,
Which the five watchful senses represent,°
She forms imaginations,° airy shapes,
Which reason joining or disjoining frames
All what we affirm or what deny, and call
Our knowledge or opinion; then retires
Into her private cell when nature rests.
Oft in her absence mimic fancy wakes
To imitate her; but misjoining shapes,
Wild work produces oft, and most in dreams,
Ill matching words and deeds long past or late.
Some such resemblances methinks I find
Of our last evening's talk in this thy dream,
But with addition strange; yet be not sad.
Evil into the mind of god or man
May come and go, so unapproved, and leave
No spot or blame behind; which gives me hope
That what in sleep thou didst abhor to dream,
Waking thou never wilt consent to do.
Be not disheartened then, nor cloud those looks
That wont to be more cheerful and serene
Than when fair morning first smiles on the world,
And let us to our fresh employments rise
Among the groves, the fountains, and the flowers
That open now their choicest bosomed smells
Reserved from night, and kept for thee in store.'

. . .

[Eve's anxiety allayed, they proceed to the first day's activities, starting with a morning hymn followed by the unfallen work of gardening. God instructs the archangel Raphael to descend to Paradise and visit Adam and Eve in the garden in order to teach them who they are and what their relation to the world is, and, most particularly, "to render man inexcusable" by telling them who their enemy is. This entails a sub-epic, Raphael's narration of all that has gone before, modeled on the flashback narration in Homer and Virgil by which we

uncouth unpleasant
lesser faculties In a brilliant parody of the story of the Fall, Chaucer's Pertelote explains to her husband Chaunteclere that his prophetic dream must have been something he ate. Here, Adam gives Eve a lecture on the psychology of the faculties, notably about fancy, or imagination (they were usually not distinguished). See *Renaissance Psychology* in the Glossary, the passage on fancy from Burton's *Anatomy of Melancholy*, and the allegory of Phantastes in *The Faerie Queene* II.ix.49–58.
represent show
imaginations visions; the objects, rather than the faculty itself

learn of all of Odysseus' adventures between Troy and Calypso's island, for example, only when he narrates them at the court of Alcinous. *Paradise Lost,* too, has started *in medias res,* and now we learn of the total time sequence stretching back behind the Fall of Satan. The promotion of the Son by God, the jealousy and scheming of Satan, and the beginning of the revolution in heaven are all unfolded.]

Book VI

[Raphael's narration continues. It describes the three days' battle in heaven in a grim and animated fashion, including the invention of "devilish engines," the first artillery, and other war matériel, "which in the second day's fight put Michael and his angels to some disorder," as Milton puts it in his prose *argument* to Book VI. The third day's victory is given not to Michael, the general, but the Son, whose thundering chariot ride routs Satan's legions; as they retreat in disarray, the wall of heaven opens, and "they leap down with horror and confusion into the place of punishment prepared for them in the deep." The Son returns to his Father in triumph.]

From *Book VII*

[Here, in the proem to Book VII, Milton finally names his "heavenly Muse." His invocation calls on her for help in making a difficult imaginative transition from the almost mock-heroic liveliness of the war in heaven in Book VI to the monumental task of revealing, through Raphael's narration, the story of creation. His poem is "descending" to earth from heavenly subjects, but his efforts and craft must rise to this harder task. This is also the midpoint of the poem, and from here the action is all downhill; there are no more scenes taking place in heaven. As always, too, there is Milton's anxiety, as a poet, about falling.]

Descend from heaven, Urania,° by that name
If rightly thou art called, whose voice divine
Following, about the Olympian hill I soar,
Above the flight of Pegasean wing.°
The meaning, not the name° I call; for thou
Nor of the Muses nine, nor on the top
Of old Olympus dwell'st, but heavenly born,
Before the hills appeared or fountain flowed,
Thou with eternal wisdom didst converse,
Wisdom thy sister, and with her didst play
In presence of the almighty father, pleased
With thy celestial song. Up led by thee
Into the heaven of heavens I have presumed,

Urania See I.6n.
Pegasean wing Pegasus, the winged horse ridden by Bellerophon when he killed the Chimera (see II.628n), thus committing an act of truth. The flying horse was symbolic of poetry itself (1) because he struck Mt. Helicon with his hoof to produce the Muses' spring and (2) from his flights above even the fountains which stood for poetic expression, for breaking out and flowing.
meaning, not the name not Urania only as one of the nine (Muse of astronomy, who will preside over the discussion of the cosmos in Bk. VII), but as a kind of Christian Muse of religious poetry

An earthly guest, and drawn empyreal air,
Thy tempering; with like safety guided down,
Return me to my native element,°
Lest from this flying steed unreined (as once
Bellerophon, though from a lower clime)
Dismounted, on the Aleian field° I fall,
Erroneous° there to wander and forlorn.
Half yet remains unsung,° but narrower bound
Within the visible diurnal° sphere;
Standing on earth, not rapt° above the pole,
More safe I sing with mortal voice, unchanged
To hoarse or mute, though fallen on evil days,°
On evil days, though fallen, and evil tongues;
In darkness,° and with dangers compassed round,
And solitude; yet not alone, while thou
Visit'st my slumbers nightly,° or when morn
Purples the east. Still govern thou my song,
Urania, and fit audience find, though few.
But drive far off the barbarous dissonance
Of Bacchus and his revellers, the race
Of that wild rout that tore the Thracian bard°
In Rhodope,° where woods and rocks had ears
To rapture, till the savage clamour drowned°
Both harp and voice; nor could the Muse defend
Her son. So fail not thou who thee implores;
For thou art heavenly, she° an empty dream.

[Book VII tells the story of Creation. Raphael tells of God's desire to create another world and "out of one man a race / Innumerable" in further despite of Satan's decimation of heaven's ranks, "there to dwell, / Not here, till by degrees of merit raised" they will become as angels (a promise Satan makes to Eve) "And Earth be changed to heaven, and heaven to earth." The Son, as the Word of God, then creates the world in six days, starting out with a pair of compasses which draw circles and boundaries of limitation, then creating light, and so on through the processes of the text in Genesis. The work culminates in the creation, among the animals, of the vertical animal, man; the Word re-ascends to heaven, and angelic rejoicing celebrates the completion of the act.

Book VIII continues the education of man, following his two heroic narrations of warfare and of creation and founding of living places with a brief

native element earth
Aleian field Bellerophon finally tried to reach heaven on Pegasus, and Zeus threw him off onto the plain of Aleia (in Greek: "error").
Erroneous Latin *error* means "wandering," and Milton plays here, as so often, on both the original and derived meanings of words.
Half . . . unsung See Headnote to Bk. VII.
diurnal rotating daily
rapt entranced, "caught up" (into heaven?)
evil days the Restoration, which commenced with an anti-Puritan reaction during which Milton felt in great danger; also, evil in that the decade of political writing and work during which he had gone blind had come to nothing
darkness his blindness; this echoes part of the meditation on light (III. 145)
nightly See III.31 and IX.21–24.
Thracian bard Orpheus, torn apart by the Bacchantes (see *Comus,* l. 550, and *Lycidas,* ll. 57–63)
Rhodope a mountain in Thrace
drowned Given the fate of the dismembered Orpheus, harp and head floating down the Hebrus, this word is doubly powerful.
she Orpheus' muse

response to Adam's questions about the relation of Paradise to the celestial phenomena apparent from it: he asks about sun, moon, and stars, and what accounts for their motions through the visible sky (an original and fruitful question for fallen man's science). Raphael instructs him to forget such pseudo-problems, implying that in Paradise the phenomena are the reality, and presenting a satiric picture of the search "through wandering mazes lost" (like the philosophy of the demons in Book II) for knowledge of reality in fallen human history. He particularly ridicules the way in which theories, or models, succeed each other in the history of science, how astronomers "build, unbuild, contrive / To save appearances, how gird the sphere / With centric and eccentric scribbled o'er, / Cycle and epicycle, orb in orb"—the picture of a Ptolemaic chart scribbled over with constant revisions. His account finished, Adam responds with one of his own, of his memories of everything since the dawn of his own consciousness, on awaking from his creation, his first sight of Eve, and so forth. Raphael, "after admonitions repeated" to Adam about not letting his feelings for Eve overcome his higher reason, departs.]

Book IX

No more of talk where God or angel guest
With man, as with his friend, familiar used
To sit indulgent, and with him partake
Rural repast, permitting him the while
Venial° discourse unblamed. I now must change
Those notes to tragic; foul distrust, and breach
Disloyal on the part of man, revolt,
And disobedience; on the part of heaven
Now alienated, distance° and distaste,°
Anger and just rebuke, and judgment given,
That brought into this world a world of woe,°
Sin and her shadow Death, and misery,
Death's harbinger. Sad task, yet argument
Not less but more heroic than the wrath°
Of stern Achilles on his foe pursued
Thrice fugitive about Troy wall; or rage
Of Turnus for Lavinia disespoused;°
Or Neptune's ire or Juno's, that so long
Perplexed the Greek° and Cytherea's son;°
If answerable style I can obtain
Of my celestial patroness,° who deigns
Her nightly visitation° unimplored,

venial allowable
distance may also have the sense "discord" or "quarrel."
distaste completes the list of hissing *"dis-"* 's starting at l. 6 with what will be the operative word in the plot now, "taste" (see I.2).
world . . . woe The two "world"'s are local and general, literal and figurative; "woe," soon after "taste," echoes I.3.
wrath the first word of the *Iliad.* Milton shifts from describing his modulating tone to the subject of epic and what its subject should be.
Turnus . . . disespoused Turnus is Aeneas' major antagonist in the latter portion of Virgil's epic; to Turnus he loses Italy, his beloved, and his life.
the Greek Odysseus
Cytherea's son Aeneas
celestial patroness Urania (see the invocations to Bks. I, III, VII)
nightly visitation Milton dictated *Paradise Lost* in the mornings from inspiration in the previous night; at any rate this is the poem's own myth of its composition, of having been sung out of darkness.

And dictates to me slumbering, or inspires
Easy my unpremeditated verse,
Since first this subject for heroic song
Pleased me long choosing, and beginning late;
Not sedulous by nature to indite
Wars, hitherto the only argument
Heroic deemed, chief maistry° to dissect
With long and tedious havoc fabled knights
In battles feigned (the better fortitude
Of patience and heroic martyrdom
Unsung), or to describe races and games,
Or tilting° furniture, emblazoned shields,
Impresses° quaint, caparisons and steeds,
Bases and tinsel trappings,° gorgeous knights
At joust and tournament; then marshalled feast
Served up in hall with sewers and seneschals;°
The skill of artifice or office mean,
Not that which justly gives heroic name
To person or to poem. Me of these
Nor skilled nor studious, higher argument
Remains, sufficient of itself to raise
That name,° unless an age too late, or cold
Climate,° or years damp my intended wing
Depressed, and much they may, if all be mine,
Not hers who brings it nightly to my ear.
　The sun was sunk,° and after him the star
Of Hesperus, whose office is to bring
Twilight upon the earth, short arbiter
'Twixt day and night, and now from end to end
Night's hemisphere had veiled the horizon round,
When Satan, who late fled before the threats
Of Gabriel out of Eden, now improved°
In meditated fraud and malice, bent
On man's destruction, maugre° what might hap
Of heavier on himself, fearless returned.°
By night he fled, and at midnight returned
From compassing the earth, cautious of day,
Since Uriel, regent of the sun, descried
His entrance, and forewarned the Cherubim
That kept their watch; thence full of anguish driven,
The space of seven continued nights he rode

maistry mastery, skill. The word has an archaic flavor, and introduces the terms associated with Renaissance epic and its world of medieval romance (Tasso, Ariosto, and Spenser).
tilting jousting
Impresses emblems or devices on shields
Bases . . . trappings draperies, caparisons, and trimmings for horses
sewers and seneschals waiters and stewards
That name epic poetry ("heroic name")
an age . . . Climate the burden of an epic tradition, even mastered, is very great. These phrases refer to a moment of Western history, Restoration England, as well as to the northern climate and the winter weather, during which, we are told, he wrote.
sun was sunk The transition to narrative is from the echoing "nightly."
improved intensified
maugre despite
returned to where the narrative left him at the end of Bk. IV

With darkness, thrice the equinoctial line
He circled, four times crossed the car° of Night
From pole to pole, traversing each colure;°
On the eighth returned, and on the coast averse°
From entrance or Cherubic watch, by stealth
Found unsuspected way. There was a place—
Now not, though sin, not time, first wrought the change—
Where Tigris at the foot of Paradise
Into a gulf shot under ground, till part
Rose up a fountain by the Tree of Life;
In with the river sunk, and with it rose
Satan, involved in rising mist, then sought
Where to lie hid; sea he had searched and land
From Eden over Pontus,° and the pool
Maeotis,° up beyond the river Ob;°
Downward as far antarctic; and in length
West from Orontes° to the ocean barred
At Darien,° thence to the land where flows
Ganges and Indus. Thus the orb he roamed
With narrow search, and with inspection deep
Considered every creature, which of all
Most opportune might serve his wiles, and found
The serpent subtlest beast of all the field.
Him after long debate, irresolute°
Of thoughts revolved,° his final sentence° chose
Fit vessel, fittest imp° of fraud, in whom
To enter, and his dark suggestions hide
From sharpest sight; for in the wily snake,
Whatever sleights none would suspicious mark,
As from his wit and native subtlety
Proceeding, which, in other beasts observed,
Doubt° might beget of diabolic power
Active within beyond the sense of brute.
Thus he resolved, but first from inward grief
His bursting passion into plaints thus poured:
'O earth, how like to heaven, if not preferred
More justly, seat worthier of gods, as built
With second thoughts, reforming what was old!°
For what God after better worse would build?

car chariot
colure one of two longitudinal circles drawn from the celestial poles, cutting the ecliptic at solstice and equinox
averse opposite
Pontus the Black Sea
Maeotis the Sea of Azov
river Ob in Siberia
Orontes Syrian river
Darien Isthmus of Panama
irresolute unresolved
thoughts revolved turned and twisted, like a serpent's motion
sentence decision
imp offshoot
Doubt suspicion
With . . . old Satan's address to the earth, paralleling his invocation of the sun in IV.32, begins here with a fallen reading of an unfallen event: wise men learn by experience, and a second version, in a technological context, improves on the first; this is not true of Creation, nor necessarily of poems.

Terrestrial heaven, danced round by other heavens
That shine, yet bear their bright officious° lamps,
Light above light, for thee alone, as seems,
In thee concentring all their precious beams
Of sacred influence! As God in heaven
Is centre, yet extends to all, so thou
Centring receivest from all those orbs; in thee,
Not in themselves, all their known virtue appears
Productive in herb, plant, and nobler birth
Of creatures animate with gradual° life
Of growth, sense, reason,° all summed up in man.
With what delight could I have walked thee round,
If I could joy in aught, sweet interchange
Of hill and valley, rivers, woods, and plains,
Now land, now sea, and shores with forest crowned,
Rocks, dens, and caves; but I in none of these
Find place or refuge; and the more I see
Pleasures about me, so much more I feel
Torment within me, as from the hateful siege°
Of contraries; all good to me becomes
Bane,° and in heaven much worse would be my state.
But neither here seek I, no nor in heaven
To dwell, unless by mastering heaven's Supreme;
Nor hope to be myself less miserable
By what I seek, but others to make such
As I, though thereby worse to me redound.
For only in destroying I find ease
To my relentless thoughts; and him destroyed,
Or won to what may work his utter loss,
For whom all this was made, all this will soon
Follow, as to him linked in weal or woe;
In woe then, that destruction wide may range.
To me shall be the glory sole among
The infernal powers, in one day to have marred
What he, almighty styled, six nights and days
Continued making, and who knows how long
Before had been contriving? Though perhaps
Not longer than since I in one night freed
From servitude inglorious well-nigh half
The angelic name, and thinner left the throng
Of his adorers. He to be avenged,
And to repair his numbers thus impaired,
Whether such virtue spent of old now failed

officious serviceable
gradual on a scale of nature
growth, sense, reason functions of the vegetable, animal, and rational souls in man; see *Renaissance Psychology* in the Glossary
siege The contraries Satan has manipulated in his dialectic are now besieging him, with the final and appropriate irony that "siege" can also mean "seat" or "throne," his internal state in which these contraries are enshrined.
all good . . . Bane "bane": "evil"; can he remember saying "Evil, be thou my good" (IV.110)? Cf. IV.32–113 and IX.467–70.

More angels to create, if they at least
Are his created, or to spite us more,
Determined to advance into our room°
A creature formed of earth, and him endow,
Exalted from so base original,
With heavenly spoils, our spoils. What he decreed
He effected; man he made, and for him built
Magnificent this world, and earth his seat,
Him lord pronounced, and, O indignity!
Subjected to his service angel wings,
And flaming ministers to watch and tend
Their earthy charge. Of these the vigilance
I dread, and to elude, thus wrapped in mist
Of midnight vapour glide obscure, and pry
In every bush and brake, where hap° may find
The serpent sleeping, in whose mazy folds
To hide me, and the dark intent I bring.
O foul descent!° that I who erst contended
With Gods to sit the highest, am now constrained
Into a beast, and mixed with bestial slime,
This essence to incarnate and imbrute,
That to the height of deity aspired;
But what will not ambition and revenge
Descend to? Who aspires must down as low
As high he soared, obnoxious° first or last
To basest things. Revenge, at first though sweet,
Bitter ere long back on itself recoils;
Let it; I reck not, so it light well aimed,
Since higher I fall short, on him who next
Provokes my envy, this new favourite
Of heaven, this man of clay, son of despite,
Whom us the more to spite his maker raised
From dust: spite then with spite is best repaid.'
So saying, through each thicket dank or dry,
Like a black mist low creeping, he held on
His midnight search, where soonest he might find
The serpent: him fast sleeping soon he found
In labyrinth of many a round self-rolled,
His head the midst, well stored with subtle wiles:
Not yet in horrid° shade or dismal den,
Nor nocent° yet, but on the grassy herb
Fearless, unfeared, he slept. In at his mouth
The devil entered, and his brutal sense,
In heart or head, possessing soon inspired

room place
hap chance
O foul descent! and a hideous parody of the other Incarnation, the other Descent (of the Holy Ghost to incarnate in Mary)
obnoxious exposed
horrid bristling
nocent harmful (snakes become poisonous only after the Fall); also, perhaps, "guilty"

With act intelligential, but his sleep
Disturbed not, waiting close° the approach of morn.
Now whenas sacred light began to dawn
In Eden on the humid flowers, that breathed
Their morning incense, when all things that breathe
From the earth's great altar send up silent praise
To the Creator, and his nostrils fill
With grateful smell, forth came the human pair
And joined their vocal worship to the quire
Of creatures wanting° voice; that done, partake
The season, prime for sweetest scents and airs;°
Then cómmune how that day they best may ply
Their growing work; for much their work outgrew
The hands' dispatch of two gardening so wide.
And Eve first to her husband thus began:
'Adam, well may we labour still to dress
This garden, still to tend plant, herb, and flower,
Our pleasant task enjoined, but till more hands
Aid us, the work under our labour grows,
Luxurious by restraint; what we by day
Lop overgrown, or prune, or prop, or bind,
One night or two with wanton growth derides,
Tending to wild. Thou therefore now advise
Or hear what to my mind first thoughts present:
Let us divide our labours, thou where choice
Leads thee, or where most needs, whether to wind
The woodbine° round this arbour, or direct
The clasping ivy where to climb, while I
In yonder spring° of roses intermixed
With myrtle, find what to redress° till noon.
For while so near each other thus all day
Our task we choose, what wonder if so near
Looks intervene and smiles, or object new
Casual discourse draw on, which intermits
Our day's work, brought to little, though begun
Early, and the hour of supper comes unearned.'
To whom mild answer Adam thus returned:
'Sole Eve,° associate sole, to me beyond
Compare above all living creatures dear,
Well hast thou motioned,° well thy thoughts employed
How we might best fulfill the work which here
God hath assigned us, nor of me shalt pass
Unpraised; for nothing lovelier can be found

close hidden
wanting lacking
airs also in a musical sense: "tunes"
wind The woodbine She leaves to Adam the intertwining plants.
spring grove of young trees or bushes
redress prop up again. The trouble with all these immensely practical suggestions is that it will leave her unpropped (ll. 432–33) by Adam.
Eve as by her epithet, "Mother of all life" (Genesis 3:2)
motioned proposed

In woman, than to study household good,
And good works in her husband to promote.
Yet not so strictly hath our Lord imposed
Labour, as to debar us when we need
Refreshment, whether food, or talk between,
Food of the mind, or this sweet intercourse
Of looks and smiles, for smiles from reason flow,
To brute denied, and are of love the food,
Love not the lowest end of human life.
For not to irksome toil, but to delight
He made us, and delight to reason joined.
These paths and bowers doubt not but our joint hands
Will keep from wilderness with ease, as wide
As we need walk, till younger hands ere long
Assist us. But if much convérse perhaps
Thee satiate, to short absence I could yield.
For solitude sometimes is best society,
And short retirement urges sweet return.
But other doubt possesses me, lest harm
Befall thee severed from me; for thou knowest
What hath been warned us, what malicious foe,
Envying our happiness, and of his own
Despairing, seeks to work us woe and shame
By sly assault; and somewhere nigh at hand
Watches, no doubt, with greedy hope to find
His wish and best advantage, us asunder,
Hopeless to circumvent us joined, where each
To other speedy aid might lend at need;
Whether his first design be to withdraw
Our fealty° from God, or to disturb
Conjugal love, than which perhaps no bliss
Enjoyed by us excites his envy more;
Or this,° or worse, leave not the faithful side
That gave thee being, still shades thee and protects.
The wife, where danger or dishonour lurks,
Safest and seemliest by her husband stays,
Who guards her, or with her the worst endures.'
   To whom the virgin° majesty of Eve,
As one who loves, and some unkindness meets,
With sweet austere composure thus replied:
   'Offspring of heaven and earth, and all earth's lord,
That such an enemy we have, who seeks
Our ruin, both by thee informed I learn,
And from the parting angel overheard
As in a shady nook I stood behind,
Just then returned at shut° of evening flowers.

fealty fidelity
Or this whether (his plan) is this
virgin innocent; but literally too: she is not a virgin, but her majesty is so far unruptured
shut folding-up time

But that thou shouldst my firmness therefore doubt
To God or thee, because we have a foe
May tempt it, I expected not to hear.
His violence thou fear'st not, being such
As we, not capable of death or pain,
Can either not receive, or can repel.
His fraud is then thy fear, which plain infers
Thy equal fear that my firm faith and love
Can by his fraud be shaken or seduced;
Thoughts, which how found they harbour in thy breast,
Adam, misthought of her to thee so dear?'
   To whom with healing words Adam replied:
'Daughter of God and man, immortal Eve,
For such thou art, from sin and blame entire;°
Not diffident of thee do I dissuade
Thy absence from my sight, but to avoid
The attempt itself, intended by our foe.
For he who tempts, though in vain, at least asperses°
The tempted with dishonour foul, supposed
Not incorruptible of faith, not proof
Against temptation. Thou thyself with scorn
And anger wouldst resent the offered wrong,
Though ineffectual found. Misdeem not then,
If such affront I labour to avert
From thee alone, which on us both at once
The enemy, though bold, will hardly dare,
Or daring, first on me the assault shall light.
Nor thou his malice and false guile contemn;
Subtle he needs must be, who could seduce
Angels, nor think superfluous others' aid.
I from the influence° of thy looks receive
Access° in every virtue, in thy sight
More wise, more watchful, stronger, if need were
Of outward strength; while shame, thou looking on,
Shame to be overcome or overreached,
Would utmost vigour raise, and raised unite.
Why shouldst not thou like sense within thee feel
When I am present, and thy trial choose
With me, best witness of thy virtue tried?'
   So spake domestic Adam in his care
And matrimonial love; but Eve, who thought
Less° attribúted to her faith sincere,
Thus her reply with accent sweet renewed:
   'If this be our condition, thus to dwell
In narrow circuit straitened° by a foe,

entire integral, untarnished
asperses sprays about
influence the beams of stars. Adam has fallen into Petrarchan poetry.
Access increase
Less too little
straitened constricted

Subtle or violent, we not endued
Single with like defence, wherever met,
How are we happy, still in fear of harm?
But harm precedes not sin: only our foe
Tempting affronts us with his foul esteem
Of our integrity; his foul esteem
Sticks no dishonour on our front,° but turns
Foul on himself; then wherefore shunned or feared
By us? Who rather double honour gain
From his surmise proved false, find peace within,
Favour from heaven, our witness, from the event.
And what is faith, love, virtue, unassayed
Alone, without exterior help sustained?
Let us not then suspect our happy state
Left so imperfect by the maker wise
As not secure to single or combined.
Frail is our happiness, if this be so,
And Eden were no Eden° thus exposed.'

To whom thus Adam fervently replied:
'O woman, best are all things as the will
Of God ordained them; his creating hand
Nothing imperfect or deficient left
Of all that he created, much less man,
Or aught that might his happy state secure,
Secure from outward force: within himself
The danger lies, yet lies within his power;
Against his will he can receive no harm.
But God left free the will, for what obeys
Reason is free, and reason he made right,°
But bid her well beware, and still erect,°
Lest by some fair appearing good surprised
She dictate false, and misinform the will
To do what God expressly hath forbid.
Not then mistrust, but tender love enjoins,
That I should mind° thee oft, and mind° thou me.
Firm we subsist, yet possible to swerve,°
Since reason not impossibly may meet
Some specious object by the foe suborned,
And fall into deception unaware,
Not keeping strictest watch, as she was warned.
Seek not temptation then, which to avoid
Were better, and most likely if from me
Thou sever not; trial will come unsought.

front brow, forehead
Eden in its Hebrew meaning of "pleasure"
right right reason, as distinguished from capable wit
erect attentive
mind remind admonishingly; but when repeated, "pay heed to"
Firm . . . swerve a subtly modulated echo of the central doctrinal statement of God: "I made him just and right, / Sufficient to have stood, though free to fall" (III.98–99)

Wouldst thou approve thy constancy, approve°
First thy obedience; the other who can know,
Not seeing thee attempted, who attest?
But if thou think trial unsought may find
Us both securer° than thus warned thou seem'st,
Go; for thy stay, not free, absents thee more;
Go in thy native innocence, rely
On what thou hast of virtue, summon all,
For God towards thee hath done his part, do thine.'
  So spake the patriarch of mankind, but Eve
Persisted; yet submiss,° though last, replied:
  'With thy permission then, and thus forewarned,
Chiefly by what thy own last reasoning words
Touched only, that our trial, when least sought,
May find us both perhaps far less prepared,
The willinger I go, nor much expect
A foe so proud will first the weaker seek;
So bent, the more shall shame him his repulse.'
  Thus saying, from her husband's hand her hand
Soft she withdrew,° and like a wood-nymph light,
Oread or Dryad, or of Delia's° train,
Betook her to the groves, but Delia's self
In gait surpassed and goddess-like deport,°
Though not as she with bow and quiver armed,
But with such gardening tools as art yet rude
—Guiltless of fire°—had formed, or angles brought.
To Pales,° or Pomona,° thus adorned,
Likest she seemed, Pomona when she fled
Vertumnus,° or to Ceres in her prime,
Yet virgin of Proserpina° from Jove.
Her long with ardent look his eye pursued
Delighted, but desiring more her stay.
Oft he to her his charge of quick return
Repeated, she to him as oft engaged
To be returned by noon amid the bower,
And all things in best order to invite
Noontide repast, or afternoon's repose.
O much deceived, much failing,° hapless Eve,
Of thy presumed return! event perverse!
Thou never from that hour in Paradise
Found'st either sweet repast or sound repose;

approve prove
Us both securer surer of ourselves (and thus, more careless)
submiss submissively
her hand . . . withdrew Casual as this detail may seem, it makes a picture of an emblem being broken (see IV.321n.).
Oread . . . Delia's mountain or tree nymph of Diana's
deport bearing
fire The fire Prometheus stole stands for all technology.
Pales Roman goddess of pastures
Pomona goddess of fruit trees
Vertumnus god of seasons, her lover
Proserpina See IV.269n.
failing to return; also, generally, "failed Eve–"

Such ambush hid, among sweet flowers and shades
Waited with hellish rancour imminent
To intercept thy way, or send thee back
Despoiled of innocence, of faith, of bliss.
For now, and since first break of dawn the fiend,
Mere serpent° in appearance, forth was come,
And on his quest, where likeliest he might find
The only two of mankind, but in them
The whole included race, his purposed prey.
In bower and field he sought, where any tuft
Of grove or garden-plot more pleasant lay,
Their tendance° or plantation for delight;
By fountain or by shady rivulet
He sought them both, but wished his hap might find
Eve separate; he wished, but not with hope
Of what so seldom chanced, when to his wish,
Beyond his hope, Eve separate he spies,
Veiled in a cloud of fragrance, where she stood,
Half spied, so thick the roses bushing round
About her glowed, oft stooping to support
Each flower of slender stalk, whose head though gay
Carnation, purple, azure, or specked with gold,
Hung drooping unsustained; them she upstays
Gently with myrtle band, mindless° the while,
Herself, though fairest unsupported flower,
From her best prop° so far, and storm so nigh.
Nearer he drew, and many a walk traversed
Of stateliest covert, cedar, pine, or palm,
Then voluble° and bold, now hid, now seen
Among thick-woven arborets° and flowers
Embordered on each bank, the hand of Eve:
Spot more delicious than those gardens feigned°
Or of revived Adonis, or renowned
Alcinous, host of old Laertes' son,°
Or that, not mystic, where the sapient king°
Held dalliance with his fair Egyptian spouse.
Much he the place admired, the person more.
As one who long in populous city pent,
Where houses thick and sewers annoy the air,
Forth issuing on a summer's morn to breathe
Among the pleasant villages and farms
Adjoined, from each thing met conceives delight,

Mere serpent He did not look like Northern Renaissance pictures of the temptation of Eve, in which the serpent has a human head.
tendance something to be tended
mindless heedless
her best prop Cf. ll. 210 and 219n.
voluble coiling; perhaps now in the sense of "glib" as well
arborets shrubs
feigned imagined; see *The Faerie Queene* III.vi, and Chapman's translation of the corresponding passage from Homer
Laertes' son Ulysses
not mystic . . . king Solomon's garden, real, historical biblical, hence not mythical like the garden of Adonis ("mystic")

The smell of grain, or tedded° grass, or kine,°
Or dairy, each rural sight, each rural sound;
If chance with nymph-like step fair virgin pass,
What pleasing seemed, for her now pleases more,
She most, and in her look sums all delight:
Such pleasure took the Serpent to behold
This flowery plat,° the sweet recess of Eve
Thus early, thus alone; her heavenly form
Angelic, but more soft and feminine,
Her graceful innocence, her every air
Of gesture or least action overawed
His malice, and with rapine sweet bereaved
His fierceness of the fierce intent it brought.
That space the evil one abstracted stood
From his own evil, and for the time remained
Stupidly° good, of enmity disarmed,
Of guile, of hate, of envy, of revenge;
But the hot hell that always in him burns,
Though in mid-heaven, soon ended his delight,
And tortures him now more, the more he sees
Of pleasure not for him ordained; then soon
Fierce hate he recollects, and all his thoughts
Of mischief, gratulating,° thus excites:
'Thoughts, whither have ye led me, with what sweet
Compulsion thus transported to forget
What hither brought us? Hate, not love, nor hope
Of Paradise for hell, hope here to taste
Of pleasure, but all pleasure to destroy,
Save what is in destroying; other joy
To me is lost. Then let me not let pass
Occasion which now smiles: behold alone
The woman, opportune° to all attempts,
Her husband, for I view far round, not nigh,
Whose higher intellectual° more I shun,
And strength, of courage haughty, and of limb
Heroic built, though of terrestrial mould,°
Foe not informidable, exempt from wound,
I not; so much hath hell debased, and pain
Enfeebled me, to what I was in heaven.
She fair, divinely fair, fit love for gods,
Not terrible, though terror be in love
And beauty, not° approached by stronger hate,
Hate stronger, under show of love well feigned,

tedded spread out for haymaking
kine cattle
plat plot of ground
Stupidly stupefied (and thus incapable, for the moment, of evil)
gratulating expressing pleasure
opportune opportunely placed
intellectual mind
terrestrial mould formed of earth
not if not

The way which to her ruin now I tend.'
  So spake the Enemy of mankind, enclosed
In serpent, inmate bad, and toward Eve
Addressed his way, not with indented wave,
Prone on the ground, as since, but on his rear,
Circular base of rising folds, that towered
Fold above fold a surging maze; his head
Crested aloft, and carbuncle his eyes;
With burnished neck of verdant gold, erect
Amidst his circling spires,° that on the grass
Floated redundant.° Pleasing was his shape,
And lovely, never since of serpent kind
Lovelier; not those that in Illyria changed
Hermione and Cadmus,° or the god
In Epidaurus;° nor to which transformed
Ammonian Jove,° or Capitoline° was seen,
He with Olympias, this with her who bore
Scipio, the highth of Rome. With tract° oblique
At first, as one who sought accéss, but feared
To interrupt, sidelong he works his way.
As when a ship by skilful steersman wrought
Nigh river's mouth or foreland, where the wind
Veers oft, as oft so steers, and shifts her sail,
So varied he, and of his tortuous train
Curled many a wanton wreath in sight of Eve,
To lure her eye; she busied heard the sound
Of rustling leaves, but minded not, as used
To such disport before her through the field
From every beast, more duteous at her call
Than at Circean call the herd disguised.°
He bolder now, uncalled before her stood,
But as in gaze admiring. Oft he bowed
His turret crest, and sleek enamelled neck,
Fawning, and licked the ground whereon she trod.
His gentle dumb expression turned at length
The eye of Eve to mark his play; he glad
Of her attention gained, with serpent tongue
Organic,° or impulse of vocal air,
His fraudulent temptation thus began:
  'Wonder not, sovereign mistress, if perhaps
Thou canst, who art sole wonder, much less arm
Thy looks, the heaven of mildness, with disdain,

spires spirals
redundant excessively flowing, wave-like
Hermione and Cadmus Hermione (Harmonia) and her king were changed into serpents.
god In Epidaurus Aesculapius' statue in Epidaurus represented the god of healing as an erect serpent.
Ammonian Jove Jupiter took Olympias, Alexander the Great's mother, in the form of a snake; Capitoline Jupiter, similarly, the father of the Roman general Scipio Africanus.
tract path
herd disguised Ulysses' men turned by Circe into pigs
Organic instrumental

Displeased that I approach thee thus, and gaze
Insatiate, I thus single, nor have feared
Thy awful brow, more awful thus retired.
Fairest resemblance of thy maker fair,
Thee all things living gaze on, all things thine
By gift, and thy celestial beauty adore,
With ravishment beheld, there best beheld
Where universally admired; but here
In this enclosure wild, these beasts among,
Beholders rude, and shallow to discern
Half what in thee is fair, one man except,
Who sees thee? (and what is one?) who shouldst be seen
A goddess among gods, adored and served
By angels numberless, thy daily train.'
  So glozed° the Tempter, and his proem tuned;
Into the heart of Eve his words made way,
Though at the voice much marvelling; at length
Not unamazed she thus in answer spake:
  'What may this mean? Language of man pronounced
By tongue of brute, and human sense expressed?
The first at least of these I thought denied
To beasts, whom God on their creation-day
Created mute to all articulate sound;
The latter I demur,° for in their looks
Much reason, and in their actions oft appears.
Thee, Serpent, subtlest beast of all the field
I knew, but not with human voice endued;
Redouble then this miracle, and say,
How cam'st thou speakable of mute,° and how
To me so friendly grown above the rest
Of brutal kind, that daily are in sight?
Say, for such wonder claims attention due.'
  To whom the guileful tempter thus replied:
'Empress of this fair world, resplendent Eve,
Easy to me it is to tell thee all
What thou command'st, and right thou shouldst be obeyed.
I was at first as other beasts that graze
The trodden herb, of abject° thoughts and low,
As was my food, nor aught but food discerned
Or sex, and apprehended nothing high:
Till on a day roving the field, I chanced
A goodly tree far distant to behold,
Loaden with fruit of fairest colours mixed,
Ruddy and gold. I nearer drew to gaze;

glozed flattered
The latter I demur I have doubts about "human sense expressed"—obviously, animals communicate, but don't have language
speakable of mute capable of speech, from being mute
abject cast down

When from the boughs a savoury odour blown,
Grateful to appetite, more pleased my sense
Than smell of sweetest fennel or the teats
Of ewe or goat dropping with milk at even,
Unsucked of lamb or kid, that tend their play.
To satisfy the sharp desire I had
Of tasting those fair apples,° I resolved
Not to defer;° hunger and thirst at once,
Powerful persuaders, quickened at the scent
Of that alluring fruit, urged me so keen.
About the mossy trunk I wound me soon,
For high from ground the branches would require
Thy utmost reach or Adam's: round the tree
All other beasts that saw, with like desire
Longing and envying stood, but could not reach.
Amid the tree now got, where plenty hung
Tempting so nigh, to pluck and eat my fill
I spared not, for such pleasure till that hour
At feed or fountain never had I found.
Sated at length, ere long I might perceive
Strange alteration in me, to degree°
Of reason in my inward powers, and speech
Wanted not long, though to this shape retained.
Thenceforth to speculations high or deep
I turned my thoughts, and with capacious mind
Considered all things visible in heaven,
Or earth, or middle,° all things fair and good;
But all that fair and good in thy divine
Semblance, and in thy beauty's heavenly ray
United I beheld; no fair to thine
Equivalent or second, which compelled
Me thus, though importune perhaps, to come
And gaze, and worship thee of right declared
Sovereign of creatures, universal dame.'°
    So talked the spirited° sly snake; and Eve
Yet more amazed unwary thus replied:
    'Serpent, thy overpraising leaves in doubt
The virtue° of that fruit, in thee first proved.
But say, where grows the tree, from hence how far?
For many are the trees of God that grow
In Paradise, and various, yet unknown
To us; in such abundance lies our choice
As leaves a greater store of fruit untouched,
Still hanging incorruptible, till men

apples The identification of the fruit with the apple is folkloristic, not biblical.
defer delay
to degree to an extent
middle the air
dame mistress
spirited animated
virtue power

Grow up to their provision, and more hands
Help to disburden Nature of her birth.'
   To whom the wily adder, blithe and glad:
'Empress, the way is ready, and not long,
Beyond a row of myrtles, on a flat,
Fast by a fountain, one small thicket past
Of blowing° myrrh and balm; if thou accept
My conduct,° I can bring thee thither soon.'
   'Lead then,' said Eve. He leading swiftly rolled
In tangles, and made intricate seem straight,°
To mischief swift. Hope elevates, and joy
Brightens his crest, as when a wandering fire,
Compact° of unctuous vapour, which the night
Condenses, and the cold environs round,
Kindled through agitation to a flame,
Which oft, they say, some evil spirit attends,°
Hovering and blazing with delusive light,
Misleads the amazed night-wanderer from his way
To bogs and mires, and oft through pond or pool,
There swallowed up and lost, from succour far.
So glistered the dire Snake, and into fraud
Led Eve our credulous mother, to the tree
Of prohibition,° root of all our woe;
Which when she saw, thus to her guide she spake:
   'Serpent, we might have spared our coming hither,
Fruitless to me, though fruit be here to excess,
The credit of whose virtue rest with thee,
Wondrous indeed, if cause of such effects.
But of this tree we may not taste nor touch;
God so commanded, and left that command
Sole daughter of his voice;° the rest, we live
Law to ourselves, our reason is our law.'
   To whom the Tempter guilefully replied:
'Indeed? Hath God then said that of the fruit
Of all these garden trees ye shall not eat,
Yet lords declared of all in earth or air?'
   To whom thus Eve yet sinless: 'Of the fruit
Of each tree in the garden we may eat,
But of the fruit of this fair tree amidst
The garden, God hath said, "Ye shall not eat
Thereof, nor shall ye touch it, lest ye die." '

blowing blooming
conduct lead (the moral sense is there, unavowed)
intricate seem straight again, his shaky motion and his moral direction. From this moment on in human history, "crooked" and "straight" will have moral connotations.
Compact composed
evil spirit attends the *ignis fatuus,* or will-o'-the-wisp, often associated with self-delusion
tree Of prohibition prohibited tree. The impact of "root," following immediately in the metaphorical sense, and "fruitless" three lines further on, is strengthened by the literalness of "tree."
daughter of his voice the only commandment He enjoined on us

She scarce had said, though brief, when now more bold
The tempter, but with show of zeal and love
To man, and indignation at his wrong,
New part puts on, and as to passion moved,
Fluctuates° disturbed, yet comely, and in act
Raised, as of some great matter to begin.
As when of old some orator renowned
In Athens or free Rome, where eloquence
Flourished, since mute, to some great cause addressed,
Stood in himself collected, while each part,
Motion, each act won audience° ere the tongue,
Sometimes in highth° began, as no delay
Of preface brooking through his zeal of right:
So standing, moving, or to highth upgrown,
The tempter all impassioned thus began:
'O sacred, wise, and wisdom-giving plant,
Mother of science,° now I feel thy power
Within me clear, not only to discern
Things in their causes, but to trace the ways
Of highest agents, deemed however wise.
Queen of this universe, do not believe
Those rigid threats of death; ye shall not die:
How should ye? By the fruit? It gives you life
To° knowledge; by the threatener? Look on me,
Me who have touched and tasted, yet both live,
And life more perfect have attained than fate
Meant me, by venturing higher than my lot.
Shall that be shut to man, which to the beast
Is open? Or will God incense his ire
For such a petty trespass, and not praise
Rather your dauntless virtue, whom the pain
Of death denounced,° whatever thing death be,
Deterred not from achieving what might lead
To happier life, knowledge of good and evil?
Of good, how just? Of evil, if what is evil
Be real, why not known, since easier shunned?
God therefore cannot hurt ye, and be just;
Not just, not God; not feared then, nor obeyed:
Your fear itself of death removes the fear.
Why then was this forbid? Why but to awe,
Why but to keep ye low and ignorant,
His worshippers? He knows that in the day
Ye eat thereof, your eyes that seem so clear,
Yet are but dim, shall perfectly be then
Opened and cleared, and ye shall be as gods,

Fluctuates changes appearance
audience attention
highth height of feeling
science knowledge
To as well as
denounced proclaimed

Knowing both good and evil as they know.
That ye should be as gods, since I as man,
Internal man,° is but proportion meet,
I of brute human, ye of human gods.
So ye shall die perhaps, by putting off
Human, to put on gods,° death to be wished,
Though threatened, which no worse than this can bring.
And what are gods that man may not become
As they, participating° godlike food?
The gods are first, and that advantage use
On our belief, that all from them proceeds;
I question it, for this fair earth I see,
Warmed by the sun, producing every kind,
Them nothing. If they° all things, who enclosed
Knowledge of good and evil in this tree,
That whoso eats thereof, forthwith attains
Wisdom without their leave? And wherein lies
The offence, that man should thus attain to know?
What can your knowledge hurt him, or this tree
Impart against his will, if all be his?
Or is it envy, and can envy dwell
In heavenly breasts? These, these and many more
Causes import° your need of this fair fruit.
Goddess humane,° reach then, and freely taste!'
He ended, and his words replete with guile
Into her heart too easy entrance won.
Fixed on the fruit she gazed, which to behold
Might tempt alone, and in her ears the sound
Yet rung of his persuasive words, impregned
With reason, to her seeming, and with truth;
Meanwhile the hour of noon° drew on, and waked
An eager appetite, raised by the smell
So savoury of that fruit, which with desire,
Inclinable now grown to touch or taste,
Solicited her longing eye; yet first
Pausing a while, thus to herself she mused:
'Great are thy virtues, doubtless, best of fruits,
Though kept from man, and worthy to be admired,
Whose taste, too long forborne, at first assay
Gave elocution° to the mute, and taught

Internal man See above, l. 600, where Satan claims that his inner state has become human through the agency of the fruit.

put on gods Satan brilliantly and nastily adapts the language of Colossians 3:9–10 to his perverse construction of spiritual regeneration: "Lie not one to another, seeing that ye have put off the old man with his deeds; And have put on the new man, which is renewed in knowledge after the image of him that created him."

participating sharing,

they they produced

import indicate

Goddess humane "Human," the first reading, concludes Satan's rhetoric with a blatant oxymoron; the second sense, "gentle," is only to mellow it in afterthought.

noon The tasting and falling must occur at noon, less light be denied, and reason be cheated.

elocution eloquence

The tongue not made for speech to speak thy praise.
Thy praise he also who forbids thy use
Conceals not from us, naming thee the Tree
Of Knowledge, knowledge both of good and evil;
Forbids us then to taste, but his forbidding
Commends thee more, while it infers the good
By thee communicated, and our want;
For good unknown sure is not had, or had
And yet unknown, is as not had at all.
In plain° then, what forbids he but to know,
Forbids us good, forbids us to be wise?
Such prohibitions bind not. But if Death
Bind us with after-bands, what profits then
Our inward freedom? In the day we eat
Of this fair fruit, our doom is, we shall die.
How dies the serpent? He hath eaten and lives,
And knows, and speaks, and reasons, and discerns,
Irrational till then. For us alone
Was death invented? Or to us denied
This intellectual food, for beasts reserved?
For beasts it seems—yet that one beast which first
Hath tasted, envies not, but brings with joy
The good befallen him, author unsuspect,°
Friendly to man, far from deceit or guile.
What fear I then, rather what know to fear
Under this ignorance of good and evil,
Of God or death, of law or penalty?
Here grows the cure° of all, this fruit divine,
Fair to the eye, inviting to the taste,
Of virtue° to make wise; what hinders then
To reach, and feed at once both body and mind?'
   So saying, her rash hand in evil hour°
Forth reaching to the fruit, she plucked, she eat.°
Earth felt the wound, and Nature from her seat
Sighing through all her works gave signs of woe,
That all was lost.° Back to the thicket slunk
The guilty Serpent, and well might, for Eve
Intent now wholly on her taste, naught else
Regarded; such delight till then, as seemed,
In fruit she never tasted, whether true
Or fancied so, through expectation high
Of knowledge, nor was godhead from her thought.
Greedily she engorged without restraint,

In plain put simply
author unsuspect unsuspected authority
cure The secondary sense is "charge, responsibility."
Of virtue able
evil hour Our sense that "evil" puns on "Eve" is confirmed at l. 1067.
eat ate
Nature . . . lost Nature only sighs in pain here, but see ll. 1000–1004.

And knew not eating death,° Satiate at length,
And heightened as with wine, jocund and boon,°
Thus to herself she pleasingly began:
'O sovereign, virtuous, precious of all trees
In Paradise, of operation° blest
To sapience, hitherto obscured, infamed,
And thy fair fruit let hang, as to no end
Created; but henceforth my early care,
Not without song, each morning, and due praise,
Shall tend thee, and the fertile burden ease
Of thy full branches offered free to all;
Till dieted by thee I grow mature
In knowledge, as the gods° who all things know;
Though others envy what they cannot give;
For had the gift been theirs, it had not here
Thus grown. Experience, next to thee I owe,
Best guide; not following thee, I had remained
In ignorance; thou open'st wisdom's way,
And giv'st accéss, though secret she retire.
And I perhaps am secret;° heaven is high,
High and remote to see from thence distinct
Each thing on earth; and other care perhaps
May have diverted from continual watch
Our Great Forbidder, safe° with all his spies
About him. But to Adam in what sort
Shall I appear? Shall I to him make known
As yet my change, and give him to partake
Full happiness with me, or rather not,
But keep the odds of knowledge in my power
Without copartner? So to add what wants
In female sex, the more to draw his love,
And render me more equal, and perhaps—
A thing not undesirable—sometime
Superior; for inferior who is free?°
This may be well. But what if God have seen,
And death ensue? Then I shall be no more,
And Adam wedded to another Eve
Shall live with her enjoying, I extinct;
A death to think.° Confirmed then I resolve,
Adam shall share with me in bliss or woe.
So dear I love him, that with him all deaths
I could endure, without him live no life.'

knew not eating death knew not that she was eating death
boon jolly
operation effectiveness
gods Echoes Satan's equivocal use of the plural in ll. 712, 718, and I.116.
secret hidden, secreted
safe of no danger
for inferior who is free? The rhetorical questioning and the political theory are both recognizably Satan's.
A death to think Having literalized death by her act, Eve's using the word figuratively is in odious taste.

So saying, from the tree her step she turned,
But first low reverence done,° as to the power
That dwelt within, whose presence had infused
Into the plant sciential° sap, derived
From nectar, drink of gods.° Adam the while
Waiting desirous her return, had wove
Of choicest flowers a garland to adorn
Her tresses, and her rural labours crown,
As reapers oft are wont their harvest queen.
Great joy he promised to his thoughts, and new
Solace in her return, so long delayed;
Yet oft his heart, divine° of something ill,
Misgave him; he the faltering measure° felt;
And forth to meet her went, the way she took
That morn when first they parted. By the Tree
Of Knowledge he must pass; there he her met,
Scarce from the tree returning; in her hand
A bough of fairest fruit that downy smiled,
New gathered, and ambrosial smell diffused.
To him she hasted; in her face excuse
Came prologue, and apology to prompt,°
Which with bland words at will she thus addressed:
'Hast thou not wondered, Adam, at my stay?
Thee I have missed, and thought it long, deprived
Thy presence, agony of love till now
Not felt, nor shall be twice, for never more
Mean I to try what rash untried I sought,
The pain of absence from thy sight. But strange
Hath been the cause, and wonderful to hear:
This tree is not as we are told, a tree
Of danger° tasted, nor to evil unknown
Opening the way, but of divine effect
To open eyes, and make them gods who taste;
And hath been tasted° such. The serpent wise,
Or° not restrained as we, or not obeying,
Hath eaten of the fruit, and is become
Not dead, as we are threatened, but thenceforth
Endued with human voice and human sense,
Reasoning to admiration, and with me
Persuasively hath so prevailed, that I
Have also tasted, and have also found

low reverence done a bow, the first act of idolatry, and the first myth. Eve is worshiping a Dryad of some sort by treating the power in the fruit in this way.
sciential knowledge-giving
nectar, drink of gods Her personal religion implies a whole pagan pantheon.
divine prophet
faltering measure irregular heartbeat
prologue . . . prompt These are theatrical terms: Eve's facial expression is visible before she speaks, like a prologue to a play; cf. IX.670–76.
Of danger of danger if
tasted tested
Or either

The effects to correspond, opener° mine eyes,
Dim erst, dilated spirits, ampler heart,
And growing up to godhead; which for thee
Chiefly I sought, without thee can despise.
For bliss, as thou hast part, to me is bliss;
Tedious, unshared with thee, and odious soon.
Thou therefore also taste, that equal lot
May join us, equal joy, as equal love;
Lest thou not tasting, different degree
Disjoin us, and I then too late renounce
Deity for thee, when fate will not permit.'
  Thus Eve with countenance blithe her story told;
But in her cheek distemper° flushing glowed.
On the other side, Adam, soon as he heard
The fatal trespass done by Eve, amazed,
Astonied° stood and blank, while horror chill
Ran through his veins, and all his joints relaxed;
From his slack hand the garland wreathed for Eve
Down dropped, and all the faded roses° shed.
Speechless he stood and pale, till thus at length
First to himself he inward silence broke:
  'O fairest of creation, last and best
Of all God's works, creature in whom excelled
Whatever can to sight or thought be formed,
Holy, divine, good, amiable,° or sweet!
How art thou lost, how on a sudden lost,
Defaced, deflowered,° and now to death devote!°
Rather how hast thou yielded to transgress
The strict forbiddance, how to violate
The sacred fruit forbidden! Some cursèd fraud
Of enemy hath beguiled thee, yet unknown,
And me with thee hath ruined, for with thee
Certain my resolution is to die;
How can I live without thee, how forgo
Thy sweet converse and love so dearly joined,
To live again in these wild woods forlorn?°
Should God create another Eve, and I
Another rib afford, yet loss of thee
Would never from my heart; no, no! I feel
The link of nature draw me: flesh of flesh,
Bone of my bone thou art,° and from thy state

opener The insistence on this word arises from Genesis 3:7, "And the eyes of them both were opened" (this is shortly to occur), but its force comes from our ironic realization that her act has closed off everything.
distemper intoxication, disorder of temperament
Astonied petrified, paralyzed
faded roses the first instance of natural cycle, of withering flowers
amiable lovely
deflowered in a host of senses, given the association of Eve with flowers throughout
devote cursed
To live . . . forlorn To see Adam think of Eden as "wild woods" is touching; to see, through the ambiguous syntax, that "forlorn" can mean the woods, Eden, as well as the speaker, is tragic.
flesh . . . art echoing IV.483

Mine never shall be parted, bliss or woe.'
  So having said, as one from sad dismay
Recomforted, and after thoughts disturbed
Submitting to what seemed remédiless,
Thus in calm mood his words to Eve he turned:
  'Bold deed thou hast presumed, adventurous Eve,
And peril great provoked, who thus hast dared
Had it been only coveting to eye
That sacred fruit, sacred to abstinence,
Much more to taste it under ban to touch.
But past who can recall, or done undo?
Not God omnipotent, nor fate. Yet so
Perhaps thou shalt not die; perhaps the fact°
Is not so heinous now, foretasted fruit,
Profaned first by the Serpent, by him first
Made common and unhallowed ere our taste,
Nor yet on him found deadly; he yet lives,
Lives, as thou saidst, and gains to live as man
Higher degree of life, inducement strong
To us, as likely tasting to attain
Proportional ascent, which cannot be
But to be gods, or angels, demi-gods.
Nor can I think that God, Creator wise,
Though threatening, will in earnest so destroy
Us his prime creatures, dignified so high,
Set over all his works, which in our fall,
For us created, needs with us must fail,
Dependent made; so God shall uncreate,
Be frustrate, do, undo, and labour lose,°
Not well conceived of God, who though his power
Creation could repeat, yet would be loth
Us to abolish, lest the adversary
Triumph and say,° *"Fickle their state whom God
Most favours, who can please him long? Me first
He ruined, now mankind; whom will he next?"*
Matter of scorn not to be given the foe;
However, I with thee have fixed my lot,
Certain° to undergo like doom: if death
Consort with thee, death is to me as life;
So forcible within my heart I feel
The bond of nature draw me to my own,
My own in thee, for what thou art is mine;
Our state cannot be severed; we are one,
One flesh; to lose thee were to lose myself.'

fact deed, crime
lose or perhaps, "loose," in the sense of "undo"
say Even before tasting the fruit himself, Adam has become sensitive to Satanic rhetoric: he parodies the adversary too well.
Certain resolved

So Adam, and thus Eve to him replied:
'O glorious trial of exceeding love,
Illustrious evidence, example high!
Engaging me to emulate, but short
Of thy perfection, how shall I attain,
Adam, from whose dear side I boast me sprung,
And gladly of our union hear thee speak,
One heart, one soul in both; whereof good proof
This day affords, declaring thee resolved,
Rather than death or aught than death more dread
Shall separate us, linked in love so dear,
To undergo with me one guilt, one crime,
If any be, of tasting this fair fruit,
Whose virtue (for of good still good proceeds,
Direct, or by occasion) hath presented
This happy trial of thy love, which else
So eminently never had been known.
Were it I thought death menaced would ensue
This my attempt, I would sustain alone
The worst, and not persuade thee, rather die
Deserted, than oblige° thee with a fact
Pernicious to thy peace, chiefly assured°
Remarkably so late of thy so true,
So faithful love unequalled; but I feel
Far otherwise the event,° not death, but life
Augmented, opened eyes, new hopes, new joys,
Taste so divine, that what of sweet before
Hath touched my sense, flat seems to this and harsh.
On my experience, Adam, freely taste,
And fear of death deliver to the winds.'
So saying, she embraced him, and for joy
Tenderly wept, much won that he his love
Had so ennobled, as of choice to incur
Divine displeasure for her sake, or death.
In recompense (for such compliance bad
Such recompense best merits) from the bough
She gave him of that fair enticing fruit
With liberal hand. He scrupled not to eat
Against his better knowledge, not deceived,
But fondly overcome with female charm.
Earth trembled from her entrails, as again
In pangs, and Nature gave a second groan;
Sky loured and, muttering thunder,° some sad drops

oblige involve in guilt
chiefly assured especially with the assurance
event result
muttering thunder the first thunderstorm, imprinting on all subsequent storms, particularly in myth (Shakespearean tempests, etc.), traces of this original rupture between man and his garden, this birth of the natural environment. From the point of view of a 16th-century usage, Nature, cracking, is decaying into "nature"—physical and biological dispositions (see Fulke Greville, "O Wearisome Condition of Humanity").

Wept at completing of the mortal sin
Original;° while Adam took no thought,
Eating his fill, nor Eve to iterate
Her former trespass feared, the more to soothe
Him with her loved society, that now
As with new wine intoxicated both
They swim in mirth, and fancy that they feel
Divinity within them breeding wings°
Wherewith to scorn the earth. But that false fruit
Far other operation first displayed,
Carnal desire inflaming: he on Eve
Began to cast lascivious eyes, she him
As wantonly repaid; in lust they burn,
Till Adam thus 'gan Eve to dalliance move:
'Eve, now I see thou art exact of taste,°
And elegant, of sapience no small part;
Since to each meaning savour we apply,
And palate call judicious; I the praise
Yield thee, so well this day thou hast purveyed.°
Much pleasure we have lost, while we abstained
From this delightful fruit, nor known till now
True relish, tasting; if such pleasure be
In things to us forbidden, it might be wished
For this one tree had been forbidden ten.°
But come, so well refreshed, now let us play,
As meet is, after such delicious fare;
For never did thy beauty since the day
I saw thee first and wedded thee, adorned
With all perfections, so inflame my sense
With ardour to enjoy thee, fairer now
Than ever, bounty of this virtuous tree.'
So said he, and forbore not glance or toy
Of amorous intent, well understood
Of Eve, whose eye darted contagious fire.
Her hand he seized,° and to a shady bank,
Thick overhead with verdant roof embowered,
He led her nothing loth; flowers were the couch,
Pansies, and violets, and asphodel,
And hyacinth, earth's freshest softest lap.
There they their fill of love and love's disport

sin Original that one, first, comprehensive disobedience, containing a host of others "which our first parents, and in them all their posterity, committed," as Milton says in the *Christian Doctrine*
breeding wings This is an expansion of Eve's first intoxication, at l. 793, and an ironic fulfillment of the trip in her dream (V.86–90).
exact of taste having "good taste" (discernment, moral and esthetic wisdom). Like so many fundamental dramatic ironies affecting the institution of human death, this word-play, unwitting on Adam's part, perhaps, is in the worst taste imaginable.
purveyed provided
ten ten times over. Now that they are mortal, number games seem appealing; now that there will never be world enough and time, the counting starts.
seized The word has all the strength of "grabbed."

Took largely,° of their mutual guilt the seal,
The solace of their sin, till dewy sleep
Oppressed them, wearied with their amorous play.°
Soon as the force of that fallacious fruit,
That with exhilarating vapour bland
About their spirits had played, and inmost powers
Made err, was now exhaled, and grosser sleep°
Bred of unkindly° fumes, with conscious dreams
Encumbered, now had left them, up they rose
As from unrest, and each the other viewing,
Soon found their eyes how opened, and their minds
How darkened; innocence, that as a veil
Had shadowed them° from knowing ill, was gone;
Just confidence, and native righteousness,
And honour from about them, naked left
To guilty shame; he covered, but his robe
Uncovered more. So rose the Danite strong,
Herculean Samson, from the harlot-lap
Of Philistéan Dálilah, and waked
Shorn of his strength, they destitute and bare
Of all their virtue. Silent, and in face
Confounded, long they sat, as strucken mute,
Till Adam, though not less than Eve abashed,
At length gave utterance to these words constrained:
'O Eve, in evil hour° thou didst give ear
To that false worm, of whomsoever taught
To counterfeit man's voice, true in our fall,
False in our promised rising; since our eyes
Opened we find indeed, and find we know
Both good and evil, good lost and evil got,
Bad fruit of knowledge, if this be to know,
Which leaves us naked thus, of honour void,
Of innocence, of faith, of purity,
Our wonted ornaments now soiled and stained,
And in our faces evident the signs
Of foul concupiscence; whence evil store,
Even shame, the last° of evils; of the first
Be sure then. How shall I behold the face
Henceforth of God or angel, erst with joy
And rapture so oft beheld? Those heavenly shapes

their fill . . . largely Milton quotes Proverbs 7:18, where a prostitute uses these phrases.
amorous play This is the first act of fallen sex, casual and desperate in its needed effects of consolation, "of their mutual guilt the seal"—and guilt for the disobedience of eating the fruit. The horror of "honour dishonourable" is that they will now feel guilt about the sex, certainly the one thing for which they should not. In their shame (ll. 1092–93) they wish not to cover the mouths that ate, but the innocent parts of love. This is the horror of the Fall, and the means by which sin infects life around it.
grosser sleep as opposed to the "airy light" sleep at V.4
unkindly unnatural
shadowed them The figurative, inner moral shade being removed, Adam and Eve will begin to feel the pain of light (ll. 1080–90).
Eve . . . hour The pun is now Adam's.
last least

Will dazzle now this earthly,° with their blaze
Insufferably bright. O might I here
In solitude live savage, in some glade
Obscured, where highest woods impenetrable
To star or sunlight, spread their umbrage° broad
And brown as evening! Cover me, ye pines,
Ye cedars, with innumerable boughs
Hide me, where I may never see them° more.
But let us now, as in bad plight, devise
What best may for the present serve to hide
The parts of each from other that seem most
To shame obnoxious,° and unseemliest seen,
Some tree whose broad smooth leaves together sewed,
And girded on our loins, may cover round
Those middle parts, that this newcomer, shame,
There sit not, and reproach us as unclean.'
  So counselled he, and both together went
Into the thickest wood; there soon they chose
The fig-tree,° not that kind for fruit renowned,
But such as at this day to Indians known
In Malabar or Deccan° spreads her arms
Branching so broad and long, that in the ground
The bended twigs take root, and daughters grow
About the mother tree, a pillared shade
High overarched, and echoing walks between;
There oft the Indian herdsman shunning heat
Shelters in cool, and tends his pasturing herds
At loop-holes cut through thickest shade. Those leaves
They gathered, broad as Amazonian targe,
And with what skill they had, together sewed,
To gird their waist, vain covering if to hide
Their guilt and dreaded shame, O how unlike
To that first naked glory! Such of late
Columbus found the American so girt
With feathered cincture, naked else and wild
Among the trees on isles and woody shores.
Thus fenced, and as they thought, their shame in part
Covered, but not at rest or ease of mind,
They sat them down to weep; nor only tears
Rained at their eyes, but high winds worse within°
Began to rise, high passions, anger, hate,

earthly earthly shape
umbrage shade
them the "heavenly shapes" of l. 1082
obnoxious exposed
fig-tree The elaborate, encyclopedic digression occurs here to reinforce the enormity of the institution of clothing; by the description of the Indian banyan tree, and by the allusion to Caribbean savages (ll. 1116–18), we now see Adam and Eve as having suddenly become not Primal man but merely Primitive man. "And with what skill they had" (l. 1112) betokens the touching but inadequate technology of paleolithic people.
Malabar or Deccan on the southwest Indian coast, or the southern peninsula of the subcontinent
Rained . . . within The first thunderstorm has been internalized, the Renaissance microcosmic view of man now becoming an adequate model for comprehending the relation of man and nature.

Mistrust, suspicion, discord, and shook sore
Their inward state of mind, calm region once
And full of peace, now tossed and turbulent;
For understanding ruled not, and the will
Heard not her lore, both in subjection now
To sensual appetite, who from beneath
Usurping over sovereign reason claimed
Superior sway.° From thus distempered breast,
Adam, estranged° in look and altered style,
Speech intermitted thus to Eve renewed:
'Would thou hadst hearkened to my words, and stayed
With me, as I besought thee, when that strange
Desire of wandering this unhappy morn,
I know not whence possessed thee; we had then
Remained still happy, not as now, despoiled
Of all our good, shamed, naked, miserable.°
Let none henceforth seek needless cause to approve°
The faith they owe;° when earnestly they seek
Such proof, conclude they then begin to fail.'
To whom, soon moved with touch of blame, thus Eve:
'What words have passed thy lips, Adam severe!
Imput'st thou that to my default, or will
Of wandering, as thou callest it, which who knows
But might as ill have happened thou being by,
Or to thyself perhaps? Hadst thou been there,
Or here the attempt, thou couldst not have discerned
Fraud in the serpent, speaking as he spake;
No ground of enmity between us known
Why he should mean me ill, or seek to harm.
Was I to have never parted from thy side?
As good have grown there still a lifeless rib.
Being as I am, why didst not thou, the head,°
Command me absolutely not to go,
Going into such danger as thou saidst?
Too facile then, thou didst not much gainsay,
Nay didst permit, approve, and fair dismiss.
Hadst thou been firm and fixed in thy dissent,
Neither had I transgressed, nor thou with me.'
To whom then first incensed Adam replied:
'Is this the love, is this the recompense
Of mine to thee, ingrateful Eve, expressed°
Immutable when thou wert lost, not I,
Who might have lived and joyed° immortal bliss,

Superior sway greater power. The imagery in ll. 1125–31 has moved from storm to political discord.
estranged changed
shamed, naked, miserable See Hobbes's characterization of the life of man in the state of nature: "Solitary, poor, nasty, brutish and short" (*Leviathan,* 1651).
approve prove
owe own
head See IV.433n.
expressed revealed
joyed enjoyed

Yet willingly chose rather death with thee?
And am I now upbraided, as the cause
Of thy transgressing? Not enough severe,
It seems, in thy restraint. What could I more?
I warned thee, I admonished thee, foretold
The danger, and the lurking enemy
That lay in wait; beyond this had been force,
And force upon free will hath here no place.
But confidence then bore thee on, secure
Either to meet no danger, or to find
Matter of glorious trial; and perhaps
I also erred in overmuch admiring
What seemed in thee so perfect, that I thought
No evil durst attempt thee, but I rue
That error now, which is become my crime,
And thou the accuser. Thus it shall befall
Him who to worth in women overtrusting
Lets her will rule; restraint she will not brook,
And left to herself, if evil thence ensue,
She first his weak indulge will accuse.'
Thus they in mutual accusation spent
The fruitless° hours, but neither self-condemning,
And of their vain contést appeared no end.

From *Book X*

[Man fallen, the guardian angels informed that it was not through their failure that the Fall occurred. Satan in triumph, Sin and Death depart from their locale at the gate of hell and enter the world. They build a broad causeway, over the realm of Chaos, connecting hell and the world, the prototype of all easy, populous routes. Satan decends to Pandemonium, where he delivers an address of victory, concluding with the exhortation, "What remains ye Gods, / But up and enter now into full bliss." As if in rhyme, applauding with a hiss, the demons (they are now serpents whose only song is hissing) they fall to a meal on the fruit of a multitude of replicas of the Forbidden Tree, but instead of fruit, they find themselves chewing "bitter ashes." Sin and Death now loose in the world, the latter to feed henceforth on all living things in order to surround man with continual emblems of his own end, God predicts the apocalypse and final revision of the created world. The details of the birth of fallen, biological nature are unfolded, and the introduction of inimical natural forces is followed by a long lament of self-recrimination from Adam which culminates in rhetoric reminiscent of Satan's: "O conscience, into what abyss of fears / And horrors hast thou driven me; out of which / I find no way, from deep to deeper plunged!"]

Thus Adam to himself lamented loud
Through the still night, not now, as ere man fell,

fruitless with the pun still working from the opening line of the poem

Wholesome and cool and mild, but with black air
Accompanied, with damps and dreadful gloom,
Which to his evil conscience represented
All things with double terror. On the ground
Outstretched he lay, on the cold ground, and oft
Cursed his creation, death as oft accused
Of tardy execution, since denounced°
The day of his offence. 'Why comes not death,'
Said he, 'with one thrice-ácceptáble stroke
To end me? Shall truth fail to keep her word,
Justice divine not hasten to be just?
But death comes not at call, justice divine
Mends not her slowest pace for prayers or cries.
O woods, O fountains, hillocks, dales, and bowers,
With other echo late I taught your shades
To answer, and resound far other song.'
Whom thus afflicted when sad Eve beheld,
Desolate where she sat, approaching nigh,
Soft words to his fierce passion she assayed:°
But her with stern regard he thus repelled:
'Out of my sight, thou serpent!° that name best
Befits thee with him leagued, thyself as false
And hateful; nothing wants, but that thy shape,
Like his, and colour serpentine, may show
Thy inward fraud, to warn all creatures from thee
Henceforth; lest that too heavenly form, pretended°
To hellish falsehood, snare them. But for thee
I had persisted happy, had not thy pride
And wandering vanity, when least was safe,
Rejected my forewarning, and disdained
Not be trusted, longing to be seen
Though by the devil himself, him overweening
To overreach, but with the serpent meeting
Fooled and beguiled, by him thou, I by thee.
To trust thee from my side, imagined wise,
Constant, mature, proof against all assaults,
And understood not all was but a show
Rather than solid virtue, all but a rib
Crooked by nature, bent, as now appears,
More to the part sinister° from me drawn;
Well if thrown out, as supernumerary
To my just° number found. O why did God,

denounced announced (on)
assayed tried out
serpent An interpretive false etymology could connect "Eve" with a word for "serpent."
pretended held out in order to screen or disguise
sinister left side, but also "evil." It is Adam, not Milton (through Raphael, in his account of the Creation in Bk. VII), who comes up with the traditional anti-feminist rhetoric and imagery here, in his self-loathing; according to some traditions, Eve came from Adam's left side where there was an extra ("supernumerary") rib.
just exact

Creator wise, that peopled highest heaven
With spirits masculine, create at last
This novelty on earth, this fair defect
Of Nature, and not fill the world at once
With men as angels without feminine,
Or find some other way to generate
Mankind? This mischief had not then befallen,
And more that shall befall, innumerable
Disturbances on earth through female snares,
And strait° conjunction with this sex. For either
He never shall find out fit mate, but such
As some misfortune brings him, or mistake,
Or whom he wishes most shall seldom gain,
Through her perverseness, but shall see her gained
By a far worse, or if she love, withheld
By parents, or his happiest choice too late
Shall meet, already linked and wedlock-bound
To a fell adversary, his hate or shame;
Which infinite calamity shall cause
To human life, and household peace confound.'
    He added not, and from her turned, but Eve,
Not so repulsed, with tears that ceased not flowing,
And tresses all disordered, at his feet
Fell humble, and embracing them, besought
His peace, and thus proceeded in her plaint:
    'Forsake me not thus, Adam, witness heaven
What love sincere and reverence in my heart
I bear thee, and unweeting° have offended,
Unhappily deceived; thy suppliant
I beg, and clasp thy knees; bereave me not
Whereon I live, thy gentle looks, thy aid,
Thy counsel in this uttermost distress,
My only strength and stay. Forlorn of thee,
Whither shall I betake me, where subsist?
While yet we live, scarce one short hour perhaps,
Between us two let there be peace, both joining,
As joined in injuries, one enmity
Against a foe by doom express assigned us,
That cruel serpent. On me exercise not
Thy hatred for this misery befallen,
On me already lost, me than thyself
More miserable. Both have sinned, but thou
Against God only, I against God and thee,
And to the place of judgment will return,
There with my cries importune heaven, that all
The sentence from thy head removed may light

strait intimate

unweeting unwitting

On me, sole cause to thee of all this woe,
Me, me only, just object of his ire.'
She ended weeping, and her lowly plight,
Immovable° till peace obtained from fault
Acknowledged and deplored, in Adam wrought
Commiseration; soon his heart relented
Towards her, his life so late and sole delight,
Now at his feet submissive in distress,
Creature so fair his reconcilement seeking,
His counsel whom she had displeased, his aid;
As one disarmed, his anger all he lost,
And thus with peaceful words upraised her soon:
'Unwary, and too desirous, as before
So now, of what thou know'st not, who desir'st
The punishment all on thyself; alas,
Bear thine own first, ill able to sustain
His full wrath whose thou feel'st as yet least part,
And my displeasure bear'st so ill. If prayers
Could alter high decrees, I to that place
Would speed before thee, and be louder heard,
That on my head all might be visited,
Thy frailty and infirmer sex forgiven,
To me committed and by me exposed.
But rise, let us no more contend, nor blame
Each other, blamed enough elsewhere,° but strive
In offices of love, how we may lighten
Each other's burden in our share of woe;
Since this day's death denounced,° if aught I see,
Will prove no sudden, but a slow-paced evil,
A long day's dying to augment our pain,
And to our seed (O hapless seed!) derived.'°
To whom thus Eve, recovering heart, replied:
'Adam, by sad experiment I know
How little weight my words with thee can find,
Found so erroneous, thence by just event
Found so unfortunate; nevertheless,
Restored by thee, vile as I am, to place
Of new acceptance, hopeful to regain
Thy love, the sole contentment of my heart
Living or dying, from thee I will not hide
What thoughts in my unquiet breast are risen,
Tending to some relief of our extremes,
Or end, though sharp and sad, yet tolerable,
As in our evils, and of easier choice.

Immovable Modifies both "plight" and "Adam."
elsewhere in heaven?

death denounced here, as at l. 853, an echo of that telling phrase in IX.695
derived descended

If care of our descent° perplex us most,
Which must be born to certain woe, devoured
By death at last (and miserable it is
To be to others cause of misery,
Our own begotten, and of our loins to bring
Into this cursèd world a woeful race,
That after wretched life must be at last
Food for so foul a monster), in thy power
It lies, yet ere conception, to prevent°
The race unblest, to being yet unbegot.
Childless thou art, childless remain; so death
Shall be deceived his glut, and with us two
Be forced to satisfy his ravenous maw.
But if thou judge it hard and difficult,
Conversing, looking, loving, to abstain
From love's due rites, nuptial embraces sweet,
And with desire to languish without hope,
Before the present object° languishing
With like desire—which would be misery
And torment less than none of what we dread
—Then both ourselves and seed at once to free
From what we fear for both, let us make short,
Let us seek death, or he not found, supply
With our own hands his office on ourselves;
Why stand we longer shivering under fears
That show no end but death, and have the power,
Of many ways to die the shortest choosing,
Destruction with destruction to destroy?'°
  She ended here, or vehement despair
Broke off the rest; so much of death her thoughts
Had entertained as dyed her cheeks with pale.
But Adam with such counsel nothing swayed,
To better hopes his more attentive mind
Labouring had raised, and thus to Eve replied:
  'Eve, thy contempt of life and pleasure seems
To argue in thee something more sublime°
And excellent than what thy mind contemns;
But self-destruction therefore sought refutes
That excellence thought in thee, and implies,
Not thy contempt, but anguish and regret
For loss of life and pleasure overloved.
Or if thou covet death, as utmost end
Of misery, so thinking to evade

descent descendants
prevent preclude
object Eve
Destruction . . . destroy This ordinarily easy paradox is more than rhetorical here, acknowledging the difficulty (". . . with destruction . . .").
Eve thy . . . sublime In this scene we have had Adam's ranting and Eve's genuine desperation; now, we have a clerical, moralizing tone from Adam at the opening of this speech.

The penalty pronounced, doubt not but God
Hath wiselier armed his vengeful ire than so
To be forestalled; much more I fear lest death
So snatched will not exempt us from the pain
We are by doom° to pay; rather such acts
Of contumácy will prove the Highest
To make death in us live. Then let us seek
Some safer resolution, which methinks
I have in view, calling to mind with heed
Part of our sentence, that thy seed shall bruise
The serpent's head;° piteous amends, unless
Be meant, whom I conjecture, our grand foe
Satan, who in the serpent hath contrived
Against us this deceit. To crush his head
Would be revenge indeed; which will be lost
By death brought on ourselves, or childless days
Resolved, as thou proposest; so our foe
Shall scape his punishment ordained, and we
Instead shall double ours upon our heads.
No more be mentioned then of violence
Against ourselves, and wilful barrenness,
That cuts us off from hope, and savours only
Rancor and pride, impatience and despite,
Reluctance° against God and his just yoke
Laid on our necks. Remember with what mild
And gracious temper he both heard and judged,
Without wrath or reviling; we expected
Immediate dissolution, which we thought
Was meant by death that day, when lo, to thee
Pains only in child-bearing were foretold,
And bringing forth, soon recompensed wth joy,
Fruit of thy womb; on me the curse aslope
Glanced on the ground: with labour I must earn
My bread; what harm? Idleness° had been worse;
My labour will sustain me; and lest cold
Or heat should injure us, his timely care
Hath unbesought provided, and his hands
Clothed us unworthy, pitying while he judged;
How much more, if we pray him, will his ear
Be open, and his heart to pity incline,
And teach us further by what means to shun
The inclement seasons, rain, ice, hail, and snow,
Which now the sky with various face begins

doom judgment
bruise The serpent's head This prophecy from Genesis 3:15 is another glimpse of Eve's compensatory fulfillment promised at X.179, outlined in detail in Bk. XII.
Reluctance struggle
Idleness Notice that with the fall from perfection into biological nature, comes not only the institution of labor, but of its complement, idleness. Both idleness and its inner state, boredom, are generally regarded as faults in most contrived Utopias; in Paradise, they are not even conceivable.

To show us in this mountain, while the winds
Blow moist and keen, shattering the graceful locks
Of these fair spreading trees; which bids us seek
Some better shroud,° some better warmth to cherish
Our limbs benumbed, ere this diurnal star°
Leave cold the night, how we his gathered beams
Reflected, may with matter sere° foment,
Or by collision of two bodies grind
The air attrite° to fire, as late the clouds,
Justling° or pushed with winds rude in their shock,
Tine° the slant lightning, whose thwart° flame driven down
Kindles the gummy bark of fir or pine,
And sends a comfortable heat from far,
Which might supply° the sun. Such fire to use,
And what may else be remedy or cure
To evils which our own misdeeds have wrought,
He will instruct us praying,° and of grace
Beseeching him, so as we need not fear
To pass commodiously this life, sustained
By him with many comforts, till we end
In dust, our final rest and native home.
What better can we do, than to the place
Repairing where he judged us, prostrate fall
Before him reverent, and there confess
Humbly our faults, and pardon beg, with tears
Watering the ground, and with our sighs the air
Frequenting,° sent from hearts contrite, in sign
Of sorrow unfeigned, and humiliation meek?
Undoubtedly he will relent and turn
From his displeasure; in whose look serene,
When angry most he seemed and most severe,
What else but favour, grace, and mercy shone?'
So spake our father penitent, nor Eve
Felt less remorse. They forthwith to the place
Repairing where he judged them, prostrate fell
Before him reverent, and both confessed
Humbly their faults, and pardon begged, with tears
Watering the ground, and with their sighs the air
Frequenting, sent from hearts contrite, in sign
Of sorrow unfeigned, and humiliation meek.

Book XI

[Books XI and XII form a reciprocal pair to the historical accounts recited by Raphael to Adam and Eve in Books VI and VII; they are revealed, not

shroud shelter
diurnal star the sun
sere dry
attrite ground down
Justling jostling
Tine kindle (hence, "tinder")
thwart transverse
supply substitute for
praying if we pray
Frequenting crowding

narrated, and they are a vision of the future, not of the past, being selected glimpses of human history leading away from the Fall and toward the redemption and fulfillment of fallen man. Michael, commissioned by God to lead Adam and Eve out of Paradise forever, takes Adam to the top of a high hill, where he sees in vision the extent of the world and a pastoral scene which ends in the first human death, in the concrete sense: Cain's murder of Abel. "Death hast thou seen / In his first shape on man," says Michael, reminding us that the original of all deaths was a murder. Other episodes from biblical history are shown, leading up to the Flood.]

From *Book XII*

[Book XII resumes the vision of the human future, starting at a point "Betwixt the world destroyed and world restored," both in the broadest sense of history as an intermediate area between loss and reconstitution, and, in particular, as applying to the Flood and subsequent history. This leads to the promise of analogous redemptive fulfillment for Eve, in that the Son will manifest himself on earth in normal human form, born of woman; the Incarnation, Death, Resurrection, and Ascension of Christ are shown, and the history of his church on earth is mapped out until the Second Coming; the final overcoming of Satan is foretold, and a promise that "then the earth / Shall be all Paradise, far happier place / Than this of Eden, and far happier days."]

So spake the Archangel Michaël, then paused,
As at the world's great period; and our sire
Replete with joy and wonder thus replied:
'O goodness infinite, goodness immense!
That all this good of evil shall produce,
And evil turn to good;° more wonderful
Than that which by creation first brought forth
Light out of darkness! Full of doubt I stand,
Whether I should repent me now of sin
By me done and occasioned, or rejoice
Much more, that much more good thereof shall spring,
To God more glory, more good will to men
From God, and over wrath grace shall abound.°
But say, if our Deliverer up to heaven
Must reascend, what will betide the few
His faithful, left among the unfaithful herd,
The enemies of truth; who then shall guide
His people, who defend? Will they not deal
Worse with his followers than with him they dealt?'

evil turn to good This whole speech is an expression of the theme of the Fortunate Fall (from the hymn *O Felix Culpa:* "O lucky sin!"), completing the reversal of, and triumph over, Satan's plan "out of good still to find means of evil" (I.165). The Fortunate Fall paradox praises the first sin on the grounds that, without it, there would have been no need for a Redeemer; it is appropriate that Adam responds to Michael's prophecy of Christ's victory over Satan by invoking the paradox.

grace shall abound an important echo: "where sin abounded, grace did much more abound" (Romans 5:20); cf. Bunyan, *Grace Abounding to the Chief of Sinners* (1666)

'Be sure they will,' said the Angel; 'but from heaven
He to his own a Comforter° will send,
The promise of the Father, who shall dwell,
His Spirit, within them, and the law of faith
Working through love, upon their hearts shall write,
To guide them in all truth, and also arm
With spiritual armour,° able to resist
Satan's assaults, and quench his fiery darts,
What man can do against them, not afraid,
Though to the death, against such cruelties
With inward consolations recompensed,
And oft supported so as shall amaze
Their proudest persecutors. For the Spirit
Poured first on his apostles, whom he sends
To evangelize the nations, then on all
Baptized, shall them with wondrous gifts endue
To speak all tongues, and do all miracles,
As did their Lord before them.° Thus they win
Great numbers of each nation to receive
With joy the tidings brought from heaven: at length
Their ministry performed, and race well run,
Their doctrine and their story written left,
They die; but in their room, as they forewarn,
Wolves° shall succeed for teachers, grievous wolves,
Who all the sacred mysteries of heaven
To their own vile advantages shall turn
Of lucre and ambition, and the truth
With superstitions and traditions taint,
Left only in those written records pure,
Though not but by the Spirit understood.
Then shall they seek to avail themselves of names,
Places and titles, and with these to join
Secular power, though feigning still to act
By spiritual, to themselves appropriating
The Spirit of God, promised alike and given
To all believers; and from that pretence,
Spiritual laws by carnal power shall force
On every conscience; laws which none shall find
Left them enrolled, or what the Spirit within
Shall on the heart engrave. What will they then
But force the Spirit of Grace itself, and bind

Comforter the Holy Spirit (sent, according to Milton, "by the Son, from the Father," and thus an emanation of his power; cf. John 15:26)

spiritual armour from Ephesians 6:11–17, the same armor the Red Cross Knight wears in Bk. I of *The Faerie Queene*. All of Michael's discourse is full of scriptural allusions and echoes, some of which will be identified.

For the Spirit . . . them (ll. 497–502) from Acts 2

Wolves from Acts 20:29, also as used in *Lycidas*, l. 128. This whole passage foresees the decline of the institutional church, first Roman, then Anglican, contrasting this with the forever uncorrupted internalized authority of conscience.

His consort Liberty,° what but unbuild
His living temples,° built by faith to stand,
Their own faith, not another's; for on earth
Who against faith and conscience can be heard
Infallible? Yet many will presume:
Whence heavy persecution shall arise
On all who in the worship persevere
Of spirit and truth; the rest, far greater part,
Will deem in outward rites and specious forms
Religion satisfied; Truth shall retire
Bestuck with slanderous darts, and works of faith
Rarely be found. So shall the world go on,
To good malignant, to bad men benign,
Under her own weight groaning,° till the day
Appear of respiration° to the just,
And vengeance to the wicked, at return
Of him so lately promised to thy aid,
The woman's seed, obscurely then foretold,
Now amplier known thy saviour and thy Lord,
Last in the clouds from heaven to be revealed
In glory of the Father, to dissolve
Satan with his perverted world; then raise
From the conflagrant mass, purged and refined,
New heavens, new earth,° ages of endless date
Founded in righteousness and peace and love,
To bring forth fruits,° joy and eternal bliss.'
He ended; and thus Adam last replied:
'How soon hath thy prediction, seer blest,
Measured this transient world, the race of time,
Till time stand fixed: beyond is all abyss,
Eternity, whose end no eye can reach.
Greatly instructed I shall hence depart,
Greatly in peace of thought, and have my fill
Of knowledge, what this vessel can contain;
Beyond which was my folly to aspire.
Henceforth I learn that to obey is best,
And love with fear the only God, to walk
As in his presence, ever to observe
His providence, and on him sole depend,
Merciful over all his works, with good
Still overcoming evil,° and by small
Accomplishing great things, by things deemed weak
Subverting worldly strong, and worldly wise

consort Liberty II Corinthians 3:17
temples I Corinthians 3:17 and 6:19
groaning Romans 8:22, perhaps also a continuation of Nature's groans (IX.783, 1001) as Eve and Adam fall
respiration refreshment, rest
new earth The final apocalypse as envisioned here culminates in an allusion to Revelation 21:1: "And I saw a new heaven and a new earth."
fruits not the fruit of I.1, followed by "taste" and "woe," but appositively here by "joy and eternal bliss"
good . . . evil Romans 12:21

By simply meek; that suffering for truth's sake
Is fortitude to highest victory,
And to the faithful death the gate of life;
Taught this by his example whom I now
Acknowledge my redeemer ever blest.'
To whom thus also the Angel last replied:
'This having learnt, thou hast attained the sum
Of wisdom; hope no higher, though all the stars
Thou knew'st by name, and all the ethereal powers,
All secrets of the deep, all Nature's works,
Or works of God in heaven, air, earth, or sea,
And all the richest of this world enjoy'dst,
And all the rule, one empire; only add
Deeds to thy knowledge answerable, add faith,
Add virtue, patience, temperance, add love,
By name to come called charity,° the soul
Of all the rest: then wilt thou not be loth
To leave this Paradise, but shalt possess
A paradise within thee, happier far.°
Let us descend now therefore from this top
Of speculation;° for the hour precise
Exacts our parting hence; and see the guards,
By me encamped on yonder hill, expect°
Their motion, at whose front a flaming sword,
In signal of remove, waves fiercely round;
We may no longer stay: go, waken Eve;
Her also I with gentle dreams have calmed,
Portending good, and all her spirits composed
To meek submission: thou at season fit
Let her with thee partake what thou hast heard,
Chiefly what may concern her faith to know,
The great deliverance by her seed to come
(For by the woman's seed) on all mankind:
That ye may live, which will be many days,°
Both in one faith unanimous though sad,
With cause for° evils past, yet much more cheered
With meditation on the happy end.'
He ended, and they both descend the hill;
Descended, Adam to the bower where Eve
Lay sleeping ran before, but found her waked;
And thus with words not sad she him received:
'Whence thou return'st, and whither went'st, I know;

charity literally "love," from the Latin *caritas,* translating Greek *agapē,* as at I Corinthians 13, especially 13:13

A paradise . . . far This final internalization of a lost exterior place also contrasts finally with Satan's "the mind is its own place" and the hell within him (IV.20); the rhythms of this authentic transfer continue into Eve's final words below.

top Of speculation mount of vision; see *Paradise Regained* IV.236n

expect await

many days 930 years, according to Genesis 5:5

With cause for in view of

For God is also in sleep, and dreams advise,
Which he hath sent propitious, some great good
Presaging, since with sorrow and heart's distress
Wearied I fell asleep. But now lead on;
In me is no delay; with thee to go,
Is to stay here;° without thee here to stay,
Is to go hence unwilling; thou to me
Art all things under heaven, all places thou,
Who for my wilful crime art banished hence.
This further consolation yet secure
I carry hence; though all by me is lost,
Such favour I unworthy am vouchsafed,
By me the promised seed shall all restore.'
  So spake our mother Eve, and Adam heard
Well pleased, but answered not; for now too nigh
The archangel stood, and from the other hill
To their fixed station, all in bright array
The Cherubim descended; on the ground
Gliding metéorous,° as evening mist
Risen from a river o'er the marish° glides,
And gathers ground fast at the labourer's heel
Homeward returning. High in front advanced,
The brandished sword of God before them blazed
Fierce as a comet; which with torrid heat,
And vapour as the Libyan air adust,°
Began to parch that temperate clime; whereat
In either hand the hastening Angel caught
Our lingering parents, and to the eastern gate
Led them direct, and down the cliff as fast
To the subjected° plain; then disappeared.
They, looking back, all the eastern side beheld
Of Paradise, so late their happy seat,
Waved over by that flaming brand, the gate
With dreadful faces thronged and fiery arms.
Some natural tears they dropped, but wiped them soon;
The world was all before them, where to choose
Their place of rest, and Providence their guide:
They hand in hand,° with wandering steps and slow,
Through Eden took their solitary° way.
1658?–1665? 1667

with thee . . . here not merely an echo of the Hebrew matriarch Ruth to her mother-in-law Naomi, "Whither thou goest, I will go, . . ." (Ruth 1:16), but an avowal of the loss the seed of compensation, and the ultimate arbitrariness of place, of location on the planet, in subsequent human history
metéorous in mid-air
marish marsh
adust parched
subjected lying below; but also subject to
hand in hand catching up the emblematic meaning present at the first appearance of the two, hand in hand (IV.321), but moving beyond hieroglyphic somehow to a larger human meaning; "wandering" and "slow" perhaps with overtones of error and hesitancy, but only with overtones
solitary They are together, which is to say, Man is alone.

Paradise Regained

Written between the publication of *Paradise Lost* (1667) and 1670, *Paradise Regained* was published with *Samson Agonistes* in 1671. It is of the genre "brief epic," of which the ultimate model was the Book of Job. Milton takes the account of the temptation in the wilderness from Luke 4:1–13, and treats it as a victory over sin which prefigures the later victory over death at the Crucifixion. He also follows a tradition of the exegetes whereby this is a *total* temptation; they built on St. Luke's words, "all the temptation" in v.13. The scheme Milton follows is almost exactly that of Marvell's *Dialogue Between the Resolved Soul and Created Pleasure,* though there are other parallels; for example, as the second Adam, Jesus rejects the temptations (gluttony, ambition, avarice) which the first accepted. Christian heroic virtue resides in "humiliation and strong sufferance" and not, like pagan heroism, in action. Consequently Jesus does nothing except decline what is offered, and finally, when swept up to the pinnacle of the temple, he simply stands still. This is his initiation into the new and higher heroism, a point which Milton enforces by frequent favorable comparisons with pagan heroes.

He first rejects the sensual banquet arranged by Satan; he prefers a celestial banquet, and gets one at the end of the poem. Then he turns down earthly honor, favoring heavenly honor, which does not depend on what fallible and foolish men say about one, but on the testimony of God. The military power of Persia he rejects "unmoved," and also the more significant power of Rome. He turns down the earthly in favor of the heavenly city. The final temptation, before the crisis at the temple, is that of knowledge. Satan, having failed with "the kingdoms of this world," tries instead, in the great encomium of Athens, the temptations of intellect. But Jesus rejects learning for the same reason he turned down the others; he already has a superior version of what the tempter offers, namely, heavenly learning. That such learning made all other kinds redundant was a common enough position in the seventeenth century and earlier; it is surprising only because we know of Milton's love of classical poetry and philosophy, which he cannot quite keep out of this very denunciation of them. But it was necessary to take a diagrammatic position here; and the hidden conflict between the needs of the work and the temper of his mind makes this the finest thing in Milton's brief epic.

From *Book IV*

Therefore let pass, as they are transitory,
The kingdoms of this world; I shall no more
Advise thee; gain them as thou canst, or not.
And thou thyself seem'st otherwise inclined
Than to a worldly crown, addicted more
To contemplation and profound dispute,
As by that early action may be judged,
When slipping from thy mother's eye thou went'st
Alone into the temple; there wast found
Among the gravest rabbis disputant
On points and questions fitting Moses' chair,
Teaching, not taught; the childhood shows the man,

As morning shows the day. Be famous then
By wisdom; as thy empire must extend,
So let extend thy mind o'er all the world,
In knowledge, all things in it comprehend.
All knowledge is not couched in Moses' Law,
The Pentateuch° or what the Prophets wrote;
The Gentiles also know, and write, and teach
To admiration,° led by nature's light;
And with the Gentiles much thou must converse,
Ruling them by persuasion as thou mean'st;
Without their learning, how wilt thou with them,
Or they with thee hold conversation meet?
How wilt thou reason with them, how refute
Their idolisms,° traditions, paradoxes?
Error by his own arms is best evinced.°
Look once more, ere we leave this specular mount,°
Westward, much nearer by southwest; behold
Where on the Aegean shore a city stands
Built nobly, pure the air, and light the soil,
Athens, the eye° of Greece, mother of arts
And eloquence, native to famous wits
Or hospitable, in her sweet recess,
City or suburban, studious walks and shades;
See there the olive grove of Academe,°
Plato's retirement, where the Attic bird°
Trills her thick-warbled notes the summer long;
There flowery hill Hymettus° with the sound
Of bees' industrious murmur oft invites
To studious musing; there Ilissus° rolls
His whispering stream. Within the walls then view
The schools of ancient sages: his° who bred
Great Alexander to subdue the world,
Lyceum° there, and painted Stoa° next.
There thou shalt hear and learn the secret power°
Of harmony in tones and numbers hit
By voice or hand, and various-measured verse,
Aeolian charms° and Dorian lyric odes,°
And his who gave them breath, but higher sung,

Pentateuch the first five books of the Old Testament
To admiration admirably
idolisms idolatries
evinced defeated
specular mount lookout hill (Latin *specula*, watchtower)
eye highest faculty, chief city
Academe Plato's Academy, a park planted with olives, just outside Athens
Attic bird nightingale
Hymettus the hills, famous for honey, in which the Ilissus rises
Ilissus stream near Athens
his Aristotle's: he was Alexander's tutor
Lyceum the park where Aristotle ran his Peripatetic School of Philosophy, so called because he and his pupils walked around as they talked
painted Stoa porch, painted with frescoes, where Zeno taught Stoicism
secret power The Greeks attributed therapeutic and other powers to music.
Aeolian charms songs in the Aeolian dialect used by Sappho
Dorian lyric odes Pindar's odes in the Dorian dialect

Blind Melesigenes,° thence° Homer called,
Whose poem Phoebus challenged for his own.°
Thence what the lofty grave tragedians taught
In chorus or iambic,° teachers best
Of moral prudence, with delight received
In brief sententious precepts, while they treat
Of fate, and chance, and change in human life,
High actions and high passions best describing.
Thence to the famous orators repair,
Those ancient, whose resistless eloquence
Wielded at will that fierce democraty,°
Shook the Arsenal° and fulmined° over Greece,
To Macedon, and Artaxerxes' throne;°
To sage philosophy next lend thine ear,
From heaven descended to the low-roofed house
Of Socrates°—see there his tenement—
Whom well inspired the oracle° pronounced
Wisest of men; from whose mouth issued forth
Mellifluous streams that watered all the schools
Of Academics old and new,° with those
Surnamed Peripatetics,° and the sect
Epicurean,° and the Stoic severe;°
These here revolve, or, as thou lik'st, at home,
Till time mature thee to a kingdom's weight;
These rules will render thee a king complete
Within thyself, much more with empire joined.'
To whom our Saviour sagely° thus replied:
'Think not but that I know these things, or think
I know them not; not therefore am I short
Of knowing what I ought. He who receives
Light from above, from the fountain of light,
No other doctrine needs, though granted true;°
But these are false, or little else but dreams,
Conjectures, fancies, built on nothing firm.
The first and wisest of them all professed

Melesigenes Homer, after his reputed birthplace near the river Meles; Milton invented this **thence** because he was blind; from the doubtful Greek word *homeros,* blind

poem . . . own An epigram in the Greek Anthology makes Apollo say "It was I who sang, but divine Homer wrote it down."

chorus or iambic Greek tragedy had choral odes, and dialogue in iambics.

democraty democracy

Arsenal naval dockyard at Piraeus near Athens, here used as military threat

fulmined hurled forth thunder and lightning

Artaxerxes' throne Artaxerxes was king of Persia, allied to Sparta.

From heaven . . . Socrates Cicero said that Socrates brought philosophy down from the heavens and made it deal with morality.

oracle The Delphic oracle said that there was no one wiser than Socrates (Plato's *Apology*).

Academics . . . new successive schools of Platonism

Peripatetics See l. 253n.

Epicurean Epicurus, 341–270 B.C. taught that happiness arose from the senses, and that virtuous pleasure was the end of life; the Stoics attacked him for debauchery.

Stoic severe Stoics thought of the soul as imprisoned in the body, and that the ideal man was totally immune to passion.

sagely Milton gives Jesus the adverb appropriate to the temptation here, as elsewhere.

He . . . true the heart of Jesus' reply; none of this knowledge is necessary, or even desirable, to those who have revealed truth

To know this only, that he nothing knew;°
The next to fabling fell and smooth conceits;°
A third sort doubted all things, though plain sense;°
Others in virtue placed felicity,°
But virtue joined with riches and long life;
In corporal pleasure he,° and careless ease;
The Stoic last in philosophic pride,
By him called virtue; and his virtuous man,
Wise, perfect in himself, and all possessing
Equal to God, oft shames not to prefer,
As fearing God nor man, contemning all
Wealth, pleasure, pain or torment, death and life,
Which when he lists, he leaves, or boasts he can;
For all his tedious talk is but vain boast,
Or subtle shifts conviction to evade.°
Alas what can they teach, and not mislead,
Ignorant of themselves, of God much more,
And how the world began, and how man fell
Degraded by himself, on grace depending?
Much of the soul they talk, but all awry,
And in themselves seek virtue, and to themselves
All glory arrogate, to God give none;°
Rather accuse him under usual names,
Fortune and fate, as one regardless quite
Of mortal things. Who therefore seeks in these
True wisdom, finds her not, or by delusion
Far worse, her false resemblance only meets,
An empty cloud.° However, many books,
Wise men have said, are wearisome;° who reads
Incessantly, and to his reading brings not
A spirit and judgment equal or superior
(And what he brings, what needs he elsewhere seek?),
Uncertain and unsettled still remains,
Deep versed in books and shallow in himself,
Crude° or intoxicate, collecting toys
And trifles for choice matters, worth a sponge,°
As children gathering pebbles on the shore.
Or if I would delight my private hours
With music or with poem, where so soon

professed . . . knew Socrates in the *Apology* said that his superiority consisted only in that he knew nothing.
To fabling . . . conceits Plato made myths in his philosophy.
doubted . . . sense the Skeptics, who did not believe that the human mind could know anything truly, and thought that a state of suspended judgment was the best
in virtue . . . felicity the Peripatetics
he Epicurus
The Stoic . . . evade The Stoics believed that the virtuous man was equal to the gods, and indifferent to pain and pleasure; he could commit suicide if he so decided.
All . . . none Cicero said that praiseworthy virtue must be a man's own, not a lucky gift of fortune.
cloud recalling the cloud embraced by Ixion in mistake for Juno
books . . . wearisome Ecclesiastes 12:12
Crude surfeited
worth a sponge worthy to be erased

As in our native language can I find
That solace? All our law and story° strewed
With hymns, our Psalms with artful terms° inscribed,
Our Hebrew songs and harps in Babylon,°
That pleased so well our victors' ear, declare
That rather Greece from us these arts derived;°
Ill imitated, while they loudest sing
The vices of their deities, and their own,
In fable, hymn, or song, so personating
Their gods ridiculous, and themselves past shame.
Remove their swelling epithets° thick laid
As varnish on a harlot's cheek, the rest,
Thin sown with aught of profit or delight,°
Will far be found unworthy to compare
With Sion's songs, to all true tastes excelling,°
Where God is praised aright, and godlike men,
The Holiest of Holies, and his saints;
Such are from God inspired, not such from thee;
Unless° where moral virtue is expressed
By light of nature not in all quite lost.
Their orators thou then extoll'st, as those
The top of eloquence, statists° indeed,
And lovers of their country, as may seem;
But herein to our Prophets far beneath,
As men divinely taught, and better teaching
The solid rules of civil government
In their majestic unaffected style
Than all the oratory of Greece and Rome.
In them is plainest taught, and easiest learnt,
What makes a nation happy, and keeps it so,
What ruins kingdoms, and lays cities flat;
These only with our Law best form a king.'

. . .

[Satan, remarking that Jesus is equally unconcerned about the active and the contemplative virtues, asks "What dost thou in this world?" and leaves him for what turns into a stormy night. Next morning he bears him by force to the highest pinnacle of the temple, telling him scornfully either to stand or to cast himself down for angels to save him. Jesus simply says "Tempt not the Lord thy God," and stands. Satan falls. Jesus, who has throughout been without divine powers or aid—like Guyon in the Cave of Mammon—is provided by angels with "a table of celestial food." Finally "he unobserved / Home to his mother's house private returned," and so the epic ends.]

story history
artful terms The Psalms were thought to originate all the arts of poetry and rhetoric.
Babylon Psalms 137:1
derived A common Renaissance opinion was that all Greek learning and poetry derived from Hebrew.
swelling epithets for example, in the odes of Pindar
profit or delight That poetry should provide both was the traditional view derived from Horace, *Ars Poetica*.
Sion's . . . excelling Sion was in this way regularly preferred to Parnassus as a source of poetry; see Sidney's *Defence of Poesie*, where the best poets are said to be biblical writers like David and Solomon.
Unless refers to "unworthy," above.
statists statesmen

Samson Agonistes

The date of *Samson Agonistes* is disputed; the argument for an early date is most fully stated in W. R. Parker's *John Milton: A Biography* (1968). The most important points are, first, there is no evidence that it was a late work except its late publication, and Milton had little time between the publication of *Paradise Lost* and that of *Paradise Regained* and *Samson Agonistes* to write more than *Paradise Regained*. Nobody ever treated it as late until Upton in 1746 said that it represented Milton after the Restoration, and Thomas Newton, on similar grounds, called it in his edition (1749) Milton's last work. Second, *Samson Agonistes* has a good deal of rhyme, which Milton rejected in a paragraph on "The Verse" affixed to *Paradise Lost*. Parker, now followed by other scholars, chooses an early date, about 1647–53, and supports it on various stylistic and autobiographical grounds. Another view, supported by the notes for tragedies surviving in Milton's Commonplace Book, is that he sketched it early and finished it late.

It does not seem impossible that Milton could have fitted the play in between 1667 and 1670; *Paradise Regained* is not so long a work. As for the rhyme, there was current a theory, as it happens erroneous, that Hebrew verse used rhymes and half-rhymes, and Milton, using a Hebrew subject and perhaps fresh from the commendation to the Psalms in *Paradise Regained* iv.334–38, could have thought it proper to use rhyme in the same irregular way; what he complains of in his note on verse is the "modern bondage of rhyming," calling it "the invention of a barbarous age"; but Hebrew rhyme was neither barbarous, nor modern, nor a bondage, since it rhymed at will and not by compulsion. Furthermore it is hard to believe (despite the tenuous parallels adduced in Milton's Latin ode *Ad Rousium*, written in 1647) that his prosodic experiments in *Samson Agonistes* should have preceded the long works in blank verse; having explored the range of effects to be had from irregular strophes —the impact of short choric lines, and the effect of such transitions as that from 79 to 80—it is highly improbable that he would return to regular blank verse without such variation. We need not give up the view that *Samson Agonistes* is a triumphant tragic conclusion to Milton's work.

Milton had explored heroism in *Paradise Lost* and *Paradise Regained*. His tragic hero is an Old Testament type of Christian heroism, though in its active mode, Christ's in *Paradise Regained* being passive. (Much of the irony turns on the apparent passivity of Samson, "vigorous most when most unactive deemed.") His subject is accordingly Hebraic. The appropriate form for tragedy is, however, Greek. Milton knew Aeschylus, Sophocles, and Euripides, and built his drama out of that knowledge. It is generally agreed that Sophocles, perhaps especially in his *Oedipus at Colonus*, affected Milton most strongly, and that the persistent ironies of the work are Sophoclean in that they depend on the ignorance of the characters as to what is to ensue. Milton Christianizes this; it is the inaccessibility of God's design to human questioning that makes everybody go wrong about the true state of affairs, at all stages up to the entry of the messenger. The plight of Samson is considered in the light of partial human explanations, some of which Milton borrowed from the exegetical tradition: Samson as a warning against pride or uxoriousness; Samson as a subject for casuistry on the subject of suicide; Samson as a case history of despair. He had formerly referred to the story (in *The Reason of Church Government*, 1641) as an allegory of the enfeebling of the king by the bishops, and there is certainly nothing implausible in the supposition that in the 1660's he was thinking of Samson's apparent eclipse and eventual triumph as an allegory of the condition, under the Restoration, of the Good Old Cause of the Puritan Commonwealth (Harapha almost certainly reflects some satirical intention). Samson proves a highly adaptable theme for exegesis and allegory.

Milton, however much he might use such interpretations as material for irony and topical comment, was primarily concerned with the relations between his hero, the elected one, and the God who seemed to have deserted him. If this is remembered, the narrative structure of the work will seem simple enough. Samson is accustomed to visitations from the spirit of God, and to "intimate impulse." In the case of the woman of Timna this impulse led him into a marriage that would ordinarily have been forbidden; the marriage was a disaster, but it furthered the ends of God. His desire for Dalila seemed to him to proceed from an exactly analogous impulse. It was another disaster, and resulted in his captivity and blindness. Therefore, he supposes, and the Israelites suppose, that he has made a mistake, for which he is now punished and abandoned. Of course this is wrong; the analogy between the two marriages is exact, but the action is not yet complete, so that God's plan cannot be seen. The completion of the action stems from a third intimate impulse, occurring between the departure and return of the Philistine Public Officer. That impulse vindicates not only itself, but also the unclean marriage to Dalila, in the destruction of the temple.

Throughout most of the work discussion of Samson's powers is erroneous simply because it is assumed that they are now forever out of use, and this accounts for the mistake of the Chorus in its comments (ll. 1268 ff.) on the heroic virtue of God's champions; they think Samson's heroism can no longer be active, and that he must now exhibit the heroism of patience. The clarification of these errors, and the motivation of the intimate impulse by God, constitute the main action of the poem. Samson begins in total suffering, lamenting the contrast with the past, blaming himself for acts which would indeed be blameworthy if God did not provide a dispensation for them as part of his plan. The important question of the marriages is brought up by Manoa, who cannot see their relation to the signs given him at Samson's birth; the Dalila marriage is agreed to have resulted from intemperance. Dalila herself continues to be the instrument of God in angering Samson, beginning the process of rousing him from his apathy which the contemptible Harapha completes. The dramatic crisis occurs at line 1382; Samson is again authorized to break the Law, take part in a heathen festival; what impels him is a force he recognizes from the past. His humility before the officer is a *conscious* irony.

There is a persistent critical charge, first made by Dr. Johnson, that whereas *Samson Agonistes* has a beginning and an end it lacks a middle, "since nothing passes between the first act and the last, that either hastens or delays the death of Samson." The criticism, which has many variants, is invalidated by such considerations as those of the preceding paragraph. Pehaps the Dalila and Harapha episodes are too long, but that is virtually the extent of the case against Milton's structure. Milton had rethought the heroic poem, and the brief heroic poem; here he rethinks tragedy. The humanist enterprise which involved the Christianizing and modernizing of the great ancient modes was at last, though at a very late date, accomplished.

Samson Agonistes [1]

A Dramatic Poem

Of That Sort of Dramatic Poem Which Is Called Tragedy

Tragedy, as it was anciently composed, hath been ever held the gravest, moralest, and most profitable of all other poems: therefore said by Aristotle to be of power, by raising pity and fear, or terror, to purge the mind of those and suchlike passions, that is, to temper and reduce them to just measure with a kind of delight, stirred up by reading or seeing those passions well imitated.[2] Nor is Nature wanting in her own effects to make good his assertion; for so in physic, things of melancholic hue and quality are used against melancholy, sour against sour, salt to remove salt humours. Hence philosophers and other gravest writers, as Cicero, Plutarch, and others, frequently cite out of tragic poets, both to adorn and illustrate their discourse. The Apostle Paul himself thought it not unworthy to insert a verse of Euripides into the text of Holy Scripture, I Cor. 15, 33,[3] and Pareus,[4] commenting on the Revelation, divides the whole book as a tragedy, into acts distinguished each by a chorus of heavenly harpings and song between. Heretofore men in highest dignity have laboured not a little to be thought able to compose a tragedy. Of that honour Dionysius the elder was no less ambitious than before of his attaining to the tyranny.[5] Augustus Caesar also had begun his *Ajax*, but, unable to please his own judgment with what he had begun, left it unfinished.[6] Seneca the philosopher is by some thought the author of those tragedies (at least the best of them) that go under that name.[7] Gregory Nazianzen, a Father of the Church, thought it not unbeseeming the sanctity of his person to write a tragedy, which he entitled *Christ Suffering*.[8] This is mentioned to vindicate tragedy from the small esteem, or rather infamy, which in the account of many it undergoes at this day with other common interludes; happening through the poet's error of intermixing comic stuff with tragic sadness and gravity, or introducing trivial and vulgar persons, which by all judicious hath been counted absurd, and brought in without discretion, corruptly to gratify the people.[9] And though

1. Samson the performer or contestant, Samson at the Games.
2. Aristotle, *Poetics* VI: "Tragedy is the imitation of a serious action, effecting through pity and terror the *catharsis* of such passions." The dispute as to what *catharsis* means here has continued since the 16th century, but Milton partly follows Italian interpretations, partly provides his own. He thinks that small doses of pity and terror in an imitated action will drive out the real dangerous passions, not only pity and terror but others ("those and suchlike"). The purgation depends on *delight* in the imitation; the medicine is pleasant.
3. Of St. Paul's references to Greek poets, Milton is thinking of "Evil communications corrupt good manners" (I Corinthians 15:33), which is from Menander. Others alluded to are Aratus, Cleanthes, and Epimenides.
4. David Paraeus (1548–1622) in his work *On the Divine Apocalypse* (1618).
5. Tyrant of Syracuse (431–367 B.C.), who sought fame as poet and playwright.
6. According to Suetonius, *Lives of the Caesars* II.85, Augustus erased what he had written of this tragedy.
7. Lucius Annaeus Seneca (3 B.C.–65 A.D.). The Renaissance distinction between Seneca the philosopher and Seneca the dramatist has since disappeared.
8. St. Gregory of Nazianzus, fourth-century bishop of Constantinople who wrote *Christus Patiens*.
9. This condemnation was made by Sir Philip Sidney in his *Defence of Poesie*.

ancient tragedy use no prologue,[10] yet using sometimes, in case of self-defence, or explanation, that which Martial calls an epistle;[11] in behalf of this tragedy, coming forth after the ancient manner, much different from what among us passes for best, thus much beforehand may be epistled: that chorus is here introduced after the Greek manner, not ancient only but modern, and still in use among the Italians.[12] In the modelling therefore of this poem, with good reason, the ancients and Italians are rather followed, as of much more authority and fame. The measure of verse used in the chorus is of all sorts, called by the Greeks *monostrophic,* or rather *apolelymenon,*[13] without regard had to strophe, antistrophe, or epode, which were a kind of stanzas framed only for the music, then used with the chorus that sung; not essential to the poem, and therefore not material; or, being divided into stanzas or pauses, they may be called *alloeostropha.*[14] Division into act and scene, referring chiefly to the stage (to which this work never was intended), is here omitted.

It suffices if the whole drama be found not produced beyond the fifth act. Of the style and uniformity, and that commonly called the plot, whether intricate or explicit[15]—which is nothing indeed but such economy, or disposition of the fable, as may stand best with verisimilitude and decorum[16]—they only will best judge who are not unacquainted with Aeschylus, Sophocles, and Euripides, the three tragic poets unequalled yet by any, and the best rule to all who endeavour to write tragedy. The circumscription of time wherein the whole drama begins and ends is, according to ancient rule and best example, within the space of twenty-four hours.[17]

The Argument

Samson, made captive, blind, and now in the prison at Gaza, there to labour as in a common workhouse, on a festival day, in the general cessation from labour, comes forth into the open air, to a place nigh, somewhat retired, there to sit a while and bemoan his condition. Where he happens at length to be visited by certain friends and equals of his tribe, which make the chorus, who seek to comfort him what they can; then by his old father, Manoa, who endeavours the like, and withal tells him his purpose to procure his liberty by ransom; lastly, that this feast was proclaimed by the Philistines as a day of thanksgiving for their deliverance from the hands of Samson, which yet more troubles him. Manoa then departs to prosecute his endeavour with the Philistian

10. Preliminary address to the audience, not the part of the tragedy which precedes the first entrance of the chorus, the sense in which it is used in Greek tragedy.
11. Martial's "Letter to the Reader" introducing his epigrams is the model.
12. Milton uses the chorus in the manner adapted by modern Italians from the Greek (in drama and opera) rather than in the original Greek way.
13. "Freed"—from the limits of a regular stanzaic pattern. In Greek drama the chorus sang the strophe as they moved or danced one way, the antistrophe as they reversed the movement, and the epode, standing still.
14. Insofar as the verse does seem to divide into stanzas, these should be regarded as "irregular strophes."
15. Referring to Aristotle's distinction between "simple" and "complex" plots (*Poetics* VI).
16. Two important aims of neoclasic thought; see *Rhetoric* in the Glossary.
17. Aristotle's words in *Poetics* V were not prescriptive, and became so only when the Unities were evolved in 16th-century Italian criticism.

lords for Samson's redemption; who in the meanwhile is visited by other persons; and lastly by a public officer to require his coming to the feast before the lords and people, to play or show his strength in their presence. He at first refuses, dismissing the public officer with absolute denial to come; at length persuaded inwardly that this was from God, he yields to go along with him, who came now the second time with great threatenings to fetch him. The chorus yet remaining on the place, Manoa returns full of joyful hope to procure ere long his son's deliverance; in the midst of which discourse an Hebrew comes in haste, confusedly at first, and afterward more distinctly, relating the catastrophe, what Samson had done to the Philistines, and by accident to himself; wherewith the tragedy ends.

THE PERSONS

SAMSON
MANOA, *the father of Samson*
DALILA, *his wife*
HARAPHA OF GATH
PUBLIC OFFICER
MESSENGER
CHORUS OF DANITES

The Scene, before the Prison in Gaza

SAMSON A little onward lend thy guiding hand
To these dark steps,° a little further on,
For yonder bank hath choice of sun or shade;
There I am wont to sit, when any chance
Relieves me from my task of servile toil,
Daily in the common prison else enjoined me,
Where I, a prisoner chained, scarce freely draw
The air imprisoned also, close and damp,
Unwholesome draught. But here I feel amends,
The breath of heaven fresh-blowing, pure and sweet,
With day-spring° born; here leave me to respire.°
This day a solemn feast the people hold
To Dagon° their sea-idol, and forbid
Laborious works; unwillingly this rest
Their superstition yields me; hence with leave
Retiring from the popular noise, I seek
This unfrequented place to find some ease,
Ease to the body some, none to the mind
From restless thoughts, that like a deadly swarm
Of hornets armed, no sooner found alone,
But rush upon me thronging, and present
Times past, what once I was, and what am now.
O wherefore was my birth from heaven foretold
Twice by an angel, who at last in sight

dark steps The very phrase echoes the language of Greek tragedy, particularly the "blind feet" of Tiresias guided by his daughter, who will be "eyes" to them, in Euripides' *Phoenissae;* one is also to think of the opening of Sophocles' *Oedipus at Colonus.*
day-spring daybreak
respire breathe
Dagon Philistine fish god, worshiped at Gaza

Of both my parents all in flames ascended
From off the altar, where an offering burned,
As in a fiery column charioting
His godlike presence, and from some great act
Or benefit revealed to Abraham's race?
Why was my breeding ordered and prescribed
As of a person separate to God,
Designed for great exploits, if I must die
Betrayed, captived, and both my eyes put out,
Made of my enemies the scorn and gaze;°
To grind in brazen fetters under task
With this heaven-gifted strength? O glorious strength,
Put to the labour of a beast, debased
Lower than bondslave! Promise was° that I
Should Israel from Philistian yoke deliver;
Ask for this great deliverer now, and find him
Eyeless in Gaza at the mill with slaves,
Himself in bonds under Philistian yoke;
Yet stay, let me not rashly call in doubt
Divine prediction; what if all foretold
Had been fulfilled but through mine own default?
Whom have I to complain of but myself?
Who this high gift of strength committed to me,
In what part lodged, how easily bereft me,
Under the seal of silence could not keep,
But weakly to a woman must reveal it,
O'ercome with importunity and tears.
O impotence of mind, in body strong!°
But what is strength without a double share
Of wisdom? Vast, unwieldy, burdensome,
Proudly secure,° yet liable to fall
By weakest subtleties; not made to rule,
But to subserve where wisdom bears command.
God, when he gave me strength, to show withal
How slight the gift was, hung it in my hair.
But peace! I must not quarrel with the will
Of highest dispensation, which herein
Haply had ends above my reach to know:
Suffices that to me strength is my bane,
And proves the source of all my miseries,
So many, and so huge, that each apart
Would ask a life to wail; but chief of all,
O loss of sight, of thee I most complain!

gaze object of jeering gazes (did Milton pronounce "Gaza" this way?)
Promise was at Judges 13:5, that he should "begin to deliver Israel out of the hands of the Philistines"

O impotence . . . strong And towering strength, like any fortress when it tumbles in, imprisons its inhabitant; see the continuation of this image in that of burial in self, ll. 101–5 and 155–56.
secure careless of danger

Blind among enemies, O worse than chains,
Dungeon, or beggary, or decrepit age!
Light, the prime work of God, to me is extinct,
And all her various objects of delight
Annulled, which might in part my grief have eased,
Inferior to the vilest now become
Of man or worm; the vilest here excel me,
They creep, yet see; I, dark in light exposed
To daily fraud, contempt, abuse and wrong,
Within doors, or without, still as a fool,
In power of others, never in my own;
Scarce half I seem to live, dead more than half.
O dark, dark, dark,° amid the blaze of noon,
Irrecoverably dark, total eclipse
Without all hope of day!
O first-created beam, and thou great Word,
'Let there be light, and light was over all';
Why am I thus bereaved thy prime decree?
The sun to me is dark
And silent° as the moon,
When she deserts the night,
Hid in her vacant° interlunar cave.
Since light so necessary is to life,
And almost life itself, if it be true
That light is in the soul,
She all in every part,° why was the sight
To such a tender ball as the eye confined?
So obvious° and so easy to be quenched,
And not, as feeling, through all parts diffused,
That she might look at will through every pore?
Then had I not been thus exiled from light,
As in the land of darkness, yet in light,
To live a life half dead, a living death,
And buried; but O yet more miserable!
Myself my sepulchre, a moving grave,
Buried, not yet exempt
By privilege of death and burial
From worst of other evils, pains and wrongs,
But made hereby obnoxious° more
To all the miseries of life,
Life in captivity

O dark, dark, dark Here Milton abandons the blank verse of the dialogue for one of the many unrhymed lyrical passages in Samson's speeches.
silent meaning the dark of the moon, but significant here in its transfer of location from the visual domain to the aural one
vacant idle, resting in her fabled cave between visible phases
all in every part The soul, in Augustinian tradition and thereafter, was not thought to be localized in any part of the body, but rather suffusing it all like warmth, until Milton's contemporary, René Descartes, decided that it was in the surgically inaccessible pineal gland.
obvious evident, thus vulnerable
obnoxious exposed to

Among inhuman foes,
But who are these? For with joint pace I hear
The tread of many feet steering this way;
Perhaps my enemies who come to stare
At my affliction, and perhaps to insult,
Their daily practice to afflict me more.
    CHORUS This, this is he; softly a while;
Let us not break in upon him.
O change beyond report, thought, or belief!
See how he lies at random, carelessly diffused,°
With languished head unpropped,
As one past hope, abandoned,
And by himself given over;
In slavish habit, ill-fitted weeds°
O'erworn and soiled;
Or do my eyes misrepresent? Can this be he,
That heroic, that renowned,
Irresistible Samson? Whom unarmed
No strength of man, or fiercest wild beast could withstand;
Who tore the lion, as the lion tears the kid,°
Ran on embattled armies clad in iron,
And, weaponless himself,
Made arms ridiculous, useless the forgery°
Of brazen shield and spear, the hammered cuirass,
Chalýbean°-tempered steel, and frock of mail
Adamantean° proof;
But safe he who stood aloof,
When insupportably° his foot advanced,
In scorn of their proud arms and warlike tools,
Spurned them to death by troops. The bold Ascalonite°
Fled from his lion ramp,° old warriors turned
Their plated° backs under his heel;
Or grovelling soiled their crested helmets in the dust.
Then with what trivial weapon came to hand,
The jaw of a dead ass, his sword of bone,
A thousand foreskins° fell, the flower of Palestine,
In Ramath-lechi, famous to this day;
Then by main force pulled up, and on his shoulders bore
The gates of Azza,° post and massy bar,
Up to the hill by Hebron, seat of giants old,
No journey of a Sabbath day,° and loaded so;

diffused spread out
weeds clothing
Who tore . . . kid See Judges 14:6.
forgery making; faking
Chalybean made by fabled metalworkers
Adamantean diamond-hard; steely
insupportably irresistibly
Ascalonite Ascalon: one of the five principal Philistine cities
lion ramp leonine, rampant posture
plated armor-clad
foreskins synecdoche for uncircumcised Philistines
Azza Gaza
No journey . . . day Jewish law permits no labor or travel on the Sabbath.

Like whom the Gentiles feign° to bear up heaven.
Which shall I first bewail,
Thy bondage or lost sight,
Prison within prison
Inseparably dark?
Thou art become (O worst imprisonment!)
The dungeon of thyself; thy soul
(Which men enjoying sight oft without cause complain)
Imprisoned now indeed,
In real darkness of the body dwells,
Shut up from outward light
To incorporate with gloomy night;
For inward light, alas,
Puts forth no visual beam.
O mirror of our fickle state,
Since man on earth unparalleled!
The rarer thy example stands,
By how much from the top of wondrous glory,
Strongest of mortal men,
To lowest pitch of abject fortune thou art fallen.
For him I reckon not in high estate
Whom long descent of birth
Or the sphere° of fortune raises;
But thee whose strength, while virtue was her mate,
Might have subdued the earth,
Universally crowned with highest praises.
SAMSON I hear the sound of words, their sense the air
Dissolves unjointed ere it reach my ear.
CHORUS He speaks, let us draw nigh. Matchless in might,
The glory late of Israel, now the grief,
We come thy friends and neighbours not unknown
From Eshtaol and Zora's fruitful vale°
To visit or bewail thee, or if better,
Counsel or consolation we may bring,
Salve to thy sores; apt words have power to 'suage
The tumours° of a troubled mind,
And are as balm to festered wounds.
SAMSON Your coming, friends, revives me, for I learn
Now of my own experience, not by talk,
How counterfeit a coin they are who friends
Bear in their superscription° (of the most
I would be understood); in prosperous days
They swarm, but in adverse withdraw their head,

feign From a Hebraic viewpoint, classical myths, like those of Atlas holding up the world, were uninterestingly fictitious.
sphere Fortune's emblematic wheel frequently became a ball, sometimes the globe, in Renaissance pictures.
Eshtaol . . . vale Samson was born at Zora; Eshtaol was near by.
tumours swellings, disturbances
superscription the legend on a coin

Not to be found, though sought. Ye see, O friends,
How many evils have enclosed me round;
Yet that which was the worst now least afflicts me,
Blindness, for had I sight, confused with shame,
How could I once look up, or heave the head,
Who like a foolish pilot have shipwrecked
My vessel trusted to me from above,
Gloriously rigged; and for a word, a tear,
Fool, have divulged the secret gift of God
To a deceitful woman: tell me, friends,
Am I not sung and proverbed° for a fool
In every street, do they not say, how well
Are come upon him his deserts? yet why?
Immeasurable strength they might behold
In me, of wisdom nothing more than mean;°
This with the other should, at least, have paired,
These two proportioned ill drove me transverse.°
CHORUS Tax not divine disposal, wisest men
Have erred, and by bad women been deceived;
And shall again, pretend they ne'er so wise.
Deject not then so overmuch thyself,
Who hast of sorrow thy full load besides;
Yet truth to say, I oft have heard men wonder
Why thou shouldst wed Philistian women rather
Than of thine own tribe fairer, or as fair,
At least of thine own nation, and as noble.
SAMSON The first I saw at Timna, and she pleased
Me, not my parents, that I sought to wed
The daughter of an infidel;° they knew not
That what I motioned was of God; I knew
From intimate impulse, and therefore urged
The marriage on; that by occasion hence
I might begin Israel's deliverance,
The work to which I was divinely called;
She proving false, the next I took to wife
(O that I never had! fond wish too late)
Was in the vale of Sorec, Dálila,°
That specious° monster, my accomplished snare.°
I thought it lawful from my former act,

proverbed made a byword
mean average
transverse astray; a nautical term, meaning "off-course"
The first . . . infidel In Judges 14:3–4 Samson's parents complain of his choice, though he insists: "she pleaseth me well." But his father and mother "knew not that it was of the Lord, that he sought an occasion [see l. 237] against the Philistines." He marries the woman, but then propounds to the Philistines the riddle of the honey which came from the lion's carcass, which they get right by making his wife pester him for the answer; whereupon Samson slays thirty Philistines, takes their clothes and pays his wager (thirty changes of garments). He breaks with his wife.
Dálila "He loved a woman in the valley of Sorek, whose name was Delilah" (Judges 16:4)
specious superficially beautiful
accomplished snare snare that has now fulfilled its task; both Dalila's accomplished charms and her accomplishment of Samson's ruin

And the same end;° still watching to oppress
Israel's oppressors: of what now I suffer
She was not the prime cause, but I myself,
Who vanquished with a peal of words° (O weakness!)
Gave up my fort of silence to a woman.
CHORUS In seeking just occasion to provoke
The Philistine, thy country's enemy,
Thou never wast remiss, I bear thee witness:
Yet Israel still serves with all his sons.
SAMSON That fault I take not on me, but transfer
On Israel's governors, and heads of tribes,
Who seeing those great acts which God had done
Singly by me against their conquerors,
Acknowledged not, or not at all considered
Deliverance offered: I on the other side
Used no ambition° to commend my deeds;
The deeds themselves, though mute, spoke loud the doer;
But they persisted deaf, and would not seem
To count them things worth notice, till at length
Their lords the Philistines with gathered powers
Entered Judea seeking me, who then
Safe to the rock of Etham° was retired,
Not flying, but forecasting in what place
To set upon them, what advantaged best;
Meanwhile the men of Judah, to prevent
The harass of their land, beset me round;
I willingly on some conditions° came
Into their hands, and they as gladly yield me
To the uncircumcised a welcome prey,
Bound with two cords; but cords to me were threads
Touched with the flame: on their whole host I flew
Unarmed, and with a trivial weapon° felled
Their choicest youth; they only lived who fled.
Had Judah that day joined, or one whole tribe,
They had by this° possessed the towers of Gath,°

I thought . . . end This is a very important source of the main ironies that animate the drama. Samson is saying that his first marriage, though a failure, was right because it was ordered by God as part of His plans, a fact he knew "by intimate impulse." But in undertaking the second, with Dalila, he now supposes that he argued wrongly from analogy; the circumstances were similar but this was *not* part of God's plan, merely an indication of his own weakness. Hence his present situation, blind, disgraced, and with no future. But the irony is that the marriage with Dalila was as much part of God's plan as that with the women of Timna. The consequences of it are not yet worked out; everybody thinks the action is over, but it is not. The provision of "just occasion to provoke / The Philistine," and of course what follows justify Samson's confidence in the inspired nature of his second marriage.
peal of words as it were, surrendering to the mere noise of the attacker's weapons
ambition canvasing (from original Latin meaning "walking around")
Etham Judges 15
conditions Samson gave himself up to the men of Judah, who wanted to hand him over to the Philistines, on a promise that they would not "fall on him." They bound him, but he burst the cords and seized the jawbone of an ass, with which he slew a thousand men (Judges 15).
trivial weapon the jawbone, casually acquired
this this time
Gath Philistian city

And lorded over them whom now they serve;
But what more oft in nations grown corrupt,
And by their vices brought to servitude,
Than to love bondage more than liberty,
Bondage with ease than strenuous liberty;
And to despise, or envy, or suspect
Whom God hath of his special favour raised
As their deliverer; if he aught begin,
How frequent° to desert him, and at last
To heap ingratitude on worthiest deeds?

CHORUS Thy words to my remembrance bring
How Succoth and the fort of Penuel
Their great deliverer contemned,
The matchless Gideon in pursuit
Of Madian and her vanquished kings:°
And how ingrateful Ephraim
Had dealt with Jephtha, who by argument,
Not worse than by his shield and spear,
Defended Israel from the Ammonite,
Had not his prowess quelled their pride
In that sore battle when so many died
Without reprieve adjudged to death,
For want of well pronouncing *Shibboleth*.°

SAMSON Of such examples add me to the roll;
Me easily indeed mine° may neglect,
But God's proposed deliverance not so.

CHORUS Just are the ways of God,
And justifiable to men;
Unless there be who think not God at all:
If any be, they walk obscure;
For of such doctrine never was there school,
But the heart of the fool,°
And no man therein doctor but himself.

Yet more there be who doubt his ways not just,
As to his own edícts, found contradicting,
Then give the reins to wandering thought,
Regardless of his glory's diminution;
Till by their own perplexities involved
They ravel° more, still less resolved,
But never find self-satisfying solution.

As if they would confine the interminable,
And tie him to his own prescript,

frequent accustomed

How Succoth . . . kings Gideon in pursuit of the enemy asked bread from Succoth and Penuel and was refused (Judges 8).

And how . . . Shibboleth The Ephraimites refused help to Jephtha, who nevertheless defeated the Ammonites. Then a quarrel grew up between the Ephraimites and Jephtha's Gileadites, and Jephtha's men used as a test the Hebrew *shibboleth*, which the Ephraimites could not pronounce; so infiltrators were detected and slain.

mine my people

heart . . . fool "The fool hath said in his heart, there is no God" (Psalms 14:1)

ravel become entangled

Who made our laws to bind us, not himself,
And hath full right to exempt
Whomso it pleases him by choice
From national obstriction,° without taint
Of sin, or legal debt;
For with his own laws he can best dispense.
He would not else, who never wanted means,
Nor in respect of the enemy just cause,
To set his people free,
Have prompted this heroic Nazarite,°
Against his vow of strictest purity,
To seek in marriage that fallacious° bride,
Unclean, unchaste.°
Down, reason, then, at least vain reasonings down,
Though reason here aver
That moral verdict quits her of unclean:
Unchaste was subsequent; her stain, not his.
But see, here comes thy reverend sire
With careful° step, locks white as down,
Old Mánoa: advise
Forthwith how thou ought'st to receive him.
SAMSON Ay me, another inward grief awaked
With mention of that name renews the assault.
MANOA Brethren and men of Dan, for such ye seem,
Though in this uncouth° place; if old respect,
As I suppose, towards your once gloried friend,
My son now captive, hither hath informed°
Your younger feet, while mine cast back with age
Came lagging after; say if he be here.
CHORUS As signal° now in low dejected state,
As erst° in highest, behold him where he lies.
MANOA O miserable change! is this the man,
That invincible Samson, far renowned,
The dread of Israel's foes, who with a strength
Equivalent to angels' walked their streets,
None offering fight;° who single combatant
Duelled their armies ranked in proud array,°
Himself an army, now unequal match
To save himself against a coward armed

obstriction obligation (the law against marriage with Gentiles)
Nazarite member of ascetic religious sect (the broken vow is not of celibacy but of impure marriage)
fallacious treacherous (referring of course to the woman of Timna)
Unclean, unchaste As the Chorus goes on to say, she was not morally unclean, only ceremonially so, as a Gentile; she was not unchaste until after the marriage and the episode of the riddle. In short, God can dispense with His own law and make any arrangements He likes without regard to such considerations; but here, as it happens, He did not make Samson marry uncleanly and unchastely.
careful full of care
uncouth unfamilar
informed directed
signal distinguished
erst formerly
The dread . . . fight presumably after his visit to the harlot of Gaza, when he went home with the town gates
Duelled . . . array in the jawbone fight

At one spear's length? O ever-failing trust
In mortal strength! and oh what not in man
Deceivable and vain! Nay, what thing good
Prayed for, but often proves our woe, our bane?
I prayed for children, and thought barrenness
In wedlock a reproach; I gained a son,
And such a son as all men hailed me happy:
Who would be now a father in my stead?
O wherefore did God grant me my request,
And as a blessing with such pomp adorned?
Why are his gifts desirable, to tempt
Our earnest prayers, then given with solemn hand
As graces,° draw a scorpion's tail behind?
For this did the angel twice descend?° For this
Ordained thy nurture holy, as of a plant;
Select and sacred, glorious for a while,
The miracle of men; then in an hour
Ensnared, assaulted, overcome, led bound,
Thy foes' derision, captive, poor, and blind,
Into a dungeon thrust, to work with slaves?
Alas, methinks whom God hath chosen once
To worthiest deeds, if he through frailty err,
He should not so o'erwhelm, and as a thrall
Subject him to so foul indignities,
Be it but for honour's sake of former deeds.°

SAMSON Appoint° not heavenly disposition, father.
Nothing of all these evils hath befallen me
But justly; I myself have brought them on,
Sole author I, sole cause: if aught seem vile,
As vile hath been my folly, who have profaned
The mystery of God given me under pledge
Of vow, and have betrayed it to a woman,
A Canaanite,° my faithless enemy.
This well I knew, nor was at all surprised,
But warned by oft experience: did not she
Of Timna first betray me, and reveal
The secret wrested from me in her highth
Of nuptial love professed, carrying it straight
To them who had corrupted her, my spies,
And rivals? In this other was there found
More faith? Who also in her prime of love,
Spousal embraces, vitiated with gold,

graces favors
twice descend He does so in Judges 13, describing the signs and admonitions accompanying the conception and prescribing the education of Samson.
former deeds Manoa thinks the story is over, and so wonders at God's desertion of his *former* champion; he does not understand that this apparent desertion is part of the arrangement for Samson's last exploit, still to come.
Appoint arraign, charge
Canaanite Philistine

Though offered only, by the scent conceived°
Her spurious first-born, treason against me.
Thrice she assayed with flattering prayer and sighs
And amorous reproaches to win from me
My capital° secret, in what part my strength
Lay stored, in what part summed, that she might know:
Thrice I deluded her, and turned to sport
Her importunity, each time perceiving
How openly, and with what impudence,
She purposed to betray me, and (which was worse
Than undissembled hate) with what contempt
She sought to make me traitor to myself;
Yet the fourth time, when mustering all her wiles,
With blandished parleys, feminine assaults,
Tongue-batteries, she surceased not day nor night
To storm me over-watched,° and wearied out,
At times when men seek most repose and rest,
I yielded, and unlocked her all my heart,
Who with a grain of manhood well resolved
Might easily have shook off all her snares;
But foul effeminacy held me yoked
Her bondslave; O indignity, O blot
To honour and religion! servile mind
Rewarded well with servile punishment!
The base degree to which I now am fallen,
These rags, this grinding,° is not yet so base
As was my former servitude, ignoble,
Unmanly, ignominious, infamous,
True slavery, and that blindness worse than this,
That saw not how degenerately I served.

MANOA I cannot praise thy marriage choices, son,
Rather approved them not; but thou didst plead
Divine impulsion prompting how thou might'st
Find some occasion to infest° our foes.
I state not that; this I am sure, our foes
Found soon occasion thereby to make thee
Their captive, and their triumph; thou the sooner
Temptation found'st, or over-potent charms,
To violate the sacred trust of silence
Deposited within thee; which to have kept
Tacit was in thy power; true; and thou bear'st
Enough, and more, the burden of that fault;
Bitterly hast thou paid, and still art paying,
That rigid score.° A worse thing yet remains:

by . . . conceived conceived, not a child from the spousal embraces, but treason from the mere promise of reward (Judges 16:5)
capital relating to the head—Samson's uncut hair; most important
over-watched too long awake. The whole story of Dalila's temptation is in Judges 16.
grinding working at the flour mill
infest harass
score account of a debt

This day the Philistines a popular feast
Here celebrate in Gaza, and proclaim
Great pomp, and sacrifice, and praises loud
To Dagon, as their god who hath delivered
Thee, Samson, bound and blind into their hands,
Them out of thine,° who slew'st them many a slain.
So Dagon shall be magnified, and God,
Besides whom is no god, compared with idols,
Disglorified, blasphemed, and had in scorn
By the idolatrous rout amidst their wine;
Which to have come to pass by means of thee,
Samson, of all thy sufferings think the heaviest,
Of all reproach the most with shame that ever
Could have befallen thee and thy father's house.
SAMSON Father, I do acknowledge and confess
That I this honour, I this pomp have brought
To Dagon, and advanced his praises high
Among the heathen round; to God have brought
Dishonour, obloquy, and oped the mouths
Of idolists° and atheists; have brought scandal
To Israel, diffidence of° God, and doubt
In feeble hearts, propense° enough before
To waver, or fall off and join with idols:
Which is my chief affliction, shame and sorrow,
The anguish of my soul, that suffers not
Mine eye to harbour sleep, or thoughts to rest.
This only hope° relieves me, that the strife
With me hath end; all the contést is now
'Twixt God and Dagon; Dagon hath presumed,
Me overthrown, to enter lists with God,
His deity comparing and preferring
Before the God of Abraham. He, be sure,
Will not connive,° or linger, thus provoked,
But will arise and his great name assert:
Dagon must stoop, and shall ere long receive
Such a discomfit,° as shall quite despoil him
Of all these boasted trophies won on me,
And with confusion blank° his worshippers.
MANOA With cause this hope relieves thee, and these words
I as a prophecy receive; for God,
Nothing more certain, will not long defer
To vindicate the glory of his name
Against all competition, nor will long
Endure it doubtful whether God be Lord,

Them . . . thine and delivered them out of your hands
idolists idolaters
diffidence of lack of faith in
propense disposed
only hope hope alone
connive acquiesce
discomfit defeat
blank confound

Or Dagon. But for thee what shall be done?
Thou must not in the meanwhile, here forgot,
Lie in this miserable loathsome plight
Neglected. I already have made way
To some Philistian lords, with whom to treat
About thy ransom:° well they may by this
Have satisfied their utmost of revenge
By pains and slaveries, worse than death, inflicted
On thee, who now no more canst do them harm.
SAMSON Spare that proposal, father, spare the trouble
Of that solicitation; let me here,
As I deserve, pay on my punishment;
And expiate, if possible, my crime,
Shameful garrulity. To have revealed
Secrets of men, the secrets of a friend,
How heinous had the fact° been, how deserving
Contempt, and scorn of all, to be excluded
All friendship, and avoided as a blab,
The mark of fool set on his front!° But I
God's counsel have not kept, his holy secret
Presumptuously have published, impiously,
Weakly at least, and shamefully: a sin
That Gentiles in their parables condemn
To their abyss and horrid pains confined.°
MANOA Be penitent and for thy fault contrite,
But act not in thy own affliction, son;
Repent the sin, but if the punishment
Thou canst avoid, self-preservation bids;
Or the execution leave to high disposal,°
And let another hand, not thine, exact
Thy penal forfeit from thyself; perhaps
God will relent, and quit thee all his debt;
Who ever more approves and more accepts
(Best pleased with humble and filial submission)
Him who imploring mercy sues for life,
Than who self-rigorous chooses death as due;
Which argues over-just, and self-displeased
For self-offence, more than for God offended.°
Reject not then what offered means who knows
But God hath set before us, to return thee
Home to thy country and his sacred house,
Where thou mayst bring thy offerings, to avert
His further ire, with prayers and vows renewed.

ransom This is an incident Milton added to the biblical account.
fact deed
front forehead
a sin . . . confined the myth of Tantalus, who was tormented in hell for having revealed the secrets of the gods (see Spenser, *The Faerie Queene* II.vii and notes)
the execution . . . disposal leave the carrying out of the punishment to God
Which . . . offended an argument against self-punishment, including suicide, used by Milton in his *Christian Doctrine*

SAMSON His pardon I implore; but as for life,
To what end should I seek it? When in strength
All mortals I excelled, and great in hopes
With youthful courage and magnanimous thoughts
Of birth from heaven foretold and high exploits,
Full of divine instinct, after some proof
Of acts indeed heroic, far beyond
The sons of Anak,° famous now and blazed,
Fearless of danger, like a petty god
I walked about admired of all and dreaded
On hostile ground, none daring my affront.
Then swollen with pride into the snare I fell
Of fair fallacious looks, venereal trains,°
Softened with pleasure and voluptuous life;
At length to lay my head and hallowed pledge
Of all my strength in the lascivious lap
Of a deceitful concubine who shore me
Like a tame wether, all my precious fleece,
Then turned me out ridiculous, despoiled,
Shaven, and disarmed among my enemies.
CHORUS Desire of wine and all delicious drinks,
Which many a famous warrior overturns,
Thou couldst repress,° nor did the dancing ruby
Sparkling outpoured, the flavour, or the smell,
Or taste that cheers the heart of gods and men,
Allure thee from the cool crystálline stream.
SAMSON Wherever fountain or fresh current flowed
Against° the eastern ray, translucent, pure
With touch ethereal of heaven's fiery rod,°
I drank, from the clear milky juice allaying
Thirst, and refreshed; nor envied them the grape
Whose heads that turbulent liquor fills with fumes.
CHORUS O madness, to think use of strongest wines
And strongest drinks our chief support of health,
When God with these forbidden made choice to rear
His mighty champion, strong above compare,
Whose drink was only from the liquid brook.
SAMSON But what availed this temperance, not complete
Against another object more enticing?
What boots it° at one gate to make defence,
And at another to let in the foe,
Effeminately vanquished? By which means,
Now blind, disheartened, shamed, dishonoured, quelled,
To what can I be useful, wherein serve

sons of Anak giants; see Numbers 13:33
venereal trains amorous snares
Desire . . . repress The Nazarites abstained from wine.
Against in the direction of (east-flowing water was thought purer)
fiery rod sun ray
What boots it what use is it?

My nation, and the work from heaven imposed,
But to sit idle on the household hearth,
A burdenous drone? To visitants a gaze,°
Or pitied object; these redundant° locks,
Robustious° to no purpose, clustering down,
Vain monument of strength; till length of years
And sedentary numbness craze° my limbs
To a contemptible old age obscure.
Here rather let me drudge and earn my bread,
Till vermin or the draff° of servile food
Consume me, and oft-invocated death
Hasten the welcome end of all my pains.
MANOA Wilt thou then serve the Philistines with that gift
Which was expressly given thee to annoy° them?
Better at home lie bed-rid, not only idle,
Inglorious, unemployed, with age outworn.
But God, who caused a fountain at thy prayer
From the dry ground to spring,° thy thirst to allay
After the brunt of battle, can as easy
Cause light again within thy eyes to spring,
Wherewith to serve him better than thou hast;
And I persuade me so; why else this strength
Miraculous yet remaining in those locks?
His might continues in thee not for naught,
Nor shall his wondrous gifts be frustrate° thus.
SAMSON All otherwise to me my thoughts portend,
That these dark orbs no more shall treat with light,
Nor the other light of life continue long,
But yield to double darkness nigh at hand:
So much I feel my genial spirits° droop,
My hopes all flat; nature within me seems
In all her functions weary of herself;
My race of glory run, and race of shame,
And I shall shortly be with them that rest.
MANOA Believe not these suggestions,° which proceed
From anguish of the mind and humours black,°
That mingle with thy fancy. I however
Must not omit a father's timely care
To prosecute the means of thy deliverance
By ransom or how else: meanwhile be calm,
And healing words from these thy friends admit.
SAMSON O that torment should not be confined
To the body's wounds and sores,

a gaze something to be stared at
redundant flowing; serving no purpose
Robustious robust, flourishing
craze enfeeble
draff refuse, garbage
annoy molest
But God . . . spring Judges 15:18–19
frustrate rendered vain
genial spirits vital and generative powers
suggestions modern sense, plus "temptations"
humours black Melancholy was the black humor.

With maladies innumerable
In heart, head, breast, and reins;°
But must secret passage find
To the inmost mind,
There exercise all his fierce accidents,°
And on her purest spirits prey,
As on entrails, joints, and limbs,
With answerable° pains, but more intense,
Though void of corporal sense.
  My griefs not only pain me
As a lingering disease,
But finding no redress, ferment and rage,
Nor less than wounds immedicable
Rankle, and fester, and gangrene,
To black mortification.°
Thoughts, my tormentors, armed with deadly stings
Mangle my apprehensive° tenderest parts,
Exasperate, exulcerate, and raise
Dire inflammation which no cooling herb
Or med'cinal liquor can assuage,
Nor breath of vernal air from snowy alp.
Sleep hath forsook and given me o'er
To death's benumbing opium as my only cure.
Thence faintings, swoonings of despair,
And sense of heaven's desertion.
  I was his nursling once and choice delight,
His destined from the womb,
Promised by heavenly message twice descending.°
Under his special eye
Abstemious I grew up and thrived amain;
He led me on to mightiest deeds
Above the nerve° of mortal arm
Against the uncircumcised, our enemies.
But now hath cast me off as never known,
And to those cruel enemies,
Whom I by his appointment had provoked,
Left me all helpless with the irreparable loss
Of sight, reserved alive to be repeated°
The subject of their cruelty or scorn.
Nor am I in the list of them that hope;
Hopeless are all my evils, all remediless;
This one prayer yet remains, might I be heard,
No long petition—speedy death,
The close of all my miseries, and the balm.

reins kidneys
accidents symptoms
answerable corresponding
mortification gangrene
apprehensive sensitive
twice descending See l. 361n.
nerve sinew; strength
repeated talked of as

CHORUS Many are the sayings of the wise
In ancient and in modern books enrolled,
Extolling patience as the truest fortitude;
And to the bearing well of all calamities,
All chances incident to man's frail life,
Consolatories° writ
With studied argument, and much persuasion sought,
Lenient° of grief and anxious thought;
But with the afflcted in his pangs their sound
Little prevails, or rather seems a tune
Harsh, and of dissonant mood° from his complaint,
Unless he feel within
Some source of consolation from above,
Secret refreshings that repair his strength,
And fainting spirits uphold.
God of our fathers, what is man!°
That thou towards him with hand so various—
Or might I say contrarious?—
Temper'st thy providence through his short course,
Not evenly, as thou rul'st
The angelic orders and inferior creatures mute,
Irrational and brute.°
Nor do I name of men the common rout,
That wandering loose about
Grow up and perish, as the summer fly,
Heads without name no more remembered;
But such as thou hast solemnly elected,
With gifts and graces eminently adorned
To some great work, thy glory,
And people's safety, which in part they effect;
Yet toward these thus dignified, thou oft
Amidst their highth of noon
Changest thy countenance and thy hand, with no regard
Of highest favours past
From thee on them, or them to thee of service.
Nor only dost degrade them, or remit
To life obscured, which were a fair dismission,°
But throw'st them lower than thou didst exalt them high,
Unseemly falls in human eye,
Too grievous for the trespass or omission;
Oft leav'st them to the hostile sword

Consolatories writings intended to console in distress
Lenient soothing
mood a pun on a term both musical and spiritual
what is man "What is man, that thou art mindful of him?" (Psalms 8:4)
That thou . . . brute (ll. 667–73) Here the uncomprehending complaint against God for maltreating his champions takes the form of the old complaint that in the orders of angel and beast, between which men stand, there is no similar problem; the angels understand intuitively their duties, and the beasts, lacking reason, are spared both moral choices and God's election.
dismission dismissal

Of heathen and profane, their carcasses
To dogs and fowls a prey, or else captívéd,
Or to the unjust tribunals, under change of times,
And condemnation of the ingrateful multitude.°
If these they scape, perhaps in poverty
With sickness and disease thou bow'st them down,
Painful diseases and deformed,
In crude° old age;
Though not disordinate, yet causeless suffering
The punishment of dissolute days;° in fine,
Just or unjust, alike seem miserable,
For oft alike, both come to evil end.
   So deal not with this once thy glorious champion,
The image of thy strength, and mighty minister.
What do I beg? How hast thou dealt already?
Behold him in this state calamitous, and turn
His labours, for thou canst, to peaceful end.
   But who is this, what thing of sea or land?
Female of sex it seems,
That so bedecked, ornate, and gay,
Comes this way sailing
Like a stately ship
Of Tarsus,° bound for the isles
Of Javan or Gadire,°
With all her bravery on, and tackle trim,
Sails filled, and streamers waving,
Courted by all the winds that hold them play,
An amber scent of odorous perfume
Her harbinger,° a damsel train behind;
Some rich Philistian matron she may seem,
And now at nearer view, no other certain
Than Dálila thy wife.
   SAMSON My wife, my traitress, let her not come near me.
   CHORUS Yet on she moves, now stands and eyes thee fixed,
About to have spoke; but now, with head declined
Like a fair flower surcharged with dew, she weeps,
And words addressed seem into tears dissolved,
Wetting the borders of her silken veil;
But now again she makes address° to speak.
   DALILA With doubtful° feet and wavering resolution

Oft leav'st . . . multitude It is often remarked (by those who take *Samson Agonistes* to be a late work) that Milton must have had in mind the sufferings of the Commonwealth leaders after the Restoration—including his own, which included diseases of the kind mentioned immediately afterward.
crude premature
Though . . . days not themselves intemperate, they nevertheless suffer diseases thought to be the penalty of dissolute living (such as Milton's gout)
Tarsus Tarshish (Isaiah 23:1), a Spanish port (Tarsus, birthplace of St. Paul, was a port in Turkey)
Javan or Gadire the Ionian isles of Greece, and Cadiz
An amber . . . harbinger scent of ambergris, which precedes her like a herald
makes address prepares
doubtful doubting

I came, still dreading thy displeasure, Samson,
Which to have merited, without excuse,
I cannot but acknowledge; yet if tears
May expiate (though the fact° more evil drew
In the perverse event° than I foresaw),
My penance° hath not slackened, though my pardon°
No way assured. But conjugal affection,
Prevailing over fear and timorous doubt,
Hath led me on, desirous to behold
Once more thy face, and know of thy estate;°
If aught in my ability may serve
To lighten what thou suffer'st, and appease
Thy mind with what amends is in my power,
Though late, yet in some part to recompense
My rash but more unfortunate misdeed.

SAMSON Out, out, hyena!° These are thy wonted arts,
And arts of every woman false like thee,
To break all faith, all vows, deceive, betray;
Then as repentant to submit, beseech,
And reconcilement move° with feigned remorse,
Confess, and promise wonders in her change,
Not truly penitent, but chief to try
Her husband, how far urged his patience bears,
His virtue or weakness which way to assail;
Then with more cautious and instructed skill
Again transgresses, and again submits;
That wisest and best men, full oft beguiled,
With goodness principled not to reject
The penitent, but ever to forgive,
Are drawn to wear out miserable days,
Entangled with a poisonous bosom snake,°
If not by quick destruction soon cut off,
As I by thee, to ages an example.

DALILA Yet hear me, Samson; not that I endeavour
To lessen or extenuate my offense,
But that on the other side if it be weighed
By itself, with aggravations° not surcharged,
Or else with just allowance counterpoised,
I may, if possible, thy pardon find
The easier towards me, or thy hatred less.
First granting, as I do, it was a weakness
In me, but incident to all our sex,
Curiosity, inquisitive, importúne

fact deed
perverse event unhappy outcome
penance penitence
pardon "Be" is understood in this latinate construction.
estate condition
hyena The hyena was thought to imitate the human voice and so lure men to destruction.
move propose
bosom snake "nourish a viper in one's bosom" (proverb)
aggravations exaggerations

Of° secrets, then with like infirmity
To publish them, both common female faults;
Was it not weakness also to make known
For importunity, that is for naught,
Wherein consisted all thy strength and safety?
To what I did thou show'dst me first the way.
But I to enemies revealed, and should not?
Nor shouldst thou have trusted that to woman's frailty:
Ere I to thee, thou to thyself wast cruel.
Let weakness then with weakness come to parle,°
So near related, or the same of kind;°
Thine forgive mine, that men may censure thine
The gentler, if severely thou exact not
More strength from me than in thyself was found.
And what if love, which thou interpret'st hate,
The jealousy of love, powerful of sway
In human hearts, nor less in mine towards thee,
Caused what I did? I saw thee mutable
Of fancy,° feared lest one day thou wouldst leave me
As her at Timna, sought by all means therefore
How to endear, and hold thee to me firmest:
No better way I saw than by impórtuning
To learn thy secrets, get into my power
Thy key of strength and safety. Thou wilt say,
'Why then revealed?' I was assured by those
Who tempted me that nothing was designed
Against thee but safe custody and hold:
That made for me;° I knew that liberty
Would draw thee forth to perilous enterprises,
While I at home sat full of cares and fears,
Wailing thy absence in my widowed bed;
Here I should still enjoy thee day and night,
Mine and love's prisoner, not the Philistines',
Whole to myself, unhazarded abroad,
Fearless at home of partners in my love.
These reasons in love's law have passed for good,
Though fond° and reasonless to some perhaps;
And love hath oft, well meaning, wrought much woe,
Yet always pity or pardon hath obtained.
Be not unlike all others, not austere
As thou art strong, inflexible as steel.
If thou in strength all mortals dost exceed,
In uncompassionate anger do not so.
SAMSON How cunningly the sorceress displays
Her own transgressions, to upbraid me mine!

importune Of persistent in inquiry concerning
parle parley
kind nature
fancy affection
made for me was to my advantage
fond foolish

That malice, not repentance, brought thee hither,
By this appears: I gave, thou say'st, the example,
I led the way—bitter reproach, but true;
I to myself was false ere thou to me;
Such pardon therefore as I give my folly,
Take to thy wicked deed; which° when thou seest
Impartial, self-severe, inexorable,
Thou wilt renounce thy seeking, and much rather
Confess it feigned. Weakness is thy excuse,
And I believe it, weakness to resist
Philistian gold; if weakness may excuse,
What murtherer, what traitor, parricide,
Incestuous, sacrilegious, but may plead it?
All wickedness is weakness: that plea therefore
With God or man will gain thee no remission.
But love constrained thee? Call it furious rage
To satisfy thy lust: love seeks to have love;
My love how couldst thou hope, who took'st the way
To raise in me inexpiable hate,
Knowing, as needs I must, by thee betrayed?°
In vain thou striv'st to cover shame with shame,
Or by evasions thy crime uncover'st more.

DALILA Since thou determin'st weakness for no plea
In man or woman, though to thy own condemning,
Hear what assaults I had, what snares besides,
What sieges girt me round, ere I consented;
Which might have awed the best-resolved of men,
The constantest, to have yielded without blame.
It was not gold, as to my charge thou lay'st,
That wrought with me: thou know'st the magistrates
And princes of my country came in person,
Solicited, commanded, threatened, urged,
Adjured by all the bonds of civil duty
And of religion, pressed how just it was,
How honourable, how glorious to entrap
A common enemy, who had destroyed
Such numbers of our nation: and the priest°
Was not behind, but ever at my ear,
Preaching how meritorious with the gods
It would be to ensnare an irreligious
Dishonourer of Dagon. What had I
To oppose against such powerful arguments?
Only my love of thee held long debate;
And combated in silence all these reasons
With hard contést. At length that grounded° maxim,

which Refers to "pardon" in l. 825.
Knowing . . . betrayed knowing myself to have beeen betrayed by you
priest an addition to the biblical story
grounded well-established

So rife and celebrated in the mouths
Of wisest men, that to the public good
Private respects° must yield, with grave authority
Took full possession of me and prevailed;
Virtue, as I thought, truth, duty, so enjoining.
SAMSON I thought where all thy circling wiles would end,
In feigned religion, smooth hypocrisy.
But had thy love, still odiously pretended,
Been, as it ought, sincere, it would have taught thee
Far other reasonings, brought forth other deeds.
I before all the daughters of my tribe
And of my nation chose thee from among
My enemies, loved thee, as too well thou knewest,
Too well; unbosomed all my secrets to thee,
Not out of levity, but overpowered
By thy request, who could deny thee nothing;
Yet now am judged an enemy. Why then
Didst thou at first receive me for thy husband,
Then, as since then, thy country's foe professed?
Being once a wife, for me thou wast to leave
Parents and country; nor was I their subject,
Nor under their protection, but my own;
Thou mine, not theirs. If aught against my life
Thy country sought of thee, it sought unjustly,
Against the law of nature, law of nations;
No more thy country, but an impious crew
Of men conspiring to uphold their state
By worse than hostile deeds, violating the ends
For which our country is a name so dear;
Not therefore to be obeyed. But zeal moved thee;
To please thy gods thou didst it; gods unable
To acquit themselves° and prosecute their foes
But by ungodly deeds, the contradiction
Of their own deity, gods cannot be:
Less therefore to be pleased, obeyed, or feared.
These false pretexts and varnished colours° failing,
Bare in thy guilt how foul must thou appear!
DALILA In argument with men a woman ever
Goes by the worse,° whatever be her cause.
SAMSON For want of words, no doubt, or lack of breath;
Witness when I was worried with thy peals.
DALILA I was a fool, too rash, and quite mistaken
In what I thought would have succeeded best.
Let me obtain forgiveness of thee, Samson;
Afford me place to show what recompense
Towards thee I intend for what I have misdone,

respects interests
acquit themselves maintain their positions
varnished colours false arguments
Goes by the worse gets the worst of it

Misguided; only what remains past cure
Bear not too sensibly,° nor still insist
To afflict thyself in vain. Though sight be lost,
Life yet hath many solaces, enjoyed
Where other senses want not their delights
At home in leisure and domestic ease,
Exempt from many a care and chance to which
Eyesight exposes daily men abroad.
I to the lords will intercede, not doubting
Their favourable ear, that I may fetch thee
From forth this loathsome prison-house, to abide
With me, where my redoubled love and care
With nursing diligence, to me glad office,
May ever tend about thee to old age
With all things grateful° cheered, and so supplied,
That what by me thou hast lost thou least shall miss.
SAMSON No, no, of my condition take no care;
It fits not; thou and I long since are twain;
Nor think me so unwary or accurst
To bring my feet again into the snare
Where once I have been caught; I know thy trains,°
Though dearly to my cost, thy gins,° and toils;
Thy fair enchanted cup and warbling charms°
No more on me have power, their force is nulled;°
So much of adder's wisdom° I have learnt
To fence my ear against thy sorceries.
If in my flower of youth and strength, when all men
Loved, honoured, feared me, thou alone could hate me,
Thy husband, slight me, sell me, and forgo me,
How wouldst thou use me now, blind, and thereby
Deceivable, in most things as a child
Helpless, thence easily contemned, and scorned,
And last neglected? How wouldst thou insult
When I must live uxorious to thy will
In perfect thraldom, how again betray me,
Bearing my words and doings to the lords
To gloss° upon, and censuring, frown or smile?
This jail I count the house of liberty
To° thine whose doors my feet shall never enter.
DALILA Let me approach at least, and touch thy hand.
SAMSON Not for thy life, lest fierce remembrance wake
My sudden rage to tear thee joint by joint.
At distance I forgive thee, go with that;

sensibly feelingly, sensitively
grateful pleasing
trains tricks
gins traps
fair . . . charms attributing to Dalila the instruments of Circe (see *Comus*, ll. 51–53, and Spenser, *The Faerie Queene* II.xii)
nulled nullified, extinguished
adder's wisdom ". . . they are like the deaf adder that stoppeth her ear; Which will not hearken to the voice of charmers" (Psalms 58: 4f.)
gloss comment
To compared with

Bewail thy falsehood, and the pious works
It hath brought forth to make thee memorable
Among illustrious women, faithful wives;
Cherish thy hastened widowhood with the gold
Of matrimonial treason: so farewell.
DALILA I see thou art implacable, more deaf
To prayers than winds and seas; yet winds to seas
Are reconciled at length, and sea to shore:
Thy anger, unappeasable, still rages,
Eternal tempest never to be calmed.
Why do I humble thus myself, and suing
For peace, reap nothing but repulse and hate?
Bid go with evil omen° and the brand
Of infamy upon my name denounced?
To mix with thy concernments I desist
Henceforth, nor too much disapprove my own.
Fame, if not double-faced, is double-mouthed,
And with contráry blast proclaims most deeds;
On both his wings, one black, the other white,
Bears greatest names in his wild airy flight.°
My name perhaps among the circumcised
In Dan,° in Judah, and the bordering tribes,
To all posterity may stand defamed,
With malediction mentioned, and the blot
Of falsehood most unconjugal traduced.
But in my country where I most desire,
In Ekron, Gaza, Asdod, and in Gath,°
I shall be named among the famousest
Of women, sung at solemn festivals,
Living and dead recorded, who, to save
Her country from a fierce destroyer, chose
Above the faith of wedlock bands, my tomb
With odours° visited and annual flowers:
Not less renowned than in Mount Ephraim
Jael, who with inhospitable guile
Smote Sisera sleeping, through the temples nailed.°
Nor shall I count it heinous to enjoy
The public marks of honour and reward
Conferred upon me for the piety°
Which to my country I was judged to have shown.
At this whoever envies or repines,
I leave him to his lot, and like my own.
CHORUS She's gone, a manifest serpent by her sting

evil omen predictions of bad luck
Fame . . . flight This allegory of Fame differs in some ways from the conventional, and Milton must have invented it.
Dan Samson's own tribe
Ekron . . . Gath principal cities of the Philistines
odours spices
Jael . . . nailed Jael allowed Sisera, a Philistine general, to hide in her tent. While he was sleeping she knocked a nail into his head; the story is in Deborah's song, Judges 5.
piety from the Latin *pietas,* meaning devotion to one's country

Discovered in the end, till now concealed.
SAMSON So let her go; God sent her to debase me,
And aggravate my folly who committed
To such a viper his most sacred trust
Of secrecy, my safety, and my life.
CHORUS Yet beauty, though injurious, hath strange power,
After offence returning, to regain
Love once possessed, nor can be easily
Repulsed, without much inward passion° felt
And secret sting of amorous remorse.
SAMSON Love-quarrels oft in pleasing concord end,
Not wedlock-treachery endangering life.
CHORUS It is not virtue, wisdom, valour, wit,
Strength, comeliness of shape, or amplest merit
That woman's love can win or long inherit;°
But what it is, hard is to say,
Harder to hit,
(Which way soever men refer it),
Much like thy riddle,° Samson, in one day
Or seven, though one should musing sit;
If any of these, or all, the Timnian bride
Had not so soon preferred
Thy paranymph,° worthless to thee compared,
Successor in thy bed,
Nor both° so loosely disallied
Their nuptials, nor this last so treacherously
Had shorn the fatal harvest of thy head.
Is it for that° such outward ornament
Was lavished on their sex, that inward gifts
Were left for haste unfinished, judgment scant,
Capacity not raised to apprehend
Or value what is best
In choice, but oftest to affect° the wrong?
Or was too much of self-love mixed,
Of constancy no root infixed,
That either they love nothing, or not long?
Whate'er it be, to wisest men and best
Seeming at first all heavenly under virgin veil,
Soft, modest, meek, demure,
Once joined, the contrary she proves, a thorn
Intestine,° far within defensive arms
A cleaving° mischief, in his way to virtue
Adverse and turbulent; or by her charms

passion suffering
inherit possess
riddle the riddle of the lion and the honeycomb, which caused the breakup of Samson's first marriage (Judges 14)
paranymph groomsman, companion of the bridegroom, to whom Samson's wife turned (Judges 14:20) for consolation
both both wives
for that because
affect desire
Intestine domestic
cleaving closely fitting, enwrapping, hindering

Draws him awry enslaved
With dotage, and his sense depraved
To folly and shameful deeds which ruin ends.
What pilot so expert but needs must wreck,
Embarked with such a steers-mate at the helm?
  Favoured of heaven who finds
One virtuous, rarely found,
That in domestic good combines:
Happy that house! his way to peace is smooth;
But virtue which breaks through all opposition,
And all temptation can remove,
Most shines and most is ácceptáble above.
  Therefore God's universal law
Gave to the man despotic power
Over his female in due awe,
Nor from that right to part an hour,
Smile she or lour:°
So shall he least confusion draw
On his whole life, not swayed
By female usurpation, nor dismayed.°
  But had we best retire? I see a storm.
  SAMSON Fair days have oft contracted wind and rain.
  CHORUS But this another kind of tempest brings.
  SAMSON Be less abstruse, my riddling days are past.
  CHORUS Look now for no enchanting voice, nor fear
The bait of honied words; a rougher tongue
Draws hitherward; I know him by his stride,
The giant Hárapha° of Gath, his look
Haughty as is his pile° high-built and proud.
Comes he in peace? What wind hath blown him hither
I less conjecture than when first I saw
The sumptuous Dálila floating this way;
His habit carries peace, his brow defiance.
  SAMSON Or peace or not, alike to me he comes.
  CHORUS His fraught° we soon shall know, he now arrives.
  HARAPHA I come not, Samson, to condole thy chance,
As these perhaps, yet wish it had not been,
Though for no friendly intent. I am of Gath;
Men call me Hárapha, of stock renowned

lour frown
Is it . . . dismayed In this "misogynist" chorus (ll. 1025–60) Milton both repeats some traditional antifeminist positions and echoes his own complaints in the pamphlets on divorce. In 1046 ff. he remembers Proverbs 31 on virtuous wives ("The heart of her husband doth safely trust in her . . . she will do him good and not evil all the days of her life," etc.). Samson was used as a negative example in discussions about good marriages. Milton, despite his own disappointments, took a more exalted view of marriage than many contemporaries, and perhaps lets the Chorus state the argument against wives as gloomily as possible for dramatic reasons: they are again showing no understanding of the reality of Samson's position, nor of the reason that he married Dalila.
Harapha not in the biblical story; Milton made him up from the Hebrew for giant and the exploits of Goliath
pile building, here probably meaning Gath
fraught freight, message

As Og or Anak and the Emims old
That Kiriathaim held;° thou knowest me now,
If thou at all art known.° Much I have heard
Of thy prodigious might and feats performed
Incredible to me, in this displeased,
That I was never present on the place
Of those encounters where we might have tried
Each other's force in camp° or listed field:°
And now am come to see of whom such noise
Hath walked° about, and each limb to survey,
If thy appearance answer loud report.
SAMSON The way to know were not to see but taste.
HARAPHA Dost thou already single° me? I thought
Gyves° and the mill had tamed thee. O that fortune
Had brought me to the field where thou art famed
To have wrought such wonders with an ass's jaw;
I should have forced thee soon wish other arms,
Or left thy carcass where the ass lay thrown:
So had the glory of prowess been recovered
To Palestine, won by a Philistine
From the unforeskinned race, of whom thou bear'st
The highest name for valiant acts; that honour,
Certain to have won by mortal duel from thee.
I lose, prevented by thy eyes put out.
SAMSON Boast not of what thou wouldst have done, but do
What then thou wouldst; thou seest it in thy hand.
HARAPHA To combat with a blind man I disdain,
And thou hast need much washing to be touched.
SAMSON Such usage as your honourable lords
Afford me, assassinated° and betrayed;
Who durst not with their whole united powers
In fight withstand me single and unarmed,
Nor in the house with chamber ambushes
Close-banded° durst attack me, no, not sleeping,
Till they had hired a woman with their gold,
Breaking her marriage faith to circumvent me.
Therefore without feigned shifts° let be assigned
Some narrow place enclosed, where sight may give thee,
Or rather flight, no great advantage on me;
Then put on all thy gorgeous arms, thy helmet
And brigandine° of brass, thy broad habergeon,°

Og . . . held "Only Og king of Bashan remained of the . . . giants" (Deuteronomy 3:11); "the giants, the sons of Anak" (Numbers 13:33); "The Emims . . . were accounted giants" (Deuteronomy 2:10–11); "the Emims in Shaveh Kiriathaim" (Genesis 14:5)
If . . . known if you know anything at all
camp field
listed field equipped with lists for jousting
walked gone
single pick me out (as opponent)
Gyves fetters
assassinated treacherously attacked
Close-banded secretly associated
shifts tricks
brigandine ringed body-armor
habergeon coat of mail

Vant-brace° and greaves,° and gauntlet; add thy spear,
A weaver's beam,° and seven-times-folded shield;°
I only with an oaken staff will meet thee,
And raise such outcries on thy clattered iron,
Which long shall not withhold me from thy head,
That in a little time while breath remains thee,
Thou oft shalt wish thyself at Gath to boast
Again in safety what thou wouldst have done
To Samson, but shalt never see Gath more.
HARAPHA Thou durst not thus disparage glorious arms
Which greatest heroes have in battle worn,
Their ornament and safety, had not spells
And black enchantments, some magician's art,
Armed thee or charmed thee strong, which thou from heaven
Feign'dst at thy birth was given thee in thy hair,
Where strength can least abide, though all thy hairs
Were bristles ranged like those that ridge the back
Of chafed° wild boars, or ruffled porcupines.
SAMSON I know no spells, use no forbidden arts;°
My trust is in the living God who gave me
At my nativity this strength, diffused
No less through all my sinews, joints and bones,
Than thine, while I preserved these locks unshorn,
The pledge of my unviolated vow.
For proof hereof, if Dagon be thy god,
Go to his temple, invocate his aid
With solemnest devotion, spread before him
How highly it concerns his glory now
To frustrate and dissolve these magic spells,
Which I to be the power of Israel's God
Avow, and challenge Dagon to the test,
Offering to combat thee, his champion bold,
With the utmost of his godhead seconded:
Then thou shalt see, or rather to thy sorrow
Soon feel, whose God is strongest, thine or mine.
HARAPHA Presume not on thy God, whate'er he be;
Thee he regards not, owns not, hath cut off
Quite from his people, and delivered up
Into thy enemies' hand; permitted them
To put out both thine eyes and fettered send thee
Into the common prison, there to grind
Among the slaves and asses, thy comrádes,
As good for nothing else, no better service
With those thy boisterous° locks; no worthy match

Vant-brace armor for forearm
greaves thigh-armor
weaver's beam wooden roller in loom (the armor comes from the description of Goliath in I Samuel 17)
shield recalling that of Ajax in Homer
chafed angry
forbidden arts Duelists were required to swear that they would use no magic.
boisterous thick-growing

For valour to assail, nor by the sword
Of noble warrior, so to stain his honour,°
But by the barber's razor best subdued.
SAMSON All these indignities, for such they are
From thine,° these evils I deserve and more,
Acknowledge them from God inflicted on me
Justly, yet despair not of his final pardon
Whose ear is ever open, and his eye
Gracious to readmit the suppliant;
In confidence whereof I once again
Defy° thee to the trial of mortal fight,
By combat to decide whose god is God,
Thine or whom I with Israel's sons adore.
HARAPHA Fair honour that thou dost thy God, in trusting
He will accept thee to defend his cause,
A murderer, a revolter, and a robber.
SAMSON Tongue-doughty° giant, how dost thou prove me these?
HARAPHA Is not thy nation subject to our lords?
Their magistrates confessed it, when they took thee
As a league-breaker and delivered bound
Into our hands:° for hadst thou not committed
Notorious murder on those thirty men
At Ascalon, who never did thee harm,
Then like a robber stripp'dst them of their robes?°
The Philistines, when thou hadst broke the league,
Went up with armèd powers thee only seeking,
To others did no violence nor spoil.
SAMSON Among the daughters of the Philistines
I chose a wife, which argued me no foe,
And in your city held my nuptial feast;
But your ill-meaning politician° lords,
Under pretence of bridal friends and guests,
Appointed to await me thirty spies,
Who threatening cruel death constrained the bride
To wring from me and tell to them my secret,
That solved the riddle which I had proposed.
When I perceived all set on enmity,
As on my enemies, wherever chanced,
I used hostility, and took their spoil
To pay my underminers in their coin.
My nation was subjected to your lords.
It was the force of conquest; force with force
Is well ejected when the conquered can.
But I a private person, whom my country

honour Milton gives Harapha some of the punctilio of the kind of courtier he hated.
thine your people
Defy challenge to combat, as in the medieval tradition of trying justice by means of a joust

Tongue-doughty brave in speech
delivered . . . hands See l. 258n.
stripp'dst . . . robes See l. 221n.
politician Machiavellian

As a league-breaker gave up bound, presumed
Single rebellion and did hostile acts.
I was no private but a person raised
With strength sufficient and command from heaven
To free my country; if their servile minds
Me their deliverer sent would not receive,
But to their masters gave me up for naught,
The unworthier they; whence to this day they serve.
I was to do my part from heaven assigned,
And had performed it if my known offence
Had not disabled me, not all your force.
These shifts° refuted, answer thy appellant,°
Though by his blindness maimed for high attempts,
Who now defies thee thrice to single fight,
As a petty enterprise of small enforce.°

HARAPHA With thee, a man condemned, a slave enrolled,
Due by the law to capital punishment?
To fight with thee no man of arms will deign.

SAMSON Cam'st thou for this, vain boaster, to survey me,
To descant° on my strength, and give thy verdict?
Come nearer, part not hence so slight informed;
But take good heed my hand survey not thee.

HARAPHA O Baal-zebub!° can my ears unused°
Hear these dishonours, and not render death?

SAMSON No man withholds thee, nothing from thy hand
Fear I incurable; bring up thy van;°
My heels are fettered, but my fist is free.

HARAPHA This insolence other kind of answer fits.

SAMSON Go, baffled coward, lest I run upon thee,
Though in these chains, bulk without spirit vast,
And with one buffet lay thy structure low,
Or swing thee in the air, then dash thee down
To the hazard of thy brains and shattered sides.

HARAPHA By Astaroth,° ere long thou shalt lament
These braveries° in irons loaden on thee.

CHORUS His giantship is gone somewhat crestfallen,
Stalking with less unconscionable° strides,
And lower looks, but in a sultry chafe.°

SAMSON I dread him not, nor all his giant brood,
Though fame divulge him father of five sons,
All of gigantic size, Goliah chief.°

CHORUS He will directly to the lords, I fear,

shifts dishonest arguments
appellant challenger
enforce effort
descant play variations on
Baal-zebub (probably) Beelzebub, lord of the flies, a Philistine idol
unused unaccustomed
van vanguard
Astaroth Philistine moon goddess
braveries boasts
unconscionable excessive
sultry chafe sullen temper
father . . . chief II Samuel 21.16 ff. describes four Philistine giants killed by David, but of course makes no mention of Harapha.

And with malicious counsel stir them up
Some way or other yet further to afflict thee.
SAMSON He must allege some cause, and offered fight
Will not dare mention, lest a question rise
Whether he durst accept the offer or not,
And that he durst not plain enough appeared.
Much more affliction than already felt
They cannot well impose, nor I sustain,
If they intend advantage of my labours,
The work of many hands, which earns my keeping
With no small profit daily to my owners.
But come what will, my deadliest foe will prove
My speediest friend, by death to rid me hence,
The worst that he can give, to me the best.
Yet so it may fall out, because their end
Is hate, not help to me, it may with mine
Draw their own ruin who attempt the deed.°
CHORUS Oh how comely it is and how reviving
To the spirits of just men long oppressed,
When God into the hands of their deliverer
Puts invincible might
To quell the mighty of the earth, the oppressor,
The brute and boisterous force of violent men,
Hardy and industrious to support
Tyrannic power, but raging to pursue
The righteous and all such as honour truth!
He all their ammunition°
And feats of war defeats
With plain heroic magnitude of mind
And celestial vigour armed;
Their armories and magazines contemns,
Renders them useless, while
With wingèd expedition
Swift as the lightning glance he executes
His errand on the wicked, who surprised
Lose their defence, distracted and amazed.
But patience is more oft the exercise
Of saints, the trial of their fortitude,°
Making them each his own deliverer,
And victor over all
That tyranny or fortune can inflict;
Either of these is in thy lot,
Samson, with might endued
Above the sons of men; but sight bereaved

yet so . . . deed Samson has a premonition of the sequel; the Chorus comments, but soon abandons the idea that this kind of heroic act is still open to Samson.

ammunition military stores

patience . . . fortitude Of the two heroisms, passive and active, the Chorus wrongly opts for the first.

May chance to number thee with those
Whom patience finally must crown.
This idol's day° hath been to thee no day of rest,
Labouring thy mind
More than the working day thy hands;
And yet perhaps more trouble is behind.
For I descry this way
Some other tending; in his hand
A sceptre or quaint° staff he bears,
Comes on amain, speed in his look.
By his habit I discern him now
A public officer, and now at hand.
His message will be short and voluble.°

OFFICER Hebrews, the prisoner Samson here I seek.

CHORUS His manacles remark° him; there he sits.

OFFICER Samson, to thee our lords thus bid me say:
This day to Dagon is a solemn feast,
With sacrifices, triumph, pomp, and games;
Thy strength they know surpassing human rate,
And now some public proof thereof require
To honour this great feast, and great assembly;
Rise therefore with all speed and come along,
Where I will see thee heartened and fresh clad
To appear as fits before the illustrious lords.

SAMSON Thou knowest I am an Hebrew, therefore tell them
Our law forbids at their religious rites
My presence; for that cause I cannot come.

OFFICER This answer, be assured, will not content them.

SAMSON Have they not sword-players, and every sort
Of gymnic artists, wrestlers, riders, runners,
Jugglers and dancers, antics,° mummers,° mimics,
But they must pick me out with shackles tired,
And over-laboured at their public mill,
To make them sport with blind activity?
Do they not seek occasion of new quarrels,
On my refusal, to distress me more,
Or make a game of my calamities?
Return the way thou cam'st; I will not come.

OFFICER Regard thyself;° this will offend them highly.

SAMSON Myself? My conscience and internal peace.
Can they think me so broken, so debased
With corporal servitude, that my mind ever
Will condescend to such absurd commands?
Although their drudge, to be their fool or jester,
And in my midst of sorrow and heart-grief

idol's day on the analogy of holy-day, holiday
quaint elaborately carved
voluble rapid
remark indicate
antics clowns
mummers actors
Regard thyself look to your own interests

To show them feats and play before their god,
The worst of all indignities, yet on me
Joined° with extreme contempt? I will not come.
OFFICER My message was imposed on me with speed,
Brooks no delay; is this thy resolution?
SAMSON So take it with what speed thy message needs.
OFFICER I am sorry what this stoutness° will produce.
SAMSON Perhaps thou shalt have cause to sorrow indeed.
CHORUS Consider, Samson; matters now are strained
Up to the highth, whether to hold or break;
He's gone, and who knows how he may report
Thy words by adding fuel to the flame?
Expect another message more imperious,
More lordly thundering than thou well wilt bear.
SAMSON Shall I abuse this consecrated gift
Of strength, again returning with my hair
After my great transgression, so requite
Favour renewed, and add a greater sin
By prostituting holy things to idols;
A Nazarite in place abominable
Vaunting my strength in honour to their Dagon?
Besides, how vile, contemptible, ridiculous,
What act more execrably unclean, profane?
CHORUS Yet with this strength thou serv'st the Philistines,
Idolatrous, uncircumcised, unclean.
SAMSON Not in their idol-worship, but by labour
Honest and lawful to deserve my food
Of those who have me in their civil power.
CHORUS Where the heart joins not, outward acts defile not.
SAMSON Where outward force constrains, the sentence° holds;
But who constrains me to the temple of Dagon,
Not dragging? The Philistian lords command.
Commands are no constraints. If I obey them,
I do it freely, venturing to displease
God for the fear of man, and man prefer,
Set God behind; which in his jealousy
Shall never, unrepented, find forgiveness.
Yet that he may dispense with° me or thee,
Present in temples at idolatrous rites
For some important cause, thou need'st not doubt.
CHORUS How thou wilt here come off surmounts my reach.
SAMSON Be of good courage; I begin to feel
Some rousing motions° in me which dispose
To something extraordinary my thoughts.

Joined enjoined, commanded
stoutness stubbornness
sentence saying, maxim
dispense with grant a dispensation to; Samson is beginning to form a different plan
rousing motions He is recognizing an "intimate impulse" like those which caused his marriages; it, too, will send him among the Philistines and put him in a position in which he seems to be breaking Hebrew law; and of course the end—the killing of Philistines—is the same, and part of God's concealed plan for his champion.

I with this messenger will go along,
Nothing to do, be sure, that may dishonour
Our law, or stain my vow of Nazarite.
If there be aught of presage in the mind,
This day will be remarkable in my life
By some great act, or of my days the last.°

CHORUS In time thou hast resolved; the man returns.

OFFICER Samson, this second message from our lords
To thee I am bid say: art thou our slave,
Our captive, at the public mill our drudge,
And dar'st thou at our sending and command
Dispute thy coming? Come without delay;
Or we shall find such engines to assail
And hamper thee, as thou shalt come of° force,
Though thou wert firmlier fastened than a rock.

SAMSON I could be well content to try their art,
Which to no few of them would prove pernicious.
Yet knowing their advantages too many,
Because° they shall not trail me through their streets
Like a wild beast, I am content to go.
Masters' commands come with a power resistless
To such as owe them absolute subjection;
And for a life who will not change his purpose?
(So mutable are all the ways of men.)°
Yet this be sure, in nothing to comply
Scandalous or forbidden in our law.

OFFICER I praise thy resolution;° doff° these links.
By this compliance thou wilt win the lords
To favour, and perhaps to set thee free.

SAMSON Brethren, farewell; your company along
I will not wish, lest it perhaps offend them
To see me girt with friends; and how the sight
Of me as of a common enemy,
So dreaded once, may now exasperate them,
I know not. Lords are lordliest in their wine;
And the well-feasted priest then soonest fired
With zeal, if aught° religion seem concerned;
No less the people on their holy-days
Impetuous, insolent, unquenchable;
Happen what may, of me expect to hear
Nothing dishonourable, impure, unworthy
Our God, our law, my nation, or myself;
The last of me or no I cannot warrant.

CHORUS Go, and the Holy One

some . . . last Samson says either-or; it turns out to be both.
of by
Because so that
Masters' . . . men all ironical
resolution decision
doff take off
aught to any degree

Of Israel be thy guide
To what may serve his glory best, and spread his name
Great among the heathen round;
Send thee the angel of thy birth, to stand
Fast by thy side, who from thy father's field
Rode up in flames after his message told
Of thy conception,° and be now a shield
Of fire; that spirit that first rushed on thee
In the camp of Dan,°
Be efficacious in thee now at need.
For never was from heaven imparted
Measure of strength so great to mortal seed,
As in thy wondrous actions hath been seen.
But wherefore comes old Mánoa in such haste
With youthful steps? Much livelier than erewhile
He seems: supposing here to find his son,
Or of him bringing to us some glad news?
MANOA Peace with you, brethren; my inducement hither
Was not at present here to find my son,
By order of the lords new parted hence
To come and play before them at their feast.
I heard all as I came, the city rings,
And numbers thither flock; I had no will,
Lest I should see him forced to things unseemly.
But that which moved my coming now was chiefly
To give ye part° with me what hope I have
With good success° to work his liberty.
CHORUS That hope would much rejoice us to partake
With thee; say, reverend sire; we thirst to hear.
MANOA I have attempted° one by one the lords,
Either at home, or through the high street passing,
With supplication prone and father's tears
To accept of ransom for my son their prisoner.
Some much averse I found and wondrous harsh,
Contemptuous, proud, set on revenge and spite;
That part most reverenced Dagon and his priests;
Others more moderate seeming, but their aim
Private reward, for which both God and State
They easily would set to sale; a third
More generous far and civil, who confessed
They had enough revenged, having reduced
Their foe to misery beneath their fears;
The rest was magnanimity to remit,
If some convenient ransom were proposed.

Rode . . . conception Judges 13:10
that spirit . . . Dan Judges 13:25. At other times the angel, or "the Spirit of the Lord," attended Samson at need.
give ye part share
success outcome
attempted appealed to

What noise or shout was that? It tore the sky.
CHORUS Doubtless the people shouting to behold
Their once great dread, captive and blind before them,
Or at some proof of strength before them shown.
MANOA His ransom, if my whole inheritance
May compass it, shall willingly be paid
And numbered down; much rather I shall choose
To live the poorest in my tribe, than richest,
And he in that calamitous prison left.°
No, I am fixed not to part hence without him.
For his redemption all my patrimony,
If need be, I am ready to forgo
And quit; not wanting him, I shall want nothing.
CHORUS Fathers are wont to lay up for their sons,
Thou for thy son art bent to lay out all;
Sons wont° to nurse their parents in old age,
Thou in old age car'st how to nurse thy son,
Made older than thy age through eyesight lost.
MANOA It shall be my delight to tend his eyes,
And view him sitting in the house, ennobled
With all those high exploits by him achieved,
And on his shoulders waving down those locks
That of a nation armed the strength contained.
And I persuade me God had not permitted
His strength again to grow up with his hair
Garrisoned round about him like a camp
Of faithful soldiery, were not his purpose
To use him further yet in some great service,
Not to sit idle with so great a gift
Useless, and thence ridiculous, about him.
And since his strength with eyesight was not lost,
God will restore him eyesight to° his strength.
CHORUS Thy hopes are not ill-founded nor seem vain
Of his delivery, and thy joy thereon
Conceived, agreeable to a father's love;
In both which we, as next,° participate.°
MANOA I know your friendly minds and—O what noise!
Mercy of heaven, what hideous noise was that!
Horribly loud, unlike the former shout.
CHORUS Noise call you it, or universal groan,
As if the whole inhabitation° perished?
Blood, death, and dreadful deeds are in that noise,
Ruin, destruction at the utmost point.

And he . . . left while he . . . is left
wont "Are" is understood.
to to match
next nearest; kinsmen, fellow tribesman
fathers . . . participate This conversation between Manoa and the Chorus (ll. 1485–1507) develops the ironical little plot of Manoa's attempts to find a human plan for the comfort of Samson despite his professed belief that God's plan is still operative. It comes to a head, and accordingly seems, like most human stratagems, ridiculous, at exactly the moment when God declares himself, and uses Samson, as before, in an actively heroic role.
inhabitation population

MANOA Of ruin indeed methought I heard the noise.
Oh it continues, they have slain my son.
CHORUS Thy son is rather slaying them; that outcry
From slaughter of one foe could not ascend.
MANOA Some dismal accident it needs must be;
What shall we do, stay here or run and see?
CHORUS Best keep together here, lest running thither
We unawares run into danger's mouth.
This evil on the Philistines is fallen;
From whom could else a general cry be heard?
The sufferers then will scarce molest us here;
From other hands we need not much to fear.
What if his eyesight (for to Israel's God
Nothing is hard) by miracle restored,
He now be dealing dole° among his foes,
And over heaps of slaughtered walk his way?
MANOA That were a joy presumptuous to be thought.
CHORUS Yet God hath wrought things as incredible
For his people of old; what hinders now?
MANOA He can I know, but doubt to think he will;
Yet hope would fain subscribe, and tempts belief.
A little stay will bring some notice hither.
CHORUS Of good or bad so great, of bad the sooner;
For evil news rides post, while good news baits.°
And to our wish I see one hither speeding,
A Hebrew, as I guess, and of our tribe.
MESSENGER° O whither shall I run, or which way fly
The sight of this so horrid spectacle
Which erst° my eyes beheld and yet behold;
For dire imagination still pursues me.
But providence or instinct of nature seems,
Or reason though disturbed, and scarce consulted
To have guided me aright, I know not how,
To thee first reverend Manoa, and to these
My countrymen, whom here I knew remaining,
As at some distance from the place of horror,
So in the sad event too much concerned.°
MANOA The accident was loud, and here before thee
With rueful cry, yet what it was we hear not,
No preface needs, thou seest we long to know.
MESSENGER It would burst forth, but I recover breath,
And sense distract,° to know well what I utter.
MANOA Tell us the sum, the circumstance defer.°

dole a pun on "that which is dealt (or doled) out" and "grief, or pain"
baits pauses for refreshment on the way
Messenger Since violent incidents were forbidden by the rules of classical tragedy, the Messenger or Nuntius is a regular feature of tragedies at this point.
erst a little while ago
As . . . concerned both removed from the scene of the occurrence and deeply concerned in it
distract distracted
Tell . . . defer give us the gist of it, leave the detail till later

MESSENGER Gaza yet stands, but all her sons are fallen,
All in a moment overwhelmed and fallen.
MANOA Sad, but thou know'st to Israelites not saddest
The desolation of a hostile city.
MESSENGER Feed on that first, there may in grief be surfeit.°
MANOA Relate by whom.
MESSENGER By Samson.
MANOA That still lessens
The sorrow, and converts it nigh to joy.
MESSENGER Ah Manoa I refrain, too suddenly
To utter what will come at last too soon;
Lest evil tidings with too rude irruption
Hitting thy agèd ear should pierce too deep.
MANOA Suspense in news is torture, speak them out.
MESSENGER Then take the worst in brief, Samson is dead.
MANOA The worst indeed, O all my hope's defeated
To free him hence! but death who sets all free
Hath paid his ransom now and full discharge.
What windy joy this day had I conceived°
Hopeful of his delivery, which now proves
Abortive as the first-born bloom of spring
Nipped with the lagging rear of winter's frost.
Yet ere I give the reins to grief, say first,
How died he? death to life is crown or shame.
All by him fell thou say'st, by whom fell he,
What glorious hand gave Samson his death's wound?
MESSENGER Unwounded of his enemies he fell.
MANOA Wearied with slaughter then or how? explain.
MESSENGER By his own hands.
MANOA Self-violence? what cause
Brought him so soon at variance with himself
Among his foes?
MESSENGER Inevitable cause
At once both to destroy and be destroyed;
The edifice where all were met to see him
Upon their heads and on his own he pulled.
MANOA O lastly over-strong against thyself!
A dreadful way thou took'st to thy revenge.
More than enough we know; but while things yet
Are in confusion, give us if thou canst,
Eye-witness of what first or last was done,
Relation more particular and distinct.
MESSENGER Occasions drew me early to this city,
And as the gates I entered with sunrise,
The morning trumpets festival proclaimed

Feed . . . surfeit digest that news first; what follows may make you sick with grief

What . . . conceived what seemed to be a pregnancy turns out to be mere flatulence

Through each high street. Little I had despatched°
When all abroad was rumoured that this day
Samson should be brought forth to show the people
Proof of his mighty strength in feats and games;
I sorrowed at his captive state, but minded°
Not to be absent at that spectacle.
The building was a spacious theatre,
Half round on two main pillars vaulted high,
With seats where all the lords, and each degree
Of sort, might sit in order to behold;
The other side was open, where the throng
On banks° and scaffolds under sky might stand;
I among these aloof obscurely stood.
The feast and noon grew high, and sacrifice
Had filled their hearts with mirth, high cheer, and wine,
When to their sports they turned. Immediately
Was Samson as a public servant brought,
In their state livery clad; before him pipes
And timbrels; on each side went armèd guards,
Both horse and foot before him and behind
Archers, and slingers, cataphracts° and spears.
At sight of him the people with a shout
Rifted the air, clamouring their god with praise,
Who had made their dreadful enemy their thrall.
He, patient but undaunted, where they led him,
Came to the place; and what was set before him,
Which without help of eye might be assayed,
To heave, pull, draw, or break, he still performed,
All with incredible, stupendious° force,
None daring to appear antagonist.
At length for intermission sake they led him
Between the pillars; he his guide requested
(For so from such as nearer stood we heard),
As over-tired, to let him lean a while
With both his arms on those two massy pillars
That to the archèd roof gave main support.
He unsuspicious led him; which when Samson
Felt in his arms, with head a while inclined,
And eyes fast fixed he stood, as one who prayed,
Or some great matter in his mind revolved.°
At last with head erect thus cried aloud:
'Hitherto, lords, what your commands imposed
I have performed, as reason was, obeying,
Not without wonder or delight beheld.

despatched done in the way of business
minded resolved
banks benches
cataphracts armored men on armored mounts
stupendious stupendous

in his mind revolved In Judges 16:30, Samson prays to be allowed to die with his enemies; Milton substitutes an inner resolution and an outer declaration to absolve Samson of suicide, a Christian sin.

Now of my own accord such other trial
I mean to show you of my strength, yet greater,
As with amaze° shall strike all who behold.'
This uttered, straining all his nerves he bowed;
As with the force of winds and waters pent
When mountains tremble, those two massy pillars
With horrible convulsion to and fro
He tugged, he shook, till down they came and drew
The whole roof after them, with burst of thunder
Upon the heads of all who sat beneath,
Lords, ladies, captains, counsellors, or priests,
Their choice nobility and flower, not only
Of this but each Philistian city round,
Met from all parts to solemnize this feast.
Samson, with these inmixed, inevitably
Pulled down the same destruction on himself;
The vulgar only scaped who stood without.

CHORUS O dearly bought revenge, yet glorious!
Living or dying thou hast fulfilled
The work for which thou wast foretold
To Israel, and now li'st victorious
Among thy slain self-killed,
Not willingly, but tangled in the fold
Of dire necessity, whose law in death conjoined
Thee with thy slaughtered foes, in number more
Than all thy life had slain before.

SEMICHORUS While their hearts were jocund and sublime,°
Drunk with idolatry, drunk with wine,
And fat regorged of bulls and goats,
Chanting their idol, and preferring
Before our living dread who dwells
In Silo,° his bright sanctuary,
Among them he a spirit of frenzy sent,
Who hurt their minds,
And urged them on with mad desire
To call in haste for their destroyer;
They only set on sport and play
Unweetingly° importuned
Their own destruction to come speedy upon them.
So fond are mortal men
Fallen into wrath divine,
As their own ruin on themselves to invite,
Insensate left, or to sense reprobate,
And with blindness internal struck.

SEMICHORUS But he, though blind of sight,

amaze confusion; cf. l. 1286
sublime elated

Silo Shiloh, where the Ark of the Covenant was set up
Unweetingly unwittingly

Despised and thought extinguished quite,
With inward eyes illuminated,
His fiery virtue roused
From under ashes into sudden flame,
And as an evening dragon° came,
Assailant on the perchèd roosts
And nests in order ranged
Of tame villatic° fowl; but as an eagle
His cloudless thunder bolted on their heads.
So virtue, given for lost,
Depressed, and overthrown, as seemed,
Like that self-begotten bird°
In the Arabian woods embost,°
That no second knows nor third,°
And lay erewhile a holocaust,°
From out her ashy womb now teemed,°
Revives, reflourishes, then vigorous most
When most unactive deemed,
And though her body die, her fame survives,
A secular° bird, ages of lives.
MANOA Come, come, no time from lamentation now,
Nor much more cause; Samson hath quit himself
Like Samson, and heroicly hath finished
A life heroic, on his enemies
Fully revenged; hath left them years of mourning,
And lamentation to the sons of Caphtor°
Through all Philistian bounds. To Israel
Honour hath left, and freedom: let but them
Find courage to lay hold on this occasion;
To himself and father's house eternal fame;
And, which is best and happiest yet, all this
With God not parted from him, as was feared,
But favouring and assisting to the end.
Nothing is here for tears, nothing to wail
Or knock the breast, no weakness, no contempt,
Dispraise, or blame, nothing but well and fair,
And what may quiet us in a death so noble.
Let us go find the body where it lies
Soaked in his enemies' blood, and from the stream
With lavers° pure and cleansing herbs wash off
The clotted gore. I with what speed° the while

dragon serpent
villatic barnyard; the Italian meaning of *villa* is farmhouse
self-begotten bird the phoenix, not used literally as an emblem of resurrection, but of fame and glory and, perhaps, some kind of spiritual regeneration; an image of Christian heroic virtue and God's use of it
embost "embosked"—hidden in woods like a hunted animal
That . . . third Only one phoenix is alive at a time.
holocaust a sacrificial animal burned entire
teemed delivered in birth
secular age-enduring
Caphtor original home of the Philistines
lavers basins
with what speed with whatever speed I can

(Gaza is not in plight° to say us nay)
Will send for all my kindred, all my friends,
To fetch him hence and solemnly attend
With silent obsequy and funeral train
Home to his father's house: there will I build him
A monument, and plant it round with shade
Of laurel ever green, and branching palm,
With all his trophies hung, and acts enrolled
In copious legend, or sweet lyric song.
Thither shall all the valiant youth resort,
And from his memory inflame their breasts
To matchless valour and adventures high;
The virgins also shall on feastful days
Visit his tomb with flowers, only bewailing
His lot unfortunate in nuptial choice,
From whence captivity and loss of eyes.
CHORUS All is best, though we oft doubt,
What the unsearchable dispose
Of highest wisdom brings about,
And ever best found in the close.
Oft he seems to hide his face,
But unexpectedly returns
And to his faithful champion hath in place°
Bore witness gloriously; whence Gaza mourns,
And all that band them to resist
His uncontrollable intent:
His servants he, with new acquist°
Of true experience from this great event,
With peace and consolation hath dismissed,
And calm of mind, all passion spent.
1647–70? 1671

Areopagitica

If *Areopagitica* is Milton's most resonant prose work, it may be because, first, its specific polemical purpose was one which still moves us today, and whose importance has not diminished, and, second, because its author evolved during the course of his argument a powerful vision of the moral life as embodied in the world of the intellect, and, particularly for Milton, in the representation of truth in terms of major fictions. Milton's essay is an address to Parliament on the subject of licensing—not censorship, to which he was by no means totally opposed, but the prior censorship imposed by requiring books to be approved before publication. Such approval had been entrusted in 1637, by Star Chamber decision, to a small group of churchmen; and a predominantly Presbyterian Parliament, in the ordinance of 1643 to which Milton is objecting, was in effect continuing the oppressive measure, which had

in plight in condition
in place at hand
acquist acquisition

given great personal licensing power to Archbishop Laud before. *Areopagitica,* like Milton's divorce tracts of the previous year, itself appeared without license. Its title derives from a famous address of the Greek orator Isocrates, to the Areopagus, or high court, which held session on the Athenian hill of Ares (Mars); like Milton's, that address was not written for oral delivery.

From Areopagitica

A Speech for the Liberty of Unlicensed Printing, to the Parliament of England

This is true liberty, when free-born men,
Having to advise the public, may speak free,
Which he who can and will, deserves high praise;
Who neither can nor will, may hold his peace;
What can be juster in a State than this?

EURIPIDES, *The Suppliants*

They who to states [1] and governors of the Commonwealth direct their speech, High Court of Parliament, or, wanting [2] such access in a private condition, write that which they foresee may advance the public good, I suppose them, as at the beginning of no mean endeavour, not a little altered [3] and moved inwardly in their minds: some with doubt of what will be the success,[4] others with fear of what will be the censure; [5] some with hope, others with confidence of what they have to speak. And me perhaps each of these dispositions, as the subject was whereon I entered, may have at other times variously affected; and likely might in these foremost expressions now also disclose which of them swayed most, but that the very attempt of this address thus made, and the thought of whom it hath recourse to, hath got the power within me to a passion far more welcome than incidental to a preface. Which though I stay not to confess ere any ask I shall be blameless, if it be no other than the joy and gratulation which it brings to all who wish and promote their country's liberty; whereof this whole discourse proposed will be a certain testimony, if not a trophy.[6] For this is not the liberty which we can hope, that no grievance ever should arise in the Commonwealth—that let no man in this world expect; but when complaints are freely heard, deeply considered, and speedily reformed, then is the utmost bound of civil liberty attained that wise men look for. . . .

Nor did they stay in matters heretical, but any subject that was not to their palate they either condemned in a Prohibition or had it straight into the new Purgatory of an Index. To fill up the measure of encroachment, their last invention was to ordain that no book, pamphlet, or paper should be printed (as

1. The three estates of lords, clergy, and commons forming the parliaments of England and France.
2. Lacking.
3. Worried.
4. Result.
5. Decision; a neutral term.
6. Of victory in his argument.

if St. Peter had bequeathed them the keys of the press also out of Paradise) unless it were approved and licensed under the hands of two or three glutton friars. For example:

> 'Let the Chancellor Cini be pleased to see if in this present work be contained aught that may withstand the printing.
>
> Vincent Rabbatta, Vicar of Florence.'

> 'I have seen this present work, and find nothing athwart the Catholic faith and good manners: in witness whereof I have given, etc.
>
> Nicolo Cini, Chancellor of Florence.'

> 'Attending the precedent relation, it is allowed that this present work of Davanzati may be printed.
>
> Vincent Rabbatta, etc.'

I deny not, but that it is of greatest concernment in the Church and Commonwealth, to have a vigilant eye how books demean themselves as well as men; and thereafter to confine, imprison, and do sharpest justice on them as malefactors. For books are not absolutely dead things, but do contain a potency of life in them to be as active as that soul was whose progeny they are; nay, they do preserve as in a vial the purest efficacy and extraction of that living intellect that bred them. I know they are as lively, and as vigorously productive, as those fabulous dragon's teeth,[7] and being sown up and down, may chance to spring up armed men. And yet, on the other hand, unless wariness be used, as good almost kill a man as kill a good book: who kills a man kills a reasonable creature, God's image; but he who destroys a good book, kills reason itself, kills the image of God, as it were in the eye.[8] Many a man lives a burden to the earth; but a good book is the precious life-blood of a master spirit, embalmed and treasured up on purpose to a life beyond life. 'Tis true, no age can restore a life, whereof perhaps there is no great loss; and revolutions of ages do not oft recover the loss of a rejected truth, for the want of which whole nations fare the worse. We should be wary therefore what persecution we raise against the living labours of public men, how we spill that seasoned life of man, preserved and stored up in books; since we see a kind of homicide may be thus committed, sometimes a martyrdom, and if it extend to the whole impression, a kind of massacre, whereof the execution ends not in the slaying of an elemental life, but strikes at that ethereal and fifth essence,[9] the breath of reason itself, slays an immortality rather than a life. But lest I should be condemned of introducing license, while I oppose licensing, I refuse not the pains to be so much historical as will serve to show what hath been done by ancient and famous commonwealths, against this disorder, till the very time that this project of licensing crept out of the Inquisition,[10] was catched up by our prelates, and

7. Cadmus and Jason both slew dragons and sowed their teeth, from which sprang up a crop of soldiers (Ovid, *Metamorphoses* III.95 ff. and VII.121 ff.).
8. In the reader's eye.
9. Beyond the four elements lay a fifth entity, ether, the heavenly essence (see Donne, "A Nocturnal upon S. Lucy's Day," l. 15n).
10. The church's inquisitorial institution rooted out heresy and heterodoxy; its powers, Milton insists, were inherited by Rome's Anglican opponents ("prelates") and, in turn, by the latter's Presbyterian antagonists ("New Presbyter is but old Priest writ large" Milton would write two years later).

hath caught some of our presbyters. [Milton now goes on to summarize the history of censorship, in Greece, Rome, and in the early days of the church, concluding with the introduction of prohibitions against reading heretical books in the 15th century, and the activities of the Spanish Inquisition and the Council of Trent (1545–63). A witty passage attacking ecclesiastical approval follows.]

'It may be printed, July 15.
Friar Simon Mompei d'Amelia,
Chancellor of the holy office in Florence.'

Sure they have a conceit, if he of the bottomless pit had not long since broke prison, that this quadruple exorcism would bar him down. I fear their next design will be to get into their custody the licensing of that which they say Claudius intended,[11] but went not through with. Vouchsafe to see another of their forms, the Roman stamp:

'Imprimatur,[12] If it seem good to the reverend master of the holy Palace,
Belcastro, Vicegerent.'

'Imprimatur, Friar Nicolo Rodolphi, Master of the holy Palace.'

Sometimes five Imprimaturs are seen together dialogue-wise in the piazza of one title-page, complimenting and ducking each to other with their shaven reverences, whether the author who stands by in perplexity at the foot of his epistle shall to the press or to the sponge.[13] These are the pretty responsories,[14] these are the dear antiphonies,[15] that so bewitched of late our prelates and their chaplains with the goodly echo they made; and besotted us to the gay imitation of a lordly Imprimatur, one from Lambeth House,[16] another from the west end of Paul's; [17] so apishly romanizing that the word of command still was set down in Latin; as if the learned grammatical pen that wrote it would cast no ink without Latin; or perhaps, as they thought, because no vulgar tongue was worthy to express the pure conceit [18] of an Imprimatur; but rather, as I hope, for that our English, the language of men ever famous and foremost in the achievements of liberty, will not easily find servile letters enow to spell such a dictatory presumption English.[19] And thus ye have the inventors and the original of book-licensing ripped up [20] and drawn as lineally as any pedigree. We have it not, that can be heard of, from any ancient state, or polity, or church, nor by any statute left us by our ancestors elder or later; nor from the

11. A license allowing one to fart at table: Milton's marginal note quotes Suetonius' *Life of Claudius* to this effect.
12. "Let it be printed"—the phrase giving official ecclesiastical permission for publication of manuscripts.
13. "To the sponge," meaning to have the contents wiped off, was an expression applied to manuscripts unworthy of publication.
14. Sections of the Psalms sung between other biblical readings in the mass.
15. Hymns or anthems sung in responsive parts by two choirs.
16. Lambeth Palace, residence of the Archbishop of Canterbury when in London.
17. This may refer either to the Bishop of London (at St. Paul's), or to the home of the Stationers' Company, who urged the enforcement of the licensing order.
18. Idea.
19. In English.
20. Revealed.

modern custom of any reformed city or church abroad; but from the most antichristian council and the most tyrannous inquisition that ever inquired. Till then books were ever as freely admitted into the world as any other birth; the issue of the brain was no more stifled than the issue of the womb: no envious Juno sat cross-legged [21] over the nativity of any man's intellectual offspring; but if it proved a monster, who denies but that it was justly burnt, or sunk into the sea. But that a book, in worse condition than a peccant soul, should be to stand before a jury ere it be born to the world, and undergo yet in darkness the judgment of Radamanth and his colleagues,[22] ere it can pass the ferry backward into light, was never heard before, till that mysterious iniquity, provoked and troubled at the first entrance of Reformation, sought out new limbos and new hells wherein they might include our books also within the number of their damned. And this was the rare morsel so officiously snatched up, and so ill-favouredly imitated by our inquisiturient [23] bishops, and the attendant minorites [24] their chaplains. That ye like not now these most certain authors of this licensing order, and that all sinister intention was far distant from your thoughts, when ye were importuned the passing it, all men who know the integrity of your actions, and how ye honour truth, will clear ye readily. [Milton then attacks the notion that there is any good in licensing itself aside from its proponents' vices, and adducing a remark of John Selden, the legal scholar (1584–1654), that "all opinions, yea errors, known, read and collated, are of main service and assistance toward the speedy attainment of what is truest," moves to the imaginative center of his argument.]

I conceive, therefore, that when God did enlarge the universal diet of man's body, saving ever the rules of temperance, he then also, as before, left arbitrary the dieting and repasting of our minds; as wherein every mature man might have to exercise his own leading capacity. How great a virtue is temperance, how much of moment through the whole life of man! Yet God commits the managing so great a trust, without particular law or prescription, wholly to the demeanour [25] of every grown man. And therefore when he himself tabled the Jews from heaven, that omer,[26] which was every man's daily portion of manna, is computed to have been more than might have well sufficed for the heartiest feeder thrice as many meals. For those actions which enter into a man, rather than issue out of him, and therefore defile not, God uses not to captivate under a perpetual childhood of prescription, but trusts him with the gift of reason to be his own chooser; there were but little work left for preaching if law and compulsion should grow so fast upon those things which heretofore were governed only by exhortation. Solomon informs us that much reading is a weariness to the flesh; but neither he nor other inspired author tells us that such or such reading is unlawful; yet certainly had God thought good to limit us herein, it had been much more expedient to have told us what was unlawful than what

21. She tried, with charms and spells, to prevent the birth of Hercules, whose mother was in labor with him for seven days.

22. Rhadamanthus, Minos, and Aeacus, the three judges of Hades.

23. Would-be inquisitors.

24. The Franciscans called themselves "minorites," alluding to their humility, with which Milton here remains unimpressed.

25. Management.

26. A biblical measure, here, of manna (Exodus 16:16 ff.), the daily ration Moses was commanded to distribute.

was wearisome. As for the burning of those Ephesian books by St. Paul's converts, 'tis replied the books were magic, the Syriac so renders them. It was a private act, a voluntary act, and leaves us to a voluntary imitation: the men in remorse burnt those books which were their own; the magistrate by this example is not appointed: these men practised the books, another might perhaps have read them in some sort usefully. Good and evil we know in the field of this world grow up together almost inseparably; and the knowledge of good is so involved and interwoven with the knowledge of evil, and in so many cunning resemblances hardly to be discerned, that those confused seeds which were imposed upon Psyche as an incessant labour to cull out, and sort asunder, were not more intermixed.[27] It was from out the rind of one apple tasted, that the knowledge of good and evil, as two twins cleaving together, leaped forth into the world. And perhaps this is that doom which Adam fell into of knowing good and evil, that is to say of knowing good by evil.[28] As therefore the state of man is, what wisdom can there be to choose, what continence to forbear, without the knowledge of evil? He that can apprehend and consider vice with all her baits and seeming pleasures, and yet abstain, and yet distinguish, and yet prefer that which is truly better, he is the true warfaring [29] Christian. I cannot praise a fugitive and cloistered virtue, unexercised and unbreathed, that never sallies out and sees her adversary, but slinks out of the race, where that immortal garland [30] is to be run for, not without dust and heat. Assuredly we bring not innocence into the world, we bring impurity much rather; that which purifies us is trial, and trial is by what is contrary. That virtue therefore which is but a youngling in the contemplation of evil, and knows not the utmost that vice promises to her followers, and rejects it, is but a blank virtue, not a pure; her whiteness is but an excremental [31] whiteness; which was the reason why our sage and serious poet Spenser, whom I dare be known to think a better teacher than Scotus or Aquinas,[32] describing true temperance under the person of Guyon, brings him in with his palmer through the cave of Mammon, and the bower of earthly bliss,[33] that he might see and know, and yet abstain. Since therefore the knowledge and survey of vice is in this world so necessary to the constituting of human virtue, and the scanning of error to the confirmation of truth, how can we more safely and with less danger scout into the regions of sin and falsity than by reading all manner of tractates and hearing all manner of reason? And this is the benefit which may be had of books promiscuously read.

. . .

27. In Apuleius' *The Golden Ass*, Venus set Psyche the task of sorting out a heap of mixed seeds, in anger at Cupid's love for her.
28. "Knowledge of good bought dear by knowing ill" (*Paradise Lost* IV.222); in his great poem, Milton expands and elaborates this theme.
29. *Wayfaring* in the first edition, but there is strong evidence for the present reading.
30. The garland is the crown of virtue; being good is likened both to medieval knight-errantry and to Greek and Roman games.
31. Superficial.
32. Duns Scotus and Thomas Aquinas, two great 13th-century logicians (the second, the master-theologian of scholasticism); they represent abstract philosophy here, as opposed to the concreteness of poetic myth.
33. See *The Faerie Queene* II. vii and xii. The Palmer does *not* accompany Guyon into the Cave of Mammon, however; Milton's memory failed him here.

Seeing, therefore, that those books, and those in great abundance which are likeliest to taint both life and doctrine, cannot be suppressed without the fall of learning, and of all ability in disputation, and that these books of either sort are most and soonest catching to the learned, from whom to the common people whatever is heretical or dissolute may quickly be conveyed, and that evil manners are as perfectly learnt without books a thousand other ways which cannot be stopped, and evil doctrine not with books can propagate, except a teacher guide, which he might also do without writing, and so beyond prohibiting, I am not unable to unfold how this cautelous [34] enterprise of licensing can be exempted from the number of vain and impossible attempts. And he who were pleasantly disposed could not well avoid to liken it to the exploit of that gallant man who thought to pound up the crows by shutting his park gate. Besides another inconvenience, if learned men be the first receivers out of books and dispreaders both of vice and error, how shall the licensers themselves be confided in, unless we can confer upon them, or they assume to themselves above all others in the land, the grace of infallibility and uncorruptedness? And again if it be true, that a wise man, like a good refiner, can gather gold out of the drossiest volume, and that a fool will be a fool with the best book, yea, or without book; there is no reason that we should deprive a wise man of any advantage to his wisdom, while we seek to restrain from a fool that which being restrained will be no hindrance to his folly. For if there should be so much exactness always used to keep that from him which is unfit for his reading, we should in the judgment of Aristotle [35] not only, but of Solomon [36] and of our Saviour,[37] not vouchsafe him good precepts, and by consequence not willingly admit him to good books; as being certain that a wise man will make better use of an idle pamphlet than a fool will do of sacred Scripture.

. . .

For if we be sure we are in the right, and do not hold the truth guiltily, which becomes not, if we ourselves condemn not our own weak and frivolous teaching, and the people for an untaught and irreligious gadding rout, what can be more fair than when a man judicious, learned, and of a conscience, for aught we know as good as theirs that taught us what we know, shall not privily from house to house, which is more dangerous, but openly by writing publish to the world what his opinion is, what his reasons, and wherefore that which is now thought cannot be sound? Christ urged it as wherewith to justify himself that he preached in public; [38] yet writing is more public than preaching; and more easy to refutation, if need be, there being so many whose business and profession merely it is to be the champions of Truth; which if they neglect, what can be imputed but their sloth, or inability?

Thus much we are hindered and disenured [39] by this course of licensing toward the true knowledge of what we seem to know. For how much it hurts

34. Tricky, liable to backfire.

35. At the end of the *Nicomachean Ethics,* rejecting the possibility that philosophy can influence ordinary men, instead of guiding the best of them.

36. Throughout the Book of Proverbs, as for example 17:24 and 26:5.

37. ". . . Neither cast ye your pearls before swine" (Matthew 7:6).

38. John 18:19–20.

39. Grown unaccustomed.

and hinders the licensers themselves in the calling of their ministry, more than any secular employment, if they will discharge that office as they ought, so that of necessity they must neglect either the one duty or the other, I insist not, because it is a particular,[40] but leave it to their own conscience, how they will decide it there.

There is yet behind of what I purposed to lay open, the incredible loss and detriment that this plot of licensing puts us to, more than if some enemy at sea should stop up all our havens and ports and creeks, it hinders and retards the importation of our richest merchandise, Truth: nay, it was first established and put in practice by anti-christian malice and mystery[41] on set purpose to extinguish, if it were possible, the light of Reformation, and to settle falsehood; little differing from that policy wherewith the Turk upholds his Alcoran, by the prohibition of Printing. 'Tis not denied, but gladly confessed, we are to send our thanks and vows to Heaven, louder than most of nations for that great measure of truth which we enjoy, especially in those main points between us and the Pope, with his appurtenances the Prelates: but he who thinks we are to pitch our tent here, and have attained the utmost prospect of reformation, that the mortal glass[42] wherein we contemplate can show us, till we come to beatific vision, that man by this very opinion declares that he is yet far short of truth.

Truth indeed came once into the world with her divine Master, and was a perfect shape most glorious to look on: but when he ascended, and his Apostles after him were laid asleep, then straight arose a wicked race of deceivers, who (as that story goes of the Egyptian Typhon with his conspirators, how they dealt with the good Osiris)[43] took the virgin Truth, hewed her lovely form into a thousand pieces, and scattered them to the four winds. From that time ever since, the sad friends of Truth, such as durst appear, imitating the careful[44] search that Isis made for the mangled body of Osiris, went up and down gathering up limb by limb still as they could find them. We have not yet found them all, Lords and Commons, nor ever shall do, till her Master's second coming; he shall bring together every joint and member, and shall mould them into an immortal feature of loveliness and perfection. Suffer not these licensing prohibitions to stand at every place of opportunity forbidding and disturbing them that continue seeking, that continue to do our obsequies to the torn body of our martyred saint. We boast our light; but if we look not wisely on the sun itself, it smites us into darkness. Who can discern those planets that are oft combust,[45] and those stars of brightest magnitude that rise and set with the sun, until the opposite motion of their orbs bring them to such a place in the firmament where they may be seen evening or morning. The light which we have gained was given us, not to be ever staring on, but by it to discover

40. Matter of particular concern.

41. Mystification.

42. Mirror (see I Corinthians 13:12).

43. Typhon, Osiris' brother, murdered and dismembered him; the body floated down the Nile and was reassembled by his wife, Isis, and Horus, their son. As early as Plutarch, this was read as a myth of the mangling and scattering of Truth, and its reconstitution, both eternal processes (compare Bacon's essay, "Of Truth").

44. Full of cares.

45. "Burnt up," figuratively, by closely approaching the sun; an astrological term.

onward things more remote from our knowledge. It is not the unfrocking of a priest, the unmitring of a bishop, and the removing him from off the Presbyterian shoulders that will make us a happy nation, no, if other things as great in the church, and in the rule of life both economical [46] and political be not looked into and reformed. We have looked so long upon the blaze that Zwinglius and Calvin [47] hath beaconed up to us that we are stark blind. There be who perpetually complain of schisms and sects, and make it such a calamity that any man dissents from their maxims. 'Tis their own pride and ignorance which causes the disturbing, who neither will hear with meekness, nor can convince, yet all must be suppressed which is not found in their syntagma.[48] They are the troublers, they are the dividers of unity, who neglect and permit not others to unite those dissevered pieces which are yet wanting to the body of Truth. To be still searching what we know not by what we know, still closing up truth to truth as we find it (for all her body is homogeneal,[49] and proportional),[50] this is the golden rule in theology as well as in arithmetic, and makes up the best harmony in a church; not the forced and outward union of cold and neutral and inwardly divided minds.

. . .

There have been not a few since the beginning of this Parliament,[51] both of the Presbytery and others, who by their unlicensed books to the contempt of an Imprimatur first broke that triple ice [52] clung about our hearts, and taught the people to see day. I hope that none of those were the persuaders to renew upon us this bondage which they themselves have wrought so much good by contemning. But if neither the check that Moses gave to young Joshua, nor the countermand which our Saviour gave to young John, who was so ready to prohibit those whom he thought unlicensed, be not enough to admonish our elders how unacceptable to God their testy mood of prohibiting is, if neither their own remembrance what evil hath abounded in the Church by this let [53] of licensing, and what good they themselves have begun by transgressing it, be not enough, but that they will persuade, and execute the most Dominican part of the Inquisition over us, and are already with one foot in the stirrup so active at suppressing, it would be no unequal distribution in the first place to suppress the suppressors themselves: whom the change of their condition hath puffed up, more than their late experience of harder times hath made wise.

And as for regulating the Press, let no man think to have the honour of advising ye better than yourselves have done in that order published next before this,[54] *'that no book be printed, unless the printer's and the author's*

46. Concerning household management, thus, here, private affairs.

47. Ulrich Zwingli (1484–1531), of Zurich; John Calvin (1509–64), of Geneva—the two Swiss reformers.

48. System of doctrine.

49. All of a piece throughout.

50. Harmoniously composed in relations of parts to whole.

51. The Long Parliament, which first assembled November 3, 1640.

52. Punning on, and nevertheless seriously alluding to, the *aes triplex* ("triple bronze"), needed, says Horace (*Odes* I.3), to gird the heart of a man setting out, for the first time, to sea.

53. Hindrance.

54. An order previous to the one (of June 14, 1643) which Milton is disputing.

name, or at least the printer's be registered.' Those which otherwise come forth, if they be found mischievous and libellous, the fire and the executioner will be the timeliest and the most effectual remedy that man's prevention can use. For this authentic [55] Spanish policy of licensing books, if I have said aught, will prove the most unlicensed book itself within a short while; and was the immediate image of a Star Chamber decree to that purpose made in those very times when that Court did the rest of those her pious works, for which she is now fallen from the stars with Lucifer. Whereby ye may guess what kind of state prudence, what love of the people, what care of Religion or good manners there was at the contriving, although with singular hypocrisy it pretended to bind books to their good behaviour. And how it got the upper hand of your precedent Order so well constituted before, if we may believe those men whose profession gives them cause to inquire most, it may be doubted there was in it the fraud of some old patentees and monopolizers in the trade of bookselling; who under pretence of the poor in their Company not to be defrauded, and the just retaining of each man his several copy, which God forbid should be gainsaid, brought divers glozing [56] colours to the House, which were indeed but colours, and serving to no end except it be to exercise a superiority over their neighbours, men who do not therefore labour in an honest profession to which learning is indebted, that they should be made other men's vassals. Another end is thought was aimed at by some of them in procuring by petition this Order, that having power in their hands, malignant books might the easier scape abroad, as the event shows. But of these sophisms and elenchs [57] of merchandise I skill not. This I know, that errors in a good government and in a bad are equally almost incident; for what Magistrate may not be misinformed, and much the sooner, if liberty of Printing be reduced into the power of a few? But to redress willingly and speedily what hath been erred, and in highest authority to esteem a plain advertisement [58] more than others have done a sumptuous bribe, is a virtue (honoured Lords and Commons) answerable to your highest actions, and whereof none can participate but greatest and wisest men.

1644 1644

55. Peculiarly.
56. Flattering.
57. Fallacious points.
58. Notification.

The Restoration and the Eighteenth Century

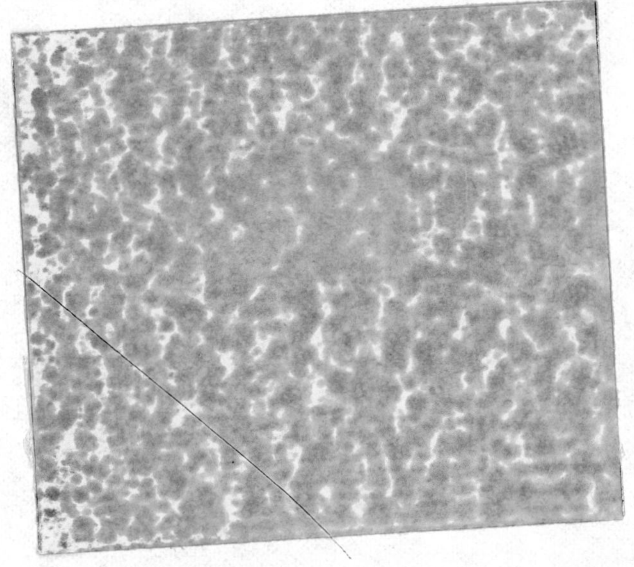

The Restoration and the Eighteenth Century

We may speak of the eighteenth century as the period of the Enlightenment, and the term carries a fairly precise meaning when it is applied to France: secular in spirit, skeptical in matters of knowledge, rationalistic only in its critique of historical institutions, devoted to the idea of justice, and jealously protective of the dignity of human nature. Not all these traits are to be found in every writer, it is true, but they serve well enough to characterize the age. When we turn from France to England, however, the idea of an Enlightenment becomes less clear.

As a predominantly Protestant nation, and one whose established church had turned away from dogmatic and evangelical extremes toward a religion of moral duty, England had less reason to be anticlerical or militantly secular. Deism became a force in the later seventeenth century and persisted as a rationalistic natural religion opposed to all dependence upon revelation; but it never achieved a highly respectable position in England. English political liberties, which served as a model for French reformers, were sufficient to make plausible the Whig trust in slow historical progression and to win loyalty, if not in fact reverence, to constitutional forms. Most of the major writers of the age, from Dryden to Dr. Johnson (and including Swift and Pope), were largely Tory in spirit: distrustful of human nature and devoted to the cause of public order.

Yet one can see a degree of secularization in England. The center of concern has shifted from the institutions that confer legitimate authority to the detached individual, from dogma to the painful quest for balance and tact. Decisions are made by man rather than for him, and they exact a new intensity of self-criticism, a wary resistance to the appeals of partiality and self-interest—a discipline, as the age would have it, of both head and heart. For while there is distrust of the private spirit and of anarchic individualism—usually shown to be based in pride—there is no easy recourse in turn to rule or formula. The distinctive spirit of the age, then, and it might be called Enlightenment, is a critical one—constantly testing through irony, purging with satire, and finding conviction in the poise of an exact antithesis or a delicate balance.

POLITICS AND MORALITY

When the Stuarts returned to the throne in 1660, the changes of two intervening decades of revolution could not simply be reversed, for the experience of power had awakened new capacities and justified new ambitions. At first there was apparent reaction. The Church of England was re-established as the state religion. But it now had to fight and intrigue with Dissenters and Roman Catholics to preserve its authority. There were strong demands for full civil rights by the Puritans, and there were grave fears of what Charles II might grant to the Catholic French monarch, Louis XIV, in return for financial subsidy. The fears of the church were only a reflection of the instability of the King's power. Charles was under constant pressure in his later years from Whig lords (whose alliances were with London merchants, middle-class Dissenters, and former Dutch allies) and from the Tory supporters of his Catholic brother and apparent heir, the Duke of York (later James II). But more fundamentally, the idea of kingship itself was in question.

In his great political work of 1651, the *Leviathan,* Thomas Hobbes had argued the need for a stable and undivided sovereignty. Hobbes opposed the growing myth of the mixed state (a balance of power among King, Lords, and Commons), but his defense of absolute sovereignty was no return to the Stuart doctrine of the divine right of kings ("right divine to govern wrong," as Pope described James I's doctrine). Hobbes based his case on natural expediency; the alternative was intolerable anarchy, in which each man warred against every other. It hardly mattered to Hobbes what form the sovereignty took so long as it could command and maintain power (and Swift, writing after the Glorious Revolution of 1688, declared that Hobbes's essential error lay in making the King rather than the Parliament the ultimate sovereign). John Locke, writing in Charles II's reign what was not to be published until 1690, insisted that the King derived his authority not from the sheer necessity of his subjects but from their active consent; should he destroy their property or enslave them, he would put himself "into a state of war with the people, who are thereupon absolved from any further obedience."

This secularized view of the state left little sanctity to the king, and Charles II was rarely the man to claim it. Urbane and cultivated, with a taste for music and wit, he inspired personal affection and public distrust in equal measure. He lacked moral depth or tenacity of purpose, and, while his love of pleasure was a welcome relief for many from the sober fanaticism of strict Puritans and surly republicans, it encouraged little repose in his strength or reliance on his word. The Marquess of Halifax wrote of Charles after his death: "It must be allowed he had a little over-balance on the well-natured side, not vigour enough to be earnest to do a kind thing, much less to do a harsh one; but if a hard thing was done to another man, he did not eat his supper the worse for it. It was rather a deadness than a severity of nature. . . ." One is struck by how often Halifax recurs to the King's physical well-being: "It may be said that his inclinations to love were the effects of health and a good constitution, with as little mixture of the seraphic part as man ever had; and though from that foundation men often raise their passions, I am apt to think his stayed as much as any man's ever did in the lower region. . . . He had more properly . . . a good stomach to his mistresses than any great passion for them. His taking them from others was never learnt in a romance, and indeed fitter for a philosopher than a knight-errant." If Charles showed no jealousy, it was "love of ease" that prevented it; for "where mere nature is the motive, it is possible for a man . . . to argue that a rival taketh away nothing but the heart and leaveth the rest."

The Glorious Revolution of 1688, which brought William III and Mary to the throne, confirmed the principle of the mixed state, a principle that was to be invoked throughout the century to follow and to be accepted as the Revolution Settlement by all but the few fanatical Jacobites (who remained loyal to James II and his heirs). There was still only a cautious assertion of constitutional changes: the fiction of James's abdication was used to soften the force of Parliament's action, and the limits set to the king's power were left implicit in his oath to govern "according to the statutes in Parliament agreed on." For years to come the full meaning of the changes remained in the process of definition, and the stability to be found in the harmony of a mixed state remained more vision than actuality.

The growth of the electorate gave more power to Commons, and the conduct of protracted wars led to the growth of the court bureaucracy. To support its program the court required more and more recourse to public loans, and with them came an increase both of an administrative cadre and of a moneyed class whose wealth came from investment rather than from rents. This erosion of the landed interest was felt most acutely by the smaller landowners, the country gentry, and they were most suspicious of the centralized power at court. The early years of the eighteenth century were a period of frequent elections and shifts of power, and the efforts of the Whig forces to enlist wider support led to more toleration for Dissenters and more dependence upon the financial power of London.

Much of the energy of the writers of the day was devoted to defending traditional attitudes or to destroying them. Daniel Defoe attacked the landed gentry in behalf of the men of wealth; Swift exposed the increasing power of men whose loyalty was claimed not by tenant and estate but by interest rates and "paper money." But meanwhile these distinctions were breaking down, as men of wealth invested in land (at times buying up the nearly bankrupt estates of small landholders) and as the landed aristocracy, through both investment and intermarriage, allied itself with the "moneyed" men. The political stability dreamed of in the mixed state was attained at last in the 1720's when Sir Robert Walpole strengthened the court by his bold use of patronage to win support, and there arose the serious question of whether the state had become a stable balance or rather a new kind of tyranny under the forms of parliamentary leadership.

If Charles II sets the note of the Restoration period, Walpole does as much for the mid-eighteenth century. Bluff, hospitable, ostentatious, he had a sufficient sense of his own power. "I am certainly at present in a situation that makes me," he said to Lord Hervey, "of consequence to more people than any man ever before me was, or perhaps than any man may ever be again." Hervey reflected on "the double vanity this great man was guilty of in believing what he said, and saying what he believed." Walpole's management of George II through Queen Caroline and of Parliament through a system of patronage made his control of England a formidable substitute for earlier and franker forms of tyranny. Walpole's control of English liberties was far less complete; but the Licensing Act of 1737, which imposed political censorship on the stage, might recall Dryden's words about Augustus, who "conscious of himself of so many crimes which he had committed, thought . . . to provide for his own reputation by making an edict against lampoons and satires."

Walpole achieved stability by freeing the court of the overriding power of Commons. In the process the Whig oligarchy, having attained a one-party system, adopted much of the traditional doctrine of the Tories. It was the so-called Patriots (led by the friend of Swift and Pope, Lord Bolingbroke) who kept alive the idea of an Opposition as a guarantor of freedom, who demanded more frequent elections and more extensive representation, and who sought to free Parliament of its control by place-holders.

In an age where power increasingly followed wealth, the highly paid sinecures that Walpole distributed were not only a reward for obedience, they were a further entrenchment of a self-perpetuating group. More appalling to men like Swift and Pope was Walpole's marshalling of a squad of hireling writers, serviceable men of limited talent, to defend his ministry and discredit his opponents. Royal patronage no longer furthered merit for its own sake but used the forms of distinction to reward subservience and intellectual dishonesty. Pope's *Dunciad* makes Colley Cibber the monarch of the dunces, the epitome of a commercialized and debased culture; he had been elevated to the post of poet-laureate less for talent than for pliability.

The opposition to Walpole was made articulate by men who had loyalties to a landed aristocracy, but those loyalties were neither felt nor expressed in limited economic terms. Rather, they were universalized as the opposition of genuine culture to sham, of free intelligence to prostitute mediocrity. For the stability that Walpole gave England was gained at the cost of moral aspiration. A man might aspire to power or wealth, but he had to leave his integrity behind when he went "to see Sir Robert." This sense of universal corruption was the specter created in the great satires of the age, and in opposition to it a new kind of heroism emerged. It included aristocratic scorn for mercantile zeal that slights honesty and justice; esteem for the "middle state" of man (above brutalizing poverty and below debilitating luxury); disdain for the mindless "mob," whether of the lower classes or the hireling nobles; nostalgia for institutions which embodied principles stabler than individual will or current fashion. One can see this as a rear-guard resistance to growing bourgeois liberalism, as reactionary appeal to a past that could not be restored and perhaps had never truly existed. But from the other end of that cycle of growth we may find it harder to call it reaction; such judgments trust history to settle issues, and history never does so for long.

The aspiration that Walpole and his chosen successors, the Pelhams, failed to satisfy found release in the leadership of the elder William Pitt, Earl of Chatham. The hero of the London merchants, he also fostered a sense of national greatness, presiding over the defeat of France on three continents and her loss of power in both Canada and India. These were triumphs of mercantile expansion which laid the groundwork for the growth of empire abroad and of industry at home; but Pitt infused them with a sense of moral purpose.

In George III, who became king in 1760, moral aspiration reached the throne itself, but his earnestness was marked by obstinacy and his devotion to duty by priggishness. The third George, unlike the first two, cultivated domestic virtues rather than foreign mistresses, and his favor was worthily conferred (with the guidance of ministers) upon such men as Dr. Johnson, Gibbon, and Rousseau. But his rigid and suspicious nature made him declare, with a sense of shock, that he had to "call in bad men to govern bad men." Among the "bad men" to be governed were the American colonists, who completed their successful revolution by 1783, and the political radicals at home, whose sympathy with the colonies was only a prelude to their support of the French Revolution a few years later.

Perhaps the best of the men George chose to govern for him was the younger William Pitt, who became chief minister in 1784 at the age of twenty-five (as Coleridge was to observe, he was "always full-grown," for he "was cast rather than grew"). Pitt had genius in administrative reform; he reduced waste in government offices, revised the tax and customs system, reduced the national debt, and stimulated trade.

These technical achievements were, however, overtaken by the war with France which followed upon the Revolution; and Pitt became, with the threat of invasion from abroad and the fear of subversion at home, all too ready to see political radicalism of any sort as potential treason and to make it so in law. Somewhat as Robert Walpole had been the object of attack by the major poets of the mid-century, so Pitt, for different reasons, was to win the scorn of Blake, Wordsworth, and Coleridge.

THE MIDDLE WAY: WIT AND DRESS

Few moments seem so decisive a break in the continuity of English literature as the Restoration. While in exile in France, the court of Charles II had acquired a new tone of worldliness and self-conscious sophistication that was to affect literary as well as social forms. The fact that Milton's *Paradise Lost* or Bunyan's *Pilgrim's Progress* was published after the Restoration seems incongruous. Yet the new tone was not simply a brittle elegance derived from French manners and turned mockingly upon sober Puritan zeal. It had its own seriousness even when it was most willfully outrageous; and it was marked by deep skepticism. The unlimited claims of religious sects and political causes had produced decades of painful division—within the nation, even within families—and they were now seen with a strong sense of their danger. Extravagant assertions of divine favor by radical Protestants and no less fanatical Royalists seemed frivolous, fevered, and deeply destructive. Skepticism turned to the practical and viable; it tested all claims and assertions for both their meaningfulness and their consequences.

One of the forms of this skepticism was the cultivation of dialectic and banter. Against each unlimited assertion one could place its contrary. Or one could frame dialogues in which the intellectual bankruptcy of the fanatics was exposed by a deadlock between extremists or by an opponent of Socratic modesty and irony. We can see the spirit of this in Dryden's *Essay of Dramatic Poesy* (1668), where four critics assert in turn the superiority of ancient or modern, French or English, literature. It is a dialogue of exceptional amiability, for these men are good-tempered and comparatively flexible; it takes place, moreover, just on the margin of an Anglo-Dutch war, a quiet retreat from public conflicts. Other dialogues were more satirical and reductive; they allowed the "enthusiast" to expand to the utmost before he was punctured and deflated by wit. Enthusiasm itself was a term of reproach; it referred to the delusion of being divinely inspired and to the self-hypnotic rhetoric of those who acted under that delusion. To show them as all the more vehement for their ignorance and superstition was the satirist's device; we see it in Samuel Butler's portrait of the radical Protestant squire Ralpho in *Hudibras* (1663–78). Another method was to study the psychopathology of enthusiasm and to trace its madness to a pride that could not endure the restraints of reason and common truths.

The retreat from public conflicts had led a group of learned men of various allegiances to gather for the discussion of scientific matters at Gresham College in London during the years of Cromwell's Protectorate; out of these meetings (from which the topics of religion and politics were barred) emerged the Royal Society, chartered by the King in 1662. The Royal Society was devoted, in a Baconian spirit, to empirical investigation, and it framed as well an influential conception of language. Joseph Glanvill, for example, could see nothing but "endless disputes and quarrels" come of devotion to the "verbal emptiness of the philosophy of the Schools," that is, the Scholasticism that sought to explain phenomena by multiplying terms: "For what else can be the fruit of a philosophy, made of occult qualities, sympathies, entelechies, elements, celestial influences, and abundance of other hard words and lazy generalities but an arrest of all ingenious and practical endeavour, and a wilderness of opinions instead of certainty and science?" What Glanvill hoped for and at last saw as possible was "a philosophy fruitful in works, not in words, and such as may accommodate the use of life, both natural and moral." And he, like others, drew a parallel for religion: the need to give up endless and insoluble controversy about doctrine, often based upon obscure texts of Scripture, and to concentrate upon the "practical and certain knowledge which will assist and promote our virtue and our happiness."

This reaction against "notion and theory" affected all realms of experience. Sir Isaac Newton boasted, "I do not frame hypotheses," and by that he meant his refusal, in contrast to Descartes, to be seduced by speculation from the essential task of empirical description. In politics and religion the men of "latitude" and moderation tried to forge a method of critical discrimination. It was typically represented as the search for a middle way between extremes. By this was meant not lukewarmness or weak compromise (what the age called "trimming") but a bold rejection of untested dogma. The middle way lacked the support of authority and precedent; it required a delicate judgment of each new situation, a weighing of values without formula, and a readiness to dwell in uncertainties rather than surrender to prejudice or cant.

We can see the theme of the middle way captured in the metaphor of dress that pervaded the writing of the age. Language has often been described as the dress of thought, and rhetoric has been treated as a wardrobe of idioms in which ideas might be clothed. In the Restoration we find a strong reaction against merely verbal wit. The attack could extend to the conceits of the metaphysical poets (and particularly the late, mannered style of a John Cleveland), to the metaphorical flights of baroque sermons, to the jargon of Scholastics or (worse) of pseudo-mystical and alchemical writers, to the "wresting of scriptures" that tortured the text of the Bible until it could serve any prejudice or party. In the realm of manners, the attack (such as we see in Restoration comedy) was turned on the coxcomb who made constant use of the "jerk and sting of an epigram" and who chased the reputation of brilliance through a thousand puns. The would-be wit was always on the stretch to show his cleverness and seldom concerned about whether truth or insight might lie below the dazzling surface. Restoration comedy tended to equate the would-be wit with the fop. The fop, too, disregards "propriety" or "decency," a sense of what belongs or is fitting. He does not dress in a manner appropriate to his rank or to the occasion but seeks only to overwhelm others with his finery. His dress is a collection of unrelated bits of brilliance—"one glaring chaos and wild heap of wit," as Pope described a poem full of conceits—whose only purpose is to dazzle.

What were the alternatives? Was not all dress a form of deception? Some believed so and insisted upon naked nature, as if that were still possible in a world of men. In Restoration comedy, the fop's opponent was often the rake, a man of frankly licentious appetite with the cunning to satisfy it, a cool Machiavellian in the world of sex and money. He enacted the unabashed animal he thought man might better be and gloried in his energy and resourcefulness. Yet neither of these extremes, fop or rake, stood up to scrutiny, for both revealed anarchic pride and self-seeking. The typical response to both was to find a middle way: to recognize the "way of the world" and to dress to meet its demands. For the true wit did not neglect the guises the world would accept; but he used them as a means of preserving his independence and integrity. This was the case of Mirabell in William Congreve's *The Way of the World* (1700), and we can see its deeper implications in Swift's *A Tale of a Tub* (1704).

Swift's allegory presented Christian teaching as a simple garment that, in the course of history, was covered with all the fashionable accessories that the world demanded. Three brothers showed the different ways of treating the garment. Peter (the Roman Catholic Church) first led the others in loading his coat with elaborate ornaments and refused, when they were criticized, to remove any. Jack (the radical Protestant church) condemned Peter's error and, in a fit of enthusiastic reformation, tore his own coat to shreds in the effort to remove whatever Peter had persuaded him to add. Only the third brother, Martin (representing the middle way of the Church of England), recognized the impossibility of restoring his coat to its original purity, accepted those additions whose removal would destroy its fabric, and carefully detached the rest stitch by stitch. Martin was concerned with the coat itself rather than its expression of his own will; and in his rejection of both imposture and brutality he showed an awareness that reached, in effect, a different level rather than lay midway on a single plane. The middle way, for Swift, is not simply a compromise between two errors but a transcendence of the vicious folly that produced both.

AN AUGUSTAN AGE

In his scorn for the verbal sophistries of false wit, the writer of this age often called them barbarous or "Gothic." By contrast he looked back to the grace and lucidity of classical writing and tried to recover its virtues in his own work. The period was one of great translation; not only did Dryden translate all of Virgil, and Pope all of Homer, but there were also the free "imitations" of Horace and Juvenal, from Rochester's early experiments to Dr. Johnson's *Vanity of Human Wishes* (1749). To write in the spirit of the ancients while adapting them to the day is perhaps a greater sign of devotion than the museum-like reproductions that were to follow once historicism, with its sense of the pastness of the past and the distinctiveness of each culture, arose in the late eighteenth century. The earlier revival of the classics was predicated on the view that these writers were more genuinely alive than the eccentric or time-bound authors of the immediate past; it was not the rust of antiquity but its relevance that was esteemed.

The period of the Restoration and early eighteenth century is now often called the Augustan age. The term arose in the period itself, but it was applied tentatively and in more than one sense. London, once called Troynovant or New Troy, came now to be called Augusta, as the heir to imperial Rome. In 1712 John Oldmixon wrote that the age of Charles II "probably may be the Augustan Age of English poetry," and Dr. Johnson applied to Dryden's role in English poetry the words once used of Augustus as the builder of Rome: "He found it brick and left it marble." The term "Augustan" was a tribute to the new urbanity and formal elegance of English verse, and it evoked as well the tradition of a ruler who gave his patronage to and won the sincere respect of his greatest writers. This role could be said to fit Charles II in some measure, but to apply it, as Pope did with brilliant irony, to George I or George II, could be nothing but a gesture of scorn. George II hated poetry and painting alike and allowed politics to dictate patronage.

There were grounds, however, for distrusting the Emperor Augustus as well; his subversion of the freedom of the Roman Republic was a constant theme of historians: Swift alluded to it in 1701, and Gibbon made it the subject of the great third chapter of his *Decline and Fall of the Roman Empire* (1776). The ambivalence felt toward an age that was at once courtly, polished, and servile awakened all the more reverence for republican Rome and praise for the stoical Horace of the Republic rather than the epicurean Horace of the court.

Still, the tribute to Rome served to evoke a common European culture beneath the accidents of time or the changing national and local customs. It was an appeal to values that had won agreement in most times and places and would be confirmed by posterity in turn. For the classical view of history saw man as constant and the accidents of time as repetitive and cyclical rather than progressive. This view provided the Enlightenment with the secular counterpart of those religious values that stood outside the world and could be used to judge it. Whatever the corruptions and blindness of the present, one could see beyond them to permanent truths.

The desire to free the general or the universal in all its grandeur from particular fashion (of dress, of manners, of language) could lead at worst to a vacuous academicism. One might remove all character in order to remove idiosyncrasy. We may recall those white marble statues (for the eighteenth century invented a white antiquity, purified of those colors that had once adorned statues and temples) in classical costume that restored contemporary statesmen (Walpole or Washington) to their universality or a poet like Pope to his role of laurel-crowned *vates*. But at their best, poets and artists achieved a nice balance between the classical form and the substantial actuality. This is most obvious in the "imitation" or in the mock form (such as mock-heroic or mock-pastoral) where the pure form is opposed to the bristling disorder of everyday life. The greatest works of the age play back and forth between the ideal form and the stubborn particular, each criticizing the other.

There is a similar interplay in the architecture of the period. When the Earl of Burlington revived the designs of Andrea Palladio as the most classical and humanistic of Renaissance architects, he was rejecting the baroque freedom of Sir Christopher Wren and in fact restoring a greater Roman severity than he could find in Palladio. Yet the Palladian country house was set in gardens which achieved the natural freedom of landscape rather than geometric formality. House and grounds were set against each other to yield a more complex harmony.

In painting no one caught the vitality and exuberance of urban life so well as William Hogarth, but he was also possessed by the desire to succeed in the high form of history-painting, with its generalized figures of heroic grandeur. Sir Joshua Reynolds, who formulated the doctrine of the grand style in his presidential addresses to the Royal Academy, created in turn witty plays upon the heroic, evoking it in teasing allusions or "quoted" poses, placing children in the heroic stances of prophets or rulers.

SATIRE AND THE NOVEL

Nowhere did the classical forms serve so well as in satire. Satire had never been so central and powerful a form of literature before in England, nor had it ever shown so great a capacity to absorb the tragic and heroic vision as well. The skeptical impetus that discredited false claims to authority found its form by inventing a ludicrous world of mock-grandeur and self-deception, where men pursued the outward forms of greatness with no sense of their meaning or their true cost. In the finest satires of the age the mantle of greatness is placed upon the fool and falls with an overwhelming weight, as if to crush an insect. The heroic vision is essential to the satiric; the satirist shows his anti-hero falling as far below the norms of decency and intelligence as the true hero rises above them. To trap an oaf in the pattern of the heroic is to define his grossness all the more sharply; his high pretensions only serve to measure his contemptible performance.

Yet the heroic works in another way, too. For while the particular object of satire may be ludicrous and transparent, he may serve to reveal a wider and deeper pattern of failure that is more commonplace and less easy to identify in actual men. When Swift embodies the history of the church in the careers of three Restoration fops, the small foreground figures serve to interpret (reductively but with frightening lucidity) vast and complex historical forces. When Pope in *The Dunciad* presents the debased culture of his day as if it were the eclipse of all culture, he is not simply attacking the corruption of the Hanoverian court or of commercialized London. He is attacking "Dulness," the chronic tendency of the mind to relapse into lazy fantasy and to give up its critical powers; the current scene is only the latest instance of a process whose dimensions extend through all history. Satire magnifies as well as reduces; it may reduce man's plausible pretexts to mechanical folly, but it makes the folly in turn a potential tragic failure and a force worthy of heroic resistance.

Once satire gives way to more neutral curiosity, what was seen as failure is regarded with more sympathy and willingness to condone or understand. In the process the very details which were an affront to the high forms of the heroic become the absorbing material of daily life. The marvelous, saintly, and heroic may be transposed to the level of the commonplace. Instead of a lonely Odysseus outwitting vengeful gods we have a sober Robinson Crusoe ingeniously transforming a lonely island into a scene of middle-class enterprise. With the rise of the novel the studied detachment of satire gives way to an exploration of the confusions and inconsistencies seen within the self. In *Robinson Crusoe* (1719) Defoe fused what might have been the material of a Puritan spiritual autobiography with the heroism of mercantile adventure. In *Moll Flanders* (1722) he went on to consider those forms of excess, the ruthlessness of theft and prostitution, that lie at the edge of mercantile zeal, and he treated them with remarkable awareness of the power of their appeal.

Defoe in his first-person narratives and, even more, Samuel Richardson in his epistolary novels, notably *Pamela* (1741) and *Clarissa* (1748), found techniques for giving their stories an air of veracity. The point was not to deceive the reader about their being fictions but to bring him into close involvement with character and event. The novel's slow unfolding and full record of both internal and external realities created a remarkable new opportunity for identification; the letters of the day record the compelling power of the novel upon the reader's feelings. Henry Fielding, particularly in *Joseph Andrews* (1742) and *Tom Jones* (1749), created a new balance between the detached satiric observer, brilliantly artful in his rhetoric, and the closely presented incident. Fielding's formalization is bold and free, and he mocks the very conventions by which the novel asserts its veracity, but he uses them too. In Laurence Sterne's *Tristram Shandy* (1759–67), the self-consciousness of the novel reaches its extreme, veering between circumstantial realism and elaborate contrivance, pushing realism to the point where it frankly topples over into *tour de force*. Sterne also carries sympathy to the point where it becomes sentimentalism, that is, the prizing of feeling and the cultivation of it for its own sake; but he mocks this, too, with a recoil into ironic detachment.

NEW FEELINGS AND FORMS

The growing esteem for sentiment and feeling in the eighteenth century was the culmination of a long process—a movement toward internalization, first from the rationalistic systems of the seventeenth century to the Augustan emphasis on immediate intuition. The Augustans were intensely distrustful of systems; their pursuit of a middle way was a matter of achieving sound feeling as well as true insight, for the two were inextricably related. Pride and self-interest distorted all awareness: the delicate balance of disinterestedness was difficult to attain, and its attainment was as much a moral achievement as an intellectual one. The action of the honest heart was more reliable than any process of reasoning; and it was not a long step to the trust in heart over head. Trust your heart, wrote the third Earl of Shaftesbury, so long as you keep it honest.

In a similar way the grandeur of the general, once derived from a vision of cosmic order, became internalized and identified with what men have generally felt. Generality became a psychological rather than a metaphysical standard. As Reynolds observed, there are illusions that all men share, such as the impression that a medieval castle is older than a classical temple, if only because its origins are more darkly shrouded in a remote but native culture. A century earlier, Sir Christopher Wren had distinguished between natural or geometric beauty and customary beauty (where "familiarity or particular inclination breeds a love to things not in themselves lovely"). Wren has no doubt that natural or geometric beauty is to be preferred; but Reynolds has come to wonder. Reality is becoming what the mind of man creates.

The imaginative power of feeling was given new stress with the doctrine of association of ideas. If men framed an image of the world through repeated and reinforced associations, the linkages were often forged and more often confirmed by the action of the feelings. That seemed true, for David Hume, of our most fundamental conceptions, such as that of causality. Hume showed in his *Treatise on Human Nature* (1739) that the necessary connection of cause and effect was a necessity of our thought rather than an objective natural process. The more distinctive structures of the literary imagination could be traced to the rapid associative movement of genius working under the guidance of strong passion, and the explanation was made complex enough to account for all that was later to be included in the idea of imagination save only conscious artistry and active control. It is interesting, in fact, that Sterne presents man alternately as a victim of his associative processes and as the creator of imagined worlds; an ironic skepticism still surrounds the creative powers of the conscious artist.

In the early stages of this cult of feeling and the exploration of its power of artistry, poetry turned away from the everyday experience that had provided the stuff of Pope's satires or Swift's occasional verse. Instead it cultivated the sublime, images that filled the mind with awe or dread by their very transcendence of its normal scope—images of vastness, of sudden rise or fall, of dark obscurity or blazing light. Before these images were given a theoretical explanation by Edmund Burke in 1757, they had become the characteristic note of such poets of the 1740's as William Collins and Thomas Gray, or of the earlier and most influential poet of the landscape,

James Thomson. These images were, as Burke made clear, supremely realized in Milton's poetry, but they bring to the fore an aspect of Milton given less stress than his moral grandeur in the criticism of Joseph Addison. For the new poetry—as later for the Gothic novel—these images seemed to well up out of the unconscious mind, unrestrained by logic or morality. Their grandeur was not the grandeur of generality, but rather a power to reduce the conscious mind and all its high achievements to triviality. They loom over the ordinary world like towering cliffs or fierce clouds; or they expose the transitoriness of man's control in the images of ruins, the sharp angles of architecture crumbling into organic forms.

Inevitably the sublime and the Gothic provided a form of play-acting, and deliberately created ruins provided a stage for meditation. Yet there was a deeper force at work. To relate man's emotions and unconscious powers to the forms of nature deepened the response to both. Nature became an object of reverence rather than exploitation, a place that both revealed man to himself and imposed limits on his will. On the other hand, the beauty as well as the terror of man's elemental feelings became clear. There were dangers in such a movement toward primitivism; as man's taste opened, it was fed by synthetic products designed to meet it more completely than the natural. If Homer seemed difficult to treat as a primitive bard, the works of the Celtic bard, Ossian, were served up through forgeries that won acclaim throughout Europe. Yet authentic folk poetry was recovered, as in collection of ballads; and the dignity of folk speech or of local dialects began to be credited. All those peculiarities which had been seen as defects of the general now began to seem expressive of a deeper humanity, one that a high culture had suppressed or undervalued.

Another way in which the particular was given new dignity was through the idea of the picturesque. This began as the effort to find (later to create) in natural landscape the designs of the painters of the seventeenth century—Claude Lorrain, Nicolas Poussin, Salvator Rosa. What it came to in time was the rejection of a landscape, however "natural," that was too simple or featureless; the picturesque sought complex relationships of form and color. This was extended from landscape to houses, to villages, to the people who inhabited them. Ironically, bandits were more complex figures—rough, colorful, energetic—than solid tradesmen. There seemed, as often with the sublime, an inverse proportion between the picturesque and the moral. So, too, squalor might provide variety of forms, but the planned town imposed tame uniformity: one might not be content to keep the squalor, but one needed to imitate the slow evolution through time and accident, as in a natural scene, in designing structures or streets. It was better, too, that a cottage reveal its various functions in its surface structure rather than be forced into a pattern of symmetry.

The titanic forces found in the sublime view of nature were found by many in the French Revolution, where oppressive and lifeless forms were thrown off by a people awakened to its own dignity and power. In England some of the enthusiasm which might have turned to revolutionary humanism was captured by Methodism. John Wesley's great evangelical revival had much of the energy of earlier Puritanism, but its anti-intellectualism and political conservatism did nothing to foster the rebellious spirit of an earlier century. Radicalism was largely the product of urban societies of artisans, small merchants, and professional men; their efforts to broaden suffrage and to reform Parliament were blocked by the war with France and the repressive measures undertaken by the younger Pitt. But by the end of the eighteenth century England was clearly moving toward change.

The population of England increased from five and a half million to nine million in the course of the century, and though London maintained its dominance there was rapid growth in the northern areas, where industry developed most rapidly and freely. The concentration of industry in the cities was marked by 1800, but technology was giving all of the landscape a new look: improved turnpikes and canals (including a triumphant aqueduct bearing a canal over a river), new steam-powered pumps for coal mines, large factories for cotton-weaving and pottery-making, and (in 1779) the first iron bridge, over the Severn in Shropshire. To support an increased population required an agricultural as well as an industrial revolution, and this was achieved through the development of new crops (notably root-vegetables), the improved breeding of cattle and sheep (doubling their average weights in the course of the century), and the enclosure of commons so as to make more efficient use of the land. The most controversial developments were the enclosures, and their cost in human displacement was recorded in Oliver Goldsmith's *The Deserted Village* (1770). Hundreds of individual acts of enclosure were approved each year by Parliament from 1760 on, and these were taking place at the time when the growth of factories was destroying the cottage industries that had supplemented farm incomes. The movement toward the towns increased; yet the new agricultural techniques managed, even with a diminished labor force, to add some two million acres of arable land during the century.

By the close of the eighteenth century, English intellectual life had begun to move outside the major cities. We find a provincial painter like Joseph Wright of Derby painting the new industrial landscape as well as portraits of its builders, sublime landscapes and scenes of popular scientific demonstrations such as an experiment with an air-pump. An industrialist like Josiah Wedgwood, properly attentive to the state of roads and canals that served his potteries in Staffordshire, was no less attentive to archaeological discoveries in Pompeii and Herculaneum, from which he adapted designs through the skills of such artists as John Flaxman. Even more, the village and countryside had found poets, and resident poets rather than nostalgic ones, in men like Crabbe, Cowper, and Burns.

JOHN DRYDEN
1631–1700

Dryden's poetic career began with a schoolboy poem, an elegy to Lord Hastings, who had died of smallpox at nineteen. Dryden wrote with hectic extravagance in the fashionable late Metaphysical manner of John Cleveland, and he did remarkable things with poor Hastings's pustules: "Each little pimple had a tear in it, / To wail the fault its rising did commit / . . . Or were these gems sent to adorn his skin, / The cabinet of a richer soul within?" His first mature poem was the *Heroic Stanzas* on the death of Cromwell, and by 1660 he welcomed the restoration of Charles II with *Astraea Redux,* the first of a series of "public" poems in celebration or defense of that monarch. When the theaters reopened, Dryden wrote the first of his twenty-eight plays and collaborated briefly with Sir Robert Howard, whose sister he was to marry. Dryden did much to create the new heroic play, that frankly artificial, rather operatic form in which spectacle alternated with the fierce and witty debates of fiery souls; the greatest of these was his double play, in ten acts, *The Conquest of Granada* (1670).

Dryden's literary reign, crowned by the wreath of the poet laureate in 1671, included several provinces: drama, criticism, both prose and verse translation, and a large body of poetry in all forms. "Perhaps no nation," Dr. Johnson wrote,

> ever produced a writer that enriched his language with such variety of models. To him we owe the improvement, perhaps the completion of our metre, the refinement of our language, and much of the correctness of our sentiments. . . . What was said of Rome adorned by Augustus may be applied by an easy metaphor to English poetry embellished by Dryden . . . he found it brick, and he left it marble.

In contrast to Johnson's splendid confidence—limited, it should be noted, to formal achievements—Dryden often expressed a double view (such as we see in the poems to Oldham and to Congreve), a sense that greater urbanity might have been gained only at the expense of vigor.

This double view is a constant element in Dryden's superb play of dialectic. As Johnson said, he taught men "to think naturally and to express forcibly"; he was "the first who joined argument with poetry." Of a skeptical turn of mind, Dryden could feel himself into any stance and imagine ideas with the intensity of one who gave them utter conviction. The splendid bravura debate between the languid courtly sensualist and the "natural" man, between the defiant atheist and the Christian saint, between the rationalistic pagan and the wily inquisitor—all these are conducted with such eloquence and cogency that they seem at once aria and argument. His comedies were not remarkable, and he felt some shame at having supplied the lubricity his times demanded; the greatest of his later plays, *All for Love* (1678) and *Don Sebastian* (1690), are tragedies, although the latter has a boldly satiric subplot.

This play of mind gave rise to a major critical essay in the form of a dialogue, *Of Dramatic Poesy: An Essay* (1668). A "sceptical" discourse, it is "sustained by persons of several opinions, all of them left doubtful." The "essay" (and the term is meant still to suggest the tentative and exploratory) is one of the first exercises of that typical Augustan effort to define issues by providing statement and counterstatement, thesis and antithesis, from which the tact of the reader must elicit the delicate and undefinable truth. Ancient and Modern, French and English, Jonson and Shakespeare are placed in an opposition that teases our judgment, just as in later critical prefaces Virgil and Ovid or Horace and Juvenal serve, through counterpoint, to suggest the true nature of metaphor or the full power of satire.

Dryden's politics show a similar dialectical movement. If he played with the ideas of Hobbes, it was usually through dubious spokesmen; if he celebrated royal authority (as in *Absalom and Achitophel*), he could strike a note of balance in a later poem to his kinsman John Driden (1700): "Betwixt the Prince and Parliament we stand; / The barriers of the state on either hand: / May neither overflow, for then they drown the land!" If he scorned the fickle and restless mob, he scorned the egocentric tyrant no less; and some of his most brilliant dramatic moments are the explosion of the power-drive into madness, an insane rage to command those imaginary subjects that alone remain obedient to the tyrant's will.

Dryden's religious attitudes were the occasion for severe doubts of his sincerity. Born into a family of Puritan sympathies, he wrote one of the great defenses of the Anglican middle way in *Religio Laici* (1682). But the restless search for an authority that would resolve doubts and establish peace—both within the mind and among men—let him finally to Roman Catholicism. That he was led there just as the Catholic James II ascended the throne inevitably aroused suspicion of motives less honorable than sincere conviction; but, whatever their mixture, his motives surely included such conviction, and it is magnificently expressed in his defense of the persecuted Roman Catholic Church in *The Hind and the Panther* (1687). There the Church of England appears as the Panther, "the lady of the spotted muff," weak and compromising in her alliance with more radical Protestant sects, ready to unsheathe her claws, for all her superficial gentility, in her use of the civil power.

In Dryden's translations we can see the full range of his power to assume different voices, styles, and visions, as he moves from superb Lucretian didacticism to Juvenalian ferocity, from Ovidian extravagance to Virgilian elegance. Not only did Dryden translate all the works of Virgil, he translated Plutarch's *Lives* as well. The last may recall, finally, Dryden's great contribution to the emergence of an urbane and easy English prose; he had models in the age of Charles I, but his own example was one of the most effective in the age to come.

Of all the major writers in the period Dryden is the most thoroughly open to the energy that outruns moderation. His Cleopatra, in *All for Love,* exclaims: "I have loved with such transcendent passion, / I soared at first quite out of reason's view, / And now am lost above it." The other side of that transcendence is the high folly or madness of Achitophel or of Alexander under the power of music. Dryden is always ready for excess, for the grand gesture or the bold metaphor; yet the excess often carries with it the levity of a holiday from restraint and the potential ironic recoil of a gesture extended an inch too far or held a moment too long. Behind all his achievements we can glimpse the self-conscious artist, fully abandoned only to art itself, and we can sense that presence in a remark that shows the amiable pride of a man nearly seventy: "Thoughts, such as they are, come crowding in so fast upon me that my only difficulty is to choose or to reject, to run them into verse or to give them the other harmony of prose."

Absalom and Achitophel

Dryden's great satire was written at a time when the crisis it presents was still unresolved. Charles II had been urged by Whig leaders, and particularly the first Earl of Shaftesbury, to exclude his Roman Catholic brother from succession to the throne. In efforts to arouse fear of Catholic power, the Whigs found explosive material in the apparent disclosures by Titus Oates, an ex-seminarian, that a Popish Plot existed to assassinate Charles (even his Catholic wife was accused of a conspiratorial role), to seize power by violent means, perhaps to burn London (the Great Fire of 1666 had been attributed by some to a Catholic plot). Oates's testimony was highly suspect, as was the man, and it showed a convenient power of expansion as his memory was stimulated by criticism. But enough shreds of confirming evidence (not least the indiscreet correspondence of the Duchess of York's secretary with Louis XIV's confessor, looking forward to the conversion of the English to the Catholic faith) could be gathered to give Oates's charges plausibility and to promote the Whig demands that Charles legitimize his bastard son, the Duke of Monmouth, and make him his successor. As the Tory observer Roger L'Estrange later described events, the Whig

> faction had the ascendant of the government, and the multitude bore all before them like a torrent; the witnesses led the rabble; the plot-managers led the witnesses; and the Devil himself led the leaders; for they were to pass to their ends through subornation, perjury, hypocrisy, sacrilege, and treason.

By the time Dryden wrote, Charles had withstood Whig demands and achieved financial independence (through the French king) of a Parliament that tried to force his hand by withholding funds. He dissolved Parliament in March 1681, and Shaftesbury, charged with treason and arrested in July, was awaiting trial at the time Dryden's poem was published. (Shaftesbury was acquitted but never regained his earlier power.)

Dryden was not the first to adduce the biblical parallel of David and Absalom to Charles and his illegitimate son, Monmouth; but he was the first to exploit it so fully and adroitly, creating a constant interplay between biblical narrative and current history. He does more than that; to the story of Absalom's rebellion and his temptation by Achitophel, he brings a resonance not unlike that of Milton's treatment of the rebel angels in *Paradise Lost*. Dryden's figures are more obviously involved in duplicity or self-deception, and the splendid portraits of Whig leaders converge in a central pattern of destructive recklessness. Achitophel sponsors Monmouth precisely because his claim to the throne is unstable; his secret object is to undo monarchy itself, and in his obsessive and theory-ridden drive he is willing to run all the risks of anarchy.

In his treatment of David, Dryden opens with a tone of amused tolerance for the expansive energies of Charles and, somewhat in the manner of Halifax, sets David's easy love of pleasure against the more dangerous intensity of Achitophel; but once the rebellion gains its own reckless force, David emerges as a figure of severity and deep concern, surrounded by figures of dedication like Barzillai and his son. The movement of the poem can almost be seen as the earning of dignity for David by conflict and by trial.

Absalom and Achitophel

In pious times, ere priestcraft did begin,
Before polygamy was made a sin;
When man on many multiplied his kind,
Ere one to one was cursedly confined;
When nature prompted, and no law denied,
Promiscuous use of concubine and bride;
Then Israel's monarch after Heaven's own heart°
His vigorous warmth did variously impart
To wives and slaves; and, wide as his command,
Scattered his Maker's image through the land.
Michal,° of royal blood, the crown did wear;

after . . . heart See I Samuel 13:14, where Samuel warns Saul, "thy Kingdom shall not continue: the Lord hath sought him a man after his own heart."

Michal alluding to the childless Catherine of Braganza, who married Charles II in 1662

A soil ungrateful to the tiller's care:
Not so the rest; for several mothers° bore
To godlike David several sons before.
But since like slaves his bed they did ascend,
No true succession could their seed attend.
Of all this numerous progeny was none
So beautiful, so brave as Absalom:°
Whether, inspired by some diviner lust,
His father got him with a greater gust;°
Or that his conscious destiny made way,
By manly beauty, to imperial sway.
Early in foreign fields° he won renown,
With kings and states allied to Israel's crown:
In peace the thoughts of war he could remove,
And seemed as he were only born for love.
Whate'er he did was done with so much ease,
In him alone 'twas natural to please,
His motions all accompanied with grace;
And paradise was opened in his face.
With secret joy indulgent David viewed
His youthful image in his son renewed:
To all his wishes nothing he denied,
And made the charming Annabel° his bride.
What faults he had (for who from faults is free?)
His father could not or he would not see.
Some warm excesses which the law forbore,
Were construed youth that purged by boiling o'er,
And Amnon's murther,° by a specious name,
Was called a just revenge for injured fame.
Thus praised and loved the noble youth remained,
While David, undisturbed, in Sion° reigned.
But life can never be sincerely° blest;
Heaven punishes the bad, and proves° the best.
The Jews,° a headstrong, moody, murmuring race
As ever tried the extent and stretch of grace;
God's pampered people, whom, debauched with ease,
No king could govern nor no God could please;
(Gods they had tried° of every shape and size,

several mothers referring to Charles II's many mistresses and his illegitimate children
Absalom James Scott (1649–85), created Duke of Monmouth in 1663, born illegitimately to a "Welsh woman of no good fame" (Clarendon); "particularly beloved by the King; but the universal terror of husbands and lovers" (Grammont); a brave commander of Charles's forces in the Scottish campaign of 1679
gust appetite, relish
foreign fields with the French against the Dutch (1672–73) and with the Dutch against the French (1678)
Annabel Anne, Countess of Buccleuch (1651–1732), of great beauty and "one of the wisest and craftiest of her sex" (John Evelyn)
Amnon's murther Absalom arranged for the death of his half-brother in revenge for the rape of his sister, Tamar (II Samuel 13:28–29). Monmouth did not murder but had his troopers attack and disfigure a man who had insulted Charles II.
Sion London
sincerely completely
proves tests
Jews English
Gods . . . tried referring to the numerous sects that arose after the Reformation

That god-smiths could produce or priests devise:)
These Adam-wits, too fortunately free,
Began to dream they wanted° liberty;
And when no rule, no precedent was found
Of men by laws less circumscribed and bound,
They led their wild desires to woods and caves,
And thought that all but savages° were slaves.
They who, when Saul° was dead, without a blow,
Made foolish Ishbosheth° the crown forego;
Who banished David did from Hebron° bring,
And with a general shout proclaimed him king:
Those very Jews, who, at their very best,
Their humour° more than loyalty expressed,
Now wondered why so long they had obeyed
An idol monarch which their hands had made;
Thought they might ruin him they could create,
Or melt him to that golden calf,° a state.°
But these were random bolts; no formed design
Nor interest made the factious crowd to join:
The sober part of Israel, free from stain,
Well knew the value of a peaceful reign;
And, looking backward with a wise affright,
Saw seams of wounds, dishonest° to the sight:
In contemplation of whose ugly scars
They cursed the memory of civil wars.
The moderate sort of men, thus qualified,
Inclined the balance to the better side;
And David's mildness managed it so well,
The bad found no occasion to rebel.
But when to sin our biased nature leans,
The careful Devil° is still at hand with means,
And providently pimps for ill desires.
The Good Old Cause° revived, a plot requires:
Plots, true or false, are necessary things
To raise up commonwealths and ruin kings.
   The inhabitants of old Jerusalem°
Were Jebusites;° the town so called from them;
And theirs the native right——
But when the chosen people° grew more strong,

wanted lacked
savages wild beasts
Saul Oliver Cromwell (1599–1658)
Ishbosheth Cromwell's son Richard (1626–1712)
Hebron Scotland, where Charles II was crowned king in 1651, long before he became King of England
humour mood
golden calf the idol worshiped by the Israelites while Moses was receiving the law on Mt. Sinai
state republic, which Dryden elsewhere scornfully describes as "that mock-appearance of a liberty, where all who have not part in the government are slaves"
dishonest shameful
careful Devil Cf. Dryden's remarks on the Devil's policy "to seduce mankind into the same rebellion with him, by telling him he might be yet freer than he was, more free than his nature would allow" (Epistle Dedicatory to *All for Love*, 1677).
Good Old Cause for the Commonwealth
Jerusalem London
Jebusites Roman Catholics
chosen people Protestants

The rightful cause at length became the wrong;
And every loss the men of Jebus bore,
They still were thought God's enemies the more.
Thus worn and weakened, well or ill content,
Submit they must to David's government:
Impoverished and deprived of all command,
Their taxes doubled as they lost their land;°
And, what was harder yet to flesh and blood,
Their gods disgraced and burnt like common wood.°
This set the heathen priesthood° in a flame,
For priests of all religions are the same:
Of whatsoe'er descent their godhead be,
Stock, stone, or other homely pedigree,
In his defence his servants are as bold
As if he had been born of beaten gold.
The Jewish rabbins,° though their enemies,
In this conclude them honest men and wise:
For 'twas their duty, all the learnèd think,
To espouse his cause by whom they eat and drink.
From hence began that Plot,° the nation's curse,
Bad in itself, but represented worse;
Raised in extremes, and in extremes decried;
With oaths affirmed, with dying vows denied;
Not weighed or winnowed° by the multitude;
But swallowed in the mass, unchewed and crude.
Some truth there was, but dashed and brewed with lies,
To please the fools and puzzle all the wise.
Succeeding times did equal folly call
Believing nothing or believing all.
The Egyptian° rites the Jebusites embraced,
Where gods were recommended by their taste.
Such savoury deities must needs be good
As served at once for worship and for food.°
By force they could not introduce these gods,
For ten to one in former days was odds;
So fraud was used (the sacrificer's° trade):
Fools are more hard to conquer than persuade.
Their busy teachers mingled with the Jews,
And raked for converts even the court and stews:°
Which Hebrew priests° the more unkindly took,

Impoverished . . . land as Roman Catholics were or might be by laws passed under Elizabeth I and still in force beyond Dryden's day
burnt . . . wood referring to the savage destruction of church images during the Commonwealth
heathen priesthood Roman Catholic priests
Jewish rabbins Church of England priests
Plot the Popish Plot (see Headnote)
winnowed sifted
Egyptian French and Roman Catholic; but also referring to Egypt as the source of mysteries and superstition
worship . . . food referring to the doctrine of transubstantiation (the real presence of the body and blood of Christ in the bread and wine of Communion), a doctrine defended by Dryden after his conversion to Catholicism in 1685
sacrificer's priest's
stews brothels
Hebrew priests Church of England clergy

Because the fleece° accompanies the flock.
Some thought they God's anointed° meant to slay
By guns, invented since full many a day:
Our author swears it not; but who can know
How far the Devil and Jebusites may go?
This Plot, which failed for want of common sense,
Had yet a deep and dangerous consequence:
For, as when raging fevers boil the blood,
The standing lake soon floats into a flood,
And every hostile° humour, which before
Slept quiet in its channels, bubbles o'er;
So several factions from this first ferment
Work up to foam, and threat the government.
Some by their friends, more by themselves thought wise,
Opposed the power to which they could not rise.
Some had in courts been great and, thrown from thence,
Like fiends were hardened in impenitence.
Some by their monarch's fatal mercy grown
From pardoned rebels kinsmen to the throne,
Were raised in power and public office high;
Strong bands, if bands ungrateful men could tie.
Of these the false Achitophel° was first;
A name to all succeeding ages curst:
For close° designs and crooked counsels fit;
Sagacious, bold, and turbulent of wit;
Restless, unfixed in principles and place;
In power unpleased, impatient of disgrace:
A fiery soul, which, working out its way,
Fretted° the pigmy body° to decay,
And o'er-informed° the tenement of clay.
A daring pilot in extremity;
Pleased with the danger, when the waves went high,
He sought the storms; but, for a calm unfit,
Would steer too nigh the sands, to boast his wit.
Great wits are sure to madness near allied,
And thin partitions do their bounds° divide;
Else why should he, with wealth and honour blest,
Refuse his age the needful hours of rest?
Punish a body which he could not please;

fleece income from tithes
God's anointed the king
hostile contentious, excessive
Achitophel Anthony Ashley Cooper (1621–83), 1st Earl of Shaftesbury, who had been one of Cromwell's council of state but helped to arrange Charles II's return; as lord chancellor an excellent jurist and reformer of the Court of Chancery; after 1673 in opposition and by 1676 leader of those opposed to popery and arbitrary royal power; a man without equal "in the art of governing parties and of making himself the head of them" (Dryden)
close secret
Fretted eroded
pigmy body in fact very small, and in any case too small for its "fiery soul"
o'er-informed filled to overflowing; that is, the soul, which should be the form of mind and body, is here too restless to serve that limited function. On the "informing soul," see Pope, *Essay on Criticism*, ll. 76–79.
bounds of genius (wit) and madness

Bankrupt of life, yet prodigal° of ease?
And all to leave what with his toil he won,
To that unfeathered two-legged thing,° a son;
Got° while his soul did huddled° notions try,
And born a shapeless lump, like anarchy.
In friendship false, implacable in hate;
Resolved to ruin or to rule the state.
To compass this the triple bond° he broke,
The pillars of the public safety shook,
And fitted Israel for a foreign yoke:°
Then seized with fear, yet still affecting fame,
Usurped a patriot's all-atoning name.
So easy still it proves in factious times
With public zeal to cancel private crimes.
How safe is treason and how sacred ill,
Where none can sin against the people's will;°
Where crowds can wink and no offence be known,
Since in another's guilt they find their own.
Yet fame deserved no enemy can grudge;
The statesman we abhor, but praise the judge.
In Israel's courts ne'er sat an Abbethdin°
With more discerning eyes or hands more clean;
Unbribed, unsought, the wretched to redress,
Swift of dispatch and easy of access.
O had he been content to serve the crown
With virtues only proper to the gown,°
Or had the rankness° of the soil been freed
From cockle° that oppressed the noble seed;
David for him his tuneful harp had strung,
And Heaven had wanted° one immortal song.
But wild ambition loves to slide, not stand,°
And fortune's ice prefers to virtue's land.
Achitophel, grown weary to possess
A lawful fame and lazy happiness,
Disdained the golden fruit to gather free,
And lent the crowd his arm to shake the tree.
Now, manifest of° crimes contrived long since,
He stood at bold defiance with his prince;
Held up the buckler of the people's cause

prodigal spendthrift
unfeathered . . . thing alluding to the famous definition of man as a "featherless biped" ascribed to Plato
Got in contrast to Absalom, ll. 17–22
huddled confused; concealed
triple bond the triple alliance of England, Holland, and Sweden against France (1668), which Shaftesbury helped to break (not without Charles's connivance, however)
foreign yoke that of France
Where none . . . will i.e. where popular approval can cancel all guilt
Abbethdin presiding judge of the Jewish civil court
gown of the judge
rankness fertility
cockle weeds found in grain fields
wanted missed, in that David, the composer of the Psalms, would have devoted one song to Achitophel rather than to God
slide, not stand as in ll. 154, 161–62
manifest of showing openly

Against the crown, and skulked behind the laws.
The wished occasion of the Plot he takes,
Some circumstances finds, but more he makes.
By buzzing emissaries fills the ears
Of listening crowds with jealousies° and fears
Of arbitrary counsels brought to light,
And proves the king himself a Jebusite.
Weak arguments! which yet he knew full well
Were strong with people easy to rebel.
For, governed by the moon, the giddy Jews
Tread the same track when she the prime° renews;
And once in twenty years,° their scribes record,
By natural instinct they change their lord.
Achitophel still wants a chief, and none
Was found so fit as warlike Absalon:
Not that he wished his greatness to create,
(For politicians neither love nor hate,)
But, for he knew his title° not allowed
Would keep him still depending on the crowd:
That kingly power, thus ebbing out, might be
Drawn to the dregs of a democracy.°
Him he attempts with studied arts to please,
And sheds his venom° in such words as these:
'Auspicious° prince, at whose nativity
Some royal° planet ruled the southern sky,
Thy longing country's darling and desire,
Their cloudy pillar and their guardian fire,°
Their second Moses,° whose extended wand
Divides the seas, and shows the promised land,
Whose dawning day in every distant age
Has exercised the sacred prophets' rage:
The people's prayer, the glad diviners' theme,
The young men's vision, and the old men's dream!°
Thee, Saviour, thee, the nation's vows confess,
And, never satisfied with seeing, bless:
Swift unbespoken° pomps thy steps proclaim,

jealousies suspicion; see Butler, *Hudibras* I.i.3
prime the beginning of a new cycle
twenty years as in Charles I's troubles with the Long Parliament about 1640, the restoration of Charles II in 1660, and the Popish Plot fever of 1678
his title to the throne (Charles II having made a formal denial in 1679 of his rumored marriage with Monmouth's mother)
democracy literally, rule of the people; regarded in classical thought as an unstable form of government, easily tending to tyranny or dictatorship
sheds his venom with suggestion of the serpent's temptation of Eve (cf. Milton, *Paradise Lost* IX)
Auspicious fortunate
royal promising kingship
cloudy pillar . . . fire In the flight of the Israelites from Egypt, the "Lord went before them by day in a pillar of cloud, to lead them the way; and by night in a pillar of fire, to give them light" (Exodus 13:21).
second Moses "And the Lord said unto Moses, wherefore criest thou unto me? . . . But lift up thy rod, and stretch out thy hand over the sea, and divide it: and the children of Israel shall go on dry ground through the midst of the sea" (Exodus 14:15–16)
The young . . . dream "Your old men shall dream dreams, your young men shall see visions" (Joel 2:28), a passage, like most of these, taken as a prophecy of Christ's reign (cf. l. 245)
unbespoken spontaneous

And stammering babes are taught to lisp thy name.
How long wilt thou the general joy detain,
Starve and defraud the people of thy reign?
Content ingloriously to pass thy days
Like one of virtue's fools that feeds on praise;
Till thy fresh glories, which now shine so bright,
Grow stale and tarnish with our daily sight.
Believe me, royal youth, thy fruit must be
Or gathered ripe or rot upon the tree.
Heaven has to all allotted, soon or late,
Some lucky revolution of their fate;
Whose motions, if we watch and guide with skill,
(For human good depends on human will,)
Our fortune rolls as from a smooth descent,
And from the first impression takes the bent;
But, if unseized, she glides away like wind
And leaves repenting folly far behind.
Now, now she meets you with a glorious prize,
And spreads her locks before her° as she flies.
Had thus old David, from whose loins you spring,
Not dared, when fortune called him, to be king,
At Gath° an exile he might still remain,
And Heaven's anointing oil had been in vain.
Let his successful youth your hopes engage;
But shun the example of declining age:
Behold him setting in his western skies,
The shadows lengthening as the vapours rise.
He is not now, as when on Jordan's sand°
The joyful people thronged to see him land,
Covering the beach and blackening all the strand;
But, like the Prince of Angels,° from his height
Comes tumbling downward with diminished light;
Betrayed by one poor plot to public scorn,
(Our only blessing since his curst return;)
Those heaps of people which one sheaf did bind,
Blown off and scattered by a puff of wind.
What strength can he to your designs oppose,
Naked of friends and round beset with foes?
If Pharaoh's° doubtful succour he should use,
A foreign aid would more incense the Jews:
Proud Egypt would dissembled friendship bring;
Foment the war, but not support the king:
Nor would the royal party e'er unite
With Pharaoh's arms to assist the Jebusite;

spreads . . . her to be seized by the forelock, like opportunity
Gath where David took refuge from Saul; Brussels, where Charles II was in exile
Jordan's sand as David crossed the river to resume his kingdom; Dover Beach, where Charles landed in 1660
Prince of Angels Satan; cf. *Paradise Lost* I. 84–87
Pharaoh's that of Louis XIV of France

Or if they should, their interest soon would break,
And with such odious aid make David weak.
All sorts of men by my successful arts,
Abhorring kings, estrange their altered hearts
From David's rule: and 'tis the general cry,
"Religion, commonwealth, and liberty."
If you, as champion of the public good,
Add to their arms a chief of royal blood,
What may not Israel hope, and what applause
Might such a general gain by such a cause?
Not barren praise alone, that gaudy flower
Fair only to the sight, but solid power;
And nobler is a limited command,
Given by the love of all your native land,
Than a successive title,° long and dark,
Drawn from the mouldy rolls of Noah's ark.'°
What cannot praise effect in mighty minds,
When flattery soothes and when ambition blinds!
Desire of power, on earth a vicious weed,
Yet, sprung from high, is of celestial seed:
In God 'tis glory; and when men aspire,
'Tis but a spark too much of heavenly fire.
The ambitious youth, too covetous of fame,
Too full of angels' metal° in his frame,
Unwarily was led from virtue's ways,
Made drunk with honour, and debauched with praise.
Half loath and half consenting to the ill,
(For loyal blood within him struggled still,)
He thus replied: 'And what pretence have I
To take up arms for public liberty?
My father governs with unquestioned right;
The faith's defender and mankind's delight;
Good, gracious, just, observant of the laws:
And Heaven by wonders° has espoused his cause.
Whom has he wronged in all his peaceful reign?
Who sues for justice to his throne in vain?
What millions has he pardoned of his foes
Whom just revenge did to his wrath expose?
Mild, easy, humble, studious of our good;
Enclined to mercy and averse from blood.
If mildness ill with stubborn Israel suit,
His crime is God's belovèd attribute.
What could he gain, his people to betray,
Or change his right for arbitrary sway?

successive title a title based on legitimate succession
Noah's ark playing with the theory that kingship has its origin in the rule of the patriarchs
angels' metal the metal of angels (gold coins); the ambition (mettle) that led the angels to rebel
wonders signs of divine favor

Let haughty Pharaoh curse with such a reign
His fruitful Nile, and yoke a servile train.
If David's rule Jerusalem displease,
The dog-star° heats their brains to this disease.
Why then should I, encouraging the bad,
Turn rebel and run popularly mad?
Were he a tyrant who by lawless might
Oppressed the Jews and raised the Jebusite,
Well might I mourn; but nature's holy bands°
Would curb my spirits and restrain my hands:
The people might assert their liberty;
But what was right in them were crime in me.
His favour leaves me nothing to require,
Prevents° my wishes and outruns desire.
What more can I expect while David lives?
All but his kingly diadem he gives:
And that'—But there he paused; then sighing, said—
'Is justly destined for a worthier head.
For when my father from his toils shall rest,
And late augment the number of the blest,
His lawful issue shall the throne ascend,
Or the collateral line,° where that shall end.
His brother, though oppressed with vulgar spite,°
Yet dauntless, and secure of native right,
Of every royal virtue stands possessed;
Still dear to all the bravest and the best.
His courage foes, his friends his truth proclaim;
His loyalty the king, the world his fame.
His mercy even the offending crowd will find;
For sure he comes of a forgiving kind.°
Why should I then repine at Heaven's decree,
Which gives me no pretence to royalty?
Yet O that fate, propitiously inclined,
Had raised my birth or had debased my mind;°
To my large soul not all her treasure lent,
And then betrayed it to a mean descent!
I find, I find my mounting spirits bold,
And David's part disdains my mother's mould.
Why am I scanted by a niggard birth?
My soul disclaims the kindred of her earth,
And, made for empire, whispers me within,
"Desire of greatness is a godlike sin." '

dog-star Sirius (in Canis Major), thought to cause heat and induce madness. See Pope, *Epistle to Dr. Arbuthnot*, ll. 3–6, on the "dog-days" of midsummer.
nature's . . . bands as son
Prevents anticipates
collateral line if not in direct descent, through the nearest legitimate kin, in this case, his brother James
vulgar spite popular opposition to his Roman Catholicism
kind family, nature
Had raised . . . mind reminiscent of Satan's great speech at the opening of *Paradise Lost*, Book IV, especially ll. 58–61

Him staggering so when Hell's dire agent found,
While fainting Virtue scarce maintained her ground,
He pours fresh forces in, and thus replies:
'The eternal God, supremely good and wise,
Imparts not these prodigious gifts in vain:
What wonders are reserved to bless your reign!
Against your will, your arguments have shown,
Such virtue's only given to guide a throne.
Not that your father's mildness I contemn;
But manly force becomes the diadem.
'Tis true he grants the people all they crave,
And more, perhaps, then subjects ought to have:
For lavish grants suppose a monarch tame,
And more his goodness than his wit proclaim.
But when should people strive their bonds to break,
If not when kings are negligent or weak?
Let him give on till he can give no more,
The thrifty Sanhedrin° shall keep him poor;
And every shekel which he can receive
Shall cost a limb of his prerogative.°
To ply him with new plots shall be my care;
Or plunge him deep in some expensive war;
Which, when his treasure can no more supply,
He must with the remains of kingship buy.
His faithful friends, our jealousies and fears
Call Jebusites and Pharaoh's pensioners;
Whom when our fury from his aid has torn,
He shall be naked left to public scorn.
The next successor, whom I fear and hate,
My arts have made obnoxious to the state;
Turned all his virtues to his overthrow,
And gained our elders° to pronounce a foe.
His right,° for sums of necessary gold,
Shall first be pawned, and afterwards be sold;
Till time shall ever-wanting David draw
To pass your doubtful title into law:
If not, the people have a right supreme
To make their kings, for kings are made for them.
All empire is no more than power in trust,
Which, when resumed, can be no longer just.
Succession, for the general good designed,
In its own wrong a nation cannot bind;
If altering that the people can relieve,
Better one suffer than a nation grieve.

Sanhedrin the supreme council of the Jews; here Parliament

prerogative those powers of the king uncircumscribed by law, which Parliament sought to limit by its control of his finances

elders rulers; here Parliament, where a bill excluding James from the throne was supported by Shaftesbury and passed Commons but was rejected by Lords through the efforts of Halifax

right to succeed Charles

The Jews well know their power: ere Saul they chose,
God was their king,° and God they durst depose.
Urge now your piety, your filial name,
A father's right, and fear of future fame;
The public good, that universal call,
To which even Heaven submitted, answers all.
Nor let his love enchant your generous mind;
'Tis Nature's trick to propagate her kind.
Our fond begetters, who would never die,
Love but themselves in their posterity.
Or let his kindness by the effects be tried,
Or let him lay his vain pretence aside.
God said he loved your father; could he bring
A better proof than to anoint him king?
It surely showed he loved the shepherd well,
Who gave so fair a flock as Israel.
Would David have you thought his darling son?
What means he then, to alienate° the crown?
The name of godly he may blush to bear:
'Tis after God's own heart° to cheat his heir.
He to his brother gives supreme command;
To you a legacy of barren land,°
Perhaps the old harp, on which he thrums his lays,°
Or some dull Hebrew ballad in your praise.
Then the next heir, a prince severe and wise,
Already looks on you with jealous eyes;
Sees through the thin disguises of your arts,
And marks your progress in the people's hearts.
Though now his mighty soul its grief contains,
He meditates revenge who least complains;
And, like a lion, slumbering in the way,
Or sleep dissembling while he waits his prey,
His fearless foes within his distance draws,
Constrains his roaring, and contracts his paws;
Till at the last, his time for fury found,
He shoots with sudden vengeance from the ground;
The prostrate vulgar° passes o'er and spares,
But with a lordly rage his hunters tears.
Your case no tame expedients will afford:
Resolve on death, or conquest by the sword,
Which for no less a stake than life you draw;
And self-defence is nature's eldest law.

God . . . king the Commonwealth, established in 1649, acknowledging only God as king (literally, a theocracy, as in l. 522), but followed in 1653 by Cromwell's Protectorate
alienate convey the title to another person
God's . . . heart See l. 7 and note.
barren land the Border estate of Monmouth's wife
lays the Psalms of David, with a reference to Charles's love of music
vulgar common people

Leave the warm people no considering time;
For then rebellion may be thought a crime.
Prevail yourself of what occasion gives,
But try your title while your father lives;
And that your arms may have a fair pretence,
Proclaim you take them in the king's defence,
Whose sacred life each minute would expose
To plots from seeming friends and secret foes.
And who can sound the depth of David's soul?
Perhaps his fear his kindness may control.
He fears his brother, though he loves his son,
For plighted vows too late to be undone.
If so, by force he wishes to be gained;
Like women's lechery, to seem constrained.
Doubt not: but, when he most affects the frown,
Commit a pleasing rape upon the crown.
Secure his person to secure your cause:
They who possess the prince, possess the laws.'
He said, and this advice above the rest
With Absalom's mild nature suited best:
Unblamed of life (ambition set aside,)
Not stained with cruelty nor puffed with pride;
How happy had he been if destiny
Had higher placed his birth, or not so high!
His kingly virtues might have claimed a throne
And blest all other countries but his own.
But charming greatness since so few refuse,
'Tis juster to lament him than accuse.
Strong were his hopes a rival to remove
With blandishments to gain the public love,
To head the faction while their zeal was hot,
And popularly prosecute the Plot.
To farther this, Achitophel unites
The malcontents of all the Israelites;
Whose differing parties he could wisely join,
For several ends, to serve the same design:
The best (and of the princes some were such)
Who thought the power of monarchy too much,
Mistaken men and patriots in their hearts,
Not wicked, but seduced by impious arts.
By these the springs of property were bent,
And wound so high they cracked the government.
The next for interest sought to embroil the state,
To sell their duty at a dearer rate,
And make their Jewish markets of the throne,
Pretending public good, to serve their own.
Others thought kings an useless heavy load,

Who cost too much and did too little good.
These were for laying honest David by,
On principles of pure good husbandry.°
With them joined all the haranguers of the throng
That thought to get preferment by the tongue.
Who follow next, a double danger bring,
Not only hating David, but the king:°
The Solymaean rout,° well-versed of old
In godly faction and in treason bold;
Cowering and quaking at a conqueror's sword,
But lofty to a lawful prince restored;
Saw with disdain an ethnic° plot begun
And scorned by Jebusites to be outdone.
Hot Levites° headed these; who, pulled before
From the ark, which in the Judges' days they bore,
Resumed their cant,° and with a zealous° cry
Pursued their old beloved Theocracy:
Where Sanhedrin and priest enslaved the nation
And justified their spoils by inspiration:
For who so fit for reign as Aaron's race,°
If once dominion they could found in grace.°
These led the pack; though not of surest scent,
Yet deepest mouthed° against the government.
A numerous host of dreaming saints° succeed
Of the true old enthusiastic° breed:
'Gainst form and order they their power employ,
Nothing to build and all things to destroy.
But far more numerous was the herd of such
Who think too little and who talk too much.
These, out of mere instinct, they knew not why,
Adored their fathers' God, and property;
And, by the same blind benefit of fate,
The Devil and the Jebusite did hate:
Born to be saved, even in their own despite,°
Because they could not help believing right.
Such were the tools; but a whole Hydra° more
Remains, of sprouting heads too long to score.
Some of their chiefs were princes of the land:

husbandry thrift
king monarchy
Solymaean rout London rabble (Solyma is Jerusalem)
ethnic Popish (or Gentile)
Levites the Presbyterian clergy, deprived of church livings by the Act of Uniformity (1662) and thus "pulled . . . from the ark" before the Plot; the "ark" being the established or state church, which in "the Judges' days" (the Commonwealth) they governed ("bore")
cant slogans, jargon
zealous fanatical
Aaron's race the priesthood
grace in purity of faith or God's election rather than natural or civil law. See Marquess of Halifax, *The Character of a Trimmer:* "Our Trimmer approveth the principles of our church, that dominion is not founded in grace."
deepest mouthed baying most loudly in the pack of hunting dogs
dreaming saints radical Protestants and visionaries
enthusiastic with, as Henry More put it, "the misconceit of being inspired"
in . . . despite because predestined to the elect
Hydra the mythical monster that grew new heads as soon as the old were cut off

In the first rank of these did Zimri° stand;
A man so various, that he seemed to be
Not one, but all mankind's epitome:
Stiff in opinions, always in the wrong;
Was everything by starts, and nothing long;
But, in the course of one revolving moon,
Was chemist,° fiddler, statesman, and buffoon:
Then all for women, painting, rhyming, drinking.
Besides ten thousand freaks° that died in thinking.
Blest madman, who could every hour employ
With something new to wish or to enjoy!
Railing and praising were his usual themes;
And both (to show his judgment) in extremes:
So over-violent or over-civil
That every man, with him, was God or Devil.
In squandering wealth was his peculiar art:
Nothing went unrewarded but desert.
Beggared by fools, whom still he found° too late,
He had his jest, and they had his estate.
He laughed himself from court; then sought relief
By forming parties, but could ne'er be chief;
For, spite of him, the weight of business fell
On Absalom and wise Achitophel:
Thus, wicked but in will, of means bereft,
He left not faction, but of that was left.
Titles and names 'twere tedious to rehearse
Of lords, below the dignity of verse.
Wits, warriors, Commonwealth's-men, were the best;
Kind husbands and mere nobles, all the rest.
And therefore, in the name of dulness, be
The well-hung Balaam° and cold Caleb,° free;
And canting Nadab° let oblivion damn,
Who made new porridge for the paschal lamb.°
Let friendship's holy band some names assure;
Some their own worth, and some let scorn secure.

Zimri George Villiers (1628–87), second Duke of Buckingham, chief minister to Charles, impeached in 1674 and active in opposition after that; a great wit, author of *The Rehearsal,* which mocked the heroic play and Dryden. "He was true to nothing, for he was not true to himself. He had no steadiness nor conduct. . . . He could never fix his thoughts, nor govern his estate" (Bishop Burnet). The biblical counterparts (there are two) are either lecherous (Numbers 25:6–15) or treacherous (I Kings 16:8–20).
chemist chemist and/or alchemist (according to Burnet, "for some years he thought he was very near finding the philosopher's stone")
freaks whims
found found out
well-hung Balaam probably Theophilus Hastings (1650–1701), 7th Earl of Huntingdon, who left Shaftesbury and returned to support the king in 1681, and may therefore be based on the diviner who is called upon by Balak to curse the Israelites but blesses them instead (Numbers 22–24); "well-hung" a tribute either to verbal fluency or sexual vigor
cold Caleb probably Arthur Capel (1632–83), Earl of Essex (Numbers 13–14)
canting Nadab Lord Howard of Escrick (1626–94), formerly an Anabaptist preacher vehement against the king and clergy
Who . . . lamb i.e. who revised the Anglican service (called a "porridge" or "hodge-podge" by Dissenters) or worship ("the paschal lamb" is Christ) by taking Communion with lamb's wool (hot ale mixed with the pulp of apples) instead of wine; so Nadab "offered strange fare before the Lord" (Leviticus 10:1)

Nor shall the rascal rabble here have place,
Whom kings no titles gave, and God no grace:
Not bull-faced Jonas,° who could statutes draw
To mean rebellion, and make treason law.
But he, though bad, is followed by a worse,
The wretch who Heaven's anointed dared to curse:
Shimei,° whose youth did early promise bring
Of zeal to God and hatred to his king;
Did wisely from expensive sins refrain,
And never broke the Sabbath but for gain;°
Nor ever was he known an oath to vent,
Or curse, unless against the government.
Thus heaping wealth, by the most ready way
Among the Jews, which was to cheat and pray,
The city, to reward his pious hate
Against his master, chose him magistrate.
His hand a vare° of justice did uphold;
His neck was loaded with a chain of gold.
During his office, treason was no crime;
The sons of Belial° had a glorious time;
For Shimei, though not prodigal of pelf,
Yet loved his wicked neighbour° as himself.
When two or three were gathered° to declaim
Against the monarch of Jerusalem,
Shimei was always in the midst of them;
And if they cursed the king when he was by,
Would rather curse than break good company.
If any durst his factious friends accuse,
He packed a jury of dissenting Jews,
Whose fellow-feeling in the godly cause
Would free the suffering saint from human laws.
For laws are only made to punish those
Who serve the king, and to protect his foes.
If any leisure time he had from power,
(Because 'tis sin to misemploy an hour,)
His business was, by writing,° to persuade
That kings were useless and a clog to trade;
And, that his noble style he might refine,

bull-faced Jonas Sir William Jones (1631–82), attorney general and prosecutor in the Popish Plot trials until 1679, involved in drafting legislation to exclude James from the throne
Shimei Slingsby Bethel (1617–97), one of the two Whig sheriffs of London, a republican bitterly opposed to the king and able to pack juries with his enemies; based on the loyal supporter of Saul who curses and stones David (II Samuel 16:5–14)
gain alluding to Puritan thrift and middle-class enterprise, raised to new heights of hypocritical miserliness by Shimei
vare staff
sons of Belial i.e. sons of wickedness, as in *Paradise Lost* I.500–502 ("And when night / Darkens the streets, then wander forth the Sons / Of Belial, flown with insolence and wine"), where Restoration court rakes may be suggested; here turned by Dryden upon Puritan rebels
wicked neighbour converting Jesus' teaching in Matthew 22:39 from charity to complicity
gathered echoing the words of Jesus, "Where two or three are gathered together in my name, there am I in the midst of them" (Matthew 18:20)
by writing pamphlets such as *The Interest of Princes and States* (1680)

No Rechabite° more shunned the fumes of wine.
Chaste were his cellars, and his shrieval° board
The grossness of a city feast° abhorred:
His cooks, with long disuse, their trade forgot;
Cool was his kitchen, though his brains were hot.
Such frugal virtue malice may accuse,
But sure 'twas necessary to the Jews;
For towns once burnt° such magistrates require
As dare not tempt God's providence by fire.
With spiritual food° he fed his servants well,
But free from flesh that made the Jews rebel;
And Moses' laws he held in more account,
For forty days of fasting in the mount.°
To speak the rest, who better are forgot,
Would tire a well-breathed° witness of the Plot.
Yet, Corah,° thou shalt from oblivion pass:
Erect thyself, thou monumental brass,°
High as the serpent° of thy metal made,
While nations stand secure beneath thy shade.
What though his birth were base, yet comets rise
From earthy vapours, ere they shine in skies.
Prodigious actions may as well be done
By weaver's issue° as by prince's son.
This arch-attestor for the public good
By that one deed ennobles all his blood.
Who ever asked the witnesses' high race
Whose oath with martyrdom did Stephen° grace?
Ours was a Levite, and as times went then,
His tribe were God Almighty's gentlemen.
Sunk were his eyes, his voice was harsh and loud,
Sure signs he neither choleric was nor proud:
His long chin proved his wit; his saintlike grace
A church vermilion and a Moses' face.°
His memory, miraculously great,
Could plots, exceeding man's belief, repeat;
Which therefore cannot be accounted lies,

Rechabite one of the sect sworn "to drink no wine all our days" (Jeremiah 35:8)
shrieval sheriff's
city feast lavish hospitality, expected of the sheriff
towns . . . burnt referring to the great fire of London (1666), often interpreted as divine punishment
spiritual food a Prayer Book term for the Lord's Supper or Communion; here a thrifty substitute for home cooking ("fire")
mount Mt. Sinai, where Moses received the Ten Commandments (Exodus 34:28)
well-breathed long-winded
Corah Titus Oates (1649–1705), chief witness of the Plot. First an Anglican clergyman, he became a Roman Catholic in 1677 and studied abroad with the Jesuits, thus acquiring some credibility as a witness against them.
brass a metal known for impenetrability; hence insensibility or shamelessness
serpent "Moses made a serpent of brass, and put it on a pole" to cure his people of the bites of fiery serpents (Numbers 21:6–9)
weaver's issue Oates was the son of a weaver turned preacher.
Stephen the first martyr of the Christian church, stoned to death on the testimony of false witnesses (Acts 6–7)
church . . . face the ruddy, well-fed look of a clergyman, the ironic counterpart of the shining face with which Moses descended from Mt. Sinai

For human wit could never such devise.
Some future truths are mingled in his book;
But where the witness failed, the prophet° spoke:
Some things like visionary flights appear;
The spirit caught him up, the Lord knows where;
And gave him his rabbinical degree,
Unknown to foreign university.°
His judgment yet his memory did excel;
Which pieced his wondrous evidence so well,
And suited to the temper of the times,
Then groaning under Jebusitic crimes.
Let Israel's foes suspect his heavenly call,
And rashly judge his writ apocryphal;°
Our laws for such affronts have forfeits° made:
He takes his life, who takes away his trade.
Were I myself in witness Corah's place,
The wretch who did me such a dire disgrace
Should whet my memory, though once forgot,
To make him an appendix of my plot.
His zeal to Heaven made him his prince despise
And load his person with indignities;
But zeal peculiar privilege affords,
Indulging latitude to deeds and words;
And Corah might for Agag's murther° call,
In terms as coarse as Samuel used to Saul.
What others in his evidence did join,
(The best that could be had for love or coin)
In Corah's own predicament will fall;
For witness is a common name to all.
   Surrounded thus with friends of every sort,
Deluded Absalom forsakes the court;
Impatient of high hopes, urged with renown,
And fired with near possession of a crown.
The admiring crowd are dazzled with surprise,
And on his goodly person feed their eyes.
His joy concealed, he sets himself to show,
On each side bowing popularly low;
His looks, his gestures, and his words he frames,
And with familiar ease repeats their names.
Thus formed by nature, furnished out with arts,
He glides unfelt into their secret hearts.
Then, with a kind compassionating look,
And sighs, bespeaking° pity ere he spoke,

prophet Oates kept recalling events he claimed to have forgotten in earlier testimony
university e.g. the University of Salamanca, which denied Oates's claim to have taken a divinity degree there
apocryphal of doubtful authenticity
forfeits fines, compensations
Agag's murther i.e. the execution of Lord Stafford, ordered on Oates's evidence in 1680. The prophet Samuel harshly ordered Saul to execute his captured enemy Agag, as the Lord had commanded (I Samuel 15).
bespeaking soliciting

Few words he said; but easy those and fit,
More slow than Hybla-drops,° and far more sweet.
'I mourn, my countrymen, your lost estate;
Though far unable to prevent your fate:
Behold a banished man,° for your dear cause
Exposed a prey to arbitrary laws!
Yet O! that I alone could be undone,
Cut off from empire, and no more a son!
Now all your liberties a spoil are made;
Egypt and Tyrus° intercept your trade,
And Jebusites your sacred rites invade.
My father, whom with reverence yet I name,
Charmed into ease, is careless of his fame;
And, bribed with petty sums of foreign gold,
Is grown in Bathsheba's° embraces old;
Exalts his enemies, his friends destroys;
And all his power against himself employs.
He gives, and let him give, my right away;
But why should he his own and yours betray?
He, only he, can make the nation bleed,
And he alone from my revenge is freed.
Take then my tears' (with that he wiped his eyes)
''Tis all the aid my present power supplies:
No court-informer can these arms accuse;
These arms may sons against their fathers use:
And 'tis my wish the next successor's reign
May make no other Israelite complain.'
Youth, beauty, graceful action seldom fail;
But common interest always will prevail,
And pity never ceases to be shown
To him who makes the people's wrongs his own.
The crowd, that still believe their kings oppress,
With lifted hands their young Messiah bless:
Who now begins his progress° to ordain
With chariots, horsemen, and a numerous train;
From east to west his glories he displays,
And, like the sun, the promised land surveys.
Fame runs before him as the morning star,°
And shouts of joy salute him from afar:

Hybla-drops drops of the honey for which Hybla in Sicily was known
banished man Monmouth was banished in September 1679, returned in November without Charles's leave, and was greeted with popular acclaim.
Tyrus Holland
Bathsheba's Louise de Kéroualle, the Duchess of Portsmouth, Charles's mistress, suspected of having a "powerful second" (Halifax) in the French court. For David's adultery with Bathsheba, see II Samuel 11.
progress Monmouth's public journey in 1680 from London to the west of England, a bid for popular support
morning star carrying on the messianic note of l. 728 with other echoes: "the Lord God is a sun and shield" (Psalms 84:11); "a land that floweth with milk and honey, as the Lord . . . hath promised thee" (Deuteronomy 27:3); "And I will give him the morning star" (Revelation 2:28)

Each house receives him as a guardian god,
And consecrates the place of his abode.
But hospitable treats did most commend
Wise Issachar,° his wealthy western friend.
This moving court, that caught the people's eyes,
And seemed but pomp, did other ends disguise:
Achitophel had formed it, with intent
To sound the depths, and fathom, where it went,
The people's hearts; distinguish friends from foes,
And try their strength, before they came to blows.
Yet all was coloured with a smooth pretence
Of specious love, and duty to their prince.
Religion and redress of grievances,
Two names that always cheat and always please,
Are often urged; and good King David's life
Endangered by a brother and a wife.°
Thus in a pageant show a plot is made,
And peace itself is war in masquerade.
O foolish Israel! never warned by ill!
Still the same bait, and circumvented still!
Did ever men forsake their present ease,
In midst of health imagine a disease,
Take pains contingent° mischiefs to foresee,
Make heirs for monarchs, and for God decree?
What shall we think! Can people give away,
Both for themselves and sons their native sway?
Then they are left defenceless to the sword
Of each unbounded, arbitrary lord:°
And laws are vain by which we right enjoy,
If kings unquestioned can those laws destroy.
Yet if the crowd be judge of fit and just,
And kings are only officers in trust,°
Then this resuming covenant° was declared
When kings were made, or is for ever barred.
If those who gave the sceptre° could not tie
By their own deed their own posterity,
How then could Adam bind his future race?
How could his forfeit on mankind° take place?
Or how could heavenly justice damn us all,
Who ne'er consented to our father's fall?

Issachar Thomas Thynne (1648–82) of Longleat (Wiltshire), the "Protestant Squire" and supporter of Monmouth
wife Oates accused the queen of high treason and of a plot to poison the king.
contingent possible
unbounded, arbitrary lord perhaps evoking the unlimited and indivisible power of the sovereign of Hobbes
in trust i.e. by contract which deputizes the sovereign power of the people to these officers
resuming covenant agreement that the people can resume their power at will in order to determine the succession to the throne
gave the sceptre the makers of the original covenant that established monarchy
forfeit on mankind alluding to the doctrine of Paul: "by one man's disobedience many were made sinners" (Romans 5:19), or "as in Adam all die, even so in Christ shall all be made alive" (I Corinthians 15:22)

Then° kings are slaves to those whom they command,
And tenants° to their people's pleasure stand.
Add, that the power for property allowed°
Is mischievously seated in the crowd;
For who can be secure of private right,
If sovereign sway may be dissolved by might?
Nor is the people's judgment always true:
The most may err as grossly as the few;
And faultless kings run down, by common cry,
For vice, oppression, and for tyranny.
What standard is there in a fickle rout,
Which, flowing to the mark, runs faster out?°
Nor only crowds, but Sanhedrins may be
Infected with this public lunacy,
And share the madness of rebellious times,
To murther monarchs for imagined crimes.
If they may give and take whene'er they please,
Not kings alone (the Godhead's images)
But government itself at length must fall
To nature's state,° where all have right to all.
Yet, grant our lords the people kings can make,
What prudent men a settled throne would shake?
For whatsoe'er their sufferings were before,
That change they covet makes them suffer more.
All other errors but disturb a state,
But innovation° is the blow of fate.
If ancient fabrics nod, and threat to fall,
To patch the flaws, and buttress up the wall,
Thus far 'tis duty: but here fix the mark;
For all beyond it is to touch our ark.°
To change foundations, cast the frame anew,
Is work for rebels, who base ends pursue,
At once divine and human laws control,°
And mend the parts by ruin of the whole.
The tampering world is subject to this curse,
To physic° their disease into a worse.
  Now what relief can righteous David bring?
How fatal 'tis to be too good a king!
Friends he has few, so high the madness grows;
Who dare be such, must be the people's foes.
Yet some there were, even in the worst of days;

Then if there is not this power to bind posterity
tenants i.e. on lease
for . . . allowed taken to be the people's property
flowing . . . out i.e. the higher the tide, the faster it runs out; an effect of the moon, literally the source of "lunacy" (l. 788 below)
nature's state Hobbes's view of the state of nature, a condition of "war of every man against every man," in which "nothing can be unjust" and all property or power is "every man's . . . for so long as he can keep it" (*Leviathan* I.13)
innovation starting anew, revolution
ark to commit sacrilege, with reference to the Ark of the Covenant
control contradict, break
physic remedy

Some let me name, and naming is to praise.
  In this short file Barzillai° first appears;
Barzillai, crowned with honour and with years.
Long since, the rising rebels he withstood
In regions waste,° beyond the Jordan's flood:
Unfortunately brave to buoy the state;
But sinking underneath his master's fate:
In exile with his godlike prince he mourned;
For him he suffered, and with him returned.
The court he practised, not the courtier's art:
Large was his wealth, but larger was his heart,
Which well the noblest objects knew to choose,
The fighting warrior and recording Muse.
His bed could once a fruitful issue boast;
Now more than half a father's name is lost.°
His eldest hope,° with every grace adorned,
By me (so Heaven will have it) always mourned,
And always honoured, snatched in manhood's prime
By unequal fates, and Providence's crime;
Yet not before the goal of honour won,
All parts fulfilled of subject and of son:
Swift was the race, but short the time to run.
O narrow circle, but of power divine,
Scanted in space, but perfect in thy line!
By sea, by land, thy matchless worth was known,
Arms thy delight, and war was all thy own:
Thy force, infused, the fainting Tyrians propped;
And haughty Pharaoh found his fortune stopped.
O ancient honour! O unconquered hand,
Whom foes unpunished never could withstand!
But Israel was unworthy of thy name;
Short is the date of all immoderate fame.
It looks as Heaven our ruin had designed,
And durst not trust thy fortune and thy mind.
Now, free from earth, thy disencumbered soul
Mounts up and leaves behind the clouds and starry pole:
From thence thy kindred legions mayst thou bring,
To aid the guardian angel of thy king.
Here stop, my Muse, here cease thy painful flight;
No pinions can pursue immortal height:
Tell good Barzillai thou canst sing no more,
And tell thy soul she should have fled before.

Barzillai James Butler (1610–88), Duke of Ormonde and Lord Lieutenant of Ireland (to whom Dryden dedicated his translation of Plutarch's *Lives*); a generous supporter of the Royalist cause, based on the aged benefactor of David (II Samuel 19:31–39)
regions waste Ireland, where Ormonde fought for Charles I
more . . . lost six of his ten children having died
eldest hope Thomas, Earl of Ossory (1634–80), who distinguished himself at sea, and in support of the Dutch on land, against Louis XIV; victim of a fever; here seen in contrast with Achitophel's son (ll. 170–72)

Or fled she with his life, and left this verse
To hang on her departed patron's hearse?°
Now take thy steepy flight from Heaven, and see
If thou canst find on earth another *he:*
Another *he* would be too hard to find;
See then whom thou canst see not far behind.
Zadoc° the priest, whom, shunning power and place,
His lowly mind advanced to David's grace.
With him the Sagan of Jerusalem,°
Of hospitable soul and noble stem;
Him of the western dome,° whose weighty sense
Flows in fit words and heavenly eloquence.
The prophets' sons,° by such example led,
To learning and to loyalty were bred:
For colleges on bounteous kings depend,
And never rebel was to arts a friend.
To these succeed the pillars of the laws;
Who best could plead, and best can judge a cause.
Next them a train of loyal peers ascend;
Sharp-judging Adriel,° the Muses' friend;
Himself a Muse—in Sanhedrin's debate
True to his prince, but not a slave of state:
Whom David's love with honours did adorn,
That from his disobedient son° were torn.
Jotham° of piercing wit, and pregnant thought;
Endued by nature, and by learning taught
To move assemblies, who but only tried
The worse a while, then chose the better side:
Nor chose alone, but turned the balance too;
So much the weight of one brave man can do.
Hushai,° the friend of David in distress;
In public storms, of manly steadfastness:
By foreign treaties he informed his youth,
And joined experience to his native truth.
His frugal care supplied the wanting throne;
Frugal for that, but bounteous of his own:
'Tis easy conduct when exchequers flow,
But hard the task to manage well the low;
For sovereign power is too depressed or high,
When kings are forced to sell, or crowds to buy.

hearse the structure over a bier where verse tributes were hung
Zadoc William Sancroft (1617–93), Archbishop of Canterbury, subject of an early ode by Swift
Sagan of Jerusalem Henry Compton (1632–1713), Bishop of London, of "noble stem" as the son of the Earl of Southampton
western dome John Dolben (1625–86), Dean of Westminster, a "most passionate and pathetic" preacher (John Evelyn)
prophets' sons boys of Westminster School
Adriel John Sheffield (1648–1721), Earl of Mulgrave, patron of Dryden's poetry, author of a well-known *Essay on Satire* (1680) and *Essay upon Poetry* (1682)
son Monmouth
Jotham George Savile, Marquess of Halifax
Hushai Laurence Hyde (1642–1711), Clarendon's son, who negotiated the Anglo-Dutch alliance of 1678

Indulge one labour more, my weary Muse,
For Amiel:° who can Amiel's praise refuse?
Of ancient race by birth, but nobler yet
In his own worth, and without title great:
The Sanhedrin long time as chief he ruled,
Their reason guided, and their passion cooled:
So dextrous was he in the crown's defence,
So formed to speak a loyal nation's sense,
That, as their band was Israel's tribes in small,
So fit was he to represent them all.
Now rasher charioteers the seat ascend,
Whose loose careers his steady skill commend:
They, like the unequal ruler° of the day,
Misguide the seasons and mistake the way;
While he withdrawn at their mad labour smiles,
And safe enjoys the sabbath of his toils.
These were the chief, a small but faithful band
Of worthies, in the breach who dared to stand,
And tempt the united fury of the land.
With grief they viewed such powerful engines bent,
To batter down the lawful government:
A numerous faction, with pretended frights,
In Sanhedrins to plume° the regal rights;
The true successor from the court removed;
The Plot, by hireling witnesses, improved.
These ills they saw, and, as their duty bound,
They showed the king the danger of the wound;
That no concessions from the throne would please,
But lenitives° fomented the disease;
That Absalom, ambitious of the crown,
Was made the lure to draw the people down;
That false Achitophel's pernicious hate
Had turned the Plot to ruin church and state;
The council violent, the rabble worse;
That Shimei taught Jerusalem to curse.
With all these loads of injuries oppressed,
And long revolving in his careful° breast
The event of things, at last, his patience tired,
Thus from his royal throne, by Heaven inspired,
The godlike David spoke: with awful fear
His train their Maker in their master hear.
'Thus long have I, by native mercy swayed,
My wrongs dissembled, my revenge delayed:
So willing to forgive the offending age;

Amiel Edward Seymour (1633–1708), Speaker of the House of Commons, 1673–78
unequal ruler Phaeton, who attempted to drive the sun chariot of his father, Apollo, across the sky and lost control, upsetting the climate and season
plume pluck away
lenitives pain killers
careful troubled

So much the father did the king assuage.
But now so far my clemency they slight,
The offenders question my forgiving right.
That one was made for many, they contend;
But 'tis to rule; for that's a monarch's end.
They call my tenderness of blood, my fear;
Though manly tempers can the longest bear.
Yet, since they will divert my native course,
'Tis time to show I am not good by force.
Those heaped affronts that haughty subjects bring,
Are burthens for a camel, not a king.
Kings are the public pillars of the state,
Born to sustain and prop the nation's weight;
If my young Samson° will pretend a call
To shake the column, let him share the fall:
But O that yet he would repent and live!
How easy 'tis for parents to forgive!
With how few tears a pardon might be won
From nature, pleading for a darling son!
Poor pitied youth, by my paternal care
Raised up to all the height his frame could bear!
Had God ordained his fate for empire born,
He would have given his soul another turn:
Gulled° with a patriot's° name, whose modern sense
Is one that would by law supplant his prince;
The people's brave,° the politician's tool;
Never was patriot yet, but was a fool.
Whence comes it that religion and the laws
Should more be Absalom's than David's cause?
His old instructor,° ere he lost his place,
Was never thought indued with so much grace.
Good heavens, how faction can a patriot paint!
My rebel ever proves my people's saint.
Would *they* impose an heir upon the throne?
Let Sanhedrins be taught to give their own.°
A king's at least a part of government,
And mine as requisite as their consent;
Without my leave a future king to choose,
Infers a right the present to depose.
True, they petition me to approve their choice;
But Esau's hands suit ill with Jacob's voice.°
My pious subjects for my safety pray;
Which to secure, they take my power away.

Samson who perished in the ruins of the temple he pulled down (Judges 16)
Gulled duped
patriot's as in l. 179 above
brave bully, champion
instructor Achitophel
their own what is in their power to give
Esau's . . . voice referring to Jacob's deception in winning his blind father's blessing: "The voice is Jacob's voice, but the hands are the hands of Esau" (Genesis 27:22)

From plots and treasons Heaven preserve my years,
But save me most from my petitioners!
Unsatiate as the barren womb or grave;
God cannot grant so much as they can crave.
What then is left but with a jealous eye
To guard the small remains of royalty?
The law shall still direct my peaceful sway,
And the same law teach rebels to obey:
Votes shall no more established power control°—
Such votes as make a part exceed the whole:
No groundless clamours shall my friends remove,
Nor crowds have power to punish ere they prove;°
For gods and godlike kings their care express,
Still to defend their servants in distress.
O that my power to saving were confined!
Why am I forced, like Heaven, against my mind,
To make examples of another kind?
Must I at length the sword of justice draw?
O curst effects of necessary law!
How ill my fear they by my mercy scan!
Beware the fury of a patient man.
Law they require, let Law then show her face;
They could not be content to look on Grace,°
Her hinder parts, but with a daring eye
To tempt the terror of her front and die.°
By their own arts, 'tis righteously decreed,
Those dire artificers of death shall bleed.
Against themselves their witnesses will swear,°
Till viper-like their mother Plot they tear,
And suck for nutriment that bloody gore,
Which was their principle of life before.°
Their Belial with their Belzebub° will fight;
Thus on my foes, my foes shall do me right.
Nor doubt the event;° for factious crowds engage,
In their first onset, all their brutal rage.
Then let 'em take an unresisted course;
Retire, and traverse, and delude their force;
But, when they stand all breathless, urge the fight,
And rise upon 'em with redoubled might;
For lawful power is still superior found;
When long driven back, at length it stands the ground.'

control contravene
No groundless . . . prove instances of arbitrary power not in the king but the parliament and the people
Grace the mercy expressed in ll. 939–44
Her hinder . . . die as God warns Moses that no man can see His face (here "front" or brow) and live: "thou shalt see my back parts; but my face shall not be seen' (Exodus 33:23)
will swear as some already had, turning upon the Whigs
Till viper-like . . . before like the offspring of the dragon Error, who "suckèd up their dying mothers blood, / Making her death their life, and eke her hurt their good" (Spenser, *The Faerie Queene* I.i.25)
Belial . . . Belzebub both among the debating leaders of the fallen angels in *Paradise Lost* II
event outcome

He said. The Almighty, nodding, gave consent;
And peals of thunder shook the firmament.
Henceforth a series of new time° began,
The mighty years in long procession ran:
Once more the godlike David was restored,
And willing nations knew their lawful lord.

1681

Mac Flecknoe

This superb mock-heroic satire, which looks ahead to Pope's achievement in *The Dunciad,* found its title in the death of a notoriously bad Irish poet, Richard Flecknoe (d. 1678). Dryden has Flecknoe choose a successor in Thomas Shadwell (1640–92), who liked to think of himself as the true heir of the great Ben Jonson (1572–1637). Shadwell, in fact, gave Jonson's plays unstinting praise and imitated them with more zeal than success; he added broader effects of bawdry and slapstick, as Dryden recalls in his satire (ll. 42, 181, 212). But, whatever his deviations from Jonson's art, Shadwell was impatient with Dryden's less than complete admiration of his master, and over ten years engaged Dryden in critical dispute on such matters as the true nature of wit. In 1673 Dryden wrote, "I know I honour Ben Jonson more than my little critics, because without vanity I may own I understand him better." In general the dispute had involved little animosity on either side, and the occasion for this poem is not altogether clear. The likeliest explanation is that Dryden resented Shadwell's praise of Buckingham's *The Rehearsal,* in which Dryden was ridiculed.

Mac Flecknoe

All human things are subject to decay,
And when fate summons, monarchs must obey.
This Flecknoe found, who, like Augustus,° young
Was called to empire, and had governed long;
In prose and verse, was owned, without dispute,
Through all the realms of *Nonsense*, absolute.
This agèd prince, now flourishing in peace,
And blest with issue of a large increase;
Worn out with business, did at length debate
To settle the succession of the state;
And, pondering which of all his sons was fit
To reign, and wage immortal war with wit,
Cried: ''Tis resolved; for nature pleads, that he
Should only rule, who most resembles me.

series of new time recalling the Virgilian prophecy in *Eclogue* IV: "Saturnian times / Roll round again, and mighty years, begun / From their first orb, in radiant circles run" (Dryden trans.)

like Augustus Octavius Caesar became first Roman emperor in 31 B.C. at the age of 32; he assumed the title of Augustus four years later and ruled for 45 years.

Sh—— alone my perfect image bears,
Mature in dulness from his tender years:
Sh—— alone, of all my sons, is he
Who stands confirmed in full stupidity.
The rest to some faint meaning make pretence,
But Sh—— never deviates into sense.
Some beams of wit on other souls may fall,
Strike through, and make a lucid interval;
But Sh——'s genuine night admits no ray,
His rising fogs prevail upon the day.
Besides, his goodly fabric° fills the eye,
And seems designed for thoughtless° majesty;
Thoughtless as monarch oaks that shade the plain,
And, spread in solemn state, supinely reign.
Heywood and Shirley° were but types° of thee,
Thou last great prophet of tautology.°
Even I, a dunce of more renown than they,
Was sent before but to prepare thy way;°
And, coarsely clad in Norwich drugget,° came
To teach the nations in thy greater name.
My warbling lute,° the lute I whilom° strung,
When to King John of Portugal° I sung,
Was but the prelude to that glorious day,
When thou on silver Thames° didst cut thy way,
With well-timed oars before the royal barge,
Swelled with the pride of thy celestial charge;
And big with hymn, commander of a host,
The like was ne'er in Epsom blankets tossed.°
Methinks I see the new Arion° sail,
The lute still trembling underneath thy nail.
At thy well-sharpened thumb from shore to shore
The treble squeaks for fear, the basses roar;
Echoes from Pissing Alley° Sh—— call,

fabric a term generally used for a building, as in l. 66 below; here a reference to Shadwell's corpulent body
thoughtless carefree; mindless
Heywood and Shirley Thomas Heywood (*c.* 1574–1641) and James Shirley (1596–1666), both popular and prolific dramatists (Heywood claiming a hand in 220 plays, Shirley the author of 36) before the closing of the theaters in 1642; held in low regard in Dryden's day
types prefigurations, as Old Testament patriarchs (Abraham, Noah), judges or kings (Samson, David, Solomon), and prophets were taken to prefigure Christ, who was their culmination (as he is the "last Adam")
tautology needless repetition in other words, here perhaps replacing "theology"
prepare thy way as John the Baptist does for Jesus (Matthew 3:3)
Norwich drugget a coarse fabric of wool and linen (like Shadwell, from Norfolk), the counterpart of John's "raiment of camel's hair" (Matthew 3:4)
lute Shadwell was ridiculed, by Andrew Marvell among others, for his musical pretensions
whilom formerly
King John of Portugal Flecknoe had visited Portugal and claimed to have been patronized by the king.
silver Thames This phrase and many in succeeding lines, as well as the allusion to Arion, echo a celebration of King Charles by Edmund Waller (1606–87).
in . . . tossed as was Sir Samuel Hearty, the self-styled wit in Shadwell's play *The Virtuoso* (1676); with reference to *Epsom Wells*, an earlier Shadwell comedy (1672)
Arion the legendary Greek musician, saved from drowning by dolphins that were charmed by his music
Pissing Alley the actual name of five streets, one near the Thames

And Sh—— they resound from Aston Hall.°
About thy boat the little fishes throng,
As at the morning toast° that floats along.
Sometimes, as prince of thy harmonious band,
Thou wieldst thy papers in thy threshing hand.
St. André's° feet ne'er kept more equal time,
Not even the feet of thy own *Psyche's* rhyme;
Though they in number° as in sense excel:
So just, so like tautology, they fell,
That, pale with envy, Singleton° forswore
The lute and sword, which he in triumph bore,
And vowed he ne'er would act Villerius° more.'
Here stopped the good old sire, and wept for joy
In silent raptures of the hopeful boy.
All arguments, but most his plays, persuade,
That for anointed° dulness° he was made.
  Close to the walls which fair Augusta° bind,
(The fair Augusta much to fears° inclined),
An ancient fabric° raised to inform the sight,
There stood of yore, and Barbican° it hight:
A watchtower once; but now, so fate ordains,
Of all the pile° an empty name remains.
From its old ruins brothel-houses rise,
Scenes of lewd loves, and of polluted joys,
Where their vast courts the mother-strumpets keep,
And, undisturbed by watch,° in silence sleep.°
Near these a Nursery° erects its head,
Where queens are formed, and future heroes bred;
Where unfledged actors learn to laugh and cry,
Where infant punks° their tender voices try,
And little Maximins° the gods defy.
Great Fletcher° never treads in buskins here,

Aston Hall unidentified
morning toast sewage, feces
St. André's a French dancing master and choreographer for Shadwell's opera *Psyche* (1675), whose flat-footed verse is described in next line
number meter; quantity
Singleton John Singleton, one of the royal musicians
Villerius a character in Sir William Davenant's *Siege of Rhodes* (1656), often ridiculed for presenting battles in recitative (requiring both "lute and sword" of the actor) and thus sacrificing sense to sound
anointed i.e. looking forward to the coronation of a new king
dulness implying not simply the power to bore but sluggishness of mind, a relapse from effort, a substitution of the cheap and easy for the excellent (cf. Pope's goddess Dulness, the daughter of Chaos and Night, in *The Dunciad*)
Augusta London
fears aroused by the Popish Plot (cf. *Absalom and Achitophel*)
fabric building
Barbican named for its former function as an outer defense of the city
pile large building
watch constables
Where their . . . sleep a parody of two lines from the epic *Davideis* (1656) by Abraham Cowley: "Where their vast court the mother-waters keep, / And undisturbed by moons in silence sleep"; as are ll. 76–77, with "punks" replacing "winds" in l. 77
Nursery a training school for actors
punks prostitutes
Maximins future performers of such heroic figures as the Roman emperor in Dryden's *Tyrannic Love* (1669), a cruel tyrant given to self-exalting rant
Fletcher John Fletcher (1579–1625), collaborator of Francis Beaumont's (*c.* 1584–1616), author of celebrated tragedies (hence "buskins," the thick-soled boots of Greek tragic actors)

Nor greater Jonson° dares in socks appear;
But gentle Simkin° just reception finds
Amidst this monument of vanished minds:°
Pure clinches° the suburbian Muse affords,
And Panton° waging harmless war with words.
Here Flecknoe, as a place to fame well known,
Ambitiously designed his Sh——'s throne;
For ancient Dekker° prophesied long since,
That in this pile should reign a mighty prince,
Born for a scourge of wit and flail of sense;
To whom true dulness should some *Psyches* owe,
But worlds of *Misers* from his pen should flow;
Humorists and *Hypocrites* it should produce,°
Whole Raymond families and tribes of Bruce.°
 Now Empress Fame had published the renown
Of Sh——'s coronation through the town.
Roused by report of Fame, the nations meet,
From near Bunhill and distant Watling Street.°
No Persian carpets spread the imperial way,
But scattered limbs of mangled poets lay;
From dusty shops neglected authors come,
Martyrs of pies, and relics of the bum.°
Much Heywood, Shirley, Ogilby° there lay,
But loads of Sh—— almost choked the way.
Bilked stationers° for yeomen stood prepared,
And Herringman° was captain of the guard.
The hoary prince in majesty appeared,
High on a throne° of his own labours reared.
At his right hand our young Ascanius° sate,
Rome's other hope,° and pillar of the state.
His brows thick fogs, instead of glories, grace,
And lambent dulness played around his face.°
As Hannibal° did to the altars come,
Sworn by his sire a mortal foe to Rome;

Jonson Ben Jonson as writer of comedy ("socks," the light shoes of the Greek comic actors)
Simkin a typical clown in farces
monument . . . minds in Davenant's *Gondibert* a phrase for a library of dead authors; here transformed by play on the word "vanished"
clinches puns
Panton another farce character, perhaps a punster
Dekker Thomas Dekker (*c.* 1572–1632), an able but often "low" playwright, satirized by Ben Jonson, here taken as a counterpart of such Old Testament prophets as Isaiah
But worlds . . . produce referring to Shadwell's early plays: the unpublished *Hypocrite; The Humorists* (1671); and *The Miser* (1672), adapted from Molière
Raymond . . . Bruce witty characters in *The Humorists* and *The Virtuoso* (1676) respectively
near . . . Street a small area in the heart of the City, the commercial center of London and, as in Pope's *Dunciad,* the center of low taste
Martyrs . . . bum their unsold books providing paper for bakers' pans and for privies
Ogilby John Ogilby (1600–1676), feeble translator of Homer and Virgil and the copious author of original epics
bilked stationers cheated publishers
Herringman Henry Herringman, publisher of both Dryden and Shadwell until 1678
High . . . throne like Milton's Satan, "High on a throne of royal state," *Paradise Lost* II.1
Ascanius Shadwell as son to Flecknoe's Aeneas
Rome's other hope translating *Aeneid* XII.168
His brows . . . his face parodying *Aeneid* II. 680–84, later translated by Dryden: "from young Iülus' head / A lambent flame arose, which gently spread / Around his brows, and on his temples fed" (II.930–32)
Hannibal forced by his father at the age of nine to swear enmity to Rome, which he almost captured in 216 B.C.

So Sh—— swore, nor should his vow be vain,
That he till death true dulness would maintain;
And, in his father's right, and realm's defence,
Ne'er to have peace with wit, nor truce with sense.
The king himself the sacred unction° made,
As king by office, and as priest by trade.°
In his sinister° hand, instead of ball,
He placed a mighty mug of potent ale;
Love's Kingdom° to his right he did convey,
At once his sceptre, and his rule of sway;
Whose righteous lore the prince had practised young,
And from whose loins recorded *Psyche* sprung.
His temples, last, with poppies° were o'erspread,
That nodding seemed to consecrate his head.
Just at that point of time, if fame not lie,
On his left hand twelve reverend owls° did fly.
So Romulus, 'tis sung, by Tiber's brook,°
Presage of sway from twice six vultures took.
The admiring throng loud acclamations make,
And omens of his future empire take.
The sire then shook the honours of his head,°
And from his brows damps of oblivion shed
Full on the filial dulness: long he stood,
Repelling from his breast the raging god;°
At length burst out in this prophetic mood:
'Heavens bless my son, from Ireland let him reign
To far Barbadoes° on the western main;
Of his dominion may no end be known,
And greater than his father's be his throne;
Beyond *Love's Kingdom* let him stretch his pen!'
He paused, and all the people cried, 'Amen.'
Then thus continued he: 'My son, advance
Still in new impudence, new ignorance.
Success let others teach, learn thou from me
Pangs without birth, and fruitless industry.
Let *Virtuosos* in five years be writ;
Yet not one thought accuse thy toil of wit.
Let gentle George° in triumph tread the stage,

unction oil for anointment
priest by trade Flecknoe was a Roman Catholic priest.
sinister left, the hand in which the British monarch holds an orb as emblem of the world, while he holds a scepter in his right
Love's Kingdom Flecknoe's "pastoral tragicomedy" of 1664
poppies as inducing sleep, but also with reference to Shadwell's use of opium
owls emblems of solemnity and gravity, either wise or stupid
Romulus . . . brook as related by Plutarch of the founder and first ruler of Rome
honours . . . head ornaments, thus locks or hair
Repelling . . . god like the Delphic priestess or the Cumaean Sibyl described in *Aeneid* VI. 46–51: "Her hair stood up; convulsive rage possessed / Her trembling limbs, and heaved her labouring breast. . . . / Her staring eyes with sparkling fury roll; / When all the god came rushing on her soul" (Dryden trans., VI.74–75, 78–79)
from Ireland . . . Barbadoes a vast empire largely of water
gentle George common nickname for Sir George Etherege (*c.* 1635–91), friend of Rochester and one of the most brilliant writers of Restoration comedies

Make Dorimant betray and Loveit rage;°
Let Cully, Cockwood, Fopling,° charm the pit,°
And in their folly show the writer's wit.
Yet still thy fools shall stand in thy defence,
And justify their author's want of sense.
Let 'em be all by thy own model made
Of dulness, and desire no foreign aid;
That they to future ages may be known,
Not copies drawn, but issue of thy own.
Nay, let thy men of wit too be the same,
All full of thee, and differing but in name.
But let no alien S-dl-y° interpose,
To lard with wit thy hungry *Epsom* prose.
And when false flowers of rhetoric thou wouldst cull,
Trust nature, do not labour to be dull;
But write thy best, and top; and, in each line,
Sir Formal's oratory° will be thine:
Sir Formal, though unsought, attends thy quill,
And does thy northern° dedications fill.
Nor let false friends seduce thy mind to fame,
By arrogating Jonson's hostile name.
Let father Flecknoe fire thy mind with praise,
And uncle Ogilby thy envy raise.
Thou art my blood, where Jonson has no part:
What share have we in nature, or in art?
Where did his wit on learning fix a brand,
And rail at arts he did not understand?
Where made he love in Prince Nicander's° vein,
Or swept the dust in *Psyche's* humble strain?
Where sold he bargains,° "whip-stitch, kiss my arse,"
Promised a play° and dwindled to a farce?
When did his Muse from Fletcher scenes purloin,
As thou whole Etherege dost transfuse to thine?
But so transfused, as oil on water's flow,
His always floats above, thine sinks below.
This is thy province, this thy wondrous way,
New humours to invent for each new play:
This is that boasted bias of thy mind,°

Make Dorimant . . . rage the rake-hero and his discarded mistress in *The Man of Mode* (1676), Etherege's finest play

Cully . . . Fopling comic fools in three of Etherege's plays

pit the floor of the theater, less fashionable than the box, more so than the gallery

S-dl-y Sir Charles Sedley (1638–1701), court wit and poet, who contributed a prologue (and many suspected more) to Shadwell's *Epsom Wells*

Sir Formal's oratory the rhetoric of that "most Ciceronian coxcomb," Sir Formal Trifle, in *The Virtuoso*

northern addressed to the Duke or Duchess of Newcastle; but also suggesting a climate where wit is scarce, what Laurence Sterne calls "Freezeland" or "Fogland" (*Tristram Shandy* VI.i)

Prince Nicander's a character in *Psyche*

sold he bargains induced a question that might be met with a coarse answer, here in the idiom of Sir Samuel Hearty of *The Virtuoso*

Promised a play as Shadwell had in the Dedication of *The Virtuoso,* where he professed to scorn "unnatural farce fools, which some intend for comical"

bias . . . mind terms from bowling (where weighting or shaping of the ball produces a curved path), recalling Shadwell's definition of humor (Epilogue, *The Humorists*): "A humour is the bias of the mind, / By which with violence

By which one way, to dulness, 'tis inclined;
Which makes thy writings lean on one side still,
And, in all changes, that way bends thy will.
Nor let thy mountain-belly make pretence
Of likeness;° thine's a tympany° of sense.
A tun° of man in thy large bulk is writ,
But sure thou art but a kilderkin° of wit.
Like mine, thy gentle numbers feebly creep;
Thy tragic Muse gives smiles, thy comic sleep.
With whate'er gall thou settest thyself to write,
Thy inoffensive satires never bite.
In thy felonious heart though venom lies,
It does but touch thy Irish° pen, and dies.
Thy genius calls thee not to purchase fame
In keen iambics,° but mild anagram.°
Leave writing plays, and choose for thy command
Some peaceful province in acrostic° land.
There thou mayst wings display and altars° raise,
And torture one poor word ten thousand ways.
Or, if thou wouldst thy different talents suit,
Set thy own songs, and sing them to thy lute.'
He said: but his last words were scarcely heard;
For Bruce and Longvil° had a trap prepared,
And down they sent the yet declaiming bard.
Sinking he left his drugget robe behind,
Borne upwards by a subterranean wind.
The mantle fell to the young prophet's part,°
With double portion of his father's art.

1678? 1682

Religio Laici

This poem, cast in a form like that of the Horatian epistle, offers a defense of a moderate (layman's) Christianity against various enemies, particularly Deism in the part given below. Later in the poem Dryden goes on to consider the implications of Father Richard Simon's *Critical History of the Old Testament,* first published in 1678 and

---

'tis one way inclined; / It makes our actions lean on one side still, / And in all changes that way bends the will." But the invention of humors was Shadwell's own bias or humor: "I may say I ne'er produced a comedy that had not some natural humour in it not represented before, nor I hope never shall."

likeness to Jonson

tympany windiness that creates unnatural swelling; hence, vacuity

tun large wine cask

kilderkin a small cask, a quarter of a tun

Irish suggesting barbarity and want of skill, inherited from father Flecknoe

keen iambics sharp satiric verse

anagram rearrangement of letters to form a new word

acrostic a poem the first letters of whose lines spell a word or name

wings . . . altars in shaped poems like those of George Herbert ("Easter Wings" and "The Altar"). All these forms of "false wit" or verbal ingenuity without real function are summed up by Joseph Addison in *Spectator* Nos. 58–61 (1711).

Bruce and Longvil characters who perform this trapdoor trick on Sir Formal Trifle in *The Virtuoso*

prophet's part as with Elisha, who "took the mantle of Elijah that fell from him" so that the sons of the prophets say, "The spirit of Elijah does rest on Elisha" (II Kings 2:14–15); whereas Elijah ascends to heaven by a whirlwind, Flecknoe's descent produces a "subterranean" wind

four years later translated into English. That work cast doubt on the reliability of scriptural texts. Dryden defends the plain meaning of Scripture against those who impose their own forced interpretations upon it and against those who use its obscurities as a pretext for divisiveness. (In this he anticipates very clearly Swift's position in *A Tale of a Tub*.) In his attack upon Deism or natural religion, he asserts that reasoning from the evidence of nature to the existence and attributes of God is really less empirical than it claims. Deism, in his view, provides "only the faint remnants or dying flames of revealed religion" that have survived from earlier patriarchal times. "[W]e have not lifted up ourselves to God by the weak pinions of our reason, but he has been pleased to descend to us," and all natural religion is "no more than the twilight of revelation after the sun of it was set in the race of Noah." In the style of his poem, Dryden attempts to be "plain and natural and yet majestic," adopting the "legislative style" of the poet as "a kind of lawgiver." He concludes his preface: "A man is to be cheated into passion, but to be reasoned into truth."

From Religio Laici
or, a Layman's Faith

Dim as the borrowed beams of moon and stars°
To lonely, weary, wandering travelers,
Is Reason to the soul; and, as on high
Those rolling fires discover° but the sky,
Not light us here, so Reason's glimmering ray
Was lent, not to assure our doubtful way,
But guide us upward to a better day.
And as those nightly tapers disappear
When day's bright lord ascends our hemisphere;
So pale grows Reason at Religion's sight;
So dies, and so dissolves in supernatural light.°
Some few,° whose lamp shone brighter, have been led
From cause to cause, to nature's secret head;
And found that one first principle must be:
But what, or who, that universal He;
Whether some soul incompassing this ball,
Unmade, unmoved, yet making, moving all;°
Or various atoms' interfering dance°
Leapt into form (the noble work of chance);

stars planets
discover reveal
supernatural light The issue is whether man's reason is self-sufficient and needs no guide from revelation or whether it is totally fallible and can provide us with no guidance at all in matters of faith; the former position leads to Deism, the latter to Fideism. Dryden insists instead upon the continuity between the "borrowed beams" of reason and the "supernatural light" to which they lead us; the dissolution of reason's light is in a light of the same kind but of greater intensity, made available through Christian revelation.
few those ancient philosophers who were led by reason to the idea of a universal God, but could not agree about his nature
Unmade . . . moving all the Platonic conception of the World Soul, with echoes of Aristotle's "unmoved mover"
interfering dance colliding movement, as in Epicurean theory about the chance formation of a cosmic order

Or this great all was from eternity;°
Not even the Stagirite himself could see,
And Epicurus guessed as well as he:
As blindly groped they for a future state;
As rashly judged of providence and fate:
But least of all could their endeavours find
What most concerned the good of humankind;
For happiness° was never to be found,
But vanished from 'em like enchanted ground.
One thought content° the good to be enjoyed;
This every little accident destroyed:
The wiser madmen did for virtue° toil,
A thorny or at best a barren soil;
In pleasure° some their glutton souls would steep,
But found their line too short, the well too deep,
And leaky vessels which no bliss could keep.
Thus anxious thoughts in endless circles° roll,
Without a centre where to fix the soul;
In this wild maze their vain endeavours end:
How can the less the greater comprehend?
Or finite reason reach Infinity?
For what could fathom God were more than He.
The Deist thinks he stands on firmer ground;
Cries: 'Eúreka! the mighty secret's° found:
God is that spring of good, supreme and best;
We, made to serve, and in that service blest.
If so, some rules of worship must be given,
Distributed alike to all by Heaven:
Else God were partial, and to some denied
The means his justice should for all provide.
This general worship is to *praise* and *pray*,
One part to borrow blessings, one to pay;
And when frail nature slides into offence,
The sacrifice for crimes is penitence.
Yet, since the effects of providence, we find,
Are variously dispensed to humankind;
That vice triumphs and virtue suffers here
(A brand that sovereign justice cannot bear),
Our reason prompts us to a future state,

from eternity a hypothesis offered by Aristotle (the "Stagirite" of the next line)

happiness The conflict about the highest good (or *summum bonum*) of man was a counterpart of the conflict in cosmic theories.

content presumably a Stoic doctrine of serenity, which could be attained only by refusing to be unsettled by accident or chance

virtue as in Aristotelian ethics

pleasure as in Epicurean doctrines

endless circles recalling the orbital movements of "moon and stars" in the first line, as opposed to their center in the sun; seen as a "wild maze" without the ordering principle that controls them (the failure of the great philosophers of antiquity to reach agreement was often used as a Christian argument against the "wisdom of this world")

mighty secret's as in Archimedes' discovery (with the exclamation, "I have found it!") of the way to determine the purity of gold by weighing its displacement of water. In what follows Dryden sums up the principal articles of Deist doctrine as set forth by Lord Herbert of Cherbury in *De Veritate* (1624) and later works by him and others.

The last appeal from fortune and from fate:
Where God's all-righteous ways will be declared,
The bad meet punishment, the good reward.'
  Thus man by his own strength to heaven would soar,
And would not be obliged to God for more.
Vain, wretched creature, how art thou misled
To think thy wit these godlike notions bred!
These truths are not the product of thy mind,
But dropped from heaven, and of a nobler kind.
Revealed Religion first informed thy sight,
And Reason saw not, till Faith sprung the light.
Hence all thy natural worship takes the source:
'Tis revelation what thou thinkest discourse.°
Else, how comest thou to see these truths so clear,
Which so obscure to heathens did appear?
Not Plato these, nor Aristotle found;
Nor he° whose wisdom oracles renowned.
Hast thou a wit so deep, or so sublime,
Or canst thou lower dive, or higher climb?°
Canst thou, by Reason, more of Godhead know
Than Plutarch, Seneca, or Cicero?°
Those giant wits, in happier ages born,
(When arms and arts did Greece and Rome adorn)
Knew no such system; no such piles° could raise
Of natural worship, built on prayer and praise,
To One Sole God:
Nor did remorse to expiate sin prescribe,
But slew their fellow creatures for a bribe:
The guiltless victim groaned for their offence,
And cruelty and blood was penitence.
If sheep and oxen could atone for men,
Ah! at how cheap a rate the rich might sin!
And great oppressors might Heaven's wrath beguile,
By offering his own creatures for a spoil!
  Darest thou, poor worm, offend Infinity?
And must the terms of peace be given by thee?
Then thou art Justice in the last appeal:
Thy easy God instructs thee to rebel;
And, like a king remote and weak, must take
What satisfaction thou art pleased to make.
  But if there be a power too just and strong
To wink at crimes and bear unpunished wrong;

discourse deliberative or discursive (as opposed to intuitive) reason
Nor he Socrates
Hast thou . . . higher climb Cf. Job 11:7–8: "Canst thou by searching find out God? canst thou find out the Almighty unto perfection? It is as high as heaven; what canst thou do? deeper than hell; what canst thou know?"
Plutarch, Seneca, or Cicero moving from Greek philosophers to those of Rome (where Plutarch, although Greek, lectured on philosophy) and of a later date (Plutarch, 46? A.D.–c. 120 A.D.; Seneca, c. 3 B.C.–65 A.D.; Cicero, 106 B.C.–43 B.C.)
piles structures

Look humbly upward, see his will disclose
The forfeit first and then the fine impose:
A mulct° thy poverty could never pay
Had not eternal wisdom found the way,
And with celestial wealth supplied thy store:
His justice makes the fine, his mercy quits the score.
See God descending in thy human frame;°
The offended suffering in the offender's name;
All thy misdeeds to him imputed see,
And all his righteousness devolved on thee.
For granting we have sinned, and that the offence
Of man is made against Omnipotence,
Some price that bears proportion must be paid,
And infinite with infinite be weighed.
See then the Deist lost: remorse for vice,
Not paid; or paid, inadequate in price:
What farther means can Reason now direct,
Or what relief from human wit expect?
That shows us sick; and sadly are we sure
Still to be sick, till Heaven reveal the cure:
If then Heaven's will must needs be understood,
(Which must, if we want cure, and Heaven be good)
Let all records of will revealed be shown;
With Scripture all in equal balance thrown,
And our one sacred book will be that one.

. . .

What then remains, but, waiving each extreme,
The tides of ignorance and pride to stem?
Neither so rich a treasure° to forego;
Nor proudly seek beyond our power to know:
Faith is not built on disquisitions vain;
The things we must believe are few and plain:
But since men will believe more than they need,
And every man will make himself a creed,
In doubtful questions 'tis the safest way
To learn what unsuspected ancients say;
For 'tis not likely we should higher soar
In search of heaven than all the Church before;
Nor can we be deceived, unless we see
The Scripture and the Fathers° disagree.
If, after all, they stand suspected still,
(For no man's faith depends upon his will)
'Tis some relief that points not clearly known

mulct fine
in thy human frame the doctrine of the Incarnation as necessary to that of Atonement, a teaching that is distinctively Christian, as are the doctrines of imputed sin and righteousness in ll. 109–10

treasure the Bible
Fathers the early Church theologians who wrote within a few centuries of the Apostles and were therefore considered purest in doctrine

Without much hazard may be let alone:
And after hearing what our Church can say,
If still our Reason runs another way,
That private Reason 'tis more just to curb
Than by disputes the public peace disturb.
For points obscure are of small use to learn,
But common quiet° is mankind's concern.
  Thus have I made my own opinions clear;
Yet neither praise expect, nor censure fear:
And this unpolished, rugged verse I chose,
As fittest for discourse and nearest prose;
For while from sacred truth I do not swerve,
Tom Sternhold's° or Tom Sha - - - ll's° rhymes will serve.

1682

To the Memory of Mr. Oldham°

Farewell, too little, and too lately known,
Whom I began to think and call my own:
For sure our souls were near allied, and thine
Cast in the same poetic mould with mine.
One common note on either lyre did strike,
And knaves and fools we both abhorred alike.
To the same goal did both our studies drive;
The last set out the soonest did arrive.
Thus Nisus° fell upon the slippery place,
While his young friend performed and won the race.
O early ripe! to thy abundant store
What could advancing age have added more?
It might (what nature never gives the young)
Have taught the numbers° of thy native tongue.
But satire needs not those, and wit will shine
Through the harsh cadence of a rugged line:
A noble error, and but seldom made,
When poets are by too much force betrayed.
Thy generous fruits, though gathered ere their prime,
Still showed a quickness;° and maturing time

common quiet Cf. Richard Hooker, *Of the Laws of Ecclesiastical Polity* (1593–97), Preface, VI. 6: "So that of peace and quietness there is not any way possible unless the probable voice of every entire society or body politic overrule all private of like nature in the same body."

Tom Sternhold's with John Hopkins author of the metrical version of the Psalms completed in 1562

Tom Sha - - - ll's for Shadwell, see the Headnote to *Mac Flecknoe*

To the Memory of Mr. Oldham John Oldham (1652–83) first attracted Rochester's attention with his manuscript poems and after some years of teaching school came to London in 1681. His *Satires upon the Jesuits* and other works had won him a reputation as a fiery writer of both odes and satires before he met Dryden, probably two years before his early death. By the time Dryden, who was twenty years older, wrote this poem, he had achieved his own reputation as a satirist with *Absalom and Achitophel*.

Nisus who with his young friend Euryalus took part in foot races at the funeral of Anchises; when Nisus slipped in the blood of a sacrifice, Euryalus won the race (*Aeneid* V.315 ff.)

numbers smoothness and control of verse

quickness vitality; playing upon the victory in the race as well

But mellows what we write to the dull sweets of rhyme.
Once more, hail and farewell; farewell, thou young,
But ah too short, Marcellus° of our tongue;
Thy brows with ivy, and with laurels° bound;
But fate and gloomy night encompass thee around.

1684

Lines on Milton°

Three poets, in three distant ages born,
Greece, Italy, and England did adorn.
The first in loftiness of thought surpassed,
The next in majesty, in both the last:
The force of Nature could no farther go;
To make a third, she joined the former two.

1688

To the Pious Memory of the Accomplished Young Lady, Mrs. Anne Killigrew

Excellent in the Two Sister-Arts
of Poesy and Painting, An Ode°

I

Thou youngest virgin-daughter° of the skies,
Made in the last promotion of the blest;
Whose palms,° new plucked from paradise,
In spreading branches more sublimely rise,
Rich with immortal green above the rest:
Whether,° adopted to some neighbouring star,
Thou rollest above us, in thy wandering race,
  Or, in procession fixed and regular,
  Moved with the heavens' majestic pace;

Marcellus the nephew and potential successor of the emperor Augustus; whose death at age twenty Virgil mourned in *Aeneid* VI.860 ff.
ivy . . . laurels the wreaths that crown the successful poet
fate and gloomy night Dryden retains a Roman idiom throughout, both in allusions and in tone; as a matter of fact, this line is a paraphrase of Virgil's line about Marcellus, VI.866
Lines on Milton first published in Tonson's illustrated edition of *Paradise Lost;* referring to Homer and Virgil as the great predecessors
Ode a free Pindaric ode, in the manner given currency by Abraham Cowley, a vehicle of sublime feeling such as could not be contained in regular forms and might be found not only in Pindar but also in the biblical prophets. This poem was praised by Dr. Johnson as "undoubtedly the noblest ode that our language ever has produced," the first part flowing "with a torrent of enthusiasm" (*Life of Dryden*).
virgin-daughter Anne Killigrew (1660–85), maid of honor to the Duchess of York, both poetess and painter, who died of smallpox at the age of 25; here she is seen promoted from her candidacy on earth (l. 21) to a place in heaven, in a way that fuses the elevation of the classical hero to the stars with that of the Christian hero to the company of saints
palms emblems of victory and rejoicing, as in Christ's entry into Jerusalem
Whether Dryden professes uncertainty (in the manner of Virgil) as to whether Anne has been placed among the nearer and lower stars (i.e. planets) as an angelic intelligence to guide their course; among the remoter fixed stars in their higher sphere; or, highest of all, among the seraphim about the throne of God.

Or, called to more superior bliss,
Thou treadest, with seraphims, the vast abyss:
Whatever happy region is thy place,
Cease thy celestial song a little space;
(Thou wilt have time enough for hymns divine,
Since heaven's eternal year is thine.)
Here then a mortal Muse thy praise rehearse,°
In no ignoble verse;
But such as thy own voice did practise here,
When thy first fruits of poesy were given,
To make thyself a welcome inmate there;
While yet a young probationer,
And candidate of heaven.

II

If by traduction° came thy mind,
Our wonder is the less to find
A soul so charming from a stock° so good;
Thy father was transfused into thy blood:
So wert thou born into the tuneful strain,
(An early, rich, and inexhausted vein.)
But if thy preëxisting soul°
Was formed, at first, with myriads more,
It did through all the mighty poets roll
Who Greek or Latin laurels wore
And was that Sappho last, which once it was before.
If so, then cease thy flight, *O heaven-born mind!*
Thou hast no dross to purge° from thy rich ore;
Nor can thy soul a fairer mansion find,
Than was the beauteous frame she left behind:
Return, to fill or mend° the choir of thy celestial kind.

III

May we presume to say that at thy birth
New joy was sprung in heaven, as well as here on earth?
For sure the milder planets did combine
On thy auspicious horoscope° to shine,
And even the most malicious were in trine.
Thy brother-angels at thy birth
Strung each his lyre and tuned it high,

rehearse repeat
traduction begotten like her body by her father (one possible origin of an immortal soul), and thus inheriting his poetic gifts
stock Dr. Henry Killigrew, chaplain to Charles I and a loyal supporter of his son, author of a tragedy praised by Ben Jonson
preëxisting soul alluding to the Pythagorean doctrine of metempsychosis, that souls go from one body to another; in this case inhabiting first the body of the splendid Greek poet Sappho and at last returning to that form in the modern Sappho, Anne Killigrew
dross to purge Plato, in the *Timaeus*, suggests that the soul undergoes repeated incarnation as a punishment until it is purged of evil or worldly appetites.
mend improve, increase
auspicious horoscope favorable because of its control by "milder" planets, with even the least favorable planets "in trine" (120 degrees distant from each other) and therefore benign

That all the people of the sky
Might know a poetess was born on earth.
And then, if ever, mortal ears
Had heard the music of the spheres!°
And if no clustering swarm of bees°
On thy sweet mouth distilled their golden dew,
'Twas that such vulgar miracles
Heaven had no leisure to renew:
For all the blest fraternity of love
Solemnized there thy birth and kept thy holiday above.

IV

O gracious God! how far have we
Profaned thy heavenly gift of poesy!
Made prostitute and profligate the Muse,
Debased to each obscene and impious use,
Whose harmony was first ordained above
For tongues of angels, and for hymns of love!
O wretched we! why were we hurried down
This lubric° and adulterate age,
(Nay, added fat° pollutions of our own,)
To increase the steaming° ordures of the stage?
What can we say to excuse our *second fall?*
Let this thy *vestal,*° Heaven, atone for all:
Her Arethusian° stream remains unsoiled,
Unmixed with foreign filth, and undefiled;
Her wit was more than man, her innocence a child!

V

Art° she had none, yet wanted° none;
For nature did that want supply:
So rich in treasures of her own,
She might our boasted stores defy:
Such noble vigour did her verse adorn
That it seemed borrowed, where 'twas only born.
Her morals too were in her bosom bred,
By great examples daily fed,
What in the best of books, her father's life, she read.
And to be read herself she need not fear;
Each test, and every light, her Muse will bear,

music of the spheres The harmony produced by the movement of the heavenly bodies was thought to be inaudible to men since the Fall, except perhaps at the birth of Christ.
bees such as gathered on the lips of the infant Plato, according to legend, and prophesied his sweetness of speech
lubric lubricious, lewd
fat gross, indecent
steaming reeking
vestal virgin, like those who served the Roman goddess Vesta
Arethusian named for the nymph whom Diana changed to a fountain to save from violation by the river god Alpheus; cf. Milton, *Lycidas,* l. 85
Art "borrowed" (l. 76) as opposed to native "vigour"; "nurture" as opposed to "nature"
wanted needed

Though Epictetus with his lamp° were there.
Even love (for love sometimes her Muse expressed)
Was but a lambent° flame which played about her breast,
Light as the vapours of a morning dream:
So cold herself, whilst she such warmth expressed,
'Twas Cupid bathing in Diana's stream.

VI

Born to the spacious empire of the Nine,°
One would have thought she should have been content
To manage well that mighty government;
But what can young ambitious souls confine?
To the next realm she stretched her sway,
For *painture* near adjoining lay,
A plenteous province, and alluring prey.
A chamber of dependences° was framed,
(As conquerors will never want pretence,
When armed, to justify the offence,)
And the whole fief in right of poetry she claimed.
The country open lay without defence;
For poets frequent inroads there had made,
And perfectly could represent
The shape, the face, with every lineament;
And all the large demains° which the *Dumb Sister*° swayed
All bowed beneath her government;
Received in triumph wheresoe'er she went.
Her pencil° drew whate'er her soul designed,
And oft the happy draught surpassed the image in her mind.
The sylvan scenes° of herds and flocks,
And fruitful plains and barren rocks,
Of shallow brooks that flowed so clear
The bottom did the top appear;
Of deeper too and ampler floods,
Which, as in mirrors, showed the woods;
Of lofty trees, with sacred shades,
And perspectives of pleasant glades,
Where nymphs of brightest form appear,
And shaggy satyrs standing near,
Which them at once admire and fear:
The ruins too of some majestic piece,
Boasting the power of ancient Rome, or Greece,

Epictetus . . . lamp i.e. it underwent the severest moral scrutiny, such as that of the Stoic philosopher of the 1st century A.D.
lambent softly flickering, as opposed to "wanton" or passionate
Nine the Muses of writing, music, and dance
chamber of dependences a device used by Louis XIV to annex new territory, inducing (by threatened force) local authorities to set up "chambers" which might cede the lands to Louis through fictions drawn from feudal claims (thus "fief" in l. 98)
demains domains
Dumb Sister Painting
pencil painter's brush
sylvan scenes The following landscapes "conquered" by Anne were the typical subjects of 17th-century painters throughout Europe.

Whose statues, friezes, columns broken lie,
And, though defaced, the wonder of the eye:
What nature, art, bold fiction e'er durst frame,
Her forming hand gave feature to the name.
So strange a concourse ne'er was seen before,
But when the peopled ark the whole creation bore.

VII

The scene then changed: with bold erected look
Our martial king° the sight with reverence strook;
For, not content to express his outward part,
Her hand called out the image of his heart:
His warlike mind, his soul devoid of fear,
His high-designing thoughts were figured there,
As when, by magic, ghosts are made appear.
Our phoenix queen° was portrayed too so bright,
Beauty alone could beauty take so right:°
Her dress, her shape, her matchless grace,
Were all observed, as well as heavenly face.
With such a peerless majesty she stands,
As in that day she took the crown° from sacred hands;
Before a train of heroines was seen,
In beauty foremost, as in rank the queen.
Thus nothing to her genius was denied,
But like a ball of fire,° the further thrown,
Still with a greater blaze she shone,
And her bright soul broke out on every side.
What next she had designed, Heaven only knows;
To such immoderate growth her conquest rose
That fate alone its progress could oppose.

VIII

Now all those charms, that blooming grace,
The well-proportioned shape and beauteous face,
Shall never more be seen by mortal eyes:
In earth the much-lamented virgin lies!
Not wit nor piety could fate prevent;
Nor was the cruel destiny content
To finish all the murder at a blow,
To sweep at once her life and beauty too;
But, like a hardened felon, took a pride
To work more mischievously slow,
And plundered first, and then destroyed.
O double sacrilege on things divine,

martial king James II
queen Mary of Modena, wife of James II, to whose beauty Dryden had earlier paid tribute
take so right represent so well
crown Mary was crowned by the Archbishop of Canterbury on April 23, 1685.
ball of fire skyrocket

To rob the relic, and deface° the shrine!
But thus Orinda° died:
Heaven, by the same disease, did both translate;
As equal were their souls, so equal was their fate.

IX

Meantime her warlike brother° on the seas
His waving streamers to the winds displays,
And vows for his return, with vain devotion, pays.
Ah, generous youth, that wish forbear,
The winds too soon will waft thee here!
Slack all thy sails, and fear to come,
Alas, thou knowst not, thou art wrecked at home!
No more shalt thou behold thy sister's face,
Thou hast already had her last embrace.
But look aloft, and if thou kennst from far
Among the Pleiads° a new kindled star;
If any sparkles than the rest more bright,
'Tis she that shines in that propitious light.

X

When in mid-air the golden trump° shall sound,
To raise the nations° under ground;
When in the Valley of Jehoshaphat
The judging God° shall close the book of fate,
And there the last assizes° keep
For those who wake and those who sleep;
When rattling bones together fly
From the four corners of the sky;
When sinews o'er the skeletons are spread,
Those clothed with flesh, and life inspires the dead;
The sacred poets first shall hear the sound,
And foremost from the tomb shall bound,
For they are covered with the lightest ground;
And straight, with inborn vigour, on the wing,
Like mounting larks, to the new morning sing.
There thou, sweet saint, before the choir shalt go,
As harbinger of heaven, the way to show,
The way which thou so well hast learned below.

1685

deface referring, as in lines above, to the disfigurement caused by smallpox
Orinda Katherine Philips (1631–64), the "Matchless Orinda," another latter-day Sappho
brother Henry Killigrew, naval captain and later admiral (d. 1712)
Pleiads the seven stars in Taurus, whose name was given to groups of poets, notably the French *Pléiade* of the 16th century, which included Ronsard and Du Bellay
trump "for the trumpet shall sound, and the dead be raised incorruptible" (I Corinthians 15:52)
nations "I will also gather all nations, and will bring them down into the valley of Jehoshaphat" (Joel 3:2)
judging God "Jehoshaphat" means "Jehovah judges."
assizes court session, i.e. the Last Judgment, for both living and dead, the latter resurrected in body as well as soul to meet their judgment

A Song for St. Cecilia's Day,° 1687

I

From harmony, from heavenly harmony
    This universal frame° began:
    When Nature underneath a heap°
        Of jarring atoms lay,
    And could not heave her head,
The tuneful voice was heard from high:
    'Arise, ye more than dead.'
Then cold, and hot, and moist, and dry,
In order to their stations° leap,
        And Music's power obey.
From harmony, from heavenly harmony
    This universal frame began:
    From harmony to harmony
Through all the compass of the notes it ran,
The diapason° closing full in Man.

II

What passion cannot Music raise and quell!°
        When Jubal° struck the corded shell,
    His listening brethren stood around,
    And, wondering, on their faces fell
    To worship that celestial sound.
Less than a god they thought there could not dwell
        Within the hollow of that shell
        That spoke so sweetly and so well.
What passion cannot Music raise and quell!

St. Cecilia's Day The celebration of the patroness of music on November 22 went back to late 16th-century France but began in England in 1683, when the Musical Society commissioned annual odes from distinguished poets and composers. Written for musical performance and to celebrate the power of music, these tended to draw on two major themes: (1) the *harmonia mundi,* or *musica mundans,* the Pythagorean and Platonic tradition that the world was designed in harmonic intervals (thus reconciling the music of the spheres in the celestial bodies with the Christian heavenly choir or the "morning stars" that "sang together" in Job 38:6–7); and (2) the *musica humana* or moral power of music to move its hearers and arouse in them varying states of the soul (each instrument best evoking a distinct emotion). This ode is the first of two Dryden wrote for such an occasion (the second, *Alexander's Feast,* followed ten years later); it was first set to music by the Italian composer, G. B. Draghi (who served Mary of Modena), and more tellingly later by Handel in 1739.

frame structure of the universe, the cosmos drawn from the chaos of "jarring atoms"

heap Nature seen as the physical world, immersed in primal chaos as imagined by the Epicureans, and notably Lucretius (see below, Dryden's version of portions of the third book of *De Rerum Natura*). Significantly, however, order exists potentially even in chaos and emerges from it not by chance but by divine fiat; here the Word as conveyed in a "tuneful voice."

stations, i.e. the four elements are assigned positions by an ordering principle, and they form a Chain of Being, each creature linked to every other in necessary sequence, creation representing the fullest of harmonies, in which all possible notes are heard

diapason the octave cadence, the consonance which is the proper close for the act of creation

raise and quell moving from the *musica mundans* to the *musica humana* and showing a progression, in successive stanzas, from martial and erotic passion to "holy love"

Jubal "the father of all such as handle the harp and organ" (Genesis 4:21), conceived as recognizing musical harmonies in the anvil blows at his brother's forge, or like Apollo finding an empty tortoise shell strung with three dry sinews, which provided him with a "corded" (but also "chorded") instrument

III

The Trumpet's loud clangour
Excites us to arms,
With shrill notes of anger
And mortal alarms.
The double double double beat
Of the thundering Drum
Cries: 'Hark! the foes come;
Charge, charge, 'tis too late to retreat.'

IV

The soft complaining Flute
In dying notes discovers
The woes of hopeless lovers,
Whose dirge is whispered by the warbling Lute.

V

Sharp Violins° proclaim
Their jealous pangs, and desperation,
Fury, frantic indignation,
Depth of pains, and height of passion,
For the fair, disdainful dame.

VI

But O! what art can teach,
What human voice can reach,
The sacred Organ's praise?
Notes inspiring holy love,
Notes that wing their heavenly ways
To mend the choirs above.

VII

Orpheus could lead the savage race;
And trees unrooted left their place,
Sequacious of the lyre;°
But bright Cecilia raised the wonder higher:
When to her Organ vocal breath° was given,
An angel heard, and straight appeared,
Mistaking earth for heaven.

GRAND CHORUS

As from the power of sacred lays°
The spheres began to move,

Sharp Violins Recently introduced into England, they seemed so in contrast to the duller viols.
lyre Orpheus, who drew beasts and trees and stones after him, figured in traditional pagan myth as the power of music; here he is surpassed by Cecilia, who can draw men to heaven (as traditionally she converted her pagan lover Valerianus to love of God) or an angel down to earth.
vocal breath suggesting, apart from its use of pipes, the power of the organ to sustain notes like the human voice and therefore its superiority (as Cecilia's instrument) to Orpheus' lyre
sacred lays the chorus of praise as both the initial ordering power of harmony and its achieved form, instituted in the music of the spheres

And sung the great Creator's praise
To all the blest above;
So, when the last and dreadful hour
This crumbling pageant° shall devour,
The Trumpet shall be heard on high,
The dead shall live, the living die,
And Music shall untune° the sky.

1687

Alexander's Feast

or, The Power of Music;°
An Ode in Honour of St. Cecilia's Day

I

'Twas at the royal feast for Persia won°
By Philip's warlike son:
Aloft in awful state
The godlike hero sate
On his imperial throne:
His valiant peers were placed around;
Their brows with roses and with myrtles° bound:
(So should desert in arms be crowned.)
The lovely Thais,° by his side,
Sat like a blooming Eastern bride
In flower of youth and beauty's pride.
Happy, happy, happy pair!
None but the brave,
None but the brave,
None but the brave deserves the fair.

CHORUS

Happy, happy, happy pair!
None but the brave,
None but the brave,
None but the brave deserves the fair.

crumbling pageant the cosmos; with probably a reference to the performance itself, as in the masque or in Prospero's remarks on "this insubstantial pageant" (Shakespeare, *The Tempest* IV.i.155); with the trumpeter of the next line placed literally above the stage as he represents the "last trump" (cf. "Killigrew" ode, l. 178) and with the players about to "untune" (slacken the strings of) their instruments

Music . . . untune the trumpet, but also the power of harmony now seen as transcending the created world

Alexander's Feast . . . Music This ode, written ten years later than the earlier "St. Cecilia" ode, devotes itself to the theme of *musica humana* announced in the subtitle and embodies it in a dramatic action rather than a series of instrumental solos. Insofar as Timotheus, the mythical court musician of Alexander the Great, had the power to conjure roles and myths as well as pure emotions, the ode becomes a celebration of poetry as well as of music. The original musical setting (now lost) was composed by Jeremiah Clarke, but the ode was reset by Handel in 1736.

Persia won Alexander, son of Philip of Macedon, celebrating the fall of Persepolis and the defeat of Darius III (331 B.C.)

roses . . . myrtles symbols of love and sensuality

Thais the Athenian courtesan

II

Timotheus, placed on high
Amid the tuneful choir,
With flying fingers touched the lyre:
The trembling notes ascend the sky,
And heavenly joys inspire.
The song began from Jove,
Who left his blissful seats above,
(Such is the power of mighty love.)
A dragon's fiery form belied the god:
Sublime on radiant spires° he rode,
When he to fair Olympia° pressed;
And while he sought her snowy breast:
Then, round her slender waist he curled,
And stamped an image of himself, a sovereign of the world.°
The listening crowd admire° the lofty sound;
'A present deity,' they shout around;
'A present deity,' the vaulted roofs rebound:
With ravished ears
The monarch hears,
Assumes the god,
Affects to nod,
And seems to shake the spheres.°

CHORUS

With ravished ears
The monarch hears,
Assumes the god,
Affects to nod,
And seems to shake the spheres.

III

The praise of Bacchus° then the sweet musician sung,
Of Bacchus ever fair and ever young:
'The jolly god in triumph comes;
Sound the trumpets; beat the drums;
Flushed with a purple grace
He shows his honest° face:
Now give the hautboys° breath; he comes, he comes.
Bacchus, ever fair and young,
Drinking joys did first ordain;

radiant spires shining coils; cf. Milton, *Paradise Lost* IX. 496–503 for the Serpent's motion "erect / Amidst his circling spires"
Olympia Olympias, the mother of Alexander, who claimed that her son was born not of Philip but of a supernatural serpent, here represented as Jove in a typical amorous disguise (that of a dragon), providing grounds for a belief in Alexander's divine origin to which Alexander readily succumbs
world as was Jove of the gods
admire wonder at, are awed by
seems . . . spheres Alexander is overcome by the fantasy of his own divinity and acts up to the role, convinced that his own nod, like Jove's, "shakes heavens's axles" (*Aeneid*, Dryden trans., X.154).
Bacchus god of wine and revelry
honest glorious
hautboys oboes

Bacchus' blessings are a treasure,
Drinking is the soldier's pleasure:
Rich the treasure,
Sweet the pleasure,
Sweet is pleasure after pain.'

CHORUS

Bacchus' blessings are a treasure,
Drinking is the soldier's pleasure:
Rich the treasure,
Sweet the pleasure,
Sweet is pleasure after pain.

IV

Soothed with the sound, the king grew vain;
Fought all his battles o'er again;
And thrice he routed all his foes; and thrice he slew the slain.
The master° saw the madness rise;
His glowing cheeks, his ardent eyes;
And, while he heaven and earth defied,
Changed his hand and checked his pride.
He chose a mournful Muse,
Soft pity to infuse:
He sung Darius great and good,
By too severe a fate,
Fallen, fallen, fallen, fallen,
Fallen from his high estate,
And weltering in his blood;°
Deserted, at his utmost need,
By those his former bounty fed;
On the bare earth exposed he lies,
With not a friend to close his eyes.
With downcast looks the joyless victor sate,
Revolving in his altered soul
The various turns of chance below;
And, now and then, a sigh he stole;
And tears began to flow.

CHORUS

Revolving in his altered soul
The various turns of chance below;
And, now and then, a sigh he stole;
And tears began to flow.

master Timotheus, as master of the master of the world, turning "his hand" (l. 72) to another tune in order to subdue Alexander's mad "pride" to "soft pity" (l. 74)

blood attacked by his own followers

V

The mighty master smiled, to see
That love was in the next degree:
'Twas but° a kindred sound to move,
For pity melts the mind to love.
Softly sweet, in Lydian° measures,
Soon he soothed his soul to pleasures.
'War,' he sung, 'is toil and trouble;
Honour but an empty bubble.
Never ending, still beginning,
Fighting still, and still destroying,
If the world be worth thy winning,
Think, O think it worth enjoying.
Lovely Thais sits beside thee,
Take the good the gods provide thee.'
The many rend the skies with loud applause;
So Love was crowned, but Music won the cause.°
The prince, unable to conceal his pain,
Gazed on the fair
Who caused his care,
And sighed and looked, sighed and looked,
Sighed and looked, and sighed again:
At length, with love and wine at once oppressed,
The vanquished victor sunk upon her breast.

CHORUS

The prince, unable to conceal his pain,
Gazed on the fair
Who caused his care,
And sighed and looked, sighed and looked,
Sighed and looked, and sighed again:
At length, with love and wine at once oppressed,
The vanquished victor sunk upon her breast.

VI

Now strike the golden lyre again:
A louder yet, and yet a louder strain.
Break his bands of sleep asunder,
And rouse him, like a rattling peal of thunder.
Hark, hark, the horrid° sound
Has raised up his head:
As awaked from the dead,
And amazed, he stares around.
'Revenge, revenge!' Timotheus cries,

'Twas but i.e. it required only
Lydian one of the "soft or drinking modes," according to Plato; cf. Milton, *L'Allegro,* ll. 136–44
Music . . . cause insisting upon the power of music to control the imagination through the passions
horrid rough, terrible

'See the Furies° arise!
See the snakes that they rear,
How they hiss in their hair,
And the sparkles that flash from their eyes!
Behold a ghastly band,
Each a torch in his hand!
Those are Grecian ghosts that in battle were slain,
And unburied remain
Inglorious on the plain:
Give the vengeance due
To the valiant crew.
Behold how they toss their torches on high,
How they point to the Persian abodes,
And glittering temples of their hostile gods!'
The princes applaud with a furious joy;
And the king seized a flambeau° with zeal to destroy;
Thais led the way,
To light him to his prey,
And, like another Helen, fired another Troy.°

CHORUS

And the king seized a flambeau with zeal to destroy;
Thais led the way,
To light him to his prey,
And, like another Helen, fired another Troy.

VII

Thus, long ago,
Ere heaving bellows learned to blow,
While organs yet were mute;
Timotheus, to his breathing flute,
And sounding lyre,
Could swell the soul to rage or kindle soft desire.
At last, divine Cecilia came,
Inventress of the vocal frame;°
The sweet enthusiast,° from her sacred store,
Enlarged the former narrow bounds,
And added length° to solemn sounds,
With nature's mother wit and arts unknown before.
Let old Timotheus yield the prize,
Or both divide the crown;

Furies the Erinyes, the three female spirits with snaky hair who punished those guilty of unavenged crimes, here demanding vengeance for Alexander's dead soldiers
flambeau torch
another Troy As Helen's passion for Paris led the Greeks to burn Troy, so Thais' zeal leads them to burn the palace of Persepolis.
vocal frame organ
enthusiast here used of one genuinely inspired by God rather than one suffering from that delusion
length through the organ's power to sustain notes

He raised a mortal to the skies;°
She drew an angel down.°

GRAND CHORUS

At last, divine Cecilia came,
Inventress of the vocal frame;
The sweet enthusiast, from her sacred store,
Enlarged the former narrow bounds,
And added length to solemn sounds,
With nature's mother wit and arts unknown before.
Let old Timotheus yield the prize,
Or both divide the crown;
He raised a mortal to the skies;
She drew an angel down.

1697

raised . . . skies caused Alexander to assume divine stature and rage, however delusively (thus music as a natural power)

drew . . . down as in the "St. Cecilia" ode, ll. 53–54, brought the full power of harmony, in the form of a guardian angel, to earth (thus music as a heavenly power)

The Secular Masque°

Enter JANUS.°

JANUS Chronos,° Chronos, mend thy pace:
An hundred times the rolling sun
Around the radiant belt° has run
In his revolving race.
Behold, behold, the goal in sight;
Spread thy fans,° and wing thy flight.

Enter CHRONOS, *with a scythe in his hand and a globe on his back, which he sets down at his entrance.*

CHRONOS Weary, weary of my weight,
Let me, let me drop my freight,
And leave the world behind.
I could not bear,
Another year,
The load of humankind.

Enter MOMUS,° *laughing.*

MOMUS Ha! ha! ha! ha! ha! ha! well hast thou done
To lay down thy pack,
And lighten thy back.
The world was a fool, e'er since it begun;
And since neither Janus, nor Chronos, nor I
Can hinder the crimes
Or mend the bad times,
'Tis better to laugh than to cry.

CHORUS OF ALL THREE 'Tis better to laugh than to cry.

JANUS Since Momus comes to laugh below,
Old Time, begin the show,
That he may see, in every scene,
What changes in this age have been.

CHRONUS Then, goddess of the silver bow, begin.

[*Horns, or hunting music within.*]

Enter DIANA.

DIANA With horns and with hounds I waken the day,
And hie to my woodland-walks away:
I tuck up my robe, and am buskined° soon,
And tie to my forehead a wexing° moon.

The Secular Masque This masque, as well as an epilogue and prologue, were added by Dryden to Sir John Vanbrugh's adaptation of John Fletcher's comedy, *The Pilgrim* (1621). The first performance was held in 1700, shortly before Dryden's death; it was not only his last work but also his retrospective view of the century in which he lived. "Secular," in fact, derives from the Latin *saeculum*, an age or a century. It has been suggested that Diana evokes the passionate hunting of James I, Mars the wars that concluded the reign of Charles I, and Venus the licentiousness and pursuit of pleasure of the court of Charles II.

Janus god of beginnings

Chronos god of time

radiant belt zodiac

fans wings of Chronos

Momus god of mockery and censure

buskined in hunting boots

wexing waxing, crescent; an attribute of Diana as goddess of the moon

I course the fleet stag, unkennel the fox,
And chase the wild goats o'er summits of rocks;
With shouting and hooting we pierce through the sky,
And Echo turns hunter, and doubles the cry.
CHORUS OF ALL With shouting and hooting we pierce through the sky,
And Echo turns hunter, and doubles the cry.
JANUS Then our age was in its prime:
CHRONOS Free from rage:
DIANA And free from crime.
MOMUS A very merry, dancing, drinking,
Laughing, quaffing, and unthinking time.
CHORUS OF ALL Then our age was in its prime,
Free from rage, and free from crime,
A very merry, dancing, drinking,
Laughing, quaffing, and unthinking time.
[*Dance of* DIANA'S *attendants.*]

Enter MARS.

MARS Inspire the vocal brass,° inspire;
The world is past its infant age:
Arms and honour,
Arms and honour,
Set the martial mind on fire,
And kindle manly rage.
Mars has looked the sky to red;
And peace, the lazy good, is fled.
Plenty, peace, and pleasure fly;
The sprightly green
In woodland-walks no more is seen;
The sprightly green has drunk the Tyrian dye.°
CHORUS OF ALL Plenty, peace, and pleasure fly;
The sprightly green
In woodland-walks no more is seen;
The sprightly green has drunk the Tyrian dye.
MARS Sound the trumpet, beat the drum;
Through all the world around,
Sound a reveille, sound, sound,
The warrior god is come.
CHORUS OF ALL Sound the trumpet, beat the drum;
Through all the world around,
Sound a reveille, sound, sound
The warrior god is come.

inspire the vocal brass sound the trumpet of war

Tyrian dye the red of blood, in particular the royal blood of Charles I, executed in 1649

MOMUS Thy sword within the scabbard keep,
And let mankind agree;
Better the world were fast asleep,
Than kept awake by thee.
The fools are only thinner,
With all our cost and care;
But neither side a winner,
For things are as they were.
CHORUS OF ALL The fools are only thinner,
With all our cost and care;
But neither side a winner,
For things are as they were.

Enter VENUS.

VENUS Calms appear when storms are past;
Love will have his hour at last:
Nature is my kindly° care;
Mars destroys, and I repair;
Take me, take me, while you may,
Venus comes not every day.
CHORUS OF ALL Take her, take her, while you may,
Venus comes not every day.
CHRONOS The world was then so light,
I scarcely felt the weight;
Joy ruled the day, and Love the night.
But, since the Queen of Pleasure left the ground,
I faint, I lag,
And feebly drag
The ponderous orb around.
MOMUS All, all of a piece throughout:
Thy chase had a beast in view;° [*Pointing to* DIANA.]
Thy wars brought nothing about; [*To* MARS.]
Thy lovers were all untrue. [*To* VENUS.]

JANUS 'Tis well an old age is out.
CHRONOS And time to begin a new.
CHORUS OF ALL All, all of a piece throughout:
Thy chase had a beast in view;
Thy wars brought nothing about;
Thy lovers were all untrue.
'Tis well an old age is out,
And time to begin a new.
[*Dance of huntsmen, nymphs, warriors, lovers.*]

1700

kindly natural
a beast in view I.e. the hunt was pursued for the sake of the quarry to be gained rather than as pure sport, for its own sake.

Translations

Dryden's translations indicate the variety of his uses of the heroic couplet, and they are often splendid poetry in their own right. Given here are translations of a portion of Lucretius' *De Rerum Natura;* a selection from Juvenal's Third Satire and the opening of his Sixth; and the tale of Baucis and Philemon from Ovid's *Metamorphoses.*

The translation from Lucretius is interesting as an example of Epicurean thought, so widely revived in the seventeenth century and particularly in Restoration England. Lucretius' great didactic poem seeks to free man from superstitious fear by presenting a view of life grounded in the theory of atoms, i.e. accounting for all nature by the chance combinations of atoms. The third book, from which this passage is taken, insists upon the mortality of the soul and tries to free man of the idea that death is an experience rather than its absence. Lucretius is one of the chief transmitters of a naturalistic view of the world and of man, one which repudiates a view of divine creation and of supernatural ends and exalts pleasure—not necessarily a gross or merely physical one—as the only true end of man. Epicurean thought like that of Lucretius is constantly contrasted by eighteenth-century writers with Stoic thought, which seems much closer to Christianity because of its belief in a rational natural order that in turn reflects man's reason, a reason most fully expressed in its conquest of passion and its intuitive recognition of duty to others.

Dryden explains in a preface that he put aside his "natural diffidence and skepticism for a while, to take up that dogmatic way" of Lucretius; but he warns against Lucretius' doctrines and defends the immortality of the soul. More interesting is his discussion of the style and tone of Lucretius in the passage that follows.

The section from Juvenal's Sixth Satire is a wonderfully urbane and amused account of a primitivistic vision.

[On Lucretius]

. . . If I am not mistaken, the distinguishing character of Lucretius (I mean of his soul and genius) is a certain kind of noble pride, and positive assertion of his opinions. He is everywhere confident of his own reason, and assuming an absolute command not only over his vulgar reader, but even his patron Memmius. For he is always bidding him attend, as if he had the rod over him; and using a magisterial authority, while he instructs him. From his time to ours, I know none so like him, as our poet and philosopher of Malmesbury. This is that perpetual dictatorship which is exercised by Lucretius; who though often in the wrong, yet seems to deal *bona fide* with his reader, and tells him nothing but what he thinks; in which plain sincerity, I believe he differs from our Hobbes, who could not but be convinced, or at least doubt of some eternal truths which he has opposed. But for Lucretius, he seems to disdain all manner of replies, and is so confident of his cause that he is beforehand with his antagonists; urging for them whatever he imagined they could say, and leaving them as he supposes, without an objection for the future. All this too, with so much scorn and indignation, as if he were assured of the triumph before he entered into the lists. From this sublime and daring genius of his, it must of necessity come to pass that his thoughts must be masculine, full of argumentation, and that sufficiently warm. From the same fiery temper proceeds the loftiness of his expressions, and the perpetual torrent of his verse, where the barrenness of his subject does not too much constrain the quickness of his fancy. For there is no doubt to be made, but that he could have been everywhere as poetical, as he is in his descriptions, and in the moral part of his philosophy, if he had not aimed more to instruct in his System of Nature, than to delight. But he was bent upon making Memmius a materialist, and teaching him to defy an invisible power. In short, he was so much an atheist that he forgot sometimes to be a poet. . . . [From Preface to *Sylvae*, 1685]

Lucretius: De Rerum Natura

From *The Latter Part of the Third Book*
Against the Fear of Death

What has this bugbear death to frighten man,
If souls can die, as well as bodies can?
For, as before our birth we felt no pain,
When Punic arms infested land and main,°
When heaven and earth were in confusion hurled,
For the debated empire of the world,
Which awed with dreadful expectation lay,
Sure to be slaves, uncertain who should sway:
So, when our mortal frame shall be disjoined,
The lifeless lump uncoupled from the mind,
From sense of grief and pain we shall be free;

Punic arms . . . main The three Punic wars between Rome and Carthage took place in 264–241 B.C., 218–201 B.C., and 149–146 B.C. Lucretius lived from *c.* 94 to 55 B.C.

We shall not feel, because we shall not *be*.
Though earth in seas, and seas in heaven were lost,
We should not move, we only should be tossed.
Nay, even suppose when we have suffered fate,
The soul could feel in her divided state,
What's that to us? for we are only we
While souls and bodies in one frame agree.
Nay, though our atoms should revolve by chance,
And matter leap into the former dance;
Though time our life and motion could restore,
And make our bodies what they were before,
What gain to us would all this bustle bring?
The new-made man would be another thing.
When once an interrupting pause is made,
That individual being is decayed.
We, who are dead and gone, shall bear no part
In all the pleasures, nor shall feel the smart
Which to that other mortal shall accrue,
Whom of our matter time shall mould anew.

. . .

And therefore if a man bemoan his lot,
That after death his mouldering limbs shall rot,
Or flames or jaws of beasts devour his mass,
Know, he's an unsincere, unthinking ass.
A secret sting remains within his mind;
The fool is to his own cast offals° kind.
He boasts no sense can after death remain,
Yet makes himself a part of life again,
As if some other He could feel the pain.
If, while he live, this thought molest his head,
What wolf or vulture shall devour me dead?
He wastes his days in idle grief, nor can
Distinguish 'twixt the body and the man;
But thinks himself can still himself survive;
And, what when dead he feels not, feels alive.
Then he repines that he was born to die,
Nor knows in death there is no other He,
No living He remains his grief to vent,
And o'er his senseless carcass to lament.
If after death 'tis painful to be torn
By birds and beasts, then why not so to burn;
Or, drenched in floods of honey, to be soaked;
Embalmed, to be at once preserved and choked;
Or on an airy mountain's top to lie,
Exposed to cold and heaven's inclemency;
Or crowded in a tomb to be oppressed

offals carrion, waste

With monumental marble on thy breast?
But to be snatched from all thy household joys,
From thy chaste wife, and thy dear prattling boys,
Whose little arms about thy legs are cast,
And climbing for a kiss prevent their mother's haste,
Inspiring secret pleasure through thy breast—
All these shall be no more: thy friends oppressed
Thy care and courage now no more shall free;
'Ah wretch!' thou criest, 'ah! miserable me!
One woeful day sweeps children, friends, and wife,
And all the brittle blessings of my life!'
Add one thing more, and all thou sayest is true;
Thy want and wish of them is vanished too:
Which, well considered, were a quick relief
To all thy vain imaginary grief.
For thou shalt sleep and never wake again,
And quitting life, shalt quit thy living pain.
But we, thy friends, shall all those sorrows find,
Which in forgetful death thou leavest behind;
No time shall dry our tears, nor drive thee from our mind.
The worst that can befall thee, measured right,
Is a sound slumber, and a long good-night.

. . .

What horror seest thou in that quiet state?
What bugbear dreams to fright thee after fate?
No ghost, no goblins, that still passage keep;
But all is there serene, in that eternal sleep.
For all the dismal tales that poets tell
Are verified on earth, and not in hell.
No Tantalus° looks up with fearful eye,
Or dreads the impending rock to crush him from on high;
But fear of chance on earth disturbs our easy hours,
Or vain imagined wrath of vain imagined powers.
No Tityus° torn by vultures lies in hell;
Nor could the lobes of his rank liver swell
To that prodigious mass for their eternal meal:
Not though his monstrous bulk had covered o'er
Nine spreading acres, or nine thousand more;
Not though the globe of earth had been the giant's floor:
Nor in eternal torments could he lie,
Nor could his corpse sufficient food supply.
But he's the Tityus, who by love oppressed,
Or tyrant passion preying on his breast,

Tantalus Punished for stealing the food of the gods, he is usually pictured as immersed in water up to his chin with fruit hanging over his head, but both water and fruit receding as he tries to assuage his thirst and hunger; Lucretius follows Pindar in seeing his punishment as a rock poised threateningly over his head but never falling.

Tityus punished for assaulting Leto by having two vultures forever tearing at his liver; as a Titan he was supposed to cover nine acres of ground

And ever-anxious thoughts, is robbed of rest.
The Sisyphus° is he, whom noise and strife
Seduce from all the soft retreats of life,
To vex the government, disturb the laws:
Drunk with the fumes of popular applause,
He courts the giddy crowd to make him great,°
And sweats and toils in vain to mount the sovereign seat.
For still to aim at power, and still to fail,
Ever to strive, and never to prevail,
What is it, but, in reason's true account,
To heave the stone against the rising mount?
Which urged, and laboured, and forced up with pain,
Recoils, and rolls impetuous down, and smokes along° the plain.
Then still to treat thy ever-craving mind
With every blessing and of every kind,
Yet never fill thy ravening appetite;
Though years and seasons vary thy delight,
Yet nothing to be seen of all the store,
But still the wolf within thee barks for more;
This is the fable's moral, which they tell
Of fifty foolish virgins° damned in hell
To leaky vessels, which the liquor spill;
To vessels of their sex, which none could ever fill.
As for the Dog,° the Furies, and their snakes,
The gloomy caverns, and the burning lakes,
And all the vain infernal trumpery,
They neither are, nor were, nor e'er can be.
But here on earth the guilty have in view
The mighty pains to mighty mischiefs due;
Racks, prisons, poisons, the Tarpeian rock,°
Stripes, hangmen, pitch, and suffocating smoke;
And last, and most, if these were cast behind,
The avenging horror of a conscious mind,
Whose deadly fear anticipates the blow,
And sees no end of punishment and woe;
But looks for more, at the last gasp of breath:
This makes a hell on earth, and life a death.

. . .

Why are we then so fond of mortal life,
Beset with dangers, and maintained with strife?
A life which all our care can never save;
One fate attends us, and one common grave.

Sisyphus punished by having always to roll a great stone uphill, only to have it roll down again before it reaches the top
He courts . . . great Dryden alters the original in ways that recall his account of Absalom.
smokes along drives at a great speed
fifty foolish virgins The Danaides, the daughters of Danaus, who at his order killed their husbands on their wedding night; they were punished by having to draw water eternally in leaky vessels (a phrase also used of women who betray confidence, as the next lines indicate).
Dog Cerberus, the three-headed guardian of the gates of the underworld
Tarpeian rock the cliff from which murderers and traitors were thrown in Rome

Besides, we tread but a perpetual round;
We ne'er strike out, but beat the former ground,
And the same mawkish joys in the same track are found.
For still we think an absent blessing best,
Which cloys, and is no blessing when possessed;
A new arising wish expels it from the breast.
The feverish thirst of life increases still;
We call for more and more, and never have our fill,
Yet know not what tomorrow we shall try,
What dregs of life in the last draught may lie:
Nor, by the longest life we can attain,
One moment from the length of death we gain;
For all behind belongs to his eternal reign.
When once the Fates have cut the mortal thread,
The man as much to all intents is dead,
Who dies today, and will as long be so,
As he who died a thousand years ago.

1685

Juvenal: Satires

From *The Third Satire*°

Return we to the dangers of the night:
And, first, behold our houses' dreadful height;
From whence come broken potsherds tumbling down;
And leaky ware, from garret windows thrown:
Well may they break our heads, that mark the flinty stone.
'Tis want of sense to sup abroad too late,
Unless thou first hast settled thy estate.
As many fates attend, thy steps to meet,
As there are waking windows in the street.
Bless the good gods, and think thy chance is rare,
To have a pisspot only for thy share.
The scouring° drunkard, if he does not fight
Before his bedtime, takes no rest that night;
Passing the tedious hours in greater pain
Than stern Achilles,° when his friend was slain:
'Tis so ridiculous, but so true withal,

The Third Satire (Juvenal) Umbricius, at the point of leaving Rome for Cumae, "reckons up the several inconveniencies which arise from a city life and the many dangers which attend it" (Dryden).

scouring given to bullying or to cruel practical jokes

Achilles mourning for the death of Patroclus

A bully cannot sleep without a brawl:
Yet though his youthful blood be fired with wine,
He wants not wit the danger to decline;
Is cautious to avoid the coach and six,
And on the lackeys will no quarrel fix.
His train of flambeaux, and embroidered coat,
May privilege my lord to walk secure on foot.
But me, who must by moonlight homeward bend,
Or lighted only with a candle's end,
Poor me he fights, if that be fighting, where
He only cudgels, and I only bear.
He stands, and bids me stand; I must abide;
For he's the stronger, and is drunk beside.
'Where did you whet your knife tonight?' he cries,
'And shred the leeks that in your stomach rise?
Whose windy beans have stuffed your guts, and where
Have your black thumbs been dipped in vinegar?
With what companion cobbler have you fed,
On old ox-cheeks, or he-goat's tougher head?
What, are you dumb? Quick, with your answer, quick,
Before my foot salutes you with a kick.
Say, in what nasty cellar, under ground,
Or what church porch, your rogueship may be found?'
Answer, or answer not, 'tis all the same:
He lays me on, and makes me bear the blame.
Before the bar, for beating him, you come;
This is a poor man's liberty in Rome.
You beg his pardon; happy to retreat
With some remaining teeth, to chew your meat.
Nor is this all; for, when retired, you think
To sleep securely; when the candles wink,
When every door with iron chains is barred,
And roaring taverns are no longer heard;
The ruffian robbers, by no justice awed,
And unpaid cutthroat soldiers are abroad,
Those venal souls, who, hardened in each ill,
To save complaints and prosecution, kill.
Chased from their woods and bogs, the padders come
To this vast city as their native home;
To live at ease, and safely skulk in Rome.
The forge in fetters only is employed;
Our iron mines exhausted and destroyed
In shackles; for these villains scarce allow
Goads for the teams, and plowshares for the plow.
O happy ages of our ancestors,
Beneath the kings and tribunitial powers!°

Beneath . . . powers in the days, long before the empire, when Rome was governed by kings, or later by consuls and tribunes of the people

One jail did all their criminals restrain,
Which, now, the walls of Rome can scarce contain.

1692

From *The Sixth Satire*°

In Saturn's reign,° at Nature's early birth,
There was that thing called chastity on earth;
When in a narrow cave, their common shade,°
The sheep, the shepherds, and their gods were laid:
When reeds, and leaves, and hides of beasts were spread
By mountain huswifes for their homely bed,
And mossy pillows raised, for the rude husband's head.
Unlike the niceness of our modern dames,
(Affected nymphs with new affected names,)
The Cynthias° and the Lesbias° of our years,
Who for a sparrow's death dissolve in tears;
Those first unpolished matrons, big and bold,
Gave suck to infants of gigantic mould;
Rough as their savage lords who ranged the wood,
And fat with acorns belched their windy food.
For when the world was buxom,° fresh, and young,
Her sons were undebauched and therefore strong;
And whether born in kindly° beds of earth,
Or struggling from the teeming oaks to birth,
Or from what other atoms they begun,
No sires they had, or, if a sire, the sun.

1693

Juvenal . . . Sixth Satire This is the longest of Juvenal's sixteen satires; written against immoral and affected women, it forms part of the high rhetorical denunciation of corrupt Rome that Dryden came so much to admire (see below, Critical Prose). Juvenal was born *c.* 50 A.D. and wrote as late as 127; his attacks upon the empire of Domitian constantly evoke an earlier, more austere virtue, but in this instance his golden age is ironically rendered as a boorish and comic one. Dryden himself translated five of Juvenal's satires, and Dr. Johnson was later to write imitations of the third and tenth, the former as *London* and the latter as *The Vanity of Human Wishes.*

Saturn's reign the golden age of innocence

shade shelter

Cynthias Cynthia was celebrated by Propertius (*c.* 54–*c.* 2 B.C.) in his account of their difficult love.

Lesbias Lesbia was the subject of many poems by Catullus (*c.* 84–*c.* 54 B.C.), including one on the death of her sparrow.

buxom wanton, jolly

kindly congenial, kindred

From Baucis and Philemon

Out of the Eighth Book of Ovid's Metamorphoses

Heaven's power is infinite; earth, air, and sea,
The manufactured mass, the making power obey.
By proof to clear your doubt: in Phrygian ground
Two neighbouring trees, with walls encompassed round,
Stand on a moderate rise, with wonder shown,
One a hard oak, a softer linden one. . . .
Not far from thence is seen a lake, the haunt
Of coots and of the fishing cormorant:
Here Jove with Hermes came; but in disguise
Of mortal men concealed their deities:
One laid aside his thunder, one his rod;
And many toilsome steps together trod;
For harbour at a thousand doors they knocked—
Not one of all the thousand but was locked.
At last an hospitable house they found,
A homely° shed; the roof, not far from ground,
Was thatched with reeds, and straw together bound.
There Baucis and Philemon lived, and there
Had lived long married, and a happy pair:
Now old in love, though little was their store,
Inured to want, their poverty they bore,
Nor aimed at wealth, professing° to be poor.
For master or for servant here to call,
Was all alike, where only two were all.
Command was none, where equal love was paid,
Or rather both commanded, both obeyed.
From lofty roofs the gods repulsed before,
Now, stooping, entered through the little door;
The man (their hearty welcome first expressed)
A common settle drew for either guest,
Inviting each his weary limbs to rest.
But e'er they sat, officious° Baucis lays
Two cushions stuffed with straw, the seat to raise;
Coarse, but the best she had; then rakes the load
Of ashes from the hearth, and spreads abroad
The living coals, and, lest they should expire,
With leaves and barks she feeds her infant fire:
It smokes, and then with trembling breath she blows,
Till in a cheerful blaze the flames arose.
With brushwood and with chips she strengthens these,
And adds at last the boughs of rotten trees.

homely humble
professing openly declaring themselves
officious full of good offices, solicitous

The fire thus formed, she sets the kettle on—
Like burnished gold the little seether shone—
Next took the coleworts° which her husband got
From his own ground (a small well-watered spot);
She stripped the stalks of all their leaves; the best
She culled, and then with handy care she dressed.
High o'er the hearth a chine of bacon hung:
Good old Philemon seized it with a prong,
And from the sooty rafter drew it down;
Then cut a slice, but scarce enough for one;
Yet a large portion of a little store,
Which for their sakes alone he wished were more.
This in the pot he plunged without delay,
To tame the flesh and drain the salt away.
The time between, before the fire they sat,
And shortened the delay by pleasing chat.
  A beam there was, on which a beechen pail
Hung by the handle, on a driven nail:
This filled with water, gently warmed, they set
Before their guests; in this they bathed their feet,
And after with clean towels dried their sweat.
This done, the host produced the genial bed,
Sallow° the feet, the borders, and the stead
Which with no costly coverlet they spread,
But coarse old garments; yet such robes as these
They laid alone° at feasts, on holidays.
The good old housewife tucking up her gown,
The table sets; the invited gods lie down.
The trivet table of a foot was lame°—
A blot which prudent Baucis overcame,
Who thrusts beneath the limping leg, a sherd;°
So was the mended board exactly reared:
Then rubbed it o'er with newly gathered mint,
A wholesome herb, that breathed a grateful scent.
Pallas° began the feast, where first was seen
The party-coloured° olive, black and green;
Autumnal cornels° next in order served,
In lees of wine° well pickled, and preserved;
A garden salad was the third supply,
Of endive, radishes, and succory;°
Then curds and cream, the flower of country fare,
And new-laid eggs, which Baucis' busy care
Turned by a gentle fire, and roasted rare.
All these in earthen ware were served to board;

coleworts cabbages
Sallow dingy
alone only
trivet . . . lame the three-legged table was short in one leg
sherd bit of earthenware
Pallas to whom the olive was sacred
party-coloured of mixed colors
cornels the red fruit of the cornelian cherry tree
lees of wine vinegary dregs of wine
succory chicory

And, next in place, an earthen pitcher, stored
With liquor of the best the cottage could afford.
This was the table's ornament and pride,
With figures wrought: like pages at his side
Stood beechen bowls; and these were shining clean,
Varnished with wax without, and lined within.
By this the boiling kettle had prepared,
And to the table sent the smoking lard,°
On which with eager appetite they dine,
A savoury bit that served to relish wine;
The wine itself was suiting to the rest,
Still working in the must,° and lately pressed.
The second course succeeds like that before;
Plums, apples, nuts, and, of their wintry store,
Dry figs and grapes, and wrinkled dates were set
In canisters, to enlarge the little treat.
All these a milk-white honeycomb surround,
Which in the midst the country banquet crowned.
But the kind hosts their entertainment grace
With hearty welcome and an open face:
In all they did you might discern with ease
A willing mind and a desire to please.
   Meantime the beechen bowls went round and still,
Though often emptied, were observed to fill;
Filled without hands, and of their own accord
Ran without feet, and danced about the board.
Devotion seized the pair, to see the feast
With wine, and of no common grape, increased;
And up they held their hands, and fell to prayer,
Excusing, as they could, their country fare.
   One goose they had ('twas all they could allow),
A wakeful sentry, and on duty now,
Whom to the gods for sacrifice they vow:
Her, with malicious zeal, the couple viewed;
She ran for life, and, limping, they pursued.
Full well the fowl perceived their bad intent,
And would not make her masters' compliment;
But, persecuted, to the powers she flies,
And close between the legs of Jove she lies.
He, with a gracious ear, the suppliant heard,
And saved her life; then what he was declared,
And owned° the god. 'The neighbourhood,' said he,
'Shall justly perish for impiety:
You stand alone exempted; but obey
With speed, and follow where we lead the way;
Leave these accurst, and to the mountain's height
Ascend, nor once look backward in your flight.'

lard bacon
working in the must fermenting
owned acknowledged himself

They haste, and what their tardy feet denied,
The trusty staff (their better leg) supplied.
An arrow's flight they wanted° to the top,
And there secure, but spent with travel, stop;
Then turn their now no more forbidden eyes:
Lost in a lake the floated level° lies;
A watery desert covers all the plains;
Their cot° alone, as in an isle, remains;
Wondering with weeping eyes, while they deplore
Their neighbours' fate and country now no more,
Their little shed, scarce large enough for two,
Seems, from the ground increased, in height and bulk to grow.
A stately temple shoots within the skies;
The crotches of their cot in columns rise;
The pavement polished marble they behold,
The gates with sculpture graced, the spires and tiles of gold.
Then thus the Sire of Gods, with look serene:
'Speak thy desire, thou only just of men;
And thou, O woman, only worthy found
To be with such a man in marriage bound.'
A while they whisper; then, to Jove addressed,
Philemon thus prefers° their joint request:
'We crave to serve before your sacred shrine,
And offer at your altars rites divine;
And since not any action of our life
Has been polluted with domestic strife,
We beg one hour of death; that neither she
With widow's tears may live to bury me,
Nor weeping I, with withered arms, may bear
My breathless Baucis to the sepulchre.'
The godheads sign their suit. They run their race
In the same tenor all the appointed space;
Then, when their hour was come, while they relate
These past adventures at the temple gate,
Old Baucis is by old Philemon seen
Sprouting with sudden leaves of sprightly green;
Old Baucis looked where old Philemon stood,
And saw his lengthened arms a sprouting wood.
New roots their fastened feet begin to bind,
Their bodies stiffen in a rising rind:
Then, ere the bark above their shoulders grew,
They give and take at once their last adieu;
At once: 'Farewell, O faithful spouse,' they said;
At once the incroaching rinds their closing lips invade.
Even yet, an ancient Tyanaean° shows
A spreading oak, that near a linden grows;

wanted had to travel
floated level flooded surface
cot dwelling
prefers offers
Tyanaean a native of Tyana (in Asia Minor)

The neighbourhood confirm the prodigy,
Grave men, not vain of tongue, or like to lie.
I saw myself the garlands on their boughs,
And tablets hung for gifts of granted vows;
And offering fresher up, with pious prayer,
'The good,' said I, 'are God's peculiar care,
And such as honour Heaven, shall heavenly honour share.'

1700

Critical Prose

Dryden's criticism was unsystematic and for the most part occasional, arising from his wide-ranging undertakings as playwright, poet, and translator. There are often allusions to the systems of classical and Renaissance critics, and Dryden shows competence in Scholastic thought as well; but he is temperamentally opposed to system for himself, preferring what he calls a skeptical method. By this he does not mean a radical skepticism but rather a dialectical openness, a balancing of contraries and opposites, that saves him from rigorous folly and produces instead generosity and readiness to risk inconsistency.

The dialectical cast of Dryden's mind is nowhere more evident than here; if sometimes at the cost of firm argument, all the more revealing of the cross-currents of his age. Thus we can see him moving back and forth between the claims of rational order and of bold fancy, between justness and liveliness, between strictness and inclusiveness of form. This becomes most apparent in those great dialectical contrasts between representative authors—a device that was to survive as late as Dr. Johnson. In his discussion of Horace and Juvenal, we can see a gradual movement toward preference for the gravity of Juvenal, and the final paragraph on Juvenal (given below) is a fine statement of what satire was to become again in the age of Walpole.

The tributes to John Oldham (see above) and to the emerging playwright William Congreve are an important part of Dryden's criticism, as is, of course, *Mac Flecknoe*. In the first two poems, to younger men, there is a warm tribute to achievements Dryden is willing to measure favorably against his own; more than that, we can see his frank acknowledgment of losses inextricable from the gains which he promoted and in which he genuinely believed. Dryden always distinguishes nicely between the "glowing" and the "glaring," between the true vigor and the false, and *Mac Flecknoe* is a poem based upon such discriminations, a splendid anatomizing of the meretricious and maudlin.

The Poetic Process
[Wit and Fancy]

. . . The composition of all poems is or ought to be of wit, and wit in the poet, or wit writing (if you will give me leave to use a school distinction[1]), is no other than the faculty of imagination in the writer, which, like a nimble spaniel, beats over and ranges through the field of memory, till it springs the quarry it hunted after; or, without metaphor, which searches over all the memory for the species or ideas of those things which it designs to represent.

1. That is, a distinction such as the Scholastics might make, on the analogy of *natura naturans* and *natura naturata*, the first a process and the second a product.

Wit written, is that which is well defined the happy result of thought, or product of that imagination. But to proceed from wit in the general notion of it to the proper wit of an heroic or historical poem, I judge it chiefly to consist in the delightful imaging of persons, actions, passions, or things. 'Tis not the jerk or sting of an epigram, nor the seeming contradiction of a poor antithesis (the delight of an ill-judging audience in a play of rhyme), nor the jingle of a more poor paranomasia:[2] neither is it so much the morality of a grave sentence,[3] affected by Lucan, but more sparingly used by Virgil; but it is some lively and apt description, dressed in such colours[4] of speech, that it sets before your eyes the absent object as perfectly and more delightfully than nature. So then, the first happiness of the poet's imagination is properly invention, or finding of the thought; the second is fancy, or the variation, driving[5] or moulding of that thought, as the judgement represents it proper to the subject; the third is elocution, or the art of clothing and adorning that thought so found and varied, in apt, significant, and sounding words: the quickness of the imagination is seen in the invention, the fertility in the fancy, and the accuracy in the expression. For the two first of these Ovid is famous amongst the poets, for the latter Virgil. Ovid images more often the movements and affections of the mind, either combating between two contrary passions, or extremely discomposed by one: his words therefore are the least part of his care, for he pictures nature in disorder, with which the study and choice of words is inconsistent. This is the proper wit of dialogue or discourse, and, consequently, of the drama, where all that is said is to be supposed the effect of sudden thought; which, though it excludes not the quickness of wit in repartees, yet admits not a too curious election of words, too frequent allusions, or use of tropes, or, in fine, anything that shows remoteness of thought, or labour in the writer. On the other side, Virgil speaks not so often to us in the person of another, like Ovid, but in his own; he relates almost all things as from himself, and thereby gains more liberty than the other to express his thoughts with all the graces of elocution, to write more figuratively, and to confess as well the labour as the force of his imagination. . . . [From "An Account of the Ensuing Poem . . .". Prefixed to *Annus Mirabilis,* 1666]

This worthless present was designed [for] you long before it was a play; when it was only a confused mass of thoughts, tumbling over one another in the dark; when the fancy was yet in its first work, moving the sleeping images of things towards the light, there to be distinguished, and then either chosen or rejected by the judgement: it was yours, my Lord, before I could call it mine. And, I confess, in that first tumult of my thoughts there appeared a disorderly kind of beauty in some of them, which gave me hope something worthy my Lord of Orrery might be drawn from them. . . . [From "To the Right Honorable Roger, Earl of Orrery." Prefixed to *The Rival Ladies,* 1664]

2. A pun or similar word play.
3. Moral axiom or maxim.
4. Figures.
5. The usual reading is "deriving," but George Watson points out that this has no authority in the editions Dryden supervised and is an unnecessary variant on "driving," which has the sense of carrying further or elaborating.

. . . Horace himself was cautious [6] to obtrude a new word on his readers, and makes custom and common use the best measure of receiving it into our writings. . . . The not observing this rule is that which the world has blamed in our satirist Cleveland;[7] to express a thing hard and unnaturally, is his new way of elocution. 'Tis true, no poet but may sometimes use a catachresis.[8]. . . But to do this always, and never be able to write a line without it, though it may be admired by some few pedants, will not pass upon those who know that wit is best conveyed to us in the most easy language and is most to be admired when a great thought comes dressed in words so commonly received that it is understood by the meanest apprehensions, as the best meat is the most easily digested: but we cannot read a verse of Cleveland's without making a face at it, as if every word were a pill to swallow. He gives us many times a hard nut to break our teeth, without a kernel for our pains.[9] So that there is this difference between his satires and Doctor Donne's, that the one gives us deep thoughts in common language, though rough cadence; the other gives us common thoughts in abstruse words: 'tis true, in some places his wit is independent of his words, as in that of the *Rebel Scot:*

> Had Cain been Scot God would have changed his doom;
> Not forced him wander, but confined him home.[10]

Si sic omnia dixisset! [11] This is wit in all languages: 'tis like mercury, never to be lost or killed;[12] and so that other:

> For beauty like white-powder makes no noise,
> And yet the silent hypocrite destroys.[13]

You see the last line is highly metaphorical, but it is so soft and gentle that it does not shock us as we read it. [From *Of Dramatic Poesy: An Essay,* 1668]

. . . Imagination in a man, or reasonable creature, is supposed to participate of reason, and when that governs, as it does in the belief of fiction, reason is not destroyed, but misled, or blinded: that can prescribe to the reason, during the time of the representation, somewhat like a weak belief of what it sees and hears; and reason suffers itself to be so hoodwinked, that it may better enjoy the pleasures of the fiction: but it is never so wholly made a captive as to be drawn headlong into a persuasion of those things which are most remote from

6. Slow or reluctant; cf. *Ars Poetica,* ll. 70–72: "Many terms will be revived which have fallen out of use, and many will fall in turn that now are current, if usage wills so, in whose power lies the judgment, the law, and the rule of speech."
7. John Cleveland (1613–58), the late Metaphysical poet and wit.
8. "The abuse of a trope, when the words are too far wrested from their native signification" (Johnson, *Dictionary*); cf. also Johnson's discussion of the Metaphysical poets.
9. In *A Tale of a Tub* Swift takes this further; he writes of wisdom as a nut "which, unless you choose with judgment, may cost you a tooth and pay you with nothing but a worm"; the figure of the rind and the kernel is a traditional means of exploring the relation of words to meaning.
10. *The Rebel Scot* (1644), ll. 63–64.
11. "If only he had always spoken this way—" (Juvenal, *Satires* X.123–24).
12. Stabilized, deprived of motion.
13. *Rupertismus,* ll. 39–40.

probability: 'tis in that case a free-born subject, not a slave; it will contribute willingly its assent, as far as it sees convenient, but will not be forced. . . . Fancy and reason go hand in hand; the first cannot leave the last behind; and though fancy, when it sees the wide gulf, would venture over, as the nimbler; yet it is withheld by reason, which will refuse to take the leap, when the distance over it appears too large. . . . [From *A Defense of an Essay of Dramatic Poesy*, 1668]

. . . Strong and glowing colours are the just resemblances[14] of bold metaphors, but both must be judiciously applied; for there is a difference betwixt daring and foolhardiness. Lucan and Statius[15] often ventured them too far; our Virgil never.

. . . 'Tis said of him that he read the second, fourth, and sixth books of his *Æneids* to Augustus Cæsar. In the sixth . . . the poet, speaking of Misenus the trumpeter, says:

quo non præstantior alter
ære ciere viros,

and broke off in the hemistich, or midst of the verse; but in the very reading, seized as it were with a divine fury, he made up the latter part of the hemistich with these following words:

Martemque accendere cantu.[16]

How warm, nay, how glowing a colouring is this! In the beginning of his verse, the word *æs*, or brass, was taken for a trumpet, because the instrument was made of that metal, which of itself was fine; but in the latter end, which was made *ex tempore*, you see three metaphors, *Martemque . . . accendere . . . cantu*. Good Heavens! how the plain sense is raised by the beauty of the words! But this was happiness; the former might be only judgement: this was the *curiosa felicitas*[17] which Petronius attributes to Horace. . . . These hits of words a true poet often finds, as I may say, without seeking; but he knows their value when he finds them, and is infinitely pleased. A bad poet may sometimes light on them, but he discerns not a diamond from a Bristol-stone;[18] and would have been of the cock's mind in Aesop; a grain of barley would have pleased him better than the jewel.

. . . As the words, etc., are evidently shown to be the clothing of the thought in the same sense as colours are the clothing of the design, so the painter and the poet ought to judge exactly when the colouring and expressions are perfect

14. Counterparts; in this *Parallel*, which accompanied his translation of Charles Alphonse du Fresnoy's Latin poem *De arte graphica* (1688), Dryden pursues analogies between the "sister arts."
15. Lucan (39–65 A.D.), author of the epic *Bellum Civile*, better known as the *Pharsalia;* Statius (45–96 A.D.), best known for the epic *Thebaid*.
16. *Aeneid* VI.164–65: "Than whom none is superior in stirring men with brass [the trumpet], and in kindling Mars [war] with his song [playing]."
17. That is, cultivated felicity or planned good luck (*Satyricon*, l. 118); cf. Pope's play on *curiosa felicitas* in the *Essay on Criticism*, l. 142: "For there's a happiness as well as care."
18. Rock-crystal.

and then to think their work is truly finished. Apelles said of Protogenes [19] that he knew not when to give over. A work may be over-wrought as well as under-wrought: too much labour often takes away the spirit by adding to the polishing, so that there remains nothing but a dull correctness, a piece without any considerable faults, but with few beauties; for when the spirits are drawn off, there is nothing but a *caput mortuum*.[20] Statius never thought an expression could be bold enough; and if a bolder could be found, he rejected the first. Virgil had judgment enough to know daring was necessary; but he knew the difference betwixt a glowing colour and a glaring. . . . [From *A Parallel Betwixt Poetry and Painting*, 1695]

Critical Issues

[Subplots and Complex Structure]

And this leads me to wonder why Lisideius and many others should cry up the barrenness of the French plots above the variety and copiousness of the English. Their plots are single, they carry on one design which is pushed forward by all the actors, every scene in the play contributing and moving towards it. Our plays besides the main design, have under-plots or by-concernments, of less considerable persons and intrigues, which are carried on with the motion of the main plot: as they say the orb of the fixed stars and those of the planets, though they have motions of their own, are whirled about by the motion of the *primum mobile*, in which they are contained:[21] that similitude expresses much of the English stage, for if contrary motions may be found in nature to agree; if a planet can go east and west at the same time, one way by virtue of his own motion, the other by the force of the first mover, it will not be difficult to imagine how the under-plot, which is only different, not contrary to the great design, may naturally be conducted along with it. [From *Of Dramatic Poesy: An Essay*, 1668]

[Comedy and Farce]

. . . Comedy consists, though of low persons, yet of natural actions and characters; I mean such humours, adventures, and designs as are to be found and met with in the world. Farce, on the other side, consists of forced humours and unnatural events. Comedy presents us with the imperfections of human nature. Farce entertains us with what is monstrous and chimerical: the one causes laughter in those who can judge of men and manners, by the lively representation of their folly or corruption; the other produces the same effect in those who can judge of neither, and that only by its extravagances. The first works on the judgement and fancy; the latter on the fancy only: there is more of satisfaction in the former kind of laughter, and in the latter more of scorn. But how it happens that an impossible adventure should cause our mirth, I cannot so easily imagine. Something there may be in the oddness of it, because on the stage it is the common effect of things unexpected to surprise us into a

19. Apelles (4th century B.C.) was court painter to Philip and Alexander of Macedon; Protogenes was a contemporary of Apelles.

20. Literally, a death's head; hence the worthless residue of a distillation.

21. Cf. the opening lines of Dryden's "Anne Killigrew" ode.

delight: and that is to be ascribed to the strange appetite, as I may call it, of the fancy; which, like that of a longing woman,[22] often runs out into the most extravagant desires; and is better satisfied sometimes with loam, or with the rinds of trees, than with the wholesome nourishments of life. In short, there is the same difference betwixt farce and comedy as betwixt an empiric and a true physician: both of them may attain their ends; but what the one performs by hazard, the other does by skill. And as the artist is often unsuccessful, while the mountebank succeeds; so farces more commonly take the people than comedies. For to write unnatural things is the most probable way of pleasing them, who understand not nature. And a true poet often misses of applause because he cannot debase himself to write so ill as to please his audience. . . . [From Preface to *An Evening's Love,* 1671]

. . . There is yet a lower sort of poetry and painting, which is out of nature; for a farce is that in poetry which grotesque is in a picture. The persons and action of a farce are all unnatural, and the manners false, that is, inconsisting with the characters of mankind. Grotesque painting is the just resemblance of this; and Horace begins his *Art of Poetry* by describing such a figure, with a man's head, a horse's neck, the wings of a bird, and a fish's tail; parts of different species jumbled together, according to the mad imagination of the dauber; and the end of all this, as he tells you afterward, to cause laughter: a very monster in a Bartholomew Fair, for the mob to gape at for their two-pence. Laughter is indeed the propriety[23] of a man, but just enough to distinguish him from his elder brother with four legs. 'Tis a kind of bastard-pleasure too, taken in at the eyes of the vulgar gazers, and at the ears of the beastly audience. Church-painters use it to divert the honest countryman at public prayers, and keep his eyes open at a heavy sermon. And farce-scribblers make use of the same noble invention to entertain citizens, country-gentlemen, and Covent Garden fops. If they are merry, all goes well on the poet's side. The better sort go thither too, but in despair of sense and the just images of nature, which are the adequate pleasures of the mind. But the author can give the stage no better than what was given him by nature; and the actors must represent such things as they are capable to perform, and by which both they and the scribbler may get their living. After all, 'tis a good thing to laugh at any rate, and if a straw can tickle a man, 'tis an instrument of happiness. Beasts can weep when they suffer, but they cannot laugh. . . . [From *A Parallel Betwixt Poetry and Painting,* 1695]

[Horace and Juvenal]

. . . Let the chastisements of Juvenal be never so necessary for his new kind of satire; let him declaim as wittily and sharply as he pleases: yet still the nicest and most delicate touches of satire consist in fine raillery. . . . How easy is it to call rogue and villain, and that wittily! But how hard to make a man appear a fool, a blockhead, or a knave, without using any of those opprobrious terms! To spare the grossness of the names, and to do the thing

22. That is, in her pregnancy.
23. Special property.

yet more severely, is to draw a full face, and to make the nose and cheeks stand out, and yet not to employ any depth of shadowing. This is the mystery of that noble trade, which yet no master can teach to his apprentice: he may give the rules, but the scholar is never the nearer in his practice. Neither is it true that this fineness of raillery is offensive. A witty man is tickled while he is hurt in this manner, and a fool feels it not. The occasion of an offence may possibly be given, but he cannot take it. If it be granted that in effect this way does more mischief; that a man is secretly wounded, and though he be not sensible himself, yet the malicious world will find it for him: yet there is still a vast difference betwixt the slovenly butchering of a man, and the fineness of a stroke that separates the head from the body, and leaves it standing in its place. . . .

. . . It must be granted by the favourers of Juvenal, that Horace is the more copious and profitable in his instructions of human life. But in my particular opinion, which I set not up for a standard to better judgements, Juvenal is the more delightful author. I am profited by both, I am pleased with both; but I owe more to Horace for my instruction, and more to Juvenal, for my pleasure. . . .

. . . I must confess, that the delight which Horace gives me is but languishing. Be pleased still to understand that I speak of my own taste only. He may ravish other men, but I am too stupid and insensible to be tickled. Where he barely grins himself, and, as Scaliger says, only shows his white teeth, he cannot provoke me to any laughter. His urbanity, that is, his good manners, are to be commended; but his wit is faint, and his salt,[24] if I may dare to say so, almost insipid. Juvenal is of a more vigorous and masculine wit; he gives me as much pleasure as I can bear. . . . Add to this, that his thoughts are as just as those of Horace, and much more elevated. His expressions are sonorous and more noble; his verse more numerous;[25] and his words are suitable to his thoughts, sublime and lofty. All these contribute to the pleasure of the reader, and the greater the soul of him who reads, his transports are the greater. Horace is always on the amble, Juvenal on the gallop, but his way is perpetually on carpet ground.[26] He goes with more impetuosity than Horace, but as securely; and the swiftness adds a more lively agitation to the spirits. . . .

The meat of Horace is more nourishing; but the cookery of Juvenal more exquisite; so that, granting Horace to be the more general philosopher, we cannot deny that Juvenal was the greater poet, I mean in satire. His thoughts are sharper, his indignation against vice is more vehement; his spirit has more of the commonwealth genius; he treats tyranny, and all the vices attending it, as they deserve, with the utmost rigour; and consequently, a noble soul is better pleased with a zealous vindicator of Roman liberty than with a temporizing poet, a well mannered court slave, and a man who is often afraid of laughing in the right place, who is ever decent because he is naturally servile. After all, Horace had the disadvantage of the times in which he lived; they were better for the man, but worse for the satirist. 'Tis generally said that those

24. Pungency.
25. Harmonious.
26. Even or smooth, as on soft turf.

enormous vices, which were practised under the reign of Domitian, were unknown in the time of Augustus Caesar, that therefore Juvenal had a larger field than Horace. Little follies were out of doors, when oppression was to be scourged instead of avarice. It was no longer time to turn into ridicule the false opinions of philosophers, when the Roman liberty was to be asserted. . . . [From *A Discourse Concerning the Original and Progress of Satire*, 1693]

Critical Judgments

[Shakespeare and Jonson]

To begin with Shakespeare; he was the man who of all modern, and perhaps ancient poets, had the largest and most comprehensive soul. All the images of nature were still present to him, and he drew them not laboriously, but luckily: when he describes anything, you more than see it, you feel it too. Those who accuse him to have wanted learning, give him the greater commendation: he was naturally learned; he needed not the spectacles of books to read nature; he looked inwards, and found her there. I cannot say he is everywhere alike; were he so, I should do him injury to compare him with the greatest of mankind. He is many times flat, insipid; his comic wit degenerating into clenches, his serious swelling into bombast. But he is always great when some great occasion is presented to him: no man can say he ever had a fit subject for his wit and did not then raise himself as high above the rest of poets,

Quantum lenta solent inter viburna cupressi.[27]

The consideration of this made Mr. Hales of Eton [28] say that there was no subject of which any poet ever writ, but he would produce it much better done in Shakespeare; and however others are now generally preferred before him, yet the age wherein he lived, which had contemporaries with him, Fletcher and Jonson, never equalled them to him in their esteem. And in the last king's Court,[29] when Ben's reputation was at highest, Sir John Suckling, and with him the greater part of the courtiers, set our Shakespeare far above him.

. . .

As for Jonson, to whose character I am now arrived, if we look upon him while he was himself (for his last plays were but his dotages), I think him the most learned and judicious writer which any theatre ever had. He was a most severe judge of himself as well as others. One cannot say he wanted wit, but rather that he was frugal of it. In his works you find little to retrench or alter. Wit and language, and humour also in some measure we had before him; but something of art was wanting to the drama till he came. He managed his strength to more advantage than any who preceded him. You seldom find him making love in any of his scenes, or endeavouring to move the passions; his genius was too sullen and saturnine to do it gracefully, especially when he knew he came after those who had performed both to such an height. Humour was his proper sphere, and in that he delighted most to represent mechanic

27. Virgil, *Eclogues* I.25: "as cypresses often do among bending osiers."
28. John Hales (1584–1656), a fellow of Eton College and a master of prose disputation; as in his *Golden Remains* (1659).
29. During the reign of Charles I (1625–49).

people. He was deeply conversant in the Ancients, both Greek and Latin, and he borrowed boldly from them. There is scarce a poet or historian among the Roman authors of those times whom he has not translated in *Sejanus* and *Catiline*. But he has done his robberies so openly, that one may see he fears not to be taxed by any law. He invades authors like a monarch, and what would be theft in other poets, is only victory in him. With the spoils of these writers he so represents old Rome to us, in its rites, ceremonies, and customs, that if one of their poets had written either of his tragedies, we had seen less of it than in him. If there was any fault in his language, 'twas that he weaved it too closely and laboriously, in his comedies especially: perhaps too, he did a little too much Romanize our tongue, leaving the words which he translated almost as much Latin as he found them: wherein though he learnedly followed their language, he did not enough comply with the idiom of ours. If I would compare him with Shakespeare, I must acknowledge him the more correct poet, but Shakespeare the greater wit. Shakespeare was the Homer, or father of our dramatic poets; Jonson was the Virgil, the pattern of elaborate writing. I admire him, but I love Shakespeare. . . . [From *Of Dramatic Poesy: An Essay*, 1668]

[Chaucer]

In the first place, as he is the father of English poetry, so I hold him in the same degree of veneration as the Grecians held Homer, or the Romans Virgil. He is a perpetual fountain of good sense; learned in all sciences; and therefore speaks properly on all subjects. As he knew what to say, so he knows also when to leave off; a continence which is practised by few writers, and scarcely by any of the Ancients, excepting Virgil and Horace. . . .

Chaucer followed nature everywhere; but was never so bold [as] to go beyond her. And there is a great difference of being *poeta* and *nimis poeta,*[30] if we may believe Catullus, as much as betwixt a modest behaviour and affectation. The verse of Chaucer, I confess, is not harmonious to us; but 'tis like the eloquence of one whom Tacitus[31] commends, it was *auribus istius temporis accommodata;* they who lived with him, and some time after him, thought it musical; and it continues so even in our judgement, if compared with the numbers of Lydgate and Gower his contemporaries. There is the rude sweetness of a Scotch tune in it, which is natural and pleasing, though not perfect. . . .

. . . He must have been a man of a most wonderful comprehensive nature, because, as it has been truly observed of him, he has taken into the compass of his *Canterbury Tales* the various manners and humours (as we now call them) of the whole English nation in his age. Not a single character has escaped him. All his pilgrims are severally distinguished from each other; and not only in their inclinations, but in their very physiognomies and persons. Baptista Porta[32] could not have described their natures better than by the marks which the poet gives them. The matter and manner of their tales and

30. Being a poet or being too much a poet; not from Catullus but from Martial, *Epigrams* III.xliv.4.

31. *De Oratoribus* XXI: "suited to the ears of another age."

32. Giambattista della Porta (1540–1615), Neapolitan physician and student of physiognomy, particularly of the influence of emotions on the face.

of their telling are so suited to their different educations, humours, and callings, that each of them would be improper in any other mouth. Even the grave and serious characters are distinguished by their several sorts of gravity. Their discourses are such as belong to their age, their calling, and their breeding; such as are becoming of them, and of them only. Some of his persons are vicious, and some virtuous; some are unlearned, or (as Chaucer calls them) lewd, and some are learned. Even the ribaldry of the low characters is different. The Reeve, the Miller, and the Cook, are several men, and distinguished from each other, as much as the mincing Lady Prioress and the broad-speaking gap-toothed Wife of Bath. But enough of this; there is such a variety of game springing up before me that I am distracted in my choice and know not which to follow. 'Tis sufficient to say according to the proverb that here is God's plenty. . . . [From Preface to *Fables, Ancient and Modern,* 1700]

JONATHAN SWIFT

1667–1745

Swift is the greatest ironist in English literature, and he has as a result been accused of all the malevolence and blindness that resentment can invent. He does not allow man much comfort or dignity, and he cruelly reduces grand pretensions to systematic follies and mechanized brutality. In fact, Swift's characteristic device is to invent some rational basis for the behavior that men fall into unthinkingly or self-indulgently; by rationalizing folly, by finding eloquent arguments for the unspeakable, Swift divorces intention (usually noble) from achievement (somewhat shabbier) and shows what one would have to intend if one were to undertake deliberately what men in fact accomplish. If we live by exploiting others, we are only a short way (just enough to save our self-esteem) from cannibalism, and Swift shocks us with that possibility in *A Modest Proposal.* If we have turned religion into an accommodation of our "schemes of wealth and power," always sure to secure a blessing for what is profitable or expedient, we are on the way to abolishing Christianity, and we need not go through the explicit motions, given our great skill at simply undermining the faith by which we might otherwise be judged. There is no wonder that Swift has aroused resentment; there are great temptations to misread him and make him a historical curiosity. The easiest way of all is to attribute his unaccommodating irony to the psychological aberrations of a disturbed or conflict-torn man.

Swift was born in Ireland of English parents and, after studying at Trinity College, Dublin, he entered the household of Sir William Temple, a retired diplomat, as a secretary. Temple lived in retirement outside of London, and he had a fine library, which Swift used well. It was in Temple's household that Swift first met Hester Johnson, with whose education he helped, and upon whose affection he depended greatly during their years together in Dublin. His relations with Temple were close but difficult, and Swift left at one point to become an Anglican parish priest in northern Ireland. Upon his return to England he remained with Temple until the latter's death, helping prepare Temple's works for publication and writing his own remarkable first volume of satire, which included *A Tale of a Tub* and *The Battle of the Books* (written in the 1690's and published in 1704). While the *Tale* had great success, its ironic treatment of the church probably hurt Swift's ecclessiastical career.

In 1707 Swift was sent by the Church of Ireland to seek financial benefits from Queen Anne; during his year's stay in London, he became accepted as a man of letters and was close to Addison's literary circle. When he returned to London in 1710, he left the Whigs and gave his support to the Tory ministry of Robert Harley, later Earl of Oxford, on the grounds that the Whigs might sell the church short in their encouragement of Dissenters. For most of the four years that followed, until the fall of the ministry with the death of the Queen, Swift became a principal spokesman and propagandist for the Tories, through such a periodical as *The Examiner* and through such political pamphlets as *The Conduct of the Allies* (1713). He became a leading spirit in the Scriblerus Club with Pope and Dr. Arbuthnot, and he was able to win patronage for friends in difficulty, Addison among them.

With the fall of the ministry, Swift (who had been appointed Dean of St. Patrick's Cathedral, Dublin, in 1713) began his long Irish exile, the hope of a bishopric in England vanishing and the visits to London growing infrequent. He became in some measure an Irish patriot, trying to stir the Irish to self-respect and to resistance against English exploitation; and he won a considerable battle against Sir Robert Walpole through his *Drapier's Letters* of 1724–25. *Gulliver's Travels* contained strong political satire, and Swift had a hand in encouraging both Gay's *Beggar's Opera* and Pope's *Dunciad* in the following years. Throughout his lifetime Swift created a body of distinctive poetry, and finally his irony turned to a compendium of "polite conversation" and a penetrating set of *Directions to Servants.* At the end Swift's mind and memory gave way after years of labyrinthine vertigo, a disease of the middle ear that disturbed his sense of balance; he was cared for by others until his death, which fell in the year after Pope's.

Swift's irony required that he write in many guises, and each of these guises (masks or *personae,* as they have been called) tends to become in some degree a fool among knaves, a man more obtuse and more innocent than the wilier and more clear-headedly vicious knaves. The fool gives them away without meaning to betray, for he guilelessly acknowledges what they know enough to conceal. This contributes to that style of cool understatement which exacts from the reader a moral judgment it does not explicitly provide; in *Gulliver's Travels* it produces a surface of meticulously realistic narration such as the novel might later use. But in Swift's hands this very precision of recorded detail is meant to strike us with its failure to judge or feel and to require us to do so instead.

The Battle of the Books

Swift carries on the wide-ranging quarrel of the Ancients and Moderns which divided scholars in seventeenth-century France. Involved in the quarrel was the whole idea of progress. Were the Moderns inferior to the great Ancients, or were they their equals or even superiors? The defenders of the Ancients could claim that writers of later ages had done little more than borrow from the greatness of Homer and Virgil, Horace and Terence. They traced a pattern of slow but steady degeneration in the history of man. The defenders of the Moderns could point to the dead hand of Aristotle upon history and science and the great achievements that arose among the Moderns with the overthrow of foolish reverence for ancient authorities.

In England the quarrel took a special turn when Sir William Temple, Swift's patron, praised the work of Aesop and Phalaris at the expense of the Moderns, only to bring down the learned criticism of Richard Bentley, the greatest classical scholar of his time, who proved that Temple's Ancients were not nearly so ancient as Temple had thought them. The conflict also represented a clash between literary humanism and philological science, and Swift entered it with an effort to show the arrogance and insensitivity of those Moderns who could date a poem accurately but could neither write nor read one well. He invented the fable of a battle (presented in mock-heroic vein) among the books in the royal library (where Bentley was keeper of books), but the finest episode in the work is an interlude in which a pompous and ill-tempered Modern, the Spider, finds his Gothic cobweb invaded by a Bee. It should be noted that Gothic architecture and scholastic disputation were cheerfully granted to the Moderns by Swift, and Horatian urbanity—so recently revived as a model of style—is a quality of his Ancients. The Ancients, for Swift, represent those who keep the past alive in the present, fostering the virtues of antiquity and not—like Cornelius Scriblerus, in another satire to which Swift contributed—revering its rust. The Moderns in their ambition to be self-sufficient risk parochial narrowness; their manners show a failure of humanity as well as of humanism.

From A Full and True Account of the Battle Fought Last Friday, Between the Ancient and Modern Books in St. James's Library

[Episode of the Spider and the Bee]

Things were at this crisis when a material accident fell out. For upon the highest corner of a large window there dwelt a certain Spider, swollen up to the first magnitude by the destruction of infinite numbers of flies, whose spoils lay scattered before the gates of his palace, like human bones before the cave of some giant.[1] The avenues to his castle were guarded with turnpikes and palisadoes, all after the modern way of fortification.[2] After you had passed several courts, you came to the centre, wherein you might behold the constable [3] himself in his own lodgings, which had windows fronting to each avenue and ports [4] to sally out upon all occasions of prey or defence. In this mansion he had for some time dwelt in peace and plenty, without danger to his person by swallows from above or to his palace by brooms from below; when it was the pleasure of Fortune to conduct thither a wandering Bee, to whose curiosity a broken pane in the glass had discovered itself, and in he went; where, expatiating a while, he at last happened to alight upon one of the outward walls of the Spider's citadel; which, yielding to the unequal weight, sunk down to the very foundation. Thrice he endeavoured to force his passage, and thrice the centre shook. The Spider within, feeling the terrible convulsion, supposed at first that Nature was approaching to her final dissolution; [5] or else that Beelzebub [6] with all his legions was come to revenge the death of many thousands of his subjects, whom his enemy had slain and devoured. However, he at length valiantly resolved to issue forth and meet his fate. Meanwhile the Bee had acquitted himself of his toils,[7] and, posted securely at some distance, was employed in cleansing his wings and disengaging them from the ragged remnants of the cobweb. By this time the Spider was adventured out, when, beholding the chasms and ruins and dilapidations of his fortress, he was very near at his wit's end; he stormed and swore like a madman and swelled till he was ready to burst. At length, casting his eye upon the Bee and wisely gathering causes from events (for they knew each other by sight): 'A plague split you,' said he, 'for a giddy son of a whore. Is it you, with a vengeance, that have made this litter here? Could not you look before you, and be d—ned? Do you think I have nothing else to do, in the devil's name, but to mend and repair after your arse?'

'Good words, friend,' said the Bee (having now pruned himself and being disposed to droll), 'I'll give you my hand and word to come near your kennel no more; I was never in such a confounded pickle since I was born.'

'Sirrah,' replied the Spider, 'if it were not for breaking an old custom in our family never to stir abroad against an enemy, I should come and teach you better manners.'

'I pray have patience,' said the Bee, 'or you will spend your substance, and, for aught I see, you may stand in need of it all towards the repair of your house.'

'Rogue, rogue,' replied the Spider, 'yet methinks you should have more respect to a person whom all the world allows to be so much your betters.'

1. With echoes of Romance literature, which was defended later in the 18th century on the analogy of Gothic architecture.

2. One of the fields in which the Moderns were generally granted eminence, as was mathematics.

3. The keeper of a royal fortress or castle.

4. Gateways.

5. Swift often satirizes the gullible and superstitious fears of scientists.

6. Literally, the god of flies.

7. Snares, nets.

'By my troth,' said the Bee, 'the comparison will amount to a very good jest, and you will do me a favour to let me know the reasons that all the world is pleased to use in so hopeful [8] a dispute.'

At this the Spider, having swelled himself into the size and posture of a disputant, began his argument in the true spirit of controversy, with a resolution to be heartily scurrilous and angry, to urge on his own reasons without the least regard to the answers or objections of his opposite, and fully predetermined in his mind against all conviction.

'Not to disparage myself,' said he, 'by the comparison with such a rascal, what art thou but a vagabond without house or home, without stock or inheritance, born to no possession of your own but a pair of wings and a drone-pipe? Your livelihood is an universal plunder upon nature, a freebooter over fields and gardens; and, for the sake of stealing, will rob a nettle as easily as a violet. Whereas I am a domestic animal, furnished with a native stock within myself. This large castle (to show my improvements in the mathematics) is all built with my own hands, and the materials extracted altogether out of my own person.'

'I am glad,' answered the Bee, 'to hear you grant at least that I am come honestly by my wings and my voice; for then, it seems, I am obliged to Heaven alone for my flights and my music; and Providence would never have bestowed on me two such gifts without designing them for the noblest ends. I visit indeed all the flowers and blossoms of the field and the garden; but whatever I collect from thence enriches myself, without the least injury to their beauty, their smell, or their taste. Now, for you and your skill in architecture and other mathematics, I have little to say. In that building of yours there might, for aught I know, have been labour and method enough; but, by woful experience for us both, 'tis too plain the materials are naught, and I hope you will henceforth take warning and consider duration and matter as well as method and art. You boast, indeed, of being obliged to no other creature but of drawing and spinning out all from yourself; that is to say, if we may judge of the liquor in the vessel by what issues out, you possess a good plentiful store of dirt and poison in your breast; and, though I would by no means lessen or disparage your genuine stock of either, yet I doubt you are somewhat obliged, for an increase of both, to a little foreign assistance. Your inherent portion of dirt does not fail of acquisitions by sweepings exhaled from below; and one insect furnishes you with a share of poison to destroy another. So that, in short, the question comes all to this: whether is the nobler being of the two that which, by a lazy contemplation of four inches round, by an overweening pride which, feeding and engendering on itself, turns all into excrement and venom, producing nothing at all but flybane and a cobweb; or that which, by an universal range, with long search, much study, true judgement, and distinction of things, brings home honey and wax.'

This dispute was managed with such eagerness, clamour, and warmth, that the two parties of Books, in arms below, stood silent a while, waiting in suspense what would be the issue, which was not long undetermined: for the Bee, grown impatient at so much loss of time, fled straight away to a bed of roses without

8. Promising.

looking for a reply, and left the Spider like an orator, collected in himself and just prepared to burst out.

It happened upon this emergency that Aesop broke silence first. He had been of late most barbarously treated by a strange effect of the regent's humanity, who had tore off his title-page, sorely defaced one half of his leaves, and chained him fast among a shelf of Moderns. Where, soon discovering how high the quarrel was like to proceed, he tried all his arts, and turned himself to a thousand forms.[9] At length, in the borrowed shape of an ass, the regent mistook him for a Modern; by which means he had time and opportunity to escape to the Ancients, just when the Spider and the Bee were entering into their contest, to which he gave his attention with a world of pleasure; and when it was ended, swore in the loudest key that in all his life he had never known two cases so parallel and adapt to each other as that in the window and this upon the shelves. 'The disputants,' said he, 'have admirably managed the dispute between them, have taken in the full strength of all that is to be said on both sides, and exhausted the substance of every argument *pro* and *con.* It is but to adjust the reasonings of both to the present quarrel, then to compare and apply the labours and fruits of each, as the Bee has learnedly deduced them, and we shall find the conclusion fall plain and close upon the Moderns and us. For, pray, gentlemen, was ever anything so modern as the Spider in his air, his turns,[10] and his paradoxes? He argues in the behalf of you his brethren and himself with many boastings of his native stock and great genius, that he spins and spits wholly from himself, and scorns to own any obligation or assistance from without. Then he displays to you his great skill in architecture and improvement in the mathematics. To all this the Bee, as an advocate retained by us the Ancients, thinks fit to answer that, if one may judge of the great genius or inventions of the Moderns by what they have produced, you will hardly have countenance to bear you out in boasting of either. Erect your schemes with as much method and skill as you please; yet, if the materials be nothing but dirt, spun out of your own entrails (the guts of modern brains), the edifice will conclude at last in a cobweb, the duration of which, like that of other spiders' webs, may be imputed to their being forgotten, or neglected, or hid in a corner. For anything else of genuine that the Moderns may pretend to, I cannot recollect, unless it be a large vein of wrangling and satire, much of a nature and substance with the Spider's poison; which, however they pretend to spit wholly out of themselves, is improved by the same arts, by feeding upon the insects and vermin of the age. As for us the Ancients, we are content with the Bee to pretend to nothing of our own beyond our wings and our voice, that is to say, our flights and our language. For the rest, whatever we have got, has been by infinite labour and search and ranging through every corner of nature; the difference is that, instead of dirt and poison, we have rather chosen to fill our hives with honey and wax, thus furnishing mankind with the two noblest of things, which are sweetness and light.'[11]

1704

9. Referring to the many animals Aesop had characterized in his fables.

10. Witty plays on words (used ironically of his spluttering abuse).

11. The terms later borrowed and extended by Matthew Arnold in *Culture and Anarchy* (1869).

A Tale of a Tub

A Tale of a Tub, originally published in one volume with *The Battle of the Books* and *The Mechanical Operation of the Spirit,* a satire on religious enthusiasm, marks a turning point in English literature. It looks back to the age of baroque and Metaphysical wit—in such prose as the sermons of John Donne or Lancelot Andrewes or the secular works of Robert Burton and Sir Thomas Browne; in such verse as that of Cowley, whom Swift imitated in his earliest poems—and in looking back, through parody, it sees false and ingenious verbal wit and self-flattering sophistry. Swift mocks the extravagant arguments through metaphor, the fanciful system-building, and the constant "wresting" of terms. Behind this last concern, which had been awakened by the preaching of witty Anglican and enthusiastic Puritan alike, lay the words of Peter (II Peter 3:16) on the epistles of Paul: "in which are some things hard to be understood, which they that are unlearned and unstable wrest, as they do also the other Scriptures, unto their own destruction."

But the *Tale* is a twofold attack: upon the corruption of religion and of learning. The counterpart of the extremes in religion—"the frenzy of Platonic visions and the lethargic ignorance of Popish dreams," as Halifax called them—is the false learning that cultivates the letter at the expense of spirit, words at the expense of meaning. Here Swift returns to the attack upon Bentley he undertook in *The Battle* but extends his attack to include the other extreme of learning as well—superficiality, gullibility, and laziness. His point is that extremes meet, that the pride in self which creates carping arrogance in some produces obtuse complacency in others. The Spider's "lazy contemplation of four inches round" is easier to maintain if the Modern is convinced of his own inherent greatness, and Swift mocks this by showing the Moderns finding "momentous truths" in their most trivial and ephemeral effusions. They do this by ingenious allegorizing, in the manner of Bunyan or his more learned scholarly counterparts, and allegory releases the will to believe, overriding all empirical evidence or restraint from outside. It becomes the vehicle of the private will and imagination, and Swift finally treats the uncontrolled fancy, as Locke and others had done before him, as a kind of madness.

The *Tale* is, in form, an ingeniously baroque structure. After many prefatory and dedicatory sections, it interweaves an allegorical tale with self-styled digressions that gradually overwhelm the tale. (As Hobbes says, in the eighth chapter of *Leviathan,* "A great fancy is one kind of madness such as they have that, entering into any discourse, are snatched from their purpose . . . into so many and so long digressions and parentheses that they utterly lose themselves.") Swift's "digressions" are, in fact, the heart of the work, and the greatest of them is given below. They embody the themes of fancy, wit, and reason in the secular world, while the allegory presents the career of the Christian church once it enters the world. It is embodied in three brothers: Peter (the Church of Rome), Martin (Luther's moderate reforming Protestantism and the Church of England in particular), and Jack (Calvinism and other forms of radical Protestantism). The brothers are meant to live together in peace, but, as they enter the world—as in Section II below—they become more and more at odds, until Peter kicks the others out of doors. Recovering his senses, Martin tries to restore the original form of his coat and realizes that he cannot achieve pristine purity without damaging the fabric. He leaves some of those accretions that cannot safely be removed; but Jack, in utter reaction, tears his to shreds rather than have it show any trace of Peter's influence. The result, ironically, is that Peter's elaborate finery and Jack's rags look—at any distance—indistinguishable, and the modest "trimmer" Martin is hated by both.

The Digression on Madness has sometimes been discussed as if it were wholly negative in implication, as if it prepared us to accept the surfaces of things, only to damn us for doing so. But one must ask whether the defense of surface is meant to be plausible, and this is best determined by asking to what surface is opposed. The speaker involves us in an impossible choice between carping and superficiality, between mangling and piercing on the one hand and skimming on the other. Between these extremes the ideal of true analysis and tactful perception is lost, just as Martin is crowded off the scene by the barbarous vigor of Peter and Jack. The same problem recurs in the fourth voyage of *Gulliver's Travels,* where we must find a norm somewhere between the undisturbed rationality of the Houyhnhnms and the savage passions of the Yahoos.

Section IX makes clear, as earlier sections of the *Tale* have revealed, that Swift is writing in the guise of a Modern hack, full of avowed respect for all forms of modernity and of scorn for old-fashioned "common forms." He writes of madness with special authority as a former inhabitant of Bedlam, and he has all the zeal of a "projector," a man with schemes for public improvements that will win him profit or praise. The guise is a transparent one, for it is clearly the vehicle of a savage irony; but it accounts for the imperturbable ease with which the author both contradicts himself and gives himself away. We see through the speaker; he is given the relative consistency of a type, both psychological and social, that is meant to be recognized and to be given only so much credit as his limitations merit. He is less obviously a *persona* (that is, a mask or assumed identity) than Lemuel Gulliver, who has a name and a fuller history, but we miss much of his meaning if we ignore the allusiveness to contemporary styles and attitudes that shapes his role.

The title of Swift's work comes from a proverbial phrase for a nonsensical *jeu d'esprit* or whimsy, but he mockingly allegorizes it as the tub seamen throw out to distract a threatening whale, the whale in this case being the dangerous doctrines of Thomas Hobbes's *Leviathan.* So influential has that work been in seducing the young wits that serious disturbances might arise if they were not kept busy with harmless tasks, Swift implies, and this book is offered as an absorbing puzzle. In fact, it mocks their modernity and seeks to recall them to sanity.

From A Tale of a Tub

Written for the Universal Improvement of Mankind

Section II

Once upon a time there was a man who had three sons by one wife, and all at a birth; neither could the midwife tell certainly which was the eldest. Their father died while they were young; and upon his deathbed, calling the lads to him, spoke thus:

'Sons, because I have purchased no estate, nor was born to any, I have long considered of some good legacies to bequeath you; and at last, with much care, as well as expense, have provided each of you (here they are) a new coat. Now, you are to understand, that these coats have two virtues contained in them: one is that with good wearing they will last you fresh and sound as long as you live; the other is that they will grow in the same proportion with your bodies, lengthening and widening of themselves, so as to be always fit. Here, let me see them on you before I die. So, very well; pray, children, wear them clean and brush them often. You will find in my will [1] (here it is) full instructions in every particular concerning the wearing and management of your coats; wherein you must be very exact, to avoid the penalties I have appointed for every transgression or neglect, upon which your future fortunes will entirely depend. I have also commanded in my will, that you should live together in one house like brethren and friends, for then you will be sure to thrive, and not otherwise.'

Here the story says this good father died, and the three sons went all together to seek their fortunes.

I shall not trouble you with recounting what adventures they met for the first seven years, any farther than by taking notice that they carefully observed their father's will and kept their coats in very good order: that they travelled through several countries, encountered a reasonable quantity of giants, and slew certain dragons.[2]

Being now arrived at the proper age for producing themselves, they came up to town and fell in love with the ladies, but especially three, who about that time were in chief reputation: the Duchess d'Argent, Madame de Grands Titres, and the Countess d'Orgueil.[3] On their first appearance our three adventurers met with a very bad reception; and soon with great sagacity guessing out the reason, they quickly began to improve in the good qualities of the town. They writ, and rallied, and rhymed, and sung, and said, and said nothing: they drank, and fought, and whored, and slept, and swore, and took snuff: they went to new plays on the first night, haunted the chocolate-houses, beat the watch, lay on bulks,[4] and got claps: they bilked [5] hackney-coachmen, ran in debt with shop-keepers, and lay with their wives: they killed bailiffs, kicked fiddlers down stairs, eat at Locket's,[6] loitered at Will's: [7] they talked of the drawing-room and never came there: dined with lords they never saw: whispered a duchess, and spoke never a word: [8] exposed the scrawls of their laundress for billetdoux of quality: came ever just from court and were never seen in it: attended the levee *sub dio:* [9] got a list of peers by heart in one company, and with great familiarity retailed them in another. Above all, they

1. That is, the New Testament, which provides all that is necessary to know for the sake of salvation (and presumably also for the sake of morality or "decency" in its fullest sense, i.e. what is "fitting"); "by the coats are meant the doctrine and faith of Christianity, by the wisdom of the Divine Founder fitted to all times, places, and circumstances." (Swift)

2. The traditional Romance elements of Christian allegory (as in *The Faerie Queene* I or Bunyan's account of Apollyon) are rapidly disposed of, and the era of "primitive Christianity" gives way to the role of the church in the world (here the world is cut to the scale of the "grand monde" or world of fashionable society).

3. Covetousness (wealth), ambition (great titles), and pride.

4. Stalls outside shops, where impoverished poets sometimes slept.

5. Cheated.

6. A fashionable tavern.

7. The well-known literary coffeehouse.

8. That is, whispered about but never spoke a word to.

9. That is, attended the official reception ("levee") only in the open air ("*sub dio*").

constantly attended those Committees of Senators who are silent in the House and loud in the coffee-house; where they nightly adjourn to chew the cud of politics and are encompassed with a ring of disciples who lie in wait to catch up their droppings. The three brothers had acquired forty other qualifications of the like stamp, too tedious to recount, and by consequence were justly reckoned the most accomplished persons in the town. But all would not suffice, and the ladies aforesaid continued still inflexible. To clear up which difficulty I must, with the reader's good leave and patience, have recourse to some points of weight, which the authors of that age have not sufficiently illustrated.

For about this time it happened a sect arose, whose tenets obtained and spread very far, especially in the *grand monde* and among everybody of good fashion. They worshipped a sort of idol, who, as their doctrine delivered, did daily create men by a kind of manufactory operation. This idol they placed in the highest parts of the house on an altar erected about three foot: he was shown in the posture of a Persian emperor, sitting on a superficies, with his legs interwoven under him.[10] This god had a goose for his ensign, whence it is that some learned men pretend to deduce his original from Jupiter Capitolinus.[11] At his left hand, beneath the altar, Hell seemed to open, and catch at the animals the idol was creating; to prevent which, certain of his priests hourly flung in pieces of the uninformed mass, or substance, and sometimes whole limbs already enlivened, which that horrid gulf insatiably swallowed, terrible to behold. The goose was also held a subaltern divinity or *deus minorum gentium,*[12] before whose shrine was sacrificed that creature whose hourly food is human gore and who is in so great renown abroad for being the delight and favourite of the Egyptian Cercopithecus.[13] Millions of these animals were cruelly slaughtered every day to appease the hunger of that consuming deity. The chief idol was also worshipped as the inventor of the yard and the needle; [14] whether as the god of seamen or on account of certain other mystical attributes hath not been sufficiently cleared.

The worshippers of this deity had also a system of their belief which seemed to turn upon the following fundamental. They held the universe to be a large suit of clothes which invests everything: that the earth is invested by the air; the air is invested by the stars; and the stars are invested by the *primum mobile*.[15] Look on this globe of earth, you will find it to be a very complete and fashionable dress. What is that which some call land, but a fine coat faced with green? or the sea, but a waistcoat of water-tabby? [16] Proceed to the par-

10. The "idol" is a tailor, the "goose" his smoothing-iron (named for the shape of its handle), and "Hell" is his receptacle for scraps of cloth (cf. Butler, *Hudibras* I.i.238).

11. Jupiter had a temple on the Capitoline Hill, where the sacred geese of Rome were also kept.

12. Subordinate deity or "god of the lesser tribes."

13. "The Egyptians worshipped a monkey, which animal is very fond of eating lice, styled here creatures that feed on human gore." (Swift)

14. Punning on the tailor's yardstick and needle as the nautical spar to hold sails and the compass needle.

15. Since the spheres of the planets and stars were seen as concentric, each might be said to be "dressed" (i.e. "invested") with the next outer one; the *primum mobile* was the outermost sphere, beyond which was the empyrean or seat of God (cf. Dryden's "Anne Killigrew" and "St. Cecilia" odes).

16. Watered silk, taffeta.

ticular works of the creation, you will find how curious[17] Journeyman Nature hath been to trim up the vegetable[18] beaux; observe how sparkish a periwig[19] adorns the head of a beech and what a fine doublet of white satin is worn by the birch. To conclude from all, what is man himself but a micro-coat,[20] or rather a complete suit of clothes with all its trimmings? As to his body, there can be no dispute; but examine even the acquirements of his mind, you will find them all contribute in their order towards furnishing out an exact dress. To instance no more: is not religion a cloak; honesty a pair of shoes worn out in the dirt; self-love a surtout;[21] vanity a shirt; and conscience a pair of breeches, which, though a cover for lewdness as well as nastiness, is easily slipped down for the service of both?

These *postulata*[22] being admitted, it will follow in due course of reasoning that those beings which the world calls improperly suits of clothes are in reality the most refined species of animals; or to proceed higher, that they are rational creatures or men. For is it not manifest that they live, and move, and talk, and perform all other offices of human life? Are not beauty, and wit, and mien, and breeding their inseparable proprieties?[23] In short, we see nothing but them, hear nothing but them. Is it not they who walk the streets, fill up parliament-, coffee-, play-, bawdy-houses? 'Tis true, indeed, that these animals, which are vulgarly called suits of clothes, or dresses, do, according to certain compositions, receive different appellations. If one of them be trimmed up with a gold chain and a red gown and a white rod and a great horse, it is called a Lord-Mayor; if certain ermines and furs be placed in a certain position, we style them a Judge; and so an apt conjunction of lawn[24] and black satin we entitle a Bishop.

Others of these professors, though agreeing in the main system, were yet more refined upon certain branches of it; and held that man was an animal compounded of two dresses, the natural and the celestial suit, which were the body and the soul: that the soul was the outward, and the body the inward clothing; that the latter was *ex traduce;*[25] but the former of daily creation and circumfusion. This last they proved by Scripture, because *in them we live, and move, and have our being;*[26] as likewise by philosophy, because they are *all in all, and all in every part.*[27] Besides, said they, separate these two, and you

17. Careful.
18. Vegetative.
19. A wig large and fashionable enough for a young fop (Swift writes of a "shrivelled beau . . . within the penthouse of a modern periwig" in *The Battle of the Books*).
20. "Alluding to the word *microcosm,* or a little world, as man hath been called by the philosophers." (Swift)
21. Loose overcoat or outer garment.
22. Assumptions, conditions (of an argument).
23. Standards.
24. Fine linen.
25. Transmitted at birth (cf. Dryden, "Anne Killigrew" ode, l. 23).
26. "In Him we live, and move, and have our being." (Acts 17:28)
27. Sir John Davies, *Nosce Teipsum* (1599), in using this phrase to describe the soul, follows Aristotelian theory. This dazzling reversal of inside and outside makes the soul (reduced to social manners and professional roles) the dress of the body and a welcome cover for its ugliness. The soul, in its traditional sense as the intellectual and moral power that resides within the body and controls it, simply disappears; for this world gives all its attention to worldly attainments or dress, and ceases, in a sense, to have a spiritual life.

will find the body to be only a senseless unsavoury carcass. By all which it is manifest that the outward dress must needs be the soul.

To this system of religion were tagged several subaltern doctrines which were entertained with great vogue; as particularly, the faculties of the mind were deduced by the learned among them in this manner: embroidery was sheer wit; [28] gold fringe was agreeable conversation; gold lace was repartee; a huge long periwig was humour; [29] and a coat full of powder was very good raillery: [30] all which required abundance of *finesse* and *delicatesse* to manage with advantage as well as a strict observance after times and fashions.[31]

I have, with much pains and reading, collected out of ancient authors, this short summary of a body of philosophy and divinity which seems to have been composed by a vein and race of thinking very different from any other systems, either ancient or modern. And it was not merely to entertain or satisfy the reader's curiosity but rather to give him light into several circumstances of the following story; that knowing the state of dispositions and opinions in an age so remote, he may better comprehend those great events which were the issue of them. I advise therefore the courteous reader to peruse with a world of application, again and again, whatever I have written upon this matter. And leaving these broken ends, I carefully gather up the chief thread of my story and proceed.

These opinions, therefore, were so universal, as well as the practices of them, among the refined part of court and town, that our three brother-adventurers, as their circumstances then stood, were strangely at a loss. For, on the one side, the three ladies they addressed themselves to (whom we have named already) were ever at the very top of the fashion and abhorred all that were below it but the breadth of a hair. On the other side, their father's will was very precise, and it was the main precept in it, with the greatest penalties annexed, not to add to, or diminish from, their coats one thread without a positive command in the will. Now, the coats their father had left them were, 'tis true, of very good cloth, and, besides, so neatly sewn, you would swear they were all of a piece; [32] but, at the same time, very plain, and with little or no ornament: and it happened that before they were a month in town, great shoulder-knots [33] came up. Straight all the world was shoulder-knots; no approaching the ladies' *ruelles* [34] without the quota of shoulder-knots. That fellow, cries one, has no soul; where is his shoulder-knot? Our three brethren soon discovered their want by sad experience, meeting in their walks with forty

28. Perhaps derived from "sheer" in the sense of "very fine" or "diaphanous" as applied to fabrics; probably implying mere verbal play without real point.

29. Probably implying mere whim or caprice.

30. Banter, good-humored teasing.

31. "Nothing is so very tender as a modern piece of wit, and which is apt to suffer so much in the carriage. Some things are extremely witty *today* or *fasting* or *in this place* or at *eight o'clock* . . . any of which, by the smallest transposal or misapplication, is utterly annihilate. . . . Such a jest there is that will not pass out of Covent Garden; and such a one that is nowhere intelligible but at Hyde Park Corner." (Preface, *A Tale of a Tub*)

32. Alluding to Christ's robe, often taken as a symbol of the Christian religion: "now the coat was without seam, woven from the top throughout" (John 19:23).

33. Knots of ribbon or lace, introduced from France about 1670; "By this is understood the first introducing of pageantry and unnecessary ornaments in the church." (Swift)

34. Bedrooms used as salons for morning receptions.

mortifications and indignities. If they went to the play-house, the doorkeeper showed them into the twelve-penny gallery. If they called a boat, says a waterman, 'I am first sculler.'[35] If they stepped to the Rose to take a bottle, the drawer would cry, 'Friend, we sell no ale.' If they went to visit a lady, a footman met them at the door with, 'Pray send up your message.' In this unhappy case, they went immediately to consult their father's will, read it over and over, but not a word of the shoulder-knot. What should they do? What temper should they find? Obedience was absolutely necessary, and yet shoulder-knots appeared extremely requisite. After much thought, one of the brothers, who happened to be more book-learned than the other two, said, he had found an expedient. ' 'Tis true,' said he, 'there is nothing here in this will, *totidem verbis*, making mention of shoulder-knots: but I dare conjecture we may find them *inclusivè*, or *totidem syllabis*.'[36] This distinction was immediately approved by all; and so they fell again to examine the will. But their evil star had so directed the matter that the first syllable was not to be found in the whole writing. Upon which disappointment he who found the former evasion took heart and said, 'Brothers, there is yet hopes; for though we cannot find them *totidem verbis*, nor *totidem syllabis*, I dare engage we shall make them out, *tertio modo*, or *totidem literis*.'[37] This discovery was also highly commended, upon which they fell once more to the scrutiny and picked out S,H,O,U,L,D,E,R; when the same planet,[38] enemy to their repose, had wonderfully contrived that a K was not to be found. Here was a weighty difficulty! But the distinguishing brother (for whom we shall hereafter find a name) now his hand was in, proved by a very good argument, that K was a modern illegitimate letter unknown to the learned ages, nor anywhere to be found in ancient manuscripts. 'Tis true, said he, the word *Calendæ* hath in Q.V.C.[39] been sometimes writ with a K, but erroneously; for in the best copies it has been ever spelt with a C. And by consequence it was a gross mistake in our language to spell Knot with a K; but that from henceforward he would take care it should be writ with a C. Upon this all farther difficulty vanished; shoulder-knots were made clearly out to be *jure paterno*:[40] and our three gentlemen swaggered with as large and as flaunting ones as the best.

But as human happiness is of a very short duration, so in those days were human fashions, upon which it entirely depends. Shoulder-knots had their time, and we must now imagine them in their decline; for a certain lord came just from Paris with fifty yards of gold lace upon his coat, exactly trimmed after the court fashion of that month. In two days all mankind appeared closed up in bars of gold lace: whoever durst peep abroad without his complement of gold lace was as scandalous as a ——, and as ill received among the women. What should our three knights do in this momentous affair? They had sufficiently strained a point already in the affair of shoulder-knots. Upon recourse to

35. That is, they are being offered the cheaper boat, a "sculler," rowed by one man rather than two; in the same way, they are offered cheap seats at the theater and ale instead of wine at the tavern, and are denied admission to the lady's salon.
36. That is, not in so many *words*, but included within them in so many *syllables*.
37. That is, by a third means, in so many *letters*.
38. That is, unfavorable destiny, the "evil star."
39. *Quibusdam veteribus codicibus* ("in some ancient manuscripts").
40. "According to paternal law," a parody of *jure divino*.

the will, nothing appeared there but *altum silentium.*[41] That of the shoulder-knots was a loose, flying, circumstantial point; but this of gold lace seemed too considerable an alteration without better warrant. It did *aliquo modo essentiæ adhærere,*[42] and therefore required a positive precept. But about this time it fell out that the learned brother aforesaid had read *Aristotelis Dialectica,*[43] and especially that wonderful piece *de Interpretatione,* which has the faculty of teaching its readers to find out a meaning in everything but itself, like commentators on the Revelations, who proceed prophets without understanding a syllable of the text. 'Brothers,' said he, 'you are to be informed that of wills *duo sunt genera,* nuncupatory and scriptory;[44] that in the scriptory will here before us, there is no precept or mention about gold lace, *conceditur:*[45] but, *si idem affirmetur de nuncupatorio, negatur.*[46] For, brothers, if you remember, we heard a fellow say, when we were boys, that he heard my father's man say that he heard my father say that he would advise his sons to get gold lace on their coats as soon as ever they could procure money to buy it.' 'By G—! that is very true,' cries the other. 'I remember it perfectly well,' said the third. And so without more ado they got the largest gold lace in the parish and walked about as fine as lords. . . .

Next winter a player, hired for the purpose by the corporation of fringe-makers, acted his part in a new comedy all covered with silver fringe and, according to the laudable custom, gave rise to that fashion. Upon which the brothers, consulting their father's will, to their great astonishment found these words; '*Item,* I charge and command my said three sons to wear no sort of silver fringe upon or about their said coats,' etc., with a penalty, in case of disobedience, too long here to insert. However, after some pause, the brother so often mentioned for his erudition, who was well skilled in criticisms, had found in a certain author, which he said should be nameless, that the same word, which in the will is called fringe, does also signify a broom-stick, and doubtless ought to have the same interpretation in this paragraph. This another of the brothers disliked, because of that epithet *silver,* which could not, he humbly conceived, in propriety of speech, be reasonably applied to a broom-stick; but it was replied upon him, that this epithet was understood in a mythological and allegorical sense. However, he objected again, why their father should forbid them to wear a broom-stick on their coats, a caution that seemed unnatural and impertinent;[47] upon which he was taken up short, as one that spoke irreverently of a mystery, which doubtless was very useful and significant, but ought not to be over-curiously pried into or nicely[48] reasoned upon. And, in short, their father's authority being now considerably sunk, this expedient was allowed to serve as a lawful dispensation for wearing their full proportion of silver fringe.

41. "Profound silence."
42. "In some manner belong to the essence."
43. A Latin compendium of Aristotle's logical treatises.
44. "There are two sorts," by word of mouth and written.
45. "It may be granted."
46. "If the same be affirmed of the oral will, it is denied." "By this is meant *tradition,* allowed to have equal authority with Scripture, or rather greater." (Swift)
47. Irrelevant.
48. Delicately, closely.

A while after was revived an old fashion, long antiquated, of embroidery with Indian figures of men, women, and children.[49] Here they had no occasion to examine the will. They remembered but too well how their father had always abhorred this fashion; that he made several paragraphs on purpose, importing his utter detestation of it and bestowing his everlasting curse to his sons whenever they should wear it. For all this, in a few days they appeared higher in the fashion than anybody else in the town. But they solved the matter by saying that these figures were not at all the same with those that were formerly worn and were meant in the will. Besides, they did not wear them in the sense as forbidden by their father; but as they were a commendable custom and of great use to the public. That these rigorous clauses in the will did therefore require some allowance and a favourable interpretation, and ought to be understood *cum grano salis*.[50]

But fashions perpetually altering in that age, the scholastic brother grew weary of searching farther evasions and solving everlasting contradictions; resolved, therefore, at all hazards to comply with the modes of the world, they concerted matters together and agreed unanimously to lock up their father's will in a strong box [51] brought out of Greece or Italy (I have forgot which), and trouble themselves no farther to examine it, but only refer to its authority whenever they thought fit. In consequence whereof, a while after, it grew a general mode to wear an infinite number of points,[52] most of them tagged with silver: upon which, the scholar pronounced *ex cathedra*,[53] that points were absolutely *jure paterno*, as they might very well remember. 'Tis true, indeed, the fashion prescribed somewhat more than were directly named in the will; however, that they, as heirs-general of their father, had power to make and add certain clauses for public emolument, though not deducible, *totidem verbis*, from the letter of the will, or else *multa absurda sequerentur*.[54] This was understood for canonical,[55] and therefore on the following Sunday they came to church all covered with points.

The learned brother, so often mentioned, was reckoned the best scholar in all that or the next street to it; insomuch as, having run something behind-hand [56] with the world, he obtained the favour from a certain lord,[57] to receive him into his house, and to teach his children. A while after the lord died, and he, by long practice upon his father's will, found the way of contriving a deed of conveyance of that house to himself and his heirs; upon which he took possession, turned the young squires out, and received his brothers in their stead.

49. "The images of saints, the Blessed Virgin, and our Savior an infant." (Swift)
50. "With a grain of salt."
51. That is, the forbidding of the use of Scripture in the vernacular, and requiring the Latin Vulgate translation or the original Greek of the New Testament.
52. Laces or ties with metal tips.
53. "From the (papal) throne."
54. "Many absurdities would follow."
55. According to church law.
56. In debt.
57. Referring to the Donation of Constantine, the alleged document by which the first Christian emperor, Constantine the Great, conferred all his rights, honors, and property as Emperor of the West on the Pope of Rome and his successors; a document "the Popes . . . have never been able to produce." (Swift)

Section IX

A Digression Concerning the Original, the Use, and Improvement of Madness, in a Commonwealth

Nor shall it any ways detract from the just reputation of this famous sect [1] that its rise and institution are owing to such an author as I have described Jack to be—a person whose intellectuals were overturned and his brain shaken out of its natural position; which we commonly suppose to be a distemper and call by the name of madness or frenzy. For if we take a survey of the greatest actions that have been performed in the world under the influence of single men, which are the establishment of new empires by conquest, the advance and progress of new schemes in philosophy, and the contriving, as well as the propagating, of new religions; we shall find the authors of them all to have been persons whose natural reason had admitted great revolutions from their diet, their education, the prevalency of some certain temper, together with the particular influence of air and climate. Besides, there is something individual in human minds that easily kindles at the accidental approach and collision of certain circumstances, which, though of paltry and mean appearance, do often flame out into the greatest emergencies of life. For great turns are not always given by strong hands but by lucky adaption and at proper seasons; and it is of no import where the fire was kindled if the vapour has once got up into the brain. For the upper region of man is furnished like the middle region of the air; the materials are formed from causes of the widest difference, yet produce at last the same substance and effect. Mists arise from the earth, steams from dunghills, exhalations from the sea, and smoke from fire; yet all clouds are the same in composition as well as consequences, and the fumes issuing from a jakes [2] will furnish as comely and useful a vapour as incense from an altar. Thus far, I suppose, will easily be granted me; and then it will follow, that, as the face of nature never produces rain but when it is overcast and disturbed, so human understanding, seated in the brain, must be troubled and overspread by vapours ascending from the lower faculties to water the invention [3] and render it fruitful. Now, although these vapours (as it hath been already said) are of as various original as those of the skies, yet the crop they produce differs both in kind and degree, merely according to the soil. I will produce two instances to prove and explain what I am now advancing.

A certain great prince [4] raised a mighty army, filled his coffers with infinite treasures, provided an invincible fleet, and all this without giving [5] the least

1. Aeolism, the worship of wind (named for the keeper of the winds in the *Odyssey* and the *Aeneid*), a system that rationalizes Jack's religious enthusiasm much as the clothes philosophy of Section II does Peter's manipulation of the words of the will.
2. Privy or cesspool.
3. The faculty for making discoveries; a term often applied in the age to poetic wit or imagination (cf. Dryden's Critical Prose, above).
4. Henry IV of France (1553–1610) was obsessed with a late passion for the young Princesse de Condé, who was taken by her husband (he was to have been only a convenient figurehead) to the Spanish Netherlands, out of Henry's reach. After a futile effort to abduct her, Henry (enraged and perhaps somewhat mad) began military preparations against the Spanish province, but he was stabbed to death before he could proceed.
5. Revealing.

part of his design to his greatest ministers or his nearest favourites. Immediately the whole world was alarmed; the neighbouring crowns in trembling expectation towards what point the storm would burst, the small politicians everywhere forming profound conjectures. Some believed he had laid a scheme for universal monarchy; others, after much insight, determined the matter to be a project for pulling down the Pope and setting up the reformed religion, which had once been his own. Some, again, of a deeper sagacity, sent him into Asia to subdue the Turk and recover Palestine. In the midst of all these projects and preparations, a certain state-surgeon, gathering the nature of the disease by these symptoms, attempted the cure, at one blow performed the operation, broke the bag, and out flew the vapour; nor did anything want to render it a complete remedy, only that the prince unfortunately happened to die in the performance. Now, is the reader exceeding curious to learn from whence this vapour took its rise which had so long set the nations at a gaze? What secret wheel, what hidden spring, could put into motion so wonderful an engine? It was afterwards discovered that the movement of this whole machine had been directed by an absent female, whose eyes had raised a protuberancy, and, before emission, she was removed into an enemy's country. What should an unhappy prince do in such ticklish circumstances as these? He tried in vain the poet's never-failing receipt of *corpora quæque;* for

> Idque petit corpus mens unde est saucia amore:
> Unde feritur, eo tendit, gestitque coire. (LUCRETIUS)[6]

Having to no purpose used all peaceable endeavours, the collected part of the semen, raised and inflamed, became adust, converted to choler, turned head upon the spinal duct[7] and ascended to the brain. The very same principle that influences a bully to break the windows of a whore who has jilted him naturally stirs up a great prince to raise mighty armies and dream of nothing but sieges, battles, and victories.

> ——Teterrima belli
> Causa.——[8]

The other instance is what I have read somewhere in a very ancient author of a mighty king who, for the space of above thirty years, amused himself to take and lose towns, beat armies and be beaten, drive princes out of their dominions; fright children from their bread and butter; burn, lay waste, plunder, dragoon, massacre subject and stranger, friend and foe, male and female. 'Tis recorded that the philosophers of each country were in grave dispute upon causes natural, moral, and political, to find out where they should assign an original solution of this phenomenon. At last the vapour or spirit which animated the hero's brain, being in perpetual circulation, seized upon that region

6. "Indulging one's lust at once with any persons at hand ["in corpore quaeque" IV.1065] so as not to allow unendurable desire to develop"; the following lines describe "that body through which the mind is wounded by love" (IV.1048) and how "each strains towards the one from whom the blow has come and struggles to unite" (IV.1055).

7. That is, became burned or parched, turned to bile (the source of anger or rage), invaded the spinal duct.

8. "For a whore had been, before Helen, a terrible cause of war." Horace, *Satires* I.iii.107.

of the human body so renowned for furnishing the *zibeta occidentalis*,[9] and, gathering there into a tumour, left the rest of the world for that time in peace. Of such mighty consequence it is where those exhalations fix and of so little from whence they proceed. The same spirits, which, in their superior progress, would conquer a kingdom, descending upon the anus, conclude in a fistula.[10]

Let us next examine the great introducers of new schemes in philosophy, and search till we can find from what faculty of the soul the disposition arises in mortal man of taking it into his head to advance new systems with such an eager zeal, in things agreed on all hands impossible to be known; from what seeds this disposition springs, and to what quality of human nature these grand innovators have been indebted for their number of disciples. Because it is plain that several of the chief among them, both ancient and modern, were usually mistaken by their adversaries, and indeed by all except their own followers, to have been persons crazed or out of their wits; having generally proceeded, in the common course of their words and actions by a method very different from the vulgar dictates of unrefined reason; agreeing for the most part in their several models with their present undoubted successors in the academy of modern Bedlam [11] (whose merits and principles I shall farther examine in due place). Of this kind were *Epicurus, Diogenes, Apollonius, Lucretius, Paracelsus, Descartes*,[12] and others, who, if they were now in the world, tied fast, and separate from their followers, would, in this our undistinguishing age, incur manifest danger of phlebotomy and whips and chains and dark chambers and straw. For what man in the natural state or course of thinking did ever conceive it in his power to reduce the notions of all mankind exactly to the same length and breadth and height of his own? Yet this is the first humble and civil design of all innovators in the empire of reason. Epicurus modestly hoped that, one time or other, a certain fortuitous concourse of all men's opinions, after perpetual justlings, the sharp with the smooth, the light and the heavy, the round and the square, would, by certain clinamina,[13] unite in the notions of atoms and void, as these did in the originals of all things. Cartesius reckoned to

9. "Paracelsus, who was so famous for chemistry, tried an experiment upon human excrement to make perfume of it, which, when he had brought to perfection, he called *Ziberta Occidentalis*, or western-civet, the back parts of a man (according to his division . . .) being the west." (Swift)

10. A pipelike ulcer with a narrow opening.

11. The Hospital of St. Mary of Bethlehem, long a madhouse, regularly open to visitors and sightseers as a public show.

12. All these men were creators or defenders of systems. Epicurus (341?–270 B.C.), the Greek philosopher, and Lucretius (96?–55 B.C.), the Roman poet, were atomists, attributing all life to the "fortuitous concourse" of atoms. Diogenes (4th century B.C.), the Greek Cynic philosopher, defied conventional rules of conduct and lived in an earthenware tub to demonstrate the austere simplicity he preached. Apollonius of Tyana (*c.* 4th century B.C.) was a wandering Pythagorean philosopher and mystic and a precursor of the occult Hermetic philosophy. Paracelsus (1490?–1541) was an alchemist as well as a chemist, a neoplatonic visionary and mystic in his system of medicine. René Descartes (1596–1650), having separated mind from extended matter (except for their interaction through the pineal gland), erected a mechanical and mathematical system of the material universe.

13. The inherent "swerves" of the atoms, which led to their varying patterns of collision and rebound, thus forming bodies of greater or lesser density; here Epicurus' material explanation is ironically applied to the interaction of minds or opinions in order to account for proselytizing.

see, before he died, the sentiments of all philosophers like so many lesser stars in his romantic system, wrapped and drawn within his own vortex.[14] Now, I would gladly be informed, how it is possible to account for such imaginations as these in particular men without recourse to my phenomenon of vapours ascending from the lower faculties to overshadow the brain, and there distilling into conceptions for which the narrowness of our mother-tongue has not yet assigned any other name besides that of madness or frenzy.

Let us therefore now conjecture how it comes to pass that none of these great prescribers do ever fail providing themselves and their notions with a number of implicit disciples. And, I think, the reason is easy to be assigned: for there is a peculiar string in the harmony of human understanding which, in several individuals, is exactly of the same tuning. This, if you can dexterously screw up to its right key and then strike gently upon it, whenever you have the good fortune to light among those of the same pitch, they will, by a secret necessary sympathy, strike exactly at the same time. And in this one circumstance lies all the skill or luck of the matter; for, if you chance to jar the string among those who are either above or below your own height, instead of subscribing to your doctrine, they will tie you fast, call you mad, and feed you with bread and water.

It is therefore a point of the nicest [15] conduct to distinguish and adapt this noble talent with respect to the differences of persons and of times. Cicero understood this very well, when writing to a friend in England, with a caution, among other matters, to beware of being cheated by our hackney-coachmen (who, it seems, in those days were as arrant [16] rascals as they are now), has these remarkable words: *Est quod gaudeas te in ista loca venisse, ubi aliquid sapere viderere.*[17] For, to speak a bold truth, it is a fatal miscarriage so ill to order affairs, as to pass for a fool in one company when in another you might be treated as a philosopher. Which I desire some certain gentlemen of my acquaintance to lay up in their hearts as a very seasonable *innuendo.*

This, indeed, was the fatal mistake of that worthy gentleman, my most ingenious friend, Mr. W-tt-n: [18] a person, in appearance, ordained for great designs as well as performances; whether you will consider his notions or his looks. Surely no man ever advanced into the public with fitter qualifications of body and mind for the propagation of a new religion. Oh, had those happy talents, misapplied to vain philosophy, been turned into their proper channels of dreams and visions, where distortion of mind and countenance are of such sovereign use, the base detracting world would not then have dared to report that something is amiss, that his brain hath undergone an unlucky shake; which

14. The *tourbillon* or whirlpool of material particles, creating a circular motion that is communicated from one body to another; it was applied to the heavenly bodies, as when one star is drawn into the stronger vortex of another's motion.

15. Subtlest.

16. Thorough.

17. "There is reason to rejoice that you have come to those places where you pass as a man of legal ability." Cicero, *Letters to Friends* VII.10 (to Trebatius). In VII.6 Cicero warns that Trebatius must look out in Britain that he is not cheated by the charioteers.

18. William Wotton had joined Bentley in the attack upon Temple; a clergyman, he also wrote what he intended as a damning explanation of Swift's meaning in *A Tale of a Tub*, but Swift used Wotton's remarks as explanatory notes in his 1710 edition.

even his brother modernists themselves, like ungrates, do whisper so loud, it reaches up to the very garret I am now writing in.

Lastly, whosoever pleases to look into the fountains of enthusiasm, from whence, in all ages, have eternally proceeded such fattening[19] streams, will find the spring-head to have been as troubled and muddy as the current. Of such great emolument is a tincture of this vapour which the world calls madness, that without its help, the world would not only be deprived of those two great blessings, conquests and systems, but even all mankind would unhappily be reduced to the same belief in things invisible. Now, the former *postulatum* being held, that it is of no import from what originals this vapour proceeds, but either in what angles it strikes and spreads over the understanding or upon what species of brain it ascends; it will be a very delicate point to cut the feather and divide the several reasons[20] to a nice and curious reader how this numerical difference in the brain can produce effects of so vast a difference from the same vapour, as to be the sole point of individuation between Alexander the Great, Jack of Leyden,[21] and Monsieur Des Cartes. The present argument is the most abstracted that ever I engaged in; it strains my faculties to their highest stretch; and I desire the reader to attend with utmost perpensity for I now proceed to unravel this knotty point.

There is in mankind a certain . . . .
. . . .
Hic multa . . . .
desiderantur.[22] . . . .
. . . . . . And this I take to be a clear solution of the matter.

Having therefore so narrowly passed through this intricate difficulty, the reader will, I am sure, agree with me in the conclusion that if the moderns mean by madness only a disturbance or transposition of the brain, by force of certain vapours issuing up from the lower faculties, then has this madness been the parent of all those mighty revolutions that have happened in empire, in philosophy, and in religion. For the brain, in its natural position and state of serenity, disposeth its owner to pass his life in the common forms, without any thought of subduing multitudes to his own power, his reasons, or his visions; and the more he shapes his understanding by the pattern of human learning, the less he is inclined to form parties after his particular notions, because that instructs him in his private infirmities as well as in the stubborn ignorance of the people.

But when a man's fancy gets astride of his reason, when imagination is at cuffs with the senses, and common understanding as well as common sense is kicked out of doors; the first proselyte he makes is himself; and when that is once compassed, the difficulty is not so great in bringing over others; a

19. Nourishing.
20. That is, to split hairs or make subtle distinctions.
21. John of Leyden (1509–36), here forming a bridge between military conquest and intellectual system, was a Dutch Anabaptist who founded a short-lived communistic and polygamous "Kingdom of Zion" in the German city of Münster.
22. "Here many things are lacking," a conventional phrase in the editing of a damaged manuscript, a technique Swift parodies throughout the *Tale* and uses, as here, to create an effect of anticlimax.

strong delusion always operating from without as vigorously as from within. For cant and vision are to the ear and the eye the same that tickling is to the touch. Those entertainments and pleasures we most value in life are such as dupe and play the wag with the senses. For, if we take an examination of what is generally understood by happiness as it has respect either to the understanding or the senses, we shall find all its properties and adjuncts [23] will herd under this short definition, that it is a perpetual possession of being well deceived.

And, first, with relation to the mind or understanding, 'tis manifest what mighty advantages fiction has over truth; and the reason is just at our elbow, because imagination can build nobler scenes and produce more wonderful revolutions than fortune or nature will be at expense to furnish. Nor is mankind so much to blame in his choice thus determining him, if we consider that the debate merely lies between things past and things conceived; and so the question is only this:—whether things that have place in the imagination may not as properly be said to exist as those that are seated in the memory, which may be justly held in the affirmative, and very much to the advantage of the former, since this is acknowledged to be the womb of things and the other allowed to be no more than the grave.

Again, if we take this definition of happiness and examine it with reference to the senses, it will be acknowledged wonderfully adapt. How fading and insipid do all objects accost us that are not conveyed in the vehicle of delusion! How shrunk is everything as it appears in the glass of nature! So that if it were not for the assistance of artificial mediums, false lights, refracted angles, varnish, and tinsel, there would be a mighty level in the felicity and enjoyments of mortal men. If this were seriously considered by the world, as I have a certain reason to suspect it hardly will, men would no longer reckon among their high points of wisdom the art of exposing weak sides and publishing infirmities; an employment, in my opinion, neither better nor worse than that of unmasking, which, I think, has never been allowed [24] fair usage, either in the world or the play-house.

In the proportion that credulity is a more peaceful possession of the mind than curiosity, so far preferable is that wisdom which converses about the surface to that pretended philosophy which enters into the depth of things and then comes gravely back with information and discoveries, that in the inside they are good for nothing. The two senses to which all objects first address themselves are the sight and the touch; these never examine farther than the colour, the shape, the size, and whatever other qualities dwell or are drawn by art upon the outward of bodies; and then comes reason officiously with tools for cutting, and opening, and mangling, and piercing, offering to demonstrate that they are not of the same consistence quite through.

Now I take all this to be the last degree of perverting nature; one of whose eternal laws it is to put her best furniture forward. And therefore, in order to save the charges of all such expensive anatomy for the time to come, I do here think fit to inform the reader, that in such conclusions as these, reason

23. Essential and nonessential characteristics.
24. Judged to be.

is certainly in the right, and that in most corporeal beings which have fallen under my cognizance the outside hath been infinitely preferable to the in; whereof I have been farther convinced from some late experiments.

Last week I saw a woman flayed, and you will hardly believe how much it altered her person for the worse. Yesterday I ordered the carcass of a beau to be stripped in my presence, when we were all amazed to find so many unsuspected faults under one suit of clothes. Then I laid open his brain, his heart, and his spleen; but I plainly perceived at every operation that the farther we proceeded, we found the defects increase upon us in number and bulk; from all which I justly formed this conclusion to myself: that whatever philosopher or projector can find out an art to sodder and patch up the flaws and imperfections of nature will deserve much better of mankind, and teach us a more useful science, than that so much in present esteem of widening and exposing them (like him who held anatomy to be the ultimate end of physic [25]). And he whose fortunes and dispositions have placed him in a convenient station to enjoy the fruits of this noble art; he that can, with Epicurus,[26] content his ideas with the films and images that fly off upon his senses from the superficies of things; such a man, truly wise, creams off nature, leaving the sour and the dregs for philosophy and reason to lap up. This is the sublime and refined point of felicity, called the possession of being well deceived; the serene peaceful state of being a fool among knaves.

But to return to madness. It is certain that, according to the system I have above deduced, every species thereof proceeds from a redundancy of vapours; therefore, as some kinds of frenzy give double strength to the sinews, so there are of other species, which add vigour and life and spirit to the brain. Now, it usually happens that these active spirits, getting possession of the brain, resemble those that haunt other waste and empty dwellings, which, for want of business, either vanish and carry away a piece of the house, or else stay at home and fling it all out of the windows. By which, are mystically displayed the two principal branches of madness, and which some philosophers, not considering so well as I, have mistaken to be different in their causes, over-hastily assigning the first to deficiency and the other to redundance.

I think it therefore manifest, from what I have here advanced, that the main point of skill and address is to furnish employment for this redundancy of vapour and prudently to adjust the season of it; by which means it may certainly become of cardinal and catholic emolument in a commonwealth. Thus one man, choosing a proper juncture, leaps into a gulf, from whence proceeds a hero, and is called the saver of his country; another achieves the same enterprise, but, unluckily timing it, has left the brand of madness fixed as a reproach upon his memory; upon so nice a distinction, are we taught to repeat the name of Curtius with reverence and love, that of Empedocles with hatred and contempt.[27] Thus also it is usually conceived that the elder

25. That is, reversing ends and means, making surgery the end for which therapy exists.

26. Who had a materialistic account of sense perception: the surfaces ("superficies") discharged fine films, which were replicas of the object and were able to penetrate the sense organs of the perceiver.

27. When a chasm suddenly opened in the Roman forum, with the prophecy that it would close only when the chief strength of Rome had been sacrificed, Marcus Curtius—

Brutus[28] only personated the fool and madman for the good of the public; but this was nothing else than a redundancy of the same vapour long misapplied, called by the Latins *ingenium par negotiis;*[29] or (to translate it as nearly as I can) a sort of frenzy, never in its right element, till you take it up in business of the state.

Upon all which, and many other reasons of equal weight though not equally curious, I do here gladly embrace an opportunity I have long sought for, of recommending it as a very noble undertaking to Sir Edward Seymour, Sir Christopher Musgrave, Sir John Bowls, John How, Esq., and other patriots[30] concerned, that they would move for leave to bring in a bill for appointing commissioners to inspect into Bedlam and the parts adjacent; who shall be empowered to send for persons, papers, and records, to examine into the merits and qualifications of every student and professor, to observe with utmost exactness their several dispositions and behaviour, by which means duly distinguishing and adapting their talents, they might produce admirable instruments for the several offices in a state, ———,[31] civil, and military, proceeding in such methods as I shall here humbly propose. And I hope the gentle reader will give some allowance to my great solicitudes in this important affair, upon account of the high esteem I have borne that honourable society, whereof I had some time the happiness to be an unworthy member.

Is any student tearing his straw in piece-meal, swearing and blaspheming, biting his grate, foaming at the mouth, and emptying his piss-pot in the spectators' faces? Let the right worshipful the commissioners of inspection give him a regiment of dragoons, and send him into Flanders among the rest. Is another eternally talking, sputtering, gaping, bawling, in a sound without period or article? What wonderful talents are here mislaid! Let him be furnished immediately with a green bag and papers, and threepence in his pocket, and away with him to Westminster Hall.[32] You will find a third gravely taking the dimensions of his kennel, a person of foresight and insight, though kept quite in the dark; for why, like Moses, *ecce cornuta erat ejus facies.*[33] He walks duly in one pace, entreats your penny with due gravity and ceremony, talks much of hard times, and taxes, and the whore of Babylon, bars up the wooden window of his cell constantly at eight o'clock, dreams of fire, and shoplifters, and court-customers, and privileged places. Now, what a figure would all these acquirements amount to, if the owner were sent into the City among his brethren![34]

---

interpreting the strength to be arms and valor—leaped in, armed and on horseback. According to some accounts, Empedocles (fl. 450), the philosopher and statesman of Sicily, threw himself into the crater of Mt. Etna so that the manner of his death might not be known and that he might later pass for a god, but the secret was revealed by Etna's rejecting one of his sandals (or casting it out in an eruption).

28. Lucius Junius Brutus, the nephew of the tyrannous Roman king Tarquin the Proud, assumed the guise of madness to avoid being killed by his uncle, as his brother had been.

29. "A head for business." Tacitus, *Annals* VI.39 and XVI.18.

30. Leading members of the House of Commons, one of them (Bowls) himself mad by 1701.

31. "Ecclesiastical" is omitted.

32. A lawyer's coach fare from the Inns of Court to the law courts at Westminster.

33. "Behold his face was shining." Vulgate text of Exodus 34:30.

34. That is, as a shopkeeper in the City, the commercial part of London.

Behold a fourth, in much and deep conversation with himself, biting his thumbs at proper junctures, his countenance checkered with business and design, sometimes walking very fast, with his eyes nailed to a paper that he holds in his hands; a great saver of time, somewhat thick of hearing, very short of sight, but more of memory; a man ever in haste, a great hatcher and breeder of business, and excellent at the famous art of whispering nothing; a huge idolater of monosyllables and procrastination, so ready to give his word to everybody that he never keeps it; one that has forgot the common meaning of words but an admirable retainer of the sound; extremely subject to the looseness,[35] for his occasions are perpetually calling him away. If you approach his grate in his familiar intervals: 'Sir,' says he, 'give me a penny, and I'll sing you a song; but give me the penny first.' (Hence comes the common saying, and commoner practice, of parting with money for a song.) What a complete system of court skill is here described in every branch of it, and all utterly lost with wrong application!

Accost the hole of another kennel, first stopping your nose; you will behold a surly, gloomy, nasty, slovenly mortal, raking in his own dung and dabbling in his urine. The best part of his diet is the reversion[36] of his own ordure, which, expiring into steams, whirls perpetually about, and at last re-infunds.[37] His complexion is of a dirty yellow, with a thin scattered beard, exactly agreeable to that of his diet upon its first declination, like other insects, who, having their birth and education in an excrement, from thence borrow their colour and their smell. The student of this apartment is very sparing of his words, but somewhat over-liberal of his breath. He holds his hand out ready to receive your penny, and immediately upon receipt withdraws to his former occupations. Now, is it not amazing to think, the society of Warwick-lane[38] should have no more concern for the recovery of so useful a member; who, if one may judge from these appearances, would become the greatest ornament to that illustrious body?

Another student struts up fiercely to your teeth, puffing with his lips, half squeezing out his eyes, and very graciously holds you out his hand to kiss. The keeper desires you not to be afraid of this professor, for he will do you no hurt; to him alone is allowed the liberty of the antechamber, and the orator of the place gives you to understand that this solemn person is a tailor run mad with pride. This considerable student is adorned with many other qualities, upon which, at present, I shall not farther enlarge . . . Hark in your ear . . . I am strangely mistaken, if all his address, his motions, and his airs, would not then be very natural, and in their proper element.[39]

I shall not descend so minutely, as to insist upon the vast number of beaux, fiddlers, poets, and politicians that the world might recover by such a reformation; but what is more material, besides the clear gain redounding to the commonwealth, by so large an acquisition of persons to employ whose talents

35. Diarrhea.
36. Return to its original state.
37. Pours in again.
38. The Royal College of Physicians.
39. "I cannot conjecture what the author means here, or how the chasm could be filled, though it is capable of more than one interpretation" (Swift).

and acquirements, if I may be so bold as to affirm it, are now buried or at least misapplied; it would be a mighty advantage accruing to the public from this inquiry that all these would very much excel and arrive at great perfection in their several kinds; which, I think, is manifest from what I have already shown and shall enforce by this one plain instance, that even I myself, the author of these momentous truths, am a person whose imaginations are hard-mouthed [40] and exceedingly disposed to run away with his reason, which I have observed from long experience to be a very light rider and easily shook off; upon which account my friends will never trust me alone without a solemn promise to vent my speculations in this or the like manner, for the universal benefit of human kind; which perhaps the gentle, courteous, and candid reader, brimful of that modern charity and tenderness usually annexed to his office, will be very hardly persuaded to believe.

1697–1704? 1704

An Argument Against Abolishing Christianity in England

The Test Act of 1673 excluded from public office those who refused the sacrament of the Church of England, but dissenters held office by taking the Anglican sacrament only once. To prevent this evasion, Tories in Commons had three times introduced a Bill for Preventing Occasional Conformity, which was defeated in each case by the Whig lords. There were, in fact, strong Whig efforts to repeal the Test Act both in Ireland and in England. Swift saw this as a real threat to the established church, for an opening of power to an alliance of Whigs and dissenters could lead to disestablishment in time. The *Argument* is presented as the cool proposal of a man who takes for granted that only "nominal" Christianity can any longer survive and argues that it does not threaten, but can even serve, "schemes of wealth and power"—presumably the only ones his public takes seriously. This dismissal of discussion of real Christianity builds up tremendous pressure, as what are taken for granted as the only acceptable terms of discussion become more and more shabbily expedient, more grossly a matter of a power calculus and of cash accounting.

An Argument

To Prove That the Abolishing of Christianity in England May, as Things Now Stand, Be Attended with Some Inconveniencies, and Perhaps, Not Produce Those Many Good Effects Proposed Thereby

I am very sensible what a weakness and presumption it is to reason against the general humour and disposition of the world. I remember it was with great justice, and a due regard to the freedom both of the public and the press, forbidden upon severe penalties to write, or discourse, or lay wagers against the Union [1] even before it was confirmed by Parliament, because that

40. Not easily controlled by bit or rein.

1. The Act of Union between England and Scotland (1707) uniting their two parliaments, opposed by Swift for its possible threat to the Sacramental Test, but also strongly opposed by the Jacobite supporters of the exiled Stuarts.

was looked upon as a design to oppose the current of the people, which besides the folly of it, is a manifest breach of the fundamental law that makes this majority of opinion the voice of God.[2] In like manner, and for the very same reasons, it may perhaps be neither safe nor prudent to argue against the abolishing of Christianity: at a juncture when all parties seem so unanimously determined upon the point, as we cannot but allow from their actions, their discourses, and their writings. However, I know not how, whether from the affectation of singularity or the perverseness of human nature, but so it unhappily falls out that I cannot be entirely of this opinion. Nay, although I were sure an order were issued out for my immediate prosecution by the Attorney-General, I should still confess that in the present posture of our affairs at home or abroad, I do not yet see the absolute necessity of extirpating the Christian religion from among us.

This perhaps may appear too great a paradox even for our wise and parodoxical age to endure; therefore I shall handle it with all tenderness, and with the utmost deference to that great and profound majority which is of another sentiment.

And yet the curious may please to observe, how much the genius of a nation is liable to alter in half an age. I have heard it affirmed for certain by some very old people that the contrary opinion was even in their memories as much in vogue as the other is now. And that a project for the abolishing of Christianity would then have appeared as singular, and been thought as absurd, as it would be at this time to write or discourse in its defence.

Therefore I freely own that all appearances are against me. The system of the gospel, after the fate of other systems, is generally antiquated and exploded; and the mass or body of the common people, among whom it seems to have had its latest credit, are now grown as much ashamed of it as their betters; opinions, like fashions, always descending from those of quality to the middle sort, and thence to the vulgar, where at length they are dropped and vanish.

But here I would not be mistaken, and must therefore be so bold as to borrow a distinction from the writers on the other side, when they make a difference between nominal and real Trinitarians. I hope no reader imagines me so weak to stand up in the defence of real Christianity, such as used, in primitive times (if we may believe the authors of those ages), to have an influence upon men's belief and actions: to offer at the restoring of that would indeed be a wild project; it would be to dig up foundations; to destroy, at one blow, all the wit, and half the learning, of the kingdom; to break the entire frame and constitution of things; to ruin trade, extinguish arts and sciences, with the professors of them; in short, to turn our courts, exchanges, and shops, into deserts; and would be full as absurd as the proposal of Horace,[3] where he advises the Romans, all in a body, to leave their city and seek a new seat in some remote part of the world, by way of cure for the corruption of their manners.

Therefore I think this caution was in itself altogether unnecessary (which I

2. Cf. Preface to *A Tale of a Tub*: "I am so entirely satisfied with the whole present procedure of human things that I have been for some years preparing materials towards *A Panegyric upon the World,* to which I intended to add a second part entitled *A Modest Defense of the Proceedings of the Rabble in All Ages.*"

3. In *Epode* XVI.

have inserted only to prevent all possibility of cavilling) since every candid reader will easily understand my discourse to be intended only in defence of nominal Christianity; the other having been for some time wholly laid aside by general consent as utterly inconsistent with our present schemes of wealth and power.

But why we should therefore cast off the name and title of Christians, although the general opinion and resolution be so violent for it, I confess I cannot (with submission) apprehend the consequence necessary. However, since the undertakers propose such wonderful advantages to the nation by this project and advance many plausible objections against the system of Christianity, I shall briefly consider the strength of both, fairly allow them their greatest weight, and offer such answers as I think most reasonable. After which I will beg leave to show what inconveniencies may possibly happen by such an innovation in the present posture of our affairs.

First, one great advantage proposed by the abolishing of Christianity is that it would very much enlarge and establish liberty of conscience, that great bulwark of our nation and of the Protestant religion; which is still too much limited by priestcraft, notwithstanding all the good intentions of the legislature, as we have lately found by a severe instance. For it is confidently reported that two young gentlemen of great hopes, bright wit, and profound judgment, who, upon a thorough examination of causes and effects, and by the mere force of natural abilities, without the least tincture of learning, having made a discovery that there was no God, and generously communicating their thoughts for the good of the public, were some time ago, by an unparalleled severity, and upon I know not what obsolete law, broke [4] for blasphemy. And as it has been wisely observed, if persecution once begins, no man alive knows how far it may reach, or where it will end.

In answer to all which, with deference to wiser judgments, I think this rather shows the necessity of a nominal religion among us. Great wits love to be free with the highest objects; and if they cannot be allowed a God to revile or renounce, they will speak evil of dignities, abuse the government, and reflect upon the Ministry; which I am sure few will deny to be of much more pernicious consequence, according to the saying of Tiberius, *deorum offensa diis curæ.*[5] As to the particular fact related, I think it is not fair to argue from one instance; perhaps another cannot be produced: yet (to the comfort of all those who may be apprehensive of persecution) blasphemy, we know, is freely spoke a million of times in every coffeehouse and tavern, or wherever else good company meet. It must be allowed, indeed, that to break an English freeborn officer only for blasphemy was, to speak the gentlest of such an action, a very high strain of absolute power. Little can be said in excuse for the general; perhaps he was afraid it might give offence to the allies,[6] among whom, for aught we know, it may be the custom of the country to believe a God. But if he argued, as some have done, upon a mistaken principle that an officer

4. Ruined.
5. Tacitus, *Annals* I.73, which reads *injurias* instead of *offensa;* when the emperor Tiberius was told that a witness had injured the divinity of Augustus by swearing a false oath in his name, the reply was, "It is for the gods to punish their own wrongs."
6. Holland, Austria, Savoy, Portugal, and many German states (in the War of the Spanish Succession, against France).

who is guilty of speaking blasphemy may some time or other proceed so far as to raise a mutiny, the consequence is by no means to be admitted; for surely the commander of an English army is likely to be but ill obeyed, whose soldiers fear and reverence him as little as they do a Deity.

It is further objected against the gospel system that it obliges men to the belief of things too difficult for freethinkers, and such who have shaken off the prejudices that usually cling to a confined education. To which I answer, that men should be cautious how they raise objections which reflect upon the wisdom of the nation. Is not everybody freely allowed to believe whatever he pleases and to publish his belief to the world whenever he thinks fit, especially if it serves to strengthen the party which is in the right? Would any indifferent foreigner who should read the trumpery lately written by Asgil, Tindal, Toland, Coward,[7] and forty more, imagine the gospel to be our rule of faith and confirmed by parliaments? Does any man either believe, or say he believes, or desire to have it thought that he says he believes, one syllable of the matter? And is any man worse received upon that score, or does he find his want of nominal faith a disadvantage to him in the pursuit of any civil or military employment? What if there be an old dormant statute or two against him, are they not now obsolete to a degree that Empson and Dudley[8] themselves, if they were now alive, would find it impossible to put them in execution?

It is likewise urged that there are, by computation, in this kingdom, above ten thousand parsons, whose revenues added to those of my lords the Bishops, would suffice to maintain at least two hundred young gentlemen of wit and pleasure and freethinking, enemies to priestcraft, narrow principles, pedantry, and prejudices; who might be an ornament to the court and town: and then again, so great a number of able [-bodied] divines might be a recruit to our fleet and armies. This indeed appears to be a consideration of some weight: but then, on the other side, several things deserve to be considered likewise: as first, whether it may not be thought necessary, that in certain tracts of country, like what we call parishes, there shall be one man at least of abilities to read and write. Then it seems a wrong computation that the revenues of the Church throughout this island, would be large enough to maintain two hundred young gentlemen, or even half that number, after the present refined way of living; that is, to allow each of them such a rent as, in the modern form of speech, would make them easy. But still there is in this project a greater mischief behind; and we ought to beware of the woman's folly who killed the hen that every morning laid her a golden egg. For, pray what would become of the race of men in the next age if we had nothing to trust to beside the scrofulous, consumptive productions furnished by our men of wit and pleasure, when,

7. John Asgil (1659–1738), an Irish lawyer, published in 1699 a work showing that man might achieve eternal life without undergoing death, a doctrine which he based on the Gospels but which caused his expulsion from Parliament. Matthew Tindal (1657–1733), earlier a Roman Catholic, later an Anglican, was the author of the extremely anticlerical *The Rights of the Christian Church Asserted*, a book burnt by order of Commons. James Junius Toland (1670–1722) carried Locke's views further toward Deism in *Christianity Not Mysterious*. William Coward (1657–1725) was a physician who held that the soul died with the body.

8. Richard Empson and Edmund Dudley were agents of Henry VII who revived obsolete statutes in order to raise new revenues.

having squandered away their vigour, health, and estates, they are forced, by some disagreeable marriage, to piece up their broken fortunes and entail[9] rottenness and politeness on their posterity? Now, here are ten thousand persons reduced, by the wise regulations of Henry the Eighth,[10] to the necessity of a low diet, and moderate exercise, who are the only great restorers of our breed, without which the nation would, in an age or two, become but one great hospital.

Another advantage proposed by the abolishing of Christianity is the clear gain of one day in seven, which is now entirely lost, and consequently the kingdom one seventh less considerable in trade, business, and pleasure; beside the loss to the public of so many stately structures, now in the hands of the clergy, which might be converted into play-houses, exchanges, market-houses, common dormitories, and other public edifices.

I hope I shall be forgiven a hard word, if I call this a perfect cavil. I readily own there has been an old custom, time out of mind, for people to assemble in the churches every Sunday, and that shops are still frequently shut in order, as it is conceived, to preserve the memory of that ancient practice; but how this can prove a hindrance to business or pleasure is hard to imagine. What if the men of pleasure are forced, one day in the week, to game at home instead of the chocolatehouse? Are not the taverns and coffeehouses open? Can there be a more convenient season for taking a dose of physic?[11] Are fewer claps[12] got upon Sundays than other days? Is not that the chief day for traders to sum up the accounts of the week, and for lawyers to prepare their briefs? But I would fain know, how it can be pretended that the churches are misapplied? Where are more appointments and rendezvouses of gallantry? Where more care to appear in the foremost box, with greater advantage of dress? Where more meetings for business? Where more bargains driven of all sorts? And where so many conveniences or enticements to sleep?

There is one advantage greater than any of the foregoing proposed by the abolishing of Christianity; that it will utterly extinguish parties among us, by removing those factious distinctions of High and Low Church, of Whig and Tory, Presbyterian and Church of England, which are now so many grievous clogs upon public proceedings, and are apt to dispose men to prefer the gratifying themselves, or depressing their adversaries, before the most important interest of the state.

I confess, if it were certain that so great an advantage would redound to the nation by this expedient, I would submit and be silent; but will any man say, that if the words *whoring, drinking, cheating, lying, stealing,* were, by act of Parliament, ejected out of the English tongue and dictionaries, we should all awake next morning chaste and temperate, honest and just, and lovers of truth? Is this a fair consequence? Or, if the physicians would forbid us to pronounce the words *pox, gout, rheumatism,* and *stone,* would that expedient serve, like so many talismans, to destroy the diseases themselves? Are party and faction rooted in men's hearts no deeper than phrases borrowed from religion, or founded upon no firmer principles? And is our language so poor

9. Impose through inheritance.

10. In plundering the monasteries and exacting from them payments to the crown; Swift loathed Henry VIII.

11. Medicine.

12. Gonorrhea.

that we cannot find other terms to express them? Are *envy, pride, avarice,* and *ambition* such ill nomenclators, that they cannot furnish appellations for their owners? Will not *heydukes* and *mamalukes, mandarins,* and *potshaws,*[13] or any other words formed at pleasure, serve to distinguish those who are in the Ministry from others who would be in it if they could? What, for instance, is easier than to vary the form of speech, and instead of the word *Church,* make it a question in politics, whether the *Monument* be in danger? [14] Because religion was nearest at hand to furnish a few convenient phrases, is our invention so barren we can find no other? Suppose, for argument sake, that the Tories favoured Margarita, the Whigs Mrs. Tofts,[15] and the Trimmers [16] Valentini; would not *Margaritians, Toftians,* and *Valentinians* be very tolerable marks of distinction? The *Prasini* and *Veniti,* two most virulent factions in Italy,[17] began (if I remember right) by a distinction of colours in ribbons; which we might do with as good a grace about the dignity of the blue and the green, and would serve as properly to divide the court, the Parliament, and the kingdom, between them, as any terms of art [18] whatsoever borrowed from religion. Therefore, I think, there is little force in this objection against Christianity, or prospect of so great an advantage as is proposed in the abolishing of it.

It is again objected, as a very absurd, ridiculous custom, that a set of men should be suffered, much less employed and hired, to bawl one day in seven against the lawfulness of those methods most in use towards the pursuit of greatness, riches, and pleasure, which are the constant practice of all men alive on the other six. But this objection is, I think, a little unworthy so refined an age as ours. Let us argue this matter calmly: I appeal to the breast of any polite freethinker whether, in the pursuit of gratifying a predominant passion, he hath not always felt a wonderful incitement by reflecting it was a thing forbidden: and, therefore, we see, in order to cultivate this taste, the wisdom of the nation hath taken special care that the ladies should be furnished with prohibited silks, and the men with prohibited wine.[19] And, indeed, it were to be wished that some other prohibitions were promoted in order to improve the pleasures of the town; which, for want of such expedients, begin already, as I am told, to flag and grow languid, giving way daily to cruel inroads from the spleen.[20]

13. Used as nonsense words, but in fact with meanings; respectively, Hungarian foot-soldiers or Polish attendants on noblemen (originally robbers or brigands and properly *hajduka*); ruling military class in Egypt; Chinese officials; Persian emperor or sultan, perhaps confused with Turkish pashas or officers.

14. The Monument, built by Sir Christopher Wren in 1666 as a memorial of the Great Fire of London, carried an inscription blaming the Catholics for the fire.

15. Margaritá and Valentini were rival Italian opera singers, and Mrs. Catherine Tofts an English competitor who sang Italian opera.

16. In English history, statesmen favoring moderation and compromise.

17. The Greens and Blues, rival factions in Roman chariot races, whose enmity was carried over to Constantinople, where it caused civil war in the reign of Justinian; also alluding to the blue ribbon of the English Order of the Garter and the green of the Scottish Order of the Thistle.

18. Technical terms, often used divisively by sectarians.

19. Prohibited by the war with France but often smuggled.

20. A melancholy affliction, ironically regarded by many as an affectation, but vaguely attributed to the mysterious secretions of the spleen.

It is likewise proposed as a great advantage to the public that if we once discard the system of the gospel, all religion will of course be banished for ever; and consequently, along with it, those grievous prejudices of education, which, under the names of *virtue, conscience, honour, justice,* and the like, are so apt to disturb the peace of human minds, and the notions whereof are so hard to be eradicated by right reason or freethinking, sometimes during the whole course of our lives.

Here first I observe how difficult it is to get rid of a phrase which the world is once grown fond of, though the occasion that first produced it be entirely taken away. For several years past, if a man had but an ill-favoured nose, the deep-thinkers of the age would, some way or other, contrive to impute the cause to the prejudice of his education. From this fountain were said to be derived all our foolish notions of justice, piety, love of our country; all our opinions of God or a future state, heaven, hell, and the like: and there might formerly perhaps have been some pretence for this charge. But so effectual care has been since taken to remove those prejudices by an entire change in the methods of education, that (with honour I mention it to our polite innovators) the young gentlemen who are now on the scene seem to have not the least tincture left of those infusions or string [21] of those weeds: and, by consequence, the reason for abolishing nominal Christianity upon that pretext is wholly ceased.

For the rest, it may perhaps admit a controversy whether the banishing all notions of religion whatsoever would be convenient for the vulgar.[22] Not that I am in the least of opinion with those who hold religion to have been the invention of politicians to keep the lower part of the world in awe by the fear of invisible powers; unless mankind were then very different from what it is now: for I look upon the mass or body of our people here in England to be as freethinkers, that is to say, as staunch unbelievers, as any of the highest rank. But I conceive some scattered notions about a superior power to be of singular use for the common people, as furnishing excellent materials to keep children quiet when they grow peevish, and providing topics of amusement in a tedious winter-night.

Lastly, it is proposed, as a singular advantage, that the abolishing of Christianity will very much contribute to the uniting of Protestants, by enlarging the terms of communion, so as to take in all sorts of dissenters, who are now shut out of the pale upon account of a few ceremonies, which all sides confess to be things indifferent; [23] that this alone will effectually answer the great ends of a scheme for comprehension, by opening a large noble gate at which all bodies may enter; whereas the chaffering with dissenters, and dodging about this or the other ceremony, is but like opening a few wickets,[24] and leaving them at jar,[25] by which no more than one can get in at a time, and that not without stooping, and sideling, and squeezing his body.

To all this I answer, that there is one darling inclination of mankind which

21. Shoots or root fibers.
22. The common people, the uneducated.
23. Matters of no importance and usually left undecided by church doctrine.
24. Small openings in large gates.
25. Ajar.

usually affects to be a retainer to religion, although she be neither its parent, its godmother, or its friend; I mean the spirit of opposition, that lived long before Christianity and can easily subsist without it. Let us, for instance, examine wherein the opposition of sectaries among us consists; we shall find Christianity to have no share in it at all. Does the gospel anywhere prescribe a starched, squeezed countenance, a stiff, formal gait, a singularity of manners and habit, or any affected modes of speech different from the reasonable part of mankind?[26] Yet, if Christianity did not lend its name to stand in the gap and to employ or divert these humours, they must of necessity be spent in contraventions to the laws of the land and disturbance of the public peace. There is a portion of enthusiasm assigned to every nation, which, if it hath not proper objects to work on, will burst out and set all in a flame. If the quiet of a state can be bought by only flinging men a few ceremonies to devour, it is a purchase no wise man would refuse. Let the mastiffs amuse themselves about a sheep's skin stuffed with hay, provided it will keep them from worrying the flock. The institution of convents abroad, seems, in one point, a strain of great wisdom; there being few irregularities in human passions that may not have recourse to vent themselves in some of those orders, which are so many retreats for the speculative, the melancholy, the proud, the silent, the politic, and the morose to spend themselves and evaporate the noxious particles; for each of whom, we, in this island, are forced to provide a several sect of religion to keep them quiet: and whenever Christianity shall be abolished, the legislature must find some other expedient to employ and entertain them. For what imports it how large a gate you open, if there will be always left a number who place a pride and a merit in refusing to enter?

Having thus considered the most important objections against Christianity and the chief advantages proposed by the abolishing thereof, I shall now, with equal deference and submission to wiser judgments as before, proceed to mention a few inconveniences that may happen, if the gospel should be repealed, which perhaps the projectors may not have sufficiently considered.

And first, I am very sensible how much the gentlemen of wit and pleasure are apt to murmur, and be choqued[27] at the sight of so many daggled-tail[28] parsons, who happen to fall in their way and offend their eyes; but, at the same time, these wise reformers do not consider what an advantage and felicity it is for great wits to be always provided with objects of scorn and contempt in order to exercise and improve their talents, and divert their spleen from falling on each other or on themselves; especially when all this may be done without the least imaginable danger to their persons.

And to urge another argument of a parallel nature: if Christianity were once abolished, how could the freethinkers, the strong reasoners, and the men of profound learning be able to find another subject so calculated in all points whereon to display their abilities? what wonderful productions of wit should we be deprived of from those whose genius, by continual practice, hath been wholly turned upon raillery and invectives against religion, and would there-

26. Typical manners of the Puritan sects; for this view of "affected modes of speech" see the criticism of Christian in Vanity Fair (Bunyan, *The Pilgrim's Progress*).
27. Shocked (taken from the French form).
28. Mud-bespattered.

fore never be able to shine or distinguish themselves upon any other subject! We are daily complaining of the great decline of wit among us, and would we take away the greatest, perhaps the only, topic we have left? Who would ever have suspected Asgil for a wit, or Toland for a philosopher, if the inexhaustible stock of Christianity had not been at hand to provide them with materials? What other subject, through all art or nature, could have produced Tindal for a profound author or furnished him with readers? It is the wise choice of the subject that alone adorns and distinguishes the writer. For, had an hundred such pens as these been employed on the side of religion, they would have immediately sunk into silence and oblivion.

Nor do I think it wholly groundless, or my fears altogether imaginary, that the abolishing Christianity may perhaps bring the Church in danger, or at least put the senate to the trouble of another securing vote.[29] I desire I may not be mistaken; I am far from presuming to affirm, or think, that the Church is in danger at present or as things now stand; but we know not how soon it may be so when the Christian religion is repealed. As plausible as this project seems, there may a dangerous design lurk under it. Nothing can be more notorious than that the Atheists, Deists, Socinians,[30] Anti-trinitarians, and other subdivisions of freethinkers are persons of little zeal for the present ecclesiastical establishment: their declared opinion is for repealing the Sacramental Test; they are very indifferent with regard to ceremonies; nor do they hold the *jus divinum*[31] of episcopacy; therefore this may be intended as one politic step towards altering the constitution of the Church established, and setting up Presbytery in the stead, which I leave to be further considered by those at the helm.

In the last place, I think nothing can be more plain than that, by this expedient, we shall run into the evil we chiefly pretend to avoid: and that the abolishment of the Christian religion will be the readiest course we can take to introduce Popery. And I am the more inclined to this opinion because we know it has been the constant practice of the Jesuits to send over emissaries with instructions to personate themselves members of the several prevailing sects among us. So it is recorded, that they have at sundry times appeared in the guise of Presbyterians, Anabaptists, Independents, and Quakers, according as any of these were most in credit; so, since the fashion hath been taken up of exploding religion, the popish missionaries have not been wanting[32] to mix with the freethinkers; among whom Toland, the great oracle of the Anti-christians, is an Irish priest, the son of an Irish priest; and the most learned and ingenious author of a book called *The Rights of the Christian Church* was in a proper juncture reconciled to the Romish faith, whose true son, as appears by an hundred passages in his treatise he still continues. Perhaps I could add some others to the number; but the fact is beyond dispute and the reasoning they proceed by is right: for, supposing Christianity to be extinguished, the

29. Such as the resolution Commons passed in 1701 for "the securing of the Protestant religion, by law established."

30. Followers of Laelius and Faustus Socinus, Italian theologians of the 16th century who denied the divinity of Christ and the supernatural status of the sacraments.

31. "Divine right" (claiming the example of the Apostles).

32. Lacking.

people will never be at ease till they find out some other method of worship; which will as infallibly produce superstition as this will end in Popery.

And therefore, if, notwithstanding all I have said, it shall still be thought necessary to have a bill brought in for repealing Christianity, I would humbly offer an amendment that instead of the word, Christianity, may be put religion in general; which, I conceive, will much better answer all the good ends proposed by the projectors of it. For, as long as we leave in being a God and his Providence, with all the necessary consequences which curious and inquisitive men will be apt to draw from such premises, we do not strike at the root of the evil, although we should ever so effectually annihilate the present scheme of the gospel: for, of what use is freedom of thought if it will not produce freedom of action, which is the sole end, how remote soever in appearance, of all objections against Christianity; and therefore, the freethinkers consider it as a sort of edifice wherein all the parts have such a mutual dependence on each other that if you happen to pull out one single nail, the whole fabric must fall to the ground. This was happily expressed by him who had heard of a text brought for proof of the Trinity, which in an ancient manuscript was differently read; he thereupon immediately took the hint, and by a sudden deduction of a long *sorites*,[33] most logically concluded; 'Why, if it be as you say, I may safely whore and drink on, and defy the parson.' From which, and many the like instances easy to be produced, I think nothing can be more manifest than that the quarrel is not against any particular points of hard digestion in the Christian system but against religion in general; which, by laying restraints on human nature, is supposed the great enemy to the freedom of thought and action.

Upon the whole, if it shall still be thought for the benefit of church and state that Christianity be abolished, I conceive, however, it may be more convenient to defer the execution to a time of peace; and not venture in this conjuncture to disoblige our allies, who, as it falls out, are all Christians, and many of them, by the prejudices of their education, so bigoted as to place a sort of pride in the appellation. If upon being rejected by them, we are to trust to an alliance with the Turk, we shall find ourselves much deceived: for, as he is too remote and generally engaged in war with the Persian emperor, so his people would be more scandalized at our infidelity than our Christian neighbours. Because the Turks are not only strict observers of religious worship but, what is worse, believe a God; which is more than is required of us even while we preserve the name of Christians.

To conclude: whatever some may think of the great advantages to trade by this favourite scheme, I do very much apprehend that in six months' time after the act is passed for the extirpation of the gospel, the Bank and East India stock may fall at least one *per cent*.[34] And since that is fifty times more than ever the wisdom of our age thought fit to venture for the preservation of Christianity, there is no reason we should be at so great a loss merely for the sake of destroying it.

1708 1711

33. A long and tenuous chain of reasoning.

34. The Bank of England (founded in 1695 by William III) and the East India Company, both largely Whig concerns.

A Modest Proposal

This concise and fiercely ironic tract is based upon England's exploitation of Ireland, which was forbidden to trade on its own with other countries but used as a source of raw materials and cheap food. Swift writes as an eager collaborator, an Irish projector who at last finds a scheme that will enrich Ireland without offending the English; it will, moreover, at last make Ireland's people "the riches of a nation," as a large working force was traditionally believed to be. The projector in whose guise Swift writes can sustain without conflict an idiom of humane tenderness, somewhat cloying in fact, with the zeal of a ruthlessly commercial breeder of beef. Clearly, the cannibalism that solves Ireland's problem is simply a metaphor for the exploitation that has created it, and "dressing them hot under the knife" shows insensibility only different in degree from counting on the poor to die "as fast as they reasonably can." The tract does not spare the Irish, either, for one of the worst evils of exploitation is that it degrades and brutalizes its victims; Swift is enraged by their passivity, and that too requires its terrible metaphors.

A Modest Proposal

for

Preventing the Children of Poor People in Ireland from Being a Burden to Their Parents or Country, and for Making Them Beneficial to the Public

It is a melancholy object to those who walk through this great town, or travel in the country, when they see the streets, the roads, and cabin-doors crowded with beggars of the female sex, followed by three, four, or six children, all in rags, and importuning every passenger for an alms. These mothers, instead of being able to work for their honest livelihood, are forced to employ all their time in strolling to beg sustenance for their helpless infants: who, as they grow up, either turn thieves for want of work, or leave their dear native country to fight for the Pretender in Spain, or sell themselves to the Barbadoes.[1]

I think it is agreed by all parties, that this prodigious number of children in the arms, or on the backs, or at the heels of their mothers, and frequently of their fathers, is, in the present deplorable state of the kingdom, a very great additional grievance; and, therefore, whoever could find out a fair, cheap, and easy method of making these children sound and useful members of the commonwealth, would deserve so well of the public, as to have his statue set up for a preserver of the nation.[2]

But my intention is very far from being confined to provide only for the children of professed beggars; it is of a much greater extent, and shall take in the

1. Many Irish Catholics enlisted in French and Spanish forces, the latter employed in the effort to restore the Stuart Pretender to the English throne in 1718; emigration to the West Indies from Ireland had reached the rate of almost fifteen hundred a year (and often led to desperate servitude).

2. The idiom of the "projector," the enthusiastic proponent of public remedies (often suspected of having an eye on his own glory).

whole number of infants at a certain age, who are born of parents in effect as little able to support them as those who demand our charity in the streets.

As to my own part, having turned my thoughts for many years upon this important subject, and maturely weighed the several schemes of other projectors, I have always found them grossly mistaken in their computation. It is true, a child, just dropped from its dam,[3] may be supported by her milk for a solar year with little other nourishment; at most, not above the value of two shillings, which the mother may certainly get, or the value in scraps, by her lawful occupation of begging; and it is exactly at one year old that I propose to provide for them in such a manner, as, instead of being a charge upon their parents or the parish, or wanting food and raiment for the rest of their lives, they shall, on the contrary, contribute to the feeding, and partly to the clothing, of many thousands.

There is likewise another great advantage in my scheme, that it will prevent those voluntary abortions, and that horrid practice of women murdering their bastard children, alas, too frequent among us, sacrificing the poor innocent babes, I doubt more to avoid the expense than the shame, which would move tears and pity in the most savage and inhuman breast.

The number of souls in this kingdom being usually reckoned one millon and a half, of these I calculate there may be about two hundred thousand couple whose wives are breeders; from which number I subtract thirty thousand couple, who are able to maintain their own children (although I apprehend there cannot be so many, under the present distresses of the kingdom); but this being granted, there will remain an hundred and seventy thousand breeders. I again subtract fifty thousand for those women who miscarry, or whose children die by accident or disease within the year. There only remain a hundred and twenty thousand children of poor parents annually born. The question therefore is how this number shall be reared and provided for? which, as I have already said, under the present situation of affairs, is utterly impossible by all the methods hitherto proposed. For we can neither employ them in handicraft or agriculture; we neither build houses (I mean in the country) nor cultivate land: they can very seldom pick up a livelihood by stealing until they arrive at six years old, except where they are of towardly parts; although I confess they learn the rudiments much earlier; during which time they can, however, be properly looked upon only as probationers; as I have been informed by a principal gentleman in the county of Cavan,[4] who protested to me, that he never knew above one or two instances under the age of six, even in a part of the kingdom so renowned for the quickest proficiency in that art.

I am assured by our merchants that a boy or a girl before twelve years old is no saleable commodity; and even when they come to this age they will not yield above three pounds or three pounds and half-a-crown at most, on the exchange; which cannot turn to account either to the parents or kingdom, the charge of nutriment and rags having been at least four times that value.

I shall now, therefore, humbly propose my own thoughts, which I hope will not be liable to the least objection.

3. The idiom now of the cattle breeder.
4. One of the poorest districts of Ireland.

I have been assured by a very knowing American [5] of my acquaintance in London, that a young healthy child, well nursed, is, at a year old, a most delicious, nourishing, and wholesome food, whether stewed, roasted, baked, or boiled; and I make no doubt that it will equally serve in a fricassee or a ragout.[6]

I do therefore humbly offer it to public consideration, that of the hundred and twenty thousand children already computed, twenty thousand may be reserved for breed, whereof only one-fourth part to be males; which is more than we allow to sheep, black cattle, or swine; and my reason is, that these children are seldom the fruits of marriage, a circumstance not much regarded by our savages, therefore one male will be sufficient to serve four females. That the remaining hundred thousand may, at a year old, be offered in sale to the persons of quality and fortune through the kingdom; always advising the mother to let them suck plentifully in the last month, so as to render them plump and fat for a good table. A child will make two dishes at an entertainment for friends; and when the family dines alone, the fore or hind quarter will make a reasonable dish, and, seasoned with a little pepper or salt, will be very good boiled on the fourth day, especially in winter.

I have reckoned, upon a medium, that a child just born will weigh twelve pounds, and in a solar year, if tolerably nursed, increaseth to twenty-eight pounds.

I grant this food will be somewhat dear, and therefore very proper for landlords, who, as they have already devoured most of the parents, seem to have the best title to the children.

Infants' flesh will be in season throughout the year, but more plentifully in March, and a little before and after: for we are told by a grave author, an eminent French physician,[7] that fish being a prolific [8] diet, there are more children born in Roman Catholic countries about nine months after Lent than at any other season; therefore, reckoning a year after Lent, the markets will be more glutted than usual, because the number of popish infants is at least three to one in this kingdom; and therefore it will have one other collateral advantage, by lessening the number of papists among us.

I have already computed the charge of nursing a beggar's child (in which list I reckon all cottagers, labourers, and four-fifths of the farmers) to be about two shillings per annum, rags included; and I believe no gentleman would repine to give ten shillings for the carcass of a good fat child, which, as I have said, will make four dishes of excellent nutritive meat, when he has only some particular friend, or his own family, to dine with him. Thus the squire will learn to be a good landlord, and grow popular among his tenants; the mother will have eight shillings net profit, and be fit for work till she produces another child.

Those who are more thrifty (as I must confess the times require) may flay

5. Presumably American Indian, many of whom were believed by the English to enjoy cannibalism.

6. A French stew, one of the foreign dishes ("olios and ragouts") Swift mocks elsewhere as affectations.

7. François Rabelais (*c.* 1494–1553), *Gargantua and Pantagruel* V.29.

8. Generative.

the carcass; the skin of which, artificially dressed, will make admirable gloves for ladies, and summer-boots for fine gentlemen.

As to our city of Dublin, shambles [9] may be appointed for this purpose in the most convenient parts of it, and butchers we may be assured will not be wanting; although I rather recommend buying the children alive, and dressing them hot from the knife, as we do roasting pigs.

A very worthy person, a true lover of his country, and whose virtues I highly esteem, was lately pleased, in discoursing on this matter, to offer a refinement upon my scheme. He said, that many gentlemen of this kingdom, having of late destroyed their deer, he conceived that the want of venison might be well supplied by the bodies of young lads and maidens, not exceeding fourteen years of age, nor under twelve; so great a number of both sexes in every country being now ready to starve for want of work and service; and these to be disposed of by their parents, if alive, or otherwise by their nearest relations. But, with due deference to so excellent a friend, and so deserving a patriot, I cannot be altogether in his sentiments; for as to the males, my American acquaintance assured me from frequent experience, that their flesh was generally tough and lean, like that of our schoolboys, by continual exercise, and their taste disagreeable; and to fatten them would not answer the charge. Then as to the females, it would, I think, with humble submission, be a loss to the public, because they soon would become breeders themselves: and besides, it is not improbable that some scrupulous people might be apt to censure such a practice (although indeed very unjustly) as a little bordering upon cruelty; which, I confess hath always been with me the strongest objection against any project, how well soever intended.

But in order to justify my friend, he confessed that this expedient was put into his head by the famous Psalmanazar,[10] a native of the island Formosa, who came from thence to London above twenty years ago; and in conversation told my friend, that in his country, when any young person happened to be put to death, the executioner sold the carcass to persons of quality as a prime dainty; and that in his time the body of a plump girl of fifteen, who was crucified for an attempt to poison the emperor, was sold to his Imperial Majesty's prime minister of state,[11] and other great mandarins of the court, in joints from the gibbet, at four hundred crowns. Neither indeed can I deny, that if the same use were made of several plump young girls in this town, who, without one single groat to their fortunes, cannot stir abroad without a chair, and appear at playhouse and assemblies [12] in foreign fineries which they never will pay for, the kingdom would not be the worse.

Some persons of a desponding spirit are in great concern about that vast number of poor people who are aged, diseased, or maimed; and I have been desired to employ my thoughts what course may be taken to ease the nation of so grievous an encumbrance. But I am not in the least pain upon that matter,

9. Slaughterhouses.

10. George Psalmanazar (1679-1763), a Frenchman who pretended to be a Formosan and wrote (in English) a fraudulent book about his "native" land.

11. Probably a reference to Walpole.

12. Social gatherings (Swift had sought an Irish boycott of all such foreign luxuries of dress or diet).

because it is very well known, that they are every day dying, and rotting, by cold and famine, and filth and vermin, as fast as can be reasonably expected. And as to the younger labourers, they are now in almost as hopeful a condition: they cannot get work, and consequently pine away for want of nourishment, to a degree, that if at any time they are accidentally hired to common labour, they have not strength to perform it; and thus the country and themselves are happily delivered from the evils to come.

I have too long digressed, and therefore shall return to my subject. I think the advantages by the proposal which I have made are obvious and many, as well as of the highest importance.

For first, as I have already observed, it would greatly lessen the number of papists, with whom we are yearly overrun, being the principal breeders of the nation as well as our most dangerous enemies; and who stay at home on purpose with a design to deliver the kingdom to the Pretender, hoping to take their advantage by the absence of so many good Protestants, who have chosen rather to leave their country than stay at home and pay tithes against their conscience to an idolatrous Episcopal curate.[13]

Secondly, the poorer tenants will have something valuable of their own, which by law may be made liable to distress, and help to pay their landlord's rent; their corn and cattle being already seized, and money a thing unknown.

Thirdly, whereas the maintenance of an hundred thousand children, from two years old and upwards, cannot be computed at less than ten shillings a piece per annum, the nation's stock will be thereby increased fifty thousand pounds per annum; besides the profit of a new dish introduced to the tables of all gentlemen of fortune in the kingdom who have any refinement in taste. And the money will circulate among ourselves, the goods being entirely of our own growth and manufacture.

Fourthly, the constant breeders, besides the gain of eight shillings sterling per annum by the sale of their children, will be rid of the charge of maintaining them after the first year.

Fifthly, this food would likewise bring great custom to taverns; where the vintners will certainly be so prudent as to procure the best receipts for dressing it to perfection, and, consequently, have their houses frequented by all the fine gentlemen, who justly value themselves upon their knowledge in good eating: and a skilful cook, who understands how to oblige his guests, will contrive to make it as expensive as they please.

Sixthly, this would be a great inducement to marriage, which all wise nations have either encouraged by rewards, or enforced by laws and penalties. It would increase the care and tenderness of mothers towards their children, when they were sure of a settlement for life to the poor babes, provided in some sort by the public, to their annual profit instead of expense. We should soon see an honest emulation among the married women, which of them could bring the

13. Swift is mocking the castigation of the Catholics, for he regarded it as a typical propaganda device of the Whigs and Protestants; his own experience as a clergyman in northern Ireland had given him reason to fear and distrust the energies of the dissenting Protestants, and he questions their motives (money or conscience) for leaving Ireland. The word "idolatrous" was added in 1735 after renewed agitation to remove the Sacramental Test, with the implication that Anglican forms and doctrines were intolerable to other Protestants.

fattest child to the market. Men would become as fond of their wives during the time of their pregnancy, as they are now of their mares in foal, their cows in calf, or sows when they are ready to farrow; nor offer to beat or kick them (as is too frequent a practice) for fear of a miscarriage.

Many other advantages might be enumerated. For instance, the addition of some thousand carcasses in our exportation of barrelled beef; the propagation of swine's flesh, and improvement in the art of making good bacon, so much wanted among us by the great destruction of pigs, too frequent at our tables, which are no way comparable in taste or magnificence to a well-grown, fat yearling child, which, roasted whole, will make a considerable figure at a Lord Mayor's feast, or any other public entertainment. But this, and many others, I omit, being studious of brevity.

Supposing that one thousand families in this city would be constant customers for infants' flesh, besides others who might have it at merry meetings, particularly weddings and christenings, I compute that Dublin would take off annually about twenty thousand carcasses; and the rest of the kingdom (where probably they will be sold somewhat cheaper) the remaining eighty thousand.

I can think of no one objection that will possibly be raised against this proposal, unless it should be urged, that the number of people will be thereby much lessened in the kingdom. This I freely own, and it was indeed one principal design in offering it to the world. I desire the reader will observe that I calculate my remedy for this one individual kingdom of Ireland, and for no other that ever was, is, or I think ever can be, upon earth. Therefore let no man talk to me of other expedients: [14] of taxing our absentees at five shillings a pound: of using neither clothes nor household-furniture except what is of our own growth and manufacture: of utterly rejecting the materials and instruments that promote foreign luxury: of curing the expensiveness of pride, vanity, idleness, and gaming in our women; of introducing a vein of parsimony, prudence, and temperance: of learning to love our country, wherein we differ even from Laplanders, and the inhabitants of Topinamboo: [15] of quitting our animosities and factions, nor act any longer like the Jews, who were murdering one another at the very moment their city was taken: [16] of being a little cautious not to sell our country and consciences for nothing: of teaching landlords to have at least one degree of mercy towards their tenants: lastly, of putting a spirit of honesty, industry, and skill into our shopkeepers; who, if a resolution could now be taken to buy only our native goods, would immediately unite to cheat and exact upon us in the price, the measure, and the goodness, nor could ever yet be brought to make one fair proposal of just dealing, though often and earnestly invited to it.

Therefore I repeat, let no man talk to me of these and the like expedients, till he hath at least some glimpse of hope that there will ever be some hearty and sincere attempt to put them in practice.

But, as to myself, having been wearied out for many years with offering vain, idle, visionary thoughts, and at length utterly despairing of success, I

14. The following are, of course, Swift's own genuine proposals for Ireland.
15. A region of Brazil known for wildness and barbarous stupidity.
16. When Jerusalem fell to Nebuchadnezzar (II Kings 24, 25; II Chronicles 36), with the suggestion that English domination is Ireland's Babylonian captivity.

fortunately fell upon this proposal; which, as it is wholly new, so it hath something solid and real, of no expense and little trouble, full in our own power, and whereby we can incur no danger in disobliging England. For this kind of commodity will not bear exportation, the flesh being of too tender a consistence to admit a long continuance in salt, although perhaps I could name a country which would be glad to eat up our whole nation without it.

After all, I am not so violently bent upon my own opinion as to reject any offer proposed by wise men which shall be found equally innocent, cheap, easy, and effectual. But before something of that kind shall be advanced in contradiction to my scheme, and offering a better, I desire the author, or authors, will be pleased maturely to consider two points. First, as things now stand, how they will be able to find food and raiment for a hundred thousand useless mouths and backs? And, secondly, there being a round million of creatures in human figure throughout this kingdom, whose whole subsistence put into a common stock would leave them in debt two millions of pounds sterling, adding those who are beggars by profession, to the bulk of farmers, cottagers, and labourers, with the wives and children who are beggars in effect; I desire those politicians who dislike my overture, and may perhaps be so bold as to attempt an answer, that they will first ask the parents of these mortals, whether they would not at this day think it a great happiness to have been sold for food at a year old, in the manner I prescribe, and thereby have avoided such a perpetual scene of misfortunes as they have since gone through, by the oppression of landlords, the impossibility of paying rent without money or trade, the want of common sustenance, with neither house nor clothes to cover them from the inclemencies of weather, and the most inevitable prospect of entailing the like, or greater miseries, upon their breed for ever.

I profess, in the sincerity of my heart, that I have not the least personal interest in endeavouring to promote this necessary work, having no other motive than the public good of my country, by advancing our trade, providing for infants, relieving the poor, and giving some pleasure to the rich. I have no children by which I can propose to get a single penny; the youngest being nine years old, and my wife past child-bearing.

1729

Swift's Poems

Swift began his poetic career with Pindaric odes in the manner of Abraham Cowley, but he soon found his characteristic idiom in the Hudibrastic tetrameter couplet. His poetry is a constant warfare against the false sublime and other forms of specious exaltation, and his dry, colloquial undercutting of pretension is to be seen alike in "Baucis and Philemon," in the birthday poems to Stella (tender and warm as they are), and in caustic or scatological satires such as "The Day of Judgment" and "Cassinus and Peter." The two "city" poems, written in pentameter to burlesque the current form of pastoral and georgic poetry, are further examples of Swift's reduction of unthinking celebration and of his opposition of the commonplace lowness of everyday life to the conventions of literary style.

Baucis and Philemon

Imitated from the Eighth Book of Ovid

In ancient times, as story tells,
The saints would often leave their cells,
And stroll about, but hide their quality,
To try good people's hospitality.
  It happened on a winter night,
As authors of the legend write,
Two brother hermits, saints by trade,
Taking their tour in masquerade,
Disguised in tattered habits, went
To a small village down in Kent;
Where, in the strollers' canting strain,
They begged from door to door in vain,
Tried every tone might pity win;
But not a soul would let them in.
  Our wandering saints, in woeful state,
Treated at this ungodly rate,
Having through all the village passed,
To a small cottage came at last
Where dwelt a good old honest yeoman,
Called in the neighbourhood Philemon;
Who kindly did these saints invite
In his poor hut to pass the night;
And then the hospitable sire
Bid Goody° Baucis mend the fire
While he from out the chimney took
A flitch of bacon off the hook,
And freely from the fattest side
Cut out large slices to be fried;
Then stepped aside to fetch 'em drink,
Filled a large jug up to the brink,
And saw it fairly twice go round;
Yet (what was wonderful) they found
'Twas still replenished to the top,
As if they ne'er had touched a drop.
The good old couple were amazed,
And often on each other gazed;
For both were frightened to the heart,
And just began to cry, 'What ar't!'
Then softly turned aside, to view
Whether the lights were burning blue.°
The gentle pilgrims, soon aware on't,
Told 'em their calling and their errand:

Goody a contracted form of goodwife

burning blue as candles were believed to do in the presence of evil spirits

'Good folks, you need not be afraid,
We are but saints,' the hermits said;
'No hurt shall come to you or yours:
But, for that pack of churlish boors,
Not fit to live on Christian ground,
They and their houses shall be drowned:
While you shall see your cottage rise,
And grow a church before your eyes.'
  They scarce had spoke, when fair and soft,
The roof began to mount aloft;
Aloft rose every beam and rafter;
The heavy wall climbed slowly after.
  The chimney widened, and grew higher,
Became a steeple with a spire.
  The kettle to the top was hoist,
And there stood fastened to a joist,
But with the upside down, to show
Its inclinations for below:
In vain; for a superior force
Applied at bottom stops its course:
Doomed ever in suspense to dwell,
'Tis now no kettle, but a bell.
  A wooden jack,° which had almost
Lost by disuse the art to roast,
A sudden alteration feels,
Increased by new intestine wheels;
And, what exalts the wonder more,
The number made the motion slower.
The flier, though it had leaden feet,
Turned round so quick you scarce could see't;
But, slackened by some secret power,
Now hardly moves an inch an hour.
The jack and chimney, near allied,
Had never left each other's side;
The chimney to a steeple grown,
The jack would not be left alone;
But, up against the steeple reared,
Became a clock, and still adhered;
And still its love to household cares
By a shrill voice at noon declares,
Warning the cookmaid not to burn
That roast meat which it cannot turn.
  The groaning chair began to crawl
Like an huge snail along the wall;
There stuck aloft in public view,
And with small change, a pulpit grew.

jack a device for turning the roasting spit

The porringers, that in a row
Hung high, and made a glittering show,
To a less noble substance changed,
Were now but leathern buckets° ranged.
The ballads, pasted on the wall,
Of Joan of France, and English Moll,°
Fair Rosamond,° and Robin Hood,
The little Children in the Wood,
Now seemed to look abundance better,
Improved in picture, size and letter:
And, high in order placed, describe
The heraldry of every tribe.°
A bedstead of the antique mode,
Compact of timber many a load,
Such as our ancestors did use,
Was metamorphosed into pews;
Which still their ancient nature keep
By lodging folks disposed to sleep.
The cottage, by such feats as these,
Grown to a church by just degrees,
The hermits then desired their host
To ask for what he fancied most.
Philemon, having paused a while,
Returned 'em thanks in homely style;
Then said, 'My house is grown so fine,
Methinks, I still would call it mine.
I'm old, and fain would live at ease;
Make me the parson, if you please.'
He spoke, and presently he feels
His grazier's° coat fall down his heels:
He sees, yet hardly can believe,
About each arm a pudding sleeve;°
His waistcoat to a cassock grew,
And both assumed a sable hue;
But, being old, continued just
As threadbare and as full of dust.
His talk was now of tithes and dues:
He smoked his pipe and read the news;
Knew how to preach old sermons next,
Vamped° in the preface and the text;
At christenings well could act his part,
And had the service all by heart:
Wished women might have children fast,

buckets for putting out fires
English Moll a heroine who fought at the siege of Ghent, 1584; here paired with Joan of Arc
Rosamond daughter of Lord Clifford and mistress of Henry II, subject of a famous ballad
heraldry . . . tribe ensigns of the twelve tribes of Israel, common in country churches
grazier's one who feeds cattle for market
pudding sleeve a full, bulging (perhaps padded) sleeve
Vamped reworked (the "text" here being the scriptural topic)

And thought whose sow had farrowed last;
Against dissenters would repine,
And stood up firm for right divine;°
Found his head filled with many a system;
But classic authors,—he ne'er missed 'em.
  Thus having furbished up a parson,
Dame Baucis next they played their farce on.
Instead of homespun coifs,° were seen
Good pinners edged with colberteen;°
Her petticoat transformed apace,
Became black satin, flounced° with lace.
Plain 'Goody' would no longer down,
'Twas 'Madam,' in her grogram° gown.
Philemon was in great surprise,
And hardly could believe his eyes.
Amazed to see her look so prim,°
And she admired as much at him.
  Thus happy in their change of life,
Were several years this man and wife:
When on a day, which proved their last,
Discoursing on old stories past,
They went by chance, amidst their talk,
To the churchyard to take a walk;
When Baucis hastily cried out,
'My dear, I see your forehead sprout!'
'Sprout,' quoth the man; 'what's this you tell us?
I hope you don't believe me jealous!°
But yet, methinks I feel it true,
And really yours is budding too—
Nay,—now I cannot stir my foot;
It feels as if 'twere taking root.'
  Description would but tire my Muse,
In short, they both were turned to yews.
Old Goodman Dobson of the green
Remembers he the trees has seen;
He'll talk of them from noon till night,
And goes with folks to show the sight;
On Sundays, after evening prayer,
He gathers all the parish there;
Points out the place of either yew,
Here Baucis, there Philemon, grew:

right divine i.e. the church structure as derived from the Apostles; perhaps also showing the Tory political cast of the lower clergy, as opposed to many Whig bishops
coifs close-fitting caps
pinners . . . colberteen caps with flaps edged with lace
flounced covered with a second tier
grogram grosgrain, a fabric all or partly of silk
prim smart
jealous referring to cuckold's horns, often called "branches" for antlers

Till once a parson of our town,
To mend his barn, cut Baucis down;
At which, 'tis hard to be believed
How much the other tree was grieved,
Grew scrubby, died a-top, was stunted;
So the next parson stubbed and burnt it.

1708

A Description of the Morning

Now hardly here and there a hackney-coach
Appearing, showed the ruddy morn's approach.
Now Betty° from her master's bed had flown,
And softly stole to discompose her own;
The slip-shod 'prentice from his master's door
Had pared the dirt and sprinkled° round the floor.
Now Moll had whirled her mop with dext'rous airs,
Prepared to scrub the entry and the stairs.
The youth with broomy stumps began to trace
The kennel-edge,° where wheels had worn the place.
The small-coal man° was heard with cadence deep,
Till drowned in shriller notes of chimney-sweep:
Duns° at his lordship's gate began to meet;
And brickdust Moll° had screamed through half the street.
The turnkey° now his flock returning sees,
Duly let out a-nights to steal for fees:
The watchful bailiffs take their silent stands,
And schoolboys lag with satchels in their hands.

1709

A Description of a City Shower

In Imitation of Virgil's Georgics

Careful observers may foretell the hour
(By sure prognostics) when to dread a shower.
While rain depends,° the pensive cat gives o'er
Her frolics and pursues her tail no more.

Betty like Aurora, the goddess of the dawn, who must leave each morning the bed of her lover Tithonus

sprinkled suggesting the conventional morning shower, as Moll's mop does the gentle breeze

kennel-edge the curb of the road, where he is looking for old nails

small-coal man vendor of charcoal, beginning the sequence of urban counterparts to braying animals and singing birds

Duns bill collectors

brickdust Moll a woman selling powdered brick for cleaning knives

turnkey the jailer who lets his prisoners steal to earn the fees he exacts

depends impends

Returning home at night, you'll find the sink°
Strike your offended sense with double stink.
If you be wise, then go not far to dine:
You'll spend in coach-hire more than save in wine.
A coming shower your shooting corns presage,
Old aches° throb, your hollow tooth will rage;
Sauntering in coffeehouse is Dulman seen;
He damns the climate, and complains of spleen.°
And bear their trophies with them as they go:
Filth of all hues and odour seem to tell
What street they sailed from by their sight and smell.
They, as each torrent drives with rapid force,
From Smithfield° or St. Pulchre's° shape their course,
And in huge confluent join at Snow Hill Ridge,
Fall from the conduit prone to Holborn bridge.
Sweepings from butchers' stalls, dung, guts, and blood,
Drowned puppies, stinking sprats,° all drenched in mud,
Dead cats, and turnip-tops, come tumbling down the flood.°

1710

sink sewer
aches pronounced "aitches"
spleen melancholy, "vapours"
Smithfield the cattle market
St. Pulchre's the church of St. Sepulchre on Snow Hill
sprats small fish
Dead cats . . . flood The last three lines are Swift's parody of the triplet (which Dryden and others favored, especially in poetry of a high style) and the last line a parody of the extended (twelve-syllable) Alexandrine, with which the triplet often concluded.

Phyllis
Or, The Progress of Love

Desponding Phyllis was endued
With every talent of a prude:
She trembled when a man drew near;
Salute her, and she turned her ear:
If o'er against her you were placed,
She durst not look above your waist:
She'd rather take you to her bed,
Than let you see her dress her head;
In church you heard her, through the crowd,
Repeat the absolution loud:
In church, secure behind her fan,
She durst behold that monster, man:
There practised how to place her head,
And bit her lips to make them red;
Or, on the mat devoutly kneeling,
Would lift her eyes up to the ceiling.
And heave her bosom unaware,
For neighbouring beaux to see it bare.
    At length a lucky lover came,
And found admittance from the dame.
Suppose all parties now agreed,
The writings drawn, the lawyer fee'd,
The vicar and the ring bespoke:
Guess, how could such a match be broke?
See then what mortals place their bliss in!
Next morn betimes the bride was missing:
The mother screamed, the father chid;
Where can this idle wench be hid?
No news of Phyl! the bridegroom came,
And thought his bride had skulked for shame;
Because her father used to say
The girl had such a bashful way.
    Now John the butler must be sent
To learn the way that Phyllis went:
The groom was wished to saddle Crop;
For John must neither light nor stop,
But find her whereso'er she fled,
And bring her back alive or dead.
See here again the devil to do;
For truly John was missing too:
The horse and pillion° both were gone!
Phyllis, it seems, was fled with John.
Old Madam, who went up to find

pillion saddle for the person who rode behind (usually a woman)

What papers Phyl had left behind,
A letter on the toilet° sees,
'To my much-honoured father—these—'
('Tis always done, romances tell us,
When daughters run away with fellows)
Filled with the choicest commonplaces,
By others used in the like cases.
'That long ago a fortune-teller
Exactly said what now befell her;
And in a glass had made her see
A serving-man of low degree.
It was her fate, must be forgiven;
For marriages are made in Heaven:
His pardon begged: but, to be plain,
She'd do't if 'twere to do again:
Thank God, 'twas neither shame nor sin,
For John was come of honest kin.
Love never thinks of rich and poor;
She'd beg with John from door to door.
Forgive her, if it be a crime;
She'll never do't another time.
She ne'er before in all her life
Once disobeyed him, maid nor wife.'
One argument she summed up all in,
'The thing was done and past recalling;
And therefore hoped she would recover
His favour, when his passion's over.
She valued not what others thought her,
And was—his most obedient daughter.'
Fair maidens all, attend the Muse,
Who now the wandering pair pursues:
Away they rode in homely° sort,
Their journey long, their money short;
The loving couple well bemired;
The horse and both the riders tired:
Their victuals bad, their lodging worse;
Phyl cried, and John began to curse:
Phyl wished that she had strained a limb,
When first she ventured out with him;
John wished that he had broke a leg,
When first for her he quitted Peg.
But what adventures more befell 'em,
The Muse has now no time to tell 'em;
How Johnny wheedled, threatened, fawned,
Till Phyllis all her trinkets pawned:
How oft she broke her marriage vows,

toilet dressing table

homely simple, plain

In kindness to maintain her spouse,
Till swains unwholesome° spoiled the trade;
For now the surgeon must be paid,
To whom those perquisites are gone,
In Christian justice due to John.
  When food and raiment now grew scarce,
Fate put a period° to the farce,
And with exact poetic justice;
For John is landlord, Phyllis hostess;
They keep, at Staines, the Old Blue Boar,
Are cat and dog, and rogue and whore.
1719 1727

On Stella's Birthday°

Stella this day is thirty-four,
(We won't dispute a year or more:)
However, Stella, be not troubled,
Although thy size and years are doubled
Since first I saw thee at sixteen,
The brightest virgin on the green;
So little is thy form declined,
Made up so largely in thy mind.
  O, would it please the gods to split
Thy beauty, size, and years, and wit,
No age could furnish out a pair
Of nymphs so graceful, wise, and fair;
With half the lustre of your eyes,
With half your wit, your years, and size.
And then, before it grew too late,
How should I beg of gentle fate,
(That either nymph might have her swain,)
To split my worship too in twain.
1719 1727

Stella's Birthday°

March 13, 1727

This day, whate'er the fates decree,
Shall still° be kept with joy by me:
This day then let us not be told,

unwholesome diseased
period end
On Stella's Birthday This is the first of a series of birthday poems Swift wrote for Hester Johnson; it was written in fact for her thirty-eighth birthday on March 13, 1719. We can see here the tenderness and gentle mockery that characterize these poems as they do Swift's letters in the so-called *Journal to Stella*.
Stella's Birthday This is the last of the series; Stella died on January 28, 1728.
still always

That you are sick, and I grown old;
Nor think on our approaching ills,
And talk of spectacles and pills;
Tomorrow will be time enough
To hear such mortifying° stuff.
Yet, since from reason may be brought
A better and more pleasing thought,
Which can, in spite of all decays,
Support a few remaining days;
From not the gravest of divines
Accept for once some serious lines.
Although we now can form no more
Long schemes of life, as heretofore;
Yet you, while time is running fast,
Can look with joy on what is past.
Were future happiness and pain
A mere contrivance of the brain;
As atheists argue, to entice
And fit their proselytes for vice;
(The only comfort they propose,
To have companions in their woes)
Grant this the case; yet sure 'tis hard
That virtue, styled its own reward,
And by all sages understood
To be the chief of human good,
Should acting die, nor leave behind
Some lasting pleasure in the mind,
Which, by remembrance, will assuage
Grief, sickness, poverty, and age;
And strongly shoot a radiant dart
To shine through life's declining part.
Say, Stella, feel you no content,
Reflecting on a life well spent?
Your skilful hand employed to save
Despairing wretches from the grave;
And then supporting with your store
Those whom you dragged from death before: °
So Providence on mortals waits,
Preserving what it first creates.
Your generous boldness to defend
An innocent and absent friend;
That courage which can make you just
To merit humbled in the dust;
The detestation you express
For vice in all its glittering dress;

mortifying humbling, but also destroying vital or active powers
from death before Swift is eloquent in his tributes to Stella's charity, both in nursing the sick and in supporting them from her limited income.

That patience under torturing pain,
Where stubborn Stoics would complain:
  Must these like empty shadows pass,
Or forms reflected from a glass?
Or mere chimeras in the mind,
That fly and leave no marks behind?
Does not the body thrive and grow
By food of twenty years ago?
And, had it not been still supplied,
It must a thousand times have died.
Then who with reason can maintain
That no effects of food remain?
And is not virtue in mankind
The nutriment that feeds the mind;
Upheld by each good action past,
And still continued by the last?
Then, who with reason can pretend
That all effects of virtue end?
  Believe me, Stella, when you show
That true contempt for things below,
Nor prize your life for other ends,
Than merely to oblige your friends;
Your former actions claim their part;
And join to fortify your heart.
For Virtue in her daily race,
Like Janus,° bears a double face;
Looks back with joy where she has gone,
And therefore goes with courage on:
She at your sickly couch will wait,
And guide you to a better state.
  O then, whatever Heaven intends,
Take pity on your pitying friends!
Nor let your ills affect your mind,
To fancy they can be unkind.
Me, surely me, you ought to spare,
Who gladly would your suffering share;
Or give my scrap of life to you,
And think it far beneath your due;
You, to whose care so oft I owe
That I'm alive to tell you so.

1727 1727

Janus the god of beginnings, his symbol a double-faced head, looking both forward and backward

The Day of Judgment

With a whirl of thought oppressed,
I sunk from reverie to rest.
A horrid vision seized my head,
I saw the graves give up their dead!
Jove, armed with terrors, bursts the skies,
And thunder roars and lightning flies!
Amazed, confused, its fate unknown,
The world stands trembling at his throne!
While each pale sinner hangs his head,
Jove, nodding, shook the heavens, and said:
'Offending race of human kind,
By nature, reason, learning, blind;
You who, through frailty, stepped aside;
And you who never fell—through pride:
You who in different sects have shammed,
And come to see each other damned;
(So some folk told you, but they knew
No more of Jove's designs than you)
The world's mad business now is o'er,
And I resent these pranks no more.
I to such blockheads set my wit!
I damn such fools!—Go, go, you're bit.'

1731? 1774

Cassinus and Peter°

A Tragical Elegy

Two college sophs of Cambridge growth,
Both special wits and lovers both,
Conferring, as they used to meet,
On love and books, in rapture sweet;
(Muse find me names to fix my metre,
Cassinus this, and t'other Peter.)
Friend Peter to Cassinus goes,
To chat a while and warm his nose:
But such a sight was never seen,
The lad lay swallowed up in spleen.°
He seemed as just crept out of bed;
One greasy stocking round his head,
The t'other he sat down to darn,

Cassinus and Peter This poem deserves study rather than the curious notoriety it has received. The last line is often cited as evidence of Swift's horror of bodily functions, as if the poem were not a consistent mockery of the fatuously romantic idealist, down to his own slovenliness (only in part the result of distraction) and his visionary mad fit in ll. 79–88, similar to those of Dryden's heroic plays or of later 18th-century odes.

spleen melancholy, "vapors"; as the ensuing picture reveals, the image of a distracted lover

With threads of different coloured yarn;
His breeches torn, exposing wide
A ragged shirt and tawny hide.
Scorched were his shins, his legs were bare,
But well embrowned with dirt and hair.
A rug was o'er his shoulders thrown,
(A rug, for nightgown he had none,)
His jordan° stood in manner fitting
Between his legs, to spew° or spit in;
His ancient pipe, in sable dyed,
And half unsmoked, lay by his side.
Him thus accoutred Peter found,
With eyes in smoke and weeping drowned;
The leavings of his last night's pot°
On embers placed, to drink it hot.
'Why, Cassy, thou wilt doze thy pate:
What makes thee lie a-bed so late?
The finch, the linnet, and the thrush,
Their matins chant in every bush;
And I have heard thee oft salute
Aurora with thy early flute.
Heaven send thou hast not got the hyps!°
How! not a word come from thy lips?'
Then gave him some familiar thumps,
A college joke to cure the dumps.
The swain at last, with grief oppressed,
Cried, 'Celia!' thrice, and sighed the rest.
'Dear Cassy, though to ask I dread,
Yet ask I must—is Celia dead?'
'How happy I, were that the worst!
But I was fated to be curst!'
'Come, tell us, has she played the whore?'
'O Peter, would it were no more!'
'Why, plague confound her sandy locks!
Say, has the small or greater pox°
Sunk down her nose, or seamed her face?
Be easy, 'tis a common case.'
'O Peter! beauty's but a varnish,
Which time and accidents will tarnish:
But Celia has contrived to blast
Those beauties that might ever last.
Nor can imagination guess,
Nor eloquence divine express,
How that ungrateful charming maid

jordan chamber pot
spew vomit
pot of wine
hyps hypochondria
small . . . pox smallpox or syphilis, the latter causing collapse of the bridge of the nose in advanced stages

My purest passion has betrayed:
Conceive the most envenomed dart
To pierce an injured lover's heart.'
'Why, hang her; though she seemed so coy,
I know, she loves the barber's boy.'
'Friend Peter, this I could excuse,
For every nymph has leave to choose;
Nor have I reason to complain,
She loves a more deserving swain.
But oh! how ill hast thou divined
A crime that shocks all humankind;
A deed unknown to female race,
At which the sun should hide his face:
Advice in vain you would apply—
Then leave me to despair and die.
Yet, kind Arcadians,° on my urn
These elegies and sonnets burn;
And on the marble grave these rhymes,
A monument to after-times—
"Here Cassy lies, by Celia slain,
And dying, never told his pain."
Vain empty world, farewell. But hark,
The loud Cerberian triple bark;°
And there—behold Alecto° stand,
A whip of scorpions in her hand:
Lo, Charon° from his leaky wherry
Beckoning to waft me o'er the ferry:
I come! I come! Medusa° see,
Her serpents hiss direct at me.
Begone; unhand me, hellish fry:
Avaunt—ye cannot say 'twas I.'°
'Dear Cassy, thou must purge and bleed;°
I fear thou wilt be mad indeed.
But now, by friendship's sacred laws,
I here conjure thee, tell the cause;
And Celia's horrid fact relate:
Thy friend would gladly share thy fate.'
'To force it out, my heart must rend;
Yet when conjured by such a friend—
Think, Peter, how my soul is racked!
These eyes, these eyes, beheld the fact.

Arcadians the shepherds of pastoral Greece. A famous subject of paintings and prints is a group of shepherds peering at a gravestone that reads "Et in Arcadia ego," interpreted as Death's saying, "Even in Arcadia I am."
Cerberian . . . bark the bark of three-headed Cerberus at the gates of the underworld
Alecto one of the three Furies
Charon the ferryman of the dead across the Styx
Medusa the gorgon whose locks are snakes and whose gaze can turn anything to stone
Avaunt . . . 'twas I "See *Macbeth*" (Swift); a condensation of two outcries of Macbeth upon seeing Banquo's ghost: "Thou canst not say I did it" and "Avaunt! and quit my sight!" (III.IV.50, 93)
purge and bleed laxatives and blood-letting as cures for the spleen

Now bend thine ear, since out it must;
But, when thou seest me laid in dust,
The secret thou shalt ne'er impart,
Not to the nymph that keeps thy heart;
(How would her virgin soul bemoan
A crime to all her sex unknown!)
Nor whisper to the tattling reeds°
The blackest of all female deeds;
Nor blab it on the lonely rocks,
Where Echo sits, and listening mocks;°
Nor let the zephyr's treacherous gale
Through Cambridge waft the direful tale;
Nor to the chattering feathered race°
Discover° Celia's foul disgrace.
But, if you fail, my spectre dread,
Attending nightly round your bed—
And yet I dare confide in you;
So take my secret, and adieu:
  Nor wonder how I lost my wits;
Oh! Celia, Celia, Celia shits!'

1734

Gulliver's Travels

Gulliver's Travels (as the book has come to be known) was probably begun by 1720 and completed in the summer of 1725; the publisher received the manuscript "he knew not whence, nor from whom, dropped at his house in the dark, from a hackney-coach." The book had immediate success. "From the highest to the lowest it is universally read," Gay wrote to Swift in Ireland, "from the cabinet-council to the nursery." And Pope wrote, "The countenance with which it is received by some statesmen is delightful; I wish I could tell you how every single man looks upon it, to observe which has been my whole diversion this fortnight." In 1735, when Swift supervised a new edition, he added the letter from Gulliver to his cousin Sympson which is given here; and the lament of Mary Gulliver is one of a series of poems inspired by the *Travels* and written in all probability by Gay, perhaps with Pope's collaboration.

Swift's great satire is recounted by a stolid, unimaginative, decent man who can, under the stress of pride, become arrogantly complacent or—once he has suffered disenchantment—arrogantly misanthropic. "I tell you after all that I do not hate mankind," Swift wrote to Pope in 1725; "it is *vous autres* who hate them because you would have them reasonable animals, and are angry for being disappointed." "You others" includes Gulliver himself, who seems blandly persuaded that man is a rational animal until he discovers what a truly rational animal is (in the form of a

the tattling reeds to which Midas' wife confided the terrible secret that he had ass's ears
listening mocks The nymph Echo was punished (for impeding Hera's investigation of Zeus' adulteries) by being denied all speech except what she could repeat of others' words.
chattering . . . race e.g. parrots
Discover disclose

horse) and what kind of animal man can be at worst (in the form, unfortunately, of man). Swift's own definition of man is a creature *rationis capax,* that is, capable of reason, but not at all securely in possession of it. What he presents in the great fourth voyage is the image of man in a state of full degeneration, his bestiality only intensified by his vestigial powers of mind; the Yahoo is offered as a limiting case of what man can become, and he inevitably raises the question of how far man has moved toward that limit already.

The Houyhnhnm, in contrast, is a thoroughly rational animal. He is no more than an animal in that he has no intimations of immortality or of divinity; Nature is the First Mother to whom in death he returns, and he can boast of himself as "the Perfection of Nature" but cannot imagine that he might be something more. His life is mild and temperate, for his passions are thoroughly in the control of his reason; and his reason is an immediate, practical, intuitive power for discerning what is right as well as what is efficient. Houyhnhnm life, then, is neither spirited nor spiritual; it has the virtues of simplicity, honesty, and peacefulness. These are virtues man rarely attains and often wishes he could, but they are not the virtues he celebrates in his heroic, erotic, or visionary art. It is to be expected, then, that that life would not finally have great appeal to man's nature, and Swift teases us with the fact—that rational goodness is something we cannot long endure.

Is the alternative to be a Yahoo? Gulliver, once he awakens to disenchantment with men, cannot really imagine more than these two alternatives and ignores the extent to which he differs from either. Resolved to pass as a Houyhnhnm and affecting the outward mannerisms (of neigh and canter), he desperately seeks to dissociate himself from the Yahoos and is mortified by their attraction to him as one of their kind. By the time of his return, when he encounters a friendly and generous Portuguese captain, Gulliver can only see a Yahoo (as, with terror and disgust, he does in his mirror); even more, he retreats in disgust from his family and seeks solace with horses, if only because they look and smell like Houyhnhnms. Having come belatedly to see below the surfaces he once unquestioningly accepted, Gulliver has not achieved discrimination; instead, he becomes devoted to a new surface.

How does this come about? In the first voyage, Gulliver finds himself among the Lilliputians, one-twelfth his bulk, and gradually adjusts to their scale of vision; for, while he decently refuses to enslave their enemies in Blefuscu (the only other island in their world and therefore the object of conquest), he rather proudly accepts the court honor of being named a *nardac.* And when he is accused of adultery with a minister's wife, he does not laugh at the incongruity, but solemnly defends himself against the charges. In Lilliput he discovers a people who once lived by rational institutions but have learned to pervert their laws into instruments of domination and self-seeking. Words have become emptied of meaning even as they remain full of prestige; the Emperor's subjects have learned to scamper for safety when he speaks of his mercy or lenity, and Gulliver must finally flee to save his own life.

In his second voyage, to Brobdingnag, the proportions are reversed, and Gulliver finds himself a Lilliputian in a land of giants. They are a mixed lot, but the King is, in contrast to George I of England, the best of them—large-souled, generous, with intellectual curiosity and an acute sense of justice. When Gulliver describes to him the institutions of England, the King easily perceives what Gulliver does not mention—the way in which they are open to corruption and the travesty they readily become. As the King sums it up, "By what I have gathered from your own relation, and the answers I have with much pains wringed and extorted from you, I cannot but conclude the bulk of your natives to be the most pernicious race of little odious vermin that nature ever suffered to crawl upon the surface of the earth." Undeterred, in fact stirred to pride, Gulliver offers to give the King the secret of gunpowder so that he can maim and destroy his enemies and gain absolute power; he does this with no active evil intent, but with the single-minded obliviousness that Swift so brilliantly catches in his satires (notably in the speaker of *A Modest Proposal*). When the King refuses with horror, Gulliver describes with scorn the limited culture of Brobdingnag: short clear laws and no need for lawyers, no tolerance for metaphysics and (it is implied) religious mystery, a balanced ("mixed") state without internal factions or rivalries, a lucid prose and the refusal to write unnecessary books. It is hardly what a European would call "civilization," and it looks ahead (as a fallible but reformed society) to the devastating rationality of the Houyhnhnms.

The third voyage takes Gulliver to Laputa, the flying island, where everyone who counts is addicted to "pure" pursuits—astronomy and music—and utterly divorced from the practical life around him. With one telling exception: the island is a portable court and descends over any province that aspires to freedom, denying it light or rainfall, even ready to crush it to earth in order to maintain power. On the mainland Gulliver encounters Lord Munodi (who, as his name indicates, hates this world), a man of taste and judgment, who must bow to the fashions for experiment and innovation. Whatever is done must be done with the greatest possible show of ingenuity (if pincushions are needed, they must be made out of marble), and the Grand Academy of Lagado (a satire on the Royal Society of England) is devoted to elaborate pseudo-science, designed not for use but for show. Among his other adventures, Gulliver encounters the Struldbruggs, a special race blessed with immortality, or rather cursed with it, for they are not free of degeneration; instead of being oracles of wisdom, they soon descend into a bickering, avaricious, melancholy senility.

At every point Gulliver is confronted with the distinction between idea and execution, the rational possibility and the corrupt practice, the capacity for reason and the passionate degeneracy that overtakes it. His responses are never acute; he may resent an injury or an insult, sidestep a larcenous or murderous gesture, but he remains essentially uncritical and unreflective. In the fourth voyage all that he has seen is made inescapable, and he moves from an insensitive complacency to an unthinking misanthropy, simply redirecting his pride from identification with his kind to hatred of them and to a new and impossible effort at identification with the Houyhnhnms. What Swift means us to conclude has been much debated by scholars. Is he ridiculing a naïve trust in reason and presenting us with a horrible rationalistic utopia of horses, or is he rather showing us how little we really want to be reasonable and how easily we allow the glamour of our corruption to persuade us of its greatness (in contrast with its ugly enactment by the Yahoos)? However one resolves the questions, one can see why a modern critic (T. S. Eliot) refers to Swift's account of Gulliver's fourth voyage as one of the greatest triumphs of the human spirit.

Travels into Several Remote Nations of the World

The Publisher to the Reader

The author of these *Travels,* Mr. Lemuel Gulliver, is my ancient and intimate friend; there is likewise some relation between us by the mother's side. About three years ago Mr. Gulliver, growing weary of the concourse of curious people coming to him at his house in Redriff,[1] made a small purchase of land, with a convenient house, near Newark in Nottinghamshire, his native country; where he now lives retired, yet in good esteem among his neighbours.

Although Mr. Gulliver was born in Nottinghamshire, where his father dwelt, yet I have heard him say his family came from Oxfordshire; to confirm which, I have observed in the churchyard at Banbury, in that county, several tombs and monuments of the Gullivers.

Before he quitted Redriff, he left the custody of the following papers in my hands, with the liberty to dispose of them as I should think fit. I have carefully perused them three times: the style is very plain and simple; and the only fault I find is that the author, after the manner of travellers, is a little too circumstantial. There is an air of truth apparent through the whole; and indeed, the author was so distinguished for his veracity that it became a sort of proverb among his neighbours at Redriff, when anyone affirmed a thing, to say it was as true as if Mr. Gulliver had spoke it.

By the advice of several worthy persons to whom, with the author's permission, I communicated these papers, I now venture to send them into the world, hoping they may be at least for some time a better entertainment to our young noblemen than the common scribbles of politics and party.

This volume would have been at least twice as large if I had not made bold to strike out innumerable passages relating to the winds and tides, as well as to the variations and bearings in the several voyages; together with the minute descriptions of the management of the ship in storms, in the style of sailors: likewise the account of the longitudes and latitudes; wherein I have reason to apprehend that Mr. Gulliver may be a little dissatisfied: but I was resolved to fit the work as much as possible to the general capacity of readers. However, if my own ignorance in sea-affairs shall have led me to commit some mistakes, I alone am answerable for them: and if any traveller hath a curiosity to see the whole work at large, as it came from the hand of the author, I will be ready to gratify him.

As for any further particulars relating to the author, the reader will receive satisfaction from the first pages of the book.

Richard Sympson.[2]

1. Rotherhithe, dock section of East London south of the Thames.
2. Gulliver's angry letter to his "publisher" follows Part IV.

Part One: A Voyage to Lilliput

Chapter One: The author gives some account of himself and family; his first inducements to travel. He is shipwrecked, and swims for his life, gets safe on shore in the country of Lilliput, is made a prisoner, and carried up the country.

My father had a small estate in Nottinghamshire; I was the third of five sons. He sent me to Emmanuel College in Cambridge at fourteen years old, where I resided three years, and applied myself close to my studies: but the charge of maintaining me (although I had a very scanty allowance) being too great for a narrow fortune, I was bound apprentice to Mr. James Bates, an eminent surgeon in London, with whom I continued four years; and my father now and then sending me small sums of money, I laid them out in learning navigation and other parts of the mathematics useful to those who intend to travel, as I always believed it would be some time or other my fortune to do. When I left Mr. Bates, I went down to my father; where, by the assistance of him and my uncle John and some other relations, I got forty pounds and a promise of thirty pounds a year to maintain me at Leyden;[1] there I studied physic two years and seven months, knowing it would be useful in long voyages.

Soon after my return from Leyden, I was recommended by my good master, Mr. Bates, to be surgeon[2] to the *Swallow,* Captain Abraham Pannell commander; with whom I continued three years and a half, making a voyage or two into the Levant[3] and some other parts. When I came back, I resolved to settle in London, to which Mr. Bates, my master, encouraged me, and by him I was recommended to several patients. I took part of a small house in the Old Jury,[4] and, being advised to alter my condition, I married Mrs.[5] Mary Burton, second daughter to Mr. Edmond Burton, hosier in Newgate Street, with whom I received four hundred pounds for a portion.[6]

But, my good master Bates dying in two years after and I having few friends, my business began to fail, for my conscience would not suffer me to imitate the bad practice of too many among my brethren. Having therefore consulted with my wife and some of my acquaintance, I determined to go again to sea. I was surgeon successively in two ships, and made several voyages, for six years, to the East and West Indies, by which I got some addition to my fortune. My hours of leisure I spent in reading the best authors ancient and modern, being always provided with a good number of books; and when I was ashore, in observing the manners and dispositions of the people, as well as learning their language, wherein I had a great facility by the strength of my memory.

The last of these voyages not proving very fortunate, I grew weary of the sea, and intended to stay at home with my wife and family. I removed from the Old Jury to Fetter Lane and from thence to Wapping, hoping to get business among the sailors; but it would not turn to account. After three years' expectation that things would mend, I accepted an advantageous offer from

1. The Dutch University of Leyden, famous for the study of medicine ("physic").
2. Ship's medical officer.
3. Eastern Mediterranean.
4. I.e. "Old Jewry," a street in the City of London.
5. Mistress, a title applied to any woman, single or married.
6. Dowry.

Captain William Prichard, master of the *Antelope,* who was making a voyage to the South Sea. We set sail from Bristol May 4th, 1699, and our voyage at first was very prosperous.

It would not be proper, for some reasons, to trouble the reader with the particulars of our adventures in those seas: let it suffice to inform him that in our passage from thence to the East Indies we were driven by a violent storm to the northwest of Van Diemen's Land.[7] By an observation, we found ourselves in the latitude of 30 degrees 2 minutes south. Twelve of our crew were dead by immoderate labour and ill food; the rest were in a very weak condition. On the fifth of November, which was the beginning of summer in those parts, the weather being very hazy, the seamen spied a rock within half a cable's length [8] of the ship; but the wind was so strong that we were driven directly upon it and immediately split. Six of the crew, of whom I was one, having let down the boat into the sea, made a shift to get clear of the ship and the rock. We rowed by my computation about three leagues,[9] till we were able to work no longer, being already spent with labour while we were in the ship. We therefore trusted ourselves to the mercy of the waves, and in about half an hour the boat was overset by a sudden flurry from the north. What became of my companions in the boat, as well as of those who escaped on the rock or were left in the vessel, I cannot tell; but conclude they were all lost.

For my own part, I swam as fortune directed me, and was pushed forward by wind and tide. I often let my legs drop and could feel no bottom: but when I was almost gone and able to struggle no longer, I found myself within my depth; and by this time the storm was much abated. The declivity was so small that I walked near a mile before I got to the shore, which I conjectured was about eight o'clock in the evening. I then advanced forward near half a mile but could not discover any sign of houses or inhabitants; at least I was in so weak a condition that I did not observe them. I was extremely tired, and with that, and the heat of the weather, and about half a pint of brandy that I drank as I left the ship, I found myself much inclined to sleep. I lay down on the grass, which was very short and soft, where I slept sounder than ever I remember to have done in my life, and, as I reckoned, above nine hours; for when I awaked, it was just daylight. I attempted to rise but was not able to stir: for as I happened to lie on my back, I found my arms and legs were strongly fastened on each side to the ground; and my hair, which was long and thick, tied down in the same manner. I likewise felt several slender ligatures across my body from my armpits to my thighs. I could only look upwards, the sun began to grow hot, and the light offended my eyes. I heard a confused noise about me, but, in the posture I lay, could see nothing except the sky.

In a little time I felt something alive moving on my left leg, which, advancing gently forward over my breast, came almost up to my chin; when, bending my eyes downwards as much as I could, I perceived it to be a human creature not six inches high,[10] with a bow and arrow in his hands, and a quiver

7. Anthony Van Dieman (1593–1645) was a Dutch explorer whose name was given both to northwestern Australia and to Tasmania.

8. About 300 feet.

9. About nine miles.

10. The scale in Lilliput is roughly one-twelfth of normal measurements (as in Brobdingnag it will be twelve times).

at his back. In the meantime I felt at least forty more of the same kind (as I conjectured) following the first. I was in the utmost astonishment, and roared so loud that they all ran back in a fright; and some of them, as I was afterwards told, were hurt with the falls they got by leaping from my sides upon the ground. However, they soon returned, and one of them, who ventured so far as to get a full sight of my face, lifting up his hands and eyes by way of admiration,[11] cried out in a shrill but distinct voice, *Hekinah degul:* the others repeated the same words several times, but I then knew not what they meant.

I lay all this while, as the reader may believe, in great uneasiness: at length, struggling to get loose, I had the fortune to break the strings and wrench out the pegs that fastened my left arm to the ground; for, by lifting it up to my face, I discovered the methods they had taken to bind me; and, at the same time, with a violent pull which gave me excessive pain, I a little loosened the strings that tied down my hair on the left side, so that I was just able to turn my head about two inches. But the creatures ran off a second time, before I could seize them; whereupon there was a great shout in a very shrill accent, and after it ceased, I heard one of them cry aloud, *Tolgo phonac;* when in an instant I felt above an hundred arrows discharged on my left hand, which pricked me like so many needles; and besides they shot another flight into the air, as we do bombs in Europe, whereof many, I suppose, fell on my body (though I felt them not) and some on my face, which I immediately covered with my left hand. When this shower of arrows was over, I fell a-groaning with grief and pain, and then striving again to get loose, they discharged another volley larger than the first, and some of them attempted with spears to stick me in the sides; but, by good luck I had on me a buff jerkin,[12] which they could not pierce.

I thought it the most prudent method to lie still, and my design was to continue so till night, when, my left hand being already loose, I could easily free myself: and as for the inhabitants, I had reason to believe I might be a match for the greatest armies they could bring against me, if they were all of the same size with him that I saw. But fortune disposed otherwise of me. When the people observed I was quiet, they discharged no more arrows: but by the noise increasing, I knew their numbers were greater; and about four yards from me, over-against my right ear, I heard a knocking for above an hour, like people at work; when, turning my head that way as well as the pegs and strings would permit me, I saw a stage erected about a foot and a half from the ground, capable of holding four of the inhabitants, with two or three ladders to mount it: from whence one of them, who seemed to be a person of quality,[13] made me a long speech, whereof I understood not one syllable. But I should have mentioned that before the principal person began his oration, he cried out three times, *Langro dehul san* (these words and the former were afterwards repeated and explained to me). Whereupon immediately about fifty of the inhabitants came, and cut the strings that fastened the left side of my head, which gave me the liberty of turning it to the right and of observing the person and gesture of him who was to speak.

11. "Admiration" and related words are used throughout in the Latinate sense of astonishment, with no implication of approval.
12. Leather jacket.
13. Nobility or high social rank.

He appeared to be of a middle age and taller than any of the other three who attended him, whereof one was a page who held up his train and seemed to be somewhat longer than my middle finger; the other two stood one on each side to support him. He acted every part of an orator, and I could observe many periods[14] of threatenings, and others of promises, pity, and kindness. I answered in a few words but in the most submissive manner, lifting up my left hand and both eyes to the sun, as calling him for a witness; and being almost famished with hunger, having not eaten a morsel for some hours before I left the ship, I found the demands of nature so strong upon me that I could not forbear showing my impatience (perhaps against the strict rules of decency) by putting my finger frequently on my mouth, to signify that I wanted food. The *Hurgo* (for so they call a great lord, as I afterwards learnt) understood me very well. He descended from the stage and commanded that several ladders should be applied to my sides, on which above an hundred of the inhabitants mounted and walked towards my mouth, laden with baskets full of meat, which had been provided and sent thither by the King's orders upon the first intelligence he received of me. I observed there was the flesh of several animals, but could not distinguish them by the taste. There were shoulders, legs, and loins shaped like those of mutton, and very well dressed, but smaller than the wings of a lark. I eat [15] them by two or three at a mouthful, and took three loaves at a time, about the bigness of musket bullets.

They supplied me as fast as they could, showing a thousand marks of wonder and astonishment at my bulk and appetite. I then made another sign that I wanted drink. They found by my eating that a small quantity would not suffice me, and, being a most ingenious people, they slung up with great dexterity one of their largest hogsheads, then rolled it towards my hand, and beat out the top; I drank it off at a draught, which I might well do, for it hardly held half a pint, and tasted like a small wine of Burgundy but much more delicious. They brought me a second hogshead, which I drank in the same manner, and made signs for more, but they had none to give me. When I had performed these wonders, they shouted for joy and danced upon my breast, repeating several times as they did at first, *Hekinah degul*. They made me a sign that I should throw down the two hogsheads, but first warned the people below to stand out of the way, crying aloud, *Borach mivola*, and, when they saw the vessels in the air, there was an universal shout of *Hekinah degul*. I confess I was often tempted, while they were passing backwards and forwards on my body, to seize forty or fifty of the first that came in my reach and dash them against the ground. But the remembrance of what I had felt, which probably might not be the worst they could do, and the promise of honour I made them, for so I interpreted my submissive behaviour, soon drove out those imaginations. Besides, I now considered myself as bound by the laws of hospitality to a people who had treated me with so much expense and magnificence. However, in my thoughts I could not sufficiently wonder at the intrepidity of these diminutive mortals, who durst venture to mount and walk on my body, while one of my hands was at liberty, without trembling at the very sight of so prodigious a creature as I must appear to them.

After some time, when they observed that I made no more demands for

14. Sentences.
15. Pronounced "ett" and meaning "ate," as elsewhere in the book.

meat, there appeared before me a person of high rank from his Imperial Majesty. His Excellency, having mounted on the small of my right leg, advanced forwards up to my face, with about a dozen of his retinue. And producing his credentials under the Signet Royal, which he applied close to my eyes, spoke about ten minutes, without any signs of anger but with a kind of determinate resolution; often pointing forwards, which, as I afterwards found, was towards the capital city about half a mile distant, whither it was agreed by his Majesty in council that I must be conveyed. I answered in few words but to no purpose, and made a sign with my hand that was loose, putting it to the other (but over his Excellency's head, for fear of hurting him or his train) and then to my own head and body, to signify that I desired my liberty. It appeared that he understood me well enough, for he shook his head by way of disapprobation, and held his hand in a posture to show that I must be carried as a prisoner. However, he made other signs to let me understand that I should have meat and drink enough and very good treatment. Whereupon I once more thought of attempting to break my bonds, but again, when I felt the smart of their arrows upon my face and hands, which were all in blisters, and many of the darts still sticking in them, and observing likewise that the number of my enemies increased, I gave tokens to let them know that they might do with me what they pleased. Upon this the *Hurgo* and his train withdrew with much civility and cheerful countenances. Soon after I heard a general shout, with frequent repetitions of the words, *Peplom selan,* and I felt great numbers of the people on my left side relaxing the cords to such a degree that I was able to turn upon my right and to ease myself with making water; which I very plentifully did, to the great astonishment of the people, who conjecturing by my motions what I was going to do, immediately opened to the right and left on that side to avoid the torrent which fell with such noise and violence from me. But before this, they had daubed my face and both my hands with a sort of ointment very pleasant to the smell, which in a few minutes removed all the smart of their arrows. These circumstances, added to the refreshment I had received by their victuals and drink, which were very nourishing, disposed me to sleep. I slept about eight hours, as I was afterwards assured; and it was no wonder, for the physicians, by the Emperor's order, had mingled a sleeping potion in the hogsheads of wine.

It seems that upon the first moment I was discovered sleeping on the ground after my landing, the Emperor had early notice of it by an express,[16] and determined in council that I should be tied in the manner I have related (which was done in the night while I slept), that plenty of meat and drink should be sent me, and a machine prepared to carry me to the capital city.

This resolution perhaps may appear very bold and dangerous, and I am confident would not be imitated by any prince in Europe on the like occasion; however, in my opinion, it was extremely prudent as well as generous. For supposing these people had endeavoured to kill me with their spears and arrows while I was asleep, I should certainly have awaked with the first sense of smart, which might so far have roused my rage and strength as to enable me to break the strings wherewith I was tied; after which, as they were not able to make resistance, so they could expect no mercy.

16. Rapid messenger.

These people are most excellent mathematicians, and arrived to a great perfection in mechanics by the countenance and encouragement of the Emperor, who is a renowned patron of learning. This prince hath several machines fixed on wheels for the carriage of trees and other great weights. He often builds his largest men of war, whereof some are nine foot long, in the woods where the timber grows, and has them carried on these engines [17] three or four hundred yards to the sea. Five hundred carpenters and engineers were immediately set at work to prepare the greatest engine they had. It was a frame of wood raised three inches from the ground, about seven foot long and four wide, moving upon twenty-two wheels. The shout I heard was upon the arrival of this engine, which it seems set out in four hours after my landing. It was brought parallel to me as I lay. But the principal difficulty was to raise and place me in this vehicle. Eighty poles, each of one foot high, were erected for this purpose, and very strong cords of the bigness of packthread were fastened by hooks to many bandages, which the workmen had girt round my neck, my hands, my body, and my legs. Nine hundred of the strongest men were employed to draw up these cords by many pulleys fastened on the poles, and thus, in less than three hours, I was raised and slung into the engine and there tied fast. All this I was told, for while the whole operation was performing, I lay in a profound sleep by the force of that soporiferous medicine infused into my liquor. Fifteen hundred of the Emperor's largest horses, each about four inches and a half high, were employed to draw me towards the metropolis, which, as I said, was half a mile distant.

About four hours after we began our journey, I awaked by a very ridiculous accident; for, the carriage being stopped a while to adjust something that was out of order, two or three of the young natives had the curiosity to see how I looked when I was asleep; they climbed up into the engine, and, advancing very softly to my face, one of them, an officer in the guards, put the sharp end of his half-pike [18] a good way up into my left nostril, which tickled my nose like a straw and made me sneeze violently: whereupon they stole off unperceived, and it was three weeks before I knew the cause of my awaking so suddenly. We made a long march the remaining part of the day, and rested at night with five hundred guards on each side of me, half with torches and half with bows and arrows, ready to shoot me if I should offer to stir. The next morning at sunrise we continued our march, and arrived within two hundred yards of the city gates about noon. The Emperor and all his court came out to meet us, but his great officers would by no means suffer his Majesty to endanger his person by mounting on my body.

At the place where the carriage stopped, there stood an ancient temple, esteemed to be the largest in the whole kingdom, which, having been polluted some years before by an unnatural murder, was, according to the zeal of those people, looked on as profane, and therefore had been applied to common use, and all the ornaments and furniture carried away.[19] In this edifice it was determined I should lodge. The great gate fronting to the north was about four foot high and almost two foot wide, through which I could easily creep.

17. Machines, devices.
18. Short spear-like staff.
19. The temple suggests Westminster Hall, where King Charles I was condemned to death in 1648.

themselves to me, and I spoke to them in as many languages as I had the least smattering of, which were High and Low Dutch, Latin, French, Spanish, Italian, and Lingua Franca;[4] but all to no purpose.

After about two hours the court retired, and I was left with a strong guard to prevent the impertinence and probably the malice of the rabble, who were very impatient to crowd about me as near as they durst, and some of them had the impudence to shoot their arrows at me as I sat on the ground by the door of my house, whereof one very narrowly missed my left eye. But the colonel ordered six of the ringleaders to be seized, and thought no punishment so proper as to deliver them bound into my hands, which some of his soldiers accordingly did, pushing them forwards with the butt-ends of their pikes into my reach. I took them all in my right hand, put five of them into my coat-pocket, and, as to the sixth, I made a countenance as if I would eat him alive. The poor man squalled terribly, and the colonel and his officers were in much pain, especially when they saw me take out my penknife: but I soon put them out of fear; for, looking mildly, and immediately cutting the strings he was bound with, I set him gently on the ground, and away he ran. I treated the rest in the same manner, taking them one by one out of my pocket, and I observed both the soldiers and people were highly obliged at this mark of my clemency, which was represented very much to my advantage at court.

Towards night I got with some difficulty into my house, where I lay on the ground, and continued to do so about a fortnight; during which time the Emperor gave orders to have a bed prepared for me. Six hundred beds of the common measure were brought in carriages, and worked up in my house; an hundred and fifty of their beds sewn together made up the breadth and length, and these were four double, which however kept me but very indifferently from the hardness of the floor, that was of smooth stone. By the same computation they provided me with sheets, blankets, and coverlets tolerable enough for one who had been so long enured to hardships as I.

As the news of my arrival spread through the kingdom, it brought prodigious numbers of rich, idle, and curious people to see me; so that the villages were almost emptied, and great neglect of tillage and household affairs must have ensued if his Imperial Majesty had not provided by several proclamations and orders of state against this inconveniency. He directed that those who had already beheld me should return home, and not presume to come within fifty yards of my house without licence from court: whereby the secretaries of state got considerable fees.

In the meantime, the Emperor held frequent councils to debate what course should be taken with me; and I was afterwards assured by a particular friend, a person of great quality, who was as much in the secret as any, that the court was under many difficulties concerning me. They apprehended my breaking loose, that my diet would be very expensive, and might cause a famine. Sometimes they determined to starve me, or at least to shoot me in the face and hands with poisoned arrows, which would soon dispatch me: but again they considered that the stench of so large a carcass might produce a plague in the metropolis and probably spread through the whole kingdom. In the midst of

4. "High Dutch" is German and "Low Dutch" is Dutch; "Lingua Franca" is the mixture of tongues used as a jargon by Mediterranean traders.

these consultations, several officers of the army went to the door of the great council-chamber; and two of them being admitted, gave an account of my behaviour to the six criminals above-mentioned, which made so favourable an impression in the breast of his Majesty and the whole board in my behalf, that an imperial commission was issued out obliging all the villages nine hundred yards round the city to deliver in every morning six beeves, forty sheep, and other victuals for my sustenance; together with a proportionable quantity of bread and wine and other liquors: for the due payment of which his Majesty gave assignments upon his treasury. For this prince lives chiefly upon his own demesnes,[5] seldom except upon great occasions raising any subsidies upon his subjects, who are bound to attend him in his wars at their own expense. An establishment was also made of six hundred persons to be my domestics, who had board-wages allowed for their maintenance and tents built for them very conveniently on each side of my door. It was likewise ordered, that three hundred tailors should make me a suit of clothes after the fashion of the country: that six of his Majesty's greatest scholars should be employed to instruct me in their language: and, lastly, that the Emperor's horses, and those of the nobility and troops of guards, should be exercised in my sight, to accustom themselves to me.

All these orders were duly put in execution, and in about three weeks I made a great progress in learning their language; during which time the Emperor frequently honoured me with his visits, and was pleased to assist my masters in teaching me. We began already to converse together in some sort; and the first words I learnt were to express my desire that he would please to give me my liberty, which I every day repeated on my knees. His answer, as I could apprehend, was that this must be a work of time, not to be thought on without the advice of his council, and that first I must *lumos kelmin pesso desmar lon emposo;* that is, swear a peace with him and his kingdom. However, that I should be used with all kindness; and he advised me to acquire, by my patience and discreet behaviour, the good opinion of himself and his subjects. He desired I would not take it ill if he gave orders to certain proper officers to search me; for probably I might carry about me several weapons, which must needs be dangerous things if they answered the bulk of so prodigious a person. I said his Majesty should be satisfied, for I was ready to strip myself and turn up my pockets before him. This I delivered part in words and part in signs. He replied that by the laws of the kingdom I must be searched by two of his officers; that he knew this could not be done without my consent and assistance; that he had so good an opinion of my generosity and justice as to trust their persons in my hands: that whatever they took from me should be returned when I left the country, or paid for at the rate which I would set upon them. I took up the two officers in my hands, put them first into my coat-pockets, and then into every other pocket about me, except my two fobs, and another secret pocket which I had no mind should be searched, wherein I had some little necessaries of no consequence to any but myself. In one of my fobs there was a silver watch, and in the other a small quantity of gold in a purse. These gentlemen, having pen, ink, and paper about them, made an exact inventory of everything they saw, and when they had done, desired I would set them

5. On the income from royal estates.

down that they might deliver it to the Emperor. This inventory I afterwards translated into English, and is word for word as follows:

"*Imprimis,* In the right coat-pocket of the Great Man-Mountain (for so I interpret the words *Quinbus Flestrin*) after the strictest search, we found only one great piece of coarse cloth, large enough to be a foot-cloth for your Majesty's chief room of state. In the left pocket, we saw a huge silver chest, with a cover of the same metal, which we the searchers were not able to lift. We desired it should be opened, and one of us, stepping into it, found himself up to the mid leg in a sort of dust, some part whereof, flying up to our faces, set us both a-sneezing for several times together. In his right waistcoat-pocket, we found a prodigious bundle of white thin substances, folded one over another, about the bigness of three men, tied with a strong cable, and marked with black figures; which we humbly conceive to be writings, every letter almost half as large as the palm of our hands. In the left, there was a sort of engine, from the back of which were extended twenty long poles, resembling the palisados before your Majesty's court; wherewith we conjecture the Man-Mountain combs his head, for we did not always trouble him with questions, because we found it a great difficulty to make him understand us. In the large pocket on the right side of his middle cover (so I translate the word *ranfu-lo,* by which they meant my breeches) we saw a hollow pillar of iron, about the length of a man, fastened to a strong piece of timber, larger than the pillar; and upon one side of the pillar were huge pieces of iron sticking out, cut into strange figures, which we know not what to make of. In the left pocket, another engine of the same kind. In the smaller pocket on the right side were several round flat pieces of white and red metal of different bulk; some of the white, which seemed to be silver, were so large and heavy that my comrade and I could hardly lift them. In the left pocket were two black pillars irregularly shaped: we could not, without difficulty, reach the top of them as we stood at the bottom of his pocket. One of them was covered and seemed all of a piece: but at the upper end of the other there appeared a white round substance, about twice the bigness of our heads. Within each of these was enclosed a prodigious plate of steel; which, by our orders, we obliged him to show us, because we apprehended they might be dangerous engines. He took them out of their cases, and told us, that in his own country his practice was to shave his beard with one of these and to cut his meat with the other.

There were two pockets which we could not enter: these he called his fobs; they were two large slits cut into the top of his middle cover, but squeezed close by the pressure of his belly. Out of the right fob hung a great silver chain, with a wonderful kind of engine at the bottom. We directed him to draw out whatever was at the end of that chain; which appeared to be a globe, half silver and half of some transparent metal: for on the transparent side we saw certain strange figures circularly drawn, and thought we could touch them, until we found our fingers stopped with that lucid substance. He put this engine to our ears, which made an incessant noise like that of a watermill. And we conjecture it is either some unknown animal, or the god that he worships: but we are more inclined to the latter opinion, because he assured us (if we understood him right, for he expressed himself very imperfectly) that he seldom did anything without consulting it. He called it his oracle, and said it pointed out the time for every action of his life. From the left fob he took out a net almost large enough for a fisherman, but contrived to open and shut like a purse, and served him for the same use: we found therein several massy pieces of yellow metal, which, if they be of real gold, must be of immense value.

"Having thus, in obedience to your Majesty's commands, diligently searched all his pockets, we observed a girdle about his waist made of the hide of some prodigious animal; from which, on the left side, hung a sword of the length of five men, and on the right, a bag or pouch divided into two cells, each cell capable of holding three of your Majesty's subjects. In one of these cells were several globes or balls of a most ponderous metal, about the bigness of our heads, and required a strong hand to lift them: the other cell contained a heap of certain black grains, but of no great bulk or weight, for we could hold above fifty of them in the palms of our hands.

"This is an exact inventory of what we found about the body of the Man-Mountain, who used us with great civility and due respect to your Majesty's commission. Signed and sealed on the fourth day of the eighty-ninth moon of your Majesty's auspicious reign,

Clefren Frelock, Marsi Frelock."

When this inventory was read over to the Emperor, he directed me to deliver up the several particulars. He first called for my scimitar, which I took out, scabbard and all. In the meantime he ordered three thousand of his choicest troops (who then attended him) to surround me at a distance, with their bows and arrows just ready to discharge: but I did not observe it, for my eyes were wholly fixed upon his Majesty. He then desired me to draw my scimitar, which, although it had got some rust by the seawater, was in most parts exceeding bright. I did so, and immediately all the troops gave a shout between terror and surprise; for the sun shone clear, and the reflection dazzled their eyes as I waved the scimitar to and fro in my hand. His Majesty, who is a most magnanimous [6] prince, was less daunted than I could expect; he ordered me to return it into the scabbard and cast it on the ground as gently as I could, about six foot from the end of my chain.

The next thing he demanded was one of the hollow iron pillars, by which he meant my pocket-pistols. I drew it out, and at his desire, as well as I could, expressed to him the use of it; and charging it only with powder, which by the closeness of my pouch happened to escape wetting in the sea (an inconvenience that all prudent mariners take special care to provide against), I first cautioned the Emperor not to be afraid, and then I let it off in the air. The astonishment here was much greater than at the sight of my scimitar. Hundreds fell down as if they had been struck dead; and even the Emperor, although

6. Courageous; *lit.*, great in spirit.

he stood his ground, could not recover himself in some time. I delivered up both my pistols in the same manner as I had done my scimitar, and then my pouch of powder and bullets; begging him that the former might be kept from fire, for it would kindle with the smallest spark, and blow up his imperial palace into the air. I likewise delivered up my watch, which the Emperor was very curious to see, and commanded two of his tallest yeomen of the guards to bear it on a pole upon their shoulders, as draymen in England do a barrel of ale. He was amazed at the continual noise it made, and the motion of the minute-hand, which he could easily discern; for their sight is much more acute than ours: he asked the opinions of his learned men about him, which were various and remote, as the reader may well imagine without my repeating, although indeed I could not very perfectly understand them. I then gave up my silver and copper money, my purse with nine large pieces of gold and some smaller ones, my knife and razor, my comb and silver snuff-box, my handkerchief and journal book. My scimitar, pistols, and pouch were conveyed in carriages to his Majesty's stores; but the rest of my goods were returned me.

I had, as I before observed, one private pocket which escaped their search, wherein there was a pair of spectacles (which I sometimes use for the weakness of my eyes), a pocket perspective,[7] and several other little conveniences; which, being of no consequence to the Emperor, I did not think myself bound in honour to discover, and I apprehended they might be lost or spoiled if I ventured them out of my possession.

Chapter Three: The author diverts the Emperor and his nobility of both sexes in a very uncommon manner. The diversions of the court of Lilliput described. The author hath his liberty granted him upon certain conditions.

My gentleness and good behaviour had gained so far on the Emperor and his court, and indeed upon the army and people in general, that I began to conceive hopes of getting my liberty in a short time. I took all possible methods to cultivate this favourable disposition. The natives came by degrees to be less apprehensive of any danger from me. I would sometimes lie down and let five or six of them dance on my hand. And at last the boys and girls would venture to come and play at hide and seek in my hair. I had now made a good progress in understanding and speaking their language. The Emperor had a mind one day to entertain me with several of the country shows, wherein they exceed all nations I have known, both for dexterity and magnificence. I was diverted with none so much as that of the rope-dancers, performed upon a slender white thread, extended about two foot, and twelve inches from the ground. Upon which I shall desire liberty, with the reader's patience, to enlarge a little.

This diversion is only practised by those persons who are candidates for great employments and high favour at court. They are trained in this art from their youth, and are not always of noble birth or liberal education. When a great office is vacant either by death or disgrace (which often happens) five or six of those candidates petition the Emperor to entertain his Majesty and the court with a dance on the rope, and whoever jumps the highest without falling,

7. Telescope.

succeeds in the office.[1] Very often the chief ministers themselves are commanded to show their skill, and to convince the Emperor that they have not lost their faculty. Flimnap, the Treasurer, is allowed to cut a caper on the strait rope at least an inch higher than any other lord in the whole empire. I have seen him do the summerset several times together upon a trencher fixed on the rope, which is no thicker than a common packthread in England. My friend Reldresal, Principal Secretary for Private Affairs, is, in my opinion, if I am not partial, the second after the Treasurer; the rest of the great officers are much upon a par.

These diversions are often attended with fatal accidents, whereof great numbers are on record. I myself have seen two or three candidates break a limb. But the danger is much greater when the ministers are commanded to show their dexterity; for by contending to excel themselves and their fellows, they strain so far that there is hardly one of them who hath not received a fall, and some of them two or three. I was assured that a year or two before my arrival, Flimnap would have infallibly broke his neck, if one of the King's cushions, that accidentally lay on the ground, had not weakened the force of his fall.[2]

There is likewise another diversion, which is only shown before the Emperor and Empress and first minister upon particular occasions. The Emperor lays on a table three fine silken threads of six inches long. One is blue, the other red, and the third green.[3] These threads are proposed as prizes for those persons whom the Emperor hath a mind to distinguish by a peculiar mark of his favour. The ceremony is performed in his Majesty's great chamber of state, where the candidates are to undergo a trial of dexterity very different from the former, and such as I have not observed the least resemblance of in any other country of the old or the new world. The Emperor holds a stick in his hands, both ends parallel to the horizon, while the candidates, advancing one by one, sometimes leap over the stick, sometimes creep under it backwards and forwards several times, according as the stick is advanced or depressed. Sometimes the Emperor holds one end of the stick and his first minister the other; sometimes the minister has it entirely to himself. Whoever performs his part with most agility, and holds out the longest in leaping and creeping, is rewarded with the blue-coloured silk; the red is given to the next, and the green to the third, which they all wear girt twice round about the middle; and you see few great persons about this court who are not adorned with one of these girdles.

The horses of the army and those of the royal stables, having been daily led before me, were no longer shy, but would come up to my very feet without starting. The riders would leap them over my head as I held it on the ground, and one of the Emperor's huntsmen, upon a large courser, took my foot, shoe and all; which was indeed a prodigious leap. I had the good fortune to divert

1. In the arts of political competition and survival the master was Sir Robert Walpole, chief minister under George I and George II, 1715–17 and again 1721–42.

2. Probably a reference to George I's mistress, the Duchess of Kendal, who helped Walpole regain power in 1721.

3. Ribbons of the Orders of the Garter, the Bath, and the Thistle, honors for service to the King, or, in the case of Walpole, to his chief minister. Walpole was given the blue ribbon of the Garter in 1726; as the first commoner to hold that honor since 1660, he was mockingly addressed as "Sir Bluestring."

the Emperor one day after a very extraordinary manner. I desired he would order several sticks of two foot high, and the thickness of an ordinary cane, to be brought me; whereupon his Majesty commanded the master of his woods to give directions accordingly, and the next morning six woodmen arrived with as many carriages, drawn by eight horses to each. I took nine of these sticks, and, fixing them firmly in the ground in a quadrangle figure, two foot and a half square, I took four sticks and tied them parallel at each corner, about two foot from the ground; then I fastened my handkerchief to the nine sticks that stood erect and extended it on all sides till it was as tight as the top of a drum; and the four parallel sticks, rising about five inches higher than the handkerchief, served as ledges on each side.

When I had finished my work, I desired the Emperor to let a troop of his best horse, twenty-four in number, come and exercise upon this plain. His Majesty approved of the proposal, and I took them up one by one in my hands, ready mounted and armed, with the proper officers to exercise them. As soon as they got into order, they divided into two parties, performed mock skirmishes, discharged blunt arrows, drew their swords, fled and pursued, attacked and retired, and in short discovered the best military discipline I ever beheld. The parallel sticks secured them and their horses from falling over the stage; and the Emperor was so much delighted that he ordered this entertainment to be repeated several days, and once was pleased to be lifted up and give the word of command; and, with great difficulty, persuaded even the Empress herself to let me hold her in her close chair [4] within two yards of the stage, from whence she was able to take a full view of the whole performance. It was my good fortune that no ill accident happened in these entertainments; only once a fiery horse that belonged to one of the captains, pawing with his hoof, struck a hole in my handkerchief, and, his foot slipping, he overthrew his rider and himself; but I immediately relieved them both, for covering the hole with one hand, I set down the troop with the other in the same manner as I took them up. The horse that fell was strained in the left shoulder, but the rider got no hurt, and I repaired my handkerchief as well as I could; however, I would not trust to the strength of it any more in such dangerous enterprises.

About two or three days before I was set at liberty, as I was entertaining the court with these kinds of feats, there arrived an express to inform his Majesty that some of his subjects, riding near the place where I was first taken up, had seen a great black substance lying on the ground, very oddly shaped, extending its edges round as wide as his Majesty's bedchamber, and rising up in the middle as high as a man; that it was no living creature, as they at first apprehended, for it lay on the grass without motion, and some of them had walked round it several times; that by mounting upon each others' shoulders, they had got to the top, which was flat and even, and stamping upon it they found it was hollow within; that they humbly conceived it might be something belonging to the Man-Mountain, and if his Majesty pleased, they would undertake to bring it with only five horses. I presently knew what they meant, and was glad at heart to receive this intelligence. It seems upon my first reaching the shore after our shipwreck, I was in such confusion that, before I came to the place where I went to sleep, my hat, which I had fastened with a string

4. Enclosed sedan chair.

to my head while I was rowing and had stuck on all the time I was swimming, fell off after I came to land; the string, as I conjecture, breaking by some accident which I never observed, but thought my hat had been lost at sea. I entreated his Imperial Majesty to give orders it might be brought to me as soon as possible, describing to him the use and the nature of it: and the next day the waggoners arrived with it, but not in a very good condition; they had bored two holes in the brim within an inch and a half of the edge, and fastened two hooks in the holes; these hooks were tied by a long cord to the harness, and thus my hat was dragged along for above half an English mile: but the ground in that country being extremely smooth and level, it received less damage than I expected.

Two days after this adventure, the Emperor, having ordered that part of his army which quarters in and about his metropolis to be in a readiness, took a fancy of diverting himself in a very singular manner. He desired I would stand like a Colossus,[5] with my legs as far asunder as I conveniently could. He then commanded his general (who was an old experienced leader and a great patron of mine) to draw up the troops in close order and march them under me, the foot by twenty-four in a breast, and the horse by sixteen, with drums beating, colours flying, and pikes advanced. This body consisted of three thousand foot and a thousand horse. His Majesty gave orders, upon pain of death, that every soldier in his march should observe the strictest decency with regard to my person; which, however, could not prevent some of the younger officers from turning up their eyes as they passed under me. And, to confess the truth, my breeches were at that time in so ill a condition that they afforded some opportunities for laughter and admiration.

I had sent so many memorials and petitions for my liberty that his Majesty at length mentioned the matter, first in the cabinet and then in a full council; where it was opposed by none except Skyresh Bolgolam, who was pleased, without any provocation, to be my mortal enemy. But it was carried against him by the whole board and confirmed by the Emperor. That minister was *Galbet,* or Admiral of the Realm, very much in his master's confidence, and a person well versed in affairs, but of a morose and sour complexion.[6] However, he was at length persuaded to comply; but prevailed that the articles and conditions upon which I should be set free, and to which I must swear, should be drawn up by himself. These articles were brought to me by Skyresh Bolgolam in person, attended by two under-secretaries and several persons of distinction. After they were read, I was demanded to swear to the performance of them; first in the manner of my own country, and afterwards in the method prescribed by their laws; which was to hold my right foot in my left hand, to place the middle finger of my right hand on the crown of my head, and my thumb on the tip of my right ear. But because the reader may perhaps be curious to have some idea of the style and manner of expression peculiar to that people, as well as to know the articles upon which I recovered my liberty, I have made a translation of the whole instrument [7] word for word, as near as I was able, which I here offer to the public.

5. The statue, 100 feet high, supposedly standing astride the harbor at Rhodes; between its legs all vessels had to pass.
6. Disposition.
7. Document.

GOLBASTO MOMAREN EVLAME GURDILO SHEFIN MULLY ULLY GUE, most mighty Emperor of Lilliput, Delight and Terror of the Universe, whose dominions extend five thousand blustrugs (about twelve miles in circumference) to the extremities of the globe; Monarch of all Monarchs, taller than the sons of men; whose feet press down to the centre, and whose head strikes against the sun: at whose nod the princes of the earth shake their knees; pleasant as the spring, comfortable as the summer, fruitful as autumn, dreadful as winter. His most sublime Majesty proposeth to the Man-Mountain, lately arrived at our celestial dominions, the following articles, which by a solemn oath he shall be obliged to perform.

First, The Man-Mountain shall not depart from our dominions, without our licence under our great seal.

Secondly, He shall not presume to come into our metropolis without our express order; at which time the inhabitants shall have two hours warning to keep within their doors.

Thirdly, The said Man-Mountain shall confine his walks to our principal high roads and not offer to walk or lie down in a meadow or field of corn.[8]

Fourthly, As he walks the said roads, he shall take the utmost care not to trample upon the bodies of any of our loving subjects, their horses, or carriages, nor take any of our said subjects into his hands without their own consent.

Fifthly, If an express require extraordinary dispatch, the Man-Mountain shall be obliged to carry in his pocket the messenger and horse a six days' journey once in every moon, and return the said messenger back (if so required) safe to our Imperial Presence.

Sixthly, He shall be our ally against our enemies in the island of Blefuscu, and do his utmost to destroy their fleet, which is now preparing to invade us.

Seventhly, That the said Man-Mountain shall, at his times of leisure, be aiding and assisting to our workmen in helping to raise certain great stones, towards covering the wall of the principal park and other our royal buildings.

Eighthly, That the said Man-Mountain shall, in two moons' time, deliver in an exact survey of the circumference of our dominions by a computation of his own paces round the coast.

Lastly, That upon his solemn oath to observe all the above articles, the said Man-Mountain shall have a daily allowance of meat and drink sufficient for the support of 1728 of our subjects, with free access to our Royal Person, and other marks of our favour. Given at our palace at Belfaborac the twelfth day of the ninety-first moon of our reign.

I swore and subscribed to these articles with great cheerfulness and content, although some of them were not so honourable as I could have wished; which proceeded wholly from the malice of Skyresh Bolgolam, the High Admiral: whereupon my chains were immediately unlocked and I was at full liberty;

8. Grain, presumably wheat.

the Emperor himself in person did me the honour to be by at the whole ceremony. I made my acknowledgements by prostrating myself at his Majesty's feet: but he commanded me to rise; and after many gracious expressions, which, to avoid the censure of vanity, I shall not repeat, he added that he hoped I should prove a useful servant, and well deserve all the favours he had already conferred upon me, or might do for the future.

The reader may please to observe that, in the last article for the recovery of my liberty, the Emperor stipulates to allow me a quantity of meat and drink sufficient for the support of 1728 Lilliputians. Some time after, asking a friend at court how they came to fix on that determinate number, he told me that his Majesty's mathematicians, having taken the height of my body by the help of a quadrant, and finding it to exceed theirs in the proportion of twelve to one, they concluded from the similarity of their bodies that mine must contain at least 1728 of theirs, and consequently would require as much food as was necessary to support that number of Lilliputians. By which the reader may conceive an idea of the ingenuity of that people, as well as the prudent and exact economy of so great a prince.

Chapter Four: Mildendo, the metropolis of Lilliput, described, together with the Emperor's palace. A conversation between the author and a principal secretary concerning the affairs of that empire. The author's offers to serve the Emperor in his wars.

The first request I made after I had obtained my liberty was that I might have licence to see Mildendo, the metropolis; which the Emperor easily granted me, but with a special charge to do no hurt, either to the inhabitants or their houses. The people had notice by proclamation of my design to visit the town. The wall which encompassed it is two foot and an half high and at least eleven inches broad, so that a coach and horses may be driven very safely round it; and it is flanked with strong towers at ten foot distance. I stepped over the great western gate, and passed very gently, and sideling [1] through the two principal streets, only in my short waistcoat, for fear of damaging the roofs and eaves of the houses with the skirts of my coat. I walked with the utmost circumspection to avoid treading on any stragglers who might remain in the streets, although the orders were very strict that all people should keep in their houses, at their own peril. The garret windows and tops of houses were so crowded with spectators that I thought in all my travels I had not seen a more populous place. The city is an exact square, each side of the wall being five hundred foot long. The two great streets, which run cross and divide it into four quarters, are five foot wide. The lanes and alleys, which I could not enter but only viewed them as I passed, are from twelve to eighteen inches. The town is capable of holding five hundred thousand souls. The houses are from three to five stories; the shops and markets well provided.

The Emperor's palace is in the center of the city, where the two great streets meet. It is enclosed by a wall of two foot high, and twenty foot distant from the buildings. I had his Majesty's permission to step over this wall; and

1. Sideways.

the space being so wide between that and the palace, I could easily view it on every side. The outward court is a square of forty foot and includes two other courts: in the inmost are the royal apartments, which I was very desirous to see, but found it extremely difficult; for the great gates, from one square into another, were but eighteen inches high and seven inches wide. Now the buildings of the outer court were at least five foot high, and it was impossible for me to stride over them without infinite damage to the pile, although the walls were strongly built of hewn stone and four inches thick. At the same time the Emperor had a great desire that I should see the magnificence of his palace; but this I was not able to do till three days after, which I spent in cutting down with my knife some of the largest trees in the royal park, about an hundred yards distant from the city. Of these trees I made two stools, each about three foot high, and strong enough to bear my weight. The people having received notice a second time, I went again through the city to the palace, with my two stools in my hands. When I came to the side of the outer court, I stood upon one stool, and took the other in my hand: this I lifted over the roof, and gently set it down on the space between the first and second court, which was eight foot wide. I then stepped over the buildings very conveniently from one stool to the other, and drew up the first after me with a hooked stick. By this contrivance I got into the inmost court; and lying down upon my side, I applied my face to the windows of the middle stories, which were left open on purpose, and discovered the most splendid apartments that can be imagined. There I saw the Empress and the young princes in their several lodgings, with their chief attendants about them. Her Imperial Majesty was pleased to smile very graciously upon me, and gave me out of the window her hand to kiss.

But I shall not anticipate the reader with farther descriptions of this kind, because I reserve them for a greater work which is now almost ready for the press, containing a general description of this empire from its first erection through a long series of princes, with a particular account of their wars and politics, laws, learning, and religion; their plants and animals, their peculiar manners and customs, with other matters very curious and useful; my chief design at present being only to relate such events and transactions as happened to the public or to myself during a residence of about nine months in that empire.

One morning, about a fortnight after I had obtained my liberty, Reldresal, Principal Secretary (as they style him) of Private Affairs, came to my house, attended only by one servant. He ordered his coach to wait at a distance and desired I would give him an hour's audience; which I readily consented to, on account of his quality and personal merits as well as of the many good offices he had done me during my solicitations at court. I offered to lie down that he might the more conveniently reach my ear; but he chose rather to let me hold him in my hand during our conversation. He began with compliments on my liberty, said he might pretend to some merit in it; but, however, added, that if it had not been for the present situation of things at court, perhaps I might not have obtained it so soon. For, said he, as flourishing a condition as we appear to be in to foreigners, we labour under two mighty evils: a violent faction at home, and the danger of an invasion by a most potent enemy from abroad. As to the first, you are to understand that, for above seventy moons past, there have been two struggling parties in the empire, under the names of *Tramecksan* and *Slamecksan,* from the high and low heels on their shoes, by which they distinguish themselves.[2] It is alleged, indeed, that the high heels are most agreeable to our ancient constitution: but however this be, his Majesty hath determined to make use of only low heels in the administration of the government and all offices in the gift of the Crown, as you cannot but observe; and particularly, that his Majesty's imperial heels are lower at least by a *drurr* than any of his court (*drurr* is a measure about the fourteenth part of an inch). The animosities between these two parties run so high that they will neither eat nor drink nor talk with each other. We compute the *Tramecksan,* or High-Heels, to exceed us in number; but the power is wholly on our side. We apprehend his Imperial Highness, the heir to the crown, to have some tendency towards the High-Heels; at least we can plainly discover one of his heels higher than the other, which gives him a hobble in his gait.

Now, in the midst of these intestine [3] disquiets, we are threatened with an invasion from the island of Blefuscu,[4] which is the other great empire of the universe, almost as large and powerful as this of his Majesty. For as to what we have heard you affirm, that there are other kingdoms and states in the world, inhabited by human creatures as large as yourself, our philosophers are in much doubt, and would rather conjecture that you dropped from the moon or one of the stars; because it is certain that an hundred mortals of your bulk would, in a short time, destroy all the fruits and cattle of his Majesty's dominions. Besides, our histories of six thousand moons make no mention of any other regions than the two great empires of Lilliput and Blefuscu. Which two mighty powers have, as I was going to tell you, been engaged in a most obstinate war for six and thirty moons past. It began upon the following occasion. It is allowed on all hands that the primitive way of breaking eggs before we eat them was upon the larger end: but his present Majesty's grandfather, while he was a boy, going to eat an egg and breaking it according to the ancient practice, happened to cut one of his fingers. Whereupon the Emperor his father published an edict commanding all his subjects, upon great penalties, to break the smaller end of their eggs.[5] The people so highly resented this law that our histories tell us there have been six rebellions raised

2. The "two struggling parties" suggest the Tories (who supported High Church views) and the Whigs (Low Church). George I supported Low Churchmen, and the Whigs generally favored toleration of (and in turn drew support from) the dissenters. The Prince of Wales, to become George II in 1727, tried to cultivate both parties; the Tories hoped for his favor because of his hostility to his father.

3. Internal.

4. Suspicions of France remained strong in England after the Peace of Utrecht of 1713, and were heightened by the efforts of the dethroned Stuarts and their Jacobite supporters to mount an invasion of England.

5. What is suggested is the conflict of Roman Catholics and Protestants, particularly over the doctrine of transubstantiation—i.e., whether the bread and wine of communion literally or only symbolically become the body and blood of Jesus Christ. The historical allegory refers to Henry VIII's break with the Roman Catholic Church and establishment of the Church of England, the conflicts of Catholic and Protestant under Mary Tudor and Elizabeth, the beheading of Charles I in 1649, and the ousting of the Roman Catholic James II in 1688. Roman Catholics, in Swift's day, were prevented (as were Protestant dissenters) from holding office by the Test Act (1673), which required acceptance of the Anglican Church as a qualification.

on that account; wherein one emperor lost his life and another his crown. These civil commotions were constantly fomented by the monarchs of Blefuscu; and, when they were quelled, the exiles always fled for refuge to that empire. It is computed that eleven thousand persons have, at several times, suffered death rather than submit to break their eggs at the smaller end. Many hundred large volumes have been published upon this controversy: but the books of the Big-Endians have been long forbidden, and the whole party rendered incapable by law of holding employments. During the course of these troubles, the emperors of Blefuscu did frequently expostulate by their ambassadors, accusing us of making a schism in religion by offending against a fundamental doctrine of our great prophet Lustrog, in the fifty-fourth chapter of the *Brundecral* (which is their Alcoran).[6] This, however, is thought to be a mere strain upon the text: for the words are these: "That all true believers shall break their eggs at the convenient end"; and which is the convenient end seems, in my humble opinion, to be left to every man's conscience, or at least in the power of the chief magistrate [7] to determine. Now the Big-Endian exiles have found so much credit in the Emperor of Blefuscu's court, and so much private assistance and encouragement from their party here at home, that a bloody war hath been carried on between the two empires for six and thirty moons with various success; during which time we have lost forty capital ships and a much greater number of smaller vessels, together with thirty thousand of our best seamen and soldiers; and the damage received by the enemy is reckoned to be somewhat greater than ours. However, they have now equipped a numerous fleet and are just preparing to make a descent upon us; and his Imperial Majesty, placing great confidence in your valour and strength, hath commanded me to lay this account of his affairs before you.

I desired the Secretary to present my humble duty to the Emperor, and to let him know that I thought it would not become me, who was a foreigner, to interfere with parties; but I was ready, with the hazard of my life, to defend his person and state against all invaders.

Chapter Five: The author by an extraordinary stratagem prevents an invasion. A high title of honour is conferred upon him. Ambassadors arrive from the Emperor of Blefuscu and sue for peace. The Empress's apartment on fire by an accident. The author instrumental in saving the rest of the palace.

The empire of Blefuscu is an island situated to the north-northeast side of Lilliput, from whence it is parted only by a channel of eight hundred yards wide. I had not yet seen it, and upon this notice of an intended invasion, I avoided appearing on that side of the coast, for fear of being discovered by some of the enemy's ships, who had received no intelligence of me, all intercourse between the two empires having been strictly forbidden during the war upon pain of death, and an embargo laid by our Emperor upon all vessels whatsoever. I communicated to his Majesty a project I had formed of seizing the enemy's whole fleet; which, as our scouts assured us, lay at anchor in the

6. Their Koran or Bible; Swift is mocking these disputes over dogma and ritual which come from the "wresting"—i.e. the forced interpretation—of Scripture.
7. The ultimate authority of the state; in the case of Lilliput, the Emperor.

harbour ready to sail with the first fair wind. I consulted the most experienced seamen upon the depth of the channel, which they had often plumbed; who told me that in the middle at high water it was seventy *glumgluffs* deep, which is about six foot of European measure, and the rest of it fifty *glumgluffs* at most.

I walked to the northeast coast over against Blefuscu; where, lying down behind a hillock, I took out my small pocket perspective-glass, and viewed the enemy's fleet at anchor, consisting of about fifty men-of-war and a great number of transports: I then came back to my house and gave order (for which I had a warrant) for a great quantity of the strongest cable and bars of iron. The cable was about as thick as packthread, and the bars of the length and size of a knitting-needle. I trebled the cable to make it stronger, and for the same reason I twisted three of the iron bars together, bending the extremities into a hook. Having thus fixed fifty hooks to as many cables, I went back to the northeast coast and, putting off my coat, shoes, and stockings, walked into the sea in my leathern jerkin, about half an hour before high water. I waded with what haste I could, and swam in the middle about thirty yards until I felt ground; I arrived at the fleet in less than half an hour. The enemy was so frighted when they saw me that they leaped out of their ships and swam to shore, where there could not be fewer than thirty thousand souls. I then took my tackling and, fastening a hook to the hole at the prow of each, I tied all the cords together at the end. While I was thus employed, the enemy discharged several thousand arrows, many of which stuck in my hands and face and, besides the excessive smart, gave me much disturbance in my work. My greatest apprehension was for my eyes, which I should have infallibly lost if I had not suddenly thought of an expedient. I kept among other little necessaries a pair of spectacles in a private pocket, which, as I observed before, had escaped the Emperor's searchers. These I took out and fastened as strongly as I could upon my nose, and thus armed went on boldly with my work in spite of the enemy's arrows, many of which struck against the glasses of my spectacles, but without any other effect further than a little to discompose them. I had now fastened all the hooks and, taking the knot in my hand, began to pull; but not a ship would stir, for they were all too fast held by their anchors, so that the boldest part of my enterprise remained. I therefore let go the cord and, leaving the hooks fixed to the ships, I resolutely cut with my knife the cables that fastened the anchors, receiving above two hundred shots in my face and hands; then I took up the knotted end of the cables to which my hooks were tied, and with great ease drew fifty of the enemy's largest men-of-war after me.

The Blefuscudians, who had not the least imagination of what I intended, were at first confounded with astonishment. They had seen me cut the cables, and thought my design was only to let the ships run adrift or fall foul on each other: but when they perceived the whole fleet moving in order, and saw me pulling at the end, they set up such a scream of grief and despair that it is almost impossible to describe or conceive. When I had got out of danger, I stopped a while to pick out the arrows that stuck in my hands and face, and rubbed on some of the same ointment that was given me at my first arrival, as I have formerly mentioned. I then took off my spectacles and, waiting about an hour until the tide was a little fallen, I waded through the middle with my cargo, and arrived safe at the royal port of Lilliput.

The Emperor and his whole court stood on the shore expecting [1] the issue of this great adventure. They saw the ships move forward in a large half-moon, but could not discern me, who was up to my breast in water. When I advanced to the middle of the channel, they were yet more in pain, because I was under water to my neck. The Emperor concluded me to be drowned, and that the enemy's fleet was approaching in a hostile manner: but he was soon eased of his fears, for, the channel growing shallower every step I made, I came in a short time within hearing, and, holding up the end of the cable by which the fleet was fastened, I cried in a loud voice, "Long live the most puissant Emperor of Lilliput!" This great prince received me at my landing with all possible encomiums, and created me a *Nardac* upon the spot, which is the highest title of honour among them.

His Majesty desired I would take some other opportunity of bringing all the rest of his enemy's ships into his ports. And so unmeasurable is the ambition of princes that he seemed to think of nothing less than reducing the whole empire of Blefuscu into a province and governing it by a viceroy; of destroying the Big-Endian exiles and compelling that people to break the smaller end of their eggs, by which he would remain sole monarch of the whole world. But I endeavoured to divert him from this design by many arguments drawn from the topics of policy as well as justice: and I plainly protested that I would never be an instrument of bringing a free and brave people into slavery. And when the matter was debated in council, the wisest part of the ministry were of my opinion.

This open bold declaration of mine was so opposite to the schemes and politics of his Imperial Majesty that he could never forgive me; he mentioned it in a very artful manner at council, where I was told that some of the wisest appeared, at least by their silence, to be of my opinion; but others, who were my secret enemies, could not forbear some expressions which by a side-wind reflected on me. And from this time began an intrigue between his Majesty and a junta of ministers maliciously bent against me, which broke out in less than two months, and had like to have ended in my utter destruction. Of so little weight are the greatest services to princes when put into the balance with a refusal to gratify their passions.

About three weeks after this exploit, there arrived a solemn embassy from Blefuscu with humble offers of a peace; which was soon concluded upon conditions very advantageous to our Emperor, wherewith I shall not trouble the reader. There were six ambassadors with a train of about five hundred persons, and their entry was very magnificent, suitable to the grandeur of their master and the importance of their business. When their treaty was finished, wherein I did them several good offices by the credit I now had, or at least appeared to have, at court, their Excellencies, who were privately told how much I had been their friend, made me a visit in form. They began with many compliments upon my valour and generosity, invited me to that kingdom in the Emperor their master's name, and desired me to show them some proofs of my prodigious strength, of which they had heard so many wonders; wherein I readily obliged them, but shall not interrupt the reader with the particulars.

When I had for some time entertained their Excellencies to their infinite

1. Awaiting.

satisfaction and surprise, I desired they would do me the honour to present my most humble respects to the Emperor their master, the renown of whose virtues had so justly filled the whole world with admiration, and whose royal person I resolved to attend before I returned to my own country: accordingly, the next time I had the honour to see our Emperor, I desired his general licence to wait on the Blefuscudian monarch, which he was pleased to grant me, as I could plainly perceive, in a very cold manner; but could not guess the reason till I had a whisper from a certain person that Flimnap and Bolgolam had represented my intercourse with those ambassadors as a mark of disaffection, from which I am sure my heart was wholly free. And this was the first time I began to conceive some imperfect idea of courts and ministers.

It is to be observed that these ambassadors spoke to me by an interpreter, the languages of both empires differing as much from each other as any two in Europe, and each nation priding itself upon the antiquity, beauty, and energy of their own tongues, with an avowed contempt for that of their neighbour; yet our Emperor, standing upon the advantage he had got by the seizure of their fleet, obliged them to deliver their credentials and make their speech in the Lilliputian tongue. And it must be confessed, that from the great intercourse of trade and commerce between both realms, from the continual reception of exiles, which is mutual among them, and from the custom in each empire to send their young nobility and richer gentry to the other, in order to polish themselves by seeing the world and understanding men and manners, there are few persons of distinction, or merchants, or seamen, who dwell in the maritime parts, but what can hold conversation in both tongues; as I found some weeks after, when I went to pay my respects to the Emperor of Blefuscu, which in the midst of great misfortunes through the malice of my enemies, proved a very happy adventure to me, as I shall relate in its proper place.

The reader may remember that, when I signed those articles upon which I recovered my liberty, there were some which I disliked upon account of their being too servile; neither could anything but an extreme necessity have forced me to submit. But being now a *Nardac*, of the highest rank in that empire, such offices were looked upon as below my dignity, and the Emperor (to do him justice) never once mentioned them to me. However, it was not long before I had an opportunity of doing his Majesty, at least as I then thought, a most signal service. I was alarmed at midnight with the cries of many hundred people at my door; by which being suddenly awaked, I was in some kind of terror. I heard the word *burglum* repeated incessantly: several of the Emperor's court, making their way through the crowd, entreated me to come immediately to the palace, where her Imperial Majesty's apartment was on fire, by the carelessness of a maid of honour who fell asleep while she was reading a romance. I got up in an instant; and, orders being given to clear the way before me, and it being likewise a moonshine night, I made a shift to get to the palace without trampling on any of the people. I found they had already applied ladders to the walls of the apartment, and were well provided with buckets, but the water was at some distance. These buckets were about the size of a large thimble, and the poor people supplied me with them as fast as they could; but the flame was so violent that they did little good. I might easily have stifled it with my coat, which I unfortunately left behind me for haste, and came away only in my leathern jerkin. The case seemed wholly desperate and deplorable, and this magnificent palace would have infallibly been burnt down to the ground if, by a presence of mind unusual to me, I had not suddenly thought of an expedient. I had the evening before drank plentifully of a most delicious wine called *glimigrim* (the Blefuscudians call it *flunec,* but ours is esteemed the better sort), which is very diuretic. By the luckiest chance in the world, I had not discharged myself of any part of it. The heat I had contracted by coming very near the flames and by my labouring to quench them, made the wine begin to operate by urine; which I voided in such a quantity, and applied so well to the proper places, that in three minutes the fire was wholly extinguished, and the rest of that noble pile, which had cost so many ages in erecting, preserved from destruction.

It was now daylight, and I returned to my house without waiting to congratulate with the Emperor; because, although I had done a very eminent piece of service, yet I could not tell how his Majesty might resent the manner by which I had performed it: for, by the fundamental laws of the realm, it is capital in any person, of what quality soever, to make water within the precincts of the palace.[2] But I was a little comforted by a message from his Majesty that he would give orders to the Grand Justiciary for passing my pardon in form; which, however, I could not obtain. And I was privately assured that the Empress, conceiving the greatest abhorrence of what I had done, removed to the most distant side of the court, firmly resolved that those buildings should never be repaired for her use; and, in the presence of her chief confidants, could not forbear vowing revenge.

Chapter Six: Of the inhabitants of Lilliput; their learning, laws, and customs. The manner of educating their children. The author's way of living in that country. His vindication of a great lady.

Although I intend to leave the description of this empire to a particular treatise, yet in the meantime I am content to gratify the curious reader with some general ideas. As the common size of the natives is somewhat under six inches, so there is an exact proportion in all other animals as well as plants and trees: for instance, the tallest horses and oxen are between four and five inches in height, the sheep an inch and a half, more or less; their geese about the bigness of a sparrow, and so the several gradations downwards till you come to the smallest, which, to my sight, were almost invisible; but Nature hath adapted the eyes of the Lilliputians to all objects proper for their view: they see with great exactness, but at no great distance. And to show the sharpness of their sight towards objects that are near, I have been much pleased with observing a cook pulling[1] a lark which was not so large as a common fly; and a young girl threading an invisible needle with invisible silk. Their tallest trees are about seven foot high; I mean some of those in the great royal park, the tops

2. Finding such an act worthy of capital punishment is, among other things, a satire on the elaborate formal etiquette maintained at Versailles under Louis XIV. The passage has often been taken to refer to Queen Anne's reputed offense at the boldness of *A Tale of a Tub* and her refusal to make Swift a bishop.

1. Plucking.

whereof I could but just reach with my fist clenched. The other vegetables [2] are in the same proportion; but this I leave to the reader's imagination.

I shall say but little at present of their learning, which for many ages hath flourished in all its branches among them: but their manner of writing is very peculiar, being neither from the left to the right, like the Europeans; nor from the right to the left, like the Arabians; nor from up to down, like the Chinese; nor from down to up, like the Cascagians;[3] but aslant from one corner of the paper to the other, like ladies in England.

They bury their dead with their heads directly downwards, because they hold an opinion that in eleven thousand moons they are all to rise again, in which period the earth (which they conceive to be flat) will turn upside down; and by this means they shall, at their resurrection, be found ready standing on their feet. The learned among them confess the absurdity of this doctrine, but the practice still continues, in compliance to the vulgar.

There are some laws and customs in this empire very peculiar, and, if they were not so directly contrary to those of my own dear country, I should be tempted to say a little in their justification. It is only to be wished that they were as well executed. The first I shall mention relates to informers. All crimes against the state are punished here with the utmost severity; but, if the person accused make his innocence plainly to appear upon his trial, the accuser is immediately put to an ignominious death; and out of his goods or lands, the innocent person is quadruply recompensed for the loss of his time, for the danger he underwent, for the hardship of his imprisonment, and for all the charges he hath been at in making his defence. Or, if that fund be deficient, it is largely [4] supplied by the crown. The Emperor doth also confer on him some public mark of his favour, and proclamation is made of his innocence through the whole city.

They look upon fraud as a greater crime than theft, and therefore seldom fail to punish it with death; for they allege that care and vigilance, with a very common understanding, may preserve a man's goods from thieves, but honesty hath no fence against superior cunning: and since it is necessary that there should be a perpetual intercourse of buying and selling and dealing upon credit, where fraud is permitted and connived at or hath no law to punish it, the honest dealer is always undone, and the knave gets the advantage. I remember when I was once interceding with the King for a criminal who had wronged his master of a great sum of money, which he had received by order and ran away with; and happening to tell his Majesty, by way of extenuation, that it was only a breach of trust, the Emperor thought it monstrous in me to offer as a defence the greatest aggravation of the crime: and truly I had little to say in return farther than the common answer that different nations had different customs; for, I confess, I was heartily ashamed.

Although we usually call reward and punishment the two hinges upon which all government turns, yet I could never observe this maxim to be put in practice by any nation except that of Lilliput. Whoever can there bring sufficient proof that he hath strictly observed the laws of his country for seventy-

2. Plants.
3. An imaginary people; much of this is parody of travel literature.
4. Amply.

three moons, hath a claim to certain privileges according to his quality and condition of life, with a proportionable sum of money out of a fund appropriated for that use: he likewise acquires the title of *Snilpall*, or *Legal*, which is added to his name but doth not descend to his posterity. And these people thought it a prodigious defect of policy among us when I told them that our laws were enforced only by penalties without any mention of reward. It is upon this account that the image of Justice, in their courts of judicature, is formed with six eyes, two before, as many behind, and on each side one, to signify circumspection; with a bag of gold open in her right hand and a sword sheathed in her left, to show she is more disposed to reward than to punish.

In choosing persons for all employments, they have more regard to good morals than to great abilities; for, since government is necessary to mankind, they believe that the common size of human understandings is fitted to some station or other, and that Providence never intended to make the management of public affairs a mystery to be comprehended only by a few persons of sublime genius, of which there seldom are three born in an age: but they suppose truth, justice, temperance, and the like to be in every man's power; the practice of which virtues, assisted by experience and a good intention, would qualify any man for the service of his country, except where a course of study is required. But they thought the want of moral virtues was so far from being supplied by superior endowments of the mind, that employments could never be put into such dangerous hands as those of persons so qualified; and at least, that the mistakes committed by ignorance in a virtuous disposition would never be of such fatal consequence to the public weal as the practices of a man whose inclinations led him to be corrupt, and had great abilities to manage, to multiply, and defend his corruptions.

In like manner, the disbelief of a divine Providence renders a man uncapable of holding any public station; for, since kings avow themselves to be the deputies of Providence, the Lilliputians think nothing can be more absurd than for a prince to employ such men as disown the authority under which he acts.

In relating these and the following laws, I would only be understood to mean the original institutions, and not the most scandalous corruptions into which these people are fallen by the degenerate nature of man. For as to that infamous practice of acquiring great employments by dancing on the ropes, or badges of favour and distinction by leaping over sticks and creeping under them, the reader is to observe that they were first introduced by the grandfather of the Emperor now reigning, and grew to the present height by the gradual increase of party and faction.

Ingratitude is among them a capital crime, as we read it to have been in some other countries; for they reason thus, that whoever makes ill returns to his benefactor must needs be a common enemy to the rest of mankind, from whom he hath received no obligation, and therefore such a man is not fit to live.

Their notions relating to the duties of parents and children differ extremely from ours. For, since the conjunction of male and female is founded upon the great law of nature, in order to propagate and continue the species, the Lilliputians will needs have it that men and women are joined together like other animals by the motives of concupiscence; and that their tenderness towards their young proceeds from the like natural principle: for which reason they will never allow that a child is under any obligation to his father for begetting him or to his mother for bringing him into the world; which, considering the miseries of human life, was neither a benefit in itself nor intended so by his parents, whose thoughts in their love-encounters were otherwise employed. Upon these and the like reasonings, their opinion is that parents are the last of all others to be trusted with the education of their own children: and therefore they have in every town public nurseries,[5] where all parents, except cottagers and labourers, are obliged to send their infants of both sexes to be reared and educated when they come to the age of twenty moons, at which time they are supposed to have some rudiments of docility. These schools are of several kinds, suited to different qualities and to both sexes. They have certain professors well skilled in preparing children for such a condition of life as befits the rank of their parents and their own capacities as well as inclinations. I shall first say something of the male nurseries and then of the female.

The nurseries for males of noble or eminent birth are provided with grave and learned professors and their several deputies. The clothes and food of the children are plain and simple. They are bred up in the principles of honour, justice, courage, modesty, clemency, religion, and love of their country; they are always employed in some business except in the times of eating and sleeping, which are very short, and two hours for diversions, consisting of bodily exercises. They are dressed by men until four years of age, and then are obliged to dress themselves although their quality be ever so great; and the women attendants, who are aged proportionably to ours at fifty, perform only the most menial offices. They are never suffered to converse with servants, but go together in small or greater numbers to take their diversions, and always in the presence of a professor or one of his deputies; whereby they avoid those early bad impressions of folly and vice to which our children are subject. Their parents are suffered to see them only twice a year; the visit is not to last above an hour. They are allowed to kiss the child at meeting and parting; but a professor, who always stands by on those occasions, will not suffer them to whisper or use any fondling expressions, or bring any presents of toys, sweetmeats, and the like.

The pension from each family for the education and entertainment[6] of a child, upon failure of due payment, is levied by the Emperor's officers.

The nurseries for children of ordinary gentlemen, merchants, traders, and handicrafts, are managed proportionably after the same manner; only, those designed for trades are put out apprentices at seven years old, whereas those of persons of quality continue in their nurseries till fifteen, which answers to one and twenty with us: but the confinement is gradually lessened for the last three years.

In the female nurseries, the young girls of quality are educated much like the males; only, they are dressed by orderly servants of their own sex, but always in the presence of a professor or deputy, until they come to dress themselves, which is at five years old. And if it be found that these nurses ever presume to entertain the girls with frightful or foolish stories, or the common

5. Schools for children of all ages and all but the lowest classes. There are suggestions in what follows of Plato's system of education in *The Republic*.
6. Sustenance.

follies practiced by chambermaids among us, they are publicly whipped thrice about the city, imprisoned for a year, and banished for life to the most desolate parts of the country. Thus the young ladies there are as much ashamed of being cowards and fools as the men, and despise all personal ornaments beyond decency and cleanliness: neither did I perceive any difference in their education made by their difference of sex, only that the exercises of the females were not altogether so robust, and that some rules were given them relating to domestic life, and a smaller compass of learning was enjoined them: for their maxim is that among people of quality a wife should be always a reasonable and agreeable companion, because she cannot always be young. When the girls are twelve years old, which among them is the marriageable age, their parents or guardians take them home, with great expressions of gratitude to the professors, and seldom without tears of the young lady and her companions.

In the nurseries of females of the meaner sort,[7] the children are instructed in all kinds of works proper for their sex and their several degrees: those intended for apprentices are dismissed at seven years old; the rest are kept to eleven.

The meaner families who have children at these nurseries are obliged, besides their annual pension, which is as low as possible, to return to the steward of the nursery a small monthly share of their gettings, to be a portion for the child; and therefore all parents are limited in their expenses by the law. For the Lilliputians think nothing can be more unjust than that people, in subservience to their own appetites, should bring children into the world and leave the burthen of supporting them on the public. As to persons of quality, they give security to appropriate a certain sum for each child, suitable to their condition; and these funds are always managed with good husbandry and the most exact justice.

The cottagers and labourers keep their children at home, their business being only to till and cultivate the earth, and therefore their education is of little consequence to the public; but the old and diseased among them are supported by hospitals:[8] for begging is a trade unknown in this empire.

And here it may perhaps divert the curious reader to give some account of my domestic,[9] and my manner of living in this country, during a residence of nine months and thirteen days. Having a head mechanically turned and being likewise forced by necessity, I had made for myself a table and chair convenient enough out of the largest trees in the royal park. Two hundred sempstresses were employed to make me shirts and linen for my bed and table, all of the strongest and coarsest kind they could get; which, however, they were forced to quilt together in several folds, for the thickest was some degrees finer than lawn. Their linen is usually three inches wide, and three foot make a piece. The sempstresses took my measure as I lay on the ground, one standing at my neck and another at my midleg, with a strong cord extended that each held by the end, while the third measured the length of the cord with a rule of an inch long. Then they measured my right thumb and desired no more; for, by a mathematical computation that twice round the thumb is once round the wrist and so on to the neck and the waist, and by the help of my old shirt,

7. Humbler social rank.
8. Public "homes" for the aged or infirm.
9. Household.

which I displayed on the ground before them for a pattern, they fitted me exactly. Three hundred tailors were employed in the same manner to make me clothes; but they had another contrivance for taking my measure. I kneeled down, and they raised a ladder from the ground to my neck; upon this ladder one of them mounted and let fall a plumb-line from my collar to the floor, which just answered the length of my coat; but my waist and arms I measured myself. When my clothes were finished, which was done in my house (for the largest of theirs would not have been able to hold them) they looked like the patchwork made by the ladies in England, only that mine were all of a colour.

I had three hundred cooks to dress my victuals in little convenient huts built about my house, where they and their families lived and prepared me two dishes apiece. I took up twenty waiters in my hand and placed them on the table; an hundred more attended below on the ground, some with dishes of meat and some with barrels of wine and other liquors slung on their shoulders; all which the waiters above drew up as I wanted, in a very ingenious manner by certain cords, as we draw the bucket up a well in Europe. A dish of their meat was a good mouthful, and a barrel of their liquor a reasonable draught. Their mutton yields to ours, but their beef is excellent. I have had a sirloin so large that I have been forced to make three bits of it; but this is rare. My servants were astonished to see me eat it bones and all, as in our country we do the leg of a lark. Their geese and turkeys I usually eat at a mouthful, and I must confess they far exceed ours. Of their smaller fowl I could take up twenty or thirty at the end of my knife.

One day his Imperial Majesty, being informed of my way of living, desired that himself and his royal consort, with the young princes of the blood of both sexes, might have the happiness (as he was pleased to call it) of dining with me. They came accordingly, and I placed them upon chairs of state on my table, just over-against me, with their guards about them. Flimnap, the Lord High Treasurer, attended there likewise with his white staff,[10] and I observed he often looked on me with a sour countenance, which I would not seem to regard, but eat more than usual, in honour to my dear country as well as to fill the court with admiration. I have some private reasons to believe that this visit from His Majesty gave Flimnap an opportunity of doing me ill offices to his master. That minister had always been my secret enemy, although he outwardly caressed me more than was usual to the moroseness of his nature. He represented to the Emperor the low condition of his treasury; that he was forced to take up money at great discount; that exchequer bills would not circulate under nine per cent below par; that I had cost his Majesty above a million and a half of *sprugs* (their greatest gold coin, about the bigness of a spangle); and upon the whole, that it would be advisable in the Emperor to take the first fair occasion of dismissing me.

I am here obliged to vindicate the reputation of an excellent lady who was an innocent sufferer upon my account. The Treasurer took a fancy to be jealous of his wife, from the malice of some evil tongues who informed him that her Grace had taken a violent affection for my person, and the court-scandal ran for some time that she once came privately to my lodging. This I solemnly declare to be a most infamous falsehood, without any grounds, farther than

10. Symbol of office of the Lord Treasurer in England.

that her Grace was pleased to treat me with all innocent marks of freedom and friendship. I own she came often to my house, but always publicly, nor ever without three more in the coach, who were usually her sister and young daughter and some particular acquaintance; but this was common to many other ladies of the court. And I still appeal to my servants round, whether they at any time saw a coach at my door without knowing what persons were in it. On those occasions when a servant had given me notice, my custom was to go immediately to the door; and, after paying my respects, to take up the coach and two horses very carefully in my hands (for if there were six horses, the postillion always unharnessed four) and place them on a table where I had fixed a movable rim quite round, of five inches high, to prevent accidents. And I have often had four coaches and horses at once on my table full of company, while I sat in my chair leaning my face towards them; and when I was engaged with one set, the coachmen would gently drive the others round my table. I have passed many an afternoon very agreeably in these conversations. But I defy the Treasurer, or his two informers (I will name them, and let them make their best of it), Clustril and Drunlo, to prove that any person ever came to me *incognito,* except the Secretary Reldresal, who was sent by express command of his Imperial Majesty, as I have before related. I should not have dwelt so long upon this particular if it had not been a point wherein the reputation of a great lady is so nearly concerned, to say nothing of my own; although I had the honour to be a *Nardac,* which the Treasurer himself is not; for all the world knows he is only a *Clumglum,* a title inferior by one degree, as that of a marquis is to a duke in England, yet I allow he preceded me in right of his post. These false informations, which I afterwards came to the knowledge of by an accident not proper to mention, made the Treasurer show his lady for some time an ill countenance, and me a worse. For although he were at last undeceived and reconciled to her, yet I lost all credit with him, and found my interest decline very fast with the Emperor himself, who was indeed too much governed by that favourite.

Chapter Seven: The author, being informed of a design to accuse him of high treason, makes his escape to Blefuscu. His reception there.

Before I proceed to give an account of my leaving this kingdom, it may be proper to inform the reader of a private intrigue which had been for two months forming against me.

I had been hitherto all my life a stranger to courts, for which I was unqualified by the meanness of my condition. I had indeed heard and read enough of the dispositions of great princes and ministers; but never expected to have found such terrible effects of them in so remote a country, governed, as I thought, by very different maxims from those in Europe.

When I was just preparing to pay my attendance on the Emperor of Blefuscu, a considerable person at court (to whom I had been very serviceable at a time when he lay under the highest displeasure of his Imperial Majesty) came to my house very privately at night in a close chair and, without sending his name, desired admittance: the chairmen were dismissed; I put the chair, with his Lordship in it, into my coat-pocket; and giving orders to a trusty servant to say I was indisposed and gone to sleep, I fastened the door of my house, placed the chair on the table, according to my usual custom, and sat down by it. After the common salutations were over, observing his Lordship's countenance full of concern and inquiring into the reason, he desired I would hear him with patience in a matter that highly concerned my honour and my life. His speech was to the following effect, for I took notes of it as soon as he left me.

"You are to know," said he, "that several committees of council have been lately called in the most private manner on your account: and it is but two days since his Majesty came to a full resolution.

"You are very sensible that Skyresh Bolgolam (*Galbet,* or High Admiral) hath been your mortal enemy almost ever since your arrival. His original reasons I know not, but his hatred is much increased since your great success against Blefuscu, by which his glory as Admiral is obscured. This lord, in conjunction with Flimnap the High Treasurer, whose enmity against you is notorious on account of his lady, Limtoc the General, Lalcon the Chamberlain, and Balmuff the Grand Justiciary, have prepared articles of impeachment against you for treason and other capital crimes."

This preface made me so impatient, being conscious of my own merits and innocence, that I was going to interrupt; when he entreated me to be silent, and thus proceeded.

"Out of gratitude for the favours you have done me, I procured information of the whole proceedings, and a copy of the articles, wherein I venture my head for your service."

Articles of Impeachment [1] *against* Quinbus Flestrin (*the* Man-Mountain).

ARTICLE I

Whereas, by a statute made in the reign of his Imperial Majesty *Calin Deffar Plune,* it is enacted that whoever shall make water within the precincts of the royal palace shall be liable to the pains and penalties of high treason: notwithstanding, the said *Quinbus Flestrin,* in open breach of the said law, under colour of extinguishing the fire kindled in the apartment of his Majesty's most dear imperial consort, did maliciously, traitorously, and devilishly, by discharge of his urine, put out the said fire kindled in the said apartment, lying and being within the precincts of the said royal palace, against the statute in that case provided, etc., against the duty, etc.

ARTICLE II

That the said *Quinbus Flestrin,* having brought the imperial fleet of Blefuscu into the royal port, and being afterwards commanded by his Imperial Majesty to seize all the other ships of the said empire of Blefuscu and reduce that empire to a province, to be governed by a

1. When the Whigs came to power in 1714, the former Tory ministers Oxford and Bolingbroke were impeached for high treason, a charge based on their supposed sympathy with the Jacobites and the French during negotiation of the Treaty of Utrecht. Bolingbroke fled to France before trial, and the charges against Oxford were later dropped.

viceroy from hence, and to destroy and put to death not only all the Big-Endian exiles but likewise all the people of that empire who would not immediately forsake the Big-Endian heresy: he, the said *Flestrin*, like a false traitor against his most Auspicious, Serene, Imperial Majesty, did petition to be excused from the said service, upon pretence of unwillingness to force the consciences or destroy the liberties and lives of an innocent people.

ARTICLE III

That whereas certain ambassadors arrived from the court of Blefuscu to sue for peace in his Majesty's court: he the said *Flestrin* did, like a false traitor, aid, abet, comfort, and divert the said ambassadors, although he knew them to be servants to a prince who was lately an open enemy to his Imperial Majesty and in open war against his said Majesty.

ARTICLE IV

That the said *Quinbus Flestrin*, contrary to the duty of a faithful subject, is now preparing to make a voyage to the court and empire of Blefuscu, for which he hath received only verbal licence from his Imperial Majesty; and under colour of the said licence, doth falsely and traitorously intend to take the said voyage, and thereby to aid, comfort, and abet the Emperor of Blefuscu, so late an enemy and in open war with his Imperial Majesty aforesaid.

"There are some other articles, but these are the most important, of which I have read you an abstract.

"In the several debates upon this impeachment, it must be confessed that his Majesty gave many marks of his great lenity, often urging the services you had done him, and endeavouring to extenuate your crimes. The Treasurer and Admiral insisted that you should be put to the most painful and ignominious death, by setting fire on your house at night, and the General was to attend with twenty thousand men armed with poisoned arrows to shoot you on the face and hands. Some of your servants were to have private orders to strew a poisonous juice on your shirts and sheets, which would soon make you tear your own flesh and die in the utmost torture. The General came into the same opinion, so that for a long time there was a majority against you. But his Majesty resolving, if possible, to spare your life, at last brought off the Chamberlain.

"Upon this incident, Reldresal, Principal Secretary for Private Affairs, who always approved himself your true friend, was commanded by the Emperor to deliver his opinion, which he accordingly did; and therein justified the good thoughts you have of him. He allowed your crimes to be great, but that still there was room for mercy, the most commendable virtue in a prince, and for which his Majesty was so justly celebrated. He said the friendship between you and him was so well known to the world that perhaps the most honourable board might think him partial: however, in obedience to the command he had received, he would freely offer his sentiments. That if his Majesty, in consideration of your services and pursuant to his own merciful disposition, would please to spare your life and only give order to put out both your eyes, he humbly conceived that by this expedient justice might in some measure be satisfied, and all the world would applaud the *lenity* of the Emperor, as well as the fair and generous proceedings of those who have the honour to be his counsellors. That the loss of your eyes would be no impediment to your bodily strength, by which you might still be useful to his Majesty. That blindness is an addition to courage, by concealing dangers from us; that the fear you had for your eyes was the greatest difficulty in bringing over the enemy's fleet, and it would be sufficient for you to see by the eyes of the ministers, since the greatest princes do no more.

"This proposal was received with the utmost disapprobation by the whole board. Bolgolam the Admiral could not preserve his temper but, rising up in fury, said he wondered how the Secretary durst presume to give his opinion for preserving the life of a traitor: that the services you had performed were, by all true reasons of state, the great aggravation of your crimes; that you, who were able to extinguish the fire by discharge of urine in her Majesty's apartment (which he mentioned with horror), might, at another time, raise an inundation by the same means to drown the whole palace; and the same strength which enabled you to bring over the enemy's fleet might serve, upon the first discontent, to carry it back: that he had good reasons to think you were a Big-Endian in your heart; and as treason begins in the heart before it appears in overt acts, so he accused you as a traitor on that account, and therefore insisted you should be put to death.

"The Treasurer was of the same opinion; he showed to what straits his Majesty's revenue was reduced by the charge of maintaining you, which would soon grow insupportable: that the Secretary's expedient of putting out your eyes was so far from being a remedy against this evil that it would probably increase it, as it is manifest from the common practice of blinding some kind of fowl, after which they fed the faster and grew sooner fat: that his sacred Majesty and the council, who are your judges, were in their own consciences fully convinced of your guilt, which was a sufficient argument to condemn you to death, without the formal proofs required by the strict letter of the law.

"But his Imperial Majesty, fully determined against capital punishment, was graciously pleased to say that since the council thought the loss of your eyes too easy a censure, some other may be inflicted hereafter. And your friend the Secretary humbly desiring to be heard again, in answer to what the Treasurer had objected concerning the great charge his Majesty was at in maintaining you, said that his Excellency, who had the sole disposal of the Emperor's revenue, might easily provide against this evil by gradually lessening your establishment; by which, for want of sufficient food, you would grow weak and faint and lose your appetite, and consequently decay and consume in a few months; neither would the stench of your carcass be then so dangerous when it should become more than half diminished; and immediately upon your death, five or six thousand of his Majesty's subjects might, in two or three days, cut your flesh from your bones, take it away by cartloads, and bury it in distant parts to prevent infection, leaving the skeleton as a monument of admiration to posterity.

"Thus by the great friendship of the Secretary, the whole affair was compromised. It was strictly enjoined that the project of starving you by degrees should be kept a secret, but the sentence of putting out your eyes was entered on the books; none dissenting except Bolgolam the Admiral, who, being a creature of the Empress, was perpetually instigated by her Majesty to insist upon your death, she having borne perpetual malice against you on account of that infamous and illegal method you took to extinguish the fire in her apartment.

"In three days your friend the Secretary will be directed to come to your house and read before you the articles of impeachment; and then to signify the great lenity and favour of his Majesty and council, whereby you are only condemned to the loss of your eyes, which his Majesty doth not question you will gratefully and humbly submit to; and twenty of his Majesty's surgeons will attend in order to see the operation well performed, by discharging very sharp-pointed arrows into the balls of your eyes as you lie on the ground.

"I leave to your prudence what measures you will take; and to avoid suspicion, I must immediately return in as private a manner as I came."

His Lordship did so, and I remained alone, under many doubts and perplexities of mind.

It was a custom introduced by this prince and his ministry (very different, as I have been assured, from the practices of former times) that after the court had decreed any cruel execution, either to gratify the monarch's resentment or the malice of a favourite, the Emperor always made a speech to his whole council, expressing his great lenity and tenderness, as qualities known and confessed by all the world. This speech was immediately published through the kingdom; nor did anything terrify the people so much as those encomiums on his Majesty's mercy; because it was observed that the more these praises were enlarged and insisted on, the more inhuman was the punishment, and the sufferer more innocent. Yet as to myself, I must confess, having never been designed for a courtier either by my birth or education, I was so ill a judge of things that I could not discover the lenity and favour of this sentence, but conceived it (perhaps erroneously) rather to be rigorous than gentle. I sometimes thought of standing my trial, for although I could not deny the facts alleged in the several articles, yet I hoped they would admit of some extenuations. But having in my life perused many state trials, which I ever observed to terminate as the judges thought fit to direct, I durst not rely on so dangerous a decision in so critical a juncture and against such powerful enemies. Once I was strongly bent upon resistance, for, while I had liberty, the whole strength of that empire could hardly subdue me, and I might easily with stones pelt the metropolis to pieces; but I soon rejected that project with horror, by remembering the oath I had made to the Emperor, the favours I received from him, and the high title of *Nardac* he conferred upon me. Neither had I so soon learned the gratitude of courtiers to persuade myself that his Majesty's present severities acquitted me of all past obligations.

At last I fixed upon a resolution for which it is probable I may incur some censure, and not unjustly; for I confess I owe the preserving my eyes, and consequently my liberty, to my own great rashness and want of experience: because if I had then known the nature of princes and ministers, which I have since observed in many other courts, and their methods of treating criminals less obnoxious than myself, I should with great alacrity and readiness have submitted to so easy a punishment. But hurried on by the precipitancy of youth, and having his Imperial Majesty's licence to pay my attendance upon the Emperor of Blefuscu, I took this opportunity, before the three days were elapsed, to send a letter to my friend the Secretary, signifying my resolution of setting out that morning for Blefuscu pursuant to the leave I had got; and without waiting for an answer, I went to that side of the island where our fleet lay. I seized a large man-of-war, tied a cable to the prow, and, lifting up the anchors, I stripped myself, put my clothes (together with my coverlet, which I carried under my arm) into the vessel, and drawing it after me, between wading and swimming arrived at the royal port of Blefuscu, where the people had long expected me; they lent me two guides to direct me to the capital city, which is of the same name. I held them in my hands until I came within two hundred yards of the gate, and desired them to signify my arrival to one of the secretaries, and let him know I there waited his Majesty's commands. I had an answer in about an hour that his Majesty, attended by the royal family and great officers of the court, was coming out to receive me. I advanced a hundred yards. The Emperor and his train alighted from their horses, the Empress and ladies from their coaches, and I did not perceive they were in any fright or concern. I lay on the ground to kiss his Majesty's and the Empress's hand. I told his Majesty that I was come according to my promise, and with the licence of the Emperor my master, to have the honour of seeing so mighty a monarch, and to offer him any service in my power consistent with my duty to my own prince; not mentioning a word of my disgrace, because I had hitherto no regular information of it and might suppose myself wholly ignorant of any such design; neither could I reasonably conceive that the Emperor would discover [2] the secret while I was out of his power: wherein, however, it soon appeared I was deceived.

I shall not trouble the reader with the particular account of my reception at this court, which was suitable to the generosity of so great a prince; nor of the difficulties I was in for want of a house and bed, being forced to lie on the ground, wrapped up in my coverlet.

Chapter Eight: The author, by a lucky accident, finds means to leave Blefuscu, and after some difficulties returns safe to his native country.

Three days after my arrival, walking out of curiosity to the northeast coast of the island, I observed, about half a league off in the sea, somewhat that looked like a boat overturned. I pulled off my shoes and stockings and, wading two or three hundred yards, I found the object to approach nearer by force of the tide, and then plainly saw it to be a real boat, which I supposed might by some tempest have been driven from a ship; whereupon I returned immediately towards the city, and desired his Imperial Majesty to lend me twenty of the tallest vessels he had left after the loss of his fleet, and three thousand seamen under the command of his Vice-Admiral. This fleet sailed round, while I went back the shortest way to the coast where I first discovered the boat; I found the tide had driven it still nearer. The seamen were all provided with cordage, which I had beforehand twisted to a sufficient strength. When the ships came

2. Reveal.

up, I stripped myself and waded till I came within an hundred yards of the boat, after which I was forced to swim till I got up to it. The seamen threw me the end of the cord, which I fastened to a hole in the fore-part of the boat and the other end to a man-of-war: but I found all my labour to little purpose; for, being out of my depth, I was not able to work. In this necessity, I was forced to swim behind, and push the boat forwards as often as I could with one of my hands; and, the tide favouring me, I advanced so far that I could just hold up my chin and feel the ground. I rested two or three minutes and then gave the boat another shove, and so on till the sea was no higher than my armpits; and now, the most laborious part being over, I took out my other cables, which were stowed in one of the ships, and, fastening them first to the boat and then to nine of the vessels which attended me, the wind being favourable, the seamen towed and I shoved till we arrived within forty yards of the shore; and waiting till the tide was out, I got dry to the boat, and by the assistance of two thousand men, with ropes and engines, I made a shift to turn it on its bottom and found it was but little damaged.

I shall not trouble the reader with the difficulties I was under by the help of certain paddles, which cost me ten days making, to get my boat to the royal port of Blefuscu, where a mighty concourse of people appeared upon my arrival, full of wonder at the sight of so prodigious a vessel. I told the Emperor that my good fortune had thrown this boat in my way, to carry me to some place from whence I might return into my native country, and begged his Majesty's orders for getting materials to fit it up, together with his licence to depart; which, after some kind expostulations, he was pleased to grant.

I did very much wonder, in all this time, not to have heard of any express relating to me from our Emperor to the court of Blefuscu. But I was afterwards given privately to understand that his Imperial Majesty, never imagining I had the least notice of his designs, believed I was only gone to Blefuscu in performance of my promise, according to the licence he had given me, which was well known at our court, and would return in a few days when that ceremony was ended. But he was at last in pain at my long absence; and after consulting with the Treasurer and the rest of that cabal, a person of quality was dispatched with the copy of the articles against me. This envoy had instructions to represent to the monarch of Blefuscu the great *lenity* of his master, who was content to punish me no further than with the loss of my eyes; that I had fled from justice, and if I did not return in two hours, I should be deprived of my title of *Nardac* and declared a traitor. The envoy further added that, in order to maintain the peace and amity between both empires, his master expected that his brother of Blefuscu would give orders to have me sent back to Lilliput, bound hand and foot, to be punished as a traitor.

The Emperor of Blefuscu, having taken three days to consult, returned an answer consisting of many civilities and excuses. He said that, as for sending me bound, his brother knew it was impossible; that although I had deprived him of his fleet, yet he owed great obligations to me for many good offices I had done him in making the peace. That, however, both their Majesties would soon be made easy; for I had found a prodigious vessel on the shore, able to carry me on the sea, which he had given order to fit up with my own assistance and direction, and he hoped in a few weeks both empires would be freed from so insupportable an incumbrance.

With this answer the envoy returned to Lilliput, and the monarch of Blefuscu related to me all that had passed, offering me at the same time (but under strictest confidence) his gracious protection if I would continue in his service; wherein although I believed him sincere, yet I resolved never more to put any confidence in princes or ministers where I could possibly avoid it; and therefore, with all due acknowledgments for his favourable intentions, I humbly begged to be excused. I told him that, since fortune, whether good or evil, had thrown a vessel in my way, I was resolved to venture myself in the ocean, rather than be an occasion of difference between two such mighty monarchs. Neither did I find the Emperor at all displeased; and I discovered by a certain accident that he was very glad of my resolution, and so were most of his ministers.

These considerations moved me to hasten my departure somewhat sooner than I intended; to which the court, impatient to have me gone, very readily contributed. Five hundred workmen were employed to make two sails to my boat, according to my directions, by quilting thirteen fold of their strongest linen together. I was at the pains of making ropes and cables by twisting ten, twenty, or thirty of the thickest and strongest of theirs. A great stone that I happened to find after a long search by the seashore served me for an anchor. I had the tallow of three hundred cows for greasing my boat and other uses. I was at incredible pains in cutting down some of the largest timber trees for oars and masts, wherein I was, however, much assisted by his Majesty's ship-carpenters, who helped me in smoothing them after I had done the rough work.

In about a month, when all was prepared, I sent to receive his Majesty's commands and to take my leave. The Emperor and royal family came out of the palace; I lay down on my face to kiss his hand, which he very graciously gave me: so did the Empress and young princes of the blood. His Majesty presented me with fifty purses of two hundred *sprugs* apiece, together with his picture at full length, which I put immediately into one of my gloves to keep it from being hurt. The ceremonies at my departure were too many to trouble the reader with at this time.

I stored the boat with the carcasses of an hundred oxen and three hundred sheep, with bread and drink proportionable, and as much meat ready dressed as four hundred cooks could provide. I took with me six cows and two bulls alive, with as many ewes and rams, intending to carry them into my own country and propagate the breed. And to feed them on board, I had a good bundle of hay and a bag of corn. I would gladly have taken a dozen of the natives, but this was a thing the Emperor would by no means permit; and besides a diligent search into my pockets, his Majesty engaged my honour not to carry away any of his subjects, although with their own consent and desire.

Having thus prepared all things as well as I was able, I set sail on the twenty-fourth day of September, 1701, at six in the morning; and when I had gone about four leagues to the northward, the wind being at southeast, at six in the evening, I descried a small island about half a league to the northwest. I advanced forward and cast anchor on the lee-side of the island, which seemed to be uninhabited. I then took some refreshment and went to my rest. I slept well, and as I conjecture at least six hours, for I found the day broke in two hours after I awaked. It was a clear night. I eat my breakfast before the sun was up; and heaving anchor, the wind being favourable, I steered the same course that I had done the day before, wherein I was directed by my pocket-compass. My intention was to reach, if possible, one of those islands which I had reason to believe lay to the northeast of Van Diemen's Land. I discovered nothing all that day; but upon the next, about three in the afternoon, when I had by my computation made twenty-four leagues from Blefuscu, I descried a sail steering to the southeast; my course was due east. I hailed her but could get no answer; yet I found I gained upon her, for the wind slackened. I made all the sail I could, and in half an hour she spied me, then hung out her ancient,[1] and discharged a gun. It is not easy to express the joy I was in upon the unexpected hope of once more seeing my beloved country and the dear pledges [2] I had left in it. The ship slackened her sails, and I came up with her between five and six in the evening, September 26; but my heart leapt within me to see her English colours. I put my cows and sheep into my coat-pockets, and got on board with all my little cargo of provisions. The vessel was an English merchantman, returning from Japan by the North and South Seas,[3] the captain, Mr. John Biddel of Deptford, a very civil man and an excellent sailor. We were now in the latitude of 30 degrees south; there were about fifty men in the ship; and here I met an old comrade of mine, one Peter Williams, who gave me a good character to the captain. This gentleman treated me with kindness, and desired I would let him know what place I came from last, and whither I was bound; which I did in few words, but he thought I was raving, and that the dangers I underwent had disturbed my head; whereupon I took my black cattle and sheep out of my pocket, which, after great astonishment, clearly convinced him of my veracity. I then showed him the gold given me by the Emperor of Blefuscu, together with his Majesty's picture at full length, and some other rarities of that country. I gave him two purses of two hundred *sprugs* each, and promised, when we arrived in England, to make him a present of a cow and a sheep big with young.

I shall not trouble the reader with a particular account of this voyage, which was very prosperous for the most part. We arrived in the Downs [4] on the 13th of April, 1702. I had only one misfortune, that the rats on board carried away one of my sheep; I found her bones in a hole, picked clean from the flesh. The rest of my cattle I got safe on shore, and set them agrazing in a bowling-green at Greenwich, where the fineness of the grass made them feed very heartily, though I had always feared the contrary; neither could I possibly have preserved them in so long a voyage if the captain had not allowed me some of his best biscuit, which, rubbed to powder and mingled with water, was their constant food. The short time I continued in England, I made a considerable profit by showing my cattle to many persons of quality and others: and before I began my second voyage, I sold them for six hundred pounds. Since my last return, I find the breed is considerably increased, especially the sheep; which I hope will prove much to the advantage of the woollen manufacture by the fineness of the fleeces.

I stayed but two months with my wife and family; for my insatiable desire

1. Flag.
2. Hostages, loved ones.
3. Pacific Ocean.
4. Anchorage near Dover where passengers might disembark.

of seeing foreign countries would suffer me to continue no longer. I left fifteen hundred pounds with my wife and fixed her in a good house at Redriff. My remaining stock I carried with me, part in money and part in goods, in hopes to improve my fortunes. My eldest uncle John had left me an estate in land near Epping, of about thirty pounds a year; and I had a long lease of the Black Bull in Fetter Lane, which yielded me as much more: so that I was not in any danger of leaving my family upon the parish.[5] My son Johnny, named so after his uncle, was at the grammar school and a towardly [6] child. My daughter Betty (who is now well married and has children) was then at her needlework. I took leave of my wife and boy and girl with tears on both sides and went on board the *Adventure,* a merchant-ship of three hundred tons, bound for Surat,[7] Captain John Nicholas of Liverpool commander. But my account of this voyage must be referred to the second part of my *Travels.*

Part Two: A Voyage to Brobdingnag

Chapter One: A great storm described. The long-boat sent to fetch water, the author goes with it to discover the country. He is left on shore, is seized by one of the natives, and carried to a farmer's house. His reception there, with several accidents that happened there. A description of the inhabitants.

Having been condemned by nature and fortune to an active and restless life, in two months after my return I again left my native country and took shipping in the Downs on the 20th day of June, 1702, in the *Adventure,* Capt. John Nicholas, a Cornish man, commander, bound for Surat. We had a very prosperous gale till we arrived at the Cape of Good Hope, where we landed for fresh water, but, discovering a leak we unshipped our goods and wintered there; for the captain falling sick of an ague, we could not leave the Cape till the end of March. We then set sail and had a good voyage till we passed the Straits of Madagascar; but having got northward of that island, and to about five degrees south latitude, the winds, which in those seas are observed to blow a constant equal gale between the north and west from the beginning of December to the beginning of May, on the 19th of April began to blow with much greater violence, and more westerly than usual, continuing so for twenty days together, during which time we were driven a little to the east of the Molucca Islands and about three degrees northward of the Line,[1] as our captain found by an observation he took the 2nd of May, at which time the wind ceased, and it was a perfect calm, whereat I was not a little rejoiced. But he, being a man well experienced in the navigation of those seas, bid us all prepare against a storm, which accordingly happened the day following: for a southern wind, called the southern monsoon, began to set in.

Finding it was like to overblow, we took in our spritsail, and stood by to hand the foresail; but making foul weather, we looked the guns were all fast,

5. Dependent on parish support as paupers.
6. Promising.
7. Port north of Bombay in western India.

1. Equator.

and handed the mizzen.[2] The ship lay very broad off, so we thought it better spooning before the sea than trying or hulling. We reefed the foresail and set him, we hauled aft the fore-sheet; the helm was hard aweather. The ship wore bravely. We belayed the fore-downhaul; but the sail was split, and we hauled down the yard, and got the sail into the ship, and unbound all the things clear of it. It was a very fierce storm; the sea broke strange and dangerous. We hauled off upon the lanyard of the whipstaff, and helped the man at helm. We would not get down our topmast, but let all stand, because she scudded before the sea very well, and we knew that, the topmast being aloft, the ship was the wholesomer, and made better way through the sea, seeing we had searoom. When the storm was over, we set foresail and mainsail and brought the ship to. Then we set the mizzen, main-topsail, and the fore-topsail. Our course was east-northeast, the wind was at southwest. We got the starboard tacks aboard, we cast off our weatherbraces and lifts; we set in the lee braces, and hauled forward by the weather bowlings, and hauled them tight, and belayed them, and hauled over the mizzen tack to windward, and kept her full and by as near as she would lie.

During this storm, which was followed by a strong west-southwest, we were carried by my computation about five hundred leagues to the east, so that the oldest sailor on board could not tell in what part of the world we were. Our provisions held out well, our ship was staunch, and our crew all in good health; but we lay in the utmost distress for water. We thought it best to hold on the same course rather than turn more northerly, which might have brought us to the northwest parts of Great Tartary and into the frozen sea.[3]

On the 16th day of June, 1703, a boy on the topmast discovered land. On the 17th we came in full view of a great island or continent (for we knew not whether) on the south side whereof was a small neck of land jutting out into the sea, and a creek too shallow to hold a ship of above one hundred tons. We cast anchor within a league of this creek, and our captain sent a dozen of his men well armed in the long-boat with vessels for water if any could be found. I desired his leave to go with them that I might see the country and make what discoveries I could. When we came to land we saw no river or spring, nor any sign of inhabitants. Our men therefore wandered on the shore to find out some fresh water near the sea, and I walked alone about a mile on the other side, where I observed the country all barren and rocky. I now began to be weary and, seeing nothing to entertain my curiosity, I returned gently down towards the creek; and the sea being full in my view, I saw our men already got into the boat and rowing for life to the ship. I was going to holloa after them, although it had been to little purpose, when I observed a huge creature walking after them in the sea as fast as he could: he waded not much deeper than his knees and took prodigious strides: but our men had the start of him half a league, and, the thereabouts being full of sharp pointed rocks, the monster was not able to overtake the boat. This I was afterwards told, for I durst not stay to see the issue of that adventure, but ran as fast as I could the way I first

2. This paragraph, so loaded with nautical jargon, is borrowed almost entirely by Swift (for the sake of parody) from Samuel Sturmy's *Mariner's Magazine* (1669).

3. The ship is brought past northwestern Siberia into the Arctic Sea. Brobdingnag is a peninsula roughly in the position of Alaska, cut off from the mainland by impassable mountains.

went; and then climbed up a steep hill which gave me some prospect of the country. I found it fully cultivated; but that which first surprised me was the length of the grass, which in those grounds that seemed to be kept for hay was above twenty foot high.

I fell into a high road, for so I took it to be, although it served to the inhabitants only as a footpath through a field of barley. Here I walked on for some time, but could see little on either side, it being now near harvest, and the corn rising at least forty foot. I was an hour walking to the end of this field, which was fenced in with a hedge of at least one hundred and twenty foot high, and the trees so lofty that I could make no computation of their altitude. There was a stile to pass from this field into the next. It had four steps, and a stone to cross over when you came to the uppermost. It was impossible for me to climb this stile, because every step was six foot high and the upper stone above twenty. I was endeavouring to find some gap in the hedge when I discovered one of the inhabitants in the next field advancing towards the stile, of the same size with him whom I saw in the sea pursuing our boat. He appeared as tall as an ordinary spire-steeple, and took about ten yards at every stride, as near as I could guess. I was struck with the utmost fear and astonishment, and ran to hide myself in the corn, from whence I saw him at the top of the stile, looking back into the next field on the right hand, and heard him call in a voice many degrees louder than a speaking-trumpet; but the noise was so high in the air that at first I certainly thought it was thunder. Whereupon seven monsters like himself came towards him with reaping-hooks in their hands, each hook about the largeness of six scythes. These people were not so well clad as the first, whose servants or labourers they seemed to be. For upon some words he spoke, they went to reap the corn in the field where I lay. I kept from them at as great a distance as I could, but was forced to move with extreme difficulty, for the stalks of the corn were sometimes not above a foot distant, so that I could hardly squeeze my body betwixt them. However, I made a shift to go forward till I came to a part of the field where the corn had been laid by the rain and wind. Here it was impossible for me to advance a step: for the stalks were so interwoven that I could not creep through, and the beards of the fallen ears so strong and pointed that they pierced through my clothes into my flesh. At the same time I heard the reapers not above an hundred yards behind me.

Being quite dispirited with toil, and wholly overcome by grief and despair, I lay down between two ridges, and heartily wished I might there end my days. I bemoaned my desolate widow and fatherless children. I lamented my own folly and wilfulness in attempting a second voyage against the advice of all my friends and relations. In this terrible agitation of mind I could not forbear thinking of Lilliput, whose inhabitants looked upon me as the greatest prodigy that ever appeared in the world: where I was able to draw an imperial fleet in my hand, and perform those other actions which will be recorded for ever in the chronicles of that empire, while posterity shall hardly believe them, although attested by millions. I reflected what a mortification it must prove to me to appear as inconsiderable in this nation as one single Lilliputian would be among us. But this I conceived was to be the least of my misfortunes: for, as human creatures are observed to be more savage and cruel in proportion to their bulk, what could I expect but to be a morsel in the mouth of the first among these enormous barbarians who should happen to seize me? Undoubtedly philosophers are in the right when they tell us that nothing is great or little otherwise than by comparison. It might have pleased fortune to let the Lilliputians find some nation where the people were as diminutive with respect to them as they were to me. And who knows but that even this prodigious race of mortals might be equally overmatched in some distant part of the world whereof we have yet no discovery?

Scared and confounded as I was, I could not forbear going on with these reflections, when one of the reapers, approaching within ten yards of the ridge where I lay, made me apprehend that with the next step I should be squashed to death under his foot, or cut in two with his reaping hook. And therefore, when he was again about to move, I screamed as loud as fear could make me. Whereupon the huge creature trod short, and, looking round about under him for some time, at last espied me as I lay on the ground. He considered a while with the caution of one who endeavours to lay hold on a small dangerous animal in such a manner that it shall not be able either to scratch or bite him, as I myself have sometimes done with a weasel in England. At length he ventured to take me up behind by the middle between his forefinger and thumb, and brought me within three yards of his eyes, that he might behold my shape more perfectly. I guessed his meaning, and my good fortune gave me so much presence of mind that I resolved not to struggle in the least as he held me in the air above sixty foot from the ground, although he grievously pinched my sides, for fear I should slip through his fingers. All I ventured was to raise my eyes towards the sun and place my hands together in a supplicating posture, and to speak some words in an humble melancholy tone suitable to the condition I then was in. For I apprehended every moment that he would dash me against the ground, as we usually do any little hateful animal which we have a mind to destroy. But my good star would have it that he appeared pleased with my voice and gestures, and began to look upon me as a curiosity, much wondering to hear me pronounce articulate words, although he could not understand them. In the meantime I was not able to forbear groaning and shedding tears and turning my head towards my sides; letting him know, as well as I could, how cruelly I was hurt by the pressure of his thumb and finger. He seemed to apprehend my meaning; for, lifting up the lappet of his coat, he put me gently into it, and immediately ran along with me to his master, who was a substantial farmer and the same person I had first seen in the field.

The farmer, having (as I supposed by their talk) received such an account of me as his servant could give him, took a piece of a small straw about the size of a walking staff, and therewith lifted up the lappets of my coat; which it seems he thought to be some kind of covering that nature had given me. He blew my hairs aside to take a better view of my face. He called his hinds [4] about him and asked them (as I afterwards learned) whether they had ever seen in the fields any little creature that resembled me. He then placed me softly on the ground upon all four, but I got immediately up and walked slowly backwards and forwards, to let those people see I had no intent to run away. They all sat down in a circle about me, the better to observe my motions. I pulled off my hat and made a low bow towards the farmer. I fell on my knees

4. Farm laborers.

and lifted up my hands and eyes, and spoke several words as loud as I could: I took a purse of gold out of my pocket and humbly presented it to him. He received it on the palm of his hand, then applied it close to his eye, to see what it was, and afterwards turned it several times with the point of a pin (which he took out of his sleeve), but could make nothing of it. Whereupon I made a sign that he should place his hand on the ground. I then took the purse and, opening it, poured all the gold into his palm. There were six Spanish pieces of four pistoles each,[5] beside twenty or thirty smaller coins. I saw him wet the tip of his little finger upon his tongue and take up one of my largest pieces and then another, but he seemed to be wholly ignorant what they were. He made me a sign to put them again into my purse, and the purse again into my pocket, which, after offering to him several times, I thought it best to do.

The farmer by this time was convinced I must be a rational creature. He spoke often to me, but the sound of his voice pierced my ears like that of a watermill, yet his words were articulate enough. I answered as loud as I could, in several languages, and he often laid his ear within two yards of me, but all in vain, for we were wholly unintelligible to each other. He then sent his servants to their work, and, taking his handkerchief out of his pocket, he doubled and spread it on his hand, which he placed flat on the ground, with the palm upwards, making me a sign to step into it, as I could easily do, for it was not above a foot in thickness. I thought it my part to obey and, for fear of falling, laid myself at full length upon the handkerchief, with the remainder of which he lapped me up to the head for further security, and in this manner carried me home to his house. There he called his wife and showed me to her; but she screamed and ran back as women in England do at the sight of a toad or a spider. However, when she had a while seen my behaviour, and how well I observed the signs her husband made, she was soon reconciled, and by degrees grew extremely tender of me.

It was about twelve at noon, and a servant brought in dinner. It was only one substantial dish of meat (fit for the plain condition of an husbandman) in a dish of about four and twenty foot diameter. The company were the farmer and his wife, three children, and an old grandmother: when they were sat down, the farmer placed me at some distance from him on the table, which was thirty foot high from the floor. I was in a terrible fright, and kept as far as I could from the edge for fear of falling. The wife minced a bit of meat, then crumbled some bread on a trencher, and placed it before me. I made her a low bow, took out my knife and fork, and fell to eat, which gave them exceeding delight. The mistress sent her maid for a small dram cup, which held about two gallons, and filled it with drink; I took up the vessel with much difficulty in both hands, and in a most respectful manner drank to her ladyship's health, expressing the words as loud as I could in English, which made the company laugh so heartily that I was almost deafened with the noise. This liquor tasted like a small cider, and was not unpleasant. Then the master made me a sign to come to his trencher side; but as I walked on the table, being in great surprise all the time, as the indulgent reader will easily conceive and excuse, I happened to stumble against a crust, and fell flat on my face, but received no hurt. I got up immediately, and observing the good people to be

5. The coins were large enough to be of considerable value in Europe.

in much concern, I took my hat (which I held under my arm out of good manners) and waving it over my head, made three huzzas to show I had got no mischief by the fall. But advancing forwards towards my master (as I shall henceforth call him) his youngest son who sat next him, an arch boy of about ten years old, took me up by the legs, and held me so high in the air, that I trembled every limb; but his father snatched me from him, and at the same time gave him such a box on the left ear as would have felled an European troop of horse to the earth, ordering him to be taken from the table. But being afraid the boy might owe me a spite,[6] and well remembering how mischievous all children among us naturally are to sparrows, rabbits, young kittens, and puppy dogs, I fell on my knees and, pointing to the boy, made my master understand as well as I could that I desired his son might be pardoned. The father complied, and the lad took his seat again; whereupon I went to him and kissed his hand, which my master took, and made him stroke me gently with it.

In the midst of dinner, my mistress's favourite cat leapt into her lap. I heard a noise behind me like that of a dozen stocking-weavers at work;[7] and turning my head I found it proceeded from the purring of this animal, who seemed to be three times larger than an ox, as I computed by the view of her head and one of her paws, which her mistress was feeding and stroking her. The fierceness of this creature's countenance altogether discomposed me; although I stood at the further end of the table, above fifty foot off, and although my mistress held her fast for fear she might give a spring and seize me in her talons. But it happened there was no danger; for the cat took not the least notice of me when my master placed me within three yards of her. And as I have been always told, and found true by experience in my travels, that flying or discovering fear before a fierce animal is a certain way to make it pursue or attack you, so I resolved in this dangerous juncture to show no manner of concern. I walked with intrepidity five or six times before the very head of the cat, and came within half a yard of her; whereupon she drew herself back, as if she were more afraid of me: I had less apprehension concerning the dogs, whereof three or four came into the room, as it is usual in farmers' houses; one of which was a mastiff equal in bulk to four elephants, and a greyhound somewhat taller than the mastiff but not so large.

When dinner was almost done, the nurse came in with a child of a year old in her arms, who immediately spied me and began a squall that you might have heard from London Bridge to Chelsea,[8] after the usual oratory of infants, to get me for a plaything. The mother out of pure indulgence took me up and put me towards the child, who presently seized me by the middle and got my head in his mouth, where I roared so loud that the urchin was frighted and let me drop, and I should infallibly have broke my neck if the mother had not held her apron under me. The nurse to quiet her babe made use of a rattle, which was a kind of hollow vessel filled with great stones and fastened by a cable to the child's waist: but all in vain, so that she was forced to apply the last remedy by giving it suck. I must confess no object ever disgusted me so much as the sight of her monstrous breast, which I cannot tell what to compare with so as to give the curious reader an idea of its bulk, shape and colour. It

6. Hold a grudge against me.
7. At mechanical looms.
8. I.e., about five miles.

stood prominent six foot and could not be less than sixteen in circumference. The nipple was about half the bigness of my head, and the hue both of that and the dug so varified with spots, pimples, and freckles that nothing could appear more nauseous: for I had a near sight of her, she sitting down the more conveniently to give suck and I standing on the table. This made me reflect upon the fair skins of our English ladies, who appear so beautiful to us only because they are of our own size, and their defects not to be seen but through a magnifying glass, where we find by experiment that the smoothest and whitest skins look rough and coarse and ill-coloured.

I remember when I was at Lilliput the complexions of those diminutive people appeared to me the fairest in the world; and talking upon this subject with a person of learning there, who was an intimate friend of mine, he said that my face appeared much fairer and smoother when he looked on me from the ground than it did upon a nearer view when I took him up in my hand and brought him close, which he confessed was at first a very shocking sight. He said he could discover great holes in my skin, that the stumps of my beard were ten times stronger than the bristles of a boar, and my complexion made up of several colours altogether disagreeable: although I must beg leave to say for myself that I am as fair as most of my sex and country, and very little sunburnt by all my travels. On the other side, discoursing of the ladies in that emperor's court, he used to tell me one had freckles, another too wide a mouth, a third too large a nose, nothing of which I was able to distinguish. I confess this reflection was obvious enough; which however I could not forbear, lest the reader might think those vast creatures were actually deformed: for I must do them justice to say they are a comely race of people; and particularly the features of my master's countenance, although he were but a farmer, when I beheld him from the height of sixty foot, appeared very well proportioned.

When dinner was done, my master went out to his labourers, and, as I could discover by his voice and gesture, gave his wife a strict charge to take care of me. I was very much tired and disposed to sleep, which, my mistress perceiving, she put me on her own bed and covered me with a clean white handkerchief, but larger and coarser than the mainsail of a man-of-war.

I slept about two hours and dreamed I was at home with my wife and children, which aggravated my sorrows when I awaked and found myself alone in a vast room between two and three hundred foot wide and above two hundred high, lying in a bed twenty yards wide. My mistress was gone about her household affairs and had locked me in. The bed was eight yards from the floor. Some natural necessities required me to get down; I durst not presume to call, and if I had, it would have been in vain with such a voice as mine at so great a distance from the room where I lay to the kitchen where the family kept. While I was under these circumstances two rats crept up the curtains and ran smelling backwards and forwards on the bed. One of them came up almost to my face, whereupon I rose in a fright and drew out my hanger [9] to defend myself. These horrible animals had the boldness to attack me on both sides, and one of them held his fore-feet at my collar; but I had the good fortune to rip up his belly before he could do me any mischief. He fell down at my feet, and the other, seeing the fate of his comrade, made his escape, but not without one good wound on the back, which I gave him as he fled, and

9. Short broad sword hanging from his belt.

made the blood run trickling from him. After this exploit, I walked gently to and fro on the bed, to recover my breath and loss of spirits. These creatures were of the size of a large mastiff, but infinitely more nimble and fierce, so that, if I had taken off my belt before I went to sleep, I must have infallibly been torn to pieces and devoured. I measured the tail of the dead rat and found it to be two yards long, wanting an inch; but it went against my stomach to drag the carcass off the bed, where it lay still bleeding; I observed it had yet some life, but with a strong slash cross the neck, I thoroughly dispatched it.

Soon after my mistress came into the room, who, seeing me all bloody, ran and took me up in her hand. I pointed to the dead rat, smiling and making other signs to show I was not hurt, whereat she was extremely rejoiced, calling the maid to take up the dead rat with a pair of tongs and throw it out of the window. Then she set me on a table, where I showed her my hanger all bloody and, wiping it on the lappet of my coat, returned it to the scabbard. I was pressed to do more than one thing which another could not do for me, and therefore endeavoured to make my mistress understand that I desired to be set down on the floor; which, after she had done, my bashfulness would not suffer me to express myself farther than by pointing to the door and bowing several times. The good woman with much difficulty at last perceived what I would be at and, taking me up again in her hand, walked into the garden, where she set me down. I went on one side about two hundred yards, and, beckoning to her not to look or to follow me, I hid myself between two leaves of sorrel and there discharged the necessities of nature.

I hope the gentle reader will excuse me for dwelling on these and the like particulars, which, however insignificant they may appear to grovelling vulgar minds, yet will certainly help a philosopher [10] to enlarge his thoughts and imagination and apply them to the benefit of public as well as private life, which was my sole design in presenting this and other accounts of my travels to the world; wherein I have been chiefly studious of truth, without affecting any ornaments of learning or of style. But the whole scene of this voyage made so strong an impression on my mind, and is so deeply fixed in my memory, that in committing it to paper I did not omit one material circumstance: however, upon a strict review, I blotted out several passages of less moment which were in my first copy for fear of being censured as tedious and trifling, whereof travellers are often, perhaps not without justice, accused.

Chapter Two: A description of the farmer's daughter. The author carried to a market-town, and then to the metropolis. The particulars of his journey.

My mistress had a daughter of nine years old, a child of forward parts [1] for her age, very dextrous at her needle and skilful in dressing her baby.[2] Her mother and she contrived to fit up the baby's cradle for me against night: the cradle

10. Common minds are opposed to that of a natural philosopher or scientist. Swift is mocking the highly detailed records collected by such scientific bodies as the Royal Society and often published in their Transactions. Travelers like Gulliver were urged to make such records, and the stolid, impassive observation of Gulliver is, whatever more, a parody of this procedure.

1. Precocious abilities.
2. Doll.

was put into a small drawer of a cabinet, and the drawer placed upon a hanging shelf for fear of the rats. This was my bed all the time I stayed with those people, although made more convenient by degrees, as I began to learn their language and make my wants known. This young girl was so handy that after I had once or twice pulled off my clothes before her, she was able to dress and undress me, although I never gave her that trouble when she would let me do either myself. She made me seven shirts and some other linen, of as fine cloth as could be got, which indeed was coarser than sackcloth; and these she constantly washed for me with her own hands. She was likewise my schoolmistress to teach me the language: when I pointed to anything, she told me the name of it in her own tongue, so that in a few days I was able to call for whatever I had a mind to. She was very good-natured, and not above forty foot high, being little for her age. She gave me the name of *Grildrig,* which the family took up, and afterwards the whole kingdom. The word imports what the Latins call *nanunculus,* the Italians *homunceletino,* and the English *mannikin.*[3] To her I chiefly owe my preservation in that country: we never parted while I was there; I called her my *glumdalclitch,* or *little nurse:* and I should be guilty of great ingratitude if I omitted this honourable mention of her care and affection towards me, which I heartily wish it lay in my power to requite as she deserves, instead of being the innocent but unhappy instrument of her disgrace, as I have too much reason to fear.

It now began to be known and talked of in the neighbourhood that my master had found a strange animal in the field, about the bigness of a *splacknuck,* but exactly shaped in every part like a human creature; which it likewise imitated in all its actions; seemed to speak in a little language of its own, had already learned several words of theirs, went erect upon two legs, was tame and gentle, would come when it was called, do whatever it was bid, had the finest limbs in the world, and a complexion fairer than a nobleman's daughter of three years old. Another farmer who lived hard by, and was a particular friend of my master, came on a visit on purpose to inquire into the truth of this story. I was immediately produced and placed upon a table, where I walked as I was commanded, drew my hanger, put it up again, made my reverence to my master's guest, asked him in his own language how he did, and told him he was welcome, just as my little nurse had instructed me. This man, who was old and dim-sighted, put on his spectacles to behold me better, at which I could not forbear laughing very heartily, for his eyes appeared like the full moon shining into a chamber at two windows. Our people, who discovered the cause of my mirth, bore me company in laughing, at which the old fellow was fool enough to be angry and out of countenance. He had the character of a great miser, and to my misfortune he well deserved it, by the cursed advice he gave my master to show me as a sight upon a market-day in the next town, which was half an hour's riding, about two and twenty miles from our house.

I guessed there was some mischief contriving when I observed my master and his friend whispering long together, sometimes pointing at me; and my fears made me fancy that I overheard and understood some of their words. But the next morning Glumdalclitch my little nurse told me the whole matter,

3. The Latin and Italian terms are Gulliver's own coinage, although they derive from Latin *nanus* (dwarf) and *homunculus* (mannikin).

which she had cunningly picked out from her mother. The poor girl laid me on her bosom and fell a-weeping with shame and grief. She apprehended some mischief would happen to me from rude vulgar folks, who might squeeze me to death or break one of my limbs by taking me in their hands. She had also observed how modest I was in my nature, how nicely I regarded my honour, and what an indignity I should conceive it to be exposed for money as a public spectacle to the meanest of the people. She said her papa and mamma had promised that Grildrig should be hers; but now she found they meant to serve her as they did last year, when they pretended to give her a lamb and yet, as soon as it was fat, sold it to a butcher. For my own part, I may truly affirm that I was less concerned than my nurse. I had a strong hope, which never left me, that I should one day recover my liberty; and, as to the ignominy of being carried about for a monster, I considered myself to be a perfect stranger in the country, and that such a misfortune could never be charged upon me as a reproach if ever I should return to England; since the King of Great Britain himself, in my condition, must have undergone the same distress.

My master, pursuant to the advice of his friend, carried me in a box the next market-day to the neighbouring town, and took along with him his little daughter my nurse upon a pillion behind him. The box was close on every side, with a little door for me to go in and out, and a few gimlet-holes to let in air. The girl had been so careful to put the quilt of her baby's bed into it, for me to lie down on. However, I was terribly shaken and discomposed in this journey, although it were but of half an hour. For the horse went about forty foot at every step, and trotted so high that the agitation was equal to the rising and falling of a ship in a great storm, but much more frequent: our journey was somewhat further than from London to St. Albans.[4] My master alighted at an inn which he used to frequent; and, after consulting a while with the innkeeper and making some necessary preparations, he hired the *Grultrud,* or *crier,* to give notice through the town of a strange creature to be seen at the sign of the Green Eagle, not so big as a *splacknuck* (an animal in that country very finely shaped, about six foot long) and in every part of the body resembling an human creature; could speak several words, and perform an hundred diverting tricks.

I was placed upon a table in the largest room of the inn, which might be near three hundred foot square. My little nurse stood on a low stool close to the table, to take care of me and direct what I should do. My master, to avoid a crowd, would suffer only thirty people at a time to see me. I walked about on the table as the girl commanded; she asked me questions as far as she knew my understanding of the language reached, and I answered them as loud as I could. I turned about several times to the company, paid my humble respects, said they were welcome, and used some other speeches I had been taught. I took up a thimble filled with liquor, which Glumdalclitch had given me for a cup, and drank their health. I drew out my hanger, and flourished with it after the manner of fencers in England. My nurse gave me part of a straw, which I exercised as a pike, having learned the art in my youth. I was that day shown to twelve sets of company, and as often forced to go over again with the same fopperies,[5] till I was half dead with weariness and vexa-

4. About 20 miles.
5. Follies.

tion. For those who had seen me made such wonderful reports that the people were ready to break down the doors to come in. My master, for his own interest, would not suffer any one to touch me except my nurse; and, to prevent danger, benches were set round the table at such a distance as put me out of everybody's reach. However, an unlucky schoolboy aimed a hazel nut directly at my head, which very narrowly missed me; otherwise, it came with so much violence that it would have infallibly knocked out my brains, for it was almost as large as a small pumpion:[6] but I had the satisfaction to see the young rogue well beaten and turned out of the room.

My master gave public notice that he would show me again the next market-day, and in the meantime he prepared a more convenient vehicle for me; which he had reason enough to do, for I was so tired with my first journey, and with entertaining company eight hours together, that I could hardly stand upon my legs or speak a word. It was at least three days before I recovered my strength; and, that I might have no rest at home, all the neighbouring gentlemen from an hundred miles round, hearing of my fame, came to see me at my master's own house. There could not be fewer than thirty persons with their wives and children (for the country is very populous); and my master demanded the rate of a full room whenever he showed me at home, although it were only to a single family. So that for some time I had but little ease every day of the week (except Wednesday, which is their Sabbath) although I were not carried to the town.

My master, finding how profitable I was like to be, resolved to carry me to the most considerable cities of the kingdom. Having therefore provided himself with all things necessary for a long journey, and settled his affairs at home, he took leave of his wife, and upon the 17th of August, 1703, about two months after my arrival, we set out for the metropolis, situated near the middle of that empire and about three thousand miles distance from our house: my master made his daughter Glumdalclitch ride behind him. She carried me on her lap in a box tied about her waist. The girl had lined it on all sides with the softest cloth she could get, well quilted underneath, furnished it with her baby's bed, provided me with linen and other necessaries, and made everything as convenient as she could. We had no other company but a boy of the house, who rode after us with the luggage.

My master's design was to show me in all the towns by the way, and to step out of the road for fifty or an hundred miles to any village or person of quality's house where he might expect custom. We made easy journeys of not above seven or eight-score miles a day: for Glumdalclitch, on purpose to spare me, complained she was tired with the trotting of the horse. She often took me out of my box at my own desire, to give me air and show me the country, but always held me fast by leading-strings. We passed over five or six rivers many degrees broader and deeper than the Nile or the Ganges; and there was hardly a rivulet so small as the Thames at London Bridge.[7] We were ten weeks in our journeys, and I was shown in eighteen large towns besides many villages and private families.

On the 26th day of October, we arrived at the metropolis, called in their

6. Pumpkin.
7. I.e., only 750 feet wide.

language *Lorbrulgrud*, or *Pride of the Universe*. My master took a lodging in the principal street of the city, not far from the royal palace, and put out bills in the usual form, containing an exact description of my person and parts. He hired a large room between three and four hundred foot wide. He provided a table sixty foot in diameter, upon which I was to act my part, and palisadoed it round three feet from the edge, and as many high, to prevent my falling over. I was shown ten times a day to the wonder and satisfaction of all people. I could now speak the language tolerably well, and perfectly understood every word that was spoken to me. Besides, I had learnt their alphabet, and could make a shift to explain a sentence here and there; for Glumdalclitch had been my instructor while we were at home and at leisure hours during our journey. She carried a little book in her pocket, not much larger than a Sanson's *Atlas;*[8] it was a common treatise for the use of young girls, giving a short account of their religion; out of this she taught me my letters and interpreted the words.

Chapter Three: The author sent for to court. The Queen buys him of his master the farmer, and presents him to the King. He disputes with his Majesty's great scholars. An apartment at court provided for the author. He is in high favour with the Queen. He stands up for the honour of his own country. His quarrels with the Queen's dwarf.

The frequent labours I underwent every day made in a few weeks a very considerable change in my health: the more my master got by me, the more unsatiable he grew. I had quite lost my stomach, and was almost reduced to a skeleton. The farmer observed it and, concluding I soon must die, resolved to make as good a hand of me as he could. While he was thus reasoning and resolving with himself, a *slardal*, or *gentleman usher*, came from court, commanding my master to bring me immediately thither for the diversion of the Queen and her ladies. Some of the latter had already been to see me and reported strange things of my beauty, behaviour, and good sense. Her Majesty and those who attended her were beyond measure delighted with my demeanor. I fell on my knees and begged the honour of kissing her imperial foot; but this gracious princess held out her little finger towards me (after I was set on a table), which I embraced in both my arms, and put the tip of it, with the utmost respect, to my lip. She made me some general questions about my country and my travels, which I answered as distinctly and in as few words as I could. She asked whether I would be content to live at court. I bowed down to the board of the table, and humbly answered that I was my master's slave, but if I were at my own disposal, I should be proud to devote my life to her Majesty's service. She then asked my master whether he were willing to sell me at a good price. He, who apprehended I could not live a month, was ready enough to part with me, and demanded a thousand pieces of gold, which were ordered him on the spot, each piece being about the bigness of eight hundred moidores,[1] but, allowing for the proportion of all things between that country and Europe, and the high price of gold among them, was hardly so great a

8. Sanson's *Atlas* was close to two feet square.

1. Portuguese gold coins, each worth more than an English pound.

sum as a thousand guineas would be in England. I then said to the Queen, since I was now her Majesty's most humble creature and vassal, I must beg the favour that Glumdalclitch, who had always tended me with so much care and kindness and understood to do it so well, might be admitted into her service and continue to be my nurse and instructor. Her Majesty agreed to my petition and easily got the farmer's consent, who was glad enough to have his daughter preferred at court: and the poor girl herself was not able to hide her joy: my late master withdrew, bidding me farewell and saying he had left me in a good service; to which I replied not a word, only making him a slight bow.

The Queen observed my coldness and, when the farmer was gone out of the apartment, asked me the reason. I made bold to tell her Majesty that I owed no other obligation to my late master than his not dashing out the brains of a poor harmless creature found by chance in his field; which obligation was amply recompensed by the gain he had made in showing me through half the kingdom, and the price he had now sold me for. That the life I had since led was laborious enough to kill an animal of ten times my strength. That my health was much impaired by the continual drudgery of entertaining the rabble every hour of the day, and that if my master had not thought my life in danger, her Majesty perhaps would not have got so cheap a bargain. But as I was out of all fear of being ill treated under the protection of so great and good an empress, the Ornament of Nature, the Darling of the World, the Delight of her Subjects, the Phoenix of the Creation; so, I hoped my late master's apprehensions would appear to be groundless, for I already found my spirits to revive by the influence of her most august presence.

This was the sum of my speech, delivered with great improprieties and hesitation; the latter part was altogether framed in the style peculiar to that people, whereof I learned some phrases from Glumdalclitch while she was carrying me to court.

The Queen, giving great allowance for my defectiveness in speaking, was however surprised at so much wit and good sense in so diminutive an animal. She took me in her own hand and carried me to the King, who was then retired to his cabinet.[2] His Majesty, a prince of much gravity and austere countenance, not well observing my shape at first view, asked the Queen after a cold manner how long it was since she grew fond of a *splacknuck;* for such it seems he took me to be as I lay upon my breast in her Majesty's right hand. But this princess, who hath an infinite deal of wit and humour, set me gently on my feet upon the scrutore,[3] and commanded me to give his Majesty an account of myself, which I did in a very few words; and Glumdalclitch, who attended at the cabinet door, and could not endure I should be out of her sight, being admitted, confirmed all that had passed from my arrival at her father's house.

The King, although he be as learned a person as any in his dominions, and had been educated in the study of philosophy, and particularly mathematics, yet when he observed my shape exactly and saw me walk erect, before I began to speak, conceived I might be a piece of clock-work (which is in that country arrived to a very great perfection), contrived by some ingenious artist. But,

2. Small private apartment.
3. Escritoire, writing desk.

when he heard my voice and found what I delivered to be regular and rational, he could not conceal his astonishment. He was by no means satisfied with the relation I gave him of the manner I came into his kingdom, but thought it a story concerted between Glumdalclitch and her father, who had taught me a set of words to make me sell at a higher price. Upon this imagination he put several other questions to me and still received rational answers, no otherwise defective than by a foreign accent and an imperfect knowledge in the language, with some rustic phrases which I had learned at the farmer's house and did not suit the polite style of a court.

His Majesty sent for three great scholars who were then in their weekly waiting (according to the custom in that country). These gentlemen, after they had a while examined my shape with much nicety, were of different opinions concerning me. They all agreed that I could not be produced according to the regular laws of nature because I was not framed with a capacity of preserving my life, either by swiftness, or climbing of trees, or digging holes in the earth. They observed by my teeth, which they viewed with great exactness, that I was a carnivorous animal; yet, most quadrupeds being an over-match for me, and field mice with some others too nimble, they could not imagine how I should be able to support myself unless I fed upon snails and other insects, which they offered by many learned arguments to evince that I could not possibly do. One of them seemed to think that I might be an embryo, or abortive birth. But this opinion was rejected by the other two, who observed my limbs to be perfect and finished and that I had lived several years, as it was manifested from my beard, the stumps whereof they plainly discovered through a magnifying-glass. They would not allow me to be a dwarf because my littleness was beyond all degrees of comparison; for the Queen's favourite dwarf, the smallest every known in that kingdom, was near thirty foot high. After much debate, they concluded unanimously that I was only *relplum scalcath*, which is, interpreted literally, *lusus natūrae;*[4] a determination exactly agreeable to the modern philosophy of Europe, whose professors, disdaining the old evasion of *occult causes,*[5] whereby the followers of Aristotle endeavour in vain to disguise their ignorance, have invented this wonderful solution of all difficulties, to the unspeakable advancement of human knowledge.

After this decisive conclusion, I entreated to be heard a word or two. I applied myself to the King and assured his Majesty that I came from a country which abounded with several millions of both sexes and of my own stature; where the animals, trees, and houses were all in proportion, and where by consequence I might be as able to defend myself, and to find sustenance, as any of his Majesty's subjects could do here; which I took for a full answer to those gentlemen's arguments. To this they only replied with a smile of contempt, saying that the farmer had instructed me very well in my lesson. The King, who had a much better understanding, dismissing his learned men, sent for the farmer, who by good fortune was not yet gone out of town; having there-

4. Sport of nature.
5. Thomas Hobbes, in *Leviathan* (1651), IV. 46, writes of such evasions: "And in many occasions they put for cause of natural events their own ignorance, but disguised in other words . . . as when they attribute many effects to *occult qualities*; that is, qualities not known to them; and therefore also, as they think, to no man else."

fore first examined him privately, and then confronted him with me and the young girl, his Majesty began to think that what we told him might possibly be true. He desired the Queen to order that a particular care should be taken of me, and was of opinion that Glumdalclitch should still continue in her office of tending me, because he observed we had a great affection for each other. A convenient apartment was provided for her at court; she had a sort of governess appointed to take care of her education, a maid to dress her, and two other servants for menial offices; but the care of me was wholly appropriated to herself.

The Queen commanded her own cabinet-maker to contrive a box that might serve me for a bed-chamber, after the model that Glumdalclitch and I should agree upon. This man was a most ingenious artist and, according to my directions, in three weeks finished for me a wooden chamber of sixteen foot square and twelve high, with sash-windows, a door, and two closets, like a London bed-chamber. The board that made the ceiling was to be lifted up and down by two hinges, to put in a bed ready furnished by her Majesty's upholsterer, which Glumdalclitch took out every day to air, made it with her own hands, and letting it down at night, locked up the roof over me. A nice workman, who was famous for little curiosities, undertook to make me two chairs, with backs and frames of a substance not unlike ivory, and two tables, with a cabinet to put my things in. The room was quilted on all sides as well as the floor and the ceiling, to prevent any accident from the carelessness of those who carried me and to break the force of a jolt when I went in a coach. I desired a lock for my door to prevent rats and mice from coming in: the smith after several attempts made the smallest that was ever seen among them, for I have known a larger at the gate of a gentleman's house in England. I made a shift to keep the key in a pocket of my own, fearing Glumdalclitch might lose it. The Queen likewise ordered the thinnest silks that could be gotten, to make me clothes, not much thicker than an English blanket, very cumbersome till I was accustomed to them. They were after the fashion of the kingdom, partly resembling the Persian and partly the Chinese, and are a very grave decent habit.

The Queen became so fond of my company that she could not dine without me. I had a table placed upon the same at which her Majesty eat, just at her left elbow, and a chair to sit on. Glumdalclitch stood upon a stool on the floor, near my table, to assist and take care of me. I had an entire set of silver dishes and plates and other necessaries, which, in proportion to those of the Queen, were not much bigger than what I have seen in a London toy-shop for the furniture of a baby-house: these my little nurse kept in her pocket in a silver box, and gave me at meals as I wanted them, always cleaning them herself. No person dined with the Queen but the two princesses royal, the elder sixteen years old and the younger at that time thirteen and a month. Her Majesty used to put a bit of meat upon one of my dishes, out of which I carved for myself; and her diversion was to see me eat in miniature. For the Queen (who had indeed but a weak stomach) took up at one mouthful as much as a dozen English farmers could eat at a meal, which to me was for some time a very nauseous sight. She would craunch the wing of a lark, bones and all, between her teeth, although it were nine times as large as that of a full-grown turkey;

and put a bit of bread in her mouth as big as two twelve-penny loaves.[6] She drank out of a golden cup, above a hogshead at a draught. Her knives were twice as long as a scythe set straight upon the handle. The spoons, forks, and other instruments were all in the same proportion. I remember when Glumdalclitch carried me out of curiosity to see some of the tables at court, where ten or a dozen of these enormous knives and forks were lifted up together, I thought I had never till then beheld so terrible a sight.

It is the custom that every Wednesday (which, as I have before observed, was their Sabbath) the King and Queen, with the royal issue of both sexes, dine together in the apartment of his Majesty, to whom I was now become a favourite; and at these times my little chair and table were placed at his left hand before one of the salt-cellars. This prince took a pleasure in conversing with me, inquiring into the manners, religion, laws, government, and learning of Europe; wherein I gave him the best account I was able. His apprehension was so clear, and his judgment so exact, that he made very wise reflections and observations upon all I said. But I confess that after I had been a little too copious in talking of my own beloved country, of our trade, and wars by sea and land, of our schisms in religion, and parties in the state, the prejudices of his education prevailed so far that he could not forbear taking me up in his right hand and, stroking me gently with the other, after an hearty fit of laughing, asked me whether I were a Whig or a Tory. Then turning to his first minister, who waited behind him with a white staff, near as tall as the mainmast of the *Royal Sovereign*,[7] he observed how contemptible a thing was human grandeur, which could be mimicked by such diminutive insects as I: "And yet," said he, "I dare engage, those creatures have their titles and distinctions of honour, they contrive little nests and burrows that they call houses and cities; they make a figure in dress and equipage;[8] they love, they fight, they dispute, they cheat, they betray." And thus he continued on, while my colour came and went several times, with indignation to hear our noble country, the mistress of arts and arms, the scourge of France, the arbitress of Europe, the seat of virtue, piety, honour, and truth, the pride and envy of the world, so contemptuously treated.[9]

But, as I was not in a condition to resent injuries, so, upon mature thoughts, I began to doubt whether I were injured or no. For, after having been accustomed several months to the sight and converse of this people, and observed every object upon which I cast my eyes to be of proportionable magnitude, the horror I had first conceived from their bulk and aspect was so far worn off that, if I had then beheld a company of English lords and ladies in their finery and birthday clothes,[10] acting their several parts in the most courtly manner of strutting and bowing and prating, to say the truth, I should have been strongly tempted to laugh as much at them as this king and his grandees did at me. Neither indeed could I forbear smiling at myself, when the Queen

6. Very large loaves. One may compare the account of Gulliver's own meals in Lilliput (Part I, Chapter 1).
7. One of the largest ships in the English navy. Compare Flimnap's white staff in Part I, Chapter 6.
8. Carriage and footmen; in general, retinue.
9. Gulliver unconsciously echoes the court rhetoric of Lilliput in Part I, Chapter 3.
10. Splendid clothing worn at court on the royal birthday.

used to place me upon her hand towards a looking-glass, by which both our persons appeared before me in full view together; and there could nothing be more ridiculous than the comparison: so that I really began to imagine myself dwindled many degrees below my usual size.[11]

Nothing angered and mortified me so much as the Queen's dwarf, who, being of the lowest stature that was ever in that country (for I verily think he was not full thirty foot high), became so insolent at seeing a creature so much beneath him that he would always affect to swagger and look big as he passed by me in the Queen's antechamber, while I was standing on some table talking with the lords or ladies of the court; and he seldom failed of a smart word or two upon my littleness; against which I could only revenge myself by calling him brother, challenging him to wrestle, and such repartees as are usual in the mouths of court pages. One day at dinner this malicious little cub was so nettled with something I had said to him that, raising himself upon the frame of her Majesty's chair, he took me up by the middle as I was sitting down, not thinking any harm, and let me drop into a large silver bowl of cream, and then ran away as fast as he could. I fell over head and ears, and if I had not been a good swimmer, it might have gone very hard with me; for Glumdalclitch in that instant happened to be at the other end of the room, and the Queen was in such a fright that she wanted presence of mind to assist me. But my little nurse ran to my relief, and took me out, after I had swallowed above a quart of cream. I was put to bed; however, I received no other damage than the loss of a suit of clothes, which was utterly spoiled. The dwarf was soundly whipped and, as a further punishment, forced to drink up the bowl of cream into which he had thrown me; neither was he ever restored to favour: for, soon after, the Queen bestowed him to a lady of high quality, so that I saw him no more, to my very great satisfaction; for I could not tell to what extremity such a malicious urchin might have carried his resentment.

He had before served me a scurvy trick which set the Queen a-laughing, although at the same time she were heartily vexed, and would have immediately cashiered him if I had not been so generous as to intercede. Her Majesty had taken a marrow-bone upon her plate and, after knocking out the marrow, placed the bone again in the dish erect as it stood before; the dwarf watching his opportunity, while Glumdalclitch was gone to the sideboard, mounted the stool she stood on to take care of me at meals, took me up in both hands, and squeezing my legs together, wedged them into the marrow-bone above my waist, where I stuck for some time and made a very ridiculous figure. I believe it was near a minute before anyone knew what was become of me, for I thought it below me to cry out. But, as princes seldom get their meat hot,[12] my legs were not scalded; only my stockings and breeches in a sad condition. The dwarf at my entreaty had no other punishment than a sound whipping.

11. A telling instance of Gulliver's adaptation to the point of view of others. Just as he accepts Lilliputian honors with full gravity, so here he begins to see himself as a dwarf; later, in the Fourth Voyage, he will come to see himself, to his horror, as a Yahoo. On the other hand, he can look down on his fellow humans like a Brobdingnagian (in the final chapter of this voyage) or later scorn them as Yahoos.

12. With elaborate building in 18th-century England, the distances between kitchen and dining room became vast. See Pope's account of Timon's Villa in *To . . . Burlington* (1731), esp. ll. 151–68.

I was frequently rallied by the Queen upon account of my fearfulness, and she used to ask me whether the people of my country were as great cowards as myself. The occasion was this. The kingdom is much pestered with flies in summer, and odious insects, each of them as big as a Dunstable lark,[13] hardly gave me any rest while I sat at dinner, with their continual humming and buzzing about my ears. They would sometimes alight upon my victuals and leave their loathsome excrement or spawn behind, which to me was very visible, although not to the natives of that country, whose large optics were not so acute as mine in viewing smaller objects. Sometimes they would fix upon my nose or forehead, where they stung me to the quick, smelling very offensively, and I could easily trace that viscous matter which our naturalists tell us enables those creatures to walk with their feet upwards upon a ceiling. I had much ado to defend myself against these detestable animals, and could not forbear starting when they came on my face. It was the common practice of the dwarf to catch a number of these insects in his hand, as schoolboys do among us, and let them out suddenly under my nose on purpose to frighten me and divert the Queen. My remedy was to cut them in pieces with my knife as they flew in the air, wherein my dexterity was much admired.

I remember one morning when Glumdalclitch had set me in my box upon a window, as she usually did in fair days to give me air (for I durst not venture to let the box be hung on a nail out of the window, as we do with cages in England), after I had lifted up one of my sashes and sat down at my table to eat a piece of sweet-cake for my breakfast, above twenty wasps, allured by the smell, came flying into the room, humming louder than the drones of as many bagpipes. Some of them seized my cake and carried it piecemeal away, others flew about my head and face, confounding me with the noise and putting me in the utmost terror of their stings. However I had the courage to rise and draw my hanger, and attack them in the air. I dispatched four of them, but the rest got away, and I presently shut my window. These insects were as large as partridges: I took out their stings, found them an inch and a half long, and as sharp as needles. I carefully preserved them all, and, having since shown them with some other curiosities in several parts of Europe, upon my return to England I gave three of them to Gresham College,[14] and kept the fourth for myself.

Chapter Four: The country described. A proposal for correcting modern maps. The King's palace, and some account of the metropolis. The author's way of travelling. The chief temple described.

I now intend to give the reader a short description of this country as far as I travelled in it, which was not above two thousand miles round Lorbrulgrud, the metropolis. For the Queen, whom I always attended, never went further when she accompanied the King in his progresses,[1] and there stayed till his

13. A lark large enough to serve as a table delicacy.

14. First home of the Royal Society, which in 1666 founded a museum with a "collection of rarities."

1. Official journeys.

Majesty returned from viewing his frontiers. The whole extent of this prince's dominions reacheth about six thousand miles in length, and from three to five in breadth. From whence I cannot but conclude that our geographers of Europe are in a great error by supposing nothing but sea between Japan and California; for it was ever my opinion that there must be a balance of earth to counterpoise the great continent of Tartary;[2] and therefore they ought to correct their maps and charts by joining this vast tract of land to the northwest parts of America, wherein I shall be ready to lend them my assistance.

The kingdom is a peninsula, terminated to the northeast by a ridge of mountains thirty miles high, which are altogether impassable by reason of the volcanoes upon the tops. Neither do the most learned know what sort of mortals inhabit beyond these mountains or whether they be inhabited at all. On the three other sides it is bounded by the ocean. There is not one seaport in the whole kingdom, and those parts of the coasts into which the rivers issue are so full of pointed rocks, and the sea generally so rough, that there is no venturing with the smallest of their boats; so that these people are wholly excluded from any commerce with the rest of the world. But the large rivers are full of vessels and abound with excellent fish, for they seldom get any from the sea, because the sea-fish are of the same size with those in Europe and consequently not worth catching; whereby it is manifest that nature in the production of plants and animals of so extraordinary a bulk is wholly confined to this continent, of which I leave the reasons to be determined by philosophers. However, now and then they take a whale that happens to be dashed against the rocks, which the common people feed on heartily. These whales I have known so large that a man could hardly carry one upon his shoulders; and sometimes for curiosity they are brought in hampers to Lorbrulgrud. I saw one of them in a dish at the King's table, which passed for a rarity, but I did not observe he was fond of it; for I think indeed the bigness disgusted him, although I have seen one somewhat larger in Greenland.

The country is well inhabited, for it contains fifty-one cities, near an hundred walled towns, and a great number of villages. To satisfy my curious reader, it may be sufficient to describe Lorbrulgrud. This city stands upon almost two equal parts on each side the river that passes through. It contains above eighty thousand houses, and about six hundred thousand inhabitants. It is in length three *glonglungs* (which make about fifty-four English miles) and two and a half in breadth, as I measured it myself in the royal map made by the King's order, which was laid on the ground on purpose for me, and extended an hundred feet; I paced the diameter and circumference several times barefoot and, computing by the scale, measured it pretty exactly.[3]

The King's palace is no regular edifice, but an heap of buildings about seven miles round: the chief rooms are generally two hundred and forty foot high, and broad and long in proportion. A coach was allowed to Glumdalclitch and me, wherein her governess frequently took her out to see the town or go among the shops; and I was always of the party, carried in my box; although the girl at my own desire would often take me out and hold me in her hand

2. Land mass of Asia.
3. Compare the stipulation that Gulliver "deliver an exact survey" of Lilliput "by computation of his own paces round the coast" (Part I, Chapter 3).

that I might more conveniently view the houses and the people as we passed along the streets. I reckoned our coach to be about a square of Westminster Hall,[4] but not altogether so high; however, I cannot be very exact. One day the governess ordered our coachman to stop at several shops, where the beggars, watching their opportunity, crowded to the sides of the coach, and gave me the most horrible spectacles that ever an European eye beheld. There was a woman with a cancer in her breast, swelled to a monstrous size, full of holes, in two or three of which I could have easily crept and covered my whole body. There was a fellow with a wen in his neck, larger than five woolpacks, and another with a couple of wooden legs, each about twenty foot high. But the most hateful sight of all was the lice crawling on their clothes. I could see distinctly the limbs of these vermin with my naked eye, much better than those of an European louse through a microscope, and their snouts with which they rooted like swine. They were the first I had ever beheld, and I should have been curious enough to dissect one of them, if I had proper instruments (which I unluckily left behind me in the ship), although indeed the sight was so nauseous that it perfectly turned my stomach.

Beside the large box in which I was usually carried, the Queen ordered a smaller one to be made for me, of about twelve foot square and ten high, for the convenience of travelling, because the other was somewhat too large for Glumdalclitch's lap and cumbersome in the coach; it was made by the same artist, whom I directed in the whole contrivance. This travelling closet was an exact square[5] with a window in the middle of three of the squares, and each window was latticed with iron wire on the outside to prevent accidents in long journeys. On the fourth side, which had no window, two strong staples were fixed, through which the person that carried me, when I had a mind to be on horseback, put in a leathern belt and buckled it about his waist. This was always the office of some grave trusty servant in which I could confide, whether I attended the King and Queen in their progresses, or were disposed to see the gardens, or pay a visit to some great lady or minister of state in the court, when Glumdalclitch happened to be out of order: for I soon began to be known and esteemed among the greatest officers, I suppose more upon account of their Majesties' favour than any merit of my own. In journeys, when I was weary of the coach, a servant on horseback would buckle my box and place it on a cushion before him; and there I had a full prospect of the country on three sides from my three windows. I had in this closet a field-bed and a hammock hung from the ceiling, two chairs and a table neatly screwed to the floor, to prevent being tossed about by the agitation of the horse or the coach. And having been long used to sea-voyages, those motions, although sometimes very violent, did not much discompose me.

Whenever I had a mind to see the town, it was always in my travelling-closet, which Glumdalclitch held in her lap in a kind of open sedan, after the fashion of the country, borne by four men, and attended by two others in the Queen's livery. The people, who had often heard of me, were very curious to crowd about the sedan, and the girl was complaisant enough to make the

4. The area of Westminster Hall was the equivalent of 140 feet square, its height about 90 feet.
5. Cube, with six square sides.

bearers stop and to take me in her hand that I might be more conveniently seen.

I was very desirous to see the chief temple, and particularly the tower belonging to it, which is reckoned the highest in the kingdom. Accordingly one day my nurse carried me thither, but I may truly say I came back disappointed; for the height is not above three thousand foot, reckoning from the ground to the highest pinnacle top; which, allowing for the difference between the size of those people and us in Europe, is no great matter for admiration, nor at all equal in proportion (if I rightly remember) to Salisbury steeple.[6] But, not to detract from a nation to which during my life I shall acknowledge myself extremely obliged, it must be allowed that whatever this famous tower wants in height is amply made up in beauty and strength. For the walls are near an hundred foot thick, built of hewn stone, whereof each is about forty foot square, and adorned on all sides with statues of gods and emperors cut in marble larger than the life, placed in their several niches. I measured a little finger which had fallen down from one of these statues and lay unperceived among some rubbish, and found it exactly four foot and an inch in length. Glumdalclitch wrapped it up in a handkerchief, and carried it home in her pocket to keep among other trinkets, of which the girl was very fond, as children at her age usually are.

The King's kitchen is indeed a noble building, vaulted at top, and about six hundred foot high. The great oven is not so wide by ten paces as the cupola at St. Paul's:[7] for I measured the latter on purpose ofter my return. But if I should describe the kitchen-grate, the prodigious pots and kettles, the joints of meat turning on the spits, with many other particulars, perhaps I should be hardly believed; at least a severe critic would be apt to think I enlarged a little, as travellers are often suspected to do. To avoid which censure, I fear I have run too much into the other extreme; and that if this treatise should happen to be translated into the language of Brobdingnag (which is the general name of that kingdom) and transmitted thither, the King and his people would have reason to complain that I had done them an injury by a false and diminutive representation.

His Majesty seldom keeps above six hundred horses in his stables: they are generally from fifty-four to sixty foot high. But when he goes abroad on solemn days, he is attended for state by a militia guard of five hundred horse, which indeed I thought was the most splendid sight that could be ever beheld, till I saw part of his army in battalia,[8] whereof I shall find another occasion to speak.

Chapter Five: Several adventures that happened to the author. The execution of a criminal. The author shows his skill in navigation.

I should have lived happy enough in that country, if my littleness had not exposed me to several ridiculous and troublesome accidents, some of which I shall venture to relate. Glumdalclitch often carried me into the gardens of the

6. Tallest spire in England, 404 feet in height.
7. The dome of St. Paul's Cathedral, London, is 112 feet in diameter at its base.
8. Battle array.

court in my smaller box, and would sometimes take me out of it and hold me in her hand or set me down to walk. I remember, before the dwarf left the Queen, he followed us one day into those gardens, and, my nurse having set me down, he and I being close together near some dwarf apple-trees, I must needs show my wit by a silly allusion between him and the trees, which happens to hold in their language as it doth in ours. Whereupon the malicious rogue, watching his opportunity, when I was walking under one of them, shook it directly over my head, by which a dozen apples, each of them near as large as a Bristol barrel,[1] came tumbling about my ears. One of them hit me on the back as I chanced to stoop and knocked me down flat on my face, but I received no other hurt; and the dwarf was pardoned at my desire, because I had given the provocation.

Another day Glumdalclitch left me on a smooth grass-plot to divert myself while she walked at some distance with her governess. In the meantime there suddenly fell such a violent shower of hail that I was immediately by the force of it struck to the ground: and when I was down, the hailstones gave me such cruel bangs all over the body as if I had been pelted with tennis-balls; however I made a shift to creep on all four and shelter myself by lying flat on my face on the lee-side of a border of lemon thyme, but so bruised from head to foot that I could not go abroad in ten days. Neither is this at all to be wondered at because, nature in that country observing the same proportion through all her operations, a hailstone is near eighteen hundred times as large as one in Europe, which I can assert upon experience, having been so curious to weigh and measure them.

But a more dangerous accident happened to me in the same garden when my little nurse, believing she had put me in a secure place, which I often entreated her to do that I might enjoy my own thoughts, and having left my box at home to avoid the trouble of carrying it, went to another part of the gardens with her governess and some ladies of her acquaintance. While she was absent and out of hearing, a small white spaniel belonging to one of the chief gardeners, having got by accident into the garden, happened to range near the place where I lay. The dog, following the scent, came directly up, and taking me in his mouth ran straight to his master, wagging his tail, and set me gently on the ground. By good fortune he had been so well taught that I was carried between his teeth without the least hurt, or even tearing my clothes. But the poor gardener, who knew me well and had a great kindness for me, was in a terrible fright. He gently took me up in both his hands and asked me how I did; but I was so amazed and out of breath that I could not speak a word. In a few minutes I came to myself, and he carried me safe to my little nurse, who by this time had returned to the place where she left me, and was in cruel agonies when I did not appear nor answer when she called: she severely reprimanded the gardener on account of his dog. But the thing was hushed up and never known at court; for the girl was afraid of the Queen's anger, and truly, as to myself, I thought it would not be for my reputation that such a story should go about.

This accident absolutely determined Glumdalclitch never to trust me abroad for the future out of her sight. I had been long afraid of this resolution, and

1. Hogshead.

therefore concealed from her some little unlucky adventures that happened in those times when I was left by myself. Once a kite hovering over the garden made a stoop [2] at me, and if I had not resolutely drawn my hanger, and run under a thick espalier, he would have certainly carried me away in his talons. Another time walking to the top of a fresh mole-hill, I fell to my neck in the hole through which that animal had cast up the earth, and coined some lie not worth remembering, to excuse myself for spoiling my clothes. I likewise broke [3] my right shin against the shell of a snail, which I happened to stumble over as I was walking alone and thinking on poor England.

I cannot tell whether I were more pleased or mortified to observe, in those solitary walks, that the smaller birds did not appear to be at all afraid of me, but would hop about within a yard distance, looking for worms and other food with as much indifference and security as if no creature at all were near them. I remember a thrush had the confidence to snatch out of my hand with his bill a piece of cake that Glumdalclitch had just given me for my breakfast. When I attempted to catch any of these birds, they would boldly turn against me, endevouring to pick my fingers, which I durst not venture within their reach; and then they would hop back unconcerned to hunt for worms or snails as they did before. But one day I took a thick cudgel, and threw it with all my strength so luckily at a linnet that I knocked him down, and seizing him by the neck with both my hands, ran with him in triumph to my nurse. However, the bird, who had only been stunned, recovering himself, gave me so many boxes with his wings on both sides of my head and body, although I held him at arm's length and was out of reach of his claws, that I was twenty times thinking to let him go. But I was soon relieved by one of our servants, who wrung off the bird's neck, and I had him next day for dinner by the Queen's command. This linnet, as near as I can remember, seemed to be somewhat larger than an English swan.

The maids of honour often invited Glumdalclitch to their apartments, and desired she would bring me along with her, on purpose to have the pleasure of seeing and touching me. They would often strip me naked from top to toe, and lay me at full length in their bosoms; wherewith I was much disgusted; because, to say the truth, a very offensive smell came from their skins; which I do not mention or intend to the disadvantage of those excellent ladies, for whom I have all manner of respect; but I conceive that my sense was more acute in proportion to my littleness, and that those illustrious persons were no more disagreeable to their lovers, or to each other, than people of the same quality are with us in England. And, after all, I found their natural smell was much more supportable than when they used perfumes, under which I immediately swooned away. I cannot forget that an intimate friend of mine in Lilliput took the freedom, in a warm day, when I had used a good deal of exercise, to complain of a strong smell about me, although I am as little faulty that way as most of my sex: but I suppose his faculty of smelling was as nice with regard to me as mine was to that of this people. Upon this point, I cannot forbear doing justice to the Queen my mistress, and Glumdalclitch my nurse, whose persons were as sweet as those of any lady in England.

2. Dive.
3. Bruised.

That which gave me most uneasiness among these maids of honour, when my nurse carried me to visit them, was to see them use me without any manner of ceremony, like a creature who had no sort of consequence. For they would strip themselves to the skin and put on their smocks in my presence, while I was placed on their toilet [4] directly before their naked bodies, which, I am sure, to me was very far from being a tempting sight or from giving me any other emotions than those of horror and disgust. Their skins appeared so coarse and uneven, so variously coloured, when I saw them near, with a mole here and there as broad as a trencher, and hairs hanging from it thicker than pack-threads; to say nothing further concerning the rest of their persons. Neither did they at all scruple while I was by to discharge what they had drunk, to the quantity of at least two hogsheads, in a vessel that held above three tuns. The handsomest among these maids of honour, a pleasant frolicsome girl of sixteen, would sometimes set me astride upon one of her nipples, with many other tricks, wherein the reader will excuse me for not being over particular. But I was so much displeased that I entreated Glumdalclitch to contrive some excuse for not seeing that young lady any more.

One day a young gentleman, who was nephew to my nurse's governess, came and pressed them both to see an execution. It was of a man who had murdered one of that gentleman's intimate acquaintance. Glumdalclitch was prevailed on to be of the company, very much against her inclination, for she was naturally tender-hearted: and as for myself, although I abhorred such kind of spectacles, yet my curiosity tempted me to see something that I thought must be extraordinary. The malefactor was fixed in a chair upon a scaffold erected for the purpose, and his head cut off at one blow with a sword of about forty foot long. The veins and arteries spouted up such a prodigious quantity of blood, and so high in the air, that the great *jet d'eau* at Versailles [5] was not equal for the time it lasted; and the head, when it fell on the scaffold floor, gave such a bounce as made me start, although I was at least an English mile distant.

The Queen, who often used to hear me talk of my sea-voyages, and took all occasions to divert me when I was melancholy, asked me whether I understood how to handle a sail or an oar, and whether a little exercise of rowing might not be convenient for my health. I answered that I understood both very well. For although my proper employment had been to be surgeon or doctor to the ship, yet often, upon a pinch, I was forced to work like a common mariner. But I could not see how this could be done in their country, where the smallest wherry was equal to a first-rate man-of-war among us, and such a boat as I could manage would never live in any of their rivers: her Majesty said, if I would contrive a boat, her own joiner [6] should make it, and she would provide a place for me to sail in. The fellow was an ingenious workman, and by my instructions in ten days finished a pleasure-boat with all its tackling, able conveniently to hold eight Europeans. When it was finished, the Queen was so delighted that she ran with it in her lap to the King, who ordered it to be put in a cistern full of water, with me in it, by way of trial, where I could not

4. Dressing table.
5. The largest fountain at Versailles spouted over 70 feet into the air.
6. Carpenter.

manage my two sculls or little oars for want of room. But the Queen had before contrived another project. She ordered the joiner to make a wooden trough of three hundred foot long, fifty broad, and eight deep; which being well pitched to prevent leaking, was placed on the floor along the wall in an outer room of the palace. It had a cock near the bottom to let out the water when it began to grow stale, and two servants could easily fill it in half an hour. Here I often used to row for my diversion, as well as that of the Queen and her ladies, who thought themselves agreeably entertained with my skill and agility. Sometimes I would put up my sail, and then my business was only to steer, while the ladies gave me a gale with their fans; and when they were weary, some of the pages would blow my sail forward with their breath, while I showed my art by steering starboard and larboard as I pleased. When I had done, Glumdalclitch always carried back my boat into her closet [7] and hung it on a nail to dry.

In this exercise I once met an accident which had like to have cost me my life. For, one of the pages having put my boat into the trough, the governess who attended Glumdalclitch very officiously [8] lifted me up to place me in the boat, but I happened to slip through her fingers, and should have infallibly fallen down forty foot upon the floor if, by the luckiest chance in the world, I had not been stopped by a corking-pin [9] that stuck in the good gentlewoman's stomacher; the head of the pin passed between my shirt and the waistband of my breeches, and thus I was held by the middle in the air till Glumdalclitch ran to my relief.

Another time one of the servants, whose office it was to fill my trough every third day with fresh water, was so careless to let a huge frog (not perceiving it) slip out of his pail. The frog lay concealed till I was put into my boat, but then seeing a resting place, climbed up, and made it lean so much on one side that I was forced to balance it with all my weight on the other to prevent overturning. When the frog was got in, it hopped at once half the length of the boat, and then over my head backwards and forwards, daubing my face and clothes with its odious slime. The largeness of its features made it appear the most deformed animal that can be conceived. However, I desired Glumdalclitch to let me deal with it alone. I banged it a good while with one of my sculls, and at last forced it to leap out of the beat.

But the greatest danger I ever underwent in that kingdom was from a monkey who belonged to one of the clerks of the kitchen. Glumdalclitch had locked me up in her closet while she went somewhere upon business or a visit. The weather being very warm, the closest window was left open, as well as the windows and the door of my bigger box, in which I usually lived because of its largeness and conveniency. As I sat quietly meditating at my table, I heard something bounce in at the closet window and skip about from one side to the other; whereat, although I were much alarmed, yet I ventured to look out, but not stirring from my seat; and then I saw this frolicsome animal frisking and leaping up and down till at last he came to my box, which he seemed to view with great pleasure and curiosity, peeping in at the door and every

7. Small private room.
8. Solicitously.
9. Very large pin.

window. I retreated to the farther corner of my room, or box, but the monkey, looking in at every side, put me into such a fright that I wanted presence of mind to conceal myself under the bed, as I might easily have done. After some time spent in peeping, grinning, and chattering, he at last espied me, and reaching one of his paws in at the door, as a cat does when she plays with a mouse, although I often shifted place to avoid him, he at length seized the lappet of my coat (which being made of that country silk, was very thick and strong) and dragged me out. He took me up in his right forefoot, and held me as a nurse does a child she is going to suckle, just as I have seen the same sort of creature do with a kitten in Europe: and when I offered to struggle, he squeezed me so hard that I thought it more prudent to submit.

I have good reason to believe that he took me for a young one of his own species, by his often stroking my face very gently with his other paw. In these diversions he was interrupted by a noise at the closet door, as if somebody were opening it; whereupon he suddenly leaped up to the window at which he had come in and thence upon the leads and gutters, walking upon three legs and holding me in the fourth, till he clambered up to a roof that was next to ours. I heard Glumdalclitch give a shriek at the moment he was carrying me out. The poor girl was almost distracted: that quarter of the palace was all in an uproar; the servants ran for ladders; the monkey was seen by hundreds in the court sitting upon the ridge of a building, holding me like a baby in one of his fore-paws, and feeding me with the other, by cramming into my mouth some victuals he had squeezed out of the bag on one side of his chaps, and patting me when I would not eat; whereat many of the rabble below could not forbear laughing; neither do I think they justly ought to be blamed, for without question the sight was ridiculous enough to everybody but myself. Some of the people threw up stones, hoping to drive the monkey down; but this was strictly forbidden, or else very probably my brains had been dashed out.

The ladders were now applied and mounted by several men, which the monkey observing, and finding himself almost encompassed, not being able to make speed enough with his three legs, let me drop on a ridge tile, and made his escape. Here I sat for some time five hundred yards from the ground, expecting every moment to be blown down by the wind, or to fall by my own giddiness, and come tumbling over and over from the ridge to the eaves. But an honest lad, one of my nurse's footmen, climbed up, and putting me into his breeches pocket, brought me down safe.

I was almost choked with the filthy stuff the monkey had crammed down my throat; but my dear little nurse picked it out of my mouth with a small needle, and then I fell a-vomiting, which gave me great relief. Yet I was so weak and bruised in the sides with the squeezes given me by this odious animal that I was forced to keep my bed a fortnight. The King, Queen and all the court sent every day to enquire after my health, and her Majesty made me several visits during my sickness. The monkey was killed, and an order made that no such animal should be kept about the palace.

When I attended the King after my recovery, to return him thanks for his favours, he was pleased to rally[10] me a good deal upon this adventure. He

10. Tease, joke with.

asked me what my thoughts and speculations were while I lay in the monkey's paw, how I liked the victuals he gave me, his manner of feeding, and whether the fresh air on the roof had sharpened my stomach.[11] He desired to know what I would have done upon such an occasion in my own country. I told his Majesty that in Europe we had no monkeys, except such as were brought for curiosities from other places, and so small that I could deal with a dozen of them together if they presumed to attack me. And as for that monstrous animal with whom I was so lately engaged (it was indeed as large as an elephant), if my fears had suffered me to think so far as to make use of my hanger (looking fiercely and clapping my hand upon the hilt as I spoke) when he poked his paw into my chamber, perhaps I should have given him such a wound as would have made him glad to withdraw it with more haste than he put it in. This I delivered in a firm tone, like a person who was jealous lest his courage should be called in question. However, my speech produced nothing else besides a loud laughter, which all the respect due to his Majesty from those about him could not make them contain. This made me reflect how vain an attempt it is for a man to endeavour doing himself honour among those who are out of all degree of equality or comparison with him. And yet I have seen the moral of my own behaviour very frequent in England since my return, where a little contemptible varlet, without the least title to birth, person, wit, or common sense, shall presume to look with importance and put himself upon a foot with the greatest persons of the kingdom.

I was every day furnishing the court with some ridiculous story; and Glumdalclitch, although she loved me to excess, yet was arch enough to inform the Queen whenever I committed any folly that she thought would be diverting to her Majesty. The girl, who had been out of order, was carried by her governess to take the air about an hour's distance, or thirty miles, from town. They alighted out of the coach near a small foot-path in a field, and, Glumdalclitch setting down my travelling box, I went out of it to walk. There was a cow-dung in the path, and I must needs try my activity by attempting to leap over it. I took a run, but unfortunately jumped short, and found myself just in the middle up to my knees. I waded through with some difficulty, and one of the footmen wiped me as clean as he could with his handkerchief; for I was filthily bemired, and my nurse confined me to my box till we returned home; where the Queen was soon informed of what had passed, and the footmen spread it about the court, so that all the mirth for some days was at my expense.

Chapter Six: Several contrivances of the author to please the King and Queen. He shows his skill in music. The King inquires into the state of Europe, which the author relates to him. The King's observations thereon.

I used to attend the King's levee [1] once or twice a week, and had often seen him under the barber's hand, which indeed was at first very terrible to behold. For the razor was almost twice as long as an ordinary scythe. His Majesty

11. Appetite.

1. Formal reception held at the King's rising from bed, attended by members of the royal household and ministers.

according to the custom of the country was only shaved twice a week. I once prevailed on the barber to give me some of the suds or lather, out of which I picked forty or fifty of the strongest stumps of hair. I then took a piece of fine wood and cut it like the back of a comb, making several holes in it at equal distance with as small a needle as I could get from Glumdalclitch. I fixed in the stumps so artificially,[2] scraping and sloping them with my knife towards the points, that I made a very tolerable comb; which was a seasonable supply, my own being so much broken in the teeth that it was almost useless: neither did I know any artist in that country so nice and exact as would undertake to make me another.

And this puts me in mind of an amusement wherein I spent many of my leisure hours. I desired the Queen's woman to save for me the combings of her Majesty's hair, whereof in time I got a good quantity, and consulting with my friend the cabinetmaker, who had received general orders to do little jobs for me, I directed him to make two chair-frames no larger than those I had in my box, and then to bore little holes with a fine awl round those parts where I designed the backs and seats; through these holes I wove the strongest hairs I could pick out, just after the manner of cane-chairs in England. When they were finished, I made a present of them to her Majesty, who kept them in her cabinet and used to show them for curiosities, as indeed they were the wonder of everyone who beheld them. The Queen would have had me sit upon one of these chairs, but I absolutely refused to obey her, protesting I would rather die a thousand deaths than place a dishonourable part of my body on those precious hairs that once adorned her Majesty's head. Of these hairs (as I had always a mechanical genius) I likewise made a neat little purse about five foot long, with her Majesty's name deciphered [3] in gold letters, which I gave to Glumdalclitch by the Queen's consent. To say the truth, it was more for show than use, being not of strength to bear the weight of the larger coins, and therefore she kept nothing in it but some little toys that girls are fond of.

The King, who delighted in music, had frequent consorts [4] at court, to which I was sometimes carried and set in my box on a table to hear them: but the noise was so great that I could hardly distinguish the tunes. I am confident that all the drums and trumpets of a royal army, beating and sounding together just at your ears, could not equal it. My practice was to have my box removed from the places where the performers sat as far as I could, then to shut the doors and windows of it and draw the window curtains; after which I found their music not disagreeable.

I had learned in my youth to play a little upon the spinet. Glumdalclitch kept one in her chamber, and a master attended twice a week to teach her: I call it a spinet, because it somewhat resembled that instrument and was played upon in the same manner. A fancy came into my head that I would entertain the King and Queen with an English tune upon this instrument. But this appeared extremely difficult: for the spinet was near sixty foot long, each key being almost a foot wide, so that, with my arms extended, I could not reach to above five keys, and to press them down required a good smart stroke with

2. Artfully.
3. Inscribed, woven.
4. Concerts.

my fist, which would be too great a labour, and to no purpose. The method I contrived was this. I prepared two round sticks about the bigness of common cudgels; they were thicker at one end than the other, and I covered the thicker ends with a piece of a mouse's skin, that by rapping on them I might neither damage the tops of the keys nor interrupt the sound. Before the spinet a bench was placed about four foot below the keys, and I was put upon the bench. I ran sideling upon it that way and this as fast as I could, banging the proper keys with my two sticks, and made a shift to play a jig to the great satisfaction of both their Majesties: but it was the most violent exercise I ever underwent, and yet I could not strike above sixteen keys nor, consequently, play the bass and treble together as other artists do; which was a great disadvantage to my performance.

The King, who, as I before observed, was a prince of excellent understanding, would frequently order that I should be brought in my box and set upon the table in his closet. He would then command me to bring one of my chairs out of the box and sit down within three yards distance upon the top of the cabinet, which brought me almost to a level with his face. In this manner I had several conversations with him. I one day took the freedom to tell his Majesty that the contempt he discovered towards Europe and the rest of the world did not seem answerable to[5] those excellent qualities of mind that he was master of. That reason did not extend itself with the bulk of the body: on the contrary, we observed in our country that the tallest persons were usually least provided with it. That among other animals bees and ants had the reputation of more industry, art, and sagacity than many of the larger kinds. And that, as inconsiderable as he took me to be, I hoped I might live to do his Majesty some signal service. The King heard me with attention and began to conceive a much better opinion of me than he had ever before. He desired I would give him as exact an account of the government of England as I possibly could; because, as fond as princes commonly are of their own customs (for so he conjectured of other monarchs by my former discourses), he should be glad to hear of anything that might deserve imitation.

Imagine with thyself, courteous reader, how often I then wished for the tongue of Demosthenes or Cicero,[6] that might have enabled me to celebrate the praise of my own dear native country in a style equal to its merits and felicity.

I began my discourse by informing his Majesty that our dominions consisted of two islands, which composed three mighty kingdoms under one sovereign, besides our plantations[7] in America. I dwelt long upon the fertility of our soil and the temperature[8] of our climate. I then spoke at large upon the constitution of an English Parliament, partly made up of an illustrious body called the House of Peers, persons of the noblest blood and of the most ancient and ample patrimonies. I described that extraordinary care always taken of their education in arts and arms to qualify them for being counsellors born to the king and kingdom, to have a share in the legislature, to be members of the

5. Consistent with.
6. Both as great orators and as defenders of their nation: Demosthenes of Greece against Philip of Macedon, and Cicero of Republican Rome against Mark Antony.
7. Colonies.
8. Temperateness.

highest court of judicature from whence there could be no appeal; and to be champions always ready for the defence of their prince and country by their valour, conduct, and fidelity. That these were the ornament and bulwark of the kingdom, worthy followers of their most renowned ancestors, whose honour had been the reward of their virtue, from which their posterity were never once known to degenerate. To these were joined several holy persons as part of that assembly, under the title of bishops,[9] whose peculiar business it is to take care of religion and of those who instruct the people therein. These were searched and sought out through the whole nation, by the prince and wisest counsellors, among such of the priesthood as were most deservedly distinguished by the sanctity of their lives and the depth of their erudition; who were indeed the spiritual fathers of the clergy and the people.

That the other part of the Parliament consisted of an assembly called the House of Commons, who were all principal gentlemen, *freely* picked and culled out by the people themselves, for their great abilities and love of their country, to represent the wisdom of the whole nation. And these two bodies make up the most august assembly in Europe, to whom, in conjunction with the prince, the whole legislature [10] is committed.

I then descended to the courts of justice, over which the judges, those venerable sages and interpreters of the law, presided, for determining the disputed rights and properties of men, as well as for the punishment of vice and protection of innocence. I mentioned the prudent management of our treasury, the valour and achievements of our forces by sea and land. I computed the number of our people by reckoning how many millions there might be of each religious sect or political party among us. I did not omit even our sports and pastimes, or any other particular which I thought might redound to the honour of my country. And I finished all with a brief historical account of affairs and events in England for about an hundred years past.

This conversation was not ended under five audiences, each of several hours, and the King heard the whole with great attention, frequently taking notes of what I spoke, as well as memorandums of what questions he intended to ask me.

When I had put an end to these long discourses, his Majesty in a sixth audience, consulting his notes, proposed many doubts, queries, and objections upon every article. He asked what methods were used to cultivate the minds and bodies of our young nobility, and in what kind of business they commonly spent the first and teachable part of their lives. What course was taken to supply that assembly when any noble family became extinct. What qualifications were necessary in those who are to be created new lords: whether the humour of the prince, a sum of money to a court-lady or a prime minister, or a design of strengthening a party opposite to the public interest ever happened to be motives in those advancements. What share of knowledge these lords had in the laws of their country, and how they came by it, so as to enable them to decide the properties of their fellow-subjects in the last resort. Whether they were always so free from avarice, partialities, or want that a bribe, or

9. Bishops sit in the House of Lords.
10. Law-making function.

some other sinister view, could have no place among them. Whether those holy lords I spoke of were constantly promoted to that rank upon account of their knowledge in religious matters and the sanctity of their lives, had never been compliers with the times while they were common priests, or slavish prostitute chaplains to some nobleman whose opinions they continued servilely to follow after they were admitted into that assembly.

He then desired to know what arts were practised in electing those whom I called Commoners. Whether a stranger with a strong purse might not influence the vulgar voters to choose him before their own landlord or the most considerable gentleman in the neighbourhood. How it came to pass that people were so violently bent upon getting into this assembly, which I allowed to be a great trouble and expense, often to the ruin of their families, without any salary or pension: because this appeared such an exalted strain of virtue and public spirit that his Majesty seemed to doubt [11] it might possibly not be always sincere: and he desired to know whether such zealous gentlemen could have any views of refunding themselves for the charges and trouble they were at, by sacrificing the public good to the designs of a weak and vicious prince in conjunction with a corrupted ministry. He multiplied his questions and sifted me thoroughly upon every part of this head, proposing numberless inquiries and objections which I think it not prudent or convenient to repeat.

Upon what I said in relation to our courts of justice, his Majesty desired to be satisfied in several points: and this I was the better able to do, having been formerly almost ruined by a long suit in Chancery, which was decreed for me with costs. He asked what time was usually spent in determining between right and wrong, and what degree of expense. Whether advocates and orators had liberty to plead in causes manifestly known to be unjust, vexatious, or oppressive. Whether party in religion or politics were observed to be of any weight in the scale of justice. Whether those pleading orators were persons educated in the general knowledge of equity or only in provincial, national, and other local customs. Whether they or their judges had any part in penning those laws which they assumed the liberty of interpreting and glossing upon at their pleasure. Whether they had ever at different times pleaded for and against the same cause, and cited precedents to prove contrary opinions. Whether they were a rich or a poor corporation.[12] Whether they received any pecuniary reward for pleading or delivering their opinions. And particularly whether they were ever admitted as members in the lower senate.

He fell next upon the management of our treasury, and said he thought my memory had failed me, because I computed our taxes at about five or six millions a year, and, when I came to mention the issues,[13] he found they sometimes amounted to more than double; for the notes he had taken were very particular in this point, because he hoped, as he told me, that the knowledge of our conduct might be useful to him, and he could not be deceived in his calculations. But, if what I told him were true, he was still at a loss how a kingdom could run out of its estate like a private person. He asked me who

11. Suspect.
12. Profession.
13. Expenditures.

were our creditors, and where we found money to pay them.[14] He wondered to hear me talk of such chargeable and extensive wars; that certainly we must be quarrelsome people or live among very bad neighbours, and that our generals must needs be richer than our kings.[15] He asked what business we had out of our own islands, unless upon the score of trade or treaty or to defend the coasts with our fleet.[16] Above all, he was amazed to hear me talk of a mercenary standing army in the midst of peace and among a free people.[17] He said, if we were governed by our own consent in the persons of our representatives, he could not imagine of whom we were afraid or against whom we were to fight, and would hear my opinion whether a private man's house might not better be defended by himself, his children, and family than by a half a dozen rascals picked up at a venture in the streets for small wages, who might get an hundred times more by cutting their throats.

He laughed at my odd kind of arithmetic (as he was pleased to call it) in reckoning the numbers of our people by a computation drawn from the several sects among us in religion and politics.[18] He said he knew no reason why those who entertain opinions prejudicial to the public should be obliged to change or should not be obliged to conceal them. And as it was tyranny in any government to require the first, so it was weakness not to enforce the second: for a man may be allowed to keep poisons in his closets but not to vend them about as cordials.[19]

He observed that among the diversions of our nobility and gentry I had mentioned gaming.[20] He desired to know at what age this entertainment was usually taken up and when it was laid down. How much of their time it employed; whether it ever went so high as to affect their fortunes. Whether mean vicious people by their dexterity in that art might not arrive at great riches, and sometimes keep our very nobles in dependence as well as habituate them to vile companions, wholly take them from the improvement of their minds, and force them, by the losses they received, to learn and practice that infamous dexterity upon others.

He was perfectly astonished with the historical account I gave him of our affairs during the last century, protesting it was only an heap of conspiracies, rebellions, murders, massacres, revolutions, banishments; the very worst effects

14. The national debt first became a permanent part of English policy during the wars conducted by William III, and its great increase under Queen Anne (during the War of the Spanish Succession) led Swift to fear the growth of a powerful "moneyed interest, that might in time vie with the landed."
15. The first Duke of Marlborough (1650–1722) amassed a tremendous fortune during the great military campaigns he conducted on the Continent; he was accused of dishonesty and finally dismissed from office.
16. Campaigns in the most recent war had been carried out in Spain, Italy, the Low Countries, and the American continent. The Tories, with Swift's active support, brought the costly and extended war to an end with the Peace of Utrecht in 1713.
17. Among policies attacked by the Tories and especially by Swift was the maintenance of a standing army; it was feared as a threat to English liberties, and the Brobdingnagian substitute is a militia or citizen army (as the following chapter shows).
18. This method of compiling demographic statistics (known as "political arithmetic") was first devised by Sir William Petty (1623–87) in a study of London and Dublin.
19. Medicines. This principle of freedom of thought but controlled public expression was a doctrine of Oliver Cromwell that Swift approved.
20. Gambling.

that avarice, faction, hypocrisy, perfidiousness, cruelty, rage, madness, hatred, envy, lust, malice, and ambition could produce.

His Majesty in another audience was at the pains to recapitulate the sum of all I had spoken, compared the questions he made with the answers I had given; then taking me into his hands and stroking me gently, delivered himself in these words, which I shall never forget, nor the manner he spoke them in: "My little friend Grildrig, you have made a most admirable panegyric upon your country. You have clearly proved that ignorance, idleness, and vice are the proper ingredients for qualifying a legislator. That laws are best explained, interpreted, and applied by those whose interest and abilities lie in perverting, confounding, and eluding them. I observe among you some lines of an institution which in its original might have been tolerable, but these half erased, and the rest wholly blurred and blotted by corruptions. It doth not appear from all you have said how any one perfection is required towards the procurement of any one station among you, much less that men are ennobled on account of their virtue, that priests are advanced for their piety or learning, soldiers for their conduct or valour, judges for their integrity, senators for the love of their country, or counsellors for their wisdom. As for yourself," continued the King, "who have spent the greatest part of your life in travelling, I am well disposed to hope you may hitherto have escaped many vices of your country. But, by what I have gathered from your own relation, and the answers I have with much pains wringed and extorted from you, I cannot but conclude the bulk of your natives to be the most pernicious race of little odious vermin that nature ever suffered to crawl upon the surface of the earth."

Chapter Seven: The author's love of his country. He makes a proposal of much advantage to the King, which is rejected. The King's great ignorance in politics. The learning of that country very imperfect and confined. Their laws and military affairs, and parties in the state.

Nothing but an extreme love of truth could have hindered me from concealing this part of my story. It was in vain to discover my resentments, which were always turned into ridicule; and I was forced to rest with patience while my noble and most beloved country was so injuriously treated. I am heartily sorry as any of my readers can possibly be that such an occasion was given: but this prince happened to be so curious and inquisitive upon every particular that it could not consist either with gratitude or good manners to refuse giving him what satisfaction I was able. Yet thus much I may be allowed to say in my own vindication, that I artfully eluded many of his questions and gave to every point a more favourable turn by many degrees than the strictness of truth would allow. For I have always borne that laudable partiality to my own country which Dionysius Halicarnassensis with so much justice recommends to an historian.[1] I would hide the frailties and deformities of my political mother and place her virtues and beauties in the most advantageous light. This was my

1. Dionysius of Halicarnassus (1st century B.C.), a Greek historian who wrote the *Antiquities of Rome* to persuade his Greek countrymen to accept Roman rule. Dionysius also attacked the Greek historian Thucydides for being too critical of his country.

sincere endeavour in those many discourses I had with that mighty monarch, although it unfortunately failed of success.

But great allowances should be given to a king who lives wholly secluded from the rest of the world and must therefore be altogether unacquainted with the manners and customs that most prevail in other nations: the want of which knowledge will ever produce many prejudices and a certain narrowness of thinking, from which we and the politer countries of Europe are wholly exempted. And it would be hard indeed if so remote a prince's notions of virtue and vice were to be offered as a standard for all mankind.

To confirm what I have now said and further to show the miserable effects of a confined education, I shall here insert a passage which will hardly obtain belief. In hopes to ingratiate myself farther into his Majesty's favour, I told him of an invention discovered between three and four hundred years ago, to make a certain powder, into an heap of which the smallest spark of fire falling would kindle the whole in a moment, although it were as big as a mountain, and make it all fly up in the air together, with a noise and agitation greater than thunder. That a proper quantity of this powder rammed into an hollow tube of brass or iron, according to its bigness, would drive a ball of iron or lead with such violence and speed as nothing was able to sustain its force. That the largest balls, thus discharged, would not only destroy whole ranks of an army at once but batter the strongest walls to the ground, sink down ships, with a thousand men in each, to the bottom of the sea; and when linked together by a chain, would cut through masts and rigging, divide hundreds of bodies in the middle, and lay all waste before them. That we often put his powder into large hollow balls of iron, and discharged them by an engine into some city we were besieging, which would rip up the pavement, tear the houses to pieces, burst and throw splinters on every side, dashing out the brains of all who came near. That I knew the ingredients very well, which were cheap and common; I understood the manner of compounding them and could direct his workmen how to make those tubes of a size proportionable to all other things in his Majesty's kingdom, and the largest need not be above two hundred foot long; twenty or thirty of which tubes, charged with the proper quantity of powder and balls, would batter down the walls of the strongest town in his dominions in a few hours or destroy the whole metropolis, if ever it should pretend to dispute his absolute commands. This I humbly offered to his Majesty as a small tribute of acknowledgment in return of so many marks that I had received of his royal favour and protection.

The King was struck with horror at the description I had given of those terrible engines and the proposal I had made. He was amazed how so impotent and groveling an insect as I (these were his expressions) could entertain such inhuman ideas, and in so familiar a manner as to appear wholly unmoved at all the scenes of blood and desolation which I had painted as the common effects of those destructive machines; whereof he said, some evil genius, enemy to mankind, must have been the first contriver. As for himself, he protested that although few things delighted him so much as new discoveries in art or in nature, yet he would rather lose half his kingdom than be privy to such a secret, which he commanded me, as I valued my life, never to mention any more.

A strange effect of narrow principles and short views! that a prince possessed of every quality which procures veneration, love, and esteem; of strong parts, great wisdom, and profound learning, endued with admirable talents for government, and almost adored by his subjects, should from a nice [2] unnecessary scruple, whereof in Europe we can have no conception, let slip an opportunity put into his hands that would have made him absolute master of the lives, the liberties, and the fortunes of his people. Neither do I say this with the least intention to detract from the many virtues of that excellent king, whose character I am sensible will on this account be very much lessened in the opinion of an English reader: but I take this defect among them to have risen from their ignorance, by not having hitherto reduced politics into a science, as the more acute wits of Europe have done.[3] For I remember very well, in a discourse one day with the King, when I happened to say there were several thousand books among us written upon the art of government, it gave him (directly contrary to my intention) a very mean opinion of our understandings. He professed both to abominate and despise all mystery, refinement, and intrigue, either in a prince or a minister. He could not tell what I meant by secrets of state where an enemy or some rival nation were not in the case. He confined the knowledge of governing within very narrow bounds; to common sense and reason, to justice and lenity, to the speedy determination of civil and criminal causes, with some other obvious topics which are not worth considering. And he gave it for his opinion that whoever could make two ears of corn or two blades of grass to grow upon a spot of ground where only one grew before, would deserve better of mankind, and do more essential service to his country, than the whole race of politicians put together.

The learning of this people is very defective, consisting only in morality, history, poetry, and mathematics, wherein they must be allowed to excel. But the last of these is wholly applied to what may be useful in life, to the improvement of agriculture and all mechanical arts; so that among us it would be little esteemed. And as to ideas, entities, abstractions, and transcendentals,[4] I could never drive the least conception into their heads.

No law of that country must exceed in words the number of letters in their alphabet, which consists only of two and twenty. But indeed few of them extend even to that length. They are expressed in the most plain and simple terms, wherein those people are not mercurial enough to discover above one interpretation. And to write a comment upon any law is a capital crime. As to the decision of civil causes or proceedings against criminals, their precedents are so few that they have little reason to boast of any extraordinary skill in either.

They have had the art of printing, as well as the Chinese, time out of mind. But their libraries are not very large; for that of the King's, which is reckoned the largest, doth not amount to above a thousand volumes, placed in a gallery

2. Excessively delicate.

3. Gulliver is holding up for admiration Niccolò Machiavelli (1469–1527) and his followers, who studied with scientific detachment the methods of gaining and wielding political power. Such a "science" aroused horror through its neglect of moral concerns and its advocacy of cruelty and deception ("mystery, refinement, and intrigue"). One may compare the King's "narrow bounds" of "justice and lenity" with the Lilliputian Emperor's cruel demonstrations of his so-called "lenity" (Part I, Chapter 7).

4. Metaphysical terms such as appeared in the jargon of Scholasticism, whose technicalities Swift, an admirer of Francis Bacon, despised.

of twelve hundred foot long, from whence I had liberty to borrow what books I pleased. The Queen's joiner had contrived in one of Glumdalclitch's rooms a kind of wooden machine five and twenty foot high, formed like a standing ladder; the steps were each fifty foot long. It was indeed a moveable pair of stairs, the lowest end placed at ten foot distance from the wall of the chamber. The book I had a mind to read was put up leaning against the wall. I first mounted to the upper step of the ladder and, turning my face towards the book, began at the top of the page, and so walking to the right and left about eight or ten paces, according to the length of the lines, till I had gotten a little below the level of my eyes, and then descending gradually till I came to the bottom: after which I mounted again and began the other page in the same manner, and so turned over the leaf, which I could easily do with both my hands, for it was as thick and stiff as a pasteboard, and in the largest folios not above eighteen or twenty foot long.

Their style is clear, masculine, and smooth, but not florid, for they avoid nothing more than multiplying unnecessary words or using various expressions. I have perused many of their books, especially those in history and morality. Among the latter I was much diverted with a little old treatise which always lay in Glumdalclitch's bedchamber, and belonged to her governess, a grave elderly gentlewoman, who dealt in writings of morality and devotion. The book treats of the weakness of human kind and is in little esteem except among women and the vulgar. However, I was curious to see what an author of that country could say upon such a subject. This writer went through all the usual topics of European moralists, showing how diminutive, contemptible, and helpless an animal was man in his own nature; how unable to defend himself from the inclemencies of the air or the fury of wild beasts. How much he was excelled by one creature in strength, by another in speed, by a third in foresight, by a fourth in industry. He added that Nature was degenerated in these latter declining ages of the world, and could now produce only small abortive births in comparison of those in ancient times. He said it was very reasonable to think not only that the species of men were originally much larger, but also that there must have been giants in former ages, which, as it is asserted by history and tradition, so it hath been confirmed by huge bones and skulls casually dug up in several parts of the kingdom, far exceeding the common dwindled race of man in our days. He argued that the very laws of nature absolutely required we should have been made, in the beginning, of a size more large and robust, not so liable to destruction from every little accident of a tile falling from an house or a stone cast from the hand of a boy, or of being drowned in a little brook. From this way of reasoning the author drew several moral applications useful in the conduct of life, but needless here to repeat. For my own part, I could not avoid reflecting how universally this talent was spread of drawing lectures in morality, or indeed rather matter of discontent and repining, from the quarrels we raise with Nature. And, I believe, upon a strict enquiry those quarrels might be shown as ill-grounded among us as they are among that people.[5]

5. The "little old treatise" resembles 17th-century works stressing the decay of Nature and the growth of corruption with mutability. Gulliver characteristically dismisses the idea. Yet one can see in the treatise also a somewhat ludicrous overstatement of that theme, which sees even in the enormous Brobdingnagians a petty, dwindled race. The irony seems, as often in Swift, to cut both ways.

As to their military affairs, they boast that the King's army consists of an hundred and seventy-six thousand foot and thirty-two thousand horses, if that may be called an army which is made up of tradesmen in the several cities and farmers in the country, whose commanders are only the nobility and gentry without pay or reward. They are indeed perfect enough in their exercises and under very good discipline, wherein I saw no great merit; for how should it be otherwise where every farmer is under the command of his own landlord, and every citizen under that of the principal men in his own city, chosen after the manner of Venice by ballot?[6]

I have often seen the militia of Lorbrulgrud drawn out to exercise in a great field near the city, of twenty miles square. They were in all not above twenty-five thousand foot and six thousand horse; but it was impossible for me to compute their number, considering the space of ground they took up. A cavalier mounted on a large steed might be about ninety foot high. I have seen this whole body of horse upon the word of command draw their swords at once and brandish them in the air. Imagination can figure nothing so grand, so surprising, and so astonishing. It looked as if ten thousand flashes of lightning were darting at the same time from every quarter of the sky.

I was curious to know how this prince, to whose dominions there is no access from any other country, came to think of armies or to teach his people the practice of military discipline. But I was soon informed, both by conversation and reading their histories. For in the course of many ages they have been troubled with the same disease to which the whole race of mankind is subject; the nobility often contending for power, the people for liberty, and the king for absolute dominion. All which, however happily tempered by the laws of that kingdom, have been sometimes violated by each of the three parties, and have more than once occasioned civil wars, the last whereof was happily put an end to by this prince's grandfather in a general composition;[7] and the militia then settled with common consent hath been ever since kept in the strictest duty.

Chapter Eight: The King and Queen make a progress to the frontiers. The author attends them. The manner in which he leaves the country very particularly related. He returns to England.

I had always a strong impulse that I should sometime recover my liberty, although it were impossible to conjecture by what means or to form any project with the least hope of succeeding. The ship in which I sailed was the first ever known to be driven within sight of that coast, and the King had given strict orders that, if at any time another appeared, it should be taken ashore and with all its crew and passengers brought in a tumbril[1] to Lorbrulgrud. He was strongly bent to get me a woman of my own size by whom I

6. The citizen army or militia was first devised by Machiavelli in Florence, but, like the secret ballot, first introduced by Venice, it was an institution much admired by defenders of freedom in England.

7. Political settlement or agreement. The Brobdingnagians have reconciled the interests of parties in a mixed state, a political structure in which Swift strongly believed and which Pope celebrated as well, in *Essay on Man* III.294.

1. Cart, wagon.

might propagate the breed: but I think I should rather have died than undergone the disgrace of leaving a posterity to be kept in cages like tame canary birds, and perhaps in time sold about the kingdom to persons of quality for curiosities.[2] I was indeed treated with much kindness; I was the favourite of a great king and queen and the delight of the whole court, but it was upon such a foot as ill became the dignity of humankind. I could never forget those domestic pledges I had left behind me. I wanted to be among people with whom I could converse upon even terms, and walk about the streets and fields without fear of being trod to death like a frog or young puppy. But my deliverance came sooner than I expected, and in a manner not very common: the whole story and circumstances of which I shall faithfully relate.

I had now been two years in this country; and about the beginning of the third, Glumdalclitch and I attended the King and Queen in a progress to the south coast of the kingdom. I was carried as usual in my travelling-box, which, as I have already described, was a very convenient closet of twelve foot wide. I had ordered a hammock to be fixed by silken ropes from the four corners at the top, to break the jolts when a servant carried me before him on horseback, as I sometimes desired; and would often sleep in my hammock while we were upon the road. On the roof of my closet, just over the middle of the hammock, I ordered the joiner to cut out a hole of a foot square to give me air in hot weather as I slept, which hole I shut at pleasure with a board that drew backwards and forwards through a groove.

When we came to our journey's end, the King thought proper to pass a few days at a palace he hath near Flanflasnic, a city within eighteen English miles of the seaside. Glumdalclitch and I were much fatigued; I had gotten a small cold, but the poor girl was so ill as to be confined to her chamber. I longed to see the ocean, which must be the only scene of my escape, if ever it should happen. I pretended to be worse than I really was and desired leave to take the fresh air of the sea, with a page whom I was very fond of and who had sometimes been trusted with me. I shall never forget with what unwillingness Glumdalclitch consented, nor the strict charge she gave the page to be careful of me, bursting at the same time into a flood of tears as if she had some foreboding of what was to happen. The boy took me out in my box about half an hour's walk from the palace towards the rocks on the seashore. I ordered him to set me down and, lifting up one of my sashes, cast many a wistful melancholy look towards the sea. I found myself not very well and told the page that I had a mind to take a nap in my hammock, which I hoped would do me good. I got in, and the boy shut the window close down to keep out the cold. I soon fell asleep, and all I can conjecture is that while I slept the page, thinking no danger could happen, went among the rocks to look for birds' eggs, having before observed him from my window searching about and picking up one or two in the clefts. Be that as it will, I found myself suddenly awaked with a violent pull upon the ring which was fastened at the top of my box for the conveniency of carriage. I felt the box raised very high in the air and then borne forward with prodigious speed. The first jolt had like to have shaken me out of my hammock, but afterwards the motion was easy enough. I called out

2. Compare Gulliver's readiness to take Blefuscudian natives back to England (Part I, Chapter 8).

several times as loud as I could raise my voice, but all to no purpose. I looked towards my windows and could see nothing but the clouds and sky. I heard a noise just over my head like the clapping of wings, and then began to perceive the woeful condition I was in; that some eagle had got the ring of my box in his beak, with an intent to let fall on a rock like a tortoise in a shell, and then pick out my body and devour it. For the sagacity and smell of this bird enable him to discover his quarry at a great distance, although better concealed than I could be within a two-inch board.

In a little time I observed the noise and flutter of wings to increase very fast, and my box was tossed up and down like a signpost in a windy day. I heard several bangs or buffets, as I thought, given to the eagle (for such I am certain it must have been that held the ring of my box in his beak), and then all on a sudden felt myself falling perpendicularly down for above a minute, but with such incredible swiftness that I almost lost my breath. My fall was stopped by a terrible squash, that sounded louder to my ears than the cataract of Niagara; after which I was quite in the dark for another minute, and then my box began to rise so high that I could see light from the tops of my windows. I now perceived that I was fallen into the sea. My box, by the weight of my body, the goods that were in, and the broad plates of iron fixed for strength at the four corners of the top and bottom, floated about five foot deep in water. I did then, and do now suppose, that the eagle which flew away with my box was pursued by two or three others, and forced to let me drop while he was defending himself against the rest, who hoped to share in the prey. The plates of iron fastened at the bottom of the box (for those were the strongest) preserved the balance while it fell, and hindered it from being broken on the surface of the water. Every joint of it was well grooved, and the door did not move on hinges, but up and down like a sash, which kept my closet so tight that very little water came in. I got with much difficulty out of my hammock, having first ventured to draw back the slip-board on the roof already mentioned, contrived on purpose to let in air, for want of which I found myself almost stifled.

How often did I then wish myself with my dear Glumdalclitch, from whom one single hour had so far divided me! And I may say with truth that in the midst of my own misfortune I could not forbear lamenting my poor nurse, the grief she would suffer for my loss, the displeasure of the Queen, and the ruin of her fortune. Perhaps many travellers have not been under greater difficulties and distress than I was at this juncture, expecting every moment to see my box dashed in pieces or at least overset by the first violent blast or a rising wave. A breach in one single pane of glass would have been immediate death: nor could anything have preserved the windows but the strong lattice wires placed on the outside against accidents in travelling. I saw the water ooze in at several crannies, although the leaks were not considerable, and I endeavoured to stop them as well as I could. I was not able to lift up the roof of my closet, which otherwise I certainly should have done and sat on the top of it, where I might at least preserve myself from being shut up, as I may call it, in the hold. Or, if I escaped these dangers for a day or two, what could I expect but a miserable death of cold and hunger! I was four hours under these circumstances, expecting and indeed wishing every moment to be my last.

I have already told the reader that there were two strong staples fixed upon the side of my box which had no window, and into which the servant who used to carry me on horseback would put a leathern belt and buckle it about his waist. Being in this disconsolate state, I heard or at least thought I heard some kind of grating noise on that side of my box where the staples were fixed, and soon after I began to fancy that the box was pulled or towed along in the sea; for I now and then felt a sort of tugging which made the waves rise near the tops of my windows, leaving me almost in the dark. This gave me some faint hopes of relief, although I were not able to imagine how it could be brought about. I ventured to unscrew one of my chairs, which were always fastened to the floor; and, having made a hard shift to screw it down again directly under the slipping-board that I had lately opened, I mounted on the chair and, putting my mouth as near as I could to the hole, I called for help in a loud voice and in all the languages I understood. I then fastened my handkerchief to a stick I usually carried and, thrusting it up the hole, waved it several times in the air, that if any boat or ship were near, the seamen might conjecture some unhappy mortal to be shut up in the box.

I found no effect from all I could do, but plainly perceived my closet to be moved along; and in the space of an hour or better, that side of the box where the staples were and had no window struck against something that was hard. I apprehended it to be a rock, and found myself tossed more than ever. I plainly heard a noise upon the cover of my closet like that of a cable, and the grating of it as it passed through the ring. I then found myself hoisted up by degrees at least three foot higher than I was before. Whereupon I again thrust up my stick and handkerchief, calling for help till I was almost hoarse. In return to which I heard a great shout repeated three times, giving me such transports of joy as are not to be conceived but by those who feel them. I now heard a trampling over my head, and somebody calling through the hole with a loud voice in the English tongue, "If there be anybody below let them speak." I answered I was an Englishman drawn by ill fortune into the greatest calamity that ever any creature underwent, and begged, by all that was moving, to be delivered out of the dungeon I was in. The voice replied I was safe, for my box was fastened to their ship; and the carpenter should immediately come and saw an hole in the cover large enough to pull me out. I answered that was needless and would take up too much time, for there was no more to be done but let one of the crew put his finger into the ring and take the box out of the sea into the ship, and so into the captain's cabin. Some of them upon hearing me talk so wildly thought I was mad; others laughed; for indeed it never came into my head that I was now got among people of my own stature and strength. The carpenter came, and in a few minutes sawed a passage about four foot square, then let down a small ladder, upon which I mounted, and from thence was taken into the ship in a very weak condition.

The sailors were all in amazement and asked me a thousand questions, which I had no inclination to answer. I was equally confounded at the sight of so many pigmies, for such I took them to be after having so long accustomed my eyes to the monstrous objects I had left. But the captain, Mr. Thomas Wilcocks, an honest worthy Shropshire man, observing I was ready to faint, took me into his cabin, gave me a cordial to comfort me, and made me turn in upon his own bed, advising me to take a little rest, of which I had great need. Before I went to sleep I gave him to understand that I had some valuable furniture in my box, too good to be lost; a fine hammock, an handsome field-bed, two chairs, a table, and a cabinet: that my closet was hung on all sides, or rather quilted, with silk and cotton: that if he would let one of the crew bring my closet into his cabin, I would open it there before him and show him my goods. The captain, hearing me utter these absurdities, concluded I was raving: however (I suppose to pacify me), he promised to give order as I desired and, going upon deck sent some of his men down into my closet, from whence (as I afterwards found) they drew up all my goods and stripped off the quilting; but the chairs, cabinet, and bedstead, being screwed to the floor, were much damaged by the ignorance of the seamen, who tore them up by force. Then they knocked off some of the boards for the use of the ship and, when they had got all they had a mind for, let the hulk drop into the sea, which, by reason of many breaches made in the bottom and sides, sunk to rights. And indeed I was glad not to have been a spectator of the havoc they made; because I am confident it would have sensibly touched me, by bringing former passages into my mind which I had rather forget.

I slept some hours, but perpetually disturbed with dreams of the place I had left and the dangers I had escaped. However, upon waking I found myself much recovered. It was now about eight o'clock at night, and the captain ordered supper immediately, thinking I had already fasted too long. He entertained me with great kindness, observing me not to look wildly or talk inconsistently; and when we were left alone, desired I would give him a relation of my travels, and by what accident I came to be set adrift in that monstrous wooden chest. He said that about twelve o'clock at noon, as he was looking through his glass, he spied it at a distance and thought it was a sail, which he had a mind to make, being not much out of his course, in hopes of buying some biscuit, his own beginning to fall short. That upon coming nearer and finding his error, he sent out his longboat to discover what I was; that his men came back in a fright, swearing they had seen a swimming house. That he laughed at their folly and went himself in the boat, ordering his men to take a strong cable along with them. That the weather being calm, he rowed round me several times, observed my windows, and the wire lattices that defended them. That he discovered two staples upon one side, which was all of boards without any passage for light. He then commanded his men to row up to that side, and fastening a cable to one of the staples, ordered his men to tow my chest (as he called it) towards the ship. When it was there, he gave directions to fasten another cable to the ring fixed in the cover, and to raise up my chest with pulleys, which all the sailors were not able to do above two or three foot. He said they saw my stick and handkerchief thrust out of the hole, and concluded that some unhappy man must be shut up in the cavity. I asked whether he or the crew had seen any prodigious birds in the air about the time he first discovered me. To which he answered that, discoursing this matter with the sailors while I was asleep, one of them said he had observed three eagles flying towards the north, but remarked nothing of their being larger than the usual size, which I suppose must be imputed to the great height they were at: and he could not guess the reason of my question.

I then asked the captain how far he reckoned we might be from land; he said, by the best computation he could make, we were at least an hundred leagues. I assured him that he must be mistaken by almost half, for I had not left the country from whence I came above two hours before I dropped into the sea. Whereupon he began again to think that my brain was disturbed, of which he gave me a hint, and advised me to go to bed in a cabin he had provided. I assured him I was well refreshed with his good entertainment and company and as much in my senses as ever I was in my life. He then grew serious and desired to ask me freely whether I were not troubled in mind by the consciousness of some enormous crime, for which I was punished at the command of some prince by exposing me in that chest, as great criminals in other countries have been forced to sea in a leaky vessel without provisions: for although he should be sorry to have taken so ill [3] a man into his ship, yet he would engage his word to set me safe on shore in the first port where we arrived. He added that his suspicions were much increased by some very absurd speeches I had delivered at first to the sailors and afterwards to himself, in relation to my closet or chest, as well as by my odd looks and behaviour while I was at supper.

I begged his patience to hear me tell my story, which I faithfully did from the last time I left England to the moment he first discovered me. And, as truth always forceth its way into rational minds, so this honest worthy gentleman, who had some tincture of learning and very good sense, was immediately convinced of my candor and veracity. But further to confirm all I had said, I entreated him to give order that my cabinet should be brought, of which I kept the key in my pocket (for he had already informed me how the seamen disposed of my closet); I opened it in his presence and showed him the small collection of rarities I made in the country from whence I had been so strangely delivered. There was the comb I had contrived out of the stumps of the King's beard, and another of the same materials but fixed into a paring of her Majesty's thumb-nail which served for the back. There was a collection of needles and pins from a foot to half a yard long. Four wasp-stings, like joiners' tacks; some combings of the Queen's hair; a gold ring which one day she made me a present of in a most obliging manner, taking it from her little finger and throwing it over my head like a collar. I desired the captain would please to accept this ring in return of his civilities, which he absolutely refused. I showed him a corn that I had cut off with my own hand from a maid of honour's toe; it was about the bigness of a Kentish pippin, and grown so hard that, when I returned to England, I got it hollowed into a cup and set in silver. Lastly, I desired him to see the breeches I had then on, which were made of a mouse's skin.

I could force nothing on him but a footman's tooth, which I observed him to examine with great curiosity, and found he had a fancy for it. He received it with abundance of thanks, more than such a trifle could deserve. It was drawn by an unskilful surgeon in a mistake from one of Glumdalclitch's men who was afflicted with the toothache, but it was as sound as any in his head. I got it cleaned and put it into my cabinet. It was about a foot long and four inches in diameter.

The captain was very well satisfied with this plain relation I had given him; and said he hoped, when we returned to England, I would oblige the world

3. Evil.

by putting it in paper and making it public. My answer was that I thought we were already overstocked with books of travels: that nothing could now pass which was not extraordinary, wherein I doubted some authors less consulted truth than their own vanity or interest or the diversion of ignorant readers. That my story could contain little besides common events, without those ornamental descriptions of strange plants, trees, birds, and other animals, or the barbarous customs and idolatry of savage people, with which most writers abound. However, I thanked him for his good opinion and promised to take the matter into my thoughts.

He said he wondered at one thing very much, which was to hear me speak so loud, asking me whether the King or Queen of that country were thick of hearing. I told him it was what I had been used to for above two years past, and that I admired as much at the voices of him and his men, who seemed to me only to whisper, and yet I could hear them well enough. But when I spoke in that country, it was like a man talking in the street to another looking out from the top of a steeple, unless when I was placed on a table or held in any person's hand. I told him I had likewise observed another thing, that, when I first got into the ship and the sailors stood all about me, I thought they were the most little contemptible creatures I had ever beheld. For, indeed, while I was in that prince's country, I could never endure to look in a glass after my eyes had been accustomed to such prodigious objects, because the comparison gave me so despicable a conceit [4] of myself. The captain said that while we were at supper he observed me to look at everything with a sort of wonder, and that I often seemed hardly able to contain my laughter, which he knew not well how to take, but imputed it to some disorder in my brain. I answered, it was very true, and I wondered how I could forbear, when I saw his dishes of the size of a silver threepence, a leg of pork hardly a mouthful, a cup not so big as a nutshell; and so I went on, describing the rest of his household-stuff and provisions after the same manner. For although the Queen had ordered a little equipage of all things necessary for me while I was in her service, yet my ideas were wholly taken up with what I saw on every side of me, and I winked at my own littleness as people do at their own faults. The captain understood my raillery very well and merrily replied with the old English proverb, that he doubted my eyes were bigger than my belly, for he did not observe my stomach so good, although I had fasted all day; and, continuing in his mirth, protested he would have gladly given an hundred pounds to have seen my closet in the eagle's bill and afterwards in its fall from so great an height into the sea; which would certainly have been a most astonishing object, worthy to have the description of it transmitted to future ages: and the comparison of Phaeton [5] was so obvious, that he could not forbear applying it, although I did not much admire the conceit.

The captain, having been at Tonquin,[6] was in his return to England driven northeastward to the latitude of 44 degrees and of longitude 143. But meeting a trade wind two days after I came on board him, we sailed southward a long

4. Conception, image.

5. The son of Apollo seized the chariot of the sun and tried to drive it through the heavens but could not control it. After having scorched and frozen portions of the earth, he was struck down by a thunderbolt of Zeus.

6. Indo-China or Vietnam.

time, and coasting New Holland [7] kept our course west-southwest, and then south-southwest till we doubled the Cape of Good Hope. Our voyage was very prosperous, but I shall not trouble the reader with a journal of it. The captain called in at one or two ports and sent in his longboat for provisions and fresh water, but I never went out of the ship till we came into the Downs, which was on the 3d day of June, 1706, about nine months after my escape. I offered to leave my goods in security for payment of my freight;[8] but the captain protested he would not receive one farthing. We took kind leave of each other, and I made him promise he would come to see me at my house in Redriff. I hired a horse and guide for five shillings, which I borrowed of the captain.

As I was on the road, observing the littleness of the houses, the trees, the cattle, and the people, I began to think myself in Lilliput. I was afraid of trampling on every traveller I met, and often called aloud to have them stand out of the way, so that I had like to have gotten one or two broken heads for my impertinence.

When I came to my own house, for which I was forced to inquire, one of the servants opening the door, I bent down to go in (like a goose under a gate) for fear of striking my head. My wife ran out to embrace me, but I stooped lower than her knees, thinking she could otherwise never be able to reach my mouth. My daughter kneeled to ask me blessing, but I could not see her till she arose, having been so long used to stand with my head and eyes erect to above sixty foot; and then I went to take her up with one hand by the waist. I looked down upon the servants and one or two friends who were in the house, as if they had been pigmies and I a giant. I told my wife she had been too thrifty, for I found she had starved herself and her daughter to nothing. In short, I behaved myself so unaccountably that they were all of the captain's opinion when he first saw me and concluded I had lost my wits. This I mention as an instance of the great power of habit and prejudice.

In a little time I and my family and friends came to a right understanding: but my wife protested I should never go to sea any more; although my evil destiny so ordered that she had not power to hinder me, as the reader may know hereafter. In the meantime I here conclude the second part of my unfortunate voyages.

Part Three: A Voyage to Laputa, Balnibarbi, Luggnagg, Glubbdubdrib, and Japan

Chapter One: The author sets out on his third voyage. Is taken by pirates. The malice of a Dutchman. His arrival at an island. He is received into Laputa.

I had not been at home above ten days when Captain William Robinson, a Cornish man, commander of the *Hope-well,* a stout ship of three hundred tons, came to my house. I had formerly been surgeon of another ship where he was master, and a fourth part owner, in a voyage to the Levant; he had always treated me more like a brother than an inferior officer, and hearing of my arrival made me a visit, as I apprehended, only out of friendship, for nothing passed more than what is usual after long absence. But repeating his visits

7. Australia.
8. Passage.

often, expressing his joy to find me in good health, asking whether I were now settled for life, adding that he intended a voyage to the East Indies in two months, at last plainly invited me, although with some apologies, to be surgeon of the ship; that I should have another surgeon under me besides our two mates; that my salary should be double to the usual pay; and that having experienced my knowledge in sea-affairs to be at least equal to his, he would enter into any engagement to follow my advice as much as if I had share in the command.

He said so many other obliging things, and I knew him to be so honest a man, that I could not reject his proposal; the thirst I had of seeing the world, notwithstanding my past misfortunes, continuing as violent as ever. The only difficulty that remained was to persuade my wife, whose consent however I at last obtained, by the prospect of advantage she proposed [1] to her children.

We set out the 5th day of August, 1706, and arrived at Fort St. George [2] the 11th of April, 1707. We stayed there three weeks to refresh our crew, many of whom were sick. From thence we went to Tonquin, where the captain resolved to continue some time, because many of the goods he intended to buy were not ready, nor could he expect to be dispatched in several months. Therefore in hopes to defray some of the charges he must be at, he bought a sloop, loaded it with several sorts of goods wherewith the Tonquinese usually trade to the neighbouring islands; and, putting fourteen men on board, whereof three were of the country, he appointed me master of the sloop and gave me power to traffic while he transacted his affairs at Tonquin.

We had not sailed above three days when, a great storm arising, we were driven five days to the north-northeast and then to the east, after which we had fair weather, but still with a pretty strong gale from the west. Upon the tenth day we were chased by two pirates who soon overtook us; for my sloop was so deep loaden that she sailed very slow, neither were we in a condition to defend ourselves.

We were boarded about the same time by both the pirates, who entered furiously at the head of their men, but, finding us all prostrate upon our faces (for so I gave order), they pinioned us with strong ropes and, setting a guard upon us, went to search the sloop.

I observed among them a Dutchman who seemed to be of some authority, although he were not commander of either ship. He knew us by our countenances to be Englishmen and, jabbering to us in his own language, swore we should be tied back to back and thrown into the sea. I spoke Dutch tolerably well; I told him who we were and begged him, in consideration of our being Christians and Protestants, of neighbouring countries in strict alliance, that he would move the captains to take some pity on us.[3] This inflamed his rage, he repeated his threatenings, and turning to his companions, spoke with great vehemence in the Japanese language, as I suppose, often using the word *Christianos*.

The largest of the two pirate ships was commanded by a Japanese captain,

1. Anticipated.
2. Madras, on the eastern coast of India.
3. England and Holland were members of the Grand Alliance and at war with France; but they remained bitter commercial rivals.

who spoke a little Dutch, but very imperfectly. He came up to me, and, after several questions which I answered in great humility, he said we should not die. I made the captain a very low bow and, then turning to the Dutchman, said I was sorry to find more mercy in a heathen than in a brother Christian. But I had soon reason to repent those foolish words; for that malicious reprobate, having often endeavoured in vain to persuade both the captains that I might be thrown into the sea (which they would not yield to after the promise made me that I should not die), however prevailed so far as to have a punishment inflicted on me worse in all human appearance than death itself. My men were sent by an equal division into both the pirate ships, and my sloop new manned. As to myself, it was determined that I should be set adrift in a small canoe with paddles and a sail and four days' provisions, which last the Japanese captain was so kind to double out of his own stores, and would permit no man to search me. I got down into the canoe while the Dutchman, standing upon the deck, loaded me with all the curses and injurious terms his language could afford.

About an hour before we saw the pirates, I had taken an observation and found we were in the latitude of 46 N. and of longitude 183.[4] When I was at some distance from the pirates, I discovered by my pocket-glass several islands to the southeast. I set up my sail, the wind being fair, with a design to reach the nearest of those islands, which I made a shift to do in about three hours. It was all rocky; however I got many birds' eggs, and, striking fire, I kindled some heath and dry seaweed, by which I roasted my eggs. I eat no other supper, being resolved to spare my provisions as much as I could. I passed the night under the shelter of a rock, strowing some heath under me, and slept pretty well.

The next day I sailed to another island, and thence to a third and fourth, sometimes using my sail and sometimes my paddles. But not to trouble the reader with a particular account of my distresses, let it suffice that on the fifth day I arrived at the last island in my sight, which lay south-southeast to the former.

This island was at a greater distance than I expected, and I did not reach it in less than five hours. I encompassed it almost round before I could find a convenient place to land in, which was a small creek about three times the wideness of my canoe. I found the island to be all rocky, only a little intermingled with tufts of grass and sweet-smelling herbs. I took out my small provisions, and, after having refreshed myself, I secured the remainder in a cave, whereof there were great numbers. I gathered plenty of eggs upon the rocks and got a quantity of dry seaweed and parched grass, which I designed to kindle the next day and roast my eggs as well as I could. (For I had about me my flint, steel, match,[5] and burning-glass.) I lay all night in the cave where I had lodged my provisions. My bed was the same dry grass and seaweed which I intended for fuel. I slept very little, for the disquiets of my mind prevailed over my weariness and kept me awake. I considered how impossible it was to preserve my life in so desolate a place and how miserable my end must be. Yet I found myself so listless and desponding that I had not the heart to

4. In the Pacific Ocean east of Japan and south of the Aleutians.

5. Small piece of cord or wood dipped in sulphur and easily set aflame by a tinder box.

rise, and, before I could get spirits enough to creep out of my cave, the day was far advanced. I walked a while among the rocks; the sky was perfectly clear and the sun so hot that I was forced to turn my face from it: when all on a sudden it became obscured, as I thought, in a manner very different from what happens by the interposition of a cloud. I turned back and perceived a vast opaque body between me and the sun, moving forwards towards the island: it seemed to be about two miles high and hid the sun six or seven minutes, but I did not observe the air to be much colder or the sky more darkened than if I had stood under the shade of a mountain. As it approached nearer over the place where I was, it appeared to be a firm substance, the bottom flat, smooth, and shining very bright from the reflection of the sea below. I stood upon a height about two hundred yards from the shore and saw this vast body descending almost to a parallel with me, at less than an English mile distance. I took out my pocket-perspective and could plainly discover numbers of people moving up and down the sides of it, which appeared to be sloping, but what those people were doing I was not able to distinguish.

The natural love of life gave me some inward motions of joy, and I was ready to entertain a hope that this adventure might some way or other help to deliver me from the desolate place and condition I was in. But at the same time the reader can hardly conceive my astonishment to behold an island in the air, inhabited by men, who were able (as it should seem) to raise, or sink, or put it into a progressive motion, as they pleased. But not being at that time in a disposition to philosophize upon this phenomenon, I rather chose to observe what course the island would take, because it seemed for a while to stand still. Yet soon after it advanced nearer, and I could see the sides of it, encompassed with several gradations of galleries, and stairs at certain intervals to descend from one to the other. In the lowest gallery, I beheld some people fishing with long angling rods, and others looking on. I waved my cap (for my hat was long since worn out) and my handkerchief towards the island; and upon its nearer approach I called and shouted with the utmost strength of my voice; and then looking circumspectly, I beheld a crowd gathered to that side which was most in my view. I found by their pointing towards me and to each other that they plainly discovered me, although they made no return to my shouting. But I could see four or five men running in great haste up the stairs to the top of the island, who then disappeared. I happened rightly to conjecture that these were sent for orders to some person in authority upon this occasion.

The number of people increased, and in less than half an hour the island was moved and raised in such a manner that the lowest gallery appeared in a parallel of less than an hundred yards' distance from the height where I stood. I then put myself into the most supplicating postures and spoke in the humblest accent, but received no answer. Those who stood nearest over-against me seemed to be persons of distinction, as I supposed by their habit. They conferred earnestly with each other, looking often upon me. At length one of them called out in a clear, polite, smooth dialect, not unlike in sound to the Italian; and therefore I returned an answer in that language, hoping at least that the cadence might be more agreeable to his ears. Although neither of us understood the other, yet my meaning was easily known, for the people saw the distress I was in.

They made signs for me to come down from the rock and go towards the shore, which I accordingly did; and the flying island being raised to a convenient height, the verge directly over me, a chain was let down from the lowest gallery, with a seat fastened to the bottom, to which I fixed myself, and was drawn up by pulleys.

Chapter Two: The humours and dispositions of the Laputans described. An account of their learning. Of the King and his court. The author's reception there. The inhabitants subject to fears and disquietudes. An account of the women.

At my alighting I was surrounded by a crowd of people, but those who stood nearest seemed to be of better quality. They beheld me with all the marks and circumstances of wonder; neither indeed was I much in their debt, having never till then seen a race of mortals so singular in their shapes, habits, and countenances. Their heads were all reclined either to the right or the left, one of their eyes turned inward, and the other directly up to the zenith. Their outward garments were adorned with the figures of suns, moons, and stars, interwoven with those of fiddles, flutes, harps, trumpets, guitars, harpsichords, and many more instruments of music unknown to us in Europe.[1] I observed here and there many in the habits of servants, with a blown bladder fastened like a flail to the end of a short stick, which they carried in their hands. In each bladder was a small quantity of dried pease or little pebbles (as I was afterwards informed). With these bladders they now and then flapped the mouths and ears of those who stood near them, of which practice I could not then conceive the meaning; it seems, the minds of these people are so taken up with intense speculations, that they neither can speak nor attend to the discourses of others without being roused by some external taction[2] upon the organs of speech and hearing; for which reason those persons who are able to afford it always keep a flapper (the original is *climenole*) in their family as one of their domestics, nor ever walk abroad or make visits without him. And the business of this officer is, when two or more persons are in company, gently to strike with his bladder the mouth of him who is to speak, and the right ear of him or them to whom the speaker addresseth himself. This flapper is likewise employed diligently to attend his master in his walks and upon occasion to give him a soft flap on his eyes, because he is always so wrapped up in cogitation that he is in manifest danger of falling down every precipice and

1. The obsession with music and astronomy marks the Laputans' devotion to theory and divorce from practical knowledge. We soon see how dismal are their efforts to apply theoretical principles to actual life, and their normal state is one of abstraction from the world, except when they are pursuing a program of political oppression. The wedding of music and mathematics goes back to Pythagorean doctrines, which construe the cosmos in terms of musical relationships (as in the music of the spheres). These doctrines continued to affect speculative thought well beyond the Renaissance; but increasingly, with the growth of modern science, they were relegated to "occult" thinkers such as Swift ridiculed as "dark authors" in *A Tale of a Tub*. Swift is also mocking the court of George I; that monarch, with an imperfect command of the English language, gave artistic patronage to music while he neglected literature. "As for the reigning amusement of the town, 'tis entirely music," John Gay wrote Swift from London in 1723.
2. Touch.

bouncing his head against every post, and in the streets of jostling others or being jostled himself into the kennel.[3]

It was necessary to give the reader this information, without which he would be at the same loss with me, to understand the proceedings of these people as they conducted me up the stairs to the top of the island, and from thence to the royal palace. While we were ascending, they forgot several times what they were about and left me to myself, till their memories were again roused by their flappers; for they appeared altogether unmoved by the sight of my foreign habit and countenance and by the shouts of the vulgar, whose thoughts and minds were more disengaged.

At last we entered the palace and proceeded into the chamber of presence, where I saw the King seated on his throne, attended on each side by persons of prime quality. Before the throne was a large table filled with globes and spheres and mathematical instruments of all kinds. His Majesty took not the least notice of us, although our entrance were not without sufficient noise, by the concourse of all persons belonging to the court. But he was then deep in a problem, and we attended at least an hour before he could solve it. There stood by him, on each side, a young page with flaps in their hands; and when they saw he was at leisure, one of them gently struck his mouth and the other his right ear; at which he started like one awaked on the sudden, and, looking towards me and the company I was in, recollected the occasion of our coming, whereof he had been informed before. He spoke some words, whereupon immediately a young man with a flap came up to my side and flapped me gently on the right ear; but I made signs as well as I could that I had no occasion for such an instrument; which as I afterwards found gave his Majesty and the whole court a very mean opinion of my understanding. The King, as far as I could conjecture, asked me several questions, and I addressed myself to him in all the languages I had. When it was found that I could neither understand nor be understood, I was conducted by his order to an apartment in his palace (this prince being distinguished above all his predecessors for his hospitality to strangers), where two servants were appointed to attend me. My dinner was brought, and four persons of quality, whom I remembered to have seen very near the King's person, did me the honour to dine with me. We had two courses of three dishes each. In the first course there was a shoulder of mutton cut into an equilateral triangle, a piece of beef into a rhomboides, and a pudding into a cycloid.[4] The second course was two ducks trussed up into the form of fiddles, sausages and puddings resembling flutes and hautboys,[5] and a breast of veal in the shape of a harp. The servants cut our bread into cones, cylinders, parallelograms, and several other mathematical figures.

While we were at dinner I made bold to ask the names of several things in their language, and those noble persons, by the assistance of their flappers, delighted to give me answers, hoping to raise my admiration of their great abilities if I could be brought to converse with them. I was soon able to call for bread and drink or whatever else I wanted.

3. Gutter.
4. Cut into geometrical patterns, including a parallelogram (rhomboid) and circle (cycloid).
5. Oboes.

After dinner my company withdrew, and a person was sent to me by the King's order, attended by a flapper. He brought with him pen, ink, and paper, and three or four books, giving me to understand by signs that he was sent to teach me the language. We sat together four hours, in which time I wrote down a great number of words in columns, with the translations over against them. I likewise made a shift to learn several short sentences. For my tutor would order one of my servants to fetch something, to turn about, to make a bow, to sit or stand or walk and the like. Then I took down the sentence in writing. He showed me also in one of his books the figures of the sun, moon, and stars, the zodiac, the tropics,[6] and polar circles, together with the denominations of many figures of planes and solids. He gave me the names and descriptions of all the musical instruments, and the general terms of art[7] in playing on each of them. After he had left me, I placed all my words with their interpretations in alphabetical order. And thus in a few days, by the help of a very faithful memory, I got some insight into their language.

The word which I interpret the *Flying* or *Floating Island* is in the original *Laputa,* whereof I could never learn the true etymology. *Lap* in the old obsolete language signifieth *high,* and *untuh* a *governor,* from which they say by corruption was derived *Laputa,* from *Lapuntuh.* But I do not approve of this derivation, which seems to be a little strained. I ventured to offer to the learned among them a conjecture of my own, that *Laputa* was *quasi*[8] *Lap outed; Lap* signifying properly the dancing of the sunbeams in the sea, and *outed* a wing, which however I shall not obtrude but submit to the judicious reader.

Those to whom the King had entrusted me, observing how ill I was clad, ordered a tailor to come next morning and take my measure for a suit of clothes. This operator did his office after a different manner from those of his trade in Europe. He first took my altitude by a quadrant, and then with rule and compasses described the dimensions and outlines of my whole body, all which he entered upon paper, and in six days brought my clothes very ill made and quite out of shape, by happening to mistake a figure in the calculation.[9] But my comfort was that I observed such accidents very frequent and little regarded.

During my confinement for want of clothes, and by an indisposition that held me some days longer, I much enlarged my dictionary; and when I went next to court was able to understand many things the King spoke and to return him some kind of answers. His Majesty had given orders that the island should move northeast and by east, to the vertical point over Lagado, the metropolis of the whole kingdom below upon the firm earth. It was about ninety leagues distant, and our voyage lasted four days and a half. I was not in the least sensible of the progressive motion made in the air by the island. On the second

6. That is, of Cancer and Capricorn.
7. Technical terms.
8. Seemingly. The paragraph is a parody of strained, pedantic, and often pseudo-scientific philology. Modern students have sometimes suggested Swift's source of the term to be *la puta,* Spanish for "the whore" and one way of regarding a "high governor."
9. The Lilliputians have shown similar ingenuity (I.vi) but far greater competence. In this world of theory, practical errors are magnified—as when a printer mistakenly added an extra zero to Newton's estimate of the distance of the sun from the earth.

morning about eleven o'clock the King himself in person, attended by his nobility, courtiers, and officers, having prepared all their musical instruments, played on them for three hours without intermission, so that I was quite stunned with the noise; neither could I possibly guess the meaning till my tutor informed me. He said that the people of their island had their ears adapted to hear the music of the spheres,[10] which always played at certain periods, and the court was now prepared to bear their part in whatever instrument they most excelled.

In our journey towards Lagado, the capital city, his Majesty ordered that the island should stop over certain towns and villages, from whence he might receive the petitions of his subjects. And to this purpose several packthreads were let down with small weights at the bottom. On these packthreads the people strung their petitions, which mounted up directly like the scraps of paper fastened by schoolboys at the end of the string that holds their kite. Sometimes we received wine and victuals from below, which were drawn up by pulleys.

The knowledge I had in mathematics gave me great assistance in acquiring their phraseology, which depended much upon that science and music; and in the latter I was not unskilled. Their ideas are perpetually conversant in lines and figures. If they would, for example, praise the beauty of a woman or any other animal, they describe it by rhombs, circles, parallelograms, ellipses, and other geometrical terms, or else by words of art drawn from music, needless here to repeat. I observed in the King's kitchen all sorts of mathematical and musical instruments, after the figures of which they cut up the joints that were served to his Majesty's table.

Their houses are very ill built, the walls bevil,[11] without one right angle in any apartment; and this defect ariseth from the contempt they bear for practical geometry, which they despise as vulgar and mechanic; those instructions they give being too refined for the intellectuals of their workmen, which occasions perpetual mistakes. And although they are dextrous enough upon a piece of paper in the management of the rule, the pencil, and the divider, yet in the common actions and behaviour of life I have not seen a more clumsy, awkward, and unhandy people, nor so slow and perplexed in their conceptions upon all other subjects except those of mathematics and music. They are very bad reasoners and vehemently given to opposition, unless when they happen to be of the right opinion, which is seldom their case. Imagination, fancy, and invention they are wholly strangers to, nor have any words in their language by which those ideas can be expressed; the whole compass of their thoughts and mind being shut up within the two forementioned sciences.

Most of them, and especially those who deal in the astronomical part, have great faith in judicial astrology,[12] although they are ashamed to own it publicly. But what I chiefly admired, and thought altogether unaccountable, was the strong disposition I observed in them towards news and politics, perpetually enquiring into public affairs, giving their judgments in matters of

10. See Glossary (*Music of the Spheres*) and John Dryden's *A Song for St. Cecilia's Day, 1687*, and notes.
11. Crooked, leaning at an angle.
12. The study of the influence of the stars on human affairs, as opposed to "natural astrology," which foretold natural phenomena such as tides and eclipses.

state, and passionately disputing every inch of a party opinion. I have indeed observed the same disposition among most of the mathematicians I have known in Europe, although I could never discover the least analogy between the two sciences; unless those people suppose that, because the smallest circle hath as many degrees as the largest, therefore the regulation and management of the world require no more abilities than the handling and turning of a globe. But I rather take this quality to spring from a very common infirmity of human nature, inclining us to be more curious and conceited in matters where we have least concern and for which we are least adapted either by study or nature.

These people are under continual disquietudes, never enjoying a minute's peace of mind; and their disturbances proceed from causes which very little affect the rest of mortals. Their apprehensions arise from several changes they dread in the celestial bodies. For instance, that the earth, by the continual approaches of the sun towards it, must in course of time be absorbed or swallowed up.[13] That the face of the sun will by degrees be encrusted with its own effluvia and give no more light to the world. That the earth very narrowly escaped a brush from the tail of the last comet, which would have infallibly reduced it to ashes; and that the next, which they have calculated for one and thirty years hence, will probably destroy us. For, if in its perihelion it should approach within a certain degree of the sun (as by their calculations they have reason to dread), it will conceive a degree of heat ten thousand times more intense than that of red-hot glowing iron; and in its absence from the sun carry a blazing tail ten hundred thousand and fourteen miles long; through which if the earth should pass at the distance of one hundred thousand miles from the nucleus or main body of the comet, it must in its passage be set on fire and reduced to ashes. That the sun, daily spending its rays without any nutriment to supply them, will at last be wholly consumed and annihilated; which must be attended with the destruction of this earth and of all the planets that receive their light from it.

They are so perpetually alarmed with the apprehensions of these and the like impending dangers that they can neither sleep quietly in their beds nor have any relish for the common pleasures or amusements of life. When they meet an acquaintance in the morning the first question is about the sun's health, how he looked at his setting and rising, and what hopes they have to avoid the stroke of the approaching comet. This conversation they are apt to run into with the same temper that boys discover in delighting to hear terrible stories of sprites and hobgoblins, which they greedily listen to and dare not go to bed for fear.

The women of the island have abundance of vivacity; they contemn their

13. Such cosmic catastrophes were an inevitable subject of speculation among such astronomers as Edmund Halley (1656–1742) and Sir Isaac Newton (1642–1727). Newton foresaw at least the theoretical possibility of the earth's being drawn into the sun, and Descartes had earlier made the encrustation of the sun (of which sun spots were taken as a symptom) an important part of his theory of vortices. Halley's comet of 1682 had awakened new fears, and in 1724 Halley himself read a paper on the Biblical flood of Noah's time in which he explored the question of how violent a disruption might be caused on earth by collision with a comet. Swift is, of course, making much of the way in which novel scientific theories can, as in some modern science fiction, awaken or reinforce primitive fear and superstition.

husbands and are exceedingly fond of strangers, whereof there is always a considerable number from the continent below attending at court, either upon affairs of the several towns and corporations or their own particular occasions, but are much despised, because they want the same endowments. Among these the ladies choose their gallants: but the vexation is that they act with too much ease and security, for the husband is always so wrapped in speculation that the mistress and lover may proceed to the greatest familiarities before his face, if he be but provided with paper and implements and without his flapper at his side.

The wives and daughters lament their confinement to the island, although I think it the most delicious spot of ground in the world; and, although they live here in the greatest plenty and magnificence and are allowed to do whatever they please, they long to see the world and take the diversions of the metropolis, which they are not allowed to do without a particular licence from the King; and this is not easy to be obtained because the people of quality have found by frequent experience how hard it is to persuade their women to return from below. I was told that a great court lady, who had several children, is married to the Prime Minister, the richest subject in the kingdom, a very graceful person extremely fond of her, and lives in the finest palace of the island, went down to Lagado on the pretence of health, there hid herself for several months, till the King sent a warrant to search for her; and she was found in an obscure eating house all in rags, having pawned her clothes to maintain an old deformed footman, who beat her every day, and in whose company she was taken much against her will. And although her husband received her with all possible kindness and without the least reproach, she soon after contrived to steal down again with all her jewels to the same gallant, and hath not been heard of since.

This may perhaps pass with the reader rather for an European or English story than for one of a country so remote. But he may please to consider that the caprices of womankind are not limited by any climate or nation and that they are much more uniform than can be easily imagined.

In about a month's time I had made a tolerably proficiency in their language and was able to answer most of the King's questions when I had the honour to attend him. His Majesty discovered not the least curiosity to enquire into the laws, government, history, religion, or manners of the countries where I had been, but confined his questions to the state of mathematics, and received the account I gave him with great contempt and indifference, though often roused by his flapper on each side.

Chapter Three: A phenomenon solved by modern philosophy and astronomy. The Laputans' great improvements in the latter. The King's method of suppressing insurrections.

I desired leave of this prince to see the curiosities of the island, which he was graciously pleased to grant, and ordered my tutor to attend me. I chiefly wanted to know to what cause in art or in nature it owed its several motions, whereof I will now give a philosophical account to the reader.[1]

1. In the following paragraphs Swift creates a dense parody of the technical idiom and detailed precision of scientific papers published in the *Transactions of the Royal Society*.

The Flying or Floating Island is exactly circular, its diameter 7,837 yards, or about four miles and an half, and consequently contains ten thousand acres. It is three hundred yards thick. The bottom or under surface, which appears to those who view it from below, is one even regular plate of adamant, shooting up to the height of about two hundred yards. Above it lie the several minerals in their usual order, and over all is a coat of rich mould ten or twelve foot deep. The declivity of the upper surface, from the circumference to the center, is the natural cause why all the dews and rains which fall upon the island are conveyed in small rivulets towards the middle, where they are emptied into four large basins, each of about half a mile in circuit and two hundred yards distant from the center. From these basins the water is continually exhaled by the sun in the daytime, which effectually prevents their overflowing. Besides, as it is in the power of the monarch to raise the island above the region of clouds and vapours, he can prevent the falling of dews and rains whenever he pleases. For the highest clouds cannot rise above two miles, as naturalists agree; at least they were never known to do so in that country.

At the center of the island there is a chasm about fifty yards in diameter, from whence the astronomers descend into a large dome, which is therefore Called *Flandona Gagnole,* or the *Astronomer's Cave,* situated at the depth of an hundred yards beneath the upper surface of the adamant. In this cave are twenty lamps continually burning, which from the reflection of the adamant cast a strong light into every part. The place is stored with great variety of sextants, quadrants, telescopes, astrolabes, and other astronomical instruments. But the greatest curiosity, upon which the fate of the island depends, is a lodestone of a prodigious size, in shape resembling a weaver's shuttle. It is in length six yards, and in the thickest part at least three yards over. This magnet is sustained by a very strong axle of adamant passing through its middle, upon which it plays, and is poised so exactly that the weakest hand can turn it. It is hooped round with an hollow cylinder of adamant, four foot deep, as many thick, and twelve yards in diameter, placed horizontally, and supported by eight adamantine feet, each six yards high. In the middle of the concave side there is a groove twelve inches deep, in which the extremities of the axle are lodged, and turned round as there is occasion.

This stone cannot be moved from its place by any force, because the hoop and its feet are one continued piece with that body of adamant which constitutes the bottom of the island.

By means of this lodestone the island is made to rise and fall and move from one place to another. For, with respect to that part of the earth over which the monarch presides, the stone is endued at one of its sides with an attractive power and at the other with a repulsive. Upon placing the magnet erect with its attracting end towards the earth, the island descends; but when the repelling extremity points downwards, the island mounts directly upwards. When the position of the stone is oblique, the motion of the island is so too. For in this magnet the forces always act in lines parallel to its direction.

By this oblique motion the island is conveyed to different parts of the monarch's dominions. To explain the manner of its progress, let *A B* represent a line drawn cross the dominions of Balnibarbi, let the line *c d* represent the lodestone, of which let *d* be the repelling end, and *c* the attracting end, the island being over *C;* let the stone be placed in the position *c d* with its repelling end downwards; then the island will be driven upwards obliquely towards *D*. When it is arrived at *D*, let the stone be turned upon its axle till its attracting end points towards *E*, and then the island will be carried obliquely towards *E;* where if the stone be again turned upon its axle till it stands in the position *E F*, with its repelling point downwards, the island will rise obliquely towards *F*, where by directing the attracting end towards *G*, the island may be carried to *G*, and from *G* to *H*, by turning the stone so as to make its repelling extremity point directly downwards. And thus by changing the situation of the stone as often as there is occasion, the island is made to rise and fall by turns in an oblique direction, and by those alternate risings and fallings (the obliquity being not considerable) is conveyed from one part of the dominions to the other.

But it must be observed that this island cannot move beyond the extent of the dominions below, nor can it rise above the height of four miles. For which the astronomers (who have written large systems concerning the stone) assign the following reason: that the magnetic virtue does not extend beyond the distance of four miles, and that the mineral which acts upon the stone in the bowels of the earth, and in the sea about six leagues distant from the shore, is not diffused through the whole globe, but terminated with the limits of the King's dominions; and it was easy, from the great advantage of such a superior situation, for a prince to bring under his obedience whatever country lay within the attraction of that magnet.

When the stone is put parallel to the plane of the horizon, the island standeth still; for in that case the extremities of it, being at equal distance from the earth, act with equal force, the one in drawing downwards, the other in pushing upwards, and consequently no motion can ensue.

This lodestone is under the care of certain astronomers, who from time to time give it such positions as the monarch directs. They spend the greatest part of their lives in observing the celestial bodies, which they do by the assistance of glasses far excelling ours in goodness. For although their largest telescopes do not exceed three feet, they magnify much more than those of an hundred yards among us, and at the same time show the stars with greater clearness. This advantage hath enabled them to extend their discoveries much farther than our astronomers in Europe. They have made a catalogue of ten thousand fixed stars, whereas the largest of ours do not contain above one third part of that number.[2] They have likewise discovered two lesser stars, or *satellites*, which revolve about Mars, whereof the innermost is distant from the center of the primary planet exactly three of his diameters, and the outermost five; the former revolves in the space of ten hours, and the latter in twenty-one and an half; so that the squares of their periodical times are very near in the same proportion with the cubes of their distance from the center of Mars, which evidently shows them to be governed by the same law of gravitation that influences the other heavenly bodies.[3]

They have observed ninety-three different comets, and settled their periods with great exactness. If this be true (and they affirm it with great confidence),

2. John Flamsteed's *British Catalogue of Stars*, 1725, included less than three thousand.
3. Two such satellites were first observed in 1877; Swift presumably gave Mars two moons on Kepler's principle that each planet should have twice as many moons as the one next closest to the sun.

it is much to be wished that their observations were made public, whereby the theory of comets, which at present is very lame and defective, might be brought to the same perfection with other parts of astronomy.[4]

The King would be the most absolute prince in the universe if he could but prevail on a ministry to join with him; but these, having their estates below on the continent and considering that the office of a favourite hath a very uncertain tenure, would never consent to the enslaving their country.

If any town should engage in rebellion or mutiny, fall into violent factions, or refuse to pay the usual tribute, the King hath two methods of reducing them to obedience. The first and the mildest course is by keeping the island hovering over such a town and the lands about it, whereby he can deprive them of the benefit of the sun and the rain and consequently afflict the inhabitants with dearth and diseases. And if the crime deserve it, they are at the same time pelted from above with great stones, against which they have no defence but by creeping into cellars or caves while the roofs of their houses are beaten to pieces. But if they still continue obstinate or offer to raise insurrections, he proceeds to the last remedy, by letting the island drop directly upon their heads, which makes a universal destruction both of houses and men. However, this is an extremity to which the prince is seldom driven; neither indeed is he willing to put it in execution, nor dare his ministers advise him to an action which, as it would render them odious to the people, so it would be a great damage to their own estates, that lie all below, for the island is the King's demesne.[5]

But there is still indeed a more weighty reason why the kings of this country have been always averse from executing so terrible an action, unless upon the utmost necessity. For if the town intended to be destroyed should have in it any tall rocks, as it generally falls out in the larger cities, a situation probably chosen at first with a view to prevent such a catastrophe, or if it abound in high spires or pillars of stone, a sudden fall might endanger the bottom or under surface of the island; which although it consist, as I have said, of one entire adamant two hundred yards thick, might happen to crack by too great a shock, or burst by approaching too near the fires from the houses below, as the backs both of iron and stone will often do in our chimneys. Of all this the people are well apprised, and understand how far to carry their obstinacy where their liberty or property is concerned. And the King, when he is highest provoked and most determined to press a city to rubbish, orders the island to descend with great gentleness, out of a pretence of tenderness to his people, but indeed for fear of breaking the adamantine bottom; in which case it is the opinion of all their philosophers that the lodestone could no longer hold it up, and the whole mass would fall to the ground.

4. Halley in 1704 calculated the orbits of 24 comets and was the first to make a successful prediction of a comet's return, confirmed when Halley's Comet reappeared in 1759.

5. The Flying Island with its adamantine bottom suggests the royal prerogative (those powers of the Crown unlimited by law) with which Swift had been concerned in *The Drapier's Letters* (1724–25). There Swift attacked a royal warrant to coin copper halfpence for Ireland that seemed to Swift a drain upon its gold and silver. Ireland was particularly victimized by absentee landlordism and (as we see in *A Modest Proposal*) by English commercial exploitation. The power of the Flying Island is limited only by the interest of those ministers whose landed wealth makes them concerned for the prosperity of the country below.

About three years before my arrival among them, while the King was in his progress over his dominions, there happened an extraordinary accident which had like to have put a period to the fate of that monarchy, at least as it is now instituted. Lindalino, the second city in the kingdom,[6] was the first his Majesty visited in his progress. Three days after his departure, the inhabitants, who had often complained of great oppressions, shut the town gates, seized on the governor, and with incredible speed and labour erected four large towers, one at every corner of the city (which is an exact square), equal in height to a strong pointed rock that stands directly in the center of the city. Upon the top of each tower, as well as upon the rock, they fixed a great lodestone; and in case their design should fail, they had provided a vast quantity of the most combustible fuel, hoping to burst therewith the adamantine bottom of the island if the lodestone project should miscarry.

It was eight months before the King had perfect notice that the Lindalinians were in rebellion. He then commanded that the island should be wafted over the city. The people were unanimous and had laid in store of provisions, and a great river runs through the middle of the town. The King hovered over them several days to deprive them of the sun and the rain. He ordered many packthreads to be let down, yet not a person offered to send up a petition, but instead thereof, very bold demands: the redress of all their grievances, great immunities, the choice of their own governor, and other the like exorbitances.[7] Upon which his Majesty commanded all the inhabitants of the island to cast great stones from the lower gallery into the town; but the citizens had provided against this mischief by conveying their persons and effects into the four towers, and other strong buildings, and vaults underground.

The King, being now determined to reduce this proud people, ordered that the island should descend gently within forty yards of the top of the towers and rock. This was accordingly done; but the officers employed in that work found the descent much speedier than usual, and by turning the lodestone could not without great difficulty keep it in a firm position, but found the island inclining to fall. They sent the King immediate intelligence of this astonishing event and begged his Majesty's permission to raise the island higher; the King consented, a general council was called, and the officers of the lodestone ordered to attend. One of the oldest and expertest among them obtained leave to try an experiment. He took a strong line of an hundred yards; and, the island being raised over the town above the attracting power they had felt, he fastened a piece of adamant to the end of his line which had in it a mixture of iron mineral, of the same nature with that whereof the bottom or lower surface of the island is composed, and from the lower gallery let it down slowly towards the top of the towers. The adamant was not descended four yards before the officer felt it drawn so strongly downwards, that he could hardly pull it back. He then threw down several small pieces of adamant and observed that they were all violently attracted by the top of the

6. Clearly a reference to Dublin, where Swift was Dean of St. Patrick's Cathedral.

7. Irish resistance to the copper halfpiece, led by Swift in his anonymous *Drapier's Letters*, caused a reward of £300 to be offered for identification of the author. Everyone knew that Swift was the Drapier, but no one claimed the reward; eventually the coinage was withdrawn.

tower. The same experiment was made on the other three towers and on the rock with the same effect.

This incident broke entirely the King's measures and (to dwell no longer on other circumstances) he was forced to give the town their own conditions.

I was assured by a great minister that, if the island had descended so near the town as not to be able to raise itself, the citizens were determined to fix it forever, to kill the King and all his servants, and entirely change the government.

By a fundamental law of this realm neither King nor either of his two elder sons are permitted to leave the island, nor the Queen till she is past child-bearing.[8]

Chapter Four: The author leaves Laputa, is conveyed to Balnibarbi, arrives at the metropolis. A description of the metropolis and the country adjoining. The author hospitably received by a great lord. His conversation with that lord.

Although I cannot say that I was ill treated in this island, yet I must confess I thought myself too much neglected, not without some degree of contempt. For neither prince nor people appeared to be curious in any part of knowledge, except mathematics and music, wherein I was far their inferior and upon that account very little regarded.

On the other side, after having seen all the curiosities of the island, I was very desirous to leave it, being heartily weary of those people. They were indeed excellent in two sciences for which I have great esteem and wherein I am not unversed, but at the same time so abstracted and involved in speculation that I never met with such disagreeable companions. I conversed only with women, tradesmen, flappers, and court-pages during two months of my abode there, by which at last I rendered myself extremely contemptible; yet these were the only people from whom I could ever receive a reasonable answer.

I had obtained by hard study a good degree of knowledge in their language; I was weary of being confined to an island where I received so little countenance, and resolved to leave it with the first opportunity.

There was a great lord at court, nearly related to the King, and for that reason alone used with respect. He was universally reckoned the most ignorant and stupid person among them. He had performed many eminent services for the crown, had great natural and acquired parts, adorned with integrity and honour, but so ill an ear for music that his detractors reported he had been often known to beat time in the wrong place; neither could his tutors without extreme difficulty teach him to demonstrate the most easy proposition in the mathematics. He was pleased to show me many marks of favour, often did me the honour of a visit, desired to be informed in the affairs of Europe, the laws and customs, the manners and learning of the several countries where I had

8. The Act of Settlement of 1701 forbade the King to leave England without the consent of Parliament. George I secured the repeal of this provision in 1716 and spent much time in his native Hanover thereafter. The danger to the Laputan royal family, however, lies more in domestic than in foreign travel.

travelled. He listened to me with great attention and made very wise observations on all I spoke. He had two flappers attending him for state, but never made use of them except at court and in visits of ceremony, and would always command them to withdraw when we were alone together.

I entreated this illustrious person to intercede in my behalf with his Majesty for leave to depart, which he accordingly did, as he was pleased to tell me, with regret: for indeed he had made me several offers very advantageous, which however I refused with expressions of the highest acknowledgement.

On the 16th day of February I took leave of his Majesty and the court. The King made me a present to the value of about two hundred pounds English, and my protector his kinsman as much more, together with a letter of recommendation to a friend of his in Lagado, the metropolis. The island being then hovering over a mountain about two miles from it, I was let down from the lowest gallery in the same manner as I had been taken up.

The continent, as far as it is subject to the monarch of the Flying Island, passes under the general name of Balnibarbi, and the metropolis, as I said before, is called Lagado. I felt some little satisfaction in finding myself on firm ground. I walked to the city without any concern, being clad like one of the natives and sufficiently instructed to converse with them. I soon found out the person's house to whom I was recommended, presented my letter from his friend, the grandee in the island, and was received with much kindness. This great lord, whose name was Munodi,[1] ordered me an apartment in his own house, where I continued during my stay, and was entertained in a most hospitable manner.

The next morning after my arrival he took me in his chariot to see the town, which is about half the bigness of London, but the houses very strangely built, and most of them out of repair. The people in the streets walked fast, looked wild, their eyes fixed, and were generally in rags. We passed through one of the town gates and went about three miles into the country, where I saw many labourers working with several sorts of tools in the ground, but was not able to conjecture what they were about; neither did I observe any expectation either of corn or grass, although the soil appeared to be excellent. I could not forbear admiring at these odd appearances both in town and country, and I made bold to desire my conductor that he would be pleased to explain to me what could be meant by so many busy heads, hands, and faces, both in the streets and the fields, because I did not discover any good effects they produced; but on the contrary, I never knew a soil so unhappily cultivated, houses so ill contrived and so ruinous, or a people whose countenance and habit expressed so much misery and want.

This Lord Munodi was a person of the first rank and had been some years Governor of Lagado, but by a cabal of ministers was discharged for insufficiency. However, the King treated him with tenderness, as a well-meaning man, but of a low contemptible understanding.[2]

1. From *mundum odi,* "I hate the world."

2. While the reference need not be to either, it is telling that Bolingbroke returned from exile to a rural life in 1723, and Robert Harley, the Earl of Oxford, Bolingbroke's fellow Tory minister, withdrew entirely from public life after charges of treason against him were dropped by the Whigs in 1717.

When I gave that free censure of the country and its inhabitants, he made no further answer than by telling me that I had not been long enough among them to form a judgment and that the different nations of the world had different customs, with other common topics to the same purpose. But when we returned to his palace, he asked me how I liked the building, what absurdities I observed, and what quarrel I had with the dress and looks of his domestics. This he might safely do, because everything about him was magnificent, regular, and polite. I answered that his Excellency's prudence, quality, and fortune had exempted him from those defects which folly and beggary had produced in others. He said if I would go with him to his country house, about twenty miles distant, where his estate lay, there would be more leisure for this kind of conversation. I told his Excellency that I was entirely at his disposal, and accordingly we set out next morning.

During our journey he made me observe the several methods used by farmers in managing their lands, which to me were wholly unaccountable, for, except in some very few places, I could not discover one ear of corn or blade of grass. But in three hours' travelling the scene was wholly altered; we came into a most beautiful country; farmers' houses at small distances, neatly built, the fields enclosed, containing vineyards, corn-grounds, and meadows. Neither do I remember to have seen a more delightful prospect. His Excellency observed my countenance to clear up; he told me with a sigh that there his estate began and would continue the same till we should come to his house. That his countrymen ridiculed and despised him for managing his affairs no better and for setting so ill an example to the kingdom, which however was followed by very few, such as were old and wilful, and weak like himself.

We came at length to the house, which was indeed a noble structure, built according to the best rules of ancient architecture. The fountains, gardens, walks, avenues, and groves were all disposed with exact judgment and taste. I gave due praises to everything I saw, whereof his Excellency took not the least notice till after supper, when, there being no third companion, he told me with a very melancholy air, that he doubted he must throw down his houses in town and country, to rebuild them after the present mode, destroy all his plantations, and cast others into such a form as modern usage required, and give the same directions to all his tenants, unless he would submit to incur the censure of pride, singularity, affectation, ignorance, caprice, and perhaps increase his Majesty's displeasure.

That the admiration I appeared to be under would cease or diminish when he had informed me of some particulars which probably I never heard of at court, the people there being too much taken up in their own speculations to have regard to what passed here below.

The sum of his discourse was to this effect. That about forty years ago, certain persons went up to Laputa either upon business or diversion, and after five months' continuance came back with a very little smattering in mathematics, but full of volatile spirits acquired in that airy region. That these persons upon their return began to dislike the management of everything below and fell into schemes of putting all arts, sciences, languages, and mechanics upon a new foot. To this end they procured a royal patent for erecting an

Academy of Projectors in Lagado;[3] and the humour prevailed so strongly among the people that there is not a town of any consequence in the kingdom without such an academy. In these colleges the professors contrive new rules and methods of agriculture and building, and new instruments and tools for all trades and manufactures; whereby, as they undertake, one man shall do the work of ten, a palace may be built in a week of materials so durable as to last forever without repairing. All the fruits of the earth shall come to maturity at whatever season we think fit to choose, and increase an hundred fold more than they do at present, with innumerable other happy proposals. The only inconvenience is that none of these projects are yet brought to perfection, and in the meantime the whole country lies miserably waste, the houses in ruins, and the people without food or clothes. By all which, instead of being discouraged, they are fifty times more violently bent upon prosecuting their schemes, driven equally on by hope and despair; that as for himself, being not of an enterprising spirit, he was content to go on in the old forms, to live in the houses his ancestors had built, and act as they did in every part of life without innovation. That some few other persons of quality and gentry had done the same but were looked on with an eye of contempt and ill will, as enemies to art, ignorant, and ill commonwealthsmen, preferring their own ease and sloth before the general improvement of their country.

His Lordship added that he would not be any further particulars prevent[4] the pleasure I should certainly take in viewing the Grand Academy, whither he was resolved I should go. He only desired me to observe a ruined building upon the side of a mountain about three miles distant, of which he gave me this account. That he had a very convenient mill within half a mile of his house, turned by a current from a large river, and sufficient for his own family as well as a great number of his tenants. That about seven years ago a club of those projectors came to him with proposals to destroy this mill and build another on the side of that mountain, on the long ridge whereof a long canal must be cut for a repository of water, to be conveyed up by pipes and engines to supply the mill: because the wind and air upon a height agitated the water and thereby made it fitter for motion, and because the water descending down a declivity would turn the mill with half the current of a river whose course is more upon a level. He said that, being then not very well with the court and pressed by many of his friends, he complied with the proposal; and after employing an hundred men for two years, the work miscarried, the projectors went off, laying the blame entirely upon him, railing at him ever since, and putting others upon the same experiment, with equal assurance of success, as well as equal disappointment.

In a few days we came back to town, and his Excellency, considering the

3. The Royal Society (of which the Academy is a satirical exaggeration) was given its charter by Charles II in 1662. Many of the experiments described here are only slight distortions of actual efforts by real "projectors" (that is, impractical or speculative thinkers, whether scientific or social). Here, as above, Swift draws freely upon the published *Transactions*. Just as he has earlier drawn a connection between the newest scientific theories and the most barbarous superstition, so here he suggests one between avowed empiricism and aggressive dogmatism.

4. Forestall.

bad character he had in the Academy, would not go with me himself, but recommended me to a friend of his to bear me company thither. My Lord was pleased to represent me as a great admirer of projects and a person of much curiosity and easy belief, which indeed was not without truth, for I had myself been a sort of projector in my younger days.

Chapter Five: The author permitted to see the Grand Academy of Lagado. The Academy largely described. The arts wherein the professors employ themselves.

This academy is not an entire single building but a continuation of several houses on both sides of a street, which, growing waste, was purchased and applied to that use.

I was received very kindly by the Warden and went for many days to the Academy. Every room hath in it one or more projectors, and I believe I could not be in fewer than five hundred rooms.

The first man I saw was of a meagre aspect, with sooty hands and face, his hair and beard long, ragged, and singed in several places. His clothes, shirt, and skin were all of the same colour. He had been eight years upon a project for extracting sunbeams out of cucumbers, which were to be put into vials hermetically sealed, and let out to warm the air in raw inclement summers. He told me he did not doubt in eight years more that he should be able to supply the Governor's gardens with sunshine at a reasonable rate; but he complained that his stock was low and entreated me to give him something as an encouragement to ingenuity, especially since this had been a very dear season for cucumbers. I made him a small present, for my Lord had furnished me with money on purpose, because he knew their practice of begging from all who go to see them.

I went into another chamber, but was ready to hasten back, being almost overcome with a horrible stink. My conductor pressed me forward, conjuring me in a whisper to give no offence, which would be highly resented, and therefore I durst not so much as stop my nose. The projector of this cell was the most ancient student of the Academy. His face and beard were of a pale yellow, his hands and clothes daubed over with filth. When I was presented to him, he gave me a very close embrace (a compliment I could well have excused). His employment from his first coming into the Academy was an operation to reduce human excrement to its original food, by separating the several parts, removing the tincture which it receives from the gall, making the odour exhale, and scumming off the saliva. He had a weekly allowance from the society of a vessel filled with human ordure, about the bigness of a Bristol barrel.

I saw another at work to calcine ice into gunpowder, who likewise showed me a treatise he had written concerning the malleability of fire, which he intended to publish.

There was a most ingenious architect who had contrived a new method for building houses, by beginning at the roof and working downwards to the foundation, which he justified to me by the like practice of those two prudent insects, the bee and the spider.

There was a man born blind, who had several apprentices in his own condition: their employment was to mix colours for painters, which their master taught them to distinguish by feeling and smelling. It was indeed my misfortune to find them at that time not very perfect in their lessons, and the professor himself happened to be generally mistaken. This artist is much encouraged and esteemed by the whole fraternity.

In another apartment I was highly pleased with a projector who had found a device of plowing the ground with hogs, to save the charges of plows, cattle, and labour. The method is this: in an acre of ground you bury, at six inches distance and eight deep, a quantity of acorns, dates, chestnuts, and other mast or vegetables whereof these animals are fondest: then you drive six hundred or more of them into the field, where in a few days they will root up the whole ground in search of their food, and make it fit for sowing, at the same time manuring it with their dung; it is true upon experiment they found the charge and trouble very great, and they had little or no crop. However, it is not doubted that this invention may be capable of great improvement.

I went into another room, where the walls and ceiling were all hung round with cobwebs, except a narrow passage for the artist to go in and out. At my entrance he called aloud to me not to disturb his webs. He lamented the fatal mistake the world had been so long in of using silkworms while we had such plenty of domestic insects who infinitely excelled the former, because they understood how to weave as well as spin. And he proposed farther that by employing spiders the charge of dyeing silks would be wholly saved, whereof I was fully convinced when he showed me a vast number of flies most beautifully coloured, wherewith he fed his spiders, assuring us that the webs would take a tincture from them; and as he had them of all hues, he hoped to fit everybody's fancy as soon as he could find proper food for the flies, of certain gums, oils, and other glutinous matter, to give a strength and consistence to the threads.

There was an astronomer who had undertaken to place a sundial upon the great weathercock on the town-house, by adjusting the annual and diurnal motions of the earth and sun, so as to answer and coincide with all accidental turnings by the wind.

I was complaining of a small fit of the colic, upon which my conductor led me into a room, where a great physician resided, who was famous for curing that disease by contrary operations from the same instrument. He had a large pair of bellows with a long slender muzzle of ivory. This he conveyed eight inches up the anus, and drawing in the wind, he affirmed he could make the guts as lank as a dried bladder. But when the disease was more stubborn and violent, he let in the muzzle while the bellows was full of wind, which he discharged into the body of the patient, then withdrew the instrument to replenish it, clapping his thumb strongly against the orifice of the fundament; and this being repeated three or four times, the adventitious wind would rush out, bringing the noxious along with it (like water put into a pump), and the patient recovers. I saw him try both experiments upon a dog, but could not discern any effect from the former. After the latter, the animal was ready to burst, and made so violent a discharge as was very offensive to me and my companions. The dog died on the spot, and we left the doctor endeavouring to recover him by the same operation.

I visited many other apartments, but shall not trouble my reader with all the curiosities I observed, being studious of brevity.

I had hitherto seen only one side of the Academy, the other being appropriated to the advancers of speculative learning, of whom I shall say something when I have mentioned one illustrious person more, who is called among them *the universal artist.* He told us he had been thirty years employing his thoughts for the improvement of human life. He had two large rooms full of wonderful curiosities and fifty men at work. Some were condensing air into a dry tangible substance by extracting the nitre and letting the aqueous or fluid particles percolate; others softening marble for pillows and pincushions; others petrifying the hoofs of a living horse to preserve them from foundering. The artist himself was at that time busy upon two great designs; the first, to sow land with chaff, wherein he affirmed the true seminal virtue to be contained, as he demonstrated by several experiments which I was not skilful enough to comprehend. The other was, by a certain composition of gums, minerals, and vegetables outwardly applied, to prevent the growth of wool upon two young lambs; and he hoped in a reasonable time to propagate the breed of naked sheep all over the kingdom.

We crossed a walk to the other part of the Academy, where, as I have already said, the projectors in speculative learning resided.

The first professor I saw was in a very large room, with forty pupils about him. After salutation, observing me to look earnestly upon a frame, which took up the greatest part of both the length and breadth of the room, he said perhaps I might wonder to see him employed in a project for improving speculative knowledge by practical and mechanical operations. But the world would soon be sensible of its usefulness, and he flattered himself that a more noble, exalted thought never sprang in any other man's head. Everyone knows how laborious the usual method is of attaining to arts and sciences; whereas by his contrivance the most ignorant person, at a reasonable charge, and with a little bodily labour, may write books in philosophy, poetry, politics, law, mathematics, and theology, without the least assistance from genius or study. He then led me to the frame, about the sides whereof all his pupils stood in ranks. It was twenty foot square, placed in the middle of the room. The superfices was composed of several bits of wood, about the bigness of a die, but some larger than others. They were all linked together by slender wires. These bits of wood were covered on every square [1] with paper pasted on them, and on these papers were written all the words of their language in their several moods, tenses, and declensions, but without any order. The professor then desired me to observe, for he was going to set his engine at work. The pupils at his command took each of them hold of an iron handle, whereof there were forty fixed round the edges of the frame, and, giving them a sudden turn, the whole disposition of the words was entirely changed. He then commanded six and thirty of the lads to read the several lines softly as they appeared upon the frame; and, where they found three or four words together that might make part of a sentence, they dictated to the four remaining boys who were scribes. This work was repeated three or four times, and at every turn the engine was

1. That is, every surface of the cubes.

so contrived that the words shifted into new places as the square bits of wood moved upside down.

Six hours a day the young students were employed in this labour, and the professor showed me several volumes in large folio, already collected, of broken sentences which he intended to piece together, and out of those rich materials to give the world a complete body of all arts and sciences; which however might be still improved, and much expedited, if the public would raise a fund for making and employing five hundred such frames in Lagado, and oblige the managers to contribute in common their several collections.

He assured me that this invention had employed all his thoughts from his youth, that he had emptied the whole vocabulary into his frame, and made the strictest computation of the general proportion there is in books between the numbers of particles, nouns, and verbs, and other parts of speech.

I made my humblest acknowledgements to this illustrious person for his great communicativeness and promised, if ever I had the good fortune to return to my native country, that I would do him justice as the sole inventor of this wonderful machine; the form and contrivance of which I desired leave to delineate upon paper . . . [drawing omitted in this text]. I told him, although it were the custom of our learned in Europe to steal inventions from each other, who had thereby at least this advantage, that it became a controversy which was the right owner, yet I would take such caution that he should have the honour entire without a rival.

We next went to the School of Languages, where three professors sat in consultation upon improving that of their own country.

The first project was to shorten discourse by cutting polysyllables into one, and leaving out verbs and participles, because in reality all things imaginable are but nouns.

The other was a scheme for entirely abolishing all words whatsoever; and this was urged as a great advantage in point of health as well as brevity. For it is plain that every word we speak is in some degree a diminution of our lungs by corrosion and consequently contributes to the shortening of our lives. An expedient was therefore offered that, since words are only names for *things*, it would be more convenient for all men to carry about them such *things* as were necessary to express the particular business they are to discourse on.[2] And this invention would certainly have taken place, to the great ease as well as health of the subject, if the women, in conjunction with the vulgar and illiterate, had not threatened to raise a rebellion unless they might be allowed the liberty to speak with their tongues after the manner of their forefathers; such constant irreconcilable enemies to science are the common people. However, many of the most learned and wise adhere to the new scheme of expressing themselves by *things*, which hath only this inconvenience attending it, that if a man's business be very great and of various kinds, he must be obliged in proportion to carry a greater bundle of *things* upon his back, unless

2. Swift is mocking the Royal Society's interest in the reformation of language or in the creation of artificial languages that would avoid the vagueness and imprecision of ordinary speech. Thomas Sprat in his *History of the Royal Society* (1667) asked for a purified language in which men "delivered so many things, almost in an equal number of words." Swift has earlier shown a wholesome simplification of language in Brobdingnag (II.vii); here he mocks the extremes to which distrust of language could be carried.

he can afford one or two strong servants to attend him. I have often beheld two of those sages almost sinking under the weight of their packs, like pedlars among us; who when they met in the street would lay down their loads, open their sacks, and hold conversation for an hour together; then put up their implements, help each other to resume their burthens, and take their leave.

But for short conversations a man may carry implements in his pockets and under his arms, enough to supply him, and in his house he cannot be at a loss; therefore the room where company meet who practice this art is full of all *things* ready at hand requisite to furnish matter for this kind of artificial converse.

Another great advantage proposed by this invention was that it would serve as an universal language to be understood in all civilised nations, whose goods and utensils are generally of the same kind or nearly resembling, so that their uses might easily be comprehended. And thus ambassadors would be qualified to treat with foreign princes or ministers of state to whose tongues they were utter strangers.

I was at the Mathematical School, where the master taught his pupils after a method scarce imaginable to us in Europe. The proposition and demonstration were fairly written on a thin wafer, with ink composed of a cephalic tincture.[3] This the student was to swallow upon a fasting stomach, and for three days following eat nothing but bread and water. As the wafer digested, the tincture mounted to his brain, bearing the proposition along with it. But the success hath not hitherto been answerable, partly by some error in the *quantum* or composition, and partly by the perverseness of lads, to whom this bolus is so nauseous that they generally steal aside and discharge it upwards before it can operate; neither have they been yet persuaded to use so long an abstinence as the prescription requires.

Chapter Six: A further account of the Academy. The author proposes some improvements, which are honourably received.

In the School of Political Projectors I was but ill entertained, the professors appearing in my judgment wholly out of their senses, which is a scene that never fails to make me melancholy. These unhappy people were proposing schemes for persuading monarchs to choose favourites upon the score of their wisdom, capacity, and virtue; of teaching ministers to consult the public good; of rewarding merit, great abilities, and eminent services; of instructing princes to know their true interest by placing it on the same foundation with that of their people; of choosing for employments persons qualified to exercise them; with many other wild impossible chimeras that never entered before into the heart of man to conceive, and confirmed in me the old observation that there is nothing so extravagant and irrational which some philosophers have not maintained for truth.

But, however, I shall so far do justice to this part of the Academy as to acknowledge that all of them were not so visionary. There was a most in-

3. A solution of brain tissue which would seek its natural place in the body.

genious doctor who seemed to be perfectly versed in the whole nature and system of government. This illustrious person had very usefully employed his studies in finding out effectual remedies for all diseases and corruptions to which the several kinds of public administration are subject by the vices or infirmities of those who govern, as well as by the licentiousness of those who are to obey. For instance: whereas all writers and reasoners have agreed that there is a strict universal resemblance between the natural and the political body, can there be anything more evident, than that the health of both must be preserved, and the diseases cured, by the same prescriptions? It is allowed that senates and great councils are often troubled with redundant, ebullient, and other peccant humours,[1] with many diseases of the head and more of the heart; with strong convulsions, with grievous contractions of the nerves and sinews in both hands, but especially the right;[2] with spleen, flatus, vertigos, and deliriums; with scrofulous tumours full of foetid purulent matter; with sour frothy ructations, with canine [3] appetites and crudeness of digestion, besides many others needless to mention. This doctor therefore proposed, that upon the meeting of a senate certain physicians should attend at the three first days of their sitting, and, at the close of each day's debate, feel the pulses of every senator; after which, having maturely considered and consulted upon the nature of the several maladies and the methods of cure, they should on the fourth day return to the senate house, attended by their apothecaries stored with proper medicines and, before the members sat, administer to each of them lenitives, aperitives, abstersives, corrosives, restringents, palliatives, laxatives, cephalagics, icterics, apophlegmatics, acoustics,[4] as their several cases required; and according as these medicines should operate, repeat, alter, or omit them at the next meeting.

This project could not be of any great expense to the public and might, in my poor opinion, be of much use for the dispatch of business in those countries where senates have any share in the legislative power: beget unanimity, shorten debates, open a few mouths which are now closed, and close many more which are now open; curb the petulancy of the young and correct the positiveness of the old; rouse the stupid and damp the pert.

Again, because it is a general complaint that the favourites of princes are troubled with short and weak memories, the same doctor proposed that whoever attended a first minister, after having told his business with the utmost brevity and in the plainest words, should at his departure give the said minister a tweak by the nose or a kick in the belly, or tread on his corns, or lug him thrice by both ears, or run a pin into his breech, or pinch his arm black and blue, to prevent forgetfulness; and at every levee day repeat the same operation till the business were done or absolutely refused.

He likewise directed that every senator in the great council of a nation, after he had delivered his opinion and argued in the defence of it, should be obliged to give his vote directly contrary; because if that were done the result would infallibly terminate in the good of the public.

1. See Glossary for *Humors*.
2. Which grasps more securely.
3. Morbid, indiscriminate, voracious.
4. Medicines for soothing, awakening, cleansing, consuming, curbing, moderation, loosening, relieving headaches, curing jaundice, stirring to action, and improving hearing.

When parties in a state are violent, he offered a wonderful contrivance to reconcile them. The method is this. You take an hundred leaders of each party, you dispose them into couples of such whose heads are nearest of a size; then let two nice[5] operators saw off the occiput of each couple at the same time, in such a manner that the brain may be equally divided. Let the occiputs thus cut off be interchanged, applying each to the head of his opposite party-man. It seems indeed to be a work that requireth some exactness, but the professor assured us; that if it were dextrously performed the cure would be infallible. For he argued thus: that the two half brains, being left to debate the matter between themselves within the space of one skull, would soon come to a good understanding and produce that moderation as well as regularity of thinking so much to be wished for in the heads of those who imagine they came into the world only to watch and govern its motion: and as to the difference of brains in quantity or quality among those who are directors in faction, the doctor assured us from his own knowledge that it was a perfect trifle.

I heard a very warm debate between two professors about the most commodious and effectual ways and means of raising money without grieving the subject. The first affirmed the justest method would be to lay a certain tax upon vices and folly, and the sum fixed upon every man to be rated after the fairest manner by a jury of his neighbours. The second was of an opinion directly contrary, to tax those qualities of body and mind for which men chiefly value themselves, the rate to be more or less according to the degrees of excelling, the decision whereof should be left entirely to their own breast. The highest tax was upon men who are the greatest favourites of the other sex, and the assessments according to the number and natures of the favours they have received, for which they are allowed to be their own vouchers. Wit, valour, and politeness were likewise proposed to be largely taxed and collected in the same manner, by every person giving his own word for the quantum of what he possessed. But as to honour, justice, wisdom, and learning, they should not be taxed at all, because they are qualifications of so singular a kind that no man will either allow them in his neighbour or value them in himself.

The women were proposed to be taxed according to their beauty and skill in dressing, wherein they had the same privilege with the men to be determined by their own judgment. But constancy, chastity, good sense, and good nature were not rated, because they would not bear the charge of collecting.

To keep senators in the interest of the crown it was proposed that the members should raffle for employments, every man first taking an oath and giving security that he would vote for the court whether he won or no, after which the losers had in their turn the liberty of raffling upon the next vacancy. Thus hope and expectation would be kept alive, none would complain of broken promises, but impute their disappointments wholly to Fortune, whose shoulders are broader and stronger than those of a ministry.

Another professor showed me a large paper of instructions for discovering plots and conspiracies against the government. He advised great statesmen to examine into the diet of all suspected persons; their times of eating; upon which side they lay in bed; with which hand they wiped their posteriors; to take a strict view of their excrements, and from the colour, the odour, the

5. Deft, delicate.

taste, the consistence, the crudeness or maturity of digestion, form a judgment of their thoughts and designs. Because men are never so serious, thoughtful, and intent, as when they are at stool, which he found by frequent experiment: for in such conjunctures, when he used merely as a trial to consider which was the best way of murdering the King, his ordure would have a tincture of green, but quite different when he thought only of raising an insurrection or burning the metropolis.

The whole discourse was written with great acuteness, containing many observations both curious and useful for politicians, but, as I conceived, not altogether complete. This I ventured to tell the author and offered, if he pleased, to supply him with some additions. He received my proposition with more compliance than is usual among writers, especially those of the projecting species, professing he would be glad to receive farther information.

I told him that in the kingdom of Tribnia, by the natives called Langden,[6] where I had long sojourned, the bulk of the people consisted wholly of discoverers, witnesses, informers, accusers, prosecutors, evidences, swearers, together with their several subservient and subaltern instruments, all under the colours, the conduct, and pay of ministers and their deputies. The plots in that kingdom are usually the workmanship of those persons who desire to raise their own characters of profound politicians, to restore new vigour to a crazy[7] administration, to stifle or divert general discontents, to fill their coffers with forfeitures, and raise or sink the opinion of public credit, as either shall best answer their private advantage. It is first agreed and settled among them what suspected persons shall be accused of a plot; then effectual care is taken to secure all their letters and other papers, and put the owners in chains. These papers are delivered to a set of artists, very dextrous in finding out the mysterious meanings of words, syllables, and letters.[8] For instance, they can decipher a close-stool to signify a privy-council, a flock of geese a senate, a lame dog an invader, a codshead a ———, the plague a standing army, a buzzard a prime minister, the gout a high priest, a gibbet a secretary of state, a chamberpot a committee of grandees, a sieve a court lady, a broom a revolution, a mousetrap an employment, a bottomless pit the treasury, a sink a court, a cap and bells a favourite, a broken reed a court of justice, an empty tun a general, a running sore the administration.

When this method fails, they have two others more effectual, which the learned among them call acrostics and anagrams. First, they can decipher all initial letters into political meanings. Thus N shall signify a plot, B a regiment of horse, L a fleet at sea. Or, secondly, by transposing the letters of the alphabet in any suspected paper, they can lay open the deepest designs of a discontented party. So, for example, if I should say in a letter to a friend, "Our brother Tom has just got the piles," a man of skill in this art would discover how the same letters which compose that sentence may be analyzed into the

6. Anagrams for Britain and England.

7. Sick, rotten.

8. In the trial (1723) of Francis Atterbury, Bishop of Rochester and a friend of Swift and Pope, for treasonous support of the Jacobites, there were efforts to interpret passages in his letters that seemed to use codes and ciphers. Swift gives each of his arbitrary code words a secondary satiric aptness. For a "codshead" (that is, blockhead), the missing word may be "King."

following words: "Resist—a plot is brought home—The Tour."[9] And this is the anagrammatic method.

The professor made me great acknowledgments for communicating these observations and promised to make honourable mention of me in his treatise.

I saw nothing in this country that could invite me to a longer continuance and began to think of returning home to England.

Chapter Seven: The author leaves Lagado, arrives at Maldonada. No ship ready. He takes a short voyage to Glubbdubdrib. His reception by the Governor.

The continent of which this kingdom is a part extends itself, as I have reason to believe, eastward to that unknown tract of America, westward of California and north to the Pacific Ocean, which is not above an hundred and fifty miles from Lagado, where there is a good port and much commerce with the great island of Luggnagg, situated to the northwest about 29 degrees north latitude and 140 longtitude. This island of Luggnagg stands southeastwards of Japan about an hundred leagues distant. There is a strict alliance between the Japanese Emperor and the King of Luggnagg, which affords frequent opportunities of sailing from one island to the other. I determined therefore to direct my course this way in order to direct my return to Europe. I hired two mules with a guide to show me the way and carry my small baggage. I took leave of my noble protector, who had shown me so much favour, and made me a generous present at my departure.

My journey was without any accident or adventure worth relating. When I arrived at the port of Maldonada (for so it is called) there was no ship in the harbour bound for Luggnagg, nor like to be in some time. The town is about as large as Portsmouth.[1] I soon fell into some acquaintance and was very hospitably received. A gentleman of distinction said to me that, since the ships bound for Luggnagg could not be ready in less than a month, it might be no disagreeable amusement for me to take a trip to the little island of Glubbdubdrib, about five leagues off to the southwest. He offered himself and a friend to accompany me, and that I should be provided with a small convenient barque for the voyage.

Glubbdubdrib, as nearly as I can interpret the word, signifies The Island of Sorcerers or Magicians. It is about one third as large as the Isle of Wight,[2] and extremely fruitful: it is governed by the head of a certain tribe who are all magicians. This tribe marries only among each other, and the eldest in succes-

9. "M. La Tour" was a code-name for the Stuart heir, "James III," in correspondence of 1715–16. "Tour" as an English word would also rhyme in Swift's day with "tower," and the capture of the Tower of London was the first goal of the proposed Jacobite invasion of England. But, if Swift is creating plausible interpretations, he is also ridiculing a method that cannot fail to yield some results if carried on with enough industry and disregard for truth.

1. The great naval base on the south coast had grown enormously during the wars with Holland and France.

2. Therefore, with an area of 50 square miles.

sion is prince or governor. He hath a noble palace and a park of about three thousand acres, surrounded by a wall of hewn stone twenty foot high. In this park are several smaller enclosures for cattle, corn, and gardening.

The Governor and his family are served and attended by domestics of a kind somewhat unusual. By his skill in necromancy, he hath power of calling whom he pleaseth from the dead and commanding their service for twenty-four hours, but no longer; nor can he call the same persons up again in less than three months, except upon very extraordinary occasions.

When we arrived at the island, which was about eleven in the morning, one of the gentlemen who accompanied me went to the Governor and desired admittance for a stranger who came on purpose to have the honour of attending on his Highness. This was immediately granted, and we all three entered the gate of the palace between two rows of guards, armed and dressed after a very antic [3] manner, and something in their countenances that made my flesh creep with a horror I cannot express. We passed through several apartments between servants of the same sort, ranked on each side as before, till we came to the Chamber of Presence, where, after three profound obeisances and a few general questions, we were permitted to sit on three stools near the lowest step of his Highness's throne. He understood the language of Balnibarbi, although it were different from that of his island. He desired me to give him some account of my travels; and, to let me see that I should be treated without ceremony, he dismissed all his attendants with a turn of his finger, at which to my great astonishment they vanished in an instant, like visions in a dream when we awake on a sudden. I could not recover myself in some time, till the Governor assured me that I should receive no hurt; and, observing my two companions to be under no concern, who had been often entertained in the same manner, I began to take courage and relate to his Highess a short history of my several adventures, yet not without some hesitation, and frequently looking behind me to the place where I had seen those domestic spectres. I had the honour to dine with the Governor, where a new set of ghosts served up the meat and waited at table. I now observed myself to be less terrified than I had been in the morning. I stayed till sunset but humbly desired his Highness to excuse me for not accepting his invitation of lodging in the palace. My two friends and I lay at a private house in the town adjoining, which is the capital of this little island; and the next morning we returned to pay our duty to the Governor, as he was pleased to command us.

After this manner we continued in the island for ten days, most part of every day with the Governor and at night in our lodging. I soon grew so familiarized to the sight of spirits that after the third or fourth time they gave me no emotion at all; or if I had any apprehensions left, my curiosity prevailed over them. For his Highness the Governor ordered me to call up whatever persons I would choose to name, and in whatever numbers among all the dead from the beginning of the world to the present time, and command them to answer any questions I should think fit to ask; with this condition, that my questions must be confined within the compass of the times they lived in. And one thing I might depend upon, that they would certainly tell me truth, for lying was a talent of no use in the lower world.

3. Odd, grotesque.

I made my humble acknowledgments to his Highness for so great a favour. We were in a chamber, from whence there was a fair prospect into the park. And because my first inclination was to be entertained with scenes of pomp and magnificence, I desired to see Alexander the Great at the head of his army just after the battle of Arbela,[4] which upon a motion of the Governor's finger immediately appeared in a large field under the window where we stood. Alexander was called up into the room: it was with great difficulty that I understood his Greek, and had but little of my own. He assured me upon his honour that he was not poisoned, but died of a fever by excessive drinking.

Next I saw Hannibal passing the Alps, who told me he had not a drop of vinegar in his camp.[5]

I saw Caesar and Pompey at the head of their troops, just ready to engage.[6] I saw the former in his last great triumph. I desired that the Senate of Rome might appear before me in one large chamber, and a modern representative[7] in counter-view in another. The first seemed to be an assembly of heroes and demigods; the other a knot of pedlars, pickpockets, highwaymen, and bullies.

The Governor at my request gave the sign for Caesar and Brutus to advance towards us. I was struck with a profound veneration at the sight of Brutus and could easily discover the most consummate virtue, the greatest intrepidity and firmness of mind, the truest love of his country and general benevolence for mankind in every lineament of his countenance. I observed with much pleasure that these two persons were in good intelligence with each other, and Caesar freely confessed to me that the greatest actions of his own life were not equal by many degrees to the glory of taking it away. I had the honour to have much conversation with Brutus; and was told that his ancestor Junius, Socrates, Epaminondas, Cato the younger, Sir Thomas More, and himself were perpetually together: a sextumvirate to which all the ages of the world cannot add a seventh.[8]

It would be tedious to trouble the reader with relating what vast numbers of illustrious persons were called up to gratify that insatiable desire I had to see the world in every period of antiquity placed before me. I chiefly fed my eyes with beholding the destroyers of tyrants and usurpers and the restorers of liberty to oppressed and injured nations. But it is impossible to express the satisfaction I received in my own mind after such a manner as to make it a suitable entertainment to the reader.

4. Where Alexander finally defeated the Persian Emperor Darius in 331 B.C.

5. According to Livy, Hannibal softened rocks by heating them and pouring vinegar over them; he could then cut through them.

6. The Battle of Pharsalia, where Julius Caesar defeated Pompey in 48 B.C., four years before Caesar's death.

7. Representative assembly or legislature; for example, Parliament.

8. Lucius Junius Brutus avenged his sister Lucretia by helping drive the Tarquins from Rome, and later put his own sons to death for plotting the Tarquins' return. Marcus Junius Brutus, friend and assassin of Julius Caesar, killed himself in 42 B.C. Socrates was put to death for his teachings in 399 B.C. Epaminondas led Thebes against the domination of Sparta and died in the victory at Mantinea, 362 B.C. Cato the Younger, a Stoic moralist, fought against Julius Caesar and committed suicide after his defeat at Thapsus, 46 B.C. Sir Thomas More, now canonized, was beheaded by Henry VIII in 1535. Swift called More "a person of the greatest virtue this Kingdom ever produced."

Chapter Eight: A further account of Glubbdubdrib. Ancient and modern history corrected.

Having a desire to see those ancients who were most renowned for wit and learning, I set apart one day on purpose. I proposed that Homer and Aristotle might appear at the head of all their commentators; but these were so numerous that some hundreds were forced to attend in the court and outward rooms of the palace. I knew and could distinguish those two heroes at first sight, not only from the crowd, but from each other. Homer was the taller and comelier person of the two, walked very erect for one of his age, and his eyes were the most quick and piercing I ever beheld. Aristotle stooped much and made use of a staff. His visage was meagre, his hair lank and thin, and his voice hollow.[1] I soon discovered that both of them were perfect strangers to the rest of the company and had never seen or heard of them before. And I had a whisper from a ghost, who shall be nameless, that these commentators always kept in the most distant quarters from their principals in the lower world, through a consciousness of shame and guilt, because they had so horribly misrepresented the meaning of those authors to posterity. I introduced Didymus and Eustathius[2] to Homer and prevailed on him to treat them better than perhaps they deserved, for he soon found they wanted a genius to enter into the spirit of a poet. But Aristotle was out of all patience with the account I gave him of Scotus and Ramus,[3] as I presented them to him, and he asked them whether the rest of the tribe were as great dunces as themselves.

I then desired the Governor to call up Descartes and Gassendi,[4] with whom I prevailed to explain their systems to Aristotle. This great philosopher freely acknowledged his own mistakes in natural philosophy, because he proceeded in many things upon conjecture, as all men must do; and he found that Gassendi, who had made the doctrine of Epicurus as palatable as he could, and the *vortices* of Descartes, were equally exploded. He predicted the same fate to *attraction*, whereof the present learned are such zealous asserters. He said, that new systems of nature were but new fashions which would vary in every age; and even those who pretend to demonstrate them from mathematical principles would flourish but a short period of time and be out of vogue when that was determined.[5]

I spent five days in conversing with many others of the ancient learned. I saw most of the first Roman emperors. I prevailed on the Governor to call up

1. Just as Gulliver destroys the traditional legend of Homer's blindness, he disproves the accounts of Aristotle as bald, handsome, elegantly dressed, and with a tendency to lisp.
2. Homeric commentators of the first and twelfth centuries A.D.
3. Duns Scotus (d. 1308), a major Scholastic philosopher and commentator on Aristotle (also the source of the word "dunce"). Petrus Ramus, or Pierre de la Ramée (1515–72), sought to correct Aristotelian logic and rhetoric; he had great influence, especially among the Puritans.
4. René Descartes (1596–1650), French philosopher and mathematician, propounded the theory of vortices, or whirlpools of material particles, in order to explain the origin of motion in all parts of the universe. Pierre Gassendi (1592–1655), French philosopher, scientist, and mathematician, revived and adapted to modern use the atomism of the Greek philosopher Epicurus. Newton's theory of gravitation (*attraction*) was the current orthodoxy whose passing Aristotle foresees.
5. Concluded.

Eliogabalus's cooks [6] to dress us a dinner, but they could not show us much of their skill for want of materials. A helot of Agesilaus [7] made us a dish of Spartan broth, but I was not able to get down a second spoonful.

The two gentlemen who conducted me to the island were pressed by their affairs to return in three days, which I employed in seeing some of the modern dead who had made the greatest figure for two or three hundred years past in our own and other countries of Europe; and having been always a great admirer of old illustrious families, I desired the Governor would call up a dozen or two of kings, with their ancestors in order for eight or nine generations. But my disappointment was grievous and unexpected. For instead of a long train with royal diadems, I saw in one family two fiddlers, three spruce courtiers, and an Italian prelate. In another, a barber, an abbot, and two cardinals. I have too great a veneration for crowned heads to dwell any longer on so nice a subject. But as to counts, marquesses, dukes, earls, and the like, I was not so scrupulous. And I confess it was not without some pleasure that I found myself able to trace the particular features by which certain families are distinguished, up to their originals. I could plainly discover from whence one family derives a long chin, why a second hath abounded with knaves for two generations, and fools for two more; why a third happened to be crack-brained, and a fourth to be sharpers. Whence it came what Polydore Virgil says of a certain great house, *Nec vir fortis, nec femina casta*.[8] How cruelty, falsehood, and cowardice grew to be characteristics by which certain families are distinguished as much as by their coat of arms. Who first brought the pox [9] into a noble house, which hath lineally descended in scrofulous tumours to their posterity. Neither could I wonder at all this when I saw such an interruption of lineages by pages, lackeys, valets, coachmen, gamesters, fiddlers, players, captains, and pickpockets.

I was chiefly disgusted with modern history. For having strictly examined all the persons of greatest name in the courts of princes for an hundred years past, I found how the world had been misled by prostitute writers to ascribe the greatest exploits in war to cowards, the wisest counsel to fools, sincerity to flatterers, Roman virtue to betrayers of their country, piety to atheists, chastity to sodomites, truth to informers. How many innocent and excellent persons had been condemned to death or banishment by the practising of great ministers upon the corruption of judges and the malice of factions. How many villains had been exalted to the highest places of trust, power, dignity, and profit: how great a share in the motions and events of courts, councils, and senates might be challenged by bawds, whores, pimps, parasites, and buffoons: how low an opinion I had of human wisdom and integrity when I was truly informed of the springs and motives of great enterprises and revolutions in the world, and of the contemptible accidents to which they owed their success.

Here I discovered the roguery and ignorance of those who pretend to write *anecdotes*, or secret history, who send so many kings to their graves with a

6. Roman emperor of the third century, notorious both for his profligacy and for the splendor of his feasts and ceremonies.
7. King of Sparta, 4th century B.C.
8. "Neither a man of them brave, nor a woman chaste." Polydore Virgil (*c.* 1470–1555) was an Italian churchman who lived in England; in 1534 he published a *Historia Anglica*.
9. Syphilis.

cup of poison; will repeat the discourse between a prince and chief minister where no witness was by; unlock the thoughts and cabinets of ambassadors and secretaries of state, and have the perpetual misfortune to be mistaken. Here I discovered the true causes of many great events that have surprised the world: how a whore can govern the back-stairs, the back-stairs a council, and the council a senate. A general confessed in my presence that he got a victory purely by the force of cowardice and ill conduct; and an admiral that for want of proper intelligence he beat the enemy to whom he intended to betray the fleet. Three kings protested to me that in their whole reigns they did never once prefer any person of merit, unless by mistake or treachery of some minister in whom they confided; neither would they do it if they were to live again; and they showed, with great strength of reason, that the royal throne could not be supported without corruption, because that positive, confident, restive temper which virtue infused into man was a perpetual clog to public business.

I had the curiosity to inquire in a particular manner by what method great numbers had procured to themselves high titles of honour and prodigious estates; and I confined my enquiry to a very modern period: however, without grating upon present times, because I would be sure to give no offence even to foreigners (for I hope the reader need not be told that I do not in the least intend my own country in what I say upon this occasion), a great number of persons concerned were called up and, upon a very slight examination, discovered such a scene of infamy that I cannot reflect upon it without some seriousness. Perjury, oppression, subornation, fraud, pandarism, and the like infirmities were amongst the most excusable arts they had to mention, and for these I gave, as it was reasonable, due allowance. But when some confessed they owed their greatness and wealth to sodomy or incest, others to the prostituting of their own wives and daughters; others to the betraying their country or their prince; some to poisoning, more to the perverting of justice in order to destroy the innocent: I hope I may be pardoned if these discoveries inclined me a little to abate of that profound veneration which I am naturally apt to pay to persons of high rank, who ought to be treated with the utmost respect due to their sublime dignity by us their inferiors.

I had often read of some great services done to princes and states and desired to see the persons by whom those services were performed. Upon enquiry I was told that their names were to be found on no record, except a few of them whom history hath represented as the vilest rogues and traitors. As to the rest, I had never once heard of them. They all appeared with dejected looks and in the meanest habit, most of them telling me they died in poverty and disgrace, and the rest on a scaffold or a gibbet.

Among others there was one person whose case appeared a little singular. He had a youth about eighteen years old standing by his side. He told me he had for many years been commander of a ship, and in the sea fight at Actium [10] had the good fortune to break through the enemy's great line of battle, sink three of their capital ships, and take a fourth, which was the sole cause of Antony's flight and of the victory that ensued; that the youth standing by him,

10. Naval battle (31 B.C.) in which Antony and Cleopatra were defeated by Octavius Caesar, later Augustus.

his only son, was killed in the action. He added, that upon the confidence of some merit, the war being at an end, he went to Rome, and solicited at the court of Augustus to be preferred to a greater ship, whose commander had been killed; but without any regard to his pretensions, it was given to a boy who had never seen the sea, the son of a Libertina,[11] who waited on one of the Emperor's mistresses. Returning back to his own vessel, he was charged with neglect of duty, and the ship given to a favourite page of Publicola, the Vice-Admiral;[12] whereupon he retired to a poor farm at a great distance from Rome, and there ended his life. I was so curious to know the truth of this story that I desired Agrippa might be called, who was admiral in that fight.[13] He appeared and confirmed the whole account, but with much more advantage to the captain, whose modesty had extenuated or concealed a great part of his merit.

I was surprised to find corruption grown so high and so quick in that empire, by the force of luxury so lately introduced, which made me less wonder at many parallel cases in other countries, where vices of all kinds have reigned so much longer, and where the whole praise as well as pillage hath been engrossed by the chief commander, who perhaps had the least title to either.

As every person called up made exactly the same appearance he had done in the world, it gave me melancholy reflections to observe how much the race of human kind was degenerate among us within these hundred years past. How the pox under all its consequences and denominations had altered every lineament of an English countenance, shortened the size of bodies, unbraced the nerves, relaxed the sinews and muscles, introduced a sallow complexion, and rendered the flesh loose and rancid.

I descended so low as to desire that some English yeomen [14] of the old stamp might be summoned to appear, once so famous for the simplicity of their manners, diet, and dress; for justice in their dealings, for their true spirit of liberty, for their valour and love of their country. Neither could I be wholly unmoved after comparing the living with the dead, when I considered how all these pure native virtues were prostituted for a piece of money by their grandchildren, who, in selling their votes and managing at elections,[15] have acquired every vice and corruption that can possibly be learned in a court.

Chapter Nine: The author's return to Maldonada. Sails to the kingdom of Luggnagg. The author confined. He is sent for to court. The manner of his admittance. The King's great lenity to his subjects.

The day of our departure being come, I took leave of his Highness the Governor of Glubbdubdrib and returned with my two companions to Maldonada, where after a fortnight's waiting a ship was ready to sail for Luggnagg. The

11. Although a proper name, this suggests (1) a freedwoman; (2) a prostitute.
12. L. Gellius Publicola, commander of the right wing of Antony's fleet at Actium.
13. Marcus Vipsanius Agrippa (63–12 B.C.), the officer principally responsible for Octavius's victory at Actium.
14. Freeholders or independent farmers.
15. The control of votes through bribery or reward was common in 18th-century England and was systematically used by Walpole to maintain power.

two gentlemen and some others were so generous and kind as to furnish me with provisions and see me on board. I was a month in this voyage. We had one violent storm and were under a necessity of steering westward to get into the trade wind, which holds for above sixty leagues. On the 21st of April, 1708, we sailed in the river of Clumegnig, which is a seaport town at the southeast point of Luggnagg. We cast anchor within a league of the town and made a signal for a pilot. Two of them came on board in less than half an hour, by whom we were guided between certain shoals and rocks, which are very dangerous in the passage, to a large basin where a fleet may ride in safety within a cable's length of the town wall.

Some of our sailors, whether out of treachery or inadvertence, had informed the pilots that I was a stranger and a great traveller, whereof these gave notice to a custom-house officer, by whom I was examined very strictly upon my landing. This officer spoke to me in the language of Balnibarbi, which by the force of much commerce is generally understood in that town, especially by seamen and those employed in the customs. I gave him a short account of some particulars, and made my story as plausible and consistent as I could; but I thought it necessary to disguise my country and call myself a Hollander, because my intentions were for Japan, and I knew the Dutch were the only Europeans permitted to enter into that kingdom.[1] I therefore told the officer that, having been shipwrecked on the coast of Balnibarbi and cast on a rock, I was received up into Laputa, or the Flying Island (of which he had often heard), and was now endeavouring to get to Japan, from whence I might find a convenience of returning to my own country. The officer said I must be confined till he could receive orders from court, for which he would write immediately and hoped to receive an answer in a fortnight. I was carried to a convenient lodging with a sentry placed at the door; however I had the liberty of a large garden and was treated with humanity enough, being maintained all the time at the King's charge. I was visited by several persons, chiefly out of curiosity, because it was reported I came from countries very remote, of which they had never heard.

I hired a young man who came in the same ship to be an interpreter; he was a native of Luggnagg but had lived some years at Maldonada and was a perfect master of both languages. By his assistance I was able to hold a conversation with those that came to visit me; but this consisted only of their questions and my answers.

The dispatch came from court about the time we expected. It contained a warrant for conducting me and my retinue to Traldragdubb or Trildrogdrib, for it is pronounced both ways as near as I can remember, by a party of ten horse. All my retinue was that poor lad for an interpreter, whom I persuaded into my service. At my humble request we had each of us a mule to ride on. A messenger was dispatched half a day's journey before us to give the King notice of my approach and to desire that his Majesty would please to appoint a day and hour when it would be his gracious pleasure that I might have the honour to "lick the dust before his footstool." This is the court style, and I

1. After the suppression of the Christian revolt of 1638, the Japanese closed their country to European traders, except for the Dutch, who were rewarded for their bombardment of the Christian rebels by admission to the port of Nagasaki.

found it to be more than matter of form. For upon my admittance two days after my arrival, I was commanded to crawl upon my belly and lick the floor as I advanced; but on account of my being a stranger, care was taken to have it so clean that the dust was not offensive. However, this was a peculiar grace, not allowed to any but persons of the highest rank, when they desire an admittance. Nay, sometimes the floor is strewed with dust on purpose when the person to be admitted happens to have powerful enemies at court. And I have seen a great lord with his mouth so crammed that, when he had crept to the proper distance from the throne, he was not able to speak a word. Neither is there any remedy, because it is capital for those who receive an audience to spit or wipe their mouths in his Majesty's presence.

There is indeed another custom which I cannot altogether approve of. When the King hath a mind to put any of his nobles to death in a gentle indulgent manner, he commands to have the floor strowed with a certain brown powder of a deadly composition, which being licked up infallibly kills him in twenty-four hours. But in justice to this prince's great clemency and the care he hath of his subjects' lives (wherein it were much to be wished that the monarchs of Europe would imitate him), it must be mentioned for his honour that strict orders are given to have the infected parts of the floor well washed after every such execution, which, if his domestics neglect, they are in danger of incurring his royal displeasure. I myself heard him give directions that one of his pages should be whipped, whose turn it was to give notice about washing the floor after an execution but maliciously had omitted it, by which neglect a young lord of great hopes coming to an audience, was unfortunately poisoned, although the King at that time had no design against his life. But this good prince was so gracious as to forgive the page his whipping, upon promise that he would do so no more, without special orders.

To return from this digression: when I had crept within four yards of the throne, I raised myself gently upon my knees, and then striking my forehead seven times against the ground, I pronounced the following words, as they had been taught me the night before, *Ickpling Gloffthrobb Squutserumm blhiop Mlashnalt Zwin tnodbalkguffh Slhiophad Gurdlubh Asht*. This is the compliment established by the laws of the land for all persons admitted to the King's presence. It may be rendered into English thus: May your Celestial Majesty outlive the sun, eleven moons and an half. To this the King returned some answer, which although I could not understand, yet I replied as I had been directed: *Fluft drin Yalerick Dwuldum prastrad mirplush*, which properly signifies, "My tongue is in the mouth of my friend," and by this expression was meant that I desired leave to bring my interpreter; whereupon the young man already mentioned was accordingly introduced, by whose intervention I answered as many questions as his Majesty could put in above an hour. I spoke in the Balnibarbian tongue, and my interpreter delivered my meaning in that of Luggnagg.

The King was much delighted with my company, and ordered his *Bliffmarklub* or high chamberlain to appoint a lodging in the court for me and my interpreter, with a daily allowance for my table and a large purse of gold for my common expenses.

I stayed three months in this country out of perfect obedience to his Majesty, who was pleased highly to favour me and made me very honourable offers.

But I thought it more consistent with prudence and justice to pass the remainder of my days with my wife and family.

Chapter Ten: The Luggnaggians commended. A particular description of the Struldbruggs, with many conversations between the author and some eminent persons upon that subject.

The Luggnaggians are a polite and generous people, and although they are not without some share of that pride which is peculiar to all eastern countries, yet they show themselves courteous to strangers, especially such who are countenanced by the court. I had many acquaintance among persons of the best fashion, and, being always attended by my interpreter, the conversation we had was not disagreeable.

One day in much good company I was asked by a person of quality whether I had seen any of their *Struldbruggs* or *immortals*. I said I had not, and desired he would explain to me what he meant by such an appellation applied to a mortal creature. He told me, that sometimes, although very rarely, a child happened to be born in a family with a red circular spot in the forehead directly over the left eyebrow, which was an infallible mark that it should never die. The spot, as he described it, was about the compass of a silver threepence, but in the course of time grew larger and changed its colour; for at twelve years old it became green, so continued till five and twenty, then turned to a deep blue; at five and forty it grew coal black, and as large as an English shilling, but never admitted any farther alteration. He said these births were so rare that he did not believe there could be above eleven hundred *Struldbruggs* of both sexes in the whole kingdom, of which he computed about fifty in the metropolis, and among the rest a young girl born about three years ago. That these productions were not peculiar to any family but a mere effect of chance, and the children of the *Struldbruggs* themselves were equally mortal with the rest of the people.

I freely own myself to have been struck with inexpressible delight upon hearing this account: and the person who gave it me happening to understand the Balnibarbian language, which I spoke very well, I could not forbear breaking out into expressions perhaps a little too extravagant. I cried out as in a rapture: "Happy nation where every child hath at least a chance for being immortal! Happy people who enjoy so many living examples of ancient virtue and have masters ready to instruct them in the wisdom of all former ages! But happiest beyond all comparison are those excellent *Struldbruggs*, who, being born exempt from that universal calamity of human nature, have their minds free and disengaged, without the weight and depression of spirits caused by the continual apprehension of death."

I discovered my admiration that I had not observed any of these illustrious persons at court, the black spot on the forehead being so remarkable a distinction that I could not have easily overlooked it, and it was impossible that his Majesty, a most judicious prince, should not provide himself with a good number of such wise and able counsellors. Yet perhaps the virtue of those reverend sages was too strict for the corrupt and libertine manners of a court. And we often find by experience that young men are too opinionative and volatile to be guided by the sober dictates of their seniors. However, since the King was pleased to allow me access to his royal person, I was resolved upon the very first occasion to deliver my opinion to him on this matter freely and at large by the help of my interpreter; and, whether he would please to take my advice or no, yet in one thing I was determined, that his Majesty having frequently offered me an establishment in this country, I would with great thankfulness accept the favour, and pass my life here in the conversation of those superior beings the *Struldbruggs*, if they would please to admit me.

The gentleman to whom I addressed my discourse, because (as I have already observed) he spoke the language of Balnibarbi, said to me with a sort of smile, which usually ariseth from pity to the ignorant, that he was glad of any occasion to keep me among them, and desired my permission to explain to the company what I had spoke. He did so, and they talked together for some time in their own language, whereof I understood not a syllable; neither could I observe by their countenances what impression my discourse had made on them. After a short silence the same person told me that his friends and mine (so he thought fit to express himself) were very much pleased with the judicious remarks I had made on the great happiness and advantages of immortal life, and they were desirous to know in a particular manner what scheme of living I should have formed to myself if it had fallen to my lot to have been born a *Struldbrugg*.

I answered it was easy to be eloquent on so copious and delightful a subject, especially to me who have been often apt to amuse myself with visions of what I should do if I were a king, a general, or a great lord; and upon this very case I had frequently run over the whole system how I should employ myself and pass the time if I were sure to live forever.

That if it had been my good fortune to come into the world a *Struldbrugg*, as soon as I could discover my own happiness by understanding the difference between life and death, I would first resolve by all arts and methods whatsoever to procure myself riches. In the pursuit of which by thrift and management, I might reasonably expect in about two hundred years to be the wealthiest man in the kingdom. In the second place, I would from my earliest youth apply myself to the study of arts and sciences, by which I should arrive in time to excel all others in learning. Lastly, I would carefully record every action and event of consequence that happened in the public, impartially draw the characters of the several successions of princes and great ministers of state, with my own observations on every point. I would exactly set down the several changes in customs, language, fashion of dress, diet, and diversions. By all which acquirements, I should be a living treasury of knowledge and wisdom, and certainly become the oracle of the nation.

I would never marry after threescore, but live in an hospitable manner, yet still on the saving side. I would entertain myself in forming and directing the minds of hopeful young men, by convincing them from my own remembrance, experience, and observation, fortified by numerous examples, of the usefulness of virtue in public and private life. But my choice and constant companions should be a set of my own immortal brotherhood, among whom I would elect a dozen from the most ancient down to my own contemporaries. Where any of these wanted fortunes, I would provide them with convenient lodges round my own estate and have some of them always at my table, only mingling a few of the most valuable among you mortals, whom length of time would harden me to lose with little or no reluctance, and treat your posterity after the same manner, just as a man diverts himself with the annual succession of pinks and tulips in his garden, without regretting the loss of those which withered the preceding year.

These *Struldbruggs* and I would mutually communicate our observations and memorials through the course of time, remark the several gradations by which corruption steals into the world, and oppose it in every step by giving perpetual warning and instruction to mankind; which, added to the strong influence of our own example, would probably prevent that continual degeneracy of human nature so justly complained of in all ages.

Add to all this, the pleasure of seeing the various revolutions of states and empires, the changes in the lower and upper world, ancient cities in ruins, and obscure villages become the seats of kings. Famous rivers lessening into shallow brooks; the ocean leaving one coast dry and overwhelming another; the discovery of many countries yet unknown. Barbarity overrunning the politest nations, and the most barbarous becoming civilized. I should then see the discovery of the longitude,[1] the perpetual motion, the universal medicine, and many other great inventions brought to the utmost perfection.

What wonderful discoveries should we make in astronomy, by outliving and confirming our own predictions, by observing the progress and returns of comets, with the changes of motion in the sun, moon, and stars.

I enlarged upon many other topics which the natural desire of endless life and sublunary [2] happiness could easily furnish me with. When I had ended, and the sum of my discourse had been interpreted as before to the rest of the company, there was a good deal of talk among them in the language of the country, not without some laughter at my expense. At last the same gentleman who had been my interpreter said, he was desired by the rest to set me right in a few mistakes, which I had fallen into through the common imbecility [3] of human nature, and upon that allowance was less answerable for them. That this breed of *Struldbruggs* was peculiar to their country, for there were no such people either in Balnibarbi or Japan, where he had the honour to be ambassadour from his Majesty, and found the natives in both those kingdoms very hard to believe that the fact was possible; and it appeared from my astonishment when he first mentioned the matter to me that I received it as a thing wholly new and scarcely to be credited. That in the two kingdoms above mentioned, where during his residence he had conversed very much, he observed long life to be the universal desire and wish of mankind. That whoever had one foot in the grave was sure to hold back the other as strongly as he could. That the oldest had still hopes of living one day longer and

1. Prizes had been offered for more than a century to anyone who could find a way of determining the longitude at sea; in 1714 Parliament established a reward of £20,000. The Greenwich Observatory was founded in 1674 to aid navigation by providing lunar tables; but the invention of the sextant and the chronometer in the 1730s met the difficulty. Swift considered the quest as futile as the old alchemical search for the philosopher's stone or the pursuit of other panaceas for human ills.

2. Traditionally, whatever existed below the sphere of the moon was subject to change and decay.

3. Weakness.

looked on death as the greatest evil, from which nature always prompted him to retreat; only in this island of Luggnagg the appetite for living was not so eager, from the continual example of the *Struldbruggs* before their eyes.

That the system of living contrived by me was unreasonable and unjust because it supposed a perpetuity of youth, health, and vigour, which no man could be so foolish to hope, however extravagant he might be in his wishes. That the question therefore was not whether a man would choose to be always in the prime of youth, attended with prosperity and health, but how he would pass a perpetual life under all the usual disadvantages which old age brings along with it. For although few men will avow their desires of being immortal upon such hard conditions, yet in the two kingdoms before-mentioned of Balnibarbi and Japan he observed that every man desired to put off death for some time longer, let it approach ever so late, and he rarely heard of any man who died willingly, except he were incited by the extremity of grief or torture. And he appealed to me whether in those countries I had travelled, as well as my own, I had not observed the same general disposition.

After this preface he gave me a particular account of the *Struldbruggs* among them. He said they commonly acted like mortals till about thirty years old, after which by degrees they grew melancholy and dejected, increasing in both till they came to fourscore. This he learned from their own confession; for otherwise there not being above two or three of that species born in an age, they were too few to form a general observation by. When they came to fourscore years, which is reckoned the extremity of living in this country, they had not only all the follies and infirmities of other old men, but many more which arose from the dreadful prospect of never dying. They were not only opinionative, peevish, covetous, morose, vain, talkative, but uncapable of friendship and dead to all natural affection, which never descended below their grandchildren. Envy and impotent desires are their prevailing passions. But those objects against which their envy seems principally directed are the vices of the younger sort and the deaths of the old. By reflecting on the former, they find themselves cut off from all possibility of pleasure; and, whenever they see a funeral, they lament and repine that others are gone to an harbour of rest to which they themselves never can hope to arrive. They have no remembrance of anything but what they learned and observed in their youth and middle age, and even that is very imperfect. And for the truth or particulars of any fact, it is safer to depend on common traditions than upon their best recollections. The least miserable among them appear to be those who turn to dotage and entirely lose their memories; these meet with more pity and assistance, because they want many bad qualities which abound in others.

If a *Struldbrugg* happen to marry one of his own kind, the marriage is dissolved of course by the courtesy of the kingdom, as soon as the younger of the two comes to be fourscore. For the law thinks it a reasonable indulgence that those who are condemned without any fault of their own to a perpetual continuance in the world should not have their misery doubled by the load of a wife.

As soon as they have completed the term of eighty years, they are looked on as dead in law; their heirs immediately succeed to their estates, only a small pittance is reserved for their support, and the poor ones are maintained at the public charge. After that period they are held incapable of any employment of trust or profit; they cannot purchase lands or take leases, neither are they allowed to be witnesses in any cause, either civil or criminal, not even for the decision of meres and bounds.

At ninety they lose their teeth and hair; they have at that age no distinction of taste, but eat and drink whatever they can get, without relish or appetite. The diseases they were subject to still continue without encreasing or diminishing. In talking they forget the common appellation of things and the names of persons, even of those who are their nearest friends and relations. For the same reason they never can amuse themselves with reading, because their memory will not serve to carry them from the beginning of a sentence to the end; and by this defect they are deprived of the only entertainment whereof they might otherwise be capable.

The language of this country being always upon the flux, the *Struldbruggs* of one age do not understand those of another, neither are they able after two hundred years to hold any conversation (farther than by a few general words) with their neighbours the mortals, and thus they lie under the disadvantage of living like foreigners in their own country.

This was the account given me of the *Struldbruggs,* as near as I can remember. I afterwards saw five or six of different ages, the youngest not above two hundred years old, who were brought to me at several times by some of my friends; but although they were told that I was a great traveller and had seen all the world, they had not the least curiosity to ask me a question; only desired I would give them *slumskudask,* or a token of remembrance, which is a modest way of begging, to avoid the law that strictly forbids it, because they are provided for by the public, although indeed with a very scanty allowance.

They are despised and hated by all sorts of people; when one of them is born, it is reckoned ominous, and their birth is recorded very particularly; so that you may know their age by consulting the registry, which however hath not been kept above a thousand years past, or at least hath been destroyed by time or public disturbances. But the usual way of computing how old they are is by asking them what kings or great persons they can remember, and then consulting history, for infallibly the last prince in their mind did not begin his reign after they were fourscore years old.

They were the most mortifying sight I ever beheld, and the women more horrible than the men. Besides the usual deformities in extreme old age, they acquired an additional ghastliness in proportion to their number of years, which is not to be described; and among half a dozen I soon distinguished which was the eldest, although there was not above a century or two between them.

The reader will easily believe that from what I had heard and seen my keen appetite for perpetuity of life was much abated. I grew heartily ashamed of the pleasing visions I had formed and thought no tyrant could invent a death into which I would not run with pleasure from such a life. The King heard of all that had passed between me and my friends upon this occasion, and rallied me very pleasantly, wishing I would send a couple of *Struldbruggs* to my own country to arm our people against the fear of death; but this it seems is forbidden by the fundamental laws of the kingdom, or else I should have been well content with the trouble and expense of transporting them.

I could not but agree that the laws of this kingdom, relating to the *Struld-*

bruggs, were founded upon the strongest reasons, and such as any other country would be under the necessity of enacting in the like circumstances. Otherwise, as avarice is the necessary consequent of old age, those immortals would in time become proprietors of the whole nation and engross the civil power, which, for want of abilities to manage, must end in the ruin of the public.

Chapter Eleven: The author leaves Luggnagg, and sails to Japan. From thence he returns in a Dutch ship to Amsterdam, and from Amsterdam to England.

I thought this account of the *Struldbruggs* might be some entertainment to the reader, because it seems to be a little out of the common way; at least, I do not remember to have met the like in any book of travels that hath come to my hands: and if I am deceived, my excuse must be that it is necessary for travellers who describe the same country very often to agree in dwelling on the same particulars, without deserving the censure of having borrowed or transcribed from those who wrote before them.

There is indeed a perpetual commerce between this kingdom and the great empire of Japan, and it is very probable that the Japanese authors may have given some account of the *Struldbruggs;* but my stay in Japan was so short, and I was so entirely a stranger to the language, that I was not qualified to make any enquiries. But I hope the Dutch upon this notice will be curious and able enough to supply my defects.

His Majesty having often pressed me to accept some employment in his court, and finding me absolutely determined to return to my native country, was pleased to give me his licence to depart, and honoured me with a letter of recommendation under his own hand to the Emperor of Japan. He likewise presented me with four hundred forty-four large pieces of gold (this nation delighting in even numbers) and a red diamond which I sold in England for eleven hundred pounds.

On the 6th day of May, 1709, I took a solemn leave of his Majesty, and all my friends. This prince was so gracious as to order a guard to conduct me to Glanguenstald, which is a royal port to the southwest part of the island. In six days I found a vessel ready to carry me to Japan, and spent fifteen days in the voyage. We landed at a small port-town called Xamoschi, situated on the southeast part of Japan. The town lies on the western point, where there is a narrow strait leading northward into a long arm of the sea, upon the northwest part of which Yedo,[1] the metropolis, stands. At landing I showed the custom-house officers my letter from the King of Luggnagg to his Imperial Majesty. They knew the seal perfectly well; it was as broad as the palm of my hand. The impression was *a king lifting up a lame beggar from the earth.* The magistrates of the town, hearing of my letter, received me as a public minister; they provided me with carriages and servants and bore my charges to Yedo, where I was admitted to an audience and delivered my letter, which was opened with great ceremony and explained to the Emperor by an interpreter, who gave me notice of his Majesty's order that I should signify my request, and, whatever it were, it should be granted for the sake of his royal brother of Luggnagg.

1. The old name (until 1868) for Tokyo.

This interpreter was a person employed to transact affairs with the Hollanders; he soon conjectured by my countenance that I was an European, and therefore repeated his Majesty's commands in Low Dutch, which he spoke perfectly well. I answered (as I had before determined) that I was a Dutch merchant, shipwrecked in a very remote country, from whence I travelled by sea and land to Luggnagg, and then took shipping for Japan, where I knew my countrymen often traded, and with some of these I hoped to get an opportunity of returning into Europe. I therefore most humbly entreated his royal favour to give order that I should be conducted in safety to Nangasac:[2] to this I added another petition, that for the sake of my patron the King of Luggnagg his Majesty would condescend to excuse my performing the ceremony imposed on my countrymen of *trampling upon the crucifix,*[3] because I had been thrown into his kingdom by my misfortunes without any intention of trading. When this latter petition was interpreted to the Emperor, he seemed a little surprised and said he believed I was the first of my countrymen who ever made any scruple in this point, and that he began to doubt whether I was a real Hollander or no, but rather suspected I must be a Christian.[4] However, for the reasons I had offered, but chiefly to gratify the King of Luggnagg, by an uncommon mark of his favour, he would comply with the singularity of my humour; but the affair must be managed with dexterity, and his officers should be commanded to let me pass as it were by forgetfulness. For he assured me, that if the secret should be discovered by my countrymen, the Dutch, they would cut my throat in the voyage. I returned my thanks by the interpreter for so unusual a favour, and, some troops being at that time on their march to Nangasac, the commanding officer had orders to convey me safe thither, with particular instructions about the business of the crucifix.

On the 9th day of June, 1709, I arrived at Nangasac, after a very long and troublesome journey. I soon fell into company of some Dutch sailors belonging to the *Amboyna* of Amsterdam, a stout ship of 450 tons. I had lived long in Holland, pursuing my studies at Leyden, and I spoke Dutch well. The seamen soon knew from whence I came last; they were curious to enquire into my voyage and course of life. I made up a story as short and probable as I could, but concealed the greatest part. I knew many persons in Holland; I was able to invent names for my parents, whom I pretended to be obscure people in the province of Gelderland. I would have given the captain (one Theodorus Vangrult) what he pleased to ask for my voyage to Holland; but, understanding I was a surgeon, he was contented to take half the usual rate on condition that I would serve him in the way of my calling. Before we took shipping I was often asked by some of the crew whether I had performed the ceremony above-mentioned. I evaded the question by general answers that I had satisfied the Emperor and court in all particulars. However, a malicious rogue of a

2. Nagasaki.

3. This was a test applied to Japanese suspected of being Christians, but not, so far as is known, to foreigners.

4. See the note to Chapter 9 above. Swift's distrust of the Dutch arose in part from their practice of religious toleration and their hospitality to all liberal and skeptical movements of thought. More than that, however, he tended to see this toleration as the product of commercial opportunism, which was often ruthless toward competitors and acquiescent to the most humiliating terms set by the Japanese.

skipper[5] went to an officer and, pointing to me, told him I had not yet *trampled on the crucifix;* but the other, who had received instructions to let me pass, gave the rascal twenty strokes on the shoulders with a bamboo, after which I was no more troubled with such questions.

Nothing happened worth mentioning in this voyage. We sailed with a fair wind to the Cape of Good Hope, where we stayed only to take in fresh water. On the 6th of April we arrived safe at Amsterdam, having lost only three men by sickness in the voyage, and a fourth who fell from the foremast into the sea, not far from the coast of Guinea. From Amsterdam I soon after set sail for England in a small vessel belonging to that city.

On the 10th of April, 1710, we put in at the Downs. I landed the next morning and saw once more my native country after an absence of five years and six months complete. I went straight to Redriff, whither I arrived the same day at two in the afternoon, and found my wife and family in good health.

Part Four: A Voyage to the Country of the Houyhnhnms

Chapter One: The author sets out as captain of a ship. His men conspire against him, confine him a long time to his cabin. Set him on shore in an unknown land. He travels up into the country. The Yahoos, a strange sort of animal, described. The author meets two Houyhnhnms.

I continued at home with my wife and children about five months in a very happy condition, if I could have learned the lesson of knowing when I was well. I left my poor wife big with child and accepted an advantageous offer made me to be captain of the *Adventure*, a stout merchantman of 350 tons: for I understood navigation well, and being grown weary of a surgeon's employment at sea, which however I could exercise upon occasion, I took a skilful young man of that calling, one Robert Purefoy, into my ship. We set sail for Portsmouth upon the 7th day of September, 1710; on the 14th, we met with Captain Pocock of Bristol, at Teneriffe,[1] who was going to the bay of Campechy, to cut logwood.[2] On the 16th, he was parted from us by a storm; I heard since my return that his ship foundered and none escaped but one cabin-boy. He was an honest man and a good sailor but a little too positive in his own opinions, which was the cause of his destruction, as it hath been of several others. For if he had followed my advice, he might at this time have been safe at home with his family as well as myself.

5. Seaman (not captain).

1. The largest of the Canary Islands.
2. On the Gulf of Mexico in Yucatán; a source of "campeachy wood," used for making dyes.

I had several men died in my ship of calentures,[3] so that I was forced to get recruits out of Barbadoes and the Leeward Islands,[4] where I touched by the direction of the merchants who employed me, which I had soon too much cause to repent; for I found afterwards that most of them had been buccaneers. I had fifty hands on board, and my orders were that I should trade with the Indians in the South Sea and make what discoveries I could. These rogues whom I had picked up debauched my other men, and they all formed a conspiracy to seize the ship and secure me; which they did one morning, rushing into my cabin and binding me hand and foot, threatening to throw me overboard if I offered to stir. I told them I was their prisoner and would submit. This they made me swear to do, and then unbound me, only fastening one of my legs with a chain near my bed, and placed a sentry at my door with his piece charged, who was commanded to shoot me dead if I attempted my liberty. They sent me down victuals and drink and took the government of the ship to themselves. Their design was to turn pirates and plunder the Spaniards, which they could not do till they got more men. But first they resolved to sell the goods in the ship and then go to Madagascar for recruits, several among them having died since my confinement. They sailed many weeks and traded with the Indians, but I knew not what course they took, being kept close prisoner in my cabin and expecting nothing less than to be murdered, as they often threatened me.

Upon the 9th day of May, 1711, one James Welch came down to my cabin and said he had orders from the captain to set me ashore. I expostulated with him, but in vain; neither would he so much as tell me who their new captain was. They forced me into the long-boat, letting me put on my best suit of clothes, which were as good as new, and a small bundle of linen, but no arms except my hanger; [5] and they were so civil as not to search my pockets, into which I conveyed what money I had, with some other little necessaries. They rowed about a league and then set me down on a strand. I desired them to tell me what country it was. They all swore they knew no more than myself, but said that the captain (as they called him) was resolved, after they had sold the lading,[6] to get rid of me in the first place where they discovered land. They pushed off immediately, advising me to make haste for fear of being overtaken by the tide, and bade me farewell.[7]

In this desolate condition I advanced forward and soon got upon firm ground, where I sat down on a bank to rest myself and consider what I had best to do. When I was a little refreshed I went up into the country, resolving to deliver myself to the first savages I should meet and purchase my life from them by some bracelets, glass rings, and other toys [8] which sailors usually provide themselves with in those voyages, and whereof I had some about me. The land was divided by long rows of trees, not regularly planted, but naturally growing;

3. Tropical fevers.
4. In the West Indies.
5. A short broad sword.
6. Cargo.
7. In his first voyage, Gulliver is shipwrecked in a storm; in his second, left behind by his shipmates; in the third, set adrift by pirates; in the fourth, abandoned by mutineers. There is clear progression from natural causes to deliberate evil.
8. Trinkets.

there was great plenty of grass, and several fields of oats. I walked very circumspectly for fear of being surprised or suddenly shot with an arrow from behind or on either side. I fell into a beaten road, where I saw many tracks of human feet, and some of cows, but most of horses.

At last I beheld several animals in a field, and one or two of the same kind sitting in trees. Their shape was very singular and deformed, which a little discomposed me, so that I lay down behind a thicket to observe them better. Some of them coming forward near the place where I lay, gave me an opportunity of distinctly marking their form. Their heads and breasts were covered with a thick hair, some frizzled and others lank; they had beards like goats, and a long ridge of hair down their backs and the foreparts of their legs and feet, but the rest of their bodies were bare, so that I might see their skins, which were of a brown buff colour. They had no tails, nor any hair at all on their buttocks, except about the anus; which, I presume, nature had placed there to defend them as they sat on the ground; for this posture they used, as well as lying down, and often stood on their hind feet. They climbed high trees as nimbly as a squirrel, for they had strong extended claws before and behind, terminating in sharp points, and hooked. They would often spring and bound and leap with prodigious agility. The females were not so large as the males; they had long lank hair on their heads, but none on their faces, nor anything more than a sort of down on the rest of their bodies, except about the anus and pudenda. Their dugs hung between their fore-feet and often reached almost to the ground as they walked. The hair of both sexes was of several colours, brown, red, black, and yellow. Upon the whole, I never beheld in all my travels so disagreeable an animal or one against which I naturally conceived so strong an antipathy. So that thinking I had seen enough, full of contempt and aversion, I got up and pursued the beaten road, hoping it might direct me to the cabin of some Indian.

I had not gone far when I met one of these creatures full in my way and coming up directly to me. The ugly monster, when he saw me, distorted several ways every feature of his visage and stared as at an object he had never seen before; then approaching nearer, lifted up his forepaw, whether out of curiosity or mischief, I could not tell. But I drew my hanger and gave him a good blow with the flat side of it, for I durst not strike him with the edge, fearing the inhabitants might be provoked against me if they should come to know that I had killed or maimed any of their cattle. When the beast felt the smart, he drew back and roared so loud that a herd of at least forty came flocking about me from the next field, howling and making odious faces; but I ran to the body of a tree and, leaning my back against it, kept them off by waving my hanger. Several of this cursed brood, getting hold of the branches behind, leaped up into the tree, from whence they began to discharge their excrements on my head: however, I escaped pretty well by sticking close to the stem of the tree, but was almost stifled with the filth, which fell about me on every side.

In the midst of this distress, I observed them all to run away on a sudden as fast as they could, at which I ventured to leave the tree and pursue the road, wondering what it was that could put them into this fright. But looking on my left hand, I saw a horse walking softly in the field, which, my persecutors having sooner discovered, was the cause of their flight. The horse started a little when he came near me but, soon recovering himself, looked full in my face with manifest tokens of wonder: he viewed my hands and feet, walking round me several times. I would have pursued my journey, but he placed himself directly in the way, yet looking with a very mild aspect, never offering the least violence. We stood gazing at each other for some time; at last I took the boldness to reach my hand towards his neck with a design to stroke it, using the common style and whistle of jockeys when they are going to handle a strange horse. But this animal, seeming to receive my civilities with disdain, shook his head and bent his brows, softly raising up his left forefoot to remove my hand. Then he neighed three or four times, but in so different a cadence that I almost began to think he was speaking to himself in some language of his own.

While he and I were thus employed, another horse came up; who applying himself to [9] the first in a very formal manner, they gently struck each other's right hoof before, neighing several times by turns and varying the sound, which seemed to be almost articulate.[10] They went some paces off as if it were to confer together, walking side by side, backward and forward, like persons deliberating upon some affair of weight, but often turning their eyes towards me as it were to watch that I might not escape. I was amazed to see such actions and behaviour in brute beasts, and concluded with myself that, if the inhabitants of this country were endued with a proportionable degree of reason, they must needs be the wisest people upon earth. This thought gave me so much comfort that I resolved to go forward until I could discover some house or village or meet with any of the natives, leaving the two horses to discourse together as they pleased. But the first, who was a dapple grey, observing me to steal off, neighed after me in so expressive a tone that I fancied myself to understand what he meant; whereupon I turned back and came near him, to expect [11] his farther commands: but concealing my fear as much as I could, for I began to be in some pain how this adventure might terminate; and the reader will easily believe I did not much like my present situation.

The two horses came up close to me, looking with great earnestness upon my face and hands. The grey steed rubbed my hat all around with his right fore-hoof and discomposed it so much that I was forced to adjust it better by taking it off and settling it again; whereat both he and his companion (who was a brown bay) appeared to be much surprised. The latter felt the lappet [12] of my coat, and finding it to hang loose about me, they both looked with new signs of wonder. He stroked my right hand, seeming to admire [13] the softness and colour; but he squeezed it so hard between his hoof and his pastern [14] that I was forced to roar; after which they both touched me with all possible tenderness. They were under great perplexity about my shoes and stockings, which they felt very often, neighing to each other and using various gestures,

9. Accosting, approaching.
10. Meaningful.
11. Await.
12. Flap or lapel.
13. Wonder at.
14. The joint at the back of a horse's leg, just above the hoof.

not unlike those of a philosopher [15] when he would attempt to solve some new and difficult phenomenon.

Upon the whole, the behaviour of these animals was so orderly and rational, so acute and judicious, that I at last concluded they must needs be magicians who had thus metamorphosed themselves upon some design, and, seeing a stranger in the way, were resolved to divert themselves with him; or perhaps were really amazed at the sight of a man so very different in habit, feature, and complexion from those who might probably live in so remote a climate. Upon the strength of this reasoning, I ventured to address them in the following manner: 'Gentlemen, if you be conjurers, as I have good cause to believe, you can understand any language; therefore I make bold to let your Worships know that I am a poor distressed Englishman driven by his misfortunes upon your coast, and I entreat one of you to let me ride upon his back, as if he were a real horse, to some house or village where I can be relieved. In return of which favour, I will make you a present of this knife and bracelet' (taking them out of my pocket). The two creatures stood silent while I spoke, seeming to listen with great attention; and when I had ended they neighed frequently towards each other, as if they were engaged in serious conversation. I plainly observed that their language expressed the passions very well, and the words might with little pains be resolved into an alphabet more easily than the Chinese.

I could frequently distinguish the word *Yahoo*, which was repeated by each of them several times; and, although it was impossible for me to conjecture what it meant, yet while the two horses were busy in conversation I endeavoured to practice this word upon my tongue; and as soon as they were silent, I boldly pronounced *Yahoo* in a loud voice, imitating, at the same time, as near as I could, the neighing of a horse; at which they were both visibly surprised, and the grey repeated the same word twice, as if he meant to teach me the right accent, wherein I spoke after him as well as I could and found myself perceivably to improve every time, although very far from any degree of perfection. Then the bay tried me with a second word much harder to be pronounced; but reducing it to the English orthography, may be spelt thus, *Houyhnhnm*. I did not succeed in this so well as the former, but after two or three farther trials I had better fortune; and they both appeared amazed at my capacity.

After some farther discourse, which I then conjectured might relate to me, the two friends took their leaves, with the same compliment of striking each other's hoof; and the grey made me signs that I should walk before him, wherein I thought it prudent to comply till I could find a better director. When I offered to slacken my pace, he would cry *Hhuun, Hhuun;* I guessed his meaning and gave him to understand, as well as I could, that I was weary and not able to walk faster; upon which he would stand a while to let me rest.

15. That is, natural philosopher or scientist.

Chapter Two: The author conducted by a Houyhnhnm to his house. The house described. The author's reception. The food of the Houyhnhnms. The author, in distress for want of meat, is at last relieved. His manner of feeding in that country.

Having travelled about three miles, we came to a long kind of building, made of timber stuck in the ground and wattled across;[1] the roof was low and covered with straw. I now began to be a little comforted and took out some toys which travellers usually carry for presents to the savage Indians of America and other parts, in hopes the people of the house would be thereby encouraged to receive me kindly. The horse made me a sign to go in first; it was a large room with a smooth clay floor and a rack and manger extending the whole length on one side. There were three nags and two mares, not eating, but some of them sitting down upon their hams, which I very much wondered at; but wondered more to see the rest employed in domestic business. The last seemed but ordinary cattle; however, this confirmed my first opinion, that a people who could so far civilize brute animals must needs excel in wisdom all the nations of the world. The grey came in just after and thereby prevented any ill treatment which the others might have given me. He neighed to them several times in a style of authority and received answers.

Beyond this room there were three others, reaching the length of the house, to which you passed through three doors, opposite to each other in the manner of a vista.[2] We went through the second room towards the third; here the grey walked in first, beckoning me to attend. I waited in the second room and got ready my presents for the master and mistress of the house: they were two knives, three bracelets of false pearl, a small looking-glass, and a bead necklace. The horse neighed three or four times, and I waited to hear some answers in human voice; but I heard no other returns than in the same dialect, only one or two a little shriller than his. I began to think that this house must belong to some person of great note among them, because there appeared so much ceremony before I could gain admittance. But that a man of quality should be served all by horses was beyond my comprehension. I feared my brain was disturbed by my sufferings and misfortunes: I roused myself, and looked about me in the room where I was left alone; this was furnished as the first, only after a more elegant manner. I rubbed my eyes often, but the same objects still occurred. I pinched my arms and sides to awake myself, hoping I might be in a dream. I then absolutely concluded that all these appearances could be nothing else but necromancy[3] and magic. But I had no time to pursue these reflections; for the grey horse came to the door and made me a sign to follow him into the third room, where I saw a very comely mare, together with a colt and foal, sitting on their haunches, upon mats of straw not unartfully made and perfectly neat and clean.

The mare, soon after my entrance, rose from her mat, and coming up close, after having nicely[4] observed my hands and face, gave me a most con-

1. Woven across with twigs or light branches.
2. An opening that allows an extended view.
3. Enchantment.
4. Carefully.

temptuous look; then turning to the horse, I heard the word *Yahoo* often repeated betwixt them; the meaning of which word I could not then comprehend, although it were the first I had learned to pronounce. But I was soon better informed, to my everlasting mortification: for the horse beckoning to me with his head, and repeating the word *Hhuun, Hhuun,* as he did upon the road, which I understood was to attend him, led me out into a kind of court, where was another building at some distance from the house. Here we entered, and I saw three of those detestable creatures which I first met after my landing, feeding upon roots and the flesh of some animals, which I afterwards found to be that of asses and dogs, and now and then a cow dead by accident or disease. They were all tied by the neck with strong withes[5] fastened to a beam; they held their food between the claws of their forefeet and tore it with their teeth.

The master horse ordered a sorrel nag, one of his servants, to untie the largest of these animals and take him into the yard. The beast and I were brought close together, and our countenances diligently compared both by master and servant, who thereupon repeated several times the word *Yahoo.* My horror and astonishment are not to be described when I observed, in this abominable animal, a perfect human figure. The face of it indeed was flat and broad, the nose depressed, the lips large, and the mouth wide. But these differences are common to all savage nations, where the lineaments of the countenance are distorted by the natives suffering their infants to lie grovelling on the earth, or by carrying them on their backs, nuzzling with their face against the mother's shoulders. The forefeet of the Yahoo differed from my hands in nothing else but the length of the nails, the coarseness and brownness of the palms, and the hairiness on the backs. There was the same resemblance between our feet, with the same differences, which I knew very well, although the horses did not, because of my shoes and stockings; the same in every part of our bodies, except as to hairiness and colour, which I have already described.

The great difficulty that seemed to stick with the two horses was to see the rest of my body so very different from that of a Yahoo; for which I was obliged to my clothes, whereof they had no conception. The sorrel nag offered me a root, which he held (after their manner, as we shall describe in its proper place) between his hoof and pastern.[6] I took it in my hand and, having smelt it, returned it to him as civilly as I could. He brought out of the Yahoo's kennel a piece of ass's flesh, but it smelt so offensively that I turned from it with loathing. He then threw it to the Yahoo, by whom it was greedily devoured. He afterwards showed me a wisp of hay and a fetlock full of oats; but I shook my head to signify that neither of these were food for me. And indeed, I now apprehended that I must absolutely starve if I did not get to some of my own species: for as to those filthy Yahoos, although there were few greater lovers of mankind, at that time, than myself, yet I confess I never saw any sensitive[7] being so detestable on all accounts; and the more I came near them, the more hateful they grew, while I stayed in that country. This the master horse ob-

5. Flexible willow branches.
6. The joint at the back of a horse's leg, just above the hoof.
7. With power of the senses.

served by my behaviour, and therefore sent the Yahoo back to his kennel. He then put his fore-hoof to his mouth, at which I was much surprised, although he did it with ease and with a motion that appeared perfectly natural, and made other signs to know what I would eat; but I could not return him such an answer as he was able to apprehend; and if he had understood me, I did not see how it was possible to contrive any way for finding myself nourishment. While we were thus engaged, I observed a cow passing by, whereupon I pointed to her and expressed a desire to let me go and milk her. This had its effect; for he led me back into the house and ordered a mare-servant to open a room where a good store of milk lay in earthen and wooden vessels, after a very orderly and cleanly manner. She gave me a large bowl full, of which I drank very heartily, and found myself well refreshed.

About noon I saw coming towards the house a kind of vehicle drawn like a sledge by four Yahoos. There was in it an old steed, who seemed to be of quality; [8] he alighted with his hind feet forward, having by accident got a hurt in his left forefoot. He came to dine with our horse, who received him with great civility. They dined in the best room and had oats boiled in milk for the second course, which the old horse eat [9] warm, but the rest cold. Their mangers were placed circular in the middle of the room and divided into several partitions, round which they sat on their haunches upon bosses [10] of straw. In the middle was a large rack with angles answering to every partition of the manger. So that each horse and mare eat their own hay and their own mash of oats and milk, with much decency and regularity. The behaviour of the young colt and foal appeared very modest, and that of the master and mistress extremely cheerful and complaisant [11] to their guest. The grey ordered me to stand by him, and much discourse passed between him and his friend concerning me, as I found by the stranger's often looking on me, and the frequent repetition of the word *Yahoo*.

I happened to wear my gloves, which the master grey observing, seemed perplexed, discovering signs of wonder what I had done to my forefeet. He put his hoof three or four times to them, as if he would signify that I should reduce them to their former shape, which I presently did, pulling off both my gloves and putting them into my pocket. This occasioned farther talk, and I saw the company was pleased with my behaviour, whereof I soon found the good effects. I was ordered to speak the few words I understood, and while they were at dinner, the master taught me the names for oats, milk, fire, water, and some others: which I could readily pronounce after him, having from my youth a great facility in learning languages.[12]

When dinner was done, the master horse took me aside, and by signs and words made me understand the concern he was in that I had nothing to eat. Oats in their tongue are called *hlunnh*. This word I pronounced two or three times; for although I had refused them at first, yet upon second thoughts, I

8. High rank.
9. The normal past form, the counterpart of modern "ate" and pronounced "ett."
10. Hassocks.
11. Courteous.
12. Gulliver's facility with strange languages is part of his pattern of adaptability to external circumstances, but it is seldom accompanied by penetration into their moral implications.

considered that I could contrive to make of them a kind of bread, which might be sufficient with milk to keep me alive till I could make my escape to some other country and to creatures of my own species. The horse immediately ordered a white mare-servant of his family to bring me a good quantity of oats in a sort of wooden tray. These I heated before the fire as well as I could, and rubbed them till the husks came off, which I made a shift to winnow from the grain. I ground and beat them between two stones, then took water and made them into a paste or cake, which I toasted at the fire and eat warm with milk. It was at first a very insipid diet, although common enough in many parts of Europe, but grew tolerable by time; and having been often reduced to hard fare in my life, this was not the first experiment I had made how easily nature is satisfied. And I cannot but observe that I never had one hour's sickness while I stayed in this island. It is true, I sometimes made a shift to catch a rabbit or bird, by springes[13] made of Yahoos' hairs; and I often gathered wholesome herbs, which I boiled or eat as salads with my bread; and now and then, for a rarity, I made a little butter and drank the whey. I was at first at a great loss for salt; but custom soon reconciled the want of it; and I am confident that the frequent use of salt among us is an effect of luxury and was first introduced only as a provocative to drink; except where it is necessary for preserving of flesh in long voyages or in places remote from great markets. For we observe no animal to be fond of it but man:[14] and as to myself, when I left this country, it was a great while before I could endure the taste of it in anything that I eat.

This is enough to say upon the subject of my diet, wherewith other travellers fill their books, as if the readers were personally concerned whether we fare well or ill.[15] However, it was necessary to mention this matter lest the world should think it impossible that I could find sustenance for three years in such a country and among such inhabitants.

When it grew towards evening, the master horse ordered a place for me to lodge in; it was but six yards from the house, and separated from the stable of the Yahoos. Here I got some straw and, covering myself with my own clothes, slept very sound. But I was in a short time better accommodated, as the reader shall know hereafter, when I come to treat more particularly about my way of living.

Chapter Three: The author studious to learn the language, the Houyhnhnm his master assists in teaching him. The language described. Several Houyhnhnms of quality come out of curiosity to see the author. He gives his master a short account of his voyage.

My principal endeavour was to learn the language, which my master (for so I shall henceforth call him) and his children, and every servant of his house,

13. Snares.

14. This error may be Swift's but is more likely a deliberate sign of Gulliver's unreliability in his enthusiasm for a simple "natural" life and a forecast of his soon-to-be-avowed adoration of the Houyhnhnms (Chapter 7).

15. If there is a greater and more frequent fault than this self-importance in travel books, it is the needless putting down of other writers; Swift's book is, whatever else, in part a satire upon the form.

were desirous to teach me. For they looked upon it as a prodigy that a brute animal should discover such marks of a rational creature. I pointed to everything and inquired the name of it, which I wrote down in my journal-book when I was alone, and corrected my bad accent by desiring those of the family to pronounce it often. In this employment a sorrel nag, one of the under-servants, was very ready to assist me.

In speaking, they pronounce through the nose and throat; and their language approaches nearest to the High Dutch or German of any I know in Europe, but is much more graceful and significant. The Emperor Charles V made almost the same observation when he said that, if he were to speak to his horse, it should be in High Dutch.[1]

The curiosity and impatience of my master were so great that he spent many hours of his leisure to instruct me. He was convinced (as he afterwards told me) that I must be a Yahoo, but my teachableness, civility, and cleanliness astonished him, which were qualities altogether so opposite to those animals. He was most perplexed about my clothes, reasoning sometimes with himself whether they were a part of my body; for I never pulled them off till the family were asleep and got them on before they waked in the morning. My master was eager to learn from whence I came, how I acquired those appearances of reason which I discovered in all my actions, and to know my story from my own mouth, which he hoped he should soon do by the great proficiency I made in learning and pronouncing their words and sentences. To help my memory, I formed all I learned into the English alphabet and writ the words down with the translations. This last, after some time, I ventured to do in my master's presence. It cost me much trouble to explain to him what I was doing; for the inhabitants have not the least idea of books or literature.[2]

In about ten weeks time I was able to understand most of his questions, and in three months could give him some tolerable answers. He was extremely curious to know from what part of the country I came and how I was taught to imitate a rational creature, because the Yahoos (whom he saw I exactly resembled in my head, hands, and face, that were only visible), with some appearance of cunning and the strongest disposition to mischief, were observed to be the most unteachable of all brutes. I answered that I came over the sea from a far place, with many others of my own kind, in a great hollow vessel made of the bodies of trees; that my companions forced me to land on this coast and then left me to shift for myself. It was with some difficulty and by the help of many signs that I brought him to understand me. He replied that I must needs be mistaken, or that I 'said the thing which was not.' (For they have no words in their language to express lying or falsehood.) He knew it was impossible that there could be a country beyond the sea, or that a parcel of brutes could move a wooden vessel whither they pleased upon water. He was sure no Houyhnhnm alive could make such a vessel, or would trust Yahoos to manage it.

1. Charles V (1500–1558), King of Spain and ruler of the Holy Roman Empire, is reported to have said that he would address his God in Spanish, his mistress in Italian, and his horse in German.
2. In the more limited sense of writing, for they have some poetic and rhetorical powers.

The word *Houyhnhnm,* in their tongue, signifies a *horse,* and in its etymology, *the Perfection of Nature.*[3] I told my master, that I was at a loss for expression but would improve as fast as I could; and hoped in a short time I should be able to tell him wonders. He was pleased to direct his own mare, his colt and foal, and the servants of the family to take all opportunities of instructing me, and every day for two or three hours he was at the same pains himself. Several horses and mares of quality in the neighbourhood came often to our house upon the report spread of a wonderful Yahoo that could speak like a Houyhnhnm and seemed in his words and actions to discover some glimmerings of reason. These delighted to converse with me; they put many questions and received such answers as I was able to return. By all which advantages I made so great a progress that in five months from my arrival I understood whatever was spoke and could express myself tolerably well.

The Houyhnhnms who came to visit my master out of a design of seeing and talking with me could hardly believe me to be a right[4] Yahoo, because my body had a different covering from others of my kind. They were astonished to observe me without the usual hair or skin except on my head, face, and hands; but I discovered that secret to my master, upon an accident which happened about a fortnight before.

I have already told the reader that every night, when the family were gone to bed, it was my custom to strip and cover myself with clothes. It happened one morning early that my master sent for me by the sorrel nag, who was his valet. When he came, I was fast asleep, my clothes fallen off on one side and my shirt above my waist. I awaked at the noise he made and observed him to deliver his message in some disorder; after which he went to my master and in a great fright gave him a very confused account of what he had seen. This I presently discovered; for going, as soon as I was dressed, to pay my attendance upon his Honour, he asked me the meaning of what his servant had reported, that I was not the same thing when I slept as I appeared to be at other times; that his valet assured him some part of me was white, some yellow, at least not so white, and some brown.

I had hitherto concealed the secret of my dress in order to distinguish myself as much as possible from that cursed race of Yahoos; but now I found it in vain to do so any longer. Besides, I considered that my clothes and shoes would soon wear out, which already were in a declining condition, and must be supplied by some contrivance from the hides of Yahoos or other brutes; whereby the whole secret would be known. I therefore told my master that, in the country from whence I came, those of my kind always covered their bodies with the hairs of certain animals prepared by art, as well for decency as to avoid inclemencies of air both hot and cold; of which, as to my own person, I would give him immediate conviction if he pleased to command me, only desiring his excuse if I did not expose those parts that nature taught us to conceal. He said my discourse was all very strange, but especially the last part; for he

3. That is, as the culmination and master of all natural life, as man has traditionally regarded himself; unlike man, they have no conception of anything supernatural or of a deity other than Nature itself, nor do they have any experience of a "fallen" Nature (except in the Yahoos).

4. True, genuine.

could not understand why nature should teach us to conceal what nature had given. That neither himself nor family were ashamed of any parts of their bodies; but however I might do as I pleased. Whereupon, I first unbuttoned my coat and pulled it off. I did the same with my waistcoat; I drew off my shoes, stockings, and breeches. I let my shirt down to my waist and drew up the bottom, fastening it like a girdle about my middle to hide my nakedness.

My master observed the whole performance with great signs of curiosity and admiration. He took up all my clothes in his pastern, one piece after another, and examined them diligently. He then stroked my body very gently and looked around me several times, after which he said it was plain I must be a perfect Yahoo; but that I differed very much from the rest of my species in the whiteness and smoothness of my skin, my want of hair in several parts of my body, the shape and shortness of my claws behind and before, and my affectation of walking continually on my two hinder feet. He desired to see no more and gave me leave to put on my clothes again, for I was shuddering with cold.

I expressed my uneasiness at his giving me so often the appellation of *Yahoo,* an odious animal for which I had so utter an hatred and contempt. I begged he would forbear applying that word to me and take the same order in his family and among his friends whom he suffered to see me. I requested likewise that the secret of my having a false covering to my body might be known to none but himself, at least as long as my present clothing should last; for as to what the sorrel nag his valet had observed, his Honour might command him to conceal it.

All this my master very graciously consented to, and thus the secret was kept till my clothes began to wear out, which I was forced to supply by several contrivances that shall hereafter be mentioned. In the meantime he desired I would go on with my utmost diligence to learn their language, because he was more astonished at my capacity for speech and reason than at the figure of my body, whether it were covered or no; adding that he waited with some impatience to hear the wonders which I promised to tell him.

From thenceforward he doubled the pains he had been at to instruct me. He brought me into all company and made them treat me with civility, because, as he told them privately, this would put me into good humour and make me more diverting.

Every day when I waited on him, beside the trouble he was at in teaching, he would ask me several questions concerning myself, which I answered as well as I could; and by those means he had already received some general ideas, although very imperfect. It would be tedious to relate the several steps by which I advanced to a more regular conversation: but the first account I gave of myself in any order and length was to this purpose:

That I came from a very far country, as I already had attempted to tell him, with about fifty more of my own species; that we travelled upon the seas in a great hollow vessel made of wood and larger than his Honour's house. I described the ship to him in the best terms I could and explained by the help of my handkerchief displayed how it was driven forward by the wind; that upon a quarrel among us, I was set on shore on this coast, where I walked forward without knowing whither, till he delivered me from the persecution of those execrable Yahoos. He asked me who made the ship, and how it was possible that the Houyhnhnms of my country would leave it to the management of brutes? My answer was that I durst proceed no farther in my relation unless he would give me his word and honour that he would not be offended, and then I would tell him the wonders I had so often promised. He agreed; and I went on by assuring him that the ship was made by creatures like myself, who in all the countries I had travelled, as well as in my own, were the only governing, rational animals; and that upon my arrival hither I was as much astonished to see the Houyhnhnms act like rational beings as he or his friends could be in finding some marks of reason in a creature he was pleased to call a Yahoo, to which I owned my resemblance in every part, but could not account for their degenerate and brutal nature. I said farther, that if good fortune ever restored me to my native country to relate my travels hither, as I resolved to do, everybody would believe that I 'said the thing which was not'; that I invented the story out of my own head; and with all possible respect to himself, his family, and friends, and under his promise of not being offended, our countrymen would hardly think it probable that a Houyhnhnm should be the presiding creature of a nation and a Yahoo the brute.

Chapter Four: The Houyhnhnms' notion of truth and falsehood. The author's discourse disapproved by his master. The author gives a more particular account of himself and the accidents of his voyage.

My master heard me with great appearances of uneasiness in his countenance, because *doubting* or *not believing* are so little known in this country that the inhabitants cannot tell how to behave themselves under such circumstances. And I remember, in frequent discourses with my master concerning the nature of manhood in other parts of the world, having occasion to talk of *lying* and *false representation,* it was with much difficulty that he comprehended what I meant, although he had otherwise a most acute judgment. For he argued thus: that the use of speech was to make us understand one another and to receive information of facts; now if any one *said the thing which was not,* these ends were defeated; because I cannot properly be said to understand him, and I am so far from receiving information that he leaves me worse than in ignorance, for I am led to believe a thing *black* when it is *white* and *short* when it is *long.* And these were all the notions he had concerning that faculty of *lying,* so perfectly well understood and so universally practised among human creatures.

To return from this digression, when I asserted that the Yahoos were the only governing animals in my country, which my master said was altogether past his conception, he desired to know whether we had Houyhnhnms among us and what was their employment. I told him, we had great numbers, that in summer they grazed in the fields and in winter were kept in houses with hay and oats, where Yahoo servants were employed to rub their skins smooth, comb their manes, pick their feet, serve them with food, and make their beds. 'I understand you well,' said my master, 'it is now very plain from all you have spoken that, whatever share of reason the Yahoos pretend to, the Houyhnhnms are your masters. I heartily wish our Yahoos would be so tractable.' I begged his Honour would please to excuse me from proceeding any farther, because I was very certain that the account he expected from me would be highly displeasing. But he insisted in commanding me to let him know the best and the worst. I told him he should be obeyed. I owned that the Houyhnhnms among us, whom we called horses,[1] were the most generous [2] and comely animal we had, that they excelled in strength and swiftness; and when they belonged to persons of quality, employed in travelling, racing, and drawing chariots, they were treated with much kindness and care, till they fell into diseases or became foundered in the feet; but then they were sold and used to all kind of drudgery till they died; after which their skins were stripped and sold for what they were worth, and their bodies left to be devoured by dogs and birds of prey.[3] But the common race of horses had not so good fortune, being kept by farmers and carriers and other mean people, who put them to greater labour and feed them worse. I described, as well as I could, our way of riding, the shape and use of a bridle, a saddle, a spur, and a whip, of harness and wheels. I added, that we fastened plates of a certain hard substance called *iron* at the bottom of their feet, to preserve their hoofs from being broken by the stony ways on which we often travelled.

My master, after some expressions of great indignation, wondered how we dared to venture upon a Houyhnhnm's back, for he was sure that the weakest servant in his house would be able to shake off the strongest Yahoo, or by lying down and rolling upon his back squeeze the brute to death. I answered that our horses were trained up from three or four years old to the several uses we intended them for; that if any of them proved intolerably vicious, they were employed for carriages; that they were severely beaten while they were young for any mischievous tricks; that the males, designed for the common use of riding or draught, were generally castrated about two years after their birth to take down their spirits and make them more tame and gentle; that they were indeed sensible of [4] rewards and punishments; but his Honour would please to consider that they had not the least tincture of reason any more than the Yahoos in this country.

It put me to the pains of many circumlocutions to give my master a right idea of what I spoke; for their language doth not abound in variety of words, because their wants and passions are fewer than among us. But it is impossible to express his noble resentment at our savage treatment of the Houyhnhnm race, particularly after I had explained the manner and use of castrating horses among us to hinder them from propagating their kind and to render them more servile. He said, if it were possible there could be any country where Yahoos alone were endued with reason, they certainly must be the governing animal, because reason will in time always prevail against brutal strength. But, considering the frame of our bodies, and especially of mine, he thought no creature of equal bulk was so ill contrived for employing that reason in the common

1. Gulliver collapses the distinction between horses and Houyhnhnms, as he has between men and Yahoos, placing external resemblances above the differences of inner capacity.
2. Noble.
3. Ironically echoing the phrase Homer applies to unburied warriors.
4. Responsive to.

offices of life; whereupon he desired to know whether those among whom I lived resembled me or the Yahoos of his country.

I assured him that I was as well shaped as most of my age: but the younger and the females were much more soft and tender, and the skins of the latter generally as white as milk. He said I differed indeed from other Yahoos, being much more cleanly and not altogether so deformed; but in point of real advantage he thought I differed for the worse. That my nails were of no use either to my fore or hinder feet; as to my forefeet, he could not properly call them by that name, for he never observed me to walk upon them; that they were too soft to bear the ground; that I generally went with them uncovered, neither was the covering I sometimes wore on them of the same shape or so strong as that on my feet behind. That I could not walk with any security, for if either of my hinder feet slipped, I must inevitably fall. He then began to find fault with other parts of my body, the flatness of my face, the prominence of my nose, my eyes placed directly in front, so that I could not look on either side without turning my head: that I was not able to feed myself without lifting one of my forefeet to my mouth: and therefore nature had placed those joints to answer that necessity. He knew not what could be the use of those several clefts and divisions in my feet behind; that these were too soft to bear the hardness and sharpness of stones without a covering made from the skin of some other brute; that my whole body wanted a fence against heat and cold, which I was forced to put on and off every day with tediousness and trouble. And lastly that he observed every animal in this country naturally to abhor the Yahoos, whom the weaker avoided and the stronger drove from them. So that supposing us to have the gift of reason, he could not see how it were possible to cure that natural antipathy which every creature discovered[5] against us; nor consequently how we could tame and render them serviceable. However, he would (as he said) debate the matter no farther, because he was more desirous to know my own story, the country where I was born, and the several actions and events of my life before I came hither.

I assured him how extremely desirous I was that he should be satisfied in every point; but I doubted much whether it would be possible for me to explain myself on several subjects whereof his Honour could have no conception, because I saw nothing in his country to which I could resemble[6] them. That, however, I would do my best and strive to express myself by similitudes, humbly, desiring his assistance when I wanted proper words, which he was pleased to promise me.

I said my birth was of honest parents, in an island called England, which was remote from this country as many days' journey as the strongest of his Honour's servants could travel in the annual course of the sun. That I was bred a surgeon, whose trade it is to cure wounds and hurts in the body got by accident or violence; that my country was governed by a female man, whom we called a *queen*.[7] That I left it to get riches, whereby I might maintain myself and family when I should return. That in my last voyage I was

5. Revealed.
6. Compare.
7. Queen Anne, who ruled from 1702 to 1714.

commander of the ship, and had about fifty Yahoos under me, many of which died at sea, and I was forced to supply them by others picked out from several nations. That our ship was twice in danger of being sunk; the first time by a great storm and the second by striking against a rock. Here my master interposed by asking me how I could persuade strangers out of different countries to venture with me after the losses I had sustained and the hazards I had run. I said they were fellows of desperate fortunes, forced to fly from the places of their birth on account of their poverty or their crimes. Some were undone by lawsuits; others spent all they had in drinking, whoring, and gaming; others fled for treason; many for murder, theft, poisoning, robbery, perjury, forgery, coining false money, for committing rapes or sodomy, for flying from their colours or deserting to the enemy, and most of them had broken prison. None of these durst return to their native countries for fear of being hanged or of starving in a jail; and therefore were under a necessity of seeking a livelihood in other places.

During this discourse, my master was pleased often to interrupt me; I had made use of many circumlocutions in describing to him the nature of the several crimes for which most of our crew had been forced to fly their country. This labour took up several days' conversation before he was able to comprehend me. He was wholly at a loss to know what could be the use or necessity of practising those vices. To clear up which I endeavoured to give him some ideas of the desire of power and riches; of the terrible effects of lust, intemperance, malice, and envy. All this I was forced to define and describe by putting of cases and making suppositions. After which, like one whose imagination was struck with something never seen or heard of before, he would lift up his eyes with amazement and indignation. Power, government, war, law, punishment, and a thousand other things had no terms wherein that language could express them, which made the difficulty almost insuperable to give my master any conception of what I meant. But being of an excellent understanding, much improved by contemplation and converse, he at last arrived at a competent knowledge of what human nature in our parts of the world is capable to perform, and desired I would give him some particular account of that land which we call Europe, especially of my own country.

Chapter Five: The author at his master's command informs him of the state of England. The causes of war among the princes of Europe. The author begins to explain the English constitution.

The reader may please to observe, that the following extract of many conversations I had with my master contains a summary of the most material points which were discoursed at several times for above two years; his Honour often desiring fuller satisfaction as I farther improved in the Houyhnhnm tongue. I laid before him, as well as I could, the whole state of Europe; I discoursed of trade and manufactures, of arts and sciences; and the answers I gave to all the questions he made, as they arose upon several subjects, were a fund of conversation not to be exhausted. But I shall here only set down the substance of what passed between us concerning my own country, reducing it into order as well as I can, without any regard to time or other circumstances, while I strictly adhere to truth. My only concern is that I shall hardly be able to do justice to my master's arguments and expressions, which must needs suffer by any want of capacity, as well as by a translation into our barbarous English.[1]

In obedience therefore to his Honour's commands, I related to him the Revolution under the Prince of Orange; the long war with France entered into by the said prince and renewed by his successor the present queen, wherein the greatest powers of Christendom were engaged, and which still continued.[2] I computed, at his request, that about a million of Yahoos might have been killed in the whole progress of it, and perhaps a hundred or more cities taken, and five times as many ships burnt or sunk.

He asked me what were the usual causes or motives that made one country go to war with another. I answered they were innumerable, but I should only mention a few of the chief: sometimes the ambition of princes, who never think they have land or people enough to govern: sometimes the corruption of ministers, who engage their master in a war in order to stifle or divert the clamour of the subjects against their evil administration. Difference in opinions[3] hath cost many millions of lives: for instance, whether *flesh* be *bread* or *bread* be *flesh;* whether the juice of a certain *berry* be *blood* or *wine;* whether *whistling* be a vice or a virtue; whether it be better to *kiss a post* or throw it into the fire; what is the best colour for a *coat,* whether *black, white, red,* or *grey;* and whether it should be *long* or *short, narrow* or *wide, dirty* or *clean,* with many more. Neither are any wars so furious and bloody or of so long continuance as those occasioned by difference in opinion, especially if it be in things indifferent.[4]

Sometimes the quarrel between two princes is to decide which of them shall dispossess a third of his dominions, where neither of them pretend to any right. Sometimes one prince quarrelleth with another for fear the other should quarrel with him. Sometimes a war is entered upon because the enemy is too *strong,* and sometimes because he is too *weak.* Sometimes our neighbours *want* the things which we *have,* or *have* the things which we *want;* and we both fight till they take ours or give us theirs. It is a very justifiable cause of war to invade a country after the people have been wasted by famine, destroyed by pestilence, or embroiled by factions amongst themselves. It is justifiable to enter into a war against our nearest ally when one of his towns

1. Gulliver's first overt revulsion from European culture.

2. William of Orange (1605–1702) succeeded James II as William III of England in the Glorious Revolution of 1688. He fought against France until 1697, when Louis XIV acknowledged his claim to the English throne, but resumed the war in 1701, when Louis gave his recognition to James's heir, the Stuart Pretender. Anne (1665–1714) carried on the War of the Spanish Succession, which ended in 1713, while Gulliver was still among the Houyhnhnms.

3. Alluding to such doctrinal quarrels among the churches as that of transubstantiation (whether the body and blood of Christ are really or only symbolically present in the Eucharistic bread and wine), the use of music in worship (offensive to some radical Protestants), the veneration of an image or crucifix (condemned by Calvinists), and the proper form of church vestments.

4. Matters not essential to belief; technically, upon which the church has not chosen to give a decision.

lies convenient for us, or a territory of land that would render our dominions round and compact. If a prince send forces into a nation where the people are poor and ignorant, he may lawfully put half of them to death and make slaves of the rest, in order to civilize and reduce them from their barbarous way of living. It is a very kingly, honourable, and frequent practice, when one prince desires the assistance of another to secure him against an invasion, that the assistant, when he hath driven out the invader, should seize on the dominions himself, and kill, imprison, or banish the prince he came to relieve. Alliance by blood or marriage is a sufficient cause of war between princes, and, the nearer the kindred is, the greater is their disposition to quarrel: *poor* nations are *hungry* and *rich* nations are *proud,* and pride and hunger will ever be at variance. For these reasons, the trade of a soldier is held the most honourable of all others: because a soldier is a Yahoo hired to kill in cold blood as many of his own species, who have never offended him, as possibly he can.

There is likewise a kind of beggarly princes in Europe, not able to make war by themselves, who hire out their troops to richer nations, for so much a day to each man; of which they keep three-fourths to themselves, and it is the best part of their maintenance; such are those in Germany and many northern parts of Europe.[5]

What you have told me (said my master) upon the subject of war does indeed discover most admirably the effects of that reason you pretend to: however, it is happy that the *shame* is greater than the *danger,* and that nature hath left you utterly uncapable of doing much mischief. For your mouths lying flat with your faces, you can hardly bite each other to any purpose unless by consent. Then as to the claws upon your feet before and behind, they are so short and tender that one of our Yahoos would drive a dozen of yours before him. And therefore in recounting the numbers of those who have been killed in battle, I cannot but think that you have *said the thing which is not.*

I could not forbear shaking my head and smiling a little at his ignorance. And being no stranger to the art of war, I gave him a description of cannons, culverins,[6] muskets, carabines,[7] pistols, bullets, powder, swords, bayonets, battles, sieges, retreats, attacks, undermines, countermines,[8] bombardments, sea-fights; ships sunk with a thousand men; twenty thousand killed on each side; dying groans, limbs flying in the air, smoke, noise, confusion, trampling to death under horses' feet; flight, pursuit, victory; fields strewed with carcasses left for food to dogs and wolves and birds of prey; plundering, stripping, ravishing, burning, and destroying. And to set forth the valour of my own dear countrymen, I assured him, that I had seen them blow up a hundred enemies at once in a siege, and as many in a ship, and beheld the dead bodies drop down in pieces from the clouds, to the great diversion of all the spectators.

I was going on to more particulars when my master commanded me silence.

5. George I of England, who ruled from 1714 to 1727, had supplied mercenaries to other nations while still Elector of Hanover.

6. Very long cannons.

7. Carbines, firearms used by the cavalry.

8. Excavations made under the walls of a fortress and those made as a defensive countermeasure.

He said whoever understood the nature of Yahoos might easily believe it possible for so vile an animal to be capable of every action I had named, if their strength and cunning equalled their malice. But as my discourse had increased his abhorrence of the whole species, so he found it gave him a disturbance in his mind to which he was wholly a stranger before. He thought his ears being used to such abominable words might by degrees admit them with less detestation. That although he hated the Yahoos of this country, yet he no more blamed them for their odious qualities than he did a *gnnayh* (a bird of prey) for its cruelty or a sharp stone for cutting his hoof. But when a creature pretending to reason could be capable of such enormities, he dreaded lest the corruption of that faculty might be worse than brutality[9] itself. He seemed therefore confident that, instead of reason, we were only possessed of some quality fitted to increase our natural vices; as the reflection from a troubled stream returns the image of an ill-shapen body not only *larger* but more *distorted.*

He added that he had heard too much upon the subject of war both in this and some former discourses. There was another point which a little perplexed him at present. I had said, that some of our crew left their country on account of being ruined by *law;* that I had already explained the meaning of the word; but he was at loss how it should come to pass that the *law,* which was intended for every man's preservation, should be any man's ruin. Therefore he desired to be farther satisfied what I meant by law, and the dispensers thereof according to the present practice in my own country; because he thought nature and reason were sufficient guides for a reasonable animal, as we pretended to be, in showing us what we ought to do and what to avoid.

I assured his Honour that law was a science wherein I had not much conversed further than by employing advocates, in vain, upon some injustices that had been done me. However, I would give him all the satisfaction I was able.

I said there was a society of men among us bred up from their youth in the art of proving by words multiplied for the purpose, that white is black and black is white, according as they are paid. To this society all the rest of the people are slaves.

For example, if my neighbour hath a mind to my cow, he hires a lawyer to prove that he ought to have my cow from me. I must then hire another to defend my right, it being against all rules of law that any man should be allowed to speak for himself. Now in this case, I who am the true owner lie under two great disadvantages. First, my lawyer, being practised almost from his cradle in defending falsehood, is quite out of his element when he would be an advocate for justice, which as an office unnatural he always attempts with great awkwardness, if not with ill will. The second disadvantage is, that my lawyer must proceed with great caution, or else he will be reprimanded by the judges, and abhorred by his brethren, as one that would lessen the practice of the law. And therefore I have but two methods to preserve my cow. The first is to gain over my adversary's lawyer with a double fee, who will then betray his client by insinuating that he hath justice on his side. The second

9. That is, brute insensibility.

way is for my lawyer to make my cause appear as unjust as he can, by allowing the cow to belong to my adversary; and this if it be skilfully done will certainly bespeak the favour of the bench.

Now, your Honour is to know that these judges are persons appointed to decide all controversies of property as well as for the trial of criminals, and picked out from the most dextrous lawyers who are grown old or lazy and, having been biassed all their lives against truth and equity, lie under such a fatal necessity of favouring fraud, perjury, and oppression, that I have known some of them to have refused a large bribe from the side where justice lay, rather than injure the faculty [10] by doing anything unbecoming their nature or their office.

It is a maxim among these lawyers that whatever hath been done before may legally be done again: and therefore they take special care to record all the decisions formerly made against common justice and the general reason of mankind. These, under the name of *precedents*, they produce as authorities to justify the most iniquitous opinions; and the judges never fail of decreeing accordingly.

In pleading, they studiously avoid entering into the merits of the cause, but are loud, violent, and tedious in dwelling upon all circumstances which are not to the purpose. For instance, in the case already mentioned; they never desire to know what claim or title my adversary hath to my cow, but whether the said cow were red or black, her horns long or short; whether the field I graze her in be round or square, whether she were milked at home or abroad, what diseases she is subject to, and the like; after which they consult precedents, adjourn the cause from time to time, and in ten, twenty, or thirty years come to an issue.[11]

It is likewise to be observed that this society hath a peculiar cant and jargon of their own that no other mortal can understand and wherein all their laws are written, which they take special care to multiply; whereby they have wholly confounded the very essence of truth and falsehood, of right and wrong; so that it will take thirty years to decide whether the field left me by my ancestors for six generations belongs to me or to a stranger three hundred miles off.

In the trial of persons accused for crimes against the state the method is much more short and commendable: the judge first sends to sound the disposition of those in power, after which he can easily hang or save the criminal, strictly preserving all due forms of law.

Here my master, interposing, said it was a pity that creatures endowed with such prodigious abilities of mind as these lawyers, by the description I gave of them, must certainly be, were not rather encouraged to be instructors of others in wisdom and knowledge. In answer to which I assured his Honour that in all points out of their own trade they were usually the most ignorant and stupid generation [12] among us, the most despicable in common conversation, avowed enemies to all knowledge and learning, and equally disposed to

10. Profession.
11. Decision, result.
12. Breed.

pervert the general reason of mankind in every other subject of discourse as in that of their own profession.

Chapter Six: A continuation of the state of England. The character of a first minister.

My master was yet wholly at a loss to understand what motives could incite this race of lawyers to perplex, disquiet, and weary themselves by engaging in a confederacy of injustice, merely for the sake of injuring their fellow-animals; neither could he comprehend what I meant in saying they did it for hire. Whereupon I was at much pains to describe to him the use of money, the materials it was made of, and the value of the metals; that when a Yahoo had got a great store of this precious substance, he was able to purchase whatever he had a mind to, the finest clothing, the noblest houses, great tracts of land, the most costly meats and drinks, and have his choice of the most beautiful females. Therefore since money alone was able to perform all these feats, our Yahoos thought they could never have enough of it to spend or to save, as they found themselves inclined from their natural bent either to profusion or avarice. That the rich man enjoyed the fruit of the poor man's labour, and the latter were a thousand to one in proportion to the former. That the bulk of our people was forced to live miserably, by labouring every day for small wages to make a few live plentifully.

I enlarged myself much on these and many other particulars to the same purpose: but his Honour was still to seek;[1] for he went upon a supposition that all animals had a title to their share in the productions of the earth, and especially those who presided over the rest. Therefore he desired I would let him know what these costly meats were, and how any of us happened to want[2] them. Whereupon I enumerated as many sorts as came into my head, with the various methods of dressing them, which could not be done without sending vessels by sea to every part of the world, as well for liquors to drink as for sauces and innumerable other conveniencies. I assured him that this whole globe of earth must be at least three times gone round before one of our better female Yahoos could get her breakfast or a cup to put it in. He said that must needs be a miserable country which cannot furnish food for its own inhabitants.

But what he chiefly wondered at was how such vast tracts of ground as I described should be wholly without fresh water, and the people put to the necessity of sending over the sea for drink. I replied that England (the dear place of my nativity) was computed to produce three times the quantity of food more than its inhabitants are able to consume, as well as liquors extracted from grain or pressed out of the fruit of certain trees, which made excellent drink, and the same proportion in every other convenience of life. But in order to feed the luxury and intemperance of the males and the vanity of the females, we sent away the greatest part of our necessary things to other countries, from whence in return we brought the materials of diseases, folly, and vice, to spend among ourselves. Hence it follows of necessity that vast

1. At a loss to understand.
2. Lack.

numbers of our people are compelled to seek their livelihood by begging, robbing, stealing, cheating, pimping, forswearing, flattering, suborning, forging, gaming, lying, fawning, hectoring, voting, scribbling, star-gazing, poisoning, whoring, canting, libelling, free-thinking, and the like occupations: every one of which terms I was at much pains to make him understand.

That wine was not imported among us from foreign countries to supply the want of water or other drinks, but because it was a sort of liquid which made us merry by putting us out of our senses; diverted all melancholy thoughts, begat wild extravagant imaginations in the brain, raised our hopes, and banished our fears, suspended every office of reason for a time, and deprived us of the use of our limbs, until we fell into a profound sleep; although it must be confessed that we always awaked sick and dispirited, and that the use of this liquor filled us with diseases which made our lives uncomfortable and short.

But beside all this, the bulk of our people supported themselves by furnishing the necessities or conveniences of life to the rich and to each other. For instance, when I am at home and dressed as I ought to be, I carry on my body the workmanship of an hundred tradesmen; the building and furniture of my house employ as many more, and five times the number to adorn my wife.

I was going on to tell him of another sort of people who get their livelihood by attending the sick, having upon some occasions informed his Honour that many of my crew had died of diseases. But here it was with the utmost difficulty that I brought him to apprehend what I meant. He could easily conceive that a Houyhnhnm grew weak and heavy a few days before his death, or by some accident might hurt a limb. But that nature, who works all things to perfection, should suffer any pains to breed in our bodies, he thought impossible, and desired to know the reason of so unaccountable an evil. I told him we fed on a thousand things which operated contrary to each other; that we eat when we were not hungry and drank without the provocation of thirst; that we sat whole nights drinking strong liquors without eating a bit, which disposed us to sloth, enflamed our bodies, and precipitated or prevented digestion. That prostitute female Yahoos acquired a certain malady which bred rottenness in the bones of those who fell into their embraces; that this and many other diseases were propagated from father to son, so that great numbers come into the world with complicated maladies upon them. That it would be endless to give him a catalogue of all diseases incident to human bodies; for they could not be fewer than five or six hundred, spread over every limb and joint; in short, every part, external and intestine, having diseases appropriated to each. To remedy which, there was a sort of people bred up among us in the profession or pretence of curing the sick. And because I had some skill in the faculty, I would, in gratitude to his Honour, let him know the whole mystery[3] and method by which they proceed.

Their fundamental is that all diseases arise from repletion, from whence they conclude that a great evacuation of the body is necessary, either through the natural passage or upwards at the mouth. Their next business is, from herbs,

3. Trade secret.

minerals, gums, oils, shells, salts, juices, seaweed, excrements, barks of trees, serpents, toads, frogs, spiders, dead men's flesh and bones, birds, beasts, and fishes, to form a composition for smell and taste the most abominable, nauseous, and detestable that they can possibly contrive, which the stomach immediately rejects with loathing, and this they call a vomit; or else from the same storehouse, with some other poisonous additions, they command us to take in at the orifice above or below (just as the physician then happens to be disposed) a medicine equally annoying and disgustful to the bowels, which, relaxing the belly, drives down all before it, and this they call a purge or a clyster.[4] For nature (as the physicians allege) having intended the superior anterior orifice only for the intromission of solids and liquids and the inferior posterior for ejection, these artists, ingeniously considering that in all diseases nature is forced out of her seat, therefore to replace her in it, the body must be treated in a manner directly contrary, by interchanging the use of each orifice, forcing solids and liquids in at the anus and making evacuations at the mouth.

But besides real diseases we are subject to many that are only imaginary, for which the physicians have invented imaginary cures; these have their several names, and so have the drugs that are proper for them, and with these our female Yahoos are always infested.

One great excellency in this tribe is their skill at prognostics, wherein they seldom fail; their predictions in real diseases, when they rise to any degree of malignity, generally portending death, which is always in their power when recovery is not: and therefore, upon any unexpected signs of amendment, after they have pronounced their sentence, rather than be accused as false prophets, they know how to approve[5] their sagacity to the world by a seasonable dose.

They are likewise of special use to husbands and wives who are grown weary of their mates, to eldest sons, to great ministers of state, and often to princes.

I had formerly upon occasion discoursed with my master upon the nature of our government in general, and particularly of our own excellent constitution, deservedly the wonder and envy of the whole world. But having here accidentally mentioned a *minister of state,* he commanded me some time after to inform him, what species of Yahoo I particularly meant by that appellation.

I told him that a *first* or *chief minister of state,*[6] whom I intended to describe, was a creature wholly exempt from joy and grief, love and hatred, pity and anger; at least makes use of no other passions but a violent desire of wealth, power, and titles; that he applies his words to all uses except to the indication of his mind; that he never tells a *truth* but with an intent that you should take it for a *lie,* nor a *lie* but with a design that you should take it for a *truth;* that those he speaks worst of behind their backs are in the surest way to preferment; and whenever he begins to praise you to others or to yourself, you are from

4. Enema.

5. Demonstrate.

6. Clearly a reference to Sir Robert Walpole (1676–1745), the first minister to be called "prime" (not an official title) because of his pre-eminence under the rule of George I and later, with the co-operation of Queen Caroline, of George II as well; the object of attacks by Swift, Pope, and Gay—on the score not only of his tyrannical political control but also of his use of writers as paid hacks of official policy.

that day forlorn.[7] The worst mark you can receive is a *promise,* especially when it is confirmed with an oath; after which every wise man retires and gives over all hopes.

There are three methods by which a man may rise to be chief minister: the first is by knowing how with prudence to dispose of a wife, a daughter, or a sister; the second, by betraying or undermining his predecessor; and the third is by a *furious zeal* in public assemblies against the corruptions of the court. But a wise prince would rather choose to employ those who practise the last of these methods; because such zealots prove always the most obsequious and subservient to the will and passions of their master. That these *ministers,* having all employments at their disposal, preserve themselves in power by bribing the majority of a senate or great council; and at last, by an expedient called an *act of indemnity* [8] (whereof I described the nature to him) they secure themselves from after reckonings, and retire from the public laden with the spoils of the nation.

The palace of a chief minister is a seminary to breed up others in his own trade: the pages, lackeys, and porter, by imitating their master, become ministers of state in their several districts, and learn to excel in the three principal ingredients, of *insolence, lying,* and *bribery.* Accordingly, they have a subaltern [9] court paid to them by persons of the best rank, and sometimes by the force of dexterity and impudence arrive through several gradations to be successors to their lord.

He is usually governed by a decayed wench or favourite footman, who are the tunnels through which all graces [10] are conveyed and may properly be called, in the last resort, the governors of the kingdom.

One day my master, having heard me mention the nobility of my country, was pleased to make me a compliment which I could not pretend to deserve: that he was sure I must have been born of some noble family, because I far exceeded in shape, colour, and cleanliness all the Yahoos of his nation, although I seemed to fail in strength and agility, which must be imputed to my different way of living from those other brutes; and, besides, I was not only endowed with the faculty of speech, but likewise with some rudiments of reason, to a degree that with all his acquaintance I passed for a prodigy.[11]

He made me observe, that among the Houyhnhnms, the *white,* the *sorrel,* and the *iron-grey,* were not so exactly shaped as the *bay,* the *dapple-grey,* and the *black,* nor born with equal talents of mind or a capacity to improve them; and therefore continued always in the condition of servants without ever aspiring to match out of their own race, which in that country would be reckoned monstrous and unnatural.

I made his Honour my most humble acknowledgments for the good opinion

7. Doomed, lost.

8. Such acts were often passed (with good reason) to free ministers from being prosecuted for actions in office by those who succeeded them to power; but they could become, as Swift pointed out in 1710, laws "enacted to take away the force of all laws whatsoever, by which a man may safely commit upon the last of June what he would be infallibly hanged for if he committed on the first of July" (*Examiner,* No. 18).

9. Subordinate.

10. Favors.

11. Wonder.

he was pleased to conceive of me; but assured him at the same time that my birth was of the lower sort, having been born of plain honest parents who were just able to give me a tolerable education: that *nobility* among us was altogether a different thing from the idea he had of it; that our young noblemen are bred from their childhood in idleness and luxury; that as soon as years will permit, they consume their vigour and contract odious diseases among lewd females; and when their fortunes are almost ruined, they marry some woman of mean birth, disagreeable person, and unsound constitution, merely for the sake of money, whom they hate and despise. That the productions of such marriages are generally scrofulous, rickety, or deformed children, by which means the family seldom continues above three generations, unless the wife take care to provide a healthy father among her neighbours or domestics, in order to improve and continue the breed. That a weak diseased body, a meagre countenance, and sallow complexion are the true marks of noble blood; and a healthy robust appearance is so disgraceful in a man of quality that the world concludes his real father to have been a groom or a coachman. The imperfections of his mind run parallel with those of his body, being a composition of spleen,[12] dullness, ignorance, caprice, sensuality, and pride.

Without the consent of this illustrious body[13] no law can be enacted, repealed, or altered, and these nobles have likewise the decision of all our possessions without appeal.

Chapter Seven: The author's great love of his native country. His master's observations upon the constitution and administration of England, as described by the author, with parallel cases and comparisons. His master's observations upon human nature.

The reader may be disposed to wonder how I could prevail on myself to give so free a representation of my own species among a race of mortals who were already too apt to conceive the vilest opinion of humankind from the entire congruity betwixt me and their Yahoos. But I must freely confess that the many virtues of those excellent quadrupeds, placed in opposite view to human corruptions, had so far opened my eyes and enlarged my understanding that I began to view the actions and passions of man in a very different light, and to think the honour of my own kind not worth managing;[1] which, besides, it was impossible for me to do before a person of so acute a judgment as my master, who daily convinced me of a thousand faults in myself whereof I had not the least perception before, and which with us would never be numbered even among human infirmities. I had likewise learned from his example an utter detestation of all falsehood or disguise; and truth appeared so amiable to me that I determined upon sacrificing everything to it.

Let me deal so candidly with the reader as to confess that there was yet a

12. Temper or passion; the function of the spleen was not known in Swift's age, and to it was attributed a variety of psychosomatic symptoms—melancholy, gloom, ennui, hypochondria, the "vapors"—which were often fashionable, as is pointed out later in the chapter, among "the lazy, the luxurious, and the rich."
13. The House of Lords.

1. Protecting.

much stronger motive for the freedom I took in my representation of things. I had not been a year in this country before I contracted such a love and veneration for the inhabitants that I entered on a firm resolution never to return to humankind, but to pass the rest of my life among these admirable Houyhnhnms in the contemplation and practice of every virtue; where I could have no example or incitement to vice. But it was decreed by Fortune, my perpetual enemy, that so great a felicity should not fall to my share. However, it is now some comfort to reflect that in what I said of my countrymen I extenuated their faults as much as I durst before so strict an examiner, and upon every article gave as favourable a turn as the matter would bear. For, indeed, who is there alive that will not be swayed by his bias and partiality to the place of his birth?

I have related the substance of several conversations I had with my master, during the greatest part of the time I had the honour to be in his service, but have indeed for brevity sake omitted much more than is here set down.

When I had answered all his questions, and his curiosity seemed to be fully satisfied, he sent for me one morning early and, commanding me to sit down at some distance (an honour which he had never before conferred upon me), he said he had been very seriously considering my whole story, as far as it related both to myself and my country: that he looked upon us as a sort of animals to whose share, by what accident he could not conjecture, some small pittance of reason had fallen, whereof we made no other use than by its assistance to aggravate our natural corruptions and to acquire new ones which nature had not given us. That we disarmed ourselves of the few abilities she had bestowed, had been very successful in multiplying our original wants, and seemed to spend our whole lives in vain endeavours to supply them by our own inventions. That as to myself, it was manifest I had neither the strength or agility of a common Yahoo, that I walked infirmly on my hinder feet, had found out a contrivance to make my claws of no use or defence and to remove the hair from my chin, which was intended as a shelter from the sun and the weather. Lastly, that I could neither run with speed nor climb trees like my brethren (as he called them), the Yahoos in this country.

That our institutions of government and law were plainly owing to our gross defects in reason and, by consequence, in virtue; because reason alone is sufficient to govern a rational creature; which was therefore a character we had no pretence to challenge, even from the account I had given of my own people, although he manifestly perceived that in order to favour them I had concealed many particulars and often *said the thing which was not*.

He was the more confirmed in this opinion because he observed that, as I agreed in every feature of my body with other Yahoos, except where it was to my real disadvantage in point of strength, speed, and activity, the shortness of my claws, and some other particulars where nature had no part; so from the representation I had given him of our lives, our manners, and our actions, he found as near a resemblance in the disposition of our minds. He said the Yahoos were known to hate one another more than they did any different species of animals; and the reason usually assigned was the odiousness of their own shapes, which all could see in the rest but not in themselves. He had therefore begun to think it not unwise in us to cover our bodies and, by that invention, conceal many of our deformities from each other, which would else be hardly supportable. But he now found he had been mistaken and that the dissensions of those brutes in his country were owing to the same cause with ours, as I had described them. For if (said he) you throw among five Yahoos as much food as would be sufficient for fifty, they will, instead of eating peaceably, fall together by the ears, each single one impatient to have all to itself; and therefore a servant was usually employed to stand by while they were feeding abroad, and those kept at home were tied at a distance from each other. That if a cow died of age or accident before a Houyhnhnm could secure it for his own Yahoos, those in the neighbourhood would come in herds to seize it, and then would ensue such a battle as I had described, with terrible wounds made by their claws on both sides, although they seldom were able to kill one another for want of such convenient instruments of death as we had invented. At other times the like battles have been fought between the Yahoos of several neighbourhoods without any visible cause; those of one district watching all opportunities to surprise the next before they are prepared. But if they find their project hath miscarried, they return home, and, for want of enemies, engage in what I call a civil war among themselves.

That in some fields of this country there are certain shining stones of several colours, whereof the Yahoos are violently fond, and when part of these stones are fixed in the earth, as it sometimes happeneth, they will dig with their claws for whole days to get them out, and carry them away, and hide them by heaps in their kennels; but still looking round with great caution for fear their comrades should find out their treasure. My master said he could never discover the reason of this unnatural appetite or how these stones could be of any use to a Yahoo; but now he believed it might proceed from the same principle of avarice which I had ascribed to mankind; that he had once, by way of experiment, privately removed a heap of these stones from the place where one of his Yahoos had buried it: whereupon the sordid animal, missing his treasure, by his loud lamenting brought the whole herd to the place, there miserably howled, then fell to biting and tearing the rest, began to pine away, would neither eat, nor sleep, nor work, till he ordered a servant privately to convey the stones into the same hole and hide them as before; which when his Yahoo had found, he presently recovered his spirits and good humour, but took care to remove them to a better hiding-place, and hath ever since been a very serviceable brute.

My master farther assured me, which I also observed myself, that in the fields where these shining stones abound, the fiercest and most frequent battles are fought, occasioned by perpetual inroads of the neighbouring Yahoos.

He said it was common when two Yahoos discovered such a stone in a field and were contending which of them should be the proprietor, a third would take the advantage and carry it away from them both; which my master would needs contend to have some resemblance with our *suits at law;* wherein I thought it for our credit not to undeceive him; since the decision he mentioned was much more equitable than many decrees among us: because the plaintiff and defendant there lost nothing beside the stone they contended for, whereas our *courts of equity* would never have dismissed the cause while either of them had anything left.

My master, continuing his discourse, said, there was nothing that rendered the Yahoos more odious than their undistinguishing appetite to devour everything that came in their way, whether herbs, roots, berries, corrupted flesh of animals, or all mingled together: and it was peculiar in their temper that they were fonder of what they could get by rapine or stealth at a greater distance than much better food provided for them at home. If their prey held out, they would eat till they were ready to burst, after which nature had pointed out to them a certain root that gave them a general evacuation.

There was also another kind of root very juicy, but something rare and difficult to be found, which the Yahoos sought for with much eagerness and would suck it with great delight; and it produced in them the same effects that wine hath upon us. It would make them sometimes hug and sometimes tear one another; they would howl and grin, and chatter, and reel, and tumble, and then fall asleep in the mud.

I did indeed observe that the Yahoos were the only animals in this country subject to any diseases; which, however, were much fewer than horses have among us, and contracted not by any ill treatment they meet with but by the nastiness and greediness of that sordid brute. Neither has their language any more than a general appellation for those maladies, which is borrowed from the name of the beast, and called *Hnea Yahoo,* or the *Yahoo's Evil;* and the cure prescribed is a mixture of their own dung and urine forcibly put down the Yahoo's throat. This I have since often known to have been taken with success and do here freely recommend it to my countrymen for the public good, as an admirable specific against all diseases produced by repletion.

As to learning, government, arts, manufactures, and the like, my master confessed he could find little or no resemblance between the Yahoos of that country and those in ours. For he only meant to observe what parity there was in our natures. He had heard indeed some curious Houyhnhnms observe that in most herds there was a sort of ruling Yahoo (as among us there is generally some leading or principal stag in a park), who was always more deformed in body and mischievous in disposition than any of the rest. That this leader had usually a favourite as like himself as he could get, whose employment was to lick his master's feet and posteriors and drive the female Yahoos to his kennel; for which he was now and then rewarded with a piece of ass's flesh. This favourite is hated by the whole herd, and therefore to protect himself keeps always near the person of his leader. He usually continues in office till a worse can be found; but the very moment he is discarded, his successor, at the head of all the Yahoos in that district, young and old, male and female, come in a body and discharge their excrements upon him from head to foot. But how far this might be applicable to our *courts* and *favourites,* and *ministers of state,* my master said I could best determine.

I durst make no return to this malicious insinuation, which debased human understanding below the sagacity of a common *hound,* who has judgment enough to distinguish and follow the cry of the ablest dog in the pack without being ever mistaken.

My master told me there were some qualities remarkable in the Yahoos which he had not observed me to mention, or at least very slightly, in the accounts I had given him of humankind. He said those animals, like other brutes, had their females in common; but in this they differed, that the she-Yahoo would admit the male while she was pregnant and that the hees would quarrel and fight with the females as fiercely as with each other. Both which practices were such degrees of infamous brutality that no other sensitive creature ever arrived at.

Another thing he wondered at in the Yahoos was their strange disposition to nastiness and dirt, whereas there appears to be a natural love of cleanliness in all other animals. As to the two former accusations, I was glad to let them pass without any reply because I had not a word to offer upon them in defence of my species, which otherwise I certainly had done from my own inclinations. But I could have easily vindicated humankind from the imputation of singularity upon the last article if there had been any *swine* in that country (as unluckily for me there were not), which, although it may be a sweeter quadruped than a Yahoo, cannot, I humbly conceive, in justice pretend to more cleanliness; and so his Honour himself must have owned, if he had seen their filthy way of feeding and their custom of wallowing and sleeping in the mud.

My master likewise mentioned another quality which his servants had discovered in several Yahoos and to him was wholly unaccountable. He said a fancy would sometimes take a Yahoo to retire into a corner, to lie down and howl, and groan, and spurn away all that came near him, although he were young and fat, and wanted neither food nor water; nor did the servants imagine what could possibly ail him. And the only remedy they found was to set him to hard work, after which he would infallibly come to himself. To this I was silent out of partiality to my own kind; yet here I could plainly discover the true seeds of *spleen,* which only seizeth on the *lazy,* the *luxurious,* and the *rich;* who, if they were forced to undergo the same regimen, I would undertake for the cure.

His Honour had farther observed that a female Yahoo would often stand behind a bank or a bush, to gaze on the young males passing by, and then appear and hide, using many antic gestures and grimaces, at which time it was observed that she had a most offensive smell; and when any of the males advanced, would slowly retire, looking often back, and with a counterfeit show of fear run off into some convenient place where she knew the male would follow her.

At other times if a female stranger came among them, three or four of her own sex would get about her and stare and chatter, and grin, and smell her all over, and then turn off with gestures that seemed to express contempt and disdain.

Perhaps my master might refine a little in these speculations, which he had drawn from what he observed himself or had been told him by others: however, I could not reflect without some amazement, and much sorrow, that the rudiments of *lewdness, coquetry, censure,* and *scandal* should have place by instinct in womankind.

I expected every moment that my master would accuse the Yahoos of those unnatural appetites in both sexes so common among us. But nature, it seems, hath not been so expert a schoolmistress; and these politer pleasures are entirely the productions of art and reason, on our side of the globe.

Chapter Eight: The author relateth several particulars of the Yahoos. The great virtues of the Houyhnhnms. The education and exercise of their youth. Their General Assembly.

As I ought to have understood human nature much better than I supposed it possible for my master to do, so it was easy to apply the character he gave of the Yahoos to myself and my countrymen, and I believed I could yet make farther discoveries from my own observation. I therefore often begged his Honour to let me go among the herds of Yahoos in the neighbourhood, to which he always very graciously consented, being perfectly convinced that the hatred I bore those brutes would never suffer me to be corrupted by them; and his Honour ordered one of his servants, a strong sorrel nag, very honest and good-natured, to be my guard, without whose protection I durst not undertake such adventures. For I have already told the reader how much I was pestered by those odious animals upon my first arrival. And I afterwards failed very narrowly three or four times of falling into their clutches, when I happened to stray at any distance without my hanger. And I have reason to believe they had some imagination that I was of their own species, which I often assisted myself by stripping up my sleeves and showing my naked arms and breast in their sight, when my protector was with me. At which times they would approach as near as they durst and imitate my actions after the manner of monkeys but ever with great signs of hatred, as a tame jackdaw, with cap and stockings, is always persecuted by the wild ones when he happens to be got among them.

They are prodigiously nimble from their infancy; however, I once caught a young male of three years old, and endeavoured by all marks of tenderness to make it quiet; but the little imp fell a-squalling, and scratching, and biting with such violence, that I was forced to let it go; and it was high time, for a whole troop of old ones came about us at the noise, but finding the cub was safe (for away it ran), and my sorrel nag being by, they durst not venture near us. I observed the young animal's flesh to smell very rank, and the stink was somewhat between a weasel and a fox, but much more disagreeable. I forgot another circumstance (and perhaps I might have the reader's pardon if it were wholly omitted) that while I held the odious vermin in my hands, it voided its filthy excrement of a yellow liquid substance all over my clothes; but by good fortune there was a small brook hard by where I washed myself as clean as I could, although I durst not come into my master's presence until I were sufficiently aired.

By what I could discover, the Yahoos appear to be the most unteachable of all animals, their capacities never reaching higher than to draw or carry burthens. Yet I am of opinion this defect ariseth chiefly from a perverse, restive disposition. For they are cunning, malicious, treacherous, and revengeful. They are strong and hardy, but of a cowardly spirit, and by consequence insolent, abject, and cruel. It is observed, that the red-haired of both sexes are more libidinous and mischievous than the rest, whom yet they much exceed in strength and activity.

The Houyhnhnms keep the Yahoos for present use in huts not far from the house; but the rest are sent abroad to certain fields where they dig up roots, eat several kinds of herbs, and search about for carrion, or sometimes catch weasels and *luhimuhs* (a sort of wild rat), which they greedily devour. Nature hath taught them to dig deep holes with their nails on the side of a rising ground, wherein they lie by themselves; only the kennels of the females are larger, sufficient to hold two or three cubs.

They swim from their infancy like frogs and are able to continue long under water, where they often take fish, which the females carry home to their young. And upon this occasion, I hope the reader will pardon my relating an odd adventure.

Being one day abroad with my protector the sorrel nag, and the weather exceeding hot, I entreated him to let me bathe in a river that was near. He consented, and I immediately stripped myself stark naked and went down softly into the stream. It happened that a young female Yahoo, standing behind a bank, saw the whole proceeding and, inflamed by desire, as the nag and I conjectured, came running with all speed and leaped into the water within five yards of the place where I bathed. I was never in my life so terribly frighted; the nag was grazing at some distance, not suspecting any harm. She embraced me after a most fulsome manner; I roared as loud as I could, and the nag came galloping towards me, whereupon she quitted her grasp, with the utmost reluctancy, and leaped upon the opposite bank, where she stood gazing and howling all the time I was putting on my clothes.

This was matter of diversion to my master and his family, as well as of mortification to myself. For now I could no longer deny that I was a real Yahoo in every limb and feature, since the females had a natural propensity to me as one of their own species: neither was the hair of this brute of a red colour (which might have been some excuse for an appetite a little irregular) but black as a sloe, and her countenance did not make an appearance altogether so hideous as the rest of the kind; for I think she could not be above eleven years old.

Having already lived three years in this country, the reader I suppose will expect that I should, like other travellers, give him some account of the manners and customs of its inhabitants, which it was indeed my principal study to learn.

As these noble Houyhnhnms are endowed by nature with a general disposition to all virtues and have no conceptions or ideas of what is evil in a rational creature, so their grand maxim is to cultivate reason and to be wholly governed by it. Neither is reason among them a point problematical as with us, where men can argue with plausibility on both sides of a question, but strikes you with immediate conviction, as it must needs do where it is not mingled, obscured, or discoloured by passion and interest. I remember it was with extreme difficulty that I could bring my master to understand the meaning of the word *opinion* or how a point could be disputable; because reason taught us to affirm or deny only where we are certain, and beyond our knowledge we cannot do either. So that controversies, wranglings, disputes, and positiveness in false or dubious propositions are evils unknown among the Houyhnhnms. In the like manner, when I used to explain to him our several systems of *natural philosophy,* he would laugh that a creature pretending to *reason* should value itself upon the knowledge of other people's conjectures and in things where that knowledge, if it were certain, could be of no use. Wherein he agreed entirely with the sentiments of Socrates, as Plato delivers them;[1] which I mention as the highest honour I can do that prince of philosophers. I have often since reflected what destruction such a doctrine would make in the libraries of Europe, and how many paths to fame would be then shut up in the learned world.

Friendship and *benevolence* are the two principal virtues among the Houyhnhnms, and these not confined to particular objects, but universal to the whole race. For a stranger from the remotest part is equally treated with the nearest neighbour, and wherever he goes looks upon himself as at home. They preserve *decency* and *civility* in the highest degrees, but are altogether ignorant of *ceremony*. They have no fondness[2] for their colts or foals, but the care they take in educating them proceeds entirely from the dictates of reason. And I observed my master to show the same affection to his neighbour's issue that he had for his own. They will have it that nature teaches them to love the whole species, and it is reason only that maketh a distinction of persons, where there is a superior degree of virtue.

When the matron Houyhnhnms have produced one of each sex, they no longer accompany with their consorts except they lose one of their issue by some casualty, which very seldom happens: but in such a case they meet again, or, when the like accident befalls a person whose wife is past bearing, some other couple bestows on him one of their own colts, and then go together a second time till the mother be pregnant. This caution is necessary to prevent the country from being overburthened with numbers. But the race of inferior Houyhnhnms bred up to be servants is not so strictly limited upon this article; these are allowed to produce three of each sex to be domestics in the noble families.

In their marriages they are exactly careful to choose such colours as will not make any disagreeable mixture in the breed. *Strength* is chiefly valued in the male, and *comeliness* in the female, not upon the account of *love*, but to preserve the race from degenerating; for where a female happens to excel in strength, a consort is chosen with regard to *comeliness*. Courtship, love, presents, jointures, settlements, have no place in their thoughts or terms whereby to express them in their language. The young couple meet and are joined merely because it is the determination of their parents and friends: it is what they see done every day, and they look upon it as one of the necessary actions in a reasonable being. But the violation of marriage, or any other unchastity, was never heard of: and the married pair pass their lives with the same friendship and mutual benevolence that they bear to all others of the same species who come in their way; without jealousy, fondness, quarrelling, or discontent.

In educating the youth of both sexes, their method is admirable and highly deserves our imitation. These are not suffered to taste a grain of oats, except upon certain days, till eighteen years old; nor milk but very rarely; and in summer they graze two hours in the morning and as many in the evening, which their parents likewise observe, but the servants are not allowed above half that time, and a great part of their grass is brought home, which they eat at the most convenient hours, when they can be best spared from work.

1. Perhaps a reference to Plato's *Phaedo* 97–98, where Socrates describes his high hopes upon hearing of Anaxagoras' doctrines and his disappointment on learning more.
2. Doting or foolish affection.

Temperance, industry, exercise and *cleanliness*, are the lessons equally enjoined to the young ones of both sexes: and my master thought it monstrous in us to give the females a different kind of education from the males except in some articles of domestic management; whereby, as he truly observed, one half of our natives were good for nothing but bringing children into the world: and to trust the care of their children to such useless animals, he said, was yet a greater instance of brutality.

But the Houyhnhnms train up their youth to strength, speed, and hardiness by exercising them in running races up and down steep hills or over hard stony grounds; and when they are all in a sweat, they are ordered to leap over head and ears into a pond or a river. Four times a year the youth of certain districts meet to show their proficiency in running and leaping and other feats of strength or agility, where the victor is rewarded with a song made in his or her praise. On this festival the servants drive a herd of Yahoos into the field, laden with hay and oats and milk for a repast to the Houyhnhnms; after which these brutes are immediately driven back again for fear of being noisome to the assembly.

Every fourth year, at the vernal equinox, there is a representative council of the whole nation, which meets in a plain about twenty miles from our house, and continues about five or six days. Here they inquire into the state and condition of the several districts: whether they abound or be deficient in hay or oats, or cows or Yahoos. And wherever there is any want (which is but seldom) it is immediately supplied by unanimous consent and contribution. Here likewise the regulation of children is settled: as for instance, if a Houyhnhnm hath two males, he changeth one of them with another who hath two females; and when a child hath been lost by any casualty, where the mother is past breeding, it is determind what family in the district shall breed another to supply the loss.

Chapter Nine: A grand debate at the General Assembly of the Houyhnhnms, and how it was determined. The learning of the Houyhnhnms. Their buildings. Their manner of burials. The defectiveness of their language.

One of these grand assemblies was held in my time, about three months before my departure, whither my master went as the representative of our district. In this council was resumed their old debate, and indeed the only debate that ever happened in their country; whereof my master after his return gave me a very particular account.

The question to be debated was whether the Yahoos should be exterminated from the face of the earth. One of the members for the affirmative offered several arguments of great strength and weight, alleging that, as the Yahoos were the most filthy, noisome, and deformed animal which nature ever produced, so they were the most restive and indocible, mischievous and malicious: they would privately suck the teats of the Houyhnhnms' cows, kill and devour their cats, trample down their oats and grass, if they were not continually watched, and commit a thousand other extravagancies. He took notice of a general tradition that Yahoos had not been always in their country: but that many ages ago two of these brutes appeared together upon a mountain,[1] whether produced by the heat of the sun upon corrupted mud and slime or from the ooze and froth of the sea was never known. That these Yahoos engendered, and their brood in a short time grew so numerous as to overrun and infest the whole nation. That the Houyhnhnms, to get rid of this evil, made a general hunting, and at last enclosed the whole herd; and, destroying the elder, every Houyhnhnm kept two young ones in a kennel and brought them to such a degree of tameness as an animal so savage by nature can be capable of acquiring, using them for draft and carriage. That there seemed to be much truth in this tradition, and that those creatures could not be *ylnhniamshy* (or *aborigines* of the land) because of the violent hatred the Houyhnhnms, as well as all other animals, bore them; which although their evil disposition sufficiently deserved, could never have arrived at so high a degree if they had been aborigines, or else they would have long since been rooted out. That the inhabitants, taking a fancy to use the service of the Yahoos, had very imprudently neglected to cultivate the breed of asses, which were a comely animal, easily kept, more tame and orderly, without any offensive smell, strong enough for labour, although they yield to the other in agility of body; and if their braying be no agreeable sound, it is far preferable to the horrible howlings of the Yahoos.

Several others declared their sentiments to the same purpose, when my master proposed an expedient to the assembly, whereof he had indeed borrowed the hint from me. He approved of the tradition mentioned by the honourable member who spoke before, and affirmed that the two Yahoos said to be first seen among them had been driven thither over the sea; that coming to land and being forsaken by their companions, they retired to the mountains and, degenerating by degrees, became in process of time much more savage than those of their own species in the country from whence these two originals came. The reason of his assertion was that he had now in his possession a certain wonderful Yahoo (meaning myself) which most of them had heard of and many of them had seen. He then related to them how he first found me; that my body was all covered with an artificial composure [2] of the skins and hairs of other animals: that I spoke in a language of my own and had thoroughly learned theirs: that I had related to him the accidents which brought me thither: that when he saw me without my covering, I was an exact Yahoo in every part, only of a whiter colour, less hairy, and with shorter claws. He added, how I had endeavoured to persuade him that in my own and other countries the Yahoos acted as the governing, rational animal, and held the Houyhnhnms in servitude: that he observed in me all the qualities of a Yahoo, only a little more civilized by some tincture of reason, which however was in a degree as far inferior to the Houyhnhnm race as the Yahoos of their country were to me: that, among other things, I mentioned a custom we had of castrating Houyhnhnms when they were young in order to render them tame; that the operation was easy and safe; that it was no shame to learn wisdom from brutes, as industry is taught by the ant and building by the swallow. (For so I translate the word *lyhannh*, although it be a much larger fowl.) That this

1. Perhaps offered by Swift with some ironic suggestion of the fallen Adam and Eve descending from the "mountain" where Milton placed the Garden of Eden (*Paradise Lost* IV.226); but, of course, all nature falls with man in Milton's poem.
2. Composition.

invention might be practised upon the younger Yahoos here, which, besides rendering them tractable and fitter for use, would in an age put an end to the whole species without destroying life. That in the meantime the Houyhnhnms should be *exhorted* to cultivate the breed of asses, which, as they are in all respects more valuable brutes, so they have this advantage, to be fit for service at five years old, which the others are not till twelve.

This was all my master thought fit to tell me at that time of what passed in the grand council. But he was pleased to conceal one particular which related personally to myself, whereof I soon felt the unhappy effect, as the reader will know in its proper place, and from whence I date all the succeeding misfortunes of my life.

The Houyhnhnms have no letters, and consequently their knowledge is all traditional. But there happening few events of any moment among a people so well united, naturally disposed to every virtue, wholly governed by reason, and cut off from all commerce with other nations, the historical part is easily preserved without burthening their memories. I have already observed that they are subject to no diseases, and therefore can have no need of physicians. However, they have excellent medicines composed of herbs, to cure accidental bruises and cuts in the pastern or frog [3] of the foot by sharp stones, as well as other maims and hurts in the several parts of the body.

They calculate the year by the revolution of the sun and the moon, but use no subdivisions into weeks. They are well enough acquainted with the motions of those two luminaries and understand the nature of eclipses; and this is the utmost progress of their astronomy.

In poetry they must be allowed to excel all other mortals; wherein the justness of their similes and the minuteness as well as exactness of their descriptions are indeed inimitable. Their verses abound very much in both of these and usually contain either some exalted notions of friendship and benevolence, or the praises of those who were victors in races and other bodily exercises. Their buildings, although very rude and simple, are not inconvenient, but well contrived to defend them from all injuries of cold and heat. They have a kind of tree which at forty years old loosens in the root and falls with the first storm; it grows very straight and, being pointed like stakes with a sharp stone (for the Houyhnhnms know not the use of iron), they stick them erect in the ground about ten inches asunder, and then weave in oat-straw or sometimes wattles betwixt them. The roof is made after the same manner and so are the doors.

The Houyhnhnms use the hollow part between the pastern and the hoof of their forefeet as we do our hands, and this with greater dexterity than I could at first imagine. I have seen a white mare of our family thread a needle (which I lent her on purpose) with that joint. They milk their cows, reap their oats, and do all the work which requires hands, in the same manner. They have a kind of hard flints, which, by grinding against other stones, they form into instruments that serve instead of wedges, axes, and hammers. With tools made of these flints they likewise cut their hay and reap their oats, which there groweth naturally in several fields: the Yahoos draw home the sheaves in carriages, and the servants tread them in certain covered huts, to get out the

3. The horny sole.

grain, which is kept in stores. They make a rude kind of earthen and wooden vessels and bake the former in the sun.

If they can avoid casualties, they die only of old age, and are buried in the obscurest places that can be found, their friends and relations expressing neither joy nor grief at their departure; nor does the dying person discover the least regret that he is leaving the world, any more than if he were upon returning home from a visit to one of his neighbours. I remember my master having once made an appointment with a friend and his family to come to his house upon some affair of importance; on the day fixed, the mistress and her two children came very late. She made two excuses, first for her husband, who, as she said, happened that very morning to *lhnuwnh*. The word is strongly expressive in their language but not easily rendered into English; it signifies, *to retire to his first mother*. Her excuse for not coming sooner was that, her husband dying late in the morning, she was a good while consulting her servants about a convenient place where his body should be laid; and I observed she behaved herself at our house as cheerfully as the rest; she died about three months after.

They live generally to seventy or seventy-five years, very seldom to fourscore; some weeks before their death they feel a gradual decay, but without pain. During this time they are much visited by their friends because they cannot go abroad with their usual ease and satisfaction. However, about ten days before their death, which they seldom fail in computing, they return the visits that have been made them by those who are nearest in the neighbourhood, being carried in a convenient sledge drawn by Yahoos, which vehicle they use, not only upon this occasion but when they grow old, upon long journeys, or when they are lamed by any accident. And therefore when the dying Houyhnhnms return those visits, they take a solemn leave of their friends, as if they were going to some remote part of the country where they designed to pass the rest of their lives.

I know not whether it may be worth observing that the Houyhnhnms have no word in their language to express anything that is evil, except what they borrow from the deformities or ill qualities of the Yahoos. Thus they denote the folly of a servant, an omission of a child, a stone that cuts their feet, a continuance of foul or unseasonable weather, and the like, by adding to each the epithet of *yahoo*. For instance, *hhnm yahoo, whnaholm yahoo, ynlhmnawihlma yahoo,* and an ill-contrived house *ynholmhnmrohlnw yahoo.*

I could with great pleasure enlarge farther upon the manners and virtues of this excellent people; but, intending in a short time to publish a volume by itself expressly upon that subject, I refer the reader thither; and in the meantime, proceed to relate my own sad catastrophe.

Chapter Ten: The author's economy and happy life among the Houyhnhnms. His great improvement in virtue by conversing with them. Their conversations. The author hath notice given him by his master that he must depart from the country. He falls into a swoon for grief, but submits. He contrives and finishes a canoe, by the help of a fellow servant, and puts to sea at a venture.

I had settled my little economy to my own heart's content. My master had ordered a room to be made for me after their manner about six yards from the house, the sides and floors of which I plastered with clay and covered with rush mats of my own contriving; I had beaten hemp, which there grows wild, and made of it a sort of ticking: this I filled with the feathers of several birds I had taken with springes made of Yahoos' hairs, and were excellent food. I had worked two chairs with my knife, the sorrel nag helping me in the grosser and more laborious part. When my clothes were worn to rags, I made myself others with the skins of rabbits and of a certain beautiful animal about the same size, called *nnuhnoh*, the skin of which is covered with a fine down. Of these I likewise made very tolerable stockings. I soled my shoes with wood which I cut from a tree and fitted to the upper leather; and when this was worn out, I supplied it with the skins of Yahoos dried in the sun. I often got honey out of hollow trees, which I mingled with water, or eat it with my bread. No man could more verify the truth of these two maxims, *That nature is very easily satisfied* and *That necessity is the mother of invention.* I enjoyed perfect health of body and tranquillity of mind; I did not feel the treachery or inconstancy of a friend, nor the injuries of a secret or open enemy. I had no occasion of bribing, flattering, or pimping to procure the favour of any great man or of his minion. I wanted no fence against fraud or oppression; here was neither physician to destroy my body, nor lawyer to ruin my fortune; no informer to watch my words and actions or forge accusations against me for hire: here were no gibers, censurers, backbiters, pickpockets, highwaymen, housebreakers, attorneys, bawds, buffoons, gamesters, politicians, wits, splenetics, tedious talkers, controvertists, ravishers, murderers, robbers, virtuosos: [1] no leaders or followers of party and faction: no encouragers to vice by seducement or examples: no dungeon, axes, gibbets, whipping-posts, or pillories: no cheating shopkeepers or mechanics: no pride, vanity, or affectation: no fops, bullies, drunkards, strolling whores, or poxes: [2] no ranting, lewd, expensive wives: no stupid, proud pedants: no importunate, overbearing, quarrelsome, noisy, roaring, empty, conceited, swearing companions: no scoundrels raised from the dust upon the merit of their vices, or nobility thrown into it on account of their virtues: no lords, fiddlers, judges, or dancing-masters.

I had the favour of being admitted to several Houyhnhnms who came to visit or dine with my master; where his Honour graciously suffered me to wait in the room and listen to their discourse. Both he and his company would often descend to ask me questions and receive my answers. I had also sometimes the honour of attending my master in his visits to others. I never presumed to speak except in answer to a question, and then I did it with inward regret, because it was a loss of so much time for improving myself: but I was infinitely delighted with the station of an humble auditor in such conversations, where nothing passed but what was useful, expressed in the fewest and most significant words: where (as I have already said) the greatest decency [3] was observed without the least degree of ceremony; where no person spoke without being pleased himself and pleasing his companions; where there was no interruptions, tediousness, heat, or difference of sentiments. They have a notion that, when people are met together, a short silence doth much improve conversation: this

1. Amateur scientists.
2. Venereal diseases.
3. Decorum, sense of form.

I found to be true; for during those little intermissions of talk, new ideas would arise in their minds, which very much enlivened the discourse. Their subjects are generally on friendship and benevolence, on order and economy, sometimes upon the visible operations of nature or ancient traditions, upon the bounds and limits of virtue, upon the unerring rules of reason, or upon some determinations to be taken at the next Great Assembly, and often upon the various excellencies of poetry. I may add without vanity that my presence often gave them sufficient matter for discourse, because it afforded my master an occasion of letting his friends into the history of me and my country, upon which they were all pleased to descant in a manner not very advantageous to humankind; and for that reason I shall not repeat what they said: only I may be allowed to observe, that his Honour, to my great admiration, appeared to understand the nature of Yahoos much better than myself. He went through all our vices and follies and discovered many which I had never mentioned to him, by only supposing what qualities a Yahoo of their country, with a small proportion of reason, might be capable of exerting; and concluded, with too much probability, how vile as well as miserable such a creature must be.

I freely confess that all the little knowledge I have of any value was acquired by the lectures I received from my master and from hearing the discourses of him and his friends; to which I should be prouder to listen than to dictate to the greatest and wisest assembly in Europe. I admired the strength, comeliness, and speed of the inhabitants; and such a constellation of virtues in such amiable persons produced in me the highest veneration. At first, indeed, I did not feel that natural awe which the Yahoos and all other animals bear towards them; but it grew upon me by degrees, much sooner than I imagined, and was mingled with a respectiful love and gratitude, that they would condescend to distinguish me from the rest of my species.

When I thought of my family, my friends, my countrymen, or human race in general, I considered them as they really were, Yahoos in shape and disposition, perhaps a little more civilized and qualified with the gift of speech, but making no other use of reason than to improve and multiply those vices whereof their brethren in this country had only the share that nature allotted them. When I happened to behold the reflection of my own form in a lake or fountain, I turned away my face in horror and detestation of myself, and could better endure the sight of a common Yahoo than of my own person. By conversing with the Houyhnhnms and looking upon them with delight, I fell to imitate their gait and gesture, which is now grown into a habit, and my friends often tell me in a blunt way that I *trot like a horse;* which, however, I take for a great compliment: neither shall I disown that in speaking I am apt to fall into the voice and manner of the Houyhnhnms, and hear myself ridiculed on that account without the least mortification.

In the midst of this happiness, when I looked upon myself to be fully settled for life, my master sent for me one morning a little earlier than his usual hour. I observed by his countenance that he was in some perplexity and at a loss how to begin what he had to speak. After a short silence he told me he did not know how I would take what he was going to say; that in the last General Assembly, when the affair of the Yahoos was entered upon, the representatives had taken offence at his keeping a Yahoo (meaning myself) in his family more like a

Houyhnhnm than a brute animal. That he was known frequently to converse with me, as if he could receive some advantage or pleasure in my company: that such a practice was not agreeable to reason or nature, or a thing ever heard of before among them. The assembly did therefore *exhort* him either to employ me like the rest of my species or command me to swim back to the place from whence I came. That the first of these expedients was utterly rejected by all the Houyhnhnms who had ever seen me at his house or their own: for they alleged that, because I had some rudiments of reason, added to the natural pravity [4] of those animals, it was to be feared I might be able to seduce them into the woody and mountainous parts of the country and bring them in troops by night to destroy the Houyhnhnms' cattle, as being naturally of the ravenous kind and averse from labour.

My master added that he was daily pressed by the Houyhnhnms of the neighbourhood to have the assembly's *exhortation* executed, which he could not put off much longer. He doubted it would be impossible for me to swim to another country, and therefore wished I would contrive some sort of vehicle, resembling those I had described to him, that might carry me on the sea, in which work I should have the assistance of his own servants, as well as those of his neighbours. He concluded that for his own part he could have been content to keep me in his service as long as I lived, because he found I had cured myself of some bad habits and dispositions by endeavouring, as far as my inferior nature was capable, to imitate the Houyhnhnms.

I should here observe to the reader that a decree of the General Assembly in this country is expressed by the word *hnhloayn,* which signifies an *exhortation,* as near as I can render it: for they have no conception how a rational creature can be *compelled,* but only advised or *exhorted,* because no person can disobey reason without giving up his claim to be a rational creature.

I was struck with the utmost grief and despair at my master's discourse, and, being unable to support the agonies I was under, I fell into a swoon at his feet. When I came to myself he told me that he concluded I had been dead. (For these people are subject to no such imbecilities [5] of nature.) I answered, in a faint voice, that death would have been too great an happiness; that although I could not blame the assembly's *exhortation* or the urgency of his friends, yet, in my weak and corrupt judgment, I thought it might consist with reason to have been less rigorous. That I could not swim a league, and probably the nearest land to theirs might be distant above an hundred; that many materials, necessary for making a small vessel to carry me off, were wholly wanting in this country, which, however, I would attempt in obedience and gratitude to his Honour, although I concluded the thing to be impossible, and therefore looked on myself as already devoted [6] to destruction. That the certain prospect of an unnatural death was the least of my evils: for, supposing I should escape with life by some strange adventure, how could I think with temper [7] of passing my days among Yahoos and relapsing into my old corruptions for want of examples to lead and keep me within the paths of virtue?

4. Viciousness.
5. Frailties, weaknesses.
6. Doomed.
7. Equanimity.

That I knew too well upon what solid reasons all the determinations of the wise Houyhnhnms were founded not to be shaken by arguments of mine, a miserable Yahoo; and therefore, after presenting him with my humble thanks for the offer of his servants' assistance in making a vessel and desiring a reasonable time for so difficult a work, I told him I would endeavour to preserve a wretched being; and, if ever I returned to England, was not without hopes of being useful to my own species by celebrating the praises of the renowned Houyhnhnms and proposing their virtues to the imitation of mankind.

My master in a few words made me a very gracious reply, allowed me the space of two months to finish my boat, and ordered the sorrel nag, my fellow-servant (for so at this distance I may presume to call him) to follow my instructions, because I told my master that his help would be sufficient, and I knew he had a tenderness for me.

In his company my first business was to go to that part of the coast where my rebellious crew had ordered me to be set on shore. I got upon a height and, looking on every side into the sea, fancied I saw a small island towards the northeast. I took out my pocket-glass and could then clearly distinguish it about five leagues off, as I computed; but it appeared to the sorrel nag to be only a blue cloud: for, as he had no conception of any country beside his own, so he could not be as expert in distinguishing remote objects at sea as we who so much converse in that element.

After I had discovered this island, I considered no farther; but resolved it should, if possible, be the first place of my banishment, leaving the consequence to fortune.

I returned home and, consulting with the sorrel nag, we went into a copse at some distance, where I with my knife, and he with a sharp flint fastened very artificially,[8] after their manner, to a wooden handle, cut down several oak wattles about the thickness of a walking-staff, and some larger pieces. But I shall not trouble the reader with a particular description of my own mechanics; let it suffice to say that in six weeks' time, with the help of the sorrel nag, who performed the parts that required most labour, I finished a sort of Indian canoe, but much larger, covering it with the skins of Yahoos well stitched together with hempen threads of my own making. My sail was likewise composed of the skins of the same animal; but I made use of the youngest I could get, the older being too tough and thick, and I likewise provided myself with four paddles. I laid in a stock of boiled flesh of rabbits and fowls, and took with me two vessels, one filled with milk and the other with water.

I tried my canoe in a large pond near my master's house and then corrected in it what was amiss; stopping all the chinks with Yahoos' tallow till I found it staunch and able to bear me and my freight. And when it was as complete as I could possibly make it, I had it drawn on a carriage very gently by Yahoos to the seaside, under the conduct of the sorrel nag and another servant.

When all was ready and the day came for my departure, I took leave of my master and lady and the whole family, my eyes flowing with tears and my heart quite sunk with grief. But his Honour, out of curiosity, and perhaps (if I may speak it without vanity) partly out of kindness, was determined to

8. Artfully.

see me in my canoe and got several of his neighbouring friends to accompany him. I was forced to wait above an hour for the tide, and then observing the wind very fortunately bearing towards the island to which I intended to steer my course, I took a second leave of my master: but as I was going to prostrate myself to kiss his hoof, he did me the honour to raise it gently to my mouth. I am not ignorant how much I have been censured for mentioning this last particular. Detractors are pleased to think it improbable that so illustrious a person should descend to give so great a mark of distinction to a creature so inferior as I. Neither have I forgot how apt some travellers are to boast of extraordinary favours they have received. But if these censurers were better acquainted with the noble and courteous disposition of the Houyhnhnms, they would soon change their opinion.

I paid my respects to the rest of the Houyhnhnms in his Honour's company; then getting into my canoe, I pushed off from shore.

Chapter Eleven: The author's dangerous voyage. He arrives at New Holland, hoping to settle there. Is wounded with an arrow by one of the natives. Is seized and carried by force into a Portuguese ship. The great civilities of the captain. The author arrives at England.

I began this desperate voyage on February 15, 1714–5;[1] at 9 o'clock in the morning. The wind was very favourable; however, I made use at first only of my paddles, but considering I should soon be weary and that the wind might probably chop about, I ventured to set up my little sail; and thus with the help of the tide I went at the rate of a league and a half an hour, as near as I could guess. My master and his friends continued on the shore till I was almost out of sight; and I often heard the sorrel nag (who always loved me) crying out, *Hnuy illa nyha maiah Yahoo,* Take care of thyself, gentle Yahoo.

My design was, if possible, to discover some small island uninhabited, yet sufficient by my labour to furnish me with necessaries of life; which I would have thought a greater happiness than to be first minister in the politest court of Europe, so horrible was the idea I conceived of returning to live in the society and under the government of Yahoos. For in such a solitude as I desired, I could at least enjoy my own thoughts and reflect with delight on the virtues of those inimitable Houyhnhnms, without any opportunity of degenerating into the vices and corruptions of my own species.

The reader may remember what I related when my crew conspired against me and confined me to my cabin. How I continued there several weeks without knowing what course we took, and when I was put ashore in the long-boat how the sailors told me with oaths, whether true or false, that they knew not in what part of the world we were. However, I did then believe us to be about ten degrees southward of the Cape of Good Hope, or about 45 degrees southern latitude, as I gathered from some general words I overheard among them, being, I supposed, to the southeast in their intended voyage to Madagascar. And although this were but little better than conjecture, yet I resolved to steer my course eastward, hoping to reach the southwest coast of New Holland,[2]

1. That is, in 1715; in England, the legal year began on March 25 until 1753.
2. Tasmania.

and perhaps some such island as I desired lying westward of it. The wind was full west, and by six in the evening I computed I had gone eastward at least eighteen leagues, when I spied a very small island about half a league off, which I soon reached. It was nothing but a rock, with one creek, naturally arched by the force of tempests. Here I put in my canoe and, climbing a part of the rock, I could plainly discover land to the east, extending from south to north. I lay all night in my canoe and, repeating my voyage early in the morning, I arrived in seven hours to the southeast point of New Holland. This confirmed me in the opinion I have long entertained that the maps and charts place this country at least three degrees more to the east than it really is; which thought I communicated many years ago to my worthy friend Mr. Herman Moll [3] and gave him my reasons for it, although he hath rather chosen to follow other authors.

I saw no inhabitants in the place where I landed and, being unarmed, I was afraid of venturing far into the country. I found some shellfish on the shore and eat them raw, not daring to kindle a fire for fear of being discovered by the natives. I continued three days feeding on oysters and limpets, to save my own provisions, and I fortunately found a brook of excellent water, which gave me great relief.

On the fourth day, venturing out early a little too far, I saw twenty or thirty natives upon a height not above five hundred yards from me. They were stark naked, men, women, and children, round a fire, as I could discover by the smoke. One of them spied me and gave notice to the rest; five of them advanced towards me, leaving the women and children at the fire. I made what haste I could to the shore and, getting into my canoe, shoved off: the savages, observing me retreat, ran after me; and before I could get far enough into the sea, discharged an arrow which wounded me deeply on the inside of my left knee (I shall carry the mark to my grave). I apprehended the arrow might be poisoned and, paddling out of the reach of their darts (being a calm day), I made a shift to suck the wound and dress it as well as I could.

I was at a loss what to do, for I durst not return to the same landing-place, but stood to the north, and was forced to paddle; for the wind, although very gentle, was against me, blowing northwest. As I was looking about for a secure landing-place, I saw a sail to the north-northeast, which appearing every minute more visible, I was in some doubt whether I should wait for them or no; but at last my detestation of the Yahoo race prevailed and, turning my canoe, I sailed and paddled together to the south and got into the same creek from whence I set out in the morning, choosing rather to trust myself among these barbarians than live with European Yahoos. I drew up my canoe as close as I could to the shore and hid myself behind a stone by the little brook, which, as I have already said, was excellent water.

The ship came within a half a league of this creek, and sent out her longboat with vessels to take in fresh water (for the place, it seems, was very well known), but I did not observe it until the boat was almost on shore and it was too late to seek another hiding-place. The seamen at their landing observed my

3. Herman Moll (d. 1732), a Dutch mapmaker who settled in England about 1698 and whose maps became widely accepted there, providing the basis for the imaginary maps that accompanied the original editions of *Gulliver's Travels*.

canoe and, rummaging it all over, easily conjectured that the owner could not be far off. Four of them well armed searched every cranny and lurking-hole, till at last they found me flat on my face behind the stone. They gazed a while in admiration at my strange uncouth dress, my coat made of skins, my wooden-soled shoes, and my furred stockings; from whence, however, they concluded I was not a native of the place, who all go naked. One of the seamen in Portuguese bid me rise, and asked who I was. I understood that language very well and, getting upon my feet, said I was a poor Yahoo, banished from the Houyhnhnms, and desired they would please to let me depart. They admired to hear me answer them in their own tongue, and saw by my complexion I must be an European, but were at loss to know what I meant by Yahoos and Houyhnhnms; and at the same time fell a-laughing at my strange tone in speaking, which resembled the neighing of a horse. I trembled all the while betwixt fear and hatred: I again desired leave to depart and was gently moving to my canoe; but they laid hold on me, desiring to know what country I was of, whence I came, with many other questions. I told them I was born in England, from whence I came about five years ago, and then their country and ours were at peace. I therefore hoped they would not treat me as an enemy since I meant them no harm, but was a poor Yahoo seeking some desolate place where to pass the remainder of his unfortunate life.

When they began to talk, I thought I never heard or saw anything so unnatural; for it appeared to me as monstrous as if a dog or a cow should speak in England, or a Yahoo in Houyhnhnmland. The honest Portuguese were equally amazed at my strange dress and the odd manner of delivering my words, which however they understood very well. They spoke to me with great humanity and said they were sure their captain would carry me *gratis* to Lisbon, from whence I might return to my own country; that two of the seamen would go back to the ship, inform the captain of what they had seen, and receive his orders; in the meantime, unless I would give my solemn oath not to fly, they would secure me by force. I thought it best to comply with their proposal. They were very curious to know my story, but I gave them very little satisfaction; and they all conjectured that my misfortunes had impaired my reason. In two hours the boat, which went loaden with vessels of water, returned with the captain's commands to fetch me on board. I fell on my knees to preserve my liberty; but all was in vain, and the men, having tied me with cords, heaved me into the boat, from whence I was taken into the ship and from thence into the captain's cabin.

His name was Pedro de Mendez; he was a very courteous and generous person. He entreated me to give some account of myself, and desired to know what I would eat or drink; said I should be used as well as himself, and spoke so many obliging things that I wondered to find such civilities from a Yahoo. However, I remained silent and sullen; I was ready to faint at the very smell of him and his men. At last I desired something to eat out of my own canoe; but he ordered me a chicken and some excellent wine, and then directed that I should be put to bed in a very clean cabin. I would not undress myself but lay on the bed-clothes, and in half an hour stole out, when I thought the crew was at dinner, and getting to the side of the ship was going to leap into the sea and swim for my life rather than continue among Yahoos. But one of the seamen prevented me, and having informed the captain, I was chained to my cabin.

After dinner Don Pedro came to me and desired to know my reason for so desperate an attempt: assured me he only meant to do me all the service he was able, and spoke so very movingly that at last I descended to treat him like an animal which had some little portion of reason. I gave him a very short relation of my voyage, of the conspiracy against me by my own men, of the country where they set me on shore, and of my three years' residence there. All which he looked upon as if it were a dream or a vision; whereat I took great offence; for I had quite forgot the faculty of lying, so peculiar to Yahoos in all countries where they preside, and, consequently, the disposition of suspecting truth in others of their own species. I asked him whether it were the custom of his country to *say the thing that was not*. I assured him I had almost forgot what he meant by falsehood, and, if I had lived a thousand years in Houyhnhnmland, I should never have heard a lie from the meanest servant; that I was altogether indifferent whether he believed me or no; but however, in return for his favours, I would give so much allowance to the corruption of his nature as to answer any objection he would please to make, and he might easily discover the truth.

The captain, a wise man, after many endeavours to catch me tripping in some part of my story, at last began to have a better opinion of my veracity, and the rather because, he confessed, he met with a Dutch skipper, who pretended to have landed with five others of his crew upon a certain island or continent south of New Holland, where they went for fresh water, and observed a horse driving before him several animals exactly resembling those I described under the name of Yahoos, with some other particulars, which the captain said he had forgot, because he then concluded them all to be lies. But he added that since I professed so inviolable an attachment to truth, I must give him my word of honour to bear him company in this voyage without attempting anything against my life, or else he would continue me a prisoner till we arrived in Lisbon. I gave him the promise he required; but at the same time protested that I would suffer the greatest hardships rather than return to live among Yahoos.

Our voyage passed without any considerable accident. In gratitude to the captain I sometimes sat with him at his earnest request and strove to conceal my antipathy against humankind, although it often broke out, which he suffered to pass without observation. But the greatest part of the day I confined myself to my cabin to avoid seeing any of the crew. The captain had often entreated me to strip myself of my savage dress, and offered to lend me the best suit of clothes he had. This I would not be prevailed on to accept, abhorring to cover myself with anything that had been on the back of a Yahoo. I only desired he would lend me two clean shirts, which having been washed since he wore them, I believed would not so much defile me. These I changed every second day, and washed them myself.

We arrived at Lisbon, Nov. 5, 1715. At our landing the captain forced me to cover myself with his cloak, to prevent the rabble from crowding about me. I was conveyed to his own house, and, at my earnest request, he led me up to the highest room backwards.[4] I conjured him to conceal from all persons

4. At the back of the house.

what I had told him of the Houyhnhnms, because the least hint of such a story would not only draw numbers of people to see me, but probably put me in danger of being imprisoned or burnt by the Inquisition. The captain persuaded me to accept a suit of clothes newly made, but I would not suffer the tailor to take my measure; however, Don Pedro being almost of my size, they fitted me well enough. He accoutred me with other necessaries all new, which I aired for twenty-four hours before I would use them.

The captain had no wife, nor above three servants, none of which were suffered to attend at meals, and his whole deportment was so obliging, added to very good *human* understanding, that I really began to tolerate his company. He gained so far upon me that I ventured to look out of the back window. By degrees I was brought into another room, from whence I peeped into the street, but drew my head back in a fright. In a week's time he seduced me down to the door. I found my terror gradually lessened, but my hatred and contempt seemed to increase. I was at last bold enough to walk the street in his company, but kept my nose well stopped with rue,[5] or sometimes with tobacco.

In ten days Don Pedro, to whom I had given some account of my domestic affairs, put it upon me as a point of honour and conscience that I ought to return to my native country and live at home with my wife and children. He told me there was an English ship in the port just ready to sail, and he would furnish me with all things necessary. It would be tedious to repeat his arguments and my contradictions. He said it was altogether impossible to find such a solitary island as I had desired to live in; but I might command in my own house and pass my time in a manner as recluse as I pleased.

I complied at last, finding I could not do better. I left Lisbon the 24th day of November in an English merchantman, but who was the master I never inquired. Don Pedro accompanied me to the ship and lent me twenty pounds. He took kind leave of me and embraced me at parting, which I bore as well as I could. During this last voyage I had no commerce with the master or any of his men, but pretending I was sick kept close in my cabin. On the fifth of December, 1715, we cast anchor in the Downs[6] about nine in the morning, and at three in the afternoon I got safe to my house at Redriff.[7]

My wife and family received me with great surprise and joy, because they concluded me certainly dead; but I must freely confess the sight of them filled me only with hatred, disgust, and contempt, and the more by reflecting on the near alliance I had to them. For although, since my unfortunate exile from the Houyhnhnm country, I had compelled myself to tolerate the sight of Yahoos, and to converse with Don Pedro de Mendez, yet my memory and imaginations were perpetually filled with the virtues and ideas of those exalted Houyhnhnms. And when I began to consider that by copulating with one of the Yahoo species I had become a parent of more, it struck me with the utmost shame, confusion, and horror.

As soon as I entered the house, my wife took me in her arms and kissed me, at which, having not been used to the touch of that odious animal for so many

5. A strong-scented herb.
6. An anchorage near Dover where ships might discharge passengers and take on pilots for the navigation of the Thames estuary.
7. Rotherhithe, the dock section of East London south of the Thames.

years, I fell in a swoon for almost an hour. At the time I am writing it is five years since my last return to England: during the first year I could not endure my wife or children in my presence; the very smell of them was intolerable, much less could I suffer them to eat in the same room. To this hour they dare not presume to touch my bread or drink out of the same cup, neither was I ever able to let one of them take me by the hand. The first money I laid out was to buy two young stone-horses; [8] which I keep in a good stable, and next to them the groom is my greatest favourite; for I feel my spirits revived by the smell he contracts in the stable. My horses understand me tolerably well; I converse with them at least four hours every day. They are strangers to bridle or saddle; they live in great amity with me and friendship to each other.

Chapter Twelve: The author's veracity. His design in publishing this work. His censure of those travellers who swerve from the truth. The author clears himself from any sinister ends in writing. An objection answered. The method of planting colonies. His native country commended. The right of the Crown to those countries described by the author is justified. The difficulty of conquering them. The author takes his last leave of the reader, proposeth his manner of living for the future, gives good advice, and concludeth.

Thus, gentle reader, I have given thee a faithful history of my travels for sixteen years and above seven months, wherein I have not been so studious of ornament as of truth. I could perhaps like others have astonished thee with strange improbable tales; but I rather chose to relate plain matter of fact in the simplest manner and style, because my principal design was to inform and not to amuse thee.

It is easy for us who travel into remote countries, which are seldom visited by Englishmen or other Europeans, to form descriptions of wonderful animals both at sea and land; whereas a traveller's chief aim should be to make men wiser and better and to improve their minds by the bad as well as good example of what they deliver concerning foreign places.

I could heartily wish a law were enacted that every traveller, before he were permitted to publish his voyages, should be obliged to make oath before the Lord High Chancellor that all he intended to print was absolutely true to the best of his knowledge; for then the world would no longer be deceived as it usually is while some writers, to make their works pass the better upon the public, impose the grossest falsities on the unwary reader. I have perused several books of travels with great delight in my younger days; but having since gone over most parts of the globe and been able to contradict many fabulous accounts from my own observation, it hath given me a great disgust against this part of reading, and some indignation to see the credulity of mankind so impudently abused. Therefore since my acquaintance were pleased to think my poor endeavours might not be unacceptable to my country, I imposed on myself as a maxim, never to be swerved from, that I would *strictly adhere to truth;* neither indeed can I be ever under the least temptation to vary from it, while I retain in my mind the lectures and example of my noble

8. Stallions.

master and the other illustrious Houyhnhnms, of whom I had so long the honour to be an humble hearer.

—Nec si miserum Fortuna Sinonem
Finxit, vanum etiam mendacemque improba finget.[1]

I know very well how little reputation is to be got by writings which require neither genius nor learning, nor indeed any other talent, except a good memory or an exact journal. I know likewise that writers of travels, like dictionary-makers, are sunk into oblivion by the weight and bulk of those who come last and therefore lie uppermost. And it is highly probable that such travellers who shall hereafter visit the countries described in this work of mine, may, by detecting my errors (if there be any) and adding many new discoveries of their own, jostle me out of vogue and stand in my place, making the world forget that ever I was an author. This indeed would be too great a mortification if I wrote for fame: but, as my sole intention was the *public good*,[2] I cannot be altogether disappointed. For who can read of the virtues I have mentioned in the glorious Houyhnhnms without being ashamed of his own vices, when he considers himself as the reasoning, governing animal of his country? I shall say nothing of those remote nations where Yahoos preside, amongst which the least corrupted are the Brobdingnagians, whose wise maxims in morality and government it would be our happiness to observe. But I forbear descanting further and rather leave the judicious reader to his own remarks and applications.

I am not a little pleased that this work of mine can possibly meet with no censurers: for what objections can be made against a writer who relates only plain facts that happened in such distant countries, where we have not the least interest with respect either to trade or negotiations? I have carefully avoided every fault with which common writers of travels are often too justly charged. Besides, I meddle not the least with any *party*, but write without passion, prejudice, or ill-will against any man or number of men whatsoever. I write for the noblest end, to inform and instruct mankind, over whom I may, without breach of modesty, pretend to some superiority from the advantages I received by conversing so long among the most accomplished Houyhnhnms. I write without any view towards profit or praise. I never suffer a word to pass that may look like reflection or possibly give the least offence even to those who are most ready to take it. So that I hope I may with justice pronounce myself an author perfectly blameless, against whom the tribes of answerers, considerers, observers, reflecters, detecters, remarkers,[3] will never be able to find matter for exercising their talents.

I confess it was whispered to me that I was bound in duty, as a subject of England, to have given in a memorial to a secretary of state at my first coming

1. "Nor, if false Fortune has made Sinon wretched, shall she make him empty and deceitful as well," Virgil, *Aeneid* II.79–80; but Sinon is the treacherous Greek who is about to persuade the Trojans to admit the wooden horse into their city.
2. Often a suspect claim (cf. the opening of *A Modest Proposal*) on the grounds of outright hypocrisy or zealous self-deception; Gulliver's pride is implied, however genuine his sincerity.
3. The usual terms by which authors of hostile replies were designated.

over; because whatever lands are discovered by a subject belong to the Crown. But I doubt whether our conquests in the countries I treat of would be as easy as those of Ferdinando Cortez over the naked Americans.[4] The Lilliputians, I think, are hardly worth the charge of a fleet and army to reduce them, and I question whether it might be prudent or safe to attempt the Brobdingnagians. Or whether an English army would be much at their ease with the Flying Island over their heads. The Houyhnhnms, indeed, appear not to be so well prepared for war, a science to which they are perfect strangers, and especially against missive weapons.[5] However, supposing myself to be a minister of state, I could never give my advice for invading them. Their prudence, unanimity, unacquaintedness with fear, and their love of their country would amply supply all defects in the military art. Imagine twenty thousand of them breaking into the midst of an European army, confounding the ranks, overturning the carriages,[6] battering the warriors' faces into mummy [7] by terrible yerks [8] from their hinder hoofs. For they would well deserve the character given to Augustus: *Recalcitrat undique tutus.*[9] But instead of proposals for conquering that magnanimous [10] nation, I rather wish they were in a capacity or disposition to send a sufficient number of their inhabitants for civilizing Europe, by teaching us the first principles of honour, justice, truth, temperance, public spirit, fortitude, chastity, friendship, benevolence, and fidelity. The *names* of all which virtues are still retained among us in most languages and are to be met with in modern as well as ancient authors; which I am able to assert from my own small reading.

But I had another reason which made me less forward to enlarge his Majesty's dominions by my discoveries. To say the truth, I had conceived a few scruples with relation to the distributive justice of princes upon those occasions. For instance, a crew of pirates are driven by a storm they know not whither, at length a boy discovers land from the topmast, they go on shore to rob and plunder, they see an harmless people, are entertained with kindness, they give the country a new name, they take formal possession of it for the king, they set up a rotten plank or a stone for a memorial, they murder two or three dozen of the natives, bring away a couple more by force for a sample, return home, and get their pardon. Here commences a new dominion acquired with a title by *divine right.*[11] Ships are sent with the first opportunity, the natives driven out or destroyed, their princes tortured to discover their gold, a free license given to all acts of inhumanity and lust, the earth reeking with the blood of its inhabitants: and this execrable crew of butchers em-

4. Cortez succeeded so easily in his conquest of Mexico (1519) because the Aztecs were awed by the ships and firearms of the Spaniards and by the fact that they were mounted on horses.

5. Those thrown or shot, rather than hand weapons.

6. Gun carriages.

7. Pulp.

8. Kicks.

9. "He kicks back with safety on every side." Horace, *Satires* II.i.20.

10. Large-souled, noble.

11. The doctrine of divine right of kings (discussed earlier by Halifax and Dryden) had been current in England since James I and was defended by many so long as the Stuarts held the throne; here it is applied to the specious justification of rule by conquest, as it had been by Spain in the New World.

ployed in so pious an expedition is a *modern colony* sent to convert and civilize an idolatrous and barbarous people.

But this description, I confess, doth by no means affect the British nation, who may be an example to the whole world for their wisdom, care, and justice in planting colonies; their liberal endowments for the advancement of religion and learning; their choice of devout and able pastors to propagate Christianity; their caution in stocking their provinces with people of sober lives and conversations from this, the mother kingdom; [12] their strict regard to the distribution of justice in supplying the civil administration through all their colonies with officers of the greatest abilities, utter strangers to corruption; and to crown all, by sending the most vigilant and virtuous governors, who have no other views than the happiness of the people over whom they preside, and the honour of the king their master.

But as those countries which I have described do not appear to have any desire of being conquered and enslaved, murdered, or driven out by colonies, nor abound either in gold, silver, sugar, or tobacco; I did humbly conceive they were by no means proper objects of our zeal, our valour, or our interest. However, if those whom it more concerns think fit to be of another opinion, I am ready to depose, when I shall be lawfully called, that no European did ever visit these countries before me. I mean, if the inhabitants ought to be believed; unless a dispute may arise about the two Yahoos, said to have been seen many ages ago on a mountain in Houyhnhnmland, from whence, the opinion is, that the race of those brutes hath descended; and these, for anything I know, may have been English, which indeed I was apt to suspect from the lineaments of their posterity's countenances, although very much defaced. But how far that will go to make out a title, I leave to the learned in colony-law.

But as to the formality of taking possession in my sovereign's name, it never came once into my thoughts; and if it had, yet as my affairs then stood, I should perhaps, in point of prudence and self-preservation, have put it off to a better opportunity.

Having thus answered the *only* objection that can be raised against me as a traveller, I here take a final leave of my courteous readers, and return to enjoy my own speculations in my little garden at Redriff, to apply those excellent lessons of virtue which I learned among the Houyhnhnms, to instruct the Yahoos of my own family as far as I shall find them docible [13] animals, to behold my figure often in a glass, and thus if possible habituate myself by time to tolerate the sight of a human creature; to lament the brutality [14] of Houyhnhnms in my own country, but always treat their persons with respect for the sake of my noble master, his family, his friends, and the whole Houyhnhnm race, whom these of ours have the honour to resemble in all their lineaments, however their intellectuals came to degenerate.

I began last week to permit my wife to sit at dinner with me, at the farthest end of a long table, and to answer (but with the utmost brevity) the few questions I asked her. Yet the smell of a Yahoo continuing very offensive, I

12. Transportation to the colonies was an alternative to hanging for many serious crimes, and it was used to supply the colonists with a labor force.

13. Teachable.

14. That is, animality.

always keep my nose well stopped with rue, lavender, or tobacco leaves. And although it be hard for a man late in life to remove old habits, I am not altogether out of hopes in some time to suffer a neighbour Yahoo in my company without the apprehensions I am yet under of his teeth or his claws.

My reconcilement to the Yahoo-kind in general might not be so difficult if they would be content with those vices and follies only which nature hath entitled them to. I am not in the least provoked at the sight of a lawyer, a pickpocket, a colonel, a fool, a lord, a gamester, a politician, a whoremonger, a physician, an evidence,[15] a suborner, an attorney, a traitor, or the like; this is all according to the due course of things: but when I behold a lump of deformity and diseases both in body and mind, smitten with *pride*, it immediately breaks all the measures of my patience; neither shall I be ever able to comprehend how such an animal and such a vice could tally together. The wise and virtuous Houyhnhnms, who abound in all excellencies that can adorn a rational creature, have no name for this vice in their language, which hath no terms to express anything that is evil except those whereby they describe the detestable qualities of their Yahoos, among which they were not able to distinguish this of pride, for want of thoroughly understanding human nature as it showeth itself in other countries where that animal presides. But I, who had more experience, could plainly observe some rudiments of it among the wild Yahoos.

But the Houyhnhnms, who live under the government of reason, are no more proud of the good qualities they possess than I should be for not wanting a leg or an arm; which no man in his wits would boast of, although he must be miserable without them. I dwell the longer upon this subject from the desire I have to make the society of an English Yahoo by any means not insupportable, and therefore I here entreat those who have any tincture of this absurd vice that they will not presume to appear in my sight.

1726

A Letter from Capt. Gulliver to His Cousin Sympson [1]

I hope you will be ready to own publicly, whenever you shall be called to it, that by your great and frequent urgency you prevailed on me to publish a very loose and uncorrect account of my travels; with direction to hire some young gentlemen of either university to put them in order and correct the style, as my cousin Dampier did by my advice, in his book called *A Voyage Round the World*.[2] But I do not remember I gave you power to consent that anything should be omitted, and much less that anything should be inserted: [3] therefore, as to the latter, I do here renounce everything of that kind; particularly a paragraph about her Majesty, the late Queen Anne, of most pious and glorious memory; although I did reverence and esteem her more than any of human species. But you or your interpolator ought to have considered that,

15. Paid informer.

1. This letter first appeared in Faulkner's edition of 1735 and was probably written close to that year rather than in 1727, as it was dated; Sympson was the fictitious name under which negotiations were first made to publish the book.

2. William Dampier (1652–1715), whose very popular work *A New Voyage Round the World* appeared in 1697 and is often parodied in *Gulliver's Travels*.

3. As was done, to moderate the satire, by the first publisher, Benjamin Motte.

as it was not my inclination, so was it not decent to praise any animal of our composition[4] before my master Houyhnhnm: and besides, the fact was altogether false; for to my knowledge, being in England during some part of her Majesty's reign, she did govern by a chief minister; nay, even by two successively; the first whereof was the Lord of Godolphin, and the second the Lord of Oxford;[5] so that you have made me *say the thing that was not.* Likewise, in the account of the Academy of Projectors and several passages of my discourse to my master Houyhnhnm, you have either omitted some material circumstances, or minced or changed them in such a manner that I do hardly know mine own work. When I formerly hinted to you something of this in a letter, you were pleased to answer that you were afraid of giving offence; that people in power were very watchful over the press and apt not only to interpret but to punish everything which looked like an *innuendo* (as I think you called it). But pray, how could that which I spoke so many years ago and at above five thousand leagues distance, in another reign, be applied to any of the Yahoos who now are said to govern the herd,[6] especially at a time when I little thought on or feared the unhappiness of living under them? Have not I the most reason to complain when I see these very Yahoos carried by Houyhnhnms in a vehicle, as if these were brutes and those the rational creatures? And, indeed, to avoid so monstrous and detestable a sight was one principal motive of my retirement hither.

Thus much I thought proper to tell you in relation to your self and to the trust I reposed in you.

I do in the next place complain of my own great want of judgment in being prevailed upon by the intreaties and false reasonings of you and some others, very much against mine own opinion, to suffer my travels to be published. Pray bring to your mind how often I desired you to consider, when you insisted on the motive of public good, that the Yahoos were a species of animals utterly incapable of amendment by precepts or examples, and so it hath proved; for instead of seeing a full stop put to all abuses and corruptions, at least in this little island, as I had reason to expect: behold, after above six months' warning, I cannot learn that my book hath produced one single effect according to mine intentions. I desired you would let me know by a letter when party and faction were extinguished; judges learned and upright; pleaders honest and modest, with some tincture of common sense; and Smithfield[7] blazing with pyramids of law-books; the young nobility's education entirely changed; the physicians banished; the female Yahoos abounding in virtue, honour, truth and good sense; courts and levees of great ministers thoroughly weeded and swept; wit, merit and learning rewarded; all disgracers of the press in prose and verse condemned to eat nothing but their own cotton[8] and

4. Kind.

5. The 1st Earl of Godolphin from 1702 until 1710; thereafter Robert Harley, 1st Earl of Oxford and the friend of Swift and Pope, until 1714.

6. An ironic reference to the highly topical satire against Walpole and the court of George I that runs through the book.

7. The London cattle market where heretics and murderers had been burned; Gulliver seems to call for a burning of false books such as Savonarola conducted in 15th-century Florence and the Inquisition did later.

8. Paper.

quench their thirst with their own ink. These and a thousand other reformations I firmly counted upon by your encouragement, as indeed they were plainly deducible from the precepts delivered in my book. And it must be owned that seven months were a sufficient time to correct every vice and folly to which Yahoos are subject, if their natures had been capable of the least disposition to virtue or wisdom; yet so far have you been from answering mine expectation in any of your letters, that on the contrary you are loading our carrier every week with libels, and keys, and reflections, and memoirs, and second parts; wherein I see myself accused of reflecting upon great statesfolk; of degrading human nature (for so they have still the confidence to style it), and of abusing the female sex. I find likewise that the writers of those bundles are not agreed among themselves; for some of them will not allow me to be author of mine own travels, and others make me author of books to which I am wholly a stranger.[9]

I find likewise that your printer hath been so careless as to confound the times and mistake the dates of my several voyages and returns, neither assigning the true year or the true month or day of the month; and I hear the original manuscript is all destroyed since the publication of my book. Neither have I any copy left; however, I have sent you some corrections, which you may insert if ever there should be a second edition: and yet I cannot stand to[10] them, but shall leave that matter to my judicious and candid readers to adjust it as they please.

I hear some of our sea-Yahoos find fault with my sea-language, as not proper in many parts nor now in use. I cannot help it. In my first voyages, while I was young, I was instructed by the oldest mariners and learned to speak as they did. But I have since found that the sea-Yahoos are apt, like the land ones, to become new-fangled in their words; which the latter change every year, insomuch as I remember upon each return to mine own country, their old dialect was so altered that I could hardly understand the new. And I observe, when any Yahoo comes from London out of curiosity to visit me at mine own house, we neither of us are able to deliver our conceptions in a manner intelligible to the other.

If the censure of Yahoos could any way affect me, I should have great reason to complain that some of them are so bold as to think my book of travels a mere fiction out of mine own brain; and have gone so far as to drop hints that the Houyhnhnms and Yahoos have no more existence than the inhabitants of Utopia.[11]

Indeed I must confess, that as to the people of Lilliput, Brobdingrag (for so the word should have been spelt, and not erroneously *Brobdingnag*), and Laputa, I have never yet heard of any Yahoo so presumptuous as to dispute their being or the facts I have related concerning them; because the truth immediately strikes every reader with conviction. And is there less probability in my account of the Houyhnhnms or Yahoos when it is manifest as to the latter, there are so many thousands even in this city who only differ from their

9. Referring to the numerous spurious "continuations" and imitations, as well as a "complete key."

10. Insist upon.

11. Utopia (from the Greek for "nowhere") was the name Sir Thomas More gave to his "ideal" commonwealth, and his great ironic work (1516) immensely influenced Swift.

brother brutes in Houyhnhnmland because they use a sort of a jabber and do not go naked? I wrote for their amendment and not their approbation. The united praise of the whole race would be of less consequence to me than the neighing of those two degenerate Houyhnhnms I keep in my stable; because from these, degenerate as they are, I still improve in some virtues, without any mixture of vice.

Do these miserable animals presume to think that I am so far degenerated as to defend my veracity? Yahoo as I am, it is well known through all Houyhnhnmland that, by the instructions and example of my illustrious master, I was able in the compass of two years (although I confess with the utmost difficulty) to remove that infernal habit of lying, shuffling, deceiving, and equivocating so deeply rooted in the very souls of all my species, especially the Europeans.

I have other complaints to make upon this vexatious occasion; but I forbear troubling myself or you any further. I must freely confess that since my last return some corruptions of my Yahoo nature have revived in me by conversing with a few of your species, and particularly those of mine own family, by an unavoidable necessity; else I should never have attempted so absurd a project as that of reforming the Yahoo race in this kingdom; but I have now done with all such visionary schemes forever.

1735

From John Gay and Alexander Pope: Mary Gulliver to Captain Lemuel Gulliver

Welcome, thrice welcome to thy native place!
—What, touch me not? what, shun a wife's embrace?
Have I for this thy tedious absence borne
And waked and wished whole nights for thy return?
In five long years I took no second spouse;
What Redriff wife so long hath kept her vows?
Your eyes, your nose, inconstancy betray;
Your nose you stop, your eyes you turn away.
'Tis said, that thou shouldst cleave unto thy wife;
Once *thou* didst cleave, and *I* could cleave for life.
Hear and relent! hark, how thy children moan;
Be kind at least to these, they are thy own:
Behold, and count them all; secure to find
The honest number that you left behind.
See how they pat thee with their pretty paws:
Why start you? are they snakes? or have they claws?
Thy Christian seed, our mutual flesh and bone:
Be kind at least to these, they are thy own.

· · ·

My bed (the scene of all our former joys,
Witness two lovely girls, two lovely boys)
Alone I press; in dreams I call my dear,
I stretch my hand, no Gulliver is there!

I wake, I rise, and shivering with the frost,
Search all the house; my Gulliver is lost!
Forth in the street I rush with frantic cries:
The windows open; all the neighbours rise:
Where sleeps my Gulliver? *O tell me where?*
The neighbours answer, *With the sorrel mare.*

At early morn, I to the market haste,
(Studious in everything to please thy taste)
A curious fowl and sparagrass I chose,
(For I remember you were fond of those),
Three shillings cost the first, the last seven groats;
Sullen you turn from both, and call for *oats.*

. . .

Nay, would kind *Jove* my organs so dispose,
To hymn harmonious *Houyhnhnm* through the nose,
I'd call thee *Houyhnhnm,* that high sounding name,
Thy children's noses all should twang the same,
So might I find my loving spouse of course
Endued with all the virtues of a horse.

1727

ALEXANDER POPE

1688–1744

Pope was the great poet of his age, and he made that role a more exacting and influential one than it had ever been before in England. Chaucer had been a court poet and had served as a diplomat; Milton had been virtually foreign minister under Cromwell. But Pope commanded hatred and admiration, both as poet and as man, throughout his career of private citizen and public conscience. He could boast in a late poem, "I must be proud to see / Men not afraid of God, afraid of me." And while he fully earned the right to make the boast, he often doubted the wisdom of his engagement. We can see in his career a constant division between the attraction of a retired life and the claims, early, of literary ambition and, late, of active political concern—a political life such as only a man too independent to be bought and too gifted to be suppressed could maintain in Walpole's England.

Those who wish to find disabilities for which ambition compensates can find more than his share in Pope. Born to Catholic parents and, however heterodox at moments, loyal to their faith, he suffered first of all the penalties of being a Catholic in a country easily alarmed by the threat of intrigue and invasion. Catholics were forbidden by law to own land or to live within ten miles of London, and, if the laws were rarely enforced, they could be invoked in times of panic. Pope's parents moved near the time of his birth to Binfield in Windsor Forest, and later Pope rented a villa at Twickenham, near London but outside the ten-mile limit. As a Catholic he was denied admission to a university or the right to hold public office, and he was subject as well to double taxation. Nor did his enemies ever allow him to forget his status as a Catholic; but they made even more of his dwarf-like stature and of his crooked body, misshapen from adolescence by a tubercular ailment ("little Alexander," he described himself to a friend, whom "the women laugh at").

The compensations took various forms, occasionally the unconvincing posture of a rake, more often precocious literary skill and application and a great talent for friendship. His early friendships with distinguished elderly writers and retired statesmen (which combined charming deference with intellectual equality) were the first of a long series that took the place of more intimate ties. There was a rather romantic, somewhat histrionic attachment to the witty and ultimately spiteful Lady Mary Wortley Montagu (once a candidate for Congreve's affection), and there was something like real intimacy with Martha Blount; but the friendships seem, at this remove, the more essential attachments.

Pope divided his works at one point into "pure description" and "sense"; and, if those terms mean anything, they mark a movement in the late 1720's from a career of intense literary concerns to one of deeper moral engagement. There is no very sharp distinction, for such early works as the *Essay on Criticism* and *Windsor Forest* show moral and even political concern. The earlier career reached its culmination in the great labor of translating Homer, an undertaking that demanded all of Pope's energies and that rewarded him with financial independence. In the course of his earlier career, Pope had become deeply involved in the literary politics of the day, which were neither distinct from nor less vicious than those of the larger public sphere. His very talent was taken as arrogance by some; and Pope, through eagerness for fame and a certain bravado of manner, did little to make his superiority easy to ignore, or even to endure. In his difficult relations with Joseph Addison, who received literary adulation at Button's coffeehouse and could reward it with Whig patronage, Pope may have seemed a self-seeking outsider or even the instrument of his Tory friends. At any rate, Addison condoned strong efforts by his followers to smother Pope's reputation and to kill the prospects of his Homer.

In 1728 Pope paid off scores with *The Dunciad*. He created a brilliant mock-epic framework within which to gather and display—like a collection of butterflies, wasps, and spiders—all those who had maligned him without cause. Thereafter, each gesture he made could be read as defense or attack, and it was only by concealing his authorship that he could get a fair (and favorable) reception for so impersonal a work as the *Essay on Man* (1733–34). The *Essay* marks the last full effort of the contemplative poet: it is a work in a Socratic spirit, seeking to undo the quarrels men make with themselves and their world. This was to have been the first part of a large philosophic work, but the rest finally emerged as a series of "moral essays" or "ethic epistles" (of which *To Burlington* and *To a Lady* are two) and in the satire on false learning in the *New Dunciad* (1743).

The themes of *The Dunciad* looked back to Swift's great early satire, *A Tale of a Tub;* Pope's poem was written in part during a visit from Swift and, when completed, dedicated to him. The two men had met by 1712; and in the next few years, with Dr. John Arbuthnot (who had created the character of John Bull in a series of political satires) and with others—John Gay among them—they undertook the project of ridiculing false learning in a series of papers purportedly written by Martinus Scriblerus, a leaden-witted, pedantic, and indefatigable searcher after natural curiosities and verbal subtleties. The Scriblerus papers, begun about 1714, were not published till years later, but the project was important for providing an imaginative form which could yield Pope's "variorum" edition of *The Dunciad* with Scriblerian commentary, or perhaps even that more modest and less sedentary kin to Scriblerus, Lemuel Gulliver.

Pope's loyalty to these Tory friends—as well as to Queen Anne's chief ministers, Oxford and Bolingbroke—moved him more and more toward a political role. He had been on good personal terms with Sir Robert Walpole, but increasingly he became offended by the ways in which Walpole promoted and embodied the corruptions of the time: the systematic control of power through bribery, the use of hirelings and hacks to malign or silence the opposition, the awarding of honors for serviceable mediocrity, the insatiable appetite for ostentatious grandeur. Pope may well have exaggerated the threat that Walpole represented and have been somewhat eager to see apocalypse where there was only muddle. As Gibbon put it, "The fall of an unpopular Minister was not succeeded, according to general expectation, by a millennium of happiness and virtue." But Pope erected an image of Walpole and his England to stand beside Juvenal's vision of Rome under the rule of Domitian or Byron's and Stendhal's vision of the reaction that followed the French Revolution and Napoleon. The historicity of Pope's world is not our primary concern today, but rather the powerful and all-embracing imaginative form into which he built the details of his time as he did shells and minerals into the arches of his grotto at Twickenham. If the grotto was the retreat of the contemplative private man, and its natural beauties framed the life of retirement, so the greater poetic structure of the satires served no less to exercise the public conscience and to voice an outrage too strong to condone either pretext or pretension.

Pope gained a reputation for deviousness from which his reputation as a poet has often suffered. It arose in part because, like Halifax, he respected men more than parties; in part because he would damn in one withering line a fool who felt he had a claim to two; in part because he was attentive to his own image, editing and revising his letters before he published them, claiming the advantage of second thoughts and of nobler impulses than were spontaneously given. Yet the self-defense was a proportionate reaction to the abuse; and if Pope may be said to have created himself anew for posterity, the creation was still his. John Ruskin, the Victorian critic, pays tribute to his concise and forceful expression of a "benevolence, humble, rational, and resigned"; it is not all of Pope nor even his greatest achievement, but it is a part of all the rest.

An Essay on Criticism

This Horatian essay, Pope's first major poem, is the culmination of those years of literary study and discussion that Pope conducted at Binfield. His choice of criticism as its subject reflects the concern with self-definition of an age that had reacted against baroque wit and sought to cultivate the urbanity of Roman (as well as modern French) models. But a more immediate concern was the social one of how writers and critics were to behave in the new open forum that replaced gentlemanly amateurism and patronage. Critics were more numerous than ever before. As one of the least amiable of them, Thomas Rymer, complained, "till of late years England was as free from critics as it is from wolves," but now "they who are least acquainted with the game are aptest to bark at everything that comes in their way." Swift complained of those critics who read only to damn: "as barbarous as a judge who should take up a resolution to hang all men that came before him upon trial." And Dryden had traced the most malevolent criticism to failed writers: "the corruption of a poet is the generation of a critic."

Pope writes in a spirit of moderation, trying to free criticism of its partiality and its animosity. He offers a generous account of the value and limits of rules and a warning above all against the pride that sets self against nature, the fashionable against the universal. The theme of pride, whether of the individual or the coterie, creates a pattern of imagery that underlies the poem at every point and gives it more strength than its casual surface might suggest. We see the light of heaven descending into the "glimmering light" of the individual mind, as it once did more strikingly in the "celestial fire" of ancient genius. We see the light of nature as "clear, unchanged, and universal," opposed to the glaring, refracted light of false wit. The light of nature, like that of true expression, "clears and improves"—that is, dresses to advantage—"whate'er it shines upon," self-effacing in order to bring each object to its full realization. In contrast, the glitter of false wit conceals the "naked nature" (or rather hopes to conceal its absence) and buries what might have been "living grace" in a tawdry display of verbal wit. Behind these images there may be traces of an implicit scheme familiar in neoplatonic thought: the light of the One descends through emanation, forming and beautifying the Many. As it informs the individual soul and awakens it to the radiance of beauty in the world, it stirs the soul to reascend toward the One. Such a system is explicit in Shaftesbury's *The Moralists;* in Pope's less rhapsodic "essay" there are only glimpses and vestiges, just as in Dryden's urbane and "skeptical" criticism there are only occasional evocations of neoplatonism (except for the extended quotation from Giovanni Bellori in *The Parallel Betwixt Painting and Poetry*) or as in Reynolds's *Discourses* we see the translation of a neoplatonic scheme into empirical terms.

From An Essay on Criticism

'Tis hard to say, if greater want of skill
Appear in writing or in judging ill;
But, of the two, less dangerous is the offence
To tire our patience, than mislead our sense.
Some few in that, but numbers err in this,
Ten censure wrong for one who writes amiss;
A fool might once himself alone expose,
Now one in verse makes many more in prose.
'Tis with our judgments as our watches; none
Go just alike, yet each believes his own.
In poets as true genius is but rare,
True taste as seldom is the critic's share;
Both must alike from Heaven derive their light,
These born to judge, as well as those to write.
Let such teach others who themselves excel,
And censure freely who have written well.
Authors are partial to their wit, 'tis true,

But are not critics to their judgment too?
  Yet if we look more closely, we shall find
Most have the seeds of judgment in their mind;
Nature affords at least a glimmering light;°
The lines, though touched but faintly, are drawn right.
But as the slightest sketch, if justly traced,
Is by ill colouring but the more disgraced,
So by false learning is good sense° defaced;
Some are bewildered in the maze of schools,°
And some made coxcombs° Nature meant but fools.
In search of wit these lose their common sense,
And then turn critics in their own defence.
Each burns alike, who can, or cannot write,
Or with a rival's or an eunuch's spite.
All fools have still an itching to deride,
And fain would be upon the laughing side;
If Maevius° scribble in Apollo's° spite,
There are who judge still worse than he can write.
  Some have at first for wits, then poets past,
Turned critics next, and proved plain fools at last;
Some neither can for wits nor critics pass,
As heavy mules are neither horse nor ass.
Those half-learned witlings, numerous in our isle,
As half-formed insects on the banks of Nile;
Unfinished things, one knows not what to call,
Their generation's so equivocal:°
To tell° 'em, would a hundred tongues require,
Or one vain wit's, that might a hundred tire.
  But you who seek to give and merit fame,
And justly bear a critic's noble name,
Be sure yourself and your own reach to know,
How far your genius, taste, and learning go;
Launch not beyond your depth, but be discreet,
And mark that point where sense and dulness meet.
  Nature to all things fixed the limits fit,
And wisely curbed proud man's pretending wit:

glimmering light Sir William Temple (*Of Poetry*) describes poetic inspiration as "the pure and free gift of Heaven or of Nature . . . a fire kindled out of some hidden spark of the very first conception." So, too, Shaftesbury in *The Moralists* III.ii speaks of the "conceptions" of the mind and its "mental children": "Nor could it ever have been thus impregnated by any other mind than that which formed it at the beginning; and which . . . is original to all mental as well as other beauty." For a further development of this theme, which insists upon the divine source of man's powers of creation (or, in Pope, judgment), see also William Collins, *Ode on the Poetical Character*.

good sense related to the "glimmering light" and "seeds of judgment" (ll. 20–21) which may be fulfilled through true learning (as the sketch may be realized by proper coloring) or may be destroyed through false

schools of thought or criticism, the very existence of "schools" implying a diffraction of the light of heaven into self-limiting partisanship

coxcombs fops, superficial pretenders

Maevius a bad poet of Virgil's age

Apollo's as god and inspirer of true poetry

Those . . . equivocal referring to the belief that insects and vermin were spontaneously generated by the mud of the Nile; they are described by Dryden as "part kindled into life, and part a lump of unformed unanimated matter" (Dedication, *Aeneid*)

tell count

As on the land while here the ocean gains,
In other parts it leaves wide sandy plains;
Thus in the soul while memory prevails,
The solid power of understanding fails;
Where beams of warm imagination play,
The memory's soft figures melt away.
One science° only will one genius fit,
So vast is art, so narrow human wit;°
Not only bounded to peculiar arts,
But oft in those confined to single parts.
Like kings we lose the conquests gained before,
By vain ambition still to make them more;
Each might his several province well command,
Would all but stoop to what they understand.
    First follow Nature, and your judgment frame
By her just standard, which is still° the same:
Unerring Nature, still divinely bright,
One clear, unchanged, and universal light,
Life, force, and beauty, must to all impart,
At once the source, and end, and test of art.
Art from that fund each just supply provides,
Works without show, and without pomp presides:
In some fair body thus the informing soul°
With spirits feeds, with vigour fills the whole,
Each motion guides, and every nerve sustains;
Itself unseen, but in the effects, remains.
Some to whom Heaven in wit has been profuse,
Want as much more,° to turn it to its use;
For wit and judgment often are at strife,
Though meant each other's aid, like man and wife.
'Tis more to guide than spur the Muse's steed;°
Restrain his fury, than provoke his speed;
The wingèd courser, like a generous° horse,
Shows most true mettle when you check his course.
    Those Rules of old discovered, not devised,
Are Nature still, but Nature methodized;
Nature, like liberty,° is but restrained

science form of learning or knowledge
So vast . . . wit recalling the maxim of Hippocrates, "Life is short, but art is long" or, in the Latin version, "Ars longa, vita brevis est" (*Aphorisms* I.i)
still always; cf. Dryden, "For Nature is still the same in all ages, and can never be contrary to herself" (*Parallel Betwixt Poetry and Painting*, 1695)
informing soul the animating power and governing structure; cf. Dryden, *Absalom and Achitophel*, ll. 157–59, for ironic account of the "fiery soul" that "o'er-informs"
as much more distinguishing implicitly between wit as invention and fancy ("quickness" and "fertility") and wit as elocution or expression ("accuracy") as in Dryden's preface to *Annus Mirabilis* (see above, his Critical Prose); or, to put it another way, insisting upon the interdependence of wit and judgment, for if like man and wife they become one, each implies the other and may be called by the same name
Muse's steed Pegasus, the winged horse
generous spirited
liberty in early editions "monarchy"; in both cases implying that the sovereign power, whether the king or the people, limits itself willingly as the condition of its rule, just as God is often conceived as limiting himself to rational rather than merely arbitrary exercise of power (for the exception, see l. 162)

By the same laws which first herself ordained.
Hear how learnèd Greece her useful rules indites,
When to repress, and when indulge our flights:
High on Parnassus'° top her sons she showed,
And pointed out those arduous paths they trod,
Held from afar, aloft, the immortal prize,
And urged the rest by equal steps to rise;
Just precepts thus from great examples given,
She drew from them what they derived from Heaven.
The generous critic fanned the poet's fire,
And taught the world with reason to admire.
Then criticism the Muses' handmaid proved,
To dress her charms,° and make her more beloved;
But following wits from that intention strayed,
Who could not win the mistress, wooed the maid;
Against the poets their own arms they turned,
Sure to hate most the men from whom they learned.
So modern 'pothecaries, taught the art
By doctor's bills° to play the doctor's part,
Bold in the practice of mistaken° rules,
Prescribed, apply, and call their masters fools.
Some on the leaves° of ancient authors prey,
Nor time nor moths e'er spoiled so much as they:
Some drily plain, without invention's° aid,
Write dull receipts° how poems may be made:
These leave the sense, their learning to display,
And those explain the meaning quite away.
You then whose judgment the right course would steer,
Know well each ancient's proper character;
His fable,° subject, scope° in every page;
Religion, country, genius of his age:
Without all these at once before your eyes,
Cavil you may, but never criticize.
Be Homer's works your study and delight,
Read them by day, and meditate by night;
Thence form your judgment, thence your maxims bring,
And trace the Muses upward to their spring;
Still with itself compared, his text peruse;
And let your comment be the Mantuan Muse.°
When first young Maro° in his boundless mind

Parnassus' the sacred mountain of the Muses
dress her charms implying both to clothe or interpret and to rectify or adjust; the former action making them more apparent, the latter bringing them to fuller realization; cf. *The Rape of the Lock* I.139–44
bills prescriptions
mistaken misunderstood
leaves textual emendators and commentators seen as devouring grubs
invention's imagination, wit
receipts formulae, recipes. Pope later wrote a mocking "receipt" for cooking up an epic poem.
fable plot
scope "aim, final end" (Johnson)
Mantuan Muse Virgil's *Aeneid,* the best commentary on Homer
Maro Virgil

A work to outlast immortal Rome designed,
Perhaps he seemed° above the critic's law,
And but from Nature's fountains scorned to draw:
But when to examine every part he came,
Nature and Homer were, he found, the same:
Convinced, amazed, he checks the bold design,
And rules as strict his laboured work confine,
As if the Stagirite° o'erlooked each line.
Learn hence for ancient rules a just esteem;
To copy nature is to copy them.
Some beauties yet no precepts can declare,
For there's a happiness° as well as care.
Music resembles poetry, in each
Are nameless graces° which no methods teach,
And which a master hand alone can reach.
If, where the rules not far enough extend,
(Since rules were made but to promote their end)
Some lucky licence answer to the full
The intent proposed, that licence is a rule.
Thus Pegasus, a nearer way to take,
May boldly deviate from the common track;
From vulgar bounds with brave° disorder part,
And snatch a grace beyond the reach of art,
Which, without passing through the judgment, gains
The heart, and all its end at once attains.
In prospects, thus, some objects please our eyes,
Which out of nature's common order rise,
The shapeless rock, or hanging precipice.
Great wits sometimes may gloriously offend,
And rise to faults true critics dare not mend.
But though the ancients thus their rules invade,
(As kings dispense with laws themselves have made)
Moderns, beware! or if you must offend
Against the precept, ne'er transgress its end;
Let it be seldom, and compelled by need,
And have, at least, their precedent to plead.
The critic else proceeds without remorse,
Seizes your fame, and puts his laws in force.
I know there are, to whose presumptuous thoughts
Those freer beauties, even in them, seem faults:
Some figures monstrous and misshaped appear,
Considered singly, or beheld too near,

seemed i.e. to himself
Stagirite Aristotle, whose *Poetics* analyzed the forms of epic and tragedy
happiness felicity, good fortune (as opposed to "care"), as in "lucky license," l. 148
nameless graces alluding to the expression "je ne sais quoi," which had gained currency in French criticism as a tribute to the value which eludes categorizing; thus René Rapin speaks of "mysteries" which there is "no method to teach"—"the hidden graces, the insensible charms, and all that secret power of poetry which passes to the heart" (1674)
brave daring; but also magnificent, brilliant

Which, but proportioned to their light or place,
Due distance reconciles to form and grace.
A prudent chief not always must display
His powers in equal ranks, and fair array,
But with the occasion and the place comply,
Conceal his force, nay seem sometimes to fly.
Those oft are stratagems which error seem,
Nor is it Homer nods, but we that dream.
  Still green with bays° each ancient altar° stands,
Above the reach of sacrilegious hands,
Secure from flames, from envy's fiercer rage,
Destructive war, and all-involving age.
See, from each clime the learned their incense bring!
Hear, in all tongues consenting° paeans ring!
In praise so just, let every voice be joined,
And fill the general chorus of mankind!
Hail Bards triumphant! born in happier days;
Immortal heirs of universal praise!
Whose honours with increase of ages grow,
As streams roll down, enlarging as they flow!
Nations unborn your mighty names shall sound,
And worlds applaud that must not yet be found!
Oh may some spark of your celestial fire,
The last, the meanest of your sons inspire,
(That on weak wings, from far, pursues your flights;
Glows while he reads, but trembles as he writes)
To teach vain wits a science little known,
To admire superior sense, and doubt their own!
  Of all the causes which conspire to blind
Man's erring judgment, and misguide the mind,
What the weak head with strongest bias rules,
Is *pride*, the never-failing vice of fools.
Whatever Nature has in worth denied,
She gives in large recruits° of needful° pride;
For as in bodies, thus in souls, we find
What wants° in blood and spirits, swelled with wind;
Pride, where wit fails, steps in to our defence,
And fills up all the mighty void of sense.
If once right reason drives that cloud away,
Truth breaks upon us with resistless day;
Trust not yourself; but your defects to know,
Make use of every friend—and every foe.
  A *little learning* is a dangerous thing;
Drink deep, or taste not the Pierian spring:°

bays the laurel that crowns the poet
altar the works of the ancients
consenting harmonious, unanimous
recruits additional supplies
needful needed (in the absence of "worth"); but also demanding, or arrogant
wants is lacking
Pierian spring a spring sacred to the Muses

There shallow draughts intoxicate the brain,
And drinking largely° sobers us again.
Fired at first sight with what the Muse imparts,
In fearless youth we tempt the heights of arts,
While from the bounded level of our mind,
Short views we take, nor see the lengths behind,
But more advanced, behold with strange surprise
New, distant scenes of endless science° rise!
So pleased at first, the towering Alps we try,
Mount o'er the vales, and seem to tread the sky;
The eternal snows appear already past,
And the first clouds and mountains seem the last:
But those attained, we tremble to survey
The growing labours of the lengthened way,
The increasing prospect tires our wandering eyes,
Hills peep o'er hills, and Alps on Alps arise!
A perfect judge will read each work of wit
With the same spirit that its author writ:
Survey the WHOLE, nor seek slight faults to find,
Where nature moves, and rapture warms the mind;
Nor lose, for that malignant dull delight,
The generous pleasure to be charmed with wit.
But in such lays as neither ebb, nor flow,
Correctly cold, and regularly° low,
That shunning faults, one quiet tenor keep;
We cannot blame indeed—but we may sleep.
In wit, as nature, what affects our hearts
Is not the exactness° of peculiar° parts;
'Tis not a lip, or eye, we beauty call,
But the joint force and full result of all.
Thus when we view some well-proportioned dome,°
(The world's just wonder, and even thine O Rome!)
No single parts unequally surprise;
All comes united to the admiring° eyes;
No monstrous height, or breadth, or length appear;
The whole at once is bold, and regular.
Whoever thinks a faultless piece to see,
Thinks what ne'er was, nor is, nor e'er shall be.
In every work regard the writer's end,
Since none can compass more than they intend;
And if the means be just, the conduct° true,
Applause, in spite of trivial faults, is due.

largely deeply
science knowledge
Correctly . . . regularly obedient to the rules but without the vigor of imagination
exactness correctness, strict conformity to rule
peculiar particular, or separate
dome building, whether domed or not; but the dome of such a cathedral as St. Peter's in Rome or St. Paul's in London provides a fine instance of unifying design
admiring wondering or awe-struck as well as approving
conduct execution

As men of breeding, sometimes men of wit,°
To avoid great errors, must the less commit,
Neglect the rules each verbal critic° lays,
For not to know some trifles, is a praise.
Most critics, fond of some subservient art,
Still make the whole depend upon a part,
They talk of principles, but notions° prize,
And all to one loved folly sacrifice.

. . .

Thus critics, of less judgment than caprice,
Curious,° not knowing, not exact, but nice,°
Form short ideas; and offend in arts
(As most in manners) by a love to parts.°
Some to *conceit*° alone their taste confine,
And glittering thoughts struck out at every line;
Pleased with a work where nothing's just or fit;
One glaring chaos and wild heap of wit:
Poets like painters, thus, unskilled to trace
The naked nature and the living grace,
With gold and jewels cover every part,
And hide with ornaments their want of art.
True wit is nature to advantage dressed,
What oft was thought, but ne'er so well expressed,
Something, whose truth convinced at sight we find,
That gives us back the image of our mind:
As shades° more sweetly recommend the light,
So modest plainness sets off sprightly wit:
For works may have more wit than does 'em good,
As bodies perish through excess of blood.°
Others for *language* all their care express,
And value books, as women men, for dress:
Their praise is still—the style is excellent:
The sense, they humbly take upon content.°
Words are like leaves; and where they most abound,
Much fruit of sense beneath is rarely found.
False eloquence, like the prismatic glass,
Its gaudy colours spreads on every place;
The face of nature we no more survey,
All glares alike, without distinction gay:

breeding . . . wit playing on the analogy between the tact of good manners and that of art
verbal critic those concerned with details of language to the neglect of larger function
notions prejudices, unexamined ideas
Curious difficult to please
nice squeamish, overly fastidious
parts isolated gifts; in criticism, the "one loved folly"; in manners, one's pleasure in one's own talents (as in "a man of parts")
conceit farfetched comparison or metaphor, such as had been favored by the Metaphysical poets; see Dryden's Critical Prose and Johnson on the Metaphysical poets
shades Cf. *Windsor Forest*, ll. 17–18, and *Epistle to Burlington*, ll. 53–56.
excess of blood as, it was believed, in apoplexy
upon content on trust

But true expression, like the unchanging sun,
Clears and improves whate'er it shines upon,
It gilds all objects, but it alters none.
Expression is the dress of thought, and still
Appears more decent° as more suitable;
A vile° conceit in pompous words expressed,
Is like a clown° in regal purple dressed;
For different styles with different subjects sort,
As several garbs with country, town, and court.
Some by old words° to fame have made pretence;
Ancients in phrase, mere moderns in their sense!
Such laboured nothings, in so strange a style,
Amaze the unlearned, and make the learnèd smile.
Unlucky, as Fungoso in the play,°
These sparks° with awkward vanity display
What the fine gentleman wore yesterday;
And but so mimic ancient wits at best,
As apes° our grandsires in their doublets drest.
In words, as fashions, the same rule will hold;
Alike fantastic, if too new, or old;
Be not the first by whom the new are tried,
Nor yet the last to lay the old aside.
  But most by *numbers*° judge a poet's song,
And smooth or rough, with them, is right or wrong;
In the bright Muse though thousand charms conspire,
Her voice is all these tuneful fools admire,
Who haunt Parnassus but to please their ear,
Not mend their minds; as some to church repair,
Not for the doctrine but the music there.
These equal syllables alone require,
Though oft the ear the open vowels tire,°
While expletives their feeble aid do join,
And ten low words oft creep in one dull line,
While they ring round the same unvaried chimes,
With sure returns of still expected rhymes.
Where'er you find 'the cooling western breeze,'
In the next line, it 'whispers through the trees';
If crystal streams 'with pleasing murmurs creep,'
The reader's threatened (not in vain) with 'sleep.'
Then, at the last and only couplet fraught

decent appropriate, becoming. In a letter to Pope in 1706 William Walsh had written that expression is "indeed the same thing to wit, as dress is to beauty."
vile low or inept
clown rustic, peasant
old words archaic diction such as Spenser uses at times, clumsily imitated by Ambrose Philips in his pastorals and parodied by John Gay in *The Shepherd's Week*
play Ben Jonson's *Every Man out of His Humour* (1599); Fungoso cannot keep up with current fashions
sparks fops, beaux
apes monkeys dressed elaborately to provide amusement
numbers versification, sound patterns
Though . . . tire This is the first of a series of parodies wherein Pope illustrates the excesses each critical prejudice encourages; here "equal syllables" are rendered.

With some unmeaning thing they call a thought,
A needless Alexandrine° ends the song,
That, like a wounded snake, drags its slow length along.
Leave such to tune their own dull rhymes, and know
What's roundly smooth, or languishingly slow;
And praise the easy vigour of a line
Where Denham's strength, and Waller's sweetness° join.
True ease in writing comes from art, not chance,
As those move easiest who have learned to dance.
'Tis not enough no harshness gives offence,
The sound must seem an echo to the sense.
Soft is the strain° when Zephyr° gently blows,
And the smooth stream in smoother numbers flows;
But when loud surges lash the sounding shore,
The hoarse, rough verse should like the torrent roar.
When Ajax° strives, some rock's vast weight to throw,
The line too labours, and the words move slow;
Not so, when swift Camilla° scours the plain,
Flies o'er the unbending corn, and skims along the main.
Hear how Timotheus'° varied lays surprise,
And bid alternate passions fall and rise!
While, at each change, the son of Libyan Jove°
Now burns with glory, and then melts with love;
Now his fierce eyes with sparkling fury glow;
Now sighs steal out, and tears begin to flow:
Persians and Greeks like turns° of nature found,
And the world's victor stood subdued by sound!
The power of music all our hearts allow,
And what Timotheus was, is DRYDEN now.

. . .

1711

The Rape of the Lock

Pope's friend John Caryll was concerned about the estrangement between two prominent Roman Catholic families caused when Robert, Lord Petre, cut off a lock of hair from the head of Arabella Fermor (known as "Belle"). As Pope explained it, Caryll, "a common acquaintance and well-wisher to both, desired me to write a poem and make a jest of it, and laugh them together again." Pope's poem failed to persuade Arabella to resume her engagement to Lord Petre, and it soon outgrew its occasion.

Alexandrine a line of twelve syllables and six stresses, illustrated in the following line

Denham's . . . sweetness These two 17th-century poets were often praised for complementary virtues (conciseness to the point of harshness, "strong lines" as opposed to harmonious musicality) which the Augustans sought to fuse.

Soft is the strain illustrating, as do the next eight lines, the maxim of l. 365

Zephyr the west wind

Ajax the rough hero in Homer's *Iliad* XII.378–86

Camilla the female warrior in Virgil's *Aeneid* VII.808 ff.

Timotheus' the bard as shown in Dryden's *Alexander's Feast*

son . . . Jove Alexander the Great

like turns similar alternations

Originally written in two cantos in 1712, it was amplified with mock-epic "machinery" and new incidents and appeared in five cantos in 1714 (Clarissa's speech in Canto V was not added until 1717).

The poem exults in the very triviality of its action, stressing the charm of a light, gay, and thoughtless world, upon which it lavishes all the gravity of tone and diction that might be allowed Achilles or Aeneas. Pope constantly plays games with scale. The sylphs—drawn from the occult and fantastic Rosicrucian mythology—are diminutive counterparts of classical deities or Miltonic angels, and they bring all the solicitude of solemn guardians to Belinda's petticoat and her hair. So, too, the full intensity of epic combat takes place not on the windy plains of Troy but on the "velvet plain" of the card table, where heroic battles are tricks in the game of ombre, and regal warriors defend the honor of their suits. The charm of this world deflects the contempt that Butler confers upon the manikins of *Hudibras,* misshapen as they are in mind and body; it exacts an attitude more subtle than moral superiority, more complicated than moral censure. Part of that attitude involves the recognition that the sylphs and gnomes are not so much external guardians as projections outward of states of mind, from coquettish concern with one's appearance to the self-pitying rancor of the spoilsport; and the ideal of good humor, explicity introduced by Clarissa but in fact everywhere present, has its own seriousness as a call to candor, warmth, and tolerance. There is a sense in which the poem is mocking neither its own world nor the imaginative world of the epic but simply putting them side by side, small and great, with a quizzical sense of their parallelism as well as their conflict.

The Rape of the Lock

An Heroi-Comical Poem

Canto I

What dire offence from amorous causes springs,
What mighty contests rise from trivial things,
I sing—This verse to CARYLL, Muse! is due;
This, even Belinda may vouchsafe to view:
Slight is the subject, but not so the praise,
If she inspire, and he approve my lays.
Say what strange motive, Goddess! could compel
A well-bred Lord to assault a gentle Belle?
O say what stranger cause, yet unexplored,
Could make a gentle Belle reject a Lord?
In tasks so bold, can little men engage,
And in soft bosoms dwells such mighty rage?°
Sol through white curtains shot a timorous ray,
And oped those eyes that must eclipse the day:
Now lapdogs give themselves the rousing shake,

in soft . . . rage Having opened with traditional epic "proposition" and invocation, Pope imitates as well the epic questions, here parodying Virgil's *Aeneid* I.ii, "Can heavenly minds such high resentment show?" (Dryden trans.). So in the following lines (13–14) he plays upon Petrarchan conventions to elevate Belinda.

And sleepless lovers, just at twelve, awake:
Thrice rung the bell, the slipper knocked the ground,
And the pressed watch° returned a silver sound.
Belinda still her downy pillow prest,
Her guardian Sylph° prolonged the balmy rest.
'Twas he had summoned to her silent bed
The morning dream that hovered o'er her head.
A youth more glittering than a birth-night beau°
(That even in slumber caused her cheek to glow)
Seemed to her ear his winning lips to lay,
And thus in whispers said, or seemed to say:
'Fairest of mortals, thou distinguished care
Of thousand bright inhabitants of air!
If e'er one vision touched thy infant thought,
Of all the nurse and all the priest° have taught,
Of airy elves by moonlight shadows seen,
The silver token, and the circled green,°
Or virgins visited by angel powers,°
With golden crowns and wreaths of heavenly flowers,
Hear and believe! thy own importance know,
Nor bound thy narrow views to things below.
Some secret truths, from learnèd pride concealed,
To maids alone and children are revealed:
What though no credit doubting wits may give?
The fair and innocent shall still believe.
Know, then, unnumbered spirits round thee fly,
The light militia of the lower sky;
These, though unseen, are ever on the wing,
Hang o'er the box, and hover round the Ring.°
Think what an equipage° thou hast in air,
And view with scorn two pages and a chair.°
As now your own, our beings were of old,
And once enclosed in woman's beauteous mould;
Thence, by a soft transition, we repair
From earthly vehicles° to these of air.

pressed watch It responds with chimes for the nearest hour and quarter-hour.
Sylph One of the spirits inhabiting the four elements (sylphs the air, gnomes the earth, nymphs water, and salamanders fire); the Sylphs "are the best-conditioned creatures imaginable," serving faithfully "upon a condition very easy to all true adepts, an inviolate preservation of chastity" (Pope). While the Sylph appears as a guardian angel, his whisper (ll. 25–26) may recall Satan's early temptation of Eve in *Paradise Lost* IV and his later successful appeal to her pride in Book IX.
birth-night beau courtier splendidly dressed for the king's birthday. For this guise, one may compare the dream used by Archimago to tempt the Red Cross Knight in *The Faerie Queene* I.i.
nurse . . . priest considered as sources of superstition, the nurse contributing the elves, the priest the angels
circled green referring to the phosphoric light ("fairy sparks") and the withered circles in the grass ("fairy rings") that were taken as signs of the fairies' presence
virgins . . . powers invoking the Annunciation to the Virgin but also the mystical experience of many saints, such as Teresa of Avila; clearly a romantic dream of glory for a young girl
Ring a circular drive in Hyde Park; like the theater box, a common scene of flirtation
equipage carriage with horses and footmen
chair a sedan chair, in which passengers were carried
vehicles both the "equipage" and the terrestrial form in which the soul was embodied

Think not, when woman's transient breath is fled,
That all her vanities at once are dead:
Succeeding vanities she still regards,
And though she plays no more, o'erlooks the cards.
Her joy in gilded chariots, when alive,
And love of ombre,° after death survive.
For when the fair in all their pride expire,
To their first elements° their souls retire:
The sprites of fiery termagants in flame
Mount up, and take a Salamander's° name.
Soft yielding minds to water glide away,
And sip, with Nymphs, their elemental tea.°
The graver prude sinks downward to a Gnome,°
In search of mischief still on earth to roam.
The light coquettes in Sylphs aloft repair,
And sport and flutter in the fields of air.
'Know farther yet; whoever fair and chaste
Rejects mankind, is by some Sylph embraced:
For spirits, freed from mortal laws, with ease
Assume what sexes and what shapes they please.°
What guards the purity of melting maids,
In courtly balls and midnight masquerades,
Safe from the treacherous friend, the daring spark,
The glance by day, the whisper in the dark;
When kind occasion prompts their warm desires,
When music softens, and when dancing fires?
'Tis but their Sylph, the wise celestials know,
Though *honour* is the word with men below.
'Some nymphs there are, too conscious of their face,
For life predestined to the Gnomes' embrace.
These swell their prospects and exalt their pride,
When offers are disdained, and love denied.
Then gay ideas crowd the vacant brain,
While peers and dukes, and all their sweeping train,
And garters, stars, and coronets° appear,
And in soft sounds, *Your Grace*° salutes their ear.
'Tis these that early taint the female soul,
Instruct the eyes of young coquettes to roll,
Teach infant cheeks a bidden blush to know,
And little hearts to flutter at a beau.
'Oft when the world imagine women stray,

ombre a popular card game similar to whist or bridge; see note to III.27 below. Another Virgilian echo: "The love of horses which they had alive, / And care of chariots after death survive" (Dryden trans. VI.890 ff.).
first elements the four (earth, air, fire, water) of which all material things are composed
Salamander's named for the animal which was believed to live unharmed in the midst of fire
tea pronounced "tay"
Gnome one of the "demons of earth" which "delight in mischief" (Pope)
what sexes . . . please as can the angels in *Paradise Lost* I.427–31
garters . . . coronets emblems of high court honors
Your Grace the address to a peeress

The Sylphs through mystic mazes guide their way,
Through all the giddy circle they pursue,
And old impertinence° expel by new.
What tender maid but must a victim fall
To one man's treat, but for another's ball?
When Florio speaks, what virgin could withstand,
If gentle Damon did not squeeze her hand?
With varying vanities, from every part,
They shift the moving toyshop° of their heart;
Where wigs with wigs, with sword-knots sword-knots strive,
Beaux banish beaux, and coaches coaches drive.°
This erring mortals levity may call,
Oh blind to truth! the Sylphs contrive it all.
'Of these am I, who thy protection claim,
A watchful sprite, and Ariel is my name.
Late, as I ranged the crystal wilds of air,
In the clear mirror of thy ruling star
I saw, alas! some dread event impend,
Ere to the main this morning sun descend.
But heaven reveals not what, or how, or where:
Warned by the Sylph, oh pious maid, beware!
This to disclose is all thy guardian can:
Beware of all, but most beware of man!'
He said; when Shock,° who thought she slept too long,
Leaped up, and waked his mistress with his tongue.
'Twas then, Belinda, if report say true,
Thy eyes first opened on a billet-doux;
Wounds, charms and ardours were no sooner read,
But all the vision vanished from thy head.
And now, unveiled, the toilet° stands displayed,
Each silver vase in mystic order laid.
First, robed in white, the nymph intent adores,
With head uncovered, the cosmetic powers.
A heavenly image in the glass appears,
To that she bends, to that her eyes she rears;
The inferior priestess,° at her altar's side,
Trembling, begins the sacred rites of pride.
Unnumbered treasures ope at once, and here
The various offerings of the world appear;
From each she nicely culls with curious° toil,

impertinence trifle, frivolity
toyshop "where playthings and little nice manufactures are sold" (Johnson)
Where wigs . . . drive Cf. Homer, *Iliad* IV. 508–9: "Now shield with shield, with helmet helmet closed, / To armor armor, lance to lance opposed" (Pope trans.). "Sword knots" were ribbons tied to hilts; they help reduce the scale qualitatively from use to decoration.

Shock name for a lapdog with very long hair
toilet The dressing-table is ironically presented as an altar, where "cosmetic powers" (l. 124) displace "cosmic."
inferior priestess the maid Betty; Belinda is the high priestess as well as the source of the "heavenly image" (l. 125)
curious careful, full of nicety

And decks the goddess with the glittering spoil.
This casket India's glowing gems unlocks,
And all Arabia° breathes from yonder box.
The tortoise here and elephant unite,
Transformed to combs, the speckled and the white.°
Here files° of pins extend their shining rows,
Puffs, powder, patches,° bibles, billet-doux.
Now awful° beauty puts on all its arms;
The fair each moment rises in her charms,
Repairs her smiles, awakens every grace,
And calls forth all the wonders of her face;
Sees by degrees a purer blush° arise,
And keener lightnings° quicken in her eyes.
The busy Sylphs surround their darling care;
These set the head, and those divide the hair,
Some fold the sleeve, whilst others plait the gown;
And Betty's praised for labours not her own.

Canto II

Not with more glories, in the ethereal plain,°
The sun first rises o'er the purpled main,°
Than issuing forth, the rival of his beams
Launched on the bosom of the silver Thames.°
Fair nymphs and well-dressed youths around her shone,
But every eye was fixed on her alone.
On her white breast a sparkling cross she wore,
Which Jews might kiss, and infidels adore.°
Her lively looks a sprightly mind disclose,
Quick as her eyes, and as unfixed as those:
Favours to none, to all she smiles extends,
Oft she rejects, but never once offends.
Bright as the sun, her eyes the gazers strike,
And, like the sun, they shine on all alike.
Yet graceful ease, and sweetness void of pride,
Might hide her faults, if belles had faults to hide:
If to her share some female errors fall,
Look on her face, and you'll forget 'em all.
  This nymph, to the destruction of mankind,
Nourished two locks, which graceful hung behind
In equal curls, and well conspired to deck
With shining ringlets the smooth ivory neck.
Love in these labyrinths his slaves detains,

Arabia the source of perfumes
speckled . . . white tortoise-shell and ivory
files as of soldiers on parade
patches tiny pieces of black silk pasted on the face to enhance the skin's whiteness
awful awe-inspiring, like the epic hero arming himself
purer blush a more even redness, the result of rouge
lightnings induced by drops of belladonna
ethereal plain the sky
purpled main the sea reddened by dawn to a "royal purple"
silver Thames Belinda is taking a boat from London to Hampton Court.
Jews . . . adore the kissing or adoration of the cross marking conversion to a new faith

And mighty hearts are held in slender chains.
With hairy springes° we the birds betray,
Slight lines of hair surprise the finny prey,
Fair tresses man's imperial race ensnare,
And beauty draws us with a single hair.
 The adventurous Baron the bright locks admired,
He saw, he wished, and to the prize aspired:
Resolved to win, he meditates the way,
By force to ravish, or by fraud betray;
For when success a lover's toil attends,
Few ask, if fraud or force attained his ends.
 For this, ere Phoebus rose,° he had implored
Propitious heaven, and every power adored,
But chiefly Love—to Love an altar built,
Of twelve vast French romances,° neatly gilt.
There lay three garters, half a pair of gloves;
And all the trophies of his former loves.
With tender billets-doux he lights the pyre,
And breathes three amorous sighs to raise the fire;
Then prostrate falls, and begs with ardent eyes
Soon to obtain, and long possess, the prize:
The powers gave ear, and granted half his prayer;
The rest, the winds dispersed in empty air.°
 But now secure the painted vessel glides,
The sunbeams trembling on the floating tides,
While melting music steals upon the sky,
And softened sounds along the waters die.
Smooth flow the waves, the zephyrs gently play,
Belinda smiled, and all the world was gay.
All but the Sylph—with careful thoughts oppress't,
The impending woe sat heavy on his breast.
He summons strait his denizens° of air;
The lucid squadrons round the sails repair:
Soft o'er the shrouds° aërial whispers breathe,
That seemed but zephrys to the train beneath.
Some to the sun their insect wings unfold,
Waft on the breeze, or sink in clouds of gold;
Transparent forms, too fine for mortal sight,
Their fluid bodies half dissolved in light.
Loose to the wind their airy garments flew,
Thin glittering textures of the filmy dew;
Dipped in the richest tincture of the skies,
Where light disports in ever-mingling dyes,

springes snares
ere . . . rose before sunrise
French romances notoriously long and highly conventionalized love stories, here handsomely bound in leather with gold titles and ornaments
The powers . . . air Cf. Virgil, *Aeneid* II.794–95: "Apollo heard, and granting half his prayer, / Shuffled in winds the rest, and tossed in empty air" (Dryden trans.).
denizens inhabitants
shrouds ropes (appropriate to a greater vessel than the river boat)

While every beam new transient colours flings,
Colours that change whene'er they wave their wings.
Amid the circle, on the gilded mast,
Superior by the head,° was Ariel placed;
His purple pinions opening to the sun,
He raised his azure wand, and thus begun.
'Ye Sylphs and Sylphids, to your chief give ear,
Fays, Fairies, Genii, Elves, and Daemons, hear!°
Ye know the spheres and various tasks assigned
By laws eternal to the aërial kind.
Some in the fields of purest aether° play,
And bask and whiten in the blaze of day.
Some guide the course of wandering orbs° on high,
Or roll the planets through the boundless sky.
Some less refined, beneath the moon's pale light
Pursue the stars that shoot athwart the night,
Or suck the mists in grosser air below,
Or dip their pinions in the painted bow,°
Or brew fierce tempests on the wintry main,
Or o'er the glebe° distil the kindly rain.
Others on earth o'er human race preside,
Watch all their ways, and all their actions guide:
Of these the chief the care of nations own,
And guard with arms divine the British throne.
'Our humbler province is to tend the fair,
Not a less pleasing, though less glorious care.
To save the powder from too rude a gale,°
Nor let the imprisoned essences° exhale,
To draw fresh colours from the vernal flowers,
To steal from rainbows e'er they drop in showers
A brighter wash;° to curl their waving hairs,
Assist their blushes, and inspire their airs;
Nay oft, in dreams, invention we bestow,
To change a flounce, or add a furbelow.°
'This day, black omens threat the brightest fair
That e'er deserved a watchful spirit's care;
Some dire disaster, or by force, or sleight,
But what, or where, the fates have wrapped in night:
Whether the nymph shall break Diana's law,°
Or some frail China jar receive a flaw,
Or stain her honour, or her new brocade,

Superior . . . head taller, like the typical epic hero
Ye Sylphs . . . hear Cf. *Paradise Lost* V.600–602: "Hear all ye Angels, progeny of light, / Thrones, Dominations, Princedoms, Virtues, Powers, / Hear my decree. . . ."
purest aether the air above the moon
wandering orbs comets, sometimes regarded as wandering planets
painted bow rainbow
glebe farmland
too rude a gale too rough a breeze
essences bottled perfumes
wash tinting rinse
furbelow ruffle
Diana's law virginity

Forget her prayers, or miss a masquerade,
Or lose her heart, or necklace, at a ball;
Or whether Heaven has doomed that Shock must fall.
Haste then, ye spirits! to your charge repair:
The fluttering fan be Zephyretta's care;
The drops° to thee, Brillante, we consign;
And, Momentilla, let the watch be thine;
Do thou, Crispissa,° tend her favourite lock;
Ariel himself shall be the guard of Shock.
'To fifty chosen Sylphs, of special note,
We trust the important charge, the petticoat:
Oft have we known that sevenfold fence to fail,
Though stiff with hoops, and armed with ribs of whale.°
Form a strong line° about the silver bound,
And guard the wide circumference around.
'Whatever spirit, careless of his charge,
His post neglects, or leaves the fair at large,
Shall feel sharp vengeance soon o'ertake his sins,
Be stopped in vials, or transfixed with pins;
Or plunged in lakes of bitter washes lie,
Or wedged whole ages in a bodkin's° eye:
Gums and pomatums° shall his flight restrain,
While clogged he beats his silken wings in vain;
Or alum styptics with contracting power
Shrink his thin essence like a rivelled flower.
Or as Ixion° fixed, the wretch shall feel
The giddy motion of the whirling mill,°
In fumes of burning chocolate shall glow,
And tremble at the sea that froths below!'
He spoke; the spirits from the sails descend;
Some, orb in orb, around the nymph extend,
Some thrid the mazy ringlets of her hair,
Some hang upon the pendants of her ear;
With beating hearts the dire event they wait,
Anxious, and trembling for the birth of fate.°

Canto III

Close by those meads, for ever crowned with flowers,
Where Thames with pride surveys his rising towers,
There stands a structure° of majestic frame,
Which from the neighbouring Hampton takes its name.
Here Britain's statesmen oft the fall foredoom

drops diamond earrings
Crispissa from "crisp," in its old sense of "curl"
whale whalebone
line i.e. of defense; the petticoat is described in terms used for an epic shield
bodkin's needle's
Gums and pomatums cosmetic ointments
Ixion the King of Thessaly who sought to seduce the goddess Hera and was bound by Zeus in hell to an eternally revolving wheel
mill for beating chocolate
birth of fate Cf. Homer, *Iliad* IV.112: "And fate now labours with some vast event" (Pope trans.).
structure Hampton Court, the largest of the royal palaces

Of foreign tyrants, and of nymphs at home;
Here thou, great Anna!° whom three realms obey,
Dost sometimes counsel take—and sometimes tea.
Hither the heroes and the nymphs resort,
To taste awhile the pleasures of a court;
In various talk the instructive hours they past,
Who gave the ball, or paid the visit last;
One speaks the glory of the British queen,
And one describes a charming Indian screen;
A third interprets motions, looks, and eyes;
At every word a reputation dies.
Snuff, or the fan, supply each pause of chat,
With singing, laughing, ogling, *and all that.*
Meanwhile, declining from the noon of day,
The sun obliquely shoots his burning ray;
The hungry judges soon the sentence sign,
And wretches hang that jurymen may dine;
The merchant from the Exchange returns in peace,
And the long labours of the toilet cease—
Belinda now, whom thirst of fame invites,
Burns to encounter two adventurous knights,
At ombre° singly to decide their doom;
And swells her breast with conquests yet to come.
Straight the three bands prepare in arms to join,
Each band the number of the sacred nine.
Soon as she spread her hand, the aërial guard
Descend, and sit on each important card:
First Ariel perched upon a Matadore,°
Then each, according to the rank they bore;
For Sylphs, yet mindful of their ancient race,
Are, as when women, wondrous fond of place.°
Behold, four Kings in majesty revered,°
With hoary whiskers and a forky beard;
And four fair Queens whose hands sustain a flower,
The expressive emblem of their softer power;
Four Knaves in garbs succinct,° a trusty band,
Caps on their heads, and halberts° in their hand;
And particoloured troops, a shining train,
Draw forth to combat on the velvet plain.°
The skilful nymph reviews her force with care;

Anna Queen Anne, ruler of Great Britain and Ireland as well as claimant to France
ombre a card game related to whist or modern bridge, played with forty cards—the 10's, 9's, and 8's being removed from the deck; there are three players, each holding nine cards, and the one who contracts to take most tricks is called the "ombre" (from Spanish for "man") and chooses the trumps
Matadore one of the three cards of highest value
place rank
revered There follows a parody of the traditional epic review of forces, in which the royal figures are given the appearance they bear on playing cards.
succinct tucked up
halberts battle axes fixed to long poles
velvet plain typical poetic diction for a smooth grassy field, here applied to the card table covered with green velvet; cf. also "verdant field" (l. 52) and "level green" (l. 80)

'Let spades be trumps!' she said, and trumps they were.°
Now move to war her sable Matadores,°
In show like leaders of the swarthy Moors.
Spadillio first, unconquerable lord!
Led off two captive trumps, and swept the board.
As many more Manillio forced to yield,
And marched a victor from the verdant field.
Him Basto followed, but his fate more hard
Gained but one trump and one plebeian card.
With his broad sabre next, a chief in years,
The hoary Majesty of Spades appears,
Puts forth one manly leg,° to sight revealed;
The rest, his many-coloured robe concealed.
The rebel Knave, who dares his prince engage,
Proves the just victim of his royal rage.
Even mighty Pam,° that kings and queens o'erthrew,
And mowed down armies in the fights of Lu,
Sad chance of war! now, destitute of aid,
Falls undistinguished by the victor spade!
Thus far both armies to Belinda yield;
Now to the Baron fate inclines the field.
His warlike Amazon° her host invades,
The imperial consort of the crown of spades.
The club's black tyrant first her victim died,
Spite of his haughty mien and barbarous pride:
What boots° the regal circle on his head,
His giant limbs in state unwieldy spread?
That long behind he trails his pompous robe,
And of all monarchs only grasps the globe?
The Baron now his diamonds pours apace;
The embroidered King who shows but half his face,
And his refulgent Queen, with powers combined,
Of broken troops an easy conquest find.
Clubs, diamonds, hearts, in wild disorder seen,
With throngs promiscuous strew the level green.
Thus when dispersed a routed army runs,
Of Asia's troops, and Afric's sable sons,
With like confusion different nations fly,
Of various habit and of various dye,
The pierced battalions disunited fall,

Let spades . . . were Cf. Genesis 1:3: "And God said, Let there be light; and there was light."

Matadores The highest cards (determined by choice of trumps) are seen as epic heroes taking the field; they are the ace of spades (Spadillio), the two of spades (Manillio), and the ace of clubs (Basto).

Puts forth . . . leg as pictured on the playing card

Pam knave of clubs, strongest card in the game of loo

Amazon the queen of spades seen as a female warrior; giving the Baron the first of four successive tricks

What boots introducing a typical epic lament for the decline of greatness (here symbolized in the "globe" the monarch holds as an emblem of his realm)

In heaps on heaps; one fate o'erwhelms them all.
The Knave of Diamonds tries his wily arts,
And wins (oh shameful chance!) the Queen of Hearts.
At this, the blood the virgin's cheek forsook,
A livid paleness spreads o'er all her look;
She sees, and trembles at the approaching ill,
Just in the jaws of ruin, and Codille.°
And now (as oft in some distempered state)
On one nice trick° depends the general fate.
An Ace of Hearts steps forth: the King unseen
Lurked in her hand, and mourned his captive Queen.
He springs to vengeance with an eager pace,
And falls like thunder on the prostrate Ace.°
The nymph exulting fills with shouts the sky,
The walls, the woods, and long canals reply.
Oh thoughtless mortals! ever blind to fate,°
Too soon dejected, and too soon elate!
Sudden these honours shall be snatched away,
And cursed for ever this victorious day.
For lo! the board with cups and spoons is crowned,
The berries° crackle, and the mill turns round.
On shining altars of Japan° they raise
The silver lamp; the fiery spirits° blaze.
From silver spouts the grateful° liquors glide,
While China's earth° receives the smoking tide.
At once they gratify their scent and taste,
And frequent cups prolong the rich repast.
Straight hover round the fair her airy band;
Some, as she sipped, the fuming liquor fanned,
Some o'er her lap their careful plumes displayed,
Trembling, and conscious of the rich brocade.
Coffee (which makes the politician wise,
And see through all things with his half-shut eyes)
Sent up in vapours to the Baron's brain
New stratagems, the radiant lock to gain.
Ah cease, rash youth! desist ere 'tis too late,
Fear the just gods, and think of Scylla's fate!°
Changed to a bird, and sent to flit in air,
She dearly pays for Nisus' injured hair!
But when to mischief mortals bend their will,
How soon they find fit instruments of ill!

Codille literally "elbow"; defeat, if the Baron wins a fifth trick
nice trick precise or careful play, with suggestion of political intrigue in "some distempered state" (l. 93)
Ace outranked by the king in the red suits; Belinda takes the trick and the game
blind to fate part of the typical epic warning in the moment of pride
berries coffee beans being ground
Japan japanned or lacquered tables
spirits in the spirit lamps that heat the coffee
grateful pleasing
China's earth the cups of earthenware or China
Scylla's fate Scylla plucked the purple hair (which was the source of his power) from the head of her royal father, Nisus, in order to give it to her lover, Minos. Her lover was shocked and refused it, and she was changed into a sea bird (see Ovid, *Metamorphoses* VIII).

Just then, Clarissa drew with tempting grace
A two-edged weapon from her shining case;
So ladies in romance assist their knight,
Present the spear, and arm him for the fight.
He takes the gift with reverence, and extends
The little engine on his fingers' ends;
This just behind Belinda's neck he spread,
As o'er the fragrant steams she bends her head.
Swift to the lock a thousand sprites repair,
A thousand wings, by turns, blow back the hair,
And thrice they twitched the diamond in her ear;
Thrice she looked back, and thrice the foe drew near.
Just in that instant, anxious Ariel sought
The close recesses of the virgin's thought;
As, on the nosegay° in her breast reclined,
He watched the ideas rising in her mind,
Sudden he viewed, in spite of all her art,
An earthly lover lurking at her heart.
Amazed, confused, he found his power expired,
Resigned to fate, and with a sigh retired.
The peer now spreads the glittering forfex° wide,
To enclose the lock; now joins it, to divide.
Even then, before the fatal engine closed,
A wretched Sylph too fondly interposed;
Fate urged the shears, and cut the Sylph in twain
(But airy substance soon unites° again),
The meeting points the sacred hair dissever
From the fair head, for ever and for ever!
Then flashed the living lightning from her eyes,
And screams of horror rend the affrighted skies.
Not louder shrieks to pitying heaven are cast,
When husbands or when lapdogs breathe their last,
Or when rich China vessels, fallen from high,
In glittering dust and painted fragments lie!
'Let wreaths of triumph now my temples twine,'
(The victor cried) 'the glorious prize is mine!
While fish in streams, or birds delight in air,
Or in a coach and six the British fair,
As long as Atalantis° shall be read,
Or the small pillow grace a lady's bed,
While visits shall be paid on solemn days,
When numerous wax-lights in bright order blaze,
While nymphs take treats, or assignations give,
So long my honour, name, and praise shall live!'
What time would spare, from steel° receives its date,

nosegay corsage of flowers
forfex Latinate diction for the pair of scissors
soon unites Cf. Milton's account of Satan pierced by Michael's sword: "but the ethereal substance closed / Not long divisible" (*Paradise Lost* VI. 330–31).
Atalantis a popular book of the day, full of court scandal
steel the fatal power of arms, which destroys even the Troy built by Apollo and Poseidon

And monuments, like men, submit to fate!
Steel could the labour of the gods destroy,
And strike to dust the imperial towers of Troy;
Steel could the works of mortal pride confound,
And hew triumphal arches to the ground.
What wonder then, fair nymph! thy hairs should feel
The conquering force of unresisted steel?

Canto IV

But anxious cares the pensive nymph oppressed,°
And secret passions laboured in her breast.
Not youthful kings in battle seized alive,
Not scornful virgins who their charms survive,
Not ardent lovers robbed of all their bliss,
Not ancient ladies when refused a kiss,
Not tyrants fierce that unrepenting die,
Not Cynthia when her manteau's° pinned awry,
E'er felt such rage, resentment, and despair,
As thou, sad virgin! for thy ravished hair.
  For, that sad moment, when the Sylphs withdrew,
And Ariel weeping from Belinda flew,
Umbriel,° a dusky melancholy sprite
As ever sullied the fair face of light,
Down to the central earth, his proper scene,
Repaired to search the gloomy Cave of Spleen.°
  Swift on his sooty pinions flits the Gnome,
And in a vapour reached the dismal dome.°
No cheerful breeze this sullen region knows,
The dreaded East° is all the wind that blows.
Here, in a grotto, sheltered close from air,
And screened in shades from day's detested glare,
She sighs for ever on her pensive bed,
Pain at her side, and Megrim° at her head.
  Two handmaids wait the throne: alike in place,
But differing far in figure and in face.
Here stood Ill Nature like an ancient maid,
Her wrinkled form in black and white arrayed;
With store of prayers, for mornings, nights, and noons,
Her hand is filled; her bosom with lampoons.°
  There Affectation, with a sickly mien
Shows in her cheek the roses of eighteen,

But anxious . . . oppressed Cf. *Aeneid* IV.1 "But anxious cares already seized the Queen" (Dryden trans.).
manteau's mantua, loose robe or hood
Umbriel a gnome and former prude, named for "umbra," Latin for "shadow"
Cave of Spleen an epic visit to the underworld; suggestive of Spenser's caves of Mammon, Despair, and Night. Spleen was the name (drawn from the bodily organ, whose function was not clearly understood) for the fashionable psychosomatic ailment of the day, involving melancholy, self-pity, and hypochondria; particularly rife among those who could afford it.
dome dwelling
East The east wind was taken as a cause of spleen.
Megrim migraine headache
lampoons ill-tempered satires or caricatures

Practiced to lisp, and hang the head aside,
Faints into airs, and languishes with pride;
On the rich quilt sinks with becoming woe,
Wrapped in a gown for sickness, and for show.
The fair ones feel such maladies as these,
When each new nightdress gives a new disease.
A constant vapour o'er the palace flies;
Strange phantoms° rising as the mists arise;
Dreadful, as hermit's dreams in haunted shades,
Or bright as visions of expiring° maids.
Now glaring fiends, and snakes on rolling spires,°
Pale spectres, gaping tombs, and purple fires:
Now lakes of liquid gold, Elysian scenes,°
And crystal domes, and angels in machines.
Unnumbered throngs on every side are seen
Of bodies changed° to various forms by Spleen.
Here living teapots stand, one arm held out,
One bent; the handle this, and that the spout:
A pipkin° there like Homer's tripod walks;
Here sighs a jar, and there a goose-pie° talks;
Men prove with child, as powerful fancy works,
And maids, turned bottles, call aloud for corks.
Safe passed the Gnome through this fantastic band,
A branch of healing spleenwort° in his hand.
Then thus addressed the power: 'Hail, wayward Queen!
Who rule the sex to fifty from fifteen,
Parent of vapours° and of female wit,
Who give the hysteric, or poetic fit,
On various tempers act by various ways,
Make some take physic,° others scribble plays;
Who cause the proud their visits to delay,
And send the godly in a pet to pray.
A nymph there is, that all thy power disdains,
And thousands more in equal mirth maintains.
But oh! if e'er thy Gnome could spoil a grace,
Or raise a pimple on a beauteous face,
Like citron-waters° matrons' cheeks inflame,
Or change complexions at a losing game;
If e'er with airy horns° I planted heads,

phantoms fantasies
expiring literally, dying; in the traditionally punning sense, coming to sexual climax (as might be suggested in the erotic intensity with which saints' raptures were sometimes presented)
spires coils
Elysian scenes not only fantasies of bliss but scenes such as contemporary opera and pantomime lavishly presented ("angels in machines")
bodies changed in fantasies that seem psychotic and clearly sexual in some cases, such as the repressed lives of prudes might have engendered
pipkin small earthenware boiler on a tripod; for Hephaistos' "walking" tripods, see **Homer,** *Iliad* XVIII.439 ff.
goose-pie "alludes to a real fact; a lady of distinction imagined herself in this condition" (Pope)
spleenwort a fern that protected one against the excesses of the spleen
vapours roughly the same ailment as spleen, melancholy moodiness, here identified with hysteria
physic medicine
citron-waters brandy flavored with lemon
airy horns the sign of the cuckold

Or rumpled petticoats, or tumbled beds,
Or caused suspicion when no soul was rude,
Or discomposed the headdress of a prude,
Or e'er to costive° lapdog gave disease,
Which not the tears of brightest eyes could ease:
Hear me, and touch Belinda with chagrin;
That single act gives half the world the spleen.'
The goddess with a discontented air
Seems to reject him, though she grants his prayer.
A wondrous bag with both her hands she binds,
Like that where once Ulysses° held the winds;
There she collects the force of female lungs,
Sighs, sobs, and passions, and the war of tongues.
A vial next she fills with fainting fears,
Soft sorrows, melting griefs, and flowing tears.
The Gnome rejoicing bears her gifts away,
Spreads his black wings, and slowly mounts to day.
Sunk in Thalestris'° arms the nymph he found,
Her eyes dejected and her hair unbound.
Full o'er their heads the swelling bag he rent,
And all the furies issued at the vent.
Belinda burns with more than mortal ire,
And fierce Thalestris fans the rising fire.
'O wretched maid!' she spread her hands, and cried,
(While Hampton's echoes, 'Wretched maid!' replied)
'Was it for this you took such constant care
The bodkin,° comb, and essence to prepare;
For this your locks in paper durance° bound,
For this with torturing irons wreathed around?
For this with fillets° strained your tender head,
And bravely bore the double loads of lead?
Gods! shall the ravisher display your hair,
While the fops envy, and the ladies stare!
Honour forbid! at whose unrivalled shrine
Ease, pleasure, virtue, all, our sex resign.
Methinks already I your tears survey,
Already hear the horrid things they say,
Already see you a degraded toast,°
And all your honour in a whisper lost!
How shall I, then, your helpless fame defend?
'Twill then be infamy to seem your friend!
And shall this prize,° the inestimable prize,

costive constipated
Ulysses when given a bag filled with the winds by Aeolus (*Odyssey* X.19 ff.)
Thalestris' named for a queen of the Amazons, thus fiercely militant
bodkin hairpin
paper durance heroic diction for curling papers as for curling ("torturing") irons in the next line
fillets headbands, worn by priestesses in the *Aeneid*, but here part of the machinery of hair-dressing, as are the "loads of lead" in the next line
toast "a celebrated woman whose health is often drunk" (Johnson); the "degraded" implies some boastfulness in the toaster
prize the lock of her hair encased in a ring

Exposed through crystal to the gazing eyes,
And heightened by the diamond's circling rays,
On that rapacious hand for ever blaze?
Sooner shall grass in Hyde Park Circus° grow,
And wits take lodgings in the sound of Bow;°
Sooner let earth, air, sea, to chaos fall,
Men, monkeys, lapdogs, parrots, perish all!'
She said; then raging to Sir Plume repairs,
And bids her beau demand the precious hairs:
(Sir Plume, of amber snuffbox justly vain,
And the nice conduct of a clouded° cane)
With earnest eyes, and round unthinking face,
He first the snuffbox opened, then the case,
And thus broke out—'My Lord, why, what the devil?
Z—ds! damn the lock! 'fore Gad, you must be civil!
Plague on't! 'tis past a jest—nay prithee, pox!
Give her the hair'—he spoke, and rapped his box.
'It grieves me much' (replied the peer again)
'Who speaks so well should ever speak in vain.
But by this lock, this sacred lock I swear,°
(Which never more shall join its parted hair,
Which never more its honours shall renew,
Clipped from the lovely head where late it grew)
That while my nostrils draw the vital air,
This hand, which won it, shall for ever wear.'
He spoke, and speaking, in proud triumph spread
The long-contended honours° of her head.
But Umbriel, hateful Gnome! forbears not so;
He breaks the vial whence the sorrows flow.
Then see! the nymph in beauteous grief appears,
Her eyes half languishing, half drowned in tears;
On her heaved bosom hung her drooping head,
Which, with a sigh, she raised; and thus she said:
'For ever cursed be this detested day,°
Which snatched my best, my favourite curl away!
Happy! ah ten times happy had I been,
If Hampton Court these eyes had never seen!
Yet am not I the first mistaken maid,
By love of courts to numerous ills betrayed.
Oh had I rather unadmired remained
In some lone isle, or distant northern land;
Where the gilt chariot never marks the way,
Where none learn ombre; none e'er taste bohea!°

Hyde Park Circus the Ring (see I.44), where carriages kept the grass from growing
Bow near St. Mary-le-Bow, in the unfashionable merchants' quarter of London as opposed to the polite (west) end
clouded fashionably mottled or veined
this lock . . . swear Cf. Achilles' oath: "Now by this sacred sceptre, hear me swear, / Which never more shall leaves or blossoms bear . . ." (Pope trans., *Iliad* I.309–10).
honours beauties
For ever . . . day This speech is based on Achilles' lament for Patroclus (*Illiad* XVIII. 107 ff.).
bohea a kind of tea

There kept my charms concealed from mortal eye,
Like roses that in deserts bloom and die.
What moved my mind with youthful lords to roam?
O had I stayed, and said my prayers at home!
'Twas this, the morning omens seemed to tell;
Thrice from my trembling hand the patch box fell;
The tottering china shook without a wind,
Nay, Poll sat mute, and Shock was most unkind!
A Sylph too warned me of the threats of fate,
In mystic visions, now believed too late!
See the poor remnants of these slighted hairs!
My hands shall rend what even thy rapine spares:
These, in two sable ringlets taught to break,
Once gave new beauties to the snowy neck;
The sister lock now sits uncouth, alone,
And in its fellow's fate foresees its own;
Uncurled it hangs, the fatal shears demands;
And tempts once more thy sacrilegious hands.
Oh hadst thou, cruel! been content to seize
Hairs less in sight, or any hairs but these!'°

Canto V

She said: the pitying audience melt in tears,
But fate and Jove had stopped the Baron's ears.
In vain Thalestris with reproach assails,
For who can move when fair Belinda fails?
Not half so fixed the Trojan could remain,
While Anna° begged and Dido raged in vain.
Then grave Clarissa° graceful waved her fan;
Silence ensued, and thus the nymph began.
'Say why are beauties praised and honoured most,
The wise man's passion, and the vain° man's toast?
Why decked with all that land and sea afford,
Why angels called, and angel-like adored?
Why round our coaches crowd the white-gloved beaux,
Why bows the side-box from its inmost rows?
How vain are all these glories, all our pains,
Unless good sense preserve what beauty gains:
That men may say, when we the front-box grace,
"Behold the first in virtue, as in face!"
Oh! if to dance all night, and dress all day,

any . . . these The joke here is that while Belinda doesn't mean her pubic hair, her whole rhetoric of honor (exteriors and reputations matter more than interior truths) leads her to invoke it inadvertently; the poet's wit traps her, much as Malvolio, in *Twelfth Night* (III.iv) is trapped into saying a bit of bawdry his Puritanism would never allow him consciously to utter.

Anna who failed to persuade Aeneas to remain faithful to her sister Dido (*Aeneid* IV)

Clarissa "A new character introduced in the subsequent editions, to open more clearly the moral of the poem, in a parody of the speech of Sarpedon to Glaucus in Homer" (Pope); cf. especially the final lines of the speech: "But since, alas! ignoble age must come, / Disease, and death's inexorable doom; / The life which others pay, let us bestow, / And give to Fame what we to Nature owe; / Brave though we fall, and honoured if we live, / Or let us glory gain, or glory give!" (Pope trans., *Iliad* XII. 391–96). The transposition of scale moves from "valour" as a source of merit to "good humour."

vain both foolish and boastful

Charmed the smallpox,° or chased old age away,
Who would not scorn what housewife's cares produce,
Or who would learn one earthly thing of use?
To patch, nay ogle, might become a saint,
Nor could it sure be such a sin to paint.
But since, alas! frail beauty must decay,
Curled or uncurled, since locks will turn to grey;
Since painted or not painted, all shall fade,
And she who scorns a man, must die a maid;
What then remains, but well our power to use,
And keep good humour still whate'er we lose?
And trust me, dear! good humour can prevail,
When airs, and flights, and screams, and scolding fail.
Beauties in vain their pretty eyes may roll;
Charms strike the sight, but merit wins the soul.'
   So spoke the dame, but no applause ensued;
Belinda frowned, Thalestris called her prude.
'To arms, to arms!' the fierce virago° cries,
And swift as lightning to the combat flies.
All side in parties, and begin the attack;
Fans clap, silks rustle, and tough whalebones crack;
Heroes' and heroines' shouts confusedly rise,
And bass and treble voices strike the skies.
No common weapons in their hands are found;
Like gods they fight, nor dread a mortal wound.
   So when bold Homer makes the gods engage,
And heavenly breasts with human passions rage;
'Gainst Pallas,° Mars; Latona,° Hermes arms;
And all Olympus rings with loud alarms.
Jove's thunder roars, heaven trembles all around;
Blue Neptune storms, the bellowing deeps resound;
Earth shakes her nodding towers, the ground gives way;
And the pale ghosts start at the flash of day!
   Triumphant Umbriel on a sconce's height
Clapped his glad wings, and sat to view the fight:
Propped on their bodkin spears, the sprites survey
The growing combat, or assist the fray.
   While through the press enraged Thalestris flies,
And scatters death around from both her eyes,
A beau and witling perished in the throng;
One died in metaphor, and one in song.
'O cruel nymph! a living death I bear,'
Cried Dapperwit,° and sunk beside his chair.
A mournful glance Sir Fopling upwards cast,
'Those eyes are made so killing'—was his last.

smallpox common and disfiguring disease at the time
virago man-like woman
Latona the mother of Apollo and Diana (Pope latinized Greek names in his translations)
Pallas Athena
Dapperwit like "Sir Fopling" below, the typical name of a false wit or fop in Restoration comedy

Thus on Maeander's flowery margin lies
The expiring swan,° and as he sings he dies.
 When bold Sir Plume had drawn Clarissa down,
Chloe stepped in, and killed him with a frown;
She smiled to see the doughty hero slain,
But at her smile, the beau revived again.
 Now Jove suspends his golden scales° in air,
Weighs the men's wits against the lady's hair;
The doubtful beam long nods from side to side;
At length the wits mount up, the hairs subside.
 See, fierce Belinda on the Baron flies,
With more than usual lightning in her eyes;
Nor feared the Chief the unequal fight to try,
Who sought no more than on his foe to die.°
But this bold lord, with manly strength endued,
She with one finger and a thumb subdued:
Just where the breath of life his nostrils drew,
A charge of snuff the wily virgin threw;
The Gnomes direct, to every atom just,
The pungent grains of titillating dust.
Sudden, with starting tears each eye o'erflows,
And the high dome re-echoes to his nose.
 'Now meet thy fate,' incensed Belinda cried,
And drew a deadly bodkin from her side.
(The same,° his ancient personage to deck,
Her great great grandsire wore about his neck
In three seal rings; which after, melted down,
Formed a vast buckle for his widow's gown:
Her infant grandame's° whistle next it grew,
The bells she jingled, and the whistle blew;
Then in a bodkin graced her mother's hairs,
Which long she wore, and now Belinda wears.)
 'Boast not my fall' (he cried) 'insulting foe!
Thou by some other shalt be laid as low.
Nor think, to die dejects my lofty mind;
All that I dread is leaving you behind!
Rather than so, ah let me still survive,
And burn in Cupid's flames—but burn alive.'
 'Restore the lock!' she cries; and all around
'Restore the lock!' the vaulted roofs rebound.
Not fierce Othello in so loud a strain
Roared for the handkerchief° that caused his pain.

expiring swan The swan, on the banks of the wandering river Maeander, sings most sweetly as he dies.
golden scales an epic convention in both Homer and Virgil
to die in the double sense of "expiring" (IV.42), as elsewhere in this section, e.g. "laid as low" (l. 98)
The same a parody of epic accounts of the descent of armor or of Agamemnon's scepter
grandame's grandmother's
Roared . . . handkerchief perhaps evoking Thomas Rymer's famous objections to the triviality of the occasion in Shakespeare's play: "So much ado, so much stress, so much passion and repetition about an handkerchief!" (*A Short View of Tragedy*, 1693)

But see how oft ambitious aims are crossed,
And chiefs contend till all the prize is lost!
The lock, obtained with guilt, and kept with pain,
In every place is sought, but sought in vain:
With such a prize no mortal must be blest,
So heaven decrees! with heaven who can contest?
Some thought it mounted to the lunar sphere,°
Since all things lost on earth are treasured there.
There heroes' wits are kept in ponderous vases,
And beaus' in snuffboxes and tweezer cases.
There broken vows, and deathbed alms are found,
And lovers' hearts with ends of riband bound;
The courtier's promises, and sick man's prayers,
The smiles of harlots, and the tears of heirs,
Cages for gnats, and chains to yoke a flea,
Dried butterflies, and tomes of casuistry.°
But trust the Muse—she saw it upward rise,
Though marked by none but quick, poetic eyes:
(So Rome's great founder° to the heavens withdrew,
To Proculus alone confessed in view.)
A sudden star, it shot through liquid° air,
And drew behind a radiant trail of hair.°
Not Berenice's locks° first rose so bright,
The heavens bespangling with dishevelled light.
The Sylphs behold it kindling as it flies,
And pleased pursue its progress through the skies.
This the beau monde° shall from the Mall° survey,
And hail with music its propitious ray.
This, the blest lover shall for Venus take,
And send up vows from Rosamonda's lake.°
This Partridge° soon shall view in cloudless skies,
When next he looks through Galileo's eyes;°
And hence the egregious wizard shall foredoom
The fate of Louis, and the fall of Rome.
Then cease, bright nymph! to mourn thy ravished hair
Which adds new glory to the shining sphere!
Not all the tresses that fair head can boast

lunar sphere reminiscent of Milton's Limbo of Vanity in *Paradise Lost* III.445–46, "Up hither like aerial vapours flew / All things transitory and vain," but even more of Milton's source in Ariosto, *Orlando Furioso* XXXIV.lxviii ff., where the moral tone is lighter and the objects more trivial and minutely specified

casuistry Pope wrote in a letter of 1708 about "deep divines, profound casuists, grave philosophers who have written . . . whole tomes and voluminous treatises about nothing"; casuistry was the difficult (and sometimes hair-splitting) application of general ethical rules to individual cases.

founder Romulus, who disappeared in a storm and whose ascent to the heavens was attested only by the senator Proculus

liquid clear

trail of hair like the tail of a comet, whose name means "hairy star"

Berenice's locks The queen's hair, offered to Aphrodite to ensure her husband's safe return from battle, disappeared from the temple and was transformed into a constellation.

beau monde fashionable world

Mall the promenade in St. James's Park

Rosamonda's lake a pond in the same park, associated with unhappy lovers

Partridge a notorious astrologer (ridiculed by Swift) who predicted public events, such as those in l. 140

Galileo's eyes telescope

Shall draw such envy as the lock you lost.
For, after all the murders of your eye,
When, after millions slain, yourself shall die;
When those fair suns shall set, as set they must,
And all those tresses shall be laid in dust;
This lock, the Muse shall consecrate to fame,
And midst the stars inscribe Belinda's name!

1712–14

The Gardens of Alcinoüs°

Close to the gates a spacious garden lies,
From storms defended, and inclement skies:
Four acres was the allotted space of ground,
Fenced with a green enclosure all around.
Tall thriving trees confessed the fruitful mould;
The redening apple ripens here to gold,
Here the blue fig with luscious juice o'erflows,
With deeper red the full pomegranate glows,
Then branch here bends beneath the weighty pear,
And verdant olives flourish round the year.
The balmy spirit of the western gale
Eternal breathes on fruits untaught to fail:
Each dropping pear a following pear supplies,
On apples apples, figs on figs arise:
The same mild season gives the blooms to blow,°
The buds to harden, and the fruits to grow.
  Here ordered vines in equal ranks appear
With all the united labours of the year;
Some to unload the fertile branches run,
Some dry the blackening clusters in the sun,
Others to tread the liquid harvest join,
The groaning presses foam with floods of wine.
Here are the vines in early flower descried,
Here grapes discoloured on the sunny side,
And there in autumn's richest purple dyed.
  Beds of all various herbs, forever green,
In beauteous order terminate the scene.
  Two plenteous fountains the whole prospect crowned;
This through the gardens leads its streams around,
Visits each plant, and waters all the ground:

The Gardens of Alcinous This translation from *Odyssey* VII was first published in *Guardian*, No. 173 and later included in the full translation of 1725 as VII.142–75. It represents one of the chief classical counterparts of the garden of Eden; it is various and fruitful but also significantly orderly, like Milton's version of Eden in *Paradise Lost* IV.

blow blossom

While that in pipes beneath the palace flows,
And thence its current on the town bestows;
To various use their various streams they bring,
The people one, and one supplies the King.

1713

From Windsor Forest°

The groves of Eden,° vanished now so long,
Live in description, and look green in song:
These, were my breast inspired with equal flame,
Like them in beauty, should be like in fame.
Here hills and vales, the woodland and the plain,
Here earth and water seem to strive again;
Not chaos-like together crushed and bruised,
But, as the world, harmoniously confused:°
Where order in variety we see,
And where, though all things differ, all agree.
Here waving groves a chequered scene display,
And part admit and part exclude the day;
As some coy nymph her lover's warm address
Nor quite indulges, nor can quite repress.°
There, interspersed in lawns and opening glades,
Thin trees arise that shun each other's shades.
Here in full light the russet plains extend:
There wrapped in clouds the bluish hills ascend.
Even the wild heath displays her purple dyes,
And midst the desert° fruitful fields arise,
That crowned with tufted trees and springing corn,
Like verdant isles the sable waste adorn.
Let India boast her plants, nor envy we
The weeping amber or the balmy tree,°
While by our oaks° the precious loads are borne,
And realms commanded which those trees adorn.
Not proud Olympus° yields a nobler sight,
Though gods assembled grace his towering height,
Than what more humble mountains offer here,

Windsor Forest This poem treats the Forest ("At once the Monarch's and the Muse's seats") not merely as a royal forest preserve but as a center of England's natural beauty and its culture; in the early section given below, Pope creates an example of "picturesque" landscape, that is, a landscape seen as it might be in a painting, with interwoven colors and well-defined receding space.

groves of Eden an evocation of Milton, *Paradise Lost* IV

harmoniously confused echoing Ovid's *discors concordia* (*Metamorphoses* I.433), anticipating the larger cosmic application of the theme in the *Essay on Man:* "But all subsists by elemental strife" (I.169); "the lights and shades, whose well accorded strife / Gives all the strength and colour of our life" (II.121–22); "all nature's difference keeps all nature's peace" (IV.56)

Nor quite . . . repress Cf. John Keats's "Ode on a Grecian Urn": "Bold lover, never, never canst thou kiss, / Though winning near the goal . . . "; or "Ode to Psyche": "Their lips touched not, but had not bade adieu."

desert barrenness, wild (cf. "waste" in l. 28)

weeping . . . tree Cf. *Paradise Lost* IV.248: "Groves whose rich trees wept odorous gums and balm."

oaks in the form of ships of trade or war

Olympus the Greek mountain where the gods had their home

Where, in their blessings,° all those gods appear.
See Pan° with flocks, with fruits Pomona° crowned,
Here blushing Flora paints the enamelled ground,°
Here Ceres' gifts° in waving prospect stand,
And nodding tempt the joyful reaper's hand;
Rich Industry° sits smiling on the plains,
And peace and plenty tell, a Stuart reigns.

1704–13 1713

Eloïsa to Abelard

In form Pope's poem is based upon Ovid's *Heroides,* a series of heroic verse epistles written in lament or reproach by women to lovers who have forsaken them. In content the poem derives from the supposed letters of Eloïsa and Abelard, first published in Latin in 1616, freely translated and adapted (with new romantic emphases) into French and, in 1713, into English by John Hughes. This last version seems the basis of Pope's poem.

Peter Abelard (1079–1142) was a brilliant teacher of logic and theology at Notre Dame in Paris. Asked by a canon of the cathedral, Fulbert, to serve as tutor to his young niece, Eloïsa, Abelard became her lover as well. When the affair was exposed, Fulbert arranged to have Abelard emasculated as punishment. Abelard became a monk, and Eloïsa a nun. Years later, when the nuns of whom Eloïsa was prioress were forced to leave their abbey, Abelard offered them the Paraclete (a title of the Holy Spirit, usually meaning the Comforter), a religious community he had earlier founded and had since left.

The poem takes place in the Paraclete when Eloïsa comes upon a letter written by Abelard to a friend. The passion she has continued to feel for him is reawakened, and the violent struggle of "grace and nature," as Pope puts it, resumes. It is a struggle not unlike that of Racine's Phèdre. Eloïsa's passion constantly subverts her religious vision, and her most devout aspirations take on the tincture of sexual rather than spiritual ecstasy. The internal struggle becomes sheer torture as she tries to hold apart the images of God and of Abelard, and the torment of her spirit is caught in the violent contrasts of a dark, shaggy Gothic setting and of visions of blazing and streaming light. It is a poem that looks back to high Baroque art and anticipates in turn the violent intensity of the "sublime" literature of the latter part of the century.

ARGUMENT

Abelard and Eloïsa flourished in the twelfth century; they were two of the most distinguished persons of their age in learning and beauty, but for nothing more famous than for their unfortunate passion. After a long course of calamities, they retired each to a several convent, and consecrated the remainder of their days to religion. It was many years after this separation, that a letter of

in their blessings in the form of their natural gifts
Pan as shepherd
Pomona as goddess of orchards and fruit
blushing Flora . . . ground The goddess of flowers, herself suffused with their color, paints the earth as if it were a painter's surface, prepared with a "ground" or coating of paint.
Ceres' gifts grain
Industry Here Pope turns Virgil's account of the Golden Age in *Eclogue* IV to a vision of English life in a time of peace, newly realized with Stuart Queen Anne's Peace of Utrecht (1713), which ended the War of the Spanish Succession begun under William III in 1701.

Abelard's to a friend, which contained the history of his misfortune, fell into the hands of Eloïsa. This awakening all her tenderness, occasioned those celebrated letters (out of which the following is partly extracted) which give so lively a picture of the struggles of grace and nature, virtue and passion.

In these deep solitudes and awful cells,
Where heavenly-pensive contemplation dwells,
And ever-musing melancholy reigns,
What means this tumult in a vestal's° veins?
Why rove my thoughts beyond this last retreat?
Why feels my heart its long-forgotten heat?
Yet, yet I love!—From Abelard it came,°
And Eloïsa yet must kiss the name.
  Dear fatal name! rest ever unrevealed,
Nor pass these lips in holy silence sealed:
Hide it, my heart, within that close disguise,
Where, mixed with God's, his loved idea° lies:
O write it not, my hand—the name appears
Already written—wash it out, my tears!
In vain lost Eloïsa weeps and prays,
Her heart still dictates, and her hand obeys.
  Relentless walls! whose darksome round contains
Repentant sighs and voluntary pains:
Ye rugged rocks! which holy knees have worn;
Ye grots and caverns shagged with horrid thorn!°
Shrines! where their vigils pale-eyed virgins keep,
And pitying saints, whose statues learn to weep!°
Though cold like you, unmoved and silent grown,
I have not yet forgot myself to stone.°
All is not Heaven's while Abelard has part,
Still rebel nature holds out half my heart;
Nor prayers nor fasts its stubborn pulse restrain,
Nor tears for ages taught to flow in vain.
  Soon as thy letters trembling I unclose,
That well-known name awakens all my woes.
Oh name for ever sad! for ever dear!
Still breathed in sighs, still ushered with a tear.
I tremble too where'er my own I find,
Some dire misfortune follows close behind.
Line after line my gushing eyes o'erflow,
Led through a sad variety of woe:
Now warm in love, now withering in thy bloom,
Lost in a convent's solitary gloom!
There stern religion quenched the unwilling flame,

vestal's nun's
it came letter that Abelard had written to a friend and Eloïsa happens to discover
idea image
horrid thorn The "Gothic" details of both the architectural and the natural setting look ahead to poetry of the later 18th century, but they draw upon sources like Richard Crashaw and Milton's early poems. Cf. "By grots, and caverns shagg'd with horrid shades," *Comus*, l. 429.
learn to weep a frequently used image, based on the condensation of moisture on stone
stone Cf. Milton, *Il Penseroso*, l. 42: "Forget thy self to marble."

There died the best of passions, love and fame.
Yet write, oh write me all, that I may join
Griefs to thy griefs, and echo sighs to thine.
Nor foes nor fortune take this power away;
And is my Abelard less kind than they?
Tears still are mine, and those I need not spare,
Love but demands what else were shed in prayer;
No happier task these faded eyes pursue;
To read and weep is all they now can do.
Then share thy pain, allow that sad relief;
Ah, more than share it, give me all thy grief.
Heaven first taught letters for some wretch's aid,
Some banished lover, or some captive maid;
They live, they speak, they breathe what love inspires,
Warm from the soul, and faithful to its fires,
The virgin's wish without her fears impart,
Excuse° the blush, and pour out all the heart;
Speed the soft intercourse from soul to soul,
And waft a sigh from Indus to the Pole.
Thou knowst how guiltless first I met thy flame,
When love approached me under friendship's name;
My fancy formed thee of angelic kind,
Some emanation of the all-beauteous Mind.
Those smiling eyes, attempering every ray,
Shone sweetly lambent with celestial day.
Guiltless I gazed; heaven listened while you sung;
And truths divine came mended° from that tongue.
From lips like those what precept failed to move?
Too soon they taught me 'twas no sin to love:
Back through the paths of pleasing sense I ran,
Nor wished an angel whom I loved a man.
Dim and remote the joys of saints I see;
Nor envy them that heaven I lose for thee.
How oft, when pressed to marriage, have I said,
Curse on all laws but those which love has made?
Love, free as air, at sight of human ties,
Spreads his light wings; and in a moment flies.°
Let wealth, let honour, wait the wedded dame,
August her deed, and sacred be her fame;
Before true passion all those views remove;
Fame, wealth, and honour! what are you to Love?
The jealous God, when we profane his fires,
Those restless passions in revenge inspires,
And bids them make mistaken mortals groan,
Who seek in love for aught but love alone.
Should at my feet the world's great master fall,

excuse free one from the need for
mended improved, made more appealing

Love . . . flies paraphrase of Chaucer, *The Franklin's Tale,* ll. 36–38

Himself, his throne, his world, I'd scorn 'em all:
Not Cæsar's empress would I deign to prove;
No, make me mistress to the man I love;
If there be yet another name more free,
More fond than mistress, make me that to thee!
Oh! happy state! when souls each other draw,
When love is liberty, and nature, law:°
All then is full, possessing and possessed,
No craving void left aching in the breast:
Even thought meets thought ere from the lips it part,
And each warm wish springs mutual from the heart.
This sure is bliss (if bliss on earth there be)
And once the lot of Abelard and me.
  Alas, how changed! what sudden horrors rise!
A naked lover bound and bleeding lies!
Where, where was Eloïse? her voice, her hand,
Her poniard,° had opposed the dire command.
Barbarian, stay! that bloody stroke restrain;
The crime was common, common be the pain.°
I can no more; by shame, by rage suppressed,
Let tears and burning blushes speak the rest.
  Canst thou forget that sad, that solemn day,
When victims° at yon altar's foot we lay?
Canst thou forget what tears that moment fell,
When, warm in youth, I bade the world farewell?
As with cold lips I kissed the sacred veil,
The shrines all trembled, and the lamps grew pale:
Heaven scarce believed the conquest it surveyed,
And saints with wonder heard the vows I made.
Yet then, to those dread altars as I drew,
Not on the cross my eyes were fixed, but you:
Not grace or zeal, love only was my call,
And if I lose thy love, I lose my all.
Come! with thy looks, thy words, relieve my woe;
Those still at least are left thee to bestow.
Still on that breast enamoured let me lie,
Still drink delicious poison from thy eye,
Pant on thy lip, and to thy heart be pressed;
Give all thou canst—and let me dream the rest.
Ah no! instruct me other joys to prize,
With other beauties charm my partial eyes;
Full in my view set all the bright abode,
And make my soul quit Abelard for God.
  Ah, think at least thy flock deserves thy care,
Plants of thy hand, and children of thy prayer.
From the false world in early youth they fled,

When love . . . law Cf. Dryden, *Absalom and Achitophel*, ll. 5–6.
poniard dagger
pain punishment
victims she as postulant, he as spectator (their vows were taken at different times)

By thee to mountains, wilds, and deserts led.
You raised these hallowed walls; the desert smiled,
And paradise was opened in the wild.°
No weeping orphan saw his father's stores
Our shrines irradiate, or emblaze the floors;
No silver saints, by dying misers given,
Here bribed the rage of ill-requited heaven:
But such plain roofs as piety could raise,
And only vocal with the Maker's praise.
In these lone walls (their day's eternal bound)
These moss-grown domes° with spiry turrets crowned,
Where awful arches make a noonday night,
And the dim windows shed a solemn light;
Thy eyes diffused a reconciling ray,
And gleams of glory brightened all the day.
But now no face divine contentment wears,
'Tis all blank sadness or continual tears.
See how the force of others' prayers I try,°
(O pious fraud of amorous charity!)
But why should I on others' prayers depend?
Come thou, my father, brother, husband, friend!
Ah let thy handmaid, sister, daughter move,
And all those tender names in one, thy love!
The darksome pines that o'er yon rocks reclined
Wave high, and murmur to the hollow wind,
The wandering streams that shine between the hills,
The grots that echo to the tinkling rills,
The dying gales that pant upon the trees,
The lakes that quiver to the curling breeze;
No more these scenes my meditation aid,
Or lull to rest the visionary maid.
But o'er the twilight groves and dusky caves,
Long-sounding aisles, and intermingled graves,
Black Melancholy sits, and round her throws
A deathlike silence and a dread repose:
Her gloomy presence saddens all the scene,
Shades every flower, and darkens every green,
Deepens the murmur of the falling floods,
And breathes a browner horror on the woods.

Yet here for ever, ever must I stay;
Sad proof how well a lover can obey!
Death, only death, can break the lasting chain;
And here, even then, shall my cold dust remain,
Here all its frailties, all its flames resign,
And wait till 'tis no sin to mix with thine.

Ah wretch! believed the spouse of God in vain,
Confessed within the slave of love and man.

You raised . . . the wild Abelard founded an oratory, the Paraclete, in a remote place as a kind of retreat without splendor or elaboration.

domes buildings

See how . . . I try by asking Abelard in the name of her sister-nuns to visit the Paraclete

Assist me, heaven! But whence arose that prayer?
Sprung it from piety, or from despair?
Even here, where frozen chastity retires,
Love finds an altar for forbidden fires.
I ought to grieve, but cannot what I ought;
I mourn the lover, not lament the fault;
I view my crime, but kindle at the view,
Repent old pleasures, and solicit new;
Now turned to heaven, I weep my past offence,
Now think of thee, and curse my innocence.
Of all affliction taught a lover yet,
'Tis sure the hardest science° to forget!
How shall I lose the sin, yet keep the sense,
And love the offender, yet detest the offence?
How the dear object from the crime remove,
Or how distinguish penitence from love?
Unequal task! a passion to resign,
For hearts so touched, so pierced, so lost as mine.
Ere such a soul regains its peaceful state,
How often must it love, how often hate!
How often hope, despair, resent, regret,
Conceal, disdain,—do all things but forget.
But let heaven seize it, all at once 'tis fired;
Not touched, but rapt;° not wakened, but inspired!
Oh come! oh teach me nature to subdue,
Renounce my love, my life, myself—and you.
Fill my fond heart with God alone, for he
Alone can rival, can succeed to thee.

How happy is the blameless vestal's lot!
The world forgetting, by the world forgot:
Eternal sunshine of the spotless mind!
Each prayer accepted, and each wish resigned;
Labour and rest, that equal periods keep;
'Obedient slumbers that can wake and weep;'°
Desires composed, affections ever even,
Tears that delight, and sighs that waft to heaven.
Grace shines around her with serenest beams,
And whispering angels prompt her golden dreams.
For her the unfading rose of Eden blooms,
And wings of seraphs shed divine perfumes,
For her the Spouse prepares the bridal ring,
For her white virgins hymeneals° sing,
To sounds of heavenly harps she dies away,
And melts° in visions of eternal day.

Far other dreams my erring soul employ,
Far other raptures, of unholy joy:

science knowledge
rapt enraptured
Obedient . . . weep from Richard Crashaw, "Description of a Religious House," l. 16
hymeneals wedding songs
melts Like *dies* in the preceding line, this carries erotic suggestions; but here, as in Bernini's famous statue of St. Teresa in ecstasy, the erotic is absorbed into and supports (rather than fights) the spiritual.

1. John Dryden, 1693, by Sir Godfrey Kneller (1649?–1723). *National Portrait Gallery*, London.

2. Charles II, c. 1660-65, ?studio of John Michael Wright (1617–1700). *National Portrait Gallery*.

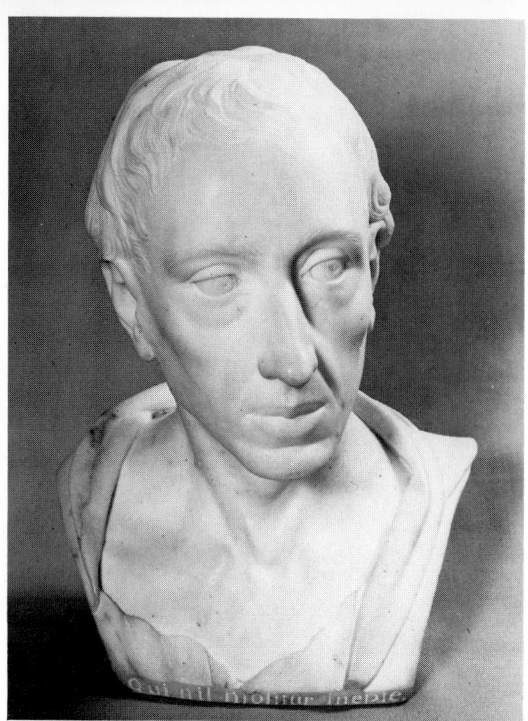

3. Alexander Pope, ?1741, by L. F. Roubiliac (c. 1705–62).
Leeds City Art Galleries.

4. Sir Robert Walpole, 1738, by J. M. Rysbrack (1694–1770).
National Portrait Gallery.

5. Jonathan Swift, by L. F. Roubiliac.
Trinity College, Dublin.

6. St. Paul's from the northwest.
A. F. Kersting.

7. The West Towers.

ENGLISH BAROQUE ARCHITECTURE

Sir Christopher Wren (1632–1723) came to architecture, at the prompting of Charles II, from a distinguished career in mathematics and astronomy. During a visit to Paris in 1665–66 he met the great Italian baroque architect Gianlorenzo Bernini (1598–1680), and brought back with him "almost all France in paper," i.e. in prints and architectural books. His designs included Hampton Court and the royal hospitals at Chelsea and Greenwich, university buildings at Oxford and Cambridge, and nearly fifty churches in London to replace or restore those damaged in the Great Fire of 1666. Of the last the most ambitious was St. Paul's Cathedral, begun in 1675 and completed in 1710. The bold and intricate west towers engage in constantly changing interplay with the massive dome as the viewer's perspective shifts. They are among the finest of the numerous and remarkably varied spires that were to dominate the London skyline for more than two centuries.

8. St. Bride, c. 1700.
A. F. Kersting.

9. St. Magnus-the-Martyr, 1705

10. St. Mary-le-Bow, completed 1680.

11. St. Vedast, 1694–97.

12. Christ Church, Spitalfields.

13. St. Anne, Limehouse.
A. F. Kersting.

Nicholas Hawksmoor (1661–1736), Wren's chief assistant, later worked closely with Sir John Vanbrugh (1664–1726) on such buildings as Blenheim Palace and Castle Howard (see Fig. 16). The two East London churches shown here were begun in 1714 and completed in the late 1720's. Hawksmoor's intense and often somber art turned conventional forms to strikingly novel uses. In Christ Church he used the Palladian form, an arch flanked by two rectangular openings (as in the so-called Venetian window), first magnifying it to the scale of a triumphal arch in the lower storeys, then varying the pattern in shallower and more attenuated forms above. St. Anne, Limehouse, plays with concave and convex forms and concludes in a tower whose angularity suggests Gothic steeples without in fact using any Gothic forms.

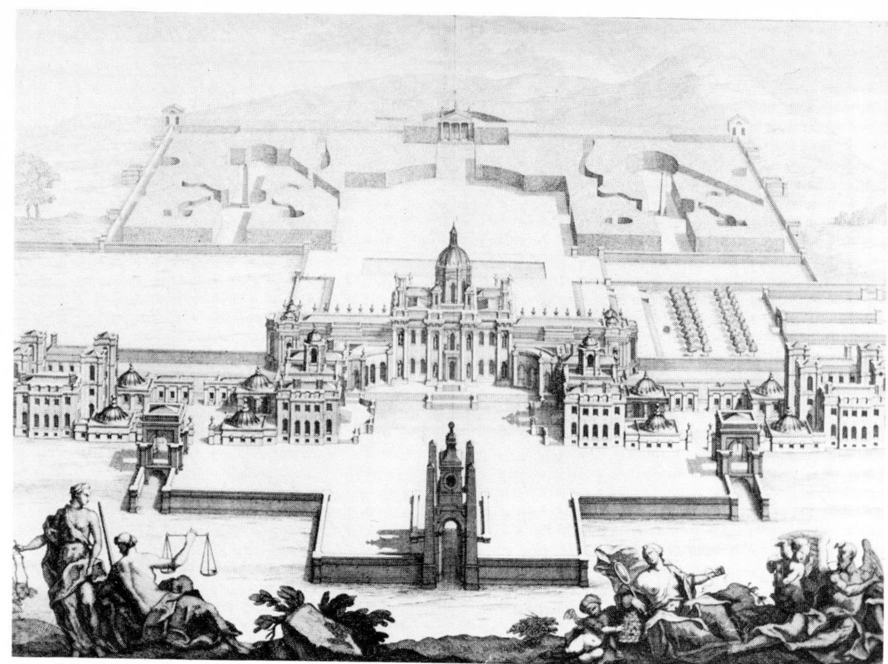

14. Vanbrugh and Hawksmoor, Castle Howard (begun c. 1699). From Colin Campbell, *Vitruvius Britannicus,* 1715. *The New York Public Library.*

Castle Howard, Yorkshire, is one of the most lavish and brilliant of baroque country houses, and its grounds are varied with ornamental buildings in bold shapes. Sir John Vanbrugh's Temple of the Winds was a belvedere; the porticos were designed to prevent direct sunlight but to admit "light of the most pleasing kind." Nicholas Hawksmoor's Mausoleum is set on a rise a mile from the house, its silhouette visible from great distances. Its exterior has twenty Doric columns whose spacing was criticized by Lord Burlington as unclassical in its closeness (see in contrast William Kent's Temple of Ancient Virtue, Fig. 20); and it was one of Burlington's protégés who added later the steps modeled on those at Chiswick House. Hawksmoor's building has survived Palladian criticism and improvement; it remains as he intended: self-enclosed, unaccommodating, formidably severe.

15. Vanbrugh, Temple of the Winds, built in the 1720's. *Country Life*, London.

16. Hawksmoor, Mausoleum, begun in 1729. *Country Life*.

17. Chiswick House, designed before 1727. *A. F. Kersting.*

PALLADIANISM

Lord Burlington (Richard Boyle, 1694–1753; see Pope's *Essay* to him), like the third Earl of Shaftesbury, reacted against Wren and English baroque architecture. Upon his return from Italy, Burlington undertook, with the assistance of William Kent (1685–1748), to work toward a more chaste, more authentic classicism than England had achieved before. He found his models in the Italian Renaissance architect Andrea Palladio (1508–80) and in Palladio's chief English follower, Inigo Jones (1573–1652); Burlington sponsored the publication of their designs and imitated their work, at times moving even closer to their Roman sources. Chiswick House, a country villa at Twickenham, derives in part from Palladio's Villa Rotonda at Vicenza. The austerity of the building itself is offset by the opulent decoration within and the natural, irregular gardens that surround it.

18. William Kent, Temple of Ancient Virtue in the gardens at Stowe.
Courtauld Institute of Art, London.

19. Henry Flitcroft (1697–1769), The Temple of Flora, c. 1745–50. *Country Life.*

20. The approach to the Pantheon (Flitcroft, c. 1752–56). *Country Life.*

THE GARDENS AT STOURHEAD

Stourhead, near the Wiltshire-Dorset border, was cultivated by banker Henry Hoare, from 1741. By 1765 Horace Walpole could declare it "one of the most picturesque scenes in the world." It was in part a Claude landscape realized in what had been originally barren downs; in fact, Claude's *Coast View of Delos with Aeneas* could have provided the elements of the design and perhaps the implicit theme of the founding of Rome.

21. Claude Lorrain, *Coast View of Delos with Aeneas,* c. 1672.
The National Gallery, London.

22. *The Marriage Contract*

The groom's father, Lord Squander, relieves his gout while he negotiates a dowry for his son's marriage to a City merchant's daughter. Visible through the window is a half-finished Palladian building (Hogarth loathed William Kent and his sponsor, Lord Burlington) which has helped to impoverish him, but he ignores the mortgage debts the clerk holds out before him. The groom gazes at his true love in a mirror, while the bride flirts with the lawyer Silvertongue. The chains on the dogs suggest their bondage.

HOGARTH ON HIGH LIFE

William Hogarth (1697–1764) invented the narrative sequence of paintings that could in turn be engraved and sold widely as sets of prints. Although he attempted more solemn and ambitious "history" painting (that is, historical, biblical, or mythological subjects in the grand style), it was in "comic history" (as Henry Fielding named it in *Joseph Andrews,* 1742) that he achieved his greatest and most characteristic work. Earlier sequences like *The Harlot's Progress* and *The Rake's Progress* had enormous success; in *Marriage à la Mode,* 1743–45, Hogarth attempted to present a more refined, if scarcely more creditable, society. (See Figs. 24–30.) *The National Gallery.*

23. *Shortly after the Marriage*

The wife lazily, but seductively, stretches at breakfast after her late card party (it is now just past noon), but the exhausted young Viscount has just come in from a night on the town. His pursuits are indicated by the woman's cap the dog is pulling from his pocket. The pious steward indicates despair at the neglected household and the unpaid bills, both reflections of the marriage itself.

24. *The Visit to the Quack Doctor*

The Viscount cheerfully brings his childlike mistress for a cure of the venereal disease he has presumably given her. The cabinets of curiosities and the monstrous machines are only less sinister than the woman with the clasp-knife (the quack's assistant or possibly the brothel-keeper).

25. *The Countess's Morning Levée*

Since Lord Squander has died and her husband has inherited the title, the wife can now adorn her dressing-table with an Earl's coronet. She is receiving morning guests while her hair is dressed. The most intimate is lawyer Silvertongue, sprawling on the sofa beside Crébillon's notorious erotic novel *Le Sopha*. The page unpacks a statue of Actaeon, given a stag's head for seeing Diana naked but here suggesting the cuckold's horns. Among other guests are a fop in curling papers and a melodious *castrato*. Over their heads hangs a painting of Jupiter snatching up Ganymede; over the Countess's, one of Jupiter descending as a cloud to embrace Io.

26. *The Killing of the Earl*

The Earl has surprised his wife with Silvertongue in a hired room after the masquerade, and has been fatally wounded by the fleeing lawyer. The owner rushes in with the guard of the watch. Emblems of disguise are everywhere on floors and walls.

27. *The Suicide of the Countess*

The lawyer has been captured, tried, and executed; a printed copy of his dying speech lies beside the poison bottle of the Countess. As she dies the nurse brings her crippled child, and her thrifty merchant father removes her ring (since a suicide's property was forfeit to the state). The apothecary upbraids the foolish servant who bought the poison; the dog enjoys the meal; and the open window discloses the City of London, where buying and selling continue.

28. *Gin Lane,* 1751. Hogarth's attack on the ravages of gin drinking was paired with a print showing the decent and moderate life of Beer Street. Physical corruption and moral insensibility are reflected in decaying streets and in the ascendancy of the pawnbroker's sign over the steeple (topped with the grandiose figure of George I) of Hawksmoor's parish church of St. George, Bloomsbury. *Courtauld Institute of Art.*

29. *Chairing the Member.* The fourth picture of Hogarth's *Election* series, c. 1754, shows the bloated victor carried in triumph while battles still rage, and the pigs rush to perdition like the Gadarene swine of the biblical parable. *Sir John Soane Museum,* London.

30. *The Beggar's Opera,* Act III, Scene xi, 1729, with Macheath between Lucy Lockit and Polly Peachum. With an ironic use of allusion that anticipates Reynolds (see Fig. 39), Hogarth sets Peachum in the stance with which Christ confronts Mary Magdalene in traditional versions of the *Noli me tangere* motif. *Collection Mr. and Mrs. Paul Mellon.*

CONVERSATION PIECES

31. Hogarth, *The Graham Children*, 1742. These children of the apothecary to the Royal Hospital, Chelsea, are occupied with keeping the infant quiet and intent on teaching the bird to sing (means of a bird-organ), while the cat bristles with a fierce interest of its own. *The Tate Gallery*, London.

32. Joseph Highmore (1692-1780), *Mr. Oldham and His Guests*, c. 1750. Oldham, arriving late, found his dinner guests "so comfortably seated with their pipes over a bowl of negus" that he commissioned a painting of the scene. In it the artist appears between farmer and schoolmaster, with Oldham behind. Highmore became a friend of Samuel Richardson, and painted scenes from Richardson's novels and a portrait of their author. *The Tate Gallery*, London.

33. Samuel Johnson, after Sir Joshua Reynolds. *National Portrait Gallery.*

34. James Boswell, 1765, in the costume of his visit to Rousseau, by George Willison (1741–97). *National Galleries of Scotland,* Edinburgh.

35. Sir Joshua Reynolds (1723–92), *Garrick between Tragedy and Comedy,* 1762. *Rothschild Collection.*

When Reynolds painted a boy in the costume and stance of Henry VIII, Horace Walpole remarked, "Is not there humour and satire in Sir Joshua's reducing Holbein's swaggering and colossal haughtiness of Henry VIII to the boyish jollity of Master Crewe?" Here Reynolds's treatment of Garrick is based on the traditional choice of Hercules. Just as Pleasure is usually represented by an erotic Venus, and Virtue by a martial Athena, so Comedy is painted in the manner of Correggio, and Tragedy in the manner of Guido Reni. Benjamin West based much of his heroic painting on a work of Poussin; but he borrowed the gesture of Tragedy from Reynolds's ironic pastiche of Guido.

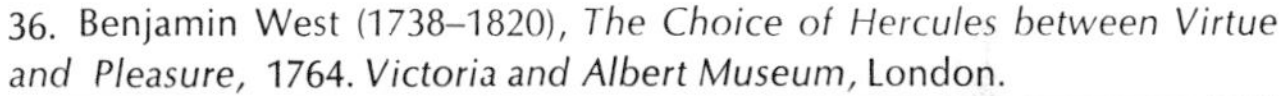

36. Benjamin West (1738–1820), *The Choice of Hercules between Virtue and Pleasure,* 1764. *Victoria and Albert Museum,* London.

37. Admiral Viscount Keppel, 1780.
The Tate Gallery, London.

The extremes of Reynolds's vision: the heroic portrait and the pathetic but amusing image of a terrified child.

38. *The Strawberry Girl*, 1773.
The Wallace Collection, London
(Crown Copyright).

39. *Circa* 1773. *Royal Academy of Arts,* London.

40. Study for a Self Portrait, c. 1780. *Collection Mr. and Mrs. Paul Mellon.*

First we see the artist as hero, Reynolds as he might aspire to be, a painter in the costume of Rembrandt, with a head of Michelangelo beside him. Below is a self-portrait of the young artist, and above right is a self-portrait of the man whom the artist inhabits.

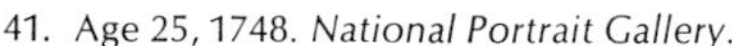

41. Age 25, 1748. *National Portrait Gallery.*

Thomas Gainsborough (1727–88) became a fashionable portrait painter, but he complained, "I'm sick of portraits and wish very much to take my viol da gamba and walk off to some sweet village where I can paint landscapes and enjoy the fag end of life in quietness and ease." He resisted even more the program of the "history" painter, for whom "there is no call in this country." Gainsborough's treatment of texture and surface made his portraits brilliant and flattering. At the same time he could cultivate a simplicity that was unheroic and singularly delicate.

42. The Honourable Mrs. Graham, 1777. *National Galleries of Scotland.*

43. *The Housemaid* (unfinished), *c.* 1786. *The Tate Gallery.*

44. William Blake, illustration for Gray's *The Bard*.

THE BARD

Thomas Gray's poem of 1757 inspired many painters and illustrators. Typically, William Blake was less concerned with natural setting than with the human form of the prophet-poet. John Martin (1789–1854) transcended the natural scene in his customary pursuit of colossal dimension and sublime intensity. What is striking in Martin's picture is that the landscape is at least as expressive as the human figure and becomes the symbol of human passion and energy at their utmost.

45. John Martin, *The Bard. Collection Mr. and Mrs. Paul Mellon.*

46. Wren, Tom Tower, 1681–82, Christ Church College, Oxford. *A. F. Kersting.*

GOTHIC TO GOTHICK

When Sir Christopher Wren was asked to complete Tom Tower at Christ Church College, Oxford, he "resolved it ought to be Gothic to agree with the founder's work; yet I have not continued so busy as he began." Hawksmoor, who completed the towers of Westminster Abbey as well as the court of All Souls College, Oxford (1715–40), used Gothic with a similar mixture of respect and freedom. The brilliant staccato style of the All Souls towers uses Gothic elements for effects that are typical of Hawksmoor, such as the light-holding angular surface of sharp recession and projection. In his Gothic garden temple, James Gibbs (1682–1754), trained in the Italian baroque and proficient as well in Palladian works (exemplified by St. Mary-le-Strand and St. Martin-in-the-Fields in London, the Radcliffe Camera at Oxford, and the Senate House at Cambridge), creates a work appropriately evocative: more a theater set than a true building. By the time Horace Walpole rebuilt his Twickenham house, Strawberry Hill (1750), in a Gothic idiom, the details—however authentic in many cases, such as the fan vaulting of the gallery—became decorative surface, akin to the irregular low-relief ornament of rococo vegetable forms.

47. Hawksmoor, Fellows' Buildings, All Souls College, Oxford.
Courtauld Institute of Art.

48. James Gibbs, Gothic Temple, c. 1740, in the gardens of Stowe.
Courtauld Institute of Art.

49. The Gallery, Strawberry Hill.
Country Life.

50. Henry Fuseli, *The Artist Moved by the Magnitude of Antique Fragments*, 1778–80. *Kunsthaus*, Zürich.

RUINS

As the art historian Nikolaus Pevsner puts it, for "a generalizing view of the style of 1750 a Chinese bridge, a miniature Pantheon, and a Gothic ruin all belong together. In fact . . . even Robert Adam enjoyed drawing ruins . . . and occasionally designed domestic work in a mildly medieval taste." Increasingly, archeological explorations of classical ruins were recorded in excellent prints. Robert Adam had explored Diocletian's Palace at Split in Yugoslavia; James ("Athenian") Stuart with his fellow architect Nicholas Revett spent five years in Greece and brought back careful studies of the Acropolis. As Fuseli's drawing shows, the interest was as romantic as it was scholarly; moreover, picturesque ruins were frequently constructed—as we see in the designs of Adam and Chambers. In Chambers's design, "There is a great quantity of cornices, and other fragments, spread over the ground, seemingly fallen from the buildings."

51. Robert Adam (1728–92), Design for a ruin to be built at Mistley Hall, 1761.
Victoria and Albert Museum.

52. Sir William Chambers (1723–96), Roman ruins at Kew Gardens, 1763.
Engraving by Woolett in Chambers's *Plans . . . of Gardens and Buildings at Kew*, 1763.

53. *The Green Monkey*, 1799. *Walker Art Gallery*, Liverpool.

George Stubbs (1724–1806) resolved "to look into nature for himself, and consult and study *her only*." In Italy he made no studies from the antique, and "differed always in opinion from his companions." He became a brilliant student of anatomy, performing elaborate dissections, on which he based his *Anatomy of the Horse* (1759). Noted as a portrait painter of race horses as well as of their owners, Stubbs also made remarkable studies of tigers, monkeys, and even a kangaroo.

54. *A Lion Attacking a Horse. Collection Mr. and Mrs. Paul Mellon.*

Joseph Wright of Derby (1734–94) was the first painter of distinction to celebrate the new industrial leaders, their buildings, and their technological concerns. The experiment with the air pump involves withdrawing air from the glass bell that holds the bird and then replenishing it just in time to save the bird's life; the children betray their fears, but the boy on the right is lowering a cage to hold the revived bird.

55. *An Experiment on a Bird in the Air Pump* (c. 1767–68).
The Tate Gallery.

56. Joseph Wright of Derby, *The Old Man and Death*, 1773.
Wadsworth Atheneum, Hartford.

DEATH IN THE EIGHTEENTH CENTURY

Wright's picture draws on Aesop's fable of the old woodgatherer who calls for death to free him of his burdens but is appalled and reluctant to receive what he asks for. The engraving by Thomas Patch (1725–82) catches the appearance of Sterne in the spirit of Tristram Shandy and Yorick.

57. Thomas Patch, *Sterne and Death*, 1768.
Courtauld Institute of Art.

When at the close of each sad, sorrowing day,
Fancy restores what vengeance snatched away;
Then conscience sleeps, and leaving nature free,
All my loose soul unbounded springs to thee.
Oh cursed, dear horrors of all-conscious° night!
How glowing guilt exalts the keen delight!
Provoking demons all restraint remove,
And stir within me every source of love.
I hear thee, view thee, gaze o'er all thy charms,
And round thy phantom glue my clasping arms.
I wake—no more I hear, no more I view;
The phantom flies me, as unkind as you.
I call aloud; it hears not what I say:
I stretch my empty arms; it glides away.
To dream once more I close my willing eyes;
Ye soft illusions, dear deceits, arise!
Alas, no more! Methinks we wandering go
Through dreary wastes, and weep each other's woe,
Where round some mouldering tower pale ivy creeps,
And low-browed rocks hang nodding o'er the deeps.
Sudden you mount, you beckon from the skies;
Clouds interpose, waves roar, and winds arise.
I shriek, start up, the same sad prospect° find,
And wake to all the griefs I left behind.
  For thee the fates, severely kind, ordain
A cool suspense from pleasure and from pain;
Thy life a long dead calm of fixed repose;
No pulse that riots, and no blood that glows.
Still as the sea, ere winds were taught to blow,
Or moving spirit bade the waters flow;
Soft as the slumbers of a saint forgiven,
And mild as opening gleams of promised heaven.
  Come, Abelard! for what hast thou to dread?
The torch of Venus burns not for the dead.
Nature stands checked; Religion disapproves;
Even thou art cold—yet Eloïsa loves.
Ah hopeless, lasting flames!° like those that burn
To light the dead, and warm the unfruitful urn.
  What scenes appear where'er I turn my view?
The dear ideas, where I fly, pursue,
Rise in the grove, before the altar rise,
Stain all my soul, and wanton in my eyes.
I waste the matin lamp in sighs for thee,
Thy image steals between my God and me,
Thy voice I seem in every hymn to hear,
With every bead I drop too soft a tear.
When from the censer clouds of fragrance roll,
And swelling organs lift the rising soul,

all-conscious as if sharing guilty knowledge
prospect view, surroundings
lasting flames like the perpetual fires in ancient tombs

One thought of thee puts all the pomp to flight.
Priests, tapers, temples, swim before my sight:
In seas of flame my plunging soul is drowned,
While altars blaze, and angels tremble round.
  While prostrate here in humble grief I lie,
Kind, virtuous drops just gathering in my eye,
While praying, trembling, in the dust I roll,
And dawning grace is opening on my soul:
Come, if thou darest, all charming as thou art!
Oppose thyself to heaven; dispute my heart;
Come, with one glance of those deluding eyes
Blot out each bright idea of the skies.
Take back that grace, those sorrows, and those tears;
Take back my fruitless penitence and prayers;
Snatch me, just mounting, from the blest abode;
Assist the fiends, and tear me from my God!
  No, fly me, fly me, far as pole from pole;
Rise Alps between us! and whole oceans roll!
Ah, come not, write not, think not once of me,
Nor share one pang of all I felt for thee.
Thy oaths I quit,° thy memory resign;
Forget, renounce me, hate whate'er was mine.
Fair eyes, and tempting looks (which yet I view!)
Long loved, adored ideas, all adieu!
Oh Grace serene! oh virtue heavenly fair!
Divine oblivion of low-thoughted care!
Fresh blooming Hope, gay daughter of the sky!
And Faith, our early immortality!
Enter, each mild, each amicable guest;
Receive, and wrap me in eternal rest!
  See in her cell sad Eloïsa spread,
Propped on some tomb, a neighbour of the dead.
In each low wind methinks a spirit calls,
And more than echoes talk along the walls.
Here, as I watched the dying lamps around,
From yonder shrine I heard a hollow sound.
'Come, sister, come!' (it said, or seemed to say)
'Thy place is here, sad sister, come away!
Once like thyself, I trembled, wept, and prayed,
Love's victim then, though now a sainted maid:
But all is calm in this eternal sleep;
Here grief forgets to groan, and love to weep,
Even superstition loses every fear:
For God, not man, absolves our frailties here.'
  I come, I come! prepare your roseate bowers,
Celestial palms, and ever-blooming flowers.
Thither, where sinners may have rest, I go,
Where flames refined in breasts seraphic glow:

quit absolve

Thou, Abelard! the last sad office pay,
And smooth my passage to the realms of day;
See my lips tremble and my eyeballs roll,
Suck my last breath and catch my flying soul!
Ah no—in sacred vestments mayst thou stand,
The hallowed taper trembling in thy hand,
Present the cross before my lifted eye,
Teach me at once, and learn of me to die.
Ah then, thy once-loved Eloïsa see!
It will be then no crime to gaze on me.
See from my cheek the transient roses fly!
See the last sparkle languish in my eye!
Till every motion, pulse, and breath be o'er;
And even my Abelard be loved no more.
O death all-eloquent! you only prove
What dust we dote on, when 'tis man we love.

Then too, when fate shall thy fair frame destroy,
(That cause of all my guilt, and all my joy)
In trance ecstatic may thy pangs be drowned,
Bright clouds descend, and angels watch thee round;
From opening skies may streaming glories shine,
And saints embrace thee with a love like mine.

May one kind grave unite each hapless name,°
And graft my love immortal on thy fame!
Then, ages hence, when all my woes are o'er,
When this rebellious heart shall beat no more;
If ever chance two wandering lovers brings
To Paraclete's white walls and silver springs,
O'er the pale marble shall they join their heads,
And drink the falling tears each other sheds;
Then sadly say, with mutual pity moved,
'Oh may we never love as these have loved!'
From the full choir when loud hosannas rise,
And swell the pomp of dreadful sacrifice,
Amid that scene if some relenting eye
Glance on the stone where our cold relics lie,
Devotion's self shall steal a thought from heaven,
One human tear shall drop, and be forgiven.
And sure, if fate some future bard shall join
In sad similitude of griefs to mine,
Condemned whole years in absence to deplore,
And image charms he must behold no more;
Such if there be, who loves so long, so well;
Let him our sad, our tender story tell;
The well-sung woes will soothe my pensive ghost;
He best can paint 'em who shall feel 'em most.

1716–17 1717

May . . . name "Abelard and Eloïsa were interred in the same grave, or in monuments adjoining, in the monastery of the Paraclete. He died in the year 1142, she in 1163." (Pope)

Elegy to the Memory of an Unfortunate Lady

With *Eloisa to Abelard,* also published in 1717, this represents the most romantic strain in Pope's poetry, and the defense of a "brave disorder" is more thoroughgoing here than in *Eloisa.* (These poems, it should be said, were chosen for highest, and at times for exclusive, praise among Pope's works by some later eighteenth-century critics who reacted against Pope's involvement in the daily life of his time.) The poem draws upon the pattern of Roman elegy, notably in Ovid, Tibullus, and Propertius; and it creates a situation comparable to those presented in Ovid's *Heroides,* where women spoke with deep feeling of the wrongs done them, or in Nicholas Rowe's "she-tragedies" (such as *The Fair Penitent* of 1703, *Jane Shore* of 1714, *or Lady Jane Grey* of 1715), which turned from the more heroic vein to the pathetic and drew upon such sources as Thomas Otway and Racine.

The identity of the lady has aroused much futile speculation. All we need to know about her can be surmised from the poet's lament. That opens with the vision of a ghost who still bears the wound and the weapon of her suicide, as if she had been rejected by heaven as she had by her guardian before. Her wandering the earth after death seems the counterpart of her burial abroad in unhallowed ground. Tellingly, as the poet asserts her dignity and even her sanctity, he laments as well her mortality and his own, stressing both the threats that beset human feeling and the grandeur of its intensity, moving from heroic passion to tender compassion.

Elegy to the Memory of an Unfortunate Lady

What beckoning ghost, along the moonlight shade
Invites my steps, and points to yonder glade?
'Tis she!—but why that bleeding bosom gored,
Why dimly gleams the visionary sword?
Oh ever beauteous, ever friendly! tell,
Is it, in heaven, a crime to love too well?
To bear too tender, or too firm a heart,
To act a lover's or a Roman's part?°
Is there no bright reversion° in the sky,
For those who greatly think, or bravely die?
Why bade ye else, ye Powers! her soul aspire
Above the vulgar flight of low desire?
Ambition first sprung from your blest abodes;
The glorious fault of angels and of gods:°
Thence to their images on earth it flows,
And in the breasts of kings and heroes glows.
Most souls, 'tis true, but peep out once an age,

Roman's part commit suicide
reversion literally, a property one expects to obtain; something restored after a period to its true owner
glorious fault . . . gods referring to the rebellion of heavenly angels (as in *Paradise Lost*) or of the Titans against Zeus, but also recalling the discussion of ambition as a "spark too much of heavenly fire" in Dryden, *Absalom and Achitophel,* l. 307, or those "great wits" who "gloriously offend" in Pope, *Essay on Criticism,* l. 152

Dull sullen prisoners in the body's cage:
Dim lights of life, that burn a length of years
Useless, unseen, as lamps in sepulchres;
Like eastern kings° a lazy state they keep,
And close confined to their own palace, sleep.
From these perhaps (ere nature bade her die)
Fate snatched her early to the pitying sky.
As into air the purer spirits flow,
And separate from their kindred dregs below;°
So flew the soul to its congenial place,
Nor left one virtue to redeem her race.
But thou, false guardian of a charge too good,
Thou, mean deserter of thy brother's blood!
See on these ruby lips the trembling breath,
These cheeks, now fading at the blast of death;
Cold is that breast which warmed the world before,
And those love-darting eyes must roll no more.
Thus, if eternal justice rules the ball,
Thus shall your wives, and thus your children fall:
On all the line a sudden vengeance waits,
And frequent hearses shall besiege your gates.
There passengers shall stand, and pointing say,
(While the long funerals blacken all the way)
Lo these were they, whose souls the Furies° steeled,
And cursed with hearts unknowing how to yield.
Thus unlamented pass the proud away,
The gaze of fools, and pageant of a day!
So perish all, whose breast ne'er learned to glow
For others' good, or melt at others' woe.
What can atone (oh ever-injured shade!)
Thy fate unpitied, and thy rites unpaid?
No friend's complaint, no kind domestic tear
Pleased thy pale ghost, or graced thy mournful bier.
By foreign hands thy dying eyes were closed,
By foreign hands thy decent limbs composed,
By foreign hands thy humble grave adorned,
By strangers honoured, and by strangers mourned!
What though no friends in sable weeds appear,
Grieve for an hour, perhaps, then mourn a year,
And bear about the mockery of woe
To midnight dances, and the public show?
What though no weeping Loves° thy ashes grace,
Nor polished marble emulate° thy face?

Like eastern kings Cf. *Epistle to Dr. Arbuthnot*, l. 220.
separate . . . below the purification process of chemical distillation
Furies the avenging goddesses, here punishing the guardian's family for cruelty by cursing them with unremitting obduracy
Loves funerary monuments in the form of mourning cupids
emulate rival, reproduce

What though no sacred earth° allow thee room,
Nor hallowed dirge be muttered o'er thy tomb?
Yet shall thy grave with rising flowers be drest,
And the green turf lie lightly on thy breast:
There shall the morn her earliest tears bestow,
There the first roses of the year shall blow;°
While angels with their silver wings o'ershade
The ground, now sacred by thy reliques° made.
So peaceful rests, without a stone, a name,
What once had beauty, titles, wealth, and fame.
How loved, how honoured once, avails thee not,
To whom related, or by whom begot;
A heap of dust alone remains of thee,
'Tis all thou art, and all the proud shall be!
Poets themselves must fall, like those they sung,
Deaf the praised ear, and mute the tuneful tongue.
Even he, whose soul now melts in mournful lays,
Shall shortly want the generous tear he pays;
Then from his closing eyes thy form shall part,
And the last pang shall tear thee from his heart,
Life's idle business at one gasp be o'er,
The Muse forgot, and thou beloved no more!

1717

sacred earth Presumably because of her suicide, the lady is denied burial in consecrated ground and the performance of Christian rites ("hallowed dirge"); in contrast, Nature pays her honors in flowers, turf, and the "tears" of morning dew.

blow blossom

reliques remains, often used of a saint's remains; here making sacred the ground in which they lie

An Essay on Man

This is Pope's effort to recall man to those truths he professes to believe but finds hard to live by. The essay deals with the complaints that man raises against his nature and his fate, complaints that grow out of the false expectations of pride: that man is the sole end of the universe and that he can enjoy stable self-mastery. The lesson he must relearn is that of God's impartial order—the Great Chain of Being, linking every kind of creature from lowest to highest—and of his place within it. Man is the most dangerous link, neither securely rational nor governed by sure instinct, a volatile mixture (as the opening passage of the second epistle of the *Essay* reveals) and therefore an unstable one. The *Essay* insists upon man's incompleteness, upon his dependent existence within a vast harmony in which nothing can quite subsist without the support of all other creatures. In the final epistle man is taught to find his happiness not in externals but in humility, not in expansion and conquest but in the contraction that opens out in turn as love rather than possession, admitting all creatures into the spreading circle of one's love. Man finds himself, as in traditional Christianity, by losing himself; as he takes "every creature in, of every kind," he finds his earth a new Eden and becomes once more a creature in God's image: "Earth smiles around, with boundless bounty blest, / And Heaven beholds its image in his breast."

In the third epistle Pope treats man's political and social order, and in the passage given below he traces man's career from the state of nature, through the fall into superstition and tyranny, to the ultimate recovery of order through human institutions. Pope differs from the Epicureans, and from Hobbes and Mandeville, in seeing the state of nature as one of society rather than of chaotic individual impulse and appetite. The recovery of political order is for Pope, as for Hobbes and Mandeville, forced upon man by the intolerable insecurity of that state that they call natural but Pope regards as a fallen one; in the process, as Pope presents it, man rediscovers what is inherently natural. The political state is not, therefore, a mere work of artifice, nor is its authority the merely arbitrary one of established power. It is an embodiment, however imperfect, of a natural order and can claim legitimacy by an appeal to natural law.

An Essay on Man

From *Epistle II*

I. Know then thyself, presume not God to scan;°
The proper study of mankind is Man.
Placed on this isthmus of a middle state,
A being darkly wise, and rudely° great:
With too much knowledge for the Sceptic side,°
With too much weakness for the Stoic's pride,°
He hangs between; in doubt to act, or rest,
In doubt to deem himself a god, or beast;

scan criticize, judge
rudely turbulently, roughly
Sceptic side the distrust of the possibility of certain knowledge
Stoic's pride the mastery of all passions

In doubt his mind or body to prefer,
Born but to die, and reasoning but to err;
Alike in ignorance, his reason such,
Whether he thinks too little, or too much:
Chaos of thought and passion, all confused;
Still by himself abused, or disabused;
Created half to rise, and half to fall;
Great lord of all things, yet a prey to all;
Sole judge of truth, in endless error hurled:
The glory, jest, and riddle of the world! . . .

From *Epistle III*

IV. Nor think, in NATURE'S STATE they blindly trod;
The state of nature° was the reign of God:
Self-love and social at her birth began,
Union the bond of all things, and of man.
Pride then was not; nor arts, that pride to aid;
Man walked with beast, joint tenant of the shade;
The same his table, and the same his bed;
No murder clothed him, and no murder fed.
In the same temple, the resounding wood,
All vocal beings hymned their equal° God:
The shrine with gore unstained, with gold undressed,
Unbribed, unbloody,° stood the blameless priest:
Heaven's attribute was universal care,
And man's prerogative to rule, but spare.
Ah! how unlike the man of times to come!
Of half that live the butcher and the tomb;°
Who, foe to nature, hears the general groan,
Murders their species and betrays his own.
But just disease to luxury succeeds,
And every death its own avenger breeds;
The fury-passions from that blood began,
And turned on man a fiercer savage,° man.
See him from nature rising slow to art!
To copy instinct then was reason's part;
Thus then to man the voice of Nature spake—
'Go, from the creatures thy instructions take:
Learn from the birds what food the thickets yield;
Learn from the beasts the physic° of the field;
Thy arts of building from the bee° receive;
Learn of the mole to plough, the worm° to weave;

state of nature rejecting Hobbes's view of it as a state of war in which man was a "wolf to man" and human life was "nasty, brutish, and short"; social love is not artificial but natural, and order or union is part of the frame of nature
equal common, impartial
unbloody not yet sacrificing animals or fellow men
butcher . . . tomb slayer and devourer
savage wild animal
physic medicinal herbs
bee as architect of honeycombed hives
worm silkworm

Learn of the little nautilus° to sail,
Spread the thin oar, and catch the driving gale.
Here too all forms of social union find,
And hence let reason, late, instruct mankind:
Here subterranean works° and cities see;
There towns aerial° on the waving tree.
Learn each small people's genius, policies,
The ant's republic, and the realm of bees;°
How those in common all their wealth bestow,
And anarchy without confusion know;
And these for ever, though a monarch reign,
Their separate cells and properties maintain.
Mark what unvaried laws preserve each state,
Laws wise as nature, and as fixed as fate.
In vain thy reason finer webs shall draw,
Entangle justice in her net of law,
And right, too rigid, harden into wrong;
Still for the strong too weak, the weak too strong.
Yet go! and thus o'er all the creatures sway,
Thus let the wiser make the rest obey,
And, for those arts mere instinct could afford,
Be crowned as monarchs, or as gods adored.'

V. Great Nature spoke; observant men obeyed;
Cities were built, societies were made:
Here rose one little state; another near
Grew by like means, and joined, through love or fear.
Did here the trees with ruddier burdens bend,
And there the streams in purer rills descend?
What war could ravish, commerce could bestow,
And he returned a friend, who came a foe.
Converse and love mankind might strongly draw,
When love was liberty, and nature law.
Thus states were formed; the name of king unknown,
Till common interest placed the sway in one.
'Twas virtue only (or in arts or arms,
Diffusing blessings, or averting harms)
The same which in a sire the sons obeyed,
A prince the father of a people made.

VI. Till then, by nature crowned, each patriarch sate,
King, priest, and parent of his growing state;
On him, their second providence, they hung,
Their law his eye, their oracle his tongue.

nautilus "They swim on the surface of the sea, on the back of their shells, which exactly resemble the hulk of a ship; they raise two feet like masts and extend a membrane between them which serves as a sail; the other two feet they employ as oars at the side" (Pope).

subterranean works anthills

towns aerial beehives

ant's republic . . . bees representing egalitarian and monarchical states, respectively, in the next four lines

He from the wondering° furrow called the food,
Taught to command the fire, control the flood,
Draw forth the monsters of the abyss profound,
Or fetch the aërial eagle to the ground.
Till drooping, sickening, dying they began
Whom they revered as god to mourn as man:
Then, looking up from sire to sire, explored°
One great first father, and that first adored.
Or plain tradition that this All begun,°
Conveyed unbroken faith from sire to son,
The worker from the work distinct was known,
And simple reason never sought but one:
Ere wit oblique° had broke that steady light,
Man, like his Maker, saw that all was right,°
To virtue, in the paths of pleasure, trod,
And owned a Father when he owned a God.
Love all the faith, and all the allegiance then;
For nature knew no right divine° in men,
No ill could fear in God; and understood
A sovereign being but a sovereign good.
True faith, true policy,° united ran,
This was but love of God, and this of man.
 Who first taught souls enslaved, and realms undone,
The enormous° faith of many made for one;°
That proud exception to all nature's laws,
To invert the world, and counterwork its Cause?°
Force first made conquest, and that conquest, law;
Till superstition taught the tyrant awe,
Then shared the tyranny, then lent it aid,
And gods of conquerors, slaves of subjects made:
She,° midst the lightning's blaze, and thunder's sound,
When rocked the mountains, and when groaned the ground,
She taught the weak to bend, the proud to pray,
To power unseen, and mightier far than they:
She, from the rending earth and bursting skies,
Saw gods descend and fiends infernal rise:
Here fixed the dreadful, there the blest abodes;
Fear made her devils, and weak hope her gods;
Gods partial, changeful, passionate, unjust,

wondering sharing the amazement of the people
explored discovered by inference
this All begun the world as created rather than eternal and self-subsistent, a theistic rather than a pantheistic view, which leads man to distinguish the creature from the Creator (l. 229)
wit oblique prismatically breaking the "steady light," as in the *Essay on Criticism*, ll. 311–12
all was right Cf. Genesis 1:31: "And God saw every thing that he had made, and, behold, it was very good."
right divine arbitrary power conferred upon specific men by God, as was claimed by the divine right of kings
policy government
enormous monstrous
many made for one "In this Aristotle placeth the difference between a king and a tyrant, that the first supposeth himself made for the people, the other that the people are made for him" (William Warburton, citing *Politics* V.10).
To invert . . . Cause repudiating God's design that all creatures serve each other
She superstition

Whose attributes were rage, revenge, or lust;
Such as the souls of cowards might conceive,
And, formed like tyrants, tyrants would believe.°
Zeal° then, not charity, became the guide,
And hell was built on spite, and heaven on pride.
Then sacred seemed the ethereal vault no more;
Altars grew marble then, and reeked with gore:
Then first the flamen° tasted living food;
Next his grim idol smeared with human blood;°
With heaven's own thunders shook the world below,
And played the god an engine on his foe.°
So drives self-love, through just and through unjust,
To one man's power, ambition, lucre, lust:
The same self-love, in all, becomes the cause
Of what restrains him, government and laws.
For, what one likes if others like as well,
What serves one will,° when many wills rebel?
How shall he keep, what, sleeping or awake,
A weaker may surprise, a stronger take?
His safety must his liberty restrain:
All join to guard what each desires to gain.
Forced into virtue thus by self-defence,
Even kings learned justice and benevolence:
Self-love forsook the path it first pursued,
And found the private in the public good.
'Twas then, the studious head or generous mind,
Follower of God or friend of humankind,
Poet or patriot, rose but to restore
The faith and moral,° Nature gave before;
Relumed her ancient light, not kindled new;°
If not God's image, yet his shadow drew:
Taught power's due use to people and to kings,
Taught nor to slack, nor strain its tender strings,°
The less, or greater, set so justly true,
That touching one must strike° the other too;
Till jarring° interests of themselves create
The according music of a well-mixed state.°

formed . . . believe A worship "grounded not on love but fear," for "the superstitious man looks on the Great Father of all as a tyrant. . . . Accordingly he serves his Maker but as slaves do their tyrants, with a gloomy savage zeal against his fellow-creatures . . . though at the same time he trembles with the dread of being ill-used himself." (Pope)
Zeal fanaticism
flamen priest
smeared . . . blood Cf. Milton, *Paradise Lost* I.392–93: "First Moloch, horrid king, besmeared with blood / Of human sacrifice . . .".
played . . . foe i.e. turned God into a piece of artillery, an instrument of man's own will and vengeance
What . . . will of what force is one will?
moral moral principles, as above in ll. 235–40
Relumed . . . new revived the natural order rather than invented society for the first time
tender strings as in musical instruments, whose harmony was a common analogy for political order
strike cause to reverberate
jarring conflicting, discordant
well-mixed state The mixed state was a balance of the power of the One, the Few, and the Many; such a balance was believed to give the state the stability to endure, and to withstand the claims of rival factions within it.

Such is the world's great harmony, that springs
From order, union, full consent of things!
Where small and great, where weak and mighty, made
To serve, not suffer, strengthen, not invade,
More powerful each as needful to the rest,
And, in proportion as it blesses, blest,
Draw to one point, and to one centre bring
Beast, man, or angel, servant, lord, or king,
For forms of government let fools contest;
Whate'er is best administered is best:°
For modes of faith, let graceless° zealots fight;
His can't be wrong whose life is in the right:
In faith and hope the world will disagree,
But all mankind's concern is charity:
All must be false that thwart this one great end,
And all of God, that bless mankind or mend.
Man, like the generous vine,° supported lives;
The strength he gains is from the embrace he gives.
On their own axis as the planets run,°
Yet make at once their circle round the sun:
So two consistent motions act the soul;
And one regards itself, and one the Whole.
Thus God and Nature linked the general frame,
And bade self-love and social be the same.

1731? 1733

To Richard Boyle, Earl of Burlington

Richard Boyle, third Earl of Burlington (1695–1753), studied architecture in Italy, designed buildings himself and commissioned works by others, and sponsored publication of the designs of Andrea Palladio and Inigo Jones. In opposition to the baroque of Sir Christopher Wren and Sir John Vanbrugh, he promoted a more severe classicism and spent great sums on public buildings in that spirit. This epistle is an important document of eighteenth-century taste. It sets forth a theory of landscape gardening that Pope had already begun to apply in his own estate and, even more, in his advice to affluent landowners. What he recommends is a "natural" garden, which came to be known through Europe as an "English garden"; that is, one which does not disdain artifice (as no garden can) but seeks to adjust its improvements to the tendencies of the landscape and to bring to fulfillment what is latently there rather than impose a formal design upon it. It is a garden of concealed boundaries, of variety of light and shade, and with the power to evoke the landscapes

Whate'er . . . best Pope later explained that he did not mean "that no one form of government is, in itself, better than another . . . but that no form of government, however excellent or preferable in itself, can be sufficient to make a people happy, unless it be administered with integrity."

graceless crude; but also, without divine grace

generous vine as in traditional fables of the love of the vine and the elm, "generous" in giving of oneself to another

run rotate

painted by the great masters of the seventeenth century—Nicolas Poussin, Claude Lorrain, and others (see below, The Garden and the Wild).

The poem is also an interesting discussion of architectural form and function, and, most generally, of the relationship between taste and morality—a problem first raised in the *Essay on Criticism*. Pride is once more a central theme; here, too, it creates objects that are meant to stun, to astonish, to captivate by size or cost, and it neglects the function of part in a whole. The whole is hospitality in Timon's villa; but, more than that, it is generosity and concern for others, even concern for a reality that bounds, limits, and—in the good man—extends and fulfills the self. We can see that whole restored when "laughing Ceres" reassumes Timon's land or when Burlington sponsors, in contrast to the ornamental projects of "imitating fools," public works that gain their dignity, and even their beauty, from solid public use.

The identity of Timon caused Pope much pain; Timon was claimed by the malice of others to refer to Lord Chandos, who had befriended Pope and who, it should be said, dismissed the rumors himself. There now seems reason to see behind Timon, or at least some aspects of him, the figure of Walpole—at his huge house at Houghton—imposing his will in displays of magnificence (which Pope treats as unwitting self-exposure) and turning away Pope's satire by having his supporters direct it to Chandos. If Timon be taken as Walpole, he is only one aspect of that "great man" and a contemptibly trivialized version at that; but he serves to relate the realms of art and politics, and to show the opposition of the tyrannous private will to the generous harmony of a natural order.

The essay was first called *Of Taste* and later *Of False Taste*.

To Richard Boyle, Earl of Burlington

Of the Use of Riches

'Tis strange, the miser should his cares employ
To gain those riches he can ne'er enjoy:
Is it less strange, the prodigal should waste
His wealth, to purchase what he ne'er can taste?
Not for himself he sees, or hears, or eats;
Artists must choose his pictures, music, meats:
He buys for Topham,° drawings and designs,
For Pembroke,° statues, dirty gods, and coins;
Rare monkish manuscripts for Hearne° alone,
And books for Mead,° and butterflies for Sloane.°
Think we all these are for himself! no more
Than his fine wife, alas! or finer whore.

Topham Richard Topham (d. 1735), a "gentleman famous for a judicious collection of drawings" (Pope)
Pembroke Thomas Herbert, 8th Earl of Pembroke (1656–1733), had large collections of statues, pictures, and coins at Wilton House.
Hearne Thomas Hearne (1678–1735), eminent medievalist and editor of early English chronicles
Mead Richard Mead (1673–1754), royal physician and friend of Pope, collector of some 30,000 books
Sloane Sir Hans Sloane (1660–1753), also royal physician and master of "the finest collection in Europe of natural curiosities" (Pope)

For what has Virro° painted, built, and planted?
Only to show, how many tastes he wanted.°
What brought Sir Visto's° ill got wealth to waste?
Some demon whispered, 'Visto! have a taste.'
Heaven visits with a taste the wealthy fool,
And needs no rod° but Ripley° with a rule.°
See! sportive fate, to punish awkward pride,
Bids Bubo° build, and sends him such a guide:
A standing sermon, at each year's expense,
That never coxcomb° reached magnificence!°
You° show us, Rome was glorious, not profuse,
And pompous buildings once were things of use.
Yet shall (my Lord) your just, your noble rules
Fill half the land with imitating fools;
Who random drawings from your sheets shall take,
And of one beauty many blunders make;
Load some vain church with old theatric state,°
Turn arcs of triumph° to a garden gate;
Reverse your ornaments, and hang them all
On some patched dog-hole eked with ends of wall;
Then clap four slices of pilaster° on't,
That, laced with bits of rustic,° makes a front;°
Shall call the winds through long arcades to roar,
Proud to catch cold at a Venetian door;°
Conscious they act a true Palladian part,
And, if they starve,° they starve by rules of art.
Oft have you hinted to your brother peer,
A certain truth, which many buy too dear:
Something there is more needful than expense,
And something previous even to taste—'tis sense:
Good sense, which only is the gift of Heaven,°
And though no science, fairly worth the seven:

Virro named for the contemptible rich patron in Juvenal's Fifth Satire
wanted lacked
Visto's named for a vista, a long view through an avenue of trees
rod punishment
Ripley Thomas Ripley (d. 1758), a mediocre but politically favored architect, a protégé of Walpole, hired to execute others' plans for Walpole's hall at Houghton; as Pope put it, "a carpenter employed by a First Minister, who raised him into an architect without any genius in the art"
rule carpenter's rule, as a form of "rod"; also a misapplied principle, as in ll. 25–26
Bubo Latin for owl; a reference to Bubb Dodington, a Whig politician who spent £140,000 completing a country house designed by Sir John Vanbrugh
coxcomb fop, pretender
magnificence not merely splendor but, according to Aristotle (*Nicomachean Ethics* IV.2), spending generously on public works rather than on one's own
You Burlington, then publishing the *Antiquities of Rome* by the great Italian architect Andrea Palladio (1518–80), and other architectural drawings whose "sheets" (l. 27) might be searched for ornamental details by those without a true sense of their "use" (l. 24)
theatric state the misapplied details of a Roman amphitheater; the use of classical detail to achieve baroque theatricality
arcs of triumph Roman triumphal arches reduced in scale and used as models for ornamental gateways
pilaster a column attached to a wall
laced . . . rustic embellished with rustication, the imitation of naturally rough stones
front "frontispiece," the formal entrance to a building
Venetian door Palladio invented the Venetian door and window, consisting of an opening with an arched top set between two smaller rectangular openings; these, originally essential to the structural design of Palladio's buildings, became isolated decorative elements.
starve because of cost and the great distances that food had to be brought
gift of Heaven Cf. *Essay on Criticism,* l. 13.

A light, which in yourself you must perceive;
Jones° and Le Nôtre° have it not to give.
To build, to plant, whatever you intend,
To rear the column, or the arch to bend,
To swell the terrace, or to sink the grot;°
In all, let Nature never be forgot.
But treat the goddess like a modest fair,
Nor overdress, nor leave her wholly bare;
Let not each beauty everywhere be spied,
Where half the skill is decently° to hide.
He gains all points, who pleasingly confounds,
Surprises, varies, and conceals the bounds.
Consult the genius of the place° in all;
That tells the waters or to rise, or fall;
Or helps the ambitious hill the heavens to scale,
Or scoops in circling theatres° the vale;
Calls in the country, catches opening glades,
Joins willing woods, and varies shades from shades;
Now breaks, or now directs, the intending lines;°
Paints° as you plant, and, as you work, designs.
Still follow sense, of every art the soul,
Parts answering parts shall slide into a whole,
Spontaneous beauties all around advance,
Start even from difficulty, strike from chance;
Nature shall join you; time shall make it grow
A work to wonder at—perhaps a Stowe.°
Without it, proud Versailles!° thy glory falls;
And Nero's terraces° desert their walls:
The vast parterres° a thousand hands shall make,
Lo! Cobham comes, and floats° them with a lake:
Or cut wide views° through mountains to the plains,
You'll wish your hill or sheltered seat° again.
Even in an ornament its place remark,
Nor in an Hermitage set Dr. Clarke.°
Behold Villario's ten years' toil complete;

Jones Inigo Jones (1573–1652), the distinguished architect and scene designer
Le Nôtre André Le Nôtre (1613–1700), the great French designer of formal gardens, notably those at Versailles
grot grotto, artificial cave
decently modestly, appropriately
genius of the place the character of the natural landscape; also the tutelary deity or *genius loci* who inhabited each place and guarded it
theatres the curving slopes of classical amphitheaters
intending lines which lead the eye forward
Paints with color, and perhaps composes in such designs as landscape painters had used
Stowe the house and gardens of Richard Temple, Lord Cobham (1675–1749), of which Pope wrote at the time, "if anything under Paradise could set me beyond all earthly cogitations, Stowe might do it"
Versailles the formal gardens of Louis XIV's palace
Nero's terraces the elaborate works of the Golden House of Nero, in Rome
parterres formal terraces
floats floods
cut wide views "This was done . . . by a wealthy citizen . . . by which means (merely to overlook a dead plain) he let in the north wind upon his house and parterre, which were before adorned and defended by beautiful woods" (Pope).
seat country house
Hermitage . . . Dr. Clarke Samuel Clarke (1675–1729) was a liberal theologian and student of science, rationalistic and unorthodox, hardly the man for a "hermitage." That is the name of an ornamental building in Richmond Park where Queen Caroline placed busts of Clarke, her favorite, as well as of Locke, Newton, and others.

His quincunx° darkens, his espaliers° meet;
The wood supports the plain, the parts unite,
And strength of shade contends with strength of light;
A waving glow the bloomy beds display,
Blushing in bright diversities of day,
With silver-quivering rills meandered o'er—
Enjoy them, you! Villario can no more;
Tired of the scene parterres and fountains yield,
He finds at last he better likes a field.
Through his young woods how pleased Sabinus strayed,
Or sat delighted in the thickening shade,
With annual joy the reddening shoots to greet,
Or see the stretching branches long to meet!
His son's fine taste an opener vista loves,
Foe to the dryads° of his father's groves;
One boundless green, or flourished carpet° views,
With all the mournful family of yews;°
The thriving plants ignoble broomsticks made,
Now sweep those alleys they were born to shade.
At Timon's Villa let us pass a day,
Where all cry out, 'What sums are thrown away!'
So proud, so grand; of that stupendous air,
Soft and agreeable come never there.
Greatness, with Timon, dwells in such a draught
As brings all Brobdingnag° before your thought.
To compass this, his building is a town,
His pond an ocean, his parterre a down:
Who but must laugh, the master when he sees,
A puny insect, shivering at a breeze!
Lo, what huge heaps of littleness around!
The whole, a laboured quarry above ground.
Two cupids squirt before: a lake behind
Improves the keenness of the northern wind.°
His gardens next your admiration call,
On every side you look, behold the wall!
No pleasing intricacies intervene,
No artful wildness to perplex the scene;
Grove nods at grove, each alley has a brother,
And half the platform just reflects the other.
The suffering eye inverted Nature sees,
Trees cut to statues,° statues thick as trees;

quincunx a planting of five trees, four at the corners and one in the center
espaliers trees fastened to a wall
dryads tree nymphs
flourished carpet a terrace with elaborate scrolled beds, here opposed to the contrary vice, the nakedness of a "boundless green"
yews typical planting in cemeteries; here simply forming "pyramids of dark green continually repeated, not unlike a funeral procession" (Pope)
Brobdingnag the land of giants (in the proportion of 12:1 to man) in the second voyage of Swift's *Gulliver's Travels;* all this emphasizing the irony of calling Timon's sprawling palace a "villa"
northern wind an instance of the neglect of function in the "improvement" of landscape; cf. l. 75
Trees . . . statues referring to the topiary art of trimming trees or hedges into sculpturesque shapes

With here a fountain, never to be played;
And there a summerhouse, that knows no shade;
Here Amphitrite° sails through myrtle bowers;
There gladiators fight, or die in flowers;
Unwatered see the drooping sea-horse mourn,
And swallows roost in Nilus' dusty urn.°
  My Lord advances with majestic mien,
Smit with the mighty pleasure, to be seen:
But soft—by regular approach—not yet—
First through the length of yon hot terrace sweat;
And when up ten steep slopes you've dragged your thighs,
Just at his study door he'll bless your eyes.
  His study! with what authors is it stored?
In books, not authors, curious is my Lord;
To all their dated backs° he turns you round:
These Aldus° printed, those Du Sueil° has bound.
Lo, some are vellum, and the rest as good
For all his Lordship knows, but they are wood.
For Locke or Milton 'tis in vain to look,
These shelves admit not any modern book.
  And now the chapel's silver bell you hear,
That summons you to all the pride of prayer:
Light quirks of music, broken and uneven,
Make the soul dance upon a jig to Heaven.
On painted ceilings you devoutly stare,
Where sprawl the saints of Verrio or Laguerre,°
On gilded clouds in fair expansion lie,
And bring all Paradise before your eye.
To rest, the cushion and soft dean° invite,
Who never mentions Hell to ears polite.
  But hark! the chiming clocks to dinner call;
A hundred footsteps scrape the marble hall:
The rich buffet well-coloured serpents grace,
And gaping tritons° spew to wash your face.
Is this a dinner? this a genial room?
No, 'tis a temple, and a hecatomb.°
A solemn sacrifice, performed in state,

Amphitrite a sea nymph, wife of Poseidon and mother of Triton
Nilus' . . . urn the urn that accompanies the statue of the reclining river god and from which the waters of the river should pour forth
dated backs early or rare editions with the date stamped in gold on the spine of the binding. "Many delight chiefly in the elegance of the print or the binding; some have carried it so far as to cause the upper shelves to be filled with painted books of wood" (Pope).
Aldus Aldus Manutius (1450–1515), the great Venetian printer
Du Sueil Augustin Desueil (1673–1746), a Parisian bookbinder of note
Verrio or Laguerre Antonio Verrio (1639–1707) and Louis Laguerre (1663–1721) were fashionable court artists, here creators of baroque ceiling paintings.
soft dean "This is a fact; a reverend Dean preaching at Court, threatened the sinner with punishment in 'a place which he thought it not decent to name in so polite an assembly'" (Pope).
gaping tritons "Taxes the incongruity of ornaments . . . where an open mouth ejects the water into a fountain or where shocking images of serpents, etc. are introduced in grottos or buffets" (Pope). "Tritons" have an upper human form and a lower fishy one, like mermaids.
hecatomb sacrificial slaughter of a hundred oxen

You drink by measure, and to minutes eat.
So quick retires each flying course, you'd swear
Sancho's dread Doctor and his wand° were there.
Between each act the trembling salvers ring,
From soup to sweet wine, and God bless the King.°
In plenty starving, tantalized in state,
And complaisantly helped to all I hate,
Treated, caressed, and tired, I take my leave,
Sick of his civil pride from morn to eve;
I curse such lavish cost, and little skill,
And swear no day was ever passed so ill.
  Yet hence the poor are clothed, the hungry fed;
Health to himself, and to his infants bread
The labourer bears: what his hard heart denies,
His charitable vanity supplies.°
  Another age shall see the golden ear°
Embrown the slope, and nod on the parterre,
Deep harvests bury all his pride has planned,
And laughing Ceres° reassume° the land.
  Who then shall grace, or who improve the soil?
Who plants like Bathurst,° or who builds like Boyle.°
'Tis use alone that sanctifies expense,
And splendour borrows all her rays from sense.
  His father's acres who enjoys in peace,
Or makes his neighbours glad, if he increase:
Whose cheerful tenants bless their yearly toil,
Yet to their Lord owe more than to the soil;
Whose ample lawns are not ashamed to feed
The milky heifer and deserving steed;
Whose rising forests, not for pride or show,
But future buildings, future navies, grow:
Let his plantations stretch from down to down,
First shade a country, and then raise a town.
  You too proceed! make falling arts your care,
Erect new wonders, and the old repair;
Jones and Palladio to themselves restore,
And be whate'er Vitruvius° was before:
Till kings call forth the ideas of your mind,
Proud to accomplish what such hands designed,
Bid harbours open, public ways extend,

Sancho's . . . wand Cf. Cervantes, *Don Quixote* II.xlvii, where the doctor has the food Sancho yearns for whisked away before he can eat it.
From soup . . . King from the beginning of the meal to the concluding toast in port
charitable . . . supplies Cf. Atossa in *To a Lady*, ll. 149–50.
golden ear of wheat
laughing Ceres the Roman goddess of agriculture, cheerfully bounteous and/or scornfully amused by Timon's unnatural art
reassume regain possession, as a monarch does a kingdom
Bathurst Allen, Lord Bathurst, (1685–1775), friend of Congreve, Swift, Pope, and (years later) of Laurence Sterne; an enthusiastic landscape gardener
Boyle Lord Burlington
Vitruvius Marcus Vitruvius Pollio (1st century B.C.), the author of the most influential classical work on architecture

Bid temples,° worthier of the God, ascend;
Bid the broad arch° the dangerous flood contain,
The mole projected break the roaring main;
Back to his bounds their subject sea command,
And roll obedient rivers through the land:
These honours, peace to happy Britain brings,
These are imperial works, and worthy kings.°

1731

To a Lady

Of the Characters of Women

Nothing so true as what you once let fall,
'Most women have no characters at all.'
Matter too soft a lasting mark to bear,
And best distinguished by black, brown, or fair.
  How many pictures° of one nymph we view,
All how unlike each other, all how true!
Arcardia's countess,° here, in ermined pride,
Is, there, Pastora° by a fountain side:
Here Fannia,° leering on her own good man,
And there, a naked Leda° with a swan.
Let then the fair one beautifully cry,
In Magdalen's loose hair and lifted eye,°
Or dressed in smiles of sweet Cecilia° shine,
With simpering angels, palms, and harps divine;
Whether the charmer sinner it, or saint it,
If folly grow romantic,° I must paint it.
  Come then, the colours and the ground° prepare!
Dip in the rainbow, trick her off° in air,

temples churches. Pope explains that because of graft and misuse of funds "some new-built churches . . . were ready to fall, being founded in boggy land . . . others were vilely executed."
broad arch A proposal to build a new Westminster Bridge was rejected, then its execution entrusted to Ripley, "the carpenter . . . who would have made it a wooden one," but finally built of stone with Burlington as a commissioner (Pope).
imperial . . . kings recalling *Aeneid* VI.852, where Anchises sums up his prophecy to Aeneas of the future of Rome: let others pursue sculpture, rhetoric, or astronomy; Rome has as its task "to tame the proud, the fettered slave to free; / These are imperial arts, and worthy thee"
pictures "Attitudes in which several ladies affected to be drawn, and sometimes one lady in them all" (Pope)
Arcadia's countess suggested by Sir Philip Sidney's romance, *The Countess of Pembroke's Arcadia* (1590), and perhaps referring to the wife of Thomas, Earl of Pembroke (1656–1733), a great collector and patron of art
Pastora a shepherdess, in contrast with "ermined pride"
Fannia the name of a Roman adulteress
Leda a popular Renaissance subject, as in the painting (now lost) by Leonardo da Vinci, a copy of which hung at Wilton House, the Pembroke seat
loose hair . . . eye typical attributes of the Magdalene in Renaissance painting; the loose hair recalling her drying of Christ's feet with it but also (as in Titian's version) only partially concealing her bare bosom
Cecilia the patron saint of music (celebrated in an ode by Dryden; see above), often shown in her ascent to heaven
romantic extravagant
ground the prepared surface to which paints will be applied
trick her off sketch her

Choose a firm cloud, before it fall, and in it
Catch, ere she change, the Cynthia° of this minute.
  Rufa,° whose eye quick-glancing o'er the park,
Attracts each light gay meteor of a spark,°
Agrees as ill with Rufa studying Locke,°
As Sappho's diamonds with her dirty smock,
Or Sappho° at her toilet's greasy task,
With Sappho fragrant at an evening mask:°
So morning insects that in muck° begun,
Shine, buzz, and flyblow° in the setting sun.
  How soft is Silia! fearful to offend,
The frail one's advocate, the weak one's friend:
To her, Calista proved her conduct nice,°
And good Simplicius asks of her advice.
Sudden, she storms! she raves! You tip the wink,°
But spare your censure; Silia does not drink.
All eyes may see from what the change arose,
All eyes may see—a pimple on her nose.
  Papillia,° wedded to her amorous spark,
Sighs for the shades—'How charming is a park!'
A park is purchased, but the fair he sees
All bathed in tears—'Oh, odious, odious trees!'
  Ladies, like variegated° tulips, show;
'Tis to their changes half their charms we owe;
Fine by defect, and delicately weak,
Their happy spots the nice° admirer take,
'Twas thus Calypso° once each heart alarmed,
Awed without virtue, without beauty charmed;
Her tongue bewitched as oddly as her eyes,
Less wit than mimic, more a wit than wise;
Strange graces still, and stranger flights she had,
Was just not ugly, and was just not mad;
Yet ne'er so sure our passion to create,
As when she touched the brink of all we hate.
  Narcissa's° nature, tolerably mild,
To make a wash,° would hardly stew a child;
Has even been proved to grant a lover's prayer,
And paid a tradesman once to make him stare;
Gave alms at Easter, in a Christian trim,°

Cynthia Diana, here the fickle goddess of the constantly changing moon
Rufa so named for her red hair, regarded as a sign of wantonness
spark beau
Locke The philosophy of John Locke (1632–1704) was made a fashionable study by Addison and Steele in the *Spectator* papers.
Sappho a woman poet (cf. Dryden's "Anne Killigrew" ode for this usage), probably Lady Mary Wortley Montagu, notorious for slovenliness
mask masked ball
muck referring to the belief that insects were generated by corruption; cf. *Essay on Criticism*, ll. 41–43
flyblow generate
nice proper, punctilious
tip the wink make a surmise
Papillia Latin for butterfly
variegated streaked, varied in color
nice discriminating
Calypso named for the nymph who detained Odysseus for seven years
Narcissa's whose name suggests vanity
wash for complexion or hair
trim dress, manner

And made a widow happy, for a whim.
Why then declare good-nature is her scorn,
When 'tis by that alone she can be borne?
Why pique all mortals, yet affect a name?
A fool to pleasure, yet a slave to fame:
Now deep in Taylor° and the Book of Martyrs,°
Now drinking citron° with his Grace° and Chartres:°
Now conscience chills her, and now passion burns;
And atheism and religion take their turns;
A very heathen in the carnal part,
Yet still a sad,° good Christian at her heart.
See Sin in state, majestically drunk;
Proud as a peeress, prouder as a punk;°
Chaste to her husband, frank° to all beside,
A teeming mistress, but a barren bride.
What then? let blood and body bear the fault,
Her head's untouched, that noble seat of thought:
Such this day's doctrine—in another fit
She sins with poets through pure love of wit.
What has not fired her bosom or her brain?
Caesar and Tallboy,° Charles° and Charlemagne.
As Helluo,° late dictator of the feast,
The nose of hautgout,° and the tip of taste,
Critiqued your wine, and analyzed your meat,
Yet on plain pudding deigned at home to eat;
So Philomedé, lecturing all mankind
On the soft passion, and the taste refined,
The address, the delicacy—stoops at once,
And makes her hearty meal upon a dunce.
Flavia's° a wit, has too much sense to pray;
To toast our wants and wishes, is her way;
Nor asks of God, but of her stars, to give
The mighty blessing, 'while we live, to live.'
Then all for death, that opiate of the soul!
Lucretia's° dagger, Rosamonda's° bowl.
Say, what can cause such impotence of mind?
A spark too fickle, or a spouse too kind.
Wise wretch! with pleasures too refined to please;
With too much spirit to be e'er at ease;
With too much quickness ever to be taught;

Taylor Jeremy Taylor (1613–67), whose *Holy Living* and *Holy Dying* were extremely popular devotional works
Book of Martyrs the popular title of the work by John Foxe (1516–87)
citron brandy flavored with lemon peel
his Grace a duke, perhaps her lover
Chartres usurer and libertine (cf. *Satires* II.i)
sad sober
punk whore
frank free
Tallboy a booby lover in Richard Brome's *The Jovial Crew* (1641)
Charles a common name for a footman
Helluo Latin for glutton
hautgout anything with a strong scent or flavor
Flavia's named for blond hair
Lucretia's the Roman matron who committed suicide when she was raped by Tarquin
Rosamonda's Rosamond Clifford (d. 1177), mistress of Henry II, forced by his queen to drink poison

With too much thinking to have common thought:
You purchase pain with all that joy can give,
And die of nothing but a rage to live.
  Turn then from wits; and look on Simo's mate,
No ass so meek, no ass so obstinate.
Or her, that owns her faults, but never mends,
Because she's honest, and the best of friends.
Or her, whose life the Church and scandal share,
For ever in a passion, or a prayer.
Or her, who laughs at Hell, but (like her Grace)
Cries, 'Ah! how charming, if there's no such place!'
Or who in sweet vicissitude appears
Of mirth and opium, ratafie° and tears,
The daily anodyne, and nightly draught,
To kill those foes to fair ones, time and thought.
Woman and fool are two hard things to hit;
For true no-meaning puzzles more than wit.
  But what are these to great Atossa's° mind?
Scarce once herself, by turns all womankind!
Who, with herself, or others, from her birth
Finds all her life one warfare upon earth:
Shines in exposing knaves and painting fools,
Yet is whate'er she hates and ridicules.
No thought advances, but her eddy brain
Whisks it about, and down it goes again.
Full sixty years the world has been her trade,
The wisest fool much time has ever made.
From loveless youth to unrespected age,
No passion gratified except her rage.
So much the fury still outran the wit,
The pleasure missed her, and the scandal hit.
Who breaks with her provokes revenge from hell,
But he's a bolder man who dares be well.
Her every turn with violence pursued,
Nor more a storm her hate than gratitude:
To that each passion turns, or soon or late;
Love, if it makes her yield, must make her hate:
Superiors? death! and equals? what a curse!
But an inferior not dependent? worse.
Offend her, and she knows not to forgive;
Oblige her, and she'll hate you while you live:
But die, and she'll adore you—Then the bust°
And temple° rise—then fall again to dust.
Last night, her Lord was all that's good and great;

ratafie fruit-flavored liqueur with a brandy base
Atossa's named for the daughter of the Persian emperor Cyrus the Great and the mother of Xerxes; probably based upon Katharine Darnley, Duchess of Buckinghamshire (1682?–1743) and daughter of James II (although long believed to be Sarah, Duchess of Marlborough)
bust funerary monument
temple sepulcher

A knave this morning, and his will a cheat.
Strange! by the means defeated of the ends,
By spirit robbed of power, by warmth of friends,
By wealth of followers! without one distress,
Sick of herself through very selfishness!
Atossa, cursed with every granted prayer,
Childless with all her children, wants an heir.
To heirs unknown descends the unguarded store,
Or wanders, Heaven-directed, to the poor.
  Pictures like these, dear Madam, to design,
Asks no firm hand, and no unerring line;
Some wandering touches, some reflected light,
Some flying stroke alone can hit 'em right:
For how should equal° colours do the knack?
Chameleons who can paint in white and black?
  'Yet Chloe sure was formed without a spot'—
Nature in her then erred not, but forgot.
'With every pleasing, every prudent part,
Say, what can Chloe want?'—She wants a heart.
She speaks, behaves, and acts just as she ought;
But never, never, reached one generous thought.
Virtue she finds too painful an endeavour,
Content to dwell in decencies° for ever.
So very reasonable, so unmoved,
As never yet to love, or to be loved.
She, while her lover pants upon her breast,
Can mark the figures on an Indian chest;
And when she sees her friend in deep despair,
Observes how much a chintz exceeds mohair.
Forbid it Heaven, a favour or a debt
She e'er should cancel—but she may forget.
Safe is your secret still in Chloe's ear;
But none of Chloe's shall you ever hear.
Of all her dears she never slandered one,
But cares not if a thousand are undone.
Would Chloe know if you're alive or dead?
She bids her footman put it in her head.
Chloe is prudent—Would you too be wise?
Then never break your heart when Chloe dies.
  One certain portrait may (I grant) be seen,
Which Heaven has varnished out, and made a *Queen:*°
The same for ever! and described by all
With truth and goodness, as with crown and ball.°
Poets heap virtues, painters gems at will,

equal solid, unvaried
decencies proprieties
Queen Caroline, who exercised her influence over George II in alliance with Sir Robert Walpole and favored Lord Hervey, the Sporus of Pope's *Epistle to Dr. Arbuthnot*
ball one of the symbols of rule

And show their zeal, and hide their want of skill.°
'Tis well—but, artists! who can paint or write,
To draw the naked is your true delight.
That robe of quality so struts and swells,
None see what parts of nature it conceals:
The exactest traits of body or of mind,
We owe to models of an humble kind.
If Queensberry° to strip there's no compelling,
'Tis from a handmaid we must take a Helen.°
From peer or bishop 'tis no easy thing
To draw the man who loves his God, or king:
Alas! I copy (or my draught° would fail)
From honest Mah'met,° or plain Parson Hale.°
  But grant, in public men sometimes are shown,
A woman's seen in private life alone:
Our bolder talents in full light displayed;
Your virtues open fairest in the shade.
Bred to disguise, in public 'tis you hide;
There, none distinguish twixt your shame or pride,
Weakness or delicacy; all so nice,
That each may seem a virtue, or a vice.
  In men, we various ruling passions° find;
In women, two almost divide the kind;
Those, only fixed, they first or last obey,
The love of pleasure, and the love of sway.
  That, Nature gives; and where the lesson taught
Is but to please, can pleasure seem a fault?
Experience, this; by man's oppression curst,
They seek the second not to lose the first.
  Men, some to business, some to pleasure take;
But every woman is at heart a rake:
Men, some to quiet, some to public strife;
But every lady would be queen for life.
  Yet mark the fate of a whole sex of queens!
Power all their end, but beauty all the means:
In youth they conquer, with so wild a rage,
As leaves them scarce a subject in their age:
For foreign glory, foreign joy, they roam;
No thought of peace or happiness at home.
But wisdom's triumph is well-timed retreat,
As hard a science to the fair as great!

hide . . . skill Cf. *Essay on Criticism*, ll. 293–96.
Queensberry Catherine Hyde, Duchess of Queensberry (1700–1777), friend and protectress of John Gay, and one of the most beautiful women of her day
Helen of Troy
draught sketch
Mah'met "Servant to the late King, said to be the son of a Turkish Bassa, whom he took at the siege of Buda, and constantly kept about his person" (Pope)
Parson Hale Dr. Stephen Hales (1677–1761), physiologist and admirable parish priest, a friend of Pope
ruling passions The ruling passions, for Pope, were ineradicable drives which might take disguised forms as they bent other passions to their control and which proved, upon scrutiny, to underlie all other motives. See *Essay on Man* II.123 ff.

Beauties, like tyrants, old and friendless grown,
Yet hate repose, and dread to be alone,
Worn out in public, weary every eye,
Nor leave one sigh behind them when they die.
 Pleasures the sex, as children birds, pursue,
Still out of reach, yet never out of view;
Sure, if they catch, to spoil the toy° at most,
To covet flying, and regret when lost:
At last, to follies youth could scarce defend,
It grows their age's prudence to pretend;
Ashamed to own they gave delight before,
Reduced to feign it, when they give no more:
As hags° hold sabbaths, less for joy than spite,
So these their merry, miserable night;°
Still round and round the ghosts of beauty glide,
And haunt the places where their honour died.
 See how the world its veterans rewards!
A youth of frolics, an old age of cards;
Fair to no purpose, artful to no end,
Young without lovers, old without a friend;
A fop their passion, but their prize a sot;
Alive, ridiculous, and dead, forgot!
 Ah! Friend!° to dazzle let the vain design;
To raise the thought, and touch the heart be thine!
That charm shall grow, while what fatigues the Ring°
Flaunts and goes down, an unregarded thing:
So when the sun's broad beam has tired the sight,
All mild ascends the moon's more sober light,
Serene in virgin modesty° she shines,
And unobserved the glaring orb declines.
 Oh! blest with temper whose unclouded ray
Can make tomorrow cheerful as today;
She, who can love a sister's charms, or hear
Sighs for a daughter with unwounded ear;
She, who ne'er answers till a husband cools,
Or, if she rules him, never shows she rules;
Charms by accepting, by submitting sways,
Yet has her humour most when she obeys;
Let fops or fortune fly which way they will;
Disdains all loss of tickets,° or Codille;°
Spleen, vapours,° or smallpox,° above them all,
And mistress of herself, though China° fall.

toy plaything
hags witches, whose sabbaths (held at midnight) were orgies with demons and sorcerers
night visiting night
Friend Martha Blount (1690–1763), whom Pope knew all his mature life and honored in his will; they were close friends and were believed by some to be lovers
Ring the fashionable drive in Hyde Park
virgin modesty alluding to Diana as the virgin goddess of the moon as well as to its silver light
tickets in lotteries
Codille a lost game of ombre (cf. *The Rape of the Lock* III.92)
Spleen, vapours fashionable forms of melancholy or moodiness
smallpox whose scars had disfigured Martha Blount's face
China For its double sense, see *The Rape of the Lock* III.110.

And yet, believe me, good as well as ill,
Woman's at best a contradiction still.
Heaven, when it strives to polish all it can
Its last best work, but forms a softer man;
Picks from each sex, to make the favourite blest,
Your love of pleasure, our desire of rest:
Blends, in exception to all general rules,
Your taste of follies, with our scorn of fools:
Reserve with frankness, art with truth allied,
Courage with softness, modesty with pride;
Fixed principles, with fancy ever new;
Shakes all together, and produces—You.
Be this a woman's fame: with this unblest,
Toasts live a scorn, and queens may die a jest.
This Phoebus° promised (I forget the year)
When those blue eyes first opened on the sphere;
Ascendant Phoebus watched that hour with care,
Averted half your parents' simple prayer;
And gave you beauty, but denied the pelf°
That buys your sex a tyrant o'er itself.
The generous god,° who wit and gold refines,
And ripens spirits as he ripens mines,
Kept dross for duchesses, the world shall know it,
To you gave sense, good humour,° and a poet.

1735

Imitations of Horace

Pope's "imitations of Horace" are among his finest works. Some of the poems are direct imitations and were published with the text of Horace beside them (or the text of Donne for the two satires of his that Pope "versified" in more regular couplets). Others are written in the manner of Horace but without precise models. One of these, originally described as "a Dialogue Something like Horace," became, with its companion poem, the Epilogue to the Satires in 1740; the *Epistle to Dr. Arbuthnot* has also been printed as a Prologue to the Satires.

The term "imitation" was first given currency by Dryden, when he distinguished among three kinds of translation: metaphrase, or word-by-word literal translation; paraphrase, or a translation that retains the meaning of the original but does so by departing from strict literalness; and finally imitation (of which Dryden was suspicious), which departs freely from the original text to create a new poem in its spirit, using the experience of a new age to take the place of earlier material. (One may compare "paraphrase" and "imitation" in two instances given here: Dryden's and Swift's versions of Ovid's tale of Baucis and Philemon, and Dryden's and Johnson's versions of Juvenal's Third Satire.)

Phoebus as god of prophecy
pelf wealth
generous god Phoebus as god of poetry, which fosters true wit, and as god of the sun, by which gold is generated and "ripens" in the earth
good humour Cf. *The Rape of the Lock* V.29–34.

The imitation emerged in England (perhaps furthered through Boileau's example) in the work of Abraham Cowley and Sir John Denham, as Dryden recognized, and one can perhaps read Rochester's *Satire Against Mankind* as an "imitation" of Boileau's Eighth Satire. At any rate, it is part of the effect of an imitation that the reader be potentially aware of the text from which the poet departs and recognize the variation upon the original, as one does in a parody. Pope, in fact, applied the phrase "a parody from Horace" to *Satire* II.i given here; and he used the term all but interchangeably with imitation. Yet the imitation, while it cannot be fully grasped without some knowledge of the original, can in considerable measure stand on its own, and it is not a great leap from those imitations which have a specific model in Horace to those which have only the generalized one of Horace's satires and epistles.

Finally, one must ask what that generalized example implied. In Dryden's *Discourse* on satire (passages from which are given above in his Critical Prose section) Juvenal is exalted over Horace: "a noble soul is better pleased with a zealous vindication of Roman liberty than with a temporizing poet, a well mannered court slave, and a man . . . who is ever decent, because he is naturally servile." These charges against Horace haunt the age, but Shaftesbury distinguishes between Horace's "debauched, slavish, courtly state" and his "returning, recovering state." In the latter he returned to a "Socratic" philosophy and left Epicureanism behind him, and in his revived moral severity (with its elements of Stoicism) he put the appeal of the court behind him. It is in this later state that the conversational poems—the *sermones*—were written, and they can be seen as an expression of it. Pope tends to carry Horace's Socratic morality to a stage of deeper intensity, perhaps more readily comparable to that of Juvenal; and he dramatizes the poet's rising to superb indignation, even prophetic rage, as he creates his vision of triumphant Vice (in *Epilogue* I) or defends himself against resentful libels. The modulation of tone is remarkable in all these poems, from the seemingly timid and naïve victim to the morally outraged patriot, from the public wrath of satiric engagement to the personal warmth of friendship in retirement.

Epistle to Dr. Arbuthnot

Being the Prologue to the Satires

P. Shut, shut the door, good John!° fatigued, I said,
Tie up the knocker, say I'm sick, I'm dead.
The Dog-star° rages! nay 'tis past a doubt,
All Bedlam, or Parnassus,° is let out:
Fire in each eye, and papers in each hand,
They rave, recite, and madden round the land.
What walls can guard me, or what shades can hide?
They pierce my thickets, through my grot° they glide;

good John Pope's servant John Serle
Dog-star Sirius, which reappears at the time of late summer heat; for Juvenal the season for the reading of new poems, whose pomposity and incompetence stung him to rage (see "Parnassus," l. 4)
Bedlam, or Parnassus inhabitants of the madhouse or (as they imagine) the mountain of the Muses
grot Pope's grotto at Twickenham was an underground retreat, an artificial cave encrusted with shells and minerals.

By land, by water,° they renew the charge;
They stop the chariot, and they board the barge.
No place is sacred, not the church is free;
Even Sunday shines no sabbath-day to me:
Then from the Mint° walks forth the man of rhyme,
Happy! to catch me just at dinner time.
  Is there a parson, much bemused in° beer,
A maudlin poetess, a rhyming peer,
A clerk, foredoomed his father's soul to cross,
Who pens a stanza, when he should *engross*.°
Is there, who, locked from ink and paper, scrawls
With desperate charcoal round his darkened walls?°
All fly to TWIT'NAM,° and in humble strain
Apply to me, to keep them mad or vain.
Arthur,° whose giddy son neglects the Laws,
Imputes to me and my damned works the cause:
Poor Cornus° sees his frantic wife elope,
And curses wit, and poetry, and Pope.°
  Friend to my life! (which did not you prolong,
The world had wanted many an idle song)
What drop or nostrum° can this plague remove?
Or which must end me, a fool's wrath or love?
A dire dilemma! either way I'm sped;°
If foes, they write, if friends, they read me dead.
Seized and tied down to judge, how wretched I!
Who can't be silent, and who will not lie;
To laugh were want of goodness and of grace,
And to be grave exceeds all power of face.
I sit with sad civility, I read
With honest anguish, and an aching head;
And drop at last, but in unwilling ears,
This saving counsel, 'Keep your piece nine years.'°
  'Nine years!' cries he, who high in Drury Lane,°
Lulled by soft zephyrs through the broken pane,
Rhymes ere he wakes, and prints before Term° ends,
Obliged by hunger, and request of friends:°
'The piece, you think, is incorrect? why, take it,

water Pope's house was on the Thames, and one could be rowed from London by scullers; "chariot" and "barge" suggest land and sea battles.
Mint a section of Southwark where debtors could stay without fear of arrest; on Sundays, however, there were no arrests anywhere
bemused in rhyming with the name of Laurence Eusden (1688–1730), a parson and poet laureate notoriously fond of drink
engross copy a legal document
darkened walls i.e. in confinement, probably in Bedlam
Twit'nam i.e. Twickenham, Pope's home
Arthur perhaps Arthur Moore, whose son (eager to shine as a wit) had plagiarized from Pope; but the name is generic, like "Cornus" below
Cornus from Latin for a horn; hence a cuckold
Pope As a Roman Catholic, Pope could enjoy parodying the hysterical charges against all forms of popery.
drop or nostrum cures
sped i.e. to my grave
nine years the advice of Horace to the poet, *Ars Poetica*, ll. 386–89
Drury Lane street of theaters, prostitutes, and—here—writers in garrets
Term law court term, also the publishing season
Obliged . . . friends offering the second reason to conceal the first, a common procedure in prefaces

I'm all submission; what you'd have it, make it.'
  Three things another's modest wishes bound:
My friendship, and a prologue,° and ten pound.
  Pitholeon° sends to me: 'You know his Grace;
I want a patron; ask him for a place.'°
Pitholeon libelled me—'but here's a letter
Informs you, sir, 'twas when he knew no better.
Dare you refuse him? Curll° invites to dine;
He'll write a Journal, or he'll turn divine.'°
  Bless me! a packet.—' 'Tis a stranger sues,
A virgin tragedy, an orphan Muse.'
If I dislike it, 'Furies, death and rage!'
If I approve, 'Commend it to the stage.'
There (thank my stars) my whole commission ends,
The players and I are, luckily, no friends.
Fired that the house° reject him, ' 'Sdeath I'll print it,
And shame the fools—Your Interest, sir, with Lintot.'°
Lintot, dull rogue! will think your price too much:
'Not, sir, if you revise it, and retouch.'
All my demurs but double his attacks;
At last he whispers, 'Do; and we go snacks.'°
Glad of a quarrel, straight I clap the door,
'Sir, let me see your works and you no more.'
'Tis sung, when Midas' ears° began to spring,
(Midas, a sacred person and a King)
His very Minister who spied them first,
(Some say his Queen) was forced to speak, or burst.
And is not mine, my friend, a sorer case,
When every coxcomb perks them in my face?
  'Good friend, forbear! you deal in dangerous things.
I'd never name Queens, Ministers, or Kings;
Keep close to ears, and those let asses prick;
'Tis nothing—' Nothing? if they bite and kick?
Out with it, DUNCIAD! let the secret pass,
That secret to each fool, that he's an ass:
The truth once told (and wherefore should we lie?)
The Queen of Midas slept, and so may I.
  You think this cruel? take it for a rule,
No creature smarts so little as a fool.

prologue often sought from well-known writers to help a play succeed
Pitholeon a foolish and pretentious poet mentioned by Horace, here a modern counterpart seeking influence with a nobleman
place position or sinecure
Curll Edmund Curll, notorious publisher of hacks, might commission him to write new libels or forge works in your name.
Journal . . . divine sell his talents in party politics or religious controversy
house theater
Lintot Bernard Lintot, who published many of Pope's works
snacks shares
Midas' ears the ass's ears given him by Apollo for preferring Pan's music. Midas' wife (in some versions, his chief minister or barber) could not keep the secret entirely and whispered it into a hole in the earth, but the reeds that grew there repeated the message in the wind. (Since Walpole as chief minister and Caroline as queen virtually ruled in George II's place, they would have most reason to conceal the full extent of that King's stupidity.)

Let peals of laughter, Codrus!° round thee break,
Thou unconcerned canst hear the mighty crack:°
Pit, box, and gallery in convulsions hurled,
Thou standst unshook amidst a bursting world.
Who shames a scribbler? break one cobweb through,
He spins the slight, self-pleasing thread anew:
Destroy his fib or sophistry; in vain,
The creature's at his dirty work° again,
Throned in the centre of his thin designs,
Proud of a vast extent of flimsy lines!
Whom have I hurt? has poet yet or peer
Lost the arched eyebrow or Parnassian sneer?°
And has not Colley still his Lord and whore?
His butchers Henley,° his Freemasons Moore?°
Does not one table Bavius° still admit?
Still to one bishop Philips° seem a wit?
Still Sappho°—'Hold! for God's sake—you'll offend,
No names—be calm—learn prudence of a friend:
I too could write, and I am twice as tall;
But foes like these—' One flatterer's worse than all.
Of all mad creatures, if the learned are right,
It is the slaver kills, and not the bite.
A fool quite angry is quite innocent:
Alas! 'tis ten times worse when they *repent*.
One dedicates in high heroic prose,
And ridicules beyond a hundred foes:
One from all Grubstreet° will my fame defend,
And, more abusive, calls himself my friend.
This prints my *Letters*,° that expects a bribe,
And others roar aloud, 'Subscribe, subscribe.'°
There are, who to my person pay their court:
I cough like Horace, and, though lean, am short,
Ammon's great son° one shoulder had too high,
Such Ovid's nose, and 'Sir! you have an eye'—
Go on, obliging creatures, make me see
All that disgraced my betters, met in me.

Codrus a poet ridiculed by Virgil and Juvenal
mighty crack This phrase of Joseph Addison's amused Pope by its total inadequacy to the idea of cosmic catastrophe, and here Pope applies it to stage thunder as Codrus's play is produced and proves a catastrophe of a lesser sort.
dirty work since, like Swift's Spider in *The Battle of the Books*, he spins a structure out of his own excrement
Parnassian sneer referring to the current poet laureate, Colley Cibber (as the phrase once had to Lewis Theobald, *The Dunciad* II.5)
Henley See *Epilogue to the Satires* I.66 and note.
Moore James Moore-Smythe whom Pope regarded as a plagiarist, here cited as a leader of Freemasons' processions
Bavius the bad poet of Virgil's and Horace's day
Philips Ambrose Philips (1674–1749), notorious for his rustic pastoral and his mock-naïve children's verse (which won him the name of Namby-Pamby), was secretary to Hugh Boulter, Bishop of Armagh.
Sappho immediately invoking Pope's enemy, Lady Mary Wortley Montagu, and implying her support (like Philips's by the bishop) by Walpole
Grubstreet the center and symbol of hack writers
Letters pirated (as some of Pope's were by Curll) or forged
subscribe Books were often published with the financial support of advance subscriptions.
Ammon's . . . son Alexander the Great, claiming descent from Jupiter Ammon

Say for my comfort, languishing in bed,
'Just so immortal Maro° held his head':
And when I die, be sure you let me know
Great Homer died three thousand years ago.
  Why did I write? what sin to me unknown
Dipped me in ink, my parents' or my own?
As yet a child, nor yet a fool to fame,
I lisped in numbers,° for the numbers came.
I left no calling for this idle trade,
No duty broke, no father disobeyed.
The Muse but served to ease some friend, not wife,
To help me through this long disease, my life,
To second, ARBUTHNOT! thy art and care,
And teach the being you preserved, to bear.
  But why then publish? Granville° the polite,
And knowing Walsh, would tell me I could write;
Well-natured Garth inflamed with early praise;
And Congreve loved, and Swift endured my lays;
The courtly Talbot, Somers, Sheffield read,
Even mitred Rochester would nod the head,
And St. John's self (great Dryden's friends before)
With open arms received one poet more.
Happy my studies, when by these approved!
Happier their author, when by these beloved!
From these the world will judge of men and books,
Not from the Burnets, Oldmixons, and Cookes.°
  Soft were my numbers; who could take offence
While pure description held the place of sense?
Like gentle Fanny's° was my flowery theme,
A painted mistress, or a purling stream.
Yet then did Gildon° draw his venal quill;
I wished the man a dinner, and sat still.
Yet then did Dennis° rave in furious fret;
I never answered—I was not in debt.

Maro Virgil
numbers meter, verses
Granville The first of a series of statesmen, poets, critics, and patrons—all of high reputation—with whom Pope associates Dryden and himself (and thus himself with Dryden) in opposition to the hacks mentioned above; they are George Granville, Baron Lansdowne (1666–1735), to whom Pope dedicated *Windsor Forest;* William Walsh (1663–1708), his early literary adviser; Sir Samuel Garth (1661–1719), physician and poet; William Congreve; Jonathan Swift; Charles Talbot, Duke of Shrewsbury (1660–1718), statesman and sponsor of Pope's "versification" of Donne's satires; John Lord Somers (1651–1716), the Whig leader to whom Swift dedicated *A Tale of a Tub;* John Sheffield, Duke of Buckinghamshire and Normanby (1648–1721), whose poems Pope edited and to whom Dryden dedicated important work; Francis Atterbury, Bishop of Rochester (1662–1732), friend of Swift and Pope and himself a distinguished writer; and Henry St. John, Viscount Bolingbroke (1678–1751), chief minister under Anne, political theorist, close friend of Swift and Pope for many years.
Burnets . . . Cookes Thomas Burnet, John Oldmixon, and Thomas Cooke; "authors of secret and scandalous history" (Pope)
gentle Fanny's any conventional poet's, but also with special reference to John, Lord Hervey, who appears below as Sporus, ll. 305–33
Gildon Charles Gildon (1665–1724), a critic who had attacked Pope personally, perhaps (as Pope believed) at the instigation of Joseph Addison (the "Atticus" of ll. 193–214); hence a hireling or "venal" writer
Dennis John Dennis (1657–1734), critic and dramatist, abusively personal in his attacks on Pope; also suspected by Pope of selling his services to Addison

If want provoked, or madness made them print,
I waged no war with Bedlam or the Mint.
 Did some more sober critic come abroad;
If wrong, I smiled; if right, I kissed the rod.
Pains, reading, study, are their just pretence,
And all they want is spirit, taste, and sense.
Commas and points° they set exactly right,
And 'twere a sin to rob them of their mite.
Yet ne'er one sprig of laurel° graced these ribalds,°
From slashing Bentley down to piddling Tibalds:°
Each wight, who reads not, and but scans and spells,
Each word-catcher, that lives on syllables,
Even such small critics some regard may claim,
Preserved in Milton's or in Shakespeare's name.
Pretty! in amber° to observe the forms
Of hairs, or straws, or dirt, or grubs, or worms!
The things, we know, are neither rich nor rare,
But wonder how the devil they got there.
 Were others angry? I excused them too;
Well might they rage; I gave them but their due.
A man's true merit 'tis not hard to find;
But each man's secret standard in his mind,
That casting-weight° pride adds to emptiness,
This, who can gratify? for who can guess?
The bard° whom pilfered pastorals renown,
Who turns a Persian tale for half a crown,°
Just writes to make his barrenness appear,
And strains, from hard-bound brains, eight lines a year;
He, who still wanting, though he lives on theft,
Steals much, spends little, yet has nothing left:
And he, who now to sense, now nonsense leaning,
Means not, but blunders round about a meaning:
And he, whose fustian's so sublimely bad,
It is not poetry, but prose run mad:
All these, my modest satire bade translate,
And owned that nine such poets made a Tate.°

points periods, the concern of these "more sober" verbal critics
laurel the bay with which the true poet was crowned
ribalds buffoons
slashing Bentley . . . piddling Tibalds Richard Bentley (the subject of Swift's earlier attack in *The Battle of the Books* and *A Tale of a Tub*) and Lewis Theobald (1688–1744) were, among other things, textual scholars. Bentley's great learning was accompanied by ill temper toward his colleagues and arrogance toward the authors he edited. Theobald had properly exposed Pope's weaknesses as an editor of Shakespeare, but his own emendations of the text are a mixture of brilliant intuition and heavy self-display; like Bentley's, his literary sense is much less secure than his historical information. Theobald was the king of the dunces in the first version of *The Dunciad* (1728), but he was supplanted by Colley Cibber in the revision of 1743; Bentley preserved his place through all editions.
in amber as flies and other insects have been decoratively preserved
casting-weight that turns the balance
bard Ambrose Philips, whose pastoral poems were clumsily based on Spenser's and who also translated a book of *Persian Tales*
half a crown a prostitute's customary fee
Tate Nahum Tate (1652–1715), former poet laureate, "a cold writer of no invention" (Pope); the line is based on the saying that it takes nine tailors to make a man.

How did they fume, and stamp, and roar, and chafe!
And swear, not *Addison* himself was safe.
  Peace to all such! but were there one° whose fires
True genius kindles, and fair fame inspires;
Blest with each talent and each art to please,
And born to write, converse, and live with ease:
Should such a man, too fond to rule alone,
Bear, like the Turk,° no brother near the throne,
View him with scornful, yet with jealous eyes,
And hate for arts that caused himself to rise;
Damn with faint praise, assent with civil leer,
And without sneering, teach the rest to sneer;
Willing to wound, and yet afraid to strike,
Just hint a fault, and hesitate dislike;
Alike reserved to blame, or to commend,
A timorous foe, and a suspicious friend;
Dreading even fools, by flatterers besieged,
And so obliging, that he ne'er obliged;
Like Cato,° give his little Senate laws,
And sit attentive to his own applause;
While wits and templars° every sentence raise,
And wonder with a foolish face of praise—
Who but must laugh, if such a man there be?
Who would not weep, if Atticus were he?
  What though my name stood rubric° on the walls,
Or plastered posts, with claps,° in capitals?
Or smoking forth, a hundred hawkers' load,
On wings of wind came flying all abroad?
I sought no homage from the race that write;
I kept, like Asian monarchs,° from their sight:
Poems I heeded (now berhymed so long)
No more than thou, great GEORGE! a birthday song.°
I ne'er with wits or witlings passed my days,
To spread about the itch of verse and praise;
Nor like a puppy, daggled° through the town,

one In this portrait of Atticus, which had appeared earlier by itself, Pope is clearly suggesting Joseph Addison (1672–1719), the author of the tragedy *Cato* as well as of the *Tatler* and *Spectator*. Addison and Pope had considerable respect for each other's powers, but Pope had some reason to feel Addison's jealousy or at least lack of generosity toward a young writer who stood outside his circle and failed to do homage to him. The original Atticus was a man of letters and friend of Cicero.
like the Turk the Turkish rulers, who in fact had often executed close kinsmen to avoid the threat of rivalry
Cato In his prologue to Addison's play (1713), Pope had written "While Cato gives his little senate laws, / What bosom beats not in his country's cause? / Who sees him act, but envies every deed? / Who hears him groan, and does not wish to bleed?" (ll. 23–26) Here those questions are echoed with a difference, and the august Roman senate is replaced by the coffee-house hangers-on whom Addison rules as a literary dictator.
templars law students, who often cultivated literary ambitions
stood rubric was posted in red letters in booksellers' advertisements
with claps on posters; also with advertisements for cures for gonorrhea
like . . . monarchs in their withdrawal; cf. *Elegy to the Memory of an Unfortunate Lady*, ll. 21–22
birthday song the official ode of the laureate
daggled splashed in mud

To fetch and carry singsong up and down;
Nor at rehearsals sweat, and mouthed, and cried,
With handkerchief and orange° at my side;
But sick of fops, and poetry, and prate,
To *Bufo*° left the whole Castalian state.°
  Proud as Apollo on his forkèd hill,
Sat full-blown Bufo, puffed by every quill;
Fed with soft dedication all day long,
Horace and he° went hand in hand in song.
His library (where busts of poets dead
And a true Pindar stood without a head)
Received of wits an undistinguished race,
Who first his judgment asked, and then a place:
Much they extolled his pictures, much his seat,°
And flattered every day, and some days eat:
Till grown more frugal in his riper days,
He paid some bards with port, and some with praise;
To some a dry rehearsal was assigned,
And others (harder still) he paid in kind.°
Dryden alone (what wonder?) came not nigh,
Dryden alone escaped this judging eye:
But still the Great have kindness in reserve,
He helped to bury° whom he helped to starve.
  May some choice patron bless each gray goose quill!
May every Bavius have his Bufo still!
So, when a statesman wants a day's defence,
Or envy holds a whole week's war with sense,
Or simple pride for flattery makes demands,
May dunce by dunce be whistled off my hands!
Blest be the Great! for those they take away,°
And those they left me; for they left me GAY,°
Left me to see neglected genius bloom,
Neglected die, and tell it on his tomb:°
Of all thy blameless life the sole return
My Verse, and QUEENSBERRY° weeping o'er thy urn!
  Oh let me live my own, and die so too!
(To live and die is all I have to do:)°

orange sold in the theater as refreshment
Bufo a patron, his name taken from the Latin word for a toad, a creature that swells up with air
Castalian state poetry; named for the Muses' sacred spring on the "forkèd hill," Parnassus
Horace and he i.e. with Bufo as a modern Maecenas, replacing Horace's patron
seat estate
in kind with his own poems
helped to bury Dryden, who was poor most of his life, was given a lavish funeral; Bufo feels more secure with "poets dead" or with assured reputations.
take away "The Lord gave and the Lord hath taken away; blessed be the name of the Lord" (Job 1:21)
Gay John Gay, author of *The Beggar's Opera* and many poems, a close friend of Pope, Swift, and Arbuthnot
on his tomb Pope wrote Gay's epitaph.
Queensberry Charles Douglas, 3rd Duke of Queensberry (1698–1778), was, with his beautiful and witty wife, Gay's patron and friend.
To live . . . do a line adapted from Sir John Denham's poem *Of Prudence*

Maintain a poet's dignity and ease,
And see what friends, and read what books I please:
Above a patron, though I condescend
Some times to call a Minister my friend.
I was not born for courts or great affairs;
I pay my debts, believe, and say my prayers;
Can sleep without a poem in my head,
Nor know, if Dennis be alive or dead.
  Why am I asked what next shall see the light?
Heavens! was I born for nothing but to write?
Has life no joys for me? or (to be grave)
Have I no friend to serve, no soul to save?
'I found him close with Swift'—'Indeed? no doubt,'
(Cries prating Balbus) 'something will come out.'
'Tis all in vain, deny it as I will.
'No, such a Genius never can lie still';
And then for mine obligingly mistakes
The first Lampoon Sir *Will.* or *Bubo*° makes.
Poor guiltless I! and can I choose but smile,
When every coxcomb knows me by my *style*?
  Cursed be the verse, how well soe'er it flow,
That tends to make one worthy man my foe,
Give Virtue scandal, Innocence a fear,
Or from the soft-eyed virgin steal a tear!
But he who hurts a harmless neighbour's peace,
Insults fallen worth, or beauty in distress,
Who loves a lie, lame slander helps about,
Who writes a libel, or who copies out:
That fop, whose pride affects a patron's name,
Yet absent, wounds an author's honest fame:
Who can your merit selfishly approve,
And show the sense of it without the love;°
Who has the vanity to call you friend,
Yet wants the honour, injured, to defend;°
Who tells whate'er you think, whate'er you say,
And, if he lie not, must at least betray:
Who to the *Dean*, and *silver bell* can swear,
And sees at *Cannons* what was never there;°
Who reads, but with a lust to misapply,
Make satire a lampoon, and fiction, lie.
A lash like mine no honest man shall dread,

Sir Will. or Bubo Sir William Yonge or George Bubb Dodington, the one known as a wit, the other a wealthy patron; but any feeble writer is meant

And show . . . love i.e. demonstrate his taste without real affection or generosity

the honour . . . defend i.e. and lacks the honor to defend the poet (whom he calls friend) against slander or attack

Who . . . there i.e. who makes false identifications of characters and places in Pope's *Epistle to Burlington.* Pope was falsely charged with ingratitude as a result of others' malicious linking of Timon's villa with Cannons, the estate of the Duke of Chandos.

But all such babbling blockheads in his stead.
  Let *Sporus*° tremble—'What? that thing of silk,
Sporus, that mere white curd of ass's milk?
Satire or sense, alas! can Sporus feel?
Who breaks a butterfly upon a wheel?'°
Yet let me flap this bug with gilded wings,
This painted child of dirt that stinks and stings;
Whose buzz the witty and the fair annoys,
Yet wit ne'er tastes, and beauty ne'er enjoys:
So well-bred spaniels civilly delight
In mumbling of the game they dare not bite.
Eternal smiles his emptiness betray,
As shallow streams run dimpling all the way.
Whether in florid impotence he speaks,
And, as the prompter breathes, the puppet squeaks;
Or at the ear of Eve,° familiar toad,
Half froth, half venom, spits himself abroad,
In puns, or politics, or tales, or lies,
Or spite, or smut, or rhymes, or blasphemies.
His wit all seesaw, between *that* and *this,*
Now high, now low, now master up, now miss,
And he himself one vile antithesis.
Amphibious thing! that acting either part,
The trifling head, or the corrupted heart,
Fop at the toilet, flatterer at the board,
Now trips a Lady, and now struts a Lord.
Eve's tempter thus the Rabbins° have exprest,
A cherub's face, a reptile all the rest;
Beauty that shocks you, parts that none will trust,
Wit that can creep, and pride that licks the dust.
  Not Fortune's worshipper, nor fashion's fool,
Not lucre's madman, nor ambition's tool,
Not proud, nor servile; be one poet's praise,
That, if he pleased, he pleased by manly ways:
That flattery, even to kings, he held a shame,
And thought a lie in verse or prose the same.
That not in fancy's maze he wandered long,
But stooped° to truth and moralized his song:
That not for fame, but virtue's better end,
He stood° the furious foe, the timid friend,

Sporus Nero's homosexual favorite, a boy to whom he was married in public; appropriately used for Lord Hervey (1696–1743), prominent in the court of George II and especially close to Queen Caroline; a long-time confederate of Lady Mary Wortley Montagu in attacks upon Pope (Hervey's brilliant *Memoirs of the Reign of King George II* were not published until 1848)
wheel the rack or instrument of torture on which men were disjointed
Eve alluding to the early temptation, with Satan "squat like a toad, close at the ear of Eve" (*Paradise Lost* IV.800)
Rabbins rabbis, scholars of the Old Testament, whose image of Satan has often been represented in paintings of the temptation of Eve
stooped as a falcon is said to "stoop" to its prey
stood withstood, endured

The damning critic, half-approving wit,
The coxcomb hit, or fearing to be hit;
Laughed at the loss of friends he never had,
The dull, the proud, the wicked, and the mad;
The distant threats of vengeance on his head,
The blow unfelt, the tear he never shed;°
The tale revived, the lie so oft o'erthrown,
The imputed trash,° and dulness not his own;
The morals blackened when the writings 'scape,
The libeled person, and the pictured shape;°
Abuse, on all he loved, or loved him, spread,
A friend in exile, or a father, dead;
The whisper,° that to greatness still too near,
Perhaps, yet vibrates on his SOVEREIGN's ear—
Welcome for thee, fair Virtue! all the past:
For thee, fair Virtue! welcome even the *last!*
'But why insult the poor, affront the great?'
A knave's a knave, to me, in every state:
Alike my scorn, if he succeed or fail,
Sporus at court, or Japhet° in a jail,
A hireling scribbler, or a hireling peer,
Knight of the post° corrupt, or of the shire;
If on a pillory, or near a throne,
He gain his Prince's ear, or lose his own.°
Yet soft by nature, more a dupe than wit,
Sappho° can tell you how this man was bit:°
This dreaded satirist Dennis will confess
Foe to his pride, but friend to his distress,°
So humble, he has knocked at Tibbald's door,
Has drunk with Cibber, nay, has rhymed for Moore.°
Full ten years slandered, did he once reply?
Three thousand suns went down on Welsted's lie.
To please a mistress one aspersed his life;
He lashed him not, but let her be his wife:
Let Budgell charge low Grubstreet° on his quill,
And write whate'er he pleased, except his will;
Let the two Curlls° of town and court, abuse

blow . . . shed the false report, circulated in the pamphlet *A Pop upon Pope* (1728), that Pope had been subjected to a whipping
trash scandalous works published as his by Curll
pictured shape as when he was shown as a hunchbacked ape in the pamphlet *Pope Alexander's Supremacy and Infallibility Examined* (1729)
whisper by Lord Hervey
Japhet Japhet Crook, a forger
Knight . . . post a term for one who made his living by giving false evidence, as opposed to a legitimate knight (of the shire or county), who might also be corrupt
lose his own as Japhet Crook did by way of punishment before he was exposed in the pillory or stocks
Sappho Lady Mary Wortley Montagu, to whom Pope once had been very close, after their estrangement joined Lord Hervey in attacking him.
bit deceived, fooled
his distress Pope had been helpful in Dennis's last years.
Moore unintentionally, for Moore-Smythe plagiarized from Pope
low Grubstreet contributions to the *Grub Street Journal* that accused Budgell of forging a will and making himself heir
two Curlls the publisher (l. 53), and Lord Hervey, his counterpart at court

His father, mother, body, soul, and Muse.
Yet why? that father held it for a rule,
It was a sin to call our neighbour fool:
That harmless mother thought no wife a whore:
Hear this, and spare his family, *James Moore!*
Unspotted names, and memorable long!
If there be force in virtue or in song.
  Of gentle blood (part shed in honour's cause,
While yet in *Britain* honour had applause)
Each parent sprung—'What fortune, pray?'—Their own,
And better got, than Bestia's° from the throne.
Born to no pride, inheriting no Strife,
Nor marrying discord in a noble wife,
Stranger to civil and religious rage,
The good man walked innoxious through his age.
No courts he saw, no suits would ever try,
Nor dared an oath, nor hazarded a lie.
Unlearned, he knew no schoolman's subtle art,°
No language, but the language of the heart.
By nature honest, by experience wise,
Healthy by temperance and by exercise;
His life, though long, to sickness passed unknown,
His death was instant, and without a groan.
O grant me, thus to live, and thus to die!
Who sprung from kings shall know less joy than I.
  O Friend!° may each domestic bliss be thine!
Be no unpleasing melancholy mine:
Me, let the tender office long engage,
To rock the cradle of reposing age,
With lenient° arts extend a mother's breath,°
Make Languor smile, and smooth the bed of Death,
Explore the thought, explain the asking eye,
And keep a while one parent from the sky!
On cares like these if length of days attend,
May Heaven, to bless those days, preserve my friend,
Preserve him social, cheerful, and serene,
And just as rich as when he served a Queen.°
Whether that blessing be denied or given,
Thus far was right, the rest belongs to Heaven.

1735

Bestia's a Roman consul bribed into a dishonorable peace; perhaps referring to the enormous grants made by Queen Anne to the victorious Duke of Marlborough
art i.e. casuistry, which might find ingenious reasons for condoning false actions. Pope's father refused to gain relief from anti-Catholic measures by taking an oath against the pope.
Friend Arbuthnot
lenient relieving
mother's breath Pope's mother died at an advanced age before this poem was published, but these lines had been written some years earlier; Pope's account of his solicitude and devotion seems to be an accurate one.
Queen Anne, to whom Arbuthnot had been court physician

The First Satire of the Second Book of Horace

To Mr. Fortescue°

P. There are (I scarce can think it, but am told),
There are, to whom my satire seems too bold:
Scarce to wise Peter° complaisant enough,
And something said of Chartres° much too rough.
The lines are weak, another's pleased to say,
Lord Fanny° spins a thousand such a day.
Timorous by nature, of the rich in awe,
I come to counsel learned in the law:
You'll give me, like a friend, both sage and free,°
Advice; and (as you use) without a fee.
F. I'd write no more.
P. Not write? but then I *think*,
And for my soul I cannot sleep a wink.
I nod in company, I wake at night,
Fools rush into my head, and so I write.
F. You could not do a worse thing for your life.
Why, if the nights seem tedious, take a wife;
Or rather truly, if your point be rest,
Lettuce and cowslip wine;° *Probatum est.*°
But talk with Celsus,° Celsus will advise
Hartshorn,° or something that shall close your eyes.
Or, if you needs must write, write Caesar's° praise,
You'll gain at least a *knighthood*, or the *bays*.°
P. What? like Sir Richard,° rumbling, rough, and fierce,
With Arms, and George, and Brunswick° crowd the verse,
Rend with tremendous sound your ears asunder,
With gun, drum, trumpet, blunderbuss, and thunder?
Or nobly wild, with Budgell's° fire and force,
Paint angels trembling round his falling horse?
F. Then all your Muse's softer art display,
Let Carolina° smooth the tuneful lay,

To Mr. Fortescue William Fortescue, a friend and legal adviser of Pope (as well as a friend and supporter of Sir Robert Walpole), replaces the celebrated Roman lawyer Trebatius of Horace's poem.
Peter Peter Walter (1664?–1746) was notorious as a moneylender to the aristocracy and was said to be worth £300,000 at his death; as Swift describes him, "That rogue, of genuine ministerial kind, / Can half the peerage by his arts bewitch" (*Epistle to Mr. Gay*, 1731); and Pope cites him often as the crassest commercial spirit of the age (cf. *Epilogue to the Satires* I.121; II.57).
Chartres Francis Charteris (1675–1732), gambler, usurer, debauchee
Lord Fanny Fannius was a foolish critic and enemy of Horace, and Pope regularly applied his version of the name to John, Lord Hervey, the Sporus of the *Epistle to Dr. Arbuthnot*.
free generous, open
Lettuce . . . wine Both were believed to induce sleep, and lettuce to counteract sexual desire.
Probatum est "it is proved" (to work)
Celsus a physician, named for the chief Roman writer on medicine
Hartshorn ammonia, used in sleeping potions
Caesar's King George II
bays poet laureateship
Sir Richard Blackmore, poet and physician (1655–1729), author of several wretched epics
Brunswick George II's inherited title, from the German duchy his family had ruled
Budgell's Eustace Budgell (1686–1737), cousin and protégé of Addison, who wrote a ludicrous celebration of George and of the horse shot out from under him in battle
Carolina Queen Caroline

Lull with Amelia's° liquid name the Nine,°
And sweetly flow through all the royal line.
 P. Alas! few verses touch their nicer° ear;
They scarce can bear their *laureate* twice a year;°
And justly Caesar scorns the poet's lays,°
It is to *history* he trusts for praise.
 F. Better be Cibber, I'll maintain it still,
Than ridicule all taste, blaspheme quadrille,°
Abuse the City's best good men° in metre,
And laugh at peers that put their trust in Peter.
Even those you touch not, hate you.
 P. What should ail them?
 F. A hundred smart in Timon and in Balaam.°
The fewer still you name, you wound the more;
Bond° is but one, but Harpax° is a score.
 P. Each mortal has his pleasure: none deny
Scarsdale° his bottle, Darty° his ham-pie;
Ridotta° sips and dances, till she see
The doubling lustres° dance as fast as she;
Fox° loves the Senate, Hockley Hole° his brother,
Like in all else, as one egg to another.
I love to pour out all my self, as plain
As downright Shippen° or as old Montaigne:°
In them, as certain to be loved as seen,
The soul stood forth, nor kept a thought within;
In me what spots (for spots I have) appear,
Will prove at least the medium must be clear.
In this impartial glass, my Muse intends
Fair to expose myself, my foes, my friends;
Publish the present age; but where my text
Is vice too high,° reserve it for the next:
My foes shall wish my life a longer date,
And every friend the less lament my fate.
My head and heart thus flowing through my quill,

Amelia's the third of the royal children
Nine the Muses
nicer more delicate
twice a year at the New Year and the king's birthday, occasions for obligatory odes
poet's lays George II had a well-known dislike of poetry and was supposed to have complained of Pope, "Why will not my subjects write in prose?" With Colley Cibber as laureate, he had better grounds than usual.
quadrille a fashionable card game
City's . . . men prosperous merchants or financiers (cf. ll. 3 and 4 above)
Timon . . . Balaam fictitious characters in the *Epistle to Burlington*, ll. 99 ff., and another satire, the *Epistle to Bathurst*
Bond Denis Bond (d. 1747), expelled from Parliament for a breach of trust and convicted of embezzlement as well
Harpax from Greek for "robber," a name that could be widely applied
Scarsdale the Earl of Scarsdale, well known for his love of drink
Darty Charles Dartineuf, a celebrated epicure
Ridotta a type of society woman
lustres crystals in chandeliers
Fox Stephen Fox, friend of Lord Hervey and loyal supporter of Walpole
Hockley Hole where bear-baiting took place, a resort of Henry Fox, also a Walpole supporter
Shippen William Shippen, a leading Jacobite and opponent of Walpole, outspoken and incorruptible
Montaigne whose essays are candidly self-revealing, open, and free
high in rank or power

Verse-man or prose-man, term me which you will,
Papist or Protestant, or both between,
Like good Erasmus° in an honest mean,
In moderation placing all my glory,
While Tories call me Whig, and Whigs a Tory.
Satire's my weapon, but I'm too discreet
To run amuck and tilt at all I meet;
I only wear it in a land of hectors,°
Thieves, supercargoes,° sharpers, and directors.°
Save but our army! and let Jove encrust
Swords, pikes, and guns, with everlasting rust!
Peace is my dear delight—not Fleury's° more:
But touch me, and no Minister so sore.
Whoe'er offends, at some unlucky time
Slides into verse, and hitches in a rhyme,
Sacred to ridicule his whole life long,
And the sad burden° of some merry song.
  Slander or poison dread from Delia's rage,
Hard words or hanging, if your judge be Page.°
From furious Sappho° scarce a milder fate,
Poxed° by her love, or libelled by her hate.
Its proper power to hurt, each creature feels;
Bulls aim their horns, and asses lift their heels;
'Tis a bear's talent not to kick but hug;
And no man wonders he's not stung by Pug.°
So drink with Walters or with Chartres eat,
They'll never poison you, they'll only cheat.
  Then, learnèd sir! (to cut the matter short)
Whate'er my fate, or well or ill at Court,
Whether old age, with faint but cheerful ray,
Attends to gild the evening of my day,
Or death's black wing already be displayed,
To wrap me in the universal shade;
Whether the darkened room to muse invite,
Or whitened wall provoke the skewer to write:°
In durance, exile, Bedlam, or the Mint,°
Like Lee or Budgell,° I will rhyme and print.
  F. Alas, young man! your days can ne'er be long,

Erasmus the detached scholar and humanist, who refused to involve himself in the controversies of the Reformation
hectors bullies
supercargoes officers aboard ship who were concerned only with the cargo and were proverbial for their wealth
directors Those of the South Sea Company had been notorious for fraud.
Fleury's the French cardinal (1653–1743) who pursued, under Louis XV, a policy of peace
burden refrain
Page Sir Francis Page, a judge quick to see guilt and to punish severely
Sappho probably referring to Lady Mary Wortley Montagu, but no doubt to others as well
Poxed infected with syphilis
Pug a common name for a pet dog
provoke . . . write with whatever instruments are available in a madhouse or prison
Mint the sanctuary for debtors
Lee or Budgell The playwright Nathanael Lee (1653–92) and Budgell (l. 27) were both insane for a time.

In flower of age you perish for a song!
Plums° and directors, Shylock° and his wife,
Will club their testers,° now, to take your life!
  P. What? armed for virtue when I point the pen,
Brand the bold front° of shameless guilty men;
Dash the proud gamester in his gilded car;
Bare the mean heart that lurks beneath a star;°
Can there be wanting, to defend her cause,
Lights of the Church, or guardians of the laws?
Could pensioned Boileau° lash in honest strain
Flatterers and bigots even in Louis' reign?
Could laureate Dryden pimp and friar° engage,
Yet neither Charles nor James° be in a rage?
And I not strip the gilding off a knave,
Unplaced, unpensioned, no man's heir or slave?
I will, or perish in the generous cause:
Hear this, and tremble! you who 'scape the laws.
Yes, while I live, no rich or noble knave
Shall walk the world, in credit, to his grave.
To Virtue only and her friends a friend,
The world beside may murmur or commend.
Know, all the distant din that world can keep,
Rolls o'er my grotto,° and but soothes my sleep.
There, my retreat the best companions grace,
Chiefs out of war and statesmen out of place.°
There St. John° mingles with my friendly bowl,
The feast of reason and the flow of soul:
And he, whose lightning pierced the Iberian lines,°
Now forms my quincunx,° and now ranks my vines,
Or tames the genius of the stubborn plain,
Almost as quickly as he conquered Spain.
  Envy must own, I live among the great,
No pimp of pleasure, and no spy of state,
With eyes that pry not, tongue that ne'er repeats,
Fond to spread friendships, but to cover heats;
To help who want, to forward who excel;
This, all who know me, know; who love me, tell;

Plums those who had acquired the sum of £100,000
Shylock any usurer, but also an adaptation of the name of the Earl of Selkirk, a widely unloved Scottish peer
club their testers pool their wealth
front brow, where criminals were branded
star the decoration for Knight of the Garter
Boileau Nicolas Boileau-Despréaux (1636–1711), eminent poet and critic, a fierce satirist even in the royal post of historiographer and in the absolute monarchy of Louis XIV
pimp and friar combined in Friar Dominick, in Dryden's comedy *The Spanish Friar* (1680)
Charles nor James Charles had made Dryden laureate in 1670 and James II retained him in that post, although the Catholic monarch banned the play for its satire on the Roman clergy.
grotto the artificial cave on Pope's estate at Twickenham
place office
St. John Bolingbroke, formerly with Harley at the head of Queen Anne's government, for a long time in self-imposed exile abroad
he . . . Iberian lines Charles Mordaunt (1658–1735), Earl of Peterborough, who captured Barcelona and Valencia in 1705–6
quincunx a planting of five trees, one at the center of the square formed by the rest

And who unknown defame me, let them be
Scribblers or peers, alike are *mob* to me.
This is my plea, on this I rest my cause—
What saith my counsel, learnèd in the laws?
F. Your plea is good; but still I say, beware!
Laws are explained by men—so have a care.
It stands on record, that in Richard's° times
A man was hanged for very honest rhymes.
Consult the statute: *quart*. I think, it is,
Edwardi sext. or *prim. et quint. Eliz.*
See *Libels, Satires*—here you have it—read.
P. *Libels* and *satires!* lawless things indeed!
But grave *epistles*, bringing vice to light,
Such as a King might read, a Bishop write,
Such as Sir ROBERT° would approve—
F. Indeed?
The case is altered—you may then proceed;
In such a cause the plaintiff will be hissed,
My Lords the Judges laugh, and you're dismissed.

1733

Epilogue to the Satires

In Two Dialogues

Dialogue I

Fr[iend]. Not twice a twelvemonth you appear in print,
And when it comes, the court see nothing in't.
You grow correct, that once with rapture writ,
And are, besides, too *moral* for a wit.
Decay of parts, alas! we all must feel—
Why now, this moment, don't I see you steal?
'Tis all from Horace; Horace long before ye
Said, 'Tories called him Whig, and Whigs a Tory;'°
And taught his Romans, in much better metre,
'To laugh at fools who put their trust in Peter.'°
But Horace, sir, was delicate, was nice;
Bubo° observes, he lashed no sort of *vice:*
Horace would say, Sir Billy° *served the crown,*
Blunt° could *do business*, Huggins° *knew the town;*

Richard's Richard III
Sir Robert Walpole
Tories called . . . Tory Cf. *Satire* II.i.68.
To laugh . . . Peter Peter Walter, the money-lender; see l. 121 below; Epilogue II. 57–58 and note; and, above, Satire II.i.3 and note, and II.i.40.
Bubo "Some guilty person very fond of making such an observation" (Pope); cf. *Epistle to Dr. Arbuthnot*, l. 280
Sir Billy Sir William Yonge (d. 1755), a prominent Whig of whom Lord Hervey wrote, "His name was proverbially used to express everything pitiful, corrupt, and contemptible"
Blunt Sir John Blunt (1665–1733), director of the South Sea Company, upon whose collapse he was forced to render his estate of almost £200,000
Huggins John Huggins (d. 1745), warden of Fleet Prison. Found guilty of extortion and cruelty and tried for the murder of a prisoner, he was acquitted because of the testimony of prominent character witnesses.

In Sappho° touch the *failings of the sex,*
In reverend bishops note some *small neglects,*
And own, the Spaniard° did a *waggish thing,*
Who cropped our ears, and sent them to the king.
His sly, polite, insinuating style
Could please at court, and make Augustus smile:
An artful manager, that crept between
His friend and shame, and was a kind of *screen.*°
But 'faith your very friends will soon be sore;
Patriots° there are, who wish you'd jest no more—
And where's the glory? 'twill be only thought
The Great Man° never offered you a groat.
Go see Sir Robert——
  P. See Sir Robert!—hum—
And never laugh—for all my life to come?
Seen him I have, but in his happier hour
Of social pleasure, ill-exchanged for power;
Seen him, uncumbered with the venal tribe,
Smile without art, and win without a bribe.
Would he oblige me? let me only find,
He does not think me what he thinks mankind.°
Come, come, at all I laugh he laughs, no doubt;
The only difference is, I dare laugh out.
  F. Why yes: with *Scripture* still you may be free;
A horselaugh, if you please, at *honesty;*
A joke on Jekyl,° or some odd *Old Whig*
Who never changed his principles, or wig:°
A patriot is a fool in every age,
Whom all Lord Chamberlains° allow the stage:
These nothing hurts; they keep their fashion still,
And wear their strange old virtue, as they will.
  If any ask you, 'Who's the man, so near
His prince, that writes in verse, and has his ear?'
Why, answer Lyttleton,° and I'll engage

Sappho Cf. *Satire* II.i.83.
Spaniard The captain of a Spanish ship cut off the ear of an English ship captain, Jenkins, and told him to carry it to his master, the king. While this eventually helped bring on war with Spain, it was still being investigated at the time the poem appeared, and Pope's irony is directed in part at Walpole's extreme reluctance to risk war.
screen a "metaphor peculiarly appropriated to a certain person in power" (Pope); i.e. Walpole, who opposed parliamentary inquiries into public frauds and was accused of being a "corrupt and all-screening minister"
Patriots a term applied to those in opposition to Walpole "though some of them . . . had views too mean and interested to deserve that name" (Pope)
Great Man a common phrase for Walpole as first minister
what . . . mankind alluding to Walpole's reported maxim, "All men have their price"
Jekyl Sir Joseph Jekyl (1663–1738), "a true Whig in his principles, and a man of the utmost probity. He sometimes voted against the Court, which drew upon him the laugh here described of *one* who bestowed it equally upon religion and honesty." (Pope)
wig still wearing the full-bottomed wig, at that time out of fashion with younger men
Lord Chamberlains given authority by Walpole's Licensing Act (1737) to forbid performances of politically dangerous plays
Lyttleton George, Baron Lyttleton (1709–73), secretary to the Prince of Wales and a strong opponent of Walpole, "distinguished for both his writings and speeches in the spirit of liberty" (Pope)

The worthy youth shall ne'er be in a rage:
But were his verses vile, his whisper base,
You'd quickly find him in Lord Fanny's° case.
Sejanus, Wolsey,° hurt not honest Fleury,°
But well may put some statesmen in a fury.
  Laugh then at any, but at fools or foes;
These you but anger, and you mend not those.
Laugh at your friends, and, if your friends are sore,
So much the better, you may laugh the more;
To vice and folly to confine the jest,
Sets half the world, God knows, against the rest,
Did not the sneer of more impartial men
At sense and virtue, balance all again.
Judicious wits spread wide the ridicule,
And charitably comfort knave and fool.
  P. Dear sir, forgive the prejudice of youth:
Adieu distinction, satire, warmth, and truth!
Come, harmless characters that no one hit;
Come, Henley's oratory,° Osborn's wit!°
The honey dropping from Favonio's° tongue,
The flowers of Bubo, and the flow of Young!°
The gracious dew of pulpit eloquence,°
And all the well-whipped cream of courtly sense,
That first was Hervey's, Fox's next, and then
The Senate's, and then Hervey's once again.
O come, that easy Ciceronian style,
So Latin, yet so English all the while,
As, though the pride of Middleton and Bland,°
All boys may read, and girls may understand!
Then might I sing without the least offence,
And all I sung should be the *Nation's Sense;*°

Lord Fanny's John, Lord Hervey; cf. *Epistle to Dr. Arbuthnot,* ll.305–33

Sejanus, Wolsey "The one the wicked minister of Tiberius; the other, of Henry VIII. The writers against the Court usually bestowed these and other odious names on the Minister" (Pope). For such names applied to Walpole, see *Epilogue* II.137.

Fleury cardinal and minister to Louis XV of France, praised by the Patriots for his wisdom and honesty; cf. *Satire* II.i.75.

Henley's oratory John Henley, a popular preacher who called himself the "restorer of ancient eloquence," charged a shilling for admission, and trained gentlemen in elocution.

Osborn's wit James Pitt, a journalist and political hireling, wrote in defense of Walpole under many names, among them Socrates and Francis Osborne; known for the "heaviness of his style" as Mother Osborne.

Favonio's from Favonius, the gentle west wind

The flowers . . . Young so coupled in the *Epistle to Dr. Arbuthnot,* l. 280. Dodington was not only dishonest but pretentious; Yonge (Young) was described by Lord Hervey as "talking eloquently without a meaning and expatiating agreeably upon nothing."

pulpit eloquence In this and the following lines Pope refers to some florid flattery that he believed Lord Hervey had composed. It was delivered by Henry Fox as a parliamentary address on the occasion of Queen Caroline's death and became "The Senate's" (l. 72) when Commons approved it and sent it to the king. It later reappeared in Hervey's Latin epitaph for the Queen. Cf. *Epilogue* II.164–80.

Middleton and Bland Conyers Middleton, theologian and librarian at Cambridge, was writing a life of Cicero, dedicated to Hervey in 1741. He helped correct the Latin of Hervey's epitaph, described by Pope as "between Latin and English." Henry Bland, Provost of Eton, translated the last act of Addison's *Cato* into Latin and published it through Walpole's help. He may have helped with the epitaph, too; both men would represent learning used (even hired) to give pretentious form to court flattery.

Nation's Sense the official view, Walpole's word for "consensus"

Or teach the melancholy Muse to mourn,
Hang the sad verse on Carolina's urn,
And hail her passage to the realms of rest,
All parts performed, and *all* her children blest![°]
So—satire is no more—I feel it die—
No *gazetteer*[°] more innocent than I—
And let, a-God's name, every fool and knave
Be graced through life, and flattered in his grave.
F. Why so? If satire knows its time and place,
You still may lash the greatest—in disgrace:
For merit will by turns forsake them all.
Would you know when? exactly when they fall.
But let all satire in all changes spare
Immortal Selkirk,[°] and grave De la Ware.[°]
Silent and soft, as saints remove to Heaven,
All ties dissolved, and every sin forgiven,
These may some gentle ministerial wing
Receive, and place forever near a king!
There, where no passion, pride, or shame transport,
Lulled with the sweet nepenthe[°] of a court;
There, where no father's, brother's, friend's disgrace
Once break their rest, or stir them from their place:[°]
But past the sense of human miseries,
All tears are wiped for ever from all eyes;[°]
No cheek is known to blush, no heart to throb,
Save when they lose a question,[°] or a job.[°]
P. Good Heaven forbid, that I should blast their glory,
Who know how like Whig ministers to Tory,
And when three sovereigns died, could scarce be vext,
Considering what a *gracious Prince* was next.
Have I, in silent wonder, seen such things
As pride in slaves, and avarice in kings;
And at a peer or peeress shall I fret
Who starves a sister, or forswears a debt?
Virtue, I grant you, is an empty boast;
But shall the dignity of *vice* be lost?
Ye Gods! shall Cibber's son[°] without rebuke,

All parts . . . blest Queen Caroline was reported to have died without taking the last sacrament and without being reconciled with her son, the Prince of Wales.
gazetteer a journalist hired by the government to present its view
Immortal Selkirk Charles Douglas, Earl of Selkirk (1663–1739). "He was of the Bedchamber to King William; he was so to King George I; he was so to King George II" (Pope).
grave De la Ware John West, 1st Earl De la Ware (1693–1766), an indefatigable supporter of Walpole, "very skillful in all the forms of the House, in which he discharged himself with great gravity" (Pope)
nepenthe a potion that brings forgetfulness of grief or suffering
place with a punning reference to political appointment
All tears . . . eyes Cf. "and the Lord God will wipe away tears from off all faces" (Isaiah 25:8).
question parliamentary motion
job opportunity for bribery or profit
Cibber's son Colley Cibber's son Theophilus, the actor

Swear like a lord, or Rich° outwhore a duke?
A favourite's porter with his master vie,
Be bribed as often, and as often lie?
Shall Ward° draw contracts with a statesman's skill?
Or Japhet° pocket, like his Grace,° a Will?
Is it for Bond,° or Peter,° (paltry things)
To pay their debts, or keep their faith, like kings?
If Blount° dispatched himself, he played the man,
And so mayst thou, illustrious Passeran!°
But shall a printer,° weary of his life,
Learn from their books, to hang himself and wife?
This, this, my friend, I cannot, must not bear;
Vice thus abused, demands a nation's care:
This calls the Church to deprecate our sin,
And hurls the thunder of the laws on *gin.*°
  Let modest Foster,° if he will, excel
Ten metropolitans° in preaching well;
A simple Quaker, or a Quaker's wife,
Outdo Landaffe° in doctrine,—yea in life:
Let humble Allen,° with an awkward shame,
Do good by stealth, and blush to find it fame.
Virtue may choose the high or low degree,
'Tis just alike to Virtue, and to me;
Dwell in a monk, or light upon a king,
She's still the same, beloved, contented thing.
Vice is undone, if she forgets her birth,
And stoops from angels to the dregs of earth:
But 'tis the *fall* degrades her to a whore;
Let *greatness* own her, and she's mean no more:
Her birth, her beauty, crowds and courts confess,
Chaste matrons praise her, and grave bishops bless;°
In golden chains the willing world she draws,

Rich John Rich, theatrical manager; producer of pantomimes and of Gay's *The Beggar's Opera* (1728)
Ward John Ward (d. 1755), convicted of forgery and expelled from Commons in 1726
Japhet Japhet Crook, convicted in 1731 of forgery and of fraud in obtaining a will; condemned to stand in the pillory, have his ears cut off and his nose slit, forfeit his goods, and be imprisoned for life
his Grace Archbishop Wake handed the will of George I to his son, who suppressed it.
Bond Denis Bond, who embezzled the funds of the Charitable Corporation
Peter Peter Walter. See l. 10 above and note; Epilogue II.57–58 and note.
Blount Charles Blount (1654–93), deistic or freethinking writer who stabbed himself out of disappointed love and died of the wound
Passeran Alberto Radicati, Count of Passerano, a Piedmontese freethinker who fled to England, where he wrote a notorious defense of suicide
printer as in fact happened in 1732
gin whose excessive use was not successfully restrained by an Act of 1736
Foster James Foster, an Anabaptist minister and brilliant preacher whom Pope, it was reported, went to hear
metropolitans bishops
Landaffe the holder of a "poor bishopric in Wales, as poorly supplied" (Pope); i.e. both poor and poorly filled
humble Allen Ralph Allen of Bath (1694–1764), friend of Pope and Henry Fielding, reformer of the postal service, famous for his philanthropy
Chaste matrons . . . bless alluding to: (1) Justinian's elevation of the prostitute and entertainer Theodora as his empress; (2) Walpole's belated but scandalous marriage in 1738 to Molly Skerrett, his mistress of many years and the mother of two of his children; (3) in the following lines, the Scarlet Whore of Revelation 17

And hers the gospel is, and hers the laws,
Mounts the tribunal, lifts her scarlet head,
And sees pale Virtue carted° in her stead.
Lo! at the wheels of her triumphal car,°
Old England's Genius, rough with many a scar,
Dragged in the dust! his arms hang idly round,
His flag inverted° trails along the ground!
Our youth, all liveried° o'er with foreign gold,
Before her dance: behind her, crawl the old!
See thronging millions to the pagod° run,
And offer country, parent, wife, or son!
Hear her black trumpet through the land proclaim,
That 'Not to be corrupted is the shame.'
In soldier, churchman, patriot, man in power,
'Tis avarice all, ambition is no more!
See, all our nobles begging to be slaves!
See, all our fools aspiring to be knaves!
The wit of cheats, the courage of a whore,
Are what ten thousand envy and adore.
All, all look up, with reverential awe,
On crimes that scape, or triumph o'er the law:
While truth, worth, wisdom, daily they decry—
'Nothing is sacred now but villainy.'
Yet may this verse (if such a verse remain)
Show there was one who held it in disdain.

Dialogue II

Fr[iend], 'Tis all a libel—Paxton° (sir) will say.
P. Not yet, my friend! tomorrow faith it may;
And for that very cause I print today.
How should I fret to mangle every line,
In reverence to the sins of *Thirty-nine!*°
Vice with such giant strides comes on amain,
Invention strives to be before in vain;
Feign what I will, and paint it e'er so strong,
Some rising genius sins up to my song.
F. Yet none but you by name the guilty lash;
Even Guthry° saves half Newgate by a dash.
Spare then the person, and expose the vice.
P. How, sir! not damn the sharper, but the dice?
Come on then, satire! general, unconfined,

carted exhibited as prostitutes were, or carried to execution
triumphal car the conqueror's chariot
flag inverted another reference (cf. ll. 17–18) to Walpole's foreign policy of peace at any price
liveried wearing the uniforms of service
pagod shrine or pagoda
Paxton Nicholas Paxton (d. 1744), an official appointed to scan new publications for slurs or libels upon Walpole's government
Thirty-nine The poem was originally published under the title *One Thousand Seven Hundred and Thirty-Eight*.
Guthry the ordinary or chaplain of Newgate Prison, who published the memoirs or confessions of criminals, "often prevailed upon to be so tender of their reputation as to set down no more than the initials of their name" (Pope)

Spread thy broad wing, and souse° on all the kind.
Ye statesmen, priests, of one religion all!
Ye tradesmen, vile, in army, court, or hall!°
Ye reverend atheists. F. Scandal! name them, who?
P. Why that's the thing you bid me not to do.
Who starved a sister, who forswore a debt,
I never named; the town's inquiring yet.
The poisoning dame— F. You mean—
P. I don't.— F. You do.
P. See, now I keep the secret, and not you!
The bribing statesmen— F. Hold! too high you go.
P. The bribed elector— F. There you stoop too low.
P. I fain would please you, if I knew with what:
Tell me, which knave is lawful game, which not?
Must great offenders, once escaped the crown,
Like royal harts, be never more run down?
Admit your law to spare the knight requires,
As beasts of nature may we hunt the squires?
Suppose I censure—you know what I mean—
To save a bishop, may I name a dean?°
F. A dean, sir? no: his fortune is not made;
You hurt a man that's rising in the trade.
P. If not the tradesman who set up today,
Much less the prentice who tomorrow may.
Down, down, proud satire! though a realm be spoiled,°
Arraign no mightier thief than wretched Wild;°
Or, if a court or country's made a job,°
Go drench° a pickpocket, and join the mob.
But, sir, I beg you (for the love of vice!)
The matter's weighty, pray consider twice;
Have you less pity for the needy cheat,
The poor and friendless villain, than the great?
Alas! the small discredit of a bribe
Scarce hurts the lawyer, but undoes the scribe.°
Then better sure it charity becomes
To tax directors, who (thank God) have plums;°
Still better, ministers; or, if the thing
May pinch even there—why, lay it on a king.
F. Stop! stop!
P. Must satire, then, nor rise nor fall?
Speak out, and bid me blame no rogues at all.
F. Yes, strike that Wild, I'll justify the blow.

souse swoop like a hawk on its prey
hall Westminster Hall, the chief law court of England
dean chief officer of a cathedral chapter, of lower rank than a bishop
spoiled despoiled
Wild Jonathan Wild, thief, fence, and informer, hanged in 1725 (see l. 55); cf. Gay, *The Beggar's Opera* (whose character of Peachum is based on Wild) and accompanying selections from Defoe and Fielding
made a job turned to personal gain
drench a common punishment, by ducking or under the public pump
scribe the scrivener or copyist, law clerk
plums large sums, usually £100,000

P. Strike? why, the man was hanged ten years ago:
Who now that obsolete example fears?
Even Peter° trembles only for his ears.
F. What, always Peter? Peter thinks you mad,
You make men desperate, if they once are bad:
Else might he take to virtue some years hence—
P. As Selkirk, if he lives, will love the Prince.°
F. Strange spleen to Selkirk!
P. Do I wrong the man?
God knows, I praise a courtier where I can.
When I confess, there is who feels for fame
And melts to goodness, need I Scarborough° name?
Pleased let me own, in Esher's peaceful grove°
(Where Kent° and Nature vie for Pelham's love)
The scene, the master, opening to my view,
I sit and dream I see my Craggs° anew!
Even in a bishop I can spy desert;
Secker° is decent, Rundle° has a heart,
Manners with candour are to Benson° given,
To Berkeley,° every virtue under heaven.
But does the court a worthy man remove?
That instant, I declare, he has my love:
I shun his zenith, court his mild decline;
Thus Somers° once, and Halifax,° were mine.
Oft, in the clear, still mirror of retreat,
I studied Shrewsbury,° the wise and great:
Carleton's° calm sense, and Stanhope's° noble flame,
Compared, and knew their generous end the same:
How pleasing Atterbury's° softer hour!

Peter Peter Walter (*Epilogue* I.10, 121), who had just escaped the pillory the year before
As Selkirk . . . Prince Cf. "immortal Selkirk," *Epilogue* I.92 ff. Because of the hostility between the king and his son, Selkirk (always true to the man in power) cannot love the prince, but he will do so as soon as the prince in turn becomes king.
Scarborough an earl who was a steady adherent to the royal interest but "whose known honour and virtue made him esteemed by all parties" (Pope)
Esher's . . . Grove the estate in Surrey of Henry Pelham, a loyal Whig who succeeded Walpole to power in 1746
Kent William Kent (1685–1748), the architect, painter, and landscape gardener, a friend of Pope and protégé of Burlington. With Pope's advice he did much to promote the "natural" garden, and Esher was one of his finest works of "improvement"; see Headnote to *To . . . Burlington*.
Craggs "There never lived a more worthy nature, a more disinterested mind, a more open and friendly temper" (Pope)
Secker Thomas Secker, Bishop of Oxford and later Archbishop of Canterbury, famous for moderation, tolerance, and discretion
Rundle Thomas Rundle, Bishop of Derry, of whom Pope wrote, "I never saw a man so seldom whom I like so much"
Benson Martin Benson, Bishop of Gloucester
Berkeley George Berkeley (1685–1753), Bishop of Cloyne, philosopher, friend of Swift and Pope
Somers John, Lord Somers, Lord Keeper under William III. Pope, who knew him after his retirement, found Somers both "a consummate politician" and "a man of learning and politeness"; cf. the *Epistle to Dr. Arbuthnot*, l. 139 and note.
Halifax Charles Montagu, 1st Earl of Halifax (1661–1715), statesman, poet, and patron; a supporter of Pope's translation of Homer
Shrewsbury minister in three reigns and Lord Lieutenant of Ireland; cf. "Courtly Talbot" in the *Epistle to Dr. Arbuthnot*, l. 139 and note
Carleton's Henry Boyle, Baron Carleton, held many offices, including President of the Council, under William III and Anne.
Stanhope's James, Earl Stanhope, commander of the British forces in Spain in 1708; "a nobleman of equal courage, spirit, and learning" (Pope)
Atterbury's Bishop of Rochester, imprisoned in 1722 for his correspondence with the Pretender, convicted of treason and banished. Pope testified in his behalf at the trial.

How shined the soul, unconquered in the Tower!
How can I Pulteney,° Chesterfield° forget,
While Roman spirit charms, and Attic wit:
Argyle,° the state's whole thunder born to wield,
And shake alike the senate and the field:
Or Wyndham,° just to freedom and the throne,
The master of our passions, and his own.
Names, which I long have loved, nor loved in vain,
Ranked with their friends, not numbered with their train;
And if yet higher° the proud list should end,
Still let me say! No follower, but a friend.
  Yet think not, friendship only prompts my lays;
I follow *virtue;* where she shines, I praise:
Point she to priest or elder, Whig or Tory,
Or round a Quater's beaver cast a glory.
I never (to my sorrow I declare)
Dined with the Man of Ross,° or my Lord Mayor.°
Some, in their choice of friends (nay, look not grave)
Have still a secret bias to a knave:
To find an honest man I beat about,
And love him, court him, praise him, in or out.
  F. Then why so few commended?
  P. Not so fierce;
Find you the virtue, and I'll find the verse.
But random praise—the task can ne'er be done;
Each mother asks it for her booby son,
Each widow asks it for *the best of men,*
For him she weeps, and him she weds again.
Praise cannot stoop, like satire, to the ground;
The number° may be hanged, but not be crowned.
Enough for half the greatest of these days,
To scape my censure, not expect my praise.
Are they not rich? what more can they pretend?
Dare they to hope a poet for their friend?
What Richelieu° wanted, Louis° scarce could gain,
And what young Ammon° wished, but wished in vain.
No power the muse's friendship can command;
No power, when virtue claims it, can withstand:

Pulteney William Pulteney (1686–1764), a leading opponent of Walpole and brilliant orator in Commons
Chesterfield Philip Dormer Stanhope, 4th Earl of Chesterfield (1694–1773) and grandson of Halifax, the Trimmer; another opponent of Walpole and friend of Pope; later author of famous letters to his son
Argyle John Campbell, 2nd Duke of Argyle, earlier a general, later an influential convert to the opposition to Walpole
Wyndham Sir William, a leader of the Tory opposition, a man of "the utmost judgment and temper" (Pope)
yet higher perhaps referring to Pope's friendship with the Prince of Wales
Man of Ross John Kyrle, celebrated by Pope in an earlier poem for the great public benefits he performed on an income of only £500 a year
my Lord Mayor Sir John Barnard, religious, modest, an example of both private and public virtue
number multitude, the many
Richelieu (1585–1642) French cardinal and statesman; principal minister of Louis XIII
Louis Louis XIV, patron of such poets as Boileau (cf. l. 231)
Ammon Alexander the Great, who envied Achilles the fame that Homer had bestowed

To Cato, Virgil paid one honest line;°
O let my country's friends illumine mine!
—What are you thinking? F. Faith, the thought's no sin,
I think your friends are out, and would be in.
P. If merely to come in, sir, they go out,
The way they take is strangely round about.
F. They too may be corrupted, you'll allow?
P. I only call those knaves who are so now.
Is that too little? Come then, I'll comply—
Spirit of Arnall!° aid me while I lie.
Cobham's° a coward, Polwarth° is a slave,
And Lyttleton° a dark, designing knave,
St. John° has ever been a wealthy fool—
But let me add, Sir Robert's° mighty dull,
Has never made a friend in private life,
And was, besides, a tyrant to his wife.
But, pray, when others praise him, do I blame?
Call Verres, Wolsey,° any odious name?
Why rail they then, if but a wreath of mine,
Oh all-accomplished° St. John! deck thy shrine?
What! shall each spur-galled hackney° of the day,
When Paxton° gives him double pots° and pay,
Or each new-pensioned sycophant, pretend°
To break my windows if I treat a friend?°
Then wisely plead, to me they meant no hurt,
But 'twas my guest at whom they threw the dirt?
Sure, if I spare the minister, no rules
Of honour bind me, not to maul his tools;
Sure, if they cannot cut, it may be said
His saws are toothless, and his hatchet's lead.
It angered Turenne,° once upon a day,
To see a footman kicked that took his pay:

line *Aeneid* VIII.670, "And far apart the good, and Cato giving them laws," perhaps in praise of Cato Uticensis, who upheld republican ideals; cf. Pope's adaptation of that line in an ironic vein (*Epistle to Dr. Arbuthnot*, l. 209 and note)
Arnall William Arnall, a hireling political journalist
Cobham's friend of Pope and the builder of Stowe (*Epistle to Burlington*, l. 70), a distinguished general discharged for opposing Walpole's screening of the South Sea Company directors; thereupon a leading opposition Whig
Polwarth Hugh Hume, 3rd Earl of Marchmont (1708–94), one of the "boy patriots" in the Whig opposition. Walpole respected his abilities and regretted his intransigent probity.
Lyttleton Cf. *Epilogue* I.29 and note; a patron of Fielding, who was to dedicate *Tom Jones* to him in 1749.
St. John Henry, Viscount Bolingbroke (1678–1751), friend of Pope, Swift, and Gay; leader with Harley of the Tory government under Anne and of the opposition to Walpole later; a brilliant orator and man of learning, to whom Pope addressed the *Essay on Man*
Sir Robert's Walpole, ironically denied his real attributes. He was personally attractive and totally indifferent to his first wife's infidelities.
Verres, Wolsey Cf. *Epilogue* I.51 and note; both "names" were derived from men who had used their office to gain great personal wealth.
all-accomplished "Lord Bolingbroke is something superior to anything I have seen in human nature" (Pope).
hackney hack writer, hireling
Paxton The censor of l. 1 was also in charge of Walpole's patronage to hired journalists.
pots of ale
pretend attempt
treat a friend as happened at Twickenham when Pope was entertaining Bolingbroke and Lord Bathurst
Turenne (1611–75), Henri, vicomte de, Marshal of France

But when he heard the affront the fellow gave,
Knew one a man of honour, one a knave;
The prudent general turned it to a jest,
And begged, he'd take the pains to kick the rest.
Which not at present having time to do—
F. Hold, sir! for God's sake, where's the affront to you?
Against your worship when had Selkirk writ?
Or Page° poured forth the torrent of his wit?
Or grant the bard whose distich all commend
[*In power a servant, out of power a friend*]°
To Walpole guilty of some venial sin,
What's that to you who ne'er was out nor in?
The priest whose flattery bedropped the crown,
How hurt he you? he only stained the gown.
And how did, pray, the florid youth° offend,
Whose speech you took, and gave it to a friend?
P. Faith, it imports not much from whom it came;
Whoever borrowed, could not be to blame,
Since the whole House did afterwards the same.
Let courtly wits to wits afford supply,
As hog to hog in huts of Westphaly;
If one, through nature's bounty or his lord's,
Has what the frugal, dirty soil affords,
From him the next receives it, thick or thin,°
As pure a mess almost as it came in;
The blessed benefit, not there confined,
Drops to the third, who nuzzles close behind;
From tail to mouth, they feed and they carouse:
The last full fairly gives it to the *House*.
F. This filthy simile, this beastly line,
Quite turns my stomach—
P. So does flattery mine;
And all your courtly civet cats can vent,
Perfume° to you, to me is excrement.
But hear me further—Japhet,° 'tis agreed,
Writ not, and Chartres° scarce could write or read,
In all the courts of Pindus° guiltless quite;
But pens can forge, my friend, that cannot write.
And must no egg in Japhet's face be thrown,
Because the deed he forged was not my own?
Must never patriot then declaim at gin,

Page Cf. *Satire* II.i.82.
In power . . . friend a line from Bubb Dodington's flattering verse epistle to Walpole, 1726. Dodington had for a time become adviser to the Prince of Wales, who was opposed to Walpole.
florid youth Cf. *Epilogue* I.71–72.
From him . . . thin Pope had earlier (1715) used the simile elsewhere: "Now will gain praise by copying other wits / As one hog lives on what another shits."
Perfume made from a substance with a musky odor secreted by the anal scent glands of the civet cat
Japhet Japhet Crook the forger; cf. *Epilogue* I. 120 and *Epistle to Dr. Arbuthnot,* l. 363
Chartres Francis Charteris, gambler, usurer, debauchee; cf. *Satire* II.i.4
Pindus mountain in Thessaly, a seat of the Muses; thus, in any literary judgment

Unless, good man! he has been fairly in?
No zealous pastor blame a failing spouse,
Without a staring reason° on his brows?
And each blasphemer quite escape the rod,
Because the insult's not on man, but God?
 Ask you what provocation I have had?
The strong antipathy of good to bad.
When truth or virtue an affront endures,
The affront is mine, my friend, and should be yours.
Mine, as a foe professed to false pretence,
Who think a coxcomb's honour like his sense;
Mine, as a friend to every worthy mind;
And mine as man, who feel for all mankind.°
 F. You're strangely proud.
 P. So proud, I am no slave:
So impudent, I own myself no knave:
So odd, my country's ruin makes me grave.
Yes, I am proud; I must be proud to see
Men not afraid of God, afraid of me:
Safe from the bar, the pulpit, and the throne,
Yet touched and shamed by ridicule alone.
 O sacred weapon! left for truth's defence,
Sole dread of folly, vice, and insolence!
To all but heaven-directed hands denied,
The muse may give thee, but the gods must guide.
Reverent I touch thee! but with honest zeal;
To rouse the watchmen of the public weal,
To virtue's work provoke the tardy Hall,°
And goad the prelate slumbering in his stall.
Ye tinsel insects! whom a court maintains,
That counts your beauties only by your stains,
Spin all your cobwebs o'er the eye of day!
The muse's wing shall brush you all away:
All his Grace preaches, all his Lordship° sings,
All that makes saints of queens, and gods of kings,
All, all but truth, drops deadborn from the press,
Like the last gazette,° or the last address.°
 When black ambition stains a public cause,
A monarch's sword when mad vainglory draws,
Not Waller's wreath° can hide the nation's scar,
Nor Boileau° turn the feather to a star.
Not so, when diademed with rays divine,

staring reason cuckold's horns
And mine . . . mankind an adaptation of Terence: "I am a man, and I think nothing human indifferent to me"
Hall Westminster Hall, as the seat of justice
Grace . . . Lordship bishop and peer
gazette official government journal
address the formal reply of Parliament to the king's opening speech
Waller's wreath Edmund Waller's panegyrics to Oliver Cromwell
Boileau who, in celebration of Louis XIV's conquest of the Lowlands, suggested that the feather in Louis's hat would be a comet or star portending disaster to his enemies

Touched with the flame that breaks from virtue's shrine,
Her priestess Muse forbids the good to die,
And opes the Temple of Eternity.
There, other trophies deck the truly brave,
Than such as Anstis° casts into the grave;
Far other stars° than * and * * wear,
And may descend to Mordington from Stair:°
(Such as on Hough's unsullied mitre shine,
Or beam, good Digby, from a heart like thine).°
Let Envy howl, while Heaven's whole chorus sings,
And bark at honour not conferred by kings;
Let Flattery sickening see the incense rise,
Sweet to the world, and grateful to the skies:
Truth guards the poet, sanctifies the line,
And makes immortal, verse as mean as mine.
Yes, the last pen for freedom let me draw,
When truth stands trembling on the edge of law;
Here, last of Britons! let your names be read;
Are none, none living? let me praise the dead,
And for that cause which made your fathers shine,
Fall by the votes of their degenerate line.
F. Alas! alas! pray end what you began,
And write next winter° more *Essays on Man.*

1738

The Dunciad

The poem was first published in three books in 1728, shortly after *Gulliver's Travels* and *The Beggar's Opera;* it was written in part during Swift's visit to England, and it was dedicated to Swift. In 1729 Pope amplified it as *The Dunciad Variorum* with prefaces and notes of an elaborate pseudo-scholarly sort, incorporating the forms of Dulness into the work, and he included an anthology of the scurrilous comments published about him by the dunces. Twelve years later Pope wrote a new fourth book and revised the poem, replacing the poet-critic Lewis Theobald with the playwright-actor-laureate Colley Cibber as the chief of the dunces. The dunces are, in fact, all those forces making for the debasement of English culture, and the action of the poem shows them moving westward, leaving the low scenes of the Smithfield Fair to take over the court (where George II presides in sublime indifference to questions

Anstis John Anstis, chief herald at arms, who devised symbols of honors that were often cast into the graves of great peers

stars symbols of the Order of the Garter; supply the names of (King) George and (Prince) Frederick

descend to . . . Stair from the Earl of Stair, a distinguished soldier and envoy, to Lord Mordington, whose wife kept a gambling house

Such as . . . thine "The one [John Hough, Bishop of Worcester] an assertor of the Church of England in opposition to the false measures of King James II; the other [William, Lord Digby] as firmly attached to the cause of that king; both acting out of principle, and equally men of honour and virtue" (Pope)

write next winter "This was the last poem of the kind printed by our author, with a resolution to publish no more, but to enter thus, in the most plain and solemn manner he could, a sort of *protest* against that insuperable corruption and depravity of manners which he had been so unhappy as to live to see" (Pope).

of value). This westward movement from the City to Westminster is the ironic counterpart of Aeneas' bearing the culture of fallen Troy to Latium, to found a new empire which would culminate in the Augustan Age of Virgil.

The mythic action of the poem is the subversion of high by low, as the Titan daughter Dulness reclaims the ordered realms of the Olympian deities for original darkness. She is a vast bloated deity swathed in fogs, pent up in her own world like Swift's Spider; but she is also a projection into the form of divinity of those forces of sluggish inertia, relaxation of effort and thought, and selfish indolence that inhabit every man. To worship her is to choose something easier than excellence and something less than full humanity. In the first three books Pope shows the archetypal dunce, the poet laureate Cibber; the epic games involving authors, publishers, and patrons (the games are debased and excremental, the physical index of moral and intellectual corruption); and the prophetic vision of Dulness's gradual movement from China to the West, marked by the fall of cultures in Greece and Rome and now England.

In the new fourth book Pope moves into the intellectual pursuits of man, reviving an earlier plan to deal with education and extending it to include politics and religion as well. At every point he shows the substitution of triviality for substance, of verbalism for wisdom, of relaxation for vigilance. The poem ends in a great yawn and a nation reduced to sleep, with only the poet himself awake to behold the eclipse of light and the triumph of the "uncreating word." This tragic close achieves a peculiar force: suddenly we see in all the minutiae of pedantry and frivolity a larger pattern, of mind surrendering its powers and of man subsiding—for all his refinements of pleasure—into barbarism.

From The Dunciad°

Book the Fourth

Yet, yet a moment, one dim ray of light
Indulge, dread Chaos, and eternal Night!°
Of darkness visible° so much be lent,
As half to show, half veil, the deep intent.
Ye Powers! whose mysteries restored I sing,
To whom Time bears me on his rapid wing,
Suspend a while your force inertly strong,
Then take at once the poet and the song.
  Now flamed the Dog-star's° unpropitious ray,
Smote every brain and withered every bay;

Dunciad The title is formed on the analogy of *Iliad* or *Aeneid;* its great subject is the dunce (whose name derived from that of the scholastic philosopher Duns Scotus) in all his manifestations, from the simple blockhead to the vast force of Dulness itself.
dread Chaos . . . Night Chaos was, according to Hesiod, the progenitor of all the gods. In *Paradise Lost* II, Chaos and Night rule that portion of the universe that God has not yet ordered; so here they are the rulers "of ancient night," seeking to reclaim (through their daughter Dulness) the realms that have been seized from them for light and order. The "restoration of this empire is the action of the poem" (Pope-Warburton); hereafter "P-W" will be used for those notes that Warburton provided on his own or from Pope's manuscripts.
darkness visible used of hell in *Paradise Lost* I.63
Dog-star's of Sirius, visible in the hot late summer; cf. *Epistle to Dr. Arbuthnot,* l.3

Sick was the sun, the owl forsook his bower,
The moon-struck prophet felt the madding hour:
Then rose the seed of Chaos, and of Night,
To blot out order and extinguish light,
Of dull and venal a new world to mould,
And bring Saturnian days of lead and gold.°
She mounts the throne: her head a cloud concealed,
In broad effulgence all below revealed;°
('Tis thus aspiring Dulness ever shines)
Soft on her lap her laureate son reclines.
Beneath her footstool, *Science* groans in chains,
And *Wit* dreads exile, penalties, and pains.
There foamed rebellious *Logic*, gagged and bound,
There, stripped, fair *Rhetoric* languished on the ground;
His blunted arms by *Sophistry*° are borne,
And shameless *Billingsgate* her robes adorn.
Morality, by her false guardians drawn,
Chicane in furs, and *Casuistry* in lawn,°
Gasps, as they straiten° at each end the cord,
And dies, when Dulness gives her Page° the word.
Mad *Máthesis*° alone was unconfined,
Too mad for mere material chains to bind,
Now to pure space lifts her ecstatic stare,
Now running round the circle, finds it square.
But held in tenfold bonds the *Muses* lie,
Watched both by Envy's and by Flattery's eye:
There to her heart sad Tragedy addrest
The dagger wont to pierce the tyrant's breast;
But sober History restrained her rage,
And promised vengeance on a barbarous age.
There sunk Thalia,° nerveless, cold, and dead,
Had not her sister Satire held her head:
Nor couldst thou, Chesterfield!° a tear refuse,
Thou weptst, and with thee wept each gentle° Muse.
When lo! a harlot form° soft sliding by,

lead and gold The age of Saturn was traditionally the Golden Age, but Saturn was also an alchemical symbol for lead; here lead represents the "dull," and gold, as in the Satires, the "venal" or corrupted.
all below revealed recalling the old adage, cited by P-W, "The higher you climb, the more you show your arse"
Sophistry Dulness "admits something *like* each science" (P-W); thus Sophistry for Logic, Billingsgate (the shrill abuse of fishwives) for Rhetoric, etc.
furs . . . lawn law (the ermine robes of the judge) and church (the fine linen sleeves of a bishop), each corrupted into its characteristic substitute for morality; for "Casuistry," cf. *The Rape of the Lock* V.122
straiten tighten
Page punning on Sir Francis Page, the famous "hanging judge"; cf. *Satire* II.i.82
Máthesis pure mathematics, unlimited by application; suggestive of its mystical Pythagorean uses, here madly ambitious and deluded
Thalia Muse of comedy, all but killed by the censorship of Walpole's Licensing Act of 1737
Chesterfield who spoke eloquently against the Act; cf. *Epilogue* II.84
gentle as opposed to the low substitutes, e.g. Billingsgate
harlot form opera, which had gained new favor with the importation of Italian singers; resented for its spectacle and other excesses but chiefly for destroying the fusion of sound and sense that had been achieved in the English song tradition of the Renaissance; here presented with "affected airs"

With mincing step, small voice, and languid eye;
Foreign her air, her robe's discordant pride
In patchwork fluttering, and her head aside.
By singing peers upheld on either hand,
She tripped and laughed, too pretty much to stand;
Cast on the prostrate Nine a scornful look,
Then thus in quaint recitativo° spoke:
'O *Cara! Cara!* silence all that train:
Joy to great Chaos! let Division° reign:
Chromatic tortures° soon shall drive them hence,
Break all their nerves, and fritter all their sense:
One trill shall harmonize joy, grief, and rage,
Wake the dull Church, and lull the ranting stage;
To the same notes thy sons shall hum, or snore,
And all thy yawning daughters cry, *encore*.
Another Phoebus, thy own Phoebus,° reigns,
Joys in my jigs, and dances in my chains.
But soon, ah soon, rebellion will commence,
If music meanly borrows aid from sense:
Strong in new arms, lo! giant Handel° stands,
Like bold Briareus,° with a hundred hands;
To stir, to rouse, to shake the soul he comes,
And Jove's own thunders follow Mars's drums.
Arrest him, Empress; or you sleep no more—'
She heard, and drove him to the Hibernian shore.
And now had Fame's posterior trumpet° blown,
And all the nations summoned to the throne.
The young, the old, who feel her inward sway,
One instinct seizes, and transports away.
None need a guide, by sure attraction led,
And strong impulsive gravity° of head:
None want° a place, for all their centre found,
Hung to the goddess, and cohered around.
Not closer, orb in orb,° conglobed are seen
The buzzing bees about their dusky queen.
The gathering number, as it moves along,

recitativo musical declamation, neither quite spoken nor quite sung
Division i.e. breaking up long notes into a succession of short ones and so dwelling on a single syllable of the word being sung; parodied by Swift in a mock-cantata
Chromatic tortures elaborate variations introducing notes that do not belong to the diatonic scale; "the Spartans forbade the use of it as languid and effeminate" (P-W)
thy own Phoebus i.e. the Apollo of *this* pseudo-art, but also referring to the French term *phébus*, "an appearance of light glimmering over the obscurity, a semblance of meaning without any real sense" (P-W, citing Bouhours)
Handel whose increase in "hands" in orchestra and chorus (see next line) "proved so much too manly for the fine gentlemen of his age that he was obliged to remove his music into Ireland" (P-W), on whose "Hibernian shore" (Dublin) *The Messiah* was first performed in 1741. The power of Handel, as opposed to precious and feminine opera, is made clear in l. 67.
Briareus the giant of a hundred hands who fought for Zeus and the Olympians against the Titans
posterior trumpet "her second or more certain report" (P-W), but cf. also l.18 and note above
gravity solemnity; but also gravitational attraction or impulsion, as in ll.81–84
want lack
orb in orb Cf. Milton's account of the angels in Heaven: "Thus when in orbs / Of circuit inexpressible they stood, / Orb within orb" (*Paradise Lost* V.594–96).

Involves a vast involuntary throng,
Who gently drawn, and struggling less and less,
Roll in her vortex,° and her power confess.
Not those alone who passive own her laws,
But who, weak rebels,° more advance her cause:
Whate'er of dunce in college or in town
Sneers at another, in toupee or gown;°
Whate'er of mongrel no one class admits,
A wit with dunces, and a dunce with wits.
  Nor absent they, no members of her state,
Who pay her homage in her sons, the Great;°
Who, false to Phoebus, bow the knee to Baal;°
Or, impious, preach his word without a call.
Patrons, who sneak from living worth to dead,
Withhold the pension, and set up the head;°
Or vest dull Flattery in the sacred gown;°
Or give from fool to fool the laurel crown.
And (last and worst) with all the cant of wit,
Without the soul, the Muse's hypocrite.°
  There marched the bard and blockhead, side by side,
Who rhymed for hire, and patronized for pride.
Narcissus,° praised with all a parson's power,
Looked a white lily sunk beneath a shower.
There moved Montalto° with superior air;
His stretched-out arm displayed a volume fair;
Courtiers and patriots in two ranks divide,
Through both he passed, and bowed from side to side:
But as in graceful act, with awful eye
Composed he stood, bold Benson° thrust him by:
On two unequal crutches propped he came,
Milton's on this, on that one Johnston's name.
The decent knight retired with sober rage,
Withdrew his hand, and closed the pompous page.
But (happy for him as the times went then)
Appeared Apollo's mayor and aldermen,°
On whom three hundred gold-capped youths° await,

Roll . . . vortex eddy around her
weak rebels those petty critics who do little to suppress Dulness but in fact only increase her power
toupee or gown in curled periwig (fops) or in academic gown (scholars)
Great the king and nobility
Baal any false god, presumably wealth or power
Withhold . . . head i.e. fail to support while alive and parasitically honor after death
vest . . . gown confer an ecclesiastical gown (with its income) upon a flatterer
Muse's hypocrite "He who thinks the only end of poetry is to be witty . . . who cultivates only such trifling talents in himself and encourages only such in others" (P-W)
Narcissus Lord Hervey, an epileptic, had a very white face; he was heavily flattered in the dedication of Dr. Middleton's *Life of Cicero* (1741); cf. *Epilogue* I.69–76.
Montalto Sir Thomas Hanmer, pompous and portly, published a lavish edition of Shakespeare at his own expense and for his own glory.
Benson William Benson, for political reasons and in spite of incompetence, succeeded Sir Christopher Wren as royal architect. He built a lavish monument to Milton in Westminster Abbey and commissioned a Latin translation of *Paradise Lost;* he also published several editions of Arthur Johnston's Latin version of the Psalms.
Apollo's . . . aldermen dignitaries of Oxford, whose press agreed to publish Hanmer's Shakespeare
gold-capped youths with the gold tassel of gentlemen-commoners, students who paid higher fees in return for special privileges and dress

To lug the ponderous volume off in state.
When Dulness, smiling—'Thus revive the wits!
But murder first, and mince them all to bits;
As erst Medea° (cruel, so to save!)
A new edition of old Aeson gave;
Let standard authors, thus, like trophies born,
Appear more glorious as more hacked and torn,
And you, my critics! in the chequered shade,
Admire new light through holes yourselves have made.
'Leave not a foot of verse, a foot of stone,
A page, a grave, that they can call their own;
But spread, my sons, your glory thin or thick,
On passive paper, or on solid brick.
So by each bard an alderman° shall sit,
A heavy lord shall hang at every wit,
And while on Fame's triumphal car they ride,
Some slave of mine° be pinioned to their side.'
Now crowds on crowds around the goddess press,
Each eager to present their first address.
Dunce scorning dunce beholds the next advance,
But fop shows fop superior complaisance.°
When lo! a spectre° rose, whose index hand
Held forth the virtue of the dreadful wand;
His beavered brow a birchen garland wears,
Dropping with infant's blood, and mother's tears.
O'er every vein a shuddering horror runs;
Eton and Winton° shake through all their sons.
All flesh is humbled, Westminster's bold race
Shrink, and confess the genius° of the place:
The pale boy senator yet tingling stands,
And holds his breeches close with both his hands.
Then thus: 'Since man from beast by words is known,
Words are man's province, words we teach alone.°
When reason doubtful, like the Samian letter,°
Points him two ways, the narrower is the better.
Placed at the door of learning, youth to guide,
We never suffer it to stand too wide.
To ask, to guess, to know, as they commence,
As fancy opens the quick spring of sense,

Medea who, in one version of the legend, had Aeson's daughters cut their father into pieces and cast them into a cauldron, whence, with Medea's magic, he emerged restored to youth
alderman such as Alderman Barber, who proudly placed his own name on the monument he erected to Samuel Butler
slave of mine as in Rome, where a slave was chained beside the triumphant victor (to remind him of the mutability of fortune) while he rode through the city
complaisance tolerance
spectre Dr. Richard Busby (1605–95), the famous headmaster of Westminster School, carrying his birch cane ("dreadful wand") for discipline (whence the "infant's blood"); cf. *Paradise Lost* I.392–93 for Moloch
Eton and Winton the latter Winchester; schools where Busby's influence still prevails
genius presiding deity
Since man . . . alone The humanist doctrine that eloquence is wisdom expressed now becomes a concern with words to the neglect of thought.
the Samian letter the letter Y, emblem of the crossroads of choice

We ply the memory, we load the brain,
Bind rebel wit, and double chain on chain,
Confine the thought to exercise the breath;
And keep them in the pale of words till death.
Whate'er the talents or howe'er designed,
We hang one jingling padlock° on the mind:
A poet the first day he dips his quill;
And what the last? a very poet still.
Pity! the charm works only in our wall,
Lost, lost too soon in yonder House or Hall.°
There truant Wyndham every Muse gave o'er,
There Talbot° sunk, and was a wit no more!
How sweet an Ovid, Murray° was our boast!
How many Martials were in Pulteney° lost!
Else sure some bard, to our eternal praise,
In twice ten thousand rhyming nights and days,
Had reached the work, the all that mortal can;
And South° beheld that masterpiece of man.'
'Oh' (cried the goddess) 'for some pedant reign!
Some gentle James,° to bless the land again;
To stick the doctor's° chair into the throne,
Give law to words, or war with words alone,
Senates and courts with Greek and Latin rule,
And turn the Council to a grammar school!
For sure, if Dulness sees a grateful day,
'Tis in the shade of arbitrary sway.°
O! if my sons may learn one earthly thing,
Teach but that one, sufficient for a king:
That which my priests, and mine alone, maintain,
Which as it dies, or lives, we fall, or reign:
May you, may Cam and Isis,° preach it long!
The RIGHT DIVINE of kings to govern wrong.'
Prompt at the call, around the goddess roll
Broad hats, and hoods, and caps, a sable shoal:
Thick and more thick the black blockade extends,

jingling padlock exercises in composing Greek and Latin verses
House or Hall Westminster Hall (the courts) or Parliament
Wyndham . . . Talbot two brilliant members of Parliament; cf. *Epilogue* II.79, 88
Murray William Murray (1705–93), later Lord Chief Justice and Earl of Mansfield; awarded a prize for a Latin poem by Busby ("our boast"), he became a distinguished statesman, jurist, and orator
Pulteney gifted in epigram like the Roman Martial, he became instead a political writer and leader in opposition to Walpole
South Dr. Robert South "declared a perfect epigram as difficult a performance as an epic poem, and the critics"—particularly Dryden—"say, 'an epic poem is the greatest work human nature is capable of," (P-W). The epigram becomes the culmination of Busby's and Dulness's verbalism.
James James I was both a famous pedant and the first English monarch to claim the divine right of kings
doctor's teacher's
For sure . . . sway "no branch of learning thrives well under arbitrary government but verbal" (P-W). Timeliness is given by the charges of the opposition that Walpole's monarch was seeking to subject Parliament to "dependence on the Crown"; thus the pedant Stuart—heavy and dull—becomes the counterpart of the heavier Hanoverian (manipulated as he is by Walpole).
Cam and Isis the universities of Cambridge and Oxford, named here for their rivers

A hundred head° of Aristotle's friends.°
Nor wert thou, Isis! wanting to the day,
Though Christ Church° long kept prudishly away.
Each staunch polemic,° stubborn as a rock,
Each fierce logician, still expelling Locke,°
Came whip and spur, and dashed through thin and thick
On German Crousaz, and Dutch Burgersdyck.°
As many quit the streams that murmuring fall
To lull the sons of Margaret and Clare Hall,°
Where Bentley° late tempestuous wont to sport
In troubled waters, but now sleeps in port.
Before them marched that awful Aristarch;°
Ploughed was his front with many a deep remark:°
His hat, which never vailed° to human pride,
Walker° with reverence took, and laid aside.
Low bowed the rest: he, kingly, did but nod;
So upright° Quakers please both man and God.
'Mistress! dismiss that rabble from your throne:
Avaunt——is Aristarchus yet unknown?
Thy mighty scholiast,° whose unwearied pains
Made Horace dull, and humbled Milton's strains.°
Turn what they will to verse, their toil is vain,
Critics like me shall make it prose again.
Roman and Greek grammarians! know your better:
Author of something yet more great than letter;
While towering o'er your alphabet, like Saul,
Stands our Digamma,° and o'ertops them all.
'Tis true, on words is still our whole debate,
Disputes of *Me* or *Te*, of *aut* or *at*,
To sound° or sink in *cano*, O or A,
Or give up Cicero° to C or K.
Let Freind affect to speak as Terence spoke,

head a term suggestive of cattle
Aristotle's friends those "faithful followers" who, in spite of Cartesian and Newtonian science, "never bowed the knee to Baal nor acknowledged any strange god in philosophy" (P-W)
Christ Church the one college at Oxford whose dons were least under the spell of Dulness
polemic controversialist
still expelling Locke whose work was censured in 1703 by the heads of Oxford
German . . . Burgersdyck cited as two instances of Aristotelian logicians
Margaret and Clare Hall St. John's and Clare colleges in Cambridge, "particularly famous for their skill in disputation" (P-W)
Bentley As master of Trinity College, Cambridge, Richard Bentley, the classical scholar so long a target of Swift and Pope, had been at odds with his fellows but was now at rest; with a pun on "port," the wine plentifully drunk after dinner.
Aristarch Bentley in the guise of Aristarchus, the Homeric commentator and corrector (d. 150 B.C.)
remark a term used for a note or commentary in Bentley's work
vailed yielded, was lowered
Walker the vice-master of Trinity
upright honest; also not bowing in prayer, as Bentley will not bow before Dulness
scholiast commentator
humbled Milton's strains Bentley, as editor of Milton, boldly "corrected" the text (and "humbled" its greatness) on the assumption that Milton's blindness allowed numerous errors to appear; he edited Horace also with arrogance and insensitivity.
Digamma a letter restored by Bentley in his projected edition of Homer. Since it was one gamma set upon another, it was like Saul, who was "higher than any of the people" (I Samuel 9:2).
sound stress
Cicero the pronunciation of whose name was disputed (as was that of Latin generally)

And Alsop° never but like Horace joke:
For me, what Virgil, Pliny may deny,
Manilius or Solinus° shall supply:
For Attic phrase in Plato let them seek,
I poach in Suidas° for unlicensed Greek.
In ancient sense if any needs will deal,
Be sure I give them fragments, not a meal:
What Gellius or Stobaeus° hashed before,
Or chewed by blind old scholiasts o'er and o'er.
The critic eye, that microscope of wit,
Sees hairs and pores, examines bit by bit;
How parts relate to parts, or they to whole,
The body's harmony, the beaming soul,°
Are things which Kuster, Burman, Wasse° shall see,
When man's whole frame is obvious to a *flea*.
'Ah, think not, Mistress! more true Dulness lies
In folly's cap, than wisdom's grave disguise.
Like buoys that never sink into the flood,
On learning's surface we but lie and nod.
Thine is the genuine head of many a house,
And much divinity without a Νοῦς.°
Nor could a Barrow work on every block,
Nor has one Atterbury° spoiled the flock.
See! still thy own, the heavy canon° roll,
And metaphysic smokes involve the pole.°
For thee we dim the eyes, and stuff the head
With all such reading as was never read:
For thee explain a thing till all men doubt it,
And write about it, Goddess, and about it:
So spins the silkworm small its slender store,
And labours till it clouds itself all o'er.
'What though we let some better sort of fool
Thrid° every science, run through every school?
Never by tumbler through the hoops was shown
Such skill in passing all, and touching none.
He may indeed (if sober all this time)
Plague with dispute, or persecute with rhyme.

Freind . . . Alsop Robert Freind and Anthony Alsop, two scholars who grasped the true spirit of classical literature rather than its letter
Manilius or Solinus As a philologist, Bentley is interested not in literature but in words; for his purposes minor authors are as useful as major and as important.
Suidas (*c.* 1100 A.D.) a "dictionary writer, a collector of impertinent facts and barbarous words" (P-W)
Gellius or Stobaeus the former a Roman grammarian (d. 165 A.D.), the latter a Greek compiler of extracts from ancient authors (*c.* 400 A.D.)
the beaming soul i.e. irradiating the body with form
Kuster . . . Wasse classical scholars and editors of lesser writers
without a Νοῦς Νοῦς was the Platonic word for mind, or the first cause, and that system of divinity is here hinted at which terminates in blind nature without a νοῦς (P-W); cf. ll. 487–92 below.
Barrow . . . Atterbury Isaac Barrow (1630–77) and Atterbury were brilliant scholars and eloquent preachers, the former a fine mathematician, the latter a classical scholar; for the "block," cf. l. 270 below.
canon churchman, but also artillery (cannon)
pole sky, heavens
Thrid thread, trace

We only furnish what he cannot use,
Or wed to what he must divorce, a Muse:
Full in the midst of Euclid dip at once,
And petrify a genius to a dunce:
Or set on metaphysic ground to prance,
Show all his paces, not a step advance.
With the same cement, ever sure to bind,
We bring to one dead level every mind.
Then take him to develop, if you can,
And hew the block off, and get out the man.°
But wherefore waste I words? I see advance
Whore, pupil, and laced governor° from France.
Walker! our hat'——nor more he deigned to say,
But, stern as Ajax' spectre,° strode away.
  In flowed at once a gay embroidered race,
And tittering pushed the pedants off the place:
Some would have spoken, but the voice was drowned
By the French horn, or by the opening° hound.
The first came forwards, with as easy mien,
As if he saw St. James's° and the Queen.
When thus the attendant orator° begun:
'Receive, great Empress! thy accomplished son,
Thine from the birth, and sacred° from the rod,
A dauntless infant! never scared with God.
The sire saw, one by one, his virtues wake:
The mother begged the blessing of a rake.
Thou gavest that ripeness, which so soon began,
And ceased so soon, he ne'er was boy, nor man.
Through school and college, thy kind cloud o'ercast,
Safe and unseen° the young Aeneas past:
Thence bursting glorious, all at once let down,°
Stunned with his giddy larum° half the town.
Intrepid then, o'er seas and lands he flew:°
Europe he saw, and Europe saw him too.
There all thy gifts and graces we display,
Thou, only thou, directing all our way!
To where the Seine, obsequious as she runs,
Pours at great Bourbon's feet her silken sons;°
Or Tiber, now no longer Roman, rolls,
Vain of Italian arts, Italian° souls:
To happy convents, bosomed deep in vines,

get out the man referring to the belief that in every block of stone there is a statue waiting to be freed
governor tutor
Ajax' spectre which turns sullenly from Odysseus in the underworld
opening baying, giving tongue
St. James's the royal palace
orator the tutor or governor of l. 272
sacred exempt
unseen veiled in a cloud as was Aeneas by Venus when he entered Carthage (*Aeneid* I)
let down freed, released
larum commotion
flew on the Grand Tour
her silken sons France is seen as an absolute monarchy encouraging luxury or effeminacy.
Italian as opposed to Roman

Where slumber abbots, purple as their wines:
To isles of fragrance, lily-silvered vales,
Diffusing languor in the panting gales:
To lands of singing, or of dancing slaves,
Love-whispering woods, and lute-resounding waves.
But chief her shrine where naked Venus keeps,
And Cupids ride the Lion of the Deeps;°
Where, eased of fleets, the Adriatic main
Wafts the smooth eunuch and enamoured swain.
Led by my hand, he sauntered Europe round,
And gathered every vice on Christian ground;
Saw every court, heard every king declare
His royal sense of operas or the fair;°
The stews° and palace equally explored,
Intrigued with glory, and with spirit whored;
Tried all *hors d'oeuvres,* all *liqueurs* defined,
Judicious drank, and greatly daring dined;
Dropped the dull lumber of the Latin store,°
Spoiled his own language, and acquired no more;
All classic learning lost on classic ground;
And last turned *air,* the echo of a sound!
See now, half-cured and perfectly well-bred,
With nothing but a solo in his head;
As much estate, and principle, and wit,
As Jansen, Fleetwood, Cibber° shall think fit;
Stolen° from a duel, followed by a nun,
And, if a borough choose him,° not undone;
See, to my country happy I restore
This glorious youth, and add one Venus more.
Her too receive (for her my soul adores)°
So may the sons of sons of sons of whores,
Prop thine, O Empress! like each neighbour throne,
And make a long posterity thy own.'
Pleased, she accepts the hero, and the dame,
Wraps in her veil, and frees from sense of shame.
  Then looked, and saw a lazy, lolling sort,
Unseen at church, at senate, or at court,
Of ever-listless loiterers, that attend
No cause, no trust, no duty, and no friend.
Thee too, my Paridel!° she marked thee there,
Stretched on the rack of a too easy chair,

Lion of the Deeps the winged lion, emblem of Venice as a great mercantile and naval power; famous at this time as the "brothel of Europe"
operas . . . fair typical conversational topics of George II of England
stews brothels
Latin store classical learning
Jansen . . . Cibber all gamblers and the last two theater managers, hence stewards and tutors to youth
Stolen escaped
borough choose him because members of Parliament could not be arrested for debt
my soul adores Both pupil and tutor seem attached to the former nun and new Venus.
Paridel Spenser's name for an amorous wandering squire (*The Faerie Queene* III.ix–x)

And heard thy everlasting yawn confess
The pains and penalties of idleness.
She pitied! but her pity only shed
Benigner influence on thy nodding head.
But Annius,° crafty seer, with ebon wand,
And well-dissembled emerald on his hand,
False as his gems, and cankered° as his coins,
Came, crammed with capon, from where Pollio° dines.
Soft, as the wily fox is seen to creep,
Where bask on sunny banks the simple sheep,
Walk round and round, now prying here, now there;
So he; but pious, whispered first his prayer:
'Grant, gracious Goddess! grant me still to cheat,
O may thy cloud still cover the deceit!
Thy choicer mists on this assembly shed,
But pour them thickest on the noble head.
So shall each youth, assisted by our eyes,
See other Caesars, other Homers° rise;
Through twilight ages hunt the Athenian fowl,°
Which chalcis gods, and mortals call an owl,°
Now see an Attys, now a Cecrops° clear,
Nay, Mahomet!° the pigeon at thine ear;
Be rich in ancient brass, though not in gold,
And keep his Lares,° though his house be sold;
To headless Phoebe° his fair bride postpone,
Honour a Syrian prince° above his own;
Lord of an Otho,° if I vouch it true;
Blest in one Niger,° till he knows of two.'
Mummius° o'erheard him; Mummius, fool-renowned,°
Who like his Cheops stinks above the ground,
Fierce as a startled adder, swelled, and said,
Rattling an ancient sistrum° at his head:
'Speakst thou of Syrian princes? Traitor base!
Mine, Goddess! mine is all the hornèd race.°

Annius named for a monk of Viterbo (1432–1502) famous for many forgeries of ancient manuscripts and inscriptions, committed out of vanity. His modern counterpart is more mercenary.
cankered corrupt
Pollio named for the Roman patron
other Caesars . . . Homers forged coins; here also a substitute form of greatness, such as the heroics of collecting and the artistry of acquisition
Athenian fowl the owl stamped on the coins of ancient Athens
Which chalcis . . . owl a line from Hobbes's flat-footed rendering of Homer, "chalcis" being Greek for a bird of prey
Attys . . . Cecrops forgeries of coins professedly issued by mythical kings of Athens
Mahomet Mohammed, who forbade all images, is here represented with the white pigeon that brought him divine messages and which he claimed to be the angel Gabriel.
Lares Roman statues of household gods
headless Phoebe a mutilated statue of Diana, which pre-empts the place and affection due a living bride
Syrian prince presumably as represented on a medal
Otho coin of a Roman emperor who ruled very briefly
Niger another emperor of short reign, whose coins would be very rare
Mummius a dealer in Egyptian antiquities
fool-renowned "a compound epithet in the Greek manner, *renowned by fools* or *renowned for making fools*" (P-W)
sistrum a percussion instrument used in Egyptian religious rites
hornèd race the successors of Alexander, supposedly born of the gods, represented with horns

True, he had wit, to make their value rise;
From foolish Greeks to steal them, was as wise;
More glorious yet, from barbarous hands to keep,
When Sallee rovers° chased him on the deep.
Then taught by Hermes,° and divinely bold,
Down his own throat he risked the Grecian gold;
Received each demigod,° with pious care,
Deep in his entrails—I revered them there,
I bought them, shrouded in that living shrine,
And, at their second birth, they issue mine.'
'Witness, great Ammon!° by whose horns I swore,'
(Replied soft Annius) 'this our paunch before
Still bears them, faithful; and that thus I eat,
Is to refund the medals with the meat.
To prove me, Goddess! clear of all design,
Bid me with Pollio sup, as well as dine:
There all the learned shall at the labour stand,
And Douglas° lend his soft, obstetric hand.'
The goddess smiling seemed to give consent;
So back to Pollio, hand in hand, they went.
Then thick as locusts blackening all the ground,
A tribe, with weeds and shells fantastic crowned,
Each with some wondrous gift approached the Power,
A nest, a toad, a fungus, or a flower.
But far the foremost, two, with earnest zeal,
And aspect ardent to the throne appeal.
The first thus opened: 'Hear thy suppliant's call,
Great Queen, and common Mother of us all!
Fair from its humble bed I reared this flower,°
Suckled and cheered, with air, and sun, and shower,
Soft on the paper ruff its leaves° I spread,
Bright with the gilded button tipped its head,
Then throned in glass, and named it Caroline:°
Each maid cried, charming! and each youth, divine!
Did nature's pencil° ever blend such rays,
Such varied light in one promiscuous blaze?
Now prostrate! dead! behold that Caroline:
No maid cries, charming! and no youth, divine!
And lo the wretch! whose vile, whose insect lust
Laid this gay daughter of the spring in dust.
Oh punish him, or to the Elysian shades

Sallee rovers pirates from Morocco
Hermes as god of commerce but also patron of thieves
demigod coins of emperors who claimed that status; with suggestions of the Eucharist that are sustained by "pious care" and culminate in the Second Coming of l. 386
Ammon Jupiter Ammon, from whom Alexander and his heirs claimed descent
Douglas James Douglas, a famous obstetrician and himself a collector of editions of Horace
flower a reference to the efforts in the age to produce a perfect carnation
leaves petals
Caroline for the queen, an ardent gardener; P-W pursue the theme of idolatry set forth in ll. 359–86 by citing a gardener who advertised his favorite flower as "*my* Queen Caroline"
pencil paintbrush

Dismiss my soul, where no carnation fades!'°
He ceased, and wept. With innocence of mien,
The accused stood forth, and thus addressed the queen:
'Of all the enamelled race,° whose silvery wing
Waves to the tepid zephyrs of the spring,
Or swims along the fluid atmosphere,
Once brightest shined this child of heat and air.
I saw, and started from its vernal bower
The rising game,° and chased from flower to flower.
It fled, I followed; now in hope, now pain;
It stopped, I stopped; it moved, I moved again.°
At last it fixed, 'twas on what plant it pleased,
And where it fixed, the beauteous bird° I seized:
Rose or carnation was below my care;
I meddle, Goddess! only in my sphere.
I tell the naked fact without disguise,
And, to excuse it, need but show the prize;
Whose spoils this paper° offers to your eye,
Fair even in death! this peerless *butterfly*.'
'My sons!' (she answered) 'both have done your parts:
Live happy both, and long promote our arts!
But hear a mother, when she recommends
To your fraternal care, our sleeping friends.°
The common soul, of Heaven's more frugal make,
Serves but to keep fools pert, and knaves awake:
A drowsy watchman, that just gives a knock,
And breaks our rest, to tell us what's a-clock.
Yet by some object every brain is stirred;
The dull may waken to a hummingbird;
The most recluse, discreetly opened find
Congenial matter in the cockle kind;°
The mind, in metaphysics at a loss,
May wander in a wilderness of moss;°
The head that turns at superlunar things,
Poised with a tail, may steer on Wilkins' wings.°
'O! would the sons of men once think their eyes
And reason given them but to study *flies!*
See nature in some partial narrow shape,
And let the author of the whole escape:
Learn but to trifle; or, who most observe,

no . . . fades Cf. I Peter 1:4 "To an inheritance incorruptible, and undefiled, and that fadeth not away, reserved in heaven for you."
enamelled race colorful butterflies
started . . . game idiom of the huntsman
It fled . . . again Cf. Eve's words (*Paradise Lost* IV.462–63) on first seeing her reflection in the water, failing, like Narcissus, to recognize what it is, and adoring it: "I started back, / It started back; but pleased I soon returned, / Pleased it returned as soon."
bird any winged creature; here the butterfly
this paper i.e. on which the butterfly is mounted
sleeping friends Cf. ll. 337–46 above.
cockle kind collections of scallop shells
moss of which three hundred species had been identified
Wilkins' wings John Wilkins (1614–72), bishop and first secretary of the Royal Society, proposed flights to the moon and started "some volatile geniuses upon making wings for that purpose" (P-W).

To wonder at their maker, not to serve!'°
'Be that my task' (replies a gloomy clerk,
Sworn foe to mystery,° yet divinely dark;
Whose pious hope aspires to see the day
When moral evidence° shall quite decay,
And damns implicit faith,° and holy lies,
Prompt to impose, and fond to dogmatize:)°
'Let others creep by timid steps, and slow,
On plain experience lay foundations low,
By common sense to common knowledge bred,
And last, to Nature's Cause through Nature led.°
All-seeing in thy mists, we want no guide,
Mother of arrogance, and source of pride!
We nobly take the high priori road,°
And reason downward, till we doubt of God:
Make Nature still encroach° upon his plan;
And shove him off as far as e'er we can:
Thrust some mechanic cause into his place,
Or bind in matter, or diffuse in space.°
Or, at one bound o'erleaping° all his laws,
Make God man's image, man the final cause,°
Find virtue local, all relation scorn,°
See all in *self*,° and but for self be born:
Of naught so certain as our *reason* still,
Of naught so doubtful as of *soul* and *will*.°

wonder . . . serve to lose themselves in the wonders of God's creation and to neglect his moral teaching
mystery religious mystery, doctrine that defies clear rational explanation, such as the Trinity
moral evidence the probability of the historical facts of the Bible, believed by some to decay as the events became more remote in time
implicit faith belief upon authority, unquestioning adherence without comprehension
Prompt . . . dogmatize the freethinker seen as dogmatically rejecting dogma, self-deceiving and complacently deductive even as he attacks "holy lies"
Nature's Cause . . . led Cf. *Essay on Man* IV. 331–32: "Slave to no sect, who takes no private road, / But looks through Nature, up to Nature's God."
high priori road the deductive or *a priori* method taken by Descartes in his *Meditations*, Spinoza in his *Ethics*, and Hobbes in his *Leviathan*
Nature . . . encroach explain away Providence by natural ("mechanic") causes, or create a metaphysical principle (such as Ralph Cudworth's "plastic nature") to displace or delimit a theistic God. God's "second causes" (those explicable in mechanical terms) assume more and more of the role once given to his "plan" or active ordering.
Thrust . . . space "The first of these follies is that of Descartes; the second of Hobbes; the third of some succeeding philosophers" (P-W). The last may include such as Henry More (1614–87), the Cambridge Platonist, who separated extension from matter in order to attribute extension or pure space to spirit; space for More is "an obscure representation of the essential presence of the divine being." More in turn influenced Sir Isaac Newton's conception of absolute space, and it may be to the consequence of the Newtonian mechanical view (rather than its intention) that Pope is alluding so discreetly.
o'erleaping like Satan overleaping the walls of Eden (*Paradise Lost* IV.181)
man the final cause i.e. see human happiness as the sole end of the universe and see God and his varied creation as a means to that end
Find virtue . . . scorn Here the process of contraction continues; given man as the sole end of creation, the idea of "man" gives way to "men" and morality becomes relative to local customs rather than universal, absolute, or dependent on God's will.
self the final contraction of scale, in contrast to the movement of the *Essay on Man* IV.361–72 where the soul rises "from individual to the whole," from self to "friend, parent, neighbour," thence to "country" and "next all human race," until "every creature . . . of every kind" is loved. At that point instead of God's being made in man's image (l. 478 above)—"Heaven beholds its image in his breast"—man has absorbed the capacity for divine love.
soul and will The metaphysical and moral principles of human nature are neglected by the dogmatic rationalism of the freethinkers or deists.

Oh hide the God still more! and make us see
Such as Lucretius° drew, a God like Thee:
Wrapped up in self, a God without a thought,
Regardless of our merit or default.
Or that bright image to our fancy draw,
Which Theocles° in raptured vision saw,
While through poetic scenes the Genius roves,
Or wanders wild in academic groves;
That NATURE our society° adores,
Where Tindal° dictates, and Silenus° snores.'
  Roused at his name, up rose the bousy sire,
And shook from out his pipe the seeds of fire;°
Then snapped his box,° and stroked his belly down:
Rosy and reverend, though without a gown.°
Bland and familiar to the throne he came,
Led up the Youth, and called the goddess *Dame*.
Then thus: 'From priestcraft happily set free,
Lo! every finished son returns to thee:
First slave to words, then vassal to a name,°
Then dupe to party; child and man the same;
Bounded by nature, narrowed still by art,
A trifling head, and a contracted heart.
Thus bred, thus taught, how many have I seen,
Smiling on all, and smiled on by a queen.
Marked out for honours, honoured for their birth,
To thee the most rebellious things on earth:
Now to thy gentle shadow all are shrunk,
All melted down, in pension, or in punk!°
So Kent, so Berkeley° sneaked into the grave,
A monarch's half, and half a harlot's slave.
Poor W——° nipped in folly's broadest bloom,

Lucretius (*c.* 94 B.C.–55 B.C.) whose philosophical poem *De Rerum Natura* (following Epicurean thought) seeks to free man of his fears of anthropomorphic gods and presents nature as an impartial force, free of the concerns that vex man (therefore, like Dulness, sublimely indifferent to all distinctions of value)
Theocles the philosophical visionary in the Earl of Shaftesbury's *The Moralists* (1709), here made into a simple worshiper of Nature (his "Genius"), cultivating Platonic ecstasy in the wild landscape
our society the association of freethinkers
Tindal Matthew Tindal (1657–1733), a leading deist
Silenus the fat, drunken, and debauched companion of Dionysus who appears in Virgil's Sixth Eclogue, where he is made a spokesman of the Epicurean philosophy; here also associated with Thomas Gordon, a political writer whom Walpole made Commissioner of the Wine Licenses
seeds of fire parodying Epicurean language for atoms
box snuffbox
without a gown not a priest; Silenus is usually pictured naked
First slave . . . name There follows a "recapitulation of the whole course of modern education . . . which confines youth to the study of *words* only in schools, subjects them to the authority of *systems* in the universities, and deludes them with the names of *party-distinctions* in the world; all equally concurring to narrow the understanding and establish slavery and error in literature, philosophy, and politics. The whole finished in modern free-thinking; the completion of whatever is vain, wrong, and destructive to the happiness of mankind, as it establishes *self-love* for the sole principle of action" (P-W).
punk whore
So Kent, so Berkeley the Duke of Kent and Earl of Berkeley, both holders of the highest royal honor, Knight of the Garter; possibly indebted to one of George I's mistresses ("harlot's slave")
W_____ perhaps the dissipated young Earl of Warwick

Who praises now? his chaplain on his tomb.
Then take them all, oh take them to thy breast!
Thy *Magus,*° Goddess! shall perform the rest.'
With that, a WIZARD OLD his *Cup* extends;
Which whoso tastes, forgets his former friends,
Sire, ancestors, himself. One casts his eyes
Up to a *star,*° and like Endymion° dies:
A *feather,*° shooting from another's head,
Extracts his brain; and principle is fled;
Lost is his God, his country, everything;
And nothing left but homage to a king!
The vulgar herd turn off to roll with hogs,°
To run with horses, or to hunt with dogs;
But, sad example! never to escape
Their infamy, still keep the human shape.
But she, good goddess, sent to every child
Firm impudence, or stupefaction mild;
And straight succeeded, leaving shame no room,
Cibberian forehead,° or Cimmerian gloom.°
Kind self-conceit to some her glass° applies,
Which no one looks in with another's eyes,
But, as the flatterer or dependent paint,
Beholds himself a patriot, chief, or saint.
On others Interest her gay livery° flings,
Interest that waves on party-coloured° wings:
Turned to the sun, she casts a thousand dyes,
And, as she turns, the colours fall or rise.
Others the Siren Sisters° warble round,
And empty heads console with empty sound.
No more, alas! the voice of fame they hear,
The balm of Dulness trickling in their ear.
Great C——, H——, P——, R——, K——,°
Why all your toils? your sons have learned to sing.
How quick ambition hastes to ridicule!
The sire is made a peer, the son a fool.
On some, a priest succinct in amice white°

Magus adept in occult arts, high priest, "wizard"; Walpole is suggested, his use of bribery embodied in the "Cup of Self-love," as P-W call it, of the next line
star worn by Knights of the Garter or of the Bath
Endymion loved by the Moon, thrown into perpetual sleep and visited by her each night
feather worn in the cap of Knights of the Garter
roll with hogs like the Prodigal Son (Luke 15:11) or like those transformed by Circe; but her enchantment "took away the shape and left the human mind," whereas the Magus's cup "takes away the mind and leaves the human shape" (P-W)
Cibberian forehead the brazenness of Colley Cibber (1671–1757), the poet laureate of George II and King of the Dunces in the revised *Dunciad,* particularly as shown in his autobiographical *Apology* (1740)
Cimmerian gloom referring to Homer's mythical land of constant mists and darkness, the appropriate habitat of the followers of Dulness
glass mirror
livery costume worn by retainers, whether courtiers or servants or both
party-coloured a pun on "parti-colored"; i.e. vari-colored
Siren Sisters the devotees of opera; cf. ll. 45 ff. and 324
Great . . . K—— noblemen ambitious for their families
priest . . . white a chef dressed in a white apron and cap, the counterpart of the priest's "amice" worn over head and shoulders with white vestments

Attends; all flesh is nothing in his sight!
Beeves, at his touch, at once to jelly turn,
And the huge boar is shrunk into an urn:°
The board with specious° miracles he loads,
Turns hares to larks, and pigeons into toads.
Another (for in all what one can shine?)
Explains the *sève* and *verdeur*° of the vine.
What cannot copious sacrifice atone?°
Thy truffles, Perigord! thy hams, Bayonne!
With French libation, and Italian strain,
Wash Bladen white, and expiate Hays's° stain.
Knight° lifts the head, for what are crowds undone
To three essential partridges in one?°
Gone every blush, and silent all reproach,
Contending princes mount them in their coach.
Next bidding all draw near on bended knees,
The Queen confers her *titles* and *degrees.*
Her children first of more distinguished sort,
Who study Shakespeare at the Inns of Court,°
Impale a glowworm, or virtú° profess,
Shine in the dignity of F.R.S.°
Some, deep Freemasons,° join the silent race
Worthy to fill Pythagoras's place:°
Some botanists, or florists at the least;
Or issue members of an annual feast.°
Nor passed the meanest unregarded; one
Rose a Gregorian, one a Gormogon.°
The last, not least in honour or applause,
Isis and Cam made Doctors of her Laws.°
Then, blessing all, 'Go, children of my care!
To practice now from theory repair.
All my commands are easy, short, and full:
My sons! be proud, be selfish, and be dull.

Beeves . . . urn culinary miracles, where beef is reduced (by a form of mock-transubstantiation) to jelly, or boned meats are given decorative and amusing shapes by ingenious transformations as in l. 554
specious "showy; superficially, not solidly right" (Johnson)
sève . . . verdeur fineness of flavor and briskness of sparkling wines
sacrifice atone the yield of luxuries by famous French regions (Perigord, Bayonne) seen as religious offerings, with libations accompanied by operatic music in l. 559
Bladen . . . Hays's two notorious gamblers who "lived with utmost magnificence at Paris and kept open tables frequented by persons of the first quality of England and even by princes of the blood of France" (P-W)
Knight Robert Knight, cashier of the South Sea Company, who fled England after its collapse in 1720, causing many to be "undone"
three . . . one two partridges dissolved into sauce for a third, with clear reference to the mystery of the Trinity ("the incomprehensible union of the three persons in the Godhead," as Dr. Johnson defines it)
Shakespeare . . . Court lawyers who neglect their duties or studies to dabble in Shakespeare criticism
virtú amateur pursuit of arts or sciences; hence *virtuoso*
F.R.S. Fellow of the Royal Society, a title often granted at the time to untrained noblemen
Freemasons "where taciturnity is the *only* essential qualification, as it was the *chief* of the disciples of Pythagoras" (P-W)
Pythagoras's place referring to the ascetic brotherhood which pursued mathematical and religious mysteries at Croton in southern Italy, *c.* 600–450 B.C.; cf. l. 31 above
annual feast yearly banquet such as was held by the Freemasons or the Royal Society
Gregorian . . . Gormogon members of societies founded in ridicule of Freemasons
Isis and Cam . . . Laws Oxford and Cambridge bestowed honorary degrees.

Guard my prerogative, assert my throne:
This nod confirms each privilege your own.
The cap and switch° be sacred to his Grace;
With staff and pumps° the Marquis lead the race;
From stage to stage° the licensed° Earl may run,
Paired with his fellow charioteer the sun;
The learnèd Baron butterflies design,°
Or draw to silk Arachne's subtile line,°
The Judge to dance his brother Sergeant° call;
The Senator at cricket urge the ball;
The Bishop stow (pontific luxury!)°
An hundred souls of turkeys in a pie;
The sturdy Squire to Gallic masters° stoop,
And drown his lands and manors in a soup.
Others import yet nobler arts from France,
Teach kings to fiddle, and make senates dance.°
Perhaps more high some daring son may soar,°
Proud to my list to add one monarch more;
And nobly conscious, princes are but things
Born for first ministers, as slaves for kings,
Tyrant supreme! shall three estates° command,
And MAKE ONE MIGHTY DUNCIAD OF THE LAND!'
  More she had spoke, but yawned—all nature nods:
What mortal can resist the yawn of gods?°
Churches and chapels° instantly it reached;
(St. James's first, for leaden Gilbert° preached)
Then catched the schools;° the Hall scarce kept awake;
The convocation gaped, but could not speak:
Lost was the nation's sense, nor could be found,
While the long solemn unison went round:
Wide, and more wide, it spread o'er all the realm;

cap and switch of a jockey, here awarded to a lord devoted to horse racing
staff and pumps equipment of footmen or grooms, at the time a fashion among young gentlemen
stage to stage driving a stagecoach, as the Earl of Salisbury did
licensed as coach owners were; also "privileged"
design study and draw
draw . . . line try to obtain silken thread from spiders' webs (as Swift has the experimenters do in the Grand Academy of Lagado, *Gulliver's Travels* III.v)
Sergeant barrister; the "call of sergeants" involved ceremonies much like a dance
pontific luxury such as was in fact enjoyed at the time by the Bishop of Durham
Gallic masters who will introduce fashionable foreign tastes (here a costly "soup") to traditionally conservative country squires
dance perhaps "after their Prince" (P-W); in *Gulliver's Travels* I.iii Lilliputian courtiers are chosen for office by their agility in dancing on a tightrope
more high . . . soar referring to Walpole's virtual rule of England as first minister from 1721 until his fall in 1742, shortly before this was published
three estates Dulness subdues (as Walpole controlled through appointment, bribery, and appeal to interest) the three estates of nobility, clergy, and commoners.
yawn of gods "The Great Mother composes all, in the same manner as Minerva at the period of the *Odyssey*" (P-W)
chapels places of Dissenters' worship
leaden Gilbert Dr. John Gilbert, Dean of Exeter, was eloquent enough in manner; "leaden" is "an epithet from the age" Dulness "had just then restored" (P-W)
Then . . . schools "The progress of this yawn is judicious, natural, and worthy to be noted. First it seizeth the churches and chapels; then catcheth the schools, where, though the boys be unwilling to sleep, the masters are not; next Westminster Hall [the chief law courts], much more hard indeed to subdue, and not put totally to silence even by the Goddess; then the Convocation [of the clergy], which though extremely desirous to speak yet cannot; even the House of Commons, justly called the Sense of the Nation, is *lost* (that is to say *suspended*) during the yawn" (P-W).

Even Palinurus° nodded at the helm:
The vapour mild o'er each committee crept;
Unfinished treaties in each office slept;
And chiefless armies dozed out the campaign;
And navies yawned for orders on the main.
O Muse! relate (for you can tell alone,
Wits have short memories, and dunces none)
Relate, who first, who last resigned to rest;
Whose heads she partly, whose completely blessed;
What charms could faction, what ambition lull,
The venal quiet, and entrance the dull;
Till drowned was sense, and shame, and right, and wrong—
O sing, and hush the nations with thy song!

* * *

In vain, in vain—the all-composing hour
Resistless falls: the Muse obeys the power.
She comes! she comes! the sable throne behold
Of *Night* primeval, and of *Chaos* old!
Before her, *Fancy's* gilded clouds decay,
And all its varying rainbows die away.
Wit shoots in vain its momentary fires,
The meteor drops, and in a flash expires.
As one by one, at dread Medea's strain,°
The sickening stars fade off the ethereal plain;
As Argus' eyes° by Hermes' wand opprest,
Closed one by one to everlasting rest;
Thus at her felt approach, and secret might,
Art after *Art* goes out, and all is night.
See skulking *Truth* to her old cavern° fled,
Mountains of casuistry heaped o'er her head!
Philosophy, that leaned on Heaven before,
Shrinks to her second cause,° and is no more.
Physic of *Metaphysic*° begs defence,
And *Metaphysic* calls for aid on *Sense!*°
See *Mystery* to *Mathematics*° fly!
In vain! they gaze, turn giddy, rave, and die.
Religion blushing veils her sacred fires,
And unawares *Morality* expires.
Nor public flame, nor private, dares to shine;

Palinurus the pilot of Aeneas' ship; here Walpole, pilot of the ship of state and, in the following lines, exhibiting passivity in foreign policy
dread Medea's strain In Seneca's *Medea* the enchantress, seeking revenge for Jason's desertion, calls back to life all the monstrous serpents and sings an incantation that causes the sun to halt and the stars to fall.
Argus' eyes placed all over his body so that some might always remain open; but he was slain by Hermes
Truth . . . cavern "alludes to the saying of Democritus, that truth lay at the bottom of a deep well" (P-W)
Shrinks . . . cause explains away divinity by natural causes; cf. ll. 471–82 above
Physic of Metaphysic natural science turning to traditional speculative metaphysics for its ground. Pope had originally written "the Stagirite's defense," suggesting the clinging to Aristotle he ridiculed in the universities.
Metaphysic . . . Sense metaphysics in turn depending upon sense data or empirical findings, completing, with the previous line, a vicious circle
Mystery to Mathematics religious mystery seeking deductive mathematical demonstration, perhaps infecting mathematics with an occult and mystical strain such as that of the Pythagoreans

Nor human spark is left, nor glimpse divine!
Lo! thy dread empire, CHAOS! is restored;
Light dies before thy uncreating word:°
Thy hand, great anarch! lets the curtain fall;
And universal darkness buries all.

1741 1743

JAMES BOSWELL

1740–1795

Boswell's father was the eighth Laird of Auchinleck, a distinguished jurist, and a man with a strong feeling for the continuity of his family. His eldest son James resisted a legal career but agreed to prepare for the bar before going to London to obtain a commission in a fashionable regiment. Self-indulgent, capricious, and eager for literary fame, James Boswell danced at the end of a tether. His efforts to obtain a commission failed, and he won only a deferment of his legal career in the form of a grand tour of the Continent. Before he left London, however, he met Samuel Johnson, to whom he turned as a more tolerant and affectionate paternal authority. Johnson's influence reinforced, even if it moderated, his father's, and Boswell—in spite of an early literary success with his *Account of Corsica* (1768), based on a visit to the heroic defender of liberty, General Paoli—settled into a legal career in Scotland, breaking out of its confinement only in bouts of self-indulgence and, more important, in the remarkable journal he kept with Johnson's approval. The extracts from the journal show him in his early London years, in his swaggering but somewhat timid visit to Rousseau, and in a typically reflective moment during a darker and later phase. But the journals were also to yield the brilliant account of his 1773 tour of the Hebrides with Johnson, and the success of its publication the year after Johnson's death encouraged him to complete the great *Life* four years before his own death.

It is only in recent years, since the discovery and publication of his journals, that Boswell has come to be recognized as a major literary artist. His openness to every nuance of feeling, his delicacy in capturing (with something of Sterne's skill) fugitive sentiments and revealing gestures, his comic self-regard and (at times) self-contempt—all these have transformed the earlier view of Boswell as alternately a servile buffoon and a mere camera eye. Clearly he induced Johnson's characteristic postures and declarations just as he induced his own, with bold experimental curiosity and a willingness to record what others repress. At times he may have lived in order to record and acted in order to be able to study himself; his journal, as Frederick Pottle has shown, is a fascinating compromise between the freshness of emerging experience and the ironic hindsight of a recorder who (with the advantage of a few days' delay and a concealed knowledge of what will ensue) can intensify naïve expectation and the shock of the real.

From the *Life* a number of extracts have been chosen to illustrate the range of techniques (as well as to suggest the dimensions of the Johnson who is, however real, a work of Boswell's imagination): the reconstruction of Johnson's early life, the dramatic encounters which Boswell attended, the final retrospective view (of which an earlier version had appeared in the Hebrides *Tour*).

uncreating word referring to the terms "wisdom" and "word" (based on the Greek *logos*) for Christ as creator and orderer; here Dulness represents "uncreation," the restoration of Chaos

From The Journals [1]

[1762–63: Farewell to Louisa]

Wednesday 22 December I stood and chatted a while with the sentries before Buckingham House. One of them, an old fellow, said he was in all the last war. 'At the battle of Dettingen,' said he, 'I saw our cannon make a lane through the French army as broad as that' (pointing to the Mall), 'which was filled up in as short time as I'm telling you it.' They asked me for a pint of beer, which I gave them. I talked on the sad mischief of war and on the frequency of poverty. 'Why, Sir,' said he, 'God made all right at first when he made mankind. ('I believe,' said the other, 'he made but few of them.') But, Sir, if God was to make the world today, it would be crooked again tomorrow. But the time will come when we shall all be rich enough. To be sure, salvation is promised to those that die in the field.' I have great pleasure in conversing with the lower part of mankind, who have very curious ideas.

This forenoon I went to Louisa's [2] in full expectation of consummate bliss. I was in a strange flutter of feeling. I was ravished at the prospect of joy, and yet I had such an anxiety upon me that I was afraid that my powers would be enervated. I almost wished to be free of this assignation. I entered her apartment in a sort of confusion. She was elegantly dressed in the morning fashion, and looked delightfully well. I felt the tormenting anxiety of serious love. I sat down and I talked with the distance of a new acquaintance and not with the ease and ardour of a lover, or rather a gallant. I talked of her lodgings being neat, opened the door of her bedchamber, looked into it. Then sat down by her in a most melancholy plight. I would have given a good deal to be out of the room.

We talked of religion. Said she, 'People who deny that, show a want of sense.' 'For my own part, Madam, I look upon the adoration of the Supreme Being as one of the greatest enjoyments we have. I would not choose to get rid of my religious notions. I have read books that staggered me. But I was glad to find myself regain my former opinions.' 'Nay, Sir, what do you think of the Scriptures having stood the test of ages?' 'Are you a Roman Catholic, Madam?' 'No, Sir. Though I like some parts of their religion, in particular, confession; not that I think the priest can remit sins, but because the notion that we are to confess to a decent clergyman may make us cautious what we do.' 'Madam,' said I, 'I would ask you to do nothing that you should be sorry to confess. Indeed I have a great deal of principle in matters of gallantry, and never yet led any woman to do what might afterwards make her uneasy. If she thinks it wrong, I never insist.' She asked me some questions about my intrigues, which I nicely eluded.

1. Boswell's journals, which have been recovered only in the 20th century, provide an extraordinary record of a man of intense sensibility and remarkable candor of self-analysis. The first excerpt is from the London Journal, which records Boswell's futile quest for a commission, his first meeting with Johnson, and his eventual departure for Holland. The second excerpt, drawn from the record of the grand tour, records Boswell's visit to Rousseau in Switzerland. The third, which takes us beyond the time of the tour of the Hebrides, shows a typical instance of the metaphysical concerns that troubled him throughout his life.

2. Louisa was Mrs. Lewis, an actress, of whom little is known but her relationship with Boswell.

I then sat near her and began to talk softly, but finding myself quite dejected with love, I really cried out and told her that I was miserable; and as I was stupid, would go away. I rose, but saluting her with warmth, my powers were excited, I felt myself vigorous. I sat down again. I beseeched her, 'You know, Madam, you said you was not a Platonist. I beg it of you to be so kind. You said you are above the finesse of your sex.' (Be sure always to make a woman better than her sex.) 'I adore you.' 'Nay, dear Sir' (I pressing her to me and kissing her now and then), 'pray be quiet. Such a thing requires time to consider of.' 'Madam, I own this would be necessary for any man but me. But you must take my character from myself. I am very good-tempered, very honest, and have little money. I should have some reward for my particular honesty.' 'But, Sir, give me time to recollect myself.' 'Well then, Madam, when shall I see you?' 'On Friday, Sir.' 'A thousand thanks.' I left her and came home and took my bread and cheese with great contentment. . . .

Thursday 20 January I then went to Louisa.[3] With excellent address did I carry on this interview, as the following scene, I trust, will make appear.

LOUISA My dear Sir! I hope you are well today.

BOSWELL Excessively well, I thank you. I hope I find you so.

LOUISA No, really, Sir. I am distressed with a thousand things. (Cunning jade, her circumstances!) I really don't know what to do.

BOSWELL Do you know that I have been very unhappy since I saw you?

LOUISA How so, Sir?

BOSWELL Why, I am afraid that you don't love me so well, nor have not such a regard for me, as I thought you had.

LOUISA Nay, dear Sir! (Seeming unconcerned.)

BOSWELL Pray, Madam, have I no reason?

LOUISA No, indeed, Sir, you have not.

BOSWELL Have I no reason, Madam? Pray think.

LOUISA Sir!

BOSWELL Pray, Madam, in what state of health have you been in for some time?

LOUISA Sir, you amaze me.

BOSWELL I have but too strong, too plain reason to doubt of your regard. I have for some days observed the symptoms of disease, but was unwilling to believe you so very ungenerous. But now, Madam, I am thoroughly convinced.

LOUISA Sir, you have terrified me. I protest I know nothing of the matter.

BOSWELL Madam, I have had no connection with any woman but you these two months. I was with my surgeon this morning, who declared I had got a strong infection, and that she from whom I had it could not be ignorant of it. Madam, such a thing in this case is worse than from a woman of the town, as from her you may expect it. You have used me very ill. I did not deserve it. You know you said where there was no confidence, there was no breach of trust. But surely I placed some confidence in you. I am sorry that I was mistaken.

3. On January 18 Boswell first discovers "a little heat in the members of my body sacred to Cupid," and on January 19, "Too, too plain was Signor Gonorrhoea."

LOUISA Sir, I will confess to you that about three years ago I was very bad. But for these fifteen months I have been quite well. I appeal to GOD Almighty that I am speaking true; and for these six months I have had to do with no man but yourself.

BOSWELL But by G—D, Madam, I have been with none but you, and here am I very bad.

LOUISA Well, Sir, by the same solemn oath I protest that I was ignorant of it.

BOSWELL Madam, I wish much to believe you. But I own I cannot upon this occasion believe a miracle.

LOUISA Sir, I cannot say more to you. But you will leave me in the greatest misery. I shall lose your esteem. I shall be hurt in the opinion of everybody, and in my circumstances.

BOSWELL (to himself) What the devil does the confounded jilt mean by being hurt in her circumstances? This is the grossest cunning. But I won't take notice of that at all.—Madam, as to the opinion of everybody, you need not be afraid. I was going to joke and say that I never boast of a lady's *favours*. But I give you my word of honour that you shall not be discovered.

LOUISA Sir, this is being more generous than I could expect.

BOSWELL I hope, Madam, you will own that since I have been with you I have always behaved like a man of honour.

LOUISA You have indeed, Sir.

BOSWELL (rising) Madam, your most obedient servant.

During all this conversation I really behaved with a manly composure and polite dignity that could not fail to inspire an awe, and she was pale as ashes and trembled and faltered. Thrice did she insist on my staying a little longer, as it was probably the last time that I should be with her. She could say nothing to the purpose. And I sat silent. As I was going, said she, 'I hope, Sir, you will give me leave to inquire after your health.' 'Madam,' said I, archly, 'I fancy it will be needless for some weeks.' She again renewed her request. But unwilling to be plagued any more with her, I put her off by saying I might perhaps go to the country, and left her. I was really confounded at her behaviour. There is scarcely a possibility that she could be innocent of the crime of horrid imposition. And yet her positive asseverations really stunned me. She is in all probability a most consummate dissembling whore.

Thus ended my intrigue with the fair Louisa, which I flattered myself so much with, and from which I expected at least a winter's safe copulation. It is indeed very hard. I cannot say, like young fellows who get themselves clapped in a bawdy-house, that I will take better care again. For I really did take care. However, since I am fairly trapped, let me make the best of it. I have not got it from imprudence. It is merely the chance of war.

I then called at Drury Lane for Mr. Garrick.[4] He was vastly good to me. 'Sir,' said he, 'you will be a very great man. And when you are so, remember the year 1763. I want to contribute my part towards saving you. And pray, will you fix a day when I shall have the pleasure of treating you with tea?' I

4. David Garrick (1717–79), Johnson's former pupil who was recognized early as the finest actor in England.

fixed next day. 'Then, Sir,' said he, 'the cups shall dance and the saucers skip.'

What he meant by my being a great man I can understand. For really, to speak seriously, I think there is a blossom about me of something more distinguished than the generality of mankind. But I am much afraid that this blossom will never swell into fruit, but will be nipped and destroyed by many a blighting heat and chilling frost. Indeed, I sometimes indulge noble reveries of having a regiment, of getting into Parliament, making a figure, and becoming a man of consequence in the state. But these are checked by dispiriting reflections on my melancholy temper and imbecility [5] of mind. Yet I may probably become sounder and stronger as I grow up. Heaven knows. I am resigned. I trust to Providence. I was quite in raptures with Garrick's kindness —the man whom from a boy I used to adore and look upon as a heathen god —to find him paying me so much respect! How amiable is he in comparison of Sheridan! [6] I was this day with him what the French call *un étourdi.*[7] I gave free vent to my feelings. Love [8] was by, to whom I cried, 'This, Sir, is the real scene.' And taking Mr. Garrick cordially by the hand, 'Thou greatest of men,' said I, 'I cannot express how happy you make me.' This, upon my soul, was no flattery. He saw it was not. And the dear great man was truly pleased with it. This scene gave me a charming flutter of spirits and dispelled my former gloom.

[1764: The Visit to Rousseau [9]]

Monday 3 December To prepare myself for the great interview, I walked out alone. I strolled pensive by the side of the river Reuse in a beautiful wild valley surrounded by immense mountains, some covered with frowning rocks, others with clustering pines, and others with glittering snow. The fresh, healthful air and the romantic prospect around me gave me a vigorous and solemn tone. I recalled all my former ideas of J. J. Rousseau, the admiration with which he is regarded over all Europe, his *Héloïse,* his *Émile:* in short, a crowd of great thoughts. This half hour was one of the most remarkable that I ever passed.

I returned to my inn, and the maid delivered to me a card with the following answer from Monsieur Rousseau: 'I am ill, in pain, really in no state to receive visits. Yet I cannot deprive myself of Mr. Boswell's, provided that out of consideration for the state of my health, he is willing to make it short.'

My sensibility dreaded the word 'short.' But I took courage, and went im-

5. Stupefaction.
6. Thomas Sheridan (1719–88), actor and teacher of elocution.
7. A giddy creature.
8. James Love, an English actor who had given Boswell lessons in elocution.
9. Jean Jacques Rousseau was at the height of his fame, but he was under steady pressure from authority. Having left Paris to settle in Switzerland, he found that the Genevan authorities sought his expulsion; he took refuge in the mountain village of Môtiers in the independent territory of Neuchâtel. When Boswell visited him, Rousseau was living in retirement, attended by his mistress Therèse Le Vasseur (then 43, in spite of Boswell's impression). The text of Boswell's conversation was written in his journal in French, and this translated text (in large part the work of Geoffrey Scott) is reprinted from the edition of Frederick A. Pottle.

mediately. I found at the street door Mademoiselle Le Vasseur waiting for me. She was a little, lively, neat French girl and did not increase my fear. She conducted me up a darkish stair, then opened a door. I expected, 'Now I shall see him'—but it was not so. I entered a room which serves for vestibule and for kitchen. My fancy formed many, many a portrait of the wild philosopher. At length his door opened and I beheld him, a genteel black man in the dress of an Armenian. I entered saying, 'Many, many thanks.' After the first looks and bows were over, he said, 'Will you be seated? Or would you rather take a turn with me in the room?' I chose the last, and happy I was to escape being formally placed upon a chair. I asked him how he was. 'Very ill. But I have given up doctors.' 'Yes, yes; you have no love for them.' As it is impossible for me to relate exactly our conversation, I shall not endeavour at order, but give sentences as I recollect them.

BOSWELL. 'The thought of your books, Sir, is a great source of pleasure to you?' ROUSSEAU. 'I am fond of them; but when I think of my books, so many misfortunes which they have brought upon me are revived in my memory that really I cannot answer you. And yet my books have saved my life.' He spoke of the Parlement of Paris: 'If any company could be covered with disgrace, that would be. I could plunge them into deep disgrace simply by printing their edict against me on one side, and the law of nations and equity on the side opposite. But I have reasons against doing so at present.' BOSWELL. 'We shall have it one day, perhaps?' ROUSSEAU. 'Perhaps.'

I was dressed in a coat and waistcoat, scarlet with gold lace, buckskin breeches, and boots. Above all I wore a greatcoat of green camlet [10] lined with fox-skin fur, with the collar and cuffs of the same fur. I held under my arm a hat with a solid gold lace, at least with the air of being solid. I had it last winter at The Hague. I had a free air and spoke well, and when Monsieur Rousseau said what touched me more than ordinary, I seized his hand, I thumped him on the shoulder. I was without restraint. When I found that I really pleased him, I said, 'Are you aware, Sir, that I am recommended to you by a man you hold in high regard?'

ROUSSEAU. 'Ah! My Lord Marischal?' [11] BOSWELL. 'Yes, Sir; my Lord furnished me with a note to introduce me to you.' ROUSSEAU. 'And you were unwilling to take advantage of it?' BOSWELL. 'Nay, Sir; I wished to have proof of my own merits.' ROUSSEAU. 'Sir, there would have been no kind of merit in gaining access to me by a note of Lord Marischal's. Whatever he sends will always find a welcome from me. He is my protector, my father; I would venture to say, my friend.' One circumstance embarrassed me a little: I had forgotten to bring with me from Neuchâtel my Lord's billet. But a generous consciousness of innocence and honesty gives a freedom which cannot be counterfeited. I told Monsieur Rousseau, 'To speak truly, I have forgotten to bring his letter with me; but you accept my word for it?'

10. A costly fabric of satin weave, originally of angora wool. (For Boswell in this costume see Fig. 36.)

11. George Keith, 10th Earl Marischal of Scotland (d. 1778); a distinguished soldier and disenchanted Jacobite, he served Frederick the Great of Prussia; as governor of Neuchâtel he became a friend and protector of Rousseau. Boswell had traveled with him in Germany earlier in the year.

ROUSSEAU. 'Why, certainly. Numbers of people have shown themselves ready to serve me in their own fashion; my Lord Marischal has served me in mine. He is the only man on earth to whom I owe an obligation.' He went on, 'When I speak of kings, I do not include the King of Prussia. He is a king quite alone and apart. That force of his! Sir, there's the great matter, to have force—revenge, even. You can always find stuff to make something out of. But when force is lacking, when everything is small and split up, there's no hope. The French, for example, are a contemptible nation.' BOSWELL. 'But the Spaniards, Sir?' ROUSSEAU. 'Yes, you will find great souls in Spain.' BOSWELL. 'And in the mountains of Scotland. But since our cursed Union,[12] ah—' ROUSSEAU. 'You undid yourselves. . . .'

'Sir, you don't see before you the bear you have heard tell of. Sir, I have no liking for the world. I live here in a world of fantasies, and I cannot tolerate the world as it is.' BOSWELL. 'But when you come across fantastical men, are they not to your liking?' ROUSSEAU. 'Why, Sir, they have not the same fantasies as myself.—Sir, your country is formed for liberty. I like your habits. You and I feel free to stroll here together without talking. That is more than two Frenchmen can do. Mankind disgusts me. And my housekeeper tells me that I am in far better humour on the days when I have been alone than on those when I have been in company.' BOSWELL. 'There has been a great deal written against you, Sir.' ROUSSEAU. 'They have not understood me. As for Monsieur Vernet at Geneva, he is an Arch-Jesuit, that is all I can say of him.'

BOSWELL. 'Tell me, Sir, do you not find that I answer to the description I gave you of myself?' ROUSSEAU. 'Sir, it is too early for me to judge. But all appearances are in your favour.' BOSWELL. 'I fear I have stayed too long. I shall take the honour of returning tomorrow.' ROUSSEAU. 'Oh, as to that, I can't tell.' BOSWELL. 'Sir, I shall stay quietly here in the village. If you are able to see me, I shall be enchanted; if not, I shall make no complaint.' ROUSSEAU. 'My Lord Marischal has a perfect understanding of man's feelings, in solitude no less than in society. I am overwhelmed with visits from idle people.' BOSWELL. 'And how do they spend their time?' ROUSSEAU. 'In paying compliments. Also I get a prodigious quantity of letters. And the writer of each of them believes that he is the only one.' BOSWELL. 'You must be greatly surprised, Sir, that a man who has not the honour of your acquaintance should take the liberty of writing to you?' ROUSSEAU. 'No. I am not at all surprised. For I got a letter like it yesterday, and one the day before yesterday, and others many times before that.' BOSWELL. 'Sir, your very humble servant.—What, you are coming further?' ROUSSEAU. 'I am not coming with you. I am going for a walk in the passage. Good-bye.'

I had great satisfaction after finding that I could support the character which I had given of myself, after finding that I should most certainly be regarded by the illustrious Rousseau. I had a strange kind of feeling after having at last seen the author of whom I had thought so much.

Wednesday 5 December When I waited upon Monsieur Rousseau this morning, he said, 'My dear Sir, I am sorry not to be able to talk with you as I would wish.' I took care to waive such excuses, and immediately set conversation a-going. I told him how I had turned Roman Catholic and had intended

12. The union of England and Scotland under one parliament in 1707.

to hide myself in a convent in France. He said, 'What folly! I too was Catholic in my youth.[13] I changed, and then I changed back again. I returned to Geneva and was readmitted to the Protestant faith. I went again among Catholics, and used to say to them, "I am no longer one of you"; and I got on with them excellently.' I stopped him in the middle of the room and I said to him, 'But tell me sincerely, are you a Christian?' I looked at him with a searching eye. His countenance was no less animated. Each stood steady and watched the other's looks. He struck his breast, and replied. 'Yes. I pique myself upon being one.' BOSWELL. 'Sir, the soul can be sustained by nothing save the Gospel.' ROUSSEAU. 'I feel that. I am unaffected by all the objections. I am weak; there may be things beyond my reach; or perhaps the man who recorded them made a mistake. I say, God the Father, God the Son, God the Holy Ghost.'

BOSWELL. 'But tell me, do you suffer from melancholy?' ROUSSEAU. 'I was born placid. I have no natural disposition to melancholy. My misfortunes have infected me with it.' BOSWELL. 'I, for my part, suffer from it severely. And how can I be happy, I, who have done so much evil?' ROUSSEAU. 'Begin your life anew. God is good, for he is just. Do good. You will cancel all the debt of evil. Say to yourself in the morning, "Come now, I am going to *pay off* so much evil." Six well-spent years will pay off all the evil you have committed.' BOSWELL. 'But what do you think of cloisters, penances, and remedies of that sort?' ROUSSEAU. 'Mummeries, all of them, invented by men. Do not be guided by men's judgments, or you will find yourself tossed to and fro perpetually. Do not base your life on the judgments of others; first, because they are as likely to be mistaken as you are, and further, because you cannot know that they are telling you their true thoughts; they may be impelled by motives of interest or convention to talk to you in a way not corresponding to what they really think.' BOSWELL. 'Will you, Sir, assume direction of me?' ROUSSEAU. 'I cannot. I can be responsible only for myself.' BOSWELL. 'But I shall come back.' ROUSSEAU. 'I don't promise to see you. I am in pain. I need a chamber-pot every minute.'[14] BOSWELL. 'Yes, you will see me.' ROUSSEAU. 'Be off; and a good journey to you.'

About six I set out.

[1776: Reflections on Man]

Sunday 31 December (I am now writing on Tuesday 2 January 1776.) My cold and sprained ankle were worse. I lay in bed but did not enjoy that tranquillity which I have formerly done in that state of indolence. I read in *The Critical Review* an account of Priestley's edition of Hartley's *Observations on Man*[15] with some essays of his own relative to the subject of that book. While

13. For Rousseau's conversion, see his *Confessions*; of Boswell's nothing is known. While he was in Holland, Boswell had found relief from some of his own Calvinistic severities of self-reproach in reading Rousseau's "Creed of a Savoyard Vicar," in *Émile*.

14. Rousseau was suffering from a congestion or constriction of the urethra.

15. David Hartley (1705–57) was trained in both medicine and divinity although he did not take either a medical degree or holy orders; his *Observations on Man* (1749) derived all religious and moral ideas from association of sense perceptions, and all thought processes from mechanical vibrations in the nerves and brain. While Hartley denied free will he claimed not to be a materialist and remained a devout Christian. Joseph Priestley abridged his work in 1775, omitting the theory of vibrations as too obscure, and gained great popularity for Hartley (whose influence on Coleridge and Wordsworth was great).

I was carried into metaphysical abstraction, and felt that *perhaps* all our thinking of every kind was only a variety of modification upon matter, I was in a sort of amaze; but I must observe that it did not affect me with 'that secret dread and inward horror' [16] which it has occasioned at other times. There is no accounting for our feelings, but certain it is that what strikes us strongly at one time will have little influence at another. Speculation of this kind relieved me from the vexation of family differences, by changing objects and by making me consider, 'If all thought and all volition and all that we denominate spirit be only properties of matter, why should I distress myself at present, while in full consciousness, about eventual successions of machines?' I however thought that philosophical theories were transient, whereas feudal principles remained for ages. In truth the mortality or immortality of the soul can make no difference on the enthusiasm for supporting a family, for, in either case, the matter must be of no moment to those who have departed this life. If they have ceased to exist, they know nothing of it. If they exist in another state, they perhaps even then know not what passes here, and, if they do, it is perhaps as trifling in their eyes as our childish concerns are in ours when we have arrived at manhood. How strange is it, then, that a man will toil all his life and deny himself satisfactions in order to aggrandize his posterity after he is dead. It is, I fancy, from a kind of delusion in the imagination, which makes us figure ourselves contemplating for ages our own magnificence in a succession of descendants. So strong is this delusion with me that I would suffer death rather than let the estate of Auchinleck be sold; and this must be from an enthusiasm for an *idea* for *the Family*.[17] The founder of it I never saw, so how can I be zealous for his race? and were I to be a martyr, I should only be reckoned a madman. But an *idea* will produce the highest enthusiasm. Witness the ardour which the individuals at the time have for the glory of their regiment, though they have no line of connexion with it, being picked out from all parts of the kingdom. The officers and soldiers of the Scots Greys boast that '*We* were never known to fly.'—'*We* gained distinguished honour at such a battle.' Yet the officers and soldiers under that *name* at former periods were as different from its officers and soldiers now as the Romans were. I don't mean that they were different in body or in mind, in any remarkable degree, but that there is not a trace of identity, unless that there is always a remain of a regiment to communicate the same discipline and gallantry of sentiment to those who come into it, so that *l'esprit du corps,* like the fire of Vesta,[18] is kept incessantly burning, though the materials are different. I thought for a little that a man should place his pride and his happiness in his own individuality, and endeavour to be as rich and as renowned and as happy as he can. I considered that Dr. Johnson is as well as if he belonged to a *family*. Priestley's *material* system affected me less that he declared his belief in Christianity, which teaches us that God bestows a future life. However, I thought myself strongly conscious of an immaterial something—of a soul. I read a pamphlet today, which I remember having looked at about twenty years ago: *The Trial of the Witnesses for the Resurrection of Jesus*.[19] I found it to be a

16. "Whence this secret dread, and inward horror, of falling into naught?" Addison, *Cato* V.i.4–5.
17. Perhaps "an *idea* of the *Family*" or "for an *idea*, for the *Family*."
18. Whose perpetual flame was kept by the Vestal Virgins in her temple at Rome.
19. (1729) by Thomas Sherlock, later Bishop of London.

piece of very good argument which confirmed me in my faith; but I was a little disgusted with its author's affecting a sort of easy smartness of dialogue in some places. . . .

Wednesday 3 January. . . . My state of mind today was still affected by Hartley and Priestley's metaphysics, and was continually trying to perceive my faculties operating as machinery. My animal spirits were so light now that such sort of thinking did not distress me as it has done when I was more atrabilious.[20] I felt an easy indifference as to what was my mental system. I liked present consciousness. Man's continuation of existence is a flux of ideas in the same body, like the flux of a river in the same channel. Even our bodies are perpetually changing. What then is the subject of praise or blame upon the whole? what of love or hatred when we are to contemplate a character? There *must* be *something*, which we understand by a *spirit* or a *soul*, which is permanent. And yet I must own that except the sense or perception of identity, I cannot say that there is any sameness in my soul now and my soul twenty years ago, or surely none thirty years ago. Though souls may be in a flux, each may have a distinct character as rivers have: one rapid, one smooth, etc. I read a little of Lord Hailes's *Annals*. . . .

Tuesday 9 January In the intervals while Mr. Lawrie copied passages, I read *The Monthly Review* on Priestley's edition of Hartley, and found his *material* system refuted with ability and spirit. I was much pleased, and wished to be acquainted with the writer of the article. I could not but think what a strange life a man would lead who should fairly act according to metaphysical conviction or impression at the time. What inconsistency and extravagance should we find! Sometimes he would be rigidly virtuous, at other times abandoned to extreme licentiousness; and at both times acting from *principle*. I have thought of writing a kind of novel to show this: 'Memoirs of a Practical Metaphysician.' I remember I mentioned this to Dr. Reid,[21] who writes on the mind according to common sense. He told me the same thought had occurred to him. Maclaurin observed very well, when he was last with me, that thinking metaphysically destroys the principles of morality; and indeed when a man analyses virtues and vices as a chemist does material substances, they lose their value as well as their odiousness. . . .

From The Life of Samuel Johnson, LL.D.

[1729: "Morbid Melancholy"]

The 'morbid melancholy,' which was lurking in his constitution, and to which we may ascribe those particularities, and that aversion to regular life, which, at a very early period, marked his character, gathered such strength in his twentieth year, as to afflict him in a dreadful manner. While he was at Lich-

20. Afflicted by black bile or melancholy.
21. Dr. Thomas Reid (1710–96), Professor of Moral Philosophy at the University of Glasgow, a leader of the Common Sense school of philosophy and an opponent of David Hume; his *Inquiry into the Human Mind* (1764) had freed Boswell from the "sceptical cobweb" of Hume during Boswell's stay in Berlin.

field, in the college vacation of the year 1729, he felt himself overwhelmed with an horrible hypochondria, with perpetual irritation, fretfulness, and impatience; and with a dejection, gloom, and despair, which made existence misery. From this dismal malady he never afterwards was perfectly relieved; and all his labours, and all his enjoyments, were but temporary interruptions of its baleful influence. How wonderful, how unsearchable are the ways of God! Johnson, who was blest with all the powers of genius and understanding in a degree far above the ordinary state of human nature, was at the same time visited with a disorder so afflictive, that they who know it by dire experience, will not envy his exalted endowments. That it was, in some degree, occasioned by a defect in his nervous system, that inexplicable part of our frame, appears highly probable. He told Mr. Paradise that he was sometimes so languid and inefficient, that he could not distinguish the hour upon the town-clock.

Johnson, upon the first violent attack of this disorder, strove to overcome it by forcible exertions. He frequently walked to Birmingham and back again,[1] and tried many other expedients, but all in vain. His expression concerning it to me was, 'I did not then know how to manage it.' His distress became so intolerable, that he applied to Dr. Swinfen, physician in Lichfield, his god-father, and put into his hands a state of his case, written in Latin. Dr. Swinfen was so much struck with the extraordinary acuteness, research, and eloquence of this paper, that in his zeal for his godson he showed it to several people. His daughter, Mrs. Desmoulins, who was many years humanely supported in Dr. Johnson's house in London, told me that upon his discovering that Dr. Swinfen had communicated his case, he was so much offended, that he was never after-wards fully reconciled to him. He indeed had good reason to be offended; for though Dr. Swinfen's motive was good, he inconsiderately betrayed a matter deeply interesting and of great delicacy, which had been entrusted to him in confidence; and exposed a complaint of his young friend and patient, which, in the superficial opinion of the generality of mankind, is attended with contempt and disgrace.

But let not little men triumph upon knowing that Johnson was an Hypochondriac, was subject to what the learned, philosophical, and pious Dr. Cheyne has so well treated under the title of 'The English Malady.'[2] Though he suffered severely from it, he was not therefore degraded. The powers of his great mind might be troubled, and their full exercise suspended at times; but the mind itself was ever entire. As a proof of this, it is only necessary to consider, that, when he was at the very worst, he composed that state of his own case, which showed an uncommon vigour, not only of fancy and taste, but of judgement. I am aware that he himself was too ready to call such a complaint by the name of *madness*; in conformity with which notion, he has traced its gradations, with exquisite nicety, in one of the chapters of his *Rasselas*. But there is surely a clear distinction between a disorder which affects only the imagination and spirits, while the judgement is sound, and a disorder by which the judgement itself is impaired. . . .

. . . To Johnson, whose supreme enjoyment was the exercise of his reason,

1. Thirty-two miles in all.
2. Dr. George Cheyne (1671–1743), *The English Malady, or a Treatise of Nervous Diseases of All Kinds* (1733), a book Johnson twice recommended to Boswell.

the disturbance or obscuration of that faculty was the evil most to be dreaded. Insanity, therefore, was the object of his most dismal apprehension; and he fancied himself seized by it, or approaching to it, at the very time when he was giving proofs of a more than ordinary soundness and vigour of judgement. That his own diseased imagination should have so far deceived him is strange; but it is stranger still that some of his friends should have given credit to his groundless opinion when they had such undoubted proofs that it was totally fallacious; though it is by no means surprising that those who wish to depreciate him should, since his death, have laid hold of his circumstance and insisted upon it with very unfair aggravation.

Amidst the oppression and distraction of a disease which very few have felt in its full extent, but many have experienced in a slighter degree, Johnson, in his writings, and in his conversation, never failed to display all the varieties of intellectual excellence. In his march through this world to a better, his mind still appeared grand and brilliant, and impressed all around him with the truth of Virgil's noble sentiment—

Igneus est ollis vigor et cœlestis origo.[3]

The history of his mind as to religion is an important article. I have mentioned the early impressions made upon his tender imagination by his mother, who continued her pious care with assiduity, but, in his opinion, not with judgement. 'Sunday (said he) was a heavy day to me when I was a boy. My mother confined me on that day, and made me read "The Whole Duty of Man," [4] from a great part of which I could derive no instruction. When, for instance, I had read the chapter on theft, which from my infancy I had been taught was wrong, I was no more convinced that theft was wrong than before; so there was no accession of knowledge. A boy should be introduced to such books by having his attention directed to the arrangement, to the style, and other excellencies of composition; that the mind being thus engaged by an amusing variety of objects, may not grow weary.'

He communicated to me the following particulars upon the subject of his religious progress. 'I fell into an inattention to religion, or an indifference about it, in my ninth year. The church at Lichfield, in which we had a seat, wanted reparation, so I was to go and find a seat in other churches; and having bad eyes, and being awkward about this, I used to go and read in the fields on Sunday. This habit continued till my fourteenth year; and still I find a great reluctance to go to church. I then became a sort of lax *talker* against religion, for I did not much *think* against it; and this lasted till I went to Oxford, where it would not be *suffered.* When at Oxford, I took up Law's *Serious Call to a Holy Life,*[5] expecting to find it a dull book (as such books generally are), and perhaps to laugh at it. But I found Law quite an over-match for me; and this was the first occasion of my thinking in earnest of religion, after I became

3. "Quick in these seeds is might of fire and birth of heavenly place" (*Aeneid,* Morris trans., VI.730).

4. The popular moral work attributed to Dr. Richard Allestree (1619–81).

5. William Law's work had great influence upon both John Wesley and George Whitefield, the founders of Methodism.

capable of rational inquiry.' From this time forward religion was the predominant object of his thoughts; though, with the just sentiments of a conscientious Christian, he lamented that his practice of its duties fell far short of what it ought to be. . . .

How seriously Johnson was impressed with a sense of religion, even in the vigour of his youth, appears from the following passage in his minutes kept by way of diary: Sept. 7, 1736. I have this day entered upon my twenty-eighth year. 'Mayest thou, O God, enable me, for Jesus Christ's sake, to spend this in such a manner that I may receive comfort from it at the hour of death, and in the day of judgement! Amen.'

The particular course of his reading while at Oxford, and during the time of vacation which he passed at home, cannot be traced. Enough has been said of his irregular mode of study. He told me that from his earliest years he loved to read poetry, but hardly ever read any poem to an end; that he read Shakespeare at a period so early, that the speech of the ghost in Hamlet terrified him when he was alone; that Horace's Odes were the compositions in which he took most delight, and it was long before he liked his Epistles and Satires. He told me what he read *solidly* at Oxford was Greek; not the Grecian historians, but Homer and Euripides, and now and then a little Epigram; that the study of which he was the most fond was Metaphysics, but he had not read much, even in that way. I always thought that he did himself injustice in his account of what he had read, and that he must have been speaking with reference to the vast portion of study which is possible, and to which a few scholars in the whole history of literature have attained; for when I once asked him whether a person, whose name I have now forgotten, studied hard, he answered 'No, Sir; I do not believe he studied hard. I never knew a man who studied hard. I conclude, indeed, from the effects, that some men have studied hard, as Bentley and Clarke.' [6] Trying him by that criterion upon which he formed his judgement of others, we may be absolutely certain, both from his writings and his conversation, that his reading was very extensive. Dr. Adam Smith,[7] than whom few were better judges on this subject, once observed to me that 'Johnson knew more books than any man alive.' He had a peculiar facility in seizing at once what was valuable in any book, without submitting to the labour of perusing it from beginning to end. He had, from the irritability of his constitution, at all times, an impatience and hurry when he either read or wrote. A certain apprehension, arising from novelty, made him write his first exercise at College twice over; but he never took that trouble with any other composition; and we shall see that his most excellent works were struck off at a heat, with rapid exertion.

Yet he appears, from his early notes or memorandums in my possession, to have at various times attempted, or at least planned, a methodical course of study, according to computation, of which he was all his life fond, as it fixed

6. Richard Bentley (1662–1742), the great classical scholar attacked by Swift in *The Battle of the Books* and Pope in *The Dunciad* IV; Samuel Clarke (1675–1729), distinguished metaphysician and moral philosopher, who gave the Boyle Lectures in 1704–1705 and engaged in a celebrated correspondence with Leibnitz.

7. Adam Smith (1723–90), the Scottish professor of logic and moral philosopher, now best known for his work of economics, *The Wealth of Nations* (1776).

his attention steadily upon something without, and prevented his mind from preying upon itself. Thus I find in his handwriting the number of lines in each of two of Euripides' Tragedies, of the Georgics of Virgil, of the first six books of the Aeneid, of Horace's Art of Poetry, of three of the books of Ovid's Metamorphosis, of some parts of Theocritus, and of the tenth Satire of Juvenal; and a table, showing at the rate of various numbers a day (I suppose verses to be read), what would be, in each case, the total amount in a week, month, and year.

No man had a more ardent love of literature, or a higher respect for it than Johnson. His apartment in Pembroke College was that upon the second floor, over the gateway. The enthusiasts of learning will ever contemplate it with veneration. One day, while he was sitting in it quite alone, Dr. Panting, then master of the College, whom he called 'a fine Jacobite fellow,' overheard him uttering this soliloquy in his strong, emphatic voice: 'Well, I have a mind to see what is done in other places of learning. I'll go and visit the Universities abroad. I'll go to France and Italy. I'll go to Padua.—And I'll mind my business. For an *Athenian* blockhead is the worst of all blockheads.'

Dr. Adams told me that Johnson, while he was at Pembroke College, 'was caressed and loved by all about him, was a gay and frolicsome fellow, and passed there the happiest part of his life.' But this is a striking proof of the fallacy of appearances, and how little any of us know of the real internal state even of those whom we see most frequently; for the truth is, that he was then depressed by poverty, and irritated by disease. When I mentioned to him this account as given me by Dr. Adams, he said, 'Ah, Sir, I was mad and violent. It was bitterness which they mistook for frolic. I was miserably poor, and I thought to fight my way by my literature and my wit; so I disregarded all power and all authority.'

[1754: The *Dictionary* and Lord Chesterfield]

The *Dictionary*, we may believe, afforded Johnson full occupation this year. As it approached to its conclusion, he probably worked with redoubled vigour, as seamen increase their exertion and alacrity when they have a near prospect of their haven.

Lord Chesterfield, to whom Johnson had paid the high compliment of addressing to his Lordship the *Plan* of his *Dictionary*, had behaved to him in such a manner as to excite his contempt and indignation. The world has been for many years amused with a story confidently told, and as confidently repeated with additional circumstances, that a sudden disgust was taken by Johnson upon occasion of his having been one day kept long in waiting in his Lordship's antechamber, for which the reason assigned was, that he had company with him; and that at last, when the door opened, out walked Colley Cibber; [8] and that Johnson was so violently provoked when he found for whom he had been so long excluded, that he went away in a passion, and never would return . . . but Johnson himself assured me, that there was not the least foundation for it.

8. Colley Cibber (1671–1757), dramatist and actor, poet laureate 1730–57, the mock-hero of Pope's revised *Dunciad;* Johnson scorned his ignorance and "impenetrable impudence."

He told me, that there never was any particular incident which produced a quarrel between Lord Chesterfield and him; but that his Lordship's continued neglect was the reason why he resolved to have no connection with him. When the *Dictionary* was upon the eve of publication, Lord Chesterfield, who, it is said, had flattered himself with expectations that Johnson would dedicate the work to him, attempted, in a courtly manner, to soothe, and insinuate himself with the Sage, conscious, as it should seem, of the cold indifference with which he had treated its learned author; and further attempted to conciliate him, by writing two papers in *The World,* in recommendation of the work; and it must be confessed, that they contain some studied compliments, so finely turned, that if there had been no previous offence, it is probable that Johnson would have been highly delighted. Praise, in general, was pleasing to him; but by praise from a man of rank and elegant accomplishments, he was peculiarly gratified. . . .

This courtly device failed of its effect. Johnson, who thought that 'all was false and hollow,' despised the honeyed words, and was even indignant that Lord Chesterfield should, for a moment, imagine that he could be the dupe of such an artifice. His expression to me concerning Lord Chesterfield, upon this occasion, was, 'Sir, after making great professions, he had, for many years, taken no notice of me; but when my *Dictionary* was coming out, he fell a scribbling in *The World* about it. Upon which, I wrote him a letter expressed in civil terms, but such as might show him that I did not mind what he said or wrote, and that I had done with him.'

This is that celebrated letter of which so much has been said, and about which curiosity has been so long excited, without being gratified. . . .

'*To* The Right Honourable the Earl of Chesterfield

'My Lord, February 1755

'I have been lately informed, by the proprietor of *The World,* that two papers, in which my Dictionary is recommended to the public, were written by your Lordship. To be so distinguished, is an honour, which, being very little accustomed to favours from the great, I know not well how to receive, or in what terms to acknowledge.

'When, upon some slight encouragement, I first visited your Lordship, I was overpowered, like the rest of mankind, by the enchantment of your address; and could not forbear to wish that I might boast myself *Le vainqueur du vainqueur de la terre;* [9]—that I might obtain that regard for which I saw the world contending; but I found my attendance so little encouraged, that neither pride nor modesty would suffer me to continue it. When I had once addressed your Lordship in public, I had exhausted all the art of pleasing which a retired and uncourtly scholar can possess. I had done all that I could; and no man is well pleased to have his all neglected, be it ever so little.

'Seven years, my Lord, have now past, since I waited in your outward rooms, or was repulsed from your door; during which time I have been pushing on my work through difficulties, of which it is useless to complain, and have brought it, at last, to the verge of publication, without one act of assistance,

9. "The conqueror of the conqueror of the earth."

one word of encouragement, or one smile of favour. Such treatment I did not expect, for I never had a Patron before.

'The shepherd in Virgil grew at last acquainted with Love, and found him a native of the rocks.[10]

'Is not a Patron, my Lord, one who looks with unconcern on a man struggling for life in the water, and, when he has reached ground, encumbers him with help? The notice which you have been pleased to take of my labours, had it been early, had been kind; but it has been delayed till I am indifferent, and cannot enjoy it; till I am solitary, and cannot impart it; [11] till I am known, and do not want it. I hope it is no very cynical asperity not to confess obligations where no benefit has been received, or to be unwilling that the Public should consider me as owing that to a Patron which Providence has enabled me to do for myself.

'Having carried on my work thus far with so little obligation to any favourer of learning, I shall not be disappointed though I should conclude it, if less be possible, with less; for I have been long wakened from that dream of hope, in which I once boasted myself with so much exultation, my Lord, your Lordship's most humble, most obedient servant,

SAM. JOHNSON.'

. . . There is a curious minute circumstance which struck me, in comparing the various editions of Johnson's imitations of Juvenal. In the tenth Satire, one of the couplets upon the vanity of wishes even for literary distinction stood thus:

Yet think what ills the scholar's life assail,
Pride, envy, want, the *garret*, and the jail.

But after experiencing the uneasiness which Lord Chesterfield's fallacious patronage made him feel, he dismissed the word *garret* from the sad group, and in all the subsequent editions the line stands

Toil, envy, want, the *Patron*, and the jail.[12]

[1763: The Meeting with Boswell]

. . . Mr. Davies [13] recollected several of Johnson's remarkable sayings, and was one of the best of the many imitators of his voice and manner, while relating them. He increased my impatience more and more to see the extraordinary man whose works I highly valued, and whose conversation was reported to be so peculiarly excellent.

At last, on Monday the 16th of May, when I was sitting in Mr. Davies's back-parlour, after having drunk tea with him and Mrs. Davies, Johnson unexpectedly came into the shop; and Mr. Davies having perceived him through the glass door in the room in which we were sitting, advancing towards us,—he an-

10. *Eclogues* VIII.43: "I know thee, Love; in deserts thou wast bred" (Dryden trans.).
11. Referring to the death of his wife, March 17, 1752.
12. In his *Dictionary* Johnson defined *patron* as "commonly a wretch who supports with insolence and is paid with flattery."
13. Thomas Davies, actor and bookseller, "a man of good understanding and talents, with the advantage of a liberal education"; "a friendly and very hospitable man" whom Johnson visited freely.

nounced his aweful approach to me, somewhat in the manner of an actor in the part of Horatio, when he addresses Hamlet on the appearance of his father's ghost, 'Look, my Lord, it comes.' I found that I had a very perfect idea of Johnson's figure from the portrait of him painted by Sir Joshua Reynolds soon after he had published his *Dictionary*, in the attitude of sitting in his easy chair in deep meditation. . . . Mr. Davies mentioned my name, and respectfully introduced me to him. I was much agitated; and recollecting his prejudice against the Scotch, of which I had heard much, I said to Davies, 'Don't tell where I come from.'—'From Scotland,' cried Davies roguishly. 'Mr. Johnson, (said I) I do indeed come from Scotland, but I cannot help it.' I am willing to flatter myself that I meant this as light pleasantry to soothe and conciliate him, and not as an humiliating abasement at the expence of my country. But however that might be, this speech was somewhat unlucky; for with that quickness of wit for which he was so remarkable, he seized the expression 'come from Scotland,' which I used in the sense of being of that country, and, as if I had said that I had come away from it, or left it, retorted, 'That, Sir, I find, is what a very great many of your countrymen cannot help.' This stroke stunned me a good deal; and when we had sat down, I felt myself not a little embarrassed, and apprehensive of what might come next. He then addressed himself to Davies: 'What do you think of Garrick? [14] He has refused me an order for the play for Miss Williams,[15] because he knows the house will be full, and that an order would be worth three shillings.' Eager to take any opening to get into conversation with him, I ventured to say, 'O, Sir, I cannot think Mr. Garrick would grudge such a trifle to you.' 'Sir, (said he, with a stern look,) I have known David Garrick longer than you have done: and I know no right you have to talk to me on the subject.' Perhaps I deserved this check; for it was rather presumptuous in me, an entire stranger, to express any doubt of the justice of his animadversion upon his old acquaintance and pupil. I now felt myself much mortified, and began to think that the hope which I had long indulged of obtaining his acquaintance was blasted. And, in truth, had not my ardour been uncommonly strong, and my resolution uncommonly persevering, so rough a reception might have deterred me for ever from making any further attempts. Fortunately, however, I remained upon the field not wholly discomfited; and was soon rewarded by hearing some of his conversation, of which I preserved the following short minute, without marking the questions and observations by which it was produced.

'People (he remarked) may be taken in once, who imagine that an author is greater in private life than other men. Uncommon parts require uncommon opportunities for their exertion.

'In barbarous society, superiority of parts is of real consequence. Great strength or great wisdom is of much value to an individual. But in more polished times there are people to do every thing for money; and then there are a number of other superiorities, such as those of birth and fortune, and

14. David Garrick, the great actor, had been a pupil of Johnson in his school at Edial (1736–37).

15. Anna Williams (1706–83), Johnson's friend and protégée, for whom David Garrick gave a benefit at Drury Lane.

rank, that dissipate men's attention, and leave no extraordinary share of respect for personal and intellectual superiority. This is wisely ordered by Providence, to preserve some equality among mankind.

'Sir, this book (*The Elements of Criticism*,[16] which he had taken up,) is a pretty essay, and deserves to be held in some estimation, though much of it is chimerical.'

Speaking of one [17] who with more than ordinary boldness attacked public measures and the royal family, he said,

'I think he is safe from the law, but he is an abusive scoundrel; and instead of applying to my Lord Chief Justice to punish him, I would send half a dozen footmen and have him well ducked.'

'The notion of liberty amuses the people of England, and helps to keep off the *tædium vitae*. When a butcher tells you that *his heart bleeds for his country*, he has, in fact, no uneasy feeling.

'Sheridan [18] will not succeed at Bath with his oratory. Ridicule has gone down before him, and, I doubt, Derrick is his enemy.

'Derrick may do very well, as long as he can outrun his character; but the moment his character gets up with him, it is all over.'

It is, however, but just to record, that some years afterwards, when I reminded him of this sarcasm, he said, 'Well, but Derrick has now got a character that he need not run away from.'

I was highly pleased with the extraordinary vigour of his conversation, and regretted that I was drawn away from it by an engagement at another place. I had, for a part of the evening, been left alone with him, and had ventured to make an observation now and then, which he received very civilly; so that I was satisfied that though there was a roughness in his manner, there was no ill-nature in his disposition. Davies followed me to the door, and when I complained to him a little of the hard blows which the great man had given me, he kindly took upon him to console me by saying, 'Don't be uneasy. I can see he likes you very well.'

A few days afterwards I called on Davies, and asked him if he thought I might take the liberty of waiting on Mr. Johnson at his Chambers in the Temple. He said I certainly might, and that Mr. Johnson would take it as a compliment. So upon Tuesday the 24th of May, after having been enlivened by the witty sallies of Messieurs Thornton, Wilkes, Churchill [19] and Lloyd, with whom I had passed the morning, I boldly repaired to Johnson. His Chambers were on the first floor of No. 1, Inner-Temple-lane, and I entered them with

16. By Henry Home, Lord Kames, published in Edinburgh in 1762.
17. John Wilkes (1727–97), in 1762 founded *The North Briton*, a journal in which he attacked the ministry of Lord Bute. He was prosecuted for libel and, as a result of an obscene article, expelled from Commons and declared an outlaw. He fled to Paris and returned in 1768 to resume his parliamentary career. His famous meeting with Johnson took place in 1776, two years after he served as Lord Mayor of London.
18. Thomas Sheridan (1719–88), actor, author, father of the playwright, and lecturer on elocution—at the moment at Bath, where Samuel Derrick was Master of Ceremonies, "or as the phrase is, King" (Boswell).
19. Charles Churchill (1731–64), the satiric poet, who had attacked Johnson "violently" (in Boswell's view).

an impression given me by the Reverend Dr. Blair, of Edinburgh,[20] who had been introduced to him not long before, and described his having 'found the Giant in his den'; an expression, which, when I came to be pretty well acquainted with Johnson, I repeated to him, and he was diverted at this picturesque account of himself. Dr. Blair had been presented to him by Dr. James Fordyce. At this time the controversy concerning the pieces published by Mr. James Macpherson, as translations of *Ossian*, was at its height. Johnson had all along denied their authenticity; and, what was still more provoking to their admirers, maintained that they had no merit. The subject having been introduced by Dr. Fordyce, Dr. Blair, relying on the internal evidence of their antiquity, asked Dr. Johnson whether he thought any man of a modern age could have written such poems? Johnson replied, 'Yes, Sir, many men, many women, and many children.' Johnson, at this time, did not know that Dr. Blair had just published a *Dissertation*, not only defending their authenticity, but seriously ranking them with the poems of Homer and Virgil; and when he was afterwards informed of this circumstance, he expressed some displeasure at Dr. Fordyce's having suggested the topic, and said, 'I am not sorry that they got thus much for their pains. Sir, it was like leading one to talk of a book when the author is concealed behind the door.'

He received me very courteously; but, it must be confessed, that his apartment, and furniture, and morning dress, were sufficiently uncouth. His brown suit of clothes looked very rusty; he had on a little old shrivelled unpowdered wig which was too small for his head; his shirt-neck and knees of his breeches were loose; his black worsted stockings ill drawn up; and he had a pair of unbuckled shoes by way of slippers. But all these slovenly particularities were forgotten the moment that he began to talk. Some gentlemen, whom I do not recollect, were sitting with him; and when they went away, I also rose; but he said to me, 'Nay, don't go.' 'Sir, (said I,) I am afraid that I intrude upon you. It is benevolent to allow me to sit and hear you.' He seemed pleased with this compliment, which I sincerely paid him, and answered, 'Sir, I am obliged to any man who visits me.' I have preserved the following short minute of what passed this day:—

'Madness frequently discovers itself merely by unnecessary deviation from the usual modes of the world. My poor friend Smart showed the disturbance of his mind, by falling upon his knees, and saying his prayers in the street, or in any other unusual place. Now although, rationally speaking, it is greater madness not to pray at all, than to pray as Smart did, I am afraid there are so many who do not pray, that their understanding is not called in question.'

Concerning this unfortunate poet, Christopher Smart, who was confined in a mad-house, he had, at another time, the following conversation with Dr.

20. Dr. Hugh Blair (1718–1800), a clergyman well known for his sermons and a critic of rhetoric and literature; introduced to Johnson by his friend the physician Fordyce. The controversy concerning Macpherson's alleged translations from Ossian was settled by a committee that, after his death, declared them in part free versions of traditional poems with much original matter added. The Ossianic poems, purporting to be Gaelic epics, gained enormous vogue throughout Europe and were highly esteemed by Goethe among others. William Blake insisted upon their authenticity; Dr. Johnson remarked in 1783, "Sir, a man might write such stuff for ever, if he would *abandon* his mind to it."

Burney:[21]—BURNEY. 'How does poor Smart do, Sir; is he likely to recover?' JOHNSON. 'It seems as if his mind had ceased to struggle with the disease; for he grows fat upon it.' BURNEY. 'Perhaps, Sir, that may be from want of exercise.' JOHNSON. 'No, Sir; he has partly as much exercise as he used to have, for he digs in the garden. Indeed, before his confinement, he used for exercise to walk to the ale-house; but he was *carried* back again. I did not think he ought to be shut up. His infirmities were not noxious to society. He insisted on people praying with him; and I'd as lief pray with Kit Smart as any one else. Another charge was, that he did not love clean linen; and I have no passion for it.'—Johnson continued. 'Mankind have a great aversion to intellectual labour; but even supposing knowledge to be easily attainable, more people would be content to be ignorant than would take even a little trouble to acquire it.'

'The morality of an action depends on the motive from which we act. If I fling half a crown to a beggar with intention to break his head, and he picks it up and buys victuals with it, the physical effect is good; but, with respect to me, the action is very wrong. So, religious exercises, if not performed with an intention to please GOD, avail us nothing. As our Saviour says of those who perform them from other motives, "Verily they have their reward.". . .'[22]

When I rose a second time he again pressed me to stay, which I did.

He told me, that he generally went abroad at four in the afternoon, and seldom came home till two in the morning. I took the liberty to ask if he did not think it wrong to live thus, and not make more use of his great talents. He owned it was a bad habit. On reviewing, at the distance of many years, my journal of this period, I wonder how, at my first visit, I ventured to talk to him so freely, and that he bore it with so much indulgence.

Before we parted, he was so good as to promise to favour me with his company one evening at my lodgings; and, as I took my leave, shook me cordially by the hand. It is almost needless to add, that I felt no little elation at having now so happily established an acquaintance of which I had been so long ambitious. . . .

I did not visit him again till Monday, June 13, at which time I recollect no part of his conversation, except that when I told him I had been to see Johnson ride upon three horses,[23] he said, 'Such a man, Sir, should be encouraged; for his performances show the extent of the human powers in one instance, and thus tend to raise our opinion of the faculties of man. He shows what may be attained by persevering application; so that every man may hope, that by giving as much application, although perhaps he may never ride three horses at a time, or dance upon a wire, yet he may be equally expert in whatever profession he has chosen to pursue.'

He again shook me by the hand at parting, and asked me why I did not come oftener to him. Trusting that I was now in his good graces, I answered, that he had not given me much encouragement, and reminded him of the check I had received from him at our first interview. 'Poh, poh! (said he, with

21. Dr. Charles Burney (1726–1814), musician and historian of music, who helped raise a subscription for Smart during his final confinement in 1771.
22. Matthew 6:16.
23. A famous exhibition of riding by a Johnson of whom only the last name is known.

a complacent smile,) never mind these things. Come to me as often as you can. I shall be glad to see you.'

[1776: The Meeting with Wilkes]

I am now to record a very curious incident in Dr. Johnson's Life, which fell under my own observation; of which *pars magna fui*,[24] and which I am persuaded will, with the liberal-minded, be much to his credit.

My desire of being acquainted with celebrated men of every description, had made me, much about the same time, obtain an introduction to Dr. Samuel Johnson and to John Wilkes, Esq. Two men more different could perhaps not be selected out of all mankind. They had even attacked one another with some asperity in their writings; yet I lived in habits of friendship with both. I could fully relish the excellence of each; for I have ever delighted in that intellectual chemistry, which can separate good qualities from evil in the same person. . . .

Notwithstanding the high veneration which I entertained for Dr. Johnson, I was sensible that he was sometimes a little actuated by the spirit of contradiction, and by means of that I hoped I should gain my point. I was persuaded that if I had come upon him with a direct proposal, 'Sir, will you dine in company with Jack Wilkes?' he would have flown into a passion, and would probably have answered, 'Dine with Jack Wilkes, Sir! I'd as soon dine with Jack Ketch.' [25] I therefore, while we were sitting quietly by ourselves at his house in an evening, took occasion to open my plan thus:—'Mr. Dilly,[26] Sir, sends his respectful compliments to you, and would be happy if you would do him the honour to dine with him on Wednesday next along with me, as I must soon go to Scotland.' JOHNSON. 'Sir, I am obliged to Mr. Dilly. I will wait upon him—' BOSWELL. 'Provided, Sir, I suppose, that the company which he is to have is agreeable to you.' JOHNSON. 'What do you mean, Sir? What do you take me for? Do you think I am so ignorant of the world, as to imagine that I am to prescribe to a gentleman what company he is to have at his table?' BOSWELL. 'I beg your pardon, Sir, for wishing to prevent you from meeting people whom you might not like. Perhaps he may have some of what he calls his patriotic[27] friends with him.' JOHNSON. 'Well, Sir, and what then? What care *I* for his *patriotic friends*? Poh!' BOSWELL. 'I should not be surprised to find Jack Wilkes there.' JOHNSON. 'And if Jack Wilkes *should* be there, what is that to *me*, Sir? My dear friend, let us have no more of this. I am sorry to be angry with you; but really it is treating me strangely to talk to me as if I could not meet any company whatever, occasionally.' BOSWELL. 'Pray forgive me, Sir: I meant well. But you shall meet whoever comes, for me.' Thus I secured him, and told Dilly that he would find him very well pleased to be one of his guests on the day appointed. . . .

When we entered Mr. Dilly's drawing room, he found himself in the midst of a company he did not know. I kept myself snug and silent, watching how

24. "I was a great part," *Aeneid* II.5.
25. That is, the hangman.
26. Edward Dilly (1732–79), the bookseller.
27. Referring to the government opposition; in 1773 Johnson added a new definition of patriot: "It is sometimes used for a factious disturber of the government."

he would conduct himself. I observed him whispering to Mr. Dilly, 'Who is that gentleman, Sir?'—'Mr. Arthur Lee.'—JOHNSON. 'Too, too, too,' (under his breath,) which was one of his habitual mutterings. Mr. Arthur Lee could not but be very obnoxious to Johnson, for he was not only a *patriot* but an *American*. He was afterwards minister from the United States at the court of Madrid. 'And who is the gentleman in lace?'—'Mr. Wilkes, Sir.' This information confounded him still more; he had some difficulty to restrain himself, and taking up a book, sat down upon a window-seat and read, or at least kept his eye upon it intently for some time, till he composed himself. His feelings, I dare say, were awkward enough. But he no doubt recollected his having rated me for supposing that he could be at all disconcerted by any company, and he, therefore, resolutely set himself to behave quite as an easy man of the world, who could adapt himself at once to the disposition and manners of those whom he might chance to meet.

The cheering sound of 'Dinner is upon the table,' dissolved his reverie, and we *all* sat down without any symptom of ill humour. There were present, besides Mr. Wilkes, and Mr. Arthur Lee, who was an old compaion of mine when he studied physic at Edinburgh, Mr. (now Sir John) Miller, Dr. Lettsom, and Mr. Slater the druggist. Mr. Wilkes placed himself next to Dr. Johnson, and behaved to him with so much attention and politeness that he gained upon him insensibly. No man eat [28] more heartily than Johnson, or loved better what was nice and delicate. Mr. Wilkes was very assiduous in helping him to some fine veal. 'Pray give me leave, Sir:—It is better here—A little of the brown—Some fat, Sir—A little of the stuffing—Some gravy—Let me have the pleasure of giving you some butter—Allow me to recommend a squeeze of this orange;—or the lemon, perhaps, may have more zest.'—'Sir, Sir, I am obliged to you, Sir,' cried Johnson, bowing, and turning his head to him with a look for some time of 'surly virtue,' [29] but, in a short while, of complacency.

Foote [30] being mentioned, Johnson said, 'He is not a good mimic.' One of the company added, 'A merry Andrew, a buffoon.' JOHNSON. 'But he has wit too, and is not deficient in ideas, or in fertility and variety of imagery, and not empty of reading; he has knowledge enough to fill up his part. One species of wit he has in an eminent degree, that of escape. You drive him into a corner with both hands; but he's gone, Sir, when you think you have got him—like an animal that jumps over your head. Then he has a great range for his wit; he never lets truth stand between him and a jest, and he is sometimes mighty coarse. Garrick is under many restraints from which Foote is free.' WILKES. 'Garrick's wit is more like Lord Chesterfield's.' JOHNSON. 'The first time I was in company with Foote was at Fitzherbert's. Having no good opinion of the fellow, I was resolved not to be pleased; and it is very difficult to please a man against his will. I went on eating my dinner pretty sullenly, affecting not to mind him. But the dog was so very comical, that I was obliged to lay down my knife and fork, throw myself back upon my chair, and fairly laugh it out.

28. "Eat" (pronounced *ett*) was a standard past form.

29. Boswell cites Johnson's *London*, ll. 144–45: "How, when competitors like these contend, / Can surly virtue hope to fix a friend?"

30. Samuel Foote (1720–77), actor and dramatist, of whom Johnson said, "For loud obstreperous broadfaced mirth, I know not his equal."

No, Sir, he was irresistible. He upon one occasion experienced, in an extraordinary degree, the efficacy of his powers of entertaining. Amongst the many and various modes which he tried of getting money, he became a partner with a small-beer [31] brewer, and he was to have a share of the profits for procuring customers amongst his numerous acquaintance. Fitzherbert was one who took his small-beer; but it was so bad that the servants resolved not to drink it. They were at some loss how to notify their resolution, being afraid of offending their master, who they knew liked Foote much as a companion. At last they fixed upon a little black boy, who was rather a favourite, to be their deputy, and deliver their remonstrance; and having invested him with the whole authority of the kitchen, he was to inform Mr. Fitzherbert, in all their names, upon a certain day, that they would drink Foote's small-beer no longer. On that day Foote happened to dine at Fitzherbert's, and this boy served at table; he was so delighted with Foote's stories, and merriment, and grimace, that when he went down stairs, he told them, "This is the finest man I have ever seen. I will not deliver your message. I will drink his small-beer." '

Somebody observed that Garrick could not have done this. WILKES. 'Garrick would have made the small-beer still smaller. He is now leaving the stage; but he will play *Scrub* all his life.' [32] I knew that Johnson would let nobody attack Garrick but himself, as Garrick once said to me, and I had heard him praise his liberality; so to bring out his commendation of his celebrated pupil, I said, loudly, 'I have heard Garrick is liberal.' JOHNSON. 'Yes, Sir, I know that Garrick has given away more money than any man in England that I am acquainted with, and that not from ostentatious views. Garrick was very poor when he began life; so when he came to have money, he probably was very unskilful in giving away, and saved when he should not. But Garrick began to be liberal as soon as he could; and I am of opinion, the reputation of avarice which he has had, has been very lucky for him, and prevented his having many enemies. You despise a man for avarice, but do not hate him. Garrick might have been much better attacked for living with more splendour than is suitable to a player: if they had had the wit to have assaulted him in that quarter, they might have galled him more. But they have kept clamouring about his avarice, which has rescued him from much obloquy and envy.' . . .

Mr. Arthur Lee mentioned some Scotch who had taken possession of a barren part of America, and wondered why they should choose it. JOHNSON. 'Why, Sir, all barrenness is comparative. The *Scotch* would not know it to be barren.' BOSWELL. 'Come, come, he is flattering the English. You have now been in Scotland, Sir, and say if you did not see meat and drink enough there.' JOHNSON. 'Why yes, Sir; meat and drink enough to give the inhabitants sufficient strength to run away from home.' All these quick and lively sallies were said sportively, quite in jest, and with a smile, which showed that he meant only wit. Upon this topic he and Mr. Wilkes could perfectly assimilate; here was a bond of union between them, and I was conscious that as

31. A weak or inferior beer.

32. Scrub is the servant to Sullen in George Farquhar's comedy *The Beaux' Stratagem* (1707); he has a different duty each day (that of butler on Sundays) and supplies a full staff in himself.

both of them had visited Caledonia, both were fully satisfied of the strange narrow ignorance of those who imagine that it is a land of famine. But they amused themselves with persevering in the old jokes. When I claimed a superiority for Scotland over England in one respect, that no man can be arrested there for a debt merely because another swears it against him; but there must first be the judgement of a court of law ascertaining its justice; and that a seizure of the person, before judgement is obtained, can take place only, if his creditor should swear that he is about to fly from the country, or, as it is technically expressed, is *in meditatione fugæ*:[33] WILKES. 'That, I should think, may be safely sworn of all the Scotch nation.' JOHNSON. (to Mr. Wilkes,) 'You must know, Sir, I lately took my friend Boswell and showed him genuine civilised life in an English provincial town. I turned him loose at Lichfield, my native city, that he might see for once real civility: for you know he lives among savages in Scotland and among rakes in London.' WILKES. 'Except when he is with grave, sober, decent people like you and me.' JOHNSON. (smiling,) 'And we ashamed of him.'

They were quite frank and easy. Johnson told the story of his asking Mrs. Macaulay to allow her footman to sit down with them,[34] to prove the ridiculousness of the argument for the equality of mankind; and he said to me afterwards, with a nod of satisfaction, 'You saw Mr. Wilkes acquiesced.' Wilkes talked with all imaginable freedom of the ludicrous title given to the Attorney-General, *Diabolus Regis;*[35] adding, 'I have reason to know something about that officer; for I was prosecuted for a libel.' Johnson, who many people would have supposed must have been furiously angry at hearing this talked of so lightly, said not a word. He was now, *indeed*, 'a good-humoured fellow.' . . .

This record, though by no means so perfect as I could wish, will serve to give a notion of a very curious interview, which was not only pleasing at the time, but had the agreeable and benignant effect of reconciling any animosity, and sweetening any acidity, which in the various bustle of political contest, had been produced in the minds of two men, who though widely different, had so many things in common—classical learning, modern literature, wit, and humour, and ready repartee—that it would have been much to be regretted if they had been for ever at a distance from each other.

Mr. Burke gave me much credit for this successful *negotiation;* and pleasantly said, that 'there was nothing to equal it in the whole history of the *Corps Diplomatique*.' . . .

On the evening of the next day I took leave of him, being to set out for Scotland. I thanked him with great warmth for all his kindness. 'Sir, (said he,) you are very welcome. Nobody repays it with more.'

How very false is the notion which has gone round the world of the rough, and passionate, and harsh manners of this great and good man. That he had occasional sallies of heat of temper, and that he was sometimes, perhaps, too

33. "Meditating flight."
34. That proposal silenced the "great republican" but, Johnson reported, "She has never liked me since. Sir, your levellers wish to level *down* as far as themselves; but they cannot bear levelling *up* to themselves."
35. "The King's Devil."

'easily provoked' by absurdity and folly, and sometimes too desirous of triumph in colloquial contest, must be allowed. The quickness both of his perception and sensibility disposed him to sudden explosions of satire; to which his extraordinary readiness of wit was a strong and almost irresistible incitement. To adopt one of the finest images in Mr. Home's *Douglas*,

> On each glance of thought
> Decision followed, as the thunderbolt
> Pursues the flash! [36]

I admit that the beadle [37] within him was often so eager to apply the lash, that the Judge had not time to consider the case with sufficient deliberation.

That he was occasionally remarkable for violence of temper may be granted: but let us ascertain the degree, and not let it be supposed that he was in a perpetual rage, and never without a club in his hand, to knock down every one who approached him. On the contrary, the truth is, that by much the greatest part of his time he was civil, obliging, nay, polite in the true sense of the word; so much so, that many gentlemen, who were long acquainted with him, never received, or even heard a strong expression from him.

[1777: The Fear of Death]

I mentioned to Dr. Johnson, that David Hume's persisting in his infidelity, when he was dying, shocked me much.[38] JOHNSON. 'Why should it shock you, Sir? Hume owned he had never read the New Testament with attention. Here then was a man, who had been at no pains to inquire into the truth of religion, and had continually turned his mind the other way. It was not to be expected that the prospect of death would alter his way of thinking, unless GOD should send an angel to set him right.' I said, I had reason to believe that the thought of annihilation gave Hume no pain. JOHNSON. 'It was not so, Sir. He had a vanity in being thought easy. It is more probable that he should assume an appearance of ease, than that so very improbable a thing should be as a man not afraid of going (as, in spite of his delusive theory, he cannot be sure but he may go,) into an unknown state, and not being uneasy at leaving all he knew. And you are to consider, that upon his own principle of annihilation he had no motive to speak the truth.' The horror of death which I had always observed in Dr. Johnson, appeared strong tonight. I ventured to tell him, that I had been, for moments in my life, not afraid of death; therefore I could suppose another man in that state of mind for a considerable space of time. He said, 'he never had a moment in which death was not terrible to him.' He added, that it had been observed, that scarce any man dies in public, but with apparent resolution; from that desire of praise

36. *Douglas* was the very popular tragedy by John Home (1722–1808), dramatist and friend of the poet William Collins.
37. A minor official who keeps order.
38. Boswell had an interview with Hume seven weeks before his death in 1776 and wrote an account of his own sense of danger in the face of Hume's obdurate disbelief in personal immortality ("But I maintained my faith"); still, Boswell admits that Hume was so good-humored that "Death for the time did not seem dismal."

which never quits us. I said, Dr. Dodd[39] seemed to be willing to die, and full of hopes of happiness. 'Sir, (said he,) Dr. Dodd would have given both his hands and both his legs to have lived. The better a man is, the more afraid he is of death, having a clearer view of infinite purity.' He owned, that our being in an unhappy uncertainty as to our salvation, was mysterious; and said, 'Ah! we must wait till we are in another state of being to have many things explained to us.' Even the powerful mind of Johnson seemed foiled by futurity. But I thought, that the gloom of uncertainty in solemn religious speculation, being mingled with hope, was yet more consolatory than the emptiness of infidelity. A man can live in thick air, but perishes in an exhausted receiver.

Dr. Johnson was much pleased with a remark which I told him was made to me by General Paoli: [40]—'That it is impossible not to be afraid of death; and that those who at the time of dying are not afraid, are not thinking of death, but of applause, or something else, which keeps death out of their sight: so that all men are equally afraid of death when they see it; only some have a power of turning their sight away from it better than others.' . . .

Some ladies, who had been present yesterday when I mentioned his birthday, came to dinner today, and plagued him unintentionally, by wishing him joy. I know not why he disliked having his birthday mentioned, unless it were that it reminded him of his approaching nearer to death, of which he had a constant dread.

I mentioned to him a friend of mine who was formerly gloomy from low spirits, and much distressed by the fear of death, but was now uniformly placid, and contemplated his dissolution without any perturbation. 'Sir, (said Johnson,) this is only a disordered imagination taking a different turn.' . . .

He observed, that a gentleman of eminence in literature[41] had got into a bad style of poetry of late. 'He puts (said he,) a very common thing in a strange dress till he does not know it himself, and thinks other people do not know it.' BOSWELL. 'That is owing to his being so much versant in old English poetry.' JOHNSON. 'What is that to the purpose, Sir? If I say a man is drunk, and you tell me it is owing to his taking much drink, the matter is not mended. No, Sir,———has taken to an odd mode. For example, he'd write thus:

> Hermit hoar, in solemn cell,
> Wearing out life's evening gray.

Gray evening is common enough; but *evening gray* he'd think fine.[42]—Stay;—we'll make out the stanza:

39. Dr. William Dodd (1729–77), king's chaplain and a popular preacher, forged a bond in the name of Lord Chesterfield, his former pupil; before his execution for this crime, Johnson did much for him and wrote several documents for him, including a "last solemn declaration." Dodd wrote Johnson at the very last: "Admitted, as I trust I shall be, to the realms of bliss before you, I shall hail *your* arrival there with transport. . . ."
40. General Pasquale Paoli (1725–1807), the Corsican general and patriot who had found asylum in England.
41. Thomas Warton (1728–90), who had just published a volume of poems.
42. Writing later in his life of Collins, Johnson complained of similar affectations in Warton's friend: "he puts his words out of the common order, seeming to think . . . that not to write prose is certainly to write poetry."

Hermit hoar, in solemn cell,
Wearing out life's evening gray;
Smite thy bosom, sage, and tell,
What is bliss? and which the way?

BOSWELL. 'But why smite his bosom, Sir?' JOHNSON. 'Why, to show he was in earnest,' (smiling.)—He at an after period added the following stanza:

Thus I spoke; and speaking sighed;
—Scarce repressed the starting tear;—
When the smiling sage replied—
—Come, my lad, and drink some beer.

I cannot help thinking the first stanza very good solemn poetry, as also the three first lines of the second. Its last line is an excellent burlesque surprise on gloomy sentimental enquirers. And, perhaps, the advice is as good as can be given to a low-spirited dissatisfied being:—'Don't trouble your head with sickly thinking: take a cup, and be merry.'

[The Character of Samuel Johnson]

The character of SAMUEL JOHNSON has, I trust, been so developed in the course of this work, that they who have honoured it with a perusal, may be considered as well acquainted with him. As, however, it may be expected that I should collect into one view the capital and distinguishing features of this extraordinary man, I shall endeavour to acquit myself of that part of my biographical undertaking, however difficult it may be to do that which many of my readers will do better for themselves.

His figure was large and well formed, and his countenance of the cast of an ancient statue; yet his appearance was rendered strange and somewhat uncouth by convulsive cramps, by the scars of that distemper [43] which it was once imagined the royal touch could cure, and by a slovenly mode of dress. He had the use only of one eye; yet so much does mind govern and even supply the deficiency of organs that his visual perceptions, as far as they extended, were uncommonly quick and accurate. So morbid was his temperament that he never knew the natural joy of a free and vigorous use of his limbs: when he walked, it was like the struggling gait of one in fetters; when he rode, he had no command or direction of his horse, but was carried as if in a balloon. That with his constitution and habits of life he should have lived seventy-five years, is a proof that an inherent *vivida vis* [44] is a powerful preservative of the human frame.

Man is, in general, made up of contradictory qualities; and these will ever show themselves in strange succession, where a consistency in appearance at least, if not in reality, has not been attained by long habits of philosophical discipline. In proportion to the native vigour of the mind, the contradictory qualities will be the more prominent, and more difficult to be adjusted; and, therefore, we are not to wonder, that Johnson exhibited an eminent example of

43. Scrofula.
44. Lively force.

this remark which I have made upon human nature. At different times, he seemed a different man, in some respects; not, however, in any great or essential article upon which he had fully employed his mind and settled certain principles of duty, but only in his manners and in the display of argument and fancy in his talk. He was prone to superstition, but not to credulity. Though his imagination might incline him to a belief of the marvellous and the mysterious, his vigorous reason examined the evidence with jealousy. He was a sincere and zealous Christian, of high Church-of-England and monarchical principles, which he would not tamely suffer to be questioned; and had, perhaps, at an early period, narrowed his mind somewhat too much, both as to religion and politics. His being impressed with the danger of extreme latitude in either, though he was of a very independent spirit, occasioned his appearing somewhat unfavourable to the prevalence of that noble freedom of sentiment which is the best possession of man. Nor can it be denied that he had many prejudices; which, however, frequently suggested many of his pointed sayings, that rather show a playfulness of fancy than any settled malignity. He was steady and inflexible in maintaining the obligations of religion and morality; both from a regard for the order of society, and from a veneration for the Great Source of all order; correct, nay stern in his taste; hard to please, and easily offended; impetuous and irritable in his temper, but of a most humane and benevolent heart, which showed itself not only in a most liberal charity, as far as his circumstances would allow, but in a thousand instances of active benevolence. He was afflicted with a bodily disease which made him often restless and fretful; and with a constitutional melancholy, the clouds of which darkened the brightness of his fancy and gave a gloomy cast to his whole course of thinking: we, therefore, ought not to wonder at his sallies of impatience and passion at any time; especially when provoked by obtrusive ignorance or presuming petulance; and allowance must be made for his uttering hasty and satirical sallies, even against his best friends. And, surely, when it is considered, that, 'amidst sickness and sorrow,' he exerted his faculties in so many works for the benefit of mankind, and particularly that he achieved the great and admirable DICTIONARY of our language, we must be astonished at his resolution. The solemn text, 'of him to whom much is given, much will be required,' [45] seems to have been ever present to his mind, in a rigorous sense, and to have made him dissatisfied with his labours and acts of goodness, however comparatively great; so that the unavoidable consciousness of his superiority was, in that respect, a cause of disquiet. He suffered so much from this, and from the gloom which perpetually haunted him and made solitude frightful, that it may be said of him, 'If in this life only he had hope, he was of all men most miserable.' [46] He loved praise, when it was brought to him; but was too proud to seek for it. He was somewhat susceptible of flattery. As he was general and unconfined in his studies, he cannot be considered as master of any one particular science; but he had accumulated a vast and various collection of learning and knowledge, which was so arranged in his mind, as to be ever in readiness to be brought forth. But his superiority over other learned men consisted chiefly in what may be called the art of

45. A close paraphrase of Luke 12:48.
46. Adapting I Corinthians 15:19.

thinking, the art of using his mind; a certain continual power of seizing the useful substance of all that he knew and exhibiting it in a clear and forcible manner; so that knowledge, which we often see to be no better than lumber in men of dull understanding, was, in him, true, evident, and actual wisdom. His moral precepts are practical; for they are drawn from an intimate acquaintance with human nature. His maxims carry conviction; for they are founded on the basis of common sense, and a very attentive and minute survey of real life. His mind was so full of imagery that he might have been perpetually a poet; yet it is remarkable that, however rich his prose is in this respect, his poetical pieces, in general, have not much of that splendour, but are rather distinguished by strong sentiment and acute observation, conveyed in harmonious and energetic verse, particularly in heroic couplets. Though usually grave, and even awful, in his deportment, he possessed uncommon and peculiar powers of wit and humour; he frequently indulged himself in colloquial pleasantry; and the heartiest merriment was often enjoyed in his company; with this great advantage, that as it was entirely free from any poisonous tincture of vice or impiety, it was salutary to those who shared in it. He had accustomed himself to such accuracy in his common conversation, that he at all times expressed his thoughts with great force, and an elegant choice of language, the effect of which was aided by his having a loud voice and a slow deliberate utterance. In him were united a most logical head with a most fertile imagination, which gave him an extraordinary advantage in arguing: for he could reason close or wide, as he saw best for the moment. Exulting in his intellectual strength and dexterity, he could, when he pleased, be the greatest sophist that ever contended in the lists of declamation; and, from a spirit of contradiction and a delight in showing his powers, he would often maintain the wrong side with equal warmth and ingenuity; so that when there was an audience, his real opinions could seldom be gathered from his talk; though when he was in company with a single friend, he would discuss a subject with genuine fairness: but he was too conscientious to make error permanent and pernicious by deliberately writing it; and, in all his numerous works, he earnestly inculcated what appeared to him to be the truth; his piety being constant, and the ruling principle of all his conduct.

Such was SAMUEL JOHNSON, a man whose talents, acquirements, and virtues, were so extraordinary, that the more his character is considered, the more he will be regarded by the present age, and by posterity, with admiration and reverence.

1791

From The Journal of a Tour to the Hebrides with Samuel Johnson, LL.D.

Wednesday, 1st September, 1773 I awaked very early. I began to imagine that the landlord,[1] being about to emigrate, might murder us to get our money, and lay it upon the soldiers in the barn. Such groundless fears will arise in the

1. This was written of the stay at Anoch in Glenmorison, the occasion for Johnson's description of the Highlands in his *Journey to the Western Islands.*

mind, before it has resumed its vigour after sleep! Dr. Johnson had had the same kind of ideas; for he told me afterwards, that he considered so many soldiers, having seen us, would be witnesses, should any harm be done, and that circumstance, I suppose, he considered as a security. When I got up, I found him sound asleep in his miserable sty, as I may call it, with a coloured handkerchief tied round his head. With difficulty could I awaken him. It reminded me of Henry the Fourth's fine soliloquy on sleep; for there was here as *uneasy a pallet* as the poet's imagination could possibly conceive.[2]

A redcoat of the 15th regiment, whether officer or only sergeant I could not be sure, came to the house in his way to the mountains to shoot deer, which it seems the Laird of Glenmorison does not hinder anybody to do. Few, indeed, can do them harm. We had him to breakfast with us. We got away about eight. M'Queen[3] walked some miles to give us a convoy. He had, in 1745, joined the Highland army at Fort Augustus, and continued in it till after battle of Culloden.[4] As he narrated the particulars of that ill-advised but brave attempt, I could not refrain from tears. There is a certain association of ideas in my mind upon that subject, by which I am strongly affected. The very Highland names, or the sound of a bagpipe, will stir my blood, and fill me with a mixture of melancholy and respect for courage; with pity for the unfortunate, and superstitious regard for antiquity, and thoughtless inclination for war; in short, with a crowd of sensations with which sober rationality has nothing to do.

We passed through Glensheal, with prodigious mountains on each side. We saw where the battle was fought in the year 1719.[5] Dr. Johnson owned he was now in a scene of as wild nature as he could see; but he corrected me sometimes in my inaccurate observations.—'There (said I) is a mountain like a cone.'—*Johnson.* 'No, sir. It would be called so in a book; and when a man comes to look at it, he sees it is not so. It is indeed pointed at the top; but one side of it is larger than the other.'—Another mountain I called immense.—*Johnson.* 'No; it is no more than a considerable protuberance.'

Sunday, 12th September . . . We spoke of Death. Dr. Johnson on this subject observed, that the boastings of some men as to dying easily were idle talk, proceeding from partial views. I mentioned Hawthornden's Cypress-grove,[6] where it is said that the world is a mere show; and that it is unreasonable for a man to wish to continue in the show-room, after he has seen it. Let him go cheerfully out, and give place to other spectators.—*Johnson.* 'Yes, sir, if he is sure he is to be well, after he goes out of it. But if he is to grow blind after he goes out of the show-room, and never to see any thing again; or if he does not know whither he is to go next, a man will not go cheerfully out of a show-room. No wise man will be contented to die, if he thinks he is to go into

2. See II *Henry IV* III.i for the soliloquy.
3. The landlord at Anoch.
4. The decisive defeat, April 16, 1746, of the Highlanders under the Jacobite Prince Charles Edward by the English troops under the Duke of Cumberland.
5. The battle of Glensheal (or Glenshiel) was lost to the British by a Jacobite force of Highlanders and Spaniards.
6. "The Cypress Grove" was a prose meditation on death by William Drummond of Hawthornden (1585–1649). For similar reflections by Johnson, see the passage from Boswell's *Life* for 1777 given above.

a state of punishment. Nay, no wise man will be contented to die, if he thinks he is to fall into annihilation: for however unhappy any man's existence may be, he yet would rather have it, than not exist at all. No; there is no rational principle by which a man can die contented, but a trust in the mercy of God, through the merits of Jesus Christ.'—This short sermon, delivered with an earnest tone, in a boat upon the sea, which was perfectly calm, on a day appropriated to religious worship, while every one listened with an air of satisfaction, had a most pleasing effect upon my mind.

Pursuing the same train of serious reflection, he added, that it seemed certain that happiness could not be found in this life, because so many had tried to find it, in such a variety of ways, and had not found it. . . .

Monday and Tuesday, September 13–14 . . . We arrived at Dunvegan late in the afternoon. The great size of the castle, which is partly old and partly new, and is built upon a rock close to the sea, while the land around it presents nothing but wild, moorish, hilly, and craggy appearances, gave a rude magnificence to the scene. . . . We were introduced into a stately dining-room, and received by Lady Macleod,[7] mother of the laird, who, with his friend Talisker, having been detained on the road, did not arrive till some time after us.

We found the lady of the house a very polite and sensible woman, who had lived for some time in London, and had there been in Dr. Johnson's company. . . .

Dr. Johnson said in the morning, 'Is not this a fine lady?'—There was not a word now of his 'impatience to be in civilized life';—though indeed I should beg pardon,—he found it here. We had slept well, and lain long. After breakfast we surveyed the castle, and the garden. . . . M'Leod started the subject of making women do penance in the church for fornication.—*Johnson.* 'It is right, sir. Infamy is attached to the crime, by universal opinion, as soon as it is known. I would not be the man who would discover it, if I alone knew it, for a woman may reform; nor would I commend a parson who divulges a woman's first offence; but being once divulged, it ought to be infamous. Consider of what importance to society the chastity of women is. Upon that all the property in the world depends. We hang a thief for stealing a sheep; but the unchastity of a woman transfers sheep, and farm and all, from the right owner. I have much more reverence for a common prostitute than for a woman who conceals her guilt. The prostitute is known. She cannot deceive: she cannot bring a strumpet into the arms of an honest man, without his knowledge.'—*Boswell.* 'There is, however, a great difference between the licentiousness of a single woman and that of a married woman.'—*Johnson.* 'Yes, sir; there is a great difference between stealing a shilling and stealing a thousand pounds; between simply taking a man's purse, and murdering him first, and then taking it. But when one begins to be vicious, it is easy to go on. Where single women are licentious, you rarely find faithful married women.'—*Boswell.* 'And yet we are told that in some nations in India, the distinction is strictly observed.'—*Johnson.* 'Nay, don't give us India. That puts me in mind of

7. John McLeod (d. 1786) was 9th Laird of Raasay; his son, Colonel John McLeod (1718–98), and the latter's wife also entertained Boswell and Johnson.

Montesquieu,[8] who is really a fellow of genius too in many respects; whenever he wants to support a strange opinion, he quotes you the practice of Japan or of some other distant country, of which he knows nothing. To support polygamy, he tells you of the island of Formosa, where there are ten women born for one man. He had but to suppose another island, where there are ten men born for one woman, and so make a marriage between them.'

At supper, Lady M'Leod mentioned Dr. Cadogan's book on the gout.[9] Lady M'Leod objected that the author does not practice what he teaches.—*Johnson.* 'I cannot help that, madam. That does not make his book the worse. People are influenced more by what a man says if his practice is suitable to it,—because they are blockheads. The more intellectual people are, the readier will they attend to what a man tells them. If it is just, they will follow it, be his practice what it will. No man practises so well as he writes. I have, all my life long, been lying till noon; yet I tell all young men, and tell them with great sincerity, that nobody who does not rise early will ever do any good. Only consider! You read a book; you are convinced by it; you do not know the author. Suppose you afterwards know him, and find that he does not practise what he teaches; are you to give up your former conviction? At this rate you would be kept in a state of equilibrium, when reading every book, till you knew how the author practised.'—'But,' said Lady M'Leod, 'you would think better of Dr. Cadogan, if he acted according to his principles.'—*Johnson.* 'Why, madam, to be sure, a man who acts in the face of light is worse than a man who does not know so much; yet I think no man should be the worse thought of for publishing good principles. There is something noble in publishing truth, though it condemns one's self.'—I expressed some surprize at Cadogan's recommending good humour, as if it were quite in our own power to attain it. —*Johnson.* 'Why, sir, a man grows better humoured as he grows older. He improves by experience. When young, he thinks himself of great consequence, and every thing of importance. As he advances in life, he learns to think himself of no consequence, and little things of little importance; and so he becomes more patient, and better pleased. All good-humour and complaisance are acquired. Naturally a child seizes directly what it sees, and thinks of pleasing itself only. By degrees, it is taught to please others, and to prefer others; and that this will ultimately produce the greatest happiness. If a man is not convinced of that, he never will practise it. Common language speaks the truth as to this: we say, a person is well *bred.* As it is said, that all material motion is primarily in a right line, and is never *per circuitum,* never in another form, unless by some particular cause; so it may be said intellectual motion is.' —Lady M'Leod asked, if no man was naturally good?—*Johnson.* 'No, madam, no more than a wolf.'—*Boswell.* 'Nor no woman, sir?'—*Johnson.* 'No, sir.'—Lady M'Leod started at this, saying, in a low voice, 'This is worse than Swift.'

Tuesday, October 19 . . . We continued to coast along Mull, and passed

8. Referring to the use of comparative evidence (such as had earlier been made by John Locke) by the Baron de Montesquieu (1689–1755) in *The Spirit of Laws* (1748); here a probable allusion to XVI.iv.

9. *A Dissertation on the Gout* (1771), a very popular work (nine printings in its first year). Dr. Cadogan was believed (perhaps falsely) to drink more than he could recommend in his book.

by Nuns' Island, which, it is said, belonged to the nuns of Icolmkill, and from which, we were told, the stone for the buildings there was taken. As we sailed along by moonlight, in a sea somewhat rough, and often between black and gloomy rocks, Dr. Johnson said, 'If this be not *roving among the Hebrides*, nothing is.'—The repetition of words which he had so often previously used, made a strong impression on my imagination; and, by a natural course of thinking, led me to consider how our present adventures would appear to me at a future period.

I have often experienced, that scenes through which a man has passed, improve by lying in the memory: they grow mellow. *Acti labores sunt jucundi.*[10] This may be owing to comparing them with present listless ease. Even harsh scenes acquire a softness by length of time; and some are like very loud sounds, which do not please, or at least do not please so much, till you are removed to a certain distance. They may be compared to strong coarse pictures, which will not bear to be viewed near. Even pleasing scenes improve by time, and seem more exquisite in recollection than when they were present; if they have not faded to dimness in the memory. Perhaps, there is so much evil in every human enjoyment when present,—so much dross mixed with it, that it requires to be refined by time; and yet I do not see why time should not melt away the good and the evil in equal proportions;—why the shade should decay, and the light remain in preservation.

After a tedious sail, which, by our following various turnings of the coast of Mull, was extended to about forty miles, it gave us no small pleasure to perceive a light in the village at Icolmkill, in which almost all the inhabitants of the island live, close to where the ancient buildings stood. As we approached the shore, the tower of the cathedral, just discernible in the air, was a picturesque object.

When we had landed upon the sacred place, which, as long as I can remember, I had thought on with veneration, Dr. Johnson and I cordially embraced. We had long talked of visiting Icolmkill; and, from the lateness of the season, were at times very doubtful whether we should be able to effect our purpose. To have seen it, even alone, would have given me great satisfaction; but the venerable scene was rendered much more pleasing by the company of my great and pious friend, who was no less affected by it than I was; and who has described the impressions it should make on the mind, with such strength of thought, and energy of language, that I shall quote his words, as conveying my own sensations much more forcibly than I am capable of doing:

'We were now treading that illustrious Island, which was once the luminary of the Caledonian regions, whence savage clans and roving barbarians derived the benefits of knowledge, and the blessings of religion. To abstract the mind from all local emotion would be impossible, if it were endeavoured, and would be foolish, if it were possible. Whatever withdraws us from the power of our senses, whatever makes the past, the distant, or the future, predominate over the present, advances us in the dignity of thinking beings. Far from me, and from my friends, be such frigid philosophy as may conduct us indifferent and

10. "Past labors are sweet," Cicero, *De Finibus* II.32.

unmoved over any ground which has been dignified by wisdom, bravery, or virtue. That man is little to be envied, whose patriotism would not gain force upon the plain of *Marathon*, or whose piety would not grow warmer among the ruins of *Iona!*' [11]

1773 1785

SAMUEL JOHNSON

1709–1784

Samuel Johnson dominates the English literary scene of the later eighteenth century and has, as well, become one of the mythical heroes of British common sense. Because of Boswell's remarkable *Life* we know him in more vividly intimate detail than most men of any age, and we are rarely without a sense of his personal presence as we read his works. While the range of Johnson's work is great, it has remarkable unity; for, whatever the stretch of his mind into natural science, philology, or history, it returns insistently to central moral themes, and notably to his favorite one, the efforts of the mind to escape the limitations of the actual. Whether in stupor or fantasy, in self-deception or in distraction, the mind seeks to elude that reality that stands outside it and rebuffs its systems. We see this in Johnson's attack upon the rules by which Shakespeare was foolishly judged, but we see it also in his identification of Shakespeare's "fatal Cleopatra" (an uncontrolled indulgence in verbal play). We see it ironically presented in Rasselas's fruitless quest for an ideal "choice of life," or in Johnson's acknowledgment of man's need for hope, however delusive. We see it in the "vanity" that overleaps the given, in the easy consolation that mistakes intention for act, in idleness and the fear of the self that seeks refuge in procrastination.

Johnson was born the son of a Lichfield bookseller, attended Oxford, and set up as a schoolmaster upon his marriage to Elizabeth Jervis Porter. In 1737 he went to London with his pupil David Garrick and began a literary career of translation, scholarship, and journalism. Among his remarkable feats was the reconstruction from notes of parliamentary debates for the *Gentleman's Magazine* (1741–44). His career was marked by three great projects. The first was the *Dictionary of the English Language* (1755), the second the edition of Shakespeare with preface and notes (1765), the third the *Lives of the Poets* written to accompany a printing of their works. But these projects were accompanied as well by the remarkable poems; the extensive series of essays that filled the *Rambler* twice a week (1750–52), and later *The Adventurer* (1753) and the *Idler* (1758–60); and the philosophical tale *Rasselas* (1759). In 1763 he met James Boswell and ten years later toured Scotland and the Hebrides with him, producing the *Journey to the Western Islands of Scotland* in 1775.

Johnson became the center of a group that included David Garrick, Edmund Burke, Sir Joshua Reynolds, Oliver Goldsmith, and others; and he often contributed encouragement, advice, and even revisions to the works of his contemporaries—notably Goldsmith, Reynolds, and Crabbe. In his conversation as well as his writing, Johnson exhibits different aspects, or perhaps different degrees of intensity. He could, with a strong histrionic sense and the levity of a debater, adopt an outrageous stance and

11. "Had our tour produced nothing but this sublime passage, the world must have acknowledged that it was not made in vain." (Boswell)

win the pleasures of domination; Johnson's nature demanded power, and he never questioned its appeal. He could, at other times, show a more defensive assertiveness, a bravado, in the face of his own doubts or fears, which insisted upon what he needed to believe in defiance of what, at a deeper level, he genuinely could. But more impressive than either is the empiricism that can be called common sense but is in fact something more radical: a recognition of the reality of the actual and a refusal to let it be dissolved in theory or masked in convention. "Liberty is the birthright of man, and where obedience is compelled, there is no liberty." This he takes to be the argument of the American revolutionaries. "The answer is equally simple. Government is necessary to man, and where obedience is not compelled, there is no government." This positivistic recognition of the fact of power is typical: "It is not infallible, for it may do wrong; but it is irresistible, for it can be resisted only by rebellion, by an act which makes it questionable what shall be thenceforward the supreme power." These three stances—the histrionic, the defensive, and the empirical—are hard to separate, and Johnson's tone must always be considered. He is a great ironist, and yet he is not the kind of skeptic who can remain uncommitted; he asserts with absoluteness what must not be ignored, however easily or little it can be wedded with its contraries or reconciled with our desires.

From London: A Poem

In Imitation of the Third Satire of Juvenal°

Prepare for death, if here at night you roam,
And sign your will before you sup from home.
Some fiery fop, with new commission vain,
Who sleeps on brambles till he kills his man;
Some frolic drunkard, reeling from a feast,
Provokes a broil, and stabs you for a jest.
Yet even these heroes, mischievously gay,
Lords of the street, and terrors of the way;
Flushed as they are with folly, youth, and wine,
Their prudent insults to the poor confine;
Afar they mark the flambeau's bright approach,
And shun the shining train, and golden coach:
In vain, these dangers past, your doors you close,
And hope the balmy blessings of repose:
Cruel with guilt, and daring with despair,
The midnight murderer bursts the faithless bar;
Invades the sacred hour of silent rest,
And leaves, unseen, a dagger in your breast.

Imitation . . . Juvenal For the meaning of "imitation" see the Headnote on Pope, Imitations of Horace. This passage in Johnson's version corresponds to the closer translation by Dryden; Johnson adapts Juvenal's satire more fully to a London setting.

Scarce can our fields, such crowds at Tyburn die,
With hemp° the gallows and the fleet supply.
Propose your schemes, ye Senatorian band,
Whose Ways and Means support the sinking land;
Lest ropes be wanting in the tempting spring,
To rig another convoy for the k—g.
A single jail, in ALFRED's golden reign,
Could half the nation's criminals contain;
Fair Justice then, without constraint adored,
Held high the steady scale, but deeped° the sword;
No spies were paid, no special juries known,
Blest age! but ah! how different from our own!

. . .

1738

The Vanity of Human Wishes

Like Pope's Horatian imitations, Johnson's is a free adaptation of Juvenal's poem to his own time and to his own frame of thought. This is nowhere clearer than in the closing lines, where Juvenal writes, "You would have no divinity if there were wisdom; it is we who make a goddess of you, Fortune, and place you in the heavens." Johnson sees instead the force of "celestial wisdom" saving man from himself, making the good fortune ("happiness") man cannot create for himself or even ask for properly. We have contemporary reactions to the difficulty of Johnson's condensed verse; David Garrick judged it "as hard as Greek." Johnson found in Juvenal a "mixture of gaiety and stateliness, of pointed sentences" (i.e. *sententiae* or maxims) "and declamatory grandeur." His version is more formal and austere than Dryden's, using the spacious generalization to indicate the ludicrous folly, as in the brilliant lines on the displaced favorite, whose image has lost its goodness with its greatness. The removal of the portrait is not presented dramatically or pictorially but in all the irony of its elaborate rationalization: "The form distorted justifies the fall, / And detestation rids the indignant wall." It is as if the very wall cannot bear his presence, as if his distortion of form is so strikingly evident to all that it cannot expect a moment's further tolerance; such, Johnson implies, is the cost of losing power in a world that knows no other standard. One can see "gaiety" in this rendering of lunacy as well as "stateliness" in the solemn recording of its pretexts, and even more in the deeper sense of its universal prevalence. The density of Johnson's diction is best seen in such compressed phrases, from which numerous particulars can be surmised, as "The general massacre of gold" or "dubious title shakes the madded land."

hemp the material for the hangman's rope (used in the gallows at Tyburn) or for the ship's ropes necessary for the frequent journeys of George II to Hanover and his mistress there (ll. 246–47), an expense supported by the House of Commons, whose "Ways and Means" are methods of raising money

deeped turned down

The Vanity of Human Wishes

The Tenth Satire of Juvenal Imitated

Let observation with extensive view,
Survey mankind, from China to Peru;
Remark each anxious toil, each eager strife,
And watch the busy scenes of crowded life;
Then say how hope and fear, desire and hate,
O'erspread with snares the clouded maze of fate,
Where wavering man, betrayed by venturous pride,
To tread the dreary paths without a guide,
As treacherous phantoms in the mist delude,
Shuns fancied ills, or chases airy good;
How rarely reason guides the stubborn choice,
Rules the bold hand, or prompts the suppliant voice;
How nations sink, by darling schemes oppressed,
When vengeance listens to the fool's request.°
Fate wings with every wish the afflictive dart,°
Each gift of nature, and each grace of art,
With fatal heat impetuous courage glows,
With fatal sweetness elocution flows,
Impeachment° stops the speaker's powerful breath,
And restless fire precipitates° on death.
But scarce observed, the knowing and the bold
Fall in the general massacre of gold;
Wide-wasting pest! that rages unconfined,
And crowds with crimes the records of mankind;
For gold his sword the hireling ruffian draws,
For gold the hireling judge distorts the laws;
Wealth heaped on wealth, nor truth nor safety buys,
The dangers gather° as the treasures rise.
Let history tell where rival kings command,
And dubious title shakes the madded land,
When statutes glean the refuse of the sword,°
How much more safe the vassal than the lord;
Low skulks the hind° beneath the rage of power,
And leaves the wealthy traitor° in the Tower,
Untouched his cottage, and his slumbers sound,

When vengeance . . . request i.e. the harshest vengeance is to give what the fool seeks, here a favorite ("darling") scheme

Fate wings . . . dart i.e. the dart is given flight (feathered) by every wish, gift, or "grace of art"

Impeachment public accusation

precipitates rushes or falls headlong; with perhaps the chemical sense of falling to the bottom as a sediment (the opposite of chemical sublimation)

The dangers gather Cf. Matthew 24:28: "For wheresoever the carcass is, there will the eagles be gathered together"; cf. the "vultures" of l. 36.

When statutes . . . sword i.e. when new laws undo those spared by open conflict; cf. l. 59

hind peasant

wealthy traitor perhaps the overthrown leader, now declared a "traitor" and imprisoned in the Tower of London, as Robert Harley, Earl of Oxford, chief minister of Queen Anne, was upon the accession of George I and Whig power in 1714 (see l. 130 below). More recent instances were the imprisonment and execution of Scottish lords after the Jacobite rising of 1745, and Johnson had originally written "bonny traitor."

Though confiscation's vultures hover round.
The needy traveller, serene and gay,
Walks the wild heath, and sings his toil away.
Does envy seize thee? crush the upbraiding joy,
Increase his riches and his peace destroy;
Now fears in dire vicissitude invade,
The rustling brake° alarms, and quivering shade,
Nor light nor darkness bring his pain relief,
One shows the plunder, and one hides the thief.
Yet still one general cry the skies assails,
And gain and grandeur load the tainted gales;°
Few know the toiling statesman's fear or care,
The insidious rival and the gaping heir.
Once more, Democritus,° arise on earth,
With cheerful wisdom and instructive mirth,
See motley° life in modern trappings dressed,
And feed with varied fools the eternal jest:
Thou who couldst laugh where want enchained caprice,
Toil crushed conceit,° and man was of a piece;
Where wealth unloved without a mourner died,
And scarce a sycophant was fed by pride;
Where ne'er was known the form of mock debate,
Or seen a new-made mayor's unwieldy state;°
Where change of favorites made no change of laws,
And senates heard before they judged a cause;
How wouldst thou shake at Britain's modish tribe,
Dart the quick taunt, and edge the piercing gibe,
Attentive truth and nature to descry,
And pierce each scene with philosophic eye.
To thee were solemn toys or empty show
The robes of pleasure and the veils of woe:
All aid the farce, and all thy mirth maintain,
Whose joys are causeless or whose griefs are vain.
Such was the scorn that filled the sage's mind,
Renewed at every glance on humankind;
How just that scorn ere yet thy voice declare,
Search every state, and canvass every prayer.
Unnumbered suppliants crowd Preferment's gate,°
Athirst for wealth, and burning to be great;
Delusive Fortune hears the incessant call,
They mount, they shine, evaporate, and fall.
On every stage the foes of peace attend,

brake thicket
tainted gales breezes carrying the scent of the hunted quarry
Democritus (*c.* 460–370 B.C.) known as the "laughing philosopher." Robert Burton wrote as Democritus Junior in *The Anatomy of Melancholy* (1621), one of Johnson's favorite books.
motley of various colors, like the traditional Fool's costume
conceit imagination
unwieldy state referring to the gilt coach and elaborate rituals of the Lord Mayor's procession
Preferment's gate the gate of a lord who can grant posts of office

Hate dogs their flight, and insult mocks their end.
Love ends with hope, the sinking statesman's door
Pours in the morning worshipper° no more;
For growing names the weekly scribbler° lies,
To growing wealth the dedicator flies,
From every room descends the painted face,
That hung the bright Palladium° of the place,
And smoked in kitchens, or in auctions sold,
To better features yields the frame of gold;
For now no more we trace in every line
Heroic worth, benevolence divine:
The form distorted justifies the fall,
And detestation rids the indignant wall.
　But will not Britain hear the last appeal,
Sign her foes' doom, or guard her favourites' zeal?
Through Freedom's sons no more remonstrance° rings,
Degrading nobles and controlling kings;
Our supple tribes repress their patriot throats,
And ask no questions but the price of votes;
With weekly libels and septennial ale,°
Their wish is full to riot and to rail.
　In full-blown dignity, see Wolsey° stand,
Law in his voice, and fortune in his hand:
To him the church, the realm, their powers consign,
Through him the rays of regal bounty shine,
Turned by his nod the stream of honour flows,
His smile alone security bestows:
Still to new heights his restless wishes tower,
Claim leads to claim, and power advances power;
Till conquest unresisted ceased to please,
And rights submitted left him none to seize.
At length his sovereign frowns—the train of state
Mark the keen glance and watch the sign to hate.
Where'er he turns he meets a stranger's eye,
His suppliants scorn him and his followers fly;
At once is lost the pride of awful state,
The golden canopy, the glittering plate,
The regal palace, the luxurious board,

morning worshipper the assiduous attendant at levees (or morning receptions)
the weekly scribbler in the political journals
Palladium the statue of Pallas Athena that supposedly conferred safety upon the city of Troy and was stolen by Diomedes so that Troy might be taken. The portrait which served this protective purpose has now been banished to the smoky kitchen or sold off and only the frame preserved.
remonstrance alluding to the Grand Remonstrance of 1641 demanding that Charles I's council be chosen from men approved by Parliament
septennial ale provided at parliamentary elections (held at least every seven years) to attract votes, as were more substantial bribes and the demagoguery of newspaper campaigns ("weekly libels"). Thus parliamentary "questions" and debate give way, through corruption, to demonstrations and slanderous railing.
Wolsey Thomas Wolsey (*c.* 1475–1530), cardinal and Lord Chancellor of Henry VIII, replacing Juvenal's Sejanus, the favorite of the emperor Tiberius

The liveried army° and the menial lord.
With age, with cares, with maladies oppressed,
He seeks the refuge of monastic rest.
Grief aids disease, remembered folly stings,
And his last sighs reproach the faith of kings.
Speak thou, whose thoughts at humble peace repine,
Shall Wolsey's wealth with Wolsey's end be thine?
Or livest thou now, with safer pride content,
The wisest justice on the banks of Trent?°
For why did Wolsey near the steeps of fate,
On weak foundations raise the enormous weight?
Why but to sink beneath misfortune's blow,
With louder ruin to the gulfs below?
What gave great Villiers° to the assassin's knife,
And fixed disease on Harley's° closing life?
What murdered Wentworth, and what exiled Hyde,°
By kings protected, and to kings allied?
What but their wish indulged in courts to shine,
And power too great to keep, or to resign?
When first the college rolls receive his name,
The young enthusiast quits his ease for fame;
Through all his veins the fever of renown
Burns from the strong contagion of the gown;°
O'er Bodley's dome° his future labours spread,
And Bacon's mansion° trembles o'er his head.
Are these thy views? proceed, illustrious youth,
And virtue guard thee to the throne of Truth!
Yet should thy soul indulge the generous heat,
Till captive Science yields her last retreat;
Should Reason guide thee with her brightest ray,
And pour on misty Doubt resistless day;°
Should no false Kindness lure to loose delight,
Nor Praise relax, nor Difficulty fright;
Should tempting Novelty thy cell refrain,
And Sloth effuse her opiate fumes in vain;
Should Beauty blunt on fops her fatal dart,
Nor claim the triumph of a lettered heart;
Should no Disease thy torpid veins invade,

liveried army an army of servants, or officers behaving as servants

on the banks of Trent any provincial scene, but here referring to Johnson's own birthplace, Lichfield

great Villiers George Villiers, 1st Duke of Buckingham, favorite of James I and Charles I, murdered in 1628

Harley's See above l. 34 and note; Harley later suffered bad health, perhaps because of his confinement in the Tower.

Wentworth . . . Hyde Thomas Wentworth, Earl of Strafford, advisor of Charles I, impeached and executed in 1641; Edward Hyde, Earl of Clarendon, Lord Chancellor to Charles II but impeached and banished in 1667 ("to kings allied" as father-in-law of James II and grandfather of Queen Mary and Queen Anne)

the strong . . . gown with the suggestion of Nessus' shirt, the poisoned robe that caused Hercules so much torture that he tore away his flesh in trying to remove it

Bodley's dome the Bodleian Library at Oxford; "dome" is used in the sense of a building

Bacon's mansion referring to the tradition that the study of Roger Bacon, the medieval Oxford philosopher and scientist, built on an arch over a bridge, would fall when a greater man than Bacon passed under it

resistless day Cf. Pope, *Essay on Criticism*, ll. 211–12.

Nor Melancholy's phantoms haunt thy shade;
Yet hope not life from grief or danger free,
Nor think the doom of man reversed for thee:
Deign on the passing world to turn thine eyes,
And pause awhile from letters to be wise;
There mark what ills the scholar's life assail,
Toil, envy, want, the patron,° and the jail.
See nations slowly wise, and meanly just,
To buried merit raise the tardy bust.°
If dreams yet flatter, once again attend,
Hear Lydiat's life, and Galileo's end.°
  Nor deem, when learning her last prize bestows,
The glittering eminence exempt from foes;
See when the vulgar 'scape, despised or awed,
Rebellion's vengeful talons seize on Laud.°
From meaner minds, though smaller fines content,
The plundered palace or sequestered rent;°
Marked out by dangerous parts he meets the shock,
And fatal Learning leads him to the block:
Around his tomb let Art and Genius weep,
But hear his death, ye blockheads, hear and sleep.
  The festal blazes, the triumphal show,
The ravished standard, and the captive foe,
The senate's thanks, the gazette's° pompous tale,
With force resistless o'er the brave prevail.
Such bribes the rapid Greek° o'er Asia whirled,
For such the steady Romans shook the world;°
For such in distant lands the Britons° shine,
And stain with blood the Danube or the Rhine;
This power has praise that virtue scarce can warm,
Till fame supplies the universal charm.
Yet Reason frowns on War's unequal game,
Where wasted nations raise a single name,
And mortgaged states their grandsires' wreaths regret,°
From age to age in everlasting debt;

patron For this substitution for "garret" see James Boswell's *Life of Johnson* on the publication of the *Dictionary*, where a patron is defined as "commonly a wretch who supports with insolence and is paid with flattery."
tardy bust e.g. that of John Milton, not placed in Westminster Abbey until 1737; but also late monuments to Dryden (1720), Samuel Butler (1721), and Shakespeare (1741)
Lydiat's . . . end Thomas Lydiat (1572–1646), a brilliant scholar ranked with Francis Bacon in his day but poor and forgotten at the time of his death. Galileo (1564–1642) was declared a heretic and imprisoned by the Inquisition in 1633 and later became blind (Mrs. Piozzi recorded that Johnson "burst into a passion of tears" one day as he read aloud this passage on the scholar's life).
Laud William Laud, Archbishop of Canterbury under Charles I, was executed by Parliament in 1645; Johnson attributes his high-church policies to his "Learning" and his gifts ("parts").
sequestered rent confiscated income, sufficient to "content" the persecutors of lesser men
gazette's official court record
rapid Greek Alexander the Great
shook the world perhaps evoking the famous long marches of the Roman legions
Britons referring to the Duke of Marlborough's campaigns in Austria and Bavaria, particularly the great victory of Blenheim (1704) in the War of the Spanish Succession
mortgaged states . . . regret Cf. Swift in *The Conduct of the Allies* (1711): "It will, no doubt, be a mighty comfort to our grandchildren, when they see a few rags hang up in Westminster Hall which cost an hundred millions, whereof they are paying the arrears, and boasting, as beggars do, that their grandfathers were rich and great."

Wreathes which at last the dear-bought right convey
To rust on medals, or on stones decay.
On what foundation stands the warrior's pride,
How just his hopes let Swedish Charles° decide;
A frame of adamant, a soul of fire,
No dangers fright him, and no labours tire;
O'er love, o'er fear, extends his wide domain,
Unconquered lord of pleasure and of pain;
No joys to him pacific sceptres yield,
War sounds the trump, he rushes to the field;
Behold surrounding kings their power combine,
And one capitulate, and one resign;°
Peace courts his hand, but spreads her charms in vain;
'Think nothing gained,' he cries, 'till nought remain,
On Moscow's walls till Gothic° standards fly,
And all be mine beneath the polar sky.'
The march begins in military state,
And nations on his eye suspended wait;
Stern Famine guards the solitary coast,
And Winter barricades the realms of Frost;
He comes, not want and cold his course delay;—
Hide, blushing Glory, hide Pultowa's day:°
The vanquished hero leaves his broken bands,
And shows his miseries in distant lands;
Condemned a needy supplicant to wait,
While ladies interpose, and slaves debate.
But did not Chance at length for error mend?
Did no subverted empire mark his end?
Did rival monarchs give the fatal wound?
Or hostile millions press him to the ground?
His fall was destined to a barren strand,
A petty fortress, and a dubious hand;°
He left the name, at which the world grew pale,
To point a moral, or adorn a tale.
All times their scenes of pompous woes afford,
From Persia's tyrant to Bavaria's lord.
In gay hostility, and barbarous pride,
With half mankind embattled at his side,
Great Xerxes° comes to seize the certain prey,
And starves exhausted regions in his way;
Attendant Flattery counts his myriads o'er,
Till counted myriads soothe his pride no more;
Fresh praise is tried till madness fires his mind,

Swedish Charles Charles XII of Sweden (1682–1718), replacing Juvenal's Hannibal
one capitulate . . . resign Frederick IV of Denmark in 1700 and Augustus II of Poland in 1704
Gothic Swedish
Pultowa's day the defeat by Peter the Great in 1709 at Poltava in Russia, followed by Charles's flight to Turkey
dubious hand Charles was killed in Norway, perhaps by the hand of his own officer.
Xerxes who invaded Greece and was defeated at the sea battles at Salamis in 480 B.C.

The waves he lashes, and enchains the wind;
New powers are claimed, new powers are still bestowed,
Till rude resistance lops the spreading god;°
The daring Greeks deride the martial show,
And heap their valleys with the gaudy foe;
The insulted sea with humbler thoughts he gains,
A single skiff to speed his flight remains;
The incumbered oar scarce leaves the dreaded coast
Through purple billows and a floating host.°
  The bold Bavarian,° in a luckless hour,
Tries the dread summits of Cesarean power,
With unexpected legions bursts away,
And sees defenceless realms receive his sway;
Short sway! fair Austria spreads her mournful charms,
The queen, the beauty, sets the world in arms;
From hill to hill the beacons' rousing blaze
Spreads wide the hope of plunder and of praise;
The fierce Croatian, and the wild Hussar,°
And all the sons of ravage crowd the war;
The baffled prince in honour's flattering bloom
Of hasty greatness finds the fatal doom,
His foes' derision, and his subjects' blame,
And steals to death from anguish and from shame.
  'Enlarge my life with multitude of days,'
In health, in sickness, thus the suppliant prays;
Hides from himself his state, and shuns to know,
That life protracted is protracted woe.
Time hovers o'er, impatient to destroy,
And shuts up all the passages of joy:
In vain their gifts the bounteous seasons pour,
The fruit autumnal, and the vernal flower,
With listless eyes the dotard views the store,
He views, and wonders that they please no more;
Now pall the tasteless meats and joyless wines,
And Luxury with sighs her slave resigns.
Approach, ye minstrels, try the soothing strain,
Diffuse the tuneful lenitives° of pain:
No sounds, alas, would touch the impervious ear,
Though dancing mountains witnessed Orpheus° near;
Nor lute nor lyre his feeble powers attend,
Nor sweeter music of a virtuous friend,
But everlasting dictates crowd his tongue,

lops . . . god i.e. as the branches of an over-arching tree
The incumbered . . . host This account of Xerxes' flight through a sea dyed with blood and thick with corpses was reported to be Johnson's own favorite couplet.
bold Bavarian Charles Albert, Elector of Bavaria, claimed the Holy Roman Empire against Maria Theresa ("fair Austria"); he was crowned Charles VII (1742) but became a puppet of his allies and died in 1745.
Hussar Hungarian light-horseman; like the Croatian, recruited in Austria's defense
lenitives easers, anodynes
Orpheus the legendary Greek bard whose music made mountains dance

Perversely grave, or positively° wrong.
The still returning tale and lingering jest
Perplex the fawning niece and pampered guest,
While growing hopes scarce awe the gathering sneer,
And scarce a legacy can bribe to hear;
The watchful guests still hint the last offence,
The daughter's petulance, the son's expense,
Improve° his heady rage with treacherous skill,
And mould his passions till they make his will.
  Unnumbered maladies his joints invade,
Lay siege to life, and press the dire blockade;
But unextinguished Avarice still remains,
And dreaded losses aggravate his pains;
He turns, with anxious heart and crippled hands,
His bonds of debt and mortgages of lands;
Or views his coffers with suspicious eyes,
Unlocks his gold, and counts it till he dies.
  But grant, the virtues of a temperate prime
Bless with an age exempt from scorn or crime;
An age that melts with unperceived decay,
And glides in modest innocence away;
Whose peaceful day Benevolence endears,
Whose night congratulating Conscience cheers;
The general favourite as the general friend:
Such age there is, and who shall wish its end?
  Yet even on this her load Misfortune flings,
To press the weary minutes' flagging wings:
New sorrow rises as the day returns,
A sister sickens, or a daughter mourns.
Now kindred Merit fills the sable bier,
Now lacerated Friendship claims a tear.
Year chases year, decay pursues decay,
Still drops some joy from withering life away;
New forms arise, and different views engage,
Superfluous lags the veteran on the stage,
Till pitying Nature signs the last release,
And bids afflicted worth retire to peace.
  But few there are whom hours like these await,
Who set unclouded in the gulfs of fate.
From Lydia's monarch° should the search descend,
By Solon cautioned to regard his end,
In life's last scene what prodigies surprise,
Fears of the brave, and follies of the wise?
From Marlborough's° eyes the streams of dotage flow,

positively peremptorily, in strong terms
Improve increase
Lydia's monarch Croesus, warned by Solon to consider no man happy while he was living
Marlborough John Churchill (1650–1722), 1st Duke of Marlborough, the great military leader and victor of Blenheim, suffered paralytic strokes in his last years.

And Swift° expires a driveller and a show.
The teeming mother, anxious for her race,
Begs for each birth the fortune of a face:
Yet Vane° could tell what ills from beauty spring;
And Sedley° cursed the form that pleased a king.
Ye nymphs of rosy lips and radiant eyes,
Whom Pleasure keeps too busy to be wise,
Whom Joys with soft varieties invite,
By day the frolic, and the dance by night,
Who frown with vanity, who smile with art,
And ask the latest fashion of the heart,
What care, what rules your heedless charms shall save,
Each nymph your rival, and each youth your slave?
Against your fame with fondness hate combines,
The rival batters, and the lover mines.
With distant voice neglected Virtue calls,
Less heard and less, the faint remonstrance falls;
Tired with contempt, she quits the slippery reign,
And Pride and Prudence take her seat in vain.
In crowd at once, where none the pass defend,
The harmless freedom and the private friend.
The guardians yield, by force superior plied;
By Interest, Prudence; and by Flattery, Pride.
Now Beauty falls betrayed, despised, distressed,
And hissing Infamy proclaims the rest.
Where then shall Hope and Fear their objects find?
Must dull Suspense° corrupt the stagnant mind?
Must helpless man, in ignorance sedate,
Roll darkling down the torrent of his fate?
Must no dislike alarm, no wishes rise,
No cries attempt the mercies of the skies?
Enquirer, cease, petitions yet remain,
Which heaven may hear; nor deem religion vain.
Still raise for good the supplicating voice,
But leave to heaven the measure and the choice,
Safe in his power, whose eyes discern afar
The secret ambush° of a specious prayer.
Implore his aid, in his decisions rest,
Secure whate'er he gives, he gives the best.
Yet when the sense of sacred presence fires,
And strong devotion to the skies aspires,
Pour forth thy fervours for a healthful mind,

Swift Swift's final madness (he was placed under the care of guardians from 1741 until his death in 1745) was "compounded of rage and fatuity"; except for a few intervals, he "sunk into lethargic stupidity, motionless, heedless, and speechless" (Johnson, *Life of Swift*).

Vane Anne Vane, mistress of Frederick, Prince of Wales, who deserted her

Sedley Catherine Sedley, mistress to the Duke of York, but abandoned when he became James II

Suspense i.e. a suspension of all moral choice, producing stagnancy

Sedley Catherine Sedley, mistress to the Duke through avowed sincerity

Obedient passions, and a will resigned;
For love, which scarce collective man can fill;°
For patience sovereign o'er transmuted° ill;
For faith, that panting for a happier seat,
Counts death kind Nature's signal of retreat:
These goods for man the laws of heaven ordain,
These goods he grants, who grants the power to gain;
With these celestial wisdom calms the mind,
And makes the happiness she does not find.°

1748 1749

On the Death of Dr. Robert Levet°

Condemned to hope's delusive mine,
  As on we toil from day to day,
By sudden blasts, or slow decline,
  Our social comforts drop away.

Well tried through many a varying year,
  See Levet to the grave descend;
Officious,° innocent, sincere,
  Of every friendless name the friend.

Yet still he fills affection's eye,
  Obscurely wise and coarsely kind;
Nor, lettered Arrogance, deny
  Thy praise to merit unrefined.

When fainting Nature called for aid,
  And hovering Death prepared the blow,
His vigorous remedy displayed
  The power of art without the show.

In misery's darkest caverns known,
  His useful care was ever nigh,
Where hopeless Anguish poured his groan,
  And lonely Want retired to die.

No summons mocked by chill delay,
  No petty gain disdained by pride,
The modest wants of every day
  The toil of every day supplied.

For love . . . fill Cf. Pope, *Essay on Man* IV. 369–70: "Wide and more wide, the o'erflowings of the mind / Take every creature in, of every kind."

transmuted i.e. altered or transformed by the very patience that meets it, as in the next lines

makes . . . find i.e. once absorbed into the mind, such wisdom has the power to create its own happiness by seeking only those objects which (in Johnson's words) are "always to be obtained"

On . . . Levet Levet (1705–82) lived as part of Johnson's household for many years, a poor man without a medical degree, somewhat stiff and silent in manner, but generous in treating others for little or no money.

Officious full of good offices

His virtues walked their narrow round,
Nor made a pause, nor left a void;
And sure the Eternal Master found
The single talent well employed.

The busy day, the peaceful night,
Unfelt, uncounted, glided by;
His frame was firm, his powers were bright,
Though now his eightieth year was nigh.

Then with no throbbing fiery pain,
No cold gradations of decay,
Death broke at once the vital chain,
And freed his soul the nearest way.
1782 1782

The History of Rasselas, Prince of Abyssinia

This Oriental tale was written "in the evenings of one week" to defray the expense of Johnson's mother's funeral and to pay off her few small debts. Its elevated, highly formalized narrative is always tinged with an ironic sense of the ludicrous, and its hero—the young Prince Rasselas—is a solemn, rather priggish idealist who seeks to make "the choice of life." But, as his guide Imlac points out, "Very few live by choice." Rasselas and his sister Nekayah are too inexperienced, too demanding, and too hopeful to accept the imperfections of a deluded or meaningless life. They must undergo the quest that Imlac has already exhausted; yet he cannot resist accompanying them, almost as though he cannot resist the vicarious enjoyment of their hope. Johnson wrote elsewhere (*Idler* No. 58): "It is necessary to hope, though hope should always be deluded; for hope itself is happiness, and its frustrations, however frequent, are yet less dreadful than its extinction."

Rasselas and Nekayah must learn to accept life as it is offered, however little it accommodates either our desires or our logic. Nekayah comes to see that "by too much prudence" we may avoid extremes but also be cheated of life itself in the process: "Of the blessings set before you, make your choice, and be content."

The tale is essentially a comic one, as we see in its gently preposterous Oriental setting, the self-mocking formality of its dialogue, the balance of characters and ideas, and the circularity of its total structure. Yet the comedy is sad, too; for its disenchantment resists all easy solutions, including even the willingness "to be driven along the stream of life" without direction. Johnson's tale was written almost precisely at the same time as Voltaire's *Candide,* with which it shares an ironic view of man's dream of finding a providential design in his life or of making a fully rational choice for himself.

The History of Rasselas, Prince of Abyssinia

Chapter I: Description of a Palace in a Valley

Ye who listen with credulity to the whispers of fancy, and pursue with eagerness the phantoms of hope; who expect that age will perform the promises of youth, and that the deficiencies of the present day will be supplied by the morrow; attend to the history of Rasselas prince of Abyssinia.

Rasselas was the fourth son of the mighty emperour, in whose dominions the father of waters [1] begins his course; whose bounty pours down the streams of plenty, and scatters over half the world the harvests of Egypt.

According to the custom which has descended from age to age among the monarchs of the torrid zone, Rasselas was confined in a private palace, with the other sons and daughters of Abyssinian royalty, till the order of succession should call him to the throne.

The place, which the wisdom or policy of antiquity had destined for the residence of the Abyssinian princes, was a spacious valley in the kingdom of Amhara, surrounded on every side by mountains, of which the summits overhang the middle part. The only passage by which it could be entered was a cavern that passed under a rock, of which it has long been disputed whether it was the work of nature or of human industry. The outlet of the cavern was concealed by a thick wood, and the mouth which opened into the valley was closed with gates of iron, forged by the artificers of ancient days, so massy that no man could, without the help of engines, open or shut them.

From the mountains on every side, rivulets descended that filled all the valley with verdure and fertility; and formed a lake in the middle inhabited by fish of every species, and frequented by every fowl whom nature has taught to dip the wing in water. This lake discharged its superfluities by a stream which entered a dark cleft of the mountain on the northern side and fell with dreadful noise from precipice to precipice till it was heard no more.

The sides of the mountains were covered with trees, the banks of the brooks were diversified with flowers; every blast shook spices from the rocks, and every month dropped fruits upon the ground. All animals that bite the grass or browse the shrub, whether wild or tame, wandered in this extensive circuit, secured from beasts of prey by the mountains which confined them. On one part were flocks and herds feeding in the pastures, on another all the beasts of chase frisking in the lawns; the sprightly kid was bounding on the rocks, the subtle monkey frolicking in the trees, and the solemn elephant reposing in the shade. All the diversities of the world were brought together, the blessings of nature were collected, and its evils extracted and excluded.[2]

The valley, wide and fruitful, supplied its inhabitants with the necessaries of life, and all delights and superfluities were added at the annual visit which the emperour paid his children, when the iron gate was opened to the sound of music; and during eight days every one that resided in the valley was required to propose whatever might contribute to make seclusion pleasant, to fill up the

1. Nile River.
2. Johnson's description of the Happy Valley, while drawn from earlier accounts of Abyssinia, also ironically evokes Milton's vision of Eden in *Paradise Lost* Bk. IV.

vacancies of attention, and lessen the tediousness of time. Every desire was immediately granted. All the artificers of pleasure were called to gladden the festivity; the musicians exerted the power of harmony, and the dancers showed their activity before the princes, in hope that they should pass their lives in this blissful captivity, to which these only were admitted whose performance was thought able to add novelty to luxury. Such was the appearance of security and delight which this retirement afforded, that they to whom it was new always desired that it might be perpetual; and as those, on whom the iron gate had once closed, were never suffered to return, the effect of longer experience could not be known. Thus every year produced new schemes of delight and new competitors for imprisonment.

The palace stood on an eminence raised about thirty paces above the surface of the lake. It was divided into many squares or courts, built with greater or less magnificence according to the rank of those for whom they were designed. The roofs were turned into arches of massy stone joined with a cement that grew harder by time, and the building stood from century to century, deriding the solstitial rains and equinoctial hurricanes, without need of reparation.[3]

This house, which was so large as to be fully known to none but some ancient officers who successively inherited the secrets of the place, was built as if suspicion herself had dictated the plan. To every room there was an open and secret passage; every square had a communication with the rest, either from the upper stories by private galleries, or by subterranean passages from the lower apartments. Many of the columns had unsuspected cavities, in which a long race of monarchs had reposited their treasures. They then closed up the opening with marble, which was never to be removed but in the utmost exigencies of the kingdom; and recorded their accumulations in a book which was itself concealed in a tower not entered but by the emperour, attended by the prince who stood next in succession.

Chapter II: The Discontent of Rasselas in the Happy Valley

Here the sons and daughters of Abyssinia lived only to know the soft vicissitudes of pleasure and repose, attended by all that were skilful to delight, and gratified with whatever the senses can enjoy. They wandered in gardens of fragrance and slept in the fortresses of security. Every art was practised to make them pleased with their own condition. The sages who instructed them told them of nothing but the miseries of public life, and described all beyond the mountains as regions of calamity, where discord was always raging and where man preyed upon man.

To heighten their opinion of their own felicity, they were daily entertained with songs, the subject of which was the *happy valley.* Their appetites were excited by frequent enumerations of different enjoyments, and revelry and merriment was the business of every hour from the dawn of morning to the close of even.

These methods were generally successful; few of the princes had ever wished to enlarge their bounds, but passed their lives in full conviction that they had all within their reach that art or nature could bestow, and pitied those

3. "The act of repairing; supply of what is wasted" (Johnson, *Dictionary*).

whom fate had excluded from this seat of tranquility, as the sport of chance and the slaves of misery.

Thus they rose in the morning and lay down at night pleased with each other and with themselves; all but Rasselas, who, in the twenty-sixth year of his age, began to withdraw himself from their pastimes and assemblies and to delight in solitary walks and silent meditation. He often sat before tables covered with luxury and forgot to taste the dainties that were placed before him: he rose abruptly in the midst of the song and hastily retired beyond the sound of music. His attendants observed the change and endeavoured to renew his love of pleasure: he neglected their officiousness, repulsed their invitations, and spent day after day on the banks of rivulets sheltered with trees, where he sometimes listened to the birds in the branches, sometimes observed the fish playing in the stream, and anon cast his eyes upon the pastures and mountains filled with animals, of which some were biting the herbage and some sleeping among the bushes.

This singularity of his humour made him much observed. One of the Sages, in whose conversation he had formerly delighted, followed him secretly in hope of discovering the cause of his disquiet. Rasselas, who knew not that any one was near him, having for some time fixed his eyes upon the goats that were browsing among the rocks, began to compare their condition with his own.

'What,' said he, 'makes the difference between man and all the rest of the animal creation? Every beast that strays beside me has the same corporal necessities with myself; he is hungry and crops the grass, he is thirsty and drinks the stream, his thirst and hunger are appeased, he is satisfied and sleeps; he rises again and is hungry, he is again fed and is at rest. I am hungry and thirsty like him, but when thirst and hunger cease I am not at rest; I am, like him, pained with want, but am not, like him, satisfied with fulness. The intermediate hours are tedious and gloomy; I long again to be hungry that I may again quicken my attention. The birds peck the berries or the corn, and fly away to the groves where they sit in seeming happiness on the branches, and waste their lives in tuning one unvaried series of sounds. I likewise can call the lutanist and the singer, but the sounds that pleased me yesterday weary me today, and will grow yet more wearisome tomorrow. I can discover within me no power of perception which is not glutted with its proper pleasure, yet I do not feel myself delighted. Man has surely some latent sense for which this place affords no gratification, or he has some desires distinct from sense which must be satisfied before he can be happy.'

After this he lifted up his head and, seeing the moon rising, walked towards the palace. As he passed through the fields and saw the animals around him, 'Ye,' said he, 'are happy, and need not envy me that walk thus among you, burthened with myself; nor do I, ye gentle beings, envy your felicity; for it is not the felicity of man. I have many distresses from which ye are free; I fear pain when I do not feel it; I sometimes shrink at evils recollected and sometimes start at evils anticipated: surely the equity of providence has balanced peculiar sufferings with peculiar enjoyments.'

With observations like these the prince amused himself as he returned, uttering them with a plaintive voice, yet with a look that discovered him to feel some complacence in his own perspicacity, and to receive some solace of the miseries of life from consciousness of the delicacy with which he felt, and the eloquence with which he bewailed, them. He mingled cheerfully in the diversions of the evening, and all rejoiced to find that his heart was lightened.

Chapter III: The Wants of Him That Wants Nothing

On the next day his old instructor, imagining that he had now made himself acquainted with his disease of mind, was in hope of curing it by counsel, and officiously sought an opportunity of conference, which the prince, having long considered him as one whose intellects were exhausted, was not very willing to afford: 'Why,' said he, 'does this man thus intrude upon me; shall I be never suffered to forget those lectures which pleased only while they were new, and to become new again must be forgotten?' He then walked into the wood, and composed himself to his usual meditations; when, before his thoughts had taken any settled form, he perceived his pursuer at his side, and was at first prompted by his impatience to go hastily away; but, being unwilling to offend a man whom he had once reverenced and still loved, he invited him to sit down with him on the bank.

The old man, thus encouraged, began to lament the change which had been lately observed in the prince, and to enquire why he so often retired from the pleasures of the palace to loneliness and silence. 'I fly from pleasure,' said the prince, 'because pleasure has ceased to please; I am lonely because I am miserable, and am unwilling to cloud with my presence the happiness of others.'

'You, Sir,' said the sage, 'are the first who has complained of misery in the *happy valley*. I hope to convince you that your complaints have no real cause. You are here in full possession of all that the emperour of Abyssinia can bestow; here is neither labour to be endured nor danger to be dreaded, yet here is all that labour or danger can procure or purchase. Look round and tell me which of your wants is without supply: if you want nothing, how are you unhappy?'

'That I want nothing', said the prince, 'or that I know not what I want, is the cause of my complaint; if I had any known want, I should have a certain wish; that wish would excite endeavour, and I should not then repine to see the sun move so slowly towards the western mountain, or lament when the day breaks and sleep will no longer hide me from myself. When I see the kids and the lambs chasing one another, I fancy that I should be happy if I had something to pursue. But, possessing all that I can want, I find one day and one hour exactly like another, except that the latter is still more tedious than the former. Let your experience inform me how the day may now seem as short as in my childhood, while nature was yet fresh, and every moment showed me what I never had observed before. I have already enjoyed too much; give me something to desire.'

The old man was surprised at this new species of affliction and knew not what to reply, yet was unwilling to be silent. 'Sir,' said he, 'if you had seen the miseries of the world, you would know how to value your present state.'

'Now,' said the prince, 'you have given me something to desire; I shall long to see the miseries of the world, since the sight of them is necessary to happiness.'

Chapter IV: The Prince Continues To Grieve and Muse

At this time the sound of music proclaimed the hour of repast, and the conversation was concluded. The old man went away sufficiently discontented to find that his reasonings had produced the only conclusion which they were intended to prevent. But in the decline of life shame and grief are of short duration; whether it be that we bear easily what we have borne long, or that, finding ourselves in age less regarded, we less regard others; or, that we look with slight regard upon afflictions, to which we know that the hand of death is about to put an end.

The prince, whose views were extended to a wider space, could not speedily quiet his emotions. He had been before terrified at the length of life which nature promised him, because he considered that in a long time much must be endured; he now rejoiced in his youth, because in many years much might be done.

This first beam of hope that had been ever darted into his mind rekindled youth in his cheeks and doubled the lustre of his eyes. He was fired with the desire of doing something, though he knew not yet with distinctness either end or means.

He was now no longer gloomy and unsocial; but, considering himself as master of a secret stock of happiness which he could enjoy only by concealing it, he affected to be busy in all schemes of diversion, and endeavoured to make others pleased with the state of which he himself was weary. But pleasures never can be so multiplied or continued as not to leave much of life unemployed; there were many hours, both of the night and day, which he could spend without suspicion in solitary thought. The load of life was much lightened: he went eagerly into the assemblies because he supposed the frequency of his presence necessary to the success of his purposes; he retired gladly to privacy because he had now a subject of thought.

His chief amusement was to picture to himself that world which he had never seen; to place himself in various conditions; to be entangled in imaginary difficulties, and to be engaged in wild adventures: but his benevolence always terminated his projects in the relief of distress, the detection of fraud, the defeat of oppression, and the diffusion of happiness.

Thus passed twenty months of the life of Rasselas. He busied himself so intensely in visionary bustle that he forgot his real solitude; and, amidst hourly preparations for the various incidents of human affairs, neglected to consider by what means he should mingle with mankind.

One day, as he was sitting on a bank, he feigned to himself an orphan virgin robbed of her little portion by a treacherous lover and crying after him for restitution and redress. So strongly was the image impressed upon his mind that he started up in the maid's defence, and run forward to seize the plunderer with all the eagerness of real pursuit. Fear naturally quickens the flight of guilt. Rasselas could not catch the fugitive with his utmost efforts; but, resolving to weary by perseverance him whom he could not surpass in speed, he pressed on till the foot of the mountain stopped his course.

Here he recollected himself and smiled at his own useless impetuosity. Then raising his eyes to the mountain, 'This,' said he, 'is the fatal obstacle that hinders at once the enjoyment of pleasure and the exercise of virtue. How long is it that my hopes and wishes have flown beyond this boundary of my life, which yet I never have attempted to surmount!'

Struck with this reflection, he sat down to muse, and remembered that, since he first resolved to escape from his confinement, the sun had passed twice over him in his annual course. He now felt a degree of regret with which he had never been before acquainted. He considered how much might have been done in the time which had passed and left nothing real behind it. He compared twenty months with the life of man. 'In life,' said he, 'is not to be counted the ignorance of infancy or imbecility of age. We are long before we are able to think, and we soon cease from the power of acting. The true period of human existence may be reasonably estimated as forty years, of which I have mused away the four and twentieth part. What I have lost was certain, for I have certainly possessed it; but of twenty months to come who can assure me?'

The consciousness of his own folly pierced him deeply, and he was long before he could be reconciled to himself. 'The rest of my time,' said he, 'has been lost by the crime or folly of my ancestors, and the absurd institutions of my country; I remember it with disgust, yet without remorse: but the months that have passed since new light darted into my soul, since I formed a scheme of reasonable felicity, have been squandered by my own fault. I have lost that which can never be restored: I have seen the sun rise and set for twenty months, an idle gazer on the light of heaven. In this time the birds have left the nest of their mother and committed themselves to the woods and to the skies: the kid has forsaken the teat and learned by degrees to climb the rocks in quest of independent sustenance. I only have made no advances, but am still helpless and ignorant. The moon by more than twenty changes admonished me of the flux of life; the stream that rolled before my feet upbraided my inactivity. I sat feasting on intellectual luxury,[4] regardless alike of the examples of the earth and the instructions of the planets. Twenty months are past; who shall restore them?'

These sorrowful meditations fastened upon his mind; he passed four months in resolving to lose no more time in idle resolves, and was awakened to more vigorous exertion by hearing a maid, who had broken a porcelain cup, remark that what cannot be repaired is not to be regretted.

This was obvious; and Rasselas reproached himself that he had not discovered it, having not known, or not considered, how many useful hints are obtained by chance, and how often the mind, hurried by her own ardour to distant views, neglects the truths that lie open before her. He for a few hours regretted his regret, and from that time bent his whole mind upon the means of escaping from the valley of happiness.

Chapter V: The Prince Meditates His Escape

He now found that it would be very difficult to effect that which it was very easy to suppose effected. When he looked round about him, he saw himself confined by the bars of nature which had never yet been broken, and by the gate through which none that once had passed it were ever able to return. He

4. Indulgence in imagination.

was now impatient as an eagle in a grate.[5] He passed week after week in clambering the mountains to see if there was any aperture which the bushes might conceal, but found all the summits inaccessible by their prominence.[6] The iron gate he despaired to open; for it was not only secured with all the power of art, but was always watched by successive sentinels, and was by its position exposed to the perpetual observation of all the inhabitants.

He then examined the cavern through which the waters of the lake were discharged; and, looking down at a time when the sun shone strongly upon its mouth, he discovered it to be full of broken rocks, which, though they permitted the stream to flow through many narrow passages, would stop any body of solid bulk. He returned discouraged and dejected; but, having now known the blessing of hope, resolved never to despair.

In these fruitless searches he spent ten months. The time, however, passed cheerfully away: in the morning he rose with new hope, in the evening applauded his own diligence, and in the night slept sound after his fatigue. He met a thousand amusements which beguiled his labour and diversified his thoughts. He discerned the various instincts of animals and properties of plants, and found the place replete with wonders, of which he purposed to solace himself with the contemplation if he should never be able to accomplish his flight; rejoicing that his endeavours, though yet unsuccessful, had supplied him with a source of inexhaustible enquiry.

But his original curiosity was not yet abated; he resolved to obtain some knowledge of the ways of men. His wish still continued, but his hope grew less. He ceased to survey any longer the walls of his prison, and spared to search by new toils for interstices which he knew could not be found, yet determined to keep his design always in view and lay hold on any expedient that time should offer.

Chapter VI: A Dissertation on the Art of Flying

Among the artists that had been allured into the happy valley, to labour for the accommodation and pleasure of its inhabitants, was a man eminent for his knowledge of the mechanic powers, who had contrived many engines both of use and recreation. By a wheel which the stream turned, he forced the water into a tower, whence it was distributed to all the apartments of the palace. He erected a pavilion in the garden, around which he kept the air always cool by artificial showers. One of the groves, appropriated to the ladies, was ventilated by fans, to which the rivulet that run through it gave a constant motion; and instruments of soft music were placed at proper distances, of which some played by the impulse of the wind and some by the power of the stream.

This artist was sometimes visited by Rasselas, who was pleased with every kind of knowledge, imagining that the time would come when all his acquisitions should be of use to him in the open world. He came one day to amuse himself in his usual manner, and found the master busy in building a sailing chariot: he saw that the design was practicable upon a level surface, and with expressions of great esteem solicited its completion. The workman was pleased

5. Cage.
6. Overhanging projection.

to find himself so much regarded by the prince, and resolved to gain yet higher honours. 'Sir,' said he, 'you have seen but a small part of what the mechanic sciences can perform. I have been long of opinion, that, instead of the tardy conveyance of ships and chariots, man might use the swifter migration of wings; that the fields of air are open to knowledge, and that only ignorance and idleness need crawl upon the ground.'

This hint rekindled the prince's desire of passing the mountains; having seen what the mechanist had already performed, he was willing to fancy that he could do more; yet resolved to enquire further before he suffered hope to afflict him by disappointment. 'I am afraid,' said he to the artist, 'that your imagination prevails over your skill, and that you now tell me rather what you wish than what you know. Every animal has his element assigned him; the birds have the air, and man and beasts the earth.'

'So,' replied the mechanist, 'fishes have the water, in which yet beasts can swim by nature and men by art. He that can swim needs not despair to fly: to swim is to fly in a grosser fluid, and to fly is to swim in a subtler. We are only to proportion our power of resistance to the different density of the matter through which we are to pass. You will be necessarily upborne by the air, if you can renew any impulse upon it, faster than the air can recede from the pressure.'

'But the exercise of swimming,' said the prince, 'is very laborious; the strongest limbs are soon wearied; I am afraid the act of flying will be yet more violent, and wings will be of no great use unless we can fly further than we can swim.'

'The labour of rising from the ground,' said the artist, 'will be great, as we see it in the heavier domestic fowls; but, as we mount higher, the earth's attraction and the body's gravity will be gradually diminished, till we shall arrive at a region where the man will float in the air without any tendency to fall: no care will then be necessary but to move forwards, which the gentlest impulse will effect. You, Sir, whose curiosity is so extensive, will easily conceive with what pleasure a philosopher,[7] furnished with wings and hovering in the sky, would see the earth and all its inhabitants rolling beneath him, and presenting to him successively by its diurnal motion all the countries within the same parallel. How must it amuse the pendent spectator to see the moving scene of land and ocean, cities and deserts! To survey with equal security the marts of trade and the fields of battle; mountains infested by barbarians, and fruitful regions gladdened by plenty and lulled by peace! How easily shall we then trace the Nile through all his passage,[8] pass over to distant regions, and examine the face of nature from one extremity of the earth to the other!'

'All this,' said the prince, 'is much to be desired, but I am afraid that no man will be able to breathe in these regions of speculation and tranquility. I have been told that respiration is difficult upon lofty mountains, yet from these precipices, though so high as to produce great tenuity of the air, it is very easy to fall: therefore I suspect that from any height where life can be supported, there may be danger of too quick descent.'

7. Natural philosopher, i.e. scientist.

8. The source of the Nile remained a matter of speculation until it was discovered by Robert Speke in 1858.

'Nothing,' replied the artist, 'will ever be attempted if all possible objections must be first overcome. If you will favour my project I will try the first flight at my own hazard. I have considered the structure of all volant [9] animals, and find the folding continuity of the bat's wings most easily accommodated to the human form. Upon this model I shall begin my task tomorrow, and in a year expect to tower into the air beyond the malice or pursuit of man. But I will work only on this condition, that the art shall not be divulged and that you shall not require me to make wings for any but ourselves.'

'Why,' said Rasselas, 'should you envy others so great an advantage? All skill ought to be exerted for universal good; every man has owed much to others, and ought to repay the kindness that he has received.'

'If men were all virtuous,' returned the artist, 'I should with great alacrity teach them all to fly. But what would be the security of the good if the bad could at pleasure invade them from the sky? Against an army sailing through the clouds neither walls, nor mountains, nor seas, could afford any security. A flight of northern savages might hover in the wind, and light at once with irresistible violence upon the capital of a fruitful region that was rolling under them. Even this valley, the retreat of princes, the abode of happiness, might be violated by the sudden descent of some of the naked nations that swarm on the coast of the southern sea.'

The prince promised secrecy and waited for the performance, not wholly hopeless of success. He visited the work from time to time, observed its progress, and remarked many ingenious contrivances to facilitate motion and unite levity [10] with strength. The artist was every day more certain that he should leave vultures and eagles behind him, and the contagion of his confidence seized upon the prince.

In a year the wings were finished, and, on a morning appointed, the maker appeared furnished for flight on a little promontory: he waved his pinions a while to gather air, then leaped from his stand, and in an instant dropped into the lake. His wings, which were of no use in the air, sustained him in the water, and the prince drew him to land, half dead with terrour and vexation.

Chapter VII: The Prince Finds a Man of Learning

The prince was not much afflicted by this disaster, having suffered himself to hope for a happier event only because he had no other means of escape in view. He still persisted in his design to leave the happy valley by the first opportunity.

His imagination was now at a stand; he had no prospect of entering into the world; and, notwithstanding all his endeavours to support himself, discontent by degrees preyed upon him, and he began again to lose his thoughts in sadness, when the rainy season, which in these countries is periodical, made it inconvenient to wander in the woods.

The rain continued longer and with more violence than had been ever known: the clouds broke on the surrounding mountains, and the torrents streamed into the plain on every side, till the cavern was too narrow to dis-

9. Flying.
10. Lightness.

charge the water. The lake overflowed its banks, and all the level of the valley was covered with the inundation. The eminence, on which the palace was built, and some other spots of rising ground, were all that the eye could now discover. The herds and flocks left the pastures, and both the wild beasts and the tame retreated to the mountains.

This inundation confined all the princes to domestic amusements, and the attention of Rasselas was particularly seized by a poem which Imlac rehearsed upon the various conditions of humanity. He commanded the poet to attend him in his apartment and recite his verses a second time; then entering into familiar talk, he thought himself happy in having found a man who knew the world so well and could so skilfully paint the scenes of life. He asked a thousand questions about things to which, though common to all other mortals, his confinement from childhood had kept him a stranger. The poet pitied his ignorance and loved his curiosity, and entertained him from day to day with novelty and instruction, so that the prince regretted the necessity of sleep and longed till the morning should renew his pleasure.

As they were sitting together, the prince commanded Imlac to relate his history, and to tell by what accident he was forced, or by what motive induced, to close his life in the happy valley. As he was going to begin his narrative, Rasselas was called to a concert, and obliged to restrain his curiosity till the evening.

Chapter VIII: The History of Imlac

The close of the day is, in the regions of the torrid zone, the only season of diversion and entertainment, and it was therefore midnight before the music ceased, and the princesses retired. Rasselas then called for his companion, and required him to begin the story of his life.

'Sir,' said Imlac, 'my history will not be long: the life that is devoted to knowledge passes silently away, and is very little diversified by events. To talk in public, to think in solitude, to read and to hear, to inquire and answer inquiries, is the business of a scholar. He wanders about the world without pomp or terror, and is neither known nor valued but by men like himself.

'I was born in the kingdom of Goiama,[11] at no great distance from the fountain of the Nile. My father was a wealthy merchant, who traded between the inland countries of Africk and the ports of the Red Sea. He was honest, frugal, and diligent, but of mean sentiments and narrow comprehension: he desired only to be rich, and to conceal his riches, lest he should be spoiled [12] by the governors of the province.'

'Surely,' said the prince, 'my father must be negligent of his charge, if any man in his dominions dares take that which belongs to another. Does he not know that kings are accountable for injustice permitted as well as done? If I were emperor, not the meanest of my subjects should be oppressed with impunity. My blood boils when I am told that a merchant durst not enjoy his

11. "One of the most fruitful provinces of all the Abyssinian dominions"; Johnson had in 1735 translated the *Voyage to Abyssinia* by the Portuguese Jesuit Father Jerome Lobo (1595–1678), and many of his geographical references derive from that work.
12. Despoiled, plundered.

honest gains, for fear of losing them by the rapacity of power. Name the governor who robbed the people, that I may declare his crimes to the emperor.'

'Sir,' said Imlac, 'your ardour is the natural effect of virtue animated by youth: the time will come when you will acquit your father, and perhaps hear with less impatience of the governor. Oppression is, in the Abyssinian dominions, neither frequent nor tolerated; but no form of government has been yet discovered, by which cruelty can be wholly prevented. Subordination supposes power on one part, and subjection on the other; and if power be in the hands of men, it will sometimes be abused. The vigilance of the supreme magistrate may do much, but much will still remain undone. He can never know all the crimes that are committed, and can seldom punish all that he knows.'

'This,' said the prince, 'I do not understand; but I had rather hear thee than dispute. Continue thy narration.'

'My father,' proceeded Imlac, 'originally intended that I should have no other education, than such as might qualify me for commerce; and discovering in me great strength of memory and quickness of apprehension, often declared his hope that I should be some time the richest man in Abyssinia.'

'Why,' said the prince, 'did thy father desire the increase of his wealth, when it was already greater than he durst discover or enjoy? I am unwilling to doubt thy veracity, yet inconsistencies cannot both be true.'

'Inconsistencies,' answered Imlac, 'cannot both be right, but, imputed to man, they may both be true. Yet diversity is not inconsistency. My father might expect a time of greater security. However, some desire is necessary to keep life in motion; and he whose real wants are supplied, must admit those of fancy.'

'This,' said the prince, 'I can in some measure conceive. I repent that I interrupted thee.'

'With this hope,' proceeded Imlac, 'he sent me to school; but when I had once found the delight of knowledge, and felt the pleasure of intelligence and the pride of invention,[13] I began silently to despise riches, and determined to disappoint the purpose of my father, whose grossness of conception raised my pity. I was twenty years old before his tenderness would expose me to the fatigue of travel, in which time I had been instructed, by successive masters, in all the literature of my native country. As every hour taught me something new, I lived in a continual course of gratification; but, as I advanced towards manhood, I lost much of the reverence with which I had been used to look on my instructors; because when the lesson was ended, I did not find them wiser or better than common men.

'At length my father resolved to initiate me in commerce, and opening one of his subterranean treasuries, counted out ten thousand pieces of gold. "This, young man," said he, "is the stock with which you must negotiate. I began with less than the fifth part, and you see how diligence and parsimony have increased it. This is your own to waste or to improve. If you squander it by negligence or caprice, you must wait for my death before you will be rich;

13. Imagination.

if in four years you double your stock, we will thenceforward let subordination cease, and live together as friends and partners; for he shall always be equal with me, who is equally skilled in the art of growing rich."

'We laid our money upon camels, concealed in bales of cheap goods, and travelled to the shore of the Red Sea. When I cast my eye on the expanse of waters, my heart bounded like that of a prisoner escaped. I felt an unextinguishable curiosity kindle in my mind, and resolved to snatch this opportunity of seeing the manners of other nations, and of learning sciences unknown in Abyssinia.

'I remembered that my father had obliged me to the improvement of my stock, not by a promise which I ought not to violate, but by a penalty which I was at liberty to incur; and therefore determined to gratify my predominant desire, and, by drinking at the fountains of knowledge, to quench the thirst of curiosity.

'As I was supposed to trade without connexion with my father, it was easy for me to become acquainted with the master of a ship, and procure a passage to some other country. I had no motives of choice to regulate my voyage; it was sufficient for me that, wherever I wandered, I should see a country which I had not seen before. I therefore entered a ship bound for Surat,[14] having left a letter for my father declaring my intention.

Chapter IX: The History of Imlac Continued

'When I first entered upon the world of waters, and lost sight of land, I looked round about me with pleasing terror, and thinking my soul enlarged by the boundless prospect, imagined that I could gaze round for ever without satiety; but in a short time I grew weary of looking on barren uniformity, where I could only see again what I had already seen. I then descended into the ship, and doubted for awhile whether all my future pleasures would not end like this, in disgust and disappointment. Yet, surely, said I, the ocean and the land are very different; the only variety of water is rest and motion, but the earth has mountains and valleys, deserts and cities; it is inhabited by men of different customs and contrary opinions; and I may hope to find variety in life, though I should miss it in nature.

'With this thought I quieted my mind; and amused myself during the voyage, sometimes by learning from the sailors the art of navigation, which I have never practised, and sometimes by forming schemes for my conduct in different situations, in not one of which I have been ever placed.

'I was almost weary of my naval amusements when we landed safely at Surat. I secured my money, and purchasing some commodities for show, joined myself to a caravan that was passing into the inland country. My companions, for some reason or other, conjecturing that I was rich, and, by my inquiries and admiration, finding that I was ignorant, considered me as a novice whom they had a right to cheat, and who was to learn at the usual expense the art of fraud. They exposed me to the theft of servants and the exaction of officers, and saw me plundered upon false pretences, without any

14. Indian seaport 150 miles north of Bombay.

advantage to themselves but that of rejoicing in the superiority of their own knowledge.'

'Stop a moment,' said the prince. 'Is there such depravity in man, as that he should injure another without benefit to himself? I can easily conceive that all are pleased with superiority; but your ignorance was merely accidental, which, being neither your crime nor your folly, could afford them no reason to applaud themselves; and the knowledge which they had, and which you wanted, they might as effectually have shown by warning, as betraying you.'

'Pride,' said Imlac, 'is seldom delicate, it will please itself with very mean advantages; and envy feels not its own happiness, but when it may be compared with the misery of others. They were my enemies, because they grieved to think me rich; and my oppressors, because they delighted to find me weak.'

'Proceed,' said the prince: 'I doubt not of the facts which you relate, but imagine that you impute them to mistaken motives.'

'In this company,' said Imlac, 'I arrived at Agra, the capital of Indostan, the city in which the great Mogul [15] commonly resides. I applied myself to the language of the country, and in a few months was able to converse with the learned men; some of whom I found morose and reserved, and others easy and communicative; some were unwilling to teach another what they had with difficulty learned themselves; and some showed that the end of their studies was to gain the dignity of instructing.

'To the tutor of the young princes I recommended myself so much, that I was presented to the emperor as a man of uncommon knowledge. The emperor asked me many questions concerning my country and my travels; and though I cannot now recollect any thing that he uttered above the power of a common man, he dismissed me astonished at his wisdom, and enamoured of his goodness.

'My credit was now so high, that the merchants with whom I had travelled, applied to me for recommendations to the ladies of the court. I was surprised at their confidence of solicitation, and gently reproached them with their practices on the road. They heard me with cold indifference, and showed no tokens of shame or sorrow.

'They then urged their request with the offer of a bribe; but what I would not do for kindness, I would not do for money, and refused them, not because they had injured me, but because I would not enable them to injure others; for I knew they would have made use of my credit to cheat those who should buy their wares.

'Having resided at Agra till there was no more to be learned, I travelled into Persia, where I saw many remains of ancient magnificence, and observed many new accommodations of life. The Persians are a nation eminently social, and their assemblies afforded me daily opportunities of remarking characters and manners, and of tracing human nature through all its variations.

'From Persia I passed into Arabia, where I saw a nation at once pastoral and warlike; who live without any settled habitation; whose only wealth is their flocks and herds; and who have yet carried on through all ages an hereditary war with all mankind, though they neither covet nor envy their possessions.'

15. Ruler of the Mohammedan empire established in India by Akbar the Great; his capital was at Agra.

Chapter X: Imlac's History Continued. A Dissertation upon Poetry

'Wherever I went, I found that poetry was considered as the highest learning, and regarded with a veneration somewhat approaching to that which man would pay to the angelic nature. And yet it fills me with wonder, that, in almost all countries, the most ancient poets are considered as the best: whether it be that every other kind of knowledge is an acquisition gradually attained, and poetry is a gift conferred at once; or that the first poetry of every nation surprised them as a novelty, and retained the credit by consent, which it received by accident at first; or whether, as the province of poetry is to describe nature and passion, which are always the same, the first writers took possession of the most striking objects for description, and the most probable occurrences for fiction, and left nothing to those that followed them but transcription of the same events, and new combinations of the same images:—whatever be the reason, it is commonly observed that the early writers are in possession of nature, and their followers of art; that the first excel in strength and invention, and the latter in elegance and refinement.

'I was desirous to add my name to this illustrious fraternity. I read all the poets of Persia and Arabia, and was able to repeat by memory the volumes that are suspended in the mosque of Mecca.[16] But I soon found that no man was ever great by imitation. My desire of excellence impelled me to transfer my attention to nature and to life. Nature was to be my subject, and men to be my auditors: I could never describe what I had not seen; I could not hope to move those with delight or terror, whose interests and opinions I did not understand.

'Being now resolved to be a poet, I saw everything with a new purpose; my sphere of attention was suddenly magnified; no kind of knowledge was to be overlooked. I ranged mountains and deserts for images and resemblances, and pictured upon my mind every tree of the forest and flower of the valley. I observed with equal care the crags of the rock and the pinnacles of the palace. Sometimes I wandered along the mazes of the rivulet, and sometimes watched the changes of the summer clouds. To a poet nothing can be useless. Whatever is beautiful, and whatever is dreadful, must be familiar to his imagination: he must be conversant with all that is awfully[17] vast or elegantly little. The plants of the garden, the animals of the wood, the minerals of the earth, and meteors of the sky must all concur to store his mind with inexhaustible variety: for every idea is useful for the enforcement or decoration of moral or religious truth; and he who knows most, will have most power of diversifying his scenes, and of gratifying his reader with remote allusions and unexpected instruction.

'All the appearances of nature I was therefore careful to study; and every country which I have surveyed has contributed something to my poetical powers.'

'In so wide a survey,' said the prince, 'you must surely have left much unobserved. I have lived, till now, within the circuit of these mountains, and

16. Illuminated manuscripts, chiefly of the *Koran* and other religious books, hung as sacred texts.

17. Awe-inspiringly; cf. Burke's work on the Sublime, which had been published two years earlier than *Rasselas*.

yet cannot walk abroad without the sight of something which I had never beheld before, or never heeded.'

'The business of a poet,' said Imlac, 'is to examine, not the individual, but the species; to remark general properties and large appearances. He does not number the streaks of the tulip, or describe the different shades in the verdure of the forest: he is to exhibit in his portraits of nature such prominent and striking features, as recall the original to every mind; and must neglect the minuter discriminations, which one may have remarked, and another have neglected, for those characteristics which are alike obvious to vigilance and carelessness.

'But the knowledge of nature is only half the task of a poet: he must be acquainted likewise with all the modes of life. His character requires that he estimate the happiness and misery of every condition, observe the power of all the passions in all their combinations, and trace the changes of the human mind as they are modified by various institutions and accidental influences of climate or custom, from the sprightliness of infancy to the despondence of decrepitude. He must divest himself of the prejudices of his age and country; he must consider right and wrong in their abstracted and invariable state; he must disregard present laws and opinions, and rise to general and transcendental truths, which will always be the same. He must therefore content himself with the slow progress of his name, contemn the applause of his own time, and commit his claims to the justice of posterity. He must write as the interpreter of nature, and the legislator of mankind,[18] and consider himself as presiding over the thoughts and manners of future generations; as a being superior to time and place.

'His labour is not yet at an end; he must know many languages and many sciences; and, that his style may be worthy of his thoughts, must, by incessant practice, familiarise to himself every delicacy of speech and grace of harmony.'

Chapter XI: Imlac's Narrative Continued. A Hint on Pilgrimage

Imlac now felt the enthusiastic fit, and was proceeding to aggrandize his own profession, when the prince cried out, 'Enough! thou hast convinced me that no human being can ever be a poet. Proceed with thy narration.'

'To be a poet,' said Imlac, 'is indeed very difficult.'

'So difficult,' returned the prince, 'that I will at present hear no more of his labours. Tell me whither you went when you had seen Persia.'

'From Persia,' said the poet, 'I travelled through Syria, and for three years resided in Palestine, where I conversed with great numbers of the northern and western nations of Europe; the nations which are now in possession of all power and all knowledge; whose armies are irresistible, and whose fleets command the remotest parts of the globe. When I compared these men with the natives of our own kingdom, and those that surround us, they appeared almost another order of beings. In their countries it is difficult to wish for anything that may not be obtained: a thousand arts, of which we never heard,

18. Compare the famous close of Percy Bysshe Shelley's *A Defence of Poetry* (1821): "Poets are the unacknowledged legislators of the world."

are continually labouring for their convenience and pleasure; and whatever their own climate has denied them is supplied by their commerce.'

'By what means,' said the prince, 'are the Europeans thus powerful; or why, since they can so easily visit Asia and Africa for trade or conquest, cannot the Asiatics and Africans invade their coasts, plant colonies in their ports, and give laws to their natural princes? The same wind that carries them back, would bring us thither.'

'They are more powerful, sir, than we,' answered Imlac, 'because they are wiser; knowledge will always predominate over ignorance, as man governs the other animals. But why their knowledge is more than ours, I know not what reason can be given, but the unsearchable will of the Supreme Being.'

'When,' said the prince with a sigh, 'shall I be able to visit Palestine, and mingle with this mighty confluence of nations? Till that happy moment shall arrive, let me fill up the time with such representations as thou canst give me. I am not ignorant of the motive that assembles such numbers in that place, and cannot but consider it as the centre of wisdom and piety, to which the best and wisest men of every land must be continually resorting.'

'There are some nations,' said Imlac, 'that send few visitants to Palestine; for many numerous and learned sects in Europe concur to censure pilgrimage as superstitious, or deride it as ridiculous.'

'You know,' said the prince, 'how little my life has made me acquainted with diversity of opinions; it will be too long to hear the arguments on both sides; you, that have considered them, tell me the result.'

'Pilgrimage,' said Imlac, 'like many other acts of piety, may be reasonable or superstitious, according to the principles upon which it is performed. Long journeys in search of truth are not commanded. Truth, such as is necessary to the regulation of life, is always found where it is honestly sought. Change of place is no natural cause of the increase of piety, for it inevitably produces dissipation of mind. Yet, since men go every day to view the fields where great actions have been performed, and return with stronger impressions of the event, curiosity of the same kind may naturally dispose us to view that country whence our religion had its beginning; and I believe no man surveys those awful scenes without some confirmation of holy resolutions. That the Supreme Being may be more easily propitiated in one place than in another is the dream of idle superstition; but that some places may operate upon our own minds in an uncommon manner is an opinion which hourly experience will justify. He who supposes that his vices may be more successfully combatted in Palestine, will, perhaps, find himself mistaken; yet he may go thither without folly: he who thinks they will be more freely pardoned dishonours at once his reason and religion.'

'These,' said the prince, 'are European distinctions. I will consider them another time. What have you found to be the effect of knowledge? Are those nations happier than we?'

'There is so much infelicity,' said the poet, 'in the world, that scarce any man has leisure from his own distresses to estimate the comparative happiness of others. Knowledge is certainly one of the means of pleasure, as is confessed by the natural desire which every mind feels of increasing its ideas. Ignorance is mere privation, by which nothing can be produced: it is a vacuity in which the soul sits motionless and torpid for want of attraction; and, without knowing why, we always rejoice when we learn and grieve when we forget. I am therefore inclined to conclude, that if nothing counteracts the natural consequence of learning, we grow more happy as our minds take a wider range.'

'In enumerating the particular comforts of life, we shall find many advantages on the side of the Europeans. They cure wounds and diseases with which we languish and perish. We suffer inclemencies of weather which they can obviate. They have engines for the despatch of many laborious works which we must perform by manual industry. There is such communication between distant places, that one friend can hardly be said to be absent from another. Their policy removes all public inconveniences; they have roads cut through their mountains, and bridges laid upon their rivers. And, if we descend to the privacies of life, their habitations are more commodious, and their possessions are more secure.'

'They are surely happy,' said the prince, 'who have all these conveniences, of which I envy none so much as the facility with which separated friends interchange their thoughts.'

'The Europeans,' answered Imlac, 'are less unhappy than we; but they are not happy. Human life is every where a state in which much is to be endured, and little to be enjoyed.'

Chapter XII: The Story of Imlac Continued

'I am not yet willing,' said the prince, 'to suppose that happiness is so parsimoniously distributed to mortals; nor can believe but that, if I had the choice of life, I should be able to fill every day with pleasure. I would injure no man, and should provoke no resentment; I would relieve every distress, and should enjoy the benedictions of gratitude. I would choose my friends among the wise, and my wife among the virtuous; and therefore should be in no danger from treachery or unkindness. My children should, by my care, be learned and pious, and would repay to my age what their childhood had received. What would dare to molest him who might call on every side to thousands enriched by his bounty, or assisted by his power? And why should not life glide quietly away in the soft reciprocation of protection and reverence? All this may be done without the help of European refinements, which appear by their effects to be rather specious than useful. Let us leave them, and pursue our journey.'

'From Palestine,' said Imlac, 'I passed through many regions of Asia; in the more civilized kingdoms as a trader, and among the barbarians of the mountains as a pilgrim. At last I began to long for my native country, that I might repose, after my travels and fatigues, in the places where I had spent my earliest years, and gladden my old companions with the recital of my adventures. Often did I figure to myself those with whom I had sported away the gay hours of dawning life, sitting round me in its evening, wondering at my tales, and listening to my counsels.

'When this thought had taken possession of my mind, I considered every moment as wasted which did not bring me nearer to Abyssinia. I hastened into Egypt, and notwithstanding my impatience, was detained ten months in the contemplation of its ancient magnificence, and in inquiries after the remains of its ancient learning. I found in Cairo a mixture of all nations; some brought thither by the love of knowledge, some by the hope of gain, and many by the desire of living after their own manner without observation, and of lying hid in the obscurity of multitudes: for in a city, populous as Cairo, it is possible to obtain at the same time the gratifications of society, and the secrecy of solitude.

'From Cairo I travelled to Suez, and embarked on the Red Sea, passing along the coast till I arrived at the port from which I had departed twenty years before. Here I joined myself to a caravan, and re-entered my native country.

'I now expected the caresses of my kinsmen, and the congratulations of my friends, and was not without hope that my father, whatever value he had set upon riches, would own with gladness and pride a son who was able to add to the felicity and honour of the nation. But I was soon convinced that my thoughts were vain. My father had been dead fourteen years, having divided his wealth among my brothers, who were removed to some other provinces. Of my companions, the greater part were in the grave; of the rest, some could with difficulty remember me, and some considered me as one corrupted by foreign manners.

'A man used to vicissitudes is not easily dejected. I forgot, after a time, my disappointment, and endeavoured to recommend myself to the nobles of the kingdom; they admitted me to their tables, heard my story, and dismissed me. I opened a school, and was prohibited to teach. I then resolved to sit down in the quiet of domestic life, and addressed a lady that was fond of my conversation but rejected my suit because my father was a merchant.

'Wearied at last with solicitation and repulses, I resolved to hide myself for ever from the world, and depend no longer on the opinion or caprice of others. I waited for the time when the gate of the *happy valley* should open, that I might bid farewell to hope and fear: the day came; my performance was distinguished with favour; and I resigned myself with joy to perpetual confinement.'

'Hast thou here found happiness at last?' said Rasselas. 'Tell me without reserve; art thou content with thy condition? or, dost thou wish to be again wandering and inquiring? All the inhabitants of this valley celebrate their lot, and at the annual visit of the emperor, invite others to partake of their felicity.'

'Great prince,' said Imlac, 'I shall speak the truth; I know not one of all your attendants, who does not lament the hour when he entered this retreat. I am less unhappy than the rest, because I have a mind replete with images, which I can vary and combine at pleasure. I can amuse my solitude by the renovation of the knowledge which begins to fade from my memory, and by recollection of the incidents of my past life. Yet all this ends in the sorrowful consideration, that my acquirements are now useless, and that none of my pleasures can be again enjoyed. The rest, whose minds have no impression but of the present moment, are either corroded by malignant passions, or sit stupid in the gloom of perpetual vacancy.'

'What passions can infest those,' said the prince, 'who have no rivals? We are in a place where impotence precludes malice, and where all envy is repressed by community of enjoyments.'

'There may be community,' said Imlac, 'of material possessions, but there can never be community of love or of esteem. It must happen that one will please more than another; he that knows himself despised will always be envious; and still more envious and malevolent, if he is condemned to live in the presence of those who despise him. The invitations by which they allure others, to a state which they feel to be wretched, proceed from the natural malignity of hopeless misery. They are weary of themselves and of each other, and expect to find relief in new companions. They envy the liberty which their folly has forfeited, and would gladly see all mankind imprisoned like themselves.

'From this crime, however, I am wholly free. No man can say that he is wretched by my persuasion. I look with pity on the crowds who are annually soliciting admission to captivity, and wish that it were lawful for me to warn them of their danger.'

'My dear Imlac,' said the prince, 'I will open to thee my whole heart. I have long meditated an escape from the *happy valley*. I have examined the mountains on every side, but find myself insuperably barred: teach me the way to break my prison; thou shalt be the companion of my flight, the guide of my rambles, the partner of my fortune, and my sole director in the *choice of life*.'

'Sir,' answered the poet, 'your escape will be difficult, and, perhaps, you may soon repent your curiosity. The world, which you figure to yourself smooth and quiet as the lake in the valley, you will find a sea foaming with tempests, and boiling with whirlpools: you will be sometimes overwhelmed by the waves of violence, and sometimes dashed against the rocks of treachery. Amidst wrongs and frauds, competitions and anxieties, you will wish a thousand times for these seats of quiet, and willingly quit hope to be free from fear.'

'Do not seek to deter me from my purpose,' said the prince; 'I am impatient to see what thou hast seen; and, since thou art thyself weary of the valley, it is evident that thy former state was better than this. Whatever be the consequence of my experiment, I am resolved to judge with mine own eyes of the various conditions of men, and then to make deliberately my *choice of life*.'

'I am afraid,' said Imlac, 'you are hindered by stronger restraints than my persuasions; yet, if your determination is fixed, I do not counsel you to despair. Few things are impossible to diligence and skill.'

Chapter XIII: Rasselas Discovers the Means of Escape

The prince now dismissed his favourite to rest, but the narrative of wonders and novelties filled his mind with perturbation. He revolved all that he had heard, and prepared innumerable questions for the morning.

Much of his uneasiness was now removed. He had a friend to whom he could impart his thoughts and whose experience could assist him in his designs. His heart was no longer condemned to swell with silent vexation. He thought that even the *happy valley* might be endured with such a companion, and that, if they could range the world together, he should have nothing further to desire.

In a few days the water was discharged and the ground dried. The prince and Imlac then walked out together to converse without the notice of the rest. The prince, whose thoughts were always on the wing, as he passed by the gate, said, with a countenance of sorrow, 'Why art thou so strong, and why is man so weak?'

'Man is not weak,' answered his companion; 'knowledge is more than equivalent to force. The master of mechanics laughs at strength. I can burst the gate, but cannot do it secretly. Some other expedient must be tried.'

As they were walking on the side of the mountain, they observed that the conies,[19] which the rain had driven from their burrows, had taken shelter among the bushes and formed holes behind them, tending upwards in an oblique line. 'It has been the opinion of antiquity,' said Imlac, 'that human reason borrowed many arts from the instinct of animals; let us, therefore, not think ourselves degraded by learning from the coney. We may escape by piercing the mountain in the same direction. We will begin where the summit hangs over the middle part, and labour upward till we shall issue out beyond the prominence.'

The eyes of the prince, when he heard this proposal, sparkled with joy. The execution was easy, and the success certain.

No time was now lost. They hastened early in the morning to choose a place proper for their mine. They clambered with great fatigue among crags and brambles, and returned without having discovered any part that favoured their design. The second and the third day were spent in the same manner and with the same frustration. But, on the fourth, they found a small cavern concealed by a thicket, where they resolved to make their experiment.

Imlac procured instruments proper to hew stone and remove earth, and they fell to their work on the next day with more eagerness than vigour. They were presently exhausted by their efforts, and sat down to pant upon the grass. The prince, for a moment, appeared to be discouraged. 'Sir,' said his companion, 'practice will enable us to continue our labour for a longer time; mark, however, how far we have advanced, and you will find that our toil will some time have an end. Great works are performed not by strength, but perseverance: yonder palace was raised by single stones, yet you see its height and spaciousness. He that shall walk with vigour three hours a day will pass in seven years a space equal to the circumference of the globe.'

They returned to their work day after day, and, in a short time, found a fissure in the rock, which enabled them to pass far with very little obstruction. This Rasselas considered as a good omen. 'Do not disturb your mind,' said Imlac, 'with other hopes or fears than reason may suggest: if you are pleased with prognostics of good, you will be terrified likewise with tokens of evil, and your whole life will be a prey to superstition. Whatever facilitates our work is more than an omen; it is a cause of success. This is one of those pleasing surprises which often happen to active resolution. Many things difficult to design prove easy to performance.'

Chapter XIV: Rasselas and Imlac Receive an Unexpected Visit

They had now wrought their way to the middle and solaced their toil with the approach of liberty, when the prince, coming down to refresh himself with air, found his sister Nekayah standing before the mouth of the cavity. He started

19. Rabbits.

and stood confused, afraid to tell his design and yet hopeless to conceal it. A few moments determined him to repose on her fidelity and secure her secrecy by a declaration without reserve.

'Do not imagine,' said the princess, 'that I came hither as a spy: I had long observed from my window, that you and Imlac directed your walk every day towards the same point, but I did not suppose you had any better reason for the preference than a cooler shade or more fragrant bank; nor followed you with any other design than to partake of your conversation. Since then not suspicion but fondness has detected you, let me not lose the advantage of my discovery. I am equally weary of confinement with yourself, and not less desirous of knowing what is done or suffered in the world. Permit me to fly with you from this tasteless tranquility, which will yet grow more loathsome when you have left me. You may deny me to accompany you, but cannot hinder me from following.'

The prince, who loved Nekayah above his other sisters, had no inclination to refuse her request, and grieved that he had lost an opportunity of showing his confidence by a voluntary communication. It was therefore agreed that she should leave the valley with them; and that, in the meantime, she should watch lest any other straggler should, by chance or curiosity, follow them to the mountain.

At length their labour was at an end; they saw light beyond the prominence, and, issuing to the top of the mountain, beheld the Nile, yet a narrow current, wandering beneath them.

The prince looked round with rapture, anticipated all the pleasures of travel, and in thought was already transported beyond his father's dominions. Imlac, though very joyful at his escape, had less expectation of pleasure in the world, which he had before tried, and of which he had been weary.

Rasselas was so much delighted with a wider horizon that he could not soon be persuaded to return into the valley. He informed his sister that the way was open and that nothing now remained but to prepare for their departure.

Chapter XV: The Prince and Princess Leave the Valley, and See Many Wonders

The prince and princess had jewels sufficient to make them rich whenever they came into a place of commerce, which, by Imlac's direction, they hid in their clothes; and, on the night of the next full moon, all left the valley. The princess was followed only by a single favourite who did not know whither she was going.

They clambered through the cavity, and began to go down on the other side. The princess and her maid turned their eyes towards every part, and, seeing nothing to bound their prospect, considered themselves as in danger of being lost in a dreary vacuity. They stopped and trembled. 'I am almost afraid,' said the princess, 'to begin a journey of which I cannot perceive an end, and to venture into this immense plain where I may be approached on every side by men whom I never saw.' The prince felt nearly the same emotions, though he thought it more manly to conceal them.

Imlac smiled at their terrours and encouraged them to proceed; but the princess continued irresolute till she had been imperceptibly drawn forward too far to return.

In the morning they found some shepherds in the field, who set milk and fruits before them. The princess wondered that she did not see a palace ready for her reception and a table spread with delicacies; but, being faint and hungry, she drank the milk and eat [20] the fruits, and thought them of a higher flavour than the products of the valley.

They travelled forward by easy journeys, being all unaccustomed to toil or difficulty, and knowing that, though they might be missed, they could not be pursued. In a few days they came into a more populous region, where Imlac was diverted with the admiration which his companions expressed at the diversity of manners, stations, and employments.

Their dress was such as might not bring upon them the suspicion of having anything to conceal; yet the prince, wherever he came, expected to be obeyed, and the princess was frighted because those that came into her presence did not prostrate themselves before her. Imlac was forced to observe them with great vigilance lest they should betray their rank by their unusual behaviour, and detained them several weeks in the first village to accustom them to the sight of common mortals.

By degrees the royal wanderers were taught to understand that they had for a time laid aside their dignity, and were to expect only such regard as liberality and courtesy could procure. And Imlac, having by many admonitions prepared them to endure the tumults of a port and the ruggedness of the commercial race, brought them down to the seacoast.

The prince and his sister, to whom everything was new, were gratified equally at all places, and therefore remained for some months at the port without any inclination to pass further. Imlac was content with their stay because he did not think it safe to expose them, unpractised in the world, to the hazards of a foreign country.

At last he began to fear lest they should be discovered and proposed to fix a day for their departure. They had no pretensions to judge for themselves, and referred the whole scheme to his direction. He therefore took passage in a ship to Suez; and, when the time came, with great difficulty prevailed on the princess to enter the vessel. They had a quick and prosperous voyage, and from Suez travelled by land to Cairo.

Chapter XVI: They Enter Cairo and Find Every Man Happy

As they approached the city, which filled the strangers with astonishment, 'This,' said Imlac to the prince, 'is the place where travellers and merchants assemble from all the corners of the earth. You will here find men of every character and every occupation. Commerce is here honourable: I will act as a merchant, and you shall live as strangers who have no other end of travel than curiosity; it will soon be observed that we are rich; our reputation will procure us access to all whom we shall desire to know; you will see all the conditions of humanity and enable yourself at leisure to make your *choice of life.*'

They now entered the town, stunned by the noise, and offended by the crowds. Instruction had not yet so prevailed over habit but that they wondered to see themselves pass undistinguished along the street and met by the lowest of the people without reverence or notice. The princess could not at first bear

20. Pronounced "ett" and meaning "ate."

the thought of being levelled with the vulgar, and for some days continued in her chamber, where she was served by her favourite Pekuah as in the palace of the valley.

Imlac, who understood traffic,[21] sold part of the jewels the next day and hired a house, which he adorned with such magnificence that he was immediately considered as a merchant of great wealth. His politeness attracted many acquaintance, and his generosity made him courted by many dependents. His table was crowded by men of every nation, who all admired his knowledge and solicited his favour. His companions, not being able to mix in the conversation, could make no discovery of their ignorance or surprise, and were gradually initiated in the world as they gained knowledge of the language.

The prince had, by frequent lectures, been taught the use and nature of money; but the ladies could not, for a long time, comprehend what the merchants did with small pieces of gold and silver, or why things of so little use should be received as equivalent to the necessaries of life.

They studied the language two years, while Imlac was preparing to set before them the various ranks and conditions of mankind. He grew acquainted with all who had anything uncommon in their fortune or conduct. He frequented the voluptuous and the frugal, the idle and the busy, the merchants and the men of learning.

The prince, being now able to converse with fluency, and having learned the caution necessary to be observed in his intercourse with strangers, began to accompany Imlac to places of resort and to enter into all assemblies, that he might make his *choice of life*.

For some time he thought choice needless, because all appeared to him equally happy. Wherever he went he met gaiety and kindness, and heard the song of joy or the laugh of carelessness. He began to believe that the world overflowed with universal plenty and that nothing was withheld either from want or merit; that every hand showered liberality, and every heart melted with benevolence: 'and who then,' says he, 'will be suffered to be wretched?'

Imlac permitted the pleasing delusion and was unwilling to crush the hope of inexperience; till one day, having sat a while silent, 'I know not,' said the prince, 'what can be the reason that I am more unhappy than any of our friends. I see them perpetually and unalterably cheerful, but feel my own mind restless and uneasy. I am unsatisfied with those pleasures which I seem most to court; I live in the crowds of jollity, not so much to enjoy company as to shun myself, and am only loud and merry to conceal my sadness.'

'Every man,' said Imlac, 'may, by examining his own mind, guess what passes in the minds of others: when you feel that your own gaiety is counterfeit, it may justly lead you to suspect that of your companions not to be sincere. Envy is commonly reciprocal. We are long before we are convinced that happiness is never to be found, and each believes it possessed by others, to keep alive the hope of obtaining it for himself. In the assembly where you passed the last night, there appeared such sprightliness of air and volatility of fancy as might have suited beings of an higher order, formed to inhabit serener regions inaccessible to care or sorrow: yet, believe me, prince, there

21. Commerce.

was not one who did not dread the moment when solitude should deliver him to the tyranny of reflection.'

'This,' said the prince, 'may be true of others, since it is true of me; yet, whatever be the general infelicity of man, one condition is more happy than another, and wisdom surely directs us to take the least evil in the *choice of life*.'

'The causes of good and evil,' answered Imlac, 'are so various and uncertain, so often entangled with each other, so diversified by various relations, and so much subject to accidents which cannot be foreseen, that he who would fix his condition upon incontestable reasons of preference, must live and die inquiring and deliberating.'

'But surely,' said Rasselas, 'the wise men to whom we listen with reverence and wonder chose that mode of life for themselves which they thought most likely to make them happy.'

'Very few,' said the poet, 'live by choice. Every man is placed in his present condition by causes which acted without his foresight, and with which he did not always willingly co-operate; and therefore you will rarely meet one who does not think the lot of his neighbour better than his own.'

'I am pleased to think,' said the prince, 'that my birth has given me at least one advantage over others, by enabling me to determine for myself. I have here the world before me; I will review it at leisure: surely happiness is somewhere to be found.'

Chapter XVII: The Prince Associates with Young Men of Spirit and Gaiety

Rasselas rose next day and resolved to begin his experiments upon life. 'Youth,' cried he, 'is the time of gladness: I will join myself to the young men, whose only business is to gratify their desires, and whose time is all spent in a succession of enjoyments.'

To such societies he was readily admitted, but a few days brought him back weary and disgusted. Their mirth was without images, their laughter without motive; their pleasures were gross and sensual, in which the mind had no part; their conduct was at once wild and mean; they laughed at order and at law, but the frown of power dejected, and the eye of wisdom abashed them.

The prince soon concluded that he should never be happy in a course of life of which he was ashamed. He thought it unsuitable to a reasonable being to act without a plan and to be sad or cheerful only by chance. 'Happiness,' said he, 'must be something solid and permanent, without fear and without uncertainty.'

But his young companions had gained so much of his regard by their frankness and courtesy that he could not leave them without warning and remonstrance. 'My friends,' said he, 'I have seriously considered our manners and our prospects, and find that we have mistaken our own interest. The first years of man must make provision for the last. He that never thinks never can be wise. Perpetual levity must end in ignorance; and intemperance, though it may fire the spirits for an hour, will make life short or miserable. Let us consider that youth is of no long duration, and that in maturer age, when the enchantments of fancy shall cease and phantoms of delight dance no more about us, we shall have no comforts but the esteem of wise men and the means of doing good.

Let us, therefore, stop, while to stop is in our power: let us live as men who are sometime to grow old, and to whom it will be the most dreadful of all evils not to count their past years but by follies, and to be reminded of their former luxuriance of health only by the maladies which riot has produced.'

They stared a while in silence one upon another, and, at last, drove him away by a general chorus of continued laughter.

The consciousness that his sentiments were just and his intentions kind was scarcely sufficient to support him against the horrour of derision. But he recovered his tranquility and pursued his search.

Chapter XVIII: The Prince Finds a Wise and Happy Man

As he was one day walking in the street, he saw a spacious building which all were, by the open doors, invited to enter: he followed the stream of people and found it a hall or school of declamation, in which professors read lectures to their auditory. He fixed his eye upon a sage raised above the rest, who discoursed with great energy on the government of the passions. His look was venerable, his action graceful, his pronunciation clear, and his diction elegant. He showed, with great strength of sentiment and variety of illustration, that human nature is degraded and debased when the lower faculties predominate over the higher; that when fancy, the parent of passion, usurps the dominion of the mind, nothing ensues but the natural effect of unlawful government, perturbation, and confusion; that she betrays the fortresses of the intellect to rebels and excites her children to sedition against reason, their lawful sovereign. He compared reason to the sun, of which the light is constant, uniform, and lasting; and fancy to a meteor, of bright but transitory lustre, irregular in its motion and delusive in its direction.

He then communicated the various precepts given from time to time for the conquest of passion and displayed the happiness of those who had obtained the important victory, after which man is no longer the slave of fear nor the fool of hope; is no more emaciated by envy, inflamed by anger, emasculated by tenderness, or depressed by grief; but walks on calmly through the tumults or the privacies of life as the sun pursues alike his course through the calm or the stormy sky.

He enumerated many examples of heroes immovable by pain or pleasure, who looked with indifference on those modes or accidents to which the vulgar give the names of good and evil. He exhorted his hearers to lay aside their prejudices and arm themselves against the shafts of malice or misfortune by invulnerable patience; concluding that this state only was happiness and that this happiness was in every one's power.

Rasselas listened to him with the veneration due to the instructions of a superior being, and, waiting for him at the door, humbly implored the liberty of visiting so great a master of true wisdom. The lecturer hesitated a moment, when Rasselas put a purse of gold into his hand, which he received with a mixture of joy and wonder.

'I have found,' said the prince, at his return to Imlac, 'a man who can teach all that is necessary to be known, who, from the unshaken throne of rational fortitude, looks down on the scenes of life changing beneath him. He speaks, and attention watches his lips. He reasons, and conviction closes his periods.

This man shall be my future guide: I will learn his doctrines, and imitate his life.'

'Be not too hasty,' said Imlac, 'to trust or to admire the teachers of morality: they discourse like angels, but they live like men.'

Rasselas, who could not conceive how any man could reason so forcibly without feeling the cogency of his own arguments, paid his visit in a few days, and was denied admission. He had now learned the power of money, and made his way by a piece of gold to the inner apartment, where he found the philosopher in a room half darkened, with his eyes misty and his face pale. 'Sir,' said he, 'you are come at a time when all human friendship is useless; what I suffer cannot be remedied, what I have lost cannot be supplied. My daughter, my only daughter, from whose tenderness I expected all the comforts of my age, died last night of a fever. My views, my purposes, my hopes are at an end: I am now a lonely being disunited from society.'

'Sir,' said the prince, 'mortality is an event by which a wise man can never be surprised: we know that death is always near, and it should therefore always be expected.'

'Young man,' answered the philosopher, 'you speak like one that has never felt the pangs of separation.'

'Have you then forgot the precepts,' said Rasselas, 'which you so powerfully enforced? Has wisdom no strength to arm the heart against calamity? Consider that external things are naturally variable, but truth and reason are always the same.'

'What comfort,' said the mourner, 'can truth and reason afford me? Of what effect are they now, but to tell me that my daughter will not be restored?'

The prince, whose humanity would not suffer him to insult misery with reproof, went away convinced of the emptiness of rhetorical sound and the inefficacy of polished periods and studied sentences.

Chapter XIX: A Glimpse of Pastoral Life

He was still eager upon the same enquiry; and, having heard of a hermit that lived near the lowest cataract of the Nile and filled the whole country with the fame of his sanctity, resolved to visit his retreat and enquire whether that felicity, which public life could not afford, was to be found in solitude; and whether a man, whose age and virtue made him venerable, could teach any peculiar art of shunning evils or enduring them.

Imlac and the princess agreed to accompany him, and, after the necessary preparations, they began their journey. Their way lay through fields where shepherds tended their flocks and the lambs were playing upon the pasture. 'This,' said the poet, 'is the life which has been often celebrated for its innocence and quiet: let us pass the heat of the day among the shepherds' tents, and know whether all our searches are not to terminate in pastoral simplicity.'

The proposal pleased them, and they induced the shepherds, by small presents and familiar questions, to tell their opinion of their own state: they were so rude and ignorant, so little able to compare the good with the evil of the occupation, and so indistinct in their narratives and descriptions, that very little could be learned from them. But it was evident that their hearts were cankered with discontent; that they considered themselves as condemned to labour for the luxury of the rich, and looked up with stupid malevolence toward those that were placed above them.

The princess pronounced with vehemence that she would never suffer these envious savages to be her companions, and that she should not soon be desirous of seeing any more specimens of rustic happiness; but could not believe that all the accounts of primeval pleasures were fabulous, and was yet in doubt whether life had anything that could be justly preferred to the placid gratifications of fields and woods. She hoped that the time would come when, with a few virtuous and elegant companions, she should gather flowers planted by her own hand, fondle the lambs of her own ewe, and listen, without care, among brooks and breezes, to one of her maidens reading in the shade.

Chapter XX: The Danger of Prosperity

On the next day they continued their journey till the heat compelled them to look round for shelter. At a small distance they saw a thick wood, which they no sooner entered than they perceived that they were approaching the habitations of men. The shrubs were diligently cut away to open walks where the shades were darkest; the boughs of opposite trees were artificially interwoven; seats of flowery turf were raised in vacant spaces, and a rivulet, that wantoned along the side of a winding path, had its banks sometimes opened into small basins and its stream sometimes obstructed by little mounds of stone heaped together to increase its murmurs.

They passed slowly through the wood, delighted with such unexpected accommodations, and entertained each other with conjecturing what or who he could be that, in those rude and unfrequented regions, had leisure and art for such harmless luxury.

As they advanced, they heard the sound of music and saw youths and virgins dancing in the grove; and, going still further, beheld a stately palace built upon a hill surrounded with woods. The laws of eastern hospitality allowed them to enter, and the master welcomed them like a man liberal and wealthy.

He was skilful enough in appearances soon to discern that they were no common guests, and spread his table with magnificence. The eloquence of Imlac caught his attention, and the lofty courtesy of the princess excited his respect. When they offered to depart he entreated their stay, and was the next day still more unwilling to dismiss them than before. They were easily persuaded to stop, and civility grew up in time to freedom and confidence.

The prince now saw all the domestics cheerful and all the face of nature smiling round the place, and could not forbear to hope that he should find here what he was seeking; but when he was congratulating the master upon his possessions, he answered with a sigh, 'My condition has indeed the appearance of happiness, but appearances are delusive. My prosperity puts my life in danger; the Bassa[22] of Egypt is my enemy, incensed only by my wealth and popularity. I have been hitherto protected against him by the princes of the country; but, as the favour of the great is uncertain, I know not how soon my defenders may be persuaded to share the plunder with the Bassa. I have sent

22. "*Bashaw,* a title of honour and command among the Turks, the viceroy of a province" (Johnson, *Dictionary*).

my treasures into a distant country, and, upon the first alarm, am prepared to follow them. Then will my enemies riot in my mansion, and enjoy the gardens which I have planted.'

They all joined in lamenting his danger and deprecating his exile; and the princess was so much disturbed with the tumult of grief and indignation, that she retired to her apartment. They continued with their kind inviter a few days longer, and then went forward to find the hermit.

Chapter XXI: The Happiness of Solitude. The Hermit's History

They came on the third day, by the direction of the peasants, to the hermit's cell: it was a cavern in the side of a mountain, overshadowed with palm trees; at such a distance from the cataract that nothing more was heard than a gentle uniform murmur, such as composed the mind to pensive meditation, especially when it was assisted by the wind whistling among the branches. The first rude essay of nature had been so much improved by human labour that the cave contained several apartments appropriated to different uses, and often afforded lodging to travellers whom darkness or tempests happened to overtake.

The hermit sat on a bench at the door to enjoy the coolness of the evening. On one side lay a book with pens and papers, on the other mechanical instruments of various kinds. As they approached him unregarded, the princess observed that he had not the countenance of a man that had found, or could teach, the way to happiness.

They saluted him with great respect, which he repaid like a man not unaccustomed to the forms of courts. 'My children,' said he, 'if you have lost your way, you shall be willingly supplied with such conveniencies for the night as this cavern will afford. I have all that nature requires, and you will not expect delicacies in a hermit's cell.'

They thanked him, and, entering, were pleased with the neatness and regularity of the place. The hermit set flesh and wine before them, though he fed only upon fruits and water. His discourse was cheerful without levity, and pious without enthusiasm.[23] He soon gained the esteem of his guests, and the princess repented of her hasty censure.

At last Imlac began thus: 'I do not now wonder that your reputation is so far extended; we have heard at Cairo of your wisdom, and came hither to implore your direction for this young man and maiden in the *choice of life*.'

'To him that lives well,' answered the hermit, 'every form of life is good; nor can I give any other rule for choice, than to remove from all apparent evil.'

'He will remove most certainly from evil,' said the prince, 'who shall devote himself to that solitude which you have recommended by your example.'

'I have indeed lived fifteen years in solitude,' said the hermit, 'but have no desire that my example should gain any imitators. In my youth I professed arms and was raised by degrees to the highest military rank. I have traversed wide countries at the head of my troops and seen many battles and sieges. At last, being disgusted by the preferment of a younger officer and feeling that my vigour was beginning to decay, I resolved to close my life in peace, having found the world full of snares, discord, and misery. I had once escaped from

23. A "vain belief of private revelation" (Johnson, *Dictionary*); here, as is Swift's *A Tale of a Tub*, extravagant or ostentatious devotion.

the pursuit of the enemy by the shelter of this cavern, and therefore chose it for my final residence. I employed artificers to form it into chambers and stored it with all that I was likely to want.

'For some time after my retreat, I rejoiced like a tempest-beaten sailor at his entrance into the harbour, being delighted with the sudden change of the noise and hurry of war to stillness and repose. When the pleasure of novelty went away, I employed my hours in examining the plants which grow in the valley and the minerals which I collected from the rocks. But that enquiry is now grown tasteless and irksome. I have been for some time unsettled and distracted: my mind is disturbed with a thousand perplexities of doubt and vanities of imagination which hourly prevail upon me, because I have no opportunities of relaxation or diversion. I am sometimes ashamed to think that I could not secure myself from vice but by retiring from the exercise of virtue, and begin to suspect that I was rather impelled by resentment, than led by devotion, into solitude. My fancy riots in scenes of folly, and I lament that I have lost so much and have gained so little. In solitude, if I escape the example of bad men, I want likewise the counsel and conversation of the good. I have been long comparing the evils with the advantages of society, and resolve to return into the world tomorrow. The life of a solitary man will be certainly miserable, but not certainly devout.'

They heard his resolution with surprise, but, after a short pause, offered to conduct him to Cairo. He dug up a considerable treasure which he had hid among the rocks, and accompanied them to the city, on which, as he approached it, he gazed with rapture.

Chapter XXII: The Happiness of a Life Led According to Nature

Rasselas went often to an assembly of learned men, who met at stated times to unbend their minds and compare their opinions. Their manners were somewhat coarse, but their conversation was instructive and their disputations acute, though sometimes too violent, and often continued till neither controvertist remembered upon what question they began. Some faults were almost general among them: every one was desirous to dictate to the rest, and every one was pleased to hear the genius or knowledge of another depreciated.

In this assembly Rasselas was relating his interview with the hermit and the wonder with which he heard him censure a course of life which he had so deliberately chosen and so laudably followed. The sentiments of the hearers were various. Some were of opinion that the folly of his choice had been justly punished by condemnation to perpetual perseverance. One of the youngest among them, with great vehemence, pronounced him an hypocrite. Some talked of the right of society to the labour of individuals and considered retirement as a desertion of duty. Others readily allowed that there was a time when the claims of the public were satisfied and when a man might properly sequester himself, to review his life and purify his heart.

One, who appeared more affected with the narrative than the rest, thought it likely that the hermit would, in a few years, go back to his retreat, and, perhaps, if shame did not restrain or death intercept him, return once more from his retreat into the world: 'For the hope of happiness,' said he, 'is so strongly impressed, that the longest experience is not able to efface it. Of the present state, whatever it be, we feel, and are forced to confess, the misery; yet, when the same state is again at a distance, imagination paints it as desirable. But the time will surely come when desire will be no longer our torment and no man shall be wretched but by his own fault.'

'This,' said a philosopher,[24] who had heard him with tokens of great impatience, 'is the present condition of a wise man. The time is already come when none are wretched but by their own fault. Nothing is more idle than to inquire after happiness, which nature has kindly placed within our reach. The way to be happy is to live according to nature, in obedience to that universal and unalterable law with which every heart is originally impressed; which is not written on it by precept but engraven by destiny, not instilled by education, but infused at our nativity. He that lives according to nature will suffer nothing from the delusions of hope or importunities of desire: he will receive and reject with equability of temper; and act or suffer as the reason of things shall alternately prescribe. Other men may amuse themselves with subtle definitions or intricate ratiocination. Let them learn to be wise by easier means: let them consider the life of animals, whose motions are regulated by instinct; they obey their guide and are happy. Let us therefore, at length, cease to dispute, and learn to live; throw away the incumbrance of precepts, which they who utter them with so much pride and pomp do not understand, and carry with us this simple and intelligible maxim, the deviation from nature is deviation from happiness.'

When he had spoken, he looked round him with a placid air, and enjoyed the consciousness of his own beneficence. 'Sir,' said the prince with great modesty, 'as I, like all the rest of mankind, am desirous of felicity, my closest attention has been fixed upon your discourse: I doubt not the truth of a position which a man so learned has so confidently advanced. Let me only know what it is to live according to nature.'

'When I find young men so humble and so docile,' said the philosopher, 'I can deny them no information which my studies have enabled me to afford. To live according to nature is to act always with due regard to the fitness arising from the relations and qualities of causes and effects; to concur with the great and unchangeable scheme of universal felicity; to co-operate with the general disposition and tendency of the present system of things.'

The prince soon found that this was one of the sages whom he should understand less as he heard him longer. He therefore bowed and was silent, and the philosopher, supposing him satisfied and the rest vanquished, rose up and departed with the air of a man that had co-operated with the present system.

Chapter XXIII: The Prince and His Sister Divide between Them the Work of Observation

Rasselas returned home full of reflections, doubtful how to direct his future steps. Of the way to happiness he found the learned and simple equally ignorant; but, as he was yet young, he flattered himself that he had time remaining for more experiments and further enquiries. He communicated to Imlac

24. The philosopher is apparently based on Jean Jacques Rousseau (1712–78), whose praise of the state of nature as happier than civilization Johnson ridiculed: "Why, Sir, a man who talks nonsense so well must know that he is talking nonsense."

his observations and his doubts, but was answered by him with new doubts, and remarks that gave him no comfort. He therefore discoursed more frequently and freely with his sister, who had yet the same hope with himself, and always assisted him to give some reason why, though he had been hitherto frustrated, he might succeed at last.

'We have hitherto,' said she, 'known but little of the world: we have never yet been either great or mean. In our own country, though we had royalty, we had no power, and in this we have not yet seen the private recesses of domestic peace. Imlac favours not our search lest we should in time find him mistaken. We will divide the task between us: you shall try what is to be found in the splendour of courts, and I will range the shades of humbler life. Perhaps command and authority may be the supreme blessings, as they afford most opportunities of doing good: or, perhaps, what this world can give may be found in the modest habitations of middle fortune; too low for great designs and too high for penury and distress.'

Chapter XXIV: The Prince Examines the Happiness of High Stations

Rasselas applauded the design, and appeared next day with a splendid retinue at the court of the Bassa. He was soon distinguished for his magnificence, and admitted, as a prince whose curiosity had brought him from distant countries, to an intimacy with the great officers, and frequent conversation with the Bassa himself.

He was at first inclined to believe that the man must be pleased with his own condition whom all approached with reverence and heard with obedience, and who had the power to extend his edicts to a whole kingdom. 'There can be no pleasure,' said he, 'equal to that of feeling at once the joy of thousands all made happy by wise administration. Yet, since, by the law of subordination, this sublime delight can be in one nation but the lot of one, it is surely reasonable to think that there is some satisfaction more popular and accessible, and that millions can hardly be subjected to the will of a single man, only to fill his particular breast with incommunicable content.'

These thoughts were often in his mind, and he found no solution of the difficulty. But as presents and civilities gained him more familiarity, he found that almost every man who stood high in employment hated all the rest and was hated by them, and that their lives were a continual succession of plots and detections, stratagems and escapes, faction and treachery. Many of those who surrounded the Bassa were sent only to watch and report his conduct; every tongue was muttering censure and every eye was searching for a fault.

At last the letters of revocation arrived; the Bassa was carried in chains to Constantinople, and his name was mentioned no more.

'What are we now to think of the prerogatives of power?' said Rasselas to his sister. 'Is it without any efficacy to good? Or, is the subordinate degree only dangerous and the supreme safe and glorious? Is the Sultan the only happy man in his dominions, or is the Sultan himself subject to the torments of suspicion and the dread of enemies?'

In a short time the second Bassa was deposed. The Sultan that had advanced him was murdered by the Janisaries,[25] and his successor had other views and different favourites.

25. The Sultan's guard, part of the standing army.

Chapter XXV: The Princess Pursues Her Enquiry with More Diligence than Success

The princess, in the meantime, insinuated herself into many families; for there are few doors through which liberality, joined with good humour, cannot find its way. The daughters of many houses were airy[26] and cheerful, but Nekayah had been too long accustomed to the conversation of Imlac and her brother to be much pleased with childish levity and prattle which had no meaning. She found their thoughts narrow, their wishes low, and their merriment often artificial. Their pleasures, poor as they were, could not be preserved pure, but were embittered by petty competitions and worthless emulation. They were always jealous of the beauty of each other; of a quality to which solicitude can add nothing, and from which detraction can take nothing away. Many were in love with triflers like themselves, and many fancied that they were in love when in truth they were only idle. Their affection was seldom fixed on sense or virtue, and therefore seldom ended but in vexation. Their grief, however, like their joy, was transient; everything floated in their mind unconnected with the past or future, so that one desire easily gave way to another, as a second stone cast into the water effaces and confounds the circles of the first.

With these girls she played as with inoffensive animals, and found them proud of her countenance[27] and weary of her company.

But her purpose was to examine more deeply, and her affability easily persuaded the hearts that were swelling with sorrow to discharge their secrets in her ear: and those whom hope flattered, or prosperity delighted, often courted her to partake their pleasures.

The princess and her brother commonly met in the evening in a private summer-house on the bank of the Nile, and related to each other the occurrences of the day. As they were sitting together, the princess cast her eyes upon the river that flowed before her. 'Answer,' said she, 'great father of waters, thou that rollest thy floods through eighty nations, to the invocations of the daughter of thy native king. Tell me if thou waterest, through all thy course, a single habitation from which thou dost not hear the murmurs of complaint?'

'You are then,' said Rasselas, 'not more successful in private houses than I have been in courts.'

'I have, since the last partition of our provinces,' [28] said the princess, 'enabled myself to enter familiarly into many families where there was the fairest show of prosperity and peace, and know not one house that is not haunted by some fury that destroys its quiet.

'I did not seek ease among the poor, because I concluded that there it could not be found. But I saw many poor whom I had supposed to live in affluence. Poverty has, in large cities, very different appearances: it is often concealed in splendour, and often in extravagance. It is the care of a very great part of mankind to conceal their indigence from the rest: they support themselves by temporary expedients, and every day is lost in contriving for the morrow.

'This, however, was an evil which, though frequent, I saw with less pain, because I could relieve it. Yet some have refused my bounties; more offended

26. "Sprightly, full of mirth" (Johnson, *Dictionary*).
27. "Patronage, appearance of favour" (Johnson, *Dictionary*).
28. Division of our labors in the quest.

with my quickness to detect their wants, than pleased with my readiness to succour them: and others, whose exigencies compelled them to admit my kindness, have never been able to forgive their benefactress. Many, however, have been sincerely grateful without the ostentation of gratitude or the hope of other favours.'

Chapter XXVI: The Princess Continues Her Remarks upon Private Life

Nekayah, perceiving her brother's attention fixed, proceeded in her narrative.

'In families, where there is or is not poverty, there is commonly discord: if a kingdom be, as Imlac tells us, a great family, a family likewise is a little kingdom, torn with factions and exposed to revolutions. An unpractised observer expects the love of parents and children to be constant and equal; but this kindness seldom continues beyond the years of infancy: in a short time the children become rivals to their parents. Benefits are allayed[29] by reproaches, and gratitude debased by envy.

'Parents and children seldom act in concert: each child endeavours to appropriate the esteem or fondness of the parents; and the parents, with yet less temptation, betray each other to their children; thus some place their confidence in the father, and some in the mother, and, by degrees, the house is filled with artifices and feuds.

'The opinions of children and parents, of the young and the old, are naturally opposite, by the contrary effects of hope and despondence, of expectation and experience, without crime or folly on either side. The colours of life in youth and age appear different, as the face of nature in spring and winter. And how can children credit the assertions of parents which their own eyes show them to be false?

'Few parents act in such a manner as much to enforce their maxims by the credit of their lives. The old man trusts wholly to slow contrivance and gradual progression: the youth expects to force his way by genius, vigour, and precipitance. The old man pays regard to riches, and the youth reverences virtue. The old man deifies prudence: the youth commits himself to magnanimity and chance. The young man, who intends no ill, believes that none is intended, and therefore acts with openness and candour: but his father, having suffered the injuries of fraud, is impelled to suspect, and too often allured to practice it. Age looks with anger on the temerity of youth, and youth with contempt on the scrupulosity of age. Thus parents and children, for the greatest part, live on to love less and less: and, if those whom nature has thus closely united are the torments of each other, where shall we look for tenderness and consolation?'

'Surely,' said the prince, 'you must have been unfortunate in your choice of acquaintance: I am unwilling to believe that the most tender of all relations is thus impeded in its effects by natural necessity.'

'Domestic discord,' answered she, 'is not inevitably and fatally necessary; but yet is not easily avoided. We seldom see that a whole family is virtuous: the good and evil cannot well agree; and the evil can yet less agree with one another: even the virtuous fall sometimes to variance, when their virtues are

29. Alloyed, corrupted.

of different kinds and tending to extremes. In general, those parents have most reverence who most deserve it: for he that lives well cannot be despised.

'Many other evils infest private life. Some are the slaves of servants whom they have trusted with their affairs. Some are kept in continual anxiety to the caprice of rich relations, whom they cannot please and dare not offend. Some husbands are imperious, and some wives perverse: and, as it is always more easy to do evil than good, though the wisdom or virtue of one can very rarely make many happy, the folly or vice of one may often make many miserable.'

'If such be the general effect of marriage,' said the prince, 'I shall, for the future, think it dangerous to connect my interest with that of another, lest I should be unhappy by my partner's fault.'

'I have met,' said the princess, 'with many who live single for that reason; but I never found that their prudence ought to raise envy. They dream away their time without friendship, without fondness, and are driven to rid themselves of the day, for which they have no use, by childish amusements or vicious delights. They act as beings under the constant sense of some known inferiority, that fills their minds with rancour and their tongues with censure. They are peevish at home and malevolent abroad; and, as the outlaws of human nature, make it their business and their pleasure to disturb that society which debars them from its privileges. To live without feeling or exciting sympathy, to be fortunate without adding to the felicity of others, or afflicted without tasting the balm of pity, is a state more gloomy than solitude: it is not retreat but exclusion from mankind. Marriage has many pains, but celibacy has no pleasures.'

'What then is to be done?' said Rasselas. 'The more we enquire, the less we can resolve. Surely he is most likely to please himself that has no other inclination to regard.'

Chapter XXVII: Disquisition upon Greatness

The conversation had a short pause. The prince, having considered his sister's observations, told her that she had surveyed life with prejudice and supposed misery where she did not find it. 'Your narrative,' says he, 'throws yet a darker gloom upon the prospects of futurity: the predictions of Imlac were but faint sketches of the evils painted by Nekayah. I have been lately convinced that quiet is not the daughter of grandeur or of power: that her presence is not to be bought by wealth nor enforced by conquest. It is evident that, as any man acts in a wider compass, he must be more exposed to opposition from enmity or miscarriage from chance; whoever has many to please or to govern must use the ministry of many agents, some of whom will be wicked and some ignorant; by some he will be misled, and by others betrayed. If he gratifies one he will offend another: those that are not favoured will think themselves injured; and, since favours can be conferred but upon few, the greater number will be always discontented.'

'The discontent,' said the princess, 'which is thus unreasonable, I hope that I shall always have spirit to despise, and you power to repress.'

'Discontent,' answered Rasselas, 'will not always be without reason under the most just or vigilant administration of public affairs. None, however attentive, can always discover that merit which indigence or faction may happen to obscure; and none, however powerful, can always reward it. Yet, he that sees inferiour desert advanced above him will naturally impute that preference to partiality or caprice; and, indeed, it can scarcely be hoped that any man, however magnanimous by nature or exalted by condition, will be able to persist forever in fixed and inexorable justice of distribution: he will sometimes indulge his own affections, and sometimes those of his favourites; he will permit some to please him who can never serve him; he will discover in those whom he loves qualities which in reality they do not possess; and to those from whom he receives pleasure, he will in his turn endeavour to give it. Thus will recommendations sometimes prevail which were purchased by money or by the more destructive bribery of flattery and servility.

'He that has much to do will do something wrong, and of that wrong must suffer the consequences; and, if it were possible that he should always act rightly, yet when such numbers are to judge of his conduct, the bad will censure and obstruct him by malevolence, and the good sometimes by mistake.

'The highest stations cannot therefore hope to be the abodes of happiness, which I would willingly believe to have fled from thrones and palaces to seats of humble privacy and placid obscurity. For what can hinder the satisfaction, or intercept the expectations, of him whose abilities are adequate to his employments, who sees with his own eyes the whole circuit of his influence, who chooses by his own knowledge all whom he trusts, and whom none are tempted to deceive by hope or fear? Surely he has nothing to do but to love and to be loved, to be virtuous and to be happy.'

'Whether perfect happiness would be procured by perfect goodness,' said Nekayah, 'this world will never afford an opportunity of deciding. But this, at least, may be maintained, that we do not always find visible happiness in proportion to visible virtue. All natural and almost all political evils are incident alike to the bad and good: they are confounded in the misery of a famine and not much distinguished in the fury of a faction; they sink together in a tempest and are driven together from their country by invaders. All that virtue can afford is quietness of conscience, a steady prospect of a happier state; this may enable us to endure calamity with patience; but remember that patience must suppose pain.'

Chapter XXVIII: Rasselas and Nekayah Continue Their Conversation

'Dear princess,' said Rasselas, 'you fall into the common errours of exaggeratory declamation by producing, in a familiar disquisition, examples of national calamities and scenes of extensive misery, which are found in books rather than in the world, and which, as they are horrid, are ordained to be rare. Let us not imagine evils which we do not feel, nor injure life by misrepresentations. I cannot bear that querulous eloquence which threatens every city with a siege like that of Jerusalem, that makes famine attend on every flight of locusts, and suspends pestilence on the wing of every blast that issues from the south.

'On necessary and inevitable evils, which overwhelm kingdoms at once, all disputation is vain: when they happen they must be endured. But it is evident that these bursts of universal distress are more dreaded than felt: thousands and ten thousands flourish in youth and wither in age, without the knowledge of any other than domestic evils, and share the same pleasures and vexations whether their kings are mild or cruel, whether the armies of their country pursue their enemies or retreat before them. While courts are disturbed with intestine competitions and ambassadours are negotiating in foreign countries, the smith still plies his anvil, and the husbandman drives his plow forward; the necessaries of life are required and obtained, and the successive business of the seasons continues to make its wonted revolutions.

'Let us cease to consider what, perhaps, may never happen, and what, when it shall happen, will laugh at human speculation. We will not endeavour to modify the motions of the elements or to fix the destiny of kingdoms. It is our business to consider what beings like us may perform; each labouring for his own happiness, by promoting within his circle, however narrow, the happiness of others.

'Marriage is evidently the dictate of nature; men and women were made to be companions of each other, and therefore I cannot be persuaded but that marriage is one of the means of happiness.'

'I know not,' said the princess, 'whether marriage be more than one of the innumerable modes of human misery. When I see and reckon the various forms of connubial infelicity, the unexpected causes of lasting discord, the diversities of temper, the oppositions of opinion, the rude collisions of contrary desire where both are urged by violent impulses, the obstinate contests of disagreeing virtues, where both are supported by consciousness of good intention, I am sometimes disposed to think with the severer casuists[30] of most nations, that marriage is rather permitted than approved, and that none, but by the instigation of a passion too much indulged, entangle themselves with indissoluble compacts.'

'You seem to forget,' replied Rasselas, 'that you have, even now, represented celibacy as less happy than marriage. Both conditions may be bad, but they cannot both be worst. Thus it happens, when wrong opinions are entertained, that they mutually destroy each other and leave the mind open to truth.'

'I did not expect,' answered the princess, 'to hear that imputed to falsehood which is the consequence only of frailty. To the mind, as to the eye, it is difficult to compare with exactness objects vast in their extent and various in their parts. Where we see or conceive the whole at once we readily note the discriminations and decide the preference: but of two systems, of which neither can be surveyed by any human being in its full compass of magnitude and multiplicity of complication, where is the wonder that, judging of the whole by parts, I am alternately affected by one and the other as either presses on my memory or fancy? We differ from ourselves just as we differ from each other, when we see only part of the question, as in the multifarious relations of politics and morality: but when we perceive the whole at once, as in numerical computations, all agree in one judgment, and none ever varies his opinion.'

'Let us not add,' said the prince, 'to the other evils of life the bitterness of controversy, nor endeavour to vie with each other in subtilties of argument. We are employed in a search of which both are equally to enjoy the success, or suffer by the miscarriage. It is therefore fit that we assist each other. You surely conclude too hastily from the infelicity of marriage against its institu-

30. Moralists; those who settle cases of conscience.

tion; will not the misery of life prove equally that life cannot be the gift of heaven? The world must be peopled by marriage, or peopled without it.'

'How the world is to be peopled,' returned Nekayah, 'is not my care, and needs not be yours. I see no danger that the present generation should omit to leave successors behind them: we are not now enquiring for the world, but for ourselves.'

Chapter XXIX: The Debate on Marriage Continued

'The good of the whole,' says Rasselas, 'is the same with the good of all its parts. If marriage be best for mankind it must be evidently best for individuals, or a permanent and necessary duty must be the cause of evil, and some must be inevitably sacrificed to the convenience of others. In the estimate which you have made of the two states, it appears that the incommodities of a single life are, in a great measure, necessary and certain, but those of the conjugal state accidental and avoidable.

'I cannot forbear to flatter myself that prudence and benevolence will make marriage happy. The general folly of mankind is the cause of general complaint. What can be expected but disappointment and repentance from a choice made in the immaturity of youth, in the ardour of desire, without judgment, without foresight, without enquiry after conformity of opinions, similarity of manners, rectitude of judgment, or purity of sentiment.

'Such is the common process of marriage. A youth and maiden meeting by chance, or brought together by artifice, exchange glances, reciprocate civilities, go home, and dream of one another. Having little to divert attention or diversify thought, they find themselves uneasy when they are apart, and therefore conclude that they shall be happy together. They marry, and discover what nothing but voluntary blindness had before concealed; they wear out life in altercations, and charge nature with cruelty.

'From those early marriages proceeds likewise the rivalry of parents and children: the son is eager to enjoy the world before the father is willing to forsake it, and there is hardly room at once for two generations. The daughter begins to bloom before the mother can be content to fade, and neither can forbear to wish for the absence of the other.

'Surely all these evils may be avoided by that deliberation and delay which prudence prescribes to irrevocable choice. In the variety and jollity of youthful pleasures life may be well enough supported without the help of a partner. Longer time will increase experience, and wider views will allow better opportunities of enquiry and selection: one advantage, at least, will be certain; the parents will be visibly older than their children.'

'What reason cannot collect,' said Nekayah, 'and what experiment has not yet taught can be known only from the report of others. I have been told that late marriages are not eminently happy. This is a question too important to be neglected, and I have often proposed it to those whose accuracy of remark and comprehensiveness of knowledge made their suffrages worthy of regard. They have generally determined that it is dangerous for a man and woman to suspend their fate upon each other at a time when opinions are fixed and habits are established; when friendships have been contracted on both sides, when life has been planned into method, and the mind has long enjoyed the contemplation of its own prospects.

'It is scarcely possible that two travelling through the world under the conduct of chance should have been both directed to the same path, and it will not often happen that either will quit the track which custom has made pleasing. When the desultory levity of youth has settled into regularity, it is soon succeeded by pride ashamed to yield, or obstinacy delighting to contend. And even though mutual esteem produces mutual desire to please, time itself, as it modifies unchangeably the external mien, determines likewise the direction of the passions, and gives an inflexible rigidity to the manners. Long customs are not easily broken: he that attempts to change the course of his own life very often labours in vain; and how shall we do that for others which we are seldom able to do for ourselves?'

'But surely,' interposed the prince, 'you suppose the chief motive of choice forgotten or neglected. Whenever I shall seek a wife, it shall be my first question whether she be willing to be led by reason?'

'Thus it is,' said Nekayah, 'that philosophers are deceived. There are a thousand familiar disputes which reason never can decide; questions that elude investigation, and make logic ridiculous; cases where something must be done and where little can be said. Consider the state of mankind, and enquire how few can be supposed to act upon any occasions, whether small or great, with all the reasons of action present to their minds. Wretched would be the pair above all names of wretchedness, who should be doomed to adjust by reason every morning all the minute detail of a domestic day.

'Those who marry at an advanced age will probably escape the encroachments of their children; but, in diminution of this advantage, they will be likely to leave them, ignorant and helpless, to a guardian's mercy: or, if that should not happen, they must at least go out of the world before they see those whom they love best either wise or great.

'From their children, if they have less to fear, they have less also to hope, and they lose, without equivalent, the joys of early love, and the convenience of uniting with manners pliant and minds susceptible of new impressions, which might wear away their dissimilitudes by long cohabitation, as soft bodies, by continual attrition, conform their surfaces to each other.

'I believe it will be found that those who marry late are best pleased with their children, and those who marry early with their partners.'

'The union of these two affections,' said Rasselas, 'would produce all that could be wished. Perhaps there is a time when marriage might unite them, a time neither too early for the father, nor too late for the husband.'

'Every hour,' answered the princess, 'confirms my prejudice in favour of the position so often uttered by the mouth of Imlac, "that nature sets her gifts on the right hand and on the left." Those conditions which flatter hope and attract desire are so constituted that, as we approach one, we recede from another. There are goods so opposed that we cannot seize both, but, by too much prudence, may pass between them at too great a distance to reach either. This is often the fate of long consideration; he does nothing who endeavours to do more than is allowed to humanity. Flatter not yourself with contrarieties of pleasure. Of the blessings set before you make your choice, and be content. No man can taste the fruits of autumn while he is delighting his scent with the flowers of the spring: no man can, at the same time, fill his cup from the source and from the mouth of the Nile.'

Chapter XXX: Imlac Enters, and Changes the Conversation

Here Imlac entered and interrupted them. 'Imlac,' said Rasselas, 'I have been taking from the princess the dismal history of private life, and am almost discouraged from further search.'

'It seems to me,' said Imlac, 'that while you are making the choice of life, you neglect to live. You wander about a single city which, however large and diversified, can now afford few novelties, and forget that you are in a country famous among the earliest monarchies for the power and wisdom of its inhabitants; a country where the sciences first dawned that illuminate the world, and beyond which the arts cannot be traced of civil society or domestic life.

'The old Egyptians have left behind them monuments of industry and power before which all European magnificence is confessed to fade away. The ruins of their architecture are the schools of modern builders, and from the wonders which time has spared we may conjecture, though uncertainly, what it has destroyed.'

'My curiosity,' said Rasselas, 'does not very strongly lead me to survey piles of stone or mounds of earth; my business is with man. I came hither not to measure fragments of temples or trace choked aqueducts, but to look upon the various scenes of the present world.'

'The things that are now before us,' said the princess, 'require attention and deserve it. What have I to do with the heroes or the monuments of ancient times? with times which never can return, and heroes, whose form of life was different from all that the present condition of mankind requires or allows.'

'To know anything,' returned the poet, 'we must know its effects; to see men we must see their works, that we may learn what reason has dictated or passion has incited, and find what are the most powerful motives of action. To judge rightly of the present we must oppose it to the past; for all judgment is comparative, and of the future nothing can be known. The truth is that no mind is much employed upon the present: recollection and anticipation fill up almost all our moments. Our passions are joy and grief, love and hatred, hope and fear. Of joy and grief the past is the object, and the future of hope and fear; even love and hatred respect the past, for the cause must have been before the effect.

'The present state of things is the consequence of the former, and it is natural to inquire what were the sources of the good that we enjoy or of the evil that we suffer. If we act only for ourselves, to neglect the study of history is not prudent: if we are entrusted with the care of others, it is not just. Ignorance, when it is voluntary, is criminal; and he may properly be charged with evil who refused to learn how he might prevent it.

'There is no part of history so generally useful as that which relates the progress of the human mind, the gradual improvement of reason, the successive advances of science, the vicissitudes of learning and ignorance, which are the light and darkness of thinking beings, the extinction and resuscitation of arts, and all the revolutions of the intellectual world. If accounts of battles and invasions are peculiarly the business of princes, the useful or elegant arts are not to be neglected; those who have kingdoms to govern have understandings to cultivate.

'Example is always more efficacious than precept. A soldier is formed in war, and a painter must copy pictures. In this, contemplative life has the advantage: great actions are seldom seen, but the labours of art are always at hand for those who desire to know what art has been able to perform.

'When the eye or the imagination is struck with any uncommon work, the next transition of an active mind is to the means by which it was performed. Here begins the true use of such contemplation; we enlarge our comprehension by new ideas, and perhaps recover some art lost to mankind, or learn what is less perfectly known in our own country. At least we compare our own with former times, and either rejoice at our improvements, or, what is the first motion towards good, discover our defects.'

'I am willing,' said the prince, 'to see all that can deserve my search.' 'And I,' said the princess, 'shall rejoice to learn something of the manners of antiquity.'

'The most pompous monument of Egyptian greatness, and one of the most bulky works of manual industry,' said Imlac, 'are the pyramids; fabrics raised before the time of history, and of which the earliest narratives afford us only uncertain traditions. Of these the greatest is still standing, very little injured by time.'

'Let us visit them tomorrow,' said Nekayah. 'I have often heard of the pyramids and shall not rest till I have seen them within and without with my own eyes.'

Chapter XXXI: They Visit the Pyramids

The resolution being thus taken, they set out the next day. They laid tents upon their camels, being resolved to stay among the pyramids till their curiosity was fully satisfied. They travelled gently, turned aside to everything remarkable, stopped from time to time and conversed with the inhabitants, and observed the various appearances of towns, ruined and inhabited, of wild and cultivated nature.

When they came to the great pyramid they were astonished at the extent of the base and the height of the top. Imlac explained to them the principles upon which the pyramidal form was chosen for a fabric intended to co-extend its duration with that of the world: he showed that its gradual diminution gave it such stability as defeated all the common attacks of the elements, and could scarcely be overthrown by earthquakes themselves, the least resistible of natural violence. A concussion that should shatter the pyramid would threaten the dissolution of the continent.

They measured all its dimensions, and pitched their tents at its foot. Next day they prepared to enter its interiour apartments and, having hired the common guides, climbed up to the first passage, when the favourite of the princess, looking into the cavity, stepped back and trembled. 'Pekuah,' said the princess, 'of what art thou afraid?'

'Of the narrow entrance,' answered the lady, 'and of the dreadful gloom. I dare not enter a place which must surely be inhabited by unquiet souls. The original possessors of these dreadful vaults will start up before us, and, perhaps, shut us in for ever.' She spoke, and threw her arms round the neck of her mistress.

'If all your fear be of apparitions," said the prince, 'I will promise you safety:

there is no danger from the dead; he that is once buried will be seen no more.'

'That the dead are seen no more,' said Imlac, 'I will not undertake to maintain against the concurrent and unvaried testimony of all ages, and of all nations. There is no people, rude or learned, among whom apparitions of the dead are not related and believed. This opinion, which, perhaps, prevails as far as human nature is diffused, could become universal only by its truth: those that never heard of one another would not have agreed in a tale which nothing but experience can make credible. That it is doubted by single cavillers can very little weaken the general evidence, and some who deny it with their tongues confess it by their fears.

'Yet I do not mean to add new terrours to those which have already seized upon Pekuah. There can be no reason why spectres should haunt the pyramid more than other places, or why they should have power or will to hurt innocence and purity. Our entrance is no violation of their privileges; we can take nothing from them, how then can we offend them?'

'My dear Pekuah,' said the princess, 'I will always go before you, and Imlac shall follow you. Remember that you are the companion of the princess of Abyssinia.'

'If the princess is pleased that her servant should die,' returned the lady, 'let her command some death less dreadful than enclosure in this horrid cavern. You know I dare not disobey you: I must go if you command me; but, if I once enter, I never shall come back.'

The princess saw that her fear was too strong for expostulation or reproof, and, embracing her, told her that she should stay in the tent till their return. Pekuah was yet not satisfied, but entreated the princess not to pursue so dreadful a purpose as that of entering the recesses of the pyramid. 'Though I cannot teach courage,' said Nekayah, 'I must not learn cowardice; nor leave at last undone what I came hither only to do.'

Chapter XXXII: They Enter the Pyramid

Pekuah descended to the tents, and the rest entered the pyramid: they passed through the galleries, surveyed the vaults of marble, and examined the chest in which the body of the founder is supposed to have been reposited. They then sat down in one of the most spacious chambers to rest a while before they attempted to return.

'We have now,' said Imlac, 'gratified our minds with an exact view of the greatest work of man, except the wall of China.

'Of the wall it is very easy to assign the motives. It secured a wealthy and timorous nation from the incursions of barbarians whose unskilfulness in arts made it easier for them to supply their wants by rapine than by industry, and who from time to time poured in upon the habitations of peaceful commerce, as vultures descend upon domestic fowl. Their celerity and fierceness made the wall necessary, and their ignorance made it efficacious.

'But for the pyramids no reason has ever been given adequate to the cost and labour of the work. The narrowness of the chambers proves that it could afford no retreat from enemies, and treasures might have been reposited at far less expence with equal security. It seems to have been erected only in compliance with that hunger of imagination which preys incessantly upon life, and must be always appeased by some employment. Those who have already all that they can enjoy, must enlarge their desires. He that has built for use, till use is supplied, must begin to build for vanity, and extend his plan to the utmost power of human performance, that he may not be soon reduced to form another wish.

'I consider this mighty structure as a monument of the insufficiency of human enjoyments. A king, whose power is unlimited, and whose treasures surmount all real and imaginary wants, is compelled to solace, by the erection of a pyramid, the satiety of dominion and tastelessness of pleasures, and to amuse the tediousness of declining life by seeing thousands labouring without end, and one stone, for no purpose, laid upon another. Whoever thou art, that, not content with a moderate condition, imaginest happiness in royal magnificence, and dreamest that command or riches can feed the appetite of novelty with perpetual gratifications, survey the pyramids, and confess thy folly!'

Chapter XXXIII: The Princess Meets with an Unexpected Misfortune

They rose up, and returned through the cavity at which they had entered, and the princess prepared for her favourite a long narrative of dark labyrinths and costly rooms, and of the different impressions which the varieties of the way had made upon her. But, when they came to their train, they found every one silent and dejected: the men discovered shame and fear in their countenances, and the women were weeping in the tents.

What had happened they did not try to conjecture, but immediately enquired. 'You had scarcely entered into the pyramid,' said one of the attendants, 'when a troop of Arabs rushed upon us: we were too few to resist them, and too slow to escape. They were about to search the tents, set us on our camels, and drive us along before them, when the approach of some Turkish horsemen put them to flight; but they seized the lady Pekuah with her two maids, and carried them away: the Turks are now pursuing them by our instigation, but I fear they will not be able to overtake them.'

The princess was overpowered with surprise and grief. Rasselas, in the first heat of his resentment, ordered his servants to follow him, and prepared to pursue the robbers with his sabre in his hand. 'Sir,' said Imlac, 'what can you hope from violence or valour? The Arabs are mounted on horses trained to battle and retreat; we have only beasts of burden. By leaving our present station we may lose the princess, but cannot hope to regain Pekuah.'

In a short time the Turks returned, having not been able to reach the enemy. The princess burst out into new lamentations, and Rasselas could scarcely forbear to reproach them with cowardice; but Imlac was of opinion that the escape of the Arabs was no addition to their misfortune, for, perhaps, they would have killed their captives rather than have resigned them.

Chapter XXXIV: They Return to Cairo without Pekuah

There was nothing to be hoped from longer stay. They returned to Cairo repenting of their curiosity, censuring the negligence of the government, lamenting their own rashness which had neglected to procure a guard, imagining many expedients by which the loss of Pekuah might have been prevented, and resolving to do something for her recovery, though none could find anything proper to be done.

Nekayah retired to her chamber, where her women attempted to comfort her by telling her that all had their troubles, and that lady Pekuah had enjoyed much happiness in the world for a long time, and might reasonably expect a change of fortune. They hoped that some good would befall her wheresoever she was, and that their mistress would find another friend who might supply her place.

The princess made them no answer, and they continued the form of condolence, not much grieved in their hearts that the favourite was lost.

Next day the prince presented to the Bassa a memorial of the wrong which he had suffered, and a petition for redress. The Bassa threatened to punish the robbers, but did not attempt to catch them, nor, indeed, could any account or description be given by which he might direct the pursuit.

It soon appeared that nothing would be done by authority. Governors, being accustomed to hear of more crimes than they can punish and more wrongs than they can redress, set themselves at ease by indiscriminate negligence, and presently forget the request when they lose sight of the petitioner.

Imlac then endeavoured to gain some intelligence by private agents. He found many who pretended to an exact knowledge of all the haunts of the Arabs, and to regular correspondence with their chiefs, and who readily undertook the recovery of Pekuah. Of these, some were furnished with money for their journey and came back no more; some were liberally paid for accounts which a few days discovered to be false. But the princess would not suffer any means, however improbable, to be left untried. While she was doing something she kept her hope alive. As one expedient failed, another was suggested; when one messenger returned unsuccessful, another was despatched to a different quarter.

Two months had now passed, and of Pekuah nothing had been heard; the hopes which they had endeavoured to raise in each other grew more languid, and the princess, when she saw nothing more to be tried, sunk down inconsolable in hopeless dejection. A thousand times she reproached herself with the easy compliance by which she permitted her favourite to stay behind her. 'Had not my fondness,' said she, 'lessened my authority, Pekuah had not dared to talk of her terrours. She ought to have feared me more than spectres. A severe look would have overpowered her; a peremptory command would have compelled obedience. Why did foolish indulgence prevail upon me? Why did I not speak and refuse to hear?'

'Great princess,' said Imlac, 'do not reproach yourself for your virtue, or consider that as blameable by which evil has accidentally been caused. Your tenderness for the timidity of Pekuah was generous and kind. When we act according to our duty, we commit the event to him by whose laws our actions are governed, and who will suffer none to be finally punished for obedience. When, in prospect of some good, whether natural or moral, we break the rules prescribed us, we withdraw from the direction of superiour wisdom, and take all consequences upon ourselves. Man cannot so far know the connexion of causes and events, as that he may venture to do wrong in order to do right. When we pursue our end by lawful means, we may always console our miscarriage by the hope of future recompense. When we consult only our own policy, and attempt to find a nearer way to good by overleaping the settled boundaries of right and wrong, we cannot be happy even by success because we cannot escape the consciousness of our fault; but, if we miscarry, the disappointment is irremediably embittered. How comfortless is the sorrow of him who feels at once the pangs of guilt and the vexation of calamity which guilt has brought upon him?

'Consider, princess, what would have been your condition, if the lady Pekuah had entreated to accompany you, and, being compelled to stay in the tents, had been carried away; or how would you have borne the thought, if you had forced her into the pyramid, and she had died before you in agonies of terrour.'

'Had either happened,' said Nekayah, 'I could not have endured life till now: I should have been tortured to madness by the remembrance of such cruelty, or must have pined away in abhorrence of myself.'

'This at least,' said Imlac, 'is the present reward of virtuous conduct, that no unlucky consequence can oblige us to repent it.'

Chapter XXXV: The Princess Languishes for Want of Pekuah

Nekayah, being thus reconciled to herself, found that no evil is insupportable but that which is accompanied with consciousness of wrong. She was, from that time, delivered from the violence of tempestuous sorrow, and sunk into silent pensiveness and gloomy tranquility. She sat from morning to evening recollecting all that had been done or said by her Pekuah, treasured up with care every trifle on which Pekuah had set an accidental value, and which might recall to mind any little incident or careless conversation. The sentiments of her whom she now expected to see no more were treasured in her memory as rules of life, and she deliberated to no other end than to conjecture on any occasion what would have been the opinion and counsel of Pekuah.

The women by whom she was attended knew nothing of her real condition, and therefore she could not talk to them but with caution and reserve. She began to remit her curiosity, having no great care to collect notions which she had no convenience of uttering. Rasselas endeavoured first to comfort and afterwards to divert her; he hired musicians, to whom she seemed to listen, but did not hear them, and procured masters to instruct her in various arts, whose lectures, when they visited her again, were again to be repeated. She had lost her taste of pleasure and her ambition of excellence. And her mind, though forced into short excursions, always recurred to the image of her friend.

Imlac was every morning earnestly enjoined to renew his enquiries, and was asked every night whether he had yet heard of Pekuah, till not being able to return the princess the answer that she desired, he was less and less willing to come into her presence. She observed his backwardness, and commanded him to attend her. 'You are not,' said she, 'to confound impatience with resentment, or to suppose that I charge you with negligence, because I repine at your unsuccessfulness. I do not much wonder at your absence; I know that the unhappy are never pleasing, and that all naturally avoid the contagion of misery. To hear complaints is wearisome alike to the wretched and the happy; for who would cloud by adventitious grief the short gleams of gaiety which life allows us? or who, that is struggling under his own evils, will add to them the miseries of another?

'The time is at hand, when none shall be disturbed any longer by the sighs of Nekayah: my search after happiness is now at an end. I am resolved to retire from the world with all its flatteries and deceits, and will hide myself in solitude, without any other care than to compose my thoughts and regulate my hours by a constant succession of innocent occupations, till, with a mind purified from all earthly desires, I shall enter into that state to which all are hastening and in which I hope again to enjoy the friendship of Pekuah.'

'Do not entangle your mind,' said Imlac, 'by irrevocable determinations, nor increase the burthen of life by a voluntary accumulation of misery: the weariness of retirement will continue or increase when the loss of Pekuah is forgotten. That you have been deprived of one pleasure is no very good reason for rejection of the rest.'

'Since Pekuah was taken from me,' said the princess, 'I have no pleasure to reject or to retain. She that has no one to love or trust has little to hope. She wants the radical principle of happiness. We may, perhaps, allow that what satisfaction this world can afford must arise from the conjunction of wealth, knowledge, and goodness: wealth is nothing but as it is bestowed, and knowledge nothing but as it is communicated: they must therefore be imparted to others, and to whom could I now delight to impart them? Goodness affords the only comfort which can be enjoyed without a partner, and goodness may be practised in retirement.'

'How far solitude may admit goodness, or advance it, I shall not,' replied Imlac, 'dispute at present. Remember the confession of the pious hermit. You will wish to return into the world, when the image of your companion has left your thoughts.'

'That time,' said Nekayah, 'will never come. The generous frankness, the modest obsequiousness, and the faithful secrecy of my dear Pekuah, will always be more missed, as I shall live longer to see vice and folly.'

'The state of a mind oppressed with a sudden calamity,' said Imlac, 'is like that of the fabulous inhabitants of the new created earth, who, when the first night came upon them, supposed that day never would return. When the clouds of sorrow gather over us, we see nothing beyond them, nor can imagine how they will be dispelled: yet a new day succeeded to the night, and sorrow is never long without a dawn of ease. But they who restrain themselves from receiving comfort do as the savages would have done, had they put out their eyes when it was dark. Our minds, like our bodies, are in continual flux; something is hourly lost, and something acquired. To lose much at once is inconvenient to either, but while the vital powers remain uninjured, nature will find the means of reparation. Distance has the same effect on the mind as on the eye, and while we glide along the stream of time, whatever we leave behind us is always lessening, and that which we approach increasing in magnitude. Do not suffer life to stagnate; it will grow muddy for want of motion: commit yourself again to the current of the world; Pekuah will vanish by degrees; you will meet in your way some other favourite, or learn to diffuse yourself in general conversation.'

'At least,' said the prince, 'do not despair before all remedies have been tried: the enquiry after the unfortunate lady is still continued, and shall be carried on with yet greater diligence, on condition that you will promise to wait a year for the event without any unalterable resolution.'

Nekayah thought this a reasonable demand, and made the promise to her brother, who had been advised by Imlac to require it. Imlac had, indeed, no great hope of regaining Pekuah, but he supposed that, if he could secure the interval of a year, the princess would be then in no danger of a cloister.

Chapter XXXVI: Pekuah is Still Remembered. The Progress of Sorrow

Nekayah, seeing that nothing was omitted for the recovery of her favourite, and having, by her promise, set her intention of retirement at a distance, began imperceptibly to return to common cares and common pleasures. She rejoiced without her own consent at the suspension of her sorrows, and sometimes caught herself with indignation in the act of turning away her mind from the remembrance of her whom yet she resolved never to forget.

She then appointed a certain hour of the day for meditation on the merits and fondness of Pekuah, and for some weeks retired constantly at the time fixed, and returned with her eyes swollen and her countenance clouded. By degrees she grew less scrupulous, and suffered any important and pressing avocation to delay the tribute of daily tears. She then yielded to less occasions; sometimes forgot what she was indeed afraid to remember, and, at last, wholly released herself from the duty of periodical affliction.

Her real love of Pekuah was yet not diminished. A thousand occurrences brought her back to memory; and a thousands wants, which nothing but the confidence of friendship can supply, made her frequently regretted. She therefore solicited Imlac never to desist from enquiry and to leave no art of intelligence untried, that, at least, she might have the comfort of knowing that she did not suffer by negligence or sluggishness. 'Yet what,' said she, 'is to be expected from our pursuit of happiness, when we find the state of life to be such that happiness itself is the cause of misery? Why should we endeavour to attain that of which the possession cannot be secured? I shall henceforward fear to yield my heart to excellence, however bright, or to fondness, however tender, lest I should lose again what I have lost in Pekuah.'

Chapter XXXVII: The Princess Hears News of Pekuah

In seven months, one of the messengers, who had been sent away upon the day when the promise was drawn from the princess, returned, after many unsuccessful rambles, from the borders of Nubia, with an account that Pekuah was in the hands of an Arab chief who possessed a castle or fortress on the extremity of Egypt. The Arab, whose revenue was plunder, was willing to restore her, with her two attendants, for two hundred ounces of gold.

The price was no subject of debate. The princess was in ecstasies when she heard that her favourite was alive, and might so cheaply be ransomed. She could not think of delaying for a moment Pekuah's happiness or her own, but entreated her brother to send back the messenger with the sum required. Imlac, being consulted, was not very confident of the veracity of the relator, and was still more doubtful of the Arab's faith, who might, if he were too liberally trusted, detain at once the money and the captives. He thought it dangerous to put themselves in the power of the Arab by going into his district, and could not expect that the rover would so much expose himself as to come into the lower country, where he might be seized by the forces of the Bassa.

It is difficult to negotiate where neither will trust. But Imlac, after some deliberation, directed the messenger to propose that Pekuah should be conducted by ten horsemen to the monastery of St. Anthony, which is situated in the deserts of Upper Egypt, where she should be met by the same number, and her ransom should be paid.

That no time might be lost, as they expected that the proposal would not be refused, they immediately began their journey to the monastery; and, when they arrived, Imlac went forward with the former messenger to the Arab's fortress. Rasselas was desirous to go with them, but neither his sister nor Imlac would consent. The Arab, according to the custom of his nation, observed the laws of hospitality with great exactness to those who put themselves into his power, and, in a few days, brought Pekuah with her maids, by easy journeys, to their place appointed; where receiving the stipulated price, he restored her with great respect to liberty and her friends, and undertook to conduct them back towards Cairo beyond all danger of robbery or violence.

The princess and her favourite embraced each other with transport too violent to be expressed, and went out together to pour the tears of tenderness in secret, and exchange professions of kindness and gratitude. After a few hours they returned into the refectory of the convent, where, in the presence of the prior and his brethren, the prince required of Pekuah the history of her adventures.

Chapter XXXVIII: The Adventures of the Lady Pekuah

'At what time, and in what manner, I was forced away,' said Pekuah, 'your servants have told you. The suddenness of the event struck me with surprise, and I was at first rather stupefied than agitated with any passion of either fear or sorrow. My confusion was increased by the speed and tumult of our flight while we were followed by the Turks, who, as it seemed, soon despaired to overtake us, or were afraid of those whom they made a show of menacing.

'When the Arabs saw themselves out of danger they slackened their course, and, as I was less harassed by external violence, I began to feel more uneasiness in my mind. After some time we stopped near a spring shaded with trees in a pleasant meadow, where we were set upon the ground, and offered such refreshments as our masters were partaking. I was suffered to sit with my maids apart from the rest, and none attempted to comfort or insult us. Here I first began to feel the full weight of my misery. The girls sat weeping in silence, and from time to time looked on me for succour. I knew not to what condition we were doomed, nor could conjecture where would be the place of our captivity, or whence to draw any hope of deliverance. I was in the hands of robbers and savages, and had no reason to suppose that their pity was more than their justice, or that they would forbear the gratification of any ardour of desire or caprice of cruelty. I, however, kissed my maids, and endeavoured to pacify them by remarking that we were yet treated with decency, and that, since we were now carried beyond pursuit, there was no danger of violence to our lives.

'When we were to be set again on horseback, my maids clung round me and refused to be parted, but I commanded them not to irritate those who had us in their power. We travelled the remaining part of the day through an unfrequented and pathless country, and came by moonlight to the side of a hill where the rest of the troop was stationed. Their tents were pitched, and their fires kindled, and our chief was welcomed as a man much beloved by his dependents.

'We were received into a large tent, where we found women who had attended their husbands in the expedition. They set before us the supper which they had provided, and I eat it rather to encourage my maids than to comply with any appetite of my own. When the meat was taken away they spread the carpets for repose. I was weary, and hoped to find in sleep that remission of distress which nature seldom denies. Ordering myself therefore to be undressed, I observed that the women looked very earnestly upon me, not expecting, I suppose, to see me so submissively attended. When my upper vest was taken off, they were apparently struck with the splendour of my clothes, and one of them timorously laid her hand upon the embroidery. She then went out, and in a short time came back with another woman who seemed to be of higher rank and greater authority. She did at her entrance the usual act of reverence, and, taking me by the hand, placed me in a smaller tent, spread with finer carpets, where I spent the night quietly with my maids.

'In the morning, as I was sitting on the grass, the chief of the troop came towards me. I rose up to receive him, and he bowed with great respect. "Illustrious lady," said he, "my fortune is better than I had presumed to hope; I am told by my women, that I have a princess in my camp."

' "Sir," answered I, "your women have deceived themselves and you; I am not a princess, but an unhappy stranger who intended soon to have left this country, in which I am now to be imprisoned for ever."

' "Whoever, or whencesoever, you are," returned the Arab, "your dress and that of your servants show your rank to be high and your wealth to be great. Why should you, who can so easily procure your ransom, think yourself in danger of perpetual captivity? The purpose of my incursions is to increase my riches, or more properly to gather tribute. The sons of Ishmael[31] are the natural and hereditary lords of this part of the continent, which is usurped by late invaders, and low-born tyrants, from whom we are compelled to take by the sword what is denied to justice. The violence of war admits no distinction; the lance that is lifted at guilt and power will sometimes fall on innocence and gentleness."

' "How little," said I, "did I expect that yesterday it should have fallen upon me."

' "Misfortunes," answered the Arab, "should always be expected. If the eye of hostility could learn reverence or pity, excellence like yours had been exempt from injury. But the angels of affliction spread their toils alike for the virtuous

31. The Arabs, who claim descent from Ishmael, the son of Hagar born in the wilderness (Genesis 21:9–21).

and the wicked, for the mighty and the mean. Do not be disconsolate; I am not one of the lawless and cruel rovers of the desert; I know the rules of civil life: I will fix your ransom, give a passport to your messenger, and perform my stipulation with nice punctuality."[32]

'You will easily believe that I was pleased with his courtesy; and finding that his predominant passion was desire of money, I began now to think my danger less, for I knew that no sum would be thought too great for the release of Pekuah. I told him that he should have no reason to charge me with ingratitude if I was used with kindness, and that any ransom which could be expected for a maid of common rank would be paid, but that he must not persist to rate me as a princess. He said he would consider what he should demand and then, smiling, bowed and retired.

'Soon after the women came about me, each contending to be more officious[33] than the other, and my maids themselves were served with reverence. We travelled onward by short journeys. On the fourth day the chief told me that my ransom must be two hundred ounces of gold, which I not only promised him, but told him that I would add fifty more if I and my maids were honourably treated.

'I never knew the power of gold before. From that time I was the leader of the troop. The march of every day was longer or shorter as I commanded, and the tents were pitched where I chose to rest. We now had camels and other conveniencies for travel; my own women were always at my side; and I amused myself with observing the manners of the vagrant nations and with viewing remains of ancient edifices with which these deserted countries appear to have been, in some distant age, lavishly embellished.

'The chief of the band was a man far from illiterate: he was able to travel by the stars or the compass, and had marked in his erratic[34] expeditions such places as are most worthy the notice of a passenger. He observed to me that buildings are always best preserved in places little frequented and difficult of access: for, when once a country declines from its primitive splendour, the more inhabitants are left, the quicker ruin will be made. Walls supply stones more easily than quarries, and palaces and temples will be demolished to make stables of granite, and cottages of porphyry.'

Chapter XXXIX: The Adventures of Pekuah Continued

'We wandered about in this manner for some weeks, whether, as our chief pretended, for my gratification, or, as I rather suspected, for some convenience of his own. I endeavoured to appear contented where sullenness and resentment would have been of no use, and that endeavour conduced much to the calmness of my mind; but my heart was always with Nekayah, and the troubles of the night much overbalanced the amusements of the day. My women, who threw all their cares upon their mistress, set their minds at ease from the time when they saw me treated with respect, and gave themselves up to the incidental alleviations of our fatigue without solicitude or sorrow. I was pleased with their pleasure and animated with their confidence. My condition had lost

32. Scrupulous exactness.
33. Helpful, solicitous.
34. Nomadic, wandering.

much of its terrour since I found that the Arab ranged the country merely to get riches. Avarice is an uniform and tractable vice: other intellectual distempers are different in different constitutions of mind; that which soothes the pride of one will offend the pride of another; but to the favour of the covetous there is a ready way: bring money and nothing is denied.

'At last we came to the dwelling of our chief, a strong and spacious house built with stone in an island of the Nile, which lies, as I was told, under the tropic.[35] "Lady," said the Arab, "you shall rest after your journey a few weeks in this place, where you are to consider yourself as sovereign. My occupation is war: I have therefore chosen this obscure residence, from which I can issue unexpected and to which I can retire unpursued. You may now repose in security: here are few pleasures, but here is no danger." He then led me into the inner apartments, and seating me on the richest couch, bowed to the ground. His women, who considered me as a rival, looked on me with malignity; but, being soon informed that I was a great lady detained only for my ransom, they began to vie with each other in obsequiousness and reverence.

'Being again comforted with new assurances of speedy liberty, I was for some days diverted from impatience by the novelty of the place. The turrets overlooked the country to a great distance and afforded a view of many windings of the stream. In the day I wandered from one place to another as the course of the sun varied the splendour of the prospect, and saw many things which I had never seen before. The crocodiles and river-horses[36] are common in this unpeopled region, and I often looked upon them with terrour, though I knew that they could not hurt me. For some time I expected to see mermaids and tritons, which, as Imlac has told me, the European travellers have stationed in the Nile; but no such beings ever appeared, and the Arab, when I enquired after them, laughed at my credulity.

'At night the Arab always attended me to a tower set apart for celestial observations, where he endeavoured to teach me the names and courses of the stars. I had no great inclination to this study, but an appearance of attention was necessary to please my instructor, who valued himself for his skill; and, in a little while, I found some employment requisite to beguile the tediousness of time which was to be passed always amidst the same objects. I was weary of looking in the morning on things from which I had turned away weary in the evening: I therefore was at last willing to observe the stars rather than do nothing, but could not always compose my thoughts, and was very often thinking on Nekayah when others imagined me contemplating the sky. Soon after the Arab went upon another expedition, and then my only pleasure was to talk with my maids about the accident by which we were carried away and the happiness that we should all enjoy at the end of our captivity.

'There were women in your Arab's fortress,' said the princess. 'Why did you not make them your companions, enjoy their conversation, and partake their diversions? In a place where they found business or amusement, why should you alone sit corroded with idle melancholy? or why could not you bear for a few months that condition to which they were condemned for life?'

'The diversions of the women,' answered Pekuah, 'were only childish play,

35. South of the Tropic of Cancer.
36. Hippopotamuses.

by which the mind accustomed to stronger operations could not be kept busy. I could do all which they delighted in doing by powers merely sensitive,[37] while my intellectual faculties were flown to Cairo. They ran from room to room as a bird hops from wire to wire in his cage. They danced for the sake of motion, as lambs frisk in a meadow. One sometimes pretended to be hurt that the rest might be alarmed or hid herself that another might seek her. Part of their time passed in watching the progress of light bodies that floated on the river, and part in marking the various forms into which clouds broke in the sky.

'Their business was only needlework, in which I and my maids sometimes helped them; but you know that the mind will easily straggle from the fingers, nor will you suspect that captivity and absence from Nekayah could receive solace from silken flowers.

'Nor was much satisfaction to be hoped from their conversation: for of what could they be expected to talk? They had seen nothing; for they had lived from early youth in that narrow spot: of what they had not seen they could have no knowledge, for they could not read. They had no ideas but of the few things that were within their view, and had hardly names for anything but their clothes and their food. As I bore a superiour character, I was often called to terminate their quarrels, which I decided as equitably as I could. If it could have amused me to hear the complaints of each against the rest, I might have been often detained by long stories, but the motives of their animosity were so small that I could not listen without intercepting the tale.'

'How,' said Rasselas, 'can the Arab, whom you represented as a man of more than common accomplishments, take any pleasure in his seraglio, when it is filled only with women like these. Are they exquisitely beautiful?'

'They do not,' said Pekuah, 'want that unaffecting and ignoble beauty which may subsist without sprightliness or sublimity, without energy of thought or dignity of virtue. But to a man like the Arab such beauty was only a flower casually plucked and carelessly thrown away. Whatever pleasures he might find among them, they were not those of friendship or society. When they were playing about him he looked on them with inattentive superiority: when they vied for his regard he sometimes turned away disgusted. As they had no knowledge, their talk could take nothing from the tediousness of life: as they had no choice, their fondness, or appearance of fondness, excited in him neither pride nor gratitude; he was not exalted in his own esteem by the smiles of a woman who saw no other man, nor was much obliged by that regard, of which he could never know the sincerity, and which he might often perceive to be exerted not so much to delight him as to pain a rival. That which he gave, and they received, as love, was only a careless distribution of superfluous time, such love as man can bestow upon that which he despises, such as has neither hope nor fear, neither joy nor sorrow.'

'You have reason, lady, to think yourself happy,' said Imlac, 'that you have been thus easily dismissed. How could a mind hungry for knowledge be willing, in an intellectual famine, to lose such a banquet as Pekuah's conversation?'

'I am inclined to believe,' answered Pekuah, 'that he was for some time in

37. Sensuous, i.e. of sensation rather than thought.

suspense; for, notwithstanding his promise, whenever I proposed to dispatch a messenger to Cairo, he found some excuse for delay. While I was detained in his house he made many incursions into the neighbouring countries, and, perhaps, he would have refused to discharge me had his plunder been equal to his wishes. He returned always courteous, related his adventures, delighted to hear my observations, and endeavoured to advance my acquaintance with the stars. When I importuned him to send away my letters, he soothed me with professions of honour and sincerity; and, when I could be no longer decently denied, put his troop again in motion and left me to govern in his absence. I was much afflicted by this studied procrastination, and was sometimes afraid that I should be forgotten; that you would leave Cairo, and I must end my my days in an island of the Nile.

'I grew at last hopeless and dejected, and cared so little to entertain him that he for a while more frequently talked with my maids. That he should fall in love with them or with me might have been equally fatal, and I was not much pleased with the growing friendship. My anxiety was not long; for, as I recovered some degree of cheerfulness, he returned to me, and I could not forbear to despise my former uneasiness.

'He still delayed to send for my ransom, and would, perhaps, never have determined, had not your agent found his way to him. The gold which he would not fetch, he could not reject when it was offered. He hastened to prepare for our journey hither, like a man delivered from the pain of an intestine[38] conflict. I took leave of my companions in the house, who dismissed me with cold indifference.'

Nekayah, having heard her favourite's relation, rose and embraced her, and Rasselas gave her an hundred ounces of gold, which she presented to the Arab for the fifty that were promised.

Chapter XL: The History of a Man of Learning

They returned to Cairo, and were so well pleased at finding themselves together that none of them went much abroad. The prince began to love learning, and one day declared to Imlac that he intended to devote himself to science[39] and pass the rest of his days in literary solitude.

'Before you make your final choice,' answered Imlac, 'you ought to examine its hazards, and converse with some of those who are grown old in the company of themselves. I have just left the observatory of one of the most learned astronomers in the world, who has spent forty years in unwearied attention to the motions and appearances of the celestial bodies, and has drawn out his soul in endless calculations. He admits a few friends once a month to hear his deductions and enjoy his discoveries. I was introduced as a man of knowledge worthy of his notice. Men of various ideas and fluent conversation are commonly welcome to those whose thoughts have been long fixed upon a single point and who find the images of other things stealing away. I delighted him with my remarks; he smiled at the narrative of my travels, and was glad to forget the constellations, and descend for a moment into the lower world.

38. Internal.
39. Study, knowledge.

'On the next day of vacation I renewed my visit, and was so fortunate as to please him again. He relaxed from that time the severity of his rule and permitted me to enter at my own choice. I found him always busy, and always glad to be relieved. As each knew much which the other was desirous of learning, we exchanged our notions with great delight. I perceived that I had every day more of his confidence, and always found new cause of admiration in the profundity of his mind. His comprehension is vast, his memory capacious and retentive, his discourse is methodical, and his expression clear.

'His integrity and benevolence are equal to his learning. His deepest researches and most favourite studies are willingly interrupted for any opportunity of doing good by his counsel or his riches. To his closest retreat, at his most busy moments, all are admitted that want his assistance: "For though I exclude idleness and pleasure, I will never," says he, "bar my doors against charity. To man is permitted the contemplation of the skies, but the practice of virtue is commanded." '

'Surely,' said the princess, 'this man is happy.'

'I visited him,' said Imlac, 'with more and more frequency, and was every time more enamoured of his conversation: he was sublime without haughtiness, courteous without formality, and communicative without ostentation. I was at first, great princess, of your opinion, thought him the happiest of mankind, and often congratulated him on the blessing that he enjoyed. He seemed to hear nothing with indifference but the praises of his condition, to which he always returned a general answer, and diverted the conversation to some other topic.

'Amidst this willingness to be pleased, and labour to please, I had quickly reason to imagine that some painful sentiment pressed upon his mind. He often looked up earnestly towards the sun, and let his voice fall in the midst of his discourse. He would sometimes, when we were alone, gaze upon me in silence with the air of a man who longed to speak what he was yet resolved to suppress. He would often send for me with vehement injunctions of haste, though, when I came to him, he had nothing extraordinary to say. And sometimes, when I was leaving him, would call me back, pause a few moments and then dismiss me.'

Chapter XLI: The Astronomer Discovers[40] the Cause of His Uneasiness

'At last the time came when the secret burst his reserve. We were sitting together last night in the turret of his house, watching the emersion[41] of a satellite of Jupiter. A sudden tempest clouded the sky and disappointed our observation. We sat a while silent in the dark, and then he addressed himself to me in these words: "Imlac, I have long considered thy friendship as the greatest blessing of my life. Integrity without knowledge is weak and useless, and knowledge without integrity is dangerous and dreadful. I have found in thee all the qualities requisite for trust, benevolence, experience, and fortitude. I have long discharged an office which I must soon quit at the call of nature, and shall rejoice in the hour of imbecility and pain to devolve it upon thee."

'I thought myself honoured by this testimony, and protested that whatever could conduce to his happiness would add likewise to mine.

40. Discloses.
41. Reappearance after obscurity or eclipse.

'"Hear, Imlac, what thou wilt not without difficulty credit. I have possessed for five years the regulation of weather, and the distribution of the seasons: the sun has listened to my dictates, and passed from tropic to tropic by my direction; the clouds, at my call, have poured their waters, and the Nile has overflowed at my command; I have restrained the rage of the dog-star, and mitigated the fervours of the crab.[42] The winds alone, of all the elemental powers, have hitherto refused my authority, and multitudes have perished by equinoctial tempests which I found myself unable to prohibit or restrain. I have administered this great office with exact justice, and made to the different nations of the earth an impartial dividend of rain and sunshine. What must have been the misery of half the globe, if I had limited the clouds to particular regions, or confined the sun to either side of the equator?"'

Chapter XLII: The Opinion of the Astronomer Is Explained and Justified

'I suppose he discovered in me, through the obscurity of the room, some tokens of amazement and doubt, for after a short pause he proceeded thus:

'"Not to be easily credited will neither surprise nor offend me; for I am, probably, the first of human beings to whom this trust has been imparted. Nor do I know whether to deem this distinction a reward or punishment; since I have possessed it I have been far less happy than before, and nothing but the consciousness of good intention could have enabled me to support the weariness of unremitted vigilance."

'"How long, Sir," said I, "has this great office been in your hands?"

'"About ten years ago," said he, "my daily observations of the changes of the sky led me to consider whether, if I had the power of the seasons, I could confer greater plenty upon the inhabitants of the earth. This contemplation fastened on my mind, and I sat days and nights in imaginary dominion, pouring upon this country and that the showers of fertility, and seconding every fall of rain with a due proportion of sunshine. I had yet only the will to do good, and did not imagine that I should ever have the power.

'"One day as I was looking on the fields withering with heat, I felt in my mind a sudden wish that I could send rain on the southern mountains and raise the Nile to an inundation. In the hurry of my imagination I commanded rain to fall, and, by comparing the time of my command with that of the inundation, I found that the clouds had listened to my lips."

'"Might not some other cause," said I, "produce this concurrence? the Nile does not always rise on the same day."

'"Do not believe," said he with impatience, "that such objections could escape me: I reasoned long against my own conviction, and laboured against truth with the utmost obstinacy. I sometimes suspected myself of madness, and should not have dared to impart this secret but to a man like you, capable of distinguishing the wonderful from the impossible, and the incredible from the false."

'"Why, Sir," said I, "do you call that incredible, which you know, or think you know, to be true?"

42. Both Sirius, the "dog-star," and Cancer, the constellation of "the crab," were associated with great heat.

'"Because," said he, "I cannot prove it by any external evidence; and I know too well the laws of demonstration to think that my conviction ought to influence another, who cannot, like me, be conscious of its force. I, therefore, shall not attempt to gain credit by disputation. It is sufficient that I feel this power, that I have long possessed and every day exerted it. But the life of man is short, the infirmities of age increase upon me, and the time will soon come when the regulator of the year must mingle with the dust. The care of appointing a successor has long disturbed me; the night and the day have been spent in comparisons of all the characters which have come to my knowledge, and I have yet found none so worthy as thyself."'

Chapter XLIII: The Astronomer Leaves Imlac His Directions

'"Hear therefore, what I shall impart with attention such as the welfare of a world requires. If the task of a king be considered as difficult, who has the care only of a few millions, to whom he cannot do much good or harm, what must be the anxiety of him, on whom depend the action of the elements, and the great gifts of light and heat!—Hear me therefore with attention.

'"I have diligently considered the position of the earth and sun, and formed innumerable schemes in which I changed their situation. I have sometimes turned aside the axis of the earth, and sometimes varied the ecliptic[43] of the sun: but I have found it impossible to make a disposition by which the world may be advantaged; what one region gains, another loses by any imaginable alteration, even without considering the distant parts of the solar system with which we are unacquainted. Do not, therefore, in thy administration of the year, indulge thy pride by innovation; do not please thyself with thinking that thou canst make thyself renowned to all future ages by disordering the seasons. The memory of mischief is no desirable fame. Much less will it become thee to let kindness or interest prevail. Never rob other countries of rain to pour it on thine own. For us the Nile is sufficient."

'I promised that when I possessed the power, I would use it with inflexible integrity, and he dismissed me, pressing my hand. "My heart," said he, "will be now at rest, and my benevolence will not more destroy my quiet: I have found a man of wisdom and virtue, to whom I can cheerfully bequeath the inheritance of the sun."'

The prince heard this narration with very serious regard, but the princess smiled, and Pekuah convulsed herself with laughter. 'Ladies,' said Imlac, 'to mock the heaviest of human afflictions is neither charitable nor wise. Few can attain this man's knowledge, and few practise his virtues; but all may suffer his calamity. Of the uncertainties of our present state, the most dreadful and alarming is the uncertain continuance of reason.'

The princess was recollected, and the favourite was abashed. Rasselas, more deeply affected, enquired of Imlac, whether he thought such maladies of the mind frequent, and how they were contracted.

Chapter XLIV: The Dangerous Prevalence of Imagination

'Disorders of intellect,' answered Imlac, 'happen much more often than superficial observers will easily believe. Perhaps, if we speak with rigorous exactness,

43. The apparent orbit, in Ptolemaic astronomy, of the sun around the earth.

no human mind is in its right state. There is no man whose imagination does not sometimes predominate over his reason, who can regulate his attention wholly by his will, and whose ideas will come and go at his command. No man will be found in whose mind airy notions do not sometimes tyrannise, and force him to hope or fear beyond the limits of sober probability. All power of fancy over reason is a degree of insanity; but while this power is such as we can control and repress, it is not visible to others, nor considered as any depravation of the mental faculties: it is not pronounced madness but when it comes ungovernable, and apparently influences speech or action.

'To indulge the power of fiction, and send imagination out upon the wing, is often the sport of those who delight too much in silent speculation. When we are alone we are not always busy; the labour of excogitation is too violent to last long; the ardour of enquiry will sometimes give way to idleness or satiety. He who has nothing external that can divert him must find pleasure in his own thoughts, and must conceive himself what he is not; for who is pleased with what he is? He then expatiates[44] in boundless futurity and culls from all imaginable conditions that which for the present moment he should most desire, amuses his desires with impossible enjoyments, and confers upon his pride unattainable dominion. The mind dances from scene to scene, unites all pleasures in all combinations, and riots in delights which nature and fortune, with all their bounty, cannot bestow.

'In time some particular train of ideas fixes the attention, all other intellectual gratifications are rejected; the mind, in weariness or leisure, recurs constantly to the favourite conception, and feasts on the luscious falsehood whenever she is offended with the bitterness of truth. By degrees the reign of fancy is confirmed; she grows first imperious, and in time despotic. Then fictions begin to operate as realities, false opinions fasten upon the mind, and life passes in dreams of rapture or of anguish.

'This, Sir, is one of the dangers of solitude, which the hermit has confessed not always to promote goodness, and the astronomer's misery has proved to be not always propitious to wisdom.'

'I will no more,' said the favourite, 'imagine myself the queen of Abyssinia. I have often spent the hours, which the princess gave to my own disposal, in adjusting ceremonies and regulating the court; I have repressed the pride of the powerful and granted the petitions of the poor; I have built new palaces in more happy situations, planted groves upon the tops of mountains, and have exulted in the beneficence of royalty, till, when the princess entered, I had almost forgotten to bow down before her.'

'And I,' said the princess, 'will not allow myself any more to play the shepherdess in my waking dreams. I have often soothed my thoughts with the quiet and innocence of pastoral employments, till I have in my chamber heard the winds whistle and the sheep bleat; sometimes freed the lamb entangled in the thicket, and sometimes with my crook encountered the wolf. I have a dress like that of the village maids, which I put on to help my imagination, and a pipe on which I play softly, and suppose myself followed by my flocks.'

'I will confess,' said the prince, 'an indulgence of fantastic delight more dangerous than yours. I have frequently endeavoured to image the possibility

44. Wanders, roams.

of a perfect government, by which all wrong should be restrained, all vice reformed, and all the subjects preserved in tranquility and innocence. This thought produced innumerable schemes of reformation, and dictated many useful regulations and salutary edicts. This has been the sport and sometimes the labour of my solitude; and I start when I think with how little anguish I once supposed the death of my father and my brothers.'

'Such,' says Imlac, 'are the effects of visionary schemes: when we first form them we know them to be absurd, but familiarise them by degrees, and in time lose sight of their folly.'

Chapter XLV: They Discourse with an Old Man

The evening was now far past, and they rose to return home. As they walked along the bank of the Nile, delighted with the beams of the moon quivering on the water, they saw at a small distance an old man whom the prince had often heard in the assembly of the sages. 'Yonder,' said he, 'is one whose years have calmed his passions, but not clouded his reason: let us close the disquisitions of the night by enquiring what are his sentiments of his own state, that we may know whether youth alone is to struggle with vexation, and whether any better hope remains for the latter part of life.'

Here the sage approached and saluted them. They invited him to join their walk, and prattled a while as acquaintance that had unexpectedly met one another. The old man was cheerful and talkative, and the way seemed short in his company. He was pleased to find himself not disregarded, accompanied them to their house, and, at the prince's request, entered with them. They placed him in the seat of honour, and set wine and conserves before him.

'Sir,' said the princess, 'an evening walk must give to a man of learning like you pleasures which ignorance and youth can hardly conceive. You know the qualities and the causes of all that you behold, the laws by which the river flows, the periods in which the planets perform their revolutions. Every thing must supply you with contemplation, and renew the consciousness of your own dignity.'

'Lady,' answered he, 'let the gay and the vigorous expect pleasure in their excursions, it is enough that age can obtain ease. To me the world has lost its novelty: I look round, and see what I remember to have seen in happier days. I rest against a tree, and consider that in the same shade I once disputed upon the annual overflow of the Nile with a friend who is now silent in the grave. I cast my eyes upwards, fix them on the changing moon, and think with pain on the vicissitudes of life. I have ceased to take much delight in physical truth; for what have I to do with those things which I am soon to leave?'

'You may at least recreate yourself,' said Imlac, 'with the recollection of an honourable and useful life, and enjoy the praise which all agree to give you.'

'Praise,' said the sage, 'with a sigh, is to an old man an empty sound. I have neither mother to be delighted with the reputation of her son, nor wife to partake the honours of her husband. I have outlived my friends and my rivals. Nothing is now of much importance; for I cannot extend my interest beyond myself. Youth is delighted with applause because it is considered as the earnest of some future good, and because the prospect of life is far extended: but to me, who am now declining to decrepitude, there is little to be feared from the malevolence of men, and yet less to be hoped from their affection or esteem. Something they may yet take away, but they can give me nothing. Riches would now be useless, and high employment would be pain. My retrospect of life recalls to my view many opportunities of good neglected, much time squandered upon trifles, and more lost in idleness and vacancy. I leave many great designs unattempted, and many great attempts unfinished. My mind is burthened with no heavy crime, and therefore I compose myself to tranquility; endeavour to abstract my thoughts from hopes and cares, which, though reason knows them to be vain, still try to keep their old possession of the heart; expect, with serene humility, that hour which nature cannot long delay; and hope to possess in a better state that happiness which here I could not find, and that virtue which here I have not attained.'

He rose and went away, leaving his audience not much elated with the hope of long life. The prince consoled himself with remarking that it was not reasonable to be disappointed by this account; for age had never been considered as the season of felicity, and, if it was possible to be easy in decline and weakness, it was likely that the days of vigour and alacrity might be happy: that the moon of life might be bright, if the evening could be calm.

The princess suspected that age was querulous and malignant, and delighted to repress the expectations of those who had newly entered the world. She had seen the possessors of estates look with envy on their heirs, and known many who enjoy pleasure no longer than they can confine it to themselves.

Pekuah conjectured that the man was older than he appeared, and was willing to impute his complaints to delirious dejection; or else supposed that he had been unfortunate, and was therefore discontented: 'For nothing,' said she, 'is more common than to call our own condition the condition of life.'

Imlac, who had no desire to see them depressed, smiled at the comforts which they could so readily procure to themselves, and remembered that at the same age he was equally confident of unmingled prosperity, and equally fertile of consolatory expedients. He forbore to force upon them unwelcome knowledge, which time itself would too soon impress. The princess and her lady retired; the madness of the astronomer hung upon their minds, and they desired Imlac to enter upon his office and delay next morning the rising of the sun.

Chapter XLVI: The Princess and Pekuah Visit the Astronomer

The princess and Pekuah, having talked in private of Imlac's astronomer, thought his character at once so amiable and so strange that they could not be satisfied without a nearer knowledge, and Imlac was requested to find the means of bringing them together.

This was somewhat difficult; the philosopher had never received any visits from women, though he lived in a city that had in it many Europeans who followed the manners of their own countries, and many from other parts of the world that lived there with European liberty. The ladies would not be refused, and several schemes were proposed for the accomplishment of their design. It was proposed to introduce them as strangers in distress, to whom the sage was always accessible; but, after some deliberation, it appeared that by this artifice no acquaintance could be formed, for their conversation would be short, and they could not decently importune him often. 'This,' said Rasselas, 'is true; but I have yet a stronger objection against the misrepresentation of your state. I have always considered it as treason against the great republic of human nature, to make any man's virtues the means of deceiving him, whether on great or little occasions. All imposture weakens confidence and chills benevolence. When the sage finds that you are not what you seemed, he will feel the resentment natural to a man who, conscious of great abilities, discovers that he has been tricked by understandings meaner than his own, and, perhaps, the distrust, which he can never afterwards wholly lay aside, may stop the voice of counsel and close the hand of charity; and where will you find the power of restoring his benefactions to mankind, or his peace to himself?'

To this no reply was attempted, and Imlac began to hope that their curiosity would subside; but, next day, Pekuah told him she had now found an honest pretence for a visit to the astronomer, for she would solicit permission to continue under him the studies in which she had been initiated by the Arab; and the princess might go with her either as a fellow-student, or because a woman could not decently come alone. 'I am afraid,' said Imlac, 'that he will be soon weary of your company: men advanced far in knowledge do not love to repeat the elements of their art, and I am not certain that even of the elements, as he will deliver them connected with inferences and mingled with reflections, you are a very capable auditress.'

'That,' said Pekuah, 'must be my care: I ask of you only to take me thither. My knowledge is, perhaps, more than you imagine it, and by concurring always with his opinions I shall make him think it greater than it is.'

The astronomer, in pursuance of this resolution, was told that a foreign lady, travelling in search of knowledge, had heard of his reputation and was desirous to become his scholar. The uncommonness of the proposal raised at once his surprise and curiosity, and when, after a short deliberation, he consented to admit her, he could not stay without impatience till the next day.

The ladies dressed themselves magnificently, and were attended by Imlac to the astronomer, who was pleased to see himself approached with respect by persons of so splendid an appearance. In the exchange of the first civilities he was timorous and bashful; but when the talk became regular, he recollected his powers, and justified the character which Imlac had given. Enquiring of Pekuah what could have turned her inclination towards astronomy, he received from her a history of her adventure at the pyramid, and of the time passed in the Arab's island. She told her tale with ease and elegance, and her conversation took possession of his heart. The discourse was then turned to astronomy: Pekuah displayed what she knew: he looked upon her as a prodigy of genius, and entreated her not to desist from a study which she had so happily begun.

They came again and again, and were every time more welcome than before. The sage endeavoured to amuse them, that they might prolong their visits, for he found his thoughts grow brighter in their company; the clouds of solicitude vanished by degrees, as he forced himself to entertain them, and he grieved when he was left at their departure to his old employment of regulating the seasons.

The princess and her favourite had now watched his lips for several months, and could not catch a single word from which they could judge whether he continued, or not, in the opinion of his preternatural commission. They often contrived to bring him to an open declaration, but he easily eluded all their attacks, and on which side soever they pressed him escaped from them to some other topic.

As their familiarity increased they invited him often to the house of Imlac, where they distinguished him by extraordinary respect. He began gradually to delight in sublunary pleasures. He came early and departed late; laboured to recommend himself by assiduity and compliance; excited their curiosity after new arts, that they might still want his assistance; and when they made any excursion of pleasure or enquiry, entreated to attend them.

By long experience of his integrity and wisdom, the prince and his sister were convinced that he might be trusted without danger; and lest he should draw any false hopes from the civilities which he received, discovered to him their condition, with the motives of their journey, and required his opinion on the choice of life.

'Of the various conditions which the world spreads before you, which you shall prefer,' said the sage, 'I am not able to instruct you. I can only tell that I have chosen wrong. I have passed my time in study without experience; in the attainment of sciences which can, for the most part, be but remotely useful to mankind. I have purchased knowledge at the expense of all the common comforts of life: I have missed the endearing elegance of female friendship and the happy commerce of domestic tenderness. If I have obtained any prerogatives above other students, they have been accompanied with fear, disquiet, and scrupulosity; but even of these prerogatives, whatever they were, I have, since my thoughts have been diversified by more intercourse with the world, begun to question the reality. When I have been for a few days lost in pleasing dissipation, I am always tempted to think that my enquiries have ended in errour, and that I have suffered much, and suffered it in vain.'

Imlac was delighted to find that the sage's understanding was breaking through its mists, and resolved to detain him from the planets till he should forget his task of ruling them, and reason should recover its original influence.

From this time the astronomer was received into familiar friendship, and partook of all their projects and pleasures: his respect kept him attentive, and the activity of Rasselas did not leave much time unengaged. Something was always to be done; the day was spent in making observations which furnished talk for the evening, and the evening was closed with a scheme for the morrow.

The sage confessed to Imlac that, since he had mingled in the gay tumults of life and divided his hours by a succession of amusements, he found the conviction of his authority over the skies fade gradually from his mind, and began to trust less to an opinion which he never could prove to others, and which he now found subject to variation from causes in which reason had no part. 'If I am accidentally left alone for a few hours,' said he, 'my inveterate persuasion rushes upon my soul, and my thoughts are chained down by some irresistible violence, but they are soon disentangled by the prince's conversation, and instantaneously released at the entrance of Pekuah. I am like a man habitually afraid of spectres who is set at ease by a lamp, and wonders at the dread which harrassed him in the dark, yet, if his lamp be extinguished, feels again the terrours which he knows that when it is light he shall feel no more. But I am sometimes afraid lest I indulge my quiet by criminal negligence, and voluntarily forget the great charge with which I am entrusted. If I favour myself in a known errour, or am determined by my own ease in a doubtful question of this importance, how dreadful is my crime!'

'No disease of the imagination,' answered Imlac, 'is so difficult of cure, as that which is complicated with the dread of guilt: fancy and conscience then act interchangeably upon us, and so often shift their places that the illusions of one are not distinguished from the dictates of the other. If fancy presents images not moral or religious, the mind drives them away when they give it pain, but when melancholic notions take the form of duty, they lay hold on the faculties without opposition, because we are afraid to exclude or banish them. For this reason the superstitious are often melancholy, and the melancholy almost always superstitious.

'But do not let the suggestions of timidity overpower your better reason: the danger of neglect can be but as the probability of the obligation, which when you consider it with freedom, you find very little, and that little growing every day less. Open your heart to the influence of the light, which, from time to time, breaks in upon you: when scruples importune you, which you in your lucid moments know to be vain, do not stand to parley, but fly to business or to Pekuah; and keep this thought always prevalent, that you are only one atom of the mass of humanity, and have neither such virtue nor vice as that you should be singled out for supernatural favours or afflictions.'

Chapter XLVII: The Prince Enters and Brings a New Topic

'All this,' said the astronomer, 'I have often thought, but my reason has been so long subjugated by an uncontrollable and overwhelming idea that it durst not confide in its own decisions. I now see how fatally I betrayed my quiet by suffering chimeras to prey upon me in secret; but melancholy shrinks from communication, and I never found a man before to whom I could impart my troubles, though I had been certain of relief. I rejoice to find my own sentiments confirmed by yours, who are not easily deceived and can have no motive or purpose to deceive. I hope that time and variety will dissipate the gloom that has so long surrounded me, and the latter part of my days will be spent in peace.'

'Your learning and virtue,' said Imlac, 'may justly give you hopes.'

Rasselas then entered with the princess and Pekuah, and enquired whether they had contrived any new diversion for the next day. 'Such,' said Nekayah, 'is the state of life that none are happy but by the anticipation of change: the change itself is nothing; when we have made it, the next wish is to change again. The world is not yet exhausted; let me see something tomorrow which I never saw before.'

'Variety,' said Rasselas, 'is so necessary to content, that even the happy valley disgusted me by the recurrence of its luxuries; yet I could not forbear to reproach myself with impatience, when I saw the monks of St. Anthony support without complaint a life not of uniform delight but uniform hardship.'

'Those men,' answered Imlac, 'are less wretched in their silent convent than the Abyssinian princes in their prison of pleasure. Whatever is done by the monks is incited by an adequate and reasonable motive. Their labour supplies them with necessaries; it therefore cannot be omitted and is certainly rewarded. Their devotion prepares them for another state and reminds them of its approach while it fits them for it. Their time is regularly distributed; one duty succeeds another, so that they are not left open to the distraction of unguided choice, nor lost in the shades of listless inactivity. There is a certain task to be performed at an appropriated hour; and their toils are cheerful, because they consider them as acts of piety, by which they are always advancing towards endless felicity.'

'Do you think,' said Nekayah, 'that the monastic rule is a more holy and less imperfect state than any other? May not he equally hope for future happiness who converses openly with mankind, who succours the distressed by his charity, instructs the ignorant by his learning, and contributes by his industry to the general system of life; even though he should omit some of the mortifications which are practised in the cloister, and allow himself such harmless delights as his condition may place within his reach?'

'This,' said Imlac, 'is a question which has long divided the wise, and perplexed the good. I am afraid to decide on either part. He that lives well in the world is better than he that lives well in a monastery. But, perhaps, every one is not able to stem the temptations of public life; and, if he cannot conquer, he may properly retreat. Some have little power to do good, and have likewise little strength to resist evil. Many are weary of their conflicts with adversity, and are willing to eject those passions which have long busied them in vain. And many are dismissed by age and diseases from the more laborious duties of society. In monasteries the weak and timorous may be happily sheltered, the weary may repose, and the penitent may meditate. Those retreats of prayer and contemplation have something so congenial to the mind of man that, perhaps, there is scarcely one that does not purpose to close his life in pious abstraction with a few associates serious as himself.'

'Such,' said Pekuah, 'has often been my wish, and I have heard the princess declare that she should not willingly die in a crowd.'

'The liberty of using harmless pleasures,' proceeded Imlac, 'will not be disputed; but it is still to be examined what pleasures are harmless. The evil of any pleasure that Nekayah can image is not in the act itself but in its consequences. Pleasure, in itself harmless, may become mischievous by endearing to us a state which we know to be transient and probatory, and withdrawing our thoughts from that of which every hour brings us nearer to the beginning, and of which no length of time will bring us to the end. Mortification is not virtuous in itself, nor has any other use but that it disengages us from the allurements of sense. In the state of future perfection, to which we all aspire, there will be pleasure without danger and security without restraint.'

The princess was silent, and Rasselas, turning to the astronomer, asked him whether he could not delay her retreat by showing her something which she had not seen before.

'Your curiosity,' said the sage, 'has been so general, and your pursuit of knowledge so vigorous, that novelties are not now very easily to be found: but what you can no longer procure from the living may be given by the dead. Among the wonders of this country are the catacombs, or the ancient repositories, in which the bodies of the earliest generations were lodged, and where, by the virtue of the gums which embalmed them, they yet remain without corruption.'

'I know not,' said Rasselas, 'what pleasure the sight of the catacombs can afford; but, since nothing else is offered, I am resolved to view them, and shall place this with many other things which I have done because I would do something.'

They hired a guard of horsemen, and the next day visited the catacombs. When they were about to descend into the sepulchral caves, 'Pekuah,' said the princess, 'we are now again invading the habitations of the dead; I know that you will stay behind; let me find you safe when I return.'

'No, I will not be left,' answered Pekuah; 'I will go down between you and the prince.'

They then all descended, and roved with wonder through the labyrinth of subterraneous passages, where the bodies were laid in rows on either side.

Chapter XLVIII: Imlac Discourses on the Nature of the Soul

'What reason,' said the prince, 'can be given why the Egyptians should thus expensively preserve those carcasses which some nations consume with fire, others lay to mingle with the earth, and all agree to remove from their sight as soon as decent rites can be performed?'

'The original of ancient customs,' said Imlac, 'is commonly unknown; for the practice often continues when the cause has ceased; and concerning superstitious ceremonies it is vain to conjecture; for what reason did not dictate reason cannot explain. I have long believed that the practice of embalming arose only from tenderness to the remains of relations or friends, and to this opinion I am more inclined, because it seems impossible that this care should have been general: had all the dead been embalmed, their repositories must in time have been more spacious than the dwellings of the living. I suppose only the rich or honourable were secured from corruption, and the rest left to the course of nature.

'But it is commonly supposed that the Egyptians believed the soul to live as long as the body continued undissolved, and therefore tried this method of eluding death.'

'Could the wise Egyptians,' said Nekayah, 'think so grossly of the soul? If the soul could once survive its separation, what could it afterwards receive or suffer from the body?'

'The Egyptians would doubtless think erroneously,' said the astronomer, 'in the darkness of heathenism and the first dawn of philosophy. The nature of the soul is still disputed amidst all our opportunities of clearer knowledge: some yet say that it may be material who, nevertheless, believe it to be immortal.'

'Some,' answered Imlac, 'have indeed said that the soul is material, but I can scarcely believe that any man has thought it who knew how to think; for all the conclusions of reason enforce the immateriality of mind, and all the notices of sense and investigations of science concur to prove the unconsciousness of matter.

'It was never supposed that cogitation is inherent in matter, or that every particle is a thinking being. Yet, if any part of matter be devoid of thought, what part can we suppose to think? Matter can differ from matter only in form, density, bulk, motion, and direction of motion: to which of these, however varied or combined, can consciousness be annexed? To be round or square, to be solid or fluid, to be great or little, to be moved slowly or swiftly one way or another, are modes of material existence, all equally alien from the nature of cogitation. If matter be once without thought, it can only be made to think by some new modification, but all the modifications which it can admit are equally unconnected with cogitative powers.'

'But the materialists,' said the astronomer, 'urge that matter may have qualities with which we are unacquainted.'

'He who will determine,' returned Imlac, 'against that which he knows because there may be something which he knows not, he that can set hypothetical possibility against acknowledged certainty, is not to be admitted among reasonable beings. All that we know of matter is that matter is inert, senseless, and lifeless; and if this conviction cannot be opposed but by referring us to something that we know not, we have all the evidence that human intellect can admit. If that which is known may be overruled by that which is unknown, no being not omniscient can arrive at certainty.'

'Yet let us not,' said the astronomer, 'too arrogantly limit the Creator's power.'

'It is no limitation of omnipotence,' replied the poet, 'to suppose that one thing is not consistent with another, that the same proposition cannot be at once true and false, that the same number cannot be even and odd, that cogitation cannot be conferred on that which is created incapable of cogitation.'

'I know not,' said Nekayah, 'any great use of this question. Does that immateriality, which in my opinion you have sufficiently proved, necessarily include eternal duration?'

'Of immateriality,' said Imlac, 'our ideas are negative and therefore obscure. Immateriality seems to imply a natural power of perpetual duration as a consequence of exemption from all causes of decay: whatever perishes is destroyed by the solution[45] of its contexture and separation of its parts; nor can we conceive how that which has no parts, and therefore admits no solution, can be naturally corrupted or impaired.'

'I know not,' said Rasselas, 'how to conceive anything without extension: what is extended must have parts, and you allow that whatever has parts may be destroyed.'

'Consider your own conceptions,' replied Imlac, 'and the difficulty will be less. You will find substance without extension. An ideal form is no less real than material bulk: yet an ideal form has no extension. It is no less certain, when you think on a pyramid, that your mind possesses the idea of a pyramid than that the pyramid itself is standing. What space does the idea of a pyramid occupy more than the idea of a grain of corn? or how can either idea suffer laceration? As is the effect such is the cause; as thought is, such is the power that thinks: a power impassive and indiscerptible.'[46]

'But the Being,' said Nekayah, 'whom I fear to name, the Being which made the soul, can destroy it.'

'He, surely, can destroy it,' answered Imlac, 'since, however unperishable, it receives from a superiour nature its power of duration. That it will not perish by any inherent cause of decay or principle of corruption may be shown by philosophy; but philosophy can tell no more. That it will not be

45. Dissolution.
46. Not susceptible to injury or to dissolution.

annihilated by him that made it, we must humbly learn from higher authority.'

The whole assembly stood a while silent and collected. 'Let us return,' said Rasselas, 'from this scene of mortality. How gloomy would be these mansions of the dead to him who did not know that he shall never die; that what now acts shall continue its agency, and what now thinks shall think on for ever. Those that lie here stretched before us, the wise and the powerful of ancient times, warn us to remember the shortness of our present state; they were, perhaps, snatched away while they were busy, like us, in the choice of life.'

'To me,' said the princess, 'the choice of life is become less important; I hope hereafter to think only on the choice of eternity.'

They then hastened out of the caverns, and, under the protection of their guard, returned to Cairo.

Chapter XLIX: The Conclusion, in Which Nothing Is Concluded

It was now the time of the inundation of the Nile: a few days after their visit to the catacombs, the river began to rise.

They were confined to their house. The whole region being under water gave them no invitation to any excursions, and, being well supplied with materials for talk, they diverted themselves with comparisons of the different forms of life which they had observed, and with various schemes of happiness which each of them had formed.

Pekuah was never so much charmed with any place as the convent of St. Anthony, where the Arab restored her to the princess, and wished only to fill it with pious maidens and to be made prioress of the order: she was weary of expectation and disgust, and would gladly be fixed in some unvariable state.

The princess thought that of all sublunary things knowledge was the best. She desired first to learn all sciences, and then purposed to found a college of learned women in which she would preside, that, by conversing with the old and educating the young, she might divide her time between the acquisition and communication of wisdom, and raise up for the next age models of prudence and patterns of piety.

The prince desired a little kingdom in which he might administer justice in his own person, and see all the parts of government with his own eyes; but he could never fix the limits of his dominion and was always adding to the number of his subjects.

Imlac and the astronomer were contented to be driven along the stream of life without directing their course to any particular port.

Of these wishes that they had formed they well knew that none could be obtained. They deliberated a while what was to be done, and resolved, when the inundation should cease, to return to Abyssinia.

1759

From The Rambler

Quis scit, an adjiciant hodiernae crastina summae
Tempora Dî superi! HORACE, *Odes*, IV.7.17–18

Who knows if Heaven, with ever-bounteous power,
Shall add tomorrow to the present hour?
(trans. FRANCIS)

I sat yesterday morning employed in deliberating on which, among the various subjects that occurred to my imagination, I should bestow the paper of today. After a short effort of meditation by which nothing was determined, I grew every moment more irresolute, my ideas wandered from the first intention, and I rather wished to think, than thought, upon any settled subject; till at last I was awakened from this dream of study by a summons from the press: the time was come for which I had been thus negligently purposing to provide, and, however dubious or sluggish, I was now necessitated to write.

Though to a writer whose design is so comprehensive and miscellaneous that he may accommodate himself with a topic from every scene of life, or view of nature, it is no great aggravation of his task to be obliged to a sudden composition, yet I could not forbear to reproach myself for having so long neglected what was unavoidably to be done, and of which every moment's idleness increased the difficulty. There was however some pleasure in reflecting that I, who had only trifled till diligence was necessary, might still congratulate myself upon my superiority to multitudes, who have trifled till diligence is vain; who can by no degree of activity or resolution recover the opportunities which have slipped away; and who are condemned by their own carelessness to hopeless calamity and barren sorrow.

The folly of allowing ourselves to delay what we know cannot be finally escaped, is one of the general weaknesses, which, in spite of the instruction of moralists, and the remonstrances of reason, prevail to a greater or less degree in every mind: even they who most steadily withstand it, find it, if not the most violent, the most pertinacious of their passions, always renewing its attacks, and though often vanquished, never destroyed.

It is indeed natural to have particular regard to the time present, and to be most solicitous for that which is by its nearness enabled to make the strongest impressions. When therefore any sharp pain is to be suffered or any formidable danger to be incurred, we can scarcely exempt ourselves wholly from the seducements of imagination; we readily believe that another day will bring some support or advantage which we now want; and are easily persuaded that the moment of necessity which we desire never to arrive is at a great distance from us.

Thus life is languished away in the gloom of anxiety, and consumed in collecting resolutions which the next morning dissipates; in forming purposes which we scarcely hope to keep, and reconciling ourselves to our own cowardice by excuses, which, while we admit them, we know to be absurd. Our firmness is by the continual contemplation of misery hourly impaired; every submission to our fear enlarges its dominion; we not only waste that time in which the evil we dread might have been suffered and surmounted, but even where procrastination produces no absolute encrease of our difficulties, make them less superable to ourselves by habitual terrors. When evils cannot be avoided, it is wise to contract the interval of expectation; to meet the mischiefs which will overtake us if we fly; and suffer only their real malignity without the conflicts of doubt and anguish of anticipation.

To act is far easier than to suffer, yet we every day see the progress of life retarded by the *vis inertiae*,[1] the mere repugnance to motion, and find multitudes repining at the want of that which nothing but idleness hinders them from enjoying. The case of Tantalus, in the region of poetic punishment, was somewhat to be pitied, because the fruits that hung about him retired from his hand; [2] but what tenderness can be claimed by those who though perhaps they suffer the pains of Tantalus will never lift their hands for their own relief?

There is nothing more common among this torpid generation than murmurs and complaints; murmurs at uneasiness which only vacancy [3] and suspicion expose them to feel, and complaints of distresses which it is in their own power to remove. Laziness is commonly associated with timidity. Either fear originally prohibits endeavours by infusing despair of success; or the frequent failure of irresolute struggles, and the constant desire of avoiding labour, impress by degrees false terrors on the mind. But fear, whether natural or acquired, when once it has full possession of the fancy, never fails to employ it upon visions of calamity, such as if they are not dissipated by useful employment, will soon overcast it with horrors, and imbitter life not only with those miseries by which all earthly beings are really more or less tormented, but with those which do not yet exist, and which can only be discerned by the perspicacity of cowardice.

Among all who sacrifice future advantage to present inclination, scarcely any gain so little as those that suffer themselves to freeze in idleness. Others are corrupted by some enjoyment of more or less power to gratify the passions; but to neglect our duties, merely to avoid the labour of performing them, a labour which is always punctually rewarded, is surely to sink under weak temptations. Idleness never can secure tranquillity; the call of reason and of conscience will pierce the closest pavilion of the sluggard, and, though it may not have force to drive him from his down,[4] will be loud enough to hinder him from sleep. Those moments which he cannot resolve to make useful by devoting them to the great business of his being, will still be usurped by powers that will not leave them to his disposal; remorse and vexation will seize upon them, and forbid him to enjoy what he is so desirous to appropriate.

There are other causes of inactivity incident to more active faculties and more acute discernment. He to whom many objects of pursuit arise at the same time, will frequently hesitate between different desires, till a rival has precluded him, or change his course as new attractions prevail, and harass himself without advancing. He who sees different ways to the same end, will, unless he watches carefully over his own conduct, lay out too much of his attention upon the comparison of probabilities and the adjustment of expedients, and

1. "Force of inertia."
2. Tantalus was tortured when the fruit receded, as he advanced his hand, and the water as he advanced his lips.
3. Idleness.
4. That is, from his pillow.

pause in the choice of his road till some accident intercepts his journey. He whose penetration extends to remote consequences and who, whenever he applies his attention to any design, discovers new prospects of advantage and possibilities of improvement, will not easily be persuaded that his project is ripe for execution; but will superadd one contrivance to another, endeavour to unite various purposes in one operation, multiply complications, and refine niceties, till he is entangled in his own scheme, and bewildered in the perplexity of various intentions. He that resolves to unite all the beauties of situation in a new purchase, must waste his life in roving to no purpose from province to province. He that hopes in the same house to obtain every convenience, may draw plans and study Palladio,[5] but will never lay a stone. He will attempt a treatise on some important subject, and amass materials, consult authors, and study all the dependent and collateral parts of learning, but never conclude himself qualified to write. He that has abilities to conceive perfection, will not easily be content without it; and since perfection cannot be reached, will lose the opportunity of doing well in the vain hope of unattainable excellence.

The certainty that life cannot be long, and the probability that it will be much shorter than nature allows, ought to awaken every man to the active prosecution of whatever he is desirous to perform. It is true that no diligence can ascertain success; death may intercept the swiftest career; but he who is cut off in the execution of an honest undertaking has at least the honour of falling in his rank, and has fought the battle, though he missed the victory. [No. 134, Saturday, June 29, 1751]

Nulla fides regni sociis, omnisque potestas
Impatiens consortis erat. LUCAN, I.92–93

No faith of partnership dominion owns;
Still discord hovers o'er divided thrones.

The hostility perpetually exercised between one man and another is caused by the desire of many for that which only few can possess. Every man would be rich, powerful, and famous; yet fame, power, and riches, are only the names of relative conditions, which imply the obscurity, dependence, and poverty of greater numbers.

This universal and incessant competition, produces injury and malice by two motives, interest and envy; the prospect of adding to our possessions what we can take from others, and the hope of alleviating the sense of our disparity by lessening others, though we gain nothing to ourselves.

Of these two malignant and destructive powers, it seems probable at the first view that interest has the strongest and most extensive influence. It is easy to conceive that opportunities to seize what has been long wanted may excite desires almost irresistible; but surely, the same eagerness cannot be kindled by an accidental power of destroying that which gives happiness to another. It must be more natural to rob for gain than to ravage only for mischief.

Yet I am inclined to believe that the great law of mutual benevolence is oftener violated by envy than by interest, and that most of the misery which

5. Andrea Palladio, the influential Italian Renaissance architect; cf. Pope, *Epistle to Burlington.*

the defamation of blameless actions or the obstruction of honest endeavours brings upon the world is inflicted by men that propose no advantage to themselves but the satisfaction of poisoning the banquet which they cannot taste, and blasting the harvest which they have no right to reap.

Interest can diffuse itself but to a narrow compass. The number is never large of those who can hope to fill the posts of degraded power, catch the fragments of shattered fortune, or succeed to the honours of depreciated beauty. But the empire of envy has no limits, as it requires to its influence very little help from external circumstances. Envy may always be produced by idleness and pride, and in what place will not they be found?

Interest requires some qualities not universally bestowed. The ruin of another will produce no profit to him who has not discernment to mark his advantage, courage to seize, and activity to pursue it; but the cold malignity of envy may be exerted in a torpid and quiescent state, amidst the gloom of stupidity, in the coverts of cowardice. He that falls by the attacks of interest is torn by hungry tigers; he may discover and resist his enemies. He that perishes in the ambushes of envy is destroyed by unknown and invisible assailants, and dies like a man suffocated by a poisonous vapour, without knowledge of his danger or possibility of contest.

Interest is seldom pursued but at some hazard. He that hopes to gain much has commonly something to lose, and when he ventures to attack superiority, if he fails to conquer, is irrecoverably crushed. But envy may act without expence or danger. To spread suspicion, to invent calumnies, to propagate scandal, requires neither labour nor courage. It is easy for the author of a lie, however malignant, to escape detection, and infamy needs very little industry to assist its circulation.

Envy is almost the only vice which is practicable at all times and in every place; the only passion which can never lie quiet for want of irritation; its effects therefore are everywhere discoverable, and its attempts always to be dreaded.

It is impossible to mention a name which any advantageous distinction has made eminent, but some latent animosity will burst out. The wealthy trader, however he may abstract himself from public affairs, will never want those who hint, with Shylock,[6] that ships are but boards. The beauty, adorned only with the unambitious graces of innocence and modesty, provokes whenever she appears a thousand murmurs of detraction. The genius, even when he endeavours only to entertain or instruct, yet suffers persecution from innumerable critics whose acrimony is excited merely by the pain of seeing others pleased, and of hearing applauses which another enjoys.

The frequency of envy makes it so familiar that it escapes our notice; nor do we often reflect upon its turpitude or malignity till we happen to feel its influence. When he that has given no provocation to malice, but by attempting to excel, finds himself pursued by multitudes whom he never saw with all the implacability of personal resentment; when he perceives clamour and malice let loose upon him as a public enemy, and incited by every stratagem of defamation; when he hears the misfortunes of his family, or the follies of his youth

6. Shakespeare, *Merchant of Venice* I.iii.20.

exposed to the world; and every failure of conduct, or defect of nature aggravated and ridiculed; he then learns to abhor those artifices at which he only laughed before, and discovers how much the happiness of life would be advanced by the eradication of envy from the human heart.

Envy is, indeed, a stubborn weed of the mind, and seldom yields to the culture [7] of philosophy. There are, however, considerations, which if carefully implanted and diligently propagated, might in time overpower and repress it, since no one can nurse it for the sake of pleasure, as its effects are only shame, anguish, and perturbation.

It is above all other vices inconsistent with the character of a social being, because it sacrifices truth and kindness to very weak temptations. He that plunders a wealthy neighbour gains as much as he takes away, and may improve his own condition in the same proportion as he impairs another's; but he that blasts a flourishing reputation must be content with a small dividend of additional fame, so small as can afford very little consolation to balance the guilt by which it is obtained.

I have hitherto avoided that dangerous and empirical morality, which cures one vice by means of another. But envy is so base and detestable, so vile in its original, and so pernicious in its effects, that the predominance of almost any other quality is to be preferred. It is one of those lawless enemies of society against which poisoned arrows may honestly be used. Let it, therefore, be constantly remembered that whoever envies another, confesses his superiority, and let those be reformed by their pride who have lost their virtue.

It is no slight aggravation of the injuries which envy incites that they are committed against those who have given no intentional provocation; and that the sufferer is often marked out for ruin, not because he has failed in any duty, but because he has dared to do more than was required.

Almost every other crime is practised by the help of some quality which might have produced esteem or love if it had been well employed; but envy is mere unmixed and genuine evil; it pursues a hateful end by despicable means, and desires not so much its own happiness as another's misery. To avoid depravity like this, it is not necessary that any one should aspire to heroism or sanctity, but only that he should resolve not to quit the rank which nature assigns him, and wish to maintain the dignity of a human being. [No. 183, Tuesday, December 17, 1751]

7. Cultivation (in its literal sense; a metaphor pursued in the next sentence).

From The Idler

Among the innumerable mortifications that waylay human arrogance on every side may well be reckoned our ignorance of the most common objects and effects, a defect of which we become more sensible by every attempt to supply it. Vulgar and inactive minds confound familiarity with knowledge, and conceive themselves informed of the whole nature of things when they are shown their form or told their use; but the speculatist, who is not content with superficial views, harasses himself with fruitless curiosity, and still as he enquires more perceives only that he knows less.

Sleep is a state in which a great part of every life is passed. No animal has been yet discovered whose existence is not varied with intervals of insensibility; and some late philosophers have extended the empire of sleep over the vegetable world.

Yet of this change so frequent, so great, so general, and so necessary, no searcher has yet found either the efficient or final cause; [8] or can tell by what power the mind and the body are thus chained down in irresistible stupefaction; or what benefits the animal receives from this alternate suspension of its active powers.

Whatever may be the multiplicity or contrariety of opinions upon this subject, nature has taken sufficient care that theory shall have little influence on practice. The most diligent enquirer is not able long to keep his eyes open; the most eager disputant will begin about midnight to desert his argument, and once in four and twenty hours, the gay and the gloomy, the witty and the dull, the clamorous and the silent, the busy and the idle, are all overpowered by the gentle tyrant, and all lie down in the equality of sleep.

Philosophy has often attempted to repress insolence by asserting that all conditions are levelled by death; a position which, however it may deject the happy, will seldom afford much comfort to the wretched. It is far more pleasing to consider that sleep is equally a leveller with death; that the time is never at a great distance when the balm of rest shall be effused alike upon every head, when the diversities of life shall stop their operation, and the high and the low shall lie down together.

It is somewhere recorded of Alexander, that in the pride of conquests and intoxication of flattery, he declared that he only perceived himself to be a man by the necessity of sleep.[9] Whether he considered sleep as necessary to his mind or body it was indeed a sufficient evidence of human infirmity; the body which required such frequency of renovation gave but faint promises of immortality; and the mind which, from time to time, sunk gladly into insensibility had made no very near approaches to the felicity of the supreme and self-sufficient nature.

I know not what can tend more to repress all the passions that disturb the peace of the world than the consideration that there is no height of happiness or honour from which man does not eagerly descend to a state of unconscious repose; that the best condition of life is such that we contentedly quit its good

8. That is, that which brings it about or the end it may be supposed to serve.
9. In Plutarch's life, XXII.3–4; Johnson refers to Alexander's conviction of his divine origin (see Dryden, *Alexander's Feast*).

to be disentangled from its evils; that in a few hours splendour fades before the eye and praise itself deadens in the ear; the senses withdraw from their objects, and reason favours the retreat.

What then are the hopes and prospects of covetousness, ambition and rapacity? Let him that desires most have all his desires gratified, he never shall attain a state which he can, for a day and a night, contemplate with satisfaction, or from which, if he had the power of perpetual vigilance, he would not long for periodical separations.

All envy would be extinguished if it were universally known that there are none to be envied, and surely none can be much envied who are not pleased with themselves. There is reason to suspect that the distinctions of mankind have more show than value when it is found that all agree to be weary alike of pleasures and of cares, that the powerful and the weak, the celebrated and obscure, join in one common wish, and implore from nature's hand the nectar of oblivion.

Such is our desire of abstraction from ourselves that very few are satisfied with the quantity of stupefaction which the needs of the body force upon the mind. Alexander himself added intemperance to sleep, and solaced with the fumes of wine the sovereignty of the world. And almost every man has some art by which he steals his thoughts away from his present state.

It is not much of life that is spent in close attention to any important duty. Many hours of every day are suffered to fly away without any traces left upon the intellects. We suffer phantoms to rise up before us, and amuse ourselves with the dance of airy images, which after a time we dismiss for ever, and know not how we have been busied.

Many have no happier moments than those that they pass in solitude, abandoned to their own imagination, which sometimes puts sceptres in their hands or mitres on their heads, shifts the scene of pleasure with endless variety, bids all the forms of beauty sparkle before them, and gluts them with every change of visionary luxury.

It is easy in these semi-slumbers to collect all the possibilities of happiness, to alter the course of the sun, to bring back the past, and anticipate the future, to unite all the beauties of all seasons, and all the blessings of all climates, to receive and bestow felicity, and forget that misery is the lot of man. All this is a voluntary dream, a temporary recession from the realities of life to airy fictions; an habitual subjection of reason to fancy.

Others are afraid to be alone, and amuse themselves by a perpetual succession of companions, but the difference is not great; in solitude we have our dreams to ourselves, and in company we agree to dream in concert. The end sought in both is forgetfulness of ourselves. [No. 32, Saturday, November 25, 1758]

Respicere ad longae jussit spatia ultima vitae.
JUVENAL, X.275 [10]

Much of the pain and pleasure of mankind arises from the conjectures which every one makes of the thoughts of others; we all enjoy praise which we do not

10. "Bidden to look at the last lap of a long life."

hear, and resent contempt which we do not see. The Idler may therefore be forgiven if he suffers his imagination to represent to him what his readers will say or think when they are informed that they have now his last paper in their hands.

Value is more frequently raised by scarcity than by use. That which lay neglected when it was common rises in estimation as its quantity becomes less. We seldom learn the true want of what we have till it is discovered that we can have no more.

This essay will, perhaps, be read with care even by those who have not yet attended to any other; and he that finds this late attention recompensed will not forbear to wish that he had bestowed it sooner.

Though the Idler and his readers have contracted no close friendship they are perhaps both unwilling to part. There are few things not purely evil of which we can say, without some emotion of uneasiness, 'this is the last.' Those who never could agree together shed tears when mutual discontent has determined them to final separation; of a place which has been frequently visited, though without pleasure, the last look is taken with heaviness of heart; and the Idler, with all his chillness of tranquillity, is not wholly unaffected by the thought that his last essay is now before him.

This secret horror of the last is inseparable from a thinking being whose life is limited, and to whom death is dreadful. We always make a secret comparison between a part and the whole; the termination of any period of life reminds us that life itself has likewise its termination; when we have done anything for the last time, we involuntarily reflect that a part of the days allotted us is past, and that as more is past there is less remaining.

It is very happily and kindly provided that in every life there are certain pauses and interruptions, which force consideration upon the careless and seriousness upon the light; points of time where one course of action ends and another begins; and by vicissitude of fortune, or alteration of employment, by change of place, or loss of friendship, we are forced to say of something, 'this is the last.'

An even and unvaried tenor of life always hides from our apprehension the approach of its end. Succession is not perceived but by variation; he that lives today as he lived yesterday, and expects that, as the present day is, such will be the morrow, easily conceives time as running in a circle and returning to itself. The uncertainty of our duration is impressed commonly by dissimilitude of condition; it is only by finding life changeable that we are reminded of its shortness.

This conviction, however forcible at every new impression, is every moment fading from the mind; and partly by the inevitable incursion of new images, and partly by voluntary exclusion of unwelcome thoughts, we are again exposed to the universal fallacy; and we must do another thing for the last time, before we consider that the time is nigh when we shall do no more.

As the last *Idler* is published in that solemn week [11] which the Christian world has always set apart for the examination of the conscience, the review of life, the extinction of earthly desires and the renovation of holy purposes, I

11. On Holy Saturday of Easter week.

hope that my readers are already disposed to view every incident with seriousness and improve it by meditation; and that when they see this series of trifles brought to a conclusion, they will consider that by outliving the *Idler* they have past weeks, months, and years which are now no longer in their power; that an end must in time be put to everything great as to everything little; that to life must come its last hour, and to this system of being its last day, the hour at which probation ceases, and repentance will be vain; the day in which every work of the hand and imagination of the heart shall be brought to judgment, and an everlasting futurity shall be determined by the past. [No. 103, Saturday, April 5, 1760]

From The Preface to Shakespeare [1]

Nothing can please many, and please long, but just representations of general nature. Particular manners can be known to few, and therefore few only can judge how nearly they are copied. The irregular combinations of fanciful invention may delight awhile by that novelty of which the common satiety of life sends us all in quest; but the pleasures of sudden wonder are soon exhausted, and the mind can only repose on the stability of truth.

Shakespeare is, above all writers, at least above all modern writers, the poet of nature, the poet that holds up to his readers a faithful mirror of manners and of life. His characters are not modified by the customs of particular places, unpractised by the rest of the world; by the peculiarities of studies or professions which can operate but upon small numbers; or by the accidents of transient fashions or temporary opinions: they are the genuine progeny of common humanity, such as the world will always supply, and observation will always find. His persons act and speak by the influence of those general passions and principles by which all minds are agitated and the whole system of life is continued in motion. In the writings of other poets a character is too often an individual; in those of Shakespeare it is commonly a species.

It is from this wide extension of design that so much instruction is derived. It is this which fills the plays of Shakespeare with practical axioms and domestic wisdom. It was said of Euripides that every verse was a precept; [2] and it may be said of Shakespeare that from his works may be collected a system of civil and economical prudence. Yet his real power is not shown in the splendour of particular passages, but by the progress of his fable and the tenor of his dia-

1. The Preface and Notes to Shakespeare are part of an edition Johnson undertook almost a decade earlier and finally completed in 1765. It need hardly be said that Johnson was not the first in his age to denounce the "rules" (in this case, the unity of time and place) derived on slender grounds from Aristotle. Addison had written a half-century before: "There is sometimes a greater judgment shown in deviating from the rules of art than in adhering to them" (*Spectator* No. 592). But Johnson uses his discussion to explore, as Dryden had before and Reynolds was to do in his thirteenth Discourse (1786), the nature of art and illusion; and he provides the most telling discussion before (or even including) Coleridge of the "willing suspension of disbelief." In his appeal from art to nature (i.e. from rules to experience) and in his notes on characters, Johnson shows the moral centrality of his literary criticism, the constant inquiry as to what human ends art can be said to serve.
2. By Cicero, *Familiar Letters* XVI.8.

logue; and he that tries to recommend him by select quotations will succeed like the pedant in Hierocles,[3] who, when he offered his house to sale, carried a brick in his pocket as a specimen.

It will not easily be imagined how much Shakespeare excels in accommodating his sentiments to real life but by comparing him with other authors. It was observed of the ancient schools of declamation that the more diligently they were frequented, the more was the student disqualified for the world, because he found nothing there which he should ever meet in any other place.[4] The same remark may be applied to every stage but that of Shakespeare. The theatre, when it is under any other direction, is peopled by such characters as were never seen, conversing in a language which was never heard, upon topics which will never arise in the commerce of mankind. But the dialogue of this author is often so evidently determined by the incident which produces it, and is pursued with so much ease and simplicity, that it seems scarcely to claim the merit of fiction, but to have been gleaned by diligent selection out of common conversation and common occurrences.

Upon every other stage the universal agent is love, by whose power all good and evil is distributed and every action quickened or retarded. To bring a lover, a lady, and a rival into the fable; to entangle them in contradictory obligations, perplex them with oppositions of interest, and harass them with violence of desires inconsistent with each other; to make them meet in rapture and part in agony, to fill their mouths with hyperbolical joy and outrageous sorrow, to distress them as nothing human ever was distressed, to deliver them as nothing human ever was delivered, is the business of a modern dramatist. For this, probability is violated, life is misrepresented, and language is depraved. But love is only one of many passions; and as it has no great influence upon the sum of life, it has little operation in the dramas of a poet who caught his ideas from the living world and exhibited only what he saw before him. He knew that any other passion, as it was regular or exorbitant, was a cause of happiness or calamity.

Characters thus ample and general were not easily discriminated and preserved, yet perhaps no poet ever kept his personages more distinct from each other. I will not say with Pope that every speech may be assigned to the proper speaker,[5] because many speeches there are which have nothing characteristical; but, perhaps, though some may be equally adapted to every person, it will be difficult to find any that can be properly transferred from the present possessor to another claimant. The choice is right, when there is reason for choice.

Other dramatists can only gain attention by hyperbolical or aggravated characters, by fabulous and unexampled excellence or depravity, as the writers of barbarous romances invigorated the reader by a giant and a dwarf; and he that should form his expectations of human affairs from the play, or from the tale, would be equally deceived. Shakespeare has no heroes; his scenes are occupied only by men, who act and speak as the reader thinks that he should

3. Hierocles was an Alexandrian of the 5th century A.D.; his "jests" were freely translated in 1741, possibly by Johnson.

4. Petronius, *Satyricon* I.i.

5. In his Preface to Shakespeare (1725).

himself have spoken or acted on the same occasion. Even where the agency is supernatural, the dialogue is level with life. Other writers disguise the most natural passions and most frequent incidents; so that he who contemplates them in the book will not know them in the world. Shakespeare approximates the remote and familiarizes the wonderful; the event which he represents will not happen, but, if it were possible, its effects would probably be such as he has assigned; and it may be said that he has not only shown human nature as it acts in real exigences, but as it would be found in trials to which it cannot be exposed.

This, therefore, is the praise of Shakespeare, that his drama is the mirror of life; that he who has mazed his imagination in following the phantoms which other writers raise up before him, may here be cured of his delirious ecstasies by reading human sentiments in human language, by scenes from which a hermit may estimate the transactions of the world and a confessor predict the progress of the passions.

. . .

Shakespeare's plays are not in the rigorous and critical sense either tragedies or comedies, but compositions of a distinct kind; exhibiting the real state of sublunary [6] nature, which partakes of good and evil, joy and sorrow, mingled with endless variety of proportion and innumerable modes of combination; and expressing the course of the world, in which the loss of one is the gain of another; in which, at the same time, the reveller is hasting to his wine, and the mourner burying his friend; in which the malignity of one is sometimes defeated by the frolic of another; and many mischiefs and many benefits are done and hindered without design.

Out of this chaos of mingled purposes and casualties the ancient poets, according to the laws which custom had prescribed, selected some the crimes of men, and some their absurdities; some the momentous vicissitudes of life, and some the lighter occurrences; some the terrors of distress, and some the gaieties of prosperity. Thus rose the two modes of imitation, known by the names of *tragedy* and *comedy*, compositions intended to promote different ends by contrary means, and considered as so little allied that I do not recollect among the Greeks or Romans a single writer who attempted both.

Shakespeare has united the powers of exciting laughter and sorrow not only in one mind but in one composition. Almost all his plays are divided between serious and ludicrous characters, and, in the successive evolutions of the design, sometimes produce seriousness and sorrow, and sometimes levity and laughter.

That this is a practice contrary to the rules of criticism will be readily allowed; but there is always an appeal open from criticism to nature. The end of writing is to instruct; the end of poetry is to instruct by pleasing. That the mingled drama may convey all the instruction of tragedy or comedy cannot be denied, because it includes both in its alternations of exhibition and approaches nearer than either to the appearance of life, by showing how great machinations and slender designs may promote or obviate one another, and the high and the low cooperate in the general system by unavoidable concatenation.

It is objected that by this change of scenes the passions are interrupted in

6. That is, beneath the celestial realms; on earth.

their progression, and that the principal event, being not advanced by a due gradation of preparatory incidents, wants at last the power to move, which constitutes the perfection of dramatic poetry. This reasoning is so specious [7] that it is received as true even by those who in daily experience feel it to be false. The interchanges of mingled scenes seldom fail to produce the intended vicissitudes of passion. Fiction cannot move so much but that the attention may be easily transferred; and though it must be allowed that pleasing melancholy be sometimes interrupted by unwelcome levity, yet let it be considered likewise that melancholy is often not pleasing, and that the disturbance of one man may be the relief of another; that different auditors have different habitudes; and that, upon the whole, all pleasure consists in variety.

. . .

Shakespeare with his excellencies has likewise faults, and faults sufficient to obscure and overwhelm any other merit. I shall show them in the proportion in which they appear to me, without envious malignity or superstitious veneration. No question can be more innocently discussed than a dead poet's pretensions to renown; and little regard is due to that bigotry which sets candour [8] higher than truth.

His first defect is that to which may be imputed most of the evil in books or in men. He sacrifices virtue to convenience and is so much more careful to please than to instruct that he seems to write without any moral purpose. From his writings indeed a system of social duty may be selected, for he that thinks reasonably must think morally; but his precepts and axioms drop casually from him; he makes no just distribution of good or evil, nor is always careful to show in the virtuous a disapprobation of the wicked; he carries his persons indifferently through right and wrong and at the close dismisses them without further care and leaves their examples to operate by chance. This fault the barbarity of his age cannot extenuate; for it is always a writer's duty to make the world better, and justice is a virtue independent on time or place.

The plots are often so loosely formed that a very slight consideration may improve them, and so carelessly pursued that he seems not always fully to comprehend his own design. He omits opportunities of instructing or delighting which the train of his story seems to force upon him, and apparently rejects those exhibitions which would be more affecting, for the sake of those which are more easy.

. . .

It is incident to him to be now and then entangled with an unwieldy sentiment, which he cannot well express and will not reject; he struggles with it a while, and, if it continues stubborn, comprises it in words such as occur and leaves it to be disentangled and evolved by those who have more leisure to bestow upon it.

Not that always where the language is intricate the thought is subtle, or the image always great where the line is bulky; the equality of words to things is very often neglected, and trivial sentiments and vulgar ideas disappoint the attention to which they are recommended by sonorous epithets and swelling figures.

7. Plausible.
8. Sympathy, kindness.

But the admirers of this great poet have most reason to complain when he approaches nearest to his highest excellence and seems fully resolved to sink them in dejection [9] and mollify them with tender emotions by the fall of greatness, the danger of innocence, or the crosses of love. What he does best, he soon ceases to do. He is not long soft and pathetic without some idle conceit or contemptible equivocation.[10] He no sooner begins to move than he counteracts himself; and terror and pity, as they are rising in the mind, are checked and blasted by sudden frigidity.

A quibble is to Shakespeare what luminous vapours are to the traveller; he follows it at all adventures; it is sure to lead him out of his way and sure to engulf him in the mire. It has some malignant power over his mind, and its fascinations are irresistible. Whatever be the dignity or profundity of his disquisition, whether he be enlarging knowledge or exalting affection, whether he be amusing attention with incidents or enchaining it in suspense, let but a quibble spring up before him, and he leaves his work unfinished. A quibble is the golden apple [11] for which he will always turn aside from his career or stoop from his elevation. A quibble, poor and barren as it is, gave him such delight that he was content to purchase it by the sacrifice of reason, propriety, and truth. A quibble was to him the fatal Cleopatra for which he lost the world and was content to lose it.

It will be thought strange that in enumerating the defects of this writer, I have not yet mentioned his neglect of the unities, his violation of those laws which have been instituted and established by the joint authority of poets and of critics.

For his other deviations from the art of writing, I resign him to critical justice, without making any other demand in his favour than that which must be indulged to all human excellence: that his virtues be rated with his failings. But from the censure which this irregularity may bring upon him, I shall, with due reverence to that learning which I must oppose, adventure to try how I can defend him.

His histories, being neither tragedies nor comedies, are not subject to any of their laws; nothing more is necessary to all the praise which they expect than that the changes of action be so prepared as to be understood, that the incidents be various and affecting, and the characters consistent, natural, and distinct. No other unity is intended, and therefore none is to be sought.

In his other works he has well enough preserved the unity of action. He has not, indeed, an intrigue regularly perplexed and regularly unravelled; he does not endeavour to hide his design only to discover it, for this is seldom the order

9. While Johnson sees this power as a strength, he associates it with a sense of justice ("which all reasonable beings naturally love") and cannot condone the death of Cordelia. He cites the version of Nahum Tate which permits her survival: "In the present case the public has decided. Cordelia, from the time of Tate, has always retired with victory and felicity. And, if my sensations could add anything to the general suffrage, I might relate that I was many years ago so shocked by Cordelia's death that I know not whether I ever endured to read again the last scenes of the play till I undertook to revise them as an editor."

10. On the "conceit," see Johnson on the Metaphysical poets in the *Life of Cowley;* by "equivocation" he means pun or quibble (the latter defined by him as "a low conceit depending on the sound of words; a pun").

11. Referring to Atalanta, the fleet princess who was overtaken when Meleager (or Melanion) cast a golden apple in her path.

of real events, and Shakespeare is the poet of nature; but his plan has commonly, what Aristotle requires, a beginning, a middle, and an end; one event is concatenated with another, and the conclusion follows by easy consequence. There are perhaps some incidents that might be spared, as in other poets there is much talk that only fills up time upon the stage; but the general system makes gradual advances, and the end of the play is the end of expectation.

To the unities of time and place he has shown no regard; and perhaps a nearer view of the principles on which they stand will diminish their value and withdraw from them the veneration which, from the time of Corneille,[12] they have very generally received, by discovering that they have given more trouble to the poet than pleasure to the auditor.

The necessity of observing the unities of time and place arises from the supposed necessity of making the drama credible. The critics hold it impossible that an action of months or years can be possibly believed to pass in three hours; or that the spectator can suppose himself to sit in the theatre while ambassadors go and return between distant kings, while armies are levied and towns besieged, while an exile wanders and returns, or till he whom they saw courting his mistress shall lament the untimely fall of his son. The mind revolts from evident falsehood, and fiction loses its force when it departs from the resemblance of reality.

From the narrow limitation of time necessarily arises the contraction of place. The spectator, who knows that he saw the first act at Alexandria, cannot suppose that he sees the next at Rome, at a distance to which not the dragons of Medea [13] could, in so short a time, have transported him; he knows with certainty that he has not changed his place; and he knows that place cannot change itself; that what was a house cannot become a plain; that what was Thebes can never be Persepolis.

Such is the triumphant language with which a critic exults over the misery of an irregular poet and exults commonly without resistance or reply. It is time, therefore, to tell him by the authority of Shakespeare that he assumes, as an unquestionable principle, a position which, while his breath is forming it into words, his understanding pronounces to be false. It is false, that any representation is mistaken for reality; that any dramatic fable in its materiality was ever credible, or, for a single moment, was ever credited.

The objection arising from the impossibility of passing the first hour at Alexandria and the next at Rome, supposes that when the play opens the spectator really imagines himself at Alexandria and believes that his walk to the theatre has been a voyage to Egypt and that he lives in the days of Antony and Cleopatra. Surely he that imagines this may imagine more. He that can take the stage at one time for the palace of the Ptolemies may take it in half an hour for the promontory of Actium. Delusion, if delusion be admitted, has no certain limitation; if the spectator can be once persuaded that his old acquaintance are Alexander and Caesar, that a room illuminated with candles is the plain of Pharsalia or the bank of Granicus,[14] he is in a state of

12. Pierre Corneille in the 1660 edition of his plays included a discourse on the unities and also *examens* of each of his plays in which he discussed such problems.

13. They draw the chariot in which she flees from Corinth after killing Jason's new wife Creusa and her own children.

14. Alexander fought a battle near the river Granicus, Caesar on the plains of Pharsalia.

elevation above the reach of reason or of truth, and from the heights of empyrean poetry may despise the circumscriptions of terrestrial nature. There is no reason why a mind thus wandering in ecstasy should count the clock, or why an hour should not be a century in that calenture [15] of the brains that can make the stage a field.

The truth is that the spectators are always in their senses and know, from the first act to the last, that the stage is only a stage, and that the players are only players. They come to hear a certain number of lines recited with just gesture and elegant modulation. The lines relate to some action, and an action must be in some place; but the different actions that complete a story may be in places very remote from each other; and where is the absurdity of allowing that space to represent first Athens and then Sicily which was always known to be neither Sicily nor Athens, but a modern theatre.

By supposition, as place is introduced, time may be extended; the time required by the fable elapses for the most part between the acts; for, of so much of the action as is represented, the real and poetical duration is the same. If in the first act preparations for war against Mithridates are represented to be made in Rome, the event of the war may, without absurdity, be represented in the catastrophe as happening in Pontus; we know that there is neither war nor preparation for war; we know that we are neither in Rome nor Pontus; that neither Mithridates nor Lucullus are before us.[16] The drama exhibits successive imitations of successive actions; and why may not the second imitation represent an action that happened years after the first, if it be so connected with it that nothing but time can be supposed to intervene? Time is, of all modes of existence, most obsequious [17] to the imagination; a lapse of years is as easily conceived as a passage of hours. In contemplation we easily contract the time of real actions and therefore willingly permit it to be contracted when we only see their imitation.

It will be asked how the drama moves if it is not credited. It is credited with all the credit due to a drama. It is credited, whenever it moves, as a just picture of a real original; as representing to the auditor what he would himself feel if he were to do or suffer what is there feigned to be suffered or to be done. The reflection that strikes the heart is not that the evils before us are real evils, but that they are evils to which we ourselves may be exposed. If there be any fallacy, it is not that we fancy the players, but that we fancy ourselves, unhappy for a moment; but we rather lament the possibility than suppose the presence of misery, as a mother weeps over her babe when she remembers that death may take it from her. The delight of tragedy proceeds from our consciousness of fiction; if we thought murders and treasons real, they would please no more.

Imitations produce pain or pleasure, not because they are mistaken for realities, but because they bring realities to mind. When the imagination is recreated [18] by a painted landscape, the trees are not supposed capable to

15. Fever.
16. Mithridates the Great (*c.* 130–63 B.C.), ruler of Pontus and conqueror of much of the rest of Asia Minor; attacked with temporary success by the Romans under Lucullus (73–66 B.C.) and finally defeated by the forces of Pompey.
17. Yielding, submissive.
18. Gratified.

give us shade, or the fountains coolness; but we consider how we should be pleased with such fountains playing beside us and such woods waving over us. We are agitated in reading the history of *Henry the Fifth,* yet no man takes his book for the field of Agincourt. A dramatic exhibition is a book recited with concomitants that increase or diminish its effect. Familiar comedy is often more powerful in the theatre than on the page; imperial tragedy is always less. The humour of Petruchio may be heightened by grimace; but what voice or what gesture can hope to add dignity or force to the soliloquy of Cato? [19]

A play read affects the mind like a play acted. It is therefore evident that the action is not supposed to be real; and it follows that between the acts a longer or shorter time may be allowed to pass, and that no more account of space or duration is to be taken by the auditor of a drama than by the reader of a narrative, before whom may pass in an hour the life of a hero or the revolutions of an empire.

. . .

He that, without diminution of any other excellence, shall preserve all the unities unbroken deserves the like applause with the architect who shall display all the orders of architecture in a citadel without any deduction from its strength; but the principal beauty of a citadel is to exclude the enemy, and the greatest graces of a play are to copy nature and instruct life.

Perhaps what I have here not dogmatically but deliberatively written may recall the principles of the drama to a new examination. I am almost frighted at my own temerity and, when I estimate the fame and the strength of those that maintain the contrary opinion, am ready to sink down in reverential silence; as Aeneas withdrew from the defence of Troy when he saw Neptune shaking the wall and Juno heading the besiegers.[20]

Those whom my arguments cannot persuade to give their approbation to the judgement of Shakespeare will easily, if they consider the condition of his life, make some allowance for his ignorance.

Every man's performances, to be rightly estimated, must be compared with the state of the age in which he lived and with his own particular opportunities; and though to the reader a book be not worse or better for the circumstances of the author, yet as there is always a silent reference of human works to human abilities, and as the inquiry how far man may extend his designs, or how high he may rate his native force, is of far greater dignity than in what rank we shall place any particular performance, curiosity is always busy to discover the instruments as well as to survey the workmanship, to know how much is to be ascribed to original powers and how much to casual and adventitious help. The palaces of Peru or Mexico were certainly mean and incommodious habitations if compared to the houses of European monarchs; yet who could forbear to view them with astonishment who remembered that they were built without the use of iron? . . .

19. Referring to Joseph Addison's tragedy of 1713.
20. *Aeneid* II.610–14.

From The Notes to Shakespeare

[Falstaff]

But Falstaff, unimitated, unimitable Falstaff, how shall I describe thee? Thou compound of sense and vice; of sense which may be admired but not esteemed, of vice which may be despised but hardly detested. Falstaff is a character loaded with faults, and with those faults which naturally produce contempt. He is a thief and a glutton, a coward and a boaster, always ready to cheat the weak and prey upon the poor; to terrify the timorous and insult the defenceless. At once obsequious and malignant, he satirizes in their absence those whom he lives by flattering. He is familiar with the prince only as an agent of vice, but of this familiarity he is so proud as not only to be supercilious and haughty with common men but to think his interest of importance to the Duke of Lancaster. Yet the man thus corrupt, thus despicable, makes himself necessary to the prince that despises him, by the most pleasing of all qualities, perpetual gaiety, by an unfailing power of exciting laughter, which is the more freely indulged as his wit is not of the splendid or ambitious kind but consists in easy escapes and sallies of levity, which make sport but raise no envy. It must be observed that he is stained with no enormous or sanguinary crimes, so that his licentiousness is not so offensive but that it may be borne for his mirth.

The moral to be drawn from this representation is that no man is more dangerous than he that, with a will to corrupt, hath the power to please; and that neither wit nor honesty ought to think themselves safe with such a companion when they see Henry seduced by Falstaff.

[Polonius]

The commentator makes the character of Polonius a character only of manners, discriminated by properties superficial, accidental, and acquired. The poet intended a nobler delineation of a mixed character of manners and of nature. Polonius is a man bred in courts, exercised in business, stored with observation, confident of his knowledge, proud of his eloquence, and declining into dotage. His mode of oratory is truly represented as designed to ridicule the practice of those times, of prefaces that made no introduction, and of method that embarrassed rather than explained. This part of his character is accidental, the rest is natural. Such a man is positive and confident, because he knows that his mind was once strong and knows not that it is become weak. Such a man excels in general principles but fails in the particular application. He is knowing in retrospect and ignorant in foresight. While he depends upon his memory and can draw from his repositories of knowledge, he utters weighty sentences and gives useful counsel; but as the mind in its enfeebled state cannot be kept long busy and intent, the old man is subject to sudden dereliction of his faculties, he loses the order of his ideas and entangles himself in his own thoughts, till he recovers the leading principle and falls again into his former train. This idea of dotage encroaching upon wisdom will solve all the phenomena of the character of Polonius.

[Lady Macbeth]

. . . The arguments by which Lady Macbeth persuades her husband to commit the murder afford a proof of Shakespeare's knowledge of human nature. She urges the excellence and dignity of courage, a glittering idea which has dazzled mankind from age to age and animated sometimes the housebreaker and sometimes the conqueror; but this sophism Macbeth has for ever destroyed, by distinguishing true from false fortitude, in a line and a half; of which it may almost be said that they ought to bestow immortality on the author, though all his other productions had been lost;

> I dare do all that may become a man,
> Who dares do more, is none.

This topic, which has been always employed with too much success, is used in this scene with peculiar propriety, to a soldier by a woman. Courage is the distinguishing virtue of a soldier, and the reproach of cowardice cannot be borne by any man from a woman, without great impatience.

She then urges the oaths by which he had bound himself to murder Duncan, another art of sophistry by which men have sometimes deluded their consciences and persuaded themselves that what would be criminal in others is virtuous in them; this argument Shakespeare, whose plan obliged him to make Macbeth yield, has not confuted, though he might easily have shown that a former obligation could not be vacated by a latter; that obligations laid on us by a higher power could not be overruled by obligations which we lay upon ourselves.

1765

From A Journey to the Western Islands [1]

. . . We were now in the bosom of the Highlands, with full leisure to contemplate the appearance and properties of mountainous regions, such as have been, in many countries, the last shelters of national distress, and are every where the scenes of adventures, stratagems, surprises and escapes.

Mountainous countries are not passed but with difficulty, not merely from the labour of climbing; for to climb is not always necessary: but because that which is not mountain is commonly bog, through which the way must be picked with caution. Where there are hills, there is much rain, and the torrents pouring down into the intermediate spaces, seldom find so ready an outlet, as not to stagnate, till they have broken the texture of the ground.

Of the hills, which our journey offered to the view on either side, we did

fiat . . . sound i.e. the first (Creation) and last (Judgment)

1. This is from Johnson's record of the tour that was also recorded by Boswell in his *Tour to the Hebrides with Samuel Johnson* (published after Johnson's death). Johnson's imagination had been stirred by the Hebrides in his boyhood reading of Martin Martin's *Description of the Western Islands of Scotland* (1703), and he spent a hundred days on the tour with Boswell in the autumn of 1773. This section comes from the account of the mainland of Scotland and describes the area near Anoch in Glenmorison.

not take the height, nor did we see any that astonished us with their loftiness. Towards the summit of one, there was a white spot, which I should have called a naked rock, but the guides, who had better eyes, and were acquainted with the phenomena of the country, declared it to be snow. It had already lasted to the end of August, and was likely to maintain its contest with the sun, till it should be reinforced by winter.

The height of mountains philosophically considered is properly computed from the surface of the next sea; but as it affects the eye or imagination of the passenger, as it makes either a spectacle or an obstruction, it must be reckoned from the place where the rise begins to make a considerable angle with the plain. In extensive continents the land may, by gradual elevation, attain great height, without any other appearance than that of a plane gently inclined, and if a hill placed upon such raised ground be described, as having its altitude equal to the whole space above the sea, the representation will be fallacious.

These mountains may be properly enough measured from the inland base; for it is not much above the sea. As we advanced at evening towards the western coast, I did not observe the declivity to be greater than is necessary for the discharge of the inland waters.

We passed many rivers and rivulets, which commonly ran with a clear shallow stream over a hard pebbly bottom. These channels, which seem so much wider than the water that they convey would naturally require, are formed by the violence of wintry floods, produced by the accumulation of innumerable streams that fall in rainy weather from the hills, and bursting away with resistless impetuosity, make themselves a passage proportionate to their mass.

Such capricious and temporary waters cannot be expected to produce many fish. The rapidity of the wintry deluge sweeps them away, and the scantiness of the summer stream would hardly sustain them above the ground. This is the reason why in fording the northern rivers, no fishes are seen, as in England, wandering in the water.

Of the hills many may be called with Homer's Ida 'abundant in springs,' but few can deserve the epithet which he bestows upon Pelion by 'waving their leaves.' [2] They exhibit very little variety; being almost wholly covered with dark heath, and even that seems to be checked in its growth. What is not heath is nakedness, a little diversified by now and then a stream rushing down the steep. An eye accustomed to flowery pastures and waving harvests is astonished and repelled by this wide extent of hopeless sterility. The appearance is that of matter incapable of form or usefulness, dismissed by nature from her care and disinherited of her favours, left in its original elemental state, or quickened only with one sullen power of useless vegetation.

It will very readily occur, that this uniformity of barrenness can afford very little amusement to the traveller; that it is easy to sit at home and conceive rocks and heath, and waterfalls; and that these journeys are useless labours, which neither impregnate the imagination, nor enlarge the understanding. It is true that of far the greater part of things, we must content ourselves with such knowledge as description may exhibit, or analogy supply; but it is true likewise,

2. Cf. Homer, *Iliad* XXIII.117 and II.757.

that these ideas are always incomplete, and that at least, till we have compared them with realities, we do not know them to be just. As we see more, we become possessed of more certainties, and consequently gain more principles of reasoning, and found a wider basis of analogy.

Regions mountainous and wild, thinly inhabited, and little cultivated, make a great part of the earth, and he that has never seen them, must live unacquainted with much of the face of nature, and with one of the great scenes of human existence.

As the day advanced towards noon, we entered a narrow valley not very flowery, but sufficiently verdant. Our guides told us, that the horses could not travel all day without rest or meat, and entreated us to stop here, because no grass would be found in any other place. The request was reasonable and the argument cogent. We therefore willingly dismounted and diverted ourselves as the place gave us opportunity.

I sat down on a bank, such as a writer of romance might have delighted to feign. I had indeed no trees to whisper over my head, but a clear rivulet streamed at my feet. The day was calm, the air soft, and all was rudeness,[3] silence, and solitude. Before me, and on either side, were high hills, which by hindering the eye from ranging, forced the mind to find entertainment for itself. Whether I spent the hour well I know not; for here I first conceived the thought of this narration.

We were in this place at ease and by choice, and had no evils to suffer or to fear; yet the imaginations excited by the view of an unknown and untravelled wilderness are not such as arise in the artificial solitude of parks and gardens, a flattering notion of self-sufficiency, a placid indulgence of voluntary delusions, a secure expansion of the fancy, or a cool concentration of the mental powers. The phantoms which haunt a desert are want, and misery, and danger; the evils of dereliction rush upon the thoughts; man is made unwillingly acquainted with his own weakness, and meditation shews him only how little he can sustain, and how little he can perform. There were no traces of inhabitants, except perhaps a rude pile of clods called a summer hut, in which a herdsman had rested in the favourable seasons. Whoever had been in the place where I then sat, unprovided with provisions and ignorant of the country, might, at least before the roads were made, have wandered among the rocks, till he had perished with hardship, before he could have found either food or shelter. Yet what are these hillocks to the ridges of Taurus,[4] or these spots of wildness to the deserts of America? . . .

1775

The Lives of the Poets

Johnson had planned biographical studies of English writers for many years, but the enterprise was given shape by an agreement with thirty-six London booksellers to supply lives to accompany the selections from fifty-two poets (from Cowley to Gray) who were no longer alive. The first four volumes appeared in 1779, the remaining six in 1781; the lives were collected in the latter year and have since acquired the unofficial but familiar title given above. The *Life of Cowley* provided Johnson with an occasion for a general discussion of the Metaphysical poets, given below. All the lives contain a balance, usually clearly demarcated, of biographical and critical writing; but in both, Johnson remains a profound, acutely aphoristic moralist.

From The Lives of the Poets

[Cowley and the Metaphysical Poets [1]]

The metaphysical poets were men of learning, and to show their learning was their whole endeavour; but, unluckily resolving to show it in rhyme, instead of writing poetry they only wrote verses, and very often such verses as stood the trial of the finger better than of the ear; for the modulation was so imperfect, that they were only found to be verses by counting the syllables.

If the father of criticism has rightly denominated poetry τέχνη μιμητικὴ, *an imitative art*,[2] these writers will, without great wrong, lose their right to the name of poets, for they cannot be said to have imitated anything; they neither copied nature nor life, neither painted the forms of matter, nor represented the operations of intellect.

Those, however, who deny them to be poets, allow them to be wits. Dryden confesses of himself and his contemporaries, that they fall below Donne in wit, but maintains that they surpass him in poetry.[3]

If wit be well described by Pope, as being 'that which has been often thought, but was never before so well expressed,' [4] they certainly never attained, nor ever sought it; for they endeavoured to be singular in their thoughts, and were careless of their diction. But Pope's account of wit is

1. Johnson used the *Life of Cowley* as an occasion for reviewing the methods of all the Metaphysical poets. While he cited many of the excesses of John Donne, whose work he knew well, the most outrageous instances are cited from such late Metaphysical poets as Cowley and John Cleveland. By Johnson's day these poets (whom Coleridge later called "witty logicians") had fallen greatly in reputation; we can see that decline begin with Dryden's remarks on Cleveland and continue in Pope's censure of those who pursue "conceit alone" (*Essay on Criticism,* ll.289 ff.). When Pope "versified" two of Donne's satires, he demonstrated by his changes his own definition of "true Wit": "a justness of thought and a facility of expression, or (in the midwives' phrase) a perfect conception with an easy delivery."
2. Aristotle in the *Poetics.*
3. In *Of Dramatic Poesy: An Essay;* see above, the section Dryden's Critical Prose.
4. Paraphrased from the *Essay on Criticism,* ll. 297–98.

undoubtedly erroneous: he depresses it below its natural dignity, and reduces it from strength of thought to happiness [5] of language.

If by a more noble and more adequate conception that be considered as wit which is at once natural and new, that which, though not obvious, is, upon its first production, acknowledged to be just; if it be that which he that never found it wonders how he missed, to wit of this kind the metaphysical poets have seldom risen. Their thoughts are often new, but seldom natural; they are not obvious, but neither are they just; and the reader, far from wondering that he missed them, wonders more frequently by what perverseness of industry they were ever found.

But wit, abstracted from its effects upon the hearer, may be more rigorously and philosophically considered as a kind of *discordia concors;* a combination of dissimilar images, or discovery of occult resemblances in things apparently unlike. Of wit, thus defined, they have more than enough. The most heterogeneous ideas are yoked by violence together; nature and art are ransacked for illustrations, comparisons, and allusions; their learning instructs, and their subtlety surprises; but the reader commonly thinks his improvement dearly bought, and, though he sometimes admires, is seldom pleased.

From this account of their compositions it will be readily inferred that they were not successful in representing or moving the affections. As they were wholly employed on something unexpected and surprising, they had no regard to that uniformity of sentiment which enables us to conceive and to excite the pains and the pleasure of other minds: they never inquired what, on any occasion, they should have said or done, but wrote rather as beholders than partakers of human nature; as beings looking upon good and evil, impassive and at leisure; as Epicurean deities, making remarks on the actions of men and the vicissitudes of life, without interest and without emotion. Their courtship was void of fondness, and their lamentation of sorrow. Their wish was only to say what they hoped had been never said before.

Nor was the sublime more within their reach than the pathetic; for they never attempted that comprehension and expanse of thought which at once fills the whole mind, and of which the first effect is sudden astonishment, and the second rational admiration.[6] Sublimity is produced by aggregation, and littleness by dispersion. Great thoughts are always general, and consist in positions not limited by exceptions, and in descriptions not descending to minuteness. It is with great propriety that subtlety, which in its original import means exility [7] of particles, is taken in its metaphorical meaning for nicety of distinction. Those writers who lay on the watch for novelty could have little hope of greatness; for great things cannot have escaped former observation. Their attempts were always analytic; they broke every image into fragments; and could no more represent, by their slender conceits and laboured particularities, the prospects of nature, or the scenes of life, than he who dissects a sunbeam with a prism can exhibit the wide effulgence of a summer noon.

What they wanted however of the sublime, they endeavoured to supply by

5. Felicity; implying chance as well as success.
6. See Edmund Burke's *Enquiry into the Origin of Our Ideas of the Sublime and Beautiful.*
7. Smallness of number, meagerness.

hyperbole; their amplification had no limits; they left not only reason but fancy behind them; and produced combinations of confused magnificence, that not only could not be credited, but could not be imagined.

Yet great labour, directed by great abilities, is never wholly lost: if they frequently threw away their wit upon false conceits, they likewise sometimes struck out unexpected truth; if their conceits were far-fetched, they were often worth the carriage. To write on their plan, it was at least necessary to read and think. No man could be born a metaphysical poet, nor assume the dignity of a writer, by descriptions copied from descriptions, by imitations borrowed from imitations, by traditional imagery, and hereditary similes, by readiness of rhyme, and volubility of syllables.

In perusing the works of this race of authors, the mind is exercised either by recollection or inquiry; either something already learned is to be retrieved, or something new is to be examined. If their greatness seldom elevates, their acuteness often surprises; if the imagination is not always gratified, at least the powers of reflection and comparison are employed; and in the mass of materials which ingenious absurdity has thrown together, genuine wit and useful knowledge may be sometimes found buried perhaps in grossness of expression, but useful to those who know their value; and such as, when they are expanded to perspicuity, and polished to elegance, may give lustre to works which have more propriety though less copiousness of sentiment.

[Milton [8]]

His political notions were those of an acrimonious and surly republican, for which it is not known that he gave any better reason than that *a popular government was the most frugal; for the trappings of a monarchy would set up an ordinary commonwealth.* It is surely very shallow policy that supposes money to be the chief good; and even this, without considering that the support and expense of a court is, for the most part, only a particular kind of traffic, for which money is circulated without any national impoverishment.

Milton's republicanism was, I am afraid, founded in an envious hatred of greatness, and a sullen desire of independence; in petulance impatient of control, and pride disdainful of superiority. He hated monarchs in the State, and prelates in the Church; for he hated all whom he was required to obey. It is to be suspected that his predominant desire was to destroy rather than establish, and that he felt not so much the love of liberty as repugnance to authority.

It has been observed that they who most loudly clamour for liberty do not most liberally grant it. What we know of Milton's character in domestic relations is that he was severe and arbitrary. His family consisted of women; and there appears in his books something like a Turkish contempt of females, as subordinate and inferior beings. That his own daughters might not break the ranks, he suffered them to be depressed by a mean and penurious education. He thought woman made only for obedience, and man only for rebellion.

8. These paragraphs, however unfair, are refreshing in an age of "candour" (to use the term, as Johnson does, in opposition to "truth") and highly characteristic of their author.

[Richard Savage [9]]

Such were the life and death of Richard Savage, a man equally distinguished by his virtues and vices, and at once remarkable for his weaknesses and abilities.

He was of a middle stature, of a thin habit of body, a long visage, coarse features, and melancholy aspect; of a grave and manly deportment, a solemn dignity of mien, but which, upon a nearer acquaintance, softened into an engaging easiness of manners. His walk was slow, and his voice tremulous and mournful. He was easily excited to smiles, but very seldom provoked to laughter.

His mind was in an uncommon degree vigorous and active. His judgment was accurate, his apprehension quick, and his memory so tenacious that he was frequently observed to know what he had learned from others in a short time, better than those by whom he was informed, and could frequently recollect incidents, with all their combination of circumstances, which few would have regarded at the present time, but which the quickness of his apprehension impressed upon him. He had the art of escaping from his own reflections, and accommodating himself to every new scene.

. . .

His method of life particularly qualified him for conversation, of which he knew how to practise all the graces. He was never vehement or loud, but at once modest and easy, open and respectful; his language was vivacious or elegant, and equally happy upon grave and humorous subjects. He was generally censured for not knowing when to retire; but that was not the defect of his judgment, but of his fortune; when he left his company, he was frequently to spend the remaining part of the night in the street, or at least was abandoned to gloomy reflections, which it is not strange that he delayed as long as he could; and sometimes forgot that he gave others pain to avoid it himself.

It cannot be said that he made use of his abilities for the direction of his own conduct: an irregular and dissipated manner of life had made him the slave of every passion that happened to be excited by the presence of its object, and that slavery to his passions reciprocally produced a life irregular and dissipated. He was not master of his own motions, nor could promise anything for the next day.

With regard to his economy, nothing can be added to the relation of his life. He appeared to think himself born to be supported by others, and dispensed from all necessity of providing for himself; he therefore never prosecuted any scheme of advantage, nor endeavoured even to secure the profits which his writings might have afforded him. His temper was, in consequence of the dominion of his passions, uncertain and capricious; he was easily engaged, and easily disgusted; but he is accused of retaining his hatred more tenaciously than his benevolence.

He was compassionate both by nature and principle, and always ready to perform offices of humanity; but when he was provoked (and very small

9. Richard Savage (1697–1743) was a close friend of Johnson, and his is the fullest and most intimate of all the *Lives;* originally composed and published in 1744.

offences were sufficient to provoke him), he would prosecute his revenge with the utmost acrimony till his passion had subsided.

His friendship was therefore of little value; for though he was zealous in the support or vindication of those whom he loved, yet it was always dangerous to trust him, because he considered himself as discharged by the first quarrel from all ties of honour or gratitude, and would betray those secrets which in the warmth of confidence had been imparted to him. This practice drew upon him an universal accusation of ingratitude: nor can it be denied that he was very ready to set himself free from the load of an obligation; for he could not bear to conceive himself in a state of dependence, his pride being equally powerful with his other passions, and appearing in the form of insolence at one time, and of vanity at another. Vanity, the most innocent species of pride, was most frequently predominant: he could not easily leave off when he had once begun to mention himself or his works; nor ever read his verses without stealing his eyes from the page, to discover in the faces of his audience how they were affected with any favourite passage.

. . .

For his life, or for his writings, none, who candidly consider his fortune, will think an apology either necessary or difficult. If he was not always sufficiently instructed in his subject, his knowledge was at least greater than could have been attained by others in the same state. If his works were sometimes unfinished, accuracy cannot reasonably be exacted from a man oppressed with want, which he has no hope of relieving but by a speedy publication. The insolence and resentment of which he is accused were not easily to be avoided by a great mind, irritated by perpetual hardships, and constrained hourly to return the spurns of contempt, and repress the insolence of prosperity; and vanity surely may be readily pardoned in him to whom life afforded no other comforts than barren praises, and the consciousness of deserving them.

Those are no proper judges of his conduct who have slumbered away their time on the down of plenty; nor will any wise man easily presume to say, 'Had I been in Savage's condition, I should have lived or written better than Savage.'

[Dryden and Pope [10]]

Integrity of understanding and nicety of discernment were not allotted in a less proportion to Dryden than to Pope. The rectitude of Dryden's mind was sufficiently shown by the dismission of his poetical prejudices, and the rejection of unnatural thoughts and rugged numbers.[11] But Dryden never desired to apply all the judgment that he had. He wrote, and professed to write, merely for the people; and when he pleased others, he contented himself. He spent no time in struggles to rouse latent powers; he never attempted to make that better which was already good, nor often to mend what he must have known to be faulty. He wrote, as he tells us, with very little consideration; when

10. This method of comparison is to be seen in Dryden's discussion of Shakespeare and Jonson or Horace and Juvenal; another example, Pope's comparison of Homer and Virgil, is given below.

11. Harsh versification.

occasion or necessity called upon him, he poured out what the present moment happened to supply, and, when once it had passed the press, ejected it from his mind; for when he had no pecuniary interest, he had no further solicitude.

Pope was not content to satisfy; he desired to excel, and therefore always endeavoured to do his best: he did not court the candour, but dared the judgment of his reader, and, expecting no indulgence from others, he showed none to himself. He examined lines and words with minute and punctilious observation, and retouched every part with indefatigable diligence, till he had left nothing to be forgiven.

For this reason he kept his pieces very long in his hands, while he considered and reconsidered them. The only poems which can be supposed to have been written with such regard to the times as might hasten their publication were the two satires of *Thirty-eight;* [12] of which Dodsley [13] told me that they were brought to him by the author, that they might be fairly copied. 'Almost every line,' he said, 'was then written twice over; I gave him a clean transcript, which he sent some time afterwards to me for the press, with almost every line written twice over a second time.'

His declaration that his care for his works ceased at their publication was not strictly true. His parental attention never abandoned them; what he found amiss in the first edition, he silently corrected in those that followed. He appears to have revised the Iliad, and freed it from some of its imperfections; and the *Essay on Criticism* received many improvements after its first appearance. It will seldom be found that he altered without adding clearness, elegance, or vigour. Pope had perhaps the judgment of Dryden; but Dryden certainly wanted the diligence of Pope.

In acquired knowledge, the superiority must be allowed to Dryden, whose education was more scholastic, and who before he became an author had been allowed more time for study, with better means of information. His mind has a larger range, and he collects his images and illustrations from a more extensive circumference of science. Dryden knew more of man in his general nature, and Pope in his local manners. The notions of Dryden were formed by comprehensive speculation, and those of Pope by minute attention. There is more dignity in the knowledge of Dryden, and more certainty in that of Pope.

Poetry was not the sole praise of either; for both excelled likewise in prose; but Pope did not borrow his prose from his predecessor. The style of Dryden is capricious and varied; that of Pope is cautious and uniform. Dryden observes the motions of his own mind; Pope constrains his mind to his own rules of composition. Dryden is sometimes vehement and rapid; Pope is always smooth, uniform, and gentle. Dryden's page is a natural field, rising into inequalities, and diversified by the varied exuberance of abundant vegetation; Pope's is a velvet lawn, shaven by the scythe, and levelled by the roller.

Of genius, that power which constitutes a poet; that quality without which judgment is cold, and knowledge is inert; that energy which collects, combines, amplifies, and animates; the superiority must, with some hesitation, be

12. Later entitled the *Epilogue to the Satires.*
13. Robert Dodsley (1703–64), the publisher.

allowed to Dryden. It is not to be inferred that of this poetical vigour Pope had only a little, because Dryden had more; for every other writer since Milton must give place to Pope; and even of Dryden it must be said, that, if he has brighter paragraphs, he has not better poems. Dryden's performances were always hasty, either excited by some external occasion, or extorted by domestic necessity; he composed without consideration, and published without correction. What his mind could supply at call, or gather in one excursion, was all that he sought, and all that he gave. The dilatory caution of Pope enabled him to condense his sentiments, to multiply his images, and to accumulate all that study might produce or chance might supply. If the flights of Dryden therefore are higher, Pope continues longer on the wing. If of Dryden's fire the blaze is brighter, of Pope's the heat is more regular and constant. Dryden often surpasses expectation, and Pope never falls below it. Dryden is read with frequent astonishment, and Pope with perpetual delight.

This parallel will, I hope, when it is well considered, be found just; and if the reader should suspect me, as I suspect myself, of some partial fondness for the memory of Dryden, let him not too hastily condemn me; for meditation and inquiry may, perhaps, show him the reasonableness of my determination.

1779–81

Glossary

A Commentary on Selected Literary and Historical Terms

Airs (1) Songs, or tunes in general. (2) The songs for solo voice with lute accompaniment, as opposed to the polyphonic madrigals (*q.v.*) of the late 16th and early 17th centuries. Airs were strophic, and the successive strophes, or stanzas, of a poem were set to the same melody.

Alchemy The predecessor of chemistry, based upon classical and medieval mythological notions of the structure of matter; it was a study that nevertheless produced a great deal of practical chemical knowledge. Believing in the ancient notion of the relative nobility of metals—for example, from gold down to "baser" substances like lead—alchemists sought to discover a mysterious *philosopher's* (i.e. "scientist's") *stone* enabling them to perform transmutations of baser metals into gold. Since it thus constituted reversing a natural order, it could be thought of as theologically subversive. Alchemists themselves were by way of being practitioners of a hermetic (*q.v.*) religion, and transmuting metals was by no means their sole aim. Alchemical theory employed what would be today regarded as poetic concepts: e.g. sexual combination for chemical compounding, where today one might think of valence or charge. During the 17th century, when chemistry evolved as a science, alchemical lore and language, alluded to in poetry, became part of the body of myth, like Ptolemaic astronomy and the astrological theory it supported.

Allegory Literally, "other reading"; originally a way of interpreting a narrative or other text in order to extract a more general, or a less literal, meaning from it, e.g. reading Homer's *Odyssey* as the universal voyage of human life—with Odysseus standing for all men–which must be made toward a final goal. In the Middle Ages allegory came to be associated with ways of reading the Bible, particularly the Old Testament in relation to the New. In addition, stories came to be written with the intention of being interpreted symbolically; thus e.g. the *Psychomachia* or "battle for the soul" of Prudentius (b. 348 A.D.) figured the virtues and vices as contending soldiers in a battle (see *Personification*). There is allegorical lyric poetry and allegorical drama as well as allegorical narrative. In works such as Spenser's *The Faerie Queene* and Bunyan's *Pilgrim's Progress* allegory becomes a dominant literary form. See also *Dream Vision; Figure; Type, Typology.*

Alliteration A repeated initial consonant in successive words. In Old English verse, any vowel alliterates with any other, and alliteration is not an unusual or expressive phenomenon but a regularly recurring structural feature of the verse, occurring on the first and third, and often on the first, second, and third, primary-stressed syllables of the four-stressed line. Thus, from "The Seafarer":

> hréran mid hóndum hrímcælde sǽ
> ("to stir with his hand the rime-cold sea")

In later English verse tradition, alliteration becomes expressive in a variety of ways. Spenser uses it decoratively, or to link adjective and noun, verb and object, as in the line: "Much daunted with that dint, her sense was dazed." In the 18th and 19th centuries it becomes even less systematic and more "musical."

Amplificatio, Amplifying The rhetorical enlargement of a statement or dilation of an argument, especially used in tragedy or epic (*q.v.*) poetry or in mock-heroic (*q.v.*). Language and stylistic ornament are deployed so as to increase the importance of a subject or to raise the level of its treatment.

Assonance A repeated vowel sound, a part-rhyme, which has great expressive effect when used internally (within lines), e.g. "An old, mad, blind, despised and dying king,—" (Shelley, "Sonnet: England in 1819").

Astronomy and Astrology Astrology may be regarded as an earlier phase or state of the science of astronomy—with an added normative provision in the notion that the *apparent* positions of the heavenly bodies, when viewed from a central earth about which all were thought to move, determined the shape of human life. (See *Zodiac.*) The geocentric astronomy of Ptolemy, wrong as it was about the relation between what was seen by an observer on earth and what caused him to see what he saw, nevertheless enabled men to predict with some accuracy events such as eclipses. In the microcosmic-macrocosmic world-view of the Middle Ages and the Renaissance, in which perspective the microcosm, or little world of man, constituted a miniature version of the whole cosmos, the relations between patterns discernible in the heavens and those of the four elements (*q.v.*), or the humors of the human constitution (*q.v.*), came to have great meaning. Specifically, the stars (meaning sun, moon, planets, fixed stars) were thought to radiate non-material substances called influences (literally, "in flowings") that beamed down to earth and affected human lives. Although the new astronomy of Copernicus, Kepler, and Galileo helped to destroy the conceptual basis for the belief in stellar influence, it is improper to think of a 16th- or 17th-century intellectual (and far less, a medieval man of letters and learning) as being superstitious in his use of astrological lore that was losing its centrality only with acceptance of the new ideas.

Aubade The French form of the Provençal *alba* ("dawn"), the morning song complementary to the evening *serenade;* it took its name from the word *alba* in the refrain (e.g. that of a famous anonymous poem, *L'alba, l'alba, oc l'alba, tan tost ve* ("the dawn, the dawn, o the dawn, it comes too soon"). In English such a song as Shakespeare's "Hark, hark, the lark / At heaven's gate sings" (from *Cymbeline*) exemplifies this tradition.

Aureate Literally, "golden"; used of the poetic and sometimes the prose language of 14th- and 15th-century England and Scotland; an idiom highly wrought and specializing in vernacular coinages from Latin.

Baroque (1) Originally (and still), an oddly shaped rather than a spherical pearl, and hence something twisted, contorted, involuted. (2) By a complicated analogy, a term designating stylistic periods in art, music, and literature during the 16th and 17th centuries in Europe. The analogies among the arts are frequently strained, and the stylistic periods by no means completely coincide. But the relation between the poetry of Richard Crashaw in English and Latin, and the sculpture and architecture of Gianlorenzo Bernini (1598–1680), is frequently taken to typify the spirit of the baroque. (See Wylie Sypher, *Four Stages of Renaissance Style,* 1955.)

Balade, Ballade The dominant lyric form in French poetry of the 14th and 15th centuries; a strict form consisting of three stanzas of eight lines each, with an *envoi* (*q.v.*), or four-line conclusion, addressing either a person of importance or a personification. Each stanza, including the *envoi,* ends in a refrain.

Ballad Meter Or *common meter;* four-lined stanzas, rhyming *abab,* the first and third lines in iambic tetrameter (four beats), and the second and fourth lines in iambic trimeter (three beats). See *Meter.*

Blazon, Blason (*Fr.*) A poetic genre cataloguing the parts or attributes of an object in order to praise it (or, in its satirical form, to condemn it). The first type, most influential chiefly on English Renaissance poetry, had its origin in a poem by Clément Marot in 1536 in praise of a beautiful breast. The English verb, *to blazon,* thus came to mean to catalogue poetically.

Bob and Wheel The bob (usually consisting of a two-syllable line) and the wheel (a brief set of short lines) are used either singly or together as a kind of *envoi* (*q.v.*) or comment on the action of the stanza preceding them. See *Sir Gawain and the Green Knight* for a prime example.

Calvin, Calvinist John Calvin (1509–64), French organizer of the strict religious discipline of Geneva (Switzerland), and author of its *Institutes* (1st ed., 1536). Calvin's teachings include among other things, the doctrine of Scripture as the sole rule of faith, the denial of free will in fallen man, and God's absolute predestination of every man, before his creation, to salvation or to damnation. There are Calvinist elements in the Thirty-Nine Articles (1563) of the Church of England, but the English (as opposed to the Scottish) tradition modified the rigor of the doctrine; Milton passed through a phase of strict Calvinism into greater independence and a rejection of absolute predestination.

Carol, Carole Originally (apparently) a song sung to an accompaniment of dance, and often set out in ballad meter and uniform stanzas of which the leader probably sang the verse and the dancers a refrain; later, generally, a song of religious joy, usually rapid in pace.

Carpe Diem Literally, "seize the day"; from Horace's Ode I.xi, which ends, *Dum loquimur, fugerit invida / aetas: carpe diem, quam minimum credula postero* ("Even while we're talking, envious Time runs by: seize the day, putting a minimum of trust in tomorrow"). This became a standard theme of Renaissance erotic verse, as in Robert Herrick's "Gather ye rosebuds while ye may."

Cavalier Designating the supporters of Charles I and of the Anglican church establishment, in opposition to the Puritans, or Roundheads, during the English Civil War. In a literary context, the lyric poetry of some of these so-named soldier-lover-poets (e.g. Thomas Carew, Richard Lovelace) is implied with its elegant wit (*q.v.*) and grace. (See *Civil War.*)

Chanson d'aventure A French poetic form describing a conversation about love or between lovers, and represented as overheard by the poet.

Civil War The struggle between Charles I and his Parliament came to a head in 1641, when the King tried forcibly to arrest five dissident members of Parliament. He failed, and in April 1642 raised his standard at Northampton, intending to advance on London. For some time there was a military deadlock, but in January 1644 the Parliamentary forces, allied with the Scots, defeated the King at Marston Moor. The Parliament men now controlled the North, but not until they instituted major military reforms did they overcome the King decisively at Naseby in June 1645. Charles became the captive of Parliament in January 1647 and was executed two years later. In 1653 Oliver Cromwell expelled the "Rump" of the Long Parliament (*q.v.*), which had survived since 1640, and became Lord Protector.

The terms "Cavalier" and "Roundhead," implying respectively aristocratic dash and middle-class puritanism, are not wholly misleading as descriptive of the Royalist and Parliamentary sides in the war; but the fact of new money and religious fervor on the winning side was not the whole story. The split between "Presbyterian" and "Independent" in the Parliament faction was partly religious, partly a division between the affluent and the enthusiastic; and with the victory of the "monied" interest the Revolution itself became conservative. But the execution of the King was an event that for a century or more resonated throughout the course of English history, and, as Marvell understood (see his "Horation Ode"), ended a whole phase of civilization.

Complaint Short poetic monologue, expressing the poet's sorrow at unrequited love or other pains and ending with a request for relief from them.

Complexion See *Temperaments.*

Conceit From the Italian *concetto,* "concept" or "idea"; used in Renaissance poetry to mean a precise and detailed comparison of something more remote or abstract with something more present or concrete, and often detailed through a chain of metaphors or similes (see *Rhetoric*). In Petrarchan (*q.v.*) poetry, certain conceits became conventionalized and were used again and again in various versions. The connection between the Lady's eyes and the Sun, so typical of these, was based on the proportion *her gaze : love's life and day :: sun's shining: world's life and daylight.* Conceits were closely linked to emblems (*q.v.*), to the degree that the verbal connection between the emblem picture and its *significatio,* or meaning, was detailed in an interpretive conceit. See also *Personification.*

Contemptus Mundi Contempt for the world, i.e. rejection of temporal and transitory pleasures and values in favor of the spiritual and eternal.

Contraries See *Qualities.*

Courtly Love Modern scholarship has coined this name for a set of conventions around which medieval love-poetry was written. It was essentially chivalric and a product of 12th-century France, especially of the troubadours. This poetry involves an idealization of the beloved woman, whose love, like all love, refines and ennobles the lover so that the union of their minds and/or bodies—a union that ought not to be apparent to others—allows them to attain excellence of character.

Dance of Death Poem accompanied by illustrations on the inevitability and universality of death, which is shown seizing men and women of all ranks and occupations, one after the other.

Decorum Propriety of discourse; what is becoming in action, character, and style; the avoidance of impossibilities and incongruities in action, style, and character: "the good grace of everything after his kind" and the "great masterpiece to observe." More formally, a neoclassical doctrine maintaining that literary style—grand, or high, middle, and low—be appropriate to the subject, occasion, and genre. Thus Milton, in *Paradise Lost* (I.13–14), invokes his "adventurous song, / That with no middle flight intends to soar. . . ." See also *Rhetoric*.

Digressio Interpolated story or description in a poem or oration, introduced for ornamentation or some structural purpose.

Dissenters In England, members of Protestant churches and sects that do not conform to the doctrines of the established Church of England; from the 16th century on, this would include Baptists, Puritans of various sorts within the Anglican Church, Presbyterians, Congregationalists, and (in the 18th century) Methodists. Another term, more current in the 19th century, is *Nonconformist.*

Dream Vision, Dream Allegory A popular medieval poetic form. Its fictional time is usually Spring; as the poet falls alseep in some pleasant place—a wood or garden—to the music of a stream and the song of birds, he dreams of "real" people or personified abstractions, who illuminate for him the nature of some aspect of knowledge, mode of behavior, or social or political question. See also *Allegory.*

Elegy Originally, in Greek and Latin poetry, a poem composed not in the hexameter lines of epic (*q.v.*) and, later, of pastoral, but in the elegiac couplets consisting of one hexameter line followed by a pentameter. Elegiac poetry was amatory, epigrammatic. By the end of the 16th century, English poets were using heroic couplets (*q.v.*), to stand for both hexameters and elegiacs; and an elegiac poem was any serious meditative piece. Perhaps because of the tradition of the pastoral elegy (*q.v.*), the general term "elegy" came to be reserved, in modern terminology, for an elaborate and formal lament, longer than a *dirge* or *threnody,* for a dead person. By extension, "elegiac" has come to mean, in general speech, broodingly sad.

Elements In ancient and medieval science, the four basic substances of which all matter was composed: earth, water, air, fire—in order of density and heaviness. They are often pictured in that order in diagrams of the universe. All four elements, being material, are below the sphere of the moon (above, there is a fifth: the quintessence). The elements are formed of combinations of the

Qualities (*q.v.*) or Contraries: the union of hot and dry makes fire; of hot and moist, air; of cold and moist, water; of cold and dry, earth.

Emblem A simple allegorical picture, or *impresa,* labeled with a motto to show its significance, and usually accompanied by a poetic description that connects the picture or "device" with the meaning, frequently by means of elaborate conceits (*q.v.*), sometimes with more obvious moralizing. Many Renaissance paintings are emblems, without the text. The first Renaissance emblem book was that of the Venetian lawyer Andrea Alciati, in 1531; for the next century and one-half, the pictures and verses were copied, translated, expanded upon, added to, and adapted in French, Dutch, Spanish, German, and Italian as well as his original Latin. Famous English books of emblems were those of Geoffrey Whitney (1586), Henry Peacham (*Minerva Brittana,* or *A Garden of Heroical Devices,* 1612), George Wither (1635), and Francis Quarles (1635). Based originally on classical mythography, an interest in ancient coins and statuary, as well as "hieroglyphics" in all ancient art, emblem traditions generally divided, in the 17th century, into "Jesuitical" types (involving precise and intense images such as tears, wings, hearts, and classical Cupids signifying not *amor,* but *caritas*), and more pragmatic Protestant emblems (particularly in the Dutch tradition), which tend toward genre scenes of everyday life illustrating proverbs in the text. In the Renaissance, pictures were to be *read* and understood, like texts; and this kind of reading of hieroglyphics extends, in a writer like Sir Thomas Browne, to all of creation:

> The world's a book in folio, printed all
> With God's great works in letters capital:
> Each creature is a page, and each effect
> A fair character, void of all defect.

These lines of Joshua Sylvester are a commonplace. See also *Conceit; Symbolism;* and Figs. 16–21 in illustrations for the Renaissance section of this Anthology.

Enjambment The "straddling" of a clause or sentence across two lines of verse, as opposed to closed, or end-stopped, lines. Thus, in the opening lines of Shakespeare's *Twelfth Night:*

> If music be the food of love, play on!
> Give me excess of it, that, surfeiting
> The appetite may sicken and so die . . .

the first line is stopped, the second enjambed. When enjambment becomes strong or violent, it may have an ironic or comic effect.

The Enlightenment A term used very generally, to refer to the late 17th and the 18th century in Europe, a period characterized by a programmatic rationalism—i.e. a belief in the ability of human reason to understand the world and thereby to transform whatever in it needed transforming; an age in which ideas of science and progress accompanied the rise of new philosophies of the relation of man to the state, an age which saw many of its hopes for human betterment fulfilled in the French Revolution.

Envoi, Envoy Short concluding stanza found in certain French poetic forms and their English imitations, e.g. the *ballade* (*q.v.*). It serves as a dedicatory postscript, and a summing up of the poem of which it repeats the refrain.

Epic Or, *heroic poetry;* originally, oral narrative delivered in a style different from that of normal discourse by reason of verse, music, and heightened diction, and concerning the great deeds of a central heroic figure, or group of figures, usually having to do with a crisis in the history of a race or culture. Its setting lies in this earlier "heroic" period, and it will often have been written down only after a long period of oral transmission. The Greek *Iliad* and *Odyssey* and the Old English *Beowulf* are examples of this, in their narration mixing details from both the heroic period described and the actual time of their own composition and narration. What is called *secondary* or *literary* epic is a long, ambitious poem, composed by a single poet on the model of the older, primary forms, and of necessity being more allusive and figurative than its predecessors. Homer's poems lead to Virgil's *Aeneid,* which leads to Milton's *Paradise Lost,* in a chain of literary dependency. Spenser's *Faerie Queene* might be called *romantic epic* of the secondary sort, and Dante's *Divine Comedy* might also be assimilated to post-Virgilian epic tradition.

Epic Simile An extended comparison, in Homeric and subsequently in Virgilian and later epic poetry, between an event in the story (the *fable*) and something in the experience of the epic audience, to the effect of making the fabulous comprehensible in terms of the familiar. From the Renaissance on, additional complications have emerged from the fact that what is the familiar for the classical audience becomes, because of historical change, itself fabled (usually, pastoral) for the modern audience. Epic similes compare the fabled with the familiar usually with respect to one property or element; thus, in the *Odyssey,* when the stalwart forward motion of a ship in high winds is described, the simile goes:

And as amids a fair field four brave horse
Before a chariot, stung into their course
With fervent lashes of the smarting scourge
That all their fire blows high, and makes them rise
To utmost speed the measure of their ground:
So bore the ship aloft her fiery bound
About whom rushed the billows, black and vast
In which the sea-roars burst . . .
(*Chapman translation*)

Notice the formal order of presentation: "even as . . .": *the familiar event, often described in detail;* "just so . . .": *the fabled one.*

Epicureanism A system of philosophy founded by the Greek Epicurus (342–270 B.C.), who taught that the five senses are the sole source of ideas and sole criterion of truth, and that the goal of human life is pleasure (i.e. hedonism), though this can be achieved only by practicing moderation. Later the term came to connote bestial self-indulgence, which Epicurus had clearly rejected.

Exclamatio Rhetorical figure representing a cry of admiration or grief.

Exemplum A short narrative used to illustrate a moral point in didactic literature (especially sermons) or in historical writing. Its function is to recommend or dissuade from a particular course of conduct.

Fabliau A short story in verse, comic in character, its subject matter often indecent, and the joke hinging on sex or excretion. The plot usually involves a witty turn or practical joke, the motive of which is love or revenge. See The Miller's Tale of Chaucer.

Fathers of the Church The earliest Christian theologians and ecclesiastical writers (also referred to as "patristic"), flourishing from the late 1st century through the 8th, composing severally in Greek or Latin. Well-known "Fathers" are St. Augustine, St. Jerome, Tertullian.

Feudal System The system of land tenure and political allegiance characteristic of Europe during the Middle Ages. The king, as owner of all land, gives portions of it to his vassals, by whom it can be passed on to heirs, in return for their pledge of loyalty and of specified military service. These nobles divide their land among their followers, the subdivision continuing until it reaches the serfs, who cultivate the land but must hand over most of their produce to the lord.

Figurative Language In a general sense, any shift away from a literal meaning of words, brought about by the use of tropes (*q.v.*) or other rhetorical devices. See *Rhetoric.*

Figure As defined by Erich Auerbach in his essay "Figura," a mode of interpretation establishing a connection between two events or persons, the first of which signifies both itself and the second, while the second encompasses or fulfills the first—e.g. the Eucharist, which is the "figure" of Christ. See *Allegory.*

Free Verse, Vers Libre Generally, any English verse form whose lines are measured neither by the number of 1) stressed syllables (see *Meter* §3, accentual verse), 2) alternations of stressed and unstressed syllables (§4, accentual-syllabic verse), nor syllables alone (§2, syllabic verse). The earliest English free verse —that of Christopher Smart in *Jubilate Agno* (18th century)—imitates the prosody of Hebrew poetry (reflected also in the translation of the English Bible), in maintaining unmeasured units marked by syntactic parallelism. While many free-verse traditions (e.g. that of Walt Whitman) remain close to the impulses of this biblical poetry, yet others, in the 20th century, have developed new *ad hoc* patternings of their own. *Vers libre* usually refers to the experimental, frequently very short unmeasured lines favored by poets of the World War I period, although the term, rather than the form, was adopted from French poetry of the 19th century.

Gothic Term (originally pejorative, as alluding to the Teutonic barbarians) designating the architectural style of the Middle Ages. The revival of interest in medieval architecture in the later 18th century produced not only pseudo-Gothic castles like Horace Walpole's "Strawberry Hill", and more modest artificial ruins on modern estates, but also a vogue for atmospheric prose romances set in medieval surroundings and involving improbable terrors, and known as Gothic novels. The taste for the Gothic, arising during the Age of Sensibility (*q.v.*), is another reflection of a reaction against earlier 18th-century neoclassicism (*q.v*).

Hermetic, Hermeticism, Hermetist Terms referring to a synthesis of Neoplatonic and other occult philosophies, founded on a collection of writings attributed to Hermes Trismegistus ("Thrice-greatest Hermes"—a name given the Egyptian god Thoth), but which in fact date from the 2nd and 3rd centuries A.D. An important doctrine was that of correspondences between earthly and heavenly things. By studying these correspondences, a man might "walk to the sky" (in the words of Henry Vaughan) in his lifetime. Hermetic tradition favored *esoteric* or forbidden knowledge, over what could be more publicly avowed.

Heroic Couplet In English prosody, a pair of rhyming, iambic pentameter lines, used at first for closure—as at the end of the Shakespearean sonnet (*q.v.*)—or to terminate a scene in blank-verse drama; later adapted to correspond in English poetry to the elegiac couplet of classical verse as well as to the heroic, unrhymed, Greek and Latin hexameter. Octosyllabic couplets, with four stresses (eight syllables) to the line, are a minor, shorter, jumpier form, used satirically unless in implicit allusion to the form of Milton's "Il Penseroso," in which they develop great lyrical power. (See *Meter.*)

Humors The combinations, in men and women (the *microcosm*) of the qualities (*q.v.*), or contraries. In primitive physiology, the four principal bodily fluids in their combinations produce the temperaments (*q.v.*) or "complexions" These "humors," with their properties and effects—at least in the Middle Ages—are, respectively: Blood (hot and moist)—cheerfulness, warmth of feeling; Choler (hot and dry)—a quick, angry temper; Phlegm (cold and moist)—dull sluggishness; Melancholy (cold and dry)—fretful depression. The Renaissance introduced the concept of "artificial" humors—e.g. scholars' and artists' melancholy, creative brooding. The humors, the temperaments, and the four elements (*q.v.*) of the macrocosm, or universe, were all looked upon as interrelated. See *Renaissance Psychology.*

Irony Generally, a mode of saying one thing to mean another. *Sarcasm,* in which one means exactly the opposite of what one says, is the easiest and cheapest form; thus, e.g. "Yeah, it's a *nice day!*" when one means that it's a miserable one. But serious literature produces ironies of a much more complex and revealing sort. *Dramatic irony* occurs when a character in a play or story asserts something whose meaning the audience or reader knows will change in time. Thus, in Genesis when Abraham assures his son Isaac (whom he is about to sacrifice) that "God will provide his own lamb," the statement is lighted with dramatic irony when a sacrificial ram is actually provided at the last minute to save Isaac. Or, in the case of Sophocles' *Oedipus,* when almost everything the protagonist says about the predicament of his city is hideously ironic in view of the fact (which he does not know) that he is responsible therefor. The ironies generated by the acknowledged use of non-literal language (see *Rhetoric*) and fictions in drama, song, and narrative are at the core of imaginative literature.

Judgment In Catholic doctrine, God's retributive judgment, which decides the fate of rational creatures according to their merits and faults. Particular judgment is the decision about the eternal destiny of each soul made immediately after death; General (Last) Judgment is at the Second Coming of Christ as God and Man, when all men will be judged again in the sight of all the world. See Fig. 50 in illustrations for the Medieval section of this anthology.

Kenning An Old Norse form designating, strictly, a condensed simile or metaphor of the kind frequently used in Old Germanic poetry; a figurative circumlocution for a thing not actually named—e.g. "swan's path" for sea; "world-candle" or "sky-candle" for sun. More loosely, often used to mean also a metaphorical compound word or phrase such as "ring-necked" or "foamy-necked" for a ship, these being descriptive rather than figurative in character.

Lancastrians See *Wars of the Roses.*

Locus Amoenus Literally, "pleasant place"; a garden, either Paradise, the most perfect of all gardens, or its pagan equivalent, or the later literary garden that was a figure (*q.v.*) of Paradise. See *Topos.*

Long Parliament The Parliament summoned by Charles I on November 3, 1640; the last remnant, not dissolved until 1660, opposed the King and brought about his downfall and execution. See *Civil War.*

Macaronic Verse in which two languages are mingled, usually for burlesque purposes.

Machiavelli, Niccolò Italian diplomat, historian, and political theorist (1469–1527), whose chief work, *Il Principe* (*The Prince,* 1513), based in part on the career of Cesare Borgia, outlines a pragmatic rule of conduct for a ruler; thus, politics should have nothing to do with morality; the prince should be an exponent of ruthless power in behalf of his people. In England his theories were put into practice by Thomas Cromwell in the reign of Henry VIII; his writings, however, were not translated until the 17th century, and his image in England, based on rumor and the reports of his adversaries, fostered a myth of the evil "Machiavel" as he appears in Marlowe (*Titus Andronicus*) and Shakespeare (*Richard III*).

Madrigal Polyphonic setting of a poem, in the 16th and 17th centuries, for several voice parts, unaccompanied or with instruments. Because of the contrapuntal texture, the words were frequently obscured for a listener, though not for the performers.

Meter Verse may be made to differ from prose and from ordinary speech in a number of ways, and in various languages these ways may be very different. Broadly speaking, lines of verse may be marked out by the following regularities of pattern:

1. *Quantitative Verse,* used in ancient Greek poetry and adopted by the Romans, used a fixed number of what were almost musical measures, called *feet;* they were built up of long and short syllables (like half- and quarter-notes in music), which depended on the vowel and consonants in them. *Stress accent* (the *word* stress which, when accompanied by vowel reduction, distinguishes the English noun "*con*tent" from the adjective "con*tent*") did not exist in ancient Greek, and played no part in the rhythm of the poetic line. Thus, the first line of the *Odyssey: Andra moi ennepe mousa, polytropon hos mala polla* ("Sing me, O muse, of that man of many resources who, after great hardship . . .") is composed in *dactyls* of one long syllable followed by two shorts (but, as in musical rhythm, replaceable by two longs, a *spondee*).

With six dactyls to a line, the resulting meter is called *dactylic hexameter* (*hexameter,* for short), the standard form for epic poetry. Other kinds of foot or measure were: the *anapest* (◡ ◡ –); the *iamb* (◡ –); the *trochee* (– ◡); and a host of complex patterns used in lyric poetry. Because of substitutions, however, the number of syllables in a classical line was not fixed, only the number of measures.

2. *Syllabic Verse,* used in French, Japanese, and many other languages, and in English poetry of the mid-20th century, measures only the *number* of syllables per line with no regard to considerations of *quantity* or *stress.* Because of the prominence of stress in the English language, two lines of the same purely syllabic length may not necessarily sound at all as though they were in the same meter, e.g.:

> These two incommensurably sounding
> Lines are both written with ten syllables.

3. *Accentual Verse,* used in early Germanic poetry, and thus in Old English poetry, depended upon the number of strong *stress accents* per line. These accents were four in number, with no fixed number of unstressed. Folk poetry and nursery rhymes often preserve this accentual verse, e.g.:

> Sing, sing, what shall I sing?
> The cat's run away with the pudding-bag string

The first line has six syllables, the second, eleven, but they sound more alike (and not merely by reason of their rhyme) than the two syllabic lines quoted above.

4. *Accentual-Syllabic Verse,* the traditional meter of English poetry from Chaucer on, depends upon both numbered *stresses* and numbered *syllables,* a standard form consisting of ten syllables alternately stressed and unstressed, and having five stresses; thus it may be said to consist of five syllable pairs.

For complex historical reasons, accentual-syllabic groups of stressed and unstressed syllables came to be known by the names used for Greek and Latin feet—which can be very confusing. The analogy was made between *long* syllables in the classical languages, and *stressed* syllables in English. Thus, the pair of syllables in the adjective "con*tent*" is called an *iamb,* and in the noun "*con*tent," a *trochee;* the word "classical" is a *dactyll,* and the phrase "of the best," an *anapest.* When English poetry is being discussed, these terms are always used in their adapted, accentual-syllabic meanings, and hence the ten-syllable line mentioned earlier is called "iambic pentameter" in English. The phrase "high-tide" would be a *spondee* (as would, in general, two monosyllables comprising a proper name, e.g. "John Smith"); whereas compound nouns like "highway" would be *trochaic.* In this adaptation of classical nomenclature, the terms *dimeter, trimeter, tetrameter, pentameter, hexameter* refer not to the number of quantitative feet but to the number of syllable-groups (pairs or triplets, from one to six) composing the line. Iambic pentameter and tetrameter lines are frequently also called *decasyllabic* and *octosyllabic* respectively.

5. *Versification.* In verse, lines may be arranged in patterns called *stichic*

or *strophic,* that is, the same linear form (say, iambic pentameter) repeated without grouping by rhyme or interlarded lines of another form, or varied in just such a way into *stanzas* or *strophes* ("turns"). Unrhymed iambic pentameter, called *blank verse,* is the English stichic form that Milton thought most similar to classic hexameter or *heroic* verse. But in the Augustan period iambic pentameter rhymed pairs, called heroic couplets (*q.v.*), came to stand for this ancient form as well as for the classical elegiac verse (*q.v.*). Taking couplets as the simplest strophic unit, we may proceed to *tercets* (groups of three lines) and to *quatrains* (groups of four), rhymed *abab* or *abcb,* and with equal or unequal line lengths. Other stanzaic forms: *ottava rima,* an eight-line, iambic pentameter stanza, rhyming *abababcc; Spenserian stanza,* rhyming *ababbcbcc,* all pentameter save for the last line, an iambic hexameter, or *alexandrine.* There have been adaptations in English (by Shelley, notably, and without rhyme by T. S. Eliot) of the Italian *terza rima* used by Dante in *The Divine Comedy,* interlocking tercets rhyming *aba bcb cdc ded,* etc. More elaborate stanza forms developed in the texts of some Elizabethan songs and in connection with the ode (*q.v.*).

Microcosm Literally, "the small world"—man. See also *Astronomy and Astrology; Humors; Qualities.*

Mirror for Princes A treatise setting out the education necessary to make a ruler and the modes of mental, moral, and physical activity that befitted him.

Mock-heroic, Mock-epic The literary mode resulting when low or trivial subjects are treated in the high, artificial literary language of classical epic (*q.v.*) poetry. The point of the joke is usually to expose not the inadequacies of the style but those of the subject, although occasionally the style may be caricatured, and the joke made about decorum (*q.v.*) itself. Alexander Pope's *The Rape of the Lock* is a famous example.

Music of the Spheres The ancient fiction held that the celestial spheres made musical sounds, either by rubbing against the ether, or because an angel—the Christian replacement for the Intelligence which in Plato's *Timaeus* guided each one—sang while riding on his charge. The inaudibility of this music was ascribed by later Platonism (*q.v.*) to the imprisonment of the soul in the body, and by Christian writers, to man's fallen state. Frequent attempts were made to preserve some meaning for this beautiful idea: thus, Aristotle's conclusion that the continuous presence of such sounds would make them inaudible to habituated ears (a sophisticated prefiguration of the modern notion of background noise). And thus the belief of the Ptolemaic astronomy that at a certain point the ratios of the diameters of the spheres of the various heavenly bodies were "harmonious" in that they would generate the overtone series. Even Kepler, who demonstrated that the planetary orbits, let alone non-existent spheres, could not be circular, suggested that the ratios of the angular velocities of the planets would generate a series of melodies; he then proceeded to put them together contrapuntally. See *Astronomy and Astrology.*

Myth A primitive story explaining the origins of certain phenomena in the world and in human life, and usually embodying gods or other supernatural forces, heroes (men who are either part human and part divine, or are placed between an ordinary mortal and a divine being), men, and animals. Literature continues to incorporate myths long after the mythology (the system of stories containing them) ceases to be a matter of actual belief. Moreover, discarded beliefs of all sorts tend to become myths when they are remembered but no longer literally clung to, and are used in literature in a similar way. The classical mythology of the Greeks and Romans was apprehended in this literary, or interpreted, way, even in ancient times. The gods and heroes and their deeds came to be read as allegory (*q.v.*). During the Renaissance, *mythography*—the interpretation of myths in order to make them reveal a moral or historical significance (rather than merely remaining entertaining but insignificant stories)—was extremely important, both for literature and for painting and sculpture. In modern criticism, mythical or *archetypal* situations and personages have been interpreted as being central objects of the work of the imagination.

Neoclassicism (1) In general the term refers to Renaissance and post-Renaissance attempts to model enterprises in the various arts on Roman and Greek originals—or as much as was known of them. Thus, in the late Renaissance, the architectural innovations of Andrea Palladio may be called "neoclassic," as may Ben Jonson's relation, and Alexander Pope's as well, to the Roman poet Horace. The whole Augustan period in English literary history (1660–1740) was a deliberately neoclassical one.

(2) More specifically, neoclassicism refers to that period in the history of all European art spanning the very late 18th and early 19th century, which period may be seen as accompanying the fulfillment, and the termination, of the Enlightenment (*q.v.*). In England such neoclassic artists as Henry Fuseli, John Flaxman, George Romney, and even, in some measure, William Blake, are close to the origins of pictorial and literary Romanticism itself.

Neoplatonism See *Platonism.*

Nonconformist See *Dissenters.*

Octosyllabic Couplet See *Heroic Couplet; Meter.*

Ode A basic poetic form, originating in Greek antiquity. The *choral ode* was a public event, sung and danced, at a large ceremony, or as part of the tragic and comic drama. Often called *Pindaric ode,* after a great Greek poet, the form consisted of *triads* (groups of three sections each). These were units of song and dance, and had the form *aab*—that is, a *strophe* (or "turn"), an *antistrophe* (or "counter-turn"), and an *epode* (or "stand"), the first two being identical musically and metrically, the third different. In English poetry, the Pindaric ode form, only in its metrical aspects, became in the 17th century a mode for almost essayistic poetic comment, and was often used also as a kind of cantata libretto, in praise of music and poetry (the so-called *musical ode*). By the 18th century the ode became the form for a certain kind of personal, visionary poem, and it is this form that Wordsworth and Coleridge transmitted to Romantic tradition. A second English form, known as *Horatian ode,* was based on the lyric (not choral) poems of Horace, and is written in *aabb* quatrains, with the last two lines shorter than the first two by a pair of syllables or more.

Oral Formula A conventional, fossilized phrase common in poetry composed as it was recited, or composed to be recited, and repeated frequently in a single poem. It serves as either a means of slowing or even stopping the action momentarily, or of filling out a verse: e.g. "Beowulf, son of Ecgtheow," or "go or ride"—i.e. "whatever you do."

Paradox In logic, a self-contradictory statement, hence meaningless (or a situation producing one), with an indication that something is wrong with the language in which such a situation can occur, e.g. the famous paradox of Epimenedes the Cretan, who held that all Cretans are liars (and thus could be lying if—and only if—he wasn't), or that of Zeno, of the arrow in flight: since at any instant of time the point of the arrow can always be said to be at one precise point, therefore it is continually at rest at a continuous sequence of such points, and therefore never moves. In literature, however, particularly in the language of lyric poetry, paradox plays another role. From the beginnings of lyric poetry, paradox has been deemed necessary to express feelings and other aspects of human inner states, e.g. Sappho's invention of the Greek word *glykypikron* ("bittersweet") to describe love, or her assertion that she was freezing and burning at the same time. So too the Latin poet Catullus, in his famous couplet

> I'm in hate and I'm in love; why do I? you may ask.
> Well, I don't know, but I feel it, and I'm in agony.

may be declaring thereby that true love poetry must be illogical.

In Elizabethan poetry, paradoxes were frequently baldly laid out in the rhetorical form called *oxymoron* (see *Rhetoric*), as in "the victor-victim," or across a fairly mechanical sentence structure, as in "My feast of joy is but a dish of pain." In the highest poetic art, however, the seeming self-contradiction is removed when one realizes that either, or both, of the conflicting terms is to be taken figuratively, rather than literally. The apparent absurdity, or strangeness, thus gives rhetorical power to the utterance. Elaborate and sophisticated paradoxes, insisting on their own absurdity, typify the poetic idiom of the tradition of John Donne.

Pastoral A literary mode in which the lives of simple country people are celebrated, described, and used allegorically by sophisticated urban poets and writers. The *idylls* of Sicilian poet Theocritus (3rd century B.C.) were imitated and made more symbolic in Virgil's *eclogues;* shepherds in an Arcadian landscape stood for literary and political personages, and the Renaissance adapted these narrative and lyric pieces for moral and aesthetic discussion. Spenser's *Shepheardes Calendar* is an experimental collection of eclogues involving an array of forms and subjects. In subsequent literary tradition, the pastoral imagery of both Old and New Testaments (Psalms, Song of Songs, priest as *pastor* or shepherd of his flock, and so on) joins with the classical mode. Modern critics, William Empson in particular, have seen the continuation of pastoral tradition in other versions of the country-city confrontation, such as child-adult and criminal-businessman. See *Pastoral Elegy*.

Pastoral Elegy A form of lament for the death of a poet, originating in Greek bucolic tradition (Bion's lament for Adonis, a lament for Bion by a fellow poet, Theocritus' first idyll, Virgil's tenth eclogue) and continued in use by Renaissance poets as a public mode for the presentation of private, inner, and even coterie matters affecting poets and their lives, while conventionally treating questions of general human importance. At a death one is moved to ask, "Why this death? Why now?" and funeral elegy must always confront these questions, avoiding easy resignation as an answer. Pastoral elegy handled these questions with formal mythological apparatus, such as the Muses, who should have protected their dead poet, local spirits, and other presences appropriate to the circumstances of the life and death, and perhaps figures of more general mythological power. The end of such poems is the eternalization of the dead poet in a monument of myth, stronger than stone or bronze: Spenser's *Astrophel,* a lament for Sir Philip Sidney, concludes with an Ovidian change—the dead poet's harp, like Orpheus' lyre, becomes the constellation Lyra. Milton's *Lycidas* both exemplifies and transforms the convention. Later examples include Shelley's *Adonais* (for Keats), Arnold's *Thyrsis* (for Clough), and Swinburne's *Ave Atque Vale* (for Baudelaire).

Penance In Catholic doctrine, the moral virtue by which a sinner is disposed to hate his sin as an offense against God; and the sacrament, of which the outward signs are the acknowledgment of sin, self-presentation of the sinner to priest to confess his sins, the absolution pronounced by the priest, and the satisfaction (penance) imposed on the sinner by the priest and to be performed before the sinner is delivered from his guilt. See Figs. 32 and 52 in illustrations for the Medieval section of this Anthology.

Peroration Final part of an oration, reviewing and summarizing the argument, often in an impassioned form. (See also *Rhetoric.*)

Personification Treating a thing or, more properly, an abstract quality, as though it were a person. Thus, "Surely *goodness* and *mercy* shall follow me all the days of my life" tends to personify the italicized terms by reason of the metaphoric use of "follow me." On the other hand, a conventional, complete personification, like *Justice* (whom we recognize by her *attributes*—she is blindfolded, she has scales and a sword) might also be called an *allegorical figure* in her own right, and her attributes *symbols* (blindness = impartiality; scales = justly deciding; sword = power to mete out what is deserved). Often the term "personification" applies to momentary, or *ad hoc,* humanizations.

Petrarch, Petrarchan Francesco Petrarca (1304–74), the Italian founder of humanistic studies, with their revival of Greek and Latin literature, was influential in Renaissance England chiefly for his *Rime sparse,* the collection of love sonnets in praise of his muse, Laura. These poems, translated and adapted in England from the 1530's on, provided not only the sonnet (*q.v.*) form but also many devices of imagery widely used by English poets of the 16th and 17th centuries.

Physiognomics The "art to read the mind's complexion in the face." From ancient times to the Renaissance, it was believed possible to gauge a person's character precisely from his outward appearance and physical characteristics.

Platonism The legacy of Plato (429–347 B.C.) is virtually the history of philosophy. His *Timaeus* was an important source of later cosmology; his doctrine of ideas is central to Platonic tradition. His doctrine of love (especially in the *Symposium*) had enormous influence in the Renaissance, at which time its applicability was shifted to heterosexual love specifically. The *Republic* and the *Laws* underlie a vast amount of political thought, and the *Republic* contains also a philosophical attack on poetry (fiction) which defenders of the arts have always had to answer. Neoplatonism—a synthesis of Platonism, Pythagoreanism, and Aristotelianism—was dominant in the 3rd century A.D.; and the whole tradition was revived in the 15th and 16th centuries. The medieval Plato was Latinized, largely at second-hand; the revival of Greek learning in the 15th century led to another Neoplatonism: a synthesis of Platonism, the medieval Christian Aristotle, and Christian doctrine. Out of this came the doctrines of love we associate with some Renaissance poetry; a sophisticated version of older systems of allegory and symbol; and notions of the relation of spirit and matter reflected in Marvell and many other poets.

Prayer Book The Book of Common Prayer, containing the order of services in the Church of England. Based on translations from medieval service books, it first appeared in 1549, under the direction of Thomas Cranmer (1489–1556), Archbishop of Canterbury. It was much revised, partly to meet Puritan complaints, but in 1662 achieved the form it has since kept, with only slight alteration.

Purgatory According to Catholic doctrine, a place or condition of temporal punishment for those who die in the grace of God, but without having made full satisfaction for their transgressions. In Purgatory they are purified so as to be fit to come into God's presence.

Quadrivium The second division of the seven liberal arts, which together with the trivium (*q.v.*) comprised the full course of a medieval education and fitted a man to study theology, the crown of the arts and sciences. The quadrivium consisted of music, arithmetic, geometry, and astronomy.

Qualities Or **Contraries**; the properties of all material things, the various combinations of which were held to determine their nature. They were four in number, in two contrasting pairs: hot and cold; moist and dry. See *Elements; Humors; Temperaments.*

Recusant Literally, "refuser"; in the Elizabethan period, anyone who refused to join the Church of England—although now the term is commonly used to allude to "popish recusants," i.e. Roman Catholics, and "recusancy," to English writings of certain Catholics during the late 16th century.

Renaissance Psychology Poetic language, particularly that of lyric poetry, is always implicitly raising assumptions about inner states of people who have feelings and who wish to express them. In the Renaissance, several informal ways coexisted of talking about the relation which we now see as one of mind and body. From Aristotelian tradition the concept of three orders of soul was maintained: in ascending order these were the *vegetable* (the "life," immobile and inactive, of plants), the *animal* (accounting for the behavior of beasts), and the *rational* (the power of reason, often associated with language as well as thought, in men). On the other hand, *wit* (*q.v.*) meant intellect, and in Elizabethan language, the conflict of *wit* and *will* correspond roughly, but not precisely, to a modern opposition of reason and emotion. Physical, as well as psychological, human diversity was explained by the theory of the humors and temperaments (*qq.v.*). On the other hand, there were mysterious entities called *spirits* (associated with the Latin root, meaning "breath," and its application to alcoholic fluids: waters that "breathe" and "burn"). Spirits were fine vapors mediating between the body and the soul, and patching up a connection which scientific psychology is still trying to make. *Natural spirits* came from the liver and circulated through the veins. *Vital spirits* came from the heart and circulated arterially. *Animal spirits* were distilled from the vital spirits (which can be associated with blood) and went to the brain through the nerves, which were thought to be conducting vessels. Other faculties of the soul included the power of *fancy* or *fantasy* (the word "imagination" most often referred to something imagined, rather than to a faculty).

Reverdie Old French dance poem imitated in other languages, usually consisting of five or six stanzas without refrain, in joyful celebration of the coming of Spring.

Rhetoric In classical times, rhetoric was the art of persuading through the use of language. The major treatises on style and structure of discourse—Aristotle's *Rhetoric,* Quintilian's *Institutes of Oratory,* the *Rhetorica ad Herrenium* ascribed for centuries to Cicero—were concerned with the "arts" of language in the older sense of "skills." In the Middle Ages the *trivium* (*q.v.*), or program that led to the degree of Bachelor of Arts, consisted of grammar, logic, and rhetoric, but it was an abstract study, based on the Roman tradition. In the Renaissance, classical rhetorical study became a matter of the first importance, and it led to the study of literary stylistics and the application of principles and concepts of the production and structure of eloquence to the higher eloquence of poetry.

Rhetoricians distinguished three stages in the production of discourse: *inventio* (finding or discovery), *dispositio* (arranging), and *elocutio* (style). Since the classical discipline aimed always at practical oratory (e.g. winning a case in court, or making a point effectively in council), *memoria* (memory) and *pronuntiatio* (delivery) were added. For the Renaissance, however, rhetoric became the art of writing. Under the heading of *elocutio,* style became stratified into three levels, *elevated* or high, *elegant* or middle, and *plain* or low. The proper fitting of these styles to the subject of discourse comprised the subject of decorum (*q.v.*).

Another area of rhetorical theory was concerned with classification of devices of language into *schemes, tropes,* and *figures.* A basic but somewhat confused distinction between figures of speech and figures of thought need not concern us here, but we may roughly distinguish between schemes (or patterns) of words, and tropes as manipulations of meanings, and of making words non-literal.

Common Schemes

anadiplosis repeating the terminal word in a clause as the start of the next one: "Pleasure might cause her read; reading might cause her know; / Knowledge might pity win, and pity grace obtain" (Sidney, *Astrophel and Stella*).

anaphora the repetition of a word or phrase at the openings of successive clauses, e.g. "The Lord sitteth above the water floods. The Lord remaineth King forever. The Lord shall give strength unto his people. The Lord shall give his people the blessing of peace."

chiasmus a pattern of criss-crossing a syntactic structure, whether of noun and adjective, e.g. "Empty his bottle, and his girlfriend gone," or of a reversal of normal syntax with similar effect, e.g. "A fop her passion, and her prize, a sot," reinforced by assonance (*q.v.*). Chiasmus may even extend to assonance, as in Coleridge's line "In Xanadu did Kubla Khan."

Common Tropes

metaphor and simile both involve comparison of one thing to another, the difference being that the *simile* will actually compare, using the words "like" or "as," while the metaphor identifies one with the other, thus producing a non-literal use of a word or attribution. Thus, Robert Burns's "O, my love is like a red, red rose / That's newly sprung in June" is a simile; had Burns written, "My love, thou art a red, red rose . . .", it would have been a metaphor—and indeed, it would not mean that the lady had acquired petals. In modern critical theory, *metaphor* has come to stand for various non-expository kinds of evocative signification. I. A. Richards, the modern critic most interested in a general theory of metaphor in this sense, has contributed the terms *tenor* (as in the case above, the girl) and *vehicle* (the rose) to designate the components. See also *Epic Simile.*

metonymy a trope in which the vehicle is closely and conventionally associated with the tenor, e.g. "crown" and "king," "pen" and "writing," "pencil" and "drawing," "sword" and "warfare."

synecdoche a trope in which the part stands for the whole, e.g. "sail" for "ship."

hyperbole intensifying exaggeration, e.g. the combined synecdoche and hyperbole in which Christopher Marlowe's Faustus asks of Helen of Troy "Is this the face that launched a thousand ships / And burned the topless towers of Ilium?"

oxymoron literally, sharp-dull; a figure of speech involving a witty paradox, e.g. "sweet harm"; "darkness visible" (Milton, *Paradise Lost* I.63).

Rhyme Royal See *Troilus stanza.*

Right Reason A natural faculty of intelligence in man, his capability of choosing between moral alternatives. In the humanism of the Renaissance, Aristotle's term, *orthos logos,* associated with the Latin word *ratio,* was thought of as having preceded the fallen knowledge acquired in Paradise by Adam and Eve's first sin.

Romance (1) A medieval tale of chivalric or amorous adventure, in prose or verse, with the specification that the material be fictional. Later on, there developed cycles of stories, such as those involving Arthurian material or the legends of Charlemagne. Many of these, particularly the Arthurian, came to involve the theme of courtly love (*q.v.*)

(2) In the Renaissance, romance becomes more complex and literary, involving some degree of consciousness on the part of the author that he was reworking medieval materials (Spenser's *Faerie Queene,* of Arthurian legends; Ariosto's *Orlando Furioso,* of Charlemagne's heroic knight; Tasso's *Gerusalemme Liberata,* of stories of the Crusades).

(3) Prose romance, the 19th-century outgrowth of earlier essays into the

Gothic (*q.v.*) tale, represents a poetic kind of narrative to be clearly distinguished (in England if not in America) from the mode of the novel (e.g. Mary Shelley's *Frankenstein* and Hawthorne's *The Scarlet Letter* are both prose romance).

Rondeau, Roundel A strict French poetic form, thirteen lines of eight to ten syllables, divided into stanzas of five, three, and five lines, using two rhymes only and repeating the first word or first few words of line one after the second and third stanzas. The two terms are used interchangeably in the Middle Ages.

Satire A literary mode painting a distorted verbal picture of part of the world in order to show its true moral, as opposed merely to its physical, nature. In this sense, Circe, the enchantress in Homer's *Odyssey* who changed Odysseus' men into pigs (because they made pigs of themselves while eating) and would have changed Odysseus into a fox (for he was indeed foxy), was the first satirist. Originally the Latin word *satura* meant a kind of literary grab bag, or medley, and a satire was a fanciful kind of tale in mixed prose and verse; but later a false etymology connected the word with *satyr* and thus with the grotesque. Satire may be in verse or in prose; in the 16th and 17th centuries, the Roman poets Horace and Juvenal were imitated and expanded upon by writers of satiric moral verse, the tone of the verse being wise, smooth, skeptical, and urbane, that of the prose, sharp, harsh, and sometimes nasty. A tradition of English verse satire runs through Donne, Jonson, Dryden, Pope, and Samuel Johnson; of prose satire, Addison, Swift, and Fielding.

Scholasticism, Schoolmen Scholasticism is the term used for the philosophy and theology of the Middle Ages. This consisted of rational inquiry into revealed truth; for it was important to understand what one believed. This technique of disposition was developed by the Schoolmen over a long period, reaching its perfection in Peter Abelard (1079–1142). In the 13th century it absorbed the newly discovered Aristotelian philosophy and method. In this phase its greatest exponent was St. Thomas Aquinas (*c.* 1225–74), who became the chief medieval philosopher and theologian; his authority, challenged in the 16th century, was more seriously contested in the 17th century by the adherents of the "new science."

Seneca Lucius Annaeus Seneca (4 B.C.–65 A.D.) was an important source of Renaissance stoicism (*q.v.*), a model for the "closet" drama of the period, and an exemplar for the kind of prose that shunned the Ciceronian loquacity of early humanism and cultivated terseness. He was Nero's tutor; in 62 A.D. he retired from public life, and in 65 was compelled to commit suicide for taking part in a political conspiracy. He produced writings on ethics and physics, as well as ten tragedies often imitated in the Renaissance.

Sensibility (1) In the mid-18th century, the term came to be used in a literary context to refer to a susceptibility to fine or tender feelings, particularly involving the feelings and sorrows of others. This became a quality to be cultivated in despite of stoical rejections of unreasonable emotion which the neoclassicism (*q.v.*) of the earlier Augustan age had prized. The meaning of the word blended easily into "sentimentality"; but the literary period in England characterized by the work of writers such as Sterne, Goldsmith, Gray, Collins, and Cowper is often called the Age of Sensibility.

(2) A meaning more important for modern literature is that of a special kind of total awareness, an ability to make the finest discriminations in its perception of the world, and yet at the same time not lacking in a kind of force by the very virtue of its own receptive power. The varieties of awareness celebrated in French literature from Baudelaire through Marcel Proust have been adapted by modernist English critics, notably T. S. Eliot, for a fuller extension of the meaning of *sensibility.* By the term "dissociation of sensibility," Eliot implied the split between the sensuous and the intellectual faculties which he thought characterized English poetry after the Restoration (1660).

Sententia A wise, fruitful saying, functioning as a guide to morally correct thought or action.

Sestina Originally a Provençal lyric form supposedly invented by Arnaut Daniel in the 12th century, and one of the most complex of those structures. It has six stanzas of six lines each, followed by an *envoi* (*q.v.*) or *tornada* of three lines. Instead of rhyming, the end-words of the lines of the first stanza are all repeated in the following stanzas, but in a constant set of permutations. The *envoi* contains all six words, three in the middle of each line. D. G. Rossetti, Swinburne, Pound, Auden, and other modern poets have used the form, and Sir Philip Sidney composed a magnificent double-sestina, "Ye Goat-herd Gods."

Skepticism A philosophy that denies the possibility of certain knowledge, and, although opposed to Stoicism and Epicureanism (*q.v.*), advocated *ataraxy,* imperturbability of mind. Skepticism originated with Pyrrhon (*c.* 360–270 B.C.), and its chief transmitter was Sextus Empiricus (*c.* 200 B.C.). In the Renaissance, skepticism had importance as questioning the power of the human mind to know truly (for a classic exposition see Donne's *Second Anniversary,* ll. 254–300), and became a powerful influence in morals and religion through the advocacy of Montaigne.

Sonnet A basic lyric form, consisting of fourteen lines of iambic pentameter rhymed in various patterns. The *Italian* or *Petrarchan* sonnet is divided clearly into *octave* and *sestet,* the first rhyming *abba abba* and the second in a pattern such as *cdc dcd.* The *Shakespearean* sonnet consists of three quatrains followed by a couplet: *abab cdcd efef gg.* In the late 16th century in England, sonnets were written either independently as short epigrammatic forms, or grouped in sonnet sequences, i.e. collections of upwards of a hundred poems, in imitation of Petrarch, purportedly addressed to one central figure or muse—a lady usually with a symbolic name like "Stella" or "Idea." Milton made a new kind of use of the Petrarchan form, and the Romantic poets continued in the Miltonic tradition. Several variations have been devised, including the addition of "tails" or extra lines, or the recasting into sixteen lines, instead of fourteen.

Stoicism, Stoics Philosophy founded by Zeno (335–263 B.C.), and opposing the hedonistic tendencies of Epicureanism (*q.v.*). The Stoics' world-view was pantheistic: God was the energy that formed and maintained the world, and wisdom lay in obedience to this law of nature as revealed by the conscience. Moreover, every man is free because the life according to nature and conscience is available to all; so too is suicide—a natural right. Certain Stoics saw the end of the world as caused by fire. In the Renaissance, Latin Stoicism, especially that of Seneca (*q.v.*), had a revival of influence and was Christianized in various ways.

Strong Lines The term used in the 17th century to refer to the tough, tense conceit (*q.v.*)-laden verse of Donne and his followers.

Style See *Decorum.*

Sublime "Lofty"; as a literary idea, originally the basic concept of a Greek treatise (by the so-called "Longinus") on style. In the 18th century, however, the *sublime* came to mean a loftiness perceivable in nature, and sometimes in art—a loftiness different from the composed vision of landscape known as the *picturesque,* because of the element of wildness, power, and even terror. The *beautiful,* the picturesque, and the sublime became three modes for the perception of nature.

Symbolism (1) Broadly, the process by which one phenomenon, in literature, stands for another, or group of others, and usually of a different sort. Clear-cut cases of this in medieval and Renaissance literature are *emblems* or *attributes* (see *Personification; Allegory*). Sometimes conventional symbols may be used in more than one way, e.g. a mirror betokening both truth and vanity. See also *Figure; Emblem.*

(2) In a specific sense (and often given in its French form, *symbolisme*), an important esthetic concept for modern literature, formulated by French poets and critics of the later 19th century following Baudelaire. In this view, the literary symbol becomes something closer to a kind of commanding, central metaphor, taking precedence over any more discursive linguistic mode for poetic communication. The effects of this concept on literature in English have been immense; and some version of the concept survives in modern notions of the poetic *image,* or *fiction.*

Temperaments The balance of combinations of humors (*q.v.*) which in the medieval and Renaissance periods was believed to determine the psychosomatic make-up or "complexion" of a man or a woman. See *Renaissance Psychology.*

Topographical Poem A descriptive poem popular in the 17th and 18th centuries and devoted to a specific scene or landscape with the addition (in the words of Samuel Johnson in 1799) of "historical retrospection or incidental meditation." Sir John Denham's "Cooper's Hill" (1642) is an influential example of the tradition (which includes also Pope's "Windsor Forest") and sometimes blends with the genre of a poem in praise of a particular house or garden.

Topos Greek for "place," commonplace; in rhetoric (*q.v.*), either a general argument, description, or observation that could serve for various occasions; or a method of inventing arguments on a statement or contention. It is often used now to mean a basic literary topic (either a proposition such as the superiority of a life of action to that of contemplation, or vice versa; of old age vs. youth; or a description, such as that of the *locus amoenus* (*q.v.*), the pleasant garden place, Paradise, which allows many variations of thought and language.

Trivium The course of study in the first three of the seven liberal arts—grammar, rhetoric, and logic (or dialectic): the basis of the medieval educational program in school and university. See also *Quadrivium*.

***Troilus* stanza** Or *rhyme royal;* iambic pentameters in stanzas of seven lines, rhyming *ababbcc*, popularized by Chaucer in his poem *Troilus and Criseyde* and called *rhyme royal* supposedly on account of its use by James I of Scotland, king and poet.

Trope (1) See *Rhetoric*. (2) In the liturgy of the Catholic Church, a phrase, sentence, or verse with its musical setting, introduced to amplify or embellish some part of the text of the mass or the office (i.e. the prayers and Scripture readings recited daily by priests, religious, and even laymen) when chanted in choir. Tropes of this second kind were discontinued in 1570 by the authority of Pope Pius V. Troping new material into older or conventional patterns seems to have been, in a general way, a basic device of medieval literature, and was the genesis of modern drama.

Type, Typology (1) Strictly, in medieval biblical interpretation, the prefiguration of the persons and events of the New Testament by persons and events of the Old, the Old Testament being fulfilled in, but not entirely superseded by, the New. Thus, the Temptation and Fall of Man were held to prefigure the first Temptation of Christ, pride in each case being the root of the temptation, and a warning against gluttony the moral lesson to be drawn from both. The Brazen Serpent raised up by Moses was held to prefigure the crucifixion of Christ; Isaac, as a sacrificial victim ("God will provide his own Lamb," says Abraham to him) is a *type* of Christ. The forty days and nights of the Deluge, the forty years of Israel's wandering in the desert, Moses' forty days in the desert are all typologically related.

(2) In a looser sense, a person or event seen as a model or paradigm. See also *Figure*.

Ubi Sunt . . . A motif introducing a lament for the passing of all mortal and material things: e.g. "*Ubi sunt qui ante nos in mundo fuere?*" (Where are they who went before us in this world?), or "Where are the snows of yesteryear?" (Swinburne's translation from the French of Villon's *ballade*).

Virelay A French poetic form, a dance song; short, with two or three rhymes, and two lines of the first stanza as a refrain.

Wars of the Roses Series of encounters between the house of Lancaster (whose emblem was the red rose) and the house of York (whose emblem was the white), which took place between 1455 and 1485 to decide the right of possession of the English throne. At the Battle of Bosworth Field in 1485 the Lancastrian Henry Tudor defeated the Yorkist Richard III and was proclaimed king as Henry VII. He married Elizabeth of York, daughter of King Edward IV.

Worthies, Nine Nine exemplary heroes, three from the Bible (Joshua, David, Judas Maccabaeus); three from pagan antiquity (Hector of Troy, Alexander the Great, Julius Caesar), and three from "Christian" romance (King Arthur, the Emperor Charlemagne, and Godfrey of Bouillon, a leader of the First Crusade and King of Jerusalem). They were favorite figures for tapestries (see Fig. 46 in illustrations for the Medieval section of this Anthology) and pageants.

Wit (1) Originally, "intellect," "intelligence"; later, "creative intelligence," or poetical rather than merely mechanical intellectual power. Thus, during the age of Dryden and Pope, a poet might be called a wit without any compromising sense. In the 19th century, "wit" came to mean verbal agility or cleverness, as opposed to the more creative powers of the mind. (2) More specifically, in literary history, as characterizing the poetic style of John Donne and his 17th-century followers. The Augustan age would contrast this with the "true wit" of *neoclassical* (*q.v.*) poetry.

Yorkists See *Wars of the Roses.*

Zodiac In astrology, a belt of the celestial sphere, about eight or nine degrees to either side of the ecliptic (the apparent orbit of the sun), within which the apparent motions of the sun, moon, and planets take place. It is divided into twelve equal parts, the signs, through each of which the sun passes in a month. Each division once coincided with one of the constellations after which the signs are named: Aries (Ram)—in Chaucer's time the sun entered this sign on 12 March; Taurus (Bull); Gemini (Twins); Cancer (Crab); Leo (Lion); Virgo (Virgin); Libra (Scales); Scorpio; Sagittarius (Archer); Capricornus (Goat); Aquarius (Water-Carrier); Pisces (Fishes). Each zodiacal sign was believed to govern a part of the human body. See *Astronomy and Astrology.*

Suggestions for Further Reading

MEDIEVAL ENGLISH LITERATURE

This reading list is deliberately summary: it cites the books most immediately helpful in providing a text or an introductory study. From the bibliographies and footnotes contained in these, the student can find his way to the more elaborate text editions and the more extended critical and historical studies.

General Backgrounds: Europe Medieval English literature is part of a larger European unit: its relations with both the classical and the medieval vernacular literatures of the Continent should always be kept in mind. The themes and modes of these literatures are splendidly treated in the first ten essays—three of them concerned with Antiquity—of Erich Auerbach, *Mimesis: The Representation of Reality in Western Literature* (trans. Willard R. Trask), 1957. Auerbach's long paper "Figura," in his *Scenes from the Drama of European Literature*, 1959, is also important. An older work, well worth reading, on European literature from the sixth century to the twelfth, is W. P. Ker's *The Dark Ages*, 1904.

For the wider context of medieval thought, Gordon Leff's *Medieval Thought: St. Augustine to Ockham*, 1958, is informative. The most stimulating general introduction oriented toward literature is C. S. Lewis's *The Discarded Image: An Introduction to Medieval and Renaissance Literature*, 1964.

The interrelations of European literature, thought, and art during the medieval period are treated by George Henderson in his lively companion volumes *Early Medieval*, 1972, and *Gothic*, 1967, in the series Style and Civilization.

For the intellectual and material conditions of life in Europe during the later Middle Ages, with their antecedents, the classic study is Johan Huizinga's *The Waning of the Middle Ages*, 1924. The best preliminary account of medieval daily life is Eileen Power's *Medieval People*, 1924.

Backgrounds: England The best introduction to the literature of England from Anglo-Saxon times to the end of the Middle Ages is still W. P. Ker's *Medieval English Literature*, 1912. Longer and more exhaustive is A. C. Baugh, ed., *A Literary History of England*, 1948; a useful survey, with bibliographies, is W. L. Renwick and H. Orton, *The Beginnings of English Literature to Skelton*, 3rd ed., revised by M. F. Wakelin, 1966.

The social and political background is treated in companion volumes by C. N. L. Brooke, *From Alfred to Henry III, 871–1272*, 1961, and George Holmes, *The Later*

Middle Ages, 1272–1485, 1962. G. M. Trevelyan's *Illustrated Social History of England,* 1949, is less satisfactory on the Middle Ages than on other periods, but is useful.

For the artistic achievement of England in the Middle Ages, consult Margaret Rickert, *Painting in Britain: The Middle Ages,* 2nd ed., 1965; Lawrence Stone, *Sculpture in Britain: The Middle Ages,* 1955; and G. F. Webb, *Architecture in Britain: The Middle Ages,* 1959—all valuable and fully illustrated volumes in the Pelican History of Art.

Anglo-Saxon England and Old English Literature A classic study is H. M. Chadwick's *The Heroic Age,* 1912; but the best and fullest general history is Sir Frank Stenton's *Anglo-Saxon England,* 3rd ed., 1971, one of the finest volumes in the Oxford History of England. P. Hunter Blair's *An Introduction to Anglo-Saxon England,* 1956, is a useful shorter survey, with illustrations, but the best introduction is Dorothy Whitelock's *The Beginnings of English Society,* 1952. For art and archaeology this can be supplemented by the best preliminary study of the subject, David M. Wilson's *The Anglo-Saxons,* 1960.

Of primary sources, *The Anglo-Saxon Chronicle* has been well translated by G. N. Garmonsway, 1953; and Venerable Bede's *Ecclesiastical History of the English People,* by L. Sherley-Price, 1955.

For Old English literature, the best survey is C. L. Wrenn's *A Study of Old English Literature,* 1967; while S. B. Greenfield's *A Critical History of Old English Literature,* 1965, is useful.

BEOWULF

Editions The standard edition of the text is F. Klaeber, ed., *Beowulf and the Fight at Finnesburh,* 3rd ed., 1950; but C. L. Wrenn, ed., *Beowulf, with the Finnesburh Fragment,* 3rd ed., 1973, is more up-to-date and often easier to use. Neither edition has a translation, but both are very fully annotated. There are prose translations by J. R. Clark Hall, with introduction and notes by C. L. Wrenn, and preface by J. R. R. Tolkien, 1950; and by E. Talbot Donaldson, 1966 (excellent). Besides the verse translation by Charles W. Kennedy used in this volume, there is a fine poetic version by Kevin Crossley-Holland, with helpful introduction and notes by Bruce Mitchell, 1968.

Critical Studies R. W. Chambers's *Beowulf: An Introduction,* 3rd ed., with Supplement by C. L. Wrenn, 1959, is the basic and encyclopedic work on *Beowulf.* Good selections of critical essays are Lewis E. Nicholson, ed., *An Anthology of Beowulf Criticism,* and Donald K. Fry, ed., *The Beowulf Poet: A Collection of Critical Essays,* 1968, which both include the most important and influential article so far published on the poem, J. R. R. Tolkien's "Beowulf: The Monsters and the Critics," from *Proceedings of the British Academy* XXII, 1936. J. C. Pope's *The Rhythm of Beowulf,* 1942, is the most elaborate study of the meter; and Dorothy Whitelock's *The Audience of Beowulf,* 1951, the best study of its social and cultural setting.

Recordings Readings from *Beowulf,* in the original Old English, are available in recordings by Jess B. Bessinger, Jr., *Beowulf, Cædmon's Hymn,* and *Other Old English Poems,* Cædmon TC 1161; by Nevill Coghill and Norman Davis, *Beowulf,* with introductory material, Spoken Arts 918; by Charles W. Dunn, *Early English*

Poetry, Folkways FL 9851; and by J. C. Pope and H. Kökeritz, *Beowulf and Chaucer,* Lexington 5505.

GEOFFREY CHAUCER

Editions Still basic is W. W. Skeat, ed., *The Works of Geoffrey Chaucer,* in six volumes and a further collection, *Chaucerian and Other Pieces,* 1894–97, with extensive commentary; but the most informative single-volume edition is F. N. Robinson, ed., *The Complete Works,* 2nd ed., 1957, with explanatory notes and glossary. The most helpful substantial selection is E. Talbot Donaldson, ed., *Chaucer's Poetry: An Anthology for the Modern Reader,* 1958. The Penguin translation by Michael Alexander, 1973, is also recommendable.

Critical Studies and Handbooks The best collections for the history of Chaucer criticism are J. A. Burrow, ed., *Geoffrey Chaucer,* in the Penguin Critical Anthologies series, 1969 (excerpts); and, for the *Canterbury Tales,* J. J. Anderson's *Chaucer: The Canterbury Tales, a Casebook,* 1974. Among other collections of modern critical essays, ed. by E. C. Wagenknecht, *Chaucer: Modern Essays in Criticism,* 1959; by R. J. Schoeck and Jerome Taylor, *Chaucer Criticism,* two vols., 1960–61; and by C. J. Owen, *Discussions of the Canterbury Tales,* 1961, all give a representative selection. The most rewarding group of essays by a single author and the best guide to the character of Chaucer's poems is E. Talbot Donaldson, *Speaking of Chaucer,* 1970.

Among monographs, John Livingston Lowes, *Geoffrey Chaucer,* 1934, remains the best introduction, especially to Chaucer's reading and his thought world. Useful additional materials are Charles Muscatine, *Chaucer and the French Tradition: A Study in Style and Meaning,* 1957, and Walter Clyde Curry, *Chaucer and the Medieval Sciences,* 2nd ed., 1960, the standard account of this special aspect. D. W. Robertson, Jr., *A Preface to Chaucer: Studies in Medieval Perspectives,* 1969, is the most lively and controversial of modern studies on Chaucer. A thorough and interesting introduction to the General Prologue of the *Canterbury Tales* is Muriel Bowden's *Commentary on the General Prologue to the Canterbury Tales,* 1967.

R. D. French, *A Chaucer Handbook,* 2nd ed., 1947, is a handy reference book; but for up-to-date essays, with excellent bibliographies, on all aspects of Chaucer, the most useful manuals are Beryl Rowland, ed., *Companion to Chaucer Studies,* 1968; and D. S. Brewer, ed., *Chaucer,* in the series *Writers and Their Background,* 1974.

The best short work on Chaucerian speech is Helge Kökeritz's *A Guide to Chaucer's Pronunciation,* 1954. *Chaucer's World,* ed. E. Rickert, C. C. Olson, and M. M. Crow, 1948, is excellent background reading, with contemporary accounts of events and many documents. Roger S. Loomis, ed., *A Mirror of Chaucer's World,* 1965, is a handsome picture book.

Recordings Readings on records are given in Chaucerian pronunciation by Nevill Coghill, Norman Davis, and J. A. Burrow, of the General Prologue, Argo RG 401; by the same, with L. Davis, of the Nun's Priest's Tale, ll. 1–625 and some shorter poems, Argo RG 466; and by N. Coghill and N. Davis, the Pardoner's Tale, ll. 739–894, Spoken Arts 919.

THE RENAISSANCE

General Historical Works J. Burckhardt, *The Civilization of the Renaissance in Italy* (1860), tr. S. G. C. Middleman, two vols., 1958. J. D. Mackie, *The Early Tudors,* 1952. J. B. Black, *The Reign of Elizabeth,* 2nd ed., 1959. A. L. Rowse, *The England of Elizabeth,* 1950. Garrett Mattingly, *The Armada,* 1959. R. H. Tawney, *Religion and the Rise of Capitalism,* 1926, *Shakespeare's England,* 1916. William Haller, *The Rise of Puritanism,* 1938. Louis B. Wright, *Middle-Class Culture in Elizabethan England,* 1935. Godfrey Davies, *The Early Stuarts,* rev. ed., 1959. Carl J. Friedrich, *The Age of the Baroque,* 1952. G. M. Trevelyan, *England under the Stuarts,* 21st ed., 1949. Christopher Hill, *Puritanism and Revolution,* 1958, *A Century of Revolution,* 1961, *Intellectual Origins of the English Revolution,* 1965, and *God's Englishman* 1970, a study of Cromwell: all brilliant and Marxist. Different approaches are represented by C. V. Wedgwood's *The Great Rebellion: The King's Peace* (1955), and *The King's War* (1958); and by Perez Zagorin's *The Court and the Country,* 1970.

Intellectual and Cultural History Arthur O. Lovejoy, *The Great Chain of Being,* 1936. E. M. W. Tillyard, *The Elizabethan World Picture,* rev. ed., 1956. C. S. Lewis, *The Discarded Image,* 1964. E. A. Burtt, *Metaphysical Foundations of Modern Science,* rev. ed., 1932. Sir Herbert Butterfield, *The Origins of Modern Science,* 1957. Donald S. Westfall, *Science and Religion in Seventeenth-Century England,* 1958. Thomas S. Kuhn, *The Copernican Revolution,* 1959. Charles Singer, *A Short History of Scientific Ideas to 1900,* 1959. Basil Willey, *The Seventeenth Century Background,* 1934. H. H. Rhys ed., *XVII Century Science and the Arts,* 1961. Norman Davy ed., *British Scientific Literature in the XVIIth Century,* 1953. Wilbur S. Howell, *Logic and Rhetoric in England,* 1956. Kitty Scoular, *Natural Magic,* 1965. J. A. Mazzeo, *Renaissance and Revolution,* 1965. John R. Mulder, *The Temple of the Mind,* 1969.

Literary History C. S. Lewis, *English Literature in the Sixteenth Century, excluding Drama,* 1954. Douglas Bush, *English Literature in the Earlier Seventeenth Century,* (2nd rev. ed., 1962. Hallett Smith, *Elizabethan Poetry,* 1952. Frank Kermode, *English Pastoral Poetry from the Beginnings to Marvell,* 1952. F. P. Wilson, *Elizabethan and Jacobean,* 1945. J. W. Lever, *The Elizabethan Love Sonnet,* 1956. Wylie Sypher, *Four Stages of Renaissance Style,* 1955.

Critical Studies (**Early**) *Elizabethan Critical Essays,* ed. G. G. Smith, two vols., 1904; and *Critical Essays of the Seventeenth Century,* three vols., 1908–1909, are important collections of texts. (**Modern**) Helpful anthologies are *Elizabethan Poetry: Modern Essays in Criticism,* ed. Paul J. Alpers, 1967; *Seventeenth-Century English Poetry: Modern Essays in Criticism,* ed. William R. Keast, rev. ed., 1971; *Seventeenth Century Prose: Modern Essays in Criticism,* ed. Stanley Fish, 1971; *The Metaphysical Poets,* ed. Frank Kermode, 1969. *Literary English Since Shakespeare,* ed. George Watson, 1970, is a useful guide. Works of one author include Mario Praz, *Studies in Seventeenth-Century Imagery,* 1939 (2nd ed., 1964); Rosamond Tuve, *Elizabethan and Metaphysical Imagery,* 1947; Austin Warren, *Rage for Order,* 1948; Ruth C. Wallerstein, *Studies in Seventeenth Century Poetic,* 1950; Odette de Mourgues, *Metaphysical, Baroque and Précieux Poetry,* 1953; M. M. Mahood, *Poetry and Humanism,* 1950; Marjorie Hope Nicolson, *The Breaking of the Circle,* 1960; Don Cameron

Allen, *Image and Meaning*, 1960; A. Alvarez, *The School of Donne*, 1961; J. A. Mazzeo ed., *Reason and Imagination*, 1962; John Hollander, *The Untuning of the Sky*, 1961; Stanley Stewart, *The Enclosed Garden*, 1966.

On Prose Writing Donald A. Stauffer, *English Biography before 1700*, 1930; George Williamson, *Seventeenth-Century Contexts*, 1960; F. P. Wilson, *Seventeenth-Century Prose: Five Lectures*, 1960; Joan Webber, *The Eloquent I*, 1968.

On Mythology Douglas Bush, *Mythology and the Renaissance Tradition in English Poetry*, 1932 (rev. ed., 1936). Jean Seznec, *The Survival of the Pagan Gods*, 1953. Harry Levin, *The Myth of the Golden Age in the Renaissance*, 1969. John Armstrong, *The Paradise Myth*, 1969. Don Cameron Allen, *Mysteriously Meant*, 1970.

On Pictures and Images Rosemary Freeman, *English Emblem Books*, 1967, is, along with Mario Praz (see above), the best introduction to what is becoming an important study. Geoffrey Whitney's *A Choice of Emblems*, 1586, Henry Peacham's *Minerva Brittana*, 1610, and George Wither's *A Collection of Emblems*, 1635, are all available in facsimile. E. H. Gombrich's *Symbolic Images*, 1972, provides theoretical backgrounds.

The Visual Arts in England Ellis Waterhouse, *Painting in Britain 1530–1790*, 1953. John Summerson, *Architecture in Britain 1530–1830*, 4th ed., 1963; and *Inigo Jones*, 1966. Jean H. Hagstrum, *The Sister Arts*, 1958, and Mario Praz, *Mnemosyne*, 1970, are both good introductions to the relation of art and poetry. John Shearman's *Mannerism*, 1967, is a good corrective to some of the uneasy generalities of Wylie Sypher's *Four Stages of Renaissance Style* mentioned above. Edward Hyams, *The English Garden*, 1964, provides background material for a major poetic theme. Roy Strong, *The English Icon*, 1969, and his catalogue of *Tudor and Jacobean Portraits*, 1969, are both excellent, as is Marcia R. Poynton's *Milton and English Art*, 1970.

The English Bible V. F. Storr, *The English Bible*, 1938. E. E. Willoughby, *The Making of the English Bible*, 1956. G. S. Paine, *The Learned Men*, 1959. F. F. Bruce, *The English Bible: A History of Translations . . .*, rev. ed. 1970.

EDMUND SPENSER

Editions *The Poetical Works*, ed. J. C. Smith and E. de Selincourt, three vols., 1909–10; and in one vol., 1912. *Variorum* Edition, ten vols., 1932–49. *Selections . . .* (with commentary), edited by F. Kermode, 1965.

Critical Studies W. L. Renwick, *Edmund Spenser*, 1925. E. Greenlaw, *Spenser's Historical Allegory*, 1932. C. B. Millican, *Spenser and the Table Round*, 1934. I. E. Rathborne, *The Meaning of Spenser's Fairyland*, 1937. C. S. Lewis, *The Allegory of Love*, 1936, and later editions; see also his *English Literature in the Sixteenth Century, excluding Drama* (Vol. III of the Oxford History of English Literature), 1954, and the posthumous *Spenser's Images of Life*, 1967. J. W. Bennett, *The Evolution of the Faerie Queene*, 1942. V. K. Whitaker, *The Religious Basis of Spenser's Thought*, 1950. A. K. Hieatt, *Short Time's Endless Monument*, 1960. A. C. Hamilton, *Structure of Allegory in Faerie Queene*, 1961. G. Hough, *A Preface to The Faerie Queene*, 1962. R. Ellrodt, *Neoplatonism in the Poetry of Spenser*, 1960. D. S. Cheney, *Spenser's*

Image of Nature, 1966. William Nelson, *The Poetry of Edmund Spenser* (dealing with all the poetry), 1963. A. Fowler, *Spenser and the Numbers of Time,* 1964. R. Tuve, *Allegorical Imagery,* 1966. P. Alpers, *The Poetry of the Faerie Queene,* 1967. H. Tonkin, *Spenser's Courteous Pastoral,* 1972. Angus Fletcher, *The Prophetic Moment,* 1972. F. Kermode, *Shakespeare, Spenser, Donne,* 1971. An article of high interest is F. Yates's "Queen Elizabeth as Astraea," in *Journal of the Warburg and Courtauld Institutes,* X (1947), 27–82. See also Roy C. Strong, *Portraits of Queen Elizabeth,* 1963.

WILLIAM SHAKESPEARE

Editions Standard editions, one volume per play, are the Arden, the Yale, the Pelican, and the Signet, all annotated. The best one-volume text is the Houghton Mifflin (the "Riverside") Shakespeare, 1973, to which the six-volume *Concordance* of Marvin Spevack, 1970, is keyed.

Critical Studies Two very different critical approaches (out of very many) to the sonnets are G. Wilson Knight's *The Mutual Flame,* 1955, and Stephen Booth's *An Essay on Shakespeare's Sonnets,* 1969. Knight deals also with *The Phoenix and Turtle,* on which see also F. Kermode, *Shakespeare, Spenser, Donne,* 1971. On *Othello* see W. H. Auden, *The Dyer's Hand,* 1962; John Bayley, *The Characters of Love,* 1960; A. C. Bradley, *Shakespearean Tragedy,* 1904; William Empson, *The Structure of Complex Words,* 1951; Helen Gardner, "Othello: a Retrospect," *Shakespeare Survey* 21 (1968); R. B. Heilman, *Magic in the Web,* 1956; John Holloway, *The Story of the Night,* 1961; Joseph Kerman, *Opera as Drama,* 1956 (on Shakespeare and Verdi); G. Wilson Knight, *The Wheel of Fire* (1930); Marvin Rosenberg, *The Masks of Othello* (1961); Bernard Spivack, *Shakespeare and the Allegory of Evil,* 1958. Kermode discusses *The Tempest* in the Arden edition (1954, and later revisions), and in *Shakespeare, Spenser, Donne.* See also N. Frye, *A Natural Perspective,* 1965, and A. D. Nuttall, *Two Concepts of Allegory,* 1967; and, on the songs, Peter Seng, *The Vocal Songs in the Plays of Shakespeare,* 1967.

Biographies While the major work in Shakespearean biography is Samuel Schoenbaum, *Shakespeare's Lives,* 1970, the most useful brief work on Shakespeare's life is G. E. Bentley, *Shakespeare: A Biographical Handbook,* 1961.

JOHN DONNE

Editions H. J. C. Grierson's 1912 edition of the *Poems* is supplemented rather than superseded by the editions of H. Gardner, *Divine Poems,* 1952, and *Elegies and the Songs and Sonnets,* 1965; and of W. Milgate, *Satires, Epigrams, and Verse Letters,* 1967. There is a separate edition of *Anniversaries* by F. Manley, 1963; of *Sermons,* in ten volumes, by G. R. Potter and E. Simpson, 1953–62; of the *Devotions,* by J. Sparrow, 1923. The best selection, with complete verse and selected prose, was prepared by J. Hayward, 1929. Among other collections are *Complete Poetry,* ed. J. T. Shawcross, 1967; *Selected Prose,* chosen by E. Simpson and edited by H. Gardner and T. Healy, 1967; and *Poems,* ed. with commentary by A. J. Smith, 1970.

Critical Studies For the history of Donne criticism see J. E. Duncan, *The Revival of Metaphysical Poetry*, 1959, as well as the selections in F. Kermode ed., *Discussions of John Donne*, 1962. For specialized commentary, see P. Legouis, *Donne the Craftsman*, 1928; R. Tuve, *Elizabethan and Metaphysical Imagery*, 1947; J. B. Leishman, *The Monarch of Wit*, 1951 (1962); L. Unger, *The Man in the Name*, 1956. G. Williamson, *The Donne Tradition*, 1930, supports the orthodoxy founded on Eliot's essays, shaken by Tuve and others. Among shorter introductions are K. W. Gransden's *John Donne*, 1954; F. Kermode's *John Donne*, 1957; and also his *Shakespeare, Spenser, Donne*, 1971. The Twentieth Century Views collection of critiques was edited by Helen Gardner, 1962. On prose, see E. Simpson, *A Study of the Prose Works of John Donne*, 1948; and Joan Webber, *Contrary Music*, 1963. *Bibliography* by Geoffrey Keynes, 1914, 1932, 1958.

Biography Standard biography is *John Donne: A Life*, by R. C. Bald, 1970.

JOHN MILTON

The Columbia Milton (eighteen vols., 1931–38) is still the standard edition of the complete verse and prose, although it is being replaced, for the prose, by the Yale Edition, currently in process of publication. Helen Darbishire's text of the *Poems*, 1952–55 (rev. ed., 1958), is somewhat eccentric. The students will find most helpful the texts edited by Merritt Y. Hughes in *Complete Poems and Major Prose*, 1957, and by John Carey and Alistair Fowler, *Poems*, 1968. Douglas Bush has done a *Complete Poetical Works*, 1965, but it is less heavily annotated than either of the above. A. W. Verity's 1910 text of *Paradise Lost* in separate volumes is unusually helpful. Perhaps the most exciting new edition of Milton will be the *Cambridge Milton for Schools and Colleges*, under the general editorship of J. B. Broadbent, appearing in separate volumes (1972–). Good selections of prose appear in Hughes's edition and in *Prose of John Milton*, by J. Max Patrick, 1965.

Critical Studies The volume of critical literature since 1950 alone is overwhelming, but excellent selections have been made by Frank Kermode in *The Living Milton*, 1960; by Arthur Barker, in *John Milton: Modern Essays in Criticism*, 1965; by C. A. Patrides, in *Milton's Epic Poetry*, 1967, and *Approaches to Paradise Lost*, 1968; and by B. Rajan, *Paradise Lost: A Tercentenary Tribute*, 1969. Central major studies are C. S. Lewis, *A Preface to Paradise Lost*, 1942; William Empson, *Milton's God*, 1961; A. J. A. Waldock, *Paradise Lost and Its Critics*, 1947; Isabel G. MacCaffrey, *Paradise Lost as "Myth,"* 1959; J. B. Broadbent, *Some Graver Subject*, 1967; Christopher Ricks, *Milton's Grand Style*, 1963; and Northrop Frye, *The Return of Eden*, 1965. On Milton's prose work, and intellectual background in general, see Arthur Barker, *Milton and the Puritan Dilemma*, 1942, and Michael J. Fixler, *Milton and the Kingdoms of God*, 1964. On *Paradise Regained:* Barbara K. Lewalski, *Milton's Brief Epic*, 1966. On *Samson Agonistes:* the edition of F. T. Prince (1957) and Arnold Stein, *Heroic Knowledge*, 1957. On *Comus:* John Arthos, *On A Masque Presented at Ludlow-Castle*, 1954, and Angus Fletcher, *The Transcendental Masque*, 1972. Other studies of the minor poems: F. T. Prince, *The Italian Element in Milton's Verse*, 1954; D. C. Allen, *The Harmonious Vision*, 1954; Rosamund Tuve, *Images* *and Themes in Five Poems by Milton,* 1957; C. A. Patrides ed., *Lycidas: The Tradition and the Poem,* 1961; and J. H. Summers ed., *The Lyric and Dramatic Milton,* 1965; E. A. Honigmann ed., *Milton's Sonnets,* 1966.

Biography The standard life is now that of William Riley Parker, *Milton: A Biography,* two vols., 1968, superseding the older work by David Masson, *Life of John Milton: Narrated in Connection with . . . the History of His Time,* rev. ed., eight vols., 1881–96.

THE RESTORATION AND THE EIGHTEENTH CENTURY

Social and Political History Three volumes of the Oxford History of England cover this period: Sir George Clark, *The Later Stuarts 1660–1714,* 2nd ed., 1956; Basil Williams, *The Whig Supremacy 1714–1760,* 2nd ed. revised by C. H. Stuart, 1961; and J. Steven Watson, *The Reign of George III 1760–1815,* 1960. For the earlier period see also J. R. Western, *Monarchy and Revolution: The English State in the 1680s,* 1972; J. H. Plumb, *The Growth of Political Stability in England 1675–1725,* 1967; David Ogg, *England in the Reign of Charles II,* 2nd ed., and *England in the Reigns of James II and William III,* 1955; and the three volumes by G. M. Trevelyan, *England under Queen Anne,* 1930–34. For the later period see the important biography by J. H. Plumb, *Sir Robert Walpole,* 1956; Caroline Robbins, *The Eighteenth-Century Commonwealthman,* 1959; Isaac Kramnick, *Bolingbroke and His Circle: The Politics of Nostalgia in the Age of Walpole,* 1968; R. J. White, *The Age of George III,* 1968.

For social history, see M. Dorothy George, *London Life in the Eighteenth Century,* 1925; Dorthy Marshall, *English People in the Eighteenth Century,* 1969; A. S. Turberville ed., *Johnson's England* (excellent essays on all aspects of English life), 1933; A. R. Humphreys, *The Augustan World,* 1954; J. L. Clifford ed., *Man versus Society in Eighteenth-Century Britain,* 1968. On political radicalism, see George Rudé, *Wilkes and Liberty,* 1962; S. Maccoby, *English Radicalism 1762–1785,* 1935; H. Butterfield, *George III, Lord North, and the People 1779–80,* 1949; Carl B. Cone, *The English Jacobins,* 1968.

Literary History George Sherburn, "The Restoration and Eighteenth Century," in A. C. Baugh ed., *A Literary History of England,* 1948; two volumes of The Oxford History of English Literature, both of which contain substantial bibliographies: James Sutherland, *English Literature of the Late Seventeenth Century,* 1969, and Bonamy Dobrée, *English Literature in the Early Eighteenth Century,* 1959; and the fourth volume in the Sphere History of Literature in the English Language, *Dryden to Johnson,* ed. Roger Lonsdale, 1971. Valuable for reference is George Watson ed., *The New Cambridge Bibliography of English Literature,* Vol. II, *1660–1800,* 1971; and still useful is Leslie Stephen's *History of English Thought in the Eighteenth Century,* two vols., 1876.

Critical Studies (General) There is a good collection of recent work in James L. Clifford ed., *Eighteenth Century English Literature: Modern Essays in Criticism,* 1959. For introduction to the literary forms of the age, see James Sutherland, *A*

Preface to Eighteenth Century Poetry, 1948; Ian Jack, *Augustan Satire,* 1952; R. P. Bond, *English Burlesque Poetry 1700–1750,* 1932; Donald Davie, *Purity of Diction in English Verse,* 1952. For critical thought of the period, see the collection by Scott Elledge, *Eighteenth Century Critical Essays,* two vols., 1961, and the following studies: W. J. Bate, *From Classic to Romantic,* 1946; S. H. Monk, *The Sublime,* 1935; M. H. Abrams, *The Mirror and the Lamp,* 1953; P. W. R. Stone, *The Art of Poetry 1750–1820,* 1967; Lawrence Lipking, *The Ordering of the Arts in Eighteenth-Century England,* 1970; René Wellek, *A History of Modern Criticism,* Vol. I, 1955.

For thematic studies relating literary forms to ideas of the period, see Paul Fussell, *The Rhetorical World of Augustan Humanism,* 1965; Martin Price, *To the Palace of Wisdom: Studies in Order and Energy from Dryden to Blake,* 1964; J. W. Johnson, *The Formation of Neo-Classical Thought,* 1967 (particularly concerned with ideas of history); Patricia M. Spacks, *The Poetry of Vision,* 1967 (on Thomson, Collins, Gray, Smart, and Cowper); and the collection of essays in honor of F. A. Pottle, *From Sensibility to Romanticism,* ed. F. W. Hilles and Harold Bloom, 1965.

On the relations of poetry and the arts in the age, see Jean H. Hagstrum, *The Sister Arts,* 1958; Edward Malins, *English Landscaping and Literature, 1660–1840,* 1966; on related arts, see Sir John Summerson, *Architecture in Britain, 1530 to 1830,* 1953; Ellis K. Waterhouse, *Painting in Britain, 1530 to 1790,* 1953; M. D. Whinney, *Sculpture in Britain, 1530–1830,* 1964; M. D. Whinney and Oliver Millar, *English Art 1625–1714,* 1957; David G. Irwin, *English Neoclassical Art,* 1966.

The Novel The best introduction is A. D. McKillop's *The Early Masters of English Fiction,* 1956. Important general studies are Ian Watt, *The Rise of the Novel,* 1957 (particularly good on the realism of Defoe and Richardson), and Ronald Paulson, *Satire and the Novel in Eighteenth-Century England,* 1967. There are valuable sections in Dorothy Van Ghent, *The English Novel,* 1953, and Wayne C. Booth, *The Rhetoric of Fiction,* 1961.

The Drama For history, Allardyce Nicoll, *A History of English Drama,* Vols. I–III, 1952; for records of performances, and other data, *The London Stage 1660–1800,* ed. W. Van Lennep, E. L. Avery, A. H. Scouten, G. W. Stone, C. B. Hogan, eleven vols., 1960–68.

On the relation of the drama to the times, see two works by John Loftis, *Comedy and Society from Congreve to Fielding,* 1959, and *The Politics of Drama in Augustan England,* 1963.

On the heroic plays of the Restoration, see Arthur C. Kirsch, *Dryden's Heroic Drama,* 1965, and two works by Eugene M. Waith, *The Herculean Hero,* 1962, and *Ideas of Greatness: Heroic Drama in England,* 1971.

On Restoration comedy, see especially Thomas H. Fujimura, *The Restoration Comedy of Wit,* 1952; Norman H. Holland, *The First Modern Comedies,* 1959, and, particularly for its general introductory chapters, Dale Underwood, *Etherege and the Seventeenth-Century Comedy of Manners,* 1957. For the later period, there is F. W. Bateson, *English Comic Drama 1700–50,* 1929.

JOHN DRYDEN

Editions The best complete edition of the poetry is by James Kinsley, four vols., 1958. In process is the careful and richly annotated edition of all the works, known as the California Dryden, ed. E. N. Hooker, H. T. Swedenberg, and others, from 1956. For the critical essays the once-standard edition of W. P. Ker (1900, 1926) is now superseded by that of George Watson, *Of Dramatic Poetry and Other Critical Writings*, two vols., 1962.

Critical Studies Louis I. Bredvold's *The Intellectual Milieu of Dryden's Thought*, 1934, is corrected and amplified by Philip Harth, *Contexts of Dryden's Thought*, 1968 (on the religious thought). The first modern critical study of the poetry, by Mark Van Doren (1920), has been succeeded by recent works of importance: William Frost, *Dryden and the Art of Translation*, 1955; A. W. Hoffman, *Dryden's Imagery*, 1962; A. H. Roper, *Dryden's Poetic Kingdoms*, 1965; and Earl Miner, *Dryden's Poetry*, 1967.

Biography The standard life (1961) is that of C. E. Ward, who also edited the *Letters*, 1952.

JONATHAN SWIFT

Editions *Prose Works*, ed. Herbert Davis, 1939–68; *Poems*, ed. Harold Williams, 1937 (rev. 1958); *Correspondence*, ed. Harold Williams, 1963–65; *A Tale of a Tub* [and shorter prose works], ed. A. C. Guthkelch and D. N. Smith, 1920 (rev. 1958); *Gulliver's Travels*, in various editions by Harold Williams (1926), A. E. Case (1936), L. A. Landa (1960).

Critical Studies Kathleen Williams, *Swift and the Age of Compromise*, 1958; Martin Price, *Swift's Rhetorical Art*, 1953; W. B. Ewald, *The Masks of Jonathan Swift*, 1954; Ronald Paulson, *Theme and Structure in Swift's Tale of a Tub*, 1960; Edward R. Rosenheim, *Swift and the Satirist's Art*, 1965. Important works on Swift's thought are Ricardo Quintana, *The Mind and Art of Jonathan Swift*, 1936 (rev. 1953); Miriam Starkman, *Swift's Satire on Learning in A Tale of a Tub*, 1950; and Philip Harth, *Swift and Anglican Rationalism*, 1961. There is a survey of recent studies in M. Voigt, *Swift and the Twentieth Century*, 1964, and among collections of essays is *The World of Jonathan Swift*, ed. Brian Vickers, 1968.

Biography Irvin Ehrenpreis, *Swift: The Man, His Works, and the Age* (to be completed in three volumes, 1962–), L. Landa, *Swift and the Church of Ireland*, 1954.

ALEXANDER POPE

Editions Standard for the poetry, including the translations, is the Twickenham Edition, ed. John Butt and others, 1940–67. The *Correspondence* is well edited by George Sherburn, 1956; and there is a useful collection of the *Literary Criticism*, ed. B. A. Goldgar, 1965.

Critical Studies Among the best are Geoffrey Tillotson, *On the Poetry of Pope*, 1938 (rev. 1950); Reuben A. Brower, *Alexander Pope: The Poetry of Allusion*, 1959; T. R. Edwards, *This Dark Estate*, 1963; and Aubrey Williams, *Pope's Dunciad*, 1955.

Biography The standard account to 1728 is George Sherburn, *The Early Career of Alexander Pope*, and there is a valuable record of the poet in Joseph Spence's *Obser-*

vations, Anecdotes, and Characters of Books and Men, ed. J. M. Osborn, 1966. These may be supplemented by Robert W. Rogers, *The Major Satires of Alexander Pope,* 1955 (in large part biographical), and Maynard Mack, *The Garden and the City,* 1970 (a searching study of Pope's imagination).

JAMES BOSWELL

Miscellaneous writings are collected in *Private Papers,* ed. Geoffrey Scott and F. A. Pottle, 1928–34; and *The Yale Editions of the Private Papers,* ed. F. A. Pottle and others, from 1950 (the Research Edition began to appear in 1966). For biography see F. A. Pottle, *James Boswell: The Earlier Years,* 1966 (to be completed in a second volume); Frank Brady, *Boswell's Political Career,* 1965.

SAMUEL JOHNSON

Editions *Works* (The Yale Edition), ed. A. T. Hazen and others, 1958– ; *Letters,* ed. R. W. Chapman, 1952. For Boswell's *Life,* the standard edition is the revision of G. B. Hill by L. F. Powell, 1934–64; this may be supplemented by J. L. Clifford, *Young Sam Johnson* (up to 1749), 1955, and two penetrating general studies, W. J. Bate, *The Achievement of Samuel Johnson,* 1955, and B. H. Bronson, *Johnson and Boswell,* 1944.

Special Topics Richard Voitle, *Johnson the Moralist,* 1961; Arieh Sachs, *Passionate Intelligence: Imagination and Reason in the Work of Samuel Johnson,* 1967; J. H. Hagstrum, *Samuel Johnson's Literary Criticism,* 1952; D. J. Greene, *The Politics of Johnson,* 1960; and a masterful study by W. K. Wimsatt, *The Prose Style of Samuel Johnson,* 1941. A useful index and collection is *The Critical Opinions of Samuel Johnson,* ed. J. E. Brown, 1926.

Author and Title Index

First-Line Index

MONTGOMERY COLLEGE LIBRARIES
germ, circ
PR 1105.09 1975
The Oxford an
0 0000 00147077 2